Definition of the Six Trigonometric Functions

Right triangle definitions, where $0 < \theta < \pi/2$

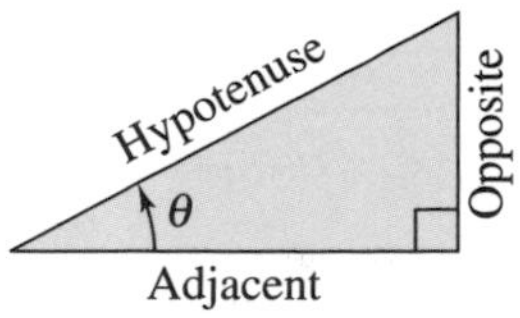

$$\sin\theta = \frac{\text{opp.}}{\text{hyp.}} \qquad \csc\theta = \frac{\text{hyp.}}{\text{opp.}}$$

$$\cos\theta = \frac{\text{adj.}}{\text{hyp.}} \qquad \sec\theta = \frac{\text{hyp.}}{\text{adj.}}$$

$$\tan\theta = \frac{\text{opp.}}{\text{adj.}} \qquad \cot\theta = \frac{\text{adj.}}{\text{opp.}}$$

Circular function definitions, where θ *is any angle*

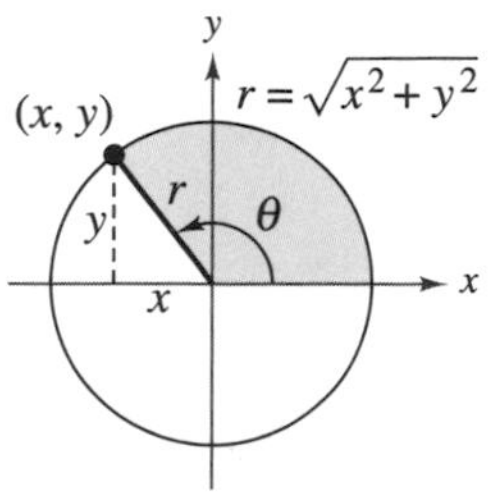

$$\sin\theta = \frac{y}{r} \qquad \csc\theta = \frac{r}{y}$$

$$\cos\theta = \frac{x}{r} \qquad \sec\theta = \frac{r}{x}$$

$$\tan\theta = \frac{y}{x} \qquad \cot\theta = \frac{x}{y}$$

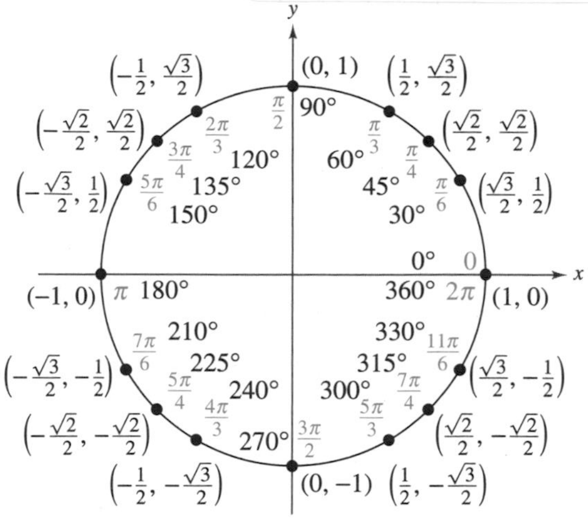

Reciprocal Identities

$$\sin u = \frac{1}{\csc u} \qquad \cos u = \frac{1}{\sec u} \qquad \tan u = \frac{1}{\cot u}$$

$$\csc u = \frac{1}{\sin u} \qquad \sec u = \frac{1}{\cos u} \qquad \cot u = \frac{1}{\tan u}$$

Quotient Identities

$$\tan u = \frac{\sin u}{\cos u} \qquad \cot u = \frac{\cos u}{\sin u}$$

Pythagorean Identities

$$\sin^2 u + \cos^2 u = 1$$

$$1 + \tan^2 u = \sec^2 u \qquad 1 + \cot^2 u = \csc^2 u$$

Cofunction Identities

$$\sin\left(\frac{\pi}{2} - u\right) = \cos u \qquad \cot\left(\frac{\pi}{2} - u\right) = \tan u$$

$$\cos\left(\frac{\pi}{2} - u\right) = \sin u \qquad \sec\left(\frac{\pi}{2} - u\right) = \csc u$$

$$\tan\left(\frac{\pi}{2} - u\right) = \cot u \qquad \csc\left(\frac{\pi}{2} - u\right) = \sec u$$

Even/Odd Identities

$$\sin(-u) = -\sin u \qquad \cot(-u) = -\cot u$$

$$\cos(-u) = \cos u \qquad \sec(-u) = \sec u$$

$$\tan(-u) = -\tan u \qquad \csc(-u) = -\csc u$$

Sum and Difference Formulas

$$\sin(u \pm v) = \sin u \cos v \pm \cos u \sin v$$

$$\cos(u \pm v) = \cos u \cos v \mp \sin u \sin v$$

$$\tan(u \pm v) = \frac{\tan u \pm \tan v}{1 \mp \tan u \tan v}$$

Double-Angle Formulas

$$\sin 2u = 2 \sin u \cos u$$

$$\cos 2u = \cos^2 u - \sin^2 u = 2\cos^2 u - 1 = 1 - 2\sin^2 u$$

$$\tan 2u = \frac{2 \tan u}{1 - \tan^2 u}$$

Power-Reducing Formulas

$$\sin^2 u = \frac{1 - \cos 2u}{2}$$

$$\cos^2 u = \frac{1 + \cos 2u}{2}$$

$$\tan^2 u = \frac{1 - \cos 2u}{1 + \cos 2u}$$

Sum-to-Product Formulas

$$\sin u + \sin v = 2 \sin\left(\frac{u + v}{2}\right)\cos\left(\frac{u - v}{2}\right)$$

$$\sin u - \sin v = 2 \cos\left(\frac{u + v}{2}\right)\sin\left(\frac{u - v}{2}\right)$$

$$\cos u + \cos v = 2 \cos\left(\frac{u + v}{2}\right)\cos\left(\frac{u - v}{2}\right)$$

$$\cos u - \cos v = -2 \sin\left(\frac{u + v}{2}\right)\sin\left(\frac{u - v}{2}\right)$$

Product-to-Sum Formulas

$$\sin u \sin v = \frac{1}{2}[\cos(u - v) - \cos(u + v)]$$

$$\cos u \cos v = \frac{1}{2}[\cos(u - v) + \cos(u + v)]$$

$$\sin u \cos v = \frac{1}{2}[\sin(u + v) + \sin(u - v)]$$

$$\cos u \sin v = \frac{1}{2}[\sin(u + v) - \sin(u - v)]$$

P423 cos of a sum

FORMULAS FROM GEOMETRY

Triangle:

$h = a \sin \theta$

Area $= \frac{1}{2}bh$

$c^2 = a^2 + b^2 - 2ab \cos \theta$ (Law of Cosines)

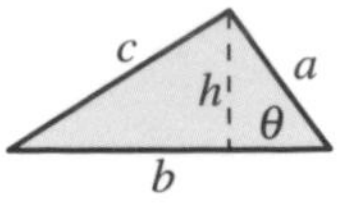

Right Triangle:

Pythagorean Theorem
$c^2 = a^2 + b^2$

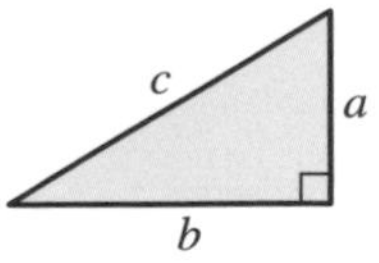

Equilateral Triangle:

$h = \frac{\sqrt{3}s}{2}$

Area $= \frac{\sqrt{3}s^2}{4}$

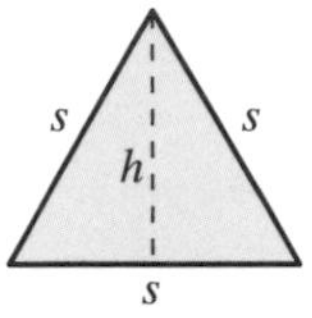

Parallelogram:

Area $= bh$

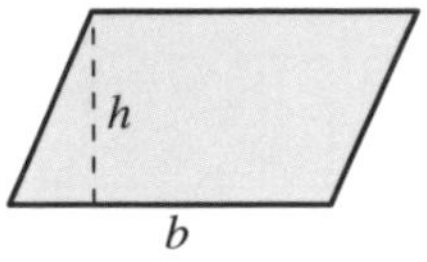

Trapezoid:

Area $= \frac{h}{2}(a + b)$

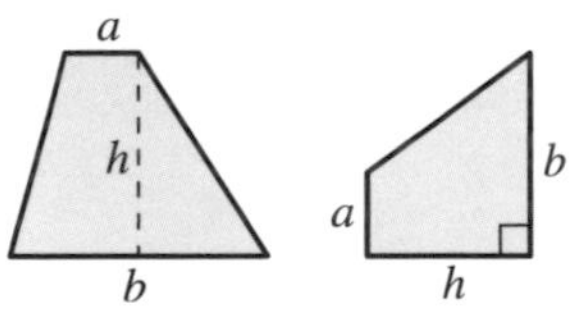

Circle:

Area $= \pi r^2$

Circumference $= 2\pi r$

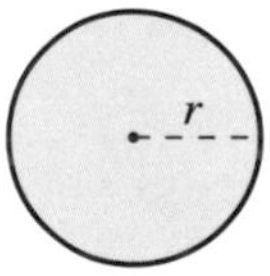

Sector of Circle:

Area $= \frac{\theta r^2}{2}$

$s = r\theta$

θ in radians

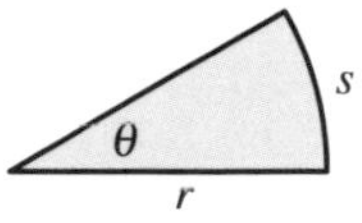

Circular Ring:

Area $= \pi(R^2 - r^2)$

$= 2\pi pw$

p = average radius,

w = width of ring

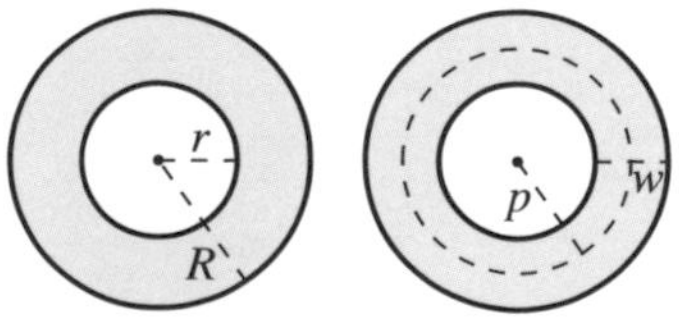

Sector of Circular Ring:

Area $= \theta pw$

p = average radius,

w = width of ring,

θ in radians

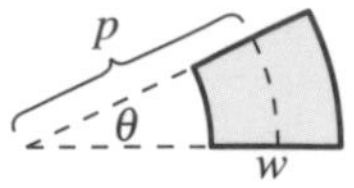

Ellipse:

Area $= \pi ab$

Circumference $\approx 2\pi\sqrt{\frac{a^2 + b^2}{2}}$

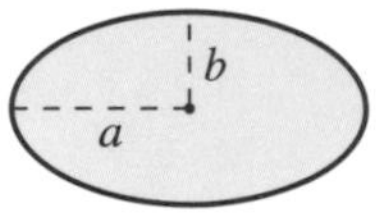

Cone:

Volume $= \frac{Ah}{3}$

A = area of base

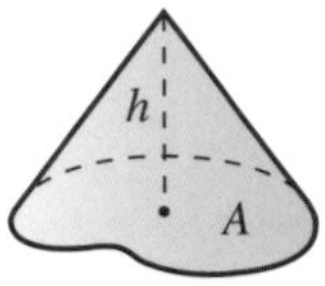

Right Circular Cone:

Volume $= \frac{\pi r^2 h}{3}$

Lateral Surface Area $= \pi r\sqrt{r^2 + h^2}$

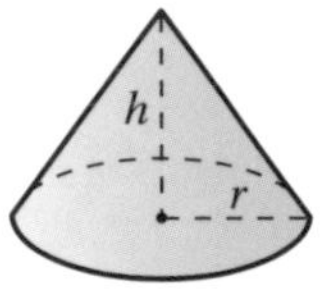

Frustum of Right Circular Cone:

Volume $= \frac{\pi(r^2 + rR + R^2)h}{3}$

Lateral Surface Area $= \pi s(R + r)$

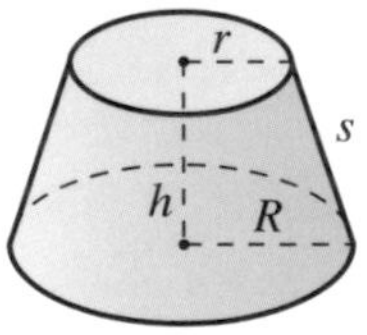

Right Circular Cylinder:

Volume $= \pi r^2 h$

Lateral Surface Area $= 2\pi rh$

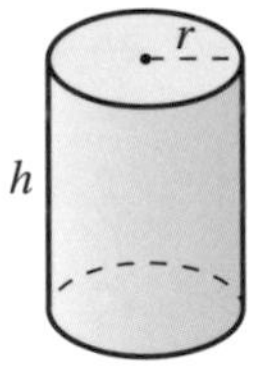

Sphere:

Volume $= \frac{4}{3}\pi r^3$

Surface Area $= 4\pi r^2$

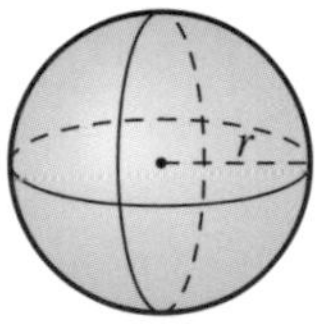

Wedge:

$A = B \sec \theta$

A = area of upper face,

B = area of base

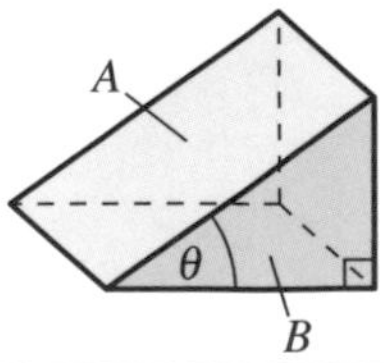

Precalculus with Limits

Precalculus with Limits

Ron Larson

The Pennsylvania State University
The Behrend College

Robert Hostetler

The Pennsylvania State University
The Behrend College

With the assistance of David C. Falvo

The Pennsylvania State University
The Behrend College

Houghton Mifflin Company Boston New York

Publisher: Richard Stratton
Sponsoring Editor: Cathy Cantin
Development Manager: Maureen Ross
Development Editor: Lisa Collette
Editorial Associate: Elizabeth Kassab
Supervising Editor: Karen Carter
Senior Project Editor: Patty Bergin
Development Editor: Yen Tieu
Editorial Assistant: Julia Keller
Art and Design Manager: Gary Crespo
Executive Marketing Manager: Brenda Bravener-Greville
Director of Manufacturing: Priscilla Manchester
Cover Design Manager: Tony Saizon

Cover Image: Ryuichi Okano/Photonica

Printed in the U.S.A.

Library of Congress Catalog Card Number: 2005938692

ISBN 13: 978-0-618-75171-6
ISBN 10: 0-618-75171-8

123456789–DOW–10 09 08 07 06

Contents

A Word from the Authors (Preface) ix
Textbook Features and Highlights xiii
Texas Applications and Problem Solving xxi

Chapter 1 Functions and Their Graphs 1

1.1 Rectangular Coordinates 2
1.2 Graphs of Equations 14
1.3 Linear Equations in Two Variables 25
1.4 Functions 40
1.5 Analyzing Graphs of Functions 54
1.6 A Library of Parent Functions 66
1.7 Transformations of Functions 74
1.8 Combinations of Functions: Composite Functions 84
1.9 Inverse Functions 93
1.10 Mathematical Modeling and Variation 103
Chapter Summary 115
Review Exercises 117
Chapter Test 123
Proofs in Mathematics 124
P.S. Problem Solving 125

Chapter 2 Polynomial and Rational Functions 127

2.1 Quadratic Functions and Models 128
2.2 Polynomial Functions of Higher Degree 139
2.3 Polynomial and Synthetic Division 153
2.4 Complex Numbers 162
2.5 Zeros of Polynomial Functions 169
2.6 Rational Functions 184
2.7 Nonlinear Inequalities 197
Chapter Summary 207
Review Exercises 208
Chapter Test 212
Proofs in Mathematics 213
P.S. Problem Solving 215

Chapter 3 Exponential and Logarithmic Functions 217

3.1 Exponential Functions and Their Graphs 218
3.2 Logarithmic Functions and Their Graphs 229
3.3 Properties of Logarithms 239
3.4 Exponential and Logarithmic Equations 246
3.5 Exponential and Logarithmic Models 257
Chapter Summary 270
Review Exercises 271
Chapter Test 275
Cumulative Test: Chapters 1–3 276
Proofs in Mathematics 278
P.S. Problem Solving 279

Chapter 4 Trigonometry 281

4.1 Radian and Degree Measure 282
4.2 Trigonometric Functions: The Unit Circle 294
4.3 Right Triangle Trigonometry 301
4.4 Trigonometric Functions of Any Angle 312
4.5 Graphs of Sine and Cosine Functions 321
4.6 Graphs of Other Trigonometric Functions 332
4.7 Inverse Trigonometric Functions 343
4.8 Applications and Models 353
Chapter Summary 364
Review Exercises 365
Chapter Test 369
Proofs in Mathematics 370
P.S. Problem Solving 371

Chapter 5 Analytic Trigonometry 373

5.1 Using Fundamental Identities 374
5.2 Verifying Trigonometric Identities 382
5.3 Solving Trigonometric Equations 389
5.4 Sum and Difference Formulas 400
5.5 Multiple-Angle and Product-to-Sum Formulas 407
Chapter Summary 419
Review Exercises 420
Chapter Test 423
Proofs in Mathematics 424
P.S. Problem Solving 427

Chapter 6 Additional Topics in Trigonometry 429

6.1 Law of Sines 430
6.2 Law of Cosines 439
6.3 Vectors in the Plane 447
6.4 Vectors and Dot Products 460
6.5 Trigonometric Form of a Complex Number 470
Chapter Summary 481
Review Exercises 482
Chapter Test 486
Cumulative Test: Chapters 4–6 487
Proofs in Mathematics 489
P.S. Problem Solving 493

Chapter 7 Systems of Equations and Inequalities 495

7.1 Linear and Nonlinear Systems of Equations 496
7.2 Two-Variable Linear Systems 507
7.3 Multivariable Linear Systems 519
7.4 Partial Fractions 533
7.5 Systems of Inequalities 541
7.6 Linear Programming 552
Chapter Summary 562
Review Exercises 563
Chapter Test 567
Proofs in Mathematics 568
P.S. Problem Solving 569

Chapter 8 Matrices and Determinants 571

8.1 Matrices and Systems of Equations 572
8.2 Operations with Matrices 587
8.3 The Inverse of a Square Matrix 602
8.4 The Determinant of a Square Matrix 611
8.5 Applications of Matrices and Determinants 619

Chapter Summary 631
Review Exercises 632
Chapter Test 637
Proofs in Mathematics 638
P.S. Problem Solving 639

Chapter 9 Sequences, Series, and Probability 641

9.1 Sequences and Series 642
9.2 Arithmetic Sequences and Partial Sums 653
9.3 Geometric Sequences and Series 663
9.4 Mathematical Induction 673
9.5 The Binomial Theorem 683
9.6 Counting Principles 691
9.7 Probability 701

Chapter Summary 714
Review Exercises 715
Chapter Test 719
Cumulative Test: Chapters 7–9 720
Proofs in Mathematics 722
P.S. Problem Solving 725

Chapter 10 Topics in Analytic Geometry 727

10.1 Lines 728
10.2 Introduction to Conics: Parabolas 735
10.3 Ellipses 744
10.4 Hyperbolas 753
10.5 Rotation of Conics 763
10.6 Parametric Equations 771
10.7 Polar Coordinates 779
10.8 Graphs of Polar Equations 785
10.9 Polar Equations of Conics 793

Chapter Summary 800
Review Exercises 801
Chapter Test 805
Proofs in Mathematics 806
P.S. Problem Solving 809

Chapter 11 Analytic Geometry in Three Dimensions 811

11.1 The Three-Dimensional Coordinate System 812
11.2 Vectors in Space 820
11.3 The Cross Product of Two Vectors 827
11.4 Lines and Planes in Space 834
Chapter Summary 843
Review Exercises 844
Chapter Test 846
Proofs in Mathematics 847
P.S. Problem Solving 849

Chapter 12 Limits and an Introduction to Calculus 851

12.1 Introduction to Limits 852
12.2 Techniques for Evaluating Limits 863
12.3 The Tangent Line Problem 873
12.4 Limits at Infinity and Limits of Sequences 883
12.5 The Area Problem 892
Chapter Summary 900
Review Exercises 901
Chapter Test 904
Cumulative Test: Chapters 10–12 905
Proofs in Mathematics 907
P.S. Problem Solving 908

Appendix A Review of Fundamental Concepts of Algebra A1

A.1 Real Numbers and Their Properties A1
A.2 Exponents and Radicals A11
A.3 Polynomials and Factoring A23
A.4 Rational Expressions A36
A.5 Solving Equations A46
A.6 Linear Inequalities in One Variable A60
A.7 Errors and the Algebra of Calculus A70

Answers to Odd-Numbered Exercises and Tests A77

Index A225

Index of Applications (Web: *college.hmco.com*)

Appendix B Concepts in Statistics (Web: *college.hmco.com*)

B.1 Representing Data
B.2 Measures of Central Tendency and Dispersion
B.3 Least Squares Regression

A Word from the Authors

Welcome to *Precalculus with Limits*. We are pleased to present this new precalculus textbook in which we focus on making the mathematics accessible, supporting student success, and offering teachers flexible teaching options. The purpose of this text is to thoroughly cover the topics of a traditional precalculus text with the addition of two new chapters. Chapter 11 encompasses analytic geometry in three dimensions and Chapter 12 introduces students to the key calculus topics, including limits, the tangent line problem, and the area problem.

Accessible to Students

We have taken care to write this text with the student in mind. Paying careful attention to the presentation, we use precise mathematical language and a clear writing style to develop an effective learning tool. We believe that every student can learn mathematics, and we are committed to providing a text that makes the mathematics of the precalculus course accessible to all students.

Throughout the text, solutions to many examples are presented from multiple perspectives—algebraically, graphically, and numerically. The side-by-side format of this pedagogical feature helps students to see that a problem can be solved in more than one way and to see that different methods yield the same result. The side-by-side format also addresses many different learning styles.

We have found that many precalculus students grasp mathematical concepts more easily when they work with them in the context of real-life situations. Students have numerous opportunities to do this throughout this text. The *Make a Decision* feature further connects real-life data and applications and motivates students. They also offer students the opportunity to generate and analyze mathematical models from large data sets. To reinforce the concept of functions, each function is introduced at the first point of use in the text with a definition and description of basic characteristics. Also, all elementary functions are presented in a summary on the endpapers of the text for convenient reference.

We have carefully written and designed each page to make the book readable and accessible to students. For example, to avoid unnecessary page turning and disruptions to students' thought processes, each example and corresponding solution begins and ends on the same page.

Supports Student Success

During more than 30 years of teaching and writing, we have learned many things about the teaching and learning of mathematics. We have found that students are most successful when they know what they are expected to learn and why it is important to learn the concepts. With that in mind, we have incorporated a thematic study thread throughout the text.

Each chapter begins with a list of applications that are covered in the chapter and serve as a motivational tool by connecting section content to real-life situations. Using the same pedagogical theme, each section begins with a set of section learning objectives—*What You Should Learn*. These are followed by an engaging real-life application—*Why You Should Learn It*—that motivates students and illustrates an area where the mathematical concepts will be applied in an example or exercise in the section. The *Chapter Summary—What Did You Learn?*—at the end of each chapter is a section-by-section overview that ties the learning objectives from the chapter to sets of *Review Exercises* at the end of each chapter.

Throughout the text, other features further improve accessibility. *Study Tips* are provided throughout the text at point-of-use to reinforce concepts and to help students learn how to study mathematics. *Technology, Writing About Mathematics, Historical Notes,* and *Explorations* reinforce mathematical concepts. Each example with worked-out solution is followed by a *Checkpoint*, which directs the student to work a similar exercise from the exercise set. The *Section Exercises* begin with a *Vocabulary Check*, which gives the students an opportunity to test their understanding of the important terms in the section. *Synthesis Exercises* check students' conceptual understanding of the topics in each section. The *Make a Decision* exercises further connect real-life data and applications and motivate students. *Skills Review Exercises* provide additional practice with the concepts in the chapter or previous chapters. *Chapter Tests*, at the end of each chapter, and periodic *Cumulative Tests* offer students frequent opportunities for self-assessment and to develop strong study- and test-taking skills.

The use of technology also supports students with different learning styles. *Technology* notes are provided throughout the text at point-of-use. These notes call attention to the strengths and weaknesses of graphing technology, as well as offer alternative methods for solving or checking a problem using technology. These notes also direct students to the *Graphing Technology Guide*, on the textbook website, for keystroke support that is available for numerous calculator models. The use of technology is optional. This feature and related exercises can be omitted without the loss of continuity in coverage of topics.

Numerous additional text-specific resources are available to help students succeed in the precalculus course. These include "live" online tutoring, instructional DVDs, and a variety of other resources, such as tutorial support and self-assessment, which are available on the HM mathSpace® CD-ROM and the Web. In addition, the *Notetaking Guide* helps students organize their class notes and create an effective study and review tool.

Flexible Options for Teachers

From the time we first began writing textbooks in the early 1970s, we have always considered it a critical part of our role as authors to provide teachers with flexible programs. In addition to addressing a variety of learning styles, the optional features within the text allow teachers to design their courses to meet their instructional needs and the needs of their students. For example, the *Explorations* throughout the text can be used as a quick introduction to concepts or as a way to reinforce student understanding.

Our goal when developing the exercise sets was to address a wide variety of learning styles and teaching preferences. The *Vocabulary Check* questions are provided at the beginning of every exercise set to help students learn proper mathematical terminology. In each exercise set we have included a variety of exercise types, including questions requiring writing and critical thinking, as well as real-data applications. The problems are carefully graded in difficulty from mastery of basic skills to more challenging exercises. Some of the more challenging exercises include the *Synthesis Exercises* that combine skills and are used to check for conceptual understanding and the *Make a Decision* exercises that further connect real-life data and applications and motivate students. *Skills Review Exercises*, placed at the end of each exercise set, reinforce previously learned skills.

Several other print and media resources are also available to support teachers. The online *Instructor Success Organizer* includes suggested lesson plans that will help guide teachers through the text. The *Notetaking Guide IAE* can be used as a lecture outline for every section of the text and includes additional examples for classroom discussion and important definitions. This is another valuable resource for schools trying to have consistent instruction and it can be used as a resource to support less experienced teachers. When used in conjunction with the *Notetaking Guide*, these resources can save teachers preparation time and help students concentrate on important concepts.

Teachers who stress applications and problem solving, or exploration and technology, coupled with more traditional methods, will be able to use this text successfully.

We hope you will enjoy using *Precalculus with Limits* in your precalculus class.

Ron Larson
Robert Hostetler

Acknowledgments

We would like to thank the many people who have helped us prepare the text and the supplements package. Their encouragement, criticisms, and suggestions have been invaluable to us.

Reviewers

Arun Agarwal, *Grambling State University*; Jean Claude Antoine, *Bunker Hill Community College*; W. Edward Bolton, *East Georgia College*; Joanne Brunner, *Joliet Junior College*; Luajean Bryan, *Walker Valley High School*; Nancy Cholvin, *Antelope Valley College*; Amy Daniel, *University of New Orleans*; Nerissa Felder, *Polk Community College*; Kathi Fields, *Blue Ridge Community College*; Edward Green, *North Georgia College & State University*; Karen Guinn, *University of South Carolina Beaufort*; Duane Larson, *Bevill State Community College*; Babette Lowe, *Victoria College (TX)*; Rudy Maglio, *Northwestern University*; Antonio Mazza, *University of Toronto*; Robin McNally, *Reinhardt College*; Constance Meade, *College of Southern Idaho*; Matt Mitchell, *American River College*; Claude Moore, *Danville Community College*; Mark Naber, *Monroe Community College*; Paul Olsen, *Wesley College*; Yewande Olubummo, *Spelman College*; Claudia Pacioni, *Washington State University*; Gary Parker, *Blue Mountain Community College*; Kevin Ratliff, *Blue Ridge Community College*; Michael Simon, *Southern Connecticut State University*; Rick Simon, *University of La Verne*; Delores Smith, *Coppin State University*; Kostas Stroumbakis, *DeVry Institute of Technology*; Michael Tedder, *Jefferson Davis Community College*; Ellen Turnell, *North Harris College*; Pamela Weston, *Tennessee Wesleyan College*

We would like to thank the staff of Larson Texts, Inc. who assisted in preparing the manuscript, rendering the art package, and typesetting and proofreading the pages and supplements.

On a personal level, we are grateful to our wives, Deanna Gilbert Larson and Eloise Hostetler, for their love, patience, and support. Also, a special thanks goes to R. Scott O'Neil.

If you have suggestions for improving this text, please feel free to write us. Over the past three decades we have received many useful comments from both teachers and students, and we value these very much.

Ron Larson
Robert Hostetler

Textbook Features and Highlights

Exponential and Logarithmic Functions

3

3.1 Exponential Functions and Their Graphs
3.2 Logarithmic Functions and Their Graphs
3.3 Properties of Logarithms
3.4 Exponential and Logarithmic Equations
3.5 Exponential and Logarithmic Models

Carbon dating is a method used to determine the ages of archeological artifacts up to 50,000 years old. For example, archeologists are using carbon dating to determine the ages of the great pyramids of Egypt.

© Sylvain Grandadam/Getty Images

SELECTED APPLICATIONS

Exponential and logarithmic functions have many real-life applications. The applications listed below represent a small sample of the applications in this chapter.

- Computer Virus, Exercise 65, page 227
- Data Analysis: Meteorology, Exercise 70, page 228
- Sound Intensity, Exercise 90, page 238
- Galloping Speeds of Animals, Exercise 85, page 244
- Average Heights, Exercise 115, page 255
- Carbon Dating, Exercise 41, page 266
- IQ Scores, Exercise 47, page 266
- Forensics, Exercise 63, page 268
- Compound Interest, Exercise 135, page 273

217

• Chapter Opener

Each chapter begins with a comprehensive overview of the chapter concepts. The photograph and caption illustrate a real-life application of a key concept. Section references help students prepare for the chapter.

• Applications List

An abridged list of applications covered in the chapter serves as a motivational tool by connecting section content to real-life situations.

• "What You Should Learn" and "Why You Should Learn It"

Sections begin with *What You Should Learn*, an outline of the main concepts covered in the section, and *Why You Should Learn It*, a real-life application or mathematical reference that illustrates the relevance of the section content.

Section 3.3 Properties of Logarithms 239

3.3 Properties of Logarithms

What you should learn

- Use the change-of-base formula to rewrite and evaluate logarithmic expressions.
- Use properties of logarithms to evaluate or rewrite logarithmic expressions.
- Use properties of logarithms to expand or condense logarithmic expressions.
- Use logarithmic functions to model and solve real-life problems.

Why you should learn it

Logarithmic functions can be used to model and solve real-life problems. For instance, in Exercises 81–83 on page 244, a logarithmic function is used to model the relationship between the number of decibels and the intensity of a sound.

AP Photo/Stephen Chernin

Change of Base

Most calculators have only two types of log keys, one for common logarithms (base 10) and one for natural logarithms (base e). Although common logs and natural logs are the most frequently used, you may occasionally need to evaluate logarithms to other bases. To do this, you can use the following **change-of-base formula.**

Change-of-Base Formula

Let a, b, and x be positive real numbers such that $a \neq 1$ and $b \neq 1$. Then $\log_a x$ can be converted to a different base as follows.

Base b	*Base 10*	*Base e*
$\log_a x = \dfrac{\log_b x}{\log_b a}$	$\log_a x = \dfrac{\log x}{\log a}$	$\log_a x = \dfrac{\ln x}{\ln a}$

One way to look at the change-of-base formula is that logarithms to base a are simply *constant multiples* of logarithms to base b. The constant multiplier is $1/(\log_b a)$.

Example 1 Changing Bases Using Common Logarithms

a. $\log_4 25 = \dfrac{\log 25}{\log 4}$ $\quad \log_a x = \dfrac{\log x}{\log a}$

$\approx \dfrac{1.39794}{0.60206}$ Use a calculator.

≈ 2.3219 Simplify.

b. $\log_2 12 = \dfrac{\log 12}{\log 2} \approx \dfrac{1.07918}{0.30103} \approx 3.5850$

✓CHECKPOINT Now try Exercise 1(a).

Example 2 Changing Bases Using Natural Logarithms

a. $\log_4 25 = \dfrac{\ln 25}{\ln 4}$ $\quad \log_a x = \dfrac{\ln x}{\ln a}$

$\approx \dfrac{3.21888}{1.38629}$ Use a calculator.

≈ 2.3219 Simplify.

b. $\log_2 12 = \dfrac{\ln 12}{\ln 2} \approx \dfrac{2.48491}{0.69315} \approx 3.5850$

✓CHECKPOINT Now try Exercise 1(b).

FEATURES

Example 7 **Movie Ticket Sales**

The weekly ticket sales for a new comedy movie decreased each week. At the same time, the weekly ticket sales for a new drama movie increased each week. Models that approximate the weekly ticket sales S (in millions of dollars) for each movie are

$$\begin{cases} S = 60 - 8x & \text{Comedy} \\ S = 10 + 4.5x & \text{Drama} \end{cases}$$

where x represents the number of weeks each movie was in theaters, with $x = 0$ corresponding to the ticket sales during the opening weekend. After how many weeks will the ticket sales for the two movies be equal?

Algebraic Solution

Because the second equation has already been solved for S in terms of x, substitute this value into the first equation and solve for x, as follows.

$10 + 4.5x = 60 - 8x$ Substitute for S in Equation 1.

$4.5x + 8x = 60 - 10$ Add $8x$ and -10 to each side.

$12.5x = 50$ Combine like terms.

$x = 4$ Divide each side by 12.5.

So, the weekly ticket sales for the two movies will be equal after 4 weeks.

✓CHECKPOINT Now try Exercise 65.

Numerical Solution

You can create a table of values for each model to determine when the ticket sales for the two movies will be equal.

Number of weeks, x	0	1	2	3	4	5	6
Sales, S (comedy)	60	52	44	36	28	20	12
Sales, S (drama)	10	14.5	19	23.5	28	32.5	37

So, from the table above, you can see that the weekly ticket sales for the two movies will be equal after 4 weeks.

WRITING ABOUT MATHEMATICS

Interpreting Points of Intersection You plan to rent a 14-foot truck for a two-day local move. At truck rental agency A, you can rent a truck for $29.95 per day plus $0.49 per mile. At agency B, you can rent a truck for $50 per day plus $0.25 per mile.

a. Write a total cost equation in terms of x and y for the total cost of renting the truck from each agency.

b. Use a graphing utility to graph the two equations in the same viewing window and find the point of intersection. Interpret the meaning of the point of intersection in the context of the problem.

c. Which agency should you choose if you plan to travel a total of 100 miles during the two-day move? Why?

d. How does the situation change if you plan to drive 200 miles during the two-day move?

• Examples

Many examples present side-by-side solutions with multiple approaches—algebraic, graphical, and numerical. This format addresses a variety of learning styles and shows students that different solution methods yield the same result.

• Checkpoint

The *Checkpoint* directs students to work a similar problem in the exercise set for extra practice.

• Explorations

The *Exploration* engages students in active discovery of mathematical concepts, strengthens critical thinking skills, and helps them to develop an intuitive understanding of theoretical concepts.

• Study Tips

Study Tips reinforce concepts and help students learn how to study mathematics.

• Technology

The *Technology* feature gives instructions for graphing utilities at point of use.

• Additional Features

Additional carefully crafted learning tools, designed to connect concepts, are placed throughout the text. These learning tools include *Writing About Mathematics*, *Historical Notes,* and an extensive art program.

Exploration

Write out the first five terms of the sequence whose nth term is

$$a_n = \frac{(-1)^{n+1}}{2n - 1}.$$

Are they the same as the first five terms of the sequence in Example 2? If not, how do they differ?

Example 2 **A Sequence Whose Terms Alternate in Sign**

Write the first five terms of the sequence given by $a_n = \dfrac{(-1)^n}{2n - 1}$.

Solution

The first five terms of the sequence are as follows.

$a_1 = \dfrac{(-1)^1}{2(1) - 1} = \dfrac{-1}{2 - 1} = -1$ 1st term

$a_2 = \dfrac{(-1)^2}{2(2) - 1} = \dfrac{1}{4 - 1} = \dfrac{1}{3}$ 2nd term

$a_3 = \dfrac{(-1)^3}{2(3) - 1} = \dfrac{-1}{6 - 1} = -\dfrac{1}{5}$ 3rd term

$a_4 = \dfrac{(-1)^4}{2(4) - 1} = \dfrac{1}{8 - 1} = \dfrac{1}{7}$ 4th term

$a_5 = \dfrac{(-1)^5}{2(5) - 1} = \dfrac{-1}{10 - 1} = -\dfrac{1}{9}$ 5th term

✓CHECKPOINT Now try Exercise 17.

Simply listing the first few terms is not sufficient to define a unique sequence—the nth term *must be given*. To see this, consider the following sequences, both of which have the same first three terms.

$$\frac{1}{2}, \frac{1}{4}, \frac{1}{8}, \frac{1}{16}, \ldots, \frac{1}{2^n}, \ldots$$

$$\frac{1}{2}, \frac{1}{4}, \frac{1}{8}, \frac{1}{15}, \ldots, \frac{6}{(n+1)(n^2 - n + 6)}, \ldots$$

Technology

To graph a sequence using a graphing utility, set the mode to *sequence* and *dot* and enter the sequence. The graph of the sequence in Example 3(a) is shown below. You can use the *trace* feature or *value* feature to identify the terms.

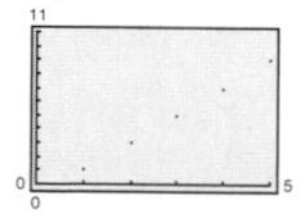

Example 3 **Finding the nth Term of a Sequence**

Write an expression for the apparent nth term (a_n) of each sequence.

a. 1, 3, 5, 7, . . . **b.** 2, −5, 10, −17, . . .

Solution

a. n: 1 2 3 4 . . . n
Terms: 1 3 5 7 . . . a_n
Apparent pattern: Each term is 1 less than twice n, which implies that

$a_n = 2n - 1.$

b. n: 1 2 3 4 . . . n
Terms: 2 −5 10 −17 . . . a_n
Apparent pattern: The terms have alternating signs with those in the even positions being negative. Each term is 1 more than the square of n, which implies that

$a_n = (-1)^{n+1}(n^2 + 1)$

✓CHECKPOINT Now try Exercise 37.

- # Real-Life Applications

A wide variety of real-life applications, many using current real data, are integrated throughout the examples and exercises. The (globe icon) indicates an example that involves a real-life application.

- # Algebra of Calculus

Throughout the text, special emphasis is given to the algebraic techniques used in calculus. Algebra of Calculus examples and exercises are integrated throughout the text and are identified by the symbol ∫.

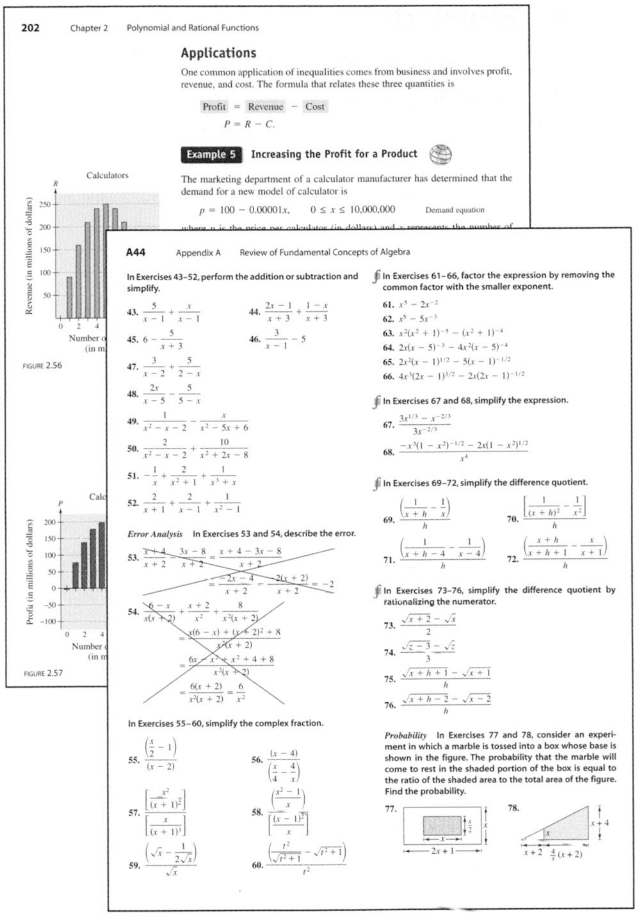
202 Chapter 2 Polynomial and Rational Functions

Applications

One common application of inequalities comes from business and involves profit, revenue, and cost. The formula that relates these three quantities is

Profit = Revenue − Cost

$P = R - C.$

Example 5 Increasing the Profit for a Product

The marketing department of a calculator manufacturer has determined that the demand for a new model of calculator is

$p = 100 - 0.00001x, \quad 0 \le x \le 10{,}000{,}000$ Demand equation

FIGURE 2.56

FIGURE 2.57

A44 Appendix A Review of Fundamental Concepts of Algebra

In Exercises 43–52, perform the addition or subtraction and simplify.

43. $\frac{5}{x-1} + \frac{x}{x-1}$ 44. $\frac{2x-1}{x+3} + \frac{1-x}{x+3}$

45. $6 - \frac{5}{x+3}$ 46. $\frac{3}{x-1} - 5$

47. $\frac{3}{x-2} + \frac{5}{2-x}$

48. $\frac{2x}{x-5} - \frac{5}{5-x}$

49. $\frac{1}{x^2-x-2} - \frac{x}{x^2-5x+6}$

50. $\frac{2}{x^2-x-2} + \frac{10}{x^2+2x-8}$

51. $-\frac{1}{x} + \frac{2}{x^2+1} + \frac{1}{x^3+x}$

52. $\frac{2}{x+1} + \frac{2}{x-1} + \frac{1}{x^2-1}$

Error Analysis In Exercises 53 and 54, describe the error.

In Exercises 55–60, simplify the complex fraction.

∫ In Exercises 61–66, factor the expression by removing the common factor with the smaller exponent.

61. $x^5 - 2x^{-2}$

62. $x^5 - 5x^{-3}$

63. $x^2(x^2+1)^{-5} - (x^2+1)^{-4}$

64. $2x(x-5)^{-3} - 4x^2(x-5)^{-4}$

65. $2x^2(x-1)^{1/2} - 5(x-1)^{-1/2}$

66. $4x^3(2x-1)^{3/2} - 2x(2x-1)^{-1/2}$

∫ In Exercises 67 and 68, simplify the expression.

67. $\frac{3x^{1/3} - x^{-2/3}}{3x^{-2/3}}$

68. $\frac{-x^3(1-x^2)^{-1/2} - 2x(1-x^2)^{1/2}}{x^4}$

∫ In Exercises 69–72, simplify the difference quotient.

∫ In Exercises 73–76, simplify the difference quotient by rationalizing the numerator.

73. $\frac{\sqrt{x+2} - \sqrt{x}}{2}$

74. $\frac{\sqrt{z-3} - \sqrt{z}}{3}$

75. $\frac{\sqrt{x+h+1} - \sqrt{x+1}}{h}$

76. $\frac{\sqrt{x+h-2} - \sqrt{x-2}}{h}$

Probability In Exercises 77 and 78, consider an experiment in which a marble is tossed into a box whose base is shown in the figure. The probability that the marble will come to rest in the shaded portion of the box is equal to the ratio of the shaded area to the total area of the figure. Find the probability.

- # Section Exercises

The section exercise sets consist of a variety of computational, conceptual, and applied problems.

- # Vocabulary Check

Section exercises begin with a *Vocabulary Check* that serves as a review of the important mathematical terms in each section.

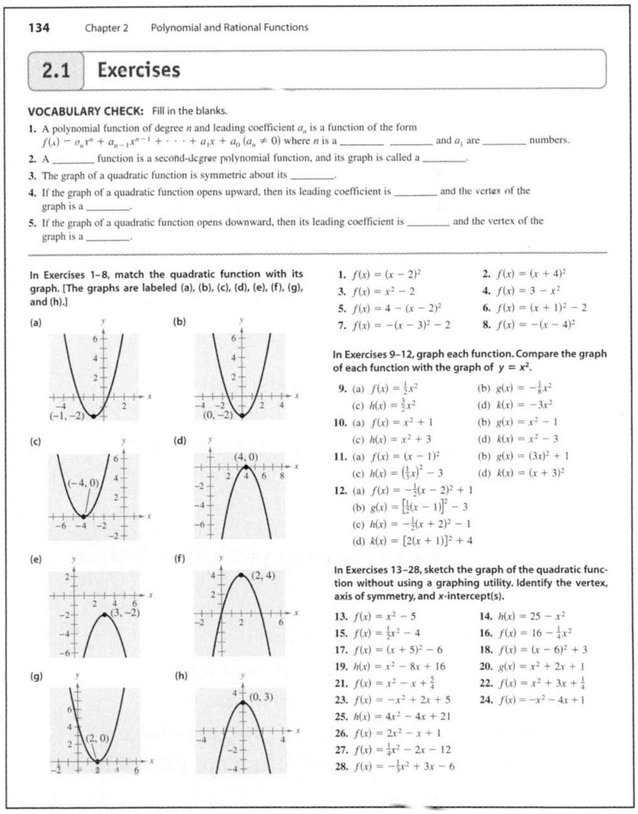
134 Chapter 2 Polynomial and Rational Functions

2.1 Exercises

VOCABULARY CHECK: Fill in the blanks.

1. A polynomial function of degree n and leading coefficient a_n is a function of the form $f(x) = a_nx^n + a_{n-1}x^{n-1} + \cdots + a_1x + a_0$ $(a_n \ne 0)$ where n is a ________ ________ and a_i are ________ numbers.
2. A ________ function is a second-degree polynomial function, and its graph is called a ________.
3. The graph of a quadratic function is symmetric about its ________.
4. If the graph of a quadratic function opens upward, then its leading coefficient is ________ and the vertex of the graph is a ________.
5. If the graph of a quadratic function opens downward, then its leading coefficient is ________ and the vertex of the graph is a ________.

In Exercises 1–8, match the quadratic function with its graph. [The graphs are labeled (a), (b), (c), (d), (e), (f), (g), and (h).]

1. $f(x) = (x-2)^2$ 2. $f(x) = (x+4)^2$
3. $f(x) = x^2 - 2$ 4. $f(x) = 3 - x^2$
5. $f(x) = 4 - (x-2)^2$ 6. $f(x) = (x+1)^2 - 2$
7. $f(x) = -(x-3)^2 - 2$ 8. $f(x) = -(x-4)^2$

In Exercises 9–12, graph each function. Compare the graph of each function with the graph of $y = x^2$.

9. (a) $f(x) = \frac{1}{2}x^2$ (b) $g(x) = -\frac{1}{8}x^2$ (c) $h(x) = \frac{3}{2}x^2$ (d) $k(x) = -3x^2$
10. (a) $f(x) = x^2 + 1$ (b) $g(x) = x^2 - 1$ (c) $h(x) = x^2 + 3$ (d) $k(x) = x^2 - 3$
11. (a) $f(x) = (x-1)^2$ (b) $g(x) = (3x)^2 + 1$ (c) $h(x) = (\frac{1}{3}x)^2 - 3$ (d) $k(x) = (x+3)^2$
12. (a) $f(x) = -\frac{1}{2}(x-2)^2 + 1$ (b) $g(x) = [\frac{1}{2}(x-1)]^2 - 3$ (c) $h(x) = -\frac{1}{2}(x+2)^2 - 1$ (d) $k(x) = [2(x+1)]^2 + 4$

In Exercises 13–28, sketch the graph of the quadratic function without using a graphing utility. Identify the vertex, axis of symmetry, and x-intercept(s).

13. $f(x) = x^2 - 5$ 14. $h(x) = 25 - x^2$
15. $f(x) = \frac{1}{2}x^2 - 4$ 16. $f(x) = 16 - \frac{1}{4}x^2$
17. $f(x) = (x+5)^2 - 6$ 18. $f(x) = (x-6)^2 + 3$
19. $h(x) = x^2 - 8x + 16$ 20. $g(x) = x^2 + 2x + 1$
21. $f(x) = x^2 - x + \frac{5}{4}$ 22. $f(x) = x^2 + 3x + \frac{1}{4}$
23. $f(x) = -x^2 + 2x + 5$ 24. $f(x) = -x^2 - 4x + 1$
25. $h(x) = 4x^2 - 4x + 21$
26. $f(x) = 2x^2 - x + 1$
27. $f(x) = \frac{1}{4}x^2 - 2x - 12$
28. $f(x) = -\frac{1}{3}x^2 + 3x - 6$

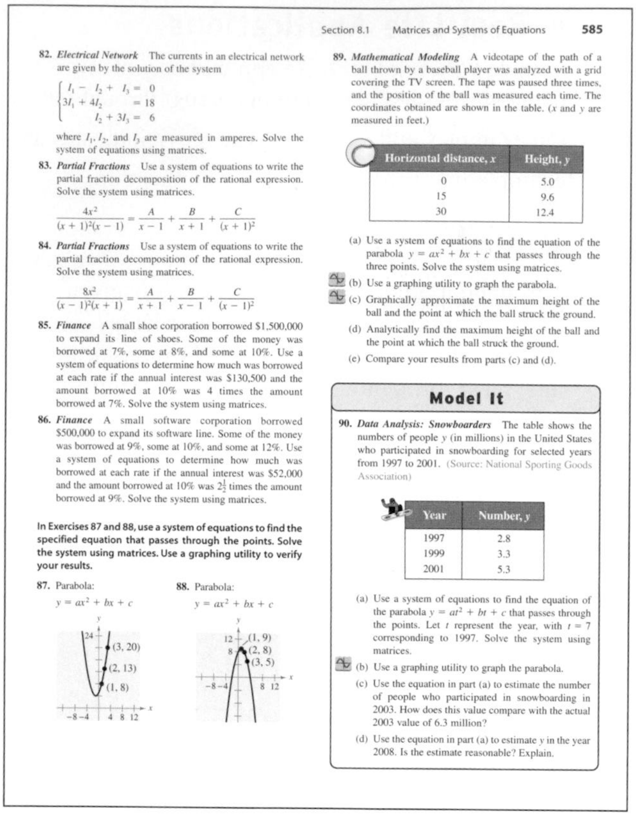

Section 8.1 Matrices and Systems of Equations 585

82. ***Electrical Network*** The currents in an electrical network are given by the solution of the system

$$\begin{cases} I_1 - I_2 + I_3 = 0 \\ 3I_1 + 4I_2 = 18 \\ I_2 + 3I_3 = 6 \end{cases}$$

where I_1, I_2, and I_3 are measured in amperes. Solve the system of equations using matrices.

83. ***Partial Fractions*** Use a system of equations to write the partial fraction decomposition of the rational expression. Solve the system using matrices.

$$\frac{4x^2}{(x+1)^2(x-1)} = \frac{A}{x-1} + \frac{B}{x+1} + \frac{C}{(x+1)^2}$$

84. ***Partial Fractions*** Use a system of equations to write the partial fraction decomposition of the rational expression. Solve the system using matrices.

$$\frac{8x^2}{(x-1)^2(x+1)} = \frac{A}{x+1} + \frac{B}{x-1} + \frac{C}{(x-1)^2}$$

85. ***Finance*** A small shoe corporation borrowed $1,500,000 to expand its line of shoes. Some of the money was borrowed at 7%, some at 8%, and some at 10%. Use a system of equations to determine how much was borrowed at each rate if the annual interest was $130,500 and the amount borrowed at 10% was 4 times the amount borrowed at 7%. Solve the system using matrices.

86. ***Finance*** A small software corporation borrowed $500,000 to expand its software line. Some of the money was borrowed at 9%, some at 10%, and some at 12%. Use a system of equations to determine how much was borrowed at each rate if the annual interest was $52,000 and the amount borrowed at 10% was $2\frac{1}{2}$ times the amount borrowed at 9%. Solve the system using matrices.

In Exercises 87 and 88, use a system of equations to find the specified equation that passes through the points. Solve the system using matrices. Use a graphing utility to verify your results.

87. Parabola: $y = ax^2 + bx + c$

88. Parabola: $y = ax^2 + bx + c$

89. ***Mathematical Modeling*** A videotape of the path of a ball thrown by a baseball player was analyzed with a grid covering the TV screen. The tape was paused three times, and the position of the ball was measured each time. The coordinates obtained are shown in the table. (x and y are measured in feet.)

Horizontal distance, x	Height, y
0	5.0
15	9.6
30	12.4

(a) Use a system of equations to find the equation of the parabola $y = ax^2 + bx + c$ that passes through the three points. Solve the system using matrices.

(b) Use a graphing utility to graph the parabola.

(c) Graphically approximate the maximum height of the ball and the point at which the ball struck the ground.

(d) Analytically find the maximum height of the ball and the point at which the ball struck the ground.

(e) Compare your results from parts (c) and (d).

Model It

90. ***Data Analysis: Snowboarders*** The table shows the numbers of people y (in millions) in the United States who participated in snowboarding for selected years from 1997 to 2001. (Source: National Sporting Goods Association)

Year	Number, y
1997	2.8
1999	3.3
2001	5.3

(a) Use a system of equations to find the equation of the parabola $y = at^2 + bt + c$ that passes through the points. Let t represent the year, with $t = 7$ corresponding to 1997. Solve the system using matrices.

(b) Use a graphing utility to graph the parabola.

(c) Use the equation in part (a) to estimate the number of people who participated in snowboarding in 2003. How does this value compare with the actual 2003 value of 6.3 million?

(d) Use the equation in part (a) to estimate y in the year 2008. Is the estimate reasonable? Explain.

• Model It

These multi-part applications that involve real data offer students the opportunity to generate and analyze mathematical models.

• Synthesis and Skills Review Exercises

Each exercise set concludes with the two types of exercises.

Synthesis exercises promote further exploration of mathematical concepts, critical thinking skills, and writing about mathematics. The exercises require students to show their understanding of the relationships between many concepts in the section.

Skills Review Exercises reinforce previously learned skills and concepts.

Make a Decision exercises, found in selected sections, further connect real-life data and applications and motivate students. They also offer students the opportunity to generate and analyze mathematical models from large data sets.

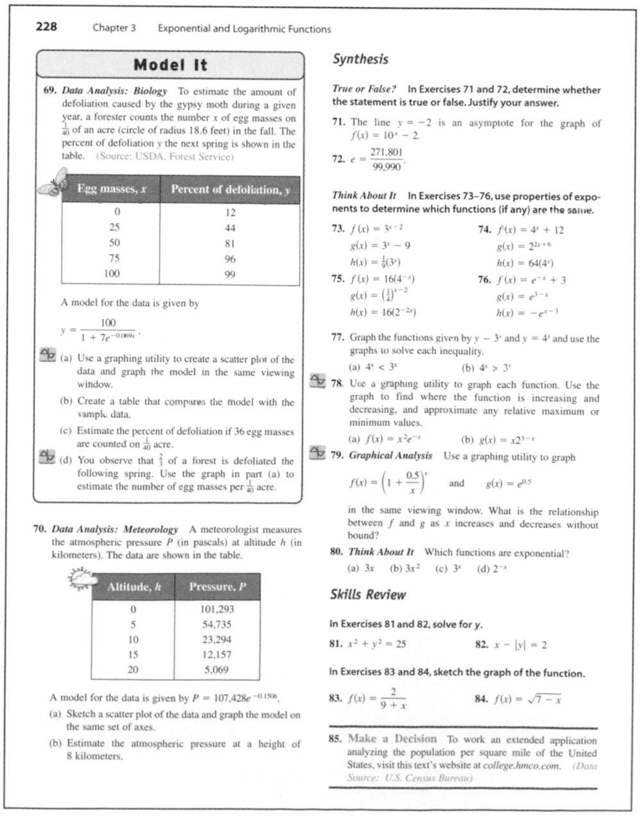

228 Chapter 3 Exponential and Logarithmic Functions

Model It

69. ***Data Analysis: Biology*** To estimate the amount of defoliation caused by the gypsy moth during a given year, a forester counts the number x of egg masses on $\frac{1}{40}$ of an acre (circle of radius 18.6 feet) in the fall. The percent of defoliation y the next spring is shown in the table. (Source: USDA, Forest Service)

Egg masses, x	Percent of defoliation, y
0	12
25	44
50	81
75	96
100	99

A model for the data is given by

$$y = \frac{100}{1 + 7e^{-0.069x}}.$$

(a) Use a graphing utility to create a scatter plot of the data and graph the model in the same viewing window.

(b) Create a table that compares the model with the sample data.

(c) Estimate the percent of defoliation if 36 egg masses are counted on $\frac{1}{40}$ acre.

(d) You observe that $\frac{2}{3}$ of a forest is defoliated the following spring. Use the graph in part (a) to estimate the number of egg masses per $\frac{1}{40}$ acre.

70. ***Data Analysis: Meteorology*** A meteorologist measures the atmospheric pressure P (in pascals) at altitude h (in kilometers). The data are shown in the table.

Altitude, h	Pressure, P
0	101,293
5	54,735
10	23,294
15	12,157
20	5,069

A model for the data is given by $P = 107{,}428e^{-0.150h}$.

(a) Sketch a scatter plot of the data and graph the model on the same set of axes.

(b) Estimate the atmospheric pressure at a height of 8 kilometers.

Synthesis

True or False? **In Exercises 71 and 72, determine whether the statement is true or false. Justify your answer.**

71. The line $y = -2$ is an asymptote for the graph of $f(x) = 10^x - 2$.

72. $e = \frac{271{,}801}{99{,}990}$.

Think About It **In Exercises 73–76, use properties of exponents to determine which functions (if any) are the same.**

73. $f(x) = 3^{x-2}$
$g(x) = 3^x - 9$
$h(x) = \frac{1}{9}(3^x)$

74. $f(x) = 4^x + 12$
$g(x) = 2^{2x+6}$
$h(x) = 64(4^x)$

75. $f(x) = 16(4^{-x})$
$g(x) = \left(\frac{1}{4}\right)^{x-2}$
$h(x) = 16(2^{-2x})$

76. $f(x) = e^{-x} + 3$
$g(x) = e^{3-x}$
$h(x) = -e^{x-3}$

77. Graph the functions given by $y = 3^x$ and $y = 4^x$ and use the graphs to solve each inequality.
(a) $4^x < 3^x$ (b) $4^x > 3^x$

78. Use a graphing utility to graph each function. Use the graph to find where the function is increasing and decreasing, and approximate any relative maximum or minimum values.
(a) $f(x) = x^2e^{-x}$ (b) $g(x) = x2^{3-x}$

79. ***Graphical Analysis*** Use a graphing utility to graph

$$f(x) = \left(1 + \frac{0.5}{x}\right)^x \quad \text{and} \quad g(x) = e^{0.5}$$

in the same viewing window. What is the relationship between f and g as x increases and decreases without bound?

80. ***Think About It*** Which functions are exponential?
(a) $3x$ (b) $3x^2$ (c) 3^x (d) 2^{-x}

Skills Review

In Exercises 81 and 82, solve for y.

81. $x^2 + y^2 = 25$

82. $x - |y| = 2$

In Exercises 83 and 84, sketch the graph of the function.

83. $f(x) = \frac{2}{9 + x}$

84. $f(x) = \sqrt{7 - x}$

85. Make a Decision To work an extended application analyzing the population per square mile of the United States, visit this text's website at *college.hmco.com*. (*Data Source: U.S. Census Bureau*)

• Chapter Summary

The *Chapter Summary* "*What Did You Learn?*" is a section-by-section overview that ties the learning objectives from the chapter to sets of Review Exercises for extra practice.

• Review Exercises

The chapter *Review Exercises* provide additional practice with the concepts covered in the chapter.

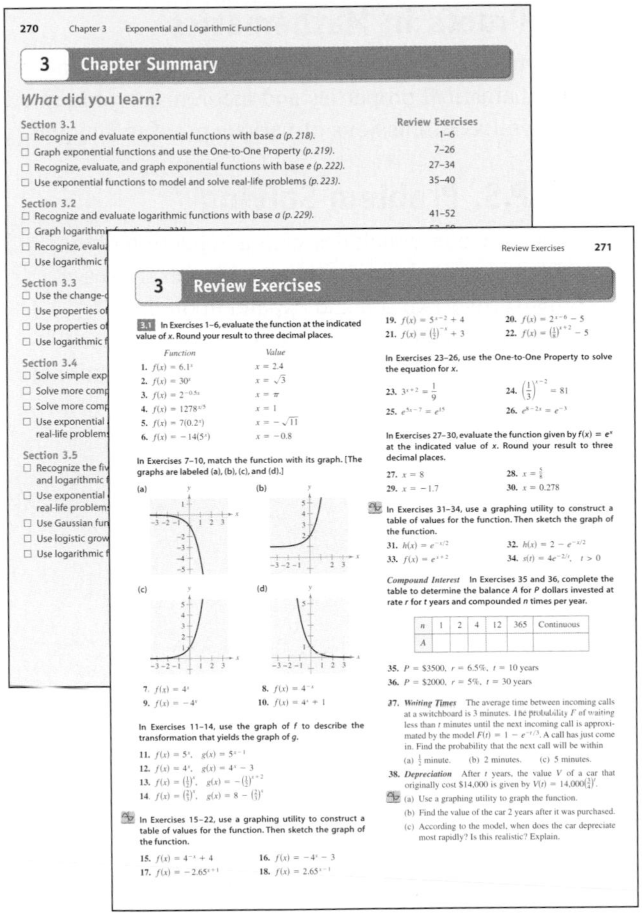

• Chapter Tests and Cumulative Tests

Chapter Tests, at the end of each chapter, and periodic *Cumulative Tests* offer students frequent opportunities for self-assessment and to develop strong study and test-taking skills.

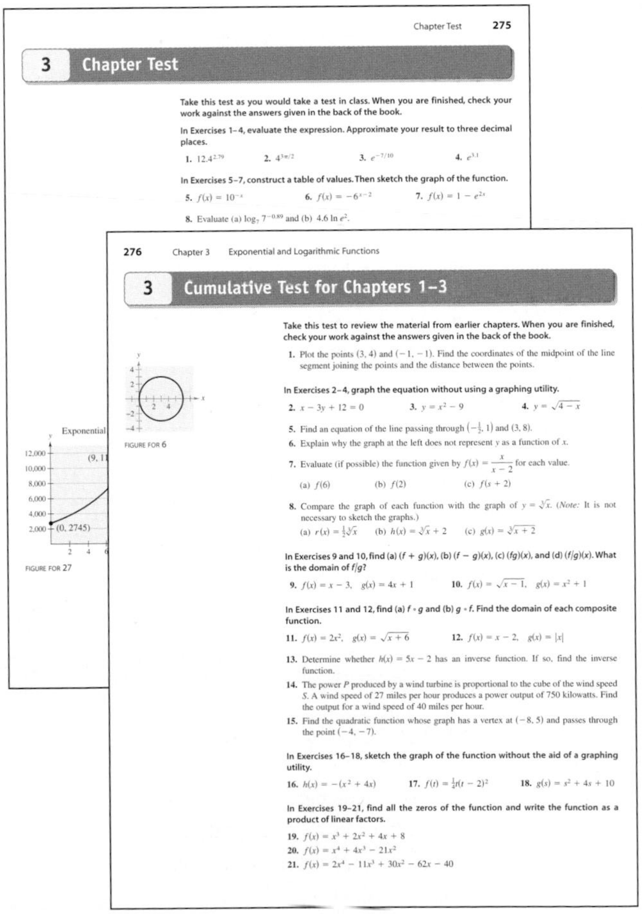

FEATURES

- **Proofs in Mathematics**

At the end of every chapter, proofs of important mathematical properties and theorems are presented as well as discussions of various proof techniques.

- **P.S. Problem Solving**

Each chapter concludes with a collection of thought-provoking and challenging exercises that further explore and expand upon the chapter concepts. These exercises have unusual characteristics that set them apart from traditional text exercises.

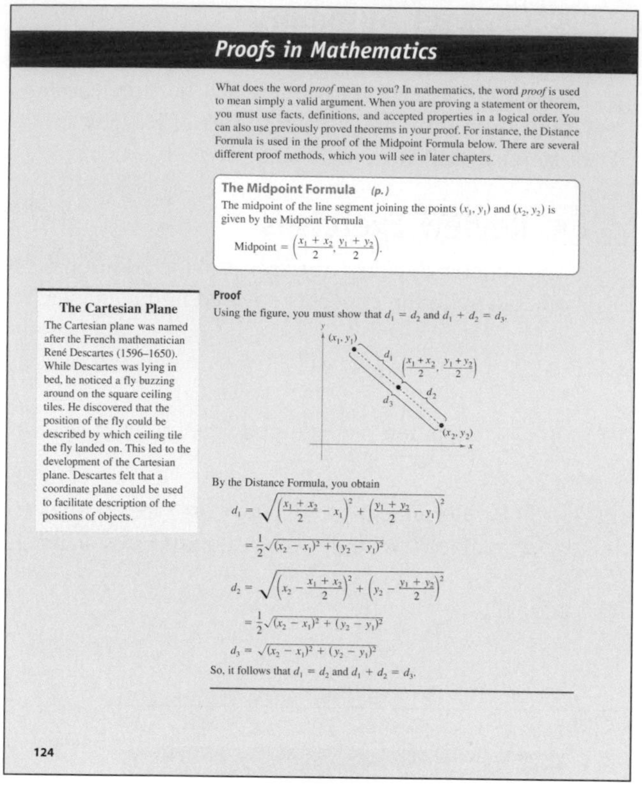

Proofs in Mathematics

What does the word *proof* mean to you? In mathematics, the word *proof* is used to mean simply a valid argument. When you are proving a statement or theorem, you must use facts, definitions, and accepted properties in a logical order. You can also use previously proved theorems in your proof. For instance, the Distance Formula is used in the proof of the Midpoint Formula below. There are several different proof methods, which you will see in later chapters.

The Midpoint Formula *(p.)*

The midpoint of the line segment joining the points (x_1, y_1) and (x_2, y_2) is given by the Midpoint Formula

$$\text{Midpoint} = \left(\frac{x_1 + x_2}{2}, \frac{y_1 + y_2}{2}\right).$$

The Cartesian Plane

The Cartesian plane was named after the French mathematician René Descartes (1596–1650). While Descartes was lying in bed, he noticed a fly buzzing around on the square ceiling tiles. He discovered that the position of the fly could be described by which ceiling tile the fly landed on. This led to the development of the Cartesian plane. Descartes felt that a coordinate plane could be used to facilitate description of the positions of objects.

Proof

Using the figure, you must show that $d_1 = d_2$ and $d_1 + d_2 = d_3$.

By the Distance Formula, you obtain

$$d_1 = \sqrt{\left(\frac{x_1 + x_2}{2} - x_1\right)^2 + \left(\frac{y_1 + y_2}{2} - y_1\right)^2}$$

$$= \frac{1}{2}\sqrt{(x_2 - x_1)^2 + (y_2 - y_1)^2}$$

$$d_2 = \sqrt{\left(x_2 - \frac{x_1 + x_2}{2}\right)^2 + \left(y_2 - \frac{y_1 + y_2}{2}\right)^2}$$

$$= \frac{1}{2}\sqrt{(x_2 - x_1)^2 + (y_2 - y_1)^2}$$

$$d_3 = \sqrt{(x_2 - x_1)^2 + (y_2 - y_1)^2}$$

So, it follows that $d_1 = d_2$ and $d_1 + d_2 = d_3$.

124

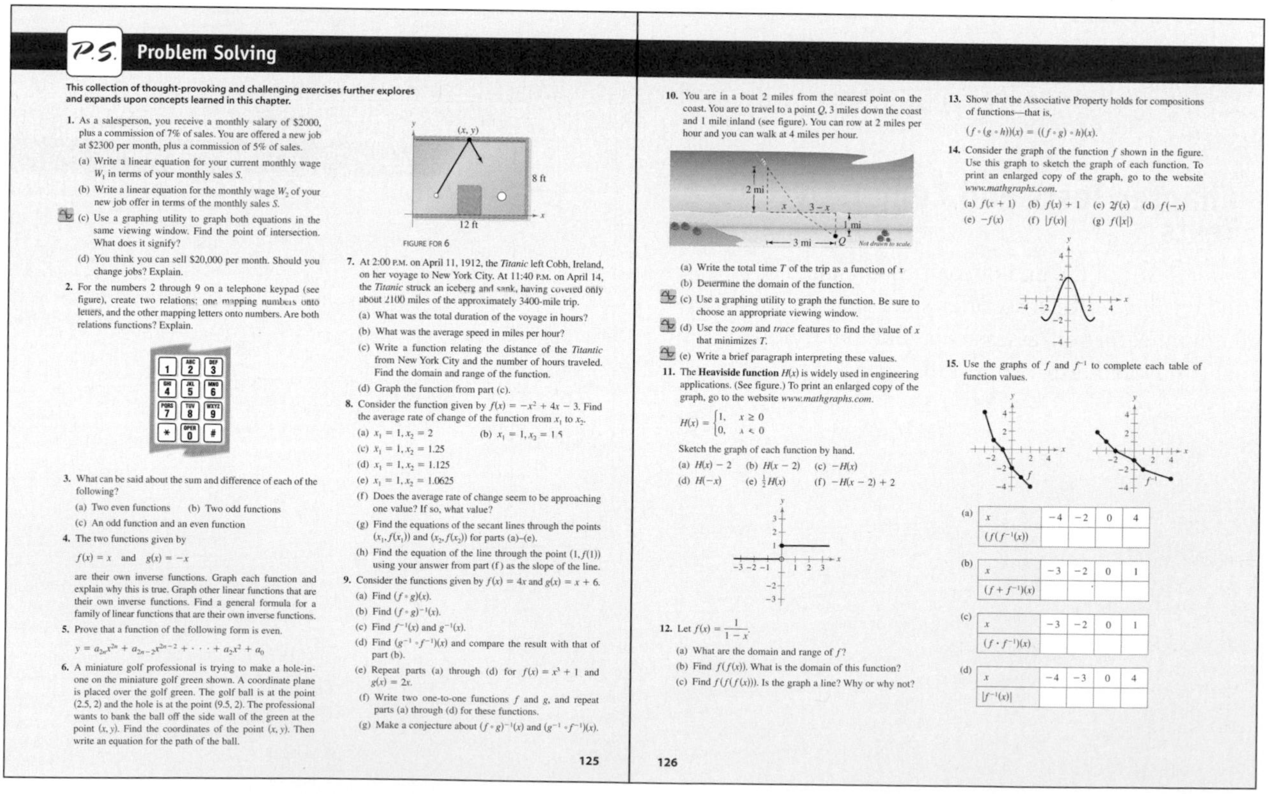

P.S. Problem Solving

This collection of thought-provoking and challenging exercises further explores and expands upon concepts learned in this chapter.

1. As a salesperson, you receive a monthly salary of \$2000, plus a commission of 7% of sales. You are offered a new job at \$2300 per month, plus a commission of 5% of sales.
   (a) Write a linear equation for your current monthly wage W_1 in terms of your monthly sales S.
   (b) Write a linear equation for the monthly wage W_2 of your new job offer in terms of the monthly sales S.
   (c) Use a graphing utility to graph both equations in the same viewing window. Find the point of intersection. What does it signify?
   (d) You think you can sell \$20,000 per month. Should you change jobs? Explain.
2. For the numbers 2 through 9 on a telephone keypad (see figure), create two relations: one mapping numbers onto letters, and the other mapping letters onto numbers. Are both relations functions? Explain.
3. What can be said about the sum and difference of each of the following?
   (a) Two even functions (b) Two odd functions
   (c) An odd function and an even function
4. The two functions given by
   $f(x) = x$ and $g(x) = -x$
   are their own inverse functions. Graph each function and explain why this is true. Graph other linear functions that are their own inverse functions. Find a general formula for a family of linear functions that are their own inverse functions.
5. Prove that a function of the following form is even.
   $y = a_{2n}x^{2n} + a_{2n-2}x^{2n-2} + \cdots + a_2x^2 + a_0$
6. A miniature golf professional is trying to make a hole-in-one on the miniature golf green shown. A coordinate plane is placed over the golf green. The golf ball is at the point (2.5, 2) and the hole is at the point (9.5, 2). The professional wants to bank the ball off the side wall of the green at the point (x, y). Find the coordinates of the point (x, y). Then write an equation for the path of the ball.

FIGURE FOR 6

7. At 2:00 P.M. on April 11, 1912, the *Titanic* left Cobh, Ireland, on her voyage to New York City. At 11:40 P.M. on April 14, the *Titanic* struck an iceberg and sank, having covered only about 2100 miles of the approximately 3400-mile trip.
   (a) What was the total duration of the voyage in hours?
   (b) What was the average speed in miles per hour?
   (c) Write a function relating the distance of the *Titanic* from New York City and the number of hours traveled. Find the domain and range of the function.
   (d) Graph the function from part (c).
8. Consider the function given by $f(x) = -x^2 + 4x - 3$. Find the average rate of change of the function from x_1 to x_2.
   (a) $x_1 = 1, x_2 = 2$ (b) $x_1 = 1, x_2 = 1.5$
   (c) $x_1 = 1, x_2 = 1.25$
   (d) $x_1 = 1, x_2 = 1.125$
   (e) $x_1 = 1, x_2 = 1.0625$
   (f) Does the average rate of change seem to be approaching one value? If so, what value?
   (g) Find the equations of the secant lines through the points $(x_1, f(x_1))$ and $(x_2, f(x_2))$ for parts (a)–(e).
   (h) Find the equation of the line through the point $(1, f(1))$ using your answer from part (f) as the slope of the line.
9. Consider the functions given by $f(x) = 4x$ and $g(x) = x + 6$.
   (a) Find $(f \circ g)(x)$.
   (b) Find $(f \circ g)^{-1}(x)$.
   (c) Find $f^{-1}(x)$ and $g^{-1}(x)$.
   (d) Find $(g^{-1} \circ f^{-1})(x)$ and compare the result with that of part (b).
   (e) Repeat parts (a) through (d) for $f(x) = x^3 + 1$ and $g(x) = 2x$.
   (f) Write two one-to-one functions f and g, and repeat parts (a) through (d) for these functions.
   (g) Make a conjecture about $(f \circ g)^{-1}(x)$ and $(g^{-1} \circ f^{-1})(x)$.

125

10. You are in a boat 2 miles from the nearest point on the coast. You are to travel to a point Q, 3 miles down the coast and 1 mile inland (see figure). You can row at 2 miles per hour and you can walk at 4 miles per hour.
    (a) Write the total time T of the trip as a function of x.
    (b) Determine the domain of the function.
    (c) Use a graphing utility to graph the function. Be sure to choose an appropriate viewing window.
    (d) Use the *zoom* and *trace* features to find the value of x that minimizes T.
    (e) Write a brief paragraph interpreting these values.
11. The **Heaviside function** $H(x)$ is widely used in engineering applications. (See figure.) To print an enlarged copy of the graph, go to the website *www.mathgraphs.com*.
    $H(x) = \begin{cases} 1, & x \ge 0 \\ 0, & x < 0 \end{cases}$
    Sketch the graph of each function by hand.
    (a) $H(x) - 2$ (b) $H(x - 2)$ (c) $-H(x)$
    (d) $H(-x)$ (e) $\frac{1}{2}H(x)$ (f) $-H(x - 2) + 2$
12. Let $f(x) = \dfrac{1}{1 - x}$.
    (a) What are the domain and range of f?
    (b) Find $f(f(x))$. What is the domain of this function?
    (c) Find $f(f(f(x)))$. Is the graph a line? Why or why not?
13. Show that the Associative Property holds for compositions of functions—that is,
    $(f \circ (g \circ h))(x) = ((f \circ g) \circ h)(x)$.
14. Consider the graph of the function f shown in the figure. Use this graph to sketch the graph of each function. To print an enlarged copy of the graph, go to the website *www.mathgraphs.com*.
    (a) $f(x + 1)$ (b) $f(x) + 1$ (c) $2f(x)$ (d) $f(-x)$
    (e) $-f(x)$ (f) $|f(x)|$ (g) $f(|x|)$
15. Use the graphs of f and f^{-1} to complete each table of function values.

(a)

x	-4	-2	0	4
$(f(f^{-1}(x))$				

(b)

x	-3	-2	0	1
$(f + f^{-1})(x)$				

(c)

x	-3	-2	0	1
$(f \cdot f^{-1})(x)$				

(d)

x	-4	-3	0	4
$\lvert f^{-1}(x) \rvert$				

126

Supplements

Supplements for the Student

Precalculus with Limits has an extensive support package for the student that includes:

Study and Solutions Guide

Notetaking Guide

Instructional DVDs

Online Study Center**:** This free companion website contains an abundance of student resources.

HM mathSpace® CD-ROM**:** This tutorial CD-ROM provides opportunities for self-paced review and practice with algorithmically generated exercises and step-by-step solutions.

Texas Applications and Problem Solving

Contents

Chapter 1 Students in Texas xxiii
Chapter 2 Employment in Texas xxiv
Chapter 3 Home Prices in Texas xxv
Chapter 4 Temperatures in Dallas and San Antonio xxvi
Chapter 5 Texas Unemployment Rate xxvii
Chapter 6 Grades of Interstates xxviii
Chapter 7 Texas School Budgets xxix
Chapter 8 Injuries in Texas Prisons xxx
Chapter 9 Record-Based Football Probabilities xxxi
Chapter 10 Hitting a Home Run xxxii
Chapter 11 A Model of Farm Expenses xxxiii
Chapter 12 Jobs in Texas xxxiv

Chapter 1 Texas Applications and Problem Solving

Students in Texas

School administrators estimate the number of students who will be attending school in order to hire teachers, buy books, build new buildings, and plan how many school meals to serve. In order to predict the number of students who will be attending school each year, they write models based on the historic trends in enrollment.

Some factors in determining enrollment are the number of students graduating, the number of children entering preschool, and the number of students moving into or out of the state. A simple model, however, can be obtained from enrollment data for the past several years. The table gives the number of students enrolled in Texas schools from the 1999–2000 school year to the 2004–2005 school year.

School Year	Enrollment
1999–2000	4,002,227
2000–2001	4,071,433
2001–2002	4,160,968
2002–2003	4,255,821
2003–2004	4,328,028
2004–2005	4,400,644

(*Source:* Texas Education Authority)

A linear model for the enrollment E in Texas schools is

$$E = 81{,}620t + 4{,}000{,}000$$

where t represents the school year with $t = 0$ corresponding to the 1999–2000 school year.

In Exercises 1–4, use the table of data and model given above.

1. Let t represent the school year with $t = 0$ corresponding to the 1999–2000 school year and let E represent enrollment. Sketch a scatter plot of the data using ordered pairs of the form (t, E). Sketch the model on the same set of coordinate axes.
2. For which year is the difference between the actual enrollment and the model's predicted enrollment the greatest? What is the difference between actual and predicted enrollment in that year? What is this difference as a percentage of the actual enrollment in that year?
3. Use the model to predict enrollment in the 2010–2011 school year.
4. Do you think that this is a good model for school enrollment? Explain.

Chapter 2 Texas Applications and Problem Solving

Employment in Texas

Economists frequently estimate the number of people employed in Texas. They are interested in how many people are employed in each industry, and in the total number employed in all industries combined. State and national leaders make policy decisions and business people make plans on the basis of these numbers.

Traditionally, people working on farms are not included in the commonly used total employment data statistics. There was a time in the past when most Texans lived and worked on farms and ranches, and economists found it particularly informative to count just those people who took other jobs. The table gives the seasonally adjusted non-farm total employment data for Texas for the years 2004 and 2005.

Month/Year	Employment
January 2004	9,414,800
April 2004	9,464,800
July 2004	9,501,600
October 2004	9,513,600
January 2005	9,553,300
April 2005	9,574,400
July 2005	9,613,200
October 2005	9,645,900

(*Source:* Texas Workforce Commission)

Two models that approximate the Texas non-farm employment E are

$$E = 5500t^2 + 9{,}414{,}500 \qquad \text{and} \qquad E = 33{,}010t + 9{,}414{,}000$$

where t represents the month with $t = 0$ corresponding to January 2004 and $t = 1$ corresponding to April 2004.

In Exercises 1–4, use the table of data and models given above.

1. Let t represent the month with $t = 0$ corresponding to January 2004 and $t = 1$ corresponding to April 2004, and let E represent the number of people employed. Make a scatter plot of the data using ordered pairs of the form (t, E). Then graph the two models on the same set of coordinate axes.
2. For each model, in which month is the difference between the actual employment and the predicted employment the greatest?
3. Which model do you think best represents the data? Explain.
4. Predict the Texas non-farm employment for January 2006. Explain your method.

Chapter 3 Texas Applications and Problem Solving

Home Prices in Texas

In recent years, home prices in Texas have increased rapidly. This often makes it more difficult for young families to buy their first home. The state and federal government attempt to encourage home ownership. Policy makers want to make owning a home affordable for most Texans.

The average price of a home in Texas is an important number that realtors and homeowners keep in mind when determining the value of individual homes. The table gives the average price of a home in Texas from 1980 to 2005.

Year	Average Home Price
1980	$ 61,300
1984	$ 90,000
1987	$ 88,700
1990	$ 87,300
1993	$ 99,300
1996	$110,800
1999	$132,200
2002	$155,600
2005	$174,400

(*Source:* Texas A&M University, Real Estate Center)

In Exercises 1–4, use the table of data given above.

1. Use a graphing utility to create a scatter plot of the data. Let t represent the year with $t = 0$ corresponding to 1980.
2. Use the *regression* feature of the graphing utility to find an exponential model for the data.
3. Use the graphing utility to graph the model in the same viewing window as the scatter plot. How well does the model fit the data?
4. Predict the average home price in Texas for 2010. Does your answer seem reasonable? Explain.

Chapter 4 Texas Applications and Problem Solving

Temperatures in Dallas and San Antonio

The National Oceanic and Atmospheric Administration keeps track of the average temperature in cities such as Dallas and San Antonio for each month of the year. This information is useful to utility companies planning how much energy will be used for heating or cooling during a particular period and for travelers deciding what they will bring when they visit a city.

The temperatures rise and fall in a cyclical pattern as the seasons change. This implies that the temperatures are best modeled by trigonometric functions. The table gives the average temperature (in degrees Fahrenheit) in Dallas and San Antonio for each month of the year.

Month	Dallas	San Antonio
Jan.	55.4	62.1
Feb.	61.0	67.1
Mar.	69.1	74.3
Apr.	76.5	80.4
May	83.8	86.0
June	91.6	91.4
July	96.1	94.6
Aug.	95.8	94.7
Sep.	88.5	90.0
Oct.	78.6	82.0
Nov.	66.0	71.4
Dec.	57.4	64.0

(*Source:* National Oceanic and Atmospheric Administration)

A model for the temperature T in Dallas is given by

$$T(t) = 20.4 \sin(0.5t - 1.9) + 75.6$$

where t represents the month with $t = 1$ corresponding to January.

In Exercises 1–6, use the table of data and model given above.

1. Use a graphing utility to graph the data points for Dallas. Let t represent the month with $t = 1$ corresponding to January.
2. Graph the model for the Dallas temperatures. How well does the model fit the data?
3. Use a graphing utility to graph the data points for San Antonio. Let t represent the month with $t = 1$ corresponding to January.
4. Use the graphing utility to find and graph a trigonometric model for the San Antonio data. How well does the model fit the data?
5. What is the period of each model? Are the periods what you expected? Explain.
6. Which city has the greater variability in temperature throughout the year? Which factor in the equations determines this variability? Explain.

Chapter 5 Texas Applications and Problem Solving

Texas Unemployment Rate

Economists think that unemployment is cyclical. This means that the percentage of people unemployed (the unemployment rate) rises and falls in a cyclical pattern and can be modeled by a trigonometric function. The table gives the Texas unemployment rate for the month of September from 1995 to 2005.

Year	Unemployment Rate (%)
1995	6.1
1996	5.7
1997	5.3
1998	4.9
1999	4.6
2000	4.3
2001	5.3
2002	6.5
2003	6.7
2004	6.0
2005	5.3

(*Source:* U.S. Dept. of Labor, Bureau of Labor Statistics)

In Exercises 1–6, use the table of data given above.

1. Let t represent the year with $t = 0$ corresponding to 1995 and let r represent the unemployment rate. Make a scatter plot of the data using ordered pairs of the form (t, r).
2. Without actually graphing, which of the following models best represents the data? Explain your reasoning.
   A. $r = \sin(0.78t + 0.87) + 5.35$
   B. $r = \sin(0.8t + 0.40) + 4$
   C. $r = \sin(0.3t + 0.85) + 5.9$
   D. $r = \sin(1.8t - 0.05) - 1.4$
3. What term in the best model approximates the average unemployment rate? What is the rate?
4. According to the best model, what is the length of one cycle?
5. Graph the best model for the data to verify your observations.
6. What does the best model predict for the Texas unemployment rate in 2010?

Chapter 6 Texas Applications and Problem Solving

Grades of Interstates

The average grade (or slope) of a road can be found by dividing the change in elevation between two points by the horizontal distance between the points. The direction of each interstate can be expressed in the form of a vector with horizontal and vertical components. Three of the major interstates in Texas connect the cities of Dallas, San Antonio, and Houston. The following information describes the cities and interstates.

- The elevation of San Antonio is 800 feet above sea level.
- The part of Interstate 35 from San Antonio to Dallas can be represented by a vector with a horizontal component of 275 miles and a vertical component of –0.06 mile.
- The part of Interstate 45 from Dallas to Houston can be represented by a vector with a horizontal component of 239 miles and a vertical component of –0.08 mile.
- The distance along Interstate 10 from San Antonio to Houston is 197 miles.

(*Source:* Texas Business and Industry Data Center)

In Exercises 1–4, use the information given above.

1. Use vector addition to calculate the change in horizontal distance and elevation on a trip from San Antonio to Houston via Dallas.
2. What is the elevation of Dallas? of Houston?
3. What is the average grade of each of the interstates to the nearest hundredth of a percent?
4. What conclusions can you make about the terrain of Texas between San Antonio, Houston, and Dallas?

Chapter 7 Texas Applications and Problem Solving

Texas School Budgets

Each school district in Texas has a budget by which to operate. School administrators plan spending so that the expenses for a school are less than the revenue. The greatest yearly expense for a school is *payroll* for teachers and other staff. The cost of building new schools, buying school buses, or other long-term expenses are called *capital expenses*. Schools may also have to pay out money for loans or to people who have bought bonds, which support the schools. These are called *debt service expenses*.

The amount of revenue R per student to Texas schools for the 1999–2000 school year to the 2003–2004 school year can be approximated by

Revenue: $R = 5732(1.025)^t$

where t represents the school year with $t = 0$ corresponding to the 1999–2000 school year. For the same time period, expenses per student for Texas schools can be represented by the following formulas:

Payroll expenses:	$P = 115t + 4598$
Capital expenses:	$C = 18t + 191$
Debt service expenses:	$D = 2t^2 + 8t + 37$
Miscellaneous expenses:	$M = 19t + 894$

(*Source:* Texas Education Agency)

In Exercises 1–5, use the information given above.

1. Find an equation that represents the total expenses E per student.
2. Graph the models for the revenue per student and the total expenses per student on the same set of coordinate axes.
3. In which school year is the revenue per student approximately equal to the total expenses per student? Explain.
4. In which school year is the difference between the revenue per student and the expenses per student the greatest? What is the difference?
5. In which school year is the percentage that capital expenses are of total expenses the greatest? What is the percentage?

Chapter 8 Texas Applications and Problem Solving

Injuries in Texas Prisons

The Texas Department of Criminal Justice attempts to prevent injuries to both employees and prisoners in the system. It tracks the number of injuries each month as part of its effort to find ways to prevent future injuries. The table gives the number of injuries incurred by Texas prisoners in each of the first three months of 2005.

Month	**Number of prisoner injuries, y**
January	1002
February	938
March	1150

(*Source:* Texas Department of Criminal Justice)

In Exercises 1–4, use the table of data given above.

1. Let x represent the month with $x = 1$ corresponding to January of 2005. Create a system of linear equations for the data by substituting each of the coordinates (x, y) into the equation $y = ax^2 + bx + c$.
2. Use Cramer's rule to solve the system of equations from Exercise 1 and find the least squares regression parabola $y = ax^2 + bx + c$.
3. Use a graphing utility to graph the parabola from Exercise 2.
4. Use the graph from Exercise 3 to estimate in what month the number of prison injuries will reach 2400. Does this seem reasonable? Explain.

Chapter 9 Texas Applications and Problem Solving

Record-Based Football Probabilities

One way to predict which of two football teams will win a future game is by comparing the historic win/loss records of the teams. The win/loss record can be calculated by dividing the number of wins by the total number of wins and losses (ignore the ties). A simple formula for the probability P that a team will win a football game is:

$$P = \frac{1 + H - A}{2}$$

where H is the team's win/loss record and A is the opposing team's win/loss record. The table gives the historic records of some college football teams in Texas.

Team	Wins	Losses	Ties
University of Texas	800	313	34
Texas A&M	639	415	48
Baylor	510	497	43
Texas Tech	474	378	32
North Texas	458	403	33
Rice	406	520	32
Texas El Paso	340	491	29

(*Source:* College Football Data Warehouse)

In Exercises 1–5, use the model and table of data given above.

1. Calculate the win/loss record for each team in the table. Round answers to the nearest thousandth.
2. Which match-up of two teams would give the highest probability of one team winning? What is that probability?
3. In which match-up of two teams would there be the least difference in the probabilities of the two teams winning? What are those probabilities?
4. Explain why this method for predicting the winner of a football game might be appropriate. What factors might it overlook?
5. Assume that *Texas El Paso* plays 12 games per season and begins a winning streak in which it wins every game. If *University of Texas* maintains its current win/loss record, after how many seasons would the win/loss record of *Texas El Paso* be better than that of *University of Texas*?

Chapter 10 Texas Applications and Problem Solving

Hitting a Home Run

Not all baseball parks have the same dimensions or the same outfield wall height. This makes hitting a home run more challenging in some parks than in others. Ameriquest Field is home to the Texas Rangers baseball team. The table gives some facts about the size of the playing field at Ameriquest Field.

Part of field	Distance from home plate	Height of outfield wall
left field	332 ft	14 ft
center field	400 ft	8 ft
right field	325 ft	8 ft

(*Source:* Texas Rangers)

Suppose a projectile, such as a baseball, is launched at a height of h feet above the ground at an angle of θ with the horizontal. The initial velocity is v_0 feet per second and the path of the projectile can be modeled by the parametric equations

$$x = (v_0 \cos \theta)t \qquad \text{and} \qquad y = h + (v_0 \sin \theta)t - 16t^2.$$

A baseball player at Ameriquest Field hits a baseball in the direction of center field at a point 3.25 feet above the ground. The ball leaves the bat at an angle of θ degrees with the horizontal at a speed of 98 miles per hour.

In Exercises 1–4, use the information given above.

1. Write a set of parametric equations that model the path of the baseball.
2. Use a graphing utility to graph the path of the baseball when $\theta = 16°$. Is the hit a home run?
3. Use a graphing utility to graph the path of the baseball when $\theta = 24°$. Is the hit a home run?
4. Find the minimum angle required for the hit to be a home run.

Chapter 11 Texas Applications and Problem Solving

A Model of Farm Expenses

The table gives the average value of farmland, the number of workers employed on farms, and the total revenue from agriculture in Texas from 2000–2004.

Year	Average value, V, of farmland (in dollars per acre)	Farm employment, E (in thousands)	Total revenue, R (in millions of dollars)
2000	680	1002	12,925
2001	730	886	13,627
2002	775	1242	12,537
2003	810	1450	14,879
2004	855	1569	16,055

(*Source:* Bureau of Labor Statistics, Federal Census Bureau, and Texas Comptroller of Public Accounts)

In Exercises 1–4, use the table of data given above.

1. Use the regression feature of a graphing utility to find quadratic models for each column of data in the table. Let t represent the year with $t = 0$ corresponding to the year 2000.
2. Do the models suggest that the productivity (revenue per worker) of Texas farms will increase or decrease in the future? Explain.
3. Is total revenue increasing faster than the average value of farmland?
4. Find a quadratic model for the total revenue in terms of the farm employment. Does the model make reasonable predictions about how the two variables relate? Explain.

Jobs in Texas

The federal government takes an economic census of the United States, which includes statistics on how many Texans are employed in different industries. The trends shown by the data allow economists to predict what industries will have the most available jobs in the future, and high school counselors use those predictions when they talk to students about their career plans. The table gives the number of employees in five large industry groups in Texas for each of three years.

Industry	1992	1997	2002
Mining	106,018	106,954	113,494
Manufacturing	887,814	985,731	855,658
Transportation and Communication	334,567	423,790	554,638
Retail	1,230,404	1,464,183	1,026,326
Service	1,430,220	1,968,608	1,739,925

(*Source:* Federal Census Bureau)

In Exercises 1–5, use the table of data given above.

1. Use the regression feature of a graphing utility to find linear models for the number N of employees in each industry group. Let t represent the year with $t = 0$ corresponding to 1992. Then graph all five models in the same viewing window.
2. Which industry group shows the fastest growth?
3. What is the limit for the number of manufacturing employees in Texas as time approaches infinity? How does this answer change if you assume the number of employees must be greater than or equal to zero?
4. Which of these industry groups might have the greatest number of employees in 2007?
5. Does the prediction that you made in Exercise 4 seem reasonable? Why or why not?

Functions and Their Graphs

1

1.1 Rectangular Coordinates

1.2 Graphs of Equations

1.3 Linear Equations in Two Variables

1.4 Functions

1.5 Analyzing Graphs of Functions

1.6 A Library of Parent Functions

1.7 Transformation of Functions

1.8 Combinations of Functions: Composite Functions

1.9 Inverse Functions

1.10 Mathematical Modeling and Variation

Functions play a primary role in modeling real-life situations. The estimated growth in the number of digital music sales in the United States can be modeled by a cubic function.

SELECTED APPLICATIONS

Functions have many real-life applications. The applications listed below represent a small sample of the applications in this chapter.

- Data Analysis: Mail, Exercise 69, page 12
- Population Statistics, Exercise 75, page 24
- College Enrollment, Exercise 109, page 37
- Cost, Revenue, and Profit, Exercise 97, page 52
- Digital Music Sales, Exercise 89, page 64
- Fluid Flow, Exercise 70, page 68
- Fuel Use, Exercise 67, page 82
- Consumer Awareness, Exercise 68, page 92
- Diesel Mechanics, Exercise 83, page 102

1.1 Rectangular Coordinates

What you should learn

- Plot points in the Cartesian plane.
- Use the Distance Formula to find the distance between two points.
- Use the Midpoint Formula to find the midpoint of a line segment.
- Use a coordinate plane and geometric formulas to model and solve real-life problems.

Why you should learn it

The Cartesian plane can be used to represent relationships between two variables. For instance, in Exercise 60 on page 12, a graph represents the minimum wage in the United States from 1950 to 2004.

The Cartesian Plane

Just as you can represent real numbers by points on a real number line, you can represent ordered pairs of real numbers by points in a plane called the **rectangular coordinate system,** or the **Cartesian plane,** named after the French mathematician René Descartes (1596–1650).

The Cartesian plane is formed by using two real number lines intersecting at right angles, as shown in Figure 1.1. The horizontal real number line is usually called the ***x*-axis,** and the vertical real number line is usually called the ***y*-axis.** The point of intersection of these two axes is the **origin,** and the two axes divide the plane into four parts called **quadrants.**

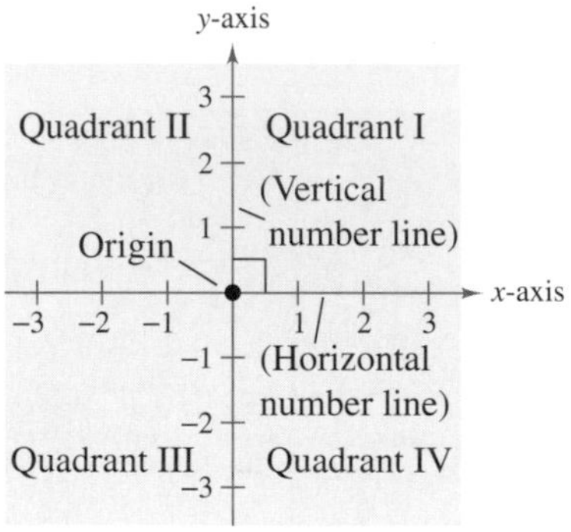

FIGURE 1.1

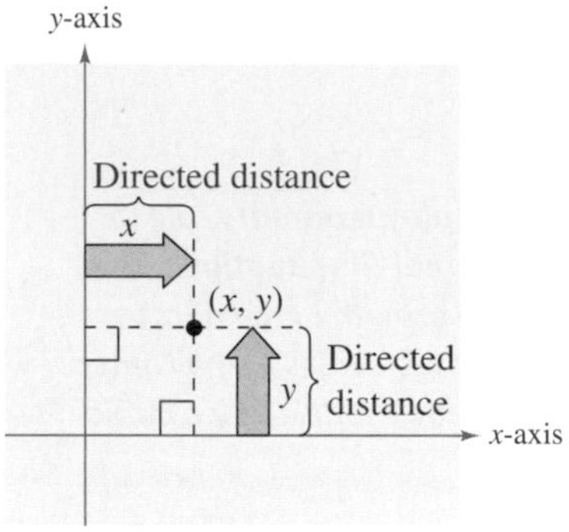

FIGURE 1.2

Each point in the plane corresponds to an **ordered pair** (x, y) of real numbers x and y, called **coordinates** of the point. The ***x*-coordinate** represents the directed distance from the y-axis to the point, and the ***y*-coordinate** represents the directed distance from the x-axis to the point, as shown in Figure 1.2.

Directed distance from y-axis → (x, y) ← Directed distance from x-axis

The notation (x, y) denotes both a point in the plane and an open interval on the real number line. The context will tell you which meaning is intended.

Example 1 Plotting Points in the Cartesian Plane

Plot the points $(-1, 2)$, $(3, 4)$, $(0, 0)$, $(3, 0)$, and $(-2, -3)$.

Solution

To plot the point $(-1, 2)$, imagine a vertical line through -1 on the x-axis and a horizontal line through 2 on the y-axis. The intersection of these two lines is the point $(-1, 2)$. The other four points can be plotted in a similar way, as shown in Figure 1.3.

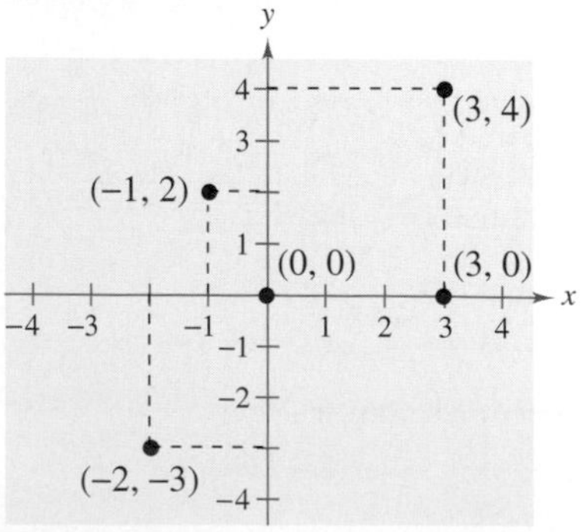

FIGURE 1.3

✓CHECKPOINT Now try Exercise 3.

The beauty of a rectangular coordinate system is that it allows you to *see* relationships between two variables. It would be difficult to overestimate the importance of Descartes's introduction of coordinates in the plane. Today, his ideas are in common use in virtually every scientific and business-related field.

Example 2 Sketching a Scatter Plot

Year, t	Amount, A
1990	475
1991	577
1992	521
1993	569
1994	609
1995	562
1996	707
1997	723
1998	718
1999	648
2000	495
2001	476
2002	527
2003	464

From 1990 through 2003, the amounts A (in millions of dollars) spent on skiing equipment in the United States are shown in the table, where t represents the year. Sketch a scatter plot of the data. (Source: National Sporting Goods Association)

Solution

To sketch a *scatter plot* of the data shown in the table, you simply represent each pair of values by an ordered pair (t, A) and plot the resulting points, as shown in Figure 1.4. For instance, the first pair of values is represented by the ordered pair (1990, 475). Note that the break in the t-axis indicates that the numbers between 0 and 1990 have been omitted.

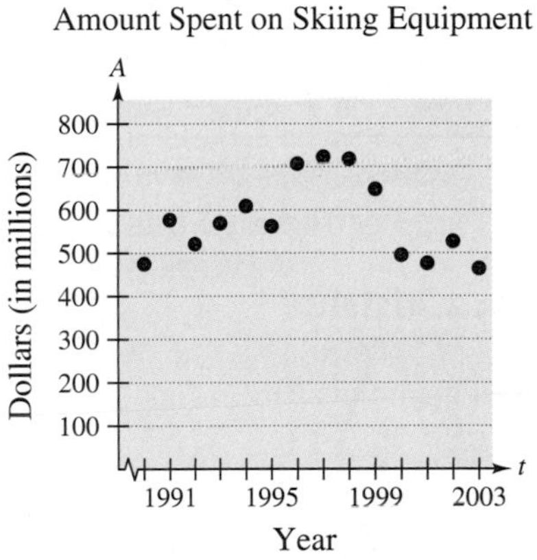

FIGURE 1.4

CHECKPOINT Now try Exercise 21.

In Example 2, you could have let $t = 1$ represent the year 1990. In that case, the horizontal axis would not have been broken, and the tick marks would have been labeled 1 through 14 (instead of 1990 through 2003).

Technology

The scatter plot in Example 2 is only one way to represent the data graphically. You could also represent the data using a bar graph and a line graph. If you have access to a graphing utility, try using it to represent graphically the data given in Example 2.

The Pythagorean Theorem and the Distance Formula

The following famous theorem is used extensively throughout this course.

> **Pythagorean Theorem**
>
> For a right triangle with hypotenuse of length c and sides of lengths a and b, you have $a^2 + b^2 = c^2$, as shown in Figure 1.5. (The converse is also true. That is, if $a^2 + b^2 = c^2$, then the triangle is a right triangle.)

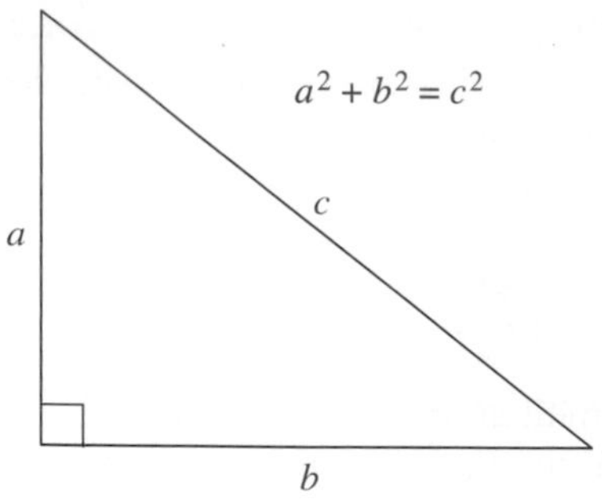

FIGURE 1.5

Suppose you want to determine the distance d between two points (x_1, y_1) and (x_2, y_2) in the plane. With these two points, a right triangle can be formed, as shown in Figure 1.6. The length of the vertical side of the triangle is $|y_2 - y_1|$, and the length of the horizontal side is $|x_2 - x_1|$. By the Pythagorean Theorem, you can write

$$d^2 = |x_2 - x_1|^2 + |y_2 - y_1|^2$$

$$d = \sqrt{|x_2 - x_1|^2 + |y_2 - y_1|^2} = \sqrt{(x_2 - x_1)^2 + (y_2 - y_1)^2}.$$

This result is the **Distance Formula.**

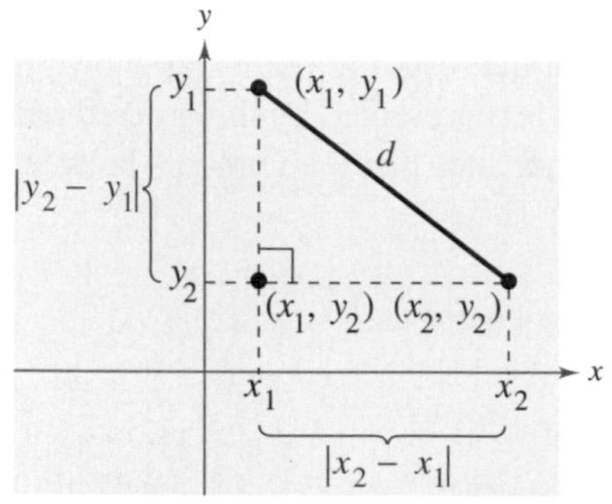

FIGURE 1.6

> **The Distance Formula**
>
> The distance d between the points (x_1, y_1) and (x_2, y_2) in the plane is
>
> $$d = \sqrt{(x_2 - x_1)^2 + (y_2 - y_1)^2}.$$

Example 3 Finding a Distance

Find the distance between the points $(-2, 1)$ and $(3, 4)$.

Algebraic Solution

Let $(x_1, y_1) = (-2, 1)$ and $(x_2, y_2) = (3, 4)$. Then apply the Distance Formula.

$d = \sqrt{(x_2 - x_1)^2 + (y_2 - y_1)^2}$	Distance Formula
$= \sqrt{[3 - (-2)]^2 + (4 - 1)^2}$	Substitute for $x_1, y_1, x_2,$ and y_2.
$= \sqrt{(5)^2 + (3)^2}$	Simplify.
$= \sqrt{34}$	Simplify.
≈ 5.83	Use a calculator.

So, the distance between the points is about 5.83 units. You can use the Pythagorean Theorem to check that the distance is correct.

$d^2 \stackrel{?}{=} 3^2 + 5^2$	Pythagorean Theorem
$(\sqrt{34})^2 \stackrel{?}{=} 3^2 + 5^2$	Substitute for d.
$34 = 34$	Distance checks. ✓

Graphical Solution

Use centimeter graph paper to plot the points $A(-2, 1)$ and $B(3, 4)$. Carefully sketch the line segment from A to B. Then use a centimeter ruler to measure the length of the segment.

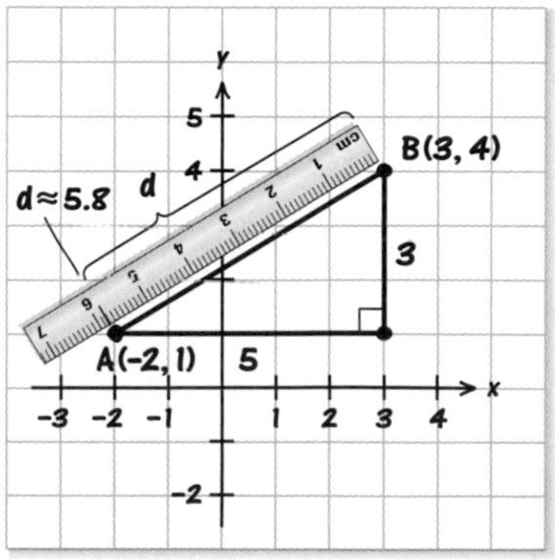

FIGURE 1.7

The line segment measures about 5.8 centimeters, as shown in Figure 1.7. So, the distance between the points is about 5.8 units.

✓CHECKPOINT Now try Exercises 31(a) and (b).

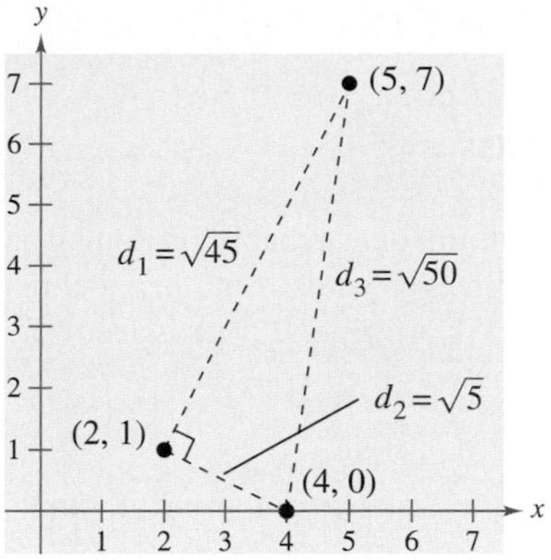

FIGURE 1.8

Example 4 **Verifying a Right Triangle**

Show that the points (2, 1), (4, 0), and (5, 7) are vertices of a right triangle.

Solution

The three points are plotted in Figure 1.8. Using the Distance Formula, you can find the lengths of the three sides as follows.

$$d_1 = \sqrt{(5-2)^2 + (7-1)^2} = \sqrt{9+36} = \sqrt{45}$$

$$d_2 = \sqrt{(4-2)^2 + (0-1)^2} = \sqrt{4+1} = \sqrt{5}$$

$$d_3 = \sqrt{(5-4)^2 + (7-0)^2} = \sqrt{1+49} = \sqrt{50}$$

Because

$$(d_1)^2 + (d_2)^2 = 45 + 5 = 50 = (d_3)^2$$

you can conclude by the Pythagorean Theorem that the triangle must be a right triangle.

CHECKPOINT Now try Exercise 41.

The Midpoint Formula

To find the **midpoint** of the line segment that joins two points in a coordinate plane, you can simply find the average values of the respective coordinates of the two endpoints using the **Midpoint Formula.**

The Midpoint Formula

The midpoint of the line segment joining the points (x_1, y_1) and (x_2, y_2) is given by the Midpoint Formula

$$\text{Midpoint} = \left(\frac{x_1 + x_2}{2}, \frac{y_1 + y_2}{2}\right).$$

For a proof of the Midpoint Formula, see Proofs in Mathematics on page 124.

Example 5 **Finding a Line Segment's Midpoint**

Find the midpoint of the line segment joining the points $(-5, -3)$ and $(9, 3)$.

Solution

Let $(x_1, y_1) = (-5, -3)$ and $(x_2, y_2) = (9, 3)$.

$$\text{Midpoint} = \left(\frac{x_1 + x_2}{2}, \frac{y_1 + y_2}{2}\right) \quad \text{Midpoint Formula}$$

$$= \left(\frac{-5 + 9}{2}, \frac{-3 + 3}{2}\right) \quad \text{Substitute for } x_1, y_1, x_2, \text{ and } y_2.$$

$$= (2, 0) \quad \text{Simplify.}$$

The midpoint of the line segment is (2, 0), as shown in Figure 1.9.

CHECKPOINT Now try Exercise 31(c).

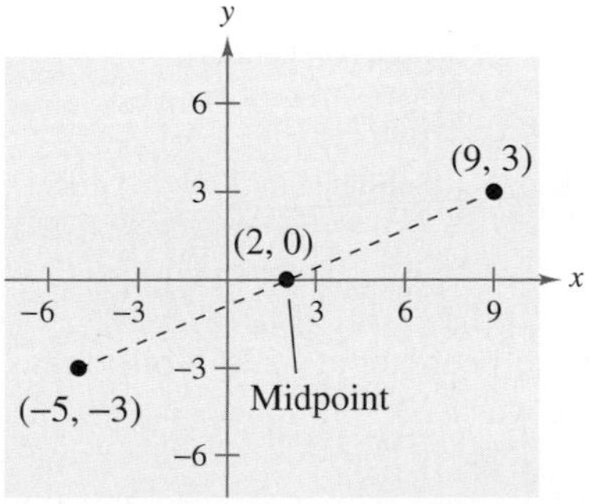

FIGURE 1.9

Applications

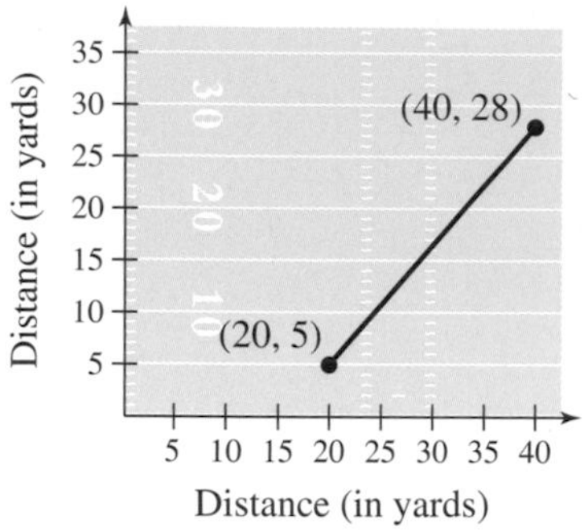

FIGURE 1.10

Example 6 Finding the Length of a Pass

During the third quarter of the 2004 Sugar Bowl, the quarterback for Louisiana State University threw a pass from the 28-yard line, 40 yards from the sideline. The pass was caught by a wide receiver on the 5-yard line, 20 yards from the same sideline, as shown in Figure 1.10. How long was the pass?

Solution

You can find the length of the pass by finding the distance between the points (40, 28) and (20, 5).

$$d = \sqrt{(x_2 - x_1)^2 + (y_2 - y_1)^2} \qquad \text{Distance Formula}$$

$$= \sqrt{(40 - 20)^2 + (28 - 5)^2} \qquad \text{Substitute for } x_1, y_1, x_2, \text{ and } y_2.$$

$$= \sqrt{400 + 529} \qquad \text{Simplify.}$$

$$= \sqrt{929} \qquad \text{Simplify.}$$

$$\approx 30 \qquad \text{Use a calculator.}$$

So, the pass was about 30 yards long.

CHECKPOINT Now try Exercise 47.

In Example 6, the scale along the goal line does not normally appear on a football field. However, when you use coordinate geometry to solve real-life problems, you are free to place the coordinate system in any way that is convenient for the solution of the problem.

Example 7 Estimating Annual Revenue

FedEx Corporation had annual revenues of \$20.6 billion in 2002 and \$24.7 billion in 2004. Without knowing any additional information, what would you estimate the 2003 revenue to have been? (Source: FedEx Corp.)

Solution

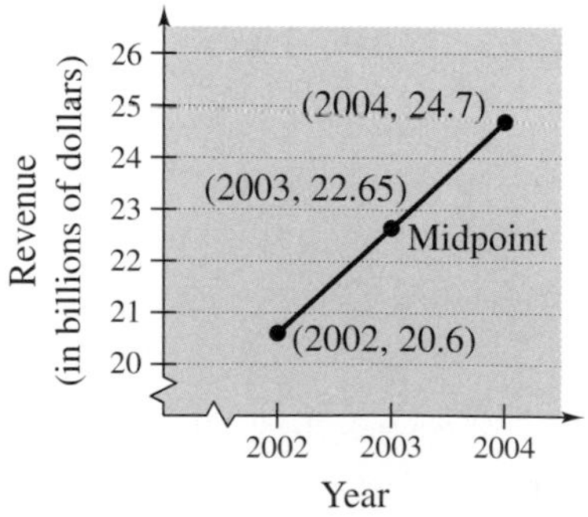

FIGURE 1.11

One solution to the problem is to assume that revenue followed a linear pattern. With this assumption, you can estimate the 2003 revenue by finding the midpoint of the line segment connecting the points (2002, 20.6) and (2004, 24.7).

$$\text{Midpoint} = \left(\frac{x_1 + x_2}{2}, \frac{y_1 + y_2}{2}\right) \qquad \text{Midpoint Formula}$$

$$= \left(\frac{2002 + 2004}{2}, \frac{20.6 + 24.7}{2}\right) \qquad \text{Substitute for } x_1, y_1, x_2, \text{ and } y_2.$$

$$= (2003, 22.65) \qquad \text{Simplify.}$$

So, you would estimate the 2003 revenue to have been about \$22.65 billion, as shown in Figure 1.11. (The actual 2003 revenue was \$22.5 billion.)

CHECKPOINT Now try Exercise 49.

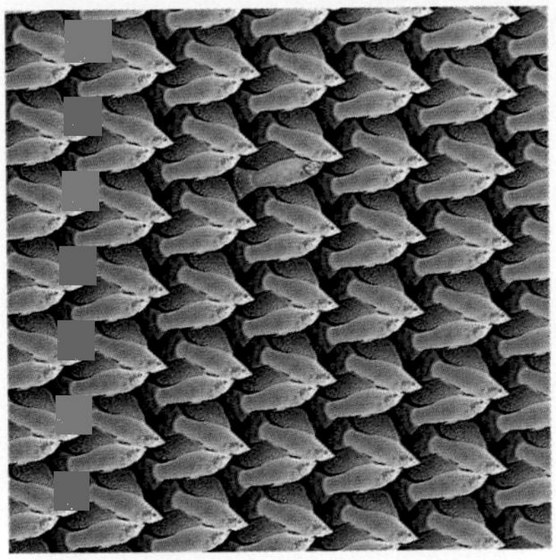

Paul Morrell

Much of computer graphics, including this computer-generated goldfish tessellation, consists of transformations of points in a coordinate plane. One type of transformation, a translation, is illustrated in Example 8. Other types include reflections, rotations, and stretches.

Example 8 Translating Points in the Plane

The triangle in Figure 1.12 has vertices at the points $(-1, 2)$, $(1, -4)$, and $(2, 3)$. Shift the triangle three units to the right and two units upward and find the vertices of the shifted triangle, as shown in Figure 1.13.

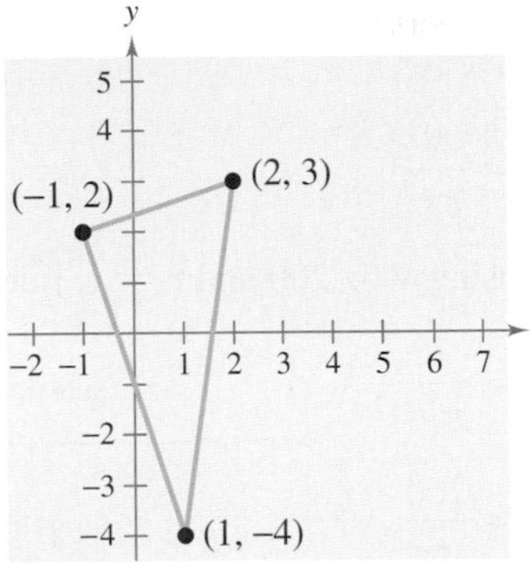

FIGURE 1.12

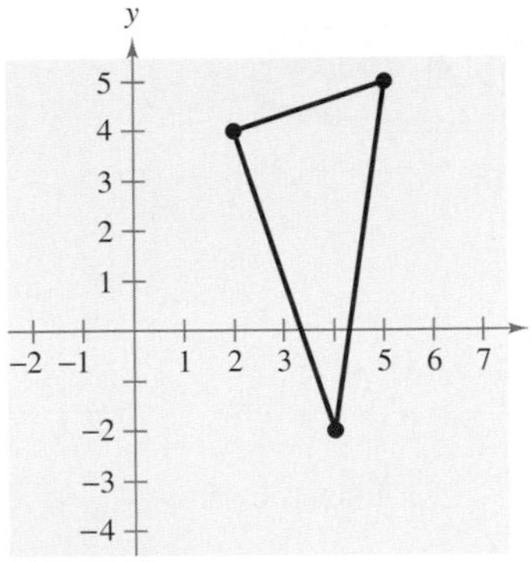

FIGURE 1.13

Solution

To shift the vertices three units to the right, add 3 to each of the x-coordinates. To shift the vertices two units upward, add 2 to each of the y-coordinates.

Original Point	*Translated Point*
$(-1, 2)$	$(-1 + 3, 2 + 2) = (2, 4)$
$(1, -4)$	$(1 + 3, -4 + 2) = (4, -2)$
$(2, 3)$	$(2 + 3, 3 + 2) = (5, 5)$

CHECKPOINT Now try Exercise 51.

The figures provided with Example 8 were not really essential to the solution. Nevertheless, it is strongly recommended that you develop the habit of including sketches with your solutions—even if they are not required.

The following geometric formulas are used at various times throughout this course. For your convenience, these formulas along with several others are also provided on the inside back cover of this text.

Common Formulas for Area *A*, Perimeter *P*, Circumference *C*, and Volume *V*

Rectangle	*Circle*	*Triangle*	*Rectangular Solid*	*Circular Cylinder*	*Sphere*
$A = lw$	$A = \pi r^2$	$A = \frac{1}{2}bh$	$V = lwh$	$V = \pi r^2 h$	$V = \frac{4}{3}\pi r^3$
$P = 2l + 2w$	$C = 2\pi r$	$P = a + b + c$			
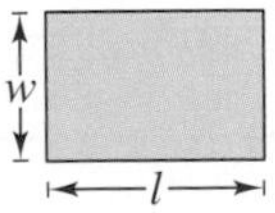	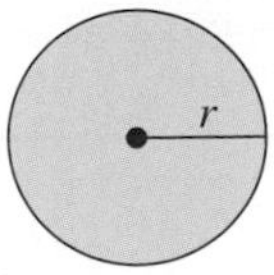	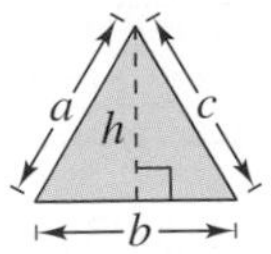	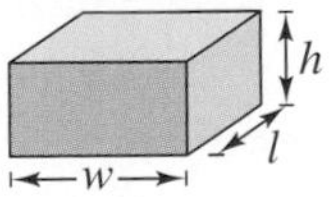	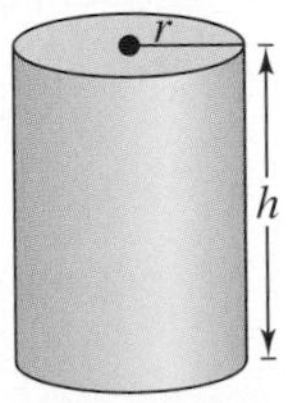	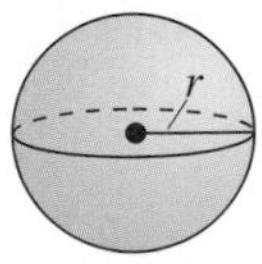

Example 9 Using a Geometric Formula

FIGURE 1.14

A cylindrical can has a volume of 200 cubic centimeters (cm^3) and a radius of 4 centimeters (cm), as shown in Figure 1.14. Find the height of the can.

Solution

The formula for the *volume of a cylinder* is $V = \pi r^2 h$. To find the height of the can, solve for h.

$$h = \frac{V}{\pi r^2}$$

Then, using $V = 200$ and $r = 4$, find the height.

$$h = \frac{200}{\pi(4)^2} \quad \text{Substitute 200 for } V \text{ and 4 for } r.$$

$$= \frac{200}{16\pi} \quad \text{Simplify denominator.}$$

$$\approx 3.98 \quad \text{Use a calculator.}$$

Because the value of h was rounded in the solution, a check of the solution will not result in an equality. If the solution is valid, the expressions on each side of the equal sign will be approximately equal to each other.

$$V = \pi r^2 h \quad \text{Write original equation.}$$

$$200 \stackrel{?}{\approx} \pi(4)^2(3.98) \quad \text{Substitute 200 for } V\text{, 4 for } r\text{, and 3.98 for } h.$$

$$200 \approx 200.06 \quad \text{Solution checks. ✓}$$

You can also use unit analysis to check that your answer is reasonable.

$$\frac{200\ \cancel{cm}^3}{16\pi\ \cancel{cm^2}} \approx 3.98 \text{ cm}$$

✓CHECKPOINT Now try Exercise 63.

WRITING ABOUT MATHEMATICS

Extending the Example Example 8 shows how to translate points in a coordinate plane. Write a short paragraph describing how each of the following transformed points is related to the original point.

Original Point	*Transformed Point*
(x, y)	$(-x, y)$
(x, y)	$(x, -y)$
(x, y)	$(-x, -y)$

1.1 Exercises

VOCABULARY CHECK

1. Match each term with its definition.

(a) x-axis	(i) point of intersection of vertical axis and horizontal axis
(b) y-axis	(ii) directed distance from the x-axis
(c) origin	(iii) directed distance from the y-axis
(d) quadrants	(iv) four regions of the coordinate plane
(e) x-coordinate	(v) horizontal real number line
(f) y-coordinate	(vi) vertical real number line

In Exercises 2–4, fill in the blanks.

2. An ordered pair of real numbers can be represented in a plane called the rectangular coordinate system or the ________ plane.
3. The ________ ________ is a result derived from the Pythagorean Theorem.
4. Finding the average values of the representative coordinates of the two endpoints of a line segment in a coordinate plane is also known as using the ________ ________.

In Exercises 1 and 2, approximate the coordinates of the points.

1.

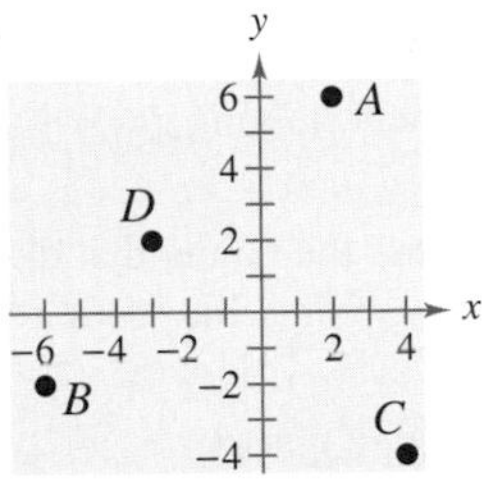

2.

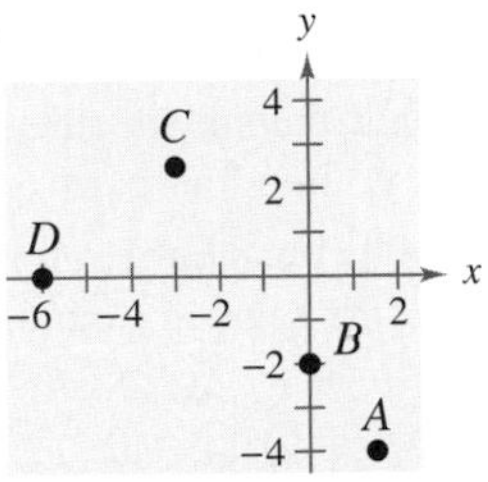

In Exercises 3–6, plot the points in the Cartesian plane.

3. $(-4, 2), (-3, -6), (0, 5), (1, -4)$
4. $(0, 0), (3, 1), (-2, 4), (1, -1)$
5. $(3, 8), (0.5, -1), (5, -6), (-2, 2.5)$
6. $\left(1, -\frac{1}{3}\right), \left(\frac{3}{4}, 3\right), (-3, 4), \left(-\frac{4}{3}, -\frac{3}{2}\right)$

In Exercises 7–10, find the coordinates of the point.

7. The point is located three units to the left of the y-axis and four units above the x-axis.
8. The point is located eight units below the x-axis and four units to the right of the y-axis.
9. The point is located five units below the x-axis and the coordinates of the point are equal.
10. The point is on the x-axis and 12 units to the left of the y-axis.

In Exercises 11–20, determine the quadrant(s) in which (x, y) is located so that the condition(s) is (are) satisfied.

11. $x > 0$ and $y < 0$
12. $x < 0$ and $y < 0$
13. $x = -4$ and $y > 0$
14. $x > 2$ and $y = 3$
15. $y < -5$
16. $x > 4$
17. $x < 0$ and $-y > 0$
18. $-x > 0$ and $y < 0$
19. $xy > 0$
20. $xy < 0$

In Exercises 21 and 22, sketch a scatter plot of the data shown in the table.

21. *Number of Stores* The table shows the number y of Wal-Mart stores for each year x from 1996 through 2003. (Source: Wal-Mart Stores, Inc.)

Year, x	Number of stores, y
1996	3054
1997	3406
1998	3599
1999	3985
2000	4189
2001	4414
2002	4688
2003	4906

22. ***Meteorology*** The table shows the lowest temperature on record y (in degrees Fahrenheit) in Duluth, Minnesota for each month x, where $x = 1$ represents January. (Source: NOAA)

Month, x	Temperature, y
1	−39
2	−39
3	−29
4	−5
5	17
6	27
7	35
8	32
9	22
10	8
11	−23
12	−34

In Exercises 23–26, find the distance between the points. (*Note:* In each case, the two points lie on the same horizontal or vertical line.)

23. $(6, -3), (6, 5)$

24. $(1, 4), (8, 4)$

25. $(-3, -1), (2, -1)$

26. $(-3, -4), (-3, 6)$

In Exercises 27–30, (a) find the length of each side of the right triangle, and (b) show that these lengths satisfy the Pythagorean Theorem.

27.

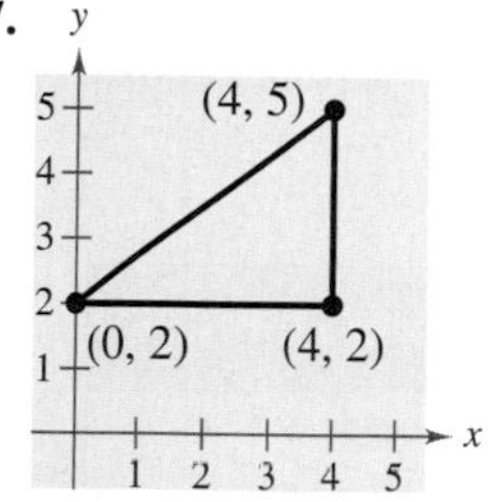

28.

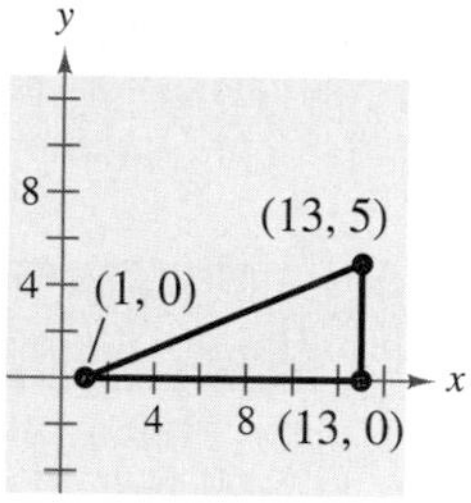

29.

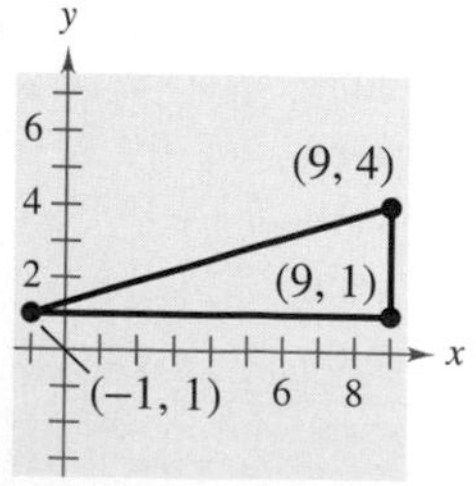

30.

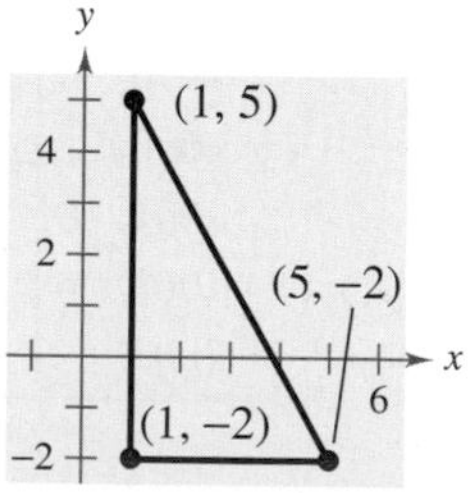

In Exercises 31–40, (a) plot the points, (b) find the distance between the points, and (c) find the midpoint of the line segment joining the points.

31. $(1, 1), (9, 7)$

32. $(1, 12), (6, 0)$

33. $(-4, 10), (4, -5)$

34. $(-7, -4), (2, 8)$

35. $(-1, 2), (5, 4)$

36. $(2, 10), (10, 2)$

37. $\left(\frac{1}{2}, 1\right), \left(-\frac{5}{2}, \frac{4}{3}\right)$

38. $\left(-\frac{1}{3}, -\frac{1}{3}\right), \left(-\frac{1}{6}, -\frac{1}{2}\right)$

39. $(6.2, 5.4), (-3.7, 1.8)$

40. $(-16.8, 12.3), (5.6, 4.9)$

In Exercises 41 and 42, show that the points form the vertices of the indicated polygon.

41. Right triangle: $(4, 0), (2, 1), (-1, -5)$

42. Isosceles triangle: $(1, -3), (3, 2), (-2, 4)$

43. A line segment has (x_1, y_1) as one endpoint and (x_m, y_m) as its midpoint. Find the other endpoint (x_2, y_2) of the line segment in terms of x_1, y_1, x_m, and y_m.

44. Use the result of Exercise 43 to find the coordinates of the endpoint of a line segment if the coordinates of the other endpoint and midpoint are, respectively,

(a) $(1, -2), (4, -1)$ and (b) $(-5, 11), (2, 4)$.

45. Use the Midpoint Formula three times to find the three points that divide the line segment joining (x_1, y_1) and (x_2, y_2) into four parts.

46. Use the result of Exercise 45 to find the points that divide the line segment joining the given points into four equal parts.

(a) $(1, -2), (4, -1)$ (b) $(-2, -3), (0, 0)$

47. ***Sports*** A soccer player passes the ball from a point that is 18 yards from the endline and 12 yards from the sideline. The pass is received by a teammate who is 42 yards from the same endline and 50 yards from the same sideline, as shown in the figure. How long is the pass?

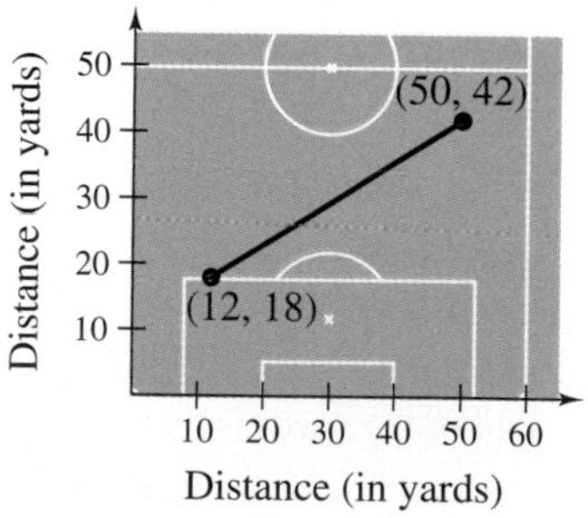

48. ***Flying Distance*** An airplane flies from Naples, Italy in a straight line to Rome, Italy, which is 120 kilometers north and 150 kilometers west of Naples. How far does the plane fly?

Sales **In Exercises 49 and 50, use the Midpoint Formula to estimate the sales of Big Lots, Inc. and Dollar Tree Stores, Inc. in 2002, given the sales in 2001 and 2003. Assume that the sales followed a linear pattern.** (Source: Big Lots, Inc.; Dollar Tree Stores, Inc.)

49. Big Lots

Year	Sales (in millions)
2001	\$3433
2003	\$4174

50. Dollar Tree

Year	Sales (in millions)
2001	\$1987
2003	\$2800

In Exercises 51–54, the polygon is shifted to a new position in the plane. Find the coordinates of the vertices of the polygon in its new position.

51.

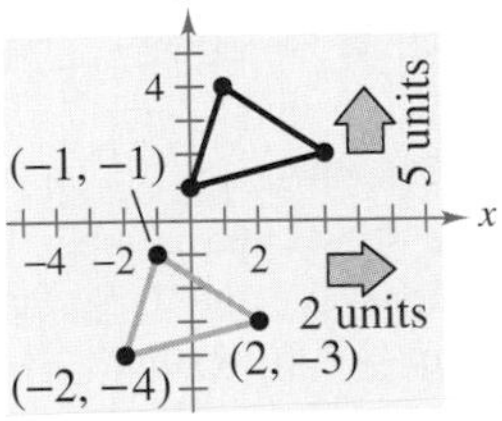

52.

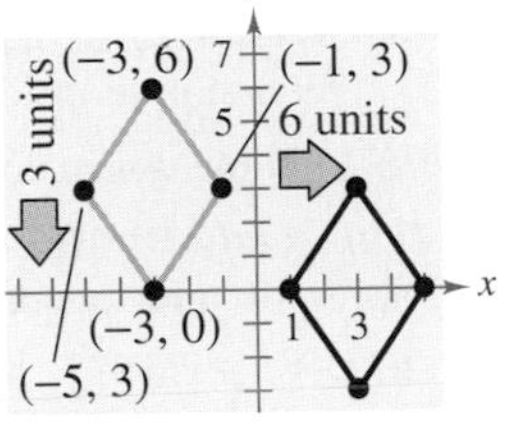

53. Original coordinates of vertices: $(-7, -2), (-2, 2), (-2, -4), (-7, -4)$

Shift: eight units upward, four units to the right

54. Original coordinates of vertices: $(5, 8), (3, 6), (7, 6), (5, 2)$

Shift: 6 units downward, 10 units to the left

Retail Price **In Exercises 55 and 56, use the graph below, which shows the average retail price of 1 pound of butter from 1995 to 2003.** (Source: U.S. Bureau of Labor Statistics)

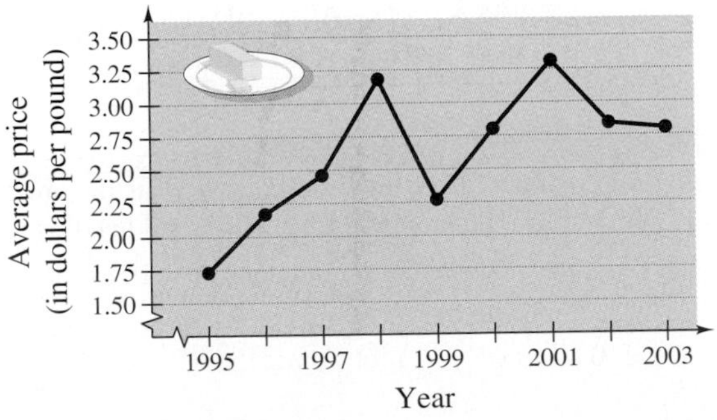

55. Approximate the highest price of a pound of butter shown in the graph. When did this occur?

56. Approximate the percent change in the price of butter from the price in 1995 to the highest price shown in the graph.

Advertising **In Exercises 57 and 58, use the graph below, which shows the cost of a 30-second television spot (in thousands of dollars) during the Super Bowl from 1989 to 2003.** (Source: USA Today Research and CNN)

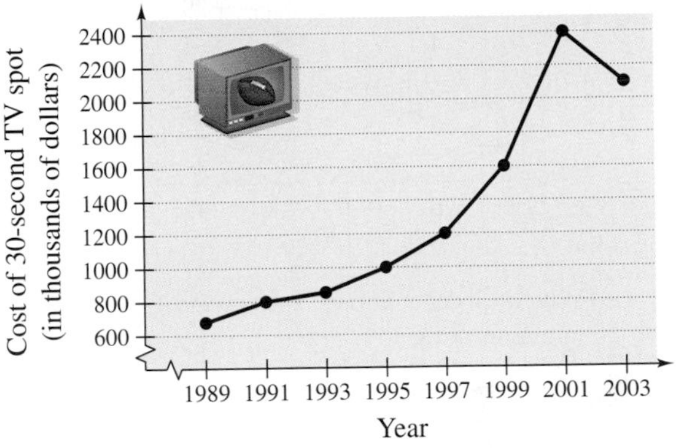

57. Approximate the percent increase in the cost of a 30-second spot from Super Bowl XXIII in 1989 to Super Bowl XXXV in 2001.

58. Estimate the percent increase in the cost of a 30-second spot (a) from Super Bowl XXIII in 1989 to Super Bowl XXVII in 1993 and (b) from Super Bowl XXVII in 1993 to Super Bowl XXXVII in 2003.

59. *Music* The graph shows the numbers of recording artists who were elected to the Rock and Roll Hall of Fame from 1986 to 2004.

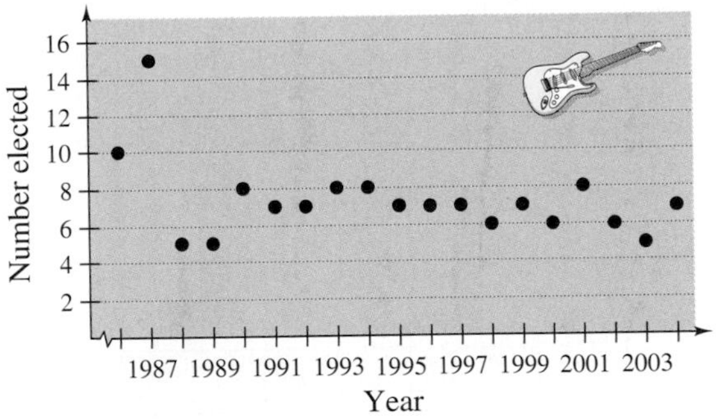

(a) Describe any trends in the data. From these trends, predict the number of artists elected in 2008.

(b) Why do you think the numbers elected in 1986 and 1987 were greater in other years?

Model It

60. *Labor Force* Use the graph below, which shows the minimum wage in the United States (in dollars) from 1950 to 2004. (Source: U.S. Department of Labor)

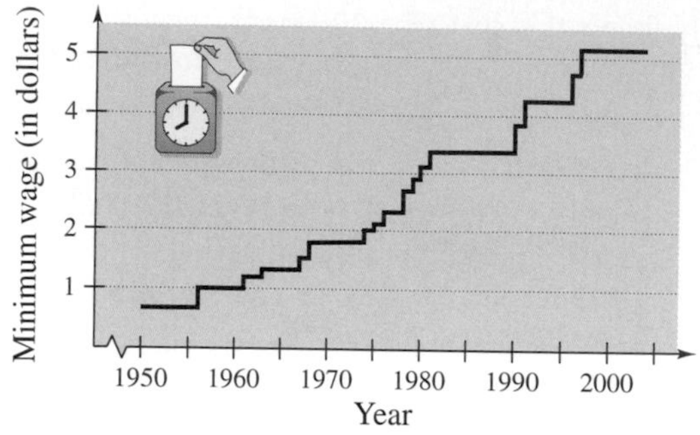

(a) Which decade shows the greatest increase in minimum wage?

(b) Approximate the percent increases in the minimum wage from 1990 to 1995 and from 1995 to 2004.

(c) Use the percent increase from 1995 to 2004 to predict the minimum wage in 2008.

(d) Do you believe that your prediction in part (c) is reasonable? Explain.

61. *Sales* The Coca-Cola Company had sales of \$18,546 million in 1996 and \$21,900 million in 2004. Use the Midpoint Formula to estimate the sales in 1998, 2000, and 2002. Assume that the sales followed a linear pattern. (Source: The Coca-Cola Company)

62. *Data Analysis: Exam Scores* The table shows the mathematics entrance test scores x and the final examination scores y in an algebra course for a sample of 10 students.

x	22	29	35	40	44
y	53	74	57	66	79

x	48	53	58	65	76
y	90	76	93	83	99

(a) Sketch a scatter plot of the data.

(b) Find the entrance exam score of any student with a final exam score in the 80s.

(c) Does a higher entrance exam score imply a higher final exam score? Explain.

63. *Volume of a Billiard Ball* A billiard ball has a volume of 5.96 cubic inches. Find the radius of a billiard ball.

64. *Length of a Tank* The diameter of a cylindrical propane gas tank is 4 feet. The total volume of the tank is 603.2 cubic feet. Find the length of the tank.

65. *Geometry* A "Slow Moving Vehicle" sign has the shape of an equilateral triangle. The sign has a perimeter of 129 centimeters. Find the length of each side of the sign. Find the area of the sign.

66. *Geometry* The radius of a traffic cone is 14 centimeters and the lateral surface of the cone is 1617 square centimeters. Find the height of the cone.

67. *Dimensions of a Room* A room is 1.5 times as long as it is wide, and its perimeter is 25 meters.

(a) Draw a diagram that represents the problem. Identify the length as l and the width as w.

(b) Write l in terms of w and write an equation for the perimeter in terms of w.

(c) Find the dimensions of the room.

68. *Dimensions of a Container* The width of a rectangular storage container is 1.25 times its height. The length of the container is 16 inches and the volume of the container is 2000 cubic inches.

(a) Draw a diagram that represents the problem. Label the height, width, and length accordingly.

(b) Write w in terms of h and write an equation for the volume in terms of h.

(c) Find the dimensions of the container.

69. *Data Analysis: Mail* The table shows the number y of pieces of mail handled (in billions) by the U.S. Postal Service for each year x from 1996 through 2003. (Source: U.S. Postal Service)

Year, x	Pieces of mail, y
1996	183
1997	191
1998	197
1999	202
2000	208
2001	207
2002	203
2003	202

(a) Sketch a scatter plot of the data.

(b) Approximate the year in which there was the greatest decrease in the number of pieces of mail handled.

(c) Why do you think the number of pieces of mail handled decreased?

70. ***Data Analysis: Athletics*** The table shows the numbers of men's M and women's W college basketball teams for each year x from 1994 through 2003. (Source: National Collegiate Athletic Association)

Year, x	Men's teams, M	Women's teams, W
1994	858	859
1995	868	864
1996	866	874
1997	865	879
1998	895	911
1999	926	940
2000	932	956
2001	937	958
2002	936	975
2003	967	1009

(a) Sketch scatter plots of these two sets of data on the same set of coordinate axes.

(b) Find the year in which the numbers of men's and women's teams were nearly equal.

(c) Find the year in which the difference between the numbers of men's and women's teams was the greatest. What was this difference?

71. ***Make a Conjecture*** Plot the points $(2, 1)$, $(-3, 5)$, and $(7, -3)$ on a rectangular coordinate system. Then change the sign of the x-coordinate of each point and plot the three new points on the same rectangular coordinate system. Make a conjecture about the location of a point when each of the following occurs.

(a) The sign of the x-coordinate is changed.

(b) The sign of the y-coordinate is changed.

(c) The signs of both the x- and y-coordinates are changed.

72. ***Collinear Points*** Three or more points are *collinear* if they all lie on the same line. Use the steps below to determine if the set of points $\{A(2, 3), B(2, 6), C(6, 3)\}$ and the set of points $\{A(8, 3), B(5, 2), C(2, 1)\}$ are collinear.

(a) For each set of points, use the Distance Formula to find the distances from A to B, from B to C, and from A to C. What relationship exists among these distances for each set of points?

(b) Plot each set of points in the Cartesian plane. Do all the points of either set appear to lie on the same line?

(c) Compare your conclusions from part (a) with the conclusions you made from the graphs in part (b). Make a general statement about how to use the Distance Formula to determine collinearity.

Synthesis

True or False? **In Exercises 73 and 74, determine whether the statement is true or false. Justify your answer.**

73. In order to divide a line segment into 16 equal parts, you would have to use the Midpoint Formula 16 times.

74. The points $(-8, 4)$, $(2, 11)$, and $(-5, 1)$ represent the vertices of an isosceles triangle.

75. ***Think About It*** When plotting points on the rectangular coordinate system, is it true that the scales on the x- and y-axes must be the same? Explain.

76. ***Proof*** Prove that the diagonals of the parallelogram in the figure intersect at their midpoints.

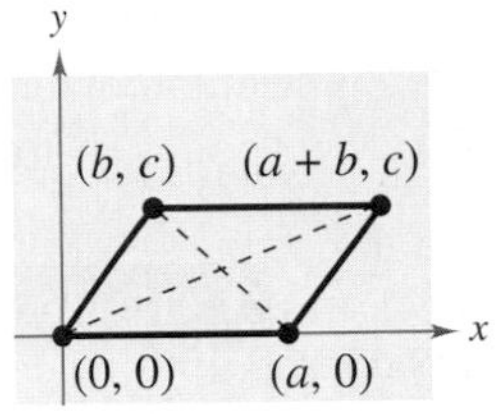

FIGURE FOR 76

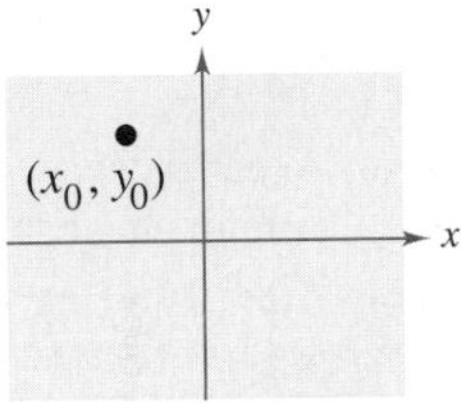

FIGURE FOR 77–80

In Exercises 77–80, use the plot of the point (x_0, y_0) in the figure. Match the transformation of the point with the correct plot. [The plots are labeled (a), (b), (c), and (d).]

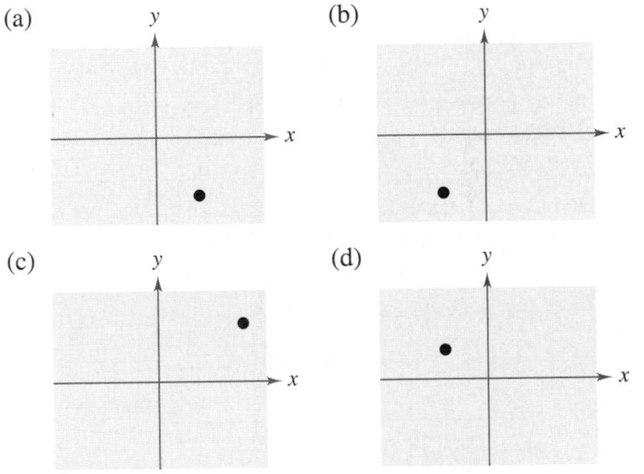

77. $(x_0, -y_0)$

78. $(-2x_0, y_0)$

79. $\left(x_0, \frac{1}{2}y_0\right)$

80. $(-x_0, -y_0)$

Skills Review

In Exercises 81–88, solve the equation or inequality.

81. $2x + 1 = 7x - 4$

82. $\frac{1}{3}x + 2 = 5 - \frac{1}{6}x$

83. $x^2 - 4x - 7 = 0$

84. $2x^2 + 3x - 8 = 0$

85. $3x + 1 < 2(2 - x)$

86. $3x - 8 \geq \frac{1}{2}(10x + 7)$

87. $|x - 18| < 4$

88. $|2x + 15| \geq 11$

1.2 Graphs of Equations

What you should learn

- Sketch graphs of equations.
- Find x- and y-intercepts of graphs of equations.
- Use symmetry to sketch graphs of equations.
- Find equations of and sketch graphs of circles.
- Use graphs of equations in solving real-life problems.

Why you should learn it

The graph of an equation can help you see relationships between real-life quantities. For example, in Exercise 75 on page 24, a graph can be used to estimate the life expectancies of children who are born in the years 2005 and 2010.

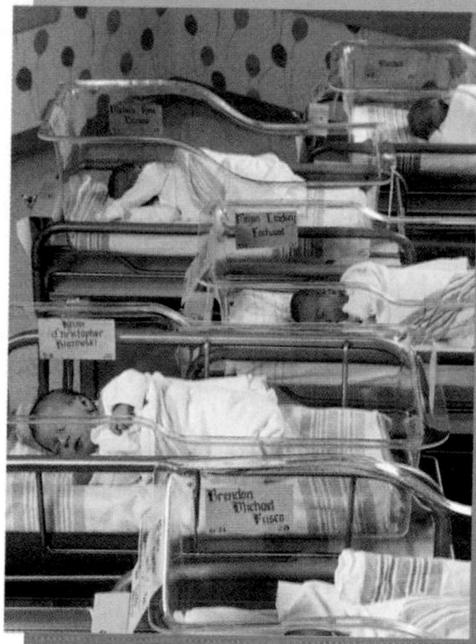

© John Griffin/The Image Works

The Graph of an Equation

In Section 1.1, you used a coordinate system to represent graphically the relationship between two quantities. There, the graphical picture consisted of a collection of points in a coordinate plane.

Frequently, a relationship between two quantities is expressed as an **equation in two variables.** For instance, $y = 7 - 3x$ is an equation in x and y. An ordered pair (a, b) is a **solution** or **solution point** of an equation in x and y if the equation is true when a is substituted for x and b is substituted for y. For instance, $(1, 4)$ is a solution of $y = 7 - 3x$ because $4 = 7 - 3(1)$ is a true statement.

In this section you will review some basic procedures for sketching the graph of an equation in two variables. The **graph of an equation** is the set of all points that are solutions of the equation.

Example 1 **Determining Solutions**

Determine whether (a) $(2, 13)$ and (b) $(-1, -3)$ are solutions of the equation $y = 10x - 7$.

Solution

a.
$y = 10x - 7$ Write original equation.

$13 \stackrel{?}{=} 10(2) - 7$ Substitute 2 for x and 13 for y.

$13 = 13$ $(2, 13)$ is a solution. ✓

Because the substitution does satisfy the original equation, you can conclude that the ordered pair $(2, 13)$ *is* a solution of the original equation.

b.
$y = 10x - 7$ Write original equation.

$-3 \stackrel{?}{=} 10(-1) - 7$ Substitute -1 for x and -3 for y.

$-3 \neq -17$ $(-1, -3)$ is not a solution.

Because the substitution does not satisfy the original equation, you can conclude that the ordered pair $(-1, -3)$ *is not* a solution of the original equation.

✓CHECKPOINT Now try Exercise 1.

The basic technique used for sketching the graph of an equation is the **point-plotting method.**

Sketching the Graph of an Equation by Point Plotting

1. If possible, rewrite the equation so that one of the variables is isolated on one side of the equation.
2. Make a table of values showing several solution points.
3. Plot these points on a rectangular coordinate system.
4. Connect the points with a smooth curve or line.

Example 2 Sketching the Graph of an Equation

Sketch the graph of

$$y = 7 - 3x.$$

Solution

Because the equation is already solved for y, construct a table of values that consists of several solution points of the equation. For instance, when $x = -1$,

$$y = 7 - 3(-1)$$
$$= 10$$

which implies that $(-1, 10)$ is a solution point of the graph.

x	$y = 7 - 3x$	(x, y)
-1	10	$(-1, 10)$
0	7	$(0, 7)$
1	4	$(1, 4)$
2	1	$(2, 1)$
3	-2	$(3, -2)$
4	-5	$(4, -5)$

From the table, it follows that

$$(-1, 10), (0, 7), (1, 4), (2, 1), (3, -2), \text{ and } (4, -5)$$

are solution points of the equation. After plotting these points, you can see that they appear to lie on a line, as shown in Figure 1.15. The graph of the equation is the line that passes through the six plotted points.

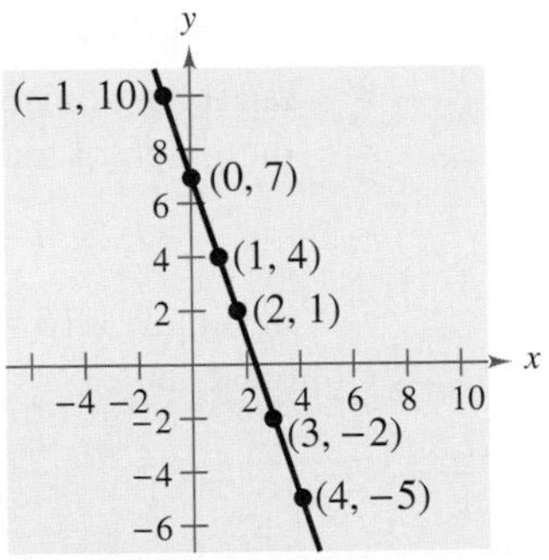

FIGURE 1.15

✓CHECKPOINT Now try Exercise 5.

Example 3 Sketching the Graph of an Equation

Sketch the graph of

$$y = x^2 - 2.$$

Solution

Because the equation is already solved for y, begin by constructing a table of values.

x	-2	-1	0	1	2	3
$y = x^2 - 2$	2	-1	-2	-1	2	7
(x, y)	$(-2, 2)$	$(-1, -1)$	$(0, -2)$	$(1, -1)$	$(2, 2)$	$(3, 7)$

Next, plot the points given in the table, as shown in Figure 1.16. Finally, connect the points with a smooth curve, as shown in Figure 1.17.

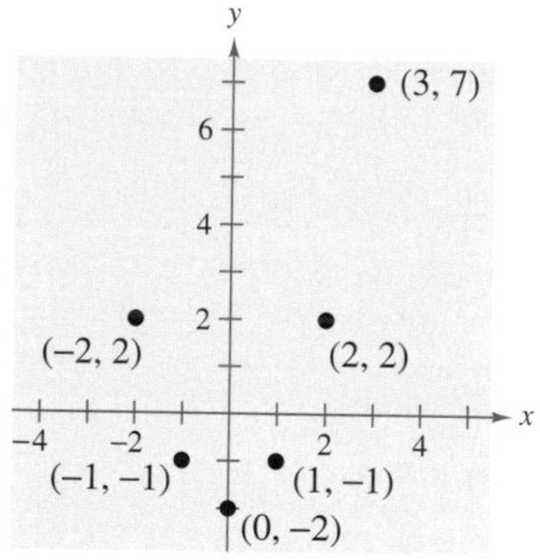

FIGURE 1.16

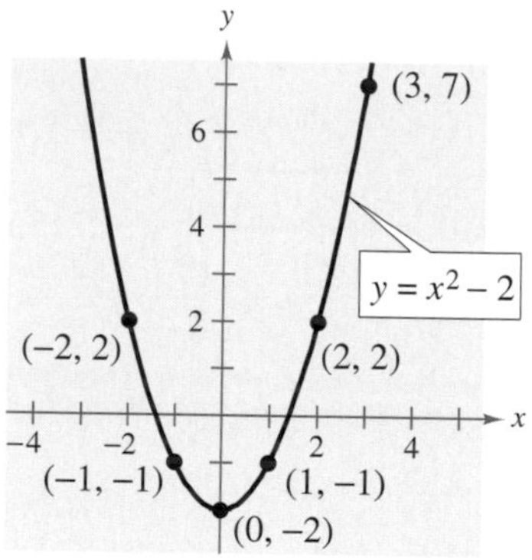

FIGURE 1.17

✓CHECKPOINT Now try Exercise 7.

The point-plotting method demonstrated in Examples 2 and 3 is easy to use, but it has some shortcomings. With too few solution points, you can misrepresent the graph of an equation. For instance, if only the four points

$$(-2, 2), (-1, -1), (1, -1), \text{ and } (2, 2)$$

in Figure 1.16 were plotted, any one of the three graphs in Figure 1.18 would be reasonable.

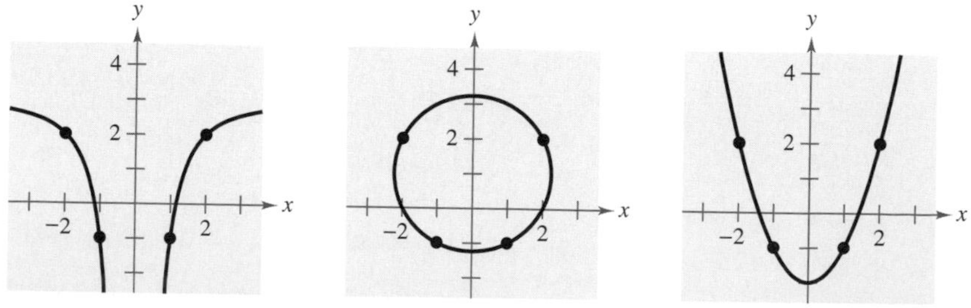

FIGURE 1.18

STUDY TIP

One of your goals in this course is to learn to classify the basic shape of a graph from its equation. For instance, you will learn that the *linear equation* in Example 2 has the form

$$y = mx + b$$

and its graph is a line. Similarly, the *quadratic equation* in Example 3 has the form

$$y = ax^2 + bx + c$$

and its graph is a parabola.

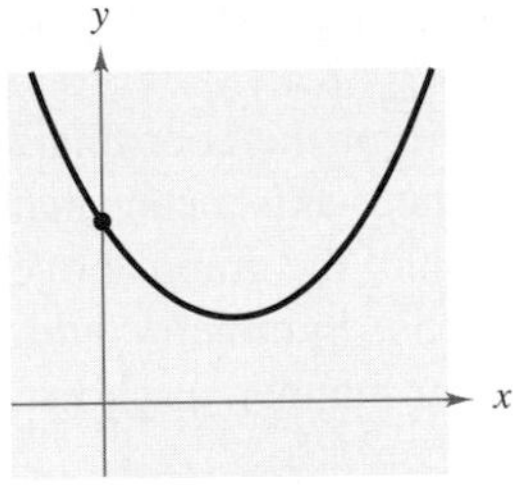

No x-intercepts; one y-intercept

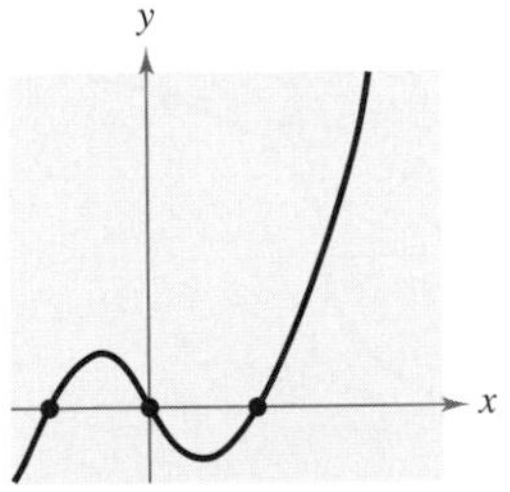

Three x-intercepts; one y-intercept

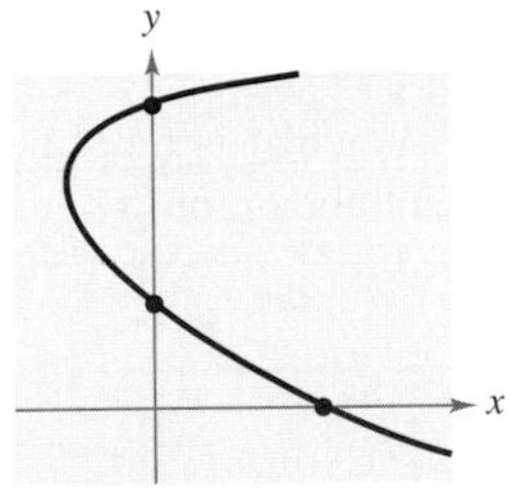

One x-intercept; two y-intercepts

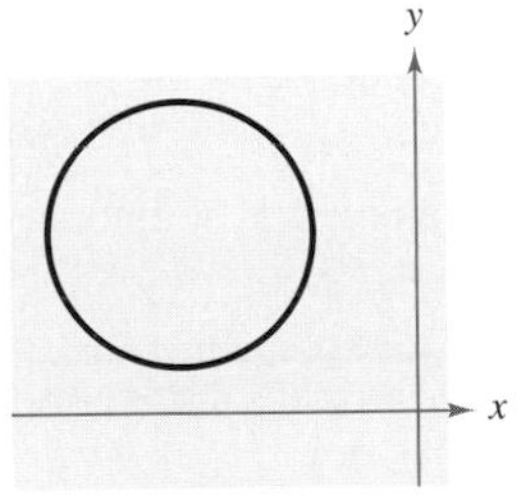

No intercepts
FIGURE 1.19

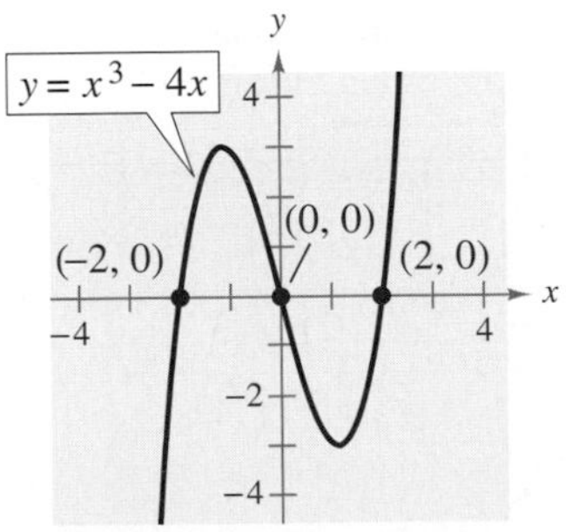

FIGURE 1.20

Technology

To graph an equation involving x and y on a graphing utility, use the following procedure.

1. Rewrite the equation so that y is isolated on the left side.
2. Enter the equation into the graphing utility.
3. Determine a *viewing window* that shows all important features of the graph.
4. Graph the equation.

For more extensive instructions on how to use a graphing utility to graph an equation, see the *Graphing Technology Guide* on the text website at *college.hmco.com.*

Intercepts of a Graph

It is often easy to determine the solution points that have zero as either the x-coordinate or the y-coordinate. These points are called **intercepts** because they are the points at which the graph intersects or touches the x- or y-axis. It is possible for a graph to have no intercepts, one intercept, or several intercepts, as shown in Figure 1.19.

Note that an x-intercept can be written as the ordered pair $(x, 0)$ and a y-intercept can be written as the ordered pair $(0, y)$. Some texts denote the x-intercept as the x-coordinate of the point $(a, 0)$ [and the y-intercept as the y-coordinate of the point $(0, b)$] rather than the point itself. Unless it is necessary to make a distinction, we will use the term *intercept* to mean either the point or the coordinate.

Finding Intercepts

1. To find x-intercepts, let y be zero and solve the equation for x.
2. To find y-intercepts, let x be zero and solve the equation for y.

Example 4 Finding x- and y-Intercepts

Find the x- and y-intercepts of the graph of $y = x^3 - 4x$.

Solution

Let $y = 0$. Then

$$0 = x^3 - 4x = x(x^2 - 4)$$

has solutions $x = 0$ and $x = \pm 2$.

$$x\text{-intercepts: } (0, 0), (2, 0), (-2, 0)$$

Let $x = 0$. Then

$$y = (0)^3 - 4(0)$$

has one solution, $y = 0$.

y-intercept: $(0, 0)$ See Figure 1.20.

✓CHECKPOINT Now try Exercise 11.

Symmetry

Graphs of equations can have **symmetry** with respect to one of the coordinate axes or with respect to the origin. Symmetry with respect to the x-axis means that if the Cartesian plane were folded along the x-axis, the portion of the graph above the x-axis would coincide with the portion below the x-axis. Symmetry with respect to the y-axis or the origin can be described in a similar manner, as shown in Figure 1.21.

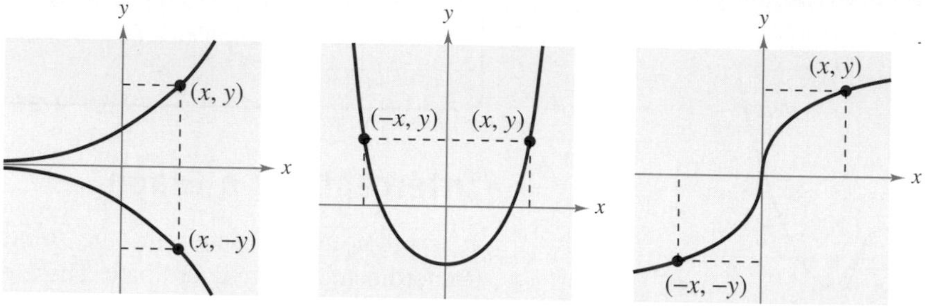

x-axis symmetry *y-axis symmetry* *Origin symmetry*

FIGURE 1.21

Knowing the symmetry of a graph *before* attempting to sketch it is helpful, because then you need only half as many solution points to sketch the graph. There are three basic types of symmetry, described as follows.

Graphical Tests for Symmetry

1. A graph is **symmetric with respect to the x-axis** if, whenever (x, y) is on the graph, $(x, -y)$ is also on the graph.
2. A graph is **symmetric with respect to the y-axis** if, whenever (x, y) is on the graph, $(-x, y)$ is also on the graph.
3. A graph is **symmetric with respect to the origin** if, whenever (x, y) is on the graph, $(-x, -y)$ is also on the graph.

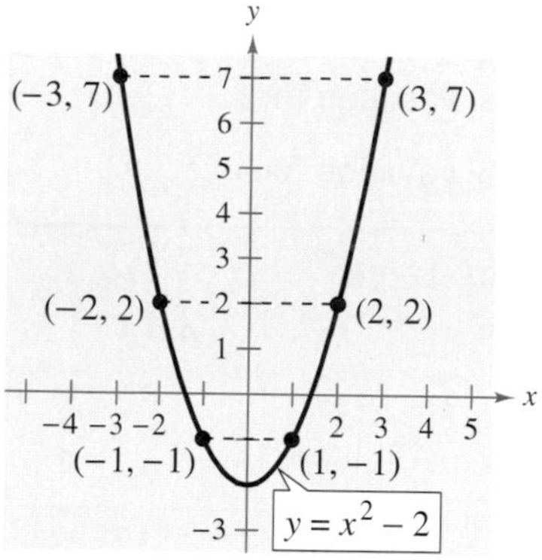

FIGURE 1.22 *y-axis symmetry*

Example 5 **Testing for Symmetry**

The graph of $y = x^2 - 2$ is symmetric with respect to the y-axis because the point $(-x, y)$ is also on the graph of $y = x^2 - 2$. (See Figure 1.22.) The table below confirms that the graph is symmetric with respect to the y-axis.

x	-3	-2	-1	1	2	3
y	7	2	-1	-1	2	7
(x, y)	$(-3, 7)$	$(-2, 2)$	$(-1, -1)$	$(1, -1)$	$(2, 2)$	$(3, 7)$

✓CHECKPOINT Now try Exercise 23.

Algebraic Tests for Symmetry

1. The graph of an equation is symmetric with respect to the x-axis if replacing y with $-y$ yields an equivalent equation.
2. The graph of an equation is symmetric with respect to the y-axis if replacing x with $-x$ yields an equivalent equation.
3. The graph of an equation is symmetric with respect to the origin if replacing x with $-x$ and y with $-y$ yields an equivalent equation.

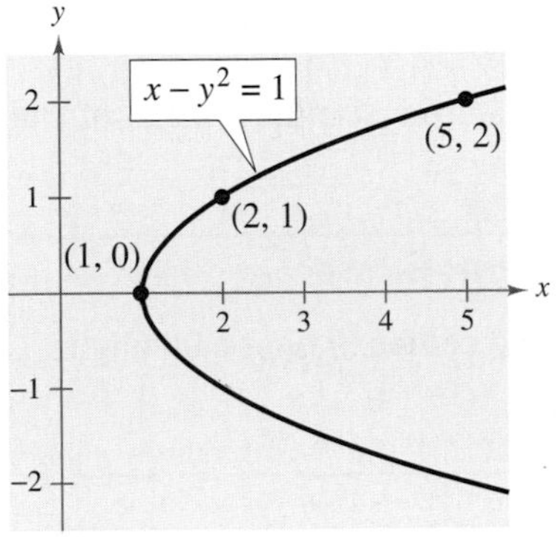

FIGURE 1.23

Example 6 Using Symmetry as a Sketching Aid

Use symmetry to sketch the graph of

$$x - y^2 = 1.$$

Solution

Of the three tests for symmetry, the only one that is satisfied is the test for x-axis symmetry because $x - (-y)^2 = 1$ is equivalent to $x - y^2 = 1$. So, the graph is symmetric with respect to the x-axis. Using symmetry, you only need to find the solution points above the x-axis and then reflect them to obtain the graph, as shown in Figure 1.23.

y	$x = y^2 + 1$	(x, y)
0	1	(1, 0)
1	2	(2, 1)
2	5	(5, 2)

STUDY TIP

Notice that when creating the table in Example 6, it is easier to choose y-values and then find the corresponding x-values of the ordered pairs.

CHECKPOINT Now try Exercise 37.

Example 7 Sketching the Graph of an Equation

Sketch the graph of

$$y = |x - 1|.$$

Solution

This equation fails all three tests for symmetry and consequently its graph is not symmetric with respect to either axis or to the origin. The absolute value sign indicates that y is always nonnegative. Create a table of values and plot the points as shown in Figure 1.24. From the table, you can see that $x = 0$ when $y = 1$. So, the y-intercept is $(0, 1)$. Similarly, $y = 0$ when $x = 1$. So, the x-intercept is $(1, 0)$.

x	-2	-1	0	1	2	3	4
$y = \|x - 1\|$	3	2	1	0	1	2	3
(x, y)	$(-2, 3)$	$(-1, 2)$	$(0, 1)$	$(1, 0)$	$(2, 1)$	$(3, 2)$	$(4, 3)$

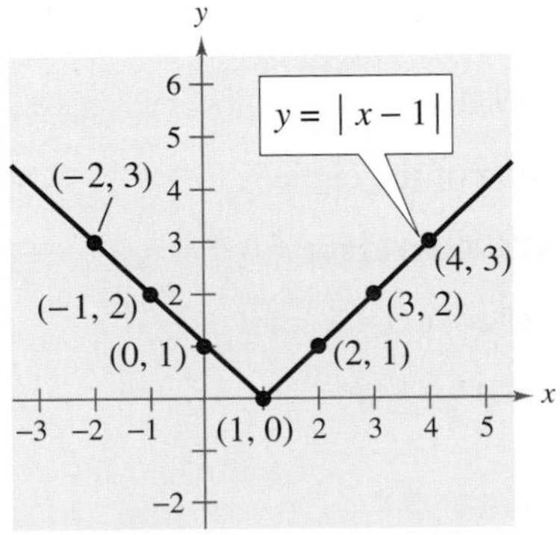

FIGURE 1.24

CHECKPOINT Now try Exercise 41.

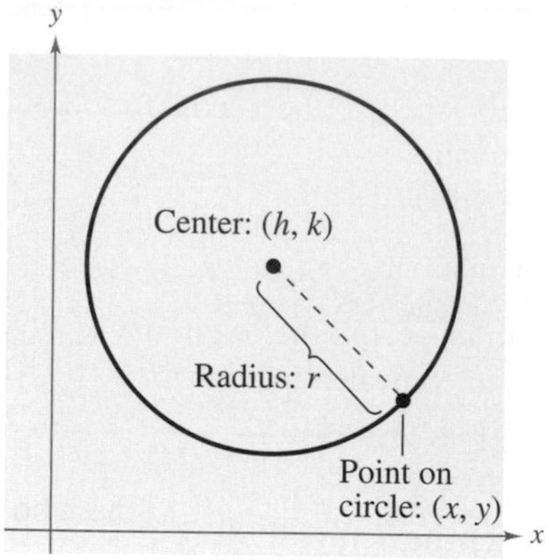

FIGURE 1.25

Throughout this course, you will learn to recognize several types of graphs from their equations. For instance, you will learn to recognize that the graph of a second-degree equation of the form

$$y = ax^2 + bx + c$$

is a parabola (see Example 3). The graph of a **circle** is also easy to recognize.

Circles

Consider the circle shown in Figure 1.25. A point (x, y) is on the circle if and only if its distance from the center (h, k) is r. By the Distance Formula,

$$\sqrt{(x - h)^2 + (y - k)^2} = r.$$

By squaring each side of this equation, you obtain the **standard form of the equation of a circle.**

Standard Form of the Equation of a Circle

The point (x, y) lies on the circle of **radius** r and **center** (h, k) if and only if

$$(x - h)^2 + (y - k)^2 = r^2.$$

STUDY TIP

To find the correct h and k, from the equation of the circle in Example 8, it may be helpful to rewrite the quantities $(x + 1)^2$ and $(y - 2)^2$, using subtraction.

$$(x + 1)^2 = [x - (-1)]^2,$$

$$(y - 2)^2 = [y - (2)]^2$$

So, $h = -1$ and $k = 2$.

From this result, you can see that the standard form of the equation of a circle *with its center at the origin,* $(h, k) = (0, 0)$, is simply

$$x^2 + y^2 = r^2. \quad \text{Circle with center at origin}$$

Example 8 Finding the Equation of a Circle

The point $(3, 4)$ lies on a circle whose center is at $(-1, 2)$, as shown in Figure 1.26. Write the standard form of the equation of this circle.

Solution

The radius of the circle is the distance between $(-1, 2)$ and $(3, 4)$.

$$r = \sqrt{(x - h)^2 + (y - k)^2} \quad \text{Distance Formula}$$

$$= \sqrt{[3 - (-1)]^2 + (4 - 2)^2} \quad \text{Substitute for } x, y, h, \text{ and } k.$$

$$= \sqrt{4^2 + 2^2} \quad \text{Simplify.}$$

$$= \sqrt{16 + 4} \quad \text{Simplify.}$$

$$= \sqrt{20} \quad \text{Radius}$$

Using $(h, k) = (-1, 2)$ and $r = \sqrt{20}$, the equation of the circle is

$$(x - h)^2 + (y - k)^2 = r^2 \quad \text{Equation of circle}$$

$$[x - (-1)]^2 + (y - 2)^2 = \left(\sqrt{20}\right)^2 \quad \text{Substitute for } h, k, \text{ and } r.$$

$$(x + 1)^2 + (y - 2)^2 = 20. \quad \text{Standard form}$$

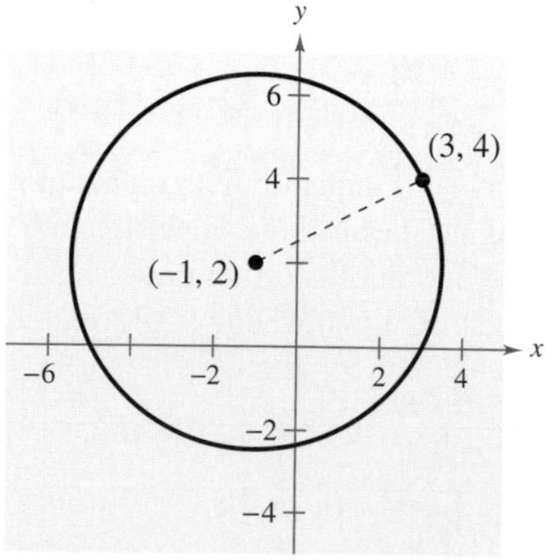

FIGURE 1.26

CHECKPOINT Now try Exercise 61.

STUDY TIP

You should develop the habit of using at least two approaches to solve every problem. This helps build your intuition and helps you check that your answer is reasonable.

Application

In this course, you will learn that there are many ways to approach a problem. Three common approaches are illustrated in Example 9.

A *Numerical Approach:* Construct and use a table.
A *Graphical Approach:* Draw and use a graph.
An *Algebraic Approach:* Use the rules of algebra.

Example 9 Recommended Weight

The median recommended weight y (in pounds) for men of medium frame who are 25 to 59 years old can be approximated by the mathematical model

$$y = 0.073x^2 - 6.99x + 289.0, \quad 62 \le x \le 76$$

where x is the man's height (in inches). (Source: Metropolitan Life Insurance Company)

a. Construct a table of values that shows the median recommended weights for men with heights of 62, 64, 66, 68, 70, 72, 74, and 76 inches.

b. Use the table of values to sketch a graph of the model. Then use the graph to estimate *graphically* the median recommended weight for a man whose height is 71 inches.

c. Use the model to confirm *algebraically* the estimate you found in part (b).

Solution

a. You can use a calculator to complete the table, as shown at the left.

Height, x	Weight, y
62	136.2
64	140.6
66	145.6
68	151.2
70	157.4
72	164.2
74	171.5
76	179.4

b. The table of values can be used to sketch the graph of the equation, as shown in Figure 1.27. From the graph, you can estimate that a height of 71 inches corresponds to a weight of about 161 pounds.

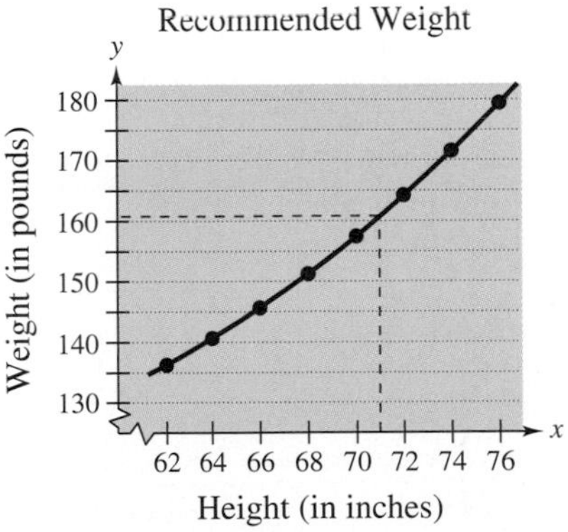

FIGURE 1.27

c. To confirm algebraically the estimate found in part (b), you can substitute 71 for x in the model.

$$y = 0.073(71)^2 - 6.99(71) + 289.0 \approx 160.70$$

So, the graphical estimate of 161 pounds is fairly good.

CHECKPOINT Now try Exercise 75.

1.2 Exercises

VOCABULARY CHECK: Fill in the blanks.

1. An ordered pair (a, b) is a ________ of an equation in x and y if the equation is true when a is substituted for x and b is substituted for y.
2. The set of all solution points of an equation is the ________ of the equation.
3. The points at which a graph intersects or touches an axis are called the ________ of the graph.
4. A graph is symmetric with respect to the ________ if, whenever (x, y) is on the graph, $(-x, y)$ is also on the graph.
5. The equation $(x - h)^2 + (y - k)^2 = r^2$ is the standard form of the equation of a ________ with center ________ and radius ________.
6. When you construct and use a table to solve a problem, you are using a ________ approach.

In Exercises 1–4, determine whether each point lies on the graph of the equation.

	Equation	*Points*	
1.	$y = \sqrt{x + 4}$	(a) $(0, 2)$	(b) $(5, 3)$
2.	$y = x^2 - 3x + 2$	(a) $(2, 0)$	(b) $(-2, 8)$
3.	$y = 4 - \lvert x - 2 \rvert$	(a) $(1, 5)$	(b) $(6, 0)$
4.	$y = \frac{1}{3}x^3 - 2x^2$	(a) $\left(2, -\frac{16}{3}\right)$	(b) $(-3, 9)$

In Exercises 5–8, complete the table. Use the resulting solution points to sketch the graph of the equation.

5. $y = -2x + 5$

x	-1	0	1	2	$\frac{5}{2}$
y					
(x, y)					

6. $y = \frac{3}{4}x - 1$

x	-2	0	1	$\frac{4}{3}$	2
y					
(x, y)					

7. $y = x^2 - 3x$

x	-1	0	1	2	3
y					
(x, y)					

8. $y = 5 - x^2$

x	-2	-1	0	1	2
y					
(x, y)					

In Exercises 9–20, find the *x*- and *y*-intercepts of the graph of the equation.

9. $y = 16 - 4x^2$

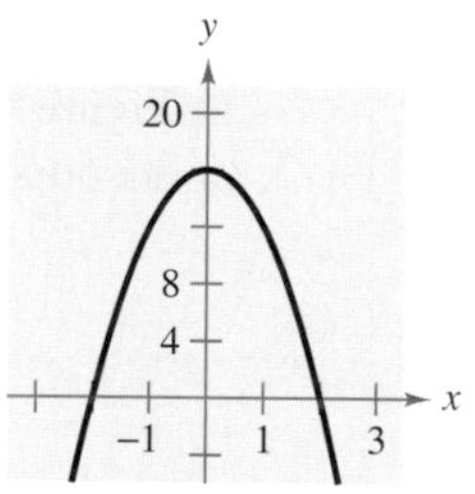

10. $y = (x + 3)^2$

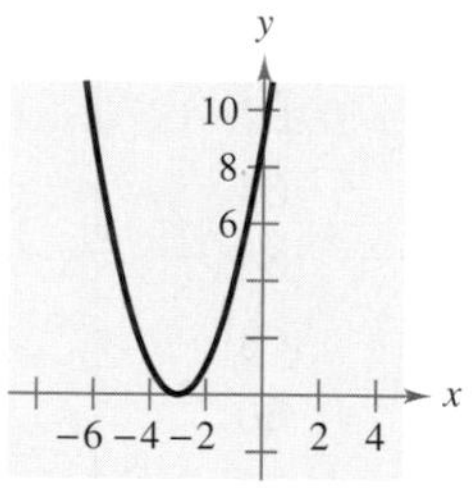

11. $y = 5x - 6$

12. $y = 8 - 3x$

13. $y = \sqrt{x + 4}$

14. $y = \sqrt{2x - 1}$

15. $y = \lvert 3x - 7 \rvert$

16. $y = -\lvert x + 10 \rvert$

17. $y = 2x^3 - 4x^2$

18. $y = x^4 - 25$

19. $y^2 = 6 - x$

20. $y^2 = x + 1$

In Exercises 21–24, assume that the graph has the indicated type of symmetry. Sketch the complete graph of the equation. To print an enlarged copy of the graph, go to the website *www.mathgraphs.com*.

21.

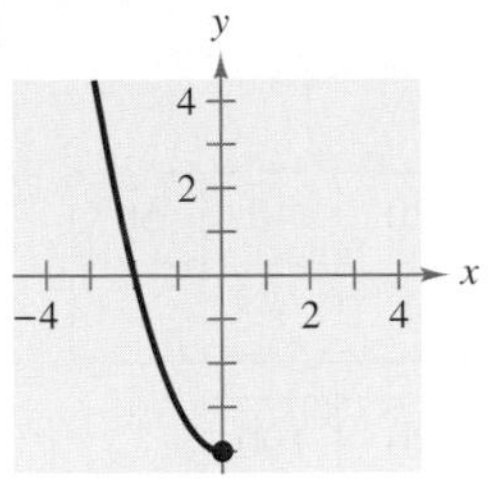

y-axis symmetry

22.

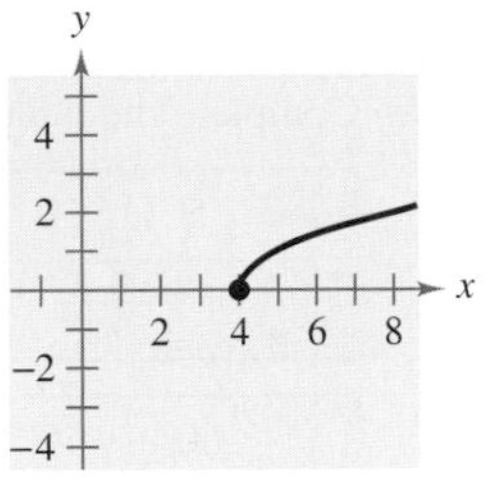

x-axis symmetry

23.

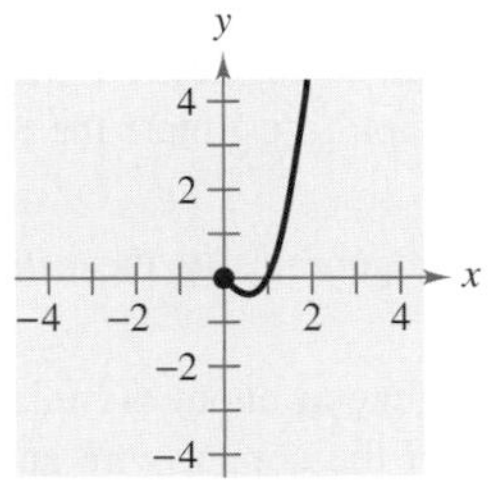

Origin symmetry

24.

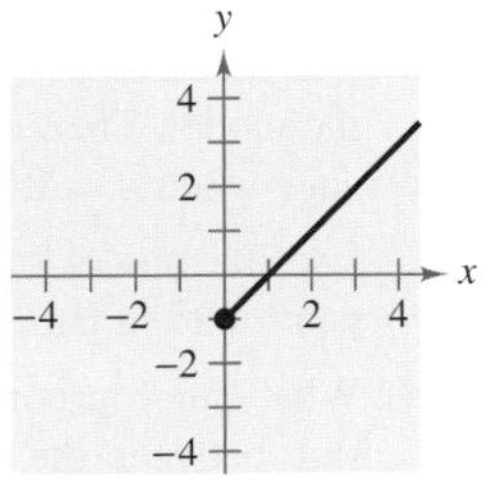

y-axis symmetry

In Exercises 25–32, use the algebraic tests to check for symmetry with respect to both axes and the origin.

25. $x^2 - y = 0$ **26.** $x - y^2 = 0$

27. $y = x^3$ **28.** $y = x^4 - x^2 + 3$

29. $y = \dfrac{x}{x^2 + 1}$ **30.** $y = \dfrac{1}{x^2 + 1}$

31. $xy^2 + 10 = 0$ **32.** $xy = 4$

In Exercises 33–44, use symmetry to sketch the graph of the equation.

33. $y = -3x + 1$ **34.** $y = 2x - 3$

35. $y = x^2 - 2x$ **36.** $y = -x^2 - 2x$

37. $y = x^3 + 3$ **38.** $y = x^3 - 1$

39. $y = \sqrt{x - 3}$ **40.** $y = \sqrt{1 - x}$

41. $y = |x - 6|$ **42.** $y = 1 - |x|$

43. $x = y^2 - 1$ **44.** $x = y^2 - 5$

In Exercises 45–56, use a graphing utility to graph the equation. Use a standard setting. Approximate any intercepts.

45. $y = 3 - \frac{1}{2}x$ **46.** $y = \frac{2}{3}x - 1$

47. $y = x^2 - 4x + 3$ **48.** $y = x^2 + x - 2$

49. $y = \dfrac{2x}{x - 1}$ **50.** $y = \dfrac{4}{x^2 + 1}$

51. $y = \sqrt[3]{x}$ **52.** $y = \sqrt[3]{x + 1}$

53. $y = x\sqrt{x + 6}$ **54.** $y = (6 - x)\sqrt{x}$

55. $y = |x + 3|$ **56.** $y = 2 - |x|$

In Exercises 57–64, write the standard form of the equation of the circle with the given characteristics.

57. Center: (0, 0); radius: 4 **58.** Center: (0, 0); radius: 5

59. Center: (2, −1); radius: 4

60. Center: (−7, −4); radius: 7

61. Center: (−1, 2); solution point: (0, 0)

62. Center: (3, −2); solution point: (−1, 1)

63. Endpoints of a diameter: (0, 0), (6, 8)

64. Endpoints of a diameter: (−4, −1), (4, 1)

In Exercises 65–70, find the center and radius of the circle, and sketch its graph.

65. $x^2 + y^2 = 25$ **66.** $x^2 + y^2 = 16$

67. $(x - 1)^2 + (y + 3)^2 = 9$

68. $x^2 + (y - 1)^2 = 1$

69. $\left(x - \frac{1}{2}\right)^2 + \left(y - \frac{1}{2}\right)^2 = \frac{9}{4}$

70. $(x - 2)^2 + (y + 3)^2 = \frac{16}{9}$

71. ***Depreciation*** A manufacturing plant purchases a new molding machine for \$225,000. The depreciated value y (reduced value) after t years is given by $y = 225{,}000 - 20{,}000t, 0 \le t \le 8$. Sketch the graph of the equation.

72. ***Consumerism*** You purchase a jet ski for \$8100. The depreciated value y after t years is given by $y = 8100 - 929t, \; 0 \le t \le 6$. Sketch the graph of the equation.

73. ***Geometry*** A regulation NFL playing field (including the end zones) of length x and width y has a perimeter of $346\frac{2}{3}$ or $\frac{1040}{3}$ yards.

(a) Draw a rectangle that gives a visual representation of the problem. Use the specified variables to label the sides of the rectangle.

(b) Show that the width of the rectangle is $y = \frac{520}{3} - x$ and its area is $A = x\left(\frac{520}{3} - x\right)$.

(c) Use a graphing utility to graph the area equation. Be sure to adjust your window settings.

(d) From the graph in part (c), estimate the dimensions of the rectangle that yield a maximum area.

(e) Use your school's library, the Internet, or some other reference source to find the actual dimensions and area of a regulation NFL playing field and compare your findings with the results of part (d).

The symbol indicates an exercise or a part of an exercise in which you are instructed to use a graphing utility.

74. ***Geometry*** A soccer playing field of length x and width y has a perimeter of 360 meters.

(a) Draw a rectangle that gives a visual representation of the problem. Use the specified variables to label the sides of the rectangle.

(b) Show that the width of the rectangle is $w = 180 - x$ and its area is $A = x(180 - x)$.

(c) Use a graphing utility to graph the area equation. Be sure to adjust your window settings.

(d) From the graph in part (c), estimate the dimensions of the rectangle that yield a maximum area.

(e) Use your school's library, the Internet, or some other reference source to find the actual dimensions and area of a regulation Major League Soccer field and compare your findings with the results of part(d).

Model It

75. ***Population Statistics*** The table shows the life expectancies of a child (at birth) in the United States for selected years from 1920 to 2000. (Source: U.S. National Center for Health Statistics)

Year	Life expectancy, y
1920	54.1
1930	59.7
1940	62.9
1950	68.2
1960	69.7
1970	70.8
1980	73.7
1990	75.4
2000	77.0

A model for the life expectancy during this period is

$$y = -0.0025t^2 + 0.574t + 44.25, \quad 20 \le t \le 100$$

where y represents the life expectancy and t is the time in years, with $t = 20$ corresponding to 1920.

(a) Sketch a scatter plot of the data.

(b) Graph the model for the data and compare the scatter plot and the graph.

(c) Determine the life expectancy in 1948 both graphically and algebraically.

(d) Use the graph of the model to estimate the life expectancies of a child for the years 2005 and 2010.

(e) Do you think this model can be used to predict the life expectancy of a child 50 years from now? Explain.

76. ***Electronics*** The resistance y (in ohms) of 1000 feet of solid copper wire at 68 degrees Fahrenheit can be approximated by the model $y = \frac{10{,}770}{x^2} - 0.37$, $5 \le x \le 100$ where x is the diameter of the wire in mils (0.001 inch). (Source: American Wire Gage)

(a) Complete the table.

x	5	10	20	30	40	50
y						

x	60	70	80	90	100
y					

(b) Use the table of values in part (a) to sketch a graph of the model. Then use your graph to estimate the resistance when $x = 85.5$.

(c) Use the model to confirm algebraically the estimate you found in part (b).

(d) What can you conclude in general about the relationship between the diameter of the copper wire and the resistance?

Synthesis

True or False? **In Exercises 77 and 78, determine whether the statement is true or false. Justify your answer.**

77. A graph is symmetric with respect to the x-axis if, whenever (x, y) is on the graph, $(-x, y)$ is also on the graph.

78. A graph of an equation can have more than one y-intercept.

79. ***Think About It*** Suppose you correctly enter an expression for the variable y on a graphing utility. However, no graph appears on the display when you graph the equation. Give a possible explanation and the steps you could take to remedy the problem. Illustrate your explanation with an example.

80. ***Think About It*** Find a and b if the graph of $y = ax^2 + bx^3$ is symmetric with respect to (a) the y-axis and (b) the origin. (There are many correct answers.)

Skills Review

81. Identify the terms: $9x^5 + 4x^3 - 7$.

82. Rewrite the expression using exponential notation.

$-(7 \times 7 \times 7 \times 7)$

In Exercises 83–88, simplify the expression.

83. $\sqrt{18x} - \sqrt{2x}$

84. $\sqrt[4]{x^5}$

85. $\dfrac{70}{\sqrt{7x}}$

86. $\dfrac{55}{\sqrt{20} - 3}$

87. $\sqrt[6]{t^2}$

88. $\sqrt[3]{\sqrt{y}}$

1.3 Linear Equations in Two Variables

What you should learn

- Use slope to graph linear equations in two variables.
- Find slopes of lines.
- Write linear equations in two variables.
- Use slope to identify parallel and perpendicular lines.
- Use slope and linear equations in two variables to model and solve real-life problems.

Why you should learn it

Linear equations in two variables can be used to model and solve real-life problems. For instance, in Exercise 109 on page 37, you will use a linear equation to model student enrollment at the Pennsylvania State University.

Courtesy of Pennsylvania State University

Using Slope

The simplest mathematical model for relating two variables is the **linear equation in two variables** $y = mx + b$. The equation is called *linear* because its graph is a line. (In mathematics, the term *line* means *straight line*.) By letting $x = 0$, you can see that the line crosses the y-axis at $y = b$, as shown in Figure 1.28. In other words, the y-intercept is $(0, b)$. The steepness or slope of the line is m.

$$y = mx + b$$

Slope (m) — y-Intercept (b)

The **slope** of a nonvertical line is the number of units the line rises (or falls) vertically for each unit of horizontal change from left to right, as shown in Figure 1.28 and Figure 1.29.

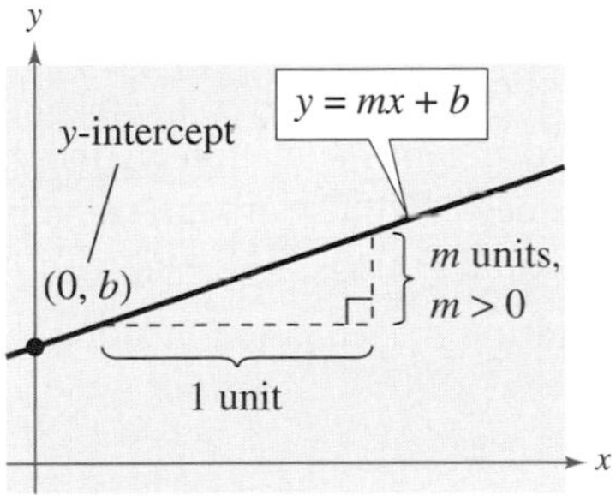

Positive slope, line rises.
FIGURE 1.28

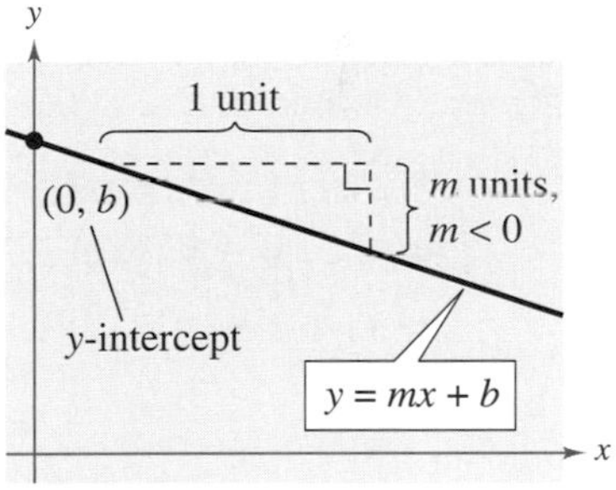

Negative slope, line falls.
FIGURE 1.29

A linear equation that is written in the form $y = mx + b$ is said to be written in **slope-intercept form.**

The Slope-Intercept Form of the Equation of a Line

The graph of the equation

$$y = mx + b$$

is a line whose slope is m and whose y-intercept is $(0, b)$.

Exploration

Use a graphing utility to compare the slopes of the lines $y = mx$, where $m = 0.5, 1, 2,$ and 4. Which line rises most quickly? Now, let $m = -0.5, -1, -2,$ and -4. Which line falls most quickly? Use a square setting to obtain a true geometric perspective. What can you conclude about the slope and the "rate" at which the line rises or falls?

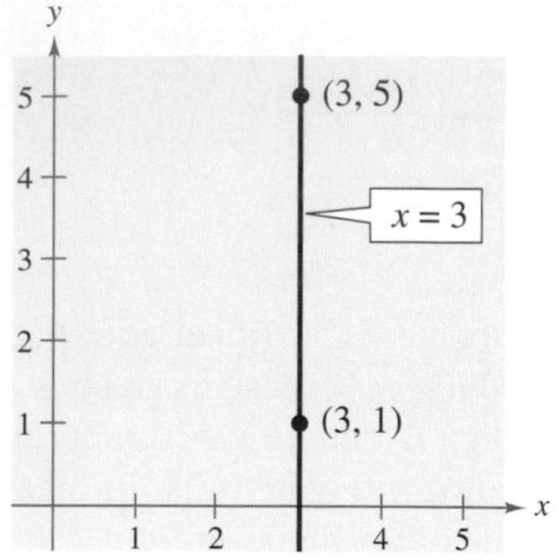

FIGURE 1.30 *Slope is undefined.*

Once you have determined the slope and the y-intercept of a line, it is a relatively simple matter to sketch its graph. In the next example, note that none of the lines is vertical. A vertical line has an equation of the form

$$x = a. \qquad \text{Vertical line}$$

The equation of a vertical line cannot be written in the form $y = mx + b$ because the slope of a vertical line is undefined, as indicated in Figure 1.30.

Example 1 Graphing a Linear Equation

Sketch the graph of each linear equation.

a. $y = 2x + 1$

b. $y = 2$

c. $x + y = 2$

Solution

a. Because $b = 1$, the y-intercept is $(0, 1)$. Moreover, because the slope is $m = 2$, the line *rises* two units for each unit the line moves to the right, as shown in Figure 1.31.

b. By writing this equation in the form $y = (0)x + 2$, you can see that the y-intercept is $(0, 2)$ and the slope is zero. A zero slope implies that the line is horizontal—that is, it doesn't rise *or* fall, as shown in Figure 1.32.

c. By writing this equation in slope-intercept form

$$x + y = 2 \qquad \text{Write original equation.}$$

$$y = -x + 2 \qquad \text{Subtract } x \text{ from each side.}$$

$$y = (-1)x + 2 \qquad \text{Write in slope-intercept form.}$$

you can see that the y-intercept is $(0, 2)$. Moreover, because the slope is $m = -1$, the line *falls* one unit for each unit the line moves to the right, as shown in Figure 1.33.

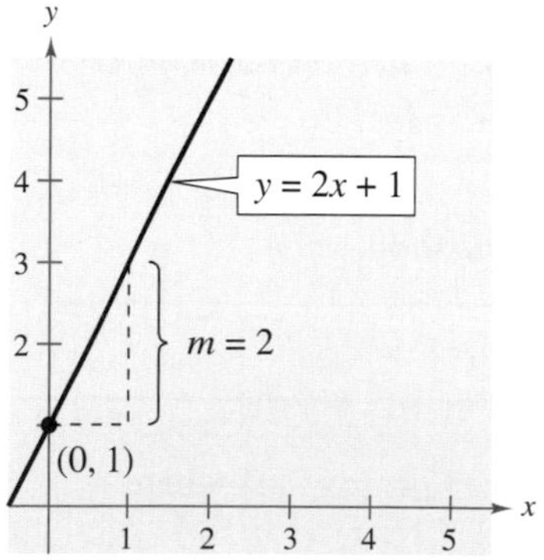

When m is positive, the line rises.
FIGURE 1.31

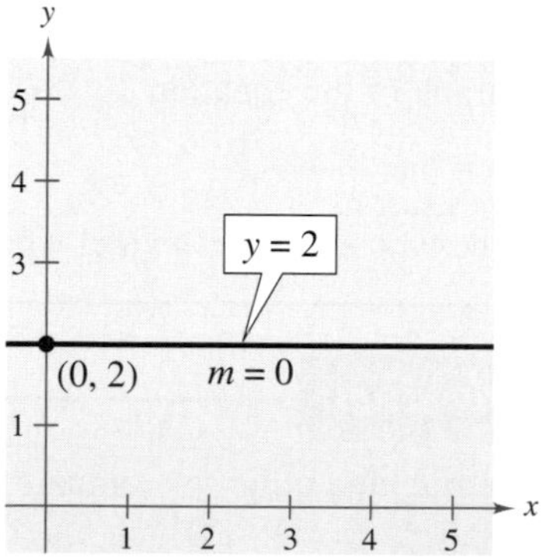

When m is 0, the line is horizontal.
FIGURE 1.32

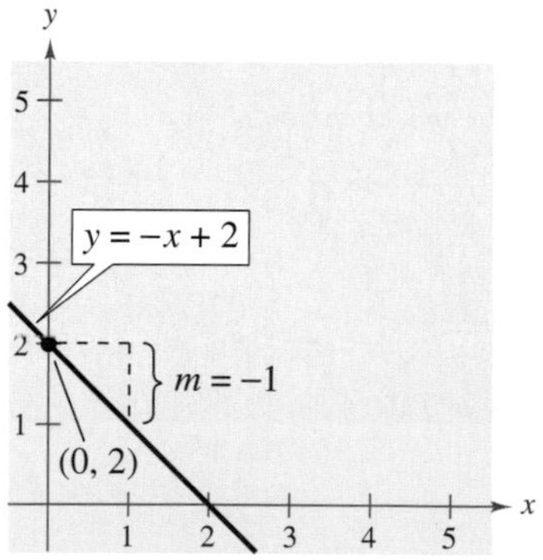

When m is negative, the line falls.
FIGURE 1.33

✓CHECKPOINT Now try Exercise 9.

Finding the Slope of a Line

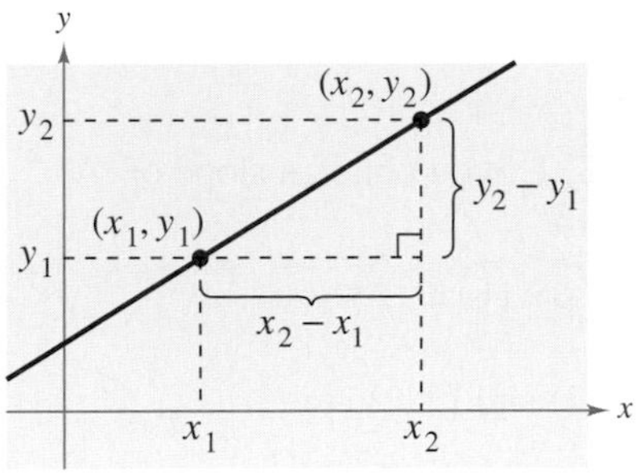

FIGURE 1.34

Given an equation of a line, you can find its slope by writing the equation in slope-intercept form. If you are not given an equation, you can still find the slope of a line. For instance, suppose you want to find the slope of the line passing through the points (x_1, y_1) and (x_2, y_2), as shown in Figure 1.34. As you move from left to right along this line, a change of $(y_2 - y_1)$ units in the vertical direction corresponds to a change of $(x_2 - x_1)$ units in the horizontal direction.

$$y_2 - y_1 = \text{the change in } y = \text{rise}$$

and

$$x_2 - x_1 = \text{the change in } x = \text{run}$$

The ratio of $(y_2 - y_1)$ to $(x_2 - x_1)$ represents the slope of the line that passes through the points (x_1, y_1) and (x_2, y_2).

$$\begin{aligned}\text{Slope} &= \frac{\text{change in } y}{\text{change in } x}\\ &= \frac{\text{rise}}{\text{run}}\\ &= \frac{y_2 - y_1}{x_2 - x_1}\end{aligned}$$

The Slope of a Line Passing Through Two Points

The **slope** m of the nonvertical line through (x_1, y_1) and (x_2, y_2) is

$$m = \frac{y_2 - y_1}{x_2 - x_1}$$

where $x_1 \neq x_2$.

When this formula is used for slope, the *order of subtraction* is important. Given two points on a line, you are free to label either one of them as (x_1, y_1) and the other as (x_2, y_2). However, once you have done this, you must form the numerator and denominator using the same order of subtraction.

$$\underbrace{m = \frac{y_2 - y_1}{x_2 - x_1}}_{\text{Correct}} \qquad \underbrace{m = \frac{y_1 - y_2}{x_1 - x_2}}_{\text{Correct}} \qquad \underbrace{\cancel{m = \frac{y_2 - y_1}{x_1 - x_2}}}_{\text{Incorrect}}$$

For instance, the slope of the line passing through the points $(3, 4)$ and $(5, 7)$ can be calculated as

$$m = \frac{7 - 4}{5 - 3} = \frac{3}{2}$$

or, reversing the subtraction order in both the numerator and denominator, as

$$m = \frac{4 - 7}{3 - 5} = \frac{-3}{-2} = \frac{3}{2}.$$

Example 2 Finding the Slope of a Line Through Two Points

Find the slope of the line passing through each pair of points.

a. $(-2, 0)$ and $(3, 1)$ **b.** $(-1, 2)$ and $(2, 2)$

c. $(0, 4)$ and $(1, -1)$ **d.** $(3, 4)$ and $(3, 1)$

Solution

a. Letting $(x_1, y_1) = (-2, 0)$ and $(x_2, y_2) = (3, 1)$, you obtain a slope of

$$m = \frac{y_2 - y_1}{x_2 - x_1} = \frac{1 - 0}{3 - (-2)} = \frac{1}{5}.$$ See Figure 1.35.

b. The slope of the line passing through $(-1, 2)$ and $(2, 2)$ is

$$m = \frac{2 - 2}{2 - (-1)} = \frac{0}{3} = 0.$$ See Figure 1.36.

c. The slope of the line passing through $(0, 4)$ and $(1, -1)$ is

$$m = \frac{-1 - 4}{1 - 0} = \frac{-5}{1} = -5.$$ See Figure 1.37.

d. The slope of the line passing through $(3, 4)$ and $(3, 1)$ is

$$m = \frac{1 - 4}{3 - 3} = \frac{-3}{0}.$$ See Figure 1.38.

Because division by 0 is undefined, the slope is undefined and the line is vertical.

STUDY TIP

In Figures 1.35 to 1.38, note the relationships between slope and the orientation of the line.

a. Positive slope: line rises from left to right

b. Zero slope: line is horizontal

c. Negative slope: line falls from left to right

d. Undefined slope: line is vertical

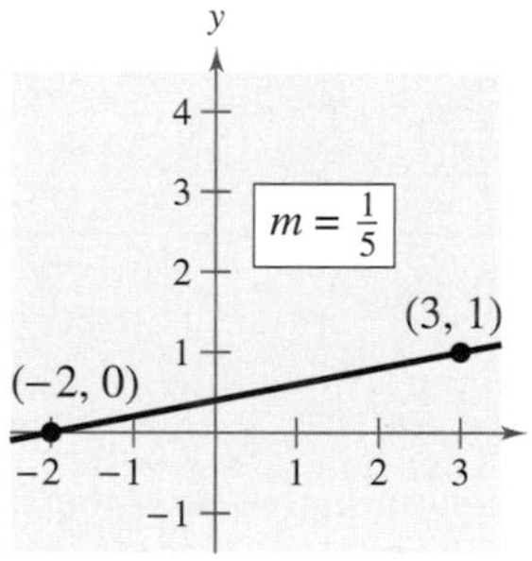

FIGURE 1.35

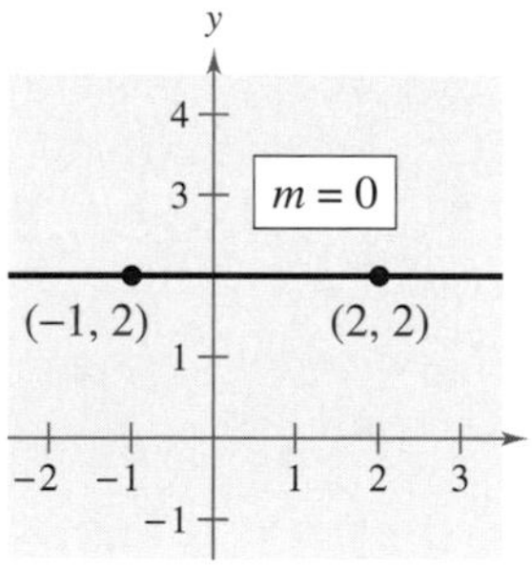

FIGURE 1.36

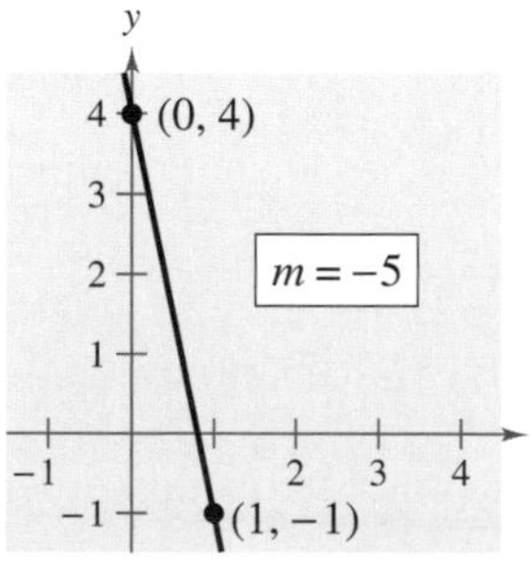

FIGURE 1.37

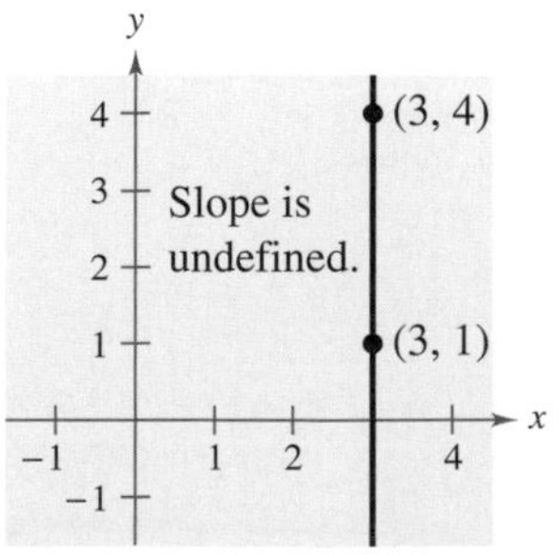

FIGURE 1.38

CHECKPOINT Now try Exercise 21.

Writing Linear Equations in Two Variables

If (x_1, y_1) is a point on a line of slope m and (x, y) is *any other* point on the line, then

$$\frac{y - y_1}{x - x_1} = m.$$

This equation, involving the variables x and y, can be rewritten in the form

$$y - y_1 = m(x - x_1)$$

which is the **point-slope form** of the equation of a line.

> **Point-Slope Form of the Equation of a Line**
>
> The equation of the line with slope m passing through the point (x_1, y_1) is
>
> $$y - y_1 = m(x - x_1).$$

The point-slope form is most useful for *finding* the equation of a line. You should remember this form.

Example 3 Using the Point-Slope Form

Find the slope-intercept form of the equation of the line that has a slope of 3 and passes through the point $(1, -2)$.

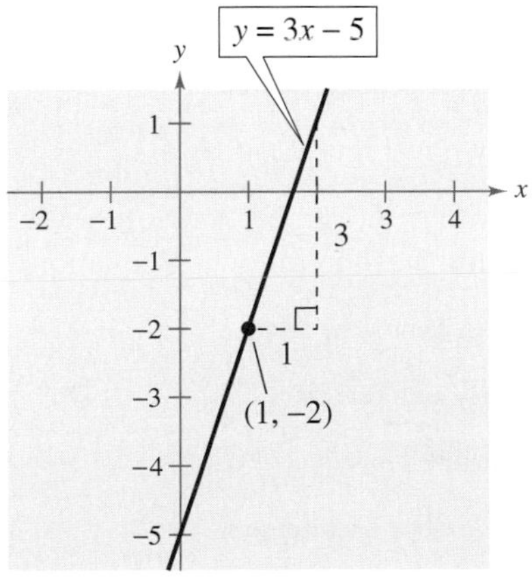

FIGURE 1.39

Solution

Use the point-slope form with $m = 3$ and $(x_1, y_1) = (1, -2)$.

$y - y_1 = m(x - x_1)$	Point-slope form
$y - (-2) = 3(x - 1)$	Substitute for m, x_1, and y_1.
$y + 2 = 3x - 3$	Simplify.
$y = 3x - 5$	Write in slope-intercept form.

The slope-intercept form of the equation of the line is $y = 3x - 5$. The graph of this line is shown in Figure 1.39.

CHECKPOINT Now try Exercise 39.

> **STUDY TIP**
>
> When you find an equation of the line that passes through two given points, you only need to substitute the coordinates of one of the points into the point-slope form. It does not matter which point you choose because both points will yield the same result.

The point-slope form can be used to find an equation of the line passing through two points (x_1, y_1) and (x_2, y_2). To do this, first find the slope of the line

$$m = \frac{y_2 - y_1}{x_2 - x_1}, \qquad x_1 \neq x_2$$

and then use the point-slope form to obtain the equation

$$y - y_1 = \frac{y_2 - y_1}{x_2 - x_1}(x - x_1). \qquad \text{Two-point form}$$

This is sometimes called the **two-point form** of the equation of a line.

Exploration

Find d_1 and d_2 in terms of m_1 and m_2, respectively (see figure). Then use the Pythagorean Theorem to find a relationship between m_1 and m_2.

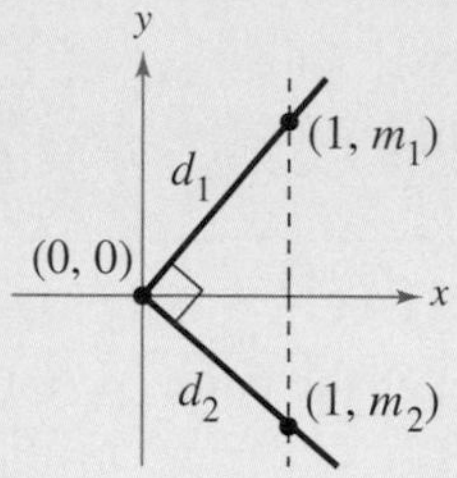

Parallel and Perpendicular Lines

Slope can be used to decide whether two nonvertical lines in a plane are parallel, perpendicular, or neither.

Parallel and Perpendicular Lines

1. Two distinct nonvertical lines are **parallel** if and only if their slopes are equal. That is, $m_1 = m_2$.
2. Two nonvertical lines are **perpendicular** if and only if their slopes are negative reciprocals of each other. That is, $m_1 = -1/m_2$.

Example 4 Finding Parallel and Perpendicular Lines

Find the slope-intercept forms of the equations of the lines that pass through the point $(2, -1)$ and are (a) parallel to and (b) perpendicular to the line $2x - 3y = 5$.

Solution

By writing the equation of the given line in slope-intercept form

$2x - 3y = 5$ Write original equation.

$-3y = -2x + 5$ Subtract $2x$ from each side.

$y = \frac{2}{3}x - \frac{5}{3}$ Write in slope-intercept form.

you can see that it has a slope of $m = \frac{2}{3}$, as shown in Figure 1.40.

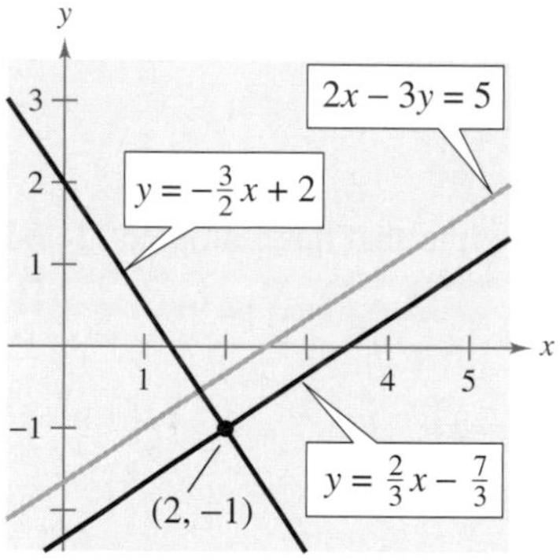

FIGURE 1.40

a. Any line parallel to the given line must also have a slope of $\frac{2}{3}$. So, the line through $(2, -1)$ that is parallel to the given line has the following equation.

$y - (-1) = \frac{2}{3}(x - 2)$ Write in point-slope form.

$3(y + 1) = 2(x - 2)$ Multiply each side by 3.

$3y + 3 = 2x - 4$ Distributive Property

$y = \frac{2}{3}x - \frac{7}{3}$ Write in slope-intercept form.

b. Any line perpendicular to the given line must have a slope of $-\frac{3}{2}$ (because $-\frac{3}{2}$ is the negative reciprocal of $\frac{2}{3}$). So, the line through $(2, -1)$ that is perpendicular to the given line has the following equation.

$y - (-1) = -\frac{3}{2}(x - 2)$ Write in point-slope form.

$2(y + 1) = -3(x - 2)$ Multiply each side by 2.

$2y + 2 = -3x + 6$ Distributive Property

$y = -\frac{3}{2}x + 2$ Write in slope-intercept form.

CHECKPOINT Now try Exercise 69.

Notice in Example 4 how the slope-intercept form is used to obtain information about the graph of a line, whereas the point-slope form is used to write the equation of a line.

Technology

On a graphing utility, lines will not appear to have the correct slope unless you use a viewing window that has a square setting. For instance, try graphing the lines in Example 4 using the standard setting $-10 \le x \le 10$ and $-10 \le y \le 10$. Then reset the viewing window with the square setting $-9 \le x \le 9$ and $-6 \le y \le 6$. On which setting do the lines $y = \frac{2}{3}x - \frac{5}{3}$ and $y = -\frac{3}{2}x + 2$ appear to be perpendicular?

Applications

In real-life problems, the slope of a line can be interpreted as either a *ratio* or a *rate*. If the x-axis and y-axis have the same unit of measure, then the slope has no units and is a **ratio.** If the x-axis and y-axis have different units of measure, then the slope is a **rate** or **rate of change.**

Example 5 Using Slope as a Ratio

The maximum recommended slope of a wheelchair ramp is $\frac{1}{12}$. A business is installing a wheelchair ramp that rises 22 inches over a horizontal length of 24 feet. Is the ramp steeper than recommended? (Source: *Americans with Disabilities Act Handbook*)

Solution

The horizontal length of the ramp is 24 feet or $12(24) = 288$ inches, as shown in Figure 1.41. So, the slope of the ramp is

$$\text{Slope} = \frac{\text{vertical change}}{\text{horizontal change}} = \frac{22 \text{ in.}}{288 \text{ in.}} \approx 0.076.$$

Because $\frac{1}{12} \approx 0.083$, the slope of the ramp is not steeper than recommended.

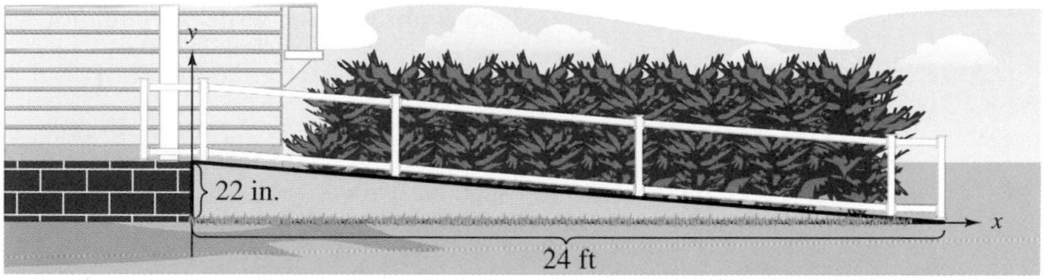

FIGURE 1.41

CHECKPOINT Now try Exercise 97.

Example 6 Using Slope as a Rate of Change

A kitchen appliance manufacturing company determines that the total cost in dollars of producing x units of a blender is

$$C = 25x + 3500. \qquad \text{Cost equation}$$

Describe the practical significance of the y-intercept and slope of this line.

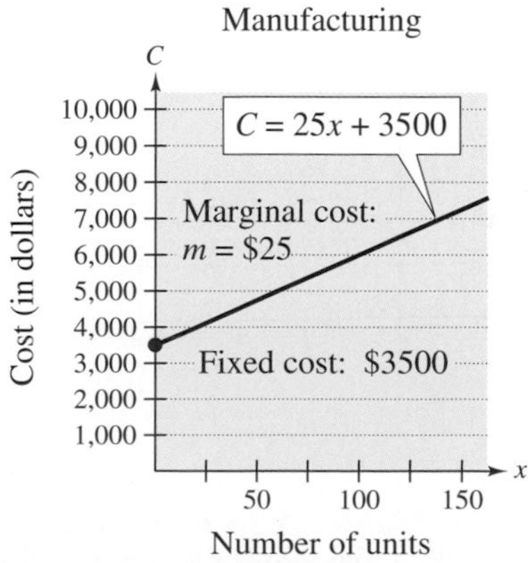

FIGURE 1.42 *Production cost*

Solution

The y-intercept $(0, 3500)$ tells you that the cost of producing zero units is \$3500. This is the *fixed cost* of production—it includes costs that must be paid regardless of the number of units produced. The slope of $m = 25$ tells you that the cost of producing each unit is \$25, as shown in Figure 1.42. Economists call the cost per unit the *marginal cost.* If the production increases by one unit, then the "margin," or extra amount of cost, is \$25. So, the cost increases at a rate of \$25 per unit.

CHECKPOINT Now try Exercise 101.

Most business expenses can be deducted in the same year they occur. One exception is the cost of property that has a useful life of more than 1 year. Such costs must be *depreciated* (decreased in value) over the useful life of the property. If the *same amount* is depreciated each year, the procedure is called *linear* or *straight-line depreciation.* The *book value* is the difference between the original value and the total amount of depreciation accumulated to date.

Example 7 Straight-Line Depreciation

A college purchased exercise equipment worth $12,000 for the new campus fitness center. The equipment has a useful life of 8 years. The salvage value at the end of 8 years is $2000. Write a linear equation that describes the book value of the equipment each year.

Solution

Let V represent the value of the equipment at the end of year t. You can represent the initial value of the equipment by the data point $(0, 12{,}000)$ and the salvage value of the equipment by the data point $(8, 2000)$. The slope of the line is

$$m = \frac{2000 - 12{,}000}{8 - 0} = -\$1250$$

which represents the annual depreciation in *dollars per year.* Using the point-slope form, you can write the equation of the line as follows.

$$V - 12{,}000 = -1250(t - 0) \qquad \text{Write in point-slope form.}$$

$$V = -1250t + 12{,}000 \qquad \text{Write in slope-intercept form.}$$

The table shows the book value at the end of each year, and the graph of the equation is shown in Figure 1.43.

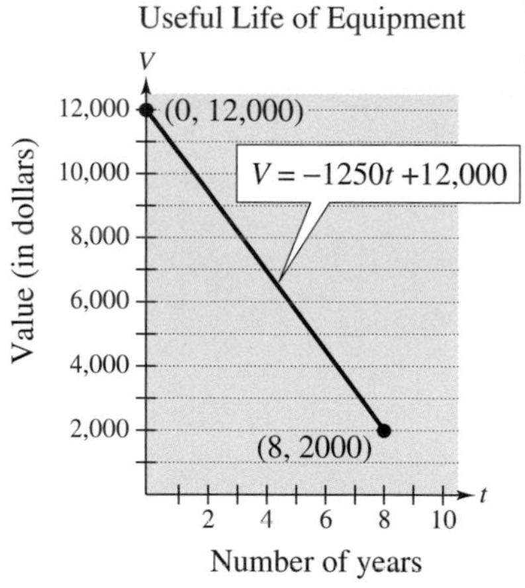

FIGURE 1.43 *Straight-line depreciation*

Year, t	Value, V
0	12,000
1	10,750
2	9,500
3	8,250
4	7,000
5	5,750
6	4,500
7	3,250
8	2,000

CHECKPOINT Now try Exercise 107.

In many real-life applications, the two data points that determine the line are often given in a disguised form. Note how the data points are described in Example 7.

Example 8 Predicting Sales per Share

The sales per share for Starbucks Corporation were \$6.97 in 2001 and \$8.47 in 2002. Using only this information, write a linear equation that gives the sales per share in terms of the year. Then predict the sales per share for 2003. (Source: Starbucks Corporation)

Solution

Let $t = 1$ represent 2001. Then the two given values are represented by the data points $(1, 6.97)$ and $(2, 8.47)$. The slope of the line through these points is

$$m = \frac{8.47 - 6.97}{2 - 1}$$

$$= 1.5.$$

Using the point-slope form, you can find the equation that relates the sales per share y and the year t to be

$$y - 6.97 = 1.5(t - 1) \qquad \text{Write in point-slope form.}$$

$$y = 1.5t + 5.47. \qquad \text{Write in slope-intercept form.}$$

According to this equation, the sales per share in 2003 was $y = 1.5(3) + 5.47 = \$9.97$, as shown in Figure 1.44. (In this case, the prediction is quite good—the actual sales per share in 2003 was \$10.35.)

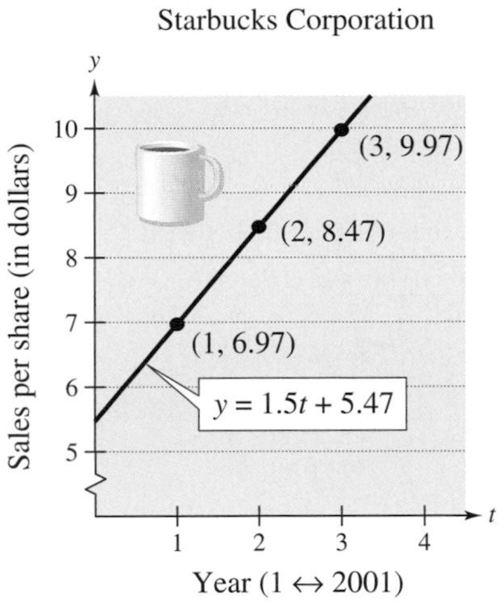

FIGURE 1.44

✓CHECKPOINT Now try Exercise 109.

The prediction method illustrated in Example 8 is called **linear extrapolation.** Note in Figure 1.45 that an extrapolated point does not lie between the given points. When the estimated point lies between two given points, as shown in Figure 1.46, the procedure is called **linear interpolation.**

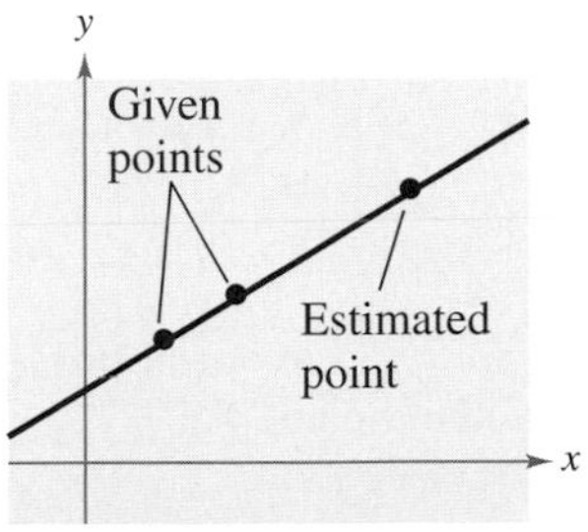

Linear extrapolation

FIGURE 1.45

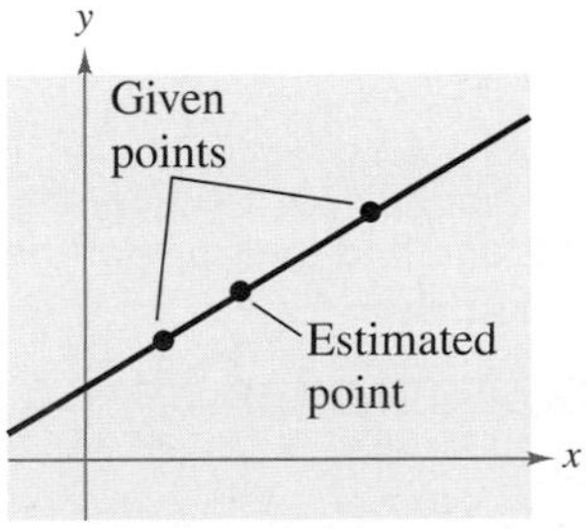

Linear interpolation

FIGURE 1.46

Because the slope of a vertical line is not defined, its equation cannot be written in slope-intercept form. However, every line has an equation that can be written in the **general form**

$$Ax + By + C = 0 \qquad \text{General form}$$

where A and B are not both zero. For instance, the vertical line given by $x = a$ can be represented by the general form $x - a = 0$.

Summary of Equations of Lines

1. General form: $Ax + By + C = 0$
2. Vertical line: $x = a$
3. Horizontal line: $y = b$
4. Slope-intercept form: $y = mx + b$
5. Point-slope form: $y - y_1 = m(x - x_1)$
6. Two-point form: $y - y_1 = \dfrac{y_2 - y_1}{x_2 - x_1}(x - x_1)$

1.3 Exercises

VOCABULARY CHECK:

In Exercises 1–6, fill in the blanks.

1. The simplest mathematical model for relating two variables is the ________ equation in two variables $y = mx + b$.
2. For a line, the ratio of the change in y to the change in x is called the ________ of the line.
3. Two lines are ________ if and only if their slopes are equal.
4. Two lines are ________ if and only if their slopes are negative reciprocals of each other.
5. When the x-axis and y-axis have different units of measure, the slope can be interpreted as a ________.
6. The prediction method ________ ________ is the method used to estimate a point on a line that does not lie between the given points.
7. Match each equation of a line with its form.

(a) $Ax + By + C = 0$	(i) Vertical line
(b) $x = a$	(ii) Slope-intercept form
(c) $y = b$	(iii) General form
(d) $y = mx + b$	(iv) Point-slope form
(e) $y - y_1 = m(x - x_1)$	(v) Horizontal line

In Exercises 1 and 2, identify the line that has each slope.

1. (a) $m = \frac{2}{3}$
   (b) m is undefined.
   (c) $m = -2$

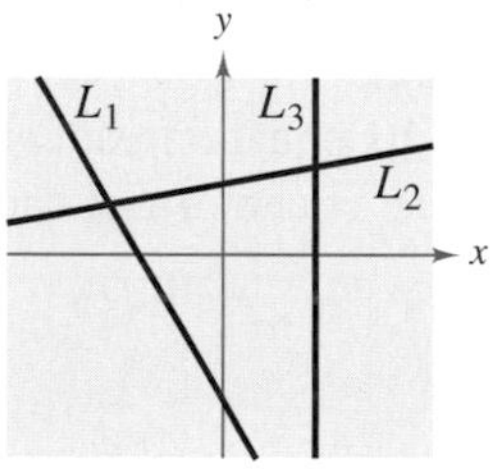

2. (a) $m = 0$
   (b) $m = -\frac{3}{4}$
   (c) $m = 1$

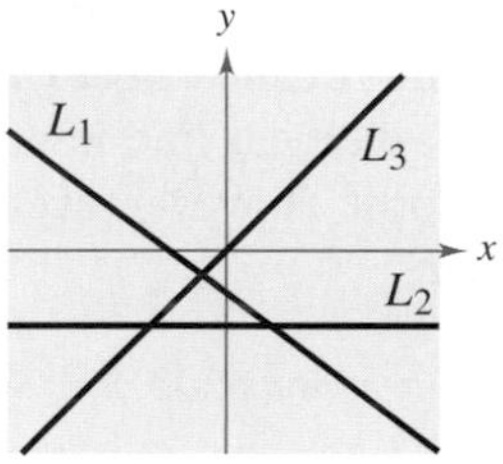

In Exercises 3 and 4, sketch the lines through the point with the indicated slopes on the same set of coordinate axes.

	Point	*Slopes*
3.	(2, 3)	(a) 0 (b) 1 (c) 2 (d) -3
4.	$(-4, 1)$	(a) 3 (b) -3 (c) $\frac{1}{2}$ (d) Undefined

In Exercises 5–8, estimate the slope of the line.

5.

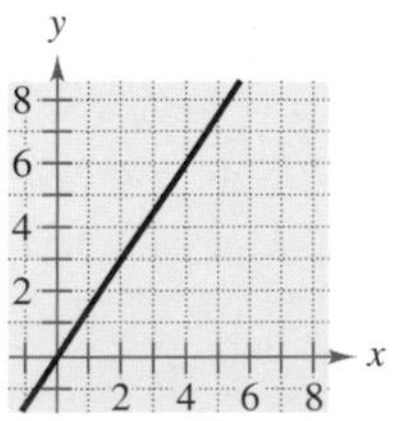

6.

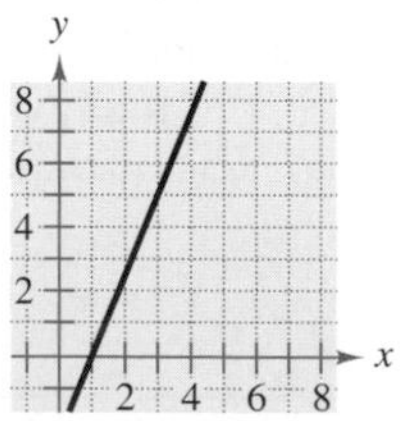

7.

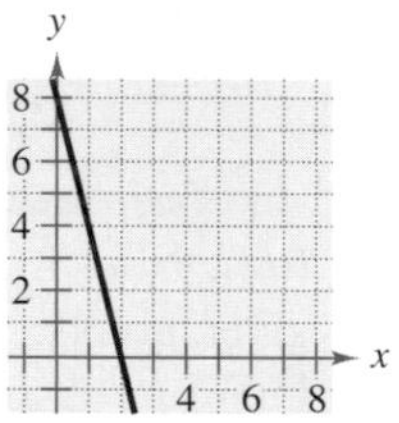

8.

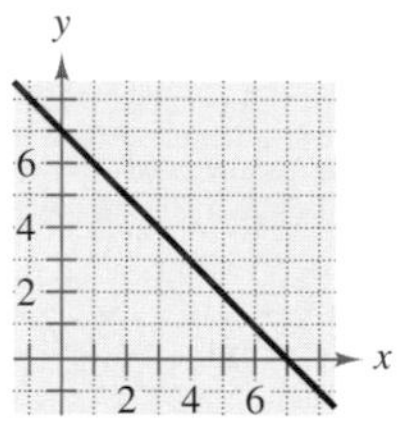

In Exercises 9–20, find the slope and y-intercept (if possible) of the equation of the line. Sketch the line.

9. $y = 5x + 3$
10. $y = x - 10$
11. $y = -\frac{1}{2}x + 4$
12. $y = -\frac{3}{2}x + 6$
13. $5x - 2 = 0$
14. $3y + 5 = 0$
15. $7x + 6y = 30$
16. $2x + 3y = 9$
17. $y - 3 = 0$
18. $y + 4 = 0$
19. $x + 5 = 0$
20. $x - 2 = 0$

In Exercises 21–28, plot the points and find the slope of the line passing through the pair of points.

21. $(-3, -2), (1, 6)$
22. $(2, 4), (4, -4)$
23. $(-6, -1), (-6, 4)$
24. $(0, -10), (-4, 0)$
25. $\left(\frac{11}{2}, -\frac{4}{3}\right), \left(-\frac{3}{2}, -\frac{1}{3}\right)$
26. $\left(\frac{7}{8}, \frac{3}{4}\right), \left(\frac{5}{4}, -\frac{1}{4}\right)$
27. $(4.8, 3.1), (-5.2, 1.6)$
28. $(-1.75, -8.3), (2.25, -2.6)$

In Exercises 29–38, use the point on the line and the slope of the line to find three additional points through which the line passes. (There are many correct answers.)

	Point	*Slope*
29.	$(2, 1)$	$m = 0$
30.	$(-4, 1)$	m is undefined.
31.	$(5, -6)$	$m = 1$
32.	$(10, -6)$	$m = -1$
33.	$(-8, 1)$	m is undefined.
34.	$(-3, -1)$	$m = 0$
35.	$(-5, 4)$	$m = 2$
36.	$(0, -9)$	$m = -2$
37.	$(7, -2)$	$m = \frac{1}{2}$
38.	$(-1, -6)$	$m = -\frac{1}{2}$

In Exercises 39–50, find the slope-intercept form of the equation of the line that passes through the given point and has the indicated slope. Sketch the line.

	Point	*Slope*
39.	$(0, -2)$	$m = 3$
40.	$(0, 10)$	$m = -1$
41.	$(-3, 6)$	$m = -2$
42.	$(0, 0)$	$m = 4$
43.	$(4, 0)$	$m = -\frac{1}{3}$
44.	$(-2, -5)$	$m = \frac{3}{4}$
45.	$(6, -1)$	m is undefined.
46.	$(-10, 4)$	m is undefined.
47.	$\left(4, \frac{5}{2}\right)$	$m = 0$
48.	$\left(-\frac{1}{2}, \frac{3}{2}\right)$	$m = 0$
49.	$(-5.1, 1.8)$	$m = 5$
50.	$(2.3, -8.5)$	$m = -\frac{5}{2}$

In Exercises 51–64, find the slope-intercept form of the equation of the line passing through the points. Sketch the line.

51. $(5, -1), (-5, 5)$

52. $(4, 3), (-4, -4)$

53. $(-8, 1), (-8, 7)$

54. $(-1, 4), (6, 4)$

55. $\left(2, \frac{1}{2}\right), \left(\frac{1}{2}, \frac{5}{4}\right)$

56. $(1, 1), \left(6, -\frac{2}{3}\right)$

57. $\left(-\frac{1}{10}, -\frac{3}{5}\right), \left(\frac{9}{10}, -\frac{9}{5}\right)$

58. $\left(\frac{3}{4}, \frac{3}{2}\right), \left(-\frac{4}{3}, \frac{7}{4}\right)$

59. $(1, 0.6), (-2, -0.6)$

60. $(-8, 0.6), (2, -2.4)$

61. $(2, -1), \left(\frac{1}{3}, -1\right)$

62. $\left(\frac{1}{5}, -2\right), (-6, -2)$

63. $\left(\frac{7}{3}, -8\right), \left(\frac{7}{3}, 1\right)$

64. $(1.5, -2), (1.5, 0.2)$

In Exercises 65–68, determine whether the lines L_1 and L_2 passing through the pairs of points are parallel, perpendicular, or neither.

65. L_1: $(0, -1), (5, 9)$
L_2: $(0, 3), (4, 1)$

66. L_1: $(-2, -1), (1, 5)$
L_2: $(1, 3), (5, -5)$

67. L_1: $(3, 6), (-6, 0)$
L_2: $(0, -1), \left(5, \frac{7}{3}\right)$

68. L_1: $(4, 8), (-4, 2)$
L_2: $(3, -5), \left(-1, \frac{1}{3}\right)$

In Exercises 69–78, write the slope-intercept forms of the equations of the lines through the given point (a) parallel to the given line and (b) perpendicular to the given line.

	Point	*Line*
69.	$(2, 1)$	$4x - 2y = 3$
70.	$(-3, 2)$	$x + y = 7$
71.	$\left(-\frac{2}{3}, \frac{7}{8}\right)$	$3x + 4y = 7$
72.	$\left(\frac{7}{8}, \frac{3}{4}\right)$	$5x + 3y = 0$
73.	$(-1, 0)$	$y = -3$
74.	$(4, -2)$	$y = 1$
75.	$(2, 5)$	$x = 4$
76.	$(-5, 1)$	$x = -2$
77.	$(2.5, 6.8)$	$x - y = 4$
78.	$(-3.9, -1.4)$	$6x + 2y = 9$

In Exercises 79–84, use the *intercept form* to find the equation of the line with the given intercepts. The intercept form of the equation of a line with intercepts $(a, 0)$ and $(0, b)$ is

$$\frac{x}{a} + \frac{y}{b} = 1, \quad a \neq 0, \quad b \neq 0.$$

79. x-intercept: $(2, 0)$
y-intercept: $(0, 3)$

80. x-intercept: $(-3, 0)$
y-intercept: $(0, 4)$

81. x-intercept: $\left(-\frac{1}{6}, 0\right)$
y-intercept: $\left(0, -\frac{2}{3}\right)$

82. x-intercept: $\left(\frac{2}{3}, 0\right)$
y-intercept: $(0, -2)$

83. Point on line: $(1, 2)$
x-intercept: $(c, 0)$
y-intercept: $(0, c)$, $c \neq 0$

84. Point on line: $(-3, 4)$
x-intercept: $(d, 0)$
y-intercept: $(0, d)$, $d \neq 0$

Graphical Interpretation **In Exercises 85–88, identify any relationships that exist among the lines, and then use a graphing utility to graph the three equations in the same viewing window. Adjust the viewing window so that the slope appears visually correct—that is, so that parallel lines appear parallel and perpendicular lines appear to intersect at right angles.**

85. (a) $y = 2x$ (b) $y = -2x$ (c) $y = \frac{1}{2}x$

86. (a) $y = \frac{2}{3}x$ (b) $y = -\frac{3}{2}x$ (c) $y = \frac{2}{3}x + 2$

87. (a) $y = -\frac{1}{2}x$ (b) $y = -\frac{1}{2}x + 3$ (c) $y = 2x - 4$

88. (a) $y = x - 8$ (b) $y = x + 1$ (c) $y = -x + 3$

In Exercises 89–92, find a relationship between x and y such that (x, y) is equidistant (the same distance) from the two points.

89. $(4, -1), (-2, 3)$

90. $(6, 5), (1, -8)$

91. $\left(3, \frac{5}{2}\right), (-7, 1)$

92. $\left(-\frac{1}{2}, -4\right), \left(\frac{7}{2}, \frac{5}{4}\right)$

93. *Sales* The following are the slopes of lines representing annual sales y in terms of time x in years. Use the slopes to interpret any change in annual sales for a one-year increase in time.

(a) The line has a slope of $m = 135$.

(b) The line has a slope of $m = 0$.

(c) The line has a slope of $m = -40$.

94. *Revenue* The following are the slopes of lines representing daily revenues y in terms of time x in days. Use the slopes to interpret any change in daily revenues for a one-day increase in time.

(a) The line has a slope of $m = 400$.

(b) The line has a slope of $m = 100$.

(c) The line has a slope of $m = 0$.

95. *Average Salary* The graph shows the average salaries for senior high school principals from 1990 through 2002. (Source: Educational Research Service)

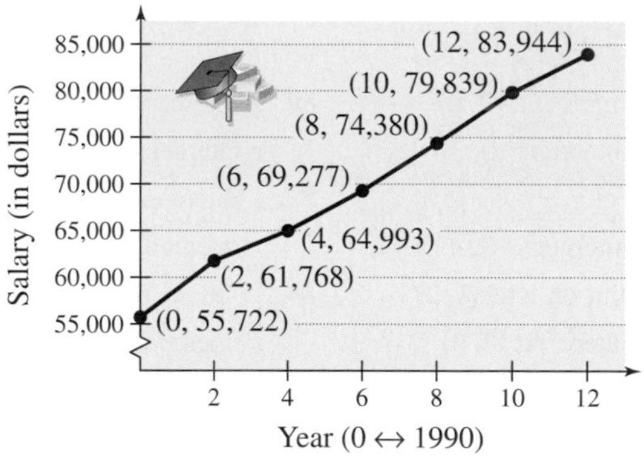

(a) Use the slopes to determine the time periods in which the average salary increased the greatest and the least.

(b) Find the slope of the line segment connecting the years 1990 and 2002.

(c) Interpret the meaning of the slope in part (b) in the context of the problem.

96. *Net Profit* The graph shows the net profits (in millions) for Applebee's International, Inc. for the years 1994 through 2003. (Source: Applebee's International, Inc.)

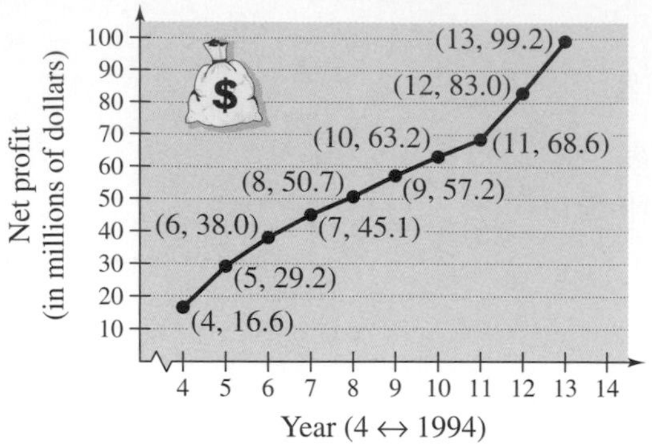

(a) Use the slopes to determine the years in which the net profit showed the greatest increase and the least increase.

(b) Find the slope of the line segment connecting the years 1994 and 2003.

(c) Interpret the meaning of the slope in part (b) in the context of the problem.

97. *Road Grade* You are driving on a road that has a 6% uphill grade (see figure). This means that the slope of the road is $\frac{6}{100}$. Approximate the amount of vertical change in your position if you drive 200 feet.

98. *Road Grade* From the top of a mountain road, a surveyor takes several horizontal measurements x and several vertical measurements y, as shown in the table (x and y are measured in feet).

x	300	600	900	1200	1500	1800	2100
y	-25	-50	-75	-100	-125	-150	-175

(a) Sketch a scatter plot of the data.

(b) Use a straightedge to sketch the line that you think best fits the data.

(c) Find an equation for the line you sketched in part (b).

(d) Interpret the meaning of the slope of the line in part (c) in the context of the problem.

(e) The surveyor needs to put up a road sign that indicates the steepness of the road. For instance, a surveyor would put up a sign that states "8% grade" on a road with a downhill grade that has a slope of $-\frac{8}{100}$. What should the sign state for the road in this problem?

Rate of Change **In Exercises 99 and 100, you are given the dollar value of a product in 2005 and the rate at which the value of the product is expected to change during the next 5 years. Use this information to write a linear equation that gives the dollar value V of the product in terms of the year t. (Let $t = 5$ represent 2005.)**

	2005 Value	*Rate*
99.	\$2540	\$125 decrease per year
100.	\$156	\$4.50 increase per year

Graphical Interpretation **In Exercises 101–104, match the description of the situation with its graph. Also determine the slope and y-intercept of each graph and interpret the slope and y-intercept in the context of the situation. [The graphs are labeled (a), (b), (c), and (d).]**

(a)

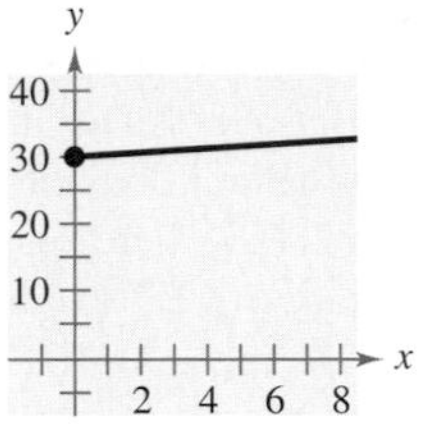

(b)

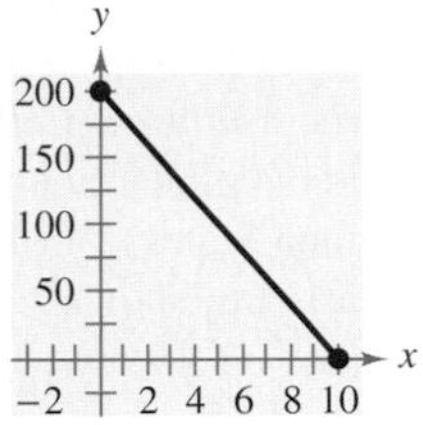

(c)

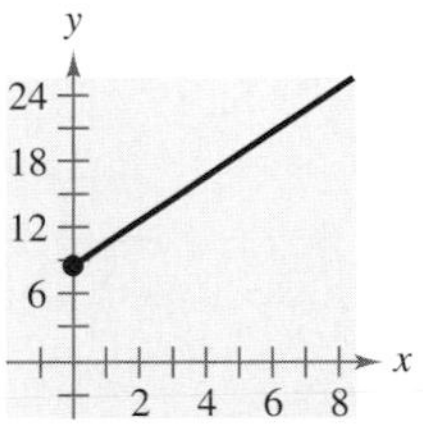

(d)

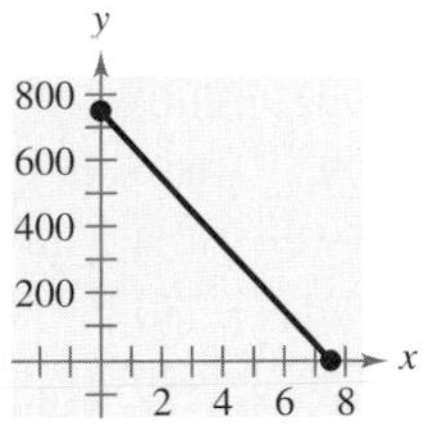

101. A person is paying \$20 per week to a friend to repay a \$200 loan.

102. An employee is paid \$8.50 per hour plus \$2 for each unit produced per hour.

103. A sales representative receives \$30 per day for food plus \$0.32 for each mile traveled.

104. A computer that was purchased for \$750 depreciates \$100 per year.

105. ***Cash Flow per Share*** The cash flow per share for the Timberland Co. was \$0.18 in 1995 and \$4.04 in 2003. Write a linear equation that gives the cash flow per share in terms of the year. Let $t = 5$ represent 1995. Then predict the cash flows for the years 2008 and 2010. (Source: The Timberland Co.)

106. ***Number of Stores*** In 1999 there were 4076 J.C. Penney stores and in 2003 there were 1078 stores. Write a linear equation that gives the number of stores in terms of the year. Let $t = 9$ represent 1999. Then predict the numbers of stores for the years 2008 and 2010. Are your answers reasonable? Explain. (Source: J.C. Penney Co.)

107. ***Depreciation*** A sub shop purchases a used pizza oven for \$875. After 5 years, the oven will have to be replaced. Write a linear equation giving the value V of the equipment during the 5 years it will be in use.

108. ***Depreciation*** A school district purchases a high-volume printer, copier, and scanner for \$25,000. After 10 years, the equipment will have to be replaced. Its value at that time is expected to be \$2000. Write a linear equation giving the value V of the equipment during the 10 years it will be in use.

109. ***College Enrollment*** The Pennsylvania State University had enrollments of 40,571 students in 2000 and 41,289 students in 2004 at its main campus in University Park, Pennsylvania. (Source: *Penn State Fact Book*)

(a) Assuming the enrollment growth is linear, find a linear model that gives the enrollment in terms of the year t, where $t = 0$ corresponds to 2000.

(b) Use your model from part (a) to predict the enrollments in 2008 and 2010.

(c) What is the slope of your model? Explain its meaning in the context of the situation.

110. ***College Enrollment*** The University of Florida had enrollments of 36,531 students in 1990 and 48,673 students in 2003. (Source: University of Florida)

(a) What was the average annual change in enrollment from 1990 to 2003?

(b) Use the average annual change in enrollment to estimate the enrollments in 1994, 1998, and 2002.

(c) Write the equation of a line that represents the given data. What is its slope? Interpret the slope in the context of the problem.

(d) Using the results of parts (a)–(c), write a short paragraph discussing the concepts of *slope* and *average rate of change*.

111. ***Sales*** A discount outlet is offering a 15% discount on all items. Write a linear equation giving the sale price S for an item with a list price L.

112. ***Hourly Wage*** A microchip manufacturer pays its assembly line workers \$11.50 per hour. In addition, workers receive a piecework rate of \$0.75 per unit produced. Write a linear equation for the hourly wage W in terms of the number of units x produced per hour.

113. ***Cost, Revenue, and Profit*** A roofing contractor purchases a shingle delivery truck with a shingle elevator for \$36,500. The vehicle requires an average expenditure of \$5.25 per hour for fuel and maintenance, and the operator is paid \$11.50 per hour.

(a) Write a linear equation giving the total cost C of operating this equipment for t hours. (Include the purchase cost of the equipment.)

(b) Assuming that customers are charged $27 per hour of machine use, write an equation for the revenue R derived from t hours of use.

(c) Use the formula for profit $(P = R - C)$ to write an equation for the profit derived from t hours of use.

(d) Use the result of part (c) to find the break-even point—that is, the number of hours this equipment must be used to yield a profit of 0 dollars.

114. ***Rental Demand*** A real estate office handles an apartment complex with 50 units. When the rent per unit is $580 per month, all 50 units are occupied. However, when the rent is $625 per month, the average number of occupied units drops to 47. Assume that the relationship between the monthly rent p and the demand x is linear.

(a) Write the equation of the line giving the demand x in terms of the rent p.

(b) Use this equation to predict the number of units occupied when the rent is $655.

(c) Predict the number of units occupied when the rent is $595.

115. ***Geometry*** The length and width of a rectangular garden are 15 meters and 10 meters, respectively. A walkway of width x surrounds the garden.

(a) Draw a diagram that gives a visual representation of the problem.

(b) Write the equation for the perimeter y of the walkway in terms of x.

(c) Use a graphing utility to graph the equation for the perimeter.

(d) Determine the slope of the graph in part (c). For each additional one-meter increase in the width of the walkway, determine the increase in its perimeter.

116. ***Monthly Salary*** A pharmaceutical salesperson receives a monthly salary of $2500 plus a commission of 7% of sales. Write a linear equation for the salesperson's monthly wage W in terms of monthly sales S.

117. ***Business Costs*** A sales representative of a company using a personal car receives $120 per day for lodging and meals plus $0.38 per mile driven. Write a linear equation giving the daily cost C to the company in terms of x, the number of miles driven.

118. ***Sports*** The median salaries (in thousands of dollars) for players on the Los Angeles Dodgers from 1996 to 2003 are shown in the scatter plot. Find the equation of the line that you think best fits these data. (Let y represent the median salary and let t represent the year, with $t = 6$ corresponding to 1996.) (Source: *USA TODAY*)

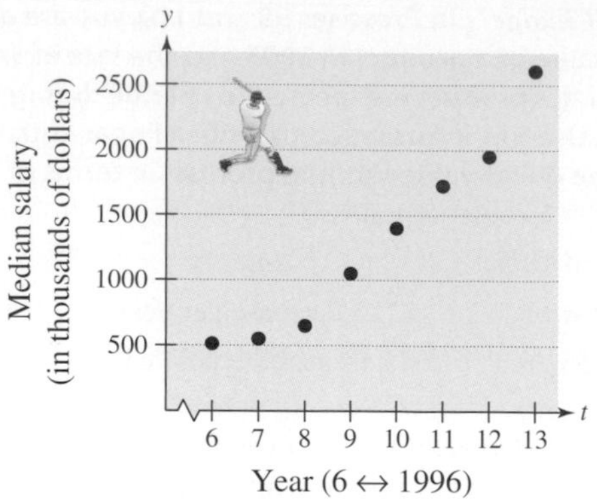

FIGURE FOR 118

Model It

119. ***Data Analysis: Cell Phone Suscribers*** The numbers of cellular phone suscribers y (in millions) in the United States from 1990 through 2002, where x is the year, are shown as data points (x, y). (Source: Cellular Telecommunications & Internet Association)

(1990, 5.3)
(1991, 7.6)
(1992, 11.0)
(1993, 16.0)
(1994, 24.1)
(1995, 33.8)
(1996, 44.0)
(1997, 55.3)
(1998, 69.2)
(1999, 86.0)
(2000, 109.5)
(2001, 128.4)
(2002, 140.8)

(a) Sketch a scatter plot of the data. Let $x = 0$ correspond to 1990.

(b) Use a straightedge to sketch the line that you think best fits the data.

(c) Find the equation of the line from part (b). Explain the procedure you used.

(d) Write a short paragraph explaining the meanings of the slope and y-intercept of the line in terms of the data.

(e) Compare the values obtained using your model with the actual values.

(f) Use your model to estimate the number of cellular phone suscribers in 2008.

120. ***Data Analysis: Average Scores*** An instructor gives regular 20-point quizzes and 100-point exams in an algebra course. Average scores for six students, given as data points (x, y) where x is the average quiz score and y is the average test score, are $(18, 87)$, $(10, 55)$, $(19, 96)$, $(16, 79)$, $(13, 76)$, and $(15, 82)$. [*Note:* There are many correct answers for parts (b)–(d).]

(a) Sketch a scatter plot of the data.

(b) Use a straightedge to sketch the line that you think best fits the data.

(c) Find an equation for the line you sketched in part (b).

(d) Use the equation in part (c) to estimate the average test score for a person with an average quiz score of 17.

(e) The instructor adds 4 points to the average test score of each student in the class. Describe the changes in the positions of the plotted points and the change in the equation of the line.

Synthesis

True or False? **In Exercises 121 and 122, determine whether the statement is true or false. Justify your answer.**

121. A line with a slope of $-\frac{5}{7}$ is steeper than a line with a slope of $-\frac{6}{7}$.

122. The line through $(-8, 2)$ and $(-1, 4)$ and the line through $(0, -4)$ and $(-7, 7)$ are parallel.

123. Explain how you could show that the points $A\ (2, 3)$, $B\ (2, 9)$, and $C\ (4, 3)$ are the vertices of a right triangle.

124. Explain why the slope of a vertical line is said to be undefined.

125. With the information shown in the graphs, is it possible to determine the slope of each line? Is it possible that the lines could have the same slope? Explain.

(a)

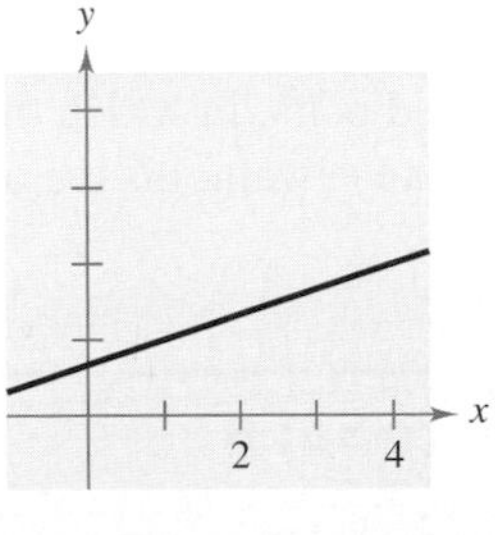

(b)

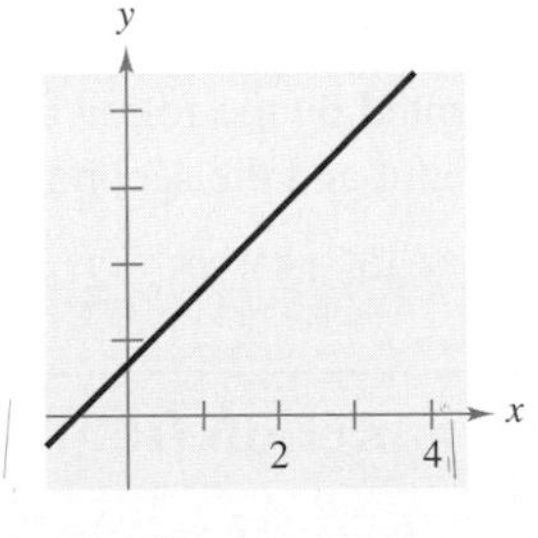

126. The slopes of two lines are -4 and $\frac{5}{2}$. Which is steeper? Explain.

127. The value V of a molding machine t years after it is purchased is

$$V = -4000t + 58{,}500, \quad 0 \le t \le 5.$$

Explain what the V-intercept and slope measure.

128. ***Think About It*** Is it possible for two lines with positive slopes to be perpendicular? Explain.

Skills Review

In Exercises 129–132, match the equation with its graph. [The graphs are labeled (a), (b), (c), and (d).]

(a)

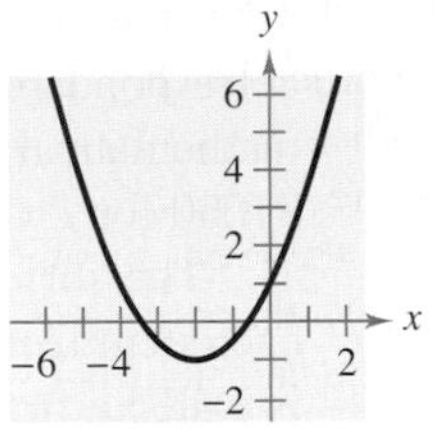

(b)

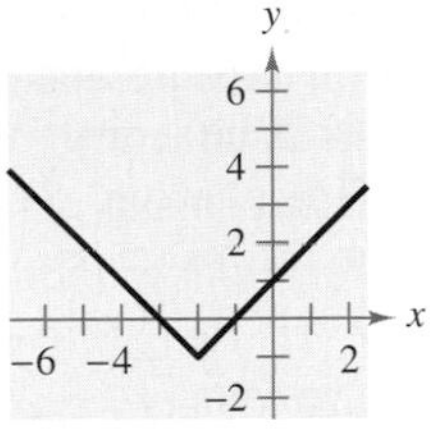

(c)

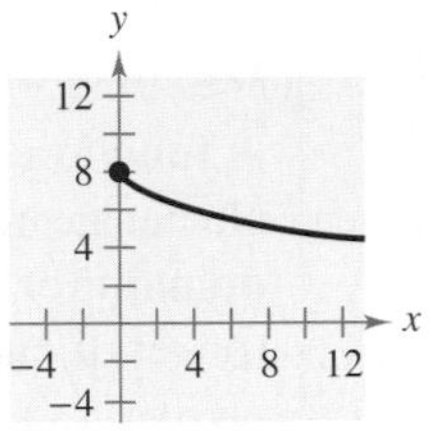

(d)

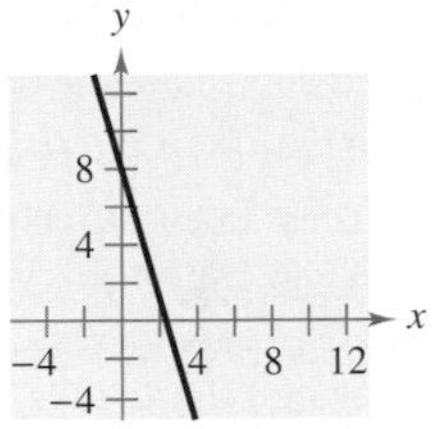

129. $y = 8 - 3x$

130. $y = 8 - \sqrt{x}$

131. $y = \frac{1}{2}x^2 + 2x + 1$

132. $y = |x + 2| - 1$

In Exercises 133–138, find all the solutions of the equation. Check your solution(s) in the original equation.

133. $-7(3 - x) = 14(x - 1)$

134. $\dfrac{8}{2x - 7} = \dfrac{4}{9 - 4x}$

135. $2x^2 - 21x + 49 = 0$

136. $x^2 - 8x + 3 = 0$

137. $\sqrt{x - 9} + 15 = 0$

138. $3x - 16\sqrt{x} + 5 = 0$

139. **Make a Decision** To work an extended application analyzing the numbers of bachelor's degrees earned by women in the United States from 1985 to 2002, visit this text's website at *college.hmco.com.* *(Data Source: U.S. Census Bureau)*

1.4 Functions

What you should learn

- Determine whether relations between two variables are functions.
- Use function notation and evaluate functions.
- Find the domains of functions.
- Use functions to model and solve real-life problems.
- Evaluate difference quotients.

Why you should learn it

Functions can be used to model and solve real-life problems. For instance, in Exercise 100 on page 52, you will use a function to model the force of water against the face of a dam.

© Lester Lefkowitz/Corbis

Introduction to Functions

Many everyday phenomena involve two quantities that are related to each other by some rule of correspondence. The mathematical term for such a rule of correspondence is a **relation.** In mathematics, relations are often represented by mathematical equations and formulas. For instance, the simple interest I earned on \$1000 for 1 year is related to the annual interest rate r by the formula $I = 1000r$.

The formula $I = 1000r$ represents a special kind of relation that matches each item from one set with *exactly one* item from a different set. Such a relation is called a **function.**

Definition of Function

A **function** f from a set A to a set B is a relation that assigns to each element x in the set A exactly one element y in the set B. The set A is the **domain** (or set of inputs) of the function f, and the set B contains the **range** (or set of outputs).

To help understand this definition, look at the function that relates the time of day to the temperature in Figure 1.47.

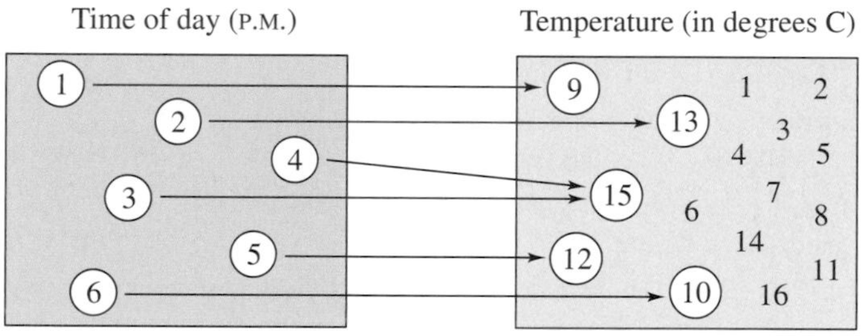

Set A is the domain.
Inputs: 1, 2, 3, 4, 5, 6

Set B contains the range.
Outputs: 9, 10, 12, 13, 15

FIGURE 1.47

This function can be represented by the following ordered pairs, in which the first coordinate (x-value) is the input and the second coordinate (y-value) is the output.

$$\{(1, 9°), (2, 13°), (3, 15°), (4, 15°), (5, 12°), (6, 10°)\}$$

Characteristics of a Function from Set A to Set B

1. Each element in A must be matched with an element in B.
2. Some elements in B may not be matched with any element in A.
3. Two or more elements in A may be matched with the same element in B.
4. An element in A (the domain) cannot be matched with two different elements in B.

Functions are commonly represented in four ways.

Four Ways to Represent a Function

1. *Verbally* by a sentence that describes how the input variable is related to the output variable
2. *Numerically* by a table or a list of ordered pairs that matches input values with output values
3. *Graphically* by points on a graph in a coordinate plane in which the input values are represented by the horizontal axis and the output values are represented by the vertical axis
4. *Algebraically* by an equation in two variables

To determine whether or not a relation is a function, you must decide whether each input value is matched with exactly one output value. If any input value is matched with two or more output values, the relation is not a function.

Example 1 Testing for Functions

Determine whether the relation represents y as a function of x.

a. The input value x is the number of representatives from a state, and the output value y is the number of senators.

b.

Input, x	Output, y
2	11
2	10
3	8
4	5
5	1

c.

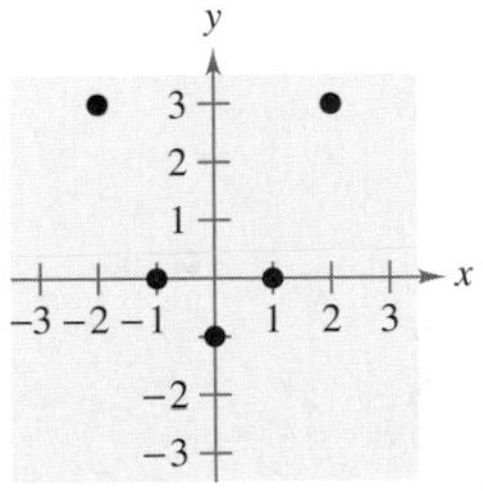

FIGURE 1.48

Solution

a. This verbal description *does* describe y as a function of x. Regardless of the value of x, the value of y is always 2. Such functions are called *constant functions*.

b. This table *does not* describe y as a function of x. The input value 2 is matched with two different y-values.

c. The graph in Figure 1.48 *does* describe y as a function of x. Each input value is matched with exactly one output value.

CHECKPOINT Now try Exercise 5.

Representing functions by sets of ordered pairs is common in *discrete mathematics*. In algebra, however, it is more common to represent functions by equations or formulas involving two variables. For instance, the equation

$$y = x^2 \qquad y \text{ is a function of } x.$$

represents the variable y as a function of the variable x. In this equation, x is

© Bettmann/Corbis

Historical Note
Leonhard Euler (1707–1783), a Swiss mathematician, is considered to have been the most prolific and productive mathematician in history. One of his greatest influences on mathematics was his use of symbols, or notation. The function notation $y = f(x)$ was introduced by Euler.

the **independent variable** and y is the **dependent variable.** The domain of the function is the set of all values taken on by the independent variable x, and the range of the function is the set of all values taken on by the dependent variable y.

Example 2 Testing for Functions Represented Algebraically

Which of the equations represent(s) y as a function of x?

a. $x^2 + y = 1$ **b.** $-x + y^2 = 1$

Solution

To determine whether y is a function of x, try to solve for y in terms of x.

a. Solving for y yields

$$x^2 + y = 1 \quad \text{Write original equation.}$$
$$y = 1 - x^2. \quad \text{Solve for } y.$$

To each value of x there corresponds exactly one value of y. So, y is a function of x.

b. Solving for y yields

$$-x + y^2 = 1 \quad \text{Write original equation.}$$
$$y^2 = 1 + x \quad \text{Add } x \text{ to each side.}$$
$$y = \pm\sqrt{1 + x}. \quad \text{Solve for } y.$$

The $\pm$ indicates that to a given value of x there correspond two values of y. So, y is not a function of x.

CHECKPOINT Now try Exercise 15.

Function Notation

When an equation is used to represent a function, it is convenient to name the function so that it can be referenced easily. For example, you know that the equation $y = 1 - x^2$ describes y as a function of x. Suppose you give this function the name "f." Then you can use the following **function notation.**

Input	*Output*	*Equation*
x	$f(x)$	$f(x) = 1 - x^2$

The symbol $f(x)$ is read as *the value of f at x* or simply *f of x*. The symbol $f(x)$ corresponds to the y-value for a given x. So, you can write $y = f(x)$. Keep in mind that f is the *name* of the function, whereas $f(x)$ is the *value* of the function at x. For instance, the function given by

$$f(x) = 3 - 2x$$

has *function values* denoted by $f(-1)$, $f(0)$, $f(2)$, and so on. To find these values, substitute the specified input values into the given equation.

For $x = -1$, $\quad f(-1) = 3 - 2(-1) = 3 + 2 = 5.$

For $x = 0$, $\quad f(0) = 3 - 2(0) = 3 - 0 = 3.$

For $x = 2$, $\quad f(2) = 3 - 2(2) = 3 - 4 = -1.$

Although f is often used as a convenient function name and x is often used as the independent variable, you can use other letters. For instance,

$$f(x) = x^2 - 4x + 7, \quad f(t) = t^2 - 4t + 7, \quad \text{and} \quad g(s) = s^2 - 4s + 7$$

all define the same function. In fact, the role of the independent variable is that of a "placeholder." Consequently, the function could be described by

$$f(\quad) = (\quad)^2 - 4(\quad) + 7.$$

STUDY TIP

In Example 3, note that $g(x + 2)$ is not equal to $g(x) + g(2)$. In general, $g(u + v) \neq g(u) + g(v)$.

Example 3 Evaluating a Function

Let $g(x) = -x^2 + 4x + 1$. Find each function value.

a. $g(2)$ **b.** $g(t)$ **c.** $g(x + 2)$

Solution

a. Replacing x with 2 in $g(x) = -x^2 + 4x + 1$ yields the following.

$$g(2) = -(2)^2 + 4(2) + 1 = -4 + 8 + 1 = 5$$

b. Replacing x with t yields the following.

$$g(t) = -(t)^2 + 4(t) + 1 = -t^2 + 4t + 1$$

c. Replacing x with $x + 2$ yields the following.

$$\begin{aligned} g(x + 2) &= -(x + 2)^2 + 4(x + 2) + 1 \\ &= -(x^2 + 4x + 4) + 4x + 8 + 1 \\ &= -x^2 - 4x - 4 + 4x + 8 + 1 \\ &= -x^2 + 5 \end{aligned}$$

✓CHECKPOINT Now try Exercise 29.

A function defined by two or more equations over a specified domain is called a **piecewise-defined function.**

Example 4 A Piecewise-Defined Function

Evaluate the function when $x = -1, 0,$ and 1.

$$f(x) = \begin{cases} x^2 + 1, & x < 0 \\ x - 1, & x \geq 0 \end{cases}$$

Solution

Because $x = -1$ is less than 0, use $f(x) = x^2 + 1$ to obtain

$$f(-1) = (-1)^2 + 1 = 2.$$

For $x = 0$, use $f(x) = x - 1$ to obtain

$$f(0) = (0) - 1 = -1.$$

For $x = 1$, use $f(x) = x - 1$ to obtain

$$f(1) = (1) - 1 = 0.$$

✓CHECKPOINT Now try Exercise 35.

Technology

Use a graphing utility to graph the functions given by $y = \sqrt{4 - x^2}$ and $y = \sqrt{x^2 - 4}$. What is the domain of each function? Do the domains of these two functions overlap? If so, for what values do the domains overlap?

The Domain of a Function

The domain of a function can be described explicitly or it can be *implied* by the expression used to define the function. The **implied domain** is the set of all real numbers for which the expression is defined. For instance, the function given by

$$f(x) = \frac{1}{x^2 - 4}$$ Domain excludes x-values that result in division by zero.

has an implied domain that consists of all real x other than $x = \pm 2$. These two values are excluded from the domain because division by zero is undefined. Another common type of implied domain is that used to avoid even roots of negative numbers. For example, the function given by

$$f(x) = \sqrt{x}$$ Domain excludes x-values that result in even roots of negative numbers.

is defined only for $x \geq 0$. So, its implied domain is the interval $[0, \infty)$. In general, the domain of a function *excludes* values that would cause division by zero *or* that would result in the even root of a negative number.

Example 5 Finding the Domain of a Function

Find the domain of each function.

a. f: $\{(-3, 0), (-1, 4), (0, 2), (2, 2), (4, -1)\}$ **b.** $g(x) = \dfrac{1}{x + 5}$

c. Volume of a sphere: $V = \frac{4}{3}\pi r^3$ **d.** $h(x) = \sqrt{4 - x^2}$

Solution

a. The domain of f consists of all first coordinates in the set of ordered pairs.

$$\text{Domain} = \{-3, -1, 0, 2, 4\}$$

b. Excluding x-values that yield zero in the denominator, the domain of g is the set of all real numbers x except $x = -5$.

c. Because this function represents the volume of a sphere, the values of the radius r must be positive. So, the domain is the set of all real numbers r such that $r > 0$.

d. This function is defined only for x-values for which

$$4 - x^2 \geq 0.$$

By solving this inequality (see Section 2.7), you can conclude that $-2 \leq x \leq 2$. So, the domain is the interval $[-2, 2]$.

CHECKPOINT Now try Exercise 59.

In Example 5(c), note that the domain of a function may be implied by the physical context. For instance, from the equation

$$V = \tfrac{4}{3}\pi r^3$$

you would have no reason to restrict r to positive values, but the physical context implies that a sphere cannot have a negative or zero radius.

FIGURE 1.49

Applications

Example 6 The Dimensions of a Container

You work in the marketing department of a soft-drink company and are experimenting with a new can for iced tea that is slightly narrower and taller than a standard can. For your experimental can, the ratio of the height to the radius is 4, as shown in Figure 1.49.

a. Write the volume of the can as a function of the radius r.

b. Write the volume of the can as a function of the height h.

Solution

a. $V(r) = \pi r^2 h = \pi r^2(4r) = 4\pi r^3$ Write V as a function of r.

b. $V(h) = \pi\left(\frac{h}{4}\right)^2 h = \frac{\pi h^3}{16}$ Write V as a function of h.

CHECKPOINT Now try Exercise 87.

Example 7 The Path of a Baseball

A baseball is hit at a point 3 feet above ground at a velocity of 100 feet per second and an angle of 45°. The path of the baseball is given by the function

$$f(x) = -0.0032x^2 + x + 3$$

where y and x are measured in feet, as shown in Figure 1.50. Will the baseball clear a 10-foot fence located 300 feet from home plate?

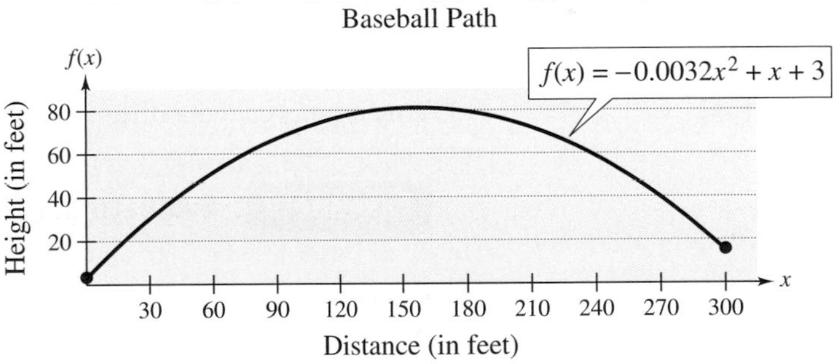

FIGURE 1.50

Solution

When $x = 300$, the height of the baseball is

$$f(300) = -0.0032(300)^2 + 300 + 3$$
$$= 15 \text{ feet.}$$

So, the baseball will clear the fence.

CHECKPOINT Now try Exercise 93.

In the equation in Example 7, the height of the baseball is a function of the distance from home plate.

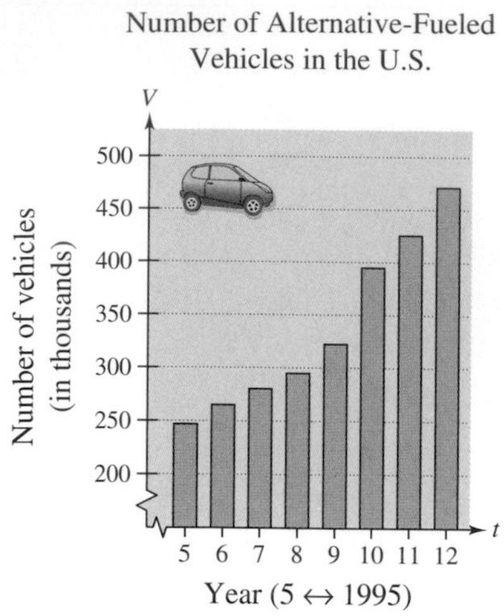

FIGURE 1.51

Example 8 Alternative-Fueled Vehicles

The number V (in thousands) of alternative-fueled vehicles in the United States increased in a linear pattern from 1995 to 1999, as shown in Figure 1.51. Then, in 2000, the number of vehicles took a jump and, until 2002, increased in a different linear pattern. These two patterns can be approximated by the function

$$V(t) = \begin{cases} 18.08t + 155.3 & 5 \le t \le 9 \\ 38.20t + 10.2, & 10 \le t \le 12 \end{cases}$$

where t represents the year, with $t = 5$ corresponding to 1995. Use this function to approximate the number of alternative-fueled vehicles for each year from 1995 to 2002. (Source: Science Applications International Corporation; Energy Information Administration)

Solution

From 1995 to 1999, use $V(t) = 18.08t + 155.3$.

$$\underbrace{245.7}_{1995} \qquad \underbrace{263.8}_{1996} \qquad \underbrace{281.9}_{1997} \qquad \underbrace{299.9}_{1998} \qquad \underbrace{318.0}_{1999}$$

From 2000 to 2002, use $V(t) = 38.20t + 10.2$.

$$\underbrace{392.2}_{2000} \qquad \underbrace{430.4}_{2001} \qquad \underbrace{468.6}_{2002}$$

CHECKPOINT Now try Exercise 95.

Difference Quotients

One of the basic definitions in calculus employs the ratio

$$\frac{f(x + h) - f(x)}{h}, \quad h \ne 0.$$

This ratio is called a **difference quotient,** as illustrated in Example 9.

Example 9 Evaluating a Difference Quotient

For $f(x) = x^2 - 4x + 7$, find $\dfrac{f(x + h) - f(x)}{h}$.

Solution

$$\begin{aligned} \frac{f(x + h) - f(x)}{h} &= \frac{[(x + h)^2 - 4(x + h) + 7] - (x^2 - 4x + 7)}{h} \\ &= \frac{x^2 + 2xh + h^2 - 4x - 4h + 7 - x^2 + 4x - 7}{h} \\ &= \frac{2xh + h^2 - 4h}{h} = \frac{h(2x + h - 4)}{h} = 2x + h - 4, \ h \ne 0 \end{aligned}$$

CHECKPOINT Now try Exercise 79.

The symbol $\int$ indicates an example or exercise that highlights algebraic techniques specifically used in calculus.

You may find it easier to calculate the difference quotient in Example 9 by first finding $f(x + h)$, and then substituting the resulting expression into the difference quotient, as follows.

$$f(x + h) = (x + h)^2 - 4(x + h) + 7 = x^2 + 2xh + h^2 - 4x - 4h + 7$$

$$\frac{f(x + h) - f(x)}{h} = \frac{(x^2 + 2xh + h^2 - 4x - 4h + 7) - (x^2 - 4x + 7)}{h}$$

$$= \frac{2xh + h^2 - 4h}{h} = \frac{h(2x + h - 4)}{h} = 2x + h - 4, h \neq 0$$

Summary of Function Terminology

Function: A **function** is a relationship between two variables such that to each value of the independent variable there corresponds exactly one value of the dependent variable.

Function Notation: $y = f(x)$

f is the *name* of the function.

y is the **dependent variable.**

x is the **independent variable.**

$f(x)$ is the *value of the function at* x.

Domain: The **domain** of a function is the set of all values (inputs) of the independent variable for which the function is defined. If x is in the domain of f, f is said to be *defined* at x. If x is not in the domain of f, f is said to be *undefined* at x.

Range: The **range** of a function is the set of all values (outputs) assumed by the dependent variable (that is, the set of all function values).

Implied Domain: If f is defined by an algebraic expression and the domain is not specified, the **implied domain** consists of all real numbers for which the expression is defined.

Writing about Mathematics

Everyday Functions In groups of two or three, identify common real-life functions. Consider everyday activities, events, and expenses, such as long distance telephone calls and car insurance. Here are two examples.

a. The statement, "Your happiness is a function of the grade you receive in this course" *is not* a correct mathematical use of the word "function." The word "happiness" is ambiguous.

b. The statement, "Your federal income tax is a function of your adjusted gross income" *is* a correct mathematical use of the word "function." Once you have determined your adjusted gross income, your income tax can be determined.

Describe your functions in words. Avoid using ambiguous words. Can you find an example of a piecewise-defined function?

1.4 Exercises

VOCABULARY CHECK: Fill in the blanks.

1. A relation that assigns to each element x from a set of inputs, or ________, exactly one element y in a set of outputs, or ________, is called a ________.
2. Functions are commonly represented in four different ways, ________, ________, ________, and ________.
3. For an equation that represents y as a function of x, the set of all values taken on by the ________ variable x is the domain, and the set of all values taken on by the ________ variable y is the range.
4. The function given by

$$f(x) = \begin{cases} 2x - 1, & x < 0 \\ x^2 + 4, & x \geq 0 \end{cases}$$

is an example of a ________ function.

5. If the domain of the function f is not given, then the set of values of the independent variable for which the expression is defined is called the ________ ________.
6. In calculus, one of the basic definitions is that of a ________ ________, given by $\dfrac{f(x+h) - f(x)}{h}$, $h \neq 0$.

In Exercises 1–4, is the relationship a function?

1. *Domain* *Range*

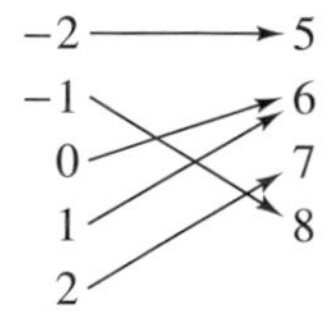

2. *Domain* *Range*

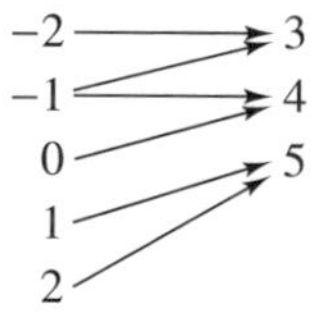

3. *Domain* *Range*

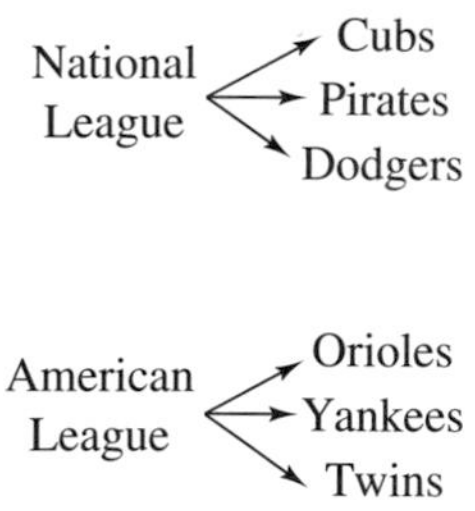

4. *Domain* (Year) *Range* (Number of North Atlantic tropical storms and hurricanes)

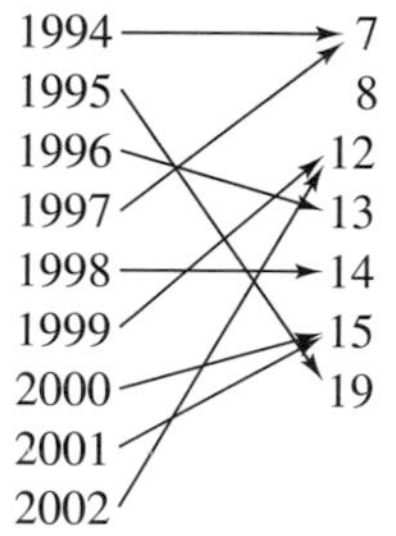

In Exercises 5–8, does the table describe a function? Explain your reasoning.

5.

Input value	−2	−1	0	1	2
Output value	−8	−1	0	1	8

6.

Input value	0	1	2	1	0
Output value	−4	−2	0	2	4

7.

Input value	10	7	4	7	10
Output value	3	6	9	12	15

8.

Input value	0	3	9	12	15
Output value	3	3	3	3	3

In Exercises 9 and 10, which sets of ordered pairs represent functions from *A* to *B*? Explain.

9. $A = \{0, 1, 2, 3\}$ and $B = \{-2, -1, 0, 1, 2\}$
   (a) $\{(0, 1), (1, -2), (2, 0), (3, 2)\}$
   (b) $\{(0, -1), (2, 2), (1, -2), (3, 0), (1, 1)\}$
   (c) $\{(0, 0), (1, 0), (2, 0), (3, 0)\}$
   (d) $\{(0, 2), (3, 0), (1, 1)\}$
10. $A = \{a, b, c\}$ and $B = \{0, 1, 2, 3\}$
   (a) $\{(a, 1), (c, 2), (c, 3), (b, 3)\}$
   (b) $\{(a, 1), (b, 2), (c, 3)\}$
   (c) $\{(1, a), (0, a), (2, c), (3, b)\}$
   (d) $\{(c, 0), (b, 0), (a, 3)\}$

Circulation of Newspapers **In Exercises 11 and 12, use the graph, which shows the circulation (in millions) of daily newspapers in the United States.** (Source: Editor & Publisher Company)

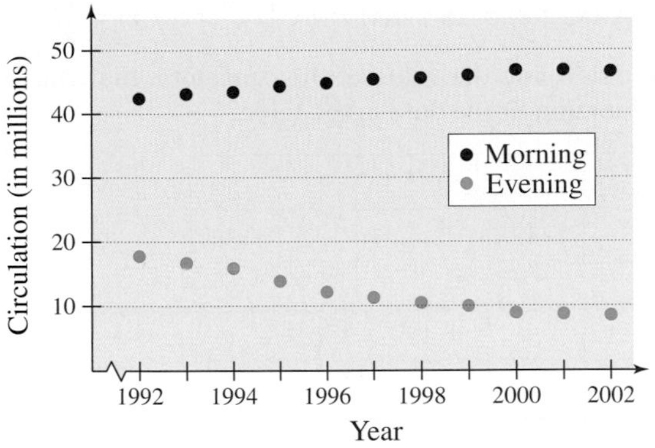

11. Is the circulation of morning newspapers a function of the year? Is the circulation of evening newspapers a function of the year? Explain.

12. Let $f(x)$ represent the circulation of evening newspapers in year x. Find $f(1998)$.

In Exercises 13–24, determine whether the equation represents y as a function of x.

13. $x^2 + y^2 = 4$
14. $x = y^2$
15. $x^2 + y = 4$
16. $x + y^2 = 4$
17. $2x + 3y = 4$
18. $(x - 2)^2 + y^2 = 4$
19. $y^2 = x^2 - 1$
20. $y = \sqrt{x + 5}$
21. $y = |4 - x|$
22. $|y| = 4 - x$
23. $x = 14$
24. $y = -75$

In Exercises 25–38, evaluate the function at each specified value of the independent variable and simplify.

25. $f(x) = 2x - 3$
(a) $f(1)$ (b) $f(-3)$ (c) $f(x - 1)$

26. $g(y) = 7 - 3y$
(a) $g(0)$ (b) $g\left(\frac{7}{3}\right)$ (c) $g(s + 2)$

27. $V(r) = \frac{4}{3}\pi r^3$
(a) $V(3)$ (b) $V\left(\frac{3}{2}\right)$ (c) $V(2r)$

28. $h(t) = t^2 - 2t$
(a) $h(2)$ (b) $h(1.5)$ (c) $h(x + 2)$

29. $f(y) = 3 - \sqrt{y}$
(a) $f(4)$ (b) $f(0.25)$ (c) $f(4x^2)$

30. $f(x) = \sqrt{x + 8} + 2$
(a) $f(-8)$ (b) $f(1)$ (c) $f(x - 8)$

31. $q(x) = \dfrac{1}{x^2 - 9}$
(a) $q(0)$ (b) $q(3)$ (c) $q(y + 3)$

32. $q(t) = \dfrac{2t^2 + 3}{t^2}$
(a) $q(2)$ (b) $q(0)$ (c) $q(-x)$

33. $f(x) = \dfrac{|x|}{x}$
(a) $f(2)$ (b) $f(-2)$ (c) $f(x - 1)$

34. $f(x) = |x| + 4$
(a) $f(2)$ (b) $f(-2)$ (c) $f(x^2)$

35. $f(x) = \begin{cases} 2x + 1, & x < 0 \\ 2x + 2, & x \geq 0 \end{cases}$
(a) $f(-1)$ (b) $f(0)$ (c) $f(2)$

36. $f(x) = \begin{cases} x^2 + 2, & x \leq 1 \\ 2x^2 + 2, & x > 1 \end{cases}$
(a) $f(-2)$ (b) $f(1)$ (c) $f(2)$

37. $f(x) = \begin{cases} 3x - 1, & x < -1 \\ 4, & -1 \leq x \leq 1 \\ x^2, & x > 1 \end{cases}$
(a) $f(-2)$ (b) $f\left(-\frac{1}{2}\right)$ (c) $f(3)$

38. $f(x) = \begin{cases} 4 - 5x, & x \leq -2 \\ 0, & -2 < x < 2 \\ x^2 + 1, & x > 2 \end{cases}$
(a) $f(-3)$ (b) $f(4)$ (c) $f(-1)$

In Exercises 39–44, complete the table.

39. $f(x) = x^2 - 3$

x	-2	-1	0	1	2
$f(x)$					

40. $g(x) = \sqrt{x - 3}$

x	3	4	5	6	7
$g(x)$					

41. $h(t) = \frac{1}{2}|t + 3|$

t	-5	-4	-3	-2	-1
$h(t)$					

42. $f(s) = \dfrac{|s - 2|}{s - 2}$

s	0	1	$\frac{3}{2}$	$\frac{5}{2}$	4
$f(s)$					

43. $f(x) = \begin{cases} -\frac{1}{2}x + 4, & x \le 0 \\ (x-2)^2, & x > 0 \end{cases}$

x	-2	-1	0	1	2
$f(x)$					

44. $f(x) = \begin{cases} 9 - x^2, & x < 3 \\ x - 3, & x \ge 3 \end{cases}$

x	1	2	3	4	5
$f(x)$					

In Exercises 45–52, find all real values of x such that $f(x) = 0$.

45. $f(x) = 15 - 3x$

46. $f(x) = 5x + 1$

47. $f(x) = \dfrac{3x - 4}{5}$

48. $f(x) = \dfrac{12 - x^2}{5}$

49. $f(x) = x^2 - 9$

50. $f(x) = x^2 - 8x + 15$

51. $f(x) = x^3 - x$

52. $f(x) = x^3 - x^2 - 4x + 4$

In Exercises 53–56, find the value(s) of x for which $f(x) = g(x)$.

53. $f(x) = x^2 + 2x + 1, \quad g(x) = 3x + 3$

54. $f(x) = x^4 - 2x^2, \quad g(x) = 2x^2$

55. $f(x) = \sqrt{3x} + 1, \quad g(x) = x + 1$

56. $f(x) = \sqrt{x} - 4, \quad g(x) = 2 - x$

In Exercises 57–70, find the domain of the function.

57. $f(x) = 5x^2 + 2x - 1$

58. $g(x) = 1 - 2x^2$

59. $h(t) = \dfrac{4}{t}$

60. $s(y) = \dfrac{3y}{y + 5}$

61. $g(y) = \sqrt{y - 10}$

62. $f(t) = \sqrt[3]{t + 4}$

63. $f(x) = \sqrt[4]{1 - x^2}$

64. $f(x) = \sqrt[4]{x^2 + 3x}$

65. $g(x) = \dfrac{1}{x} - \dfrac{3}{x + 2}$

66. $h(x) = \dfrac{10}{x^2 - 2x}$

67. $f(s) = \dfrac{\sqrt{s - 1}}{s - 4}$

68. $f(x) = \dfrac{\sqrt{x + 6}}{6 + x}$

69. $f(x) = \dfrac{x - 4}{\sqrt{x}}$

70. $f(x) = \dfrac{x - 5}{\sqrt{x^2 - 9}}$

In Exercises 71–74, assume that the domain of f is the set $A = \{-2, -1, 0, 1, 2\}$. Determine the set of ordered pairs that represents the function f.

71. $f(x) = x^2$

72. $f(x) = x^2 - 3$

73. $f(x) = |x| + 2$

74. $f(x) = |x + 1|$

Exploration **In Exercises 75–78, match the data with one of the following functions**

$$f(x) = cx, \; g(x) = cx^2, \; h(x) = c\sqrt{|x|}, \text{ and } r(x) = \frac{c}{x}$$

and determine the value of the constant c that will make the function fit the data in the table.

75.

x	-4	-1	0	1	4
y	-32	-2	0	-2	-32

76.

x	-4	-1	0	1	4
y	-1	$-\frac{1}{4}$	0	$\frac{1}{4}$	1

77.

x	-4	-1	0	1	4
y	-8	-32	Undef.	32	8

78.

x	-4	-1	0	1	4
y	6	3	0	3	6

∫ **In Exercises 79–86, find the difference quotient and simplify your answer.**

79. $f(x) = x^2 - x + 1, \quad \dfrac{f(2 + h) - f(2)}{h}, \; h \neq 0$

80. $f(x) = 5x - x^2, \quad \dfrac{f(5 + h) - f(5)}{h}, \; h \neq 0$

81. $f(x) = x^3 + 3x, \quad \dfrac{f(x + h) - f(x)}{h}, \; h \neq 0$

82. $f(x) = 4x^2 - 2x, \quad \dfrac{f(x + h) - f(x)}{h}, \; h \neq 0$

83. $g(x) = \dfrac{1}{x^2}, \quad \dfrac{g(x) - g(3)}{x - 3}, \; x \neq 3$

84. $f(t) = \dfrac{1}{t - 2}, \quad \dfrac{f(t) - f(1)}{t - 1}, \; t \neq 1$

85. $f(x) = \sqrt{5x}, \quad \dfrac{f(x) - f(5)}{x - 5}, \; x \neq 5$

86. $f(x) = x^{2/3} + 1, \quad \dfrac{f(x) - f(8)}{x - 8}, \; x \neq 8$

87. ***Geometry*** Write the area A of a square as a function of its perimeter P.

88. ***Geometry*** Write the area A of a circle as a function of its circumference C.

The symbol ∫ indicates an example or exercise that highlights algebraic techniques specifically used in calculus.

89. ***Maximum Volume*** An open box of maximum volume is to be made from a square piece of material 24 centimeters on a side by cutting equal squares from the corners and turning up the sides (see figure).

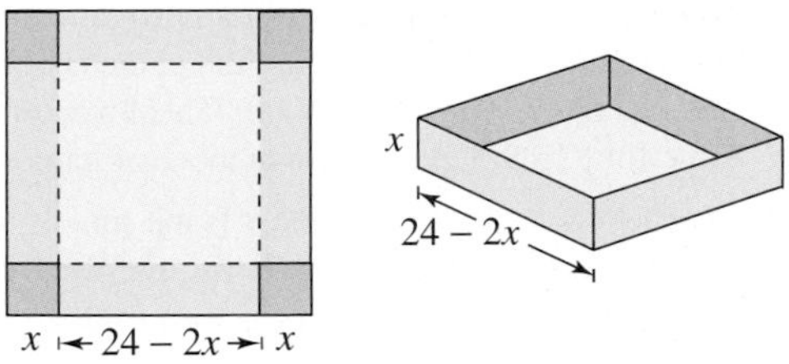

(a) The table shows the volume V (in cubic centimeters) of the box for various heights x (in centimeters). Use the table to estimate the maximum volume.

Height, x	1	2	3	4	5	6
Volume, V	484	800	972	1024	980	864

(b) Plot the points (x, V) from the table in part (a). Does the relation defined by the ordered pairs represent V as a function of x?

(c) If V is a function of x, write the function and determine its domain.

90. ***Maximum Profit*** The cost per unit in the production of a portable CD player is \$60. The manufacturer charges \$90 per unit for orders of 100 or less. To encourage large orders, the manufacturer reduces the charge by \$0.15 per CD player for each unit ordered in excess of 100 (for example, there would be a charge of \$87 per CD player for an order size of 120).

(a) The table shows the profit P (in dollars) for various numbers of units ordered, x. Use the table to estimate the maximum profit.

Units, x	110	120	130	140
Profit, P	3135	3240	3315	3360

Units, x	150	160	170
Profit, P	3375	3360	3315

(b) Plot the points (x, P) from the table in part (a). Does the relation defined by the ordered pairs represent P as a function of x?

(c) If P is a function of x, write the function and determine its domain.

91. ***Geometry*** A right triangle is formed in the first quadrant by the x- and y-axes and a line through the point $(2, 1)$ (see figure). Write the area A of the triangle as a function of x, and determine the domain of the function.

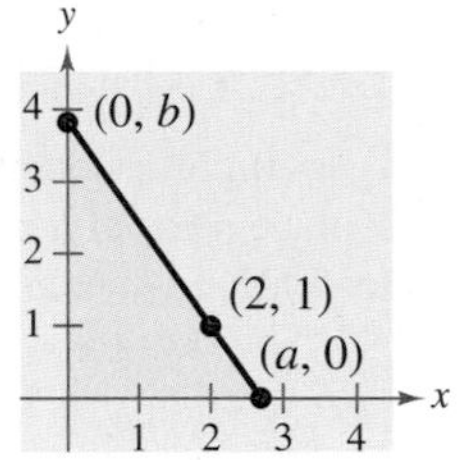

FIGURE FOR 91

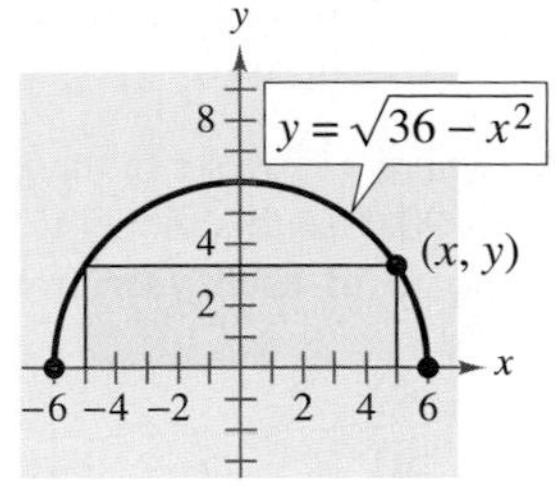

FIGURE FOR 92

92. ***Geometry*** A rectangle is bounded by the x-axis and the semicircle $y = \sqrt{36 - x^2}$ (see figure). Write the area A of the rectangle as a function of x, and determine the domain of the function.

93. ***Path of a Ball*** The height y (in feet) of a baseball thrown by a child is

$$y = -\frac{1}{10}x^2 + 3x + 6$$

where x is the horizontal distance (in feet) from where the ball was thrown. Will the ball fly over the head of another child 30 feet away trying to catch the ball? (Assume that the child who is trying to catch the ball holds a baseball glove at a height of 5 feet.)

94. ***Prescription Drugs*** The amounts d (in billions of dollars) spent on prescription drugs in the United States from 1991 to 2002 (see figure) can be approximated by the model

$$d(t) = \begin{cases} 5.0t + 37, & 1 \le t \le 7 \\ 18.7t - 64, & 8 \le t \le 12 \end{cases}$$

where t represents the year, with $t = 1$ corresponding to 1991. Use this model to find the amount spent on prescription drugs in each year from 1991 to 2002. (Source: U.S. Centers for Medicare & Medicaid Services)

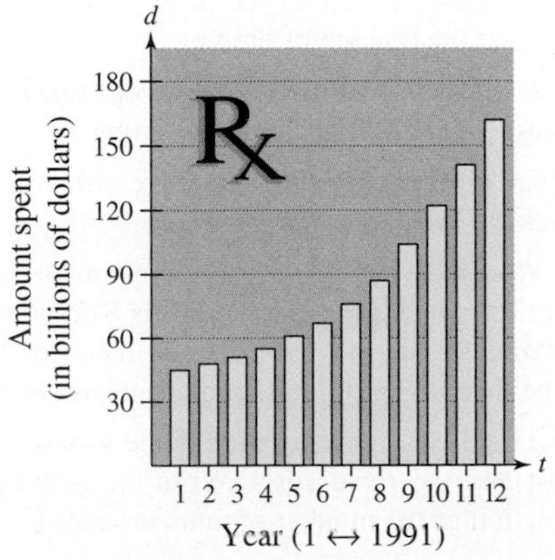

95. ***Average Price*** The average prices p (in thousands of dollars) of a new mobile home in the United States from 1990 to 2002 (see figure) can be approximated by the model

$$p(t) = \begin{cases} 0.182t^2 + 0.57t + 27.3, & 0 \le t \le 7 \\ 2.50t + 21.3, & 8 \le t \le 12 \end{cases}$$

where t represents the year, with $t = 0$ corresponding to 1990. Use this model to find the average price of a mobile home in each year from 1990 to 2002. (Source: U.S. Census Bureau)

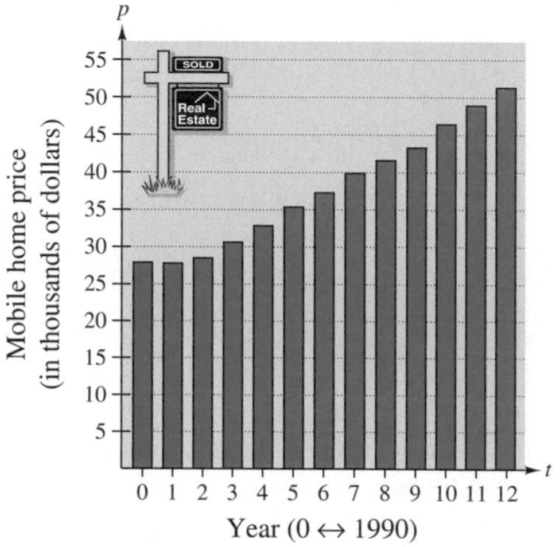

96. ***Postal Regulations*** A rectangular package to be sent by the U.S. Postal Service can have a maximum combined length and girth (perimeter of a cross section) of 108 inches (see figure).

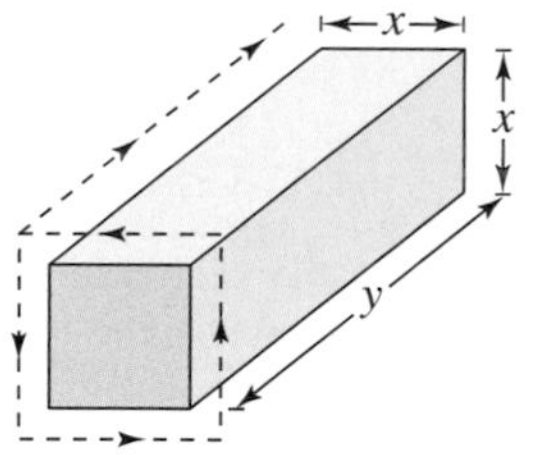

(a) Write the volume V of the package as a function of x. What is the domain of the function?

(b) Use a graphing utility to graph your function. Be sure to use an appropriate window setting.

(c) What dimensions will maximize the volume of the package? Explain your answer.

97. ***Cost, Revenue, and Profit*** A company produces a product for which the variable cost is \$12.30 per unit and the fixed costs are \$98,000. The product sells for \$17.98. Let x be the number of units produced and sold.

(a) The total cost for a business is the sum of the variable cost and the fixed costs. Write the total cost C as a function of the number of units produced.

(b) Write the revenue R as a function of the number of units sold.

(c) Write the profit P as a function of the number of units sold. (*Note:* $P = R - C$)

98. ***Average Cost*** The inventor of a new game believes that the variable cost for producing the game is \$0.95 per unit and the fixed costs are \$6000. The inventor sells each game for \$1.69. Let x be the number of games sold.

(a) The total cost for a business is the sum of the variable cost and the fixed costs. Write the total cost C as a function of the number of games sold.

(b) Write the average cost per unit $\overline{C} = C/x$ as a function of x.

99. ***Transportation*** For groups of 80 or more people, a charter bus company determines the rate per person according to the formula

$$\text{Rate} = 8 - 0.05(n - 80), \quad n \ge 80$$

where the rate is given in dollars and n is the number of people.

(a) Write the revenue R for the bus company as a function of n.

(b) Use the function in part (a) to complete the table. What can you conclude?

n	90	100	110	120	130	140	150
$R(n)$							

100. ***Physics*** The force F (in tons) of water against the face of a dam is estimated by the function $F(y) = 149.76\sqrt{10}y^{5/2}$, where y is the depth of the water (in feet).

(a) Complete the table. What can you conclude from the table?

y	5	10	20	30	40
$F(y)$					

(b) Use the table to approximate the depth at which the force against the dam is 1,000,000 tons.

(c) Find the depth at which the force against the dam is 1,000,000 tons algebraically.

101. ***Height of a Balloon*** A balloon carrying a transmitter ascends vertically from a point 3000 feet from the receiving station.

(a) Draw a diagram that gives a visual representation of the problem. Let h represent the height of the balloon and let d represent the distance between the balloon and the receiving station.

(b) Write the height of the balloon as a function of d. What is the domain of the function?

Model It

102. ***Wildlife*** The graph shows the numbers of threatened and endangered fish species in the world from 1996 through 2003. Let $f(t)$ represent the number of threatened and endangered fish species in the year t. (Source: U.S. Fish and Wildlife Service)

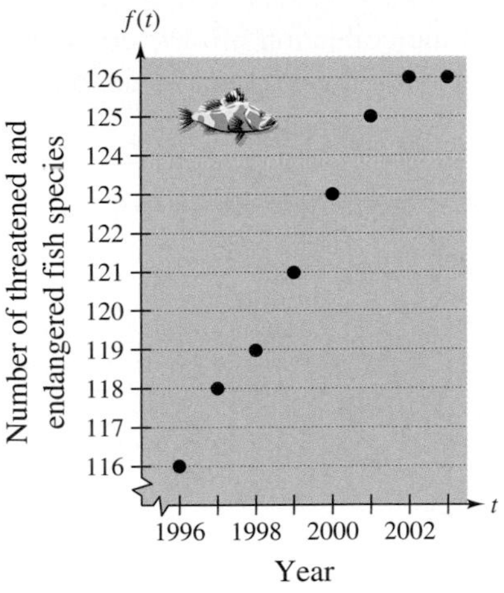

(a) Find $\dfrac{f(2003) - f(1996)}{2003 - 1996}$ and interpret the result in the context of the problem.

(b) Find a linear model for the data algebraically. Let N represent the number of threatened and endangered fish species and let $x = 6$ correspond to 1996.

(c) Use the model found in part (b) to complete the table.

x	6	7	8	9	10	11	12	13
N								

(d) Compare your results from part (c) with the actual data.

(e) Use a graphing utility to find a linear model for the data. Let $x = 6$ correspond to 1996. How does the model you found in part (b) compare with the model given by the graphing utility?

Synthesis

True or False? **In Exercises 103 and 104, determine whether the statement is true or false. Justify your answer.**

103. The domain of the function given by $f(x) = x^4 - 1$ is $(-\infty, \infty)$, and the range of $f(x)$ is $(0, \infty)$.

104. The set of ordered pairs $\{(-8, -2), (-6, 0), (-4, 0), (-2, 2), (0, 4), (2, -2)\}$ represents a function.

105. ***Writing*** In your own words, explain the meanings of *domain* and *range*.

106. ***Think About It*** Consider $f(x) = \sqrt{x - 2}$ and $g(x) = \sqrt[3]{x - 2}$. Why are the domains of f and g different?

In Exercises 107 and 108, determine whether the statements use the word *function* in ways that are mathematically correct. Explain your reasoning.

107. (a) The sales tax on a purchased item is a function of the selling price.

(b) Your score on the next algebra exam is a function of the number of hours you study the night before the exam.

108. (a) The amount in your savings account is a function of your salary.

(b) The speed at which a free-falling baseball strikes the ground is a function of the height from which it was dropped.

Skills Review

In Exercises 109–112, solve the equation.

109. $\dfrac{t}{3} + \dfrac{t}{5} = 1$

110. $\dfrac{3}{t} + \dfrac{5}{t} = 1$

111. $\dfrac{3}{x(x + 1)} - \dfrac{4}{x} = \dfrac{1}{x + 1}$

112. $\dfrac{12}{x} - 3 = \dfrac{4}{x} + 9$

In Exercises 113–116, find the equation of the line passing through the pair of points.

113. $(-2, -5), (4, -1)$

114. $(10, 0), (1, 9)$

115. $(-6, 5), (3, -5)$

116. $\left(-\frac{1}{2}, 3\right), \left(\frac{11}{2}, -\frac{1}{3}\right)$

1.5 Analyzing Graphs of Functions

What you should learn

- Use the Vertical Line Test for functions.
- Find the zeros of functions.
- Determine intervals on which functions are increasing or decreasing and determine relative maximum and relative minimum values of functions.
- Determine the average rate of change of a function.
- Identify even and odd functions.

Why you should learn it

Graphs of functions can help you visualize relationships between variables in real life. For instance, in Exercise 86 on page 64, you will use the graph of a function to represent visually the temperature for a city over a 24-hour period.

The Graph of a Function

In Section 1.4, you studied functions from an algebraic point of view. In this section, you will study functions from a graphical perspective.

The **graph of a function** f is the collection of ordered pairs $(x, f(x))$ such that x is in the domain of f. As you study this section, remember that

$x =$ the directed distance from the y-axis

$y = f(x) =$ the directed distance from the x-axis

as shown in Figure 1.52.

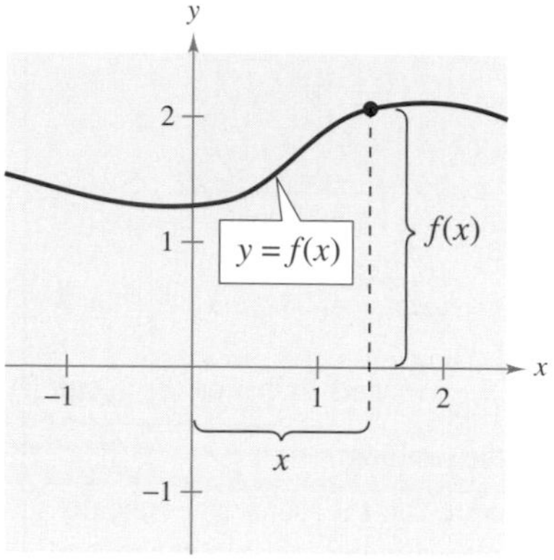

FIGURE 1.52

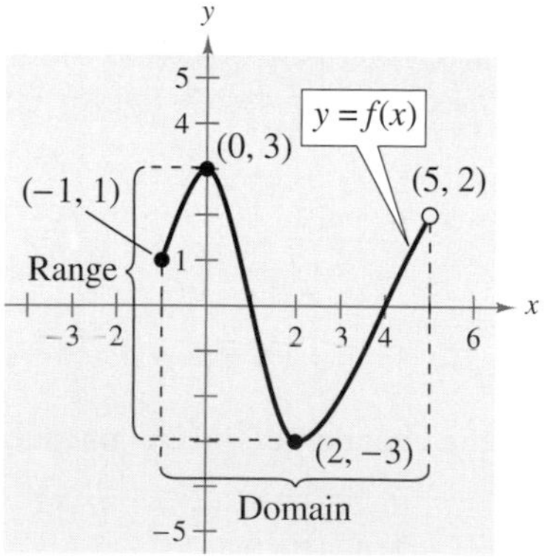

FIGURE 1.53

Example 1 Finding the Domain and Range of a Function

Use the graph of the function f, shown in Figure 1.53, to find (a) the domain of f, (b) the function values $f(-1)$ and $f(2)$, and (c) the range of f.

Solution

a. The closed dot at $(-1, 1)$ indicates that $x = -1$ is in the domain of f, whereas the open dot at $(5, 2)$ indicates that $x = 5$ is not in the domain. So, the domain of f is all x in the interval $[-1, 5)$.

b. Because $(-1, 1)$ is a point on the graph of f, it follows that $f(-1) = 1$. Similarly, because $(2, -3)$ is a point on the graph of f, it follows that $f(2) = -3$.

c. Because the graph does not extend below $f(2) = -3$ or above $f(0) = 3$, the range of f is the interval $[-3, 3]$.

✓CHECKPOINT Now try Exercise 1.

The use of dots (open or closed) at the extreme left and right points of a graph indicates that the graph does not extend beyond these points. If no such dots are shown, assume that the graph extends beyond these points.

By the definition of a function, at most one y-value corresponds to a given x-value. This means that the graph of a function cannot have two or more different points with the same x-coordinate, and no two points on the graph of a function can be vertically above or below each other. It follows, then, that a vertical line can intersect the graph of a function at most once. This observation provides a convenient visual test called the **Vertical Line Test** for functions.

Vertical Line Test for Functions

A set of points in a coordinate plane is the graph of y as a function of x if and only if no *vertical* line intersects the graph at more than one point.

Example 2 Vertical Line Test for Functions

Use the Vertical Line Test to decide whether the graphs in Figure 1.54 represent y as a function of x.

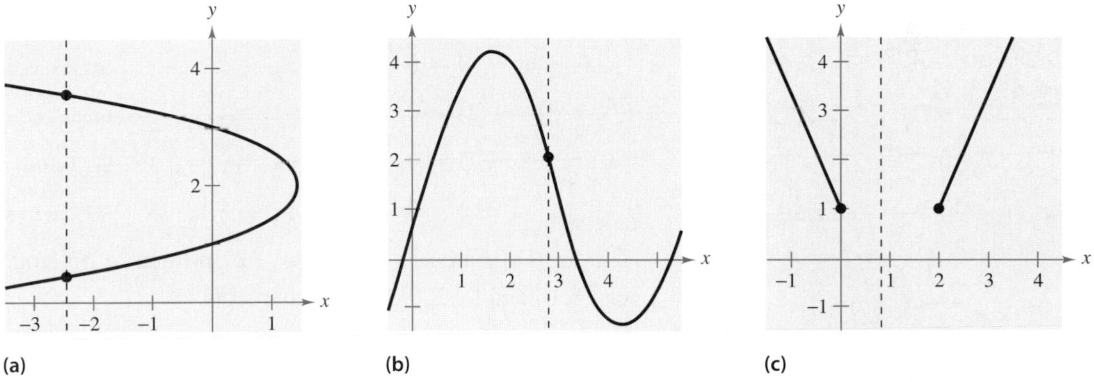

FIGURE 1.54

Solution

a. This *is not* a graph of y as a function of x, because you can find a vertical line that intersects the graph twice. That is, for a particular input x, there is more than one output y.

b. This *is* a graph of y as a function of x, because every vertical line intersects the graph at most once. That is, for a particular input x, there is at most one output y.

c. This *is* a graph of y as a function of x. (Note that if a vertical line does not intersect the graph, it simply means that the function is undefined for that particular value of x.) That is, for a particular input x, there is at most one output y.

CHECKPOINT Now try Exercise 9.

Zeros of a Function

If the graph of a function of x has an x-intercept at $(a, 0)$, then a is a **zero** of the function.

> **Zeros of a Function**
>
> The **zeros of a function** f of x are the x-values for which $f(x) = 0$.

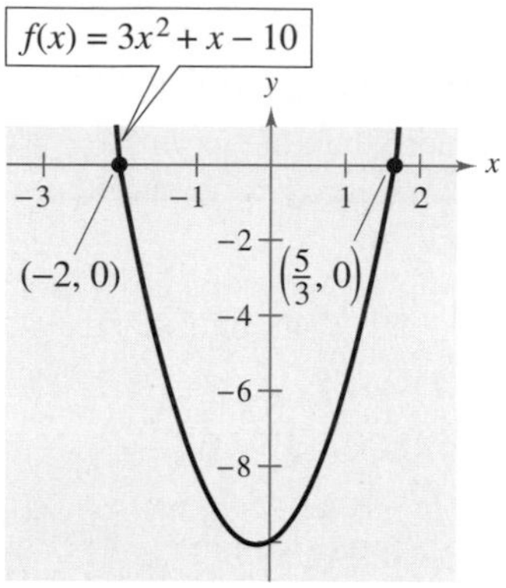

Zeros of f: $x = -2, x = \frac{5}{3}$
FIGURE 1.55

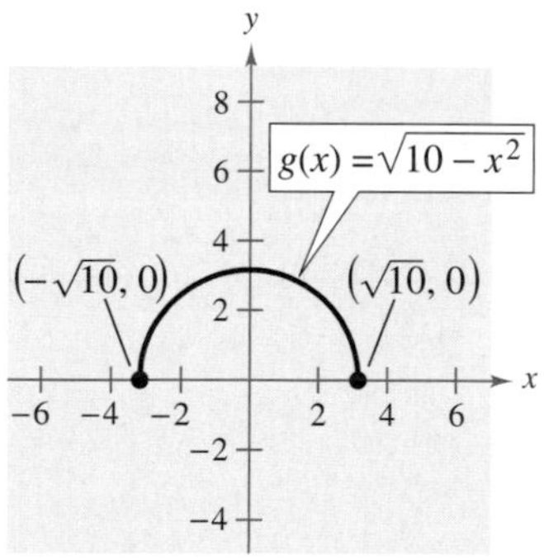

Zeros of g: $x = \pm\sqrt{10}$
FIGURE 1.56

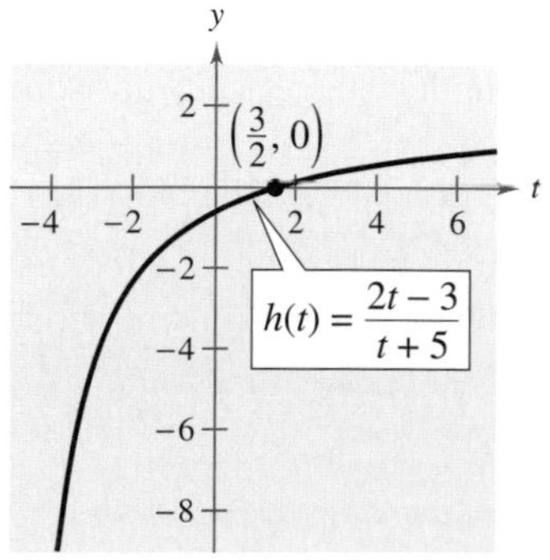

Zero of h: $t = \frac{3}{2}$
FIGURE 1.57

Example 3 Finding the Zeros of a Function

Find the zeros of each function.

a. $f(x) = 3x^2 + x - 10$ **b.** $g(x) = \sqrt{10 - x^2}$ **c.** $h(t) = \dfrac{2t - 3}{t + 5}$

Solution

To find the zeros of a function, set the function equal to zero and solve for the independent variable.

a.

$3x^2 + x - 10 = 0$		Set $f(x)$ equal to 0.
$(3x - 5)(x + 2) = 0$		Factor.
$3x - 5 = 0$	$\Rightarrow$ $x = \frac{5}{3}$	Set 1st factor equal to 0.
$x + 2 = 0$	$\Rightarrow$ $x = -2$	Set 2nd factor equal to 0.

The zeros of f are $x = \frac{5}{3}$ and $x = -2$. In Figure 1.55, note that the graph of f has $\left(\frac{5}{3}, 0\right)$ and $(-2, 0)$ as its x-intercepts.

b.

$\sqrt{10 - x^2} = 0$	Set $g(x)$ equal to 0.
$10 - x^2 = 0$	Square each side.
$10 = x^2$	Add x^2 to each side.
$\pm\sqrt{10} = x$	Extract square roots.

The zeros of g are $x = -\sqrt{10}$ and $x = \sqrt{10}$. In Figure 1.56, note that the graph of g has $\left(-\sqrt{10}, 0\right)$ and $\left(\sqrt{10}, 0\right)$ as its x-intercepts.

c.

$\dfrac{2t - 3}{t + 5} = 0$	Set $h(t)$ equal to 0.
$2t - 3 = 0$	Multiply each side by $t + 5$.
$2t = 3$	Add 3 to each side.
$t = \dfrac{3}{2}$	Divide each side by 2.

The zero of h is $t = \frac{3}{2}$. In Figure 1.57, note that the graph of h has $\left(\frac{3}{2}, 0\right)$ as its t-intercept.

CHECKPOINT Now try Exercise 15.

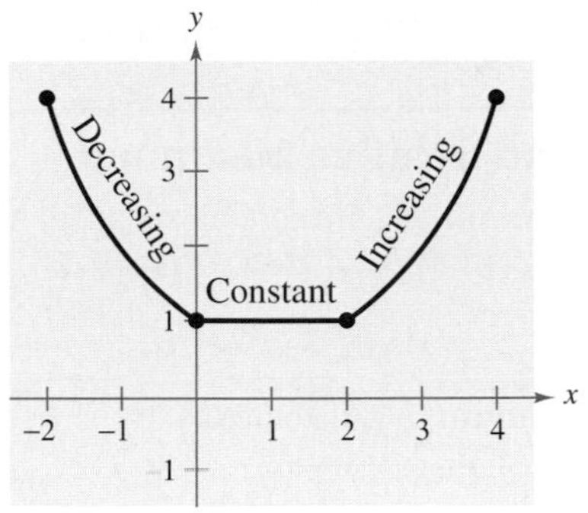

FIGURE 1.58

Increasing and Decreasing Functions

The more you know about the graph of a function, the more you know about the function itself. Consider the graph shown in Figure 1.58. As you move from *left to right*, this graph falls from $x = -2$ to $x = 0$, is constant from $x = 0$ to $x = 2$, and rises from $x = 2$ to $x = 4$.

Increasing, Decreasing, and Constant Functions

A function f is **increasing** on an interval if, for any x_1 and x_2 in the interval, $x_1 < x_2$ implies $f(x_1) < f(x_2)$.

A function f is **decreasing** on an interval if, for any x_1 and x_2 in the interval, $x_1 < x_2$ implies $f(x_1) > f(x_2)$.

A function f is **constant** on an interval if, for any x_1 and x_2 in the interval, $f(x_1) = f(x_2)$.

Example 4 Increasing and Decreasing Functions

Use the graphs in Figure 1.59 to describe the increasing or decreasing behavior of each function.

Solution

a. This function is increasing over the entire real line.

b. This function is increasing on the interval $(-\infty, -1)$, decreasing on the interval $(-1, 1)$, and increasing on the interval $(1, \infty)$.

c. This function is increasing on the interval $(-\infty, 0)$, constant on the interval $(0, 2)$, and decreasing on the interval $(2, \infty)$.

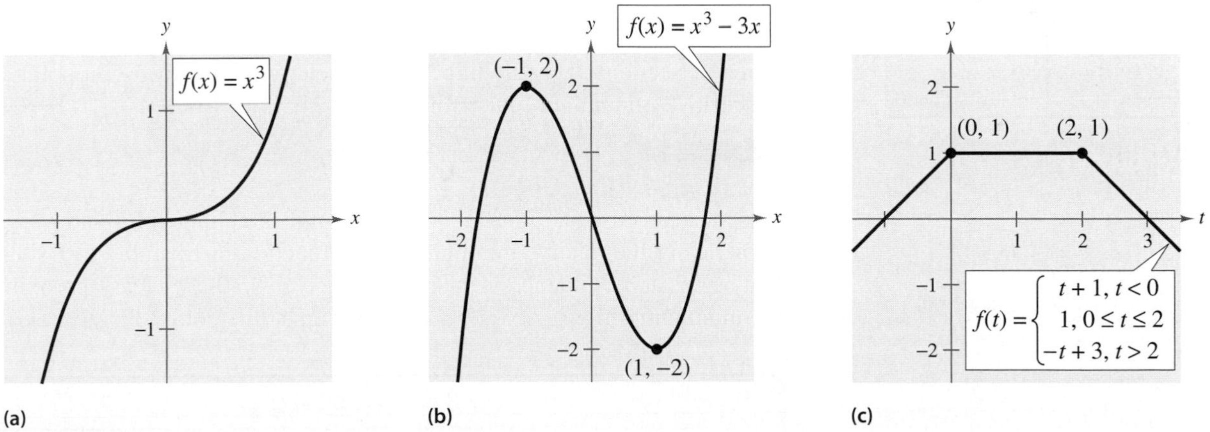

FIGURE 1.59

✓CHECKPOINT Now try Exercise 33.

To help you decide whether a function is increasing, decreasing, or constant on an interval, you can evaluate the function for several values of x. However, calculus is needed to determine, for certain, all intervals on which a function is increasing, decreasing, or constant.

STUDY TIP

A relative minimum or relative maximum is also referred to as a *local* minimum or *local* maximum.

The points at which a function changes its increasing, decreasing, or constant behavior are helpful in determining the **relative minimum** or **relative maximum** values of the function.

Definitions of Relative Minimum and Relative Maximum

A function value $f(a)$ is called a **relative minimum** of f if there exists an interval (x_1, x_2) that contains a such that

$$x_1 < x < x_2 \quad \text{implies} \quad f(a) \le f(x).$$

A function value $f(a)$ is called a **relative maximum** of f if there exists an interval (x_1, x_2) that contains a such that

$$x_1 < x < x_2 \quad \text{implies} \quad f(a) \ge f(x).$$

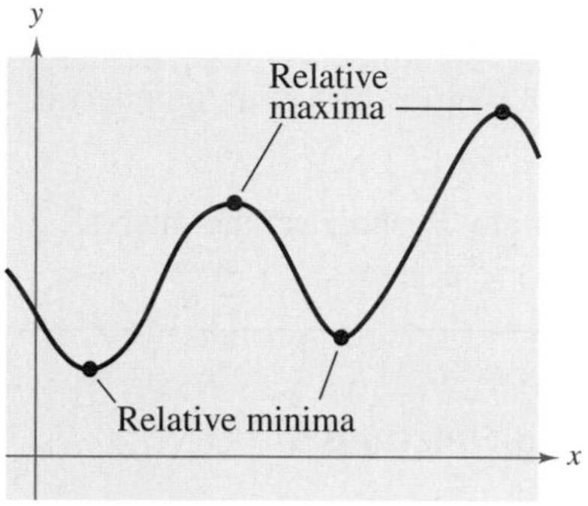

FIGURE 1.60

Figure 1.60 shows several different examples of relative minima and relative maxima. In Section 2.1, you will study a technique for finding the *exact point* at which a second-degree polynomial function has a relative minimum or relative maximum. For the time being, however, you can use a graphing utility to find reasonable approximations of these points.

Example 5 Approximating a Relative Minimum

Use a graphing utility to approximate the relative minimum of the function given by $f(x) = 3x^2 - 4x - 2$.

Solution

The graph of f is shown in Figure 1.61. By using the *zoom* and *trace* features or the *minimum* feature of a graphing utility, you can estimate that the function has a relative minimum at the point

$(0.67, -3.33)$. Relative minimum

Later, in Section 2.1, you will be able to determine that the exact point at which the relative minimum occurs is $\left(\frac{2}{3}, -\frac{10}{3}\right)$.

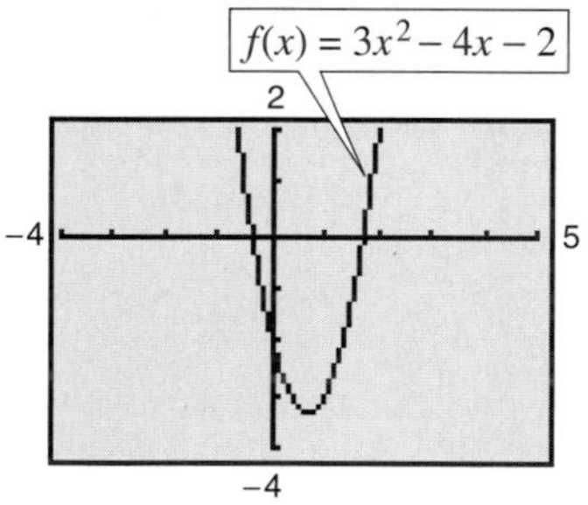

FIGURE 1.61

CHECKPOINT Now try Exercise 49.

You can also use the *table* feature of a graphing utility to approximate numerically the relative minimum of the function in Example 5. Using a table that begins at 0.6 and increments the value of x by 0.01, you can approximate that the minimum of $f(x) = 3x^2 - 4x - 2$ occurs at the point $(0.67, -3.33)$.

Technology

If you use a graphing utility to estimate the *x*- and *y*-values of a relative minimum or relative maximum, the *zoom* feature will often produce graphs that are nearly flat. To overcome this problem, you can manually change the vertical setting of the viewing window. The graph will stretch vertically if the values of Ymin and Ymax are closer together.

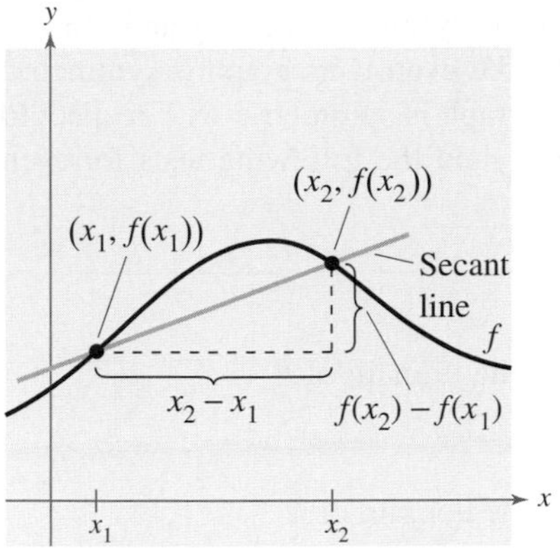

FIGURE 1.62

Average Rate of Change

In Section 1.3, you learned that the slope of a line can be interpreted as a *rate of change*. For a nonlinear graph whose slope changes at each point, the **average rate of change** between any two points $(x_1, f(x_1))$ and $(x_2, f(x_2))$ is the slope of the line through the two points (see Figure 1.62). The line through the two points is called the **secant line,** and the slope of this line is denoted as m_{sec}.

$$\text{Average rate of change of } f \text{ from } x_1 \text{ to } x_2 = \frac{f(x_2) - f(x_1)}{x_2 - x_1}$$

$$= \frac{\text{change in } y}{\text{change in } x}$$

$$= m_{sec}$$

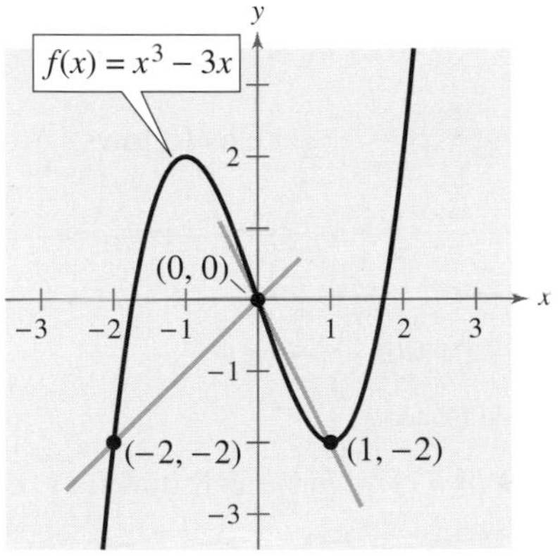

FIGURE 1.63

Example 6 Average Rate of Change of a Function

Find the average rates of change of $f(x) = x^3 - 3x$ (a) from $x_1 = -2$ to $x_2 = 0$ and (b) from $x_1 = 0$ to $x_2 = 1$ (see Figure 1.63).

Solution

a. The average rate of change of f from $x_1 = -2$ to $x_2 = 0$ is

$$\frac{f(x_2) - f(x_1)}{x_2 - x_1} = \frac{f(0) - f(-2)}{0 - (-2)} = \frac{0 - (-2)}{2} = 1.$$

Secant line has positive slope.

b. The average rate of change of f from $x_1 = 0$ to $x_2 = 1$ is

$$\frac{f(x_2) - f(x_1)}{x_2 - x_1} = \frac{f(1) - f(0)}{1 - 0} = \frac{-2 - 0}{1} = -2.$$

Secant line has negative slope.

CHECKPOINT Now try Exercise 63.

Example 7 Finding Average Speed

The distance s (in feet) a moving car is from a stoplight is given by the function $s(t) = 20t^{3/2}$, where t is the time (in seconds). Find the average speed of the car (a) from $t_1 = 0$ to $t_2 = 4$ seconds and (b) from $t_1 = 4$ to $t_2 = 9$ seconds.

Solution

a. The average speed of the car from $t_1 = 0$ to $t_2 = 4$ seconds is

$$\frac{s(t_2) - s(t_1)}{t_2 - t_1} = \frac{s(4) - s(0)}{4 - (0)} = \frac{160 - 0}{4} = 40 \text{ feet per second.}$$

b. The average speed of the car from $t_1 = 4$ to $t_2 = 9$ seconds is

$$\frac{s(t_2) - s(t_1)}{t_2 - t_1} = \frac{s(9) - s(4)}{9 - 4} = \frac{540 - 160}{5} = 76 \text{ feet per second.}$$

CHECKPOINT Now try Exercise 89.

Exploration

Use the information in Example 7 to find the average speed of the car from $t_1 = 0$ to $t_2 = 9$ seconds. Explain why the result is less than the value obtained in part (b).

Even and Odd Functions

In Section 1.2, you studied different types of symmetry of a graph. In the terminology of functions, a function is said to be **even** if its graph is symmetric with respect to the y-axis and to be **odd** if its graph is symmetric with respect to the origin. The symmetry tests in Section 1.2 yield the following tests for even and odd functions.

Exploration

Graph each of the functions with a graphing utility. Determine whether the function is *even*, *odd*, or *neither*.

$f(x) = x^2 - x^4$

$g(x) = 2x^3 + 1$

$h(x) = x^5 - 2x^3 + x$

$j(x) = 2 - x^6 - x^8$

$k(x) = x^5 - 2x^4 + x - 2$

$p(x) = x^9 + 3x^5 - x^3 + x$

What do you notice about the equations of functions that are odd? What do you notice about the equations of functions that are even? Can you describe a way to identify a function as odd or even by inspecting the equation? Can you describe a way to identify a function as neither odd nor even by inspecting the equation?

Tests for Even and Odd Functions

A function $y = f(x)$ is **even** if, for each x in the domain of f,

$$f(-x) = f(x).$$

A function $y = f(x)$ is **odd** if, for each x in the domain of f,

$$f(-x) = -f(x).$$

Example 8 Even and Odd Functions

a. The function $g(x) = x^3 - x$ is odd because $g(-x) = -g(x)$, as follows.

$$g(-x) = (-x)^3 - (-x) \qquad \text{Substitute } -x \text{ for } x.$$
$$= -x^3 + x \qquad \text{Simplify.}$$
$$= -(x^3 - x) \qquad \text{Distributive Property}$$
$$= -g(x) \qquad \text{Test for odd function}$$

b. The function $h(x) = x^2 + 1$ is even because $h(-x) = h(x)$, as follows.

$$h(-x) = (-x)^2 + 1 \qquad \text{Substitute } -x \text{ for } x.$$
$$= x^2 + 1 \qquad \text{Simplify.}$$
$$= h(x) \qquad \text{Test for even function}$$

The graphs and symmetry of these two functions are shown in Figure 1.64.

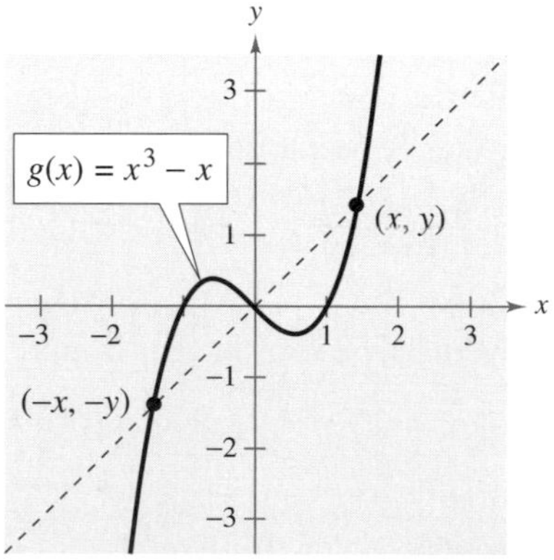

(a) Symmetric to origin: Odd Function

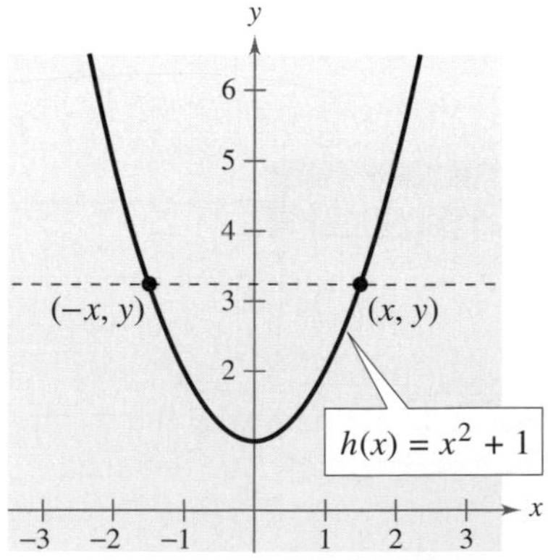

(b) Symmetric to y-axis: Even Function

FIGURE 1.64

CHECKPOINT Now try Exercise 71.

1.5 Exercises

VOCABULARY CHECK: Fill in the blanks.

1. The graph of a function f is the collection of ________ ________ or $(x, f(x))$ such that x is in the domain of f.
2. The ________ ________ ________ is used to determine whether the graph of an equation is a function of y in terms of x.
3. The ________ of a function f are the values of x for which $f(x) = 0$.
4. A function f is ________ on an interval if, for any x_1 and x_2 in the interval, $x_1 < x_2$ implies $f(x_1) > f(x_2)$.
5. A function value $f(a)$ is a relative ________ of f if there exists an interval (x_1, x_2) containing a such that $x_1 < x < x_2$ implies $f(a) \geq f(x)$.
6. The ________ ________ ________ ________ between any two points $(x_1, f(x_1))$ and $(x_2, f(x_2))$ is the slope of the line through the two points, and this line is called the ________ line.
7. A function f is ________ if for the each x in the domain of f, $f(-x) = -f(x)$.
8. A function f is ________ if its graph is symmetric with respect to the y-axis.

In Exercises 1–4, use the graph of the function to find the domain and range of *f*.

1.

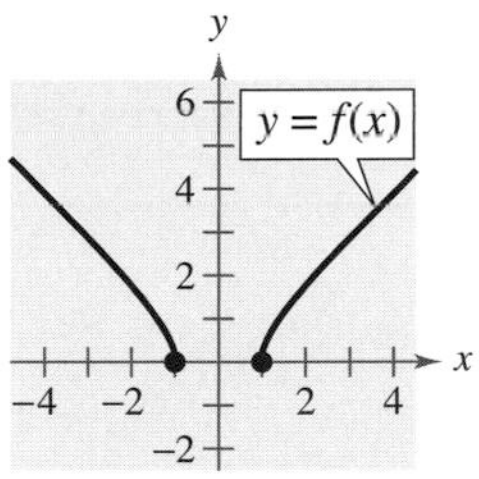

2.

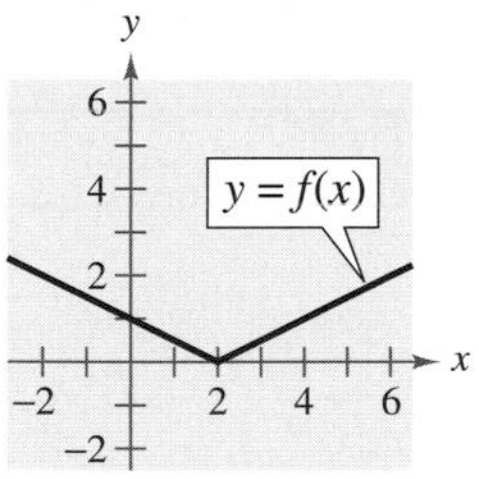

3.

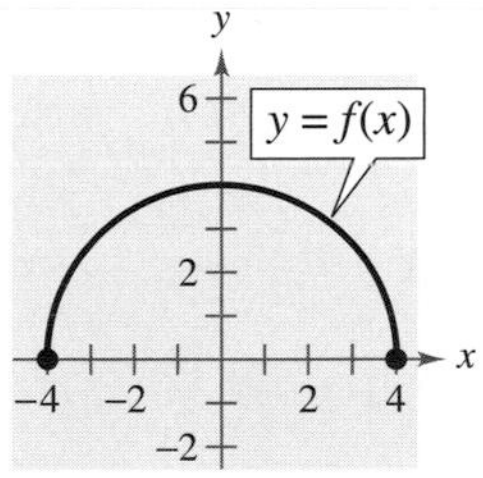

4.

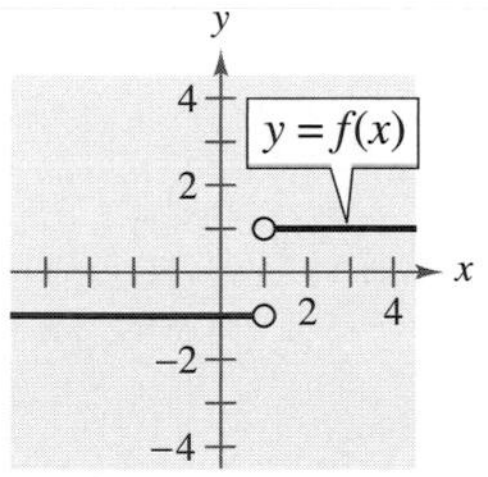

In Exercises 5–8, use the graph of the function to find the indicated function values.

5. (a) $f(-2)$ (b) $f(-1)$ (c) $f\left(\frac{1}{2}\right)$ (d) $f(1)$

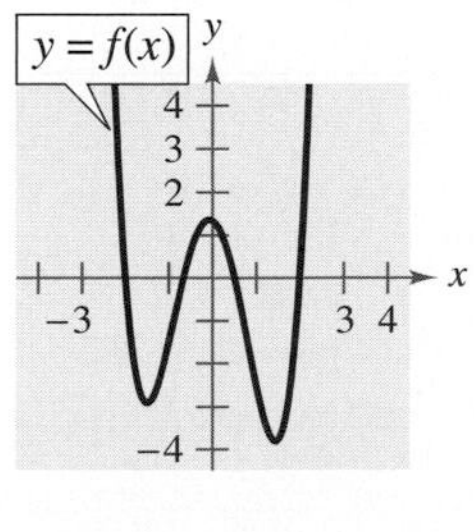

6. (a) $f(-1)$ (b) $f(2)$ (c) $f(0)$ (d) $f(1)$

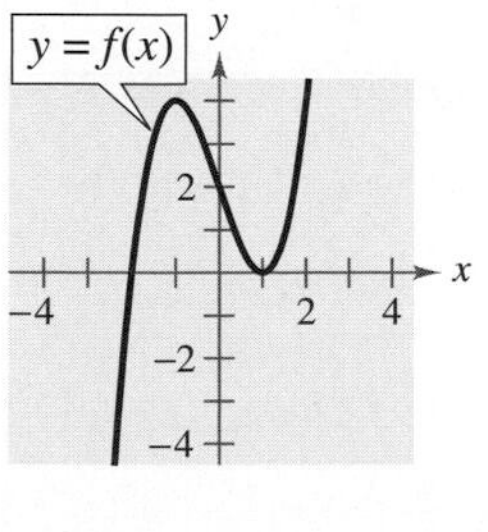

7. (a) $f(-2)$ (b) $f(1)$ (c) $f(0)$ (d) $f(2)$

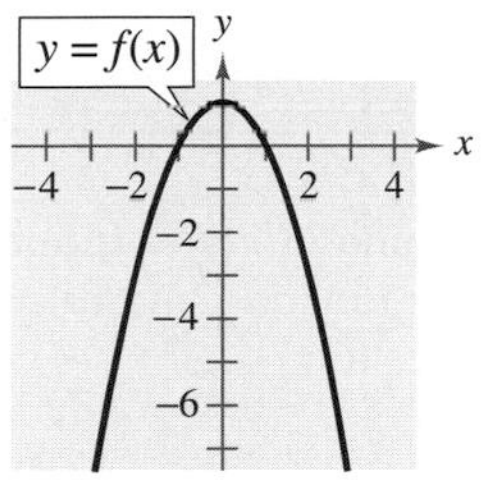

8. (a) $f(2)$ (b) $f(1)$ (c) $f(3)$ (d) $f(-1)$

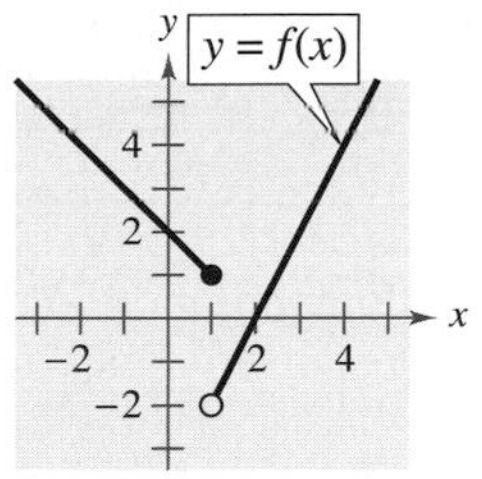

In Exercises 9–14, use the Vertical Line Test to determine whether *y* is a function of *x*. To print an enlarged copy of the graph, go to the website *www.mathgraphs.com*.

9. $y = \frac{1}{2}x^2$

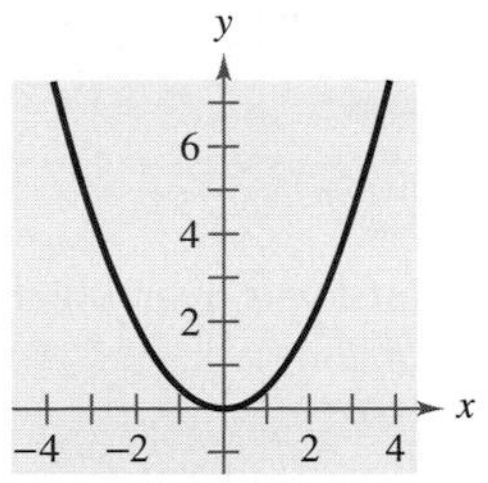

10. $y = \frac{1}{4}x^3$

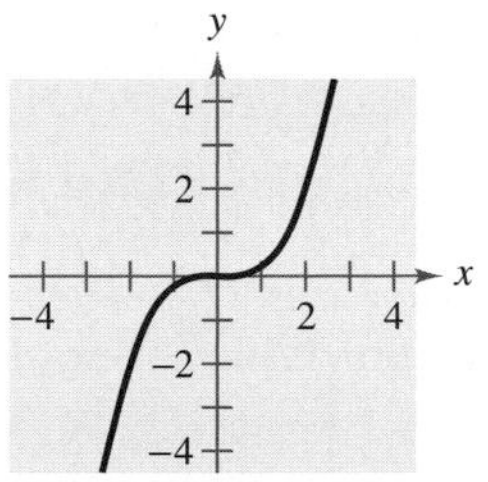

11. $x - y^2 = 1$

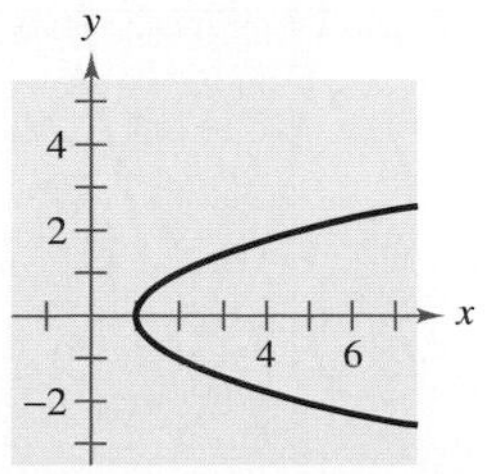

12. $x^2 + y^2 = 25$

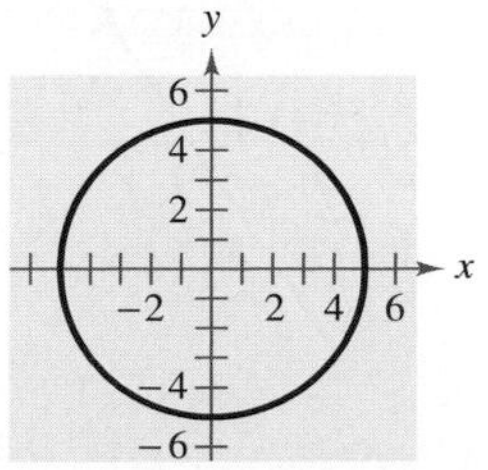

13. $x^2 = 2xy - 1$

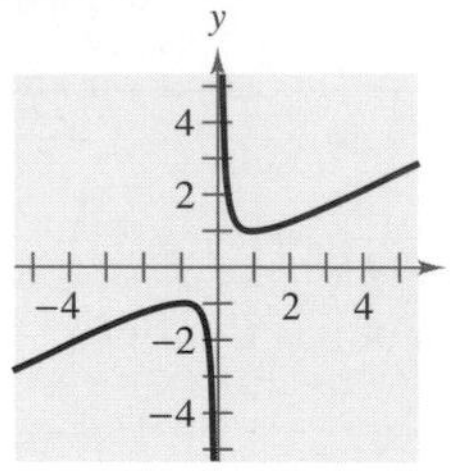

14. $x = |y + 2|$

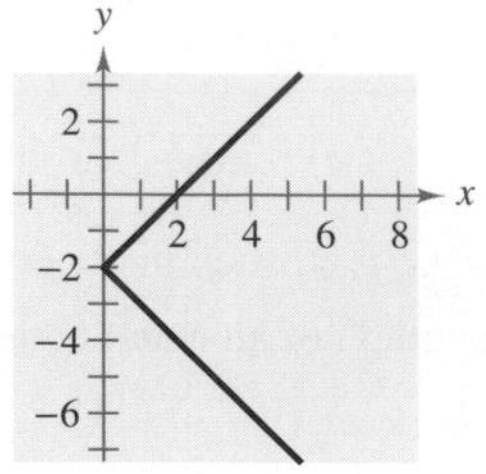

In Exercises 15–24, find the zeros of the function algebraically.

15. $f(x) = 2x^2 - 7x - 30$

16. $f(x) = 3x^2 + 22x - 16$

17. $f(x) = \dfrac{x}{9x^2 - 4}$

18. $f(x) = \dfrac{x^2 - 9x + 14}{4x}$

19. $f(x) = \frac{1}{2}x^3 - x$

20. $f(x) = x^3 - 4x^2 - 9x + 36$

21. $f(x) = 4x^3 - 24x^2 - x + 6$

22. $f(x) = 9x^4 - 25x^2$

23. $f(x) = \sqrt{2x} - 1$

24. $f(x) = \sqrt{3x + 2}$

In Exercises 25–30, (a) use a graphing utility to graph the function and find the zeros of the function and (b) verify your results from part (a) algebraically.

25. $f(x) = 3 + \dfrac{5}{x}$

26. $f(x) = x(x - 7)$

27. $f(x) = \sqrt{2x + 11}$

28. $f(x) = \sqrt{3x - 14} - 8$

29. $f(x) = \dfrac{3x - 1}{x - 6}$

30. $f(x) = \dfrac{2x^2 - 9}{3 - x}$

In Exercises 31–38, determine the intervals over which the function is increasing, decreasing, or constant.

31. $f(x) = \frac{3}{2}x$

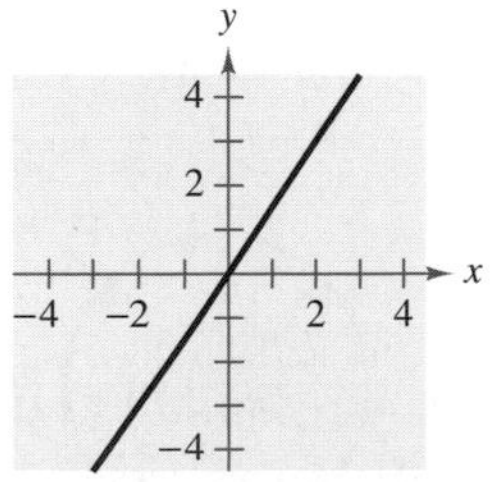

32. $f(x) = x^2 - 4x$

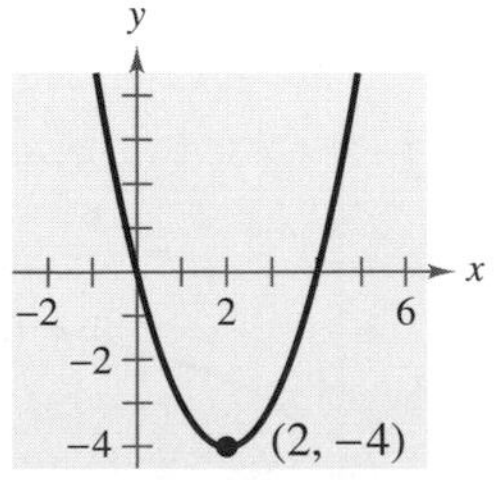

33. $f(x) = x^3 - 3x^2 + 2$

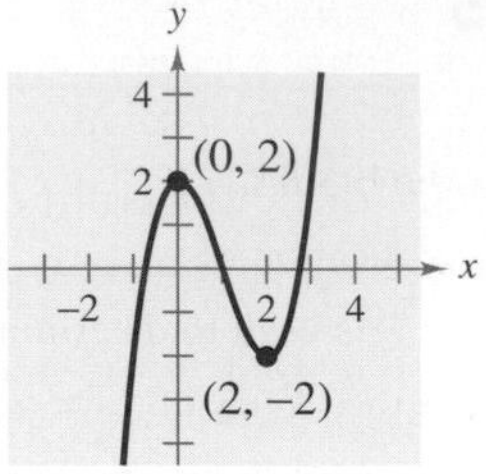

34. $f(x) = \sqrt{x^2 - 1}$

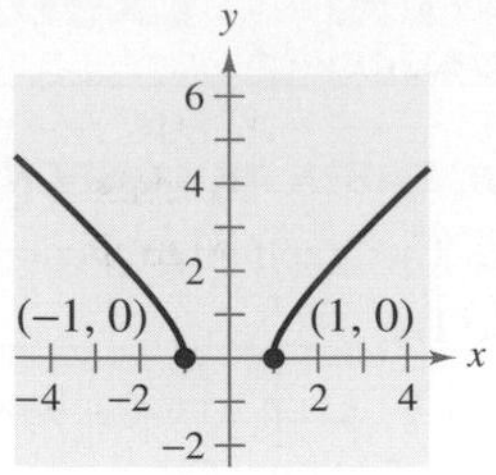

35. $f(x) = \begin{cases} x + 3, & x \le 0 \\ 3, & 0 < x \le 2 \\ 2x + 1, & x > 2 \end{cases}$

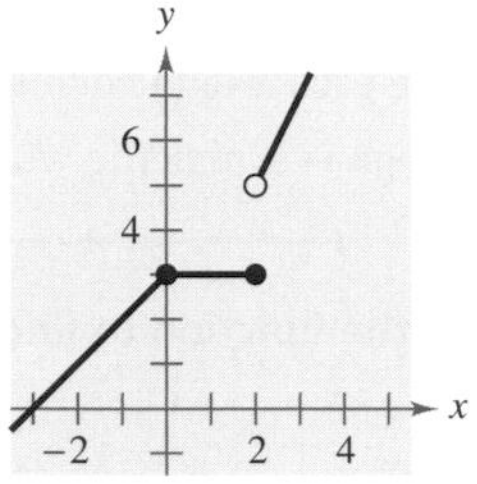

36. $f(x) = \begin{cases} 2x + 1, & x \le -1 \\ x^2 - 2, & x > -1 \end{cases}$

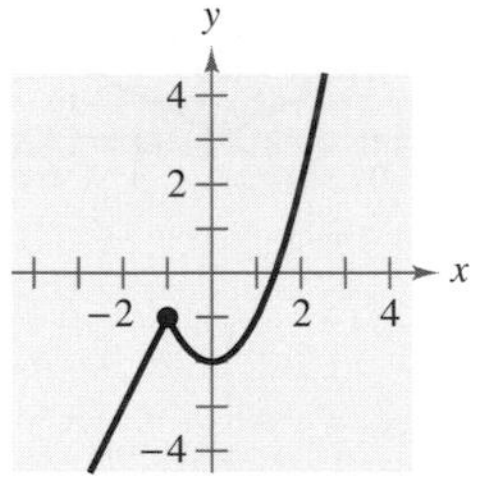

37. $f(x) = |x + 1| + |x - 1|$

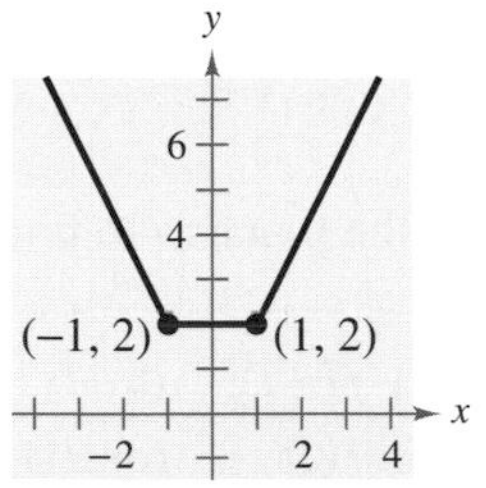

38. $f(x) = \dfrac{x^2 + x + 1}{x + 1}$

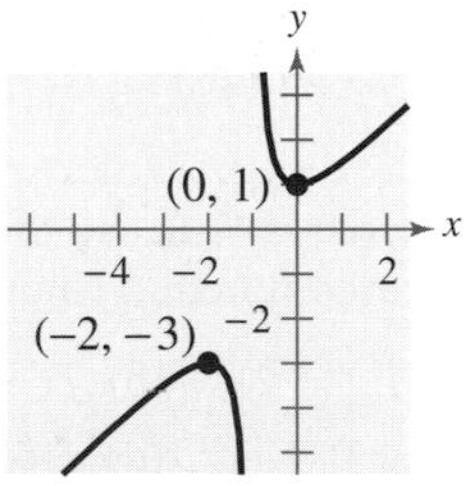

In Exercises 39–48, (a) use a graphing utility to graph the function and visually determine the intervals over which the function is increasing, decreasing, or constant, and (b) make a table of values to verify whether the function is increasing, decreasing, or constant over the intervals you identified in part (a).

39. $f(x) = 3$

40. $g(x) = x$

41. $g(s) = \frac{s^2}{4}$

42. $h(x) = x^2 - 4$

43. $f(t) = -t^4$

44. $f(x) = 3x^4 - 6x^2$

45. $f(x) = \sqrt{1 - x}$

46. $f(x) = x\sqrt{x + 3}$

47. $f(x) = x^{3/2}$

48. $f(x) = x^{2/3}$

In Exercises 49–54, use a graphing utility to graph the function and approximate (to two decimal places) any relative minimum or relative maximum values.

49. $f(x) = (x - 4)(x + 2)$

50. $f(x) = 3x^2 - 2x - 5$

51. $f(x) = -x^2 + 3x - 2$

52. $f(x) = -2x^2 + 9x$

53. $f(x) = x(x - 2)(x + 3)$

54. $f(x) = x^3 - 3x^2 - x + 1$

In Exercises 55–62, graph the function and determine the interval(s) for which $f(x) \geq 0$.

55. $f(x) = 4 - x$

56. $f(x) = 4x + 2$

57. $f(x) = x^2 + x$

58. $f(x) = x^2 - 4x$

59. $f(x) = \sqrt{x - 1}$

60. $f(x) = \sqrt{x + 2}$

61. $f(x) = -(1 + |x|)$

62. $f(x) = \frac{1}{2}(2 + |x|)$

In Exercises 63–70, find the average rate of change of the function from x_1 to x_2.

	Function	*x-Values*
63.	$f(x) = -2x + 15$	$x_1 = 0, x_2 = 3$
64.	$f(x) = 3x + 8$	$x_1 = 0, x_2 = 3$
65.	$f(x) = x^2 + 12x - 4$	$x_1 = 1, x_2 = 5$
66.	$f(x) = x^2 - 2x + 8$	$x_1 = 1, x_2 = 5$
67.	$f(x) = x^3 - 3x^2 - x$	$x_1 = 1, x_2 = 3$
68.	$f(x) = -x^3 + 6x^2 + x$	$x_1 = 1, x_2 = 6$
69.	$f(x) = -\sqrt{x - 2} + 5$	$x_1 = 3, x_2 = 11$
70.	$f(x) = -\sqrt{x + 1} + 3$	$x_1 = 3, x_2 = 8$

In Exercises 71–76, determine whether the function is even, odd, or neither. Then describe the symmetry.

71. $f(x) = x^6 - 2x^2 + 3$

72. $h(x) = x^3 - 5$

73. $g(x) = x^3 - 5x$

74. $f(x) = x\sqrt{1 - x^2}$

75. $f(t) = t^2 + 2t - 3$

76. $g(s) = 4s^{2/3}$

In Exercises 77–80, write the height h of the rectangle as a function of x.

77.

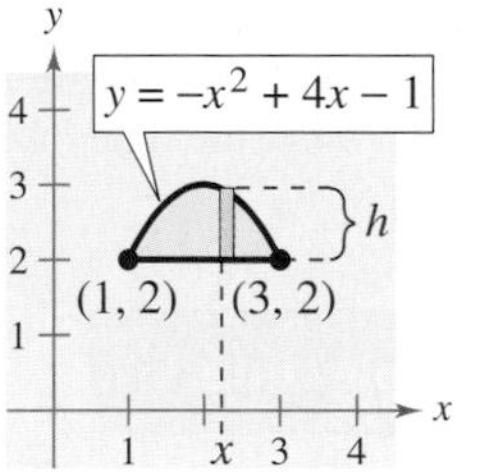

78.

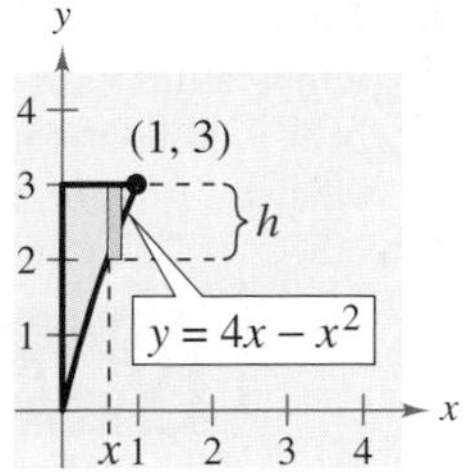

79.

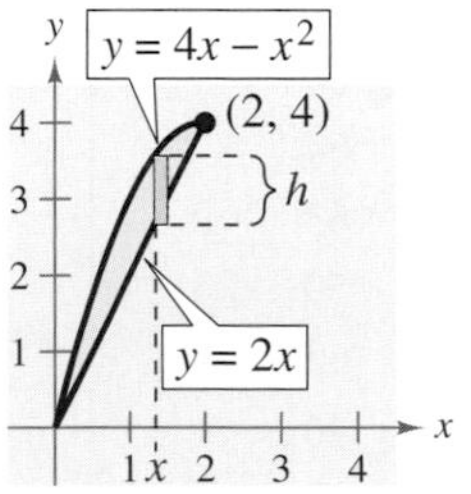

80.

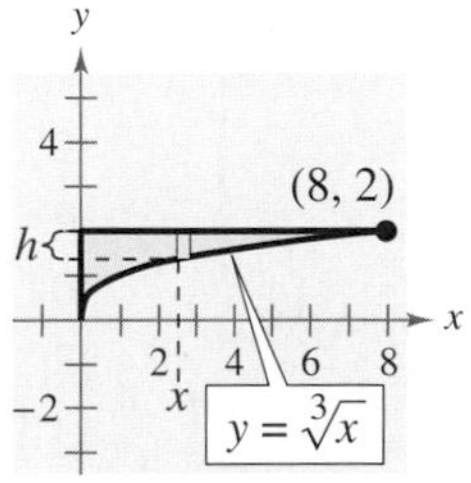

In Exercises 81–84, write the length L of the rectangle as a function of y.

81.

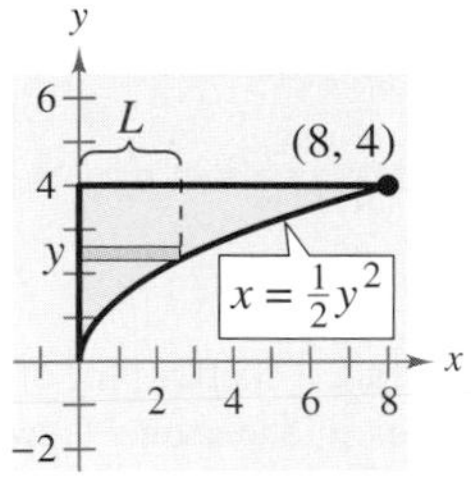

82.

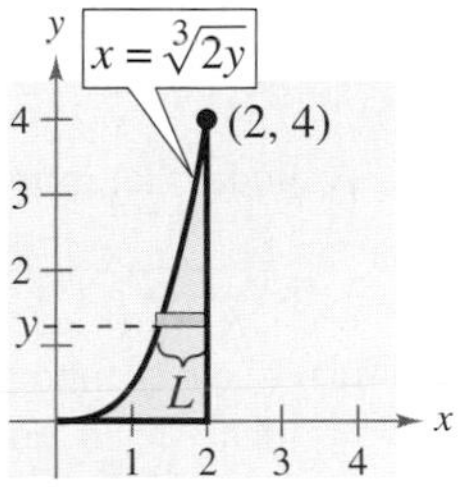

83.

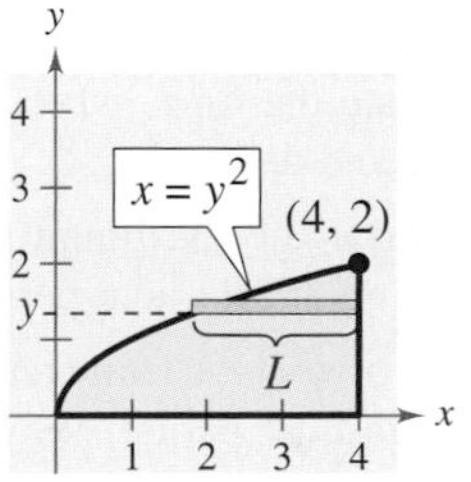

84.

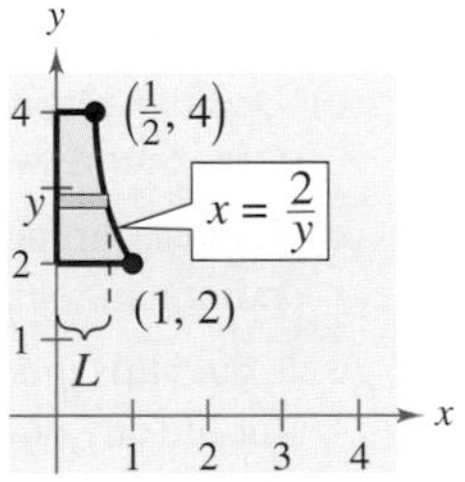

85. ***Electronics*** The number of lumens (time rate of flow of light) L from a fluorescent lamp can be approximated by the model

$$L = -0.294x^2 + 97.744x - 664.875, \quad 20 \leq x \leq 90$$

where x is the wattage of the lamp.

(a) Use a graphing utility to graph the function.

(b) Use the graph from part (a) to estimate the wattage necessary to obtain 2000 lumens.

Model It

86. *Data Analysis: Temperature* The table shows the temperature y (in degrees Fahrenheit) of a certain city over a 24-hour period. Let x represent the time of day, where $x = 0$ corresponds to 6 A.M.

Time, x	Temperature, y
0	34
2	50
4	60
6	64
8	63
10	59
12	53
14	46
16	40
18	36
20	34
22	37
24	45

A model that represents these data is given by

$$y = 0.026x^3 - 1.03x^2 + 10.2x + 34, \quad 0 \le x \le 24.$$

(a) Use a graphing utility to create a scatter plot of the data. Then graph the model in the same viewing window.

(b) How well does the model fit the data?

(c) Use the graph to approximate the times when the temperature was increasing and decreasing.

(d) Use the graph to approximate the maximum and minimum temperatures during this 24-hour period.

(e) Could this model be used to predict the temperature for the city during the next 24-hour period? Why or why not?

87. *Coordinate Axis Scale* Each function models the specified data for the years 1995 through 2005, with $t = 5$ corresponding to 1995. Estimate a reasonable scale for the vertical axis (e.g., hundreds, thousands, millions, etc.) of the graph and justify your answer. (There are many correct answers.)

(a) $f(t)$ represents the average salary of college professors.

(b) $f(t)$ represents the U.S. population.

(c) $f(t)$ represents the percent of the civilian work force that is unemployed.

88. *Geometry* Corners of equal size are cut from a square with sides of length 8 meters (see figure).

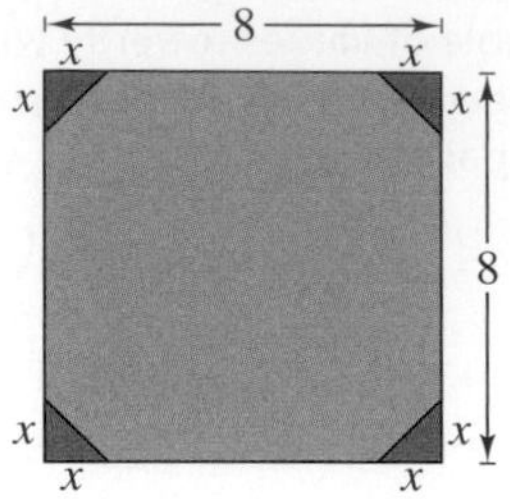

(a) Write the area A of the resulting figure as a function of x. Determine the domain of the function.

(b) Use a graphing utility to graph the area function over its domain. Use the graph to find the range of the function.

(c) Identify the figure that would result if x were chosen to be the maximum value in the domain of the function. What would be the length of each side of the figure?

89. *Digital Music Sales* The estimated revenues r (in billions of dollars) from sales of digital music from 2002 to 2007 can be approximated by the model

$$r = 15.639t^3 - 104.75t^2 + 303.5t - 301, \quad 2 \le t \le 7$$

where t represents the year, with $t = 2$ corresponding to 2002. (Source: *Fortune*)

(a) Use a graphing utility to graph the model.

(b) Find the average rate of change of the model from 2002 to 2007. Interpret your answer in the context of the problem.

90. *Foreign College Students* The numbers of foreign students F (in thousands) enrolled in colleges in the United States from 1992 to 2002 can be approximated by the model.

$$F = 0.004t^4 + 0.46t^2 + 431.6, \quad 2 \le t \le 12$$

where t represents the year, with $t = 2$ corresponding to 1992. (Source: Institute of International Education)

(a) Use a graphing utility to graph the model.

(b) Find the average rate of change of the model from 1992 to 2002. Interpret your answer in the context of the problem.

(c) Find the five-year time periods when the rate of change was the greatest and the least.

Physics **In Exercises 91–96, (a) use the position equation $s = -16t^2 + v_0t + s_0$ to write a function that represents the situation, (b) use a graphing utility to graph the function, (c) find the average rate of change of the function from t_1 to t_2, (d) interpret your answer to part (c) in the context of the problem, (e) find the equation of the secant line through t_1 and t_2, and (f) graph the secant line in the same viewing window as your position function.**

91. An object is thrown upward from a height of 6 feet at a velocity of 64 feet per second.

$t_1 = 0, t_2 = 3$

92. An object is thrown upward from a height of 6.5 feet at a velocity of 72 feet per second.

$t_1 = 0, t_2 = 4$

93. An object is thrown upward from ground level at a velocity of 120 feet per second.

$t_1 = 3, t_2 = 5$

94. An object is thrown upward from ground level at a velocity of 96 feet per second.

$t_1 = 2, t_2 = 5$

95. An object is dropped from a height of 120 feet.

$t_1 = 0, t_2 = 2$

96. An object is dropped from a height of 80 feet.

$t_1 = 1, t_2 = 2$

Synthesis

True or False? **In Exercises 97 and 98, determine whether the statement is true or false. Justify your answer.**

97. A function with a square root cannot have a domain that is the set of real numbers.

98. It is possible for an odd function to have the interval $[0, \infty)$ as its domain.

99. If f is an even function, determine whether g is even, odd, or neither. Explain.

(a) $g(x) = -f(x)$

(b) $g(x) = f(-x)$

(c) $g(x) = f(x) - 2$

(d) $g(x) = f(x - 2)$

100. ***Think About It*** Does the graph in Exercise 11 represent x as a function of y? Explain.

Think About It **In Exercises 101–104, find the coordinates of a second point on the graph of a function f if the given point is on the graph and the function is (a) even and (b) odd.**

101. $\left(-\frac{3}{2}, 4\right)$

102. $\left(-\frac{5}{3}, -7\right)$

103. $(4, 9)$

104. $(5, -1)$

105. ***Writing*** Use a graphing utility to graph each function. Write a paragraph describing any similarities and differences you observe among the graphs.

(a) $y = x$ (b) $y = x^2$

(c) $y = x^3$ (d) $y = x^4$

(e) $y = x^5$ (f) $y = x^6$

106. ***Conjecture*** Use the results of Exercise 105 to make a conjecture about the graphs of $y = x^7$ and $y = x^8$. Use a graphing utility to graph the functions and compare the results with your conjecture.

Skills Review

In Exercises 107–110, solve the equation.

107. $x^2 - 10x = 0$

108. $100 - (x - 5)^2 = 0$

109. $x^3 - x = 0$

110. $16x^2 - 40x + 25 = 0$

In Exercises 111–114, evaluate the function at each specified value of the independent variable and simplify.

111. $f(x) = 5x - 8$

(a) $f(9)$ (b) $f(-4)$ (c) $f(x - 7)$

112. $f(x) = x^2 - 10x$

(a) $f(4)$ (b) $f(-8)$ (c) $f(x - 4)$

113. $f(x) = \sqrt{x - 12} - 9$

(a) $f(12)$ (b) $f(40)$ (c) $f\left(-\sqrt{36}\right)$

114. $f(x) = x^4 - x - 5$

(a) $f(-1)$ (b) $f\left(\frac{1}{2}\right)$ (c) $f\left(2\sqrt{3}\right)$

In Exercises 115 and 116, find the difference quotient and simplify your answer.

115. $f(x) = x^2 - 2x + 9, \quad \dfrac{f(3 + h) - f(3)}{h}, \quad h \neq 0$

116. $f(x) = 5 + 6x - x^2, \quad \dfrac{f(6 + h) - f(6)}{h}, \quad h \neq 0$

1.6 A Library of Parent Functions

What you should learn

- Identify and graph linear and squaring functions.
- Identify and graph cubic, square root, and reciprocal functions.
- Identify and graph step and other piecewise-defined functions.
- Recognize graphs of parent functions.

Why you should learn it

Step functions can be used to model real-life situations. For instance, in Exercise 63 on page 72, you will use a step function to model the cost of sending an overnight package from Los Angeles to Miami.

© Getty Images

Linear and Squaring Functions

One of the goals of this text is to enable you to recognize the basic shapes of the graphs of different types of functions. For instance, you know that the graph of the **linear function** $f(x) = ax + b$ is a line with slope $m = a$ and y-intercept at $(0, b)$. The graph of the linear function has the following characteristics.

- The domain of the function is the set of all real numbers.
- The range of the function is the set of all real numbers.
- The graph has an x-intercept of $(-b/m, 0)$ and a y-intercept of $(0, b)$.
- The graph is increasing if $m > 0$, decreasing if $m < 0$, and constant if $m = 0$.

Example 1 **Writing a Linear Function**

Write the linear function f for which $f(1) = 3$ and $f(4) = 0$.

Solution

To find the equation of the line that passes through $(x_1, y_1) = (1, 3)$ and $(x_2, y_2) = (4, 0)$, first find the slope of the line.

$$m = \frac{y_2 - y_1}{x_2 - x_1} = \frac{0 - 3}{4 - 1} = \frac{-3}{3} = -1$$

Next, use the point-slope form of the equation of a line.

$y - y_1 = m(x - x_1)$ Point-slope form

$y - 3 = -1(x - 1)$ Substitute for x_1, y_1, and m.

$y = -x + 4$ Simplify.

$f(x) = -x + 4$ Function notation

The graph of this function is shown in Figure 1.65.

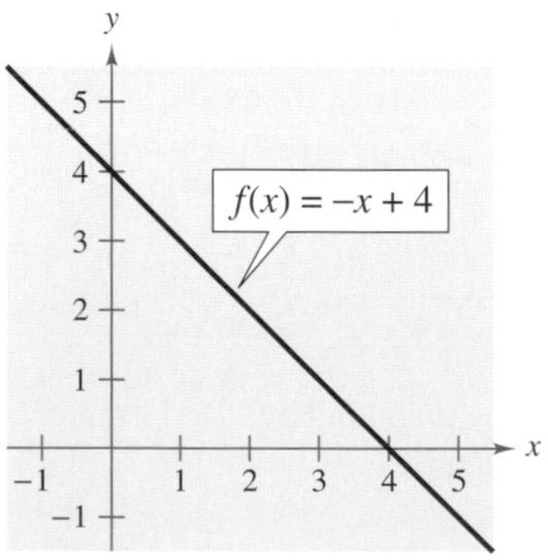

FIGURE 1.65

CHECKPOINT Now try Exercise 1.

There are two special types of linear functions, the **constant function** and the **identity function.** A constant function has the form

$$f(x) = c$$

and has the domain of all real numbers with a range consisting of a single real number c. The graph of a constant function is a horizontal line, as shown in Figure 1.66. The identity function has the form

$$f(x) = x.$$

Its domain and range are the set of all real numbers. The identity function has a slope of $m = 1$ and a y-intercept $(0, 0)$. The graph of the identity function is a line for which each x-coordinate equals the corresponding y-coordinate. The graph is always increasing, as shown in Figure 1.67

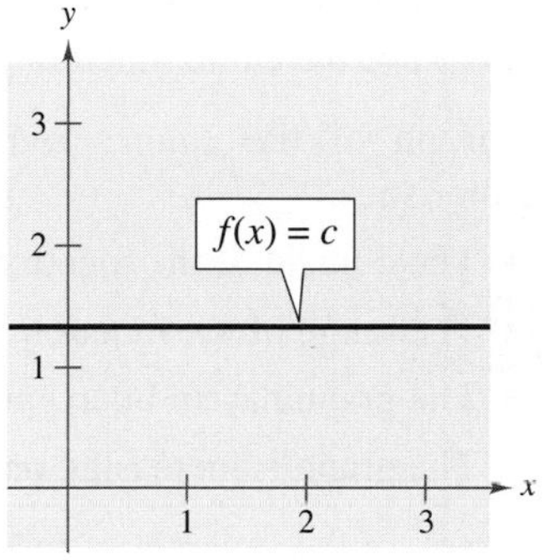

FIGURE 1.66

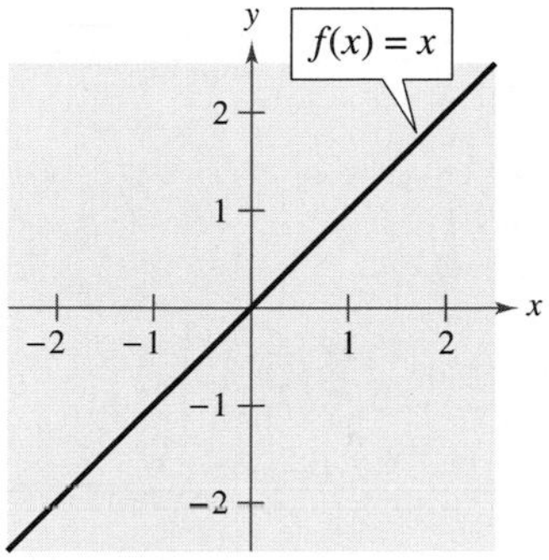

FIGURE 1.67

The graph of the **squaring function**

$$f(x) = x^2$$

is a U-shaped curve with the following characteristics.

- The domain of the function is the set of all real numbers.
- The range of the function is the set of all nonnegative real numbers.
- The function is even.
- The graph has an intercept at $(0, 0)$.
- The graph is decreasing on the interval $(-\infty, 0)$ and increasing on the interval $(0, \infty)$.
- The graph is symmetric with respect to the y-axis.
- The graph has a relative minimum at $(0, 0)$.

The graph of the squaring function is shown in Figure 1.68.

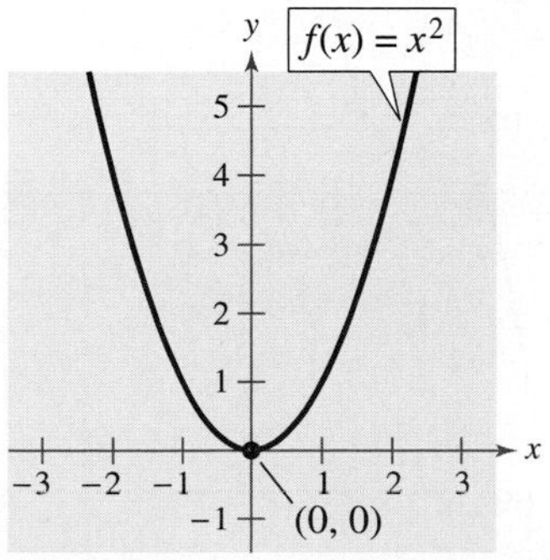

FIGURE 1.68

Cubic, Square Root, and Reciprocal Functions

The basic characteristics of the graphs of the **cubic, square root,** and **reciprocal functions** are summarized below.

1. The graph of the cubic function $f(x) = x^3$ has the following characteristics.

- The domain of the function is the set of all real numbers.
- The range of the function is the set of all real numbers.
- The function is odd.
- The graph has an intercept at $(0, 0)$.
- The graph is increasing on the interval $(-\infty, \infty)$.
- The graph is symmetric with respect to the origin.

The graph of the cubic function is shown in Figure 1.69.

2. The graph of the *square root* function $f(x) = \sqrt{x}$ has the following characteristics.

- The domain of the function is the set of all nonnegative real numbers.
- The range of the function is the set of all nonnegative real numbers.
- The graph has an intercept at $(0, 0)$.
- The graph is increasing on the interval $(0, \infty)$.

The graph of the square root function is shown in Figure 1.70.

3. The graph of the reciprocal function $f(x) = \dfrac{1}{x}$ has the following characteristics.

- The domain of the function is $(-\infty, 0) \cup (0, \infty)$.
- The range of the function is $(-\infty, 0) \cup (0, \infty)$.
- The function is odd.
- The graph does not have any intercepts.
- The graph is decreasing on the intervals $(-\infty, 0)$ and $(0, \infty)$.
- The graph is symmetric with respect to the origin.

The graph of the reciprocal function is shown in Figure 1.71.

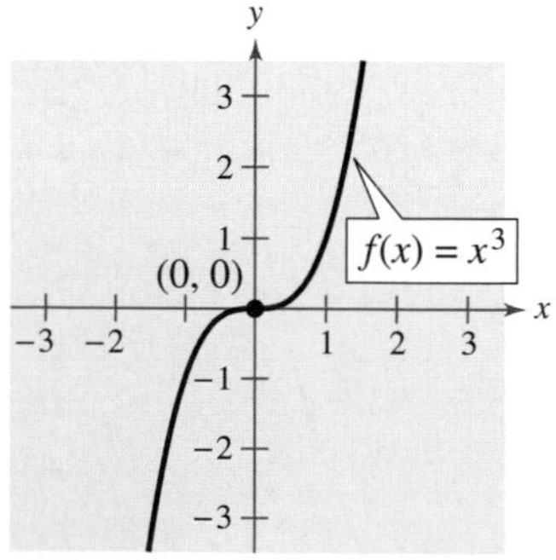

Cubic function
FIGURE 1.69

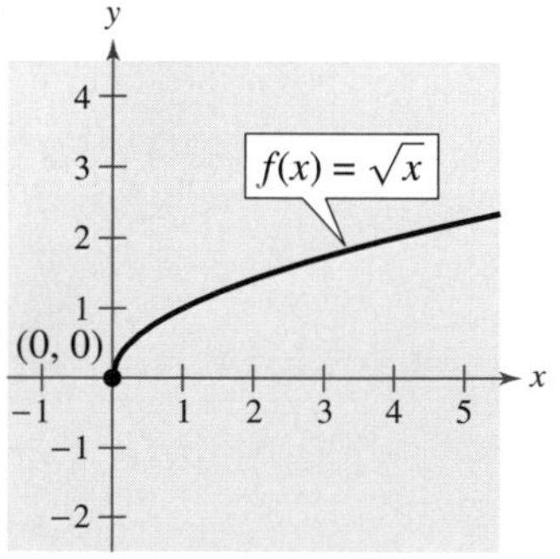

Square root function
FIGURE 1.70

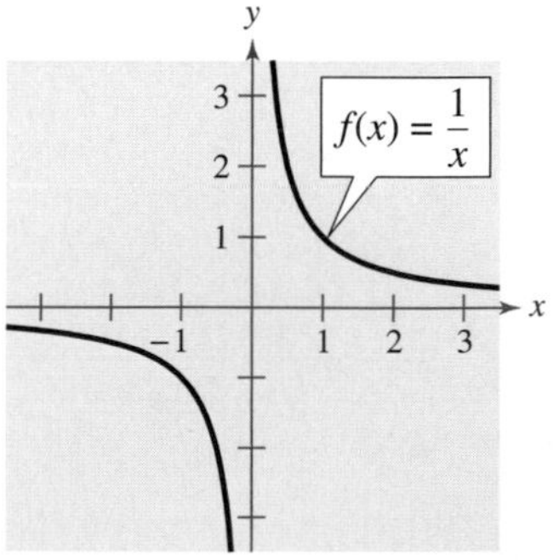

Reciprocal function
FIGURE 1.71

Step and Piecewise-Defined Functions

Functions whose graphs resemble sets of stairsteps are known as **step functions.** The most famous of the step functions is the **greatest integer function,** which is denoted by $[\![x]\!]$ and defined as

$$f(x) = [\![x]\!] = \textit{the greatest integer less than or equal to } x.$$

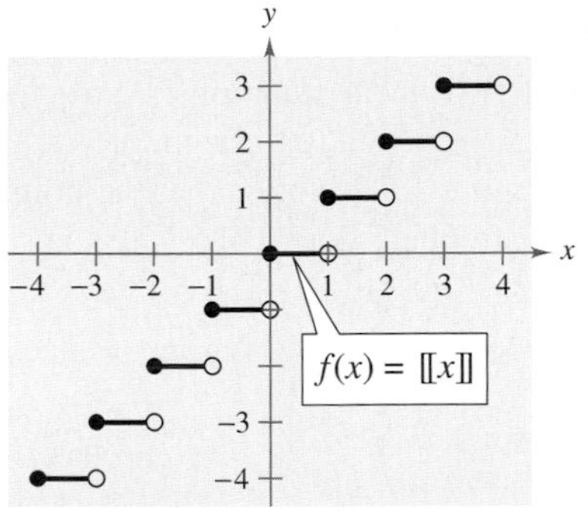

FIGURE 1.72

Some values of the greatest integer function are as follows.

$$[\![-1]\!] = (\text{greatest integer} \le -1) = -1$$

$$[\![-\tfrac{1}{2}]\!] = \left(\text{greatest integer} \le -\tfrac{1}{2}\right) = -1$$

$$[\![\tfrac{1}{10}]\!] = \left(\text{greatest integer} \le \tfrac{1}{10}\right) = 0$$

$$[\![1.5]\!] = (\text{greatest integer} \le 1.5) = 1$$

The graph of the greatest integer function

$$f(x) = [\![x]\!]$$

has the following characteristics, as shown in Figure 1.72.

- The domain of the function is the set of all real numbers.
- The range of the function is the set of all integers.
- The graph has a y-intercept at $(0, 0)$ and x-intercepts in the interval $[0, 1)$.
- The graph is constant between each pair of consecutive integers.
- The graph jumps vertically one unit at each integer value.

Technology

When graphing a step function, you should set your graphing utility to *dot* mode.

Example 2 Evaluating a Step Function

Evaluate the function when $x = -1$, 2, and $\frac{3}{2}$.

$$f(x) = [\![x]\!] + 1$$

Solution

For $x = -1$, the greatest integer ≤ -1 is -1, so

$$f(-1) = [\![-1]\!] + 1 = -1 + 1 = 0.$$

For $x = 2$, the greatest integer ≤ 2 is 2, so

$$f(2) = [\![2]\!] + 1 = 2 + 1 = 3.$$

For $x = \frac{3}{2}$, the greatest integer $\le \frac{3}{2}$ is 1, so

$$f\left(\tfrac{3}{2}\right) = [\![\tfrac{3}{2}]\!] + 1 = 1 + 1 = 2.$$

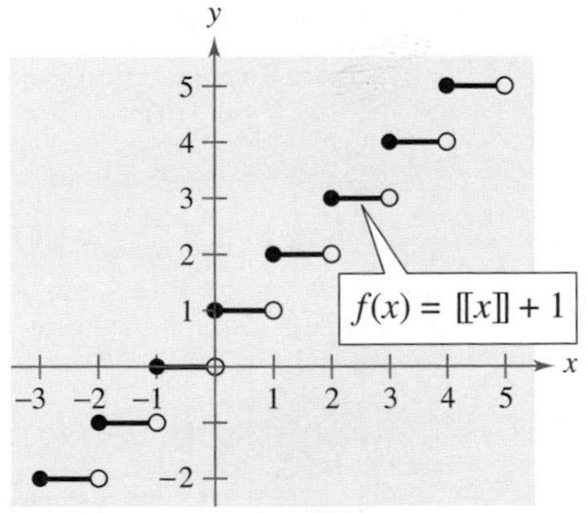

FIGURE 1.73

You can verify your answers by examining the graph of $f(x) = [\![x]\!] + 1$ shown in Figure 1.73.

CHECKPOINT Now try Exercise 29.

Recall from Section 1.4 that a piecewise-defined function is defined by two or more equations over a specified domain. To graph a piecewise-defined function, graph each equation separately over the specified domain, as shown in Example 3.

Example 3 Graphing a Piecewise-Defined Function

Sketch the graph of

$$f(x) = \begin{cases} 2x + 3, & x \le 1 \\ -x + 4, & x > 1 \end{cases}.$$

Solution

This piecewise-defined function is composed of two linear functions. At $x = 1$ and to the left of $x = 1$ the graph is the line $y = 2x + 3$, and to the right of $x = 1$ the graph is the line $y = -x + 4$, as shown in Figure 1.74. Notice that the point $(1, 5)$ is a solid dot and the point $(1, 3)$ is an open dot. This is because $f(1) = 2(1) + 3 = 5$.

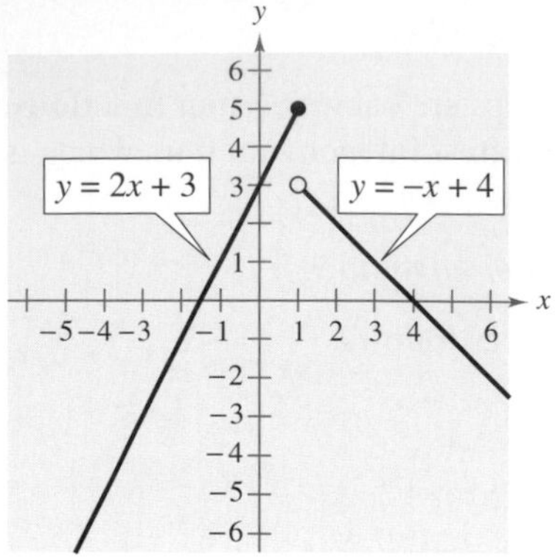

FIGURE 1.74

CHECKPOINT Now try Exercise 43.

Parent Functions

The eight graphs shown in Figure 1.75 represent the most commonly used functions in algebra. Familiarity with the basic characteristics of these simple graphs will help you analyze the shapes of more complicated graphs—in particular, graphs obtained from these graphs by the rigid and nonrigid transformations studied in the next section.

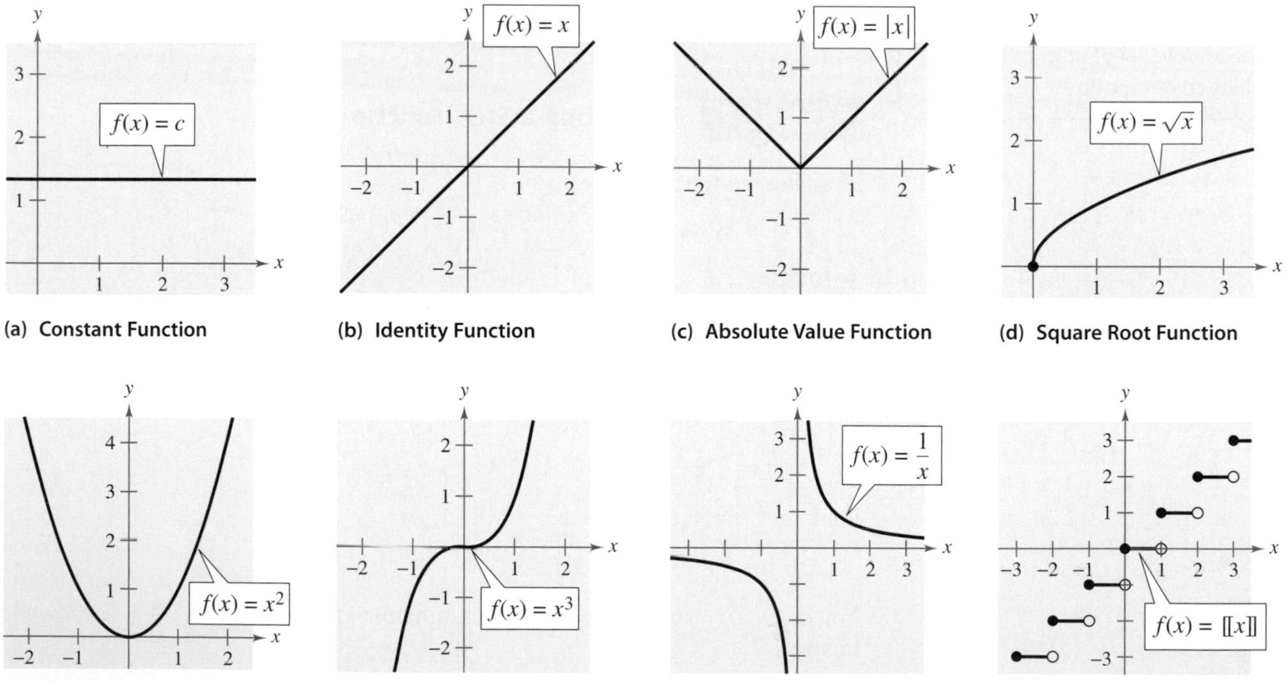

(a) Constant Function (b) Identity Function (c) Absolute Value Function (d) Square Root Function

(e) Quadratic Function (f) Cubic Function (g) Reciprocal Function (h) Greatest Integer Function

FIGURE 1.75

1.6 Exercises

VOCABULARY CHECK: Match each function with its name.

1. $f(x) = [\![x]\!]$
2. $f(x) = x$
3. $f(x) = \dfrac{1}{x}$
4. $f(x) = x^2$
5. $f(x) = \sqrt{x}$
6. $f(x) = c$
7. $f(x) = |x|$
8. $f(x) = x^3$
9. $f(x) = ax + b$

(a) squaring function
(b) square root function
(c) cubic function
(d) linear function
(e) constant function
(f) absolute value function
(e) greatest integer function
(h) reciprocal function
(i) identity function

In Exercises 1–8, (a) write the linear function f such that it has the indicated function values and (b) sketch the graph of the function.

1. $f(1) = 4, f(0) = 6$
2. $f(-3) = -8, f(1) = 2$
3. $f(5) = -4, f(-2) = 17$
4. $f(3) = 9, f(-1) = -11$
5. $f(-5) = -1, f(5) = -1$
6. $f(-10) = 12, f(16) = -1$
7. $f\left(\frac{1}{2}\right) = 6, f(4) = -3$
8. $f\left(\frac{2}{3}\right) = -\frac{15}{2}, f(-4) = -11$

In Exercises 9–28, use a graphing utility to graph the function. Be sure to choose an appropriate viewing window.

9. $f(x) = -x - \frac{3}{4}$
10. $f(x) = 3x - \frac{5}{2}$
11. $f(x) = -\frac{1}{6}x - \frac{5}{2}$
12. $f(x) = \frac{5}{6} - \frac{2}{3}x$
13. $f(x) = x^2 - 2x$
14. $f(x) = -x^2 + 8x$
15. $h(x) = -x^2 + 4x + 12$
16. $g(x) = x^2 - 6x - 16$
17. $f(x) = x^3 - 1$
18. $f(x) = 8 - x^3$
19. $f(x) = (x - 1)^3 + 2$
20. $g(x) = 2(x + 3)^3 + 1$
21. $f(x) = 4\sqrt{x}$
22. $f(x) = 4 - 2\sqrt{x}$
23. $g(x) = 2 - \sqrt{x + 4}$
24. $h(x) = \sqrt{x + 2} + 3$
25. $f(x) = -\dfrac{1}{x}$
26. $f(x) = 4 + \dfrac{1}{x}$
27. $h(x) = \dfrac{1}{x + 2}$
28. $k(x) = \dfrac{1}{x - 3}$

In Exercises 29–36, evaluate the function for the indicated values.

29. $f(x) = [\![x]\!]$
   (a) $f(2.1)$ (b) $f(2.9)$ (c) $f(-3.1)$ (d) $f\left(\frac{7}{2}\right)$
30. $g(x) = 2[\![x]\!]$
   (a) $g(-3)$ (b) $g(0.25)$ (c) $g(9.5)$ (d) $g\left(\frac{11}{3}\right)$
31. $h(x) = [\![x + 3]\!]$
   (a) $h(-2)$ (b) $h\left(\frac{1}{2}\right)$ (c) $h(4.2)$ (d) $h(-21.6)$
32. $f(x) = 4[\![x]\!] + 7$
   (a) $f(0)$ (b) $f(-1.5)$ (c) $f(6)$ (d) $f\left(\frac{5}{3}\right)$
33. $h(x) = [\![3x - 1]\!]$
   (a) $h(2.5)$ (b) $h(-3.2)$ (c) $h\left(\frac{7}{3}\right)$ (d) $h\left(-\frac{21}{3}\right)$
34. $k(x) = [\![\frac{1}{2}x + 6]\!]$
   (a) $k(5)$ (b) $k(-6.1)$ (c) $k(0.1)$ (d) $k(15)$
35. $g(x) = 3[\![x - 2]\!] + 5$
   (a) $g(-2.7)$ (b) $g(-1)$ (c) $g(0.8)$ (d) $g(14.5)$
36. $g(x) = -7[\![x + 4]\!] + 6$
   (a) $g\left(\frac{1}{8}\right)$ (b) $g(9)$ (c) $g(-4)$ (d) $g\left(\frac{3}{2}\right)$

In Exercises 37–42, sketch the graph of the function.

37. $g(x) = -[\![x]\!]$
38. $g(x) = 4[\![x]\!]$
39. $g(x) = [\![x]\!] - 2$
40. $g(x) = [\![x]\!] - 1$
41. $g(x) = [\![x + 1]\!]$
42. $g(x) = [\![x - 3]\!]$

In Exercises 43–50, graph the function.

43. $f(x) = \begin{cases} 2x + 3, & x < 0 \\ 3 - x, & x \ge 0 \end{cases}$
44. $g(x) = \begin{cases} x + 6, & x \le -4 \\ \frac{1}{2}x - 4, & x > -4 \end{cases}$
45. $f(x) = \begin{cases} \sqrt{4 + x}, & x < 0 \\ \sqrt{4 - x}, & x \ge 0 \end{cases}$
46. $f(x) = \begin{cases} 1 - (x - 1)^2, & x \le 2 \\ \sqrt{x - 2}, & x > 2 \end{cases}$
47. $f(x) = \begin{cases} x^2 + 5, & x \le 1 \\ -x^2 + 4x + 3, & x > 1 \end{cases}$

48. $h(x) = \begin{cases} 3 - x^2, & x < 0 \\ x^2 + 2, & x \geq 0 \end{cases}$

49. $h(x) = \begin{cases} 4 - x^2, & x < -2 \\ 3 + x, & -2 \leq x < 0 \\ x^2 + 1, & x \geq 0 \end{cases}$

50. $k(x) = \begin{cases} 2x + 1, & x \leq -1 \\ 2x^2 - 1, & -1 < x \leq 1 \\ 1 - x^2, & x > 1 \end{cases}$

In Exercises 51 and 52, (a) use a graphing utility to graph the function, (b) state the domain and range of the function, and (c) describe the pattern of the graph.

51. $s(x) = 2\left(\frac{1}{4}x - [\![\frac{1}{4}x]\!]\right)$ **52.** $g(x) = 2\left(\frac{1}{4}x - [\![\frac{1}{4}x]\!]\right)^2$

In Exercises 53–60, (a) identify the parent function and the transformed parent function shown in the graph, (b) write an equation for the function shown in the graph, and (c) use a graphing utility to verify your answers in parts (a) and (b).

53.

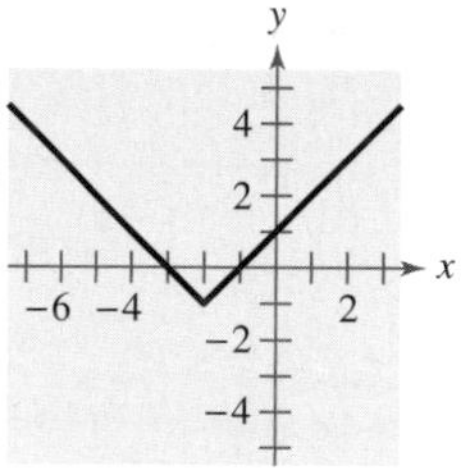

54.

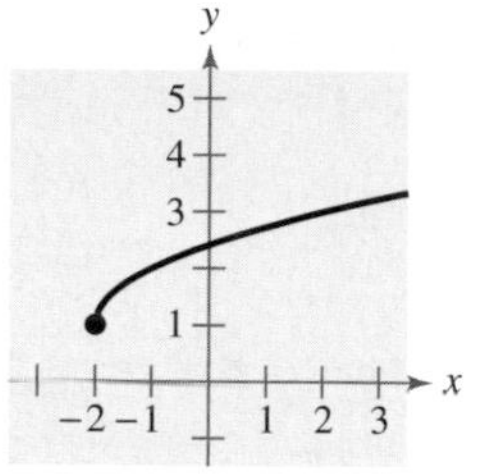

55.

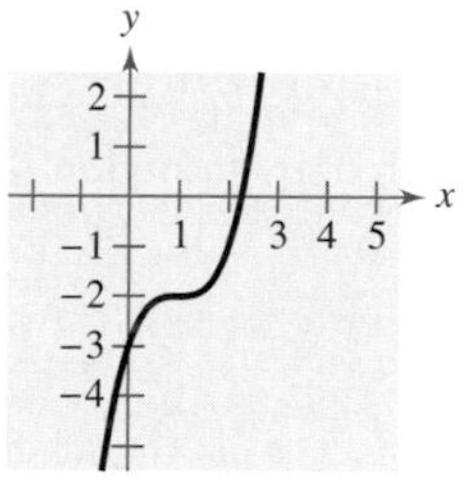

56.

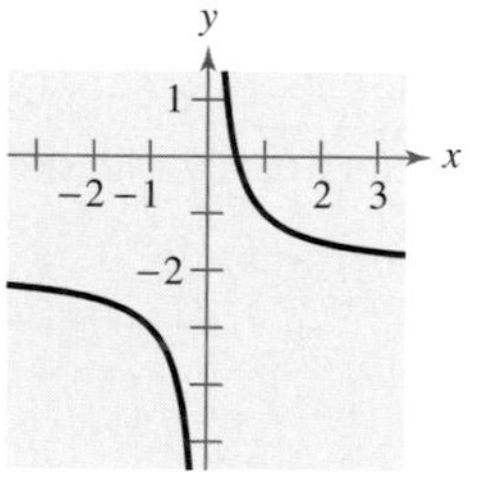

57.

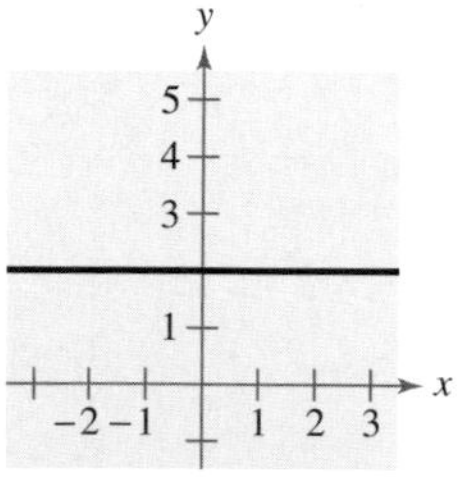

58.

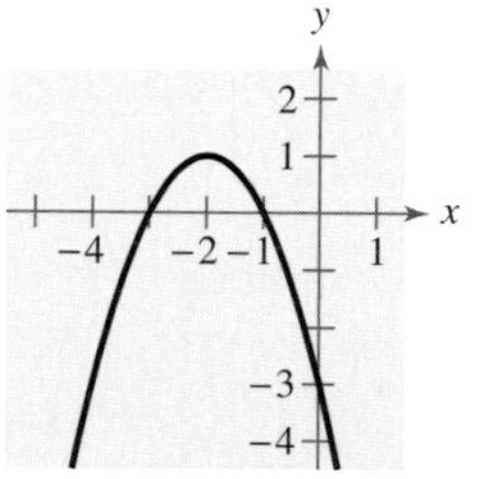

59.

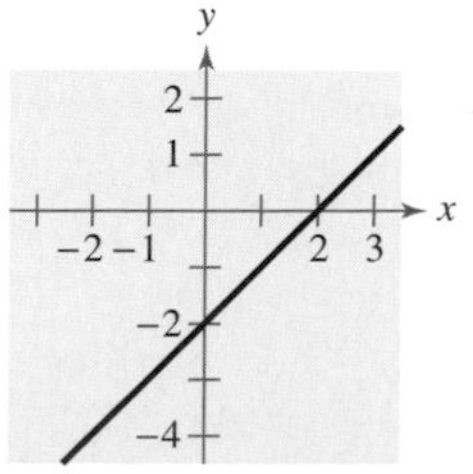

60.

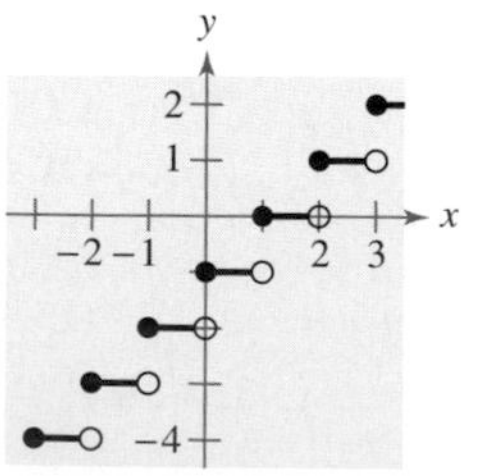

61. ***Communications*** The cost of a telephone call between Denver and Boise is \$0.60 for the first minute and \$0.42 for each additional minute or portion of a minute. A model for the total cost C (in dollars) of the phone call is $C = 0.60 - 0.42[\![1 - t]\!]$, $t > 0$ where t is the length of the phone call in minutes.

(a) Sketch the graph of the model.

(b) Determine the cost of a call lasting 12 minutes and 30 seconds.

62. ***Communications*** The cost of using a telephone calling card is \$1.05 for the first minute and \$0.38 for each additional minute or portion of a minute.

(a) A customer needs a model for the cost C of using a calling card for a call lasting t minutes. Which of the following is the appropriate model? Explain.

$C_1(t) = 1.05 + 0.38[\![t - 1]\!]$

$C_2(t) = 1.05 - 0.38[\![-(t - 1)]\!]$

(b) Graph the appropriate model. Determine the cost of a call lasting 18 minutes and 45 seconds.

63. ***Delivery Charges*** The cost of sending an overnight package from Los Angeles to Miami is \$10.75 for a package weighing up to but not including 1 pound and \$3.95 for each additional pound or portion of a pound. A model for the total cost C (in dollars) of sending the package is $C = 10.75 + 3.95[\![x]\!]$, $x > 0$ where x is the weight in pounds.

(a) Sketch a graph of the model.

(b) Determine the cost of sending a package that weighs 10.33 pounds.

64. ***Delivery Charges*** The cost of sending an overnight package from New York to Atlanta is \$9.80 for a package weighing up to but not including 1 pound and \$2.50 for each additional pound or portion of a pound.

(a) Use the greatest integer function to create a model for the cost C of overnight delivery of a package weighing x pounds, $x > 0$.

(b) Sketch the graph of the function.

65. ***Wages*** A mechanic is paid \$12.00 per hour for regular time and time-and-a-half for overtime. The weekly wage function is given by

$$W(h) = \begin{cases} 12h, & 0 < h \leq 40 \\ 18(h - 40) + 480, & h > 40 \end{cases}$$

where h is the number of hours worked in a week.

(a) Evaluate $W(30)$, $W(40)$, $W(45)$, and $W(50)$.

(b) The company increased the regular work week to 45 hours. What is the new weekly wage function?

66. *Snowstorm* During a nine-hour snowstorm, it snows at a rate of 1 inch per hour for the first 2 hours, at a rate of 2 inches per hour for the next 6 hours, and at a rate of 0.5 inch per hour for the final hour. Write and graph a piecewise-defined function that gives the depth of the snow during the snowstorm. How many inches of snow accumulated from the storm?

Model It

67. *Revenue* The table shows the monthly revenue y (in thousands of dollars) of a landscaping business for each month of the year 2005, with $x = 1$ representing January.

Month, x	Revenue, y
1	5.2
2	5.6
3	6.6
4	8.3
5	11.5
6	15.8
7	12.8
8	10.1
9	8.6
10	6.9
11	4.5
12	2.7

A mathematical model that represents these data is

$$f(x) = \begin{cases} -1.97x + 26.3 \\ 0.505x^2 - 1.47x + 6.3 \end{cases}.$$

(a) What is the domain of each part of the piecewise-defined function? How can you tell? Explain your reasoning.

(b) Sketch a graph of the model.

(c) Find $f(5)$ and $f(11)$, and interpret your results in the context of the problem.

(d) How do the values obtained from the model in part (b) compare with the actual data values?

68. *Fluid Flow* The intake pipe of a 100-gallon tank has a flow rate of 10 gallons per minute, and two drainpipes have flow rates of 5 gallons per minute each. The figure shows the volume V of fluid in the tank as a function of time t. Determine the combination of the input pipe and drain pipes in which the fluid is flowing in specific subintervals of the 1 hour of time shown on the graph. (There are many correct answers.)

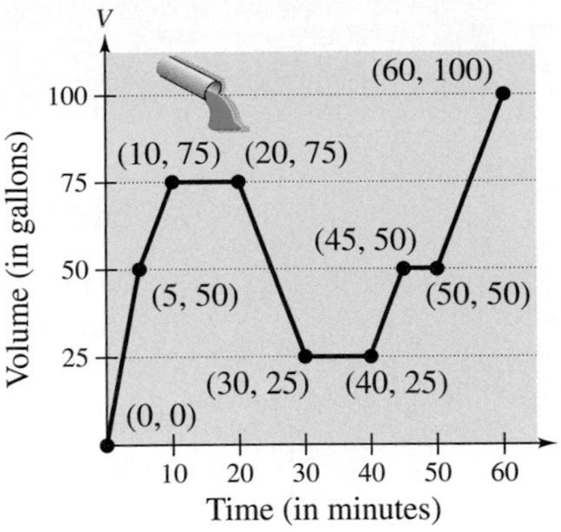

FIGURE FOR 68

Synthesis

True or False? **In Exercises 69 and 70, determine whether the statement is true or false. Justify your answer.**

69. A piecewise-defined function will always have at least one x-intercept or at least one y-intercept.

70. $f(x) = \begin{cases} 2, & 1 \le x < 2 \\ 4, & 2 \le x < 3 \\ 6, & 3 \le x < 4 \end{cases}$

can be rewritten as $f(x) = 2[\![x]\!], \quad 1 \le x < 4$.

Exploration **In Exercises 71 and 72, write equations for the piecewise-defined function shown in the graph.**

71.

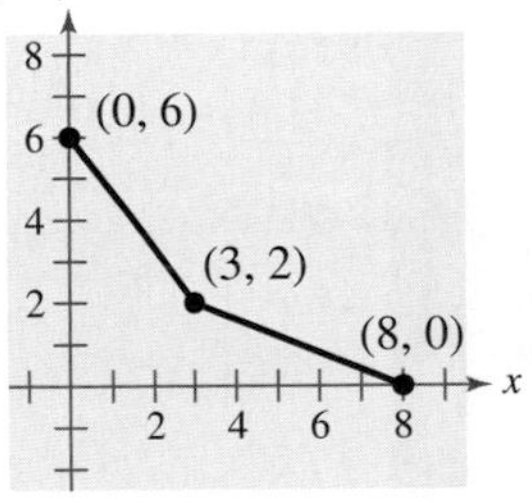

72.

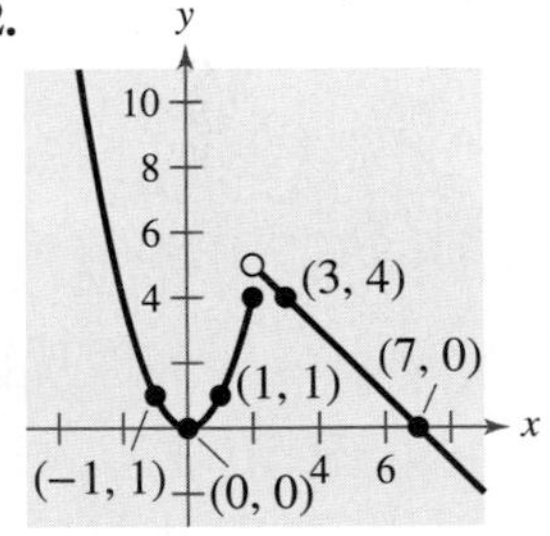

Skills Review

In Exercises 73 and 74, solve the inequality and sketch the solution on the real number line.

73. $3x + 4 \le 12 - 5x$

74. $2x + 1 > 6x - 9$

In Exercises 75 and 76, determine whether the lines L_1 and L_2 passing through the pairs of points are parallel, perpendicular, or neither.

75. L_1: $(-2, -2), (2, 10)$
L_2: $(-1, 3), (3, 9)$

76. L_1: $(-1, -7), (4, 3)$
L_2: $(1, 5), (-2, -7)$

1.7 Transformations of Functions

What you should learn

- Use vertical and horizontal shifts to sketch graphs of functions.
- Use reflections to sketch graphs of functions.
- Use nonrigid transformations to sketch graphs of functions.

Why you should learn it

Knowing the graphs of common functions and knowing how to shift, reflect, and stretch graphs of functions can help you sketch a wide variety of simple functions by hand. This skill is useful in sketching graphs of functions that model real-life data, such as in Exercise 68 on page 83, where you are asked to sketch the graph of a function that models the amounts of mortgage debt outstanding from 1990 through 2002.

Shifting Graphs

Many functions have graphs that are simple transformations of the parent graphs summarized in Section 1.6. For example, you can obtain the graph of

$$h(x) = x^2 + 2$$

by shifting the graph of $f(x) = x^2$ *upward* two units, as shown in Figure 1.76. In function notation, h and f are related as follows.

$$h(x) = x^2 + 2 = f(x) + 2 \qquad \text{Upward shift of two units}$$

Similarly, you can obtain the graph of

$$g(x) = (x - 2)^2$$

by shifting the graph of $f(x) = x^2$ to the *right* two units, as shown in Figure 1.77. In this case, the functions g and f have the following relationship.

$$g(x) = (x - 2)^2 = f(x - 2) \qquad \text{Right shift of two units}$$

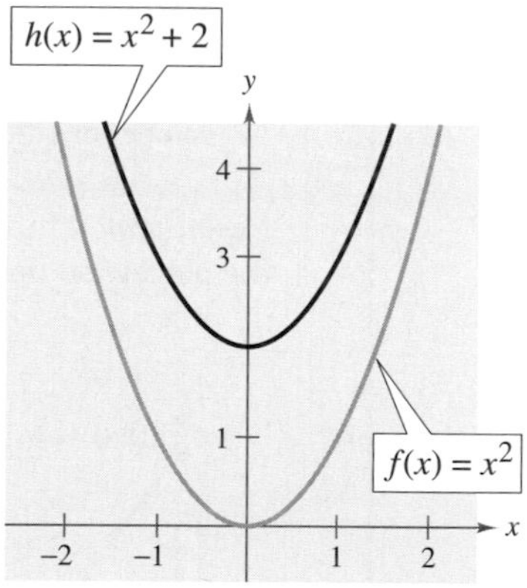

FIGURE 1.76

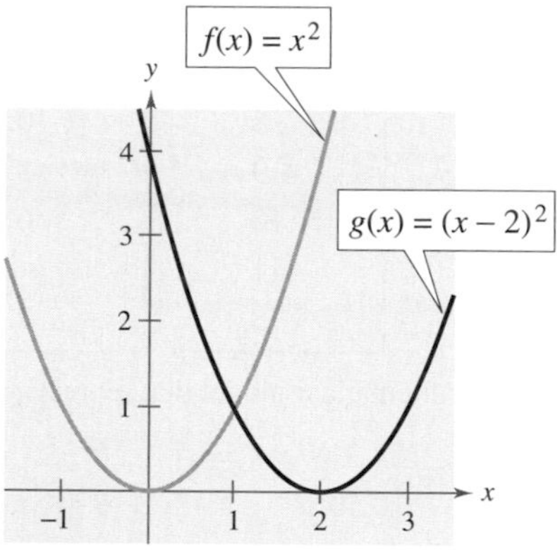

FIGURE 1.77

The following list summarizes this discussion about horizontal and vertical shifts.

Vertical and Horizontal Shifts

Let c be a positive real number. **Vertical and horizontal shifts** in the graph of $y = f(x)$ are represented as follows.

1. Vertical shift c units *upward:* $h(x) = f(x) + c$
2. Vertical shift c units *downward:* $h(x) = f(x) - c$
3. Horizontal shift c units to the *right:* $h(x) = f(x - c)$
4. Horizontal shift c units to the *left:* $h(x) = f(x + c)$

STUDY TIP

In items 3 and 4, be sure you see that $h(x) = f(x - c)$ corresponds to a *right* shift and $h(x) = f(x + c)$ corresponds to a *left* shift for $c > 0$.

Some graphs can be obtained from combinations of vertical and horizontal shifts, as demonstrated in Example 1(b). Vertical and horizontal shifts generate a *family of functions*, each with the same shape but at different locations in the plane.

Example 1 **Shifts in the Graphs of a Function**

Use the graph of $f(x) = x^3$ to sketch the graph of each function.

a. $g(x) = x^3 - 1$

b. $h(x) = (x + 2)^3 + 1$

Solution

a. Relative to the graph of $f(x) = x^3$, the graph of $g(x) = x^3 - 1$ is a downward shift of one unit, as shown in Figure 1.78.

b. Relative to the graph of $f(x) = x^3$, the graph of $h(x) = (x + 2)^3 + 1$ involves a left shift of two units and an upward shift of one unit, as shown in Figure 1.79.

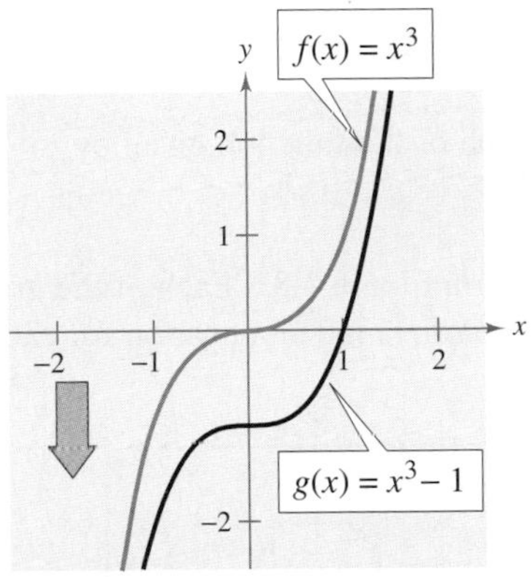

FIGURE 1.78

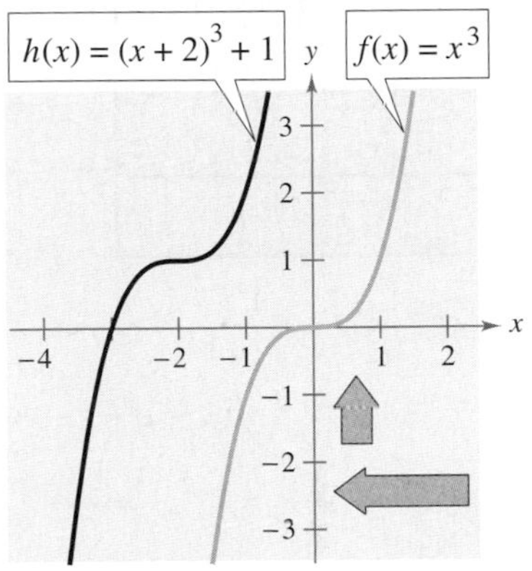

FIGURE 1.79

✓CHECKPOINT Now try Exercise 1.

In Figure 1.79, notice that the same result is obtained if the vertical shift precedes the horizontal shift *or* if the horizontal shift precedes the vertical shift.

Exploration

Graphing utilities are ideal tools for exploring translations of functions. Graph f, g, and h in same viewing window. Before looking at the graphs, try to predict how the graphs of g and h relate to the graph of f.

a. $f(x) = x^2, \quad g(x) = (x - 4)^2, \quad h(x) = (x - 4)^2 + 3$

b. $f(x) = x^2, \quad g(x) = (x + 1)^2, \quad h(x) = (x + 1)^2 - 2$

c. $f(x) = x^2, \quad g(x) = (x + 4)^2, \quad h(x) = (x + 4)^2 + 2$

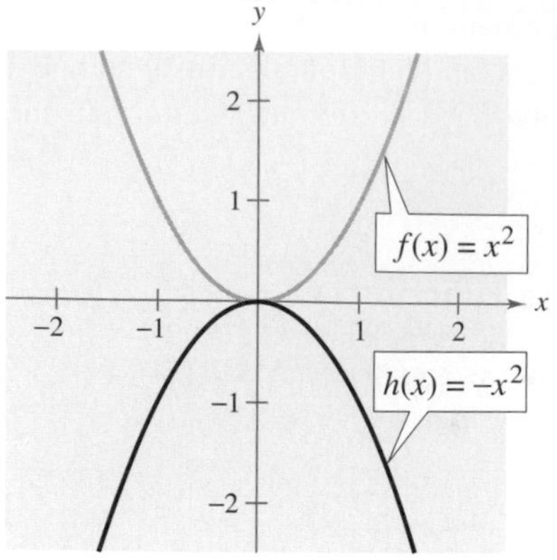

FIGURE 1.80

Reflecting Graphs

The second common type of transformation is a **reflection.** For instance, if you consider the x-axis to be a mirror, the graph of

$$h(x) = -x^2$$

is the mirror image (or reflection) of the graph of

$$f(x) = x^2,$$

as shown in Figure 1.80.

> **Reflections in the Coordinate Axes**
>
> **Reflections** in the coordinate axes of the graph of $y = f(x)$ are represented as follows.
>
> **1.** Reflection in the x-axis: $h(x) = -f(x)$
>
> **2.** Reflection in the y-axis: $h(x) = f(-x)$

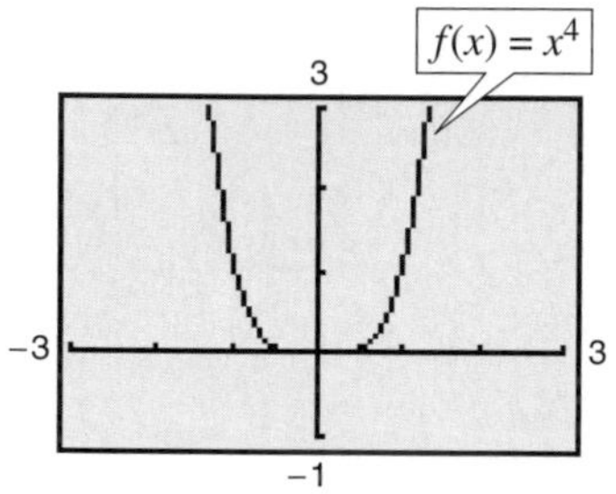

FIGURE 1.81

Example 2 Finding Equations from Graphs

The graph of the function given by

$$f(x) = x^4$$

is shown in Figure 1.81. Each of the graphs in Figure 1.82 is a transformation of the graph of f. Find an equation for each of these functions.

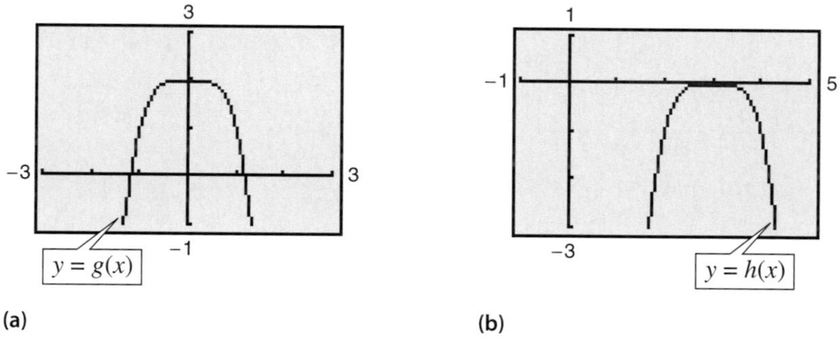

FIGURE 1.82

Solution

a. The graph of g is a reflection in the x-axis *followed by* an upward shift of two units of the graph of $f(x) = x^4$. So, the equation for g is

$$g(x) = -x^4 + 2.$$

b. The graph of h is a horizontal shift of three units to the right *followed by* a reflection in the x-axis of the graph of $f(x) = x^4$. So, the equation for h is

$$h(x) = -(x - 3)^4.$$

CHECKPOINT Now try Exercise 9.

> *Exploration*
>
> Reverse the order of transformations in Example 2(a). Do you obtain the same graph? Do the same for Example 2(b). Do you obtain the same graph? Explain.

Example 3 **Reflections and Shifts**

Compare the graph of each function with the graph of $f(x) = \sqrt{x}$.

a. $g(x) = -\sqrt{x}$ **b.** $h(x) = \sqrt{-x}$ **c.** $k(x) = -\sqrt{x+2}$

Algebraic Solution

a. The graph of g is a reflection of the graph of f in the x-axis because

$$g(x) = -\sqrt{x}$$
$$= -f(x).$$

b. The graph of h is a reflection of the graph of f in the y-axis because

$$h(x) = \sqrt{-x}$$
$$= f(-x).$$

c. The graph of k is a left shift of two units followed by a reflection in the x-axis because

$$k(x) = -\sqrt{x+2}$$
$$= -f(x+2).$$

CHECKPOINT Now try Exercise 19.

Graphical Solution

a. Graph f and g on the same set of coordinate axes. From the graph in Figure 1.83, you can see that the graph of g is a reflection of the graph of f in the x-axis.

b. Graph f and h on the same set of coordinate axes. From the graph in Figure 1.84, you can see that the graph of h is a reflection of the graph of f in the y-axis.

c. Graph f and k on the same set of coordinate axes. From the graph in Figure 1.85, you can see that the graph of k is a left shift of two units of the graph of f, followed by a reflection in the x-axis.

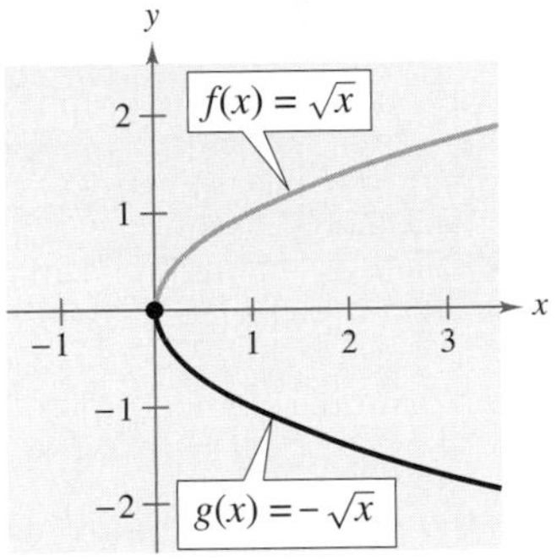

FIGURE 1.83

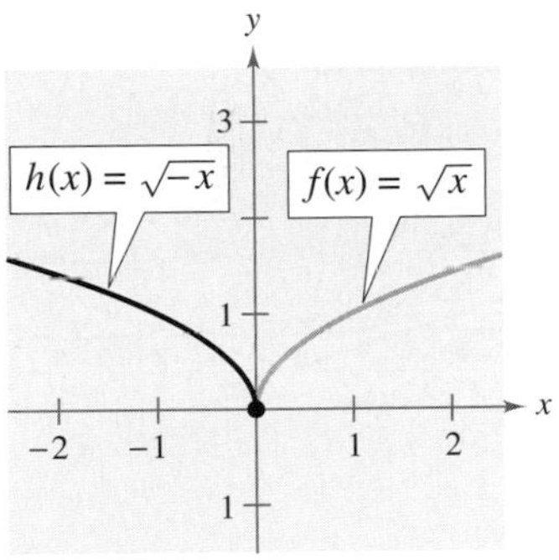

FIGURE 1.84

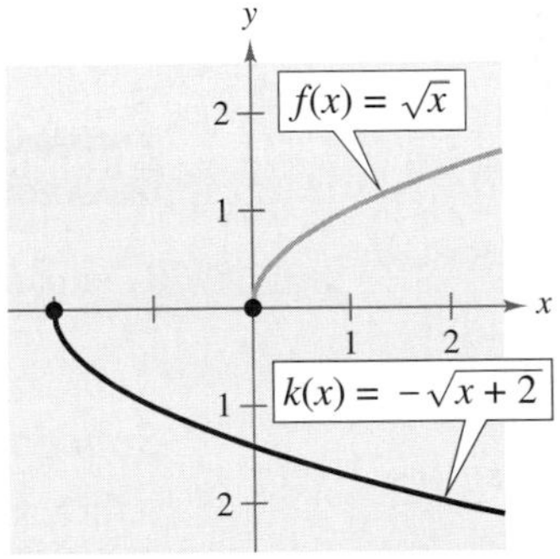

FIGURE 1.85

When sketching the graphs of functions involving square roots, remember that the domain must be restricted to exclude negative numbers inside the radical. For instance, here are the domains of the functions in Example 3.

Domain of $g(x) = -\sqrt{x}$: $\quad x \ge 0$

Domain of $h(x) = \sqrt{-x}$: $\quad x \le 0$

Domain of $k(x) = -\sqrt{x+2}$: $\quad x \ge -2$

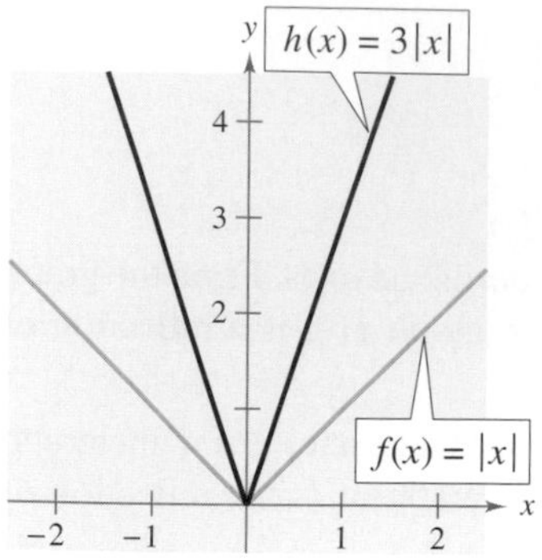

FIGURE 1.86

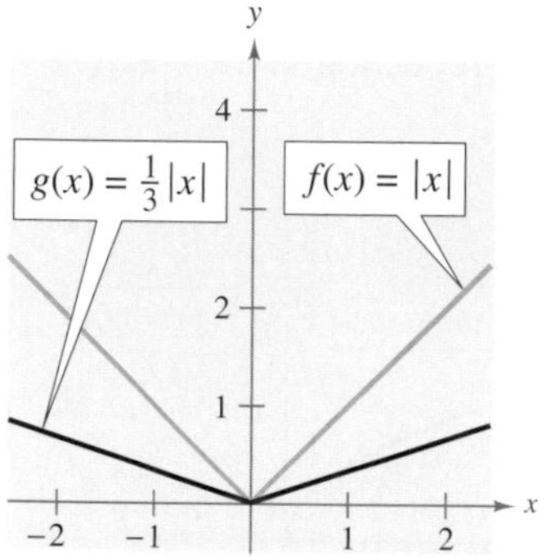

FIGURE 1.87

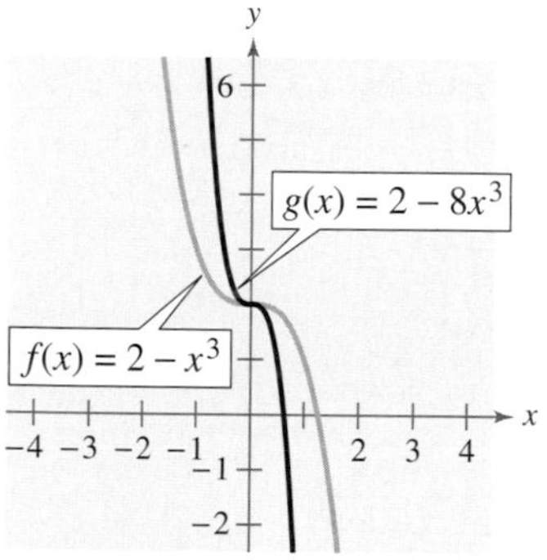

FIGURE 1.88

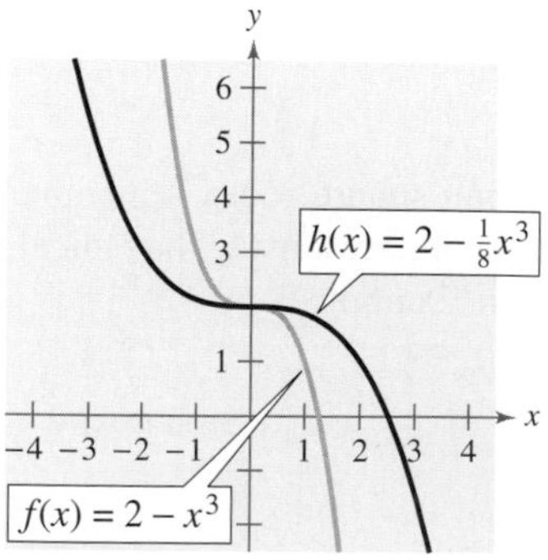

FIGURE 1.89

Nonrigid Transformations

Horizontal shifts, vertical shifts, and reflections are **rigid transformations** because the basic shape of the graph is unchanged. These transformations change only the *position* of the graph in the coordinate plane. **Nonrigid transformations** are those that cause a *distortion*—a change in the shape of the original graph. For instance, a nonrigid transformation of the graph of $y = f(x)$ is represented by $g(x) = cf(x)$, where the transformation is a **vertical stretch** if $c > 1$ and a **vertical shrink** if $0 < c < 1$. Another nonrigid transformation of the graph of $y = f(x)$ is represented by $h(x) = f(cx)$, where the transformation is a **horizontal shrink** if $c > 1$ and a **horizontal stretch** if $0 < c < 1$.

Example 4 Nonrigid Transformations

Compare the graph of each function with the graph of $f(x) = |x|$.

a. $h(x) = 3|x|$ **b.** $g(x) = \frac{1}{3}|x|$

Solution

a. Relative to the graph of $f(x) = |x|$, the graph of

$$h(x) = 3|x| = 3f(x)$$

is a vertical stretch (each y-value is multiplied by 3) of the graph of f. (See Figure 1.86.)

b. Similarly, the graph of

$$g(x) = \frac{1}{3}|x| = \frac{1}{3}f(x)$$

is a vertical shrink $\left(\text{each } y\text{-value is multiplied by } \frac{1}{3}\right)$ of the graph of f. (See Figure 1.87.)

✓CHECKPOINT Now try Exercise 23.

Example 5 Nonrigid Transformations

Compare the graph of each function with the graph of $f(x) = 2 - x^3$.

a. $g(x) = f(2x)$ **b.** $h(x) = f\left(\frac{1}{2}x\right)$

Solution

a. Relative to the graph of $f(x) = 2 - x^3$, the graph of

$$g(x) = f(2x) = 2 - (2x)^3 = 2 - 8x^3$$

is a horizontal shrink $(c > 1)$ of the graph of f. (See Figure 1.88.)

b. Similarly, the graph of

$$h(x) = f\left(\tfrac{1}{2}x\right) = 2 - \left(\tfrac{1}{2}x\right)^3 = 2 - \tfrac{1}{8}x^3$$

is a horizontal stretch $(0 < c < 1)$ of the graph of f. (See Figure 1.89.)

✓CHECKPOINT Now try Exercise 27.

1.7 Exercises

VOCABULARY CHECK:

In Exercises 1–5, fill in the blanks.

1. Horizontal shifts, vertical shifts, and reflections are called ________ transformations.
2. A reflection in the x-axis of $y = f(x)$ is represented by $h(x) =$ ________, while a reflection in the y-axis of $y = f(x)$ is represented by $h(x) =$ ________.
3. Transformations that cause a distortion in the shape of the graph of $y = f(x)$ are called ________ transformations.
4. A nonrigid transformation of $y = f(x)$ represented by $h(x) = f(cx)$ is a ________ ________ if $c > 1$ and a ________ ________ if $0 < c < 1$.
5. A nonrigid transformation of $y = f(x)$ represented by $g(x) = cf(x)$ is a ________ ________ if $c > 1$ and a ________ ________ if $0 < c < 1$.
6. Match the rigid transformation of $y = f(x)$ with the correct representation of the graph of h, where $c > 0$.

   (a) $h(x) = f(x) + c$ (i) A horizontal shift of f, c units to the right

   (b) $h(x) = f(x) - c$ (ii) A vertical shift of f, c units downward

   (c) $h(x) = f(x + c)$ (iii) A horizontal shift of f, c units to the left

   (d) $h(x) = f(x - c)$ (iv) A vertical shift of f, c units upward

---

1. For each function, sketch (on the same set of coordinate axes) a graph of each function for $c = -1, 1$, and 3.

(a) $f(x) = |x| + c$

(b) $f(x) = |x - c|$

(c) $f(x) = |x + 4| + c$

2. For each function, sketch (on the same set of coordinate axes) a graph of each function for $c = -3, -1, 1$, and 3.

(a) $f(x) = \sqrt{x} + c$

(b) $f(x) = \sqrt{x - c}$

(c) $f(x) = \sqrt{x - 3} + c$

3. For each function, sketch (on the same set of coordinate axes) a graph of each function for $c = -2, 0$, and 2.

(a) $f(x) = [\![x]\!] + c$

(b) $f(x) = [\![x + c]\!]$

(c) $f(x) = [\![x - 1]\!] + c$

4. For each function, sketch (on the same set of coordinate axes) a graph of each function for $c = -3, -1, 1$, and 3.

(a) $f(x) = \begin{cases} x^2 + c, & x < 0 \\ -x^2 + c, & x \geq 0 \end{cases}$

(b) $f(x) = \begin{cases} (x + c)^2, & x < 0 \\ -(x + c)^2, & x \geq 0 \end{cases}$

In Exercises 5–8, use the graph of *f* to sketch each graph. To print an enlarged copy of the graph go to the website *www.mathgraphs.com*.

5. (a) $y = f(x) + 2$

(b) $y = f(x - 2)$

(c) $y = 2f(x)$

(d) $y = -f(x)$

(e) $y = f(x + 3)$

(f) $y = f(-x)$

(g) $y = f\left(\frac{1}{2}x\right)$

6. (a) $y = f(-x)$

(b) $y = f(x) + 4$

(c) $y = 2f(x)$

(d) $y = -f(x - 4)$

(e) $y = f(x) - 3$

(f) $y = -f(x) - 1$

(g) $y = f(2x)$

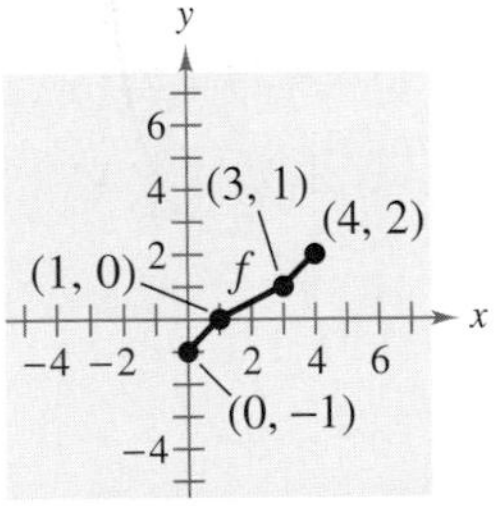

FIGURE FOR 5

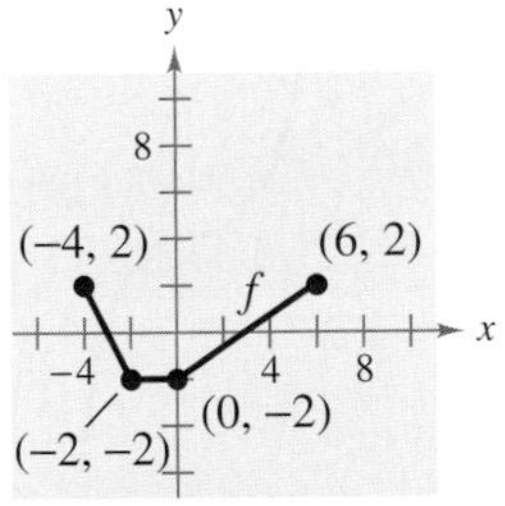

FIGURE FOR 6

7. (a) $y = f(x) - 1$

(b) $y = f(x - 1)$

(c) $y = f(-x)$

(d) $y = f(x + 1)$

(e) $y = -f(x - 2)$

(f) $y = \frac{1}{2}f(x)$

(g) $y = f(2x)$

8. (a) $y = f(x - 5)$

(b) $y = -f(x) + 3$

(c) $y = \frac{1}{3}f(x)$

(d) $y = -f(x + 1)$

(e) $y = f(-x)$

(f) $y = f(x) - 10$

(g) $y = f\left(\frac{1}{3}x\right)$

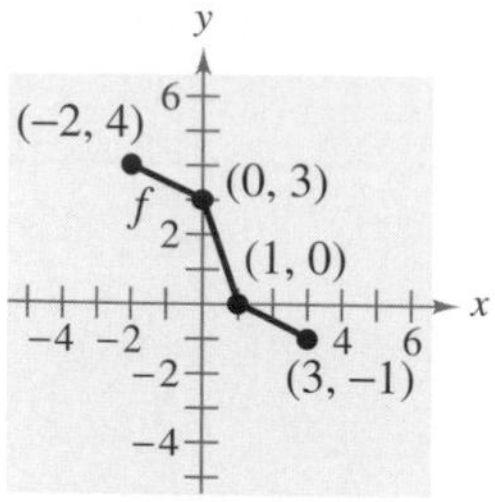

FIGURE FOR 7

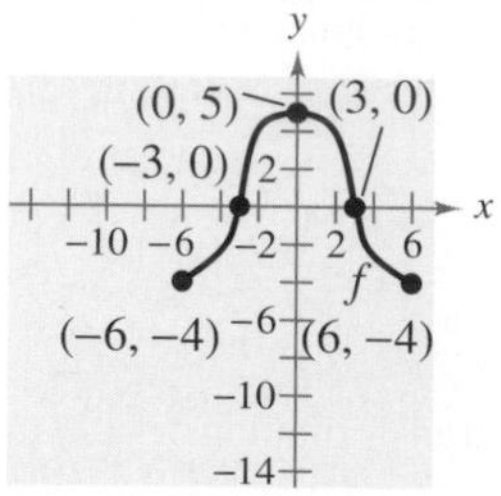

FIGURE FOR 8

9. Use the graph of $f(x) = x^2$ to write an equation for each function whose graph is shown.

(a)

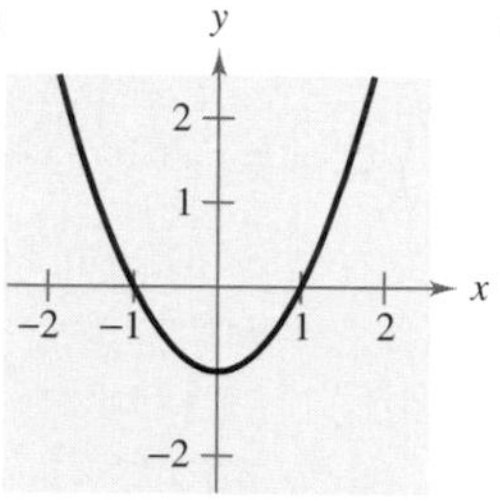

(b)

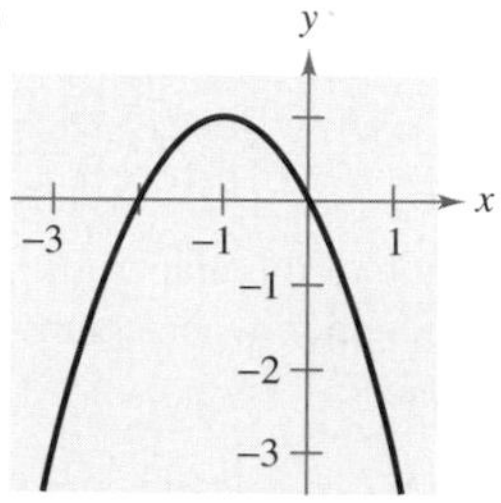

(c)

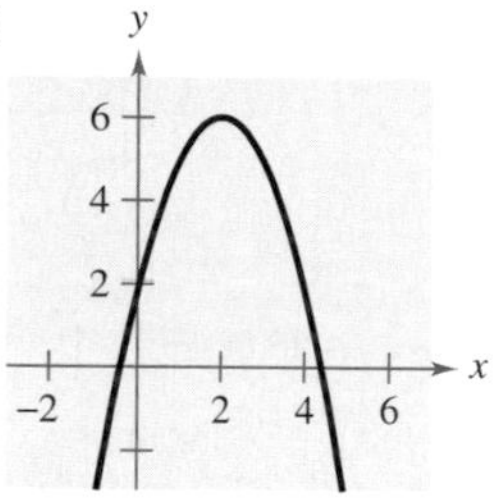

(d)

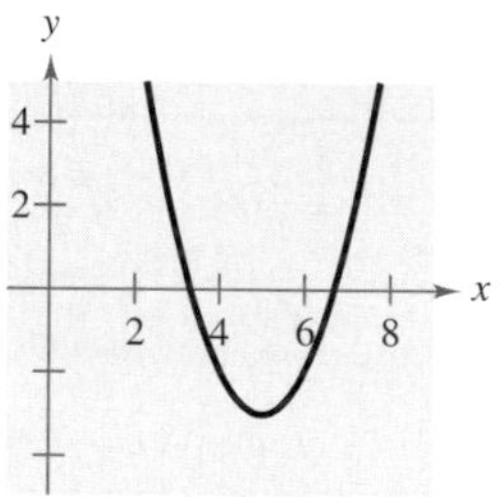

10. Use the graph of $f(x) = x^3$ to write an equation for each function whose graph is shown.

(a)

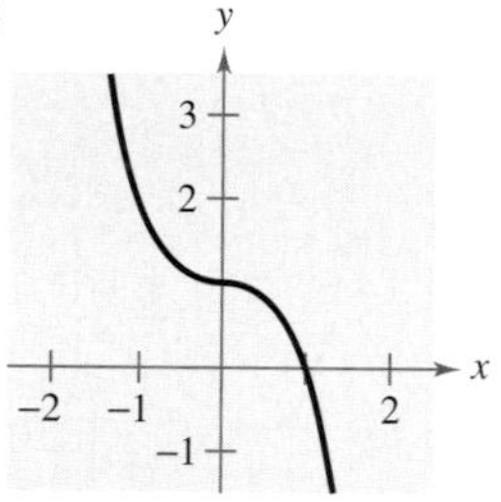

(b)

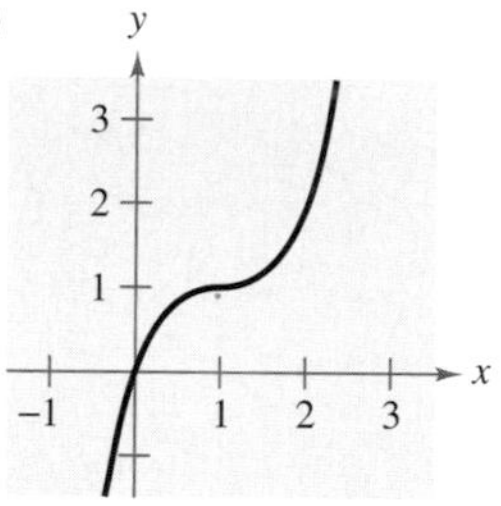

(c)

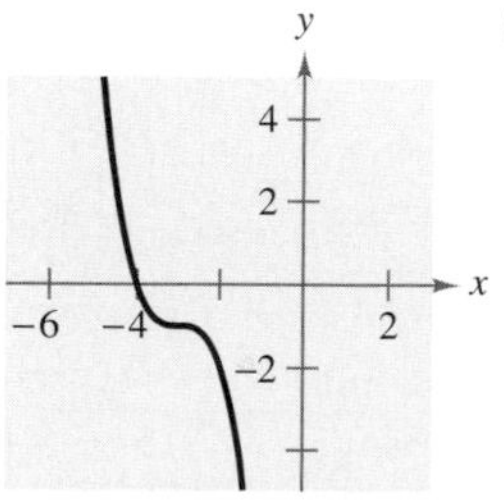

(d)

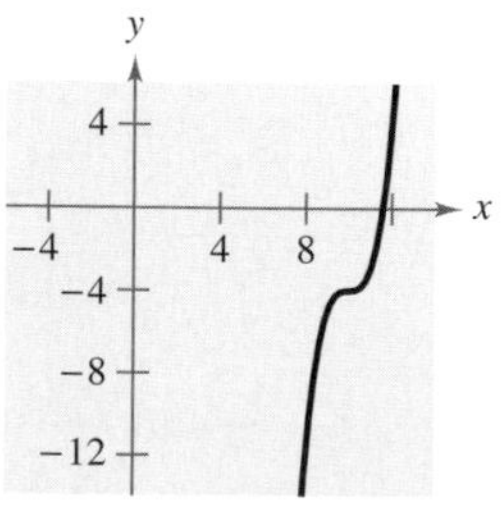

11. Use the graph of $f(x) = |x|$ to write an equation for each function whose graph is shown.

(a)

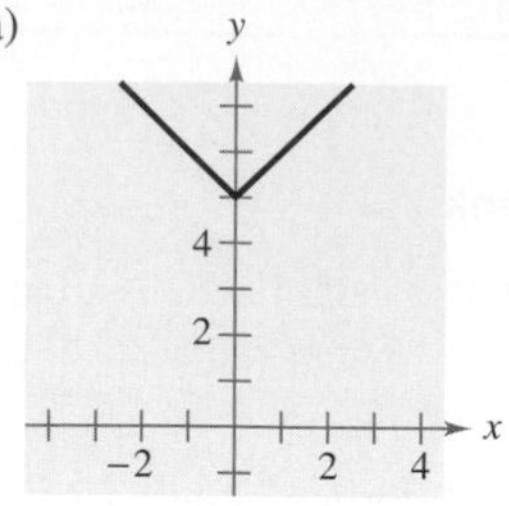

(b)

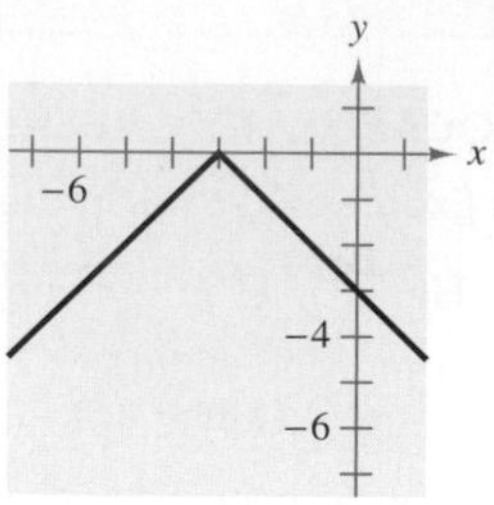

(c)

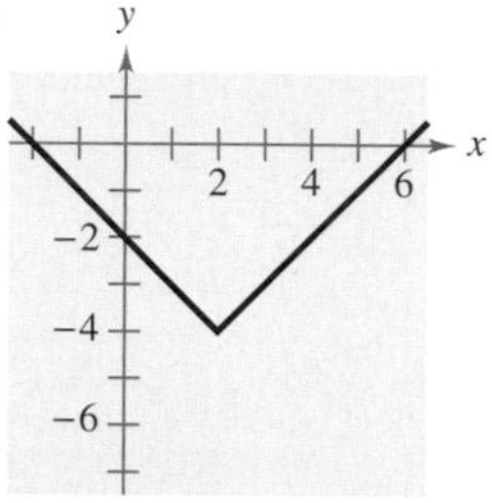

(d)

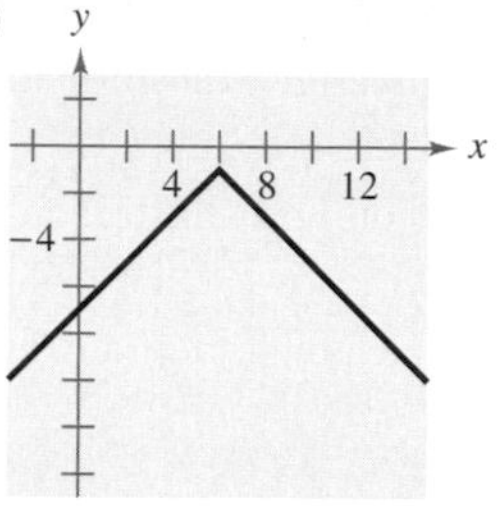

12. Use the graph of $f(x) = \sqrt{x}$ to write an equation for each function whose graph is shown.

(a)

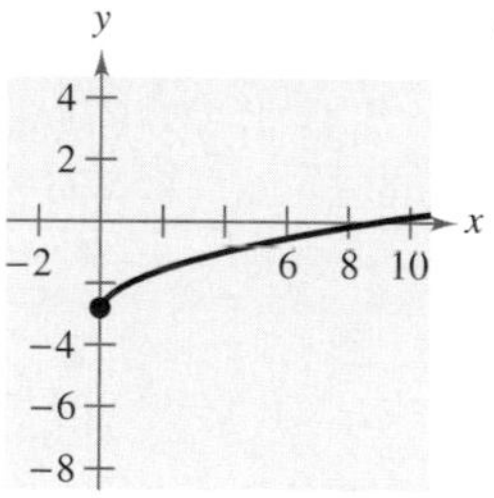

(b)

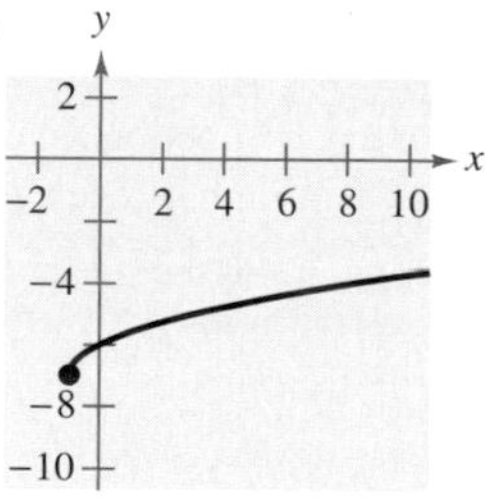

(c)

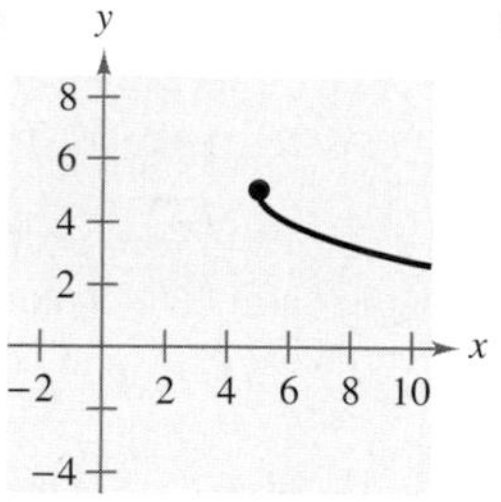

(d)

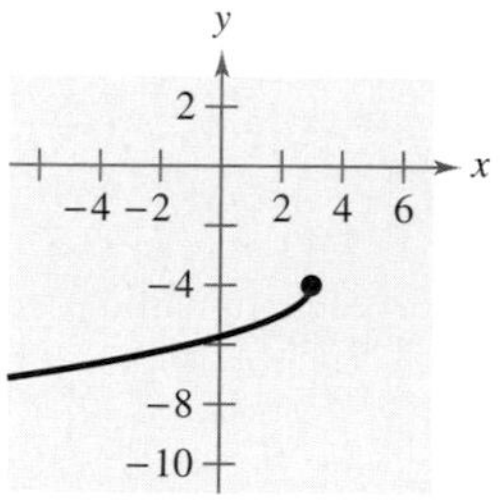

In Exercises 13–18, identify the parent function and the transformation shown in the graph. Write an equation for the function shown in the graph.

13.

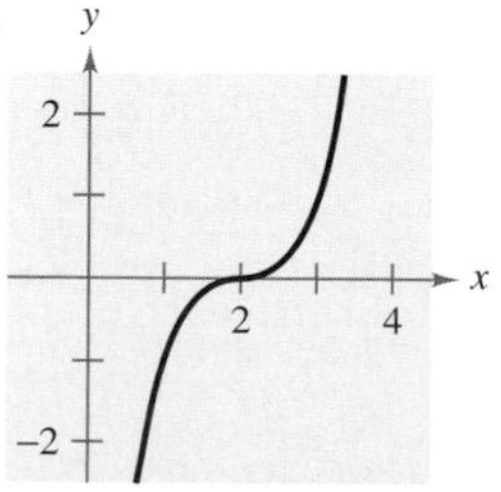

14.

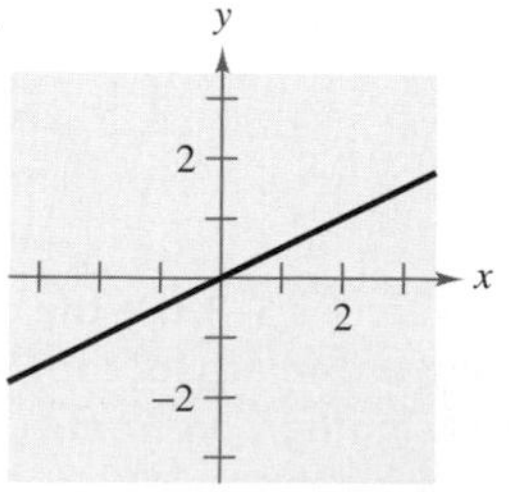

15.

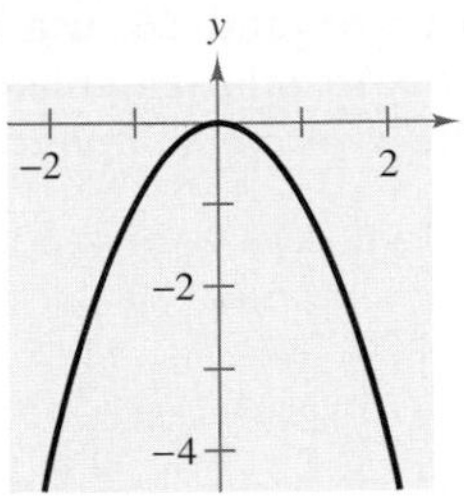

16.

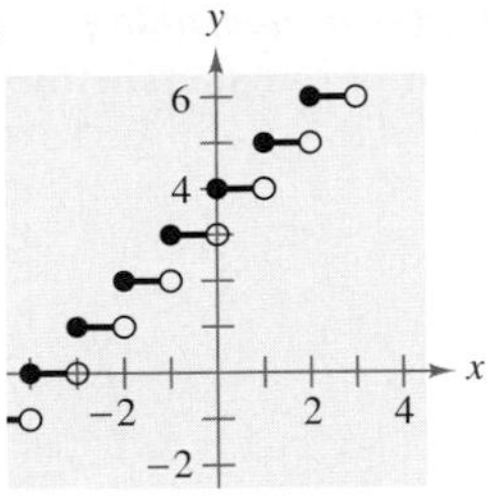

17.

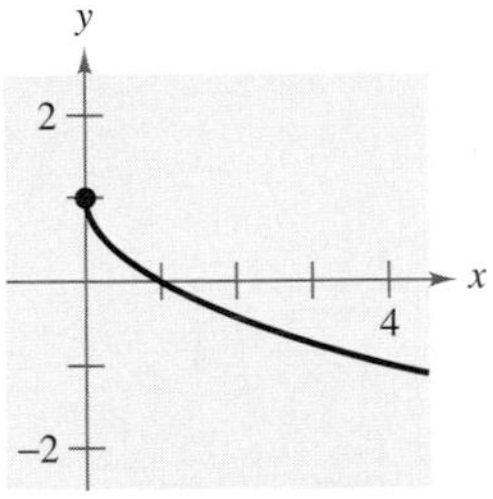

18.

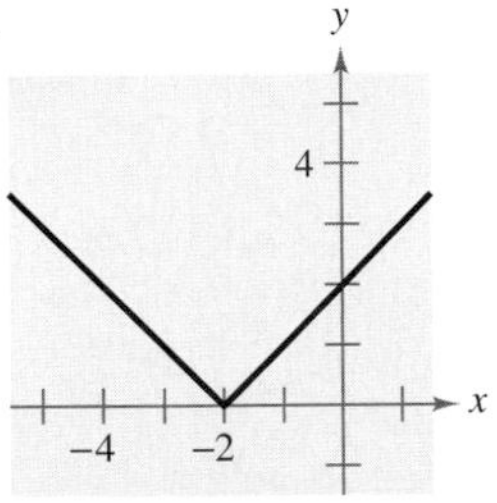

In Exercises 19–42, g is related to one of the parent functions described in this chapter. (a) Identify the parent function f. (b) Describe the sequence of tranformations from f to g. (c) Sketch the graph of g. (d) Use function notation to write g in terms of f.

19. $g(x) = 12 - x^2$

20. $g(x) = (x - 8)^2$

21. $g(x) = x^3 + 7$

22. $g(x) = -x^3 - 1$

23. $g(x) = \frac{2}{3}x^2 + 4$

24. $g(x) = 2(x - 7)^2$

25. $g(x) = 2 - (x + 5)^2$

26. $g(x) = -(x + 10)^2 + 5$

27. $g(x) = \sqrt{3x}$

28. $g(x) = \sqrt{\frac{1}{4}x}$

29. $g(x) = (x - 1)^3 + 2$

30. $g(x) = (x + 3)^3 - 10$

31. $g(x) = -|x| - 2$

32. $g(x) = 6 - |x + 5|$

33. $g(x) = -|x + 4| + 8$

34. $g(x) = |-x + 3| + 9$

35. $g(x) = 3 - [\![x]\!]$

36. $g(x) = 2[\![x + 5]\!]$

37. $g(x) = \sqrt{x - 9}$

38. $g(x) = \sqrt{x + 4} + 8$

39. $g(x) = \sqrt{7 - x} - 2$

40. $g(x) = -\sqrt{x + 1} - 6$

41. $g(x) = \sqrt{\frac{1}{2}x} - 4$

42. $g(x) = \sqrt{3x} + 1$

In Exercises 43–50, write an equation for the function that is described by the given characteristics.

43. The shape of $f(x) = x^2$, but moved two units to the right and eight units downward

44. The shape of $f(x) = x^2$, but moved three units to the left, seven units upward, and reflected in the x-axis

45. The shape of $f(x) = x^3$, but moved 13 units to the right

46. The shape of $f(x) = x^3$, but moved six units to the left, six units downward, and reflected in the y-axis

47. The shape of $f(x) = |x|$, but moved 10 units upward and reflected in the x-axis

48. The shape of $f(x) = |x|$, but moved one unit to the left and seven units downward

49. The shape of $f(x) = \sqrt{x}$, but moved six units to the left and reflected in both the x-axis and the y-axis

50. The shape of $f(x) = \sqrt{x}$, but moved nine units downward and reflected in both the x-axis and the y-axis

51. Use the graph of $f(x) = x^2$ to write an equation for each function whose graph is shown.

(a)

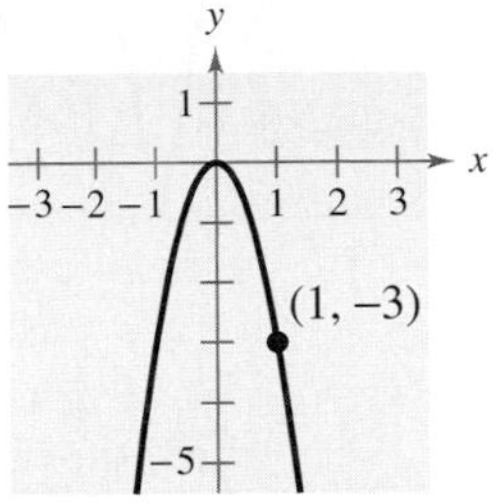

(b)

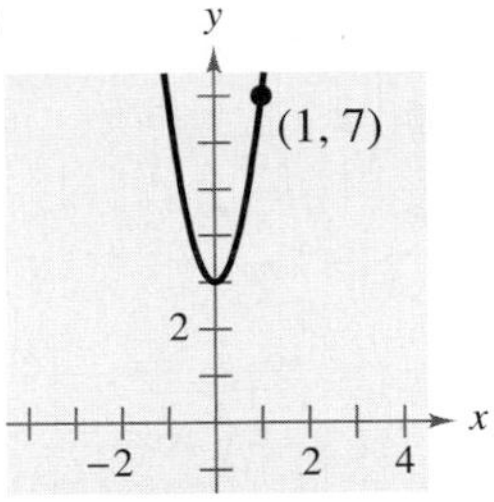

52. Use the graph of $f(x) = x^3$ to write an equation for each function whose graph is shown.

(a)

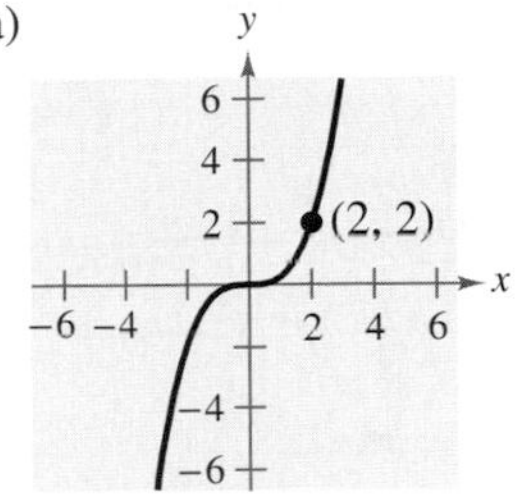

(b)

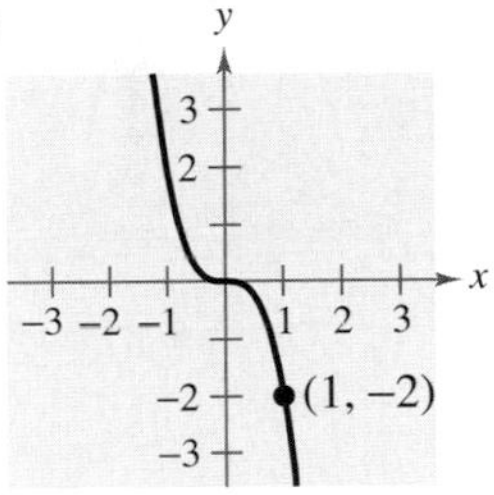

53. Use the graph of $f(x) = |x|$ to write an equation for each function whose graph is shown.

(a)

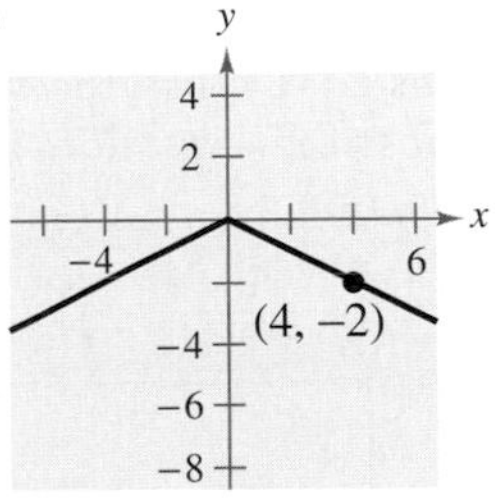

(b)

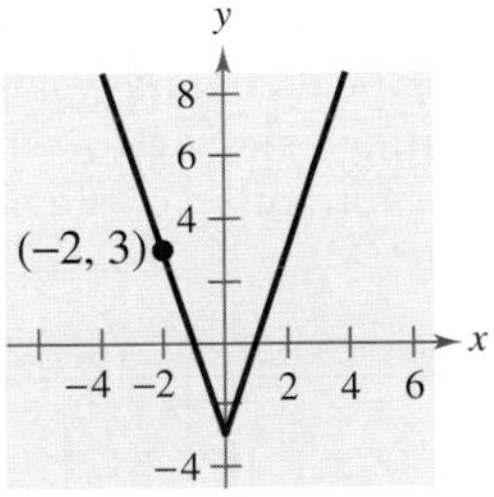

54. Use the graph of $f(x) = \sqrt{x}$ to write an equation for each function whose graph is shown.

(a)

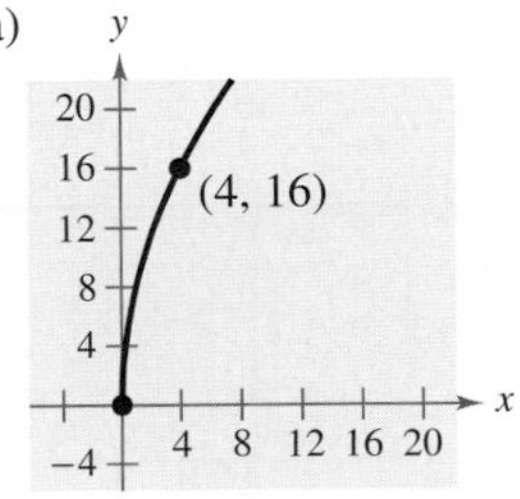

(b)

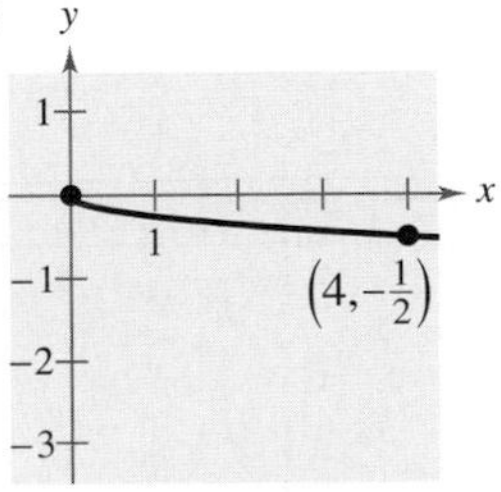

In Exercises 55–60, identify the parent function and the transformation shown in the graph. Write an equation for the function shown in the graph. Then use a graphing utility to verify your answer.

55.

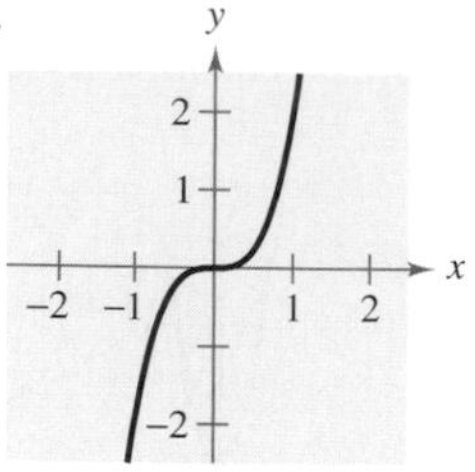

56.

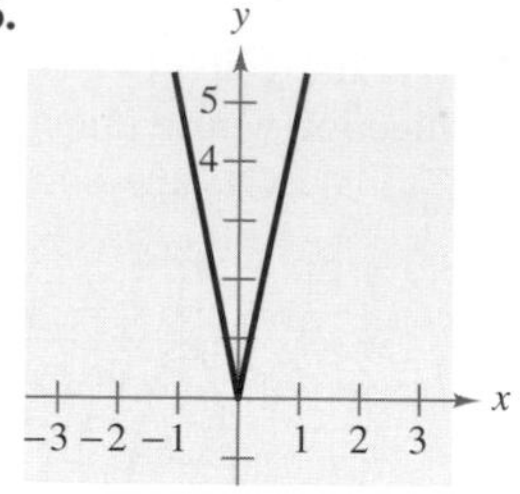

57.

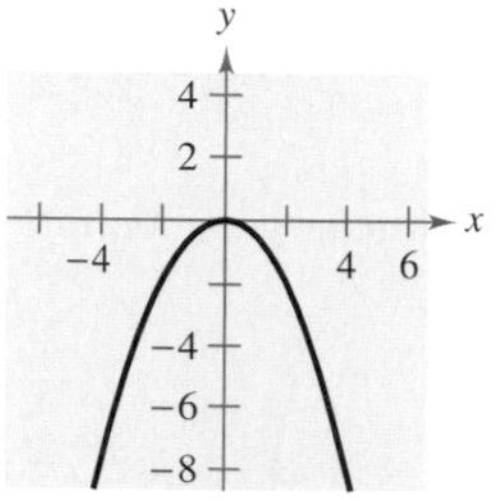

58.

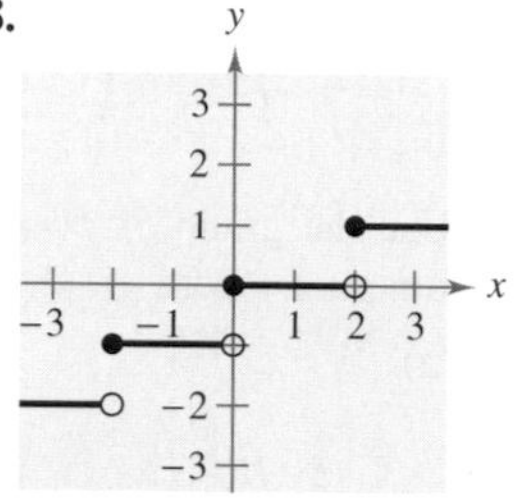

59.

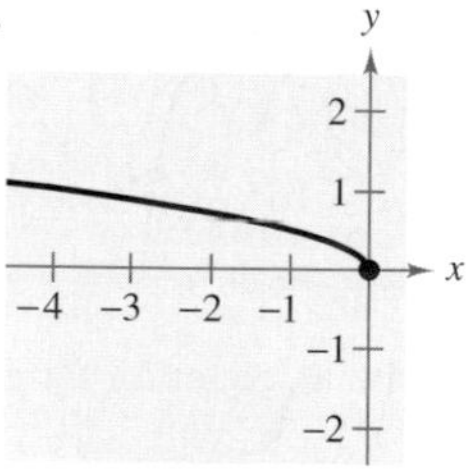

60.

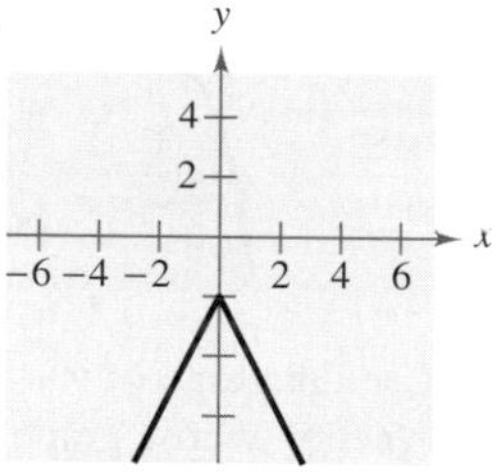

Graphical Analysis **In Exercises 61–64, use the viewing window shown to write a possible equation for the transformation of the parent function.**

61.

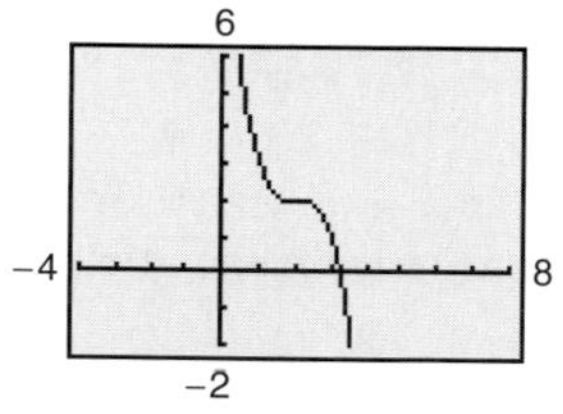

62.

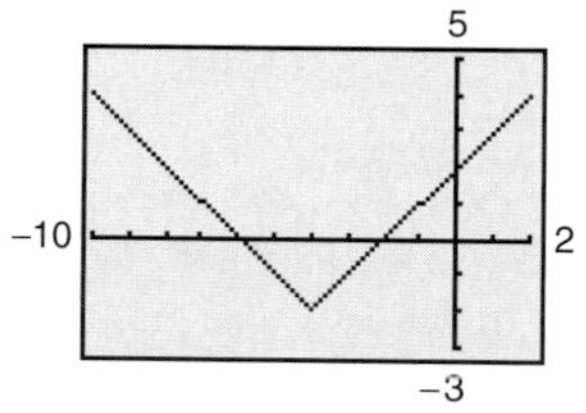

63.

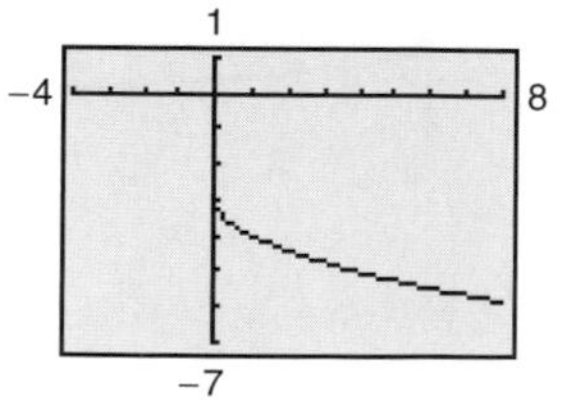

64.

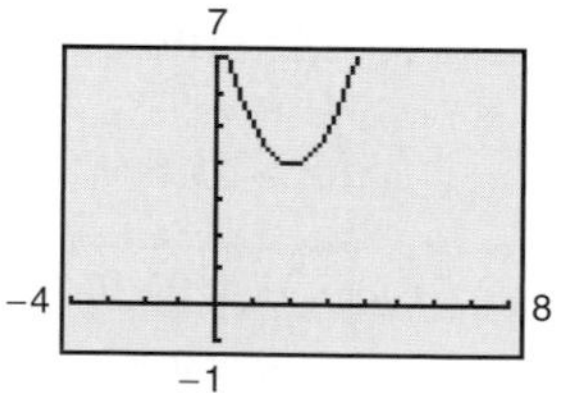

Graphical Reasoning **In Exercises 65 and 66, use the graph of f to sketch the graph of g. To print an enlarged copy of the graph, go to the website *www.mathgraphs.com*.**

65.

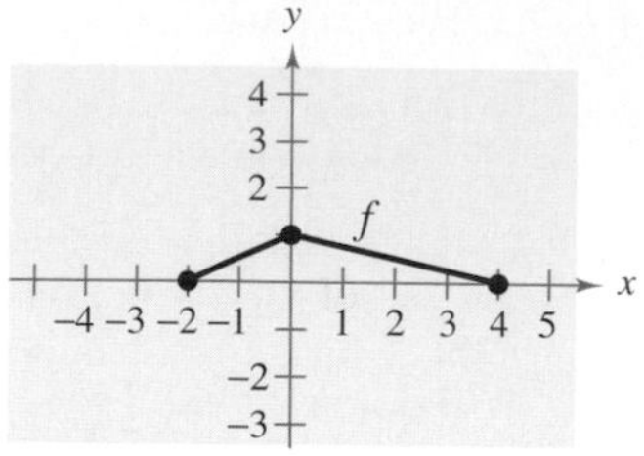

(a) $g(x) = f(x) + 2$ (b) $g(x) = f(x) - 1$

(c) $g(x) = f(-x)$ (d) $g(x) = -2f(x)$

(e) $g(x) = f(4x)$ (f) $g(x) = f\left(\frac{1}{2}x\right)$

66.

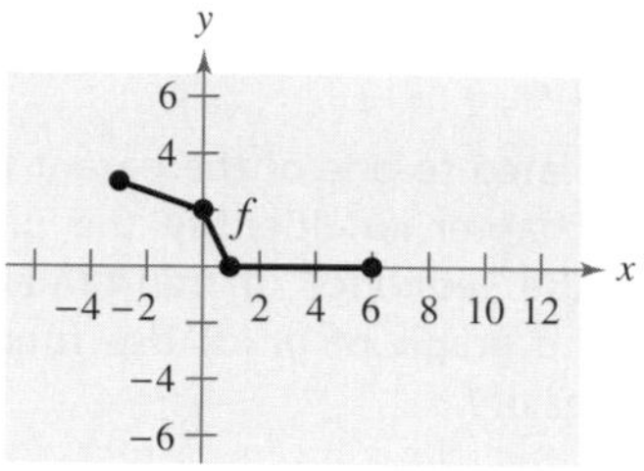

(a) $g(x) = f(x) - 5$ (b) $g(x) = f(x) + \frac{1}{2}$

(c) $g(x) = f(-x)$ (d) $g(x) = -4f(x)$

(e) $g(x) = f(2x) + 1$ (f) $g(x) = f\left(\frac{1}{4}x\right) - 2$

Model It

67. ***Fuel Use*** The amounts of fuel F (in billions of gallons) used by trucks from 1980 through 2002 can be approximated by the function

$$F = f(t) = 20.6 + 0.035t^2, \quad 0 \le t \le 22$$

where t represents the year, with $t = 0$ corresponding to 1980. (Source: U.S. Federal Highway Administration)

(a) Describe the transformation of the parent function $f(x) = x^2$. Then sketch the graph over the specified domain.

(b) Find the average rate of change of the function from 1980 to 2002. Interpret your answer in the context of the problem.

(c) Rewrite the function so that $t = 0$ represents 1990. Explain how you got your answer.

(d) Use the model from part (c) to predict the amount of fuel used by trucks in 2010. Does your answer seem reasonable? Explain.

68. ***Finance*** The amounts M (in trillions of dollars) of mortgage debt outstanding in the United States from 1990 through 2002 can be approximated by the function

$$M = f(t) = 0.0054(t + 20.396)^2, \quad 0 \le t \le 12$$

where t represents the year, with $t = 0$ corresponding to 1990. (Source: Board of Governors of the Federal Reserve System)

(a) Describe the transformation of the parent function $f(x) = x^2$. Then sketch the graph over the specified domain.

(b) Rewrite the function so that $t = 0$ represents 2000. Explain how you got your answer.

Synthesis

True or False? **In Exercises 69 and 70, determine whether the statement is true or false. Justify your answer.**

69. The graphs of

$$f(x) = |x| + 6 \quad \text{and} \quad f(x) = |-x| + 6$$

are identical.

70. If the graph of the parent function $f(x) = x^2$ is moved six units to the right, three units upward, and reflected in the x-axis, then the point $(-2, 19)$ will lie on the graph of the transformation.

71. ***Describing Profits*** Management originally predicted that the profits from the sales of a new product would be approximated by the graph of the function f shown. The actual profits are shown by the function g along with a verbal description. Use the concepts of transformations of graphs to write g in terms of f.

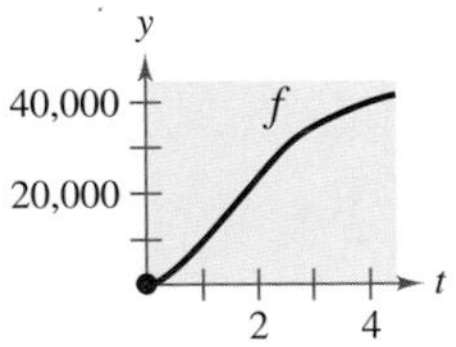

(a) The profits were only three-fourths as large as expected.

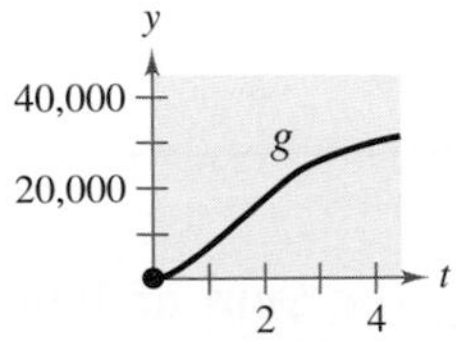

(b) The profits were consistently $10,000 greater than predicted.

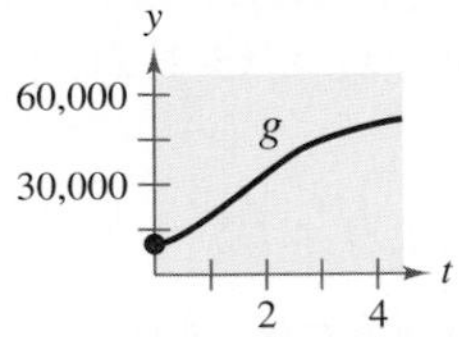

(c) There was a two-year delay in the introduction of the product. After sales began, profits grew as expected.

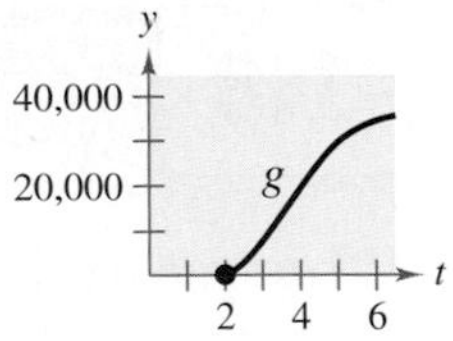

72. Explain why the graph of $y = -f(x)$ is a reflection of the graph of $y = f(x)$ about the x-axis.

73. The graph of $y = f(x)$ passes through the points $(0, 1)$, $(1, 2)$, and $(2, 3)$. Find the corresponding points on the graph of $y = f(x + 2) - 1$.

74. ***Think About It*** You can use either of two methods to graph a function: plotting points or translating a parent function as shown in this section. Which method of graphing do you prefer to use for each function? Explain.

(a) $f(x) = 3x^2 - 4x + 1$ (b) $f(x) = 2(x - 1)^2 - 6$

Skills Review

In Exercises 75–82, perform the operation and simplify.

75. $\dfrac{4}{x} + \dfrac{4}{1 - x}$

76. $\dfrac{2}{x + 5} - \dfrac{2}{x - 5}$

77. $\dfrac{3}{x - 1} - \dfrac{2}{x(x - 1)}$

78. $\dfrac{x}{x - 5} + \dfrac{1}{2}$

79. $(x - 4)\left(\dfrac{1}{\sqrt{x^2 - 4}}\right)$

80. $\left(\dfrac{x}{x^2 - 4}\right)\left(\dfrac{x^2 - x - 2}{x^2}\right)$

81. $(x^2 - 9) \div \left(\dfrac{x + 3}{5}\right)$

82. $\left(\dfrac{x}{x^2 - 3x - 28}\right) \div \left(\dfrac{x^2 + 3x}{x^2 + 5x + 4}\right)$

In Exercises 83 and 84, evaluate the function at the specified values of the independent variable and simplify.

83. $f(x) = x^2 - 6x + 11$

(a) $f(-3)$ (b) $f\left(-\frac{1}{2}\right)$ (c) $f(x - 3)$

84. $f(x) = \sqrt{x + 10} - 3$

(a) $f(-10)$ (b) $f(26)$ (c) $f(x - 10)$

In Exercises 85–88, find the domain of the function.

85. $f(x) = \dfrac{2}{11 - x}$

86. $f(x) = \dfrac{\sqrt{x - 3}}{x - 8}$

87. $f(x) = \sqrt{81 - x^2}$

88. $f(x) = \sqrt[3]{4 - x^2}$

1.8 Combinations of Functions: Composite Functions

What you should learn

- Add, subtract, multiply, and divide functions.
- Find the composition of one function with another function.
- Use combinations and compositions of functions to model and solve real-life problems.

Why you should learn it

Compositions of functions can be used to model and solve real-life problems. For instance, in Exercise 68 on page 92, compositions of functions are used to determine the price of a new hybrid car.

© Jim West/The Image Works

Arithmetic Combinations of Functions

Just as two real numbers can be combined by the operations of addition, subtraction, multiplication, and division to form other real numbers, two *functions* can be combined to create new functions. For example, the functions given by $f(x) = 2x - 3$ and $g(x) = x^2 - 1$ can be combined to form the sum, difference, product, and quotient of f and g.

$$f(x) + g(x) = (2x - 3) + (x^2 - 1)$$
$$= x^2 + 2x - 4 \qquad \text{Sum}$$
$$f(x) - g(x) = (2x - 3) - (x^2 - 1)$$
$$= -x^2 + 2x - 2 \qquad \text{Difference}$$
$$f(x)g(x) = (2x - 3)(x^2 - 1)$$
$$= 2x^3 - 3x^2 - 2x + 3 \qquad \text{Product}$$
$$\frac{f(x)}{g(x)} = \frac{2x - 3}{x^2 - 1}, \quad x \neq \pm 1 \qquad \text{Quotient}$$

The domain of an **arithmetic combination** of functions f and g consists of all real numbers that are common to the domains of f and g. In the case of the quotient $f(x)/g(x)$, there is the further restriction that $g(x) \neq 0$.

Sum, Difference, Product, and Quotient of Functions

Let f and g be two functions with overlapping domains. Then, for all x common to both domains, the *sum*, *difference*, *product*, and *quotient* of f and g are defined as follows.

1. *Sum:* $(f + g)(x) = f(x) + g(x)$
2. *Difference:* $(f - g)(x) = f(x) - g(x)$
3. *Product:* $(fg)(x) = f(x) \cdot g(x)$
4. *Quotient:* $\left(\frac{f}{g}\right)(x) = \frac{f(x)}{g(x)}, \quad g(x) \neq 0$

Example 1 Finding the Sum of Two Functions

Given $f(x) = 2x + 1$ and $g(x) = x^2 + 2x - 1$, find $(f + g)(x)$.

Solution

$$(f + g)(x) = f(x) + g(x) = (2x + 1) + (x^2 + 2x - 1) = x^2 + 4x$$

CHECKPOINT Now try Exercise 5(a).

Example 2 **Finding the Difference of Two Functions**

Given $f(x) = 2x + 1$ and $g(x) = x^2 + 2x - 1$, find $(f - g)(x)$. Then evaluate the difference when $x = 2$.

Solution

The difference of f and g is

$$\begin{aligned}(f - g)(x) &= f(x) - g(x)\\ &= (2x + 1) - (x^2 + 2x - 1)\\ &= -x^2 + 2.\end{aligned}$$

When $x = 2$, the value of this difference is

$$\begin{aligned}(f - g)(2) &= -(2)^2 + 2\\ &= -2.\end{aligned}$$

✓CHECKPOINT Now try Exercise 5(b).

In Examples 1 and 2, both f and g have domains that consist of all real numbers. So, the domains of $(f + g)$ and $(f - g)$ are also the set of all real numbers. Remember that any restrictions on the domains of f and g must be considered when forming the sum, difference, product, or quotient of f and g.

Example 3 **Finding the Domains of Quotients of Functions**

Find $\left(\frac{f}{g}\right)(x)$ and $\left(\frac{g}{f}\right)(x)$ for the functions given by

$$f(x) = \sqrt{x} \quad \text{and} \quad g(x) = \sqrt{4 - x^2}.$$

Then find the domains of f/g and g/f.

Solution

The quotient of f and g is

$$\left(\frac{f}{g}\right)(x) = \frac{f(x)}{g(x)} = \frac{\sqrt{x}}{\sqrt{4 - x^2}}$$

and the quotient of g and f is

$$\left(\frac{g}{f}\right)(x) = \frac{g(x)}{f(x)} = \frac{\sqrt{4 - x^2}}{\sqrt{x}}.$$

The domain of f is $[0, \infty)$ and the domain of g is $[-2, 2]$. The intersection of these domains is $[0, 2]$. So, the domains of $\left(\frac{f}{g}\right)$ and $\left(\frac{g}{f}\right)$ are as follows.

$$\text{Domain of } \left(\frac{f}{g}\right): [0, 2) \qquad \text{Domain of } \left(\frac{g}{f}\right): (0, 2]$$

Note that the domain of (f/g) includes $x = 0$, but not $x = 2$, because $x = 2$ yields a zero in the denominator, whereas the domain of (g/f) includes $x = 2$, but not $x = 0$, because $x = 0$ yields a zero in the denominator.

✓CHECKPOINT Now try Exercise 5(d).

Composition of Functions

Another way of combining two functions is to form the **composition** of one with the other. For instance, if $f(x) = x^2$ and $g(x) = x + 1$, the composition of f with g is

$$f(g(x)) = f(x + 1)$$
$$= (x + 1)^2.$$

This composition is denoted as $(f \circ g)$ and reads as "f composed with g."

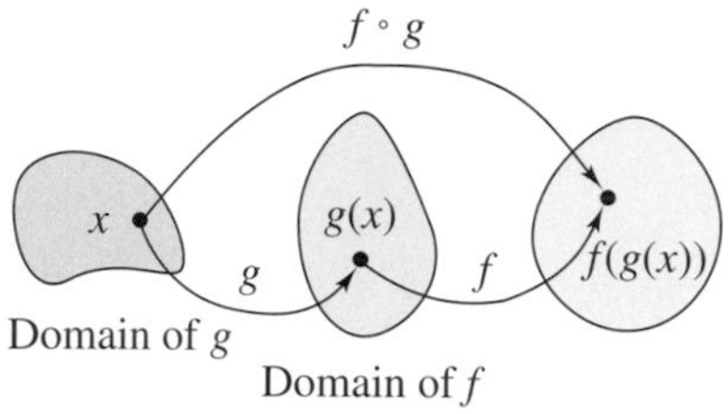

FIGURE 1.90

Definition of Composition of Two Functions

The **composition** of the function f with the function g is

$$(f \circ g)(x) = f(g(x)).$$

The domain of $(f \circ g)$ is the set of all x in the domain of g such that $g(x)$ is in the domain of f. (See Figure 1.90.)

Example 4 Composition of Functions

Given $f(x) = x + 2$ and $g(x) = 4 - x^2$, find the following.

a. $(f \circ g)(x)$ **b.** $(g \circ f)(x)$ **c.** $(g \circ f)(-2)$

Solution

a. The composition of f with g is as follows.

$$(f \circ g)(x) = f(g(x)) \qquad \text{Definition of } f \circ g$$
$$= f(4 - x^2) \qquad \text{Definition of } g(x)$$
$$= (4 - x^2) + 2 \qquad \text{Definition of } f(x)$$
$$= -x^2 + 6 \qquad \text{Simplify.}$$

b. The composition of g with f is as follows.

$$(g \circ f)(x) = g(f(x)) \qquad \text{Definition of } g \circ f$$
$$= g(x + 2) \qquad \text{Definition of } f(x)$$
$$= 4 - (x + 2)^2 \qquad \text{Definition of } g(x)$$
$$= 4 - (x^2 + 4x + 4) \qquad \text{Expand.}$$
$$= -x^2 - 4x \qquad \text{Simplify.}$$

Note that, in this case, $(f \circ g)(x) \neq (g \circ f)(x)$.

c. Using the result of part (b), you can write the following.

$$(g \circ f)(-2) = -(-2)^2 - 4(-2) \qquad \text{Substitute.}$$
$$= -4 + 8 \qquad \text{Simplify.}$$
$$= 4 \qquad \text{Simplify.}$$

CHECKPOINT Now try Exercise 31.

STUDY TIP

The following tables of values help illustrate the composition $(f \circ g)(x)$ given in Example 4.

x	0	1	2	3
$g(x)$	4	3	0	-5

$g(x)$	4	3	0	-5
$f(g(x))$	6	5	2	-3

x	0	1	2	3
$f(g(x))$	6	5	2	-3

Note that the first two tables can be combined (or "composed") to produce the values given in the third table.

Technology

You can use a graphing utility to determine the domain of a composition of functions. For the composition in Example 5, enter the function composition as

$$y = \left(\sqrt{9 - x^2}\right)^2 - 9.$$

You should obtain the graph shown below. Use the *trace* feature to determine that the x-coordinates of points on the graph extend from -3 to 3. So, the domain of $(f \circ g)(x)$ is $-3 \le x \le 3$.

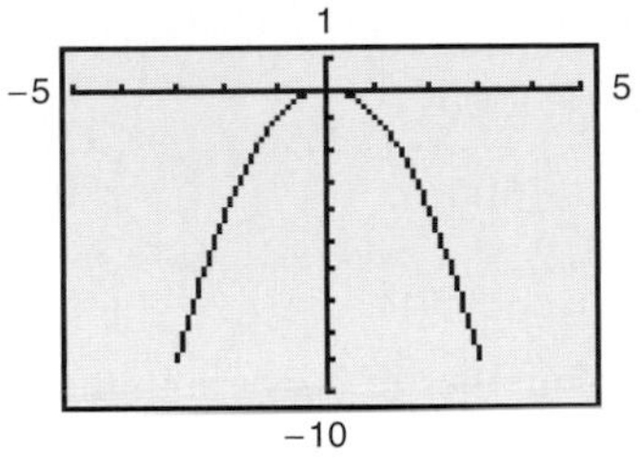

Example 5 Finding the Domain of a Composite Function

Given $f(x) = x^2 - 9$ and $g(x) = \sqrt{9 - x^2}$, find the composition $(f \circ g)(x)$. Then find the domain of $(f \circ g)$.

Solution

$$\begin{aligned}(f \circ g)(x) &= f(g(x)) \\ &= f\left(\sqrt{9 - x^2}\right) \\ &= \left(\sqrt{9 - x^2}\right)^2 - 9 \\ &= 9 - x^2 - 9 \\ &= -x^2\end{aligned}$$

From this, it might appear that the domain of the composition is the set of all real numbers. This, however is not true. Because the domain of f is the set of all real numbers and the domain of g is $-3 \le x \le 3$, the domain of $(f \circ g)$ is $-3 \le x \le 3$.

✓CHECKPOINT Now try Exercise 35.

In Examples 4 and 5, you formed the composition of two given functions. In calculus, it is also important to be able to identify two functions that make up a given composite function. For instance, the function h given by

$$h(x) = (3x - 5)^3$$

is the composition of f with g, where $f(x) = x^3$ and $g(x) = 3x - 5$. That is,

$$h(x) = (3x - 5)^3 = [g(x)]^3 = f(g(x)).$$

Basically, to "decompose" a composite function, look for an "inner" function and an "outer" function. In the function h above, $g(x) = 3x - 5$ is the inner function and $f(x) = x^3$ is the outer function.

Example 6 Decomposing a Composite Function

Write the function given by $h(x) = \dfrac{1}{(x - 2)^2}$ as a composition of two functions.

Solution

One way to write h as a composition of two functions is to take the inner function to be $g(x) = x - 2$ and the outer function to be

$$f(x) = \frac{1}{x^2} = x^{-2}.$$

Then you can write

$$h(x) = \frac{1}{(x - 2)^2} = (x - 2)^{-2} = f(x - 2) = f(g(x)).$$

✓CHECKPOINT Now try Exercise 47.

Application

Example 7 Bacteria Count

The number N of bacteria in a refrigerated food is given by

$$N(T) = 20T^2 - 80T + 500, \qquad 2 \le T \le 14$$

where T is the temperature of the food in degrees Celsius. When the food is removed from refrigeration, the temperature of the food is given by

$$T(t) = 4t + 2, \qquad 0 \le t \le 3$$

where t is the time in hours. (a) Find the composition $N(T(t))$ and interpret its meaning in context. (b) Find the time when the bacterial count reaches 2000.

Solution

a.
$$\begin{aligned} N(T(t)) &= 20(4t + 2)^2 - 80(4t + 2) + 500 \\ &= 20(16t^2 + 16t + 4) - 320t - 160 + 500 \\ &= 320t^2 + 320t + 80 - 320t - 160 + 500 \\ &= 320t^2 + 420 \end{aligned}$$

The composite function $N(T(t))$ represents the number of bacteria in the food as a function of the amount of time the food has been out of refrigeration.

b. The bacterial count will reach 2000 when $320t^2 + 420 = 2000$. Solve this equation to find that the count will reach 2000 when $t \approx 2.2$ hours. When you solve this equation, note that the negative value is rejected because it is not in the domain of the composite function.

CHECKPOINT Now try Exercise 65.

WRITING ABOUT MATHEMATICS

Analyzing Arithmetic Combinations of Functions

a. Use the graphs of f and $(f + g)$ in Figure 1.91 to make a table showing the values of $g(x)$ when $x = 1, 2, 3, 4, 5,$ and 6. Explain your reasoning.

b. Use the graphs of f and $(f - h)$ in Figure 1.91 to make a table showing the values of $h(x)$ when $x = 1, 2, 3, 4, 5,$ and 6. Explain your reasoning.

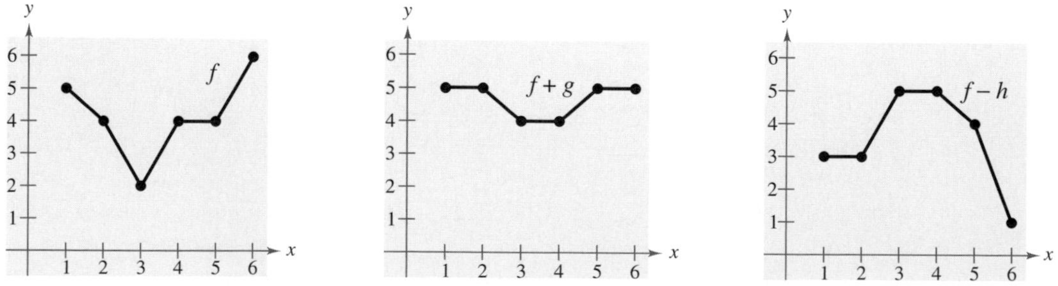

FIGURE 1.91

1.8 Exercises

VOCABULARY CHECK: Fill in the blanks.

1. Two functions f and g can be combined by the arithmetic operations of ________, ________, ________, and ________ to create new functions.
2. The ________ of the function f with g is $(f \circ g)(x) = f(g(x))$.
3. The domain of $(f \circ g)$ is all x in the domain of g such that ________ is in the domain of f.
4. To decompose a composite function, look for an ________ function and an ________ function.

In Exercises 1–4, use the graphs of f and g to graph $h(x) = (f + g)(x)$. To print an enlarged copy of the graph, go to the website *www.mathgraphs.com*.

1.
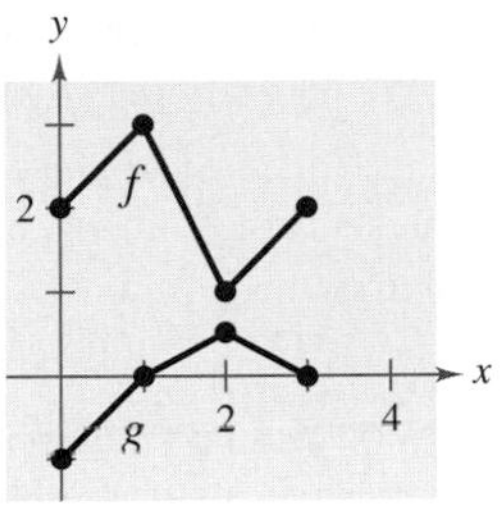

2.
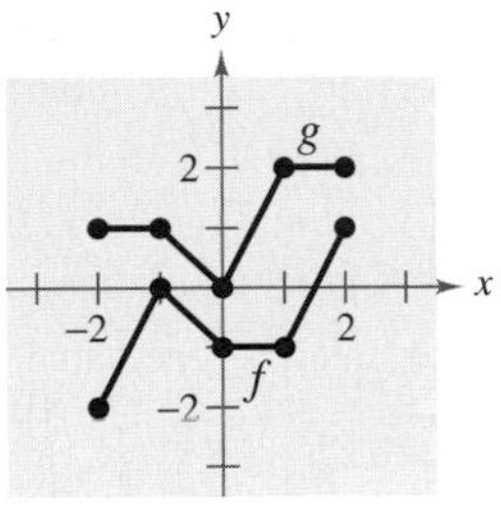

3.
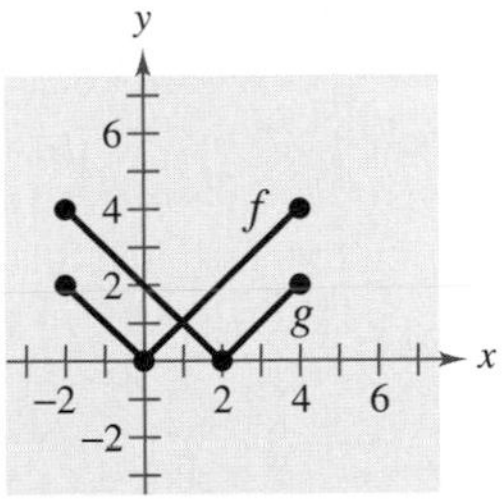

4.
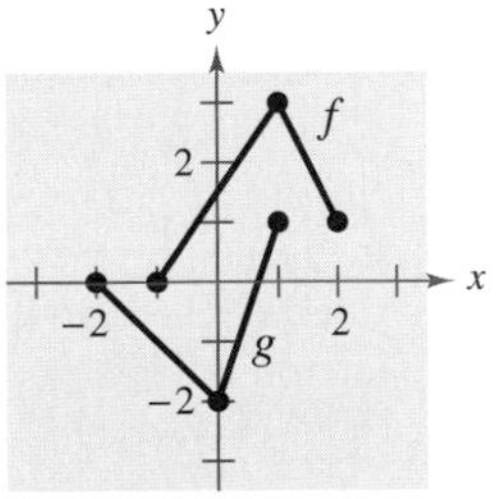

In Exercises 5–12, find (a) $(f + g)(x)$, (b) $(f - g)(x)$, (c) $(fg)(x)$, and (d) $(f/g)(x)$. What is the domain of f/g?

5. $f(x) = x + 2,\quad g(x) = x - 2$
6. $f(x) = 2x - 5,\quad g(x) = 2 - x$
7. $f(x) = x^2,\quad g(x) = 4x - 5$
8. $f(x) = 2x - 5,\quad g(x) = 4$
9. $f(x) = x^2 + 6,\quad g(x) = \sqrt{1 - x}$
10. $f(x) = \sqrt{x^2 - 4},\quad g(x) = \dfrac{x^2}{x^2 + 1}$
11. $f(x) = \dfrac{1}{x},\quad g(x) = \dfrac{1}{x^2}$
12. $f(x) = \dfrac{x}{x + 1},\quad g(x) = x^3$

In Exercises 13–24, evaluate the indicated function for $f(x) = x^2 + 1$ and $g(x) = x - 4$.

13. $(f + g)(2)$
14. $(f - g)(-1)$
15. $(f - g)(0)$
16. $(f + g)(1)$
17. $(f - g)(3t)$
18. $(f + g)(t - 2)$
19. $(fg)(6)$
20. $(fg)(-6)$
21. $\left(\dfrac{f}{g}\right)(5)$
22. $\left(\dfrac{f}{g}\right)(0)$
23. $\left(\dfrac{f}{g}\right)(-1) - g(3)$
24. $(fg)(5) + f(4)$

In Exercises 25–28, graph the functions f, g, and $f + g$ on the same set of coordinate axes.

25. $f(x) = \frac{1}{2}x,\quad g(x) = x - 1$
26. $f(x) = \frac{1}{3}x,\quad g(x) = -x + 4$
27. $f(x) = x^2,\quad g(x) = -2x$
28. $f(x) = 4 - x^2,\quad g(x) = x$

Graphical Reasoning **In Exercises 29 and 30, use a graphing utility to graph f, g, and $f + g$ in the same viewing window. Which function contributes most to the magnitude of the sum when $0 \le x \le 2$? Which function contributes most to the magnitude of the sum when $x > 6$?**

29. $f(x) = 3x,\quad g(x) = -\dfrac{x^3}{10}$
30. $f(x) = \dfrac{x}{2},\quad g(x) = \sqrt{x}$

In Exercises 31–34, find (a) $f \circ g$, (b) $g \circ f$, and (c) $f \circ f$.

31. $f(x) = x^2,\quad g(x) = x - 1$
32. $f(x) = 3x + 5,\quad g(x) = 5 - x$
33. $f(x) = \sqrt[3]{x - 1},\quad g(x) = x^3 + 1$
34. $f(x) = x^3,\quad g(x) = \dfrac{1}{x}$

In Exercises 35–42, find (a) $f \circ g$ and (b) $g \circ f$. Find the domain of each function and each composite function.

35. $f(x) = \sqrt{x + 4}$, $g(x) = x^2$
36. $f(x) = \sqrt[3]{x - 5}$, $g(x) = x^3 + 1$
37. $f(x) = x^2 + 1$, $g(x) = \sqrt{x}$
38. $f(x) = x^{2/3}$, $g(x) = x^6$
39. $f(x) = |x|$, $g(x) = x + 6$
40. $f(x) = |x - 4|$, $g(x) = 3 - x$
41. $f(x) = \dfrac{1}{x}$, $g(x) = x + 3$
42. $f(x) = \dfrac{3}{x^2 - 1}$, $g(x) = x + 1$

In Exercises 43–46, use the graphs of f and g to evaluate the functions.

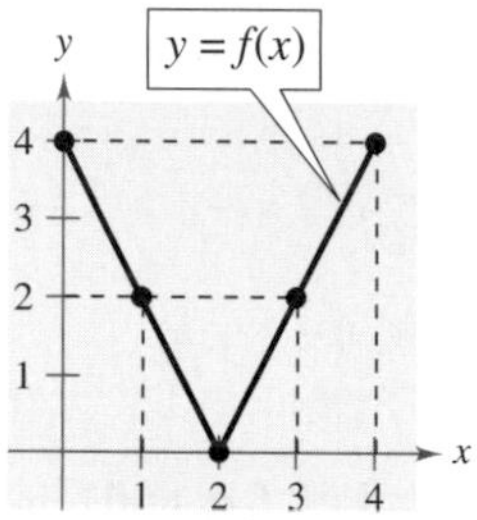

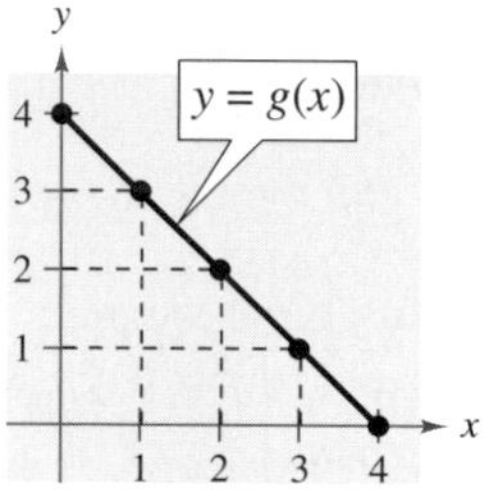

43. (a) $(f + g)(3)$ (b) $(f/g)(2)$
44. (a) $(f - g)(1)$ (b) $(fg)(4)$
45. (a) $(f \circ g)(2)$ (b) $(g \circ f)(2)$
46. (a) $(f \circ g)(1)$ (b) $(g \circ f)(3)$

In Exercises 47–54, find two functions f and g such that $(f \circ g)(x) = h(x)$. (There are many correct answers.)

47. $h(x) = (2x + 1)^2$
48. $h(x) = (1 - x)^3$
49. $h(x) = \sqrt[3]{x^2 - 4}$
50. $h(x) = \sqrt{9 - x}$
51. $h(x) = \dfrac{1}{x + 2}$
52. $h(x) = \dfrac{4}{(5x + 2)^2}$
53. $h(x) = \dfrac{-x^2 + 3}{4 - x^2}$
54. $h(x) = \dfrac{27x^3 + 6x}{10 - 27x^3}$

55. ***Stopping Distance*** The research and development department of an automobile manufacturer has determined that when a driver is required to stop quickly to avoid an accident, the distance (in feet) the car travels during the driver's reaction time is given by $R(x) = \frac{3}{4}x$, where x is the speed of the car in miles per hour. The distance (in feet) traveled while the driver is braking is given by $B(x) = \frac{1}{15}x^2$. Find the function that represents the total stopping distance T. Graph the functions R, B, and T on the same set of coordinate axes for $0 \le x \le 60$.

56. ***Sales*** From 2000 to 2005, the sales R_1 (in thousands of dollars) for one of two restaurants owned by the same parent company can be modeled by

$$R_1 = 480 - 8t - 0.8t^2, \quad t = 0, 1, 2, 3, 4, 5$$

where $t = 0$ represents 2000. During the same six-year period, the sales R_2 (in thousands of dollars) for the second restaurant can be modeled by

$$R_2 = 254 + 0.78t, \quad t = 0, 1, 2, 3, 4, 5.$$

(a) Write a function R_3 that represents the total sales of the two restaurants owned by the same parent company.

(b) Use a graphing utility to graph R_1, R_2, and R_3 in the same viewing window.

57. ***Vital Statistics*** Let $b(t)$ be the number of births in the United States in year t, and let $d(t)$ represent the number of deaths in the United States in year t, where $t = 0$ corresponds to 2000.

(a) If $p(t)$ is the population of the United States in year t, find the function $c(t)$ that represents the percent change in the population of the United States.

(b) Interpret the value of $c(5)$.

58. ***Pets*** Let $d(t)$ be the number of dogs in the United States in year t, and let $c(t)$ be the number of cats in the United States in year t, where $t = 0$ corresponds to 2000.

(a) Find the function $p(t)$ that represents the total number of dogs and cats in the United States.

(b) Interpret the value of $p(5)$.

(c) Let $n(t)$ represent the population of the United States in year t, where $t = 0$ corresponds to 2000. Find and interpret

$$h(t) = \frac{p(t)}{n(t)}.$$

59. ***Military Personnel*** The total numbers of Army personnel (in thousands) A and Navy personnel (in thousands) N from 1990 to 2002 can be approximated by the models

$$A(t) = 3.36t^2 - 59.8t + 735$$

and

$$N(t) = 1.95t^2 - 42.2t + 603$$

where t represents the year, with $t = 0$ corresponding to 1990. (Source: Department of Defense)

(a) Find and interpret $(A + N)(t)$. Evaluate this function for $t = 4$, 8, and 12.

(b) Find and interpret $(A - N)(t)$. Evaluate this function for $t = 4$, 8, and 12.

60. ***Sales*** The sales of exercise equipment E (in millions of dollars) in the United States from 1997 to 2003 can be approximated by the function

$$E(t) = 25.95t^2 - 231.2t + 3356$$

and the U.S. population P (in millions) from 1997 to 2003 can be approximated by the function

$$P(t) = 3.02t + 252.0$$

where t represents the year, with $t = 7$ corresponding to 1997. (Source: National Sporting Goods Association, U.S. Census Bureau)

(a) Find and interpret $h(t) = \dfrac{E(t)}{P(t)}$.

(b) Evaluate the function in part (a) for $t = 7$, 10, and 12.

Model It

61. ***Health Care Costs*** The table shows the total amounts (in billions of dollars) spent on health services and supplies in the United States (including Puerto Rico) for the years 1995 through 2001. The variables y_1, y_2, and y_3 represent out-of-pocket payments, insurance premiums, and other types of payments, respectively. (Source: Centers for Medicare and Medicaid Services)

Year	y_1	y_2	y_3
1995	146.2	329.1	44.8
1996	152.0	344.1	48.1
1997	162.2	359.9	52.1
1998	175.2	382.0	55.6
1999	184.4	412.1	57.8
2000	194.7	449.0	57.4
2001	205.5	496.1	57.8

(a) Use the *regression* feature of a graphing utility to find a linear model for y_1 and quadratic models for y_2 and y_3. Let $t = 5$ represent 1995.

(b) Find $y_1 + y_2 + y_3$. What does this sum represent?

(c) Use a graphing utility to graph y_1, y_2, y_3, and $y_1 + y_2 + y_3$ in the same viewing window.

(d) Use the model from part (b) to estimate the total amounts spent on health services and supplies in the years 2008 and 2010.

62. ***Graphical Reasoning*** An electronically controlled thermostat in a home is programmed to lower the temperature automatically during the night. The temperature in the house T (in degrees Fahrenheit) is given in terms of t, the time in hours on a 24-hour clock (see figure).

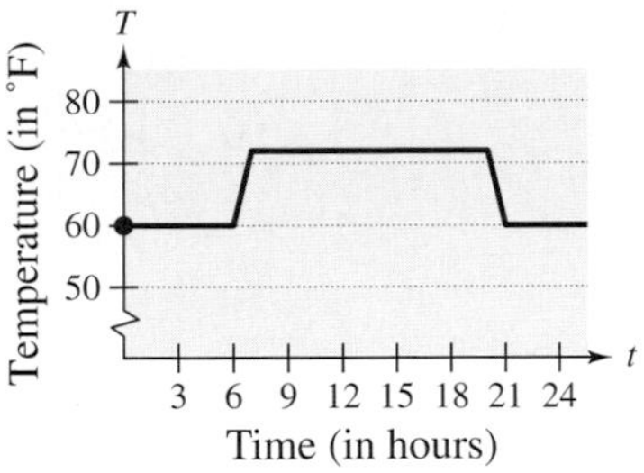

(a) Explain why T is a function of t.

(b) Approximate $T(4)$ and $T(15)$.

(c) The thermostat is reprogrammed to produce a temperature H for which $H(t) = T(t - 1)$. How does this change the temperature?

(d) The thermostat is reprogrammed to produce a temperature H for which $H(t) = T(t) - 1$. How does this change the temperature?

(e) Write a piecewise-defined function that represents the graph.

63. ***Geometry*** A square concrete foundation is prepared as a base for a cylindrical tank (see figure).

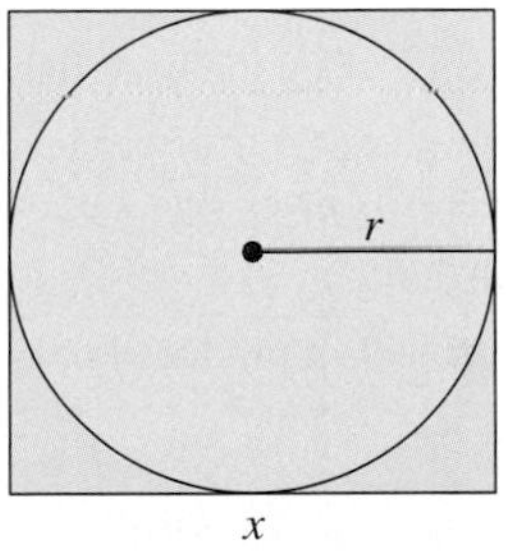

(a) Write the radius r of the tank as a function of the length x of the sides of the square.

(b) Write the area A of the circular base of the tank as a function of the radius r.

(c) Find and interpret $(A \circ r)(x)$.

64. ***Physics*** A pebble is dropped into a calm pond, causing ripples in the form of concentric circles (see figure). The radius r (in feet) of the outer ripple is $r(t) = 0.6t$, where t is the time in seconds after the pebble strikes the water. The area A of the circle is given by the function $A(r) = \pi r^2$. Find and interpret $(A \circ r)(t)$.

65. ***Bacteria Count*** The number N of bacteria in a refrigerated food is given by

$N(T) = 10T^2 - 20T + 600, \quad 1 \le T \le 20$

where T is the temperature of the food in degrees Celsius. When the food is removed from refrigeration, the temperature of the food is given by

$T(t) = 3t + 2, \quad 0 \le t \le 6$

where t is the time in hours.

(a) Find the composition $N(T(t))$ and interpret its meaning in context.

(b) Find the time when the bacterial count reaches 1500.

66. ***Cost*** The weekly cost C of producing x units in a manufacturing process is given by

$C(x) = 60x + 750.$

The number of units x produced in t hours is given by

$x(t) = 50t.$

(a) Find and interpret $(C \circ x)(t)$.

(b) Find the time that must elapse in order for the cost to increase to \$15,000.

67. ***Salary*** You are a sales representative for a clothing manufacturer. You are paid an annual salary, plus a bonus of 3% of your sales over \$500,000. Consider the two functions given by

$f(x) = x - 500{,}000$ and $g(x) = 0.03x.$

If x is greater than \$500,000, which of the following represents your bonus? Explain your reasoning.

(a) $f(g(x))$ (b) $g(f(x))$

68. ***Consumer Awareness*** The suggested retail price of a new hybrid car is p dollars. The dealership advertises a factory rebate of \$2000 and a 10% discount.

(a) Write a function R in terms of p giving the cost of the hybrid car after receiving the rebate from the factory.

(b) Write a function S in terms of p giving the cost of the hybrid car after receiving the dealership discount.

(c) Form the composite functions $(R \circ S)(p)$ and $(S \circ R)(p)$ and interpret each.

(d) Find $(R \circ S)(20{,}500)$ and $(S \circ R)(20{,}500)$. Which yields the lower cost for the hybrid car? Explain.

Synthesis

True or False? **In Exercises 69 and 70, determine whether the statement is true or false. Justify your answer.**

69. If $f(x) = x + 1$ and $g(x) = 6x$, then

$(f \circ g)(x) = (g \circ f)(x).$

70. If you are given two functions $f(x)$ and $g(x)$, you can calculate $(f \circ g)(x)$ if and only if the range of g is a subset of the domain of f.

71. ***Proof*** Prove that the product of two odd functions is an even function, and that the product of two even functions is an even function.

72. ***Conjecture*** Use examples to hypothesize whether the product of an odd function and an even function is even or odd. Then prove your hypothesis.

Skills Review

Average Rate of Change **In Exercises 73–76, find the difference quotient**

$$\frac{f(x + h) - f(x)}{h}$$

and simplify your answer.

73. $f(x) = 3x - 4$

74. $f(x) = 1 - x^2$

75. $f(x) = \frac{4}{x}$

76. $f(x) = \sqrt{2x + 1}$

In Exercises 77–80, find an equation of the line that passes through the given point and has the indicated slope. Sketch the line.

77. $(2, -4), m = 3$

78. $(-6, 3), m = -1$

79. $(8, -1), m = -\frac{3}{2}$

80. $(7, 0), m = \frac{5}{7}$

1.9 Inverse Functions

What you should learn

- Find inverse functions informally and verify that two functions are inverse functions of each other.
- Use graphs of functions to determine whether functions have inverse functions.
- Use the Horizontal Line Test to determine if functions are one-to-one.
- Find inverse functions algebraically.

Why you should learn it

Inverse functions can be used to model and solve real-life problems. For instance, in Exercise 80 on page 101, an inverse function can be used to determine the year in which there was a given dollar amount of sales of digital cameras in the United States.

Inverse Functions

Recall from Section 1.4, that a function can be represented by a set of ordered pairs. For instance, the function $f(x) = x + 4$ from the set $A = \{1, 2, 3, 4\}$ to the set $B = \{5, 6, 7, 8\}$ can be written as follows.

$$f(x) = x + 4\text{:}\quad \{(1, 5), (2, 6), (3, 7), (4, 8)\}$$

In this case, by interchanging the first and second coordinates of each of these ordered pairs, you can form the **inverse function** of f, which is denoted by f^{-1}. It is a function from the set B to the set A, and can be written as follows.

$$f^{-1}(x) = x - 4\text{:}\quad \{(5, 1), (6, 2), (7, 3), (8, 4)\}$$

Note that the domain of f is equal to the range of f^{-1}, and vice versa, as shown in Figure 1.92. Also note that the functions f and f^{-1} have the effect of "undoing" each other. In other words, when you form the composition of f with f^{-1} or the composition of f^{-1} with f, you obtain the identity function.

$$f(f^{-1}(x)) = f(x - 4) = (x - 4) + 4 = x$$

$$f^{-1}(f(x)) = f^{-1}(x + 4) = (x + 4) - 4 = x$$

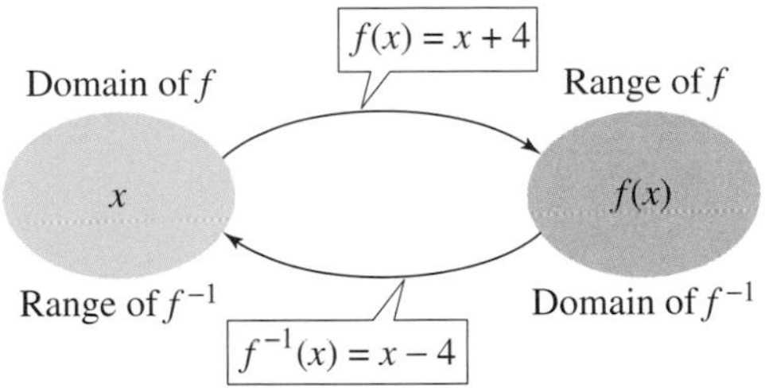

FIGURE 1.92

Example 1 Finding Inverse Functions Informally

Find the inverse function of $f(x) = 4x$. Then verify that both $f(f^{-1}(x))$ and $f^{-1}(f(x))$ are equal to the identity function.

Solution

The function f *multiplies* each input by 4. To "undo" this function, you need to *divide* each input by 4. So, the inverse function of $f(x) = 4x$ is

$$f^{-1}(x) = \frac{x}{4}.$$

You can verify that both $f(f^{-1}(x)) = x$ and $f^{-1}(f(x)) = x$ as follows.

$$f(f^{-1}(x)) = f\left(\frac{x}{4}\right) = 4\left(\frac{x}{4}\right) = x \qquad f^{-1}(f(x)) = f^{-1}(4x) = \frac{4x}{4} = x$$

CHECKPOINT Now try Exercise 1.

Exploration

Consider the functions given by

$$f(x) = x + 2$$

and

$$f^{-1}(x) = x - 2.$$

Evaluate $f(f^{-1}(x))$ and $f^{-1}(f(x))$ for the indicated values of x. What can you conclude about the functions?

x	-10	0	7	45
$f(f^{-1}(x))$				
$f^{-1}(f(x))$				

Definition of Inverse Function

Let f and g be two functions such that

$$f(g(x)) = x \qquad \text{for every } x \text{ in the domain of } g$$

and

$$g(f(x)) = x \qquad \text{for every } x \text{ in the domain of } f.$$

Under these conditions, the function g is the **inverse function** of the function f. The function g is denoted by f^{-1} (read "f-inverse"). So,

$$f(f^{-1}(x)) = x \qquad \text{and} \qquad f^{-1}(f(x)) = x.$$

The domain of f must be equal to the range of f^{-1}, and the range of f must be equal to the domain of f^{-1}.

Don't be confused by the use of -1 to denote the inverse function f^{-1}. In this text, whenever f^{-1} is written, it *always* refers to the inverse function of the function f and *not* to the reciprocal of $f(x)$.

If the function g is the inverse function of the function f, it must also be true that the function f is the inverse function of the function g. For this reason, you can say that the functions f and g are *inverse functions of each other.*

Example 2 Verifying Inverse Functions

Which of the functions is the inverse function of $f(x) = \dfrac{5}{x-2}$?

$$g(x) = \frac{x-2}{5} \qquad h(x) = \frac{5}{x} + 2$$

Solution

By forming the composition of f with g, you have

$$f(g(x)) = f\left(\frac{x-2}{5}\right)$$

$$= \frac{5}{\left(\frac{x-2}{5}\right) - 2} \qquad \text{Substitute } \frac{x-2}{5} \text{ for } x.$$

$$= \frac{25}{x-12} \neq x.$$

Because this composition is not equal to the identity function x, it follows that g *is not* the inverse function of f. By forming the composition of f with h, you have

$$f(h(x)) = f\left(\frac{5}{x} + 2\right) = \frac{5}{\left(\frac{5}{x} + 2\right) - 2} = \frac{5}{\left(\frac{5}{x}\right)} = x.$$

So, it appears that h *is* the inverse function of f. You can confirm this by showing that the composition of h with f is also equal to the identity function.

CHECKPOINT Now try Exercise 5.

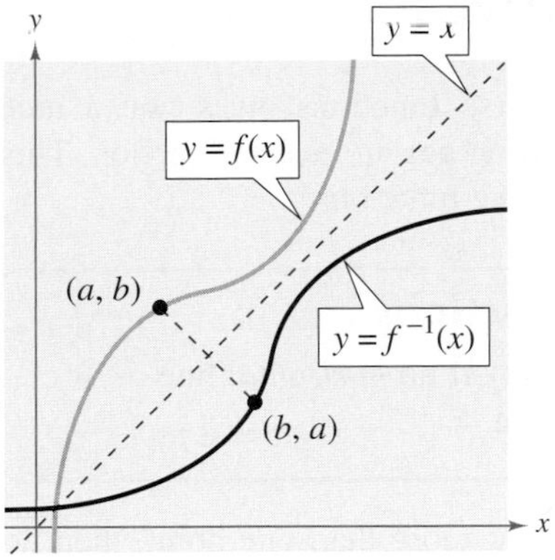

FIGURE 1.93

The Graph of an Inverse Function

The graphs of a function f and its inverse function f^{-1} are related to each other in the following way. If the point (a, b) lies on the graph of f, then the point (b, a) must lie on the graph of f^{-1}, and vice versa. This means that the graph of f^{-1} is a *reflection* of the graph of f in the line $y = x$, as shown in Figure 1.93.

Example 3 Finding Inverse Functions Graphically

Sketch the graphs of the inverse functions $f(x) = 2x - 3$ and $f^{-1}(x) = \frac{1}{2}(x + 3)$ on the same rectangular coordinate system and show that the graphs are reflections of each other in the line $y = x$.

Solution

The graphs of f and f^{-1} are shown in Figure 1.94. It appears that the graphs are reflections of each other in the line $y = x$. You can further verify this reflective property by testing a few points on each graph. Note in the following list that if the point (a, b) is on the graph of f, the point (b, a) is on the graph of f^{-1}.

Graph of $f(x) = 2x - 3$	*Graph of* $f^{-1}(x) = \frac{1}{2}(x + 3)$
$(-1, -5)$	$(-5, -1)$
$(0, -3)$	$(-3, 0)$
$(1, -1)$	$(-1, 1)$
$(2, 1)$	$(1, 2)$
$(3, 3)$	$(3, 3)$

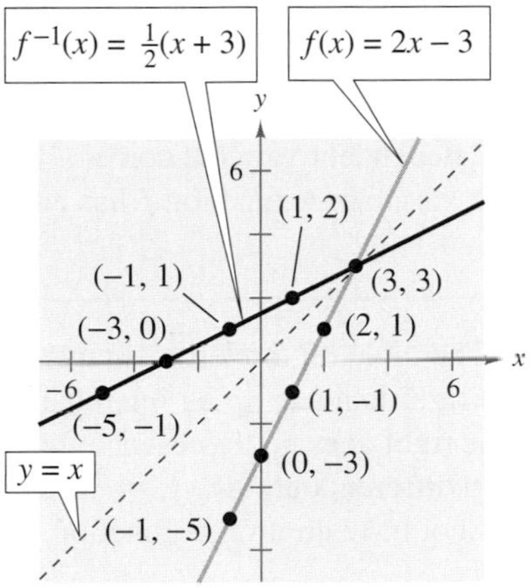

FIGURE 1.94

CHECKPOINT Now try Exercise 15.

Example 4 Finding Inverse Functions Graphically

Sketch the graphs of the inverse functions $f(x) = x^2$ $(x \geq 0)$ and $f^{-1}(x) = \sqrt{x}$ on the same rectangular coordinate system and show that the graphs are reflections of each other in the line $y = x$.

Solution

The graphs of f and f^{-1} are shown in Figure 1.95. It appears that the graphs are reflections of each other in the line $y = x$. You can further verify this reflective property by testing a few points on each graph. Note in the following list that if the point (a, b) is on the graph of f, the point (b, a) is on the graph of f^{-1}.

Graph of $f(x) = x^2, \quad x \geq 0$	*Graph of* $f^{-1}(x) = \sqrt{x}$
$(0, 0)$	$(0, 0)$
$(1, 1)$	$(1, 1)$
$(2, 4)$	$(4, 2)$
$(3, 9)$	$(9, 3)$

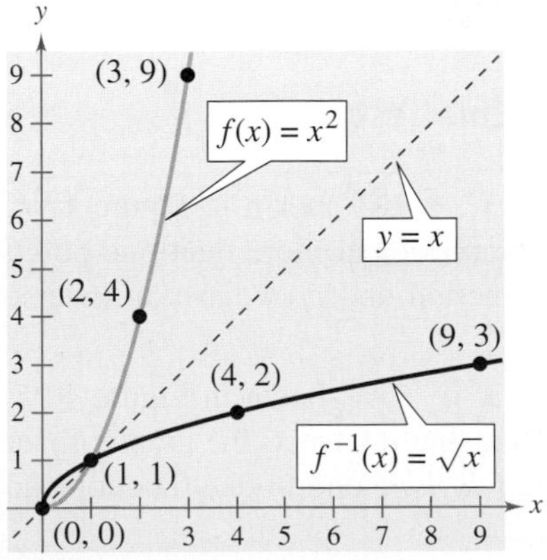

FIGURE 1.95

Try showing that $f(f^{-1}(x)) = x$ and $f^{-1}(f(x)) = x$.

CHECKPOINT Now try Exercise 17.

One-to-One Functions

The reflective property of the graphs of inverse functions gives you a nice *geometric* test for determining whether a function has an inverse function. This test is called the **Horizontal Line Test** for inverse functions.

> **Horizontal Line Test for Inverse Functions**
>
> A function f has an inverse function if and only if no *horizontal* line intersects the graph of f at more than one point.

If no horizontal line intersects the graph of f at more than one point, then no y-value is matched with more than one x-value. This is the essential characteristic of what are called **one-to-one functions.**

> **One-to-One Functions**
>
> A function f is **one-to-one** if each value of the dependent variable corresponds to exactly one value of the independent variable. A function f has an inverse function if and only if f is one-to-one.

Consider the function given by $f(x) = x^2$. The table on the left is a table of values for $f(x) = x^2$. The table of values on the right is made up by interchanging the columns of the first table. The table on the right does not represent a function because the input $x = 4$ is matched with two different outputs: $y = -2$ and $y = 2$. So, $f(x) = x^2$ is not one-to-one and does not have an inverse function.

x	$f(x) = x^2$
-2	4
-1	1
0	0
1	1
2	4
3	9

x	y
4	-2
1	-1
0	0
1	1
4	2
9	3

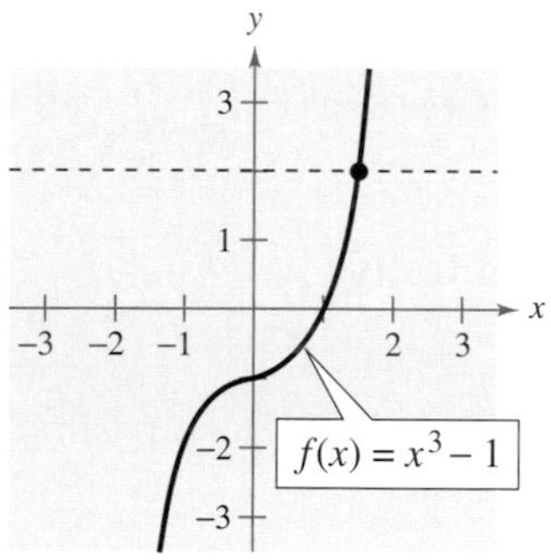

FIGURE 1.96

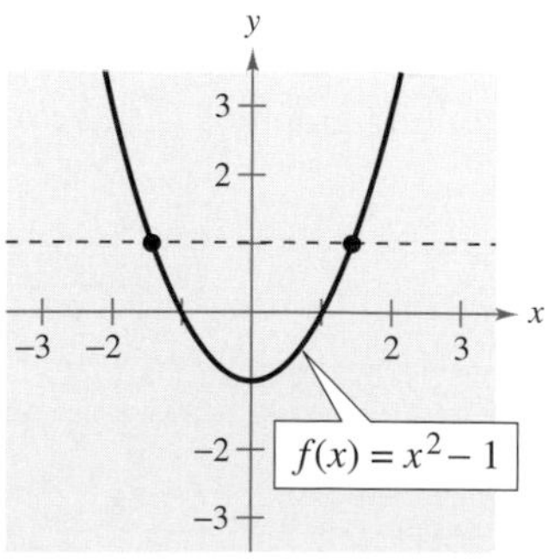

FIGURE 1.97

Example 5 Applying the Horizontal Line Test

a. The graph of the function given by $f(x) = x^3 - 1$ is shown in Figure 1.96. Because no horizontal line intersects the graph of f at more than one point, you can conclude that f *is* a one-to-one function and *does* have an inverse function.

b. The graph of the function given by $f(x) = x^2 - 1$ is shown in Figure 1.97. Because it is possible to find a horizontal line that intersects the graph of f at more than one point, you can conclude that f *is not* a one-to-one function and *does not* have an inverse function.

CHECKPOINT Now try Exercise 29.

STUDY TIP

Note what happens when you try to find the inverse function of a function that is not one-to-one.

$f(x) = x^2 + 1$	Original function
$y = x^2 + 1$	Replace $f(x)$ by y.
$x = y^2 + 1$	Interchange x and y.
$x - 1 = y^2$	Isolate y-term.
$y = \pm\sqrt{x - 1}$	Solve for y.

You obtain two y-values for each x.

Finding Inverse Functions Algebraically

For simple functions (such as the one in Example 1), you can find inverse functions by inspection. For more complicated functions, however, it is best to use the following guidelines. The key step in these guidelines is Step 3—interchanging the roles of x and y. This step corresponds to the fact that inverse functions have ordered pairs with the coordinates reversed.

Finding an Inverse Function

1. Use the Horizontal Line Test to decide whether f has an inverse function.
2. In the equation for $f(x)$, replace $f(x)$ by y.
3. Interchange the roles of x and y, and solve for y.
4. Replace y by $f^{-1}(x)$ in the new equation.
5. Verify that f and f^{-1} are inverse functions of each other by showing that the domain of f is equal to the range of f^{-1}, the range of f is equal to the domain of f^{-1}, and $f(f^{-1}(x)) = x$ and $f^{-1}(f(x)) = x$.

Example 6 Finding an Inverse Function Algebraically

Find the inverse function of

$$f(x) = \frac{5 - 3x}{2}.$$

Solution

The graph of f is a line, as shown in Figure 1.98. This graph passes the Horizontal Line Test. So, you know that f is one-to-one and has an inverse function.

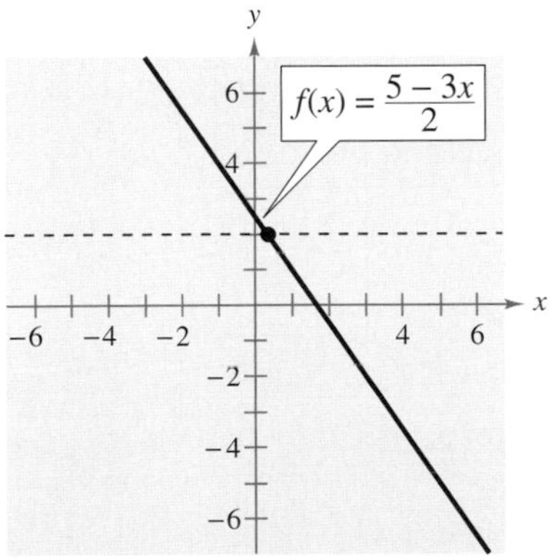

FIGURE 1.98

$f(x) = \dfrac{5 - 3x}{2}$	Write original function.
$y = \dfrac{5 - 3x}{2}$	Replace $f(x)$ by y.
$x = \dfrac{5 - 3y}{2}$	Interchange x and y.
$2x = 5 - 3y$	Multiply each side by 2.
$3y = 5 - 2x$	Isolate the y-term.
$y = \dfrac{5 - 2x}{3}$	Solve for y.
$f^{-1}(x) = \dfrac{5 - 2x}{3}$	Replace y by $f^{-1}(x)$.

Note that both f and f^{-1} have domains and ranges that consist of the entire set of real numbers. Check that $f(f^{-1}(x)) = x$ and $f^{-1}(f(x)) = x$.

✓CHECKPOINT Now try Exercise 55.

Exploration

Restrict the domain of $f(x) = x^2 + 1$ to $x \geq 0$. Use a graphing utility to graph the function. Does the restricted function have an inverse function? Explain.

Example 7 Finding an Inverse Function

Find the inverse function of

$$f(x) = \sqrt[3]{x+1}.$$

Solution

The graph of f is a curve, as shown in Figure 1.99. Because this graph passes the Horizontal Line Test, you know that f is one-to-one and has an inverse function.

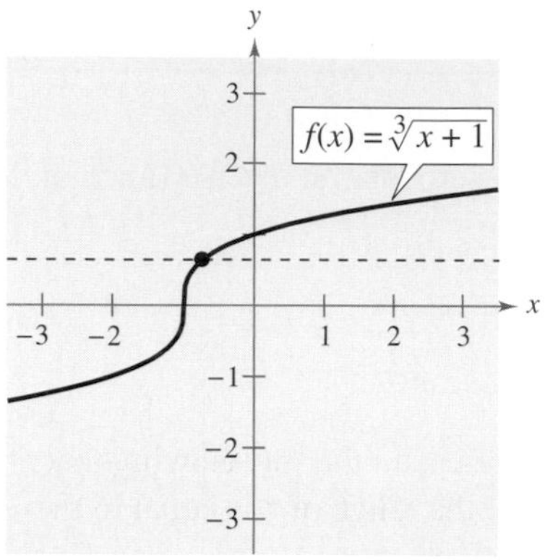

FIGURE 1.99

$f(x) = \sqrt[3]{x+1}$ Write original function.

$y = \sqrt[3]{x+1}$ Replace $f(x)$ by y.

$x = \sqrt[3]{y+1}$ Interchange x and y.

$x^3 = y + 1$ Cube each side.

$x^3 - 1 = y$ Solve for y.

$x^3 - 1 = f^{-1}(x)$ Replace y by $f^{-1}(x)$.

Both f and f^{-1} have domains and ranges that consist of the entire set of real numbers. You can verify this result numerically as shown in the tables below.

x	$f(x)$
-28	-3
-9	-2
-2	-1
-1	0
0	1
7	2
26	3

x	$f^{-1}(x)$
-3	-28
-2	-9
-1	-2
0	-1
1	0
2	7
3	26

CHECKPOINT Now try Exercise 61.

Writing About Mathematics

The Existence of an Inverse Function Write a short paragraph describing why the following functions do or do not have inverse functions.

a. Let x represent the retail price of an item (in dollars), and let $f(x)$ represent the sales tax on the item. Assume that the sales tax is 6% of the retail price *and* that the sales tax is rounded to the nearest cent. Does this function have an inverse function? (*Hint:* Can you undo this function? For instance, if you know that the sales tax is \$0.12, can you determine exactly what the retail price is?)

b. Let x represent the temperature in degrees Celsius, and let $f(x)$ represent the temperature in degrees Fahrenheit. Does this function have an inverse function? (*Hint:* The formula for converting from degrees Celsius to degrees Fahrenheit is $F = \frac{9}{5}C + 32$.)

1.9 Exercises

VOCABULARY CHECK: Fill in the blanks.

1. If the composite functions $f(g(x)) = x$ and $g(f(x)) = x$ then the function g is the ________ function of f.
2. The domain of f is the ________ of f^{-1}, and the ________ of f^{-1} is the range of f.
3. The graphs of f and f^{-1} are reflections of each other in the line ________.
4. A function f is ________ if each value of the dependent variable corresponds to exactly one value of the independent variable.
5. A graphical test for the existence of an inverse function of f is called the _______ Line Test.

In Exercises 1–8, find the inverse function of f informally. Verify that $f(f^{-1}(x)) = x$ and $f^{-1}(f(x)) = x$.

1. $f(x) = 6x$
2. $f(x) = \frac{1}{3}x$
3. $f(x) = x + 9$
4. $f(x) = x - 4$
5. $f(x) = 3x + 1$
6. $f(x) = \dfrac{x-1}{5}$
7. $f(x) = \sqrt[3]{x}$
8. $f(x) = x^5$

In Exercises 9–12, match the graph of the function with the graph of its inverse function. [The graphs of the inverse functions are labeled (a), (b), (c), and (d).]

(a)

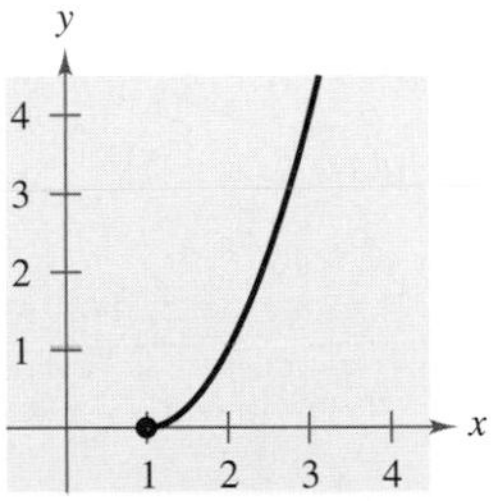

(b)

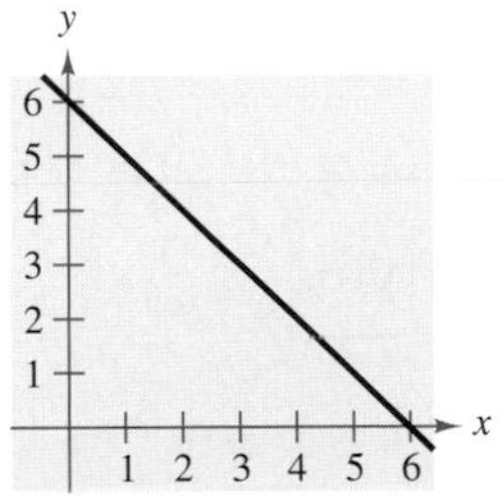

(c)

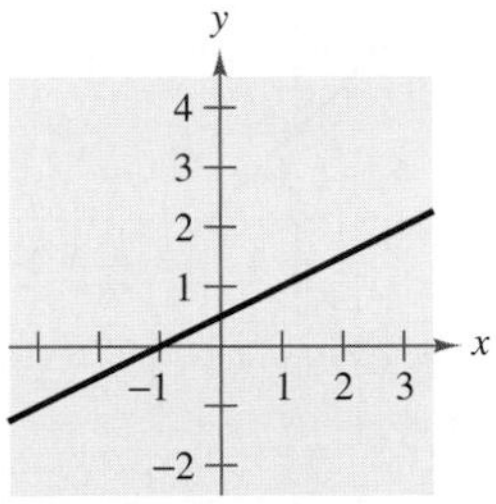

(d)

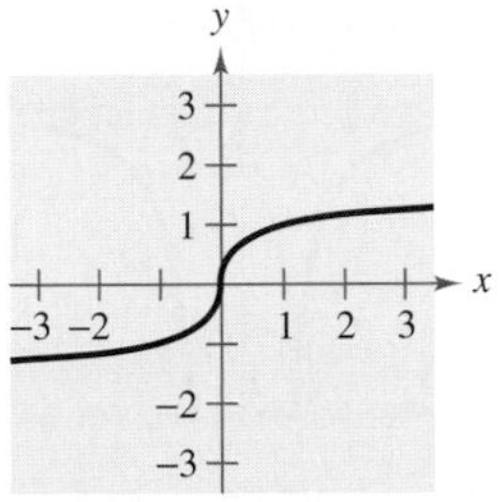

9.

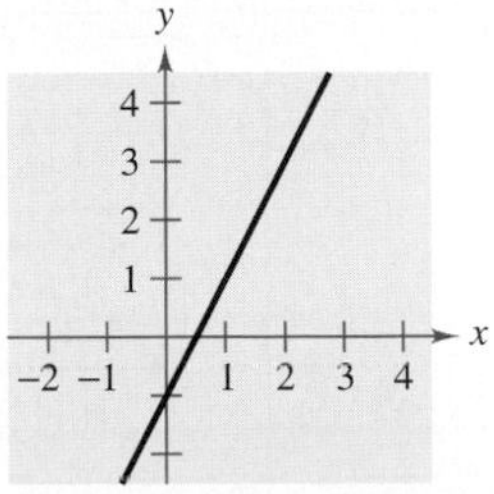

10.

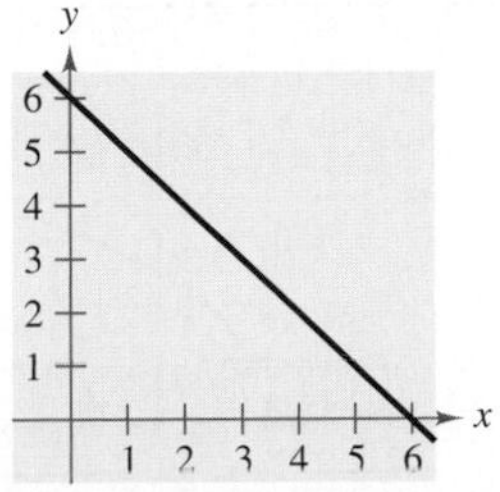

11.

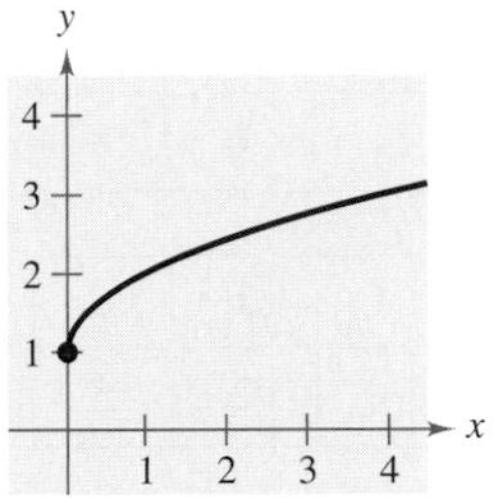

12.

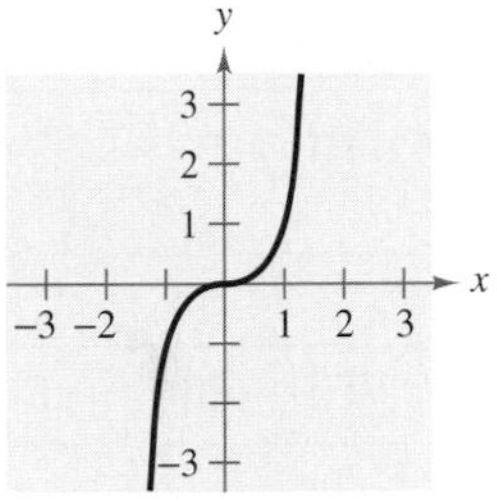

In Exercises 13–24, show that f and g are inverse functions (a) algebraically and (b) graphically.

13. $f(x) = 2x,\quad g(x) = \dfrac{x}{2}$
14. $f(x) = x - 5,\quad g(x) = x + 5$
15. $f(x) = 7x + 1,\quad g(x) = \dfrac{x-1}{7}$
16. $f(x) = 3 - 4x,\quad g(x) = \dfrac{3-x}{4}$
17. $f(x) = \dfrac{x^3}{8},\quad g(x) = \sqrt[3]{8x}$
18. $f(x) = \dfrac{1}{x},\quad g(x) = \dfrac{1}{x}$
19. $f(x) = \sqrt{x-4},\quad g(x) = x^2 + 4,\ \ x \ge 0$
20. $f(x) = 1 - x^3,\quad g(x) = \sqrt[3]{1-x}$
21. $f(x) = 9 - x^2,\ \ x \ge 0,\quad g(x) = \sqrt{9-x},\ \ x \le 9$
22. $f(x) = \dfrac{1}{1+x},\ \ x \ge 0,\quad g(x) = \dfrac{1-x}{x},\ \ 0 < x \le 1$
23. $f(x) = \dfrac{x-1}{x+5},\quad g(x) = -\dfrac{5x+1}{x-1}$
24. $f(x) = \dfrac{x+3}{x-2},\quad g(x) = \dfrac{2x+3}{x-1}$

In Exercises 25 and 26, does the function have an inverse function?

25.

x	-1	0	1	2	3	4
$f(x)$	-2	1	2	1	-2	-6

26.

x	-3	-2	-1	0	2	3
$f(x)$	10	6	4	1	-3	-10

In Exercises 27 and 28, use the table of values for $y = f(x)$ to complete a table for $y = f^{-1}(x)$.

27.

x	-2	-1	0	1	2	3
$f(x)$	-2	0	2	4	6	8

28.

x	-3	-2	-1	0	1	2
$f(x)$	-10	-7	-4	-1	2	5

In Exercises 29–32, does the function have an inverse function?

29.

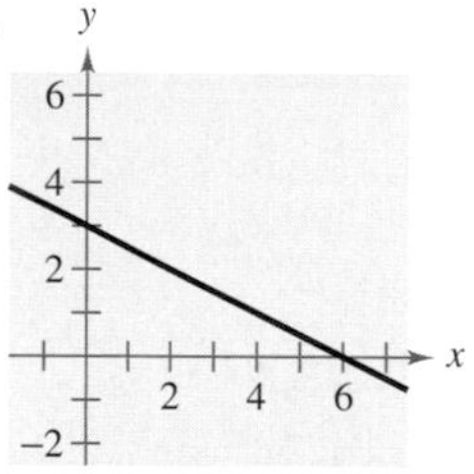

30.

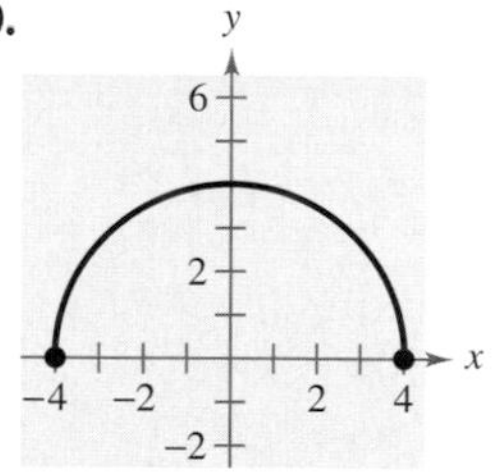

31.

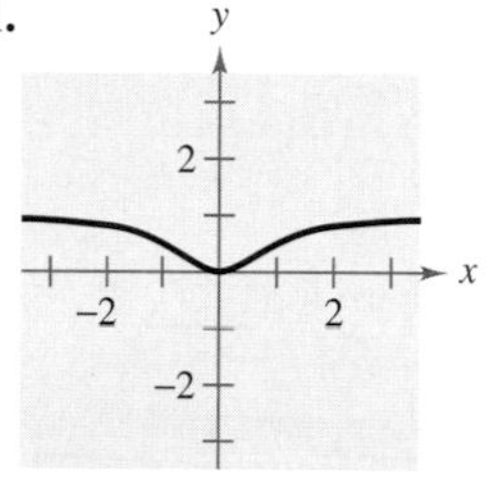

32.

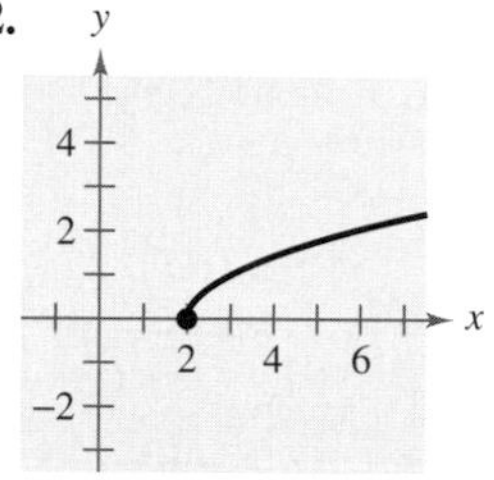

In Exercises 33–38, use a graphing utility to graph the function, and use the Horizontal Line Test to determine whether the function is one-to-one and so has an inverse function.

33. $g(x) = \dfrac{4 - x}{6}$

34. $f(x) = 10$

35. $h(x) = |x + 4| - |x - 4|$

36. $g(x) = (x + 5)^3$

37. $f(x) = -2x\sqrt{16 - x^2}$

38. $f(x) = \frac{1}{8}(x + 2)^2 - 1$

In Exercises 39–54, (a) find the inverse function of f, (b) graph both f and f^{-1} on the same set of coordinate axes, (c) describe the relationship between the graphs of f and f^{-1}, and (d) state the domain and range of f and f^{-1}.

39. $f(x) = 2x - 3$

40. $f(x) = 3x + 1$

41. $f(x) = x^5 - 2$

42. $f(x) = x^3 + 1$

43. $f(x) = \sqrt{x}$

44. $f(x) = x^2, \quad x \ge 0$

45. $f(x) = \sqrt{4 - x^2}, \quad 0 \le x \le 2$

46. $f(x) = x^2 - 2, \quad x \le 0$

47. $f(x) = \dfrac{4}{x}$

48. $f(x) = -\dfrac{2}{x}$

49. $f(x) = \dfrac{x + 1}{x - 2}$

50. $f(x) = \dfrac{x - 3}{x + 2}$

51. $f(x) = \sqrt[3]{x - 1}$

52. $f(x) = x^{3/5}$

53. $f(x) = \dfrac{6x + 4}{4x + 5}$

54. $f(x) = \dfrac{8x - 4}{2x + 6}$

In Exercises 55–68, determine whether the function has an inverse function. If it does, find the inverse function.

55. $f(x) = x^4$

56. $f(x) = \dfrac{1}{x^2}$

57. $g(x) = \dfrac{x}{8}$

58. $f(x) = 3x + 5$

59. $p(x) = -4$

60. $f(x) = \dfrac{3x + 4}{5}$

61. $f(x) = (x + 3)^2, \quad x \ge -3$

62. $q(x) = (x - 5)^2$

63. $f(x) = \begin{cases} x + 3, & x < 0 \\ 6 - x, & x \ge 0 \end{cases}$

64. $f(x) = \begin{cases} -x, & x \le 0 \\ x^2 - 3x, & x > 0 \end{cases}$

65. $h(x) = -\dfrac{4}{x^2}$

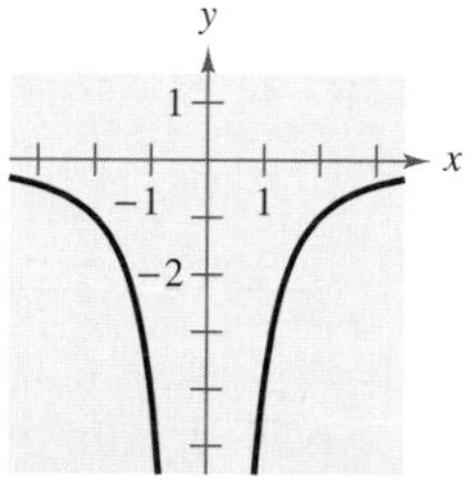

66. $f(x) = |x - 2|, \quad x \le 2$

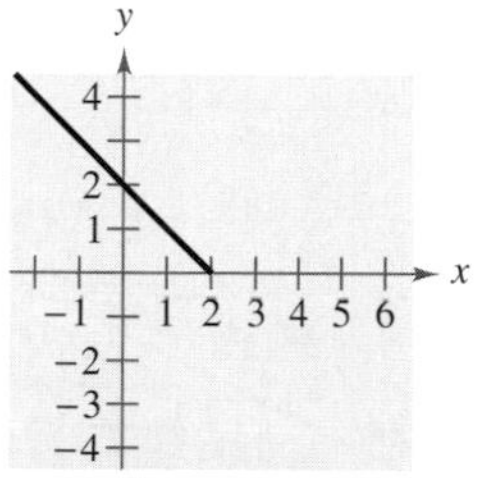

67. $f(x) = \sqrt{2x + 3}$

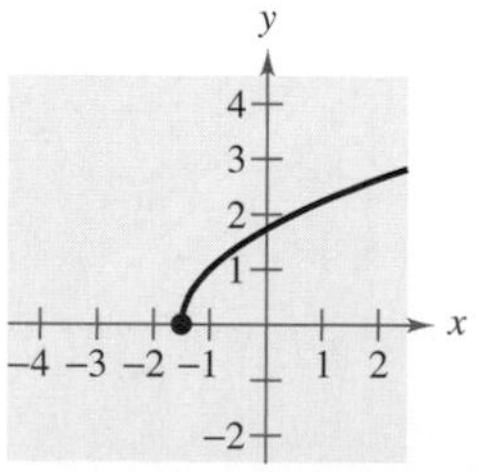

68. $f(x) = \sqrt{x - 2}$

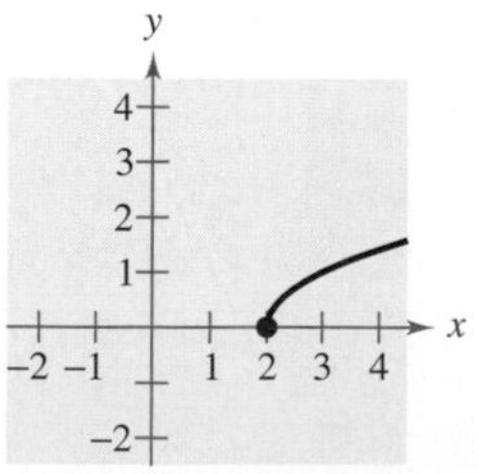

In Exercises 69–74, use the functions given by $f(x) = \frac{1}{8}x - 3$ and $g(x) = x^3$ to find the indicated value or function.

69. $(f^{-1} \circ g^{-1})(1)$

70. $(g^{-1} \circ f^{-1})(-3)$

71. $(f^{-1} \circ f^{-1})(6)$

72. $(g^{-1} \circ g^{-1})(-4)$

73. $(f \circ g)^{-1}$

74. $g^{-1} \circ f^{-1}$

In Exercises 75–78, use the functions given by $f(x) = x + 4$ and $g(x) = 2x - 5$ to find the specified function.

75. $g^{-1} \circ f^{-1}$

76. $f^{-1} \circ g^{-1}$

77. $(f \circ g)^{-1}$

78. $(g \circ f)^{-1}$

Model It

79. ***U.S. Households*** The numbers of households f (in thousands) in the United States from 1995 to 2003 are shown in the table. The time (in years) is given by t, with $t = 5$ corresponding to 1995. (Source: U.S. Census Bureau)

Year, t	Households, $f(t)$
5	98,990
6	99,627
7	101,018
8	102,528
9	103,874
10	104,705
11	108,209
12	109,297
13	111,278

(a) Find $f^{-1}(108{,}209)$.

(b) What does f^{-1} mean in the context of the problem?

(c) Use the *regression* feature of a graphing utility to find a linear model for the data, $y = mx + b$. (Round m and b to two decimal places.)

(d) Algebraically find the inverse function of the linear model in part (c).

(e) Use the inverse function of the linear model you found in part (d) to approximate $f^{-1}(117, 022)$.

(f) Use the inverse function of the linear model you found in part (d) to approximate $f^{-1}(108{,}209)$. How does this value compare with the original data shown in the table?

80. ***Digital Camera Sales*** The factory sales f (in millions of dollars) of digital cameras in the United States from 1998 through 2003 are shown in the table. The time (in years) is given by t, with $t = 8$ corresponding to 1998. (Source: Consumer Electronincs Association)

Year, t	Sales, $f(t)$
8	519
9	1209
10	1825
11	1972
12	2794
13	3421

(a) Does f^{-1} exist?

(b) If f^{-1} exists, what does it represent in the context of the problem?

(c) If f^{-1} exists, find $f^{-1}(1825)$.

(d) If the table was extended to 2004 and if the factory sales of digital cameras for that year was \$2794 million, would f^{-1} exist? Explain.

81. ***Miles Traveled*** The total numbers f (in billions) of miles traveled by motor vehicles in the United States from 1995 through 2002 are shown in the table. The time (in years) is given by t, with $t = 5$ corresponding to 1995. (Source: U.S. Federal Highway Administration)

Year, t	Miles traveled, $f(t)$
5	2423
6	2486
7	2562
8	2632
9	2691
10	2747
11	2797
12	2856

(a) Does f^{-1} exist?

(b) If f^{-1} exists, what does it mean in the context of the problem?

(c) If f^{-1} exists, find $f^{-1}(2632)$.

(d) If the table was extended to 2003 and if the total number of miles traveled by motor vehicles for that year was 2747 billion, would f^{-1} exist? Explain.

82. ***Hourly Wage*** Your wage is \$8.00 per hour plus \$0.75 for each unit produced per hour. So, your hourly wage y in terms of the number of units produced is

$$y = 8 + 0.75x.$$

(a) Find the inverse function.

(b) What does each variable represent in the inverse function?

(c) Determine the number of units produced when your hourly wage is \$22.25.

83. ***Diesel Mechanics*** The function given by

$$y = 0.03x^2 + 245.50, \qquad 0 < x < 100$$

approximates the exhaust temperature y in degrees Fahrenheit, where x is the percent load for a diesel engine.

(a) Find the inverse function. What does each variable represent in the inverse function?

(b) Use a graphing utility to graph the inverse function.

(c) The exhaust temperature of the engine must not exceed 500 degrees Fahrenheit. What is the percent load interval?

84. ***Cost*** You need a total of 50 pounds of two types of ground beef costing \$1.25 and \$1.60 per pound, respectively. A model for the total cost y of the two types of beef is

$$y = 1.25x + 1.60(50 - x)$$

where x is the number of pounds of the less expensive ground beef.

(a) Find the inverse function of the cost function. What does each variable represent in the inverse function?

(b) Use the context of the problem to determine the domain of the inverse function.

(c) Determine the number of pounds of the less expensive ground beef purchased when the total cost is \$73.

Synthesis

True or False? **In Exercises 85 and 86, determine whether the statement is true or false. Justify your answer.**

85. If f is an even function, f^{-1} exists.

86. If the inverse function of f exists and the graph of f has a y-intercept, the y-intercept of f is an x-intercept of f^{-1}.

87. ***Proof*** Prove that if f and g are one-to-one functions, then $(f \circ g)^{-1}(x) = (g^{-1} \circ f^{-1})(x)$.

88. ***Proof*** Prove that if f is a one-to-one odd function, then f^{-1} is an odd function.

In Exercises 89–92, use the graph of the function f to create a table of values for the given points. Then create a second table that can be used to find f^{-1}, and sketch the graph of f^{-1} if possible.

89.

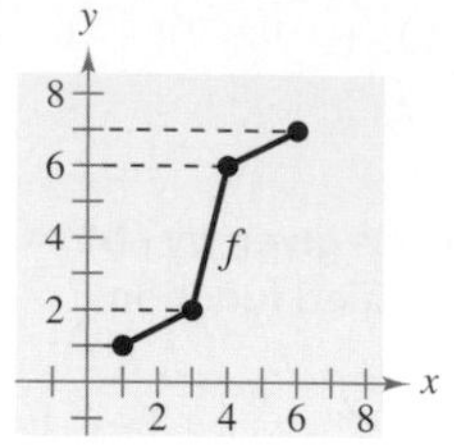

90.

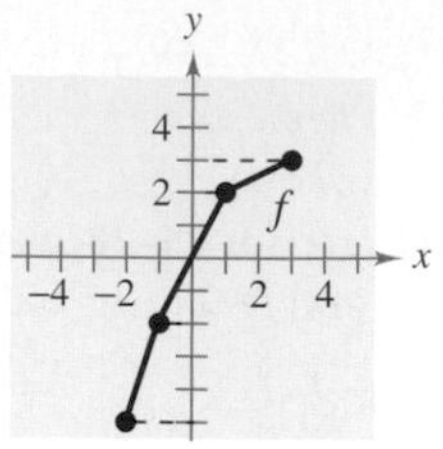

91.

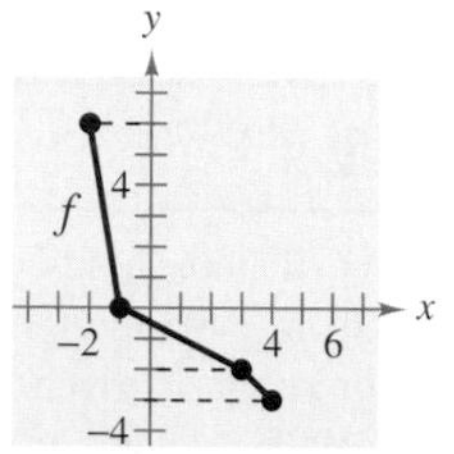

92.

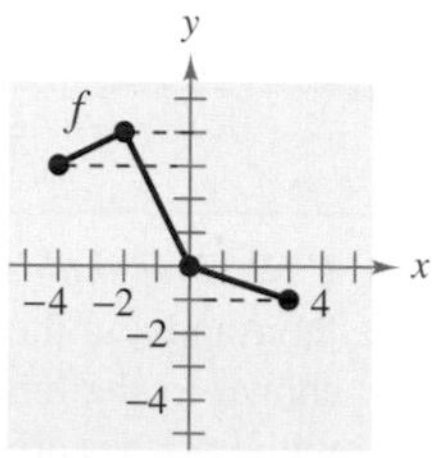

93. ***Think About It*** The function given by

$$f(x) = k(2 - x - x^3)$$

has an inverse function, and $f^{-1}(3) = -2$. Find k.

94. ***Think About It*** The function given by

$$f(x) = k(x^3 + 3x - 4)$$

has an inverse function, and $f^{-1}(-5) = 2$. Find k.

Skills Review

In Exercises 95–102, solve the equation using any convenient method.

95. $x^2 = 64$

96. $(x - 5)^2 = 8$

97. $4x^2 - 12x + 9 = 0$

98. $9x^2 + 12x + 3 = 0$

99. $x^2 - 6x + 4 = 0$

100. $2x^2 - 4x - 6 = 0$

101. $50 + 5x = 3x^2$

102. $2x^2 + 4x - 9 = 2(x - 1)^2$

103. Find two consecutive positive even integers whose product is 288.

104. ***Geometry*** A triangular sign has a height that is twice its base. The area of the sign is 10 square feet. Find the base and height of the sign.

1.10 Mathematical Modeling and Variation

What you should learn

- Use mathematical models to approximate sets of data points.
- Use the *regression* feature of a graphing utility to find the equation of a least squares regression line.
- Write mathematical models for direct variation.
- Write mathematical models for direct variation as an *n*th power.
- Write mathematical models for inverse variation.
- Write mathematical models for joint variation.

Why you should learn it

You can use functions as models to represent a wide variety of real-life data sets. For instance, in Exercise 71 on page 113, a variation model can be used to model the water temperature of the ocean at various depths.

Introduction

You have already studied some techniques for fitting models to data. For instance, in Section 1.3, you learned how to find the equation of a line that passes through two points. In this section, you will study other techniques for fitting models to data: *least squares regression* and *direct and inverse variation*. The resulting models are either polynomial functions or rational functions. (Rational functions will be studied in Chapter 2.)

Example 1 A Mathematical Model

The numbers of insured commercial banks y (in thousands) in the United States for the years 1996 to 2001 are shown in the table. (Source: Federal Deposit Insurance Corporation)

Year	Insured commercial banks, y
1996	9.53
1997	9.14
1998	8.77
1999	8.58
2000	8.32
2001	8.08

A linear model that approximates the data is $y = -0.283t + 11.14$ for $6 \le t \le 11$, where t is the year, with $t = 6$ corresponding to 1996. Plot the actual data *and* the model on the same graph. How closely does the model represent the data?

Solution

The actual data are plotted in Figure 1.100, along with the graph of the linear model. From the graph, it appears that the model is a "good fit" for the actual data. You can see how well the model fits by comparing the actual values of y with the values of y given by the model. The values given by the model are labeled y^* in the table below.

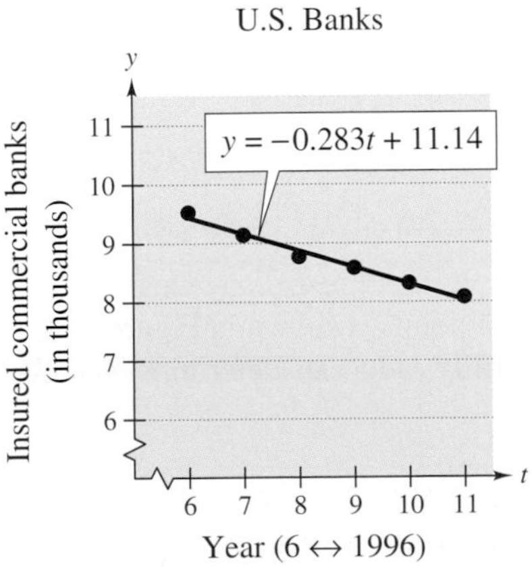

FIGURE 1.100

t	6	7	8	9	10	11
y	9.53	9.14	8.77	8.58	8.32	8.08
y^*	9.44	9.16	8.88	8.59	8.31	8.03

✓CHECKPOINT Now try Exercise 1.

Note in Example 1 that you could have chosen any two points to find a line that fits the data. However, the given linear model was found using the *regression* feature of a graphing utility and is the line that *best* fits the data. This concept of a "best-fitting" line is discussed on the next page.

Least Squares Regression and Graphing Utilities

So far in this text, you have worked with many different types of mathematical models that approximate real-life data. In some instances the model was given (as in Example 1), whereas in other instances you were asked to find the model using simple algebraic techniques or a graphing utility.

To find a model that approximates the data most accurately, statisticians use a measure called the **sum of square differences,** which is the sum of the squares of the differences between actual data values and model values. The "best-fitting" linear model, called the **least squares regression line,** is the one with the least sum of square differences. Recall that you can approximate this line visually by plotting the data points and drawing the line that appears to fit best—or you can enter the data points into a calculator or computer and use the *linear regression* feature of the calculator or computer. When you use the *regression* feauture of a graphing calculator or computer program, you will notice that the program may also output an "r-value." This r-value is the **correlation coefficient** of the data and gives a measure of how well the model fits the data. The closer the value of $|r|$ is to 1, the better the fit.

Example 2 Finding a Least Squares Regression Line

The amounts p (in millions of dollars) of total annual prize money awarded at the Indianapolis 500 race from 1995 to 2004 are shown in the table. Construct a scatter plot that represents the data and find the least squares regression line for the data. (Source: indy500.com)

Year	Prize money, p
1995	8.06
1996	8.11
1997	8.61
1998	8.72
1999	9.05
2000	9.48
2001	9.61
2002	10.03
2003	10.15
2004	10.25

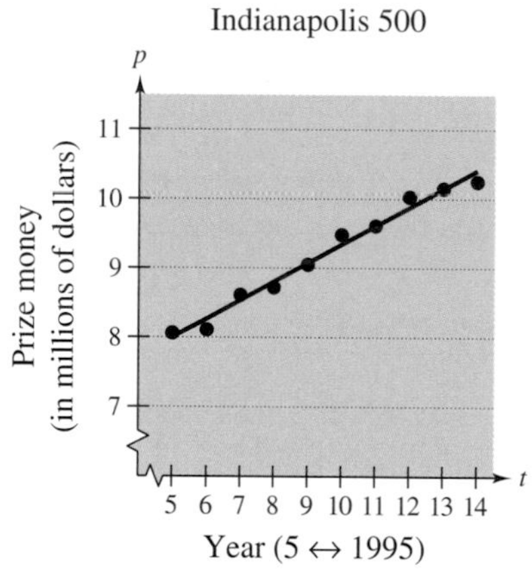

FIGURE 1.101

t	p	p^*
5	8.06	8.00
6	8.11	8.27
7	8.61	8.54
8	8.72	8.80
9	9.05	9.07
10	9.48	9.34
11	9.61	9.61
12	10.03	9.88
13	10.15	10.14
14	10.25	10.41

Solution

Let $t = 5$ represent 1995. The scatter plot for the points is shown in Figure 1.101. Using the *regression* feature of a graphing utility, you can determine that the equation of the least squares regression line is

$$p = 0.268t + 6.66.$$

To check this model, compare the actual p-values with the p-values given by the model, which are labeled $p*$ in the table at the left. The correlation coefficient for this model is $r \approx 0.991$, which implies that the model is a good fit.

CHECKPOINT Now try Exercise 7.

Direct Variation

There are two basic types of linear models. The more general model has a y-intercept that is nonzero.

$$y = mx + b, \quad b \neq 0$$

The simpler model

$$y = kx$$

has a y-intercept that is zero. In the simpler model, y is said to **vary directly** as x, or to be **directly proportional** to x.

Direct Variation

The following statements are equivalent.

1. y **varies directly** as x.
2. y is **directly proportional** to x.
3. $y = kx$ for some nonzero constant k.

k is the **constant of variation** or the **constant of proportionality.**

Example 3 Direct Variation

In Pennsylvania, the state income tax is directly proportional to *gross income*. You are working in Pennsylvania and your state income tax deduction is \$46.05 for a gross monthly income of \$1500. Find a mathematical model that gives the Pennsylvania state income tax in terms of gross income.

Solution

Verbal Model: State income tax $= k \cdot$ Gross income

Labels: State income tax $= y$ (dollars)
Gross income $= x$ (dollars)
Income tax rate $= k$ (percent in decimal form)

Equation: $y = kx$

To solve for k, substitute the given information into the equation $y = kx$, and then solve for k.

$y = kx$	Write direct variation model.
$46.05 = k(1500)$	Substitute $y = 46.05$ and $x = 1500$.
$0.0307 = k$	Simplify.

So, the equation (or model) for state income tax in Pennsylvania is

$$y = 0.0307x.$$

In other words, Pennsylvania has a state income tax rate of 3.07% of gross income. The graph of this equation is shown in Figure 1.102.

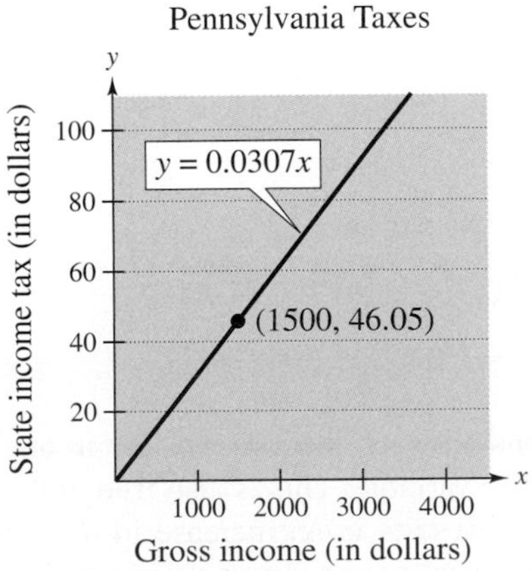

FIGURE 1.102

CHECKPOINT Now try Exercise 33.

Direct Variation as an *n*th Power

Another type of direct variation relates one variable to a *power* of another variable. For example, in the formula for the area of a circle

$$A = \pi r^2$$

the area A is directly proportional to the square of the radius r. Note that for this formula, π is the constant of proportionality.

STUDY TIP

Note that the direct variation model $y = kx$ is a special case of $y = kx^n$ with $n = 1$.

Direct Variation as an *n*th Power

The following statements are equivalent.

1. y **varies directly as the** n**th power** of x.
2. y is **directly proportional to the** n**th power** of x.
3. $y = kx^n$ for some constant k.

Example 4 Direct Variation as *n*th Power

The distance a ball rolls down an inclined plane is directly proportional to the square of the time it rolls. During the first second, the ball rolls 8 feet. (See Figure 1.103.)

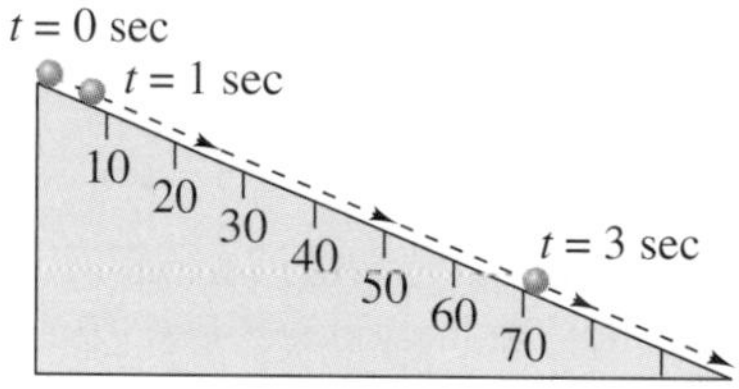

FIGURE 1.103

a. Write an equation relating the distance traveled to the time.

b. How far will the ball roll during the first 3 seconds?

Solution

a. Letting d be the distance (in feet) the ball rolls and letting t be the time (in seconds), you have

$$d = kt^2.$$

Now, because $d = 8$ when $t = 1$, you can see that $k = 8$, as follows.

$$d = kt^2$$

$$8 = k(1)^2$$

$$8 = k$$

So, the equation relating distance to time is

$$d = 8t^2.$$

b. When $t = 3$, the distance traveled is $d = 8(3)^2 = 8(9) = 72$ feet.

✓CHECKPOINT Now try Exercise 63.

In Examples 3 and 4, the direct variations are such that an *increase* in one variable corresponds to an *increase* in the other variable. This is also true in the model $d = \frac{1}{5}F$, $F > 0$, where an increase in F results in an increase in d. You should not, however, assume that this always occurs with direct variation. For example, in the model $y = -3x$, an increase in x results in a *decrease* in y, and yet y is said to vary directly as x.

Inverse Variation

Inverse Variation

The following statements are equivalent.

1. y **varies inversely** as x.
2. y is **inversely proportional** to x.
3. $y = \dfrac{k}{x}$ for some constant k.

If x and y are related by an equation of the form $y = k/x^n$, then y varies inversely as the nth power of x (or y is inversely proportional to the nth power of x).

Some applications of variation involve problems with *both* direct and inverse variation in the same model. These types of models are said to have **combined variation.**

Example 5 Direct and Inverse Variation

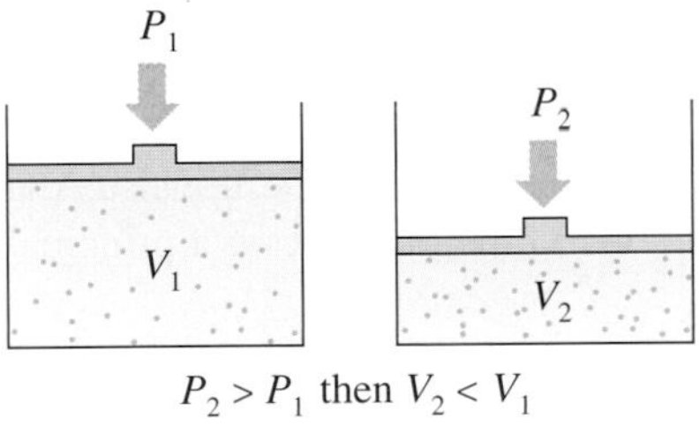

FIGURE 1.104 *If the temperature is held constant and pressure increases, volume decreases.*

A gas law states that the volume of an enclosed gas varies directly as the temperature *and* inversely as the pressure, as shown in Figure 1.104. The pressure of a gas is 0.75 kilogram per square centimeter when the temperature is 294 K and the volume is 8000 cubic centimeters. (a) Write an equation relating pressure, temperature, and volume. (b) Find the pressure when the temperature is 300 K and the volume is 7000 cubic centimeters.

Solution

a. Let V be volume (in cubic centimeters), let P be pressure (in kilograms per square centimeter), and let T be temperature (in Kelvin). Because V varies directly as T and inversely as P, you have

$$V = \frac{kT}{P}.$$

Now, because $P = 0.75$ when $T = 294$ and $V = 8000$, you have

$$8000 = \frac{k(294)}{0.75}$$

$$k = \frac{6000}{294} = \frac{1000}{49}.$$

So, the equation relating pressure, temperature, and volume is

$$V = \frac{1000}{49}\left(\frac{T}{P}\right).$$

b. When $T = 300$ and $V = 7000$, the pressure is

$$P = \frac{1000}{49}\left(\frac{300}{7000}\right) = \frac{300}{343} \approx 0.87 \text{ kilogram per square centimeter.}$$

✓CHECKPOINT Now try Exercise 65.

Joint Variation

In Example 5, note that when a direct variation and an inverse variation occur in the same statement, they are coupled with the word "and." To describe two different *direct* variations in the same statement, the word **jointly** is used.

Joint Variation

The following statements are equivalent.

1. z **varies jointly** as x and y.
2. z is **jointly proportional** to x and y.
3. $z = kxy$ for some constant k.

If x, y, and z are related by an equation of the form

$$z = kx^n y^m$$

then z varies jointly as the nth power of x and the mth power of y.

Example 6 Joint Variation

The *simple* interest for a certain savings account is jointly proportional to the time and the principal. After one quarter (3 months), the interest on a principal of \$5000 is \$43.75.

a. Write an equation relating the interest, principal, and time.

b. Find the interest after three quarters.

Solution

a. Let I = interest (in dollars), P = principal (in dollars), and t = time (in years). Because I is jointly proportional to P and t, you have

$$I = kPt.$$

For $I = 43.75$, $P = 5000$, and $t = \frac{1}{4}$, you have

$$43.75 = k(5000)\left(\frac{1}{4}\right)$$

which implies that $k = 4(43.75)/5000 = 0.035$. So, the equation relating interest, principal, and time is

$$I = 0.035Pt$$

which is the familiar equation for simple interest where the constant of proportionality, 0.035, represents an annual interest rate of 3.5%.

b. When $P = \$5000$ and $t = \frac{3}{4}$, the interest is

$$I = (0.035)(5000)\left(\frac{3}{4}\right)$$

$$= \$131.25.$$

✓CHECKPOINT Now try Exercise 67.

1.10 Exercises

VOCABULARY CHECK: Fill in the blanks.

1. Two techniques for fitting models to data are called direct ________ and least squares ________.
2. Statisticians use a measure called ________ of________ ________ to find a model that approximates a set of data most accurately.
3. An r-value of a set of data, also called a ________ ________, gives a measure of how well a model fits a set of data.
4. Direct variation models can be described as y varies directly as x, or y is ________ ________ to x.
5. In direct variation models of the form $y = kx$, k is called the ________ of ________.
6. The direct variation model $y = kx^n$ can be described as y varies directly as the nth power of x, or y is ________ ________ to the nth power of x.
7. The mathematical model $y = \dfrac{k}{x}$ is an example of ________ variation.
8. Mathematical models that involve both direct and inverse variation are said to have ________ variation.
9. The joint variation model $z = kxy$ can be described as z varies jointly as x and y, or z is ________ ________ to x and y.

---

1. ***Employment*** The total numbers of employees (in thousands) in the United States from 1992 to 2002 are given by the following ordered pairs.

   (1992, 128,105) (1998, 137,673)
   (1993, 129,200) (1999, 139,368)
   (1994, 131,056) (2000, 142,583)
   (1995, 132,304) (2001, 143,734)
   (1996, 133,943) (2002, 144,683)
   (1997, 136,297)

   A linear model that approximates the data is $y = 1767.0t + 123{,}916$, where y represents the number of employees (in thousands) and $t = 2$ represents 1992. Plot the actual data and the model on the same set of coordinate axes. How closely does the model represent the data? (Source: U.S. Bureau of Labor Statistics)

2. ***Sports*** The winning times (in minutes) in the women's 400-meter freestyle swimming event in the Olympics from 1948 to 2004 are given by the following ordered pairs.

   (1948, 5.30) (1980, 4.15)
   (1952, 5.20) (1984, 4.12)
   (1956, 4.91) (1988, 4.06)
   (1960, 4.84) (1992, 4.12)
   (1964, 4.72) (1996, 4.12)
   (1968, 4.53) (2000, 4.10)
   (1972, 4.32) (2004, 4.09)
   (1976, 4.16)

   A linear model that approximates the data is $y = -0.022t + 5.03$, where y represents the winning time (in minutes) and $t = 0$ represents 1950. Plot the actual data and the model on the same set of coordinate axes. How closely does the model represent the data? Does it appear that another type of model may be a better fit? Explain. (Source: *The World Almanac and Book of Facts*)

In Exercises 3–6, sketch the line that you think best approximates the data in the scatter plot. Then find an equation of the line. To print an enlarged copy of the graph, go to the website *www.mathgraphs.com*.

3.
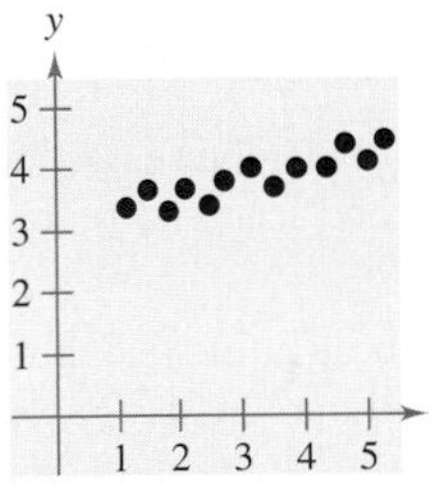

4.
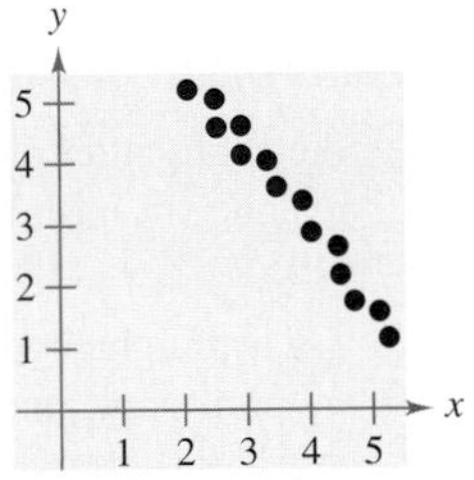

5.
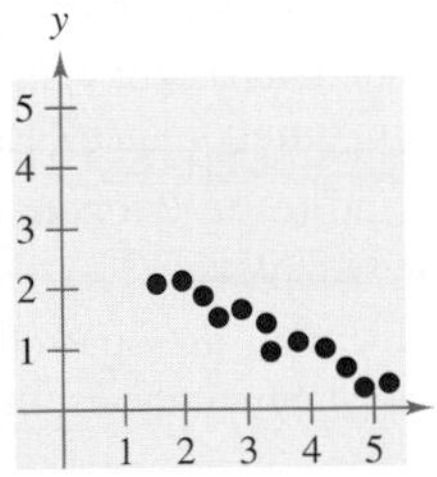

6.
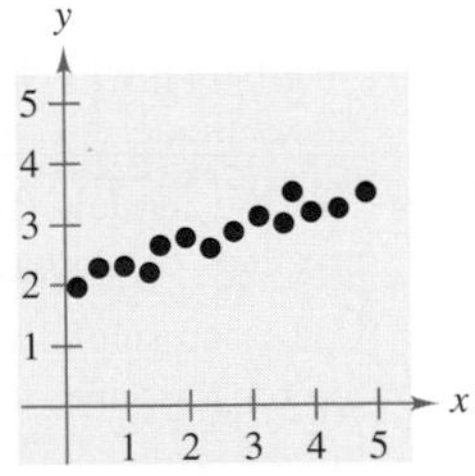

7. ***Sports*** The lengths (in feet) of the winning men's discus throws in the Olympics from 1912 to 2004 are listed below. (Source: *The World Almanac and Book of Facts*)

1912	148.3	1952	180.5	1980	218.7
1920	146.6	1956	184.9	1984	218.5
1924	151.3	1960	194.2	1988	225.8
1928	155.3	1964	200.1	1992	213.7
1932	162.3	1968	212.5	1996	227.7
1936	165.6	1972	211.3	2000	227.3
1948	173.2	1976	221.5	2004	229.3

(a) Sketch a scatter plot of the data. Let y represent the length of the winning discus throw (in feet) and let $t = 12$ represent 1912.

(b) Use a straightedge to sketch the best-fitting line through the points and find an equation of the line.

(c) Use the *regression* feature of a graphing utility to find the least squares regression line that fits the data.

(d) Compare the linear model you found in part (b) with the linear model given by the graphing utility in part (c).

(e) Use the models from parts (b) and (c) to estimate the winning men's discus throw in the year 2008.

(f) Use your school's library, the Internet, or some other reference source to analyze the accuracy of the estimate in part (e).

8. ***Revenue*** The total revenues (in millions of dollars) for Outback Steakhouse from 1995 to 2003 are listed below. (Source: Outback Steakhouse, Inc.)

1995	664.0	2000	1906.0
1996	937.4	2001	2127.0
1997	1151.6	2002	2362.1
1998	1358.9	2003	2744.4
1999	1646.0		

(a) Sketch a scatter plot of the data. Let y represent the total revenue (in millions of dollars) and let $t = 5$ represent 1995.

(b) Use a straightedge to sketch the best-fitting line through the points and find an equation of the line.

(c) Use the *regression* feature of a graphing utility to find the least squares regression line that fits the data.

(d) Compare the linear model you found in part (b) with the linear model given by the graphing utility in part (c).

(e) Use the models from parts (b) and (c) to estimate the revenues of Outback Steakhouse in 2005.

(f) Use your school's library, the Internet, or some other reference source to analyze the accuracy of the estimate in part (e).

9. ***Data Analysis: Broadway Shows*** The table shows the annual gross ticket sales S (in millions of dollars) for Broadway shows in New York City from 1995 through 2004. (Source: The League of American Theatres and Producers, Inc.)

Year	Sales, S
1995	406
1996	436
1997	499
1998	558
1999	588
2000	603
2001	666
2002	643
2003	721
2004	771

(a) Use a graphing utility to create a scatter plot of the data. Let $t = 5$ represent 1995.

(b) Use the *regression* feature of a graphing utility to find the equation of the least squares regression line that fits the data.

(c) Use the graphing utility to graph the scatter plot you found in part (a) and the model you found in part (b) in the same viewing window. How closely does the model represent the data?

(d) Use the model to estimate the annual gross ticket sales in 2005 and 2007.

(e) Interpret the meaning of the slope of the linear model in the context of the problem.

10. ***Data Analysis: Television Households*** The table shows the numbers x (in millions) of households with cable television and the numbers y (in millions) of households with color television sets in the United States from 1995 through 2002. (Source: Nielson Media Research; Television Bureau of Advertising, Inc.)

Households with cable, x	Households with color TV, y
63	94
65	95
66	97
67	98
75	99
77	101
80	102
86	105

(a) Use the *regression* feature of a graphing utility to find the equation of the least squares regression line that fits the data.

(b) Use the graphing utility to create a scatter plot of the data. Then graph the model you found in part (a) and the scatter plot in the same viewing window. How closely does the model represent the data?

(c) Use the model to estimate the number of households with color television sets if the number of households with cable television is 90 million.

(d) Interpret the meaning of the slope of the linear model in the context of the problem.

Think About It **In Exercises 11 and 12, use the graph to determine whether y varies directly as some power of x or inversely as some power of x. Explain.**

11.

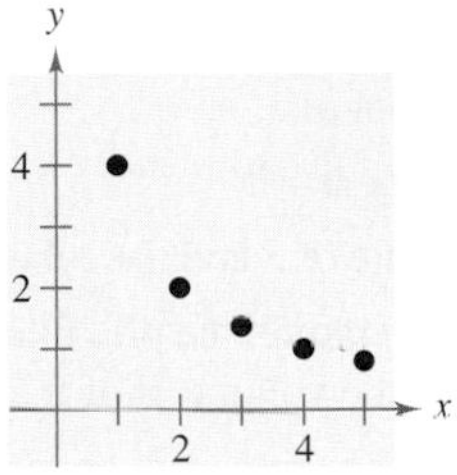

12.

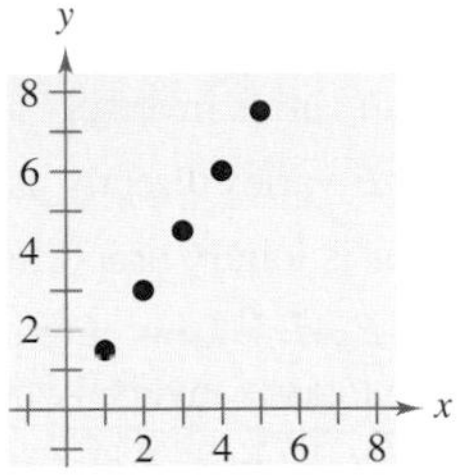

In Exercises 13–16, use the given value of k to complete the table for the direct variation model $y = kx^2$. Plot the points on a rectangular coordinate system.

x	2	4	6	8	10
$y = kx^2$					

13. $k = 1$

14. $k = 2$

15. $k = \frac{1}{2}$

16. $k = \frac{1}{4}$

In Exercises 17–20, use the given value of k to complete the table for the inverse variation model

$$y = \frac{k}{x^2}.$$

Plot the points on a rectangular coordinate system.

x	2	4	6	8	10
$y = \frac{k}{x^2}$					

17. $k = 2$

18. $k = 5$

19. $k = 10$

20. $k = 20$

In Exercises 21–24, determine whether the variation model is of the form $y = kx$ or $y = k/x$, and find k.

21.

x	5	10	15	20	25
y	1	$\frac{1}{2}$	$\frac{1}{3}$	$\frac{1}{4}$	$\frac{1}{5}$

22.

x	5	10	15	20	25
y	2	4	6	8	10

23.

x	5	10	15	20	25
y	-3.5	-7	-10.5	-14	-17.5

24.

x	5	10	15	20	25
y	24	12	8	6	$\frac{24}{5}$

Direct Variation **In Exercises 25–28, assume that y is directly proportional to x. Use the given x-value and y-value to find a linear model that relates y and x.**

25. $x = 5,\ y = 12$

26. $x = 2,\ y = 14$

27. $x = 10,\ y = 2050$

28. $x = 6,\ y = 580$

29. ***Simple Interest*** The simple interest on an investment is directly proportional to the amount of the investment. By investing $2500 in a certain bond issue, you obtained an interest payment of $87.50 after 1 year. Find a mathematical model that gives the interest I for this bond issue after 1 year in terms of the amount invested P.

30. ***Simple Interest*** The simple interest on an investment is directly proportional to the amount of the investment. By investing $5000 in a municipal bond, you obtained an interest payment of $187.50 after 1 year. Find a mathematical model that gives the interest I for this municipal bond after 1 year in terms of the amount invested P.

31. ***Measurement*** On a yardstick with scales in inches and centimeters, you notice that 13 inches is approximately the same length as 33 centimeters. Use this information to find a mathematical model that relates centimeters to inches. Then use the model to find the numbers of centimeters in 10 inches and 20 inches.

32. ***Measurement*** When buying gasoline, you notice that 14 gallons of gasoline is approximately the same amount of gasoline as 53 liters. Then use this information to find a linear model that relates gallons to liters. Then use the model to find the numbers of liters in 5 gallons and 25 gallons.

33. ***Taxes*** Property tax is based on the assessed value of a property. A house that has an assessed value of \$150,000 has a property tax of \$5520. Find a mathematical model that gives the amount of property tax y in terms of the assessed value x of the property. Use the model to find the property tax on a house that has an assessed value of \$200,000.

34. ***Taxes*** State sales tax is based on retail price. An item that sells for \$145.99 has a sales tax of \$10.22. Find a mathematical model that gives the amount of sales tax y in terms of the retail price x. Use the model to find the sales tax on a \$540.50 purchase.

Hooke's Law **In Exercises 35–38, use Hooke's Law for springs, which states that the distance a spring is stretched (or compressed) varies directly as the force on the spring.**

35. A force of 265 newtons stretches a spring 0.15 meter (see figure).

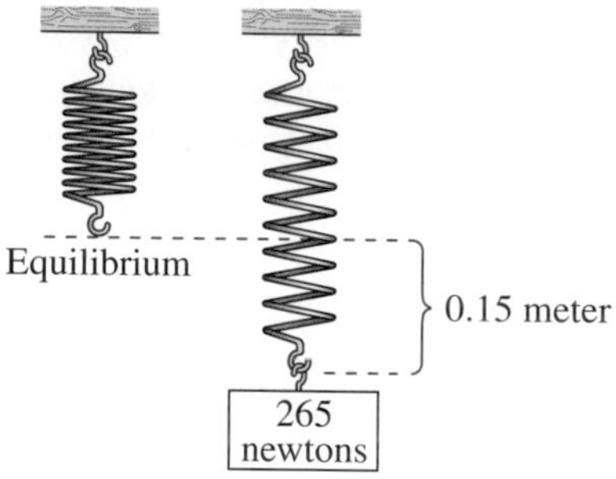

(a) How far will a force of 90 newtons stretch the spring?

(b) What force is required to stretch the spring 0.1 meter?

36. A force of 220 newtons stretches a spring 0.12 meter. What force is required to stretch the spring 0.16 meter?

37. The coiled spring of a toy supports the weight of a child. The spring is compressed a distance of 1.9 inches by the weight of a 25-pound child. The toy will not work properly if its spring is compressed more than 3 inches. What is the weight of the heaviest child who should be allowed to use the toy?

38. An overhead garage door has two springs, one on each side of the door (see figure). A force of 15 pounds is required to stretch each spring 1 foot. Because of a pulley system, the springs stretch only one-half the distance the door travels. The door moves a total of 8 feet, and the springs are at their natural length when the door is open. Find the combined lifting force applied to the door by the springs when the door is closed.

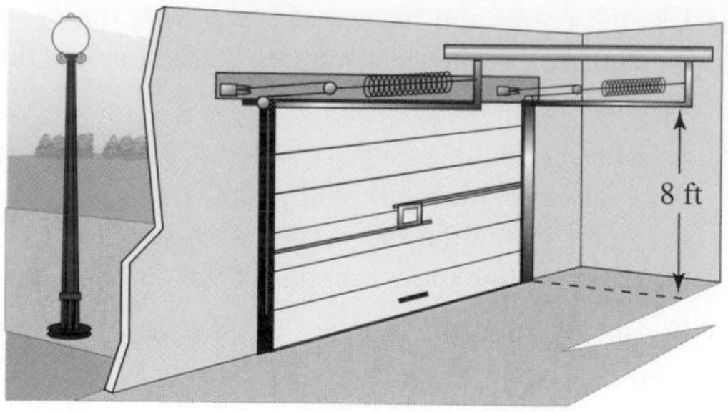

FIGURE FOR 38

In Exercises 39–48, find a mathematical model for the verbal statement.

39. A varies directly as the square of r.

40. V varies directly as the cube of e.

41. y varies inversely as the square of x.

42. h varies inversely as the square root of s.

43. F varies directly as g and inversely as r^2.

44. z is jointly proportional to the square of x and the cube of y.

45. ***Boyle's Law:*** For a constant temperature, the pressure P of a gas is inversely proportional to the volume V of the gas.

46. ***Newton's Law of Cooling:*** The rate of change R of the temperature of an object is proportional to the difference between the temperature T of the object and the temperature T_e of the environment in which the object is placed.

47. ***Newton's Law of Universal Gravitation:*** The gravitational attraction F between two objects of masses m_1 and m_2 is proportional to the product of the masses and inversely proportional to the square of the distance r between the objects.

48. ***Logistic Growth:*** The rate of growth R of a population is jointly proportional to the size S of the population and the difference between S and the maximum population size L that the environment can support.

In Exercises 49–54, write a sentence using the variation terminology of this section to describe the formula.

49. ***Area of a triangle:*** $A = \frac{1}{2}bh$

50. ***Surface area of a sphere:*** $S = 4\pi r^2$

51. ***Volume of a sphere:*** $V = \frac{4}{3}\pi r^3$

52. ***Volume of a right circular cylinder:*** $V = \pi r^2 h$

53. ***Average speed:*** $r = \dfrac{d}{t}$

54. ***Free vibrations:*** $\omega = \sqrt{\dfrac{kg}{W}}$

In Exercises 55–62, find a mathematical model representing the statement. (In each case, determine the constant of proportionality.)

55. A varies directly as r^2. ($A = 9\pi$ when $r = 3$.)

56. y varies inversely as x. ($y = 3$ when $x = 25$.)

57. y is inversely proportional to x. ($y = 7$ when $x = 4$.)

58. z varies jointly as x and y. ($z = 64$ when $x = 4$ and $y = 8$.)

59. F is jointly proportional to r and the third power of s. ($F = 4158$ when $r = 11$ and $s = 3$.)

60. P varies directly as x and inversely as the square of y. $\left(P = \frac{28}{3}\text{ when } x = 42 \text{ and } y = 9.\right)$

61. z varies directly as the square of x and inversely as y. ($z = 6$ when $x = 6$ and $y = 4$.)

62. v varies jointly as p and q and inversely as the square of s. ($v = 1.5$ when $p = 4.1$, $q = 6.3$, and $s = 1.2$.)

Ecology **In Exercises 63 and 64, use the fact that the diameter of the largest particle that can be moved by a stream varies approximately directly as the square of the velocity of the stream.**

63. A stream with a velocity of $\frac{1}{4}$ mile per hour can move coarse sand particles about 0.02 inch in diameter. Approximate the velocity required to carry particles 0.12 inch in diameter.

64. A stream of velocity v can move particles of diameter d or less. By what factor does d increase when the velocity is doubled?

Resistance **In Exercises 65 and 66, use the fact that the resistance of a wire carrying an electrical current is directly proportional to its length and inversely proportional to its cross-sectional area.**

65. If #28 copper wire (which has a diameter of 0.0126 inch) has a resistance of 66.17 ohms per thousand feet, what length of #28 copper wire will produce a resistance of 33.5 ohms?

66. A 14-foot piece of copper wire produces a resistance of 0.05 ohm. Use the constant of proportionality from Exercise 65 to find the diameter of the wire.

67. ***Work*** The work W (in joules) done when lifting an object varies jointly with the mass m (in kilograms) of the object and the height h (in meters) that the object is lifted. The work done when a 120-kilogram object is lifted 1.8 meters is 2116.8 joules. How much work is done when lifting a 100-kilogram object 1.5 meters?

68. ***Spending*** The prices of three sizes of pizza at a pizza shop are as follows.

9-inch: \$8.78, 12-inch: \$11.78, 15-inch: \$14.18

You would expect that the price of a certain size of pizza would be directly proportional to its surface area. Is that the case for this pizza shop? If not, which size of pizza is the best buy?

69. ***Fluid Flow*** The velocity v of a fluid flowing in a conduit is inversely proportional to the cross-sectional area of the conduit. (Assume that the volume of the flow per unit of time is held constant.) Determine the change in the velocity of water flowing from a hose when a person places a finger over the end of the hose to decrease its cross-sectional area by 25%.

70. ***Beam Load*** The maximum load that can be safely supported by a horizontal beam varies jointly as the width of the beam and the square of its depth, and inversely as the length of the beam. Determine the changes in the maximum safe load under the following conditions.

(a) The width and length of the beam are doubled.

(b) The width and depth of the beam are doubled.

(c) All three of the dimensions are doubled.

(d) The depth of the beam is halved.

Model It

71. ***Data Analysis: Ocean Temperatures*** An oceanographer took readings of the water temperatures C (in degrees Celsius) at several depths d (in meters). The data collected are shown in the table.

Depth, d	Temperature, C
1000	4.2°
2000	1.9°
3000	1.4°
4000	1.2°
5000	0.9°

(a) Sketch a scatter plot of the data.

(b) Does it appear that the data can be modeled by the inverse variation model $C = k/d$? If so, find k for each pair of coordinates.

(c) Determine the mean value of k from part (b) to find the inverse variation model $C = k/d$.

(d) Use a graphing utility to plot the data points and the inverse model in part (c).

(e) Use the model to approximate the depth at which the water temperature is 3°C.

72. ***Data Analysis: Physics Experiment*** An experiment in a physics lab requires a student to measure the compressed lengths y (in centimeters) of a spring when various forces of F pounds are applied. The data are shown in the table.

Force, F	Length, y
0	0
2	1.15
4	2.3
6	3.45
8	4.6
10	5.75
12	6.9

(a) Sketch a scatter plot of the data.

(b) Does it appear that the data can be modeled by Hooke's Law? If so, estimate k. (See Exercises 35–38.)

(c) Use the model in part (b) to approximate the force required to compress the spring 9 centimeters.

73. ***Data Analysis: Light Intensity*** A light probe is located x centimeters from a light source, and the intensity y (in microwatts per square centimeter) of the light is measured. The results are shown as ordered pairs (x, y).

(30, 0.1881) (34, 0.1543) (38, 0.1172)

(42, 0.0998) (46, 0.0775) (50, 0.0645)

A model for the data is $y = 262.76/x^{2.12}$.

(a) Use a graphing utility to plot the data points and the model in the same viewing window.

(b) Use the model to approximate the light intensity 25 centimeters from the light source.

74. ***Illumination*** The illumination from a light source varies inversely as the square of the distance from the light source. When the distance from a light source is doubled, how does the illumination change? Discuss this model in terms of the data given in Exercise 73. Give a possible explanation of the difference.

Synthesis

True or False? **In Exercises 75–77, decide whether the statement is true or false. Justify your answer.**

75. If y varies directly as x, then if x increases, y will increase as well.

76. In the equation for kinetic energy, $E = \frac{1}{2}mv^2$, the amount of kinetic energy E is directly proportional to the mass m of an object and the square of its velocity v.

77. If the correlation coefficient for a least squares regression line is close to -1, the regression line cannot be used to describe the data.

78. Discuss how well the data shown in each scatter plot can be approximated by a linear model.

(a)

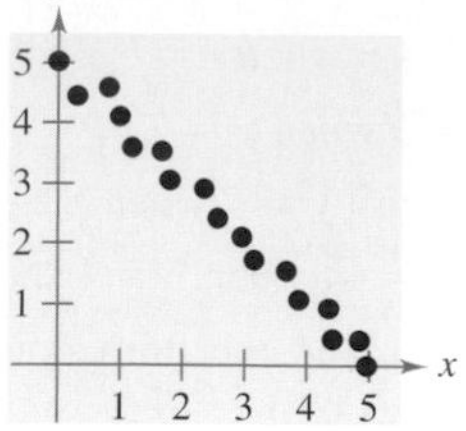

(b)

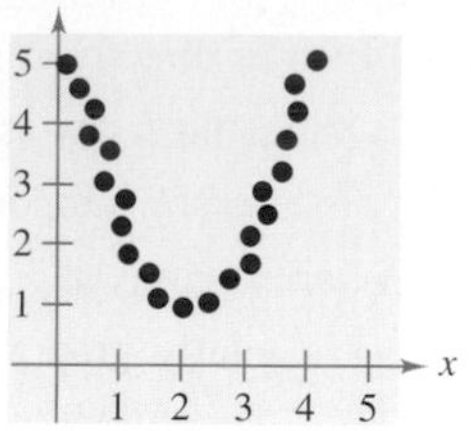

(c)

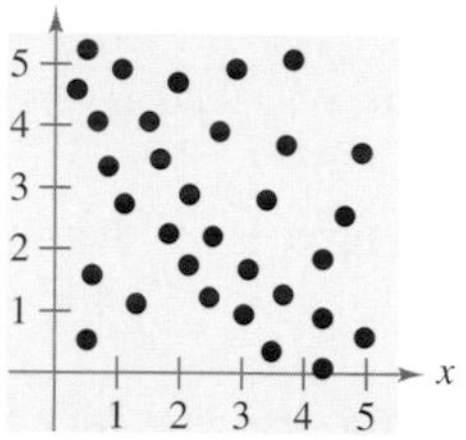

(d)

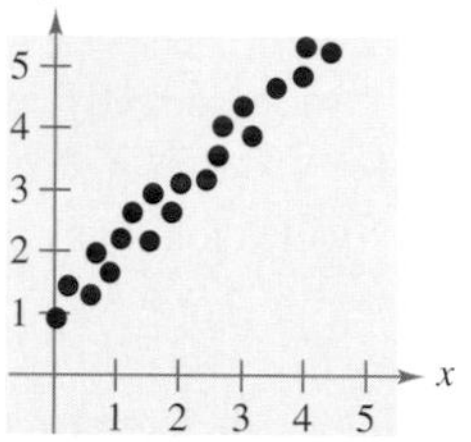

79. ***Writing*** A linear mathematical model for predicting prize winnings at a race is based on data for 3 years. Write a paragraph discussing the potential accuracy or inaccuracy of such a model.

80. ***Research Project*** Use your school's library, the Internet, or some other reference source to find data that you think describe a linear relationship. Create a scatter plot of the data and find the least squares regression line that represents the data points. Interpret the slope and y-intercept in the context of the data. Write a summary of your findings.

Skills Review

In Exercises 81–84, solve the inequality and graph the solution on the real number line.

81. $3x + 2 > 17$

82. $-7x + 10 \leq -1 + x$

83. $|2x - 1| < 9$

84. $|4 - 3x| + 7 \geq 12$

In Exercises 85 and 86, evaluate the function at each value of the independent variable and simplify.

85. $f(x) = \dfrac{x^2 + 5}{x - 3}$

(a) $f(0)$ (b) $f(-3)$ (c) $f(4)$

86. $f(x) = \begin{cases} -x^2 + 10, & x \geq -2 \\ 6x^2 - 1, & x < -2 \end{cases}$

(a) $f(-2)$ (b) $f(1)$ (c) $f(-8)$

87. **Make a Decision** To work an extended application analyzing registered voters in United States, visit this text's website at *college.hmco.com*. *(Data Source: U.S. Census Bureau)*

1 Chapter Summary

What did you learn?

	Review Exercises
Section 1.1	
☐ Plot points on the Cartesian plane *(p. 2)*.	1–4
☐ Use the Distance Formula to find the distance between two points *(p. 4)*.	5–8
☐ Use the Midpoint Formula to find the midpoint of a line segment *(p. 5)*.	5–8
☐ Use a coordinate plane and geometric formulas to model and solve real-life problems *(p. 6)*.	9–14
Section 1.2	
☐ Sketch graphs of equations *(p. 14)*.	15–24
☐ Find x- and y-intercepts of graphs of equations *(p. 17)*.	25–28
☐ Use symmetry to sketch graphs of equations *(p. 18)*.	29–36
☐ Find equations of and sketch graphs of circles *(p. 20)*.	37–44
☐ Use graphs of equations in solving real-life problems *(p. 21)*.	45, 46
Section 1.3	
☐ Use slope to graph linear equations in two variables *(p. 25)*.	47–50
☐ Find slopes of lines *(p. 27)*.	51–54
☐ Write linear equations in two variables *(p. 29)*.	55–62
☐ Use slope to identify parallel and perpendicular lines *(p. 30)*.	63, 64
☐ Use slope and linear equations in two variables to model and solve real-life problems *(p. 31)*.	65, 66
Section 1.4	
☐ Determine whether relations between two variables are functions *(p. 40)*.	67–70
☐ Use function notation and evaluate functions *(p. 42)*.	71, 72
☐ Find the domains of functions *(p. 44)*.	73–76
☐ Use functions to model and solve real-life problems *(p. 45)*.	77, 78
☐ Evaluate difference quotients *(p. 46)*.	79, 80
Section 1.5	
☐ Use the Vertical Line Test for functions *(p. 54)*.	81–84
☐ Find the zeros of functions *(p. 56)*.	85–88
☐ Determine intervals on which functions are increasing or decreasing and determine relative maximum and relative minimum values of functions *(p. 57)*.	89–94
☐ Determine the average rate of change of a function *(p. 59)*.	95–98
☐ Identify even and odd functions *(p. 60)*.	99–102

Section 1.6	
☐ Identify and graph linear, squaring *(p. 66)*, cubic, square root, reciprocal *(p. 68)*, step, and other piecewise-defined functions *(p. 69)*.	103–114
☐ Recognize graphs of parent functions *(p. 70)*.	115, 116
Section 1.7	
☐ Use vertical and horizontal shifts to sketch graphs of functions *(p. 74)*.	117–120
☐ Use reflections to sketch graphs of functions *(p. 76)*.	121–126
☐ Use nonrigid transformations to sketch graphs of functions *(p. 78)*.	127–130
Section 1.8	
☐ Add, subtract, multiply, and divide functions *(p. 84)*.	131, 132
☐ Find the composition of one function with another function *(p. 86)*.	133–136
☐ Use combinations and compositions of functions to model and solve real-life problems *(p. 88)*.	137, 138
Section 1.9	
☐ Find inverse functions informally and verify that two functions are inverse functions of each other *(p. 93)*.	139, 140
☐ Use graphs of functions to determine whether functions have inverse functions *(p. 95)*.	141, 142
☐ Use the Horizontal Line Test to determine if functions are one-to-one *(p. 96)*.	143–146
☐ Find inverse functions algebraically *(p. 97)*.	147–152
Section 1.10	
☐ Use mathematical models to approximate sets of data points *(p. 103)*.	153
☐ Use the *regression* feature of a graphing utility to find the equation of a least squares regression line *(p. 104)*.	154
☐ Write mathematical models for direct variation *(p. 105)*.	155
☐ Write mathematical models for direct variation as an nth power *(p. 106)*.	156, 157
☐ Write mathematical models for inverse variation *(p. 107)*.	158, 159
☐ Write mathematical models for joint variation *(p. 108)*.	160

1 Review Exercises

1.1 In Exercises 1 and 2, plot the points in the Cartesian plane.

1. $(2, 2), (0, -4), (-3, 6), (-1, -7)$
2. $(5, 0), (8, 1), (4, -2), (-3, -3)$

In Exercises 3 and 4, determine the quadrant(s) in which (x, y) is located so that the condition(s) is (are) satisfied.

3. $x > 0$ and $y = -2$
4. $y > 0$

In Exercises 5–8, (a) plot the points, (b) find the distance between the points, and (c) find the midpoint of the line segment joining the points.

5. $(-3, 8), (1, 5)$
6. $(-2, 6), (4, -3)$
7. $(5.6, 0), (0, 8.2)$
8. $(0, -1.2), (-3.6, 0)$

In Exercises 9 and 10, the polygon is shifted to a new position in the plane. Find the coordinates of the vertices of the polygon in its new position.

9. Original coordinates of vertices:

   $(4, 8), (6, 8), (4, 3), (6, 3)$

   Shift: three units downward, two units to the left

10. Original coordinates of vertices:

    $(0, 1), (3, 3), (0, 5), (-3, 3)$

    Shift: five units upward, four units to the left

11. ***Sales*** The Cheesecake Factory had annual sales of \$539.1 million in 2001 and \$773.8 million in 2003. Use the Midpoint Formula to estimate the sales in 2002. (Source: The Cheesecake Factory, Inc.)

12. ***Meteorology*** The apparent temperature is a measure of relative discomfort to a person from heat and high humidity. The table shows the actual temperatures x (in degrees Fahrenheit) versus the apparent temperatures y (in degrees Fahrenheit) for a relative humidity of 75%.

x	70	75	80	85	90	95	100
y	70	77	85	95	109	130	150

    (a) Sketch a scatter plot of the data shown in the table.

    (b) Find the change in the apparent temperature when the actual temperature changes from 70°F to 100°F.

13. ***Geometry*** The volume of a globe is about 47,712.94 cubic centimeters. Find the radius of the globe.

14. ***Geometry*** The volume of a rectangular package is 2304 cubic inches. The length of the package is 3 times its width, and the height is 1.5 times its width.

    (a) Draw a diagram that represents the problem. Label the height, width, and length accordingly.

    (b) Find the dimensions of the package.

1.2 In Exercises 15–18, complete a table of values. Use the solution points to sketch the graph of the equation.

15. $y = 3x - 5$
16. $y = -\frac{1}{2}x + 2$
17. $y = x^2 - 3x$
18. $y = 2x^2 - x - 9$

In Exercises 19–24, sketch the graph *by hand*.

19. $y - 2x - 3 = 0$
20. $3x + 2y + 6 = 0$
21. $y = \sqrt{5 - x}$
22. $y = \sqrt{x + 2}$
23. $y + 2x^2 = 0$
24. $y = x^2 - 4x$

In Exercises 25–28, find the x- and y-intercepts of the graph of the equation.

25. $y = 2x + 7$
26. $y = |x + 1| - 3$
27. $y = (x - 3)^2 - 4$
28. $y = x\sqrt{4 - x^2}$

In Exercises 29–36, use the algebraic tests to check for symmetry with respect to both axes and the origin. Then sketch the graph of the equation.

29. $y = -4x + 1$
30. $y = 5x - 6$
31. $y = 5 - x^2$
32. $y = x^2 - 10$
33. $y = x^3 + 3$
34. $y = -6 - x^3$
35. $y = \sqrt{x + 5}$
36. $y = |x| + 9$

In Exercises 37–42, find the center and radius of the circle and sketch its graph.

37. $x^2 + y^2 = 9$

38. $x^2 + y^2 = 4$

39. $(x + 2)^2 + y^2 = 16$

40. $x^2 + (y - 8)^2 = 81$

41. $\left(x - \frac{1}{2}\right)^2 + (y + 1)^2 = 36$

42. $(x + 4)^2 + \left(y - \frac{3}{2}\right)^2 = 100$

43. Find the standard form of the equation of the circle for which the endpoints of a diameter are $(0, 0)$ and $(4, -6)$.

44. Find the standard form of the equation of the circle for which the endpoints of a diameter are $(-2, -3)$ and $(4, -10)$.

45. ***Physics*** The force F (in pounds) required to stretch a spring x inches from its natural length (see figure) is

$$F = \frac{5}{4}x, \quad 0 \le x \le 20.$$

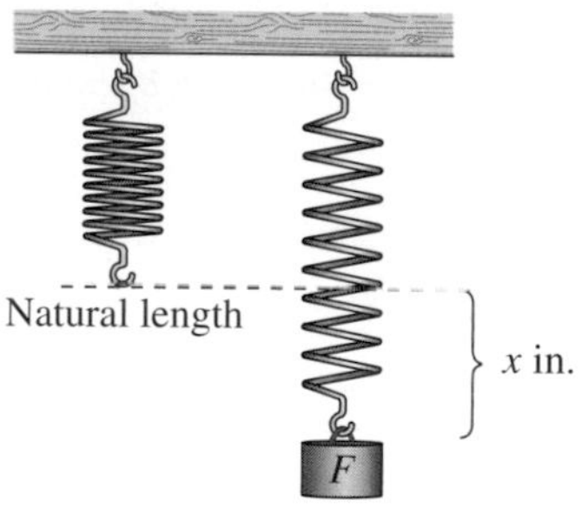

(a) Use the model to complete the table.

x	0	4	8	12	16	20
Force, F						

(b) Sketch a graph of the model.

(c) Use the graph to estimate the force necessary to stretch the spring 10 inches.

46. ***Number of Stores*** The numbers N of Target stores for the years 1994 to 2003 can be approximated by the model

$$N = 3.69t^2 + 939, \quad 4 \le t \le 13$$

where t is the time (in years), with $t = 4$ corresponding to 1994. (Source: Target Corp.)

(a) Sketch a graph of the model.

(b) Use the graph to estimate the year in which the number of stores was 1300.

1.3 In Exercises 47–50, find the slope and y-intercept (if possible) of the equation of the line. Sketch the line.

47. $y = 6$

48. $x = -3$

49. $y = 3x + 13$

50. $y = -10x + 9$

In Exercises 51–54, plot the points and find the slope of the line passing through the pair of points.

51. $(3, -4), (-7, 1)$

52. $(-1, 8), (6, 5)$

53. $(-4.5, 6), (2.1, 3)$

54. $(-3, 2), (8, 2)$

In Exercises 55–58, find the slope-intercept form of the equation of the line that passes through the given point and has the indicated slope. Sketch the line.

	Point	*Slope*
55.	$(0, -5)$	$m = \frac{3}{2}$
56.	$(-2, 6)$	$m = 0$
57.	$(10, -3)$	$m = -\frac{1}{2}$
58.	$(-8, 5)$	m is undefined.

In Exercises 59–62, find the slope-intercept form of the equation of the line passing through the points.

59. $(0, 0), (0, 10)$

60. $(2, 5), (-2, -1)$

61. $(-1, 4), (2, 0)$

62. $(11, -2), (6, -1)$

In Exercises 63 and 64, write the slope-intercept forms of the equations of the lines through the given point (a) parallel to the given line and (b) perpendicular to the given line.

	Point	*Line*
63.	$(3, -2)$	$5x - 4y = 8$
64.	$(-8, 3)$	$2x + 3y = 5$

Rate of Change **In Exercises 65 and 66, you are given the dollar value of a product in 2006 and the rate at which the value of the product is expected to change during the next 5 years. Use this information to write a linear equation that gives the dollar value V of the product in terms of the year t. (Let $t = 6$ represent 2006.)**

	2006 Value	*Rate*
65.	\$12,500	\$850 increase per year
66.	\$72.95	\$5.15 increase per year

1.4 In Exercises 67–70, determine whether the equation represents *y* as a function of *x*.

67. $16x - y^4 = 0$

68. $2x - y - 3 = 0$

69. $y = \sqrt{1 - x}$

70. $|y| = x + 2$

In Exercises 71 and 72, evaluate the function at each specified value of the independent variable and simplify.

71. $f(x) = x^2 + 1$

(a) $f(2)$ (b) $f(-4)$ (c) $f(t^2)$ (d) $f(t + 1)$

72. $h(x) = \begin{cases} 2x + 1, & x \le -1 \\ x^2 + 2, & x > -1 \end{cases}$

(a) $h(-2)$ (b) $h(-1)$ (c) $h(0)$ (d) $h(2)$

In Exercises 73–76, find the domain of the function. Verify your result with a graph.

73. $f(x) = \sqrt{25 - x^2}$

74. $f(x) = 3x + 4$

75. $h(x) = \dfrac{x}{x^2 - x - 6}$

76. $h(t) = |t + 1|$

77. ***Physics*** The velocity of a ball projected upward from ground level is given by $v(t) = -32t + 48$, where t is the time in seconds and v is the velocity in feet per second.

(a) Find the velocity when $t = 1$.

(b) Find the time when the ball reaches its maximum height. [*Hint:* Find the time when $v(t) = 0$.]

(c) Find the velocity when $t = 2$.

78. ***Mixture Problem*** From a full 50-liter container of a 40% concentration of acid, x liters is removed and replaced with 100% acid.

(a) Write the amount of acid in the final mixture as a function of x.

(b) Determine the domain and range of the function.

(c) Determine x if the final mixture is 50% acid.

In Exercises 79 and 80, find the difference quotient and simplify your answer.

79. $f(x) = 2x^2 + 3x - 1, \quad \dfrac{f(x + h) - f(x)}{h}, \quad h \neq 0$

80. $f(x) = x^3 - 5x^2 + x, \quad \dfrac{f(x + h) - f(x)}{h}, \quad h \neq 0$

1.5 In Exercises 81–84, use the Vertical Line Test to determine whether *y* is a function of *x*. To print an enlarged copy of the graph, go to the website *www.mathgraphs.com*.

81. $y = (x - 3)^2$

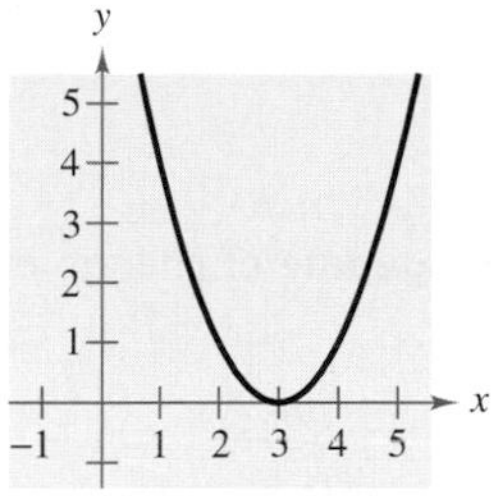

82. $y = -\frac{3}{5}x^3 - 2x + 1$

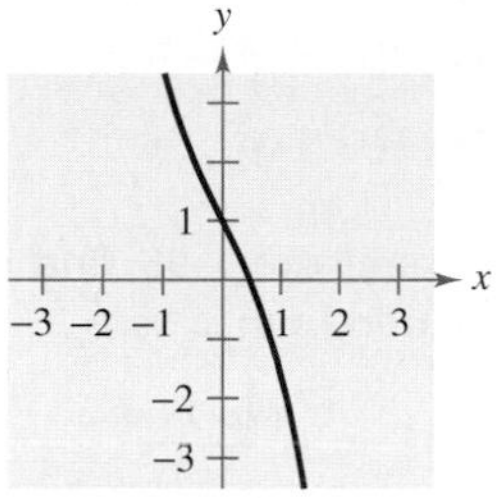

83. $x - 4 = y^2$

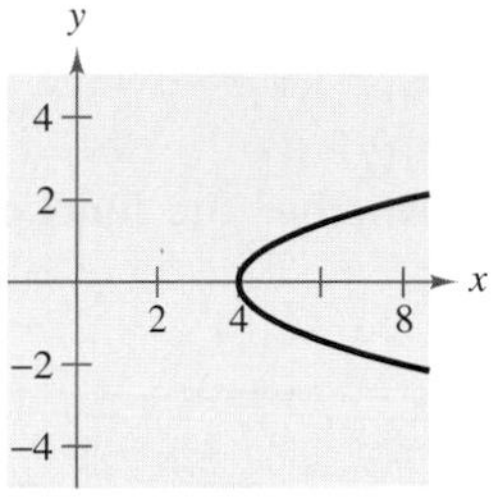

84. $x = -|4 - y|$

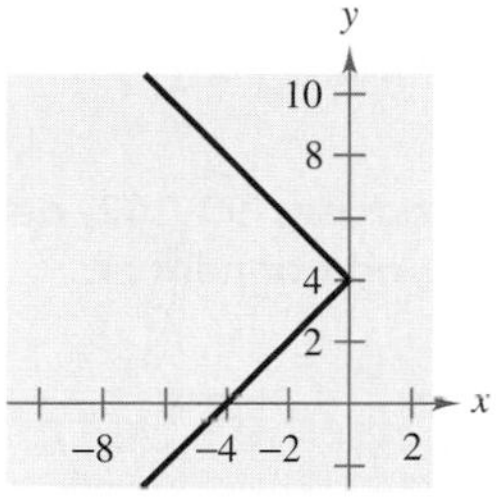

In Exercises 85–88, find the zeros of the function algebraically.

85. $f(x) = 3x^2 - 16x + 21$

86. $f(x) = 5x^2 + 4x - 1$

87. $f(x) = \dfrac{8x + 3}{11 - x}$

88. $f(x) = x^3 - x^2 - 25x + 25$

In Exercises 89 and 90, determine the intervals over which the function is increasing, decreasing, or constant.

89. $f(x) = |x| + |x + 1|$

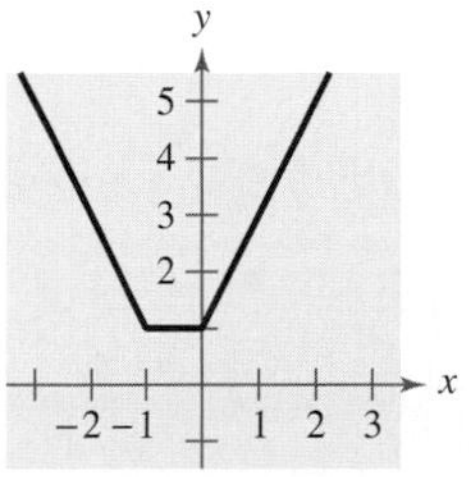

90. $f(x) = (x^2 - 4)^2$

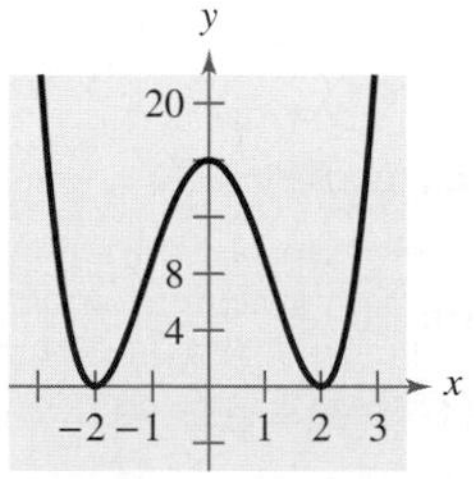

In Exercises 91–94, use a graphing utility to graph the function and approximate (to two decimal places) any relative minimum or relative maximum values.

91. $f(x) = -x^2 + 2x + 1$

92. $f(x) = x^4 - 4x^2 - 2$

93. $f(x) = x^3 - 6x^4$

94. $f(x) = x^3 - 4x^2 + x - 1$

In Exercises 95–98, find the average rate of change of the function from x_1 to x_2.

	Function	*x-Values*
95.	$f(x) = -x^2 + 8x - 4$	$x_1 = 0, x_2 = 4$
96.	$f(x) = x^3 + 12x - 2$	$x_1 = 0, x_2 = 4$
97.	$f(x) = 2 - \sqrt{x + 1}$	$x_1 = 3, x_2 = 7$
98.	$f(x) = 1 - \sqrt{x + 3}$	$x_1 = 1, x_2 = 6$

In Exercises 99–102, determine whether the function is even, odd, or neither.

99. $f(x) = x^5 + 4x - 7$

100. $f(x) = x^4 - 20x^2$

101. $f(x) = 2x\sqrt{x^2 + 3}$

102. $f(x) = \sqrt[5]{6x^2}$

1.6 **In Exercises 103–104, write the linear function f such that it has the indicated function values. Then sketch the graph of the function.**

103. $f(2) = -6, \; f(-1) = 3$

104. $f(0) = -5, \; f(4) = -8$

In Exercises 105–114, graph the function.

105. $f(x) = 3 - x^2$

106. $h(x) = x^3 - 2$

107. $f(x) = -\sqrt{x}$

108. $f(x) = \sqrt{x + 1}$

109. $g(x) = \dfrac{3}{x}$

110. $g(x) = \dfrac{1}{x + 5}$

111. $f(x) = [\![x]\!] - 2$

112. $g(x) = [\![x + 4]\!]$

113. $f(x) = \begin{cases} 5x - 3, & x \geq -1 \\ -4x + 5, & x < -1 \end{cases}$

114. $f(x) = \begin{cases} x^2 - 2, & x < -2 \\ 5, & -2 \leq x \leq 0 \\ 8x - 5, & x > 0 \end{cases}$

In Exercises 115 and 116, the figure shows the graph of a transformed parent function. Identify the parent function.

115.

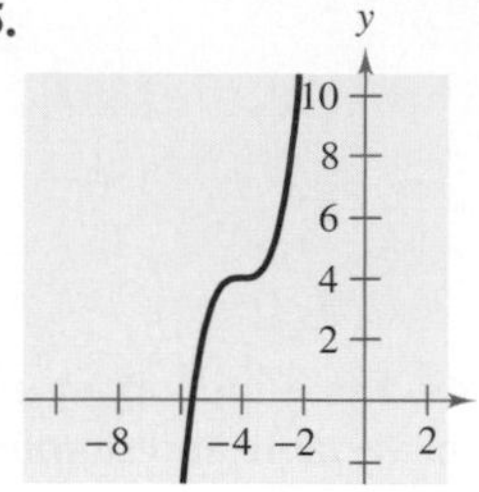

116.

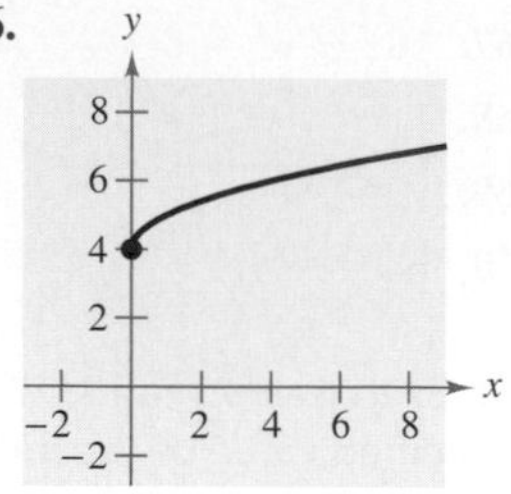

1.7 **In Exercises 117–130, h is related to one of the parent functions described in this chapter. (a) Identify the parent function f. (b) Describe the sequence of transformations from f to h. (c) Sketch the graph of h. (d) Use function notation to write h in terms of f.**

117. $h(x) = x^2 - 9$

118. $h(x) = (x - 2)^3 + 2$

119. $h(x) = \sqrt{x - 7}$

120. $h(x) = |x + 3| - 5$

121. $h(x) = -(x + 3)^2 + 1$

122. $h(x) = -(x - 5)^3 - 5$

123. $h(x) = -[\![x]\!] + 6$

124. $h(x) = -\sqrt{x + 1} + 9$

125. $h(x) = -|-x + 4| + 6$

126. $h(x) = -(x + 1)^2 - 3$

127. $h(x) = 5[\![x - 9]\!]$

128. $h(x) = -\frac{1}{3}x^3$

129. $h(x) = -2\sqrt{x - 4}$

130. $h(x) = \frac{1}{2}|x| - 1$

1.8 **In Exercises 131 and 132, find (a) $(f + g)(x)$, (b) $(f - g)(x)$, (c) $(fg)(x)$, and (d) $(f/g)(x)$. What is the domain of f/g?**

131. $f(x) = x^2 + 3, \quad g(x) = 2x - 1$

132. $f(x) = x^2 - 4, \quad g(x) = \sqrt{3 - x}$

In Exercises 133 and 134, find (a) $f \circ g$ and (b) $g \circ f$. Find the domain of each function and each composite function.

133. $f(x) = \frac{1}{3}x - 3, \quad g(x) = 3x + 1$

134. $f(x) = x^3 - 4, \quad g(x) = \sqrt[3]{x + 7}$

In Exercises 135 and 136, find two functions f and g such that $(f \circ g)(x) = h(x)$. (There are many correct answers.)

135. $h(x) = (6x - 5)^3$

136. $h(x) = \sqrt[3]{x + 2}$

137. ***Electronics Sales*** The factory sales (in millions of dollars) for VCRs $v(t)$ and DVD players $d(t)$ from 1997 to 2003 can be approximated by the functions

$$v(t) = -31.86t^2 + 233.6t + 2594$$

and

$$d(t) = -4.18t^2 + 571.0t - 3706$$

where t represents the year, with $t = 7$ corresponding to 1997. (Source: Consumer Electronics Association)

(a) Find and interpret $(v + d)(t)$.

(b) Use a graphing utility to graph $v(t)$, $d(t)$, and the function from part (a) in the same viewing window.

(c) Find $(v + d)(10)$. Use the graph in part (b) to verify your result.

138. ***Bacteria Count*** The number N of bacteria in a refrigerated food is given by

$$N(T) = 25T^2 - 50T + 300, \quad 2 \le T \le 20$$

where T is the temperature of the food in degrees Celsius. When the food is removed from refrigeration, the temperature of the food is given by

$$T(t) = 2t + 1, \quad 0 \le t \le 9$$

where t is the time in hours (a) Find the composition $N(T(t))$, and interpret its meaning in context, and (b) find the time when the bacterial count reaches 750.

1.9 In Exercises 139 and 140, find the inverse function of f informally. Verify that $f(f^{-1}(x)) = x$ and $f^{-1}(f(x)) = x$.

139. $f(x) = x - 7$

140. $f(x) = x + 5$

In Exercises 141 and 142, determine whether the function has an inverse function.

141.

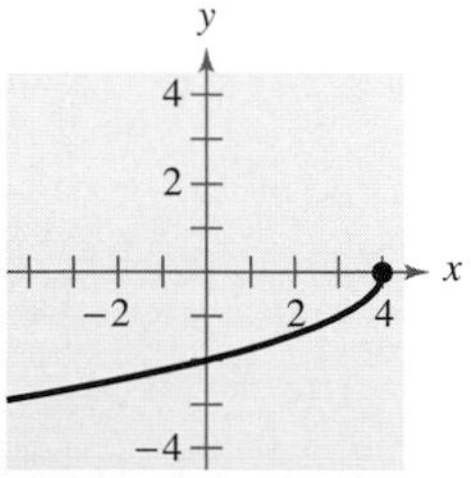

142.

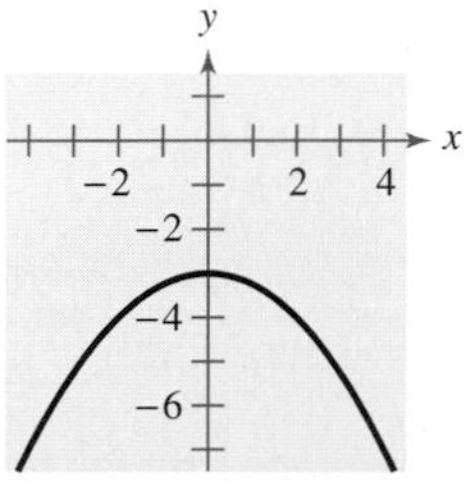

In Exercises 143–146, use a graphing utility to graph the function, and use the Horizontal Line Test to determine whether the function is one-to-one and so has an inverse function.

143. $f(x) = 4 - \frac{1}{3}x$

144. $f(x) = (x - 1)^2$

145. $h(t) = \dfrac{2}{t - 3}$

146. $g(x) = \sqrt{x + 6}$

In Exercises 147–150, (a) find the inverse function of f, (b) graph both f and f^{-1} on the same set of coordinate axes, (c) describe the relationship between the graphs of f and f^{-1}, and (d) state the domains and ranges of f and f^{-1}.

147. $f(x) = \frac{1}{2}x - 3$

148. $f(x) = 5x - 7$

149. $f(x) = \sqrt{x + 1}$

150. $f(x) = x^3 + 2$

In Exercises 151 and 152, restrict the domain of the function f to an interval over which the function is increasing and determine f^{-1} over that interval.

151. $f(x) = 2(x - 4)^2$

152. $f(x) = |x - 2|$

1.10 153. ***Median Income*** The median incomes I (in thousands of dollars) for married-couple families in the United States from 1995 through 2002 are shown in the table. A linear model that approximates these data is

$$I = 2.09t + 37.2$$

where t represents the year, with $t = 5$ corresponding to 1995. (Source: U.S. Census Bureau)

Year	Median income, I
1995	47.1
1996	49.7
1997	51.6
1998	54.2
1999	56.5
2000	59.1
2001	60.3
2002	61.1

(a) Plot the actual data and the model on the same set of coordinate axes.

(b) How closely does the model represent the data?

154. ***Data Analysis: Electronic Games*** The table shows the factory sales S (in millions of dollars) of electronic gaming software in the United States from 1995 through 2003. (Source: Consumer Electronics Association)

Year	Sales, S
1995	3000
1996	3500
1997	3900
1998	4480
1999	5100
2000	5850
2001	6725
2002	7375
2003	7744

(a) Use a graphing utility to create a scatter plot of the data. Let t represent the year, with $t = 5$ corresponding to 1995.

(b) Use the *regression* feature of the graphing utility to find the equation of the least squares regression line that fits the data. Then graph the model and the scatter plot you found in part (a) in the same viewing window. How closely does the model represent the data?

(c) Use the model to estimate the factory sales of electronic gaming software in the year 2008.

(d) Interpret the meaning of the slope of the linear model in the context of the problem.

155. ***Measurement*** You notice a billboard indicating that it is 2.5 miles or 4 kilometers to the next restaurant of a national fast-food chain. Use this information to find a mathematical model that relates miles to kilometers. Then use the model to find the numbers of kilometers in 2 miles and 10 miles.

156. ***Energy*** The power P produced by a wind turbine is proportional to the cube of the wind speed S. A wind speed of 27 miles per hour produces a power output of 750 kilowatts. Find the output for a wind speed of 40 miles per hour.

157. ***Frictional Force*** The frictional force F between the tires and the road required to keep a car on a curved section of a highway is directly proportional to the square of the speed s of the car. If the speed of the car is doubled, the force will change by what factor?

158. ***Demand*** A company has found that the daily demand x for its boxes of chocolates is inversely proportional to the price p. When the price is \$5, the demand is 800 boxes. Approximate the demand when the price is increased to \$6.

159. ***Travel Time*** The travel time between two cities is inversely proportional to the average speed. A train travels between the cities in 3 hours at an average speed of 65 miles per hour. How long would it take to travel between the cities at an average speed of 80 miles per hour?

160. ***Cost*** The cost of constructing a wooden box with a square base varies jointly as the height of the box and the square of the width of the box. A box of height 16 inches and width 6 inches costs \$28.80. How much would a box of height 14 inches and width 8 inches cost?

Synthesis

True or False? **In Exercises 161–163, determine whether the statement is true or false. Justify your answer.**

161. Relative to the graph of $f(x) = \sqrt{x}$, the function given by $h(x) = -\sqrt{x+9} - 13$ is shifted 9 units to the left and 13 units downward, then reflected in the x-axis.

162. If f and g are two inverse functions, then the domain of g is equal to the range of f.

163. If y is directly proportional to x, then x is directly proportional to y.

164. ***Writing*** Explain the difference between the Vertical Line Test and the Horizontal Line Test.

165. ***Writing*** Explain how to tell whether a relation between two variables is a function.

1 Chapter Test

Take this test as you would take a test in class. When you are finished, check your work against the answers given in the back of the book.

1. Plot the points $(-2, 5)$ and $(6, 0)$. Find the coordinates of the midpoint of the line segment joining the points and the distance between the points.
2. A cylindrical can has a volume of 600 cubic centimeters and a radius of 4 centimeters. Find the height of the can.

In Exercises 3–5, use intercepts and symmetry to sketch the graph of the equation.

3. $y = 3 - 5x$ 4. $y = 4 - |x|$ 5. $y = x^2 - 1$

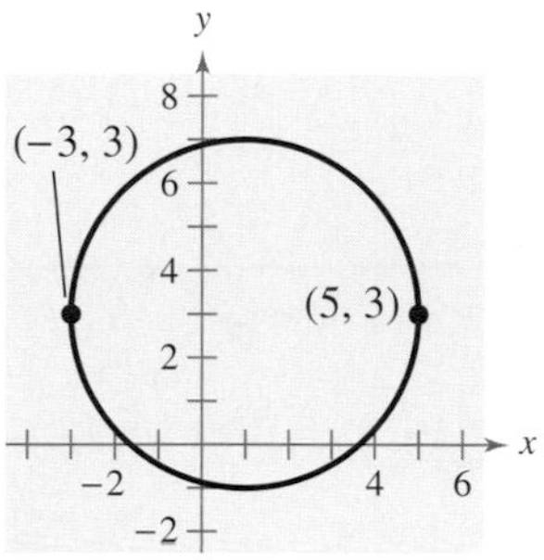

FIGURE FOR 6

6. Write the standard form of the equation of the circle shown at the left.

In Exercises 7 and 8, find an equation of the line passing through the points.

7. $(2, -3), (-4, 9)$ 8. $(3, 0.8), (7, -6)$

9. Find equations of the lines that pass through the point $(3, 8)$ and are (a) parallel to and (b) perpendicular to the line $-4x + 7y = -5$.
10. Evaluate $f(x) = \dfrac{\sqrt{x+9}}{x^2 - 81}$ at each value: (a) $f(7)$ (b) $f(-5)$ (c) $f(x - 9)$.
11. Determine the domain of $f(x) = \sqrt{100 - x^2}$.

In Exercises 12–14, (a) find the zeros of the function, (b) use a graphing utility to graph the function, (c) approximate the intervals over which the function is increasing, decreasing, or constant, and (d) determine whether the function is even, odd, or neither.

12. $f(x) = 2x^6 + 5x^4 - x^2$ 13. $f(x) = 4x\sqrt{3 - x}$ 14. $f(x) = |x + 5|$

15. Sketch the graph of $f(x) = \begin{cases} 3x + 7, & x \le -3 \\ 4x^2 - 1, & x > -3 \end{cases}$.

In Exercises 16 and 17, identify the parent function in the transformation. Then sketch a graph of the function.

16. $h(x) = -[\![x]\!]$ 17. $h(x) = -\sqrt{x + 5} + 8$

In Exercises 18 and 19, find (a) $(f + g)(x)$, (b) $(f - g)(x)$, (c) $(fg)(x)$, (d) $(f/g)(x)$, (e) $(f \circ g)(x)$, and (f) $(g \circ f)(x)$.

18. $f(x) = 3x^2 - 7,\quad g(x) = -x^2 - 4x + 5$ 19. $f(x) = \dfrac{1}{x},\quad g(x) = 2\sqrt{x}$

In Exercises 20–22, determine whether or not the function has an inverse function, and if so, find the inverse function.

20. $f(x) = x^3 + 8$ 21. $f(x) = |x^2 - 3| + 6$ 22. $f(x) = 3x\sqrt{x}$

In Exercises 23–25, find a mathematical model representing the statement. (In each case, determine the constant of proportionality.)

23. v varies directly as the square root of s. ($v = 24$ when $s = 16$.)
24. A varies jointly as x and y. ($A = 500$ when $x = 15$ and $y = 8$.)
25. b varies inversely as a. ($b = 32$ when $a = 1.5$.)

Proofs in Mathematics

What does the word *proof* mean to you? In mathematics, the word *proof* is used to mean simply a valid argument. When you are proving a statement or theorem, you must use facts, definitions, and accepted properties in a logical order. You can also use previously proved theorems in your proof. For instance, the Distance Formula is used in the proof of the Midpoint Formula below. There are several different proof methods, which you will see in later chapters.

The Midpoint Formula *(p. 5)*

The midpoint of the line segment joining the points (x_1, y_1) and (x_2, y_2) is given by the Midpoint Formula

$$\text{Midpoint} = \left(\frac{x_1 + x_2}{2}, \frac{y_1 + y_2}{2}\right).$$

The Cartesian Plane

The Cartesian plane was named after the French mathematician René Descartes (1596–1650). While Descartes was lying in bed, he noticed a fly buzzing around on the square ceiling tiles. He discovered that the position of the fly could be described by which ceiling tile the fly landed on. This led to the development of the Cartesian plane. Descartes felt that a coordinate plane could be used to facilitate description of the positions of objects.

Proof

Using the figure, you must show that $d_1 = d_2$ and $d_1 + d_2 = d_3$.

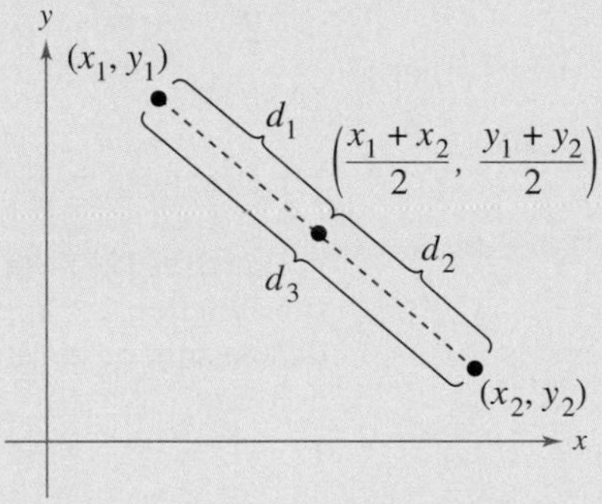

By the Distance Formula, you obtain

$$d_1 = \sqrt{\left(\frac{x_1 + x_2}{2} - x_1\right)^2 + \left(\frac{y_1 + y_2}{2} - y_1\right)^2}$$

$$= \frac{1}{2}\sqrt{(x_2 - x_1)^2 + (y_2 - y_1)^2}$$

$$d_2 = \sqrt{\left(x_2 - \frac{x_1 + x_2}{2}\right)^2 + \left(y_2 - \frac{y_1 + y_2}{2}\right)^2}$$

$$= \frac{1}{2}\sqrt{(x_2 - x_1)^2 + (y_2 - y_1)^2}$$

$$d_3 = \sqrt{(x_2 - x_1)^2 + (y_2 - y_1)^2}$$

So, it follows that $d_1 = d_2$ and $d_1 + d_2 = d_3$.

P.S. Problem Solving

This collection of thought-provoking and challenging exercises further explores and expands upon concepts learned in this chapter.

1. As a salesperson, you receive a monthly salary of \$2000, plus a commission of 7% of sales. You are offered a new job at \$2300 per month, plus a commission of 5% of sales.

(a) Write a linear equation for your current monthly wage W_1 in terms of your monthly sales S.

(b) Write a linear equation for the monthly wage W_2 of your new job offer in terms of the monthly sales S.

(c) Use a graphing utility to graph both equations in the same viewing window. Find the point of intersection. What does it signify?

(d) You think you can sell \$20,000 per month. Should you change jobs? Explain.

2. For the numbers 2 through 9 on a telephone keypad (see figure), create two relations: one mapping numbers onto letters, and the other mapping letters onto numbers. Are both relations functions? Explain.

3. What can be said about the sum and difference of each of the following?

(a) Two even functions (b) Two odd functions

(c) An odd function and an even function

4. The two functions given by

$f(x) = x$ and $g(x) = -x$

are their own inverse functions. Graph each function and explain why this is true. Graph other linear functions that are their own inverse functions. Find a general formula for a family of linear functions that are their own inverse functions.

5. Prove that a function of the following form is even.

$$y = a_{2n}x^{2n} + a_{2n-2}x^{2n-2} + \cdot \cdot \cdot + a_2x^2 + a_0$$

6. A miniature golf professional is trying to make a hole-in-one on the miniature golf green shown. A coordinate plane is placed over the golf green. The golf ball is at the point (2.5, 2) and the hole is at the point (9.5, 2). The professional wants to bank the ball off the side wall of the green at the point (x, y). Find the coordinates of the point (x, y). Then write an equation for the path of the ball.

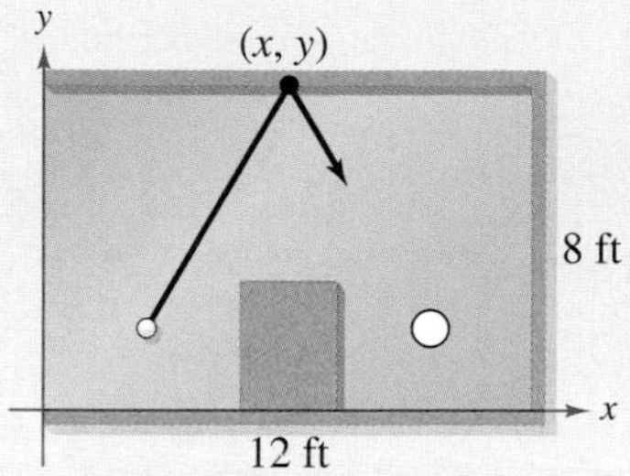

FIGURE FOR 6

7. At 2:00 P.M. on April 11, 1912, the *Titanic* left Cobh, Ireland, on her voyage to New York City. At 11:40 P.M. on April 14, the *Titanic* struck an iceberg and sank, having covered only about 2100 miles of the approximately 3400-mile trip.

(a) What was the total duration of the voyage in hours?

(b) What was the average speed in miles per hour?

(c) Write a function relating the distance of the *Titantic* from New York City and the number of hours traveled. Find the domain and range of the function.

(d) Graph the function from part (c).

8. Consider the function given by $f(x) = -x^2 + 4x - 3$. Find the average rate of change of the function from x_1 to x_2.

(a) $x_1 = 1, x_2 = 2$ (b) $x_1 = 1, x_2 = 1.5$

(c) $x_1 = 1, x_2 = 1.25$

(d) $x_1 = 1, x_2 = 1.125$

(e) $x_1 = 1, x_2 = 1.0625$

(f) Does the average rate of change seem to be approaching one value? If so, what value?

(g) Find the equations of the secant lines through the points $(x_1, f(x_1))$ and $(x_2, f(x_2))$ for parts (a)–(e).

(h) Find the equation of the line through the point $(1, f(1))$ using your answer from part (f) as the slope of the line.

9. Consider the functions given by $f(x) = 4x$ and $g(x) = x + 6$.

(a) Find $(f \circ g)(x)$.

(b) Find $(f \circ g)^{-1}(x)$.

(c) Find $f^{-1}(x)$ and $g^{-1}(x)$.

(d) Find $(g^{-1} \circ f^{-1})(x)$ and compare the result with that of part (b).

(e) Repeat parts (a) through (d) for $f(x) = x^3 + 1$ and $g(x) = 2x$.

(f) Write two one-to-one functions f and g, and repeat parts (a) through (d) for these functions.

(g) Make a conjecture about $(f \circ g)^{-1}(x)$ and $(g^{-1} \circ f^{-1})(x)$.

10. You are in a boat 2 miles from the nearest point on the coast. You are to travel to a point Q, 3 miles down the coast and 1 mile inland (see figure). You can row at 2 miles per hour and you can walk at 4 miles per hour.

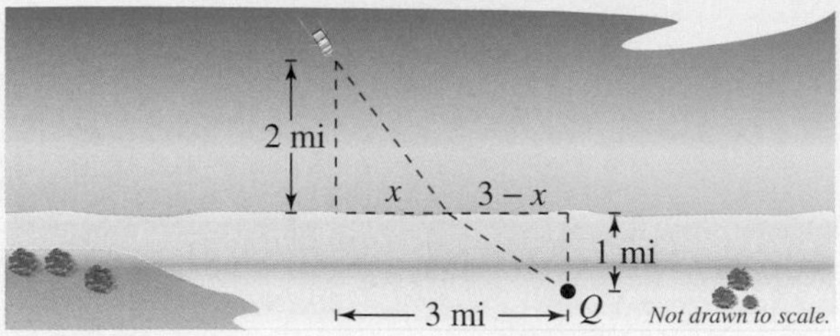

(a) Write the total time T of the trip as a function of x.

(b) Determine the domain of the function.

(c) Use a graphing utility to graph the function. Be sure to choose an appropriate viewing window.

(d) Use the *zoom* and *trace* features to find the value of x that minimizes T.

(e) Write a brief paragraph interpreting these values.

11. The **Heaviside function** $H(x)$ is widely used in engineering applications. (See figure.) To print an enlarged copy of the graph, go to the website *www.mathgraphs.com*.

$$H(x) = \begin{cases} 1, & x \geq 0 \\ 0, & x < 0 \end{cases}$$

Sketch the graph of each function by hand.

(a) $H(x) - 2$ (b) $H(x - 2)$ (c) $-H(x)$

(d) $H(-x)$ (e) $\frac{1}{2}H(x)$ (f) $-H(x - 2) + 2$

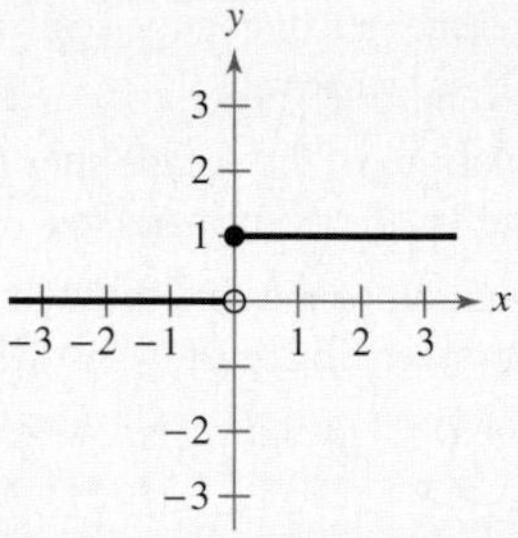

12. Let $f(x) = \dfrac{1}{1 - x}$.

(a) What are the domain and range of f?

(b) Find $f(f(x))$. What is the domain of this function?

(c) Find $f(f(f(x)))$. Is the graph a line? Why or why not?

13. Show that the Associative Property holds for compositions of functions—that is,

$$(f \circ (g \circ h))(x) = ((f \circ g) \circ h)(x).$$

14. Consider the graph of the function f shown in the figure. Use this graph to sketch the graph of each function. To print an enlarged copy of the graph, go to the website *www.mathgraphs.com*.

(a) $f(x + 1)$ (b) $f(x) + 1$ (c) $2f(x)$ (d) $f(-x)$

(e) $-f(x)$ (f) $|f(x)|$ (g) $f(|x|)$

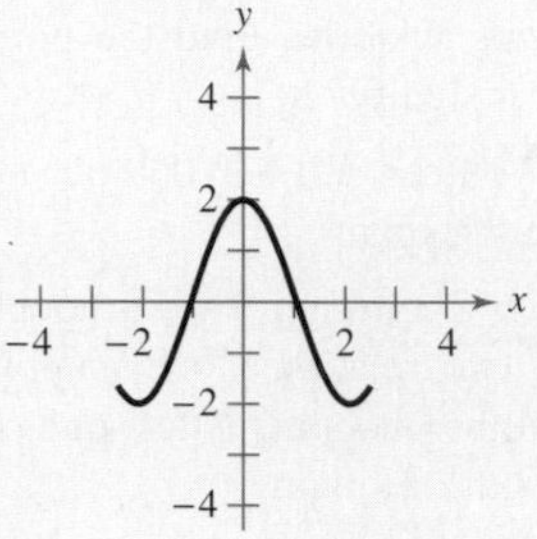

15. Use the graphs of f and f^{-1} to complete each table of function values.

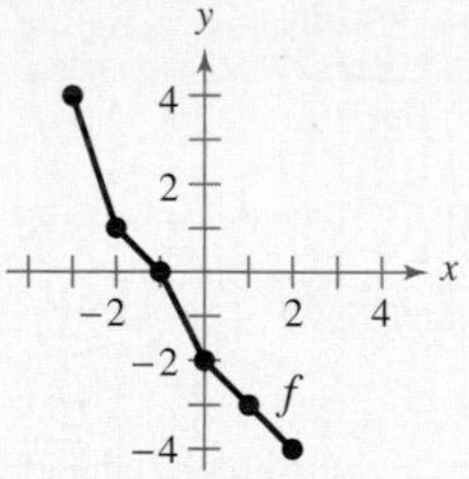

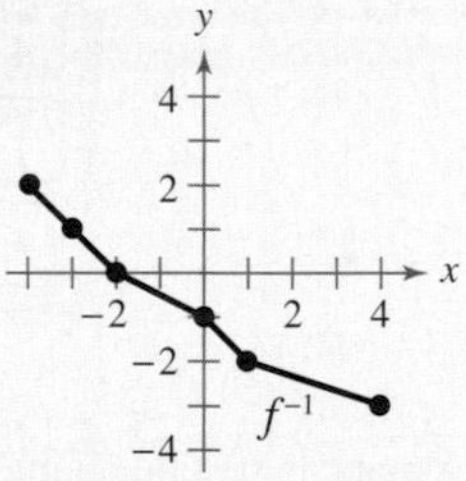

(a)

x	-4	-2	0	4
$(f(f^{-1}(x))$				

(b)

x	-3	-2	0	1
$(f + f^{-1})(x)$				

(c)

x	-3	-2	0	1
$(f \cdot f^{-1})(x)$				

(d)

x	-4	-3	0	4
$\lvert f^{-1}(x)\rvert$				

Polynomial and Rational Functions

2

2.1 Quadratic Functions and Models
2.2 Polynomial Functions of Higher Degree
2.3 Polynomial and Synthetic Division
2.4 Complex Numbers
2.5 Zeros of Polynomial Functions
2.6 Rational Functions
2.7 Nonlinear Inequalities

Quadratic functions are often used to model real-life phenomena, such as the path of a diver.

SELECTED APPLICATIONS

Polynomial and rational functions have many real-life applications. The applications listed below represent a small sample of the applications in this chapter.

- Path of a Diver, Exercise 77, page 136
- Data Analysis: Home Prices, Exercises 93–96, page 151
- Data Analysis: Cable Television, Exercise 74, page 161
- Advertising Cost, Exercise 105, page 181
- Athletics, Exercise 109, page 182
- Recycling, Exercise 112, page 195
- Average Speed, Exercise 79, page 196
- Height of a Projectile, Exercise 67, page 205

2.1 Quadratic Functions and Models

What you should learn

- Analyze graphs of quadratic functions.
- Write quadratic functions in standard form and use the results to sketch graphs of functions.
- Use quadratic functions to model and solve real-life problems.

Why you should learn it

Quadratic functions can be used to model data to analyze consumer behavior. For instance, in Exercise 83 on page 137, you will use a quadratic function to model the revenue earned from manufacturing handheld video games.

The Graph of a Quadratic Function

In this and the next section, you will study the graphs of polynomial functions. In Section 1.6, you were introduced to the following basic functions.

$f(x) = ax + b$ Linear function

$f(x) = c$ Constant function

$f(x) = x^2$ Squaring function

These functions are examples of **polynomial functions.**

Definition of Polynomial Function

Let n be a nonnegative integer and let $a_n, a_{n-1}, \ldots, a_2, a_1, a_0$ be real numbers with $a_n \neq 0$. The function given by

$$f(x) = a_n x^n + a_{n-1}x^{n-1} + \cdots + a_2x^2 + a_1x + a_0$$

is called a **polynomial function of x with degree n.**

Polynomial functions are classified by degree. For instance, a constant function has degree 0 and a linear function has degree 1. In this section, you will study second-degree polynomial functions, which are called **quadratic functions.**

For instance, each of the following functions is a quadratic function.

$$f(x) = x^2 + 6x + 2$$

$$g(x) = 2(x + 1)^2 - 3$$

$$h(x) = 9 + \tfrac{1}{4}x^2$$

$$k(x) = -3x^2 + 4$$

$$m(x) = (x - 2)(x + 1)$$

Note that the squaring function is a simple quadratic function that has degree 2.

Definition of Quadratic Function

Let a, b, and c be real numbers with $a \neq 0$. The function given by

$$f(x) = ax^2 + bx + c \qquad \text{Quadratic function}$$

is called a **quadratic function.**

The graph of a quadratic function is a special type of "U"-shaped curve called a **parabola.** Parabolas occur in many real-life applications—especially those involving reflective properties of satellite dishes and flashlight reflectors. You will study these properties in Section 10.2.

All parabolas are symmetric with respect to a line called the **axis of symmetry,** or simply the **axis** of the parabola. The point where the axis intersects the parabola is the **vertex** of the parabola, as shown in Figure 2.1. If the leading coefficient is positive, the graph of

$$f(x) = ax^2 + bx + c$$

is a parabola that opens upward. If the leading coefficient is negative, the graph of

$$f(x) = ax^2 + bx + c$$

is a parabola that opens downward.

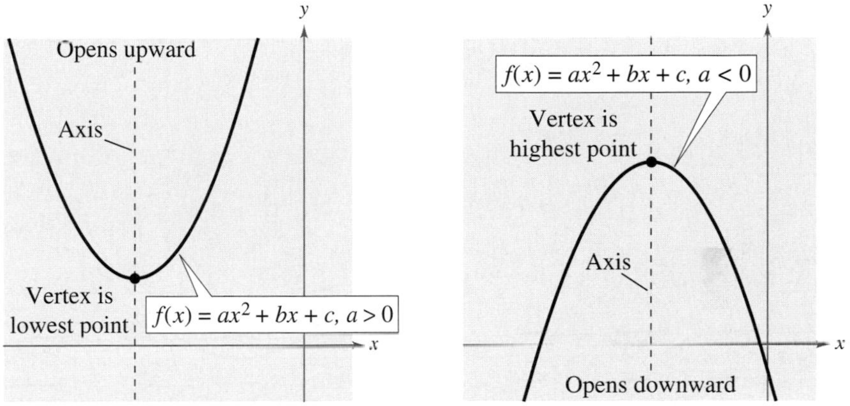

Leading coefficient is positive. *Leading coefficient is negative.*

FIGURE 2.1

The simplest type of quadratic function is

$$f(x) = ax^2.$$

Its graph is a parabola whose vertex is (0, 0). If $a > 0$, the vertex is the point with the *minimum* y-value on the graph, and if $a < 0$, the vertex is the point with the *maximum* y-value on the graph, as shown in Figure 2.2.

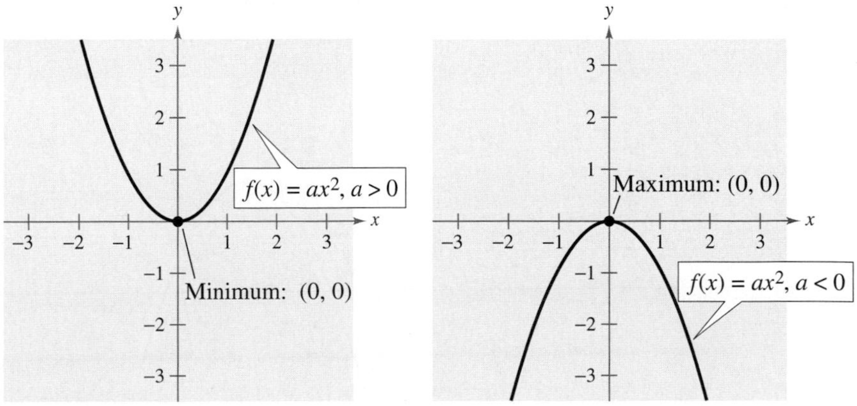

Leading coefficient is positive. *Leading coefficient is negative.*

FIGURE 2.2

When sketching the graph of $f(x) = ax^2$, it is helpful to use the graph of $y = x^2$ as a reference, as discussed in Section 1.7.

Exploration

Graph $y = ax^2$ for $a = -2, -1, -0.5, 0.5, 1,$ and 2. How does changing the value of a affect the graph?

Graph $y = (x - h)^2$ for $h = -4, -2, 2,$ and 4. How does changing the value of h affect the graph?

Graph $y = x^2 + k$ for $k = -4, -2, 2,$ and 4. How does changing the value of k affect the graph?

Example 1 Sketching Graphs of Quadratic Functions

a. Compare the graphs of $y = x^2$ and $f(x) = \frac{1}{3}x^2$.

b. Compare the graphs of $y = x^2$ and $g(x) = 2x^2$.

Solution

a. Compared with $y = x^2$, each output of $f(x) = \frac{1}{3}x^2$ "shrinks" by a factor of $\frac{1}{3}$, creating the broader parabola shown in Figure 2.3.

b. Compared with $y = x^2$, each output of $g(x) = 2x^2$ "stretches" by a factor of 2, creating the narrower parabola shown in Figure 2.4.

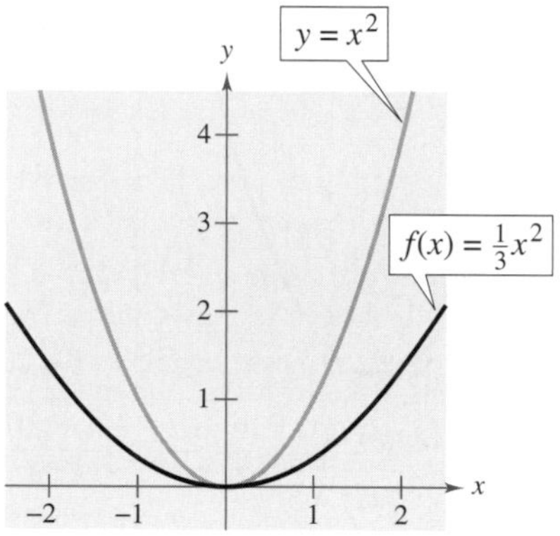

FIGURE 2.3

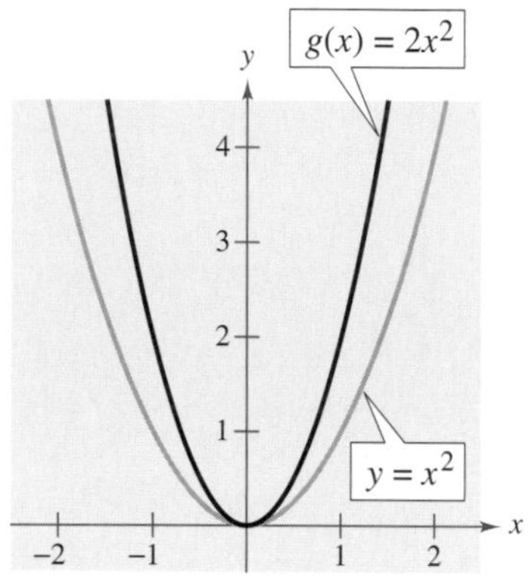

FIGURE 2.4

✓CHECKPOINT Now try Exercise 9.

In Example 1, note that the coefficient a determines how widely the parabola given by $f(x) = ax^2$ opens. If $|a|$ is small, the parabola opens more widely than if $|a|$ is large.

Recall from Section 1.7 that the graphs of $y = f(x \pm c)$, $y = f(x) \pm c$, $y = f(-x)$, and $y = -f(x)$ are rigid transformations of the graph of $y = f(x)$. For instance, in Figure 2.5, notice how the graph of $y = x^2$ can be transformed to produce the graphs of $f(x) = -x^2 + 1$ and $g(x) = (x + 2)^2 - 3$.

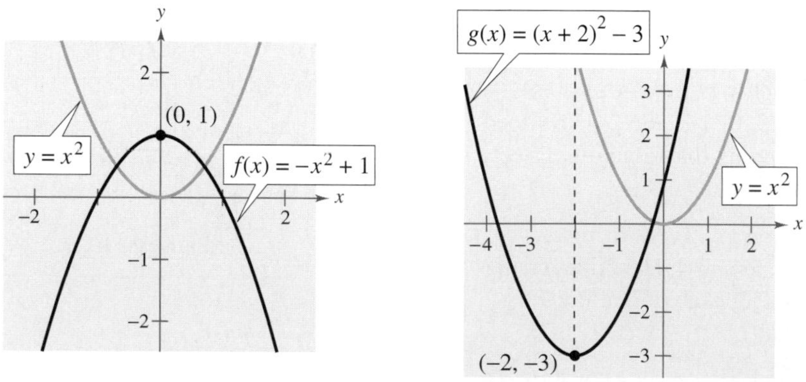

Reflection in x-axis followed by an upward shift of one unit

Left shift of two units followed by a downward shift of three units

FIGURE 2.5

STUDY TIP

The standard form of a quadratic function identifies four basic transformations of the graph of $y = x^2$.

a. The factor $|a|$ produces a vertical stretch or shrink.

b. If $a < 0$, the graph is reflected in the x-axis.

c. The factor $(x - h)^2$ represents a horizontal shift of h units.

d. The term k represents a vertical shift of k units.

The Standard Form of a Quadratic Function

The **standard form** of a quadratic function is $f(x) = a(x - h)^2 + k$. This form is especially convenient for sketching a parabola because it identifies the vertex of the parabola as (h, k).

Standard Form of a Quadratic Function

The quadratic function given by

$$f(x) = a(x - h)^2 + k, \qquad a \neq 0$$

is in **standard form.** The graph of f is a parabola whose axis is the vertical line $x = h$ and whose vertex is the point (h, k). If $a > 0$, the parabola opens upward, and if $a < 0$, the parabola opens downward.

To graph a parabola, it is helpful to begin by writing the quadratic function in standard form using the process of completing the square, as illustrated in Example 2. In this example, notice that when completing the square, you *add and subtract* the square of half the coefficient of x within the parentheses instead of adding the value to each side of the equation as is done in Appendix A.5.

Example 2 Graphing a Parabola in Standard Form

Sketch the graph of $f(x) = 2x^2 + 8x + 7$ and identify the vertex and the axis of the parabola.

Solution

Begin by writing the quadratic function in standard form. Notice that the first step in completing the square is to factor out any coefficient of x^2 that is not 1.

$f(x) = 2x^2 + 8x + 7$ Write original function.

$= 2(x^2 + 4x) + 7$ Factor 2 out of x-terms.

$= 2(x^2 + 4x + 4 - 4) + 7$ Add and subtract 4 within parentheses.

$(4/2)^2$

After adding and subtracting 4 within the parentheses, you must now regroup the terms to form a perfect square trinomial. The -4 can be removed from inside the parentheses; however, because of the 2 outside of the parentheses, you must multiply -4 by 2, as shown below.

$f(x) = 2(x^2 + 4x + 4) - 2(4) + 7$ Regroup terms.

$= 2(x^2 + 4x + 4) - 8 + 7$ Simplify.

$= 2(x + 2)^2 - 1$ Write in standard form.

From this form, you can see that the graph of f is a parabola that opens upward and has its vertex at $(-2, -1)$. This corresponds to a left shift of two units and a downward shift of one unit relative to the graph of $y = 2x^2$, as shown in Figure 2.6. In the figure, you can see that the axis of the parabola is the vertical line through the vertex, $x = -2$.

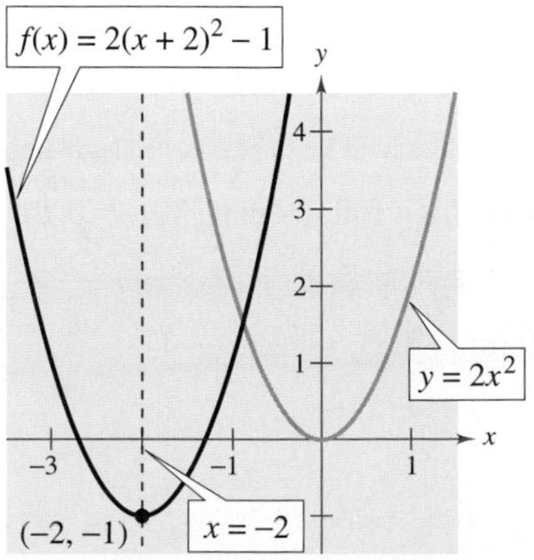

FIGURE 2.6

CHECKPOINT Now try Exercise 13.

To find the x-intercepts of the graph of $f(x) = ax^2 + bx + c$, you must solve the equation $ax^2 + bx + c = 0$. If $ax^2 + bx + c$ does not factor, you can use the Quadratic Formula to find the x-intercepts. Remember, however, that a parabola may not have x-intercepts.

Example 3 Finding the Vertex and x-Intercepts of a Parabola

Sketch the graph of $f(x) = -x^2 + 6x - 8$ and identify the vertex and x-intercepts.

Solution

$$f(x) = -x^2 + 6x - 8 \qquad \text{Write original function.}$$
$$= -(x^2 - 6x) - 8 \qquad \text{Factor } -1 \text{ out of } x\text{-terms.}$$
$$= -(x^2 - 6x + 9 - 9) - 8 \qquad \text{Add and subtract 9 within parentheses.}$$

$(-6/2)^2$

$$= -(x^2 - 6x + 9) - (-9) - 8 \qquad \text{Regroup terms.}$$
$$= -(x - 3)^2 + 1 \qquad \text{Write in standard form.}$$

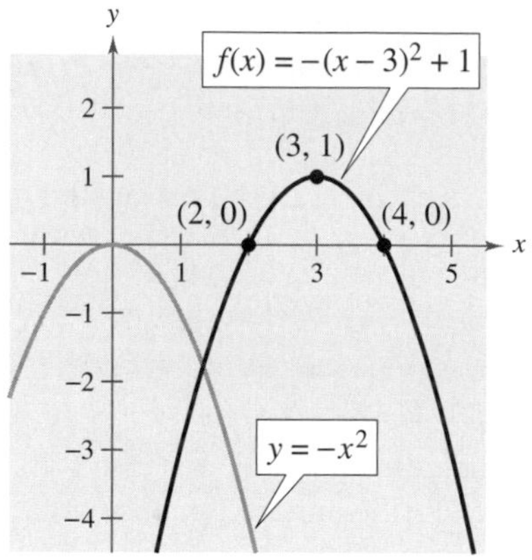

FIGURE 2.7

From this form, you can see that f is a parabola that opens downward with vertex $(3, 1)$. The x-intercepts of the graph are determined as follows.

$$-(x^2 - 6x + 8) = 0 \qquad \text{Factor out } -1.$$
$$-(x - 2)(x - 4) = 0 \qquad \text{Factor.}$$
$$x - 2 = 0 \quad \Rightarrow \quad x = 2 \qquad \text{Set 1st factor equal to 0.}$$
$$x - 4 = 0 \quad \Rightarrow \quad x = 4 \qquad \text{Set 2nd factor equal to 0.}$$

So, the x-intercepts are $(2, 0)$ and $(4, 0)$, as shown in Figure 2.7.

CHECKPOINT Now try Exercise 19.

Example 4 Writing the Equation of a Parabola

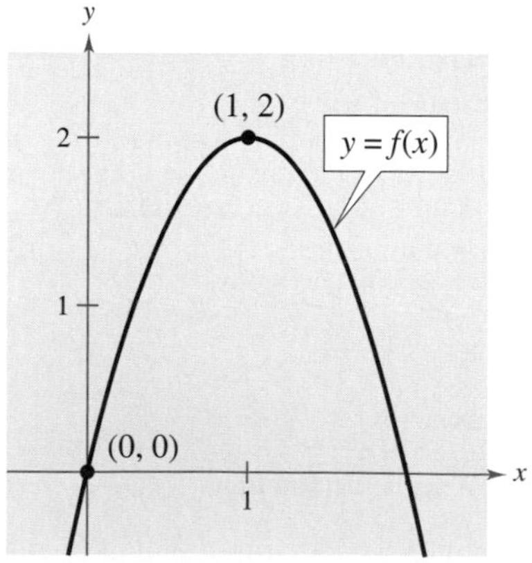

FIGURE 2.8

Write the standard form of the equation of the parabola whose vertex is $(1, 2)$ and that passes through the point $(0, 0)$, as shown in Figure 2.8.

Solution

Because the vertex of the parabola is at $(h, k) = (1, 2)$, the equation has the form

$$f(x) = a(x - 1)^2 + 2. \qquad \text{Substitute for } h \text{ and } k \text{ in standard form.}$$

Because the parabola passes through the point $(0, 0)$, it follows that $f(0) = 0$. So,

$$0 = a(0 - 1)^2 + 2 \quad \Rightarrow \quad a = -2 \qquad \text{Substitute 0 for } x\text{; solve for } a.$$

which implies that the equation in standard form is $f(x) = -2(x - 1)^2 + 2$.

CHECKPOINT Now try Exercise 43.

Applications

Many applications involve finding the maximum or minimum value of a quadratic function. You can find the maximum or minimum value of a quadratic function by locating the vertex of the graph of the function.

Vertex of a Parabola

The vertex of the graph of $f(x) = ax^2 + bx + c$ is $\left(-\frac{b}{2a}, f\left(-\frac{b}{2a}\right)\right)$.

1. If $a > 0$, has a *minimum* at $x = -\frac{b}{2a}$.
2. If $a < 0$, has a *maximum* at $x = -\frac{b}{2a}$.

Example 5 The Maximum Height of a Baseball

A baseball is hit at a point 3 feet above the ground at a velocity of 100 feet per second and at an angle of 45° with respect to the ground. The path of the baseball is given by the function $f(x) = -0.0032x^2 + x + 3$, where $f(x)$ is the height of the baseball (in feet) and x is the horizontal distance from home plate (in feet). What is the maximum height reached by the baseball?

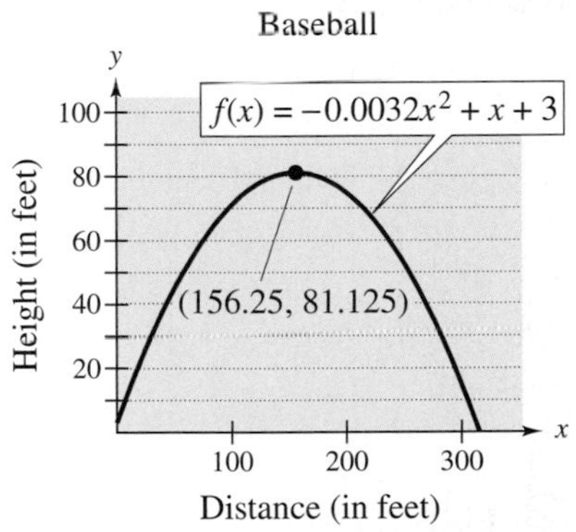

FIGURE 2.9

Solution

From the given function, you can see that $a = -0.0032$ and $b = 1$. Because the function has a maximum when $x = -b/(2a)$, you can conclude that the baseball reaches its maximum height when it is x feet from home plate, where x is

$$x = -\frac{b}{2a}x = -\frac{b}{2a} = -\frac{1}{2(-0.0032)} = 156.25 \text{ feet.}$$

At this distance, the maximum height is $f(156.25) = -0.0032(156.25)^2 + 156.25 + 3 = 81.125$ feet. The path of the baseball is shown in Figure 2.9.

✓CHECKPOINT Now try Exercise 77.

Example 6 Minimizing Cost

A small local soft-drink manufacturer has daily production costs of $C = 70{,}000 - 120x + 0.075x^2$, where C is the total cost (in dollars) and x is the number of units produced. How many units should be produced each day to yield a minimum cost?

Solution

Use the fact that the function has a minimum when $x = -b/(2a)$. From the given function you can see that $a = 0.075$ and $b = -120$. So, producing

$$x = -\frac{b}{2a} = -\frac{-120}{2(0.075)} = 800 \text{ units}$$

each day will yield a minimum cost.

✓CHECKPOINT Now try Exercise 83.

2.1 Exercises

VOCABULARY CHECK: Fill in the blanks.

1. A polynomial function of degree n and leading coefficient a_n is a function of the form $f(x) = a_n x^n + a_{n-1}x^{n-1} + \cdots + a_1 x + a_0 \ (a_n \neq 0)$ where n is a ________ ________ and a_1 are ________ numbers.
2. A ________ function is a second-degree polynomial function, and its graph is called a ________.
3. The graph of a quadratic function is symmetric about its ________.
4. If the graph of a quadratic function opens upward, then its leading coefficient is ________ and the vertex of the graph is a ________.
5. If the graph of a quadratic function opens downward, then its leading coefficient is ________ and the vertex of the graph is a ________.

In Exercises 1–8, match the quadratic function with its graph. [The graphs are labeled (a), (b), (c), (d), (e), (f), (g), and (h).]

(a)

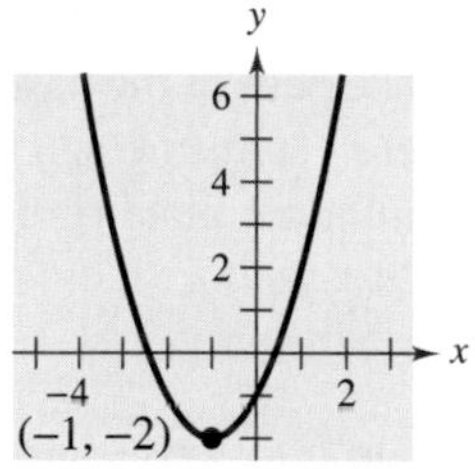

(b)

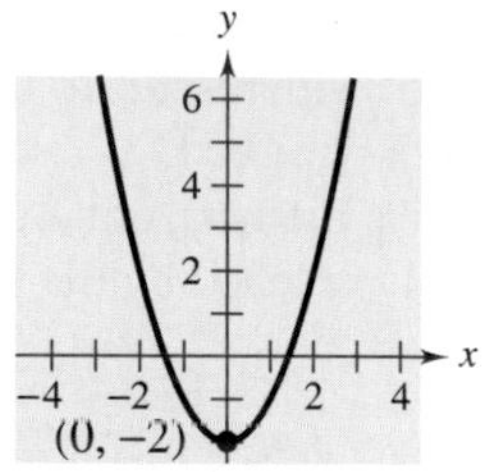

(c)

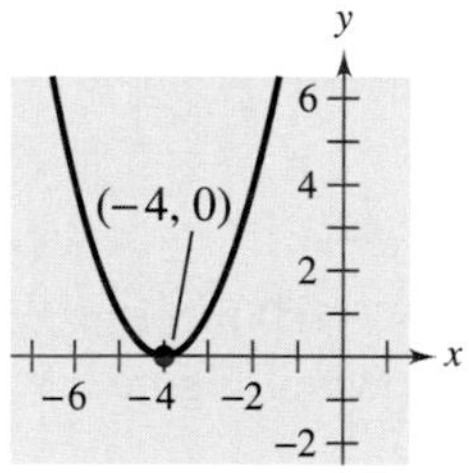

(d)

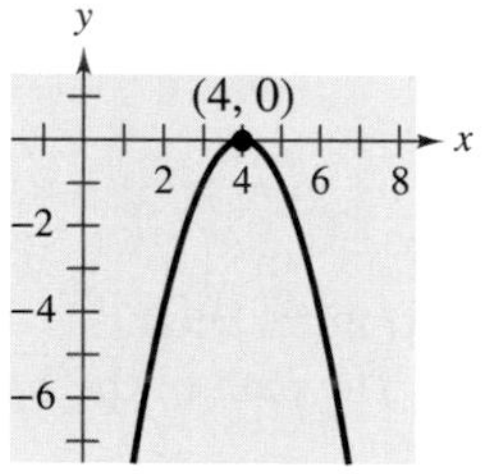

(e)

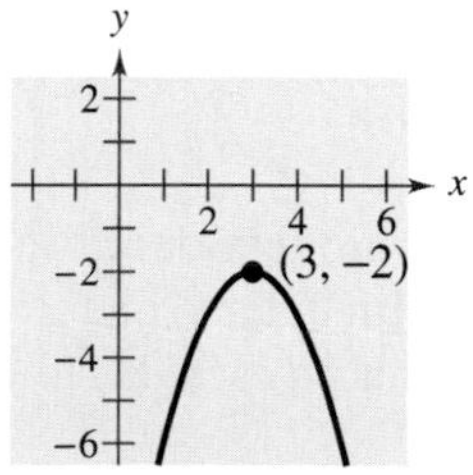

(f)

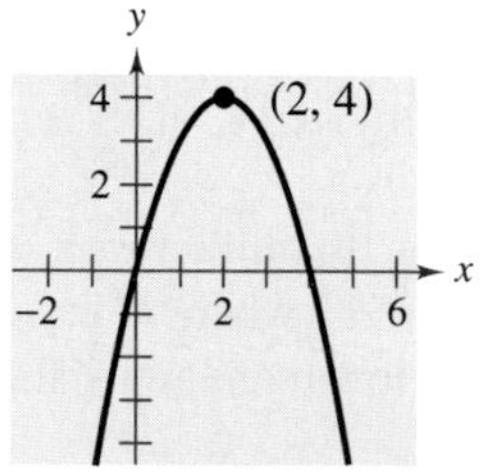

(g)

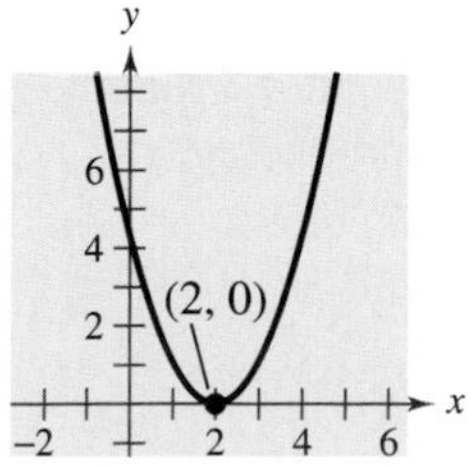

(h)

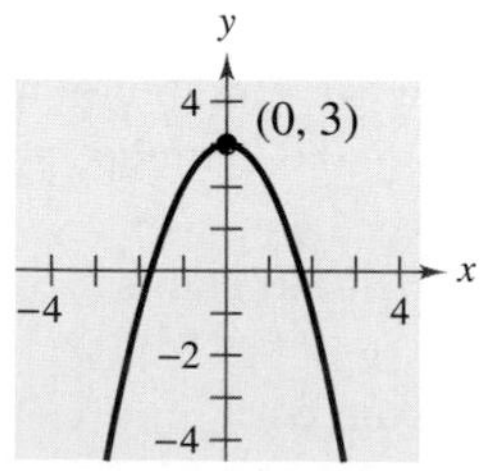

1. $f(x) = (x - 2)^2$
2. $f(x) = (x + 4)^2$
3. $f(x) = x^2 - 2$
4. $f(x) = 3 - x^2$
5. $f(x) = 4 - (x - 2)^2$
6. $f(x) = (x + 1)^2 - 2$
7. $f(x) = -(x - 3)^2 - 2$
8. $f(x) = -(x - 4)^2$

In Exercises 9–12, graph each function. Compare the graph of each function with the graph of $y = x^2$.

9. (a) $f(x) = \frac{1}{2}x^2$ (b) $g(x) = -\frac{1}{8}x^2$
   (c) $h(x) = \frac{3}{2}x^2$ (d) $k(x) = -3x^2$
10. (a) $f(x) = x^2 + 1$ (b) $g(x) = x^2 - 1$
   (c) $h(x) = x^2 + 3$ (d) $k(x) = x^2 - 3$
11. (a) $f(x) = (x - 1)^2$ (b) $g(x) = (3x)^2 + 1$
   (c) $h(x) = \left(\frac{1}{3}x\right)^2 - 3$ (d) $k(x) = (x + 3)^2$
12. (a) $f(x) = -\frac{1}{2}(x - 2)^2 + 1$
   (b) $g(x) = \left[\frac{1}{2}(x - 1)\right]^2 - 3$
   (c) $h(x) = -\frac{1}{2}(x + 2)^2 - 1$
   (d) $k(x) = [2(x + 1)]^2 + 4$

In Exercises 13–28, sketch the graph of the quadratic function without using a graphing utility. Identify the vertex, axis of symmetry, and x-intercept(s).

13. $f(x) = x^2 - 5$
14. $h(x) = 25 - x^2$
15. $f(x) = \frac{1}{2}x^2 - 4$
16. $f(x) = 16 - \frac{1}{4}x^2$
17. $f(x) = (x + 5)^2 - 6$
18. $f(x) = (x - 6)^2 + 3$
19. $h(x) = x^2 - 8x + 16$
20. $g(x) = x^2 + 2x + 1$
21. $f(x) = x^2 - x + \frac{5}{4}$
22. $f(x) = x^2 + 3x + \frac{1}{4}$
23. $f(x) = -x^2 + 2x + 5$
24. $f(x) = -x^2 - 4x + 1$
25. $h(x) = 4x^2 - 4x + 21$
26. $f(x) = 2x^2 - x + 1$
27. $f(x) = \frac{1}{4}x^2 - 2x - 12$
28. $f(x) = -\frac{1}{3}x^2 + 3x - 6$

In Exercises 29–36, use a graphing utility to graph the quadratic function. Identify the vertex, axis of symmetry, and x-intercepts. Then check your results algebraically by writing the quadratic function in standard form.

29. $f(x) = -(x^2 + 2x - 3)$

30. $f(x) = -(x^2 + x - 30)$

31. $g(x) = x^2 + 8x + 11$

32. $f(x) = x^2 + 10x + 14$

33. $f(x) = 2x^2 - 16x + 31$

34. $f(x) = -4x^2 + 24x - 41$

35. $g(x) = \frac{1}{2}(x^2 + 4x - 2)$

36. $f(x) = \frac{3}{5}(x^2 + 6x - 5)$

In Exercises 37–42, find the standard form of the quadratic function.

37.

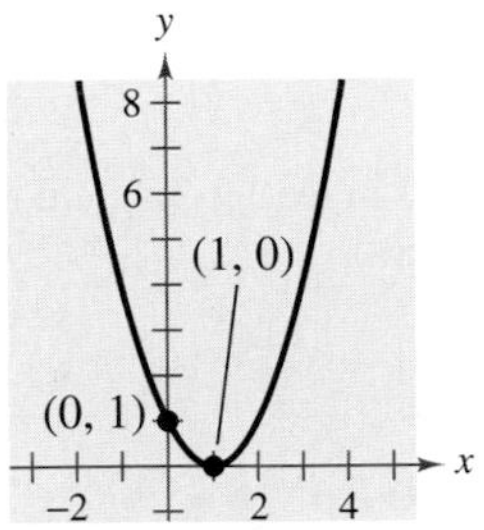

38.

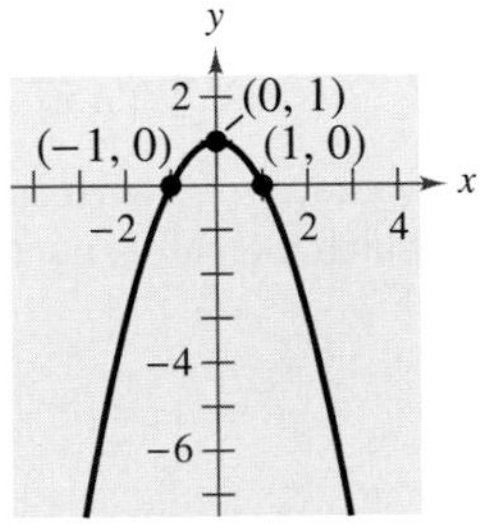

39.

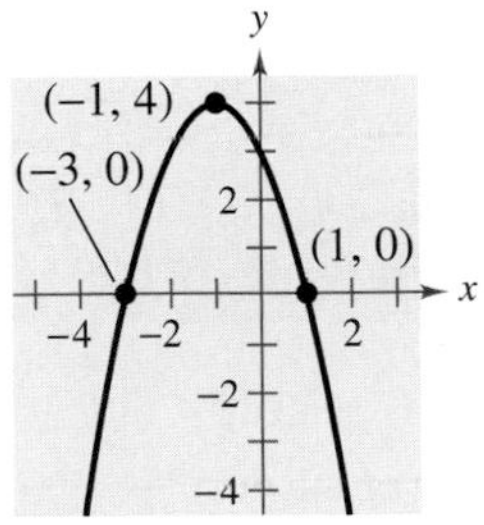

40.

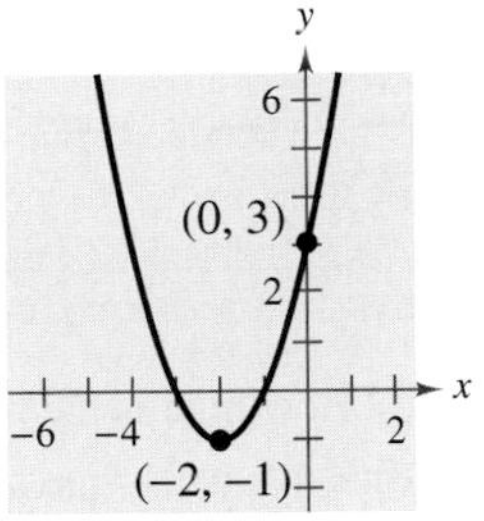

41.

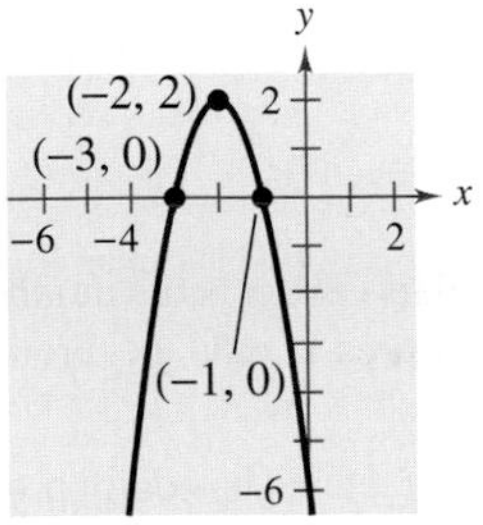

42.

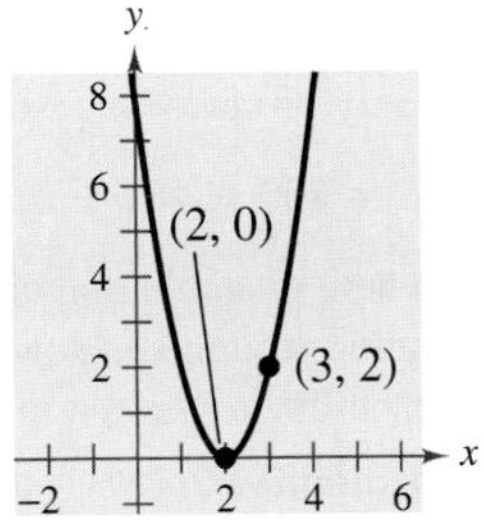

In Exercises 43–52, write the standard form of the equation of the parabola that has the indicated vertex and whose graph passes through the given point.

43. Vertex: $(-2, 5)$; point: $(0, 9)$

44. Vertex: $(4, -1)$; point: $(2, 3)$

45. Vertex: $(3, 4)$; point: $(1, 2)$

46. Vertex: $(2, 3)$; point: $(0, 2)$

47. Vertex: $(5, 12)$; point: $(7, 15)$

48. Vertex: $(-2, -2)$; point: $(-1, 0)$

49. Vertex: $\left(-\frac{1}{4}, \frac{3}{2}\right)$; point: $(-2, 0)$

50. Vertex: $\left(\frac{5}{2}, -\frac{3}{4}\right)$; point: $(-2, 4)$

51. Vertex: $\left(-\frac{5}{2}, 0\right)$; point: $\left(-\frac{7}{2}, -\frac{16}{3}\right)$

52. Vertex: $(6, 6)$; point: $\left(\frac{61}{10}, \frac{3}{2}\right)$

Graphical Reasoning **In Exercises 53–56, determine the x-intercept(s) of the graph visually. Then find the x-intercepts algebraically to confirm your results.**

53. $y = x^2 - 16$

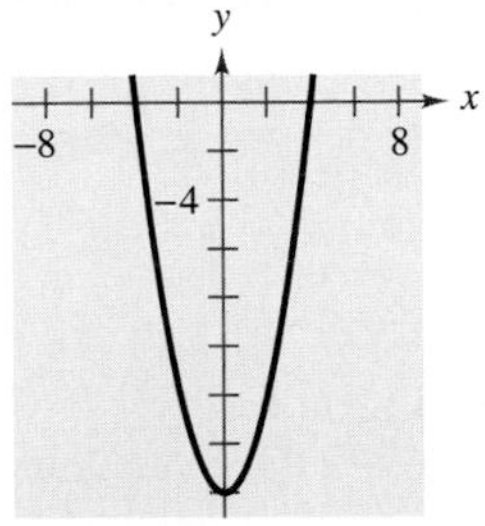

54. $y = x^2 - 6x + 9$

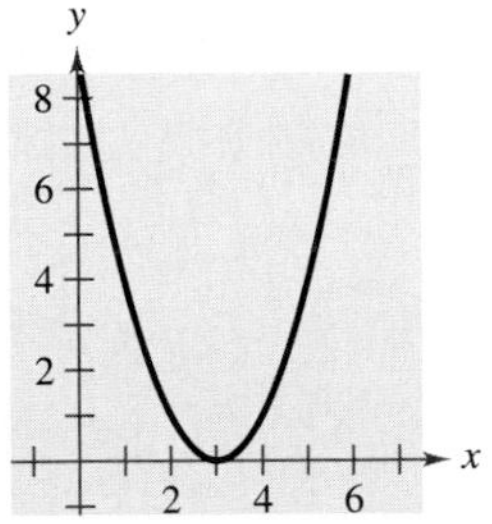

55. $y = x^2 - 4x - 5$

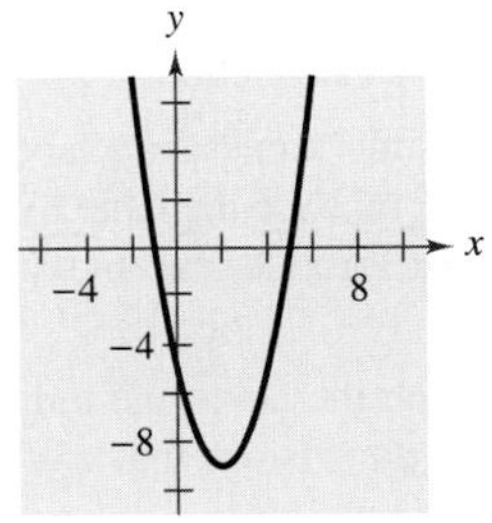

56. $y = 2x^2 + 5x - 3$

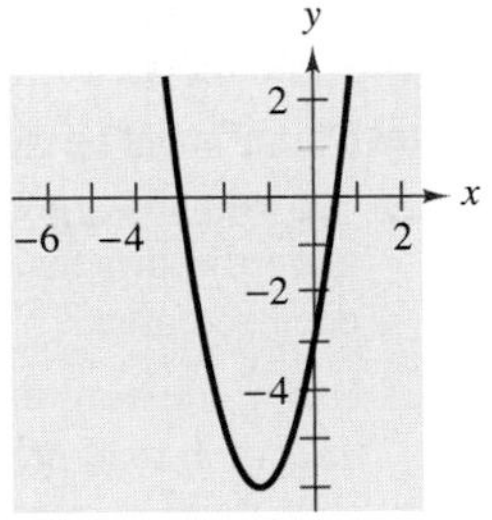

In Exercises 57–64, use a graphing utility to graph the quadratic function. Find the x-intercepts of the graph and compare them with the solutions of the corresponding quadratic equation when $f(x) = 0$.

57. $f(x) = x^2 - 4x$

58. $f(x) = -2x^2 + 10x$

59. $f(x) = x^2 - 9x + 18$

60. $f(x) = x^2 - 8x - 20$

61. $f(x) = 2x^2 - 7x - 30$

62. $f(x) = 4x^2 + 25x - 21$

63. $f(x) = -\frac{1}{2}(x^2 - 6x - 7)$

64. $f(x) = \frac{7}{10}(x^2 + 12x - 45)$

In Exercises 65–70, find two quadratic functions, one that opens upward and one that opens downward, whose graphs have the given x-intercepts. (There are many correct answers.)

65. $(-1, 0), (3, 0)$

66. $(-5, 0), (5, 0)$

67. $(0, 0), (10, 0)$

68. $(4, 0), (8, 0)$

69. $(-3, 0), \left(-\frac{1}{2}, 0\right)$

70. $\left(-\frac{5}{2}, 0\right), (2, 0)$

In Exercises 71–74, find two positive real numbers whose product is a maximum.

71. The sum is 110.

72. The sum is S.

73. The sum of the first and twice the second is 24.

74. The sum of the first and three times the second is 42.

75. ***Numerical, Graphical, and Analytical Analysis*** A rancher has 200 feet of fencing to enclose two adjacent rectangular corrals (see figure).

(a) Write the area A of the corral as a function of x.

(b) Create a table showing possible values of x and the corresponding areas of the corral. Use the table to estimate the dimensions that will produce the maximum enclosed area.

(c) Use a graphing utility to graph the area function. Use the graph to approximate the dimensions that will produce the maximum enclosed area.

(d) Write the area function in standard form to find analytically the dimensions that will produce the maximum area.

(e) Compare your results from parts (b), (c), and (d).

76. ***Geometry*** An indoor physical fitness room consists of a rectangular region with a semicircle on each end (see figure). The perimeter of the room is to be a 200-meter single-lane running track.

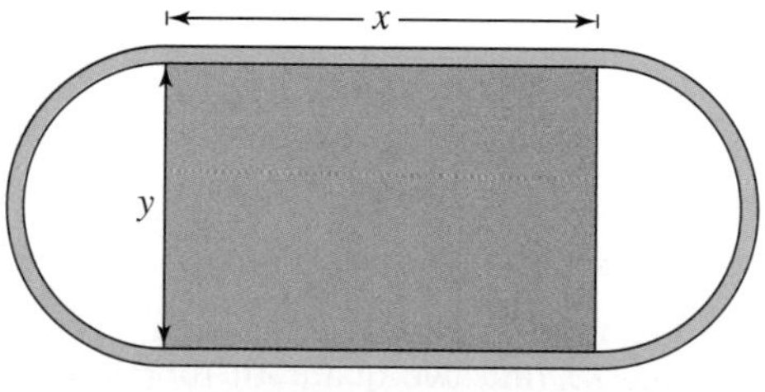

(a) Determine the radius of the semicircular ends of the room. Determine the distance, in terms of y, around the inside edge of the two semicircular parts of the track.

(b) Use the result of part (a) to write an equation, in terms of x and y, for the distance traveled in one lap around the track. Solve for y.

(c) Use the result of part (b) to write the area A of the rectangular region as a function of x. What dimensions will produce a maximum area of the rectangle?

77. ***Path of a Diver*** The path of a diver is given by

$$y = -\frac{4}{9}x^2 + \frac{24}{9}x + 12$$

where y is the height (in feet) and x is the horizontal distance from the end of the diving board (in feet). What is the maximum height of the diver?

78. ***Height of a Ball*** The height y (in feet) of a punted football is given by

$$y = -\frac{16}{2025}x^2 + \frac{9}{5}x + 1.5$$

where x is the horizontal distance (in feet) from the point at which the ball is punted (see figure).

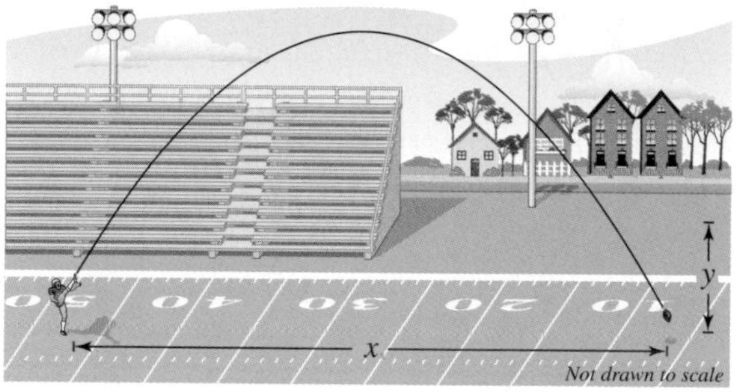

(a) How high is the ball when it is punted?

(b) What is the maximum height of the punt?

(c) How long is the punt?

79. ***Minimum Cost*** A manufacturer of lighting fixtures has daily production costs of

$$C = 800 - 10x + 0.25x^2$$

where C is the total cost (in dollars) and x is the number of units produced. How many fixtures should be produced each day to yield a minimum cost?

80. ***Minimum Cost*** A textile manufacturer has daily production costs of

$$C = 100{,}000 - 110x + 0.045x^2$$

where C is the total cost (in dollars) and x is the number of units produced. How many units should be produced each day to yield a minimum cost?

81. ***Maximum Profit*** The profit P (in dollars) for a company that produces antivirus and system utilities software is

$$P = -0.0002x^2 + 140x - 250{,}000$$

where x is the number of units sold. What sales level will yield a maximum profit?

82. ***Maximum Profit*** The profit P (in hundreds of dollars) that a company makes depends on the amount x (in hundreds of dollars) the company spends on advertising according to the model

$$P = 230 + 20x - 0.5x^2.$$

What expenditure for advertising will yield a maximum profit?

83. ***Maximum Revenue*** The total revenue R earned (in thousands of dollars) from manufacturing handheld video games is given by

$$R(p) = -25p^2 + 1200p$$

where p is the price per unit (in dollars).

(a) Find the revenue earned for each price per unit given below.

$20

$25

$30

(b) Find the unit price that will yield a maximum revenue. What is the maximum revenue? Explain your results.

84. ***Maximum Revenue*** The total revenue R earned per day (in dollars) from a pet-sitting service is given by

$$R(p) = -12p^2 + 150p$$

where p is the price charged per pet (in dollars).

(a) Find the revenue earned for each price per pet given below.

$4

$6

$8

(b) Find the price that will yield a maximum revenue. What is the maximum revenue? Explain your results.

85. ***Graphical Analysis*** From 1960 to 2003, the per capita consumption C of cigarettes by Americans (age 18 and older) can be modeled by

$$C = 4299 - 1.8t - 1.36t^2, \quad 0 \le t \le 43$$

where t is the year, with $t = 0$ corresponding to 1960. (Source: *Tobacco Outlook Report*)

(a) Use a graphing utility to graph the model.

(b) Use the graph of the model to approximate the maximum average annual consumption. Beginning in 1966, all cigarette packages were required by law to carry a health warning. Do you think the warning had any effect? Explain.

(c) In 2000, the U.S. population (age 18 and over) was 209,128,094. Of those, about 48,308,590 were smokers. What was the average annual cigarette consumption *per smoker* in 2000? What was the average daily cigarette consumption *per smoker*?

Model It

86. ***Data Analysis*** The numbers y (in thousands) of hairdressers and cosmetologists in the United States for the years 1994 through 2002 are shown in the table. (Source: U.S. Bureau of Labor Statistics)

Year	Number of hairdressers and cosmetologists, y
1994	753
1995	750
1996	737
1997	748
1998	763
1999	784
2000	820
2001	854
2002	908

(a) Use a graphing utility to create a scatter plot of the data. Let x represent the year, with $x = 4$ corresponding to 1994.

(b) Use the *regression* feature of a graphing utility to find a quadratic model for the data.

(c) Use a graphing utility to graph the model in the same viewing window as the scatter plot. How well does the model fit the data?

(d) Use the *trace* feature of the graphing utility to approximate the year in which the number of hairdressers and cosmetologists was the least.

(e) Verify your answer to part (d) algebraically.

(f) Use the model to predict the number of hairdressers and cosmetologists in 2008.

87. ***Wind Drag*** The number of horsepower y required to overcome wind drag on an automobile is approximated by

$$y = 0.002s^2 + 0.005s - 0.029, \quad 0 \le s \le 100$$

where s is the speed of the car (in miles per hour).

(a) Use a graphing utility to graph the function.

(b) Graphically estimate the maximum speed of the car if the power required to overcome wind drag is not to exceed 10 horsepower. Verify your estimate algebraically.

88. ***Maximum Fuel Economy*** A study was done to compare the speed x (in miles per hour) with the mileage y (in miles per gallon) of an automobile. The results are shown in the table. (Source: Federal Highway Administration)

Speed, x	Mileage, y
15	22.3
20	25.5
25	27.5
30	29.0
35	28.8
40	30.0
45	29.9
50	30.2
55	30.4
60	28.8
65	27.4
70	25.3
75	23.3

(a) Use a graphing utility to create a scatter plot of the data.

(b) Use the *regression* feature of a graphing utility to find a quadratic model for the data.

(c) Use a graphing utility to graph the model in the same viewing window as the scatter plot.

(d) Estimate the speed for which the miles per gallon is greatest.

Synthesis

True or False? **In Exercises 89 and 90, determine whether the statement is true or false. Justify your answer.**

89. The function given by $f(x) = -12x^2 - 1$ has no x-intercepts.

90. The graphs of

$$f(x) = -4x^2 - 10x + 7$$

and

$$g(x) = 12x^2 + 30x + 1$$

have the same axis of symmetry.

91. Write the quadratic function

$$f(x) = ax^2 + bx + c$$

in standard form to verify that the vertex occurs at

$$\left(-\frac{b}{2a}, f\left(-\frac{b}{2a}\right)\right).$$

92. ***Profit*** The profit P (in millions of dollars) for a recreational vehicle retailer is modeled by a quadratic function of the form

$$P = at^2 + bt + c$$

where t represents the year. If you were president of the company, which of the models below would you prefer? Explain your reasoning.

(a) a is positive and $-b/(2a) \le t$.

(b) a is positive and $t \le -b/(2a)$.

(c) a is negative and $-b/(2a) \le t$.

(d) a is negative and $t \le -b/(2a)$.

93. Is it possible for a quadratic equation to have only one x-intercept? Explain.

94. Assume that the function given by

$$f(x) = ax^2 + bx + c, \quad a \neq 0$$

has two real zeros. Show that the x-coordinate of the vertex of the graph is the average of the zeros of f. (*Hint:* Use the Quadratic Formula.)

Skills Review

In Exercises 95–98, find the equation of the line in slope-intercept form that has the given characteristics.

95. Passes through the points $(-4, 3)$ and $(2, 1)$

96. Passes through the point $\left(\frac{7}{2}, 2\right)$ and has a slope of $\frac{3}{2}$

97. Passes through the point $(0, 3)$ and is perpendicular to the line $4x + 5y = 10$

98. Passes through the point $(-8, 4)$ and is parallel to the line $y = -3x + 2$

In Exercises 99–104, let $f(x) = 14x - 3$ and let $g(x) = 8x^2$. Find the indicated value.

99. $(f + g)(-3)$

100. $(g - f)(2)$

101. $(fg)\left(-\frac{4}{7}\right)$

102. $\left(\frac{f}{g}\right)(-1.5)$

103. $(f \circ g)(-1)$

104. $(g \circ f)(0)$

105. Make a Decision To work an extended application analyzing the height of a basketball after it has been dropped, visit this text's website at *college.hmco.com.*

2.2 Polynomial Functions of Higher Degree

What you should learn

- Use transformations to sketch graphs of polynomial functions.
- Use the Leading Coefficient Test to determine the end behavior of graphs of polynomial functions.
- Find and use zeros of polynomial functions as sketching aids.
- Use the Intermediate Value Theorem to help locate zeros of polynomial functions.

Why you should learn it

You can use polynomial functions to analyze business situations such as how revenue is related to advertising expenses, as discussed in Exercise 98 on page 151.

Bill Aron/PhotoEdit, Inc.

Graphs of Polynomial Functions

In this section, you will study basic features of the graphs of polynomial functions. The first feature is that the graph of a polynomial function is **continuous.** Essentially, this means that the graph of a polynomial function has no breaks, holes, or gaps, as shown in Figure 2.10(a). The graph shown in Figure 2.10(b) is an example of a piecewise-defined function that is not continuous.

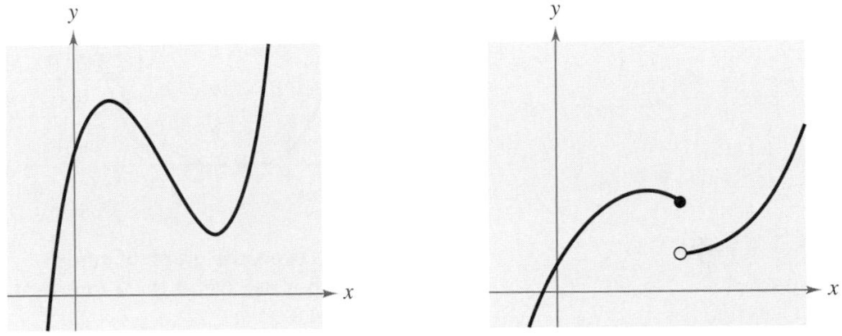

(a) Polynomial functions have continuous graphs.

(b) Functions with graphs that are not continuous are not polynomial functions.

FIGURE 2.10

The second feature is that the graph of a polynomial function has only smooth, rounded turns, as shown in Figure 2.11. A polynomial function cannot have a sharp turn. For instance, the function given by $f(x) = |x|$, which has a sharp turn at the point $(0, 0)$, as shown in Figure 2.12, is not a polynomial function.

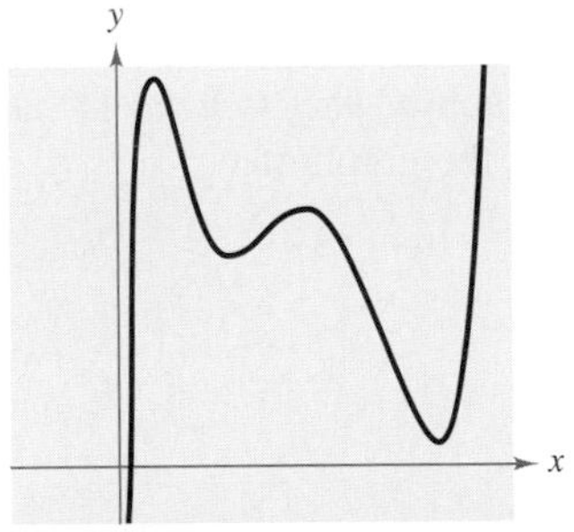

Polynomial functions have graphs with smooth rounded turns.

FIGURE 2.11

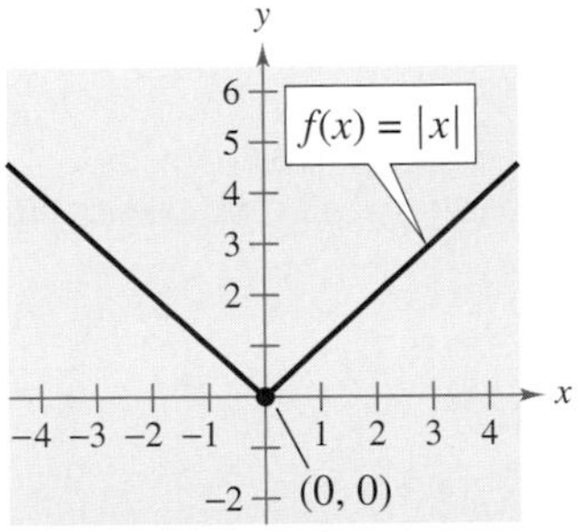

Graphs of polynomial functions cannot have sharp turns.

FIGURE 2.12

The graphs of polynomial functions of degree greater than 2 are more difficult to analyze than the graphs of polynomials of degree 0, 1, or 2. However, using the features presented in this section, coupled with your knowledge of point plotting, intercepts, and symmetry, you should be able to make reasonably accurate sketches *by hand.*

STUDY TIP

For power functions given by $f(x) = x^n$, if n is even, then the graph of the function is symmetric with respect to the y-axis, and if n is odd, then the graph of the function is symmetric with respect to the origin.

The polynomial functions that have the simplest graphs are monomials of the form $f(x) = x^n$, where n is an integer greater than zero. From Figure 2.13, you can see that when n is *even*, the graph is similar to the graph of $f(x) = x^2$, and when n is *odd*, the graph is similar to the graph of $f(x) = x^3$. Moreover, the greater the value of n, the flatter the graph near the origin. Polynomial functions of the form $f(x) = x^n$ are often referred to as **power functions.**

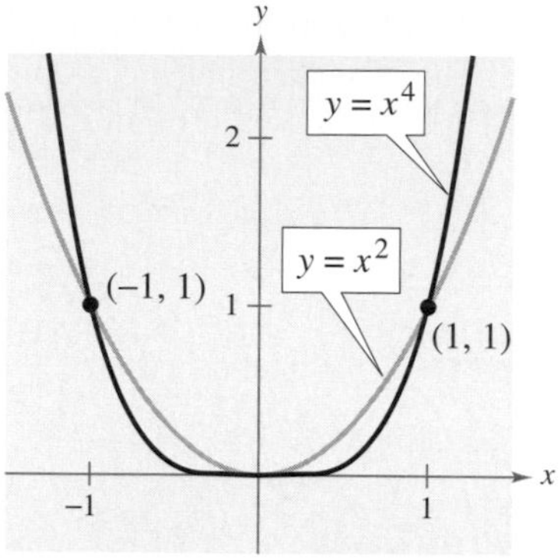

(a) If n is even, the graph of $y = x^n$ touches the axis at the x-intercept.

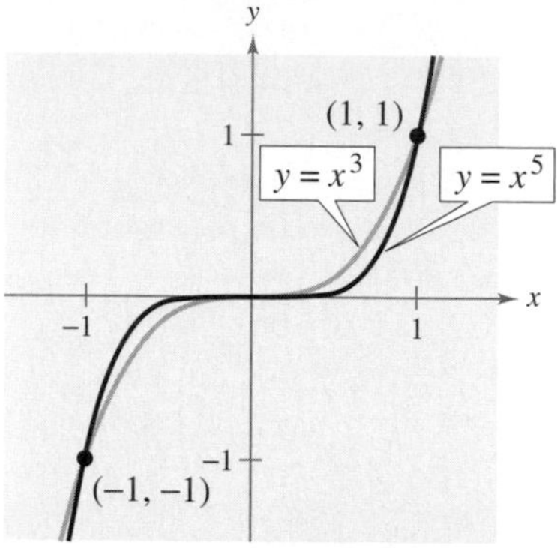

(b) If n is odd, the graph of $y = x^n$ crosses the axis at the x-intercept.

FIGURE 2.13

Example 1 Sketching Transformations of Monomial Functions

Sketch the graph of each function.

a. $f(x) = -x^5$ **b.** $h(x) = (x + 1)^4$

Solution

a. Because the degree of $f(x) = -x^5$ is odd, its graph is similar to the graph of $y = x^3$. In Figure 2.14, note that the negative coefficient has the effect of reflecting the graph in the x-axis.

b. The graph of $h(x) = (x + 1)^4$, as shown in Figure 2.15, is a left shift by one unit of the graph of $y = x^4$.

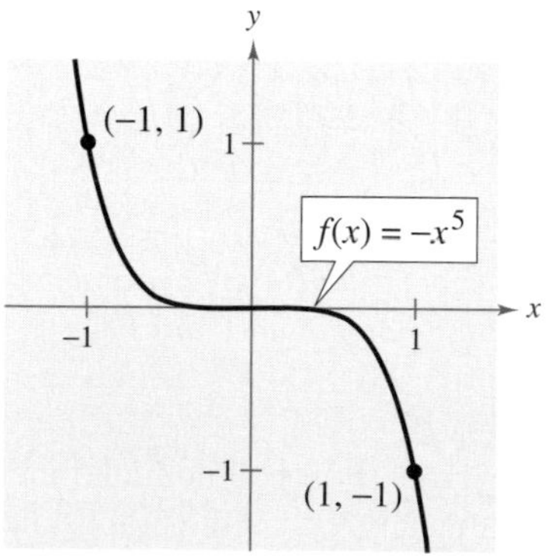

FIGURE 2.14

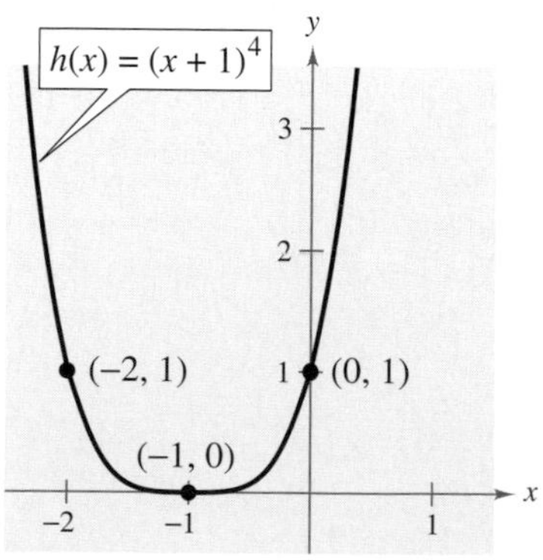

FIGURE 2.15

CHECKPOINT Now try Exercise 9.

The Leading Coefficient Test

In Example 1, note that both graphs eventually rise or fall without bound as x moves to the right. Whether the graph of a polynomial function eventually rises or falls can be determined by the function's degree (even or odd) and by its leading coefficient, as indicated in the **Leading Coefficient Test.**

Leading Coefficient Test

As x moves without bound to the left or to the right, the graph of the polynomial function $f(x) = a_n x^n + \cdot \cdot \cdot + a_1 x + a_0$ eventually rises or falls in the following manner.

1. When n is *odd:*

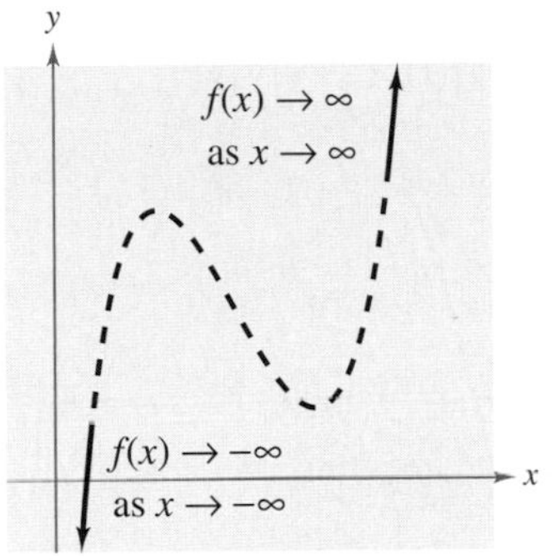

If the leading coefficient is positive ($a_n > 0$), the graph falls to the left and rises to the right.

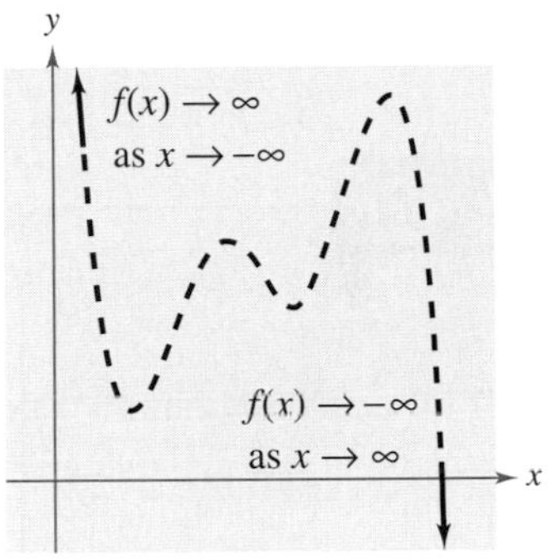

If the leading coefficient is negative ($a_n < 0$), the graph rises to the left and falls to the right.

2. When n is *even:*

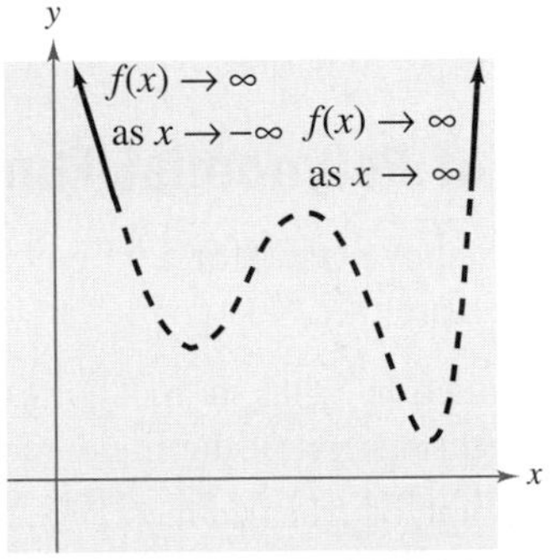

If the leading coefficient is positive ($a_n > 0$), the graph rises to the left and right.

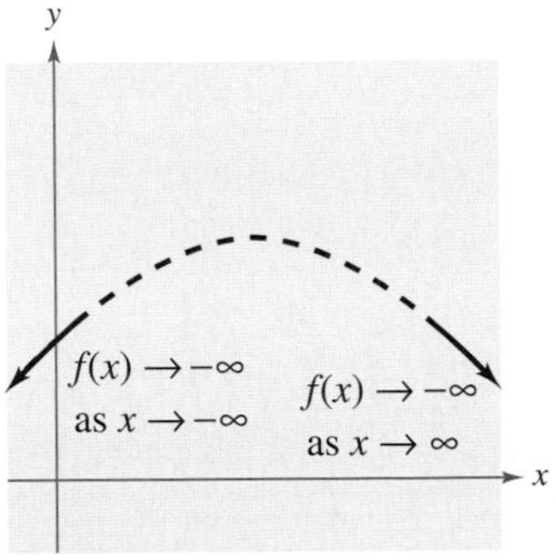

If the leading coefficient is negative ($a_n < 0$), the graph falls to the left and right.

The dashed portions of the graphs indicate that the test determines *only* the right-hand and left-hand behavior of the graph.

Exploration

For each function, identify the degree of the function and whether the degree of the function is even or odd. Identify the leading coefficient and whether the leading coefficient is positive or negative. Use a graphing utility to graph each function. Describe the relationship between the degree and the sign of the leading coefficient of the function and the right-hand and left-hand behavior of the graph of the function.

a. $f(x) = x^3 - 2x^2 - x + 1$

b. $f(x) = 2x^5 + 2x^2 - 5x + 1$

c. $f(x) = -2x^5 - x^2 + 5x + 3$

d. $f(x) = -x^3 + 5x - 2$

e. $f(x) = 2x^2 + 3x - 4$

f. $f(x) = x^4 - 3x^2 + 2x - 1$

g. $f(x) = x^2 + 3x + 2$

STUDY TIP

The notation "$f(x) \to -\infty$ as $x \to -\infty$" indicates that the graph falls to the left. The notation "$f(x) \to \infty$ as $x \to \infty$" indicates that the graph rises to the right.

STUDY TIP

A polynomial function is written in **standard form** if its terms are written in descending order of exponents from left to right. Before applying the Leading Coefficient Test to a polynomial function, it is a good idea to check that the polynomial function is written in standard form.

Example 2 **Applying the Leading Coefficient Test**

Describe the right-hand and left-hand behavior of the graph of each function.

a. $f(x) = -x^3 + 4x$ **b.** $f(x) = x^4 - 5x^2 + 4$ **c.** $f(x) = x^5 - x$

Solution

a. Because the degree is odd and the leading coefficient is negative, the graph rises to the left and falls to the right, as shown in Figure 2.16.

b. Because the degree is even and the leading coefficient is positive, the graph rises to the left and right, as shown in Figure 2.17.

c. Because the degree is odd and the leading coefficient is positive, the graph falls to the left and rises to the right, as shown in Figure 2.18.

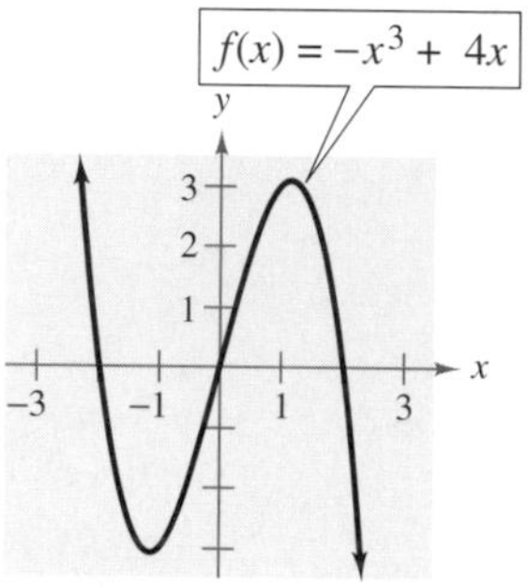

FIGURE 2.16

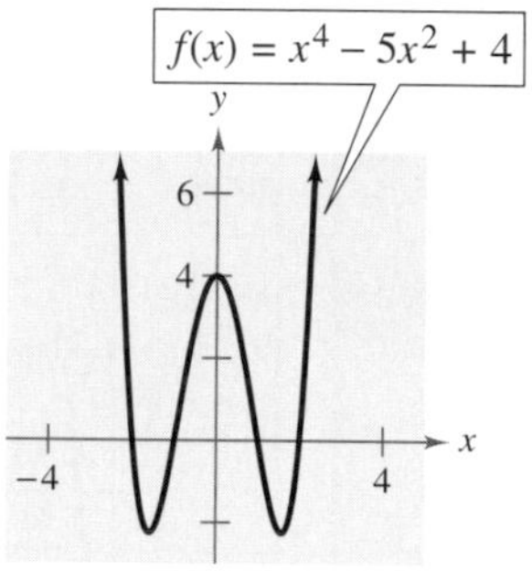

FIGURE 2.17

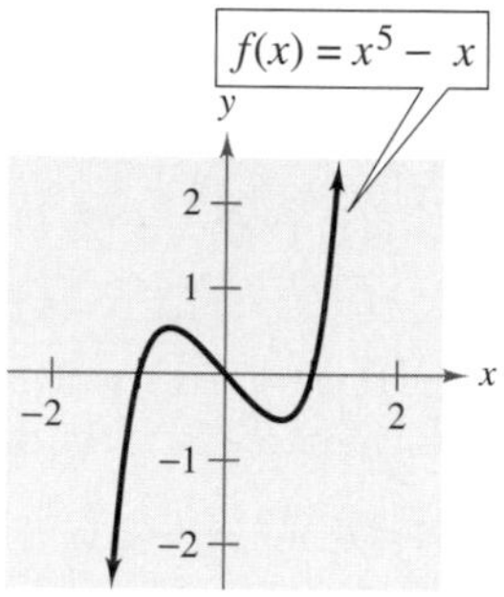

FIGURE 2.18

✓CHECKPOINT Now try Exercise 15.

Exploration

For each of the graphs in Example 2, count the number of zeros of the polynomial function and the number of relative minima and relative maxima. Compare these numbers with the degree of the polynomial. What do you observe?

In Example 2, note that the Leading Coefficient Test tells you only whether the graph *eventually* rises or falls to the right or left. Other characteristics of the graph, such as intercepts and minimum and maximum points, must be determined by other tests.

Zeros of Polynomial Functions

It can be shown that for a polynomial function f of degree n, the following statements are true.

1. The function f has, at most, n real zeros. (You will study this result in detail in the discussion of the Fundamental Theorem of Algebra in Section 2.5.)
2. The graph of f has, at most, $n - 1$ turning points. (Turning points, also called relative minima or relative maxima, are points at which the graph changes from increasing to decreasing or vice versa.)

Finding the zeros of polynomial functions is one of the most important problems in algebra. There is a strong interplay between graphical and algebraic approaches to this problem. Sometimes you can use information about the graph of a function to help find its zeros, and in other cases you can use information about the zeros of a function to help sketch its graph. Finding zeros of polynomial functions is closely related to factoring and finding x-intercepts.

STUDY TIP

Remember that the *zeros* of a function of x are the x-values for which the function is zero.

Real Zeros of Polynomial Functions

If f is a polynomial function and a is a real number, the following statements are equivalent.

1. $x = a$ is a *zero* of the function f.
2. $x = a$ is a *solution* of the polynomial equation $f(x) = 0$.
3. $(x - a)$ is a *factor* of the polynomial $f(x)$.
4. $(a, 0)$ is an *x-intercept* of the graph of f.

Example 3 **Finding the Zeros of a Polynomial Function**

Find all real zeros of

$$f(x) = -2x^4 + 2x^2.$$

Then determine the number of turning points of the graph of the function.

Algebraic Solution

To find the real zeros of the function, set $f(x)$ equal to zero and solve for x.

$$-2x^4 + 2x^2 = 0 \qquad \text{Set } f(x) \text{ equal to 0.}$$

$$-2x^2(x^2 - 1) = 0 \qquad \text{Remove common monomial factor.}$$

$$-2x^2(x - 1)(x + 1) = 0 \qquad \text{Factor completely.}$$

So, the real zeros are $x = 0$, $x = 1$, and $x = -1$. Because the function is a fourth-degree polynomial, the graph of f can have at most $4 - 1 = 3$ turning points.

Graphical Solution

Use a graphing utility to graph $y = -2x^4 + 2x^2$. In Figure 2.19, the graph appears to have zeros at $(0, 0)$, $(1, 0)$, and $(-1, 0)$. Use the *zero* or *root* feature, or the *zoom* and *trace* features, of the graphing utility to verify these zeros. So, the real zeros are $x = 0$, $x = 1$, and $x = -1$. From the figure, you can see that the graph has three turning points. This is consistent with the fact that a fourth-degree polynomial can have at most three turning points.

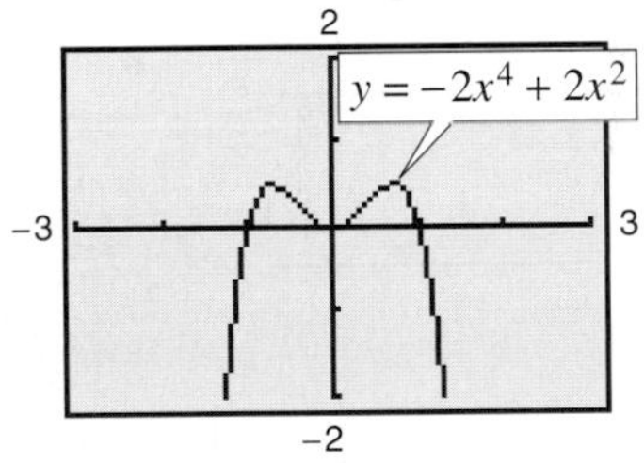

FIGURE 2.19

✓CHECKPOINT Now try Exercise 27.

In Example 3, note that because k is even, the factor $-2x^2$ yields the *repeated* zero $x = 0$. The graph touches the x-axis at $x = 0$, as shown in Figure 2.19.

Repeated Zeros

A factor $(x - a)^k$, $k > 1$, yields a **repeated zero** $x = a$ of **multiplicity** k.

1. If k is odd, the graph *crosses* the x-axis at $x = a$.
2. If k is even, the graph *touches* the x-axis (but does not cross the x-axis) at $x = a$.

Technology

Example 4 uses an *algebraic approach* to describe the graph of the function. A graphing utility is a complement to this approach. Remember that an important aspect of using a graphing utility is to find a viewing window that shows all significant features of the graph. For instance, the viewing window in part (a) illustrates all of the significant features of the function in Example 4.

a.

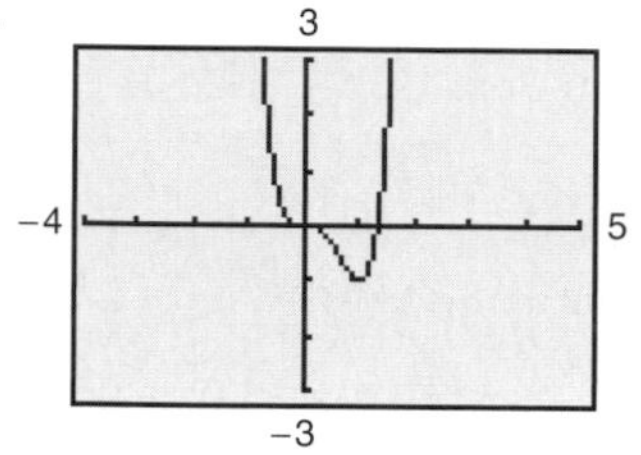

b.

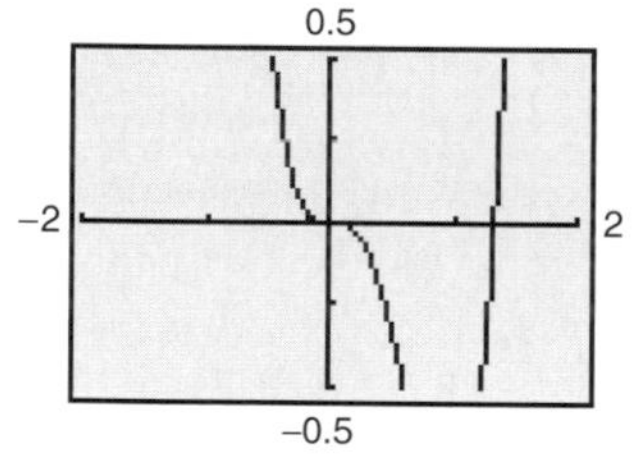

To graph polynomial functions, you can use the fact that a polynomial function can change signs only at its zeros. Between two consecutive zeros, a polynomial must be entirely positive or entirely negative. This means that when the real zeros of a polynomial function are put in order, they divide the real number line into intervals in which the function has no sign changes. These resulting intervals are **test intervals** in which a representative x-value in the interval is chosen to determine if the value of the polynomial function is positive (the graph lies above the x-axis) or negative (the graph lies below the x-axis).

Example 4 Sketching the Graph of a Polynomial Function

Sketch the graph of $f(x) = 3x^4 - 4x^3$.

Solution

1. *Apply the Leading Coefficient Test.* Because the leading coefficient is positive and the degree is even, you know that the graph eventually rises to the left and to the right (see Figure 2.20).
2. *Find the Zeros of the Polynomial.* By factoring $f(x) = 3x^4 - 4x^3$ as $f(x) = x^3(3x - 4)$, you can see that the zeros of f are $x = 0$ and $x = \frac{4}{3}$ (both of odd multiplicity). So, the x-intercepts occur at $(0, 0)$ and $\left(\frac{4}{3}, 0\right)$. Add these points to your graph, as shown in Figure 2.20.
3. *Plot a Few Additional Points.* Use the zeros of the polynomial to find the test intervals. In each test interval, choose a representative x-value and evaluate the polynomial function, as shown in the table.

Test interval	Representative x-value	Value of f	Sign	Point on graph
$(-\infty, 0)$	-1	$f(-1) = 7$	Positive	$(-1, 7)$
$\left(0, \frac{4}{3}\right)$	1	$f(1) = -1$	Negative	$(1, -1)$
$\left(\frac{4}{3}, \infty\right)$	1.5	$f(1.5) = 1.6875$	Positive	$(1.5, 1.6875)$

4. *Draw the Graph.* Draw a continuous curve through the points, as shown in Figure 2.21. Because both zeros are of odd multiplicity, you know that the graph should cross the x-axis at $x = 0$ and $x = \frac{4}{3}$.

STUDY TIP

If you are unsure of the shape of a portion of the graph of a polynomial function, plot some additional points, such as the point $(0.5, -0.3125)$ as shown in Figure 2.21.

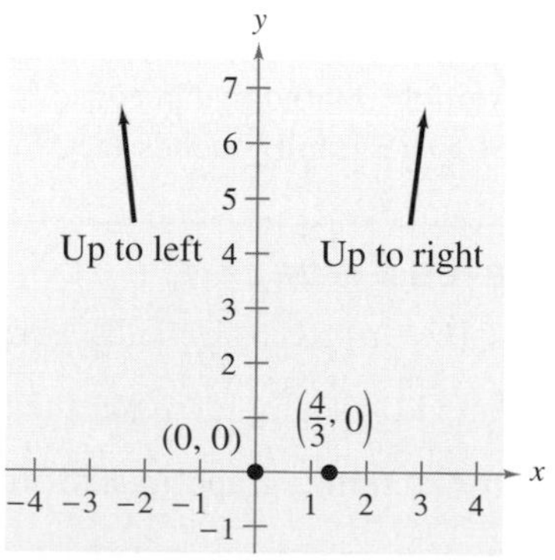

FIGURE 2.20

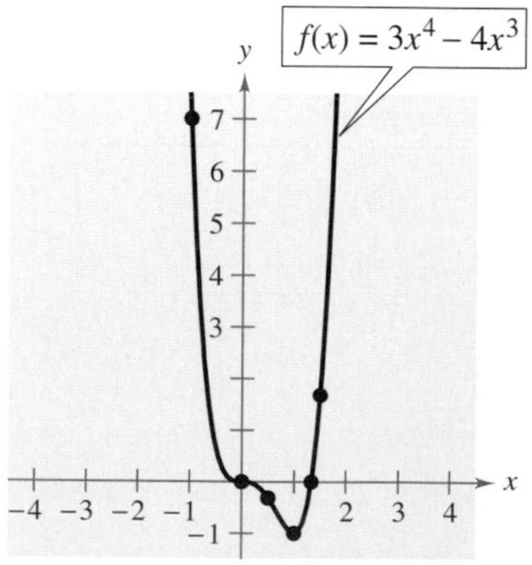

FIGURE 2.21

✓CHECKPOINT Now try Exercise 67.

Example 5 Sketching the Graph of a Polynomial Function

Sketch the graph of $f(x) = -2x^3 + 6x^2 - \frac{9}{2}x$.

Solution

1. *Apply the Leading Coefficient Test.* Because the leading coefficient is negative and the degree is odd, you know that the graph eventually rises to the left and falls to the right (see Figure 2.22).
2. *Find the Zeros of the Polynomial.* By factoring

$$\begin{aligned} f(x) &= -2x^3 + 6x^2 - \tfrac{9}{2}x \\ &= -\tfrac{1}{2}x(4x^2 - 12x + 9) \\ &= -\tfrac{1}{2}x(2x - 3)^2 \end{aligned}$$

you can see that the zeros of f are $x = 0$ (odd multiplicity) and $x = \frac{3}{2}$ (even multiplicity). So, the x-intercepts occur at $(0, 0)$ and $\left(\frac{3}{2}, 0\right)$. Add these points to your graph, as shown in Figure 2.22.

3. *Plot a Few Additional Points.* Use the zeros of the polynomial to find the test intervals. In each test interval, choose a representative x-value and evaluate the polynomial function, as shown in the table.

Test interval	Representative x-value	Value of f	Sign	Point on graph
$(-\infty, 0)$	-0.5	$f(-0.5) = 4$	Positive	$(-0.5, 4)$
$\left(0, \frac{3}{2}\right)$	0.5	$f(0.5) = -1$	Negative	$(0.5, -1)$
$\left(\frac{3}{2}, \infty\right)$	2	$f(2) = -1$	Negative	$(2, -1)$

4. *Draw the Graph.* Draw a continuous curve through the points, as shown in Figure 2.23. As indicated by the multiplicities of the zeros, the graph crosses the x-axis at $(0, 0)$ but does not cross the x-axis at $\left(\frac{3}{2}, 0\right)$.

STUDY TIP

Observe in Example 5 that the sign of $f(x)$ is positive to the left of and negative to the right of the zero $x = 0$. Similarly, the sign of $f(x)$ is negative to the left and to the right of the zero $x = \frac{3}{2}$. This suggests that if the zero of a polynomial function is of *odd* multiplicity, then the sign of $f(x)$ changes from one side of the zero to the other side. If the zero is of *even* multiplicity, then the sign of $f(x)$ does not change from one side of the zero to the other side.

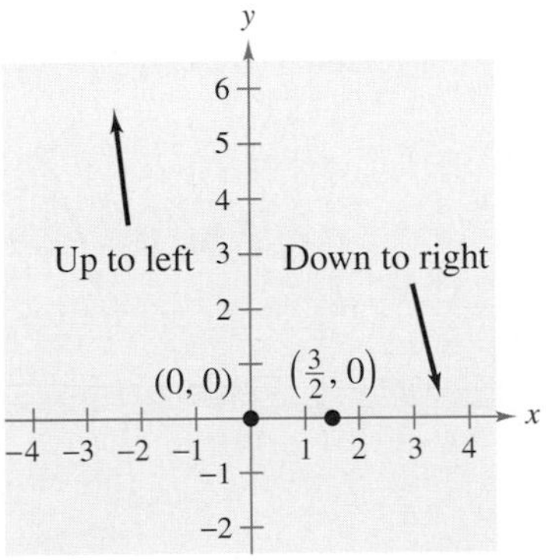

FIGURE 2.22

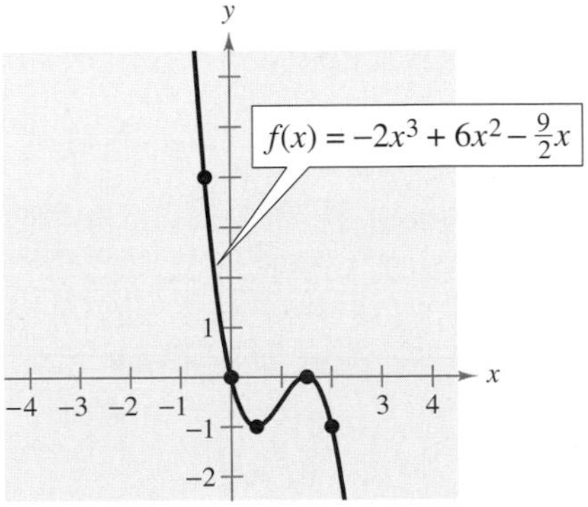

FIGURE 2.23

✓CHECKPOINT Now try Exercise 69.

The Intermediate Value Theorem

The next theorem, called the **Intermediate Value Theorem,** illustrates the existence of real zeros of polynomial functions. This theorem implies that if $(a, f(a))$ and $(b, f(b))$ are two points on the graph of a polynomial function such that $f(a) \neq f(b)$, then for any number d between $f(a)$ and $f(b)$ there must be a number c between a and b such that $f(c) = d$. (See Figure 2.24.)

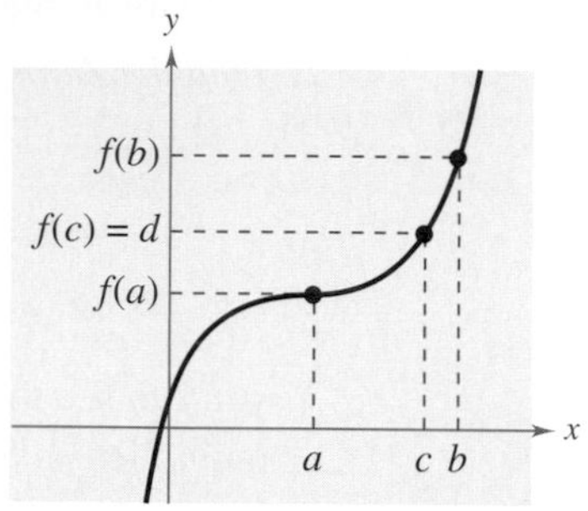

FIGURE 2.24

> **Intermediate Value Theorem**
>
> Let a and b be real numbers such that $a < b$. If f is a polynomial function such that $f(a) \neq f(b)$, then, in the interval $[a, b]$, f takes on every value between $f(a)$ and $f(b)$.

The Intermediate Value Theorem helps you locate the real zeros of a polynomial function in the following way. If you can find a value $x = a$ at which a polynomial function is positive, and another value $x = b$ at which it is negative, you can conclude that the function has at least one real zero between these two values. For example, the function given by $f(x) = x^3 + x^2 + 1$ is negative when $x = -2$ and positive when $x = -1$. Therefore, it follows from the Intermediate Value Theorem that f must have a real zero somewhere between -2 and -1, as shown in Figure 2.25.

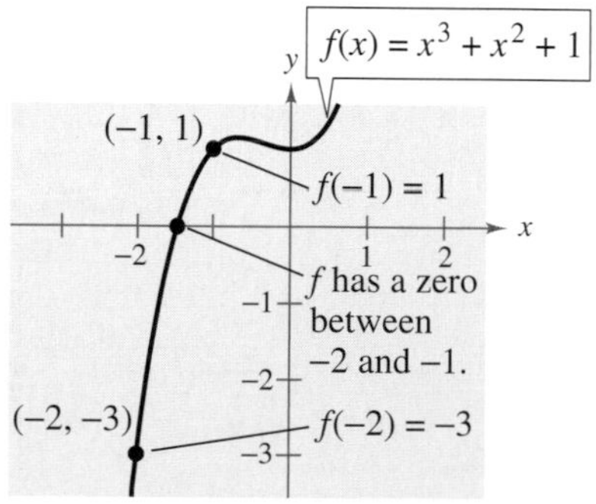

FIGURE 2.25

By continuing this line of reasoning, you can approximate any real zeros of a polynomial function to any desired accuracy. This concept is further demonstrated in Example 6.

Example 6 Approximating a Zero of a Polynomial Function

Use the Intermediate Value Theorem to approximate the real zero of

$$f(x) = x^3 - x^2 + 1.$$

Solution

Begin by computing a few function values, as follows.

x	$f(x)$
-2	-11
-1	-1
0	1
1	1

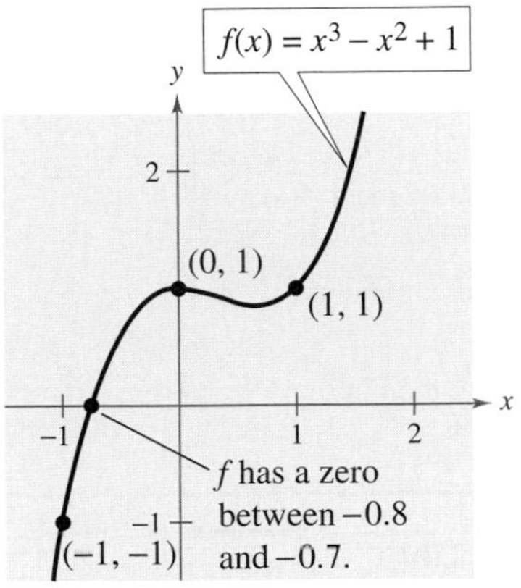

FIGURE 2.26

Because $f(-1)$ is negative and $f(0)$ is positive, you can apply the Intermediate Value Theorem to conclude that the function has a zero between -1 and 0. To pinpoint this zero more closely, divide the interval $[-1, 0]$ into tenths and evaluate the function at each point. When you do this, you will find that

$$f(-0.8) = -0.152 \quad \text{and} \quad f(-0.7) = 0.167.$$

So, f must have a zero between -0.8 and -0.7, as shown in Figure 2.26. For a more accurate approximation, compute function values between $f(-0.8)$ and $f(-0.7)$ and apply the Intermediate Value Theorem again. By continuing this process, you can approximate this zero to any desired accuracy.

CHECKPOINT Now try Exercise 85.

Technology

You can use the *table* feature of a graphing utility to approximate the zeros of a polynomial function. For instance, for the function given by

$$f(x) = -2x^3 - 3x^2 + 3$$

create a table that shows the function values for $-20 \le x \le 20$, as shown in the first table at the right. Scroll through the table looking for consecutive function values that differ in sign. From the table, you can see that $f(0)$ and $f(1)$ differ in sign. So, you can conclude from the Intermediate Value Theorem that the function has a zero between 0 and 1. You can adjust your table to show function values for $0 \le x \le 1$ using increments of 0.1, as shown in the second table at the right. By scrolling through the table you can see that $f(0.8)$ and $f(0.9)$ differ in sign. So, the function has a zero between 0.8 and 0.9. If you repeat this process several times, you should obtain $x \approx 0.806$ as the zero of the function. Use the *zero* or *root* feature of a graphing utility to confirm this result.

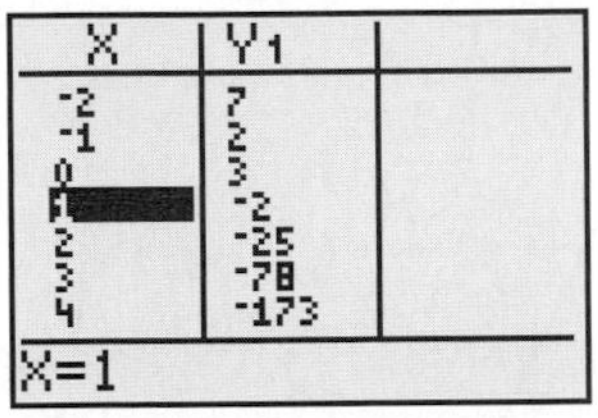

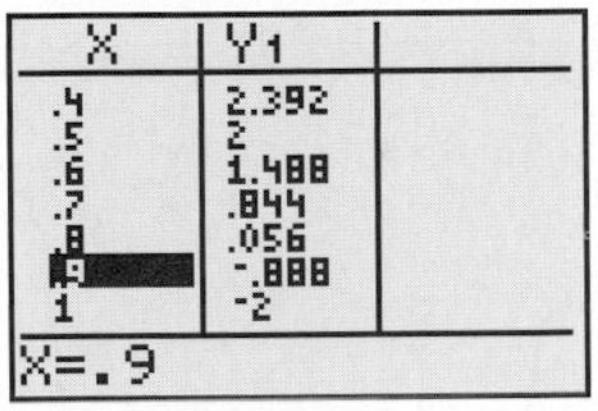

2.2 Exercises

VOCABULARY CHECK: Fill in the blanks.

1. The graphs of all polynomial functions are ________, which means that the graphs have no breaks, holes, or gaps.
2. The ________ ________ ________ is used to determine the left-hand and right-hand behavior of the graph of a polynomial function.
3. A polynomial function of degree n has at most ________ real zeros and at most ________ turning points.
4. If $x = a$ is a zero of a polynomial function f, then the following three statements are true.
   (a) $x = a$ is a ________ of the polynomial equation $f(x) = 0$.
   (b) ________ is a factor of the polynomial $f(x)$.
   (c) $(a, 0)$ is an ________ of the graph f.
5. If a real zero of a polynomial function is of even multiplicity, then the graph of f ________ the x-axis at $x = a$, and if it is of odd multiplicity then the graph of f ________ the x-axis at $x = a$.
6. A polynomial function is written in ________ form if its terms are written in descending order of exponents from left to right.
7. The ________ ________ Theorem states that if f is a polynomial function such that $f(a) \neq f(b)$, then in the interval $[a, b]$, f takes on every value between $f(a)$ and $f(b)$.

In Exercises 1–8, match the polynomial function with its graph. [The graphs are labeled (a), (b), (c), (d), (e), (f), (g), and (h).]

(a)

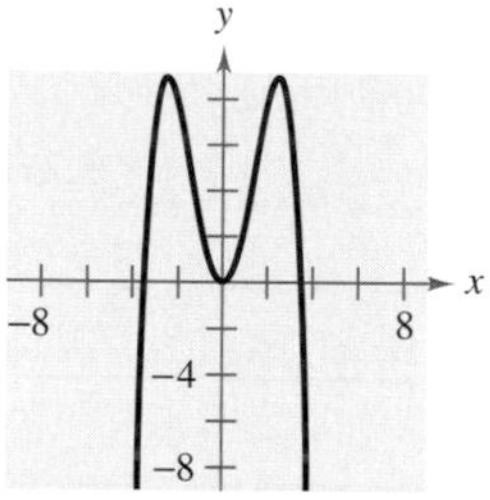

(b)

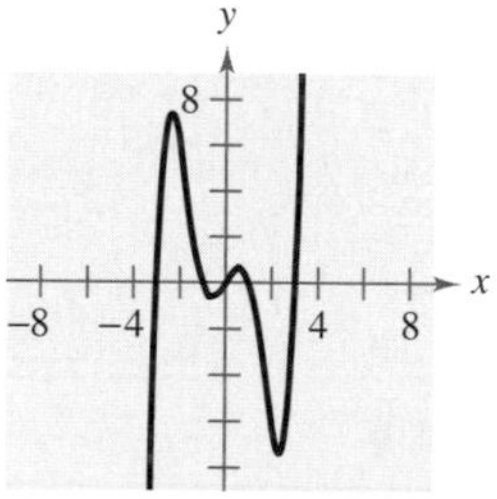

(c)

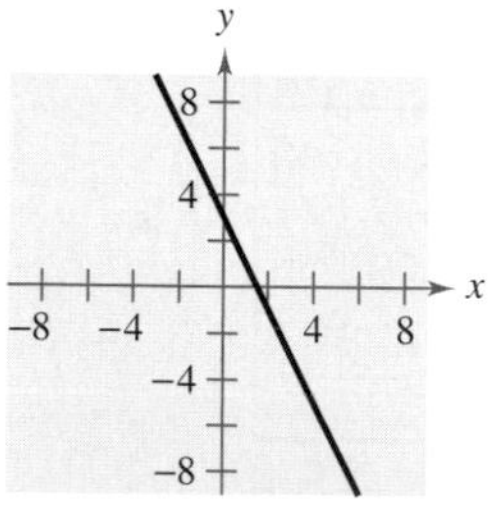

(d)

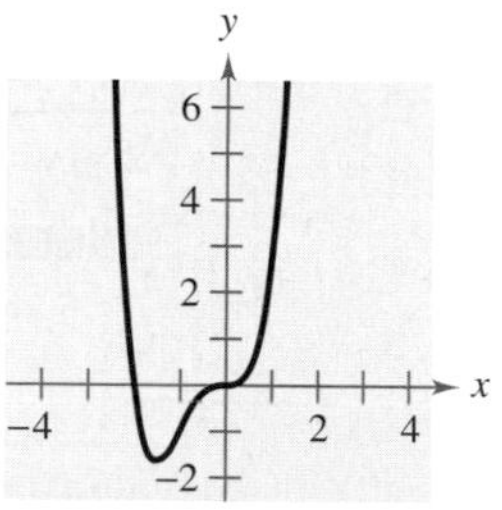

(e)

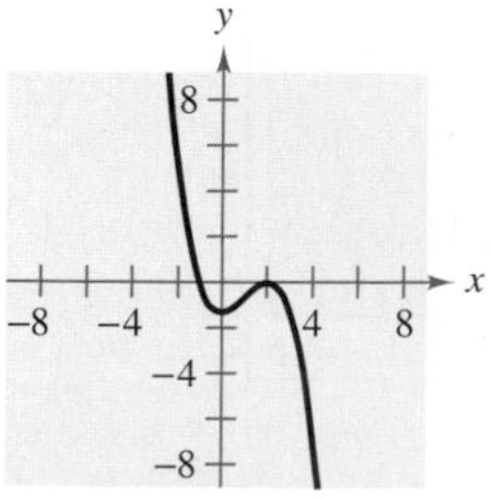

(f)

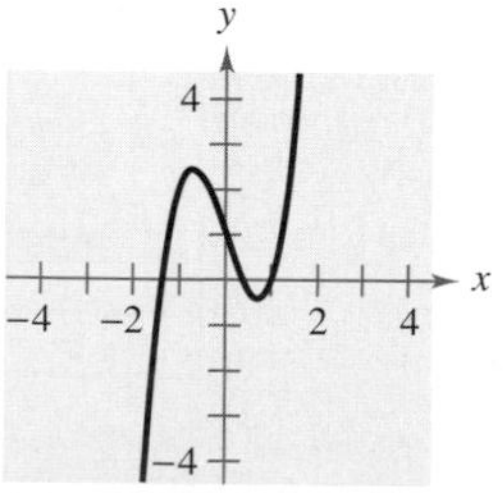

(g)

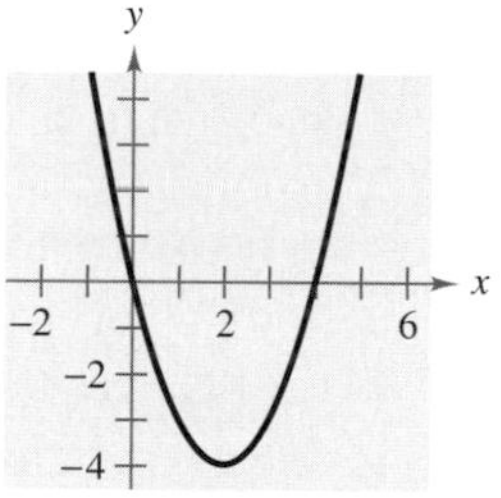

(h)

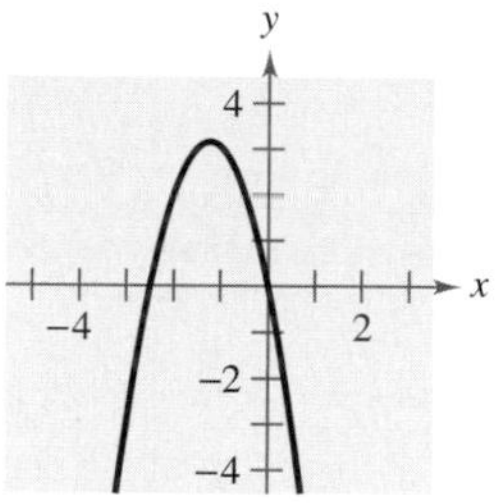

1. $f(x) = -2x + 3$
2. $f(x) = x^2 - 4x$
3. $f(x) = -2x^2 - 5x$
4. $f(x) = 2x^3 - 3x + 1$
5. $f(x) = -\frac{1}{4}x^4 + 3x^2$
6. $f(x) = -\frac{1}{3}x^3 + x^2 - \frac{4}{3}$
7. $f(x) = x^4 + 2x^3$
8. $f(x) = \frac{1}{5}x^5 - 2x^3 + \frac{9}{5}x$

In Exercises 9–12, sketch the graph of $y = x^n$ and each transformation.

9. $y = x^3$
   (a) $f(x) = (x - 2)^3$
   (b) $f(x) = x^3 - 2$
   (c) $f(x) = -\frac{1}{2}x^3$
   (d) $f(x) = (x - 2)^3 - 2$
10. $y = x^5$
   (a) $f(x) = (x + 1)^5$
   (b) $f(x) = x^5 + 1$
   (c) $f(x) = 1 - \frac{1}{2}x^5$
   (d) $f(x) = -\frac{1}{2}(x + 1)^5$
11. $y = x^4$
   (a) $f(x) = (x + 3)^4$
   (b) $f(x) = x^4 - 3$
   (c) $f(x) = 4 - x^4$
   (d) $f(x) = \frac{1}{2}(x - 1)^4$
   (e) $f(x) = (2x)^4 + 1$
   (f) $f(x) = \left(\frac{1}{2}x\right)^4 - 2$

12. $y = x^6$

(a) $f(x) = -\frac{1}{8}x^6$ (b) $f(x) = (x + 2)^6 - 4$

(c) $f(x) = x^6 - 4$ (d) $f(x) = -\frac{1}{4}x^6 + 1$

(e) $f(x) = \left(\frac{1}{4}x\right)^6 - 2$ (f) $f(x) = (2x)^6 - 1$

In Exercises 13–22, describe the right-hand and left-hand behavior of the graph of the polynomial function.

13. $f(x) = \frac{1}{3}x^3 + 5x$ **14.** $f(x) = 2x^2 - 3x + 1$

15. $g(x) = 5 - \frac{7}{2}x - 3x^2$ **16.** $h(x) = 1 - x^6$

17. $f(x) = -2.1x^5 + 4x^3 - 2$

18. $f(x) = 2x^5 - 5x + 7.5$

19. $f(x) = 6 - 2x + 4x^2 - 5x^3$

20. $f(x) = \dfrac{3x^4 - 2x + 5}{4}$

21. $h(t) = -\frac{2}{3}(t^2 - 5t + 3)$

22. $f(s) = -\frac{7}{8}(s^3 + 5s^2 - 7s + 1)$

Graphical Analysis **In Exercises 23–26, use a graphing utility to graph the functions f and g in the same viewing window. Zoom out sufficiently far to show that the right-hand and left-hand behaviors of f and g appear identical.**

23. $f(x) = 3x^3 - 9x + 1, \quad g(x) = 3x^3$

24. $f(x) = -\frac{1}{3}(x^3 - 3x + 2), \quad g(x) = -\frac{1}{3}x^3$

25. $f(x) = -(x^4 - 4x^3 + 16x), \quad g(x) = -x^4$

26. $f(x) = 3x^4 - 6x^2, \quad g(x) = 3x^4$

In Exercises 27–42, (a) find all the real zeros of the polynomial function, (b) determine the multiplicity of each zero and the number of turning points of the graph of the function, and (c) use a graphing utility to graph the function and verify your answers.

27. $f(x) = x^2 - 25$ **28.** $f(x) = 49 - x^2$

29. $h(t) = t^2 - 6t + 9$ **30.** $f(x) = x^2 + 10x + 25$

31. $f(x) = \frac{1}{3}x^2 + \frac{1}{3}x - \frac{2}{3}$

32. $f(x) = \frac{1}{2}x^2 + \frac{5}{2}x - \frac{3}{2}$

33. $f(x) = 3x^3 - 12x^2 + 3x$

34. $g(x) = 5x(x^2 - 2x - 1)$

35. $f(t) = t^3 - 4t^2 + 4t$

36. $f(x) = x^4 - x^3 - 20x^2$

37. $g(t) = t^5 - 6t^3 + 9t$

38. $f(x) = x^5 + x^3 - 6x$

39. $f(x) = 5x^4 + 15x^2 + 10$

40. $f(x) = 2x^4 - 2x^2 - 40$

41. $g(x) = x^3 + 3x^2 - 4x - 12$

42. $f(x) = x^3 - 4x^2 - 25x + 100$

Graphical Analysis **In Exercises 43–46, (a) use a graphing utility to graph the function, (b) use the graph to approximate any x-intercepts of the graph, (c) set $y = 0$ and solve the resulting equation, and (d) compare the results of part (c) with any x-intercepts of the graph.**

43. $y = 4x^3 - 20x^2 + 25x$

44. $y = 4x^3 + 4x^2 - 8x + 8$

45. $y = x^5 - 5x^3 + 4x$

46. $y = \frac{1}{4}x^3(x^2 - 9)$

In Exercises 47–56, find a polynomial function that has the given zeros. (There are many correct answers.)

47. $0, 10$ **48.** $0, -3$

49. $2, -6$ **50.** $-4, 5$

51. $0, -2, -3$ **52.** $0, 2, 5$

53. $4, -3, 3, 0$ **54.** $-2, -1, 0, 1, 2$

55. $1 + \sqrt{3}, 1 - \sqrt{3}$ **56.** $2, 4 + \sqrt{5}, 4 - \sqrt{5}$

In Exercises 57–66, find a polynomial of degree n that has the given zero(s). (There are many correct answers.)

	Zero(s)	*Degree*
57.	$x = -2$	$n = 2$
58.	$x = -8, -4$	$n = 2$
59.	$x = -3, 0, 1$	$n = 3$
60.	$x = -2, 4, 7$	$n = 3$
61.	$x = 0, \sqrt{3}, -\sqrt{3}$	$n = 3$
62.	$x = 9$	$n = 3$
63.	$x = -5, 1, 2$	$n = 4$
64.	$x = -4, -1, 3, 6$	$n = 4$
65.	$x = 0, -4$	$n = 5$
66.	$x = -3, 1, 5, 6$	$n = 5$

In Exercises 67–80, sketch the graph of the function by (a) applying the Leading Coefficient Test, (b) finding the zeros of the polynomial, (c) plotting sufficient solution points, and (d) drawing a continuous curve through the points.

67. $f(x) = x^3 - 9x$ **68.** $g(x) = x^4 - 4x^2$

69. $f(t) = \frac{1}{4}(t^2 - 2t + 15)$

70. $g(x) = -x^2 + 10x - 16$

71. $f(x) = x^3 - 3x^2$ **72.** $f(x) = 1 - x^3$

73. $f(x) = 3x^3 - 15x^2 + 18x$

74. $f(x) = -4x^3 + 4x^2 + 15x$

75. $f(x) = -5x^2 - x^3$ **76.** $f(x) = -48x^2 + 3x^4$

77. $f(x) = x^2(x - 4)$ **78.** $h(x) = \frac{1}{3}x^3(x - 4)^2$

79. $g(t) = -\frac{1}{4}(t - 2)^2(t + 2)^2$

80. $g(x) = \frac{1}{10}(x + 1)^2(x - 3)^3$

In Exercises 81–84, use a graphing utility to graph the function. Use the *zero* or *root* feature to approximate the real zeros of the function. Then determine the multiplicity of each zero.

81. $f(x) = x^3 - 4x$

82. $f(x) = \frac{1}{4}x^4 - 2x^2$

83. $g(x) = \frac{1}{5}(x + 1)^2(x - 3)(2x - 9)$

84. $h(x) = \frac{1}{5}(x + 2)^2(3x - 5)^2$

In Exercises 85–88, use the Intermediate Value Theorem and the *table* feature of a graphing utility to find intervals one unit in length in which the polynomial function is guaranteed to have a zero. Adjust the table to approximate the zeros of the function. Use the *zero* or *root* feature of a graphing utility to verify your results.

85. $f(x) = x^3 - 3x^2 + 3$

86. $f(x) = 0.11x^3 - 2.07x^2 + 9.81x - 6.88$

87. $g(x) = 3x^4 + 4x^3 - 3$

88. $h(x) = x^4 - 10x^2 + 3$

89. ***Numerical and Graphical Analysis*** An open box is to be made from a square piece of material, 36 inches on a side, by cutting equal squares with sides of length x from the corners and turning up the sides (see figure).

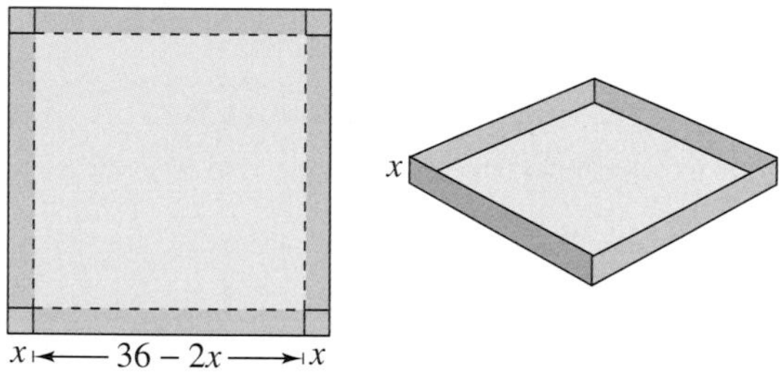

(a) Verify that the volume of the box is given by the function

$V(x) = x(36 - 2x)^2$.

(b) Determine the domain of the function.

(c) Use a graphing utility to create a table that shows the box height x and the corresponding volumes V. Use the table to estimate the dimensions that will produce a maximum volume.

(d) Use a graphing utility to graph V and use the graph to estimate the value of x for which $V(x)$ is maximum. Compare your result with that of part (c).

90. ***Maximum Volume*** An open box with locking tabs is to be made from a square piece of material 24 inches on a side. This is to be done by cutting equal squares from the corners and folding along the dashed lines shown in the figure.

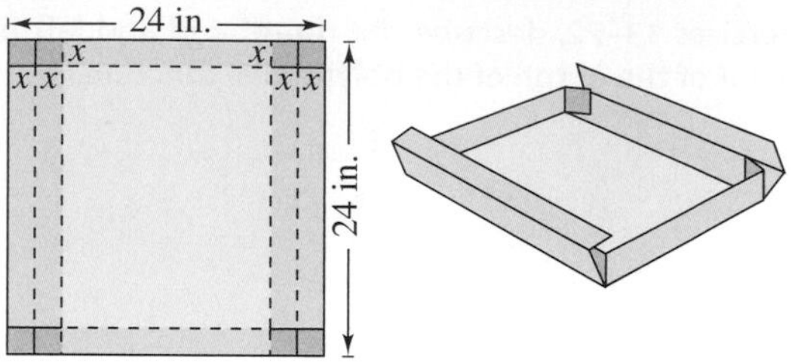

(a) Verify that the volume of the box is given by the function

$V(x) = 8x(6 - x)(12 - x)$.

(b) Determine the domain of the function V.

(c) Sketch a graph of the function and estimate the value of x for which $V(x)$ is maximum.

91. ***Construction*** A roofing contractor is fabricating gutters from 12-inch aluminum sheeting. The contractor plans to use an aluminum siding folding press to create the gutter by creasing equal lengths for the sidewalls (see figure).

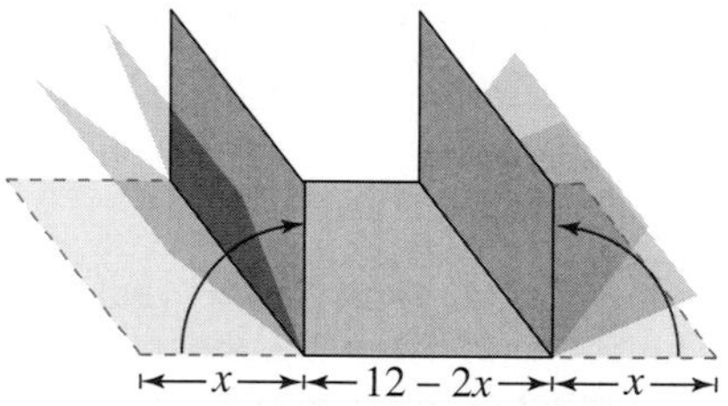

(a) Let x represent the height of the sidewall of the gutter. Write a function A that represents the cross-sectional area of the gutter.

(b) The length of the aluminum sheeting is 16 feet. Write a function V that represents the volume of one run of gutter in terms of x.

(c) Determine the domain of the function in part (b).

(d) Use a graphing utility to create a table that shows the sidewall height x and the corresponding volumes V. Use the table to estimate the dimensions that will produce a maximum volume.

(e) Use a graphing utility to graph V. Use the graph to estimate the value of x for which $V(x)$ is a maximum. Compare your result with that of part (d).

(f) Would the value of x change if the aluminum sheeting were of different lengths? Explain.

92. ***Construction*** An industrial propane tank is formed by adjoining two hemispheres to the ends of a right circular cylinder. The length of the cylindrical portion of the tank is four times the radius of the hemispherical components (see figure).

(a) Write a function that represents the total volume V of the tank in terms of r.

(b) Find the domain of the function.

(c) Use a graphing utility to graph the function.

(d) The total volume of the tank is to be 120 cubic feet. Use the graph from part (c) to estimate the radius and length of the cylindrical portion of the tank.

Data Analysis: Home Prices **In Exercise 93–96, use the table, which shows the median prices (in thousands of dollars) of new privately owned U.S. homes in the Midwest y_1 and in the South y_2 for the years 1997 through 2003. The data can be approximated by the following models.**

$$y_1 = 0.139t^3 - 4.42t^2 + 51.1t - 39$$

$$y_2 = 0.056t^3 - 1.73t^2 + 23.8t + 29$$

In the models, t represents the year, with $t = 7$ corresponding to 1997. (Source: U.S. Census Bureau; U.S. Department of Housing and Urban Development)

Year, t	y_1	y_2
7	150	130
8	158	136
9	164	146
10	170	148
11	173	155
12	178	163
13	184	168

93. Use a graphing utility to plot the data and graph the model for y_1 in the same viewing window. How closely does the model represent the data?

94. Use a graphing utility to plot the data and graph the model for y_2 in the same viewing window. How closely does the model represent the data?

95. Use the models to predict the median prices of a new privately owned home in both regions in 2008. Do your answers seem reasonable? Explain.

96. Use the graphs of the models in Exercises 93 and 94 to write a short paragraph about the relationship between the median prices of homes in the two regions.

Model It

97. ***Tree Growth*** The growth of a red oak tree is approximated by the function

$$G = -0.003t^3 + 0.137t^2 + 0.458t - 0.839$$

where G is the height of the tree (in feet) and t $(2 \le t \le 34)$ is its age (in years).

(a) Use a graphing utility to graph the function. (*Hint:* Use a viewing window in which $-10 \le x \le 45$ and $-5 \le y \le 60$.)

(b) Estimate the age of the tree when it is growing most rapidly. This point is called the *point of diminishing returns* because the increase in size will be less with each additional year.

(c) Using calculus, the point of diminishing returns can also be found by finding the vertex of the parabola given by

$$y = -0.009t^2 + 0.274t + 0.458.$$

Find the vertex of this parabola.

(d) Compare your results from parts (b) and (c).

98. ***Revenue*** The total revenue R (in millions of dollars) for a company is related to its advertising expense by the function

$$R = \frac{1}{100{,}000}(-x^3 + 600x^2), \qquad 0 \le x \le 400$$

where x is the amount spent on advertising (in tens of thousands of dollars). Use the graph of this function, shown in the figure, to estimate the point on the graph at which the function is increasing most rapidly. This point is called the *point of diminishing returns* because any expense above this amount will yield less return per dollar invested in advertising.

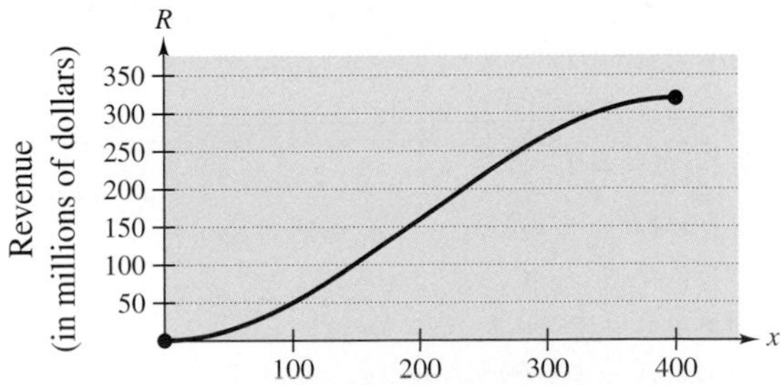

Advertising expense
(in tens of thousands of dollars)

Synthesis

True or False? **In Exercises 99–101, determine whether the statement is true or false. Justify your answer.**

99. A fifth-degree polynomial can have five turning points in its graph.

100. It is possible for a sixth-degree polynomial to have only one solution.

101. The graph of the function given by

$$f(x) = 2 + x - x^2 + x^3 - x^4 + x^5 + x^6 - x^7$$

rises to the left and falls to the right.

102. ***Graphical Analysis*** For each graph, describe a polynomial function that could represent the graph. (Indicate the degree of the function and the sign of its leading coefficient.)

(a)

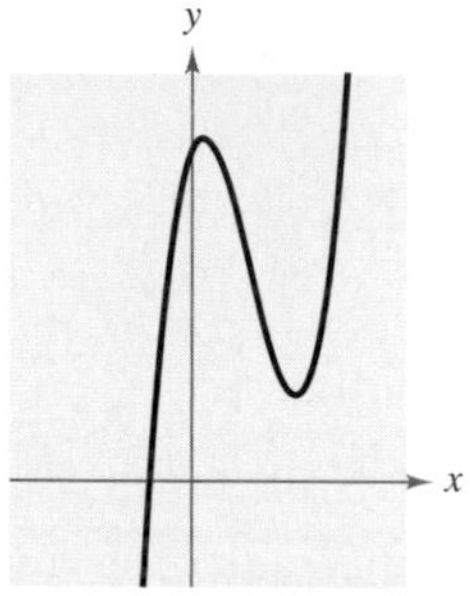

(b)

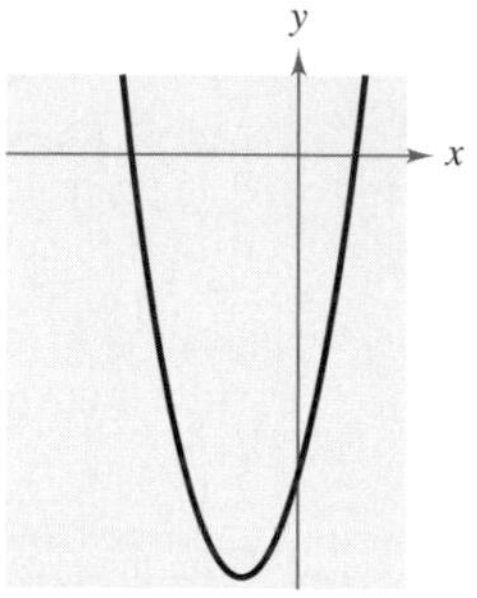

(c)

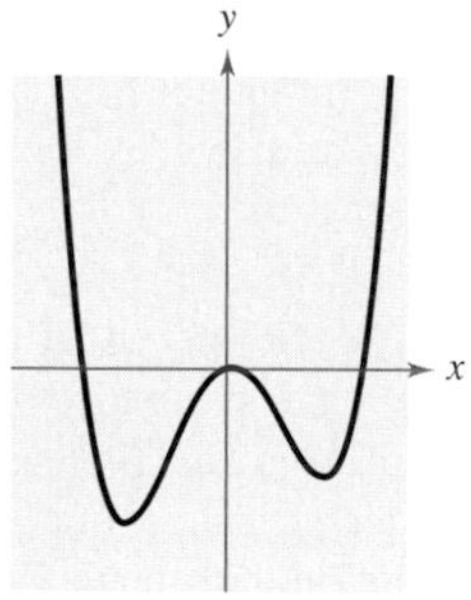

(d)

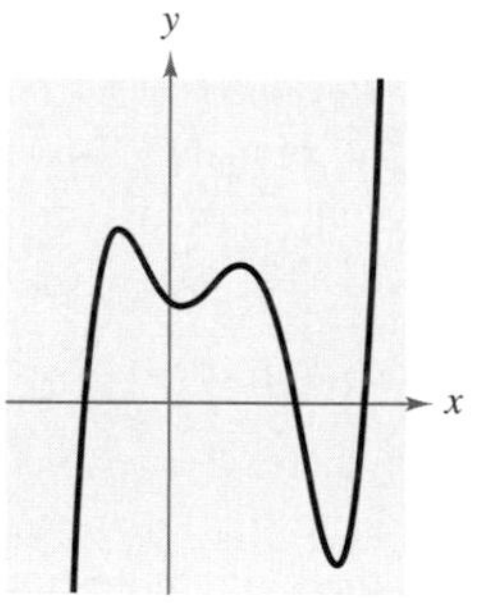

103. ***Graphical Reasoning*** Sketch a graph of the function given by $f(x) = x^4$. Explain how the graph of each function g differs (if it does) from the graph of each function f. Determine whether g is odd, even, or neither.

(a) $g(x) = f(x) + 2$

(b) $g(x) = f(x + 2)$

(c) $g(x) = f(-x)$

(d) $g(x) = -f(x)$

(e) $g(x) = f\left(\frac{1}{2}x\right)$

(f) $g(x) = \frac{1}{2}f(x)$

(g) $g(x) = f\left(x^{3/4}\right)$

(h) $g(x) = (f \circ f)(x)$

104. ***Exploration*** Explore the transformations of the form $g(x) = a(x - h)^5 + k$.

(a) Use a graphing utility to graph the functions given by

$$y_1 = -\frac{1}{3}(x - 2)^5 + 1$$

and

$$y_2 = \frac{3}{5}(x + 2)^5 - 3.$$

Determine whether the graphs are increasing or decreasing. Explain.

(b) Will the graph of g always be increasing or decreasing? If so, is this behavior determined by a, h, or k? Explain.

(c) Use a graphing utility to graph the function given by

$$H(x) = x^5 - 3x^3 + 2x + 1.$$

Use the graph and the result of part (b) to determine whether H can be written in the form $H(x) = a(x - h)^5 + k$. Explain.

Skills Review

In Exercises 105–108, factor the expression completely.

105. $5x^2 + 7x - 24$

106. $6x^3 - 61x^2 + 10x$

107. $4x^4 - 7x^3 - 15x^2$

108. $y^3 + 216$

In Exercises 109–112, solve the equation by factoring.

109. $2x^2 - x - 28 = 0$

110. $3x^2 - 22x - 16 = 0$

111. $12x^2 + 11x - 5 = 0$

112. $x^2 + 24x + 144 = 0$

In Exercises 113–116, solve the equation by completing the square.

113. $x^2 - 2x - 21 = 0$

114. $x^2 - 8x + 2 = 0$

115. $2x^2 + 5x - 20 = 0$

116. $3x^2 + 4x - 9 = 0$

In Exercises 117–122, describe the transformation from a common function that occurs in *f*(*x*). Then sketch its graph.

117. $f(x) = (x + 4)^2$

118. $f(x) = 3 - x^2$

119. $f(x) = \sqrt{x + 1} - 5$

120. $f(x) = 7 - \sqrt{x - 6}$

121. $f(x) = 2[\![x]\!] + 9$

122. $f(x) = 10 - \frac{1}{3}[\![x + 3]\!]$

2.3 Polynomial and Synthetic Division

What you should learn

- Use long division to divide polynomials by other polynomials.
- Use synthetic division to divide polynomials by binomials of the form $(x - k)$.
- Use the Remainder Theorem and the Factor Theorem.

Why you should learn it

Synthetic division can help you evaluate polynomial functions. For instance, in Exercise 73 on page 160, you will use synthetic division to determine the number of U.S. military personnel in 2008.

Long Division of Polynomials

In this section, you will study two procedures for *dividing* polynomials. These procedures are especially valuable in factoring and finding the zeros of polynomial functions. To begin, suppose you are given the graph of

$$f(x) = 6x^3 - 19x^2 + 16x - 4.$$

Notice that a zero of f occurs at $x = 2$, as shown in Figure 2.27. Because $x = 2$ is a zero of f, you know that $(x - 2)$ is a factor of $f(x)$. This means that there exists a second-degree polynomial $q(x)$ such that

$$f(x) = (x - 2) \cdot q(x).$$

To find $q(x)$, you can use **long division,** as illustrated in Example 1.

Example 1 Long Division of Polynomials

Divide $6x^3 - 19x^2 + 16x - 4$ by $x - 2$, and use the result to factor the polynomial completely.

Solution

Think $\dfrac{6x^3}{x} = 6x^2.$

Think $\dfrac{-7x^2}{x} = -7x.$

Think $\dfrac{2x}{x} = 2.$

$$\begin{array}{rll}
 & 6x^2 - 7x + 2 & \\
x - 2 \,\big) & 6x^3 - 19x^2 + 16x - 4 & \\
 & \underline{6x^3 - 12x^2} & \text{Multiply: } 6x^2(x - 2). \\
 & -7x^2 + 16x & \text{Subtract.} \\
 & \underline{-7x^2 + 14x} & \text{Multiply: } -7x(x - 2). \\
 & 2x - 4 & \text{Subtract.} \\
 & \underline{2x - 4} & \text{Multiply: } 2(x - 2). \\
 & 0 & \text{Subtract.}
\end{array}$$

From this division, you can conclude that

$$6x^3 - 19x^2 + 16x - 4 = (x - 2)(6x^2 - 7x + 2)$$

and by factoring the quadratic $6x^2 - 7x + 2$, you have

$$6x^3 - 19x^2 + 16x - 4 = (x - 2)(2x - 1)(3x - 2).$$

Note that this factorization agrees with the graph shown in Figure 2.27 in that the three x-intercepts occur at $x = 2$, $x = \frac{1}{2}$, and $x = \frac{2}{3}$.

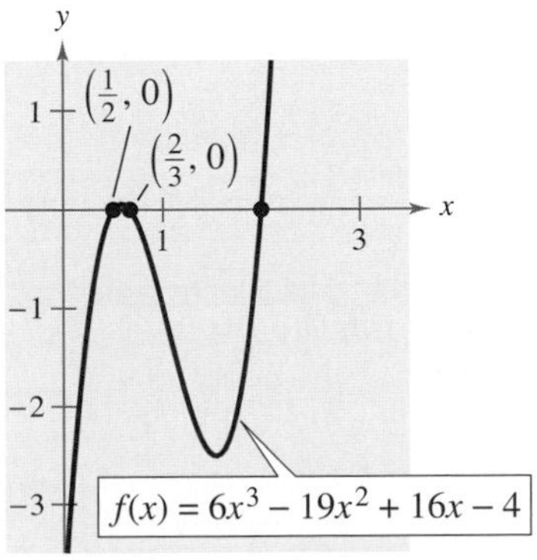

FIGURE 2.27

CHECKPOINT Now try Exercise 5.

In Example 1, $x - 2$ is a factor of the polynomial $6x^3 - 19x^2 + 16x - 4$, and the long division process produces a remainder of zero. Often, long division will produce a nonzero remainder. For instance, if you divide $x^2 + 3x + 5$ by $x + 1$, you obtain the following.

$$\begin{array}{rll} & x + 2 & \leftarrow \text{Quotient} \\ \text{Divisor} \rightarrow x + 1 \,\big)\!\!\!\! & \overline{x^2 + 3x + 5} & \leftarrow \text{Dividend} \\ & \underline{x^2 + x} & \\ & 2x + 5 & \\ & \underline{2x + 2} & \\ & 3 & \leftarrow \text{Remainder} \end{array}$$

In fractional form, you can write this result as follows.

$$\overbrace{\frac{x^2 + 3x + 5}{\underbrace{x + 1}_{\text{Divisor}}}}^{\text{Dividend}} = \overbrace{x + 2}^{\text{Quotient}} + \frac{\overset{\text{Remainder}}{3}}{\underbrace{x + 1}_{\text{Divisor}}}$$

This implies that

$$x^2 + 3x + 5 = (x + 1)(x + 2) + 3 \qquad \text{Multiply each side by } (x + 1).$$

which illustrates the following theorem, called the **Division Algorithm.**

The Division Algorithm

If $f(x)$ and $d(x)$ are polynomials such that $d(x) \neq 0$, and the degree of $d(x)$ is less than or equal to the degree of $f(x)$, there exist unique polynomials $q(x)$ and $r(x)$ such that

$$\underset{\text{Dividend}}{f(x)} = \underset{\text{Divisor}}{d(x)}\underset{\text{Quotient}}{q(x)} + \underset{\text{Remainder}}{r(x)}$$

where $r(x) = 0$ *or* the degree of $r(x)$ is less than the degree of $d(x)$. If the remainder $r(x)$ is zero, $d(x)$ *divides evenly* into $f(x)$.

The Division Algorithm can also be written as

$$\frac{f(x)}{d(x)} = q(x) + \frac{r(x)}{d(x)}.$$

In the Division Algorithm, the rational expression $f(x)/d(x)$ is **improper** because the degree of $f(x)$ is greater than or equal to the degree of $d(x)$. On the other hand, the rational expression $r(x)/d(x)$ is **proper** because the degree of $r(x)$ is less than the degree of $d(x)$.

Before you apply the Division Algorithm, follow these steps.

1. Write the dividend and divisor in descending powers of the variable.
2. Insert placeholders with zero coefficients for missing powers of the variable.

Example 2 Long Division of Polynomials

Divide $x^3 - 1$ by $x - 1$.

Solution

Because there is no x^2-term or x-term in the dividend, you need to line up the subtraction by using zero coefficients (or leaving spaces) for the missing terms.

$$\begin{array}{r}
x^2 + x + 1 \\
x - 1 \overline{) x^3 + 0x^2 + 0x - 1} \\
\underline{x^3 - x^2} \quad\quad\quad\quad \\
x^2 + 0x \quad\quad \\
\underline{x^2 - x} \quad\quad \\
x - 1 \\
\underline{x - 1} \\
0
\end{array}$$

So, $x - 1$ divides evenly into $x^3 - 1$, and you can write

$$\frac{x^3 - 1}{x - 1} = x^2 + x + 1, \quad x \neq 1.$$

✓CHECKPOINT Now try Exercise 13.

You can check the result of Example 2 by multiplying.

$$(x - 1)(x^2 + x + 1) = x^3 + x^2 + x - x^2 - x - 1 = x^3 - 1$$

Example 3 Long Division of Polynomials

Divide $2x^4 + 4x^3 - 5x^2 + 3x - 2$ by $x^2 + 2x - 3$.

Solution

$$\begin{array}{r}
2x^2 \quad\quad\quad + 1 \\
x^2 + 2x - 3 \overline{) 2x^4 + 4x^3 - 5x^2 + 3x - 2} \\
\underline{2x^4 + 4x^3 - 6x^2} \quad\quad\quad\quad \\
x^2 + 3x - 2 \\
\underline{x^2 + 2x - 3} \\
x + 1
\end{array}$$

Note that the first subtraction eliminated two terms from the dividend. When this happens, the quotient skips a term. You can write the result as

$$\frac{2x^4 + 4x^3 - 5x^2 + 3x - 2}{x^2 + 2x - 3} = 2x^2 + 1 + \frac{x + 1}{x^2 + 2x - 3}.$$

✓CHECKPOINT Now try Exercise 15.

Synthetic Division

There is a nice shortcut for long division of polynomials when dividing by divisors of the form $x - k$. This shortcut is called **synthetic division.** The pattern for synthetic division of a cubic polynomial is summarized as follows. (The pattern for higher-degree polynomials is similar.)

> **Synthetic Division (for a Cubic Polynomial)**
>
> To divide $ax^3 + bx^2 + cx + d$ by $x - k$, use the following pattern.
>
> 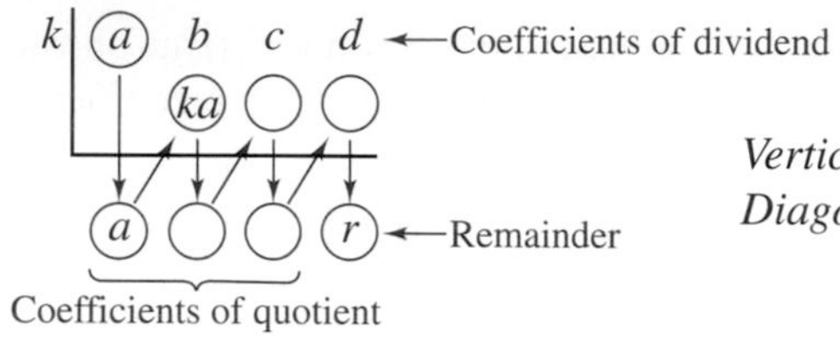
>
>
> *Vertical pattern:* Add terms.
> *Diagonal pattern:* Multiply by k.

Synthetic division works only for divisors of the form $x - k$. [Remember that $x + k = x - (-k)$.] You cannot use synthetic division to divide a polynomial by a quadratic such as $x^2 - 3$.

Example 4 Using Synthetic Division

Use synthetic division to divide $x^4 - 10x^2 - 2x + 4$ by $x + 3$.

Solution

You should set up the array as follows. Note that a zero is included for the missing x^3-term in the dividend.

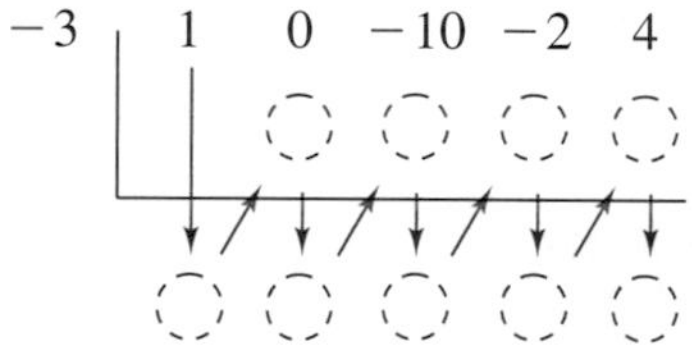

Then, use the synthetic division pattern by adding terms in columns and multiplying the results by -3.

Divisor: $x + 3$ Dividend: $x^4 - 10x^2 - 2x + 4$

$$\begin{array}{r|rrrrr} -3 & 1 & 0 & -10 & -2 & 4 \\ & & -3 & 9 & 3 & -3 \\ \hline & 1 & -3 & -1 & 1 & \boxed{1} \end{array}$$

Remainder: 1

Quotient: $x^3 - 3x^2 - x + 1$

So, you have

$$\frac{x^4 - 10x^2 - 2x + 4}{x + 3} = x^3 - 3x^2 - x + 1 + \frac{1}{x + 3}.$$

✓CHECKPOINT Now try Exercise 19.

The Remainder and Factor Theorems

The remainder obtained in the synthetic division process has an important interpretation, as described in the **Remainder Theorem.**

> **The Remainder Theorem**
>
> If a polynomial $f(x)$ is divided by $x - k$, the remainder is
>
> $$r = f(k).$$

For a proof of the Remainder Theorem, see Proofs in Mathematics on page 213.

The Remainder Theorem tells you that synthetic division can be used to evaluate a polynomial function. That is, to evaluate a polynomial function $f(x)$ when $x = k$, divide $f(x)$ by $x - k$. The remainder will be $f(k)$, as illustrated in Example 5.

Example 5 Using the Remainder Theorem

Use the Remainder Theorem to evaluate the following function at $x = -2$.

$$f(x) = 3x^3 + 8x^2 + 5x - 7$$

Solution

Using synthetic division, you obtain the following.

$$\begin{array}{r|rrrr} -2 & 3 & 8 & 5 & -7 \\ & & -6 & -4 & -2 \\ \hline & 3 & 2 & 1 & -9 \end{array}$$

Because the remainder is $r = -9$, you can conclude that

$$f(-2) = -9. \qquad r = f(k)$$

This means that $(-2, -9)$ is a point on the graph of f. You can check this by substituting $x = -2$ in the original function.

Check

$$f(-2) = 3(-2)^3 + 8(-2)^2 + 5(-2) - 7$$
$$= 3(-8) + 8(4) - 10 - 7 = -9$$

CHECKPOINT Now try Exercise 45.

Another important theorem is the **Factor Theorem,** stated below. This theorem states that you can test to see whether a polynomial has $(x - k)$ as a factor by evaluating the polynomial at $x = k$. If the result is 0, $(x - k)$ is a factor.

> **The Factor Theorem**
>
> A polynomial $f(x)$ has a factor $(x - k)$ if and only if $f(k) = 0$.

For a proof of the Factor Theorem, see Proofs in Mathematics on page 213.

Example 6 Factoring a Polynomial: Repeated Division

Show that $(x - 2)$ and $(x + 3)$ are factors of

$$f(x) = 2x^4 + 7x^3 - 4x^2 - 27x - 18.$$

Then find the remaining factors of $f(x)$.

Solution

Using synthetic division with the factor $(x - 2)$, you obtain the following.

2	2	7	−4	−27	−18
		4	22	36	18
	2	11	18	9	0

0 remainder, so $f(2) = 0$ and $(x - 2)$ is a factor.

Take the result of this division and perform synthetic division again using the factor $(x + 3)$.

−3	2	11	18	9
		−6	−15	−9
	2	5	3	0

0 remainder, so $f(-3) = 0$ and $(x + 3)$ is a factor.

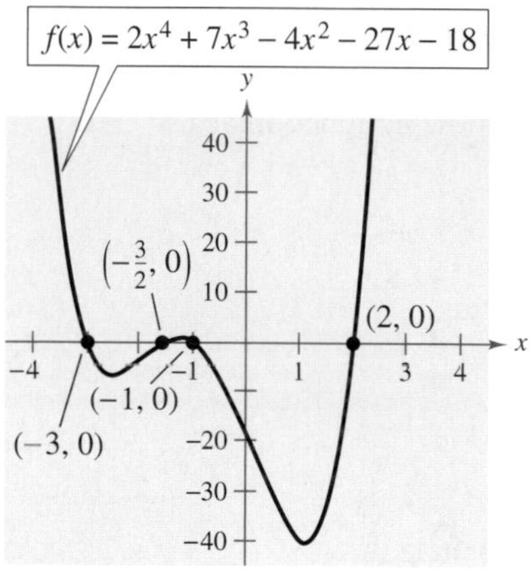

FIGURE 2.28

Because the resulting quadratic expression factors as

$$2x^2 + 5x + 3 = (2x + 3)(x + 1)$$

the complete factorization of $f(x)$ is

$$f(x) = (x - 2)(x + 3)(2x + 3)(x + 1).$$

Note that this factorization implies that f has four real zeros:

$$x = 2, x = -3, x = -\tfrac{3}{2}, \text{ and } x = -1.$$

This is confirmed by the graph of f, which is shown in Figure 2.28.

✓CHECKPOINT Now try Exercise 57.

Uses of the Remainder in Synthetic Division

The remainder r, obtained in the synthetic division of $f(x)$ by $x - k$, provides the following information.

1. The remainder r gives the value of f at $x = k$. That is, $r = f(k)$.
2. If $r = 0$, $(x - k)$ is a factor of $f(x)$.
3. If $r = 0$, $(k, 0)$ is an x-intercept of the graph of f.

Throughout this text, the importance of developing several problem-solving strategies is emphasized. In the exercises for this section, try using more than one strategy to solve several of the exercises. For instance, if you find that $x - k$ divides evenly into $f(x)$ (with no remainder), try sketching the graph of f. You should find that $(k, 0)$ is an x-intercept of the graph.

2.3 Exercises

VOCABULARY CHECK:

1. Two forms of the Division Algorithm are shown below. Identify and label each term or function.

$$f(x) = d(x)q(x) + r(x) \qquad \frac{f(x)}{d(x)} = q(x) + \frac{r(x)}{d(x)}$$

In Exercises 2–5, fill in the blanks.

2. The rational expression $p(x)/q(x)$ is called ________ if the degree of the numerator is greater than or equal to that of the denominator, and is called ________ if the degree of the numerator is less than that of the denominator.

3. An alternative method to long division of polynomials is called ________ ________, in which the divisor must be of the form $x - k$.

4. The ________ Theorem states that a polynomial $f(x)$ has a factor $(x - k)$ if and only if $f(k) = 0$.

5. The ________ Theorem states that if a polynomial $f(x)$ is divided by $x - k$, the remainder is $r = f(k)$.

Analytical Analysis **In Exercises 1 and 2, use long division to verify that $y_1 = y_2$.**

1. $y_1 = \dfrac{x^2}{x + 2}$, $y_2 = x - 2 + \dfrac{4}{x + 2}$

2. $y_1 = \dfrac{x^4 - 3x^2 - 1}{x^2 + 5}$, $y_2 = x^2 - 8 + \dfrac{39}{x^2 + 5}$

Graphical Analysis **In Exercises 3 and 4, (a) use a graphing utility to graph the two equations in the same viewing window, (b) use the graphs to verify that the expressions are equivalent, and (c) use long division to verify the results algebraically.**

3. $y_1 = \dfrac{x^5 - 3x^3}{x^2 + 1}$, $y_2 = x^3 - 4x + \dfrac{4x}{x^2 + 1}$

4. $y_1 = \dfrac{x^3 - 2x^2 + 5}{x^2 + x + 1}$, $y_2 = x - 3 + \dfrac{2(x + 4)}{x^2 + x + 1}$

In Exercises 5–18, use long division to divide.

5. $(2x^2 + 10x + 12) \div (x + 3)$

6. $(5x^2 - 17x - 12) \div (x - 4)$

7. $(4x^3 - 7x^2 - 11x + 5) \div (4x + 5)$

8. $(6x^3 - 16x^2 + 17x - 6) \div (3x - 2)$

9. $(x^4 + 5x^3 + 6x^2 - x - 2) \div (x + 2)$

10. $(x^3 + 4x^2 - 3x - 12) \div (x - 3)$

11. $(7x + 3) \div (x + 2)$

12. $(8x - 5) \div (2x + 1)$

13. $(6x^3 + 10x^2 + x + 8) \div (2x^2 + 1)$

14. $(x^3 - 9) \div (x^2 + 1)$

15. $(x^4 + 3x^2 + 1) \div (x^2 - 2x + 3)$

16. $(x^5 + 7) \div (x^3 - 1)$

17. $\dfrac{x^4}{(x - 1)^3}$

18. $\dfrac{2x^3 - 4x^2 - 15x + 5}{(x - 1)^2}$

In Exercises 19–36, use synthetic division to divide.

19. $(3x^3 - 17x^2 + 15x - 25) \div (x - 5)$

20. $(5x^3 + 18x^2 + 7x - 6) \div (x + 3)$

21. $(4x^3 - 9x + 8x^2 - 18) \div (x + 2)$

22. $(9x^3 - 16x - 18x^2 + 32) \div (x - 2)$

23. $(-x^3 + 75x - 250) \div (x + 10)$

24. $(3x^3 - 16x^2 - 72) \div (x - 6)$

25. $(5x^3 - 6x^2 + 8) \div (x - 4)$

26. $(5x^3 + 6x + 8) \div (x + 2)$

27. $\dfrac{10x^4 - 50x^3 - 800}{x - 6}$

28. $\dfrac{x^5 - 13x^4 - 120x + 80}{x + 3}$

29. $\dfrac{x^3 + 512}{x + 8}$

30. $\dfrac{x^3 - 729}{x - 9}$

31. $\dfrac{-3x^4}{x - 2}$

32. $\dfrac{-3x^4}{x + 2}$

33. $\dfrac{180x - x^4}{x - 6}$

34. $\dfrac{5 - 3x + 2x^2 - x^3}{x + 1}$

35. $\dfrac{4x^3 + 16x^2 - 23x - 15}{x + \frac{1}{2}}$

36. $\dfrac{3x^3 - 4x^2 + 5}{x - \frac{3}{2}}$

In Exercises 37–44, write the function in the form $f(x) = (x - k)q(x) + r$ for the given value of k, and demonstrate that $f(k) = r$.

	Function	*Value of k*
37.	$f(x) = x^3 - x^2 - 14x + 11$	$k = 4$
38.	$f(x) = x^3 - 5x^2 - 11x + 8$	$k = -2$

Function	*Value of k*
39. $f(x) = 15x^4 + 10x^3 - 6x^2 + 14$	$k = -\frac{2}{3}$
40. $f(x) = 10x^3 - 22x^2 - 3x + 4$	$k = \frac{1}{5}$
41. $f(x) = x^3 + 3x^2 - 2x - 14$	$k = \sqrt{2}$
42. $f(x) = x^3 + 2x^2 - 5x - 4$	$k = -\sqrt{5}$
43. $f(x) = -4x^3 + 6x^2 + 12x + 4$	$k = 1 - \sqrt{3}$
44. $f(x) = -3x^3 + 8x^2 + 10x - 8$	$k = 2 + \sqrt{2}$

In Exercises 45–48, use synthetic division to find each function value. Verify your answers using another method.

45. $f(x) = 4x^3 - 13x + 10$

(a) $f(1)$ (b) $f(-2)$ (c) $f\left(\frac{1}{2}\right)$ (d) $f(8)$

46. $g(x) = x^6 - 4x^4 + 3x^2 + 2$

(a) $g(2)$ (b) $g(-4)$ (c) $g(3)$ (d) $g(-1)$

47. $h(x) = 3x^3 + 5x^2 - 10x + 1$

(a) $h(3)$ (b) $h\left(\frac{1}{3}\right)$ (c) $h(-2)$ (d) $h(-5)$

48. $f(x) = 0.4x^4 - 1.6x^3 + 0.7x^2 - 2$

(a) $f(1)$ (b) $f(-2)$ (c) $f(5)$ (d) $f(-10)$

In Exercises 49–56, use synthetic division to show that *x* is a solution of the third-degree polynomial equation, and use the result to factor the polynomial completely. List all real solutions of the equation.

Polynomial Equation	*Value of x*
49. $x^3 - 7x + 6 = 0$	$x = 2$
50. $x^3 - 28x - 48 = 0$	$x = -4$
51. $2x^3 - 15x^2 + 27x - 10 = 0$	$x = \frac{1}{2}$
52. $48x^3 - 80x^2 + 41x - 6 = 0$	$x = \frac{2}{3}$
53. $x^3 + 2x^2 - 3x - 6 = 0$	$x = \sqrt{3}$
54. $x^3 + 2x^2 - 2x - 4 = 0$	$x = \sqrt{2}$
55. $x^3 - 3x^2 + 2 = 0$	$x = 1 + \sqrt{3}$
56. $x^3 - x^2 - 13x - 3 = 0$	$x = 2 - \sqrt{5}$

In Exercises 57–64, (a) verify the given factors of the function *f*, (b) find the remaining factors of *f*, (c) use your results to write the complete factorization of *f*, (d) list all real zeros of *f*, and (e) confirm your results by using a graphing utility to graph the function.

Function	*Factors*
57. $f(x) = 2x^3 + x^2 - 5x + 2$	$(x + 2), (x - 1)$
58. $f(x) = 3x^3 + 2x^2 - 19x + 6$	$(x + 3), (x - 2)$
59. $f(x) = x^4 - 4x^3 - 15x^2 + 58x - 40$	$(x - 5), (x + 4)$
60. $f(x) = 8x^4 - 14x^3 - 71x^2 - 10x + 24$	$(x + 2), (x - 4)$
61. $f(x) = 6x^3 + 41x^2 - 9x - 14$	$(2x + 1), (3x - 2)$
62. $f(x) = 10x^3 - 11x^2 - 72x + 45$	$(2x + 5), (5x - 3)$
63. $f(x) = 2x^3 - x^2 - 10x + 5$	$(2x - 1), (x + \sqrt{5})$
64. $f(x) = x^3 + 3x^2 - 48x - 144$	$(x + 4\sqrt{3}), (x + 3)$

Graphical Analysis **In Exercises 65–68, (a) use the *zero* or *root* feature of a graphing utility to approximate the zeros of the function accurate to three decimal places, (b) determine one of the exact zeros, and (c) use synthetic division to verify your result from part (b), and then factor the polynomial completely.**

65. $f(x) = x^3 - 2x^2 - 5x + 10$

66. $g(x) = x^3 - 4x^2 - 2x + 8$

67. $h(t) = t^3 - 2t^2 - 7t + 2$

68. $f(s) = s^3 - 12s^2 + 40s - 24$

In Exercises 69–72, simplify the rational expression by using long division or synthetic division.

69. $\dfrac{4x^3 - 8x^2 + x + 3}{2x - 3}$

70. $\dfrac{x^3 + x^2 - 64x - 64}{x + 8}$

71. $\dfrac{x^4 + 6x^3 + 11x^2 + 6x}{x^2 + 3x + 2}$

72. $\dfrac{x^4 + 9x^3 - 5x^2 - 36x + 4}{x^2 - 4}$

Model It

73. ***Data Analysis: Military Personnel*** The numbers M (in thousands) of United States military personnel on active duty for the years 1993 through 2003 are shown in the table, where t represents the year, with $t = 3$ corresponding to 1993. (Source: U.S. Department of Defense)

Year, t	Military personnel, M
3	1705
4	1611
5	1518
6	1472
7	1439
8	1407
9	1386
10	1384
11	1385
12	1412
13	1434

Model It (continued)

(a) Use a graphing utility to create a scatter plot of the data.

(b) Use the *regression* feature of the graphing utility to find a cubic model for the data. Graph the model in the same viewing window as the scatter plot.

(c) Use the model to create a table of estimated values of M. Compare the model with the original data.

(d) Use synthetic division to evaluate the model for the year 2008. Even though the model is relatively accurate for estimating the given data, would you use this model to predict the number of military personnel in the future? Explain.

74. ***Data Analysis: Cable Television*** The average monthly basic rates R (in dollars) for cable television in the United States for the years 1992 through 2002 are shown in the table, where t represents the year, with $t = 2$ corresponding to 1992. (Source: Kagan Research LLC)

Year, t	Basic rate, R
2	19.08
3	19.39
4	21.62
5	23.07
6	24.41
7	26.48
8	27.81
9	28.92
10	30.37
11	32.87
12	34.71

(a) Use a graphing utility to create a scatter plot of the data.

(b) Use the *regression* feature of the graphing utility to find a cubic model for the data. Then graph the model in the same viewing window as the scatter plot. Compare the model with the data.

(c) Use synthetic division to evaluate the model for the year 2008.

Synthesis

True or False? **In Exercises 75–77, determine whether the statement is true or false. Justify your answer.**

75. If $(7x + 4)$ is a factor of some polynomial function f, then $\frac{4}{7}$ is a zero of f.

76. $(2x - 1)$ is a factor of the polynomial

$$6x^6 + x^5 - 92x^4 + 45x^3 + 184x^2 + 4x - 48.$$

77. The rational expression

$$\frac{x^3 + 2x^2 - 13x + 10}{x^2 - 4x - 12}$$

is improper.

78. ***Exploration*** Use the form $f(x) = (x - k)q(x) + r$ to create a cubic function that (a) passes through the point $(2, 5)$ and rises to the right, and (b) passes through the point $(-3, 1)$ and falls to the right. (There are many correct answers.)

Think About It **In Exercises 79 and 80, perform the division by assuming that n is a positive integer.**

79. $\dfrac{x^{3n} + 9x^{2n} + 27x^n + 27}{x^n + 3}$ **80.** $\dfrac{x^{3n} - 3x^{2n} + 5x^n - 6}{x^n - 2}$

81. ***Writing*** Briefly explain what it means for a divisor to divide evenly into a dividend.

82. ***Writing*** Briefly explain how to check polynomial division, and justify your reasoning. Give an example.

Exploration **In Exercises 83 and 84, find the constant c such that the denominator will divide evenly into the numerator.**

83. $\dfrac{x^3 + 4x^2 - 3x + c}{x - 5}$ **84.** $\dfrac{x^5 - 2x^2 + x + c}{x + 2}$

Think About It **In Exercises 85 and 86, answer the questions about the division $f(x) \div (x - k)$, where $f(x) = (x + 3)^2(x - 3)(x + 1)^3$.**

85. What is the remainder when $k = -3$? Explain.

86. If it is necessary to find $f(2)$, is it easier to evaluate the function directly or to use synthetic division? Explain.

Skills Review

In Exercises 87–92, use any method to solve the quadratic equation.

87. $9x^2 - 25 = 0$ **88.** $16x^2 - 21 = 0$

89. $5x^2 - 3x - 14 = 0$ **90.** $8x^2 - 22x + 15 = 0$

91. $2x^2 + 6x + 3 = 0$ **92.** $x^2 + 3x - 3 = 0$

In Exercises 93–96, find a polynomial function that has the given zeros. (There are many correct answers.)

93. $0, 3, 4$ **94.** $-6, 1$

95. $-3, 1 + \sqrt{2}, 1 - \sqrt{2}$ **96.** $1, -2, 2 + \sqrt{3}, 2 - \sqrt{3}$

2.4 Complex Numbers

What you should learn

- Use the imaginary unit i to write complex numbers.
- Add, subtract, and multiply complex numbers.
- Use complex conjugates to write the quotient of two complex numbers in standard form.
- Find complex solutions of quadratic equations.

Why you should learn it

You can use complex numbers to model and solve real-life problems in electronics. For instance, in Exercise 83 on page 168, you will learn how to use complex numbers to find the impedance of an electrical circuit.

The Imaginary Unit i

You have learned that some quadratic equations have no real solutions. For instance, the quadratic equation $x^2 + 1 = 0$ has no real solution because there is no real number x that can be squared to produce -1. To overcome this deficiency, mathematicians created an expanded system of numbers using the **imaginary unit *i*,** defined as

$$i = \sqrt{-1} \qquad \text{Imaginary unit}$$

where $i^2 = -1$. By adding real numbers to real multiples of this imaginary unit, the set of **complex numbers** is obtained. Each complex number can be written in the **standard form $a + bi$.** For instance, the standard form of the complex number $-5 + \sqrt{-9}$ is $-5 + 3i$ because

$$-5 + \sqrt{-9} = -5 + \sqrt{3^2(-1)} = -5 + 3\sqrt{-1} = -5 + 3i.$$

In the standard form $a + bi$, the real number a is called the **real part** of the **complex number $a + bi$,** and the number bi (where b is a real number) is called the **imaginary part** of the complex number.

Definition of a Complex Number

If a and b are real numbers, the number $a + bi$ is a **complex number,** and it is said to be written in **standard form.** If $b = 0$, the number $a + bi = a$ is a real number. If $b \neq 0$, the number $a + bi$ is called an **imaginary number.** A number of the form bi, where $b \neq 0$, is called a **pure imaginary number.**

The set of real numbers is a subset of the set of complex numbers, as shown in Figure 2.29. This is true because every real number a can be written as a complex number using $b = 0$. That is, for every real number a, you can write $a = a + 0i$.

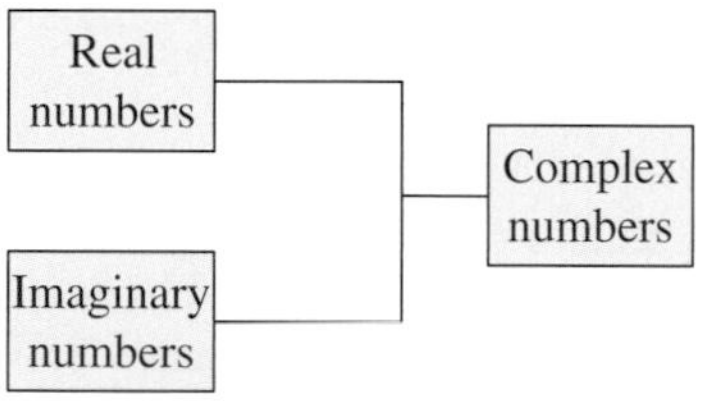

FIGURE 2.29

Equality of Complex Numbers

Two complex numbers $a + bi$ and $c + di$, written in standard form, are equal to each other

$$a + bi = c + di \qquad \text{Equality of two complex numbers}$$

if and only if $a = c$ and $b = d$.

Operations with Complex Numbers

To add (or subtract) two complex numbers, you add (or subtract) the real and imaginary parts of the numbers separately.

Addition and Subtraction of Complex Numbers

If $a + bi$ and $c + di$ are two complex numbers written in standard form, their sum and difference are defined as follows.

Sum: $(a + bi) + (c + di) = (a + c) + (b + d)i$

Difference: $(a + bi) - (c + di) = (a - c) + (b - d)i$

The **additive identity** in the complex number system is zero (the same as in the real number system). Furthermore, the **additive inverse** of the complex number $a + bi$ is

$$-(a + bi) = -a - bi. \qquad \text{Additive inverse}$$

So, you have

$$(a + bi) + (-a - bi) = 0 + 0i = 0.$$

Example 1 **Adding and Subtracting Complex Numbers**

a. $(4 + 7i) + (1 - 6i) = 4 + 7i + 1 - 6i$ Remove parentheses.

$= (4 + 1) + (7i - 6i)$ Group like terms.

$= 5 + i$ Write in standard form.

b. $(1 + 2i) - (4 + 2i) = 1 + 2i - 4 - 2i$ Remove parentheses.

$= (1 - 4) + (2i - 2i)$ Group like terms.

$= -3 + 0$ Simplify.

$= -3$ Write in standard form.

c. $3i - (-2 + 3i) - (2 + 5i) = 3i + 2 - 3i - 2 - 5i$

$= (2 - 2) + (3i - 3i - 5i)$

$= 0 - 5i$

$= -5i$

d. $(3 + 2i) + (4 - i) - (7 + i) = 3 + 2i + 4 - i - 7 - i$

$= (3 + 4 - 7) + (2i - i - i)$

$= 0 + 0i$

$= 0$

✓CHECKPOINT Now try Exercise 17.

Note in Examples 1(b) and 1(d) that the sum of two complex numbers can be a real number.

Exploration

Complete the following.

$i^1 = i$	$i^7 = \square$
$i^2 = -1$	$i^8 = \square$
$i^3 = -i$	$i^9 = \square$
$i^4 = 1$	$i^{10} = \square$
$i^5 = \square$	$i^{11} = \square$
$i^6 = \square$	$i^{12} = \square$

What pattern do you see? Write a brief description of how you would find i raised to any positive integer power.

Many of the properties of real numbers are valid for complex numbers as well. Here are some examples.

Associative Properties of Addition and Multiplication
Commutative Properties of Addition and Multiplication
Distributive Property of Multiplication Over Addition

Notice below how these properties are used when two complex numbers are multiplied.

$$(a + bi)(c + di) = a(c + di) + bi(c + di) \quad \text{Distributive Property}$$
$$= ac + (ad)i + (bc)i + (bd)i^2 \quad \text{Distributive Property}$$
$$= ac + (ad)i + (bc)i + (bd)(-1) \quad i^2 = -1$$
$$= ac - bd + (ad)i + (bc)i \quad \text{Commutative Property}$$
$$= (ac - bd) + (ad + bc)i \quad \text{Associative Property}$$

Rather than trying to memorize this multiplication rule, you should simply remember how the Distributive Property is used to multiply two complex numbers.

Example 2 Multiplying Complex Numbers

a. $4(-2 + 3i) = 4(-2) + 4(3i)$ Distributive Property
$= -8 + 12i$ Simplify.

b. $(2 - i)(4 + 3i) = 2(4 + 3i) - i(4 + 3i)$ Distributive Property
$= 8 + 6i - 4i - 3i^2$ Distributive Property
$= 8 + 6i - 4i - 3(-1)$ $i^2 = -1$
$= (8 + 3) + (6i - 4i)$ Group like terms.
$= 11 + 2i$ Write in standard form.

c. $(3 + 2i)(3 - 2i) = 3(3 - 2i) + 2i(3 - 2i)$ Distributive Property
$= 9 - 6i + 6i - 4i^2$ Distributive Property
$= 9 - 6i + 6i - 4(-1)$ $i^2 = -1$
$= 9 + 4$ Simplify.
$= 13$ Write in standard form.

d. $(3 + 2i)^2 = (3 + 2i)(3 + 2i)$ Square of a binomial
$= 3(3 + 2i) + 2i(3 + 2i)$ Distributive Property
$= 9 + 6i + 6i + 4i^2$ Distributive Property
$= 9 + 6i + 6i + 4(-1)$ $i^2 = -1$
$= 9 + 12i - 4$ Simplify.
$= 5 + 12i$ Write in standard form.

CHECKPOINT Now try Exercise 27.

STUDY TIP

The procedure described above is similar to multiplying two polynomials and combining like terms, as in the FOIL Method shown in Appendix A.3. For instance, you can use the FOIL Method to multiply the two complex numbers from Example 2(b).

$$(2 - i)(4 + 3i) = \overset{F}{8} + \overset{O}{6i} - \overset{I}{4i} - \overset{L}{3i^2}$$

Complex Conjugates

Notice in Example 2(c) that the product of two complex numbers can be a real number. This occurs with pairs of complex numbers of the form $a + bi$ and $a - bi$, called **complex conjugates.**

$$\begin{aligned}(a + bi)(a - bi) &= a^2 - abi + abi - b^2i^2\\ &= a^2 - b^2(-1)\\ &= a^2 + b^2\end{aligned}$$

Example 3 **Multiplying Conjugates**

Multiply each complex number by its complex conjugate.

a. $1 + i$ **b.** $4 - 3i$

Solution

a. The complex conjugate of $1 + i$ is $1 - i$.

$$(1 + i)(1 - i) = 1^2 - i^2 = 1 - (-1) = 2$$

b. The complex conjugate of $4 - 3i$ is $4 + 3i$.

$$(4 - 3i)(4 + 3i) = 4^2 - (3i)^2 = 16 - 9i^2 = 16 - 9(-1) = 25$$

✓CHECKPOINT Now try Exercise 37.

STUDY TIP

Note that when you multiply the numerator and denominator of a quotient of complex numbers by

$$\frac{c - di}{c - di}$$

you are actually multiplying the quotient by a form of 1. You are not changing the original expression, you are only creating an expression that is equivalent to the original expression.

To write the quotient of $a + bi$ and $c + di$ in standard form, where c and d are not both zero, multiply the numerator and denominator by the complex conjugate of the *denominator* to obtain

$$\frac{a + bi}{c + di} = \frac{a + bi}{c + di}\left(\frac{c - di}{c - di}\right)$$

$$= \frac{(ac + bd) + (bc - ad)i}{c^2 + d^2}. \qquad \text{Standard form}$$

Example 4 **Writing a Quotient of Complex Numbers in Standard Form**

$$\frac{2 + 3i}{4 - 2i} = \frac{2 + 3i}{4 - 2i}\left(\frac{4 + 2i}{4 + 2i}\right) \qquad \text{Multiply numerator and denominator by complex conjugate of denominator.}$$

$$= \frac{8 + 4i + 12i + 6i^2}{16 - 4i^2} \qquad \text{Expand.}$$

$$= \frac{8 - 6 + 16i}{16 + 4} \qquad i^2 = -1$$

$$= \frac{2 + 16i}{20} \qquad \text{Simplify.}$$

$$= \frac{1}{10} + \frac{4}{5}i \qquad \text{Write in standard form.}$$

✓CHECKPOINT Now try Exercise 49.

Complex Solutions of Quadratic Equations

When using the Quadratic Formula to solve a quadratic equation, you often obtain a result such as $\sqrt{-3}$, which you know is not a real number. By factoring out $i = \sqrt{-1}$, you can write this number in standard form.

$$\sqrt{-3} = \sqrt{3(-1)} = \sqrt{3}\sqrt{-1} = \sqrt{3}i$$

The number $\sqrt{3}i$ is called the *principal square root* of -3.

STUDY TIP

The definition of principal square root uses the rule

$$\sqrt{ab} = \sqrt{a}\sqrt{b}$$

for $a > 0$ and $b < 0$. This rule is not valid if *both* a and b are negative. For example,

$$\begin{aligned}\sqrt{-5}\sqrt{-5} &= \sqrt{5(-1)}\sqrt{5(-1)}\\ &= \sqrt{5}i\sqrt{5}i\\ &= \sqrt{25}i^2\\ &= 5i^2 = -5\end{aligned}$$

whereas

$$\sqrt{(-5)(-5)} = \sqrt{25} = 5.$$

To avoid problems with square roots of negative numbers, be sure to convert complex numbers to standard form *before* multiplying.

Principal Square Root of a Negative Number

If a is a positive number, the **principal square root** of the negative number $-a$ is defined as

$$\sqrt{-a} = \sqrt{a}i.$$

Example 5 Writing Complex Numbers in Standard Form

a. $\sqrt{-3}\sqrt{-12} = \sqrt{3}i\sqrt{12}i = \sqrt{36}i^2 = 6(-1) = -6$

b. $\sqrt{-48} - \sqrt{-27} = \sqrt{48}i - \sqrt{27}i = 4\sqrt{3}i - 3\sqrt{3}i = \sqrt{3}i$

c. $$\begin{aligned}\left(-1 + \sqrt{-3}\right)^2 &= \left(-1 + \sqrt{3}i\right)^2\\ &= (-1)^2 - 2\sqrt{3}i + \left(\sqrt{3}\right)^2(i^2)\\ &= 1 - 2\sqrt{3}i + 3(-1)\\ &= -2 - 2\sqrt{3}i\end{aligned}$$

CHECKPOINT Now try Exercise 59.

Example 6 Complex Solutions of a Quadratic Equation

Solve (a) $x^2 + 4 = 0$ and (b) $3x^2 - 2x + 5 = 0$.

Solution

a. $x^2 + 4 = 0$ Write original equation.

$x^2 = -4$ Subtract 4 from each side.

$x = \pm 2i$ Extract square roots.

b. $3x^2 - 2x + 5 = 0$ Write original equation.

$x = \dfrac{-(-2) \pm \sqrt{(-2)^2 - 4(3)(5)}}{2(3)}$ Quadratic Formula

$= \dfrac{2 \pm \sqrt{-56}}{6}$ Simplify.

$= \dfrac{2 \pm 2\sqrt{14}i}{6}$ Write $\sqrt{-56}$ in standard form.

$= \dfrac{1}{3} \pm \dfrac{\sqrt{14}}{3}i$ Write in standard form.

CHECKPOINT Now try Exercise 65.

2.4 Exercises

VOCABULARY CHECK:

1. Match the type of complex number with its definition.

(a) Real Number (i) $a + bi, \quad a \neq 0, \quad b \neq 0$

(b) Imaginary number (ii) $a + bi, \quad a = 0, \quad b \neq 0$

(c) Pure imaginary number (iii) $a + bi, \quad b = 0$

In Exercises 2–4, fill in the blanks.

2. The imaginary unit i is defined as $i =$ ________, where $i^2 =$ ________.

3. If a is a positive number, the ________ ________ root of the negative number $-a$ is defined as $\sqrt{-a} = \sqrt{a}\,i$.

4. The numbers $a + bi$ and $a - bi$ are called ________ ________, and their product is a real number $a^2 + b^2$.

In Exercises 1–4, find real numbers a and b such that the equation is true.

1. $a + bi = -10 + 6i$

2. $a + bi = 13 + 4i$

3. $(a - 1) + (b + 3)i = 5 + 8i$

4. $(a + 6) + 2bi = 6 - 5i$

In Exercises 5–16, write the complex number in standard form.

5. $4 + \sqrt{-9}$

6. $3 + \sqrt{-16}$

7. $2 - \sqrt{-27}$

8. $1 + \sqrt{-8}$

9. $\sqrt{-75}$

10. $\sqrt{-4}$

11. 8

12. 45

13. $-6i + i^2$

14. $-4i^2 + 2i$

15. $\sqrt{-0.09}$

16. $\sqrt{-0.0004}$

In Exercises 17–26, perform the addition or subtraction and write the result in standard form.

17. $(5 + i) + (6 - 2i)$

18. $(13 - 2i) + (-5 + 6i)$

19. $(8 - i) - (4 - i)$

20. $(3 + 2i) - (6 + 13i)$

21. $\left(-2 + \sqrt{-8}\right) + \left(5 - \sqrt{-50}\right)$

22. $\left(8 + \sqrt{-18}\right) - \left(4 + 3\sqrt{2}i\right)$

23. $13i - (14 - 7i)$

24. $22 + (-5 + 8i) + 10i$

25. $-\left(\frac{3}{2} + \frac{5}{2}i\right) + \left(\frac{5}{3} + \frac{11}{3}i\right)$

26. $(1.6 + 3.2i) + (-5.8 + 4.3i)$

In Exercises 27–36, perform the operation and write the result in standard form.

27. $(1 + i)(3 - 2i)$

28. $(6 - 2i)(2 - 3i)$

29. $6i(5 - 2i)$

30. $-8i(9 + 4i)$

31. $\left(\sqrt{14} + \sqrt{10}i\right)\left(\sqrt{14} - \sqrt{10}i\right)$

32. $\left(\sqrt{3} + \sqrt{15}i\right)\left(\sqrt{3} - \sqrt{15}i\right)$

33. $(4 + 5i)^2$

34. $(2 - 3i)^2$

35. $(2 + 3i)^2 + (2 - 3i)^2$

36. $(1 - 2i)^2 - (1 + 2i)^2$

In Exercises 37–44, write the complex conjugate of the complex number. Then multiply the number by its complex conjugate.

37. $6 + 3i$

38. $7 - 12i$

39. $-1 - \sqrt{5}i$

40. $-3 + \sqrt{2}i$

41. $\sqrt{-20}$

42. $\sqrt{-15}$

43. $\sqrt{8}$

44. $1 + \sqrt{8}$

In Exercises 45–54, write the quotient in standard form.

45. $\dfrac{5}{i}$

46. $-\dfrac{14}{2i}$

47. $\dfrac{2}{4 - 5i}$

48. $\dfrac{5}{1 - i}$

49. $\dfrac{3 + i}{3 - i}$

50. $\dfrac{6 - 7i}{1 - 2i}$

51. $\dfrac{6 - 5i}{i}$

52. $\dfrac{8 + 16i}{2i}$

53. $\dfrac{3i}{(4 - 5i)^2}$

54. $\dfrac{5i}{(2 + 3i)^2}$

In Exercises 55–58, perform the operation and write the result in standard form.

55. $\dfrac{2}{1 + i} - \dfrac{3}{1 - i}$

56. $\dfrac{2i}{2 + i} + \dfrac{5}{2 - i}$

57. $\dfrac{i}{3 - 2i} + \dfrac{2i}{3 + 8i}$

58. $\dfrac{1 + i}{i} - \dfrac{3}{4 - i}$

In Exercises 59–64, write the complex number in standard form.

59. $\sqrt{-6} \cdot \sqrt{-2}$ **60.** $\sqrt{-5} \cdot \sqrt{-10}$

61. $\left(\sqrt{-10}\right)^2$ **62.** $\left(\sqrt{-75}\right)^2$

63. $\left(3 + \sqrt{-5}\right)\left(7 - \sqrt{-10}\right)$ **64.** $\left(2 - \sqrt{-6}\right)^2$

In Exercises 65–74, use the Quadratic Formula to solve the quadratic equation.

65. $x^2 - 2x + 2 = 0$ **66.** $x^2 + 6x + 10 = 0$

67. $4x^2 + 16x + 17 = 0$ **68.** $9x^2 - 6x + 37 = 0$

69. $4x^2 + 16x + 15 = 0$ **70.** $16t^2 - 4t + 3 = 0$

71. $\frac{3}{2}x^2 - 6x + 9 = 0$ **72.** $\frac{7}{8}x^2 - \frac{3}{4}x + \frac{5}{16} = 0$

73. $1.4x^2 - 2x - 10 = 0$ **74.** $4.5x^2 - 3x + 12 = 0$

In Exercises 75–82, simplify the complex number and write it in standard form.

75. $-6i^3 + i^2$ **76.** $4i^2 - 2i^3$

77. $-5i^5$ **78.** $(-i)^3$

79. $\left(\sqrt{-75}\right)^3$ **80.** $\left(\sqrt{-2}\right)^6$

81. $\dfrac{1}{i^3}$ **82.** $\dfrac{1}{(2i)^3}$

Model It

83. ***Impedance*** The opposition to current in an electrical circuit is called its impedance. The impedance z in a parallel circuit with two pathways satisfies the equation

$$\frac{1}{z} = \frac{1}{z_1} + \frac{1}{z_2}$$

where z_1 is the impedance (in ohms) of pathway 1 and z_2 is the impedance of pathway 2.

(a) The impedance of each pathway in a parallel circuit is found by adding the impedances of all components in the pathway. Use the table to find z_1 and z_2.

(b) Find the impedance z.

	Resistor	Inductor	Capacitor
Symbol	$a\Omega$	$b\Omega$	$c\Omega$
Impedance	a	bi	$-ci$

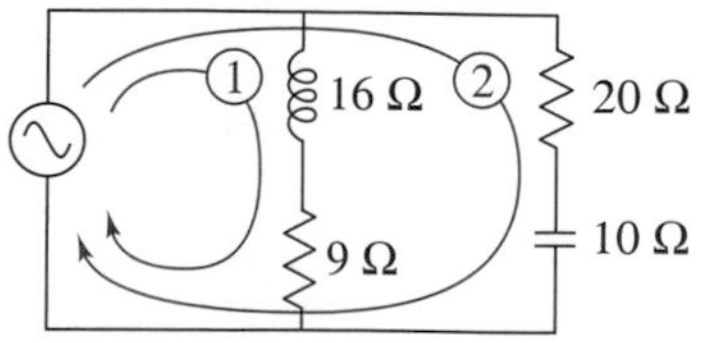

84. Cube each complex number.

(a) 2 (b) $-1 + \sqrt{3}i$ (c) $-1 - \sqrt{3}i$

85. Raise each complex number to the fourth power.

(a) 2 (b) -2 (c) $2i$ (d) $-2i$

86. Write each of the powers of i as i, $-i$, 1, or -1.

(a) i^{40} (b) i^{25} (c) i^{50} (d) i^{67}

Synthesis

True or False? **In Exercises 87–89, determine whether the statement is true or false. Justify your answer.**

87. There is no complex number that is equal to its complex conjugate.

88. $-i\sqrt{6}$ is a solution of $x^4 - x^2 + 14 = 56$.

89. $i^{44} + i^{150} - i^{74} - i^{109} + i^{61} = -1$

90. ***Error Analysis*** Describe the error.

~~$\sqrt{-6}\sqrt{-6} = \sqrt{(-6)(-6)} = \sqrt{36} = 6$~~

91. ***Proof*** Prove that the complex conjugate of the product of two complex numbers $a_1 + b_1i$ and $a_2 + b_2i$ is the product of their complex conjugates.

92. ***Proof*** Prove that the complex conjugate of the sum of two complex numbers $a_1 + b_1i$ and $a_2 + b_2i$ is the sum of their complex conjugates.

Skills Review

In Exercises 93–96, perform the operation and write the result in standard form.

93. $(4 + 3x) + (8 - 6x - x^2)$

94. $(x^3 - 3x^2) - (6 - 2x - 4x^2)$

95. $\left(3x - \frac{1}{2}\right)(x + 4)$ **96.** $(2x - 5)^2$

In Exercises 97–100, solve the equation and check your solution.

97. $-x - 12 = 19$ **98.** $8 - 3x = -34$

99. $4(5x - 6) - 3(6x + 1) = 0$

100. $5[x - (3x + 11)] = 20x - 15$

101. ***Volume of an Oblate Spheroid***

Solve for a: $V = \frac{4}{3}\pi a^2 b$

102. ***Newton's Law of Universal Gravitation***

Solve for r: $F = \alpha\dfrac{m_1 m_2}{r^2}$

103. ***Mixture Problem*** A five-liter container contains a mixture with a concentration of 50%. How much of this mixture must be withdrawn and replaced by 100% concentrate to bring the mixture up to 60% concentration?

2.5 Zeros of Polynomial Functions

What you should learn

- Use the Fundamental Theorem of Algebra to determine the number of zeros of polynomial functions.
- Find rational zeros of polynomial functions.
- Find conjugate pairs of complex zeros.
- Find zeros of polynomials by factoring.
- Use Descartes's Rule of Signs and the Upper and Lower Bound Rules to find zeros of polynomials.

Why you should learn it

Finding zeros of polynomial functions is an important part of solving real-life problems. For instance, in Exercise 112 on page 182, the zeros of a polynomial function can help you analyze the attendance at women's college basketball games.

The Fundamental Theorem of Algebra

You know that an nth-degree polynomial can have at most n real zeros. In the complex number system, this statement can be improved. That is, in the complex number system, every nth-degree polynomial function has *precisely* n zeros. This important result is derived from the **Fundamental Theorem of Algebra,** first proved by the German mathematician Carl Friedrich Gauss (1777–1855).

The Fundamental Theorem of Algebra

If $f(x)$ is a polynomial of degree n, where $n > 0$, then f has at least one zero in the complex number system.

Using the Fundamental Theorem of Algebra and the equivalence of zeros and factors, you obtain the **Linear Factorization Theorem.**

Linear Factorization Theorem

If $f(x)$ is a polynomial of degree n, where $n > 0$, then f has precisely n linear factors

$$f(x) = a_n(x - c_1)(x - c_2) \cdot \cdot \cdot (x - c_n)$$

where $c_1, c_2, \ldots, c_n$ are complex numbers.

For a proof of the Linear Factorization Theorem, see Proofs in Mathematics on page 214.

Note that the Fundamental Theorem of Algebra and the Linear Factorization Theorem tell you only that the zeros or factors of a polynomial exist, not how to find them. Such theorems are called *existence theorems.*

Example 1 Zeros of Polynomial Functions

a. The first-degree polynomial $f(x) = x - 2$ has exactly *one* zero: $x = 2$.

b. Counting multiplicity, the second-degree polynomial function

$$f(x) = x^2 - 6x + 9 = (x - 3)(x - 3)$$

has exactly *two* zeros: $x = 3$ and $x = 3$. (This is called a *repeated zero.*)

c. The third-degree polynomial function

$$f(x) = x^3 + 4x = x(x^2 + 4) = x(x - 2i)(x + 2i)$$

has exactly *three* zeros: $x = 0$, $x = 2i$, and $x = -2i$.

d. The fourth-degree polynomial function

$$f(x) = x^4 - 1 = (x - 1)(x + 1)(x - i)(x + i)$$

has exactly *four* zeros: $x = 1$, $x = -1$, $x = i$, and $x = -i$.

✓CHECKPOINT Now try Exercise 1.

STUDY TIP

Recall that in order to find the zeros of a function $f(x)$, set $f(x)$ equal to 0 and solve the resulting equation for x. For instance, the function in Example 1(a) has a zero at $x = 2$ because

$$x - 2 = 0$$
$$x = 2.$$

The Rational Zero Test

The **Rational Zero Test** relates the possible rational zeros of a polynomial (having integer coefficients) to the leading coefficient and to the constant term of the polynomial.

Historical Note
Although they were not contemporaries, Jean Le Rond d'Alembert (1717–1783) worked independently of Carl Gauss in trying to prove the Fundamental Theorem of Algebra. His efforts were such that, in France, the Fundamental Theorem of Algebra is frequently known as the Theorem of d'Alembert.

The Rational Zero Test

If the polynomial $f(x) = a_nx^n + a_{n-1}x^{n-1} + \cdot \cdot \cdot + a_2x^2 + a_1x + a_0$ has *integer* coefficients, every rational zero of f has the form

$$\text{Rational zero} = \frac{p}{q}$$

where p and q have no common factors other than 1, and

$p =$ a factor of the constant term a_0

$q =$ a factor of the leading coefficient a_n.

To use the Rational Zero Test, you should first list all rational numbers whose numerators are factors of the constant term and whose denominators are factors of the leading coefficient.

$$\text{Possible rational zeros} = \frac{\text{factors of constant term}}{\text{factors of leading coefficient}}$$

Having formed this list of *possible rational zeros*, use a trial-and-error method to determine which, if any, are actual zeros of the polynomial. Note that when the leading coefficient is 1, the possible rational zeros are simply the factors of the constant term.

Example 2 **Rational Zero Test with Leading Coefficient of 1**

Find the rational zeros of

$$f(x) = x^3 + x + 1.$$

Solution

Because the leading coefficient is 1, the possible rational zeros are ± 1, the factors of the constant term. By testing these possible zeros, you can see that neither works.

$$f(1) = (1)^3 + 1 + 1$$
$$= 3$$
$$f(-1) = (-1)^3 + (-1) + 1$$
$$= -1$$

So, you can conclude that the given polynomial has *no* rational zeros. Note from the graph of f in Figure 2.30 that f does have one real zero between -1 and 0. However, by the Rational Zero Test, you know that this real zero is *not* a rational number.

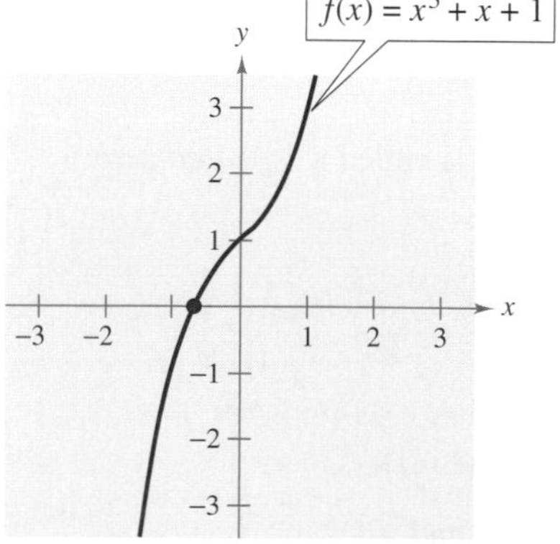

FIGURE 2.30

✓CHECKPOINT Now try Exercise 7.

> **STUDY TIP**
>
> When the list of possible rational zeros is small, as in Example 2, it may be quicker to test the zeros by evaluating the function. When the list of possible rational zeros is large, as in Example 3, it may be quicker to use a different approach to test the zeros, such as using synthetic division or sketching a graph.

Example 3 Rational Zero Test with Leading Coefficient of 1

Find the rational zeros of $f(x) = x^4 - x^3 + x^2 - 3x - 6$.

Solution

Because the leading coefficient is 1, the possible rational zeros are the factors of the constant term.

Possible rational zeros: $\pm 1, \pm 2, \pm 3, \pm 6$

By applying synthetic division successively, you can determine that $x = -1$ and $x = 2$ are the only two rational zeros.

$$\begin{array}{r|rrrrr} -1 & 1 & -1 & 1 & -3 & -6 \\ & & -1 & 2 & -3 & 6 \\ \hline & 1 & -2 & 3 & -6 & 0 \end{array} \longrightarrow \text{0 remainder, so } x = -1 \text{ is a zero.}$$

$$\begin{array}{r|rrrr} 2 & 1 & -2 & 3 & -6 \\ & & 2 & 0 & 6 \\ \hline & 1 & 0 & 3 & 0 \end{array} \longrightarrow \text{0 remainder, so } x = 2 \text{ is a zero.}$$

So, $f(x)$ factors as

$$f(x) = (x + 1)(x - 2)(x^2 + 3).$$

Because the factor $(x^2 + 3)$ produces no real zeros, you can conclude that $x = -1$ and $x = 2$ are the only *real* zeros of f, which is verified in Figure 2.31.

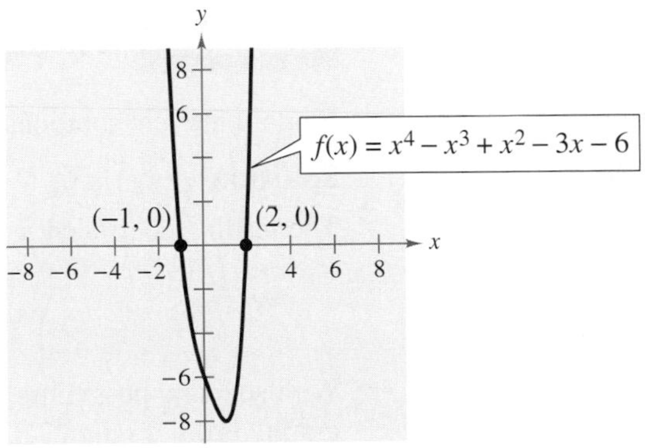

FIGURE 2.31

✓CHECKPOINT Now try Exercise 11.

If the leading coefficient of a polynomial is not 1, the list of possible rational zeros can increase dramatically. In such cases, the search can be shortened in several ways: (1) a programmable calculator can be used to speed up the calculations; (2) a graph, drawn either by hand or with a graphing utility, can give a good estimate of the locations of the zeros; (3) the Intermediate Value Theorem along with a table generated by a graphing utility can give approximations of zeros; and (4) synthetic division can be used to test the possible rational zeros.

Finding the first zero is often the most difficult part. After that, the search is simplified by working with the lower-degree polynomial obtained in synthetic division, as shown in Example 3.

STUDY TIP

Remember that when you try to find the rational zeros of a polynomial function with many possible rational zeros, as in Example 4, you must use trial and error. There is no quick algebraic method to determine which of the possibilities is an actual zero; however, sketching a graph may be helpful.

Example 4 Using the Rational Zero Test

Find the rational zeros of $f(x) = 2x^3 + 3x^2 - 8x + 3$.

Solution

The leading coefficient is 2 and the constant term is 3.

$$\textit{Possible rational zeros: } \frac{\text{Factors of } 3}{\text{Factors of } 2} = \frac{\pm 1, \pm 3}{\pm 1, \pm 2} = \pm 1, \pm 3, \pm \frac{1}{2}, \pm \frac{3}{2}$$

By synthetic division, you can determine that $x = 1$ is a rational zero.

$$\begin{array}{r|rrrr} 1 & 2 & 3 & -8 & 3 \\ & & 2 & 5 & -3 \\ \hline & 2 & 5 & -3 & 0 \end{array}$$

So, $f(x)$ factors as

$$\begin{aligned} f(x) &= (x - 1)(2x^2 + 5x - 3) \\ &= (x - 1)(2x - 1)(x + 3) \end{aligned}$$

and you can conclude that the rational zeros of f are $x = 1$, $x = \frac{1}{2}$, and $x = -3$.

CHECKPOINT Now try Exercise 17.

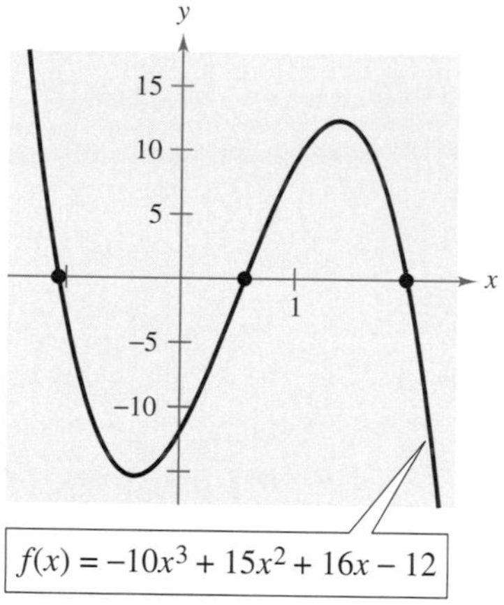

FIGURE 2.32

Recall from Section 2.2 that if $x = a$ is a zero of the polynomial function f, then $x = a$ is a solution of the polynomial equation $f(x) = 0$.

Example 5 Solving a Polynomial Equation

Find all the real solutions of $-10x^3 + 15x^2 + 16x - 12 = 0$.

Solution

The leading coefficient is -10 and the constant term is -12.

$$\textit{Possible rational solutions: } \frac{\text{Factors of } -12}{\text{Factors of } -10} = \frac{\pm 1, \pm 2, \pm 3, \pm 4, \pm 6, \pm 12}{\pm 1, \pm 2, \pm 5, \pm 10}$$

With so many possibilities (32, in fact), it is worth your time to stop and sketch a graph. From Figure 2.32, it looks like three reasonable solutions would be $x = -\frac{6}{5}$, $x = \frac{1}{2}$, and $x = 2$. Testing these by synthetic division shows that $x = 2$ is the only rational solution. So, you have

$$(x - 2)(-10x^2 - 5x + 6) = 0.$$

Using the Quadratic Formula for the second factor, you find that the two additional solutions are irrational numbers.

$$x = \frac{-5 - \sqrt{265}}{20} \approx -1.0639$$

and

$$x = \frac{-5 + \sqrt{265}}{20} \approx 0.5639$$

CHECKPOINT Now try Exercise 23.

Conjugate Pairs

In Example 1(c) and (d), note that the pairs of complex zeros are **conjugates.** That is, they are of the form $a + bi$ and $a - bi$.

Complex Zeros Occur in Conjugate Pairs

Let $f(x)$ be a polynomial function that has *real coefficients*. If $a + bi$, where $b \neq 0$, is a zero of the function, the conjugate $a - bi$ is also a zero of the function.

Be sure you see that this result is true only if the polynomial function has *real coefficients*. For instance, the result applies to the function given by $f(x) = x^2 + 1$ but not to the function given by $g(x) = x - i$.

Example 6 Finding a Polynomial with Given Zeros

Find a fourth-degree polynomial function with real coefficients that has -1, -1, and $3i$ as zeros.

Solution

Because $3i$ is a zero *and* the polynomial is stated to have real coefficients, you know that the conjugate $-3i$ must also be a zero. So, from the Linear Factorization Theorem, $f(x)$ can be written as

$$f(x) = a(x + 1)(x + 1)(x - 3i)(x + 3i).$$

For simplicity, let $a = 1$ to obtain

$$f(x) = (x^2 + 2x + 1)(x^2 + 9)$$
$$= x^4 + 2x^3 + 10x^2 + 18x + 9.$$

✓CHECKPOINT Now try Exercise 37.

Factoring a Polynomial

The Linear Factorization Theorem shows that you can write any nth-degree polynomial as the product of n linear factors.

$$f(x) = a_n(x - c_1)(x - c_2)(x - c_3) \cdot \cdot \cdot (x - c_n)$$

However, this result includes the possibility that some of the values of c_i are complex. The following theorem says that even if you do not want to get involved with "complex factors," you can still write $f(x)$ as the product of linear and/or quadratic factors. For a proof of this theorem, see Proofs in Mathematics on page 214.

Factors of a Polynomial

Every polynomial of degree $n > 0$ with real coefficients can be written as the product of linear and quadratic factors with real coefficients, where the quadratic factors have no real zeros.

A quadratic factor with no real zeros is said to be *prime* or **irreducible over the reals.** Be sure you see that this is not the same as being *irreducible over the rationals*. For example, the quadratic $x^2 + 1 = (x - i)(x + i)$ is irreducible over the reals (and therefore over the rationals). On the other hand, the quadratic $x^2 - 2 = \left(x - \sqrt{2}\right)\left(x + \sqrt{2}\right)$ is irreducible over the rationals but *reducible* over the reals.

Example 7 Finding the Zeros of a Polynomial Function

Find all the zeros of $f(x) = x^4 - 3x^3 + 6x^2 + 2x - 60$ given that $1 + 3i$ is a zero of f.

Algebraic Solution

Because complex zeros occur in conjugate pairs, you know that $1 - 3i$ is also a zero of f. This means that both

$$[x - (1 + 3i)] \quad \text{and} \quad [x - (1 - 3i)]$$

are factors of f. Multiplying these two factors produces

$$\begin{aligned}[x - (1 + 3i)][x - (1 - 3i)] &= [(x - 1) - 3i][(x - 1) + 3i] \\ &= (x - 1)^2 - 9i^2 \\ &= x^2 - 2x + 10.\end{aligned}$$

Using long division, you can divide $x^2 - 2x + 10$ into f to obtain the following.

$$\begin{array}{r} x^2 - x - 6 \\ x^2 - 2x + 10 \enclose{longdiv}{x^4 - 3x^3 + 6x^2 + 2x - 60} \\ \underline{x^4 - 2x^3 + 10x^2} \qquad\qquad \\ -x^3 - 4x^2 + 2x \qquad \\ \underline{-x^3 + 2x^2 - 10x} \qquad \\ -6x^2 + 12x - 60 \\ \underline{-6x^2 + 12x - 60} \\ 0 \end{array}$$

So, you have

$$\begin{aligned}f(x) &= (x^2 - 2x + 10)(x^2 - x - 6) \\ &= (x^2 - 2x + 10)(x - 3)(x + 2)\end{aligned}$$

and you can conclude that the zeros of f are $x = 1 + 3i$, $x = 1 - 3i$, $x = 3$, and $x = -2$.

✓CHECKPOINT Now try Exercise 47.

Graphical Solution

Because complex zeros always occur in conjugate pairs, you know that $1 - 3i$ is also a zero of f. Because the polynomial is a fourth-degree polynomial, you know that there are at most two other zeros of the function. Use a graphing utility to graph

$$y = x^4 - 3x^3 + 6x^2 + 2x - 60$$

as shown in Figure 2.33.

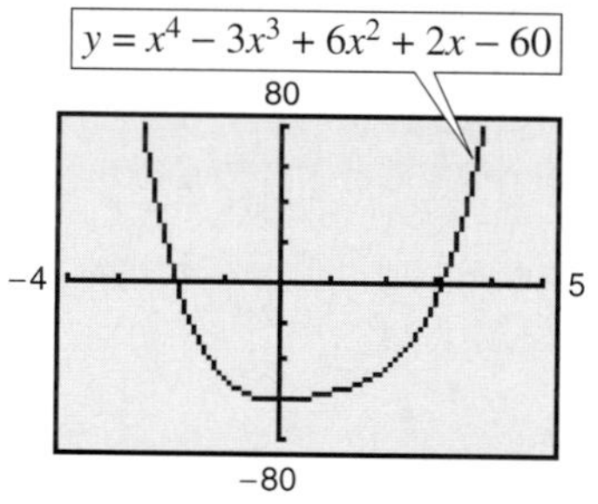

FIGURE 2.33

You can see that -2 and 3 appear to be zeros of the graph of the function. Use the *zero* or *root* feature or the *zoom* and *trace* features of the graphing utility to confirm that $x = -2$ and $x = 3$ are zeros of the graph. So, you can conclude that the zeros of f are $x = 1 + 3i$, $x = 1 - 3i$, $x = 3$, and $x = -2$.

In Example 7, if you were not told that $1 + 3i$ is a zero of f, you could still find all zeros of the function by using synthetic division to find the real zeros -2 and 3. Then you could factor the polynomial as $(x + 2)(x - 3)(x^2 - 2x + 10)$. Finally, by using the Quadratic Formula, you could determine that the zeros are $x = -2$, $x = 3$, $x = 1 + 3i$, and $x = 1 - 3i$.

STUDY TIP

In Example 8, the fifth-degree polynomial function has three real zeros. In such cases, you can use the *zoom* and *trace* features or the *zero* or *root* feature of a graphing utility to approximate the real zeros. You can then use these real zeros to determine the complex zeros algebraically.

Example 8 shows how to find all the zeros of a polynomial function, including complex zeros.

Example 8 Finding the Zeros of a Polynomial Function

Write $f(x) = x^5 + x^3 + 2x^2 - 12x + 8$ as the product of linear factors, and list all of its zeros.

Solution

The possible rational zeros are $\pm 1, \pm 2, \pm 4$, and ± 8. Synthetic division produces the following.

$$\begin{array}{r|rrrrrr} 1 & 1 & 0 & 1 & 2 & -12 & 8 \\ & & 1 & 1 & 2 & 4 & -8 \\ \hline & 1 & 1 & 2 & 4 & -8 & 0 \end{array} \longrightarrow \text{1 is a zero.}$$

$$\begin{array}{r|rrrrr} -2 & 1 & 1 & 2 & 4 & -8 \\ & & -2 & 2 & -8 & 8 \\ \hline & 1 & -1 & 4 & -4 & 0 \end{array} \longrightarrow -2 \text{ is a zero.}$$

So, you have

$$f(x) = x^5 + x^3 + 2x^2 - 12x + 8$$
$$= (x - 1)(x + 2)(x^3 - x^2 + 4x - 4).$$

You can factor $x^3 - x^2 + 4x - 4$ as $(x - 1)(x^2 + 4)$, and by factoring $x^2 + 4$ as

$$x^2 - (-4) = \left(x - \sqrt{-4}\right)\left(x + \sqrt{-4}\right)$$
$$= (x - 2i)(x + 2i)$$

you obtain

$$f(x) = (x - 1)(x - 1)(x + 2)(x - 2i)(x + 2i)$$

which gives the following five zeros of f.

$$x = 1, x = 1, x = -2, x = 2i, \quad \text{and} \quad x = -2i$$

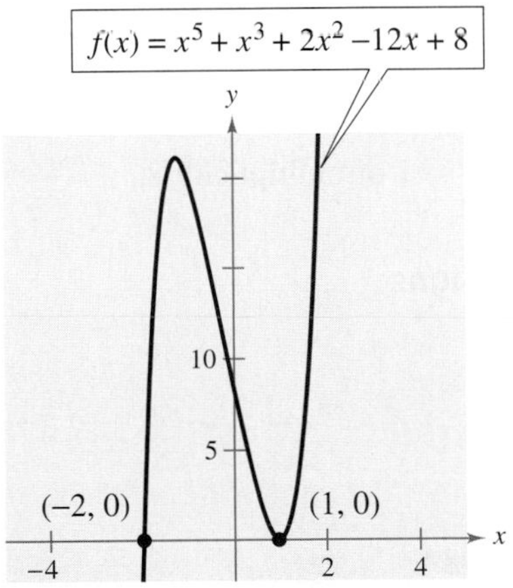

FIGURE 2.34

From the graph of f shown in Figure 2.34, you can see that the *real* zeros are the only ones that appear as x-intercepts. Note that $x = 1$ is a repeated zero.

CHECKPOINT Now try Exercise 63.

Technology

You can use the *table* feature of a graphing utility to help you determine which of the possible rational zeros are zeros of the polynomial in Example 8. The table should be set to *ask* mode. Then enter each of the possible rational zeros in the table. When you do this, you will see that there are two rational zeros, −2 and 1, as shown at the right.

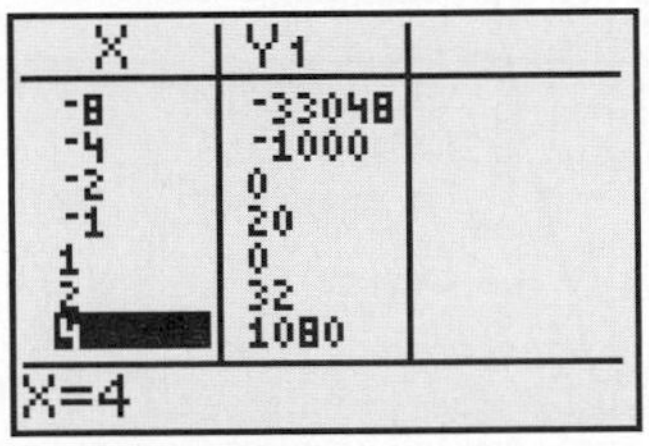

Other Tests for Zeros of Polynomials

You know that an nth-degree polynomial function can have *at most n* real zeros. Of course, many nth-degree polynomials do not have that many real zeros. For instance, $f(x) = x^2 + 1$ has no real zeros, and $f(x) = x^3 + 1$ has only one real zero. The following theorem, called **Descartes's Rule of Signs,** sheds more light on the number of real zeros of a polynomial.

> **Descartes's Rule of Signs**
>
> Let $f(x) = a_n x^n + a_{n-1}x^{n-1} + \cdot \cdot \cdot + a_2x^2 + a_1x + a_0$ be a polynomial with real coefficients and $a_0 \neq 0$.
>
> **1.** The number of *positive real zeros* of f is either equal to the number of variations in sign of $f(x)$ or less than that number by an even integer.
>
> **2.** The number of *negative real zeros* of f is either equal to the number of variations in sign of $f(-x)$ or less than that number by an even integer.

A **variation in sign** means that two consecutive coefficients have opposite signs.

When using Descartes's Rule of Signs, a zero of multiplicity k should be counted as k zeros. For instance, the polynomial $x^3 - 3x + 2$ has two variations in sign, and so has either two positive or no positive real zeros. Because

$$x^3 - 3x + 2 = (x - 1)(x - 1)(x + 2)$$

you can see that the two positive real zeros are $x = 1$ of multiplicity 2.

Example 9 Using Descartes's Rule of Signs

Describe the possible real zeros of

$$f(x) = 3x^3 - 5x^2 + 6x - 4.$$

Solution

The original polynomial has *three* variations in sign.

+ to −   + to −

$$f(x) = 3x^3 - 5x^2 + 6x - 4$$

− to +

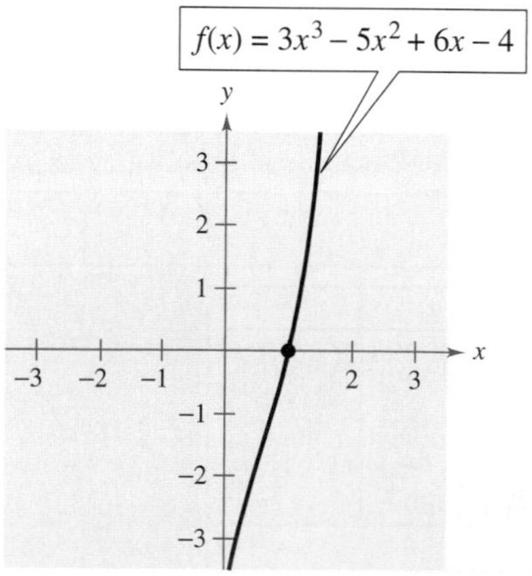

FIGURE 2.35

The polynomial

$$f(-x) = 3(-x)^3 - 5(-x)^2 + 6(-x) - 4$$

$$= -3x^3 - 5x^2 - 6x - 4$$

has no variations in sign. So, from Descartes's Rule of Signs, the polynomial $f(x) = 3x^3 - 5x^2 + 6x - 4$ has either three positive real zeros or one positive real zero, and has no negative real zeros. From the graph in Figure 2.35, you can see that the function has only one real zero (it is a positive number, near $x = 1$).

CHECKPOINT Now try Exercise 79.

Another test for zeros of a polynomial function is related to the sign pattern in the last row of the synthetic division array. This test can give you an upper or lower bound of the real zeros of f. A real number b is an **upper bound** for the real zeros of f if no zeros are greater than b. Similarly, b is a **lower bound** if no real zeros of f are less than b.

Upper and Lower Bound Rules

Let $f(x)$ be a polynomial with real coefficients and a positive leading coefficient. Suppose $f(x)$ is divided by $x - c$, using synthetic division.

1. If $c > 0$ and each number in the last row is either positive or zero, c is an **upper bound** for the real zeros of f.
2. If $c < 0$ and the numbers in the last row are alternately positive and negative (zero entries count as positive or negative), c is a **lower bound** for the real zeros of f.

Example 10 Finding the Zeros of a Polynomial Function

Find the real zeros of $f(x) = 6x^3 - 4x^2 + 3x - 2$.

Solution

The possible real zeros are as follows.

$$\frac{\text{Factors of } 2}{\text{Factors of } 6} = \frac{\pm 1, \pm 2}{\pm 1, \pm 2, \pm 3, \pm 6} = \pm 1, \pm\frac{1}{2}, \pm\frac{1}{3}, \pm\frac{1}{6}, \pm\frac{2}{3}, \pm 2$$

The original polynomial $f(x)$ has three variations in sign. The polynomial

$$\begin{aligned} f(-x) &= 6(-x)^3 - 4(-x)^2 + 3(-x) - 2 \\ &= -6x^3 - 4x^2 - 3x - 2 \end{aligned}$$

has no variations in sign. As a result of these two findings, you can apply Descartes's Rule of Signs to conclude that there are three positive real zeros or one positive real zero, and no negative zeros. Trying $x = 1$ produces the following.

$$\begin{array}{r|rrrr} 1 & 6 & -4 & 3 & -2 \\ & & 6 & 2 & 5 \\ \hline & 6 & 2 & 5 & 3 \end{array}$$

So, $x = 1$ is not a zero, but because the last row has all positive entries, you know that $x = 1$ is an upper bound for the real zeros. So, you can restrict the search to zeros between 0 and 1. By trial and error, you can determine that $x = \frac{2}{3}$ is a zero. So,

$$f(x) = \left(x - \frac{2}{3}\right)(6x^2 + 3).$$

Because $6x^2 + 3$ has no real zeros, it follows that $x = \frac{2}{3}$ is the only real zero.

✓CHECKPOINT Now try Exercise 87.

Before concluding this section, here are two additional hints that can help you find the real zeros of a polynomial.

1. If the terms of $f(x)$ have a common monomial factor, it should be factored out before applying the tests in this section. For instance, by writing

$$\begin{aligned} f(x) &= x^4 - 5x^3 + 3x^2 + x \\ &= x(x^3 - 5x^2 + 3x + 1) \end{aligned}$$

you can see that $x = 0$ is a zero of f and that the remaining zeros can be obtained by analyzing the cubic factor.

2. If you are able to find all but two zeros of $f(x)$, you can always use the Quadratic Formula on the remaining quadratic factor. For instance, if you succeeded in writing

$$\begin{aligned} f(x) &= x^4 - 5x^3 + 3x^2 + x \\ &= x(x - 1)(x^2 - 4x - 1) \end{aligned}$$

you can apply the Quadratic Formula to $x^2 - 4x - 1$ to conclude that the two remaining zeros are $x = 2 + \sqrt{5}$ and $x = 2 - \sqrt{5}$.

Example 11 Using a Polynomial Model

You are designing candle-making kits. Each kit contains 25 cubic inches of candle wax and a mold for making a pyramid-shaped candle. You want the height of the candle to be 2 inches less than the length of each side of the candle's square base. What should the dimensions of your candle mold be?

Solution

The volume of a pyramid is $V = \frac{1}{3}Bh$, where B is the area of the base and h is the height. The area of the base is x^2 and the height is $(x - 2)$. So, the volume of the pyramid is $V = \frac{1}{3}x^2(x - 2)$. Substituting 25 for the volume yields the following.

$$25 = \frac{1}{3}x^2(x - 2) \qquad \text{Substitute 25 for } V.$$

$$75 = x^3 - 2x^2 \qquad \text{Multiply each side by 3.}$$

$$0 = x^3 - 2x^2 - 75 \qquad \text{Write in general form.}$$

The possible rational solutions are $x = \pm1, \pm3, \pm5, \pm15, \pm25, \pm75$. Use synthetic division to test some of the possible solutions. Note that in this case, it makes sense to test only positive x-values. Using synthetic division, you can determine that $x = 5$ is a solution.

$$\begin{array}{r|rrrr} 5 & 1 & -2 & 0 & -75 \\ & & 5 & 15 & 75 \\ \hline & 1 & 3 & 15 & 0 \end{array}$$

The other two solutions, which satisfy $x^2 + 3x + 15 = 0$, are imaginary and can be discarded. You can conclude that the base of the candle mold should be 5 inches by 5 inches and the height of the mold should be $5 - 2 = 3$ inches.

✓CHECKPOINT Now try Exercise 107.

2.5 Exercises

VOCABULARY CHECK: Fill in the blanks.

1. The ________ ________ of ________ states that if $f(x)$ is a polynomial of degree n $(n > 0)$, then f has at least one zero in the complex number system.
2. The ________ ________ ________ states that if $f(x)$ is a polynomial of degree n $(n > 0)$, then f has precisely n linear factors $f(x) = a_n(x - c_1)(x - c_2) \cdot \cdot \cdot (x - c_n)$ where $c_1, c_2, . . . , c_n$ are complex numbers.
3. The test that gives a list of the possible rational zeros of a polynomial function is called the ________ ________ Test.
4. If $a + bi$ is a complex zero of a polynomial with real coefficients, then so is its ________, $a - bi$.
5. A quadratic factor that cannot be factored further as a product of linear factors containing real numbers is said to be ________ over the ________.
6. The theorem that can be used to determine the possible numbers of positive real zeros and negative real zeros of a function is called ________ ________ of ________.
7. A real number b is a(n) ________ bound for the real zeros of f if no real zeros are less than b, and is a(n) ________ bound if no real zeros are greater than b.

In Exercises 1–6, find all the zeros of the function.

1. $f(x) = x(x - 6)^2$
2. $f(x) = x^2(x + 3)(x^2 - 1)$
3. $g(x) = (x - 2)(x + 4)^3$
4. $f(x) = (x + 5)(x - 8)^2$
5. $f(x) = (x + 6)(x + i)(x - i)$
6. $h(t) = (t - 3)(t - 2)(t - 3i)(t + 3i)$

In Exercises 7–10, use the Rational Zero Test to list all possible rational zeros of *f*. Verify that the zeros of *f* shown on the graph are contained in the list.

7. $f(x) = x^3 + 3x^2 - x - 3$

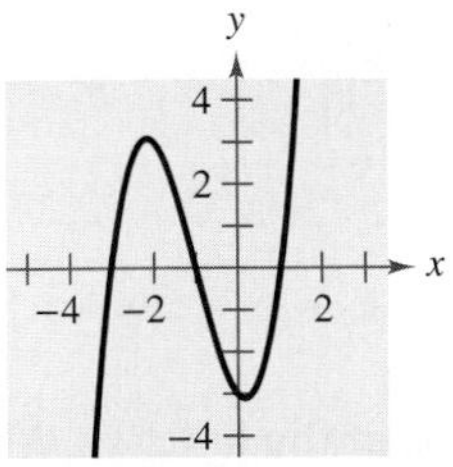

8. $f(x) = x^3 - 4x^2 - 4x + 16$

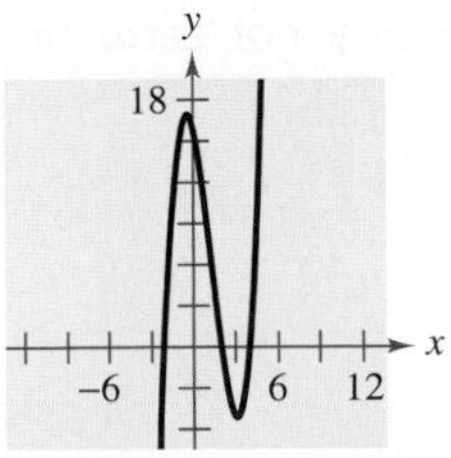

9. $f(x) = 2x^4 - 17x^3 + 35x^2 + 9x - 45$

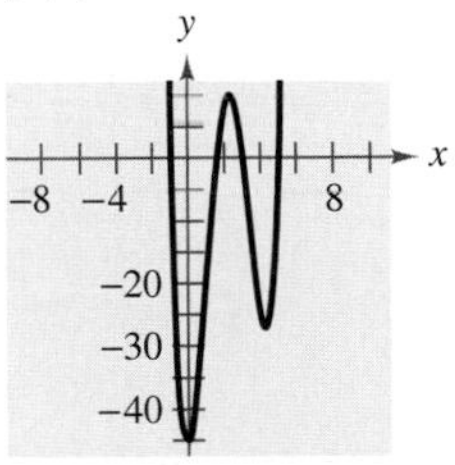

10. $f(x) = 4x^5 - 8x^4 - 5x^3 + 10x^2 + x - 2$

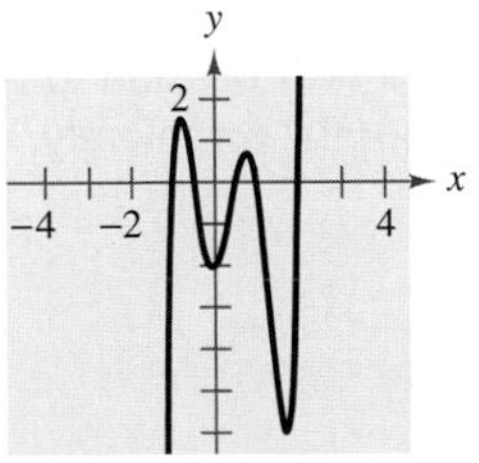

In Exercises 11–20, find all the rational zeros of the function.

11. $f(x) = x^3 - 6x^2 + 11x - 6$
12. $f(x) = x^3 - 7x - 6$
13. $g(x) = x^3 - 4x^2 - x + 4$
14. $h(x) = x^3 - 9x^2 + 20x - 12$
15. $h(t) = t^3 + 12t^2 + 21t + 10$
16. $p(x) = x^3 - 9x^2 + 27x - 27$
17. $C(x) = 2x^3 + 3x^2 - 1$
18. $f(x) = 3x^3 - 19x^2 + 33x - 9$
19. $f(x) = 9x^4 - 9x^3 - 58x^2 + 4x + 24$
20. $f(x) = 2x^4 - 15x^3 + 23x^2 + 15x - 25$

In Exercises 21–24, find all real solutions of the polynomial equation.

21. $z^4 - z^3 - 2z - 4 = 0$

22. $x^4 - 13x^2 - 12x = 0$

23. $2y^4 + 7y^3 - 26y^2 + 23y - 6 = 0$

24. $x^5 - x^4 - 3x^3 + 5x^2 - 2x = 0$

In Exercises 25–28, (a) list the possible rational zeros of *f*, (b) sketch the graph of *f* so that some of the possible zeros in part (a) can be disregarded, and then (c) determine all real zeros of *f*.

25. $f(x) = x^3 + x^2 - 4x - 4$

26. $f(x) = -3x^3 + 20x^2 - 36x + 16$

27. $f(x) = -4x^3 + 15x^2 - 8x - 3$

28. $f(x) = 4x^3 - 12x^2 - x + 15$

In Exercises 29–32, (a) list the possible rational zeros of *f*, (b) use a graphing utility to graph *f* so that some of the possible zeros in part (a) can be disregarded, and then (c) determine all real zeros of *f*.

29. $f(x) = -2x^4 + 13x^3 - 21x^2 + 2x + 8$

30. $f(x) = 4x^4 - 17x^2 + 4$

31. $f(x) = 32x^3 - 52x^2 + 17x + 3$

32. $f(x) = 4x^3 + 7x^2 - 11x - 18$

Graphical Analysis **In Exercises 33–36, (a) use the *zero* or *root* feature of a graphing utility to approximate the zeros of the function accurate to three decimal places, (b) determine one of the exact zeros (use synthetic division to verify your result), and (c) factor the polynomial completely.**

33. $f(x) = x^4 - 3x^2 + 2$

34. $P(t) = t^4 - 7t^2 + 12$

35. $h(x) = x^5 - 7x^4 + 10x^3 + 14x^2 - 24x$

36. $g(x) = 6x^4 - 11x^3 - 51x^2 + 99x - 27$

In Exercises 37–42, find a polynomial function with real coefficients that has the given zeros. (There are many correct answers.)

37. $1, 5i, -5i$

38. $4, 3i, -3i$

39. $6, -5 + 2i, -5 - 2i$

40. $2, 4 + i, 4 - i$

41. $\frac{2}{3}, -1, 3 + \sqrt{2}i$

42. $-5, -5, 1 + \sqrt{3}i$

In Exercises 43–46, write the polynomial (a) as the product of factors that are irreducible over the *rationals*, (b) as the product of linear and quadratic factors that are irreducible over the *reals*, and (c) in completely factored form.

43. $f(x) = x^4 + 6x^2 - 27$

44. $f(x) = x^4 - 2x^3 - 3x^2 + 12x - 18$
(*Hint:* One factor is $x^2 - 6$.)

45. $f(x) = x^4 - 4x^3 + 5x^2 - 2x - 6$
(*Hint:* One factor is $x^2 - 2x - 2$.)

46. $f(x) = x^4 - 3x^3 - x^2 - 12x - 20$
(*Hint:* One factor is $x^2 + 4$.)

In Exercises 47–54, use the given zero to find all the zeros of the function.

	Function	*Zero*
47.	$f(x) = 2x^3 + 3x^2 + 50x + 75$	$5i$
48.	$f(x) = x^3 + x^2 + 9x + 9$	$3i$
49.	$f(x) = 2x^4 - x^3 + 7x^2 - 4x - 4$	$2i$
50.	$g(x) = x^3 - 7x^2 - x + 87$	$5 + 2i$
51.	$g(x) = 4x^3 + 23x^2 + 34x - 10$	$-3 + i$
52.	$h(x) = 3x^3 - 4x^2 + 8x + 8$	$1 - \sqrt{3}i$
53.	$f(x) = x^4 + 3x^3 - 5x^2 - 21x + 22$	$-3 + \sqrt{2}i$
54.	$f(x) = x^3 + 4x^2 + 14x + 20$	$-1 - 3i$

In Exercises 55–72, find all the zeros of the function and write the polynomial as a product of linear factors.

55. $f(x) = x^2 + 25$

56. $f(x) = x^2 - x + 56$

57. $h(x) = x^2 - 4x + 1$

58. $g(x) = x^2 + 10x + 23$

59. $f(x) = x^4 - 81$

60. $f(y) = y^4 - 625$

61. $f(z) = z^2 - 2z + 2$

62. $h(x) = x^3 - 3x^2 + 4x - 2$

63. $g(x) = x^3 - 6x^2 + 13x - 10$

64. $f(x) = x^3 - 2x^2 - 11x + 52$

65. $h(x) = x^3 - x + 6$

66. $h(x) = x^3 + 9x^2 + 27x + 35$

67. $f(x) = 5x^3 - 9x^2 + 28x + 6$

68. $g(x) = 3x^3 - 4x^2 + 8x + 8$

69. $g(x) = x^4 - 4x^3 + 8x^2 - 16x + 16$

70. $h(x) = x^4 + 6x^3 + 10x^2 + 6x + 9$

71. $f(x) = x^4 + 10x^2 + 9$

72. $f(x) = x^4 + 29x^2 + 100$

In Exercises 73–78, find all the zeros of the function. When there is an extended list of possible rational zeros, use a graphing utility to graph the function in order to discard any rational zeros that are obviously not zeros of the function.

73. $f(x) = x^3 + 24x^2 + 214x + 740$

74. $f(s) = 2s^3 - 5s^2 + 12s - 5$

75. $f(x) = 16x^3 - 20x^2 - 4x + 15$

76. $f(x) = 9x^3 - 15x^2 + 11x - 5$

77. $f(x) = 2x^4 + 5x^3 + 4x^2 + 5x + 2$

78. $g(x) = x^5 - 8x^4 + 28x^3 - 56x^2 + 64x - 32$

In Exercises 79–86, use Descartes's Rule of Signs to determine the possible numbers of positive and negative zeros of the function.

79. $g(x) = 5x^5 + 10x$
80. $h(x) = 4x^2 - 8x + 3$
81. $h(x) = 3x^4 + 2x^2 + 1$
82. $h(x) = 2x^4 - 3x + 2$
83. $g(x) = 2x^3 - 3x^2 - 3$
84. $f(x) = 4x^3 - 3x^2 + 2x - 1$
85. $f(x) = -5x^3 + x^2 - x + 5$
86. $f(x) = 3x^3 + 2x^2 + x + 3$

In Exercises 87–90, use synthetic division to verify the upper and lower bounds of the real zeros of *f*.

87. $f(x) = x^4 - 4x^3 + 15$
(a) Upper: $x = 4$ (b) Lower: $x = -1$
88. $f(x) = 2x^3 - 3x^2 - 12x + 8$
(a) Upper: $x = 4$ (b) Lower: $x = -3$
89. $f(x) = x^4 - 4x^3 + 16x - 16$
(a) Upper: $x = 5$ (b) Lower: $x = -3$
90. $f(x) = 2x^4 - 8x + 3$
(a) Upper: $x = 3$ (b) Lower: $x = -4$

In Exercises 91–94, find all the real zeros of the function.

91. $f(x) = 4x^3 - 3x - 1$
92. $f(z) = 12z^3 - 4z^2 - 27z + 9$
93. $f(y) = 4y^3 + 3y^2 + 8y + 6$
94. $g(x) = 3x^3 - 2x^2 + 15x - 10$

In Exercises 95–98, find all the rational zeros of the polynomial function.

95. $P(x) = x^4 - \frac{25}{4}x^2 + 9 = \frac{1}{4}(4x^4 - 25x^2 + 36)$
96. $f(x) = x^3 - \frac{3}{2}x^2 - \frac{23}{2}x + 6 = \frac{1}{2}(2x^3 - 3x^2 - 23x + 12)$
97. $f(x) = x^3 - \frac{1}{4}x^2 - x + \frac{1}{4} = \frac{1}{4}(4x^3 - x^2 - 4x + 1)$
98. $f(z) = z^3 + \frac{11}{6}z^2 - \frac{1}{2}z - \frac{1}{3} = \frac{1}{6}(6z^3 + 11z^2 - 3z - 2)$

In Exercises 99–102, match the cubic function with the numbers of rational and irrational zeros.

(a) Rational zeros: 0; irrational zeros: 1
(b) Rational zeros: 3; irrational zeros: 0
(c) Rational zeros: 1; irrational zeros: 2
(d) Rational zeros: 1; irrational zeros: 0

99. $f(x) = x^3 - 1$
100. $f(x) = x^3 - 2$
101. $f(x) = x^3 - x$
102. $f(x) = x^3 - 2x$

103. ***Geometry*** An open box is to be made from a rectangular piece of material, 15 centimeters by 9 centimeters, by cutting equal squares from the corners and turning up the sides.

(a) Let x represent the length of the sides of the squares removed. Draw a diagram showing the squares removed from the original piece of material and the resulting dimensions of the open box.
(b) Use the diagram to write the volume V of the box as a function of x. Determine the domain of the function.
(c) Sketch the graph of the function and approximate the dimensions of the box that will yield a maximum volume.
(d) Find values of x such that $V = 56$. Which of these values is a physical impossibility in the construction of the box? Explain.

104. ***Geometry*** A rectangular package to be sent by a delivery service (see figure) can have a maximum combined length and girth (perimeter of a cross section) of 120 inches.

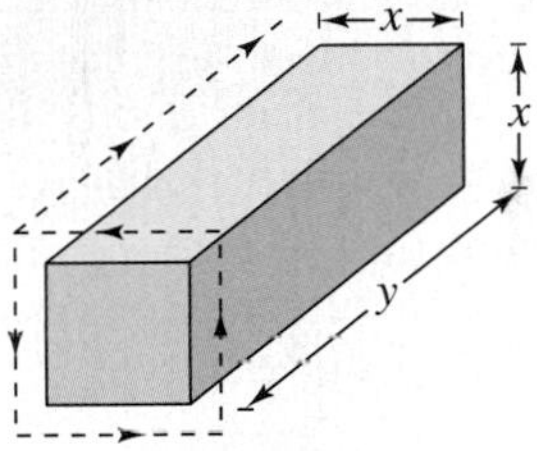

(a) Show that the volume of the package is

$$V(x) = 4x^2(30 - x).$$

(b) Use a graphing utility to graph the function and approximate the dimensions of the package that will yield a maximum volume.
(c) Find values of x such that $V = 13{,}500$. Which of these values is a physical impossibility in the construction of the package? Explain.

105. ***Advertising Cost*** A company that produces MP3 players estimates that the profit P (in dollars) for selling a particular model is given by

$$P = -76x^3 + 4830x^2 - 320{,}000, \quad 0 \le x \le 60$$

where x is the advertising expense (in tens of thousands of dollars). Using this model, find the smaller of two advertising amounts that will yield a profit of \$2,500,000.

106. ***Advertising Cost*** A company that manufactures bicycles estimates that the profit P (in dollars) for selling a particular model is given by

$$P = -45x^3 + 2500x^2 - 275{,}000, \quad 0 \le x \le 50$$

where x is the advertising expense (in tens of thousands of dollars). Using this model, find the smaller of two advertising amounts that will yield a profit of \$800,000.

107. ***Geometry*** A bulk food storage bin with dimensions 2 feet by 3 feet by 4 feet needs to be increased in size to hold five times as much food as the current bin. (Assume each dimension is increased by the same amount.)

(a) Write a function that represents the volume V of the new bin.

(b) Find the dimensions of the new bin.

108. ***Geometry*** A rancher wants to enlarge an existing rectangular corral such that the total area of the new corral is 1.5 times that of the original corral. The current corral's dimensions are 250 feet by 160 feet. The rancher wants to increase each dimension by the same amount.

(a) Write a function that represents the area A of the new corral.

(b) Find the dimensions of the new corral.

(c) A rancher wants to add a length to the sides of the corral that are 160 feet, and twice the length to the sides that are 250 feet, such that the total area of the new corral is 1.5 times that of the original corral. Repeat parts (a) and (b). Explain your results.

109. ***Cost*** The ordering and transportation cost C (in thousands of dollars) for the components used in manufacturing a product is given by

$$C = 100\left(\frac{200}{x^2} + \frac{x}{x + 30}\right), \quad x \geq 1$$

where x is the order size (in hundreds). In calculus, it can be shown that the cost is a minimum when

$$3x^3 - 40x^2 - 2400x - 36{,}000 = 0.$$

Use a calculator to approximate the optimal order size to the nearest hundred units.

110. ***Height of a Baseball*** A baseball is thrown upward from a height of 6 feet with an initial velocity of 48 feet per second, and its height h (in feet) is

$$h(t) = -16t^2 + 48t + 6, \quad 0 \leq t \leq 3$$

where t is the time (in seconds). You are told the ball reaches a height of 64 feet. Is this possible?

111. ***Profit*** The demand equation for a certain product is $p = 140 - 0.0001x$, where p is the unit price (in dollars) of the product and x is the number of units produced and sold. The cost equation for the product is $C = 80x + 150{,}000$, where C is the total cost (in dollars) and x is the number of units produced. The total profit obtained by producing and selling x units is

$$P = R - C = xp - C.$$

You are working in the marketing department of the company that produces this product, and you are asked to determine a price p that will yield a profit of 9 million dollars. Is this possible? Explain.

Model It

112. ***Athletics*** The attendance A (in millions) at NCAA women's college basketball games for the years 1997 through 2003 is shown in the table, where t represents the year, with $t = 7$ corresponding to 1997. (Source: National Collegiate Athletic Association)

Year, t	Attendance, A
7	6.7
8	7.4
9	8.0
10	8.7
11	8.8
12	9.5
13	10.2

(a) Use the *regression* feature of a graphing utility to find a cubic model for the data.

(b) Use the graphing utility to create a scatter plot of the data. Then graph the model and the scatter plot in the same viewing window. How do they compare?

(c) According to the model found in part (a), in what year did attendance reach 8.5 million?

(d) According to the model found in part (a), in what year did attendance reach 9 million?

(e) According to the right-hand behavior of the model, will the attendance continue to increase? Explain.

Synthesis

True or False? **In Exercises 113 and 114, decide whether the statement is true or false. Justify your answer.**

113. It is possible for a third-degree polynomial function with integer coefficients to have no real zeros.

114. If $x = -i$ is a zero of the function given by

$$f(x) = x^3 + ix^2 + ix - 1$$

then $x = i$ must also be a zero of f.

Think About It **In Exercises 115–120, determine (if possible) the zeros of the function g if the function f has zeros at $x = r_1$, $x = r_2$, and $x = r_3$.**

115. $g(x) = -f(x)$

116. $g(x) = 3f(x)$

117. $g(x) = f(x - 5)$

118. $g(x) = f(2x)$

119. $g(x) = 3 + f(x)$

120. $g(x) = f(-x)$

121. ***Exploration*** Use a graphing utility to graph the function given by $f(x) = x^4 - 4x^2 + k$ for different values of k. Find values of k such that the zeros of f satisfy the specified characteristics. (Some parts do not have unique answers.)

(a) Four real zeros

(b) Two real zeros, each of multiplicity 2

(c) Two real zeros and two complex zeros

(d) Four complex zeros

122. ***Think About It*** Will the answers to Exercise 121 change for the function g?

(a) $g(x) = f(x - 2)$ (b) $g(x) = f(2x)$

123. ***Think About It*** A third-degree polynomial function f has real zeros $-2, \frac{1}{2}$, and 3, and its leading coefficient is negative. Write an equation for f. Sketch the graph of f. How many different polynomial functions are possible for f?

124. ***Think About It*** Sketch the graph of a fifth-degree polynomial function whose leading coefficient is positive and that has one zero at $x = 3$ of multiplicity 2.

125. ***Writing*** Compile a list of all the various techniques for factoring a polynomial that have been covered so far in the text. Give an example illustrating each technique, and write a paragraph discussing when the use of each technique is appropriate.

126. Use the information in the table to answer each question.

Interval	Value of $f(x)$
$(-\infty, -2)$	Positive
$(-2, 1)$	Negative
$(1, 4)$	Negative
$(4, \infty)$	Positive

(a) What are the three real zeros of the polynomial function f?

(b) What can be said about the behavior of the graph of f at $x = 1$?

(c) What is the least possible degree of f? Explain. Can the degree of f ever be odd? Explain.

(d) Is the leading coefficient of f positive or negative? Explain.

(e) Write an equation for f. (There are many correct answers.)

(f) Sketch a graph of the equation you wrote in part (e).

127. (a) Find a quadratic function f (with integer coefficients) that has $\pm\sqrt{b}i$ as zeros. Assume that b is a positive integer.

(b) Find a quadratic function f (with integer coefficients) that has $a \pm bi$ as zeros. Assume that b is a positive integer.

128. ***Graphical Reasoning*** The graph of one of the following functions is shown below. Identify the function shown in the graph. Explain why each of the others is not the correct function. Use a graphing utility to verify your result.

(a) $f(x) = x^2(x + 2)(x - 3.5)$

(b) $g(x) = (x + 2)(x - 3.5)$

(c) $h(x) = (x + 2)(x - 3.5)(x^2 + 1)$

(d) $k(x) = (x + 1)(x + 2)(x - 3.5)$

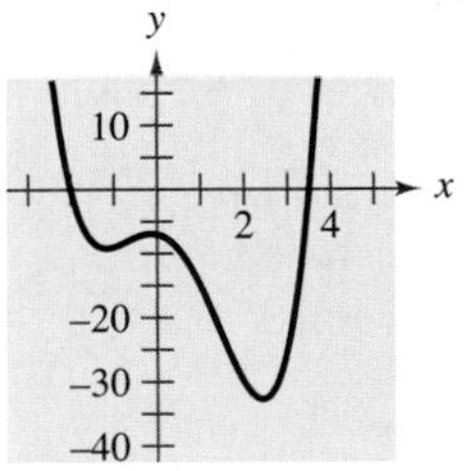

Skills Review

In Exercises 129–132, perform the operation and simplify.

129. $(-3 + 6i) - (8 - 3i)$

130. $(12 - 5i) + 16i$

131. $(6 - 2i)(1 + 7i)$

132. $(9 - 5i)(9 + 5i)$

In Exercises 133–138, use the graph of f to sketch the graph of g. To print an enlarged copy of the graph, go to the website *www.mathgraphs.com*.

133. $g(x) = f(x - 2)$

134. $g(x) = f(x) - 2$

135. $g(x) = 2f(x)$

136. $g(x) = f(-x)$

137. $g(x) = f(2x)$

138. $g(x) = f\left(\frac{1}{2}x\right)$

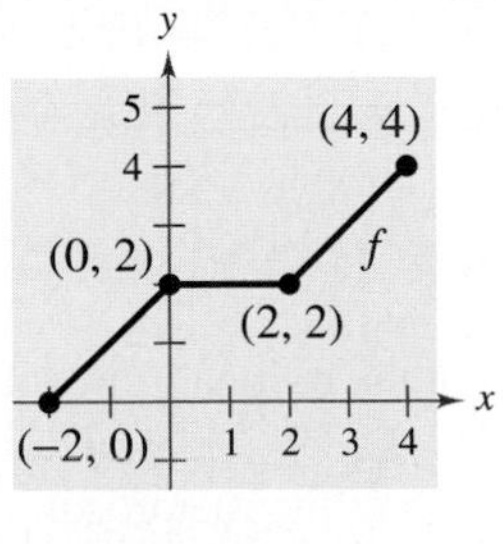

2.6 Rational Functions

What you should learn

- Find the domains of rational functions.
- Find the horizontal and vertical asymptotes of graphs of rational functions.
- Analyze and sketch graphs of rational functions.
- Sketch graphs of rational functions that have slant asymptotes.
- Use rational functions to model and solve real-life problems.

Why you should learn it

Rational functions can be used to model and solve real-life problems relating to business. For instance, in Exercise 79 on page 196, a rational function is used to model average speed over a distance.

Mike Powell/Getty Images

Introduction

A **rational function** can be written in the form

$$f(x) = \frac{N(x)}{D(x)}$$

where $N(x)$ and $D(x)$ are polynomials and $D(x)$ is not the zero polynomial.

In general, the *domain* of a rational function of x includes all real numbers except x-values that make the denominator zero. Much of the discussion of rational functions will focus on their graphical behavior near the x-values excluded from the domain.

Example 1 **Finding the Domain of a Rational Function**

Find the domain of $f(x) = \dfrac{1}{x}$ and discuss the behavior of f near any excluded x-values.

Solution

Because the denominator is zero when $x = 0$, the domain of f is all real numbers except $x = 0$. To determine the behavior of f near this excluded value, evaluate $f(x)$ to the left and right of $x = 0$, as indicated in the following tables.

x	-1	-0.5	-0.1	-0.01	-0.001	$\longrightarrow 0$
$f(x)$	-1	-2	-10	-100	-1000	$\longrightarrow -\infty$

x	$0 \longleftarrow$	0.001	0.01	0.1	0.5	1
$f(x)$	$\infty \longleftarrow$	1000	100	10	2	1

Note that as x approaches 0 *from the left*, $f(x)$ decreases without bound. In contrast, as x approaches 0 *from the right*, $f(x)$ increases without bound. The graph of f is shown in Figure 2.36.

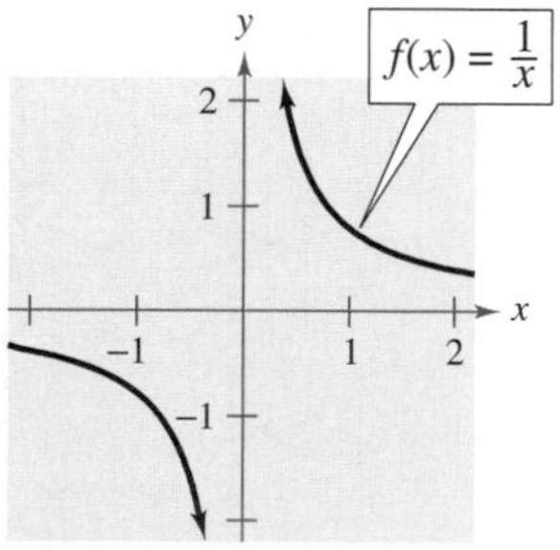

FIGURE 2.36

✓CHECKPOINT Now try Exercise 1.

STUDY TIP

Note that the rational function given by $f(x) = 1/x$ is also referred to as the reciprocal function discussed in Section 1.6.

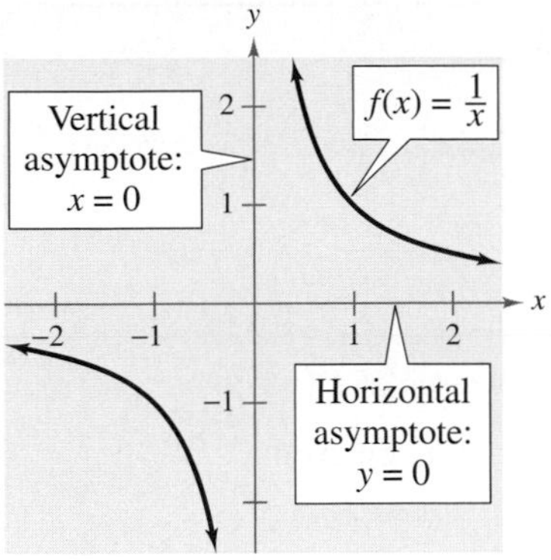

FIGURE 2.37

Horizontal and Vertical Asymptotes

In Example 1, the behavior of f near $x = 0$ is denoted as follows.

$$\underbrace{f(x) \longrightarrow -\infty \text{ as } x \longrightarrow 0^-}_{f(x) \text{ decreases without bound as } x \text{ approaches 0 from the left.}} \qquad \underbrace{f(x) \longrightarrow \infty \text{ as } x \longrightarrow 0^+}_{f(x) \text{ increases without bound as } x \text{ approaches 0 from the right.}}$$

The line $x = 0$ is a **vertical asymptote** of the graph of f, as shown in Figure 2.37. From this figure, you can see that the graph of f also has a **horizontal asymptote**—the line $y = 0$. This means that the values of $f(x) = 1/x$ approach zero as x increases or decreases without bound.

$$\underbrace{f(x) \longrightarrow 0 \text{ as } x \longrightarrow -\infty}_{f(x) \text{ approaches 0 as } x \text{ decreases without bound.}} \qquad \underbrace{f(x) \longrightarrow 0 \text{ as } x \longrightarrow \infty}_{f(x) \text{ approaches 0 as } x \text{ increases without bound.}}$$

Definitions of Vertical and Horizontal Asymptotes

1. The line $x = a$ is a **vertical asymptote** of the graph of f if

$$f(x) \longrightarrow \infty \quad \text{or} \quad f(x) \longrightarrow -\infty$$

as $x \longrightarrow a$, either from the right or from the left.

2. The line $y = b$ is a **horizontal asymptote** of the graph of f if

$$f(x) \longrightarrow b$$

as $x \longrightarrow \infty$ or $x \longrightarrow -\infty$.

Eventually (as $x \longrightarrow \infty$ or $x \longrightarrow -\infty$), the distance between the horizontal asymptote and the points on the graph must approach zero. Figure 2.38 shows the horizontal and vertical asymptotes of the graphs of three rational functions.

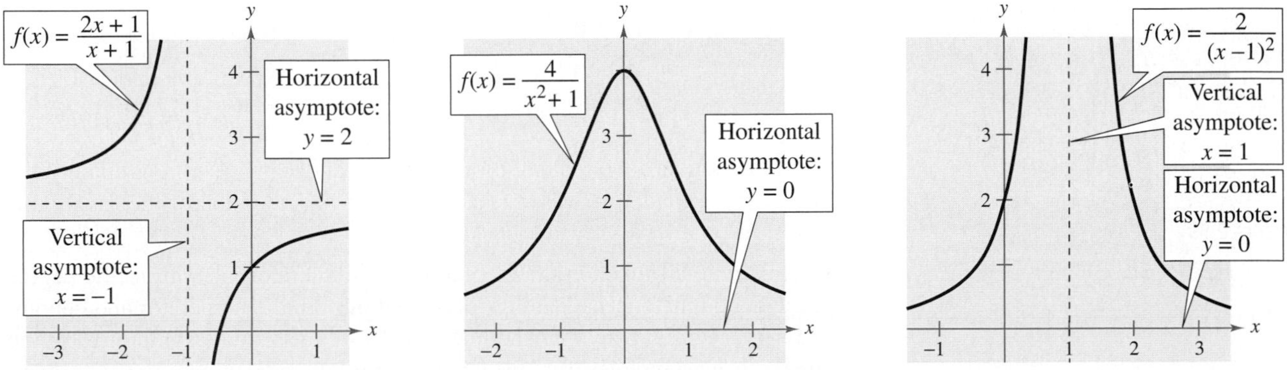

(a) (b) (c)

FIGURE 2.38

The graphs of $f(x) = 1/x$ in Figure 2.37 and $f(x) = (2x + 1)/(x + 1)$ in Figure 2.38(a) are **hyperbolas.** You will study hyperbolas in Section 10.4.

Asymptotes of a Rational Function

Let f be the rational function given by

$$f(x) = \frac{N(x)}{D(x)} = \frac{a_n x^n + a_{n-1}x^{n-1} + \cdot \cdot \cdot + a_1 x + a_0}{b_m x^m + b_{m-1}x^{m-1} + \cdot \cdot \cdot + b_1 x + b_0}$$

where $N(x)$ and $D(x)$ have no common factors.

1. The graph of f has *vertical* asymptotes at the zeros of $D(x)$.
2. The graph of f has one or no *horizontal* asymptote determined by comparing the degrees of $N(x)$ and $D(x)$.
   a. If $n < m$, the graph of f has the line $y = 0$ (the x-axis) as a horizontal asymptote.
   b. If $n = m$, the graph of f has the line $y = a_n/b_m$ (ratio of the leading coefficients) as a horizontal asymptote.
   c. If $n > m$, the graph of f has no horizontal asymptote.

Example 2 Finding Horizontal and Vertical Asymptotes

Find all horizontal and vertical asymptotes of the graph of each rational function.

a. $f(x) = \dfrac{2x^2}{x^2 - 1}$ **b.** $f(x) = \dfrac{x^2 + x - 2}{x^2 - x - 6}$

Solution

a. For this rational function, the degree of the numerator is *equal to* the degree of the denominator. The leading coefficient of the numerator is 2 and the leading coefficient of the denominator is 1, so the graph has the line $y = 2$ as a horizontal asymptote. To find any vertical asymptotes, set the denominator equal to zero and solve the resulting equation for x.

$x^2 - 1 = 0$ Set denominator equal to zero.

$(x + 1)(x - 1) = 0$ Factor.

$x + 1 = 0 \Rightarrow x = -1$ Set 1st factor equal to 0.

$x - 1 = 0 \Rightarrow x = 1$ Set 2nd factor equal to 0.

This equation has two real solutions $x = -1$ and $x = 1$, so the graph has the lines $x = -1$ and $x = 1$ as vertical asymptotes. The graph of the function is shown in Figure 2.39.

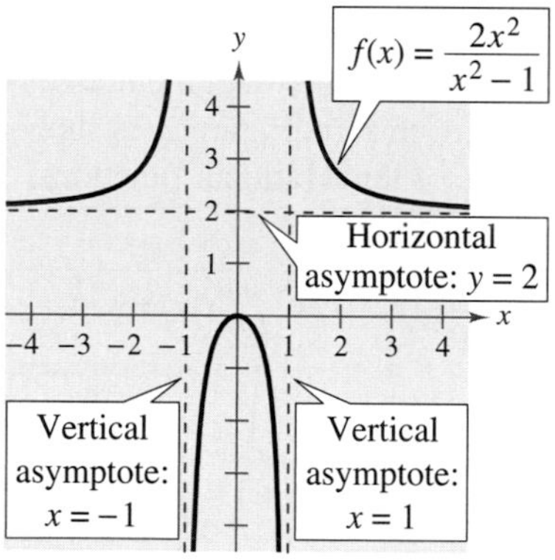

FIGURE 2.39

b. For this rational function, the degree of the numerator is *equal to* the degree of the denominator. The leading coefficient of both the numerator and denominator is 1, so the graph has the line $y = 1$ as a horizontal asymptote. To find any vertical asymptotes, first factor the numerator and denominator as follows.

$$f(x) = \frac{x^2 + x - 2}{x^2 - x - 6} = \frac{(x - 1)\cancel{(x + 2)}}{\cancel{(x + 2)}(x - 3)} = \frac{x - 1}{x - 3}, \quad x \neq 2$$

By setting the denominator $x - 3$ (of the simplified function) equal to zero, you can determine that the graph has the line $x = 3$ as a vertical asymptote.

CHECKPOINT Now try Exercise 9.

Analyzing Graphs of Rational Functions

To sketch the graph of a rational function, use the following guidelines.

STUDY TIP

You may also want to test for symmetry when graphing rational functions, especially for simple rational functions. Recall from Section 1.6 that the graph of

$$f(x) = \frac{1}{x}$$

is symmetric with respect to the origin.

Guidelines for Analyzing Graphs of Rational Functions

Let $f(x) = N(x)/D(x)$, where $N(x)$ and $D(x)$ are polynomials.

1. Simplify f, if possible.
2. Find and plot the y-intercept (if any) by evaluating $f(0)$.
3. Find the zeros of the numerator (if any) by solving the equation $N(x) = 0$. Then plot the corresponding x-intercepts.
4. Find the zeros of the denominator (if any) by solving the equation $D(x) = 0$. Then sketch the corresponding vertical asymptotes.
5. Find and sketch the horizontal asymptote (if any) by using the rule for finding the horizontal asymptote of a rational function.
6. Plot at least one point *between* and one point *beyond* each x-intercept and vertical asymptote.
7. Use smooth curves to complete the graph between and beyond the vertical asymptotes.

Technology

Some graphing utilities have difficulty graphing rational functions that have vertical asymptotes. Often, the utility will connect parts of the graph that are not supposed to be connected. For instance, the top screen on the right shows the graph of

$$f(x) = \frac{1}{x-2}.$$

Notice that the graph should consist of two unconnected portions—one to the left of $x = 2$ and the other to the right of $x = 2$. To eliminate this problem, you can try changing the mode of the graphing utility to *dot mode*. The problem with this is that the graph is then represented as a collection of dots (as shown in the bottom screen on the right) rather than as a smooth curve.

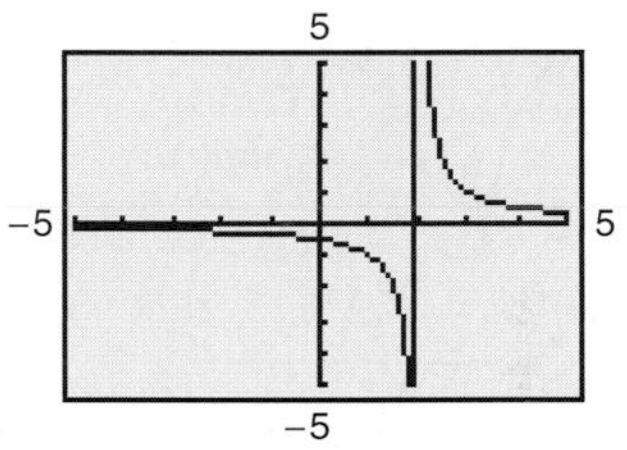

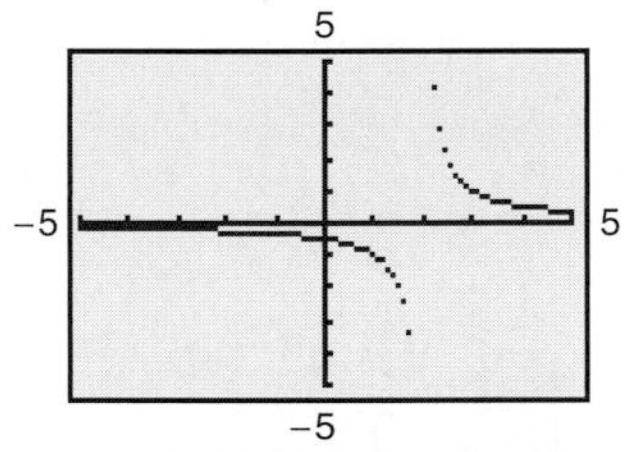

The concept of *test intervals* from Section 2.2 can be extended to graphing of rational functions. To do this, use the fact that a rational function can change signs only at its zeros and its undefined values (the x-values for which its denominator is zero). Between two consecutive zeros of the numerator and the denominator, a rational function must be entirely positive or entirely negative. This means that when the zeros of the numerator and the denominator of a rational function are put in order, they divide the real number line into test intervals in which the function has no sign changes. A representative x-value is chosen to determine if the value of the rational function is positive (the graph lies above the x-axis) or negative (the graph lies below the x-axis).

STUDY TIP

You can use transformations to help you sketch graphs of rational functions. For instance, the graph of g in Example 3 is a vertical stretch and a right shift of the graph of $f(x) = 1/x$ because

$$\begin{aligned} g(x) &= \frac{3}{x-2} \\ &= 3\left(\frac{1}{x-2}\right) \\ &= 3f(x-2). \end{aligned}$$

Example 3 Sketching the Graph of a Rational Function

Sketch the graph of $g(x) = \dfrac{3}{x-2}$ and state its domain.

Solution

y-intercept: $\left(0, -\frac{3}{2}\right)$, because $g(0) = -\frac{3}{2}$

x-intercept: None, because $3 \neq 0$

Vertical asymptote: $x = 2$, zero of denominator

Horizontal asymptote: $y = 0$, because degree of $N(x) <$ degree of $D(x)$

Additional points:

Test interval	Representative x-value	Value of g	Sign	Point on graph
$(-\infty, 2)$	-4	$g(-4) = -0.5$	Negative	$(-4, -0.5)$
$(2, \infty)$	3	$g(3) = 3$	Positive	$(3, 3)$

By plotting the intercepts, asymptotes, and a few additional points, you can obtain the graph shown in Figure 2.40. The domain of g is all real numbers x except $x = 2$.

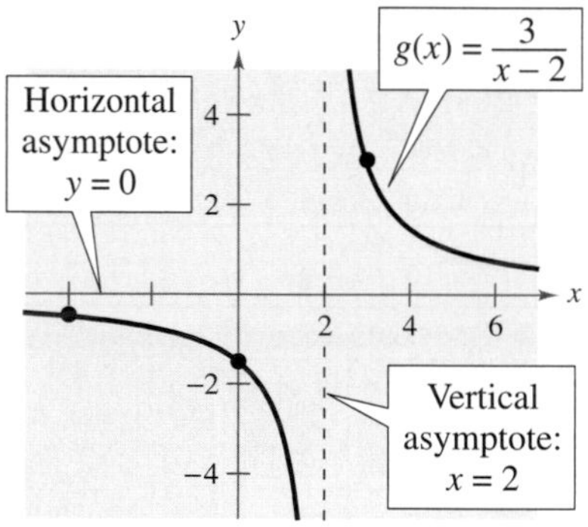

FIGURE 2.40

✓CHECKPOINT Now try Exercise 27.

Example 4 Sketching the Graph of a Rational Function

Sketch the graph of

$$f(x) = \frac{2x-1}{x}$$

and state its domain.

Solution

y-intercept: None, because $x = 0$ is not in the domain

x-intercept: $\left(\frac{1}{2}, 0\right)$, because $2x - 1 = 0$

Vertical asymptote: $x = 0$, zero of denominator

Horizontal asymptote: $y = 2$, because degree of $N(x) =$ degree of $D(x)$

Additional points:

Test interval	Representative x-value	Value of f	Sign	Point on graph
$(-\infty, 0)$	-1	$f(-1) = 3$	Positive	$(-1, 3)$
$\left(0, \frac{1}{2}\right)$	$\frac{1}{4}$	$f\left(\frac{1}{4}\right) = -2$	Negative	$\left(\frac{1}{4}, -2\right)$
$\left(\frac{1}{2}, \infty\right)$	4	$f(4) = 1.75$	Positive	$(4, 1.75)$

By plotting the intercepts, asymptotes, and a few additional points, you can obtain the graph shown in Figure 2.41. The domain of f is all real numbers x except $x = 0$.

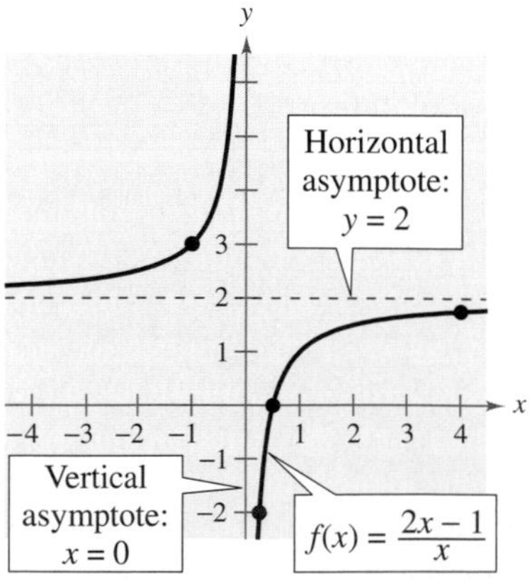

FIGURE 2.41

✓CHECKPOINT Now try Exercise 31.

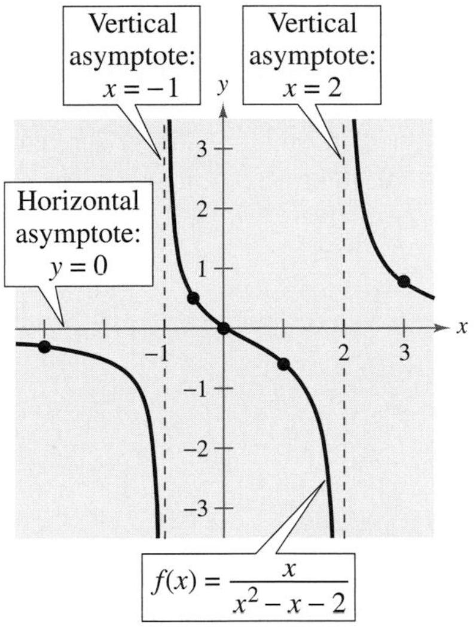

FIGURE 2.42

Example 5 Sketching the Graph of a Rational Function

Sketch the graph of $f(x) = x/(x^2 - x - 2)$.

Solution

Factoring the denominator, you have $f(x) = \dfrac{x}{(x+1)(x-2)}$.

y-intercept: (0, 0), because $f(0) = 0$

x-intercept: (0, 0)

Vertical asymptotes: $x = -1$, $x = 2$, zeros of denominator

Horizontal asymptote: $y = 0$, because degree of $N(x)$ < degree of $D(x)$

Additional points:

Test interval	Representative x-value	Value of f	Sign	Point on graph
$(-\infty, -1)$	-3	$f(-3) = -0.3$	Negative	$(-3, -0.3)$
$(-1, 0)$	-0.5	$f(-0.5) = 0.4$	Positive	$(-0.5, 0.4)$
$(0, 2)$	1	$f(1) = -0.5$	Negative	$(1, -0.5)$
$(2, \infty)$	3	$f(3) = 0.75$	Positive	$(3, 0.75)$

The graph is shown in Figure 2.42.

CHECKPOINT Now try Exercise 35.

STUDY TIP

If you are unsure of the shape of a portion of the graph of a rational function, plot some additional points. Also note that when the numerator and the denominator of a rational function have a common factor, the graph of the function has a *hole* at the zero of the common factor (see Example 6).

Example 6 A Rational Function with Common Factors

Sketch the graph of $f(x) = (x^2 - 9)/(x^2 - 2x - 3)$.

Solution

By factoring the numerator and denominator, you have

$$f(x) = \frac{x^2 - 9}{x^2 - 2x - 3} = \frac{\cancel{(x-3)}(x+3)}{\cancel{(x-3)}(x+1)} = \frac{x+3}{x+1}, \quad x \neq 3.$$

y-intercept: (0, 3), because $f(0) = 3$

x-intercept: $(-3, 0)$, because $f(-3) = 0$

Vertical asymptote: $x = -1$, zero of (simplified) denominator

Horizontal asymptote: $y = 1$, because degree of $N(x)$ = degree of $D(x)$

Additional points:

Test interval	Representative x-value	Value of f	Sign	Point on graph
$(-\infty, -3)$	-4	$f(-4) = 0.33$	Positive	$(-4, -0.33)$
$(-3, -1)$	-2	$f(-2) = -1$	Negative	$(-2, -1)$
$(-1, \infty)$	2	$f(2) = 1.67$	Positive	$(2, 1.67)$

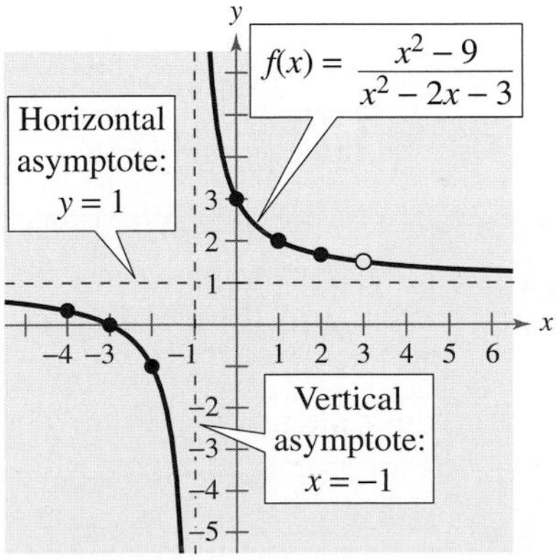

FIGURE 2.43 HOLE AT $x = 3$

The graph is shown in Figure 2.43. Notice that there is a hole in the graph at $x = 3$ because the function is not defined when $x = 3$.

CHECKPOINT Now try Exercise 41.

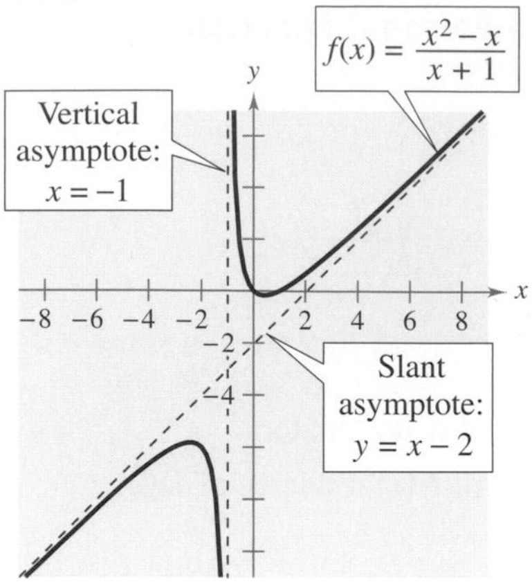

FIGURE 2.44

Slant Asymptotes

Consider a rational function whose denominator is of degree 1 or greater. If the degree of the numerator is exactly *one more* than the degree of the denominator, the graph of the function has a **slant** (or **oblique**) **asymptote.** For example, the graph of

$$f(x) = \frac{x^2 - x}{x + 1}$$

has a slant asymptote, as shown in Figure 2.44. To find the equation of a slant asymptote, use long division. For instance, by dividing $x + 1$ into $x^2 - x$, you obtain

$$f(x) = \frac{x^2 - x}{x + 1} = \underbrace{x - 2}_{\substack{\text{Slant asymptote} \\ (y = x - 2)}} + \frac{2}{x + 1}.$$

As x increases or decreases without bound, the remainder term $2/(x + 1)$ approaches 0, so the graph of f approaches the line $y = x - 2$, as shown in Figure 2.44.

Example 7 A Rational Function with a Slant Asymptote

Sketch the graph of $f(x) = (x^2 - x - 2)/(x - 1)$.

Solution

Factoring the numerator as $(x - 2)(x + 1)$ allows you to recognize the x-intercepts. Using long division

$$f(x) = \frac{x^2 - x - 2}{x - 1} = x - \frac{2}{x - 1}$$

allows you to recognize that the line $y = x$ is a slant asymptote of the graph.

y-intercept: $(0, 2)$, because $f(0) = 2$

x-intercepts: $(-1, 0)$ and $(2, 0)$

Vertical asymptote: $x = 1$, zero of denominator

Slant asymptote: $y = x$

Additional points:

Test interval	Representative x-value	Value of f	Sign	Point on graph
$(-\infty, -1)$	-2	$f(-2) = -1.33$	Negative	$(-2, -1.33)$
$(-1, 1)$	0.5	$f(0.5) = 4.5$	Positive	$(0.5, 4.5)$
$(1, 2)$	1.5	$f(1.5) = -2.5$	Negative	$(1.5, -2.5)$
$(2, \infty)$	3	$f(3) = 2$	Positive	$(3, 2)$

The graph is shown in Figure 2.45.

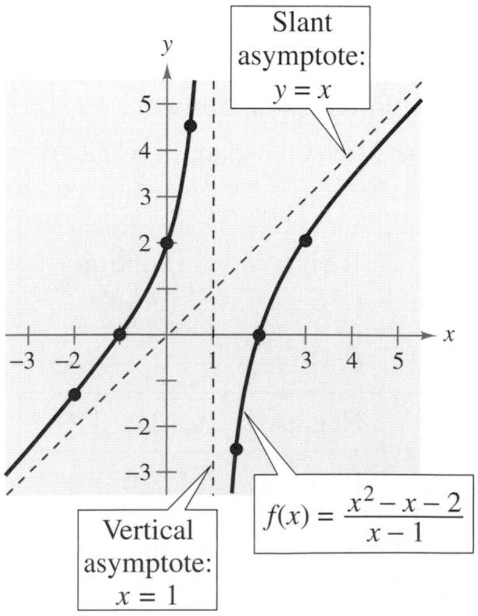

FIGURE 2.45

CHECKPOINT Now try Exercise 61.

Applications

There are many examples of asymptotic behavior in real life. For instance, Example 8 shows how a vertical asymptote can be used to analyze the cost of removing pollutants from smokestack emissions.

Example 8 Cost-Benefit Model

A utility company burns coal to generate electricity. The cost C (in dollars) of removing $p\%$ of the smokestack pollutants is given by

$$C = \frac{80{,}000p}{100 - p}$$

for $0 \le p < 100$. Sketch the graph of this function. You are a member of a state legislature considering a law that would require utility companies to remove 90% of the pollutants from their smokestack emissions. The current law requires 85% removal. How much additional cost would the utility company incur as a result of the new law?

Solution

The graph of this function is shown in Figure 2.46. Note that the graph has a vertical asymptote at $p = 100$. Because the current law requires 85% removal, the current cost to the utility company is

$$C = \frac{80{,}000(85)}{100 - 85} \approx \$453{,}333. \qquad \text{Evaluate } C \text{ when } p = 85.$$

If the new law increases the percent removal to 90%, the cost will be

$$C = \frac{80{,}000(90)}{100 - 90} = \$720{,}000. \qquad \text{Evaluate } C \text{ when } p = 90.$$

So, the new law would require the utility company to spend an additional

$$720{,}000 - 453{,}333 = \$266{,}667. \qquad \text{Subtract 85\% removal cost from 90\% removal cost.}$$

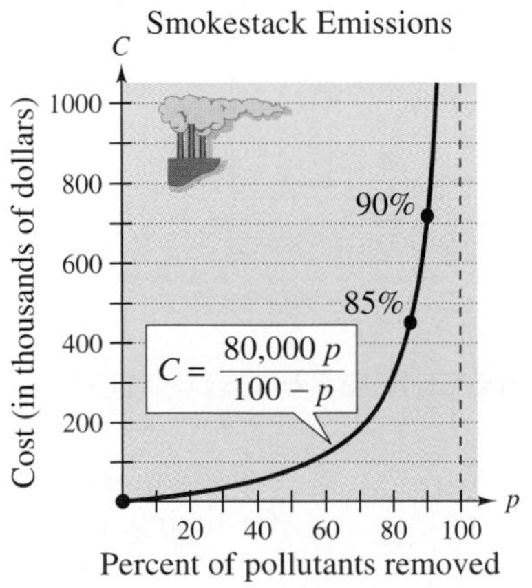

FIGURE 2.46

CHECKPOINT Now try Exercise 73.

Example 9 Finding a Minimum Area

A rectangular page is designed to contain 48 square inches of print. The margins at the top and bottom of the page are each 1 inch deep. The margins on each side are $1\frac{1}{2}$ inches wide. What should the dimensions of the page be so that the least amount of paper is used?

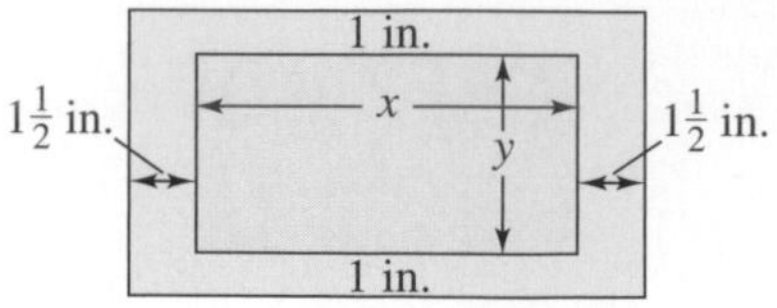

FIGURE 2.47

Graphical Solution

Let A be the area to be minimized. From Figure 2.47, you can write

$$A = (x + 3)(y + 2).$$

The printed area inside the margins is modeled by $48 = xy$ or $y = 48/x$. To find the minimum area, rewrite the equation for A in terms of just one variable by substituting $48/x$ for y.

$$A = (x + 3)\left(\frac{48}{x} + 2\right)$$

$$= \frac{(x + 3)(48 + 2x)}{x}, \quad x > 0$$

The graph of this rational function is shown in Figure 2.48. Because x represents the width of the printed area, you need consider only the portion of the graph for which x is positive. Using a graphing utility, you can approximate the minimum value of A to occur when $x \approx 8.5$ inches. The corresponding value of y is $48/8.5 \approx 5.6$ inches. So, the dimensions should be

$$x + 3 \approx 11.5 \text{ inches} \quad \text{by} \quad y + 2 \approx 7.6 \text{ inches.}$$

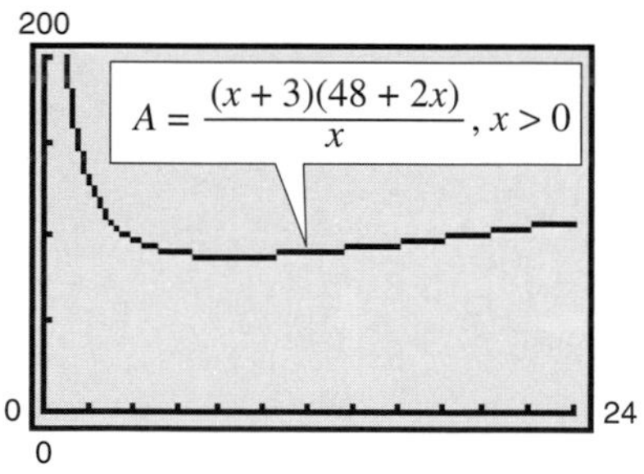

FIGURE 2.48

✓CHECKPOINT Now try Exercise 77.

Numerical Solution

Let A be the area to be minimized. From Figure 2.47, you can write

$$A = (x + 3)(y + 2).$$

The printed area inside the margins is modeled by $48 = xy$ or $y = 48/x$. To find the minimum area, rewrite the equation for A in terms of just one variable by substituting $48/x$ for y.

$$A = (x + 3)\left(\frac{48}{x} + 2\right)$$

$$= \frac{(x + 3)(48 + 2x)}{x}, \quad x > 0$$

Use the *table* feature of a graphing utility to create a table of values for the function

$$y_1 = \frac{(x + 3)(48 + 2x)}{x}$$

beginning at $x = 1$. From the table, you can see that the minimum value of y_1 occurs when x is somewhere between 8 and 9, as shown in Figure 2.49. To approximate the minimum value of y_1 to one decimal place, change the table so that it starts at $x = 8$ and increases by 0.1. The minimum value of y_1 occurs when $x \approx 8.5$, as shown in Figure 2.50. The corresponding value of y is $48/8.5 \approx 5.6$ inches. So, the dimensions should be $x + 3 \approx 11.5$ inches by $y + 2 \approx 7.6$ inches.

X	Y1
6	90
7	88.571
8	88
9	88
10	88.4
11	89.091
12	90

X=8

FIGURE 2.49

X	Y1
8.2	87.961
8.3	87.949
8.4	87.943
8.5	87.941
8.6	87.944
8.7	87.952
8.8	87.964

X=8.5

FIGURE 2.50

If you go on to take a course in calculus, you will learn an analytic technique for finding the exact value of x that produces a minimum area. In this case, that value is $x = 6\sqrt{2} \approx 8.485$.

2.6 Exercises

VOCABULARY CHECK: Fill in the blanks.

1. Functions of the form $f(x) = N(x)/D(x)$, where $N(x)$ and $D(x)$ are polynomials and $D(x)$ is not the zero polynomial, are called ________ ________.
2. If $f(x) \to \pm\infty$ as $x \to a$ from the left or the right, then $x = a$ is a ________ ________ of the graph of f.
3. If $f(x) \to b$ as $x \to \pm\infty$, then $y = b$ is a ________ ________ of the graph of f.
4. For the rational function given by $f(x) = N(x)/D(x)$, if the degree of $N(x)$ is exactly one more than the degree of $D(x)$, then the graph of f has a ________ (or oblique) ________.

In Exercises 1–4, (a) complete each table for the function, (b) determine the vertical and horizontal asymptotes of the graph of the function, and (c) find the domain of the function.

x	$f(x)$
0.5	
0.9	
0.99	
0.999	

x	$f(x)$
1.5	
1.1	
1.01	
1.001	

x	$f(x)$
5	
10	
100	
1000	

1. $f(x) = \dfrac{1}{x - 1}$

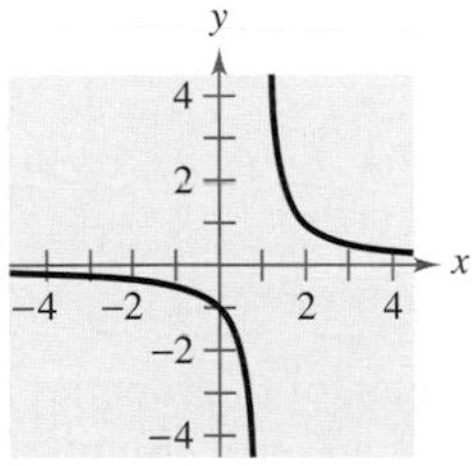

2. $f(x) = \dfrac{5x}{x - 1}$

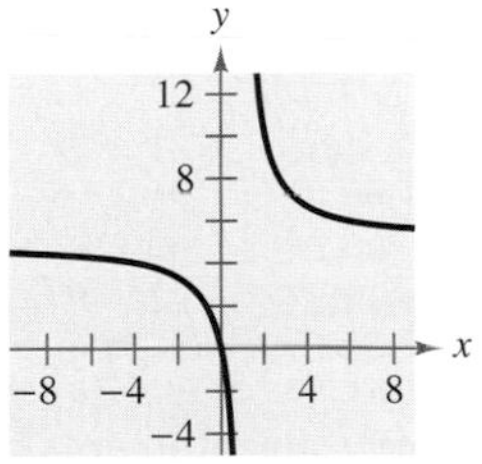

3. $f(x) = \dfrac{3x^2}{x^2 - 1}$

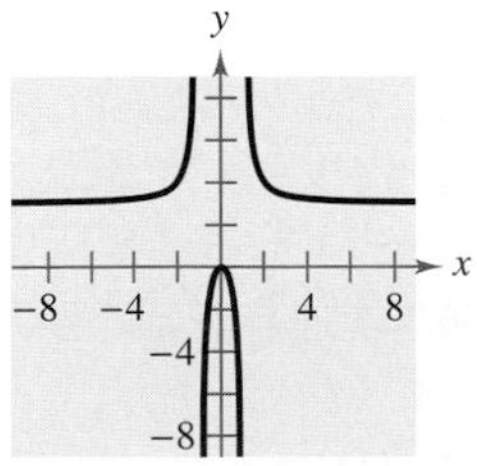

4. $f(x) = \dfrac{4x}{x^2 - 1}$

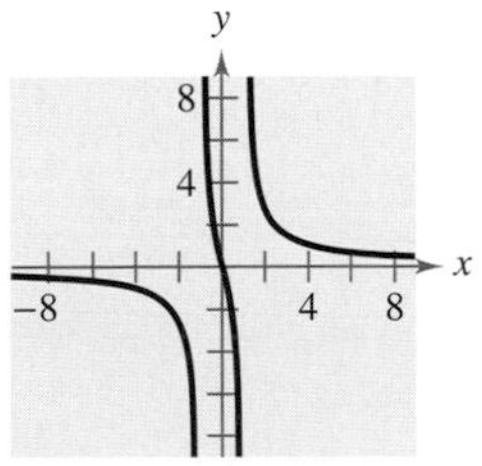

In Exercises 5–12, find the domain of the function and identify any horizontal and vertical asymptotes.

5. $f(x) = \dfrac{1}{x^2}$

6. $f(x) = \dfrac{4}{(x - 2)^3}$

7. $f(x) = \dfrac{2 + x}{2 - x}$

8. $f(x) = \dfrac{1 - 5x}{1 + 2x}$

9. $f(x) = \dfrac{x^3}{x^2 - 1}$

10. $f(x) = \dfrac{2x^2}{x + 1}$

11. $f(x) = \dfrac{3x^2 + 1}{x^2 + x + 9}$

12. $f(x) = \dfrac{3x^2 + x - 5}{x^2 + 1}$

In Exercises 13–16, match the rational function with its graph. [The graphs are labeled (a), (b), (c), and (d).]

(a)

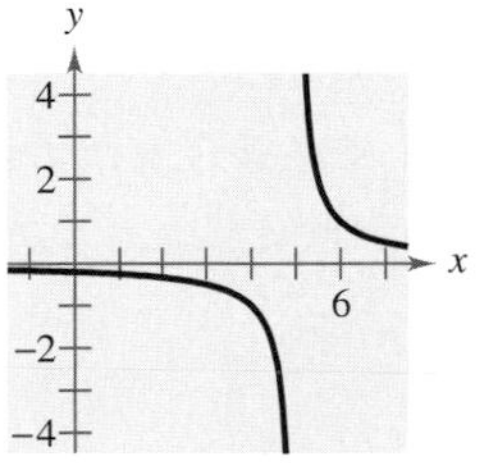

(b)

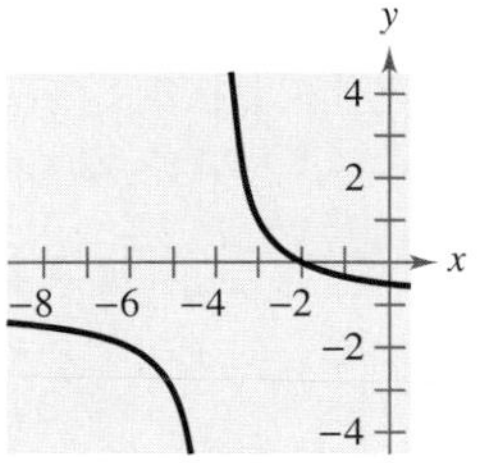

(c)

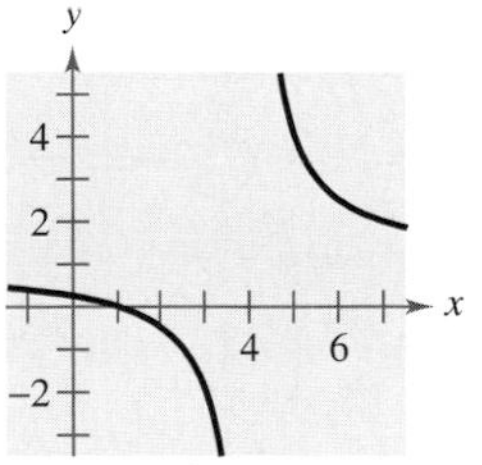

(d)

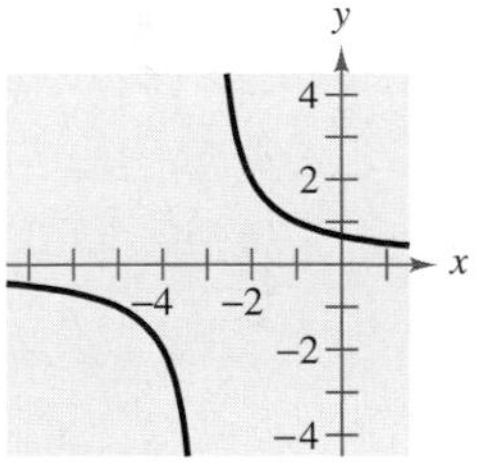

13. $f(x) = \dfrac{2}{x + 3}$

14. $f(x) = \dfrac{1}{x - 5}$

15. $f(x) = \dfrac{x - 1}{x - 4}$

16. $f(x) = -\dfrac{x + 2}{x + 4}$

In Exercises 17–20, find the zeros (if any) of the rational function.

17. $g(x) = \dfrac{x^2 - 1}{x + 1}$

18. $h(x) = 2 + \dfrac{5}{x^2 + 2}$

19. $f(x) = 1 - \dfrac{3}{x - 3}$

20. $g(x) = \dfrac{x^3 - 8}{x^2 + 1}$

In Exercises 21–26, find the domain of the function and identify any horizontal and vertical asymptotes.

21. $f(x) = \dfrac{x - 4}{x^2 - 16}$

22. $f(x) = \dfrac{x + 3}{x^2 - 9}$

23. $f(x) = \dfrac{x^2 - 1}{x^2 - 2x - 3}$

24. $f(x) = \dfrac{x^2 - 4}{x^2 - 3x + 2}$

25. $f(x) = \dfrac{x^2 - 3x - 4}{2x^2 + x - 1}$

26. $f(x) = \dfrac{6x^2 - 11x + 3}{6x^2 - 7x - 3}$

In Exercises 27–46, (a) state the domain of the function, (b) identify all intercepts, (c) find any vertical and horizontal asymptotes, and (d) plot additional solution points as needed to sketch the graph of the rational function.

27. $f(x) = \dfrac{1}{x + 2}$

28. $f(x) = \dfrac{1}{x - 3}$

29. $h(x) = \dfrac{-1}{x + 2}$

30. $g(x) = \dfrac{1}{3 - x}$

31. $C(x) = \dfrac{5 + 2x}{1 + x}$

32. $P(x) = \dfrac{1 - 3x}{1 - x}$

33. $f(x) = \dfrac{x^2}{x^2 + 9}$

34. $f(t) = \dfrac{1 - 2t}{t}$

35. $g(s) = \dfrac{s}{s^2 + 1}$

36. $f(x) = -\dfrac{1}{(x - 2)^2}$

37. $h(x) = \dfrac{x^2 - 5x + 4}{x^2 - 4}$

38. $g(x) = \dfrac{x^2 - 2x - 8}{x^2 - 9}$

39. $f(x) = \dfrac{2x^2 - 5x - 3}{x^3 - 2x^2 - x + 2}$

40. $f(x) = \dfrac{x^2 - x - 2}{x^3 - 2x^2 - 5x + 6}$

41. $f(x) = \dfrac{x^2 + 3x}{x^2 + x - 6}$

42. $f(x) = \dfrac{5(x + 4)}{x^2 + x - 12}$

43. $f(x) = \dfrac{2x^2 - 5x + 2}{2x^2 - x - 6}$

44. $f(x) = \dfrac{3x^2 - 8x + 4}{2x^2 - 3x - 2}$

45. $f(t) = \dfrac{t^2 - 1}{t + 1}$

46. $f(x) = \dfrac{x^2 - 16}{x - 4}$

Analytical, Numerical, and Graphical Analysis **In Exercises 47–50, do the following.**

(a) Determine the domains of *f* and *g*.

(b) Simplify *f* and find any vertical asymptotes of the graph of *f*.

(c) Compare the functions by completing the table.

(d) Use a graphing utility to graph *f* and *g* in the same viewing window.

(e) Explain why the graphing utility may not show the difference in the domains of *f* and *g*.

47. $f(x) = \dfrac{x^2 - 1}{x + 1}, \quad g(x) = x - 1$

x	-3	-2	-1.5	-1	-0.5	0	1
$f(x)$							
$g(x)$							

48. $f(x) = \dfrac{x^2(x - 2)}{x^2 - 2x}, \quad g(x) = x$

x	-1	0	1	1.5	2	2.5	3
$f(x)$							
$g(x)$							

49. $f(x) = \dfrac{x - 2}{x^2 - 2x}, \quad g(x) = \dfrac{1}{x}$

x	-0.5	0	0.5	1	1.5	2	3
$f(x)$							
$g(x)$							

50. $f(x) = \dfrac{2x - 6}{x^2 - 7x + 12}, \quad g(x) = \dfrac{2}{x - 4}$

x	0	1	2	3	4	5	6
$f(x)$							
$g(x)$							

In Exercises 51–64, (a) state the domain of the function, (b) identify all intercepts, (c) identify any vertical and slant asymptotes, and (d) plot additional solution points as needed to sketch the graph of the rational function.

51. $h(x) = \dfrac{x^2 - 4}{x}$

52. $g(x) = \dfrac{x^2 + 5}{x}$

53. $f(x) = \dfrac{2x^2 + 1}{x}$

54. $f(x) = \dfrac{1 - x^2}{x}$

55. $g(x) = \dfrac{x^2 + 1}{x}$

56. $h(x) = \dfrac{x^2}{x - 1}$

57. $f(t) = -\dfrac{t^2 + 1}{t + 5}$

58. $f(x) = \dfrac{x^2}{3x + 1}$

59. $f(x) = \dfrac{x^3}{x^2 - 1}$

60. $g(x) = \dfrac{x^3}{2x^2 - 8}$

61. $f(x) = \dfrac{x^2 - x + 1}{x - 1}$

62. $f(x) = \dfrac{2x^2 - 5x + 5}{x - 2}$

63. $f(x) = \dfrac{2x^3 - x^2 - 2x + 1}{x^2 + 3x + 2}$

64. $f(x) = \dfrac{2x^3 + x^2 - 8x - 4}{x^2 - 3x + 2}$

In Exercises 65–68, use a graphing utility to graph the rational function. Give the domain of the function and identify any asymptotes. Then zoom out sufficiently far so that the graph appears as a line. Identify the line.

65. $f(x) = \dfrac{x^2 + 5x + 8}{x + 3}$

66. $f(x) = \dfrac{2x^2 + x}{x + 1}$

67. $g(x) = \dfrac{1 + 3x^2 - x^3}{x^2}$

68. $h(x) = \dfrac{12 - 2x - x^2}{2(4 + x)}$

Graphical Reasoning **In Exercises 69–72, (a) use the graph to determine any x-intercepts of the graph of the rational function and (b) set $y = 0$ and solve the resulting equation to confirm your result in part (a).**

69. $y = \dfrac{x + 1}{x - 3}$

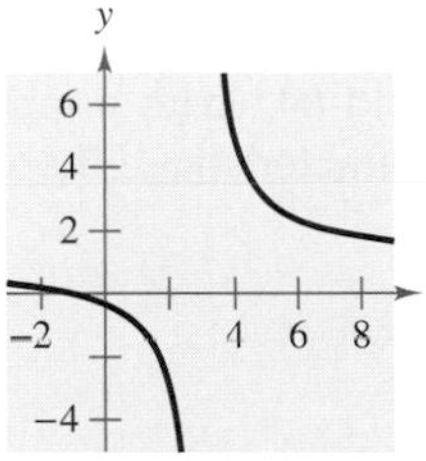

70. $y = \dfrac{2x}{x - 3}$

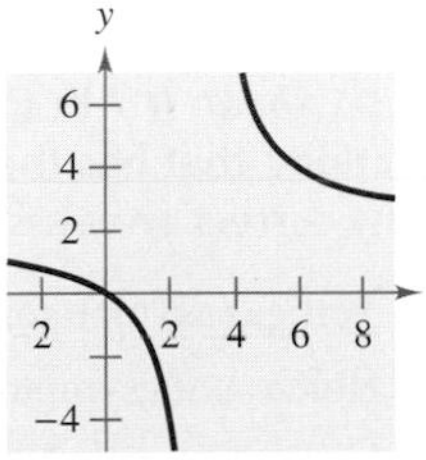

71. $y = \dfrac{1}{x} - x$

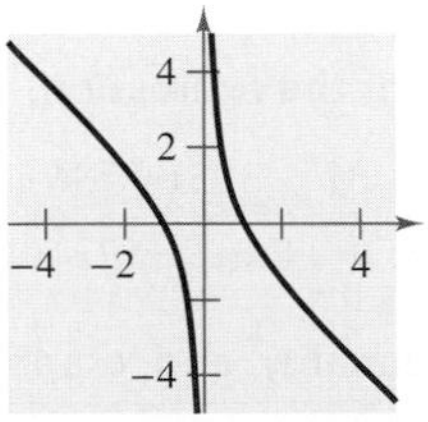

72. $y = x - 3 + \dfrac{2}{x}$

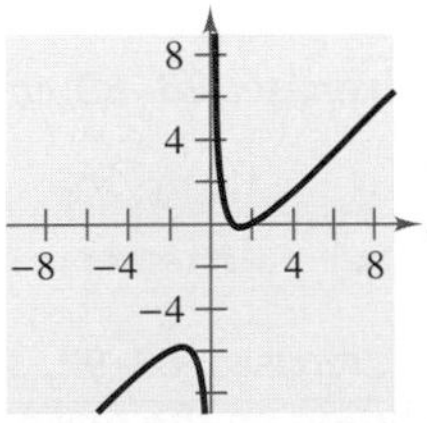

73. ***Pollution*** The cost C (in millions of dollars) of removing $p\%$ of the industrial and municipal pollutants discharged into a river is given by

$$C = \frac{255p}{100 - p}, \quad 0 \le p < 100.$$

(a) Use a graphing utility to graph the cost function.

(b) Find the costs of removing 10%, 40%, and 75% of the pollutants.

(c) According to this model, would it be possible to remove 100% of the pollutants? Explain.

74. ***Recycling*** In a pilot project, a rural township is given recycling bins for separating and storing recyclable products. The cost C (in dollars) for supplying bins to $p\%$ of the population is given by

$$C = \frac{25{,}000p}{100 - p}, \quad 0 \le p < 100.$$

(a) Use a graphing utility to graph the cost function.

(b) Find the costs of supplying bins to 15%, 50%, and 90% of the population.

(c) According to this model, would it be possible to supply bins to 100% of the residents? Explain.

75. ***Population Growth*** The game commission introduces 100 deer into newly acquired state game lands. The population N of the herd is modeled by

$$N = \frac{20(5 + 3t)}{1 + 0.04t}, \quad t \ge 0$$

where t is the time in years (see figure).

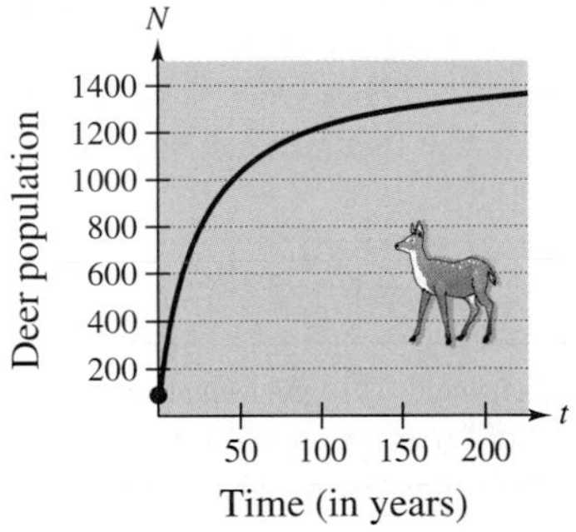

(a) Find the populations when $t = 5$, $t = 10$, and $t = 25$.

(b) What is the limiting size of the herd as time increases?

76. ***Concentration of a Mixture*** A 1000-liter tank contains 50 liters of a 25% brine solution. You add x liters of a 75% brine solution to the tank.

(a) Show that the concentration C, the proportion of brine to total solution, in the final mixture is

$$C = \frac{3x + 50}{4(x + 50)}.$$

(b) Determine the domain of the function based on the physical constraints of the problem.

(c) Sketch a graph of the concentration function.

(d) As the tank is filled, what happens to the rate at which the concentration of brine is increasing? What percent does the concentration of brine appear to approach?

77. ***Page Design*** A page that is x inches wide and y inches high contains 30 square inches of print. The top and bottom margins are 1 inch deep and the margins on each side are 2 inches wide (see figure).

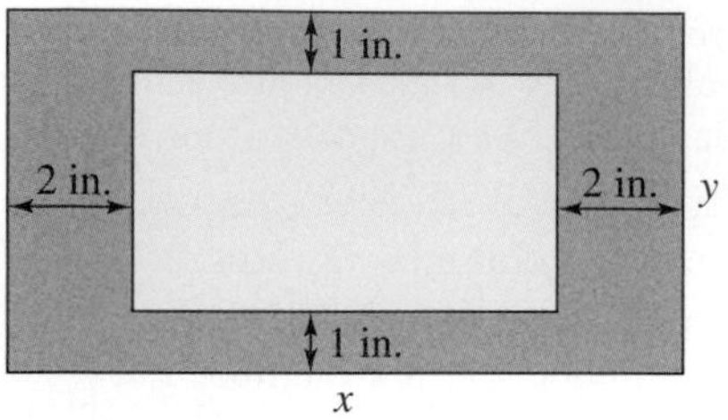

(a) Show that the total area A on the page is

$$A = \frac{2x(x + 11)}{x - 4}.$$

(b) Determine the domain of the function based on the physical constraints of the problem.

(c) Use a graphing utility to graph the area function and approximate the page size for which the least amount of paper will be used. Verify your answer numerically using the *table* feature of the graphing utility.

78. ***Page Design*** A rectangular page is designed to contain 64 square inches of print. The margins at the top and bottom of the page are each 1 inch deep. The margins on each side are $1\frac{1}{2}$ inches wide. What should the dimensions of the page be so that the least amount of paper is used?

Model It

79. ***Average Speed*** A driver averaged 50 miles per hour on the round trip between Akron, Ohio, and Columbus, Ohio, 100 miles away. The average speeds for going and returning were x and y miles per hour, respectively.

(a) Show that $y = \dfrac{25x}{x - 25}$.

(b) Determine the vertical and horizontal asymptotes of the graph of the function.

(c) Use a graphing utility to graph the function.

(d) Complete the table.

x	30	35	40	45	50	55	60
y							

(e) Are the results in the table what you expected? Explain.

(f) Is it possible to average 20 miles per hour in one direction and still average 50 miles per hour on the round trip? Explain.

80. ***Sales*** The sales S (in millions of dollars) for the Yankee Candle Company in the years 1998 through 2003 are shown in the table. (Source: The Yankee Candle Company)

1998	184.5	1999	256.6	2000	338.8
2001	379.8	2002	444.8	2003	508.6

A model for these data is given by

$$S = \frac{5.816t^2 - 130.68}{0.004t^2 + 1.00}, \quad 8 \le t \le 13$$

where t represents the year, with $t = 8$ corresponding to 1998.

(a) Use a graphing utility to plot the data and graph the model in the same viewing window. How well does the model fit the data?

(b) Use the model to estimate the sales for the Yankee Candle Company in 2008.

(c) Would this model be useful for estimating sales after 2008? Explain.

Synthesis

True or False? **In Exercises 81 and 82, determine whether the statement is true or false. Justify your answer.**

81. A polynomial can have infinitely many vertical asymptotes.

82. The graph of a rational function can never cross one of its asymptotes.

Think About It **In Exercises 83 and 84, write a rational function f that has the specified characteristics. (There are many correct answers.)**

83. Vertical asymptote: None
Horizontal asymptote: $y = 2$

84. Vertical asymptote: $x = -2, x = 1$
Horizontal asymptote: None

Skills Review

In Exercises 85–88, completely factor the expression.

85. $x^2 - 15x + 56$

86. $3x^2 + 23x - 36$

87. $x^3 - 5x^2 + 4x - 20$

88. $x^3 + 6x^2 - 2x - 12$

In Exercises 89–92, solve the inequality and graph the solution on the real number line.

89. $10 - 3x \le 0$

90. $5 - 2x > 5(x + 1)$

91. $|4(x - 2)| < 20$

92. $\frac{1}{2}|2x + 3| \ge 5$

93. **Make a Decision** To work an extended application analyzing the total manpower of the Department of Defense, visit this text's website at *college.hmco.com*. *(Data Source: U.S. Census Bureau)*

2.7 Nonlinear Inequalities

What you should learn

- Solve polynomial inequalities.
- Solve rational inequalities.
- Use inequalities to model and solve real-life problems.

Why you should learn it

Inequalities can be used to model and solve real-life problems. For instance, in Exercise 73 on page 205, a polynomial inequality is used to model the percent of households that own a television and have cable in the United States.

Polynomial Inequalities

To solve a polynomial inequality such as $x^2 - 2x - 3 < 0$, you can use the fact that a polynomial can change signs only at its zeros (the x-values that make the polynomial equal to zero). Between two consecutive zeros, a polynomial must be entirely positive or entirely negative. This means that when the real zeros of a polynomial are put in order, they divide the real number line into intervals in which the polynomial has no sign changes. These zeros are the **critical numbers** of the inequality, and the resulting intervals are the **test intervals** for the inequality. For instance, the polynomial above factors as

$$x^2 - 2x - 3 = (x + 1)(x - 3)$$

and has two zeros, $x = -1$ and $x = 3$. These zeros divide the real number line into three test intervals:

$$(-\infty, -1), \quad (-1, 3), \quad \text{and} \quad (3, \infty). \qquad \text{(See Figure 2.51.)}$$

So, to solve the inequality $x^2 - 2x - 3 < 0$, you need only test one value from each of these test intervals to determine whether the value satisfies the original inequality. If so, you can conclude that the interval is a solution of the inequality.

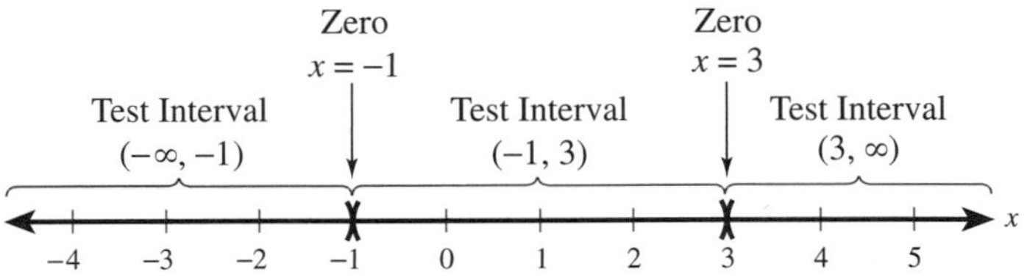

FIGURE 2.51 *Three test intervals for* $x^2 - 2x - 3$

You can use the same basic approach to determine the test intervals for any polynomial.

Finding Test Intervals for a Polynomial

To determine the intervals on which the values of a polynomial are entirely negative or entirely positive, use the following steps.

1. Find all real zeros of the polynomial, and arrange the zeros in increasing order (from smallest to largest). These zeros are the critical numbers of the polynomial.
2. Use the critical numbers of the polynomial to determine its test intervals.
3. Choose one representative x-value in each test interval and evaluate the polynomial at that value. If the value of the polynomial is negative, the polynomial will have negative values for every x-value in the interval. If the value of the polynomial is positive, the polynomial will have positive values for every x-value in the interval.

Example 1 Solving a Polynomial Inequality

Solve

$$x^2 - x - 6 < 0.$$

Solution

By factoring the polynomial as

$$x^2 - x - 6 = (x + 2)(x - 3)$$

you can see that the critical numbers are $x = -2$ and $x = 3$. So, the polynomial's test intervals are

$$(-\infty, -2), \quad (-2, 3), \quad \text{and} \quad (3, \infty). \qquad \text{Test intervals}$$

In each test interval, choose a representative x-value and evaluate the polynomial.

Test Interval	*x-Value*	*Polynomial Value*	*Conclusion*
$(-\infty, -2)$	$x = -3$	$(-3)^2 - (-3) - 6 = 6$	Positive
$(-2, 3)$	$x = 0$	$(0)^2 - (0) - 6 = -6$	Negative
$(3, \infty)$	$x = 4$	$(4)^2 - (4) - 6 = 6$	Positive

From this you can conclude that the inequality is satisfied for all x-values in $(-2, 3)$. This implies that the solution of the inequality $x^2 - x - 6 < 0$ is the interval $(-2, 3)$, as shown in Figure 2.52. Note that the original inequality contains a less than symbol. This means that the solution set does not contain the endpoints of the test interval $(-2, 3)$.

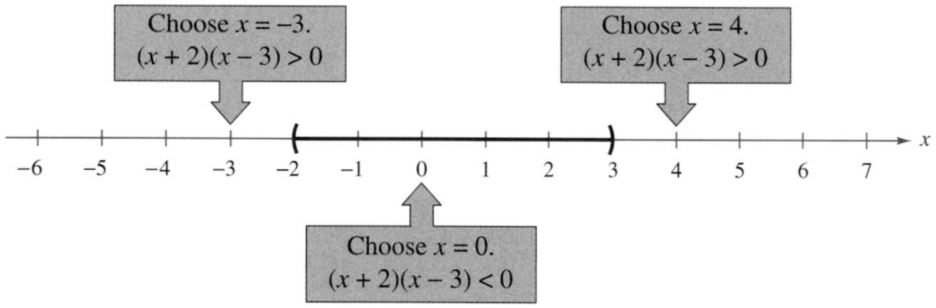

FIGURE 2.52

✓CHECKPOINT Now try Exercise 13.

As with linear inequalities, you can check the reasonableness of a solution by substituting x-values into the original inequality. For instance, to check the solution found in Example 1, try substituting several x-values from the interval $(-2, 3)$ into the inequality

$$x^2 - x - 6 < 0.$$

Regardless of which x-values you choose, the inequality should be satisfied.

You can also use a graph to check the result of Example 1. Sketch the graph of $y = x^2 - x - 6$, as shown in Figure 2.53. Notice that the graph is below the x-axis on the interval $(-2, 3)$.

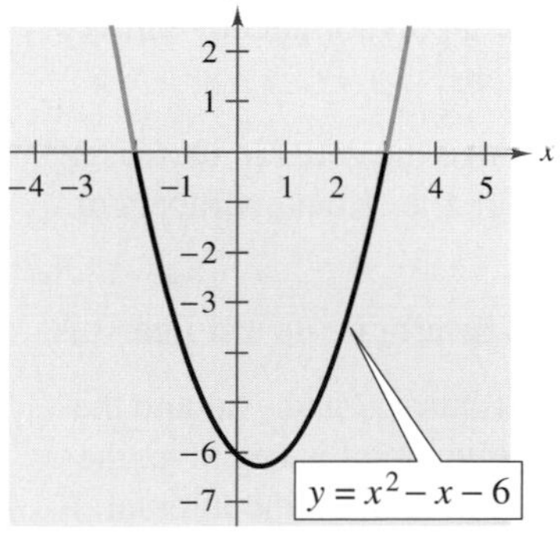

FIGURE 2.53

In Example 1, the polynomial inequality was given in general form (with the polynomial on one side and zero on the other). Whenever this is not the case, you should begin the solution process by writing the inequality in general form.

Example 2 Solving a Polynomial Inequality

Solve $2x^3 - 3x^2 - 32x > -48$.

Solution

Begin by writing the inequality in general form.

$$2x^3 - 3x^2 - 32x > -48 \quad \text{Write original inequality.}$$

$$2x^3 - 3x^2 - 32x + 48 > 0 \quad \text{Write in general form.}$$

$$(x - 4)(x + 4)(2x - 3) > 0 \quad \text{Factor.}$$

The critical numbers are $x = -4$, $x = \frac{3}{2}$, and $x = 4$, and the test intervals are $(-\infty, -4)$, $\left(-4, \frac{3}{2}\right)$, $\left(\frac{3}{2}, 4\right)$, and $(4, \infty)$.

Test Interval	*x-Value*	*Polynomial Value*	*Conclusion*
$(-\infty, -4)$	$x = -5$	$2(-5)^3 - 3(-5)^2 - 32(-5) + 48$	Negative
$\left(-4, \frac{3}{2}\right)$	$x = 0$	$2(0)^3 - 3(0)^2 - 32(0) + 48$	Positive
$\left(\frac{3}{2}, 4\right)$	$x = 2$	$2(2)^3 - 3(2)^2 - 32(2) + 48$	Negative
$(4, \infty)$	$x = 5$	$2(5)^3 - 3(5)^2 - 32(5) + 48$	Positive

From this you can conclude that the inequality is satisfied on the open intervals $\left(-4, \frac{3}{2}\right)$ and $(4, \infty)$. Therefore, the solution set consists of all real numbers in the intervals $\left(-4, \frac{3}{2}\right)$ and $(4, \infty)$, as shown in Figure 2.54.

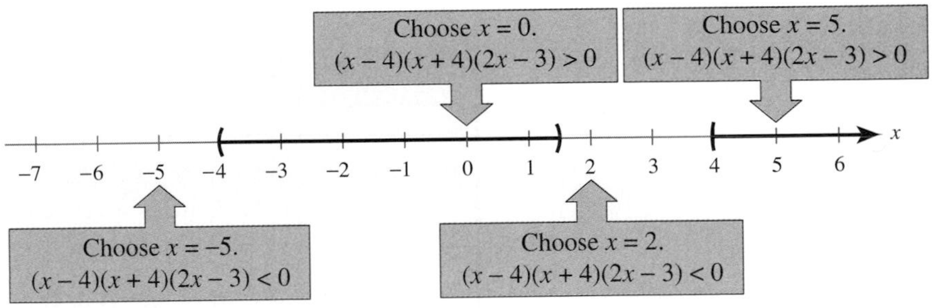

FIGURE 2.54

✓CHECKPOINT Now try Exercise 21.

When solving a polynomial inequality, be sure you have accounted for the particular type of inequality symbol given in the inequality. For instance, in Example 2, note that the original inequality contained a "greater than" symbol and the solution consisted of two open intervals. If the original inequality had been

$$2x^3 - 3x^2 - 32x \geq -48$$

the solution would have consisted of the closed interval $\left[-4, \frac{3}{2}\right]$ and the interval $[4, \infty)$.

STUDY TIP

You may find it easier to determine the sign of a polynomial from its *factored* form. For instance, in Example 2, if the test value $x = 2$ is substituted into the factored form

$$(x - 4)(x + 4)(2x - 3)$$

you can see that the sign pattern of the factors is

$$(-)(+)(+)$$

which yields a negative result. Try using the factored forms of the polynomials to determine the signs of the polynomials in the test intervals of the other examples in this section.

Each of the polynomial inequalities in Examples 1 and 2 has a solution set that consists of a single interval or the union of two intervals. When solving the exercises for this section, watch for unusual solution sets, as illustrated in Example 3.

Example 3 Unusual Solution Sets

a. The solution set of the following inequality consists of the entire set of real numbers, $(-\infty, \infty)$. In other words, the value of the quadratic $x^2 + 2x + 4$ is positive for every real value of x.

$$x^2 + 2x + 4 > 0$$

b. The solution set of the following inequality consists of the single real number $\{-1\}$, because the quadratic $x^2 + 2x + 1$ has only one critical number, $x = -1$, and it is the only value that satisfies the inequality.

$$x^2 + 2x + 1 \le 0$$

c. The solution set of the following inequality is empty. In other words, the quadratic $x^2 + 3x + 5$ is not less than zero for any value of x.

$$x^2 + 3x + 5 < 0$$

d. The solution set of the following inequality consists of all real numbers except $x = 2$. In interval notation, this solution set can be written as $(-\infty, 2) \cup (2, \infty)$.

$$x^2 - 4x + 4 > 0$$

✓CHECKPOINT Now try Exercise 25.

Exploration

You can use a graphing utility to verify the results in Example 3. For instance, the graph of $y = x^2 + 2x + 4$ is shown below. Notice that the y-values are greater than 0 for all values of x, as stated in Example 3(a). Use the graphing utility to graph the following:

$$y = x^2 + 2x + 1 \qquad y = x^2 + 3x + 5 \qquad y = x^2 - 4x + 4$$

Explain how you can use the graphs to verify the results of parts (b), (c), and (d) of Example 3.

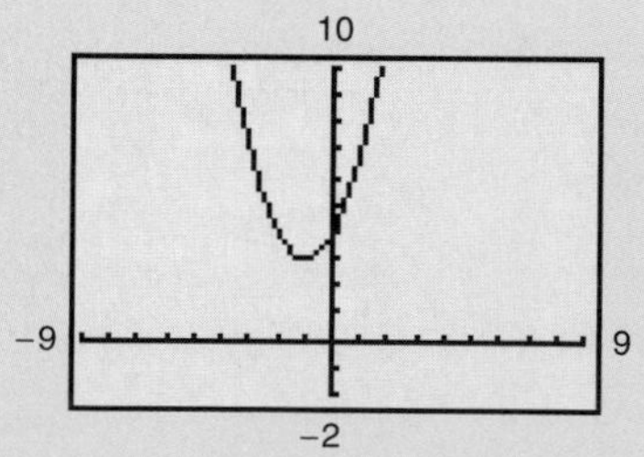

Rational Inequalities

The concepts of critical numbers and test intervals can be extended to rational inequalities. To do this, use the fact that the value of a rational expression can change sign only at its *zeros* (the x-values for which its numerator is zero) and its *undefined values* (the x-values for which its denominator is zero). These two types of numbers make up the *critical numbers* of a rational inequality. When solving a rational inequality, begin by writing the inequality in general form with the rational expression on the left and zero on the right.

Example 4 Solving a Rational Inequality

Solve $\dfrac{2x - 7}{x - 5} \le 3$.

Solution

$$\frac{2x - 7}{x - 5} \le 3$$ Write original inequality.

$$\frac{2x - 7}{x - 5} - 3 \le 0$$ Write in general form.

$$\frac{2x - 7 - 3x + 15}{x - 5} \le 0$$ Find the LCD and add fractions.

$$\frac{-x + 8}{x - 5} \le 0$$ Simplify.

Critical numbers: $x = 5, x = 8$ Zeros and undefined values of rational expression

Test intervals: $(-\infty, 5), (5, 8), (8, \infty)$

Test: Is $\dfrac{-x + 8}{x - 5} \le 0$?

After testing these intervals, as shown in Figure 2.55, you can see that the inequality is satisfied on the open intervals $(-\infty, 5)$ and $(8, \infty)$. Moreover, because $(-x + 8)/(x - 5) = 0$ when $x = 8$, you can conclude that the solution set consists of all real numbers in the intervals $(-\infty, 5) \cup [8, \infty)$. (Be sure to use a closed interval to indicate that x can equal 8.)

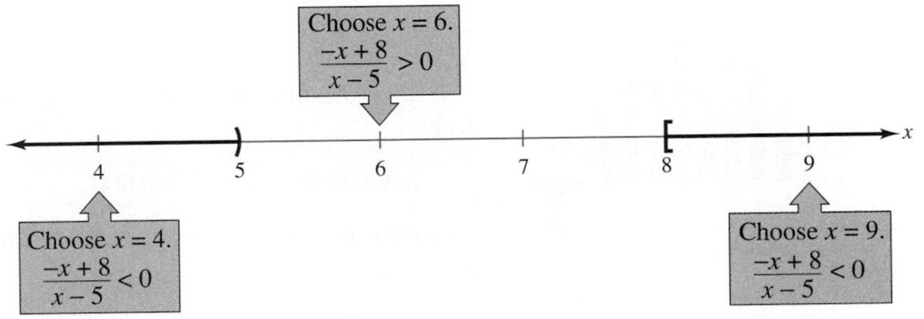

FIGURE 2.55

CHECKPOINT Now try Exercise 39.

Applications

One common application of inequalities comes from business and involves profit, revenue, and cost. The formula that relates these three quantities is

$$\text{Profit} = \text{Revenue} - \text{Cost}$$
$$P = R - C.$$

Example 5 Increasing the Profit for a Product

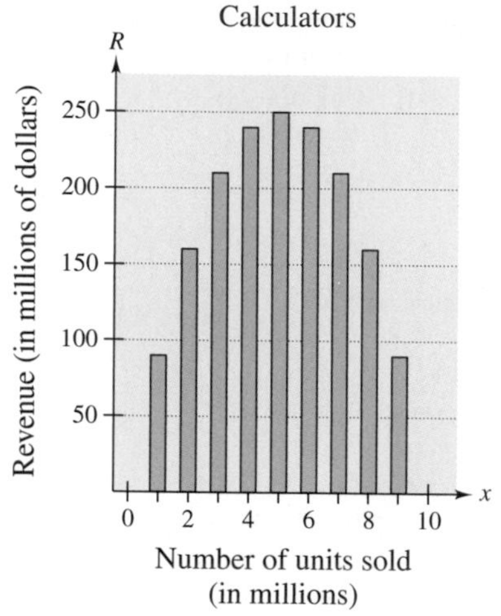

FIGURE 2.56

The marketing department of a calculator manufacturer has determined that the demand for a new model of calculator is

$$p = 100 - 0.00001x, \quad 0 \le x \le 10{,}000{,}000 \qquad \text{Demand equation}$$

where p is the price per calculator (in dollars) and x represents the number of calculators sold. (If this model is accurate, no one would be willing to pay \$100 for the calculator. At the other extreme, the company couldn't sell more than 10 million calculators.) The revenue for selling x calculators is

$$R = xp = x(100 - 0.00001x) \qquad \text{Revenue equation}$$

as shown in Figure 2.56. The total cost of producing x calculators is \$10 per calculator plus a development cost of \$2,500,000. So, the total cost is

$$C = 10x + 2{,}500{,}000. \qquad \text{Cost equation}$$

What price should the company charge per calculator to obtain a profit of at least \$190,000,000?

Solution

Verbal Model: $\text{Profit} = \text{Revenue} - \text{Cost}$

Equation: $P = R - C$

$$P = 100x - 0.00001x^2 - (10x + 2{,}500{,}000)$$
$$P = -0.00001x^2 + 90x - 2{,}500{,}000$$

To answer the question, solve the inequality

$$P \ge 190{,}000{,}000$$
$$-0.00001x^2 + 90x - 2{,}500{,}000 \ge 190{,}000{,}000.$$

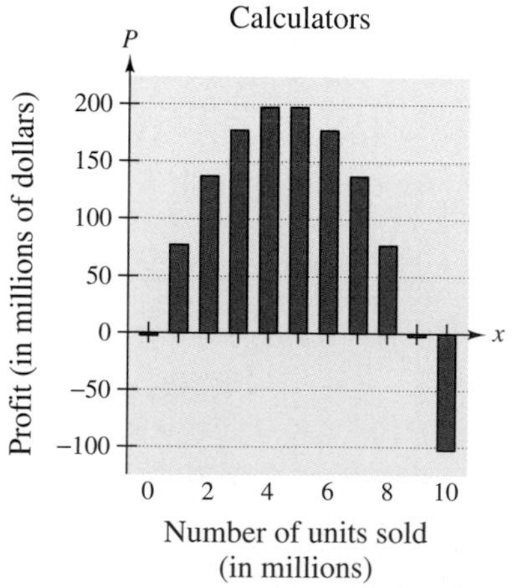

FIGURE 2.57

When you write the inequality in general form, find the critical numbers and the test intervals, and then test a value in each test interval, you can find the solution to be

$$3{,}500{,}000 \le x \le 5{,}500{,}000$$

as shown in Figure 2.57. Substituting the x-values in the original price equation shows that prices of

$$\$45.00 \le p \le \$65.00$$

will yield a profit of at least \$190,000,000.

CHECKPOINT Now try Exercise 71.

Another common application of inequalities is finding the domain of an expression that involves a square root, as shown in Example 6.

Example 6 Finding the Domain of an Expression

Find the domain of $\sqrt{64 - 4x^2}$.

Algebraic Solution

Remember that the domain of an expression is the set of all x-values for which the expression is defined. Because $\sqrt{64 - 4x^2}$ is defined (has real values) only if $64 - 4x^2$ is nonnegative, the domain is given by $64 - 4x^2 \geq 0$.

$64 - 4x^2 \geq 0$ Write in general form.

$16 - x^2 \geq 0$ Divide each side by 4.

$(4 - x)(4 + x) \geq 0$ Write in factored form.

So, the inequality has two critical numbers: $x = -4$ and $x = 4$. You can use these two numbers to test the inequality as follows.

Critical numbers: $x = -4, x = 4$

Test intervals: $(-\infty, -4), (-4, 4), (4, \infty)$

Test: For what values of x is $\sqrt{64 - 4x^2} \geq 0$?

A test shows that the inequality is satisfied in the *closed interval* $[-4, 4]$. So, the domain of the expression $\sqrt{64 - 4x^2}$ is the interval $[-4, 4]$.

Graphical Solution

Begin by sketching the graph of the equation $y = \sqrt{64 - 4x^2}$, as shown in Figure 2.58. From the graph, you can determine that the x-values extend from -4 to 4 (including -4 and 4). So, the domain of the expression $\sqrt{64 - 4x^2}$ is the interval $[-4, 4]$.

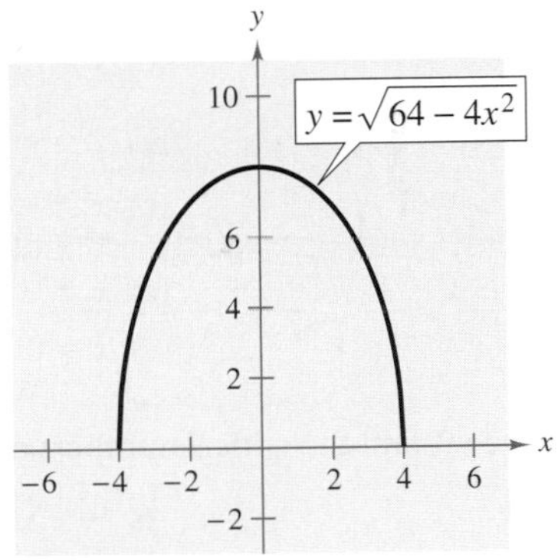

FIGURE 2.58

✓CHECKPOINT Now try Exercise 55.

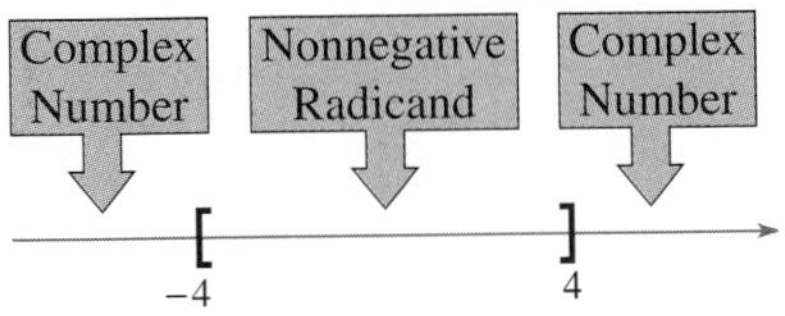

FIGURE 2.59

To analyze a test interval, choose a representative x-value in the interval and evaluate the expression at that value. For instance, in Example 6, if you substitute any number from the interval $[-4, 4]$ into the expression $\sqrt{64 - 4x^2}$ you will obtain a nonnegative number under the radical symbol that simplifies to a real number. If you substitute any number from the intervals $(-\infty, -4)$ and $(4, \infty)$ you will obtain a complex number. It might be helpful to draw a visual representation of the intervals as shown in Figure 2.59.

WRITING ABOUT MATHEMATICS

Profit Analysis Consider the relationship

$$P = R - C$$

described on page 202. Write a paragraph discussing why it might be beneficial to solve $P < 0$ if you owned a business. Use the situation described in Example 5 to illustrate your reasoning.

2.7 Exercises

VOCABULARY CHECK: Fill in the blanks.

1. To solve a polynomial inequality, find the ________ numbers of the polynomial, and use these numbers to create ________ ________ for the inequality.
2. The critical numbers of a rational expression are its ________ and its ________ ________.
3. The formula that relates cost, revenue, and profit is ________.

In Exercises 1–4, determine whether each value of x is a solution of the inequality.

Inequality	*Values*	
1. $x^2 - 3 < 0$	(a) $x = 3$	(b) $x = 0$
	(c) $x = \frac{3}{2}$	(d) $x = -5$
2. $x^2 - x - 12 \geq 0$	(a) $x = 5$	(b) $x = 0$
	(c) $x = -4$	(d) $x = -3$
3. $\dfrac{x+2}{x-4} \geq 3$	(a) $x = 5$	(b) $x = 4$
	(c) $x = -\frac{9}{2}$	(d) $x = \frac{9}{2}$
4. $\dfrac{3x^2}{x^2+4} < 1$	(a) $x = -2$	(b) $x = -1$
	(c) $x = 0$	(d) $x = 3$

In Exercises 5–8, find the critical numbers of the expression.

5. $2x^2 - x - 6$

6. $9x^3 - 25x^2$

7. $2 + \dfrac{3}{x-5}$

8. $\dfrac{x}{x+2} - \dfrac{2}{x-1}$

In Exercises 9–26, solve the inequality and graph the solution on the real number line.

9. $x^2 \leq 9$

10. $x^2 < 36$

11. $(x+2)^2 < 25$

12. $(x-3)^2 \geq 1$

13. $x^2 + 4x + 4 \geq 9$

14. $x^2 - 6x + 9 < 16$

15. $x^2 + x < 6$

16. $x^2 + 2x > 3$

17. $x^2 + 2x - 3 < 0$

18. $x^2 - 4x - 1 > 0$

19. $x^2 + 8x - 5 \geq 0$

20. $-2x^2 + 6x + 15 \leq 0$

21. $x^3 - 3x^2 - x + 3 > 0$

22. $x^3 + 2x^2 - 4x - 8 \leq 0$

23. $x^3 - 2x^2 - 9x - 2 \geq -20$

24. $2x^3 + 13x^2 - 8x - 46 \geq 6$

25. $4x^2 - 4x + 1 \leq 0$

26. $x^2 + 3x + 8 > 0$

In Exercises 27–32, solve the inequality and write the solution set in interval notation.

27. $4x^3 - 6x^2 < 0$

28. $4x^3 - 12x^2 > 0$

29. $x^3 - 4x \geq 0$

30. $2x^3 - x^4 \leq 0$

31. $(x-1)^2(x+2)^3 \geq 0$

32. $x^4(x-3) \leq 0$

Graphical Analysis **In Exercises 33–36, use a graphing utility to graph the equation. Use the graph to approximate the values of x that satisfy each inequality.**

Equation	*Inequalities*	
33. $y = -x^2 + 2x + 3$	(a) $y \leq 0$	(b) $y \geq 3$
34. $y = \frac{1}{2}x^2 - 2x + 1$	(a) $y \leq 0$	(b) $y \geq 7$
35. $y = \frac{1}{8}x^3 - \frac{1}{2}x$	(a) $y \geq 0$	(b) $y \leq 6$
36. $y = x^3 - x^2 - 16x + 16$	(a) $y \leq 0$	(b) $y \geq 36$

In Exercises 37–50, solve the inequality and graph the solution on the real number line.

37. $\dfrac{1}{x} - x > 0$

38. $\dfrac{1}{x} - 4 < 0$

39. $\dfrac{x+6}{x+1} - 2 < 0$

40. $\dfrac{x+12}{x+2} - 3 \geq 0$

41. $\dfrac{3x-5}{x-5} > 4$

42. $\dfrac{5+7x}{1+2x} < 4$

43. $\dfrac{4}{x+5} > \dfrac{1}{2x+3}$

44. $\dfrac{5}{x-6} > \dfrac{3}{x+2}$

45. $\dfrac{1}{x-3} \leq \dfrac{9}{4x+3}$

46. $\dfrac{1}{x} \geq \dfrac{1}{x+3}$

47. $\dfrac{x^2+2x}{x^2-9} \leq 0$

48. $\dfrac{x^2+x-6}{x} \geq 0$

49. $\dfrac{5}{x-1} - \dfrac{2x}{x+1} < 1$

50. $\dfrac{3x}{x-1} \leq \dfrac{x}{x+4} + 3$

Graphical Analysis **In Exercises 51–54, use a graphing utility to graph the equation. Use the graph to approximate the values of x that satisfy each inequality.**

Equation	*Inequalities*
51. $y = \dfrac{3x}{x - 2}$	(a) $y \le 0$ (b) $y \ge 6$
52. $y = \dfrac{2(x - 2)}{x + 1}$	(a) $y \le 0$ (b) $y \ge 8$
53. $y = \dfrac{2x^2}{x^2 + 4}$	(a) $y \ge 1$ (b) $y \le 2$
54. $y = \dfrac{5x}{x^2 + 4}$	(a) $y \ge 1$ (b) $y \le 0$

In Exercises 55–60, find the domain of x in the expression. Use a graphing utility to verify your result.

55. $\sqrt{4 - x^2}$

56. $\sqrt{x^2 - 4}$

57. $\sqrt{x^2 - 7x + 12}$

58. $\sqrt{144 - 9x^2}$

59. $\sqrt{\dfrac{x}{x^2 - 2x - 35}}$

60. $\sqrt{\dfrac{x}{x^2 - 9}}$

In Exercises 61–66, solve the inequality. (Round your answers to two decimal places.)

61. $0.4x^2 + 5.26 < 10.2$

62. $-1.3x^2 + 3.78 > 2.12$

63. $-0.5x^2 + 12.5x + 1.6 > 0$

64. $1.2x^2 + 4.8x + 3.1 < 5.3$

65. $\dfrac{1}{2.3x - 5.2} > 3.4$

66. $\dfrac{2}{3.1x - 3.7} > 5.8$

67. ***Height of a Projectile*** A projectile is fired straight upward from ground level with an initial velocity of 160 feet per second.

(a) At what instant will it be back at ground level?

(b) When will the height exceed 384 feet?

68. ***Height of a Projectile*** A projectile is fired straight upward from ground level with an initial velocity of 128 feet per second.

(a) At what instant will it be back at ground level?

(b) When will the height be less than 128 feet?

69. ***Geometry*** A rectangular playing field with a perimeter of 100 meters is to have an area of at least 500 square meters. Within what bounds must the length of the rectangle lie?

70. ***Geometry*** A rectangular parking lot with a perimeter of 440 feet is to have an area of at least 8000 square feet. Within what bounds must the length of the rectangle lie?

71. ***Cost, Revenue, and Profit*** The revenue and cost equations for a product are

$$R = x(75 - 0.0005x) \quad \text{and} \quad C = 30x + 250{,}000$$

where R and C are measured in dollars and x represents the number of units sold. How many units must be sold to obtain a profit of at least \$750,000? What is the price per unit?

72. ***Cost, Revenue, and Profit*** The revenue and cost equations for a product are

$$R = x(50 - 0.0002x) \quad \text{and} \quad C = 12x + 150{,}000$$

where R and C are measured in dollars and x represents the number of units sold. How many units must be sold to obtain a profit of at least \$1,650,000? What is the price per unit?

Model It

73. ***Cable Television*** The percents C of households in the United States that owned a television and had cable from 1980 to 2003 can be modeled by

$$C = 0.0031t^3 - 0.216t^2 + 5.54t + 19.1, \quad 0 \le t \le 23$$

where t is the year, with $t = 0$ corresponding to 1980. (Source: Nielsen Media Research)

(a) Use a graphing utility to graph the equation.

(b) Complete the table to determine the year in which the percent of households that own a television and have cable will exceed 75%.

t	24	26	28	30	32	34
C						

(c) Use the *trace* feature of a graphing utility to verify your answer to part (b).

(d) Complete the table to determine the years during which the percent of households that own a television and have cable will be between 85% and 100%.

t	36	37	38	39	40	41	42	43
C								

(e) Use the *trace* feature of a graphing utility to verify your answer to part (d).

(f) Explain why the model may give values greater than 100% even though such values are not reasonable.

74. ***Safe Load*** The maximum safe load uniformly distributed over a one-foot section of a two-inch-wide wooden beam is approximated by the model Load $= 168.5d^2 - 472.1$, where d is the depth of the beam.

(a) Evaluate the model for $d = 4$, $d = 6$, $d = 8$, $d = 10$, and $d = 12$. Use the results to create a bar graph.

(b) Determine the minimum depth of the beam that will safely support a load of 2000 pounds.

75. ***Resistors*** When two resistors of resistances R_1 and R_2 are connected in parallel (see figure), the total resistance R satisfies the equation

$$\frac{1}{R} = \frac{1}{R_1} + \frac{1}{R_2}.$$

Find R_1 for a parallel circuit in which $R_2 = 2$ ohms and R must be at least 1 ohm.

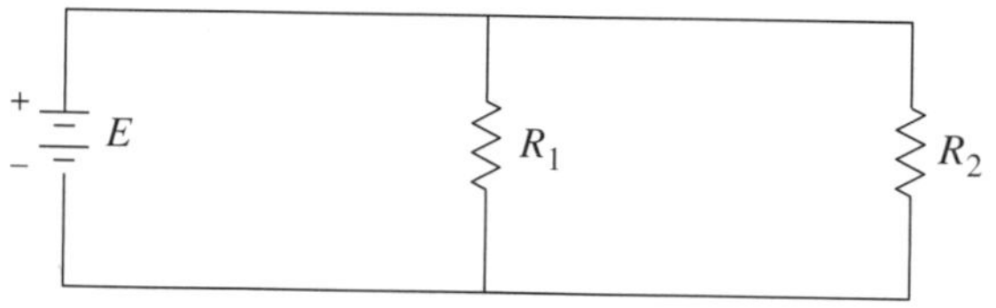

76. ***Education*** The numbers N (in thousands) of master's degrees earned by women in the United States from 1990 to 2002 are approximated by the model

$$N = -0.03t^2 + 9.6t + 172$$

where t represents the year, with $t = 0$ corresponding to 1990 (see figure). (Source: U.S. National Center for Education Statistics)

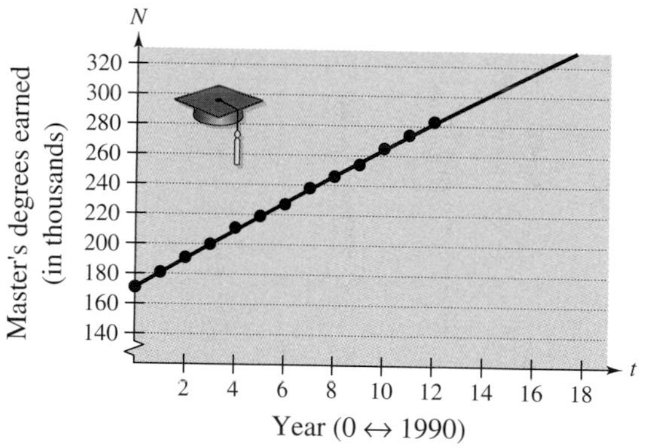

(a) According to the model, during what year did the number of master's degrees earned by women exceed 220,000?

(b) Use the graph to verify the result of part (a).

(c) According to the model, during what year will the number of master's degrees earned by women exceed 320,000?

(d) Use the graph to verify the result of part (c).

Synthesis

True or False? **In Exercises 77 and 78, determine whether the statement is true or false. Justify your answer.**

77. The zeros of the polynomial $x^3 - 2x^2 - 11x + 12 \geq 0$ divide the real number line into four test intervals.

78. The solution set of the inequality $\frac{3}{2}x^2 + 3x + 6 \geq 0$ is the entire set of real numbers.

Exploration **In Exercises 79–82, find the interval for b such that the equation has at least one real solution.**

79. $x^2 + bx + 4 = 0$

80. $x^2 + bx - 4 = 0$

81. $3x^2 + bx + 10 = 0$

82. $2x^2 + bx + 5 = 0$

83. (a) Write a conjecture about the intervals for b in Exercises 79–82. Explain your reasoning.

(b) What is the center of each interval for b in Exercises 79–82?

84. Consider the polynomial $(x - a)(x - b)$ and the real number line shown below.

(a) Identify the points on the line at which the polynomial is zero.

(b) In each of the three subintervals of the line, write the sign of each factor and the sign of the product.

(c) For what x-values does the polynomial change signs?

Skills Review

In Exercises 85–88, factor the expression completely.

85. $4x^2 + 20x + 25$

86. $(x + 3)^2 - 16$

87. $x^2(x + 3) - 4(x + 3)$

88. $2x^4 - 54x$

In Exercises 89 and 90, write an expression for the area of the region.

89.

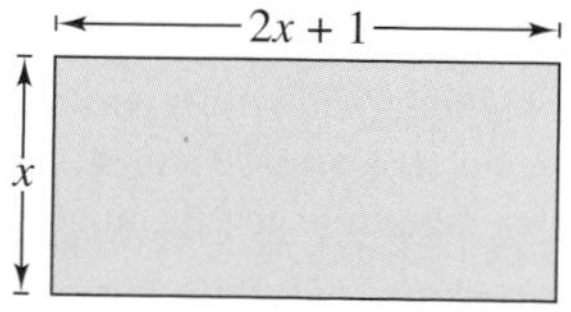

90.

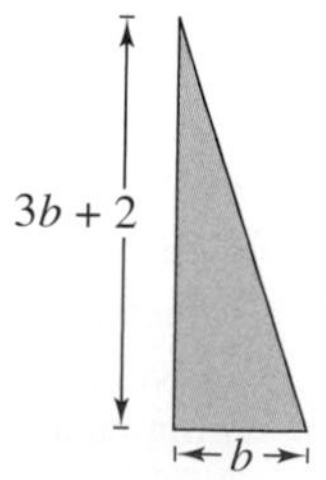

2 Chapter Summary

What did you learn?

	Review Exercises
Section 2.1	
☐ Analyze graphs of quadratic functions *(p. 128).*	1, 2
☐ Write quadratic functions in standard form and use the results to sketch graphs of functions *(p. 131).*	3–18
☐ Use quadratic functions to model and solve real-life problems *(p. 133).*	19–22
Section 2.2	
☐ Use transformations to sketch graphs of polynomial functions *(p. 139).*	23–28
☐ Use the Leading Coefficient Test to determine the end behavior of graphs of polynomial functions *(p. 141).*	29–32
☐ Find and use zeros of polynomial functions as sketching aids *(p. 142).*	33–42
☐ Use the Intermediate Value Theorem to help locate zeros of polynomial functions *(p. 146).*	43–46
Section 2.3	
☐ Use long division to divide polynomials by other polynomials *(p. 153).*	47–52
☐ Use synthetic division to divide polynomials by binomials of the form $(x - k)$ *(p. 156).*	53–60
☐ Use the Remainder Theorem and the Factor Theorem *(p. 157).*	61–64
Section 2.4	
☐ Use the imaginary unit i to write complex numbers *(p. 162).*	65–68
☐ Add, subtract, and multiply complex numbers *(p. 163).*	69–74
☐ Use complex conjugates to write the quotient of two complex numbers in standard form *(p. 165).*	75–78
☐ Find complex solutions of quadratic equations *(p. 166).*	79–82
Section 2.5	
☐ Use the Fundamental Theorem of Algebra to determine the number of zeros of polynomial functions *(p. 169).*	83–88
☐ Find rational zeros of polynomial functions *(p. 170).*	89–96
☐ Find conjugate pairs of complex zeros *(p. 173).*	97, 98
☐ Use factoring *(p. 173)*, Descartes's Rule of Signs *(p. 176)*, and the Upper and Lower Bound Rules *(p. 177)*, to find zeros of polynomials.	99–110
Section 2.6	
☐ Find the domains of rational functions *(p. 184).*	111–114
☐ Find the horizontal and vertical asymptotes of graphs of rational functions *(p. 185).*	115–118
☐ Analyze and sketch graphs of rational functions *(p. 187).*	119–130
☐ Sketch graphs of rational functions that have slant asymptotes *(p. 190).*	131–134
☐ Use rational functions to model and solve real-life problems *(p. 191).*	135–138
Section 2.7	
☐ Solve polynomial inequalities *(p. 197)*, and rational inequalities *(p. 201).*	139–146
☐ Use inequalities to model and solve real-life problems *(p. 202).*	147, 148

2 Review Exercises

2.1 In Exercises 1 and 2, graph each function. Compare the graph of each function with the graph of $y = x^2$.

1. (a) $f(x) = 2x^2$
(b) $g(x) = -2x^2$
(c) $h(x) = x^2 + 2$
(d) $k(x) = (x + 2)^2$

2. (a) $f(x) = x^2 - 4$
(b) $g(x) = 4 - x^2$
(c) $h(x) = (x - 3)^2$
(d) $k(x) = \frac{1}{2}x^2 - 1$

In Exercises 3–14, write the quadratic function in standard form and sketch its graph. Identify the vertex, axis of symmetry, and x-intercept(s).

3. $g(x) = x^2 - 2x$
4. $f(x) = 6x - x^2$
5. $f(x) = x^2 + 8x + 10$
6. $h(x) = 3 + 4x - x^2$
7. $f(t) = -2t^2 + 4t + 1$
8. $f(x) = x^2 - 8x + 12$
9. $h(x) = 4x^2 + 4x + 13$
10. $f(x) = x^2 - 6x + 1$
11. $h(x) = x^2 + 5x - 4$
12. $f(x) = 4x^2 + 4x + 5$
13. $f(x) = \frac{1}{3}(x^2 + 5x - 4)$
14. $f(x) = \frac{1}{2}(6x^2 - 24x + 22)$

In Exercises 15–18, write the standard form of the equation of the parabola that has the indicated vertex and whose graph passes through the given point.

15.

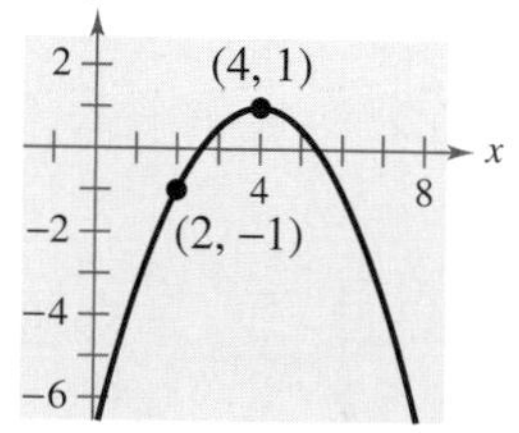

16.

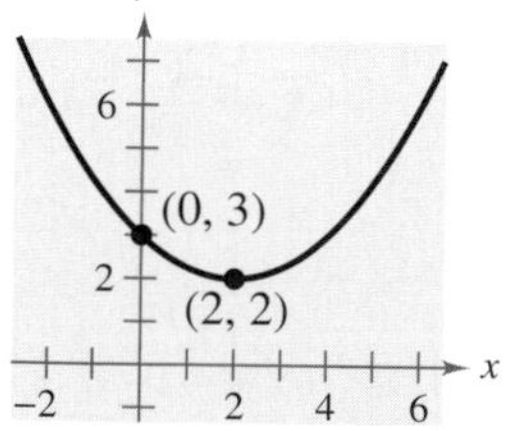

17. Vertex: $(1, -4)$; point: $(2, -3)$
18. Vertex: $(2, 3)$; point: $(-1, 6)$

19. ***Geometry*** The perimeter of a rectangle is 200 meters.
(a) Draw a diagram that gives a visual representation of the problem. Label the length and width as x and y, respectively.
(b) Write y as a function of x. Use the result to write the area as a function of x.
(c) Of all possible rectangles with perimeters of 200 meters, find the dimensions of the one with the maximum area.

20. ***Maximum Revenue*** The total revenue R earned (in dollars) from producing a gift box of candles is given by

$$R(p) = -10p^2 + 800p$$

where p is the price per unit (in dollars).
(a) Find the revenues when the prices per box are \$20, \$25, and \$30.
(b) Find the unit price that will yield a maximum revenue. What is the maximum revenue? Explain your results.

21. ***Minimum Cost*** A soft-drink manufacturer has daily production costs of

$$C = 70{,}000 - 120x + 0.055x^2$$

where C is the total cost (in dollars) and x is the number of units produced. How many units should be produced each day to yield a minimum cost?

22. ***Sociology*** The average age of the groom at a first marriage for a given age of the bride can be approximated by the model

$$y = -0.107x^2 + 5.68x - 48.5, \quad 20 \le x \le 25$$

where y is the age of the groom and x is the age of the bride. Sketch a graph of the model. For what age of the bride is the average age of the groom 26? (Source: U.S. Census Bureau)

2.2 In Exercises 23–28, sketch the graphs of $y = x^n$ and the transformation.

23. $y = x^3, \quad f(x) = -(x - 4)^3$
24. $y = x^3, \quad f(x) = -4x^3$
25. $y = x^4, \quad f(x) = 2 - x^4$
26. $y = x^4, \quad f(x) = 2(x - 2)^4$
27. $y = x^5, \quad f(x) = (x - 3)^5$
28. $y = x^5, \quad f(x) = \frac{1}{2}x^5 + 3$

In Exercises 29–32, describe the right-hand and left-hand behavior of the graph of the polynomial function.

29. $f(x) = -x^2 + 6x + 9$

30. $f(x) = \frac{1}{2}x^3 + 2x$

31. $g(x) = \frac{3}{4}(x^4 + 3x^2 + 2)$

32. $h(x) = -x^5 - 7x^2 + 10x$

In Exercises 33–38, find all the real zeros of the polynomial function. Determine the multiplicity of each zero and the number of turning points of the graph of the function. Use a graphing utility to verify your answers.

33. $f(x) = 2x^2 + 11x - 21$

34. $f(x) = x(x + 3)^2$

35. $f(t) = t^3 - 3t$

36. $f(x) = x^3 - 8x^2$

37. $f(x) = -12x^3 + 20x^2$

38. $g(x) = x^4 - x^3 - 2x^2$

In Exercises 39–42, sketch the graph of the function by (a) applying the Leading Coefficient Test, (b) finding the zeros of the polynomial, (c) plotting sufficient solution points, and (d) drawing a continuous curve through the points.

39. $f(x) = -x^3 + x^2 - 2$

40. $g(x) = 2x^3 + 4x^2$

41. $f(x) = x(x^3 + x^2 - 5x + 3)$

42. $h(x) = 3x^2 - x^4$

In Exercises 43–46, (a) use the Intermediate Value Theorem and the *table* feature of a graphing utility to find intervals one unit in length in which the polynomial function is guaranteed to have a zero. (b) Adjust the table to approximate the zeros of the function. Use the *zero* or *root* feature of the graphing utility to verify your results.

43. $f(x) = 3x^3 - x^2 + 3$

44. $f(x) = 0.25x^3 - 3.65x + 6.12$

45. $f(x) = x^4 - 5x - 1$

46. $f(x) = 7x^4 + 3x^3 - 8x^2 + 2$

2.3 In Exercises 47–52, use long division to divide.

47. $\dfrac{24x^2 - x - 8}{3x - 2}$

48. $\dfrac{4x + 7}{3x - 2}$

49. $\dfrac{5x^3 - 13x^2 - x + 2}{x^2 - 3x + 1}$

50. $\dfrac{3x^4}{x^2 - 1}$

51. $\dfrac{x^4 - 3x^3 + 4x^2 - 6x + 3}{x^2 + 2}$

52. $\dfrac{6x^4 + 10x^3 + 13x^2 - 5x + 2}{2x^2 - 1}$

In Exercises 53–56, use synthetic division to divide.

53. $\dfrac{6x^4 - 4x^3 - 27x^2 + 18x}{x - 2}$

54. $\dfrac{0.1x^3 + 0.3x^2 - 0.5}{x - 5}$

55. $\dfrac{2x^3 - 19x^2 + 38x + 24}{x - 4}$

56. $\dfrac{3x^3 + 20x^2 + 29x - 12}{x + 3}$

In Exercises 57 and 58, use synthetic division to determine whether the given values of *x* are zeros of the function.

57. $f(x) = 20x^4 + 9x^3 - 14x^2 - 3x$

(a) $x = -1$ (b) $x = \frac{3}{4}$ (c) $x = 0$ (d) $x = 1$

58. $f(x) = 3x^3 - 8x^2 - 20x + 16$

(a) $x = 4$ (b) $x = -4$ (c) $x = \frac{2}{3}$ (d) $x = -1$

In Exercises 59 and 60, use synthetic division to find each function value.

59. $f(x) = x^4 + 10x^3 - 24x^2 + 20x + 44$

(a) $f(-3)$ (b) $f(-1)$

60. $g(t) = 2t^5 - 5t^4 - 8t + 20$

(a) $g(-4)$ (b) $g(\sqrt{2})$

In Exercises 61–64, (a) verify the given factor(s) of the function *f*, (b) find the remaining factors of *f*, (c) use your results to write the complete factorization of *f*, (d) list all real zeros of *f*, and (e) confirm your results by using a graphing utility to graph the function.

	Function	*Factor(s)*
61.	$f(x) = x^3 + 4x^2 - 25x - 28$	$(x - 4)$
62.	$f(x) = 2x^3 + 11x^2 - 21x - 90$	$(x + 6)$
63.	$f(x) = x^4 - 4x^3 - 7x^2 + 22x + 24$	$(x + 2)(x - 3)$
64.	$f(x) = x^4 - 11x^3 + 41x^2 - 61x + 30$	$(x - 2)(x - 5)$

2.4 In Exercises 65–68, write the complex number in standard form.

65. $6 + \sqrt{-4}$

66. $3 - \sqrt{-25}$

67. $i^2 + 3i$

68. $-5i + i^2$

In Exercises 69–74, perform the operation and write the result in standard form.

69. $(7 + 5i) + (-4 + 2i)$

70. $\left(\dfrac{\sqrt{2}}{2} - \dfrac{\sqrt{2}}{2}i\right) - \left(\dfrac{\sqrt{2}}{2} + \dfrac{\sqrt{2}}{2}i\right)$

71. $5i(13 - 8i)$

72. $(1 + 6i)(5 - 2i)$

73. $(10 - 8i)(2 - 3i)$

74. $i(6 + i)(3 - 2i)$

In Exercises 75 and 76, write the quotient in standard form.

75. $\dfrac{6+i}{4-i}$

76. $\dfrac{3+2i}{5+i}$

In Exercises 77 and 78, perform the operation and write the result in standard form.

77. $\dfrac{4}{2-3i}+\dfrac{2}{1+i}$

78. $\dfrac{1}{2+i}-\dfrac{5}{1+4i}$

In Exercises 79–82, find all solutions of the equation.

79. $3x^2+1=0$

80. $2+8x^2=0$

81. $x^2-2x+10=0$

82. $6x^2+3x+27=0$

2.5 In Exercises 83–88, find all the zeros of the function.

83. $f(x)=3x(x-2)^2$

84. $f(x)=(x-4)(x+9)^2$

85. $f(x)=x^2-9x+8$

86. $f(x)=x^3+6x$

87. $f(x)=(x+4)(x-6)(x-2i)(x+2i)$

88. $f(x)=(x-8)(x-5)^2(x-3+i)(x-3-i)$

In Exercises 89 and 90, use the Rational Zero Test to list all possible rational zeros of *f*.

89. $f(x)=-4x^3+8x^2-3x+15$

90. $f(x)=3x^4+4x^3-5x^2-8$

In Exercises 91–96, find all the rational zeros of the function.

91. $f(x)=x^3-2x^2-21x-18$

92. $f(x)=3x^3-20x^2+7x+30$

93. $f(x)=x^3-10x^2+17x-8$

94. $f(x)=x^3+9x^2+24x+20$

95. $f(x)=x^4+x^3-11x^2+x-12$

96. $f(x)=25x^4+25x^3-154x^2-4x+24$

In Exercises 97 and 98, find a polynomial function with real coefficients that has the given zeros. (There are many correct answers.)

97. $\frac{2}{3}, 4, \sqrt{3}i$

98. $2, -3, 1-2i$

In Exercises 99–102, use the given zero to find all the zeros of the function.

	Function	*Zero*
99.	$f(x)=x^3-4x^2+x-4$	i
100.	$h(x)=-x^3+2x^2-16x+32$	$-4i$
101.	$g(x)=2x^4-3x^3-13x^2+37x-15$	$2+i$
102.	$f(x)=4x^4-11x^3+14x^2-6x$	$1-i$

In Exercises 103–106, find all the zeros of the function and write the polynomial as a product of linear factors.

103. $f(x)=x^3+4x^2-5x$

104. $g(x)=x^3-7x^2+36$

105. $g(x)=x^4+4x^3-3x^2+40x+208$

106. $f(x)=x^4+8x^3+8x^2-72x-153$

In Exercises 107 and 108, use Descartes's Rule of Signs to determine the possible numbers of positive and negative zeros of the function.

107. $g(x)=5x^3+3x^2-6x+9$

108. $h(x)=-2x^5+4x^3-2x^2+5$

In Exercises 109 and 110, use synthetic division to verify the upper and lower bounds of the real zeros of *f*.

109. $f(x)=4x^3-3x^2+4x-3$
  (a) Upper: $x=1$
  (b) Lower: $x=-\frac{1}{4}$

110. $f(x)=2x^3-5x^2-14x+8$
  (a) Upper: $x=8$
  (b) Lower: $x=-4$

2.6 In Exercises 111–114, find the domain of the rational function.

111. $f(x)=\dfrac{5x}{x+12}$

112. $f(x)=\dfrac{3x^2}{1+3x}$

113. $f(x)=\dfrac{8}{x^2-10x+24}$

114. $f(x)=\dfrac{x^2+x-2}{x^2+4}$

In Exercises 115–118, identify any horizontal or vertical asymptotes.

115. $f(x)=\dfrac{4}{x+3}$

116. $f(x)=\dfrac{2x^2+5x-3}{x^2+2}$

117. $h(x)=\dfrac{2x-10}{x^2-2x-15}$

118. $h(x)=\dfrac{x^3-4x^2}{x^2+3x+2}$

In Exercises 119–130, (a) state the domain of the function, (b) identify all intercepts, (c) find any vertical and horizontal asymptotes, and (d) plot additional solution points as needed to sketch the graph of the rational function.

119. $f(x)=\dfrac{-5}{x^2}$

120. $f(x)=\dfrac{4}{x}$

121. $g(x)=\dfrac{2+x}{1-x}$

122. $h(x)=\dfrac{x-3}{x-2}$

123. $p(x)=\dfrac{x^2}{x^2+1}$

124. $f(x)=\dfrac{2x}{x^2+4}$

125. $f(x)=\dfrac{x}{x^2+1}$

126. $h(x)=\dfrac{4}{(x-1)^2}$

127. $f(x) = \dfrac{-6x^2}{x^2 + 1}$

128. $y = \dfrac{2x^2}{x^2 - 4}$

129. $f(x) = \dfrac{6x^2 - 11x + 3}{3x^2 - x}$

130. $f(x) = \dfrac{6x^2 - 7x + 2}{4x^2 - 1}$

In Exercises 131–134, (a) state the domain of the function, (b) identify all intercepts, (c) identify any vertical and slant asymptotes, and (d) plot additional solution points as needed to sketch the graph of the rational function.

131. $f(x) = \dfrac{2x^3}{x^2 + 1}$

132. $f(x) = \dfrac{x^2 + 1}{x + 1}$

133. $f(x) = \dfrac{3x^3 - 2x^2 - 3x + 2}{3x^2 - x - 4}$

134. $f(x) = \dfrac{3x^3 - 4x^2 - 12x + 16}{3x^2 + 5x - 2}$

135. ***Average Cost*** A business has a production cost of $C = 0.5x + 500$ for producing x units of a product. The average cost per unit, $\overline{C}$, is given by

$$\overline{C} = \frac{C}{x} = \frac{0.5x + 500}{x}, \quad x > 0.$$

Determine the average cost per unit as x increases without bound. (Find the horizontal asymptote.)

136. ***Seizure of Illegal Drugs*** The cost C (in millions of dollars) for the federal government to seize $p\%$ of an illegal drug as it enters the country is given by

$$C = \frac{528p}{100 - p}, \quad 0 \le p < 100.$$

(a) Use a graphing utility to graph the cost function.

(b) Find the costs of seizing 25%, 50%, and 75% of the drug.

(c) According to this model, would it be possible to seize 100% of the drug?

137. ***Page Design*** A page that is x inches wide and y inches high contains 30 square inches of print. The top and bottom margins are 2 inches deep and the margins on each side are 2 inches wide.

(a) Draw a diagram that gives a visual representation of the problem.

(b) Show that the total area A on the page is

$$A = \frac{2x(2x + 7)}{x - 4}.$$

(c) Determine the domain of the function based on the physical constraints of the problem.

(d) Use a graphing utility to graph the area function and approximate the page size for which the least amount of paper will be used. Verify your answer numerically using the *table* feature of the graphing utility.

138. ***Photosynthesis*** The amount y of CO_2 uptake (in milligrams per square decimeter per hour) at optimal temperatures and with the natural supply of CO_2 is approximated by the model

$$y = \frac{18.47x - 2.96}{0.23x + 1}, \quad x > 0$$

where x is the light intensity (in watts per square meter). Use a graphing utility to graph the function and determine the limiting amount of CO_2 uptake.

2.7 In Exercises 139–146, solve the inequality.

139. $6x^2 + 5x < 4$

140. $2x^2 + x \ge 15$

141. $x^3 - 16x \ge 0$

142. $12x^3 - 20x^2 < 0$

143. $\dfrac{2}{x + 1} \le \dfrac{3}{x - 1}$

144. $\dfrac{x - 5}{3 - x} < 0$

145. $\dfrac{x^2 + 7x + 12}{x} \ge 0$

146. $\dfrac{1}{x - 2} > \dfrac{1}{x}$

147. ***Investment*** P dollars invested at interest rate r compounded annually increases to an amount

$$A = P(1 + r)^2$$

in 2 years. An investment of \$5000 is to increase to an amount greater than \$5500 in 2 years. The interest rate must be greater than what percent?

148. ***Population of a Species*** A biologist introduces 200 ladybugs into a crop field. The population P of the ladybugs is approximated by the model

$$P = \frac{1000(1 + 3t)}{5 + t}$$

where t is the time in days. Find the time required for the population to increase to at least 2000 ladybugs.

Synthesis

True or False? **In Exercises 149 and 150, determine whether the statement is true or false. Justify your answer.**

149. A fourth-degree polynomial with real coefficients can have -5, $-8i$, $4i$, and 5 as its zeros.

150. The domain of a rational function can never be the set of all real numbers.

151. ***Writing*** Explain how to determine the maximum or minimum value of a quadratic function.

152. ***Writing*** Explain the connections among factors of a polynomial, zeros of a polynomial function, and solutions of a polynomial equation.

153. ***Writing*** Describe what is meant by an asymptote of a graph.

2 Chapter Test

Take this test as you would take a test in class. When you are finished, check your work against the answers given in the back of the book.

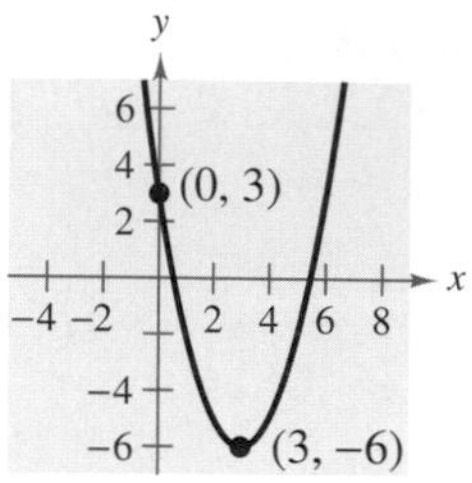

FIGURE FOR 2

1. Describe how the graph of g differs from the graph of $f(x) = x^2$.
   (a) $g(x) = 2 - x^2$ (b) $g(x) = \left(x - \frac{3}{2}\right)^2$
2. Find an equation of the parabola shown in the figure at the left.
3. The path of a ball is given by $y = -\frac{1}{20}x^2 + 3x + 5$, where y is the height (in feet) of the ball and x is the horizontal distance (in feet) from where the ball was thrown.
   (a) Find the maximum height of the ball.
   (b) Which number determines the height at which the ball was thrown? Does changing this value change the coordinates of the maximum height of the ball? Explain.
4. Determine the right-hand and left-hand behavior of the graph of the function $h(t) = -\frac{3}{4}t^5 + 2t^2$. Then sketch its graph.
5. Divide using long division.
   $$\frac{3x^3 + 4x - 1}{x^2 + 1}$$
6. Divide using synthetic division.
   $$\frac{2x^4 - 5x^2 - 3}{x - 2}$$
7. Use synthetic division to show that $x = \sqrt{3}$ is a zero of the function given by
   $f(x) = 4x^3 - x^2 - 12x + 3.$
   Use the result to factor the polynomial function completely and list all the real zeros of the function.
8. Perform each operation and write the result in standard form.
   (a) $10i - \left(3 + \sqrt{-25}\right)$ (b) $\left(2 + \sqrt{3}i\right)\left(2 - \sqrt{3}i\right)$
9. Write the quotient in standard form: $\dfrac{5}{2 + i}$.

In Exercises 10 and 11, find a polynomial function with real coefficients that has the given zeros. (There are many correct answers.)

10. $0, 3, 3 + i, 3 - i$
11. $1 + \sqrt{3}i, 1 - \sqrt{3}i, 2, 2$

In Exercises 12 and 13, find all the zeros of the function.

12. $f(x) = x^3 + 2x^2 + 5x + 10$
13. $f(x) = x^4 - 9x^2 - 22x - 24$

In Exercises 14–16, identify any intercepts and asymptotes of the graph the function. Then sketch a graph of the function.

14. $h(x) = \dfrac{4}{x^2} - 1$
15. $f(x) = \dfrac{2x^2 - 5x - 12}{x^2 - 16}$
16. $g(x) = \dfrac{x^2 + 2}{x - 1}$

In Exercises 17 and 18, solve the inequality. Sketch the solution set on the real number line.

17. $2x^2 + 5x > 12$
18. $\dfrac{2}{x} > \dfrac{5}{x + 6}$

Proofs in Mathematics

These two pages contain proofs of four important theorems about polynomial functions. The first two theorems are from Section 2.3, and the second two theorems are from Section 2.5.

The Remainder Theorem *(p. 157)*

If a polynomial $f(x)$ is divided by $x - k$, the remainder is

$$r = f(k).$$

Proof

From the Division Algorithm, you have

$$f(x) = (x - k)q(x) + r(x)$$

and because either $r(x) = 0$ or the degree of $r(x)$ is less than the degree of $x - k$, you know that $r(x)$ must be a constant. That is, $r(x) = r$. Now, by evaluating $f(x)$ at $x = k$, you have

$$f(k) = (k - k)q(k) + r$$
$$= (0)q(k) + r = r.$$

To be successful in algebra, it is important that you understand the connection among *factors* of a polynomial, *zeros* of a polynomial function, and *solutions* or *roots* of a polynomial equation. The Factor Theorem is the basis for this connection.

The Factor Theorem *(p. 157)*

A polynomial $f(x)$ has a factor $(x - k)$ if and only if $f(k) = 0$.

Proof

Using the Division Algorithm with the factor $(x - k)$, you have

$$f(x) = (x - k)q(x) + r(x).$$

By the Remainder Theorem, $r(x) = r = f(k)$, and you have

$$f(x) = (x - k)q(x) + f(k)$$

where $q(x)$ is a polynomial of lesser degree than $f(x)$. If $f(k) = 0$, then

$$f(x) = (x - k)q(x)$$

and you see that $(x - k)$ is a factor of $f(x)$. Conversely, if $(x - k)$ is a factor of $f(x)$, division of $f(x)$ by $(x - k)$ yields a remainder of 0. So, by the Remainder Theorem, you have $f(k) = 0$.

Proofs in Mathematics

The Fundamental Theorem of Algebra

The Linear Factorization Theorem is closely related to the Fundamental Theorem of Algebra. The Fundamental Theorem of Algebra has a long and interesting history. In the early work with polynomial equations, The Fundamental Theorem of Algebra was thought to have been not true, because imaginary solutions were not considered. In fact, in the very early work by mathematicians such as Abu al-Khwarizmi (c. 800 A.D.), negative solutions were also not considered.

Once imaginary numbers were accepted, several mathematicians attempted to give a general proof of the Fundamental Theorem of Algebra. These included Gottfried von Leibniz (1702), Jean d'Alembert (1746), Leonhard Euler (1749), Joseph-Louis Lagrange (1772), and Pierre Simon Laplace (1795). The mathematician usually credited with the first correct proof of the Fundamental Theorem of Algebra is Carl Friedrich Gauss, who published the proof in his doctoral thesis in 1799.

Linear Factorization Theorem *(p. 169)*

If $f(x)$ is a polynomial of degree n, where $n > 0$, then f has precisely n linear factors

$$f(x) = a_n(x - c_1)(x - c_2) \cdot \cdot \cdot (x - c_n)$$

where $c_1, c_2, \ldots, c_n$ are complex numbers.

Proof

Using the Fundamental Theorem of Algebra, you know that f must have at least one zero, c_1. Consequently, $(x - c_1)$ is a factor of $f(x)$, and you have

$$f(x) = (x - c_1)f_1(x).$$

If the degree of $f_1(x)$ is greater than zero, you again apply the Fundamental Theorem to conclude that f_1 must have a zero c_2, which implies that

$$f(x) = (x - c_1)(x - c_2)f_2(x).$$

It is clear that the degree of $f_1(x)$ is $n - 1$, that the degree of $f_2(x)$ is $n - 2$, and that you can repeatedly apply the Fundamental Theorem n times until you obtain

$$f(x) = a_n(x - c_1)(x - c_2) \cdot \cdot \cdot (x - c_n)$$

where a_n is the leading coefficient of the polynomial $f(x)$.

Factors of a Polynomial *(p. 173)*

Every polynomial of degree $n > 0$ with real coefficients can be written as the product of linear and quadratic factors with real coefficients, where the quadratic factors have no real zeros.

Proof

To begin, you use the Linear Factorization Theorem to conclude that $f(x)$ can be *completely* factored in the form

$$f(x) = d(x - c_1)(x - c_2)(x - c_3) \cdot \cdot \cdot (x - c_n).$$

If each c_i is real, there is nothing more to prove. If any c_i is complex ($c_i = a + bi$, $b \neq 0$), then, because the coefficients of $f(x)$ are real, you know that the conjugate $c_j = a - bi$ is also a zero. By multiplying the corresponding factors, you obtain

$$\begin{aligned}(x - c_i)(x - c_j) &= [x - (a + bi)][x - (a - bi)] \\ &= x^2 - 2ax + (a^2 + b^2)\end{aligned}$$

where each coefficient is real.

P.S. Problem Solving

This collection of thought-provoking and challenging exercises further explores and expands upon concepts learned in this chapter.

1. Show that if $f(x) = ax^3 + bx^2 + cx + d$ then $f(k) = r$, where $r = ak^3 + bk^2 + ck + d$ using long division. In other words, verify the Remainder Theorem for a third-degree polynomial function.

2. In 2000 B.C., the Babylonians solved polynomial equations by referring to tables of values. One such table gave the values of $y^3 + y^2$. To be able to use this table, the Babylonians sometimes had to manipulate the equation as shown below.

$$ax^3 + bx^2 = c \qquad \text{Original equation}$$

$$\frac{a^3x^3}{b^3} + \frac{a^2x^2}{b^2} = \frac{a^2c}{b^3} \qquad \text{Multiply each side by } \frac{a^2}{b^3}.$$

$$\left(\frac{ax}{b}\right)^3 + \left(\frac{ax}{b}\right)^2 = \frac{a^2c}{b^3} \qquad \text{Rewrite.}$$

Then they would find $(a^2c)/b^3$ in the $y^3 + y^2$ column of the table. Because they knew that the corresponding y-value was equal to $(ax)/b$, they could conclude that $x = (by)/a$.

(a) Calculate $y^3 + y^2$ for $y = 1, 2, 3, \ldots, 10$. Record the values in a table.

Use the table from part (a) and the method above to solve each equation.

(b) $x^3 + x^2 = 252$

(c) $x^3 + 2x^2 = 288$

(d) $3x^3 + x^2 = 90$

(e) $2x^3 + 5x^2 = 2500$

(f) $7x^3 + 6x^2 = 1728$

(g) $10x^3 + 3x^2 = 297$

Using the methods from this chapter, verify your solution to each equation.

3. At a glassware factory, molten cobalt glass is poured into molds to make paperweights. Each mold is a rectangular prism whose height is 3 inches greater than the length of each side of the square base. A machine pours 20 cubic inches of liquid glass into each mold. What are the dimensions of the mold?

4. Determine whether the statement is true or false. If false, provide one or more reasons why the statement is false and correct the statement. Let $f(x) = ax^3 + bx^2 + cx + d$, $a \neq 0$, and let $f(2) = -1$. Then

$$\frac{f(x)}{x+1} = q(x) + \frac{2}{x+1}$$

where $q(x)$ is a second-degree polynomial.

5. The parabola shown in the figure has an equation of the form $y = ax^2 + bx + c$. Find the equation of this parabola by the following methods. (a) Find the equation analytically. (b) Use the *regression* feature of a graphing utility to find the equation.

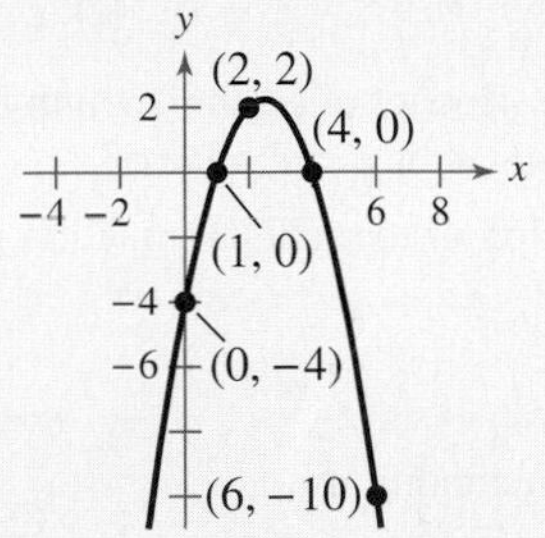

6. One of the fundamental themes of calculus is to find the slope of the tangent line to a curve at a point. To see how this can be done, consider the point (2, 4) on the graph of the quadratic function $f(x) = x^2$.

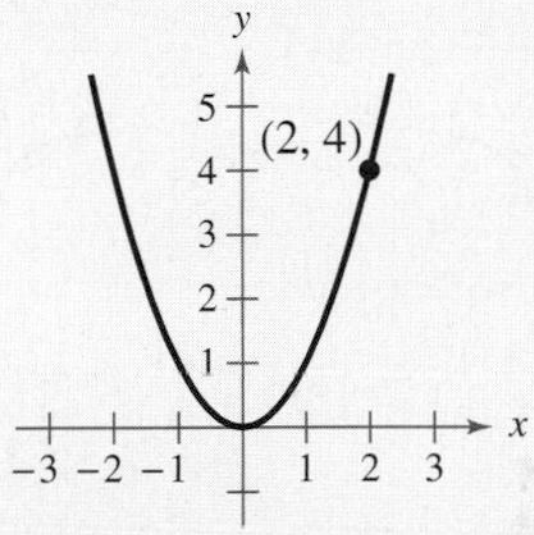

(a) Find the slope of the line joining (2, 4) and (3, 9). Is the slope of the tangent line at (2, 4) greater than or less than the slope of the line through (2, 4) and (3, 9)?

(b) Find the slope of the line joining (2, 4) and (1, 1). Is the slope of the tangent line at (2, 4) greater than or less than the slope of the line through (2, 4) and (1, 1)?

(c) Find the slope of the line joining (2, 4) and (2.1, 4.41). Is the slope of the tangent line at (2, 4) greater than or less than the slope of the line through (2, 4) and (2.1, 4.41)?

(d) Find the slope of the line joining (2, 4) and $(2 + h, f(2 + h))$ in terms of the nonzero number h.

(e) Evaluate the slope formula from part (d) for $h = -1$, 1, and 0.1. Compare these values with those in parts (a)–(c).

(f) What can you conclude the slope of the tangent line at (2, 4) to be? Explain your answer.

7. Use the form $f(x) = (x - k)q(x) + r$ to create a cubic function that (a) passes through the point $(2, 5)$ and rises to the right and (b) passes through the point $(-3, 1)$ and falls to the right. (There are many correct answers.)

8. The multiplicative inverse of z is a complex number z_m such that $z \cdot z_m = 1$. Find the multiplicative inverse of each complex number.

(a) $z = 1 + i$ (b) $z = 3 - i$ (c) $z = -2 + 8i$

9. Prove that the product of a complex number $a + bi$ and its complex conjugate is a real number.

10. Match the graph of the rational function given by

$$f(x) = \frac{ax + b}{cx + d}$$

with the given conditions.

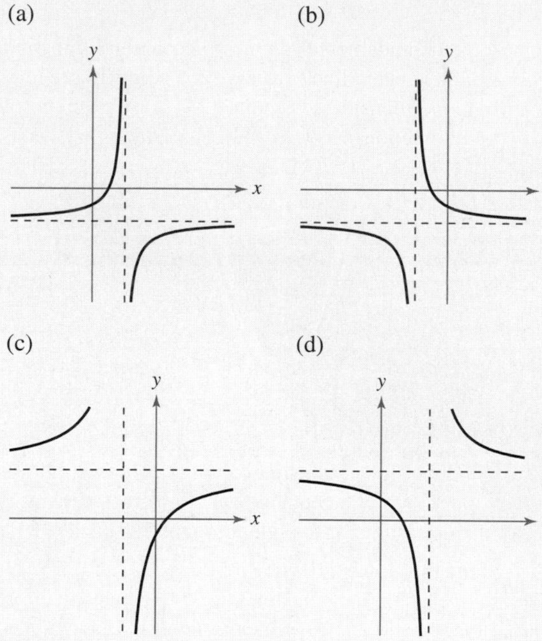

(i) $a > 0$, $b < 0$, $c > 0$, $d < 0$

(ii) $a > 0$, $b > 0$, $c < 0$, $d < 0$

(iii) $a < 0$, $b > 0$, $c > 0$, $d < 0$

(iv) $a > 0$, $b < 0$, $c > 0$, $d > 0$

11. Consider the function given by

$$f(x) = \frac{ax}{(x - b)^2}.$$

(a) Determine the effect on the graph of f if $b \neq 0$ and a is varied. Consider cases in which a is positive and a is negative.

(b) Determine the effect on the graph of f if $a \neq 0$ and b is varied.

12. The endpoints of the interval over which distinct vision is possible is called the *near point* and *far point* of the eye (see figure). With increasing age, these points normally change. The table shows the approximate near points y (in inches) for various ages x (in years).

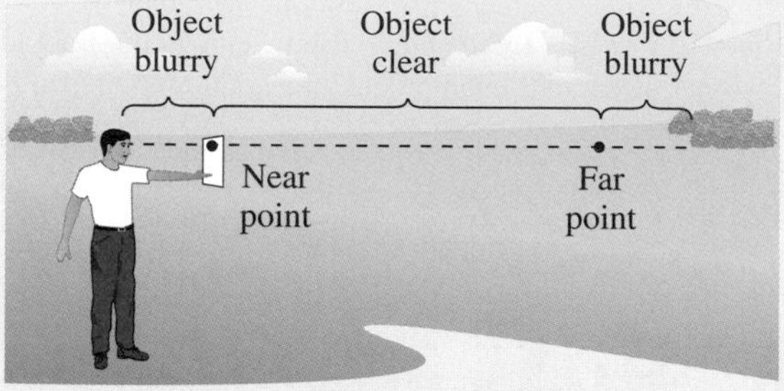

FIGURE FOR 12

Age, x	Near point, y
16	3.0
32	4.7
44	9.8
50	19.7
60	39.4

(a) Use the *regression* feature of a graphing utility to find a quadratic model for the data. Use a graphing utility to plot the data and graph the model in the same viewing window.

(b) Find a rational model for the data. Take the reciprocals of the near points to generate the points $(x, 1/y)$. Use the *regression* feature of a graphing utility to find a linear model for the data. The resulting line has the form

$$\frac{1}{y} = ax + b.$$

Solve for y. Use a graphing utility to plot the data and graph the model in the same viewing window.

(c) Use the *table* feature of a graphing utility to create a table showing the predicted near point based on each model for each of the ages in the original table. How well do the models fit the original data?

(d) Use both models to estimate the near point for a person who is 25 years old. Which model is a better fit?

(e) Do you think either model can be used to predict the near point for a person who is 70 years old? Explain.

Exponential and Logarithmic Functions

3

3.1 Exponential Functions and Their Graphs

3.2 Logarithmic Functions and Their Graphs

3.3 Properties of Logarithms

3.4 Exponential and Logarithmic Equations

3.5 Exponential and Logarithmic Models

Carbon dating is a method used to determine the ages of archeological artifacts up to 50,000 years old. For example, archeologists are using carbon dating to determine the ages of the great pyramids of Egypt.

SELECTED APPLICATIONS

Exponential and logarithmic functions have many real-life applications. The applications listed below represent a small sample of the applications in this chapter.

- Computer Virus, Exercise 65, page 227
- Data Analysis: Meteorology, Exercise 70, page 228
- Sound Intensity, Exercise 90, page 238
- Galloping Speeds of Animals, Exercise 85, page 244
- Average Heights, Exercise 115, page 255
- Carbon Dating, Exercise 41, page 266
- IQ Scores, Exercise 47, page 266
- Forensics, Exercise 63, page 268
- Compound Interest, Exercise 135, page 273

3.1 Exponential Functions and Their Graphs

What you should learn

- Recognize and evaluate exponential functions with base a.
- Graph exponential functions and use the One-to-One Property.
- Recognize, evaluate, and graph exponential functions with base e.
- Use exponential functions to model and solve real-life problems.

Why you should learn it

Exponential functions can be used to model and solve real-life problems. For instance, in Exercise 70 on page 228, an exponential function is used to model the atmospheric pressure at different altitudes.

© Comstock Images/Alamy

Exponential Functions

So far, this text has dealt mainly with **algebraic functions,** which include polynomial functions and rational functions. In this chapter, you will study two types of nonalgebraic functions—*exponential functions* and *logarithmic functions*. These functions are examples of **transcendental functions.**

Definition of Exponential Function

The **exponential function f with base a** is denoted by

$$f(x) = a^x$$

where $a > 0$, $a \neq 1$, and x is any real number.

The base $a = 1$ is excluded because it yields $f(x) = 1^x = 1$. This is a constant function, not an exponential function.

You have evaluated a^x for integer and rational values of x. For example, you know that $4^3 = 64$ and $4^{1/2} = 2$. However, to evaluate 4^x for any real number x, you need to interpret forms with *irrational* exponents. For the purposes of this text, it is sufficient to think of

$$a^{\sqrt{2}} \quad (\text{where } \sqrt{2} \approx 1.41421356)$$

as the number that has the successively closer approximations

$$a^{1.4}, a^{1.41}, a^{1.414}, a^{1.4142}, a^{1.41421}, \ldots .$$

Example 1 Evaluating Exponential Functions

Use a calculator to evaluate each function at the indicated value of x.

	Function	*Value*
a.	$f(x) = 2^x$	$x = -3.1$
b.	$f(x) = 2^{-x}$	$x = \pi$
c.	$f(x) = 0.6^x$	$x = \frac{3}{2}$

Solution

	Function Value	*Graphing Calculator Keystrokes*	*Display*
a.	$f(-3.1) = 2^{-3.1}$	2 [^] [(−)] 3.1 [ENTER]	0.1166291
b.	$f(\pi) = 2^{-\pi}$	2 [^] [(−)] π [ENTER]	0.1133147
c.	$f\left(\frac{3}{2}\right) = (0.6)^{3/2}$	.6 [^] [(] 3 [÷] 2 [)] [ENTER]	0.4647580

CHECKPOINT Now try Exercise 1.

When evaluating exponential functions with a calculator, remember to enclose fractional exponents in parentheses. Because the calculator follows the order of operations, parentheses are crucial in order to obtain the correct result.

Exploration

Note that an exponential function $f(x) = a^x$ is a constant raised to a variable power, whereas a power function $g(x) = x^n$ is a variable raised to a constant power. Use a graphing utility to graph each pair of functions in the same viewing window. Describe any similarities and differences in the graphs.

a. $y_1 = 2^x, y_2 = x^2$

b. $y_1 = 3^x, y_2 = x^3$

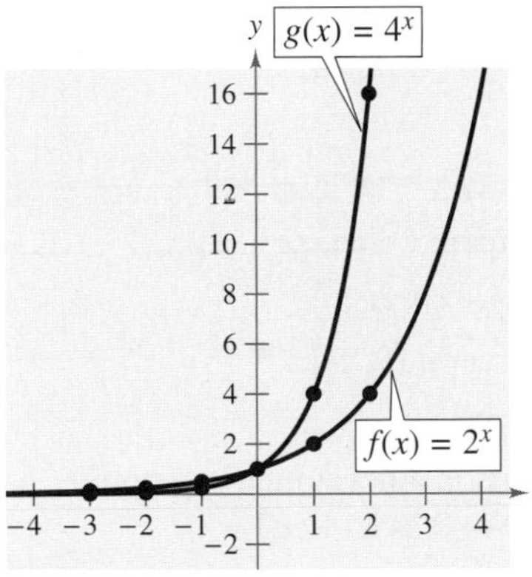

FIGURE 3.1

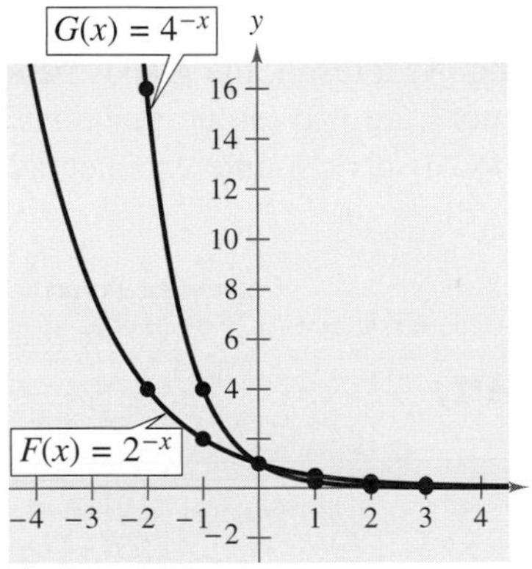

FIGURE 3.2

Graphs of Exponential Functions

The graphs of all exponential functions have similar characteristics, as shown in Examples 2, 3, and 5.

Example 2 Graphs of $y = a^x$

In the same coordinate plane, sketch the graph of each function.

a. $f(x) = 2^x$ **b.** $g(x) = 4^x$

Solution

The table below lists some values for each function, and Figure 3.1 shows the graphs of the two functions. Note that both graphs are increasing. Moreover, the graph of $g(x) = 4^x$ is increasing more rapidly than the graph of $f(x) = 2^x$.

x	-3	-2	-1	0	1	2
2^x	$\frac{1}{8}$	$\frac{1}{4}$	$\frac{1}{2}$	1	2	4
4^x	$\frac{1}{64}$	$\frac{1}{16}$	$\frac{1}{4}$	1	4	16

✓CHECKPOINT Now try Exercise 11.

The table in Example 2 was evaluated by hand. You could, of course, use a graphing utility to construct tables with even more values.

Example 3 Graphs of $y = a^{-x}$

In the same coordinate plane, sketch the graph of each function.

a. $F(x) - 2^{-x}$ **b.** $G(x) = 4^{-x}$

Solution

The table below lists some values for each function, and Figure 3.2 shows the graphs of the two functions. Note that both graphs are decreasing. Moreover, the graph of $G(x) = 4^{-x}$ is decreasing more rapidly than the graph of $F(x) = 2^{-x}$.

x	-2	-1	0	1	2	3
2^{-x}	4	2	1	$\frac{1}{2}$	$\frac{1}{4}$	$\frac{1}{8}$
4^{-x}	16	4	1	$\frac{1}{4}$	$\frac{1}{16}$	$\frac{1}{64}$

✓CHECKPOINT Now try Exercise 13.

In Example 3, note that by using one of the properties of exponents, the functions $F(x) = 2^{-x}$ and $G(x) = 4^{-x}$ can be rewritten with positive exponents.

$$F(x) = 2^{-x} = \frac{1}{2^x} = \left(\frac{1}{2}\right)^x \quad \text{and} \quad G(x) = 4^{-x} = \frac{1}{4^x} = \left(\frac{1}{4}\right)^x$$

Comparing the functions in Examples 2 and 3, observe that

$$F(x) = 2^{-x} = f(-x) \qquad \text{and} \qquad G(x) = 4^{-x} = g(-x).$$

Consequently, the graph of F is a reflection (in the y-axis) of the graph of f. The graphs of G and g have the same relationship. The graphs in Figures 3.1 and 3.2 are typical of the exponential functions $y = a^x$ and $y = a^{-x}$. They have one y-intercept and one horizontal asymptote (the x-axis), and they are continuous. The basic characteristics of these exponential functions are summarized in Figures 3.3 and 3.4.

STUDY TIP

Notice that the range of an exponential function is $(0, \infty)$, which means that $a^x > 0$ for all values of x.

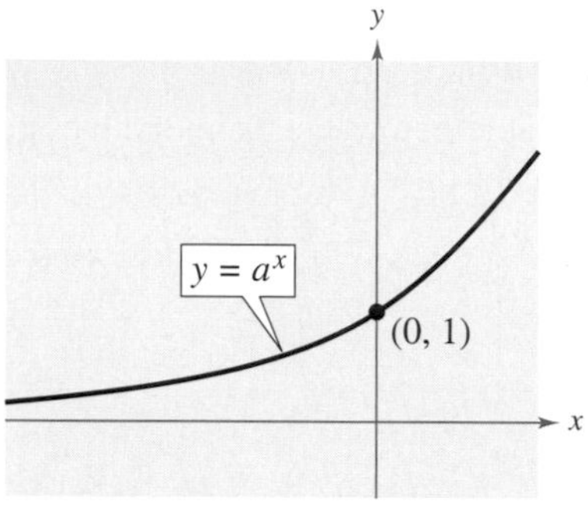

FIGURE 3.3

Graph of $y = a^x$, $a > 1$
- Domain: $(-\infty, \infty)$
- Range: $(0, \infty)$
- Intercept: $(0, 1)$
- Increasing
- x-axis is a horizontal asymptote ($a^x \rightarrow 0$ as $x \rightarrow -\infty$)
- Continuous

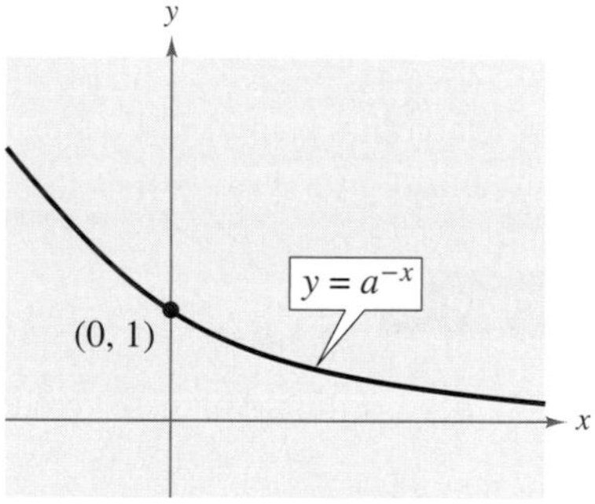

FIGURE 3.4

Graph of $y = a^{-x}$, $a > 1$
- Domain: $(-\infty, \infty)$
- Range: $(0, \infty)$
- Intercept: $(0, 1)$
- Decreasing
- x-axis is a horizontal asymptote ($a^{-x} \rightarrow 0$ as $x \rightarrow \infty$)
- Continuous

From Figures 3.3 and 3.4, you can see that the graph of an exponential function is always increasing or always decreasing. As a result, the graphs pass the Horizontal Line Test, and therefore the functions are one-to-one functions. You can use the following **One-to-One Property** to solve simple exponential equations.

For $a > 0$ and $a \neq 1$, $a^x = a^y$ if and only if $x = y$. One-to-One Property

Example 4 Using the One-to-One Property

a. $9 = 3^{x+1}$ Original equation

$3^2 = 3^{x+1}$ $9 = 3^2$

$2 = x + 1$ One-to-One Property

$1 = x$ Solve for x.

b. $\left(\frac{1}{2}\right)^x = 8 \Longrightarrow 2^{-x} = 2^3 \Longrightarrow x = -3$

CHECKPOINT Now try Exercise 45.

In the following example, notice how the graph of $y = a^x$ can be used to sketch the graphs of functions of the form $f(x) = b \pm a^{x+c}$.

Example 5 Transformations of Graphs of Exponential Functions

Each of the following graphs is a transformation of the graph of $f(x) = 3^x$.

a. Because $g(x) = 3^{x+1} = f(x + 1)$, the graph of g can be obtained by shifting the graph of f one unit to the *left*, as shown in Figure 3.5.

b. Because $h(x) = 3^x - 2 = f(x) - 2$, the graph of h can be obtained by shifting the graph of f *downward* two units, as shown in Figure 3.6.

c. Because $k(x) = -3^x = -f(x)$, the graph of k can be obtained by *reflecting* the graph of f in the x-axis, as shown in Figure 3.7.

d. Because $j(x) = 3^{-x} = f(-x)$, the graph of j can be obtained by *reflecting* the graph of f in the y-axis, as shown in Figure 3.8.

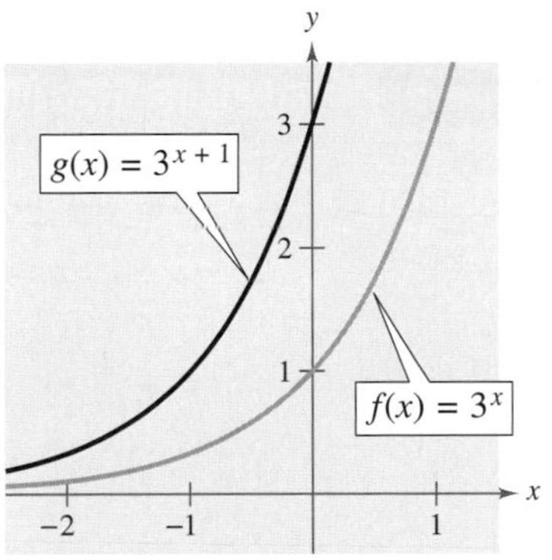

FIGURE 3.5 *Horizontal shift*

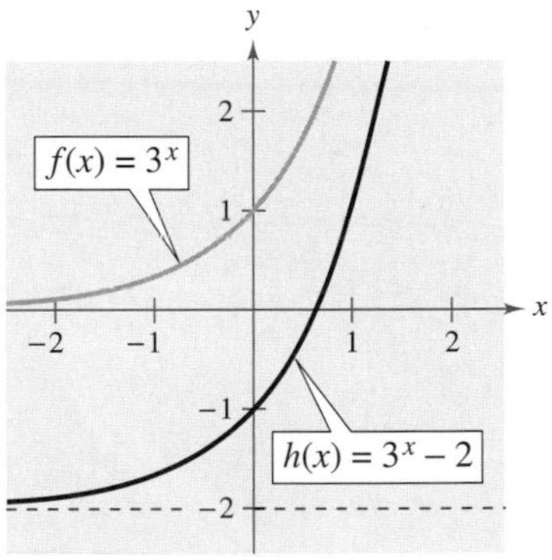

FIGURE 3.6 *Vertical shift*

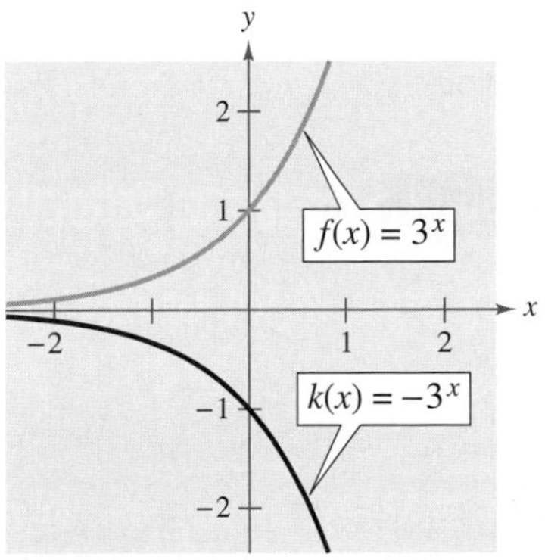

FIGURE 3.7 *Reflection in x-axis*

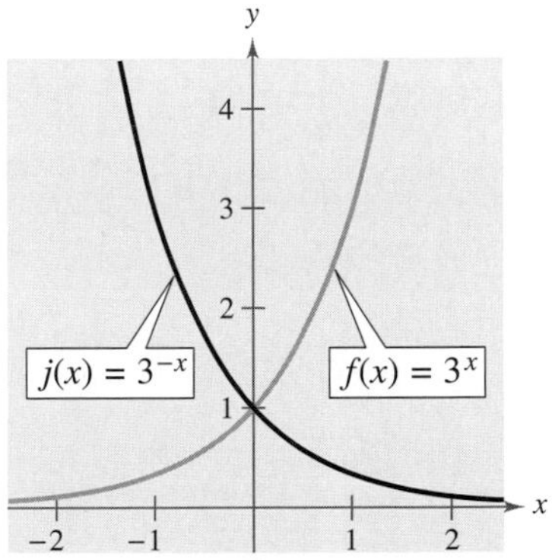

FIGURE 3.8 *Reflection in y-axis*

CHECKPOINT Now try Exercise 17.

Notice that the transformations in Figures 3.5, 3.7, and 3.8 keep the x-axis as a horizontal asymptote, but the transformation in Figure 3.6 yields a new horizontal asymptote of $y = -2$. Also, be sure to note how the y-intercept is affected by each transformation.

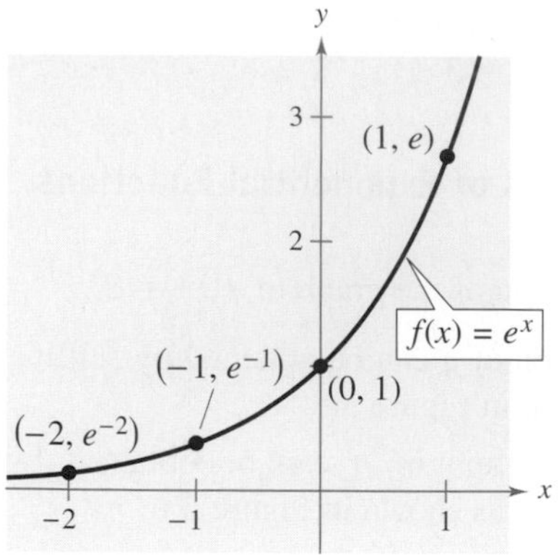

FIGURE 3.9

The Natural Base e

In many applications, the most convenient choice for a base is the irrational number

$$e \approx 2.718281828\ .\ .\ .\ .$$

This number is called the **natural base.** The function given by $f(x) = e^x$ is called the **natural exponential function.** Its graph is shown in Figure 3.9. Be sure you see that for the exponential function $f(x) = e^x$, e is the constant 2.718281828 . . . , whereas x is the variable.

Exploration

Use a graphing utility to graph $y_1 = (1 + 1/x)^x$ and $y_2 = e$ in the same viewing window. Using the *trace* feature, explain what happens to the graph of y_1 as x increases.

Example 6 Evaluating the Natural Exponential Function

Use a calculator to evaluate the function given by $f(x) = e^x$ at each indicated value of x.

a. $x = -2$ **b.** $x = -1$ **c.** $x = 0.25$ **d.** $x = -0.3$

Solution

Function Value	*Graphing Calculator Keystrokes*	*Display*
a. $f(-2) = e^{-2}$	[e^x] [(−)] 2 [ENTER]	0.1353353
b. $f(-1) = e^{-1}$	[e^x] [(−)] 1 [ENTER]	0.3678794
c. $f(0.25) = e^{0.25}$	[e^x] 0.25 [ENTER]	1.2840254
d. $f(-0.3) = e^{-0.3}$	[e^x] [(−)] 0.3 [ENTER]	0.7408182

✓CHECKPOINT Now try Exercise 27.

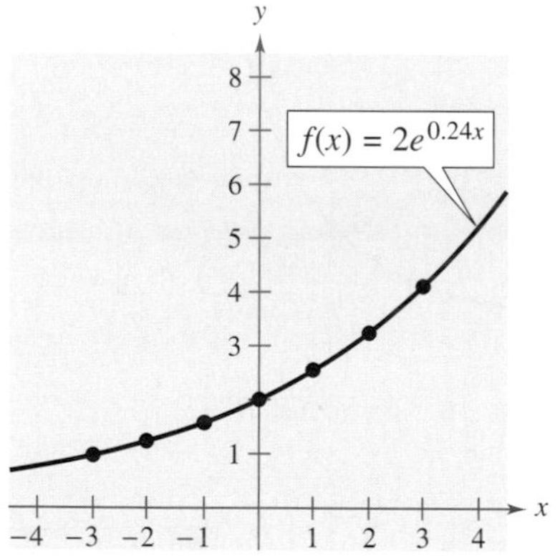

FIGURE 3.10

Example 7 Graphing Natural Exponential Functions

Sketch the graph of each natural exponential function.

a. $f(x) = 2e^{0.24x}$ **b.** $g(x) = \frac{1}{2}e^{-0.58x}$

Solution

To sketch these two graphs, you can use a graphing utility to construct a table of values, as shown below. After constructing the table, plot the points and connect them with smooth curves, as shown in Figures 3.10 and 3.11. Note that the graph in Figure 3.10 is increasing, whereas the graph in Figure 3.11 is decreasing.

x	-3	-2	-1	0	1	2	3
$f(x)$	0.974	1.238	1.573	2.000	2.542	3.232	4.109
$g(x)$	2.849	1.595	0.893	0.500	0.280	0.157	0.088

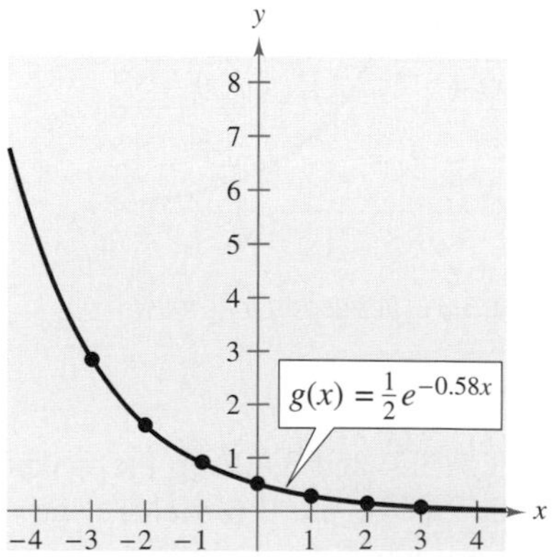

FIGURE 3.11

✓CHECKPOINT Now try Exercise 35.

Exploration

Use the formula

$$A = P\left(1 + \frac{r}{n}\right)^{nt}$$

to calculate the amount in an account when $P = \$3000$, $r = 6\%$, $t = 10$ years, and compounding is done (a) by the day, (b) by the hour, (c) by the minute, and (d) by the second. Does increasing the number of compoundings per year result in unlimited growth of the amount in the account? Explain.

Applications

One of the most familiar examples of exponential growth is that of an investment earning *continuously compounded interest*. Using exponential functions, you can *develop* a formula for interest compounded n times per year and show how it leads to continuous compounding.

Suppose a principal P is invested at an annual interest rate r, compounded once a year. If the interest is added to the principal at the end of the year, the new balance P_1 is

$$P_1 = P + Pr$$
$$= P(1 + r).$$

This pattern of multiplying the previous principal by $1 + r$ is then repeated each successive year, as shown below.

Year	*Balance After Each Compounding*
0	$P = P$
1	$P_1 = P(1 + r)$
2	$P_2 = P_1(1 + r) = P(1 + r)(1 + r) = P(1 + r)^2$
3	$P_3 = P_2(1 + r) = P(1 + r)^2(1 + r) = P(1 + r)^3$
⋮	⋮
t	$P_t = P(1 + r)^t$

To accommodate more frequent (quarterly, monthly, or daily) compounding of interest, let n be the number of compoundings per year and let t be the number of years. Then the rate per compounding is r/n and the account balance after t years is

$$A = P\left(1 + \frac{r}{n}\right)^{nt}.$$ Amount (balance) with n compoundings per year

If you let the number of compoundings n increase without bound, the process approaches what is called **continuous compounding.** In the formula for n compoundings per year, let $m = n/r$. This produces

$$A = P\left(1 + \frac{r}{n}\right)^{nt}$$ Amount with n compoundings per year

$$= P\left(1 + \frac{r}{mr}\right)^{mrt}$$ Substitute mr for n.

$$= P\left(1 + \frac{1}{m}\right)^{mrt}$$ Simplify.

$$= P\left[\left(1 + \frac{1}{m}\right)^{m}\right]^{rt}.$$ Property of exponents

m	$\left(1 + \frac{1}{m}\right)^m$
1	2
10	2.59374246
100	2.704813829
1,000	2.716923932
10,000	2.718145927
100,000	2.718268237
1,000,000	2.718280469
10,000,000	2.718281693
↓	↓
∞	e

As m increases without bound, the table at the left shows that $[1 + (1/m)]^m \to e$ as $m \to \infty$. From this, you can conclude that the formula for continuous compounding is

$$A = Pe^{rt}.$$ Substitute e for $(1 + 1/m)^m$.

STUDY TIP

Be sure you see that the annual interest rate must be written in decimal form. For instance, 6% should be written as 0.06.

Formulas for Compound Interest

After t years, the balance A in an account with principal P and annual interest rate r (in decimal form) is given by the following formulas.

1. For n compoundings per year: $A = P\left(1 + \frac{r}{n}\right)^{nt}$

2. For continuous compounding: $A = Pe^{rt}$

Example 8 Compound Interest

A total of \$12,000 is invested at an annual interest rate of 9%. Find the balance after 5 years if it is compounded

a. quarterly.

b. monthly.

c. continuously.

Solution

a. For quarterly compounding, you have $n = 4$. So, in 5 years at 9%, the balance is

$$A = P\left(1 + \frac{r}{n}\right)^{nt} \qquad \text{Formula for compound interest}$$

$$= 12{,}000\left(1 + \frac{0.09}{4}\right)^{4(5)} \qquad \text{Substitute for } P, r, n, \text{ and } t.$$

$$\approx \$18{,}726.11. \qquad \text{Use a calculator.}$$

b. For monthly compounding, you have $n = 12$. So, in 5 years at 9%, the balance is

$$A = P\left(1 + \frac{r}{n}\right)^{nt} \qquad \text{Formula for compound interest}$$

$$= 12{,}000\left(1 + \frac{0.09}{12}\right)^{12(5)} \qquad \text{Substitute for } P, r, n, \text{ and } t.$$

$$\approx \$18{,}788.17. \qquad \text{Use a calculator.}$$

c. For continuous compounding, the balance is

$$A = Pe^{rt} \qquad \text{Formula for continuous compounding}$$

$$= 12{,}000e^{0.09(5)} \qquad \text{Substitute for } P, r, \text{ and } t.$$

$$\approx \$18{,}819.75. \qquad \text{Use a calculator.}$$

✓CHECKPOINT Now try Exercise 53.

In Example 8, note that continuous compounding yields more than quarterly or monthly compounding. This is typical of the two types of compounding. That is, for a given principal, interest rate, and time, continuous compounding will always yield a larger balance than compounding n times a year.

Example 9 Radioactive Decay

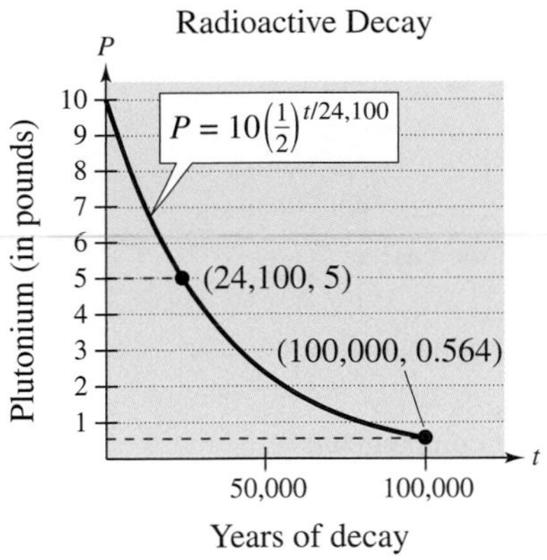

FIGURE 3.12

In 1986, a nuclear reactor accident occurred in Chernobyl in what was then the Soviet Union. The explosion spread highly toxic radioactive chemicals, such as plutonium, over hundreds of square miles, and the government evacuated the city and the surrounding area. To see why the city is now uninhabited, consider the model

$$P = 10\left(\frac{1}{2}\right)^{t/24,100}$$

which represents the amount of plutonium P that remains (from an initial amount of 10 pounds) after t years. Sketch the graph of this function over the interval from $t = 0$ to $t = 100,000$, where $t = 0$ represents 1986. How much of the 10 pounds will remain in the year 2010? How much of the 10 pounds will remain after 100,000 years?

Solution

The graph of this function is shown in Figure 3.12. Note from this graph that plutonium has a *half-life* of about 24,100 years. That is, after 24,100 years, *half* of the original amount will remain. After another 24,100 years, one-quarter of the original amount will remain, and so on. In the year 2010 ($t = 24$), there will still be

$$P = 10\left(\frac{1}{2}\right)^{24/24,100} \approx 10\left(\frac{1}{2}\right)^{0.0009959} \approx 9.993 \text{ pounds}$$

of plutonium remaining. After 100,000 years, there will still be

$$P = 10\left(\frac{1}{2}\right)^{100,000/24,100} \approx 10\left(\frac{1}{2}\right)^{4.1494} \approx 0.564 \text{ pound}$$

of plutonium remaining.

CHECKPOINT Now try Exercise 67.

WRITING ABOUT MATHEMATICS

Identifying Exponential Functions Which of the following functions generated the two tables below? Discuss how you were able to decide. What do these functions have in common? Are any of them the same? If so, explain why.

a. $f_1(x) = 2^{(x+3)}$
b. $f_2(x) = 8\left(\frac{1}{2}\right)^x$
c. $f_3(x) = \left(\frac{1}{2}\right)^{(x-3)}$
d. $f_4(x) = \left(\frac{1}{2}\right)^x + 7$
e. $f_5(x) = 7 + 2^x$
f. $f_6(x) = (8)2^x$

x	-1	0	1	2	3
$g(x)$	7.5	8	9	11	15

x	-2	-1	0	1	2
$h(x)$	32	16	8	4	2

Create two different exponential functions of the forms $y = a(b)^x$ and $y = c^x + d$ with y-intercepts of $(0, -3)$.

3.1 Exercises

VOCABULARY CHECK: Fill in the blanks.

1. Polynomials and rational functions are examples of ________ functions.
2. Exponential and logarithmic functions are examples of nonalgebraic functions, also called ________ functions.
3. The exponential function given by $f(x) = e^x$ is called the ________ ________ function, and the base e is called the ________ base.
4. To find the amount A in an account after t years with principal P and an annual interest rate r compounded n times per year, you can use the formula ________.
5. To find the amount A in an account after t years with principal P and an annual interest rate r compounded continuously, you can use the formula ________.

In Exercises 1–6, evaluate the function at the indicated value of x. Round your result to three decimal places.

Function	*Value*
1. $f(x) = 3.4^x$	$x = 5.6$
2. $f(x) = 2.3^x$	$x = \frac{3}{2}$
3. $f(x) = 5^x$	$x = -\pi$
4. $f(x) = \left(\frac{2}{3}\right)^{5x}$	$x = \frac{3}{10}$
5. $g(x) = 5000(2^x)$	$x = -1.5$
6. $f(x) = 200(1.2)^{12x}$	$x = 24$

In Exercises 7–10, match the exponential function with its graph. [The graphs are labeled (a), (b), (c), and (d).]

(a)

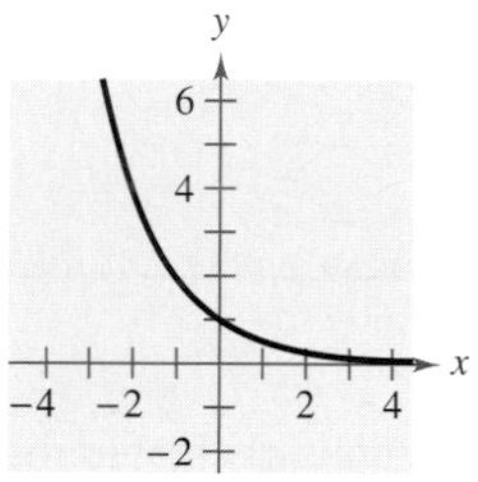

(b)

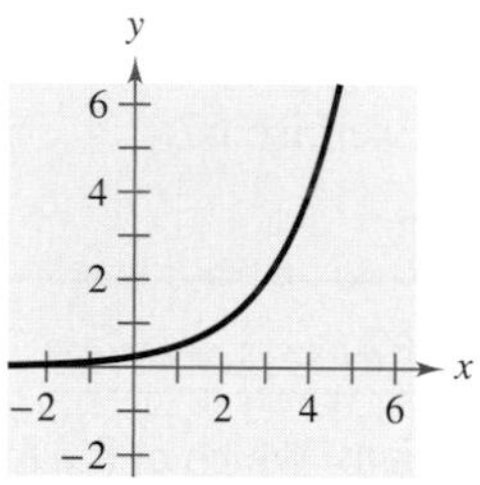

(c)

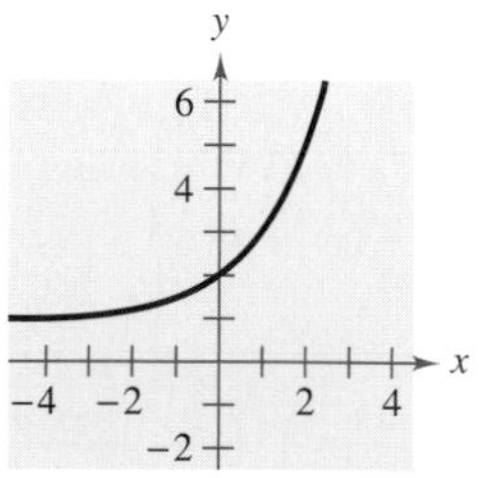

(d)

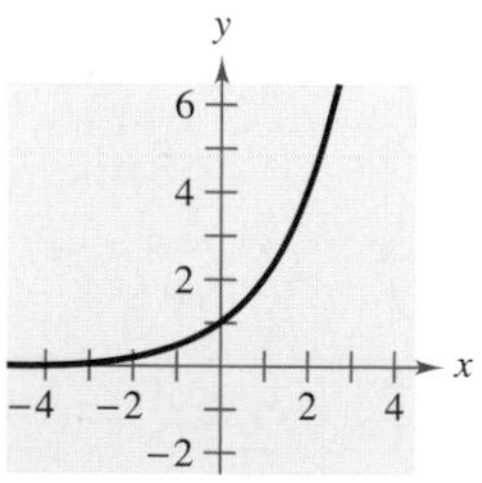

7. $f(x) = 2^x$
8. $f(x) = 2^x + 1$
9. $f(x) = 2^{-x}$
10. $f(x) = 2^{x-2}$

In Exercises 11–16, use a graphing utility to construct a table of values for the function. Then sketch the graph of the function.

11. $f(x) = \left(\frac{1}{2}\right)^x$
12. $f(x) = \left(\frac{1}{2}\right)^{-x}$
13. $f(x) = 6^{-x}$
14. $f(x) = 6^x$
15. $f(x) = 2^{x-1}$
16. $f(x) = 4^{x-3} + 3$

In Exercises 17–22, use the graph of f to describe the transformation that yields the graph of g.

17. $f(x) = 3^x, \quad g(x) = 3^{x-4}$
18. $f(x) = 4^x, \quad g(x) = 4^x + 1$
19. $f(x) = -2^x, \quad g(x) = 5 - 2^x$
20. $f(x) = 10^x, \quad g(x) = 10^{-x+3}$
21. $f(x) = \left(\frac{7}{2}\right)^x, \quad g(x) = -\left(\frac{7}{2}\right)^{-x+6}$
22. $f(x) = 0.3^x, \quad g(x) = -0.3^x + 5$

In Exercises 23–26, use a graphing utility to graph the exponential function.

23. $y = 2^{-x^2}$
24. $y = 3^{-|x|}$
25. $y = 3^{x-2} + 1$
26. $y = 4^{x+1} - 2$

In Exercises 27–32, evaluate the function at the indicated value of x. Round your result to three decimal places.

Function	*Value*
27. $h(x) = e^{-x}$	$x = \frac{3}{4}$
28. $f(x) = e^x$	$x = 3.2$
29. $f(x) = 2e^{-5x}$	$x = 10$
30. $f(x) = 1.5e^{x/2}$	$x = 240$
31. $f(x) = 5000e^{0.06x}$	$x = 6$
32. $f(x) = 250e^{0.05x}$	$x = 20$

In Exercises 33–38, use a graphing utility to construct a table of values for the function. Then sketch the graph of the function.

33. $f(x) = e^x$ **34.** $f(x) = e^{-x}$

35. $f(x) = 3e^{x+4}$ **36.** $f(x) = 2e^{-0.5x}$

37. $f(x) = 2e^{x-2} + 4$ **38.** $f(x) = 2 + e^{x-5}$

In Exercises 39–44, use a graphing utility to graph the exponential function.

39. $y = 1.08^{-5x}$ **40.** $y = 1.08^{5x}$

41. $s(t) = 2e^{0.12t}$ **42.** $s(t) = 3e^{-0.2t}$

43. $g(x) = 1 + e^{-x}$ **44.** $h(x) = e^{x-2}$

In Exercise 45–52, use the One-to-One Property to solve the equation for *x*.

45. $3^{x+1} = 27$ **46.** $2^{x-3} = 16$

47. $2^{x-2} = \frac{1}{32}$ **48.** $\left(\frac{1}{5}\right)^{x+1} = 125$

49. $e^{3x+2} = e^3$ **50.** $e^{2x-1} = e^4$

51. $e^{x^2-3} = e^{2x}$ **52.** $e^{x^2+6} = e^{5x}$

Compound Interest **In Exercises 53–56, complete the table to determine the balance *A* for *P* dollars invested at rate *r* for *t* years and compounded *n* times per year.**

n	1	2	4	12	365	Continuous
A						

53. $P = \$2500$, $r = 2.5\%$, $t = 10$ years

54. $P = \$1000$, $r = 4\%$, $t = 10$ years

55. $P = \$2500$, $r = 3\%$, $t = 20$ years

56. $P = \$1000$, $r = 6\%$, $t = 40$ years

Compound Interest **In Exercises 57–60, complete the table to determine the balance *A* for $12,000 invested at rate *r* for *t* years, compounded continuously.**

t	10	20	30	40	50
A					

57. $r = 4\%$ **58.** $r = 6\%$

59. $r = 6.5\%$ **60.** $r = 3.5\%$

61. ***Trust Fund*** On the day of a child's birth, a deposit of $25,000 is made in a trust fund that pays 8.75% interest, compounded continuously. Determine the balance in this account on the child's 25th birthday.

62. ***Trust Fund*** A deposit of $5000 is made in a trust fund that pays 7.5% interest, compounded continuously. It is specified that the balance will be given to the college from which the donor graduated after the money has earned interest for 50 years. How much will the college receive?

63. ***Inflation*** If the annual rate of inflation averages 4% over the next 10 years, the approximate costs C of goods or services during any year in that decade will be modeled by $C(t) = P(1.04)^t$, where t is the time in years and P is the present cost. The price of an oil change for your car is presently $23.95. Estimate the price 10 years from now.

64. ***Demand*** The demand equation for a product is given by

$$p = 5000\left(1 - \frac{4}{4 + e^{-0.002x}}\right)$$

where p is the price and x is the number of units.

(a) Use a graphing utility to graph the demand function for $x > 0$ and $p > 0$.

(b) Find the price p for a demand of $x = 500$ units.

(c) Use the graph in part (a) to approximate the greatest price that will still yield a demand of at least 600 units.

65. ***Computer Virus*** The number V of computers infected by a computer virus increases according to the model $V(t) = 100e^{4.6052t}$, where t is the time in hours. Find (a) $V(1)$, (b) $V(1.5)$, and (c) $V(2)$.

66. ***Population*** The population P (in millions) of Russia from 1996 to 2004 can be approximated by the model $P = 152.26e^{-0.0039t}$, where t represents the year, with $t = 6$ corresponding to 1996. (Source: Census Bureau, International Data Base)

(a) According to the model, is the population of Russia increasing or decreasing? Explain.

(b) Find the population of Russia in 1998 and 2000.

(c) Use the model to predict the population of Russia in 2010.

67. ***Radioactive Decay*** Let Q represent a mass of radioactive radium (^{226}Ra) (in grams), whose half-life is 1599 years. The quantity of radium present after t years is $Q = 25\left(\frac{1}{2}\right)^{t/1599}$.

(a) Determine the initial quantity (when $t = 0$).

(b) Determine the quantity present after 1000 years.

(c) Use a graphing utility to graph the function over the interval $t = 0$ to $t = 5000$.

68. ***Radioactive Decay*** Let Q represent a mass of carbon 14 (^{14}C) (in grams), whose half-life is 5715 years. The quantity of carbon 14 present after t years is $Q = 10\left(\frac{1}{2}\right)^{t/5715}$.

(a) Determine the initial quantity (when $t = 0$).

(b) Determine the quantity present after 2000 years.

(c) Sketch the graph of this function over the interval $t = 0$ to $t = 10{,}000$.

Model It

69. ***Data Analysis: Biology*** To estimate the amount of defoliation caused by the gypsy moth during a given year, a forester counts the number x of egg masses on $\frac{1}{40}$ of an acre (circle of radius 18.6 feet) in the fall. The percent of defoliation y the next spring is shown in the table. (Source: USDA, Forest Service)

Egg masses, x	Percent of defoliation, y
0	12
25	44
50	81
75	96
100	99

A model for the data is given by

$$y = \frac{100}{1 + 7e^{-0.069x}}.$$

(a) Use a graphing utility to create a scatter plot of the data and graph the model in the same viewing window.

(b) Create a table that compares the model with the sample data.

(c) Estimate the percent of defoliation if 36 egg masses are counted on $\frac{1}{40}$ acre.

(d) You observe that $\frac{2}{3}$ of a forest is defoliated the following spring. Use the graph in part (a) to estimate the number of egg masses per $\frac{1}{40}$ acre.

70. ***Data Analysis: Meteorology*** A meteorologist measures the atmospheric pressure P (in pascals) at altitude h (in kilometers). The data are shown in the table.

Altitude, h	Pressure, P
0	101,293
5	54,735
10	23,294
15	12,157
20	5,069

A model for the data is given by $P = 107{,}428e^{-0.150h}$.

(a) Sketch a scatter plot of the data and graph the model on the same set of axes.

(b) Estimate the atmospheric pressure at a height of 8 kilometers.

Synthesis

True or False? **In Exercises 71 and 72, determine whether the statement is true or false. Justify your answer.**

71. The line $y = -2$ is an asymptote for the graph of $f(x) = 10^x - 2$.

72. $e = \dfrac{271{,}801}{99{,}990}$.

Think About It **In Exercises 73–76, use properties of exponents to determine which functions (if any) are the same.**

73. $f(x) = 3^{x-2}$
$g(x) = 3^x - 9$
$h(x) = \frac{1}{9}(3^x)$

74. $f(x) = 4^x + 12$
$g(x) = 2^{2x+6}$
$h(x) = 64(4^x)$

75. $f(x) = 16(4^{-x})$
$g(x) = \left(\frac{1}{4}\right)^{x-2}$
$h(x) = 16(2^{-2x})$

76. $f(x) = e^{-x} + 3$
$g(x) = e^{3-x}$
$h(x) = -e^{x-3}$

77. Graph the functions given by $y = 3^x$ and $y = 4^x$ and use the graphs to solve each inequality.

(a) $4^x < 3^x$ (b) $4^x > 3^x$

78. Use a graphing utility to graph each function. Use the graph to find where the function is increasing and decreasing, and approximate any relative maximum or minimum values.

(a) $f(x) = x^2e^{-x}$ (b) $g(x) = x2^{3-x}$

79. ***Graphical Analysis*** Use a graphing utility to graph

$$f(x) = \left(1 + \frac{0.5}{x}\right)^x \quad \text{and} \quad g(x) = e^{0.5}$$

in the same viewing window. What is the relationship between f and g as x increases and decreases without bound?

80. ***Think About It*** Which functions are exponential?

(a) $3x$ (b) $3x^2$ (c) 3^x (d) 2^{-x}

Skills Review

In Exercises 81 and 82, solve for y.

81. $x^2 + y^2 = 25$

82. $x - |y| = 2$

In Exercises 83 and 84, sketch the graph of the function.

83. $f(x) = \dfrac{2}{9 + x}$

84. $f(x) = \sqrt{7 - x}$

85. **Make a Decision** To work an extended application analyzing the population per square mile of the United States, visit this text's website at *college.hmco.com*. *(Data Source: U.S. Census Bureau)*

3.2 Logarithmic Functions and Their Graphs

What you should learn

- Recognize and evaluate logarithmic functions with base *a*.
- Graph logarithmic functions.
- Recognize, evaluate, and graph natural logarithmic functions.
- Use logarithmic functions to model and solve real-life problems.

Why you should learn it

Logarithmic functions are often used to model scientific observations. For instance, in Exercise 89 on page 238, a logarithmic function is used to model human memory.

© Ariel Skelley/Corbis

Logarithmic Functions

In Section 1.9, you studied the concept of an inverse function. There, you learned that if a function is one-to-one—that is, if the function has the property that no horizontal line intersects the graph of the function more than once—the function must have an inverse function. By looking back at the graphs of the exponential functions introduced in Section 3.1, you will see that every function of the form $f(x) = a^x$ passes the Horizontal Line Test and therefore must have an inverse function. This inverse function is called the **logarithmic function with base *a*.**

Definition of Logarithmic Function with Base *a*

For $x > 0$, $a > 0$, and $a \neq 1$,

$$y = \log_a x \text{ if and only if } x = a^y.$$

The function given by

$f(x) = \log_a x$ Read as "log base *a* of *x*."

is called the **logarithmic function with base *a*.**

The equations

$$y = \log_a x \quad \text{and} \quad x = a^y$$

are equivalent. The first equation is in logarithmic form and the second is in exponential form. For example, the logarithmic equation $2 = \log_3 9$ can be rewritten in exponential form as $9 = 3^2$. The exponential equation $5^3 = 125$ can be rewritten in logarithmic form as $\log_5 125 = 3$.

When evaluating logarithms, remember that *a logarithm is an exponent*. This means that $\log_a x$ is the exponent to which *a* must be raised to obtain *x*. For instance, $\log_2 8 = 3$ because 2 must be raised to the third power to get 8.

Example 1 Evaluating Logarithms

Use the definition of logarithmic function to evaluate each logarithm at the indicated value of *x*.

a. $f(x) = \log_2 x, \quad x = 32$ **b.** $f(x) = \log_3 x, \quad x = 1$

c. $f(x) = \log_4 x, \quad x = 2$ **d.** $f(x) = \log_{10} x, \quad x = \frac{1}{100}$

Solution

a. $f(32) = \log_2 32 = 5$ because $2^5 = 32$.

b. $f(1) = \log_3 1 = 0$ because $3^0 = 1$.

c. $f(2) = \log_4 2 = \frac{1}{2}$ because $4^{1/2} = \sqrt{4} = 2$.

d. $f\left(\frac{1}{100}\right) = \log_{10} \frac{1}{100} = -2$ because $10^{-2} = \frac{1}{10^2} = \frac{1}{100}$.

✓CHECKPOINT Now try Exercise 17.

STUDY TIP

Remember that a logarithm is an exponent. So, to evaluate the logarithmic expression $\log_a x$, you need to ask the question, "To what power must *a* be raised to obtain *x*?"

Exploration

Complete the table for $f(x) = 10^x$.

x	-2	-1	0	1	2
$f(x)$					

Complete the table for $f(x) = \log x$.

x	$\frac{1}{100}$	$\frac{1}{10}$	1	10	100
$f(x)$					

Compare the two tables. What is the relationship between $f(x) = 10^x$ and $f(x) = \log x$?

The logarithmic function with base 10 is called the **common logarithmic function.** It is denoted by $\log_{10}$ or simply by log. On most calculators, this function is denoted by [LOG]. Example 2 shows how to use a calculator to evaluate common logarithmic functions. You will learn how to use a calculator to calculate logarithms to any base in the next section.

Example 2 Evaluating Common Logarithms on a Calculator

Use a calculator to evaluate the function given by $f(x) = \log x$ at each value of x.

a. $x = 10$ **b.** $x = \frac{1}{3}$ **c.** $x = 2.5$ **d.** $x = -2$

Solution

Function Value	Graphing Calculator Keystrokes	Display
a. $f(10) = \log 10$	[LOG] 10 [ENTER]	1
b. $f(\frac{1}{3}) = \log \frac{1}{3}$	[LOG] [(] 1 [÷] 3 [)] [ENTER]	-0.4771213
c. $f(2.5) = \log 2.5$	[LOG] 2.5 [ENTER]	0.3979400
d. $f(-2) = \log(-2)$	[LOG] [(−)] 2 [ENTER]	ERROR

Note that the calculator displays an error message (or a complex number) when you try to evaluate $\log(-2)$. The reason for this is that there is no real number power to which 10 can be raised to obtain -2.

CHECKPOINT Now try Exercise 23.

The following properties follow directly from the definition of the logarithmic function with base a.

Properties of Logarithms

1. $\log_a 1 = 0$ because $a^0 = 1$.
2. $\log_a a = 1$ because $a^1 = a$.
3. $\log_a a^x = x$ and $a^{\log_a x} = x$ Inverse Properties
4. If $\log_a x = \log_a y$, then $x = y$. One-to-One Property

Example 3 Using Properties of Logarithms

a. Simplify: $\log_4 1$ **b.** Simplify: $\log_{\sqrt{7}} \sqrt{7}$ **c.** Simplify: $6^{\log_6 20}$

Solution

a. Using Property 1, it follows that $\log_4 1 = 0$.

b. Using Property 2, you can conclude that $\log_{\sqrt{7}} \sqrt{7} = 1$.

c. Using the Inverse Property (Property 3), it follows that $6^{\log_6 20} = 20$.

CHECKPOINT Now try Exercise 27.

You can use the One-to-One Property (Property 4) to solve simple logarithmic equations, as shown in Example 4.

Example 4 **Using the One-to-One Property**

a. $\log_3 x = \log_3 12$ Original equation

$x = 12$ One-to-One Property

b. $\log(2x + 1) = \log x \Rightarrow 2x + 1 = x \Rightarrow x = -1$

c. $\log_4(x^2 - 6) = \log_4 10 \Rightarrow x^2 - 6 = 10 \Rightarrow x^2 = 16 \Rightarrow x = \pm 4$

✓CHECKPOINT Now try Exercise 79.

Graphs of Logarithmic Functions

To sketch the graph of $y = \log_a x$, you can use the fact that the graphs of inverse functions are reflections of each other in the line $y = x$.

Example 5 **Graphs of Exponential and Logarithmic Functions**

In the same coordinate plane, sketch the graph of each function.

a. $f(x) = 2^x$ **b.** $g(x) = \log_2 x$

Solution

a. For $f(x) = 2^x$, construct a table of values. By plotting these points and connecting them with a smooth curve, you obtain the graph shown in Figure 3.13.

x	-2	-1	0	1	2	3
$f(x) = 2^x$	$\frac{1}{4}$	$\frac{1}{2}$	1	2	4	8

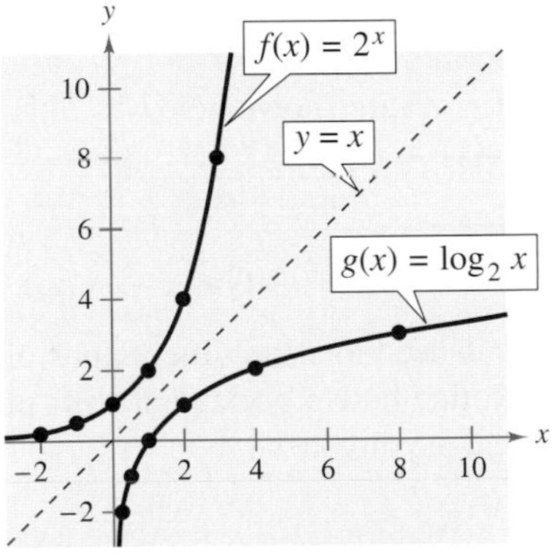

FIGURE 3.13

b. Because $g(x) = \log_2 x$ is the inverse function of $f(x) = 2^x$, the graph of g is obtained by plotting the points $(f(x), x)$ and connecting them with a smooth curve. The graph of g is a reflection of the graph of f in the line $y = x$, as shown in Figure 3.13.

✓CHECKPOINT Now try Exercise 31.

Example 6 **Sketching the Graph of a Logarithmic Function**

Sketch the graph of the common logarithmic function $f(x) = \log x$. Identify the vertical asymptote.

Solution

Begin by constructing a table of values. Note that some of the values can be obtained without a calculator by using the Inverse Property of Logarithms. Others require a calculator. Next, plot the points and connect them with a smooth curve, as shown in Figure 3.14. The vertical asymptote is $x = 0$ (y-axis).

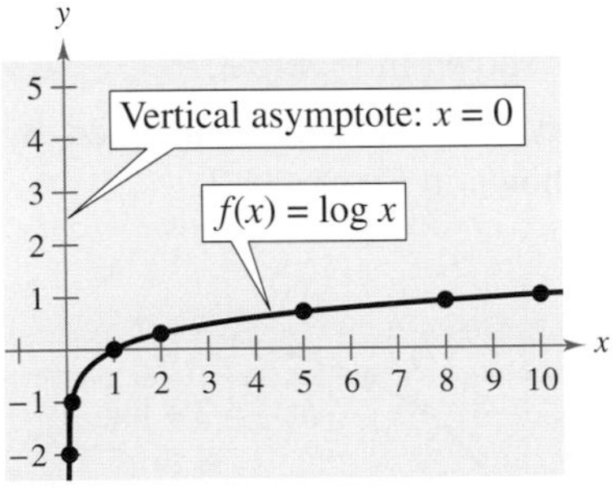

FIGURE 3.14

	Without calculator				With calculator		
x	$\frac{1}{100}$	$\frac{1}{10}$	1	10	2	5	8
$f(x) = \log x$	-2	-1	0	1	0.301	0.699	0.903

✓CHECKPOINT Now try Exercise 37.

The nature of the graph in Figure 3.14 is typical of functions of the form $f(x) = \log_a x$, $a > 1$. They have one x-intercept and one vertical asymptote. Notice how slowly the graph rises for $x > 1$. The basic characteristics of logarithmic graphs are summarized in Figure 3.15.

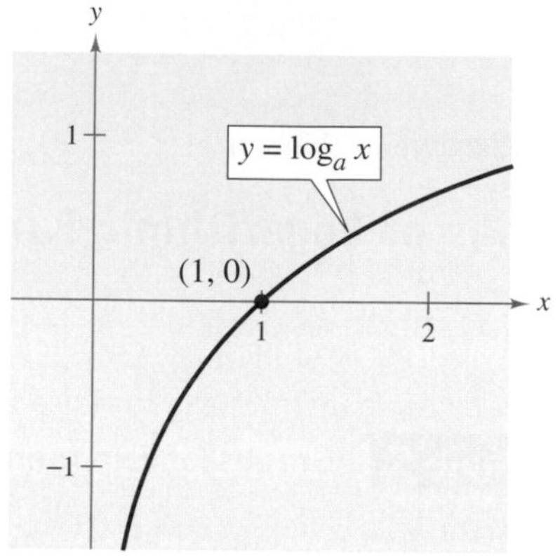

FIGURE 3.15

Graph of $y = \log_a x$, $a > 1$

- Domain: $(0, \infty)$
- Range: $(-\infty, \infty)$
- x-intercept: $(1, 0)$
- Increasing
- One-to-one, therefore has an inverse function
- y-axis is a vertical asymptote ($\log_a x \to -\infty$ as $x \to 0^+$).
- Continuous
- Reflection of graph of $y = a^x$ about the line $y = x$

The basic characteristics of the graph of $f(x) = a^x$ are shown below to illustrate the inverse relation between $f(x) = a^x$ and $g(x) = \log_a x$.

- Domain: $(-\infty, \infty)$
- Range: $(0, \infty)$
- y-intercept: $(0,1)$
- x-axis is a horizontal asymptote ($a^x \to 0$ as $x \to -\infty$).

In the next example, the graph of $y = \log_a x$ is used to sketch the graphs of functions of the form $f(x) = b \pm \log_a(x + c)$. Notice how a horizontal shift of the graph results in a horizontal shift of the vertical asymptote.

STUDY TIP

You can use your understanding of transformations to identify vertical asymptotes of logarithmic functions. For instance, in Example 7(a) the graph of $g(x) = f(x - 1)$ shifts the graph of $f(x)$ one unit to the right. So, the vertical asymptote of $g(x)$ is $x = 1$, one unit to the right of the vertical asymptote of the graph of $f(x)$.

Example 7 Shifting Graphs of Logarithmic Functions

The graph of each of the functions is similar to the graph of $f(x) = \log x$.

a. Because $g(x) = \log(x - 1) = f(x - 1)$, the graph of g can be obtained by shifting the graph of f one unit to the right, as shown in Figure 3.16.

b. Because $h(x) = 2 + \log x = 2 + f(x)$, the graph of h can be obtained by shifting the graph of f two units upward, as shown in Figure 3.17.

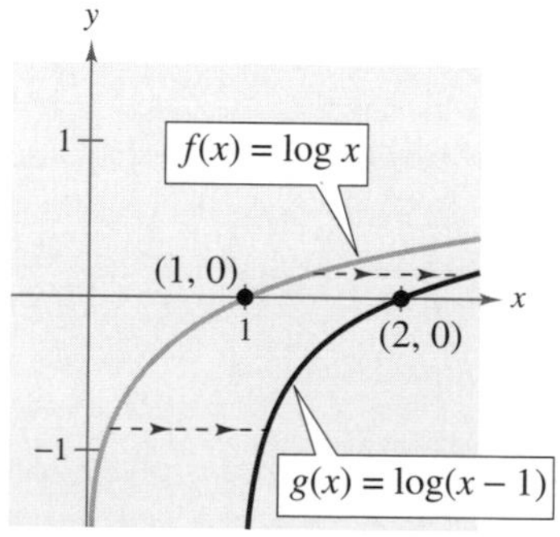

FIGURE 3.16

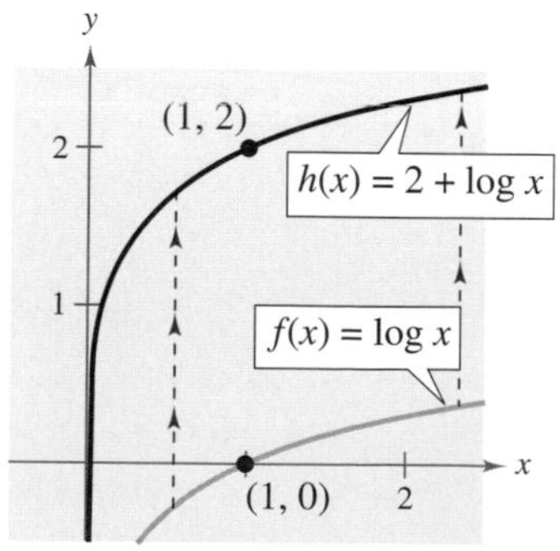

FIGURE 3.17

CHECKPOINT Now try Exercise 39.

The Natural Logarithmic Function

By looking back at the graph of the natural exponential function introduced in Section 3.1 on page 388, you will see that $f(x) = e^x$ is one-to-one and so has an inverse function. This inverse function is called the **natural logarithmic function** and is denoted by the special symbol $\ln x$, read as "the natural log of x" or "el en of x." Note that the natural logarithm is written without a base. The base is understood to be e.

> **The Natural Logarithmic Function**
>
> The function defined by
>
> $$f(x) = \log_e x = \ln x, \quad x > 0$$
>
> is called the **natural logarithmic function.**

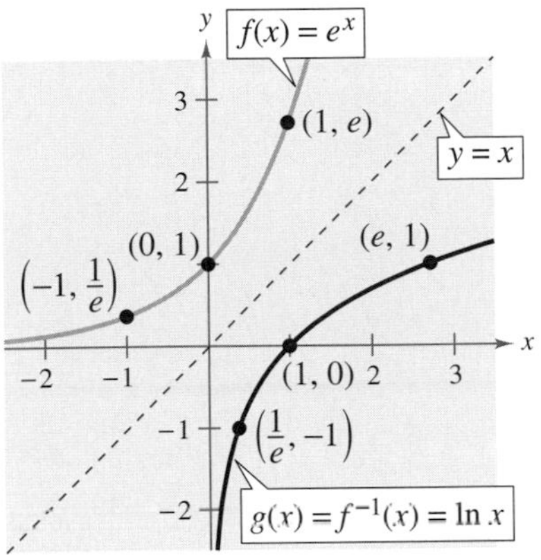

Reflection of graph of $f(x) = e^x$ about the line $y = x$
FIGURE 3.18

The definition above implies that the natural logarithmic function and the natural exponential function are inverse functions of each other. So, every logarithmic equation can be written in an equivalent exponential form and every exponential equation can be written in logarithmic form. That is, $y = \ln x$ and $x = e^y$ are equivalent equations.

Because the functions given by $f(x) = e^x$ and $g(x) = \ln x$ are inverse functions of each other, their graphs are reflections of each other in the line $y = x$. This reflective property is illustrated in Figure 3.18.

On most calculators, the natural logarithm is denoted by LN, as illustrated in Example 8.

Example 8 Evaluating the Natural Logarithmic Function

Use a calculator to evaluate the function given by $f(x) = \ln x$ for each value of x.

a. $x = 2$ **b.** $x = 0.3$ **c.** $x = -1$ **d.** $x = 1 + \sqrt{2}$

Solution

	Function Value	*Graphing Calculator Keystrokes*	*Display*
a.	$f(2) = \ln 2$	LN 2 ENTER	0.6931472
b.	$f(0.3) = \ln 0.3$	LN .3 ENTER	−1.2039728
c.	$f(-1) = \ln(-1)$	LN (−) 1 ENTER	ERROR
d.	$f(1 + \sqrt{2}) = \ln(1 + \sqrt{2})$	LN (1 + √ 2) ENTER	0.8813736

✓CHECKPOINT Now try Exercise 61.

> **STUDY TIP**
>
> Notice that as with every other logarithmic function, the domain of the natural logarithmic function is the set of *positive real numbers*—be sure you see that $\ln x$ is not defined for zero or for negative numbers.

In Example 8, be sure you see that $\ln(-1)$ gives an error message on most calculators. (Some calculators may display a complex number.) This occurs because the domain of $\ln x$ is the set of positive real numbers (see Figure 3.18). So, $\ln(-1)$ is undefined.

The four properties of logarithms listed on page 230 are also valid for natural logarithms.

Properties of Natural Logarithms

1. $\ln 1 = 0$ because $e^0 = 1$.
2. $\ln e = 1$ because $e^1 = e$.
3. $\ln e^x = x$ and $e^{\ln x} = x$ — Inverse Properties
4. If $\ln x = \ln y$, then $x = y$. — One-to-One Property

Example 9 Using Properties of Natural Logarithms

Use the properties of natural logarithms to simplify each expression.

a. $\ln \frac{1}{e}$ **b.** $e^{\ln 5}$ **c.** $\frac{\ln 1}{3}$ **d.** $2 \ln e$

Solution

a. $\ln \frac{1}{e} = \ln e^{-1} = -1$ Inverse Property **b.** $e^{\ln 5} = 5$ Inverse Property

c. $\frac{\ln 1}{3} = \frac{0}{3} = 0$ Property 1 **d.** $2 \ln e = 2(1) = 2$ Property 2

CHECKPOINT Now try Exercise 65.

Example 10 Finding the Domains of Logarithmic Functions

Find the domain of each function.

a. $f(x) = \ln(x - 2)$ **b.** $g(x) = \ln(2 - x)$ **c.** $h(x) = \ln x^2$

Solution

a. Because $\ln(x - 2)$ is defined only if $x - 2 > 0$, it follows that the domain of f is $(2, \infty)$. The graph of f is shown in Figure 3.19.

b. Because $\ln(2 - x)$ is defined only if $2 - x > 0$, it follows that the domain of g is $(-\infty, 2)$. The graph of g is shown in Figure 3.20.

c. Because $\ln x^2$ is defined only if $x^2 > 0$, it follows that the domain of h is all real numbers except $x = 0$. The graph of h is shown in Figure 3.21.

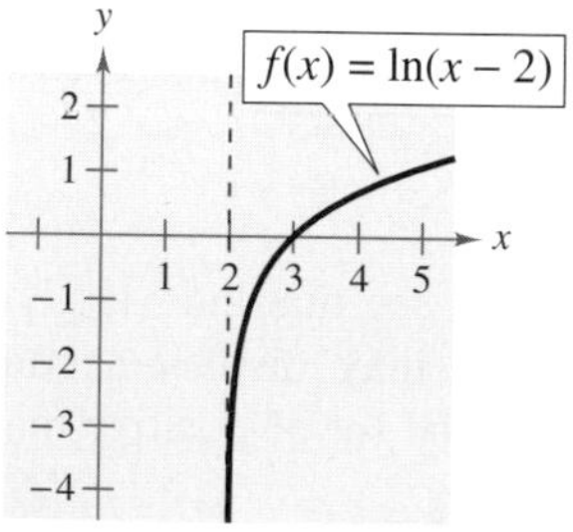

FIGURE 3.19

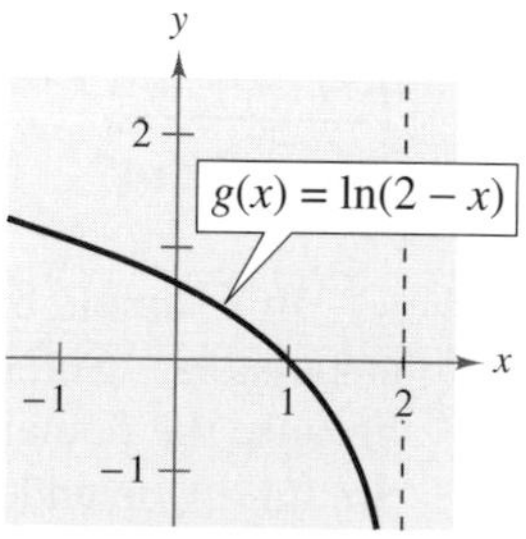

FIGURE 3.20

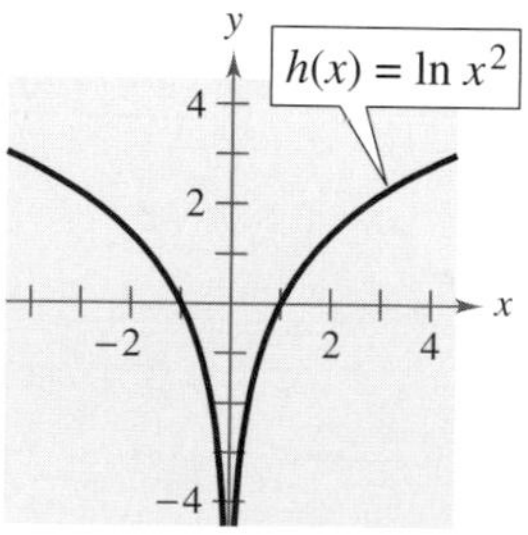

FIGURE 3.21

CHECKPOINT Now try Exercise 69.

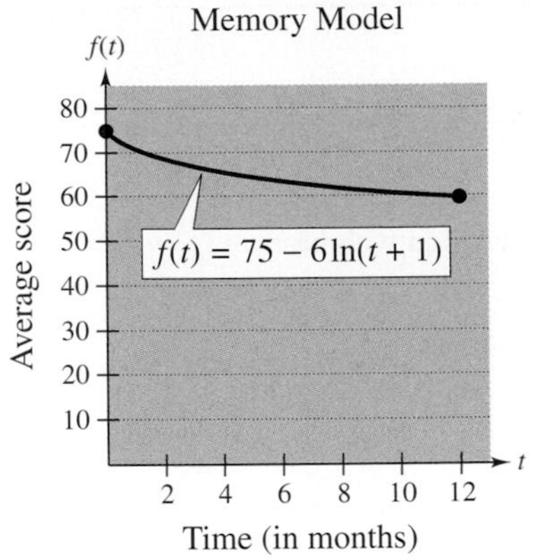

FIGURE 3.22

Application

Example 11 Human Memory Model

Students participating in a psychology experiment attended several lectures on a subject and were given an exam. Every month for a year after the exam, the students were retested to see how much of the material they remembered. The average scores for the group are given by the *human memory model*

$$f(t) = 75 - 6\ln(t + 1), \quad 0 \le t \le 12$$

where t is the time in months. The graph of f is shown in Figure 3.22.

a. What was the average score on the original ($t = 0$) exam?

b. What was the average score at the end of $t = 2$ months?

c. What was the average score at the end of $t = 6$ months?

Solution

a. The original average score was

$$f(0) = 75 - 6\ln(0 + 1) \qquad \text{Substitute 0 for } t.$$
$$= 75 - 6\ln 1 \qquad \text{Simplify.}$$
$$= 75 - 6(0) \qquad \text{Property of natural logarithms}$$
$$= 75. \qquad \text{Solution}$$

b. After 2 months, the average score was

$$f(2) = 75 - 6\ln(2 + 1) \qquad \text{Substitute 2 for } t.$$
$$= 75 - 6\ln 3 \qquad \text{Simplify.}$$
$$\approx 75 - 6(1.0986) \qquad \text{Use a calculator.}$$
$$\approx 68.4. \qquad \text{Solution}$$

c. After 6 months, the average score was

$$f(6) = 75 - 6\ln(6 + 1) \qquad \text{Substitute 6 for } t.$$
$$= 75 - 6\ln 7 \qquad \text{Simplify.}$$
$$\approx 75 - 6(1.9459) \qquad \text{Use a calculator.}$$
$$\approx 63.3. \qquad \text{Solution}$$

✓CHECKPOINT Now try Exercise 89.

WRITING ABOUT MATHEMATICS

Analyzing a Human Memory Model Use a graphing utility to determine the time in months when the average score in Example 11 was 60. Explain your method of solving the problem. Describe another way that you can use a graphing utility to determine the answer.

3.2 Exercises

VOCABULARY CHECK: Fill in the blanks.

1. The inverse function of the exponential function given by $f(x) = a^x$ is called the ________ function with base a.
2. The common logarithmic function has base ________ .
3. The logarithmic function given by $f(x) = \ln x$ is called the ________ logarithmic function and has base ________.
4. The Inverse Property of logarithms and exponentials states that $\log_a a^x = x$ and ________.
5. The One-to-One Property of natural logarithms states that if $\ln x = \ln y$, then ________.

In Exercises 1–8, write the logarithmic equation in exponential form. For example, the exponential form of $\log_5 25 = 2$ is $5^2 = 25$.

1. $\log_4 64 = 3$
2. $\log_3 81 = 4$
3. $\log_7 \frac{1}{49} = -2$
4. $\log \frac{1}{1000} = -3$
5. $\log_{32} 4 = \frac{2}{5}$
6. $\log_{16} 8 = \frac{3}{4}$
7. $\log_{36} 6 = \frac{1}{2}$
8. $\log_8 4 = \frac{2}{3}$

In Exercises 9–16, write the exponential equation in logarithmic form. For example, the logarithmic form of $2^3 = 8$ is $\log_2 8 = 3$.

9. $5^3 = 125$
10. $8^2 = 64$
11. $81^{1/4} = 3$
12. $9^{3/2} = 27$
13. $6^{-2} = \frac{1}{36}$
14. $4^{-3} = \frac{1}{64}$
15. $7^0 = 1$
16. $10^{-3} = 0.001$

In Exercises 17–22, evaluate the function at the indicated value of x without using a calculator.

	Function	*Value*
17.	$f(x) = \log_2 x$	$x = 16$
18.	$f(x) = \log_{16} x$	$x = 4$
19.	$f(x) = \log_7 x$	$x = 1$
20.	$f(x) = \log x$	$x = 10$
21.	$g(x) = \log_a x$	$x = a^2$
22.	$g(x) = \log_b x$	$x = b^{-3}$

In Exercises 23–26, use a calculator to evaluate $f(x) = \log x$ at the indicated value of x. Round your result to three decimal places.

23. $x = \frac{4}{5}$
24. $x = \frac{1}{500}$
25. $x = 12.5$
26. $x = 75.25$

In Exercises 27–30, use the properties of logarithms to simplify the expression.

27. $\log_3 3^4$
28. $\log_{1.5} 1$
29. $\log_\pi \pi$
30. $9^{\log_9 15}$

In Exercises 31–38, find the domain, x-intercept, and vertical asymptote of the logarithmic function and sketch its graph.

31. $f(x) = \log_4 x$
32. $g(x) = \log_6 x$
33. $y = -\log_3 x + 2$
34. $h(x) = \log_4(x - 3)$
35. $f(x) = -\log_6(x + 2)$
36. $y = \log_5(x - 1) + 4$
37. $y = \log\left(\frac{x}{5}\right)$
38. $y = \log(-x)$

In Exercises 39–44, use the graph of $g(x) = \log_3 x$ to match the given function with its graph. Then describe the relationship between the graphs of f and g. [The graphs are labeled (a), (b), (c), (d), (e), and (f).]

(a)

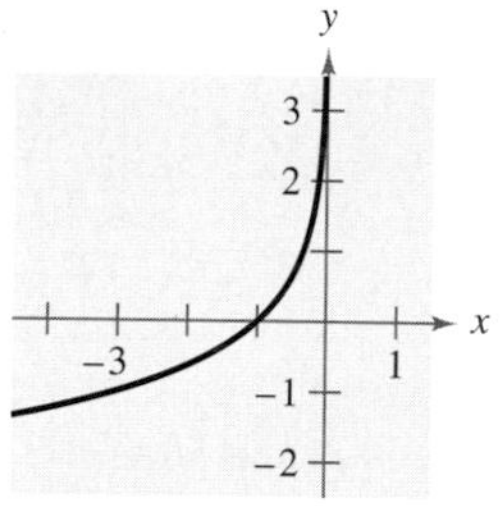

(b)

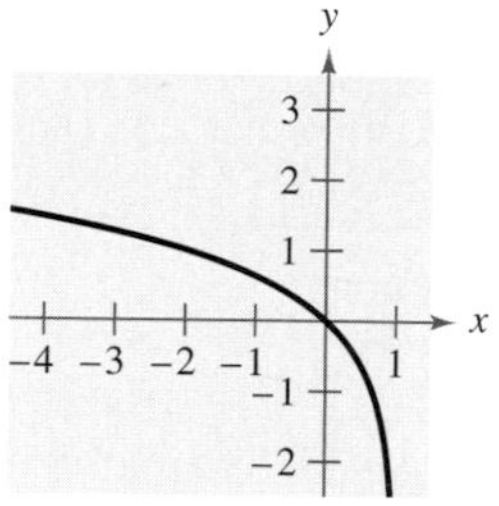

(c)

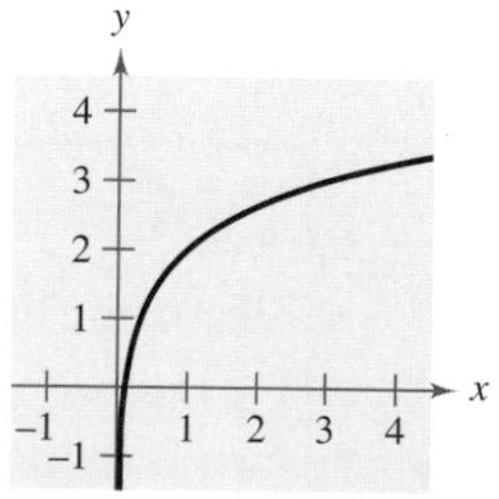

(d)

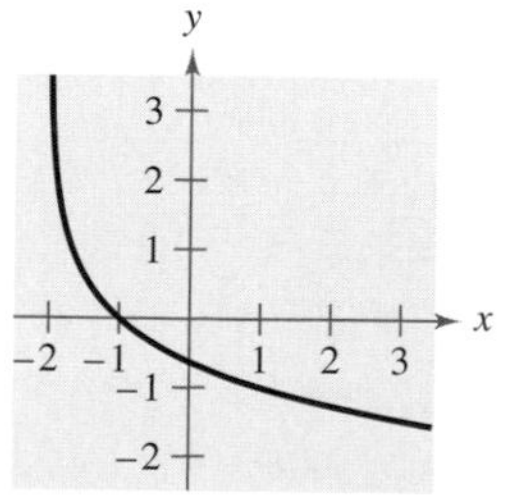

(e)

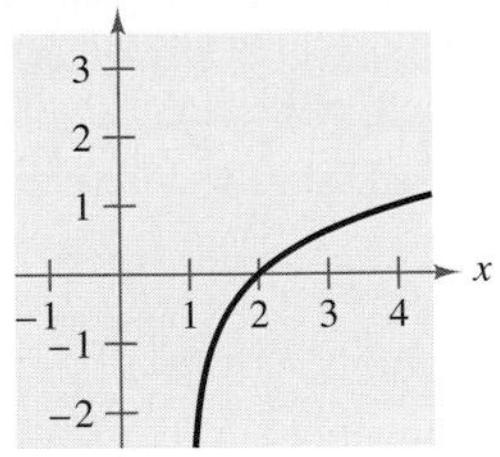

(f)

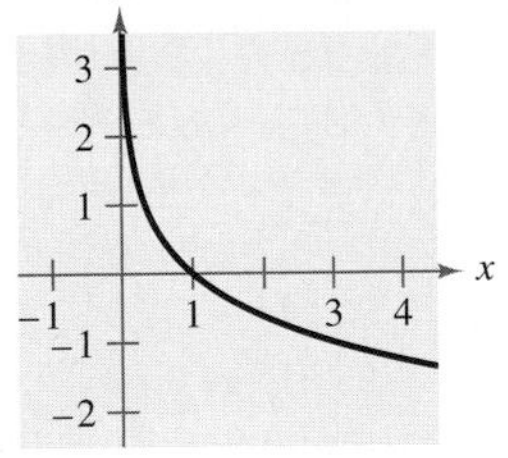

39. $f(x) = \log_3 x + 2$
40. $f(x) = -\log_3 x$
41. $f(x) = -\log_3(x + 2)$
42. $f(x) = \log_3(x - 1)$
43. $f(x) = \log_3(1 - x)$
44. $f(x) = -\log_3(-x)$

In Exercises 45–52, write the logarithmic equation in exponential form.

45. $\ln \frac{1}{2} = -0.693 \ldots$
46. $\ln \frac{2}{5} = -0.916 \ldots$
47. $\ln 4 = 1.386 \ldots$
48. $\ln 10 = 2.302 \ldots$
49. $\ln 250 = 5.521 \ldots$
50. $\ln 679 = 6.520 \ldots$
51. $\ln 1 = 0$
52. $\ln e = 1$

In Exercises 53–60, write the exponential equation in logarithmic form.

53. $e^3 = 20.0855 \ldots$
54. $e^2 = 7.3890 \ldots$
55. $e^{1/2} = 1.6487 \ldots$
56. $e^{1/3} = 1.3956 \ldots$
57. $e^{-0.5} = 0.6065 \ldots$
58. $e^{-4.1} = 0.0165 \ldots$
59. $e^x = 4$
60. $e^{2x} = 3$

In Exercises 61–64, use a calculator to evaluate the function at the indicated value of *x*. Round your result to three decimal places.

	Function	*Value*
61.	$f(x) = \ln x$	$x = 18.42$
62.	$f(x) = 3 \ln x$	$x = 0.32$
63.	$g(x) = 2 \ln x$	$x = 0.75$
64.	$g(x) = -\ln x$	$x = \frac{1}{2}$

In Exercises 65–68, evaluate $g(x) = \ln x$ at the indicated value of *x* without using a calculator.

65. $x = e^3$
66. $x = e^{-2}$
67. $x = e^{-2/3}$
68. $x = e^{-5/2}$

In Exercises 69–72, find the domain, *x*-intercept, and vertical asymptote of the logarithmic function and sketch its graph.

69. $f(x) = \ln(x - 1)$
70. $h(x) = \ln(x + 1)$
71. $g(x) = \ln(-x)$
72. $f(x) = \ln(3 - x)$

In Exercises 73–78, use a graphing utility to graph the function. Be sure to use an appropriate viewing window.

73. $f(x) = \log(x + 1)$
74. $f(x) = \log(x - 1)$
75. $f(x) = \ln(x - 1)$
76. $f(x) = \ln(x + 2)$
77. $f(x) = \ln x + 2$
78. $f(x) = 3 \ln x - 1$

In Exercises 79–86, use the One-to-One Property to solve the equation for *x*.

79. $\log_2(x + 1) = \log_2 4$
80. $\log_2(x - 3) = \log_2 9$
81. $\log(2x + 1) = \log 15$
82. $\log(5x + 3) = \log 12$
83. $\ln(x + 2) = \ln 6$
84. $\ln(x - 4) = \ln 2$
85. $\ln(x^2 - 2) = \ln 23$
86. $\ln(x^2 - x) = \ln 6$

Model It

87. ***Monthly Payment*** The model

$$t = 12.542 \ln\left(\frac{x}{x - 1000}\right), \quad x > 1000$$

approximates the length of a home mortgage of \$150,000 at 8% in terms of the monthly payment. In the model, t is the length of the mortgage in years and x is the monthly payment in dollars (see figure).

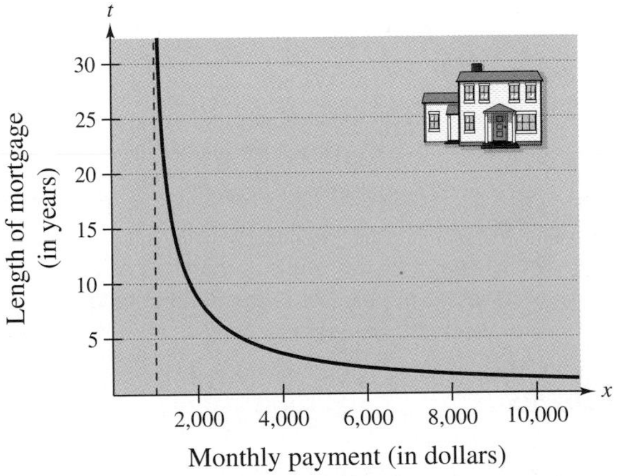

(a) Use the model to approximate the lengths of a \$150,000 mortgage at 8% when the monthly payment is \$1100.65 and when the monthly payment is \$1254.68.

(b) Approximate the total amounts paid over the term of the mortgage with a monthly payment of \$1100.65 and with a monthly payment of \$1254.68.

(c) Approximate the total interest charges for a monthly payment of \$1100.65 and for a monthly payment of \$1254.68.

(d) What is the vertical asymptote for the model? Interpret its meaning in the context of the problem.

88. ***Compound Interest*** A principal P, invested at $9\frac{1}{2}\%$ and compounded continuously, increases to an amount K times the original principal after t years, where t is given by $t = (\ln K)/0.095$.

(a) Complete the table and interpret your results.

K	1	2	4	6	8	10	12
t							

(b) Sketch a graph of the function.

89. ***Human Memory Model*** Students in a mathematics class were given an exam and then retested monthly with an equivalent exam. The average scores for the class are given by the human memory model $f(t) = 80 - 17\log(t + 1)$, $0 \le t \le 12$ where t is the time in months.

(a) Use a graphing utility to graph the model over the specified domain.

(b) What was the average score on the original exam $(t = 0)$?

(c) What was the average score after 4 months?

(d) What was the average score after 10 months?

90. ***Sound Intensity*** The relationship between the number of decibels β and the intensity of a sound I in watts per square meter is

$$\beta = 10\log\left(\frac{I}{10^{-12}}\right).$$

(a) Determine the number of decibels of a sound with an intensity of 1 watt per square meter.

(b) Determine the number of decibels of a sound with an intensity of 10^{-2} watt per square meter.

(c) The intensity of the sound in part (a) is 100 times as great as that in part (b). Is the number of decibels 100 times as great? Explain.

Synthesis

True or False? **In Exercises 91 and 92, determine whether the statement is true or false. Justify your answer.**

91. You can determine the graph of $f(x) = \log_6 x$ by graphing $g(x) = 6^x$ and reflecting it about the x-axis.

92. The graph of $f(x) = \log_3 x$ contains the point $(27, 3)$.

In Exercises 93–96, sketch the graph of f and g and describe the relationship between the graphs of f and g. What is the relationship between the functions f and g?

93. $f(x) = 3^x$, $g(x) = \log_3 x$

94. $f(x) = 5^x$, $g(x) = \log_5 x$

95. $f(x) = e^x$, $g(x) = \ln x$

96. $f(x) = 10^x$, $g(x) = \log x$

97. ***Graphical Analysis*** Use a graphing utility to graph f and g in the same viewing window and determine which is increasing at the greater rate as x approaches $+\infty$. What can you conclude about the rate of growth of the natural logarithmic function?

(a) $f(x) = \ln x$, $g(x) = \sqrt{x}$

(b) $f(x) = \ln x$, $g(x) = \sqrt[4]{x}$

98. (a) Complete the table for the function given by

$$f(x) = \frac{\ln x}{x}.$$

x	1	5	10	10^2	10^4	10^6
$f(x)$						

(b) Use the table in part (a) to determine what value $f(x)$ approaches as x increases without bound.

(c) Use a graphing utility to confirm the result of part (b).

99. ***Think About It*** The table of values was obtained by evaluating a function. Determine which of the statements may be true and which must be false.

x	1	2	8
y	0	1	3

(a) y is an exponential function of x.

(b) y is a logarithmic function of x.

(c) x is an exponential function of y.

(d) y is a linear function of x.

100. ***Writing*** Explain why $\log_a x$ is defined only for $0 < a < 1$ and $a > 1$.

In Exercises 101 and 102, (a) use a graphing utility to graph the function, (b) use the graph to determine the intervals in which the function is increasing and decreasing, and (c) approximate any relative maximum or minimum values of the function.

101. $f(x) = |\ln x|$

102. $h(x) = \ln(x^2 + 1)$

Skills Review

In Exercises 103–108, evaluate the function for $f(x) = 3x + 2$ and $g(x) = x^3 - 1$.

103. $(f + g)(2)$

104. $(f - g)(-1)$

105. $(fg)(6)$

106. $\left(\frac{f}{g}\right)(0)$

107. $(f \circ g)(7)$

108. $(g \circ f)(-3)$

3.3 Properties of Logarithms

What you should learn

- Use the change-of-base formula to rewrite and evaluate logarithmic expressions.
- Use properties of logarithms to evaluate or rewrite logarithmic expressions.
- Use properties of logarithms to expand or condense logarithmic expressions.
- Use logarithmic functions to model and solve real-life problems.

Why you should learn it

Logarithmic functions can be used to model and solve real-life problems. For instance, in Exercises 81–83 on page 244, a logarithmic function is used to model the relationship between the number of decibels and the intensity of a sound.

AP Photo/Stephen Chernin

Change of Base

Most calculators have only two types of log keys, one for common logarithms (base 10) and one for natural logarithms (base e). Although common logs and natural logs are the most frequently used, you may occasionally need to evaluate logarithms to other bases. To do this, you can use the following **change-of-base formula.**

Change-of-Base Formula

Let a, b, and x be positive real numbers such that $a \neq 1$ and $b \neq 1$. Then $\log_a x$ can be converted to a different base as follows.

Base b	*Base 10*	*Base e*
$\log_a x = \dfrac{\log_b x}{\log_b a}$	$\log_a x = \dfrac{\log x}{\log a}$	$\log_a x = \dfrac{\ln x}{\ln a}$

One way to look at the change-of-base formula is that logarithms to base a are simply *constant multiples* of logarithms to base b. The constant multiplier is $1/(\log_b a)$.

Example 1 Changing Bases Using Common Logarithms

a. $\log_4 25 = \dfrac{\log 25}{\log 4}$ $\log_a x = \dfrac{\log x}{\log a}$

$\approx \dfrac{1.39794}{0.60206}$ Use a calculator.

≈ 2.3219 Simplify.

b. $\log_2 12 = \dfrac{\log 12}{\log 2} \approx \dfrac{1.07918}{0.30103} \approx 3.5850$

✓CHECKPOINT Now try Exercise 1(a).

Example 2 Changing Bases Using Natural Logarithms

a. $\log_4 25 = \dfrac{\ln 25}{\ln 4}$ $\log_a x = \dfrac{\ln x}{\ln a}$

$\approx \dfrac{3.21888}{1.38629}$ Use a calculator.

≈ 2.3219 Simplify.

b. $\log_2 12 = \dfrac{\ln 12}{\ln 2} \approx \dfrac{2.48491}{0.69315} \approx 3.5850$

✓CHECKPOINT Now try Exercise 1(b).

Properties of Logarithms

You know from the preceding section that the logarithmic function with base a is the *inverse function* of the exponential function with base a. So, it makes sense that the properties of exponents should have corresponding properties involving logarithms. For instance, the exponential property $a^0 = 1$ has the corresponding logarithmic property $\log_a 1 = 0$.

STUDY TIP

There is no general property that can be used to rewrite $\log_a(u \pm v)$. Specifically, $\log_a(u + v)$ is *not* equal to $\log_a u + \log_a v$.

Properties of Logarithms

Let a be a positive number such that $a \neq 1$, and let n be a real number. If u and v are positive real numbers, the following properties are true.

	Logarithm with Base a	*Natural Logarithm*
1. Product Property:	$\log_a(uv) = \log_a u + \log_a v$	$\ln(uv) = \ln u + \ln v$
2. Quotient Property:	$\log_a \frac{u}{v} = \log_a u - \log_a v$	$\ln \frac{u}{v} = \ln u - \ln v$
3. Power Property:	$\log_a u^n = n \log_a u$	$\ln u^n = n \ln u$

For proofs of the properties listed above, see Proofs in Mathematics on page 278.

Example 3 Using Properties of Logarithms

Write each logarithm in terms of ln 2 and ln 3.

a. $\ln 6$ **b.** $\ln \frac{2}{27}$

Solution

a. $\ln 6 = \ln(2 \cdot 3)$ Rewrite 6 as $2 \cdot 3$.

$= \ln 2 + \ln 3$ Product Property

b. $\ln \frac{2}{27} = \ln 2 - \ln 27$ Quotient Property

$= \ln 2 - \ln 3^3$ Rewrite 27 as 3^3.

$= \ln 2 - 3 \ln 3$ Power Property

CHECKPOINT Now try Exercise 17.

The Granger Collection

Historical Note

John Napier, a Scottish mathematician, developed logarithms as a way to simplify some of the tedious calculations of his day. Beginning in 1594, Napier worked about 20 years on the invention of logarithms. Napier was only partially successful in his quest to simplify tedious calculations. Nonetheless, the development of logarithms was a step forward and received immediate recognition.

Example 4 Using Properties of Logarithms

Find the exact value of each expression without using a calculator.

a. $\log_5 \sqrt[3]{5}$ **b.** $\ln e^6 - \ln e^2$

Solution

a. $\log_5 \sqrt[3]{5} = \log_5 5^{1/3} = \frac{1}{3} \log_5 5 = \frac{1}{3}(1) = \frac{1}{3}$

b. $\ln e^6 - \ln e^2 = \ln \frac{e^6}{e^2} = \ln e^4 = 4 \ln e = 4(1) = 4$

CHECKPOINT Now try Exercise 23.

Rewriting Logarithmic Expressions

The properties of logarithms are useful for rewriting logarithmic expressions in forms that simplify the operations of algebra. This is true because these properties convert complicated products, quotients, and exponential forms into simpler sums, differences, and products, respectively.

Example 5 Expanding Logarithmic Expressions

Expand each logarithmic expression.

a. $\log_4 5x^3y$ **b.** $\ln \dfrac{\sqrt{3x-5}}{7}$

Solution

a. $\log_4 5x^3y = \log_4 5 + \log_4 x^3 + \log_4 y$ — Product Property

$= \log_4 5 + 3\log_4 x + \log_4 y$ — Power Property

b. $\ln \dfrac{\sqrt{3x-5}}{7} = \ln \dfrac{(3x-5)^{1/2}}{7}$ — Rewrite using rational exponent.

$= \ln(3x-5)^{1/2} - \ln 7$ — Quotient Property

$= \dfrac{1}{2}\ln(3x-5) - \ln 7$ — Power Property

CHECKPOINT Now try Exercise 47.

In Example 5, the properties of logarithms were used to *expand* logarithmic expressions. In Example 6, this procedure is reversed and the properties of logarithms are used to *condense* logarithmic expressions.

Exploration

Use a graphing utility to graph the functions given by

$$y_1 = \ln x - \ln(x-3)$$

and

$$y_2 = \ln \frac{x}{x-3}$$

in the same viewing window. Does the graphing utility show the functions with the same domain? If so, should it? Explain your reasoning.

Example 6 Condensing Logarithmic Expressions

Condense each logarithmic expression.

a. $\frac{1}{2}\log x + 3\log(x+1)$ **b.** $2\ln(x+2) - \ln x$

c. $\frac{1}{3}[\log_2 x + \log_2(x+1)]$

Solution

a. $\frac{1}{2}\log x + 3\log(x+1) = \log x^{1/2} + \log(x+1)^3$ — Power Property

$= \log\left[\sqrt{x}(x+1)^3\right]$ — Product Property

b. $2\ln(x+2) - \ln x = \ln(x+2)^2 - \ln x$ — Power Property

$= \ln \dfrac{(x+2)^2}{x}$ — Quotient Property

c. $\frac{1}{3}[\log_2 x + \log_2(x+1)] = \frac{1}{3}\{\log_2[x(x+1)]\}$ — Product Property

$= \log_2[x(x+1)]^{1/3}$ — Power Property

$= \log_2 \sqrt[3]{x(x+1)}$ — Rewrite with a radical.

CHECKPOINT Now try Exercise 69.

Application

One method of determining how the x- and y-values for a set of nonlinear data are related is to take the natural logarithm of each of the x- and y-values. If the points are graphed and fall on a line, then you can determine that the x- and y-values are related by the equation

$$\ln y = m \ln x$$

where m is the slope of the line.

Example 7 Finding a Mathematical Model

The table shows the mean distance x and the period (the time it takes a planet to orbit the sun) y for each of the six planets that are closest to the sun. In the table, the mean distance is given in terms of astronomical units (where Earth's mean distance is defined as 1.0), and the period is given in years. Find an equation that relates y and x.

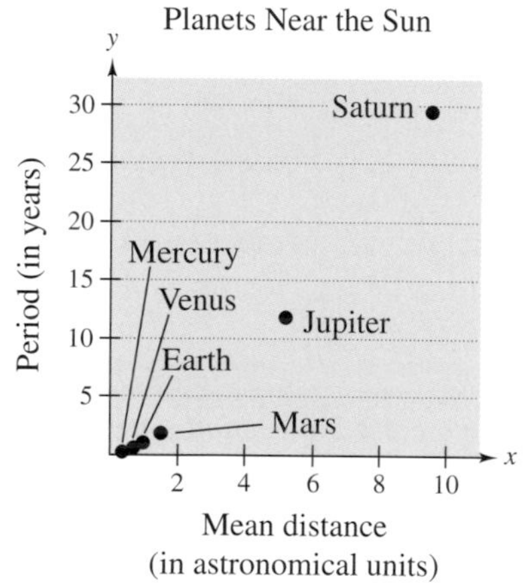

FIGURE 3.23

Planet	Mean distance, x	Period, y
Mercury	0.387	0.241
Venus	0.723	0.615
Earth	1.000	1.000
Mars	1.524	1.881
Jupiter	5.203	11.863
Saturn	9.537	29.447

Solution

The points in the table above are plotted in Figure 3.23. From this figure it is not clear how to find an equation that relates y and x. To solve this problem, take the natural logarithm of each of the x- and y-values in the table. This produces the following results.

Planet	Mercury	Venus	Earth	Mars	Jupiter	Saturn
$\ln x$	-0.949	-0.324	0.000	0.421	1.649	2.255
$\ln y$	-1.423	-0.486	0.000	0.632	2.473	3.383

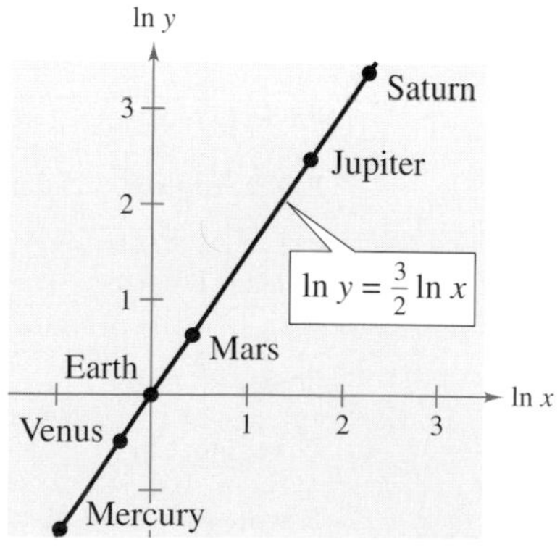

FIGURE 3.24

Now, by plotting the points in the second table, you can see that all six of the points appear to lie in a line (see Figure 3.24). Choose any two points to determine the slope of the line. Using the two points (0.421, 0.632) and (0, 0), you can determine that the slope of the line is

$$m = \frac{0.632 - 0}{0.421 - 0} \approx 1.5 = \frac{3}{2}.$$

By the point-slope form, the equation of the line is $Y = \frac{3}{2}X$, where $Y = \ln y$ and $X = \ln x$. You can therefore conclude that $\ln y = \frac{3}{2} \ln x$.

CHECKPOINT Now try Exercise 85.

3.3 Exercises

VOCABULARY CHECK:

In Exercises 1 and 2, fill in the blanks.

1. To evaluate a logarithm to any base, you can use the ________ formula.
2. The change-of-base formula for base e is given by $\log_a x =$ ________.

In Exercises 3–5, match the property of logarithms with its name.

3. $\log_a(uv) = \log_a u + \log_a v$ (a) Power Property
4. $\ln u^n = n \ln u$ (b) Quotient Property
5. $\log_a \frac{u}{v} = \log_a u - \log_a v$ (c) Product Property

---

In Exercises 1–8, rewrite the logarithm as a ratio of (a) common logarithms and (b) natural logarithms.

1. $\log_5 x$
2. $\log_3 x$
3. $\log_{1/5} x$
4. $\log_{1/3} x$
5. $\log_x \frac{3}{10}$
6. $\log_x \frac{3}{4}$
7. $\log_{2.6} x$
8. $\log_{7.1} x$

In Exercises 9–16, evaluate the logarithm using the change-of-base formula. Round your result to three decimal places.

9. $\log_3 7$
10. $\log_7 4$
11. $\log_{1/2} 4$
12. $\log_{1/4} 5$
13. $\log_9 0.4$
14. $\log_{20} 0.125$
15. $\log_{15} 1250$
16. $\log_3 0.015$

In Exercises 17–22, use the properties of logarithms to rewrite and simplify the logarithmic expression.

17. $\log_4 8$
18. $\log_2(4^2 \cdot 3^4)$
19. $\log_5 \frac{1}{250}$
20. $\log \frac{9}{300}$
21. $\ln(5e^6)$
22. $\ln \frac{6}{e^2}$

In Exercises 23–38, find the exact value of the logarithmic expression without using a calculator. (If this is not possible, state the reason.)

23. $\log_3 9$
24. $\log_5 \frac{1}{125}$
25. $\log_2 \sqrt[4]{8}$
26. $\log_6 \sqrt[3]{6}$
27. $\log_4 16^{1.2}$
28. $\log_3 81^{-0.2}$
29. $\log_3(-9)$
30. $\log_2(-16)$
31. $\ln e^{4.5}$
32. $3 \ln e^4$
33. $\ln \frac{1}{\sqrt{e}}$
34. $\ln \sqrt[4]{e^3}$
35. $\ln e^2 + \ln e^5$
36. $2 \ln e^6 - \ln e^5$
37. $\log_5 75 - \log_5 3$
38. $\log_4 2 + \log_4 32$

In Exercises 39–60, use the properties of logarithms to expand the expression as a sum, difference, and/or constant multiple of logarithms. (Assume all variables are positive.)

39. $\log_4 5x$
40. $\log_3 10z$
41. $\log_8 x^4$
42. $\log_{10} \frac{y}{2}$
43. $\log_5 \frac{5}{x}$
44. $\log_6 \frac{1}{z^3}$
45. $\ln \sqrt{z}$
46. $\ln \sqrt[3]{t}$
47. $\ln xyz^2$
48. $\log 4x^2 y$
49. $\ln z(z-1)^2,\ z > 1$
50. $\ln\left(\frac{x^2-1}{x^3}\right),\ x > 1$
51. $\log_2 \frac{\sqrt{a-1}}{9},\ a > 1$
52. $\ln \frac{6}{\sqrt{x^2+1}}$
53. $\ln \sqrt[3]{\frac{x}{y}}$
54. $\ln \sqrt{\frac{x^2}{y^3}}$
55. $\ln \frac{x^4\sqrt{y}}{z^5}$
56. $\log_2 \frac{\sqrt{x}\,y^4}{z^4}$
57. $\log_5 \frac{x^2}{y^2z^3}$
58. $\log_{10} \frac{xy^4}{z^5}$
59. $\ln \sqrt[4]{x^3(x^2+3)}$
60. $\ln \sqrt{x^2(x+2)}$

In Exercises 61–78, condense the expression to the logarithm of a single quantity.

61. $\ln x + \ln 3$

62. $\ln y + \ln t$

63. $\log_4 z - \log_4 y$

64. $\log_5 8 - \log_5 t$

65. $2 \log_2(x + 4)$

66. $\frac{2}{3} \log_7(z - 2)$

67. $\frac{1}{4} \log_3 5x$

68. $-4 \log_6 2x$

69. $\ln x - 3 \ln(x + 1)$

70. $2 \ln 8 + 5 \ln(z - 4)$

71. $\log x - 2 \log y + 3 \log z$

72. $3 \log_3 x + 4 \log_3 y - 4 \log_3 z$

73. $\ln x - 4[\ln(x + 2) + \ln(x - 2)]$

74. $4[\ln z + \ln(z + 5)] - 2 \ln(z - 5)$

75. $\frac{1}{3}[2 \ln(x + 3) + \ln x - \ln(x^2 - 1)]$

76. $2[3 \ln x - \ln(x + 1) - \ln(x - 1)]$

77. $\frac{1}{3}[\log_8 y + 2 \log_8(y + 4)] - \log_8(y - 1)$

78. $\frac{1}{2}[\log_4(x + 1) + 2 \log_4(x - 1)] + 6 \log_4 x$

In Exercises 79 and 80, compare the logarithmic quantities. If two are equal, explain why.

79. $\dfrac{\log_2 32}{\log_2 4}$, $\log_2 \dfrac{32}{4}$, $\log_2 32 - \log_2 4$

80. $\log_7 \sqrt{70}$, $\log_7 35$, $\frac{1}{2} + \log_7 \sqrt{10}$

Sound Intensity **In Exercises 81–83, use the following information. The relationship between the number of decibels β and the intensity of a sound I in watts per square meter is given by**

$$\beta = 10 \log\left(\frac{I}{10^{-12}}\right).$$

81. Use the properties of logarithms to write the formula in simpler form, and determine the number of decibels of a sound with an intensity of 10^{-6} watt per square meter.

82. Find the difference in loudness between an average office with an intensity of 1.26×10^{-7} watt per square meter and a broadcast studio with an intensity of 3.16×10^{-5} watt per square meter.

83. You and your roommate are playing your stereos at the same time and at the same intensity. How much louder is the music when both stereos are playing compared with just one stereo playing?

Model It

84. ***Human Memory Model*** Students participating in a psychology experiment attended several lectures and were given an exam. Every month for a year after the exam, the students were retested to see how much of the material they remembered. The average scores for the group can be modeled by the human memory model

$$f(t) = 90 - 15 \log(t + 1), \quad 0 \le t \le 12$$

where t is the time in months.

(a) Use the properties of logarithms to write the function in another form.

(b) What was the average score on the original exam $(t = 0)$?

(c) What was the average score after 4 months?

(d) What was the average score after 12 months?

(e) Use a graphing utility to graph the function over the specified domain.

(f) Use the graph in part (e) to determine when the average score will decrease to 75.

(g) Verify your answer to part (f) numerically.

85. ***Galloping Speeds of Animals*** Four-legged animals run with two different types of motion: trotting and galloping. An animal that is trotting has at least one foot on the ground at all times, whereas an animal that is galloping has all four feet off the ground at some point in its stride. The number of strides per minute at which an animal breaks from a trot to a gallop depends on the weight of the animal. Use the table to find a logarithmic equation that relates an animal's weight x (in pounds) and its lowest galloping speed y (in strides per minute).

Weight, x	Galloping Speed, y
25	191.5
35	182.7
50	173.8
75	164.2
500	125.9
1000	114.2

86. ***Comparing Models*** A cup of water at an initial temperature of 78° C is placed in a room at a constant temperature of 21° C. The temperature of the water is measured every 5 minutes during a half-hour period. The results are recorded as ordered pairs of the form (t, T), where t is the time (in minutes) and T is the temperature (in degrees Celsius).

(0, 78.0°), (5, 66.0°), (10, 57.5°), (15, 51.2°), (20, 46.3°), (25, 42.4°), (30, 39.6°)

(a) The graph of the model for the data should be asymptotic with the graph of the temperature of the room. Subtract the room temperature from each of the temperatures in the ordered pairs. Use a graphing utility to plot the data points (t, T) and $(t, T - 21)$.

(b) An exponential model for the data $(t, T - 21)$ is given by

$$T - 21 = 54.4(0.964)^t.$$

Solve for T and graph the model. Compare the result with the plot of the original data.

(c) Take the natural logarithms of the revised temperatures. Use a graphing utility to plot the points $(t, \ln(T - 21))$ and observe that the points appear to be linear. Use the *regression* feature of the graphing utility to fit a line to these data. This resulting line has the form

$$\ln(T - 21) = at + b.$$

Use the properties of the logarithms to solve for T. Verify that the result is equivalent to the model in part (b).

(d) Fit a rational model to the data. Take the reciprocals of the y-coordinates of the revised data points to generate the points

$$\left(t, \frac{1}{T - 21}\right).$$

Use a graphing utility to graph these points and observe that they appear to be linear. Use the *regression* feature of a graphing utility to fit a line to these data. The resulting line has the form

$$\frac{1}{T - 21} = at + b.$$

Solve for T, and use a graphing utility to graph the rational function and the original data points.

(e) Write a short paragraph explaining why the transformations of the data were necessary to obtain each model. Why did taking the logarithms of the temperatures lead to a linear scatter plot? Why did taking the reciprocals of the temperature lead to a linear scatter plot?

Synthesis

True or False? **In Exercises 87–92, determine whether the statement is true or false given that $f(x) = \ln x$. Justify your answer.**

87. $f(0) = 0$

88. $f(ax) = f(a) + f(x), \quad a > 0, x > 0$

89. $f(x - 2) = f(x) - f(2), \quad x > 2$

90. $\sqrt{f(x)} = \frac{1}{2}f(x)$

91. If $f(u) = 2f(v)$, then $v = u^2$.

92. If $f(x) < 0$, then $0 < x < 1$.

93. ***Proof*** Prove that $\log_b \dfrac{u}{v} = \log_b u - \log_b v$.

94. ***Proof*** Prove that $\log_b u^n = n \log_b u$.

In Exercises 95–100, use the change-of-base formula to rewrite the logarithm as a ratio of logarithms. Then use a graphing utility to graph both functions in the same viewing window to verify that the functions are equivalent.

95. $f(x) = \log_2 x$

96. $f(x) = \log_4 x$

97. $f(x) = \log_{1/2} x$

98. $f(x) = \log_{1/4} x$

99. $f(x) = \log_{11.8} x$

100. $f(x) = \log_{12.4} x$

101. ***Think About It*** Consider the functions below.

$$f(x) = \ln \frac{x}{2}, \quad g(x) = \frac{\ln x}{\ln 2}, \quad h(x) = \ln x - \ln 2$$

Which two functions should have identical graphs? Verify your answer by sketching the graphs of all three functions on the same set of coordinate axes.

102. ***Exploration*** For how many integers between 1 and 20 can the natural logarithms be approximated given that $\ln 2 \approx 0.6931$, $\ln 3 \approx 1.0986$, and $\ln 5 \approx 1.6094$? Approximate these logarithms (do not use a calculator).

Skills Review

In Exercises 103–106, simplify the expression.

103. $\dfrac{24xy^{-2}}{16x^{-3}y}$

104. $\left(\dfrac{2x^2}{3y}\right)^{-3}$

105. $(18x^3y^4)^{-3}(18x^3y^4)^3$

106. $xy(x^{-1} + y^{-1})^{-1}$

In Exercises 107–110, solve the equation.

107. $3x^2 + 2x - 1 = 0$

108. $4x^2 - 5x + 1 = 0$

109. $\dfrac{2}{3x + 1} = \dfrac{x}{4}$

110. $\dfrac{5}{x - 1} = \dfrac{2x}{3}$

3.4 Exponential and Logarithmic Equations

What you should learn

- Solve simple exponential and logarithmic equations.
- Solve more complicated exponential equations.
- Solve more complicated logarithmic equations.
- Use exponential and logarithmic equations to model and solve real-life problems.

Why you should learn it

Exponential and logarithmic equations are used to model and solve life science applications. For instance, in Exercise 112, on page 255, a logarithmic function is used to model the number of trees per acre given the average diameter of the trees.

© James Marshall/Corbis

Introduction

So far in this chapter, you have studied the definitions, graphs, and properties of exponential and logarithmic functions. In this section, you will study procedures for *solving equations* involving these exponential and logarithmic functions.

There are two basic strategies for solving exponential or logarithmic equations. The first is based on the One-to-One Properties and was used to solve simple exponential and logarithmic equations in Sections 3.1 and 3.2. The second is based on the Inverse Properties. For $a > 0$ and $a \neq 1$, the following properties are true for all x and y for which $\log_a x$ and $\log_a y$ are defined.

One-to-One Properties

$a^x = a^y$ if and only if $x = y$.

$\log_a x = \log_a y$ if and only if $x = y$.

Inverse Properties

$a^{\log_a x} = x$

$\log_a a^x = x$

Example 1 **Solving Simple Equations**

	Original Equation	*Rewritten Equation*	*Solution*	*Property*
a.	$2^x = 32$	$2^x = 2^5$	$x = 5$	One-to-One
b.	$\ln x - \ln 3 = 0$	$\ln x = \ln 3$	$x = 3$	One-to-One
c.	$\left(\frac{1}{3}\right)^x = 9$	$3^{-x} = 3^2$	$x = -2$	One-to-One
d.	$e^x = 7$	$\ln e^x = \ln 7$	$x = \ln 7$	Inverse
e.	$\ln x = -3$	$e^{\ln x} = e^{-3}$	$x = e^{-3}$	Inverse
f.	$\log x = -1$	$10^{\log x} = 10^{-1}$	$x = 10^{-1} = \frac{1}{10}$	Inverse

✓CHECKPOINT Now try Exercise 13.

The strategies used in Example 1 are summarized as follows.

Strategies for Solving Exponential and Logarithmic Equations

1. Rewrite the original equation in a form that allows the use of the One-to-One Properties of exponential or logarithmic functions.
2. Rewrite an *exponential* equation in logarithmic form and apply the Inverse Property of logarithmic functions.
3. Rewrite a *logarithmic* equation in exponential form and apply the Inverse Property of exponential functions.

Solving Exponential Equations

Example 2 **Solving Exponential Equations**

Solve each equation and approximate the result to three decimal places if necessary.

a. $e^{-x^2} = e^{-3x-4}$ **b.** $3(2^x) = 42$

Solution

a.

$e^{-x^2} = e^{-3x-4}$	Write original equation.
$-x^2 = -3x - 4$	One-to-One Property
$x^2 - 3x - 4 = 0$	Write in general form.
$(x + 1)(x - 4) = 0$	Factor.
$(x + 1) = 0 \Rightarrow x = -1$	Set 1st factor equal to 0.
$(x - 4) = 0 \Rightarrow x = 4$	Set 2nd factor equal to 0.

The solutions are $x = -1$ and $x = 4$. Check these in the original equation.

b.

$3(2^x) = 42$	Write original equation.
$2^x = 14$	Divide each side by 3.
$\log_2 2^x = \log_2 14$	Take log (base 2) of each side.
$x = \log_2 14$	Inverse Property
$x = \dfrac{\ln 14}{\ln 2} \approx 3.807$	Change-of-base formula

The solution is $x = \log_2 14 \approx 3.807$. Check this in the original equation.

✓CHECKPOINT Now try Exercise 25.

In Example 2(b), the exact solution is $x = \log_2 14$ and the approximate solution is $x \approx 3.807$. An exact answer is preferred when the solution is an intermediate step in a larger problem. For a final answer, an approximate solution is easier to comprehend.

Example 3 **Solving an Exponential Equation**

Solve $e^x + 5 = 60$ and approximate the result to three decimal places.

STUDY TIP

Remember that the natural logarithmic function has a base of e.

Solution

$e^x + 5 = 60$	Write original equation.
$e^x = 55$	Subtract 5 from each side.
$\ln e^x = \ln 55$	Take natural log of each side.
$x = \ln 55 \approx 4.007$	Inverse Property

The solution is $x = \ln 55 \approx 4.007$. Check this in the original equation.

✓CHECKPOINT Now try Exercise 51.

Example 4 Solving an Exponential Equation

Solve $2(3^{2t-5}) - 4 = 11$ and approximate the result to three decimal places.

Solution

$2(3^{2t-5}) - 4 = 11$	Write original equation.
$2(3^{2t-5}) = 15$	Add 4 to each side.
$3^{2t-5} = \dfrac{15}{2}$	Divide each side by 2.
$\log_3 3^{2t-5} = \log_3 \dfrac{15}{2}$	Take log (base 3) of each side.
$2t - 5 = \log_3 \dfrac{15}{2}$	Inverse Property
$2t = 5 + \log_3 7.5$	Add 5 to each side.
$t = \dfrac{5}{2} + \dfrac{1}{2}\log_3 7.5$	Divide each side by 2.
$t \approx 3.417$	Use a calculator.

The solution is $t = \frac{5}{2} + \frac{1}{2}\log_3 7.5 \approx 3.417$. Check this in the original equation.

CHECKPOINT Now try Exercise 53.

STUDY TIP

Remember that to evaluate a logarithm such as $\log_3 7.5$, you need to use the change-of-base formula.

$$\log_3 7.5 = \frac{\ln 7.5}{\ln 3} \approx 1.834$$

When an equation involves two or more exponential expressions, you can still use a procedure similar to that demonstrated in Examples 2, 3, and 4. However, the algebra is a bit more complicated.

Example 5 Solving an Exponential Equation of Quadratic Type

Solve $e^{2x} - 3e^x + 2 = 0$.

Algebraic Solution

$e^{2x} - 3e^x + 2 = 0$	Write original equation.
$(e^x)^2 - 3e^x + 2 = 0$	Write in quadratic form.
$(e^x - 2)(e^x - 1) = 0$	Factor.
$e^x - 2 = 0$	Set 1st factor equal to 0.
$x = \ln 2$	Solution
$e^x - 1 = 0$	Set 2nd factor equal to 0.
$x = 0$	Solution

The solutions are $x = \ln 2 \approx 0.693$ and $x = 0$. Check these in the original equation.

CHECKPOINT Now try Exercise 67.

Graphical Solution

Use a graphing utility to graph $y = e^{2x} - 3e^x + 2$. Use the *zero* or *root* feature or the *zoom* and *trace* features of the graphing utility to approximate the values of x for which $y = 0$. In Figure 3.25, you can see that the zeros occur at $x = 0$ and at $x \approx 0.693$. So, the solutions are $x = 0$ and $x \approx 0.693$.

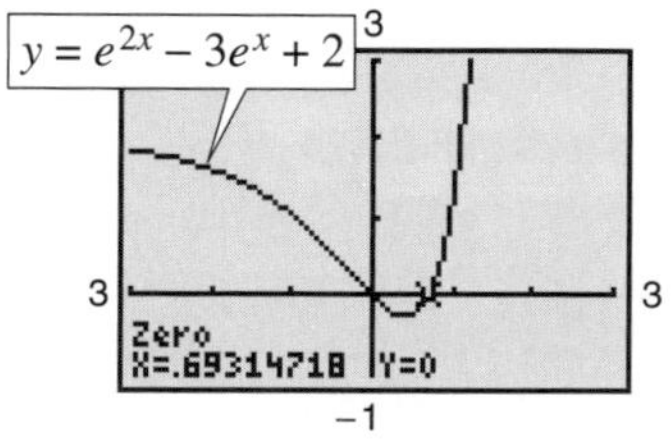

FIGURE 3.25

Solving Logarithmic Equations

To solve a logarithmic equation, you can write it in exponential form.

$\ln x = 3$ — Logarithmic form

$e^{\ln x} = e^3$ — Exponentiate each side.

$x = e^3$ — Exponential form

This procedure is called *exponentiating* each side of an equation.

Example 6 **Solving Logarithmic Equations**

> **STUDY TIP**
>
> Remember to check your solutions in the original equation when solving equations to verify that the answer is correct and to make sure that the answer lies in the domain of the original equation.

a. $\ln x = 2$ — Original equation

$e^{\ln x} = e^2$ — Exponentiate each side.

$x = e^2$ — Inverse Property

b. $\log_3(5x - 1) = \log_3(x + 7)$ — Original equation

$5x - 1 = x + 7$ — One-to-One Property

$4x = 8$ — Add $-x$ and 1 to each side.

$x = 2$ — Divide each side by 4.

c. $\log_6(3x + 14) - \log_6 5 = \log_6 2x$ — Original equation

$\log_6\left(\frac{3x + 14}{5}\right) = \log_6 2x$ — Quotient Property of Logarithms

$\frac{3x + 14}{5} = 2x$ — One-to-One Property

$3x + 14 = 10x$ — Cross multiply.

$-7x = -14$ — Isolate x.

$x = 2$ — Divide each side by -7.

CHECKPOINT Now try Exercise 77.

Example 7 **Solving a Logarithmic Equation**

Solve $5 + 2 \ln x = 4$ and approximate the result to three decimal places.

Solution

$5 + 2 \ln x = 4$ — Write original equation.

$2 \ln x = -1$ — Subtract 5 from each side.

$\ln x = -\frac{1}{2}$ — Divide each side by 2.

$e^{\ln x} = e^{-1/2}$ — Exponentiate each side.

$x = e^{-1/2}$ — Inverse Property

$x \approx 0.607$ — Use a calculator.

CHECKPOINT Now try Exercise 85.

Example 8 Solving a Logarithmic Equation

Solve $2 \log_5 3x = 4$.

Solution

$$2 \log_5 3x = 4 \qquad \text{Write original equation.}$$

$$\log_5 3x = 2 \qquad \text{Divide each side by 2.}$$

$$5^{\log_5 3x} = 5^2 \qquad \text{Exponentiate each side (base 5).}$$

$$3x = 25 \qquad \text{Inverse Property}$$

$$x = \frac{25}{3} \qquad \text{Divide each side by 3.}$$

The solution is $x = \frac{25}{3}$. Check this in the original equation.

✓CHECKPOINT Now try Exercise 87.

STUDY TIP

Notice in Example 9 that the logarithmic part of the equation is condensed into a single logarithm before exponentiating each side of the equation.

Because the domain of a logarithmic function generally does not include all real numbers, you should be sure to check for extraneous solutions of logarithmic equations.

Example 9 Checking for Extraneous Solutions

Solve $\log 5x + \log(x - 1) = 2$.

Algebraic Solution

$$\log 5x + \log(x - 1) = 2 \qquad \text{Write original equation.}$$

$$\log[5x(x - 1)] = 2 \qquad \text{Product Property of Logarithms}$$

$$10^{\log(5x^2 - 5x)} = 10^2 \qquad \text{Exponentiate each side (base 10).}$$

$$5x^2 - 5x = 100 \qquad \text{Inverse Property}$$

$$x^2 - x - 20 = 0 \qquad \text{Write in general form.}$$

$$(x - 5)(x + 4) = 0 \qquad \text{Factor.}$$

$$x - 5 = 0 \qquad \text{Set 1st factor equal to 0.}$$

$$x = 5 \qquad \text{Solution}$$

$$x + 4 = 0 \qquad \text{Set 2nd factor equal to 0.}$$

$$x = -4 \qquad \text{Solution}$$

The solutions appear to be $x = 5$ and $x = -4$. However, when you check these in the original equation, you can see that $x = 5$ is the only solution.

✓CHECKPOINT Now try Exercise 99.

Graphical Solution

Use a graphing utility to graph $y_1 = \log 5x + \log(x - 1)$ and $y_2 = 2$ in the same viewing window. From the graph shown in Figure 3.26, it appears that the graphs intersect at one point. Use the *intersect* feature or the *zoom* and *trace* features to determine that the graphs intersect at approximately $(5, 2)$. So, the solution is $x = 5$. Verify that 5 is an exact solution algebraically.

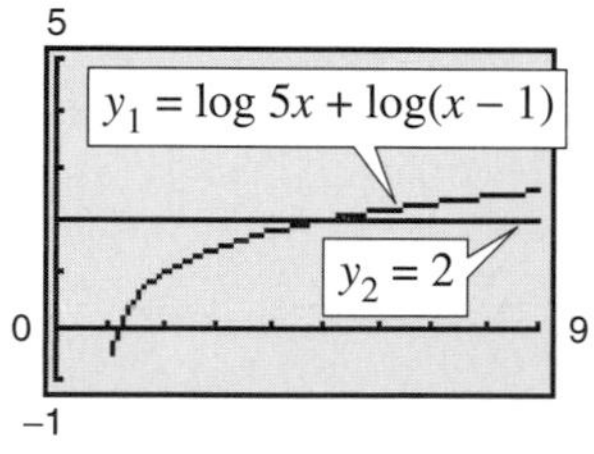

FIGURE 3.26

In Example 9, the domain of $\log 5x$ is $x > 0$ and the domain of $\log(x - 1)$ is $x > 1$, so the domain of the original equation is $x > 1$. Because the domain is all real numbers greater than 1, the solution $x = -4$ is extraneous. The graph in Figure 3.26 verifies this concept.

Applications

Example 10 Doubling an Investment

You have deposited \$500 in an account that pays 6.75% interest, compounded continuously. How long will it take your money to double?

Solution

Using the formula for continuous compounding, you can find that the balance in the account is

$$A = Pe^{rt}$$

$$A = 500e^{0.0675t}.$$

To find the time required for the balance to double, let $A = 1000$ and solve the resulting equation for t.

$500e^{0.0675t} = 1000$	Let $A = 1000$.
$e^{0.0675t} = 2$	Divide each side by 500.
$\ln e^{0.0675t} = \ln 2$	Take natural log of each side.
$0.0675t = \ln 2$	Inverse Property
$t = \dfrac{\ln 2}{0.0675}$	Divide each side by 0.0675.
$t \approx 10.27$	Use a calculator.

The balance in the account will double after approximately 10.27 years. This result is demonstrated graphically in Figure 3.27.

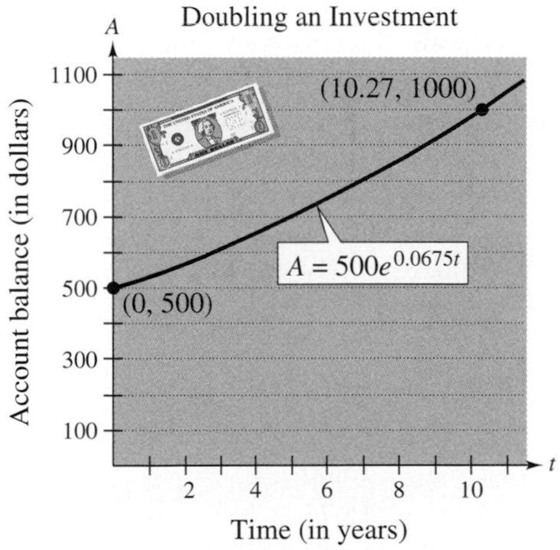

FIGURE 3.27

✓CHECKPOINT Now try Exercise 107.

In Example 10, an approximate answer of 10.27 years is given. Within the context of the problem, the exact solution, $(\ln 2)/0.0675$ years, does not make sense as an answer.

Exploration

The *effective yield* of a savings plan is the percent increase in the balance after 1 year. Find the effective yield for each savings plan when \$1000 is deposited in a savings account.

a. 7% annual interest rate, compounded annually

b. 7% annual interest rate, compounded continuously

c. 7% annual interest rate, compounded quarterly

d. 7.25% annual interest rate, compounded quarterly

Which savings plan has the greatest effective yield? Which savings plan will have the highest balance after 5 years?

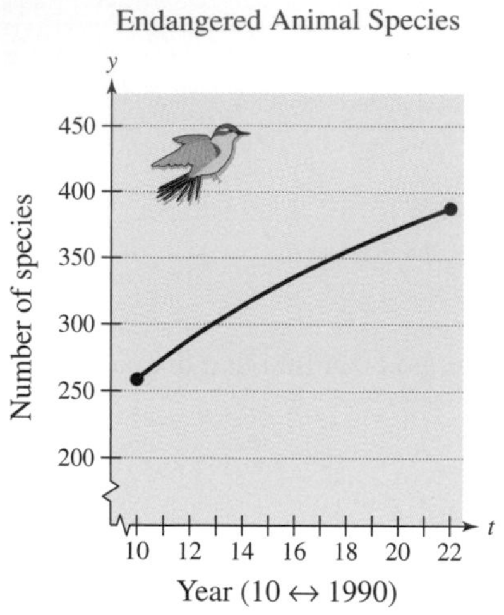

FIGURE 3.28

Example 11 Endangered Animals

The number y of endangered animal species in the United States from 1990 to 2002 can be modeled by

$$y = -119 + 164 \ln t, \quad 10 \le t \le 22$$

where t represents the year, with $t = 10$ corresponding to 1990 (see Figure 3.28). During which year did the number of endangered animal species reach 357? (Source: U.S. Fish and Wildlife Service)

Solution

$-119 + 164 \ln t = y$ — Write original equation.

$-119 + 164 \ln t = 357$ — Substitute 357 for y.

$164 \ln t = 476$ — Add 119 to each side.

$\ln t = \dfrac{476}{164}$ — Divide each side by 164.

$e^{\ln t} \approx e^{476/164}$ — Exponentiate each side.

$t \approx e^{476/164}$ — Inverse Property

$t \approx 18$ — Use a calculator.

The solution is $t \approx 18$. Because $t = 10$ represents 1990, it follows that the number of endangered animals reached 357 in 1998.

CHECKPOINT Now try Exercise 113.

WRITING ABOUT MATHEMATICS

Comparing Mathematical Models The table shows the U.S. Postal Service rates y for sending an express mail package for selected years from 1985 through 2002, where $x = 5$ represents 1985. (Source: U.S. Postal Service)

Year, x	Rate, y
5	10.75
8	12.00
11	13.95
15	15.00
19	15.75
21	16.00
22	17.85

a. Create a scatter plot of the data. Find a linear model for the data, and add its graph to your scatter plot. According to this model, when will the rate for sending an express mail package reach \$19.00?

b. Create a new table showing values for $\ln x$ and $\ln y$ and create a scatter plot of these transformed data. Use the method illustrated in Example 7 in Section 3.3 to find a model for the transformed data, and add its graph to your scatter plot. According to this model, when will the rate for sending an express mail package reach \$19.00?

c. Solve the model in part (b) for y, and add its graph to your scatter plot in part (a). Which model better fits the original data? Which model will better predict future rates? Explain.

3.4 Exercises

VOCABULARY CHECK: Fill in the blanks.

1. To ________ an equation in x means to find all values of x for which the equation is true.

2. To solve exponential and logarithmic equations, you can use the following One-to-One and Inverse Properties.

(a) $a^x = a^y$ if and only if ________.

(b) $\log_a x = \log_a y$ if and only if ________.

(c) $a^{\log_a x} =$ ________

(d) $\log_a a^x =$ ________

3. An ________ solution does not satisfy the original equation.

In Exercises 1–8, determine whether each x-value is a solution (or an approximate solution) of the equation.

1. $4^{2x-7} = 64$

(a) $x = 5$

(b) $x = 2$

2. $2^{3x+1} = 32$

(a) $x = -1$

(b) $x = 2$

3. $3e^{x+2} = 75$

(a) $x = -2 + e^{25}$

(b) $x = -2 + \ln 25$

(c) $x \approx 1.219$

4. $2e^{5x+2} = 12$

(a) $x = \frac{1}{5}(-2 + \ln 6)$

(b) $x = \dfrac{\ln 6}{5 \ln 2}$

(c) $x \approx -0.0416$

5. $\log_4(3x) = 3$

(a) $x \approx 21.333$

(b) $x = -4$

(c) $x = \frac{64}{3}$

6. $\log_2(x + 3) = 10$

(a) $x = 1021$

(b) $x = 17$

(c) $x = 10^2 - 3$

7. $\ln(2x + 3) = 5.8$

(a) $x = \frac{1}{2}(-3 + \ln 5.8)$

(b) $x = \frac{1}{2}(-3 + e^{5.8})$

(c) $x \approx 163.650$

8. $\ln(x - 1) = 3.8$

(a) $x = 1 + e^{3.8}$

(b) $x \approx 45.701$

(c) $x = 1 + \ln 3.8$

In Exercises 9–20, solve for x.

9. $4^x = 16$

10. $3^x = 243$

11. $\left(\frac{1}{2}\right)^x = 32$

12. $\left(\frac{1}{4}\right)^x = 64$

13. $\ln x - \ln 2 = 0$

14. $\ln x - \ln 5 = 0$

15. $e^x = 2$

16. $e^x = 4$

17. $\ln x = -1$

18. $\ln x = -7$

19. $\log_4 x = 3$

20. $\log_5 x = -3$

In Exercises 21–24, approximate the point of intersection of the graphs of f and g. Then solve the equation $f(x) = g(x)$ algebraically to verify your approximation.

21. $f(x) = 2^x$

$g(x) = 8$

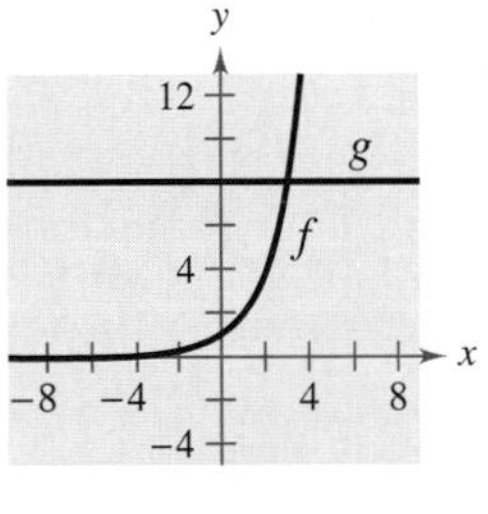

22. $f(x) = 27^x$

$g(x) = 9$

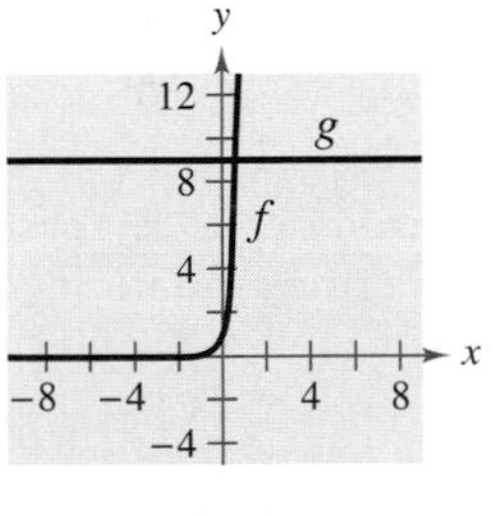

23. $f(x) = \log_3 x$

$g(x) = 2$

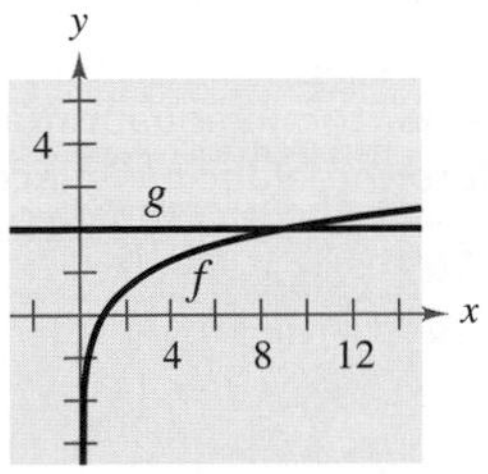

24. $f(x) = \ln(x - 4)$

$g(x) = 0$

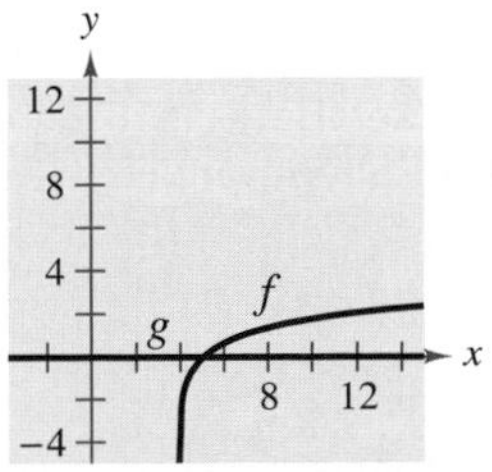

In Exercises 25–66, solve the exponential equation algebraically. Approximate the result to three decimal places.

25. $e^x = e^{x^2-2}$

26. $e^{2x} = e^{x^2-8}$

27. $e^{x^2-3} = e^{x-2}$

28. $e^{-x^2} = e^{x^2-2x}$

29. $4(3^x) = 20$

30. $2(5^x) = 32$

31. $2e^x = 10$

32. $4e^x = 91$

33. $e^x - 9 = 19$

34. $6^x + 10 = 47$

35. $3^{2x} = 80$

36. $6^{5x} = 3000$

37. $5^{-t/2} = 0.20$

38. $4^{-3t} = 0.10$

39. $3^{x-1} = 27$

40. $2^{x-3} = 32$

41. $2^{3-x} = 565$

42. $8^{-2-x} = 431$

43. $8(10^{3x}) = 12$

44. $5(10^{x-6}) = 7$

45. $3(5^{x-1}) = 21$

46. $8(3^{6-x}) = 40$

47. $e^{3x} = 12$

48. $e^{2x} = 50$

49. $500e^{-x} = 300$

50. $1000e^{-4x} = 75$

51. $7 - 2e^x = 5$

52. $-14 + 3e^x = 11$

53. $6(2^{3x-1}) - 7 = 9$

54. $8(4^{6-2x}) + 13 = 41$

55. $e^{2x} - 4e^x - 5 = 0$

56. $e^{2x} - 5e^x + 6 = 0$

57. $e^{2x} - 3e^x - 4 = 0$

58. $e^{2x} + 9e^x + 36 = 0$

59. $\dfrac{500}{100 - e^{x/2}} = 20$

60. $\dfrac{400}{1 + e^{-x}} = 350$

61. $\dfrac{3000}{2 + e^{2x}} = 2$

62. $\dfrac{119}{e^{6x} - 14} = 7$

63. $\left(1 + \dfrac{0.065}{365}\right)^{365t} = 4$

64. $\left(4 - \dfrac{2.471}{40}\right)^{9t} = 21$

65. $\left(1 + \dfrac{0.10}{12}\right)^{12t} = 2$

66. $\left(16 - \dfrac{0.878}{26}\right)^{3t} = 30$

In Exercises 67–74, use a graphing utility to graph and solve the equation. Approximate the result to three decimal places. Verify your result algebraically.

67. $6e^{1-x} = 25$

68. $-4e^{-x-1} + 15 = 0$

69. $3e^{3x/2} = 962$

70. $8e^{-2x/3} = 11$

71. $e^{0.09t} = 3$

72. $-e^{1.8x} + 7 = 0$

73. $e^{0.125t} - 8 = 0$

74. $e^{2.724x} = 29$

In Exercises 75–102, solve the logarithmic equation algebraically. Approximate the result to three decimal places.

75. $\ln x = -3$

76. $\ln x = 2$

77. $\ln 2x = 2.4$

78. $\ln 4x = 1$

79. $\log x = 6$

80. $\log 3z = 2$

81. $3 \ln 5x = 10$

82. $2 \ln x = 7$

83. $\ln\sqrt{x + 2} = 1$

84. $\ln\sqrt{x - 8} = 5$

85. $7 + 3 \ln x = 5$

86. $2 - 6 \ln x = 10$

87. $6 \log_3(0.5x) = 11$

88. $5 \log_{10}(x - 2) = 11$

89. $\ln x - \ln(x + 1) = 2$

90. $\ln x + \ln(x + 1) = 1$

91. $\ln x + \ln(x - 2) = 1$

92. $\ln x + \ln(x + 3) = 1$

93. $\ln(x + 5) = \ln(x - 1) - \ln(x + 1)$

94. $\ln(x + 1) - \ln(x - 2) = \ln x$

95. $\log_2(2x - 3) = \log_2(x + 4)$

96. $\log(x - 6) = \log(2x + 1)$

97. $\log(x + 4) - \log x = \log(x + 2)$

98. $\log_2 x + \log_2(x + 2) = \log_2(x + 6)$

99. $\log_4 x - \log_4(x - 1) = \frac{1}{2}$

100. $\log_3 x + \log_3(x - 8) = 2$

101. $\log 8x - \log\left(1 + \sqrt{x}\right) = 2$

102. $\log 4x - \log\left(12 + \sqrt{x}\right) = 2$

In Exercises 103–106, use a graphing utility to graph and solve the equation. Approximate the result to three decimal places. Verify your result algebraically.

103. $7 = 2^x$

104. $500 = 1500e^{-x/2}$

105. $3 - \ln x = 0$

106. $10 - 4 \ln(x - 2) = 0$

Compound Interest **In Exercises 107 and 108, \$2500 is invested in an account at interest rate *r*, compounded continuously. Find the time required for the amount to (a) double and (b) triple.**

107. $r = 0.085$

108. $r = 0.12$

109. ***Demand*** The demand equation for a microwave oven is given by

$$p = 500 - 0.5(e^{0.004x}).$$

Find the demand x for a price of (a) $p = \$350$ and (b) $p = \$300$.

110. ***Demand*** The demand equation for a hand-held electronic organizer is

$$p = 5000\left(1 - \frac{4}{4 + e^{-0.002x}}\right).$$

Find the demand x for a price of (a) $p = \$600$ and (b) $p = \$400$.

111. ***Forest Yield*** The yield V (in millions of cubic feet per acre) for a forest at age t years is given by

$$V = 6.7e^{-48.1/t}.$$

(a) Use a graphing utility to graph the function.

(b) Determine the horizontal asymptote of the function. Interpret its meaning in the context of the problem.

(c) Find the time necessary to obtain a yield of 1.3 million cubic feet.

112. ***Trees per Acre*** The number N of trees of a given species per acre is approximated by the model $N = 68(10^{-0.04x})$, $5 \le x \le 40$ where x is the average diameter of the trees (in inches) 3 feet above the ground. Use the model to approximate the average diameter of the trees in a test plot when $N = 21$.

113. ***Medicine*** The number y of hospitals in the United States from 1995 to 2002 can be modeled by

$$y = 7312 - 630.0 \ln t, \quad 5 \le t \le 12$$

where t represents the year, with $t = 5$ corresponding to 1995. During which year did the number of hospitals reach 5800? (Source: Health Forum)

114. ***Sports*** The number y of daily fee golf facilities in the United States from 1995 to 2003 can be modeled by $y = 4381 + 1883.6 \ln t$, $5 \le t \le 13$ where t represents the year, with $t = 5$ corresponding to 1995. During which year did the number of daily fee golf facilities reach 9000? (Source: National Golf Foundation)

115. ***Average Heights*** The percent m of American males between the ages of 18 and 24 who are no more than x inches tall is modeled by

$$m(x) = \frac{100}{1 + e^{-0.6114(x-69.71)}}$$

and the percent f of American females between the ages of 18 and 24 who are no more than x inches tall is modeled by

$$f(x) = \frac{100}{1 + e^{-0.66607(x-64.51)}}.$$

(Source: U.S. National Center for Health Statistics)

(a) Use the graph to determine any horizontal asymptotes of the graphs of the functions. Interpret the meaning in the context of the problem.

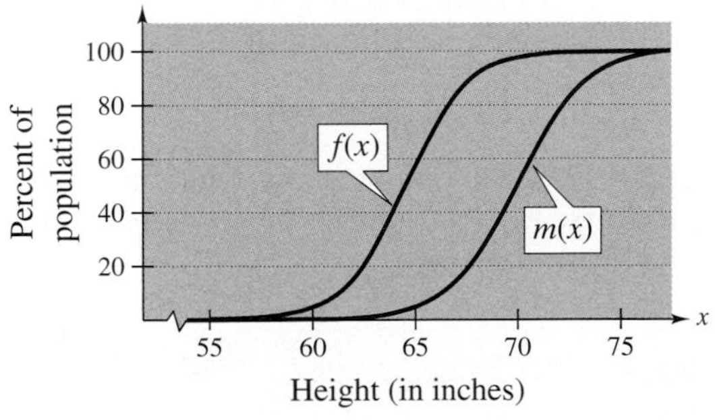

(b) What is the average height of each sex?

116. ***Learning Curve*** In a group project in learning theory, a mathematical model for the proportion P of correct responses after n trials was found to be

$$P = \frac{0.83}{1 + e^{-0.2n}}.$$

(a) Use a graphing utility to graph the function.

(b) Use the graph to determine any horizontal asymptotes of the graph of the function. Interpret the meaning of the upper asymptote in the context of this problem.

(c) After how many trials will 60% of the responses be correct?

Model It

117. ***Automobiles*** Automobiles are designed with crumple zones that help protect their occupants in crashes. The crumple zones allow the occupants to move short distances when the automobiles come to abrupt stops. The greater the distance moved, the fewer g's the crash victims experience. (One g is equal to the acceleration due to gravity. For very short periods of time, humans have withstood as much as 40 g's.) In crash tests with vehicles moving at 90 kilometers per hour, analysts measured the numbers of g's experienced during deceleration by crash dummies that were permitted to move x meters during impact. The data are shown in the table.

x	g's
0.2	158
0.4	80
0.6	53
0.8	40
1.0	32

A model for the data is given by

$$y = -3.00 + 11.88 \ln x + \frac{36.94}{x}$$

where y is the number of g's.

(a) Complete the table using the model.

x	0.2	0.4	0.6	0.8	1.0
y					

(b) Use a graphing utility to graph the data points and the model in the same viewing window. How do they compare?

(c) Use the model to estimate the distance traveled during impact if the passenger deceleration must not exceed 30 g's.

(d) Do you think it is practical to lower the number of g's experienced during impact to fewer than 23? Explain your reasoning.

118. ***Data Analysis*** An object at a temperature of 160°C was removed from a furnace and placed in a room at 20°C. The temperature T of the object was measured each hour h and recorded in the table. A model for the data is given by $T = 20[1 + 7(2^{-h})]$. The graph of this model is shown in the figure.

Hour, h	Temperature, T
0	160°
1	90°
2	56°
3	38°
4	29°
5	24°

(a) Use the graph to identify the horizontal asymptote of the model and interpret the asymptote in the context of the problem.

(b) Use the model to approximate the time when the temperature of the object was 100°C.

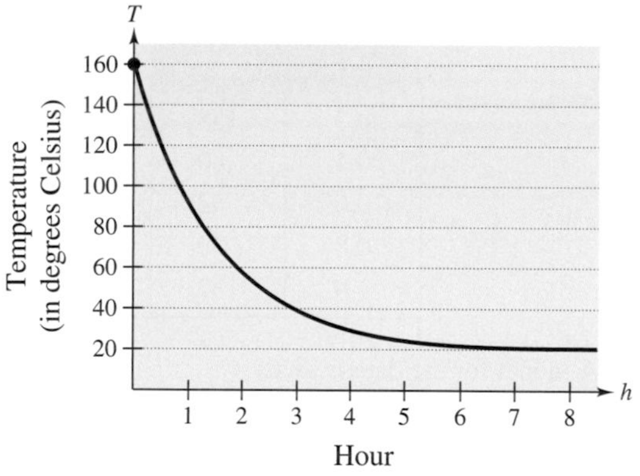

Synthesis

True or False? **In Exercises 119–122, rewrite each verbal statement as an equation. Then decide whether the statement is true or false. Justify your answer.**

119. The logarithm of the product of two numbers is equal to the sum of the logarithms of the numbers.

120. The logarithm of the sum of two numbers is equal to the product of the logarithms of the numbers.

121. The logarithm of the difference of two numbers is equal to the difference of the logarithms of the numbers.

122. The logarithm of the quotient of two numbers is equal to the difference of the logarithms of the numbers.

123. ***Think About It*** Is it possible for a logarithmic equation to have more than one extraneous solution? Explain.

124. ***Finance*** You are investing P dollars at an annual interest rate of r, compounded continuously, for t years. Which of the following would result in the highest value of the investment? Explain your reasoning.

(a) Double the amount you invest.

(b) Double your interest rate.

(c) Double the number of years.

125. ***Think About It*** Are the times required for the investments in Exercises 107 and 108 to quadruple twice as long as the times for them to double? Give a reason for your answer and verify your answer algebraically.

126. ***Writing*** Write two or three sentences stating the general guidelines that you follow when solving (a) exponential equations and (b) logarithmic equations.

Skills Review

In Exercises 127–130, simplify the expression.

127. $\sqrt{48x^2y^5}$

128. $\sqrt{32} - 2\sqrt{25}$

129. $\sqrt[3]{25} \cdot \sqrt[3]{15}$

130. $\dfrac{3}{\sqrt{10} - 2}$

In Exercises 131–134, sketch a graph of the function.

131. $f(x) = |x| + 9$

132. $f(x) = |x + 2| - 8$

133. $g(x) = \begin{cases} 2x, & x < 0 \\ -x^2 + 4, & x \geq 0 \end{cases}$

134. $g(x) = \begin{cases} x - 3, & x \leq -1 \\ x^2 + 1, & x > -1 \end{cases}$

In Exercises 135–138, evaluate the logarithm using the change-of-base formula. Approximate your result to three decimal places.

135. $\log_6 9$

136. $\log_3 4$

137. $\log_{3/4} 5$

138. $\log_8 22$

3.5 Exponential and Logarithmic Models

What you should learn

- Recognize the five most common types of models involving exponential and logarithmic functions.
- Use exponential growth and decay functions to model and solve real-life problems.
- Use Gaussian functions to model and solve real-life problems.
- Use logistic growth functions to model and solve real-life problems.
- Use logarithmic functions to model and solve real-life problems.

Why you should learn it

Exponential growth and decay models are often used to model the population of a country. For instance, in Exercise 36 on page 265, you will use exponential growth and decay models to compare the populations of several countries.

Alan Becker/Getty Images

Introduction

The five most common types of mathematical models involving exponential functions and logarithmic functions are as follows.

1. **Exponential growth model:** $y = ae^{bx}, \quad b > 0$
2. **Exponential decay model:** $y = ae^{-bx}, \quad b > 0$
3. **Gaussian model:** $y = ae^{-(x-b)^2/c}$
4. **Logistic growth model:** $y = \dfrac{a}{1 + be^{-rx}}$
5. **Logarithmic models:** $y = a + b \ln x, \quad y = a + b \log x$

The basic shapes of the graphs of these functions are shown in Figure 3.29.

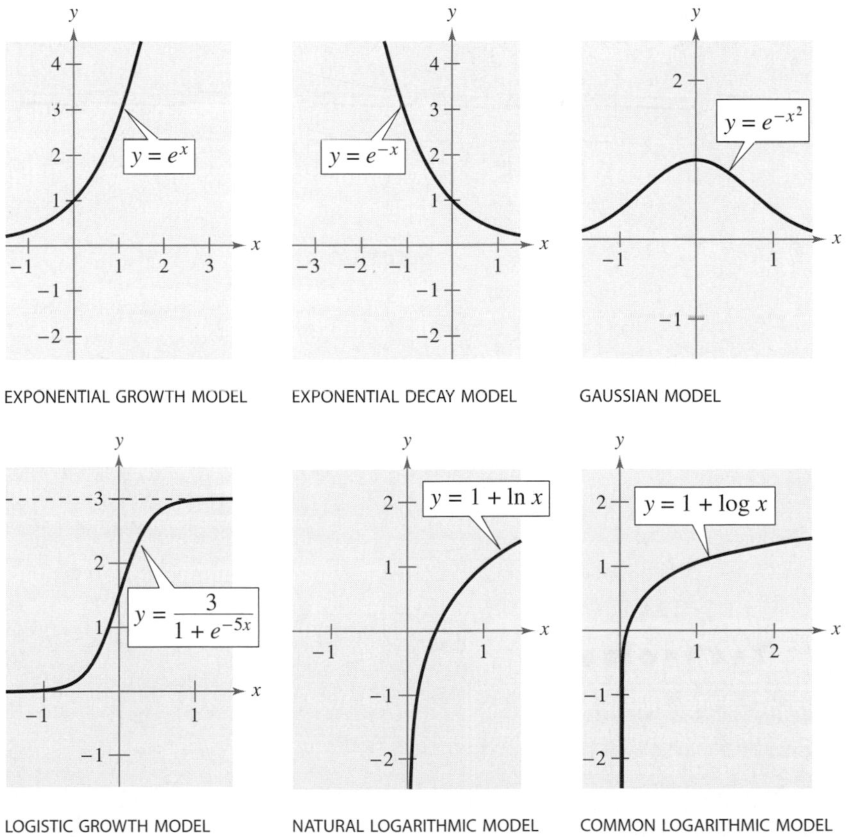

FIGURE 3.29

You can often gain quite a bit of insight into a situation modeled by an exponential or logarithmic function by identifying and interpreting the function's asymptotes. Use the graphs in Figure 3.29 to identify the asymptotes of the graph of each function.

Exponential Growth and Decay

Example 1 Digital Television

Estimates of the numbers (in millions) of U.S. households with digital television from 2003 through 2007 are shown in the table. The scatter plot of the data is shown in Figure 3.30. (Source: eMarketer)

Year	Households
2003	44.2
2004	49.0
2005	55.5
2006	62.5
2007	70.3

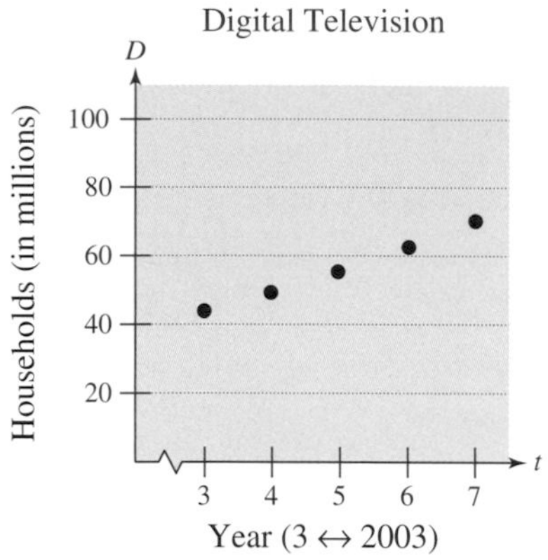

FIGURE 3.30

An exponential growth model that approximates these data is given by

$$D = 30.92e^{0.1171t}, \quad 3 \leq t \leq 7$$

where D is the number of households (in millions) and $t = 3$ represents 2003. Compare the values given by the model with the estimates shown in the table. According to this model, when will the number of U.S. households with digital television reach 100 million?

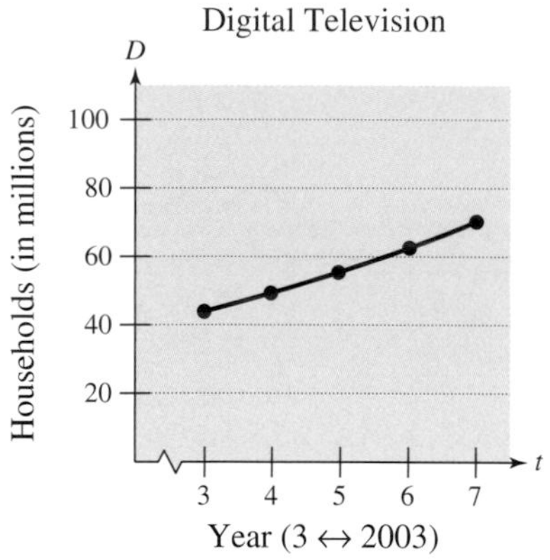

FIGURE 3.31

Solution

The following table compares the two sets of figures. The graph of the model and the original data are shown in Figure 3.31.

Year	2003	2004	2005	2006	2007
Households	44.2	49.0	55.5	62.5	70.3
Model	43.9	49.4	55.5	62.4	70.2

To find when the number of U.S. households with digital television will reach 100 million, let $D = 100$ in the model and solve for t.

$$30.92e^{0.1171t} = D \qquad \text{Write original model.}$$

$$30.92e^{0.1171t} = 100 \qquad \text{Let } D = 100.$$

$$e^{0.1171t} \approx 3.2342 \qquad \text{Divide each side by 30.92.}$$

$$\ln e^{0.1171t} \approx \ln 3.2342 \qquad \text{Take natural log of each side.}$$

$$0.1171t \approx 1.1738 \qquad \text{Inverse Property}$$

$$t \approx 10.0 \qquad \text{Divide each side by 0.1171.}$$

According to the model, the number of U.S. households with digital television will reach 100 million in 2010.

CHECKPOINT Now try Exercise 35.

Technology

Some graphing utilities have an *exponential regression* feature that can be used to find exponential models that represent data. If you have such a graphing utility, try using it to find an exponential model for the data given in Example 1. How does your model compare with the model given in Example 1?

In Example 1, you were given the exponential growth model. But suppose this model were not given; how could you find such a model? One technique for doing this is demonstrated in Example 2.

Example 2 Modeling Population Growth

In a research experiment, a population of fruit flies is increasing according to the law of exponential growth. After 2 days there are 100 flies, and after 4 days there are 300 flies. How many flies will there be after 5 days?

Solution

Let y be the number of flies at time t. From the given information, you know that $y = 100$ when $t = 2$ and $y = 300$ when $t = 4$. Substituting this information into the model $y = ae^{bt}$ produces

$$100 = ae^{2b} \quad \text{and} \quad 300 = ae^{4b}.$$

To solve for b, solve for a in the first equation.

$$100 = ae^{2b} \quad \Rightarrow \quad a = \frac{100}{e^{2b}}$$ Solve for a in the first equation.

Then substitute the result into the second equation.

$$300 = ae^{4b}$$ Write second equation.

$$300 = \left(\frac{100}{e^{2b}}\right)e^{4b}$$ Substitute $100/e^{2b}$ for a.

$$\frac{300}{100} = e^{2b}$$ Divide each side by 100.

$$\ln 3 = 2b$$ Take natural log of each side.

$$\frac{1}{2}\ln 3 = b$$ Solve for b.

Using $b = \frac{1}{2}\ln 3$ and the equation you found for a, you can determine that

$$a = \frac{100}{e^{2[(1/2)\ln 3]}}$$ Substitute $\frac{1}{2}\ln 3$ for b.

$$= \frac{100}{e^{\ln 3}}$$ Simplify.

$$= \frac{100}{3}$$ Inverse Property

$$\approx 33.33.$$ Simplify.

So, with $a \approx 33.33$ and $b = \frac{1}{2}\ln 3 \approx 0.5493$, the exponential growth model is

$$y = 33.33e^{0.5493t}$$

as shown in Figure 3.32. This implies that, after 5 days, the population will be

$$y = 33.33e^{0.5493(5)} \approx 520 \text{ flies.}$$

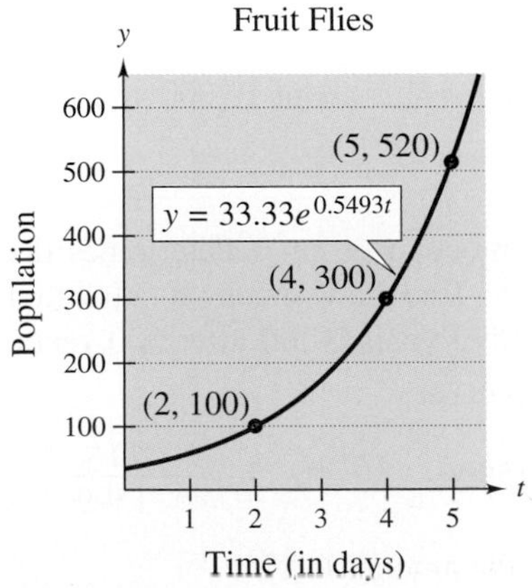

FIGURE 3.32

CHECKPOINT Now try Exercise 37.

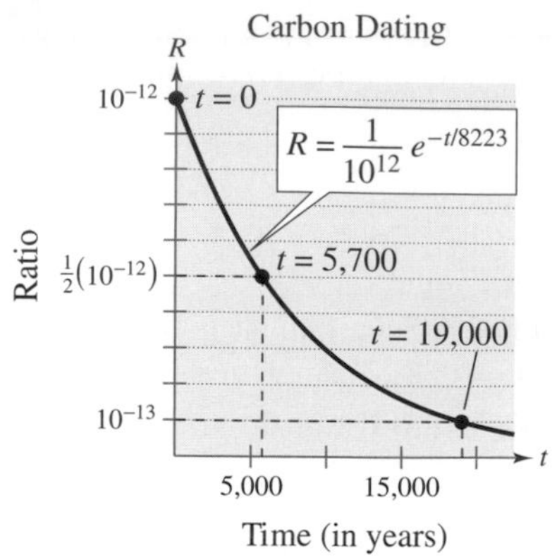

FIGURE 3.33

In living organic material, the ratio of the number of radioactive carbon isotopes (carbon 14) to the number of nonradioactive carbon isotopes (carbon 12) is about 1 to 10^{12}. When organic material dies, its carbon 12 content remains fixed, whereas its radioactive carbon 14 begins to decay with a half-life of about 5700 years. To estimate the age of dead organic material, scientists use the following formula, which denotes the ratio of carbon 14 to carbon 12 present at any time t (in years).

$$R = \frac{1}{10^{12}}e^{-t/8223} \qquad \text{Carbon dating model}$$

The graph of R is shown in Figure 3.33. Note that R decreases as t increases.

Example 3 Carbon Dating

Estimate the age of a newly discovered fossil in which the ratio of carbon 14 to carbon 12 is

$$R = \frac{1}{10^{13}}.$$

Solution

In the carbon dating model, substitute the given value of R to obtain the following.

$$\frac{1}{10^{12}}e^{-t/8223} = R \qquad \text{Write original model.}$$

$$\frac{e^{-t/8223}}{10^{12}} = \frac{1}{10^{13}} \qquad \text{Let } R = \frac{1}{10^{13}}.$$

$$e^{-t/8223} = \frac{1}{10} \qquad \text{Multiply each side by } 10^{12}.$$

$$\ln e^{-t/8223} = \ln\frac{1}{10} \qquad \text{Take natural log of each side.}$$

$$-\frac{t}{8223} \approx -2.3026 \qquad \text{Inverse Property}$$

$$t \approx 18,934 \qquad \text{Multiply each side by } -8223.$$

So, to the nearest thousand years, the age of the fossil is about 19,000 years.

CHECKPOINT Now try Exercise 41.

The value of b in the exponential decay model $y = ae^{-bt}$ determines the *decay* of radioactive isotopes. For instance, to find how much of an initial 10 grams of ^{226}Ra isotope with a half-life of 1599 years is left after 500 years, substitute this information into the model $y = ae^{-bt}$.

$$\frac{1}{2}(10) = 10e^{-b(1599)} \quad \Rightarrow \quad \ln\frac{1}{2} = -1599b \quad \Rightarrow \quad b = -\frac{\ln\frac{1}{2}}{1599}$$

Using the value of b found above and $a = 10$, the amount left is

$$y = 10e^{-[-\ln(1/2)/1599](500)} \approx 8.05 \text{ grams.}$$

STUDY TIP

The carbon dating model in Example 3 assumed that the carbon 14 to carbon 12 ratio was one part in 10,000,000,000,000. Suppose an error in measurement occurred and the actual ratio was one part in 8,000,000,000,000. The fossil age corresponding to the actual ratio would then be approximately 17,000 years. Try checking this result.

Gaussian Models

As mentioned at the beginning of this section, Gaussian models are of the form

$$y = ae^{-(x-b)^2/c}.$$

This type of model is commonly used in probability and statistics to represent populations that are **normally distributed.** The graph of a Gaussian model is called a **bell-shaped curve.** Try graphing the normal distribution with a graphing utility. Can you see why it is called a bell-shaped curve?

For *standard* normal distributions, the model takes the form

$$y = \frac{1}{\sqrt{2\pi}}e^{-x^2/2}.$$

The **average value** for a population can be found from the bell-shaped curve by observing where the maximum y-value of the function occurs. The x-value corresponding to the maximum y-value of the function represents the average value of the independent variable—in this case, x.

Example 4 **SAT Scores**

In 2004, the Scholastic Aptitude Test (SAT) math scores for college-bound seniors roughly followed the normal distribution given by

$$y = 0.0035e^{-(x-518)^2/25,992}, \quad 200 \le x \le 800$$

where x is the SAT score for mathematics. Sketch the graph of this function. From the graph, estimate the average SAT score. (Source: College Board)

Solution

The graph of the function is shown in Figure 3.34. On this bell-shaped curve, the maximum value of the curve represents the average score. From the graph, you can estimate that the average mathematics score for college-bound seniors in 2004 was 518.

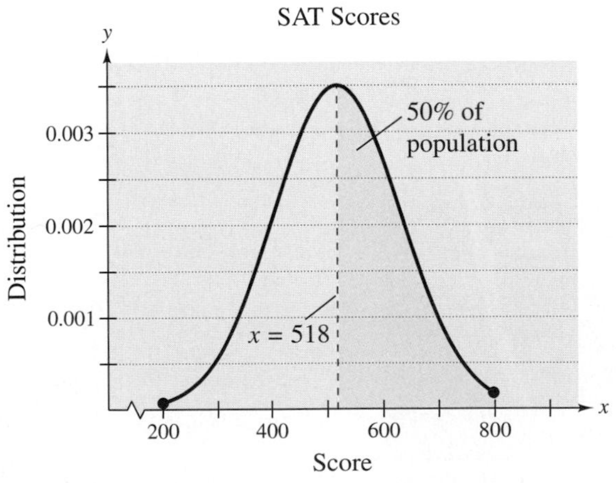

FIGURE 3.34

CHECKPOINT Now try Exercise 47.

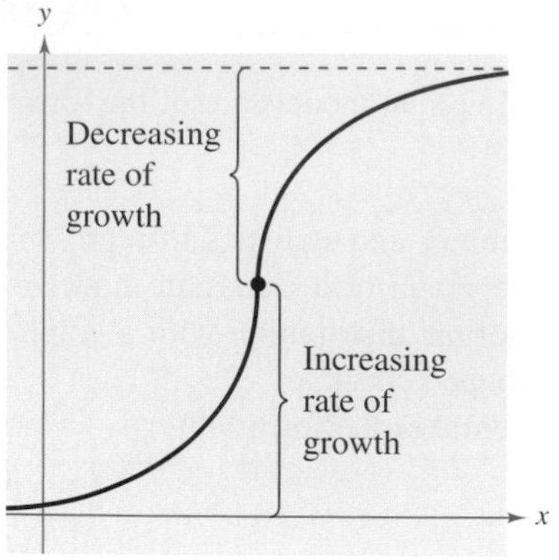

FIGURE 3.35

Logistic Growth Models

Some populations initially have rapid growth, followed by a declining rate of growth, as indicated by the graph in Figure 3.35. One model for describing this type of growth pattern is the **logistic curve** given by the function

$$y = \frac{a}{1 + be^{-rx}}$$

where y is the population size and x is the time. An example is a bacteria culture that is initially allowed to grow under ideal conditions, and then under less favorable conditions that inhibit growth. A logistic growth curve is also called a **sigmoidal curve.**

Example 5 Spread of a Virus

On a college campus of 5000 students, one student returns from vacation with a contagious and long-lasting flu virus. The spread of the virus is modeled by

$$y = \frac{5000}{1 + 4999e^{-0.8t}}, \quad t \geq 0$$

where y is the total number of students infected after t days. The college will cancel classes when 40% or more of the students are infected.

a. How many students are infected after 5 days?

b. After how many days will the college cancel classes?

Solution

a. After 5 days, the number of students infected is

$$y = \frac{5000}{1 + 4999e^{-0.8(5)}} = \frac{5000}{1 + 4999e^{-4}} \approx 54.$$

b. Classes are canceled when the number infected is $(0.40)(5000) = 2000$.

$$2000 = \frac{5000}{1 + 4999e^{-0.8t}}$$

$$1 + 4999e^{-0.8t} = 2.5$$

$$e^{-0.8t} = \frac{1.5}{4999}$$

$$\ln e^{-0.8t} = \ln \frac{1.5}{4999}$$

$$-0.8t = \ln \frac{1.5}{4999}$$

$$t = -\frac{1}{0.8} \ln \frac{1.5}{4999}$$

$$t \approx 10.1$$

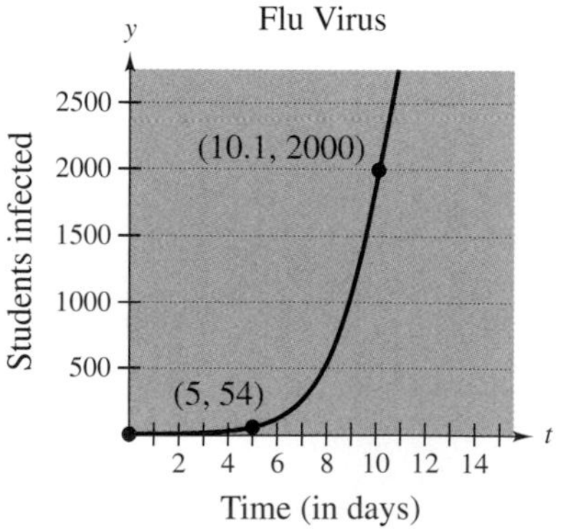

FIGURE 3.36

So, after about 10 days, at least 40% of the students will be infected, and the college will cancel classes. The graph of the function is shown in Figure 3.36.

CHECKPOINT Now try Exercise 49.

BAY ISMOYO/AFP/Getty Images

On December 26, 2004, an earthquake of magnitude 9.0 struck northern Sumatra and many other Asian countries. This earthquake caused a deadly tsunami and was the fourth largest earthquake in the world since 1900.

Logarithmic Models

Example 6 Magnitudes of Earthquakes

On the Richter scale, the magnitude R of an earthquake of intensity I is given by

$$R = \log \frac{I}{I_0}$$

where $I_0 = 1$ is the minimum intensity used for comparison. Find the intensities per unit of area for each earthquake. (Intensity is a measure of the wave energy of an earthquake.)

a. Northern Sumatra in 2004: $R = 9.0$

b. Southeastern Alaska in 2004: $R = 6.8$

Solution

a. Because $I_0 = 1$ and $R = 9.0$, you have

$$9.0 = \log \frac{I}{1} \qquad \text{Substitute 1 for } I_0 \text{ and 9.0 for } R.$$

$$10^{9.0} = 10^{\log I} \qquad \text{Exponentiate each side.}$$

$$I = 10^{9.0} \approx 100{,}000{,}000. \qquad \text{Inverse Property}$$

b. For $R = 6.8$, you have

$$6.8 = \log \frac{I}{1} \qquad \text{Substitute 1 for } I_0 \text{ and 6.8 for } R.$$

$$10^{6.8} = 10^{\log I} \qquad \text{Exponentiate each side.}$$

$$I = 10^{6.8} \approx 6{,}310{,}000. \qquad \text{Inverse Property}$$

Note that an increase of 2.2 units on the Richter scale (from 6.8 to 9.0) represents an increase in intensity by a factor of

$$\frac{1{,}000{,}000{,}000}{6{,}310{,}000} \approx 158.$$

In other words, the intensity of the earthquake in Sumatra was about 158 times greater than that of the earthquake in Alaska.

CHECKPOINT Now try Exercise 51.

t	Year	Population, P
1	1910	92.23
2	1920	106.02
3	1930	123.20
4	1940	132.16
5	1950	151.33
6	1960	179.32
7	1970	203.30
8	1980	226.54
9	1990	248.72
10	2000	281.42

WRITING ABOUT MATHEMATICS

Comparing Population Models The populations P (in millions) of the United States for the census years from 1910 to 2000 are shown in the table at the left. Least squares regression analysis gives the best quadratic model for these data as $P = 1.0328t^2 + 9.607t + 81.82$, and the best exponential model for these data as $P = 82.677e^{0.124t}$. Which model better fits the data? Describe how you reached your conclusion. (Source: U.S. Census Bureau)

3.5 Exercises

VOCABULARY CHECK: Fill in the blanks.

1. An exponential growth model has the form ________ and an exponential decay model has the form ________.
2. A logarithmic model has the form ________ or ________.
3. Gaussian models are commonly used in probability and statistics to represent populations that are ________ ________.
4. The graph of a Gaussian model is ________ shaped, where the ________ ________ is the maximum y-value of the graph.
5. A logistic curve is also called a ________ curve.

In Exercises 1–6, match the function with its graph. [The graphs are labeled (a), (b), (c), (d), (e), and (f).]

(a)

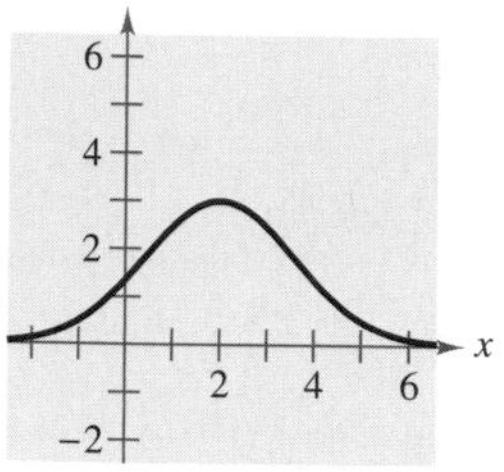

(b)

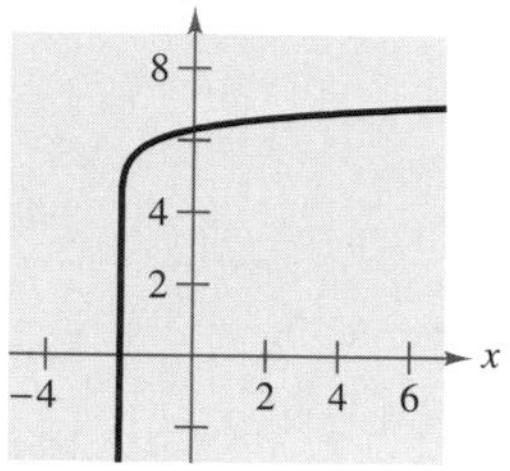

(c)

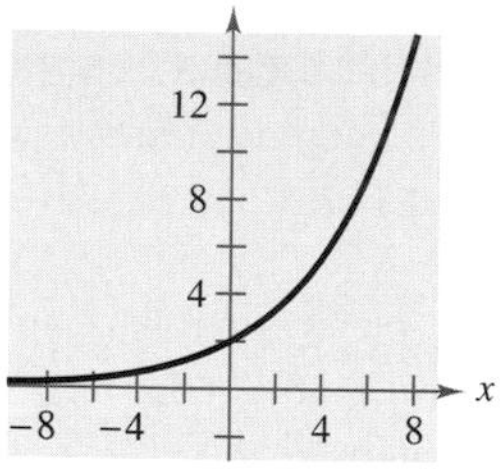

(d)

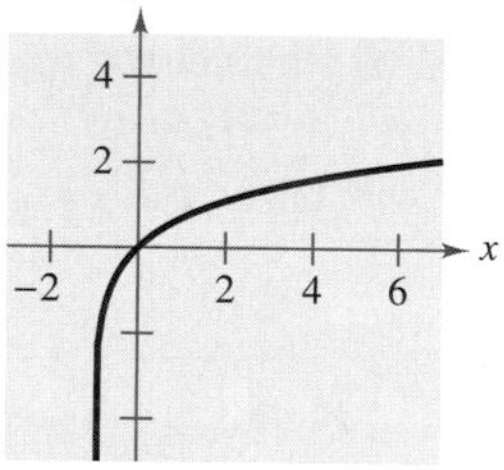

(e)

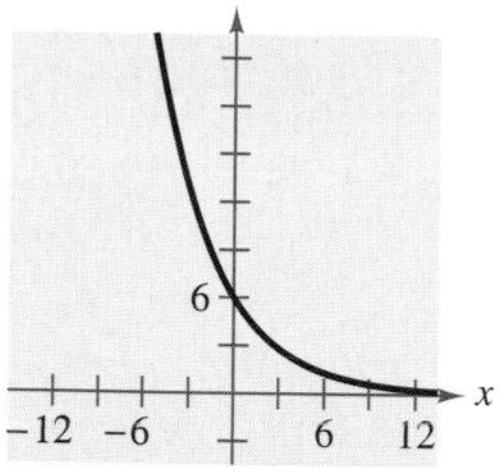

(f)

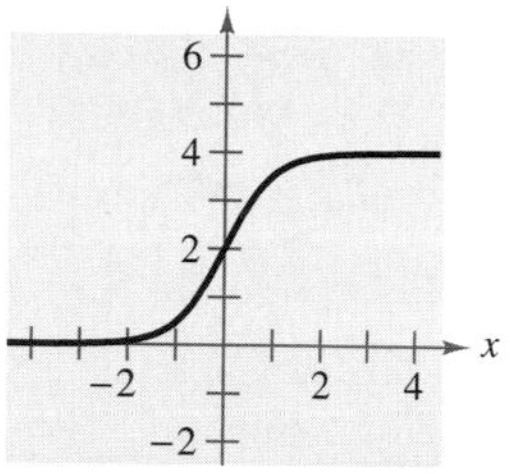

1. $y = 2e^{x/4}$
2. $y = 6e^{-x/4}$
3. $y = 6 + \log(x + 2)$
4. $y = 3e^{-(x-2)^2/5}$
5. $y = \ln(x + 1)$
6. $y = \dfrac{4}{1 + e^{-2x}}$

Compound Interest **In Exercises 7–14, complete the table for a savings account in which interest is compounded continuously.**

	Initial Investment	*Annual % Rate*	*Time to Double*	*Amount After 10 Years*
7.	\$1000	3.5%		
8.	\$750	$10\frac{1}{2}$%		
9.	\$750		$7\frac{3}{4}$ yr	
10.	\$10,000		12 yr	
11.	\$500			\$1505.00
12.	\$600			\$19,205.00
13.		4.5%		\$10,000.00
14.		2%		\$2000.00

Compound Interest **In Exercises 15 and 16, determine the principal P that must be invested at rate r, compounded monthly, so that \$500,000 will be available for retirement in t years.**

15. $r = 7\frac{1}{2}\%, t = 20$

16. $r = 12\%, t = 40$

Compound Interest **In Exercises 17 and 18, determine the time necessary for \$1000 to double if it is invested at interest rate r compounded (a) annually, (b) monthly, (c) daily, and (d) continuously.**

17. $r = 11\%$

18. $r = 10\frac{1}{2}\%$

19. ***Compound Interest*** Complete the table for the time t necessary for P dollars to triple if interest is compounded continuously at rate r.

r	2%	4%	6%	8%	10%	12%
t						

20. ***Modeling Data*** Draw a scatter plot of the data in Exercise 19. Use the *regression* feature of a graphing utility to find a model for the data.

21. ***Compound Interest*** Complete the table for the time t necessary for P dollars to triple if interest is compounded annually at rate r.

r	2%	4%	6%	8%	10%	12%
t						

22. ***Modeling Data*** Draw a scatter plot of the data in Exercise 21. Use the *regression* feature of a graphing utility to find a model for the data.

23. ***Comparing Models*** If \$1 is invested in an account over a 10-year period, the amount in the account, where t represents the time in years, is given by $A = 1 + 0.075[\![t]\!]$ or $A = e^{0.07t}$ depending on whether the account pays simple interest at $7\frac{1}{2}\%$ or continuous compound interest at 7%. Graph each function on the same set of axes. Which grows at a higher rate? (Remember that $[\![t]\!]$ is the greatest integer function discussed in Section 1.6.)

24. ***Comparing Models*** If \$1 is invested in an account over a 10-year period, the amount in the account, where t represents the time in years, is given by

$$A = 1 + 0.06[\![t]\!] \quad \text{or} \quad A = \left(1 + \frac{0.055}{365}\right)^{[\![365t]\!]}$$

depending on whether the account pays simple interest at 6% or compound interest at $5\frac{1}{2}\%$ compounded daily. Use a graphing utility to graph each function in the same viewing window. Which grows at a higher rate?

Radioactive Decay **In Exercises 25–30, complete the table for the radioactive isotope.**

	Isotope	Half-life (years)	Initial Quantity	Amount After 1000 Years
25.	^{226}Ra	1599	10 g	
26.	^{226}Ra	1599		1.5 g
27.	^{14}C	5715		2 g
28.	^{14}C	5715	3 g	
29.	^{239}Pu	24,100		2.1 g
30.	^{239}Pu	24,100		0.4 g

In Exercises 31–34, find the exponential model $y = ae^{bx}$ that fits the points shown in the graph or table.

31.

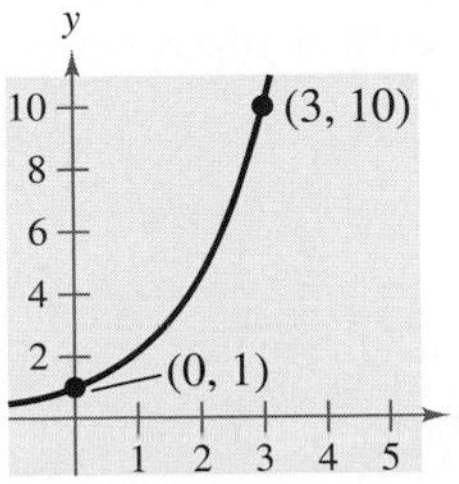

32.

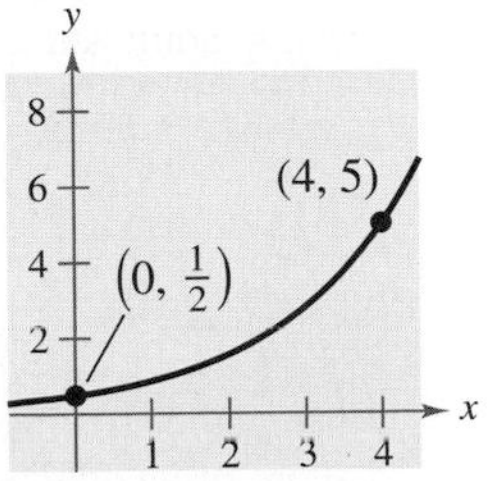

33.

x	0	4
y	5	1

34.

x	0	3
y	1	$\frac{1}{4}$

35. ***Population*** The population P (in thousands) of Pittsburgh, Pennsylvania from 2000 through 2003 can be modeled by $P = 2430e^{-0.0029t}$, where t represents the year, with $t = 0$ corresponding to 2000. (Source: U.S. Census Bureau)

(a) According to the model, was the population of Pittsburgh increasing or decreasing from 2000 to 2003? Explain your reasoning.

(b) What were the populations of Pittsburgh in 2000 and 2003?

(c) According to the model, when will the population be approximately 2.3 million?

Model It

36. ***Population*** The table shows the populations (in millions) of five countries in 2000 and the projected populations (in millions) for the year 2010. (Source: U.S. Census Bureau)

Country	2000	2010
Bulgaria	7.8	7.1
Canada	31.3	34.3
China	1268.9	1347.6
United Kingdom	59.5	61.2
United States	282.3	309.2

(a) Find the exponential growth or decay model $y = ae^{bt}$ or $y = ae^{-bt}$ for the population of each country by letting $t = 0$ correspond to 2000. Use the model to predict the population of each country in 2030.

(b) You can see that the populations of the United States and the United Kingdom are growing at different rates. What constant in the equation $y = ae^{bt}$ is determined by these different growth rates? Discuss the relationship between the different growth rates and the magnitude of the constant.

(c) You can see that the population of China is increasing while the population of Bulgaria is decreasing. What constant in the equation $y = ae^{bt}$ reflects this difference? Explain.

37. ***Website Growth*** The number y of hits a new search-engine website receives each month can be modeled by

$$y = 4080e^{kt}$$

where t represents the number of months the website has been operating. In the website's third month, there were 10,000 hits. Find the value of k, and use this result to predict the number of hits the website will receive after 24 months.

38. ***Value of a Painting*** The value V (in millions of dollars) of a famous painting can be modeled by

$$V = 10e^{kt}$$

where t represents the year, with $t = 0$ corresponding to 1990. In 2004, the same painting was sold for \$65 million. Find the value of k, and use this result to predict the value of the painting in 2010.

39. ***Bacteria Growth*** The number N of bacteria in a culture is modeled by

$$N = 100e^{kt}$$

where t is the time in hours. If $N = 300$ when $t = 5$, estimate the time required for the population to double in size.

40. ***Bacteria Growth*** The number N of bacteria in a culture is modeled by

$$N = 250e^{kt}$$

where t is the time in hours. If $N = 280$ when $t = 10$, estimate the time required for the population to double in size.

41. ***Carbon Dating***

(a) The ratio of carbon 14 to carbon 12 in a piece of wood discovered in a cave is $R = 1/8^{14}$. Estimate the age of the piece of wood.

(b) The ratio of carbon 14 to carbon 12 in a piece of paper buried in a tomb is $R = 1/13^{11}$. Estimate the age of the piece of paper.

42. ***Radioactive Decay*** Carbon 14 dating assumes that the carbon dioxide on Earth today has the same radioactive content as it did centuries ago. If this is true, the amount of ^{14}C absorbed by a tree that grew several centuries ago should be the same as the amount of ^{14}C absorbed by a tree growing today. A piece of ancient charcoal contains only 15% as much radioactive carbon as a piece of modern charcoal. How long ago was the tree burned to make the ancient charcoal if the half-life of ^{14}C is 5715 years?

43. ***Depreciation*** A 2005 Jeep Wrangler that costs \$30,788 new has a book value of \$18,000 after 2 years.

(a) Find the linear model $V = mt + b$.

(b) Find the exponential model $V = ae^{kt}$.

(c) Use a graphing utility to graph the two models in the same viewing window. Which model depreciates faster in the first 2 years?

(d) Find the book values of the vehicle after 1 year and after 3 years using each model.

(e) Explain the advantages and disadvantages of using each model to a buyer and a seller.

44. ***Depreciation*** A Dell Inspiron 8600 laptop computer that costs \$1150 new has a book value of \$550 after 2 years.

(a) Find the linear model $V = mt + b$.

(b) Find the exponential model $V = ae^{kt}$.

(c) Use a graphing utility to graph the two models in the same viewing window. Which model depreciates faster in the first 2 years?

(d) Find the book values of the computer after 1 year and after 3 years using each model.

(e) Explain the advantages and disadvantages to a buyer and a seller of using each model.

45. ***Sales*** The sales S (in thousands of units) of a new CD burner after it has been on the market for t years are modeled by

$$S(t) = 100(1 - e^{kt}).$$

Fifteen thousand units of the new product were sold the first year.

(a) Complete the model by solving for k.

(b) Sketch the graph of the model.

(c) Use the model to estimate the number of units sold after 5 years.

46. ***Learning Curve*** The management at a plastics factory has found that the maximum number of units a worker can produce in a day is 30. The learning curve for the number N of units produced per day after a new employee has worked t days is modeled by

$$N = 30(1 - e^{kt}).$$

After 20 days on the job, a new employee produces 19 units.

(a) Find the learning curve for this employee (first, find the value of k).

(b) How many days should pass before this employee is producing 25 units per day?

47. ***IQ Scores*** The IQ scores from a sample of a class of returning adult students at a small northeastern college roughly follow the normal distribution

$$y = 0.0266e^{-(x-100)^2/450}, \quad 70 \le x \le 115$$

where x is the IQ score.

(a) Use a graphing utility to graph the function.

(b) From the graph in part (a), estimate the average IQ score of an adult student.

48. ***Education*** The time (in hours per week) a student utilizes a math-tutoring center roughly follows the normal distribution

$$y = 0.7979e^{-(x-5.4)^2/0.5}, \quad 4 \le x \le 7$$

where x is the number of hours.

(a) Use a graphing utility to graph the function.

(b) From the graph in part (a), estimate the average number of hours per week a student uses the tutor center.

49. ***Population Growth*** A conservation organization releases 100 animals of an endangered species into a game preserve. The organization believes that the preserve has a carrying capacity of 1000 animals and that the growth of the pack will be modeled by the logistic curve

$$p(t) = \frac{1000}{1 + 9e^{-0.1656t}}$$

where t is measured in months (see figure).

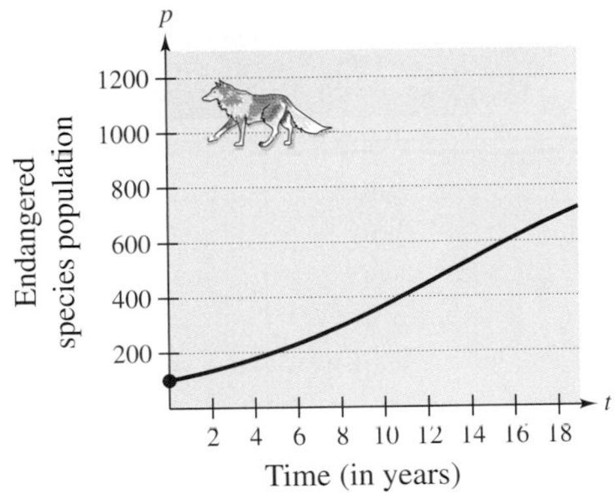

(a) Estimate the population after 5 months.

(b) After how many months will the population be 500?

(c) Use a graphing utility to graph the function. Use the graph to determine the horizontal asymptotes, and interpret the meaning of the larger p-value in the context of the problem.

50. ***Sales*** After discontinuing all advertising for a tool kit in 2000, the manufacturer noted that sales began to drop according to the model

$$S = \frac{500{,}000}{1 + 0.6e^{kt}}$$

where S represents the number of units sold and $t = 0$ represents 2000. In 2004, the company sold 300,000 units.

(a) Complete the model by solving for k.

(b) Estimate sales in 2008.

Geology **In Exercises 51 and 52, use the Richter scale**

$$R = \log \frac{I}{I_0}$$

for measuring the magnitudes of earthquakes.

51. Find the intensity I of an earthquake measuring R on the Richter scale (let $I_0 = 1$).

(a) Centeral Alaska in 2002, $R = 7.9$

(b) Hokkaido, Japan in 2003, $R = 8.3$

(c) Illinois in 2004, $R = 4.2$

52. Find the magnitude R of each earthquake of intensity I (let $I_0 = 1$).

(a) $I = 80{,}500{,}000$ (b) $I = 48{,}275{,}000$

(c) $I = 251{,}200$

Intensity of Sound **In Exercises 53–56, use the following information for determining sound intensity. The level of sound β, in decibels, with an intensity of I, is given by**

$$\beta = 10 \log \frac{I}{I_0}$$

where I_0 is an intensity of 10^{-12} watt per square meter, corresponding roughly to the faintest sound that can be heard by the human ear. In Exercises 53 and 54, find the level of sound β.

53. (a) $I = 10^{-10}$ watt per m^2 (quiet room)

(b) $I = 10^{-5}$ watt per m^2 (busy street corner)

(c) $I = 10^{-8}$ watt per m^2 (quiet radio)

(d) $I = 10^{0}$ watt per m^2 (threshold of pain)

54. (a) $I = 10^{-11}$ watt per m^2 (rustle of leaves)

(b) $I = 10^{2}$ watt per m^2 (jet at 30 meters)

(c) $I = 10^{-4}$ watt per m^2 (door slamming)

(d) $I = 10^{-2}$ watt per m^2 (siren at 30 meters)

55. Due to the installation of noise suppression materials, the noise level in an auditorium was reduced from 93 to 80 decibels. Find the percent decrease in the intensity level of the noise as a result of the installation of these materials.

56. Due to the installation of a muffler, the noise level of an engine was reduced from 88 to 72 decibels. Find the percent decrease in the intensity level of the noise as a result of the installation of the muffler.

pH Levels **In Exercises 57–62, use the acidity model given by pH $= -\log[H^+]$, where acidity (pH) is a measure of the hydrogen ion concentration $[H^+]$ (measured in moles of hydrogen per liter) of a solution.**

57. Find the pH if $[H^+] = 2.3 \times 10^{-5}$.

58. Find the pH if $[H^+] = 11.3 \times 10^{-6}$.

59. Compute $[H^+]$ for a solution in which pH = 5.8.

60. Compute $[H^+]$ for a solution in which pH = 3.2.

61. Apple juice has a pH of 2.9 and drinking water has a pH of 8.0. The hydrogen ion concentration of the apple juice is how many times the concentration of drinking water?

62. The pH of a solution is decreased by one unit. The hydrogen ion concentration is increased by what factor?

63. ***Forensics*** At 8:30 A.M., a coroner was called to the home of a person who had died during the night. In order to estimate the time of death, the coroner took the person's temperature twice. At 9:00 A.M. the temperature was 85.7°F, and at 11:00 a.m. the temperature was 82.8°F. From these two temperatures, the coroner was able to determine that the time elapsed since death and the body temperature were related by the formula

$$t = -10 \ln \frac{T - 70}{98.6 - 70}$$

where t is the time in hours elapsed since the person died and T is the temperature (in degrees Fahrenheit) of the person's body. Assume that the person had a normal body temperature of 98.6°F at death, and that the room temperature was a constant 70°F. (This formula is derived from a general cooling principle called *Newton's Law of Cooling*.) Use the formula to estimate the time of death of the person.

64. ***Home Mortgage*** A \$120,000 home mortgage for 35 years at $7\frac{1}{2}\%$ has a monthly payment of \$809.39. Part of the monthly payment is paid toward the interest charge on the unpaid balance, and the remainder of the payment is used to reduce the principal. The amount that is paid toward the interest is

$$u = M - \left(M - \frac{Pr}{12}\right)\left(1 + \frac{r}{12}\right)^{12t}$$

and the amount that is paid toward the reduction of the principal is

$$v = \left(M - \frac{Pr}{12}\right)\left(1 + \frac{r}{12}\right)^{12t}.$$

In these formulas, P is the size of the mortgage, r is the interest rate, M is the monthly payment, and t is the time in years.

(a) Use a graphing utility to graph each function in the same viewing window. (The viewing window should show all 35 years of mortgage payments.)

(b) In the early years of the mortgage, is the larger part of the monthly payment paid toward the interest or the principal? Approximate the time when the monthly payment is evenly divided between interest and principal reduction.

(c) Repeat parts (a) and (b) for a repayment period of 20 years (M = \$966.71). What can you conclude?

65. ***Home Mortgage*** The total interest u paid on a home mortgage of P dollars at interest rate r for t years is

$$u = P\left[\frac{rt}{1 - \left(\dfrac{1}{1 + r/12}\right)^{12t}} - 1\right].$$

Consider a \$120,000 home mortgage at $7\frac{1}{2}\%$.

(a) Use a graphing utility to graph the total interest function.

(b) Approximate the length of the mortgage for which the total interest paid is the same as the size of the mortgage. Is it possible that some people are paying twice as much in interest charges as the size of the mortgage?

66. ***Data Analysis*** The table shows the time t (in seconds) required to attain a speed of s miles per hour from a standing start for a car.

Speed, s	Time, t
30	3.4
40	5.0
50	7.0
60	9.3
70	12.0
80	15.8
90	20.0

Two models for these data are as follows.

$$t_1 = 40.757 + 0.556s - 15.817 \ln s$$

$$t_2 = 1.2259 + 0.0023s^2$$

(a) Use the *regression* feature of a graphing utility to find a linear model t_3 and an exponential model t_4 for the data.

(b) Use a graphing utility to graph the data and each model in the same viewing window.

(c) Create a table comparing the data with estimates obtained from each model.

(d) Use the results of part (c) to find the sum of the absolute values of the differences between the data and the estimated values given by each model. Based on the four sums, which model do you think better fits the data? Explain.

Synthesis

True or False? **In Exercises 67–70, determine whether the statement is true or false. Justify your answer.**

67. The domain of a logistic growth function cannot be the set of real numbers.

68. A logistic growth function will always have an x-intercept.

69. The graph of

$$f(x) = \frac{4}{1 + 6e^{-2x}} + 5$$

is the graph of

$$g(x) = \frac{4}{1 + 6e^{-2x}}$$

shifted to the right five units.

70. The graph of a Gaussian model will never have an x-intercept.

71. Identify each model as linear, logarithmic, exponential, logistic, or none of the above. Explain your reasoning.

(a)
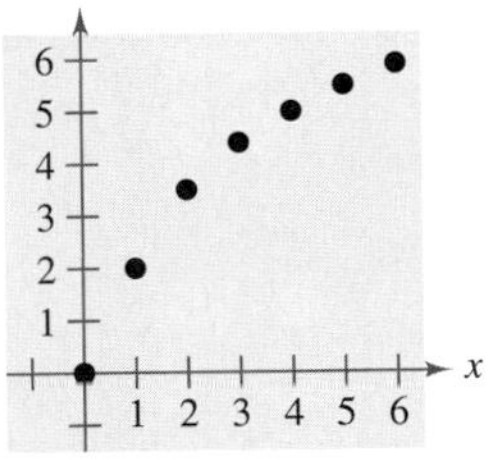

(b)
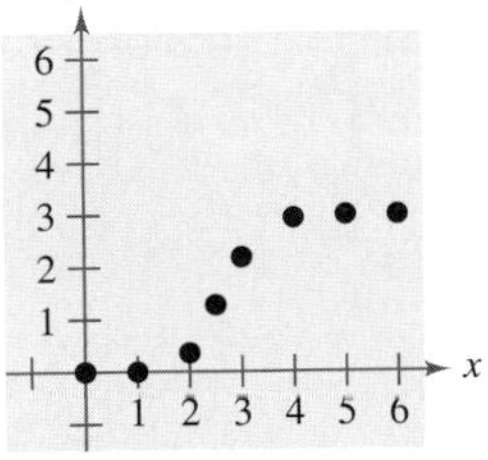

(c)
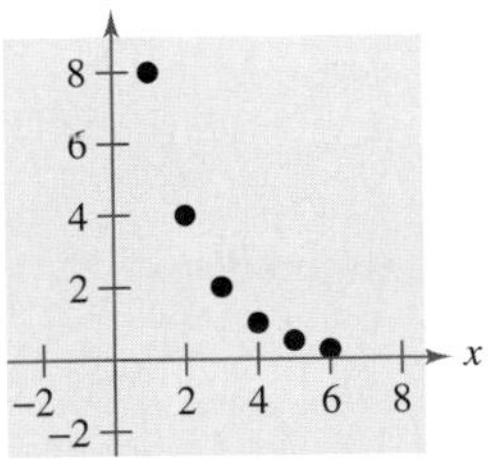

(d)
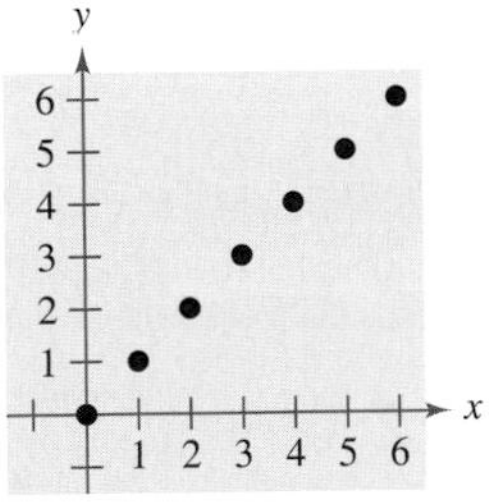

(e)
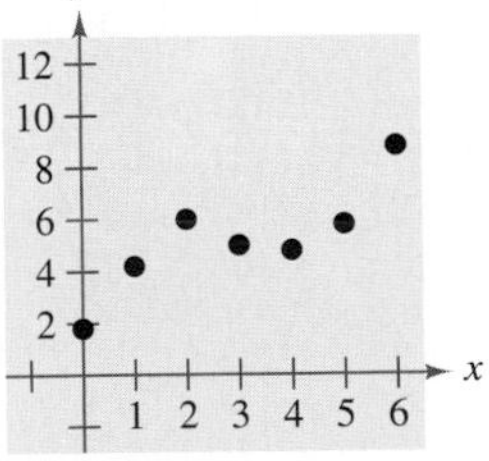

(f)
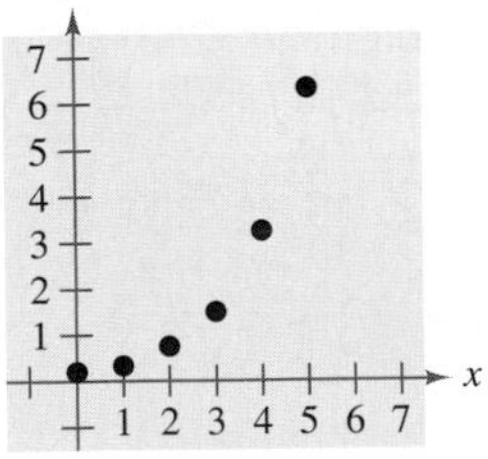

72. ***Writing*** Use your school's library, the Internet, or some other reference source to write a paper describing John Napier's work with logarithms.

Skills Review

In Exercises 73–78, (a) plot the points, (b) find the distance between the points, (c) find the midpoint of the line segment joining the points, and (d) find the slope of the line passing through the points.

73. $(-1, 2), (0, 5)$

74. $(4, -3), (-6, 1)$

75. $(3, 3), (14, -2)$

76. $(7, 0), (10, 4)$

77. $\left(\frac{1}{2}, -\frac{1}{4}\right), \left(\frac{3}{4}, 0\right)$

78. $\left(\frac{7}{3}, \frac{1}{6}\right), \left(-\frac{2}{3}, -\frac{1}{3}\right)$

In Exercises 79–88, sketch the graph of the equation.

79. $y = 10 - 3x$

80. $y = -4x - 1$

81. $y = -2x^2 - 3$

82. $y = 2x^2 - 7x - 30$

83. $3x^2 - 4y = 0$

84. $-x^2 - 8y = 0$

85. $y = \dfrac{4}{1 - 3x}$

86. $y = \dfrac{x^2}{-x - 2}$

87. $x^2 + (y - 8)^2 = 25$

88. $(x - 4)^2 + (y + 7) = 4$

In Exercises 89–92, graph the exponential function.

89. $f(x) = 2^{x-1} + 5$

90. $f(x) = -2^{-x-1} - 1$

91. $f(x) = 3^x - 4$

92. $f(x) = -3^x + 4$

93. Make a Decision To work an extended application analyzing the net sales for Kohl's Corporation from 1992 to 2004, visit this text's website at *college.hmco.com.* *(Data Source: Kohl's Illinois, Inc.)*

3 Chapter Summary

What did you learn?

	Review Exercises
Section 3.1	
☐ Recognize and evaluate exponential functions with base a *(p. 218)*.	1–6
☐ Graph exponential functions and use the One-to-One Property *(p. 219)*.	7–26
☐ Recognize, evaluate, and graph exponential functions with base e *(p. 222)*.	27–34
☐ Use exponential functions to model and solve real-life problems *(p. 223)*.	35–40
Section 3.2	
☐ Recognize and evaluate logarithmic functions with base a *(p. 229)*.	41–52
☐ Graph logarithmic functions *(p. 231)*.	53–58
☐ Recognize, evaluate, and graph natural logarithmic functions *(p. 233)*.	59–68
☐ Use logarithmic functions to model and solve real-life problems *(p. 235)*.	69, 70
Section 3.3	
☐ Use the change-of-base formula to rewrite and evaluate logarithmic expressions *(p. 239)*.	71–74
☐ Use properties of logarithms to evaluate or rewrite logarithmic expressions *(p. 240)*.	75–78
☐ Use properties of logarithms to expand or condense logarithmic expressions *(p. 241)*.	79–94
☐ Use logarithmic functions to model and solve real-life problems *(p. 242)*.	95, 96
Section 3.4	
☐ Solve simple exponential and logarithmic equations *(p. 246)*.	97–104
☐ Solve more complicated exponential equations *(p. 247)*.	105–118
☐ Solve more complicated logarithmic equations *(p. 249)*.	119–134
☐ Use exponential and logarithmic equations to model and solve real-life problems *(p. 251)*.	135, 136
Section 3.5	
☐ Recognize the five most common types of models involving exponential and logarithmic functions *(p. 257)*.	137–142
☐ Use exponential growth and decay functions to model and solve real-life problems *(p. 258)*.	143–148
☐ Use Gaussian functions to model and solve real-life problems *(p. 261)*.	149
☐ Use logistic growth functions to model and solve real-life problems *(p. 262)*.	150
☐ Use logarithmic functions to model and solve real-life problems *(p. 263)*.	151, 152

3 Review Exercises

3.1 In Exercises 1–6, evaluate the function at the indicated value of x. Round your result to three decimal places.

Function	*Value*
1. $f(x) = 6.1^x$	$x = 2.4$
2. $f(x) = 30^x$	$x = \sqrt{3}$
3. $f(x) = 2^{-0.5x}$	$x = \pi$
4. $f(x) = 1278^{x/5}$	$x = 1$
5. $f(x) = 7(0.2^x)$	$x = -\sqrt{11}$
6. $f(x) = -14(5^x)$	$x = -0.8$

In Exercises 7–10, match the function with its graph. [The graphs are labeled (a), (b), (c), and (d).]

(a)

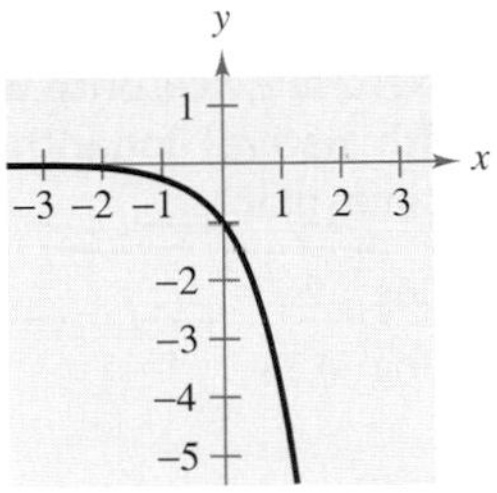

(b)

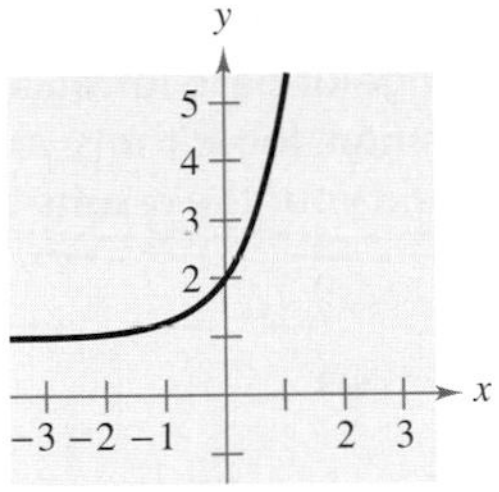

(c)

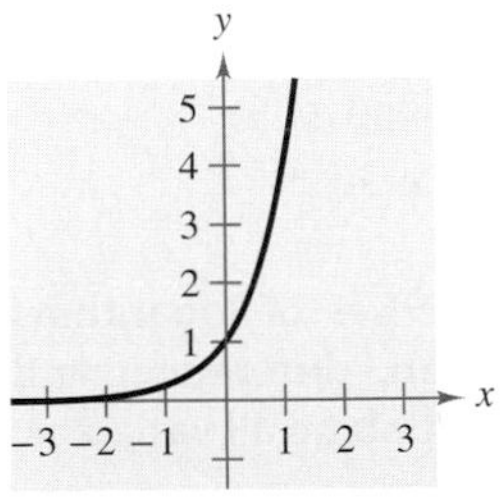

(d)

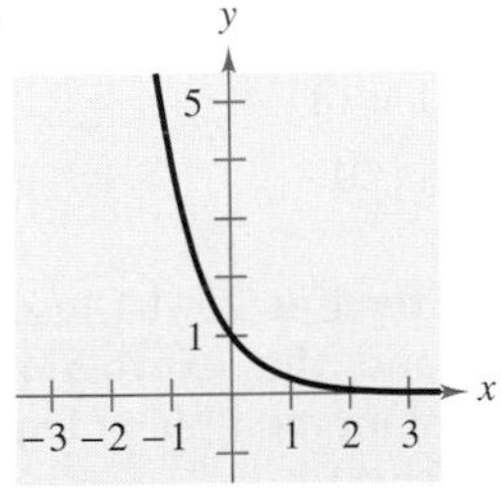

7. $f(x) = 4^x$

8. $f(x) = 4^{-x}$

9. $f(x) = -4^x$

10. $f(x) = 4^x + 1$

In Exercises 11–14, use the graph of f to describe the transformation that yields the graph of g.

11. $f(x) = 5^x, \quad g(x) = 5^{x-1}$

12. $f(x) = 4^x, \quad g(x) = 4^x - 3$

13. $f(x) = \left(\frac{1}{2}\right)^x, \quad g(x) = -\left(\frac{1}{2}\right)^{x+2}$

14. $f(x) = \left(\frac{2}{3}\right)^x, \quad g(x) = 8 - \left(\frac{2}{3}\right)^x$

In Exercises 15–22, use a graphing utility to construct a table of values for the function. Then sketch the graph of the function.

15. $f(x) = 4^{-x} + 4$

16. $f(x) = -4^x - 3$

17. $f(x) = -2.65^{x+1}$

18. $f(x) = 2.65^{x-1}$

19. $f(x) = 5^{x-2} + 4$

20. $f(x) = 2^{x-6} - 5$

21. $f(x) = \left(\frac{1}{2}\right)^{-x} + 3$

22. $f(x) = \left(\frac{1}{8}\right)^{x+2} - 5$

In Exercises 23–26, use the One-to-One Property to solve the equation for x.

23. $3^{x+2} = \dfrac{1}{9}$

24. $\left(\dfrac{1}{3}\right)^{x-2} = 81$

25. $e^{5x-7} = e^{15}$

26. $e^{8-2x} = e^{-3}$

In Exercises 27–30, evaluate the function given by $f(x) = e^x$ at the indicated value of x. Round your result to three decimal places.

27. $x = 8$

28. $x = \frac{5}{8}$

29. $x = -1.7$

30. $x = 0.278$

In Exercises 31–34, use a graphing utility to construct a table of values for the function. Then sketch the graph of the function.

31. $h(x) = e^{-x/2}$

32. $h(x) = 2 - e^{-x/2}$

33. $f(x) = e^{x+2}$

34. $s(t) = 4e^{-2/t}, \quad t > 0$

Compound Interest **In Exercises 35 and 36, complete the table to determine the balance A for P dollars invested at rate r for t years and compounded n times per year.**

n	1	2	4	12	365	Continuous
A						

35. $P = \$3500, \ r = 6.5\%, \ t = 10$ years

36. $P = \$2000, \ r = 5\%, \ t = 30$ years

37. ***Waiting Times*** The average time between incoming calls at a switchboard is 3 minutes. The probability F of waiting less than t minutes until the next incoming call is approximated by the model $F(t) = 1 - e^{-t/3}$. A call has just come in. Find the probability that the next call will be within

(a) $\frac{1}{2}$ minute. (b) 2 minutes. (c) 5 minutes.

38. ***Depreciation*** After t years, the value V of a car that originally cost \$14,000 is given by $V(t) = 14{,}000\left(\frac{3}{4}\right)^t$.

(a) Use a graphing utility to graph the function.

(b) Find the value of the car 2 years after it was purchased.

(c) According to the model, when does the car depreciate most rapidly? Is this realistic? Explain.

39. ***Trust Fund*** On the day a person is born, a deposit of \$50,000 is made in a trust fund that pays 8.75% interest, compounded continuously.

(a) Find the balance on the person's 35th birthday.

(b) How much longer would the person have to wait for the balance in the trust fund to double?

40. ***Radioactive Decay*** Let Q represent a mass of plutonium 241 (^{241}Pu) (in grams), whose half-life is 14.4 years. The quantity of plutonium 241 present after t years is given by $Q = 100\left(\frac{1}{2}\right)^{t/14.4}$.

(a) Determine the initial quantity (when $t = 0$).

(b) Determine the quantity present after 10 years.

(c) Sketch the graph of this function over the interval $t = 0$ to $t = 100$.

3.2 **In Exercises 41–44, write the exponential equation in logarithmic form.**

41. $4^3 = 64$ **42.** $25^{3/2} = 125$

43. $e^{0.8} = 2.2255 . . .$ **44.** $e^0 = 1$

In Exercises 45–48, evaluate the function at the indicated value of x without using a calculator.

Function	*Value*
45. $f(x) = \log x$	$x = 1000$
46. $g(x) = \log_9 x$	$x = 3$
47. $g(x) = \log_2 x$	$x = \frac{1}{8}$
48. $f(x) = \log_4 x$	$x = \frac{1}{4}$

In Exercises 49–52, use the One-to-One Property to solve the equation for x.

49. $\log_4(x + 7) = \log_4 14$ **50.** $\log_8(3x - 10) = \log_8 5$

51. $\ln(x + 9) = \ln 4$ **52.** $\ln(2x - 1) = \ln 11$

In Exercises 53–58, find the domain, x-intercept, and vertical asymptote of the logarithmic function and sketch its graph.

53. $g(x) = \log_7 x$ **54.** $g(x) = \log_5 x$

55. $f(x) = \log\left(\frac{x}{3}\right)$ **56.** $f(x) = 6 + \log x$

57. $f(x) = 4 - \log(x + 5)$ **58.** $f(x) = \log(x - 3) + 1$

In Exercises 59–64, use a calculator to evaluate the function given by $f(x) = \ln x$ at the indicated value of x. Round your result to three decimal places if necessary.

59. $x = 22.6$ **60.** $x = 0.98$

61. $x = e^{-12}$ **62.** $x = e^7$

63. $x = \sqrt{7} + 5$ **64.** $x = \frac{\sqrt{3}}{8}$

In Exercises 65–68, find the domain, x-intercept, and vertical asymptote of the logarithmic function and sketch its graph.

65. $f(x) = \ln x + 3$ **66.** $f(x) = \ln(x - 3)$

67. $h(x) = \ln(x^2)$ **68.** $f(x) = \frac{1}{4} \ln x$

69. ***Antler Spread*** The antler spread a (in inches) and shoulder height h (in inches) of an adult male American elk are related by the model $h = 116 \log(a + 40) - 176$. Approximate the shoulder height of a male American elk with an antler spread of 55 inches.

70. ***Snow Removal*** The number of miles s of roads cleared of snow is approximated by the model

$$s = 25 - \frac{13 \ln(h/12)}{\ln 3}, \quad 2 \le h \le 15$$

where h is the depth of the snow in inches. Use this model to find s when $h = 10$ inches.

3.3 **In Exercises 71–74, evaluate the logarithm using the change-of-base formula. Do each exercise twice, once with common logarithms and once with natural logarithms. Round your the results to three decimal places.**

71. $\log_4 9$ **72.** $\log_{12} 200$

73. $\log_{1/2} 5$ **74.** $\log_3 0.28$

In Exercises 75–78, use the properties of logarithms to rewrite and simplify the logarithmic expression.

75. $\log 18$ **76.** $\log_2\left(\frac{1}{12}\right)$

77. $\ln 20$ **78.** $\ln(3e^{-4})$

In Exercises 79–86, use the properties of logarithms to expand the expression as a sum, difference, and/or constant multiple of logarithms. (Assume all variables are positive.)

79. $\log_5 5x^2$ **80.** $\log 7x^4$

81. $\log_3 \frac{6}{\sqrt[3]{x}}$ **82.** $\log_7 \frac{\sqrt{x}}{4}$

83. $\ln x^2y^2z$ **84.** $\ln 3xy^2$

85. $\ln\left(\frac{x + 3}{xy}\right)$ **86.** $\ln\left(\frac{y - 1}{4}\right)^2, \quad y > 1$

In Exercises 87–94, condense the expression to the logarithm of a single quantity.

87. $\log_2 5 + \log_2 x$ **88.** $\log_6 y - 2 \log_6 z$

89. $\ln x - \frac{1}{4} \ln y$ **90.** $3 \ln x + 2 \ln(x + 1)$

91. $\frac{1}{3} \log_8(x + 4) + 7 \log_8 y$ **92.** $-2 \log x - 5 \log(x + 6)$

93. $\frac{1}{2} \ln(2x - 1) - 2 \ln(x + 1)$

94. $5 \ln(x - 2) - \ln(x + 2) - 3 \ln x$

95. *Climb Rate* The time t (in minutes) for a small plane to climb to an altitude of h feet is modeled by

$$t = 50 \log \frac{18{,}000}{18{,}000 - h}$$

where 18,000 feet is the plane's absolute ceiling.

(a) Determine the domain of the function in the context of the problem.

(b) Use a graphing utility to graph the function and identify any asymptotes.

(c) As the plane approaches its absolute ceiling, what can be said about the time required to increase its altitude?

(d) Find the time for the plane to climb to an altitude of 4000 feet.

96. *Human Memory Model* Students in a learning theory study were given an exam and then retested monthly for 6 months with an equivalent exam. The data obtained in the study are given as the ordered pairs (t, s), where t is the time in months after the initial exam and s is the average score for the class. Use these data to find a logarithmic equation that relates t and s.

(1, 84.2), (2, 78.4), (3, 72.1),
(4, 68.5), (5, 67.1), (6, 65.3)

3.4 In Exercises 97–104, solve for x.

97. $8^x = 512$ **98.** $6^x = \frac{1}{216}$

99. $e^x = 3$ **100.** $e^x = 6$

101. $\log_4 x = 2$ **102.** $\log_6 x = -1$

103. $\ln x = 4$ **104.** $\ln x = -3$

In Exercises 105–114, solve the exponential equation algebraically. Approximate your result to three decimal places.

105. $e^x = 12$ **106.** $e^{3x} = 25$

107. $e^{4x} = e^{x^2+3}$ **108.** $14e^{3x+2} = 560$

109. $2^x + 13 = 35$ **110.** $6^x - 28 = -8$

111. $-4(5^x) = -68$ **112.** $2(12^x) = 190$

113. $e^{2x} - 7e^x + 10 = 0$ **114.** $e^{2x} - 6e^x + 8 = 0$

In Exercises 115–118, use a graphing utility to graph and solve the equation. Approximate the result to three decimal places.

115. $2^{0.6x} - 3x = 0$ **116.** $4^{-0.2x} + x = 0$

117. $25e^{-0.3x} = 12$ **118.** $4e^{1.2x} = 9$

In Exercises 119–130, solve the logarithmic equation algebraically. Approximate the result to three decimal places.

119. $\ln 3x = 8.2$ **120.** $\ln 5x = 7.2$

121. $2 \ln 4x = 15$ **122.** $4 \ln 3x = 15$

123. $\ln x - \ln 3 = 2$ **124.** $\ln \sqrt{x + 8} = 3$

125. $\ln \sqrt{x + 1} = 2$ **126.** $\ln x - \ln 5 = 4$

127. $\log_8 (x - 1) = \log_8 (x - 2) - \log_8 (x + 2)$

128. $\log_6 (x + 2) - \log_6 x = \log_6 (x + 5)$

129. $\log(1 - x) = -1$

130. $\log(-x - 4) = 2$

In Exercises 131–134, use a graphing utility to graph and solve the equation. Approximate the result to three decimal places.

131. $2 \ln(x + 3) + 3x = 8$ **132.** $6 \log(x^2 + 1) - x = 0$

133. $4 \ln(x + 5) - x = 10$ **134.** $x - 2 \log(x + 4) = 0$

135. *Compound Interest* You deposit \$7550 in an account that pays 7.25% interest, compounded continuously. How long will it take for the money to triple?

136. *Meteorology* The speed of the wind S (in miles per hour) near the center of a tornado and the distance d (in miles) the tornado travels are related by the model $S = 93 \log d + 65$. On March 18, 1925, a large tornado struck portions of Missouri, Illinois, and Indiana with a wind speed at the center of about 283 miles per hour. Approximate the distance traveled by this tornado.

3.5 In Exercises 137–142, match the function with its graph. [The graphs are labeled (a), (b), (c), (d), (e), and (f).]

(a)

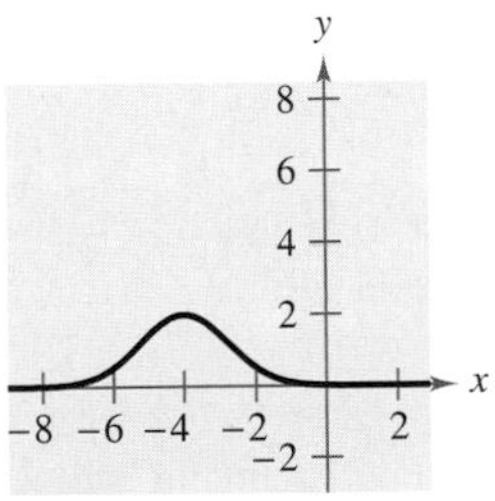

(b)

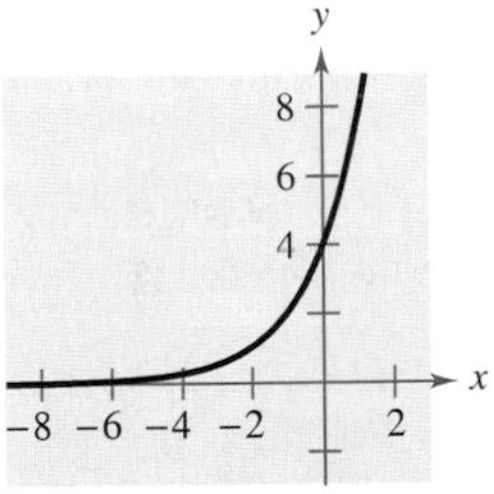

(c)

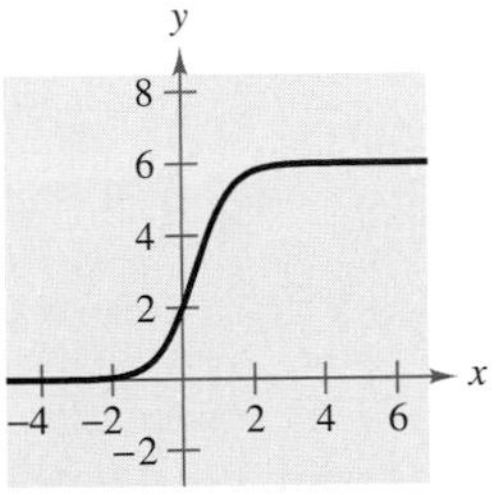

(d)

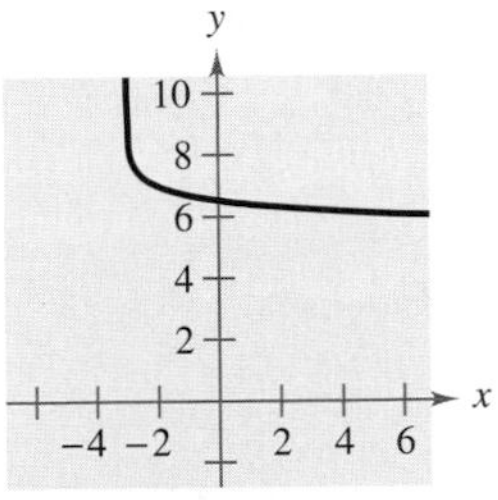

(e)

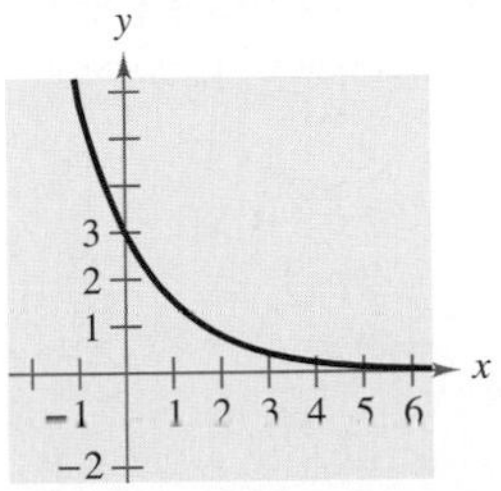

(f)

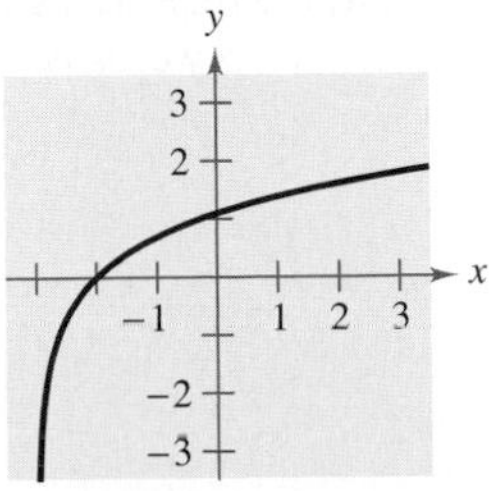

137. $y = 3e^{-2x/3}$

138. $y = 4e^{2x/3}$

139. $y = \ln(x + 3)$

140. $y = 7 - \log(x + 3)$

141. $y = 2e^{-(x+4)^2/3}$

142. $y = \dfrac{6}{1 + 2e^{-2x}}$

In Exercises 143 and 144, find the exponential model $y = ae^{bx}$ that passes through the points.

143. $(0, 2), (4, 3)$

144. $\left(0, \frac{1}{2}\right), (5, 5)$

145. ***Population*** The population P of South Carolina (in thousands) from 1990 through 2003 can be modeled by $P = 3499e^{0.0135t}$, where t represents the year, with $t = 0$ corresponding to 1990. According to this model, when will the population reach 4.5 million? (Source: U.S. Census Bureau)

146. ***Radioactive Decay*** The half-life of radioactive uranium II (^{234}U) is about 250,000 years. What percent of a present amount of radioactive uranium II will remain after 5000 years?

147. ***Compound Interest*** A deposit of $10,000 is made in a savings account for which the interest is compounded continuously. The balance will double in 5 years.

(a) What is the annual interest rate for this account?

(b) Find the balance after 1 year.

148. ***Wildlife Population*** A species of bat is in danger of becoming extinct. Five years ago, the total population of the species was 2000. Two years ago, the total population of the species was 1400. What was the total population of the species one year ago?

149. ***Test Scores*** The test scores for a biology test follow a normal distribution modeled by

$$y = 0.0499e^{-(x-71)^2/128}, \quad 40 \le x \le 100$$

where x is the test score.

(a) Use a graphing utility to graph the equation.

(b) From the graph in part (a), estimate the average test score.

150. ***Typing Speed*** In a typing class, the average number N of words per minute typed after t weeks of lessons was found to be

$$N = \frac{157}{1 + 5.4e^{-0.12t}}.$$

Find the time necessary to type (a) 50 words per minute and (b) 75 words per minute.

151. ***Sound Intensity*** The relationship between the number of decibels β and the intensity of a sound I in watts per square centimeter is

$$\beta = 10 \log\left(\frac{I}{10^{-16}}\right).$$

Determine the intensity of a sound in watts per square centimeter if the decibel level is 125.

152. ***Geology*** On the Richter scale, the magnitude R of an earthquake of intensity I is given by

$$R = \log \frac{I}{I_0}$$

where $I_0 = 1$ is the minimum intensity used for comparison. Find the intensity per unit of area for each value of R.

(a) $R = 8.4$ (b) $R = 6.85$ (c) $R = 9.1$

Synthesis

True or False? **In Exercises 153 and 154, determine whether the equation is true or false. Justify your answer.**

153. $\log_b b^{2x} = 2x$

154. $\ln(x + y) = \ln x + \ln y$

155. The graphs of $y = e^{kt}$ are shown where $k = a, b, c,$ and d. Which of the four values are negative? Which are positive? Explain your reasoning.

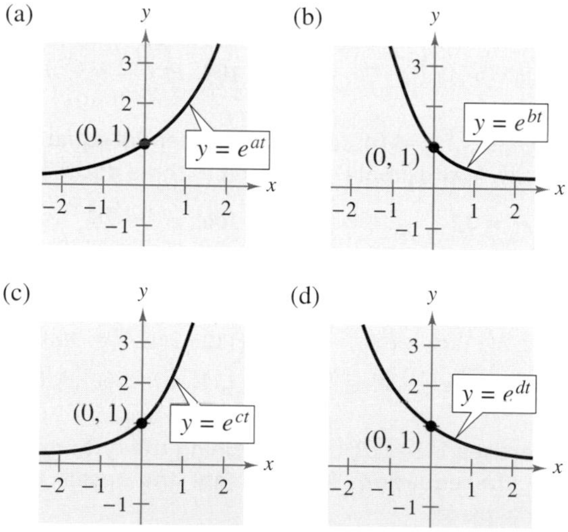

3 Chapter Test

Take this test as you would take a test in class. When you are finished, check your work against the answers given in the back of the book.

In Exercises 1–4, evaluate the expression. Approximate your result to three decimal places.

1. $12.4^{2.79}$ **2.** $4^{3\pi/2}$ **3.** $e^{-7/10}$ **4.** $e^{3.1}$

In Exercises 5–7, construct a table of values. Then sketch the graph of the function.

5. $f(x) = 10^{-x}$ **6.** $f(x) = -6^{x-2}$ **7.** $f(x) = 1 - e^{2x}$

8. Evaluate (a) $\log_7 7^{-0.89}$ and (b) $4.6 \ln e^2$.

In Exercises 9–11, construct a table of values. Then sketch the graph of the function. Identify any asymptotes.

9. $f(x) = -\log x - 6$ **10.** $f(x) = \ln(x - 4)$ **11.** $f(x) = 1 + \ln(x + 6)$

In Exercises 12–14, evaluate the logarithm using the change-of-base formula. Round your result to three decimal places.

12. $\log_7 44$ **13.** $\log_{2/5} 0.9$ **14.** $\log_{24} 68$

In Exercises 15–17, use the properties of logarithms to expand the expression as a sum, difference, and/or constant multiple of logarithms.

15. $\log_2 3a^4$ **16.** $\ln \dfrac{5\sqrt{x}}{6}$ **17.** $\log \dfrac{7x^2}{yz^3}$

In Exercises 18–20, condense the expression to the logarithm of a single quantity.

18. $\log_3 13 + \log_3 y$ **19.** $4 \ln x - 4 \ln y$

20. $2 \ln x + \ln(x - 5) - 3 \ln y$

In Exercises 21–26, solve the equation algebraically. Approximate your result to three decimal places.

21. $5^x = \dfrac{1}{25}$ **22.** $3e^{-5x} = 132$

23. $\dfrac{1025}{8 + e^{4x}} = 5$ **24.** $\ln x = \dfrac{1}{2}$

25. $18 + 4 \ln x = 7$ **26.** $\log x - \log(8 - 5x) = 2$

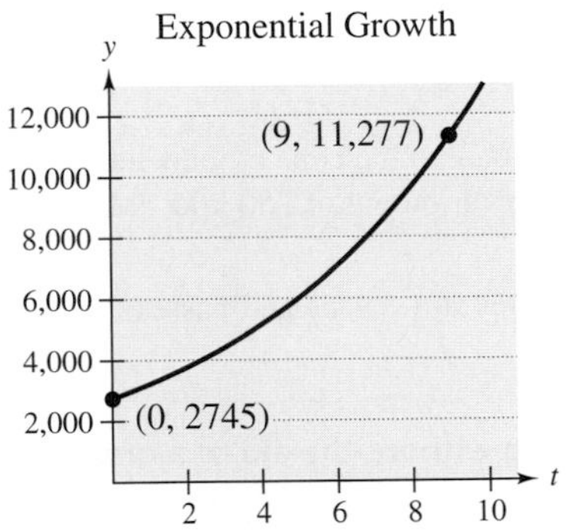

FIGURE FOR 27

27. Find an exponential growth model for the graph shown in the figure.

28. The half-life of radioactive actinium (^{227}Ac) is 21.77 years. What percent of a present amount of radioactive actinium will remain after 19 years?

29. A model that can be used for predicting the height H (in centimeters) of a child based on his or her age is $H = 70.228 + 5.104x + 9.222 \ln x$, $\frac{1}{4} \le x \le 6$, where x is the age of the child in years. (Source: Snapshots of Applications in Mathematics)

(a) Construct a table of values. Then sketch the graph of the model.

(b) Use the graph from part (a) to estimate the height of a four-year-old child. Then calculate the actual height using the model.

3 Cumulative Test for Chapters 1–3

Take this test to review the material from earlier chapters. When you are finished, check your work against the answers given in the back of the book.

1. Plot the points $(3, 4)$ and $(-1, -1)$. Find the coordinates of the midpoint of the line segment joining the points and the distance between the points.

In Exercises 2–4, graph the equation without using a graphing utility.

2. $x - 3y + 12 = 0$ 3. $y = x^2 - 9$ 4. $y = \sqrt{4 - x}$

5. Find an equation of the line passing through $\left(-\frac{1}{2}, 1\right)$ and $(3, 8)$.

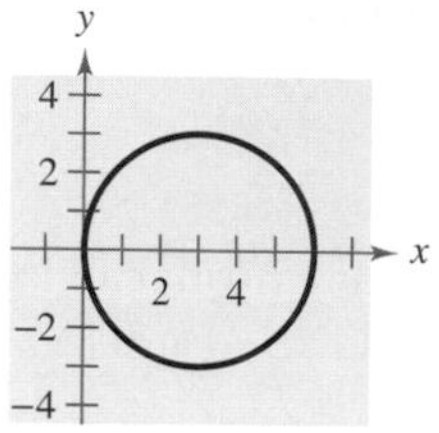

FIGURE FOR 6

6. Explain why the graph at the left does not represent y as a function of x.

7. Evaluate (if possible) the function given by $f(x) = \dfrac{x}{x - 2}$ for each value.

(a) $f(6)$ (b) $f(2)$ (c) $f(s + 2)$

8. Compare the graph of each function with the graph of $y = \sqrt[3]{x}$. (*Note:* It is not necessary to sketch the graphs.)

(a) $r(x) = \frac{1}{2}\sqrt[3]{x}$ (b) $h(x) = \sqrt[3]{x} + 2$ (c) $g(x) = \sqrt[3]{x + 2}$

In Exercises 9 and 10, find (a) $(f + g)(x)$, (b) $(f - g)(x)$, (c) $(fg)(x)$, and (d) $(f/g)(x)$. What is the domain of f/g?

9. $f(x) = x - 3,\quad g(x) = 4x + 1$ 10. $f(x) = \sqrt{x - 1},\quad g(x) = x^2 + 1$

In Exercises 11 and 12, find (a) $f \circ g$ and (b) $g \circ f$. Find the domain of each composite function.

11. $f(x) = 2x^2,\quad g(x) = \sqrt{x + 6}$ 12. $f(x) = x - 2,\quad g(x) = |x|$

13. Determine whether $h(x) = 5x - 2$ has an inverse function. If so, find the inverse function.

14. The power P produced by a wind turbine is proportional to the cube of the wind speed S. A wind speed of 27 miles per hour produces a power output of 750 kilowatts. Find the output for a wind speed of 40 miles per hour.

15. Find the quadratic function whose graph has a vertex at $(-8, 5)$ and passes through the point $(-4, -7)$.

In Exercises 16–18, sketch the graph of the function without the aid of a graphing utility.

16. $h(x) = -(x^2 + 4x)$ 17. $f(t) = \frac{1}{4}t(t - 2)^2$ 18. $g(s) = s^2 + 4s + 10$

In Exercises 19–21, find all the zeros of the function and write the function as a product of linear factors.

19. $f(x) = x^3 + 2x^2 + 4x + 8$

20. $f(x) = x^4 + 4x^3 - 21x^2$

21. $f(x) = 2x^4 - 11x^3 + 30x^2 - 62x - 40$

22. Use long division to divide $6x^3 - 4x^2$ by $2x^2 + 1$.

23. Use synthetic division to divide $2x^4 + 3x^3 - 6x + 5$ by $x + 2$.

24. Use the Intermediate Value Theorem and a graphing utility to find intervals one unit in length in which the function $g(x) = x^3 + 3x^2 - 6$ is guaranteed to have a zero. Approximate the real zeros of the function.

In Exercises 25–27, sketch the graph of the rational function by hand. Be sure to identify all intercepts and asymptotes.

25. $f(x) = \dfrac{2x}{x^2 - 9}$

26. $f(x) = \dfrac{x^2 - 4x + 3}{x^2 - 2x - 3}$

27. $f(x) = \dfrac{x^3 + 3x^2 - 4x - 12}{x^2 - x - 2}$

In Exercises 28 and 29, solve the inequality. Sketch the solution set on the real number line.

28. $3x^3 - 12x \leq 0$

29. $\dfrac{1}{x + 1} \geq \dfrac{1}{x + 5}$

In Exercises 30 and 31, use the graph of *f* to describe the transformation that yields the graph of *g*.

30. $f(x) = \left(\frac{2}{5}\right)^x, \quad g(x) = -\left(\frac{2}{5}\right)^{-x+3}$

31. $f(x) = 2.2^x, \quad g(x) = -2.2^x + 4$

In Exercises 32–35, use a calculator to evaluate the expression. Round your result to three decimal places.

32. $\log 98$

33. $\log\left(\frac{6}{7}\right)$

34. $\ln\sqrt{31}$

35. $\ln\left(\sqrt{40} - 5\right)$

36. Use the properties of logarithms to expand $\ln\left(\dfrac{x^2 - 16}{x^4}\right)$, where $x > 4$.

37. Write $2 \ln x - \frac{1}{2}\ln(x + 5)$ as a logarithm of a single quantity.

In Exercises 38–40, solve the equation algebraicially. Approximate the result to three decimal places.

38. $6e^{2x} = 72$

39. $e^{2x} - 11e^x + 24 = 0$

40. $\ln\sqrt{x + 2} = 3$

Year	Sales, *S*
1997	35.5
1998	35.6
1999	36.0
2000	37.2
2001	38.4
2002	42.0
2003	43.5

TABLE FOR 41

41. The sales S (in billions of dollars) of lottery tickets in the United States from 1997 through 2003 are shown in the table. (Source: TLF Publications, Inc.)

(a) Use a graphing utility to create a scatter plot of the data. Let t represent the year, with $t = 7$ corresponding to 1997.

(b) Use the *regression* feature of the graphing utility to find a quadratic model for the data.

(c) Use the graphing utility to graph the model in the same viewing window used for the scatter plot. How well does the model fit the data?

(d) Use the model to predict the sales of lottery tickets in 2008. Does your answer seem reasonable? Explain.

42. The number N of bacteria in a culture is given by the model $N = 175e^{kt}$, where t is the time in hours. If $N = 420$ when $t = 8$, estimate the time required for the population to double in size.

Proofs in Mathematics

Each of the following three properties of logarithms can be proved by using properties of exponential functions.

Slide Rules

The slide rule was invented by William Oughtred (1574–1660) in 1625. The slide rule is a computational device with a sliding portion and a fixed portion. A slide rule enables you to perform multiplication by using the Product Property of Logarithms. There are other slide rules that allow for the calculation of roots and trigonometric functions. Slide rules were used by mathematicians and engineers until the invention of the hand-held calculator in 1972.

Properties of Logarithms *(p. 240)*

Let a be a positive number such that $a \neq 1$, and let n be a real number. If u and v are positive real numbers, the following properties are true.

	Logarithm with Base a	*Natural Logarithm*
1. Product Property:	$\log_a(uv) = \log_a u + \log_a v$	$\ln(uv) = \ln u + \ln v$
2. Quotient Property:	$\log_a \frac{u}{v} = \log_a u - \log_a v$	$\ln \frac{u}{v} = \ln u - \ln v$
3. Power Property:	$\log_a u^n = n \log_a u$	$\ln u^n = n \ln u$

Proof

Let

$$x = \log_a u \quad \text{and} \quad y = \log_a v.$$

The corresponding exponential forms of these two equations are

$$a^x = u \quad \text{and} \quad a^y = v.$$

To prove the Product Property, multiply u and v to obtain

$$uv = a^x a^y = a^{x+y}.$$

The corresponding logarithmic form of $uv = a^{x+y}$ is $\log_a(uv) = x + y$. So,

$$\log_a(uv) = \log_a u + \log_a v.$$

To prove the Quotient Property, divide u by v to obtain

$$\frac{u}{v} = \frac{a^x}{a^y} = a^{x-y}.$$

The corresponding logarithmic form of $u/v = a^{x-y}$ is $\log_a(u/v) = x - y$. So,

$$\log_a \frac{u}{v} = \log_a u - \log_a v.$$

To prove the Power Property, substitute a^x for u in the expression $\log_a u^n$, as follows.

$\log_a u^n = \log_a(a^x)^n$	Substitute a^x for u.
$= \log_a a^{nx}$	Property of exponents
$= nx$	Inverse Property of Logarithms
$= n \log_a u$	Substitute $\log_a u$ for x.

So, $\log_a u^n = n \log_a u$.

P.S. Problem Solving

This collection of thought-provoking and challenging exercises further explores and expands upon concepts learned in this chapter.

1. Graph the exponential function given by $y = a^x$ for $a = 0.5$, 1.2, and 2.0. Which of these curves intersects the line $y = x$? Determine all positive numbers a for which the curve $y = a^x$ intersects the line $y = x$.

2. Use a graphing utility to graph $y_1 = e^x$ and each of the functions $y_2 = x^2$, $y_3 = x^3$, $y_4 = \sqrt{x}$, and $y_5 = |x|$. Which function increases at the greatest rate as x approaches $+\infty$?

3. Use the result of Exercise 2 to make a conjecture about the rate of growth of $y_1 = e^x$ and $y = x^n$, where n is a natural number and x approaches $+\infty$.

4. Use the results of Exercises 2 and 3 to describe what is implied when it is stated that a quantity is growing exponentially.

5. Given the exponential function

$$f(x) = a^x$$

show that

(a) $f(u + v) = f(u) \cdot f(v)$.

(b) $f(2x) = [f(x)]^2$.

6. Given that

$$f(x) = \frac{e^x + e^{-x}}{2} \text{ and } g(x) = \frac{e^x - e^{-x}}{2}$$

show that

$$[f(x)]^2 - [g(x)]^2 = 1.$$

7. Use a graphing utility to compare the graph of the function given by $y = e^x$ with the graph of each given function. [$n!$ (read "n factorial") is defined as $n! = 1 \cdot 2 \cdot 3 \cdots (n - 1) \cdot n$.]

(a) $y_1 = 1 + \dfrac{x}{1!}$

(b) $y_2 = 1 + \dfrac{x}{1!} + \dfrac{x^2}{2!}$

(c) $y_3 = 1 + \dfrac{x}{1!} + \dfrac{x^2}{2!} + \dfrac{x^3}{3!}$

8. Identify the pattern of successive polynomials given in Exercise 7. Extend the pattern one more term and compare the graph of the resulting polynomial function with the graph of $y = e^x$. What do you think this pattern implies?

9. Graph the function given by

$$f(x) = e^x - e^{-x}.$$

From the graph, the function appears to be one-to-one. Assuming that the function has an inverse function, find $f^{-1}(x)$.

10. Find a pattern for $f^{-1}(x)$ if

$$f(x) = \frac{a^x + 1}{a^x - 1}$$

where $a > 0$, $a \neq 1$.

11. By observation, identify the equation that corresponds to the graph. Explain your reasoning.

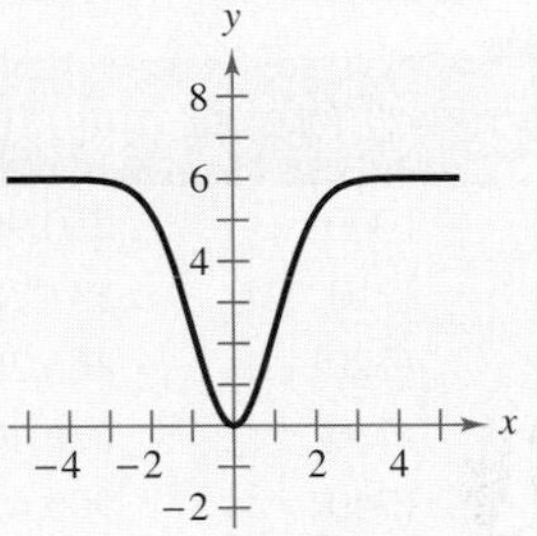

(a) $y = 6e^{-x^2/2}$

(b) $y = \dfrac{6}{1 + e^{-x/2}}$

(c) $y = 6(1 - e^{-x^2/2})$

12. You have two options for investing \$500. The first earns 7% compounded annually and the second earns 7% simple interest. The figure shows the growth of each investment over a 30-year period.

(a) Identify which graph represents each type of investment. Explain your reasoning.

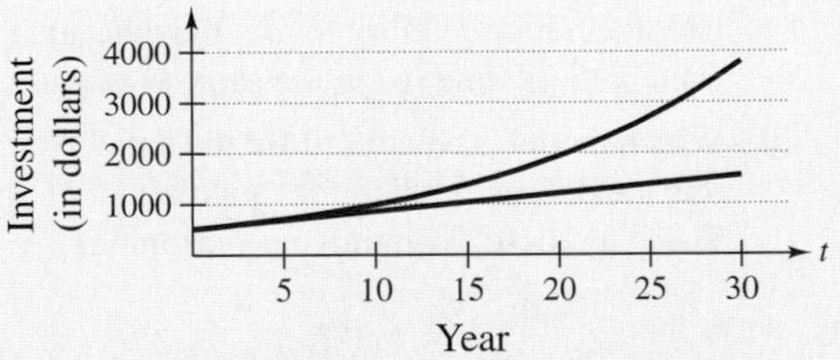

(b) Verify your answer in part (a) by finding the equations that model the investment growth and graphing the models.

(c) Which option would you choose? Explain your reasoning.

13. Two different samples of radioactive isotopes are decaying. The isotopes have initial amounts of c_1 and c_2, as well as half-lives of k_1 and k_2, respectively. Find the time required for the samples to decay to equal amounts.

14. A lab culture initially contains 500 bacteria. Two hours later, the number of bacteria has decreased to 200. Find the exponential decay model of the form

$$B = B_0 a^{kt}$$

that can be used to approximate the number of bacteria after t hours.

15. The table shows the colonial population estimates of the American colonies from 1700 to 1780. (Source: U.S. Census Bureau)

Year	Population
1700	250,900
1710	331,700
1720	466,200
1730	629,400
1740	905,600
1750	1,170,800
1760	1,593,600
1770	2,148,100
1780	2,780,400

In each of the following, let y represent the population in the year t, with $t = 0$ corresponding to 1700.

(a) Use the *regression* feature of a graphing utility to find an exponential model for the data.

(b) Use the *regression* feature of the graphing utility to find a quadratic model for the data.

(c) Use the graphing utility to plot the data and the models from parts (a) and (b) in the same viewing window.

(d) Which model is a better fit for the data? Would you use this model to predict the population of the United States in 2010? Explain your reasoning.

16. Show that $\dfrac{\log_a x}{\log_{a/b} x} = 1 + \log_a \dfrac{1}{b}$.

17. Solve $(\ln x)^2 = \ln x^2$.

18. Use a graphing utility to compare the graph of the function given by $y = \ln x$ with the graph of each given function.

(a) $y_1 = x - 1$

(b) $y_2 = (x - 1) - \frac{1}{2}(x - 1)^2$

(c) $y_3 = (x - 1) - \frac{1}{2}(x - 1)^2 + \frac{1}{3}(x - 1)^3$

19. Identify the pattern of successive polynomials given in Exercise 18. Extend the pattern one more term and compare the graph of the resulting polynomial function with the graph of $y = \ln x$. What do you think the pattern implies?

20. Using

$$y = ab^x \quad \text{and} \quad y = ax^b$$

take the natural logarithm of each side of each equation. What are the slope and y-intercept of the line relating x and $\ln y$ for $y = ab^x$? What are the slope and y-intercept of the line relating $\ln x$ and $\ln y$ for $y = ax^b$?

In Exercises 21 and 22, use the model

$$y = 80.4 - 11 \ln x, \quad 100 \le x \le 1500$$

which approximates the minimum required ventilation rate in terms of the air space per child in a public school classroom. In the model, x is the air space per child in cubic feet and y is the ventilation rate per child in cubic feet per minute.

21. Use a graphing utility to graph the model and approximate the required ventilation rate if there is 300 cubic feet of air space per child.

22. A classroom is designed for 30 students. The air conditioning system in the room has the capacity of moving 450 cubic feet of air per minute.

(a) Determine the ventilation rate per child, assuming that the room is filled to capacity.

(b) Estimate the air space required per child.

(c) Determine the minimum number of square feet of floor space required for the room if the ceiling height is 30 feet.

In Exercises 23–26, (a) use a graphing utility to create a scatter plot of the data, (b) decide whether the data could best be modeled by a linear model, an exponential model, or a logarithmic model, (c) explain why you chose the model you did in part (b), (d) use the *regression* feature of a graphing utility to find the model you chose in part (b) for the data and graph the model with the scatter plot, and (e) determine how well the model you chose fits the data.

23. (1, 2.0), (1.5, 3.5), (2, 4.0), (4, 5.8), (6, 7.0), (8, 7.8)

24. (1, 4.4), (1.5, 4.7), (2, 5.5), (4, 9.9), (6, 18.1), (8, 33.0)

25. (1, 7.5), (1.5, 7.0), (2, 6.8), (4, 5.0), (6, 3.5), (8, 2.0)

26. (1, 5.0), (1.5, 6.0), (2, 6.4), (4, 7.8), (6, 8.6), (8, 9.0)

Trigonometry

4

4.1 Radian and Degree Measure

4.2 Trigonometric Functions: The Unit Circle

4.3 Right Triangle Trigonometry

4.4 Trigonometric Functions of Any Angle

4.5 Graphs of Sine and Cosine Functions

4.6 Graphs of Other Trigonometric Functions

4.7 Inverse Trigonometric Functions

4.8 Applications and Models

Airport runways are named on the basis of the angles they form with due north, measured in a clockwise direction. These angles are called bearings and can be determined using trigonometry.

Rajs/Photonica/Getty Images

SELECTED APPLICATIONS

Trigonometric functions have many real-life applications. The applications listed below represent a small sample of the applications in this chapter.

- Speed of a Bicycle, Exercise 108, page 293
- Machine Shop Calculations, Exercise 69, page 310
- Sales, Exercise 88, page 320
- Respiratory Cycle, Exercise 73, page 330
- Data Analysis: Meteorology, Exercise 75, page 330
- Predator-Prey Model, Exercise 77, page 341
- Security Patrol, Exercise 97, page 351
- Navigation, Exercise 29, page 360
- Wave Motion, Exercise 60, page 362

4.1 Radian and Degree Measure

What you should learn

- Describe angles.
- Use radian measure.
- Use degree measure.
- Use angles to model and solve real-life problems.

Why you should learn it

You can use angles to model and solve real-life problems. For instance, in Exercise 108 on page 293, you are asked to use angles to find the speed of a bicycle.

Angles

As derived from the Greek language, the word **trigonometry** means "measurement of triangles." Initially, trigonometry dealt with relationships among the sides and angles of triangles and was used in the development of astronomy, navigation, and surveying. With the development of calculus and the physical sciences in the 17th century, a different perspective arose—one that viewed the classic trigonometric relationships as *functions* with the set of real numbers as their domains. Consequently, the applications of trigonometry expanded to include a vast number of physical phenomena involving rotations and vibrations. These phenomena include sound waves, light rays, planetary orbits, vibrating strings, pendulums, and orbits of atomic particles.

The approach in this text incorporates *both* perspectives, starting with angles and their measure.

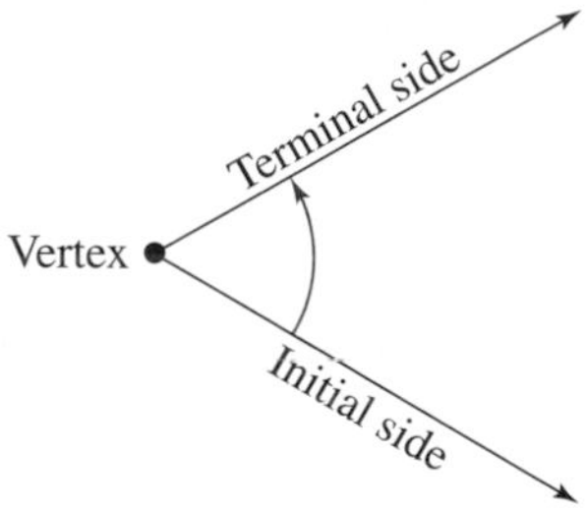

Angle
FIGURE 4.1

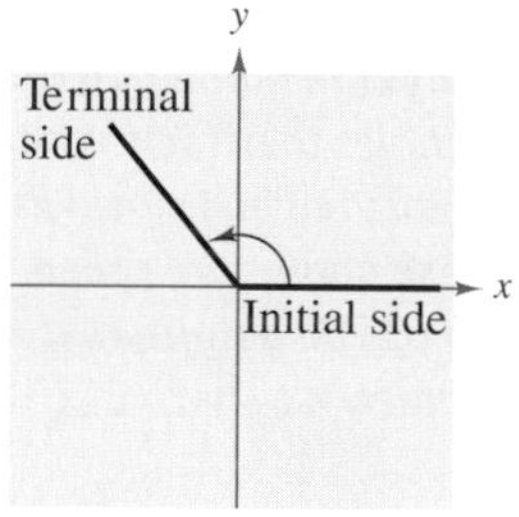

Angle in Standard Position
FIGURE 4.2

An **angle** is determined by rotating a ray (half-line) about its endpoint. The starting position of the ray is the **initial side** of the angle, and the position after rotation is the **terminal side,** as shown in Figure 4.1. The endpoint of the ray is the **vertex** of the angle. This perception of an angle fits a coordinate system in which the origin is the vertex and the initial side coincides with the positive x-axis. Such an angle is in **standard position,** as shown in Figure 4.2. **Positive angles** are generated by counterclockwise rotation, and **negative angles** by clockwise rotation, as shown in Figure 4.3. Angles are labeled with Greek letters α (alpha), β (bcta), and 0 (theta), as well as uppercase letters A, B, and C. In Figure 4.4, note that angles α and β have the same initial and terminal sides. Such angles are **coterminal.**

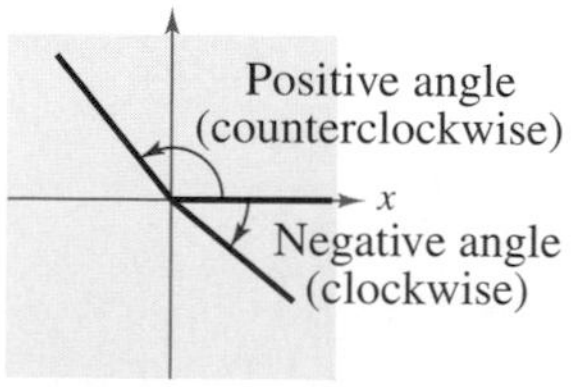

FIGURE 4.3

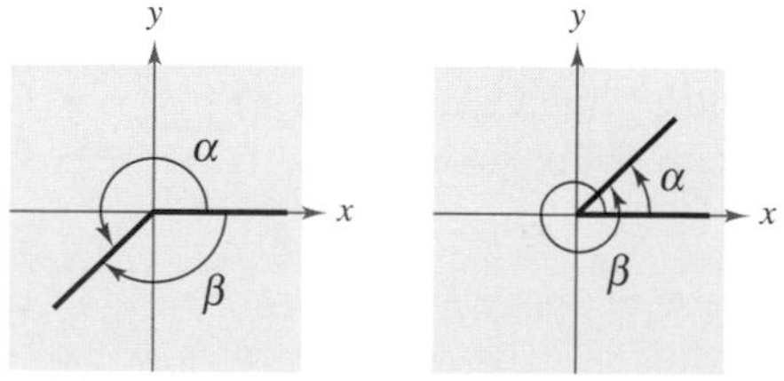

FIGURE 4.4 *Coterminal Angles*

Radian Measure

The **measure of an angle** is determined by the amount of rotation from the initial side to the terminal side. One way to measure angles is in *radians*. This type of measure is especially useful in calculus. To define a radian, you can use a **central angle** of a circle, one whose vertex is the center of the circle, as shown in Figure 4.5.

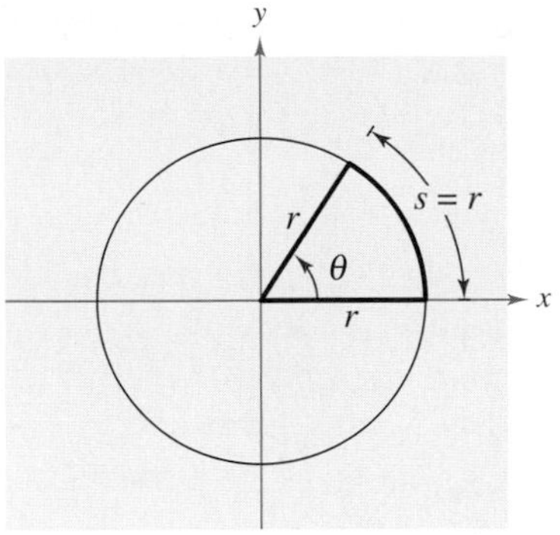

Arc length = radius when $\theta = 1$ radian
FIGURE 4.5

Definition of Radian

One **radian** is the measure of a central angle θ that intercepts an arc s equal in length to the radius r of the circle. See Figure 4.5. Algebraically, this means that

$$\theta = \frac{s}{r}$$

where θ is measured in radians.

Because the circumference of a circle is $2\pi r$ units, it follows that a central angle of one full revolution (counterclockwise) corresponds to an arc length of

$$s = 2\pi r.$$

Moreover, because $2\pi \approx 6.28$, there are just over six radius lengths in a full circle, as shown in Figure 4.6. Because the units of measure for s and r are the same, the ratio s/r has no units—it is simply a real number.

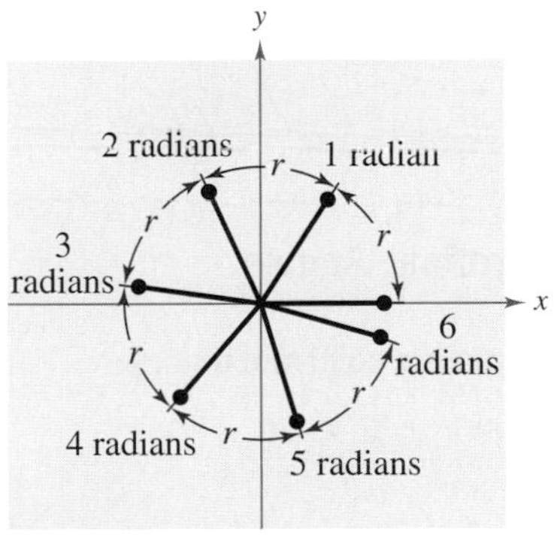

FIGURE 4.6

Because the radian measure of an angle of one full revolution is 2π, you can obtain the following.

$$\frac{1}{2} \text{ revolution} = \frac{2\pi}{2} = \pi \text{ radians}$$

$$\frac{1}{4} \text{ revolution} = \frac{2\pi}{4} = \frac{\pi}{2} \text{ radians}$$

$$\frac{1}{6} \text{ revolution} = \frac{2\pi}{6} = \frac{\pi}{3} \text{ radians}$$

These and other common angles are shown in Figure 4.7.

STUDY TIP

One revolution around a circle of radius r corresponds to an angle of 2π radians because

$$\theta = \frac{s}{r} = \frac{2\pi r}{r} = 2\pi \text{ radians.}$$

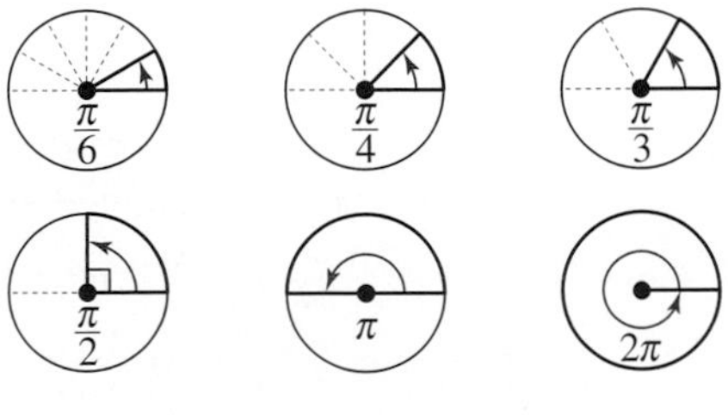

FIGURE 4.7

Recall that the four quadrants in a coordinate system are numbered I, II, III, and IV. Figure 4.8 on page 284 shows which angles between 0 and 2π lie in each of the four quadrants. Note that angles between 0 and $\pi/2$ are **acute** angles and angles between $\pi/2$ and π are **obtuse** angles.

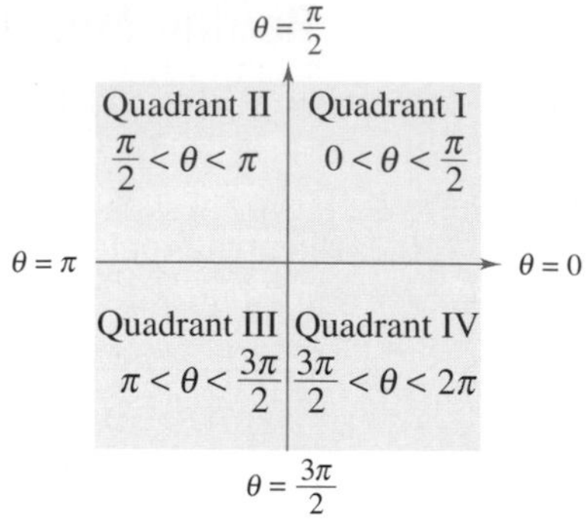

FIGURE 4.8

STUDY TIP

The phrase "the terminal side of θ lies in a quadrant" is often abbreviated by simply saying that "θ lies in a quadrant." The terminal sides of the "quadrant angles" 0, $\pi/2$, π, and $3\pi/2$ do not lie within quadrants.

Two angles are coterminal if they have the same initial and terminal sides. For instance, the angles 0 and 2π are coterminal, as are the angles $\pi/6$ and $13\pi/6$. You can find an angle that is coterminal to a given angle θ by adding or subtracting 2π (one revolution), as demonstrated in Example 1. A given angle θ has infinitely many coterminal angles. For instance, $\theta = \pi/6$ is coterminal with

$$\frac{\pi}{6} + 2n\pi$$

where n is an integer.

Example 1 Sketching and Finding Coterminal Angles

a. For the positive angle $13\pi/6$, subtract 2π to obtain a coterminal angle

$$\frac{13\pi}{6} - 2\pi = \frac{\pi}{6}.$$ See Figure 4.9.

b. For the positive angle $3\pi/4$, subtract 2π to obtain a coterminal angle

$$\frac{3\pi}{4} - 2\pi = -\frac{5\pi}{4}.$$ See Figure 4.10.

c. For the negative angle $-2\pi/3$, add 2π to obtain a coterminal angle

$$-\frac{2\pi}{3} + 2\pi = \frac{4\pi}{3}.$$ See Figure 4.11.

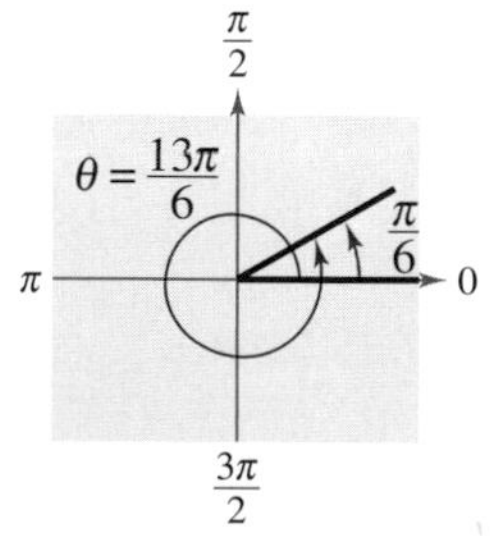

FIGURE 4.9

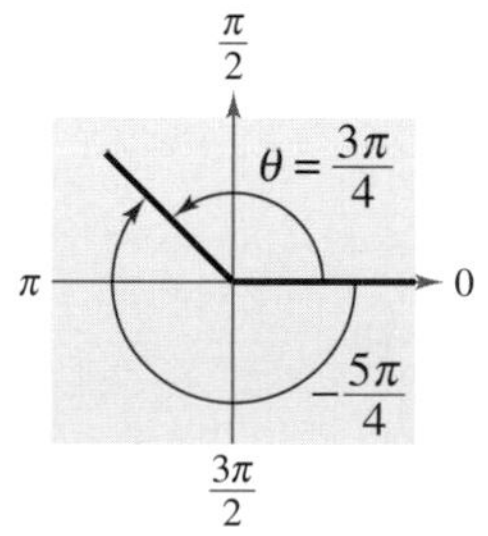

FIGURE 4.10

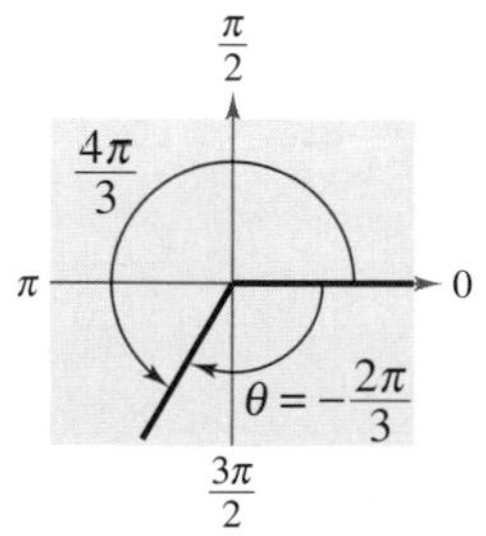

FIGURE 4.11

✓CHECKPOINT Now try Exercise 17.

Two positive angles α and β are **complementary** (complements of each other) if their sum is $\pi/2$. Two positive angles are **supplementary** (supplements of each other) if their sum is π. See Figure 4.12.

Complementary Angles *Supplementary Angles*

FIGURE 4.12

Example 2 **Complementary and Supplementary Angles**

If possible, find the complement and the supplement of (a) $2\pi/5$ and (b) $4\pi/5$.

Solution

a. The complement of $2\pi/5$ is

$$\frac{\pi}{2} - \frac{2\pi}{5} = \frac{5\pi}{10} - \frac{4\pi}{10} = \frac{\pi}{10}.$$

The supplement of $2\pi/5$ is

$$\pi - \frac{2\pi}{5} = \frac{5\pi}{5} - \frac{2\pi}{5} = \frac{3\pi}{5}.$$

b. Because $4\pi/5$ is greater than $\pi/2$, it has no complement. (Remember that complements are *positive* angles.) The supplement is

$$\pi - \frac{4\pi}{5} = \frac{5\pi}{5} - \frac{4\pi}{5} = \frac{\pi}{5}.$$

✓CHECKPOINT Now try Exercise 21.

Degree Measure

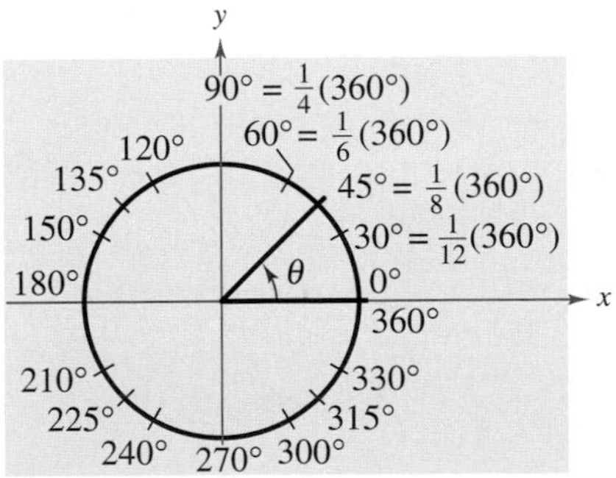

FIGURE 4.13

A second way to measure angles is in terms of **degrees,** denoted by the symbol °. A measure of one degree (1°) is equivalent to a rotation of $\frac{1}{360}$ of a complete revolution about the vertex. To measure angles, it is convenient to mark degrees on the circumference of a circle, as shown in Figure 4.13. So, a full revolution (counterclockwise) corresponds to 360°, a half revolution to 180°, a quarter revolution to 90°, and so on.

Because 2π radians corresponds to one complete revolution, degrees and radians are related by the equations

$$360° = 2\pi \text{ rad} \qquad \text{and} \qquad 180° = \pi \text{ rad}.$$

From the latter equation, you obtain

$$1° = \frac{\pi}{180} \text{ rad} \qquad \text{and} \qquad 1 \text{ rad} = \left(\frac{180°}{\pi}\right)$$

which lead to the conversion rules at the top of the next page.

Conversions Between Degrees and Radians

1. To convert degrees to radians, multiply degrees by $\dfrac{\pi \text{ rad}}{180°}$.

2. To convert radians to degrees, multiply radians by $\dfrac{180°}{\pi \text{ rad}}$.

To apply these two conversion rules, use the basic relationship π rad $= 180°$. (See Figure 4.14.)

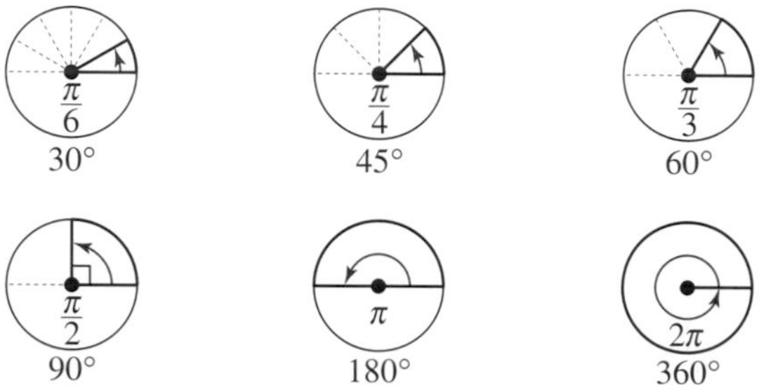

FIGURE 4.14

When no units of angle measure are specified, *radian measure is implied.* For instance, if you write $\theta = 2$, you imply that $\theta = 2$ radians.

Example 3 Converting from Degrees to Radians

a. $135° = (135 \text{ deg})\left(\dfrac{\pi \text{ rad}}{180 \text{ deg}}\right) = \dfrac{3\pi}{4}$ radians Multiply by $\pi/180$.

b. $540° = (540 \text{ deg})\left(\dfrac{\pi \text{ rad}}{180 \text{ deg}}\right) = 3\pi$ radians Multiply by $\pi/180$.

c. $-270° = (-270 \text{ deg})\left(\dfrac{\pi \text{ rad}}{180 \text{ deg}}\right) = -\dfrac{3\pi}{2}$ radians Multiply by $\pi/180$.

CHECKPOINT Now try Exercise 47.

Example 4 Converting from Radians to Degrees

a. $-\dfrac{\pi}{2} \text{ rad} = \left(-\dfrac{\pi}{2} \text{ rad}\right)\left(\dfrac{180 \text{ deg}}{\pi \text{ rad}}\right) = -90°$ Multiply by $180/\pi$.

b. $\dfrac{9\pi}{2} \text{ rad} = \left(\dfrac{9\pi}{2} \text{ rad}\right)\left(\dfrac{180 \text{ deg}}{\pi \text{ rad}}\right) = 810°$ Multiply by $180/\pi$.

c. $2 \text{ rad} = (2 \text{ rad})\left(\dfrac{180 \text{ deg}}{\pi \text{ rad}}\right) = \dfrac{360°}{\pi} \approx 114.59°$ Multiply by $180/\pi$.

CHECKPOINT Now try Exercise 51.

If you have a calculator with a "radian-to-degree" conversion key, try using it to verify the result shown in part (c) of Example 4.

Technology

With calculators it is convenient to use *decimal* degrees to denote fractional parts of degrees. Historically, however, fractional parts of degrees were expressed in *minutes* and *seconds*, using the prime (′) and double prime (″) notations, respectively. That is,

$1' = \text{one minute} = \frac{1}{60}(1°)$

$1'' = \text{one second} = \frac{1}{3600}(1°)$

Consequently, an angle of 64 degrees, 32 minutes, and 47 seconds is represented by $\theta = 64° \, 32' \, 47''$. Many calculators have special keys for converting an angle in degrees, minutes, and seconds (D° M′ S″) to decimal degree form, and vice versa.

Applications

The *radian measure* formula, $\theta = s/r$, can be used to measure arc length along a circle.

Arc Length

For a circle of radius r, a central angle θ intercepts an arc of length s given by

$$s = r\theta \qquad \text{Length of circular arc}$$

where θ is measured in radians. Note that if $r = 1$, then $s = \theta$, and the radian measure of θ equals the arc length.

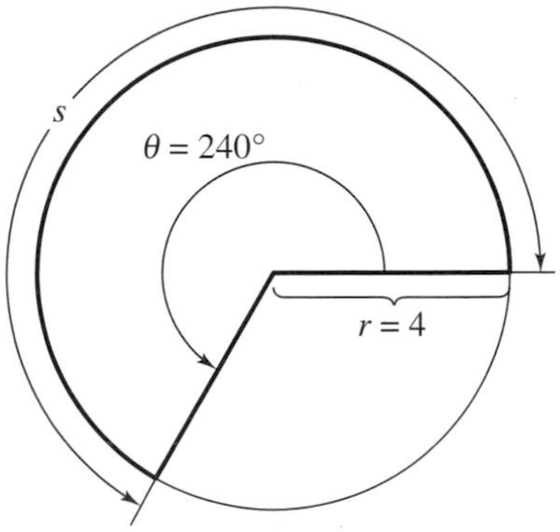

FIGURE 4.15

Example 5 Finding Arc Length

A circle has a radius of 4 inches. Find the length of the arc intercepted by a central angle of 240°, as shown in Figure 4.15.

Solution

To use the formula $s = r\theta$, first convert 240° to radian measure.

$$240° = (240 \text{ deg})\left(\frac{\pi \text{ rad}}{180 \text{ deg}}\right) = \frac{4\pi}{3} \text{ radians}$$

Then, using a radius of $r = 4$ inches, you can find the arc length to be

$$s = r\theta = 4\left(\frac{4\pi}{3}\right) = \frac{16\pi}{3} \approx 16.76 \text{ inches.}$$

Note that the units for $r\theta$ are determined by the units for r because θ is given in radian measure, which has no units.

✓CHECKPOINT Now try Exercise 87.

The formula for the length of a circular arc can be used to analyze the motion of a particle moving at a *constant speed* along a circular path.

Linear and Angular Speeds

Consider a particle moving at a constant speed along a circular arc of radius r. If s is the length of the arc traveled in time t, then the **linear speed** v of the particle is

$$\text{Linear speed } v = \frac{\text{arc length}}{\text{time}} = \frac{s}{t}.$$

Moreover, if θ is the angle (in radian measure) corresponding to the arc length s, then the **angular speed** ω (the lowercase Greek letter omega) of the particle is

$$\text{Angular speed } \omega = \frac{\text{central angle}}{\text{time}} = \frac{\theta}{t}.$$

STUDY TIP

Linear speed measures how fast the particle moves, and angular speed measures how fast the angle changes. By dividing the formula for arc length by t, you can establish a relationship between linear speed v and angular speed ω, as shown.

$$s = r\theta$$

$$\frac{s}{t} = \frac{r\theta}{t}$$

$$v = r\omega$$

FIGURE 4.16

Example 6 Finding Linear Speed

The second hand of a clock is 10.2 centimeters long, as shown in Figure 4.16. Find the linear speed of the tip of this second hand as it passes around the clock face.

Solution

In one revolution, the arc length traveled is

$$\begin{aligned} s &= 2\pi r \\ &= 2\pi(10.2) && \text{Substitute for } r. \\ &= 20.4\pi \text{ centimeters.} \end{aligned}$$

The time required for the second hand to travel this distance is

$$t = 1 \text{ minute} = 60 \text{ seconds.}$$

So, the linear speed of the tip of the second hand is

$$\begin{aligned} \text{Linear speed} &= \frac{s}{t} \\ &= \frac{20.4\pi \text{ centimeters}}{60 \text{ seconds}} \\ &\approx 1.068 \text{ centimeters per second.} \end{aligned}$$

CHECKPOINT Now try Exercise 103.

FIGURE 4.17

Example 7 Finding Angular and Linear Speeds

A Ferris wheel with a 50-foot radius (see Figure 4.17) makes 1.5 revolutions per minute.

a. Find the angular speed of the Ferris wheel in radians per minute.

b. Find the linear speed of the Ferris wheel.

Solution

a. Because each revolution generates 2π radians, it follows that the wheel turns $(1.5)(2\pi) = 3\pi$ radians per minute. In other words, the angular speed is

$$\begin{aligned} \text{Angular speed} &= \frac{\theta}{t} \\ &= \frac{3\pi \text{ radians}}{1 \text{ minute}} = 3\pi \text{ radians per minute.} \end{aligned}$$

b. The linear speed is

$$\begin{aligned} \text{Linear speed} &= \frac{s}{t} \\ &= \frac{r\theta}{t} \\ &= \frac{50(3\pi) \text{ feet}}{1 \text{ minute}} \approx 471.2 \text{ feet per minute.} \end{aligned}$$

CHECKPOINT Now try Exercise 105.

A **sector** of a circle is the region bounded by two radii of the circle and their intercepted arc (see Figure 4.18).

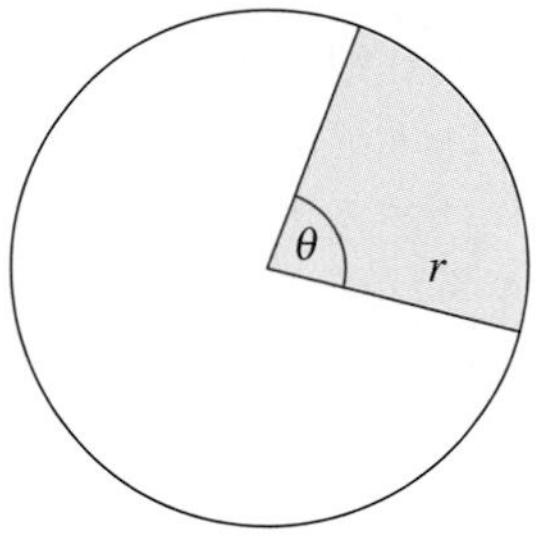

FIGURE 4.18

Area of a Sector of a Circle

For a circle of radius r, the area A of a sector of the circle with central angle θ is given by

$$A = \frac{1}{2}r^2\theta$$

where θ is measured in radians.

Example 8 Area of a Sector of a Circle

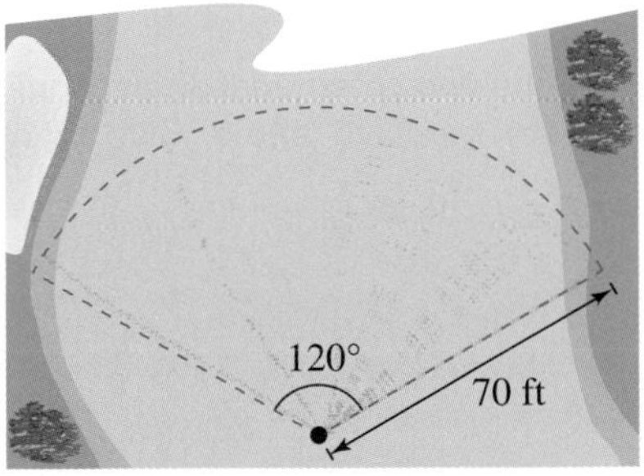

FIGURE 4.19

A sprinkler on a golf course fairway is set to spray water over a distance of 70 feet and rotates through an angle of 120° (see Figure 4.19). Find the area of the fairway watered by the sprinkler.

Solution

First convert 120° to radian measure as follows.

$$\theta = 120°$$

$$= (120 \text{ deg})\left(\frac{\pi \text{ rad}}{180 \text{ deg}}\right) \qquad \text{Multiply by } \pi/180.$$

$$= \frac{2\pi}{3} \text{ radians}$$

Then, using $\theta = 2\pi/3$ and $r = 70$, the area is

$$A = \frac{1}{2}r^2\theta \qquad \text{Formula for the area of a sector of a circle}$$

$$= \frac{1}{2}(70)^2\left(\frac{2\pi}{3}\right) \qquad \text{Substitute for } r \text{ and } \theta.$$

$$= \frac{4900\pi}{3} \qquad \text{Simplify.}$$

$$\approx 5131 \text{ square feet.} \qquad \text{Simplify.}$$

CHECKPOINT Now try Exercise 107.

4.1 Exercises

VOCABULARY CHECK: Fill in the blanks.

1. ________ means "measurement of triangles."
2. An ________ is determined by rotating a ray about its endpoint.
3. Two angles that have the same initial and terminal sides are ________.
4. One ________ is the measure of a central angle that intercepts an arc equal to the radius of the circle.
5. Angles that measure between 0 and $\pi/2$ are ________ angles, and angles that measure between $\pi/2$ and π are ________ angles.
6. Two positive angles that have a sum of $\pi/2$ are ________ angles, whereas two positive angles that have a sum of π are ________ angles.
7. The angle measure that is equivalent to $\frac{1}{360}$ of a complete revolution about an angle's vertex is one ________.
8. The ________ speed of a particle is the ratio of the arc length traveled to the time traveled.
9. The ________ speed of a particle is the ratio of the change in the central angle to time.
10. The area of a sector of a circle with radius r and central angle θ, where θ is measured in radians, is given by the formula ________.

In Exercises 1–6, estimate the angle to the nearest one-half radian.

1. 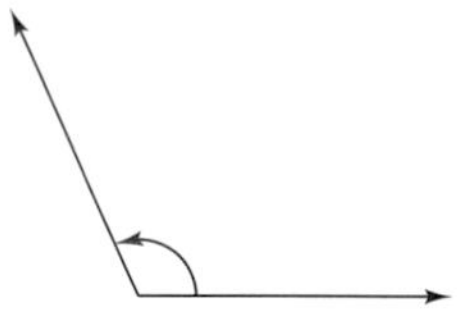

2. 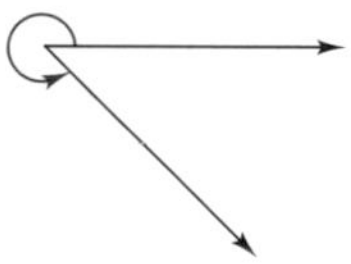

3. 

4. 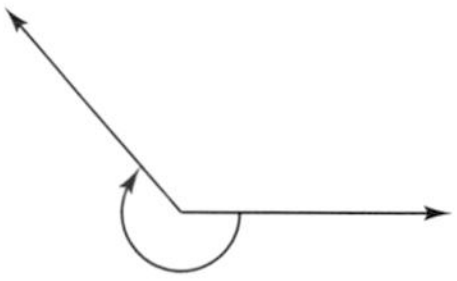

5. 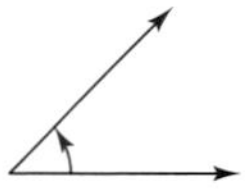

6. 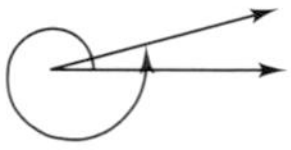

In Exercises 7–12, determine the quadrant in which each angle lies. (The angle measure is given in radians.)

7. (a) $\frac{\pi}{5}$ (b) $\frac{7\pi}{5}$
8. (a) $\frac{11\pi}{8}$ (b) $\frac{9\pi}{8}$
9. (a) $-\frac{\pi}{12}$ (b) -2
10. (a) -1 (b) $-\frac{11\pi}{9}$
11. (a) 3.5 (b) 2.25
12. (a) 6.02 (b) -4.25

In Exercises 13–16, sketch each angle in standard position.

13. (a) $\frac{5\pi}{4}$ (b) $-\frac{2\pi}{3}$
14. (a) $-\frac{7\pi}{4}$ (b) $\frac{5\pi}{2}$
15. (a) $\frac{11\pi}{6}$ (b) -3
16. (a) 4 (b) 7π

In Exercises 17–20, determine two coterminal angles (one positive and one negative) for each angle. Give your answers in radians.

17. (a) 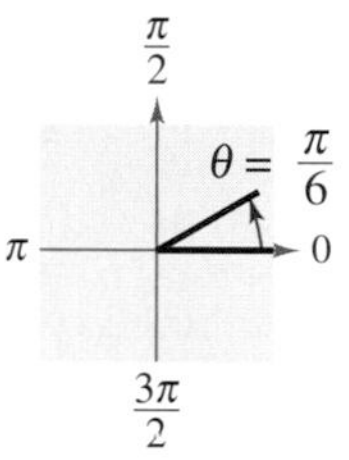

(b) 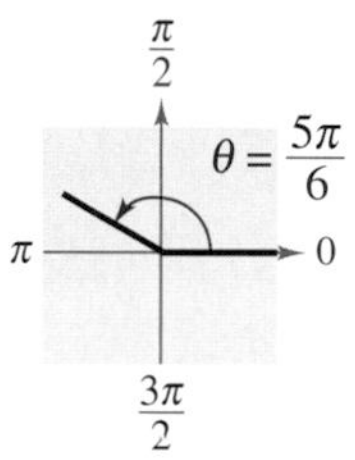

18. (a) 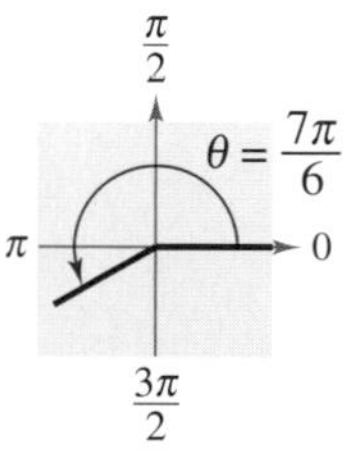

(b) 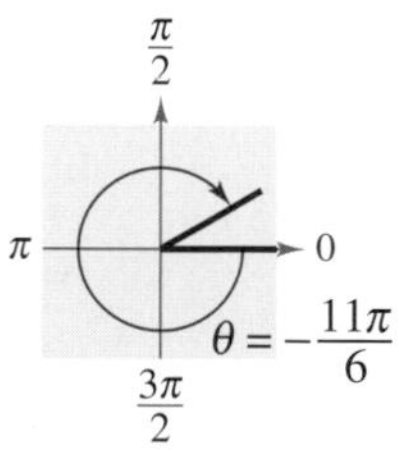

19. (a) $\theta = \frac{2\pi}{3}$ (b) $\theta = \frac{\pi}{12}$
20. (a) $\theta = -\frac{9\pi}{4}$ (b) $\theta = -\frac{2\pi}{15}$

In Exercises 21–24, find (if possible) the complement and supplement of each angle.

21. (a) $\frac{\pi}{3}$ (b) $\frac{3\pi}{4}$ **22.** (a) $\frac{\pi}{12}$ (b) $\frac{11\pi}{12}$

23. (a) 1 (b) 2 **24.** (a) 3 (b) 1.5

In Exercises 25–30, estimate the number of degrees in the angle.

25.

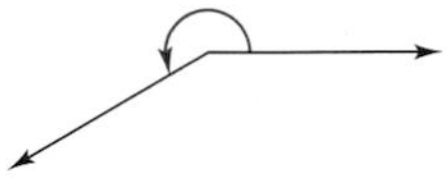

26.

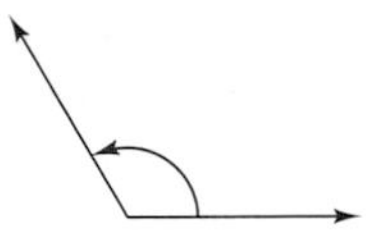

27.

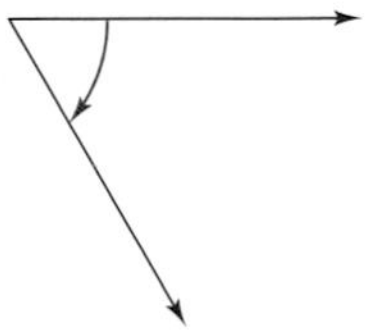

28.

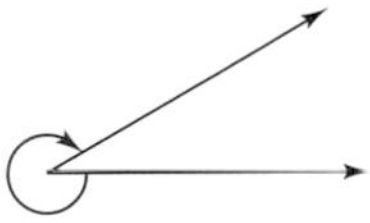

29.

30.

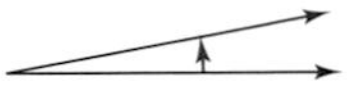

In Exercises 31–34, determine the quadrant in which each angle lies.

31. (a) $130°$ (b) $285°$

32. (a) $8.3°$ (b) $257° 30'$

33. (a) $-132° 50'$ (b) $-336°$

34. (a) $-260°$ (b) $-3.4°$

In Exercises 35–38, sketch each angle in standard position.

35. (a) $30°$ (b) $150°$ **36.** (a) $-270°$ (b) $-120°$

37. (a) $405°$ (b) $480°$ **38.** (a) $-750°$ (b) $-600°$

In Exercises 39–42, determine two coterminal angles (one positive and one negative) for each angle. Give your answers in degrees.

39. (a)

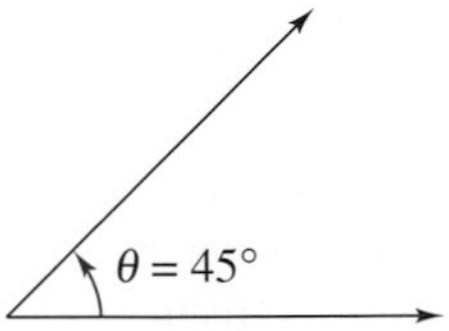

(b)

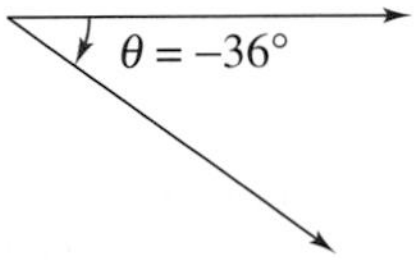

40. (a)

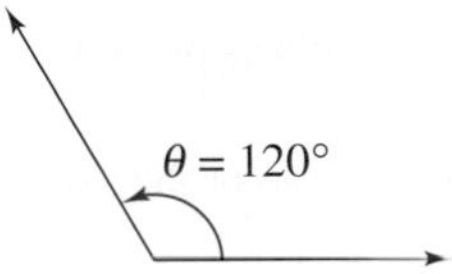

(b)

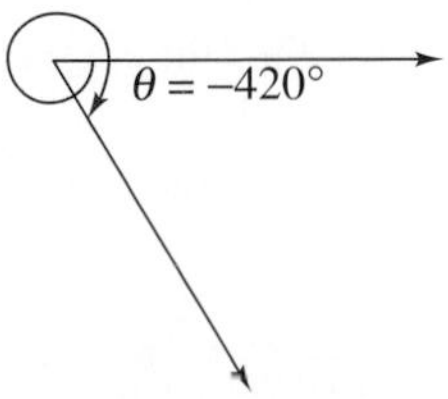

41. (a) $\theta = 240°$ (b) $\theta = -180°$

42. (a) $\theta = -420°$ (b) $\theta = 230°$

In Exercises 43–46, find (if possible) the complement and supplement of each angle.

43. (a) $18°$ (b) $115°$ **44.** (a) $3°$ (b) $64°$

45. (a) $79°$ (b) $150°$ **46.** (a) $130°$ (b) $170°$

In Exercises 47–50, rewrite each angle in radian measure as a multiple of π. (Do not use a calculator.)

47. (a) $30°$ (b) $150°$ **48.** (a) $315°$ (b) $120°$

49. (a) $-20°$ (b) $-240°$ **50.** (a) $-270°$ (b) $144°$

In Exercises 51–54, rewrite each angle in degree measure. (Do not use a calculator.)

51. (a) $\frac{3\pi}{2}$ (b) $\frac{7\pi}{6}$ **52.** (a) $-\frac{7\pi}{12}$ (b) $\frac{\pi}{9}$

53. (a) $\frac{7\pi}{3}$ (b) $-\frac{11\pi}{30}$ **54.** (a) $\frac{11\pi}{6}$ (b) $\frac{34\pi}{15}$

In Exercises 55–62, convert the angle measure from degrees to radians. Round to three decimal places.

55. $115°$ **56.** $87.4°$

57. $-216.35°$ **58.** $-48.27°$

59. $532°$ **60.** $345°$

61. $-0.83°$ **62.** $0.54°$

In Exercises 63–70, convert the angle measure from radians to degrees. Round to three decimal places.

63. $\frac{\pi}{7}$ **64.** $\frac{5\pi}{11}$

65. $\frac{15\pi}{8}$ **66.** $\frac{13\pi}{2}$

67. -4.2π **68.** 4.8π

69. -2 **70.** -0.57

In Exercises 71–74, convert each angle measure to decimal degree form.

71. (a) $54° 45'$ (b) $-128° 30'$

72. (a) $245° 10'$ (b) $2° 12'$

73. (a) $85° 18' 30''$ (b) $330° 25''$

74. (a) $-135° 36''$ (b) $-408° 16' 20''$

In Exercises 75–78, convert each angle measure to D° M′ S″ form.

75. (a) $240.6°$ (b) $-145.8°$

76. (a) $-345.12°$ (b) $0.45°$

77. (a) $2.5°$ (b) $-3.58°$

78. (a) $-0.355°$ (b) $0.7865°$

In Exercises 79–82, find the angle in radians.

79.

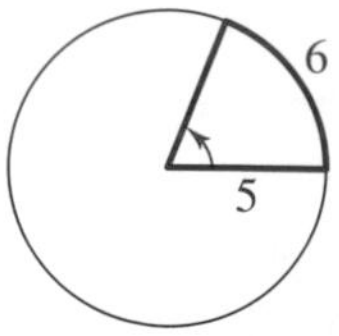

80.

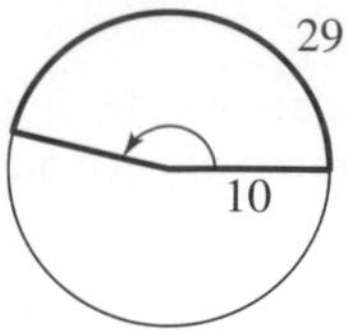

81.

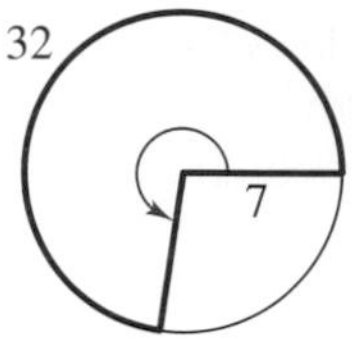

82.

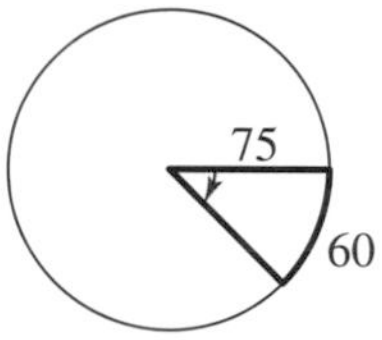

In Exercises 83–86, find the radian measure of the central angle of a circle of radius r that intercepts an arc of length s.

	Radius r	*Arc Length s*
83.	27 inches	6 inches
84.	14 feet	8 feet
85.	14.5 centimeters	25 centimeters
86.	80 kilometers	160 kilometers

In Exercises 87–90, find the length of the arc on a circle of radius r intercepted by a central angle θ.

	Radius r	*Central Angle θ*
87.	15 inches	$180°$
88.	9 feet	$60°$
89.	3 meters	1 radian
90.	20 centimeters	$\pi/4$ radian

In Exercises 91–94, find the area of the sector of the circle with radius r and central angle θ.

	Radius r	*Central Angle θ*
91.	4 inches	$\dfrac{\pi}{3}$
92.	12 millimeters	$\dfrac{\pi}{4}$
93.	2.5 feet	$225°$
94.	1.4 miles	$330°$

Distance Between Cities **In Exercises 95 and 96, find the distance between the cities. Assume that Earth is a sphere of radius 4000 miles and that the cities are on the same longitude (one city is due north of the other).**

	City	*Latitude*
95.	Dallas, Texas	$32° 47' 39''$ N
	Omaha, Nebraska	$41° 15' 50''$ N
96.	San Francisco, California	$37° 47' 36''$ N
	Seattle, Washington	$47° 37' 18''$ N

97. ***Difference in Latitudes*** Assuming that Earth is a sphere of radius 6378 kilometers, what is the difference in the latitudes of Syracuse, New York and Annapolis, Maryland, where Syracuse is 450 kilometers due north of Annapolis?

98. ***Difference in Latitudes*** Assuming that Earth is a sphere of radius 6378 kilometers, what is the difference in the latitudes of Lynchburg, Virginia and Myrtle Beach, South Carolina, where Lynchburg is 400 kilometers due north of Myrtle Beach?

99. ***Instrumentation*** The pointer on a voltmeter is 6 centimeters in length (see figure). Find the angle through which the pointer rotates when it moves 2.5 centimeters on the scale.

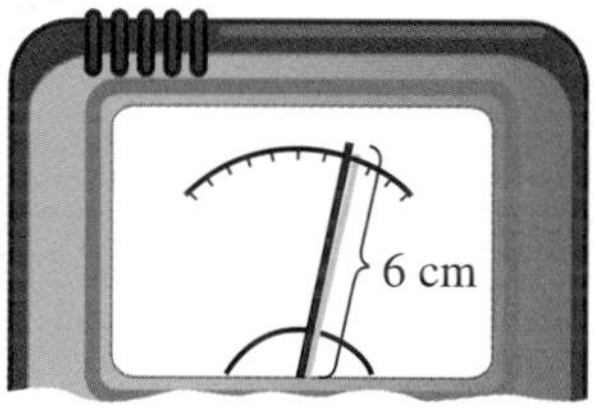

FIGURE FOR 99

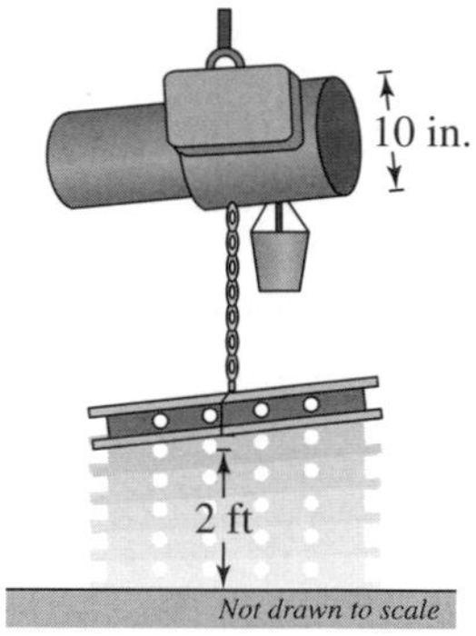

FIGURE FOR 100

100. ***Electric Hoist*** An electric hoist is being used to lift a beam (see figure). The diameter of the drum on the hoist is 10 inches, and the beam must be raised 2 feet. Find the number of degrees through which the drum must rotate.

101. ***Angular Speed*** A car is moving at a rate of 65 miles per hour, and the diameter of its wheels is 2.5 feet.

(a) Find the number of revolutions per minute the wheels are rotating.

(b) Find the angular speed of the wheels in radians per minute.

102. ***Angular Speed*** A two-inch-diameter pulley on an electric motor that runs at 1700 revolutions per minute is connected by a belt to a four-inch-diameter pulley on a saw arbor.

(a) Find the angular speed (in radians per minute) of each pulley.

(b) Find the revolutions per minute of the saw.

103. ***Linear and Angular Speeds*** A $7\frac{1}{4}$-inch circular power saw rotates at 5200 revolutions per minute.

(a) Find the angular speed of the saw blade in radians per minute.

(b) Find the linear speed (in feet per minute) of one of the 24 cutting teeth as they contact the wood being cut.

104. ***Linear and Angular Speeds*** A carousel with a 50-foot diameter makes 4 revolutions per minute.

(a) Find the angular speed of the carousel in radians per minute.

(b) Find the linear speed of the platform rim of the carousel.

105. ***Linear and Angular Speeds*** The diameter of a DVD is approximately 12 centimeters. The drive motor of the DVD player is controlled to rotate precisely between 200 and 500 revolutions per minute, depending on what track is being read.

(a) Find an interval for the angular speed of a DVD as it rotates.

(b) Find an interval for the linear speed of a point on the outermost track as the DVD rotates.

106. ***Area*** A car's rear windshield wiper rotates 125°. The total length of the wiper mechanism is 25 inches and wipes the windshield over a distance of 14 inches. Find the area covered by the wiper.

107. ***Area*** A sprinkler system on a farm is set to spray water over a distance of 35 meters and to rotate through an angle of 140°. Draw a diagram that shows the region that can be irrigated with the sprinkler. Find the area of the region.

Model It

108. ***Speed of a Bicycle*** The radii of the pedal sprocket, the wheel sprocket, and the wheel of the bicycle in the figure are 4 inches, 2 inches, and 14 inches, respectively. A cyclist is pedaling at a rate of 1 revolution per second.

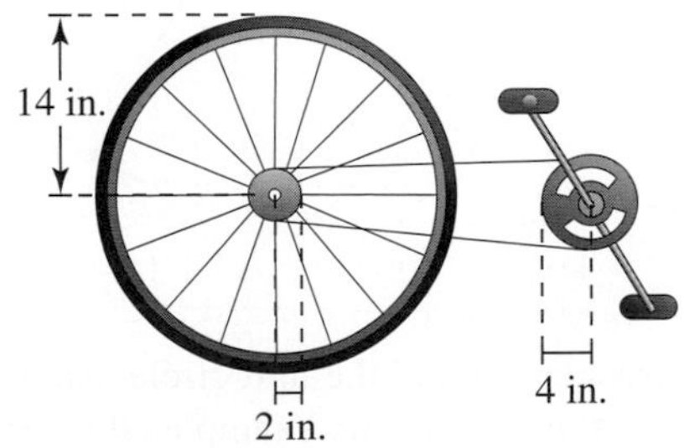

(a) Find the speed of the bicycle in feet per second and miles per hour.

(b) Use your result from part (a) to write a function for the distance d (in miles) a cyclist travels in terms of the number n of revolutions of the pedal sprocket.

Model It (continued)

(c) Write a function for the distance d (in miles) a cyclist travels in terms of the time t (in seconds). Compare this function with the function from part (b).

(d) Classify the types of functions you found in parts (b) and (c). Explain your reasoning.

Synthesis

True or False? **In Exercises 109–111, determine whether the statement is true or false. Justify your answer.**

109. A measurement of 4 radians corresponds to two complete revolutions from the initial side to the terminal side of an angle.

110. The difference between the measures of two coterminal angles is always a multiple of 360° if expressed in degrees and is always a multiple of 2π radians if expressed in radians.

111. An angle that measures $-1260°$ lies in Quadrant III.

112. ***Writing*** In your own words, explain the meanings of (a) an angle in standard position, (b) a negative angle, (c) coterminal angles, and (d) an obtuse angle.

113. ***Think About It*** A fan motor turns at a given angular speed. How does the speed of the tips of the blades change if a fan of greater diameter is installed on the motor? Explain.

114. ***Think About It*** Is a degree or a radian the larger unit of measure? Explain.

115. ***Writing*** If the radius of a circle is increasing and the magnitude of a central angle is held constant, how is the length of the intercepted arc changing? Explain your reasoning.

116. ***Proof*** Prove that the area of a circular sector of radius r with central angle θ is $A = \frac{1}{2}\theta r^2$, where θ is measured in radians.

Skills Review

In Exercises 117–120, simplify the radical expression.

117. $\dfrac{4}{4\sqrt{2}}$

118. $\dfrac{5\sqrt{5}}{2\sqrt{10}}$

119. $\sqrt{2^2 + 6^2}$

120. $\sqrt{17^2 - 9^2}$

In Exercises 121–124, sketch the graphs of $y = x^5$ and the specified transformation.

121. $f(x) = (x - 2)^5$

122. $f(x) = x^5 - 4$

123. $f(x) = 2 - x^5$

124. $f(x) = -(x + 3)^5$

4.2 Trigonometric Functions: The Unit Circle

What you should learn

- Identify a unit circle and describe its relationship to real numbers.
- Evaluate trigonometric functions using the unit circle.
- Use the domain and period to evaluate sine and cosine functions.
- Use a calculator to evaluate trigonometric functions.

Why you should learn it

Trigonometric functions are used to model the movement of an oscillating weight. For instance, in Exercise 57 on page 300, the displacement from equilibrium of an oscillating weight suspended by a spring is modeled as a function of time.

Richard Megna/Fundamental Photographs

The Unit Circle

The two historical perspectives of trigonometry incorporate different methods for introducing the trigonometric functions. Our first introduction to these functions is based on the unit circle.

Consider the **unit circle** given by

$$x^2 + y^2 = 1 \qquad \text{Unit circle}$$

as shown in Figure 4.20.

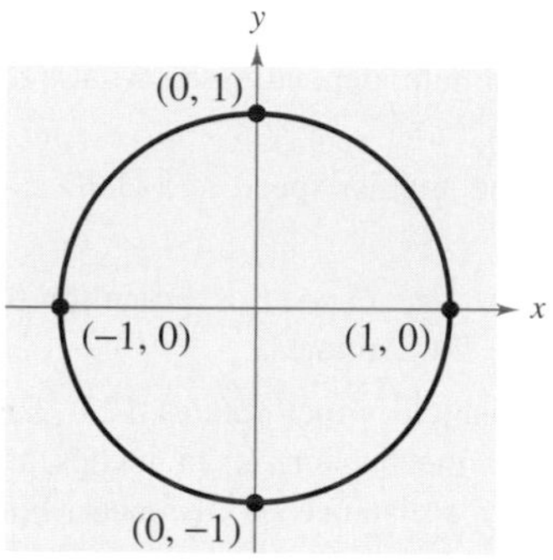

FIGURE 4.20

Imagine that the real number line is wrapped around this circle, with positive numbers corresponding to a counterclockwise wrapping and negative numbers corresponding to a clockwise wrapping, as shown in Figure 4.21.

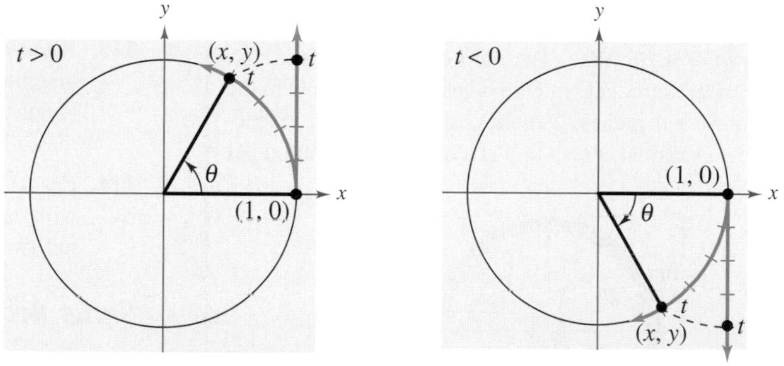

FIGURE 4.21

As the real number line is wrapped around the unit circle, each real number t corresponds to a point (x, y) on the circle. For example, the real number 0 corresponds to the point $(1, 0)$. Moreover, because the unit circle has a circumference of 2π, the real number 2π also corresponds to the point $(1, 0)$.

In general, each real number t also corresponds to a central angle θ (in standard position) whose radian measure is t. With this interpretation of t, the arc length formula $s = r\theta$ (with $r = 1$) indicates that the real number t is the length of the arc intercepted by the angle θ, given in radians.

The Trigonometric Functions

From the preceding discussion, it follows that the coordinates x and y are two functions of the real variable t. You can use these coordinates to define the six trigonometric functions of t.

sine **cosecant** **cosine** **secant** **tangent** **cotangent**

These six functions are normally abbreviated sin, csc, cos, sec, tan, and cot, respectively.

STUDY TIP

Note in the definition at the right that the functions in the second row are the *reciprocals* of the corresponding functions in the first row.

Definitions of Trigonometric Functions

Let t be a real number and let (x, y) be the point on the unit circle corresponding to t.

$\sin t = y$ $\quad$ $\cos t = x$ $\quad$ $\tan t = \frac{y}{x}, \quad x \neq 0$

$\csc t = \frac{1}{y}, \quad y \neq 0$ $\quad$ $\sec t = \frac{1}{x}, \quad x \neq 0$ $\quad$ $\cot t = \frac{x}{y}, \quad y \neq 0$

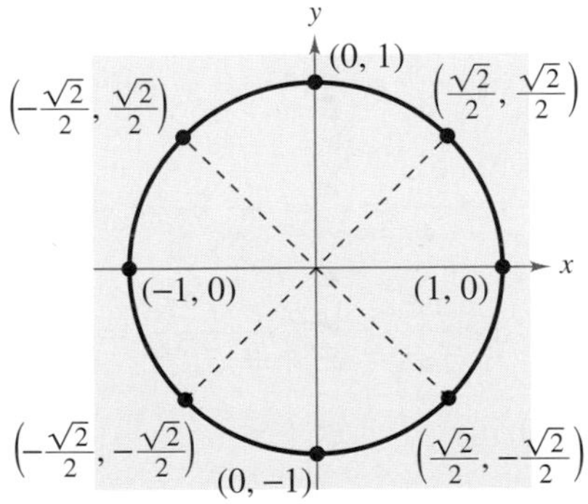

FIGURE 4.22

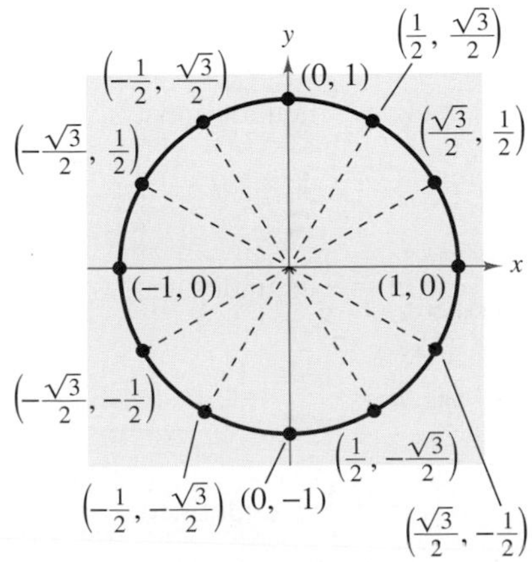

FIGURE 4.23

In the definitions of the trigonometric functions, note that the tangent and secant are not defined when $x = 0$. For instance, because $t = \pi/2$ corresponds to $(x, y) = (0, 1)$, it follows that $\tan(\pi/2)$ and $\sec(\pi/2)$ are *undefined.* Similarly, the cotangent and cosecant are not defined when $y = 0$. For instance, because $t = 0$ corresponds to $(x, y) = (1, 0)$, cot 0 and csc 0 are *undefined.*

In Figure 4.22, the unit circle has been divided into eight equal arcs, corresponding to t-values of

$$0, \frac{\pi}{4}, \frac{\pi}{2}, \frac{3\pi}{4}, \pi, \frac{5\pi}{4}, \frac{3\pi}{2}, \frac{7\pi}{4}, \text{ and } 2\pi.$$

Similarly, in Figure 4.23, the unit circle has been divided into 12 equal arcs, corresponding to t-values of

$$0, \frac{\pi}{6}, \frac{\pi}{3}, \frac{\pi}{2}, \frac{2\pi}{3}, \frac{5\pi}{6}, \pi, \frac{7\pi}{6}, \frac{4\pi}{3}, \frac{3\pi}{2}, \frac{5\pi}{3}, \frac{11\pi}{6}, \text{ and } 2\pi.$$

To verify the points on the unit circle in Figure 4.22, note that $\left(\frac{\sqrt{2}}{2}, \frac{\sqrt{2}}{2}\right)$ also lies on the line $y = x$. So, substituting x for y in the equation of the unit circle produces the following.

$$x^2 + x^2 = 1 \quad \Rightarrow \quad 2x^2 = 1 \quad \Rightarrow \quad x^2 = \frac{1}{2} \quad \Rightarrow \quad x = \pm\frac{\sqrt{2}}{2}$$

Because the point is in the first quadrant, $x = \frac{\sqrt{2}}{2}$ and because $y = x$, you also have $y = \frac{\sqrt{2}}{2}$. You can use similar reasoning to verify the rest of the points in Figure 4.22 and the points in Figure 4.23.

Using the (x, y) coordinates in Figures 4.22 and 4.23, you can easily evaluate the trigonometric functions for common t-values. This procedure is demonstrated in Examples 1 and 2. You should study and learn these exact function values for common t-values because they will help you in later sections to perform calculations quickly and easily.

Example 1 Evaluating Trigonometric Functions

Evaluate the six trigonometric functions at each real number.

a. $t = \dfrac{\pi}{6}$ **b.** $t = \dfrac{5\pi}{4}$ **c.** $t = 0$ **d.** $t = \pi$

Solution

For each t-value, begin by finding the corresponding point (x, y) on the unit circle. Then use the definitions of trigonometric functions listed on page 295.

a. $t = \dfrac{\pi}{6}$ corresponds to the point $(x, y) = \left(\dfrac{\sqrt{3}}{2}, \dfrac{1}{2}\right)$.

$$\sin\frac{\pi}{6} = y = \frac{1}{2} \qquad \csc\frac{\pi}{6} = \frac{1}{y} = \frac{1}{1/2} = 2$$

$$\cos\frac{\pi}{6} = x = \frac{\sqrt{3}}{2} \qquad \sec\frac{\pi}{6} = \frac{1}{x} = \frac{2}{\sqrt{3}} = \frac{2\sqrt{3}}{3}$$

$$\tan\frac{\pi}{6} = \frac{y}{x} = \frac{1/2}{\sqrt{3}/2} = \frac{1}{\sqrt{3}} = \frac{\sqrt{3}}{3} \qquad \cot\frac{\pi}{6} = \frac{x}{y} = \frac{\sqrt{3}/2}{1/2} = \sqrt{3}$$

b. $t = \dfrac{5\pi}{4}$ corresponds to the point $(x, y) = \left(-\dfrac{\sqrt{2}}{2}, -\dfrac{\sqrt{2}}{2}\right)$.

$$\sin\frac{5\pi}{4} = y = -\frac{\sqrt{2}}{2} \qquad \csc\frac{5\pi}{4} = \frac{1}{y} = -\frac{2}{\sqrt{2}} = -\sqrt{2}$$

$$\cos\frac{5\pi}{4} = x = -\frac{\sqrt{2}}{2} \qquad \sec\frac{5\pi}{4} = \frac{1}{x} = -\frac{2}{\sqrt{2}} = -\sqrt{2}$$

$$\tan\frac{5\pi}{4} = \frac{y}{x} = \frac{-\sqrt{2}/2}{-\sqrt{2}/2} = 1 \qquad \cot\frac{5\pi}{4} = \frac{x}{y} = \frac{-\sqrt{2}/2}{-\sqrt{2}/2} = 1$$

c. $t = 0$ corresponds to the point $(x, y) = (1, 0)$.

$$\sin 0 = y = 0 \qquad \csc 0 = \frac{1}{y} \text{ is undefined.}$$

$$\cos 0 = x = 1 \qquad \sec 0 = \frac{1}{x} = \frac{1}{1} = 1$$

$$\tan 0 = \frac{y}{x} = \frac{0}{1} = 0 \qquad \cot 0 = \frac{x}{y} \text{ is undefined.}$$

d. $t = \pi$ corresponds to the point $(x, y) = (-1, 0)$.

$$\sin \pi = y = 0 \qquad \csc \pi = \frac{1}{y} \text{ is undefined.}$$

$$\cos \pi = x = -1 \qquad \sec \pi = \frac{1}{x} = \frac{1}{-1} = -1$$

$$\tan \pi = \frac{y}{x} = \frac{0}{-1} = 0 \qquad \cot \pi = \frac{x}{y} \text{ is undefined.}$$

CHECKPOINT Now try Exercise 23.

Exploration

With your graphing utility in *radian* and *parametric* modes, enter the equations

X1T = cos T and Y1T = sin T

and use the following settings.

Tmin = 0, Tmax = 6.3,
Tstep = 0.1
Xmin = -1.5, Xmax = 1.5,
Xscl = 1
Ymin = -1, Ymax = 1,
Yscl = 1

1. Graph the entered equations and describe the graph.
2. Use the *trace* feature to move the cursor around the graph. What do the *t*-values represent? What do the *x*- and *y*-values represent?
3. What are the least and greatest values of *x* and *y*?

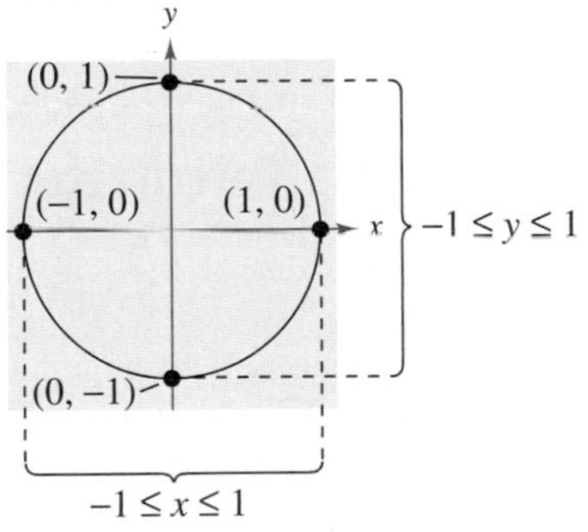

FIGURE 4.24

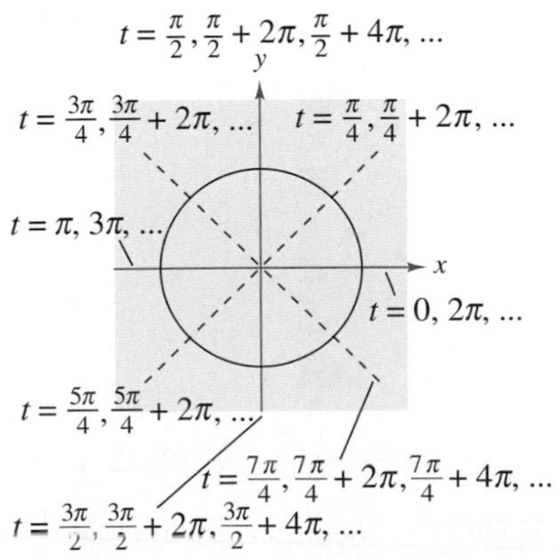

FIGURE 4.25

Example 2 Evaluating Trigonometric Functions

Evaluate the six trigonometric functions at $t = -\frac{\pi}{3}$.

Solution

Moving *clockwise* around the unit circle, it follows that $t = -\pi/3$ corresponds to the point $(x, y) = \left(1/2, -\sqrt{3}/2\right)$.

$$\sin\left(-\frac{\pi}{3}\right) = -\frac{\sqrt{3}}{2} \qquad \csc\left(-\frac{\pi}{3}\right) = -\frac{2}{\sqrt{3}} = -\frac{2\sqrt{3}}{3}$$

$$\cos\left(-\frac{\pi}{3}\right) = \frac{1}{2} \qquad \sec\left(-\frac{\pi}{3}\right) = 2$$

$$\tan\left(-\frac{\pi}{3}\right) = \frac{-\sqrt{3}/2}{1/2} = -\sqrt{3} \qquad \cot\left(-\frac{\pi}{3}\right) = \frac{1/2}{-\sqrt{3}/2} = -\frac{1}{\sqrt{3}} = -\frac{\sqrt{3}}{3}$$

CHECKPOINT Now try Exercise 25.

Domain and Period of Sine and Cosine

The *domain* of the sine and cosine functions is the set of all real numbers. To determine the *range* of these two functions, consider the unit circle shown in Figure 4.24. Because $r = 1$, it follows that $\sin t = y$ and $\cos t = x$. Moreover, because (x, y) is on the unit circle, you know that $-1 \le y \le 1$ and $-1 \le x \le 1$. So, the values of sine and cosine also range between -1 and 1.

$$\begin{array}{ccc} -1 \le y \le 1 & & -1 \le x \le 1 \\ & \text{and} & \\ -1 \le \sin t \le 1 & & -1 \le \cos t \le 1 \end{array}$$

Adding 2π to each value of t in the interval $[0, 2\pi]$ completes a second revolution around the unit circle, as shown in Figure 4.25. The values of $\sin(t + 2\pi)$ and $\cos(t + 2\pi)$ correspond to those of $\sin t$ and $\cos t$. Similar results can be obtained for repeated revolutions (positive or negative) on the unit circle. This leads to the general result

$$\sin(t + 2\pi n) = \sin t$$

and

$$\cos(t + 2\pi n) = \cos t$$

for any integer n and real number t. Functions that behave in such a repetitive (or cyclic) manner are called **periodic.**

Definition of Periodic Function

A function f is **periodic** if there exists a positive real number c such that

$$f(t + c) = f(t)$$

for all t in the domain of f. The smallest number c for which f is periodic is called the **period** of f.

Recall from Section 1.5 that a function f is *even* if $f(-t) = f(t)$, and is *odd* if $f(-t) = -f(t)$.

Even and Odd Trigonometric Functions

The cosine and secant functions are *even*.

$$\cos(-t) = \cos t \qquad \sec(-t) = \sec t$$

The sine, cosecant, tangent, and cotangent functions are *odd*.

$$\sin(-t) = -\sin t \qquad \csc(-t) = -\csc t$$

$$\tan(-t) = -\tan t \qquad \cot(-t) = -\cot t$$

STUDY TIP

From the definition of periodic function, it follows that the sine and cosine functions are periodic and have a period of 2π. The other four trigonometric functions are also periodic, and will be discussed further in Section 4.6.

Example 3 **Using the Period to Evaluate the Sine and Cosine**

a. Because $\frac{13\pi}{6} = 2\pi + \frac{\pi}{6}$, you have $\sin \frac{13\pi}{6} = \sin\left(2\pi + \frac{\pi}{6}\right) = \sin \frac{\pi}{6} = \frac{1}{2}$.

b. Because $-\frac{7\pi}{2} = -4\pi + \frac{\pi}{2}$, you have

$$\cos\left(-\frac{7\pi}{2}\right) = \cos\left(-4\pi + \frac{\pi}{2}\right) = \cos \frac{\pi}{2} = 0.$$

c. For $\sin t = \frac{4}{5}$, $\sin(-t) = -\frac{4}{5}$ because the sine function is odd.

✓CHECKPOINT Now try Exercise 31.

Evaluating Trigonometric Functions with a Calculator

When evaluating a trigonometric function with a calculator, you need to set the calculator to the desired *mode* of measurement (*degree* or *radian*).

Most calculators do not have keys for the cosecant, secant, and cotangent functions. To evaluate these functions, you can use the $\boxed{x^{-1}}$ key with their respective reciprocal functions sine, cosine, and tangent. For example, to evaluate $\csc(\pi/8)$, use the fact that

$$\csc \frac{\pi}{8} = \frac{1}{\sin(\pi/8)}$$

and enter the following keystroke sequence in *radian* mode.

(SIN (π ÷ 8)) x^{-1} ENTER   Display 2.6131259

Technology

When evaluating trigonometric functions with a calculator, remember to enclose all fractional angle measures in parentheses. For instance, if you want to evaluate $\sin \theta$ for $\theta = \pi/6$, you should enter

SIN (π ÷ 6) ENTER.

These keystrokes yield the correct value of 0.5. Note that some calculators automatically place a left parenthesis after trigonometric functions. Check the user's guide for your calculator for specific keystrokes on how to evaluate trigonometric functions.

Example 4 **Using a Calculator**

	Function	*Mode*	*Calculator Keystrokes*	*Display*
a.	$\sin \frac{2\pi}{3}$	Radian	SIN (2 π ÷ 3) ENTER	0.8660254
b.	cot 1.5	Radian	(TAN (1.5)) x^{-1} ENTER	0.0709148

✓CHECKPOINT Now try Exercise 45.

4.2 Exercises

VOCABULARY CHECK: Fill in the blanks.

1. Each real number t corresponds to a point (x, y) on the ________ ________.
2. A function f is ________ if there exists a positive real number c such that $f(t + c) = f(t)$ for all t in the domain of f.
3. The smallest number c for which a function f is periodic is called the ________ of f.
4. A function f is ________ if $f(-t) = -f(t)$ and ________ if $f(-t) = f(t)$.

In Exercises 1–4, determine the exact values of the six trigonometric functions of the angle θ.

1.
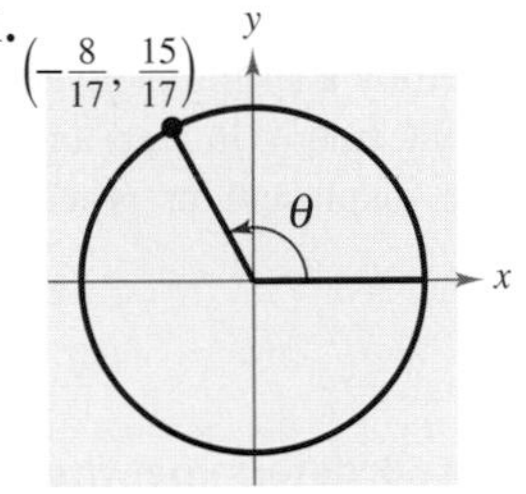

2.
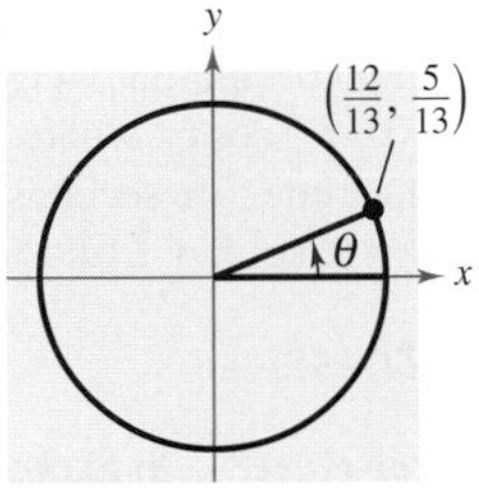

3.
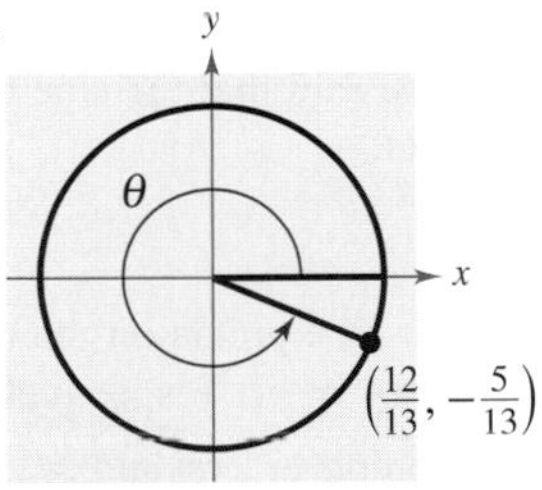

4.
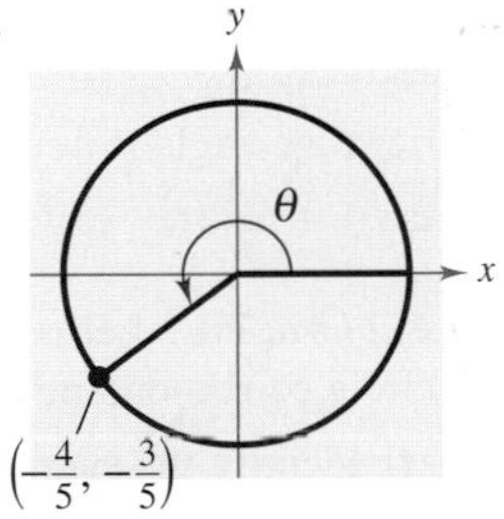

In Exercises 5–12, find the point (x, y) on the unit circle that corresponds to the real number t.

5. $t = \dfrac{\pi}{4}$
6. $t = \dfrac{\pi}{3}$
7. $t = \dfrac{7\pi}{6}$
8. $t = \dfrac{5\pi}{4}$
9. $t = \dfrac{4\pi}{3}$
10. $t = \dfrac{5\pi}{3}$
11. $t = \dfrac{3\pi}{2}$
12. $t = \pi$

In Exercises 13–22, evaluate (if possible) the sine, cosine, and tangent of the real number.

13. $t = \dfrac{\pi}{4}$
14. $t = \dfrac{\pi}{3}$
15. $t = -\dfrac{\pi}{6}$
16. $t = -\dfrac{\pi}{4}$
17. $t = -\dfrac{7\pi}{4}$
18. $t = -\dfrac{4\pi}{3}$
19. $t = \dfrac{11\pi}{6}$
20. $t = \dfrac{5\pi}{3}$
21. $t = -\dfrac{3\pi}{2}$
22. $t = -2\pi$

In Exercises 23–28, evaluate (if possible) the six trigonometric functions of the real number.

23. $t = \dfrac{3\pi}{4}$
24. $t = \dfrac{5\pi}{6}$
25. $t = -\dfrac{\pi}{2}$
26. $t = \dfrac{3\pi}{2}$
27. $t = \dfrac{4\pi}{3}$
28. $t = \dfrac{7\pi}{4}$

In Exercises 29–36, evaluate the trigonometric function using its period as an aid.

29. $\sin 5\pi$
30. $\cos 5\pi$
31. $\cos \dfrac{8\pi}{3}$
32. $\sin \dfrac{9\pi}{4}$
33. $\cos\left(-\dfrac{15\pi}{2}\right)$
34. $\sin \dfrac{19\pi}{6}$
35. $\sin\left(-\dfrac{9\pi}{4}\right)$
36. $\cos\left(-\dfrac{8\pi}{3}\right)$

In Exercises 37–42, use the value of the trigonometric function to evaluate the indicated functions.

37. $\sin t = \frac{1}{3}$
   (a) $\sin(-t)$
   (b) $\csc(-t)$
38. $\sin(-t) = \frac{3}{8}$
   (a) $\sin t$
   (b) $\csc t$
39. $\cos(-t) = -\frac{1}{5}$
   (a) $\cos t$
   (b) $\sec(-t)$
40. $\cos t = -\frac{3}{4}$
   (a) $\cos(-t)$
   (b) $\sec(-t)$
41. $\sin t = \frac{4}{5}$
   (a) $\sin(\pi - t)$
   (b) $\sin(t + \pi)$
42. $\cos t = \frac{4}{5}$
   (a) $\cos(\pi - t)$
   (b) $\cos(t + \pi)$

In Exercises 43–52, use a calculator to evaluate the trigonometric function. Round your answer to four decimal places. (Be sure the calculator is set in the correct angle mode.)

43. $\sin \frac{\pi}{4}$ **44.** $\tan \frac{\pi}{3}$

45. $\csc 1.3$ **46.** $\cot 1$

47. $\cos(-1.7)$ **48.** $\cos(-2.5)$

49. $\csc 0.8$ **50.** $\sec 1.8$

51. $\sec 22.8$ **52.** $\sin(-0.9)$

Estimation **In Exercises 53 and 54, use the figure and a straightedge to approximate the value of each trigonometric function. To print an enlarged copy of the graph, go to the website *www.mathgraphs.com*.**

53. (a) $\sin 5$ (b) $\cos 2$ **54.** (a) $\sin 0.75$ (b) $\cos 2.5$

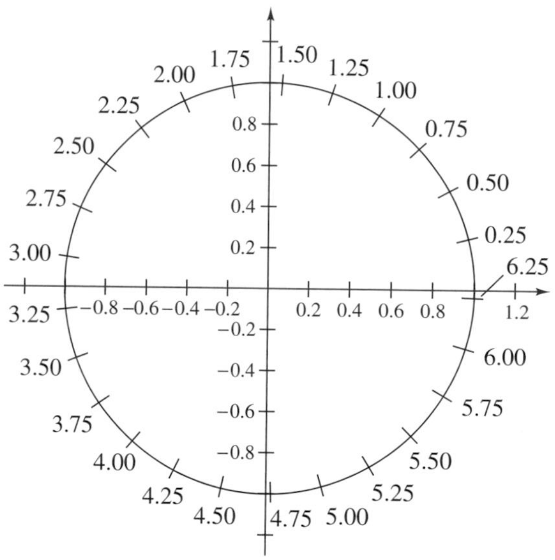

FIGURE FOR 53–56

Estimation **In Exercises 55 and 56, use the figure and a straightedge to approximate the solution of each equation, where $0 \le t < 2\pi$. To print an enlarged copy of the graph, go to the website *www.mathgraphs.com*.**

55. (a) $\sin t = 0.25$ (b) $\cos t = -0.25$

56. (a) $\sin t = -0.75$ (b) $\cos t = 0.75$

Model It

57. ***Harmonic Motion*** The displacement from equilibrium of an oscillating weight suspended by a spring and subject to the damping effect of friction is given by $y(t) = \frac{1}{4}e^{-t} \cos 6t$ where y is the displacement (in feet) and t is the time (in seconds).

Model It (continued)

(a) Complete the table.

t	0	$\frac{1}{4}$	$\frac{1}{2}$	$\frac{3}{4}$	1
y					

(b) Use the *table* feature of a graphing utility to approximate the time when the weight reaches equilibrium.

(c) What appears to happen to the displacement as t increases?

58. ***Harmonic Motion*** The displacement from equilibrium of an oscillating weight suspended by a spring is given by $y(t) = \frac{1}{4} \cos 6t$, where y is the displacement (in feet) and t is the time (in seconds). Find the displacement when (a) $t = 0$, (b) $t = \frac{1}{4}$, and (c) $t = \frac{1}{2}$.

Synthesis

True or False? **In Exercises 59 and 60, determine whether the statement is true or false. Justify your answer.**

59. Because $\sin(-t) = -\sin t$, it can be said that the sine of a negative angle is a negative number.

60. $\tan a = \tan(a - 6\pi)$

61. ***Exploration*** Let (x_1, y_1) and (x_2, y_2) be points on the unit circle corresponding to $t = t_1$ and $t = \pi - t_1$, respectively.

(a) Identify the symmetry of the points (x_1, y_1) and (x_2, y_2).

(b) Make a conjecture about any relationship between $\sin t_1$ and $\sin(\pi - t_1)$.

(c) Make a conjecture about any relationship between $\cos t_1$ and $\cos(\pi - t_1)$.

62. Use the unit circle to verify that the cosine and secant functions are even and that the sine, cosecant, tangent, and cotangent functions are odd.

Skills Review

In Exercises 63–66, find the inverse function f^{-1} of the one-to-one function f.

63. $f(x) = \frac{1}{2}(3x - 2)$ **64.** $f(x) = \frac{1}{4}x^3 + 1$

65. $f(x) = \sqrt{x^2 - 4}, \quad x \ge 2$ **66.** $f(x) = \dfrac{x + 2}{x - 4}$

In Exercises 67–70, sketch the graph of the rational function by hand. Show all asymptotes.

67. $f(x) = \dfrac{2x}{x - 3}$ **68.** $f(x) = \dfrac{5x}{x^2 + x - 6}$

69. $f(x) = \dfrac{x^2 + 3x - 10}{2x^2 - 8}$ **70.** $f(x) = \dfrac{x^3 - 6x^2 + x - 1}{2x^2 - 5x - 8}$

4.3 Right Triangle Trigonometry

What you should learn

- Evaluate trigonometric functions of acute angles.
- Use the fundamental trigonometric identities.
- Use a calculator to evaluate trigonometric functions.
- Use trigonometric functions to model and solve real-life problems.

Why you should learn it

Trigonometric functions are often used to analyze real-life situations. For instance, in Exercise 71 on page 311, you can use trigonometric functions to find the height of a helium-filled balloon.

Joseph Sohm; Chromosohm

The Six Trigonometric Functions

Our second look at the trigonometric functions is from a *right triangle* perspective. Consider a right triangle, with one acute angle labeled θ, as shown in Figure 4.26. Relative to the angle θ, the three sides of the triangle are the **hypotenuse,** the **opposite side** (the side opposite the angle θ), and the **adjacent side** (the side adjacent to the angle θ).

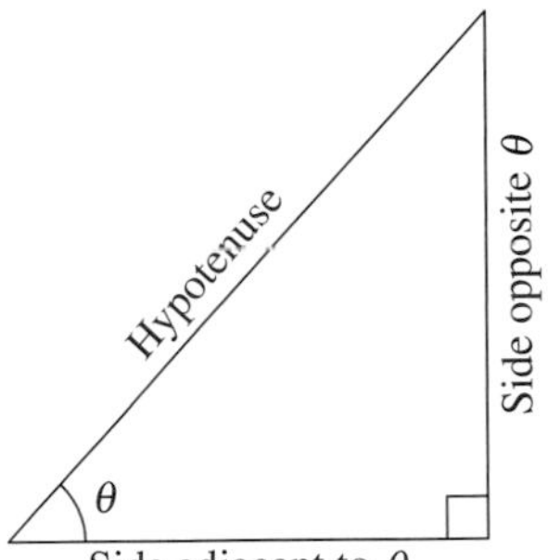

FIGURE 4.26

Using the lengths of these three sides, you can form six ratios that define the six trigonometric functions of the acute angle θ.

sine cosecant cosine secant tangent cotangent

In the following definitions, it is important to see that $0° < \theta < 90°$ (θ lies in the first quadrant) and that for such angles the value of each trigonometric function is *positive*.

Right Triangle Definitions of Trigonometric Functions

Let θ be an *acute* angle of a right triangle. The six trigonometric functions of the angle θ are defined as follows. (Note that the functions in the second row are the *reciprocals* of the corresponding functions in the first row.)

$$\sin \theta = \frac{\text{opp}}{\text{hyp}} \qquad \cos \theta = \frac{\text{adj}}{\text{hyp}} \qquad \tan \theta = \frac{\text{opp}}{\text{adj}}$$

$$\csc \theta = \frac{\text{hyp}}{\text{opp}} \qquad \sec \theta = \frac{\text{hyp}}{\text{adj}} \qquad \cot \theta = \frac{\text{adj}}{\text{opp}}$$

The abbreviations opp, adj, and hyp represent the lengths of the three sides of a right triangle.

opp = the length of the side *opposite* θ

adj = the length of the side *adjacent to* θ

hyp = the length of the *hypotenuse*

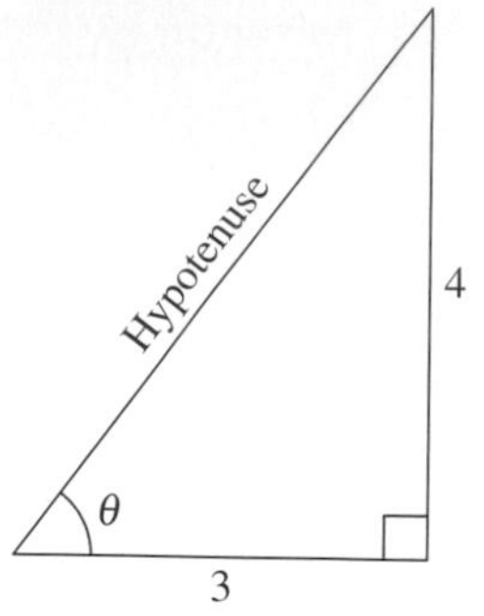

FIGURE 4.27

Example 1 **Evaluating Trigonometric Functions**

Use the triangle in Figure 4.27 to find the values of the six trigonometric functions of θ.

Solution

By the Pythagorean Theorem, $(\text{hyp})^2 = (\text{opp})^2 + (\text{adj})^2$, it follows that

$$\begin{aligned} \text{hyp} &= \sqrt{4^2 + 3^2} \\ &= \sqrt{25} \\ &= 5. \end{aligned}$$

So, the six trigonometric functions of θ are

$$\sin\theta = \frac{\text{opp}}{\text{hyp}} = \frac{4}{5} \qquad \csc\theta = \frac{\text{hyp}}{\text{opp}} = \frac{5}{4}$$

$$\cos\theta = \frac{\text{adj}}{\text{hyp}} = \frac{3}{5} \qquad \sec\theta = \frac{\text{hyp}}{\text{adj}} = \frac{5}{3}$$

$$\tan\theta = \frac{\text{opp}}{\text{adj}} = \frac{4}{3} \qquad \cot\theta = \frac{\text{adj}}{\text{opp}} = \frac{3}{4}.$$

✓CHECKPOINT Now try Exercise 3.

Historical Note
Georg Joachim Rhaeticus (1514–1576) was the leading Teutonic mathematical astronomer of the 16th century. He was the first to define the trigonometric functions as ratios of the sides of a right triangle.

In Example 1, you were given the lengths of two sides of the right triangle, but not the angle θ. Often, you will be asked to find the trigonometric functions of a *given* acute angle θ. To do this, construct a right triangle having θ as one of its angles.

Example 2 **Evaluating Trigonometric Functions of 45°**

Find the values of sin 45°, cos 45°, and tan 45°.

Solution

Construct a right triangle having 45° as one of its acute angles, as shown in Figure 4.28. Choose the length of the adjacent side to be 1. From geometry, you know that the other acute angle is also 45°. So, the triangle is isosceles and the length of the opposite side is also 1. Using the Pythagorean Theorem, you find the length of the hypotenuse to be $\sqrt{2}$.

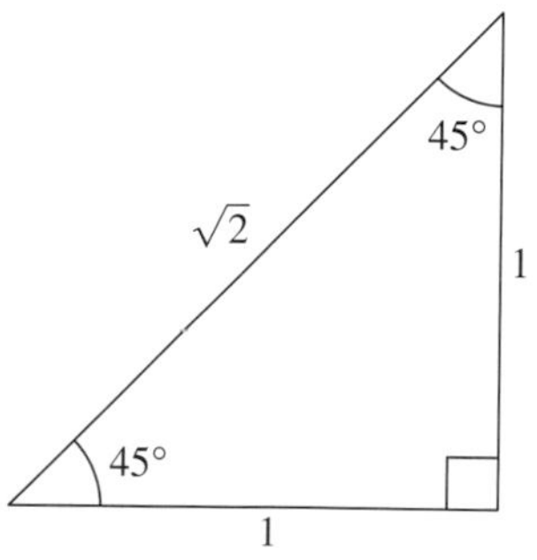

FIGURE 4.28

$$\sin 45^\circ = \frac{\text{opp}}{\text{hyp}} = \frac{1}{\sqrt{2}} = \frac{\sqrt{2}}{2}$$

$$\cos 45^\circ = \frac{\text{adj}}{\text{hyp}} = \frac{1}{\sqrt{2}} = \frac{\sqrt{2}}{2}$$

$$\tan 45^\circ = \frac{\text{opp}}{\text{adj}} = \frac{1}{1} = 1$$

✓CHECKPOINT Now try Exercise 17.

STUDY TIP

Because the angles 30°, 45°, and 60° ($\pi/6$, $\pi/4$, and $\pi/3$) occur frequently in trigonometry, you should learn to construct the triangles shown in Figures 4.28 and 4.29.

Example 3 Evaluating Trigonometric Functions of 30° and 60°

Use the equilateral triangle shown in Figure 4.29 to find the values of sin 60°, cos 60°, sin 30°, and cos 30°.

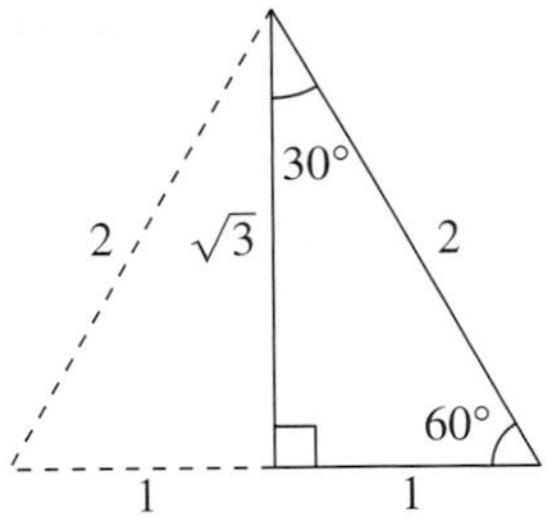

FIGURE 4.29

Solution

Use the Pythagorean Theorem and the equilateral triangle in Figure 4.29 to verify the lengths of the sides shown in the figure. For $\theta = 60°$, you have adj $= 1$, opp $= \sqrt{3}$, and hyp $= 2$. So,

$$\sin 60° = \frac{\text{opp}}{\text{hyp}} = \frac{\sqrt{3}}{2} \quad \text{and} \quad \cos 60° = \frac{\text{adj}}{\text{hyp}} = \frac{1}{2}.$$

For $\theta = 30°$, adj $= \sqrt{3}$, opp $= 1$, and hyp $= 2$. So,

$$\sin 30° = \frac{\text{opp}}{\text{hyp}} = \frac{1}{2} \quad \text{and} \quad \cos 30° = \frac{\text{adj}}{\text{hyp}} = \frac{\sqrt{3}}{2}.$$

CHECKPOINT Now try Exercise 19.

Technology

You can use a calculator to convert the answers in Example 3 to decimals. However, the radical form is the exact value and in most cases, the exact value is preferred.

Sines, Cosines, and Tangents of Special Angles

$$\sin 30° = \sin\frac{\pi}{6} = \frac{1}{2} \qquad \cos 30° = \cos\frac{\pi}{6} = \frac{\sqrt{3}}{2} \qquad \tan 30° = \tan\frac{\pi}{6} = \frac{\sqrt{3}}{3}$$

$$\sin 45° = \sin\frac{\pi}{4} = \frac{\sqrt{2}}{2} \qquad \cos 45° = \cos\frac{\pi}{4} = \frac{\sqrt{2}}{2} \qquad \tan 45° = \tan\frac{\pi}{4} = 1$$

$$\sin 60° = \sin\frac{\pi}{3} = \frac{\sqrt{3}}{2} \qquad \cos 60° = \cos\frac{\pi}{3} = \frac{1}{2} \qquad \tan 60° = \tan\frac{\pi}{3} = \sqrt{3}$$

In the box, note that $\sin 30° = \frac{1}{2} = \cos 60°$. This occurs because 30° and 60° are complementary angles. In general, it can be shown from the right triangle definitions that *cofunctions of complementary angles are equal*. That is, if θ is an acute angle, the following relationships are true.

$$\sin(90° - \theta) = \cos\theta \qquad \cos(90° - \theta) = \sin\theta$$

$$\tan(90° - \theta) = \cot\theta \qquad \cot(90° - \theta) = \tan\theta$$

$$\sec(90° - \theta) = \csc\theta \qquad \csc(90° - \theta) = \sec\theta$$

Trigonometric Identities

In trigonometry, a great deal of time is spent studying relationships between trigonometric functions (identities).

Fundamental Trigonometric Identities

Reciprocal Identities

$$\sin\theta = \frac{1}{\csc\theta} \qquad \cos\theta = \frac{1}{\sec\theta} \qquad \tan\theta = \frac{1}{\cot\theta}$$

$$\csc\theta = \frac{1}{\sin\theta} \qquad \sec\theta = \frac{1}{\cos\theta} \qquad \cot\theta = \frac{1}{\tan\theta}$$

Quotient Identities

$$\tan\theta = \frac{\sin\theta}{\cos\theta} \qquad \cot\theta = \frac{\cos\theta}{\sin\theta}$$

Pythagorean Identities

$$\sin^2\theta + \cos^2\theta = 1 \qquad 1 + \tan^2\theta = \sec^2\theta$$

$$1 + \cot^2\theta = \csc^2\theta$$

Note that $\sin^2\theta$ represents $(\sin\theta)^2$, $\cos^2\theta$ represents $(\cos\theta)^2$, and so on.

Example 4 **Applying Trigonometric Identities**

Let θ be an acute angle such that $\sin\theta = 0.6$. Find the values of (a) $\cos\theta$ and (b) $\tan\theta$ using trigonometric identities.

Solution

a. To find the value of $\cos\theta$, use the Pythagorean identity

$$\sin^2\theta + \cos^2\theta = 1.$$

So, you have

$$(0.6)^2 + \cos^2\theta = 1 \qquad \text{Substitute 0.6 for } \sin\theta.$$

$$\cos^2\theta = 1 - (0.6)^2 = 0.64 \qquad \text{Subtract } (0.6)^2 \text{ from each side.}$$

$$\cos\theta = \sqrt{0.64} = 0.8. \qquad \text{Extract the positive square root.}$$

b. Now, knowing the sine and cosine of θ, you can find the tangent of θ to be

$$\tan\theta = \frac{\sin\theta}{\cos\theta} = \frac{0.6}{0.8} = 0.75.$$

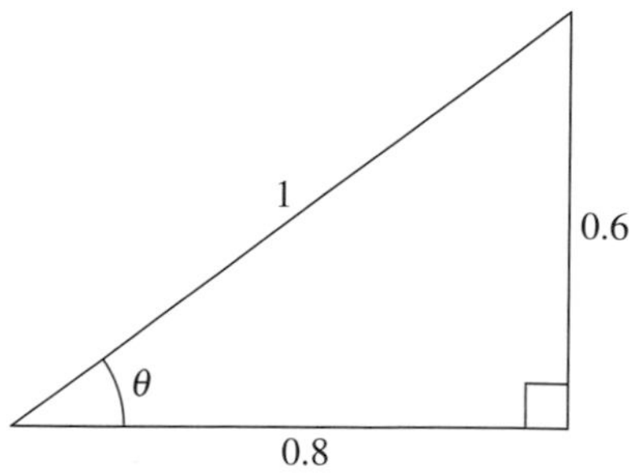

FIGURE 4.30

Use the definitions of $\cos\theta$ and $\tan\theta$, and the triangle shown in Figure 4.30, to check these results.

CHECKPOINT Now try Exercise 29.

Example 5 Applying Trigonometric Identities

Let θ be an acute angle such that $\tan \theta = 3$. Find the values of (a) $\cot \theta$ and (b) $\sec \theta$ using trigonometric identities.

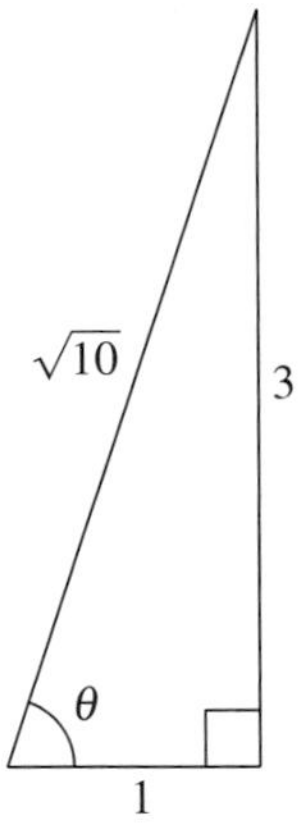

FIGURE 4.31

Solution

a. $\cot \theta = \dfrac{1}{\tan \theta}$ Reciprocal identity

$\cot \theta = \dfrac{1}{3}$

b. $\sec^2 \theta = 1 + \tan^2 \theta$ Pythagorean identity

$\sec^2 \theta = 1 + 3^2$

$\sec^2 \theta = 10$

$\sec \theta = \sqrt{10}$

Use the definitions of $\cot \theta$ and $\sec \theta$, and the triangle shown in Figure 4.31, to check these results.

CHECKPOINT Now try Exercise 31.

Evaluating Trigonometric Functions with a Calculator

To use a calculator to evaluate trigonometric functions of angles measured in degrees, first set the calculator to *degree* mode and then proceed as demonstrated in Section 4.2. For instance, you can find values of $\cos 28°$ and $\sec 28°$ as follows.

	Function	*Mode*	*Calculator Keystrokes*	*Display*
a.	$\cos 28°$	Degree	[COS] 28 [ENTER]	0.8829476
b.	$\sec 28°$	Degree	[(] [COS] [(] 28 [)] [)] [x^{-1}] [ENTER]	1.1325701

Throughout this text, angles are assumed to be measured in radians unless noted otherwise. For example, sin 1 means the sine of 1 radian and $\sin 1°$ means the sine of 1 degree.

STUDY TIP

You can also use the reciprocal identities for sine, cosine, and tangent to evaluate the cosecant, secant, and cotangent functions with a calculator. For instance, you could use the following keystroke sequence to evaluate $\sec 28°$.

1 [÷] [COS] 28 [ENTER]

The calculator should display 1.1325701.

Example 6 Using a Calculator

Use a calculator to evaluate $\sec(5° \, 40' \, 12'')$.

Solution

Begin by converting to decimal degree form. [Recall that $1' = \frac{1}{60}(1°)$ and $1'' = \frac{1}{3600}(1°)$].

$$5° \, 40' \, 12'' = 5° + \left(\frac{40}{60}\right)^{\circ} + \left(\frac{12}{3600}\right)^{\circ} = 5.67°$$

Then, use a calculator to evaluate $\sec 5.67°$.

Function	*Calculator Keystrokes*	*Display*
$\sec(5° \, 40' \, 12'') = \sec 5.67°$	[(] [COS] [(] 5.67 [)] [)] [x^{-1}] [ENTER]	1.0049166

CHECKPOINT Now try Exercise 47.

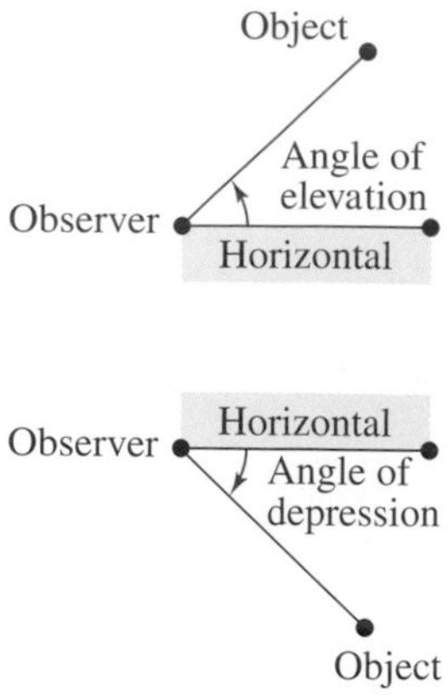

FIGURE 4.32

Applications Involving Right Triangles

Many applications of trigonometry involve a process called **solving right triangles.** In this type of application, you are usually given one side of a right triangle and one of the acute angles and are asked to find one of the other sides, *or* you are given two sides and are asked to find one of the acute angles.

In Example 7, the angle you are given is the **angle of elevation,** which represents the angle from the horizontal upward to an object. For objects that lie below the horizontal, it is common to use the term **angle of depression,** as shown in Figure 4.32.

Example 7 Using Trigonometry to Solve a Right Triangle

A surveyor is standing 115 feet from the base of the Washington Monument, as shown in Figure 4.33. The surveyor measures the angle of elevation to the top of the monument as 78.3°. How tall is the Washington Monument?

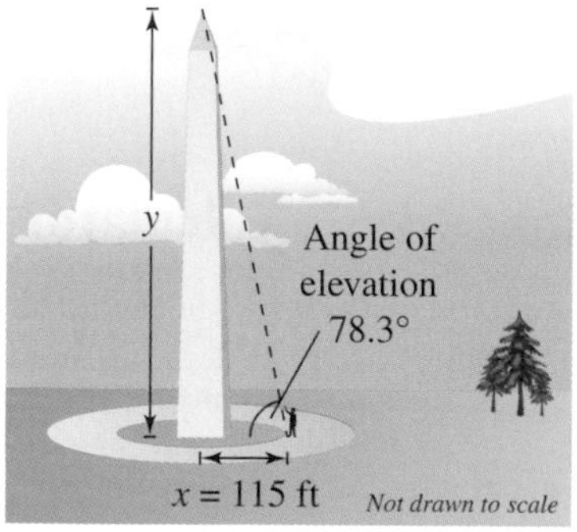

FIGURE 4.33

Solution

From Figure 4.33, you can see that

$$\tan 78.3° = \frac{\text{opp}}{\text{adj}} = \frac{y}{x}$$

where $x = 115$ and y is the height of the monument. So, the height of the Washington Monument is

$$y = x \tan 78.3° \approx 115(4.82882) \approx 555 \text{ feet.}$$

✓CHECKPOINT Now try Exercise 63.

Example 8 Using Trigonometry to Solve a Right Triangle

An historic lighthouse is 200 yards from a bike path along the edge of a lake. A walkway to the lighthouse is 400 yards long. Find the acute angle θ between the bike path and the walkway, as illustrated in Figure 4.34.

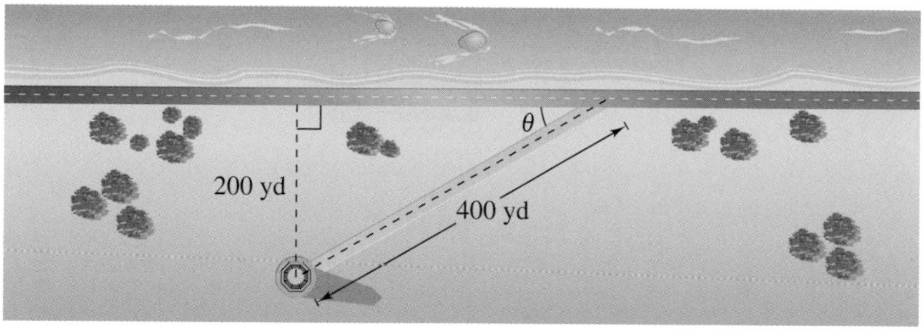

FIGURE 4.34

Solution

From Figure 4.34, you can see that the sine of the angle θ is

$$\sin \theta = \frac{\text{opp}}{\text{hyp}} = \frac{200}{400} = \frac{1}{2}.$$

Now you should recognize that $\theta = 30°$.

✓CHECKPOINT Now try Exercise 65.

By now you are able to recognize that $\theta = 30°$ is the acute angle that satisfies the equation $\sin\theta = \frac{1}{2}$. Suppose, however, that you were given the equation $\sin\theta = 0.6$ and were asked to find the acute angle θ. Because

$$\sin 30° = \frac{1}{2}$$

$$= 0.5000$$

and

$$\sin 45° = \frac{1}{\sqrt{2}}$$

$$\approx 0.7071$$

you might guess that θ lies somewhere between 30° and 45°. In a later section, you will study a method by which a more precise value of θ can be determined.

Example 9 **Solving a Right Triangle**

Find the length c of the skateboard ramp shown in Figure 4.35.

FIGURE 4.35

Solution

From Figure 4.35, you can see that

$$\sin 18.4° = \frac{\text{opp}}{\text{hyp}}$$

$$= \frac{4}{c}.$$

So, the length of the skateboard ramp is

$$c = \frac{4}{\sin 18.4°}$$

$$\approx \frac{4}{0.3156}$$

$$\approx 12.7 \text{ feet.}$$

CHECKPOINT Now try Exercise 67.

4.3 Exercises

VOCABULARY CHECK:

1. Match the trigonometric function with its right triangle definition.

(a) Sine (b) Cosine (c) Tangent (d) Cosecant (e) Secant (f) Cotangent

(i) $\dfrac{\text{hypotenuse}}{\text{adjacent}}$ (ii) $\dfrac{\text{adjacent}}{\text{opposite}}$ (iii) $\dfrac{\text{hypotenuse}}{\text{opposite}}$ (iv) $\dfrac{\text{adjacent}}{\text{hypotenuse}}$ (v) $\dfrac{\text{opposite}}{\text{hypotenuse}}$ (vi) $\dfrac{\text{opposite}}{\text{adjacent}}$

In Exercises 2 and 3, fill in the blanks.

2. Relative to the angle θ, the three sides of a right triangle are the ________ side, the ________ side, and the ________.

3. An angle that measures from the horizontal upward to an object is called the angle of ________, whereas an angle that measures from the horizontal downward to an object is called the angle of ________.

In Exercises 1–4, find the exact values of the six trigonometric functions of the angle θ shown in the figure. (Use the Pythagorean Theorem to find the third side of the triangle.)

1. 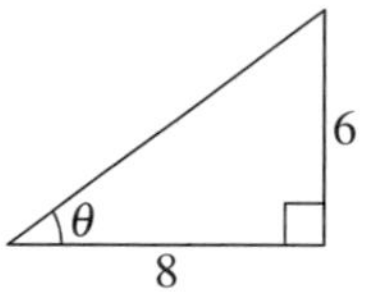

2. 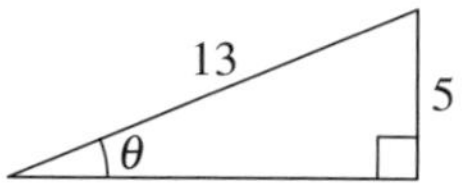

3. 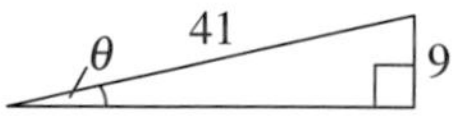

4. 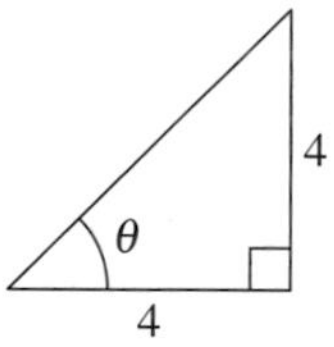

In Exercises 5–8, find the exact values of the six trigonometric functions of the angle θ for each of the two triangles. Explain why the function values are the same.

5. 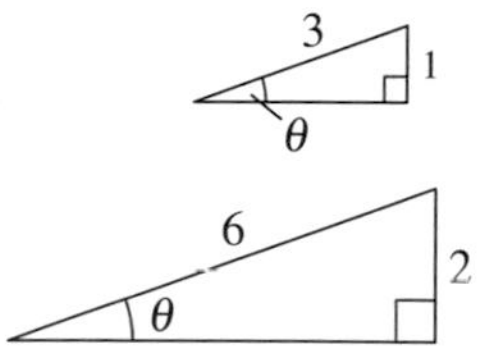

6. 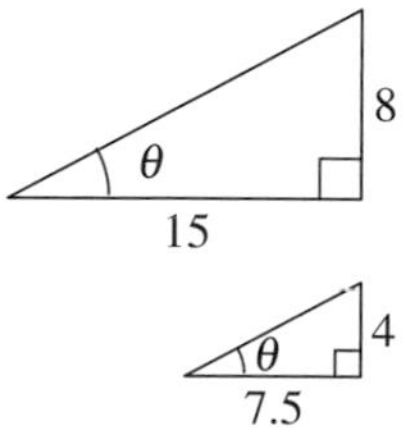

7. 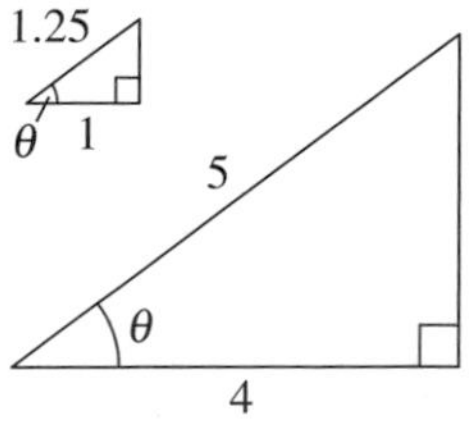

8. 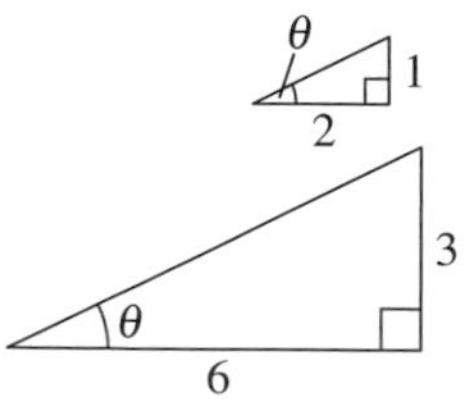

In Exercises 9–16, sketch a right triangle corresponding to the trigonometric function of the acute angle θ. Use the Pythagorean Theorem to determine the third side and then find the other five trigonometric functions of θ.

9. $\sin\theta = \frac{3}{4}$
10. $\cos\theta = \frac{5}{7}$
11. $\sec\theta = 2$
12. $\cot\theta = 5$
13. $\tan\theta = 3$
14. $\sec\theta = 6$
15. $\cot\theta = \frac{3}{2}$
16. $\csc\theta = \frac{17}{4}$

In Exercises 17–26, construct an appropriate triangle to complete the table. ($0 \le \theta \le 90°$, $0 \le \theta \le \pi/2$)

	Function	*θ (deg)*	*θ (rad)*	*Function Value*
17.	sin	30°		
18.	cos	45°		
19.	tan		$\frac{\pi}{3}$	
20.	sec		$\frac{\pi}{4}$	
21.	cot			$\frac{\sqrt{3}}{3}$
22.	csc			$\sqrt{2}$
23.	cos		$\frac{\pi}{6}$	
24.	sin		$\frac{\pi}{4}$	
25.	cot			1
26.	tan			$\frac{\sqrt{3}}{3}$

In Exercises 27–32, use the given function value(s), and trigonometric identities (including the cofunction identities), to find the indicated trigonometric functions.

27. $\sin 60° = \dfrac{\sqrt{3}}{2}$, $\cos 60° = \dfrac{1}{2}$

(a) $\tan 60°$ (b) $\sin 30°$

(c) $\cos 30°$ (d) $\cot 60°$

28. $\sin 30° = \dfrac{1}{2}$, $\tan 30° = \dfrac{\sqrt{3}}{3}$

(a) $\csc 30°$ (b) $\cot 60°$

(c) $\cos 30°$ (d) $\cot 30°$

29. $\csc \theta = \dfrac{\sqrt{13}}{2}$, $\sec \theta = \dfrac{\sqrt{13}}{3}$

(a) $\sin \theta$ (b) $\cos \theta$

(c) $\tan \theta$ (d) $\sec(90° - \theta)$

30. $\sec \theta = 5$, $\tan \theta = 2\sqrt{6}$

(a) $\cos \theta$ (b) $\cot \theta$

(c) $\cot(90° - \theta)$ (d) $\sin \theta$

31. $\cos \alpha = \frac{1}{3}$

(a) $\sec \alpha$ (b) $\sin \alpha$

(c) $\cot \alpha$ (d) $\sin(90° - \alpha)$

32. $\tan \beta = 5$

(a) $\cot \beta$ (b) $\cos \beta$

(c) $\tan(90° - \beta)$ (d) $\csc \beta$

In Exercises 33–42, use trigonometric identities to transform the left side of the equation into the right side $(0 < \theta < \pi/2)$.

33. $\tan \theta \cot \theta = 1$

34. $\cos \theta \sec \theta = 1$

35. $\tan \alpha \cos \alpha = \sin \alpha$

36. $\cot \alpha \sin \alpha = \cos \alpha$

37. $(1 + \cos \theta)(1 - \cos \theta) = \sin^2 \theta$

38. $(1 + \sin \theta)(1 - \sin \theta) = \cos^2 \theta$

39. $(\sec \theta + \tan \theta)(\sec \theta - \tan \theta) = 1$

40. $\sin^2 \theta - \cos^2 \theta = 2 \sin^2 \theta - 1$

41. $\dfrac{\sin \theta}{\cos \theta} + \dfrac{\cos \theta}{\sin \theta} = \csc \theta \sec \theta$

42. $\dfrac{\tan \beta + \cot \beta}{\tan \beta} = \csc^2 \beta$

In Exercises 43–52, use a calculator to evaluate each function. Round your answers to four decimal places. (Be sure the calculator is in the correct angle mode.)

43. (a) $\sin 10°$ (b) $\cos 80°$

44. (a) $\tan 23.5°$ (b) $\cot 66.5°$

45. (a) $\sin 16.35°$ (b) $\csc 16.35°$

46. (a) $\cos 16° 18'$ (b) $\sin 73° 56'$

47. (a) $\sec 42° 12'$ (b) $\csc 48° 7'$

48. (a) $\cos 4° 50' 15''$ (b) $\sec 4° 50' 15''$

49. (a) $\cot 11° 15'$ (b) $\tan 11° 15'$

50. (a) $\sec 56° 8 10''$ (b) $\cos 56° 8 10''$

51. (a) $\csc 32° 40' 3''$ (b) $\tan 44° 28 16''$

52. (a) $\sec\left(\frac{9}{5} \cdot 20 + 32\right)°$ (b) $\cot\left(\frac{9}{5} \cdot 30 + 32\right)°$

In Exercises 53–58, find the values of θ in degrees $(0° < \theta < 90°)$ and radians $(0 < \theta < \pi/2)$ without the aid of a calculator.

53. (a) $\sin \theta = \dfrac{1}{2}$ (b) $\csc \theta = 2$

54. (a) $\cos \theta = \dfrac{\sqrt{2}}{2}$ (b) $\tan \theta = 1$

55. (a) $\sec \theta = 2$ (b) $\cot \theta = 1$

56. (a) $\tan \theta = \sqrt{3}$ (b) $\cos \theta = \dfrac{1}{2}$

57. (a) $\csc \theta = \dfrac{2\sqrt{3}}{3}$ (b) $\sin \theta = \dfrac{\sqrt{2}}{2}$

58. (a) $\cot \theta = \dfrac{\sqrt{3}}{3}$ (b) $\sec \theta = \sqrt{2}$

In Exercises 59–62, solve for *x*, *y*, or *r* as indicated.

59. Solve for x.

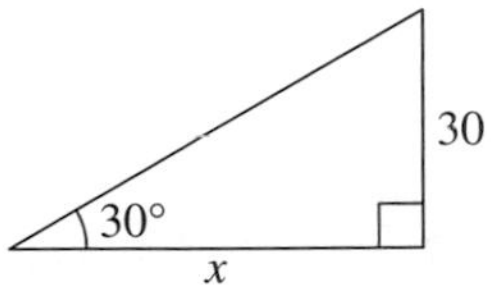

60. Solve for y.

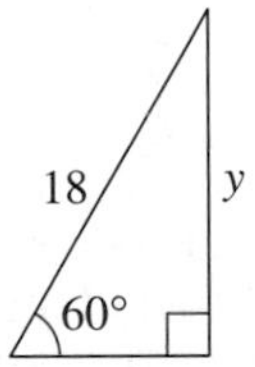

61. Solve for x.

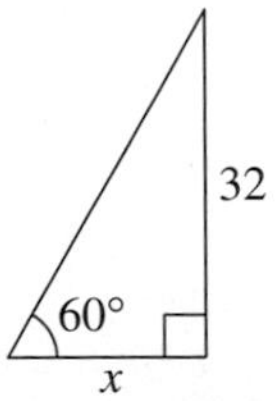

62. Solve for r.

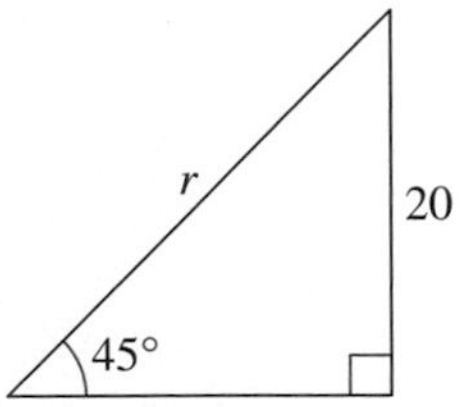

63. ***Empire State Building*** You are standing 45 meters from the base of the Empire State Building. You estimate that the angle of elevation to the top of the 86th floor (the observatory) is 82°. If the total height of the building is another 123 meters above the 86th floor, what is the approximate height of the building? One of your friends is on the 86th floor. What is the distance between you and your friend?

64. *Height* A six-foot person walks from the base of a broadcasting tower directly toward the tip of the shadow cast by the tower. When the person is 132 feet from the tower and 3 feet from the tip of the shadow, the person's shadow starts to appear beyond the tower's shadow.

(a) Draw a right triangle that gives a visual representation of the problem. Show the known quantities of the triangle and use a variable to indicate the height of the tower.

(b) Use a trigonometric function to write an equation involving the unknown quantity.

(c) What is the height of the tower?

65. *Angle of Elevation* You are skiing down a mountain with a vertical height of 1500 feet. The distance from the top of the mountain to the base is 3000 feet. What is the angle of elevation from the base to the top of the mountain?

66. *Width of a River* A biologist wants to know the width w of a river so in order to properly set instruments for studying the pollutants in the water. From point A, the biologist walks downstream 100 feet and sights to point C (see figure). From this sighting, it is determined that $\theta = 54°$. How wide is the river?

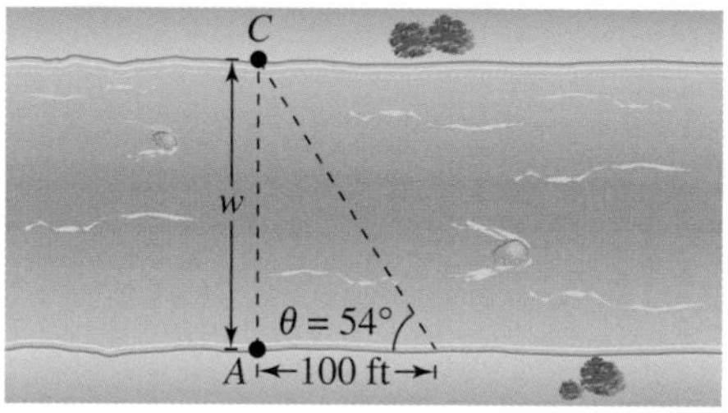

67. *Length* A steel cable zip-line is being constructed for a competition on a reality television show. One end of the zip-line is attached to a platform on top of a 150-foot pole. The other end of the zip-line is attached to the top of a 5-foot stake. The angle of elevation to the platform is 23° (see figure).

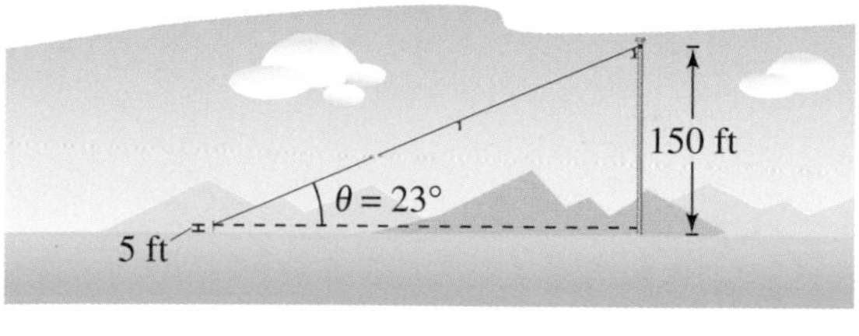

(a) How long is the zip-line?

(b) How far is the stake from the pole?

(c) Contestants take an average of 6 seconds to reach the ground from the top of the zip-line. At what rate are contestants moving down the line? At what rate are they dropping vertically?

68. *Height of a Mountain* In traveling across flat land, you notice a mountain directly in front of you. Its angle of elevation (to the peak) is 3.5°. After you drive 13 miles closer to the mountain, the angle of elevation is 9°. Approximate the height of the mountain.

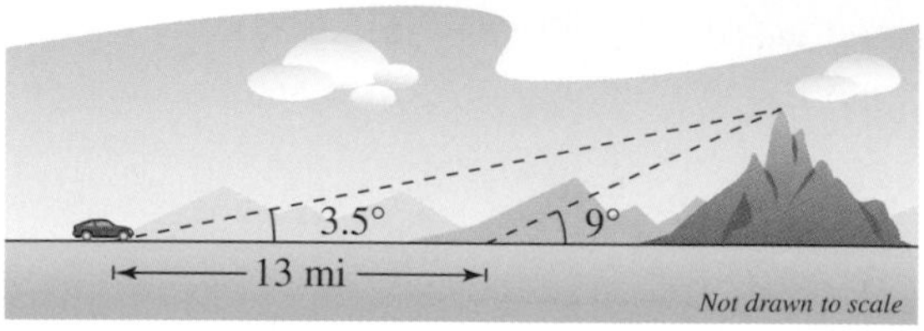

69. *Machine Shop Calculations* A steel plate has the form of one-fourth of a circle with a radius of 60 centimeters. Two two-centimeter holes are to be drilled in the plate positioned as shown in the figure. Find the coordinates of the center of each hole.

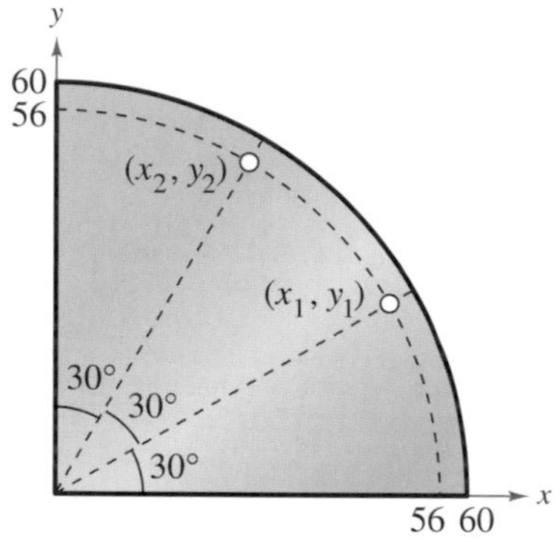

70. *Machine Shop Calculations* A tapered shaft has a diameter of 5 centimeters at the small end and is 15 centimeters long (see figure). The taper is 3°. Find the diameter d of the large end of the shaft.

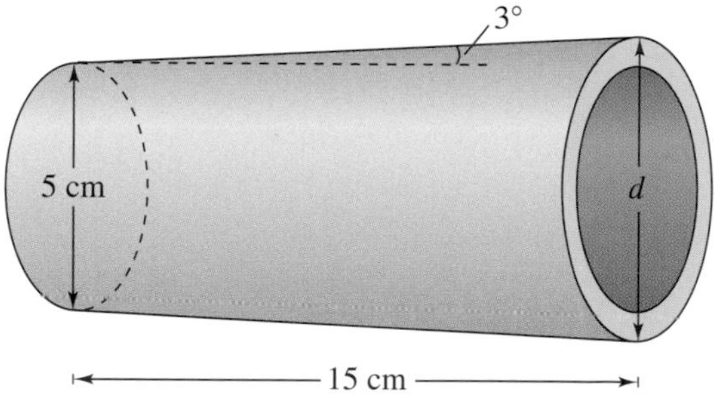

Model It

71. ***Height*** A 20-meter line is used to tether a helium-filled balloon. Because of a breeze, the line makes an angle of approximately 85° with the ground.

(a) Draw a right triangle that gives a visual representation of the problem. Show the known quantities of the triangle and use a variable to indicate the height of the balloon.

(b) Use a trigonometric function to write an equation involving the unknown quantity.

(c) What is the height of the balloon?

(d) The breeze becomes stronger and the angle the balloon makes with the ground decreases. How does this affect the triangle you drew in part (a)?

(e) Complete the table, which shows the heights (in meters) of the balloon for decreasing angle measures θ.

Angle, θ	80°	70°	60°	50°
Height				

Angle, θ	40°	30°	20°	10°
Height				

(f) As the angle the balloon makes with the ground approaches 0°, how does this affect the height of the balloon? Draw a right triangle to explain your reasoning.

72. ***Geometry*** Use a compass to sketch a quarter of a circle of radius 10 centimeters. Using a protractor, construct an angle of 20° in standard position (see figure). Drop a perpendicular line from the point of intersection of the terminal side of the angle and the arc of the circle. By actual measurement, calculate the coordinates (x, y) of the point of intersection and use these measurements to approximate the six trigonometric functions of a 20° angle.

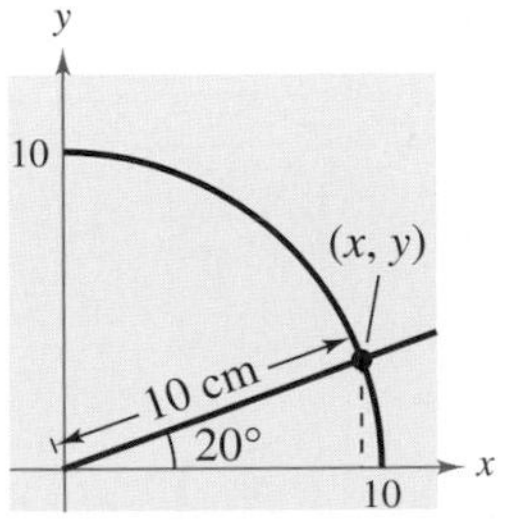

Synthesis

True or False? **In Exercises 73–78, determine whether the statement is true or false. Justify your answer.**

73. $\sin 60° \csc 60° = 1$

74. $\sec 30° = \csc 60°$

75. $\sin 45° + \cos 45° = 1$

76. $\cot^2 10° - \csc^2 10° = -1$

77. $\dfrac{\sin 60°}{\sin 30°} = \sin 2°$

78. $\tan[(5°)^2] = \tan^2(5°)$

79. ***Writing*** In right triangle trigonometry, explain why $\sin 30° = \frac{1}{2}$ regardless of the size of the triangle.

80. ***Think About It*** You are given only the value $\tan\theta$. Is it possible to find the value of $\sec\theta$ without finding the measure of θ? Explain.

81. ***Exploration***

(a) Complete the table.

θ	0.1	0.2	0.3	0.4	0.5
$\sin\theta$					

(b) Is θ or $\sin\theta$ greater for θ in the interval $(0, 0.5]$?

(c) As θ approaches 0, how do θ and $\sin\theta$ compare? Explain.

82. ***Exploration***

(a) Complete the table.

θ	0°	18°	36°	54°	72°	90°
$\sin\theta$						
$\cos\theta$						

(b) Discuss the behavior of the sine function for θ in the range from 0° to 90°.

(c) Discuss the behavior of the cosine function for θ in the range from 0° to 90°.

(d) Use the definitions of the sine and cosine functions to explain the results of parts (b) and (c).

Skills Review

In Exercises 83–86, perform the operations and simplify.

83. $\dfrac{x^2 - 6x}{x^2 + 4x - 12} \cdot \dfrac{x^2 + 12x + 36}{x^2 - 36}$

84. $\dfrac{2t^2 + 5t - 12}{9 - 4t^2} \div \dfrac{t^2 - 16}{4t^2 + 12t + 9}$

85. $\dfrac{3}{x + 2} - \dfrac{2}{x - 2} + \dfrac{x}{x^2 + 4x + 4}$

86. $\dfrac{\left(\dfrac{3}{x} - \dfrac{1}{4}\right)}{\left(\dfrac{12}{x} - 1\right)}$

4.4 Trigonometric Functions of Any Angle

What you should learn

- Evaluate trigonometric functions of any angle.
- Use reference angles to evaluate trigonometric functions.
- Evaluate trigonometric functions of real numbers.

Why you should learn it

You can use trigonometric functions to model and solve real-life problems. For instance, in Exercise 87 on page 319, you can use trigonometric functions to model the monthly normal temperatures in New York City and Fairbanks, Alaska.

James Urbach/SuperStock

Introduction

In Section 4.3, the definitions of trigonometric functions were restricted to acute angles. In this section, the definitions are extended to cover *any* angle. If θ is an *acute* angle, these definitions coincide with those given in the preceding section.

Definitions of Trigonometric Functions of Any Angle

Let θ be an angle in standard position with (x, y) a point on the terminal side of θ and $r = \sqrt{x^2 + y^2} \neq 0$.

$$\sin\theta = \frac{y}{r} \qquad \cos\theta = \frac{x}{r}$$

$$\tan\theta = \frac{y}{x}, \quad x \neq 0 \qquad \cot\theta = \frac{x}{y}, \quad y \neq 0$$

$$\sec\theta = \frac{r}{x}, \quad x \neq 0 \qquad \csc\theta = \frac{r}{y}, \quad y \neq 0$$

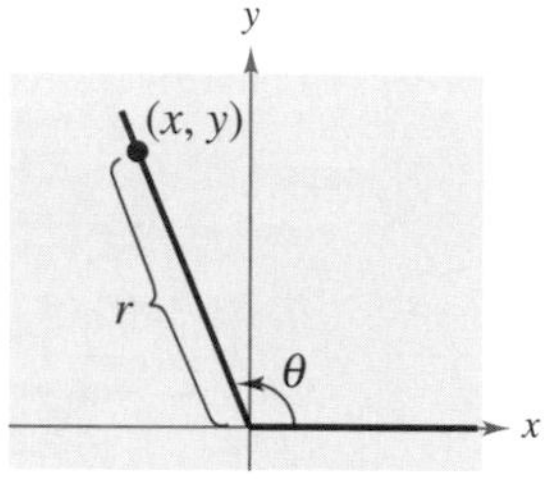

Because $r = \sqrt{x^2 + y^2}$ *cannot* be zero, it follows that the sine and cosine functions are defined for any real value of θ. However, if $x = 0$, the tangent and secant of θ are undefined. For example, the tangent of 90° is undefined. Similarly, if $y = 0$, the cotangent and cosecant of θ are undefined.

Example 1 Evaluating Trigonometric Functions

Let $(-3, 4)$ be a point on the terminal side of θ. Find the sine, cosine, and tangent of θ.

Solution

Referring to Figure 4.36, you can see that $x = -3$, $y = 4$, and

$$r = \sqrt{x^2 + y^2} = \sqrt{(-3)^2 + 4^2} = \sqrt{25} = 5.$$

So, you have the following.

$$\sin\theta = \frac{y}{r} = \frac{4}{5}$$

$$\cos\theta = \frac{x}{r} = -\frac{3}{5}$$

$$\tan\theta = \frac{y}{x} = -\frac{4}{3}$$

CHECKPOINT Now try Exercise 1.

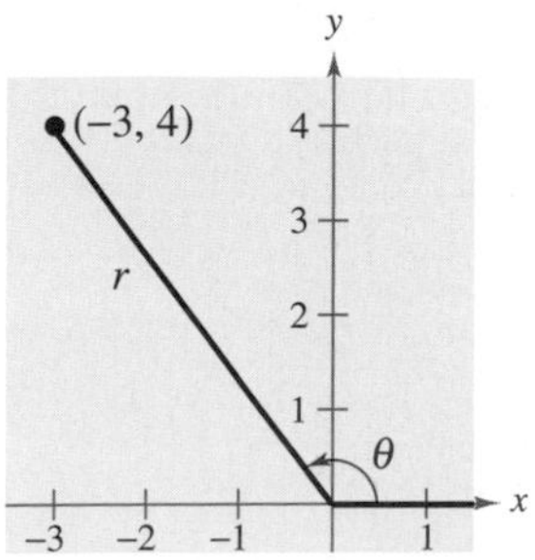

FIGURE 4.36

The *signs* of the trigonometric functions in the four quadrants can be determined easily from the definitions of the functions. For instance, because $\cos\theta = x/r$, it follows that $\cos\theta$ is positive wherever $x > 0$, which is in Quadrants I and IV. (Remember, r is always positive.) In a similar manner, you can verify the results shown in Figure 4.37.

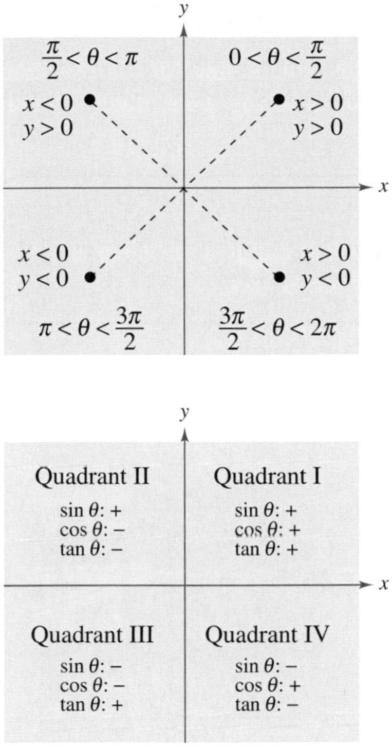

FIGURE 4.37

Example 2 Evaluating Trigonometric Functions

Given $\tan\theta = -\frac{5}{4}$ and $\cos\theta > 0$, find $\sin\theta$ and $\sec\theta$.

Solution

Note that θ lies in Quadrant IV because that is the only quadrant in which the tangent is negative and the cosine is positive. Moreover, using

$$\tan\theta = \frac{y}{x} = -\frac{5}{4}$$

and the fact that y is negative in Quadrant IV, you can let $y = -5$ and $x = 4$. So, $r = \sqrt{16 + 25} = \sqrt{41}$ and you have

$$\sin\theta = \frac{y}{r} = \frac{-5}{\sqrt{41}}$$

$$\approx -0.7809$$

$$\sec\theta = \frac{r}{x} = \frac{\sqrt{41}}{4}$$

$$\approx 1.6008.$$

CHECKPOINT Now try Exercise 17.

Example 3 Trigonometric Functions of Quadrant Angles

Evaluate the cosine and tangent functions at the four quadrant angles $0, \frac{\pi}{2}, \pi$, and $\frac{3\pi}{2}$.

Solution

To begin, choose a point on the terminal side of each angle, as shown in Figure 4.38. For each of the four points, $r = 1$, and you have the following.

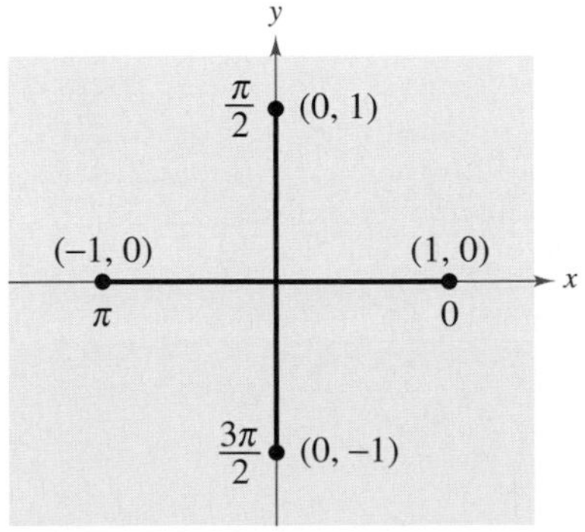

FIGURE 4.38

$$\cos 0 = \frac{x}{r} = \frac{1}{1} = 1 \qquad \tan 0 = \frac{y}{x} = \frac{0}{1} = 0 \qquad (x, y) = (1, 0)$$

$$\cos\frac{\pi}{2} = \frac{x}{r} = \frac{0}{1} = 0 \qquad \tan\frac{\pi}{2} = \frac{y}{x} = \frac{1}{0} \Rightarrow \text{undefined} \qquad (x, y) = (0, 1)$$

$$\cos\pi = \frac{x}{r} = \frac{-1}{1} = -1 \qquad \tan\pi = \frac{y}{x} = \frac{0}{-1} = 0 \qquad (x, y) = (-1, 0)$$

$$\cos\frac{3\pi}{2} = \frac{x}{r} = \frac{0}{1} = 0 \qquad \tan\frac{3\pi}{2} = \frac{y}{x} = \frac{-1}{0} \Rightarrow \text{undefined} \qquad (x, y) = (0, -1)$$

CHECKPOINT Now try Exercise 29.

Reference Angles

The values of the trigonometric functions of angles greater than 90° (or less than 0°) can be determined from their values at corresponding acute angles called **reference angles.**

> **Definition of Reference Angle**
>
> Let θ be an angle in standard position. Its **reference angle** is the acute angle θ' formed by the terminal side of θ and the horizontal axis.

Figure 4.39 shows the reference angles for θ in Quadrants II, III, and IV.

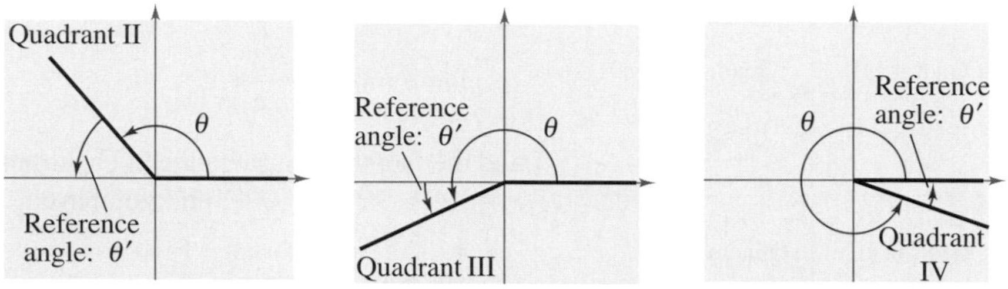

$\theta' = \pi - \theta$ (radians)
$\theta' = 180° - \theta$ (degrees)

$\theta' = \theta - \pi$ (radians)
$\theta' = \theta - 180°$ (degrees)

$\theta' = 2\pi - \theta$ (radians)
$\theta' = 360° - \theta$ (degrees)

FIGURE 4.39

Example 4 **Finding Reference Angles**

Find the reference angle θ'.

a. $\theta = 300°$ **b.** $\theta = 2.3$ **c.** $\theta = -135°$

Solution

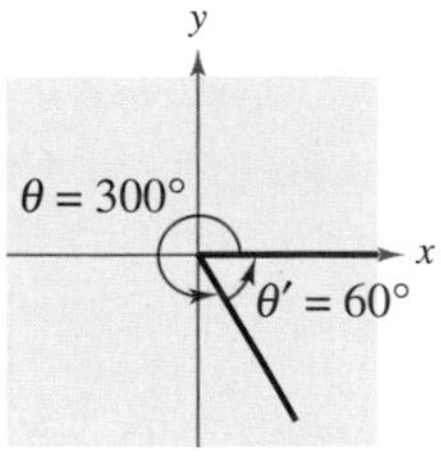

FIGURE 4.40

a. Because 300° lies in Quadrant IV, the angle it makes with the x-axis is

$$\theta' = 360° - 300°$$
$$= 60°. \quad \text{Degrees}$$

Figure 4.40 shows the angle $\theta = 300°$ and its reference angle $\theta' = 60°$.

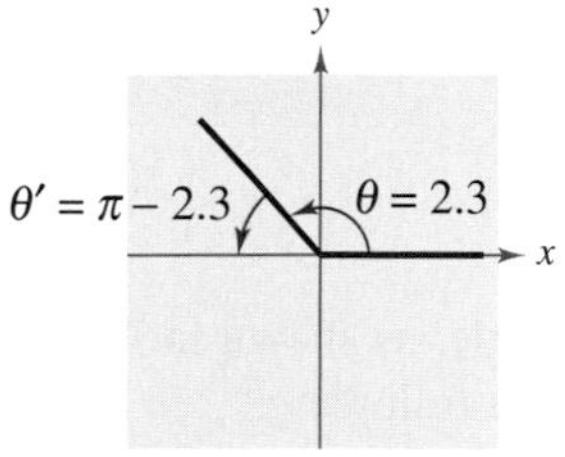

FIGURE 4.41

b. Because 2.3 lies between $\pi/2 \approx 1.5708$ and $\pi \approx 3.1416$, it follows that it is in Quadrant II and its reference angle is

$$\theta' = \pi - 2.3$$
$$\approx 0.8416. \quad \text{Radians}$$

Figure 4.41 shows the angle $\theta = 2.3$ and its reference angle $\theta' = \pi - 2.3$.

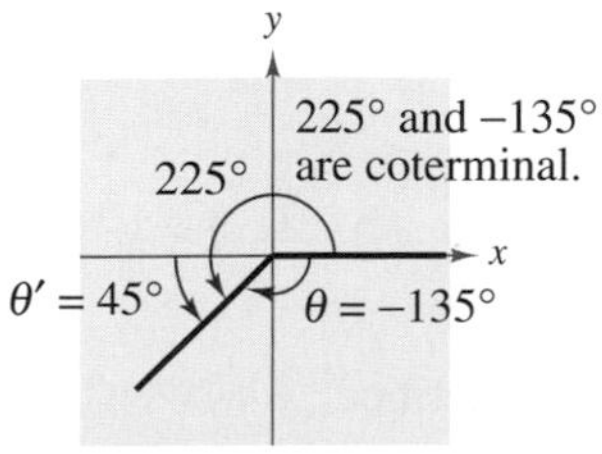

FIGURE 4.42

c. First, determine that $-135°$ is coterminal with 225°, which lies in Quadrant III. So, the reference angle is

$$\theta' = 225° - 180°$$
$$= 45°. \quad \text{Degrees}$$

Figure 4.42 shows the angle $\theta = -135°$ and its reference angle $\theta' = 45°$.

✓CHECKPOINT Now try Exercise 37.

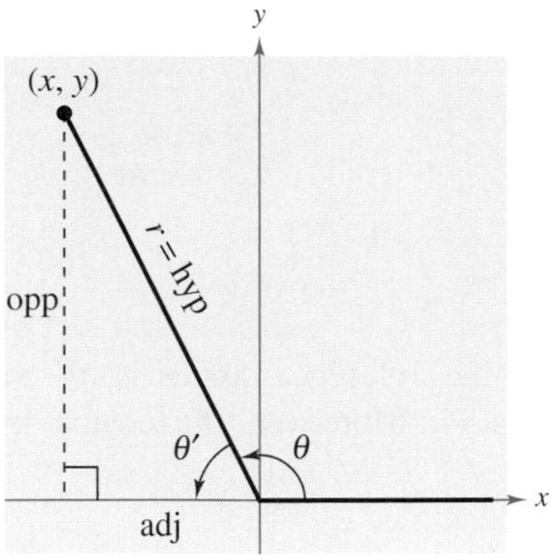

opp = |y|, adj = |x|
FIGURE 4.43

Trigonometric Functions of Real Numbers

To see how a reference angle is used to evaluate a trigonometric function, consider the point (x, y) on the terminal side of θ, as shown in Figure 4.43. By definition, you know that

$$\sin \theta = \frac{y}{r} \quad \text{and} \quad \tan \theta = \frac{y}{x}.$$

For the right triangle with acute angle θ' and sides of lengths $|x|$ and $|y|$, you have

$$\sin \theta' = \frac{\text{opp}}{\text{hyp}} = \frac{|y|}{r}$$

and

$$\tan \theta' = \frac{\text{opp}}{\text{adj}} = \frac{|y|}{|x|}.$$

So, it follows that $\sin \theta$ and $\sin \theta'$ are equal, *except possibly in sign*. The same is true for $\tan \theta$ and $\tan \theta'$ *and* for the other four trigonometric functions. In all cases, the sign of the function value can be determined by the quadrant in which θ lies.

Evaluating Trigonometric Functions of Any Angle

To find the value of a trigonometric function of any angle θ:

1. Determine the function value for the associated reference angle θ'.

2. Depending on the quadrant in which θ lies, affix the appropriate sign to the function value.

STUDY TIP

Learning the table of values at the right is worth the effort because doing so will increase both your efficiency and your confidence. Here is a pattern for the sine function that may help you remember the values.

θ	0°	30°	45°	60°	90°
$\sin \theta$	$\frac{\sqrt{0}}{2}$	$\frac{\sqrt{1}}{2}$	$\frac{\sqrt{2}}{2}$	$\frac{\sqrt{3}}{2}$	$\frac{\sqrt{4}}{2}$

Reverse the order to get cosine values of the same angles.

By using reference angles and the special angles discussed in the preceding section, you can greatly extend the scope of *exact* trigonometric values. For instance, knowing the function values of 30° means that you know the function values of all angles for which 30° is a reference angle. For convenience, the table below shows the exact values of the trigonometric functions of special angles and quadrant angles.

Trigonometric Values of Common Angles

θ (degrees)	0°	30°	45°	60°	90°	180°	270°
θ (radians)	0	$\frac{\pi}{6}$	$\frac{\pi}{4}$	$\frac{\pi}{3}$	$\frac{\pi}{2}$	π	$\frac{3\pi}{2}$
$\sin \theta$	0	$\frac{1}{2}$	$\frac{\sqrt{2}}{2}$	$\frac{\sqrt{3}}{2}$	1	0	-1
$\cos \theta$	1	$\frac{\sqrt{3}}{2}$	$\frac{\sqrt{2}}{2}$	$\frac{1}{2}$	0	-1	0
$\tan \theta$	0	$\frac{\sqrt{3}}{3}$	1	$\sqrt{3}$	Undef.	0	Undef.

Example 5 Using Reference Angles

Evaluate each trigonometric function.

a. $\cos \frac{4\pi}{3}$ **b.** $\tan(-210°)$ **c.** $\csc \frac{11\pi}{4}$

Solution

a. Because $\theta = 4\pi/3$ lies in Quadrant III, the reference angle is $\theta' = (4\pi/3) - \pi = \pi/3$, as shown in Figure 4.44. Moreover, the cosine is negative in Quadrant III, so

$$\cos \frac{4\pi}{3} = (-) \cos \frac{\pi}{3}$$
$$= -\frac{1}{2}.$$

b. Because $-210° + 360° = 150°$, it follows that $-210°$ is coterminal with the second-quadrant angle $150°$. So, the reference angle is $\theta' = 180° - 150° = 30°$, as shown in Figure 4.45. Finally, because the tangent is negative in Quadrant II, you have

$$\tan(-210°) = (-) \tan 30°$$
$$= -\frac{\sqrt{3}}{3}.$$

c. Because $(11\pi/4) - 2\pi = 3\pi/4$, it follows that $11\pi/4$ is coterminal with the second-quadrant angle $3\pi/4$. So, the reference angle is $\theta' = \pi - (3\pi/4) = \pi/4$, as shown in Figure 4.46. Because the cosecant is positive in Quadrant II, you have

$$\csc \frac{11\pi}{4} = (+) \csc \frac{\pi}{4}$$
$$= \frac{1}{\sin(\pi/4)}$$
$$= \sqrt{2}.$$

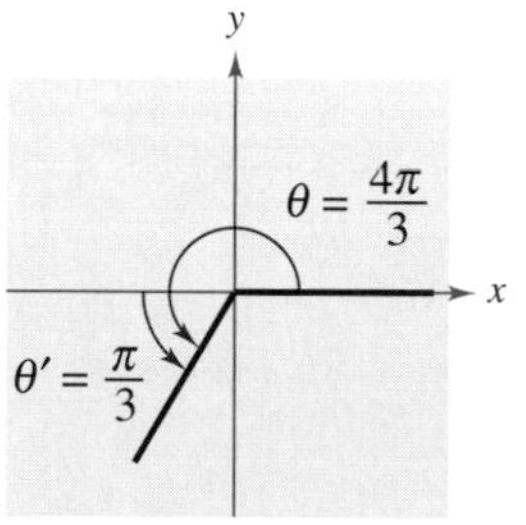

FIGURE 4.44

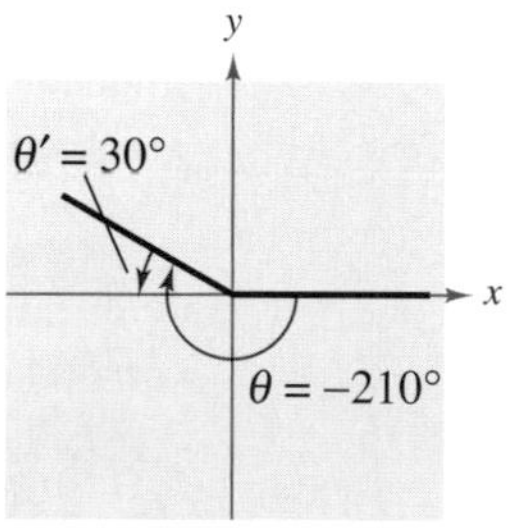

FIGURE 4.45

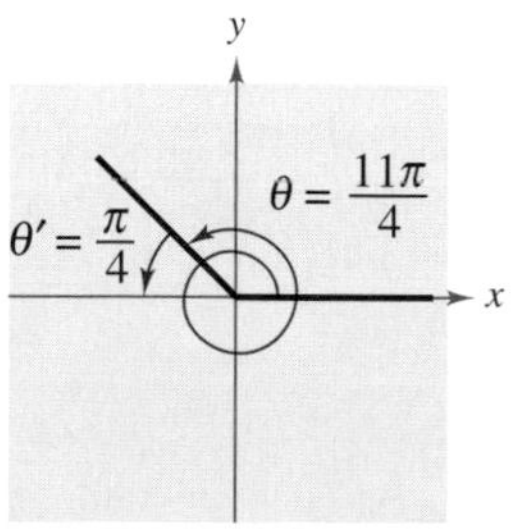

FIGURE 4.46

CHECKPOINT Now try Exercise 51.

Example 6 Using Trigonometric Identities

Let θ be an angle in Quadrant II such that $\sin\theta = \frac{1}{3}$. Find (a) $\cos\theta$ and (b) $\tan\theta$ by using trigonometric identities.

Solution

a. Using the Pythagorean identity $\sin^2\theta + \cos^2\theta = 1$, you obtain

$$\left(\frac{1}{3}\right)^2 + \cos^2\theta = 1 \qquad \text{Substitute } \tfrac{1}{3} \text{ for } \sin\theta.$$

$$\cos^2\theta = 1 - \frac{1}{9} = \frac{8}{9}.$$

Because $\cos\theta < 0$ in Quadrant II, you can use the negative root to obtain

$$\cos\theta = -\frac{\sqrt{8}}{\sqrt{9}}$$

$$= -\frac{2\sqrt{2}}{3}.$$

b. Using the trigonometric identity $\tan\theta = \dfrac{\sin\theta}{\cos\theta}$, you obtain

$$\tan\theta = \frac{1/3}{-2\sqrt{2}/3} \qquad \text{Substitute for } \sin\theta \text{ and } \cos\theta.$$

$$= -\frac{1}{2\sqrt{2}}$$

$$= -\frac{\sqrt{2}}{4}.$$

CHECKPOINT Now try Exercise 59.

You can use a calculator to evaluate trigonometric functions, as shown in the next example.

Example 7 Using a Calculator

Use a calculator to evaluate each trigonometric function.

a. $\cot 410°$ **b.** $\sin(-7)$ **c.** $\sec \dfrac{\pi}{9}$

Solution

Function	*Mode*	*Calculator Keystrokes*	*Display*
a. $\cot 410°$	Degree	(TAN (410)) x^{-1} ENTER	0.8390996
b. $\sin(-7)$	Radian	SIN ((−) 7) ENTER	−0.6569866
c. $\sec \dfrac{\pi}{9}$	Radian	(COS (π ÷ 9)) x^{-1} ENTER	1.0641778

CHECKPOINT Now try Exercise 69.

4.4 Exercises

VOCABULARY CHECK:

In Exercises 1–6, let θ be an angle in standard position, with (x, y) a point on the terminal side of θ and $r\sqrt{x^2 + y^2} \neq 0$.

1. $\sin \theta =$ ________ **2.** $\dfrac{r}{y} =$ ________

3. $\tan \theta =$ ________ **4.** $\sec \theta =$ ________

5. $\dfrac{x}{r} =$ ________ **6.** $\dfrac{x}{y} =$ ________

7. The acute positive angle that is formed by the terminal side of the angle θ and the horizontal axis is called the ________ angle of θ and is denoted by θ'.

In Exercises 1–4, determine the exact values of the six trigonometric functions of the angle θ.

1. (a)

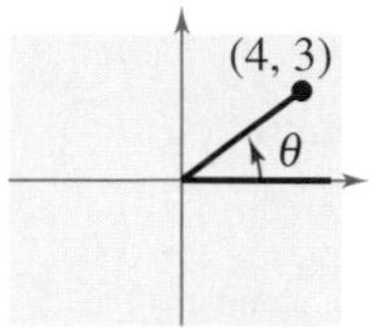

(b)

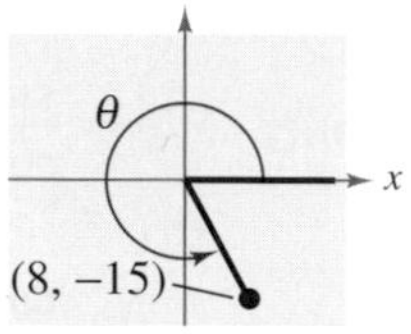

2. (a)

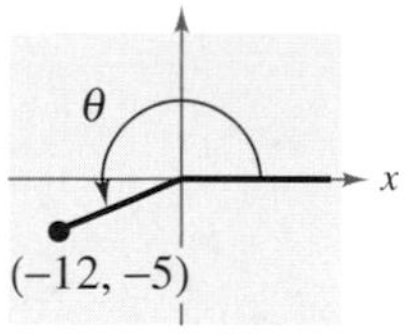

(b)

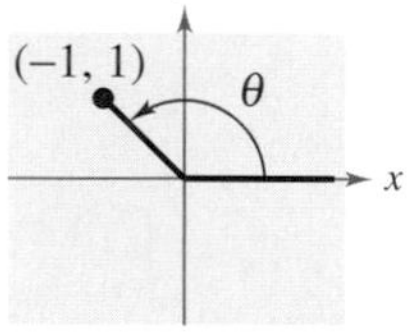

3. (a)

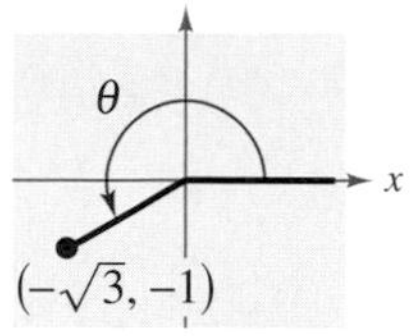

(b)

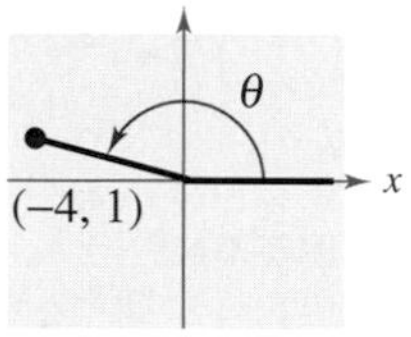

4. (a)

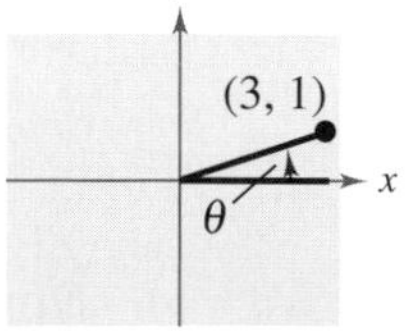

(b)

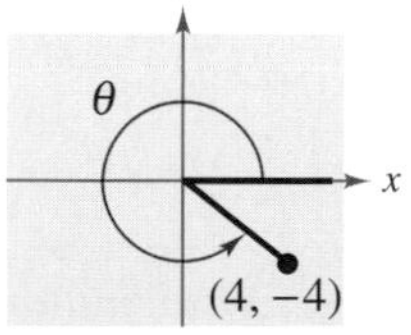

In Exercises 5–10, the point is on the terminal side of an angle in standard position. Determine the exact values of the six trigonometric functions of the angle.

5. $(7, 24)$ **6.** $(8, 15)$

7. $(-4, 10)$ **8.** $(-5, -2)$

9. $(-3.5, 6.8)$ **10.** $\left(3\frac{1}{2}, -7\frac{3}{4}\right)$

In Exercises 11–14, state the quadrant in which θ lies.

11. $\sin \theta < 0$ and $\cos \theta < 0$

12. $\sin \theta > 0$ and $\cos \theta > 0$

13. $\sin \theta > 0$ and $\tan \theta < 0$

14. $\sec \theta > 0$ and $\cot \theta < 0$

In Exercises 15–24, find the values of the six trigonometric functions of θ with the given constraint.

Function Value	*Constraint*
15. $\sin \theta = \frac{3}{5}$	θ lies in Quadrant II.
16. $\cos \theta = -\frac{4}{5}$	θ lies in Quadrant III.
17. $\tan \theta = -\frac{15}{8}$	$\sin \theta < 0$
18. $\cos \theta = \frac{8}{17}$	$\tan \theta < 0$
19. $\cot \theta = -3$	$\cos \theta > 0$
20. $\csc \theta = 4$	$\cot \theta < 0$
21. $\sec \theta = -2$	$\sin \theta > 0$
22. $\sin \theta = 0$	$\sec \theta = -1$
23. $\cot \theta$ is undefined.	$\pi/2 \leq \theta \leq 3\pi/2$
24. $\tan \theta$ is undefined.	$\pi \leq \theta \leq 2\pi$

In Exercises 25–28, the terminal side of θ lies on the given line in the specified quadrant. Find the values of the six trigonometric functions of θ by finding a point on the line.

Line	*Quadrant*
25. $y = -x$	II
26. $y = \frac{1}{3}x$	III
27. $2x - y = 0$	III
28. $4x + 3y = 0$	IV

In Exercises 29–36, evaluate the trigonometric function of the quadrant angle.

29. $\sin \pi$

30. $\csc \dfrac{3\pi}{2}$

31. $\sec \dfrac{3\pi}{2}$

32. $\sec \pi$

33. $\sin \dfrac{\pi}{2}$

34. $\cot \pi$

35. $\csc \pi$

36. $\cot \dfrac{\pi}{2}$

In Exercises 37–44, find the reference angle θ', and sketch θ and θ' in standard position.

37. $\theta = 203°$

38. $\theta = 309°$

39. $\theta = -245°$

40. $\theta = -145°$

41. $\theta = \dfrac{2\pi}{3}$

42. $\theta = \dfrac{7\pi}{4}$

43. $\theta = 3.5$

44. $\theta = \dfrac{11\pi}{3}$

In Exercises 45–58, evaluate the sine, cosine, and tangent of the angle without using a calculator.

45. $225°$

46. $300°$

47. $750°$

48. $-405°$

49. $-150°$

50. $-840°$

51. $\dfrac{4\pi}{3}$

52. $\dfrac{\pi}{4}$

53. $-\dfrac{\pi}{6}$

54. $-\dfrac{\pi}{2}$

55. $\dfrac{11\pi}{4}$

56. $\dfrac{10\pi}{3}$

57. $-\dfrac{3\pi}{2}$

58. $-\dfrac{25\pi}{4}$

In Exercises 59–64, find the indicated trigonometric value in the specified quadrant.

Function	*Quadrant*	*Trigonometric Value*
59. $\sin \theta = -\frac{3}{5}$	IV	$\cos \theta$
60. $\cot \theta = -3$	II	$\sin \theta$
61. $\tan \theta = \frac{3}{2}$	III	$\sec \theta$
62. $\csc \theta = -2$	IV	$\cot \theta$
63. $\cos \theta = \frac{5}{8}$	I	$\sec \theta$
64. $\sec \theta = -\frac{9}{4}$	III	$\tan \theta$

In Exercises 65–80, use a calculator to evaluate the trigonometric function. Round your answer to four decimal places. (Be sure the calculator is set in the correct angle mode.)

65. $\sin 10°$

66. $\sec 225°$

67. $\cos(-110°)$

68. $\csc(-330°)$

69. $\tan 304°$

70. $\cot 178°$

71. $\sec 72°$

72. $\tan(-188°)$

73. $\tan 4.5$

74. $\cot 1.35$

75. $\tan \dfrac{\pi}{9}$

76. $\tan\left(-\dfrac{\pi}{9}\right)$

77. $\sin(-0.65)$

78. $\sec 0.29$

79. $\cot\left(-\dfrac{11\pi}{8}\right)$

80. $\csc\left(-\dfrac{15\pi}{14}\right)$

In Exercises 81–86, find two solutions of the equation. Give your answers in degrees ($0° \le \theta < 360°$) and in radians ($0 \le \theta < 2\pi$). Do not use a calculator.

81. (a) $\sin \theta = \frac{1}{2}$ (b) $\sin \theta = -\frac{1}{2}$

82. (a) $\cos \theta = \dfrac{\sqrt{2}}{2}$ (b) $\cos \theta = -\dfrac{\sqrt{2}}{2}$

83. (a) $\csc \theta = \dfrac{2\sqrt{3}}{3}$ (b) $\cot \theta = -1$

84. (a) $\sec \theta = 2$ (b) $\sec \theta = -2$

85. (a) $\tan \theta = 1$ (b) $\cot \theta = -\sqrt{3}$

86. (a) $\sin \theta = \dfrac{\sqrt{3}}{2}$ (b) $\sin \theta = -\dfrac{\sqrt{3}}{2}$

Model It

87. ***Data Analysis: Meteorology*** The table shows the monthly normal temperatures (in degrees Fahrenheit) for selected months for New York City (N) and Fairbanks, Alaska (F). (Source: National Climatic Data Center)

Month	New York City, N	Fairbanks, F
January	33	−10
April	52	32
July	77	62
October	58	24
December	38	−6

(a) Use the *regression* feature of a graphing utility to find a model of the form

$$y = a \sin(bt + c) + d$$

for each city. Let t represent the month, with $t = 1$ corresponding to January.

Model It (continued)

(b) Use the models from part (a) to find the monthly normal temperatures for the two cities in February, March, May, June, August, September, and November.

(c) Compare the models for the two cities.

88. ***Sales*** A company that produces snowboards, which are seasonal products, forecasts monthly sales over the next 2 years to be

$$S = 23.1 + 0.442t + 4.3 \cos \frac{\pi t}{6}$$

where S is measured in thousands of units and t is the time in months, with $t = 1$ representing January 2006. Predict sales for each of the following months.

(a) February 2006

(b) February 2007

(c) June 2006

(d) June 2007

89. ***Harmonic Motion*** The displacement from equilibrium of an oscillating weight suspended by a spring is given by

$$y(t) = 2 \cos 6t$$

where y is the displacement (in centimeters) and t is the time (in seconds). Find the displacement when (a) $t = 0$, (b) $t = \frac{1}{4}$, and (c) $t = \frac{1}{2}$.

90. ***Harmonic Motion*** The displacement from equilibrium of an oscillating weight suspended by a spring and subject to the damping effect of friction is given by

$$y(t) = 2e^{-t} \cos 6t$$

where y is the displacement (in centimeters) and t is the time (in seconds). Find the displacement when (a) $t = 0$, (b) $t = \frac{1}{4}$, and (c) $t = \frac{1}{2}$.

91. ***Electric Circuits*** The current I (in amperes) when 100 volts is applied to a circuit is given by

$$I = 5e^{-2t} \sin t$$

where t is the time (in seconds) after the voltage is applied. Approximate the current at $t = 0.7$ second after the voltage is applied.

92. ***Distance*** An airplane, flying at an altitude of 6 miles, is on a flight path that passes directly over an observer (see figure). If θ is the angle of elevation from the observer to the plane, find the distance d from the observer to the plane when (a) $\theta = 30°$, (b) $\theta = 90°$, and (c) $\theta = 120°$.

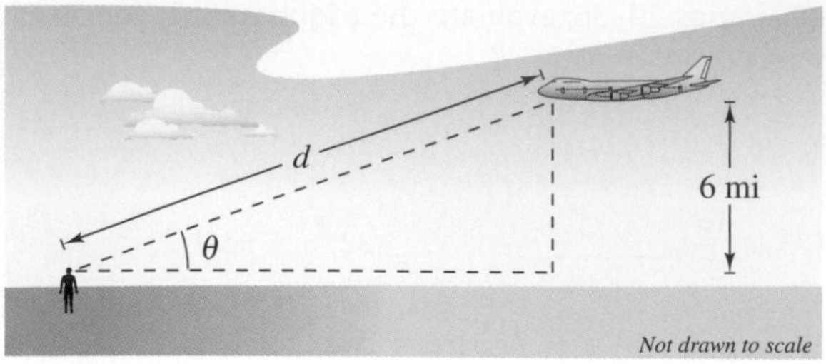

FIGURE FOR 92

Synthesis

True or False? **In Exercises 93 and 94, determine whether the statement is true or false. Justify your answer.**

93. In each of the four quadrants, the signs of the secant function and sine function will be the same.

94. To find the reference angle for an angle θ (given in degrees), find the integer n such that $0 \leq 360°n - \theta \leq 360°$. The difference $360°n - \theta$ is the reference angle.

95. ***Writing*** Consider an angle in standard position with $r = 12$ centimeters, as shown in the figure. Write a short paragraph describing the changes in the values of x, y, $\sin \theta$, $\cos \theta$, and $\tan \theta$ as θ increases continuously from 0° to 90°.

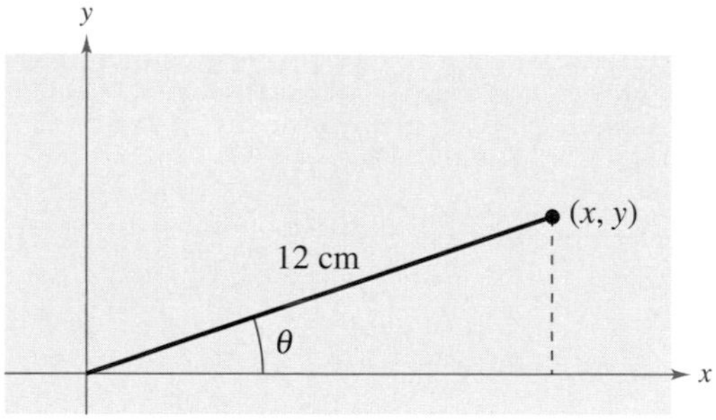

96. ***Writing*** Explain how reference angles are used to find the trigonometric functions of obtuse angles.

Skills Review

In Exercises 97–106, graph the function. Identify the domain and any intercepts and asymptotes of the function.

97. $y = x^2 + 3x - 4$

98. $y = 2x^2 - 5x$

99. $f(x) = x^3 + 8$

100. $g(x) = x^4 + 2x^2 - 3$

101. $f(x) = \dfrac{x - 7}{x^2 + 4x + 4}$

102. $h(x) = \dfrac{x^2 - 1}{x + 5}$

103. $y = 2^{x-1}$

104. $y = 3^{x+1} + 2$

105. $y = \ln x^4$

106. $y = \log_{10}(x + 2)$

4.5 Graphs of Sine and Cosine Functions

What you should learn

- Sketch the graphs of basic sine and cosine functions.
- Use amplitude and period to help sketch the graphs of sine and cosine functions.
- Sketch translations of the graphs of sine and cosine functions.
- Use sine and cosine functions to model real-life data.

Why you should learn it

Sine and cosine functions are often used in scientific calculations. For instance, in Exercise 73 on page 330, you can use a trigonometric function to model the airflow of your respiratory cycle.

© Karl Weatherly/Corbis

Basic Sine and Cosine Curves

In this section, you will study techniques for sketching the graphs of the sine and cosine functions. The graph of the sine function is a **sine curve.** In Figure 4.47, the black portion of the graph represents one period of the function and is called **one cycle** of the sine curve. The gray portion of the graph indicates that the basic sine curve repeats indefinitely in the positive and negative directions. The graph of the cosine function is shown in Figure 4.48.

Recall from Section 4.2 that the domain of the sine and cosine functions is the set of all real numbers. Moreover, the range of each function is the interval $[-1, 1]$, and each function has a period of 2π. Do you see how this information is consistent with the basic graphs shown in Figures 4.47 and 4.48?

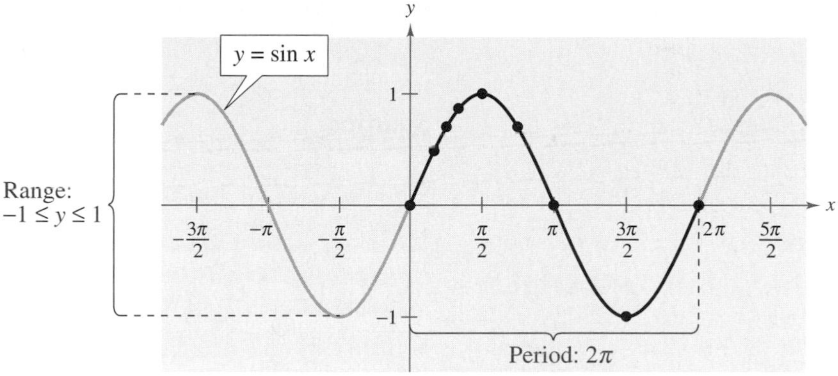

FIGURE 4.47

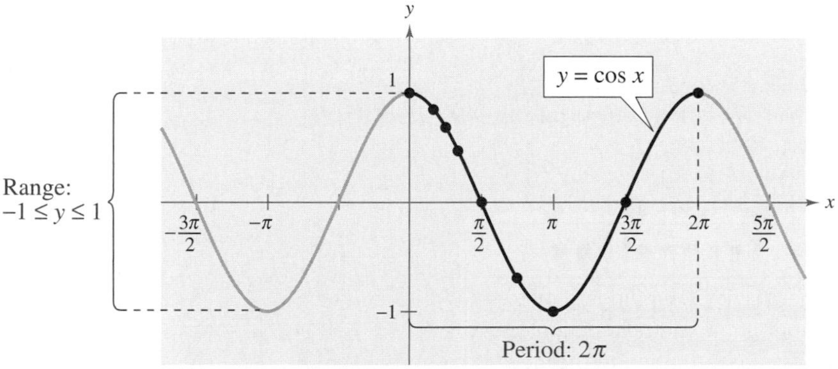

FIGURE 4.48

Note in Figures 4.47 and 4.48 that the sine curve is symmetric with respect to the *origin*, whereas the cosine curve is symmetric with respect to the *y-axis*. These properties of symmetry follow from the fact that the sine function is odd and the cosine function is even.

To sketch the graphs of the basic sine and cosine functions by hand, it helps to note five **key points** in one period of each graph: the *intercepts*, *maximum points*, and *minimum points* (see Figure 4.49).

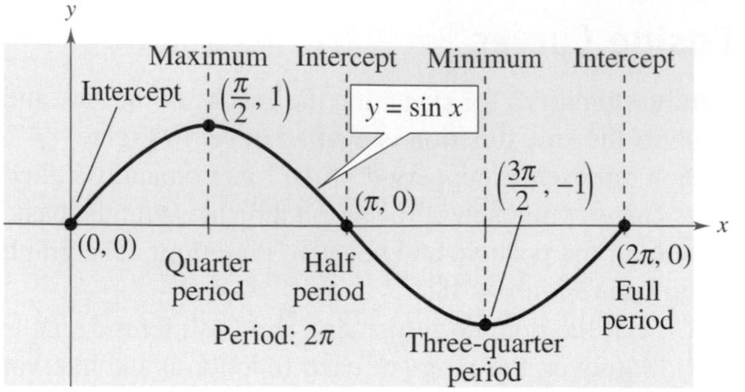

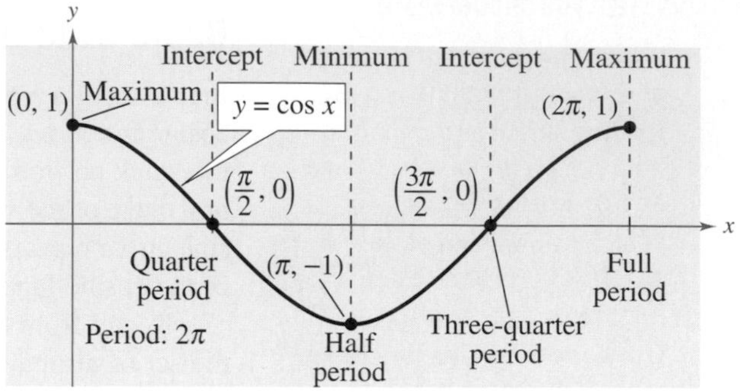

FIGURE 4.49

Example 1 Using Key Points to Sketch a Sine Curve

Sketch the graph of $y = 2 \sin x$ on the interval $[-\pi, 4\pi]$.

Solution

Note that

$$y = 2 \sin x = 2(\sin x)$$

indicates that the y-values for the key points will have twice the magnitude of those on the graph of $y = \sin x$. Divide the period 2π into four equal parts to get the key points for $y = 2 \sin x$.

Intercept	*Maximum*	*Intercept*	*Minimum*		*Intercept*
$(0, 0)$,	$\left(\frac{\pi}{2}, 2\right)$,	$(\pi, 0)$,	$\left(\frac{3\pi}{2}, -2\right)$,	and	$(2\pi, 0)$

By connecting these key points with a smooth curve and extending the curve in both directions over the interval $[-\pi, 4\pi]$, you obtain the graph shown in Figure 4.50.

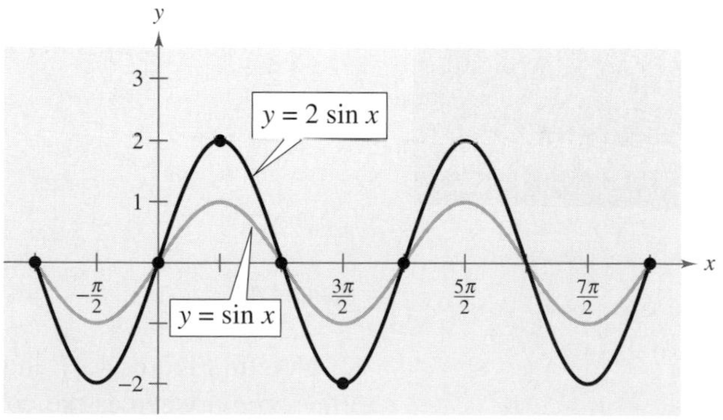

FIGURE 4.50

CHECKPOINT Now try Exercise 35.

Technology

When using a graphing utility to graph trigonometric functions, pay special attention to the viewing window you use. For instance, try graphing $y = [\sin(10x)]/10$ in the standard viewing window in *radian* mode. What do you observe? Use the *zoom* feature to find a viewing window that displays a good view of the graph.

Amplitude and Period

In the remainder of this section you will study the graphic effect of each of the constants a, b, c, and d in equations of the forms

$$y = d + a\sin(bx - c)$$

and

$$y = d + a\cos(bx - c).$$

A quick review of the transformations you studied in Section 1.7 should help in this investigation.

The constant factor a in $y = a \sin x$ acts as a *scaling factor*—a *vertical stretch* or *vertical shrink* of the basic sine curve. If $|a| > 1$, the basic sine curve is stretched, and if $|a| < 1$, the basic sine curve is shrunk. The result is that the graph of $y = a\sin x$ ranges between $-a$ and a instead of between -1 and 1. The absolute value of a is the **amplitude** of the function $y = a \sin x$. The range of the function $y = a \sin x$ for $a > 0$ is $-a \le y \le a$.

Definition of Amplitude of Sine and Cosine Curves

The **amplitude** of $y = a\sin x$ and $y = a\cos x$ represents half the distance between the maximum and minimum values of the function and is given by

$$\text{Amplitude} = |a|.$$

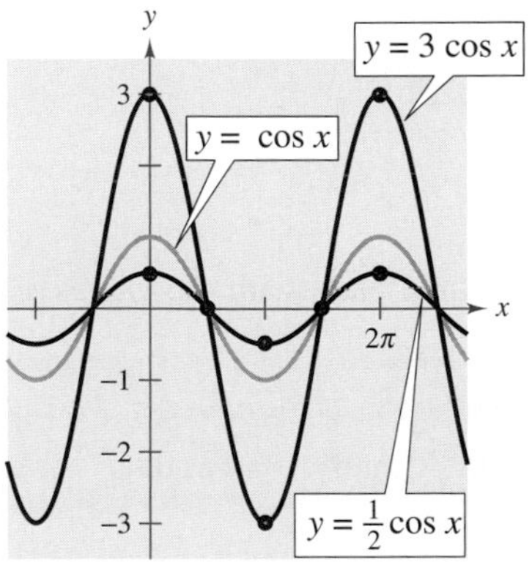

FIGURE 4.51

Example 2 **Scaling: Vertical Shrinking and Stretching**

On the same coordinate axes, sketch the graph of each function.

a. $y = \dfrac{1}{2}\cos x$ **b.** $y = 3\cos x$

Solution

a. Because the amplitude of $y = \frac{1}{2}\cos x$ is $\frac{1}{2}$, the maximum value is $\frac{1}{2}$ and the minimum value is $-\frac{1}{2}$. Divide one cycle, $0 \le x \le 2\pi$, into four equal parts to get the key points

Maximum	*Intercept*	*Minimum*	*Intercept*		*Maximum*
$\left(0, \frac{1}{2}\right)$,	$\left(\frac{\pi}{2}, 0\right)$,	$\left(\pi, -\frac{1}{2}\right)$,	$\left(\frac{3\pi}{2}, 0\right)$,	and	$\left(2\pi, \frac{1}{2}\right)$.

b. A similar analysis shows that the amplitude of $y = 3\cos x$ is 3, and the key points are

Maximum	*Intercept*	*Minimum*	*Intercept*		*Maximum*
$(0, 3)$,	$\left(\frac{\pi}{2}, 0\right)$,	$(\pi, -3)$,	$\left(\frac{3\pi}{2}, 0\right)$,	and	$(2\pi, 3)$.

The graphs of these two functions are shown in Figure 4.51. Notice that the graph of $y = \frac{1}{2}\cos x$ is a vertical *shrink* of the graph of $y = \cos x$ and the graph of $y = 3\cos x$ is a vertical *stretch* of the graph of $y = \cos x$.

CHECKPOINT Now try Exercise 37.

Exploration

Sketch the graph of $y = \cos bx$ for $b = \frac{1}{2}$, 2, and 3. How does the value of b affect the graph? How many complete cycles occur between 0 and 2π for each value of b?

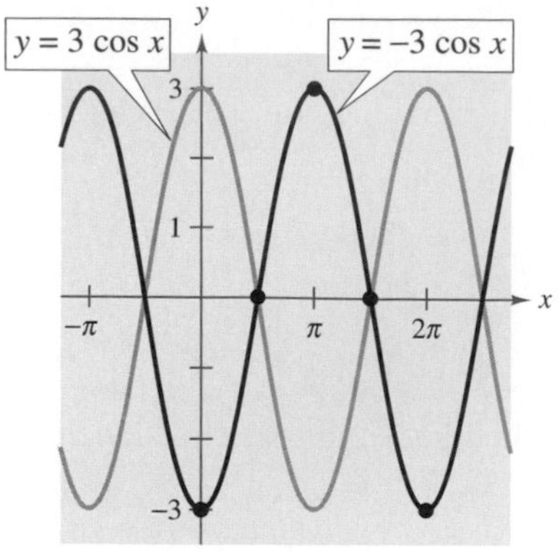

FIGURE 4.52

You know from Section 1.7 that the graph of $y = -f(x)$ is a **reflection** in the x-axis of the graph of $y = f(x)$. For instance, the graph of $y = -3 \cos x$ is a reflection of the graph of $y = 3 \cos x$, as shown in Figure 4.52.

Because $y = a \sin x$ completes one cycle from $x = 0$ to $x = 2\pi$, it follows that $y = a \sin bx$ completes one cycle from $x = 0$ to $x = 2\pi/b$.

Period of Sine and Cosine Functions

Let b be a positive real number. The **period** of $y = a \sin bx$ and $y = a \cos bx$ is given by

$$\text{Period} = \frac{2\pi}{b}.$$

Note that if $0 < b < 1$, the period of $y = a \sin bx$ is greater than 2π and represents a *horizontal stretching* of the graph of $y = a \sin x$. Similarly, if $b > 1$, the period of $y = a \sin bx$ is less than 2π and represents a *horizontal shrinking* of the graph of $y = a \sin x$. If b is negative, the identities $\sin(-x) = -\sin x$ and $\cos(-x) = \cos x$ are used to rewrite the function.

Exploration

Sketch the graph of

$$y = \sin(x - c)$$

where $c = -\pi/4$, 0, and $\pi/4$. How does the value of c affect the graph?

Example 3 Scaling: Horizontal Stretching

Sketch the graph of $y = \sin \dfrac{x}{2}$.

Solution

The amplitude is 1. Moreover, because $b = \frac{1}{2}$, the period is

$$\frac{2\pi}{b} = \frac{2\pi}{\frac{1}{2}} = 4\pi. \qquad \text{Substitute for } b.$$

Now, divide the period-interval $[0, 4\pi]$ into four equal parts with the values π, 2π, and 3π to obtain the key points on the graph.

Intercept	*Maximum*	*Intercept*	*Minimum*		*Intercept*
$(0, 0)$,	$(\pi, 1)$,	$(2\pi, 0)$,	$(3\pi, -1)$,	and	$(4\pi, 0)$

The graph is shown in Figure 4.53.

STUDY TIP

In general, to divide a period-interval into four equal parts, successively add "period/4," starting with the left endpoint of the interval. For instance, for the period-interval $[-\pi/6, \pi/2]$ of length $2\pi/3$, you would successively add

$$\frac{2\pi/3}{4} = \frac{\pi}{6}$$

to get $-\pi/6$, 0, $\pi/6$, $\pi/3$, and $\pi/2$ as the x-values for the key points on the graph.

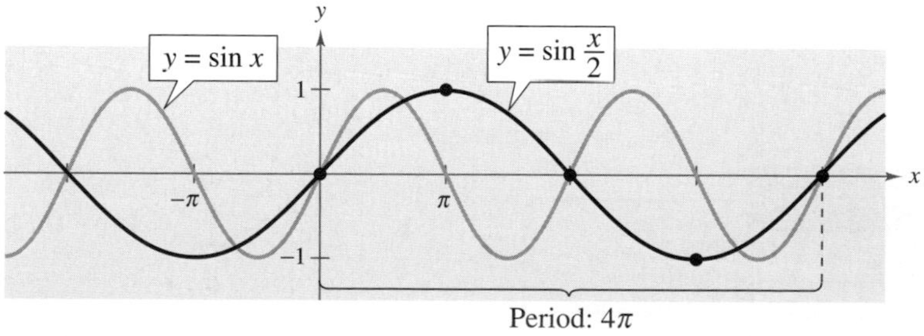

FIGURE 4.53

CHECKPOINT Now try Exercise 39.

Translations of Sine and Cosine Curves

The constant c in the general equations

$$y = a\sin(bx - c) \qquad \text{and} \qquad y = a\cos(bx - c)$$

creates a *horizontal translation* (shift) of the basic sine and cosine curves. Comparing $y = a\sin bx$ with $y = a\sin(bx - c)$, you find that the graph of $y = a\sin(bx - c)$ completes one cycle from $bx - c = 0$ to $bx - c = 2\pi$. By solving for x, you can find the interval for one cycle to be

$$\overbrace{\frac{c}{b}}^{\text{Left endpoint}} \le x \le \overbrace{\frac{c}{b} + \underbrace{\frac{2\pi}{b}}_{\text{Period}}}^{\text{Right endpoint}}.$$

This implies that the period of $y = a\sin(bx - c)$ is $2\pi/b$, and the graph of $y = a\sin bx$ is shifted by an amount c/b. The number c/b is the **phase shift.**

Graphs of Sine and Cosine Functions

The graphs of $y = a\sin(bx - c)$ and $y = a\cos(bx - c)$ have the following characteristics. (Assume $b > 0$.)

$$\text{Amplitude} = |a| \qquad \text{Period} = \frac{2\pi}{b}$$

The left and right endpoints of a one-cycle interval can be determined by solving the equations $bx - c = 0$ and $bx - c = 2\pi$.

Example 4 **Horizontal Translation**

Sketch the graph of $y = \frac{1}{2}\sin\left(x - \frac{\pi}{3}\right)$.

Solution

The amplitude is $\frac{1}{2}$ and the period is 2π. By solving the equations

$$x - \frac{\pi}{3} = 0 \quad \Rightarrow \quad x = \frac{\pi}{3}$$

and

$$x - \frac{\pi}{3} = 2\pi \quad \Rightarrow \quad x = \frac{7\pi}{3}$$

you see that the interval $[\pi/3, 7\pi/3]$ corresponds to one cycle of the graph. Dividing this interval into four equal parts produces the key points

Intercept	*Maximum*	*Intercept*	*Minimum*		*Intercept*
$\left(\frac{\pi}{3}, 0\right)$,	$\left(\frac{5\pi}{6}, \frac{1}{2}\right)$,	$\left(\frac{4\pi}{3}, 0\right)$,	$\left(\frac{11\pi}{6}, -\frac{1}{2}\right)$,	and	$\left(\frac{7\pi}{3}, 0\right)$.

The graph is shown in Figure 4.54.

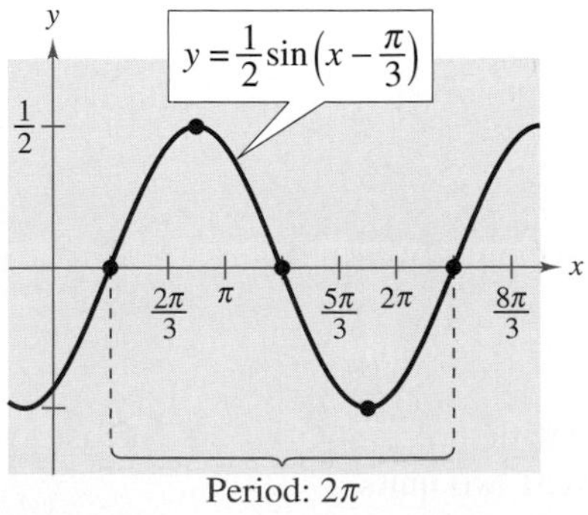

FIGURE 4.54

CHECKPOINT Now try Exercise 45.

Example 5 Horizontal Translation

Sketch the graph of

$$y = -3\cos(2\pi x + 4\pi).$$

Solution

The amplitude is 3 and the period is $2\pi/2\pi = 1$. By solving the equations

$$2\pi x + 4\pi = 0$$
$$2\pi x = -4\pi$$
$$x = -2$$

and

$$2\pi x + 4\pi = 2\pi$$
$$2\pi x = -2\pi$$
$$x = -1$$

you see that the interval $[-2, -1]$ corresponds to one cycle of the graph. Dividing this interval into four equal parts produces the key points

Minimum	*Intercept*	*Maximum*	*Intercept*		*Minimum*
$(-2, -3)$,	$\left(-\frac{7}{4}, 0\right)$,	$\left(-\frac{3}{2}, 3\right)$,	$\left(-\frac{5}{4}, 0\right)$,	and	$(-1, -3)$.

The graph is shown in Figure 4.55.

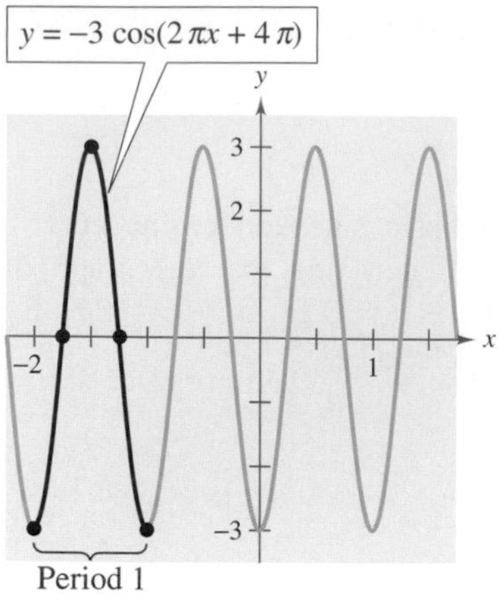

FIGURE 4.55

CHECKPOINT Now try Exercise 47.

The final type of transformation is the *vertical translation* caused by the constant d in the equations

$$y = d + a\sin(bx - c)$$

and

$$y = d + a\cos(bx - c).$$

The shift is d units upward for $d > 0$ and d units downward for $d < 0$. In other words, the graph oscillates about the horizontal line $y = d$ instead of about the x-axis.

Example 6 Vertical Translation

Sketch the graph of

$$y = 2 + 3\cos 2x.$$

Solution

The amplitude is 3 and the period is π. The key points over the interval $[0, \pi]$ are

$$(0, 5), \quad \left(\frac{\pi}{4}, 2\right), \quad \left(\frac{\pi}{2}, -1\right), \quad \left(\frac{3\pi}{4}, 2\right), \quad \text{and} \quad (\pi, 5).$$

The graph is shown in Figure 4.56. Compared with the graph of $f(x) = 3\cos 2x$, the graph of $y - 2 + 3\cos 2x$ is shifted upward two units.

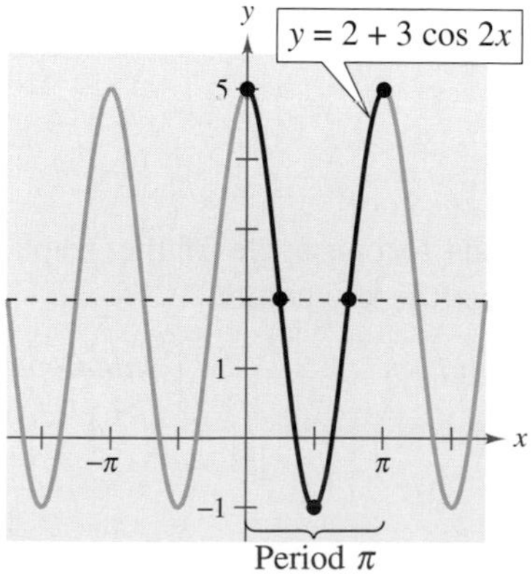

FIGURE 4.56

CHECKPOINT Now try Exercise 53.

Mathematical Modeling

Sine and cosine functions can be used to model many real-life situations, including electric currents, musical tones, radio waves, tides, and weather patterns.

Example 7 Finding a Trigonometric Model

Throughout the day, the depth of water at the end of a dock in Bar Harbor, Maine varies with the tides. The table shows the depths (in feet) at various times during the morning. (Source: Nautical Software, Inc.)

Time, t	Depth, y
Midnight	3.4
2 A.M.	8.7
4 A.M.	11.3
6 A.M.	9.1
8 A.M.	3.8
10 A.M.	0.1
Noon	1.2

a. Use a trigonometric function to model the data.

b. Find the depths at 9 A.M. and 3 P.M.

c. A boat needs at least 10 feet of water to moor at the dock. During what times in the afternoon can it safely dock?

Solution

a. Begin by graphing the data, as shown in Figure 4.57. You can use either a sine or cosine model. Suppose you use a cosine model of the form

$$y = a\cos(bt - c) + d.$$

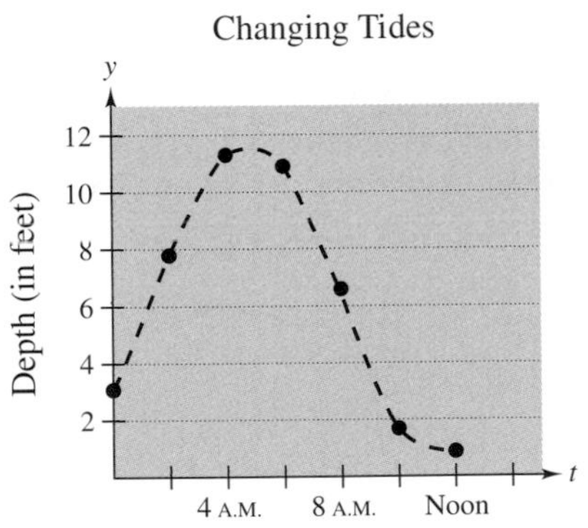

FIGURE 4.57

The difference between the maximum height and the minimum height of the graph is twice the amplitude of the function. So, the amplitude is

$$a = \frac{1}{2}[(\text{maximum depth}) - (\text{minimum depth})] = \frac{1}{2}(11.3 - 0.1) = 5.6.$$

The cosine function completes one half of a cycle between the times at which the maximum and minimum depths occur. So, the period is

$$p = 2[(\text{time of min. depth}) - (\text{time of max. depth})] = 2(10 - 4) = 12$$

which implies that $b = 2\pi/p \approx 0.524$. Because high tide occurs 4 hours after midnight, consider the left endpoint to be $c/b = 4$, so $c \approx 2.094$. Moreover, because the average depth is $\frac{1}{2}(11.3 + 0.1) = 5.7$, it follows that $d = 5.7$. So, you can model the depth with the function given by

$$y = 5.6\cos(0.524t - 2.094) + 5.7.$$

b. The depths at 9 A.M. and 3 P.M. are as follows.

$$y = 5.6\cos(0.524 \cdot 9 - 2.094) + 5.7$$
$$\approx 0.84 \text{ foot} \qquad \text{9 A.M.}$$
$$y = 5.6\cos(0.524 \cdot 15 - 2.094) + 5.7$$
$$\approx 10.57 \text{ feet} \qquad \text{3 P.M.}$$

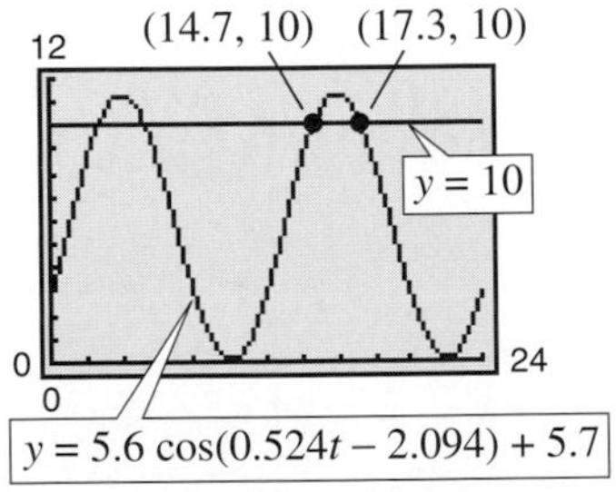

FIGURE 4.58

c. To find out when the depth y is at least 10 feet, you can graph the model with the line $y = 10$ using a graphing utility, as shown in Figure 4.58. Using the *intersect* feature, you can determine that the depth is at least 10 feet between 2:42 P.M. ($t \approx 14.7$) and 5:18 P.M. ($t \approx 17.3$).

CHECKPOINT Now try Exercise 77.

4.5 Exercises

VOCABULARY CHECK: Fill in the blanks.

1. One period of a sine or cosine function function is called one ________ of the sine curve or cosine curve.
2. The ________ of a sine or cosine curve represents half the distance between the maximum and minimum values of the function.
3. The period of a sine or cosine function is given by ________.
4. For the function given by $y = a\sin(bx - c)$, $\dfrac{c}{b}$ represents the ________ ________ of the graph of the function.
5. For the function given by $y = d + a\cos(bx - c)$, d represents a ________ ________ of the graph of the function.

In Exercises 1–14, find the period and amplitude.

1. $y = 3\sin 2x$

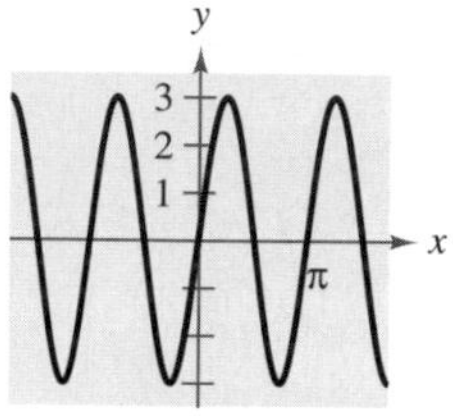

2. $y = 2\cos 3x$

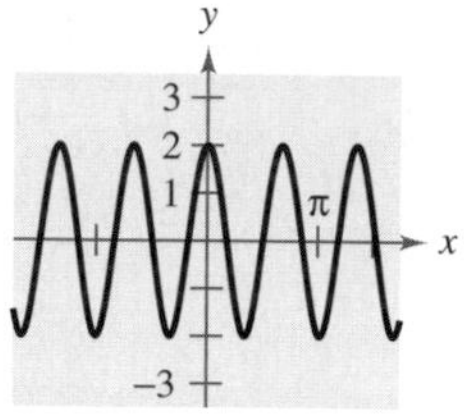

3. $y = \dfrac{5}{2}\cos\dfrac{x}{2}$

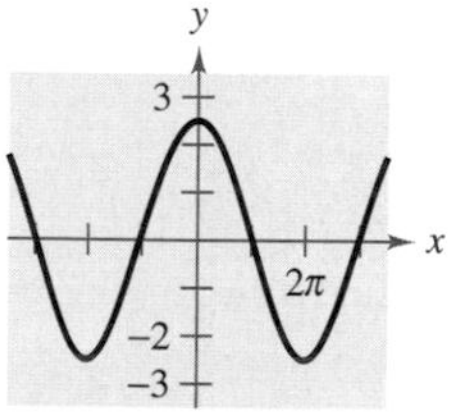

4. $y = -3\sin\dfrac{x}{3}$

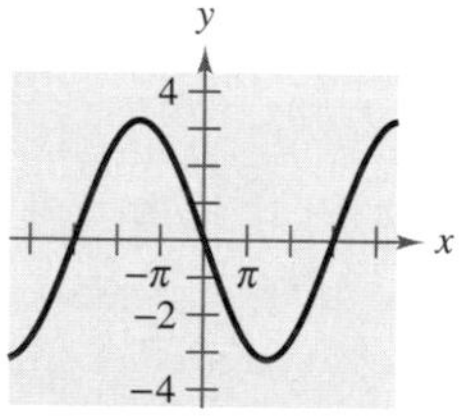

5. $y = \dfrac{1}{2}\sin\dfrac{\pi x}{3}$

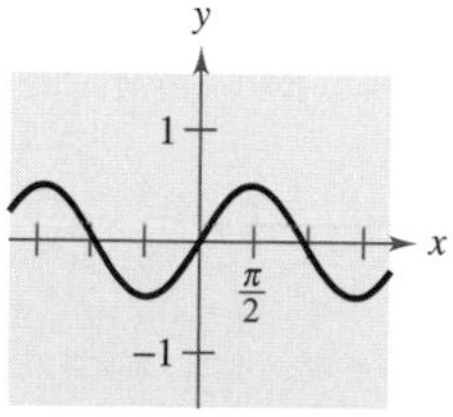

6. $y = \dfrac{3}{2}\cos\dfrac{\pi x}{2}$

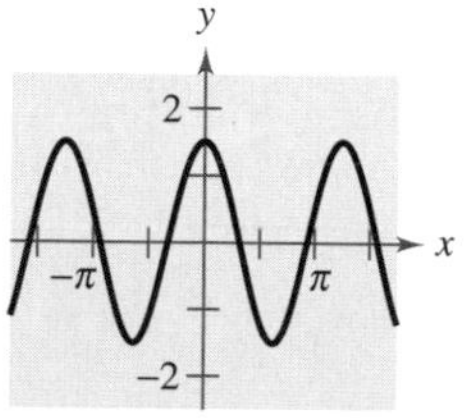

7. $y = -2\sin x$
8. $y = -\cos\dfrac{2x}{3}$
9. $y = 3\sin 10x$
10. $y = \frac{1}{3}\sin 8x$
11. $y = \dfrac{1}{2}\cos\dfrac{2x}{3}$
12. $y = \dfrac{5}{2}\cos\dfrac{x}{4}$
13. $y = \dfrac{1}{4}\sin 2\pi x$
14. $y = \dfrac{2}{3}\cos\dfrac{\pi x}{10}$

In Exercises 15–22, describe the relationship between the graphs of *f* and *g*. Consider amplitude, period, and shifts.

15. $f(x) = \sin x$
    $g(x) = \sin(x - \pi)$
16. $f(x) = \cos x$
    $g(x) = \cos(x + \pi)$
17. $f(x) = \cos 2x$
    $g(x) = -\cos 2x$
18. $f(x) = \sin 3x$
    $g(x) = \sin(-3x)$
19. $f(x) = \cos x$
    $g(x) = \cos 2x$
20. $f(x) = \sin x$
    $g(x) = \sin 3x$
21. $f(x) = \sin 2x$
    $g(x) = 3 + \sin 2x$
22. $f(x) = \cos 4x$
    $g(x) = -2 + \cos 4x$

In Exercises 23–26, describe the relationship between the graphs of *f* and *g*. Consider amplitude, period, and shifts.

23.

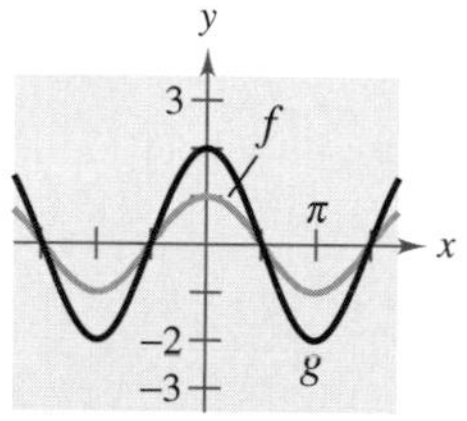

24.

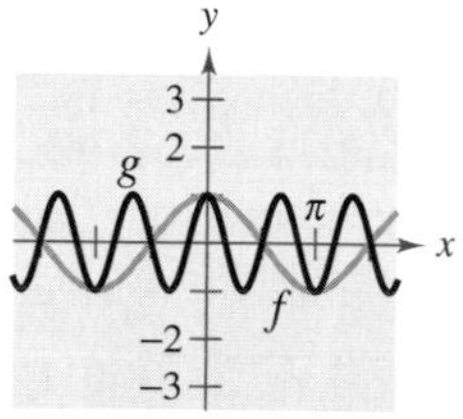

25.

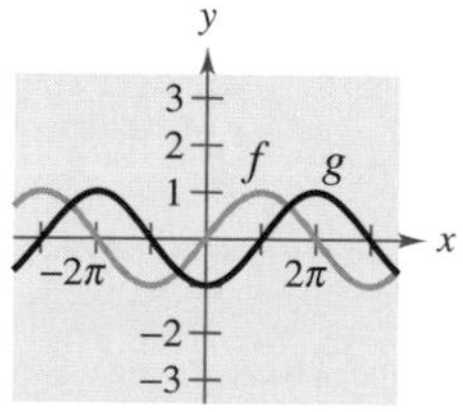

26.

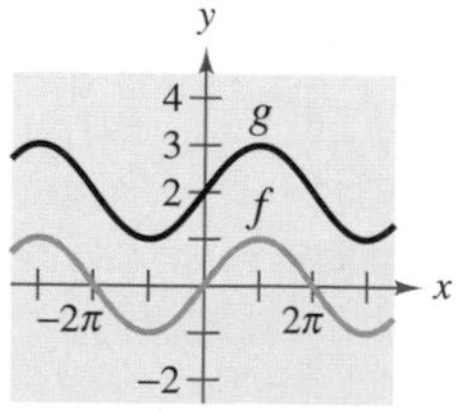

In Exercises 27–34, graph *f* and *g* on the same set of coordinate axes. (Include two full periods.)

27. $f(x) = -2 \sin x$
 $g(x) = 4 \sin x$

28. $f(x) = \sin x$
 $g(x) = \sin \dfrac{x}{3}$

29. $f(x) = \cos x$
 $g(x) = 1 + \cos x$

30. $f(x) = 2 \cos 2x$
 $g(x) = -\cos 4x$

31. $f(x) = -\dfrac{1}{2} \sin \dfrac{x}{2}$
 $g(x) = 3 - \dfrac{1}{2} \sin \dfrac{x}{2}$

32. $f(x) = 4 \sin \pi x$
 $g(x) = 4 \sin \pi x - 3$

33. $f(x) = 2 \cos x$
 $g(x) = 2 \cos(x + \pi)$

34. $f(x) = -\cos x$
 $g(x) = -\cos(x - \pi)$

In Exercises 35–56, sketch the graph of the function. (Include two full periods.)

35. $y = 3 \sin x$

36. $y = \frac{1}{4} \sin x$

37. $y = \frac{1}{3} \cos x$

38. $y = 4 \cos x$

39. $y = \cos \dfrac{x}{2}$

40. $y = \sin 4x$

41. $y = \cos 2\pi x$

42. $y = \sin \dfrac{\pi x}{4}$

43. $y = -\sin \dfrac{2\pi x}{3}$

44. $y = -10 \cos \dfrac{\pi x}{6}$

45. $y = \sin\left(x - \dfrac{\pi}{4}\right)$

46. $y = \sin(x - \pi)$

47. $y = 3 \cos(x + \pi)$

48. $y = 4 \cos\left(x + \dfrac{\pi}{4}\right)$

49. $y = 2 - \sin \dfrac{2\pi x}{3}$

50. $y = -3 + 5 \cos \dfrac{\pi t}{12}$

51. $y = 2 + \frac{1}{10} \cos 60\pi x$

52. $y = 2 \cos x - 3$

53. $y = 3 \cos(x + \pi) - 3$

54. $y = 4 \cos\left(x + \dfrac{\pi}{4}\right) + 4$

55. $y = \dfrac{2}{3} \cos\left(\dfrac{x}{2} - \dfrac{\pi}{4}\right)$

56. $y = -3 \cos(6x + \pi)$

In Exercises 57–62, use a graphing utility to graph the function. Include two full periods. Be sure to choose an appropriate viewing window.

57. $y = -2 \sin(4x + \pi)$

58. $y = -4 \sin\left(\dfrac{2}{3}x - \dfrac{\pi}{3}\right)$

59. $y = \cos\left(2\pi x - \dfrac{\pi}{2}\right) + 1$

60. $y = 3 \cos\left(\dfrac{\pi x}{2} + \dfrac{\pi}{2}\right) - 2$

61. $y = -0.1 \sin\left(\dfrac{\pi x}{10} + \pi\right)$

62. $y = \frac{1}{100} \sin 120\pi t$

Graphical Reasoning **In Exercises 63–66, find *a* and *d* for the function $f(x) = a \cos x + d$ such that the graph of *f* matches the figure.**

63.
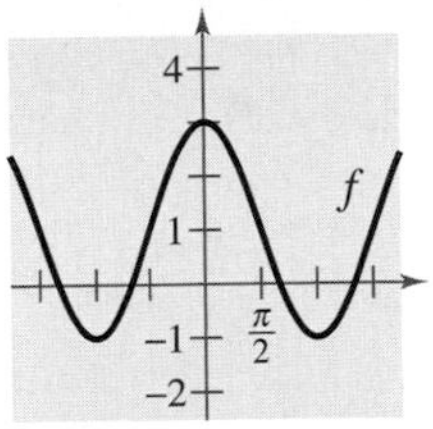

64.
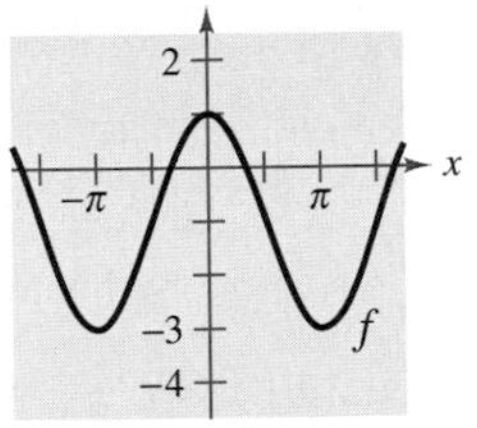

65.
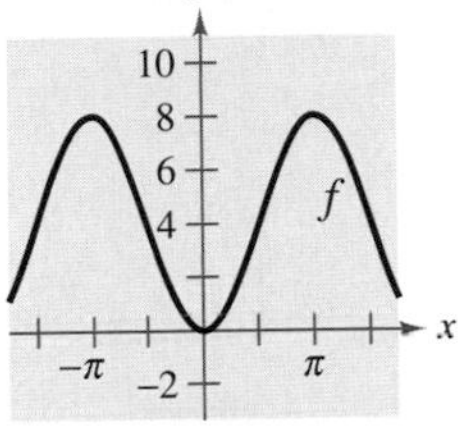

66.
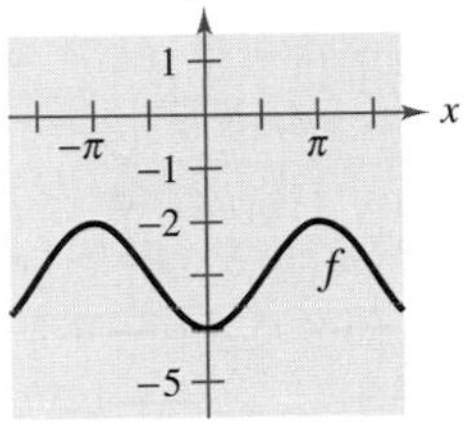

Graphical Reasoning **In Exercises 67–70, find *a*, *b*, and *c* for the function $f(x) = a \sin(bx - c)$ such that the graph of *f* matches the figure.**

67.
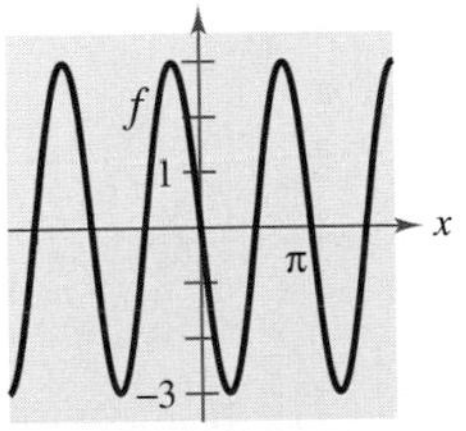

68.
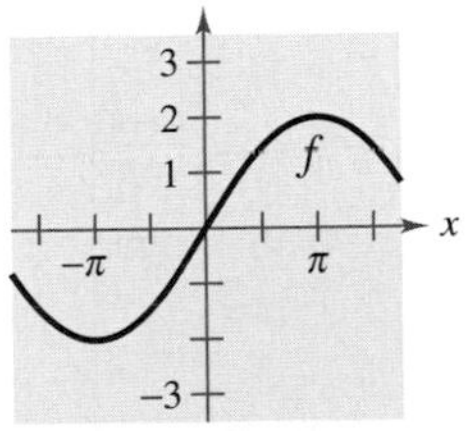

69.
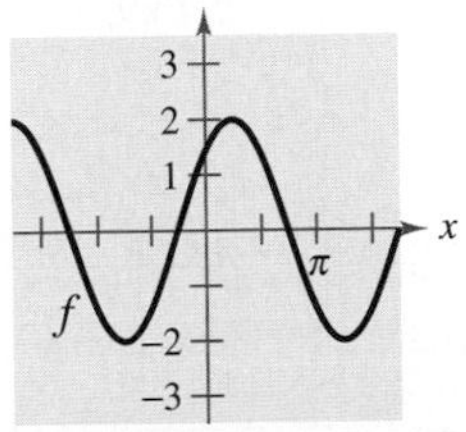

70.
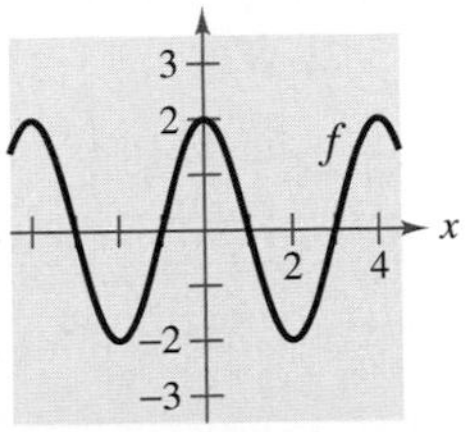

In Exercises 71 and 72, use a graphing utility to graph y_1 and y_2 in the interval $[-2\pi, 2\pi]$. Use the graphs to find real numbers *x* such that $y_1 = y_2$.

71. $y_1 = \sin x$
 $y_2 = -\frac{1}{2}$

72. $y_1 = \cos x$
 $y_2 = -1$

73. ***Respiratory Cycle*** For a person at rest, the velocity v (in liters per second) of air flow during a respiratory cycle (the time from the beginning of one breath to the beginning of the next) is given by $v = 0.85 \sin \frac{\pi t}{3}$, where t is the time (in seconds). (Inhalation occurs when $v > 0$, and exhalation occurs when $v < 0$.)

(a) Find the time for one full respiratory cycle.

(b) Find the number of cycles per minute.

(c) Sketch the graph of the velocity function.

74. ***Respiratory Cycle*** After exercising for a few minutes, a person has a respiratory cycle for which the velocity of air flow is approximated by $v = 1.75 \sin \frac{\pi t}{2}$, where t is the time (in seconds). (Inhalation occurs when $v > 0$, and exhalation occurs when $v < 0$.)

(a) Find the time for one full respiratory cycle.

(b) Find the number of cycles per minute.

(c) Sketch the graph of the velocity function.

75. ***Data Analysis: Meteorology*** The table shows the maximum daily high temperatures for Tallahassee T and Chicago C (in degrees Fahrenheit) for month t, with $t = 1$ corresponding to January. (Source: National Climatic Data Center)

Month, t	Tallahassee, T	Chicago, C
1	63.8	29.6
2	67.4	34.7
3	74.0	46.1
4	80.0	58.0
5	86.5	69.9
6	90.9	79.2
7	92.0	83.5
8	91.5	81.2
9	88.5	73.9
10	81.2	62.1
11	72.9	47.1
12	65.8	34.4

(a) A model for the temperature in Tallahassee is given by

$$T(t) = 77.90 + 14.10 \cos\left(\frac{\pi t}{6} - 3.67\right).$$

Find a trigonometric model for Chicago.

(b) Use a graphing utility to graph the data points and the model for the temperatures in Tallahassee. How well does the model fit the data?

(c) Use a graphing utility to graph the data points and the model for the temperatures in Chicago. How well does the model fit the data?

(d) Use the models to estimate the average maximum temperature in each city. Which term of the models did you use? Explain.

(e) What is the period of each model? Are the periods what you expected? Explain.

(f) Which city has the greater variability in temperature throughout the year? Which factor of the models determines this variability? Explain.

76. ***Health*** The function given by $P = 100 - 20 \cos \frac{5\pi t}{3}$ approximates the blood pressure P (in millimeters) of mercury at time t (in seconds) for a person at rest.

(a) Find the period of the function.

(b) Find the number of heartbeats per minute.

77. ***Piano Tuning*** When tuning a piano, a technician strikes a tuning fork for the A above middle C and sets up a wave motion that can be approximated by $y = 0.001 \sin 880\pi t$, where t is the time (in seconds).

(a) What is the period of the function?

(b) The frequency f is given by $f = 1/p$. What is the frequency of the note?

Model It

78. ***Data Analysis: Astronomy*** The percent y of the moon's face that is illuminated on day x of the year 2007, where $x = 1$ represents January 1, is shown in the table. (Source: U.S. Naval Observatory)

x	y
3	1.0
11	0.5
19	0.0
26	0.5
32	1.0
40	0.5

(a) Create a scatter plot of the data.

(b) Find a trigonometric model that fits the data.

(c) Add the graph of your model in part (b) to the scatter plot. How well does the model fit the data?

(d) What is the period of the model?

(e) Estimate the moon's percent illumination for March 12, 2007.

79. ***Fuel Consumption*** The daily consumption C (in gallons) of diesel fuel on a farm is modeled by

$$C = 30.3 + 21.6 \sin\left(\frac{2\pi t}{365} + 10.9\right)$$

where t is the time (in days), with $t = 1$ corresponding to January 1.

(a) What is the period of the model? Is it what you expected? Explain.

(b) What is the average daily fuel consumption? Which term of the model did you use? Explain.

(c) Use a graphing utility to graph the model. Use the graph to approximate the time of the year when consumption exceeds 40 gallons per day.

80. ***Ferris Wheel*** A Ferris wheel is built such that the height h (in feet) above ground of a seat on the wheel at time t (in seconds) can be modeled by

$$h(t) = 53 + 50 \sin\left(\frac{\pi}{10}t - \frac{\pi}{2}\right).$$

(a) Find the period of the model. What does the period tell you about the ride?

(b) Find the amplitude of the model. What does the amplitude tell you about the ride?

(c) Use a graphing utility to graph one cycle of the model.

Synthesis

True or False? **In Exercises 81–83, determine whether the statement is true or false. Justify your answer.**

81. The graph of the function given by $f(x) = \sin(x + 2\pi)$ translates the graph of $f(x) = \sin x$ exactly one period to the right so that the two graphs look identical.

82. The function given by $y = \frac{1}{2}\cos 2x$ has an amplitude that is twice that of the function given by $y = \cos x$.

83. The graph of $y = -\cos x$ is a reflection of the graph of $y = \sin(x + \pi/2)$ in the x-axis.

84. ***Writing*** Use a graphing utility to graph the function given by $y = d + a \sin(bx - c)$, for several different values of a, b, c, and d. Write a paragraph describing the changes in the graph corresponding to changes in each constant.

Conjecture **In Exercises 85 and 86, graph f and g on the same set of coordinate axes. Include two full periods. Make a conjecture about the functions.**

85. $f(x) = \sin x, \quad g(x) = \cos\left(x - \frac{\pi}{2}\right)$

86. $f(x) = \sin x, \quad g(x) = -\cos\left(x + \frac{\pi}{2}\right)$

87. ***Exploration*** Using calculus, it can be shown that the sine and cosine functions can be approximated by the polynomials

$$\sin x \approx x - \frac{x^3}{3!} + \frac{x^5}{5!} \quad \text{and} \quad \cos x \approx 1 - \frac{x^2}{2!} + \frac{x^4}{4!}$$

where x is in radians.

(a) Use a graphing utility to graph the sine function and its polynomial approximation in the same viewing window. How do the graphs compare?

(b) Use a graphing utility to graph the cosine function and its polynomial approximation in the same viewing window. How do the graphs compare?

(c) Study the patterns in the polynomial approximations of the sine and cosine functions and predict the next term in each. Then repeat parts (a) and (b). How did the accuracy of the approximations change when an additional term was added?

88. ***Exploration*** Use the polynomial approximations for the sine and cosine functions in Exercise 87 to approximate the following function values. Compare the results with those given by a calculator. Is the error in the approximation the same in each case? Explain.

(a) $\sin \frac{1}{2}$ (b) $\sin 1$ (c) $\sin \frac{\pi}{6}$

(d) $\cos(-0.5)$ (e) $\cos 1$ (f) $\cos \frac{\pi}{4}$

Skills Review

In Exercises 89–92, use the properties of logarithms to write the expression as a sum, difference, and/or constant multiple of a logarithm.

89. $\log_{10} \sqrt{x - 2}$

90. $\log_2[x^2(x - 3)]$

91. $\ln \frac{t^3}{t - 1}$

92. $\ln \sqrt{\frac{z}{z^2 + 1}}$

In Exercises 93–96, write the expression as the logarithm of a single quantity.

93. $\frac{1}{2}(\log_{10} x + \log_{10} y)$

94. $2 \log_2 x + \log_2(xy)$

95. $\ln 3x - 4 \ln y$

96. $\frac{1}{2}(\ln 2x - 2 \ln x) + 3 \ln x$

97. **Make a Decision** To work an extended application analyzing the normal daily maximum temperature and normal precipitation in Honolulu, Hawaii, visit this text's website at *college.hmco.com*. *(Data Source: NOAA)*

4.6 Graphs of Other Trigonometric Functions

What you should learn

- Sketch the graphs of tangent functions.
- Sketch the graphs of cotangent functions.
- Sketch the graphs of secant and cosecant functions.
- Sketch the graphs of damped trigonometric functions.

Why you should learn it

Trigonometric functions can be used to model real-life situations such as the distance from a television camera to a unit in a parade as in Exercise 76 on page 341.

Photodisc/Getty Images

Graph of the Tangent Function

Recall that the tangent function is odd. That is, $\tan(-x) = -\tan x$. Consequently, the graph of $y = \tan x$ is symmetric with respect to the origin. You also know from the identity $\tan x = \sin x/\cos x$ that the tangent is undefined for values at which $\cos x = 0$. Two such values are $x = \pm\pi/2 \approx \pm 1.5708$.

x	$-\frac{\pi}{2}$	-1.57	-1.5	$-\frac{\pi}{4}$	0	$\frac{\pi}{4}$	1.5	1.57	$\frac{\pi}{2}$
$\tan x$	Undef.	-1255.8	-14.1	-1	0	1	14.1	1255.8	Undef.

As indicated in the table, $\tan x$ increases without bound as x approaches $\pi/2$ from the left, and decreases without bound as x approaches $-\pi/2$ from the right. So, the graph of $y = \tan x$ has *vertical asymptotes* at $x = \pi/2$ and $x = -\pi/2$, as shown in Figure 4.59. Moreover, because the period of the tangent function is π, vertical asymptotes also occur when $x = \pi/2 + n\pi$, where n is an integer. The domain of the tangent function is the set of all real numbers other than $x = \pi/2 + n\pi$, and the range is the set of all real numbers.

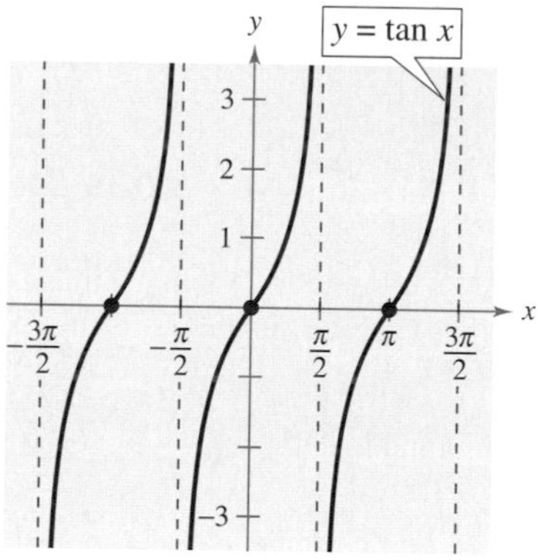

FIGURE 4.59

PERIOD: π
DOMAIN: ALL $x \neq \frac{\pi}{2} + n\pi$
RANGE: $(-\infty, \infty)$
VERTICAL ASYMPTOTES: $x = \frac{\pi}{2} + n\pi$

Sketching the graph of $y = a\tan(bx - c)$ is similar to sketching the graph of $y = a\sin(bx - c)$ in that you locate key points that identify the intercepts and asymptotes. Two consecutive vertical asymptotes can be found by solving the equations

$$bx - c = -\frac{\pi}{2} \quad \text{and} \quad bx - c = \frac{\pi}{2}.$$

The midpoint between two consecutive vertical asymptotes is an x-intercept of the graph. The period of the function $y = a\tan(bx - c)$ is the distance between two consecutive vertical asymptotes. The amplitude of a tangent function is not defined. After plotting the asymptotes and the x-intercept, plot a few additional points between the two asymptotes and sketch one cycle. Finally, sketch one or two additional cycles to the left and right.

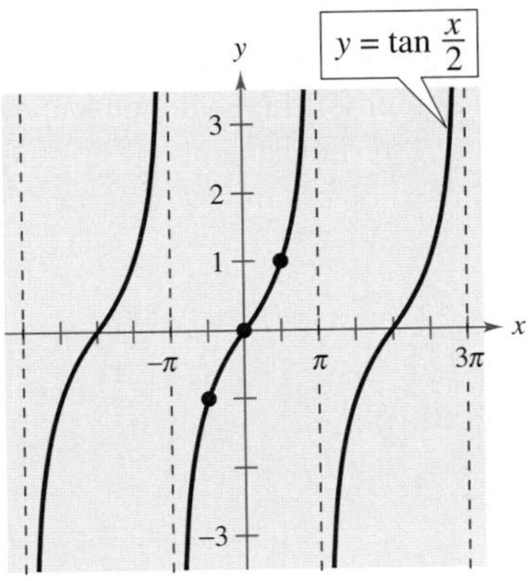

FIGURE 4.60

Example 1 Sketching the Graph of a Tangent Function

Sketch the graph of $y = \tan \frac{x}{2}$.

Solution

By solving the equations

$$\frac{x}{2} = -\frac{\pi}{2} \quad \text{and} \quad \frac{x}{2} = \frac{\pi}{2}$$

$$x = -\pi \qquad\qquad x = \pi$$

you can see that two consecutive vertical asymptotes occur at $x = -\pi$ and $x = \pi$. Between these two asymptotes, plot a few points, including the x-intercept, as shown in the table. Three cycles of the graph are shown in Figure 4.60.

x	$-\pi$	$-\frac{\pi}{2}$	0	$\frac{\pi}{2}$	π
$\tan \frac{x}{2}$	Undef.	-1	0	1	Undef.

CHECKPOINT Now try Exercise 7.

Example 2 Sketching the Graph of a Tangent Function

Sketch the graph of $y = -3 \tan 2x$.

Solution

By solving the equations

$$2x = -\frac{\pi}{2} \quad \text{and} \quad 2x = \frac{\pi}{2}$$

$$x = -\frac{\pi}{4} \qquad\qquad x = \frac{\pi}{4}$$

you can see that two consecutive vertical asymptotes occur at $x = -\pi/4$ and $x = \pi/4$. Between these two asymptotes, plot a few points, including the x-intercept, as shown in the table. Three cycles of the graph are shown in Figure 4.61.

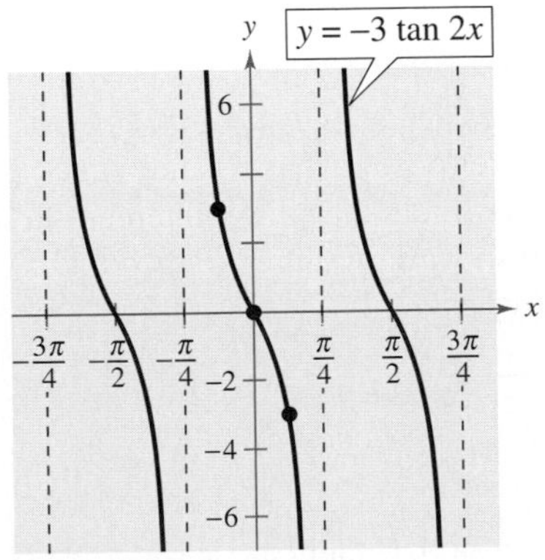

FIGURE 4.61

x	$-\frac{\pi}{4}$	$-\frac{\pi}{8}$	0	$\frac{\pi}{8}$	$\frac{\pi}{4}$
$-3 \tan 2x$	Undef.	3	0	-3	Undef.

CHECKPOINT Now try Exercise 9.

By comparing the graphs in Examples 1 and 2, you can see that the graph of $y = a \tan(bx - c)$ increases between consecutive vertical asymptotes when $a > 0$, and decreases between consecutive vertical asymptotes when $a < 0$. In other words, the graph for $a < 0$ is a reflection in the x-axis of the graph for $a > 0$.

Graph of the Cotangent Function

The graph of the cotangent function is similar to the graph of the tangent function. It also has a period of π. However, from the identity

$$y = \cot x = \frac{\cos x}{\sin x}$$

you can see that the cotangent function has vertical asymptotes when $\sin x$ is zero, which occurs at $x = n\pi$, where n is an integer. The graph of the cotangent function is shown in Figure 4.62. Note that two consecutive vertical asymptotes of the graph of $y = a\cot(bx - c)$ can be found by solving the equations $bx - c = 0$ and $bx - c = \pi$.

Technology

Some graphing utilities have difficulty graphing trigonometric functions that have vertical asymptotes. Your graphing utility may connect parts of the graphs of tangent, cotangent, secant, and cosecant functions that are not supposed to be connected. To eliminate this problem, change the mode of the graphing utility to *dot* mode.

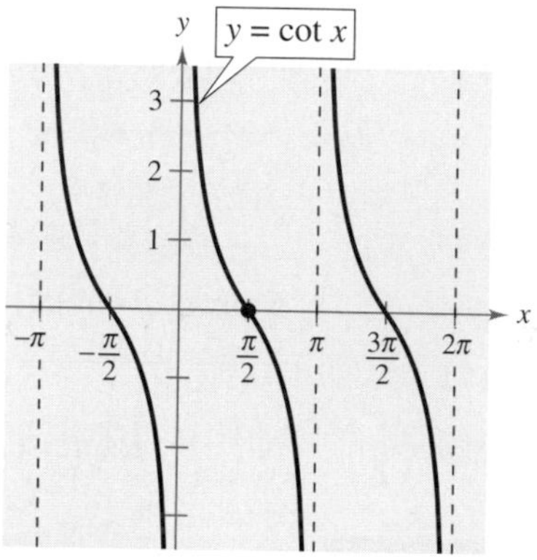

FIGURE 4.62

PERIOD: π
DOMAIN: ALL $x \neq n\pi$
RANGE: $(-\infty, \infty)$
VERTICAL ASYMPTOTES: $x = n\pi$

Example 3 Sketching the Graph of a Cotangent Function

Sketch the graph of $y = 2\cot \frac{x}{3}$.

Solution

By solving the equations

$$\frac{x}{3} = 0 \qquad \text{and} \qquad \frac{x}{3} = \pi$$

$$x = 0 \qquad\qquad x = 3\pi$$

you can see that two consecutive vertical asymptotes occur at $x = 0$ and $x = 3\pi$. Between these two asymptotes, plot a few points, including the x-intercept, as shown in the table. Three cycles of the graph are shown in Figure 4.63. Note that the period is 3π, the distance between consecutive asymptotes.

x	0	$\frac{3\pi}{4}$	$\frac{3\pi}{2}$	$\frac{9\pi}{4}$	3π
$2\cot \frac{x}{3}$	Undef.	2	0	-2	Undef.

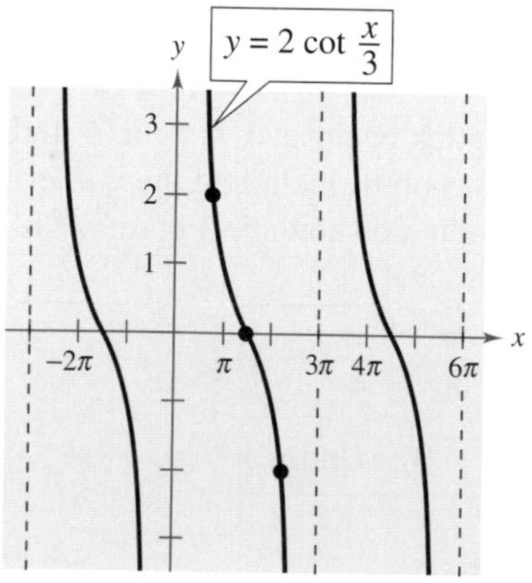

FIGURE 4.63

CHECKPOINT Now try Exercise 19.

Graphs of the Reciprocal Functions

The graphs of the two remaining trigonometric functions can be obtained from the graphs of the sine and cosine functions using the reciprocal identities

$$\csc x = \frac{1}{\sin x} \qquad \text{and} \qquad \sec x = \frac{1}{\cos x}.$$

For instance, at a given value of x, the y-coordinate of $\sec x$ is the reciprocal of the y-coordinate of $\cos x$. Of course, when $\cos x = 0$, the reciprocal does not exist. Near such values of x, the behavior of the secant function is similar to that of the tangent function. In other words, the graphs of

$$\tan x = \frac{\sin x}{\cos x} \qquad \text{and} \qquad \sec x = \frac{1}{\cos x}$$

have vertical asymptotes at $x = \pi/2 + n\pi$, where n is an integer, and the cosine is zero at these x-values. Similarly,

$$\cot x = \frac{\cos x}{\sin x} \qquad \text{and} \qquad \csc x = \frac{1}{\sin x}$$

have vertical asymptotes where $\sin x = 0$—that is, at $x = n\pi$.

To sketch the graph of a secant or cosecant function, you should first make a sketch of its reciprocal function. For instance, to sketch the graph of $y = \csc x$, first sketch the graph of $y = \sin x$. Then take reciprocals of the y-coordinates to obtain points on the graph of $y = \csc x$. This procedure is used to obtain the graphs shown in Figure 4.64.

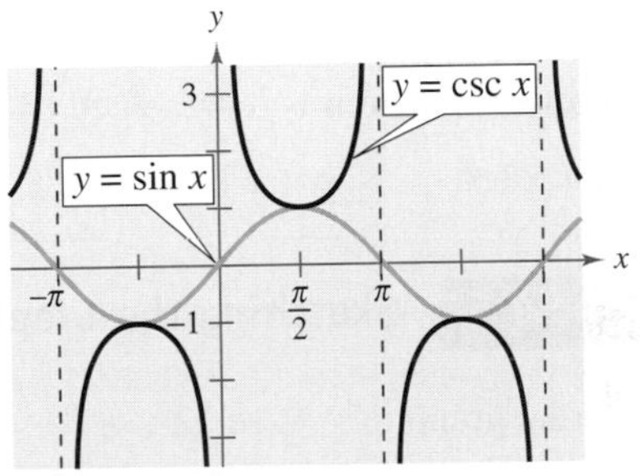

PERIOD: 2π
DOMAIN: ALL $x \neq n\pi$
RANGE: $(-\infty, -1] \cup [1, \infty)$
VERTICAL ASYMPTOTES: $x = n\pi$
SYMMETRY: ORIGIN

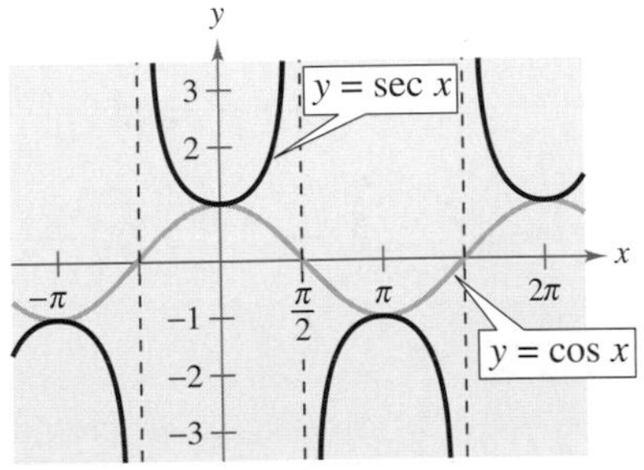

PERIOD: 2π
DOMAIN: ALL $x \neq \frac{\pi}{2} + n\pi$
RANGE: $(-\infty, -1] \cup [1, \infty)$
VERTICAL ASYMPTOTES: $x = \frac{\pi}{2} + n\pi$
SYMMETRY: y-AXIS

FIGURE 4.64

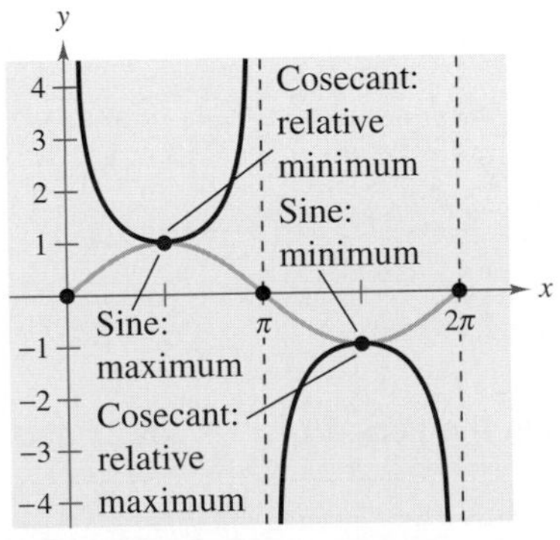

FIGURE 4.65

In comparing the graphs of the cosecant and secant functions with those of the sine and cosine functions, note that the "hills" and "valleys" are interchanged. For example, a hill (or maximum point) on the sine curve corresponds to a valley (a relative minimum) on the cosecant curve, and a valley (or minimum point) on the sine curve corresponds to a hill (a relative maximum) on the cosecant curve, as shown in Figure 4.65. Additionally, x-intercepts of the sine and cosine functions become vertical asymptotes of the cosecant and secant functions, respectively (see Figure 4.65).

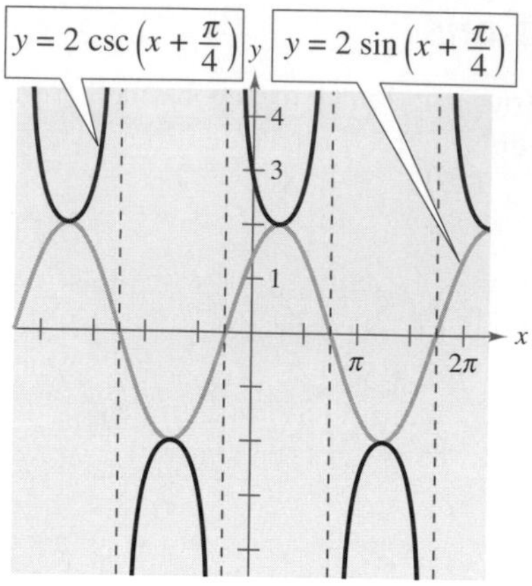

FIGURE 4.66

Example 4 Sketching the Graph of a Cosecant Function

Sketch the graph of $y = 2\csc\left(x + \frac{\pi}{4}\right)$.

Solution

Begin by sketching the graph of

$$y = 2\sin\left(x + \frac{\pi}{4}\right).$$

For this function, the amplitude is 2 and the period is 2π. By solving the equations

$$x + \frac{\pi}{4} = 0 \qquad \text{and} \qquad x + \frac{\pi}{4} = 2\pi$$

$$x = -\frac{\pi}{4} \qquad\qquad x = \frac{7\pi}{4}$$

you can see that one cycle of the sine function corresponds to the interval from $x = -\pi/4$ to $x = 7\pi/4$. The graph of this sine function is represented by the gray curve in Figure 4.66. Because the sine function is zero at the midpoint and endpoints of this interval, the corresponding cosecant function

$$y = 2\csc\left(x + \frac{\pi}{4}\right)$$

$$= 2\left(\frac{1}{\sin[x + (\pi/4)]}\right)$$

has vertical asymptotes at $x = -\pi/4$, $x = 3\pi/4$, $x = 7\pi/4$, etc. The graph of the cosecant function is represented by the black curve in Figure 4.66.

CHECKPOINT Now try Exercise 25.

Example 5 Sketching the Graph of a Secant Function

Sketch the graph of $y = \sec 2x$.

Solution

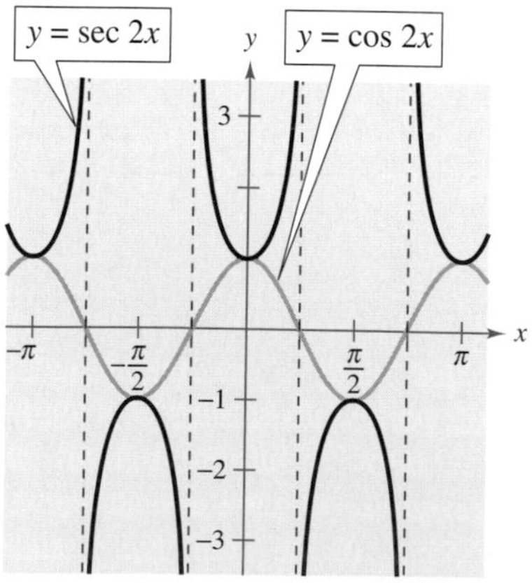

FIGURE 4.67

Begin by sketching the graph of $y = \cos 2x$, as indicated by the gray curve in Figure 4.67. Then, form the graph of $y = \sec 2x$ as the black curve in the figure. Note that the x-intercepts of $y = \cos 2x$

$$\left(-\frac{\pi}{4}, 0\right), \quad \left(\frac{\pi}{4}, 0\right), \quad \left(\frac{3\pi}{4}, 0\right), \ldots$$

correspond to the vertical asymptotes

$$x = -\frac{\pi}{4}, \quad x = \frac{\pi}{4}, \quad x = \frac{3\pi}{4}, \ldots$$

of the graph of $y = \sec 2x$. Moreover, notice that the period of $y = \cos 2x$ and $y = \sec 2x$ is π.

CHECKPOINT Now try Exercise 27.

Damped Trigonometric Graphs

A *product* of two functions can be graphed using properties of the individual functions. For instance, consider the function

$$f(x) = x \sin x$$

as the product of the functions $y = x$ and $y = \sin x$. Using properties of absolute value and the fact that $|\sin x| \leq 1$, you have $0 \leq |x||\sin x| \leq |x|$. Consequently,

$$-|x| \leq x \sin x \leq |x|$$

which means that the graph of $f(x) = x \sin x$ lies between the lines $y = -x$ and $y = x$. Furthermore, because

$$f(x) = x \sin x = \pm x \qquad \text{at} \qquad x = \frac{\pi}{2} + n\pi$$

and

$$f(x) = x \sin x = 0 \qquad \text{at} \qquad x = n\pi$$

the graph of f touches the line $y = -x$ or the line $y = x$ at $x = \pi/2 + n\pi$ and has x-intercepts at $x = n\pi$. A sketch of f is shown in Figure 4.68. In the function $f(x) = x \sin x$, the factor x is called the **damping factor.**

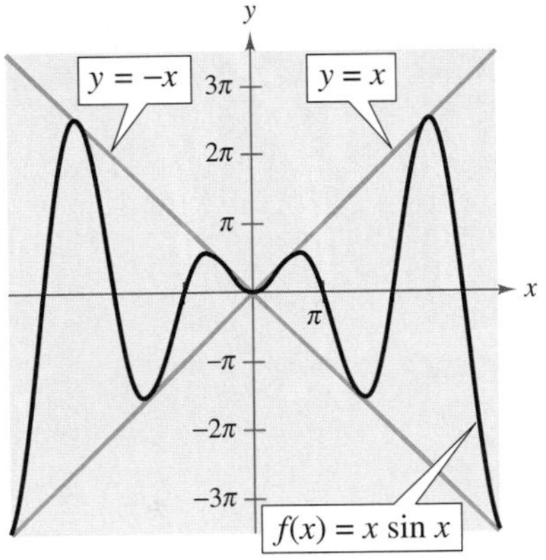

FIGURE 4.68

STUDY TIP

Do you see why the graph of $f(x) = x \sin x$ touches the lines $y = \pm x$ at $x = \pi/2 + n\pi$ and why the graph has x-intercepts at $x = n\pi$? Recall that the sine function is equal to 1 at $\pi/2$, $3\pi/2$, $5\pi/2$, . . . (odd multiples of $\pi/2$) and is equal to 0 at π, 2π, 3π, . . . (multiples of π).

Example 6 Damped Sine Wave

Sketch the graph of

$$f(x) = e^{-x} \sin 3x.$$

Solution

Consider $f(x)$ as the product of the two functions

$$y = e^{-x} \qquad \text{and} \qquad y = \sin 3x$$

each of which has the set of real numbers as its domain. For any real number x, you know that $e^{-x} \geq 0$ and $|\sin 3x| \leq 1$. So, $e^{-x}|\sin 3x| \leq e^{-x}$, which means that

$$-e^{-x} \leq e^{-x} \sin 3x \leq e^{-x}.$$

Furthermore, because

$$f(x) = e^{-x} \sin 3x = \pm e^{-x} \qquad \text{at} \qquad x = \frac{\pi}{6} + \frac{n\pi}{3}$$

and

$$f(x) = e^{-x} \sin 3x = 0 \qquad \text{at} \qquad x = \frac{n\pi}{3}$$

the graph of f touches the curves $y = -e^{-x}$ and $y = e^{-x}$ at $x = \pi/6 + n\pi/3$ and has intercepts at $x = n\pi/3$. A sketch is shown in Figure 4.69.

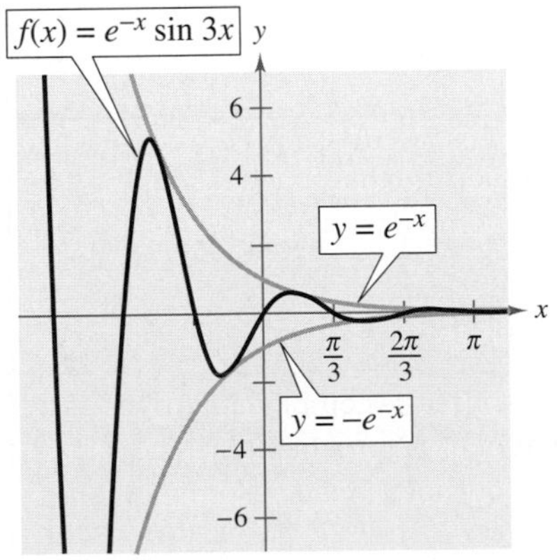

FIGURE 4.69

✓CHECKPOINT Now try Exercise 65.

Figure 4.70 summarizes the characteristics of the six basic trigonometric functions.

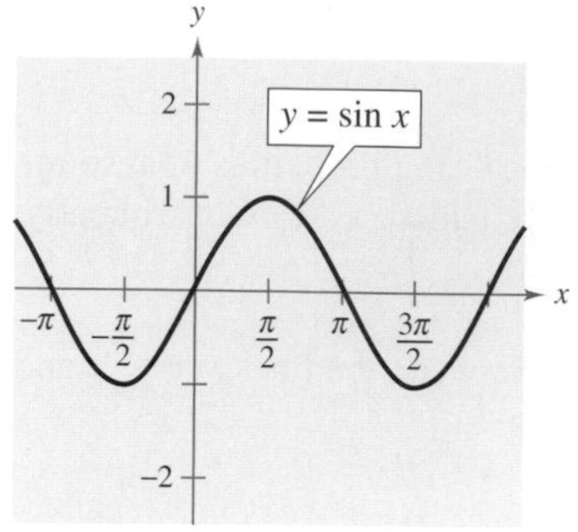

DOMAIN: ALL REALS
RANGE: $[-1, 1]$
PERIOD: 2π

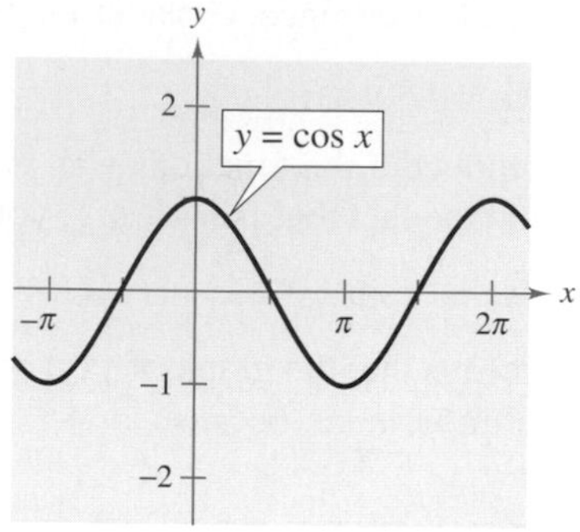

DOMAIN: ALL REALS
RANGE: $[-1, 1]$
PERIOD: 2π

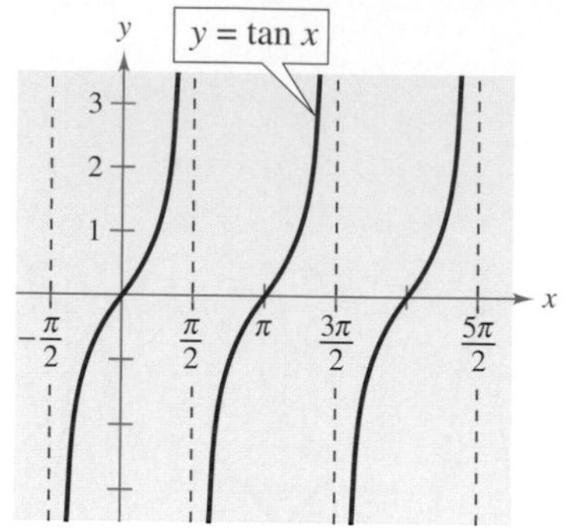

DOMAIN: ALL $x \neq \frac{\pi}{2} + n\pi$
RANGE: $(-\infty, \infty)$
PERIOD: π

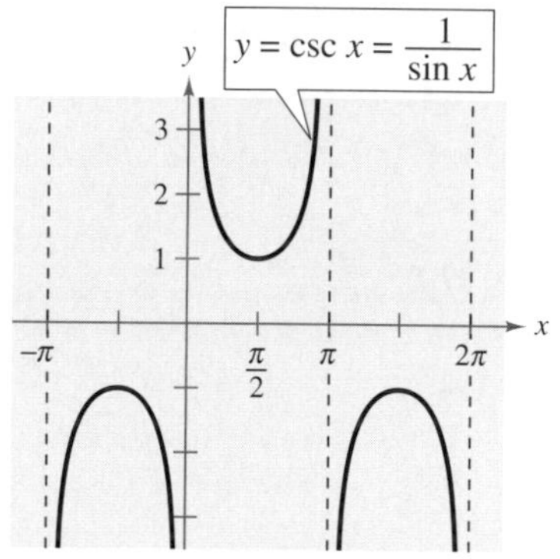

DOMAIN: ALL $x \neq n\pi$
RANGE: $(-\infty, -1] \cup [1, \infty)$
PERIOD: 2π

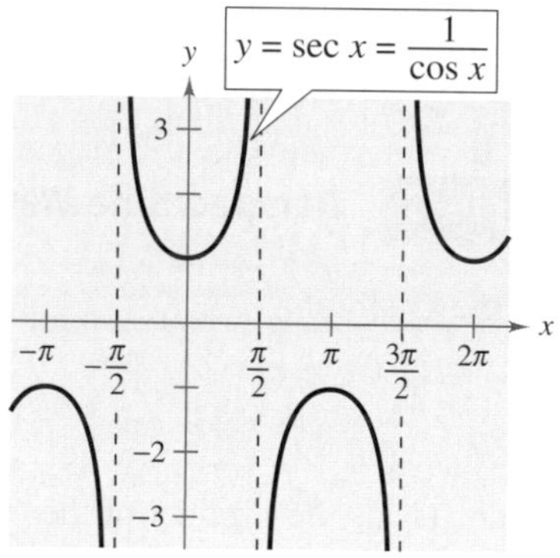

DOMAIN: ALL $x \neq \frac{\pi}{2} + n\pi$
RANGE: $(-\infty, -1] \cup [1, \infty)$
PERIOD: 2π

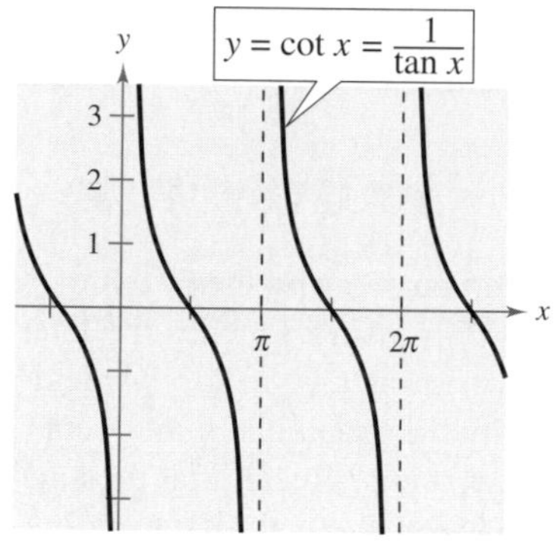

DOMAIN: ALL $x \neq n\pi$
RANGE: $(-\infty, \infty)$
PERIOD: π

FIGURE 4.70

WRITING ABOUT MATHEMATICS

Combining Trigonometric Functions Recall from Section 1.8 that functions can be combined arithmetically. This also applies to trigonometric functions. For each of the functions

$$h(x) = x + \sin x \quad \text{and} \quad h(x) = \cos x - \sin 3x$$

(a) identify two simpler functions f and g that comprise the combination, (b) use a table to show how to obtain the numerical values of $h(x)$ from the numerical values of $f(x)$ and $g(x)$, and (c) use graphs of f and g to show how h may be formed.

Can you find functions

$$f(x) = d + a \sin(bx + c) \quad \text{and} \quad g(x) = d + a \cos(bx + c)$$

such that $f(x) + g(x) = 0$ for all x?

4.6 Exercises

VOCABULARY CHECK: Fill in the blanks.

1. The graphs of the tangent, cotangent, secant, and cosecant functions all have ________ asymptotes.
2. To sketch the graph of a secant or cosecant function, first make a sketch of its corresponding ________ function.
3. For the functions given by $f(x) = g(x) \cdot \sin x$, $g(x)$ is called the ________ factor of the function $f(x)$.
4. The period of $y = \tan x$ is ________.
5. The domain of $y = \cot x$ is all real numbers such that ________.
6. The range of $y = \sec x$ is ________.
7. The period of $y = \csc x$ is ________.

In Exercises 1–6, match the function with its graph. State the period of the function. [The graphs are labeled (a), (b), (c), (d), (e), and (f).]

(a)

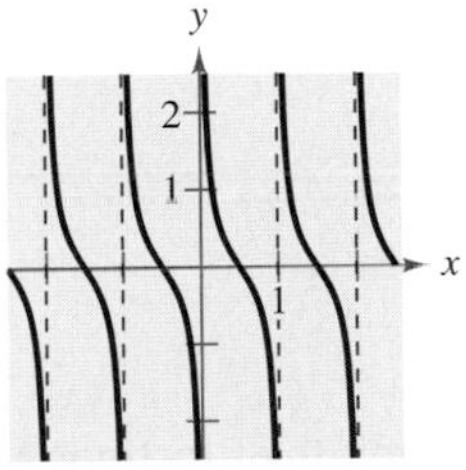

(b)

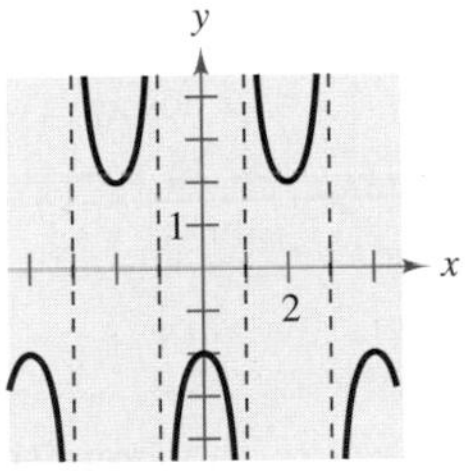

(c)

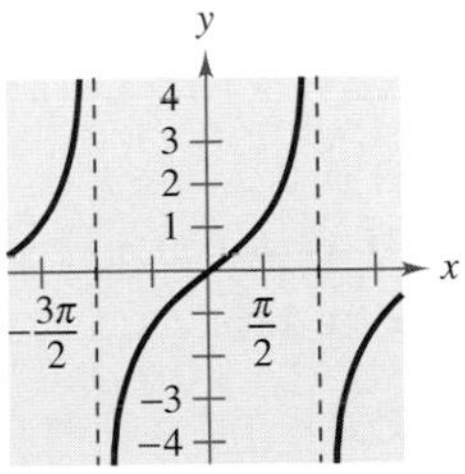

(d)

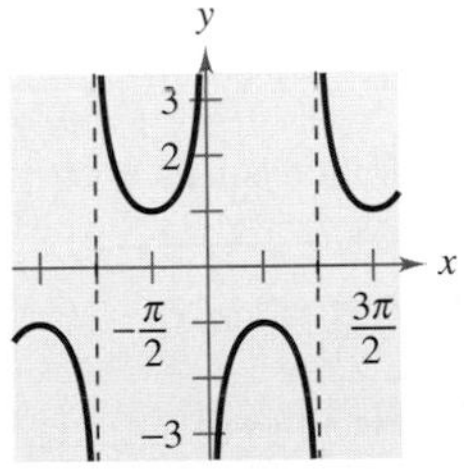

(e)

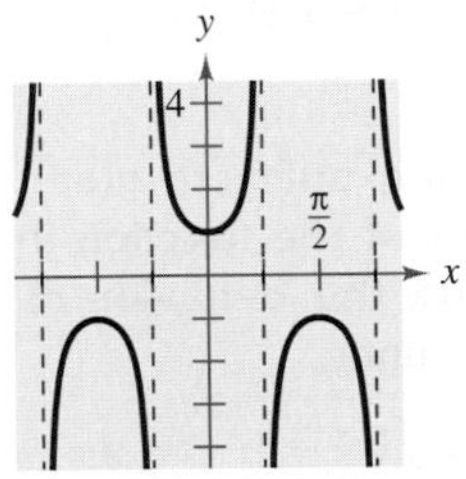

(f)

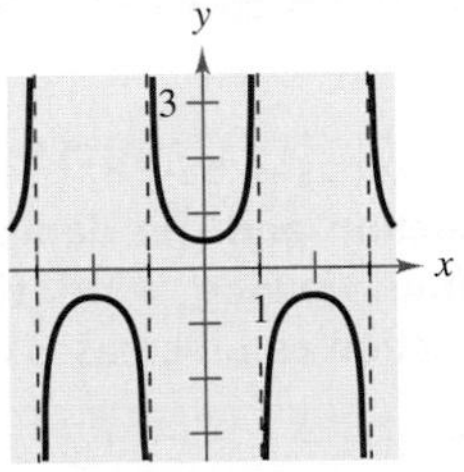

1. $y = \sec 2x$
2. $y = \tan \dfrac{x}{2}$
3. $y = \dfrac{1}{2} \cot \pi x$
4. $y = -\csc x$
5. $y = \dfrac{1}{2} \sec \dfrac{\pi x}{2}$
6. $y = -2 \sec \dfrac{\pi x}{2}$

In Exercises 7–30, sketch the graph of the function. Include two full periods.

7. $y = \frac{1}{3} \tan x$
8. $y = \frac{1}{4} \tan x$
9. $y = \tan 3x$
10. $y = -3 \tan \pi x$
11. $y = -\frac{1}{2} \sec x$
12. $y = \frac{1}{4} \sec x$
13. $y = \csc \pi x$
14. $y = 3 \csc 4x$
15. $y = \sec \pi x - 1$
16. $y = -2 \sec 4x + 2$
17. $y = \csc \dfrac{x}{2}$
18. $y = \csc \dfrac{x}{3}$
19. $y = \cot \dfrac{x}{2}$
20. $y = 3 \cot \dfrac{\pi x}{2}$
21. $y = \frac{1}{2} \sec 2x$
22. $y = -\frac{1}{2} \tan x$
23. $y = \tan \dfrac{\pi x}{4}$
24. $y = \tan(x + \pi)$
25. $y = \csc(\pi - x)$
26. $y = \csc(2x - \pi)$
27. $y = 2 \sec(x + \pi)$
28. $y = -\sec \pi x + 1$
29. $y = \dfrac{1}{4} \csc\left(x + \dfrac{\pi}{4}\right)$
30. $y = 2 \cot\left(x + \dfrac{\pi}{2}\right)$

In Exercises 31–40, use a graphing utility to graph the function. Include two full periods.

31. $y = \tan \dfrac{x}{3}$
32. $y = -\tan 2x$
33. $y = -2 \sec 4x$
34. $y = \sec \pi x$
35. $y = \tan\left(x - \dfrac{\pi}{4}\right)$
36. $y = \dfrac{1}{4} \cot\left(x - \dfrac{\pi}{2}\right)$
37. $y = -\csc(4x - \pi)$
38. $y = 2 \sec(2x - \pi)$
39. $y = 0.1 \tan\left(\dfrac{\pi x}{4} + \dfrac{\pi}{4}\right)$
40. $y = \dfrac{1}{3} \sec\left(\dfrac{\pi x}{2} + \dfrac{\pi}{2}\right)$

In Exercises 41–48, use a graph to solve the equation on the interval $[-2\pi, 2\pi]$.

41. $\tan x = 1$

42. $\tan x = \sqrt{3}$

43. $\cot x = -\dfrac{\sqrt{3}}{3}$

44. $\cot x = 1$

45. $\sec x = -2$

46. $\sec x = 2$

47. $\csc x = \sqrt{2}$

48. $\csc x = -\dfrac{2\sqrt{3}}{3}$

In Exercises 49 and 50, use the graph of the function to determine whether the function is even, odd, or neither.

49. $f(x) = \sec x$ **50.** $f(x) = \tan x$

51. ***Graphical Reasoning*** Consider the functions given by

$$f(x) = 2\sin x \quad \text{and} \quad g(x) = \frac{1}{2}\csc x$$

on the interval $(0, \pi)$.

(a) Graph f and g in the same coordinate plane.

(b) Approximate the interval in which $f > g$.

(c) Describe the behavior of each of the functions as x approaches π. How is the behavior of g related to the behavior of f as x approaches π?

52. ***Graphical Reasoning*** Consider the functions given by

$$f(x) = \tan\frac{\pi x}{2} \quad \text{and} \quad g(x) = \frac{1}{2}\sec\frac{\pi x}{2}$$

on the interval $(-1, 1)$.

(a) Use a graphing utility to graph f and g in the same viewing window.

(b) Approximate the interval in which $f < g$.

(c) Approximate the interval in which $2f < 2g$. How does the result compare with that of part (b)? Explain.

In Exercises 53–56, use a graphing utility to graph the two equations in the same viewing window. Use the graphs to determine whether the expressions are equivalent. Verify the results algebraically.

53. $y_1 = \sin x \csc x, \quad y_2 = 1$

54. $y_1 = \sin x \sec x, \quad y_2 = \tan x$

55. $y_1 = \dfrac{\cos x}{\sin x}, \quad y_2 = \cot x$

56. $y_1 = \sec^2 x - 1, \quad y_2 = \tan^2 x$

In Exercises 57–60, match the function with its graph. Describe the behavior of the function as x approaches zero. [The graphs are labeled (a), (b), (c), and (d).]

(a)

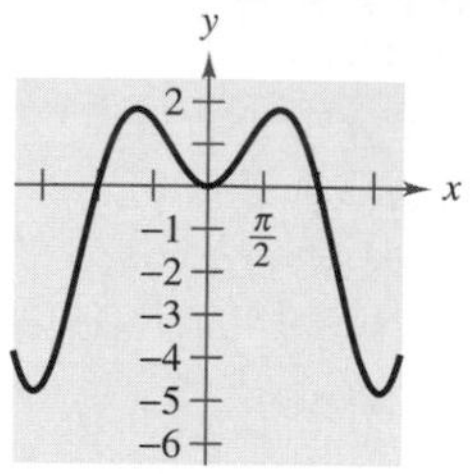

(b)

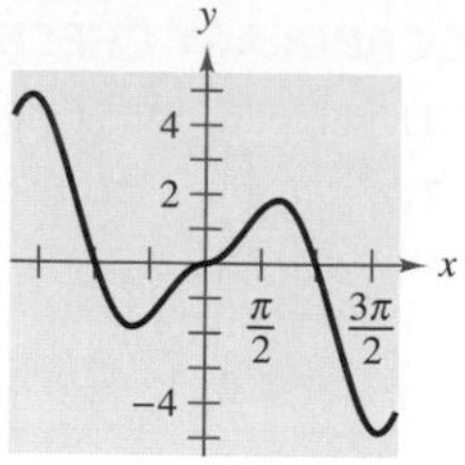

(c)

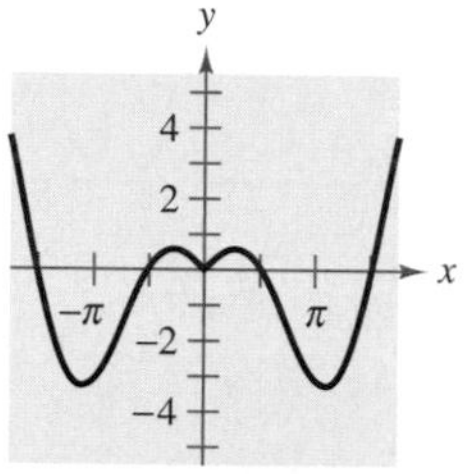

(d)

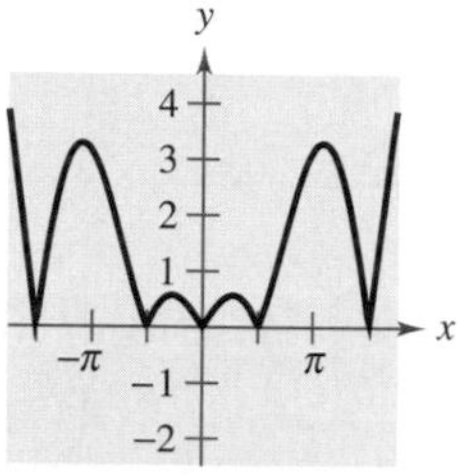

57. $f(x) = |x\cos x|$

58. $f(x) = x\sin x$

59. $g(x) = |x|\sin x$

60. $g(x) = |x|\cos x$

Conjecture **In Exercises 61–64, graph the functions f and g. Use the graphs to make a conjecture about the relationship between the functions.**

61. $f(x) = \sin x + \cos\left(x + \dfrac{\pi}{2}\right), \quad g(x) = 0$

62. $f(x) = \sin x - \cos\left(x + \dfrac{\pi}{2}\right), \quad g(x) = 2\sin x$

63. $f(x) = \sin^2 x, \quad g(x) = \frac{1}{2}(1 - \cos 2x)$

64. $f(x) = \cos^2\dfrac{\pi x}{2}, \quad g(x) = \dfrac{1}{2}(1 + \cos \pi x)$

In Exercises 65–68, use a graphing utility to graph the function and the damping factor of the function in the same viewing window. Describe the behavior of the function as x increases without bound.

65. $g(x) = e^{-x^2/2}\sin x$ **66.** $f(x) = e^{-x}\cos x$

67. $f(x) = 2^{-x/4}\cos \pi x$ **68.** $h(x) = 2^{-x^2/4}\sin x$

Exploration **In Exercises 69–74, use a graphing utility to graph the function. Describe the behavior of the function as x approaches zero.**

69. $y = \dfrac{6}{x} + \cos x, \quad x > 0$ **70.** $y = \dfrac{4}{x} + \sin 2x, \quad x > 0$

71. $g(x) = \dfrac{\sin x}{x}$

72. $f(x) = \dfrac{1 - \cos x}{x}$

73. $f(x) = \sin \dfrac{1}{x}$

74. $h(x) = x \sin \dfrac{1}{x}$

75. ***Distance*** A plane flying at an altitude of 7 miles above a radar antenna will pass directly over the radar antenna (see figure). Let d be the ground distance from the antenna to the point directly under the plane and let x be the angle of elevation to the plane from the antenna. (d is positive as the plane approaches the antenna.) Write d as a function of x and graph the function over the interval $0 < x < \pi$.

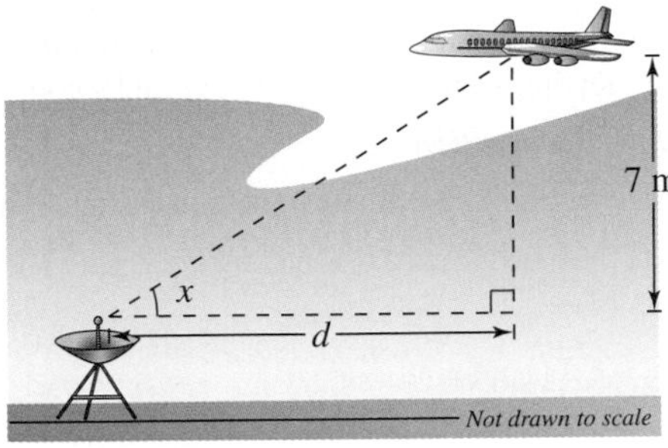

76. ***Television Coverage*** A television camera is on a reviewing platform 27 meters from the street on which a parade will be passing from left to right (see figure). Write the distance d from the camera to a particular unit in the parade as a function of the angle x, and graph the function over the interval $-\pi/2 < x < \pi/2$. (Consider x as negative when a unit in the parade approaches from the left.)

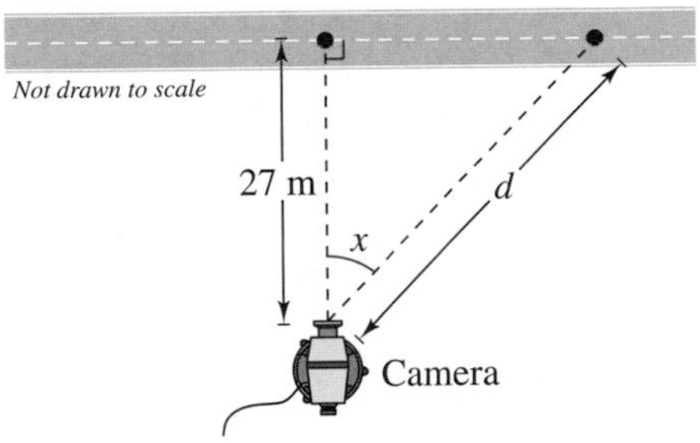

Model It

77. ***Predator-Prey Model*** The population C of coyotes (a predator) at time t (in months) in a region is estimated to be

$$C = 5000 + 2000 \sin \frac{\pi t}{12}$$

and the population R of rabbits (its prey) is estimated to be

Model It (continued)

$$R = 25{,}000 + 15{,}000 \cos \frac{\pi t}{12}.$$

(a) Use a graphing utility to graph both models in the same viewing window. Use the window setting $0 \le t \le 100$.

(b) Use the graphs of the models in part (a) to explain the oscillations in the size of each population.

(c) The cycles of each population follow a periodic pattern. Find the period of each model and describe several factors that could be contributing to the cyclical patterns.

78. ***Sales*** The projected monthly sales S (in thousands of units) of lawn mowers (a seasonal product) are modeled by $S = 74 + 3t - 40 \cos(\pi t/6)$, where t is the time (in months), with $t = 1$ corresponding to January. Graph the sales function over 1 year.

79. ***Meterology*** The normal monthly high temperatures H (in degrees Fahrenheit) for Erie, Pennsylvania are approximated by

$$H(t) = 54.33 - 20.38 \cos \frac{\pi t}{6} - 15.69 \sin \frac{\pi t}{6}$$

and the normal monthly low temperatures L are approximated by

$$L(t) = 39.36 - 15.70 \cos \frac{\pi t}{6} - 14.16 \sin \frac{\pi t}{6}$$

where t is the time (in months), with $t = 1$ corresponding to January (see figure). (Source: National Oceanic and Atmospheric Administration)

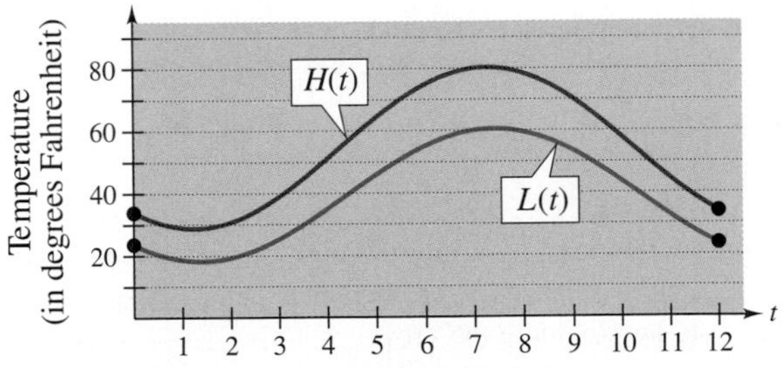

(a) What is the period of each function?

(b) During what part of the year is the difference between the normal high and normal low temperatures greatest? When is it smallest?

(c) The sun is northernmost in the sky around June 21, but the graph shows the warmest temperatures at a later date. Approximate the lag time of the temperatures relative to the position of the sun.

80. ***Harmonic Motion*** An object weighing W pounds is suspended from the ceiling by a steel spring (see figure). The weight is pulled downward (positive direction) from its equilibrium position and released. The resulting motion of the weight is described by the function

$$y = \frac{1}{2}e^{-t/4}\cos 4t, \quad t > 0$$

where y is the distance (in feet) and t is the time (in seconds).

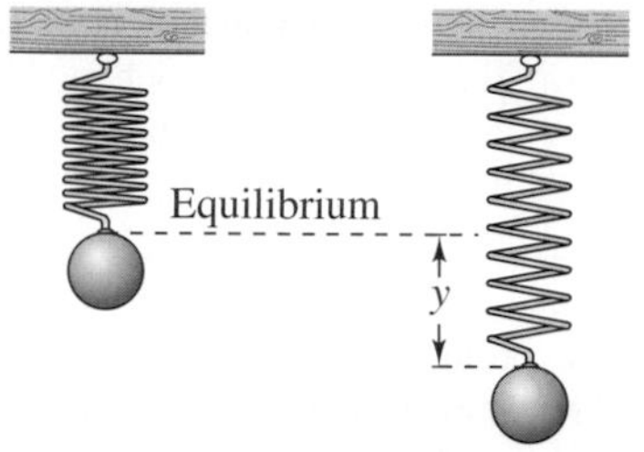

(a) Use a graphing utility to graph the function.

(b) Describe the behavior of the displacement function for increasing values of time t.

Synthesis

True or False? **In Exercises 81 and 82, determine whether the statement is true or false. Justify your answer.**

81. The graph of $y = \csc x$ can be obtained on a calculator by graphing the reciprocal of $y = \sin x$.

82. The graph of $y = \sec x$ can be obtained on a calculator by graphing a translation of the reciprocal of $y = \sin x$.

83. ***Writing*** Describe the behavior of $f(x) = \tan x$ as x approaches $\pi/2$ from the left and from the right.

84. ***Writing*** Describe the behavior of $f(x) = \csc x$ as x approaches π from the left and from the right.

85. ***Exploration*** Consider the function given by

$$f(x) = x - \cos x.$$

(a) Use a graphing utility to graph the function and verify that there exists a zero between 0 and 1. Use the graph to approximate the zero.

(b) Starting with $x_0 = 1$, generate a sequence $x_1, x_2, x_3, \ldots$, where $x_n = \cos(x_{n-1})$. For example,

$$x_0 = 1$$
$$x_1 = \cos(x_0)$$
$$x_2 = \cos(x_1)$$
$$x_3 = \cos(x_2)$$
$$\vdots$$

What value does the sequence approach?

86. ***Approximation*** Using calculus, it can be shown that the tangent function can be approximated by the polynomial

$$\tan x \approx x + \frac{2x^3}{3!} + \frac{16x^5}{5!}$$

where x is in radians. Use a graphing utility to graph the tangent function and its polynomial approximation in the same viewing window. How do the graphs compare?

87. ***Approximation*** Using calculus, it can be shown that the secant function can be approximated by the polynomial

$$\sec x \approx 1 + \frac{x^2}{2!} + \frac{5x^4}{4!}$$

where x is in radians. Use a graphing utility to graph the secant function and its polynomial approximation in the same viewing window. How do the graphs compare?

88. ***Pattern Recognition***

(a) Use a graphing utility to graph each function.

$$y_1 = \frac{4}{\pi}\left(\sin \pi x + \frac{1}{3}\sin 3\pi x\right)$$

$$y_2 = \frac{4}{\pi}\left(\sin \pi x + \frac{1}{3}\sin 3\pi x + \frac{1}{5}\sin 5\pi x\right)$$

(b) Identify the pattern started in part (a) and find a function y_3 that continues the pattern one more term. Use a graphing utility to graph y_3.

(c) The graphs in parts (a) and (b) approximate the periodic function in the figure. Find a function y_4 that is a better approximation.

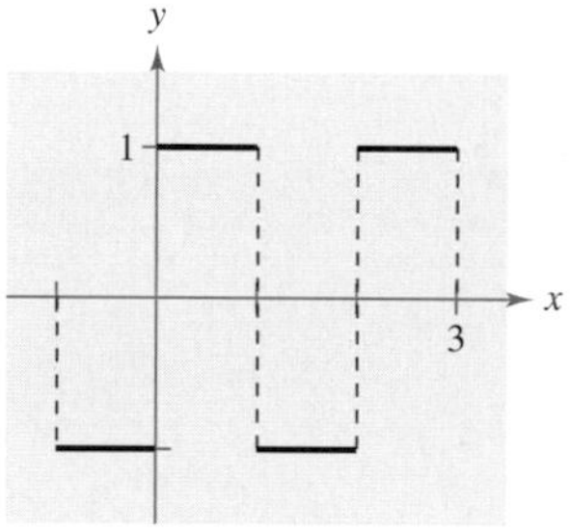

Skills Review

In Exercises 89–92, solve the exponential equation. Round your answer to three decimal places.

89. $e^{2x} = 54$

90. $8^{3x} = 98$

91. $\dfrac{300}{1 + e^{-x}} = 100$

92. $\left(1 + \dfrac{0.15}{365}\right)^{365t} = 5$

In Exercises 93–98, solve the logarithmic equation. Round your answer to three decimal places.

93. $\ln(3x - 2) = 73$

94. $\ln(14 - 2x) = 68$

95. $\ln(x^2 + 1) = 3.2$

96. $\ln \sqrt{x + 4} = 5$

97. $\log_8 x + \log_8(x - 1) = \frac{1}{3}$

98. $\log_6 x + \log_6(x^2 - 1) = \log_6 64x$

4.7 Inverse Trigonometric Functions

What you should learn

- Evaluate and graph the inverse sine function.
- Evaluate and graph the other inverse trigonometric functions.
- Evaluate and graph the compositions of trigonometric functions.

Why you should learn it

You can use inverse trigonometric functions to model and solve real-life problems. For instance, in Exercise 92 on page 351, an inverse trigonometric function can be used to model the angle of elevation from a television camera to a space shuttle launch.

NASA

STUDY TIP

When evaluating the inverse sine function, it helps to remember the phrase "the arcsine of x is the angle (or number) whose sine is x."

Inverse Sine Function

Recall from Section 1.9 that, for a function to have an inverse function, it must be one-to-one—that is, it must pass the Horizontal Line Test. From Figure 4.71, you can see that $y = \sin x$ does not pass the test because different values of x yield the same y-value.

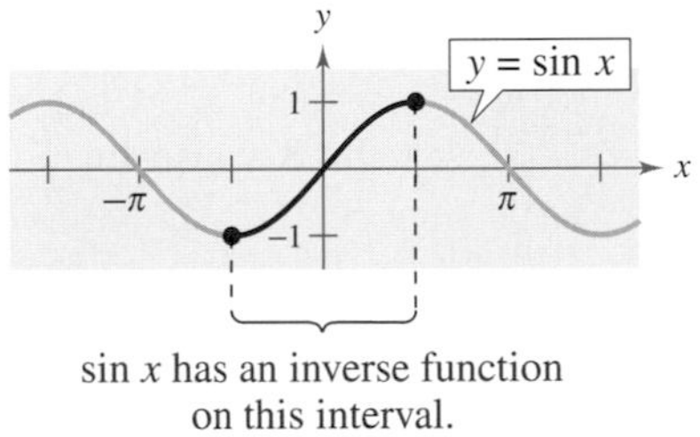

FIGURE 4.71

However, if you restrict the domain to the interval $\pi/2 \le x \le \pi/2$ (corresponding to the black portion of the graph in Figure 4.71), the following properties hold.

1. On the interval $[-\pi/2, \pi/2]$, the function $y = \sin x$ is increasing.
2. On the interval $[-\pi/2, \pi/2]$, $y = \sin x$ takes on its full range of values, $-1 \le \sin x \le 1$.
3. On the interval $[-\pi/2, \pi/2]$, $y = \sin x$ is one-to-one.

So, on the restricted domain $-\pi/2 \le x \le \pi/2$, $y = \sin x$ has a unique inverse function called the **inverse sine function.** It is denoted by

$$y = \arcsin x \qquad \text{or} \qquad y = \sin^{-1} x.$$

The notation $\sin^{-1} x$ is consistent with the inverse function notation $f^{-1}(x)$. The $\arcsin x$ notation (read as "the arcsine of x") comes from the association of a central angle with its intercepted *arc length* on a unit circle. So, $\arcsin x$ means the angle (or arc) whose sine is x. Both notations, $\arcsin x$ and $\sin^{-1} x$, are commonly used in mathematics, so remember that $\sin^{-1} x$ denotes the *inverse* sine function rather than $1/\sin x$. The values of $\arcsin x$ lie in the interval $-\pi/2 \le \arcsin x \le \pi/2$. The graph of $y = \arcsin x$ is shown in Example 2.

Definition of Inverse Sine Function

The **inverse sine function** is defined by

$$y = \arcsin x \qquad \text{if and only if} \qquad \sin y = x$$

where $-1 \le x \le 1$ and $-\pi/2 \le y \le \pi/2$. The domain of $y = \arcsin x$ is $[-1, 1]$, and the range is $[-\pi/2, \pi/2]$.

> **STUDY TIP**
>
> As with the trigonometric functions, much of the work with the inverse trigonometric functions can be done by *exact* calculations rather than by calculator approximations. Exact calculations help to increase your understanding of the inverse functions by relating them to the right triangle definitions of the trigonometric functions.

Example 1 Evaluating the Inverse Sine Function

If possible, find the exact value.

a. $\arcsin\left(-\frac{1}{2}\right)$ **b.** $\sin^{-1}\frac{\sqrt{3}}{2}$ **c.** $\sin^{-1}2$

Solution

a. Because $\sin\left(-\frac{\pi}{6}\right) = -\frac{1}{2}$ for $-\frac{\pi}{2} \le y \le \frac{\pi}{2}$, it follows that

$$\arcsin\left(-\frac{1}{2}\right) = -\frac{\pi}{6}. \qquad \text{Angle whose sine is } -\tfrac{1}{2}$$

b. Because $\sin\frac{\pi}{3} = \frac{\sqrt{3}}{2}$ for $-\frac{\pi}{2} \le y \le \frac{\pi}{2}$, it follows that

$$\sin^{-1}\frac{\sqrt{3}}{2} = \frac{\pi}{3}. \qquad \text{Angle whose sine is } \sqrt{3}/2$$

c. It is not possible to evaluate $y = \sin^{-1}x$ when $x = 2$ because there is no angle whose sine is 2. Remember that the domain of the inverse sine function is $[-1, 1]$.

✓CHECKPOINT Now try Exercise 1.

Example 2 Graphing the Arcsine Function

Sketch a graph of

$$y = \arcsin x.$$

Solution

By definition, the equations $y = \arcsin x$ and $\sin y = x$ are equivalent for $-\pi/2 \le y \le \pi/2$. So, their graphs are the same. From the interval $[-\pi/2, \pi/2]$, you can assign values to y in the second equation to make a table of values. Then plot the points and draw a smooth curve through the points.

y	$-\frac{\pi}{2}$	$-\frac{\pi}{4}$	$-\frac{\pi}{6}$	0	$\frac{\pi}{6}$	$\frac{\pi}{4}$	$\frac{\pi}{2}$
$x = \sin y$	-1	$-\frac{\sqrt{2}}{2}$	$-\frac{1}{2}$	0	$\frac{1}{2}$	$\frac{\sqrt{2}}{2}$	1

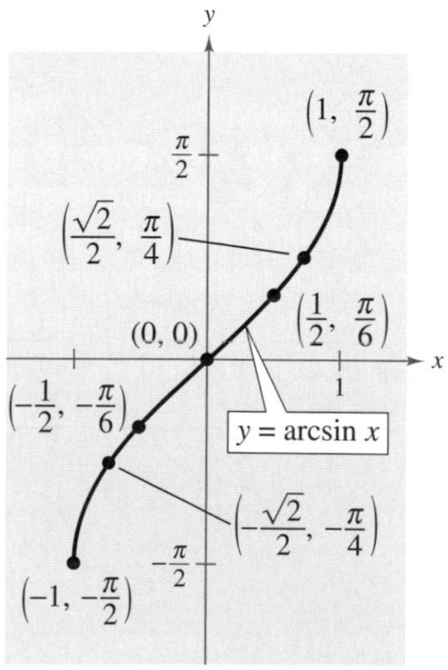

FIGURE 4.72

The resulting graph for $y = \arcsin x$ is shown in Figure 4.72. Note that it is the reflection (in the line $y = x$) of the black portion of the graph in Figure 4.71. Be sure you see that Figure 4.72 shows the *entire* graph of the inverse sine function. Remember that the domain of $y = \arcsin x$ is the closed interval $[-1, 1]$ and the range is the closed interval $[-\pi/2, \pi/2]$.

✓CHECKPOINT Now try Exercise 17.

Other Inverse Trigonometric Functions

The cosine function is decreasing and one-to-one on the interval $0 \leq x \leq \pi$, as shown in Figure 4.73.

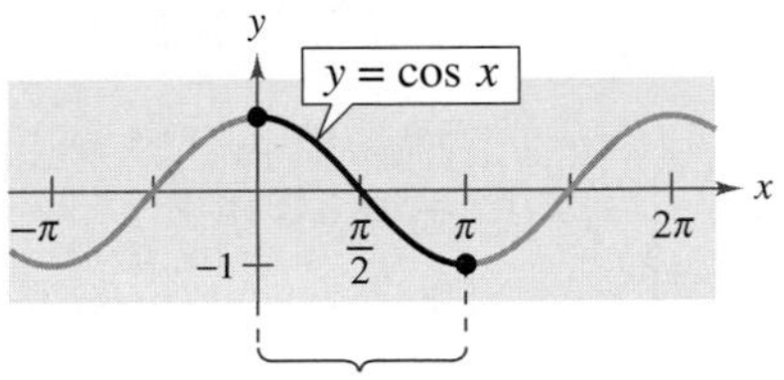

FIGURE 4.73

Consequently, on this interval the cosine function has an inverse function—the **inverse cosine function**—denoted by

$$y = \arccos x \qquad \text{or} \qquad y = \cos^{-1} x.$$

Similarly, you can define an **inverse tangent function** by restricting the domain of $y = \tan x$ to the interval $(-\pi/2, \pi/2)$. The following list summarizes the definitions of the three most common inverse trigonometric functions. The remaining three are defined in Exercises 101–103.

Definitions of the Inverse Trigonometric Functions

Function	*Domain*	*Range*
$y = \arcsin x$ if and only if $\sin y = x$	$-1 \leq x \leq 1$	$-\frac{\pi}{2} \leq y \leq \frac{\pi}{2}$
$y = \arccos x$ if and only if $\cos y = x$	$-1 \leq x \leq 1$	$0 \leq y \leq \pi$
$y = \arctan x$ if and only if $\tan y = x$	$-\infty < x < \infty$	$-\frac{\pi}{2} < y < \frac{\pi}{2}$

The graphs of these three inverse trigonometric functions are shown in Figure 4.74.

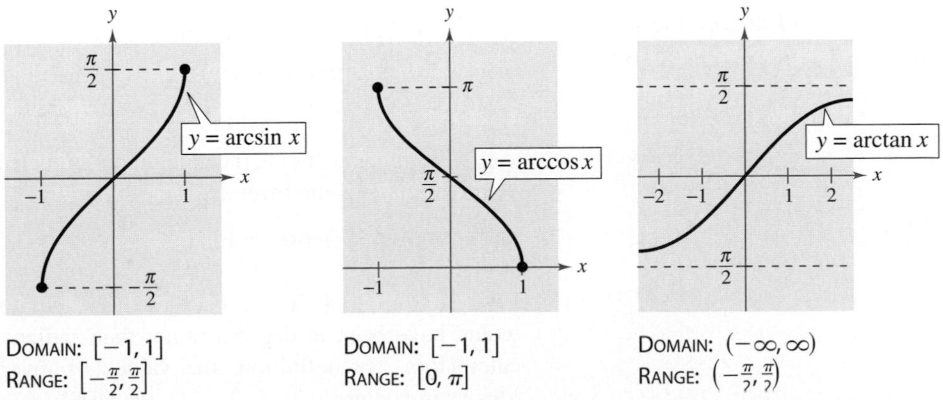

FIGURE 4.74

Example 3 Evaluating Inverse Trigonometric Functions

Find the exact value.

a. $\arccos \frac{\sqrt{2}}{2}$ **b.** $\cos^{-1}(-1)$

c. $\arctan 0$ **d.** $\tan^{-1}(-1)$

Solution

a. Because $\cos(\pi/4) = \sqrt{2}/2$, and $\pi/4$ lies in $[0, \pi]$, it follows that

$$\arccos \frac{\sqrt{2}}{2} = \frac{\pi}{4}.$$ Angle whose cosine is $\sqrt{2}/2$

b. Because $\cos \pi = -1$, and π lies in $[0, \pi]$, it follows that

$$\cos^{-1}(-1) = \pi.$$ Angle whose cosine is -1

c. Because $\tan 0 = 0$, and 0 lies in $(-\pi/2, \pi/2)$, it follows that

$$\arctan 0 = 0.$$ Angle whose tangent is 0

d. Because $\tan(-\pi/4) = -1$, and $-\pi/4$ lies in $(-\pi/2, \pi/2)$, it follows that

$$\tan^{-1}(-1) = -\frac{\pi}{4}.$$ Angle whose tangent is -1

CHECKPOINT Now try Exercise 11.

Example 4 Calculators and Inverse Trigonometric Functions

Use a calculator to approximate the value (if possible).

a. $\arctan(-8.45)$

b. $\sin^{-1} 0.2447$

c. $\arccos 2$

Solution

	Function	*Mode*	*Calculator Keystrokes*
a.	$\arctan(-8.45)$	Radian	TAN⁻¹ ((−) 8.45) ENTER

From the display, it follows that $\arctan(-8.45) \approx -1.453001$.

b.	$\sin^{-1} 0.2447$	Radian	SIN⁻¹ (0.2447) ENTER

From the display, it follows that $\sin^{-1} 0.2447 \approx 0.2472103$.

c.	$\arccos 2$	Radian	COS⁻¹ (2) ENTER

In *real number* mode, the calculator should display an *error message* because the domain of the inverse cosine function is $[-1, 1]$.

CHECKPOINT Now try Exercise 25.

STUDY TIP

It is important to remember that the domain of the inverse sine function and the inverse cosine function is $[-1, 1]$, as indicated in Example 4(c).

In Example 4, if you had set the calculator to *degree* mode, the displays would have been in degrees rather than radians. This convention is peculiar to calculators. By definition, the values of inverse trigonometric functions are *always in radians*.

Compositions of Functions

Recall from Section 1.9 that for all x in the domains of f and f^{-1}, inverse functions have the properties

$$f(f^{-1}(x)) = x \qquad \text{and} \qquad f^{-1}(f(x)) = x.$$

Inverse Properties of Trigonometric Functions

If $-1 \le x \le 1$ and $-\pi/2 \le y \le \pi/2$, then

$$\sin(\arcsin x) = x \qquad \text{and} \qquad \arcsin(\sin y) = y.$$

If $-1 \le x \le 1$ and $0 \le y \le \pi$, then

$$\cos(\arccos x) = x \qquad \text{and} \qquad \arccos(\cos y) = y.$$

If x is a real number and $-\pi/2 < y < \pi/2$, then

$$\tan(\arctan x) = x \qquad \text{and} \qquad \arctan(\tan y) = y.$$

Keep in mind that these inverse properties do not apply for arbitrary values of x and y. For instance,

$$\arcsin\left(\sin \frac{3\pi}{2}\right) = \arcsin(-1) = -\frac{\pi}{2} \neq \frac{3\pi}{2}.$$

In other words, the property

$$\arcsin(\sin y) = y$$

is not valid for values of y outside the interval $[-\pi/2, \pi/2]$.

Example 5 Using Inverse Properties

If possible, find the exact value.

a. $\tan[\arctan(-5)]$ **b.** $\arcsin\left(\sin \frac{5\pi}{3}\right)$ **c.** $\cos(\cos^{-1} \pi)$

Solution

a. Because -5 lies in the domain of the arctan function, the inverse property applies, and you have

$$\tan[\arctan(-5)] = -5.$$

b. In this case, $5\pi/3$ does not lie within the range of the arcsine function, $-\pi/2 \le y \le \pi/2$. However, $5\pi/3$ is coterminal with

$$\frac{5\pi}{3} - 2\pi = -\frac{\pi}{3}$$

which does lie in the range of the arcsine function, and you have

$$\arcsin\left(\sin \frac{5\pi}{3}\right) = \arcsin\left[\sin\left(-\frac{\pi}{3}\right)\right] = -\frac{\pi}{3}.$$

c. The expression $\cos(\cos^{-1} \pi)$ is not defined because $\cos^{-1} \pi$ is not defined. Remember that the domain of the inverse cosine function is $[-1, 1]$.

CHECKPOINT Now try Exercise 43.

Example 6 shows how to use right triangles to find exact values of compositions of inverse functions. Then, Example 7 shows how to use right triangles to convert a trigonometric expression into an algebraic expression. This conversion technique is used frequently in calculus.

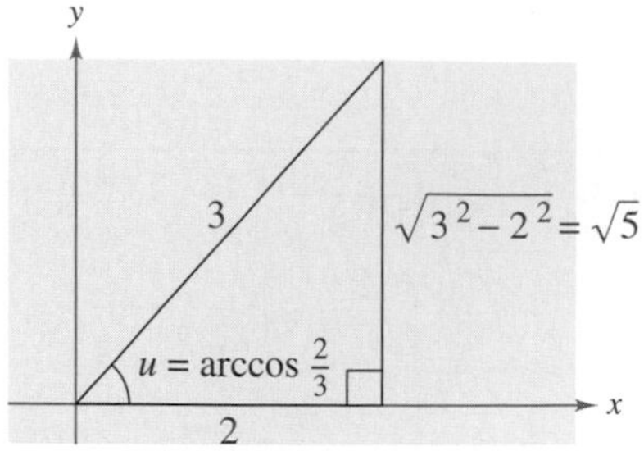

Angle whose cosine is $\frac{2}{3}$
FIGURE 4.75

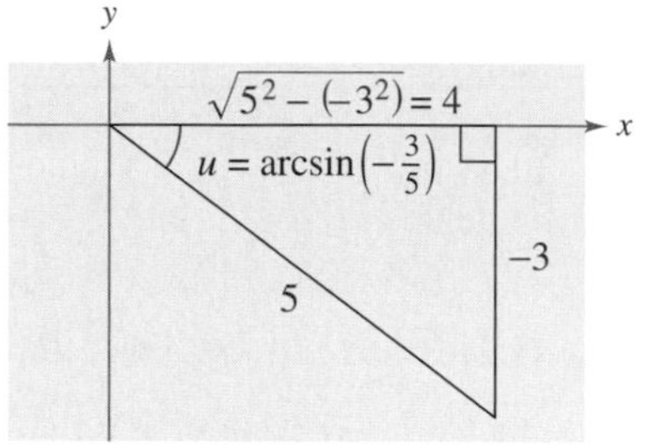

Angle whose sine is $-\frac{3}{5}$
FIGURE 4.76

Example 6 Evaluating Compositions of Functions

Find the exact value.

a. $\tan\left(\arccos \dfrac{2}{3}\right)$ **b.** $\cos\left[\arcsin\left(-\dfrac{3}{5}\right)\right]$

Solution

a. If you let $u = \arccos \frac{2}{3}$, then $\cos u = \frac{2}{3}$. Because $\cos u$ is positive, u is a *first*-quadrant angle. You can sketch and label angle u as shown in Figure 4.75. Consequently,

$$\tan\left(\arccos \frac{2}{3}\right) = \tan u = \frac{\text{opp}}{\text{adj}} = \frac{\sqrt{5}}{2}.$$

b. If you let $u = \arcsin\left(-\frac{3}{5}\right)$, then $\sin u = -\frac{3}{5}$. Because $\sin u$ is negative, u is a *fourth*-quadrant angle. You can sketch and label angle u as shown in Figure 4.76. Consequently,

$$\cos\left[\arcsin\left(-\frac{3}{5}\right)\right] = \cos u = \frac{\text{adj}}{\text{hyp}} = \frac{4}{5}.$$

CHECKPOINT Now try Exercise 51.

Example 7 Some Problems from Calculus

Write each of the following as an algebraic expression in x.

a. $\sin(\arccos 3x), \quad 0 \le x \le \dfrac{1}{3}$ **b.** $\cot(\arccos 3x), \quad 0 \le x < \dfrac{1}{3}$

Solution

If you let $u = \arccos 3x$, then $\cos u = 3x$, where $-1 \le 3x \le 1$. Because

$$\cos u = \frac{\text{adj}}{\text{hyp}} = \frac{3x}{1}$$

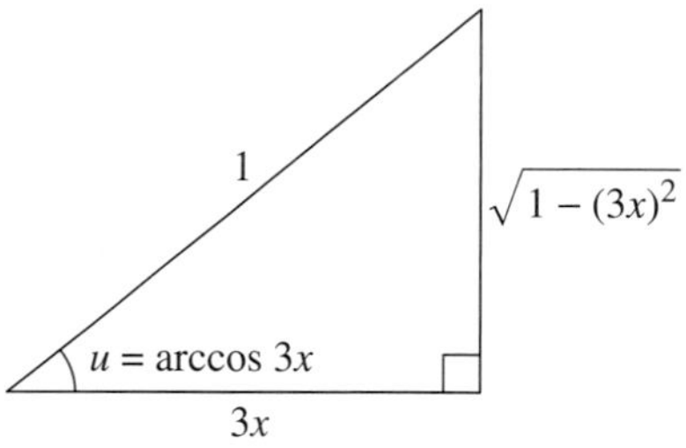

Angle whose cosine is 3x
FIGURE 4.77

you can sketch a right triangle with acute angle u, as shown in Figure 4.77. From this triangle, you can easily convert each expression to algebraic form.

a. $\sin(\arccos 3x) = \sin u = \dfrac{\text{opp}}{\text{hyp}} = \sqrt{1-9x^2}, \quad 0 \le x \le \dfrac{1}{3}$

b. $\cot(\arccos 3x) = \cot u = \dfrac{\text{adj}}{\text{opp}} = \dfrac{3x}{\sqrt{1-9x^2}}, \quad 0 \le x < \dfrac{1}{3}$

CHECKPOINT Now try Exercise 59.

In Example 7, similar arguments can be made for x-values lying in the interval $\left[-\frac{1}{3}, 0\right]$.

4.7 Exercises

VOCABULARY CHECK: Fill in the blanks.

	Function	*Alternative Notation*	*Domain*	*Range*
1.	$y = \arcsin x$	______	______	$-\frac{\pi}{2} \le y \le \frac{\pi}{2}$
2.	______	$y = \cos^{-1} x$	$-1 \le x \le 1$	______
3.	$y = \arctan x$	______	______	______

In Exercises 1–16, evaluate the expression without using a calculator.

1. $\arcsin \frac{1}{2}$
2. $\arcsin 0$
3. $\arccos \frac{1}{2}$
4. $\arccos 0$
5. $\arctan \frac{\sqrt{3}}{3}$
6. $\arctan(-1)$
7. $\cos^{-1}\left(-\frac{\sqrt{3}}{2}\right)$
8. $\sin^{-1}\left(-\frac{\sqrt{2}}{2}\right)$
9. $\arctan(-\sqrt{3})$
10. $\arctan \sqrt{3}$
11. $\arccos\left(-\frac{1}{2}\right)$
12. $\arcsin \frac{\sqrt{2}}{2}$
13. $\sin^{-1} \frac{\sqrt{3}}{2}$
14. $\tan^{-1}\left(-\frac{\sqrt{3}}{3}\right)$
15. $\tan^{-1} 0$
16. $\cos^{-1} 1$

In Exercises 17 and 18, use a graphing utility to graph f, g, and $y = x$ in the same viewing window to verify geometrically that g is the inverse function of f. (Be sure to restrict the domain of f properly.)

17. $f(x) = \sin x, \quad g(x) = \arcsin x$
18. $f(x) = \tan x, \quad g(x) = \arctan x$

In Exercises 19–34, use a calculator to evaluate the expression. Round your result to two decimal places.

19. $\arccos 0.28$
20. $\arcsin 0.45$
21. $\arcsin(-0.75)$
22. $\arccos(-0.7)$
23. $\arctan(-3)$
24. $\arctan 15$
25. $\sin^{-1} 0.31$
26. $\cos^{-1} 0.26$
27. $\arccos(-0.41)$
28. $\arcsin(-0.125)$
29. $\arctan 0.92$
30. $\arctan 2.8$
31. $\arcsin \frac{3}{4}$
32. $\arccos\left(-\frac{1}{3}\right)$
33. $\tan^{-1} \frac{7}{2}$
34. $\tan^{-1}\left(-\frac{95}{7}\right)$

In Exercises 35 and 36, determine the missing coordinates of the points on the graph of the function.

35.

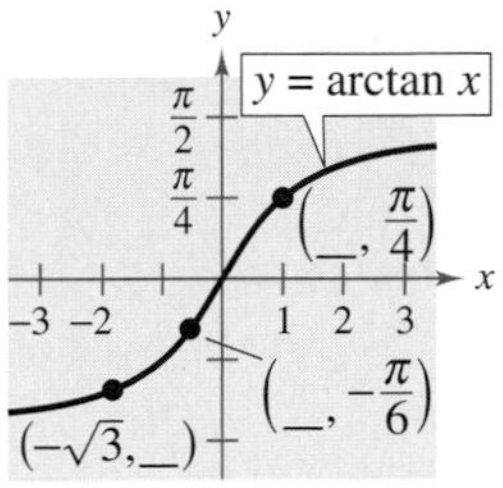

36.

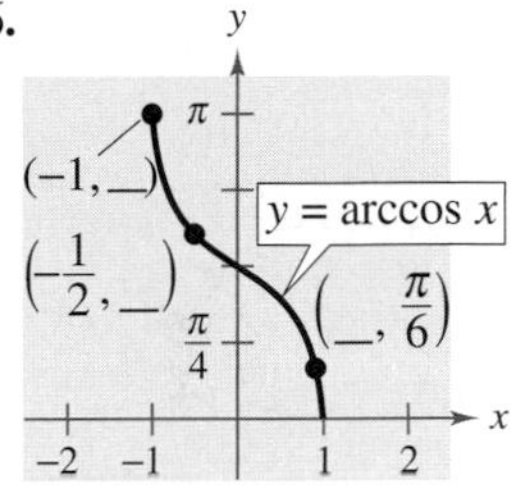

In Exercises 37–42, use an inverse trigonometric function to write θ as a function of x.

37.

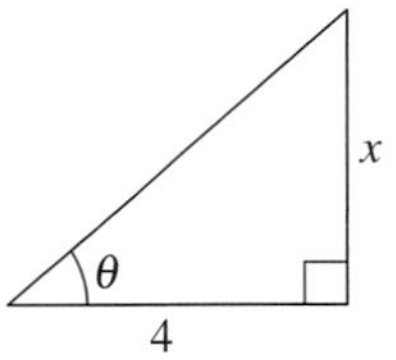

38.

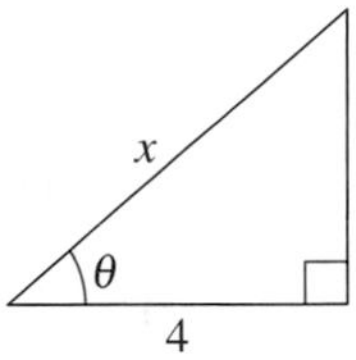

39.

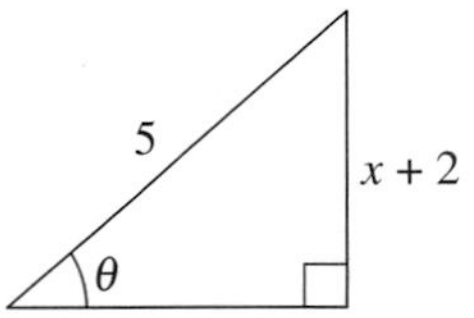

40.

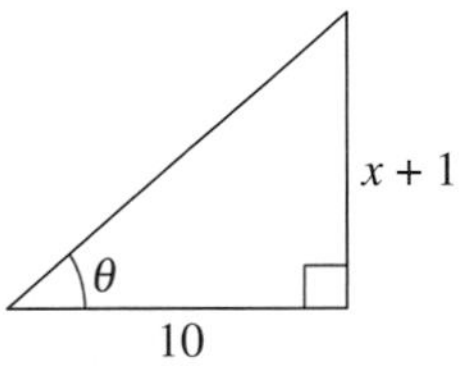

41.

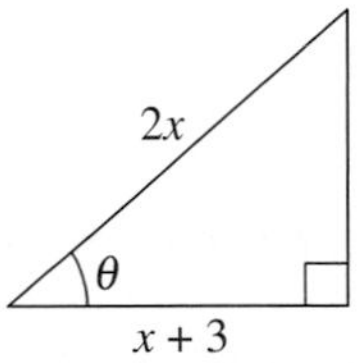

42.

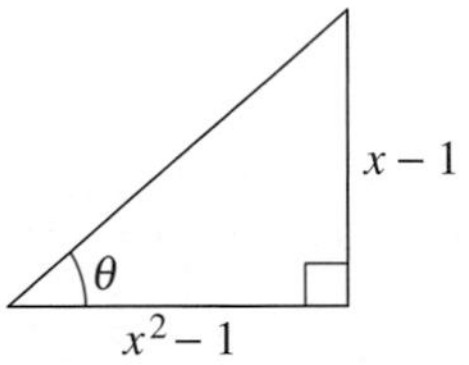

In Exercises 43–48, use the properties of inverse trigonometric functions to evaluate the expression.

43. $\sin(\arcsin 0.3)$
44. $\tan(\arctan 25)$
45. $\cos[\arccos(-0.1)]$
46. $\sin[\arcsin(-0.2)]$
47. $\arcsin(\sin 3\pi)$
48. $\arccos\left(\cos \frac{7\pi}{2}\right)$

In Exercises 49–58, find the exact value of the expression. (*Hint:* Sketch a right triangle.)

49. $\sin\left(\arctan \frac{3}{4}\right)$ **50.** $\sec\left(\arcsin \frac{4}{5}\right)$

51. $\cos(\tan^{-1} 2)$ **52.** $\sin\left(\cos^{-1} \frac{\sqrt{5}}{5}\right)$

53. $\cos\left(\arcsin \frac{5}{13}\right)$ **54.** $\csc\left[\arctan\left(-\frac{5}{12}\right)\right]$

55. $\sec\left[\arctan\left(-\frac{3}{5}\right)\right]$ **56.** $\tan\left[\arcsin\left(-\frac{3}{4}\right)\right]$

57. $\sin\left[\arccos\left(-\frac{2}{3}\right)\right]$ **58.** $\cot\left(\arctan \frac{5}{8}\right)$

In Exercises 59–68, write an algebraic expression that is equivalent to the expression. (*Hint:* Sketch a right triangle, as demonstrated in Example 7.)

59. $\cot(\arctan x)$ **60.** $\sin(\arctan x)$

61. $\cos(\arcsin 2x)$ **62.** $\sec(\arctan 3x)$

63. $\sin(\arccos x)$ **64.** $\sec[\arcsin(x - 1)]$

65. $\tan\left(\arccos \frac{x}{3}\right)$

66. $\cot\left(\arctan \frac{1}{x}\right)$

67. $\csc\left(\arctan \frac{x}{\sqrt{2}}\right)$

68. $\cos\left(\arcsin \frac{x - h}{r}\right)$

In Exercises 69 and 70, use a graphing utility to graph *f* and *g* in the same viewing window to verify that the two functions are equal. Explain why they are equal. Identify any asymptotes of the graphs.

69. $f(x) = \sin(\arctan 2x), \quad g(x) = \dfrac{2x}{\sqrt{1 + 4x^2}}$

70. $f(x) = \tan\left(\arccos \dfrac{x}{2}\right), \quad g(x) = \dfrac{\sqrt{4 - x^2}}{x}$

In Exercises 71–74, fill in the blank.

71. $\arctan \dfrac{9}{x} = \arcsin(\quad), \quad x \neq 0$

72. $\arcsin \dfrac{\sqrt{36 - x^2}}{6} = \arccos(\quad), \quad 0 \le x \le 6$

73. $\arccos \dfrac{3}{\sqrt{x^2 - 2x + 10}} = \arcsin(\quad)$

74. $\arccos \dfrac{x - 2}{2} = \arctan(\quad), \quad |x - 2| \le 2$

In Exercises 75 and 76, sketch a graph of the function and compare the graph of *g* with the graph of $f(x) = \arcsin x$.

75. $g(x) = \arcsin(x - 1)$ **76.** $g(x) = \arcsin \dfrac{x}{2}$

In Exercises 77–82, sketch a graph of the function.

77. $y = 2 \arccos x$

78. $g(t) = \arccos(t + 2)$

79. $f(x) = \arctan 2x$

80. $f(x) = \dfrac{\pi}{2} + \arctan x$

81. $h(v) = \tan(\arccos v)$

82. $f(x) = \arccos \dfrac{x}{4}$

In Exercises 83–88, use a graphing utility to graph the function.

83. $f(x) = 2 \arccos(2x)$

84. $f(x) = \pi \arcsin(4x)$

85. $f(x) = \arctan(2x - 3)$

86. $f(x) = -3 + \arctan(\pi x)$

87. $f(x) = \pi - \sin^{-1}\left(\dfrac{2}{3}\right)$

88. $f(x) = \dfrac{\pi}{2} + \cos^{-1}\left(\dfrac{1}{\pi}\right)$

In Exercises 89 and 90, write the function in terms of the sine function by using the identity

$$A \cos \omega t + B \sin \omega t = \sqrt{A^2 + B^2} \sin\left(\omega t + \arctan \frac{A}{B}\right).$$

Use a graphing utility to graph both forms of the function. What does the graph imply?

89. $f(t) = 3 \cos 2t + 3 \sin 2t$

90. $f(t) = 4 \cos \pi t + 3 \sin \pi t$

91. ***Docking a Boat*** A boat is pulled in by means of a winch located on a dock 5 feet above the deck of the boat (see figure). Let θ be the angle of elevation from the boat to the winch and let s be the length of the rope from the winch to the boat.

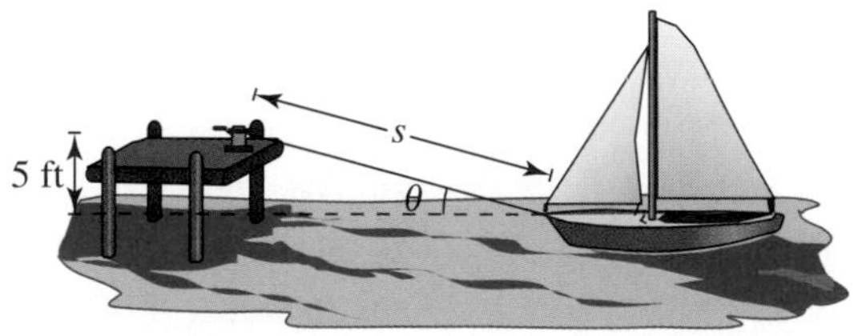

(a) Write θ as a function of s.

(b) Find θ when $s = 40$ feet and $s = 20$ feet.

92. ***Photography*** A television camera at ground level is filming the lift-off of a space shuttle at a point 750 meters from the launch pad (see figure). Let θ be the angle of elevation to the shuttle and let s be the height of the shuttle.

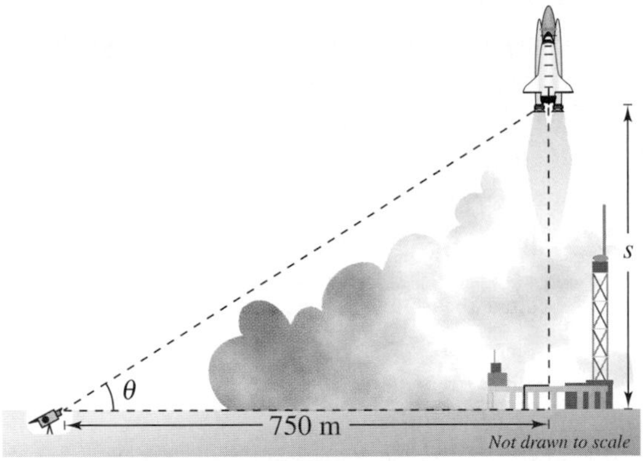

(a) Write θ as a function of s.

(b) Find θ when $s = 300$ meters and $s = 1200$ meters.

Model It

93. ***Photography*** A photographer is taking a picture of a three-foot-tall painting hung in an art gallery. The camera lens is 1 foot below the lower edge of the painting (see figure). The angle β subtended by the camera lens x feet from the painting is

$$\beta = \arctan \frac{3x}{x^2 + 4}, \quad x > 0.$$

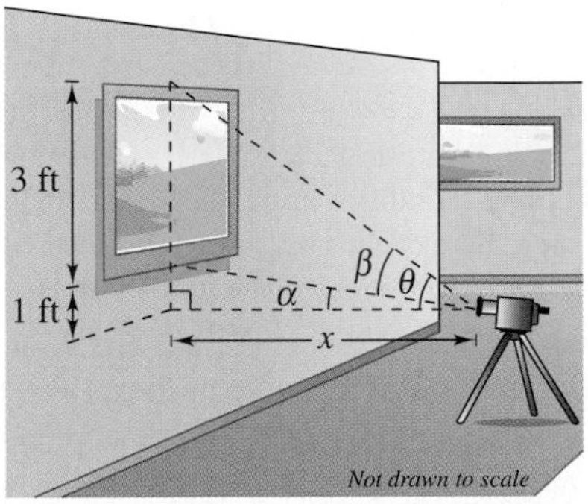

(a) Use a graphing utility to graph β as a function of x.

(b) Move the cursor along the graph to approximate the distance from the picture when β is maximum.

(c) Identify the asymptote of the graph and discuss its meaning in the context of the problem.

94. ***Granular Angle of Repose*** Different types of granular substances naturally settle at different angles when stored in cone-shaped piles. This angle θ is called the *angle of repose* (see figure). When rock salt is stored in a cone-shaped pile 11 feet high, the diameter of the pile's base is about 34 feet. (Source: Bulk-Store Structures, Inc.)

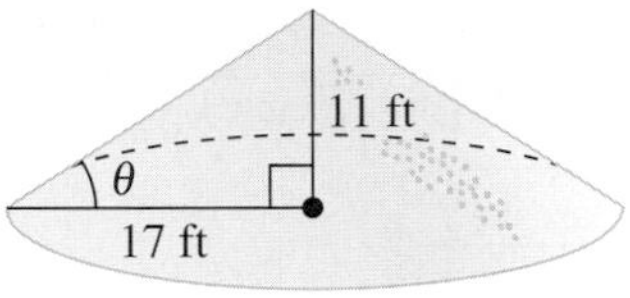

(a) Find the angle of repose for rock salt.

(b) How tall is a pile of rock salt that has a base diameter of 40 feet?

95. ***Granular Angle of Repose*** When whole corn is stored in a cone-shaped pile 20 feet high, the diameter of the pile's base is about 82 feet.

(a) Find the angle of repose for whole corn.

(b) How tall is a pile of corn that has a base diameter of 100 feet?

96. ***Angle of Elevation*** An airplane flies at an altitude of 6 miles toward a point directly over an observer. Consider θ and x as shown in the figure.

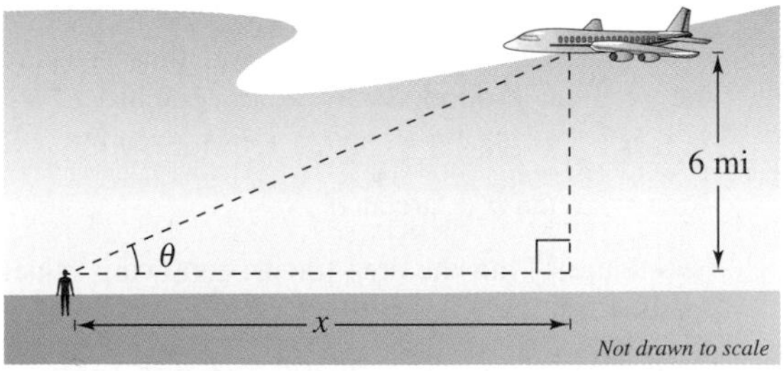

(a) Write θ as a function of x.

(b) Find θ when $x = 7$ miles and $x = 1$ mile.

97. ***Security Patrol*** A security car with its spotlight on is parked 20 meters from a warehouse. Consider θ and x as shown in the figure.

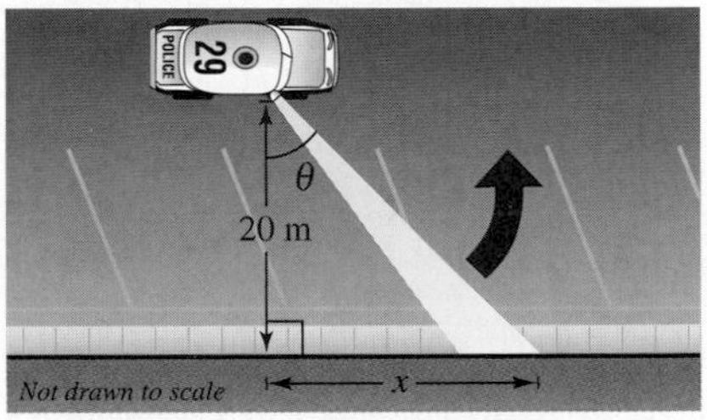

(a) Write θ as a function of x.

(b) Find θ when $x = 5$ meters and $x = 12$ meters.

Synthesis

True or False? **In Exercises 98–100, determine whether the statement is true or false. Justify your answer.**

98. $\sin \frac{5\pi}{6} = \frac{1}{2}$ ⟹ $\arcsin \frac{1}{2} = \frac{5\pi}{6}$

99. $\tan \frac{5\pi}{4} = 1$ ⟹ $\arctan 1 = \frac{5\pi}{4}$

100. $\arctan x = \dfrac{\arcsin x}{\arccos x}$

101. Define the inverse cotangent function by restricting the domain of the cotangent function to the interval $(0, \pi)$, and sketch its graph.

102. Define the inverse secant function by restricting the domain of the secant function to the intervals $[0, \pi/2)$ and $(\pi/2, \pi]$, and sketch its graph.

103. Define the inverse cosecant function by restricting the domain of the cosecant function to the intervals $[-\pi/2, 0)$ and $(0, \pi/2]$, and sketch its graph.

104. Use the results of Exercises 101–103 to evaluate each expression without using a calculator.

(a) $\operatorname{arcsec} \sqrt{2}$ (b) $\operatorname{arcsec} 1$

(c) $\operatorname{arccot}(-\sqrt{3})$ (d) $\operatorname{arccsc} 2$

105. ***Area*** In calculus, it is shown that the area of the region bounded by the graphs of $y = 0$, $y = 1/(x^2 + 1)$, $x = a$, and $x = b$ is given by

Area $= \arctan b - \arctan a$

(see figure). Find the area for the following values of a and b.

(a) $a = 0, b = 1$ (b) $a = -1, b = 1$

(c) $a = 0, b = 3$ (d) $a = -1, b = 3$

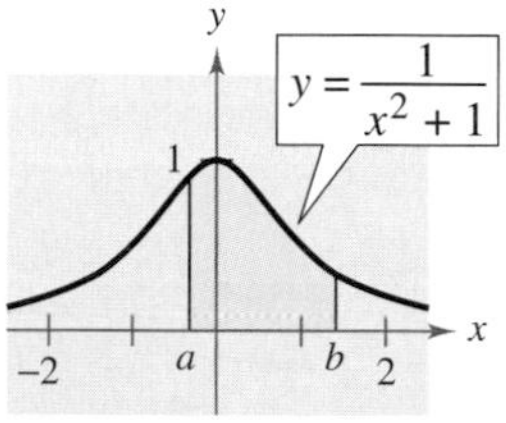

106. ***Think About It*** Use a graphing utility to graph the functions

$f(x) = \sqrt{x}$ and $g(x) = 6 \arctan x$.

For $x > 0$, it appears that $g > f$. Explain why you know that there exists a positive real number a such that $g < f$ for $x > a$. Approximate the number a.

107. ***Think About It*** Consider the functions given by

$f(x) = \sin x$ and $f^{-1}(x) = \arcsin x$.

(a) Use a graphing utility to graph the composite functions $f \circ f^{-1}$ and $f^{-1} \circ f$.

(b) Explain why the graphs in part (a) are not the graph of the line $y = x$. Why do the graphs of $f \circ f^{-1}$ and $f^{-1} \circ f$ differ?

108. ***Proof*** Prove each identity.

(a) $\arcsin(-x) = -\arcsin x$

(b) $\arctan(-x) = -\arctan x$

(c) $\arctan x + \arctan \frac{1}{x} = \frac{\pi}{2}, \quad x > 0$

(d) $\arcsin x + \arccos x = \frac{\pi}{2}$

(e) $\arcsin x = \arctan \dfrac{x}{\sqrt{1 - x^2}}$

Skills Review

In Exercises 109–112, evaluate the expression. Round your result to three decimal places.

109. $(8.2)^{3.4}$ **110.** $10(14)^{-2}$

111. $(1.1)^{50}$ **112.** $16^{-2\pi}$

In Exercises 113–116, sketch a right triangle corresponding to the trigonometric function of the acute angle θ. Use the Pythagorean Theorem to determine the third side. Then find the other five trigonometric functions of θ.

113. $\sin \theta = \frac{3}{4}$ **114.** $\tan \theta = 2$

115. $\cos \theta = \frac{5}{6}$ **116.** $\sec \theta = 3$

117. ***Partnership Costs*** A group of people agree to share equally in the cost of a \$250,000 endowment to a college. If they could find two more people to join the group, each person's share of the cost would decrease by \$6250. How many people are presently in the group?

118. ***Speed*** A boat travels at a speed of 18 miles per hour in still water. It travels 35 miles upstream and then returns to the starting point in a total of 4 hours. Find the speed of the current.

119. ***Compound Interest*** A total of \$15,000 is invested in an account that pays an annual interest rate of 3.5%. Find the balance in the account after 10 years, if interest is compounded (a) quarterly, (b) monthly, (c) daily, and (d) continuously.

120. ***Profit*** Because of a slump in the economy, a department store finds that its annual profits have dropped from \$742,000 in 2002 to \$632,000 in 2004. The profit follows an exponential pattern of decline. What is the expected profit for 2008? (Let $t = 2$ represent 2002.)

4.8 Applications and Models

What you should learn

- Solve real-life problems involving right triangles.
- Solve real-life problems involving directional bearings.
- Solve real-life problems involving harmonic motion.

Why you should learn it

Right triangles often occur in real-life situations. For instance, in Exercise 62 on page 362, right triangles are used to determine the shortest grain elevator for a grain storage bin on a farm.

Applications Involving Right Triangles

In this section, the three angles of a right triangle are denoted by the letters A, B, and C (where C is the right angle), and the lengths of the sides opposite these angles by the letters a, b, and c (where c is the hypotenuse).

Example 1 **Solving a Right Triangle**

Solve the right triangle shown in Figure 4.78 for all unknown sides and angles.

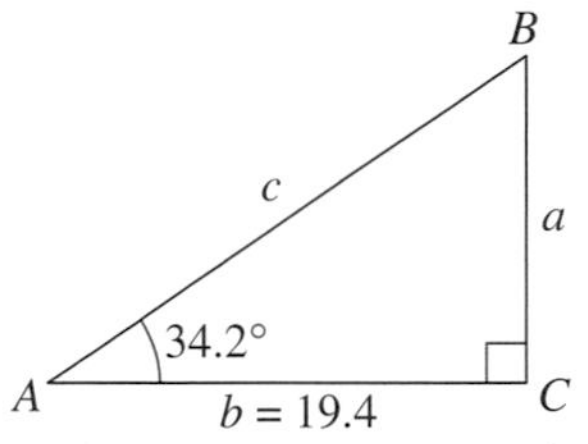

FIGURE 4.78

Solution

Because $C = 90°$, it follows that $A + B = 90°$ and $B = 90° - 34.2° = 55.8°$. To solve for a, use the fact that

$$\tan A = \frac{\text{opp}}{\text{adj}} = \frac{a}{b} \quad \Longrightarrow \quad a = b \tan A.$$

So, $a = 19.4 \tan 34.2° \approx 13.18$. Similarly, to solve for c, use the fact that

$$\cos A = \frac{\text{adj}}{\text{hyp}} = \frac{b}{c} \quad \Longrightarrow \quad c = \frac{b}{\cos A}.$$

So, $c = \dfrac{19.4}{\cos 34.2°} \approx 23.46$.

✓CHECKPOINT Now try Exercise 1.

Example 2 **Finding a Side of a Right Triangle**

A safety regulation states that the maximum angle of elevation for a rescue ladder is 72°. A fire department's longest ladder is 110 feet. What is the maximum safe rescue height?

Solution

A sketch is shown in Figure 4.79. From the equation $\sin A = a/c$, it follows that

$$a = c \sin A = 110 \sin 72° \approx 104.6.$$

So, the maximum safe rescue height is about 104.6 feet above the height of the fire truck.

✓CHECKPOINT Now try Exercise 15.

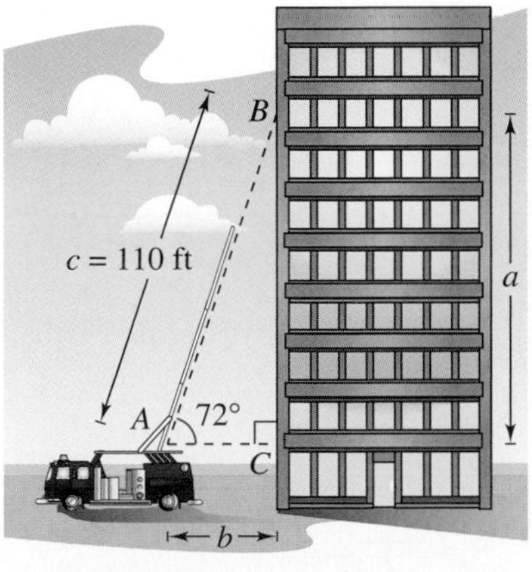

FIGURE 4.79

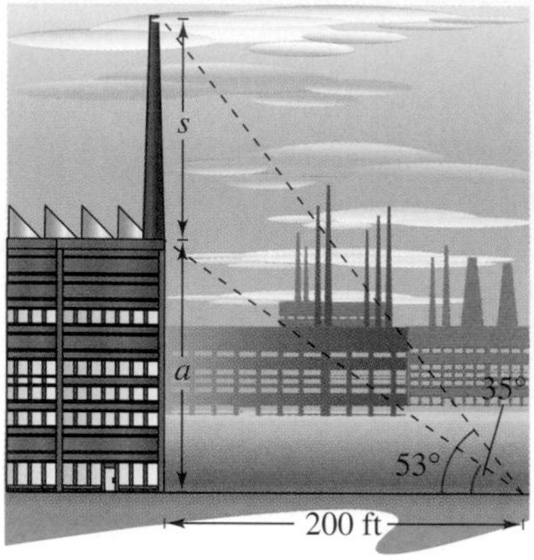

FIGURE 4.80

Example 3 Finding a Side of a Right Triangle

At a point 200 feet from the base of a building, the angle of elevation to the *bottom* of a smokestack is 35°, whereas the angle of elevation to the *top* is 53°, as shown in Figure 4.80. Find the height s of the smokestack alone.

Solution

Note from Figure 4.80 that this problem involves two right triangles. For the smaller right triangle, use the fact that

$$\tan 35° = \frac{a}{200}$$

to conclude that the height of the building is

$$a = 200 \tan 35°.$$

For the larger right triangle, use the equation

$$\tan 53° = \frac{a + s}{200}$$

to conclude that $a + s = 200 \tan 53°$. So, the height of the smokestack is

$$\begin{aligned} s &= 200 \tan 53° - a \\ &= 200 \tan 53° - 200 \tan 35° \\ &\approx 125.4 \text{ feet.} \end{aligned}$$

CHECKPOINT Now try Exercise 19.

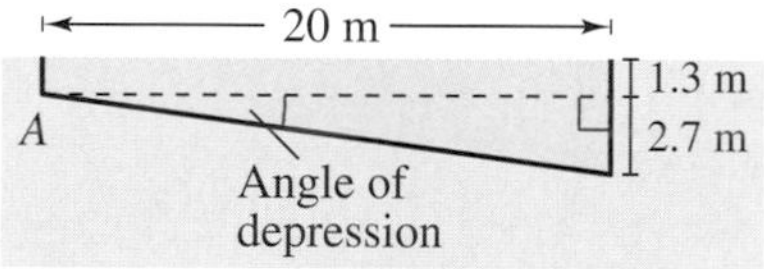

FIGURE 4.81

Example 4 Finding an Acute Angle of a Right Triangle

A swimming pool is 20 meters long and 12 meters wide. The bottom of the pool is slanted so that the water depth is 1.3 meters at the shallow end and 4 meters at the deep end, as shown in Figure 4.81. Find the angle of depression of the bottom of the pool.

Solution

Using the tangent function, you can see that

$$\begin{aligned} \tan A &= \frac{\text{opp}}{\text{adj}} \\ &= \frac{2.7}{20} \\ &= 0.135. \end{aligned}$$

So, the angle of depression is

$$\begin{aligned} A &= \arctan 0.135 \\ &\approx 0.13419 \text{ radian} \\ &\approx 7.69°. \end{aligned}$$

CHECKPOINT Now try Exercise 25.

Trigonometry and Bearings

In surveying and navigation, directions are generally given in terms of **bearings.** A bearing measures the acute angle that a path or line of sight makes with a fixed north-south line, as shown in Figure 4.82. For instance, the bearing S 35° E in Figure 4.82 means 35 degrees east of south.

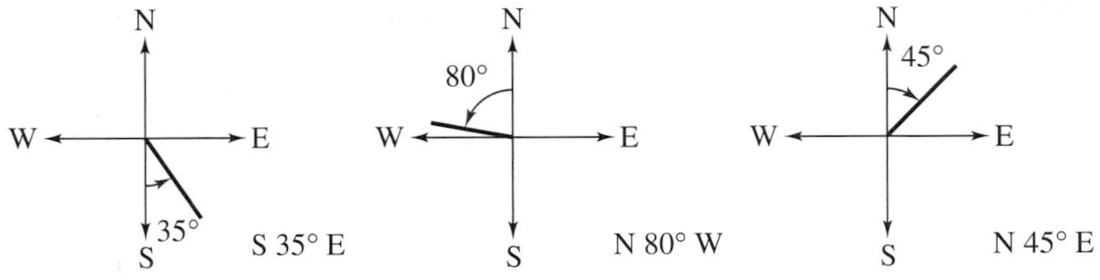

FIGURE 4.82

Example 5 **Finding Directions in Terms of Bearings**

A ship leaves port at noon and heads due west at 20 knots, or 20 nautical miles (nm) per hour. At 2 P.M. the ship changes course to N 54° W, as shown in Figure 4.83. Find the ship's bearing and distance from the port of departure at 3 P.M.

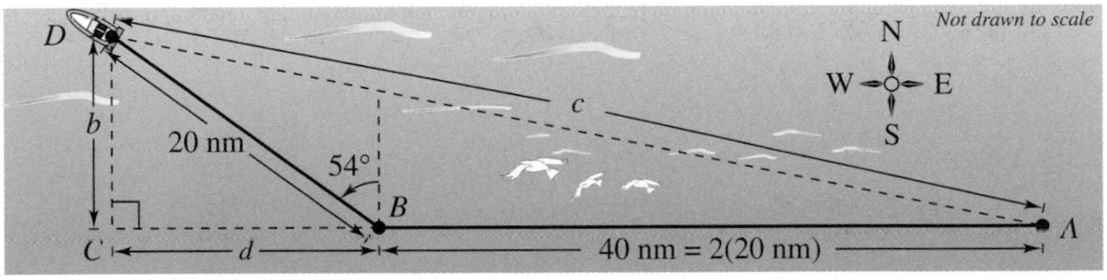

FIGURE 4.83

Solution

For triangle BCD, you have $B = 90° - 54° = 36°$. The two sides of this triangle can be determined to be

$$b = 20 \sin 36° \quad \text{and} \quad d = 20 \cos 36°.$$

For triangle ACD, you can find angle A as follows.

$$\tan A = \frac{b}{d + 40} = \frac{20 \sin 36°}{20 \cos 36° + 40} \approx 0.2092494$$

$$A \approx \arctan 0.2092494 \approx 0.2062732 \text{ radian} \approx 11.82°$$

The angle with the north-south line is $90° - 11.82° = 78.18°$. So, the bearing of the ship is N 78.18° W. Finally, from triangle ACD, you have $\sin A = b/c$, which yields

$$c = \frac{b}{\sin A} = \frac{20 \sin 36°}{\sin 11.82°}$$

$$\approx 57.4 \text{ nautical miles.} \qquad \text{Distance from port}$$

✓CHECKPOINT Now try Exercise 31.

STUDY TIP

In *air navigation*, bearings are measured in degrees *clockwise* from north. Examples of air navigation bearings are shown below.

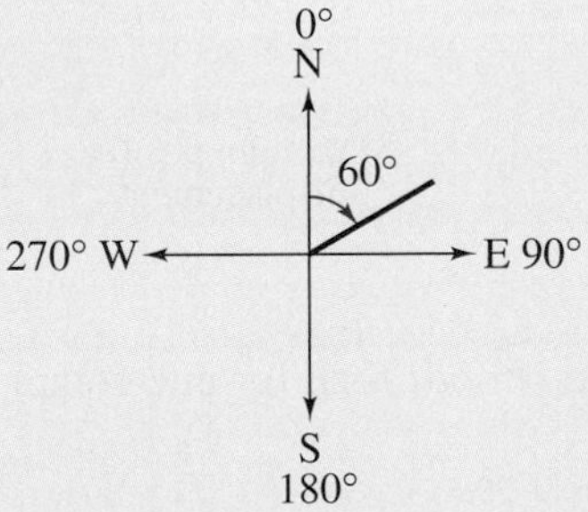

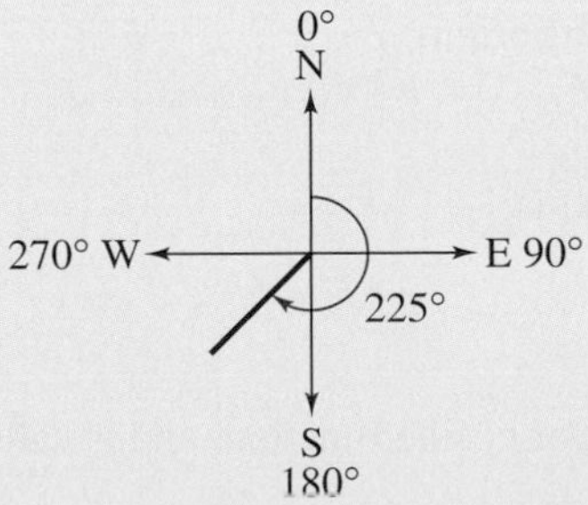

Harmonic Motion

The periodic nature of the trigonometric functions is useful for describing the motion of a point on an object that vibrates, oscillates, rotates, or is moved by wave motion.

For example, consider a ball that is bobbing up and down on the end of a spring, as shown in Figure 4.84. Suppose that 10 centimeters is the maximum distance the ball moves vertically upward or downward from its equilibrium (at rest) position. Suppose further that the time it takes for the ball to move from its maximum displacement above zero to its maximum displacement below zero and back again is $t = 4$ seconds. Assuming the ideal conditions of perfect elasticity and no friction or air resistance, the ball would continue to move up and down in a uniform and regular manner.

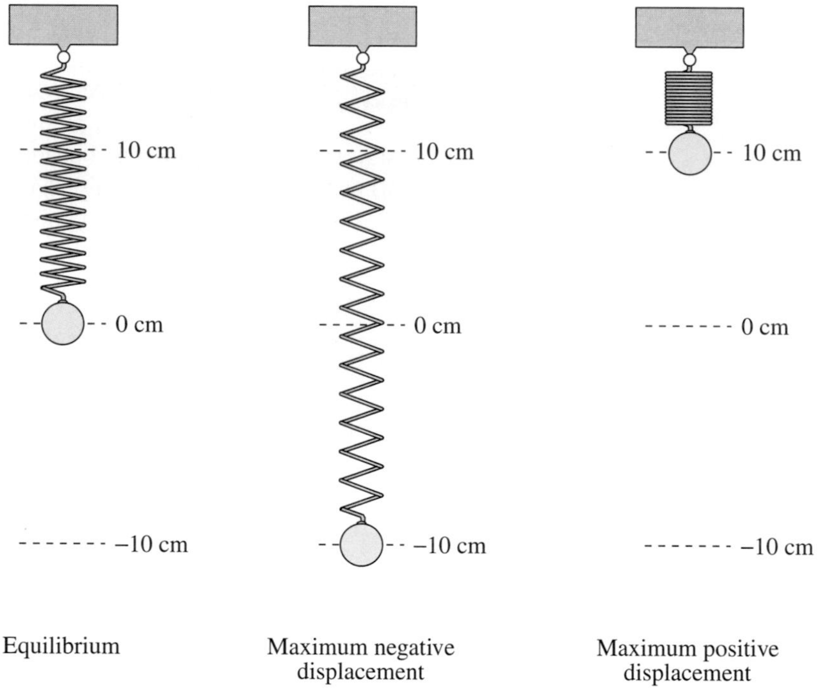

FIGURE 4.84

From this spring you can conclude that the period (time for one complete cycle) of the motion is

Period $= 4$ seconds

its amplitude (maximum displacement from equilibrium) is

Amplitude $= 10$ centimeters

and its **frequency** (number of cycles per second) is

Frequency $= \frac{1}{4}$ cycle per second.

Motion of this nature can be described by a sine or cosine function, and is called **simple harmonic motion.**

Definition of Simple Harmonic Motion

A point that moves on a coordinate line is said to be in **simple harmonic motion** if its distance d from the origin at time t is given by either

$$d = a \sin \omega t \qquad \text{or} \qquad d = a \cos \omega t$$

where a and ω are real numbers such that $\omega > 0$. The motion has amplitude $|a|$, period $2\pi/\omega$, and frequency $\omega/(2\pi)$.

Example 6 Simple Harmonic Motion

Write the equation for the simple harmonic motion of the ball described in Figure 4.84, where the period is 4 seconds. What is the frequency of this harmonic motion?

Solution

Because the spring is at equilibrium ($d = 0$) when $t = 0$, you use the equation

$$d = a \sin \omega t.$$

Moreover, because the maximum displacement from zero is 10 and the period is 4, you have

$$\text{Amplitude} = |a| = 10$$

$$\text{Period} = \frac{2\pi}{\omega} = 4 \quad \Rightarrow \quad \omega = \frac{\pi}{2}.$$

Consequently, the equation of motion is

$$d = 10 \sin \frac{\pi}{2} t.$$

Note that the choice of $a = 10$ or $a = -10$ depends on whether the ball initially moves up or down. The frequency is

$$\text{Frequency} = \frac{\omega}{2\pi}$$

$$= \frac{\pi/2}{2\pi}$$

$$= \frac{1}{4} \text{ cycle per second.}$$

FIGURE 4.85

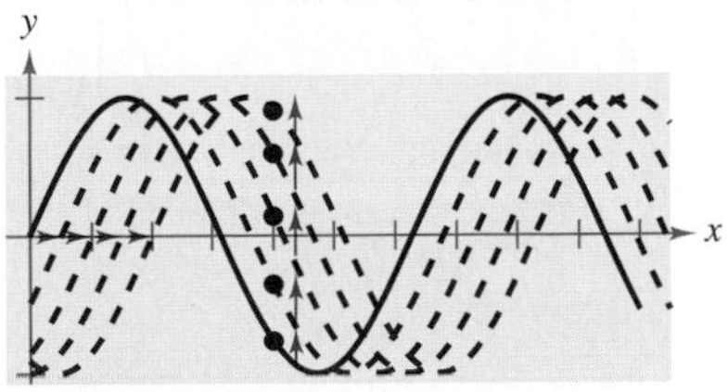

FIGURE 4.86

✓CHECKPOINT Now try Exercise 51.

One illustration of the relationship between sine waves and harmonic motion can be seen in the wave motion resulting when a stone is dropped into a calm pool of water. The waves move outward in roughly the shape of sine (or cosine) waves, as shown in Figure 4.85. As an example, suppose you are fishing and your fishing bob is attached so that it does not move horizontally. As the waves move outward from the dropped stone, your fishing bob will move up and down in simple harmonic motion, as shown in Figure 4.86.

Example 7 Simple Harmonic Motion

Given the equation for simple harmonic motion

$$d = 6\cos\frac{3\pi}{4}t$$

find (a) the maximum displacement, (b) the frequency, (c) the value of d when $t = 4$, and (d) the least positive value of t for which $d = 0$.

Algebraic Solution

The given equation has the form $d = a\cos\omega t$, with $a = 6$ and $\omega = 3\pi/4$.

a. The maximum displacement (from the point of equilibrium) is given by the amplitude. So, the maximum displacement is 6.

b. $$\text{Frequency} = \frac{\omega}{2\pi}$$

$$= \frac{3\pi/4}{2\pi} = \frac{3}{8} \text{ cycle per unit of time}$$

c. $$d = 6\cos\left[\frac{3\pi}{4}(4)\right]$$

$$= 6\cos 3\pi$$

$$= 6(-1)$$

$$= -6$$

d. To find the least positive value of t for which $d = 0$, solve the equation

$$d = 6\cos\frac{3\pi}{4}t = 0.$$

First divide each side by 6 to obtain

$$\cos\frac{3\pi}{4}t = 0.$$

This equation is satisfied when

$$\frac{3\pi}{4}t = \frac{\pi}{2}, \frac{3\pi}{2}, \frac{5\pi}{2}, \ldots.$$

Multiply these values by $4/(3\pi)$ to obtain

$$t = \frac{2}{3}, 2, \frac{10}{3}, \ldots.$$

So, the least positive value of t is $t = \frac{2}{3}$.

CHECKPOINT Now try Exercise 55.

Graphical Solution

Use a graphing utility set in *radian* mode to graph

$$y = 6\cos\frac{3\pi}{4}x.$$

a. Use the *maximum* feature of the graphing utility to estimate that the maximum displacement from the point of equilibrium $y = 0$ is 6, as shown in Figure 4.87.

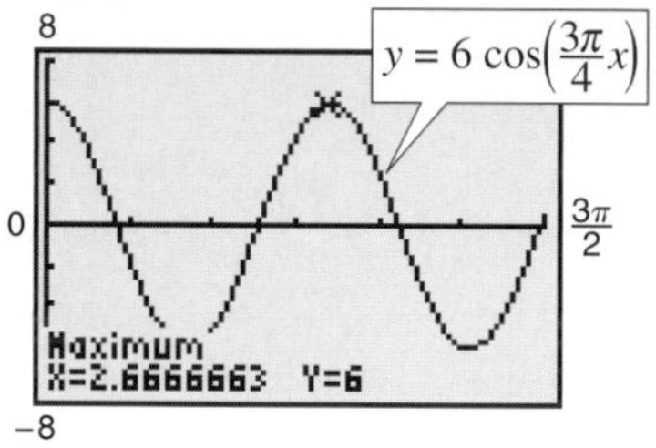

FIGURE 4.87

b. The period is the time for the graph to complete one cycle, which is $x \approx 2.667$. You can estimate the frequency as follows.

$$\text{Frequency} \approx \frac{1}{2.667} \approx 0.375 \text{ cycle per unit of time}$$

c. Use the *trace* feature to estimate that the value of y when $x = 4$ is $y = -6$, as shown in Figure 4.88.

d. Use the *zero* or *root* feature to estimate that the least positive value of x for which $y = 0$ is $x \approx 0.6667$, as shown in Figure 4.89.

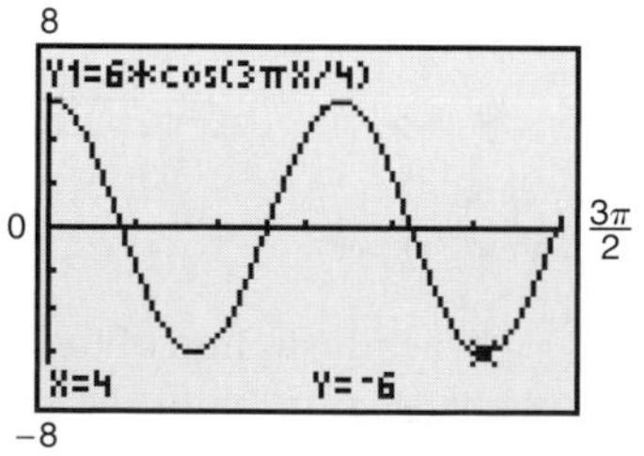

FIGURE 4.88

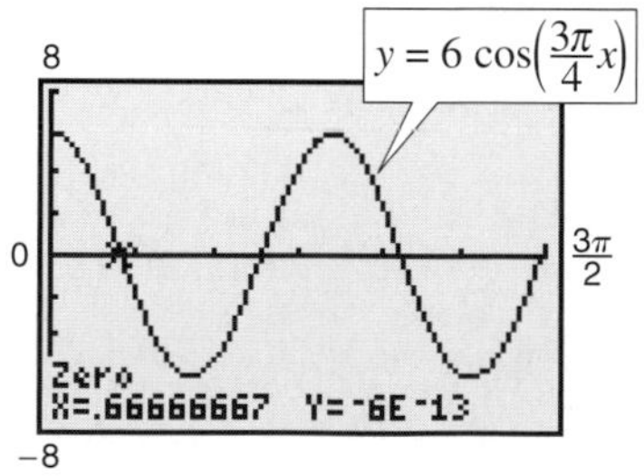

FIGURE 4.89

4.8 Exercises

VOCABULARY CHECK: Fill in the blanks.

1. An angle that measures from the horizontal upward to an object is called the angle of ________, whereas an angle that measures from the horizontal downward to an object is called the angle of ________.
2. A ________ measures the acute angle a path or line of sight makes with a fixed north-south line.
3. A point that moves on a coordinate line is said to be in simple ________ ________ if its distance d from the origin at time t is given by either $d = a \sin \omega t$ or $d = a \cos \omega t$.

In Exercises 1–10, solve the right triangle shown in the figure. Round your answers to two decimal places.

1. $A = 20°$, $b = 10$
2. $B = 54°$, $c = 15$
3. $B = 71°$, $b = 24$
4. $A = 8.4°$, $a = 40.5$
5. $a = 6$, $b = 10$
6. $a = 25$, $c = 35$
7. $b = 16$, $c = 52$
8. $b = 1.32$, $c = 9.45$
9. $A = 12°15'$, $c = 430.5$
10. $B = 65°12'$, $a = 14.2$

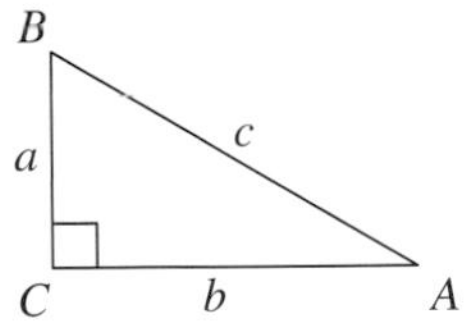

FIGURE FOR 1–10

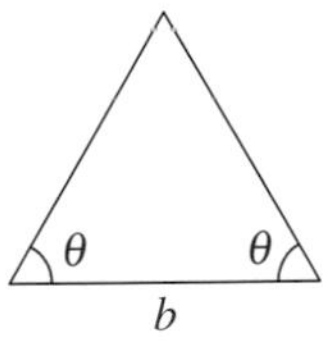

FIGURE FOR 11–14

In Exercises 11–14, find the altitude of the isosceles triangle shown in the figure. Round your answers to two decimal places.

11. $\theta = 52°$, $b = 4$ inches
12. $\theta = 18°$, $b = 10$ meters
13. $\theta = 41°$, $b = 46$ inches
14. $\theta = 27°$, $b = 11$ feet

15. ***Length*** The sun is 25° above the horizon. Find the length of a shadow cast by a silo that is 50 feet tall (see figure).

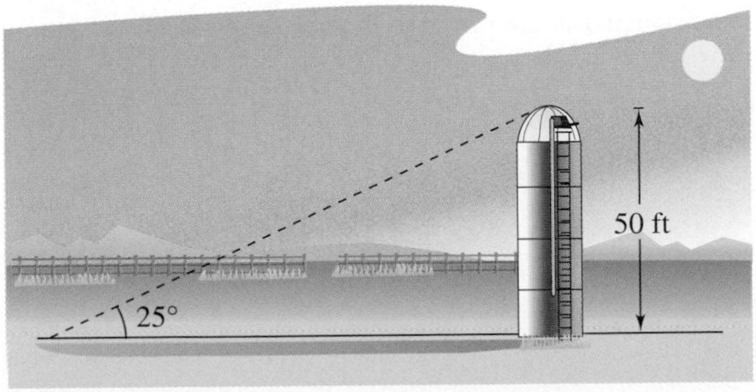

16. ***Length*** The sun is 20° above the horizon. Find the length of a shadow cast by a building that is 600 feet tall.
17. ***Height*** A ladder 20 feet long leans against the side of a house. Find the height from the top of the ladder to the ground if the angle of elevation of the ladder is 80°.
18. ***Height*** The length of a shadow of a tree is 125 feet when the angle of elevation of the sun is 33°. Approximate the height of the tree.
19. ***Height*** From a point 50 feet in front of a church, the angles of elevation to the base of the steeple and the top of the steeple are 35° and 47° 40′, respectively.
    (a) Draw right triangles that give a visual representation of the problem. Label the known and unknown quantities.
    (b) Use a trigonometric function to write an equation involving the unknown quantity.
    (c) Find the height of the steeple.
20. ***Height*** You are standing 100 feet from the base of a platform from which people are bungee jumping. The angle of elevation from your position to the top of the platform from which they jump is 51°. From what height are the people jumping?
21. ***Depth*** The sonar of a navy cruiser detects a submarine that is 4000 feet from the cruiser. The angle between the water line and the submarine is 34° (see figure). How deep is the submarine?

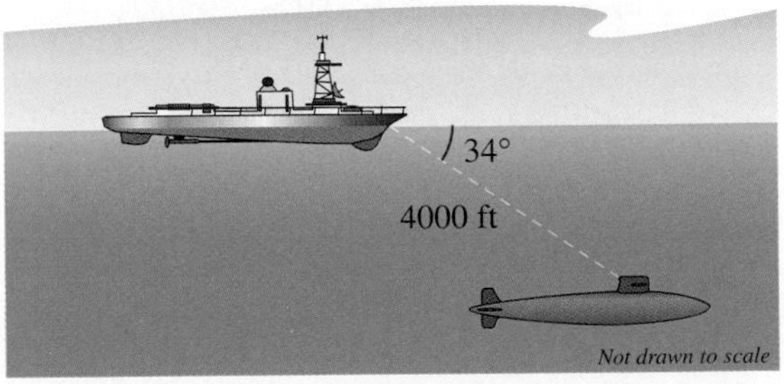

22. ***Angle of Elevation*** An engineer erects a 75-foot cellular telephone tower. Find the angle of elevation to the top of the tower at a point on level ground 50 feet from its base.

23. ***Angle of Elevation*** The height of an outdoor basketball backboard is $12\frac{1}{2}$ feet, and the backboard casts a shadow $17\frac{1}{3}$ feet long.

(a) Draw a right triangle that gives a visual representation of the problem. Label the known and unknown quantities.

(b) Use a trigonometric function to write an equation involving the unknown quantity.

(c) Find the angle of elevation of the sun.

24. ***Angle of Depression*** A Global Positioning System satellite orbits 12,500 miles above Earth's surface (see figure). Find the angle of depression from the satellite to the horizon. Assume the radius of Earth is 4000 miles.

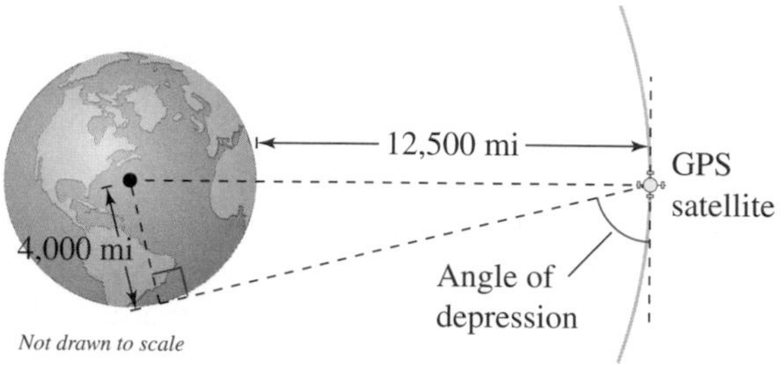

25. ***Angle of Depression*** A cellular telephone tower that is 150 feet tall is placed on top of a mountain that is 1200 feet above sea level. What is the angle of depression from the top of the tower to a cell phone user who is 5 horizontal miles away and 400 feet above sea level?

26. ***Airplane Ascent*** During takeoff, an airplane's angle of ascent is 18° and its speed is 275 feet per second.

(a) Find the plane's altitude after 1 minute.

(b) How long will it take the plane to climb to an altitude of 10,000 feet?

27. ***Mountain Descent*** A sign on a roadway at the top of a mountain indicates that for the next 4 miles the grade is 10.5° (see figure). Find the change in elevation over that distance for a car descending the mountain.

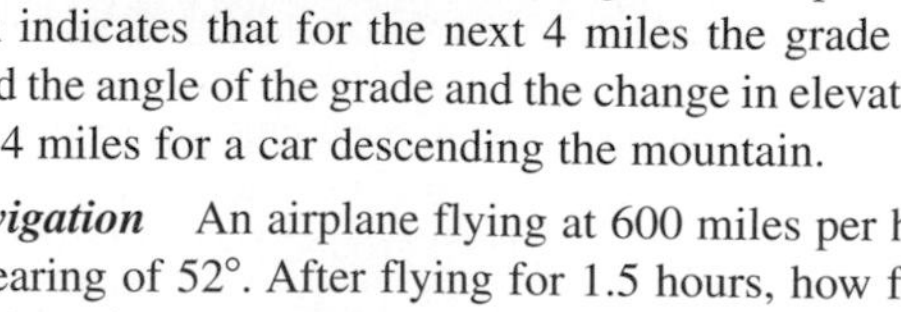

28. ***Mountain Descent*** A roadway sign at the top of a mountain indicates that for the next 4 miles the grade is 12%. Find the angle of the grade and the change in elevation over the 4 miles for a car descending the mountain.

29. ***Navigation*** An airplane flying at 600 miles per hour has a bearing of 52°. After flying for 1.5 hours, how far north and how far east will the plane have traveled from its point of departure?

30. ***Navigation*** A jet leaves Reno, Nevada and is headed toward Miami, Florida at a bearing of 100°. The distance between the two cities is approximately 2472 miles.

(a) How far north and how far west is Reno relative to Miami?

(b) If the jet is to return directly to Reno from Miami, at what bearing should it travel?

31. ***Navigation*** A ship leaves port at noon and has a bearing of S 29° W. The ship sails at 20 knots.

(a) How many nautical miles south and how many nautical miles west will the ship have traveled by 6:00 P.M.?

(b) At 6:00 P.M., the ship changes course to due west. Find the ship's bearing and distance from the port of departure at 7:00 P.M.

32. ***Navigation*** A privately owned yacht leaves a dock in Myrtle Beach, South Carolina and heads toward Freeport in the Bahamas at a bearing of S 1.4° E. The yacht averages a speed of 20 knots over the 428 nautical-mile trip.

(a) How long will it take the yacht to make the trip?

(b) How far east and south is the yacht after 12 hours?

(c) If a plane leaves Myrtle Beach to fly to Freeport, what bearing should be taken?

33. ***Surveying*** A surveyor wants to find the distance across a swamp (see figure). The bearing from A to B is N 32° W. The surveyor walks 50 meters from A, and at the point C the bearing to B is N 68° W. Find (a) the bearing from A to C and (b) the distance from A to B.

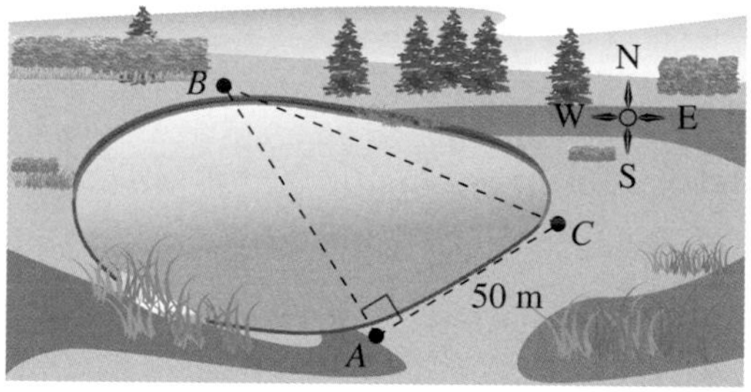

34. ***Location of a Fire*** Two fire towers are 30 kilometers apart, where tower A is due west of tower B. A fire is spotted from the towers, and the bearings from A and B are E 14° N and W 34° N, respectively (see figure). Find the distance d of the fire from the line segment AB.

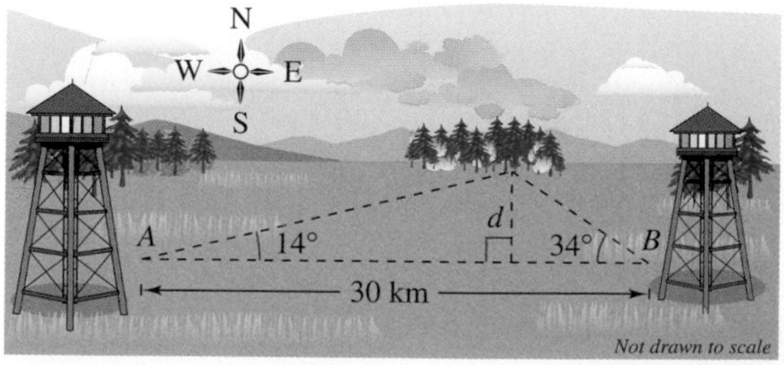

35. ***Navigation*** A ship is 45 miles east and 30 miles south of port. The captain wants to sail directly to port. What bearing should be taken?

36. ***Navigation*** An airplane is 160 miles north and 85 miles east of an airport. The pilot wants to fly directly to the airport. What bearing should be taken?

37. ***Distance*** An observer in a lighthouse 350 feet above sea level observes two ships directly offshore. The angles of depression to the ships are 4° and 6.5° (see figure). How far apart are the ships?

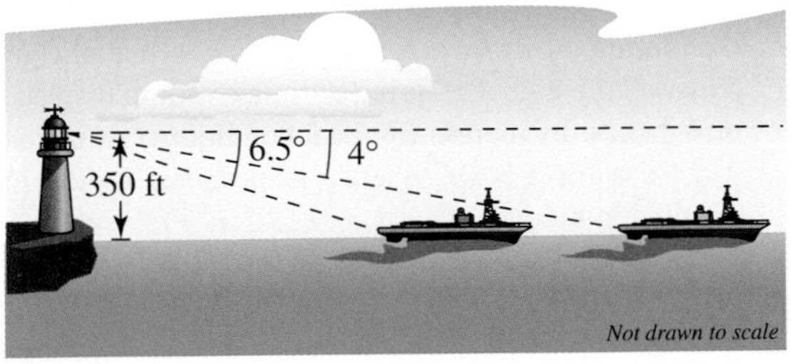

38. ***Distance*** A passenger in an airplane at an altitude of 10 kilometers sees two towns directly to the east of the plane. The angles of depression to the towns are 28° and 55° (see figure). How far apart are the towns?

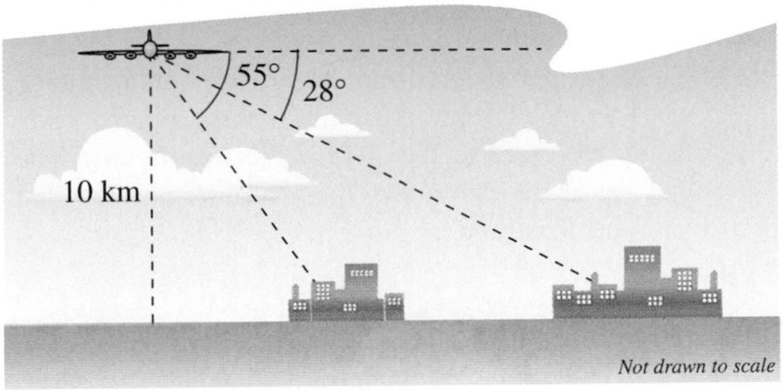

39. ***Altitude*** A plane is observed approaching your home and you assume that its speed is 550 miles per hour. The angle of elevation of the plane is 16° at one time and 57° one minute later. Approximate the altitude of the plane.

40. ***Height*** While traveling across flat land, you notice a mountain directly in front of you. The angle of elevation to the peak is 2.5°. After you drive 17 miles closer to the mountain, the angle of elevation is 9°. Approximate the height of the mountain.

Geometry **In Exercises 41 and 42, find the angle α between two nonvertical lines L_1 and L_2. The angle α satisfies the equation**

$$\tan \alpha = \left| \frac{m_2 - m_1}{1 + m_2 m_1} \right|$$

where m_1 and m_2 are the slopes of L_1 and L_2, respectively. (Assume that $m_1 m_2 \neq -1$.)

41. L_1: $3x - 2y = 5$
L_2: $x + y = 1$

42. L_1: $2x - y = 8$
L_2: $x - 5y = -4$

43. ***Geometry*** Determine the angle between the diagonal of a cube and the diagonal of its base, as shown in the figure.

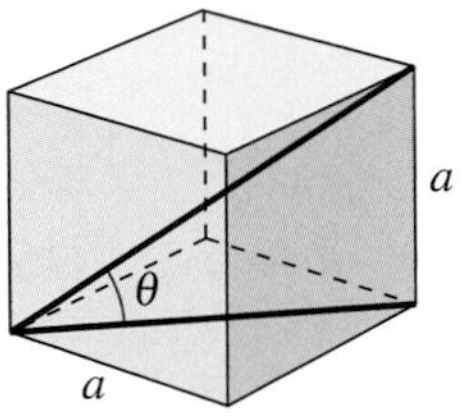

FIGURE FOR 43

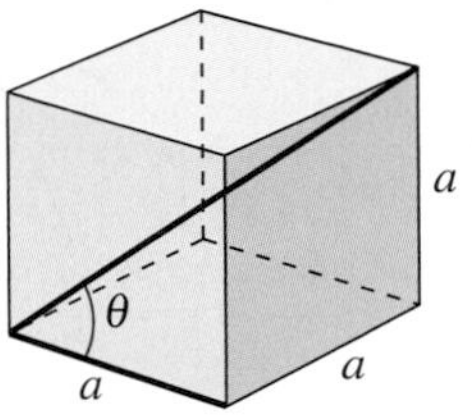

FIGURE FOR 44

44. ***Geometry*** Determine the angle between the diagonal of a cube and its edge, as shown in the figure.

45. ***Geometry*** Find the length of the sides of a regular pentagon inscribed in a circle of radius 25 inches.

46. ***Geometry*** Find the length of the sides of a regular hexagon inscribed in a circle of radius 25 inches.

47. ***Hardware*** Write the distance y across the flat sides of a hexagonal nut as a function of r, as shown in the figure.

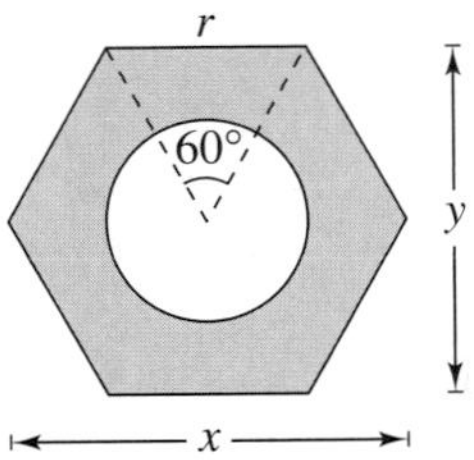

48. ***Bolt Holes*** The figure shows a circular piece of sheet metal that has a diameter of 40 centimeters and contains 12 equally spaced bolt holes. Determine the straight-line distance between the centers of consecutive bolt holes.

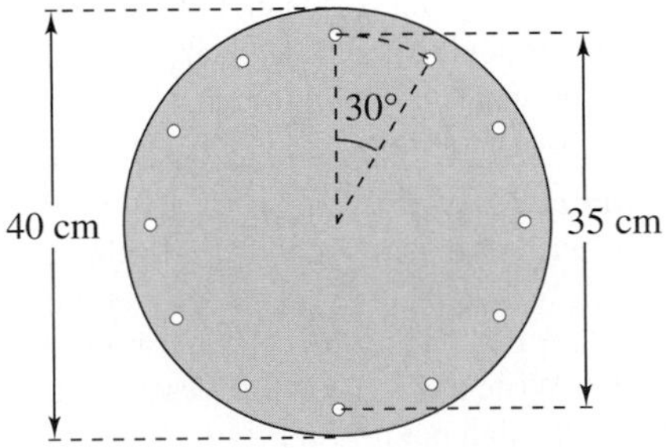

Trusses **In Exercises 49 and 50, find the lengths of all the unknown members of the truss.**

49.

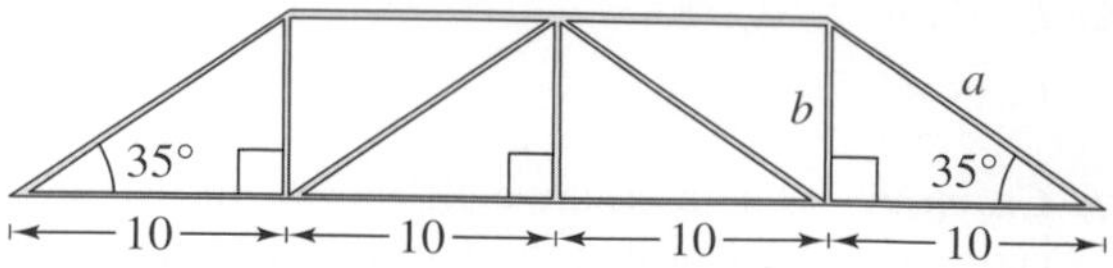

50.

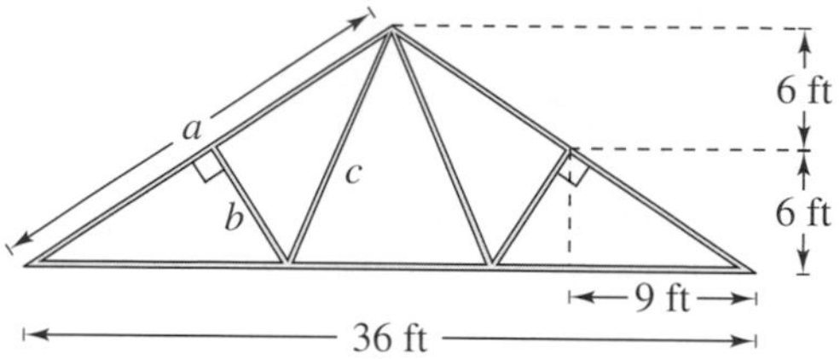

Harmonic Motion **In Exercises 51–54, find a model for simple harmonic motion satisfying the specified conditions.**

	Displacement $(t = 0)$	*Amplitude*	*Period*
51.	0	4 centimeters	2 seconds
52.	0	3 meters	6 seconds
53.	3 inches	3 inches	1.5 seconds
54.	2 feet	2 feet	10 seconds

Harmonic Motion **In Exercises 55–58, for the simple harmonic motion described by the trigonometric function, find (a) the maximum displacement, (b) the frequency, (c) the value of d when $t = 5$, and (d) the least positive value of t for which $d = 0$. Use a graphing utility to verify your results.**

55. $d = 4 \cos 8\pi t$

56. $d = \frac{1}{2} \cos 20\pi t$

57. $d = \frac{1}{16} \sin 120\pi t$

58. $d = \frac{1}{64} \sin 792\pi t$

59. ***Tuning Fork*** A point on the end of a tuning fork moves in simple harmonic motion described by $d = a \sin \omega t$. Find ω given that the tuning fork for middle C has a frequency of 264 vibrations per second.

60. ***Wave Motion*** A buoy oscillates in simple harmonic motion as waves go past. It is noted that the buoy moves a total of 3.5 feet from its low point to its high point (see figure), and that it returns to its high point every 10 seconds. Write an equation that describes the motion of the buoy if its high point is at $t = 0$.

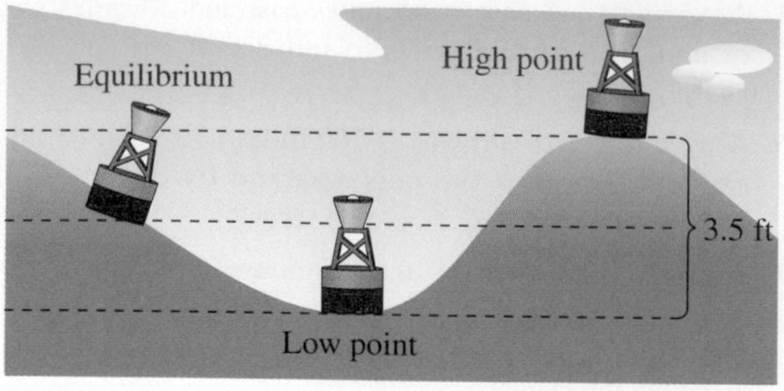

FIGURE FOR 60

61. ***Oscillation of a Spring*** A ball that is bobbing up and down on the end of a spring has a maximum displacement of 3 inches. Its motion (in ideal conditions) is modeled by $y = \frac{1}{4} \cos 16t$ $(t > 0)$, where y is measured in feet and t is the time in seconds.

(a) Graph the function.

(b) What is the period of the oscillations?

(c) Determine the first time the weight passes the point of equilibrium $(y = 0)$.

Model It

62. ***Numerical and Graphical Analysis*** A two-meter-high fence is 3 meters from the side of a grain storage bin. A grain elevator must reach from ground level outside the fence to the storage bin (see figure). The objective is to determine the shortest elevator that meets the constraints.

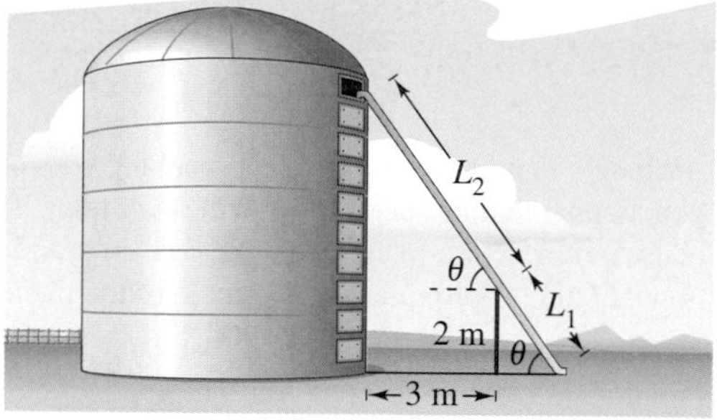

(a) Complete four rows of the table.

θ	L_1	L_2	$L_1 + L_2$
0.1	$\frac{2}{\sin 0.1}$	$\frac{3}{\cos 0.1}$	23.0
0.2	$\frac{2}{\sin 0.2}$	$\frac{3}{\cos 0.2}$	13.1

Model It (continued)

(b) Use a graphing utility to generate additional rows of the table. Use the table to estimate the minimum length of the elevator.

(c) Write the length $L_1 + L_2$ as a function of θ.

(d) Use a graphing utility to graph the function. Use the graph to estimate the minimum length. How does your estimate compare with that of part (b)?

63. *Numerical and Graphical Analysis* The cross section of an irrigation canal is an isosceles trapezoid of which three of the sides are 8 feet long (see figure). The objective is to find the angle θ that maximizes the area of the cross section. [*Hint:* The area of a trapezoid is $(h/2)(b_1 + b_2)$.]

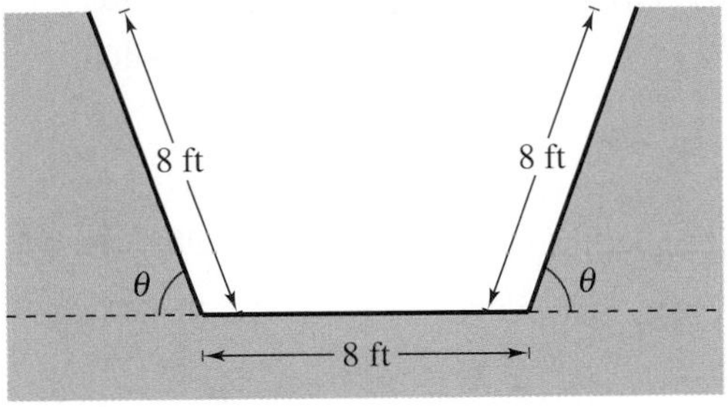

(a) Complete seven additional rows of the table.

Base 1	Base 2	Altitude	Area
8	$8 + 16 \cos 10°$	$8 \sin 10°$	22.1
8	$8 + 16 \cos 20°$	$8 \sin 20°$	42.5

(b) Use a graphing utility to generate additional rows of the table. Use the table to estimate the maximum cross-sectional area.

(c) Write the area A as a function of θ.

(d) Use a graphing utility to graph the function. Use the graph to estimate the maximum cross-sectional area. How does your estimate compare with that of part (b)?

64. *Data Analysis* The table shows the average sales S (in millions of dollars) of an outerwear manufacturer for each month t, where $t = 1$ represents January.

Time, t	1	2	3	4	5	6
Sales, s	13.46	11.15	8.00	4.85	2.54	1.70

Time, t	7	8	9	10	11	12
Sales, s	2.54	4.85	8.00	11.15	13.46	14.3

(a) Create a scatter plot of the data.

(b) Find a trigonometric model that fits the data. Graph the model with your scatter plot. How well does the model fit the data?

(c) What is the period of the model? Do you think it is reasonable given the context? Explain your reasoning.

(d) Interpret the meaning of the model's amplitude in the context of the problem.

Synthesis

True or False? **In Exercises 65 and 66, determine whether the statement is true or false. Justify your answer.**

65. The Leaning Tower of Pisa is not vertical, but if you know the exact angle of elevation θ to the 191-foot tower when you stand near it, then you can determine the exact distance to the tower d by using the formula

$$\tan \theta = \frac{191}{d}.$$

66. For the harmonic motion of a ball bobbing up and down on the end of a spring, one period can be described as the length of one coil of the spring.

67. *Writing* Is it true that N 24° E means 24 degrees north of east? Explain.

68. *Writing* Explain the difference between bearings used in nautical navigation and bearings used in air navigation.

Skills Review

In Exercises 69–72, write the slope-intercept form of the equation of the line with the specified characteristics. Then sketch the line.

69. $m = 4$, passes through $(-1, 2)$

70. $m = -\frac{1}{2}$, passes through $\left(\frac{1}{3}, 0\right)$

71. Passes through $(-2, 6)$ and $(3, 2)$

72. Passes through $\left(\frac{1}{4}, -\frac{2}{3}\right)$ and $\left(-\frac{1}{2}, \frac{1}{3}\right)$

4 Chapter Summary

What did you learn?

	Review Exercises
Section 4.1	
☐ Describe angles *(p. 282)*.	1, 2
☐ Use radian measure *(p. 283)*.	3–6, 11–18
☐ Use degree measure *(p. 285)*.	7–18
☐ Use angles to model and solve real-life problems *(p. 287)*.	19–24
Section 4.2	
☐ Identify a unit circle and describe its relationship to real numbers *(p. 294)*.	25–28
☐ Evaluate trigonometric functions using the unit circle *(p. 295)*.	29–32
☐ Use domain and period to evaluate sine and cosine functions *(p. 297)*.	33–36
☐ Use a calculator to evaluate trigonometric functions *(p. 298)*.	37–40
Section 4.3	
☐ Evaluate trigonometric functions of acute angles *(p. 301)*.	41–44
☐ Use the fundamental trigonometric identities *(p. 304)*.	45–48
☐ Use a calculator to evaluate trigonometric functions *(p. 305)*.	49–54
☐ Use trigonometric functions to model and solve real-life problems *(p. 306)*.	55, 56
Section 4.4	
☐ Evaluate trigonometric functions of any angle *(p. 312)*.	57–70
☐ Use reference angles to evaluate trigonometric functions *(p. 314)*.	71–82
☐ Evaluate trigonometric functions of real numbers *(p. 315)*.	83–88
Section 4.5	
☐ Use amplitude and period to help sketch the graphs of sine and cosine functions *(p. 323)*.	89–92
☐ Sketch translations of the graphs of sine and cosine functions *(p. 325)*.	93–96
☐ Use sine and cosine functions to model real-life data *(p. 327)*.	97, 98
Section 4.6	
☐ Sketch the graphs of tangent *(p. 332)* and cotangent *(p. 334)* functions.	99–102
☐ Sketch the graphs of secant and cosecant functions *(p. 335)*.	103–106
☐ Sketch the graphs of damped trigonometric functions *(p. 337)*.	107, 108
Section 4.7	
☐ Evaluate and graph the inverse sine function *(p. 343)*.	109–114, 123, 126
☐ Evaluate and graph the other inverse trigonometric functions *(p. 345)*.	115–122, 124, 125
☐ Evaluate compositions of trigonometric functions *(p. 347)*.	127–132
Section 4.8	
☐ Solve real-life problems involving right triangles *(p. 353)*.	133, 134
☐ Solve real-life problems involving directional bearings *(p. 355)*.	135
☐ Solve real-life problems involving harmonic motion *(p. 356)*.	136

4 Review Exercises

4.1 In Exercises 1 and 2, estimate the angle to the nearest one-half radian.

1.

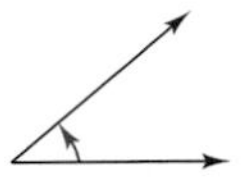

2.

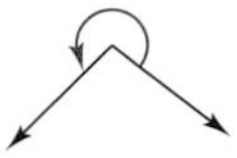

In Exercises 3–10, (a) sketch the angle in standard position, (b) determine the quadrant in which the angle lies, and (c) determine one positive and one negative coterminal angle.

3. $\frac{11\pi}{4}$

4. $\frac{2\pi}{9}$

5. $-\frac{4\pi}{3}$

6. $-\frac{23\pi}{3}$

7. $70°$

8. $280°$

9. $-110°$

10. $-405°$

In Exercises 11–14, convert the angle measure from degrees to radians. Round your answer to three decimal places.

11. $480°$

12. $-127.5°$

13. $-33° 45'$

14. $196° 77'$

In Exercises 15–18, convert the angle measure from radians to degrees. Round your answer to three decimal places.

15. $\frac{5\pi}{7}$

16. $-\frac{11\pi}{6}$

17. -3.5

18. 5.7

19. ***Arc Length*** Find the length of the arc on a circle with a radius of 20 inches intercepted by a central angle of 138°.

20. ***Arc Length*** Find the length of the arc on a circle with a radius of 11 meters intercepted by a central angle of 60°.

21. ***Phonograph*** Compact discs have all but replaced phonograph records. Phonograph records are vinyl discs that rotate on a turntable. A typical record album is 12 inches in diameter and plays at $33\frac{1}{3}$ revolutions per minute.

(a) What is the angular speed of a record album?

(b) What is the linear speed of the outer edge of a record album?

22. ***Bicycle*** At what speed is a bicyclist traveling when his 27-inch-diameter tires are rotating at an angular speed of 5π radians per second?

23. ***Circular Sector*** Find the area of the sector of a circle with a radius of 18 inches and central angle $\theta = 120°$.

24. ***Circular Sector*** Find the area of the sector of a circle with a radius of 6.5 millimeters and central angle $\theta = 5\pi/6$.

4.2 In Exercises 25–28, find the point (x, y) on the unit circle that corresponds to the real number t.

25. $t = \frac{2\pi}{3}$

26. $t = \frac{3\pi}{4}$

27. $t = \frac{5\pi}{6}$

28. $t = -\frac{4\pi}{3}$

In Exercises 29–32, evaluate (if possible) the six trigonometric functions of the real number.

29. $t = \frac{7\pi}{6}$

30. $t = \frac{\pi}{4}$

31. $t = -\frac{2\pi}{3}$

32. $t = 2\pi$

In Exercises 33–36, evaluate the trigonometric function using its period as an aid.

33. $\sin \frac{11\pi}{4}$

34. $\cos 4\pi$

35. $\sin\left(-\frac{17\pi}{6}\right)$

36. $\cos\left(-\frac{13\pi}{3}\right)$

In Exercises 37–40, use a calculator to evaluate the trigonometric function. Round your answer to four decimal places.

37. $\tan 33$

38. $\csc 10.5$

39. $\sec \frac{12\pi}{5}$

40. $\sin\left(-\frac{\pi}{9}\right)$

4.3 In Exercises 41–44, find the exact values of the six trigonometric functions of the angle θ shown in the figure.

41.

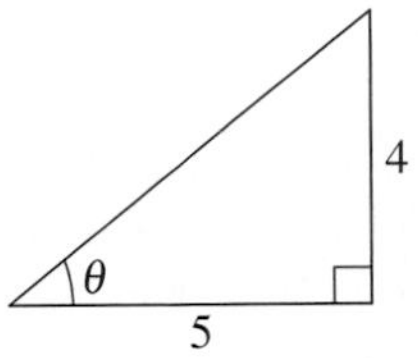

42.

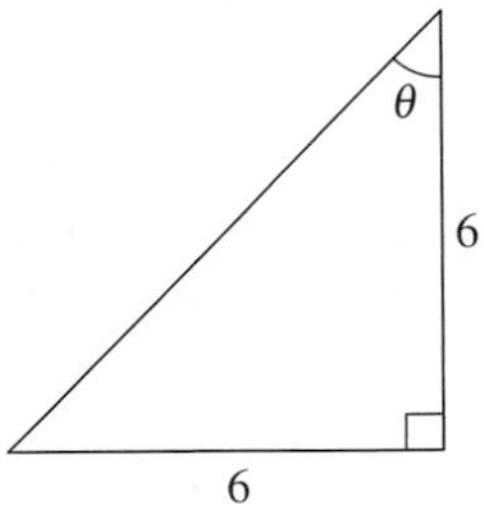

43.

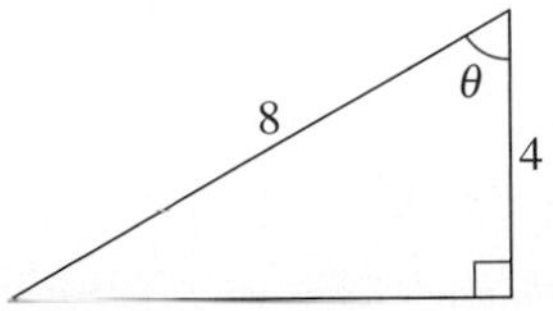

44.

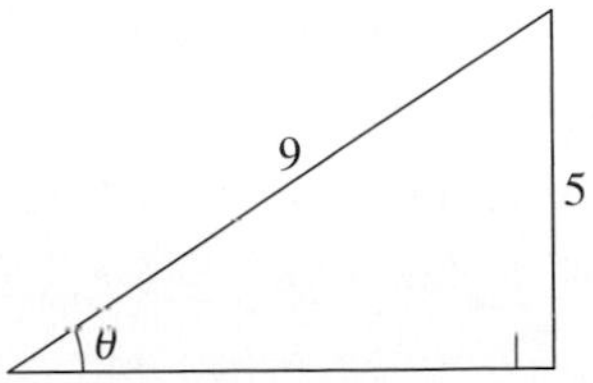

In Exercises 45–48, use the given function value and trigonometric identities (including the cofunction identities) to find the indicated trigonometric functions.

45. $\sin\theta = \frac{1}{3}$ (a) $\csc\theta$ (b) $\cos\theta$ (c) $\sec\theta$ (d) $\tan\theta$

46. $\tan\theta = 4$ (a) $\cot\theta$ (b) $\sec\theta$ (c) $\cos\theta$ (d) $\csc\theta$

47. $\csc\theta = 4$ (a) $\sin\theta$ (b) $\cos\theta$ (c) $\sec\theta$ (d) $\tan\theta$

48. $\csc\theta = 5$ (a) $\sin\theta$ (b) $\cot\theta$ (c) $\tan\theta$ (d) $\sec(90° - \theta)$

In Exercises 49–54, use a calculator to evaluate the trigonometric function. Round your answer to four decimal places.

49. $\tan 33°$

50. $\csc 11°$

51. $\sin 34.2°$

52. $\sec 79.3°$

53. $\cot 15°\,14'$

54. $\cos 78°\,11'58''$

55. ***Railroad Grade*** A train travels 3.5 kilometers on a straight track with a grade of 1° 10′ (see figure). What is the vertical rise of the train in that distance?

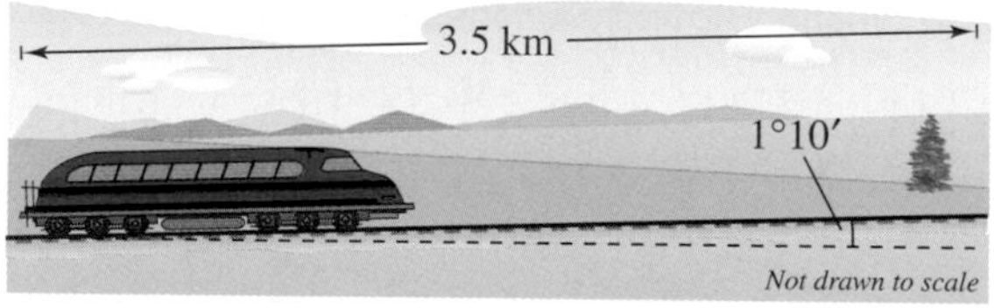

56. ***Guy Wire*** A guy wire runs from the ground to the top of a 25-foot telephone pole. The angle formed between the wire and the ground is 52°. How far from the base of the pole is the wire attached to the ground?

4.4 **In Exercises 57–64, the point is on the terminal side of an angle θ in standard position. Determine the exact values of the six trigonometric functions of the angle θ.**

57. $(12, 16)$

58. $(3, -4)$

59. $\left(\frac{2}{3}, \frac{5}{2}\right)$

60. $\left(-\frac{10}{3}, -\frac{2}{3}\right)$

61. $(-0.5, 4.5)$

62. $(0.3, 0.4)$

63. $(x, 4x),\ x > 0$

64. $(-2x, -3x),\ x > 0$

In Exercises 65–70, find the values of the six trigonometric functions of θ.

Function Value	*Constraint*
65. $\sec\theta = \frac{6}{5}$	$\tan\theta < 0$
66. $\csc\theta = \frac{3}{2}$	$\cos\theta < 0$
67. $\sin\theta = \frac{3}{8}$	$\cos\theta < 0$
68. $\tan\theta = \frac{5}{4}$	$\cos\theta < 0$
69. $\cos\theta = -\frac{2}{5}$	$\sin\theta > 0$
70. $\sin\theta = -\frac{2}{4}$	$\cos\theta > 0$

In Exercises 71–74, find the reference angle θ', and sketch θ and θ' in standard position.

71. $\theta = 264°$

72. $\theta = 635°$

73. $\theta = -\dfrac{6\pi}{5}$

74. $\theta = \dfrac{17\pi}{3}$

In Exercises 75–82, evaluate the sine, cosine, and tangent of the angle without using a calculator.

75. $\dfrac{\pi}{3}$

76. $\dfrac{\pi}{4}$

77. $-\dfrac{7\pi}{3}$

78. $-\dfrac{5\pi}{4}$

79. $495°$

80. $-150°$

81. $-240°$

82. $315°$

In Exercises 83–88, use a calculator to evaluate the trigonometric function. Round your answer to four decimal places.

83. $\sin 4$

84. $\tan 3$

85. $\sin(-3.2)$

86. $\cot(-4.8)$

85. $\sin\dfrac{12\pi}{5}$

88. $\tan\left(-\dfrac{25\pi}{7}\right)$

4.5 **In Exercises 89–96, sketch the graph of the function. Include two full periods.**

89. $y = \sin x$

90. $y = \cos x$

91. $f(x) = 5\sin\dfrac{2x}{5}$

92. $f(x) = 8\cos\left(-\dfrac{x}{4}\right)$

93. $y = 2 + \sin x$

94. $y = -4 - \cos\pi x$

95. $g(t) = \frac{5}{2}\sin(t - \pi)$

96. $g(t) = 3\cos(t + \pi)$

97. ***Sound Waves*** Sound waves can be modeled by sine functions of the form $y = a\sin bx$, where x is measured in seconds.

(a) Write an equation of a sound wave whose amplitude is 2 and whose period is $\frac{1}{264}$ second.

(b) What is the frequency of the sound wave described in part (a)?

98. ***Data Analysis: Meteorology*** The times S of sunset (Greenwich Mean Time) at 40° north latitude on the 15th of each month are: 1(16:59), 2(17:35), 3(18:06), 4(18:38), 5(19:08), 6(19:30), 7(19:28), 8(18:57), 9(18:09), 10(17:21), 11(16:44), 12(16:36). The month is represented by t, with $t = 1$ corresponding to January. A model (in which minutes have been converted to the decimal parts of an hour) for the data is

$$S(t) = 18.09 + 1.41 \sin\left(\frac{\pi t}{6} + 4.60\right).$$

(a) Use a graphing utility to graph the data points and the model in the same viewing window.

(b) What is the period of the model? Is it what you expected? Explain.

(c) What is the amplitude of the model? What does it represent in the model? Explain.

4.6 **In Exercises 99–106, sketch a graph of the function. Include two full periods.**

99. $f(x) = \tan x$ **100.** $f(t) = \tan\left(t - \frac{\pi}{4}\right)$

101. $f(x) = \cot x$

102. $g(t) = 2 \cot 2t$

103. $f(x) = \sec x$

104. $h(t) = \sec\left(t - \frac{\pi}{4}\right)$

105. $f(x) = \csc x$

106. $f(t) = 3 \csc\left(2t + \frac{\pi}{4}\right)$

In Exercises 107 and 108, use a graphing utility to graph the function and the damping factor of the function in the same viewing window. Describe the behavior of the function as *x* increases without bound.

107. $f(x) = x \cos x$ **108.** $g(x) = x^4 \cos x$

4.7 **In Exercises 109–114, evaluate the expression. If necessary, round your answer to two decimal places.**

109. $\arcsin\left(-\frac{1}{2}\right)$ **110.** $\arcsin(-1)$

111. $\arcsin 0.4$ **112.** $\arcsin 0.213$

113. $\sin^{-1}(-0.44)$ **114.** $\sin^{-1} 0.89$

In Exercises 115–118, evaluate the expression without the aid of a calculator.

115. $\arccos \frac{\sqrt{3}}{2}$ **116.** $\arccos \frac{\sqrt{2}}{2}$

117. $\cos^{-1}(-1)$ **118.** $\cos^{-1} \frac{\sqrt{3}}{2}$

In Exercises 119–122, use a calculator to evaluate the expression. Round your answer to two decimal places.

119. $\arccos 0.324$ **120.** $\arccos(-0.888)$

121. $\tan^{-1}(-1.5)$ **122.** $\tan^{-1} 8.2$

In Exercises 123–126, use a graphing utility to graph the function.

123. $f(x) = 2 \arcsin x$ **124.** $f(x) = 3 \arccos x$

125. $f(x) = \arctan \frac{x}{2}$

126. $f(x) = -\arcsin 2x$

In Exercises 127–130, find the exact value of the expression.

127. $\cos\left(\arctan \frac{3}{4}\right)$

128. $\tan\left(\arccos \frac{3}{5}\right)$

129. $\sec\left(\arctan \frac{12}{5}\right)$

130. $\cot\left[\arcsin\left(-\frac{12}{13}\right)\right]$

In Exercises 131 and 132, write an algebraic expression that is equivalent to the expression.

131. $\tan\left(\arccos \frac{x}{2}\right)$

132. $\sec[\arcsin(x - 1)]$

4.8 **133.** ***Angle of Elevation*** The height of a radio transmission tower is 70 meters, and it casts a shadow of length 30 meters (see figure). Find the angle of elevation of the sun.

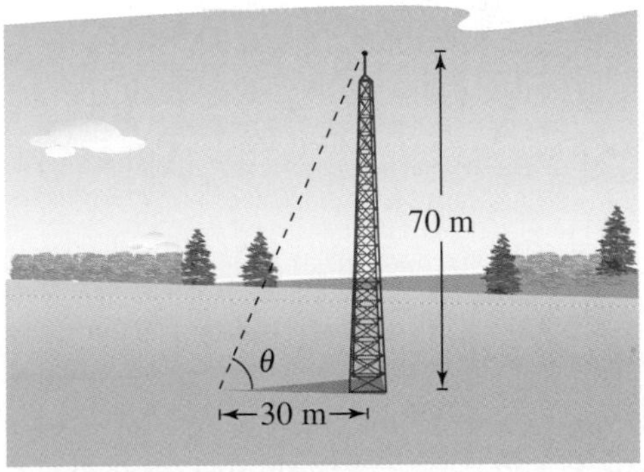

134. ***Height*** Your football has landed at the edge of the roof of your school building. When you are 25 feet from the base of the building, the angle of elevation to your football is 21°. How high off the ground is your football?

135. ***Distance*** From city A to city B, a plane flies 650 miles at a bearing of 48°. From city B to city C, the plane flies 810 miles at a bearing of 115°. Find the distance from city A to city C and the bearing from city A to city C.

136. ***Wave Motion*** Your fishing bobber oscillates in simple harmonic motion from the waves in the lake where you fish. Your bobber moves a total of 1.5 inches from its high point to its low point and returns to its high point every 3 seconds. Write an equation modeling the motion of your bobber if it is at its high point at time $t = 0$.

Synthesis

True or False? **In Exercises 137–140, determine whether the statement is true or false. Justify your answer.**

137. The tangent function is often useful for modeling simple harmonic motion.

138. The inverse sine function $y = \arcsin x$ cannot be defined as a function over any interval that is greater than the interval defined as $-\pi/2 \le y \le \pi/2$.

139. $y = \sin \theta$ is not a function because $\sin 30° = \sin 150°$.

140. Because $\tan 3\pi/4 = -1$, $\arctan(-1) = 3\pi/4$.

In Exercises 141–144, match the function $y = a \sin bx$ with its graph. Base your selection solely on your interpretation of the constants a and b. Explain your reasoning. [The graphs are labeled (a), (b), (c), and (d).]

(a)

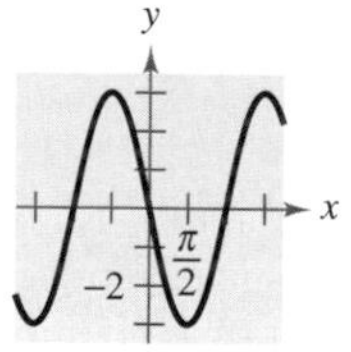

(b)

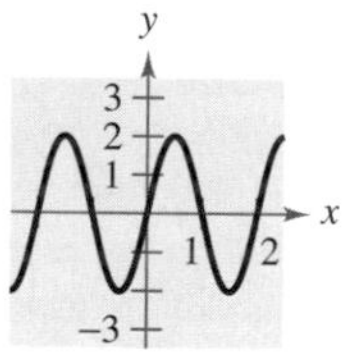

(c)

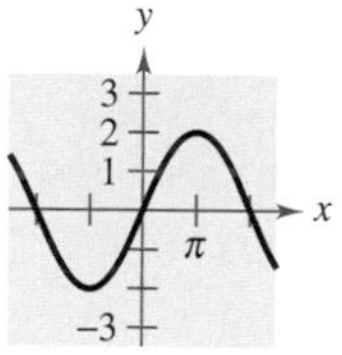

(d)

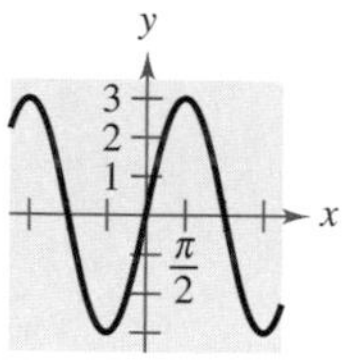

141. $y = 3 \sin x$

142. $y = -3 \sin x$

143. $y = 2 \sin \pi x$

144. $y = 2 \sin \dfrac{x}{2}$

145. ***Writing*** Describe the behavior of $f(\theta) = \sec \theta$ at the zeros of $g(\theta) = \cos \theta$. Explain your reasoning.

146. ***Conjecture***

(a) Use a graphing utility to complete the table.

θ	0.1	0.4	0.7	1.0	1.3
$\tan\left(\theta - \frac{\pi}{2}\right)$					
$-\cot \theta$					

(b) Make a conjecture about the relationship between $\tan\left(\theta - \frac{\pi}{2}\right)$ and $-\cot \theta$.

147. ***Writing*** When graphing the sine and cosine functions, determining the amplitude is part of the analysis. Explain why this is not true for the other four trigonometric functions.

148. ***Oscillation of a Spring*** A weight is suspended from a ceiling by a steel spring. The weight is lifted (positive direction) from the equilibrium position and released. The resulting motion of the weight is modeled by

$$y = Ae^{-kt} \cos bt = \tfrac{1}{5}e^{-t/10} \cos 6t$$

where y is the distance in feet from equilibrium and t is the time in seconds. The graph of the function is shown in the figure. For each of the following, describe the change in the system without graphing the resulting function.

(a) A is changed from $\frac{1}{5}$ to $\frac{1}{3}$.

(b) k is changed from $\frac{1}{10}$ to $\frac{1}{3}$.

(c) b is changed from 6 to 9.

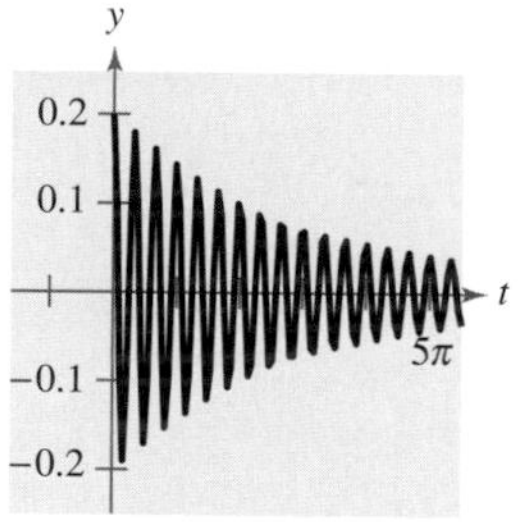

149. ***Graphical Reasoning*** The formulas for the area of a circular sector and arc length are $A = \frac{1}{2}r^2\theta$ and $s = r\theta$, respectively. (r is the radius and θ is the angle measured in radians.)

(a) For $\theta = 0.8$, write the area and arc length as functions of r. What is the domain of each function? Use a graphing utility to graph the functions. Use the graphs to determine which function changes more rapidly as r increases. Explain.

(b) For $r = 10$ centimeters, write the area and arc length as functions of θ. What is the domain of each function? Use a graphing utility to graph and identify the functions.

150. ***Writing*** Describe a real-life application that can be represented by a simple harmonic motion model and is different from any that you've seen in this chapter. Explain which function you would use to model your application and why. Explain how you would determine the amplitude, period, and frequency of the model for your application.

4 Chapter Test

Take this test as you would take a test in class. When you are finished, check your work against the answers given in the back of the book.

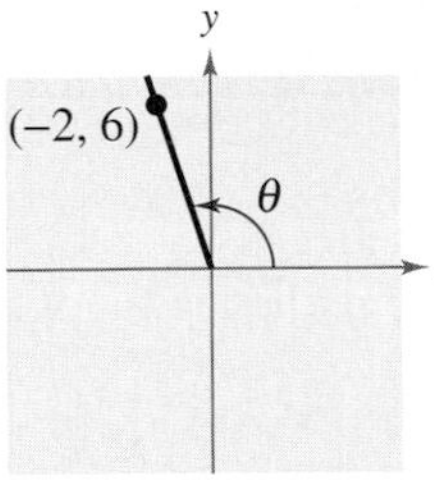

FIGURE FOR 4

1. Consider an angle that measures $\frac{5\pi}{4}$ radians.
   (a) Sketch the angle in standard position.
   (b) Determine two coterminal angles (one positive and one negative).
   (c) Convert the angle to degree measure.
2. A truck is moving at a rate of 90 kilometers per hour, and the diameter of its wheels is 1 meter. Find the angular speed of the wheels in radians per minute.
3. A water sprinkler sprays water on a lawn over a distance of 25 feet and rotates through an angle of 130°. Find the area of the lawn watered by the sprinkler.
4. Find the exact values of the six trigonometric functions of the angle θ shown in the figure.
5. Given that $\tan \theta = \frac{3}{2}$, find the other five trigonometric functions of θ.
6. Determine the reference angle θ' of the angle $\theta = 290°$ and sketch θ and θ' in standard position.
7. Determine the quadrant in which θ lies if $\sec \theta < 0$ and $\tan \theta > 0$.
8. Find two exact values of θ in degrees $(0 \le \theta < 360°)$ if $\cos \theta = -\sqrt{3}/2$. (Do not use a calculator.)
9. Use a calculator to approximate two values of θ in radians $(0 \le \theta < 2\pi)$ if $\csc \theta = 1.030$. Round the results to two decimal places.

In Exercises 10 and 11, find the remaining five trigonometric functions of θ satisfying the conditions.

10. $\cos \theta = \frac{3}{5}, \quad \tan \theta < 0$
11. $\sec \theta = -\frac{17}{8}, \quad \sin \theta > 0$

In Exercises 12 and 13, sketch the graph of the function. (Include two full periods.)

12. $g(x) = -2 \sin\left(x - \frac{\pi}{4}\right)$
13. $f(\alpha) = \frac{1}{2} \tan 2\alpha$

In Exercises 14 and 15, use a graphing utility to graph the function. If the function is periodic, find its period.

14. $y = \sin 2\pi x + 2 \cos \pi x$
15. $y = 6e^{-0.12t} \cos(0.25t), \quad 0 \le t \le 32$

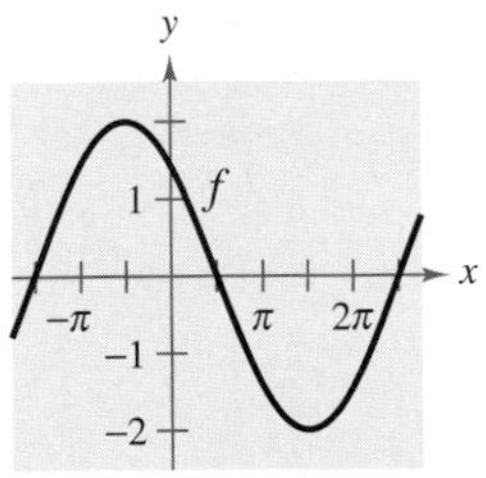

FIGURE FOR 16

16. Find a, b, and c for the function $f(x) = a \sin(bx + c)$ such that the graph of f matches the figure.
17. Find the exact value of $\tan\left(\arccos \frac{2}{3}\right)$ without the aid of a calculator.
18. Graph the function $f(x) = 2 \arcsin\left(\frac{1}{2}x\right)$.
19. A plane is 80 miles south and 95 miles east of Cleveland Hopkins International Airport. What bearing should be taken to fly directly to the airport?
20. Write the equation for the simple harmonic motion of a ball on a spring that starts at its lowest point of 6 inches below equilibrium, bounces to its maximum height of 6 inches above equilibrium, and returns to its lowest point in a total of 2 seconds.

The Pythagorean Theorem

The Pythagorean Theorem is one of the most famous theorems in mathematics. More than 100 different proofs now exist. James A. Garfield, the twentieth president of the United States, developed a proof of the Pythagorean Theorem in 1876. His proof, shown below, involved the fact that a trapezoid can be formed from two congruent right triangles and an isosceles right triangle.

The Pythagorean Theorem

In a right triangle, the sum of the squares of the lengths of the legs is equal to the square of the length of the hypotenuse, where a and b are the legs and c is the hypotenuse.

$$a^2 + b^2 = c^2$$

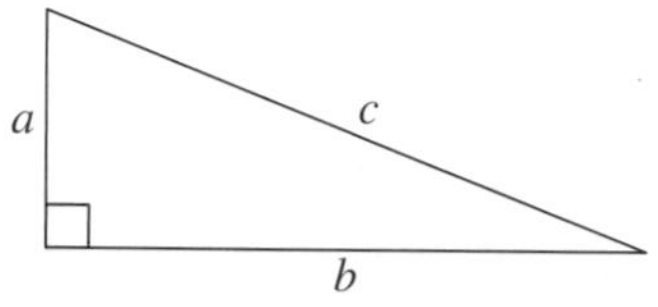

Proof

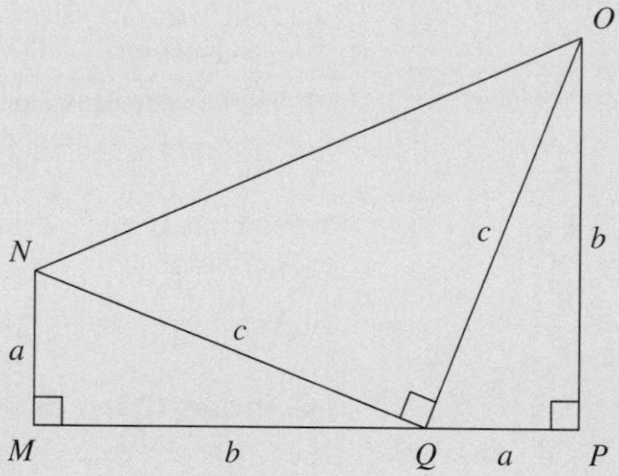

$$\text{Area of trapezoid } MNOP = \text{Area of } \triangle MNQ + \text{Area of } \triangle PQO + \text{Area of } \triangle NOQ$$

$$\frac{1}{2}(a + b)(a + b) = \frac{1}{2}ab + \frac{1}{2}ab + \frac{1}{2}c^2$$

$$\frac{1}{2}(a + b)(a + b) = ab + \frac{1}{2}c^2$$

$$(a + b)(a + b) = 2ab + c^2$$

$$a^2 + 2ab + b^2 = 2ab + c^2$$

$$a^2 + b^2 = c^2$$

P.S. Problem Solving

This collection of thought-provoking and challenging exercises further explores and expands upon concepts learned in this chapter.

1. The restaurant at the top of the Space Needle in Seattle, Washington is circular and has a radius of 47.25 feet. The dining part of the restaurant revolves, making about one complete revolution every 48 minutes. A dinner party was seated at the edge of the revolving restaurant at 6:45 P.M. and was finished at 8:57 P.M.

(a) Find the angle through which the dinner party rotated.

(b) Find the distance the party traveled during dinner.

2. A bicycle's gear ratio is the number of times the freewheel turns for every one turn of the chainwheel (see figure). The table shows the numbers of teeth in the freewheel and chainwheel for the first five gears of an 18-speed touring bicycle. The chainwheel completes one rotation for each gear. Find the angle through which the freewheel turns for each gear. Give your answers in both degrees and radians.

Gear number	Number of teeth in freewheel	Number of teeth in chainwheel
1	32	24
2	26	24
3	22	24
4	32	40
5	19	24

3. A surveyor in a helicopter is trying to determine the width of an island, as shown in the figure.

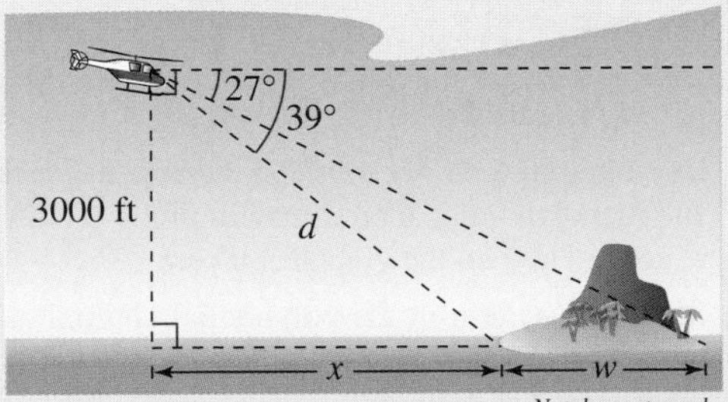

Not drawn to scale

(a) What is the shortest distance d the helicopter would have to travel to land on the island?

(b) What is the horizontal distance x that the helicopter would have to travel before it would be directly over the nearer end of the island?

(c) Find the width w of the island. Explain how you obtained your answer.

4. Use the figure below.

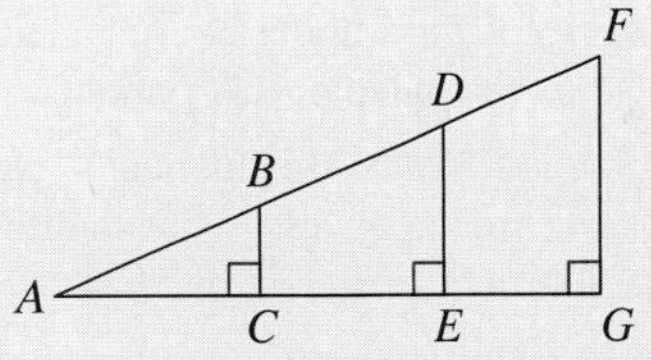

(a) Explain why $\triangle ABC$, $\triangle ADE$, and $\triangle AFG$ are similar triangles.

(b) What does similarity imply about the ratios

$$\frac{BC}{AB}, \frac{DE}{AD}, \text{ and } \frac{FG}{AF}?$$

(c) Does the value of sin A depend on which triangle from part (a) is used to calculate it? Would the value of sin A change if it were found using a different right triangle that was similar to the three given triangles?

(d) Do your conclusions from part (c) apply to the other five trigonometric functions? Explain.

5. Use a graphing utility to graph h, and use the graph to decide whether h is even, odd, or neither.

(a) $h(x) = \cos^2 x$

(b) $h(x) = \sin^2 x$

6. If f is an even function and g is an odd function, use the results of Exercise 5 to make a conjecture about h, where

(a) $h(x) = [f(x)]^2$

(b) $h(x) = [g(x)]^2$.

7. The model for the height h (in feet) of a Ferris wheel car is

$$h = 50 + 50 \sin 8\pi t$$

where t is the time (in minutes). (The Ferris wheel has a radius of 50 feet.) This model yields a height of 50 feet when $t = 0$. Alter the model so that the height of the car is 1 foot when $t = 0$.

8. The pressure P (in millimeters of mercury) against the walls of the blood vessels of a patient is modeled by

$$P = 100 - 20 \cos\left(\frac{8\pi}{3}t\right)$$

where t is time (in seconds).

(a) Use a graphing utility to graph the model.

(b) What is the period of the model? What does the period tell you about this situation?

(c) What is the amplitude of the model? What does it tell you about this situation?

(d) If one cycle of this model is equivalent to one heartbeat, what is the pulse of this patient?

(e) If a physician wants this patient's pulse rate to be 64 beats per minute or less, what should the period be? What should the coefficient of t be?

9. A popular theory that attempts to explain the ups and downs of everyday life states that each of us has three cycles, called biorhythms, which begin at birth. These three cycles can be modeled by sine waves.

Physical (23 days): $P = \sin \frac{2\pi t}{23}, \quad t \geq 0$

Emotional (28 days): $E = \sin \frac{2\pi t}{28}, \quad t \geq 0$

Intellectual (33 days): $I = \sin \frac{2\pi t}{33}, \quad t \geq 0$

where t is the number of days since birth. Consider a person who was born on July 20, 1986.

(a) Use a graphing utility to graph the three models in the same viewing window for $7300 \leq t \leq 7380$.

(b) Describe the person's biorhythms during the month of September 2006.

(c) Calculate the person's three energy levels on September 22, 2006.

10. (a) Use a graphing utility to graph the functions given by

$$f(x) = 2 \cos 2x + 3 \sin 3x$$

and

$$g(x) = 2 \cos 2x + 3 \sin 4x.$$

(b) Use the graphs from part (a) to find the period of each function.

(c) If α and β are positive integers, is the function given by

$$h(x) = A \cos \alpha x + B \sin \beta x$$

periodic? Explain your reasoning.

11. Two trigonometric functions f and g have periods of 2, and their graphs intersect at $x = 5.35$.

(a) Give one smaller and one larger positive value of x at which the functions have the same value.

(b) Determine one negative value of x at which the graphs intersect.

(c) Is it true that $f(13.35) = g(-4.65)$? Explain your reasoning.

12. The function f is periodic, with period c. So, $f(t + c) = f(t)$. Are the following equal? Explain.

(a) $f(t - 2c) = f(t)$ (b) $f\left(t + \frac{1}{2}c\right) = f\left(\frac{1}{2}t\right)$

(c) $f\left(\frac{1}{2}(t + c)\right) = f\left(\frac{1}{2}t\right)$

13. If you stand in shallow water and look at an object below the surface of the water, the object will look farther away from you than it really is. This is because when light rays pass between air and water, the water refracts, or bends, the light rays. The index of refraction for water is 1.333. This is the ratio of the sine of θ_1 and the sine of θ_2 (see figure).

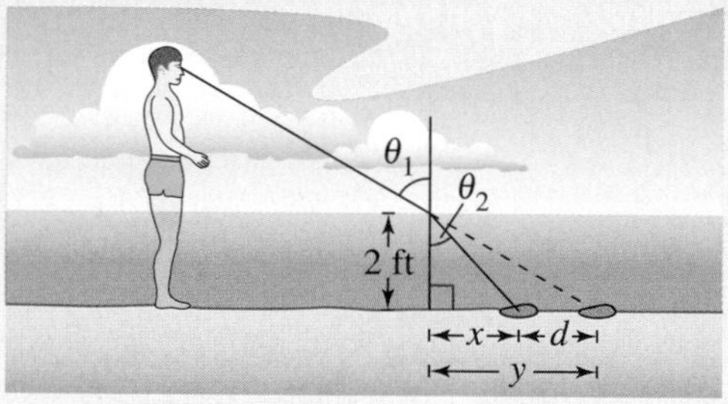

(a) You are standing in water that is 2 feet deep and are looking at a rock at angle $\theta_1 = 60°$ (measured from a line perpendicular to the surface of the water). Find θ_2.

(b) Find the distances x and y.

(c) Find the distance d between where the rock is and where it appears to be.

(d) What happens to d as you move closer to the rock? Explain your reasoning.

14. In calculus, it can be shown that the arctangent function can be approximated by the polynomial

$$\arctan x \approx x - \frac{x^3}{3} + \frac{x^5}{5} - \frac{x^7}{7}$$

where x is in radians.

(a) Use a graphing utility to graph the arctangent function and its polynomial approximation in the same viewing window. How do the graphs compare?

(b) Study the pattern in the polynomial approximation of the arctangent function and guess the next term. Then repeat part (a). How does the accuracy of the approximation change when additional terms are added?

Analytic Trigonometry

5

5.1 Using Fundamental Identities

5.2 Verifying Trigonometric Identities

5.3 Solving Trigonometric Equations

5.4 Sum and Difference Formulas

5.5 Multiple-Angle and Product-to-Sum Formula

Concepts of trigonometry can be used to model the height above ground of a seat on a Ferris wheel.

SELECTED APPLICATIONS

Trigonometric equations and identities have many real-life applications. The applications listed below represent a small sample of the applications in this chapter.

- Friction, Exercise 99, page 381
- Shadow Length, Exercise 56, page 388
- Ferris Wheel, Exercise 75, page 398
- Data Analysis: Unemployment Rate, Exercise 76, page 398
- Harmonic Motion, Exercise 75, page 405
- Mach Number, Exercise 121, page 417
- Projectile Motion, Exercise 101, page 421
- Ocean Depth, Exercise 10, page 428

5.1 Using Fundamental Identities

What you should learn

- Recognize and write the fundamental trigonometric identities.
- Use the fundamental trigonometric identities to evaluate trigonometric functions, simplify trigonometric expressions, and rewrite trigonometric expressions.

Why you should learn it

Fundamental trigonometric identities can be used to simplify trigonometric expressions. For instance, in Exercise 99 on page 381, you can use trigonometric identities to simplify an expression for the coefficient of friction.

Introduction

In Chapter 4, you studied the basic definitions, properties, graphs, and applications of the individual trigonometric functions. In this chapter, you will learn how to use the fundamental identities to do the following.

1. Evaluate trigonometric functions.
2. Simplify trigonometric expressions.
3. Develop additional trigonometric identities.
4. Solve trigonometric equations.

Fundamental Trigonometric Identities

Reciprocal Identities

$$\sin u = \frac{1}{\csc u} \qquad \cos u = \frac{1}{\sec u} \qquad \tan u = \frac{1}{\cot u}$$

$$\csc u = \frac{1}{\sin u} \qquad \sec u = \frac{1}{\cos u} \qquad \cot u = \frac{1}{\tan u}$$

Quotient Identities

$$\tan u = \frac{\sin u}{\cos u} \qquad \cot u = \frac{\cos u}{\sin u}$$

Pythagorean Identities

$$\sin^2 u + \cos^2 u = 1 \qquad 1 + \tan^2 u = \sec^2 u \qquad 1 + \cot^2 u = \csc^2 u$$

Cofunction Identities

$$\sin\left(\frac{\pi}{2} - u\right) = \cos u \qquad \cos\left(\frac{\pi}{2} - u\right) = \sin u$$

$$\tan\left(\frac{\pi}{2} - u\right) = \cot u \qquad \cot\left(\frac{\pi}{2} - u\right) = \tan u$$

$$\sec\left(\frac{\pi}{2} - u\right) = \csc u \qquad \csc\left(\frac{\pi}{2} - u\right) = \sec u$$

Even/Odd Identities

$$\sin(-u) = -\sin u \qquad \cos(-u) = \cos u \qquad \tan(-u) = -\tan u$$

$$\csc(-u) = -\csc u \qquad \sec(-u) = \sec u \qquad \cot(-u) = -\cot u$$

Pythagorean identities are sometimes used in radical form such as

$$\sin u = \pm\sqrt{1 - \cos^2 u}$$

or

$$\tan u = \pm\sqrt{\sec^2 u - 1}$$

where the sign depends on the choice of u.

STUDY TIP

You should learn the fundamental trigonometric identities well, because they are used frequently in trigonometry and they will also appear later in calculus. Note that u can be an angle, a real number, or a variable.

Using the Fundamental Identities

One common use of trigonometric identities is to use given values of trigonometric functions to evaluate other trigonometric functions.

Example 1 Using Identities to Evaluate a Function

Use the values $\sec u = -\frac{3}{2}$ and $\tan u > 0$ to find the values of all six trigonometric functions.

Solution

Using a reciprocal identity, you have

$$\cos u = \frac{1}{\sec u} = \frac{1}{-3/2} = -\frac{2}{3}.$$

Using a Pythagorean identity, you have

$$\sin^2 u = 1 - \cos^2 u \qquad \text{Pythagorean identity}$$

$$= 1 - \left(-\frac{2}{3}\right)^2 \qquad \text{Substitute } -\tfrac{2}{3} \text{ for } \cos u.$$

$$= 1 - \frac{4}{9} = \frac{5}{9}. \qquad \text{Simplify.}$$

Because $\sec u < 0$ and $\tan u > 0$, it follows that u lies in Quadrant III. Moreover, because $\sin u$ is negative when u is in Quadrant III, you can choose the negative root and obtain $\sin u = -\sqrt{5}/3$. Now, knowing the values of the sine and cosine, you can find the values of all six trigonometric functions.

$$\sin u = -\frac{\sqrt{5}}{3} \qquad \csc u = \frac{1}{\sin u} = -\frac{3}{\sqrt{5}} = -\frac{3\sqrt{5}}{5}$$

$$\cos u = -\frac{2}{3} \qquad \sec u = \frac{1}{\cos u} = -\frac{3}{2}$$

$$\tan u = \frac{\sin u}{\cos u} = \frac{-\sqrt{5}/3}{-2/3} = \frac{\sqrt{5}}{2} \qquad \cot u = \frac{1}{\tan u} = \frac{2}{\sqrt{5}} = \frac{2\sqrt{5}}{5}$$

CHECKPOINT Now try Exercise 11.

Technology

You can use a graphing utility to check the result of Example 2. To do this, graph

$$y_1 = \sin x \cos^2 x - \sin x$$

and

$$y_2 = -\sin^3 x$$

in the same viewing window, as shown below. Because Example 2 shows the equivalence algebraically and the two graphs appear to coincide, you can conclude that the expressions are equivalent.

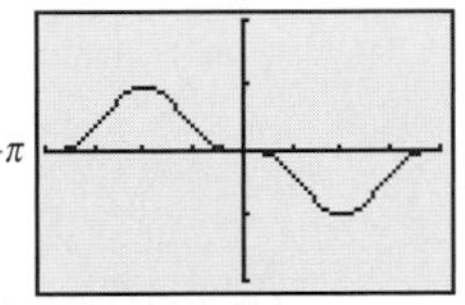

Example 2 Simplifying a Trigonometric Expression

Simplify $\sin x \cos^2 x - \sin x$.

Solution

First factor out a common monomial factor and then use a fundamental identity.

$$\sin x \cos^2 x - \sin x = \sin x(\cos^2 x - 1) \qquad \text{Factor out common monomial factor.}$$

$$= -\sin x(1 - \cos^2 x) \qquad \text{Factor out } -1.$$

$$= -\sin x(\sin^2 x) \qquad \text{Pythagorean identity}$$

$$= -\sin^3 x \qquad \text{Multiply.}$$

CHECKPOINT Now try Exercise 45.

When factoring trigonometric expressions, it is helpful to find a special polynomial factoring form that fits the expression, as shown in Example 3.

Example 3 Factoring Trigonometric Expressions

Factor each expression.

a. $\sec^2 \theta - 1$ **b.** $4 \tan^2 \theta + \tan \theta - 3$

Solution

a. Here you have the difference of two squares, which factors as

$$\sec^2 \theta - 1 = (\sec \theta - 1)(\sec \theta + 1).$$

b. This expression has the polynomial form $ax^2 + bx + c$, and it factors as

$$4 \tan^2 \theta + \tan \theta - 3 = (4 \tan \theta - 3)(\tan \theta + 1).$$

✓CHECKPOINT Now try Exercise 47.

On occasion, factoring or simplifying can best be done by first rewriting the expression in terms of just *one* trigonometric function or in terms of *sine and cosine only*. These strategies are illustrated in Examples 4 and 5, respectively.

Example 4 Factoring a Trigonometric Expression

Factor $\csc^2 x - \cot x - 3$.

Solution

Use the identity $\csc^2 x = 1 + \cot^2 x$ to rewrite the expression in terms of the cotangent.

$$\csc^2 x - \cot x - 3 = (1 + \cot^2 x) - \cot x - 3 \quad \text{Pythagorean identity}$$
$$= \cot^2 x - \cot x - 2 \quad \text{Combine like terms.}$$
$$= (\cot x - 2)(\cot x + 1) \quad \text{Factor.}$$

✓CHECKPOINT Now try Exercise 51.

Example 5 Simplifying a Trigonometric Expression

Simplify $\sin t + \cot t \cos t$.

Solution

Begin by rewriting $\cot t$ in terms of sine and cosine.

$$\sin t + \cot t \cos t = \sin t + \left(\frac{\cos t}{\sin t}\right) \cos t \quad \text{Quotient identity}$$
$$= \frac{\sin^2 t + \cos^2 t}{\sin t} \quad \text{Add fractions.}$$
$$= \frac{1}{\sin t} \quad \text{Pythagorean identity}$$
$$= \csc t \quad \text{Reciprocal identity}$$

✓CHECKPOINT Now try Exercise 57.

STUDY TIP

Remember that when adding rational expressions, you must first find the least common denominator (LCD). In Example 5, the LCD is $\sin t$.

Example 6 Adding Trigonometric Expressions

Perform the addition and simplify.

$$\frac{\sin\theta}{1+\cos\theta}+\frac{\cos\theta}{\sin\theta}$$

Solution

$$\frac{\sin\theta}{1+\cos\theta}+\frac{\cos\theta}{\sin\theta}=\frac{(\sin\theta)(\sin\theta)+(\cos\theta)(1+\cos\theta)}{(1+\cos\theta)(\sin\theta)}$$

$$=\frac{\sin^2\theta+\cos^2\theta+\cos\theta}{(1+\cos\theta)(\sin\theta)}$$ Multiply.

$$=\frac{\cancel{1+\cos\theta}}{\cancel{(1+\cos\theta)}(\sin\theta)}$$ Pythagorean identity: $\sin^2\theta+\cos^2\theta=1$

$$=\frac{1}{\sin\theta}$$ Divide out common factor.

$$=\csc\theta$$ Reciprocal identity

CHECKPOINT Now try Exercise 61.

The last two examples in this section involve techniques for rewriting expressions in forms that are used in calculus.

Example 7 Rewriting a Trigonometric Expression

Rewrite $\dfrac{1}{1+\sin x}$ so that it is *not* in fractional form.

Solution

From the Pythagorean identity $\cos^2 x = 1 - \sin^2 x = (1 - \sin x)(1 + \sin x)$, you can see that multiplying both the numerator and the denominator by $(1 - \sin x)$ will produce a monomial denominator.

$$\frac{1}{1+\sin x}=\frac{1}{1+\sin x}\cdot\frac{1-\sin x}{1-\sin x}$$ Multiply numerator and denominator by $(1-\sin x)$.

$$=\frac{1-\sin x}{1-\sin^2 x}$$ Multiply.

$$=\frac{1-\sin x}{\cos^2 x}$$ Pythagorean identity

$$=\frac{1}{\cos^2 x}-\frac{\sin x}{\cos^2 x}$$ Write as separate fractions.

$$=\frac{1}{\cos^2 x}-\frac{\sin x}{\cos x}\cdot\frac{1}{\cos x}$$ Product of fractions

$$=\sec^2 x-\tan x\sec x$$ Reciprocal and quotient identities

CHECKPOINT Now try Exercise 65.

Example 8 Trigonometric Substitution

Use the substitution $x = 2\tan\theta$, $0 < \theta < \pi/2$, to write

$$\sqrt{4 + x^2}$$

as a trigonometric function of θ.

Solution

Begin by letting $x = 2\tan\theta$. Then, you can obtain

$$\sqrt{4 + x^2} = \sqrt{4 + (2\tan\theta)^2} \quad \text{Substitute } 2\tan\theta \text{ for } x.$$
$$= \sqrt{4 + 4\tan^2\theta} \quad \text{Rule of exponents}$$
$$= \sqrt{4(1 + \tan^2\theta)} \quad \text{Factor.}$$
$$= \sqrt{4\sec^2\theta} \quad \text{Pythagorean identity}$$
$$= 2\sec\theta. \quad \sec\theta > 0 \text{ for } 0 < \theta < \pi/2$$

CHECKPOINT Now try Exercise 77.

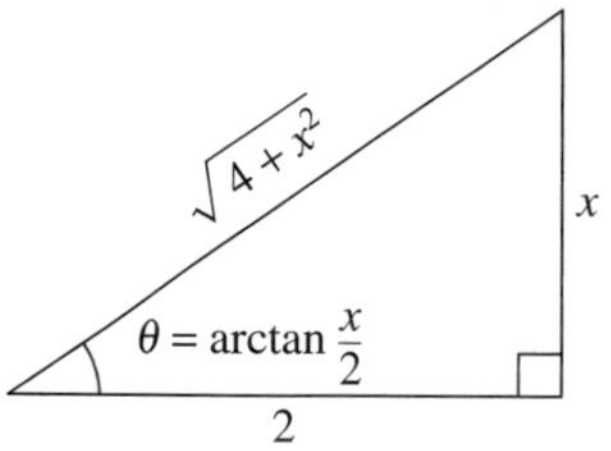

Angle whose tangent is $\frac{x}{2}$.

FIGURE 5.1

Figure 5.1 shows the right triangle illustration of the trigonometric substitution $x = 2\tan\theta$ in Example 8. You can use this triangle to check the solution of Example 8. For $0 < \theta < \pi/2$, you have

$$\text{opp} = x, \quad \text{adj} = 2, \quad \text{and} \quad \text{hyp} = \sqrt{4 + x^2}.$$

With these expressions, you can write the following.

$$\sec\theta = \frac{\text{hyp}}{\text{adj}}$$
$$\sec\theta = \frac{\sqrt{4 + x^2}}{2}$$
$$2\sec\theta = \sqrt{4 + x^2}$$

So, the solution checks.

Example 9 Rewriting a Logarithmic Expression

Rewrite $\ln|\csc\theta| + \ln|\tan\theta|$ as a single logarithm and simplify the result.

Solution

$$\ln|\csc\theta| + \ln|\tan\theta| = \ln|\csc\theta\tan\theta| \quad \text{Product Property of Logarithms}$$
$$= \ln\left|\frac{1}{\sin\theta} \cdot \frac{\sin\theta}{\cos\theta}\right| \quad \text{Reciprocal and quotient identities}$$
$$= \ln\left|\frac{1}{\cos\theta}\right| \quad \text{Simplify.}$$
$$= \ln|\sec\theta| \quad \text{Reciprocal identity}$$

CHECKPOINT Now try Exercise 91.

5.1 Exercises

VOCABULARY CHECK: Fill in the blank to complete the trigonometric identity.

1. $\dfrac{\sin u}{\cos u} = $ ________
2. $\dfrac{1}{\sec u} = $ ________
3. $\dfrac{1}{\tan u} = $ ________
4. $\dfrac{1}{\sin u} = $ ________
5. $1 + $ ________ $= \csc^2 u$
6. $1 + \tan^2 u = $ ________
7. $\sin\left(\dfrac{\pi}{2} - u\right) = $ ________
8. $\sec\left(\dfrac{\pi}{2} - u\right) = $ ________
9. $\cos(-u) = $ ________
10. $\tan(-u) = $ ________

In Exercises 1–14, use the given values to evaluate (if possible) all six trigonometric functions.

1. $\sin x = \dfrac{\sqrt{3}}{2}, \quad \cos x = -\dfrac{1}{2}$
2. $\tan x = \dfrac{\sqrt{3}}{3}, \quad \cos x = -\dfrac{\sqrt{3}}{2}$
3. $\sec \theta = \sqrt{2}, \quad \sin \theta = -\dfrac{\sqrt{2}}{2}$
4. $\csc \theta = \frac{5}{3}, \quad \tan \theta = \frac{3}{4}$
5. $\tan x = \frac{5}{12}, \quad \sec x = -\frac{13}{12}$
6. $\cot \phi = -3, \quad \sin \phi = \dfrac{\sqrt{10}}{10}$
7. $\sec \phi = \dfrac{3}{2}, \quad \csc \phi = -\dfrac{3\sqrt{5}}{5}$
8. $\cos\left(\dfrac{\pi}{2} - x\right) = \dfrac{3}{5}, \quad \cos x = \dfrac{4}{5}$
9. $\sin(-x) = -\dfrac{1}{3}, \quad \tan x = -\dfrac{\sqrt{2}}{4}$
10. $\sec x = 4, \quad \sin x > 0$
11. $\tan \theta = 2, \quad \sin \theta < 0$
12. $\csc \theta = -5, \quad \cos \theta < 0$
13. $\sin \theta = -1, \quad \cot \theta = 0$
14. $\tan \theta$ is undefined, $\quad \sin \theta > 0$

In Exercises 15–20, match the trigonometric expression with one of the following.

(a) $\sec x$ (b) -1 (c) $\cot x$
(d) 1 (e) $-\tan x$ (f) $\sin x$

15. $\sec x \cos x$
16. $\tan x \csc x$
17. $\cot^2 x - \csc^2 x$
18. $(1 - \cos^2 x)(\csc x)$
19. $\dfrac{\sin(-x)}{\cos(-x)}$
20. $\dfrac{\sin[(\pi/2) - x]}{\cos[(\pi/2) - x]}$

In Exercises 21–26, match the trigonometric expression with one of the following.

(a) $\csc x$ (b) $\tan x$ (c) $\sin^2 x$
(d) $\sin x \tan x$ (e) $\sec^2 x$ (f) $\sec^2 x + \tan^2 x$

21. $\sin x \sec x$
22. $\cos^2 x(\sec^2 x - 1)$
23. $\sec^4 x - \tan^4 x$
24. $\cot x \sec x$
25. $\dfrac{\sec^2 x - 1}{\sin^2 x}$
26. $\dfrac{\cos^2[(\pi/2) - x]}{\cos x}$

In Exercises 27–44, use the fundamental identities to simplify the expression. There is more than one correct form of each answer.

27. $\cot \theta \sec \theta$
28. $\cos \beta \tan \beta$
29. $\sin \phi(\csc \phi - \sin \phi)$
30. $\sec^2 x(1 - \sin^2 x)$
31. $\dfrac{\cot x}{\csc x}$
32. $\dfrac{\csc \theta}{\sec \theta}$
33. $\dfrac{1 - \sin^2 x}{\csc^2 x - 1}$
34. $\dfrac{1}{\tan^2 x + 1}$
35. $\sec \alpha \cdot \dfrac{\sin \alpha}{\tan \alpha}$
36. $\dfrac{\tan^2 \theta}{\sec^2 \theta}$
37. $\cos\left(\dfrac{\pi}{2} - x\right)\sec x$
38. $\cot\left(\dfrac{\pi}{2} - x\right)\cos x$
39. $\dfrac{\cos^2 y}{1 - \sin y}$
40. $\cos t(1 + \tan^2 t)$
41. $\sin \beta \tan \beta + \cos \beta$
42. $\csc \phi \tan \phi + \sec \phi$
43. $\cot u \sin u + \tan u \cos u$
44. $\sin \theta \sec \theta + \cos \theta \csc \theta$

In Exercises 45–56, factor the expression and use the fundamental identities to simplify. There is more than one correct form of each answer.

45. $\tan^2 x - \tan^2 x \sin^2 x$

46. $\sin^2 x \csc^2 x - \sin^2 x$

47. $\sin^2 x \sec^2 x - \sin^2 x$

48. $\cos^2 x + \cos^2 x \tan^2 x$

49. $\dfrac{\sec^2 x - 1}{\sec x - 1}$

50. $\dfrac{\cos^2 x - 4}{\cos x - 2}$

51. $\tan^4 x + 2\tan^2 x + 1$

52. $1 - 2\cos^2 x + \cos^4 x$

53. $\sin^4 x - \cos^4 x$

54. $\sec^4 x - \tan^4 x$

55. $\csc^3 x - \csc^2 x - \csc x + 1$

56. $\sec^3 x - \sec^2 x - \sec x + 1$

In Exercises 57–60, perform the multiplication and use the fundamental identities to simplify. There is more than one correct form of each answer.

57. $(\sin x + \cos x)^2$

58. $(\cot x + \csc x)(\cot x - \csc x)$

59. $(2\csc x + 2)(2\csc x - 2)$

60. $(3 - 3\sin x)(3 + 3\sin x)$

In Exercises 61–64, perform the addition or subtraction and use the fundamental identities to simplify. There is more than one correct form of each answer.

61. $\dfrac{1}{1 + \cos x} + \dfrac{1}{1 - \cos x}$

62. $\dfrac{1}{\sec x + 1} - \dfrac{1}{\sec x - 1}$

63. $\dfrac{\cos x}{1 + \sin x} + \dfrac{1 + \sin x}{\cos x}$

64. $\tan x - \dfrac{\sec^2 x}{\tan x}$

In Exercises 65–68, rewrite the expression so that it is not in fractional form. There is more than one correct form of each answer.

65. $\dfrac{\sin^2 y}{1 - \cos y}$

66. $\dfrac{5}{\tan x + \sec x}$

67. $\dfrac{3}{\sec x - \tan x}$

68. $\dfrac{\tan^2 x}{\csc x + 1}$

Numerical and Graphical Analysis **In Exercises 69–72, use a graphing utility to complete the table and graph the functions. Make a conjecture about y_1 and y_2.**

x	0.2	0.4	0.6	0.8	1.0	1.2	1.4
y_1							
y_2							

69. $y_1 = \cos\left(\dfrac{\pi}{2} - x\right), \quad y_2 = \sin x$

70. $y_1 = \sec x - \cos x, \quad y_2 = \sin x \tan x$

71. $y_1 = \dfrac{\cos x}{1 - \sin x}, \quad y_2 = \dfrac{1 + \sin x}{\cos x}$

72. $y_1 = \sec^4 x - \sec^2 x, \quad y_2 = \tan^2 x + \tan^4 x$

In Exercises 73–76, use a graphing utility to determine which of the six trigonometric functions is equal to the expression. Verify your answer algebraically.

73. $\cos x \cot x + \sin x$

74. $\sec x \csc x - \tan x$

75. $\dfrac{1}{\sin x}\left(\dfrac{1}{\cos x} - \cos x\right)$

76. $\dfrac{1}{2}\left(\dfrac{1 + \sin\theta}{\cos\theta} + \dfrac{\cos\theta}{1 + \sin\theta}\right)$

In Exercises 77–82, use the trigonometric substitution to write the algebraic expression as a trigonometric function of θ, where $0 < \theta < \pi/2$.

77. $\sqrt{9 - x^2}, \quad x = 3\cos\theta$

78. $\sqrt{64 - 16x^2}, \quad x = 2\cos\theta$

79. $\sqrt{x^2 - 9}, \quad x = 3\sec\theta$

80. $\sqrt{x^2 - 4}, \quad x = 2\sec\theta$

81. $\sqrt{x^2 + 25}, \quad x = 5\tan\theta$

82. $\sqrt{x^2 + 100}, \quad x = 10\tan\theta$

In Exercises 83–86, use the trigonometric substitution to write the algebraic equation as a trigonometric function of θ, where $-\pi/2 < \theta < \pi/2$. Then find $\sin\theta$ and $\cos\theta$.

83. $3 = \sqrt{9 - x^2}, \quad x = 3\sin\theta$

84. $3 = \sqrt{36 - x^2}, \quad x = 6\sin\theta$

85. $2\sqrt{2} = \sqrt{16 - 4x^2}, \quad x = 2\cos\theta$

86. $-5\sqrt{3} = \sqrt{100 - x^2}, \quad x = 10\cos\theta$

In Exercises 87–90, use a graphing utility to solve the equation for θ, where $0 \le \theta < 2\pi$.

87. $\sin\theta = \sqrt{1 - \cos^2\theta}$

88. $\cos\theta = -\sqrt{1 - \sin^2\theta}$

89. $\sec\theta = \sqrt{1 + \tan^2\theta}$

90. $\csc\theta = \sqrt{1 + \cot^2\theta}$

In Exercises 91–94, rewrite the expression as a single logarithm and simplify the result.

91. $\ln|\cos x| - \ln|\sin x|$

92. $\ln|\sec x| + \ln|\sin x|$

93. $\ln|\cot t| + \ln(1 + \tan^2 t)$

94. $\ln(\cos^2 t) + \ln(1 + \tan^2 t)$

In Exercises 95–98, use a calculator to demonstrate the identity for each value of θ.

95. $\csc^2 \theta - \cot^2 \theta = 1$

(a) $\theta = 132°$, (b) $\theta = \dfrac{2\pi}{7}$

96. $\tan^2 \theta + 1 = \sec^2 \theta$

(a) $\theta = 346°$, (b) $\theta = 3.1$

97. $\cos\left(\dfrac{\pi}{2} - \theta\right) = \sin \theta$

(a) $\theta = 80°$, (b) $\theta = 0.8$

98. $\sin(-\theta) = -\sin \theta$

(a) $\theta = 250°$, (b) $\theta = \frac{1}{2}$

99. ***Friction*** The forces acting on an object weighing W units on an inclined plane positioned at an angle of θ with the horizontal (see figure) are modeled by

$\mu W \cos \theta = W \sin \theta$

where μ is the coefficient of friction. Solve the equation for μ and simplify the result.

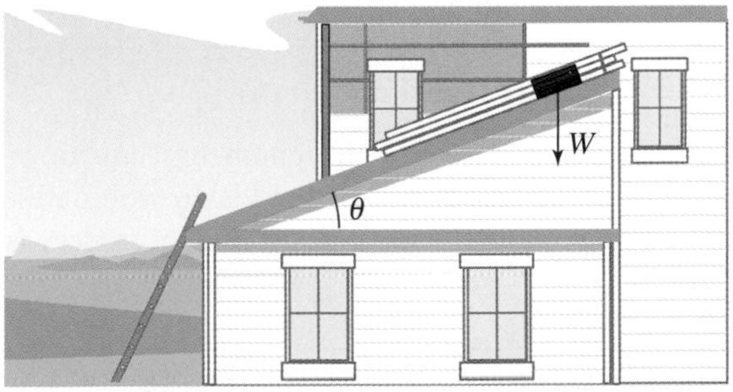

100. ***Rate of Change*** The rate of change of the function

$f(x) = -\csc x - \sin x$

is given by the expression

$\csc x \cot x - \cos x.$

Show that this expression can also be written as $\cos x \cot^2 x$.

Synthesis

True or False? **In Exercises 101 and 102, determine whether the statement is true or false. Justify your answer.**

101. The even and odd trigonometric identities are helpful for determining whether the value of a trigonometric function is positive or negative.

102. A cofunction identity can be used to transform a tangent function so that it can be represented by a cosecant function.

In Exercises 103–106, fill in the blanks. (*Note:* The notation $x \to c^+$ indicates that x approaches c from the right and $x \to c^-$ indicates that x approaches c from the left.)

103. As $x \to \dfrac{\pi}{2}^-$, $\sin x \to$ ___ and $\csc x \to$ ___.

104. As $x \to 0^+$, $\cos x \to$ ___ and $\sec x \to$ ___.

105. As $x \to \dfrac{\pi}{2}^-$, $\tan x \to$ ___ and $\cot x \to$ ___.

106. As $x \to \pi^+$, $\sin x \to$ ___ and $\csc x \to$ ___.

In Exercises 107–112, determine whether or not the equation is an identity, and give a reason for your answer.

107. $\cos \theta = \sqrt{1 - \sin^2 \theta}$ **108.** $\cot \theta = \sqrt{\csc^2 \theta + 1}$

109. $\dfrac{(\sin k\theta)}{(\cos k\theta)} = \tan \theta$, k is a constant.

110. $\dfrac{1}{(5 \cos \theta)} = 5 \sec \theta$

111. $\sin \theta \csc \theta = 1$ **112.** $\csc^2 \theta = 1$

113. Use the definitions of sine and cosine to derive the Pythagorean identity $\sin^2 \theta + \cos^2 \theta = 1$.

114. ***Writing*** Use the Pythagorean identity

$\sin^2 \theta + \cos^2 \theta = 1$

to derive the other Pythagorean identities, $1 + \tan^2 \theta = \sec^2 \theta$ and $1 + \cot^2 \theta = \csc^2 \theta$. Discuss how to remember these identities and other fundamental identities.

Skills Review

In Exercises 115 and 116, perform the operation and simplify.

115. $(\sqrt{x} + 5)(\sqrt{x} - 5)$ **116.** $(2\sqrt{z} + 3)^2$

In Exercises 117–120, perform the addition or subtraction and simplify.

117. $\dfrac{1}{x + 5} + \dfrac{x}{x - 8}$ **118.** $\dfrac{6x}{x - 4} - \dfrac{3}{4 - x}$

119. $\dfrac{2x}{x^2 - 4} - \dfrac{7}{x + 4}$ **120.** $\dfrac{x}{x^2 - 25} + \dfrac{x^2}{x - 5}$

In Exercises 121–124, sketch the graph of the function. (Include two full periods.)

121. $f(x) = \dfrac{1}{2} \sin \pi x$ **122.** $f(x) = -2 \tan \dfrac{\pi x}{2}$

123. $f(x) = \dfrac{1}{2} \sec\left(x + \dfrac{\pi}{4}\right)$ **124.** $f(x) = \dfrac{3}{2} \cos(x - \pi) + 3$

5.2 Verifying Trigonometric Identities

What you should learn

- Verify trigonometric identities.

Why you should learn it

You can use trigonometric identities to rewrite trigonometric equations that model real-life situations. For instance, in Exercise 56 on page 388, you can use trigonometric identities to simplify the equation that models the length of a shadow cast by a gnomon (a device used to tell time).

Robert Ginn/PhotoEdit

Introduction

In this section, you will study techniques for verifying trigonometric identities. In the next section, you will study techniques for solving trigonometric equations. The key to verifying identities *and* solving equations is the ability to use the fundamental identities and the rules of algebra to rewrite trigonometric expressions.

Remember that a *conditional equation* is an equation that is true for only some of the values in its domain. For example, the conditional equation

$$\sin x = 0 \qquad \text{Conditional equation}$$

is true only for $x = n\pi$, where n is an integer. When you find these values, you are *solving* the equation.

On the other hand, an equation that is true for all real values in the domain of the variable is an *identity*. For example, the familiar equation

$$\sin^2 x = 1 - \cos^2 x \qquad \text{Identity}$$

is true for all real numbers x. So, it is an identity.

Verifying Trigonometric Identities

Although there are similarities, verifying that a trigonometric equation is an identity is quite different from solving an equation. There is no well-defined set of rules to follow in verifying trigonometric identities, and the process is best learned by practice.

Guidelines for Verifying Trigonometric Identities

1. Work with one side of the equation at a time. It is often better to work with the more complicated side first.
2. Look for opportunities to factor an expression, add fractions, square a binomial, or create a monomial denominator.
3. Look for opportunities to use the fundamental identities. Note which functions are in the final expression you want. Sines and cosines pair up well, as do secants and tangents, and cosecants and cotangents.
4. If the preceding guidelines do not help, try converting all terms to sines and cosines.
5. Always try *something*. Even paths that lead to dead ends provide insights.

Verifying trigonometric identities is a useful process if you need to convert a trigonometric expression into a form that is more useful algebraically. When you verify an identity, you cannot *assume* that the two sides of the equation are equal because you are trying to verify that they *are* equal. As a result, when verifying identities, you cannot use operations such as adding the same quantity to each side of the equation or cross multiplication.

Example 1 Verifying a Trigonometric Identity

Verify the identity $\dfrac{\sec^2 \theta - 1}{\sec^2 \theta} = \sin^2 \theta.$

Solution

Because the left side is more complicated, start with it.

$$\frac{\sec^2 \theta - 1}{\sec^2 \theta} = \frac{(\tan^2 \theta + 1) - 1}{\sec^2 \theta} \qquad \text{Pythagorean identity}$$

$$= \frac{\tan^2 \theta}{\sec^2 \theta} \qquad \text{Simplify.}$$

$$= \tan^2 \theta(\cos^2 \theta) \qquad \text{Reciprocal identity}$$

$$= \frac{\sin^2 \theta}{\cancel{(\cos^2 \theta)}}\cancel{(\cos^2 \theta)} \qquad \text{Quotient identity}$$

$$= \sin^2 \theta \qquad \text{Simplify.}$$

Notice how the identity is verified. You start with the left side of the equation (the more complicated side) and use the fundamental trigonometric identities to simplify it until you obtain the right side.

CHECKPOINT Now try Exercise 5.

There is more than one way to verify an identity. Here is another way to verify the identity in Example 1.

$$\frac{\sec^2 \theta - 1}{\sec^2 \theta} = \frac{\sec^2 \theta}{\sec^2 \theta} - \frac{1}{\sec^2 \theta} \qquad \text{Rewrite as the difference of fractions.}$$

$$= 1 - \cos^2 \theta \qquad \text{Reciprocal identity}$$

$$= \sin^2 \theta \qquad \text{Pythagorean identity}$$

STUDY TIP

Remember that an identity is only true for all real values in the domain of the variable. For instance, in Example 1 the identity is not true when $\theta = \pi/2$ because $\sec^2 \theta$ is not defined when $\theta = \pi/2$.

Example 2 Combining Fractions Before Using Identities

Verify the identity $\dfrac{1}{1 - \sin \alpha} + \dfrac{1}{1 + \sin \alpha} = 2 \sec^2 \alpha.$

Solution

$$\frac{1}{1 - \sin \alpha} + \frac{1}{1 + \sin \alpha} = \frac{1 + \sin \alpha + 1 - \sin \alpha}{(1 - \sin \alpha)(1 + \sin \alpha)} \qquad \text{Add fractions.}$$

$$= \frac{2}{1 - \sin^2 \alpha} \qquad \text{Simplify.}$$

$$= \frac{2}{\cos^2 \alpha} \qquad \text{Pythagorean identity}$$

$$= 2 \sec^2 \alpha \qquad \text{Reciprocal identity}$$

CHECKPOINT Now try Exercise 19.

Example 3 Verifying Trigonometric Identity

Verify the identity $(\tan^2 x + 1)(\cos^2 x - 1) = -\tan^2 x$.

Algebraic Solution

By applying identities before multiplying, you obtain the following.

$$(\tan^2 x + 1)(\cos^2 x - 1) = (\sec^2 x)(-\sin^2 x) \qquad \text{Pythagorean identities}$$

$$= -\frac{\sin^2 x}{\cos^2 x} \qquad \text{Reciprocal identity}$$

$$= -\left(\frac{\sin x}{\cos x}\right)^2 \qquad \text{Rule of exponents}$$

$$= -\tan^2 x \qquad \text{Quotient identity}$$

✔CHECKPOINT Now try Exercise 39.

Numerical Solution

Use the *table* feature of a graphing utility set in *radian* mode to create a table that shows the values of $y_1 = (\tan^2 x + 1)(\cos^2 x - 1)$ and $y_2 = -\tan^2 x$ for different values of x, as shown in Figure 5.2. From the table you can see that the values of y_1 and y_2 appear to be identical, so $(\tan^2 x + 1)(\cos^2 x - 1) = -\tan^2 x$ appears to be an identity.

X	Y1	Y2
-.5	-.2984	-.2984
-.25	-.0652	-.0652
0	0	0
.25	-.0652	-.0652
.5	-.2984	-.2984
.75	-.8679	-.8679
1	-2.426	-2.426

X=-.5

FIGURE 5.2

Example 4 Converting to Sines and Cosines

Verify the identity $\tan x + \cot x = \sec x \csc x$.

Solution

Try converting the left side into sines and cosines.

$$\tan x + \cot x = \frac{\sin x}{\cos x} + \frac{\cos x}{\sin x} \qquad \text{Quotient identities}$$

$$= \frac{\sin^2 x + \cos^2 x}{\cos x \sin x} \qquad \text{Add fractions.}$$

$$= \frac{1}{\cos x \sin x} \qquad \text{Pythagorean identity}$$

$$= \frac{1}{\cos x} \cdot \frac{1}{\sin x} = \sec x \csc x \qquad \text{Reciprocal identities}$$

✔CHECKPOINT Now try Exercise 29.

STUDY TIP

Although a graphing utility can be useful in helping to verify an identity, you must use algebraic techniques to produce a *valid* proof.

Recall from algebra that *rationalizing the denominator* using conjugates is, on occasion, a powerful simplification technique. A related form of this technique, shown below, works for simplifying trigonometric expressions as well.

$$\frac{1}{1 - \cos x} = \frac{1}{1 - \cos x}\left(\frac{1 + \cos x}{1 + \cos x}\right) = \frac{1 + \cos x}{1 - \cos^2 x} = \frac{1 + \cos x}{\sin^2 x}$$

$$= \csc^2 x(1 + \cos x)$$

This technique is demonstrated in the next example.

STUDY TIP

As shown at the right, $\csc^2 x(1 + \cos x)$ is considered a simplified form of $1/(1 - \cos x)$ because the expression does not contain any fractions.

Example 5 Verifying Trigonometric Identities

Verify the identity $\sec y + \tan y = \dfrac{\cos y}{1 - \sin y}$.

Solution

Begin with the *right* side, because you can create a monomial denominator by multiplying the numerator and denominator by $1 + \sin y$.

$$\frac{\cos y}{1 - \sin y} = \frac{\cos y}{1 - \sin y}\left(\frac{1 + \sin y}{1 + \sin y}\right) \qquad \text{Multiply numerator and denominator by } 1 + \sin y.$$

$$= \frac{\cos y + \cos y \sin y}{1 - \sin^2 y} \qquad \text{Multiply.}$$

$$= \frac{\cos y + \cos y \sin y}{\cos^2 y} \qquad \text{Pythagorean identity}$$

$$= \frac{\cos y}{\cos^2 y} + \frac{\cos y \sin y}{\cos^2 y} \qquad \text{Write as separate fractions.}$$

$$= \frac{1}{\cos y} + \frac{\sin y}{\cos y} \qquad \text{Simplify.}$$

$$= \sec y + \tan y \qquad \text{Identities}$$

CHECKPOINT Now try Exercise 33.

In Examples 1 through 5, you have been verifying trigonometric identities by working with one side of the equation and converting to the form given on the other side. On occasion, it is practical to work with each side *separately*, to obtain one common form equivalent to both sides. This is illustrated in Example 6.

Example 6 Working with Each Side Separately

Verify the identity $\dfrac{\cot^2 \theta}{1 + \csc \theta} = \dfrac{1 - \sin \theta}{\sin \theta}$.

Solution

Working with the left side, you have

$$\frac{\cot^2 \theta}{1 + \csc \theta} = \frac{\csc^2 \theta - 1}{1 + \csc \theta} \qquad \text{Pythagorean identity}$$

$$= \frac{(\csc \theta - 1)\cancel{(\csc \theta + 1)}}{\cancel{1 + \csc \theta}} \qquad \text{Factor.}$$

$$= \csc \theta - 1. \qquad \text{Simplify.}$$

Now, simplifying the right side, you have

$$\frac{1 - \sin \theta}{\sin \theta} = \frac{1}{\sin \theta} - \frac{\sin \theta}{\sin \theta} \qquad \text{Write as separate fractions.}$$

$$= \csc \theta - 1. \qquad \text{Reciprocal identity}$$

The identity is verified because both sides are equal to $\csc \theta - 1$.

CHECKPOINT Now try Exercise 47.

In Example 7, powers of trigonometric functions are rewritten as more complicated sums of products of trigonometric functions. This is a common procedure used in calculus.

Example 7 **Three Examples from Calculus**

Verify each identity.

a. $\tan^4 x = \tan^2 x \sec^2 x - \tan^2 x$

b. $\sin^3 x \cos^4 x = (\cos^4 x - \cos^6 x) \sin x$

c. $\csc^4 x \cot x = \csc^2 x(\cot x + \cot^3 x)$

Solution

a. $\tan^4 x = (\tan^2 x)(\tan^2 x)$ — Write as separate factors.

$= \tan^2 x(\sec^2 x - 1)$ — Pythagorean identity

$= \tan^2 x \sec^2 x - \tan^2 x$ — Multiply.

b. $\sin^3 x \cos^4 x = \sin^2 x \cos^4 x \sin x$ — Write as separate factors.

$= (1 - \cos^2 x)\cos^4 x \sin x$ — Pythagorean identity

$= (\cos^4 x - \cos^6 x) \sin x$ — Multiply.

c. $\csc^4 x \cot x = \csc^2 x \csc^2 x \cot x$ — Write as separate factors.

$= \csc^2 x(1 + \cot^2 x) \cot x$ — Pythagorean identity

$= \csc^2 x(\cot x + \cot^3 x)$ — Multiply.

✓CHECKPOINT Now try Exercise 49.

WRITING ABOUT MATHEMATICS

Error Analysis You are tutoring a student in trigonometry. One of the homework problems your student encounters asks whether the following statement is an identity.

$$\tan^2 x \sin^2 x \stackrel{?}{=} \frac{5}{6} \tan^2 x$$

Your student does not attempt to verify the equivalence algebraically, but mistakenly uses only a graphical approach. Using range settings of

Xmin $= -3\pi$	Ymin $= -20$
Xmax $= 3\pi$	Ymax $= 20$
Xscl $= \pi/2$	Yscl $= 1$

your student graphs both sides of the expression on a graphing utility and concludes that the statement is an identity.

What is wrong with your student's reasoning? Explain. Discuss the limitations of verifying identities graphically.

5.2 Exercises

VOCABULARY CHECK:

In Exercises 1 and 2, fill in the blanks.

1. An equation that is true for all real values in its domain is called an ________.
2. An equation that is true for only some values in its domain is called a ________ ________.

In Exercises 3–8, fill in the blank to complete the trigonometric identity.

3. $\dfrac{1}{\cot u} =$ ________
4. $\dfrac{\cos u}{\sin u} =$ ________
5. $\sin^2 u +$ ________ $= 1$
6. $\cos\left(\dfrac{\pi}{2} - u\right) =$ ________
7. $\csc(-u) =$ ________
8. $\sec(-u) =$ ________

In Exercises 1–38, verify the identity.

1. $\sin t \csc t = 1$
2. $\sec y \cos y = 1$
3. $(1 + \sin\alpha)(1 - \sin\alpha) = \cos^2\alpha$
4. $\cot^2 y(\sec^2 y - 1) = 1$
5. $\cos^2\beta - \sin^2\beta = 1 - 2\sin^2\beta$
6. $\cos^2\beta - \sin^2\beta = 2\cos^2\beta - 1$
7. $\sin^2\alpha - \sin^4\alpha = \cos^2\alpha - \cos^4\alpha$
8. $\cos x + \sin x \tan x = \sec x$
9. $\dfrac{\csc^2\theta}{\cot\theta} = \csc\theta\sec\theta$
10. $\dfrac{\cot^3 t}{\csc t} = \cos t(\csc^2 t - 1)$
11. $\dfrac{\cot^2 t}{\csc t} = \csc t - \sin t$
12. $\dfrac{1}{\tan\beta} + \tan\beta = \dfrac{\sec^2\beta}{\tan\beta}$
13. $\sin^{1/2} x\cos x - \sin^{5/2} x\cos x = \cos^3 x\sqrt{\sin x}$
14. $\sec^6 x(\sec x\tan x) - \sec^4 x(\sec x\tan x) = \sec^5 x\tan^3 x$
15. $\dfrac{1}{\sec x\tan x} = \csc x - \sin x$
16. $\dfrac{\sec\theta - 1}{1 - \cos\theta} = \sec\theta$
17. $\csc x - \sin x = \cos x\cot x$
18. $\sec x - \cos x = \sin x\tan x$
19. $\dfrac{1}{\tan x} + \dfrac{1}{\cot x} = \tan x + \cot x$
20. $\dfrac{1}{\sin x} - \dfrac{1}{\csc x} = \csc x - \sin x$
21. $\dfrac{\cos\theta\cot\theta}{1 - \sin\theta} - 1 = \csc\theta$
22. $\dfrac{1 + \sin\theta}{\cos\theta} + \dfrac{\cos\theta}{1 + \sin\theta} = 2\sec\theta$
23. $\dfrac{1}{\sin x + 1} + \dfrac{1}{\csc x + 1} = 1$
24. $\cos x - \dfrac{\cos x}{1 - \tan x} = \dfrac{\sin x\cos x}{\sin x - \cos x}$
25. $\tan\left(\dfrac{\pi}{2} - \theta\right)\tan\theta = 1$
26. $\dfrac{\cos[(\pi/2) - x]}{\sin[(\pi/2) - x]} = \tan x$
27. $\dfrac{\csc(-x)}{\sec(-x)} = -\cot x$
28. $(1 + \sin y)[1 + \sin(-y)] = \cos^2 y$
29. $\dfrac{\tan x\cot x}{\cos x} = \sec x$
30. $\dfrac{\tan x + \tan y}{1 - \tan x\tan y} = \dfrac{\cot x + \cot y}{\cot x\cot y - 1}$
31. $\dfrac{\tan x + \cot y}{\tan x\cot y} = \tan y + \cot x$
32. $\dfrac{\cos x - \cos y}{\sin x + \sin y} + \dfrac{\sin x - \sin y}{\cos x + \cos y} = 0$
33. $\sqrt{\dfrac{1 + \sin\theta}{1 - \sin\theta}} = \dfrac{1 + \sin\theta}{|\cos\theta|}$
34. $\sqrt{\dfrac{1 - \cos\theta}{1 + \cos\theta}} = \dfrac{1 - \cos\theta}{|\sin\theta|}$
35. $\cos^2\beta + \cos^2\left(\dfrac{\pi}{2} - \beta\right) = 1$
36. $\sec^2 y - \cot^2\left(\dfrac{\pi}{2} - y\right) = 1$
37. $\sin t\csc\left(\dfrac{\pi}{2} - t\right) = \tan t$
38. $\sec^2\left(\dfrac{\pi}{2} - x\right) - 1 = \cot^2 x$

In Exercises 39–46, (a) use a graphing utility to graph each side of the equation to determine whether the equation is an identity, (b) use the *table* feature of a graphing utility to determine whether the equation is an identity, and (c) confirm the results of parts (a) and (b) algebraically.

39. $2\sec^2 x - 2\sec^2 x \sin^2 x - \sin^2 x - \cos^2 x = 1$

40. $\csc x(\csc x - \sin x) + \dfrac{\sin x - \cos x}{\sin x} + \cot x = \csc^2 x$

41. $2 + \cos^2 x - 3\cos^4 x = \sin^2 x(3 + 2\cos^2 x)$

42. $\tan^4 x + \tan^2 x - 3 = \sec^2 x(4\tan^2 x - 3)$

43. $\csc^4 x - 2\csc^2 x + 1 = \cot^4 x$

44. $(\sin^4 \beta - 2\sin^2 \beta + 1)\cos \beta = \cos^5 \beta$

45. $\dfrac{\cos x}{1 - \sin x} = \dfrac{1 - \sin x}{\cos x}$ **46.** $\dfrac{\cot \alpha}{\csc \alpha + 1} = \dfrac{\csc \alpha + 1}{\cot \alpha}$

In Exercises 47–50, verify the identity.

47. $\tan^5 x = \tan^3 x \sec^2 x - \tan^3 x$

48. $\sec^4 x \tan^2 x = (\tan^2 x + \tan^4 x)\sec^2 x$

49. $\cos^3 x \sin^2 x = (\sin^2 x - \sin^4 x)\cos x$

50. $\sin^4 x + \cos^4 x = 1 - 2\cos^2 x + 2\cos^4 x$

In Exercises 51–54, use the cofunction identities to evaluate the expression without the aid of a calculator.

51. $\sin^2 25° + \sin^2 65°$ **52.** $\cos^2 55° + \cos^2 35°$

53. $\cos^2 20° + \cos^2 52° + \cos^2 38° + \cos^2 70°$

54. $\sin^2 12° + \sin^2 40° + \sin^2 50° + \sin^2 78°$

55. ***Rate of Change*** The rate of change of the function $f(x) = \sin x + \csc x$ with respect to change in the variable x is given by the expression $\cos x - \csc x \cot x$. Show that the expression for the rate of change can also be $-\cos x \cot^2 x$.

Model It

56. ***Shadow Length*** The length s of a shadow cast by a vertical gnomon (a device used to tell time) of height h when the angle of the sun above the horizon is θ (see figure) can be modeled by the equation

$$s = \frac{h \sin(90° - \theta)}{\sin \theta}.$$

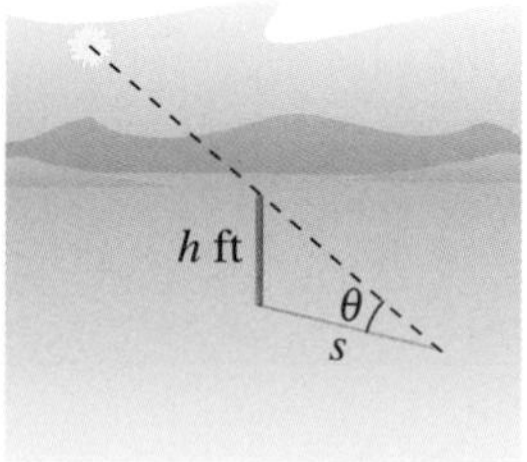

Model It (continued)

(a) Verify that the equation for s is equal to $h \cot \theta$.

(b) Use a graphing utility to complete the table. Let $h = 5$ feet.

θ	10°	20°	30°	40°	50°
s					

θ	60°	70°	80°	90°
s				

(c) Use your table from part (b) to determine the angles of the sun for which the length of the shadow is the greatest and the least.

(d) Based on your results from part (c), what time of day do you think it is when the angle of the sun above the horizon is 90°?

Synthesis

True or False? **In Exercises 57 and 58, determine whether the statement is true or false. Justify your answer.**

57. The equation $\sin^2 \theta + \cos^2 \theta = 1 + \tan^2 \theta$ is an identity, because $\sin^2(0) + \cos^2(0) = 1$ and $1 + \tan^2(0) = 1$.

58. The equation $1 + \tan^2 \theta = 1 + \cot^2 \theta$ is *not* an identity, because it is true that $1 + \tan^2(\pi/6) = 1\frac{1}{3}$, and $1 + \cot^2(\pi/6) = 4$.

Think About It **In Exercises 59 and 60, explain why the equation is not an identity and find one value of the variable for which the equation is not true.**

59. $\sin \theta = \sqrt{1 - \cos^2 \theta}$

60. $\tan \theta = \sqrt{\sec^2 \theta - 1}$

Skills Review

In Exercises 61–64, perform the operation and simplify.

61. $(2 + 3i) - \sqrt{-26}$ **62.** $(2 - 5i)^2$

63. $\sqrt{-16}\left(1 + \sqrt{-4}\right)$ **64.** $(3 + 2i)^3$

In Exercises 65–68, use the Quadratic Formula to solve the quadratic equation.

65. $x^2 + 6x - 12 = 0$ **66.** $x^2 + 5x - 7 = 0$

67. $3x^2 - 6x - 12 = 0$ **68.** $8x^2 - 4x - 3 = 0$

5.3 Solving Trigonometric Equations

What you should learn

- Use standard algebraic techniques to solve trigonometric equations.
- Solve trigonometric equations of quadratic type.
- Solve trigonometric equations involving multiple angles.
- Use inverse trigonometric functions to solve trigonometric equations.

Why you should learn it

You can use trigonometric equations to solve a variety of real-life problems. For instance, in Exercise 72 on page 398, you can solve a trigonometric equation to help answer questions about monthly sales of skiing equipment.

Tom Stillo/Index Stock Imagery

Introduction

To solve a trigonometric equation, use standard algebraic techniques such as collecting like terms and factoring. Your preliminary goal in solving a trigonometric equation is to *isolate* the trigonometric function involved in the equation. For example, to solve the equation $2 \sin x = 1$, divide each side by 2 to obtain

$$\sin x = \frac{1}{2}.$$

To solve for x, note in Figure 5.3 that the equation $\sin x = \frac{1}{2}$ has solutions $x = \pi/6$ and $x = 5\pi/6$ in the interval $[0, 2\pi)$. Moreover, because $\sin x$ has a period of 2π, there are infinitely many other solutions, which can be written as

$$x = \frac{\pi}{6} + 2n\pi \quad \text{and} \quad x = \frac{5\pi}{6} + 2n\pi \qquad \text{General solution}$$

where n is an integer, as shown in Figure 5.3.

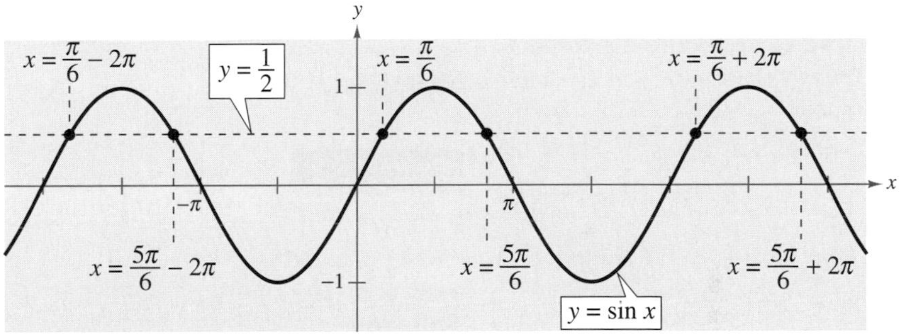

FIGURE 5.3

Another way to show that the equation $\sin x = \frac{1}{2}$ has infinitely many solutions is indicated in Figure 5.4. Any angles that are coterminal with $\pi/6$ or $5\pi/6$ will also be solutions of the equation.

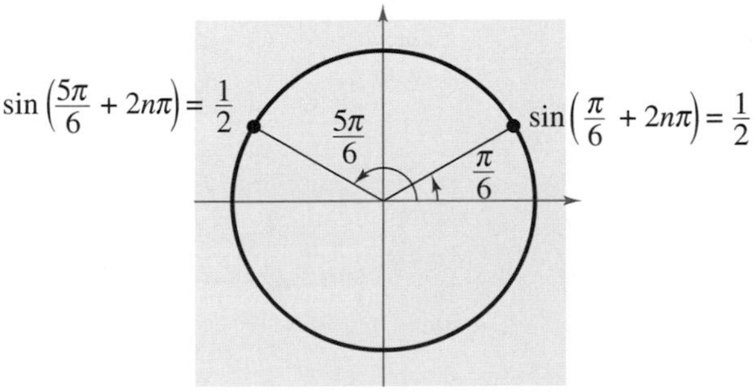

FIGURE 5.4

When solving trigonometric equations, you should write your answer(s) using exact values rather than decimal approximations.

Example 1 **Collecting Like Terms**

Solve $\sin x + \sqrt{2} = -\sin x$.

Solution

Begin by rewriting the equation so that $\sin x$ is isolated on one side of the equation.

$$\sin x + \sqrt{2} = -\sin x \qquad \text{Write original equation.}$$

$$\sin x + \sin x + \sqrt{2} = 0 \qquad \text{Add } \sin x \text{ to each side.}$$

$$\sin x + \sin x = -\sqrt{2} \qquad \text{Subtract } \sqrt{2} \text{ from each side.}$$

$$2 \sin x = -\sqrt{2} \qquad \text{Combine like terms.}$$

$$\sin x = -\frac{\sqrt{2}}{2} \qquad \text{Divide each side by 2.}$$

Because $\sin x$ has a period of 2π, first find all solutions in the interval $[0, 2\pi)$. These solutions are $x = 5\pi/4$ and $x = 7\pi/4$. Finally, add multiples of 2π to each of these solutions to get the general form

$$x = \frac{5\pi}{4} + 2n\pi \quad \text{and} \quad x = \frac{7\pi}{4} + 2n\pi \qquad \text{General solution}$$

where n is an integer.

CHECKPOINT Now try Exercise 7.

Example 2 **Extracting Square Roots**

Solve $3 \tan^2 x - 1 = 0$.

Solution

Begin by rewriting the equation so that $\tan x$ is isolated on one side of the equation.

$$3 \tan^2 x - 1 = 0 \qquad \text{Write original equation.}$$

$$3 \tan^2 x = 1 \qquad \text{Add 1 to each side.}$$

$$\tan^2 x = \frac{1}{3} \qquad \text{Divide each side by 3.}$$

$$\tan x = \pm\frac{1}{\sqrt{3}} = \pm\frac{\sqrt{3}}{3} \qquad \text{Extract square roots.}$$

Because $\tan x$ has a period of π, first find all solutions in the interval $[0, \pi)$. These solutions are $x = \pi/6$ and $x = 5\pi/6$. Finally, add multiples of π to each of these solutions to get the general form

$$x = \frac{\pi}{6} + n\pi \quad \text{and} \quad x = \frac{5\pi}{6} + n\pi \qquad \text{General solution}$$

where n is an integer.

CHECKPOINT Now try Exercise 11.

The equations in Examples 1 and 2 involved only one trigonometric function. When two or more functions occur in the same equation, collect all terms on one side and try to separate the functions by factoring or by using appropriate identities. This may produce factors that yield no solutions, as illustrated in Example 3.

Exploration

Using the equation from Example 3, explain what would happen if you divided each side of the equation by $\cot x$. Is this a correct method to use when solving equations?

Example 3 **Factoring**

Solve $\cot x \cos^2 x = 2 \cot x$.

Solution

Begin by rewriting the equation so that all terms are collected on one side of the equation.

$$\cot x \cos^2 x = 2 \cot x \qquad \text{Write original equation.}$$

$$\cot x \cos^2 x - 2 \cot x = 0 \qquad \text{Subtract } 2 \cot x \text{ from each side.}$$

$$\cot x(\cos^2 x - 2) = 0 \qquad \text{Factor.}$$

By setting each of these factors equal to zero, you obtain

$$\cot x = 0 \qquad \text{and} \qquad \cos^2 x - 2 = 0$$

$$x = \frac{\pi}{2} \qquad\qquad \cos^2 x = 2$$

$$\cos x = \pm\sqrt{2}.$$

The equation $\cot x = 0$ has the solution $x = \pi/2$ [in the interval $(0, \pi)$]. No solution is obtained for $\cos x = \pm\sqrt{2}$ because $\pm\sqrt{2}$ are outside the range of the cosine function. Because $\cot x$ has a period of π, the general form of the solution is obtained by adding multiples of π to $x = \pi/2$, to get

$$x = \frac{\pi}{2} + n\pi \qquad \text{General solution}$$

where n is an integer. You can confirm this graphically by sketching the graph of $y = \cot x \cos^2 x - 2 \cot x$, as shown in Figure 5.5. From the graph you can see that the x-intercepts occur at $-3\pi/2$, $-\pi/2$, $\pi/2$, $3\pi/2$, and so on. These x-intercepts correspond to the solutions of $\cot x \cos^2 x - 2 \cot x = 0$.

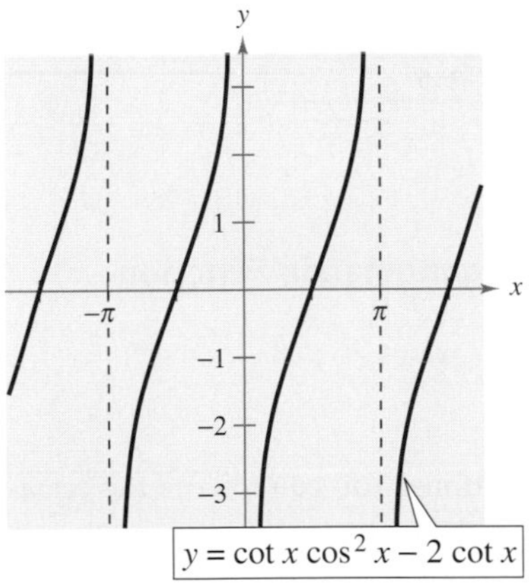

FIGURE 5.5

CHECKPOINT Now try Exercise 15.

Equations of Quadratic Type

Many trigonometric equations are of quadratic type $ax^2 + bx + c = 0$. Here are a couple of examples.

Quadratic in sin x	*Quadratic in sec x*
$2 \sin^2 x - \sin x - 1 = 0$	$\sec^2 x - 3 \sec x - 2 = 0$
$2(\sin x)^2 - \sin x - 1 = 0$	$(\sec x)^2 - 3(\sec x) - 2 = 0$

To solve equations of this type, factor the quadratic or, if this is not possible, use the Quadratic Formula.

Example 4 Factoring an Equation of Quadratic Type

Find all solutions of $2\sin^2 x - \sin x - 1 = 0$ in the interval $[0, 2\pi)$.

Algebraic Solution

Begin by treating the equation as a quadratic in $\sin x$ and factoring.

$$2\sin^2 x - \sin x - 1 = 0 \quad \text{Write original equation.}$$

$$(2\sin x + 1)(\sin x - 1) = 0 \quad \text{Factor.}$$

Setting each factor equal to zero, you obtain the following solutions in the interval $[0, 2\pi)$.

$$2\sin x + 1 = 0 \quad \text{and} \quad \sin x - 1 = 0$$

$$\sin x = -\frac{1}{2} \qquad \sin x = 1$$

$$x = \frac{7\pi}{6}, \frac{11\pi}{6} \qquad x = \frac{\pi}{2}$$

CHECKPOINT Now try Exercise 29.

Graphical Solution

Use a graphing utility set in *radian* mode to graph $y = 2\sin^2 x - \sin x - 1$ for $0 \le x < 2\pi$, as shown in Figure 5.6. Use the *zero* or *root* feature or the *zoom* and *trace* features to approximate the x-intercepts to be

$$x \approx 1.571 \approx \frac{\pi}{2}, \; x \approx 3.665 \approx \frac{7\pi}{6}, \text{ and } x \approx 5.760 \approx \frac{11\pi}{6}.$$

These values are the approximate solutions of $2\sin^2 x - \sin x - 1 = 0$ in the interval $[0, 2\pi)$.

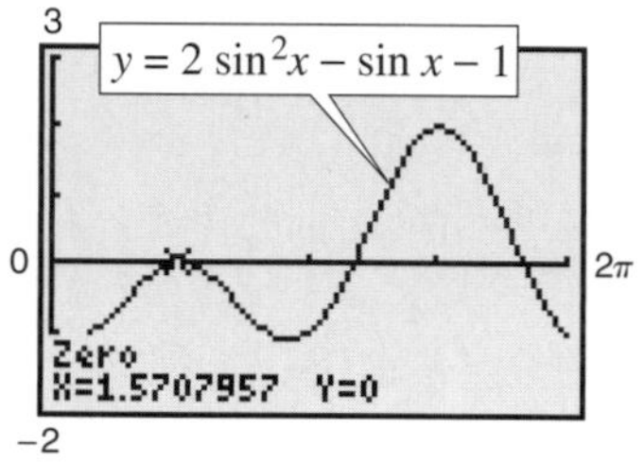

FIGURE 5.6

Example 5 Rewriting with a Single Trigonometric Function

Solve $2\sin^2 x + 3\cos x - 3 = 0$.

Solution

This equation contains both sine and cosine functions. You can rewrite the equation so that it has only cosine functions by using the identity $\sin^2 x = 1 - \cos^2 x$.

$$2\sin^2 x + 3\cos x - 3 = 0 \quad \text{Write original equation.}$$

$$2(1 - \cos^2 x) + 3\cos x - 3 = 0 \quad \text{Pythagorean identity}$$

$$2\cos^2 x - 3\cos x + 1 = 0 \quad \text{Multiply each side by } -1.$$

$$(2\cos x - 1)(\cos x - 1) = 0 \quad \text{Factor.}$$

Set each factor equal to zero to find the solutions in the interval $[0, 2\pi)$.

$$2\cos x - 1 = 0 \Rightarrow \cos x = \frac{1}{2} \Rightarrow x = \frac{\pi}{3}, \frac{5\pi}{3}$$

$$\cos x - 1 = 0 \Rightarrow \cos x = 1 \Rightarrow x = 0$$

Because $\cos x$ has a period of 2π, the general form of the solution is obtained by adding multiples of 2π to get

$$x = 2n\pi, \quad x = \frac{\pi}{3} + 2n\pi, \quad x = \frac{5\pi}{3} + 2n\pi \quad \text{General solution}$$

where n is an integer.

CHECKPOINT Now try Exercise 31.

Sometimes you must square each side of an equation to obtain a quadratic, as demonstrated in the next example. Because this procedure can introduce extraneous solutions, you should check any solutions in the original equation to see whether they are valid or extraneous.

Example 6 Squaring and Converting to Quadratic Type

Find all solutions of $\cos x + 1 = \sin x$ in the interval $[0, 2\pi)$.

Solution

It is not clear how to rewrite this equation in terms of a single trigonometric function. Notice what happens when you square each side of the equation.

$$\cos x + 1 = \sin x \quad \text{Write original equation.}$$

$$\cos^2 x + 2\cos x + 1 = \sin^2 x \quad \text{Square each side.}$$

$$\cos^2 x + 2\cos x + 1 = 1 - \cos^2 x \quad \text{Pythagorean identity}$$

$$\cos^2 x + \cos^2 x + 2\cos x + 1 - 1 = 0 \quad \text{Rewrite equation.}$$

$$2\cos^2 x + 2\cos x = 0 \quad \text{Combine like terms.}$$

$$2\cos x(\cos x + 1) = 0 \quad \text{Factor.}$$

Setting each factor equal to zero produces

$$2\cos x = 0 \qquad \text{and} \qquad \cos x + 1 = 0$$

$$\cos x = 0 \qquad\qquad \cos x = -1$$

$$x = \frac{\pi}{2}, \frac{3\pi}{2} \qquad\qquad x = \pi.$$

Because you squared the original equation, check for extraneous solutions.

Check $x = \pi/2$

$$\cos\frac{\pi}{2} + 1 \stackrel{?}{=} \sin\frac{\pi}{2} \quad \text{Substitute } \pi/2 \text{ for } x.$$

$$0 + 1 = 1 \quad \text{Solution checks. ✓}$$

Check $x = 3\pi/2$

$$\cos\frac{3\pi}{2} + 1 \stackrel{?}{=} \sin\frac{3\pi}{2} \quad \text{Substitute } 3\pi/2 \text{ for } x.$$

$$0 + 1 \neq -1 \quad \text{Solution does not check.}$$

Check $x = \pi$

$$\cos\pi + 1 \stackrel{?}{=} \sin\pi \quad \text{Substitute } \pi \text{ for } x.$$

$$-1 + 1 = 0 \quad \text{Solution checks. ✓}$$

Of the three possible solutions, $x = 3\pi/2$ is extraneous. So, in the interval $[0, 2\pi)$, the only two solutions are $x = \pi/2$ and $x = \pi$.

✓CHECKPOINT Now try Exercise 33.

STUDY TIP

You square each side of the equation in Example 6 because the squares of the sine and cosine functions are related by a Pythagorean identity. The same is true for the squares of the secant and tangent functions and the cosecant and cotangent functions.

Exploration

Use a graphing utility to confirm the solutions found in Example 6 in two different ways. Do both methods produce the same x-values? Which method do you prefer? Why?

1. Graph both sides of the equation and find the x-coordinates of the points at which the graphs intersect.

   Left side: $y = \cos x + 1$

   Right side: $y = \sin x$

2. Graph the equation

   $y = \cos x + 1 - \sin x$

   and find the x-intercepts of the graph.

Functions Involving Multiple Angles

The next two examples involve trigonometric functions of multiple angles of the forms sin *ku* and cos *ku*. To solve equations of these forms, first solve the equation for *ku*, then divide your result by *k*.

Example 7 Functions of Multiple Angles

Solve $2 \cos 3t - 1 = 0$.

Solution

$$2 \cos 3t - 1 = 0 \qquad \text{Write original equation.}$$

$$2 \cos 3t = 1 \qquad \text{Add 1 to each side.}$$

$$\cos 3t = \frac{1}{2} \qquad \text{Divide each side by 2.}$$

In the interval $[0, 2\pi)$, you know that $3t = \pi/3$ and $3t = 5\pi/3$ are the only solutions, so, in general, you have

$$3t = \frac{\pi}{3} + 2n\pi \quad \text{and} \quad 3t = \frac{5\pi}{3} + 2n\pi.$$

Dividing these results by 3, you obtain the general solution

$$t = \frac{\pi}{9} + \frac{2n\pi}{3} \quad \text{and} \quad t = \frac{5\pi}{9} + \frac{2n\pi}{3} \qquad \text{General solution}$$

where n is an integer.

CHECKPOINT Now try Exercise 35.

Example 8 Functions of Multiple Angles

Solve $3 \tan \frac{x}{2} + 3 = 0$.

Solution

$$3 \tan \frac{x}{2} + 3 = 0 \qquad \text{Write original equation.}$$

$$3 \tan \frac{x}{2} = -3 \qquad \text{Subtract 3 from each side.}$$

$$\tan \frac{x}{2} = -1 \qquad \text{Divide each side by 3.}$$

In the interval $[0, \pi)$, you know that $x/2 = 3\pi/4$ is the only solution, so, in general, you have

$$\frac{x}{2} = \frac{3\pi}{4} + n\pi.$$

Multiplying this result by 2, you obtain the general solution

$$x = \frac{3\pi}{2} + 2n\pi \qquad \text{General solution}$$

where n is an integer.

CHECKPOINT Now try Exercise 39.

Using Inverse Functions

In the next example, you will see how inverse trigonometric functions can be used to solve an equation.

Example 9 Using Inverse Functions

Solve $\sec^2 x - 2 \tan x = 4$.

Solution

$$\sec^2 x - 2 \tan x = 4$$ Write original equation.

$$1 + \tan^2 x - 2 \tan x - 4 = 0$$ Pythagorean identity

$$\tan^2 x - 2 \tan x - 3 = 0$$ Combine like terms.

$$(\tan x - 3)(\tan x + 1) = 0$$ Factor.

Setting each factor equal to zero, you obtain two solutions in the interval $(-\pi/2, \pi/2)$. [Recall that the range of the inverse tangent function is $(-\pi/2, \pi/2)$.]

$$\tan x - 3 = 0 \quad \text{and} \quad \tan x + 1 = 0$$

$$\tan x = 3 \qquad\qquad \tan x = \quad 1$$

$$x = \arctan 3 \qquad\qquad x = -\frac{\pi}{4}$$

Finally, because $\tan x$ has a period of π, you obtain the general solution by adding multiples of π

$$x = \arctan 3 + n\pi \quad \text{and} \quad x = -\frac{\pi}{4} + n\pi$$ General solution

where n is an integer. You can use a calculator to approximate the value of arctan 3.

✓CHECKPOINT Now try Exercise 59.

Writing about Mathematics

Equations with No Solutions One of the following equations has solutions and the other two do not. Which two equations do not have solutions?

a. $\sin^2 x - 5 \sin x + 6 = 0$

b. $\sin^2 x - 4 \sin x + 6 = 0$

c. $\sin^2 x - 5 \sin x - 6 = 0$

Find conditions involving the constants b and c that will guarantee that the equation

$$\sin^2 x + b \sin x + c = 0$$

has at least one solution on some interval of length 2π.

5.3 Exercises

VOCABULARY CHECK: Fill in the blanks.

1. The equation $2 \sin \theta + 1 = 0$ has the solutions $\theta = \frac{7\pi}{6} + 2n\pi$ and $\theta = \frac{11\pi}{6} + 2n\pi$, which are called ________ solutions.
2. The equation $2 \tan^2 x - 3 \tan x + 1 = 0$ is a trigonometric equation that is of ________ type.
3. A solution to an equation that does not satisfy the original equation is called an ________ solution.

In Exercises 1–6, verify that the *x*-values are solutions of the equation.

1. $2 \cos x - 1 = 0$

   (a) $x = \frac{\pi}{3}$ (b) $x = \frac{5\pi}{3}$

2. $\sec x - 2 = 0$

   (a) $x = \frac{\pi}{3}$ (b) $x = \frac{5\pi}{3}$

3. $3 \tan^2 2x - 1 = 0$

   (a) $x = \frac{\pi}{12}$ (b) $x = \frac{5\pi}{12}$

4. $2 \cos^2 4x - 1 = 0$

   (a) $x = \frac{\pi}{16}$ (b) $x = \frac{3\pi}{16}$

5. $2 \sin^2 x - \sin x - 1 = 0$

   (a) $x = \frac{\pi}{2}$ (b) $x = \frac{7\pi}{6}$

6. $\csc^4 x - 4 \csc^2 x = 0$

   (a) $x = \frac{\pi}{6}$ (b) $x = \frac{5\pi}{6}$

In Exercises 7–20, solve the equation.

7. $2 \cos x + 1 = 0$
8. $2 \sin x + 1 = 0$
9. $\sqrt{3} \csc x - 2 = 0$
10. $\tan x + \sqrt{3} = 0$
11. $3 \sec^2 x - 4 = 0$
12. $3 \cot^2 x - 1 = 0$
13. $\sin x(\sin x + 1) = 0$
14. $(3 \tan^2 x - 1)(\tan^2 x - 3) = 0$
15. $4 \cos^2 x - 1 = 0$
16. $\sin^2 x = 3 \cos^2 x$
17. $2 \sin^2 2x = 1$
18. $\tan^2 3x = 3$
19. $\tan 3x(\tan x - 1) = 0$
20. $\cos 2x(2 \cos x + 1) = 0$

In Exercises 21–34, find all solutions of the equation in the interval $[0, 2\pi)$.

21. $\cos^3 x = \cos x$
22. $\sec^2 x - 1 = 0$
23. $3 \tan^3 x = \tan x$
24. $2 \sin^2 x = 2 + \cos x$
25. $\sec^2 x - \sec x = 2$
26. $\sec x \csc x = 2 \csc x$
27. $2 \sin x + \csc x = 0$
28. $\sec x + \tan x = 1$
29. $2 \cos^2 x + \cos x - 1 = 0$
30. $2 \sin^2 x + 3 \sin x + 1 = 0$
31. $2 \sec^2 x + \tan^2 x - 3 = 0$
32. $\cos x + \sin x \tan x = 2$
33. $\csc x + \cot x = 1$
34. $\sin x - 2 = \cos x - 2$

In Exercises 35–40, solve the multiple-angle equation.

35. $\cos 2x = \frac{1}{2}$
36. $\sin 2x = -\frac{\sqrt{3}}{2}$
37. $\tan 3x = 1$
38. $\sec 4x = 2$
39. $\cos \frac{x}{2} = \frac{\sqrt{2}}{2}$
40. $\sin \frac{x}{2} = -\frac{\sqrt{3}}{2}$

In Exercises 41–44, find the *x*-intercepts of the graph.

41. $y = \sin \frac{\pi x}{2} + 1$

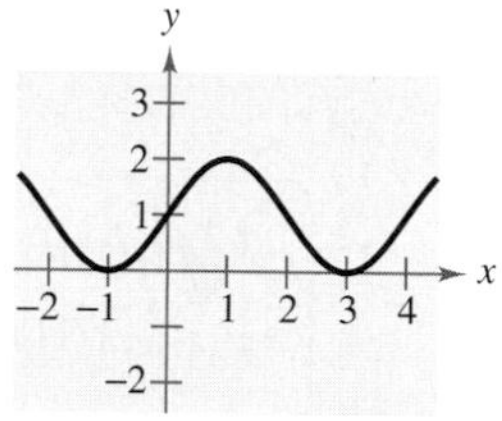

42. $y = \sin \pi x + \cos \pi x$

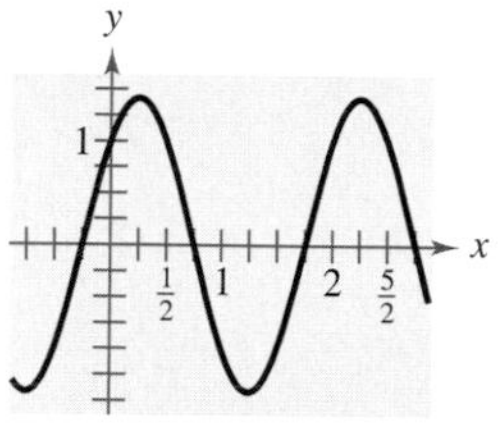

43. $y = \tan^2\left(\frac{\pi x}{6}\right) - 3$

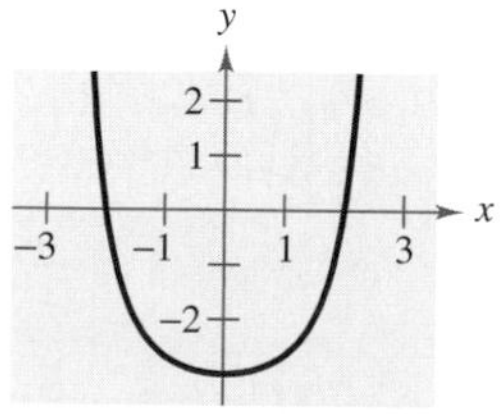

44. $y = \sec^4\left(\frac{\pi x}{8}\right) - 4$

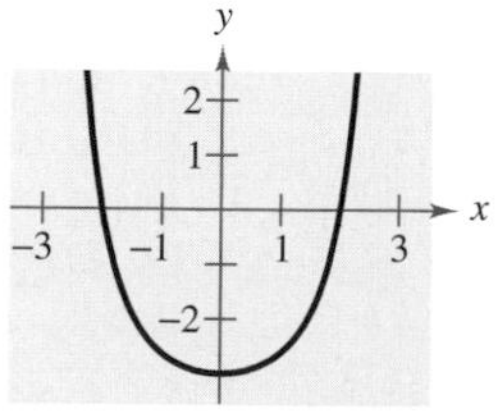

In Exercises 45–54, use a graphing utility to approximate the solutions (to three decimal places) of the equation in the interval $[0, 2\pi)$.

45. $2 \sin x + \cos x = 0$

46. $4 \sin^3 x + 2 \sin^2 x - 2 \sin x - 1 = 0$

47. $\dfrac{1 + \sin x}{\cos x} + \dfrac{\cos x}{1 + \sin x} = 4$

48. $\dfrac{\cos x \cot x}{1 - \sin x} = 3$

49. $x \tan x - 1 = 0$

50. $x \cos x - 1 = 0$

51. $\sec^2 x + 0.5 \tan x - 1 = 0$

52. $\csc^2 x + 0.5 \cot x - 5 = 0$

53. $2 \tan^2 x + 7 \tan x - 15 = 0$

54. $6 \sin^2 x - 7 \sin x + 2 = 0$

In Exercises 55–58, use the Quadratic Formula to solve the equation in the interval $[0, 2\pi)$. Then use a graphing utility to approximate the angle x.

55. $12 \sin^2 x - 13 \sin x + 3 = 0$

56. $3 \tan^2 x + 4 \tan x - 4 = 0$

57. $\tan^2 x + 3 \tan x + 1 = 0$

58. $4 \cos^2 x - 4 \cos x - 1 = 0$

In Exercises 59–62, use inverse functions where needed to find all solutions of the equation in the interval $[0, 2\pi)$.

59. $\tan^2 x - 6 \tan x + 5 = 0$

60. $\sec^2 x + \tan x - 3 = 0$

61. $2 \cos^2 x - 5 \cos x + 2 = 0$

62. $2 \sin^2 x - 7 \sin x + 3 = 0$

In Exercises 63 and 64, (a) use a graphing utility to graph the function and approximate the maximum and minimum points on the graph in the interval $[0, 2\pi)$, and (b) solve the trigonometric equation and demonstrate that its solutions are the x-coordinates of the maximum and minimum points of f. (Calculus is required to find the trigonometric equation.)

	Function	*Trigonometric Equation*
63.	$f(x) = \sin x + \cos x$	$\cos x - \sin x = 0$
64.	$f(x) = 2 \sin x + \cos 2x$	$2 \cos x - 4 \sin x \cos x = 0$

Fixed Point **In Exercises 65 and 66, find the smallest positive fixed point of the function f. [A *fixed point* of a function f is a real number c such that $f(c) = c$.]**

65. $f(x) = \tan \dfrac{\pi x}{4}$

66. $f(x) = \cos x$

67. ***Graphical Reasoning*** Consider the function given by

$$f(x) = \cos \frac{1}{x}$$

and its graph shown in the figure.

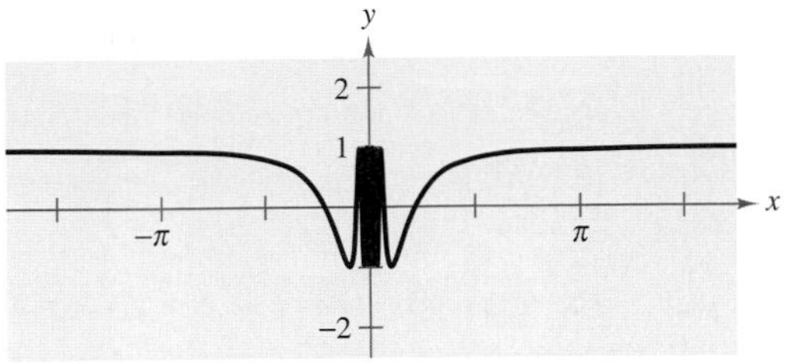

(a) What is the domain of the function?

(b) Identify any symmetry and any asymptotes of the graph.

(c) Describe the behavior of the function as $x \rightarrow 0$.

(d) How many solutions does the equation

$$\cos \frac{1}{x} = 0$$

have in the interval $[-1, 1]$? Find the solutions.

(e) Does the equation $\cos(1/x) = 0$ have a greatest solution? If so, approximate the solution. If not, explain why.

68. ***Graphical Reasoning*** Consider the function given by

$$f(x) = \frac{\sin x}{x}$$

and its graph shown in the figure.

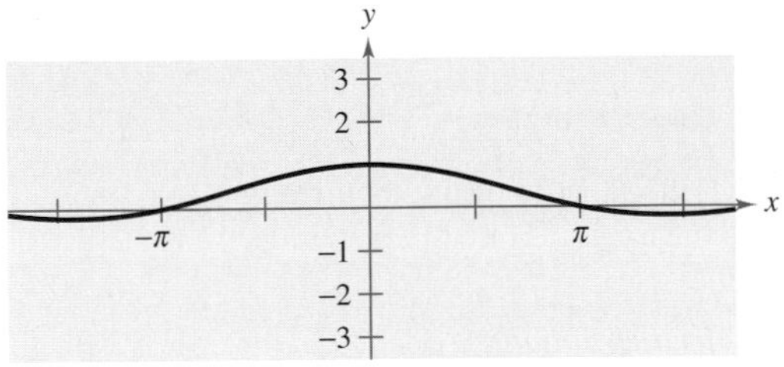

(a) What is the domain of the function?

(b) Identify any symmetry and any asymptotes of the graph.

(c) Describe the behavior of the function as $x \rightarrow 0$.

(d) How many solutions does the equation

$$\frac{\sin x}{x} = 0$$

have in the interval $[-8, 8]$? Find the solutions.

69. ***Harmonic Motion*** A weight is oscillating on the end of a spring (see figure). The position of the weight relative to the point of equilibrium is given by $y = \frac{1}{12}(\cos 8t - 3 \sin 8t)$, where y is the displacement (in meters) and t is the time (in seconds). Find the times when the weight is at the point of equilibrium $(y = 0)$ for $0 \le t \le 1$.

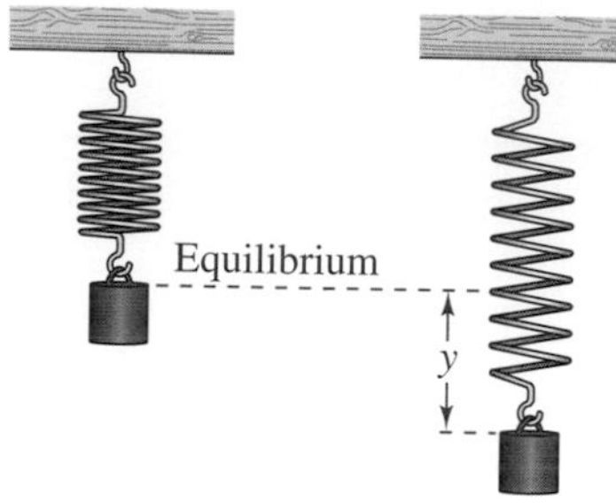

70. ***Damped Harmonic Motion*** The displacement from equilibrium of a weight oscillating on the end of a spring is given by $y = 1.56e^{-0.22t} \cos 4.9t$, where y is the displacement (in feet) and t is the time (in seconds). Use a graphing utility to graph the displacement function for $0 \le t \le 10$. Find the time beyond which the displacement does not exceed 1 foot from equilibrium.

71. ***Sales*** The monthly sales S (in thousands of units) of a seasonal product are approximated by

$$S = 74.50 + 43.75 \sin \frac{\pi t}{6}$$

where t is the time (in months), with $t = 1$ corresponding to January. Determine the months when sales exceed 100,000 units.

72. ***Sales*** The monthly sales S (in hundreds of units) of skiing equipment at a sports store are approximated by

$$S = 58.3 + 32.5 \cos \frac{\pi t}{6}$$

where t is the time (in months), with $t = 1$ corresponding to January. Determine the months when sales exceed 7500 units.

73. ***Projectile Motion*** A batted baseball leaves the bat at an angle of θ with the horizontal and an initial velocity of $v_0 = 100$ feet per second. The ball is caught by an outfielder 300 feet from home plate (see figure). Find θ if the range r of a projectile is given by $r = \frac{1}{32} v_0^2 \sin 2\theta$.

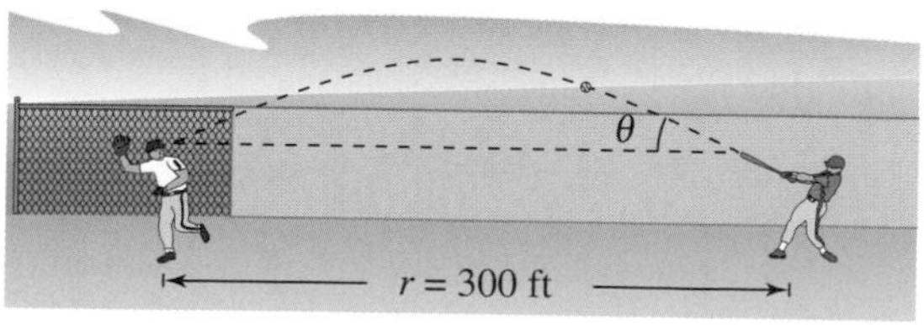

Not drawn to scale

74. ***Projectile Motion*** A sharpshooter intends to hit a target at a distance of 1000 yards with a gun that has a muzzle velocity of 1200 feet per second (see figure). Neglecting air resistance, determine the gun's minimum angle of elevation θ if the range r is given by

$$r = \frac{1}{32} v_0^2 \sin 2\theta.$$

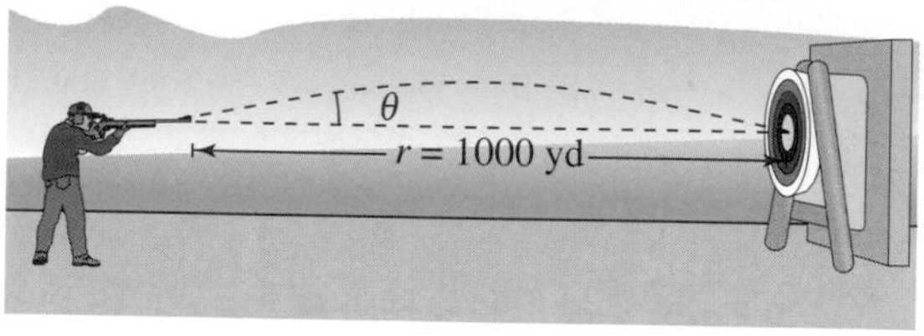

Not drawn to scale

75. ***Ferris Wheel*** A Ferris wheel is built such that the height h (in feet) above ground of a seat on the wheel at time t (in minutes) can be modeled by

$$h(t) = 53 + 50 \sin\left(\frac{\pi}{16}t - \frac{\pi}{2}\right).$$

The wheel makes one revolution every 32 seconds. The ride begins when $t = 0$.

(a) During the first 32 seconds of the ride, when will a person on the Ferris wheel be 53 feet above ground?

(b) When will a person be at the top of the Ferris wheel for the first time during the ride? If the ride lasts 160 seconds, how many times will a person be at the top of the ride, and at what times?

Model It

76. ***Data Analysis: Unemployment Rate*** The table shows the unemployment rates r in the United States for selected years from 1990 through 2004. The time t is measured in years, with $t = 0$ corresponding to 1990. (Source: U.S. Bureau of Labor Statistics)

Time, t	Rate, r	Time, t	Rate, r
0	5.6	8	4.5
2	7.5	10	4.0
4	6.1	12	5.8
6	5.4	14	5.5

(a) Create a scatter plot of the data.

Model It (continued)

(b) Which of the following models best represents the data? Explain your reasoning.

(1) $r = 1.24 \sin(0.47t + 0.40) + 5.45$

(2) $r = 1.24 \sin(0.47t - 0.01) + 5.45$

(3) $r = \sin(0.10t + 5.61) + 4.80$

(4) $r = 896 \sin(0.57t - 2.05) + 6.48$

(c) What term in the model gives the average unemployment rate? What is the rate?

(d) Economists study the lengths of business cycles such as unemployment rates. Based on this short span of time, use the model to find the length of this cycle.

(e) Use the model to estimate the next time the unemployment rate will be 5% or less.

77. ***Geometry*** The area of a rectangle (see figure) inscribed in one arc of the graph of $y = \cos x$ is given by

$$A = 2x \cos x, \quad 0 < x < \frac{\pi}{2}.$$

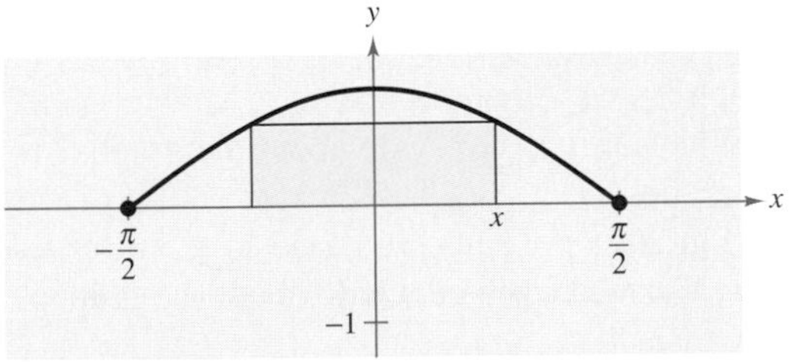

(a) Use a graphing utility to graph the area function, and approximate the area of the largest inscribed rectangle.

(b) Determine the values of x for which $A \geq 1$.

78. ***Quadratic Approximation*** Consider the function given by $f(x) = 3 \sin(0.6x - 2)$.

(a) Approximate the zero of the function in the interval $[0, 6]$.

(b) A quadratic approximation agreeing with f at $x = 5$ is $g(x) = -0.45x^2 + 5.52x - 13.70$. Use a graphing utility to graph f and g in the same viewing window. Describe the result.

(c) Use the Quadratic Formula to find the zeros of g. Compare the zero in the interval $[0, 6]$ with the result of part (a).

Synthesis

True or False? **In Exercises 79 and 80, determine whether the statement is true or false. Justify your answer.**

79. The equation $2 \sin 4t - 1 = 0$ has four times the number of solutions in the interval $[0, 2\pi)$ as the equation $2 \sin t - 1 = 0$.

80. If you correctly solve a trigonometric equation to the statement $\sin x = 3.4$, then you can finish solving the equation by using an inverse function.

In Exercises 81 and 82, use the graph to approximate the number of points of intersection of the graphs of y_1 and y_2.

81. $y_1 = 2 \sin x$
$y_2 = 3x + 1$

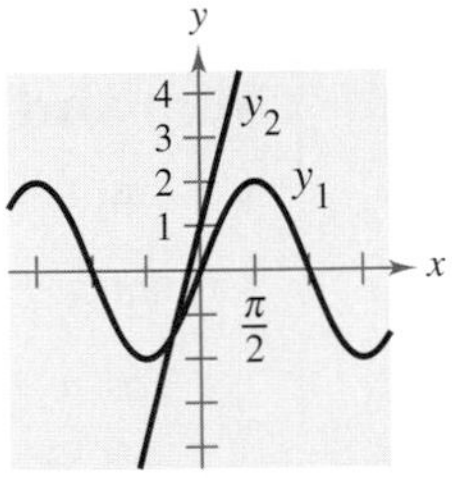

82. $y_1 = 2 \sin x$
$y_2 = \frac{1}{2}x + 1$

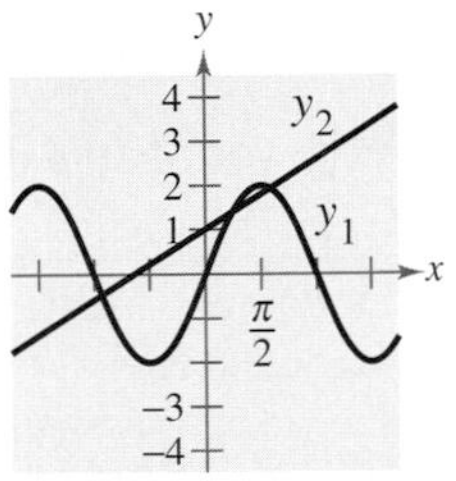

Skills Review

In Exercises 83 and 84, solve triangle *ABC* by finding all missing angle measures and side lengths.

83.

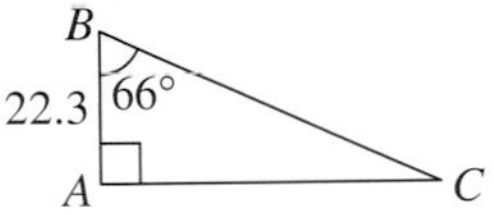

84.

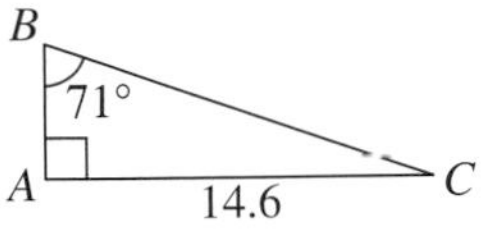

In Exercises 85–88, use reference angles to find the exact values of the sine, cosine, and tangent of the angle with the given measure.

85. 390°

86. 600°

87. −1845°

88. −1410°

89. ***Angle of Depression*** Find the angle of depression from the top of a lighthouse 250 feet above water level to the water line of a ship 2 miles offshore.

90. ***Height*** From a point 100 feet in front of a public library, the angles of elevation to the base of the flagpole and the top of the pole are 28° and 39° 45′, respectively. The flagpole is mounted on the front of the library's roof. Find the height of the flagpole.

91. **Make a Decision** To work an extended application analyzing the normal daily high temperatures in Phoenix and in Seattle, visit this text's website at *college.hmco.com.* *(Data Source: NOAA)*

5.4 Sum and Difference Formulas

What you should learn

- Use sum and difference formulas to evaluate trigonometric functions, verify identities, and solve trigonometric equations.

Why you should learn it

You can use identities to rewrite trigonometric expressions. For instance, in Exercise 75 on page 405, you can use an identity to rewrite a trigonometric expression in a form that helps you analyze a harmonic motion equation.

Richard Megna/Fundamental Photographs

Using Sum and Difference Formulas

In this and the following section, you will study the uses of several trigonometric identities and formulas.

Sum and Difference Formulas

$$\sin(u + v) = \sin u \cos v + \cos u \sin v$$

$$\sin(u - v) = \sin u \cos v - \cos u \sin v$$

$$\cos(u + v) = \cos u \cos v - \sin u \sin v$$

$$\cos(u - v) = \cos u \cos v + \sin u \sin v$$

$$\tan(u + v) = \frac{\tan u + \tan v}{1 - \tan u \tan v}$$

$$\tan(u - v) = \frac{\tan u - \tan v}{1 + \tan u \tan v}$$

For a proof of the sum and difference formulas, see Proofs in Mathematics on page 424.

Exploration

Use a graphing utility to graph $y_1 = \cos(x + 2)$ and $y_2 = \cos x + \cos 2$ in the same viewing window. What can you conclude about the graphs? Is it true that $\cos(x + 2) = \cos x + \cos 2$?

Use a graphing utility to graph $y_1 = \sin(x + 4)$ and $y_2 = \sin x + \sin 4$ in the same viewing window. What can you conclude about the graphs? Is it true that $\sin(x + 4) = \sin x + \sin 4$?

Examples 1 and 2 show how **sum and difference formulas** can be used to find exact values of trigonometric functions involving sums or differences of special angles.

Example 1 Evaluating a Trigonometric Function

Find the exact value of $\cos 75°$.

Solution

To find the *exact* value of $\cos 75°$, use the fact that $75° = 30° + 45°$. Consequently, the formula for $\cos(u + v)$ yields

$$\begin{aligned} \cos 75° &= \cos(30° + 45°) \\ &= \cos 30° \cos 45° - \sin 30° \sin 45° \\ &= \frac{\sqrt{3}}{2}\left(\frac{\sqrt{2}}{2}\right) - \frac{1}{2}\left(\frac{\sqrt{2}}{2}\right) = \frac{\sqrt{6} - \sqrt{2}}{4}. \end{aligned}$$

Try checking this result on your calculator. You will find that $\cos 75° \approx 0.259$.

CHECKPOINT Now try Exercise 1.

The Granger Collection, New York

Historical Note
Hipparchus, considered the most eminent of Greek astronomers, was born about 160 B.C. in Nicaea. He was credited with the invention of trigonometry. He also derived the sum and difference formulas for $\sin(A \pm B)$ and $\cos(A \pm B)$.

Example 2 Evaluating a Trigonometric Expression

Find the exact value of $\sin \dfrac{\pi}{12}$.

Solution

Using the fact that

$$\frac{\pi}{12} = \frac{\pi}{3} - \frac{\pi}{4}$$

together with the formula for $\sin(u - v)$, you obtain

$$\begin{aligned}\sin \frac{\pi}{12} &= \sin\left(\frac{\pi}{3} - \frac{\pi}{4}\right)\\ &= \sin \frac{\pi}{3} \cos \frac{\pi}{4} - \cos \frac{\pi}{3} \sin \frac{\pi}{4}\\ &= \frac{\sqrt{3}}{2}\left(\frac{\sqrt{2}}{2}\right) - \frac{1}{2}\left(\frac{\sqrt{2}}{2}\right)\\ &= \frac{\sqrt{6} - \sqrt{2}}{4}.\end{aligned}$$

CHECKPOINT Now try Exercise 3.

Example 3 Evaluating a Trigonometric Expression

Find the exact value of $\sin 42° \cos 12° - \cos 42° \sin 12°$.

Solution

Recognizing that this expression fits the formula for $\sin(u - v)$, you can write

$$\begin{aligned}\sin 42° \cos 12° - \cos 42° \sin 12° &= \sin(42° - 12°)\\ &= \sin 30°\\ &= \tfrac{1}{2}.\end{aligned}$$

CHECKPOINT Now try Exercise 31.

Example 4 An Application of a Sum Formula

Write $\cos(\arctan 1 + \arccos x)$ as an algebraic expression.

Solution

This expression fits the formula for $\cos(u + v)$. Angles $u = \arctan 1$ and $v = \arccos x$ are shown in Figure 5.7. So

$$\begin{aligned}\cos(u + v) &= \cos(\arctan 1) \cos(\arccos x) - \sin(\arctan 1) \sin(\arccos x)\\ &= \frac{1}{\sqrt{2}} \cdot x - \frac{1}{\sqrt{2}} \cdot \sqrt{1 - x^2}\\ &= \frac{x - \sqrt{1 - x^2}}{\sqrt{2}}.\end{aligned}$$

CHECKPOINT Now try Exercise 51.

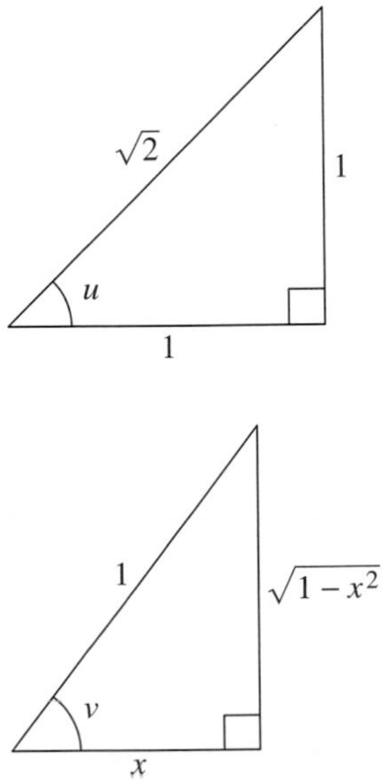

FIGURE 5.7

Example 5 shows how to use a difference formula to prove the cofunction identity

$$\cos\left(\frac{\pi}{2} - x\right) = \sin x.$$

Example 5 Proving a Cofunction Identity

Prove the cofunction identity $\cos\left(\frac{\pi}{2} - x\right) = \sin x$.

Solution

Using the formula for $\cos(u - v)$, you have

$$\begin{aligned}\cos\left(\frac{\pi}{2} - x\right) &= \cos\frac{\pi}{2}\cos x + \sin\frac{\pi}{2}\sin x\\ &= (0)(\cos x) + (1)(\sin x) = \sin x.\end{aligned}$$

CHECKPOINT Now try Exercise 55.

Sum and difference formulas can be used to rewrite expressions such as

$$\sin\left(\theta + \frac{n\pi}{2}\right) \quad \text{and} \quad \cos\left(\theta + \frac{n\pi}{2}\right), \quad \text{where } n \text{ is an integer}$$

as expressions involving only $\sin\theta$ or $\cos\theta$. The resulting formulas are called **reduction formulas.**

Example 6 Deriving Reduction Formulas

Simplify each expression.

a. $\cos\left(\theta - \frac{3\pi}{2}\right)$ **b.** $\tan(\theta + 3\pi)$

Solution

a. Using the formula for $\cos(u - v)$, you have

$$\begin{aligned}\cos\left(\theta - \frac{3\pi}{2}\right) &= \cos\theta\cos\frac{3\pi}{2} + \sin\theta\sin\frac{3\pi}{2}\\ &= (\cos\theta)(0) + (\sin\theta)(-1)\\ &= -\sin\theta.\end{aligned}$$

b. Using the formula for $\tan(u + v)$, you have

$$\begin{aligned}\tan(\theta + 3\pi) &= \frac{\tan\theta + \tan 3\pi}{1 - \tan\theta\tan 3\pi}\\ &= \frac{\tan\theta + 0}{1 - (\tan\theta)(0)}\\ &= \tan\theta.\end{aligned}$$

CHECKPOINT Now try Exercise 65.

Example 7 Solving a Trigonometric Equation

Find all solutions of $\sin\left(x + \frac{\pi}{4}\right) + \sin\left(x - \frac{\pi}{4}\right) = -1$ in the interval $[0, 2\pi)$.

Solution

Using sum and difference formulas, rewrite the equation as

$$\sin x \cos \frac{\pi}{4} + \cos x \sin \frac{\pi}{4} + \sin x \cos \frac{\pi}{4} - \cos x \sin \frac{\pi}{4} = -1$$

$$2 \sin x \cos \frac{\pi}{4} = -1$$

$$2(\sin x)\left(\frac{\sqrt{2}}{2}\right) = -1$$

$$\sin x = -\frac{1}{\sqrt{2}}$$

$$\sin x = -\frac{\sqrt{2}}{2}.$$

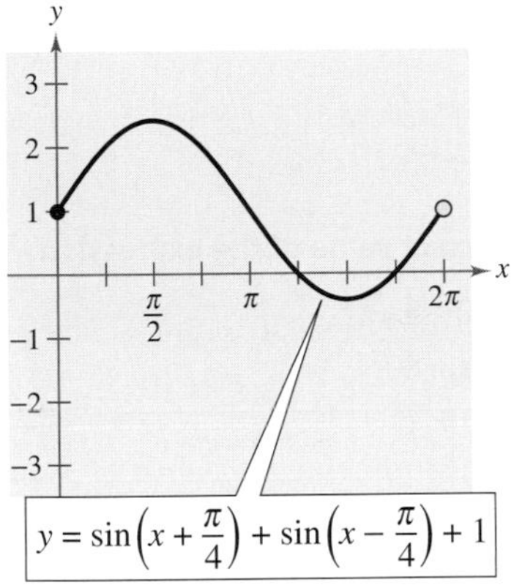

FIGURE 5.8

So, the only solutions in the interval $[0, 2\pi)$ are

$$x = \frac{5\pi}{4} \quad \text{and} \quad x = \frac{7\pi}{4}.$$

You can confirm this graphically by sketching the graph of

$$y = \sin\left(x + \frac{\pi}{4}\right) + \sin\left(x - \frac{\pi}{4}\right) + 1 \text{ for } 0 \le x < 2\pi,$$

as shown in Figure 5.8. From the graph you can see that the x-intercepts are $5\pi/4$ and $7\pi/4$.

CHECKPOINT Now try Exercise 69.

The next example was taken from calculus. It is used to derive the derivative of the sine function.

Example 8 An Application from Calculus

Verify that

$$\frac{\sin(x + h) - \sin x}{h} = (\cos x)\left(\frac{\sin h}{h}\right) - (\sin x)\left(\frac{1 - \cos h}{h}\right)$$

where $h \neq 0$.

Solution

Using the formula for $\sin(u + v)$, you have

$$\frac{\sin(x + h) - \sin x}{h} = \frac{\sin x \cos h + \cos x \sin h - \sin x}{h}$$

$$= \frac{\cos x \sin h - \sin x(1 - \cos h)}{h}$$

$$= (\cos x)\left(\frac{\sin h}{h}\right) - (\sin x)\left(\frac{1 - \cos h}{h}\right).$$

CHECKPOINT Now try Exercise 91.

5.4 Exercises

VOCABULARY CHECK: Fill in the blank to complete the trigonometric identity.

1. $\sin(u - v) =$ ________
2. $\cos(u + v) =$ ________
3. $\tan(u + v) =$ ________
4. $\sin(u + v) =$ ________
5. $\cos(u - v) =$ ________
6. $\tan(u - v) =$ ________

In Exercises 1–6, find the exact value of each expression.

1. (a) $\cos(120° + 45°)$ (b) $\cos 120° + \cos 45°$
2. (a) $\sin(135° - 30°)$ (b) $\sin 135° - \cos 30°$
3. (a) $\cos\left(\frac{\pi}{4} + \frac{\pi}{3}\right)$ (b) $\cos \frac{\pi}{4} + \cos \frac{\pi}{3}$
4. (a) $\sin\left(\frac{3\pi}{4} + \frac{5\pi}{6}\right)$ (b) $\sin \frac{3\pi}{4} + \sin \frac{5\pi}{6}$
5. (a) $\sin\left(\frac{7\pi}{6} - \frac{\pi}{3}\right)$ (b) $\sin \frac{7\pi}{6} - \sin \frac{\pi}{3}$
6. (a) $\sin(315° - 60°)$ (b) $\sin 315° - \sin 60°$

In Exercises 7–22, find the exact values of the sine, cosine, and tangent of the angle by using a sum or difference formula.

7. $105° = 60° + 45°$
8. $165° = 135° + 30°$
9. $195° = 225° - 30°$
10. $255° = 300° - 45°$
11. $\frac{11\pi}{12} = \frac{3\pi}{4} + \frac{\pi}{6}$
12. $\frac{7\pi}{12} = \frac{\pi}{3} + \frac{\pi}{4}$
13. $\frac{17\pi}{12} = \frac{9\pi}{4} - \frac{5\pi}{6}$
14. $-\frac{\pi}{12} = \frac{\pi}{6} - \frac{\pi}{4}$
15. $285°$
16. $-105°$
17. $-165°$
18. $15°$
19. $\frac{13\pi}{12}$
20. $-\frac{7\pi}{12}$
21. $-\frac{13\pi}{12}$
22. $\frac{5\pi}{12}$

In Exercises 23–30, write the expression as the sine, cosine, or tangent of an angle.

23. $\cos 25° \cos 15° - \sin 25° \sin 15°$
24. $\sin 140° \cos 50° + \cos 140° \sin 50°$
25. $\dfrac{\tan 325° - \tan 86°}{1 + \tan 325° \tan 86°}$
26. $\dfrac{\tan 140° - \tan 60°}{1 + \tan 140° \tan 60°}$
27. $\sin 3 \cos 1.2 - \cos 3 \sin 1.2$
28. $\cos \frac{\pi}{7} \cos \frac{\pi}{5} - \sin \frac{\pi}{7} \sin \frac{\pi}{5}$
29. $\dfrac{\tan 2x + \tan x}{1 - \tan 2x \tan x}$
30. $\cos 3x \cos 2y + \sin 3x \sin 2y$

In Exercises 31–36, find the exact value of the expression.

31. $\sin 330° \cos 30° - \cos 330° \sin 30°$
32. $\cos 15° \cos 60° + \sin 15° \sin 60°$
33. $\sin \frac{\pi}{12} \cos \frac{\pi}{4} + \cos \frac{\pi}{12} \sin \frac{\pi}{4}$
34. $\cos \frac{\pi}{16} \cos \frac{3\pi}{16} - \sin \frac{\pi}{16} \sin \frac{3\pi}{16}$
35. $\dfrac{\tan 25° + \tan 110°}{1 - \tan 25° \tan 110°}$
36. $\dfrac{\tan(5\pi/4) - \tan(\pi/12)}{1 + \tan(5\pi/4) \tan(\pi/12)}$

In Exercises 37–44, find the exact value of the trigonometric function given that $\sin u = \frac{5}{13}$ and $\cos v = -\frac{3}{5}$. (Both u and v are in Quadrant II.)

37. $\sin(u + v)$
38. $\cos(u - v)$
39. $\cos(u + v)$
40. $\sin(v - u)$
41. $\tan(u + v)$
42. $\csc(u - v)$
43. $\sec(v - u)$
44. $\cot(u + v)$

In Exercises 45–50, find the exact value of the trigonometric function given that $\sin u = -\frac{7}{25}$ and $\cos v = -\frac{4}{5}$. (Both u and v are in Quadrant III.)

45. $\cos(u + v)$
46. $\sin(u + v)$
47. $\tan(u - v)$
48. $\cot(v - u)$
49. $\sec(u + v)$
50. $\cos(u - v)$

In Exercises 51–54, write the trigonometric expression as an algebraic expression.

51. $\sin(\arcsin x + \arccos x)$ **52.** $\sin(\arctan 2x - \arccos x)$

53. $\cos(\arccos x + \arcsin x)$

54. $\cos(\arccos x - \arctan x)$

In Exercises 55–64, verify the identity.

55. $\sin(3\pi - x) = \sin x$ **56.** $\sin\left(\frac{\pi}{2} + x\right) = \cos x$

57. $\sin\left(\frac{\pi}{6} + x\right) = \frac{1}{2}(\cos x + \sqrt{3}\sin x)$

58. $\cos\left(\frac{5\pi}{4} - x\right) = -\frac{\sqrt{2}}{2}(\cos x + \sin x)$

59. $\cos(\pi - \theta) + \sin\left(\frac{\pi}{2} + \theta\right) = 0$

60. $\tan\left(\frac{\pi}{4} - \theta\right) = \frac{1 - \tan\theta}{1 + \tan\theta}$

61. $\cos(x + y)\cos(x - y) = \cos^2 x - \sin^2 y$

62. $\sin(x + y)\sin(x - y) = \sin^2 x - \sin^2 y$

63. $\sin(x + y) + \sin(x - y) = 2\sin x \cos y$

64. $\cos(x + y) + \cos(x - y) = 2\cos x \cos y$

In Exercises 65–68, simplify the expression algebraically and use a graphing utility to confirm your answer graphically.

65. $\cos\left(\frac{3\pi}{2} - x\right)$ **66.** $\cos(\pi + x)$

67. $\sin\left(\frac{3\pi}{2} + \theta\right)$ **68.** $\tan(\pi + \theta)$

In Exercises 69–72, find all solutions of the equation in the interval $[0, 2\pi)$.

69. $\sin\left(x + \frac{\pi}{3}\right) + \sin\left(x - \frac{\pi}{3}\right) = 1$

70. $\sin\left(x + \frac{\pi}{6}\right) - \sin\left(x - \frac{\pi}{6}\right) = \frac{1}{2}$

71. $\cos\left(x + \frac{\pi}{4}\right) - \cos\left(x - \frac{\pi}{4}\right) = 1$

72. $\tan(x + \pi) + 2\sin(x + \pi) = 0$

In Exercises 73 and 74, use a graphing utility to approximate the solutions in the interval $[0, 2\pi)$.

73. $\cos\left(x + \frac{\pi}{4}\right) + \cos\left(x - \frac{\pi}{4}\right) = 1$

74. $\tan(x + \pi) - \cos\left(x + \frac{\pi}{2}\right) = 0$

Model It

75. ***Harmonic Motion*** A weight is attached to a spring suspended vertically from a ceiling. When a driving force is applied to the system, the weight moves vertically from its equilibrium position, and this motion is modeled by

$$y = \frac{1}{3}\sin 2t + \frac{1}{4}\cos 2t$$

where y is the distance from equilibrium (in feet) and t is the time (in seconds).

(a) Use the identity

$$a\sin B\theta + b\cos B\theta = \sqrt{a^2 + b^2}\sin(B\theta + C)$$

where $C = \arctan(b/a)$, $a > 0$, to write the model in the form

$$y = \sqrt{a^2 + b^2}\sin(Bt + C).$$

(b) Find the amplitude of the oscillations of the weight.

(c) Find the frequency of the oscillations of the weight.

76. ***Standing Waves*** The equation of a standing wave is obtained by adding the displacements of two waves traveling in opposite directions (see figure). Assume that each of the waves has amplitude A, period T, and wavelength λ. If the models for these waves are

$$y_1 = A\cos 2\pi\left(\frac{t}{T} - \frac{x}{\lambda}\right) \quad \text{and} \quad y_2 = A\cos 2\pi\left(\frac{t}{T} + \frac{x}{\lambda}\right)$$

show that

$$y_1 + y_2 = 2A\cos\frac{2\pi t}{T}\cos\frac{2\pi x}{\lambda}.$$

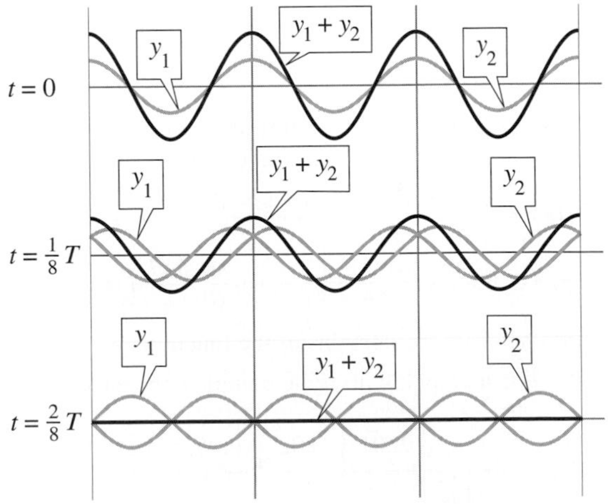

Synthesis

True or False? **In Exercises 77–80, determine whether the statement is true or false. Justify your answer.**

77. $\sin(u \pm v) = \sin u \pm \sin v$

78. $\cos(u \pm v) = \cos u \pm \cos v$

79. $\cos\left(x - \dfrac{\pi}{2}\right) = -\sin x$

80. $\sin\left(x - \dfrac{\pi}{2}\right) = -\cos x$

In Exercises 81–84, verify the identity.

81. $\cos(n\pi + \theta) = (-1)^n \cos\theta$, n is an integer

82. $\sin(n\pi + \theta) = (-1)^n \sin\theta$, n is an integer

83. $a \sin B\theta + b \cos B\theta = \sqrt{a^2 + b^2}\sin(B\theta + C)$,
where $C = \arctan(b/a)$ and $a > 0$

84. $a \sin B\theta + b \cos B\theta = \sqrt{a^2 + b^2}\cos(B\theta - C)$,
where $C = \arctan(a/b)$ and $b > 0$

In Exercises 85–88, use the formulas given in Exercises 83 and 84 to write the trigonometric expression in the following forms.

(a) $\sqrt{a^2 + b^2}\sin(B\theta + C)$ **(b)** $\sqrt{a^2 + b^2}\cos(B\theta - C)$

85. $\sin\theta + \cos\theta$

86. $3 \sin 2\theta + 4 \cos 2\theta$

87. $12 \sin 3\theta + 5 \cos 3\theta$

88. $\sin 2\theta - \cos 2\theta$

In Exercises 89 and 90, use the formulas given in Exercises 83 and 84 to write the trigonometric expression in the form $a \sin B\theta + b \cos B\theta$.

89. $2 \sin\left(\theta + \dfrac{\pi}{2}\right)$

90. $5 \cos\left(\theta + \dfrac{3\pi}{4}\right)$

91. Verify the following identity used in calculus.

$$\frac{\cos(x + h) - \cos x}{h} = \frac{\cos x(\cos h - 1)}{h} - \frac{\sin x \sin h}{h}$$

92. ***Exploration*** Let $x = \pi/6$ in the identity in Exercise 91 and define the functions f and g as follows.

$$f(h) = \frac{\cos(\pi/6 + h) - \cos(\pi/6)}{h}$$

$$g(h) = \cos\frac{\pi}{6}\left(\frac{\cos h - 1}{h}\right) - \sin\frac{\pi}{6}\left(\frac{\sin h}{h}\right)$$

(a) What are the domains of the functions f and g?

(b) Use a graphing utility to complete the table.

h	0.01	0.02	0.05	0.1	0.2	0.5
$f(h)$						
$g(h)$						

(c) Use a graphing utility to graph the functions f and g.

(d) Use the table and the graphs to make a conjecture about the values of the functions f and g as $h \to 0$.

In Exercises 93 and 94, use the figure, which shows two lines whose equations are

$$y_1 = m_1x + b_1 \quad \text{and} \quad y_2 = m_2x + b_2.$$

Assume that both lines have positive slopes. Derive a formula for the angle between the two lines. Then use your formula to find the angle between the given pair of lines.

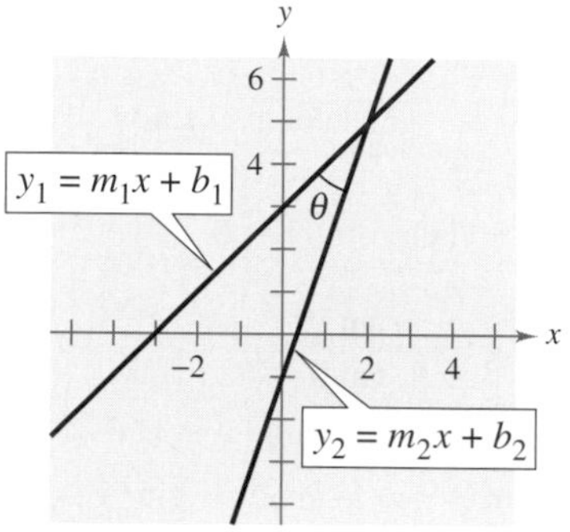

93. $y = x$ and $y = \sqrt{3}x$

94. $y = x$ and $y = \dfrac{1}{\sqrt{3}}x$

95. ***Conjecture*** Consider the function given by

$$f(\theta) = \sin^2\left(\theta + \frac{\pi}{4}\right) + \sin^2\left(\theta - \frac{\pi}{4}\right).$$

Use a graphing utility to graph the function and use the graph to create an identity. Prove your conjecture.

96. ***Proof***

(a) Write a proof of the formula for $\sin(u + v)$.

(b) Write a proof of the formula for $\sin(u - v)$.

Skills Review

In Exercises 97–100, find the inverse function of *f*. Verify that $f(f^{-1}(x)) = x$ and $f^{-1}(f(x)) = x$.

97. $f(x) = 5(x - 3)$

98. $f(x) = \dfrac{7 - x}{8}$

99. $f(x) = x^2 - 8$

100. $f(x) = \sqrt{x - 16}$

In Exercises 101–104, apply the inverse properties of $\ln x$ and e^x to simplify the expression.

101. $\log_3 3^{4x-3}$

102. $\log_8 8^{3x^2}$

103. $e^{\ln(6x-3)}$

104. $12x + e^{\ln x(x-2)}$

5.5 Multiple Angle and Product-to-Sum Formulas

What you should learn

- Use multiple-angle formulas to rewrite and evaluate trigonometric functions.
- Use power-reducing formulas to rewrite and evaluate trigonometric functions.
- Use half-angle formulas to rewrite and evaluate trigonometric functions.
- Use product-to-sum and sum-to-product formulas to rewrite and evaluate trigonometric functions.
- Use trigonometric formulas to rewrite real-life models.

Why you should learn it

You can use a variety of trigonometric formulas to rewrite trigonometric functions in more convenient forms. For instance, in Exercise 119 on page 417, you can use a double-angle formula to determine at what angle an athlete must throw a javelin.

Mark Dadswell/Getty Images

Multiple-Angle Formulas

In this section, you will study four other categories of trigonometric identities.

1. The first category involves *functions of multiple angles* such as $\sin ku$ and $\cos ku$.
2. The second category involves *squares of trigonometric functions* such as $\sin^2 u$.
3. The third category involves *functions of half-angles* such as $\sin(u/2)$.
4. The fourth category involves *products of trigonometric functions* such as $\sin u \cos v$.

You should learn the **double-angle formulas** because they are used often in trigonometry and calculus. For proofs of the formulas, see Proofs in Mathematics on page 425.

Double-Angle Formulas

$$\sin 2u = 2 \sin u \cos u \qquad \cos 2u = \cos^2 u - \sin^2 u$$

$$\tan 2u = \frac{2 \tan u}{1 - \tan^2 u} \qquad = 2\cos^2 u - 1$$

$$= 1 - 2\sin^2 u$$

Example 1 Solving a Multiple-Angle Equation

Solve $2 \cos x + \sin 2x = 0$.

Solution

Begin by rewriting the equation so that it involves functions of x (rather than $2x$). Then factor and solve as usual.

$$2 \cos x + \sin 2x = 0 \qquad \text{Write original equation.}$$

$$2 \cos x + 2 \sin x \cos x = 0 \qquad \text{Double-angle formula}$$

$$2 \cos x(1 + \sin x) = 0 \qquad \text{Factor.}$$

$$2 \cos x = 0 \quad \text{and} \quad 1 + \sin x = 0 \qquad \text{Set factors equal to zero.}$$

$$x = \frac{\pi}{2}, \frac{3\pi}{2} \qquad x = \frac{3\pi}{2} \qquad \text{Solutions in } [0, 2\pi)$$

So, the general solution is

$$x = \frac{\pi}{2} + 2n\pi \quad \text{and} \quad x = \frac{3\pi}{2} + 2n\pi$$

where n is an integer. Try verifying these solutions graphically.

CHECKPOINT Now try Exercise 9.

Example 2 Using Double-Angle Formulas to Analyze Graphs

Use a double-angle formula to rewrite the equation

$$y = 4\cos^2 x - 2.$$

Then sketch the graph of the equation over the interval $[0, 2\pi]$.

Solution

Using the double-angle formula for $\cos 2u$, you can rewrite the original equation as

$$\begin{aligned} y &= 4\cos^2 x - 2 && \text{Write original equation.} \\ &= 2(2\cos^2 x - 1) && \text{Factor.} \\ &= 2\cos 2x. && \text{Use double-angle formula.} \end{aligned}$$

Using the techniques discussed in Section 4.5, you can recognize that the graph of this function has an amplitude of 2 and a period of π. The key points in the interval $[0, \pi]$ are as follows.

Maximum	Intercept	Minimum	Intercept	Maximum
$(0, 2)$	$\left(\frac{\pi}{4}, 0\right)$	$\left(\frac{\pi}{2}, -2\right)$	$\left(\frac{3\pi}{4}, 0\right)$	$(\pi, 2)$

Two cycles of the graph are shown in Figure 5.9.

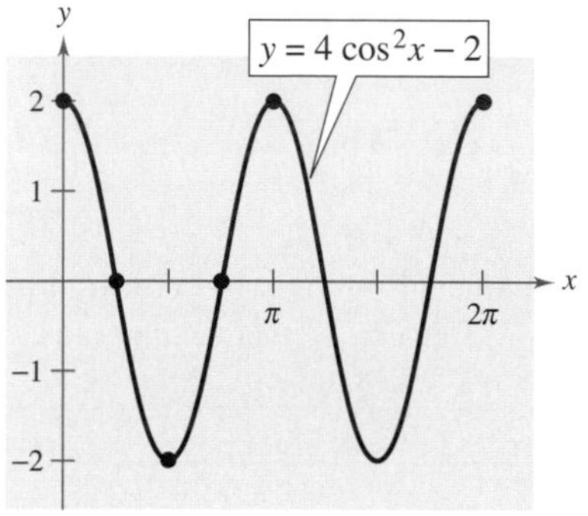

FIGURE 5.9

CHECKPOINT Now try Exercise 21.

Example 3 Evaluating Functions Involving Double Angles

Use the following to find $\sin 2\theta$, $\cos 2\theta$, and $\tan 2\theta$.

$$\cos\theta = \frac{5}{13}, \qquad \frac{3\pi}{2} < \theta < 2\pi$$

Solution

From Figure 5.10, you can see that $\sin\theta = y/r = -12/13$. Consequently, using each of the double-angle formulas, you can write

$$\sin 2\theta = 2\sin\theta\cos\theta = 2\left(-\frac{12}{13}\right)\left(\frac{5}{13}\right) = -\frac{120}{169}$$

$$\cos 2\theta = 2\cos^2\theta - 1 = 2\left(\frac{25}{169}\right) - 1 = -\frac{119}{169}$$

$$\tan 2\theta = \frac{\sin 2\theta}{\cos 2\theta} = \frac{120}{119}.$$

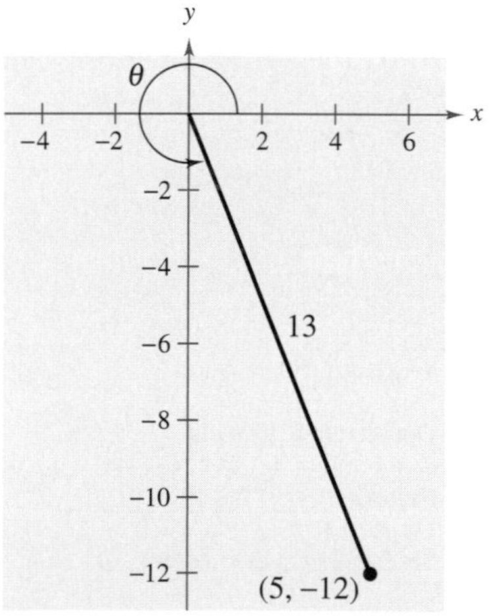

FIGURE 5.10

CHECKPOINT Now try Exercise 23.

The double-angle formulas are not restricted to angles 2θ and θ. Other *double* combinations, such as 4θ and 2θ or 6θ and 3θ, are also valid. Here are two examples.

$$\sin 4\theta = 2\sin 2\theta\cos 2\theta \qquad \text{and} \qquad \cos 6\theta = \cos^2 3\theta - \sin^2 3\theta$$

By using double-angle formulas together with the sum formulas given in the preceding section, you can form other multiple-angle formulas.

Example 4 **Deriving a Triple-Angle Formula**

$$\begin{aligned}\sin 3x &= \sin(2x + x)\\ &= \sin 2x \cos x + \cos 2x \sin x\\ &= 2 \sin x \cos x \cos x + (1 - 2 \sin^2 x)\sin x\\ &= 2 \sin x \cos^2 x + \sin x - 2 \sin^3 x\\ &= 2 \sin x(1 - \sin^2 x) + \sin x - 2 \sin^3 x\\ &= 2 \sin x - 2 \sin^3 x + \sin x - 2 \sin^3 x\\ &= 3 \sin x - 4 \sin^3 x\end{aligned}$$

✓CHECKPOINT Now try Exercise 97.

Power-Reducing Formulas

The double-angle formulas can be used to obtain the following **power-reducing formulas.** Example 5 shows a typical power reduction that is used in calculus.

Power-Reducing Formulas

$$\sin^2 u = \frac{1 - \cos 2u}{2} \qquad \cos^2 u = \frac{1 + \cos 2u}{2} \qquad \tan^2 u = \frac{1 - \cos 2u}{1 + \cos 2u}$$

For a proof of the power-reducing formulas, see Proofs in Mathematics on page 425.

Example 5 **Reducing a Power**

Rewrite $\sin^4 x$ as a sum of first powers of the cosines of multiple angles.

Solution

Note the repeated use of power-reducing formulas.

$$\begin{aligned}\sin^4 x &= (\sin^2 x)^2 && \text{Property of exponents}\\ &= \left(\frac{1 - \cos 2x}{2}\right)^2 && \text{Power-reducing formula}\\ &= \frac{1}{4}(1 - 2 \cos 2x + \cos^2 2x) && \text{Expand.}\\ &= \frac{1}{4}\left(1 - 2 \cos 2x + \frac{1 + \cos 4x}{2}\right) && \text{Power-reducing formula}\\ &= \frac{1}{4} - \frac{1}{2}\cos 2x + \frac{1}{8} + \frac{1}{8}\cos 4x && \text{Distributive Property}\\ &= \frac{1}{8}(3 - 4 \cos 2x + \cos 4x) && \text{Factor out common factor.}\end{aligned}$$

✓CHECKPOINT Now try Exercise 29.

Half-Angle Formulas

You can derive some useful alternative forms of the power-reducing formulas by replacing u with $u/2$. The results are called **half-angle formulas.**

Half-Angle Formulas

$$\sin \frac{u}{2} = \pm\sqrt{\frac{1 - \cos u}{2}}$$

$$\cos \frac{u}{2} = \pm\sqrt{\frac{1 + \cos u}{2}}$$

$$\tan \frac{u}{2} = \frac{1 - \cos u}{\sin u} = \frac{\sin u}{1 + \cos u}$$

The signs of $\sin \frac{u}{2}$ and $\cos \frac{u}{2}$ depend on the quadrant in which $\frac{u}{2}$ lies.

Example 6 **Using a Half-Angle Formula**

Find the exact value of $\sin 105°$.

Solution

Begin by noting that $105°$ is half of $210°$. Then, using the half-angle formula for $\sin(u/2)$ and the fact that $105°$ lies in Quadrant II, you have

$$\sin 105° = \sqrt{\frac{1 - \cos 210°}{2}}$$

$$= \sqrt{\frac{1 - (-\cos 30°)}{2}}$$

$$= \sqrt{\frac{1 + (\sqrt{3}/2)}{2}}$$

$$= \frac{\sqrt{2 + \sqrt{3}}}{2}.$$

The positive square root is chosen because $\sin \theta$ is positive in Quadrant II.

CHECKPOINT Now try Exercise 41.

Use your calculator to verify the result obtained in Example 6. That is, evaluate $\sin 105°$ and $\left(\sqrt{2 + \sqrt{3}}\right)/2$.

$$\sin 105° \approx 0.9659258$$

$$\frac{\sqrt{2 + \sqrt{3}}}{2} \approx 0.9659258$$

You can see that both values are approximately 0.9659258.

STUDY TIP

To find the exact value of a trigonometric function with an angle measure in D°M′S″ form using a half-angle formula, first convert the angle measure to decimal degree form. Then multiply the resulting angle measure by 2.

Example 7 Solving a Trigonometric Equation

Find all solutions of $2 - \sin^2 x = 2\cos^2 \dfrac{x}{2}$ in the interval $[0, 2\pi)$.

Algebraic Solution

$$2 - \sin^2 x = 2\cos^2 \frac{x}{2} \qquad \text{Write original equation.}$$

$$2 - \sin^2 x = 2\left(\pm\sqrt{\frac{1 + \cos x}{2}}\right)^2 \qquad \text{Half-angle formula}$$

$$2 - \sin^2 x = 2\left(\frac{1 + \cos x}{2}\right) \qquad \text{Simplify.}$$

$$2 - \sin^2 x = 1 + \cos x \qquad \text{Simplify.}$$

$$2 - (1 - \cos^2 x) = 1 + \cos x \qquad \text{Pythagorean identity}$$

$$\cos^2 x - \cos x = 0 \qquad \text{Simplify.}$$

$$\cos x(\cos x - 1) = 0 \qquad \text{Factor.}$$

By setting the factors $\cos x$ and $\cos x - 1$ equal to zero, you find that the solutions in the interval $[0, 2\pi)$ are

$$x = \frac{\pi}{2}, \quad x = \frac{3\pi}{2}, \quad \text{and} \quad x = 0.$$

CHECKPOINT Now try Exercise 59.

Graphical Solution

Use a graphing utility set in *radian* mode to graph $y = 2 - \sin^2 x - 2\cos^2(x/2)$, as shown in Figure 5.11. Use the *zero* or *root* feature or the *zoom* and *trace* features to approximate the x-intercepts in the interval $[0, 2\pi)$ to be

$$x = 0,\ x \approx 1.571 \approx \frac{\pi}{2},\ \text{and } x \approx 4.712 \approx \frac{3\pi}{2}.$$

These values are the approximate solutions of $2 - \sin^2 x - 2\cos^2(x/2) = 0$ in the interval $[0, 2\pi)$.

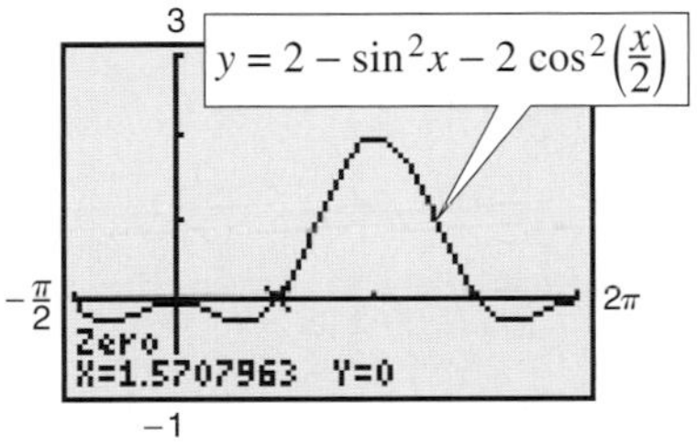

FIGURE 5.11

Product-to-Sum Formulas

Each of the following **product-to-sum formulas** is easily verified using the sum and difference formulas discussed in the preceding section.

Product-to-Sum Formulas

$$\sin u \sin v = \frac{1}{2}[\cos(u - v) - \cos(u + v)]$$

$$\cos u \cos v = \frac{1}{2}[\cos(u - v) + \cos(u + v)]$$

$$\sin u \cos v = \frac{1}{2}[\sin(u + v) + \sin(u - v)]$$

$$\cos u \sin v = \frac{1}{2}[\sin(u + v) - \sin(u - v)]$$

Product-to-sum formulas are used in calculus to evaluate integrals involving the products of sines and cosines of two different angles.

Example 8 **Writing Products as Sums**

Rewrite the product $\cos 5x \sin 4x$ as a sum or difference.

Solution

Using the appropriate product-to-sum formula, you obtain

$$\cos 5x \sin 4x = \tfrac{1}{2}[\sin(5x + 4x) - \sin(5x - 4x)]$$
$$= \tfrac{1}{2}\sin 9x - \tfrac{1}{2}\sin x.$$

✓CHECKPOINT Now try Exercise 67.

Occasionally, it is useful to reverse the procedure and write a sum of trigonometric functions as a product. This can be accomplished with the following **sum-to-product formulas.**

Sum-to-Product Formulas

$$\sin u + \sin v = 2\sin\left(\frac{u+v}{2}\right)\cos\left(\frac{u-v}{2}\right)$$

$$\sin u - \sin v = 2\cos\left(\frac{u+v}{2}\right)\sin\left(\frac{u-v}{2}\right)$$

$$\cos u + \cos v = 2\cos\left(\frac{u+v}{2}\right)\cos\left(\frac{u-v}{2}\right)$$

$$\cos u - \cos v = -2\sin\left(\frac{u+v}{2}\right)\sin\left(\frac{u-v}{2}\right)$$

For a proof of the sum-to-product formulas, see Proofs in Mathematics on page 426.

Example 9 **Using a Sum-to-Product Formula**

Find the exact value of $\cos 195° + \cos 105°$.

Solution

Using the appropriate sum-to-product formula, you obtain

$$\cos 195° + \cos 105° = 2\cos\left(\frac{195° + 105°}{2}\right)\cos\left(\frac{195° - 105°}{2}\right)$$
$$= 2\cos 150° \cos 45°$$
$$= 2\left(-\frac{\sqrt{3}}{2}\right)\left(\frac{\sqrt{2}}{2}\right)$$
$$= -\frac{\sqrt{6}}{2}.$$

✓CHECKPOINT Now try Exercise 83.

Example 10 **Solving a Trigonometric Equation**

Solve $\sin 5x + \sin 3x = 0$.

Solution

$$\sin 5x + \sin 3x = 0 \qquad \text{Write original equation.}$$

$$2 \sin\left(\frac{5x + 3x}{2}\right) \cos\left(\frac{5x - 3x}{2}\right) = 0 \qquad \text{Sum-to-product formula}$$

$$2 \sin 4x \cos x = 0 \qquad \text{Simplify.}$$

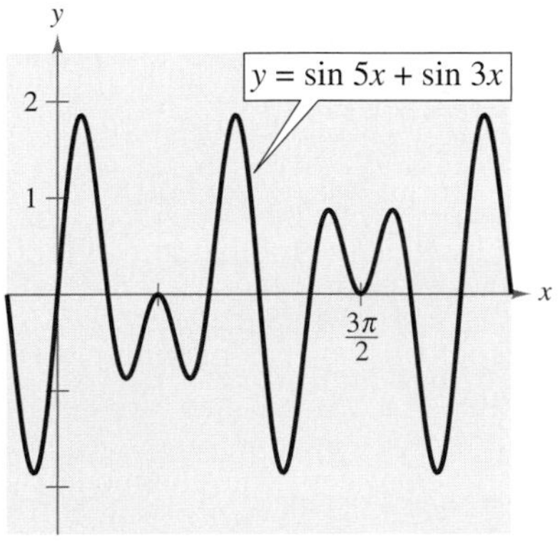

FIGURE 5.12

By setting the factor $2 \sin 4x$ equal to zero, you can find that the solutions in the interval $[0, 2\pi)$ are

$$x = 0, \frac{\pi}{4}, \frac{\pi}{2}, \frac{3\pi}{4}, \pi, \frac{5\pi}{4}, \frac{3\pi}{2}, \frac{7\pi}{4}.$$

The equation $\cos x = 0$ yields no additional solutions, and you can conclude that the solutions are of the form

$$x = \frac{n\pi}{4}$$

where n is an integer. You can confirm this graphically by sketching the graph of $y = \sin 5x + \sin 3x$, as shown in Figure 5.12. From the graph you can see that the x-intercepts occur at multiples of $\pi/4$.

✓CHECKPOINT Now try Exercise 87.

Example 11 **Verifying a Trigonometric Identity**

Verify the identity

$$\frac{\sin t + \sin 3t}{\cos t + \cos 3t} = \tan 2t.$$

Solution

Using appropriate sum-to-product formulas, you have

$$\frac{\sin t + \sin 3t}{\cos t + \cos 3t} = \frac{2 \sin\left(\frac{t + 3t}{2}\right) \cos\left(\frac{t - 3t}{2}\right)}{2 \cos\left(\frac{t + 3t}{2}\right) \cos\left(\frac{t - 3t}{2}\right)}$$

$$= \frac{2 \sin(2t) \cos(-t)}{2 \cos(2t) \cos(-t)}$$

$$= \frac{\sin 2t}{\cos 2t}$$

$$= \tan 2t.$$

✓CHECKPOINT Now try Exercise 105.

Application

Example 12 Projectile Motion

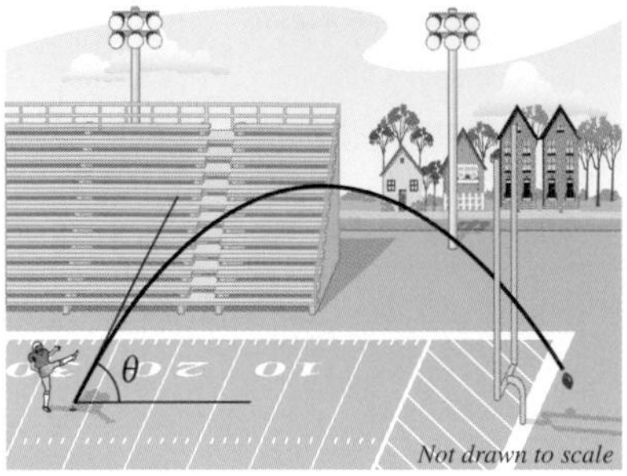

FIGURE 5.13

Ignoring air resistance, the range of a projectile fired at an angle θ with the horizontal and with an initial velocity of v_0 feet per second is given by

$$r = \frac{1}{16}v_0^2 \sin\theta\cos\theta$$

where r is the horizontal distance (in feet) that the projectile will travel. A place kicker for a football team can kick a football from ground level with an initial velocity of 80 feet per second (see Figure 5.13).

a. Write the projectile motion model in a simpler form.

b. At what angle must the player kick the football so that the football travels 200 feet?

c. For what angle is the horizontal distance the football travels a maximum?

Solution

a. You can use a double-angle formula to rewrite the projectile motion model as

$$r = \frac{1}{32}v_0^2(2\sin\theta\cos\theta) \qquad \text{Rewrite original projectile motion model.}$$

$$= \frac{1}{32}v_0^2 \sin 2\theta. \qquad \text{Rewrite model using a double-angle formula.}$$

b.

$$r = \frac{1}{32}v_0^2 \sin 2\theta \qquad \text{Write projectile motion model.}$$

$$200 = \frac{1}{32}(80)^2 \sin 2\theta \qquad \text{Substitute 200 for } r \text{ and 80 for } v_0.$$

$$200 = 200 \sin 2\theta \qquad \text{Simplify.}$$

$$1 = \sin 2\theta \qquad \text{Divide each side by 200.}$$

You know that $2\theta = \pi/2$, so dividing this result by 2 produces $\theta = \pi/4$. Because $\pi/4 = 45°$, you can conclude that the player must kick the football at an angle of 45° so that the football will travel 200 feet.

c. From the model $r = 200 \sin 2\theta$ you can see that the amplitude is 200. So the maximum range is $r = 200$ feet. From part (b), you know that this corresponds to an angle of 45°. Therefore, kicking the football at an angle of 45° will produce a maximum horizontal distance of 200 feet.

CHECKPOINT Now try Exercise 119.

WRITING ABOUT MATHEMATICS

Deriving an Area Formula Describe how you can use a double-angle formula or a half-angle formula to derive a formula for the area of an isosceles triangle. Use a labeled sketch to illustrate your derivation. Then write two examples that show how your formula can be used.

5.5 Exercises

VOCABULARY CHECK: Fill in the blank to complete the trigonometric formula.

1. $\sin 2u =$ ________
2. $\dfrac{1 + \cos 2u}{2} =$ ________
3. $\cos 2u =$ ________
4. $\dfrac{1 - \cos 2u}{1 + \cos 2u} =$ ________
5. $\sin \dfrac{u}{2} =$ ________
6. $\tan \dfrac{u}{2} =$ ________
7. $\cos u \cos v =$ ________
8. $\sin u \cos v =$ ________
9. $\sin u + \sin v =$ ________
10. $\cos u - \cos v =$ ________

In Exercises 1–8, use the figure to find the exact value of the trigonometric function.

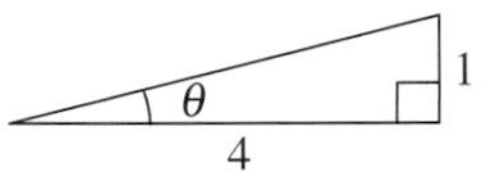

1. $\sin \theta$
2. $\tan \theta$
3. $\cos 2\theta$
4. $\sin 2\theta$
5. $\tan 2\theta$
6. $\sec 2\theta$
7. $\csc 2\theta$
8. $\cot 2\theta$

In Exercises 9–18, find the exact solutions of the equation in the interval $[0, 2\pi)$.

9. $\sin 2x - \sin x = 0$
10. $\sin 2x + \cos x = 0$
11. $4 \sin x \cos x = 1$
12. $\sin 2x \sin x = \cos x$
13. $\cos 2x - \cos x = 0$
14. $\cos 2x + \sin x = 0$
15. $\tan 2x - \cot x = 0$
16. $\tan 2x - 2 \cos x = 0$
17. $\sin 4x = -2 \sin 2x$
18. $(\sin 2x + \cos 2x)^2 = 1$

In Exercises 19–22, use a double-angle formula to rewrite the expression.

19. $6 \sin x \cos x$
20. $6 \cos^2 x - 3$
21. $4 - 8 \sin^2 x$
22. $(\cos x + \sin x)(\cos x - \sin x)$

In Exercises 23–28, find the exact values of $\sin 2u$, $\cos 2u$, and $\tan 2u$ using the double-angle formulas.

23. $\sin u = -\dfrac{4}{5}, \quad \pi < u < \dfrac{3\pi}{2}$
24. $\cos u = -\dfrac{2}{3}, \quad \dfrac{\pi}{2} < u < \pi$
25. $\tan u = \dfrac{3}{4}, \quad 0 < u < \dfrac{\pi}{2}$
26. $\cot u = -4, \quad \dfrac{3\pi}{2} < u < 2\pi$
27. $\sec u = -\dfrac{5}{2}, \quad \dfrac{\pi}{2} < u < \pi$
28. $\csc u = 3, \quad \dfrac{\pi}{2} < u < \pi$

In Exercises 29–34, use the power-reducing formulas to rewrite the expression in terms of the first power of the cosine.

29. $\cos^4 x$
30. $\sin^8 x$
31. $\sin^2 x \cos^2 x$
32. $\sin^4 x \cos^4 x$
33. $\sin^2 x \cos^4 x$
34. $\sin^4 x \cos^2 x$

In Exercises 35–40, use the figure to find the exact value of the trigonometric function.

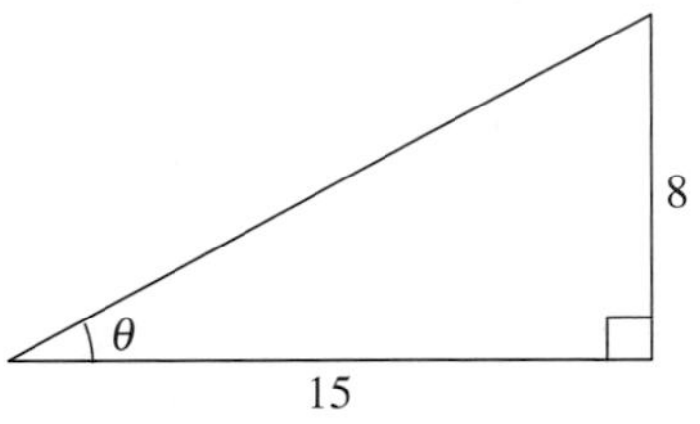

35. $\cos \dfrac{\theta}{2}$
36. $\sin \dfrac{\theta}{2}$
37. $\tan \dfrac{\theta}{2}$
38. $\sec \dfrac{\theta}{2}$
39. $\csc \dfrac{\theta}{2}$
40. $\cot \dfrac{\theta}{2}$

In Exercises 41–48, use the half-angle formulas to determine the exact values of the sine, cosine, and tangent of the angle.

41. 75°
42. 165°
43. $112^\circ\ 30'$
44. $67^\circ\ 30'$
45. $\dfrac{\pi}{8}$
46. $\dfrac{\pi}{12}$
47. $\dfrac{3\pi}{8}$
48. $\dfrac{7\pi}{12}$

In Exercises 49–54, find the exact values of sin(*u*/2), cos(*u*/2), and tan(*u*/2) using the half-angle formulas.

49. $\sin u = \dfrac{5}{13},\quad \dfrac{\pi}{2} < u < \pi$

50. $\cos u = \dfrac{3}{5},\quad 0 < u < \dfrac{\pi}{2}$

51. $\tan u = -\dfrac{5}{8},\quad \dfrac{3\pi}{2} < u < 2\pi$

52. $\cot u = 3,\quad \pi < u < \dfrac{3\pi}{2}$

53. $\csc u = -\dfrac{5}{3},\quad \pi < u < \dfrac{3\pi}{2}$

54. $\sec u = -\dfrac{7}{2},\quad \dfrac{\pi}{2} < u < \pi$

In Exercises 55–58, use the half-angle formulas to simplify the expression.

55. $\sqrt{\dfrac{1 - \cos 6x}{2}}$
56. $\sqrt{\dfrac{1 + \cos 4x}{2}}$
57. $-\sqrt{\dfrac{1 - \cos 8x}{1 + \cos 8x}}$
58. $-\sqrt{\dfrac{1 - \cos(x - 1)}{2}}$

In Exercises 59–62, find all solutions of the equation in the interval $[0, 2\pi)$. Use a graphing utility to graph the equation and verify the solutions.

59. $\sin\dfrac{x}{2} + \cos x = 0$
60. $\sin\dfrac{x}{2} + \cos x - 1 = 0$
61. $\cos\dfrac{x}{2} - \sin x = 0$
62. $\tan\dfrac{x}{2} - \sin x = 0$

In Exercises 63–74, use the product-to-sum formulas to write the product as a sum or difference.

63. $6 \sin\dfrac{\pi}{4} \cos\dfrac{\pi}{4}$
64. $4 \cos\dfrac{\pi}{3} \sin\dfrac{5\pi}{6}$
65. $10 \cos 75^\circ \cos 15^\circ$
66. $6 \sin 45^\circ \cos 15^\circ$
67. $\cos 4\theta \sin 6\theta$
68. $3 \sin 2\alpha \sin 3\alpha$
69. $5 \cos(-5\beta) \cos 3\beta$
70. $\cos 2\theta \cos 4\theta$
71. $\sin(x + y) \sin(x - y)$
72. $\sin(x + y) \cos(x - y)$
73. $\cos(\theta - \pi) \sin(\theta + \pi)$
74. $\sin(\theta + \pi) \sin(\theta - \pi)$

In Exercises 75–82, use the sum-to-product formulas to write the sum or difference as a product.

75. $\sin 5\theta - \sin 3\theta$
76. $\sin 3\theta + \sin \theta$
77. $\cos 6x + \cos 2x$
78. $\sin x + \sin 5x$
79. $\sin(\alpha + \beta) - \sin(\alpha - \beta)$
80. $\cos(\phi + 2\pi) + \cos \phi$
81. $\cos\left(\theta + \dfrac{\pi}{2}\right) - \cos\left(\theta - \dfrac{\pi}{2}\right)$
82. $\sin\left(x + \dfrac{\pi}{2}\right) + \sin\left(x - \dfrac{\pi}{2}\right)$

In Exercises 83–86, use the sum-to-product formulas to find the exact value of the expression.

83. $\sin 60^\circ + \sin 30^\circ$
84. $\cos 120^\circ + \cos 30^\circ$
85. $\cos\dfrac{3\pi}{4} - \cos\dfrac{\pi}{4}$
86. $\sin\dfrac{5\pi}{4} - \sin\dfrac{3\pi}{4}$

In Exercises 87–90, find all solutions of the equation in the interval $[0, 2\pi)$. Use a graphing utility to graph the equation and verify the solutions.

87. $\sin 6x + \sin 2x = 0$
88. $\cos 2x - \cos 6x = 0$
89. $\dfrac{\cos 2x}{\sin 3x - \sin x} - 1 = 0$
90. $\sin^2 3x - \sin^2 x = 0$

In Exercises 91–94, use the figure and trigonometric identities to find the exact value of the trigonometric function in two ways.

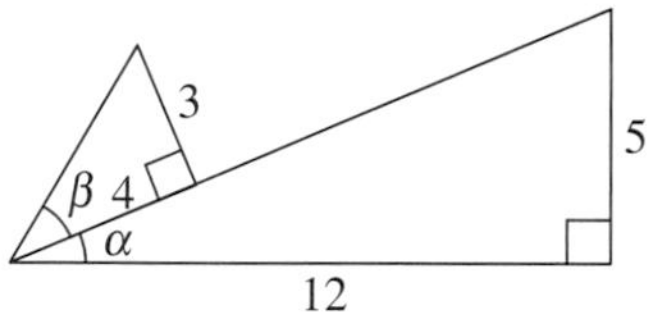

91. $\sin^2 \alpha$
92. $\cos^2 \alpha$
93. $\sin \alpha \cos \beta$
94. $\cos \alpha \sin \beta$

In Exercises 95–110, verify the identity.

95. $\csc 2\theta = \dfrac{\csc \theta}{2 \cos \theta}$

96. $\sec 2\theta = \dfrac{\sec^2 \theta}{2 - \sec^2 \theta}$

97. $\cos^2 2\alpha - \sin^2 2\alpha = \cos 4\alpha$

98. $\cos^4 x - \sin^4 x = \cos 2x$

99. $(\sin x + \cos x)^2 = 1 + \sin 2x$

100. $\sin\frac{\alpha}{3}\cos\frac{\alpha}{3} = \frac{1}{2}\sin\frac{2\alpha}{3}$

101. $1 + \cos 10y = 2\cos^2 5y$

102. $\frac{\cos 3\beta}{\cos\beta} = 1 - 4\sin^2\beta$

103. $\sec\frac{u}{2} = \pm\sqrt{\frac{2\tan u}{\tan u + \sin u}}$

104. $\tan\frac{u}{2} = \csc u - \cot u$

105. $\frac{\sin x \pm \sin y}{\cos x + \cos y} = \tan\frac{x \pm y}{2}$

106. $\frac{\sin x + \sin y}{\cos x - \cos y} = -\cot\frac{x - y}{2}$

107. $\frac{\cos 4x + \cos 2x}{\sin 4x + \sin 2x} = \cot 3x$

108. $\frac{\cos t + \cos 3t}{\sin 3t - \sin t} = \cot t$

109. $\sin\left(\frac{\pi}{6} + x\right) + \sin\left(\frac{\pi}{6} - x\right) = \cos x$

110. $\cos\left(\frac{\pi}{3} + x\right) + \cos\left(\frac{\pi}{3} - x\right) = \cos x$

In Exercises 111–114, use a graphing utility to verify the identity. Confirm that it is an identity algebraically.

111. $\cos 3\beta = \cos^3\beta - 3\sin^2\beta\cos\beta$

112. $\sin 4\beta = 4\sin\beta\cos\beta(1 - 2\sin^2\beta)$

113. $(\cos 4x - \cos 2x)/(2\sin 3x) = -\sin x$

114. $(\cos 3x - \cos x)/(\sin 3x - \sin x) = -\tan 2x$

In Exercises 115 and 116, graph the function by hand in the interval $[0, 2\pi]$ by using the power-reducing formulas.

115. $f(x) = \sin^2 x$

116. $f(x) = \cos^2 x$

In Exercises 117 and 118, write the trigonometric expression as an algebraic expression.

117. $\sin(2\arcsin x)$

118. $\cos(2\arccos x)$

119. ***Projectile Motion*** The range of a projectile fired at an angle θ with the horizontal and with an initial velocity of v_0 feet per second is

$$r = \frac{1}{32}v_0^2 \sin 2\theta$$

where r is measured in feet. An athlete throws a javelin at 75 feet per second. At what angle must the athlete throw the javelin so that the javelin travels 130 feet?

120. ***Geometry*** The length of each of the two equal sides of an isosceles triangle is 10 meters (see figure). The angle between the two sides is θ.

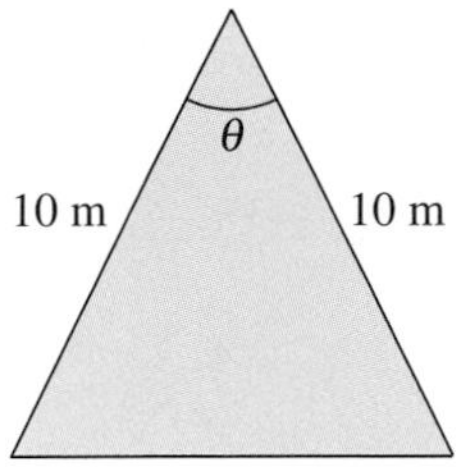

(a) Write the area of the triangle as a function of $\theta/2$.

(b) Write the area of the triangle as a function of θ. Determine the value of θ such that the area is a maximum.

Model It

121. ***Mach Number*** The mach number M of an airplane is the ratio of its speed to the speed of sound. When an airplane travels faster than the speed of sound, the sound waves form a cone behind the airplane (see figure). The mach number is related to the apex angle θ of the cone by

$$\sin\frac{\theta}{2} = \frac{1}{M}.$$

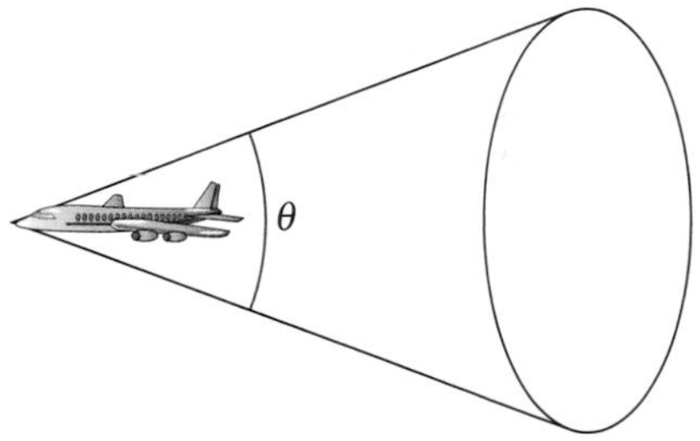

(a) Find the angle θ that corresponds to a mach number of 1.

(b) Find the angle θ that corresponds to a mach number of 4.5.

(c) The speed of sound is about 760 miles per hour. Determine the speed of an object with the mach numbers from parts (a) and (b).

(d) Rewrite the equation in terms of θ.

122. ***Railroad Track*** When two railroad tracks merge, the overlapping portions of the tracks are in the shapes of circular arcs (see figure). The radius of each arc r (in feet) and the angle θ are related by

$$\frac{x}{2} = 2r\sin^2\frac{\theta}{2}.$$

Write a formula for x in terms of $\cos\theta$.

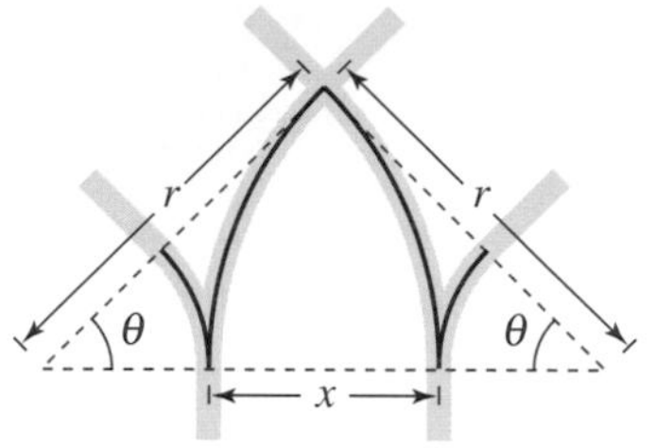

Synthesis

True or False? **In Exercises 123 and 124, determine whether the statement is true or false. Justify your answer.**

123. Because the sine function is an odd function, for a negative number u, $\sin 2u = -2\sin u\cos u$.

124. $\sin\frac{u}{2} = -\sqrt{\frac{1-\cos u}{2}}$ when u is in the second quadrant.

In Exercises 125 and 126, (a) use a graphing utility to graph the function and approximate the maximum and minimum points on the graph in the interval $[0, 2\pi)$ and (b) solve the trigonometric equation and verify that its solutions are the x-coordinates of the maximum and minimum points of f. (Calculus is required to find the trigonometric equation.)

	Function	*Trigonometric Equation*
125.	$f(x) = 4\sin\frac{x}{2} + \cos x$	$2\cos\frac{x}{2} - \sin x = 0$
126.	$f(x) = \cos 2x - 2\sin x$	$-2\cos x(2\sin x + 1) = 0$

127. ***Exploration*** Consider the function given by

$$f(x) = \sin^4 x + \cos^4 x.$$

(a) Use the power-reducing formulas to write the function in terms of cosine to the first power.

(b) Determine another way of rewriting the function. Use a graphing utility to rule out incorrectly rewritten functions.

(c) Add a trigonometric term to the function so that it becomes a perfect square trinomial. Rewrite the function as a perfect square trinomial minus the term that you added. Use a graphing utility to rule out incorrectly rewritten functions.

(d) Rewrite the result of part (c) in terms of the sine of a double angle. Use a graphing utility to rule out incorrectly rewritten functions.

(e) When you rewrite a trigonometric expression, the result may not be the same as a friend's. Does this mean that one of you is wrong? Explain.

128. ***Conjecture*** Consider the function given by

$$f(x) = 2\sin x\left(2\cos^2\frac{x}{2} - 1\right).$$

(a) Use a graphing utility to graph the function.

(b) Make a conjecture about the function that is an identity with f.

(c) Verify your conjecture analytically.

Skills Review

In Exercises 129–132, (a) plot the points, (b) find the distance between the points, and (c) find the midpoint of the line segment connecting the points.

129. $(5, 2), (-1, 4)$

130. $(-4, -3), (6, 10)$

131. $\left(0, \frac{1}{2}\right), \left(\frac{4}{3}, \frac{5}{2}\right)$

132. $\left(\frac{1}{3}, \frac{2}{3}\right), \left(-1, -\frac{3}{2}\right)$

In Exercises 133–136, find (if possible) the complement and supplement of each angle.

133. (a) 55° (b) 162°

134. (a) 109° (b) 78°

135. (a) $\frac{\pi}{18}$ (b) $\frac{9\pi}{20}$

136. (a) 0.95 (b) 2.76

137. ***Profit*** The total profit for a car manufacturer in October was 16% higher than it was in September. The total profit for the 2 months was \$507,600. Find the profit for each month.

138. ***Mixture Problem*** A 55-gallon barrel contains a mixture with a concentration of 30%. How much of this mixture must be withdrawn and replaced by 100% concentrate to bring the mixture up to 50% concentration?

139. ***Distance*** A baseball diamond has the shape of a square in which the distance between each of the consecutive bases is 90 feet. Approximate the straight-line distance from home plate to second base.

5 Chapter Summary

What did you learn?

	Review Exercises
Section 5.1	
☐ Recognize and write the fundamental trigonometric identities *(p. 374)*.	1–6
☐ Use the fundamental trigonometric identities to evaluate trigonometric functions, simplify trigonometric expressions, and rewrite trigonometric expressions *(p. 375)*.	7–24
Section 5.2	
☐ Verify trigonometric identities *(p. 382)*.	25–32
Section 5.3	
☐ Use standard algebraic techniques to solve trigonometric equations *(p. 389)*.	33–38
☐ Solve trigonometric equations of quadratic type *(p. 391)*.	39–42
☐ Solve trigonometric equations involving multiple angles *(p. 394)*.	43–46
☐ Use inverse trigonometric functions to solve trigonometric equations *(p. 395)*.	47–50
Section 5.4	
☐ Use sum and difference formulas to evaluate trigonometric functions, verify identities, and solve trigonometric equations *(p. 400)*.	51–74
Section 5.5	
☐ Use multiple-angle formulas to rewrite and evaluate trigonometric functions *(p. 407)*.	75–78
☐ Use power-reducing formulas to rewrite and evaluate trigonometric functions *(p. 409)*.	79–82
☐ Use half-angle formulas to rewrite and evaluate trigonometric functions *(p. 410)*.	83–92
☐ Use product-to-sum and sum-to-product formulas to rewrite and evaluate trigonometric functions *(p. 411)*.	93–100
☐ Use trigonometric formulas to rewrite real-life models *(p. 414)*.	101–106

5 Review Exercises

5.1 In Exercises 1–6, name the trigonometric function that is equivalent to the expression.

1. $\dfrac{1}{\cos x}$
2. $\dfrac{1}{\sin x}$
3. $\dfrac{1}{\sec x}$
4. $\dfrac{1}{\tan x}$
5. $\dfrac{\cos x}{\sin x}$
6. $\sqrt{1 + \tan^2 x}$

In Exercises 7–10, use the given values and trigonometric identities to evaluate (if possible) all six trigonometric functions.

7. $\sin x = \frac{3}{5}, \quad \cos x = \frac{4}{5}$
8. $\tan \theta = \dfrac{2}{3}, \quad \sec \theta = \dfrac{\sqrt{13}}{3}$
9. $\sin\left(\dfrac{\pi}{2} - x\right) = \dfrac{\sqrt{2}}{2}, \quad \sin x = -\dfrac{\sqrt{2}}{2}$
10. $\csc\left(\dfrac{\pi}{2} - \theta\right) = 9, \quad \sin \theta = \dfrac{4\sqrt{5}}{9}$

In Exercises 11–22, use the fundamental trigonometric identities to simplify the expression.

11. $\dfrac{1}{\cot^2 x + 1}$
12. $\dfrac{\tan \theta}{1 - \cos^2 \theta}$
13. $\tan^2 x(\csc^2 x - 1)$
14. $\cot^2 x(\sin^2 x)$
15. $\dfrac{\sin\left(\dfrac{\pi}{2} - \theta\right)}{\sin \theta}$
16. $\dfrac{\cot\left(\dfrac{\pi}{2} - u\right)}{\cos u}$
17. $\cos^2 x + \cos^2 x \cot^2 x$
18. $\tan^2 \theta \csc^2 \theta - \tan^2 \theta$
19. $(\tan x + 1)^2 \cos x$
20. $(\sec x - \tan x)^2$
21. $\dfrac{1}{\csc \theta + 1} - \dfrac{1}{\csc \theta - 1}$
22. $\dfrac{\cos^2 x}{1 - \sin x}$

23. ***Rate of Change*** The rate of change of the function $f(x) = \csc x - \cot x$ is given by the expression $\csc^2 x - \csc x \cot x$. Show that this expression can also be written as

$$\frac{1 - \cos x}{\sin^2 x}.$$

24. ***Rate of Change*** The rate of change of the function $f(x) = 2\sqrt{\sin x}$ is given by the expression $\sin^{-1/2} x \cos x$. Show that this expression can also be written as $\cot x\sqrt{\sin x}$.

5.2 In Exercises 25–32, verify the identity.

25. $\cos x(\tan^2 x + 1) = \sec x$
26. $\sec^2 x \cot x - \cot x = \tan x$
27. $\cos\left(x + \dfrac{\pi}{2}\right) = -\sin x$
28. $\cot\left(\dfrac{\pi}{2} - x\right) = \tan x$
29. $\dfrac{1}{\tan \theta \csc \theta} = \cos \theta$
30. $\dfrac{1}{\tan x \csc x \sin x} = \cot x$
31. $\sin^5 x \cos^2 x = (\cos^2 x - 2\cos^4 x + \cos^6 x)\sin x$
32. $\cos^3 x \sin^2 x = (\sin^2 x - \sin^4 x)\cos x$

5.3 In Exercises 33–38, solve the equation.

33. $\sin x = \sqrt{3} - \sin x$
34. $4\cos \theta = 1 + 2\cos \theta$
35. $3\sqrt{3}\tan u = 3$
36. $\frac{1}{2}\sec x - 1 = 0$
37. $3\csc^2 x = 4$
38. $4\tan^2 u - 1 = \tan^2 u$

In Exercises 39–46, find all solutions of the equation in the interval $[0, 2\pi)$.

39. $2\cos^2 x - \cos x = 1$
40. $2\sin^2 x - 3\sin x = -1$
41. $\cos^2 x + \sin x = 1$
42. $\sin^2 x + 2\cos x = 2$
43. $2\sin 2x - \sqrt{2} = 0$
44. $\sqrt{3}\tan 3x = 0$
45. $\cos 4x(\cos x - 1) = 0$
46. $3\csc^2 5x = -4$

In Exercises 47–50, use inverse functions where needed to find all solutions of the equation in the interval $[0, 2\pi)$.

47. $\sin^2 x - 2\sin x = 0$
48. $2\cos^2 x + 3\cos x = 0$
49. $\tan^2 \theta + \tan \theta - 12 = 0$
50. $\sec^2 x + 6\tan x + 4 = 0$

5.4 In Exercises 51–54, find the exact values of the sine, cosine, and tangent of the angle by using a sum or difference formula.

51. $285° = 315° - 30°$
52. $345° = 300° + 45°$
53. $\dfrac{25\pi}{12} = \dfrac{11\pi}{6} + \dfrac{\pi}{4}$
54. $\dfrac{19\pi}{12} = \dfrac{11\pi}{6} - \dfrac{\pi}{4}$

In Exercises 55–58, write the expression as the sine, cosine, or tangent of an angle.

55. $\sin 60° \cos 45° - \cos 60° \sin 45°$

56. $\cos 45° \cos 120° - \sin 45° \sin 120°$

57. $\dfrac{\tan 25° + \tan 10°}{1 - \tan 25° \tan 10°}$

58. $\dfrac{\tan 68° - \tan 115°}{1 + \tan 68° \tan 115°}$

In Exercises 59–64, find the exact value of the trigonometric function given that $\sin u = \frac{3}{4}$ and $\cos v = -\frac{5}{13}$. (Both u and v are in Quadrant II.)

59. $\sin(u + v)$

60. $\tan(u + v)$

61. $\cos(u - v)$

62. $\sin(u - v)$

63. $\cos(u + v)$

64. $\tan(u - v)$

In Exercises 65–70, verify the identity.

65. $\cos\left(x + \dfrac{\pi}{2}\right) = -\sin x$

66. $\sin\left(x - \dfrac{3\pi}{2}\right) = \cos x$

67. $\cot\left(\dfrac{\pi}{2} - x\right) = \tan x$

68. $\sin(\pi - x) = \sin x$

69. $\cos 3x = 4\cos^3 x - 3\cos x$

70. $\dfrac{\sin(\alpha + \beta)}{\cos \alpha \cos \beta} = \tan \alpha + \tan\beta$

In Exercises 71–74, find all solutions of the equation in the interval $[0, 2\pi)$.

71. $\sin\left(x + \dfrac{\pi}{4}\right) - \sin\left(x - \dfrac{\pi}{4}\right) = 1$

72. $\cos\left(x + \dfrac{\pi}{6}\right) - \cos\left(x - \dfrac{\pi}{6}\right) = 1$

73. $\sin\left(x + \dfrac{\pi}{2}\right) - \sin\left(x - \dfrac{\pi}{2}\right) = \sqrt{3}$

74. $\cos\left(x + \dfrac{3\pi}{4}\right) - \cos\left(x - \dfrac{3\pi}{4}\right) = 0$

5.5 **In Exercises 75 and 76, find the exact values of $\sin 2u$, $\cos 2u$, and $\tan 2u$ using the double-angle formulas.**

75. $\sin u = -\dfrac{4}{5}, \quad \pi < u < \dfrac{3\pi}{2}$

76. $\cos u = -\dfrac{2}{\sqrt{5}}, \quad \dfrac{\pi}{2} < u < \pi$

In Exercises 77 and 78, use double-angle formulas to verify the identity algebraically and use a graphing utility to confirm your result graphically.

77. $\sin 4x = 8\cos^3 x \sin x - 4\cos x \sin x$

78. $\tan^2 x = \dfrac{1 - \cos 2x}{1 + \cos 2x}$

In Exercises 79–82, use the power-reducing formulas to rewrite the expression in terms of the first power of the cosine.

79. $\tan^2 2x$

80. $\cos^2 3x$

81. $\sin^2 x \tan^2 x$

82. $\cos^2 x \tan^2 x$

In Exercises 83–86, use the half-angle formulas to determine the exact values of the sine, cosine, and tangent of the angle.

83. $-75°$

84. $15°$

85. $\dfrac{19\pi}{12}$

86. $-\dfrac{17\pi}{12}$

In Exercises 87–90, find the exact values of $\sin(u/2)$, $\cos(u/2)$, and $\tan(u/2)$ using the half-angle formulas.

87. $\sin u = \frac{3}{5}, \; 0 < u < \pi/2$

88. $\tan u = \frac{5}{8}, \; \pi < u < 3\pi/2$

89. $\cos u = -\frac{2}{7}, \; \pi/2 < u < \pi$

90. $\sec u = -6, \; \pi/2 < u < \pi$

In Exercises 91 and 92, use the half-angle formulas to simplify the expression.

91. $-\sqrt{\dfrac{1 + \cos 10x}{2}}$

92. $\dfrac{\sin 6x}{1 + \cos 6x}$

In Exercises 93–96, use the product-to-sum formulas to write the product as a sum or difference.

93. $\cos \dfrac{\pi}{6} \sin \dfrac{\pi}{6}$

94. $6 \sin 15° \sin 45°$

95. $\cos 5\theta \cos 3\theta$

96. $4 \sin 3\alpha \cos 2\alpha$

In Exercises 97–100, use the sum-to-product formulas to write the sum or difference as a product.

97. $\sin 4\theta - \sin 2\theta$

98. $\cos 3\theta + \cos 2\theta$

99. $\cos\left(x + \dfrac{\pi}{6}\right) - \cos\left(x - \dfrac{\pi}{6}\right)$

100. $\sin\left(x + \dfrac{\pi}{4}\right) - \sin\left(x - \dfrac{\pi}{4}\right)$

101. ***Projectile Motion*** A baseball leaves the hand of the person at first base at an angle of θ with the horizontal and at an initial velocity of $v_0 = 80$ feet per second. The ball is caught by the person at second base 100 feet away. Find θ if the range r of a projectile is

$$r = \frac{1}{32} v_0^2 \sin 2\theta.$$

102. ***Geometry*** A trough for feeding cattle is 4 meters long and its cross sections are isosceles triangles with the two equal sides being $\frac{1}{2}$ meter (see figure). The angle between the two sides is θ.

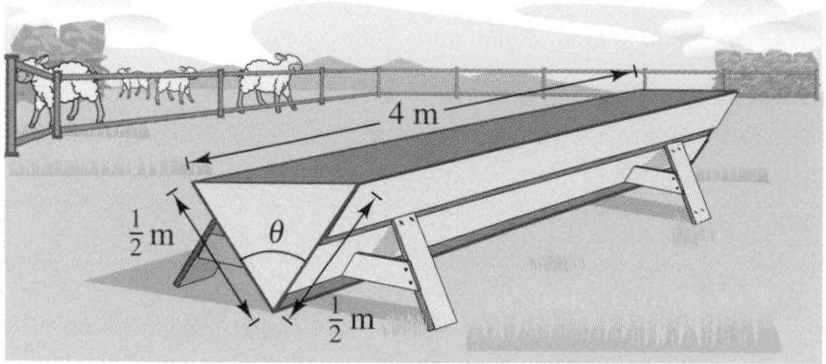

(a) Write the trough's volume as a function of $\frac{\theta}{2}$.

(b) Write the volume of the trough as a function of θ and determine the value of θ such that the volume is maximum.

Harmonic Motion **In Exercises 103–106, use the following information. A weight is attached to a spring suspended vertically from a ceiling. When a driving force is applied to the system, the weight moves vertically from its equilibrium position, and this motion is described by the model**

$$y = 1.5 \sin 8t - 0.5 \cos 8t$$

where y is the distance from equilibrium (in feet) and t is the time (in seconds).

103. Use a graphing utility to graph the model.

104. Write the model in the form

$$y = \sqrt{a^2 + b^2} \sin(Bt + C).$$

105. Find the amplitude of the oscillations of the weight.

106. Find the frequency of the oscillations of the weight.

Synthesis

True or False? **In Exercises 107–110, determine whether the statement is true or false. Justify your answer.**

107. If $\frac{\pi}{2} < \theta < \pi$, then $\cos \frac{\theta}{2} < 0$.

108. $\sin(x + y) = \sin x + \sin y$

109. $4 \sin(-x) \cos(-x) = -2 \sin 2x$

110. $4 \sin 45° \cos 15° = 1 + \sqrt{3}$

111. List the reciprocal identities, quotient identities, and Pythagorean identities from memory.

112. ***Think About It*** If a trigonometric equation has an infinite number of solutions, is it true that the equation is an identity? Explain.

113. ***Think About It*** Explain why you know from observation that the equation $a \sin x - b = 0$ has no solution if $|a| < |b|$.

114. ***Surface Area*** The surface area of a honeycomb is given by the equation

$$S = 6hs + \frac{3}{2}s^2\left(\frac{\sqrt{3} - \cos\theta}{\sin\theta}\right), \quad 0 < \theta \leq 90°$$

where $h = 2.4$ inches, $s = 0.75$ inch, and θ is the angle shown in the figure.

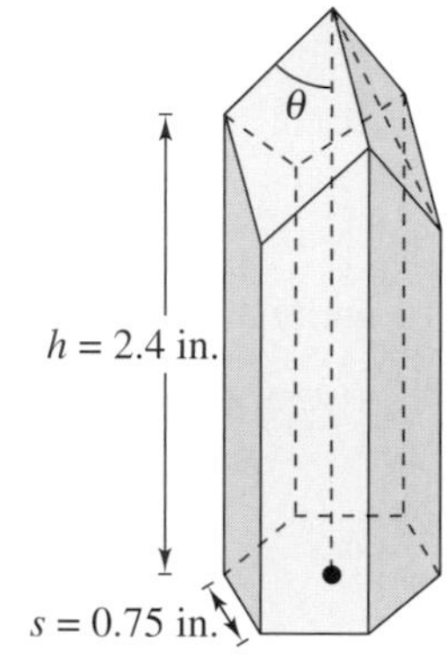

(a) For what value(s) of θ is the surface area 12 square inches?

(b) What value of θ gives the minimum surface area?

In Exercises 115 and 116, use the graphs of y_1 and y_2 to determine how to change one function to form the identity $y_1 = y_2$.

115. $y_1 = \sec^2\left(\frac{\pi}{2} - x\right)$

$y_2 = \cot^2 x$

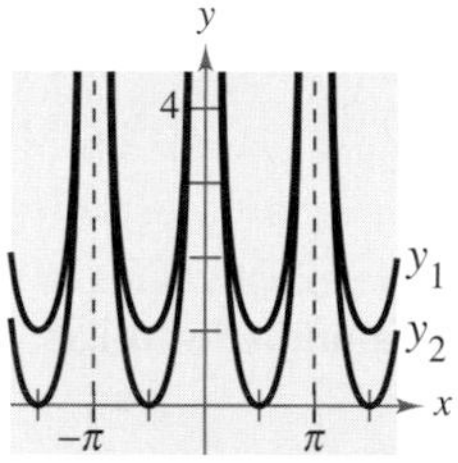

116. $y_1 = \frac{\cos 3x}{\cos x}$

$y_2 = (2 \sin x)^2$

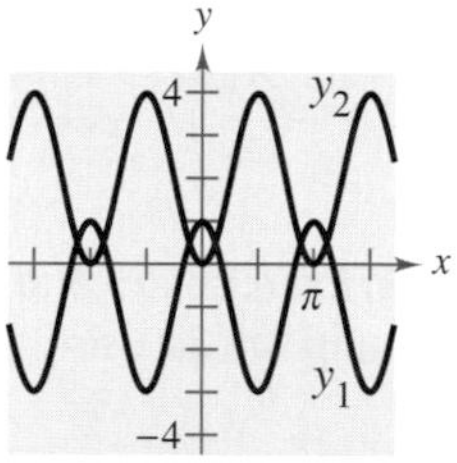

In Exercises 117 and 118, use the *zero* or *root* feature of a graphing utility to approximate the solutions of the equation.

117. $y = \sqrt{x + 3} + 4 \cos x$

118. $y = 2 - \frac{1}{2}x^2 + 3 \sin \frac{\pi x}{2}$

5 Chapter Test

Take this test as you would take a test in class. When you are finished, check your work against the answers given in the back of the book.

1. If $\tan\theta = \frac{3}{2}$ and $\cos\theta < 0$, use the fundamental identities to evaluate the other five trigonometric functions of θ.
2. Use the fundamental identities to simplify $\csc^2\beta(1 - \cos^2\beta)$.
3. Factor and simplify $\dfrac{\sec^4 x - \tan^4 x}{\sec^2 x + \tan^2 x}$.
4. Add and simplify $\dfrac{\cos\theta}{\sin\theta} + \dfrac{\sin\theta}{\cos\theta}$.
5. Determine the values of θ, $0 \le \theta < 2\pi$, for which $\tan\theta = -\sqrt{\sec^2\theta - 1}$ is true.
6. Use a graphing utility to graph the functions $y_1 = \cos x + \sin x \tan x$ and $y_2 = \sec x$. Make a conjecture about y_1 and y_2. Verify the result algebraically.

In Exercises 7–12, verify the identity.

7. $\sin\theta \sec\theta = \tan\theta$
8. $\sec^2 x \tan^2 x + \sec^2 x = \sec^4 x$
9. $\dfrac{\csc\alpha + \sec\alpha}{\sin\alpha + \cos\alpha} = \cot\alpha + \tan\alpha$
10. $\cos\left(x + \dfrac{\pi}{2}\right) = -\sin x$
11. $\sin(n\pi + \theta) = (-1)^n \sin\theta$, n is an integer.
12. $(\sin x + \cos x)^2 = 1 + \sin 2x$

13. Rewrite $\sin^4 x \tan^2 x$ in terms of the first power of the cosine.
14. Use a half-angle formula to simplify the expression $\dfrac{\sin 4\theta}{1 + \cos 4\theta}$.
15. Write $4\cos 2\theta \sin 4\theta$ as a sum or difference.
16. Write $\sin 3\theta - \sin 4\theta$ as a product.

In Exercises 17–20, find all solutions of the equation in the interval $[0, 2\pi)$.

17. $\tan^2 x + \tan x = 0$
18. $\sin 2\alpha - \cos\alpha = 0$
19. $4\cos^2 x - 3 = 0$
20. $\csc^2 x - \csc x - 2 = 0$

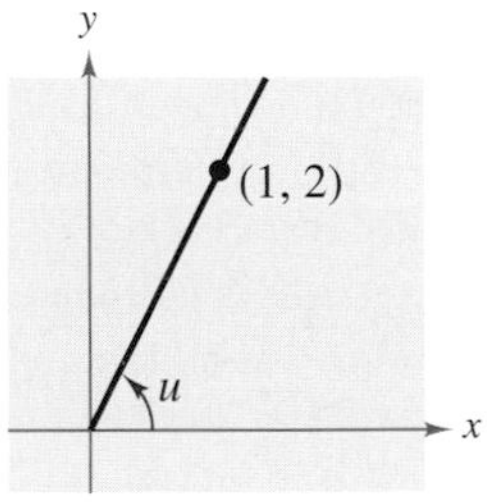

FIGURE FOR 23

21. Use a graphing utility to approximate the solutions of the equation $3\cos x - x = 0$ accurate to three decimal places.
22. Find the exact value of $\cos 105°$ using the fact that $105° = 135° - 30°$.
23. Use the figure to find the exact values of $\sin 2u$, $\cos 2u$, and $\tan 2u$.
24. Cheyenne, Wyoming has a latitude of 41°N. At this latitude, the position of the sun at sunrise can be modeled by

$$D = 31\sin\left(\frac{2\pi}{365}t - 1.4\right)$$

where t is the time (in days) and $t = 1$ represents January 1. In this model, D represents the number of degrees north or south of due east that the sun rises. Use a graphing utility to determine the days on which the sun is more than 20° north of due east at sunrise.

25. The heights h (in feet) of two people in different seats on a Ferris wheel can be modeled by

$$h_1 = 28\cos 10t + 38 \quad \text{and} \quad h_2 = 28\cos\left[10\left(t - \frac{\pi}{6}\right)\right] + 38, \ 0 \le t \le 2$$

where t is the time (in minutes). When are the two people at the same height?

Proofs in Mathematics

Sum and Difference Formulas *(p. 400)*

$$\sin(u + v) = \sin u \cos v + \cos u \sin v$$

$$\sin(u - v) = \sin u \cos v - \cos u \sin v$$

$$\cos(u + v) = \cos u \cos v - \sin u \sin v$$

$$\cos(u - v) = \cos u \cos v + \sin u \sin v$$

$$\tan(u + v) = \frac{\tan u + \tan v}{1 - \tan u \tan v}$$

$$\tan(u - v) = \frac{\tan u - \tan v}{1 + \tan u \tan v}$$

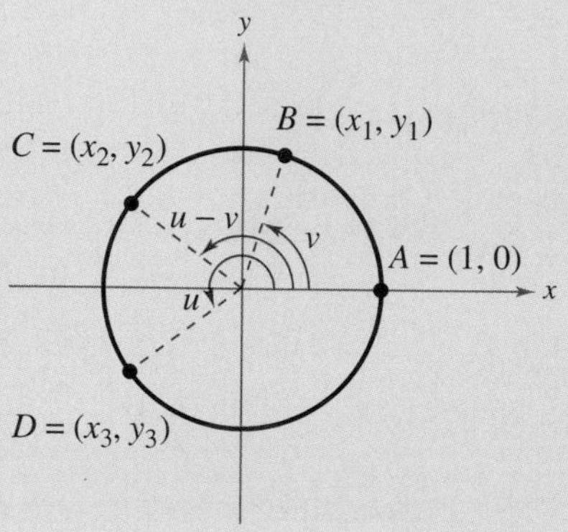

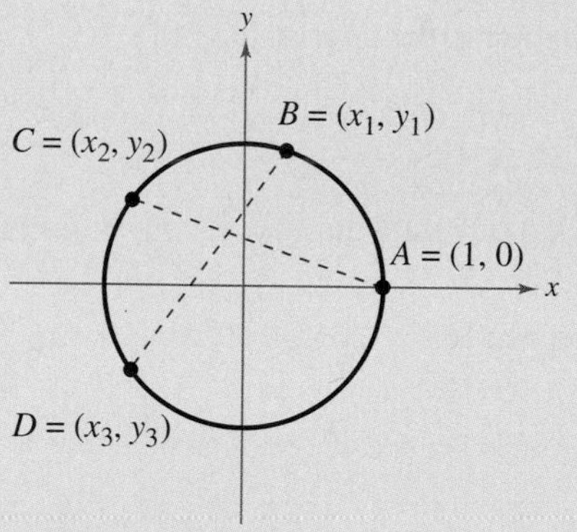

Proof

You can use the figures at the left for the proofs of the formulas for $\cos(u \pm v)$. In the top figure, let A be the point $(1, 0)$ and then use u and v to locate the points $B = (x_1, y_1)$, $C = (x_2, y_2)$, and $D = (x_3, y_3)$ on the unit circle. So, $x_i^2 + y_i^2 = 1$ for $i = 1, 2$, and 3. For convenience, assume that $0 < v < u < 2\pi$. In the bottom figure, note that arcs AC and BD have the same length. So, line segments AC and BD are also equal in length, which implies that

$$\sqrt{(x_2 - 1)^2 + (y_2 - 0)^2} = \sqrt{(x_3 - x_1)^2 + (y_3 - y_1)^2}$$

$$x_2^2 - 2x_2 + 1 + y_2^2 = x_3^2 - 2x_1x_3 + x_1^2 + y_3^2 - 2y_1y_3 + y_1^2$$

$$(x_2^2 + y_2^2) + 1 - 2x_2 = (x_3^2 + y_3^2) + (x_1^2 + y_1^2) - 2x_1x_3 - 2y_1y_3$$

$$1 + 1 - 2x_2 = 1 + 1 - 2x_1x_3 - 2y_1y_3$$

$$x_2 = x_3x_1 + y_3y_1.$$

Finally, by substituting the values $x_2 = \cos(u - v)$, $x_3 = \cos u$, $x_1 = \cos v$, $y_3 = \sin u$, and $y_1 = \sin v$, you obtain $\cos(u - v) = \cos u \cos v + \sin u \sin v$. The formula for $\cos(u + v)$ can be established by considering $u + v = u - (-v)$ and using the formula just derived to obtain

$$\cos(u + v) = \cos[u - (-v)] = \cos u \cos(-v) + \sin u \sin(-v)$$

$$= \cos u \cos v - \sin u \sin v.$$

You can use the sum and difference formulas for sine and cosine to prove the formulas for $\tan(u \pm v)$.

$$\tan(u \pm v) = \frac{\sin(u \pm v)}{\cos(u \pm v)}$$ Quotient identity

$$= \frac{\sin u \cos v \pm \cos u \sin v}{\cos u \cos v \mp \sin u \sin v}$$ Sum and difference formulas

$$= \frac{\dfrac{\sin u \cos v \pm \cos u \sin v}{\cos u \cos v}}{\dfrac{\cos u \cos v \mp \sin u \sin v}{\cos u \cos v}}$$ Divide numerator and denominator by $\cos u \cos v$.

$$= \frac{\dfrac{\sin u \cos v}{\cos u \cos v} \pm \dfrac{\cos u \sin v}{\cos u \cos v}}{\dfrac{\cos u \cos v}{\cos u \cos v} \mp \dfrac{\sin u \sin v}{\cos u \cos v}}$$ Write as separate fractions.

$$= \frac{\dfrac{\sin u}{\cos u} \pm \dfrac{\sin v}{\cos v}}{1 \mp \dfrac{\sin u}{\cos u} \cdot \dfrac{\sin v}{\cos v}}$$ Product of fractions

$$= \frac{\tan u \pm \tan v}{1 \mp \tan u \tan v}$$ Quotient identity

Trigonometry and Astronomy

Trigonometry was used by early astronomers to calculate measurements in the universe. Trigonometry was used to calculate the circumference of Earth and the distance from Earth to the moon. Another major accomplishment in astronomy using trigonometry was computing distances to stars.

Double-Angle Formulas *(p. 407)*

$$\sin 2u = 2 \sin u \cos u \qquad \cos 2u = \cos^2 u - \sin^2 u$$

$$\tan 2u = \frac{2 \tan u}{1 - \tan^2 u} \qquad = 2\cos^2 u - 1 = 1 - 2\sin^2 u$$

Proof

To prove all three formulas, let $v = u$ in the corresponding sum formulas.

$$\sin 2u = \sin(u + u) = \sin u \cos u + \cos u \sin u = 2 \sin u \cos u$$

$$\cos 2u = \cos(u + u) = \cos u \cos u - \sin u \sin u = \cos^2 u - \sin^2 u$$

$$\tan 2u = \tan(u + u) = \frac{\tan u + \tan u}{1 - \tan u \tan u} = \frac{2 \tan u}{1 - \tan^2 u}$$

Power-Reducing Formulas *(p. 409)*

$$\sin^2 u = \frac{1 - \cos 2u}{2} \qquad \cos^2 u = \frac{1 + \cos 2u}{2} \qquad \tan^2 u = \frac{1 - \cos 2u}{1 + \cos 2u}$$

Proof

To prove the first formula, solve for $\sin^2 u$ in the double-angle formula $\cos 2u = 1 - 2\sin^2 u$, as follows.

$$\cos 2u = 1 - 2\sin^2 u$$ Write double-angle formula.

$$2\sin^2 u = 1 - \cos 2u$$ Subtract $\cos 2u$ from and add $2 \sin^2 u$ to each side.

$$\sin^2 u = \frac{1 - \cos 2u}{2}$$ Divide each side by 2.

In a similar way you can prove the second formula, by solving for $\cos^2 u$ in the double-angle formula

$$\cos 2u = 2\cos^2 u - 1.$$

To prove the third formula, use a quotient identity, as follows.

$$\begin{aligned}\tan^2 u &= \frac{\sin^2 u}{\cos^2 u}\\ &= \frac{\dfrac{1-\cos 2u}{2}}{\dfrac{1+\cos 2u}{2}}\\ &= \frac{1-\cos 2u}{1+\cos 2u}\end{aligned}$$

Sum-to-Product Formulas *(p. 412)*

$$\sin u + \sin v = 2\sin\left(\frac{u+v}{2}\right)\cos\left(\frac{u-v}{2}\right)$$

$$\sin u - \sin v = 2\cos\left(\frac{u+v}{2}\right)\sin\left(\frac{u-v}{2}\right)$$

$$\cos u + \cos v = 2\cos\left(\frac{u+v}{2}\right)\cos\left(\frac{u-v}{2}\right)$$

$$\cos u - \cos v = -2\sin\left(\frac{u+v}{2}\right)\sin\left(\frac{u-v}{2}\right)$$

Proof

To prove the first formula, let $x = u + v$ and $y = u - v$. Then substitute $u = (x + y)/2$ and $v = (x - y)/2$ in the product-to-sum formula.

$$\begin{aligned}\sin u \cos v &= \frac{1}{2}[\sin(u+v) + \sin(u-v)]\\ \sin\left(\frac{x+y}{2}\right)\cos\left(\frac{x-y}{2}\right) &= \frac{1}{2}(\sin x + \sin y)\\ 2\sin\left(\frac{x+y}{2}\right)\cos\left(\frac{x-y}{2}\right) &= \sin x + \sin y\end{aligned}$$

The other sum-to-product formulas can be proved in a similar manner.

P.S. Problem Solving

This collection of thought-provoking and challenging exercises further explores and expands upon concepts learned in this chapter.

1. (a) Write each of the other trigonometric functions of θ in terms of $\sin\theta$.

(b) Write each of the other trigonometric functions of θ in terms of $\cos\theta$.

2. Verify that for all integers n,

$$\cos\left[\frac{(2n+1)\pi}{2}\right] = 0.$$

3. Verify that for all integers n,

$$\sin\left[\frac{(12n+1)\pi}{6}\right] = \frac{1}{2}.$$

4. A particular sound wave is modeled by

$$p(t) = \frac{1}{4\pi}(p_1(t) + 30p_2(t) + p_3(t) + p_5(t) + 30p_6(t))$$

where $p_n(t) = \frac{1}{n}\sin(524n\pi t)$, and t is the time (in seconds).

(a) Find the sine components $p_n(t)$ and use a graphing utility to graph each component. Then verify the graph of p that is shown.

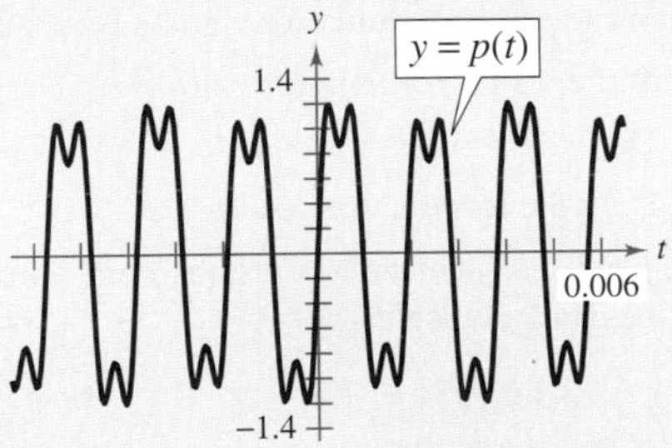

(b) Find the period of each sine component of p. Is p periodic? If so, what is its period?

(c) Use the *zero* or *root* feature or the *zoom* and *trace* features of a graphing utility to find the t-intercepts of the graph of p over one cycle.

(d) Use the *maximum* and *minimum* features of a graphing utility to approximate the absolute maximum and absolute minimum values of p over one cycle.

5. Three squares of side s are placed side by side (see figure). Make a conjecture about the relationship between the sum $u + v$ and w. Prove your conjecture by using the identity for the tangent of the sum of two angles.

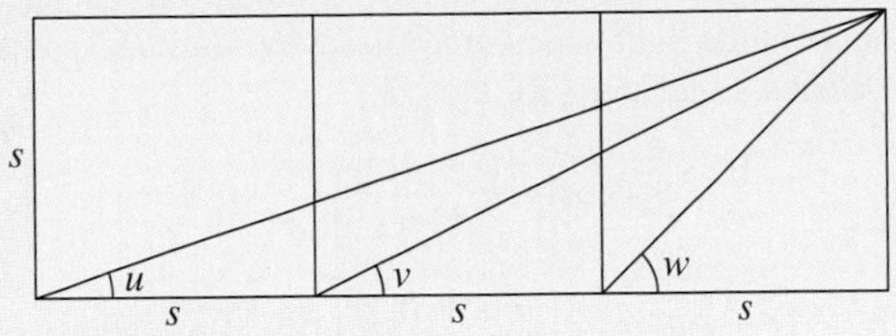

FIGURE FOR 5

6. The path traveled by an object (neglecting air resistance) that is projected at an initial height of h_0 feet, an initial velocity of v_0 feet per second, and an initial angle θ is given by

$$y = -\frac{16}{v_0^2\cos^2\theta}x^2 + (\tan\theta)x + h_0$$

where x and y are measured in feet. Find a formula for the maximum height of an object projected from ground level at velocity v_0 and angle θ. To do this, find half of the horizontal distance

$$\frac{1}{32}v_0^2\sin 2\theta$$

and then substitute it for x in the general model for the path of a projectile (where $h_0 = 0$).

7. Use the figure to derive the formulas for

$$\sin\frac{\theta}{2},\ \cos\frac{\theta}{2},\ \text{and } \tan\frac{\theta}{2}$$

where θ is an acute angle.

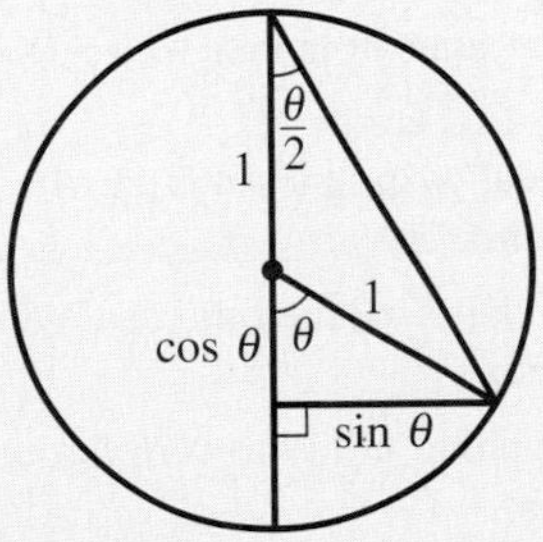

8. The force F (in pounds) on a person's back when he or she bends over at an angle θ is modeled by

$$F = \frac{0.6W\sin(\theta + 90^\circ)}{\sin 12^\circ}$$

where W is the person's weight (in pounds).

(a) Simplify the model.

(b) Use a graphing utility to graph the model, where $W = 185$ and $0^\circ < \theta < 90^\circ$.

(c) At what angle is the force a maximum? At what angle is the force a minimum?

9. The number of hours of daylight that occur at any location on Earth depends on the time of year and the latitude of the location. The following equations model the numbers of hours of daylight in Seward, Alaska (60° latitude) and New Orleans, Louisiana (30° latitude).

$$D = 12.2 - 6.4\cos\left[\frac{\pi(t + 0.2)}{182.6}\right] \qquad \text{Seward}$$

$$D = 12.2 - 1.9\cos\left[\frac{\pi(t + 0.2)}{182.6}\right] \qquad \text{New Orleans}$$

In these models, D represents the number of hours of daylight and t represents the day, with $t = 0$ corresponding to January 1.

(a) Use a graphing utility to graph both models in the same viewing window. Use a viewing window of $0 \le t \le 365$.

(b) Find the days of the year on which both cities receive the same amount of daylight. What are these days called?

(c) Which city has the greater variation in the number of daylight hours? Which constant in each model would you use to determine the difference between the greatest and least numbers of hours of daylight?

(d) Determine the period of each model.

10. The tide, or depth of the ocean near the shore, changes throughout the day. The water depth d (in feet) of a bay can be modeled by

$$d = 35 - 28\cos\frac{\pi}{6.2}t$$

where t is the time in hours, with $t = 0$ corresponding to 12:00 A.M.

(a) Algebraically find the times at which the high and low tides occur.

(b) Algebraically find the time(s) at which the water depth is 3.5 feet.

(c) Use a graphing utility to verify your results from parts (a) and (b).

11. Find the solution of each inequality in the interval $[0, 2\pi]$.

(a) $\sin x \ge 0.5$ (b) $\cos x \le -0.5$

(c) $\tan x < \sin x$ (d) $\cos x \ge \sin x$

12. The index of refraction n of a transparent material is the ratio of the speed of light in a vacuum to the speed of light in the material. Some common materials and their indices are air (1.00), water (1.33), and glass (1.50). Triangular prisms are often used to measure the index of refraction based on the formula

$$n = \frac{\sin\left(\frac{\theta}{2} + \frac{\alpha}{2}\right)}{\sin\frac{\theta}{2}}.$$

For the prism shown in the figure, $\alpha = 60°$.

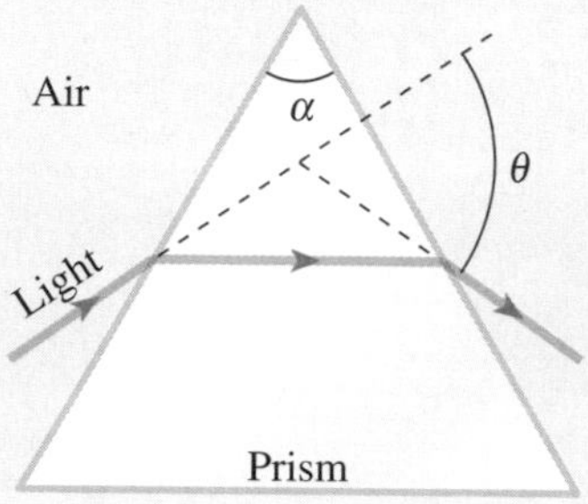

(a) Write the index of refraction as a function of $\cot(\theta/2)$.

(b) Find θ for a prism made of glass.

13. (a) Write a sum formula for $\sin(u + v + w)$.

(b) Write a sum formula for $\tan(u + v + w)$.

14. (a) Derive a formula for $\cos 3\theta$.

(b) Derive a formula for $\cos 4\theta$.

15. The heights h (in inches) of pistons 1 and 2 in an automobile engine can be modeled by

$$h_1 = 3.75\sin 733t + 7.5$$

and

$$h_2 = 3.75\sin 733\left(t + \frac{4\pi}{3}\right) + 7.5$$

where t is measured in seconds.

(a) Use a graphing utility to graph the heights of these two pistons in the same viewing window for $0 \le t \le 1$.

(b) How often are the pistons at the same height?

Additional Topics in Trigonometry

6

6.1 Law of Sines

6.2 Law of Cosines

6.3 Vectors in the Plane

6.4 Vectors and Dot Products

6.5 Trigonometric Form of a Complex Number

The work done by a force, such as pushing and pulling objects, can be calculated using vector operations.

SELECTED APPLICATIONS

Triangles and vectors have many real-life applications. The applications listed below represent a small sample of the applications in this chapter.

- Bridge Design, Exercise 39, page 437
- Glide Path, Exercise 41, page 437
- Surveying, Exercise 31, page 444
- Paper Manufacturing, Exercise 45, page 445
- Cable Tension, Exercises 79 and 80, page 458
- Navigation, Exercise 84, page 459
- Revenue, Exercise 65, page 468
- Work, Exercise 73, page 469

6.1 Law of Sines

What you should learn

- Use the Law of Sines to solve oblique triangles (AAS or ASA).
- Use the Law of Sines to solve oblique triangles (SSA).
- Find the areas of oblique triangles.
- Use the Law of Sines to model and solve real-life problems.

Why you should learn it

You can use the Law of Sines to solve real-life problems involving oblique triangles. For instance, in Exercise 44 on page 438, you can use the Law of Sines to determine the length of the shadow of the Leaning Tower of Pisa.

Hideo Kurihara/Getty Images

Introduction

In Chapter 4, you studied techniques for solving right triangles. In this section and the next, you will solve **oblique triangles**—triangles that have no right angles. As standard notation, the angles of a triangle are labeled A, B, and C, and their opposite sides are labeled a, b, and c, as shown in Figure 6.1.

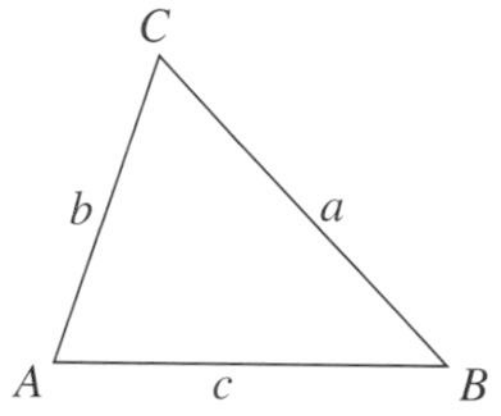

FIGURE 6.1

To solve an oblique triangle, you need to know the measure of at least one side and any two other parts of the triangle—either two sides, two angles, or one angle and one side. This breaks down into the following four cases.

1. Two angles and any side (AAS or ASA)
2. Two sides and an angle opposite one of them (SSA)
3. Three sides (SSS)
4. Two sides and their included angle (SAS)

The first two cases can be solved using the **Law of Sines,** whereas the last two cases require the Law of Cosines (see Section 6.2).

Law of Sines

If ABC is a triangle with sides a, b, and c, then

$$\frac{a}{\sin A} = \frac{b}{\sin B} = \frac{c}{\sin C}.$$

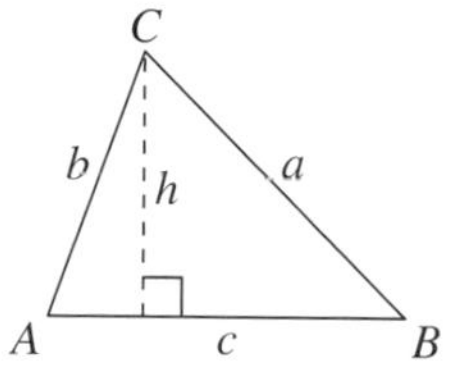

A is acute.

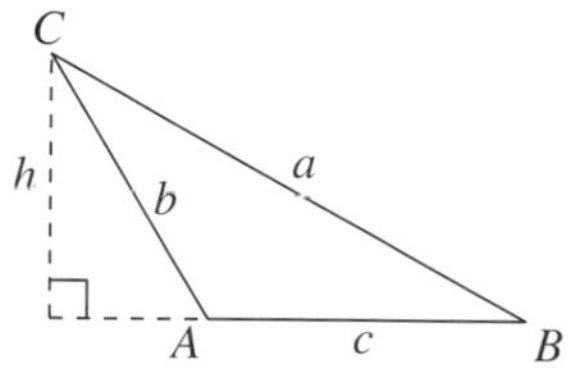

A is obtuse.

The Law of Sines can also be written in the reciprocal form

$$\frac{\sin A}{a} = \frac{\sin B}{b} = \frac{\sin C}{c}.$$

For a proof of the Law of Sines, see Proofs in Mathematics on page 489.

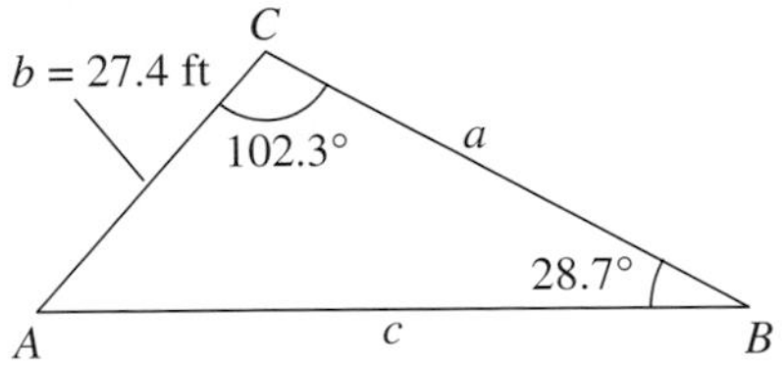

FIGURE 6.2

Example 1 Given Two Angles and One Side—AAS

For the triangle in Figure 6.2, $C = 102.3°$, $B = 28.7°$, and $b = 27.4$ feet. Find the remaining angle and sides.

Solution

The third angle of the triangle is

$$\begin{aligned} A &= 180° - B - C \\ &= 180° - 28.7° - 102.3° \\ &= 49.0°. \end{aligned}$$

By the Law of Sines, you have

$$\frac{a}{\sin A} = \frac{b}{\sin B} = \frac{c}{\sin C}.$$

Using $b = 27.4$ produces

$$a = \frac{b}{\sin B}(\sin A) = \frac{27.4}{\sin 28.7°}(\sin 49.0°) \approx 43.06 \text{ feet}$$

and

$$c = \frac{b}{\sin B}(\sin C) = \frac{27.4}{\sin 28.7°}(\sin 102.3°) \approx 55.75 \text{ feet.}$$

CHECKPOINT Now try Exercise 1.

STUDY TIP

When solving triangles, a careful sketch is useful as a quick test for the feasibility of an answer. Remember that the longest side lies opposite the largest angle, and the shortest side lies opposite the smallest angle.

Example 2 Given Two Angles and One Side—ASA

A pole tilts *toward* the sun at an 8° angle from the vertical, and it casts a 22-foot shadow. The angle of elevation from the tip of the shadow to the top of the pole is 43°. How tall is the pole?

Solution

From Figure 6.3, note that $A = 43°$ and $B = 90° + 8° = 98°$. So, the third angle is

$$\begin{aligned} C &= 180° - A - B \\ &= 180° - 43° - 98° \\ &= 39°. \end{aligned}$$

By the Law of Sines, you have

$$\frac{a}{\sin A} = \frac{c}{\sin C}.$$

Because $c = 22$ feet, the length of the pole is

$$a = \frac{c}{\sin C}(\sin A) = \frac{22}{\sin 39°}(\sin 43°) \approx 23.84 \text{ feet.}$$

CHECKPOINT Now try Exercise 35.

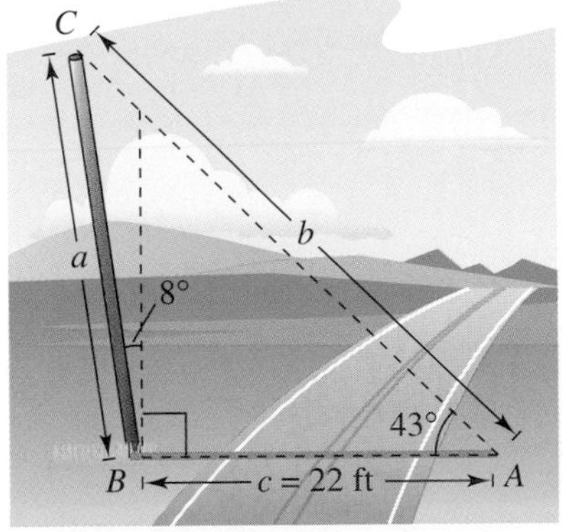

FIGURE 6.3

For practice, try reworking Example 2 for a pole that tilts *away from* the sun under the same conditions.

The Ambiguous Case (SSA)

In Examples 1 and 2 you saw that two angles and one side determine a unique triangle. However, if two sides and one opposite angle are given, three possible situations can occur: (1) no such triangle exists, (2) one such triangle exists, or (3) two distinct triangles may satisfy the conditions.

The Ambiguous Case (SSA)

Consider a triangle in which you are given a, b, and A. $(h = b \sin A)$

	A is acute.	A is acute.	A is acute.	A is acute.	A is obtuse.	A is obtuse.
Sketch	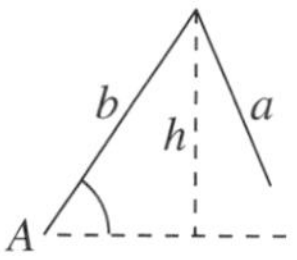	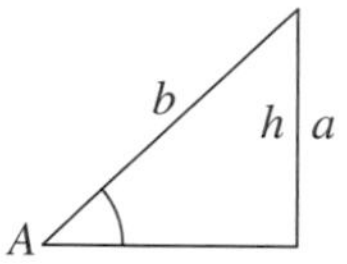	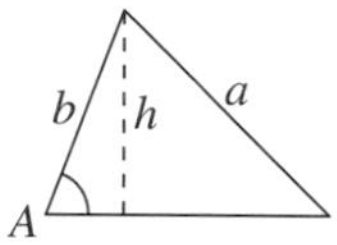	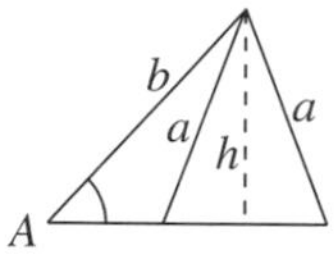	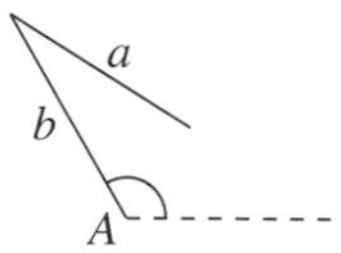	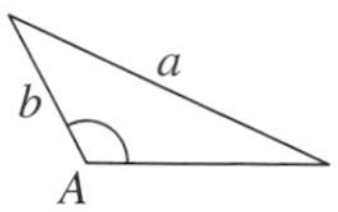
Necessary condition	$a < h$	$a = h$	$a > b$	$h < a < b$	$a \leq b$	$a > b$
Triangles possible	None	One	One	Two	None	One

Example 3 Single-Solution Case—SSA

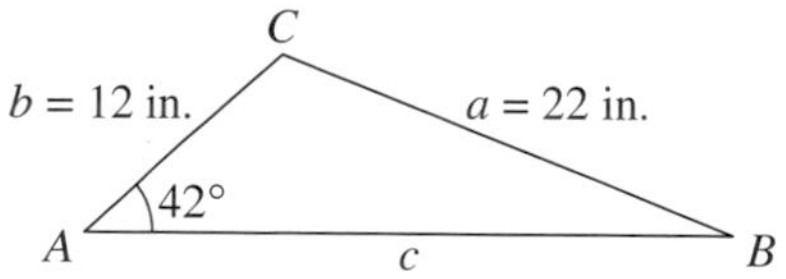

One solution: $a > b$

FIGURE 6.4

For the triangle in Figure 6.4, $a = 22$ inches, $b = 12$ inches, and $A = 42°$. Find the remaining side and angles.

Solution

By the Law of Sines, you have

$$\frac{\sin B}{b} = \frac{\sin A}{a} \qquad \text{Reciprocal form}$$

$$\sin B = b\left(\frac{\sin A}{a}\right) \qquad \text{Multiply each side by } b.$$

$$\sin B = 12\left(\frac{\sin 42°}{22}\right) \qquad \text{Substitute for } A, a, \text{ and } b.$$

$$B \approx 21.41°. \qquad B \text{ is acute.}$$

Now, you can determine that

$$C \approx 180° - 42° - 21.41° = 116.59°.$$

Then, the remaining side is

$$\frac{c}{\sin C} = \frac{a}{\sin A}$$

$$c = \frac{a}{\sin A}(\sin C) = \frac{22}{\sin 42°}(\sin 116.59°) \approx 29.40 \text{ inches.}$$

✓CHECKPOINT Now try Exercise 19.

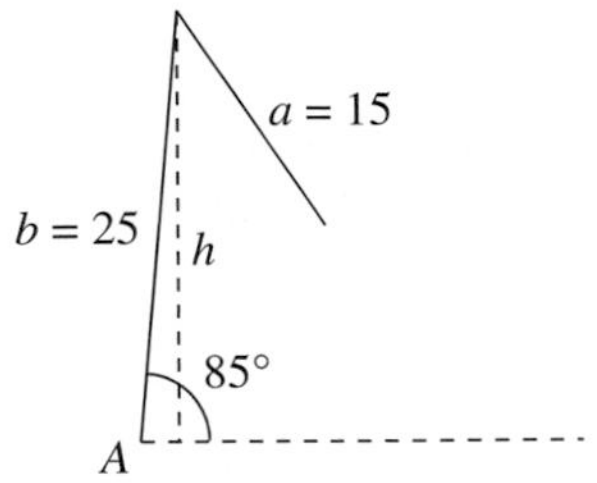

No solution: $a < h$

FIGURE 6.5

Example 4 No-Solution Case—SSA

Show that there is no triangle for which $a = 15$, $b = 25$, and $A = 85°$.

Solution

Begin by making the sketch shown in Figure 6.5. From this figure it appears that no triangle is formed. You can verify this using the Law of Sines.

$$\frac{\sin B}{b} = \frac{\sin A}{a}$$ Reciprocal form

$$\sin B = b\left(\frac{\sin A}{a}\right)$$ Multiply each side by b.

$$\sin B = 25\left(\frac{\sin 85°}{15}\right) \approx 1.660 > 1$$

This contradicts the fact that $|\sin B| \le 1$. So, no triangle can be formed having sides $a = 15$ and $b = 25$ and an angle of $A = 85°$.

✓CHECKPOINT Now try Exercise 21.

Example 5 Two-Solution Case—SSA

Find two triangles for which $a = 12$ meters, $b = 31$ meters, and $A = 20.5°$.

Solution

By the Law of Sines, you have

$$\frac{\sin B}{b} = \frac{\sin A}{a}$$ Reciprocal form

$$\sin B = b\left(\frac{\sin A}{a}\right) = 31\left(\frac{\sin 20.5°}{12}\right) \approx 0.9047.$$

There are two angles $B_1 \approx 64.8°$ and $B_2 \approx 180° - 64.8° = 115.2°$ between 0° and 180° whose sine is 0.9047. For $B_1 \approx 64.8°$, you obtain

$$C \approx 180° - 20.5° - 64.8° = 94.7°$$

$$c = \frac{a}{\sin A}(\sin C) = \frac{12}{\sin 20.5°}(\sin 94.7°) \approx 34.15 \text{ meters.}$$

For $B_2 \approx 115.2°$, you obtain

$$C \approx 180° - 20.5° - 115.2° = 44.3°$$

$$c = \frac{a}{\sin A}(\sin C) = \frac{12}{\sin 20.5°}(\sin 44.3°) \approx 23.93 \text{ meters.}$$

The resulting triangles are shown in Figure 6.6.

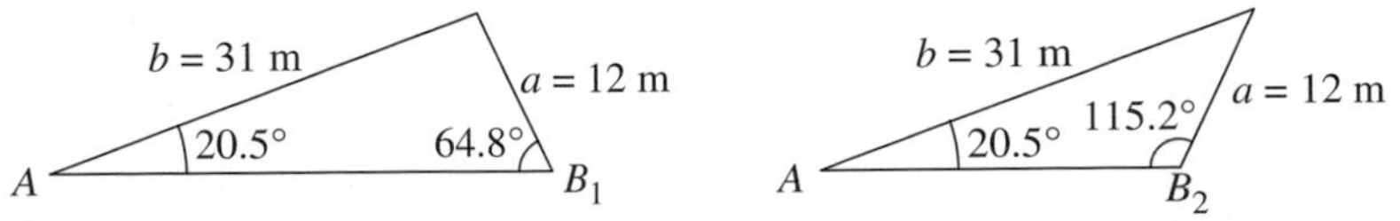

FIGURE 6.6

✓CHECKPOINT Now try Exercise 23.

> **STUDY TIP**
>
> To see how to obtain the height of the obtuse triangle in Figure 6.7, notice the use of the reference angle $180° - A$ and the difference formula for sine, as follows.
>
> $$\begin{aligned} h &= b\sin(180° - A) \\ &= b(\sin 180° \cos A \\ &\qquad - \cos 180° \sin A) \\ &= b[0 \cdot \cos A - (-1) \cdot \sin A] \\ &= b \sin A \end{aligned}$$

Area of an Oblique Triangle

The procedure used to prove the Law of Sines leads to a simple formula for the area of an oblique triangle. Referring to Figure 6.7, note that each triangle has a height of $h = b \sin A$. Consequently, the area of each triangle is

$$\text{Area} = \frac{1}{2}(\text{base})(\text{height}) = \frac{1}{2}(c)(b \sin A) = \frac{1}{2}bc \sin A.$$

By similar arguments, you can develop the formulas

$$\text{Area} = \frac{1}{2}ab \sin C = \frac{1}{2}ac \sin B.$$

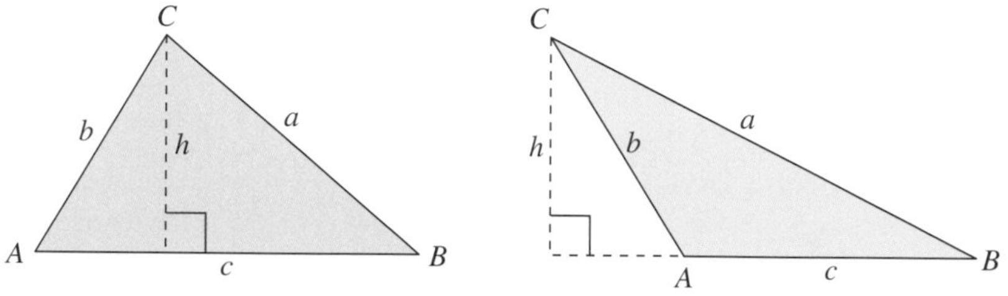

A is acute *A is obtuse*

FIGURE 6.7

> **Area of an Oblique Triangle**
>
> The area of any triangle is one-half the product of the lengths of two sides times the sine of their included angle. That is,
>
> $$\text{Area} = \frac{1}{2}bc \sin A = \frac{1}{2}ab \sin C = \frac{1}{2}ac \sin B.$$

Note that if angle A is $90°$, the formula gives the area for a right triangle:

$$\text{Area} = \frac{1}{2}bc(\sin 90°) = \frac{1}{2}bc = \frac{1}{2}(\text{base})(\text{height}). \qquad \sin 90° = 1$$

Similar results are obtained for angles C and B equal to $90°$.

Example 6 Finding the Area of a Triangular Lot

Find the area of a triangular lot having two sides of lengths 90 meters and 52 meters and an included angle of $102°$.

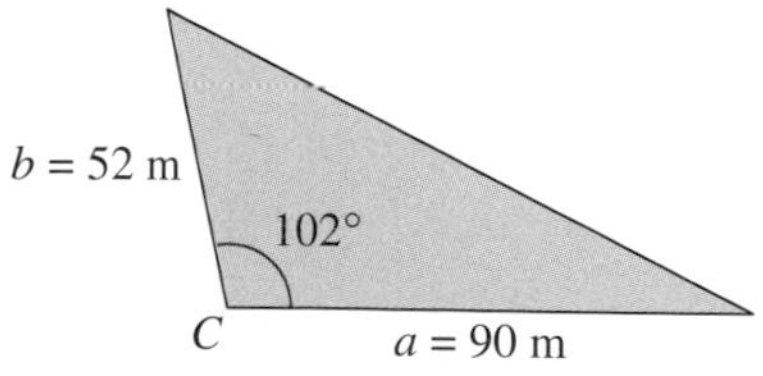

FIGURE 6.8

Solution

Consider $a = 90$ meters, $b = 52$ meters, and angle $C = 102°$, as shown in Figure 6.8. Then, the area of the triangle is

$$\text{Area} = \frac{1}{2}ab \sin C = \frac{1}{2}(90)(52)(\sin 102°) \approx 2289 \text{ square meters.}$$

CHECKPOINT Now try Exercise 29.

Application

Example 7 An Application of the Law of Sines

The course for a boat race starts at point A in Figure 6.9 and proceeds in the direction S 52° W to point B, then in the direction S 40° E to point C, and finally back to A. Point C lies 8 kilometers directly south of point A. Approximate the total distance of the race course.

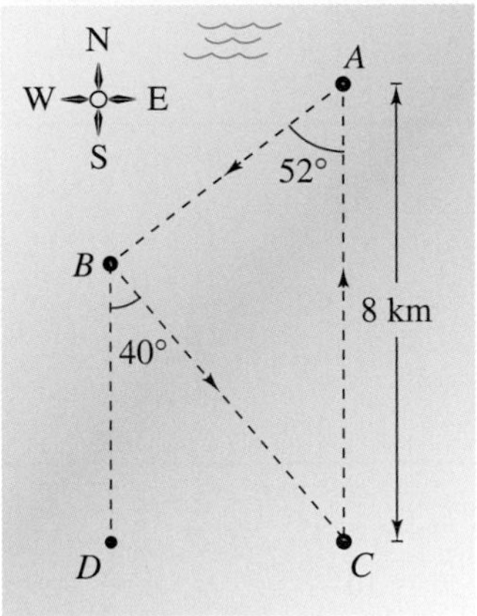

FIGURE 6.9

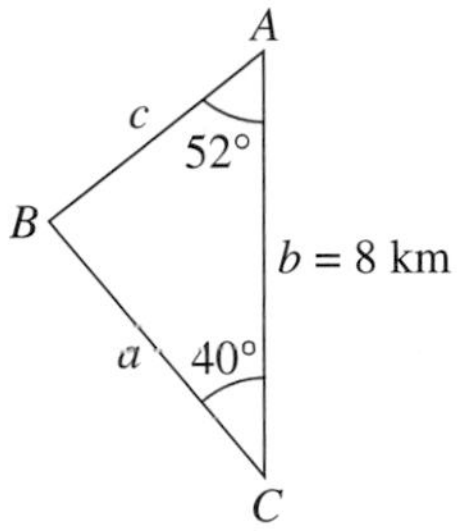

FIGURE 6.10

Solution

Because lines BD and AC are parallel, it follows that $\angle BCA \cong \angle DBC$. Consequently, triangle ABC has the measures shown in Figure 6.10. For angle B, you have $B = 180° - 52° - 40° = 88°$. Using the Law of Sines

$$\frac{a}{\sin 52°} = \frac{b}{\sin 88°} = \frac{c}{\sin 40°}$$

you can let $b = 8$ and obtain

$$a = \frac{8}{\sin 88°}(\sin 52°) \approx 6.308$$

and

$$c = \frac{8}{\sin 88°}(\sin 40°) \approx 5.145.$$

The total length of the course is approximately

$$\text{Length} \approx 8 + 6.308 + 5.145$$

$$= 19.453 \text{ kilometers.}$$

CHECKPOINT Now try Exercise 39.

WRITING ABOUT MATHEMATICS

Using the Law of Sines In this section, you have been using the Law of Sines to solve *oblique* triangles. Can the Law of Sines also be used to solve a right triangle? If so, write a short paragraph explaining how to use the Law of Sines to solve each triangle. Is there an easier way to solve these triangles?

a. (AAS)

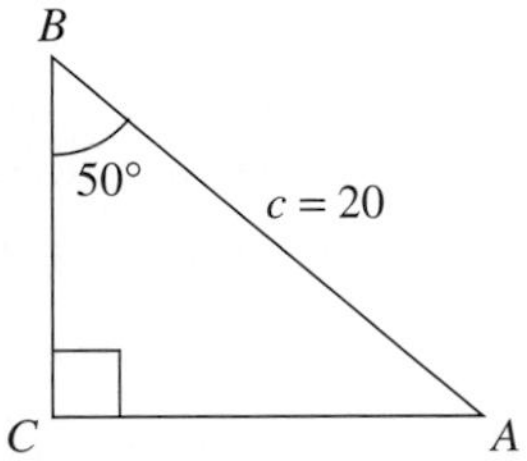

b. (ASA)

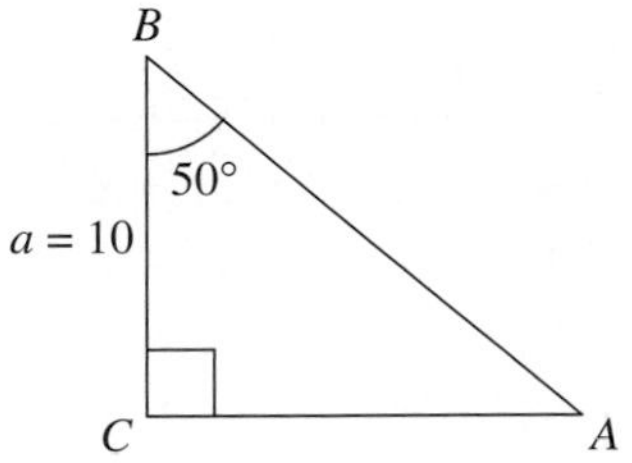

6.1 Exercises

VOCABULARY CHECK: Fill in the blanks.

1. An ________ triangle is a triangle that has no right angle.

2. For triangle ABC, the Law of Sines is given by $\frac{a}{\sin A} = $ ________ $= \frac{c}{\sin C}$.

3. The area of an oblique triangle is given by $\frac{1}{2}bc \sin A = \frac{1}{2}ab \sin C = $ ________ .

In Exercises 1–18, use the Law of Sines to solve the triangle. Round your answers to two decimal places.

1.

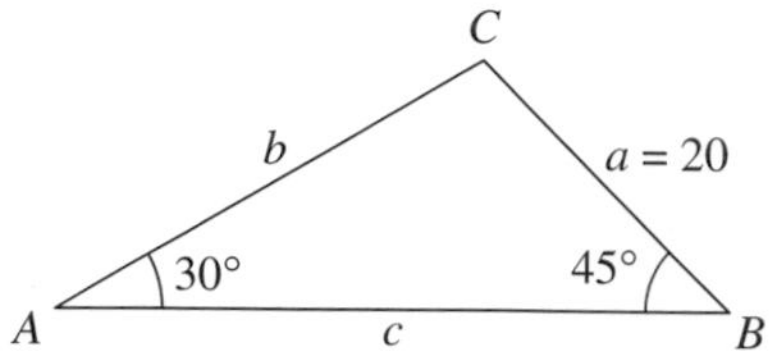

2.

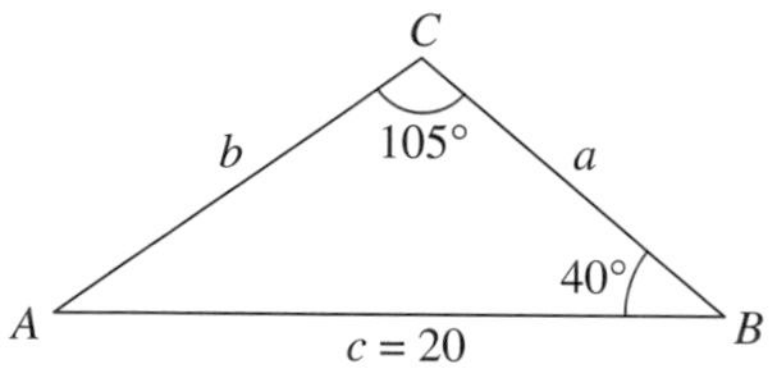

3.

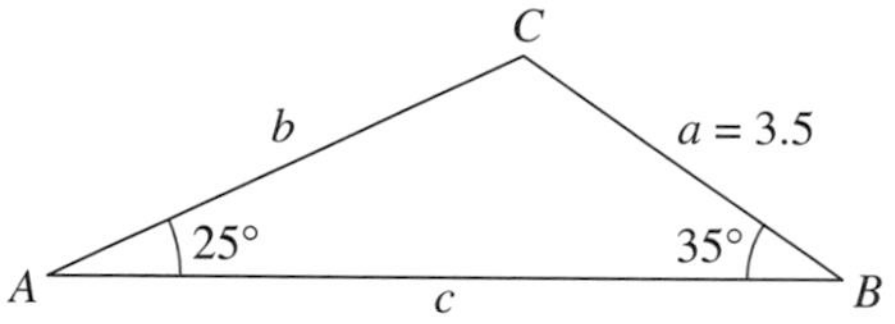

4.

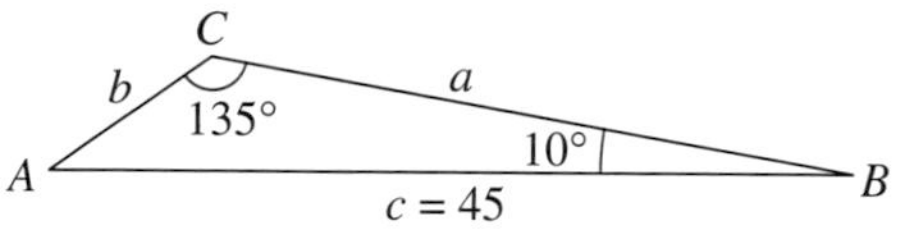

5. $A = 36°$, $a = 8$, $b = 5$
6. $A = 60°$, $a = 9$, $c = 10$
7. $A = 102.4°$, $C = 16.7°$, $a = 21.6$
8. $A = 24.3°$, $C = 54.6°$, $c = 2.68$
9. $A = 83° 20'$, $C = 54.6°$, $c = 18.1$
10. $A = 5° 40'$, $B = 8° 15'$, $b = 4.8$
11. $B = 15° 30'$, $a = 4.5$, $b = 6.8$
12. $B = 2° 45'$, $b = 6.2$, $c = 5.8$
13. $C = 145°$, $b = 4$, $c = 14$
14. $A = 100°$, $a = 125$, $c = 10$
15. $A = 110° 15'$, $a = 48$, $b = 16$
16. $C = 85° 20'$, $a = 35$, $c = 50$
17. $A = 55°$, $B = 42°$, $c = \frac{3}{4}$
18. $B = 28°$, $C = 104°$, $a = 3\frac{5}{8}$

In Exercises 19–24, use the Law of Sines to solve (if possible) the triangle. If two solutions exist, find both. Round your answers to two decimal places.

19. $A = 110°$, $a = 125$, $b = 100$
20. $A = 110°$, $a = 125$, $b = 200$
21. $A = 76°$, $a = 18$, $b = 20$
22. $A = 76°$, $a = 34$, $b = 21$
23. $A = 58°$, $a = 11.4$, $b = 12.8$
24. $A = 58°$, $a = 4.5$, $b = 12.8$

In Exercises 25–28, find values for *b* such that the triangle has (a) one solution, (b) two solutions, and (c) no solution.

25. $A = 36°$, $a = 5$
26. $A = 60°$, $a = 10$
27. $A = 10°$, $a = 10.8$
28. $A = 88°$, $a = 315.6$

In Exercises 29–34, find the area of the triangle having the indicated angle and sides.

29. $C = 120°$, $a = 4$, $b = 6$
30. $B = 130°$, $a = 62$, $c = 20$
31. $A = 43° 45'$, $b = 57$, $c = 85$
32. $A = 5° 15'$, $b = 4.5$, $c = 22$
33. $B = 72° 30'$, $a = 105$, $c = 64$
34. $C = 84° 30'$, $a = 16$, $b = 20$

35. ***Height*** Because of prevailing winds, a tree grew so that it was leaning 4° from the vertical. At a point 35 meters from the tree, the angle of elevation to the top of the tree is 23° (see figure). Find the height h of the tree.

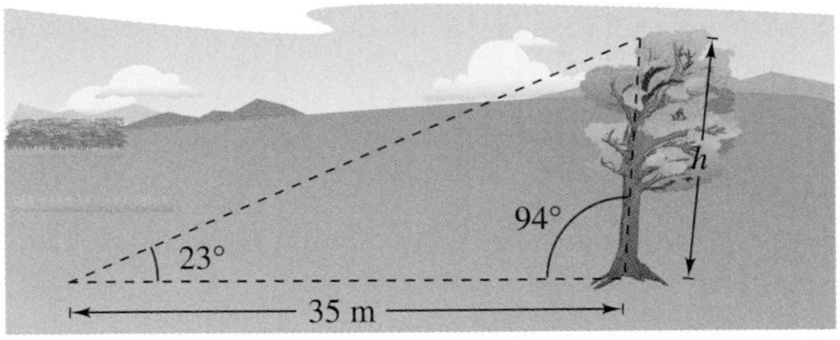

36. ***Height*** A flagpole at a right angle to the horizontal is located on a slope that makes an angle of 12° with the horizontal. The flagpole's shadow is 16 meters long and points directly up the slope. The angle of elevation from the tip of the shadow to the sun is 20°.

(a) Draw a triangle that represents the problem. Show the known quantities on the triangle and use a variable to indicate the height of the flagpole.

(b) Write an equation involving the unknown quantity.

(c) Find the height of the flagpole.

37. ***Angle of Elevation*** A 10-meter telephone pole casts a 17-meter shadow directly down a slope when the angle of elevation of the sun is 42° (see figure). Find θ, the angle of elevation of the ground.

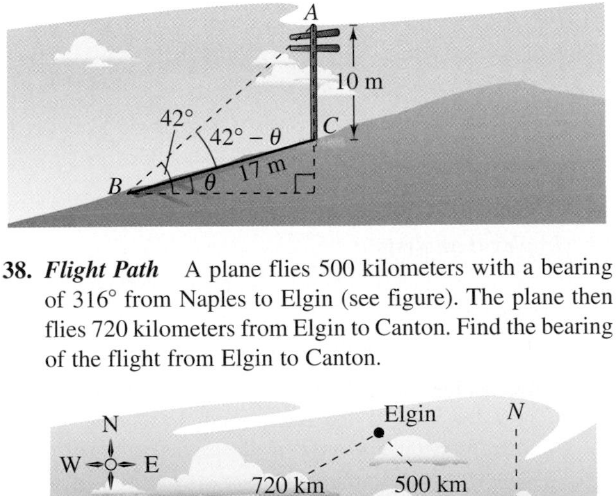

38. ***Flight Path*** A plane flies 500 kilometers with a bearing of 316° from Naples to Elgin (see figure). The plane then flies 720 kilometers from Elgin to Canton. Find the bearing of the flight from Elgin to Canton.

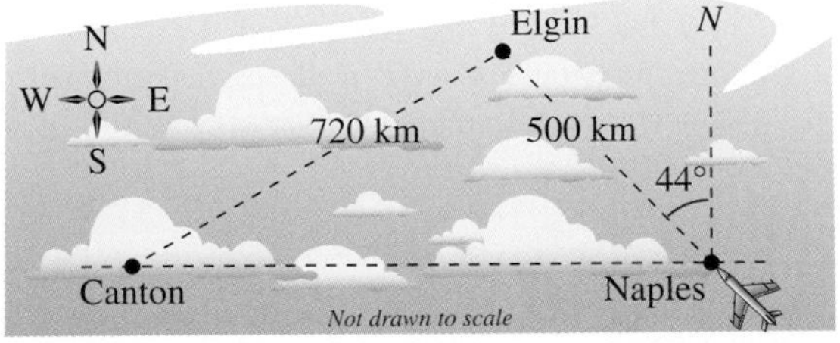

39. ***Bridge Design*** A bridge is to be built across a small lake from a gazebo to a dock (see figure). The bearing from the gazebo to the dock is S 41° W. From a tree 100 meters from the gazebo, the bearings to the gazebo and the dock are S 74° E and S 28° E, respectively. Find the distance from the gazebo to the dock.

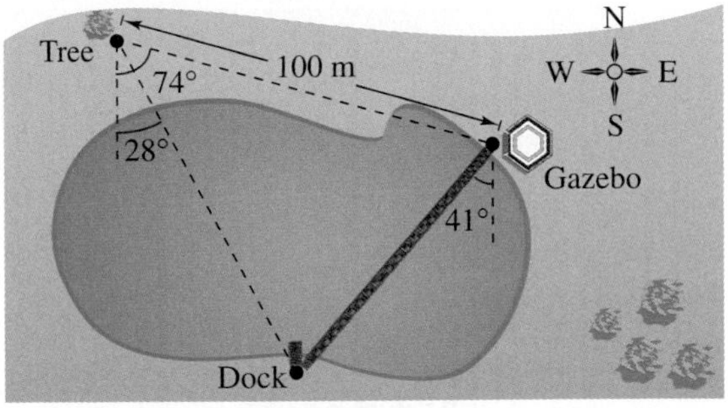

40. ***Railroad Track Design*** The circular arc of a railroad curve has a chord of length 3000 feet and a central angle of 40°.

(a) Draw a diagram that visually represents the problem. Show the known quantities on the diagram and use the variables r and s to represent the radius of the arc and the length of the arc, respectively.

(b) Find the radius r of the circular arc.

(c) Find the length s of the circular arc.

41. ***Glide Path*** A pilot has just started on the glide path for landing at an airport with a runway of length 9000 feet. The angles of depression from the plane to the ends of the runway are 17.5° and 18.8°.

(a) Draw a diagram that visually represents the problem.

(b) Find the air distance the plane must travel until touching down on the near end of the runway.

(c) Find the ground distance the plane must travel until touching down.

(d) Find the altitude of the plane when the pilot begins the descent.

42. ***Locating a Fire*** The bearing from the Pine Knob fire tower to the Colt Station fire tower is N 65° E, and the two towers are 30 kilometers apart. A fire spotted by rangers in each tower has a bearing of N 80° E from Pine Knob and S 70° E from Colt Station (see figure). Find the distance of the fire from each tower.

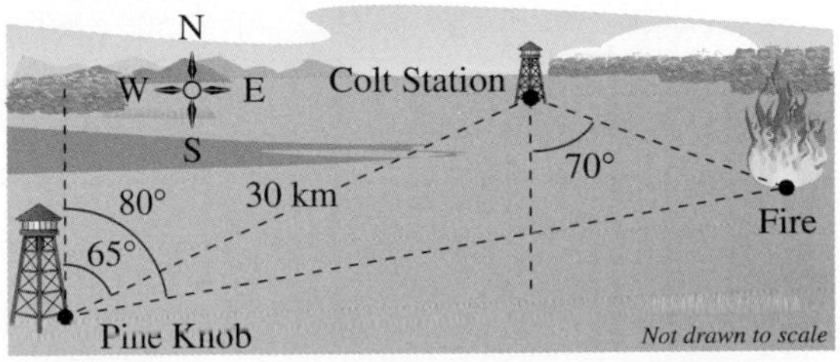

43. ***Distance*** A boat is sailing due east parallel to the shoreline at a speed of 10 miles per hour. At a given time, the bearing to the lighthouse is S 70° E, and 15 minutes later the bearing is S 63° E (see figure). The lighthouse is located at the shoreline. What is the distance from the boat to the shoreline?

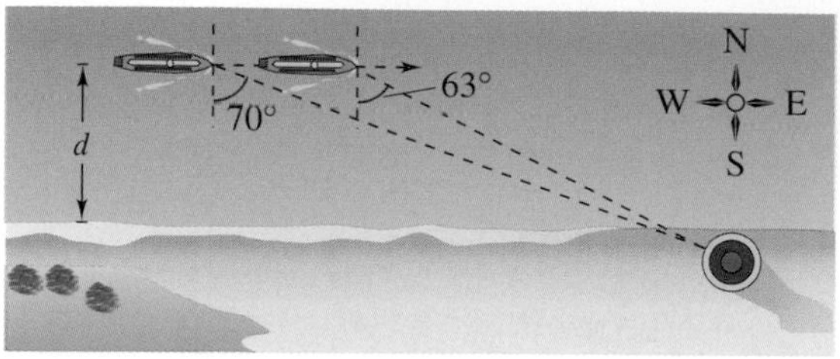

Model It

44. ***Shadow Length*** The Leaning Tower of Pisa in Italy is characterized by its tilt. The tower leans because it was built on a layer of unstable soil—clay, sand, and water. The tower is approximately 58.36 meters tall from its foundation (see figure). The top of the tower leans about 5.45 meters off center.

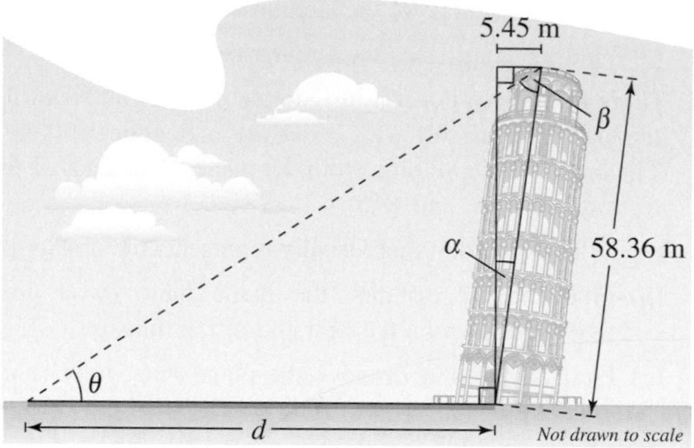

(a) Find the angle of lean α of the tower.

(b) Write β as a function of d and θ, where θ is the angle of elevation to the sun.

(c) Use the Law of Sines to write an equation for the length d of the shadow cast by the tower.

(d) Use a graphing utility to complete the table.

θ	10°	20°	30°	40°	50°	60°
d						

Synthesis

True or False? **In Exercises 45 and 46, determine whether the statement is true or false. Justify your answer.**

45. If a triangle contains an obtuse angle, then it must be oblique.

46. Two angles and one side of a triangle do not necessarily determine a unique triangle.

47. ***Graphical and Numerical Analysis*** In the figure, α and β are positive angles.

(a) Write α as a function of β.

(b) Use a graphing utility to graph the function. Determine its domain and range.

(c) Use the result of part (a) to write c as a function of β.

(d) Use a graphing utility to graph the function in part (c). Determine its domain and range.

(e) Complete the table. What can you infer?

β	0.4	0.8	1.2	1.6	2.0	2.4	2.8
α							
c							

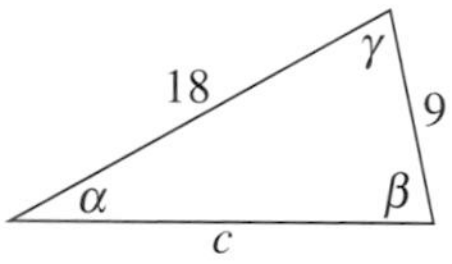

FIGURE FOR 47

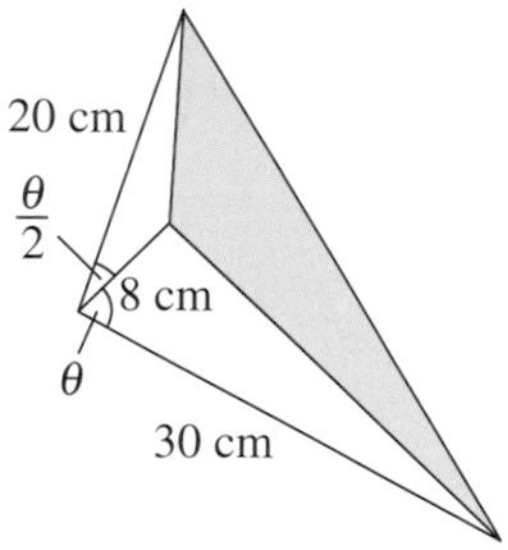

FIGURE FOR 48

48. ***Graphical Analysis***

(a) Write the area A of the shaded region in the figure as a function of θ.

(b) Use a graphing utility to graph the area function.

(c) Determine the domain of the area function. Explain how the area of the region and the domain of the function would change if the eight-centimeter line segment were decreased in length.

Skills Review

In Exercises 49–52, use the fundamental trigonometric identities to simplify the expression.

49. $\sin x \cot x$

50. $\tan x \cos x \sec x$

51. $1 - \sin^2\left(\dfrac{\pi}{2} - x\right)$

52. $1 + \cot^2\left(\dfrac{\pi}{2} - x\right)$

6.2 Law of Cosines

What you should learn

- Use the Law of Cosines to solve oblique triangles (SSS or SAS).
- Use the Law of Cosines to model and solve real-life problems.
- Use Heron's Area Formula to find the area of a triangle.

Why you should learn it

You can use the Law of Cosines to solve real-life problems involving oblique triangles. For instance, in Exercise 31 on page 444, you can use the Law of Cosines to approximate the length of a marsh.

Introduction

Two cases remain in the list of conditions needed to solve an oblique triangle—SSS and SAS. If you are given three sides (SSS), or two sides and their included angle (SAS), none of the ratios in the Law of Sines would be complete. In such cases, you can use the **Law of Cosines.**

Law of Cosines

Standard Form	*Alternative Form*
$a^2 = b^2 + c^2 - 2bc\cos A$	$\cos A = \dfrac{b^2 + c^2 - a^2}{2bc}$
$b^2 = a^2 + c^2 - 2ac\cos B$	$\cos B = \dfrac{a^2 + c^2 - b^2}{2ac}$
$c^2 = a^2 + b^2 - 2ab\cos C$	$\cos C = \dfrac{a^2 + b^2 - c^2}{2ab}$

For a proof of the Law of Cosines, see Proofs in Mathematics on page 490.

Example 1 Three Sides of a Triangle—SSS

Find the three angles of the triangle in Figure 6.11.

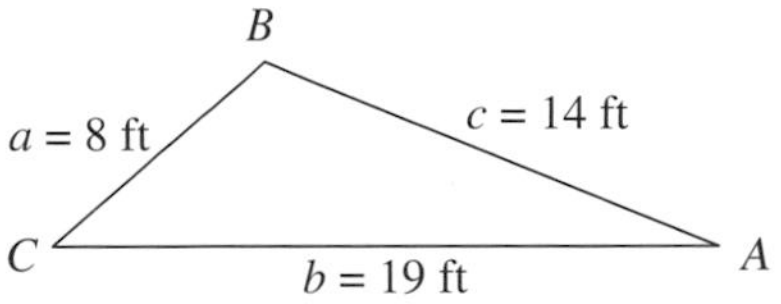

FIGURE 6.11

Solution

It is a good idea first to find the angle opposite the longest side—side b in this case. Using the alternative form of the Law of Cosines, you find that

$$\cos B = \frac{a^2 + c^2 - b^2}{2ac} = \frac{8^2 + 14^2 - 19^2}{2(8)(14)} \approx -0.45089.$$

Because $\cos B$ is negative, you know that B is an *obtuse* angle given by $B \approx 116.80°$. At this point, it is simpler to use the Law of Sines to determine A.

$$\sin A = a\left(\frac{\sin B}{b}\right) \approx 8\left(\frac{\sin 116.80°}{19}\right) \approx 0.37583$$

Because B is obtuse, A must be acute, because a triangle can have, at most, one obtuse angle. So, $A \approx 22.08°$ and $C \approx 180° - 22.08° - 116.80° = 41.12°$.

✓CHECKPOINT Now try Exercise 1.

Exploration

What familiar formula do you obtain when you use the third form of the Law of Cosines

$$c^2 = a^2 + b^2 - 2ab \cos C$$

and you let $C = 90°$? What is the relationship between the Law of Cosines and this formula?

Do you see why it was wise to find the largest angle *first* in Example 1? Knowing the cosine of an angle, you can determine whether the angle is acute or obtuse. That is,

$\cos \theta > 0$ for $0° < \theta < 90°$ Acute

$\cos \theta < 0$ for $90° < \theta < 180°.$ Obtuse

So, in Example 1, once you found that angle B was obtuse, you knew that angles A and C were both acute. If the largest angle is acute, the remaining two angles are acute also.

Example 2 Two Sides and the Included Angle—SAS

Find the remaining angles and side of the triangle in Figure 6.12.

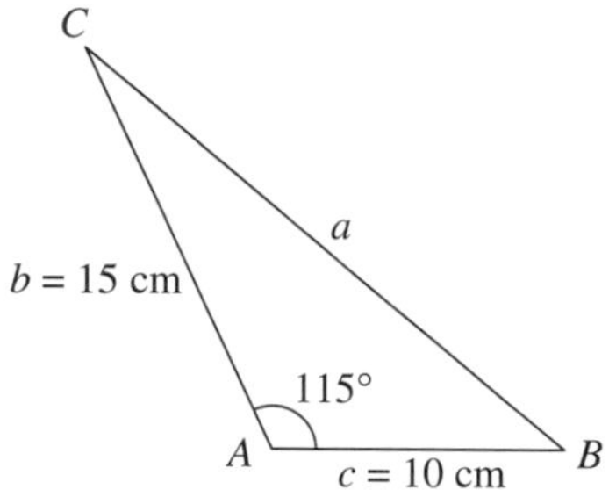

FIGURE 6.12

Solution

Use the Law of Cosines to find the unknown side a in the figure.

$$a^2 = b^2 + c^2 - 2bc \cos A$$

$$a^2 = 15^2 + 10^2 - 2(15)(10) \cos 115°$$

$$a^2 \approx 451.79$$

$$a \approx 21.26$$

Because $a \approx 21.26$ centimeters, you now know the ratio $\sin A/a$ and you can use the reciprocal form of the Law of Sines to solve for B.

$$\frac{\sin B}{b} = \frac{\sin A}{a}$$

$$\sin B = b\left(\frac{\sin A}{a}\right)$$

$$= 15\left(\frac{\sin 115°}{21.26}\right)$$

$$\approx 0.63945$$

So, $B = \arcsin 0.63945 \approx 39.75°$ and $C \approx 180° - 115° - 39.75° = 25.25°$.

✓CHECKPOINT Now try Exercise 3.

STUDY TIP

When solving an oblique triangle given three sides, you use the alternative form of the Law of Cosines to solve for an angle. When solving an oblique triangle given two sides and their included angle, you use the standard form of the Law of Cosines to solve for an unknown.

Applications

Example 3 An Application of the Law of Cosines

The pitcher's mound on a women's softball field is 43 feet from home plate and the distance between the bases is 60 feet, as shown in Figure 6.13. (The pitcher's mound is not halfway between home plate and second base.) How far is the pitcher's mound from first base?

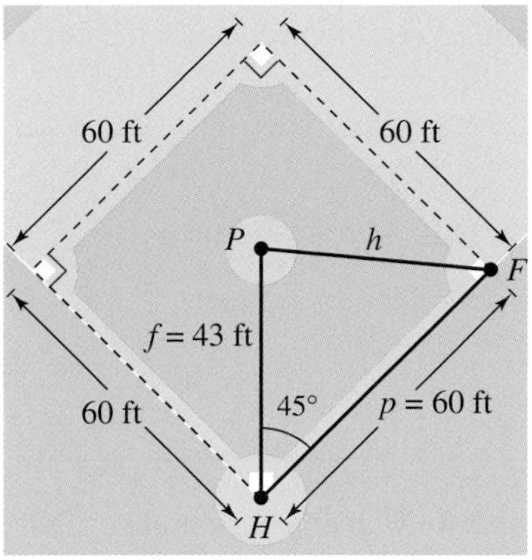

FIGURE 6.13

Solution

In triangle HPF, $H = 45°$ (line HP bisects the right angle at H), $f = 43$, and $p = 60$. Using the Law of Cosines for this SAS case, you have

$$h^2 = f^2 + p^2 - 2fp \cos H$$

$$= 43^2 + 60^2 - 2(43)(60) \cos 45° \approx 1800.3$$

So, the approximate distance from the pitcher's mound to first base is

$$h \approx \sqrt{1800.3} \approx 42.43 \text{ feet.}$$

CHECKPOINT Now try Exercise 31.

Example 4 An Application of the Law of Cosines

A ship travels 60 miles due east, then adjusts its course northward, as shown in Figure 6.14. After traveling 80 miles in that direction, the ship is 139 miles from its point of departure. Describe the bearing from point B to point C.

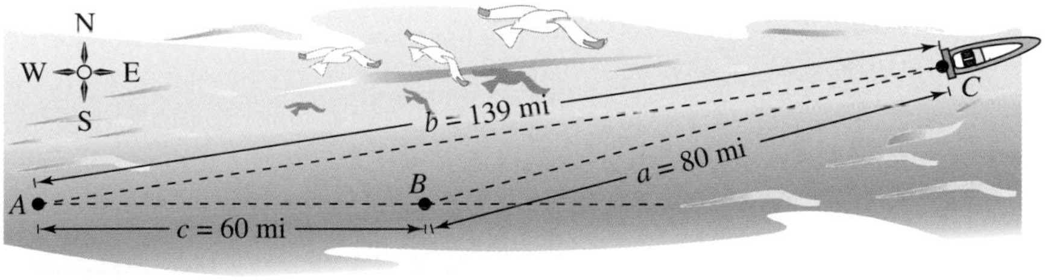

FIGURE 6.14

Solution

You have $a = 80$, $b = 139$, and $c = 60$; so, using the alternative form of the Law of Cosines, you have

$$\cos B = \frac{a^2 + c^2 - b^2}{2ac}$$

$$= \frac{80^2 + 60^2 - 139^2}{2(80)(60)}$$

$$\approx -0.97094.$$

So, $B \approx \arccos(-0.97094) \approx 166.15°$, and thus the bearing measured from due north from point B to point C is $166.15° - 90° = 76.15°$, or N 76.15° E.

CHECKPOINT Now try Exercise 37.

> ***Historical Note***
> Heron of Alexandria (c. 100 B.C.) was a Greek geometer and inventor. His works describe how to find the areas of triangles, quadrilaterals, regular polygons having 3 to 12 sides, and circles as well as the surface areas and volumes of three-dimensional objects.

Heron's Area Formula

The Law of Cosines can be used to establish the following formula for the area of a triangle. This formula is called **Heron's Area Formula** after the Greek mathematician Heron (c. 100 B.C.).

> **Heron's Area Formula**
>
> Given any triangle with sides of lengths a, b, and c, the area of the triangle is
>
> $$\text{Area} = \sqrt{s(s-a)(s-b)(s-c)}$$
>
> where $s = (a + b + c)/2$.

For a proof of Heron's Area Formula, see Proofs in Mathematics on page 491.

Example 5 Using Heron's Area Formula

Find the area of a triangle having sides of lengths $a = 43$ meters, $b = 53$ meters, and $c = 72$ meters.

Solution

Because $s = (a + b + c)/2 = 168/2 = 84$, Heron's Area Formula yields

$$\begin{aligned}\text{Area} &= \sqrt{s(s-a)(s-b)(s-c)}\\ &= \sqrt{84(41)(31)(12)} \approx 1131.89 \text{ square meters.}\end{aligned}$$

CHECKPOINT Now try Exercise 47.

You have now studied three different formulas for the area of a triangle.

Standard Formula $\quad \text{Area} = \frac{1}{2}bh$

Oblique Triangle $\quad \text{Area} = \frac{1}{2}bc \sin A = \frac{1}{2}ab \sin C = \frac{1}{2}ac \sin B$

Heron's Area Formula $\quad \text{Area} = \sqrt{s(s-a)(s-b)(s-c)}$

> **WRITING ABOUT MATHEMATICS**
>
> **The Area of a Triangle** Use the most appropriate formula to find the area of each triangle below. Show your work and give your reasons for choosing each formula.
>
> **a.**
>
> 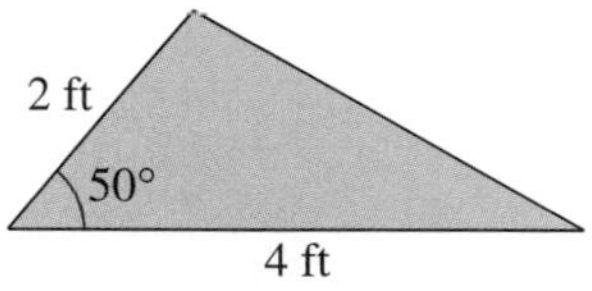
>
>
> **b.**
>
> 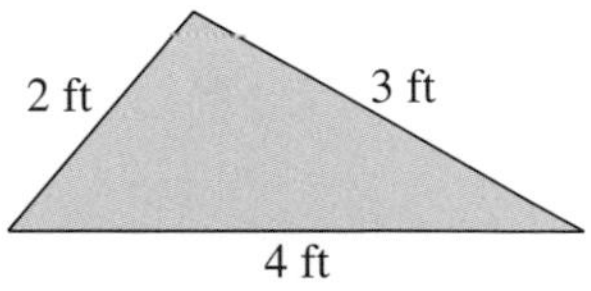
>
>
> **c.**
>
> 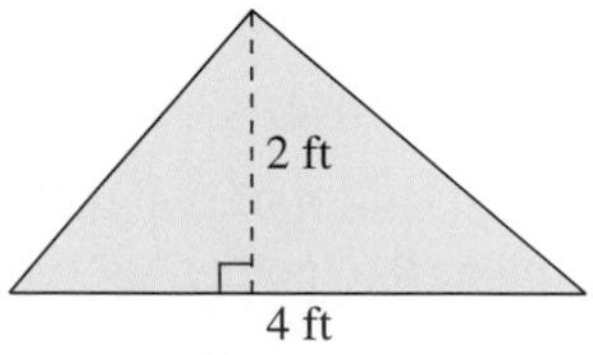
>
>
> **d.**
>
> 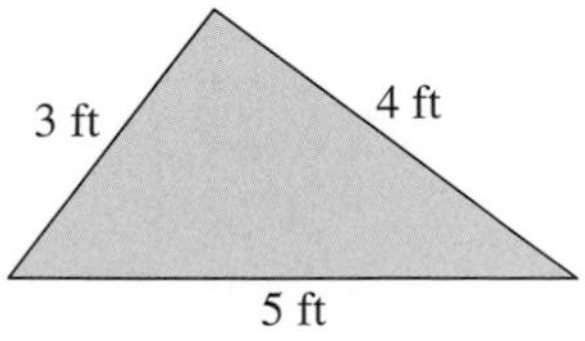
>

6.2 Exercises

VOCABULARY CHECK: Fill in the blanks.

1. If you are given three sides of a triangle, you would use the Law of ________ to find the three angles of the triangle.

2. The standard form of the Law of Cosines for $\cos B = \dfrac{a^2 + c^2 - b^2}{2ac}$ is ________ .

3. The Law of Cosines can be used to establish a formula for finding the area of a triangle called ________ ________ Formula.

In Exercises 1–16, use the Law of Cosines to solve the triangle. Round your answers to two decimal places.

1. 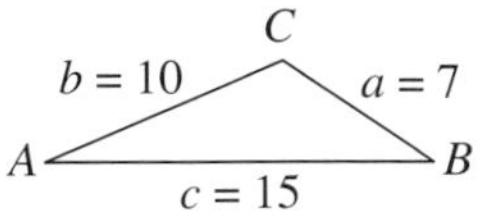

2. 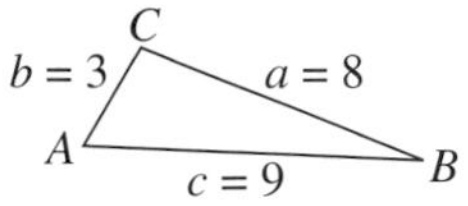

3. 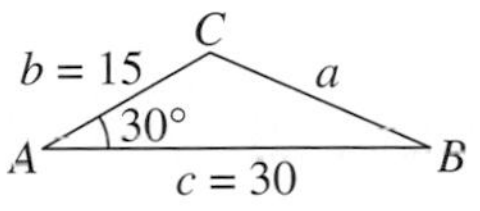

4. 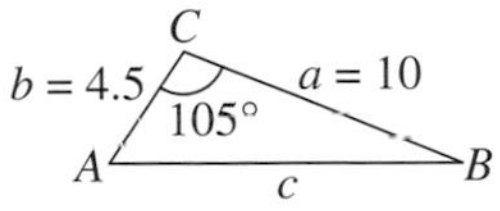

5. $a = 11,\quad b = 14,\quad c = 20$
6. $a = 55,\quad b = 25,\quad c = 72$
7. $a = 75.4,\quad b = 52,\quad c = 52$
8. $a = 1.42,\quad b = 0.75,\quad c = 1.25$
9. $A = 135°,\quad b = 4,\quad c = 9$
10. $A = 55°,\quad b = 3,\quad c = 10$
11. $B = 10° 35',\quad a = 40,\quad c = 30$
12. $B = 75° 20',\quad a = 6.2,\quad c = 9.5$
13. $B = 125° 40',\quad a = 32,\quad c = 32$
14. $C = 15° 15',\quad a = 6.25,\quad b = 2.15$
15. $C = 43°,\quad a = \frac{4}{9},\quad b = \frac{7}{9}$
16. $C = 103°,\quad a = \frac{3}{8},\quad b = \frac{3}{4}$

In Exercises 17–22, complete the table by solving the parallelogram shown in the figure. (The lengths of the diagonals are given by *c* and *d*.)

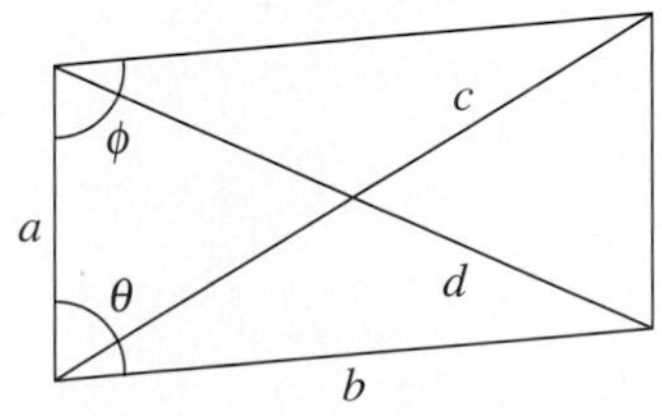

	a	b	c	d	θ	ϕ
17.	5	8			45°	
18.	25	35				120°
19.	10	14	20			
20.	40	60		80		
21.	15		25	20		
22.		25	50	35		

In Exercises 23–28, use Heron's Area Formula to find the area of the triangle.

23. $a = 5,\quad b = 7,\quad c = 10$
24. $a = 12,\quad b = 15,\quad c = 9$
25. $a = 2.5,\quad b = 10.2,\quad c = 9$
26. $a = 75.4,\quad b = 52,\quad c = 52$
27. $a = 12.32,\quad b = 8.46,\quad c = 15.05$
28. $a = 3.05,\quad b = 0.75,\quad c = 2.45$

29. ***Navigation*** A boat race runs along a triangular course marked by buoys *A*, *B*, and *C*. The race starts with the boats headed west for 3700 meters. The other two sides of the course lie to the north of the first side, and their lengths are 1700 meters and 3000 meters. Draw a figure that gives a visual representation of the problem, and find the bearings for the last two legs of the race.

30. ***Navigation*** A plane flies 810 miles from Franklin to Centerville with a bearing of 75°. Then it flies 648 miles from Centerville to Rosemount with a bearing of 32°. Draw a figure that visually represents the problem, and find the straight-line distance and bearing from Franklin to Rosemount.

31. ***Surveying*** To approximate the length of a marsh, a surveyor walks 250 meters from point A to point B, then turns 75° and walks 220 meters to point C (see figure). Approximate the length AC of the marsh.

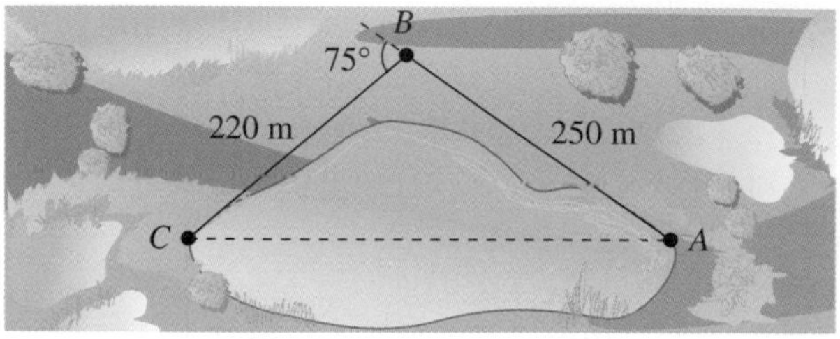

32. ***Surveying*** A triangular parcel of land has 115 meters of frontage, and the other boundaries have lengths of 76 meters and 92 meters. What angles does the frontage make with the two other boundaries?

33. ***Surveying*** A triangular parcel of ground has sides of lengths 725 feet, 650 feet, and 575 feet. Find the measure of the largest angle.

34. ***Streetlight Design*** Determine the angle θ in the design of the streetlight shown in the figure.

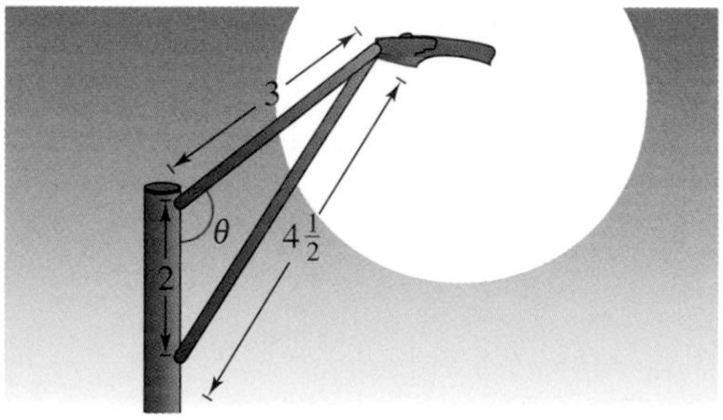

35. ***Distance*** Two ships leave a port at 9 A.M. One travels at a bearing of N 53° W at 12 miles per hour, and the other travels at a bearing of S 67° W at 16 miles per hour. Approximate how far apart they are at noon that day.

36. ***Length*** A 100-foot vertical tower is to be erected on the side of a hill that makes a 6° angle with the horizontal (see figure). Find the length of each of the two guy wires that will be anchored 75 feet uphill and downhill from the base of the tower.

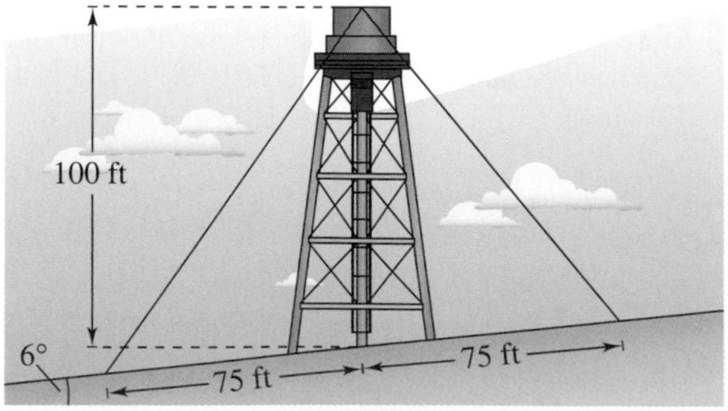

37. ***Navigation*** On a map, Orlando is 178 millimeters due south of Niagara Falls, Denver is 273 millimeters from Orlando, and Denver is 235 millimeters from Niagara Falls (see figure).

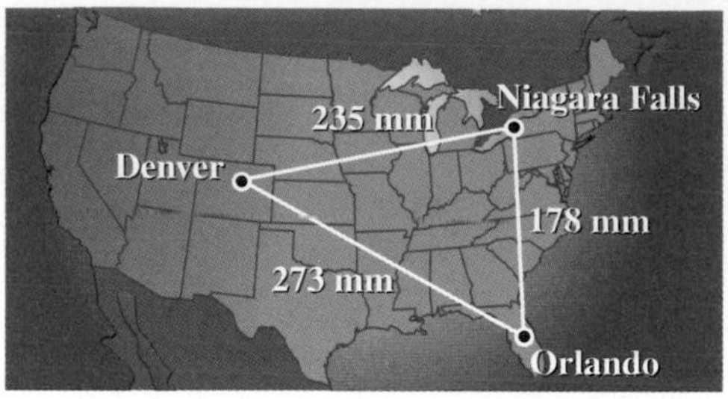

(a) Find the bearing of Denver from Orlando.

(b) Find the bearing of Denver from Niagara Falls.

38. ***Navigation*** On a map, Minneapolis is 165 millimeters due west of Albany, Phoenix is 216 millimeters from Minneapolis, and Phoenix is 368 millimeters from Albany (see figure).

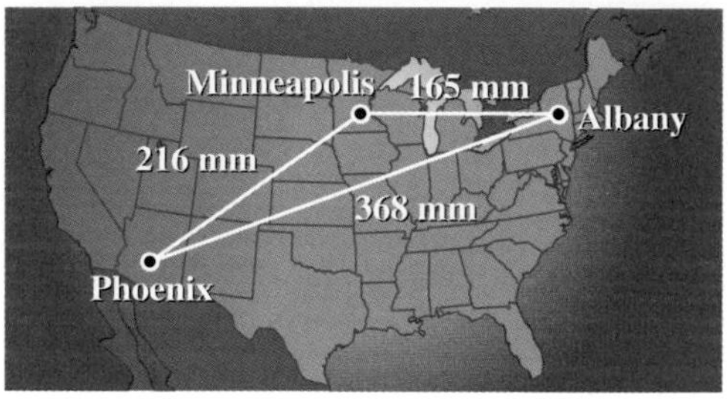

(a) Find the bearing of Minneapolis from Phoenix.

(b) Find the bearing of Albany from Phoenix.

39. ***Baseball*** On a baseball diamond with 90-foot sides, the pitcher's mound is 60.5 feet from home plate. How far is it from the pitcher's mound to third base?

40. ***Baseball*** The baseball player in center field is playing approximately 330 feet from the television camera that is behind home plate. A batter hits a fly ball that goes to the wall 420 feet from the camera (see figure). The camera turns 8° to follow the play. Approximately how far does the center fielder have to run to make the catch?

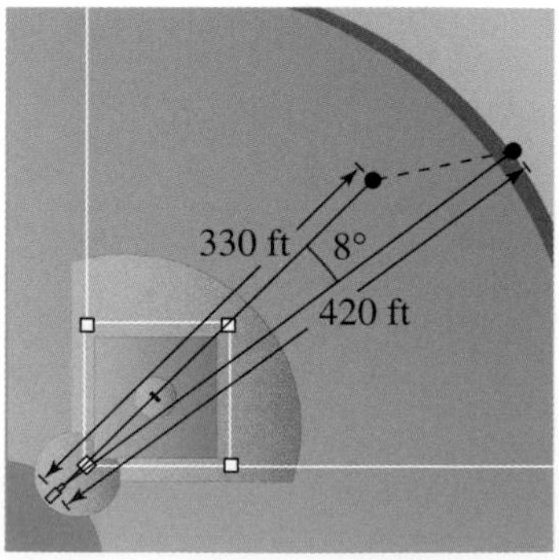

41. ***Aircraft Tracking*** To determine the distance between two aircraft, a tracking station continuously determines the distance to each aircraft and the angle A between them (see figure). Determine the distance a between the planes when $A = 42°$, $b = 35$ miles, and $c = 20$ miles.

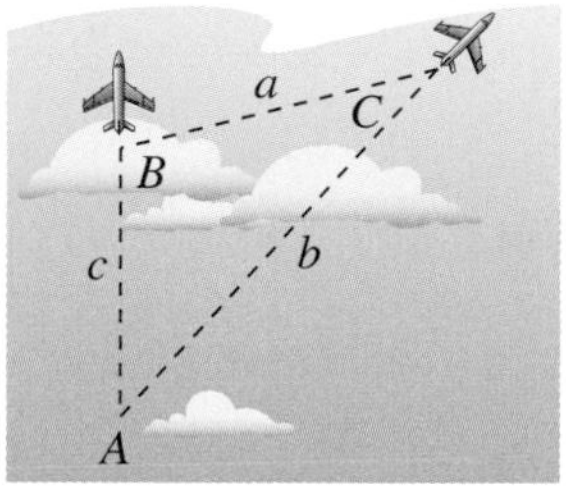

FIGURE FOR 41

42. ***Aircraft Tracking*** Use the figure for Exercise 41 to determine the distance a between the planes when $A = 11°$, $b = 20$ miles, and $c = 20$ miles.

43. ***Trusses*** Q is the midpoint of the line segment $\overline{PR}$ in the truss rafter shown in the figure. What are the lengths of the line segments $\overline{PQ}$, $\overline{QS}$, and $\overline{RS}$?

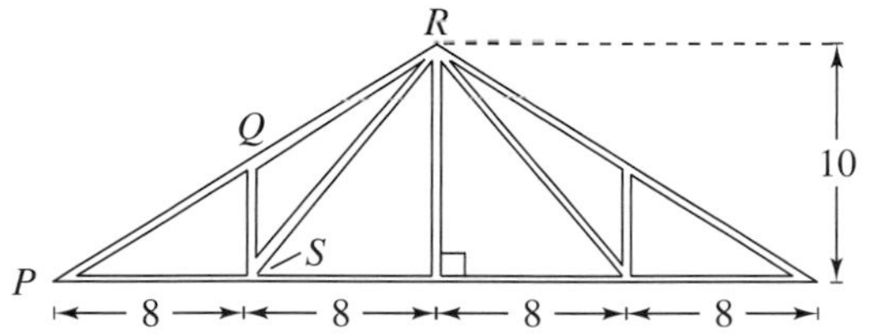

Model It

44. ***Engine Design*** An engine has a seven-inch connecting rod fastened to a crank (see figure).

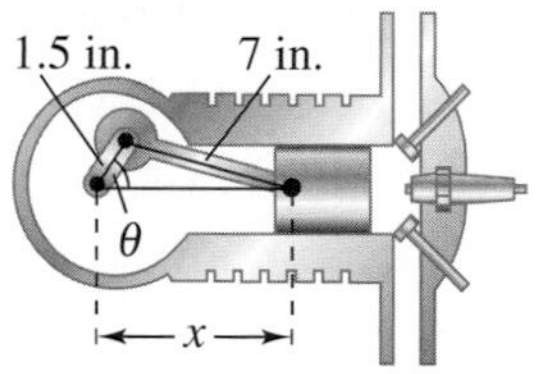

(a) Use the Law of Cosines to write an equation giving the relationship between x and θ.

(b) Write x as a function of θ. (Select the sign that yields positive values of x.)

(c) Use a graphing utility to graph the function in part (b).

(d) Use the graph in part (c) to determine the maximum distance the piston moves in one cycle.

45. ***Paper Manufacturing*** In a process with continuous paper, the paper passes across three rollers of radii 3 inches, 4 inches, and 6 inches (see figure). The centers of the three-inch and six-inch rollers are d inches apart, and the length of the arc in contact with the paper on the four-inch roller is s inches. Complete the table.

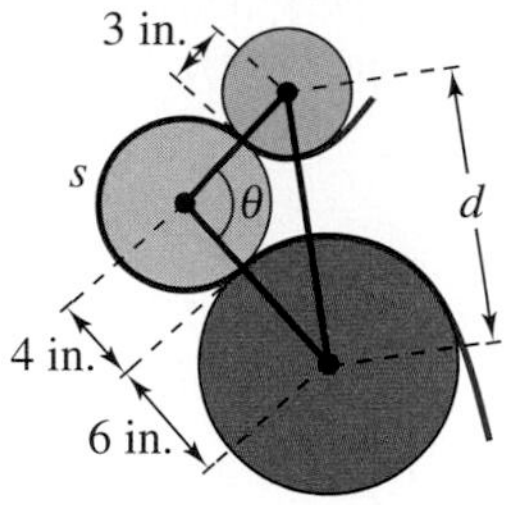

d (inches)	9	10	12	13	14	15	16
θ (degrees)							
s (inches)							

46. ***Awning Design*** A retractable awning above a patio door lowers at an angle of 50° from the exterior wall at a height of 10 feet above the ground (see figure). No direct sunlight is to enter the door when the angle of elevation of the sun is greater than 70°. What is the length x of the awning?

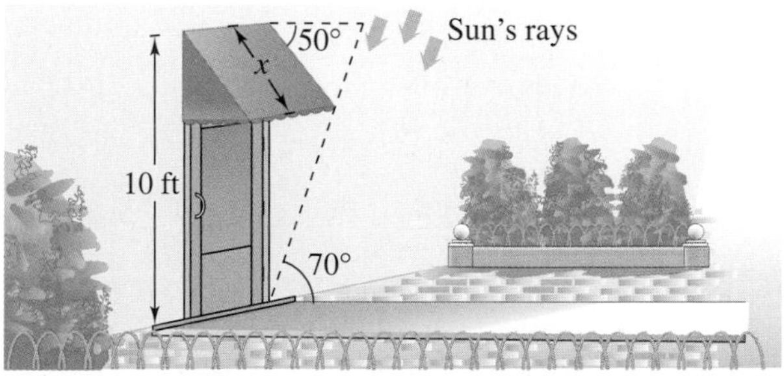

47. ***Geometry*** The lengths of the sides of a triangular parcel of land are approximately 200 feet, 500 feet, and 600 feet. Approximate the area of the parcel.

48. ***Geometry*** A parking lot has the shape of a parallelogram (see figure). The lengths of two adjacent sides are 70 meters and 100 meters. The angle between the two sides is 70°. What is the area of the parking lot?

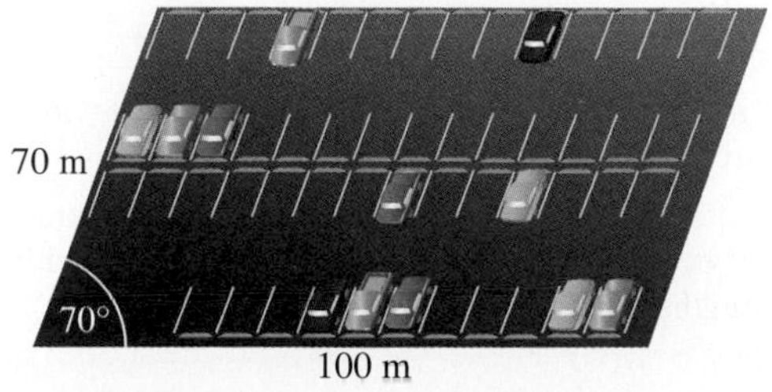

49. ***Geometry*** You want to buy a triangular lot measuring 510 yards by 840 yards by 1120 yards. The price of the land is \$2000 per acre. How much does the land cost? (*Hint:* 1 acre = 4840 square yards)

50. ***Geometry*** You want to buy a triangular lot measuring 1350 feet by 1860 feet by 2490 feet. The price of the land is \$2200 per acre. How much does the land cost? (*Hint:* 1 acre = 43,560 square feet)

Synthesis

True or False? **In Exercises 51–53, determine whether the statement is true or false. Justify your answer.**

51. In Heron's Area Formula, s is the average of the lengths of the three sides of the triangle.

52. In addition to SSS and SAS, the Law of Cosines can be used to solve triangles with SSA conditions.

53. A triangle with side lengths of 10 centimeters, 16 centimeters, and 5 centimeters can be solved using the Law of Cosines.

54. ***Circumscribed and Inscribed Circles*** Let R and r be the radii of the circumscribed and inscribed circles of a triangle ABC, respectively (see figure), and let

$$s = \frac{a+b+c}{2}.$$

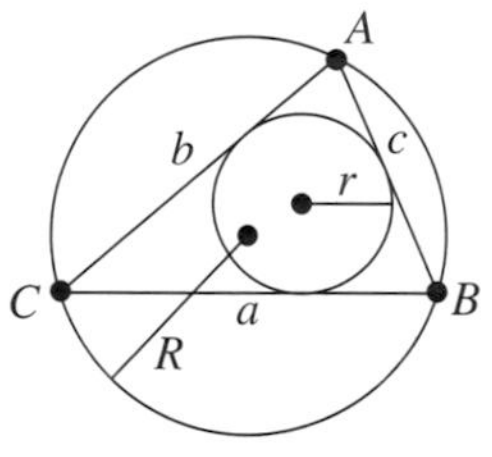

(a) Prove that $2R = \dfrac{a}{\sin A} = \dfrac{b}{\sin B} = \dfrac{c}{\sin C}$.

(b) Prove that $r = \sqrt{\dfrac{(s-a)(s-b)(s-c)}{s}}$.

Circumscribed and Inscribed Circles **In Exercises 55 and 56, use the results of Exercise 54.**

55. Given a triangle with

$a = 25$, $b = 55$, and $c = 72$

find the areas of (a) the triangle, (b) the circumscribed circle, and (c) the inscribed circle.

56. Find the length of the largest circular running track that can be built on a triangular piece of property with sides of lengths 200 feet, 250 feet, and 325 feet.

57. ***Proof*** Use the Law of Cosines to prove that

$$\frac{1}{2}bc(1+\cos A) = \frac{a+b+c}{2}\cdot\frac{-a+b+c}{2}.$$

58. ***Proof*** Use the Law of Cosines to prove that

$$\frac{1}{2}bc(1-\cos A) = \frac{a-b+c}{2}\cdot\frac{a+b-c}{2}.$$

Skills Review

In Exercises 59–64, evaluate the expression without using a calculator.

59. $\arcsin(-1)$

60. $\arccos 0$

61. $\arctan \sqrt{3}$

62. $\arctan(-\sqrt{3})$

63. $\arcsin\left(-\dfrac{\sqrt{3}}{2}\right)$

64. $\arccos\left(-\dfrac{\sqrt{3}}{2}\right)$

In Exercises 65–68, write an algebraic expression that is equivalent to the expression.

65. $\sec(\arcsin 2x)$

66. $\tan(\arccos 3x)$

67. $\cot[\arctan(x-2)]$

68. $\cos\left(\arcsin \dfrac{x-1}{2}\right)$

In Exercises 69–72, use trigonometric substitution to write the algebraic equation as a trigonometric function of θ, where $-\pi/2 < \theta < \pi/2$. Then find $\sec\theta$ and $\csc\theta$.

69. $5 = \sqrt{25 - x^2}$, $x = 5\sin\theta$

70. $-\sqrt{2} = \sqrt{4 - x^2}$, $x = 2\cos\theta$

71. $-\sqrt{3} = \sqrt{x^2 - 9}$, $x = 3\sec\theta$

72. $12 = \sqrt{36 + x^2}$, $x = 6\tan\theta$

In Exercises 73 and 74, write the sum or difference as a product.

73. $\cos\dfrac{5\pi}{6} - \cos\dfrac{\pi}{3}$

74. $\sin\left(x - \dfrac{\pi}{2}\right) - \sin\left(x + \dfrac{\pi}{2}\right)$

6.3 Vectors in the Plane

What you should learn

- Represent vectors as directed line segments.
- Write the component forms of vectors.
- Perform basic vector operations and represent them graphically.
- Write vectors as linear combinations of unit vectors.
- Find the direction angles of vectors.
- Use vectors to model and solve real-life problems.

Why you should learn it

You can use vectors to model and solve real-life problems involving magnitude and direction. For instance, in Exercise 84 on page 459, you can use vectors to determine the true direction of a commercial jet.

Bill Bachman/Photo Researchers, Inc.

Introduction

Quantities such as force and velocity involve both *magnitude* and *direction* and cannot be completely characterized by a single real number. To represent such a quantity, you can use a **directed line segment,** as shown in Figure 6.15. The directed line segment $\overrightarrow{PQ}$ has **initial point** P and **terminal point** Q. Its **magnitude** (or length) is denoted by $\|\overrightarrow{PQ}\|$ and can be found using the Distance Formula.

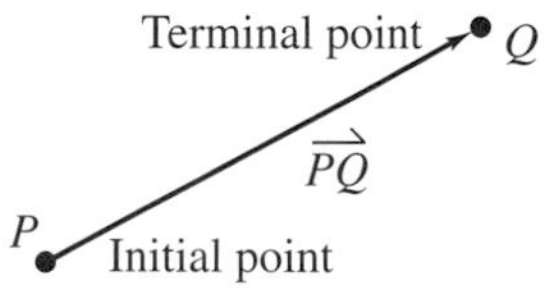

FIGURE 6.15

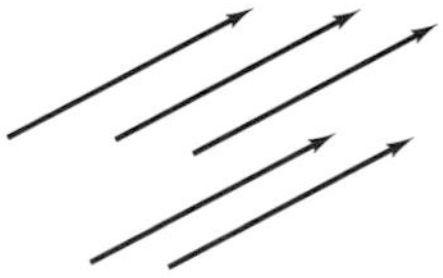

FIGURE 6.16

Two directed line segments that have the same magnitude and direction are equivalent. For example, the directed line segments in Figure 6.16 are all equivalent. The set of all directed line segments that are equivalent to the directed line segment $\overrightarrow{PQ}$ is a **vector v in the plane,** written $\mathbf{v} = \overrightarrow{PQ}$. Vectors are denoted by lowercase, boldface letters such as **u**, **v**, and **w**.

Example 1 Vector Representation by Directed Line Segments

Let **u** be represented by the directed line segment from $P = (0, 0)$ to $Q = (3, 2)$, and let **v** be represented by the directed line segment from $R = (1, 2)$ to $S = (4, 4)$, as shown in Figure 6.17. Show that $\mathbf{u} = \mathbf{v}$.

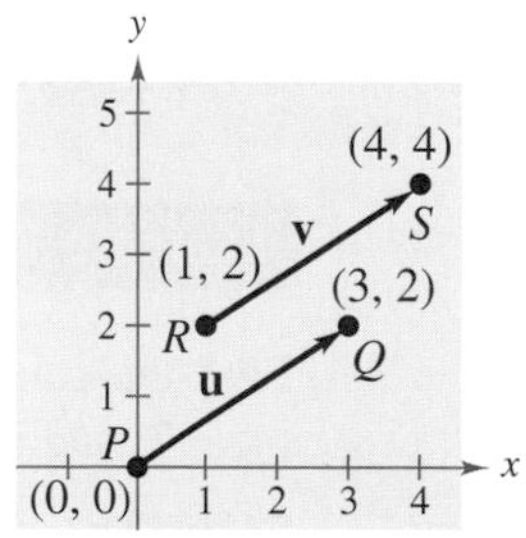

FIGURE 6.17

Solution

From the Distance Formula, it follows that $\overrightarrow{PQ}$ and $\overrightarrow{RS}$ have the *same magnitude*.

$$\|\overrightarrow{PQ}\| = \sqrt{(3-0)^2 + (2-0)^2} = \sqrt{13}$$

$$\|\overrightarrow{RS}\| = \sqrt{(4-1)^2 + (4-2)^2} = \sqrt{13}$$

Moreover, both line segments have the *same direction* because they are both directed toward the upper right on lines having a slope of $\frac{2}{3}$. So, $\overrightarrow{PQ}$ and $\overrightarrow{RS}$ have the same magnitude and direction, and it follows that $\mathbf{u} = \mathbf{v}$.

CHECKPOINT Now try Exercise 1.

Component Form of a Vector

The directed line segment whose initial point is the origin is often the most convenient representative of a set of equivalent directed line segments. This representative of the vector **v** is in **standard position.**

A vector whose initial point is the origin (0, 0) can be uniquely represented by the coordinates of its terminal point (v_1, v_2). This is the **component form of a vector v,** written as

$$\mathbf{v} = \langle v_1, v_2 \rangle.$$

The coordinates v_1 and v_2 are the *components* of **v**. If both the initial point and the terminal point lie at the origin, **v** is the **zero vector** and is denoted by $\mathbf{0} = \langle 0, 0 \rangle$.

Component Form of a Vector

The component form of the vector with initial point $P = (p_1, p_2)$ and terminal point $Q = (q_1, q_2)$ is given by

$$\overrightarrow{PQ} = \langle q_1 - p_1, q_2 - p_2 \rangle = \langle v_1, v_2 \rangle = \mathbf{v}.$$

The **magnitude** (or length) of **v** is given by

$$\|\mathbf{v}\| = \sqrt{(q_1 - p_1)^2 + (q_2 - p_2)^2} = \sqrt{v_1^2 + v_2^2}.$$

If $\|\mathbf{v}\| = 1$, **v** is a **unit vector.** Moreover, $\|\mathbf{v}\| = 0$ if and only if **v** is the zero vector **0**.

Technology

You can graph vectors with a graphing utility by graphing directed line segments. Consult the user's guide for your graphing utility for specific instructions.

Two vectors $\mathbf{u} = \langle u_1, u_2 \rangle$ and $\mathbf{v} = \langle v_1, v_2 \rangle$ are *equal* if and only if $u_1 = v_1$ and $u_2 = v_2$. For instance, in Example 1, the vector **u** from $P = (0, 0)$ to $Q = (3, 2)$ is

$$\mathbf{u} = \overrightarrow{PQ} = \langle 3 - 0, 2 - 0 \rangle = \langle 3, 2 \rangle$$

and the vector **v** from $R = (1, 2)$ to $S = (4, 4)$ is

$$\mathbf{v} = \overrightarrow{RS} = \langle 4 - 1, 4 - 2 \rangle = \langle 3, 2 \rangle.$$

Example 2 Finding the Component Form of a Vector

Find the component form and magnitude of the vector **v** that has initial point $(4, -7)$ and terminal point $(-1, 5)$.

Solution

Let $P = (4, -7) = (p_1, p_2)$ and let $Q = (-1, 5) = (q_1, q_2)$, as shown in Figure 6.18. Then, the components of $\mathbf{v} = \langle v_1, v_2 \rangle$ are

$$v_1 = q_1 - p_1 = -1 - 4 = -5$$

$$v_2 = q_2 - p_2 = 5 - (-7) = 12.$$

So, $\mathbf{v} = \langle -5, 12 \rangle$ and the magnitude of **v** is

$$\|\mathbf{v}\| = \sqrt{(-5)^2 + 12^2} = \sqrt{169} = 13.$$

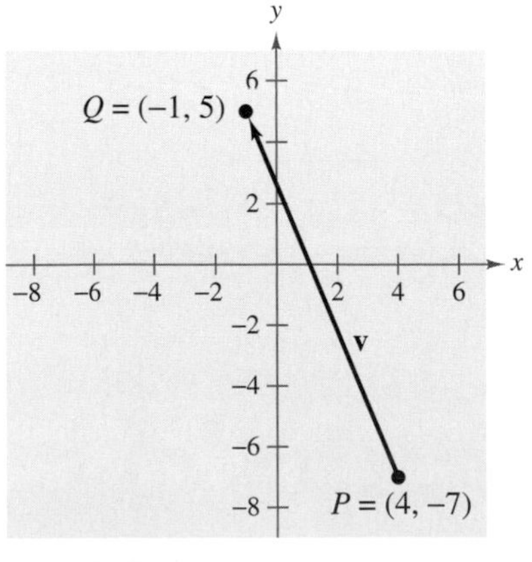

FIGURE 6.18

CHECKPOINT Now try Exercise 9.

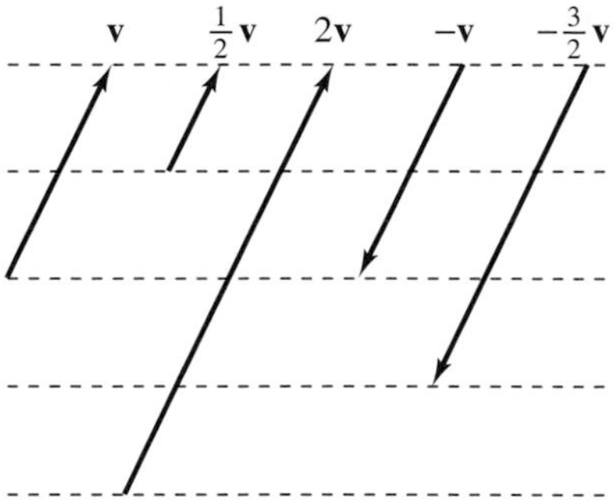

FIGURE 6.19

Vector Operations

The two basic vector operations are **scalar multiplication** and **vector addition.** In operations with vectors, numbers are usually referred to as **scalars.** In this text, scalars will always be real numbers. Geometrically, the product of a vector $\mathbf{v}$ and a scalar k is the vector that is $|k|$ times as long as $\mathbf{v}$. If k is positive, $k\mathbf{v}$ has the same direction as $\mathbf{v}$, and if k is negative, $k\mathbf{v}$ has the direction opposite that of $\mathbf{v}$, as shown in Figure 6.19.

To add two vectors geometrically, position them (without changing their lengths or directions) so that the initial point of one coincides with the terminal point of the other. The sum $\mathbf{u} + \mathbf{v}$ is formed by joining the initial point of the second vector $\mathbf{v}$ with the terminal point of the first vector $\mathbf{u}$, as shown in Figure 6.20. This technique is called the **parallelogram law** for vector addition because the vector $\mathbf{u} + \mathbf{v}$, often called the **resultant** of vector addition, is the diagonal of a parallelogram having $\mathbf{u}$ and $\mathbf{v}$ as its adjacent sides.

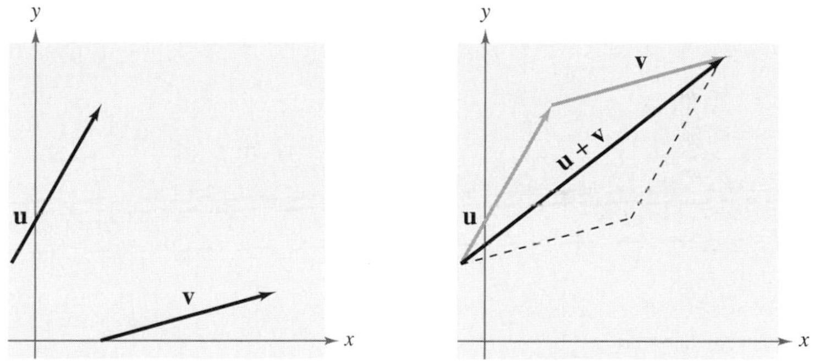

FIGURE 6.20

Definitions of Vector Addition and Scalar Multiplication

Let $\mathbf{u} = \langle u_1, u_2 \rangle$ and $\mathbf{v} = \langle v_1, v_2 \rangle$ be vectors and let k be a scalar (a real number). Then the *sum* of $\mathbf{u}$ and $\mathbf{v}$ is the vector

$$\mathbf{u} + \mathbf{v} = \langle u_1 + v_1, u_2 + v_2 \rangle \qquad \text{Sum}$$

and the *scalar multiple* of k times $\mathbf{u}$ is the vector

$$k\mathbf{u} = k\langle u_1, u_2 \rangle = \langle ku_1, ku_2 \rangle. \qquad \text{Scalar multiple}$$

The **negative** of $\mathbf{v} = \langle v_1, v_2 \rangle$ is

$$-\mathbf{v} = (-1)\mathbf{v}$$
$$= \langle -v_1, -v_2 \rangle \qquad \text{Negative}$$

and the **difference** of $\mathbf{u}$ and $\mathbf{v}$ is

$$\mathbf{u} - \mathbf{v} = \mathbf{u} + (-\mathbf{v}) \qquad \text{Add } (-\mathbf{v}). \text{ See Figure 8.21.}$$
$$= \langle u_1 - v_1, u_2 - v_2 \rangle. \qquad \text{Difference}$$

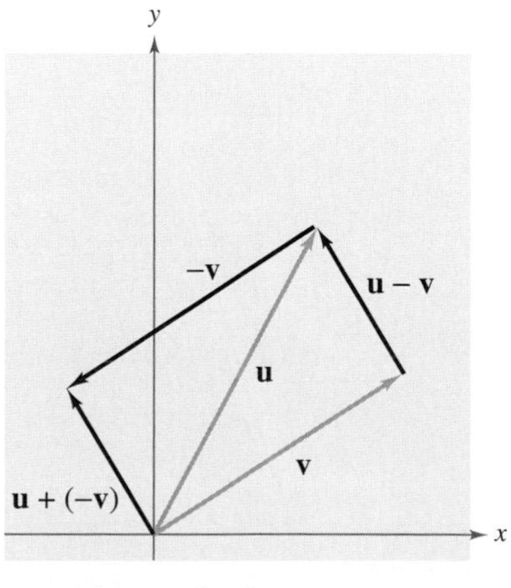

$\mathbf{u} - \mathbf{v} = \mathbf{u} + (-\mathbf{v})$
FIGURE 6.21

To represent $\mathbf{u} - \mathbf{v}$ geometrically, you can use directed line segments with the *same* initial point. The difference $\mathbf{u} - \mathbf{v}$ is the vector from the terminal point of $\mathbf{v}$ to the terminal point of $\mathbf{u}$, which is equal to $\mathbf{u} + (-\mathbf{v})$, as shown in Figure 6.21.

The component definitions of vector addition and scalar multiplication are illustrated in Example 3. In this example, notice that each of the vector operations can be interpreted geometrically.

Example 3 Vector Operations

Let $\mathbf{v} = \langle -2, 5\rangle$ and $\mathbf{w} = \langle 3, 4\rangle$, and find each of the following vectors.

a. $2\mathbf{v}$ **b.** $\mathbf{w} - \mathbf{v}$ **c.** $\mathbf{v} + 2\mathbf{w}$

Solution

a. Because $\mathbf{v} = \langle -2, 5\rangle$, you have

$$\begin{aligned} 2\mathbf{v} &= 2\langle -2, 5\rangle \\ &= \langle 2(-2), 2(5)\rangle \\ &= \langle -4, 10\rangle. \end{aligned}$$

A sketch of $2\mathbf{v}$ is shown in Figure 6.22.

b. The difference of $\mathbf{w}$ and $\mathbf{v}$ is

$$\begin{aligned} \mathbf{w} - \mathbf{v} &= \langle 3 - (-2), 4 - 5\rangle \\ &= \langle 5, -1\rangle. \end{aligned}$$

A sketch of $\mathbf{w} - \mathbf{v}$ is shown in Figure 6.23. Note that the figure shows the vector difference $\mathbf{w} - \mathbf{v}$ as the sum $\mathbf{w} + (-\mathbf{v})$.

c. The sum of $\mathbf{v}$ and $2\mathbf{w}$ is

$$\begin{aligned} \mathbf{v} + 2\mathbf{w} &= \langle -2, 5\rangle + 2\langle 3, 4\rangle \\ &= \langle -2, 5\rangle + \langle 2(3), 2(4)\rangle \\ &= \langle -2, 5\rangle + \langle 6, 8\rangle \\ &= \langle -2 + 6, 5 + 8\rangle \\ &= \langle 4, 13\rangle. \end{aligned}$$

A sketch of $\mathbf{v} + 2\mathbf{w}$ is shown in Figure 6.24.

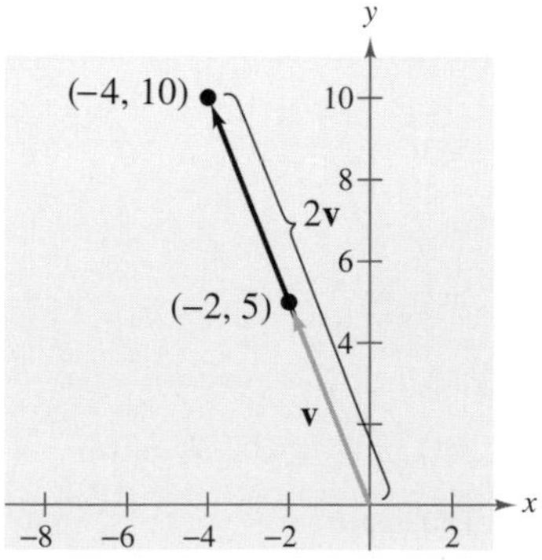

FIGURE 6.22

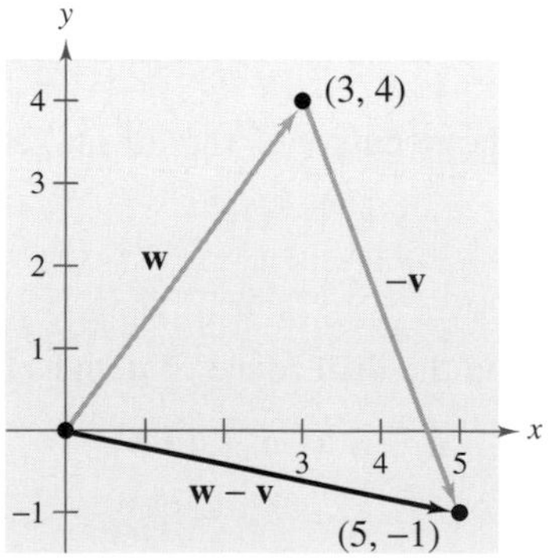

FIGURE 6.23

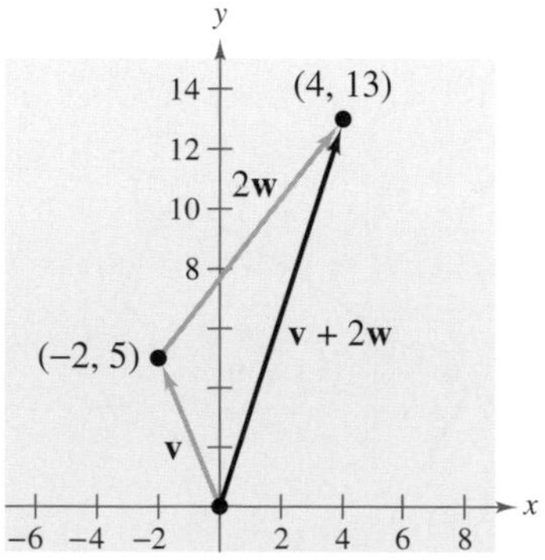

FIGURE 6.24

CHECKPOINT Now try Exercise 21.

Vector addition and scalar multiplication share many of the properties of ordinary arithmetic.

Properties of Vector Addition and Scalar Multiplication

Let $\mathbf{u}$, $\mathbf{v}$, and $\mathbf{w}$ be vectors and let c and d be scalars. Then the following properties are true.

1. $\mathbf{u} + \mathbf{v} = \mathbf{v} + \mathbf{u}$

2. $(\mathbf{u} + \mathbf{v}) + \mathbf{w} = \mathbf{u} + (\mathbf{v} + \mathbf{w})$

3. $\mathbf{u} + \mathbf{0} = \mathbf{u}$

4. $\mathbf{u} + (-\mathbf{u}) = \mathbf{0}$

5. $c(d\mathbf{u}) = (cd)\mathbf{u}$

6. $(c + d)\mathbf{u} = c\mathbf{u} + d\mathbf{u}$

7. $c(\mathbf{u} + \mathbf{v}) = c\mathbf{u} + c\mathbf{v}$

8. $1(\mathbf{u}) = \mathbf{u}, 0(\mathbf{u}) = \mathbf{0}$

9. $\|c\mathbf{v}\| = |c|\,\|\mathbf{v}\|$

Property 9 can be stated as follows: the magnitude of the vector $c\mathbf{v}$ is the absolute value of c times the magnitude of $\mathbf{v}$.

Unit Vectors

In many applications of vectors, it is useful to find a unit vector that has the same direction as a given nonzero vector $\mathbf{v}$. To do this, you can divide $\mathbf{v}$ by its magnitude to obtain

$$\mathbf{u} = \text{unit vector} = \frac{\mathbf{v}}{\|\mathbf{v}\|} = \left(\frac{1}{\|\mathbf{v}\|}\right)\mathbf{v}. \qquad \text{Unit vector in direction of } \mathbf{v}$$

Note that $\mathbf{u}$ is a scalar multiple of $\mathbf{v}$. The vector $\mathbf{u}$ has a magnitude of 1 and the same direction as $\mathbf{v}$. The vector $\mathbf{u}$ is called a **unit vector in the direction of v**.

The Granger Collection

Historical Note

William Rowan Hamilton (1805–1865), an Irish mathematician, did some of the earliest work with vectors. Hamilton spent many years developing a system of vector-like quantities called quaternions. Although Hamilton was convinced of the benefits of quaternions, the operations he defined did not produce good models for physical phenomena. It wasn't until the latter half of the nineteenth century that the Scottish physicist James Maxwell (1831–1879) restructured Hamilton's quaternions in a form useful for representing physical quantities such as force, velocity, and acceleration.

Example 4 Finding a Unit Vector

Find a unit vector in the direction of $\mathbf{v} = \langle -2, 5\rangle$ and verify that the result has a magnitude of 1.

Solution

The unit vector in the direction of $\mathbf{v}$ is

$$\frac{\mathbf{v}}{\|\mathbf{v}\|} = \frac{\langle -2, 5\rangle}{\sqrt{(-2)^2 + (5)^2}}$$

$$= \frac{1}{\sqrt{29}}\langle -2, 5\rangle$$

$$= \left\langle \frac{-2}{\sqrt{29}}, \frac{5}{\sqrt{29}}\right\rangle.$$

This vector has a magnitude of 1 because

$$\sqrt{\left(\frac{-2}{\sqrt{29}}\right)^2 + \left(\frac{5}{\sqrt{29}}\right)^2} = \sqrt{\frac{4}{29} + \frac{25}{29}} = \sqrt{\frac{29}{29}} = 1.$$

CHECKPOINT Now try Exercise 31.

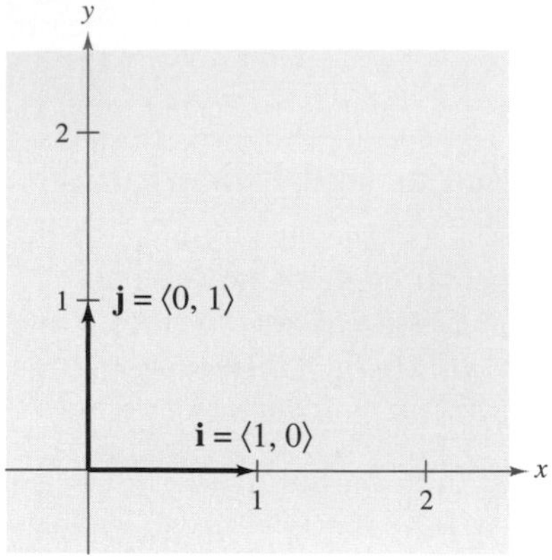

FIGURE 6.25

The unit vectors $\langle 1, 0\rangle$ and $\langle 0, 1\rangle$ are called the **standard unit vectors** and are denoted by

$$\mathbf{i} = \langle 1, 0\rangle \quad \text{and} \quad \mathbf{j} = \langle 0, 1\rangle$$

as shown in Figure 6.25. (Note that the lowercase letter **i** is written in boldface to distinguish it from the imaginary number $i = \sqrt{-1}$.) These vectors can be used to represent any vector $\mathbf{v} = \langle v_1, v_2\rangle$, as follows.

$$\begin{aligned}\mathbf{v} &= \langle v_1, v_2\rangle \\ &= v_1\langle 1, 0\rangle + v_2\langle 0, 1\rangle \\ &= v_1\mathbf{i} + v_2\mathbf{j}\end{aligned}$$

The scalars v_1 and v_2 are called the **horizontal** and **vertical components of v,** respectively. The vector sum

$$v_1\mathbf{i} + v_2\mathbf{j}$$

is called a **linear combination** of the vectors **i** and **j**. Any vector in the plane can be written as a linear combination of the standard unit vectors **i** and **j**.

Example 5 Writing a Linear Combination of Unit Vectors

Let **u** be the vector with initial point $(2, -5)$ and terminal point $(-1, 3)$. Write **u** as a linear combination of the standard unit vectors **i** and **j**.

Solution

Begin by writing the component form of the vector **u**.

$$\begin{aligned}\mathbf{u} &= \langle -1 - 2, 3 - (-5)\rangle \\ &= \langle -3, 8\rangle \\ &= -3\mathbf{i} + 8\mathbf{j}\end{aligned}$$

This result is shown graphically in Figure 6.26.

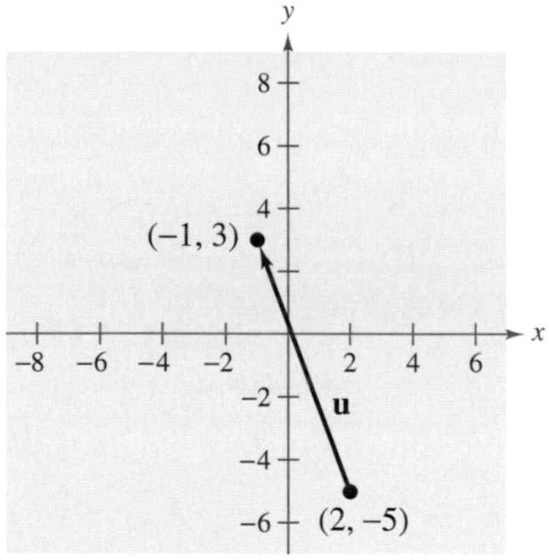

FIGURE 6.26

CHECKPOINT Now try Exercise 43.

Example 6 Vector Operations

Let $\mathbf{u} = -3\mathbf{i} + 8\mathbf{j}$ and let $\mathbf{v} = 2\mathbf{i} - \mathbf{j}$. Find $2\mathbf{u} - 3\mathbf{v}$.

Solution

You could solve this problem by converting **u** and **v** to component form. This, however, is not necessary. It is just as easy to perform the operations in unit vector form.

$$\begin{aligned}2\mathbf{u} - 3\mathbf{v} &= 2(-3\mathbf{i} + 8\mathbf{j}) - 3(2\mathbf{i} - \mathbf{j}) \\ &= -6\mathbf{i} + 16\mathbf{j} - 6\mathbf{i} + 3\mathbf{j} \\ &= -12\mathbf{i} + 19\mathbf{j}\end{aligned}$$

CHECKPOINT Now try Exercise 49.

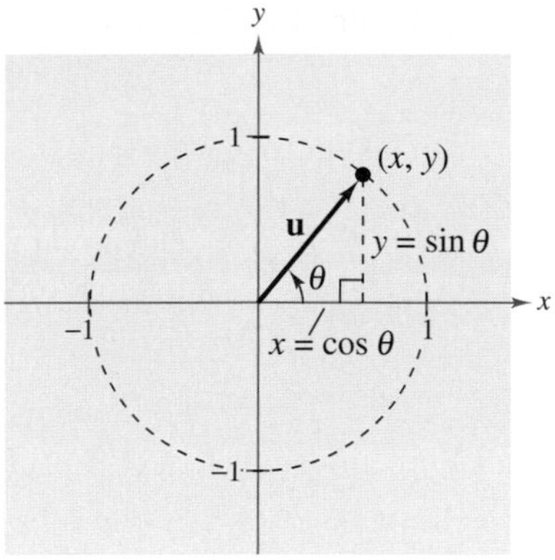

FIGURE 6.27 $\|\mathbf{u}\| = 1$

Direction Angles

If $\mathbf{u}$ is a *unit vector* such that θ is the angle (measured counterclockwise) from the positive x-axis to $\mathbf{u}$, the terminal point of $\mathbf{u}$ lies on the unit circle and you have

$$\mathbf{u} = \langle x, y \rangle = \langle \cos\theta, \sin\theta \rangle = (\cos\theta)\mathbf{i} + (\sin\theta)\mathbf{j}$$

as shown in Figure 6.27. The angle θ is the **direction angle** of the vector $\mathbf{u}$.

Suppose that $\mathbf{u}$ is a unit vector with direction angle θ. If $\mathbf{v} = a\mathbf{i} + b\mathbf{j}$ is any vector that makes an angle θ with the positive x-axis, it has the same direction as $\mathbf{u}$ and you can write

$$\mathbf{v} = \|\mathbf{v}\| \langle \cos\theta, \sin\theta \rangle$$
$$= \|\mathbf{v}\| (\cos\theta)\mathbf{i} + \|\mathbf{v}\| (\sin\theta)\mathbf{j}.$$

Because $\mathbf{v} = a\mathbf{i} + b\mathbf{j} = \|\mathbf{v}\| (\cos\theta)\mathbf{i} + \|\mathbf{v}\| (\sin\theta)\mathbf{j}$, it follows that the direction angle θ for $\mathbf{v}$ is determined from

$$\tan\theta = \frac{\sin\theta}{\cos\theta} \qquad \text{Quotient identity}$$

$$= \frac{\|\mathbf{v}\| \sin\theta}{\|\mathbf{v}\| \cos\theta} \qquad \text{Multiply numerator and denominator by } \|\mathbf{v}\|.$$

$$= \frac{b}{a}. \qquad \text{Simplify.}$$

Example 7 Finding Direction Angles of Vectors

Find the direction angle of each vector.

a. $\mathbf{u} = 3\mathbf{i} + 3\mathbf{j}$

b. $\mathbf{v} = 3\mathbf{i} - 4\mathbf{j}$

Solution

a. The direction angle is

$$\tan\theta = \frac{b}{a} = \frac{3}{3} = 1.$$

So, $\theta = 45°$, as shown in Figure 6.28.

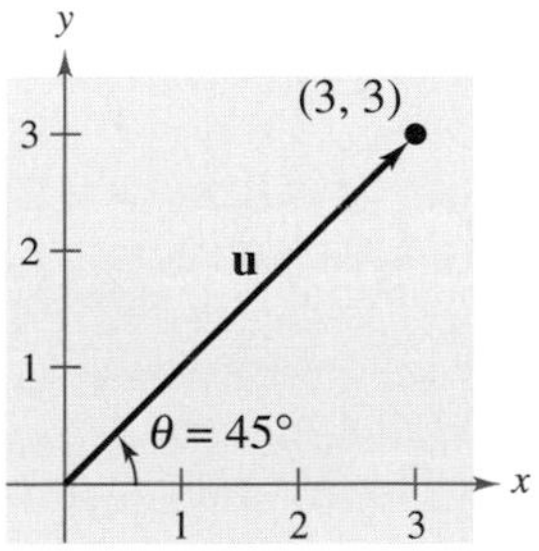

FIGURE 6.28

b. The direction angle is

$$\tan\theta = \frac{b}{a} = \frac{-4}{3}.$$

Moreover, because $\mathbf{v} = 3\mathbf{i} - 4\mathbf{j}$ lies in Quadrant IV, θ lies in Quadrant IV and its reference angle is

$$\theta = \left|\arctan\left(-\frac{4}{3}\right)\right| \approx |-53.13°| = 53.13°.$$

So, it follows that $\theta \approx 360° - 53.13° = 306.87°$, as shown in Figure 6.29.

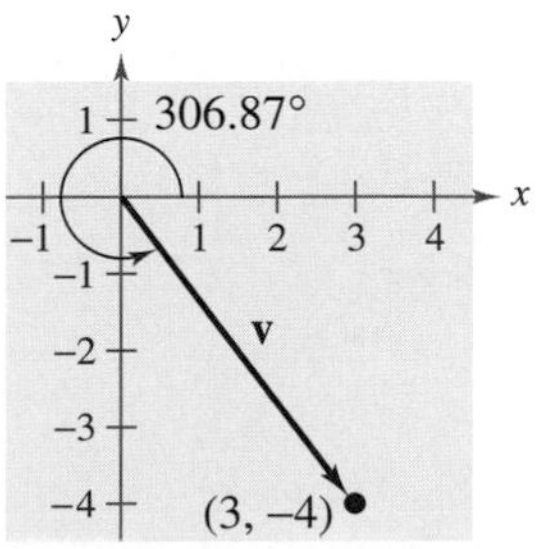

FIGURE 6.29

CHECKPOINT Now try Exercise 55.

Applications of Vectors

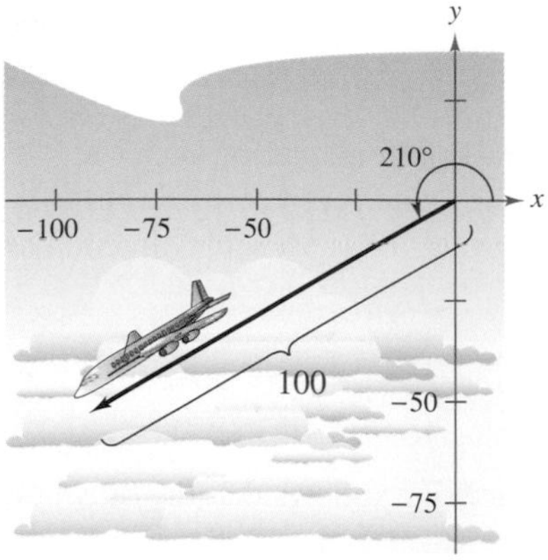

FIGURE 6.30

Example 8 Finding the Component Form of a Vector

Find the component form of the vector that represents the velocity of an airplane descending at a speed of 100 miles per hour at an angle 30° below the horizontal, as shown in Figure 6.30.

Solution

The velocity vector $\mathbf{v}$ has a magnitude of 100 and a direction angle of $\theta = 210°$.

$$\begin{aligned}\mathbf{v} &= \|\mathbf{v}\|(\cos\theta)\mathbf{i} + \|\mathbf{v}\|(\sin\theta)\mathbf{j}\\ &= 100(\cos 210°)\mathbf{i} + 100(\sin 210°)\mathbf{j}\\ &= 100\left(-\frac{\sqrt{3}}{2}\right)\mathbf{i} + 100\left(-\frac{1}{2}\right)\mathbf{j}\\ &= -50\sqrt{3}\,\mathbf{i} - 50\mathbf{j}\\ &= \langle -50\sqrt{3}, -50\rangle\end{aligned}$$

You can check that $\mathbf{v}$ has a magnitude of 100, as follows.

$$\begin{aligned}\|\mathbf{v}\| &= \sqrt{(-50\sqrt{3})^2 + (-50)^2}\\ &= \sqrt{7500 + 2500}\\ &= \sqrt{10{,}000} = 100\end{aligned}$$

CHECKPOINT Now try Exercise 77.

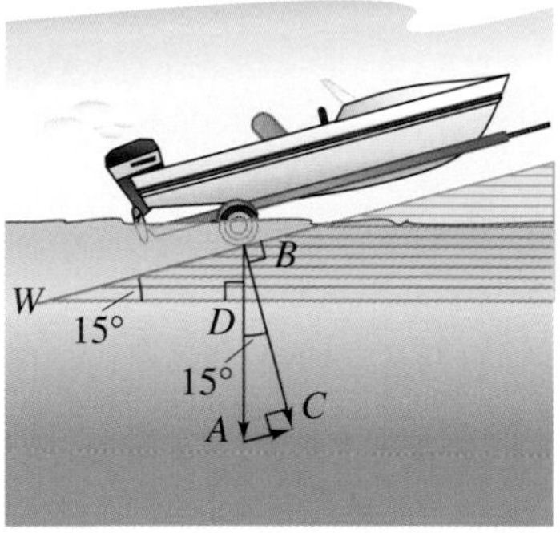

FIGURE 6.31

Example 9 Using Vectors to Determine Weight

A force of 600 pounds is required to pull a boat and trailer up a ramp inclined at 15° from the horizontal. Find the combined weight of the boat and trailer.

Solution

Based on Figure 6.31, you can make the following observations.

$\|\overrightarrow{BA}\|$ = force of gravity = combined weight of boat and trailer

$\|\overrightarrow{BC}\|$ = force against ramp

$\|\overrightarrow{AC}\|$ = force required to move boat up ramp = 600 pounds

By construction, triangles BWD and ABC are similar. So, angle ABC is 15°, and so in triangle ABC you have

$$\sin 15° = \frac{\|\overrightarrow{AC}\|}{\|\overrightarrow{BA}\|} = \frac{600}{\|\overrightarrow{BA}\|}$$

$$\|\overrightarrow{BA}\| = \frac{600}{\sin 15°} \approx 2318.$$

Consequently, the combined weight is approximately 2318 pounds. (In Figure 6.31, note that $\overrightarrow{AC}$ is parallel to the ramp.)

CHECKPOINT Now try Exercise 81.

Example 10 Using Vectors to Find Speed and Direction

> **STUDY TIP**
>
> Recall from Section 4.8 that in air navigation, bearings are measured in degrees clockwise from north.

An airplane is traveling at a speed of 500 miles per hour with a bearing of 330° at a fixed altitude with a negligible wind velocity as shown in Figure 6.32(a). When the airplane reaches a certain point, it encounters a wind with a velocity of 70 miles per hour in the direction N 45° E, as shown in Figure 6.32(b). What are the resultant speed and direction of the airplane?

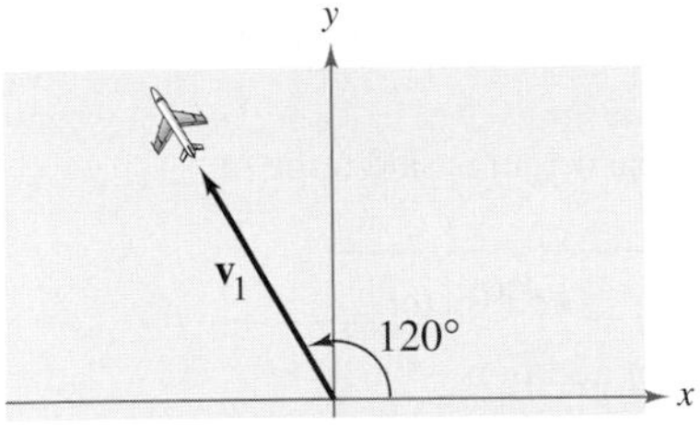

(a)

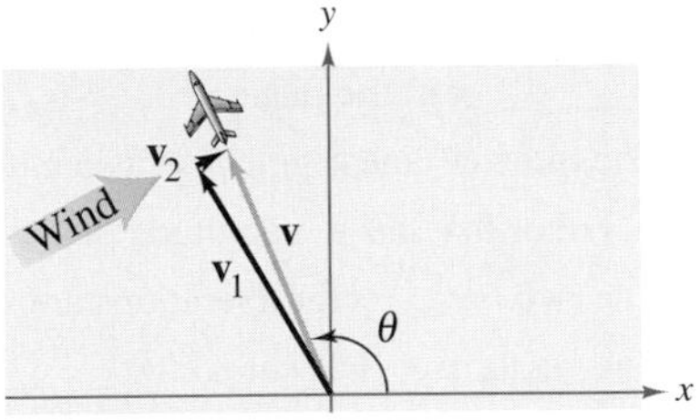

(b)

FIGURE 6.32

Solution

Using Figure 6.32, the velocity of the airplane (alone) is

$$\mathbf{v}_1 = 500\langle \cos 120°, \sin 120° \rangle$$
$$= \langle -250, 250\sqrt{3} \rangle$$

and the velocity of the wind is

$$\mathbf{v}_2 = 70\langle \cos 45°, \sin 45° \rangle$$
$$= \langle 35\sqrt{2}, 35\sqrt{2} \rangle.$$

So, the velocity of the airplane (in the wind) is

$$\mathbf{v} = \mathbf{v}_1 + \mathbf{v}_2$$
$$= \langle -250 + 35\sqrt{2}, 250\sqrt{3} + 35\sqrt{2} \rangle$$
$$\approx \langle -200.5, 482.5 \rangle$$

and the resultant speed of the airplane is

$$\|\mathbf{v}\| = \sqrt{(-200.5)^2 + (482.5)^2}$$
$$\approx 522.5 \text{ miles per hour.}$$

Finally, if θ is the direction angle of the flight path, you have

$$\tan \theta = \frac{482.5}{-200.5}$$
$$\approx -2.4065$$

which implies that

$$\theta \approx 180° + \arctan(-2.4065) \approx 180° - 67.4° = 112.6°.$$

So, the true direction of the airplane is 337.4°.

✓CHECKPOINT Now try Exercise 83.

6.3 Exercises

VOCABULARY CHECK: Fill in the blanks.

1. A ________ ________ ________ can be used to represent a quantity that involves both magnitude and direction.
2. The directed line segment $\overrightarrow{PQ}$ has ________ point P and ________ point Q.
3. The ________ of the directed line segment $\overrightarrow{PQ}$ is denoted by $\|PQ\|$.
4. The set of all directed line segments that are equivalent to a given directed line segment $\overrightarrow{PQ}$ is a ________ **v** in the plane.
5. The directed line segment whose initial point is the origin is said to be in ________ ________ .
6. A vector that has a magnitude of 1 is called a ________ ________ .
7. The two basic vector operations are scalar ________ and vector ________ .
8. The vector **u** + **v** is called the ________ of vector addition.
9. The vector sum $v_1\mathbf{i} + v_2\mathbf{j}$ is called a ________ ________ of the vectors **i** and **j**, and the scalars v_1 and v_2 are called the ________ and ________ components of **v**, respectively.

In Exercises 1 and 2, show that u = v.

1.

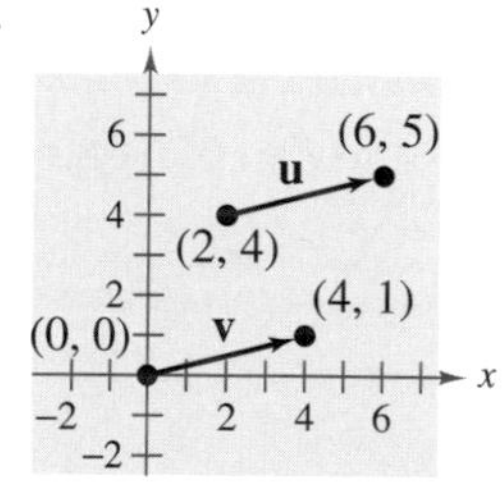

2.

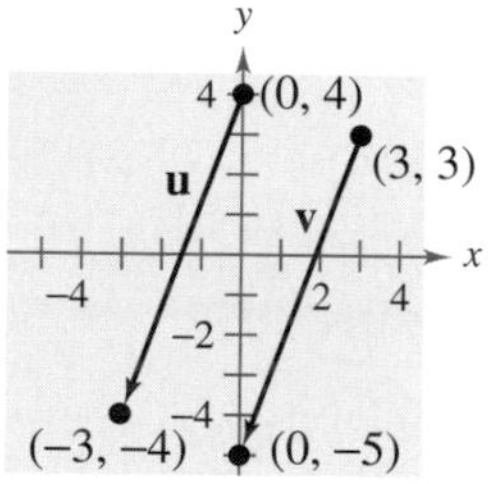

In Exercises 3–14, find the component form and the magnitude of the vector v.

3.

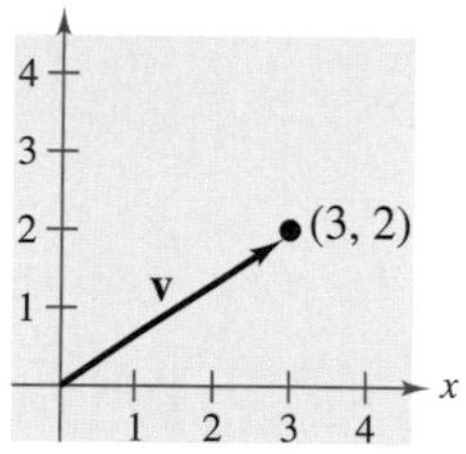

4.

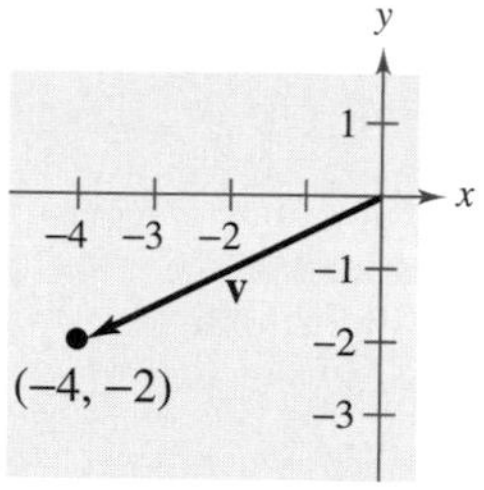

5.

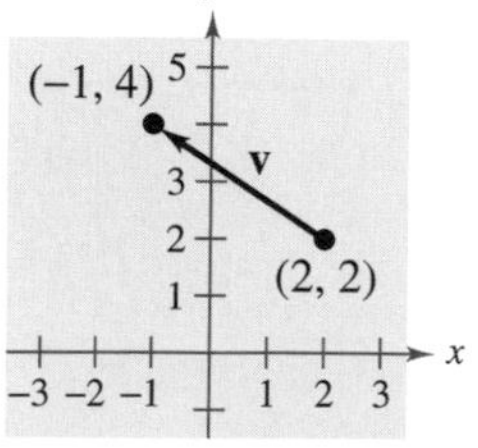

6.

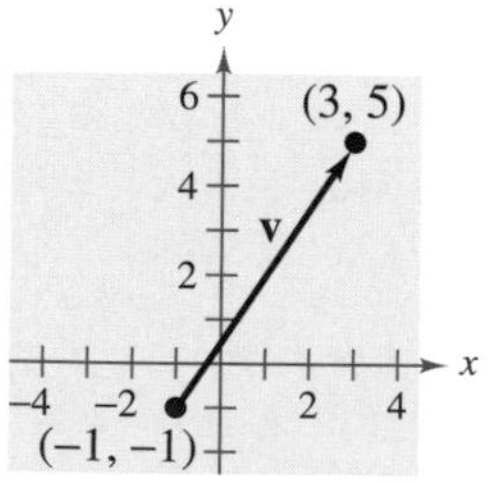

7.

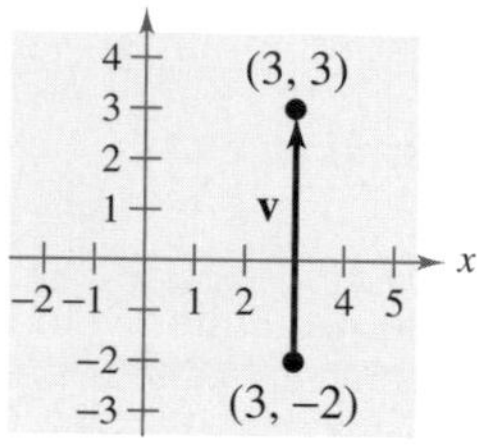

8.

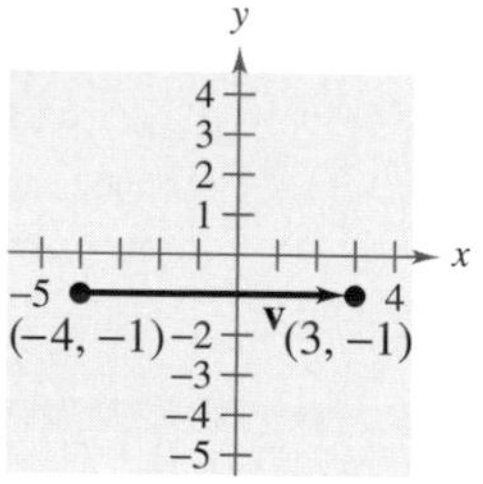

	Initial Point	*Terminal Point*
9.	$(-1, 5)$	$(15, 12)$
10.	$(1, 11)$	$(9, 3)$
11.	$(-3, -5)$	$(5, 1)$
12.	$(-3, 11)$	$(9, 40)$
13.	$(1, 3)$	$(-8, -9)$
14.	$(-2, 7)$	$(5, -17)$

In Exercises 15–20, use the figure to sketch a graph of the specified vector. To print an enlarged copy of the graph, go to the website, *www.mathgraphs.com*.

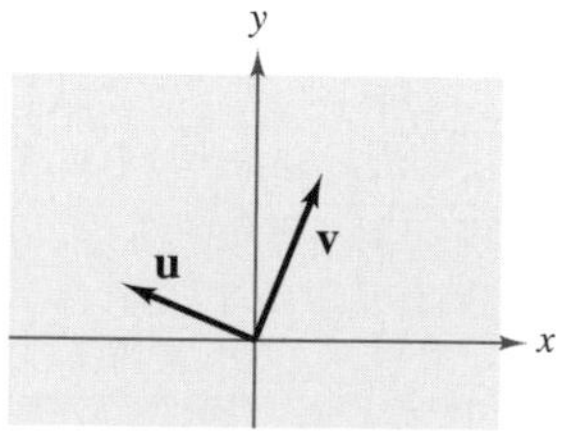

15. $-\mathbf{v}$

16. $5\mathbf{v}$

17. $\mathbf{u} + \mathbf{v}$

18. $\mathbf{u} - \mathbf{v}$

19. $\mathbf{u} + 2\mathbf{v}$

20. $\mathbf{v} - \frac{1}{2}\mathbf{u}$

In Exercises 21–28, find (a) u + v, (b) u − v, and (c) 2u − 3v. Then sketch the resultant vector.

21. $\mathbf{u} = \langle 2, 1 \rangle$, $\mathbf{v} = \langle 1, 3 \rangle$
22. $\mathbf{u} = \langle 2, 3 \rangle$, $\mathbf{v} = \langle 4, 0 \rangle$
23. $\mathbf{u} = \langle -5, 3 \rangle$, $\mathbf{v} = \langle 0, 0 \rangle$
24. $\mathbf{u} = \langle 0, 0 \rangle$, $\mathbf{v} = \langle 2, 1 \rangle$
25. $\mathbf{u} = \mathbf{i} + \mathbf{j}$, $\mathbf{v} = 2\mathbf{i} - 3\mathbf{j}$
26. $\mathbf{u} = -2\mathbf{i} + \mathbf{j}$, $\mathbf{v} = -\mathbf{i} + 2\mathbf{j}$
27. $\mathbf{u} = 2\mathbf{i}$, $\mathbf{v} = \mathbf{j}$
28. $\mathbf{u} = 3\mathbf{j}$, $\mathbf{v} = 2\mathbf{i}$

In Exercises 29–38, find a unit vector in the direction of the given vector.

29. $\mathbf{u} = \langle 3, 0 \rangle$
30. $\mathbf{u} = \langle 0, -2 \rangle$
31. $\mathbf{v} = \langle -2, 2 \rangle$
32. $\mathbf{v} = \langle 5, -12 \rangle$
33. $\mathbf{v} = 6\mathbf{i} - 2\mathbf{j}$
34. $\mathbf{v} = \mathbf{i} + \mathbf{j}$
35. $\mathbf{w} = 4\mathbf{j}$
36. $\mathbf{w} = -6\mathbf{i}$
37. $\mathbf{w} = \mathbf{i} - 2\mathbf{j}$
38. $\mathbf{w} = 7\mathbf{j} - 3\mathbf{i}$

In Exercises 39–42, find the vector v with the given magnitude and the same direction as u.

	Magnitude	*Direction*
39.	$\|\mathbf{v}\| = 5$	$\mathbf{u} = \langle 3, 3 \rangle$
40.	$\|\mathbf{v}\| = 6$	$\mathbf{u} = \langle -3, 3 \rangle$
41.	$\|\mathbf{v}\| = 9$	$\mathbf{u} = \langle 2, 5 \rangle$
42.	$\|\mathbf{v}\| = 10$	$\mathbf{u} = \langle -10, 0 \rangle$

In Exercises 43–46, the initial and terminal points of a vector are given. Write a linear combination of the standard unit vectors i and j.

	Initial Point	*Terminal Point*
43.	$(-3, 1)$	$(4, 5)$
44.	$(0, -2)$	$(3, 6)$
45.	$(-1, -5)$	$(2, 3)$
46.	$(-6, 4)$	$(0, 1)$

In Exercises 47–52, find the component form of v and sketch the specified vector operations geometrically, where u = 2i − j and w = i + 2j.

47. $\mathbf{v} = \frac{3}{2}\mathbf{u}$
48. $\mathbf{v} = \frac{3}{4}\mathbf{w}$
49. $\mathbf{v} = \mathbf{u} + 2\mathbf{w}$
50. $\mathbf{v} = -\mathbf{u} + \mathbf{w}$
51. $\mathbf{v} = \frac{1}{2}(3\mathbf{u} + \mathbf{w})$
52. $\mathbf{v} = \mathbf{u} - 2\mathbf{w}$

In Exercises 53–56, find the magnitude and direction angle of the vector v.

53. $\mathbf{v} = 3(\cos 60°\mathbf{i} + \sin 60°\mathbf{j})$
54. $\mathbf{v} = 8(\cos 135°\mathbf{i} + \sin 135°\mathbf{j})$
55. $\mathbf{v} = 6\mathbf{i} - 6\mathbf{j}$
56. $\mathbf{v} = -5\mathbf{i} + 4\mathbf{j}$

In Exercises 57–64, find the component form of v given its magnitude and the angle it makes with the positive *x*-axis. Sketch v.

	Magnitude	*Angle*
57.	$\|\mathbf{v}\| = 3$	$\theta = 0°$
58.	$\|\mathbf{v}\| = 1$	$\theta = 45°$
59.	$\|\mathbf{v}\| = \frac{7}{2}$	$\theta = 150°$
60.	$\|\mathbf{v}\| = \frac{5}{2}$	$\theta = 45°$
61.	$\|\mathbf{v}\| = 3\sqrt{2}$	$\theta = 150°$
62.	$\|\mathbf{v}\| = 4\sqrt{3}$	$\theta = 90°$
63.	$\|\mathbf{v}\| = 2$	$\mathbf{v}$ in the direction $\mathbf{i} + 3\mathbf{j}$
64.	$\|\mathbf{v}\| = 3$	$\mathbf{v}$ in the direction $3\mathbf{i} + 4\mathbf{j}$

In Exercises 65–68, find the component form of the sum of u and v with direction angles θ_u and θ_v.

	Magnitude	*Angle*
65.	$\|\mathbf{u}\| = 5$	$\theta_{\mathbf{u}} = 0°$
	$\|\mathbf{v}\| = 5$	$\theta_{\mathbf{v}} = 90°$
66.	$\|\mathbf{u}\| = 4$	$\theta_{\mathbf{u}} = 60°$
	$\|\mathbf{v}\| = 4$	$\theta_{\mathbf{v}} = 90°$
67.	$\|\mathbf{u}\| = 20$	$\theta_{\mathbf{u}} = 45°$
	$\|\mathbf{v}\| = 50$	$\theta_{\mathbf{v}} = 180°$
68.	$\|\mathbf{u}\| = 50$	$\theta_{\mathbf{u}} = 30°$
	$\|\mathbf{v}\| = 30$	$\theta_{\mathbf{v}} = 110°$

In Exercises 69 and 70, use the Law of Cosines to find the angle α between the vectors. (Assume $0° \leq \alpha \leq 180°$.)

69. $\mathbf{v} = \mathbf{i} + \mathbf{j}$, $\mathbf{w} = 2\mathbf{i} - 2\mathbf{j}$
70. $\mathbf{v} = \mathbf{i} + 2\mathbf{j}$, $\mathbf{w} = 2\mathbf{i} - \mathbf{j}$

Resultant Force **In Exercises 71 and 72, find the angle between the forces given the magnitude of their resultant. (*Hint:* Write force 1 as a vector in the direction of the positive *x*-axis and force 2 as a vector at an angle θ with the positive *x*-axis.)**

	Force 1	*Force 2*	*Resultant Force*
71.	45 pounds	60 pounds	90 pounds
72.	3000 pounds	1000 pounds	3750 pounds

73. ***Resultant Force*** Forces with magnitudes of 125 newtons and 300 newtons act on a hook (see figure). The angle between the two forces is 45°. Find the direction and magnitude of the resultant of these forces.

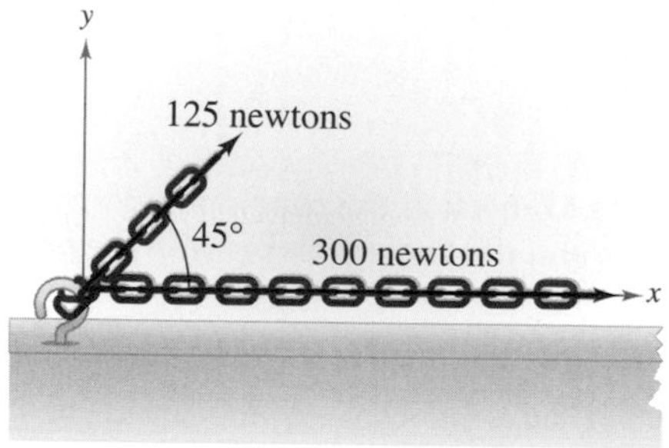

74. ***Resultant Force*** Forces with magnitudes of 2000 newtons and 900 newtons act on a machine part at angles of 30° and −45°, respectively, with the x-axis (see figure). Find the direction and magnitude of the resultant of these forces.

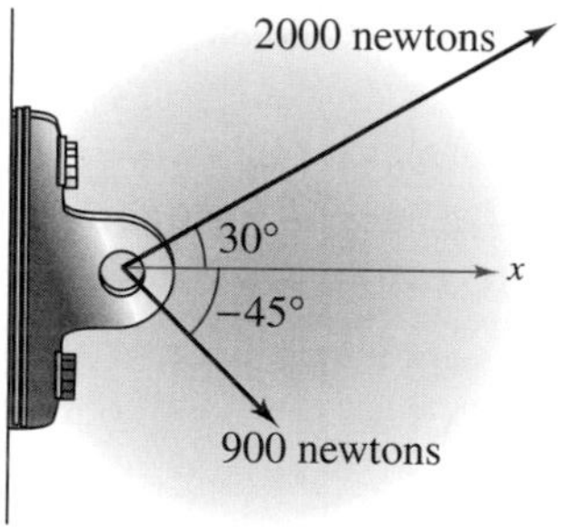

75. ***Resultant Force*** Three forces with magnitudes of 75 pounds, 100 pounds, and 125 pounds act on an object at angles of 30°, 45°, and 120°, respectively, with the positive x-axis. Find the direction and magnitude of the resultant of these forces.

76. ***Resultant Force*** Three forces with magnitudes of 70 pounds, 40 pounds, and 60 pounds act on an object at angles of −30°, 445°, and 135°, respectively, with the positive x-axis. Find the direction and magnitude of the resultant of these forces.

77. ***Velocity*** A ball is thrown with an initial velocity of 70 feet per second, at an angle of 35° with the horizontal (see figure). Find the vertical and horizontal components of the velocity.

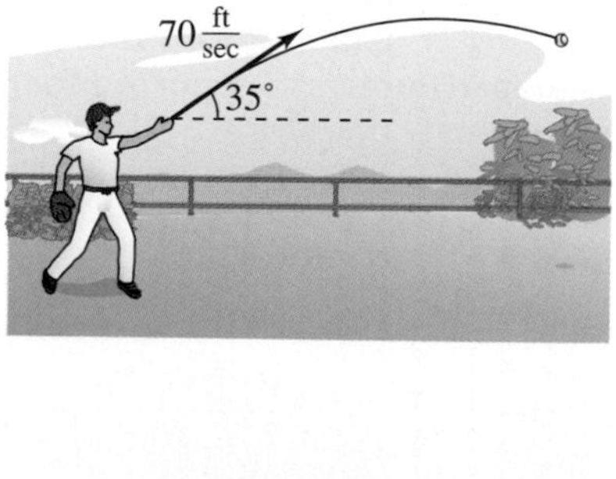

78. ***Velocity*** A gun with a muzzle velocity of 1200 feet per second is fired at an angle of 6° with the horizontal. Find the vertical and horizontal components of the velocity.

Cable Tension **In Exercises 79 and 80, use the figure to determine the tension in each cable supporting the load.**

79.

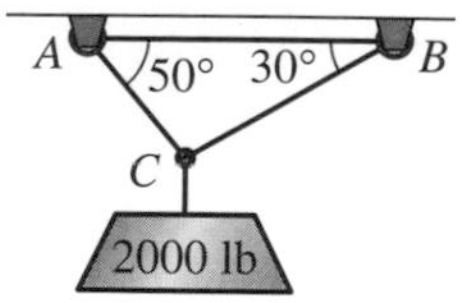

80.

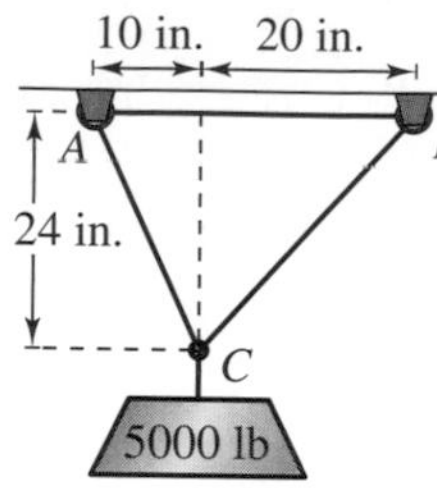

81. ***Tow Line Tension*** A loaded barge is being towed by two tugboats, and the magnitude of the resultant is 6000 pounds directed along the axis of the barge (see figure). Find the tension in the tow lines if they each make an 18° angle with the axis of the barge.

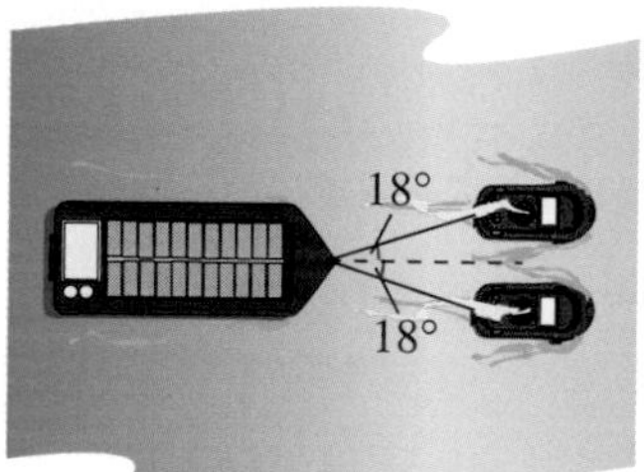

82. ***Rope Tension*** To carry a 100-pound cylindrical weight, two people lift on the ends of short ropes that are tied to an eyelet on the top center of the cylinder. Each rope makes a 20° angle with the vertical. Draw a figure that gives a visual representation of the problem, and find the tension in the ropes.

83. ***Navigation*** An airplane is flying in the direction of 148°, with an airspeed of 875 kilometers per hour. Because of the wind, its groundspeed and direction are 800 kilometers per hour and 140°, respectively (see figure). Find the direction and speed of the wind.

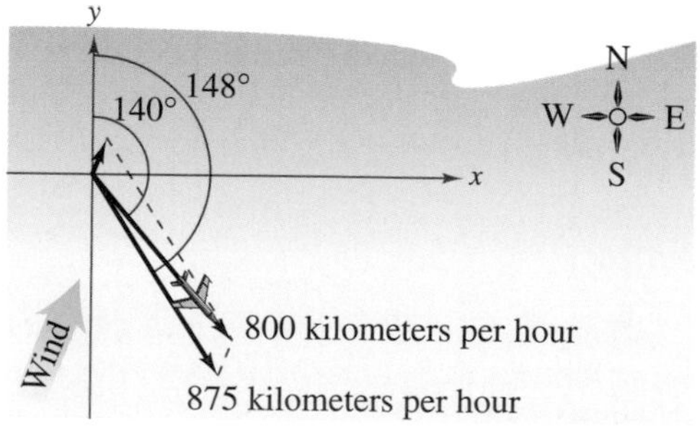

Model It

84. ***Navigation*** A commercial jet is flying from Miami to Seattle. The jet's velocity with respect to the air is 580 miles per hour, and its bearing is 332°. The wind, at the altitude of the plane, is blowing from the southwest with a velocity of 60 miles per hour.

(a) Draw a figure that gives a visual representation of the problem.

(b) Write the velocity of the wind as a vector in component form.

(c) Write the velocity of the jet relative to the air in component form.

(d) What is the speed of the jet with respect to the ground?

(e) What is the true direction of the jet?

85. ***Work*** A heavy implement is pulled 30 feet across a floor, using a force of 100 pounds. The force is exerted at an angle of 50° above the horizontal (see figure). Find the work done. (Use the formula for work, $W = FD$, where F is the component of the force in the direction of motion and D is the distance.)

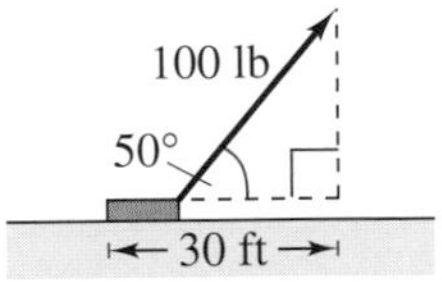

FIGURE FOR 85

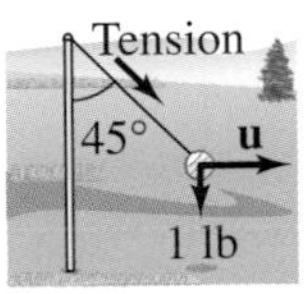

FIGURE FOR 86

86. ***Rope Tension*** A tetherball weighing 1 pound is pulled outward from the pole by a horizontal force **u** until the rope makes a 45° angle with the pole (see figure). Determine the resulting tension in the rope and the magnitude of **u**.

Synthesis

True or False? **In Exercises 87 and 88, decide whether the statement is true or false. Justify your answer.**

87. If **u** and **v** have the same magnitude and direction, then $\mathbf{u} = \mathbf{v}$.

88. If $\mathbf{u} = a\mathbf{i} + b\mathbf{j}$ is a unit vector, then $a^2 + b^2 = 1$.

89. ***Think About It*** Consider two forces of equal magnitude acting on a point.

(a) If the magnitude of the resultant is the sum of the magnitudes of the two forces, make a conjecture about the angle between the forces.

(b) If the resultant of the forces is **0**, make a conjecture about the angle between the forces.

(c) Can the magnitude of the resultant be greater than the sum of the magnitudes of the two forces? Explain.

90. ***Graphical Reasoning*** Consider two forces

$$\mathbf{F}_1 = \langle 10, 0\rangle \text{ and } \mathbf{F}_2 = 5\langle \cos\theta, \sin\theta\rangle.$$

(a) Find $\|\mathbf{F}_1 + \mathbf{F}_2\|$ as a function of θ.

(b) Use a graphing utility to graph the function in part (a) for $0 \le \theta < 2\pi$.

(c) Use the graph in part (b) to determine the range of the function. What is its maximum, and for what value of θ does it occur? What is its minimum, and for what value of θ does it occur?

(d) Explain why the magnitude of the resultant is never 0.

91. ***Proof*** Prove that $(\cos\theta)\mathbf{i} + (\sin\theta)\mathbf{j}$ is a unit vector for any value of θ.

92. ***Technology*** Write a program for your graphing utility that graphs two vectors and their difference given the vectors in component form.

In Exercises 93 and 94, use the program in Exercise 92 to find the difference of the vectors shown in the figure.

93.

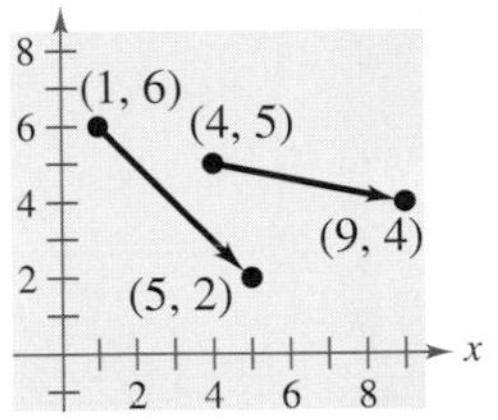

94.

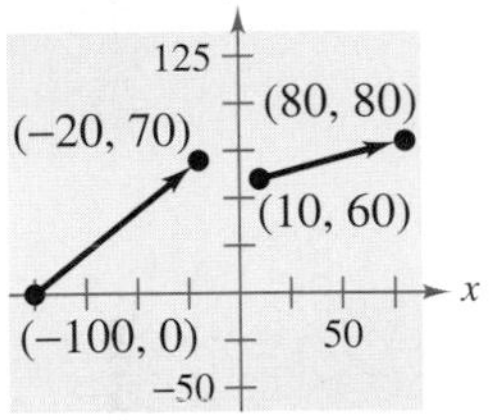

Skills Review

In Exercises 95–98, use the trigonometric substitution to write the algebraic expression as a trigonometric function of θ, where $0 < \theta < \pi/2$.

95. $\sqrt{x^2 - 64}$, $x = 8 \sec\theta$

96. $\sqrt{64 - x^2}$, $x = 8 \sin\theta$

97. $\sqrt{x^2 + 36}$, $x = 6 \tan\theta$

98. $\sqrt{(x^2 - 25)^3}$, $x = 5 \sec\theta$

In Exercises 99–102, solve the equation.

99. $\cos x(\cos x + 1) = 0$

100. $\sin x\left(2 \sin x + \sqrt{2}\right) = 0$

101. $3 \sec x \sin x - 2\sqrt{3} \sin x = 0$

102. $\cos x \csc x + \cos x\sqrt{2} = 0$

6.4 Vectors and Dot Products

What you should learn

- Find the dot product of two vectors and use the Properties of the Dot Product.
- Find the angle between two vectors and determine whether two vectors are orthogonal.
- Write a vector as the sum of two vector components.
- Use vectors to find the work done by a force.

Why you should learn it

You can use the dot product of two vectors to solve real-life problems involving two vector quantities. For instance, in Exercise 68 on page 468, you can use the dot product to find the force necessary to keep a sport utility vehicle from rolling down a hill.

Edward Ewert

The Dot Product of Two Vectors

So far you have studied two vector operations—vector addition and multiplication by a scalar—each of which yields another vector. In this section, you will study a third vector operation, the **dot product.** This product yields a scalar, rather than a vector.

Definition of the Dot Product

The **dot product** of $\mathbf{u} = \langle u_1, u_2 \rangle$ and $\mathbf{v} = \langle v_1, v_2 \rangle$ is

$$\mathbf{u} \cdot \mathbf{v} = u_1v_1 + u_2v_2.$$

Properties of the Dot Product

Let **u**, **v**, and **w** be vectors in the plane or in space and let c be a scalar.

1. $\mathbf{u} \cdot \mathbf{v} = \mathbf{v} \cdot \mathbf{u}$
2. $\mathbf{0} \cdot \mathbf{v} = 0$
3. $\mathbf{u} \cdot (\mathbf{v} + \mathbf{w}) = \mathbf{u} \cdot \mathbf{v} + \mathbf{u} \cdot \mathbf{w}$
4. $\mathbf{v} \cdot \mathbf{v} = \|\mathbf{v}\|^2$
5. $c(\mathbf{u} \cdot \mathbf{v}) = c\mathbf{u} \cdot \mathbf{v} = \mathbf{u} \cdot c\mathbf{v}$

For proofs of the properties of the dot product, see Proofs in Mathematics on page 492.

Example 1 Finding Dot Products

Find each dot product.

a. $\langle 4, 5 \rangle \cdot \langle 2, 3 \rangle$ **b.** $\langle 2, -1 \rangle \cdot \langle 1, 2 \rangle$ **c.** $\langle 0, 3 \rangle \cdot \langle 4, -2 \rangle$

Solution

a. $\langle 4, 5 \rangle \cdot \langle 2, 3 \rangle = 4(2) + 5(3)$

$= 8 + 15$

$= 23$

b. $\langle 2, -1 \rangle \cdot \langle 1, 2 \rangle = 2(1) + (-1)(2) = 2 - 2 = 0$

c. $\langle 0, 3 \rangle \cdot \langle 4, -2 \rangle = 0(4) + 3(-2) = 0 - 6 = -6$

✓CHECKPOINT Now try Exercise 1.

In Example 1, be sure you see that the dot product of two vectors is a scalar (a real number), not a vector. Moreover, notice that the dot product can be positive, zero, or negative.

Example 2 **Using Properties of Dot Products**

Let $\mathbf{u} = \langle -1, 3 \rangle$, $\mathbf{v} = \langle 2, -4 \rangle$, and $\mathbf{w} = \langle 1, -2 \rangle$. Find each dot product.

a. $(\mathbf{u} \cdot \mathbf{v})\mathbf{w}$ **b.** $\mathbf{u} \cdot 2\mathbf{v}$

Solution

Begin by finding the dot product of **u** and **v**.

$$\begin{aligned} \mathbf{u} \cdot \mathbf{v} &= \langle -1, 3 \rangle \cdot \langle 2, -4 \rangle \\ &= (-1)(2) + 3(-4) \\ &= -14 \end{aligned}$$

a. $$\begin{aligned} (\mathbf{u} \cdot \mathbf{v})\mathbf{w} &= -14\langle 1, -2 \rangle \\ &= \langle -14, 28 \rangle \end{aligned}$$

b. $$\begin{aligned} \mathbf{u} \cdot 2\mathbf{v} &= 2(\mathbf{u} \cdot \mathbf{v}) \\ &= 2(-14) \\ &= -28 \end{aligned}$$

Notice that the product in part (a) is a vector, whereas the product in part (b) is a scalar. Can you see why?

✓CHECKPOINT Now try Exercise 11.

Example 3 **Dot Product and Magnitude**

The dot product of **u** with itself is 5. What is the magnitude of **u**?

Solution

Because $\|\mathbf{u}\|^2 = \mathbf{u} \cdot \mathbf{u}$ and $\mathbf{u} \cdot \mathbf{u} = 5$, it follows that

$$\begin{aligned} \|\mathbf{u}\| &= \sqrt{\mathbf{u} \cdot \mathbf{u}} \\ &= \sqrt{5}. \end{aligned}$$

✓CHECKPOINT Now try Exercise 19.

The Angle Between Two Vectors

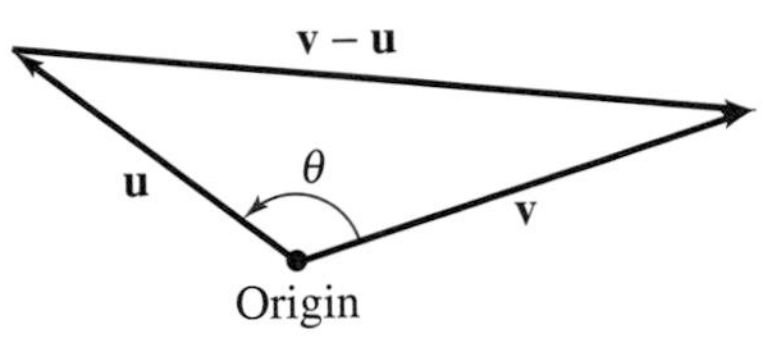

FIGURE 6.33

The **angle between two nonzero vectors** is the angle θ, $0 \le \theta \le \pi$, between their respective standard position vectors, as shown in Figure 6.33. This angle can be found using the dot product. (Note that the angle between the zero vector and another vector is not defined.)

Angle Between Two Vectors

If θ is the angle between two nonzero vectors **u** and **v**, then

$$\cos \theta = \frac{\mathbf{u} \cdot \mathbf{v}}{\|\mathbf{u}\| \, \|\mathbf{v}\|}.$$

For a proof of the angle between two vectors, see Proofs in Mathematics on page 492.

Example 4 Finding the Angle Between Two Vectors

Find the angle between $\mathbf{u} = \langle 4, 3 \rangle$ and $\mathbf{v} = \langle 3, 5 \rangle$.

Solution

$$\cos\theta = \frac{\mathbf{u}\cdot\mathbf{v}}{\|\mathbf{u}\|\,\|\mathbf{v}\|}$$

$$= \frac{\langle 4, 3\rangle \cdot \langle 3, 5\rangle}{\|\langle 4, 3\rangle\|\,\|\langle 3, 5\rangle\|}$$

$$= \frac{27}{5\sqrt{34}}$$

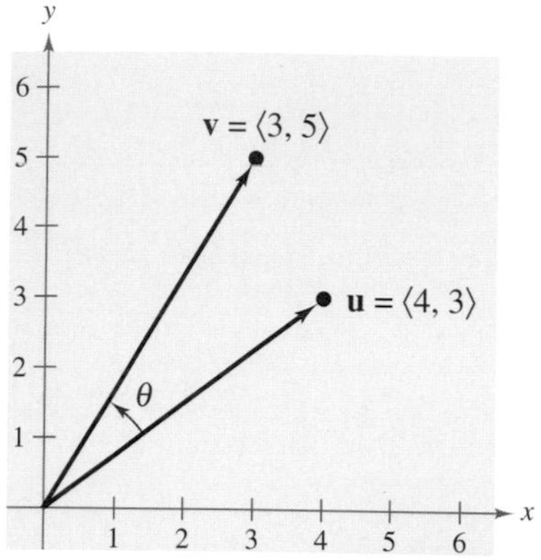

FIGURE 6.34

This implies that the angle between the two vectors is

$$\theta = \arccos\frac{27}{5\sqrt{34}} \approx 22.2^\circ$$

as shown in Figure 6.34.

✓CHECKPOINT Now try Exercise 29.

Rewriting the expression for the angle between two vectors in the form

$$\mathbf{u}\cdot\mathbf{v} = \|\mathbf{u}\|\,\|\mathbf{v}\|\cos\theta \qquad \text{Alternative form of dot product}$$

produces an alternative way to calculate the dot product. From this form, you can see that because $\|\mathbf{u}\|$ and $\|\mathbf{v}\|$ are always positive, $\mathbf{u}\cdot\mathbf{v}$ and $\cos\theta$ will always have the same sign. Figure 6.35 shows the five possible orientations of two vectors.

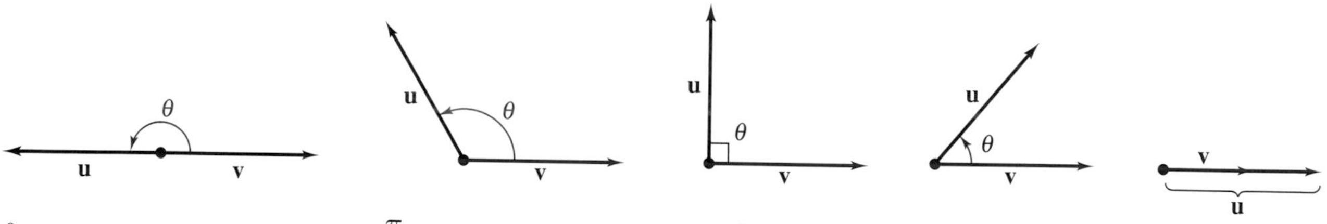

$\theta = \pi$
$\cos\theta = -1$
Opposite Direction

$\frac{\pi}{2} < \theta < \pi$
$-1 < \cos\theta < 0$
Obtuse Angle

$\theta = \frac{\pi}{2}$
$\cos\theta = 0$
90° Angle

$0 < \theta < \frac{\pi}{2}$
$0 < \cos\theta < 1$
Acute Angle

$\theta = 0$
$\cos\theta = 1$
Same Direction

FIGURE 6.35

Definition of Orthogonal Vectors

The vectors **u** and **v** are **orthogonal** if $\mathbf{u}\cdot\mathbf{v} = 0$.

The terms *orthogonal* and *perpendicular* mean essentially the same thing—meeting at right angles. Even though the angle between the zero vector and another vector is not defined, it is convenient to extend the definition of orthogonality to include the zero vector. In other words, the zero vector is orthogonal to every vector **u**, because $\mathbf{0}\cdot\mathbf{u} = 0$.

Technology

The graphing utility program Finding the Angle Between Two Vectors, found on our website *college.hmco.com*, graphs two vectors $\mathbf{u} = \langle a, b \rangle$ and $\mathbf{v} = \langle c, d \rangle$ in standard position and finds the measure of the angle between them. Use the program to verify the solutions for Examples 4 and 5.

Example 5 Determining Orthogonal Vectors

Are the vectors $\mathbf{u} = \langle 2, -3 \rangle$ and $\mathbf{v} = \langle 6, 4 \rangle$ orthogonal?

Solution

Begin by finding the dot product of the two vectors.

$$\mathbf{u} \cdot \mathbf{v} = \langle 2, -3 \rangle \cdot \langle 6, 4 \rangle = 2(6) + (-3)(4) = 0$$

Because the dot product is 0, the two vectors are orthogonal (see Figure 6.36).

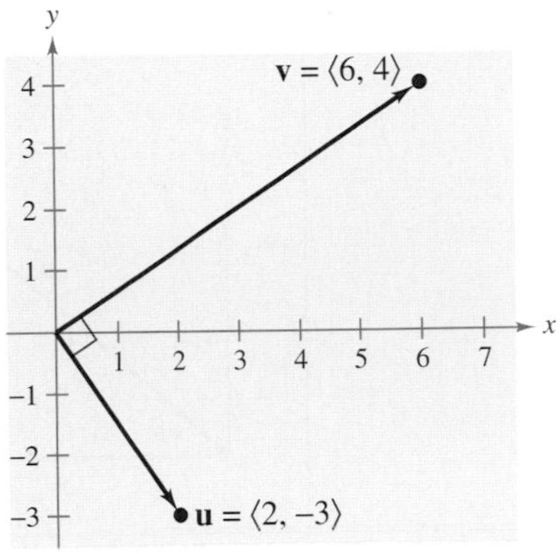

FIGURE 6.36

CHECKPOINT Now try Exercise 47.

Finding Vector Components

You have already seen applications in which two vectors are added to produce a resultant vector. Many applications in physics and engineering pose the reverse problem—decomposing a given vector into the sum of two **vector components.**

Consider a boat on an inclined ramp, as shown in Figure 6.37. The force $\mathbf{F}$ due to gravity pulls the boat *down* the ramp and *against* the ramp. These two orthogonal forces, $\mathbf{w}_1$ and $\mathbf{w}_2$, are vector components of $\mathbf{F}$. That is,

$$\mathbf{F} = \mathbf{w}_1 + \mathbf{w}_2. \qquad \text{Vector components of } \mathbf{F}$$

The negative of component $\mathbf{w}_1$ represents the force needed to keep the boat from rolling down the ramp, whereas $\mathbf{w}_2$ represents the force that the tires must withstand against the ramp. A procedure for finding $\mathbf{w}_1$ and $\mathbf{w}_2$ is shown on the following page.

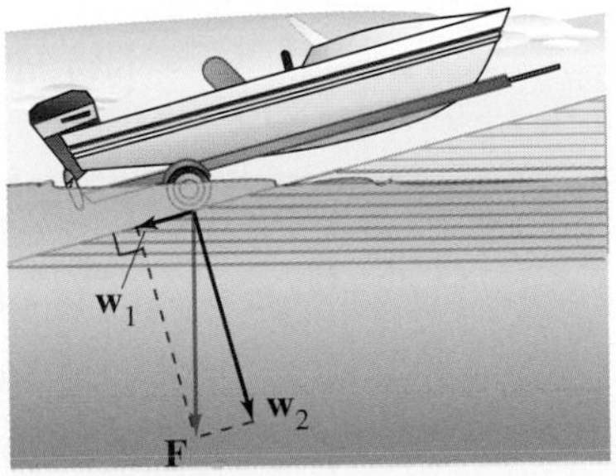

FIGURE 6.37

Definition of Vector Components

Let **u** and **v** be nonzero vectors such that

$$\mathbf{u} = \mathbf{w}_1 + \mathbf{w}_2$$

where $\mathbf{w}_1$ and $\mathbf{w}_2$ are orthogonal and $\mathbf{w}_1$ is parallel to (or a scalar multiple of) **v**, as shown in Figure 6.38. The vectors $\mathbf{w}_1$ and $\mathbf{w}_2$ are called **vector components** of **u**. The vector $\mathbf{w}_1$ is the **projection** of **u** onto **v** and is denoted by

$$\mathbf{w}_1 = \text{proj}_{\mathbf{v}}\mathbf{u}.$$

The vector $\mathbf{w}_2$ is given by $\mathbf{w}_2 = \mathbf{u} - \mathbf{w}_1$.

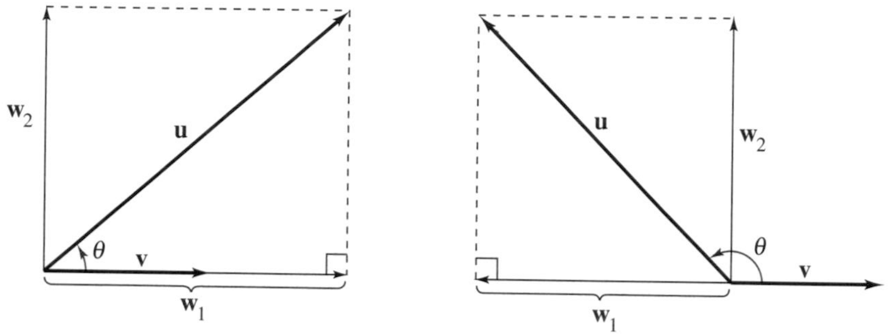

θ is acute. *θ is obtuse.*

FIGURE 6.38

From the definition of vector components, you can see that it is easy to find the component $\mathbf{w}_2$ once you have found the projection of **u** onto **v**. To find the projection, you can use the dot product, as follows.

$$\mathbf{u} = \mathbf{w}_1 + \mathbf{w}_2 = c\mathbf{v} + \mathbf{w}_2 \qquad \mathbf{w}_1 \text{ is a scalar multiple of } \mathbf{v}.$$

$$\mathbf{u} \cdot \mathbf{v} = (c\mathbf{v} + \mathbf{w}_2) \cdot \mathbf{v} \qquad \text{Take dot product of each side with } \mathbf{v}.$$

$$= c\mathbf{v} \cdot \mathbf{v} + \mathbf{w}_2 \cdot \mathbf{v}$$

$$= c\|\mathbf{v}\|^2 + 0 \qquad \mathbf{w}_2 \text{ and } \mathbf{v} \text{ are orthogonal.}$$

So,

$$c = \frac{\mathbf{u} \cdot \mathbf{v}}{\|\mathbf{v}\|^2}$$

and

$$\mathbf{w}_1 = \text{proj}_{\mathbf{v}}\,\mathbf{u} = c\mathbf{v} = \frac{\mathbf{u} \cdot \mathbf{v}}{\|\mathbf{v}\|^2}\mathbf{v}.$$

Projection of u onto v

Let **u** and **v** be nonzero vectors. The projection of **u** onto **v** is

$$\text{proj}_{\mathbf{v}}\mathbf{u} = \left(\frac{\mathbf{u} \cdot \mathbf{v}}{\|\mathbf{v}\|^2}\right)\mathbf{v}.$$

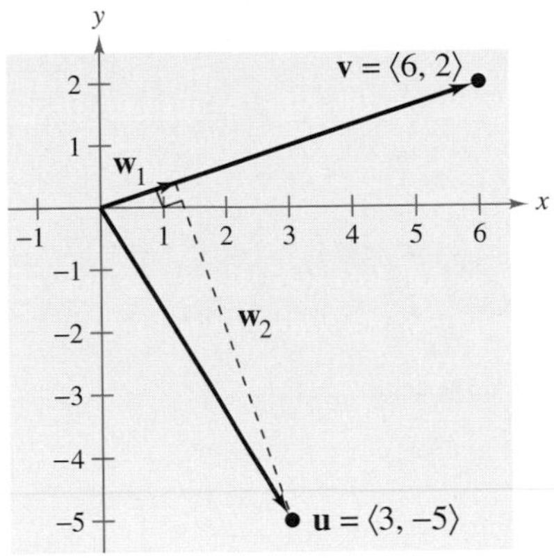

FIGURE 6.39

Example 6 Decomposing a Vector into Components

Find the projection of $\mathbf{u} = \langle 3, -5\rangle$ onto $\mathbf{v} = \langle 6, 2\rangle$. Then write $\mathbf{u}$ as the sum of two orthogonal vectors, one of which is $\text{proj}_{\mathbf{v}}\mathbf{u}$.

Solution

The projection of $\mathbf{u}$ onto $\mathbf{v}$ is

$$\mathbf{w}_1 = \text{proj}_{\mathbf{v}}\mathbf{u} = \left(\frac{\mathbf{u}\cdot\mathbf{v}}{\|\mathbf{v}\|^2}\right)\mathbf{v} = \left(\frac{8}{40}\right)\langle 6, 2\rangle = \left\langle \frac{6}{5}, \frac{2}{5}\right\rangle$$

as shown in Figure 6.39. The other component, $\mathbf{w}_2$, is

$$\mathbf{w}_2 = \mathbf{u} - \mathbf{w}_1 = \langle 3, -5\rangle - \left\langle \frac{6}{5}, \frac{2}{5}\right\rangle = \left\langle \frac{9}{5}, -\frac{27}{5}\right\rangle.$$

So,

$$\mathbf{u} = \mathbf{w}_1 + \mathbf{w}_2 = \left\langle \frac{6}{5}, \frac{2}{5}\right\rangle + \left\langle \frac{9}{5}, -\frac{27}{5}\right\rangle = \langle 3, -5\rangle.$$

CHECKPOINT Now try Exercise 53.

Example 7 Finding a Force

A 200-pound cart sits on a ramp inclined at 30°, as shown in Figure 6.40. What force is required to keep the cart from rolling down the ramp?

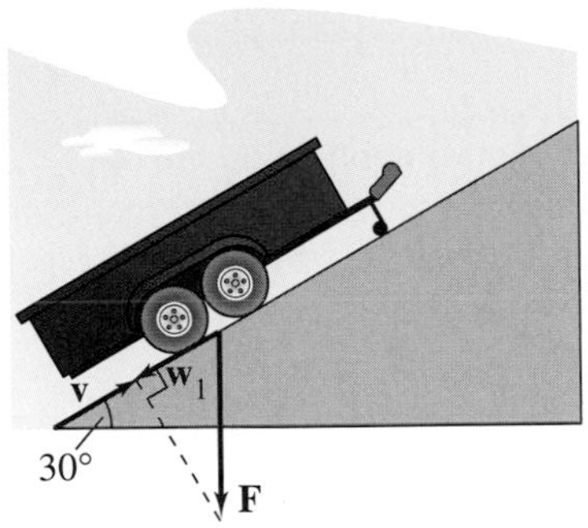

FIGURE 6.40

Solution

Because the force due to gravity is vertical and downward, you can represent the gravitational force by the vector

$$\mathbf{F} = -200\mathbf{j}.$$ Force due to gravity

To find the force required to keep the cart from rolling down the ramp, project $\mathbf{F}$ onto a unit vector $\mathbf{v}$ in the direction of the ramp, as follows.

$$\mathbf{v} = (\cos 30°)\mathbf{i} + (\sin 30°)\mathbf{j} = \frac{\sqrt{3}}{2}\mathbf{i} + \frac{1}{2}\mathbf{j}$$ Unit vector along ramp

Therefore, the projection of $\mathbf{F}$ onto $\mathbf{v}$ is

$$\begin{aligned}\mathbf{w}_1 &= \text{proj}_{\mathbf{v}}\mathbf{F}\\ &= \left(\frac{\mathbf{F}\cdot\mathbf{v}}{\|\mathbf{v}\|^2}\right)\mathbf{v}\\ &= (\mathbf{F}\cdot\mathbf{v})\mathbf{v}\\ &= (-200)\left(\frac{1}{2}\right)\mathbf{v}\\ &= -100\left(\frac{\sqrt{3}}{2}\mathbf{i} + \frac{1}{2}\mathbf{j}\right).\end{aligned}$$

The magnitude of this force is 100, and so a force of 100 pounds is required to keep the cart from rolling down the ramp.

CHECKPOINT Now try Exercise 67.

Work

The work W done by a *constant* force $\mathbf{F}$ acting along the line of motion of an object is given by

$$W = (\text{magnitude of force})(\text{distance}) = \|\mathbf{F}\|\,\|\overrightarrow{PQ}\|$$

as shown in Figure 6.41. If the constant force $\mathbf{F}$ is not directed along the line of motion, as shown in Figure 6.42, the work W done by the force is given by

$$\begin{aligned} W &= \|\text{proj}_{\overrightarrow{PQ}}\mathbf{F}\|\,\|\overrightarrow{PQ}\| && \text{Projection form for work} \\ &= (\cos\theta)\|\mathbf{F}\|\,\|\overrightarrow{PQ}\| && \|\text{proj}_{\overrightarrow{PQ}}\mathbf{F}\| = (\cos\theta)\|\mathbf{F}\| \\ &= \mathbf{F}\cdot\overrightarrow{PQ}. && \text{Alternative form of dot product} \end{aligned}$$

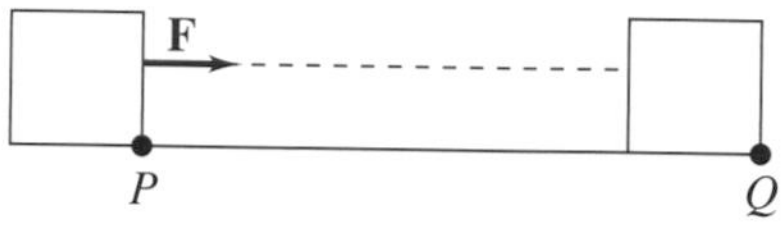

Force acts along the line of motion.
FIGURE 6.41

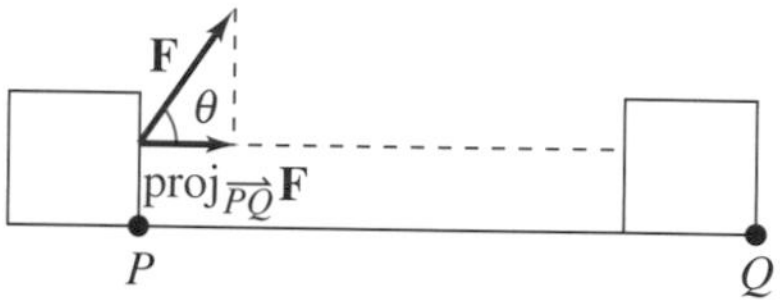

Force acts at angle θ with the line of motion.
FIGURE 6.42

This notion of work is summarized in the following definition.

Definition of Work

The **work** W done by a constant force $\mathbf{F}$ as its point of application moves along the vector $\overrightarrow{PQ}$ is given by either of the following.

1. $W = \|\text{proj}_{\overrightarrow{PQ}}\mathbf{F}\|\,\|\overrightarrow{PQ}\|$ Projection form
2. $W = \mathbf{F}\cdot\overrightarrow{PQ}$ Dot product form

Example 8 Finding Work

To close a sliding door, a person pulls on a rope with a constant force of 50 pounds at a constant angle of 60°, as shown in Figure 6.43. Find the work done in moving the door 12 feet to its closed position.

FIGURE 6.43

Solution

Using a projection, you can calculate the work as follows.

$$\begin{aligned} W &= \|\text{proj}_{\overrightarrow{PQ}}\mathbf{F}\|\,\|\overrightarrow{PQ}\| && \text{Projection form for work} \\ &= (\cos 60°)\|\mathbf{F}\|\,\|\overrightarrow{PQ}\| \\ &= \frac{1}{2}(50)(12) = 300 \text{ foot-pounds} \end{aligned}$$

So, the work done is 300 foot-pounds. You can verify this result by finding the vectors $\mathbf{F}$ and $\overrightarrow{PQ}$ and calculating their dot product.

CHECKPOINT Now try Exercise 69.

6.4 Exercises

VOCABULARY CHECK: Fill in the blanks.

1. The ________ ________ of two vectors yields a scalar, rather than a vector.
2. If θ is the angle between two nonzero vectors **u** and **v**, then $\cos\theta =$ ________ .
3. The vectors **u** and **v** are ________ if $\mathbf{u}\cdot\mathbf{v} = 0$.
4. The projection of **u** onto **v** is given by $\text{proj}_{\mathbf{v}}\mathbf{u} =$ ________ .
5. The work W done by a constant force $\mathbf{F}$ as its point of application moves along the vector $\overrightarrow{PQ}$ is given by $W =$ ________ or $W =$ ________ .

In Exercises 1–8, find the dot product of u and v.

1. $\mathbf{u} = \langle 6, 1\rangle$, $\mathbf{v} = \langle -2, 3\rangle$
2. $\mathbf{u} = \langle 5, 12\rangle$, $\mathbf{v} = \langle -3, 2\rangle$
3. $\mathbf{u} = \langle -4, 1\rangle$, $\mathbf{v} = \langle 2, -3\rangle$
4. $\mathbf{u} = \langle -2, 5\rangle$, $\mathbf{v} = \langle -1, -2\rangle$
5. $\mathbf{u} = 4\mathbf{i} - 2\mathbf{j}$, $\mathbf{v} = \mathbf{i} - \mathbf{j}$
6. $\mathbf{u} = 3\mathbf{i} + 4\mathbf{j}$, $\mathbf{v} = 7\mathbf{i} - 2\mathbf{j}$
7. $\mathbf{u} = 3\mathbf{i} + 2\mathbf{j}$, $\mathbf{v} = -2\mathbf{i} - 3\mathbf{j}$
8. $\mathbf{u} = \mathbf{i} - 2\mathbf{j}$, $\mathbf{v} = -2\mathbf{i} + \mathbf{j}$

In Exercises 9–18, use the vectors u = ⟨2, 2⟩, v = ⟨−3, 4⟩, and w = ⟨1, −2⟩ to find the indicated quantity. State whether the result is a vector or a scalar.

9. $\mathbf{u}\cdot\mathbf{u}$
10. $3\mathbf{u}\cdot\mathbf{v}$
11. $(\mathbf{u}\cdot\mathbf{v})\mathbf{v}$
12. $(\mathbf{v}\cdot\mathbf{u})\mathbf{w}$
13. $(3\mathbf{w}\cdot\mathbf{v})\mathbf{u}$
14. $(\mathbf{u}\cdot 2\mathbf{v})\mathbf{w}$
15. $\|\mathbf{w}\| - 1$
16. $2 - \|\mathbf{u}\|$
17. $(\mathbf{u}\cdot\mathbf{v}) - (\mathbf{u}\cdot\mathbf{w})$
18. $(\mathbf{v}\cdot\mathbf{u}) - (\mathbf{w}\cdot\mathbf{v})$

In Exercises 19–24, use the dot product to find the magnitude of u.

19. $\mathbf{u} = \langle -5, 12\rangle$
20. $\mathbf{u} = \langle 2, -4\rangle$
21. $\mathbf{u} = 20\mathbf{i} + 25\mathbf{j}$
22. $\mathbf{u} = 12\mathbf{i} - 16\mathbf{j}$
23. $\mathbf{u} = 6\mathbf{j}$
24. $\mathbf{u} = -21\mathbf{i}$

In Exercises 25–34, find the angle θ between the vectors.

25. $\mathbf{u} = \langle 1, 0\rangle$, $\mathbf{v} = \langle 0, -2\rangle$
26. $\mathbf{u} = \langle 3, 2\rangle$, $\mathbf{v} = \langle 4, 0\rangle$
27. $\mathbf{u} = 3\mathbf{i} + 4\mathbf{j}$, $\mathbf{v} = -2\mathbf{j}$
28. $\mathbf{u} = 2\mathbf{i} - 3\mathbf{j}$, $\mathbf{v} = \mathbf{i} - 2\mathbf{j}$
29. $\mathbf{u} = 2\mathbf{i} - \mathbf{j}$, $\mathbf{v} = 6\mathbf{i} + 4\mathbf{j}$
30. $\mathbf{u} = -6\mathbf{i} - 3\mathbf{j}$, $\mathbf{v} = -8\mathbf{i} + 4\mathbf{j}$
31. $\mathbf{u} = 5\mathbf{i} + 5\mathbf{j}$, $\mathbf{v} = -6\mathbf{i} + 6\mathbf{j}$
32. $\mathbf{u} = 2\mathbf{i} - 3\mathbf{j}$, $\mathbf{v} = 4\mathbf{i} + 3\mathbf{j}$
33. $\mathbf{u} = \cos\left(\frac{\pi}{3}\right)\mathbf{i} + \sin\left(\frac{\pi}{3}\right)\mathbf{j}$, $\mathbf{v} = \cos\left(\frac{3\pi}{4}\right)\mathbf{i} + \sin\left(\frac{3\pi}{4}\right)\mathbf{j}$
34. $\mathbf{u} = \cos\left(\frac{\pi}{4}\right)\mathbf{i} + \sin\left(\frac{\pi}{4}\right)\mathbf{j}$, $\mathbf{v} = \cos\left(\frac{\pi}{2}\right)\mathbf{i} + \sin\left(\frac{\pi}{2}\right)\mathbf{j}$

In Exercises 35–38, graph the vectors and find the degree measure of the angle θ between the vectors.

35. $\mathbf{u} = 3\mathbf{i} + 4\mathbf{j}$, $\mathbf{v} = -7\mathbf{i} + 5\mathbf{j}$
36. $\mathbf{u} = 6\mathbf{i} + 3\mathbf{j}$, $\mathbf{v} = -4\mathbf{i} + 4\mathbf{j}$
37. $\mathbf{u} = 5\mathbf{i} + 5\mathbf{j}$, $\mathbf{v} = -8\mathbf{i} + 8\mathbf{j}$
38. $\mathbf{u} = 2\mathbf{i} - 3\mathbf{j}$, $\mathbf{v} = 8\mathbf{i} + 3\mathbf{j}$

In Exercises 39–42, use vectors to find the interior angles of the triangle with the given vertices.

39. $(1, 2), (3, 4), (2, 5)$
40. $(-3, -4), (1, 7), (8, 2)$
41. $(-3, 0), (2, 2), (0, 6)$
42. $(-3, 5), (-1, 9), (7, 9)$

In Exercises 43–46, find u · v, where θ is the angle between u and v.

43. $\|\mathbf{u}\| = 4, \|\mathbf{v}\| = 10, \theta = \frac{2\pi}{3}$
44. $\|\mathbf{u}\| = 100, \|\mathbf{v}\| = 250, \theta = \frac{\pi}{6}$
45. $\|\mathbf{u}\| = 9, \|\mathbf{v}\| = 36, \theta = \frac{3\pi}{4}$
46. $\|\mathbf{u}\| = 4, \|\mathbf{v}\| = 12, \theta = \frac{\pi}{3}$

In Exercises 47–52, determine whether u and v are orthogonal, parallel, or neither.

47. $\mathbf{u} = \langle -12, 30 \rangle$
$\mathbf{v} = \left\langle \frac{1}{2}, -\frac{5}{4} \right\rangle$

48. $\mathbf{u} = \langle 3, 15 \rangle$
$\mathbf{v} = \langle -1, 5 \rangle$

49. $\mathbf{u} = \frac{1}{4}(3\mathbf{i} - \mathbf{j})$
$\mathbf{v} = 5\mathbf{i} + 6\mathbf{j}$

50. $\mathbf{u} = \mathbf{i}$
$\mathbf{v} = -2\mathbf{i} + 2\mathbf{j}$

51. $\mathbf{u} = 2\mathbf{i} - 2\mathbf{j}$
$\mathbf{v} = -\mathbf{i} - \mathbf{j}$

52. $\mathbf{u} = \langle \cos\theta, \sin\theta \rangle$
$\mathbf{v} = \langle \sin\theta, -\cos\theta \rangle$

In Exercises 53–56, find the projection of u onto v. Then write u as the sum of two orthogonal vectors, one of which is $\text{proj}_{\mathbf{v}}\mathbf{u}$.

53. $\mathbf{u} = \langle 2, 2 \rangle$
$\mathbf{v} = \langle 6, 1 \rangle$

54. $\mathbf{u} = \langle 4, 2 \rangle$
$\mathbf{v} = \langle 1, -2 \rangle$

55. $\mathbf{u} = \langle 0, 3 \rangle$
$\mathbf{v} = \langle 2, 15 \rangle$

56. $\mathbf{u} = \langle -3, -2 \rangle$
$\mathbf{v} = \langle -4, -1 \rangle$

In Exercises 57 and 58, use the graph to determine mentally the projection of u onto v. (The coordinates of the terminal points of the vectors in standard position are given.) Use the formula for the projection of u onto v to verify your result.

57.

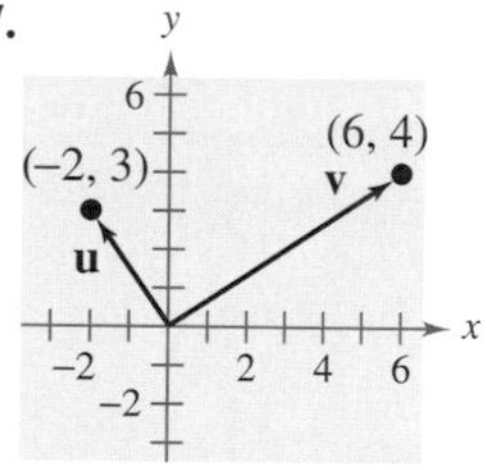

58.

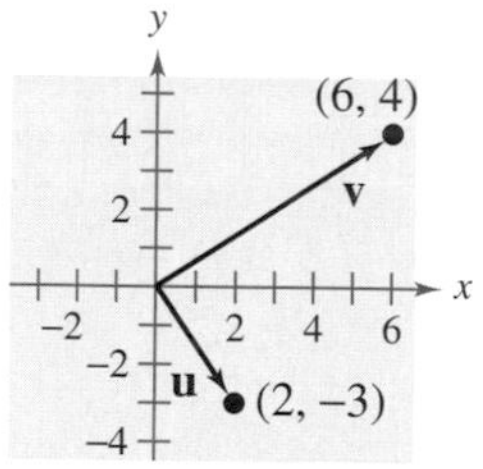

In Exercises 59–62, find two vectors in opposite directions that are orthogonal to the vector u. (There are many correct answers.)

59. $\mathbf{u} = \langle 3, 5 \rangle$

60. $\mathbf{u} = \langle -8, 3 \rangle$

61. $\mathbf{u} = \frac{1}{2}\mathbf{i} - \frac{2}{3}\mathbf{j}$

62. $\mathbf{u} - -\frac{5}{2}\mathbf{i} - 3\mathbf{j}$

Work **In Exercises 63 and 64, find the work done in moving a particle from *P* to *Q* if the magnitude and direction of the force are given by v.**

63. $P = (0, 0),\quad Q = (4, 7),\quad \mathbf{v} = \langle 1, 4 \rangle$

64. $P = (1, 3),\quad Q = (-3, 5),\quad \mathbf{v} = -2\mathbf{i} + 3\mathbf{j}$

65. ***Revenue*** The vector $\mathbf{u} = \langle 1650, 3200 \rangle$ gives the numbers of units of two types of baking pans produced by a company. The vector $\mathbf{v} = \langle 15.25, 10.50 \rangle$ gives the prices (in dollars) of the two types of pans, respectively.

(a) Find the dot product $\mathbf{u} \cdot \mathbf{v}$ and interpret the result in the context of the problem.

(b) Identify the vector operation used to increase the prices by 5%.

66. ***Revenue*** The vector $\mathbf{u} = \langle 3240, 2450 \rangle$ gives the numbers of hamburgers and hot dogs, respectively, sold at a fast-food stand in one month. The vector $\mathbf{v} = \langle 1.75, 1.25 \rangle$ gives the prices (in dollars) of the food items.

(a) Find the dot product $\mathbf{u} \cdot \mathbf{v}$ and interpret the result in the context of the problem.

(b) Identify the vector operation used to increase the prices by 2.5%.

Model It

67. ***Braking Load*** A truck with a gross weight of 30,000 pounds is parked on a slope of $d°$ (see figure). Assume that the only force to overcome is the force of gravity.

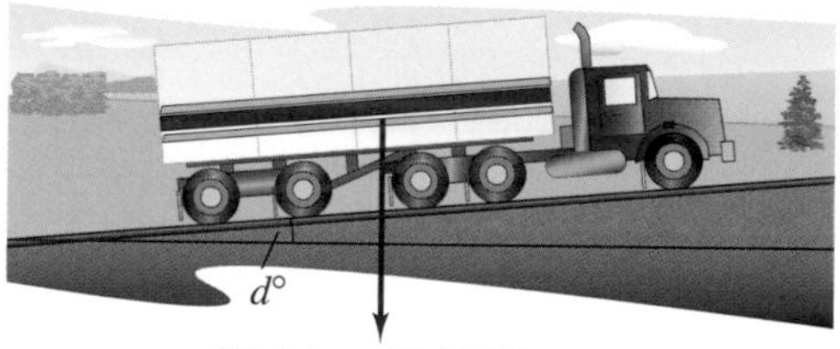

(a) Find the force required to keep the truck from rolling down the hill in terms of the slope *d*.

(b) Use a graphing utility to complete the table.

d	0°	1°	2°	3°	4°	5°
Force						

d	6°	7°	8°	9°	10°
Force					

(c) Find the force perpendicular to the hill when $d = 5°$.

68. ***Braking Load*** A sport utility vehicle with a gross weight of 5400 pounds is parked on a slope of 10°. Assume that the only force to overcome is the force of gravity. Find the force required to keep the vehicle from rolling down the hill. Find the force perpendicular to the hill.

69. ***Work*** Determine the work done by a person lifting a 25-kilogram (245-newton) bag of sugar.

70. ***Work*** Determine the work done by a crane lifting a 2400-pound car 5 feet.

71. ***Work*** A force of 45 pounds exerted at an angle of 30° above the horizontal is required to slide a table across a floor (see figure). The table is dragged 20 feet. Determine the work done in sliding the table.

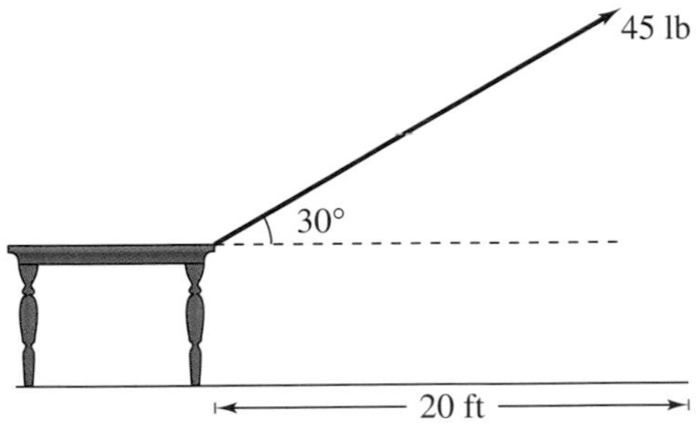

72. ***Work*** A tractor pulls a log 800 meters, and the tension in the cable connecting the tractor and log is approximately 1600 kilograms (15,691 newtons). The direction of the force is 35° above the horizontal. Approximate the work done in pulling the log.

73. ***Work*** One of the events in a local strongman contest is to pull a cement block 100 feet. One competitor pulls the block by exerting a force of 250 pounds on a rope attached to the block at an angle of 30° with the horizontal (see figure). Find the work done in pulling the block.

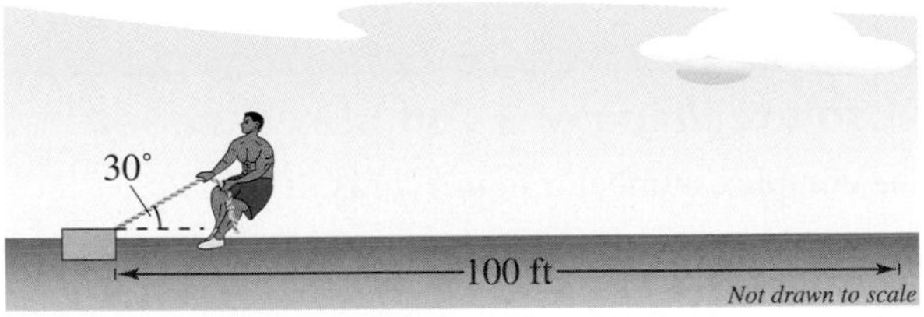

74. ***Work*** A toy wagon is pulled by exerting a force of 25 pounds on a handle that makes a 20° angle with the horizontal (see figure). Find the work done in pulling the wagon 50 feet.

Synthesis

True or False? **In Exercises 75 and 76, determine whether the statement is true or false. Justify your answer.**

75. The work W done by a constant force $\mathbf{F}$ acting along the line of motion of an object is represented by a vector.

76. A sliding door moves along the line of vector $\overrightarrow{PQ}$. If a force is applied to the door along a vector that is orthogonal to $\overrightarrow{PQ}$, then no work is done.

77. ***Think About It*** What is known about θ, the angle between two nonzero vectors $\mathbf{u}$ and $\mathbf{v}$, under each condition?

(a) $\mathbf{u} \cdot \mathbf{v} = 0$ (b) $\mathbf{u} \cdot \mathbf{v} > 0$ (c) $\mathbf{u} \cdot \mathbf{v} < 0$

78. ***Think About It*** What can be said about the vectors $\mathbf{u}$ and $\mathbf{v}$ under each condition?

(a) The projection of $\mathbf{u}$ onto $\mathbf{v}$ equals $\mathbf{u}$.

(b) The projection of $\mathbf{u}$ onto $\mathbf{v}$ equals $\mathbf{0}$.

79. ***Proof*** Use vectors to prove that the diagonals of a rhombus are perpendicular.

80. ***Proof*** Prove the following.

$$\|\mathbf{u} - \mathbf{v}\|^2 = \|\mathbf{u}\|^2 + \|\mathbf{v}\|^2 - 2\mathbf{u} \cdot \mathbf{v}$$

Skills Review

In Exercises 81–84, perform the operation and write the result in standard form.

81. $\sqrt{42} \cdot \sqrt{24}$

82. $\sqrt{18} \cdot \sqrt{112}$

83. $\sqrt{-3} \cdot \sqrt{-8}$

84. $\sqrt{-12} \cdot \sqrt{-96}$

In Exercises 85–88, find all solutions of the equation in the interval $[0, 2\pi)$.

85. $\sin 2x - \sqrt{3} \sin x = 0$

86. $\sin 2x + \sqrt{2} \cos x = 0$

87. $2 \tan x = \tan 2x$

88. $\cos 2x - 3 \sin x = 2$

In Exercises 89–92, find the exact value of the trigonometric function given that $\sin u = -\frac{12}{13}$ and $\cos v = \frac{24}{25}$. (Both u and v are in Quadrant IV.)

89. $\sin(u - v)$

90. $\sin(u + v)$

91. $\cos(v - u)$

92. $\tan(u - v)$

6.5 Trigonometric Form of a Complex Number

What you should learn

- Plot complex numbers in the complex plane and find absolute values of complex numbers.
- Write the trigonometric forms of complex numbers.
- Multiply and divide complex numbers written in trigonometric form.
- Use DeMoivre's Theorem to find powers of complex numbers.
- Find nth roots of complex numbers.

Why you should learn it

You can use the trigonometric form of a complex number to perform operations with complex numbers. For instance, in Exercises 105–112 on page 480, you can use the trigonometric forms of complex numbers to help you solve polynomial equations.

The Complex Plane

Just as real numbers can be represented by points on the real number line, you can represent a complex number

$$z = a + bi$$

as the point (a, b) in a coordinate plane (the **complex plane**). The horizontal axis is called the **real axis** and the vertical axis is called the **imaginary axis,** as shown in Figure 6.44.

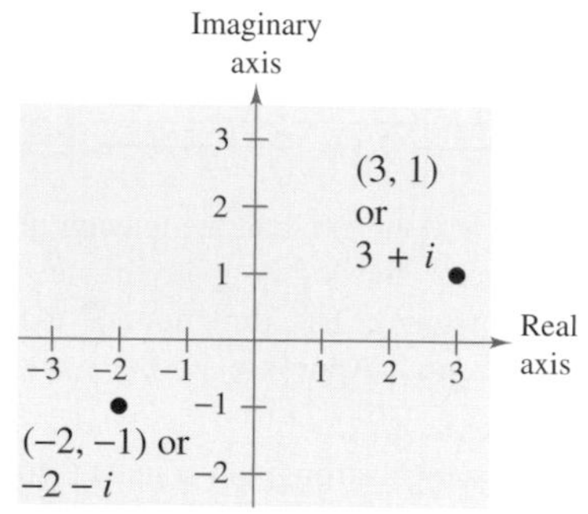

FIGURE 6.44

The **absolute value** of the complex number $a + bi$ is defined as the distance between the origin $(0, 0)$ and the point (a, b).

Definition of the Absolute Value of a Complex Number

The **absolute value** of the complex number $z = a + bi$ is

$$|a + bi| = \sqrt{a^2 + b^2}.$$

If the complex number $a + bi$ is a real number (that is, if $b = 0$), then this definition agrees with that given for the absolute value of a real number

$$|a + 0i| = \sqrt{a^2 + 0^2} = |a|.$$

Example 1 Finding the Absolute Value of a Complex Number

Plot $z = -2 + 5i$ and find its absolute value.

Solution

The number is plotted in Figure 6.45. It has an absolute value of

$$|z| = \sqrt{(-2)^2 + 5^2}$$
$$= \sqrt{29}.$$

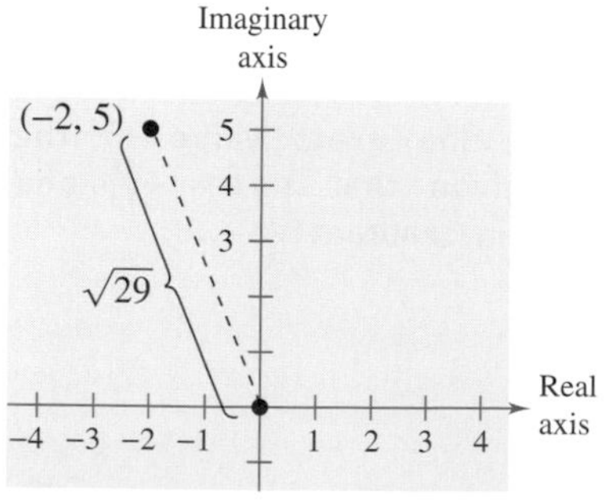

FIGURE 6.45

CHECKPOINT Now try Exercise 3.

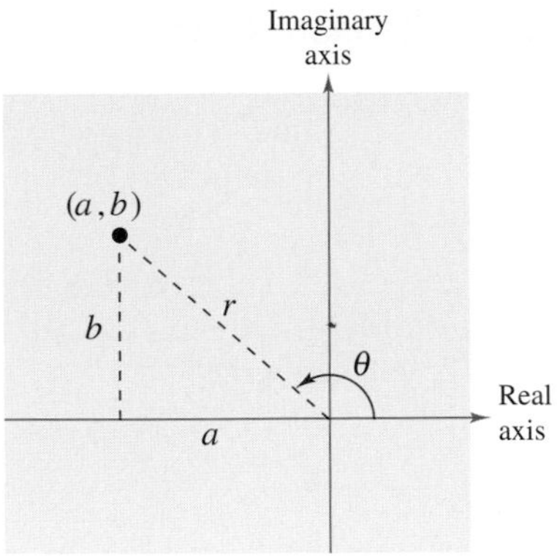

FIGURE 6.46

Trigonometric Form of a Complex Number

In Section 2.4, you learned how to add, subtract, multiply, and divide complex numbers. To work effectively with *powers* and *roots* of complex numbers, it is helpful to write complex numbers in trigonometric form. In Figure 6.46, consider the nonzero complex number $a + bi$. By letting θ be the angle from the positive real axis (measured counterclockwise) to the line segment connecting the origin and the point (a, b), you can write

$$a = r\cos\theta \qquad \text{and} \qquad b = r\sin\theta$$

where $r = \sqrt{a^2 + b^2}$. Consequently, you have

$$a + bi = (r\cos\theta) + (r\sin\theta)i$$

from which you can obtain the **trigonometric form of a complex number.**

Trigonometric Form of a Complex Number

The **trigonometric form** of the complex number $z = a + bi$ is

$$z = r(\cos\theta + i\sin\theta)$$

where $a = r\cos\theta$, $b = r\sin\theta$, $r = \sqrt{a^2 + b^2}$, and $\tan\theta = b/a$. The number r is the **modulus** of z, and θ is called an **argument** of z.

The trigonometric form of a complex number is also called the *polar form*. Because there are infinitely many choices for θ, the trigonometric form of a complex number is not unique. Normally, θ is restricted to the interval $0 \le \theta < 2\pi$, although on occasion it is convenient to use $\theta < 0$.

Example 2 Writing a Complex Number in Trigonometric Form

Write the complex number $z = -2 - 2\sqrt{3}i$ in trigonometric form.

Solution

The absolute value of z is

$$r = \left|-2 - 2\sqrt{3}i\right| = \sqrt{(-2)^2 + \left(-2\sqrt{3}\right)^2} = \sqrt{16} = 4$$

and the reference angle θ' is given by

$$\tan\theta' = \frac{b}{a} = \frac{-2\sqrt{3}}{-2} = \sqrt{3}.$$

Because $\tan(\pi/3) = \sqrt{3}$ and because $z = -2 - 2\sqrt{3}i$ lies in Quadrant III, you choose θ to be $\theta = \pi + \pi/3 = 4\pi/3$. So, the trigonometric form is

$$z = r(\cos\theta + i\sin\theta)$$

$$= 4\left(\cos\frac{4\pi}{3} + i\sin\frac{4\pi}{3}\right).$$

See Figure 6.47.

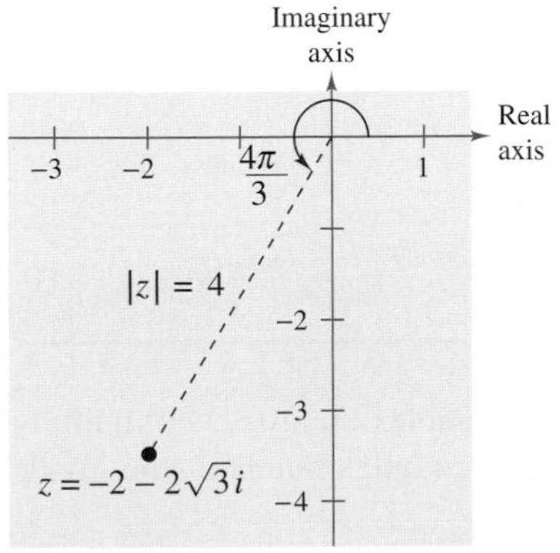

FIGURE 6.47

CHECKPOINT Now try Exercise 13.

Example 3 **Writing a Complex Number in Standard Form**

Write the complex number in standard form $a + bi$.

$$z = \sqrt{8}\left[\cos\left(-\frac{\pi}{3}\right) + i\sin\left(-\frac{\pi}{3}\right)\right]$$

Technology

A graphing utility can be used to convert a complex number in trigonometric (or polar) form to standard form. For specific keystrokes, see the user's manual for your graphing utility.

Solution

Because $\cos(-\pi/3) = \frac{1}{2}$ and $\sin(-\pi/3) = -\sqrt{3}/2$, you can write

$$z = \sqrt{8}\left[\cos\left(-\frac{\pi}{3}\right) + i\sin\left(-\frac{\pi}{3}\right)\right]$$

$$= 2\sqrt{2}\left(\frac{1}{2} - \frac{\sqrt{3}}{2}i\right)$$

$$= \sqrt{2} - \sqrt{6}i.$$

CHECKPOINT Now try Exercise 35.

Multiplication and Division of Complex Numbers

The trigonometric form adapts nicely to multiplication and division of complex numbers. Suppose you are given two complex numbers

$$z_1 = r_1(\cos\theta_1 + i\sin\theta_1) \qquad \text{and} \qquad z_2 = r_2(\cos\theta_2 + i\sin\theta_2).$$

The product of z_1 and z_2 is given by

$$z_1 z_2 = r_1 r_2(\cos\theta_1 + i\sin\theta_1)(\cos\theta_2 + i\sin\theta_2)$$

$$= r_1 r_2[(\cos\theta_1\cos\theta_2 - \sin\theta_1\sin\theta_2) + i(\sin\theta_1\cos\theta_2 + \cos\theta_1\sin\theta_2)].$$

Using the sum and difference formulas for cosine and sine, you can rewrite this equation as

$$z_1 z_2 = r_1 r_2[\cos(\theta_1 + \theta_2) + i\sin(\theta_1 + \theta_2)].$$

This establishes the first part of the following rule. The second part is left for you to verify (see Exercise 117).

Product and Quotient of Two Complex Numbers

Let $z_1 = r_1(\cos\theta_1 + i\sin\theta_1)$ and $z_2 = r_2(\cos\theta_2 + i\sin\theta_2)$ be complex numbers.

$$z_1 z_2 = r_1 r_2[\cos(\theta_1 + \theta_2) + i\sin(\theta_1 + \theta_2)] \qquad \text{Product}$$

$$\frac{z_1}{z_2} = \frac{r_1}{r_2}[\cos(\theta_1 - \theta_2) + i\sin(\theta_1 - \theta_2)], \quad z_2 \neq 0 \qquad \text{Quotient}$$

Note that this rule says that to *multiply* two complex numbers you multiply moduli and add arguments, whereas to *divide* two complex numbers you divide moduli and subtract arguments.

Example 4 Multiplying Complex Numbers

Find the product z_1z_2 of the complex numbers.

$$z_1 = 2\left(\cos\frac{2\pi}{3} + i\sin\frac{2\pi}{3}\right) \qquad z_2 = 8\left(\cos\frac{11\pi}{6} + i\sin\frac{11\pi}{6}\right)$$

Solution

$$z_1z_2 = 2\left(\cos\frac{2\pi}{3} + i\sin\frac{2\pi}{3}\right) \cdot 8\left(\cos\frac{11\pi}{6} + i\sin\frac{11\pi}{6}\right)$$

$$= 16\left[\cos\left(\frac{2\pi}{3} + \frac{11\pi}{6}\right) + i\sin\left(\frac{2\pi}{3} + \frac{11\pi}{6}\right)\right] \quad \text{Multiply moduli and add arguments.}$$

$$= 16\left(\cos\frac{5\pi}{2} + i\sin\frac{5\pi}{2}\right)$$

$$= 16\left(\cos\frac{\pi}{2} + i\sin\frac{\pi}{2}\right)$$

$$= 16[0 + i(1)]$$

$$= 16i$$

You can check this result by first converting the complex numbers to thc standard forms $z_1 = -1 + \sqrt{3}i$ and $z_2 = 4\sqrt{3} - 4i$ and then multiplying algebraically, as in Section 2.4.

$$z_1z_2 = \left(-1 + \sqrt{3}i\right)\left(4\sqrt{3} - 4i\right)$$

$$= -4\sqrt{3} + 4i + 12i + 4\sqrt{3}$$

$$= 16i$$

CHECKPOINT Now try Exercise 47.

Technology

Some graphing utilities can multiply and divide complex numbers in trigonometric form. If you have access to such a graphing utility, use it to find z_1z_2 and z_1/z_2 in Examples 4 and 5.

Example 5 Dividing Complex Numbers

Find the quotient z_1/z_2 of the complex numbers.

$$z_1 = 24(\cos 300° + i\sin 300°) \qquad z_2 = 8(\cos 75° + i\sin 75°)$$

Solution

$$\frac{z_1}{z_2} = \frac{24(\cos 300° + i\sin 300°)}{8(\cos 75° + i\sin 75°)}$$

$$= \frac{24}{8}[\cos(300° - 75°) + i\sin(300° - 75°)] \quad \text{Divide moduli and subtract arguments.}$$

$$= 3(\cos 225° + i\sin 225°)$$

$$= 3\left[\left(-\frac{\sqrt{2}}{2}\right) + i\left(-\frac{\sqrt{2}}{2}\right)\right]$$

$$= -\frac{3\sqrt{2}}{2} - \frac{3\sqrt{2}}{2}i$$

CHECKPOINT Now try Exercise 53.

Powers of Complex Numbers

The trigonometric form of a complex number is used to raise a complex number to a power. To accomplish this, consider repeated use of the multiplication rule.

$$z = r(\cos \theta + i \sin \theta)$$

$$z^2 = r(\cos \theta + i \sin \theta)r(\cos \theta + i \sin \theta) = r^2(\cos 2\theta + i \sin 2\theta)$$

$$z^3 = r^2(\cos 2\theta + i \sin 2\theta)r(\cos \theta + i \sin \theta) = r^3(\cos 3\theta + i \sin 3\theta)$$

$$z^4 = r^4(\cos 4\theta + i \sin 4\theta)$$

$$z^5 = r^5(\cos 5\theta + i \sin 5\theta)$$

$$\vdots$$

This pattern leads to DeMoivre's Theorem, which is named after the French mathematician Abraham DeMoivre (1667–1754).

The Granger Collection

Historical Note

Abraham DeMoivre (1667–1754) is remembered for his work in probability theory and DeMoivre's Theorem. His book *The Doctrine of Chances* (published in 1718) includes the theory of recurring series and the theory of partial fractions.

DeMoivre's Theorem

If $z = r(\cos \theta + i \sin \theta)$ is a complex number and n is a positive integer, then

$$z^n = [r(\cos \theta + i \sin \theta)]^n$$
$$= r^n(\cos n\theta + i \sin n\theta).$$

Example 6 Finding Powers of a Complex Number

Use DeMoivre's Theorem to find $(-1 + \sqrt{3}i)^{12}$.

Solution

First convert the complex number to trigonometric form using

$$r = \sqrt{(-1)^2 + (\sqrt{3})^2} = 2 \text{ and } \theta = \arctan \frac{\sqrt{3}}{-1} = \frac{2\pi}{3}.$$

So, the trigonometric form is

$$z = -1 + \sqrt{3}i = 2\left(\cos \frac{2\pi}{3} + i \sin \frac{2\pi}{3}\right).$$

Then, by DeMoivre's Theorem, you have

$$(-1 + \sqrt{3}i)^{12} = \left[2\left(\cos \frac{2\pi}{3} + i \sin \frac{2\pi}{3}\right)\right]^{12}$$

$$= 2^{12}\left[\cos \frac{12(2\pi)}{3} + i \sin \frac{12(2\pi)}{3}\right]$$

$$= 4096(\cos 8\pi + i \sin 8\pi)$$

$$= 4096(1 + 0)$$

$$= 4096.$$

CHECKPOINT Now try Exercise 75.

Roots of Complex Numbers

Recall that a consequence of the Fundamental Theorem of Algebra is that a polynomial equation of degree n has n solutions in the complex number system. So, the equation $x^6 = 1$ has six solutions, and in this particular case you can find the six solutions by factoring and using the Quadratic Formula.

$$\begin{aligned} x^6 - 1 &= (x^3 - 1)(x^3 + 1) \\ &= (x - 1)(x^2 + x + 1)(x + 1)(x^2 - x + 1) = 0 \end{aligned}$$

Consequently, the solutions are

$$x = \pm 1, \qquad x = \frac{-1 \pm \sqrt{3}i}{2}, \qquad \text{and} \qquad x = \frac{1 \pm \sqrt{3}i}{2}.$$

Each of these numbers is a sixth root of 1. In general, the ***n*th root of a complex number** is defined as follows.

Definition of the *n*th Root of a Complex Number

The complex number $u = a + bi$ is an ***n*th root** of the complex number z if

$$z = u^n = (a + bi)^n.$$

Exploration

The nth roots of a complex number are useful for solving some polynomial equations. For instance, explain how you can use DeMoivre's Theorem to solve the polynomial equation

$$x^4 + 16 = 0.$$

[*Hint:* Write -16 as $16(\cos \pi + i \sin \pi)$.]

To find a formula for an nth root of a complex number, let u be an nth root of z, where

$$u = s(\cos \beta + i \sin \beta)$$

and

$$z = r(\cos \theta + i \sin \theta).$$

By DeMoivre's Theorem and the fact that $u^n = z$, you have

$$s^n(\cos n\beta + i \sin n\beta) = r(\cos \theta + i \sin \theta).$$

Taking the absolute value of each side of this equation, it follows that $s^n = r$. Substituting back into the previous equation and dividing by r, you get

$$\cos n\beta + i \sin n\beta = \cos \theta + i \sin \theta.$$

So, it follows that

$$\cos n\beta = \cos \theta \qquad \text{and} \qquad \sin n\beta = \sin \theta.$$

Because both sine and cosine have a period of 2π, these last two equations have solutions if and only if the angles differ by a multiple of 2π. Consequently, there must exist an integer k such that

$$\begin{aligned} n\beta &= \theta + 2\pi k \\ \beta &= \frac{\theta + 2\pi k}{n}. \end{aligned}$$

By substituting this value of β into the trigonometric form of u, you get the result stated on the following page.

Finding *n*th Roots of a Complex Number

For a positive integer n, the complex number $z = r(\cos\theta + i\sin\theta)$ has exactly n distinct nth roots given by

$$\sqrt[n]{r}\left(\cos\frac{\theta + 2\pi k}{n} + i\sin\frac{\theta + 2\pi k}{n}\right)$$

where $k = 0, 1, 2, \ldots, n - 1$.

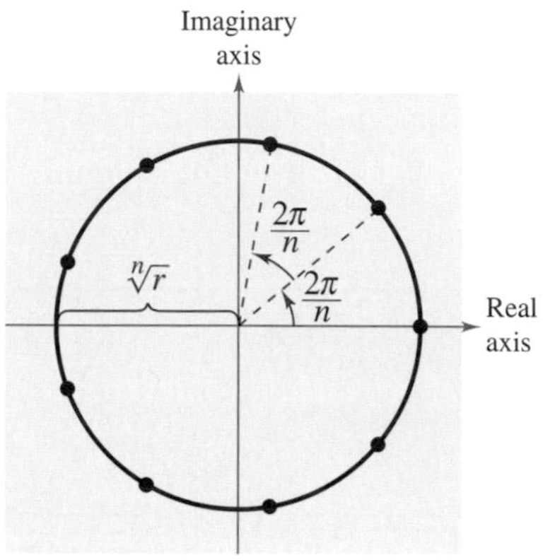

FIGURE 6.48

When k exceeds $n - 1$, the roots begin to repeat. For instance, if $k = n$, the angle

$$\frac{\theta + 2\pi n}{n} = \frac{\theta}{n} + 2\pi$$

is coterminal with θ/n, which is also obtained when $k = 0$.

The formula for the nth roots of a complex number z has a nice geometrical interpretation, as shown in Figure 6.48. Note that because the nth roots of z all have the same magnitude $\sqrt[n]{r}$, they all lie on a circle of radius $\sqrt[n]{r}$ with center at the origin. Furthermore, because successive nth roots have arguments that differ by $2\pi/n$, the n roots are equally spaced around the circle.

You have already found the sixth roots of 1 by factoring and by using the Quadratic Formula. Example 7 shows how you can solve the same problem with the formula for nth roots.

Example 7 Finding the *n*th Roots of a Real Number

Find all the sixth roots of 1.

Solution

First write 1 in the trigonometric form $1 = 1(\cos 0 + i\sin 0)$. Then, by the nth root formula, with $n = 6$ and $r = 1$, the roots have the form

$$\sqrt[6]{1}\left(\cos\frac{0 + 2\pi k}{6} + i\sin\frac{0 + 2\pi k}{6}\right) = \cos\frac{\pi k}{3} + i\sin\frac{\pi k}{3}.$$

So, for $k = 0, 1, 2, 3, 4,$ and 5, the sixth roots are as follows. (See Figure 6.49.)

$$\cos 0 + i\sin 0 = 1$$

$$\cos\frac{\pi}{3} + i\sin\frac{\pi}{3} = \frac{1}{2} + \frac{\sqrt{3}}{2}i$$

Increment by $\frac{2\pi}{n} = \frac{2\pi}{6} = \frac{\pi}{3}$

$$\cos\frac{2\pi}{3} + i\sin\frac{2\pi}{3} = -\frac{1}{2} + \frac{\sqrt{3}}{2}i$$

$$\cos\pi + i\sin\pi = -1$$

$$\cos\frac{4\pi}{3} + i\sin\frac{4\pi}{3} = -\frac{1}{2} - \frac{\sqrt{3}}{2}i$$

$$\cos\frac{5\pi}{3} + i\sin\frac{5\pi}{3} = \frac{1}{2} - \frac{\sqrt{3}}{2}i$$

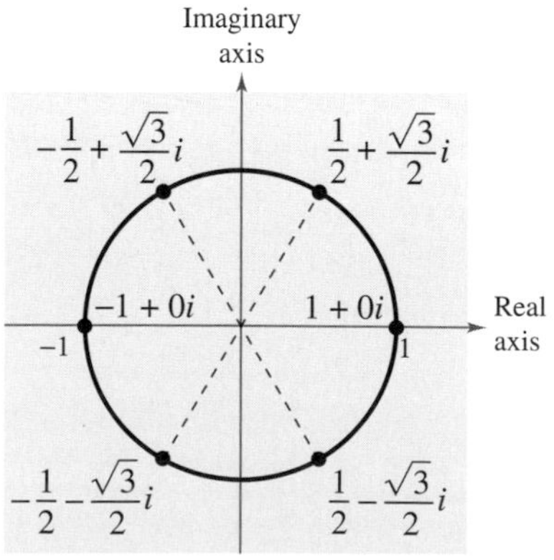

FIGURE 6.49

CHECKPOINT Now try Exercise 97.

In Figure 8.49, notice that the roots obtained in Example 7 all have a magnitude of 1 and are equally spaced around the unit circle. Also notice that the complex roots occur in conjugate pairs, as discussed in Section 2.5. The n distinct nth roots of 1 are called the ***n*th roots of unity.**

Example 8 Finding the *n*th Roots of a Complex Number

Find the three cube roots of $z = -2 + 2i$.

Solution

Because z lies in Quadrant II, the trigonometric form of z is

$$z = -2 + 2i$$
$$= \sqrt{8}\,(\cos 135° + i \sin 135°). \qquad \theta = \arctan(2/-2) = 135°$$

By the formula for nth roots, the cube roots have the form

$$\sqrt[6]{8}\left(\cos \frac{135° + 360°k}{3} + i \sin \frac{135° + 360°k}{3}\right).$$

Finally, for $k = 0, 1,$ and 2, you obtain the roots

$$\sqrt[6]{8}\left(\cos \frac{135° + 360°(0)}{3} + i \sin \frac{135° + 360°(0)}{3}\right) = \sqrt{2}(\cos 45° + i \sin 45°)$$
$$= 1 + i$$

$$\sqrt[6]{8}\left(\cos \frac{135° + 360°(1)}{3} + i \sin \frac{135° + 360°(1)}{3}\right) = \sqrt{2}(\cos 165° + i \sin 165°)$$
$$\approx -1.3660 + 0.3660i$$

$$\sqrt[6]{8}\left(\cos \frac{135° + 360°(2)}{3} + i \sin \frac{135° + 360°(2)}{3}\right) = \sqrt{2}(\cos 285° + i \sin 285°)$$
$$\approx 0.3660 - 1.3660i.$$

See Figure 6.50.

CHECKPOINT Now try Exercise 103.

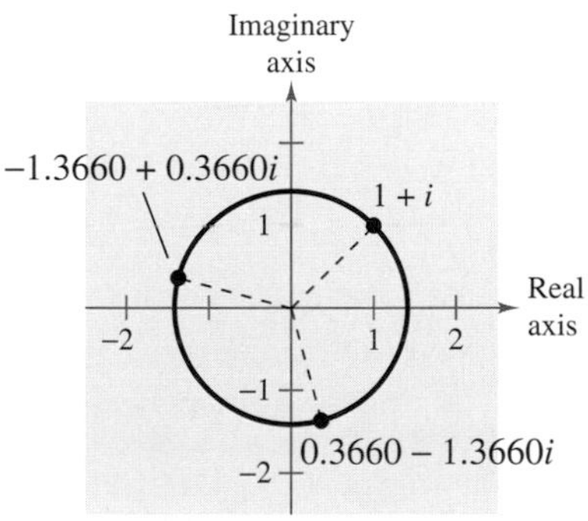

FIGURE 6.50

STUDY TIP

Note in Example 8 that the absolute value of z is

$$r = |-2 + 2i|$$
$$= \sqrt{(-2)^2 + 2^2}$$
$$= \sqrt{8}$$

and the angle θ is given by

$$\tan \theta = \frac{b}{a} = \frac{2}{-2} = -1.$$

WRITING ABOUT MATHEMATICS

A Famous Mathematical Formula The famous formula

$$e^{a+bi} = e^a(\cos b + i \sin b)$$

is called Euler's Formula, after the Swiss mathematician Leonhard Euler (1707–1783). Although the interpretation of this formula is beyond the scope of this text, we decided to include it because it gives rise to one of the most wonderful equations in mathematics.

$$e^{\pi i} + 1 = 0$$

This elegant equation relates the five most famous numbers in mathematics—0, 1, π, e, and i—in a single equation. Show how Euler's Formula can be used to derive this equation.

6.5 Exercises

VOCABULARY CHECK: Fill in the blanks.

1. The ________ ________ of a complex number $a + bi$ is the distance between the origin $(0, 0)$ and the point (a, b).
2. The ________ ________ of a complex number $z = a + bi$ is given by $z = r(\cos \theta + i \sin \theta)$, where r is the ________ of z and θ is the ________ of z.
3. ________ Theorem states that if $z = r(\cos \theta + i \sin \theta)$ is a complex number and n is a positive integer, then $z^n = r^n(\cos n\theta + i \sin n\theta)$.
4. The complex number $u = a + bi$ is an ________ ________ of the complex number z if $z = u^n = (a + bi)^n$.

In Exercises 1–6, plot the complex number and find its absolute value.

1. $-7i$
2. -7
3. $-4 + 4i$
4. $5 - 12i$
5. $6 - 7i$
6. $-8 + 3i$

In Exercises 7–10, write the complex number in trigonometric form.

7.
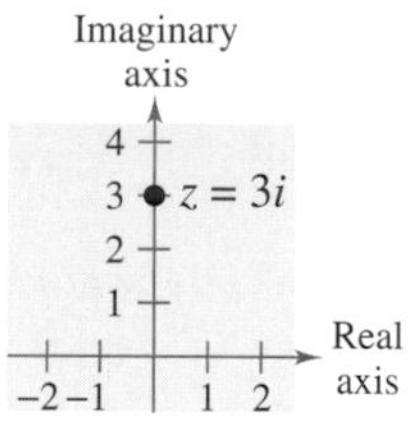

8.
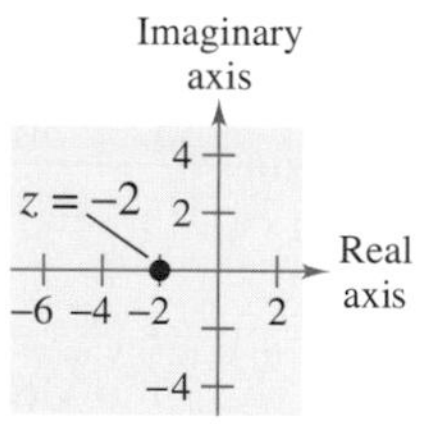

9.
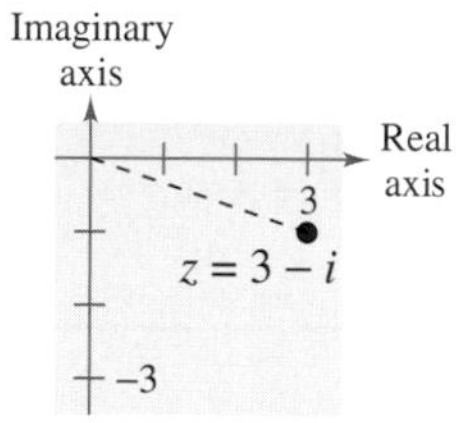

10.
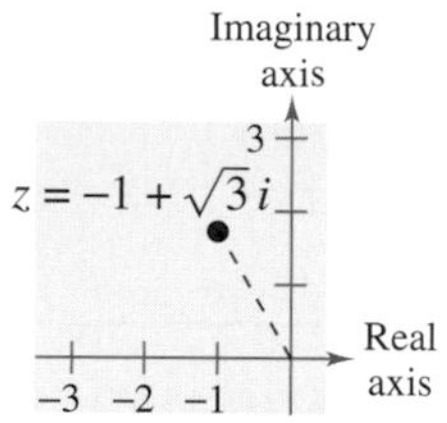

In Exercises 11–30, represent the complex number graphically, and find the trigonometric form of the number.

11. $3 - 3i$
12. $2 + 2i$
13. $\sqrt{3} + i$
14. $4 - 4\sqrt{3}i$
15. $-2(1 + \sqrt{3}i)$
16. $\frac{5}{2}(\sqrt{3} - i)$
17. $-5i$
18. $4i$
19. $-7 + 4i$
20. $3 - i$
21. 7
22. 4
23. $3 + \sqrt{3}i$
24. $2\sqrt{2} - i$
25. $-3 - i$
26. $1 + 3i$
27. $5 + 2i$
28. $8 + 3i$
29. $-8 - 5\sqrt{3}i$
30. $-9 - 2\sqrt{10}i$

In Exercises 31–40, represent the complex number graphically, and find the standard form of the number.

31. $3(\cos 120° + i \sin 120°)$
32. $5(\cos 135° + i \sin 135°)$
33. $\frac{3}{2}(\cos 300° + i \sin 300°)$
34. $\frac{1}{4}(\cos 225° + i \sin 225°)$
35. $3.75\left(\cos \frac{3\pi}{4} + i \sin \frac{3\pi}{4}\right)$
36. $6\left(\cos \frac{5\pi}{12} + i \sin \frac{5\pi}{12}\right)$
37. $8\left(\cos \frac{\pi}{2} + i \sin \frac{\pi}{2}\right)$
38. $7(\cos 0 + i \sin 0)$
39. $3[\cos(18° 45') + i \sin(18° 45')]$
40. $6[\cos(230° 30') + i \sin(230° 30')]$

In Exercises 41–44, use a graphing utility to represent the complex number in standard form.

41. $5\left(\cos \frac{\pi}{9} + i \sin \frac{\pi}{9}\right)$
42. $10\left(\cos \frac{2\pi}{5} + i \sin \frac{2\pi}{5}\right)$
43. $3(\cos 165.5° + i \sin 165.5°)$
44. $9(\cos 58° + i \sin 58°)$

In Exercises 45 and 46, represent the powers z, z^2, z^3, and z^4 graphically. Describe the pattern.

45. $z = \frac{\sqrt{2}}{2}(1 + i)$
46. $z = \frac{1}{2}(1 + \sqrt{3}i)$

In Exercises 47–58, perform the operation and leave the result in trigonometric form.

47. $\left[2\left(\cos\frac{\pi}{4} + i\sin\frac{\pi}{4}\right)\right]\left[6\left(\cos\frac{\pi}{12} + i\sin\frac{\pi}{12}\right)\right]$

48. $\left[\frac{3}{4}\left(\cos\frac{\pi}{3} + i\sin\frac{\pi}{3}\right)\right]\left[4\left(\cos\frac{3\pi}{4} + i\sin\frac{3\pi}{4}\right)\right]$

49. $\left[\frac{5}{3}(\cos 140° + i\sin 140°)\right]\left[\frac{2}{3}(\cos 60° + i\sin 60°)\right]$

50. $[0.5(\cos 100° + i\sin 100°)] \times [0.8(\cos 300° + i\sin 300°)]$

51. $[0.45(\cos 310° + i\sin 310°)] \times [0.60(\cos 200° + i\sin 200°)]$

52. $(\cos 5° + i\sin 5°)(\cos 20° + i\sin 20°)$

53. $\dfrac{\cos 50° + i\sin 50°}{\cos 20° + i\sin 20°}$

54. $\dfrac{2(\cos 120° + i\sin 120°)}{4(\cos 40° + i\sin 40°)}$

55. $\dfrac{\cos(5\pi/3) + i\sin(5\pi/3)}{\cos\pi + i\sin\pi}$

56. $\dfrac{5(\cos 4.3 + i\sin 4.3)}{4(\cos 2.1 + i\sin 2.1)}$

57. $\dfrac{12(\cos 52° + i\sin 52°)}{3(\cos 110° + i\sin 110°)}$

58. $\dfrac{6(\cos 40° + i\sin 40°)}{7(\cos 100° + i\sin 100°)}$

In Exercises 59–66, (a) write the trigonometric forms of the complex numbers, (b) perform the indicated operation using the trigonometric forms, and (c) perform the indicated operation using the standard forms, and check your result with that of part (b).

59. $(2 + 2i)(1 - i)$

60. $(\sqrt{3} + i)(1 + i)$

61. $-2i(1 + i)$

62. $4(1 - \sqrt{3}i)$

63. $\dfrac{3 + 4i}{1 - \sqrt{3}i}$

64. $\dfrac{1 + \sqrt{3}i}{6 - 3i}$

65. $\dfrac{5}{2 + 3i}$

66. $\dfrac{4i}{-4 + 2i}$

In Exercises 67–70, sketch the graph of all complex numbers z satisfying the given condition.

67. $|z| = 2$

68. $|z| = 3$

69. $\theta = \dfrac{\pi}{6}$

70. $\theta = \dfrac{5\pi}{4}$

In Exercises 71–88, use DeMoivre's Theorem to find the indicated power of the complex number. Write the result in standard form.

71. $(1 + i)^5$

72. $(2 + 2i)^6$

73. $(-1 + i)^{10}$

74. $(3 - 2i)^8$

75. $2(\sqrt{3} + i)^7$

76. $4(1 - \sqrt{3}i)^3$

77. $[5(\cos 20° + i\sin 20°)]^3$

78. $[3(\cos 150° + i\sin 150°)]^4$

79. $\left(\cos\frac{\pi}{4} + i\sin\frac{\pi}{4}\right)^{12}$

80. $\left[2\left(\cos\frac{\pi}{2} + i\sin\frac{\pi}{2}\right)\right]^8$

81. $[5(\cos 3.2 + i\sin 3.2)]^4$

82. $(\cos 0 + i\sin 0)^{20}$

83. $(3 - 2i)^5$

84. $(\sqrt{5} - 4i)^3$

85. $[3(\cos 15° + i\sin 15°)]^4$

86. $[2(\cos 10° + i\sin 10°)]^8$

87. $\left[2\left(\cos\frac{\pi}{10} + i\sin\frac{\pi}{10}\right)\right]^5$

88. $\left[2\left(\cos\frac{\pi}{8} + i\sin\frac{\pi}{8}\right)\right]^6$

In Exercises 89–104, (a) use the theorem on page 476 to find the indicated roots of the complex number, (b) represent each of the roots graphically, and (c) write each of the roots in standard form.

89. Square roots of $5(\cos 120° + i\sin 120°)$

90. Square roots of $16(\cos 60° + i\sin 60°)$

91. Cube roots of $8\left(\cos\frac{2\pi}{3} + i\sin\frac{2\pi}{3}\right)$

92. Fifth roots of $32\left(\cos\frac{5\pi}{6} + i\sin\frac{5\pi}{6}\right)$

93. Square roots of $-25i$

94. Fourth roots of $625i$

95. Cube roots of $-\frac{125}{2}(1 + \sqrt{3}i)$

96. Cube roots of $-4\sqrt{2}(1 - i)$

97. Fourth roots of 16

98. Fourth roots of i

99. Fifth roots of 1

100. Cube roots of 1000

101. Cube roots of -125

102. Fourth roots of -4

103. Fifth roots of $128(-1 + i)$

104. Sixth roots of $64i$

In Exercises 105–112, use the theorem on page 476 to find all the solutions of the equation and represent the solutions graphically.

105. $x^4 + i = 0$

106. $x^3 + 1 = 0$

107. $x^5 + 243 = 0$

108. $x^3 - 27 = 0$

109. $x^4 + 16i = 0$

110. $x^6 + 64i = 0$

111. $x^3 - (1 - i) = 0$

112. $x^4 + (1 + i) = 0$

Synthesis

True or False? **In Exercises 113–116, determine whether the statement is true or false. Justify your answer.**

113. Although the square of the complex number bi is given by $(bi)^2 = -b^2$, the absolute value of the complex number $z = a + bi$ is defined as

$$|a + bi| = \sqrt{a^2 + b^2}.$$

114. Geometrically, the nth roots of any complex number z are all equally spaced around the unit circle centered at the origin.

115. The product of two complex numbers

$$z_1 = r_1(\cos \theta_1 + i \sin \theta_1)$$

and

$$z_2 = r_2(\cos \theta_2 + i \sin \theta_2).$$

is zero only when $r_1 = 0$ and/or $r_2 = 0$.

116. By DeMoivre's Theorem,

$$\left(4 + \sqrt{6}i\right)^8 = \cos(32) + i \sin\left(8\sqrt{6}\right).$$

117. Given two complex numbers $z_1 = r_1(\cos \theta_1 + i \sin \theta_1)$ and $z_2 = r_2(\cos \theta_2 + i \sin \theta_2)$, $z_2 \neq 0$, show that

$$\frac{z_1}{z_2} = \frac{r_1}{r_2}[\cos(\theta_1 - \theta_2) + i \sin(\theta_1 - \theta_2)].$$

118. Show that $\bar{z} = r[\cos(-\theta) + i \sin(-\theta)]$ is the complex conjugate of $z = r(\cos \theta + i \sin \theta)$.

119. Use the trigonometric forms of z and $\bar{z}$ in Exercise 118 to find (a) $z\bar{z}$ and (b) $z/\bar{z}$, $\bar{z} \neq 0$.

120. Show that the negative of $z = r(\cos \theta + i \sin \theta)$ is $-z = r[\cos(\theta + \pi) + i \sin(\theta + \pi)]$.

121. Show that $-\frac{1}{2}\left(1 + \sqrt{3}i\right)$ is a sixth root of 1.

122. Show that $2^{-1/4}(1 - i)$ is a fourth root of -2.

Graphical Reasoning **In Exercises 123 and 124, use the graph of the roots of a complex number.**

(a) Write each of the roots in trigonometric form.

(b) Identify the complex number whose roots are given.

(c) Use a graphing utility to verify the results of part (b).

123.

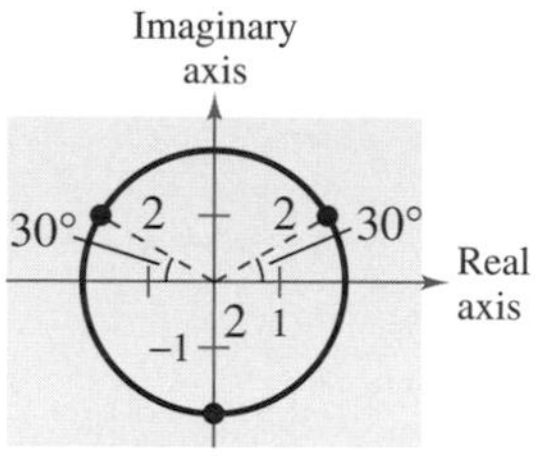

124.

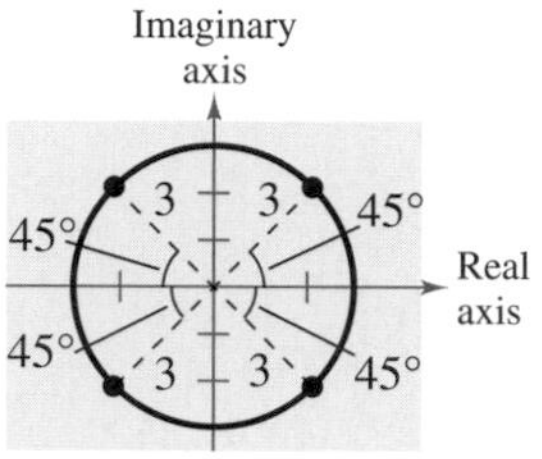

Skills Review

In Exercises 125–130, solve the right triangle shown in the figure. Round your answers to two decimal places.

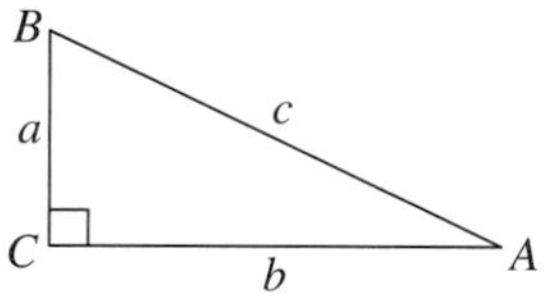

125. $A = 22°$, $a = 8$

126. $B = 66°$, $a = 33.5$

127. $A = 30°$, $b = 112.6$

128. $B = 6°$, $b = 211.2$

129. $A = 42° 15'$, $c = 11.2$

130. $B = 81° 30'$, $c = 6.8$

Harmonic Motion **In Exercises 131–134, for the simple harmonic motion described by the trigonometric function, find the maximum displacement and the least positive value of *t* for which *d* = 0.**

131. $d = 16 \cos \frac{\pi}{4}t$

132. $d = \frac{1}{8} \cos 12\pi t$

133. $d = \frac{1}{16} \sin \frac{5}{4}\pi t$

134. $d = \frac{1}{12} \sin 60\pi t$

In Exercises 135 and 136, write the product as a sum or difference.

135. $6 \sin 8\theta \cos 3\theta$

136. $2 \cos 5\theta \sin 2\theta$

6 Chapter Summary

What did you learn?

Section 6.1	Review Exercises
☐ Use the Law of Sines to solve oblique triangles (AAS, ASA, or SSA) *(p. 430, 432).*	1–12
☐ Find areas of oblique triangles *(p. 434).*	13–16
☐ Use the Law of Sines to model and solve real-life problems *(p. 435).*	17–20
Section 6.2	
☐ Use the Law of Cosines to solve oblique triangles (SSS or SAS) *(p. 439).*	21–28
☐ Use the Law of Cosines to model and solve real-life problems *(p. 441).*	29–32
☐ Use Heron's Area Formula to find areas of triangles *(p. 442).*	33–36
Section 6.3	
☐ Represent vectors as directed line segments *(p. 447).*	37, 38
☐ Write the component forms of vectors *(p. 448).*	39–44
☐ Perform basic vector operations and represent vectors graphically *(p. 449).*	45–56
☐ Write vectors as linear combinations of unit vectors *(p. 451).*	57–62
☐ Find the direction angles of vectors *(p. 453).*	63–68
☐ Use vectors to model and solve real-life problems *(p. 454).*	69–72
Section 6.4	
☐ Find the dot product of two vectors and use the properties of the dot product *(p. 460).*	73–80
☐ Find the angle between two vectors and determine whether two vectors are orthogonal *(p. 461).*	81–88
☐ Write vectors as sums of two vector components *(p. 463).*	89–92
☐ Use vectors to find the work done by a force *(p. 466).*	93–96
Section 6.5	
☐ Plot complex numbers in the complex plane and find absolute values of complex numbers *(p. 470).*	97–100
☐ Write the trigonometric forms of complex numbers *(p. 471).*	101–104
☐ Multiply and divide complex numbers written in trigonometric form *(p. 472).*	105, 106
☐ Use DeMoivre's Theorem to find powers of complex numbers *(p. 474)*	107–110
☐ Find *n*th roots of complex numbers *(p. 475).*	111–118

6 Review Exercises

6.1 In Exercises 1–12, use the Law of Sines to solve (if possible) the triangle. If two solutions exist, find both. Round your answers to two decimal places.

1.

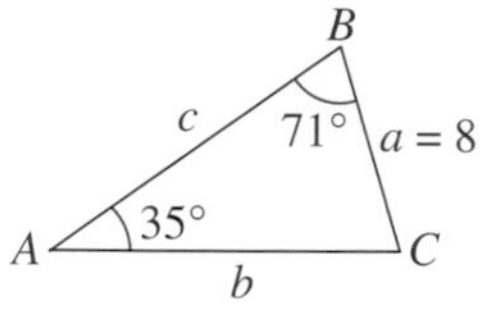

2.

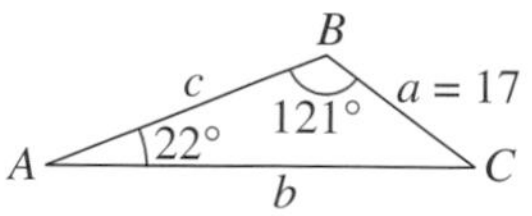

3. $B = 72°,\ C = 82°,\ b = 54$

4. $B = 10°,\ C = 20°,\ c = 33$

5. $A = 16°,\ B = 98°,\ c = 8.4$

6. $A = 95°,\ B = 45°,\ c = 104.8$

7. $A = 24°,\ C = 48°,\ b = 27.5$

8. $B = 64°,\ C = 36°,\ a = 367$

9. $B = 150°,\ b = 30,\ c = 10$

10. $B = 150°,\ a = 10,\ b = 3$

11. $A = 75°,\ a = 51.2,\ b = 33.7$

12. $B = 25°,\ a = 6.2,\ b = 4$

In Exercises 13–16, find the area of the triangle having the indicated angle and sides.

13. $A = 27°,\ b = 5,\ c = 7$

14. $B = 80°,\ a = 4,\ c = 8$

15. $C = 123°,\ a = 16,\ b = 5$

16. $A = 11°,\ b = 22,\ c = 21$

17. ***Height*** From a certain distance, the angle of elevation to the top of a building is 17°. At a point 50 meters closer to the building, the angle of elevation is 31°. Approximate the height of the building.

18. ***Geometry*** Find the length of the side w of the parallelogram.

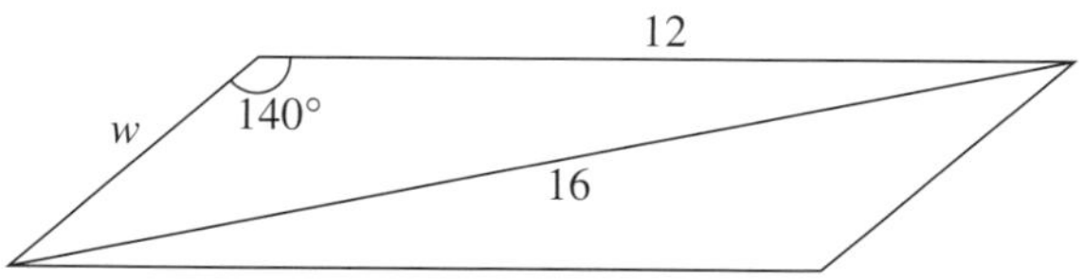

19. ***Height*** A tree stands on a hillside of slope 28° from the horizontal. From a point 75 feet down the hill, the angle of elevation to the top of the tree is 45° (see figure). Find the height of the tree.

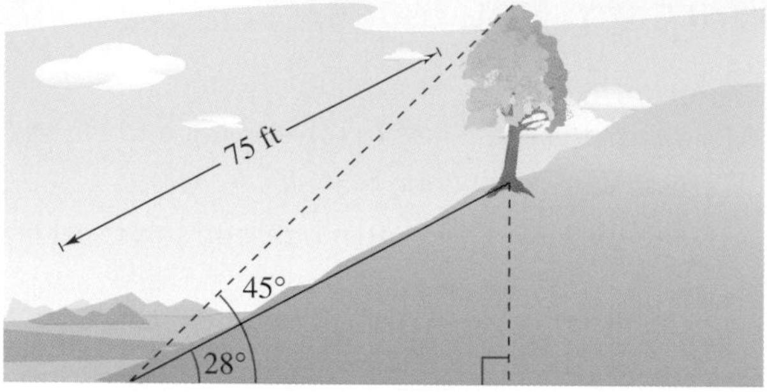

FIGURE FOR 19

20. ***River Width*** A surveyor finds that a tree on the opposite bank of a river, flowing due east, has a bearing of N 22° 30′ E from a certain point and a bearing of N 15° W from a point 400 feet downstream. Find the width of the river.

6.2 In Exercises 21–28, use the Law of Cosines to solve the triangle. Round your answers to two decimal places.

21. $a = 5,\ b = 8,\ c = 10$

22. $a = 80,\ b = 60,\ c = 100$

23. $a = 2.5,\ b = 5.0,\ c = 4.5$

24. $a = 16.4,\ b = 8.8,\ c = 12.2$

25. $B = 110°,\ a = 4,\ c = 4$

26. $B = 150°,\ a = 10,\ c = 20$

27. $C = 43°,\ a = 22.5,\ b = 31.4$

28. $A = 62°,\ b = 11.34,\ c = 19.52$

29. ***Geometry*** The lengths of the diagonals of a parallelogram are 10 feet and 16 feet. Find the lengths of the sides of the parallelogram if the diagonals intersect at an angle of 28°.

30. ***Geometry*** The lengths of the diagonals of a parallelogram are 30 meters and 40 meters. Find the lengths of the sides of the parallelogram if the diagonals intersect at an angle of 34°.

31. ***Surveying*** To approximate the length of a marsh, a surveyor walks 425 meters from point A to point B. Then the surveyor turns 65° and walks 300 meters to point C (see figure). Approximate the length AC of the marsh.

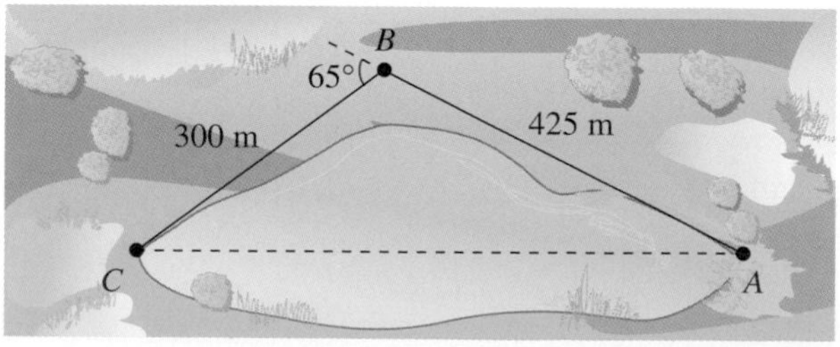

32. ***Navigation*** Two planes leave Raleigh-Durham Airport at approximately the same time. One is flying 425 miles per hour at a bearing of 355°, and the other is flying 530 miles per hour at a bearing of 67°. Draw a figure that gives a visual representation of the problem and determine the distance between the planes after they have flown for 2 hours.

In Exercises 33–36, use Heron's Area Formula to find the area of the triangle.

33. $a = 4,\ b = 5,\ c = 7$
34. $a = 15,\ b = 8,\ c = 10$
35. $a = 12.3,\ b = 15.8,\ c = 3.7$
36. $a = 38.1,\ b = 26.7,\ c = 19.4$

6.3 In Exercises 37 and 38, show that $\mathbf{u} = \mathbf{v}$.

37.

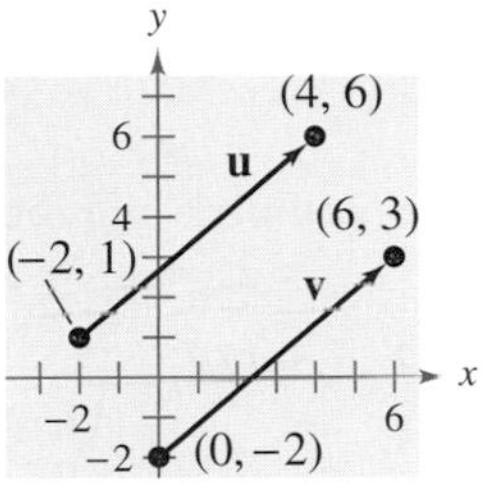

38.

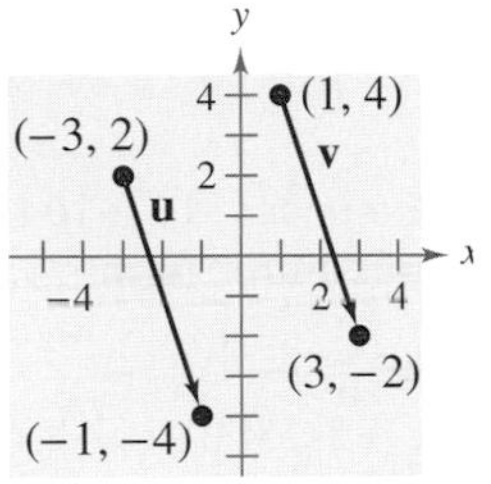

In Exercises 39–44, find the component form of the vector v satisfying the conditions.

39.

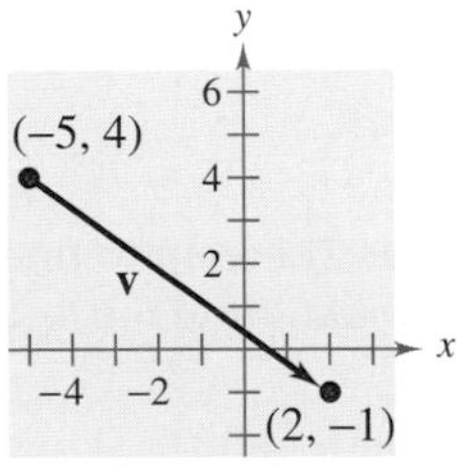

40.

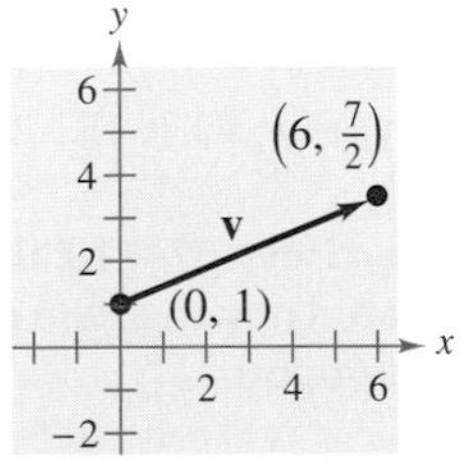

41. Initial point: (0, 10); terminal point: (7, 3)
42. Initial point: (1, 5); terminal point: (15, 9)
43. $\|\mathbf{v}\| = 8,\quad \theta = 120°$
44. $\|\mathbf{v}\| = \frac{1}{2},\quad \theta = 225°$

In Exercises 45–52, find (a) $\mathbf{u} + \mathbf{v}$, (b) $\mathbf{u} - \mathbf{v}$, (c) $3\mathbf{u}$, and (d) $2\mathbf{v} + 5\mathbf{u}$.

45. $\mathbf{u} = \langle -1, -3\rangle, \mathbf{v} = \langle -3, 6\rangle$
46. $\mathbf{u} = \langle 4, 5\rangle, \mathbf{v} = \langle 0, -1\rangle$
47. $\mathbf{u} = \langle -5, 2\rangle, \mathbf{v} = \langle 4, 4\rangle$
48. $\mathbf{u} = \langle 1, -8\rangle, \mathbf{v} = \langle 3, -2\rangle$
49. $\mathbf{u} = 2\mathbf{i} - \mathbf{j}, \mathbf{v} = 5\mathbf{i} + 3\mathbf{j}$
50. $\mathbf{u} = -7\mathbf{i} - 3\mathbf{j}, \mathbf{v} = 4\mathbf{i} - \mathbf{j}$
51. $\mathbf{u} = 4\mathbf{i}, \mathbf{v} = -\mathbf{i} + 6\mathbf{j}$
52. $\mathbf{u} = -6\mathbf{j}, \mathbf{v} = \mathbf{i} + \mathbf{j}$

In Exercises 53–56, find the component form of w and sketch the specified vector operations geometrically, where $\mathbf{u} = 6\mathbf{i} - 5\mathbf{j}$ and $\mathbf{v} = 1 - \mathbf{i} + 3\mathbf{j}$.

53. $\mathbf{w} = 2\mathbf{u} + \mathbf{v}$
54. $\mathbf{w} = 4\mathbf{u} - 5\mathbf{v}$
55. $\mathbf{w} = 3\mathbf{v}$
56. $\mathbf{w} = \frac{1}{2}\mathbf{v}$

In Exercises 57–60, write vector u as a linear combination of the standard unit vectors i and j.

57. $\mathbf{u} = \langle -3, 4\rangle$
58. $\mathbf{u} = \langle -6, -8\rangle$
59. $\mathbf{u}$ has initial point (3, 4) and terminal point (9, 8).
60. $\mathbf{u}$ has initial point (−2, 7) and terminal point (5, −9).

In Exercises 61 and 62, write the vector v in the form $\|\mathbf{v}\|(\cos\theta\mathbf{i} + \sin\theta\mathbf{j})$.

61. $\mathbf{v} = -10\mathbf{i} + 10\mathbf{j}$
62. $\mathbf{v} = 4\mathbf{i} - \mathbf{j}$

In Exercises 63–68, find the magnitude and the direction angle of the vector v.

63. $\mathbf{v} = 7(\cos 60°\mathbf{i} + \sin 60°\mathbf{j})$
64. $\mathbf{v} = 3(\cos 150°\mathbf{i} + \sin 150°\mathbf{j})$
65. $\mathbf{v} = 5\mathbf{i} + 4\mathbf{j}$
66. $\mathbf{v} = -4\mathbf{i} + 7\mathbf{j}$
67. $\mathbf{v} = -3\mathbf{i} - 3\mathbf{j}$
68. $\mathbf{v} = 8\mathbf{i} - \mathbf{j}$

69. ***Resultant Force*** Forces with magnitudes of 85 pounds and 50 pounds act on a single point. The angle between the forces is 15°. Describe the resultant force.

70. ***Rope Tension*** A 180-pound weight is supported by two ropes, as shown in the figure. Find the tension in each rope.

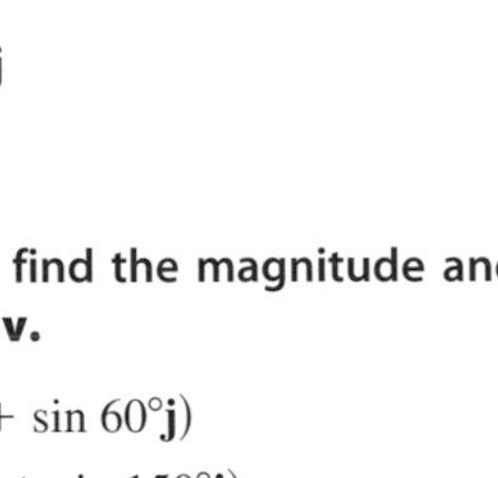

71. ***Navigation*** An airplane has an airspeed of 430 miles per hour at a bearing of 135°. The wind velocity is 35 miles per hour in the direction of N 30° E. Find the resultant speed and direction of the airplane.

72. ***Navigation*** An airplane has an airspeed of 724 kilometers per hour at a bearing of 30°. The wind velocity is 32 kilometers per hour from the west. Find the resultant speed and direction of the airplane.

6.4 **In Exercises 73–76, find the dot product of u. and v.**

73. $\mathbf{u} = \langle 6, 7 \rangle$, $\mathbf{v} = \langle -3, 9 \rangle$

74. $\mathbf{u} = \langle -7, 12 \rangle$, $\mathbf{v} = \langle -4, -14 \rangle$

75. $\mathbf{u} = 3\mathbf{i} + 7\mathbf{j}$, $\mathbf{v} = 11\mathbf{i} - 5\mathbf{j}$

76. $\mathbf{u} = -7\mathbf{i} + 2\mathbf{j}$, $\mathbf{v} = 16\mathbf{i} - 12\mathbf{j}$

In Exercises 77–80, use the vectors u = $\langle -3, 4 \rangle$ and v = $\langle 2, 1 \rangle$ to find the indicated quantity. State whether the result is a vector or a scalar.

77. $2\mathbf{u} \cdot \mathbf{u}$

78. $\|\mathbf{v}\|^2$

79. $\mathbf{u}(\mathbf{u} \cdot \mathbf{v})$

80. $3\mathbf{u} \cdot \mathbf{v}$

In Exercises 81–84, find the angle θ between the vectors.

81. $\mathbf{u} = \cos \frac{7\pi}{4}\mathbf{i} + \sin \frac{7\pi}{4}\mathbf{j}$

$\mathbf{v} = \cos \frac{5\pi}{6}\mathbf{i} + \sin \frac{5\pi}{6}\mathbf{j}$

82. $\mathbf{u} = \cos 45°\mathbf{i} + \sin 45°\mathbf{j}$

$\mathbf{v} = \cos 300°\mathbf{i} + \sin 300°\mathbf{j}$

83. $\mathbf{u} = \langle 2\sqrt{2}, -4 \rangle$, $\mathbf{v} = \langle -\sqrt{2}, 1 \rangle$

84. $\mathbf{u} = \langle 3, \sqrt{3} \rangle$, $\mathbf{v} = \langle 4, 3\sqrt{3} \rangle$

In Exercises 85–88, determine whether u and v are orthogonal, parallel, or neither.

85. $\mathbf{u} = \langle -3, 8 \rangle$, $\mathbf{v} = \langle 8, 3 \rangle$

86. $\mathbf{u} = \langle \frac{1}{4}, -\frac{1}{2} \rangle$, $\mathbf{v} = \langle -2, 4 \rangle$

87. $\mathbf{u} = -\mathbf{i}$, $\mathbf{v} = \mathbf{i} + 2\mathbf{j}$

88. $\mathbf{u} = -2\mathbf{i} + \mathbf{j}$, $\mathbf{v} = 3\mathbf{i} + 6\mathbf{j}$

In Exercises 89–92, find the projection of u onto v. Then write u as the sum of two orthogonal vectors, one of which is $\text{proj}_{\mathbf{v}}\mathbf{u}$.

89. $\mathbf{u} = \langle -4, 3 \rangle$, $\mathbf{v} = \langle -8, -2 \rangle$

90. $\mathbf{u} = \langle 5, 6 \rangle$, $\mathbf{v} = \langle 10, 0 \rangle$

91. $\mathbf{u} = \langle 2, 7 \rangle$, $\mathbf{v} = \langle 1, -1 \rangle$

92. $\mathbf{u} = \langle -3, 5 \rangle$, $\mathbf{v} = \langle -5, 2 \rangle$

Work **In Exercises 93 and 94, find the work done in moving a particle from P to Q if the magnitude and direction of the force are given by v.**

93. $P = (5, 3)$, $Q = (8, 9)$, $\mathbf{v} = \langle 2, 7 \rangle$

94. $P = (-2, -9)$, $Q = (-12, 8)$, $\mathbf{v} = 3\mathbf{i} - 6\mathbf{j}$

95. ***Work*** Determine the work done by a crane lifting an 18,000-pound truck 48 inches.

96. ***Work*** A mover exerts a horizontal force of 25 pounds on a crate as it is pushed up a ramp that is 12 feet long and inclined at an angle of 20° above the horizontal. Find the work done in pushing the crate.

6.5 **In Exercises 97–100, plot the complex number and find its absolute value.**

97. $7i$

98. $-6i$

99. $5 + 3i$

100. $-10 - 4i$

In Exercises 101–104, write the complex number in trigonometric form.

101. $5 - 5i$

102. $5 + 12i$

103. $-3\sqrt{3} + 3i$

104. -7

In Exercises 105 and 106, (a) write the two complex numbers in trigonometric form, and (b) use the trigonometric forms to find z_1z_2 and z_1/z_2, where $z_2 \neq 0$.

105. $z_1 = 2\sqrt{3} - 2i$, $z_2 = -10i$

106. $z_1 = -3(1 + i)$, $z_2 = 2(\sqrt{3} + i)$

In Exercises 107–110, use DeMoivre's Theorem to find the indicated power of the complex number. Write the result in standard form.

107. $\left[5\left(\cos \frac{\pi}{12} + i \sin \frac{\pi}{12}\right)\right]^4$

108. $\left[2\left(\cos \frac{4\pi}{15} + i \sin \frac{4\pi}{15}\right)\right]^5$

109. $(2 + 3i)^6$

110. $(1 - i)^8$

In Exercises 111–114, (a) use the theorem on page 476 to find the indicated roots of the complex number, (b) represent each of the roots graphically, and (c) write each of the roots in standard form.

111. Sixth roots of $-729i$

112. Fourth roots of $256i$

113. Cube roots of 8

114. Fifth roots of -1024

In Exercises 115–118, use the theorem on page 476 to find all solutions of the equation and represent the solutions graphically.

115. $x^4 + 81 = 0$

116. $x^5 - 32 = 0$

117. $x^3 + 8i = 0$

118. $(x^3 - 1)(x^2 + 1) = 0$

Synthesis

True or False? **In Exercises 119–123, determine whether the statement is true or false. Justify your answer.**

119. The Law of Sines is true if one of the angles in the triangle is a right angle.

120. When the Law of Sines is used, the solution is always unique.

121. If $\mathbf{u}$ is a unit vector in the direction of $\mathbf{v}$, then $\mathbf{v} = \|\mathbf{v}\|\,\mathbf{u}$.

122. If $\mathbf{v} = a\mathbf{i} + b\mathbf{j} = \mathbf{0}$, then $a = -b$.

123. $x = \sqrt{3} + i$ is a solution of the equation $x^2 - 8i = 0$.

124. State the Law of Sines from memory.

125. State the Law of Cosines from memory.

126. What characterizes a vector in the plane?

127. Which vectors in the figure appear to be equivalent?

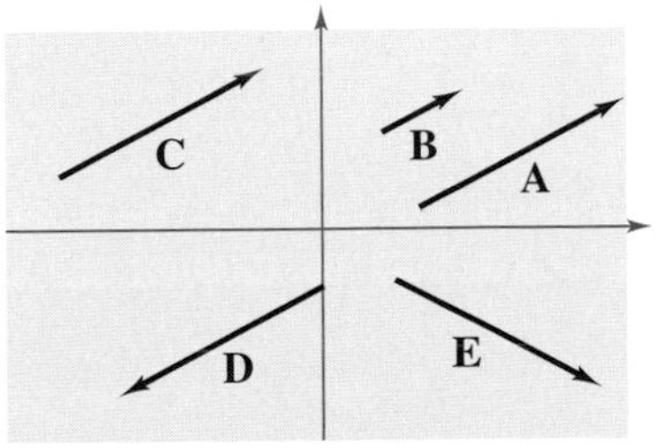

128. The vectors $\mathbf{u}$ and $\mathbf{v}$ have the same magnitudes in the two figures. In which figure will the magnitude of the sum be greater? Give a reason for your answer.

(a)

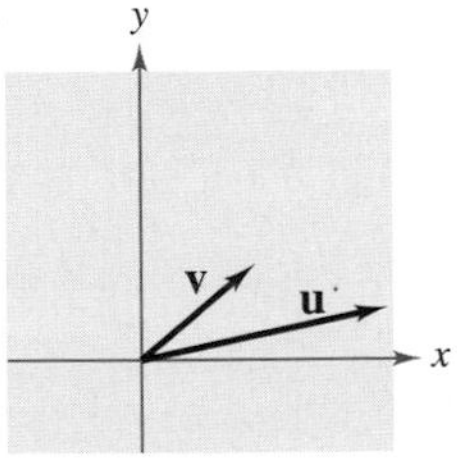

(b)

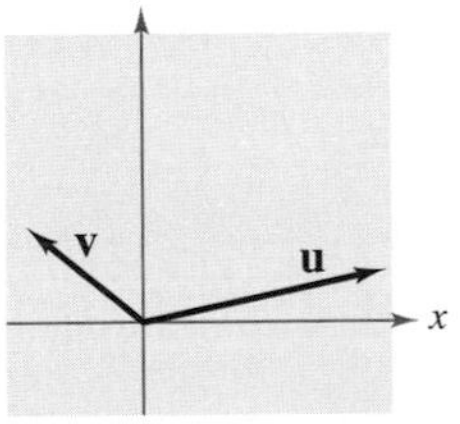

129. Give a geometric description of the scalar multiple $k\mathbf{u}$ of the vector $\mathbf{u}$, for $k > 0$ and for $k < 0$.

130. Give a geometric description of the sum of the vectors $\mathbf{u}$ and $\mathbf{v}$.

Graphical Reasoning **In Exercises 131 and 132, use the graph of the roots of a complex number.**

(a) Write each of the roots in trigonometric form.

(b) Identify the complex number whose roots are given.

(c) Use a graphing utility to verify the results of part (b).

131.

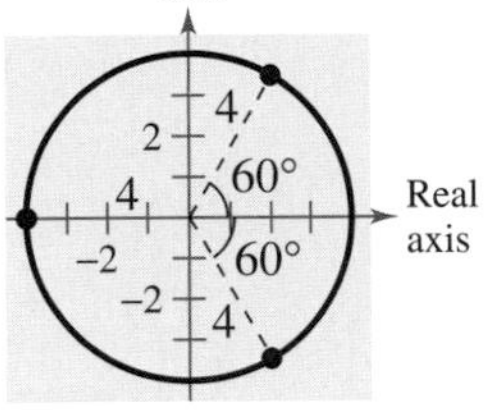

132.

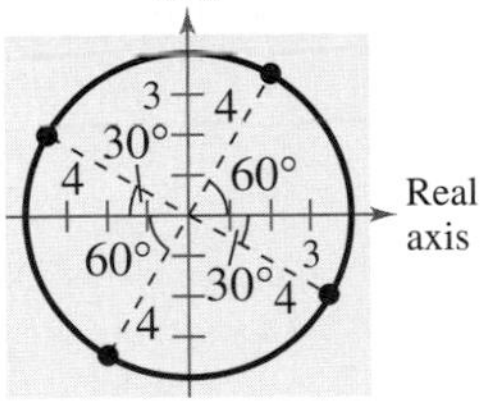

133. The figure shows z_1 and z_2. Describe $z_1 z_2$ and z_1/z_2.

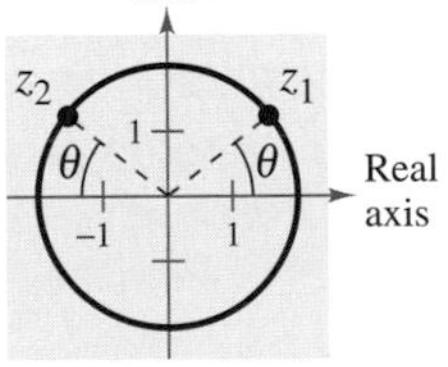

134. One of the fourth roots of a complex number z is shown in the figure.

(a) How many roots are not shown?

(b) Describe the other roots.

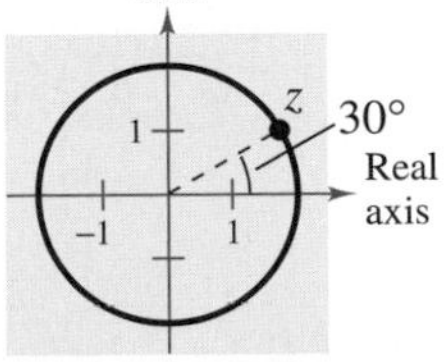

6 Chapter Test

Take this test as you would take a test in class. When you are finished, check your work against the answers given in the back of the book.

In Exercises 1–6, use the information to solve the triangle. If two solutions exist, find both solutions. Round your answers to two decimal places.

1. $A = 24°,\ B = 68°,\ a = 12.2$
2. $B = 104°,\ C = 33°,\ a = 18.1$
3. $A = 24°,\ a = 11.2,\ b = 13.4$
4. $a = 4.0,\ b = 7.3,\ c = 12.4$
5. $B = 100°,\ a = 15,\ b = 23$
6. $C = 123°,\ a = 41,\ b = 57$
7. A triangular parcel of land has borders of lengths 60 meters, 70 meters, and 82 meters. Find the area of the parcel of land.
8. An airplane flies 370 miles from point A to point B with a bearing of 24°. It then flies 240 miles from point B to point C with a bearing of 37° (see figure). Find the distance and bearing from point A to point C.

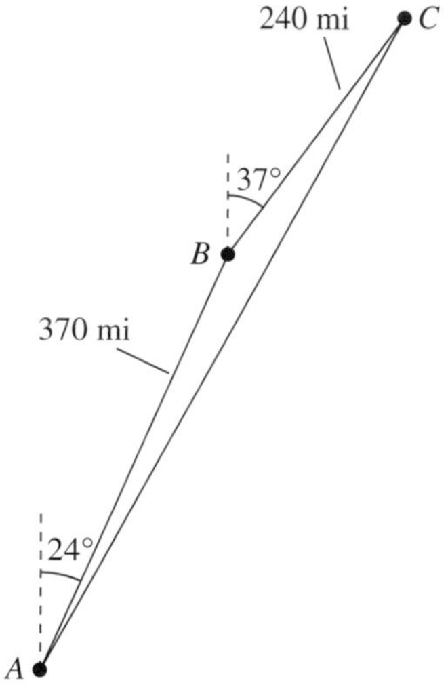

FIGURE FOR 8

In Exercises 9 and 10, find the component form of the vector v satisfying the given conditions.

9. Initial point of $\mathbf{v}$: $(-3, 7)$; terminal point of $\mathbf{v}$: $(11, -16)$
10. Magnitude of $\mathbf{v}$: $\|\mathbf{v}\| = 12$; direction of $\mathbf{v}$: $\mathbf{u} = \langle 3, -5\rangle$

In Exercises 11–13, $\mathbf{u} = \langle 3, 5\rangle$ and $\mathbf{v} = \langle -7, 1\rangle$. Find the resultant vector and sketch its graph.

11. $\mathbf{u} + \mathbf{v}$
12. $\mathbf{u} - \mathbf{v}$
13. $5\mathbf{u} - 3\mathbf{v}$
14. Find a unit vector in the direction of $\mathbf{u} = \langle 4, -3\rangle$.
15. Forces with magnitudes of 250 pounds and 130 pounds act on an object at angles of 45° and −60°, respectively, with the x-axis. Find the direction and magnitude of the resultant of these forces.
16. Find the angle between the vectors $\mathbf{u} = \langle -1, 5\rangle$ and $\mathbf{v} = \langle 3, -2\rangle$.
17. Are the vectors $\mathbf{u} = \langle 6, 10\rangle$ and $\mathbf{v} = \langle 2, 3\rangle$ orthogonal?
18. Find the projection of $\mathbf{u} = \langle 6, 7\rangle$ onto $\mathbf{v} = \langle -5, -1\rangle$. Then write $\mathbf{u}$ as the sum of two orthogonal vectors.
19. A 500-pound motorcycle is headed up a hill inclined at 12°. What force is required to keep the motorcycle from rolling down the hill when stopped at a red light?
20. Write the complex number $z = 5 - 5i$ in trigonometric form.
21. Write the complex number $z = 6(\cos 120° + i \sin 120°)$ in standard form.

In Exercises 22 and 23, use DeMoivre's Theorem to find the indicated power of the complex number. Write the result in standard form.

22. $\left[3\left(\cos \frac{7\pi}{6} + i \sin \frac{7\pi}{6}\right)\right]^8$
23. $(3 - 3i)^6$
24. Find the fourth roots of $256(1 + \sqrt{3}i)$.
25. Find all solutions of the equation $x^3 - 27i = 0$ and represent the solutions graphically.

6 Cumulative Test for Chapter 4–6

Take this test to review the material from earlier chapters. When you are finished, check your work against the answers given in the back of the book.

1. Consider the angle $\theta = -120°$.

(a) Sketch the angle in standard position.

(b) Determine a coterminal angle in the interval $[0°, 360°)$.

(c) Convert the angle to radian measure.

(d) Find the reference angle θ'.

(e) Find the exact values of the six trigonometric functions of θ.

2. Convert the angle $\theta = 2.35$ radians to degrees. Round the answer to one decimal place.

3. Find $\cos \theta$ if $\tan \theta = -\frac{4}{3}$ and $\sin \theta < 0$.

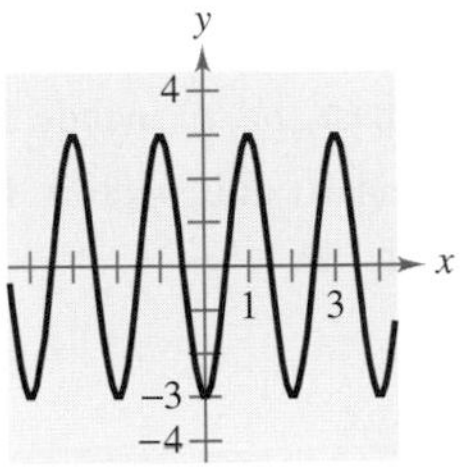

FIGURE FOR 7

In Exercises 4–6, sketch the graph of the function. (Include two full periods.)

4. $f(x) = 3 - 2 \sin \pi x$ **5.** $g(x) = \dfrac{1}{2} \tan\left(x - \dfrac{\pi}{2}\right)$ **6.** $h(x) = -\sec(x + \pi)$

7. Find a, b, and c such that the graph of the function $h(x) = a \cos(bx + c)$ matches the graph in the figure.

8. Sketch the graph of the function $f(x) = \frac{1}{2}x \sin x$ over the interval $-3\pi \le x \le 3\pi$.

In Exercises 9 and 10, find the exact value of the expression without using a calculator.

9. $\tan(\arctan 6.7)$ **10.** $\tan\left(\arcsin \frac{3}{5}\right)$

11. Write an algebraic expression equivalent to $\sin(\arccos 2x)$.

12. Use the fundamental identities to simplify: $\cos\left(\dfrac{\pi}{2} - x\right) \csc x$.

13. Subtract and simplify: $\dfrac{\sin \theta - 1}{\cos \theta} - \dfrac{\cos \theta}{\sin \theta - 1}$.

In Exercises 14–16, verify the identity.

14. $\cot^2 \alpha(\sec^2 \alpha - 1) = 1$

15. $\sin(x + y) \sin(x - y) = \sin^2 x - \sin^2 y$

16. $\sin^2 x \cos^2 x = \frac{1}{8}(1 - \cos 4x)$

In Exercises 17 and 18, find all solutions of the equation in the interval $[0, 2\pi)$.

17. $2 \cos^2 \beta - \cos \beta = 0$

18. $3 \tan \theta - \cot \theta = 0$

19. Use the Quadratic Formula to solve the equation in the interval $[0, 2\pi)$: $\sin^2 x + 2 \sin x + 1 = 0$.

20. Given that $\sin u = \frac{12}{13}$, $\cos v = \frac{3}{5}$, and angles u and v are both in Quadrant I, find $\tan(u - v)$.

21. If $\tan \theta = \frac{1}{2}$, find the exact value of $\tan(2\theta)$.

22. If $\tan \theta = \frac{4}{3}$, find the exact value of $\sin \frac{\theta}{2}$.

23. Write the product $5 \sin \frac{3\pi}{4} \cdot \cos \frac{7\pi}{4}$ as a sum or difference.

24. Write $\cos 8x + \cos 4x$ as a product.

In Exercises 25–28, use the information to solve the triangle shown in the figure. Round your answers to two decimal places.

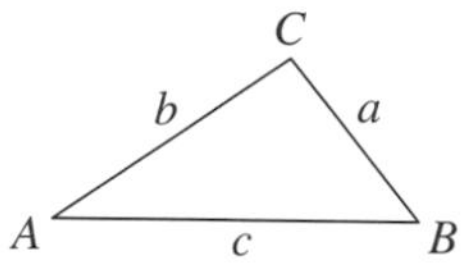

FIGURE FOR 25–28

25. $A = 30°, \ a = 9, \ b = 8$

26. $A = 30°, b = 8, \ c = 10$

27. $A = 30°, \ C = 90°, \ b = 10$

28. $a = 4, \ b = 8, \ c = 9$

29. Two sides of a triangle have lengths 7 inches and 12 inches. Their included angle measures 60°. Find the area of the triangle.

30. Find the area of a triangle with sides of lengths 11 inches, 16 inches, and 17 inches.

31. Write the vector $\mathbf{u} = \langle 3, 5 \rangle$ as a linear combination of the standard unit vectors $\mathbf{i}$ and $\mathbf{j}$.

32. Find a unit vector in the direction of $\mathbf{v} = \mathbf{i} + \mathbf{j}$.

33. Find $\mathbf{u} \cdot \mathbf{v}$ for $\mathbf{u} = 3\mathbf{i} + 4\mathbf{j}$ and $\mathbf{v} = \mathbf{i} - 2\mathbf{j}$.

34. Find the projection of $\mathbf{u} = \langle 8, -2 \rangle$ onto $\mathbf{v} = \langle 1, 5 \rangle$. Then write $\mathbf{u}$ as the sum of two orthogonal vectors.

35. Write the complex number $-2 + 2i$ in trigonometric form.

36. Find the product of $[4(\cos 30° + i \sin 30°)][6(\cos 120° + i \sin 120°)]$. Write the answer in standard form.

37. Find the three cube roots of 1.

38. Find all the solutions of the equation $x^5 + 243 = 0$.

39. A ceiling fan with 21-inch blades makes 63 revolutions per minute. Find the angular speed of the fan in radians per minute. Find the linear speed of the tips of the blades in inches per minute.

40. Find the area of the sector of a circle with a radius of 8 yards and a central angle of 114°.

41. From a point 200 feet from a flagpole, the angles of elevation to the bottom and top of the flag are 16° 45′ and 18°, respectively. Approximate the height of the flag to the nearest foot.

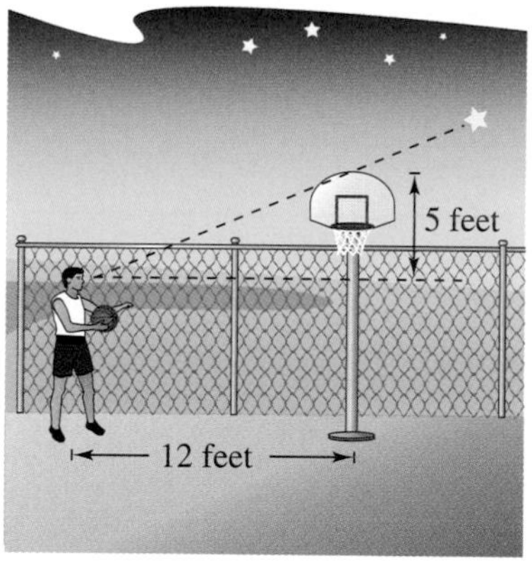

FIGURE FOR 42

42. To determine the angle of elevation of a star in the sky, you get the star in your line of vision with the backboard of a basketball hoop that is 5 feet higher than your eyes (see figure). Your horizontal distance from the backboard is 12 feet. What is the angle of elevation of the star?

43. Write a model for a particle in simple harmonic motion with a displacement of 4 inches and a period of 8 seconds.

44. An airplane's velocity with respect to the air is 500 kilometers per hour, with a bearing of 30°. The wind at the altitude of the plane has a velocity of 50 kilometers per hour with a bearing of N 60° E. What is the true direction of the plane, and what is its speed relative to the ground?

45. A force of 85 pounds exerted at an angle of 60° above the horizontal is required to slide an object across a floor. The object is dragged 10 feet. Determine the work done in sliding the object.

Proofs in Mathematics

Law of Tangents

Besides the Law of Sines and the Law of Cosines, there is also a Law of Tangents, which was developed by Francois Viète (1540–1603). The Law of Tangents follows from the Law of Sines and the sum-to-product formulas for sine and is defined as follows.

$$\frac{a+b}{a-b} = \frac{\tan[(A+B)/2]}{\tan[(A-B)/2]}$$

The Law of Tangents can be used to solve a triangle when two sides and the included angle are given (SAS). Before calculators were invented, the Law of Tangents was used to solve the SAS case instead of the Law of Cosines, because computation with a table of tangent values was easier.

Law of Sines *(p. 430)*

If ABC is a triangle with sides a, b, and c, then

$$\frac{a}{\sin A} = \frac{b}{\sin B} = \frac{c}{\sin C}.$$

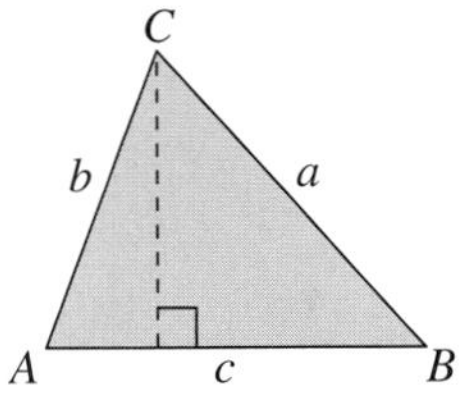

A is acute.

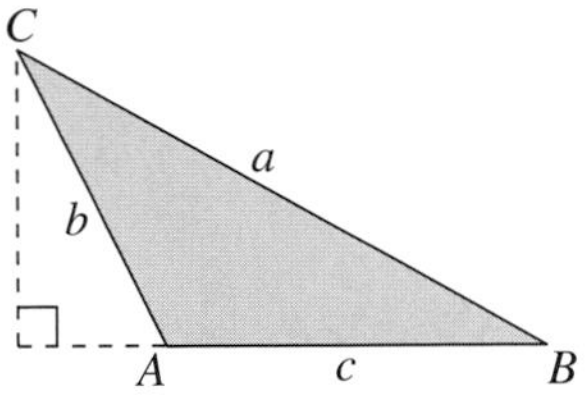

A is obtuse.

Proof

Let h be the altitude of either triangle found in the figure above. Then you have

$$\sin A = \frac{h}{b} \quad \text{or} \quad h = b \sin A$$

$$\sin B = \frac{h}{a} \quad \text{or} \quad h = a \sin B.$$

Equating these two values of h, you have

$$a \sin B = b \sin A \quad \text{or} \quad \frac{a}{\sin A} = \frac{b}{\sin B}.$$

Note that $\sin A \neq 0$ and $\sin B \neq 0$ because no angle of a triangle can have a measure of 0° or 180°. In a similar manner, construct an altitude from vertex B to side AC (extended in the obtuse triangle), as shown at the left. Then you have

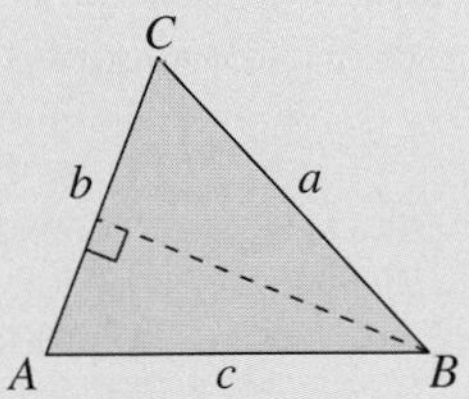

A is acute.

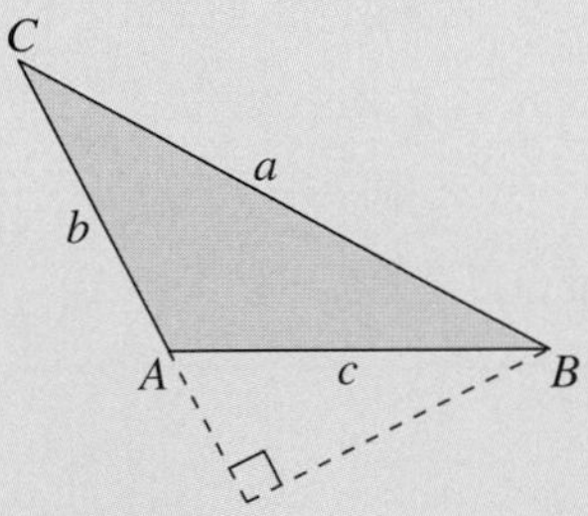

A is obtuse.

$$\sin A = \frac{h}{c} \quad \text{or} \quad h = c \sin A$$

$$\sin C = \frac{h}{a} \quad \text{or} \quad h = a \sin C.$$

Equating these two values of h, you have

$$a \sin C = c \sin A \quad \text{or} \quad \frac{a}{\sin A} = \frac{c}{\sin C}.$$

By the Transitive Property of Equality you know that

$$\frac{a}{\sin A} = \frac{b}{\sin B} = \frac{c}{\sin C}.$$

So, the Law of Sines is established.

Law of Cosines *(p. 439)*

Standard Form	*Alternative Form*
$a^2 = b^2 + c^2 - 2bc \cos A$	$\cos A = \dfrac{b^2 + c^2 - a^2}{2bc}$
$b^2 = a^2 + c^2 - 2ac \cos B$	$\cos B = \dfrac{a^2 + c^2 - b^2}{2ac}$
$c^2 = a^2 + b^2 - 2ab \cos C$	$\cos C = \dfrac{a^2 + b^2 - c^2}{2ab}$

Proof

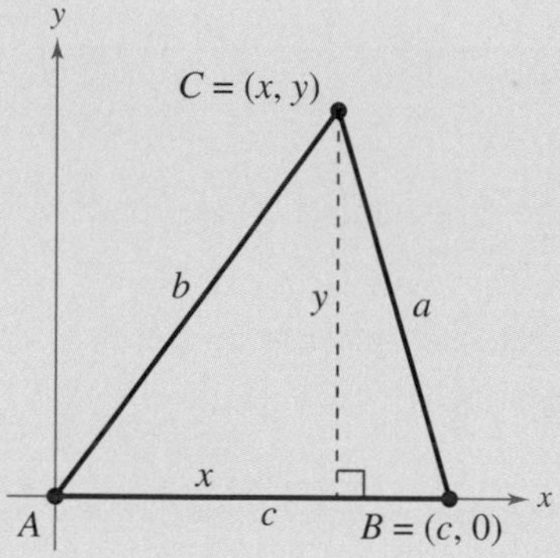

To prove the first formula, consider the top triangle at the left, which has three acute angles. Note that vertex B has coordinates $(c, 0)$. Furthermore, C has coordinates (x, y), where $x = b \cos A$ and $y = b \sin A$. Because a is the distance from vertex C to vertex B, it follows that

$$a = \sqrt{(x - c)^2 + (y - 0)^2} \qquad \text{Distance Formula}$$

$$a^2 = (x - c)^2 + (y - 0)^2 \qquad \text{Square each side.}$$

$$a^2 = (b \cos A - c)^2 + (b \sin A)^2 \qquad \text{Substitute for } x \text{ and } y.$$

$$a^2 = b^2 \cos^2 A - 2bc \cos A + c^2 + b^2 \sin^2 A \qquad \text{Expand.}$$

$$a^2 = b^2(\sin^2 A + \cos^2 A) + c^2 - 2bc \cos A \qquad \text{Factor out } b^2.$$

$$a^2 = b^2 + c^2 - 2bc \cos A. \qquad \sin^2 A + \cos^2 A = 1$$

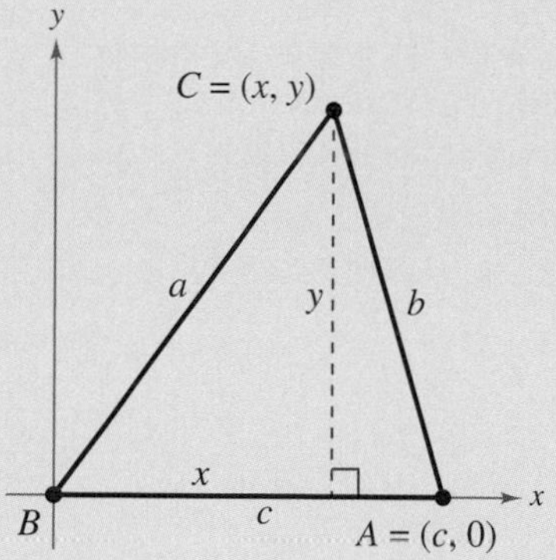

To prove the second formula, consider the bottom triangle at the left, which also has three acute angles. Note that vertex A has coordinates $(c, 0)$. Furthermore, C has coordinates (x, y), where $x = a \cos B$ and $y = a \sin B$. Because b is the distance from vertex C to vertex A, it follows that

$$b = \sqrt{(x - c)^2 + (y - 0)^2} \qquad \text{Distance Formula}$$

$$b^2 = (x - c)^2 + (y - 0)^2 \qquad \text{Square each side.}$$

$$b^2 = (a \cos B - c)^2 + (a \sin B)^2 \qquad \text{Substitute for } x \text{ and } y.$$

$$b^2 = a^2 \cos^2 B - 2ac \cos B + c^2 + a^2 \sin^2 B \qquad \text{Expand.}$$

$$b^2 = a^2(\sin^2 B + \cos^2 B) + c^2 - 2ac \cos B \qquad \text{Factor out } a^2.$$

$$b^2 = a^2 + c^2 - 2ac \cos B. \qquad \sin^2 B + \cos^2 B = 1$$

A similar argument is used to establish the third formula.

Heron's Area Formula (p. 442)

Given any triangle with sides of lengths a, b, and c, the area of the triangle is

$$\text{Area} = \sqrt{s(s-a)(s-b)(s-c)}$$

where $s = \dfrac{(a+b+c)}{2}$.

Proof

From Section 6.1, you know that

$$\text{Area} = \frac{1}{2}bc\sin A$$ Formula for the area of an oblique triangle

$$(\text{Area})^2 = \frac{1}{4}b^2c^2\sin^2 A$$ Square each side.

$$\text{Area} = \sqrt{\frac{1}{4}b^2c^2\sin^2 A}$$ Take the square root of each side.

$$= \sqrt{\frac{1}{4}b^2c^2(1-\cos^2 A)}$$ Pythagorean Identity

$$= \sqrt{\left[\frac{1}{2}bc(1+\cos A)\right]\left[\frac{1}{2}bc(1-\cos A)\right]}.$$ Factor.

Using the Law of Cosines, you can show that

$$\frac{1}{2}bc(1+\cos A) = \frac{a+b+c}{2} \cdot \frac{-a+b+c}{2}$$

and

$$\frac{1}{2}bc(1-\cos A) = \frac{a-b+c}{2} \cdot \frac{a+b-c}{2}.$$

Letting $s = (a+b+c)/2$, these two equations can be rewritten as

$$\frac{1}{2}bc(1+\cos A) = s(s-a)$$

and

$$\frac{1}{2}bc(1-\cos A) = (s-b)(s-c).$$

By substituting into the last formula for area, you can conclude that

$$\text{Area} = \sqrt{s(s-a)(s-b)(s-c)}.$$

Properties of the Dot Product (p. 460)

Let **u**, **v**, and **w** be vectors in the plane or in space and let c be a scalar.

1. $\mathbf{u} \cdot \mathbf{v} = \mathbf{v} \cdot \mathbf{u}$
2. $\mathbf{0} \cdot \mathbf{v} = 0$
3. $\mathbf{u} \cdot (\mathbf{v} + \mathbf{w}) = \mathbf{u} \cdot \mathbf{v} + \mathbf{u} \cdot \mathbf{w}$
4. $\mathbf{v} \cdot \mathbf{v} = \|\mathbf{v}\|^2$
5. $c(\mathbf{u} \cdot \mathbf{v}) = c\mathbf{u} \cdot \mathbf{v} = \mathbf{u} \cdot c\mathbf{v}$

Proof

Let $\mathbf{u} = \langle u_1, u_2 \rangle$, $\mathbf{v} = \langle v_1, v_2 \rangle$, $\mathbf{w} = \langle w_1, w_2 \rangle$, $\mathbf{0} = \langle 0, 0 \rangle$, and let c be a scalar.

1. $\mathbf{u} \cdot \mathbf{v} = u_1v_1 + u_2v_2 = v_1u_1 + v_2u_2 = \mathbf{v} \cdot \mathbf{u}$

2. $\mathbf{0} \cdot \mathbf{v} = 0 \cdot v_1 + 0 \cdot v_2 = 0$

3.
$$\begin{aligned}\mathbf{u} \cdot (\mathbf{v} + \mathbf{w}) &= \mathbf{u} \cdot \langle v_1 + w_1, v_2 + w_2 \rangle\\ &= u_1(v_1 + w_1) + u_2(v_2 + w_2)\\ &= u_1v_1 + u_1w_1 + u_2v_2 + u_2w_2\\ &= (u_1v_1 + u_2v_2) + (u_1w_1 + u_2w_2) = \mathbf{u} \cdot \mathbf{v} + \mathbf{u} \cdot \mathbf{w}\end{aligned}$$

4. $\mathbf{v} \cdot \mathbf{v} = v_1^2 + v_2^2 = \left(\sqrt{v_1^2 + v_2^2}\right)^2 = \|\mathbf{v}\|^2$

5.
$$\begin{aligned}c(\mathbf{u} \cdot \mathbf{v}) &= c(\langle u_1, u_2 \rangle \cdot \langle v_1, v_2 \rangle)\\ &= c(u_1v_1 + u_2v_2)\\ &= (cu_1)v_1 + (cu_2)v_2\\ &= \langle cu_1, cu_2 \rangle \cdot \langle v_1, v_2 \rangle\\ &= c\mathbf{u} \cdot \mathbf{v}\end{aligned}$$

Angle Between Two Vectors (p. 461)

If θ is the angle between two nonzero vectors **u** and **v**, then $\cos\theta = \dfrac{\mathbf{u} \cdot \mathbf{v}}{\|\mathbf{u}\|\,\|\mathbf{v}\|}$.

Proof

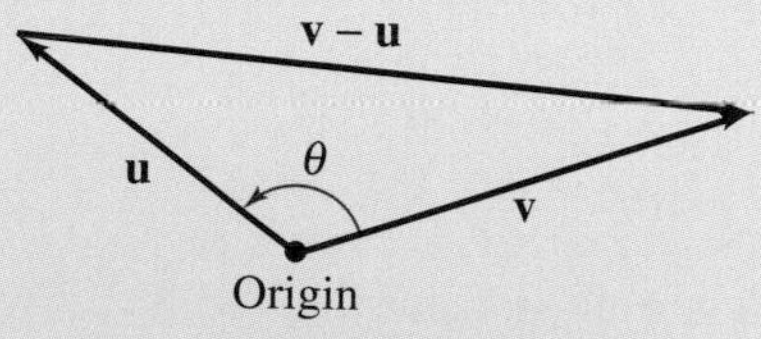

Consider the triangle determined by vectors **u, v,** and **v** − **u**, as shown in the figure. By the Law of Cosines, you can write

$$\begin{aligned}\|\mathbf{v} - \mathbf{u}\|^2 &= \|\mathbf{u}\|^2 + \|\mathbf{v}\|^2 - 2\|\mathbf{u}\|\,\|\mathbf{v}\|\cos\theta\\ (\mathbf{v} - \mathbf{u}) \cdot (\mathbf{v} - \mathbf{u}) &= \|\mathbf{u}\|^2 + \|\mathbf{v}\|^2 - 2\|\mathbf{u}\|\,\|\mathbf{v}\|\cos\theta\\ (\mathbf{v} - \mathbf{u}) \cdot \mathbf{v} - (\mathbf{v} - \mathbf{u}) \cdot \mathbf{u} &= \|\mathbf{u}\|^2 + \|\mathbf{v}\|^2 - 2\|\mathbf{u}\|\,\|\mathbf{v}\|\cos\theta\\ \mathbf{v} \cdot \mathbf{v} - \mathbf{u} \cdot \mathbf{v} - \mathbf{v} \cdot \mathbf{u} + \mathbf{u} \cdot \mathbf{u} &= \|\mathbf{u}\|^2 + \|\mathbf{v}\|^2 - 2\|\mathbf{u}\|\,\|\mathbf{v}\|\cos\theta\\ \|\mathbf{v}\|^2 - 2\mathbf{u} \cdot \mathbf{v} + \|\mathbf{u}\|^2 &= \|\mathbf{u}\|^2 + \|\mathbf{v}\|^2 - 2\|\mathbf{u}\|\,\|\mathbf{v}\|\cos\theta\\ \cos\theta &= \frac{\mathbf{u} \cdot \mathbf{v}}{\|\mathbf{u}\|\,\|\mathbf{v}\|}.\end{aligned}$$

P.S. Problem Solving

This collection of thought-provoking and challenging exercises further explores and expands upon concepts learned in this chapter.

1. In the figure, a beam of light is directed at the blue mirror, reflected to the red mirror, and then reflected back to the blue mirror. Find the distance PT that the light travels from the red mirror back to the blue mirror.

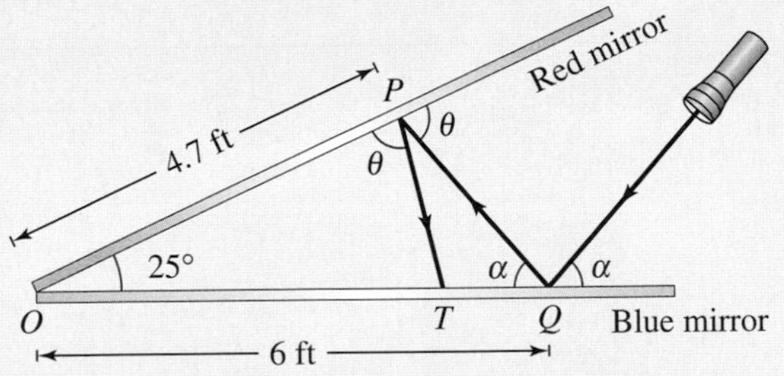

2. A triathlete sets a course to swim S 25° E from a point on shore to a buoy $\frac{3}{4}$ mile away. After swimming 300 yards through a strong current, the triathlete is off course at a bearing of S 35° E. Find the bearing and distance the triathlete needs to swim to correct her course.

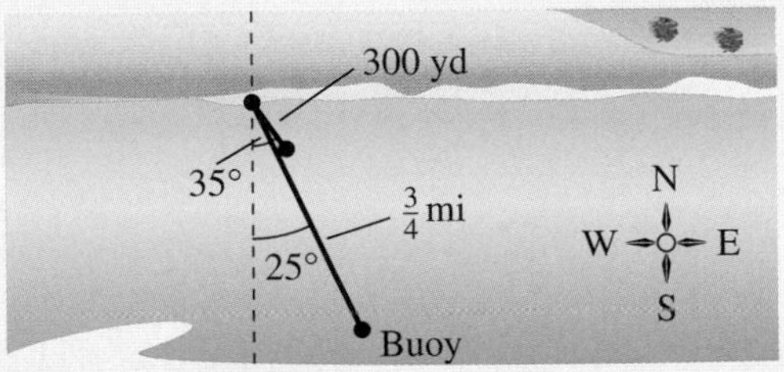

3. A hiking party is lost in a national park. Two ranger stations have received an emergency SOS signal from the party. Station B is 75 miles due east of station A. The bearing from station A to the signal is S 60° E and the bearing from station B to the signal is S 75° W.

(a) Draw a diagram that gives a visual representation of the problem.

(b) Find the distance from each station to the SOS signal.

(c) A rescue party is in the park 20 miles from station A at a bearing of S 80° E. Find the distance and the bearing the rescue party must travel to reach the lost hiking party.

4. You are seeding a triangular courtyard. One side of the courtyard is 52 feet long and another side is 46 feet long. The angle opposite the 52-foot side is 65°.

(a) Draw a diagram that gives a visual representation of the problem.

(b) How long is the third side of the courtyard?

(c) One bag of grass covers an area of 50 square feet. How many bags of grass will you need to cover the courtyard?

5. For each pair of vectors, find the following.

(i) $\|\mathbf{u}\|$ (ii) $\|\mathbf{v}\|$ (iii) $\|\mathbf{u} + \mathbf{v}\|$

(iv) $\left\|\frac{\mathbf{u}}{\|\mathbf{u}\|}\right\|$ (v) $\left\|\frac{\mathbf{v}}{\|\mathbf{v}\|}\right\|$ (vi) $\left\|\frac{\mathbf{u} + \mathbf{v}}{\|\mathbf{u} + \mathbf{v}\|}\right\|$

(a) $\mathbf{u} = \langle 1, -1 \rangle$, $\mathbf{v} = \langle -1, 2 \rangle$

(b) $\mathbf{u} = \langle 0, 1 \rangle$, $\mathbf{v} = \langle 3, -3 \rangle$

(c) $\mathbf{u} = \left\langle 1, \frac{1}{2} \right\rangle$, $\mathbf{v} = \langle 2, 3 \rangle$

(d) $\mathbf{u} = \langle 2, -4 \rangle$, $\mathbf{v} = \langle 5, 5 \rangle$

6. A skydiver is falling at a constant downward velocity of 120 miles per hour. In the figure, vector $\mathbf{u}$ represents the skydiver's velocity. A steady breeze pushes the skydiver to the east at 40 miles per hour. Vector $\mathbf{v}$ represents the wind velocity.

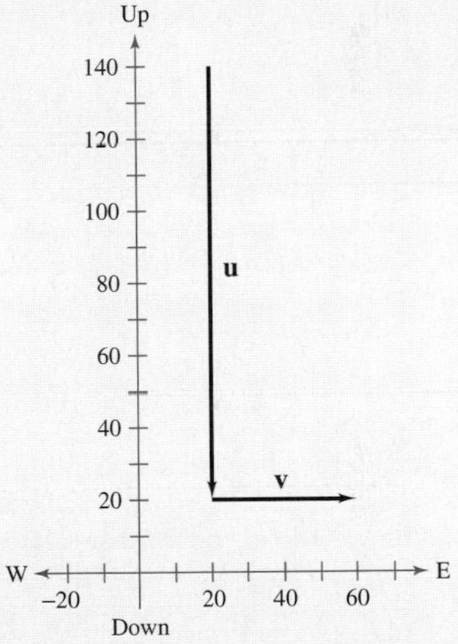

(a) Write the vectors $\mathbf{u}$ and $\mathbf{v}$ in component form.

(b) Let $\mathbf{s} = \mathbf{u} + \mathbf{v}$. Use the figure to sketch $\mathbf{s}$. To print an enlarged copy of the graph, go to the website, *www.mathgraphs.com*.

(c) Find the magnitude of $\mathbf{s}$. What information does the magnitude give you about the skydiver's fall?

(d) If there were no wind, the skydiver would fall in a path perpendicular to the ground. At what angle to the ground is the path of the skydiver when the skydiver is affected by the 40 mile per hour wind from due west?

(e) The skydiver is blown to the west at 30 miles per hour. Draw a new figure that gives a visual representation of the problem and find the skydiver's new velocity.

7. Write the vector **w** in terms of **u** and **v**, given that the terminal point of **w** bisects the line segment (see figure).

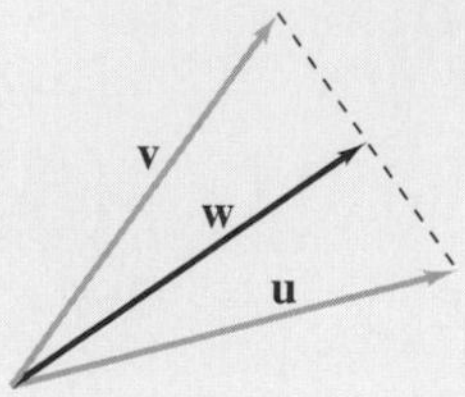

8. Prove that if **u** is orthogonal to **v** and **w**, then **u** is orthogonal to

$c\mathbf{v} + d\mathbf{w}$

for any scalars c and d (see figure).

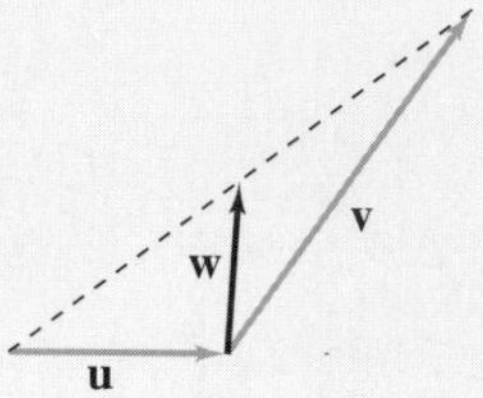

9. Two forces of the same magnitude $\mathbf{F}_1$ and $\mathbf{F}_2$ act at angles θ_1 and θ_2, respectively. Use a diagram to compare the work done by $\mathbf{F}_1$ with the work done by $\mathbf{F}_2$ in moving along the vector PQ if

(a) $\theta_1 = -\theta_2$

(b) $\theta_1 = 60°$ and $\theta_2 = 30°$.

10. Four basic forces are in action during flight: weight, lift, thrust, and drag. To fly through the air, an object must overcome its own *weight*. To do this, it must create an upward force called *lift*. To generate lift, a forward motion called *thrust* is needed. The thrust must be great enough to overcome air resistance, which is called *drag*.

For a commercial jet aircraft, a quick climb is important to maximize efficiency, because the performance of an aircraft at high altitudes is enhanced. In addition, it is necessary to clear obstacles such as buildings and mountains and reduce noise in residential areas. In the diagram, the angle θ is called the climb angle. The velocity of the plane can be represented by a vector **v** with a vertical component $\|\mathbf{v}\| \sin\theta$ (called climb speed) and a horizontal component $\|\mathbf{v}\| \cos\theta$, where $\|\mathbf{v}\|$ is the speed of the plane.

When taking off, a pilot must decide how much of the thrust to apply to each component. The more the thrust is applied to the horizontal component, the faster the airplane will gain speed. The more the thrust is applied to the vertical component, the quicker the airplane will climb.

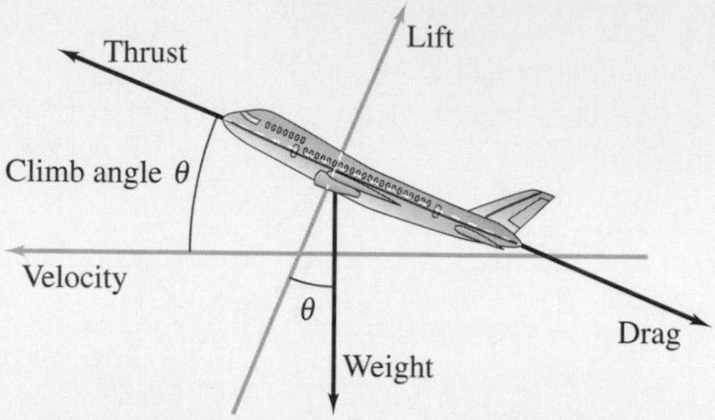

FIGURE FOR 10

(a) Complete the table for an airplane that has a speed of $\|\mathbf{v}\| = 100$ miles per hour.

θ	0.5°	1.0°	1.5°	2.0°	2.5°	3.0°
$\|\mathbf{v}\| \sin\theta$						
$\|\mathbf{v}\| \cos\theta$						

(b) Does an airplane's speed equal the sum of the vertical and horizontal components of its velocity? If not, how could you find the speed of an airplane whose velocity components were known?

(c) Use the result of part (b) to find the speed of an airplane with the given velocity components.

(i) $\|\mathbf{v}\| \sin\theta = 5.235$ miles per hour

$\|\mathbf{v}\| \cos\theta = 149.909$ miles per hour

(ii) $\|\mathbf{v}\| \sin\theta = 10.463$ miles per hour

$\|\mathbf{v}\| \cos\theta = 149.634$ miles per hour

Systems of Equations and Inequalities

7

7.1 Linear and Nonlinear Systems of Equations

7.2 Two-Variable Linear Systems

7.3 Multivariable Linear Systems

7.4 Partial Fractions

7.5 Systems of Inequalities

7.6 Linear Programming

Systems of equations can be used to determine the combinations of scoring plays for different sports, such as football.

SELECTED APPLICATIONS

Systems of equations and inequalities have many real-life applications. The applications listed below represent a small sample of the applications in this chapter.

- Break-Even Analysis, Exercises 61–64, page 504
- Data Analysis: Renewable Energy, Exercise 71, page 505
- Acid Mixture, Exercise 51, page 516
- Sports, Exercise 51, page 529
- Electrical Network, Exercise 65, page 530
- Thermodynamics, Exercise 57, page 540
- Data Analysis: Prescription Drugs, Exercise 77, page 550
- Investment Portfolio, Exercises 47 and 48, page 561
- Supply and Demand, Exercises 75 and 76, page 565

7.1 Linear and Nonlinear Systems of Equations

What you should learn

- Use the method of substitution to solve systems of linear equations in two variables.
- Use the method of substitution to solve systems of nonlinear equations in two variables.
- Use a graphical approach to solve systems of equations in two variables.
- Use systems of equations to model and solve real-life problems.

Why you should learn it

Graphs of systems of equations help you solve real-life problems. For instance, in Exercise 71 on page 505, you can use the graph of a system of equations to approximate when the consumption of wind energy exceeded the consumption of solar energy.

© ML Sinibaldi/Corbis

The Method of Substitution

Up to this point in the text, most problems have involved either a function of one variable or a single equation in two variables. However, many problems in science, business, and engineering involve two or more equations in two or more variables. To solve such problems, you need to find solutions of a **system of equations.** Here is an example of a system of two equations in two unknowns.

$$\begin{cases} 2x + y = 5 & \text{Equation 1} \\ 3x - 2y = 4 & \text{Equation 2} \end{cases}$$

A **solution** of this system is an ordered pair that satisfies each equation in the system. Finding the set of all solutions is called **solving the system of equations.** For instance, the ordered pair (2, 1) is a solution of this system. To check this, you can substitute 2 for x and 1 for y in *each* equation.

Check (2, 1) in Equation 1 and Equation 2:

$2x + y = 5$ Write Equation 1.

$2(2) + 1 \stackrel{?}{=} 5$ Substitute 2 for x and 1 for y.

$4 + 1 = 5$ Solution checks in Equation 1. ✓

$3x - 2y = 4$ Write Equation 2.

$3(2) - 2(1) \stackrel{?}{=} 4$ Substitute 2 for x and 1 for y.

$6 - 2 = 4$ Solution checks in Equation 2. ✓

In this chapter, you will study four ways to solve systems of equations, beginning with the **method of substitution.**

Method	*Section*	*Type of System*
1. Substitution	7.1	Linear or nonlinear, two variables
2. Graphical method	7.1	Linear or nonlinear, two variables
3. Elimination	7.2	Linear, two variables
4. Gaussian elimination	7.3	Linear, three or more variables

Method of Substitution

1. *Solve* one of the equations for one variable in terms of the other.
2. *Substitute* the expression found in Step 1 into the other equation to obtain an equation in one variable.
3. *Solve* the equation obtained in Step 2.
4. *Back-substitute* the value obtained in Step 3 into the expression obtained in Step 1 to find the value of the other variable.
5. *Check* that the solution satisfies *each* of the original equations.

Exploration

Use a graphing utility to graph $y_1 = 4 - x$ and $y_2 = x - 2$ in the same viewing window. Use the *zoom* and *trace* features to find the coordinates of the point of intersection. What is the relationship between the point of intersection and the solution found in Example 1?

Example 1 Solving a System of Equations by Substitution

Solve the system of equations.

$$\begin{cases} x + y = 4 & \text{Equation 1} \\ x - y = 2 & \text{Equation 2} \end{cases}$$

Solution

Begin by solving for y in Equation 1.

$y = 4 - x$ Solve for y in Equation 1.

Next, substitute this expression for y into Equation 2 and solve the resulting single-variable equation for x.

$x - y = 2$ Write Equation 2.

$x - (4 - x) = 2$ Substitute $4 - x$ for y.

$x - 4 + x = 2$ Distributive Property

$2x = 6$ Combine like terms.

$x = 3$ Divide each side by 2.

Finally, you can solve for y by *back-substituting* $x = 3$ into the equation $y = 4 - x$, to obtain

$y = 4 - x$ Write revised Equation 1.

$y = 4 - 3$ Substitute 3 for x.

$y = 1.$ Solve for y.

The solution is the ordered pair (3, 1). You can check this solution as follows.

Check

Substitute (3, 1) into Equation 1:

$x + y = 4$ Write Equation 1.

$3 + 1 \stackrel{?}{=} 4$ Substitute for x and y.

$4 = 4$ Solution checks in Equation 1. ✓

Substitute (3, 1) into Equation 2:

$x - y = 2$ Write Equation 2.

$3 - 1 \stackrel{?}{=} 2$ Substitute for x and y.

$2 = 2$ Solution checks in Equation 2. ✓

Because (3, 1) satisfies both equations in the system, it is a solution of the system of equations.

✓CHECKPOINT Now try Exercise 5.

STUDY TIP

Because many steps are required to solve a system of equations, it is very easy to make errors in arithmetic. So, you should always check your solution by substituting it into *each* equation in the original system.

The term *back-substitution* implies that you work *backwards*. First you solve for one of the variables, and then you substitute that value *back* into one of the equations in the system to find the value of the other variable.

Example 2 **Solving a System by Substitution**

A total of $12,000 is invested in two funds paying 5% and 3% simple interest. (Recall that the formula for simple interest is $I = Prt$, where P is the principal, r is the annual interest rate, and t is the time.) The yearly interest is $500. How much is invested at each rate?

Solution

Verbal Model: 5% fund + 3% fund = Total investment

5% interest + 3% interest = Total interest

Labels:

Amount in 5% fund $= x$ (dollars)

Interest for 5% fund $= 0.05x$ (dollars)

Amount in 3% fund $= y$ (dollars)

Interest for 3% fund $= 0.03y$ (dollars)

Total investment $= 12{,}000$ (dollars)

Total interest $= 500$ (dollars)

System:

$$\begin{cases} x + y = 12{,}000 & \text{Equation 1} \\ 0.05x + 0.03y = 500 & \text{Equation 2} \end{cases}$$

To begin, it is convenient to multiply each side of Equation 2 by 100. This eliminates the need to work with decimals.

$$100(0.05x + 0.03y) = 100(500) \qquad \text{Multiply each side by 100.}$$

$$5x + 3y = 50{,}000 \qquad \text{Revised Equation 2}$$

To solve this system, you can solve for x in Equation 1.

$$x = 12{,}000 - y \qquad \text{Revised Equation 1}$$

Then, substitute this expression for x into revised Equation 2 and solve the resulting equation for y.

$$5x + 3y = 50{,}000 \qquad \text{Write revised Equation 2.}$$

$$5(12{,}000 - y) + 3y = 50{,}000 \qquad \text{Substitute } 12{,}000 - y \text{ for } x.$$

$$60{,}000 - 5y + 3y = 50{,}000 \qquad \text{Distributive Property}$$

$$-2y = -10{,}000 \qquad \text{Combine like terms.}$$

$$y = 5000 \qquad \text{Divide each side by } -2.$$

Next, back-substitute the value $y = 5000$ to solve for x.

$$x = 12{,}000 - y \qquad \text{Write revised Equation 1.}$$

$$x = 12{,}000 - 5000 \qquad \text{Substitute 5000 for } y.$$

$$x = 7000 \qquad \text{Simplify.}$$

The solution is (7000, 5000). So, $7000 is invested at 5% and $5000 is invested at 3%. Check this in the original system.

✓CHECKPOINT Now try Exercise 19.

STUDY TIP

When using the method of substitution, it does not matter which variable you choose to solve for first. Whether you solve for y first or x first, you will obtain the same solution. When making your choice, you should choose the variable and equation that are easier to work with. For instance, in Example 2, solving for x in Equation 1 is easier than solving for x in Equation 2.

Technology

One way to check the answers you obtain in this section is to use a graphing utility. For instance, enter the two equations in Example 2

$$y_1 = 12{,}000 - x$$

$$y_2 = \frac{500 - 0.05x}{0.03}$$

and find an appropriate viewing window that shows where the two lines intersect. Then use the *intersect* feature or the *zoom* and *trace* features to find the point of intersection. Does this point agree with the solution obtained at the right?

Nonlinear Systems of Equations

The equations in Examples 1 and 2 are linear. The method of substitution can also be used to solve systems in which one or both of the equations are nonlinear.

Example 3 Substitution: Two-Solution Case

Solve the system of equations.

$$\begin{cases} x^2 + 4x - y = 7 & \text{Equation 1} \\ 2x - y = -1 & \text{Equation 2} \end{cases}$$

Solution

Begin by solving for y in Equation 2 to obtain $y = 2x + 1$. Next, substitute this expression for y into Equation 1 and solve for x.

$x^2 + 4x - (2x + 1) = 7$ Substitute $2x + 1$ for y into Equation 1.

$x^2 + 2x - 1 = 7$ Simplify.

$x^2 + 2x - 8 = 0$ Write in general form.

$(x + 4)(x - 2) = 0$ Factor.

$x = -4, 2$ Solve for x.

Back-substituting these values of x to solve for the corresponding values of y produces the solutions $(-4, -7)$ and $(2, 5)$. Check these in the original system.

CHECKPOINT Now try Exercise 25.

When using the method of substitution, you may encounter an equation that has no solution, as shown in Example 4.

Example 4 Substitution: No-Real-Solution Case

Solve the system of equations.

$$\begin{cases} -x + y = 4 & \text{Equation 1} \\ x^2 + y = 3 & \text{Equation 2} \end{cases}$$

Solution

Begin by solving for y in Equation 1 to obtain $y = x + 4$. Next, substitute this expression for y into Equation 2 and solve for x.

$x^2 + (x + 4) = 3$ Substitute $x + 4$ for y into Equation 2.

$x^2 + x + 1 = 0$ Simplify.

$x = \dfrac{-1 \pm \sqrt{-3}}{2}$ Use the Quadratic Formula.

Because the discriminant is negative, the equation $x^2 + x + 1 = 0$ has no (real) solution. So, the original system has no (real) solution.

CHECKPOINT Now try Exercise 27.

Exploration

Use a graphing utility to graph the two equations in Example 3

$y_1 = x^2 + 4x - 7$

$y_2 = 2x + 1$

in the same viewing window. How many solutions do you think this system has?

Repeat this experiment for the equations in Example 4. How many solutions does this system have? Explain your reasoning.

Technology

Most graphing utilities have built-in features that approximate the point(s) of intersection of two graphs. Typically, you must enter the equations of the graphs and visually locate a point of intersection before using the *intersect* feature.

Use this feature to find the points of intersection of the graphs in Figures 7.1 to 7.3. Be sure to adjust your viewing window so that you see all the points of intersection.

Graphical Approach to Finding Solutions

From Examples 2, 3, and 4, you can see that a system of two equations in two unknowns can have exactly one solution, more than one solution, or no solution. By using a **graphical method,** you can gain insight about the number of solutions and the location(s) of the solution(s) of a system of equations by graphing each of the equations in the same coordinate plane. The solutions of the system correspond to the **points of intersection** of the graphs. For instance, the two equations in Figure 7.1 graph as two lines with a *single point* of intersection; the two equations in Figure 7.2 graph as a parabola and a line with *two points* of intersection; and the two equations in Figure 7.3 graph as a line and a parabola that have *no points* of intersection.

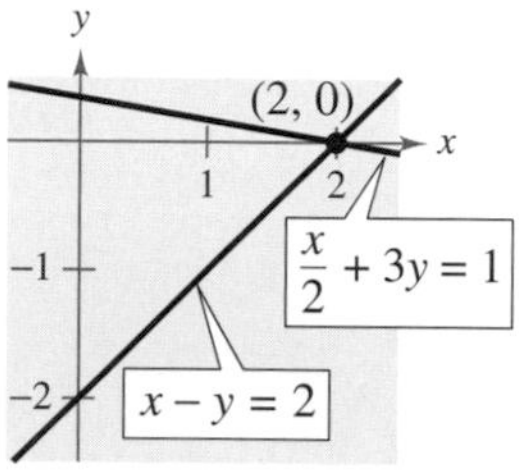

One intersection point
FIGURE 7.1

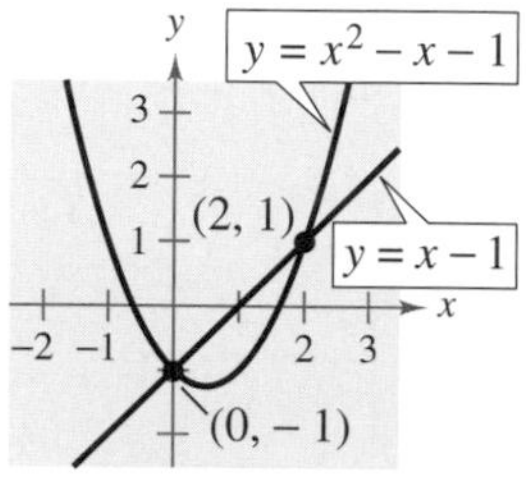

Two intersection points
FIGURE 7.2

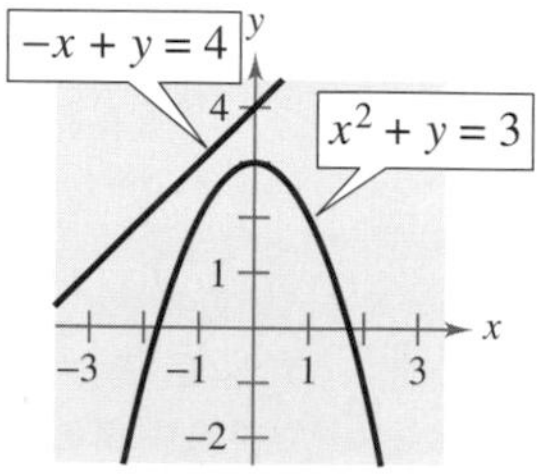

No intersection points
FIGURE 7.3

Example 5 Solving a System of Equations Graphically

Solve the system of equations.

$$\begin{cases} y = \ln x & \text{Equation 1} \\ x + y = 1 & \text{Equation 2} \end{cases}$$

Solution

Sketch the graphs of the two equations. From the graphs of these equations, it is clear that there is only one point of intersection and that $(1, 0)$ is the solution point (see Figure 7.4). You can confirm this by substituting 1 for x and 0 for y in *both* equations.

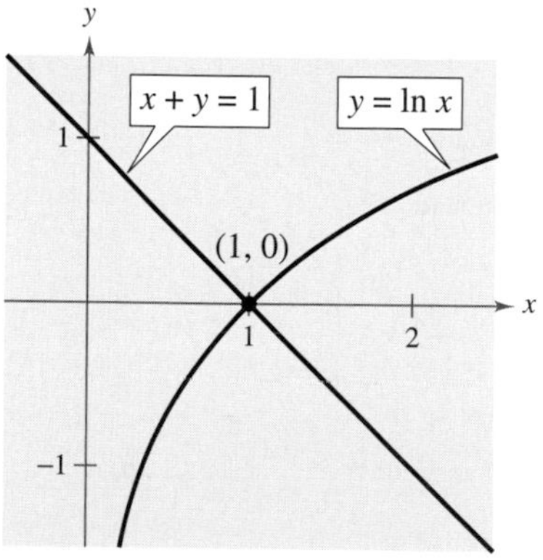

FIGURE 7.4

Check (1, 0) in Equation 1:

$y = \ln x$ Write Equation 1.

$0 = \ln 1$ Equation 1 checks. ✓

Check (1, 0) in Equation 2:

$x + y = 1$ Write Equation 2.

$1 + 0 = 1$ Equation 2 checks. ✓

✓CHECKPOINT Now try Exercise 33.

Example 5 shows the value of a graphical approach to solving systems of equations in two variables. Notice what would happen if you tried only the substitution method in Example 5. You would obtain the equation $x + \ln x = 1$. It would be difficult to solve this equation for x using standard algebraic techniques.

Applications

The total cost C of producing x units of a product typically has two components—the initial cost and the cost per unit. When enough units have been sold so that the total revenue R equals the total cost C, the sales are said to have reached the **break-even point.** You will find that the break-even point corresponds to the point of intersection of the cost and revenue curves.

Example 6 Break-Even Analysis

A shoe company invests \$300,000 in equipment to produce a new line of athletic footwear. Each pair of shoes costs \$5 to produce and is sold for \$60. How many pairs of shoes must be sold before the business breaks even?

Solution

The total cost of producing x units is

Total cost = Cost per unit · Number of units + Initial cost

$$C = 5x + 300{,}000. \qquad \text{Equation 1}$$

The revenue obtained by selling x units is

Total revenue = Price per unit · Number of units

$$R = 60x. \qquad \text{Equation 2}$$

Because the break-even point occurs when $R = C$, you have $C = 60x$, and the system of equations to solve is

$$\begin{cases} C = 5x + 300{,}000 \\ C = 60x \end{cases}.$$

Now you can solve by substitution.

$60x = 5x + 300{,}000$ Substitute $60x$ for C in Equation 1.

$55x = 300{,}000$ Subtract $5x$ from each side.

$x \approx 5455$ Divide each side by 55.

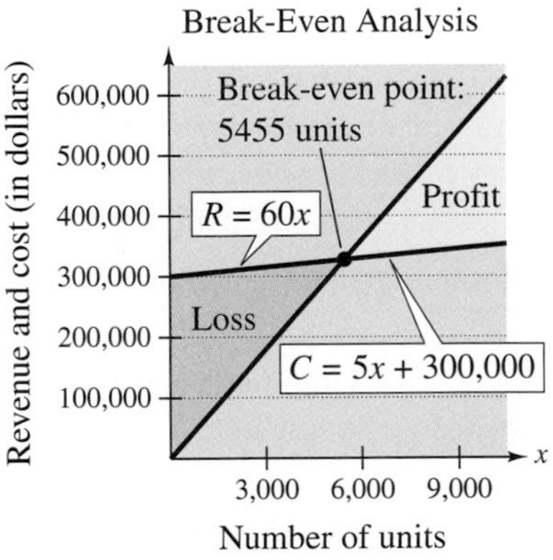

FIGURE 7.5

So, the company must sell about 5455 pairs of shoes to break even. Note in Figure 7.5 that revenue less than the break-even point corresponds to an overall loss, whereas revenue greater than the break-even point corresponds to a profit.

CHECKPOINT Now try Exercise 63.

Another way to view the solution in Example 6 is to consider the profit function

$$P = R - C.$$

The break-even point occurs when the profit is 0, which is the same as saying that $R = C$.

Example 7 **Movie Ticket Sales**

The weekly ticket sales for a new comedy movie decreased each week. At the same time, the weekly ticket sales for a new drama movie increased each week. Models that approximate the weekly ticket sales S (in millions of dollars) for each movie are

$$\begin{cases} S = 60 - 8x & \text{Comedy} \\ S = 10 + 4.5x & \text{Drama} \end{cases}$$

where x represents the number of weeks each movie was in theaters, with $x = 0$ corresponding to the ticket sales during the opening weekend. After how many weeks will the ticket sales for the two movies be equal?

Algebraic Solution

Because the second equation has already been solved for S in terms of x, substitute this value into the first equation and solve for x, as follows.

$$10 + 4.5x = 60 - 8x \quad \text{Substitute for } S \text{ in Equation 1.}$$

$$4.5x + 8x = 60 - 10 \quad \text{Add } 8x \text{ and } -10 \text{ to each side.}$$

$$12.5x = 50 \quad \text{Combine like terms.}$$

$$x = 4 \quad \text{Divide each side by 12.5.}$$

So, the weekly ticket sales for the two movies will be equal after 4 weeks.

✓CHECKPOINT Now try Exercise 65.

Numerical Solution

You can create a table of values for each model to determine when the ticket sales for the two movies will be equal.

Number of weeks, x	0	1	2	3	4	5	6
Sales, S (comedy)	60	52	44	36	28	20	12
Sales, S (drama)	10	14.5	19	23.5	28	32.5	37

So, from the table above, you can see that the weekly ticket sales for the two movies will be equal after 4 weeks.

WRITING ABOUT MATHEMATICS

Interpreting Points of Intersection You plan to rent a 14-foot truck for a two-day local move. At truck rental agency A, you can rent a truck for \$29.95 per day plus \$0.49 per mile. At agency B, you can rent a truck for \$50 per day plus \$0.25 per mile.

a. Write a total cost equation in terms of x and y for the total cost of renting the truck from each agency.

b. Use a graphing utility to graph the two equations in the same viewing window and find the point of intersection. Interpret the meaning of the point of intersection in the context of the problem.

c. Which agency should you choose if you plan to travel a total of 100 miles during the two-day move? Why?

d. How does the situation change if you plan to drive 200 miles during the two-day move?

7.1 Exercises

VOCABULARY CHECK: Fill in the blanks.

1. A set of two or more equations in two or more variables is called a ________ of ________.
2. A ________ of a system of equations is an ordered pair that satisfies each equation in the system.
3. Finding the set of all solutions to a system of equations is called ________ the system of equations.
4. The first step in solving a system of equations by the method of ________ is to solve one of the equations for one variable in terms of the other variable.
5. Graphically, the solution of a system of two equations is the ________ of ________ of the graphs of the two equations.
6. In business applications, the point at which the revenue equals costs is called the ________ point.

In Exercises 1–4, determine whether each ordered pair is a solution of the system of equations.

1. $\begin{cases} 4x - y = 1 \\ 6x + y = -6 \end{cases}$ (a) $(0, -3)$ (b) $(-1, -4)$ (c) $\left(-\frac{3}{2}, -2\right)$ (d) $\left(-\frac{1}{2}, -3\right)$

2. $\begin{cases} 4x^2 + y = 3 \\ -x - y = 11 \end{cases}$ (a) $(2, -13)$ (b) $(2, -9)$ (c) $\left(-\frac{3}{2}, -\frac{31}{3}\right)$ (d) $\left(-\frac{7}{4}, -\frac{37}{4}\right)$

3. $\begin{cases} y = -2e^x \\ 3x - y = 2 \end{cases}$ (a) $(-2, 0)$ (b) $(0, -2)$ (c) $(0, -3)$ (d) $(-1, 2)$

4. $\begin{cases} -\log x + 3 = y \\ \frac{1}{9}x + y = \frac{28}{9} \end{cases}$ (a) $\left(9, \frac{37}{9}\right)$ (b) $(10, 2)$ (c) $(1, 3)$ (d) $(2, 4)$

In Exercises 5–14, solve the system by the method of substitution. Check your solution graphically.

5. $\begin{cases} 2x + y = 6 \\ -x + y = 0 \end{cases}$

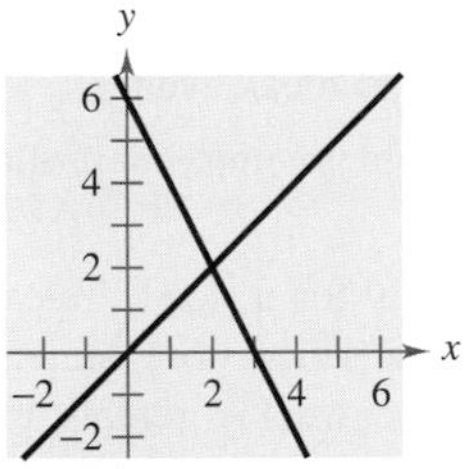

6. $\begin{cases} x - y = -4 \\ x + 2y = 5 \end{cases}$

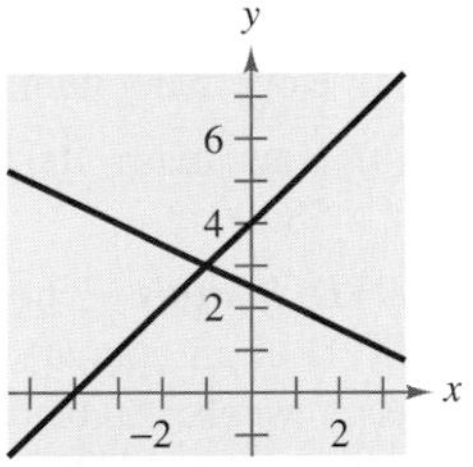

7. $\begin{cases} x - y = -4 \\ x^2 - y = -2 \end{cases}$

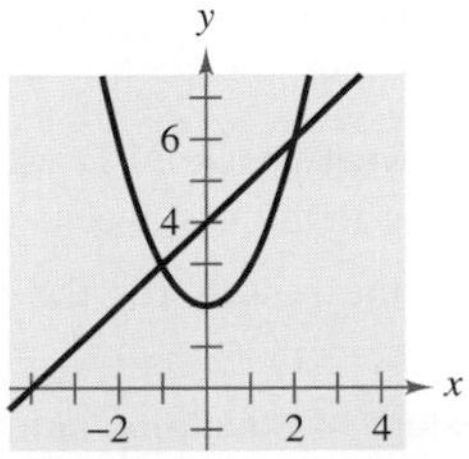

8. $\begin{cases} 3x + y = 2 \\ x^3 - 2 + y = 0 \end{cases}$

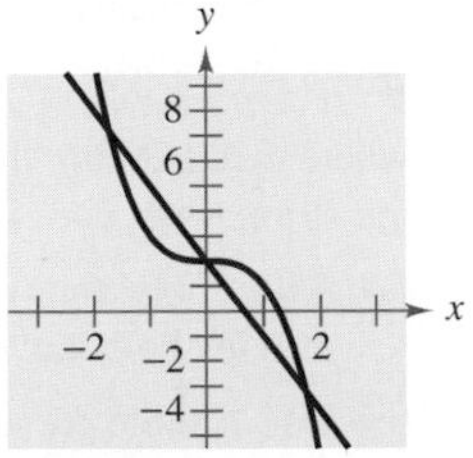

9. $\begin{cases} -2x + y = -5 \\ x^2 + y^2 = 25 \end{cases}$

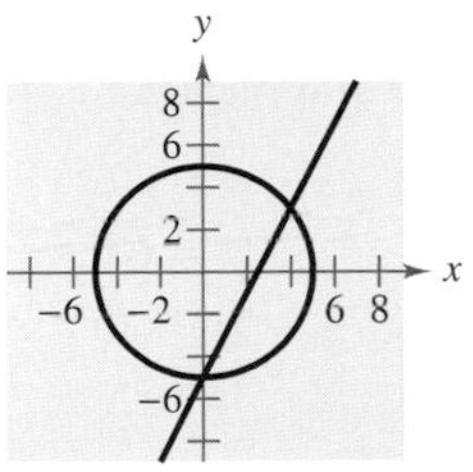

10. $\begin{cases} x + y = 0 \\ x^3 - 5x - y = 0 \end{cases}$

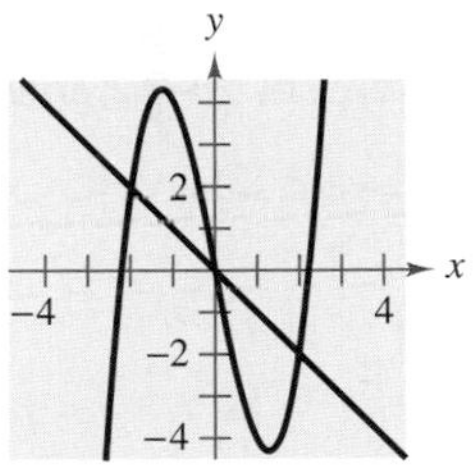

11. $\begin{cases} x^2 + y = 0 \\ x^2 - 4x - y = 0 \end{cases}$

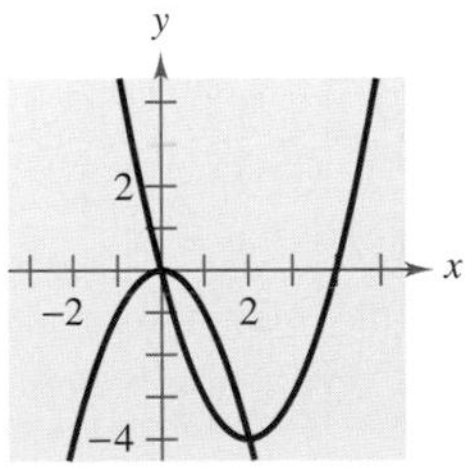

12. $\begin{cases} y = -2x^2 + 2 \\ y = 2(x^4 - 2x^2 + 1) \end{cases}$

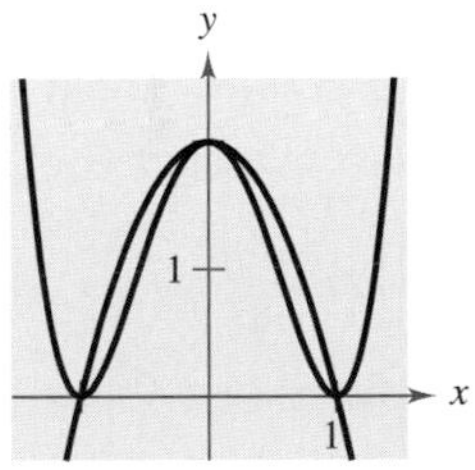

13. $\begin{cases} y = x^3 - 3x^2 + 1 \\ y = x^2 - 3x + 1 \end{cases}$

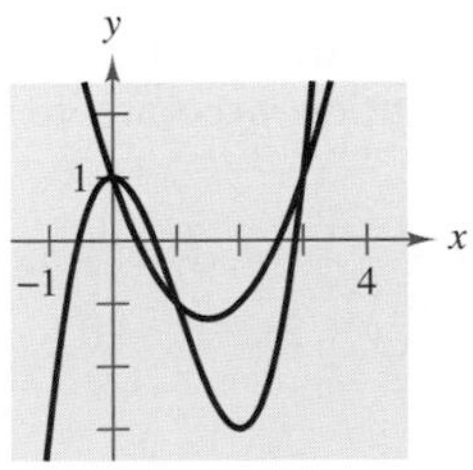

14. $\begin{cases} y = x^3 - 3x^2 + 4 \\ y = -2x + 4 \end{cases}$

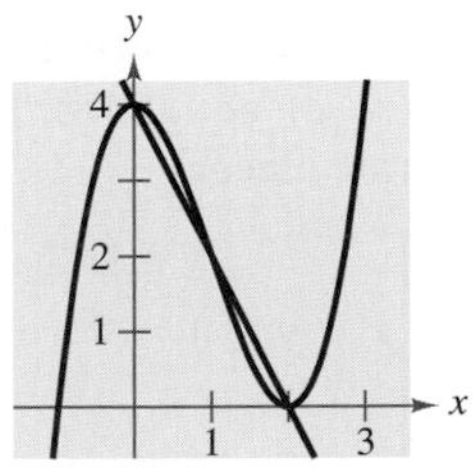

In Exercises 15–28, solve the system by the method of substitution.

15. $\begin{cases} x - y = 0 \\ 5x - 3y = 10 \end{cases}$

16. $\begin{cases} x + 2y = 1 \\ 5x - 4y = -23 \end{cases}$

17. $\begin{cases} 2x - y + 2 = 0 \\ 4x + y - 5 = 0 \end{cases}$

18. $\begin{cases} 6x - 3y - 4 = 0 \\ x + 2y - 4 = 0 \end{cases}$

19. $\begin{cases} 1.5x + 0.8y = 2.3 \\ 0.3x - 0.2y = 0.1 \end{cases}$

20. $\begin{cases} 0.5x + 3.2y = 9.0 \\ 0.2x - 1.6y = -3.6 \end{cases}$

21. $\begin{cases} \frac{1}{5}x + \frac{1}{2}y = 8 \\ x + y = 20 \end{cases}$

22. $\begin{cases} \frac{1}{2}x + \frac{3}{4}y = 10 \\ \frac{3}{4}x - y = 4 \end{cases}$

23. $\begin{cases} 6x + 5y = -3 \\ -x - \frac{5}{6}y = -7 \end{cases}$

24. $\begin{cases} -\frac{2}{3}x + y = 2 \\ 2x - 3y = 6 \end{cases}$

25. $\begin{cases} x^2 - y = 0 \\ 2x + y = 0 \end{cases}$

26. $\begin{cases} x - 2y = 0 \\ 3x - y^2 = 0 \end{cases}$

27. $\begin{cases} x - y = -1 \\ x^2 - y = -4 \end{cases}$

28. $\begin{cases} y = -x \\ y = x^3 + 3x^2 + 2x \end{cases}$

In Exercises 29–42, solve the system graphically.

29. $\begin{cases} -x + 2y = 2 \\ 3x + y = 15 \end{cases}$

30. $\begin{cases} x + y = 0 \\ 3x - 2y = 10 \end{cases}$

31. $\begin{cases} x - 3y = -2 \\ 5x + 3y = 17 \end{cases}$

32. $\begin{cases} -x + 2y = 1 \\ x - y = 2 \end{cases}$

33. $\begin{cases} x + y = 4 \\ x^2 + y^2 - 4x = 0 \end{cases}$

34. $\begin{cases} -x + y = 3 \\ x^2 - 6x - 27 + y^2 = 0 \end{cases}$

35. $\begin{cases} x - y + 3 = 0 \\ x^2 - 4x + 7 = y \end{cases}$

36. $\begin{cases} y^2 - 4x + 11 = 0 \\ -\frac{1}{2}x + y = -\frac{1}{2} \end{cases}$

37. $\begin{cases} 7x + 8y = 24 \\ x - 8y = 8 \end{cases}$

38. $\begin{cases} x - y = 0 \\ 5x - 2y = 6 \end{cases}$

39. $\begin{cases} 3x - 2y = 0 \\ x^2 - y^2 = 4 \end{cases}$

40. $\begin{cases} 2x - y + 3 = 0 \\ x^2 + y^2 - 4x = 0 \end{cases}$

41. $\begin{cases} x^2 + y^2 = 25 \\ 3x^2 - 16y = 0 \end{cases}$

42. $\begin{cases} x^2 + y^2 = 25 \\ (x - 8)^2 + y^2 = 41 \end{cases}$

In Exercises 43–48, use a graphing utility to solve the system of equations. Find the solution accurate to two decimal places.

43. $\begin{cases} y = e^x \\ x - y + 1 = 0 \end{cases}$

44. $\begin{cases} y = -4e^{-x} \\ y + 3x + 8 = 0 \end{cases}$

45. $\begin{cases} x + 2y = 8 \\ y = \log_2 x \end{cases}$

46. $\begin{cases} y = -2 + \ln(x - 1) \\ 3y + 2x = 9 \end{cases}$

47. $\begin{cases} x^2 + y^2 = 169 \\ x^2 - 8y = 104 \end{cases}$

48. $\begin{cases} x^2 + y^2 = 4 \\ 2x^2 - y = 2 \end{cases}$

In Exercises 49–60, solve the system graphically or algebraically. Explain your choice of method.

49. $\begin{cases} y = 2x \\ y = x^2 + 1 \end{cases}$

50. $\begin{cases} x + y = 4 \\ x^2 + y = 2 \end{cases}$

51. $\begin{cases} 3x - 7y + 6 = 0 \\ x^2 - y^2 = 4 \end{cases}$

52. $\begin{cases} x^2 + y^2 = 25 \\ 2x + y = 10 \end{cases}$

53. $\begin{cases} x - 2y = 4 \\ x^2 - y = 0 \end{cases}$

54. $\begin{cases} y = (x + 1)^3 \\ y = \sqrt{x - 1} \end{cases}$

55. $\begin{cases} y - e^{-x} = 1 \\ y - \ln x = 3 \end{cases}$

56. $\begin{cases} x^2 + y = 4 \\ e^x - y = 0 \end{cases}$

57. $\begin{cases} y = x^4 - 2x^2 + 1 \\ y = 1 - x^2 \end{cases}$

58. $\begin{cases} y = x^3 - 2x^2 + x - 1 \\ y = -x^2 + 3x - 1 \end{cases}$

59. $\begin{cases} xy - 1 = 0 \\ 2x - 4y + 7 = 0 \end{cases}$

60. $\begin{cases} x - 2y = 1 \\ y = \sqrt{x - 1} \end{cases}$

Break-Even Analysis **In Exercises 61 and 62, find the sales necessary to break even ($R = C$) for the cost C of producing x units and the revenue R obtained by selling x units. (Round to the nearest whole unit.)**

61. $C = 8650x + 250{,}000, \quad R = 9950x$

62. $C = 5.5\sqrt{x} + 10{,}000, \quad R = 3.29x$

63. ***Break-Even Analysis*** A small software company invests \$16,000 to produce a software package that will sell for \$55.95. Each unit can be produced for \$35.45.
    (a) How many units must be sold to break even?
    (b) How many units must be sold to make a profit of \$60,000?

64. ***Break-Even Analysis*** A small fast-food restaurant invests \$5000 to produce a new food item that will sell for \$3.49. Each item can be produced for \$2.16.
    (a) How many items must be sold to break even?
    (b) How many items must be sold to make a profit of \$8500?

65. ***DVD Rentals*** The weekly rentals for a newly released DVD of an animated film at a local video store decreased each week. At the same time, the weekly rentals for a newly released DVD of a horror film increased each week. Models that approximate the weekly rentals R for each DVD are

$$\begin{cases} R = 360 - 24x & \text{Animated film} \\ R = 24 + 18x & \text{Horror film} \end{cases}$$

where x represents the number of weeks each DVD was in the store, with $x = 1$ corresponding to the first week.
    (a) After how many weeks will the rentals for the two movies be equal?
    (b) Use a table to solve the system of equations numerically. Compare your result with that of part (a).

66. ***CD Sales*** The total weekly sales for a newly released rock CD increased each week. At the same time, the total weekly sales for a newly released rap CD decreased each week. Models that approximate the total weekly sales S (in thousands of units) for each CD are

$$\begin{cases} S = 25x + 100 & \text{Rock CD} \\ S = -50x + 475 & \text{Rap CD} \end{cases}$$

where x represents the number of weeks each CD was in stores, with $x = 0$ corresponding to the CD sales on the day each CD was first released in stores.

(a) After how many weeks will the sales for the two CDs be equal?

(b) Use a table to solve the system of equations numerically. Compare your result with that of part (a).

67. ***Choice of Two Jobs*** You are offered two jobs selling dental supplies. One company offers a straight commission of 6% of sales. The other company offers a salary of \$350 per week plus 3% of sales. How much would you have to sell in a week in order to make the straight commission offer better?

68. ***Supply and Demand*** The supply and demand curves for a business dealing with wheat are

Supply: $p = 1.45 + 0.00014x^2$

Demand: $p = (2.388 - 0.007x)^2$

where p is the price in dollars per bushel and x is the quantity in bushels per day. Use a graphing utility to graph the supply and demand equations and find the market equilibrium. (The market equilibrium is the point of intersection of the graphs for $x > 0$.)

69. ***Investment Portfolio*** A total of \$25,000 is invested in two funds paying 6% and 8.5% simple interest. (The 6% investment has a lower risk.) The investor wants a yearly interest income of \$2000 from the two investments.

(a) Write a system of equations in which one equation represents the total amount invested and the other equation represents the \$2000 required in interest. Let x and y represent the amounts invested at 6% and 8.5%, respectively.

(b) Use a graphing utility to graph the two equations in the same viewing window. As the amount invested at 6% increases, how does the amount invested at 8.5% change? How does the amount of interest income change? Explain.

(c) What amount should be invested at 6% to meet the requirement of \$2000 per year in interest?

70. ***Log Volume*** You are offered two different rules for estimating the number of board feet in a 16-foot log. (A board foot is a unit of measure for lumber equal to a board 1 foot square and 1 inch thick.) The first rule is the *Doyle Log Rule* and is modeled by

$$V_1 = (D - 4)^2, \quad 5 \le D \le 40$$

and the other is the *Scribner Log Rule* and is modeled by

$$V_2 = 0.79D^2 - 2D - 4, \quad 5 \le D \le 40$$

where D is the diameter (in inches) of the log and V is its volume (in board feet).

(a) Use a graphing utility to graph the two log rules in the same viewing window.

(b) For what diameter do the two scales agree?

(c) You are selling large logs by the board foot. Which scale would you use? Explain your reasoning.

Model It

71. ***Data Analysis: Renewable Energy*** The table shows the consumption C (in trillions of Btus) of solar energy and wind energy in the United States from 1998 to 2003. (Source: Energy Information Administration)

Year	Solar, C	Wind, C
1998	70	31
1999	69	46
2000	66	57
2001	65	68
2002	64	105
2003	63	108

(a) Use the *regression* feature of a graphing utility to find a quadratic model for the solar energy consumption data and a linear model for the wind energy consumption data. Let t represent the year, with $t = 8$ corresponding to 1998.

(b) Use a graphing utility to graph the data and the two models in the same viewing window.

(c) Use the graph from part (b) to approximate the point of intersection of the graphs of the models. Interpret your answer in the context of the problem.

(d) Approximate the point of intersection of the graphs of the models algebraically.

(e) Compare your results from parts (c) and (d).

(f) Use your school's library, the Internet, or some other reference source to research the advantages and disadvantages of using renewable energy.

72. ***Data Analysis: Population*** The table shows the populations P (in thousands) of Alabama and Colorado from 1999 to 2003. (Source: U.S. Census Bureau)

Year	Alabama, P	Colorado, P
1999	4430	4226
2000	4447	4302
2001	4466	4429
2002	4479	4501
2003	4501	4551

(a) Use the *regression* feature of a graphing utility to find linear models for each set of data. Graph the models in the same viewing window. Let t represent the year, with $t = 9$ corresponding to 1999.

(b) Use your graph from part (a) to approximate when the population of Colorado exceeded the population of Alabama.

(c) Verify your answer from part (b) algebraically.

Geometry **In Exercises 73–76, find the dimensions of the rectangle meeting the specified conditions.**

73. The perimeter is 30 meters and the length is 3 meters greater than the width.

74. The perimeter is 280 centimeters and the width is 20 centimeters less than the length.

75. The perimeter is 42 inches and the width is three-fourths the length.

76. The perimeter is 210 feet and the length is $1\frac{1}{2}$ times the width.

77. ***Geometry*** What are the dimensions of a rectangular tract of land if its perimeter is 40 kilometers and its area is 96 square kilometers?

78. ***Geometry*** What are the dimensions of an isosceles right triangle with a two-inch hypotenuse and an area of 1 square inch?

Synthesis

True or False? **In Exercises 79 and 80, determine whether the statement is true or false. Justify your answer.**

79. In order to solve a system of equations by substitution, you must always solve for y in one of the two equations and then back-substitute.

80. If a system consists of a parabola and a circle, then the system can have at most two solutions.

81. ***Writing*** List and explain the steps used to solve a system of equations by the method of substitution.

82. ***Think About It*** When solving a system of equations by substitution, how do you recognize that the system has no solution?

83. ***Exploration*** Find an equation of a line whose graph intersects the graph of the parabola $y = x^2$ at (a) two points, (b) one point, and (c) no points. (There is more than one correct answer.)

84. ***Conjecture*** Consider the system of equations

$$\begin{cases} y = b^x \\ y = x^b \end{cases}.$$

(a) Use a graphing utility to graph the system for $b = 1, 2, 3,$ and 4.

(b) For a fixed even value of $b > 1$, make a conjecture about the number of points of intersection of the graphs in part (a).

Skills Review

In Exercises 85–90, find the general form of the equation of the line passing through the two points.

85. $(-2, 7), (5, 5)$

86. $(3.5, 4), (10, 6)$

87. $(6, 3), (10, 3)$

88. $(4, -2), (4, 5)$

89. $\left(\frac{3}{5}, 0\right), (4, 6)$

90. $\left(-\frac{7}{3}, 8\right), \left(\frac{5}{2}, \frac{1}{2}\right)$

In Exercises 91–94, find the domain of the function and identify any horizontal or vertical asymptotes.

91. $f(x) = \dfrac{5}{x - 6}$

92. $f(x) = \dfrac{2x - 7}{3x + 2}$

93. $f(x) = \dfrac{x^2 + 2}{x^2 - 16}$

94. $f(x) = 3 - \dfrac{2}{x^2}$

7.2 Two-Variable Linear Systems

What you should learn

- Use the method of elimination to solve systems of linear equations in two variables.
- Interpret graphically the numbers of solutions of systems of linear equations in two variables.
- Use systems of linear equations in two variables to model and solve real-life problems.

Why you should learn it

You can use systems of equations in two variables to model and solve real-life problems. For instance, in Exercise 63 on page 517, you will solve a system of equations to find a linear model that represents the relationship between wheat yield and amount of fertilizer applied.

© Bill Stormont/Corbis

The Method of Elimination

In Section 7.1, you studied two methods for solving a system of equations: substitution and graphing. Now you will study the **method of elimination.** The key step in this method is to obtain, for one of the variables, coefficients that differ only in sign so that *adding* the equations eliminates the variable.

$$3x + 5y = 7 \qquad \text{Equation 1}$$
$$-3x - 2y = -1 \qquad \text{Equation 2}$$
$$3y = 6 \qquad \text{Add equations.}$$

Note that by adding the two equations, you eliminate the x-terms and obtain a single equation in y. Solving this equation for y produces $y = 2$, which you can then back-substitute into one of the original equations to solve for x.

Example 1 Solving a System of Equations by Elimination

Solve the system of linear equations.

$$\begin{cases} 3x + 2y = 4 & \text{Equation 1} \\ 5x - 2y = 8 & \text{Equation 2} \end{cases}$$

Solution

Because the coefficients of y differ only in sign, you can eliminate the y-terms by adding the two equations.

$$3x + 2y = 4 \qquad \text{Write Equation 1.}$$
$$5x - 2y = 8 \qquad \text{Write Equation 2.}$$
$$8x = 12 \qquad \text{Add equations.}$$

So, $x = \frac{3}{2}$. By back-substituting this value into Equation 1, you can solve for y.

$$3x + 2y = 4 \qquad \text{Write Equation 1.}$$
$$3\left(\tfrac{3}{2}\right) + 2y = 4 \qquad \text{Substitute } \tfrac{3}{2} \text{ for } x.$$
$$\tfrac{9}{2} + 2y = 4 \qquad \text{Simplify.}$$
$$y = -\tfrac{1}{4} \qquad \text{Solve for } y.$$

The solution is $\left(\frac{3}{2}, -\frac{1}{4}\right)$. Check this in the original system, as follows.

Check

$$3\left(\tfrac{3}{2}\right) + 2\left(-\tfrac{1}{4}\right) \stackrel{?}{=} 4 \qquad \text{Substitute into Equation 1.}$$
$$\tfrac{9}{2} - \tfrac{1}{2} = 4 \qquad \text{Equation 1 checks. ✓}$$
$$5\left(\tfrac{3}{2}\right) - 2\left(-\tfrac{1}{4}\right) \stackrel{?}{=} 8 \qquad \text{Substitute into Equation 2.}$$
$$\tfrac{15}{2} + \tfrac{1}{2} = 8 \qquad \text{Equation 2 checks. ✓}$$

✓CHECKPOINT Now try Exercise 11.

Exploration

Use the method of substitution to solve the system in Example 1. Which method is easier?

Method of Elimination

To use the **method of elimination** to solve a system of two linear equations in x and y, perform the following steps.

1. *Obtain coefficients* for x (or y) that differ only in sign by multiplying all terms of one or both equations by suitably chosen constants.
2. *Add* the equations to eliminate one variable, and solve the resulting equation.
3. *Back-substitute* the value obtained in Step 2 into either of the original equations and solve for the other variable.
4. *Check* your solution in both of the original equations.

Example 2 Solving a System of Equations by Elimination

Solve the system of linear equations.

$$\begin{cases} 2x - 3y = -7 & \text{Equation 1} \\ 3x + y = -5 & \text{Equation 2} \end{cases}$$

Solution

For this system, you can obtain coefficients that differ only in sign by multiplying Equation 2 by 3.

$$\begin{array}{lcll} 2x - 3y = -7 & \Rightarrow & 2x - 3y = -7 & \text{Write Equation 1.} \\ \underline{3x + y = -5} & \Rightarrow & \underline{9x + 3y = -15} & \text{Multiply Equation 2 by 3.} \\ & & 11x \qquad = -22 & \text{Add equations.} \end{array}$$

So, you can see that $x = -2$. By back-substituting this value of x into Equation 1, you can solve for y.

$$\begin{aligned} 2x - 3y &= -7 && \text{Write Equation 1.} \\ 2(-2) - 3y &= -7 && \text{Substitute } -2 \text{ for } x. \\ -3y &= -3 && \text{Combine like terms.} \\ y &= 1 && \text{Solve for } y. \end{aligned}$$

The solution is $(-2, 1)$. Check this in the original system, as follows.

Check

$$\begin{aligned} 2x - 3y &= -7 && \text{Write original Equation 1.} \\ 2(-2) - 3(1) &\stackrel{?}{=} -7 && \text{Substitute into Equation 1.} \\ -4 - 3 &= -7 && \text{Equation 1 checks. ✓} \\ 3x + y &= -5 && \text{Write original Equation 2.} \\ 3(-2) + 1 &\stackrel{?}{=} -5 && \text{Substitute into Equation 2.} \\ -6 + 1 &= -5 && \text{Equation 2 checks. ✓} \end{aligned}$$

✓CHECKPOINT Now try Exercise 13.

Exploration

Rewrite each system of equations in slope-intercept form and sketch the graph of each system. What is the relationship between the slopes of the two lines and the number of points of intersection?

a. $\begin{cases} 5x - y = -1 \\ -x + y = -5 \end{cases}$

b. $\begin{cases} 4x - 3y = 1 \\ -8x + 6y = -2 \end{cases}$

c. $\begin{cases} x + 2y = 3 \\ x + 2y = -8 \end{cases}$

In Example 2, the two systems of linear equations (the original system and the system obtained by multiplying by constants)

$$\begin{cases} 2x - 3y = -7 \\ 3x + y = -5 \end{cases} \quad \text{and} \quad \begin{cases} 2x - 3y = -7 \\ 9x + 3y = -15 \end{cases}$$

are called **equivalent systems** because they have precisely the same solution set. The operations that can be performed on a system of linear equations to produce an equivalent system are (1) interchanging any two equations, (2) multiplying an equation by a nonzero constant, and (3) adding a multiple of one equation to any other equation in the system.

Example 3 Solving the System of Equations by Elimination

Solve the system of linear equations.

$$\begin{cases} 5x + 3y = 9 & \text{Equation 1} \\ 2x - 4y = 14 & \text{Equation 2} \end{cases}$$

Algebraic Solution

You can obtain coefficients that differ only in sign by multiplying Equation 1 by 4 and multiplying Equation 2 by 3.

$5x + 3y = 9 \Rightarrow 20x + 12y = 36$ Multiply Equation 1 by 4.

$2x - 4y = 14 \Rightarrow 6x - 12y = 42$ Multiply Equation 2 by 3.

$26x = 78$ Add equations.

From this equation, you can see that $x = 3$. By back-substituting this value of x into Equation 2, you can solve for y.

$2x - 4y = 14$ Write Equation 2.

$2(3) - 4y = 14$ Substitute 3 for x.

$-4y = 8$ Combine like terms.

$y = -2$ Solve for y.

The solution is $(3, -2)$. Check this in the original system.

Graphical Solution

Solve each equation for y. Then use a graphing utility to graph $y_1 = -\frac{5}{3}x + 3$ and $y_2 = \frac{1}{2}x - \frac{7}{2}$ in the same viewing window. Use the *intersect* feature or the *zoom* and *trace* features to approximate the point of intersection of the graphs. From the graph in Figure 7.6, you can see that the point of intersection is $(3, -2)$. You can determine that this is the exact solution by checking $(3, -2)$ in both equations.

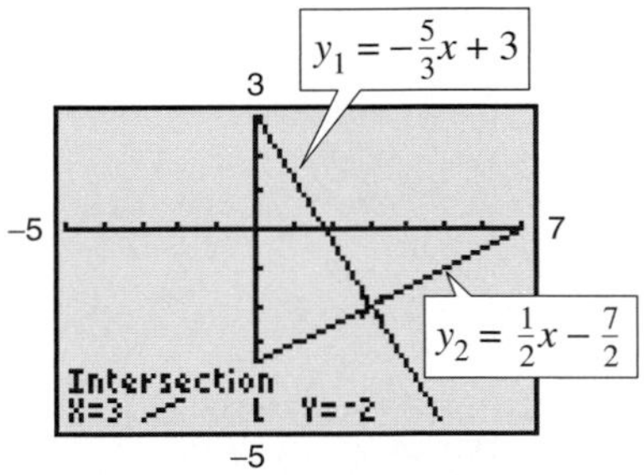

FIGURE 7.6

✓CHECKPOINT Now try Exercise 15.

You can check the solution from Example 3 as follows.

$5(3) + 3(-2) \stackrel{?}{=} 9$ Substitute 3 for x and -2 for y in Equation 1.

$15 - 6 = 9$ Equation 1 checks. ✓

$2(3) - 4(-2) \stackrel{?}{=} 14$ Substitute 3 for x and -2 for y in Equation 2.

$6 + 8 = 14$ Equation 2 checks. ✓

Keep in mind that the terminology and methods discussed in this section apply only to systems of *linear* equations.

Graphical Interpretation of Solutions

It is possible for a *general* system of equations to have exactly one solution, two or more solutions, or no solution. If a system of *linear* equations has two different solutions, it must have an *infinite* number of solutions.

Graphical Interpretations of Solutions

For a system of two linear equations in two variables, the number of solutions is one of the following.

Number of Solutions	*Graphical Interpretation*	*Slopes of Lines*
1. Exactly one solution	The two lines intersect at one point.	The slopes of the two lines are not equal.
2. Infinitely many solutions	The two lines coincide (are identical).	The slopes of the two lines are equal.
3. No solution	The two lines are parallel.	The slopes of the two lines are equal.

A system of linear equations is **consistent** if it has at least one solution. A consistent system with exactly one solution is *independent*, whereas a consistent system with infinitely many solutions is *dependent*. A system is **inconsistent** if it has no solution.

Example 4 Recognizing Graphs of Linear Systems

Match each system of linear equations with its graph in Figure 7.7. Describe the number of solutions and state whether the system is consistent or inconsistent.

a. $\begin{cases} 2x - 3y = 3 \\ -4x + 6y = 6 \end{cases}$ **b.** $\begin{cases} 2x - 3y = 3 \\ x + 2y = 5 \end{cases}$ **c.** $\begin{cases} 2x - 3y = 3 \\ -4x + 6y = -6 \end{cases}$

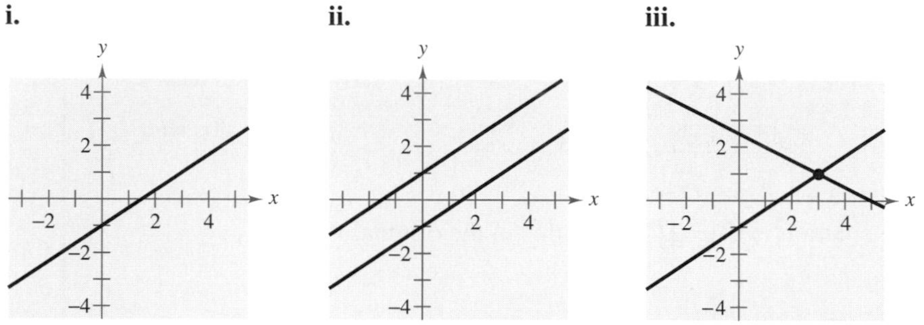

FIGURE 7.7

Solution

a. The graph of system (a) is a pair of parallel lines (ii). The lines have no point of intersection, so the system has no solution. The system is inconsistent.

b. The graph of system (b) is a pair of intersecting lines (iii). The lines have one point of intersection, so the system has exactly one solution. The system is consistent.

c. The graph of system (c) is a pair of lines that coincide (i). The lines have infinitely many points of intersection, so the system has infinitely many solutions. The system is consistent.

CHECKPOINT Now try Exercises 31–34.

STUDY TIP

A comparison of the slopes of two lines gives useful information about the number of solutions of the corresponding system of equations. To solve a system of equations graphically, it helps to begin by writing the equations in slope-intercept form. Try doing this for the systems in Example 4.

In Examples 5 and 6, note how you can use the method of elimination to determine that a system of linear equations has no solution or infinitely many solutions.

Example 5 No-Solution Case: Method of Elimination

Solve the system of linear equations.

$$\begin{cases} x - 2y = 3 & \text{Equation 1} \\ -2x + 4y = 1 & \text{Equation 2} \end{cases}$$

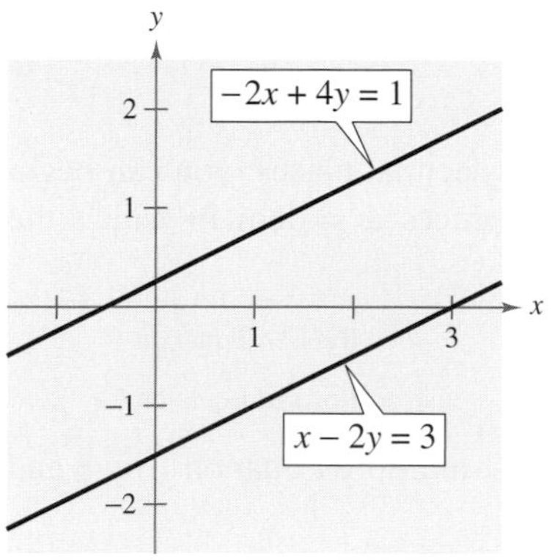

FIGURE 7.8

Solution

To obtain coefficients that differ only in sign, multiply Equation 1 by 2.

$x - 2y = 3 \Rightarrow 2x - 4y = 6$ Multiply Equation 1 by 2.

$-2x + 4y = 1 \Rightarrow -2x + 4y = 1$ Write Equation 2.

$0 = 7$ False statement

Because there are no values of x and y for which $0 = 7$, you can conclude that the system is inconsistent and has no solution. The lines corresponding to the two equations in this system are shown in Figure 7.8. Note that the two lines are parallel and therefore have no point of intersection.

✓CHECKPOINT Now try Exercise 19.

In Example 5, note that the occurrence of a false statement, such as $0 = 7$, indicates that the system has no solution. In the next example, note that the occurrence of a statement that is true for all values of the variables, such as $0 = 0$, indicates that the system has infinitely many solutions.

Example 6 Many-Solution Case: Method of Elimination

Solve the system of linear equations.

$$\begin{cases} 2x - y = 1 & \text{Equation 1} \\ 4x - 2y = 2 & \text{Equation 2} \end{cases}$$

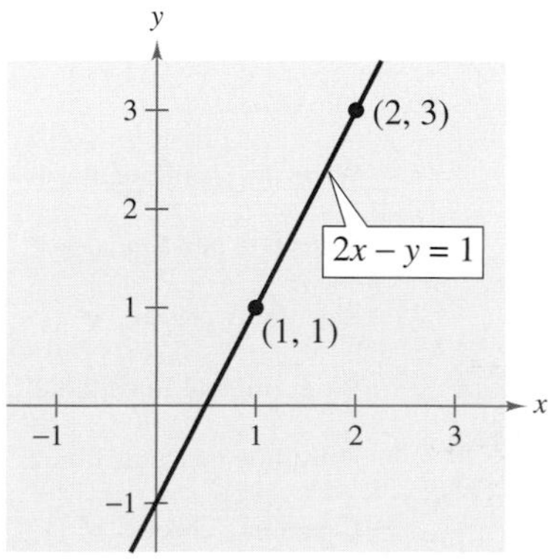

FIGURE 7.9

Solution

To obtain coefficients that differ only in sign, multiply Equation 2 by $-\frac{1}{2}$.

$2x - y = 1 \Rightarrow 2x - y = 1$ Write Equation 1.

$4x - 2y = 2 \Rightarrow -2x + y = -1$ Multiply Equation 2 by $-\frac{1}{2}$.

$0 = 0$ Add equations.

Because the two equations turn out to be equivalent (have the same solution set), you can conclude that the system has infinitely many solutions. The solution set consists of all points (x, y) lying on the line $2x - y = 1$, as shown in Figure 7.9. Letting $x = a$, where a is any real number, you can see that the solutions to the system are $(a, 2a - 1)$.

✓CHECKPOINT Now try Exercise 23.

> **Technology**
>
> The general solution of the linear system
>
> $$\begin{cases} ax + by = c \\ dx + ey = f \end{cases}$$
>
> is $x = (ce - bf)/(ae - bd)$ and $y = (af - cd)/(ae - bd)$. If $ae - bd = 0$, the system does not have a unique solution. A graphing utility program (called Systems of Linear Equations) for solving such a system can be found at our website *college.hmco.com*. Try using the program for your graphing utility to solve the system in Example 7.

Example 7 illustrates a strategy for solving a system of linear equations that has decimal coefficients.

Example 7 A Linear System Having Decimal Coefficients

Solve the system of linear equations.

$$\begin{cases} 0.02x - 0.05y = -0.38 & \text{Equation 1} \\ 0.03x + 0.04y = 1.04 & \text{Equation 2} \end{cases}$$

Solution

Because the coefficients in this system have two decimal places, you can begin by multiplying each equation by 100. This produces a system in which the coefficients are all integers.

$$\begin{cases} 2x - 5y = -38 & \text{Revised Equation 1} \\ 3x + 4y = 104 & \text{Revised Equation 2} \end{cases}$$

Now, to obtain coefficients that differ only in sign, multiply Equation 1 by 3 and multiply Equation 2 by -2.

$2x - 5y = -38 \quad \Rightarrow \quad 6x - 15y = -114$ Multiply Equation 1 by 3.

$3x + 4y = 104 \quad \Rightarrow \quad -6x - 8y = -208$ Multiply Equation 2 by -2.

$-23y = -322$ Add equations.

So, you can conclude that

$$y = \frac{-322}{-23} = 14.$$

Back-substituting this value into revised Equation 2 produces the following.

$3x + 4y = 104$ Write revised Equation 2.

$3x + 4(14) = 104$ Substitute 14 for y.

$3x = 48$ Combine like terms.

$x = 16$ Solve for x.

The solution is $(16, 14)$. Check this in the original system, as follows.

Check

$0.02x - 0.05y = -0.38$ Write original Equation 1.

$0.02(16) - 0.05(14) \stackrel{?}{=} -0.38$ Substitute into Equation 1.

$0.32 - 0.70 = -0.38$ Equation 1 checks. ✓

$0.03x + 0.04y = 1.04$ Write original Equation 2.

$0.03(16) + 0.04(14) \stackrel{?}{=} 1.04$ Substitute into Equation 2.

$0.48 + 0.56 = 1.04$ Equation 2 checks. ✓

✓CHECKPOINT Now try Exercise 25.

Applications

At this point, you may be asking the question "How can I tell which application problems can be solved using a system of linear equations?" The answer comes from the following considerations.

1. Does the problem involve more than one unknown quantity?
2. Are there two (or more) equations or conditions to be satisfied?

If one or both of these situations occur, the appropriate mathematical model for the problem may be a system of linear equations.

Example 8 An Application of a Linear System

An airplane flying into a headwind travels the 2000-mile flying distance between Chicopee, Massachusetts and Salt Lake City, Utah in 4 hours and 24 minutes. On the return flight, the same distance is traveled in 4 hours. Find the airspeed of the plane and the speed of the wind, assuming that both remain constant.

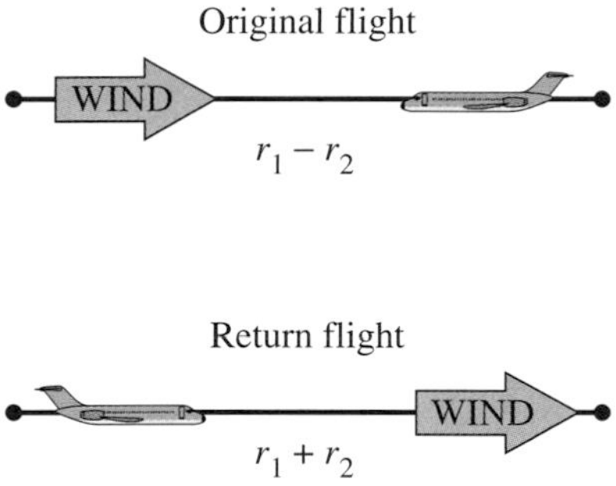

FIGURE 7.10

Solution

The two unknown quantities are the speeds of the wind and the plane. If r_1 is the speed of the plane and r_2 is the speed of the wind, then

$$r_1 - r_2 = \text{speed of the plane against the wind}$$

$$r_1 + r_2 = \text{speed of the plane with the wind}$$

as shown in Figure 7.10. Using the formula distance = (rate)(time) for these two speeds, you obtain the following equations.

$$2000 = (r_1 - r_2)\left(4 + \frac{24}{60}\right)$$

$$2000 = (r_1 + r_2)(4)$$

These two equations simplify as follows.

$$\begin{cases} 5000 = 11r_1 - 11r_2 & \text{Equation 1} \\ 500 = r_1 + r_2 & \text{Equation 2} \end{cases}$$

To solve this system by elimination, multiply Equation 2 by 11.

$$\begin{array}{lcll} 5000 = 11r_1 - 11r_2 & \Rightarrow & 5000 = 11r_1 - 11r_2 & \text{Write Equation 1.} \\ \underline{500 = r_1 + r_2} & \Rightarrow & \underline{5500 = 11r_1 + 11r_2} & \text{Multiply Equation 2 by 11.} \\ & & 10{,}500 = 22r_1 & \text{Add equations.} \end{array}$$

So,

$$r_1 = \frac{10{,}500}{22} = \frac{5250}{11} \approx 477.27 \text{ miles per hour} \qquad \text{Speed of plane}$$

$$r_2 = 500 - \frac{5250}{11} = \frac{250}{11} \approx 22.73 \text{ miles per hour.} \qquad \text{Speed of wind}$$

Check this solution in the original statement of the problem.

CHECKPOINT Now try Exercise 43.

In a free market, the demands for many products are related to the prices of the products. As the prices decrease, the demands by consumers increase and the amounts that producers are able or willing to supply decrease.

Example 9 Finding the Equilibrium Point

The demand and supply functions for a new type of personal digital assistant are

$$\begin{cases} p = 150 - 0.00001x & \text{Demand equation} \\ p = 60 + 0.00002x & \text{Supply equation} \end{cases}$$

where p is the price in dollars and x represents the number of units. Find the equilibrium point for this market. The **equilibrium point** is the price p and number of units x that satisfy both the demand and supply equations.

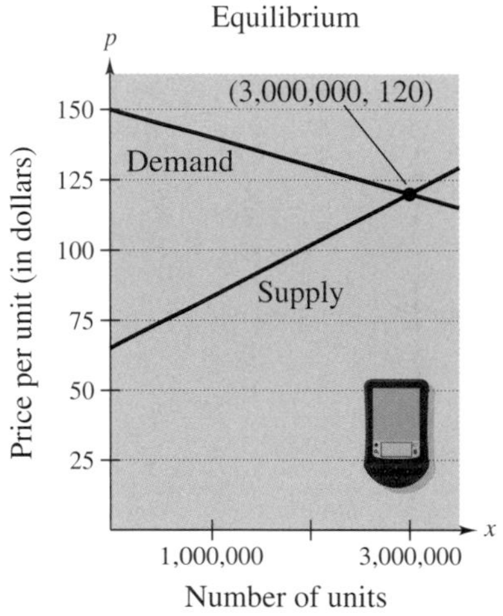

FIGURE 7.11

Solution

Because p is written in terms of x, begin by substituting the value of p given in the supply equation into the demand equation.

$$p = 150 - 0.00001x \qquad \text{Write demand equation.}$$

$$60 + 0.00002x = 150 - 0.00001x \qquad \text{Substitute } 60 + 0.00002x \text{ for } p.$$

$$0.00003x = 90 \qquad \text{Combine like terms.}$$

$$x = 3{,}000{,}000 \qquad \text{Solve for } x.$$

So, the equilibrium point occurs when the demand and supply are each 3 million units. (See Figure 7.11.) The price that corresponds to this x-value is obtained by back-substituting $x = 3{,}000{,}000$ into either of the original equations. For instance, back-substituting into the demand equation produces

$$p = 150 - 0.00001(3{,}000{,}000)$$

$$= 150 - 30$$

$$= \$120.$$

The solution is (3,000,000, 120). You can check this as follows.

Check

Substitute (3,000,000, 120) into the demand equation.

$$p = 150 - 0.00001x \qquad \text{Write demand equation.}$$

$$120 \stackrel{?}{=} 150 - 0.00001(3{,}000{,}000) \qquad \text{Substitute 120 for } p \text{ and 3,000,000 for } x.$$

$$120 = 120 \qquad \text{Solution checks in demand equation.} \checkmark$$

Substitute (3,000,000, 120) into the supply equation.

$$p = 60 + 0.00002x \qquad \text{Write supply equation.}$$

$$120 \stackrel{?}{=} 60 + 0.00002(3{,}000{,}000) \qquad \text{Substitute 120 for } p \text{ and 3,000,000 for } x.$$

$$120 = 120 \qquad \text{Solution checks in supply equation.} \checkmark$$

✓CHECKPOINT Now try Exercise 45.

7.2 Exercises

VOCABULARY CHECK: Fill in the blanks.

1. The first step in solving a system of equations by the method of ________ is to obtain coefficients for x (or y) that differ only in sign.
2. Two systems of equations that have the same solution set are called ________ systems.
3. A system of linear equations that has at least one solution is called ________, whereas a system of linear equations that has no solution is called ________.
4. In business applications, the ________ ________ is defined as the price p and the number of units x that satisfy both the demand and supply equations.

In Exercises 1–10, solve the system by the method of elimination. Label each line with its equation. To print an enlarged copy of the graph, go to the website *www.mathgraphs.com*.

1. $\begin{cases} 2x + y = 5 \\ x - y = 1 \end{cases}$

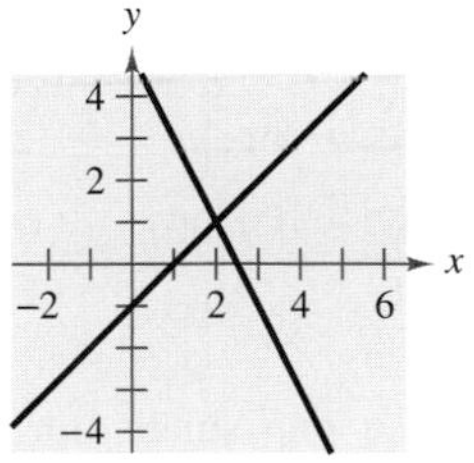

2. $\begin{cases} x + 3y = 1 \\ -x + 2y = 4 \end{cases}$

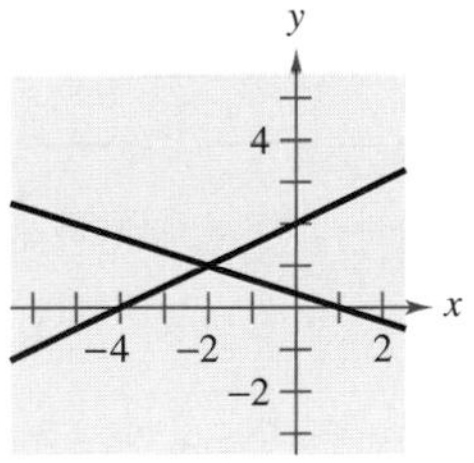

3. $\begin{cases} x + y = 0 \\ 3x + 2y = 1 \end{cases}$

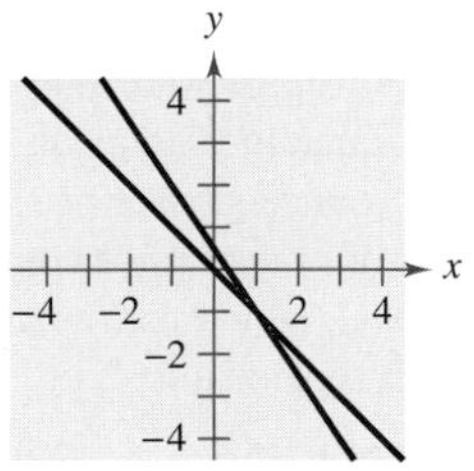

4. $\begin{cases} 2x - y = 3 \\ 4x + 3y = 21 \end{cases}$

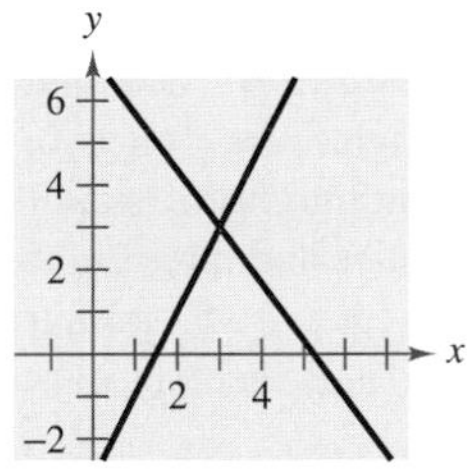

5. $\begin{cases} x - y = 2 \\ -2x + 2y = 5 \end{cases}$

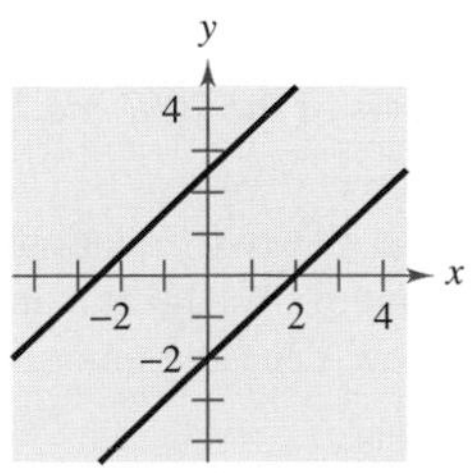

6. $\begin{cases} 3x + 2y = 3 \\ 6x + 4y = 14 \end{cases}$

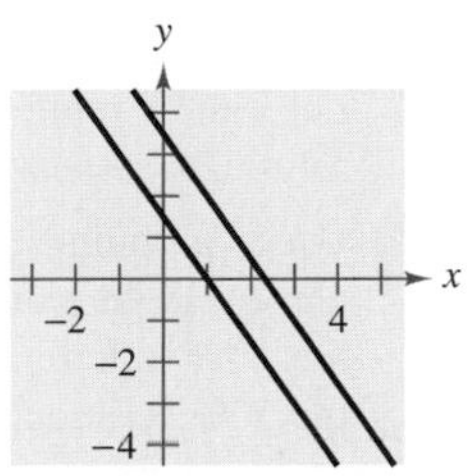

7. $\begin{cases} 3x - 2y = 5 \\ -6x + 4y = -10 \end{cases}$

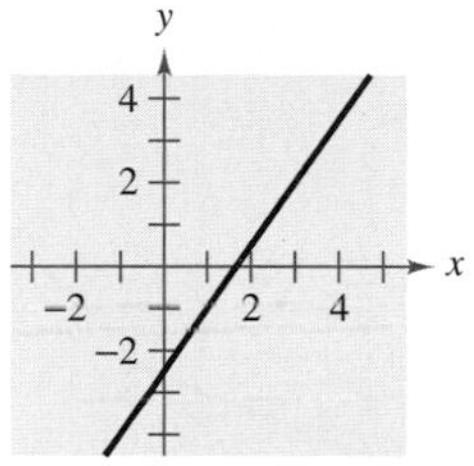

8. $\begin{cases} 9x - 3y = -15 \\ -3x + y = 5 \end{cases}$

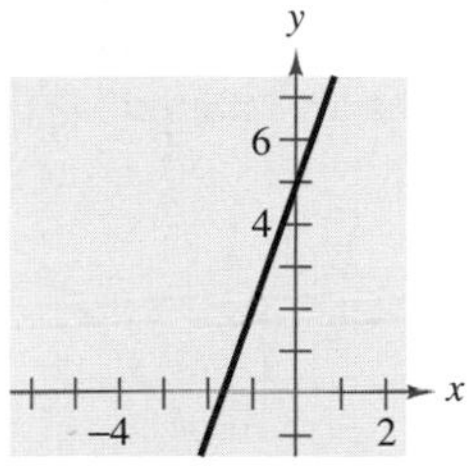

9. $\begin{cases} 9x + 3y = 1 \\ 3x - 6y = 5 \end{cases}$

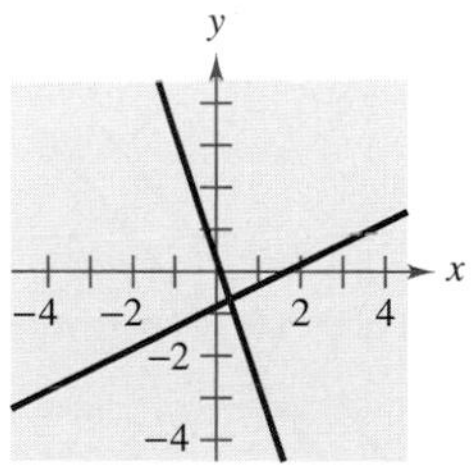

10. $\begin{cases} 5x + 3y = -18 \\ 2x - 6y = 1 \end{cases}$

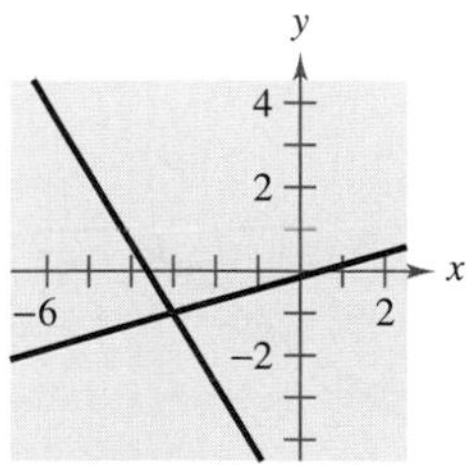

In Exercises 11–30, solve the system by the method of elimination and check any solutions algebraically.

11. $\begin{cases} x + 2y = 4 \\ x - 2y = 1 \end{cases}$

12. $\begin{cases} 3x - 5y = 2 \\ 2x + 5y = 13 \end{cases}$

13. $\begin{cases} 2x + 3y = 18 \\ 5x - y = 11 \end{cases}$

14. $\begin{cases} x + 7y = 12 \\ 3x - 5y = 10 \end{cases}$

15. $\begin{cases} 3x + 2y = 10 \\ 2x + 5y = 3 \end{cases}$

16. $\begin{cases} 2r + 4s = 5 \\ 16r + 50s = 55 \end{cases}$

17. $\begin{cases} 5u + 6v = 24 \\ 3u + 5v = 18 \end{cases}$

18. $\begin{cases} 3x + 11y = 4 \\ -2x - 5y = 9 \end{cases}$

19. $\begin{cases} \frac{9}{5}x + \frac{6}{5}y = 4 \\ 9x + 6y = 3 \end{cases}$

20. $\begin{cases} \frac{3}{4}x + y = \frac{1}{8} \\ \frac{9}{4}x + 3y = \frac{3}{8} \end{cases}$

21. $\begin{cases} \dfrac{x}{4} + \dfrac{y}{6} = 1 \\ x - y = 3 \end{cases}$

22. $\begin{cases} \dfrac{2}{3}x + \dfrac{1}{6}y = \dfrac{2}{3} \\ 4x + y = 4 \end{cases}$

23. $\begin{cases} -5x + 6y = -3 \\ 20x - 24y = 12 \end{cases}$

24. $\begin{cases} 7x + 8y = 6 \\ -14x - 16y = -12 \end{cases}$

25. $\begin{cases} 0.05x - 0.03y = 0.21 \\ 0.07x + 0.02y = 0.16 \end{cases}$

26. $\begin{cases} 0.2x - 0.5y = -27.8 \\ 0.3x + 0.4y = 68.7 \end{cases}$

27. $\begin{cases} 4b + 3m = 3 \\ 3b + 11m = 13 \end{cases}$

28. $\begin{cases} 2x + 5y = 8 \\ 5x + 8y = 10 \end{cases}$

29. $\begin{cases} \dfrac{x+3}{4} + \dfrac{y-1}{3} = 1 \\ 2x - y = 12 \end{cases}$

30. $\begin{cases} \dfrac{x-1}{2} + \dfrac{y+2}{3} = 4 \\ x - 2y = 5 \end{cases}$

In Exercises 31–34, match the system of linear equations with its graph. Describe the number of solutions and state whether the system is consistent or inconsistent. [The graphs are labeled (a), (b), (c) and (d).]

(a)

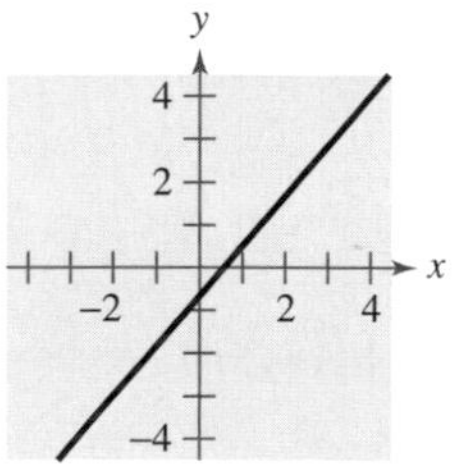

(b)

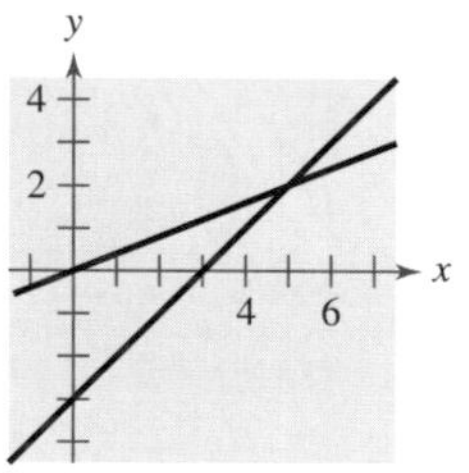

(c)

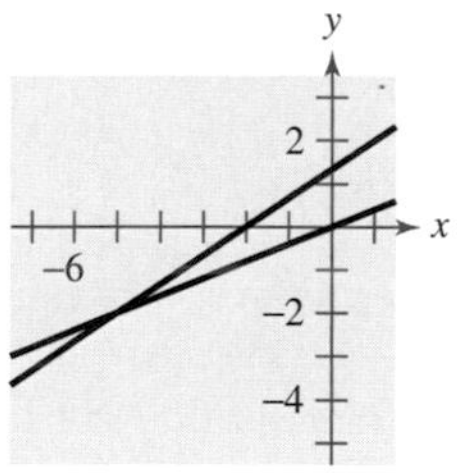

(d)

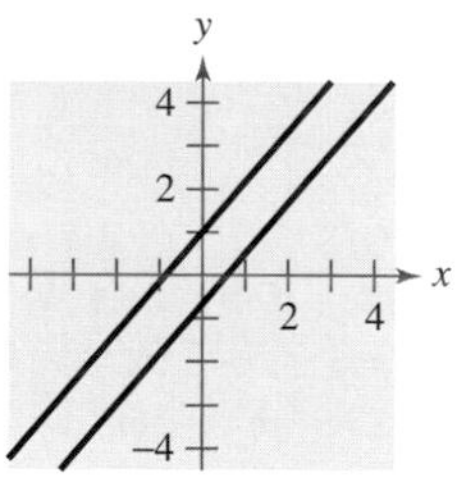

31. $\begin{cases} 2x - 5y = 0 \\ x - y = 3 \end{cases}$

32. $\begin{cases} -7x + 6y = -4 \\ 14x - 12y = 8 \end{cases}$

33. $\begin{cases} 2x - 5y = 0 \\ 2x - 3y = -4 \end{cases}$

34. $\begin{cases} 7x - 6y = -6 \\ -7x + 6y = -4 \end{cases}$

In Exercises 35–42, use any method to solve the system.

35. $\begin{cases} 3x - 5y = 7 \\ 2x + y = 9 \end{cases}$

36. $\begin{cases} -x + 3y = 17 \\ 4x + 3y = 7 \end{cases}$

37. $\begin{cases} y = 2x - 5 \\ y = 5x - 11 \end{cases}$

38. $\begin{cases} 7x + 3y = 16 \\ y = x + 2 \end{cases}$

39. $\begin{cases} x - 5y = 21 \\ 6x + 5y = 21 \end{cases}$

40. $\begin{cases} y = -3x - 8 \\ y = 15 - 2x \end{cases}$

41. $\begin{cases} -2x + 8y = 19 \\ y = x - 3 \end{cases}$

42. $\begin{cases} 4x - 3y = 6 \\ -5x + 7y = -1 \end{cases}$

43. ***Airplane Speed*** An airplane flying into a headwind travels the 1800-mile flying distance between Pittsburgh, Pennsylvania and Phoenix, Arizona in 3 hours and 36 minutes. On the return flight, the distance is traveled in 3 hours. Find the airspeed of the plane and the speed of the wind, assuming that both remain constant.

44. ***Airplane Speed*** Two planes start from Los Angeles International Airport and fly in opposite directions. The second plane starts $\frac{1}{2}$ hour after the first plane, but its speed is 80 kilometers per hour faster. Find the airspeed of each plane if 2 hours after the first plane departs the planes are 3200 kilometers apart.

Supply and Demand **In Exercises 45–48, find the equilibrium point of the demand and supply equations. The equilibrium point is the price p and number of units x that satisfy both the demand and supply equations.**

	Demand	*Supply*
45.	$p = 50 - 0.5x$	$p = 0.125x$
46.	$p = 100 - 0.05x$	$p = 25 + 0.1x$
47.	$p = 140 - 0.00002x$	$p = 80 + 0.00001x$
48.	$p = 400 - 0.0002x$	$p = 225 + 0.0005x$

49. ***Nutrition*** Two cheeseburgers and one small order of French fries from a fast-food restaurant contain a total of 850 calories. Three cheeseburgers and two small orders of French fries contain a total of 1390 calories. Find the caloric content of each item.

50. ***Nutrition*** One eight-ounce glass of apple juice and one eight-ounce glass of orange juice contain a total of 185 milligrams of vitamin C. Two eight-ounce glasses of apple juice and three eight-ounce glasses of orange juice contain a total of 452 milligrams of vitamin C. How much vitamin C is in an eight-ounce glass of each type of juice?

51. ***Acid Mixture*** Ten liters of a 30% acid solution is obtained by mixing a 20% solution with a 50% solution.

(a) Write a system of equations in which one equation represents the amount of final mixture required and the other represents the percent of acid in the final mixture. Let x and y represent the amounts of the 20% and 50% solutions, respectively.

(b) Use a graphing utility to graph the two equations in part (a) in the same viewing window. As the amount of the 20% solution increases, how does the amount of the 50% solution change?

(c) How much of each solution is required to obtain the specified concentration of the final mixture?

52. ***Fuel Mixture*** Five hundred gallons of 89 octane gasoline is obtained by mixing 87 octane gasoline with 92 octane gasoline.

(a) Write a system of equations in which one equation represents the amount of final mixture required and the other represents the amounts of 87 and 92 octane gasolines in the final mixture. Let x and y represent the numbers of gallons of 87 octane and 92 octane gasolines, respectively.

(b) Use a graphing utility to graph the two equations in part (a) in the same viewing window. As the amount of 87 octane gasoline increases, how does the amount of 92 octane gasoline change?

(c) How much of each type of gasoline is required to obtain the 500 gallons of 89 octane gasoline?

53. ***Investment Portfolio*** A total of \$12,000 is invested in two corporate bonds that pay 7.5% and 9% simple interest. The investor wants an annual interest income of \$990 from the investments. What amount should be invested in the 7.5% bond?

54. ***Investment Portfolio*** A total of \$32,000 is invested in two municipal bonds that pay 5.75% and 6.25% simple interest. The investor wants an annual interest income of \$1900 from the investments. What amount should be invested in the 5.75% bond?

55. ***Ticket Sales*** At a local high school city championship basketball game, 1435 tickets were sold. A student admission ticket cost \$1.50 and an adult admission ticket cost \$5.00. The sum of all the total ticket receipts for the basketball game were \$3552.50. How many of each type of ticket were sold?

56. ***Consumer Awareness*** A department store held a sale to sell all of the 214 winter jackets that remained after the season ended. Until noon, each jacket in the store was priced at \$31.95. At noon, the price of the jackets was further reduced to \$18.95. After the last jacket was sold, total receipts for the clearance sale were \$5108.30. How many jackets were sold before noon and how many were sold after noon?

Fitting a Line to Data **In Exercises 57–62, find the least squares regression line $y = ax + b$ for the points**

$$(x_1, y_1), (x_2, y_2), \ldots, (x_n, y_n)$$

by solving the system for a and b.

$$nb + \left(\sum_{i=1}^{n} x_i\right)a = \left(\sum_{i=1}^{n} y_i\right)$$

$$\left(\sum_{i=1}^{n} x_i\right)b + \left(\sum_{i=1}^{n} x_i^2\right)a = \left(\sum_{i=1}^{n} x_i y_i\right)$$

Then use a graphing utility to confirm the result. (If you are unfamiliar with summation notation, look at the discussion in Section 9.1 or in Appendix B at the website for this text at *college.hmco.com*.)

57. $\begin{cases} 5b + 10a = 20.2 \\ 10b + 30a = 50.1 \end{cases}$

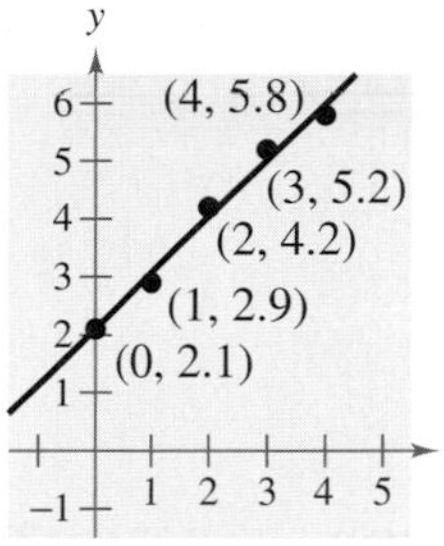

58. $\begin{cases} 5b + 10a = 11.7 \\ 10b + 30a = 25.6 \end{cases}$

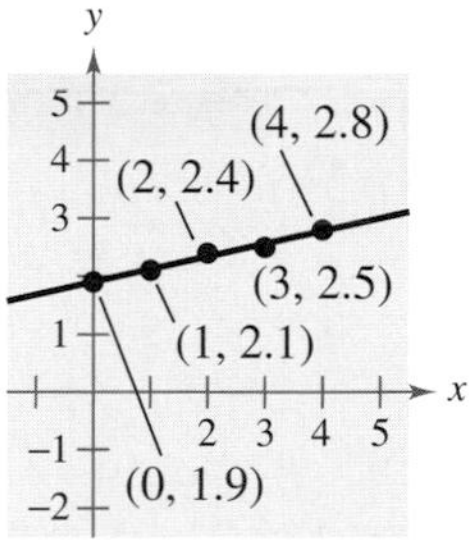

59. $\begin{cases} 7b + 21a = 35.1 \\ 21b + 91a = 114.2 \end{cases}$

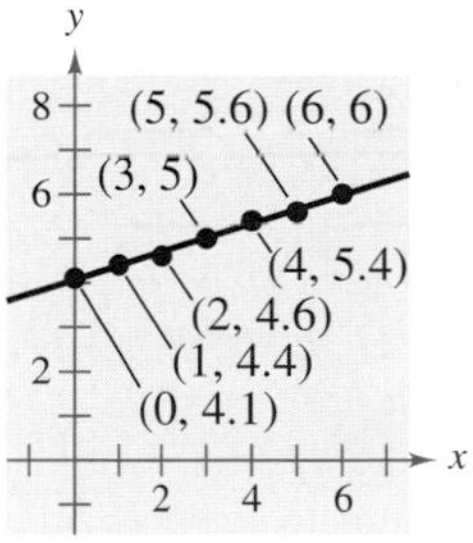

60. $\begin{cases} 6b + 15a = 23.6 \\ 15b + 55a = 48.8 \end{cases}$

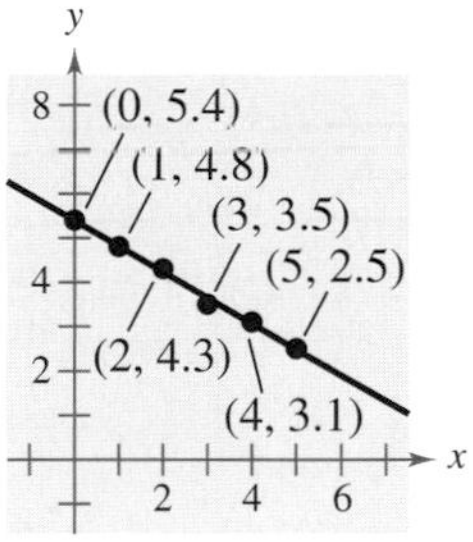

61. (0, 4), (1, 3), (1, 1), (2, 0)

62. (1, 0), (2, 0), (3, 0), (3, 1), (4, 1), (4, 2), (5, 2), (6, 2)

63. ***Data Analysis*** A farmer used four test plots to determine the relationship between wheat yield y (in bushels per acre) and the amount of fertilizer x (in hundreds of pounds per acre). The results are shown in the table.

Fertilizer, x	Yield, y
1.0	32
1.5	41
2.0	48
2.5	53

(a) Use the technique demonstrated in Exercises 57–62 to set up a system of equations for the data and to find the least squares regression line $y = ax + b$.

(b) Use the linear model to predict the yield for a fertilizer application of 160 pounds per acre.

Model It

64. ***Data Analysis*** The table shows the average room rates y for a hotel room in the United States for the years 1995 through 2001. (Source: American Hotel & Motel Association)

Year	Average room rate, y
1995	\$66.65
1996	\$70.93
1997	\$75.31
1998	\$78.62
1999	\$81.33
2000	\$85.89
2001	\$88.27

(a) Use the technique demonstrated in Exercises 57–62 to set up a system of equations for the data and to find the least squares regression line $y = at + b$. Let t represent the year, with $t = 5$ corresponding to 1995.

(b) Use the *regression* feature of a graphing utility to find a linear model for the data. How does this model compare with the model obtained in part (a)?

(c) Use the linear model to create a table of estimated values of y. Compare the estimated values with the actual data.

(d) Use the linear model to predict the average room rate in 2002. The actual average room rate in 2002 was \$83.54. How does this value compare with your prediction?

(e) Use the linear model to predict when the average room rate will be \$100.00. Using your result from part (d), do you think this prediction is accurate?

Synthesis

True or False? **In Exercises 65 and 66, determine whether the statement is true or false. Justify your answer.**

65. If two lines do not have exactly one point of intersection, then they must be parallel.

66. Solving a system of equations graphically will always give an exact solution.

67. ***Writing*** Briefly explain whether or not it is possible for a consistent system of linear equations to have exactly two solutions.

68. ***Think About It*** Give examples of a system of linear equations that has (a) no solution and (b) an infinite number of solutions.

Think About It **In Exercises 69 and 70, the graphs of the two equations appear to be parallel. Yet, when the system is solved algebraically, you find that the system does have a solution. Find the solution and explain why it does not appear on the portion of the graph that is shown.**

69. $\begin{cases} 100y - x = 200 \\ 99y - x = -198 \end{cases}$

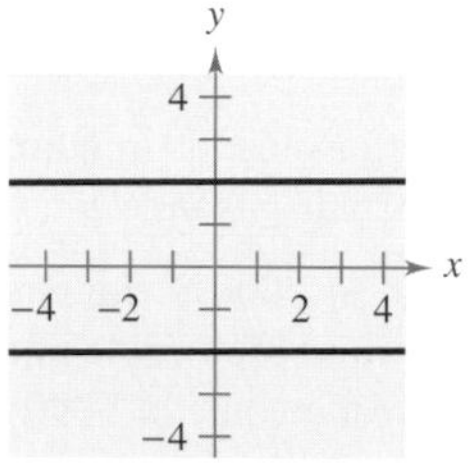

70. $\begin{cases} 21x - 20y = 0 \\ 13x - 12y = 120 \end{cases}$

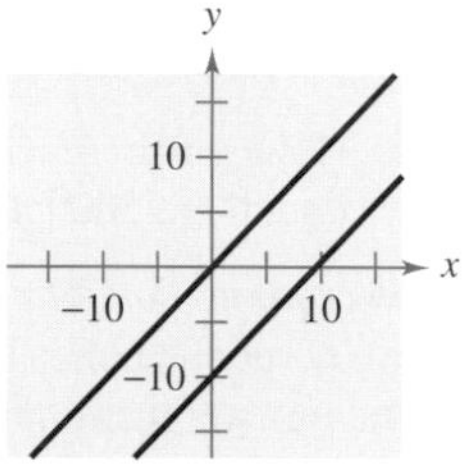

In Exercises 71 and 72, find the value of k such that the system of linear equations is inconsistent.

71. $\begin{cases} 4x - 8y = -3 \\ 2x + ky = 16 \end{cases}$

72. $\begin{cases} 15x + 3y = 6 \\ -10x + ky = 9 \end{cases}$

Skills Review

In Exercises 73–80, solve the inequality and graph the solution on the real number line.

73. $-11 - 6x \geq 33$

74. $2(x - 3) > -5x + 1$

75. $8x - 15 \leq -4(2x - 1)$

76. $-6 \leq 3x - 10 < 6$

77. $|x - 8| < 10$

78. $|x + 10| \geq -3$

79. $2x^2 + 3x - 35 < 0$

80. $3x^2 + 12x > 0$

In Exercises 81–84, write the expression as the logarithm of a single quantity.

81. $\ln x + \ln 6$

82. $\ln x - 5 \ln(x + 3)$

83. $\log_9 12 - \log_9 x$

84. $\frac{1}{4} \log_6 3x$

In Exercises 85 and 86, solve the system by the method of substitution.

85. $\begin{cases} 2x - y = 4 \\ -4x + 2y = -12 \end{cases}$

86. $\begin{cases} 30x - 40y - 33 = 0 \\ 10x + 20y - 21 = 0 \end{cases}$

87. **Make a Decision** To work an extended application analyzing the average undergraduate tuition, room, and board charges at private colleges in the United States from 1985 to 2003, visit this text's website at *college.hmco.com*. *(Data Source: U.S. Dept. of Education)*

7.3 Multivariable Linear Systems

What you should learn

- Use back-substitution to solve linear systems in row-echelon form.
- Use Gaussian elimination to solve systems of linear equations.
- Solve nonsquare systems of linear equations.
- Use systems of linear equations in three or more variables to model and solve real-life problems.

Why you should learn it

Systems of linear equations in three or more variables can be used to model and solve real-life problems. For instance, in Exercise 71 on page 531, a system of linear equations can be used to analyze the reproduction rates of deer in a wildlife preserve.

Jeanne Drake/Tony Stone Images

Row-Echelon Form and Back-Substitution

The method of elimination can be applied to a system of linear equations in more than two variables. In fact, this method easily adapts to computer use for solving linear systems with dozens of variables.

When elimination is used to solve a system of linear equations, the goal is to rewrite the system in a form to which back-substitution can be applied. To see how this works, consider the following two systems of linear equations.

System of Three Linear Equations in Three Variables: (See Example 3.)

$$\begin{cases} x - 2y + 3z = 9 \\ -x + 3y = -4 \\ 2x - 5y + 5z = 17 \end{cases}$$

Equivalent System in Row-Echelon Form: (See Example 1.)

$$\begin{cases} x - 2y + 3z = 9 \\ y + 3z = 5 \\ z = 2 \end{cases}$$

The second system is said to be in **row-echelon form,** which means that it has a "stair-step" pattern with leading coefficients of 1. After comparing the two systems, it should be clear that it is easier to solve the system in row-echelon form, using back-substitution.

Example 1 Using Back-Substitution in Row-Echelon Form

Solve the system of linear equations.

$$\begin{cases} x - 2y + 3z = 9 & \text{Equation 1} \\ y + 3z = 5 & \text{Equation 2} \\ z = 2 & \text{Equation 3} \end{cases}$$

Solution

From Equation 3, you know the value of z. To solve for y, substitute $z = 2$ into Equation 2 to obtain

$$y + 3(2) = 5 \qquad \text{Substitute 2 for } z.$$

$$y = -1. \qquad \text{Solve for } y.$$

Finally, substitute $y = -1$ and $z = 2$ into Equation 1 to obtain

$$x - 2(-1) + 3(2) = 9 \qquad \text{Substitute } -1 \text{ for } y \text{ and 2 for } z.$$

$$x = 1. \qquad \text{Solve for } x.$$

The solution is $x = 1$, $y = -1$, and $z = 2$, which can be written as the **ordered triple** $(1, -1, 2)$. Check this in the original system of equations.

✓CHECKPOINT Now try Exercise 5.

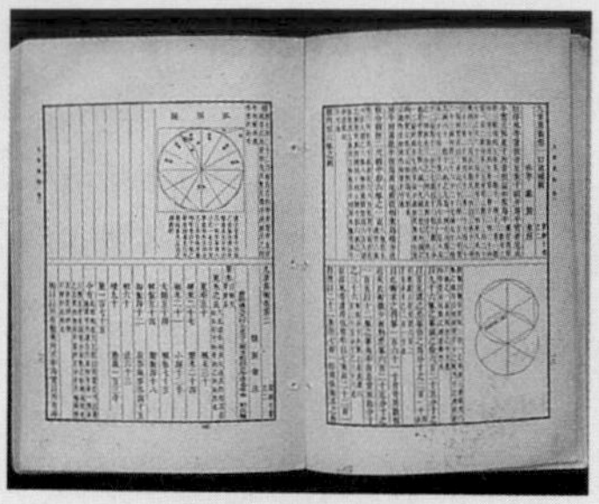

Christopher Lui/China Stock

Historical Note

One of the most influential Chinese mathematics books was the *Chui-chang suan-shu* or *Nine Chapters on the Mathematical Art* (written in approximately 250 B.C.). Chapter Eight of the *Nine Chapters* contained solutions of systems of linear equations using positive and negative numbers. One such system was as follows.

$$\begin{cases} 3x + 2y + z = 39 \\ 2x + 3y + z = 34 \\ x + 2y + 3z = 26 \end{cases}$$

This system was solved using column operations on a matrix. Matrices (plural for matrix) will be discussed in the next chapter.

Gaussian Elimination

Two systems of equations are *equivalent* if they have the same solution set. To solve a system that is not in row-echelon form, first convert it to an *equivalent* system that is in row-echelon form by using the following operations.

Operations That Produce Equivalent Systems

Each of the following **row operations** on a system of linear equations produces an *equivalent* system of linear equations.

1. Interchange two equations.
2. Multiply one of the equations by a nonzero constant.
3. Add a multiple of one of the equations to another equation to replace the latter equation.

To see how this is done, take another look at the method of elimination, as applied to a system of two linear equations.

Example 2 Using Gaussian Elimination to Solve a System

Solve the system of linear equations.

$$\begin{cases} 3x - 2y = -1 & \text{Equation 1} \\ x - y = 0 & \text{Equation 2} \end{cases}$$

Solution

There are two strategies that seem reasonable: eliminate the variable x or eliminate the variable y. The following steps show how to use the first strategy.

$$\begin{cases} x - y = 0 \\ 3x - 2y = -1 \end{cases}$$

Interchange the two equations in the system.

$$\begin{cases} -3x + 3y = 0 \\ 3x - 2y = -1 \end{cases}$$

Multiply the first equation by -3.

$$\begin{array}{r} -3x + 3y = 0 \\ \underline{3x - 2y = -1} \\ y = -1 \end{array}$$

Add the multiple of the first equation to the second equation to obtain a new second equation.

$$\begin{cases} x - y = 0 \\ y = -1 \end{cases}$$

New system in row-echelon form

Now, using back-substitution, you can determine that the solution is $y = -1$ and $x = -1$, which can be written as the ordered pair $(-1, -1)$. Check this solution in the original system of equations.

✓CHECKPOINT Now try Exercise 13.

STUDY TIP

As demonstrated in the first step in the solution of Example 2, interchanging rows is an easy way of obtaining a leading coefficient of 1.

As shown in Example 2, rewriting a system of linear equations in row-echelon form usually involves a chain of equivalent systems, each of which is obtained by using one of the three basic row operations listed on the previous page. This process is called **Gaussian elimination,** after the German mathematician Carl Friedrich Gauss (1777–1855).

STUDY TIP

Arithmetic errors are often made when performing elementary row operations. You should note the operation performed in each step so that you can go back and check your work.

Example 3 Using Gaussian Elimination to Solve a System

Solve the system of linear equations.

$$\begin{cases} x - 2y + 3z = 9 & \text{Equation 1} \\ -x + 3y = -4 & \text{Equation 2} \\ 2x - 5y + 5z = 17 & \text{Equation 3} \end{cases}$$

Solution

Because the leading coefficient of the first equation is 1, you can begin by saving the x at the upper left and eliminating the other x-terms from the first column.

$x - 2y + 3z = 9$ Write Equation 1.

$-x + 3y = -4$ Write Equation 2.

$y + 3z = 5$ Add Equation 1 to Equation 2.

$$\begin{cases} x - 2y + 3z = 9 \\ y + 3z = 5 \\ 2x - 5y + 5z = 17 \end{cases}$$

Adding the first equation to the second equation produces a new second equation.

$-2x + 4y - 6z = -18$ Multiply Equation 1 by -2.

$2x - 5y + 5z = 17$ Write Equation 3.

$-y - z = -1$ Add revised Equation 1 to Equation 3.

$$\begin{cases} x - 2y + 3z = 9 \\ y + 3z = 5 \\ -y - z = -1 \end{cases}$$

Adding -2 times the first equation to the third equation produces a new third equation.

Now that all but the first x have been eliminated from the first column, go to work on the second column. (You need to eliminate y from the third equation.)

$$\begin{cases} x - 2y + 3z = 9 \\ y + 3z = 5 \\ 2z = 4 \end{cases}$$

Adding the second equation to the third equation produces a new third equation.

Finally, you need a coefficient of 1 for z in the third equation.

$$\begin{cases} x - 2y + 3z = 9 \\ y + 3z = 5 \\ z = 2 \end{cases}$$

Multiplying the third equation by $\frac{1}{2}$ produces a new third equation.

This is the same system that was solved in Example 1, and, as in that example, you can conclude that the solution is

$$x = 1, \quad y = -1, \quad \text{and} \quad z = 2.$$

✓CHECKPOINT Now try Exercise 15.

The next example involves an inconsistent system—one that has no solution. The key to recognizing an inconsistent system is that at some stage in the elimination process you obtain a false statement such as $0 = -2$.

Example 4 An Inconsistent System

Solve the system of linear equations.

$$\begin{cases} x - 3y + z = 1 & \text{Equation 1} \\ 2x - y - 2z = 2 & \text{Equation 2} \\ x + 2y - 3z = -1 & \text{Equation 3} \end{cases}$$

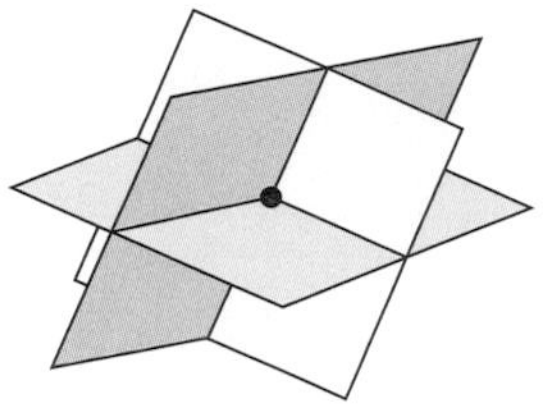

FIGURE 7.12 *Solution: one point*

Solution

$$\begin{cases} x - 3y + z = 1 \\ 5y - 4z = 0 \\ x + 2y - 3z = -1 \end{cases}$$

Adding -2 times the first equation to the second equation produces a new second equation.

$$\begin{cases} x - 3y + z = 1 \\ 5y - 4z = 0 \\ 5y - 4z = -2 \end{cases}$$

Adding -1 times the first equation to the third equation produces a new third equation.

$$\begin{cases} x - 3y + z = 1 \\ 5y - 4z = 0 \\ 0 = -2 \end{cases}$$

Adding -1 times the second equation to the third equation produces a new third equation.

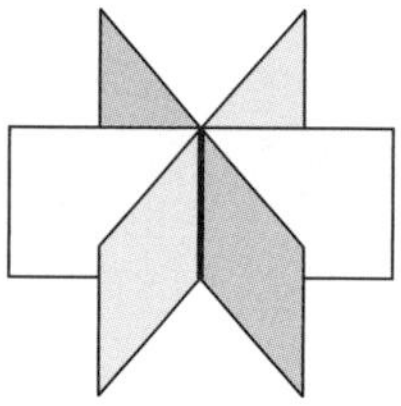

FIGURE 7.13 *Solution: one line*

Because $0 = -2$ is a false statement, you can conclude that this system is inconsistent and so has no solution. Moreover, because this system is equivalent to the original system, you can conclude that the original system also has no solution.

✓CHECKPOINT Now try Exercise 19.

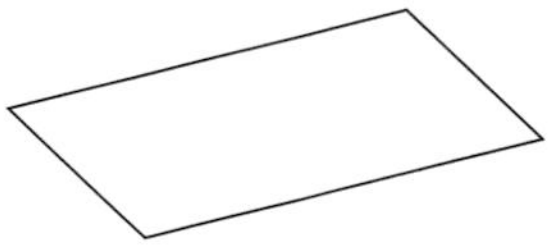

FIGURE 7.14 *Solution: one plane*

As with a system of linear equations in two variables, the solution(s) of a system of linear equations in more than two variables must fall into one of three categories.

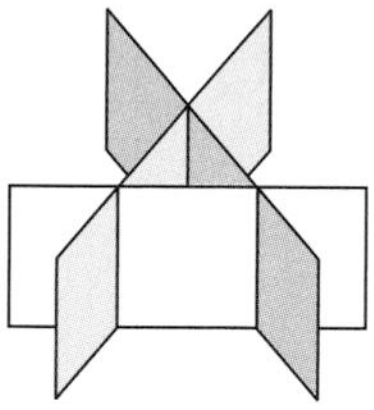

FIGURE 7.15 *Solution: none*

The Number of Solutions of a Linear System

For a system of linear equations, exactly one of the following is true.

1. There is exactly one solution.
2. There are infinitely many solutions.
3. There is no solution.

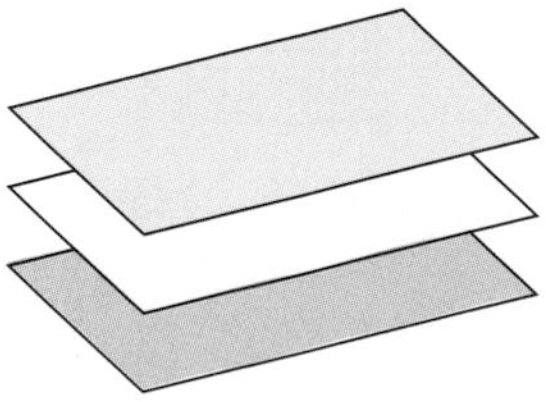

FIGURE 7.16 *Solution: none*

In Section 7.2, you learned that a system of two linear equations in two variables can be represented graphically as a pair of lines that are intersecting, coincident, or parallel. A system of three linear equations in three variables has a similar graphical representation—it can be represented as three planes in space that intersect in one point (exactly one solution) [see Figure 7.12], intersect in a line or a plane (infinitely many solutions) [see Figures 7.13 and 7.14], or have no points common to all three planes (no solution) [see Figures 7.15 and 7.16].

Example 5 **A System with Infinitely Many Solutions**

Solve the system of linear equations.

$$\begin{cases} x + y - 3z = -1 & \text{Equation 1} \\ y - z = 0 & \text{Equation 2} \\ -x + 2y = 1 & \text{Equation 3} \end{cases}$$

Solution

$$\begin{cases} x + y - 3z = -1 \\ y - z = 0 \\ 3y - 3z = 0 \end{cases}$$

Adding the first equation to the third equation produces a new third equation.

$$\begin{cases} x + y - 3z = -1 \\ y - z = 0 \\ 0 = 0 \end{cases}$$

Adding -3 times the second equation to the third equation produces a new third equation.

This result means that Equation 3 depends on Equations 1 and 2 in the sense that it gives no additional information about the variables. Because $0 = 0$ is a true statement, you can conclude that this system will have infinitely many solutions. However, it is incorrect to say simply that the solution is "infinite." You must also specify the correct form of the solution. So, the original system is equivalent to the system

$$\begin{cases} x + y - 3z = -1 \\ y - z = 0 \end{cases}.$$

In the last equation, solve for y in terms of z to obtain $y = z$. Back-substituting for y in the first equation produces $x = 2z - 1$. Finally, letting $z = a$, where a is a real number, the solutions to the given system are all of the form $x = 2a - 1$, $y = a$, and $z = a$. So, every ordered triple of the form

$$(2a - 1, a, a), \qquad a \text{ is a real number}$$

is a solution of the system.

✓CHECKPOINT Now try Exercise 23.

STUDY TIP

In Example 5, x and y are solved in terms of the third variable z. To write the correct form of the solution to the system that does not use any of the three variables of the system, let a represent any real number and let $z = a$. Then solve for x and y. The solution can then be written in terms of a, which is not one of the variables of the system.

In Example 5, there are other ways to write the same infinite set of solutions. For instance, letting $x = b$, the solutions could have been written as

$$\left(b, \tfrac{1}{2}(b + 1), \tfrac{1}{2}(b + 1)\right), \qquad b \text{ is a real number.}$$

To convince yourself that this description produces the same set of solutions, consider the following.

Substitution	*Solution*	
$a = 0$	$(2(0) - 1, 0, 0) = (-1, 0, 0)$	Same solution
$b = -1$	$\left(-1, \tfrac{1}{2}(-1 + 1), \tfrac{1}{2}(-1 + 1)\right) = (-1, 0, 0)$	
$a = 1$	$(2(1) - 1, 1, 1) = (1, 1, 1)$	Same solution
$b = 1$	$\left(1, \tfrac{1}{2}(1 + 1), \tfrac{1}{2}(1 + 1)\right) = (1, 1, 1)$	
$a = 2$	$(2(2) - 1, 2, 2) = (3, 2, 2)$	Same solution
$b = 3$	$\left(3, \tfrac{1}{2}(3 + 1), \tfrac{1}{2}(3 + 1)\right) = (3, 2, 2)$	

STUDY TIP

When comparing descriptions of an infinite solution set, keep in mind that there is more than one way to describe the set.

Nonsquare Systems

So far, each system of linear equations you have looked at has been *square*, which means that the number of equations is equal to the number of variables. In a **nonsquare** system, the number of equations differs from the number of variables. A system of linear equations cannot have a unique solution unless there are at least as many equations as there are variables in the system.

Example 6 A System with Fewer Equations than Variables

Solve the system of linear equations.

$$\begin{cases} x - 2y + z = 2 & \text{Equation 1} \\ 2x - y - z = 1 & \text{Equation 2} \end{cases}$$

Solution

Begin by rewriting the system in row-echelon form.

$$\begin{cases} x - 2y + z = 2 \\ 3y - 3z = -3 \end{cases}$$

Adding -2 times the first equation to the second equation produces a new second equation.

$$\begin{cases} x - 2y + z = 2 \\ y - z = -1 \end{cases}$$

Multiplying the second equation by $\frac{1}{3}$ produces a new second equation.

Solve for y in terms of z, to obtain

$$y = z - 1.$$

By back-substituting into Equation 1, you can solve for x, as follows.

$$x - 2y + z = 2 \quad \text{Write Equation 1.}$$

$$x - 2(z - 1) + z = 2 \quad \text{Substitute for } y \text{ in Equation 1.}$$

$$x - 2z + 2 + z = 2 \quad \text{Distributive Property}$$

$$x = z \quad \text{Solve for } x.$$

Finally, by letting $z = a$, where a is a real number, you have the solution

$$x = a, \quad y = a - 1, \quad \text{and} \quad z = a.$$

So, every ordered triple of the form

$$(a, a - 1, a), \quad a \text{ is a real number}$$

is a solution of the system. Because there were originally three variables and only two equations, the system cannot have a unique solution.

✓CHECKPOINT Now try Exercise 27.

In Example 6, try choosing some values of a to obtain different solutions of the system, such as $(1, 0, 1)$, $(2, 1, 2)$, and $(3, 2, 3)$. Then check each of the solutions in the original system to verify that they are solutions of the original system.

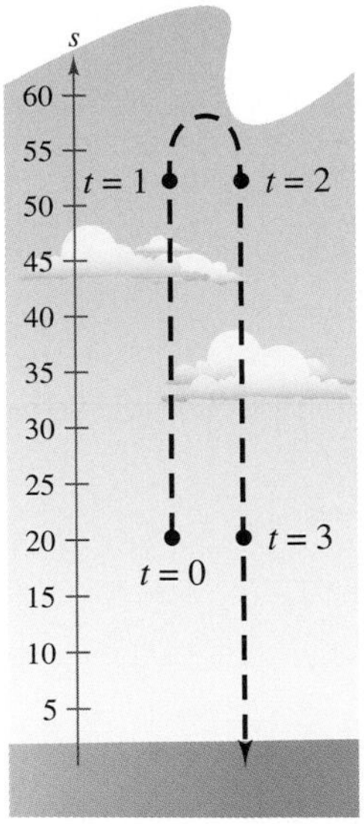

FIGURE 7.17

Applications

Example 7 Vertical Motion

The height at time t of an object that is moving in a (vertical) line with constant acceleration a is given by the **position equation**

$$s = \frac{1}{2}at^2 + v_0t + s_0.$$

The height s is measured in feet, the acceleration a is measured in feet per second squared, t is measured in seconds, v_0 is the initial velocity (at $t = 0$), and s_0 is the initial height. Find the values of a, v_0, and s_0 if $s = 52$ at $t = 1$, $s = 52$ at $t = 2$, and $s = 20$ at $t = 3$, and interpret the result. (See Figure 7.17.)

Solution

By substituting the three values of t and s into the position equation, you can obtain three linear equations in a, v_0, and s_0.

When $t = 1$: $\frac{1}{2}a(1)^2 + v_0(1) + s_0 = 52$ ⟹ $a + 2v_0 + 2s_0 = 104$

When $t = 2$: $\frac{1}{2}a(2)^2 + v_0(2) + s_0 = 52$ ⟹ $2a + 2v_0 + s_0 = 52$

When $t = 3$: $\frac{1}{2}a(3)^2 + v_0(3) + s_0 = 20$ ⟹ $9a + 6v_0 + 2s_0 = 40$

This produces the following system of linear equations.

$$\begin{cases} a + 2v_0 + 2s_0 = 104 \\ 2a + 2v_0 + s_0 = 52 \\ 9a + 6v_0 + 2s_0 = 40 \end{cases}$$

Now solve the system using Gaussian elimination.

$$\begin{cases} a + 2v_0 + 2s_0 = 104 \\ \quad - 2v_0 - 3s_0 = -156 \\ 9a + 6v_0 + 2s_0 = 40 \end{cases}$$

Adding -2 times the first equation to the second equation produces a new second equation.

$$\begin{cases} a + 2v_0 + 2s_0 = 104 \\ \quad - 2v_0 - 3s_0 = -156 \\ \quad - 12v_0 - 16s_0 = -896 \end{cases}$$

Adding -9 times the first equation to the third equation produces a new third equation.

$$\begin{cases} a + 2v_0 + 2s_0 = 104 \\ \quad - 2v_0 - 3s_0 = -156 \\ \quad 2s_0 = 40 \end{cases}$$

Adding -6 times the second equation to the third equation produces a new third equation.

$$\begin{cases} a + 2v_0 + 2s_0 = 104 \\ \quad v_0 + \frac{3}{2}s_0 = 78 \\ \quad s_0 = 20 \end{cases}$$

Multiplying the second equation by $-\frac{1}{2}$ produces a new second equation and multiplying the third equation by $\frac{1}{2}$ produces a new third equation.

So, the solution of this system is $a = -32$, $v_0 = 48$, and $s_0 = 20$. This solution results in a position equation of $s = -16t^2 + 48t + 20$ and implies that the object was thrown upward at a velocity of 48 feet per second from a height of 20 feet.

✓CHECKPOINT Now try Exercise 39.

Example 8 **Data Analysis: Curve-Fitting**

Find a quadratic equation

$$y = ax^2 + bx + c$$

whose graph passes through the points $(-1, 3)$, $(1, 1)$, and $(2, 6)$.

Solution

Because the graph of $y = ax^2 + bx + c$ passes through the points $(-1, 3)$, $(1, 1)$, and $(2, 6)$, you can write the following.

When $x = -1$, $y = 3$: $a(-1)^2 + b(-1) + c = 3$

When $x = 1$, $y = 1$: $a(1)^2 + b(1) + c = 1$

When $x = 2$, $y = 6$: $a(2)^2 + b(2) + c = 6$

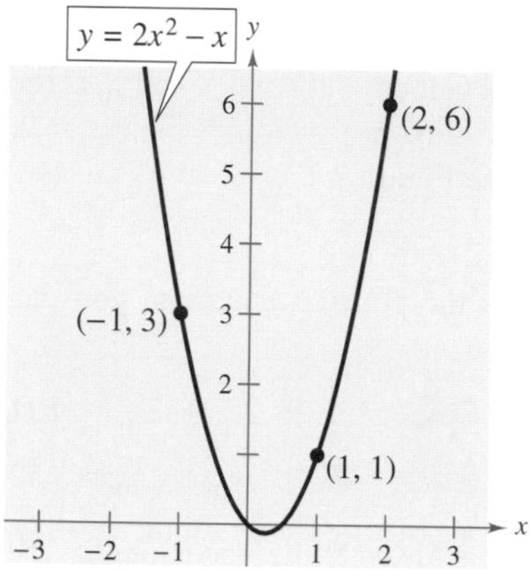

FIGURE 7.18

This produces the following system of linear equations.

$$\begin{cases} a - b + c = 3 & \text{Equation 1} \\ a + b + c = 1 & \text{Equation 2} \\ 4a + 2b + c = 6 & \text{Equation 3} \end{cases}$$

The solution of this system is $a = 2$, $b = -1$, and $c = 0$. So, the equation of the parabola is $y = 2x^2 - x$, as shown in Figure 7.18.

CHECKPOINT Now try Exercise 43.

Example 9 **Investment Analysis**

An inheritance of \$12,000 was invested among three funds: a money-market fund that paid 5% annually, municipal bonds that paid 6% annually, and mutual funds that paid 12% annually. The amount invested in mutual funds was \$4000 more than the amount invested in municipal bonds. The total interest earned during the first year was \$1120. How much was invested in each type of fund?

Solution

Let x, y, and z represent the amounts invested in the money-market fund, municipal bonds, and mutual funds, respectively. From the given information, you can write the following equations.

$$\begin{cases} x + y + z = 12{,}000 & \text{Equation 1} \\ z = y + 4000 & \text{Equation 2} \\ 0.05x + 0.06y + 0.12z = 1120 & \text{Equation 3} \end{cases}$$

Rewriting this system in standard form without decimals produces the following.

$$\begin{cases} x + y + z = 12{,}000 & \text{Equation 1} \\ -y + z = 4{,}000 & \text{Equation 2} \\ 5x + 6y + 12z = 112{,}000 & \text{Equation 3} \end{cases}$$

Using Gaussian elimination to solve this system yields $x = 2000$, $y = 3000$, and $z = 7000$. So, \$2000 was invested in the money-market fund, \$3000 was invested in municipal bonds, and \$7000 was invested in mutual funds.

CHECKPOINT Now try Exercise 53.

7.3 Exercises

VOCABULARY CHECK: Fill in the blanks.

1. A system of equations that is in ________ form has a "stair-step" pattern with leading coefficients of 1.
2. A solution to a system of three linear equations in three unknowns can be written as an ________ ________, which has the form (x, y, z).
3. The process used to write a system of linear equations in row-echelon form is called ________ elimination.
4. Interchanging two equations of a system of linear equations is a ________ ________ that produces an equivalent system.
5. A system of equations is called ________ if the number of equations differs from the number of variables in the system.
6. The equation $s = \frac{1}{2}at^2 + v_0t + s_0$ is called the ________ equation, and it models the height s of an object at time t that is moving in a vertical line with a constant acceleration a.

In Exercises 1–4, determine whether each ordered triple is a solution of the system of equations.

1. $\begin{cases} 3x - y + z = 1 \\ 2x - 3z - -14 \\ 5y + 2z = 8 \end{cases}$

(a) $(2, 0, -3)$ (b) $(-2, 0, 8)$

(c) $(0, -1, 3)$ (d) $(-1, 0, 4)$

2. $\begin{cases} 3x + 4y - z = 17 \\ 5x - y + 2z = -2 \\ 2x - 3y + 7z = -21 \end{cases}$

(a) $(3, -1, 2)$ (b) $(1, 3, -2)$

(c) $(4, 1, -3)$ (d) $(1, -2, 2)$

3. $\begin{cases} 4x + y - z = 0 \\ -8x - 6y + z = -\frac{7}{4} \\ 3x - y = -\frac{9}{4} \end{cases}$

(a) $\left(\frac{1}{2}, -\frac{3}{4}, -\frac{7}{4}\right)$ (b) $\left(-\frac{3}{2}, \frac{5}{4}, -\frac{5}{4}\right)$

(c) $\left(-\frac{1}{2}, \frac{3}{4}, -\frac{5}{4}\right)$ (d) $\left(-\frac{1}{2}, \frac{1}{6}, -\frac{3}{4}\right)$

4. $\begin{cases} -4x - y - 8z = -6 \\ y + z = 0 \\ 4x - 7y = 6 \end{cases}$

(a) $(-2, -2, 2)$ (b) $\left(-\frac{33}{2}, -10, 10\right)$

(c) $\left(\frac{1}{8}, -\frac{1}{2}, \frac{1}{2}\right)$ (d) $\left(-\frac{11}{2}, -4, 4\right)$

In Exercises 5–10, use back-substitution to solve the system of linear equations.

5. $\begin{cases} 2x - y + 5z = 24 \\ y + 2z = 6 \\ z = 4 \end{cases}$

6. $\begin{cases} 4x - 3y - 2z = 21 \\ 6y - 5z = -8 \\ z = -2 \end{cases}$

7. $\begin{cases} 2x + y - 3z = 10 \\ y + z = 12 \\ z = 2 \end{cases}$

8. $\begin{cases} x - y + 2z = 22 \\ 3y - 8z = -9 \\ z = -3 \end{cases}$

9. $\begin{cases} 4x - 2y + z = 8 \\ -y + z = 4 \\ z = 2 \end{cases}$

10. $\begin{cases} 5x - 8z = 22 \\ 3y - 5z = 10 \\ z = -4 \end{cases}$

In Exercises 11 and 12, perform the row operation and write the equivalent system.

11. Add Equation 1 to Equation 2.

$\begin{cases} x - 2y + 3z = 5 & \text{Equation 1} \\ -x + 3y - 5z = 4 & \text{Equation 2} \\ 2x - 3z = 0 & \text{Equation 3} \end{cases}$

What did this operation accomplish?

12. Add -2 times Equation 1 to Equation 3.

$\begin{cases} x - 2y + 3z = 5 & \text{Equation 1} \\ -x + 3y - 5z = 4 & \text{Equation 2} \\ 2x - 3z = 0 & \text{Equation 3} \end{cases}$

What did this operation accomplish?

In Exercises 13–38, solve the system of linear equations and check any solution algebraically.

13. $\begin{cases} x + y + z = 6 \\ 2x - y + z = 3 \\ 3x - z = 0 \end{cases}$

14. $\begin{cases} x + y + z = 3 \\ x - 2y + 4z = 5 \\ 3y + 4z = 5 \end{cases}$

15. $\begin{cases} 2x + 2z = 2 \\ 5x + 3y = 4 \\ 3y - 4z = 4 \end{cases}$

16. $\begin{cases} 2x + 4y + z = 1 \\ x - 2y - 3z = 2 \\ x + y - z = -1 \end{cases}$

17. $\begin{cases} 6y + 4z = -12 \\ 3x + 3y = 9 \\ 2x - 3z = 10 \end{cases}$

18. $\begin{cases} 2x + 4y - z = 7 \\ 2x - 4y + 2z = -6 \\ x + 4y + z = 0 \end{cases}$

19. $\begin{cases} 2x + y - z = 7 \\ x - 2y + 2z = -9 \\ 3x - y + z = 5 \end{cases}$

20. $\begin{cases} 5x - 3y + 2z = 3 \\ 2x + 4y - z = 7 \\ x - 11y + 4z = 3 \end{cases}$

21. $\begin{cases} 3x - 5y + 5z = 1 \\ 5x - 2y + 3z = 0 \\ 7x - y + 3z = 0 \end{cases}$

22. $\begin{cases} 2x + y + 3z = 1 \\ 2x + 6y + 8z = 3 \\ 6x + 8y + 18z = 5 \end{cases}$

23. $\begin{cases} x + 2y - 7z = -4 \\ 2x + y + z = 13 \\ 3x + 9y - 36z = -33 \end{cases}$

24. $\begin{cases} 2x + y - 3z = 4 \\ 4x + 2z = 10 \\ -2x + 3y - 13z = -8 \end{cases}$

25. $\begin{cases} 3x - 3y + 6z = 6 \\ x + 2y - z = 5 \\ 5x - 8y + 13z = 7 \end{cases}$

26. $\begin{cases} x + 2z = 5 \\ 3x - y - z = 1 \\ 6x - y + 5z = 16 \end{cases}$

27. $\begin{cases} x - 2y + 5z = 2 \\ 4x - z = 0 \end{cases}$

28. $\begin{cases} x - 3y + 2z = 18 \\ 5x - 13y + 12z = 80 \end{cases}$

29. $\begin{cases} 2x - 3y + z = -2 \\ -4x + 9y = 7 \end{cases}$

30. $\begin{cases} 2x + 3y + 3z = 7 \\ 4x + 18y + 15z = 44 \end{cases}$

31. $\begin{cases} x + 3w = 4 \\ 2y - z - w = 0 \\ 3y - 2w = 1 \\ 2x - y + 4z = 5 \end{cases}$

32. $\begin{cases} x + y + z + w = 6 \\ 2x + 3y - w = 0 \\ -3x + 4y + z + 2w = 4 \\ x + 2y - z + w = 0 \end{cases}$

33. $\begin{cases} x + 4z = 1 \\ x + y + 10z = 10 \\ 2x - y + 2z = -5 \end{cases}$

34. $\begin{cases} 2x - 2y - 6z = -4 \\ -3x + 2y + 6z = 1 \\ x - y - 5z = -3 \end{cases}$

35. $\begin{cases} 2x + 3y = 0 \\ 4x + 3y - z = 0 \\ 8x + 3y + 3z = 0 \end{cases}$

36. $\begin{cases} 4x + 3y + 17z = 0 \\ 5x + 4y + 22z = 0 \\ 4x + 2y + 19z = 0 \end{cases}$

37. $\begin{cases} 12x + 5y + z = 0 \\ 23x + 4y - z = 0 \end{cases}$

38. $\begin{cases} 2x - y - z = 0 \\ -2x + 6y + 4z = 2 \end{cases}$

Vertical Motion **In Exercises 39–42, an object moving vertically is at the given heights at the specified times. Find the position equation $s = \frac{1}{2}at^2 + v_0t + s_0$ for the object.**

39. At $t = 1$ second, $s = 128$ feet
At $t = 2$ seconds, $s = 80$ feet
At $t = 3$ seconds, $s = 0$ feet

40. At $t = 1$ second, $s = 48$ feet
At $t = 2$ seconds, $s = 64$ feet
At $t = 3$ seconds, $s = 48$ feet

41. At $t = 1$ second, $s = 452$ feet
At $t = 2$ seconds, $s = 372$ feet
At $t = 3$ seconds, $s = 260$ feet

42. At $t = 1$ second, $s = 132$ feet
At $t = 2$ seconds, $s = 100$ feet
At $t = 3$ seconds, $s = 36$ feet

In Exercises 43–46, find the equation of the parabola

$y = ax^2 + bx + c$

that passes through the points. To verify your result, use a graphing utility to plot the points and graph the parabola.

43. $(0, 0), (2, -2), (4, 0)$

44. $(0, 3), (1, 4), (2, 3)$

45. $(2, 0), (3, -1), (4, 0)$

46. $(1, 3), (2, 2), (3, -3)$

In Exercises 47–50, find the equation of the circle

$x^2 + y^2 + Dx + Ey + F = 0$

that passes through the points. To verify your result, use a graphing utility to plot the points and graph the circle.

47. $(0, 0), (2, 2), (4, 0)$

48. $(0, 0), (0, 6), (3, 3)$

49. $(-3, -1), (2, 4), (-6, 8)$

50. $(0, 0), (0, -2), (3, 0)$

51. ***Sports*** In Super Bowl I, on January 15, 1967, the Green Bay Packers defeated the Kansas City Chiefs by a score of 35 to 10. The total points scored came from 13 different scoring plays, which were a combination of touchdowns, extra-point kicks, and field goals, worth 6, 1, and 3 points respectively. The same number of touchdowns and extra point kicks were scored. There were six times as many touchdowns as field goals. How many touchdowns, extra-point kicks, and field goals were scored during the game? (Source: SuperBowl.com)

52. ***Sports*** In the 2004 Women's NCAA Final Four Championship game, the University of Connecticut Huskies defeated the University of Tennessee Lady Volunteers by a score of 70 to 61. The Huskies won by scoring a combination of two-point baskets, three-point baskets, and one-point free throws. The number of two-point baskets was two more than the number of free throws. The number of free throws was one more than two times the number of three-point baskets. What combination of scoring accounted for the Huskies' 70 points? (Source: National Collegiate Athletic Association)

53. ***Finance*** A small corporation borrowed \$775,000 to expand its clothing line. Some of the money was borrowed at 8%, some at 9%, and some at 10%. How much was borrowed at each rate if the annual interest owed was \$67,500 and the amount borrowed at 8% was four times the amount borrowed at 10%?

54. ***Finance*** A small corporation borrowed \$800,000 to expand its line of toys. Some of the money was borrowed at 8%, some at 9%, and some at 10%. How much was borrowed at each rate if the annual interest owed was \$67,000 and the amount borrowed at 8% was five times the amount borrowed at 10%?

Investment Portfolio **In Exercises 55 and 56, consider an investor with a portfolio totaling \$500,000 that is invested in certificates of deposit, municipal bonds, blue-chip stocks, and growth or speculative stocks. How much is invested in each type of investment?**

55. The certificates of deposit pay 10% annually, and the municipal bonds pay 8% annually. Over a five-year period, the investor expects the blue-chip stocks to return 12% annually and the growth stocks to return 13% annually. The investor wants a combined annual return of 10% and also wants to have only one-fourth of the portfolio invested in stocks.

56. The certificates of deposit pay 9% annually, and the municipal bonds pay 5% annually. Over a five-year period, the investor expects the blue-chip stocks to return 12% annually and the growth stocks to return 14% annually. The investor wants a combined annual return of 10% and also wants to have only one-fourth of the portfolio invested in stocks.

57. ***Agriculture*** A mixture of 5 pounds of fertilizer A, 13 pounds of fertilizer B, and 4 pounds of fertilizer C provides the optimal nutrients for a plant. Commercial brand X contains equal parts of fertilizer B and fertilizer C. Commercial brand Y contains one part of fertilizer A and two parts of fertilizer B. Commercial brand Z contains two parts of fertilizer A, five parts of fertilizer B, and two parts of fertilizer C. How much of each fertilizer brand is needed to obtain the desired mixture?

58. ***Agriculture*** A mixture of 12 liters of chemical A, 16 liters of chemical B, and 26 liters of chemical C is required to kill a destructive crop insect. Commercial spray X contains 1, 2, and 2 parts, respectively, of these chemicals. Commercial spray Y contains only chemical C. Commercial spray Z contains only chemicals A and B in equal amounts. How much of each type of commercial spray is needed to get the desired mixture?

59. ***Coffee Mixture*** A coffee manufacturer sells a 10-pound package of coffee that consists of three flavors of coffee. Vanilla-flavored coffee costs \$2 per pound, hazelnut-flavored coffee costs \$2.50 per pound, and mocha-flavored coffee costs \$3 per pound. The package contains the same amount of hazelnut coffee as mocha coffee. The cost of the 10-pound package is \$26. How many pounds of each type of coffee are in the package?

60. ***Floral Arrangements*** A florist is creating 10 centerpieces for a wedding. The florist can use roses that cost \$2.50 each, lilies that cost \$4 each, and irises that cost \$2 each to make the bouquets. The customer has a budget of \$300 and wants each bouquet to contain 12 flowers, with twice as many roses used as the other two types of flowers combined. How many of each type of flower should be in each centerpiece?

61. ***Advertising*** A health insurance company advertises on television, radio, and in the local newspaper. The marketing department has an advertising budget of \$42,000 per month. A television ad costs \$1000, a radio ad costs \$200, and a newspaper ad costs \$500. The department wants to run 60 ads per month, and have as many television ads as radio and newspaper ads combined. How many of each type of ad can the department run each month?

62. ***Radio*** You work as a disc jockey at your college radio station. You are supposed to play 32 songs within two hours. You are to choose the songs from the latest rock, dance, and pop albums. You want to play twice as many rock songs as pop songs and four more pop songs than dance songs. How many of each type of song will you play?

63. ***Acid Mixture*** A chemist needs 10 liters of a 25% acid solution. The solution is to be mixed from three solutions whose concentrations are 10%, 20%, and 50%. How many liters of each solution will satisfy each condition?

(a) Use 2 liters of the 50% solution.

(b) Use as little as possible of the 50% solution.

(c) Use as much as possible of the 50% solution.

64. ***Acid Mixture*** A chemist needs 12 gallons of a 20% acid solution. The solution is to be mixed from three solutions whose concentrations are 10%, 15%, and 25%. How many gallons of each solution will satisfy each condition?

(a) Use 4 gallons of the 25% solution.

(b) Use as little as possible of the 25% solution.

(c) Use as much as possible of the 25% solution.

65. ***Electrical Network*** Applying Kirchhoff's Laws to the electrical network in the figure, the currents I_1, I_2, and I_3 are the solution of the system

$$\begin{cases} I_1 - I_2 + I_3 = 0 \\ 3I_1 + 2I_2 = 7 \\ 2I_2 + 4I_3 = 8 \end{cases}$$

find the currents.

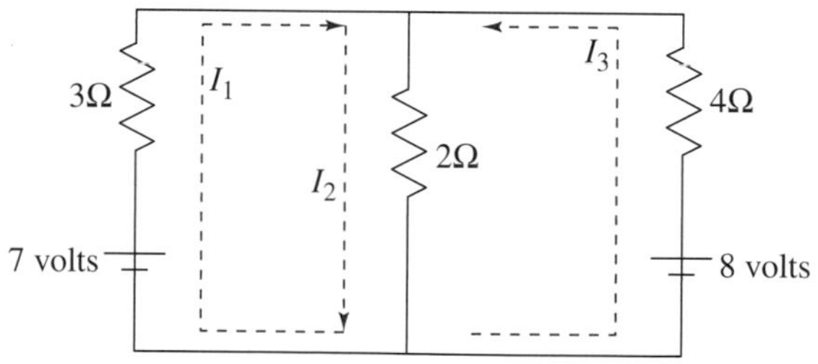

66. ***Pulley System*** A system of pulleys is loaded with 128-pound and 32-pound weights (see figure). The tensions t_1 and t_2 in the ropes and the acceleration a of the 32-pound weight are found by solving the system of equations

$$\begin{cases} t_1 - 2t_2 = 0 \\ t_1 - 2a = 128 \\ t_2 + a = 32 \end{cases}$$

where t_1 and t_2 are measured in pounds and a is measured in feet per second squared.

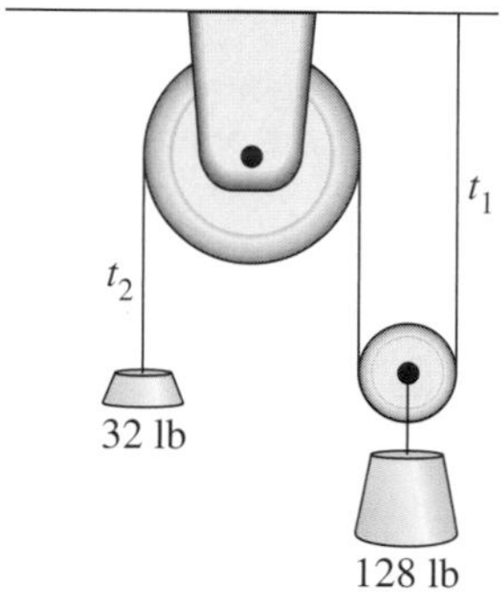

(a) Solve this system.

(b) The 32-pound weight in the pulley system is replaced by a 64-pound weight. The new pulley system will be modeled by the following system of equations.

$$\begin{cases} t_1 - 2t_2 = 0 \\ t_1 - 2a = 128 \\ t_2 + a = 64 \end{cases}$$

Solve this system and use your answer for the acceleration to describe what (if anything) is happening in the pulley system.

Fitting a Parabola **In Exercises 67–70, find the least squares regression parabola $y = ax^2 + bx + c$ for the points $(x_1, y_1), (x_2, y_2), \ldots, (x_n, y_n)$ by solving the following system of linear equations for a, b, and c. Then use the *regression* feature of a graphing utility to confirm the result. (If you are unfamiliar with summation notation, look at the discussion in Section 9.1 or in Appendix B at the website for this text at *college.hmco.com*.)**

$$nc + \left(\sum_{i=1}^{n} x_i\right)b + \left(\sum_{i=1}^{n} x_i^2\right)a = \sum_{i=1}^{n} y_i$$

$$\left(\sum_{i=1}^{n} x_i\right)c + \left(\sum_{i=1}^{n} x_i^2\right)b + \left(\sum_{i=1}^{n} x_i^3\right)a = \sum_{i=1}^{n} x_i y_i$$

$$\left(\sum_{i=1}^{n} x_i^2\right)c + \left(\sum_{i=1}^{n} x_i^3\right)b + \left(\sum_{i=1}^{n} x_i^4\right)a = \sum_{i=1}^{n} x_i^2 y_i$$

67.

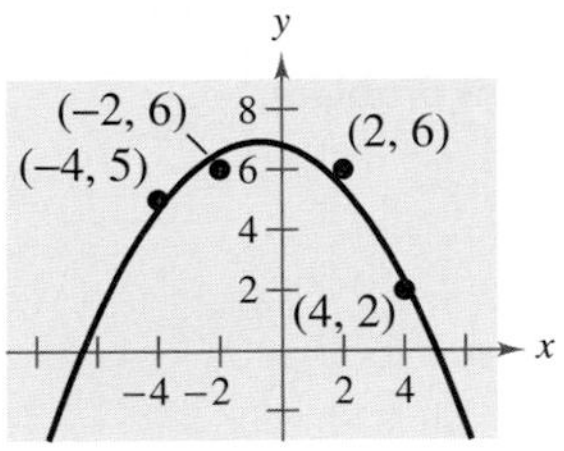

68.

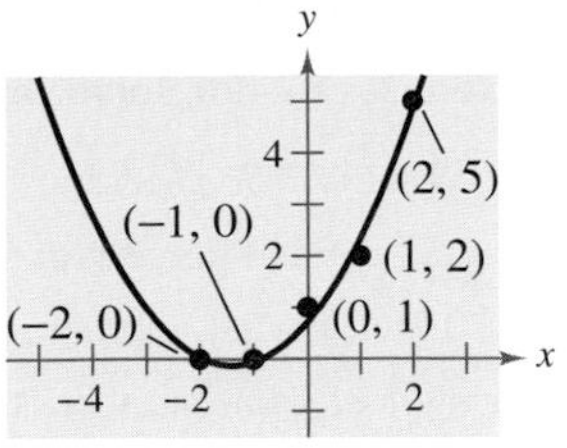

69.

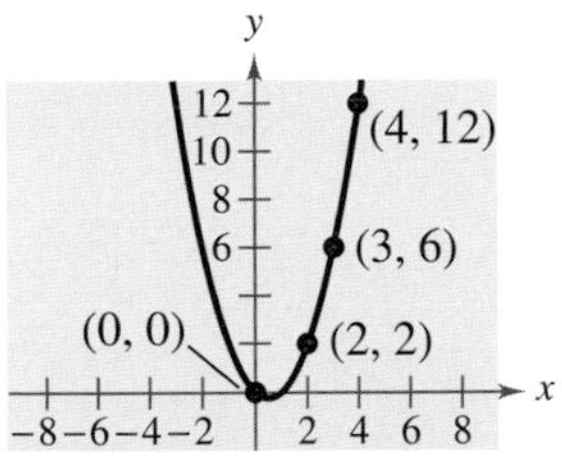

70.

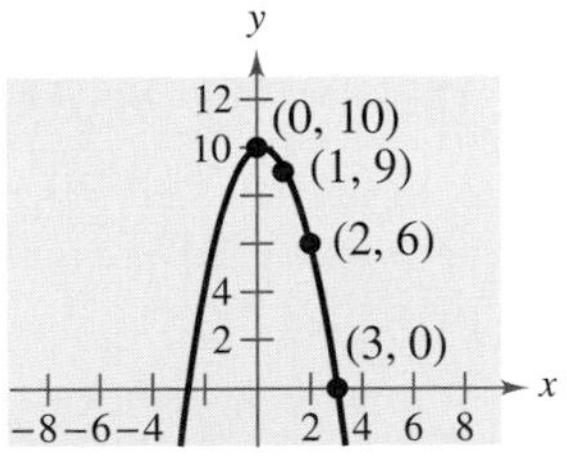

Model It

71. ***Data Analysis: Wildlife*** A wildlife management team studied the reproduction rates of deer in three tracts of a wildlife preserve. Each tract contained 5 acres. In each tract, the number of females x, and the percent of females y that had offspring the following year, were recorded. The results are shown in the table.

Number, x	Percent, y
100	75
120	68
140	55

(a) Use the technique demonstrated in Exercises 67–70 to set up a system of equations for the data and to find a least squares regression parabola that models the data.

(b) Use a graphing utility to graph the parabola and the data in the same viewing window.

(c) Use the model to create a table of estimated values of y. Compare the estimated values with the actual data.

(d) Use the model to estimate the percent of females that had offspring when there were 170 females.

(e) Use the model to estimate the number of females when 40% of the females had offspring.

72. ***Data Analysis: Stopping Distance*** In testing a new automobile braking system, the speed x (in miles per hour) and the stopping distance y (in feet) were recorded in the table.

Speed, x	Stopping distance, y
30	55
40	105
50	188

(a) Use the technique demonstrated in Exercises 67–70 to set up a system of equations for the data and to find a least squares regression parabola that models the data.

(b) Graph the parabola and the data on the same set of axes.

(c) Use the model to estimate the stopping distance when the speed is 70 miles per hour.

73. ***Sports*** In Super Bowl XXXVIII, on February 1, 2004, the New England Patriots beat the Carolina Panthers by a score of 32 to 29. The total points scored came from 16 different scoring plays, which were a combination of touchdowns, extra-point kicks, two-point conversions, and field goals, worth 6, 1, 2, and 3 points, respectively. There were four times as many touchdowns as field goals and two times as many field goals as two-point conversions. How many touchdowns, extra-point kicks, two-point conversions, and field goals were scored during the game? (Source: SuperBowl.com)

74. ***Sports*** In the 2005 Orange Bowl, the University of Southern California won the National Championship by defeating the University of Oklahoma by a score of 55 to 19. The total points scored came from 22 different scoring plays, which were a combination of touchdowns, extra-point kicks, field goals and safeties, worth 6, 1, 3, and 2 points respectively. The same number of touchdowns and extra-point kicks were scored, and there were three times as many field goals as safeties. How many touchdowns, extra-point kicks, field goals, and safeties were scored? (Source: ESPN.com)

Advanced Applications **In Exercises 75–78, find values of x, y, and λ that satisfy the system. These systems arise in certain optimization problems in calculus, and λ is called a Lagrange multiplier.**

75. $\begin{cases} y + \lambda = 0 \\ x + \lambda = 0 \\ x + y - 10 = 0 \end{cases}$

76. $\begin{cases} 2x + \lambda = 0 \\ 2y + \lambda = 0 \\ x + y - 4 = 0 \end{cases}$

77. $\begin{cases} 2x - 2x\lambda = 0 \\ -2y + \lambda = 0 \\ y - x^2 = 0 \end{cases}$

78. $\begin{cases} 2 + 2y + 2\lambda = 0 \\ 2x + 1 + \lambda = 0 \\ 2x + y - 100 = 0 \end{cases}$

Synthesis

True or False? **In Exercises 79 and 80, determine whether the statement is true or false. Justify your answer.**

79. The system

$$\begin{cases} x + 3y - 6z = -16 \\ 2y - z = -1 \\ z = 3 \end{cases}$$

is in row-echelon form.

80. If a system of three linear equations is inconsistent, then its graph has no points common to all three equations.

81. ***Think About It*** Are the following two systems of equations equivalent? Give reasons for your answer.

$$\begin{cases} x + 3y - z = 6 \\ 2x - y + 2z = 1 \\ 3x + 2y - z = 2 \end{cases} \qquad \begin{cases} x + 3y - z = 6 \\ -7y + 4z = 1 \\ -7y - 4z = -16 \end{cases}$$

82. ***Writing*** When using Gaussian elimination to solve a system of linear equations, explain how you can recognize that the system has no solution. Give an example that illustrates your answer.

In Exercises 83–86, find two systems of linear equations that have the ordered triple as a solution. (There are many correct answers.)

83. $(4, -1, 2)$ **84.** $(-5, -2, 1)$

85. $\left(3, -\frac{1}{2}, \frac{7}{4}\right)$ **86.** $\left(-\frac{3}{2}, 4, -7\right)$

Skills Review

In Exercises 87–90, solve the percent problem.

87. What is $7\frac{1}{2}\%$ of 85?

88. 225 is what percent of 150?

89. 0.5% of what number is 400?

90. 48% of what number is 132?

In Exercises 91–96, perform the operation and write the result in standard form.

91. $(7 - i) + (4 + 2i)$

92. $(-6 + 3i) - (1 + 6i)$

93. $(4 - i)(5 + 2i)$

94. $(1 + 2i)(3 - 4i)$

95. $\dfrac{i}{1 + i} + \dfrac{6}{1 - i}$

96. $\dfrac{i}{4 + i} - \dfrac{2i}{8 - 3i}$

In Exercises 97–100, (a) determine the real zeros of f and (b) sketch the graph of f.

97. $f(x) = x^3 + x^2 - 12x$

98. $f(x) = -8x^4 + 32x^2$

99. $f(x) = 2x^3 + 5x^2 - 21x - 36$

100. $f(x) = 6x^3 - 29x^2 - 6x + 5$

In Exercises 101–104, use a graphing utility to construct a table of values for the equation. Then sketch the graph of the equation by hand.

101. $y = 4^{x-4} - 5$

102. $y = \left(\frac{5}{2}\right)^{-x+1} - 4$

103. $y = 1.9^{-0.8x} + 3$

104. $y = 3.5^{-x+2} + 6$

In Exercises 105 and 106, solve the system by elimination.

105. $\begin{cases} 2x + y = 120 \\ x + 2y = 120 \end{cases}$

106. $\begin{cases} 6x - 5y = 3 \\ 10x - 12y = 5 \end{cases}$

107. Make a Decision To work an extended application analyzing the earnings per share for Wal-Mart Stores, Inc. from 1988 to 2003, visit this text's website at *college.hmco.com*. *(Data Source: Wal-Mart Stores, Inc.)*

7.4 Partial Fractions

What you should learn

- Recognize partial fraction decompositions of rational expressions.
- Find partial fraction decompositions of rational expressions.

Why you should learn it

Partial fractions can help you analyze the behavior of a rational function. For instance, in Exercise 57 on page 540, you can analyze the exhaust temperatures of a diesel engine using partial fractions.

© Michael Rosenfeld/Getty Images

Introduction

In this section, you will learn to write a rational expression as the sum of two or more simpler rational expressions. For example, the rational expression

$$\frac{x+7}{x^2-x-6}$$

can be written as the sum of two fractions with first-degree denominators. That is,

$$\frac{x+7}{x^2-x-6} = \underbrace{\overbrace{\underbrace{\frac{2}{x-3}}_{\text{Partial fraction}} + \underbrace{\frac{-1}{x+2}}_{\text{Partial fraction}}}^{\text{Partial fraction decomposition of } \frac{x+7}{x^2-x-6}}}_{}.$$

Each fraction on the right side of the equation is a **partial fraction,** and together they make up the **partial fraction decomposition** of the left side.

Decomposition of $N(x)/D(x)$ into Partial Fractions

1. *Divide if improper:* If $N(x)/D(x)$ is an improper fraction [degree of $N(x) \geq$ degree of $D(x)$], divide the denominator into the numerator to obtain

$$\frac{N(x)}{D(x)} = (\text{polynomial}) + \frac{N_1(x)}{D(x)}$$

and apply Steps 2, 3, and 4 below to the proper rational expression $N_1(x)/D(x)$. Note that $N_1(x)$ is the remainder from the division of $N(x)$ by $D(x)$.

2. *Factor the denominator:* Completely factor the denominator into factors of the form

$$(px+q)^m \quad \text{and} \quad (ax^2+bx+c)^n$$

where (ax^2+bx+c) is irreducible.

3. *Linear factors:* For *each* factor of the form $(px+q)^m$, the partial fraction decomposition must include the following sum of m fractions.

$$\frac{A_1}{(px+q)} + \frac{A_2}{(px+q)^2} + \cdot \cdot \cdot + \frac{A_m}{(px+q)^m}$$

4. *Quadratic factors:* For *each* factor of the form $(ax^2+bx+c)^n$, the partial fraction decomposition must include the following sum of n fractions.

$$\frac{B_1x+C_1}{ax^2+bx+c} + \frac{B_2x+C_2}{(ax^2+bx+c)^2} + \cdot \cdot \cdot + \frac{B_nx+C_n}{(ax^2+bx+c)^n}$$

STUDY TIP

Section A.4, shows you how to combine expressions such as

$$\frac{1}{x-2} + \frac{-1}{x+3} = \frac{5}{(x-2)(x+3)}.$$

The method of partial fractions shows you how to reverse this process.

$$\frac{5}{(x-2)(x+3)} = \frac{?}{x-2} + \frac{?}{x+3}$$

Partial Fraction Decomposition

Algebraic techniques for determining the constants in the numerators of partial fractions are demonstrated in the examples that follow. Note that the techniques vary slightly, depending on the type of factors of the denominator: linear or quadratic, distinct or repeated.

Example 1 Distinct Linear Factors

Write the partial fraction decomposition of $\dfrac{x+7}{x^2-x-6}$.

Solution

The expression is proper, so be sure to factor the denominator. Because $x^2 - x - 6 = (x-3)(x+2)$, you should include one partial fraction with a constant numerator for each linear factor of the denominator. Write the form of the decomposition as follows.

$$\frac{x+7}{x^2-x-6} = \frac{A}{x-3} + \frac{B}{x+2}$$ Write form of decomposition.

Multiplying each side of this equation by the least common denominator, $(x-3)(x+2)$, leads to the **basic equation**

$$x + 7 = A(x+2) + B(x-3).$$ Basic equation

Because this equation is true for all x, you can substitute any *convenient* values of x that will help determine the constants A and B. Values of x that are especially convenient are ones that make the factors $(x+2)$ and $(x-3)$ equal to zero. For instance, let $x = -2$. Then

$$-2 + 7 = A(-2+2) + B(-2-3)$$ Substitute -2 for x.

$$5 = A(0) + B(-5)$$

$$5 = -5B$$

$$-1 = B.$$

To solve for A, let $x = 3$ and obtain

$$3 + 7 = A(3+2) + B(3-3)$$ Substitute 3 for x.

$$10 = A(5) + B(0)$$

$$10 = 5A$$

$$2 = A.$$

So, the partial fraction decomposition is

$$\frac{x+7}{x^2-x-6} = \frac{2}{x-3} + \frac{-1}{x+2}.$$

Check this result by combining the two partial fractions on the right side of the equation, or by using your graphing utility.

✓CHECKPOINT Now try Exercise 15.

Technology

You can use a graphing utility to check *graphically* the decomposition found in Example 1. To do this, graph

$$y_1 = \frac{x+7}{x^2-x-6}$$

and

$$y_2 = \frac{2}{x-3} + \frac{-1}{x+2}$$

in the same viewing window. The graphs should be identical, as shown below.

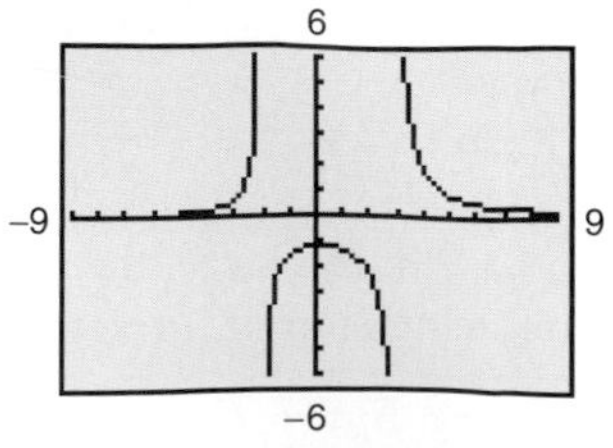

The next example shows how to find the partial fraction decomposition of a rational expression whose denominator has a *repeated* linear factor.

Example 2 Repeated Linear Factors

Write the partial fraction decomposition of $\dfrac{x^4 + 2x^3 + 6x^2 + 20x + 6}{x^3 + 2x^2 + x}$.

Solution

This rational expression is improper, so you should begin by dividing the numerator by the denominator to obtain

$$x + \frac{5x^2 + 20x + 6}{x^3 + 2x^2 + x}.$$

Because the denominator of the remainder factors as

$$x^3 + 2x^2 + x = x(x^2 + 2x + 1) = x(x + 1)^2$$

you should include one partial fraction with a constant numerator for each power of x and $(x + 1)$ and write the form of the decomposition as follows.

$$\frac{5x^2 + 20x + 6}{x(x + 1)^2} = \frac{A}{x} + \frac{B}{x + 1} + \frac{C}{(x + 1)^2}$$ Write form of decomposition.

Multiplying by the LCD, $x(x + 1)^2$, leads to the basic equation

$$5x^2 + 20x + 6 = A(x + 1)^2 + Bx(x + 1) + Cx.$$ Basic equation

Letting $x = -1$ eliminates the A- and B-terms and yields

$$5(-1)^2 + 20(-1) + 6 = A(-1 + 1)^2 + B(-1)(-1 + 1) + C(-1)$$
$$5 - 20 + 6 = 0 + 0 - C$$
$$C = 9.$$

Letting $x = 0$ eliminates the B- and C-terms and yields

$$5(0)^2 + 20(0) + 6 = A(0 + 1)^2 + B(0)(0 + 1) + C(0)$$
$$6 = A(1) + 0 + 0$$
$$6 = A.$$

At this point, you have exhausted the most convenient choices for x, so to find the value of B, use *any other value* for x along with the known values of A and C. So, using $x = 1$, $A = 6$, and $C = 9$,

$$5(1)^2 + 20(1) + 6 = 6(1 + 1)^2 + B(1)(1 + 1) + 9(1)$$
$$31 = 6(4) + 2B + 9$$
$$-2 = 2B$$
$$-1 = B.$$

So, the partial fraction decomposition is

$$\frac{x^4 + 2x^3 + 6x^2 + 20x + 6}{x^3 + 2x^2 + x} = x + \frac{6}{x} + \frac{-1}{x + 1} + \frac{9}{(x + 1)^2}.$$

CHECKPOINT Now try Exercise 27.

The procedure used to solve for the constants in Examples 1 and 2 works well when the factors of the denominator are linear. However, when the denominator contains irreducible quadratic factors, you should use a different procedure, which involves writing the right side of the basic equation in polynomial form and *equating the coefficients* of like terms. Then you can use a system of equations to solve for the coefficients.

The Granger Collection

Historical Note

John Bernoulli (1667–1748), a Swiss mathematician, introduced the method of partial fractions and was instrumental in the early development of calculus. Bernoulli was a professor at the University of Basel and taught many outstanding students, the most famous of whom was Leonhard Euler.

Example 3 **Distinct Linear and Quadratic Factors**

Write the partial fraction decomposition of

$$\frac{3x^2 + 4x + 4}{x^3 + 4x}.$$

Solution

This expression is proper, so factor the denominator. Because the denominator factors as

$$x^3 + 4x = x(x^2 + 4)$$

you should include one partial fraction with a constant numerator and one partial fraction with a linear numerator and write the form of the decomposition as follows.

$$\frac{3x^2 + 4x + 4}{x^3 + 4x} = \frac{A}{x} + \frac{Bx + C}{x^2 + 4}$$ Write form of decomposition.

Multiplying by the LCD, $x(x^2 + 4)$, yields the basic equation

$$3x^2 + 4x + 4 = A(x^2 + 4) + (Bx + C)x.$$ Basic equation

Expanding this basic equation and collecting like terms produces

$$3x^2 + 4x + 4 = Ax^2 + 4A + Bx^2 + Cx$$

$$= (A + B)x^2 + Cx + 4A.$$ Polynomial form

Finally, because two polynomials are equal if and only if the coefficients of like terms are equal, you can equate the coefficients of like terms on opposite sides of the equation.

$$3x^2 + 4x + 4 = (A + B)x^2 + Cx + 4A$$ Equate coefficients of like terms.

You can now write the following system of linear equations.

$$\begin{cases} A + B \quad = 3 & \text{Equation 1} \\ \qquad C = 4 & \text{Equation 2} \\ 4A \qquad = 4 & \text{Equation 3} \end{cases}$$

From this system you can see that $A = 1$ and $C = 4$. Moreover, substituting $A = 1$ into Equation 1 yields

$$1 + B = 3 \Longrightarrow B = 2.$$

So, the partial fraction decomposition is

$$\frac{3x^2 + 4x + 4}{x^3 + 4x} = \frac{1}{x} + \frac{2x + 4}{x^2 + 4}.$$

CHECKPOINT Now try Exercise 29.

The next example shows how to find the partial fraction decomposition of a rational expression whose denominator has a *repeated* quadratic factor.

Example 4 Repeated Quadratic Factors

Write the partial fraction decomposition of $\dfrac{8x^3 + 13x}{(x^2 + 2)^2}$.

Solution

You need to include one partial fraction with a linear numerator for each power of $(x^2 + 2)$.

$$\frac{8x^3 + 13x}{(x^2 + 2)^2} = \frac{Ax + B}{x^2 + 2} + \frac{Cx + D}{(x^2 + 2)^2} \qquad \text{Write form of decomposition.}$$

Multiplying by the LCD, $(x^2 + 2)^2$, yields the basic equation

$$\begin{aligned} 8x^3 + 13x &= (Ax + B)(x^2 + 2) + Cx + D && \text{Basic equation} \\ &= Ax^3 + 2Ax + Bx^2 + 2B + Cx + D \\ &= Ax^3 + Bx^2 + (2A + C)x + (2B + D). && \text{Polynomial form} \end{aligned}$$

Equating coefficients of like terms on opposite sides of the equation

$$8x^3 + 0x^2 + 13x + 0 = Ax^3 + Bx^2 + (2A + C)x + (2B + D)$$

produces the following system of linear equations.

$$\begin{cases} A = 8 & \text{Equation 1} \\ B = 0 & \text{Equation 2} \\ 2A + C = 13 & \text{Equation 3} \\ 2B + D = 0 & \text{Equation 4} \end{cases}$$

Finally, use the values $A = 8$ and $B = 0$ to obtain the following.

$$\begin{aligned} 2(8) + C &= 13 && \text{Substitute 8 for } A \text{ in Equation 3.} \\ C &= -3 \end{aligned}$$

$$\begin{aligned} 2(0) + D &= 0 && \text{Substitute 0 for } B \text{ in Equation 4.} \\ D &= 0 \end{aligned}$$

So, using $A = 8$, $B = 0$, $C = -3$, and $D = 0$, the partial fraction decomposition is

$$\frac{8x^3 + 13x}{(x^2 + 2)^2} = \frac{8x}{x^2 + 2} + \frac{-3x}{(x^2 + 2)^2}.$$

Check this result by combining the two partial fractions on the right side of the equation, or by using your graphing utility.

CHECKPOINT Now try Exercise 49.

Guidelines for Solving the Basic Equation

Linear Factors

1. Substitute the *zeros* of the distinct linear factors into the basic equation.
2. For repeated linear factors, use the coefficients determined in Step 1 to rewrite the basic equation. Then substitute *other* convenient values of x and solve for the remaining coefficients.

Quadratic Factors

1. Expand the basic equation.
2. Collect terms according to powers of x.
3. Equate the coefficients of like terms to obtain equations involving A, B, C, and so on.
4. Use a system of linear equations to solve for $A, B, C, \ldots$.

Keep in mind that for *improper* rational expressions such as

$$\frac{N(x)}{D(x)} = \frac{2x^3 + x^2 - 7x + 7}{x^2 + x - 2}$$

you must first divide before applying partial fraction decomposition.

Writing About Mathematics

Error Analysis You are tutoring a student in algebra. In trying to find a partial fraction decomposition, the student writes the following.

$$\frac{x^2 + 1}{x(x - 1)} = \frac{A}{x} + \frac{B}{x - 1}$$

$$\frac{x^2 + 1}{x(x - 1)} = \frac{A(x - 1)}{x(x - 1)} + \frac{Bx}{x(x - 1)}$$

$$x^2 + 1 = A(x - 1) + Bx \qquad \text{Basic equation}$$

By substituting $x = 0$ and $x = 1$ into the basic equation, the student concludes that $A = -1$ and $B = 2$. However, in checking this solution, the student obtains the following.

$$\frac{-1}{x} + \frac{2}{x - 1} = \frac{(-1)(x - 1) + 2(x)}{x(x - 1)}$$

$$= \frac{x + 1}{x(x - 1)}$$

$$\neq \frac{x^2 + 1}{x(x + 1)}$$

What has gone wrong?

7.4 Exercises

VOCABULARY CHECK: Fill in the blanks.

1. The process of writing a rational expression as the sum or difference of two or more simpler rational expressions is called ________ ________ ________.
2. If the degree of the numerator of a rational expression is greater than or equal to the degree of the denominator, then the fraction is called ________.
3. In order to find the partial fraction decomposition of a rational expression, the denominator must be completely factored into ________ factors of the form $(px + q)^m$ and ________ factors of the form $(ax^2 + bx + c)^n$, which are ________ over the rationals.
4. The ________ ________ is derived after multiplying each side of the partial fraction decomposition form by the least common denominator.

In Exercises 1–4, match the rational expression with the form of its decomposition. [The decompositions are labeled (a), (b), (c), and (d).]

(a) $\dfrac{A}{x} + \dfrac{B}{x+2} + \dfrac{C}{x-2}$ (b) $\dfrac{A}{x} + \dfrac{B}{x-4}$

(c) $\dfrac{A}{x} + \dfrac{B}{x^2} + \dfrac{C}{x-4}$ (d) $\dfrac{A}{x} + \dfrac{Bx + C}{x^2 + 4}$

1. $\dfrac{3x - 1}{x(x - 4)}$
2. $\dfrac{3x - 1}{x^2(x - 4)}$
3. $\dfrac{3x - 1}{x(x^2 + 4)}$
4. $\dfrac{3x - 1}{x(x^2 - 4)}$

In Exercises 5–14, write the form of the partial fraction decomposition of the rational expression. Do not solve for the constants.

5. $\dfrac{7}{x^2 - 14x}$
6. $\dfrac{x - 2}{x^2 + 4x + 3}$
7. $\dfrac{12}{x^3 - 10x^2}$
8. $\dfrac{x^2 - 3x + 2}{4x^3 + 11x^2}$
9. $\dfrac{4x^2 + 3}{(x - 5)^3}$
10. $\dfrac{6x + 5}{(x + 2)^4}$
11. $\dfrac{2x - 3}{x^3 + 10x}$
12. $\dfrac{x - 6}{2x^3 + 8x}$
13. $\dfrac{x - 1}{x(x^2 + 1)^2}$
14. $\dfrac{x + 4}{x^2(3x - 1)^2}$

In Exercises 15–38, write the partial fraction decomposition of the rational expression. Check your result algebraically.

15. $\dfrac{1}{x^2 - 1}$
16. $\dfrac{1}{4x^2 - 9}$
17. $\dfrac{1}{x^2 + x}$
18. $\dfrac{3}{x^2 - 3x}$
19. $\dfrac{1}{2x^2 + x}$
20. $\dfrac{5}{x^2 + x - 6}$
21. $\dfrac{3}{x^2 + x - 2}$
22. $\dfrac{x + 1}{x^2 + 4x + 3}$
23. $\dfrac{x^2 + 12x + 12}{x^3 - 4x}$
24. $\dfrac{x + 2}{x(x - 4)}$
25. $\dfrac{4x^2 + 2x - 1}{x^2(x + 1)}$
26. $\dfrac{2x - 3}{(x - 1)^2}$
27. $\dfrac{3x}{(x - 3)^2}$
28. $\dfrac{6x^2 + 1}{x^2(x - 1)^2}$
29. $\dfrac{x^2 - 1}{x(x^2 + 1)}$
30. $\dfrac{x}{(x - 1)(x^2 + x + 1)}$
31. $\dfrac{x}{x^3 - x^2 - 2x + 2}$
32. $\dfrac{x + 6}{x^3 - 3x^2 - 4x + 12}$
33. $\dfrac{x^2}{x^4 - 2x^2 - 8}$
34. $\dfrac{2x^2 + x + 8}{(x^2 + 4)^2}$
35. $\dfrac{x}{16x^4 - 1}$
36. $\dfrac{x + 1}{x^3 + x}$
37. $\dfrac{x^2 + 5}{(x + 1)(x^2 - 2x + 3)}$
38. $\dfrac{x^2 - 4x + 7}{(x + 1)(x^2 - 2x + 3)}$

In Exercises 39–44, write the partial fraction decomposition of the improper rational expression.

39. $\dfrac{x^2 - x}{x^2 + x + 1}$
40. $\dfrac{x^2 - 4x}{x^2 + x + 6}$
41. $\dfrac{2x^3 - x^2 + x + 5}{x^2 + 3x + 2}$
42. $\dfrac{x^3 + 2x^2 - x + 1}{x^2 + 3x - 4}$
43. $\dfrac{x^4}{(x - 1)^3}$
44. $\dfrac{16x^4}{(2x - 1)^3}$

In Exercises 45–52, write the partial fraction decomposition of the rational expression. Use a graphing utility to check your result graphically.

45. $\dfrac{5 - x}{2x^2 + x - 1}$

46. $\dfrac{3x^2 - 7x - 2}{x^3 - x}$

47. $\dfrac{x - 1}{x^3 + x^2}$

48. $\dfrac{4x^2 - 1}{2x(x + 1)^2}$

49. $\dfrac{x^2 + x + 2}{(x^2 + 2)^2}$

50. $\dfrac{x^3}{(x + 2)^2(x - 2)^2}$

51. $\dfrac{2x^3 - 4x^2 - 15x + 5}{x^2 - 2x - 8}$

52. $\dfrac{x^3 - x + 3}{x^2 + x - 2}$

Graphical Analysis **In Exercises 53–56, (a) write the partial fraction decomposition of the rational function, (b) identify the graph of the rational function and the graph of each term of its decomposition, and (c) state any relationship between the vertical asymptotes of the graph of the rational function and the vertical asymptotes of the graphs of the terms of the decomposition. To print an enlarged copy of the graph, go to the website *www.mathgraphs.com*.**

53. $y = \dfrac{x - 12}{x(x - 4)}$

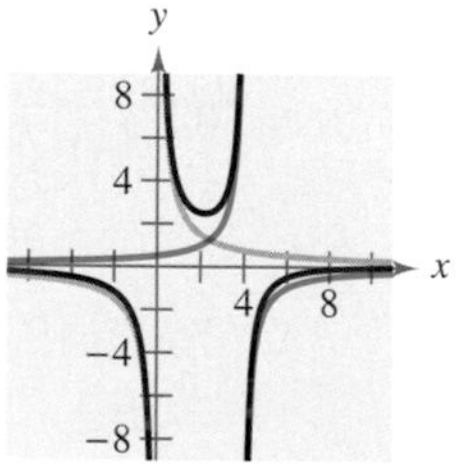

54. $y = \dfrac{2(x + 1)^2}{x(x^2 + 1)}$

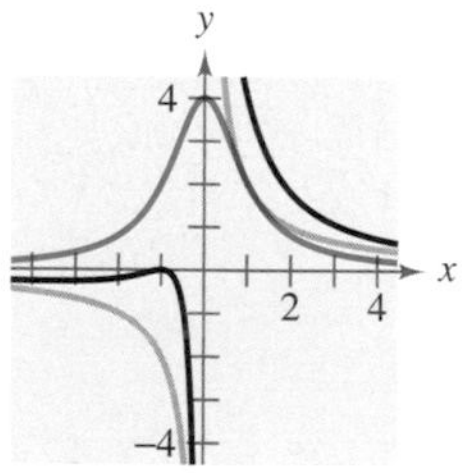

55. $y = \dfrac{2(4x - 3)}{x^2 - 9}$

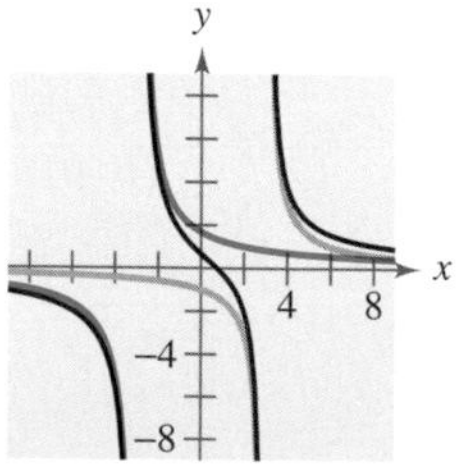

56. $y = \dfrac{2(4x^2 - 15x + 39)}{x^2(x^2 - 10x + 26)}$

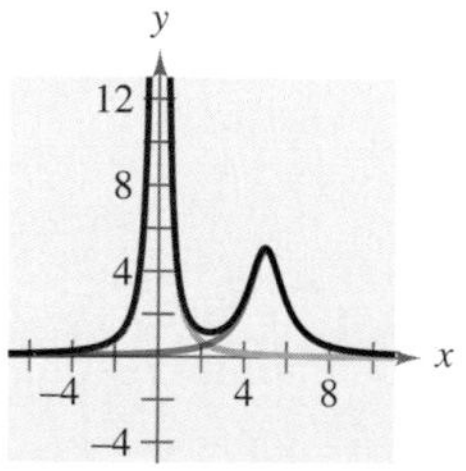

Model It

57. ***Thermodynamics*** The magnitude of the range R of exhaust temperatures (in degrees Fahrenheit) in an experimental diesel engine is approximated by the model

$$R = \frac{2000(4 - 3x)}{(11 - 7x)(7 - 4x)}, \quad 0 < x \leq 1$$

Model It (continued)

where x is the relative load (in foot-pounds).

(a) Write the partial fraction decomposition of the equation.

(b) The decomposition in part (a) is the difference of two fractions. The absolute values of the terms give the expected maximum and minimum temperatures of the exhaust gases for different loads.

Ymax = |1st term| Ymin = |2nd term|

Write the equations for Ymax and Ymin.

(c) Use a graphing utility to graph each equation from part (b) in the same viewing window.

(d) Determine the expected maximum and minimum temperatures for a relative load of 0.5.

Synthesis

58. ***Writing*** Describe two ways of solving for the constants in a partial fraction decomposition.

True or False? **In Exercises 59 and 60, determine whether the statement is true or false. Justify your answer.**

59. For the rational expression $\dfrac{x}{(x + 10)(x - 10)^2}$ the partial fraction decomposition is of the form $\dfrac{A}{x + 10} + \dfrac{B}{(x - 10)^2}$.

60. When writing the partial fraction decomposition of the expression $\dfrac{x^3 + x - 2}{x^2 - 5x - 14}$ the first step is to factor the denominator.

In Exercises 61–64, write the partial fraction decomposition of the rational expression. Check your result algebraically. Then assign a value to the constant *a* to check the result graphically.

61. $\dfrac{1}{a^2 - x^2}$

62. $\dfrac{1}{x(x + a)}$

63. $\dfrac{1}{y(a - y)}$

64. $\dfrac{1}{(x + 1)(a - x)}$

Skills Review

In Exercises 65–70, sketch the graph of the function.

65. $f(x) = x^2 - 9x + 18$

66. $f(x) = 2x^2 - 9x - 5$

67. $f(x) = -x^2(x - 3)$

68. $f(x) = \frac{1}{2}x^3 - 1$

69. $f(x) = \dfrac{x^2 + x - 6}{x + 5}$

70. $f(x) = \dfrac{3x - 1}{x^2 + 4x - 12}$

7.5 Systems of Inequalities

What you should learn

- Sketch the graphs of inequalities in two variables.
- Solve systems of inequalities.
- Use systems of inequalities in two variables to model and solve real-life problems.

Why you should learn it

You can use systems of inequalities in two variables to model and solve real-life problems. For instance, in Exercise 77 on page 550, you will use a system of inequalities to analyze the retail sales of prescription drugs.

Jon Feingersh/Masterfile

STUDY TIP

Note that when sketching the graph of an inequality in two variables, a dashed line means all points on the line or curve *are not* solutions of the inequality. A solid line means all points on the line or curve *are* solutions of the inequality.

The Graph of an Inequality

The statements $3x - 2y < 6$ and $2x^2 + 3y^2 \geq 6$ are inequalities in two variables. An ordered pair (a, b) is a **solution of an inequality** in x and y if the inequality is true when a and b are substituted for x and y, respectively. The **graph of an inequality** is the collection of all solutions of the inequality. To sketch the graph of an inequality, begin by sketching the graph of the *corresponding equation*. The graph of the equation will normally separate the plane into two or more regions. In each such region, one of the following must be true.

1. *All* points in the region are solutions of the inequality.
2. *No* point in the region is a solution of the inequality.

So, you can determine whether the points in an entire region satisfy the inequality by simply testing *one* point in the region.

Sketching the Graph of an Inequality in Two Variables

1. Replace the inequality sign by an equal sign, and sketch the graph of the resulting equation. (Use a dashed line for $<$ or $>$ and a solid line for $\leq$ or $\geq$.)
2. Test one point in each of the regions formed by the graph in Step 1. If the point satisfies the inequality, shade the entire region to denote that every point in the region satisfies the inequality.

Example 1 Sketching the Graph of an Inequality

To sketch the graph of $y \geq x^2 - 1$, begin by graphing the corresponding equation $y = x^2 - 1$, which is a parabola, as shown in Figure 7.19. By testing a point *above* the parabola $(0, 0)$ and a point *below* the parabola $(0, -2)$, you can see that the points that satisfy the inequality are those lying above (or on) the parabola.

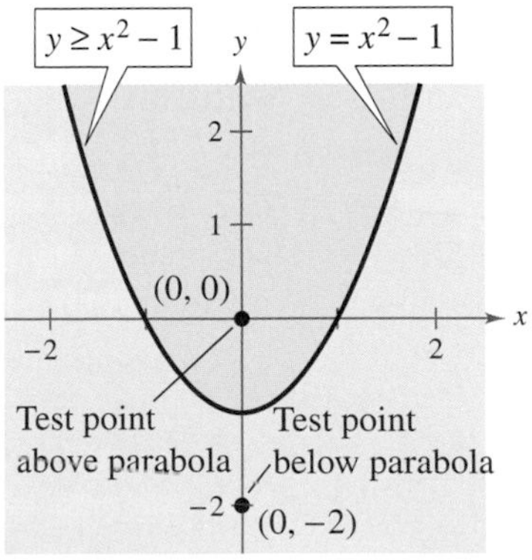

FIGURE 7.19

✓CHECKPOINT Now try Exercise 1.

The inequality in Example 1 is a nonlinear inequality in two variables. Most of the following examples involve **linear inequalities** such as $ax + by < c$ (a and b are not both zero). The graph of a linear inequality is a half-plane lying on one side of the line $ax + by = c$.

Example 2 Sketching the Graph of a Linear Inequality

Sketch the graph of each linear inequality.

a. $x > -2$ **b.** $y \le 3$

Solution

a. The graph of the corresponding equation $x = -2$ is a vertical line. The points that satisfy the inequality $x > -2$ are those lying to the right of this line, as shown in Figure 7.20.

b. The graph of the corresponding equation $y = 3$ is a horizontal line. The points that satisfy the inequality $y \le 3$ are those lying below (or on) this line, as shown in Figure 7.21.

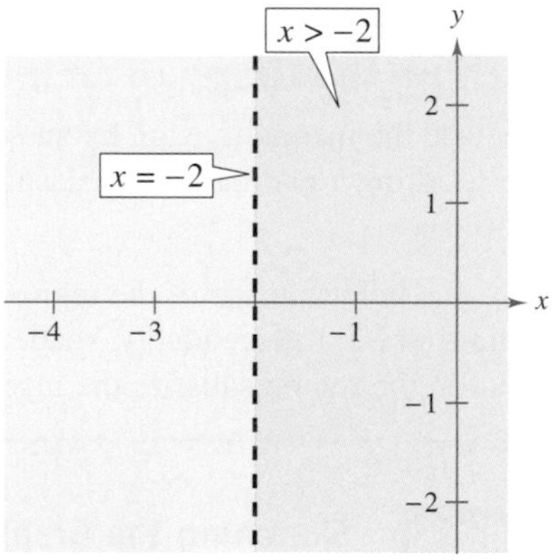

FIGURE 7.20

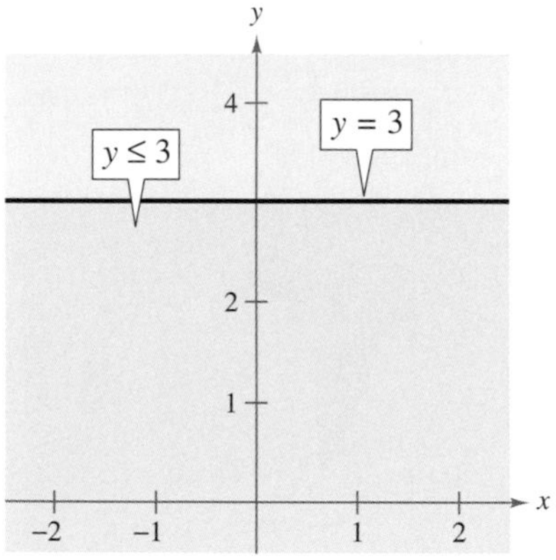

FIGURE 7.21

CHECKPOINT Now try Exercise 3.

Technology

A graphing utility can be used to graph an inequality or a system of inequalities. For instance, to graph $y \ge x - 2$, enter $y = x - 2$ and use the *shade* feature of the graphing utility to shade the correct part of the graph. You should obtain the graph below. Consult the user's guide for your graphing utility for specific keystrokes.

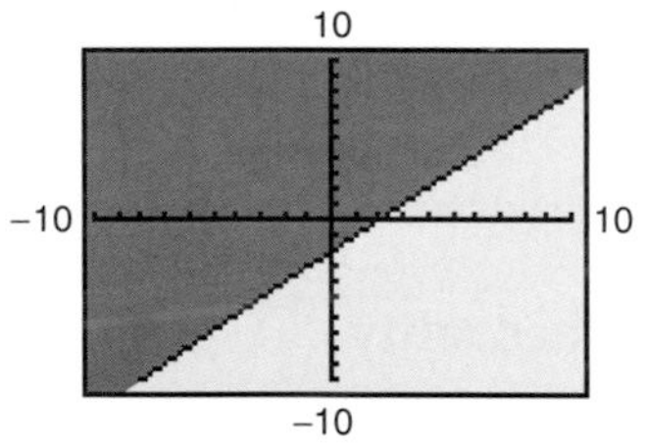

Example 3 Sketching the Graph of a Linear Inequality

Sketch the graph of $x - y < 2$.

Solution

The graph of the corresponding equation $x - y = 2$ is a line, as shown in Figure 7.22. Because the origin (0, 0) satisfies the inequality, the graph consists of the half-plane lying above the line. (Try checking a point below the line. Regardless of which point you choose, you will see that it does not satisfy the inequality.)

CHECKPOINT Now try Exercise 9.

To graph a linear inequality, it can help to write the inequality in slope-intercept form. For instance, by writing $x - y < 2$ in the form

$$y > x - 2$$

you can see that the solution points lie *above* the line $x - y = 2$ (or $y = x - 2$), as shown in Figure 7.22.

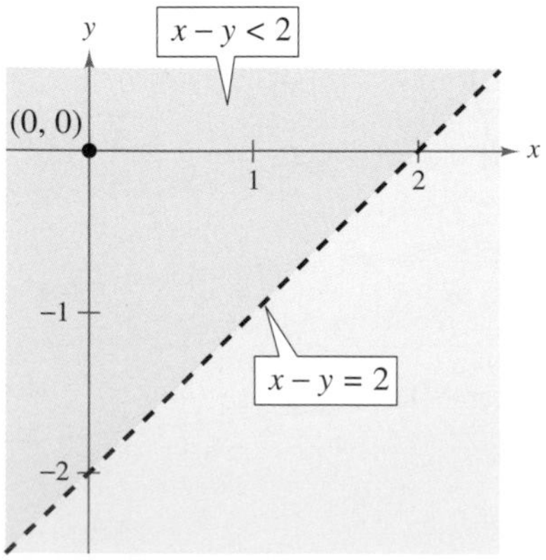

FIGURE 7.22

Systems of Inequalities

Many practical problems in business, science, and engineering involve systems of linear inequalities. A **solution** of a system of inequalities in x and y is a point (x, y) that satisfies each inequality in the system.

To sketch the graph of a system of inequalities in two variables, first sketch the graph of each individual inequality (on the same coordinate system) and then find the region that is *common* to every graph in the system. This region represents the **solution set** of the system. For systems of *linear inequalities*, it is helpful to find the vertices of the solution region.

Example 4 Solving a System of Inequalities

Sketch the graph (and label the vertices) of the solution set of the system.

$$\begin{cases} x - y < 2 & \text{Inequality 1} \\ x > -2 & \text{Inequality 2} \\ y \leq 3 & \text{Inequality 3} \end{cases}$$

Solution

The graphs of these inequalities are shown in Figures 7.22, 7.20, and 7.21, respectively, on page 542. The triangular region common to all three graphs can be found by superimposing the graphs on the same coordinate system, as shown in Figure 7.23. To find the vertices of the region, solve the three systems of corresponding equations obtained by taking *pairs* of equations representing the boundaries of the individual regions.

Vertex A: $(-2, -4)$ $\begin{cases} x - y = 2 \\ x = -2 \end{cases}$

Vertex B: $(5, 3)$ $\begin{cases} x - y = 2 \\ y = 3 \end{cases}$

Vertex C: $(-2, 3)$ $\begin{cases} x = -2 \\ y = 3 \end{cases}$

STUDY TIP

Using different colored pencils to shade the solution of each inequality in a system will make identifying the solution of the system of inequalities easier.

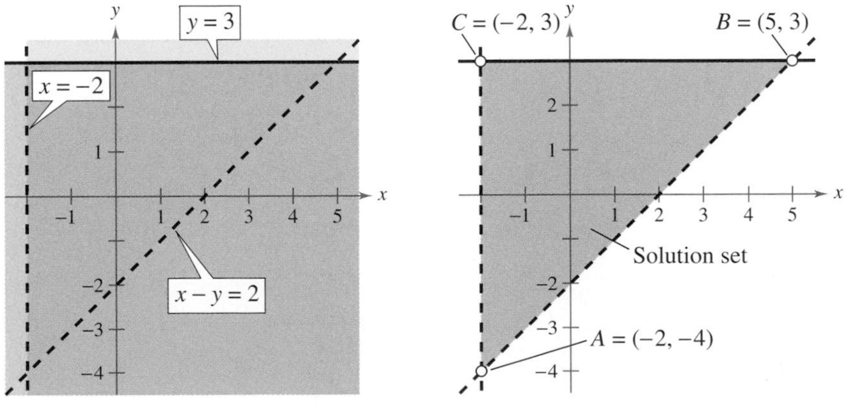

FIGURE 7.23

Note in Figure 7.23 that the vertices of the region are represented by open dots. This means that the vertices *are not* solutions of the system of inequalities.

✓CHECKPOINT Now try Exercise 35.

For the triangular region shown in Figure 7.23, each point of intersection of a pair of boundary lines corresponds to a vertex. With more complicated regions, two border lines can sometimes intersect at a point that is not a vertex of the region, as shown in Figure 7.24. To keep track of which points of intersection are actually vertices of the region, you should sketch the region and refer to your sketch as you find each point of intersection.

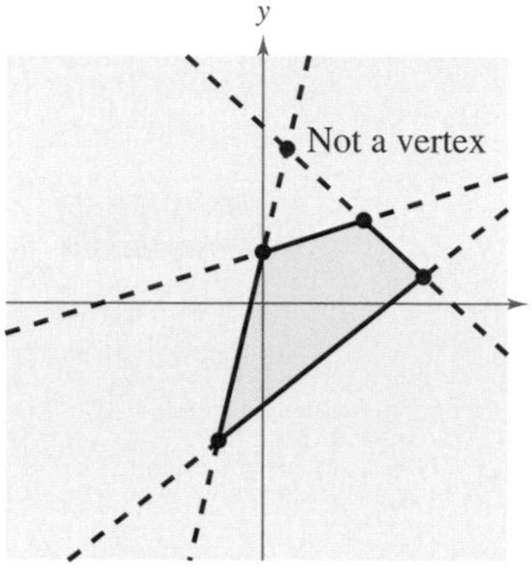

FIGURE 7.24

Example 5 Solving a System of Inequalities

Sketch the region containing all points that satisfy the system of inequalities.

$$\begin{cases} x^2 - y \le 1 & \text{Inequality 1} \\ -x + y \le 1 & \text{Inequality 2} \end{cases}$$

Solution

As shown in Figure 7.25, the points that satisfy the inequality

$$x^2 - y \le 1 \qquad \text{Inequality 1}$$

are the points lying above (or on) the parabola given by

$$y = x^2 - 1. \qquad \text{Parabola}$$

The points satisfying the inequality

$$-x + y \le 1 \qquad \text{Inequality 2}$$

are the points lying below (or on) the line given by

$$y = x + 1. \qquad \text{Line}$$

To find the points of intersection of the parabola and the line, solve the system of corresponding equations.

$$\begin{cases} x^2 - y = 1 \\ -x + y = 1 \end{cases}$$

Using the method of substitution, you can find the solutions to be $(-1, 0)$ and $(2, 3)$. So, the region containing all points that satisfy the system is indicated by the shaded region in Figure 7.25.

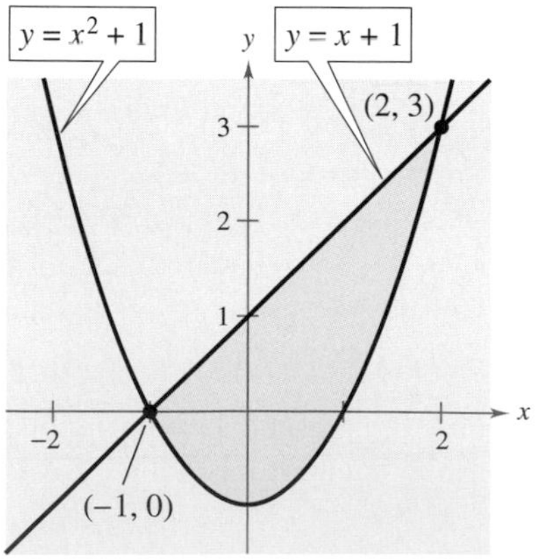

FIGURE 7.25

CHECKPOINT Now try Exercise 37.

When solving a system of inequalities, you should be aware that the system might have no solution *or* it might be represented by an unbounded region in the plane. These two possibilities are shown in Examples 6 and 7.

Example 6 A System with No Solution

Sketch the solution set of the system of inequalities.

$$\begin{cases} x + y > 3 & \text{Inequality 1} \\ x + y < -1 & \text{Inequality 2} \end{cases}$$

Solution

From the way the system is written, it is clear that the system has no solution, because the quantity $(x + y)$ cannot be both less than -1 and greater than 3. Graphically, the inequality $x + y > 3$ is represented by the half-plane lying above the line $x + y = 3$, and the inequality $x + y < -1$ is represented by the half-plane lying below the line $x + y = -1$, as shown in Figure 7.26. These two half-planes have no points in common. So, the system of inequalities has no solution.

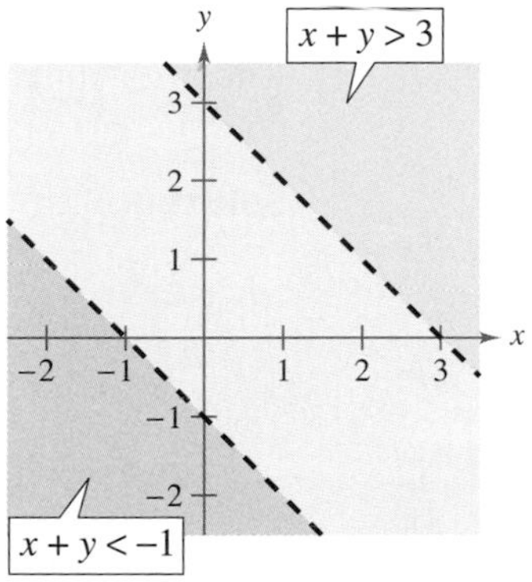

FIGURE 7.26

CHECKPOINT Now try Exercise 39.

Example 7 An Unbounded Solution Set

Sketch the solution set of the system of inequalities.

$$\begin{cases} x + y < 3 & \text{Inequality 1} \\ x + 2y > 3 & \text{Inequality 2} \end{cases}$$

Solution

The graph of the inequality $x + y < 3$ is the half-plane that lies below the line $x + y = 3$, as shown in Figure 7.27. The graph of the inequality $x + 2y > 3$ is the half-plane that lies above the line $x + 2y = 3$. The intersection of these two half-planes is an *infinite wedge* that has a vertex at $(3, 0)$. So, the solution set of the system of inequalities is unbounded.

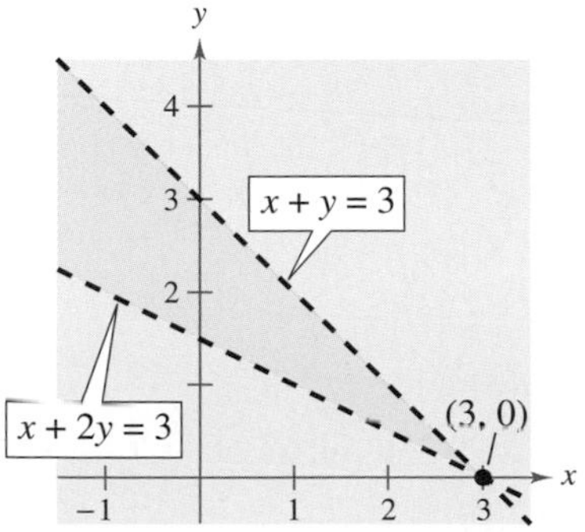

FIGURE 7.27

CHECKPOINT Now try Exercise 41.

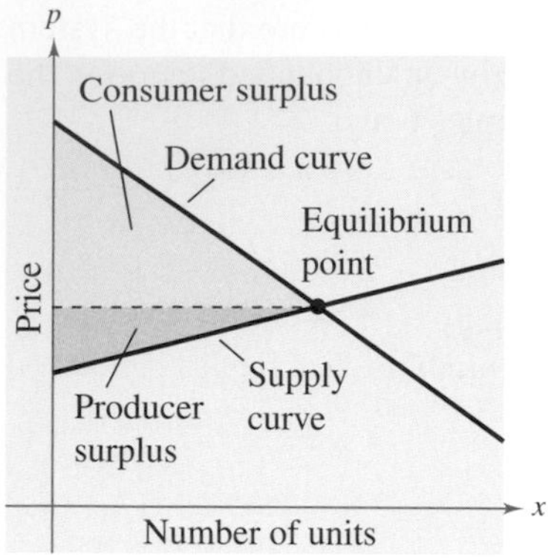

FIGURE 7.28

Applications

Example 9 in Section 7.2 discussed the *equilibrium point* for a system of demand and supply functions. The next example discusses two related concepts that economists call **consumer surplus** and **producer surplus.** As shown in Figure 7.28, the consumer surplus is defined as the area of the region that lies *below* the demand curve, *above* the horizontal line passing through the equilibrium point, and to the right of the p-axis. Similarly, the producer surplus is defined as the area of the region that lies *above* the supply curve, *below* the horizontal line passing through the equilibrium point, and to the right of the p-axis. The consumer surplus is a measure of the amount that consumers would have been willing to pay *above what they actually paid*, whereas the producer surplus is a measure of the amount that producers would have been willing to receive *below what they actually received.*

Example 8 Consumer Surplus and Producer Surplus

The demand and supply functions for a new type of personal digital assistant are given by

$$\begin{cases} p = 150 - 0.00001x & \text{Demand equation} \\ p = \ \ 60 + 0.00002x & \text{Supply equation} \end{cases}$$

where p is the price (in dollars) and x represents the number of units. Find the consumer surplus and producer surplus for these two equations.

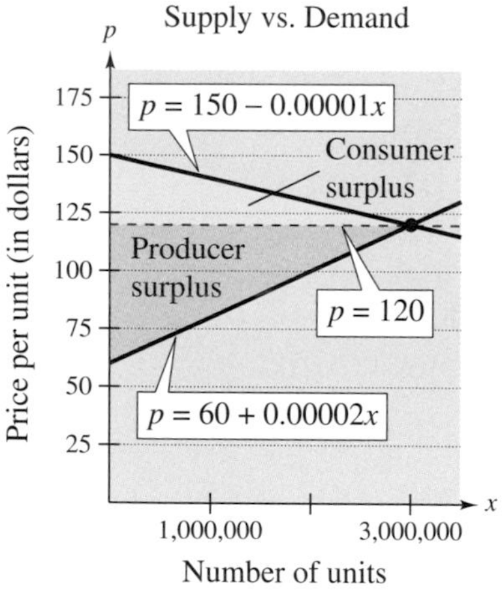

FIGURE 7.29

Solution

Begin by finding the equilibrium point (when supply and demand are equal) by solving the equation

$$60 + 0.00002x = 150 - 0.00001x.$$

In Example 9 in Section 7.2, you saw that the solution is $x = 3{,}000{,}000$ units, which corresponds to an equilibrium price of $p = \$120$. So, the consumer surplus and producer surplus are the areas of the following triangular regions.

Consumer Surplus

$$\begin{cases} p \le 150 - 0.00001x \\ p \ge 120 \\ x \ge 0 \end{cases}$$

Producer Surplus

$$\begin{cases} p \ge 60 + 0.00002x \\ p \le 120 \\ x \ge 0 \end{cases}$$

In Figure 7.29, you can see that the consumer and producer surpluses are defined as the areas of the shaded triangles.

$$\text{Consumer surplus} = \frac{1}{2}(\text{base})(\text{height})$$

$$= \frac{1}{2}(3{,}000{,}000)(30) = \$45{,}000{,}000$$

$$\text{Producer surplus} = \frac{1}{2}(\text{base})(\text{height})$$

$$= \frac{1}{2}(3{,}000{,}000)(60) = \$90{,}000{,}000$$

✓CHECKPOINT Now try Exercise 65.

Example 9 Nutrition

The liquid portion of a diet is to provide at least 300 calories, 36 units of vitamin A, and 90 units of vitamin C. A cup of dietary drink X provides 60 calories, 12 units of vitamin A, and 10 units of vitamin C. A cup of dietary drink Y provides 60 calories, 6 units of vitamin A, and 30 units of vitamin C. Set up a system of linear inequalities that describes how many cups of each drink should be consumed each day to meet or exceed the minimum daily requirements for calories and vitamins.

Solution

Begin by letting x and y represent the following.

$x =$ number of cups of dietary drink X

$y =$ number of cups of dietary drink Y

To meet or exceed the minimum daily requirements, the following inequalities must be satisfied.

$$\begin{cases} 60x + 60y \geq 300 & \text{Calories} \\ 12x + 6y \geq 36 & \text{Vitamin A} \\ 10x + 30y \geq 90 & \text{Vitamin C} \\ x \geq 0 & \\ y \geq 0 & \end{cases}$$

The last two inequalities are included because x and y cannot be negative. The graph of this system of inequalities is shown in Figure 7.30. (More is said about this application in Example 6 in Section 7.6.)

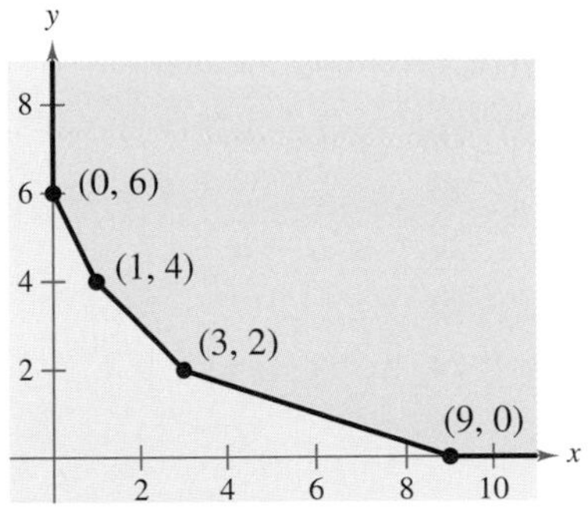

FIGURE 7.30

✓CHECKPOINT Now try Exercise 69.

WRITING ABOUT MATHEMATICS

Creating a System of Inequalities Plot the points (0, 0), (4, 0), (3, 2), and (0, 2) in a coordinate plane. Draw the quadrilateral that has these four points as its vertices. Write a system of linear inequalities that has the quadrilateral as its solution. Explain how you found the system of inequalities.

7.5 Exercises

VOCABULARY CHECK: Fill in the blanks.

1. An ordered pair (a, b) is a ________ of an inequality in x and y if the inequality is true when a and b are substituted for x and y, respectively.
2. The ________ of an inequality is the collection of all solutions of the inequality.
3. The graph of a ________ inequality is a half-plane lying on one side of the line $ax + by = c$.
4. A ________ of a system of inequalities in x and y is a point (x, y) that satisfies each inequality in the system.
5. The area of the region that lies below the demand curve, above the horizontal line passing through the equilibrium point, to the right of the p-axis is called the ________ ________.

In Exercises 1–14, sketch the graph of the inequality.

1. $y < 2 - x^2$
2. $y^2 - x < 0$
3. $x \geq 2$
4. $x \leq 4$
5. $y \geq -1$
6. $y \leq 3$
7. $y < 2 - x$
8. $y > 2x - 4$
9. $2y - x \geq 4$
10. $5x + 3y \geq -15$
11. $(x + 1)^2 + (y - 2)^2 < 9$
12. $(x - 1)^2 + (y - 4)^2 > 9$
13. $y \leq \dfrac{1}{1 + x^2}$
14. $y > \dfrac{-15}{x^2 + x + 4}$

In Exercises 15–26, use a graphing utility to graph the inequality. Shade the region representing the solution.

15. $y < \ln x$
16. $y \geq 6 - \ln(x + 5)$
17. $y < 3^{-x-4}$
18. $y \leq 2^{2x-0.5} - 7$
19. $y \geq \frac{2}{3}x - 1$
20. $y \leq 6 - \frac{3}{2}x$
21. $y < -3.8x + 1.1$
22. $y \geq -20.74 + 2.66x$
23. $x^2 + 5y - 10 \leq 0$
24. $2x^2 - y - 3 > 0$
25. $\frac{5}{2}y - 3x^2 - 6 \geq 0$
26. $-\frac{1}{10}x^2 - \frac{3}{8}y < -\frac{1}{4}$

In Exercises 27–30, write an inequality for the shaded region shown in the figure.

27.

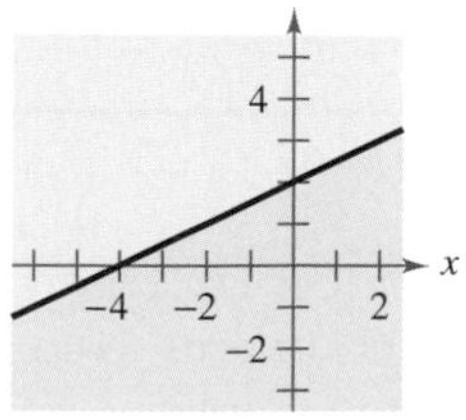

28.

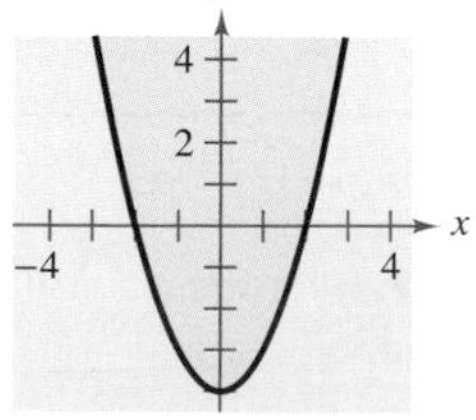

29.

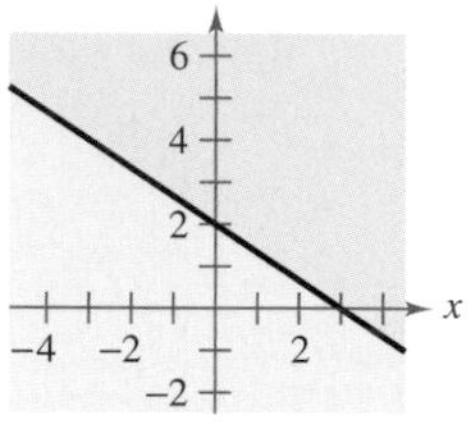

30.

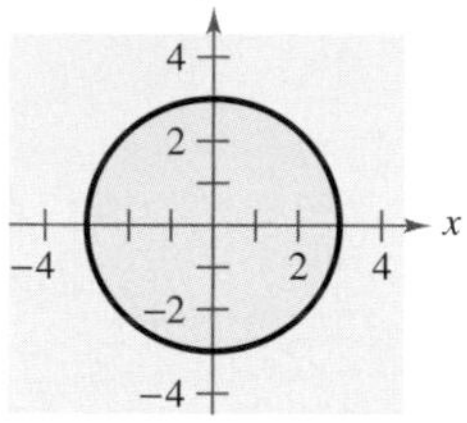

In Exercises 31–34, determine whether each ordered pair is a solution of the system of linear inequalities.

31. $\begin{cases} x \geq -4 \\ y > -3 \\ y \leq -8x - 3 \end{cases}$ (a) $(0, 0)$ (b) $(-1, -3)$ (c) $(-4, 0)$ (d) $(-3, 11)$

32. $\begin{cases} -2x + 5y \geq 3 \\ y < 4 \\ -4x + 2y < 7 \end{cases}$ (a) $(0, 2)$ (b) $(-6, 4)$ (c) $(-8, -2)$ (d) $(-3, 2)$

33. $\begin{cases} 3x + y > 1 \\ -y - \frac{1}{2}x^2 \leq -4 \\ -15x + 4y > 0 \end{cases}$ (a) $(0, 10)$ (b) $(0, -1)$ (c) $(2, 9)$ (d) $(-1, 6)$

34. $\begin{cases} x^2 + y^2 \geq 36 \\ -3x + y \leq 10 \\ \frac{2}{3}x - y \geq 5 \end{cases}$ (a) $(-1, 7)$ (b) $(-5, 1)$ (c) $(6, 0)$ (d) $(4, -8)$

In Exercises 35–48, sketch the graph and label the vertices of the solution set of the system of inequalities.

35. $\begin{cases} x + y \leq 1 \\ -x + y \leq 1 \\ y \geq 0 \end{cases}$

36. $\begin{cases} 3x + 2y < 6 \\ x > 0 \\ y > 0 \end{cases}$

37. $\begin{cases} x^2 + y \leq 5 \\ x \geq -1 \\ y \geq 0 \end{cases}$

38. $\begin{cases} 2x^2 + y \geq 2 \\ x \leq 2 \\ y \leq 1 \end{cases}$

39. $\begin{cases} 2x + y > 2 \\ 6x + 3y < 2 \end{cases}$

40. $\begin{cases} x - 7y > -36 \\ 5x + 2y > 5 \\ 6x - 5y > 6 \end{cases}$

41. $\begin{cases} -3x + 2y < 6 \\ x - 4y > -2 \\ 2x + y < 3 \end{cases}$

42. $\begin{cases} x - 2y < -6 \\ 5x - 3y > -9 \end{cases}$

43. $\begin{cases} x > y^2 \\ x < y + 2 \end{cases}$

44. $\begin{cases} x - y^2 > 0 \\ x - y > 2 \end{cases}$

45. $\begin{cases} x^2 + y^2 \le 9 \\ x^2 + y^2 \ge 1 \end{cases}$

46. $\begin{cases} x^2 + y^2 \le 25 \\ 4x - 3y \le 0 \end{cases}$

47. $\begin{cases} 3x + 4 \ge y^2 \\ x - y < 0 \end{cases}$

48. $\begin{cases} x < 2y - y^2 \\ 0 < x + y \end{cases}$

In Exercises 49–54, use a graphing utility to graph the inequalities. Shade the region representing the solution set of the system.

49. $\begin{cases} y \le \sqrt{3x} + 1 \\ y \ge x^2 + 1 \end{cases}$

50. $\begin{cases} y < -x^2 + 2x + 3 \\ y > x^2 - 4x + 3 \end{cases}$

51. $\begin{cases} y < x^3 - 2x + 1 \\ y > -2x \\ x \le 1 \end{cases}$

52. $\begin{cases} y \ge x^4 - 2x^2 + 1 \\ y \le 1 - x^2 \end{cases}$

53. $\begin{cases} x^2y \ge 1 \\ 0 < x \le 4 \\ y \le 4 \end{cases}$

54. $\begin{cases} y \le e^{-x^2/2} \\ y \ge 0 \\ -2 \le x \le 2 \end{cases}$

In Exercises 55–64, derive a set of inequalities to describe the region.

55.

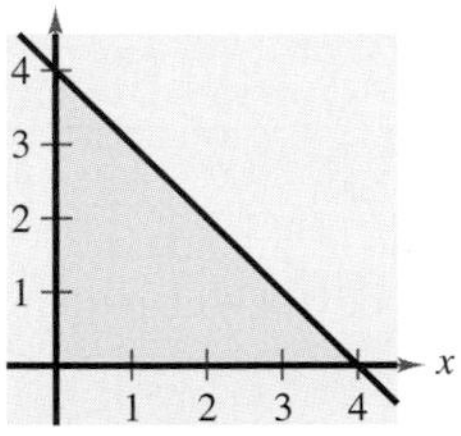

56.

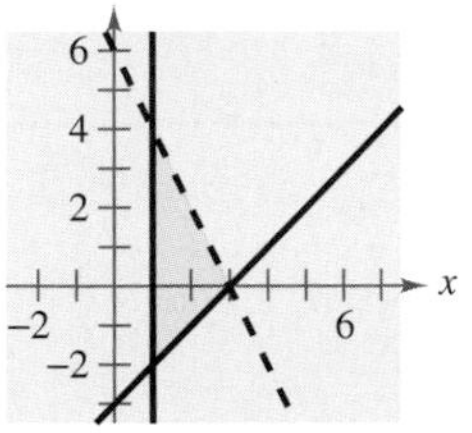

57.

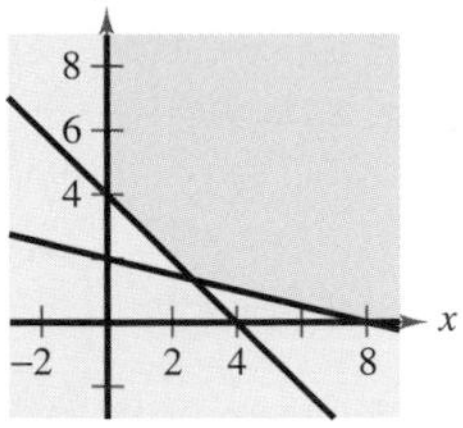

58.

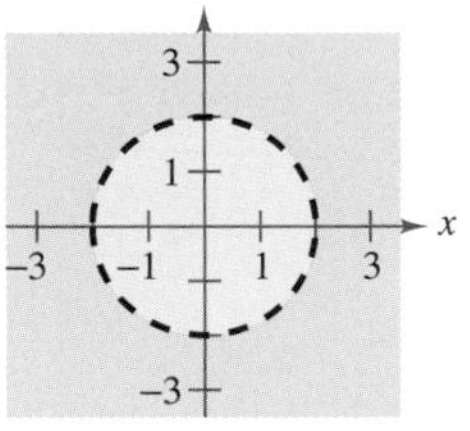

59.

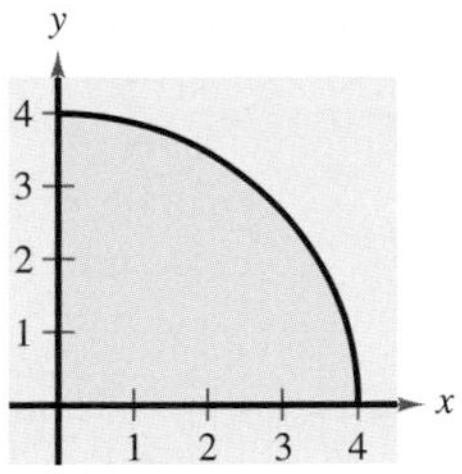

60.

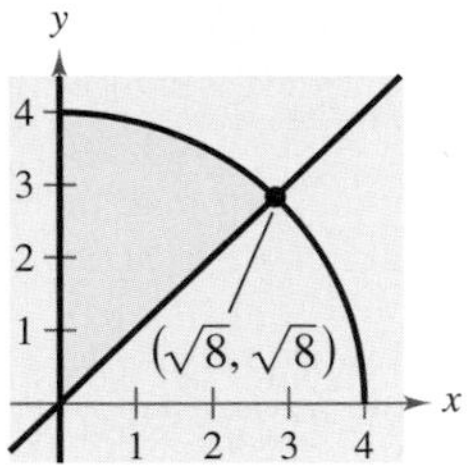

61. Rectangle: vertices at (2, 1), (5, 1), (5, 7), (2, 7)

62. Parallelogram: vertices at (0, 0), (4, 0), (1, 4), (5, 4)

63. Triangle: vertices at (0, 0), (5, 0), (2, 3)

64. Triangle: vertices at (−1, 0), (1, 0), (0, 1)

Supply and Demand **In Exercises 65–68, (a) graph the systems representing the consumer surplus and producer surplus for the supply and demand equations and (b) find the consumer surplus and producer surplus.**

	Demand	*Supply*
65.	$p = 50 - 0.5x$	$p = 0.125x$
66.	$p = 100 - 0.05x$	$p = 25 + 0.1x$
67.	$p = 140 - 0.00002x$	$p = 80 + 0.00001x$
68.	$p = 400 - 0.0002x$	$p = 225 + 0.0005x$

69. ***Production*** A furniture company can sell all the tables and chairs it produces. Each table requires 1 hour in the assembly center and $1\frac{1}{3}$ hours in the finishing center. Each chair requires $1\frac{1}{2}$ hours in the assembly center and $1\frac{1}{2}$ hours in the finishing center. The company's assembly center is available 12 hours per day, and its finishing center is available 15 hours per day. Find and graph a system of inequalities describing all possible production levels.

70. ***Inventory*** A store sells two models of computers. Because of the demand, the store stocks at least twice as many units of model A as of model B. The costs to the store for the two models are \$800 and \$1200, respectively. The management does not want more than \$20,000 in computer inventory at any one time, and it wants at least four model A computers and two model B computers in inventory at all times. Find and graph a system of inequalities describing all possible inventory levels.

71. ***Investment Analysis*** A person plans to invest up to \$20,000 in two different interest-bearing accounts. Each account is to contain at least \$5000. Moreover, the amount in one account should be at least twice the amount in the other account. Find and graph a system of inequalities to describe the various amounts that can be deposited in each account.

72. ***Ticket Sales*** For a concert event, there are \$30 reserved seat tickets and \$20 general admission tickets. There are 2000 reserved seats available, and fire regulations limit the number of paid ticket holders to 3000. The promoter must take in at least \$75,000 in ticket sales. Find and graph a system of inequalities describing the different numbers of tickets that can be sold.

73. ***Shipping*** A warehouse supervisor is told to ship at least 50 packages of gravel that weigh 55 pounds each and at least 40 bags of stone that weigh 70 pounds each. The maximum weight capacity in the truck he is loading is 7500 pounds. Find and graph a system of inequalities describing the numbers of bags of stone and gravel that he can send.

74. ***Truck Scheduling*** A small company that manufactures two models of exercise machines has an order for 15 units of the standard model and 16 units of the deluxe model. The company has trucks of two different sizes that can haul the products, as shown in the table.

Truck	Standard	Deluxe
Large	6	3
Medium	4	6

Find and graph a system of inequalities describing the numbers of trucks of each size that are needed to deliver the order.

75. ***Nutrition*** A dietitian is asked to design a special dietary supplement using two different foods. Each ounce of food X contains 20 units of calcium, 15 units of iron, and 10 units of vitamin B. Each ounce of food Y contains 10 units of calcium, 10 units of iron, and 20 units of vitamin B. The minimum daily requirements of the diet are 300 units of calcium, 150 units of iron, and 200 units of vitamin B.

(a) Write a system of inequalities describing the different amounts of food X and food Y that can be used.

(b) Sketch a graph of the region corresponding to the system in part (a).

(c) Find two solutions of the system and interpret their meanings in the context of the problem.

76. ***Health*** A person's maximum heart rate is $220 - x$, where x is the person's age in years for $20 \le x \le 70$. When a person exercises, it is recommended that the person strive for a heart rate that is at least 50% of the maximum and at most 75% of the maximum. (Source: American Heart Association)

(a) Write a system of inequalities that describes the exercise target heart rate region.

(b) Sketch a graph of the region in part (a).

(c) Find two solutions to the system and interpret their meanings in the context of the problem.

Model It

77. ***Data Analysis: Prescription Drugs*** The table shows the retail sales y (in billions of dollars) of prescription drugs in the United States from 1999 to 2003. (Source: National Association of Chain Drug Stores)

Year	Retail sales, y
1999	125.8
2000	145.6
2001	164.1
2002	182.7
2003	203.1

(a) Use the *regression* feature of a graphing utility to find a linear model for the data. Let t represent the year, with $t = 9$ corresponding to 1999.

(b) The total retail sales of prescription drugs in the United States during this five-year period can be approximated by finding the area of the trapezoid bounded by the linear model you found in part (a) and the lines $y = 0$, $t = 8.5$, and $t = 13.5$. Use a graphing utility to graph this region.

(c) Use the formula for the area of a trapezoid to approximate the total retail sales of prescription drugs.

78. ***Physical Fitness Facility*** An indoor running track is to be constructed with a space for body-building equipment inside the track (see figure). The track must be at least 125 meters long, and the body-building space must have an area of at least 500 square meters.

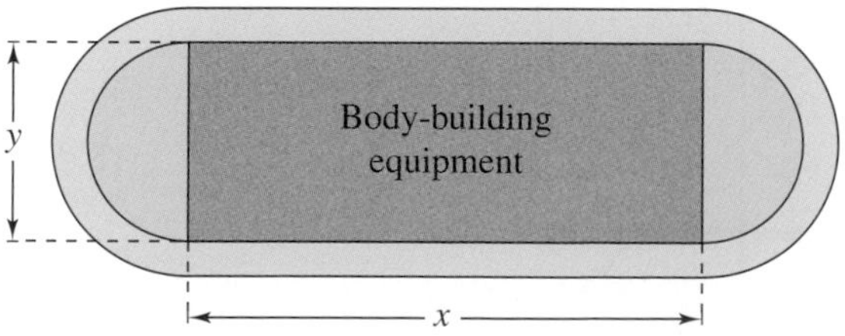

(a) Find a system of inequalities describing the requirements of the facility.

(b) Graph the system from part (a).

Synthesis

True or False? **In Exercises 79 and 80, determine whether the statement is true or false. Justify your answer.**

79. The area of the figure defined by the system

$$\begin{cases} x \geq -3 \\ x \leq 6 \\ y \leq 5 \\ y \geq -6 \end{cases}$$

is 99 square units.

80. The graph below shows the solution of the system

$$\begin{cases} y \leq 6 \\ -4x - 9y > 6. \\ 3x + y^2 \geq 2 \end{cases}$$

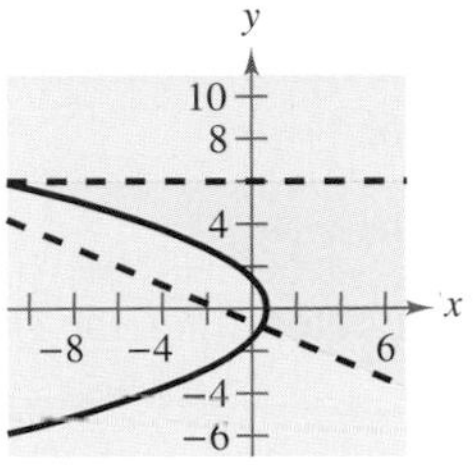

81. ***Writing*** Explain the difference between the graphs of the inequality $x \leq 4$ on the real number line and on the rectangular coordinate system.

82. ***Think About It*** After graphing the boundary of an inequality in x and y, how do you decide on which side of the boundary the solution set of the inequality lies?

83. ***Graphical Reasoning*** Two concentric circles have radii x and y, where $y > x$. The area between the circles must be at least 10 square units.

(a) Find a system of inequalities describing the constraints on the circles.

(b) Use a graphing utility to graph the system of inequalities in part (a). Graph the line $y = x$ in the same viewing window.

(c) Identify the graph of the line in relation to the boundary of the inequality. Explain its meaning in the context of the problem.

84. The graph of the solution of the inequality $x + 2y < 6$ is shown in the figure. Describe how the solution set would change for each of the following.

(a) $x + 2y \leq 6$ (b) $x + 2y > 6$

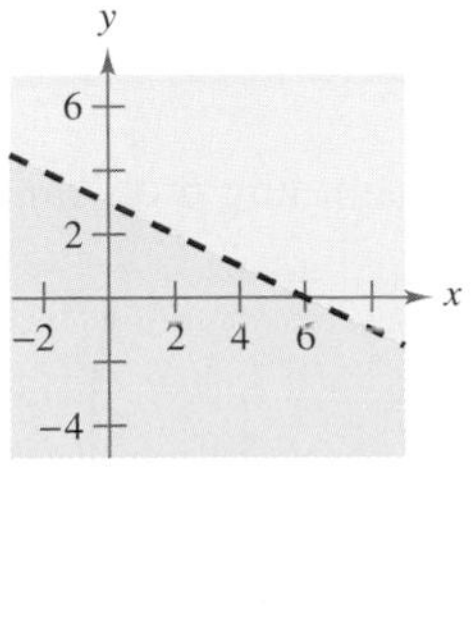

In Exercises 85–88, match the system of inequalities with the graph of its solution. [The graphs are labeled (a), (b), (c), and (d).]

(a)

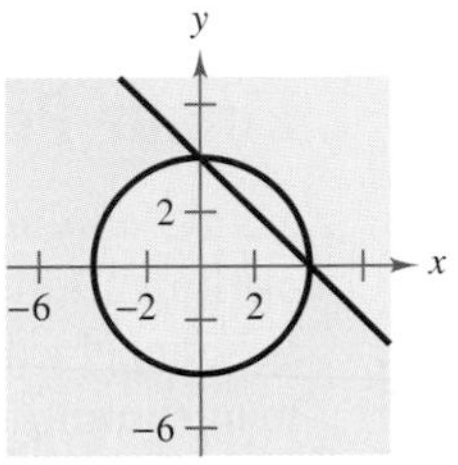

(b)

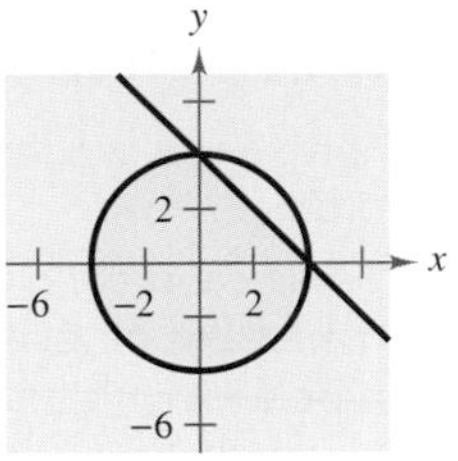

(c)

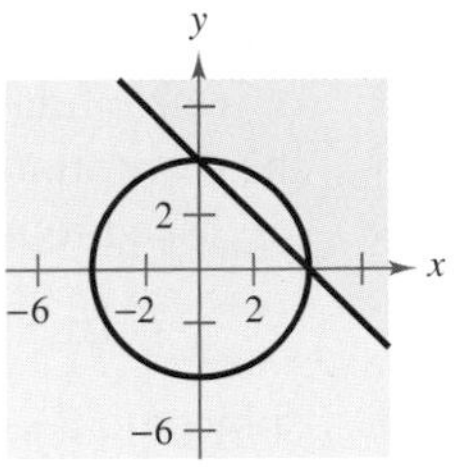

(d)

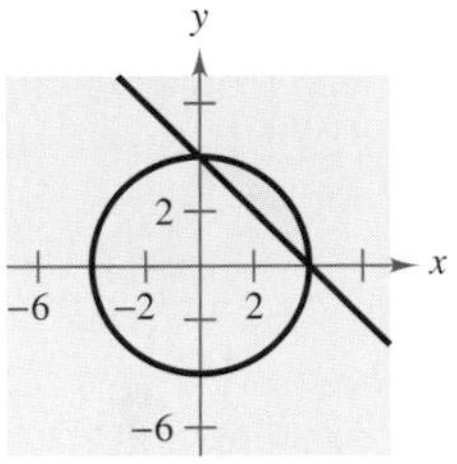

85. $\begin{cases} x^2 + y^2 \leq 16 \\ x + y \geq 4 \end{cases}$

86. $\begin{cases} x^2 + y^2 \leq 16 \\ x + y \leq 4 \end{cases}$

87. $\begin{cases} x^2 + y^2 \geq 16 \\ x + y \geq 4 \end{cases}$

88. $\begin{cases} x^2 + y^2 \geq 16 \\ x + y \leq 4 \end{cases}$

Skills Review

In Exercises 89–94, find the equation of the line passing through the two points.

89. $(-2, 6), (4, -4)$

90. $(-8, 0), (3, -1)$

91. $\left(\frac{3}{4}, -2\right), \left(-\frac{7}{2}, 5\right)$

92. $\left(-\frac{1}{2}, 0\right), \left(\frac{11}{2}, 12\right)$

93. $(3.4, -5.2), (-2.6, 0.8)$

94. $(-4.1, -3.8), (2.9, 8.2)$

95. ***Data Analysis: Cell Phone Bills*** The average monthly cell phone bills y (in dollars) in the United States from 1998 to 2003, where t is the year, are shown as data points (t, y). (Source: Cellular Telecommunications & Internet Association)

(1998, 39.43), (1999, 41.24), (2000, 45.27)

(2001, 47.37), (2002, 48.40), (2003, 49.91)

(a) Use the *regression* feature of a graphing utility to find a linear model, a quadratic model, and an exponential model for the data. Let $t = 8$ correspond to 1998.

(b) Use a graphing utility to plot the data and the models in the same viewing window.

(c) Which model is the best fit for the data?

(d) Use the model from part (c) to predict the average monthly cell phone bill in 2008.

7.6 Linear Programming

What you should learn

- Solve linear programming problems.
- Use linear programming to model and solve real-life problems.

Why you should learn it

Linear programming is often useful in making real-life economic decisions. For example, Exercise 44 on page 560 shows how you can determine the optimal cost of a blend of gasoline and compare it with the national average.

Tim Boyle/Getty Images

Linear Programming: A Graphical Approach

Many applications in business and economics involve a process called **optimization,** in which you are asked to find the minimum or maximum of a quantity. In this section, you will study an optimization strategy called **linear programming.**

A two-dimensional linear programming problem consists of a linear **objective function** and a system of linear inequalities called **constraints.** The objective function gives the quantity that is to be maximized (or minimized), and the constraints determine the set of **feasible solutions.** For example, suppose you are asked to maximize the value of

$$z = ax + by \qquad \text{Objective function}$$

subject to a set of constraints that determines the shaded region in Figure 7.31.

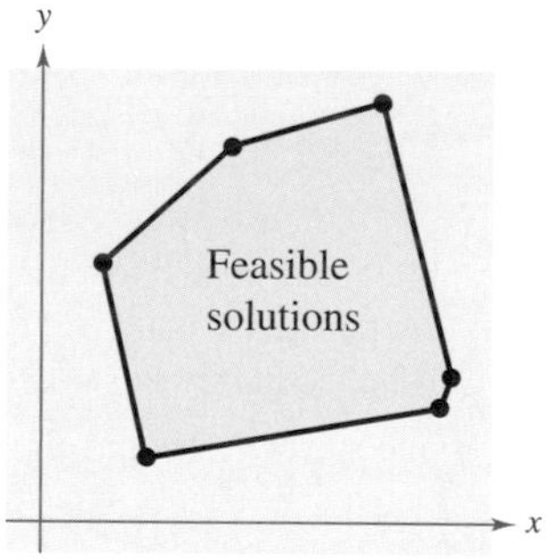

FIGURE 7.31

Because every point in the shaded region satisfies each constraint, it is not clear how you should find the point that yields a maximum value of z. Fortunately, it can be shown that if there is an optimal solution, it must occur at one of the vertices. This means that *you can find the maximum value of z by testing z at each of the vertices.*

Optimal Solution of a Linear Programming Problem

If a linear programming problem has a solution, it must occur at a vertex of the set of feasible solutions. If there is more than one solution, at least one of them must occur at such a vertex. In either case, the value of the objective function is unique.

Some guidelines for solving a linear programming problem in two variables are listed at the top of the next page.

Solving a Linear Programming Problem

1. Sketch the region corresponding to the system of constraints. (The points inside or on the boundary of the region are *feasible solutions*.)
2. Find the vertices of the region.
3. Test the objective function at each of the vertices and select the values of the variables that optimize the objective function. For a bounded region, both a minimum and a maximum value will exist. (For an unbounded region, *if* an optimal solution exists, it will occur at a vertex.)

Example 1 Solving a Linear Programming Problem

Find the maximum value of

$$z = 3x + 2y \qquad \text{Objective function}$$

subject to the following constraints.

$$\left.\begin{aligned} x &\geq 0 \\ y &\geq 0 \\ x + 2y &\leq 4 \\ x - y &\leq 1 \end{aligned}\right\} \qquad \text{Constraints}$$

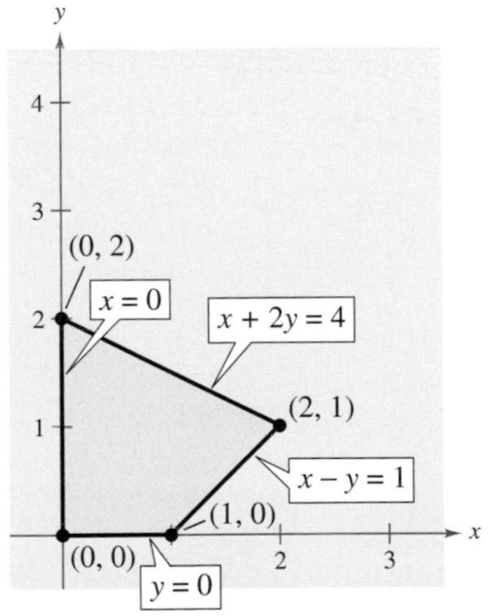

FIGURE 7.32

Solution

The constraints form the region shown in Figure 7.32. At the four vertices of this region, the objective function has the following values.

$$\begin{aligned} &\text{At } (0, 0): && z = 3(0) + 2(0) = 0 \\ &\text{At } (1, 0): && z = 3(1) + 2(0) = 3 \\ &\text{At } (2, 1): && z = 3(2) + 2(1) = 8 && \text{Maximum value of } z \\ &\text{At } (0, 2): && z = 3(0) + 2(2) = 4 \end{aligned}$$

So, the maximum value of z is 8, and this occurs when $x = 2$ and $y = 1$.

✓CHECKPOINT Now try Exercise 5.

In Example 1, try testing some of the *interior* points in the region. You will see that the corresponding values of z are less than 8. Here are some examples.

$$\text{At } (1, 1): \quad z = 3(1) + 2(1) = 5 \qquad \text{At } \left(\tfrac{1}{2}, \tfrac{3}{2}\right): \quad z = 3\left(\tfrac{1}{2}\right) + 2\left(\tfrac{3}{2}\right) = \tfrac{9}{2}$$

To see why the maximum value of the objective function in Example 1 must occur at a vertex, consider writing the objective function in slope-intercept form

$$y = -\frac{3}{2}x + \frac{z}{2} \qquad \text{Family of lines}$$

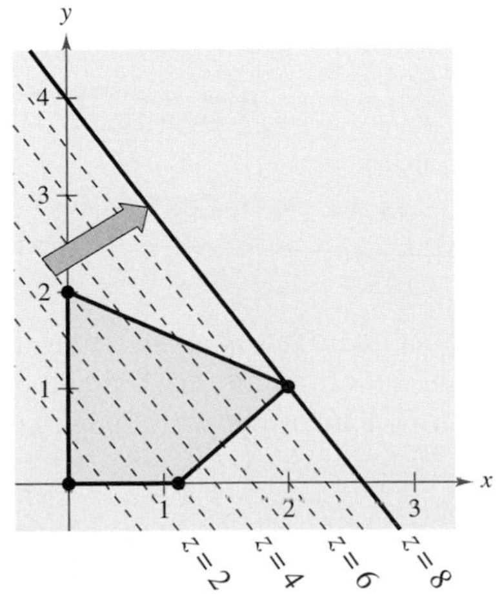

FIGURE 7.33

where $z/2$ is the y-intercept of the objective function. This equation represents a family of lines, each of slope $-\frac{3}{2}$. Of these infinitely many lines, you want the one that has the largest z-value while still intersecting the region determined by the constraints. In other words, of all the lines whose slope is $-\frac{3}{2}$, you want the one that has the largest y-intercept *and* intersects the given region, as shown in Figure 7.33. From the graph you can see that such a line will pass through one (or more) of the vertices of the region.

The next example shows that the same basic procedure can be used to solve a problem in which the objective function is to be *minimized.*

Example 2 Minimizing an Objective Function

Find the minimum value of

$z = 5x + 7y$ Objective function

where $x \geq 0$ and $y \geq 0$, subject to the following constraints.

$$\left.\begin{aligned} 2x + 3y &\geq 6 \\ 3x - y &\leq 15 \\ -x + y &\leq 4 \\ 2x + 5y &\leq 27 \end{aligned}\right\} \quad \text{Constraints}$$

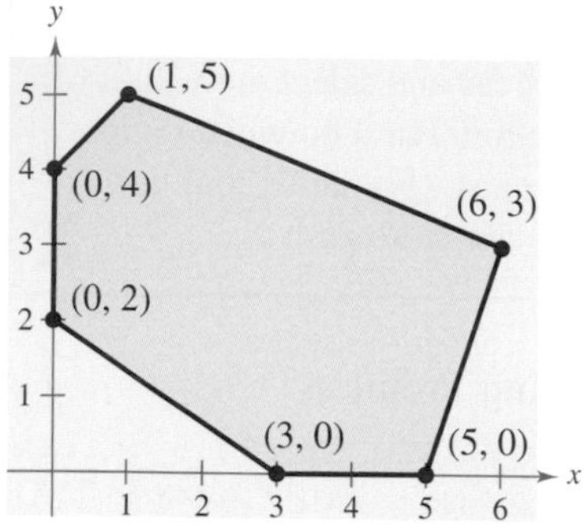

FIGURE 7.34

Solution

The region bounded by the constraints is shown in Figure 7.34. By testing the objective function at each vertex, you obtain the following.

At $(0, 2)$: $z = 5(0) + 7(2) = 14$ Minimum value of z

At $(0, 4)$: $z = 5(0) + 7(4) = 28$

At $(1, 5)$: $z = 5(1) + 7(5) = 40$

At $(6, 3)$: $z = 5(6) + 7(3) = 51$

At $(5, 0)$: $z = 5(5) + 7(0) = 25$

At $(3, 0)$: $z = 5(3) + 7(0) = 15$

So, the minimum value of z is 14, and this occurs when $x = 0$ and $y = 2$.

✓CHECKPOINT Now try Exercise 13.

Edward W. Souza/News Service/Stanford University

Historical Note
George Dantzig (1914–) was the first to propose the simplex method, or linear programming, in 1947. This technique defined the steps needed to find the optimal solution to a complex multivariable problem.

Example 3 Maximizing an Objective Function

Find the maximum value of

$z = 5x + 7y$ Objective function

where $x \geq 0$ and $y \geq 0$, subject to the following constraints.

$$\left.\begin{aligned} 2x + 3y &\geq 6 \\ 3x - y &\leq 15 \\ -x + y &\leq 4 \\ 2x + 5y &\leq 27 \end{aligned}\right\} \quad \text{Constraints}$$

Solution

This linear programming problem is identical to that given in Example 2 above, *except* that the objective function is maximized instead of minimized. Using the values of z at the vertices shown above, you can conclude that the maximum value of z is

$z = 5(6) + 7(3) = 51$

and occurs when $x = 6$ and $y = 3$.

✓CHECKPOINT Now try Exercise 15.

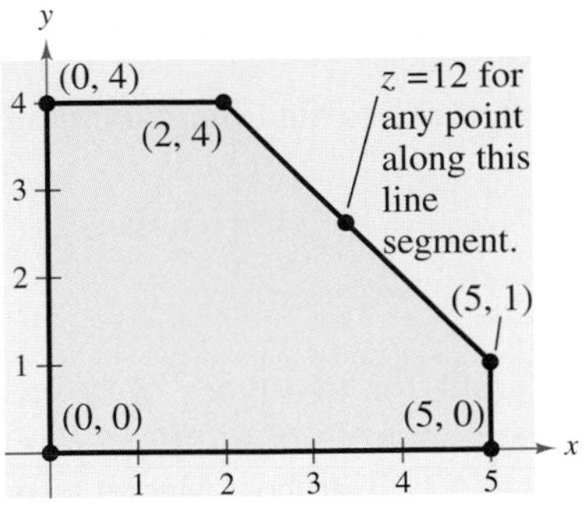

FIGURE 7.35

It is possible for the maximum (or minimum) value in a linear programming problem to occur at *two* different vertices. For instance, at the vertices of the region shown in Figure 7.35, the objective function

$z = 2x + 2y$ Objective function

has the following values.

At (0, 0): $z = 2(0) + 2(0) = 0$
At (0, 4): $z = 2(0) + 2(4) = 8$
At (2, 4): $z = 2(2) + 2(4) = 12$ Maximum value of z
At (5, 1): $z = 2(5) + 2(1) = 12$ Maximum value of z
At (5, 0): $z = 2(5) + 2(0) = 10$

In this case, you can conclude that the objective function has a maximum value not only at the vertices (2, 4) and (5, 1); it also has a maximum value (of 12) at *any point on the line segment connecting these two vertices.* Note that the objective function in slope-intercept form $y = -x + \frac{1}{2}z$ has the same slope as the line through the vertices (2, 4) and (5, 1).

Some linear programming problems have no optimal solutions. This can occur if the region determined by the constraints is *unbounded.* Example 4 illustrates such a problem.

Example 4 An Unbounded Region

Find the maximum value of

$z = 4x + 2y$ Objective function

where $x \geq 0$ and $y \geq 0$, subject to the following constraints.

$$\left.\begin{aligned} x + 2y &\geq 4 \\ 3x + y &\geq 7 \\ -x + 2y &\leq 7 \end{aligned}\right\} \quad \text{Constraints}$$

Solution

The region determined by the constraints is shown in Figure 7.36. For this unbounded region, there is no maximum value of z. To see this, note that the point $(x, 0)$ lies in the region for all values of $x \geq 4$. Substituting this point into the objective function, you get

$z = 4(x) + 2(0) = 4x.$

By choosing x to be large, you can obtain values of z that are as large as you want. So, there is no maximum value of z. However, there *is* a minimum value of z.

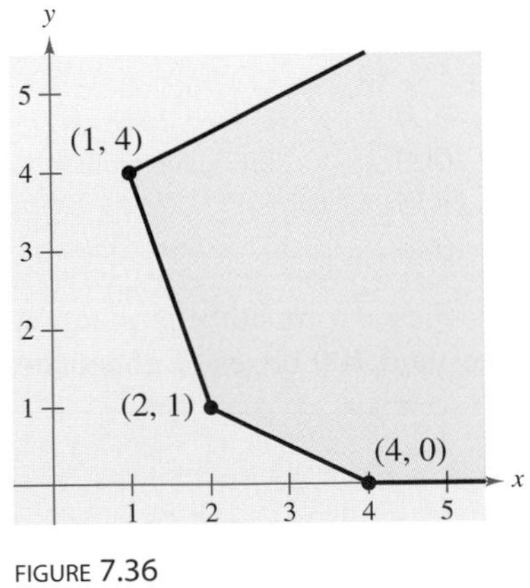

FIGURE 7.36

At (1, 4): $z = 4(1) + 2(4) = 12$
At (2, 1): $z = 4(2) + 2(1) = 10$ Minimum value of z
At (4, 0): $z = 4(4) + 2(0) = 16$

So, the minimum value of z is 10, and this occurs when $x = 2$ and $y = 1$.

CHECKPOINT Now try Exercise 17.

Applications

Example 5 shows how linear programming can be used to find the maximum profit in a business application.

Example 5 Optimal Profit

A candy manufacturer wants to maximize the profit for two types of boxed chocolates. A box of chocolate covered creams yields a profit of $1.50 per box, and a box of chocolate covered nuts yields a profit of $2.00 per box. Market tests and available resources have indicated the following constraints.

1. The combined production level should not exceed 1200 boxes per month.
2. The demand for a box of chocolate covered nuts is no more than half the demand for a box of chocolate covered creams.
3. The production level for chocolate covered creams should be less than or equal to 600 boxes plus three times the production level for chocolate covered nuts.

Solution

Let x be the number of boxes of chocolate covered creams and let y be the number of boxes of chocolate covered nuts. So, the objective function (for the combined profit) is given by

$$P = 1.5x + 2y.$$ Objective function

The three constraints translate into the following linear inequalities.

1. $x + y \le 1200 \quad \Rightarrow \quad x + y \le 1200$
2. $y \le \frac{1}{2}x \quad \Rightarrow \quad -x + 2y \le 0$
3. $x \le 600 + 3y \quad \Rightarrow \quad x - 3y \le 600$

Because neither x nor y can be negative, you also have the two additional constraints of $x \ge 0$ and $y \ge 0$. Figure 7.37 shows the region determined by the constraints. To find the maximum profit, test the values of P at the vertices of the region.

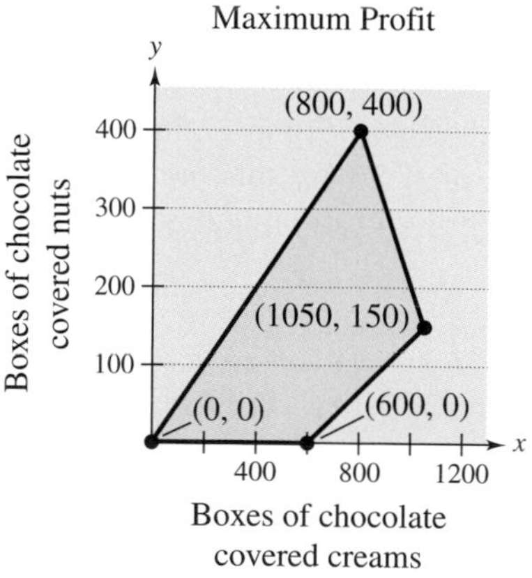

FIGURE 7.37

$$\begin{aligned}
\text{At } (0, 0)\text{:} \quad P &= 1.5(0) + 2(0) = 0 \\
\text{At } (800, 400)\text{:} \quad P &= 1.5(800) + 2(400) = 2000 \quad \text{Maximum profit} \\
\text{At } (1050, 150)\text{:} \quad P &= 1.5(1050) + 2(150) = 1875 \\
\text{At } (600, 0)\text{:} \quad P &= 1.5(600) + 2(0) = 900
\end{aligned}$$

So, the maximum profit is $2000, and it occurs when the monthly production consists of 800 boxes of chocolate covered creams and 400 boxes of chocolate covered nuts.

CHECKPOINT Now try Exercise 39.

In Example 5, if the manufacturer improved the production of chocolate covered creams so that they yielded a profit of $2.50 per unit, the maximum profit could then be found using the objective function $P = 2.5x + 2y$. By testing the values of P at the vertices of the region, you would find that the maximum profit was $2925 and that it occurred when $x = 1050$ and $y = 150$.

Example 6 Optimal Cost

The liquid portion of a diet is to provide at least 300 calories, 36 units of vitamin A, and 90 units of vitamin C. A cup of dietary drink X costs \$0.12 and provides 60 calories, 12 units of vitamin A, and 10 units of vitamin C. A cup of dietary drink Y costs \$0.15 and provides 60 calories, 6 units of vitamin A, and 30 units of vitamin C. How many cups of each drink should be consumed each day to obtain an optimal cost and still meet the daily requirements?

Solution

As in Example 9 in Section 7.5, let x be the number of cups of dietary drink X and let y be the number of cups of dietary drink Y.

$$\left.\begin{array}{lr} \text{For calories:} & 60x + 60y \geq 300 \\ \text{For vitamin A:} & 12x + 6y \geq 36 \\ \text{For vitamin C:} & 10x + 30y \geq 90 \\ & x \geq 0 \\ & y \geq 0 \end{array}\right\} \quad \text{Constraints}$$

The cost C is given by $C = 0.12x + 0.15y$. Objective function

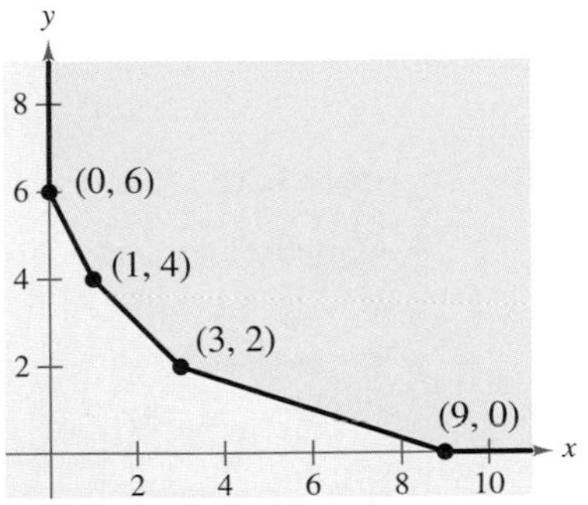

FIGURE 7.38

The graph of the region corresponding to the constraints is shown in Figure 7.38. Because you want to incur as little cost as possible, you want to determine the *minimum* cost. To determine the minimum cost, test C at each vertex of the region.

At $(0, 6)$: $C = 0.12(0) + 0.15(6) = 0.90$

At $(1, 4)$: $C = 0.12(1) + 0.15(4) = 0.72$

At $(3, 2)$: $C = 0.12(3) + 0.15(2) = 0.66$ Minimum value of C

At $(9, 0)$: $C = 0.12(9) + 0.15(0) = 1.08$

So, the minimum cost is \$0.66 per day, and this occurs when 3 cups of drink X and 2 cups of drink Y are consumed each day.

CHECKPOINT Now try Exercise 43.

Writing About Mathematics

Creating a Linear Programming Problem Sketch the region determined by the following constraints.

$$\left.\begin{array}{r} x + 2y \leq 8 \\ x + y \leq 5 \\ x \geq 0 \\ y \geq 0 \end{array}\right\} \quad \text{Constraints}$$

Find, if possible, an objective function of the form $z = ax + by$ that has a maximum at each indicated vertex of the region.

a. $(0, 4)$ **b.** $(2, 3)$ **c.** $(5, 0)$ **d.** $(0, 0)$

Explain how you found each objective function.

7.6 Exercises

VOCABULARY CHECK: Fill in the blanks.

1. In the process called ________, you are asked to find the maximum or minimum value of a quantity.
2. One type of optimization strategy is called ________ ________.
3. The ________ function of a linear programming problem gives the quantity that is to be maximized or minimized.
4. The ________ of a linear programming problem determine the set of ________ ________.
5. If a linear programming problem has a solution, it must occur at a ________ of the set of feasible solutions.

In Exercises 1–12, find the minimum and maximum values of the objective function and where they occur, subject to the indicated constraints. (For each exercise, the graph of the region determined by the constraints is provided.)

1. Objective function:

$z = 4x + 3y$

Constraints:

$x \geq 0$

$y \geq 0$

$x + y \leq 5$

2. Objective function:

$z = 2x + 8y$

Constraints:

$x \geq 0$

$y \geq 0$

$2x + y \leq 4$

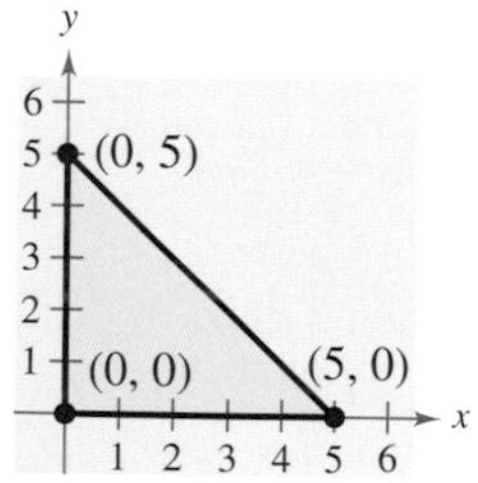

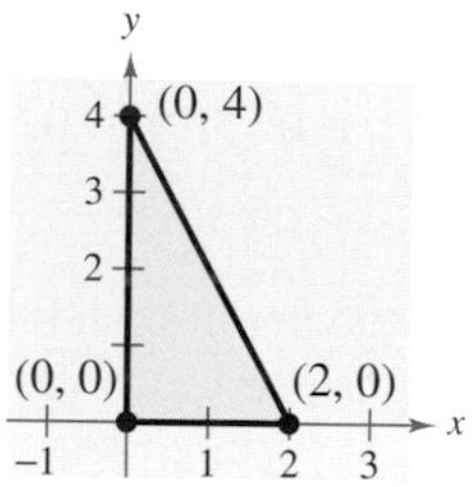

3. Objective function:

$z = 3x + 8y$

Constraints:
(See Exercise 1.)

4. Objective function:

$z = 7x + 3y$

Constraints:
(See Exercise 2.)

5. Objective function:

$z = 3x + 2y$

Constraints:

$x \geq 0$

$y \geq 0$

$x + 3y \leq 15$

$4x + y \leq 16$

6. Objective function:

$z = 4x + 5y$

Constraints:

$x \geq 0$

$2x + 3y \geq 6$

$3x - y \leq 9$

$x + 4y \leq 16$

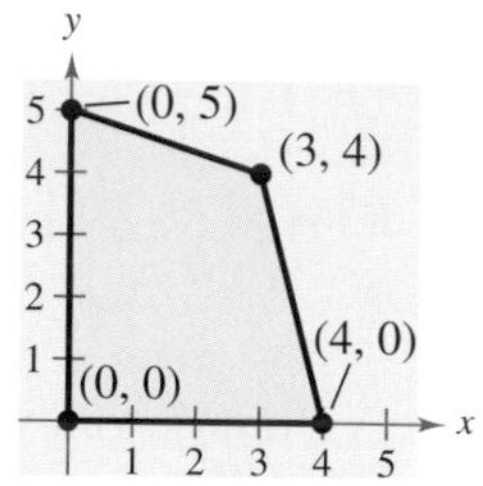

FIGURE FOR 5

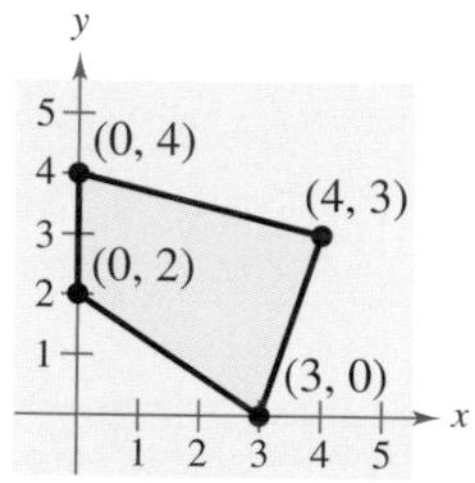

FIGURE FOR 6

7. Objective function:

$z = 5x + 0.5y$

Constraints:
(See Exercise 5.)

8. Objective function:

$z = 2x + y$

Constraints:
(See Exercise 6.)

9. Objective function:

$z = 10x + 7y$

Constraints:

$0 \leq x \leq 60$

$0 \leq y \leq 45$

$5x + 6y \leq 420$

10. Objective function:

$z = 25x + 35y$

Constraints:

$x \geq 0$

$y \geq 0$

$8x + 9y \leq 7200$

$8x + 9y \geq 3600$

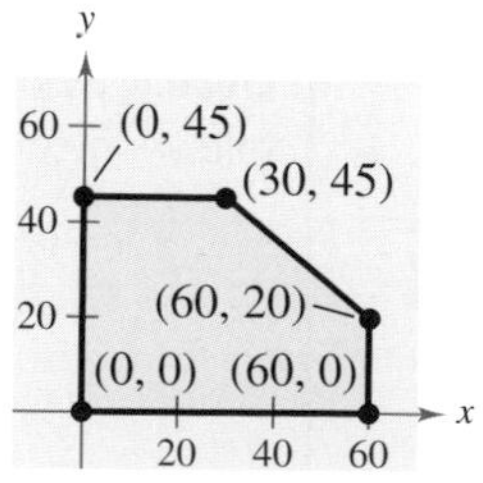

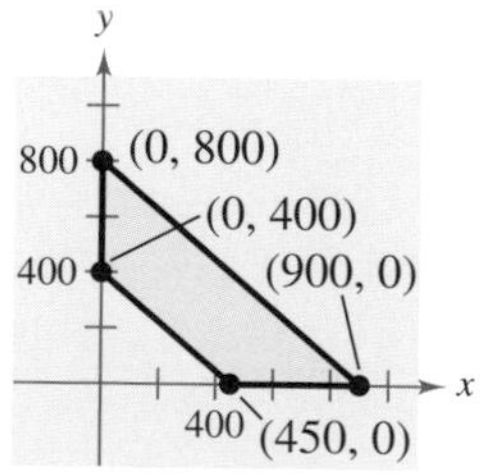

11. Objective function:

$z = 25x + 30y$

Constraints:
(See Exercise 9.)

12. Objective function:

$z = 15x + 20y$

Constraints:
(See Exercise 10.)

In Exercises 13–20, sketch the region determined by the constraints. Then find the minimum and maximum values of the objective function and where they occur, subject to the indicated constraints.

13. Objective function:

$z = 6x + 10y$

Constraints:

$x \geq 0$

$y \geq 0$

$2x + 5y \leq 10$

14. Objective function:

$z = 7x + 8y$

Constraints:

$x \geq 0$

$y \geq 0$

$x + \frac{1}{2}y \leq 4$

15. Objective function:

$z = 9x + 24y$

Constraints:
(See Exercise 13.)

16. Objective function:

$z = 7x + 2y$

Constraints:
(See Exercise 14.)

17. Objective function:

$z = 4x + 5y$

Constraints:

$x \geq 0$

$y \geq 0$

$x + y \geq 8$

$3x + 5y \geq 30$

18. Objective function:

$z = 4x + 5y$

Constraints:

$x \geq 0$

$y \geq 0$

$2x + 2y \leq 10$

$x + 2y \leq 6$

19. Objective function:

$z = 2x + 7y$

Constraints:
(See Exercise 17.)

20. Objective function:

$z = 2x - y$

Constraints:
(See Exercise 18.)

In Exercises 21–24, use a graphing utility to graph the region determined by the constraints. Then find the minimum and maximum values of the objective function and where they occur, subject to the constraints.

21. Objective function:

$z = 4x + y$

Constraints:

$x \geq 0$

$y \geq 0$

$x + 2y \leq 40$

$2x + 3y \geq 72$

22. Objective function:

$z = x$

Constraints:

$x \geq 0$

$y \geq 0$

$2x + 3y \leq 60$

$2x + y \leq 28$

$4x + y \leq 48$

23. Objective function:

$z = x + 4y$

Constraints:
(See Exercise 21.)

24. Objective function:

$z = y$

Constraints:
(See Exercise 22.)

In Exercises 25–28, find the maximum value of the objective function and where it occurs, subject to the constraints $x \geq 0$, $y \geq 0$, $3x + y \leq 15$, and $4x + 3y \leq 30$.

25. $z = 2x + y$

26. $z = 5x + y$

27. $z = x + y$

28. $z = 3x + y$

In Exercises 29–32, find the maximum value of the objective function and where it occurs, subject to the constraints $x \geq 0$, $y \geq 0$, $x + 4y \leq 20$, $x + y \leq 18$, and $2x + 2y \leq 21$.

29. $z = x + 5y$

30. $z = 2x + 4y$

31. $z = 4x + 5y$

32. $z = 4x + y$

In Exercises 33–38, the linear programming problem has an unusual characteristic. Sketch a graph of the solution region for the problem and describe the unusual characteristic. Find the maximum value of the objective function and where it occurs.

33. Objective function:

$z = 2.5x + y$

Constraints:

$x \geq 0$

$y \geq 0$

$3x + 5y \leq 15$

$5x + 2y \leq 10$

34. Objective function:

$z = x + y$

Constraints:

$x \geq 0$

$y \geq 0$

$-x + y \leq 1$

$-x + 2y \leq 4$

35. Objective function:

$z = -x + 2y$

Constraints:

$x \geq 0$

$y \geq 0$

$x \leq 10$

$x + y \leq 7$

36. Objective function:

$z = x + y$

Constraints:

$x \geq 0$

$y \geq 0$

$-x + y \leq 0$

$-3x + y \geq 3$

37. Objective function:

$z = 3x + 4y$

Constraints:

$x \geq 0$

$y \geq 0$

$x + y \leq 1$

$2x + y \leq 4$

38. Objective function:

$z = x + 2y$

Constraints:

$x \geq 0$

$y \geq 0$

$x + 2y \leq 4$

$2x + y \leq 4$

39. ***Optimal Profit*** A manufacturer produces two models of bicycles. The times (in hours) required for assembling, painting, and packaging each model are shown in the table.

Process	Hours, model A	Hours, model B
Assembling	2	2.5
Painting	4	1
Packaging	1	0.75

The total times available for assembling, painting, and packaging are 4000 hours, 4800 hours, and 1500 hours, respectively. The profits per unit are $45 for model A and $50 for model B. What is the optimal production level for each model? What is the optimal profit?

40. ***Optimal Profit*** A manufacturer produces two models of bicycles. The times (in hours) required for assembling, painting, and packaging each model are shown in the table.

Process	Hours, model A	Hours, model B
Assembling	2.5	3
Painting	2	1
Packaging	0.75	1.25

The total times available for assembling, painting, and packaging are 4000 hours, 2500 hours, and 1500 hours, respectively. The profits per unit are $50 for model A and $52 for model B. What is the optimal production level for each model? What is the optimal profit?

41. ***Optimal Profit*** A merchant plans to sell two models of MP3 players at costs of $250 and $300. The $250 model yields a profit of $25 per unit and the $300 model yields a profit of $40 per unit. The merchant estimates that the total monthly demand will not exceed 250 units. The merchant does not want to invest more than $65,000 in inventory for these products. What is the optimal inventory level for each model? What is the optimal profit?

42. ***Optimal Profit*** A fruit grower has 150 acres of land available to raise two crops, A and B. It takes 1 day to trim an acre of crop A and 2 days to trim an acre of crop B, and there are 240 days per year available for trimming. It takes 0.3 day to pick an acre of crop A and 0.1 day to pick an acre of crop B, and there are 30 days available for picking. The profit is $140 per acre for crop A and $235 per acre for crop B. What is the optimal acreage for each fruit? What is the optimal profit?

43. ***Optimal Cost*** A farming cooperative mixes two brands of cattle feed. Brand X costs $25 per bag and contains two units of nutritional element A, two units of element B, and two units of element C. Brand Y costs $20 per bag and contains one unit of nutritional element A, nine units of element B, and three units of element C. The minimum requirements of nutrients A, B, and C are 12 units, 36 units, and 24 units, respectively. What is the optimal number of bags of each brand that should be mixed? What is the optimal cost?

Model It

44. ***Optimal Cost*** According to AAA (Automobile Association of America), on January 24, 2005, the national average price per gallon for regular unleaded (87-octane) gasoline was $1.84, and the price for premium unleaded (93-octane) gasoline was $2.03.

(a) Write an objective function that models the cost of the blend of mid-grade unleaded gasoline (89-octane).

(b) Determine the constraints for the objective function in part (a).

(c) Sketch a graph of the region determined by the constraints from part (b).

(d) Determine the blend of regular and premium unleaded gasoline that results in an optimal cost of mid-grade unleaded gasoline.

(e) What is the optimal cost?

(f) Is the cost lower than the national average of $1.96 per gallon for mid-grade unleaded gasoline?

45. ***Optimal Revenue*** An accounting firm has 900 hours of staff time and 155 hours of reviewing time available each week. The firm charges $2500 for an audit and $350 for a tax return. Each audit requires 75 hours of staff time and 10 hours of review time. Each tax return requires 12.5 hours of staff time and 2.5 hours of review time. What numbers of audits and tax returns will yield an optimal revenue? What is the optimal revenue?

46. ***Optimal Revenue*** The accounting firm in Exercise 45 lowers its charge for an audit to $2000. What numbers of audits and tax returns will yield an optimal revenue? What is the optimal revenue?

47. ***Investment Portfolio*** An investor has up to \$250,000 to invest in two types of investments. Type A pays 8% annually and type B pays 10% annually. To have a well-balanced portfolio, the investor imposes the following conditions. At least one-fourth of the total portfolio is to be allocated to type A investments and at least one-fourth of the portfolio is to be allocated to type B investments. What is the optimal amount that should be invested in each type of investment? What is the optimal return?

48. ***Investment Portfolio*** An investor has up to \$450,000 to invest in two types of investments. Type A pays 6% annually and type B pays 10% annually. To have a well-balanced portfolio, the investor imposes the following conditions. At least one-half of the total portfolio is to be allocated to type A investments and at least one-fourth of the portfolio is to be allocated to type B investments. What is the optimal amount that should be invested in each type of investment? What is the optimal return?

Synthesis

True or False? **In Exercises 49 and 50, determine whether the statement is true or false. Justify your answer.**

49. If an objective function has a maximum value at the vertices (4, 7) and (8, 3), you can conclude that it also has a maximum value at the points (4.5, 6.5) and (7.8, 3.2).

50. When solving a linear programming problem, if the objective function has a maximum value at more than one vertex, you can assume that there are an infinite number of points that will produce the maximum value.

In Exercises 51 and 52, determine values of *t* such that the objective function has maximum values at the indicated vertices.

51. Objective function: $z = 3x + ty$

Constraints:

$x \geq 0$

$y \geq 0$

$x + 3y \leq 15$

$4x + y \leq 16$

(a) (0, 5)

(b) (3, 4)

52. Objective function: $z = 3x + ty$

Constraints:

$x \geq 0$

$y \geq 0$

$x + 2y \leq 4$

$x - y \leq 1$

(a) (2, 1)

(b) (0, 2)

Think About It **In Exercises 53–56, find an objective function that has a maximum or minimum value at the indicated vertex of the constraint region shown below. (There are many correct answers.)**

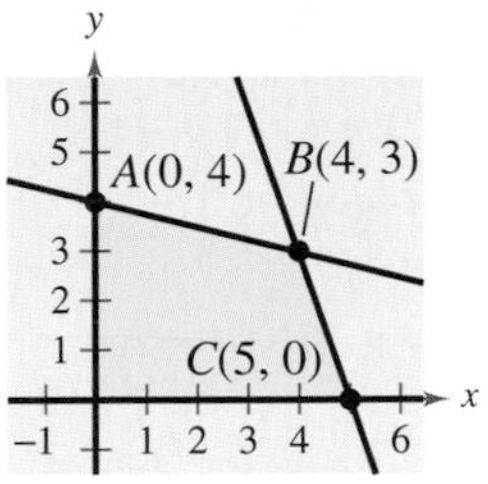

53. The maximum occurs at vertex *A*.

54. The maximum occurs at vertex *B*.

55. The maximum occurs at vertex *C*.

56. The minimum occurs at vertex *C*.

Skills Review

In Exercises 57–60, simplify the complex fraction.

57. $\dfrac{\left(\dfrac{9}{x}\right)}{\left(\dfrac{6}{x} + 2\right)}$

58. $\dfrac{\left(1 + \dfrac{2}{x}\right)}{\left(x - \dfrac{4}{x}\right)}$

59. $\dfrac{\left(\dfrac{4}{x^2 - 9} + \dfrac{2}{x - 2}\right)}{\left(\dfrac{1}{x + 3} + \dfrac{1}{x - 3}\right)}$

60. $\dfrac{\left(\dfrac{1}{x + 1} + \dfrac{1}{2}\right)}{\left(\dfrac{3}{2x^2 + 4x + 2}\right)}$

In Exercises 61–66, solve the equation algebraically. Round the result to three decimal places.

61. $e^{2x} + 2e^x - 15 = 0$

62. $e^{2x} - 10e^x + 24 = 0$

63. $8(62 - e^{x/4}) = 192$

64. $\dfrac{150}{e^{-x} - 4} = 75$

65. $7 \ln 3x = 12$

66. $\ln(x + 9)^2 = 2$

In Exercises 67 and 68, solve the system of linear equations and check any solution algebraically.

67. $\begin{cases} -x - 2y + 3z = -23 \\ 2x + 6y - z = 17 \\ 5y + z = 8 \end{cases}$

68. $\begin{cases} 7x - 3y + 5z = -28 \\ 4x + 4z = -16 \\ 7x + 2y - z = 0 \end{cases}$

7 Chapter Summary

What did you learn?

	Review Exercises
Section 7.1	
☐ Use the method of substitution to solve systems of linear equations in two variables *(p. 496)*.	1–4
☐ Use the method of substitution to solve systems of nonlinear equations in two variables *(p. 499)*.	5–8
☐ Use a graphical approach to solve systems of equations in two variables *(p. 500)*.	9–14
☐ Use systems of equations to model and solve real-life problems *(p. 501)*.	15–18
Section 7.2	
☐ Use the method of elimination to solve systems of linear equations in two variables *(p.507)*.	19–26
☐ Interpret graphically the numbers of solutions of systems of linear equations in two variables *(p. 510)*.	27–30
☐ Use systems of linear equations in two variables to model and solve real-life problems *(p. 513)*.	31, 32
Section 7.3	
☐ Use back-substitution to solve linear systems in row-echelon form *(p. 519)*.	33, 34
☐ Use Gaussian elimination to solve systems of linear equations *(p. 520)*.	35–38
☐ Solve nonsquare systems of linear equations *(p. 524)*.	39, 40
☐ Use systems of linear equations in three or more variables to model and solve real-life problems *(p. 525)*.	41–48
Section 7.4	
☐ Recognize partial fraction decompositions of rational expressions *(p. 533)*.	49–52
☐ Find partial fraction decompositions of rational expressions *(p. 534)*.	53–60
Section 7.5	
☐ Sketch the graphs of inequalities in two variables *(p. 541)*.	61–64
☐ Solve systems of inequalities *(p. 543)*.	65–72
☐ Use systems of inequalities in two variables to model and solve real-life problems *(p. 546)*.	73–76
Section 7.6	
☐ Solve linear programming problems *(p. 552)*.	77–82
☐ Use linear programming to model and solve real-life problems *(p. 556)*.	83–86

7 Review Exercises

7.1 In Exercises 1–8, solve the system by the method of substitution.

1. $\begin{cases} x + y = 2 \\ x - y = 0 \end{cases}$

2. $\begin{cases} 2x - 3y = 3 \\ x - y = 0 \end{cases}$

3. $\begin{cases} 0.5x + y = 0.75 \\ 1.25x - 4.5y = -2.5 \end{cases}$

4. $\begin{cases} -x + \frac{2}{5}y = \frac{3}{5} \\ -x + \frac{1}{5}y = -\frac{4}{5} \end{cases}$

5. $\begin{cases} x^2 - y^2 = 9 \\ x - y = 1 \end{cases}$

6. $\begin{cases} x^2 + y^2 = 169 \\ 3x + 2y = 39 \end{cases}$

7. $\begin{cases} y = 2x^2 \\ y = x^4 - 2x^2 \end{cases}$

8. $\begin{cases} x = y + 3 \\ x = y^2 + 1 \end{cases}$

In Exercises 9–12, solve the system graphically.

9. $\begin{cases} 2x - y = 10 \\ x + 5y = -6 \end{cases}$

10. $\begin{cases} 8x - 3y = -3 \\ 2x + 5y = 28 \end{cases}$

11. $\begin{cases} y = 2x^2 - 4x + 1 \\ y = x^2 - 4x + 3 \end{cases}$

12. $\begin{cases} y^2 - 2y + x = 0 \\ x + y = 0 \end{cases}$

In Exercises 13 and 14, use a graphing utility to solve the system of equations. Find the solution accurate to two decimal places.

13. $\begin{cases} y = -2e^{-x} \\ 2e^x + y = 0 \end{cases}$

14. $\begin{cases} y = \ln(x - 1) - 3 \\ y = 4 - \frac{1}{2}x \end{cases}$

15. ***Break-Even Analysis*** You set up a scrapbook business and make an initial investment of \$50,000. The unit cost of a scrapbook kit is \$12 and the selling price is \$25. How many kits must you sell to break even?

16. ***Choice of Two Jobs*** You are offered two sales jobs at a pharmaceutical company. One company offers an annual salary of \$35,000 plus a year-end bonus of 1.5% of your total sales. The other company offers an annual salary of \$32,000 plus a year-end bonus of 2% of your total sales. What amount of sales will make the second offer better? Explain.

17. ***Geometry*** The perimeter of a rectangle is 480 meters and its length is 150% of its width. Find the dimensions of the rectangle.

18. ***Geometry*** The perimeter of a rectangle is 68 feet and its width is $\frac{8}{9}$ times its length. Find the dimensions of the rectangle.

7.2 In Exercises 19–26, solve the system by the method of elimination.

19. $\begin{cases} 2x - y = 2 \\ 6x + 8y = 39 \end{cases}$

20. $\begin{cases} 40x + 30y = 24 \\ 20x - 50y = -14 \end{cases}$

21. $\begin{cases} 0.2x + 0.3y = 0.14 \\ 0.4x + 0.5y = 0.20 \end{cases}$

22. $\begin{cases} 12x + 42y = -17 \\ 30x - 18y = 19 \end{cases}$

23. $\begin{cases} 3x - 2y = 0 \\ 3x + 2(y + 5) = 10 \end{cases}$

24. $\begin{cases} 7x + 12y = 63 \\ 2x + 3(y + 2) = 21 \end{cases}$

25. $\begin{cases} 1.25x - 2y = 3.5 \\ 5x - 8y = 14 \end{cases}$

26. $\begin{cases} 1.5x + 2.5y = 8.5 \\ 6x + 10y = 24 \end{cases}$

In Exercises 27–30, match the system of linear equations with its graph. Describe the number of solutions and state whether the system is consistent or inconsistent. [The graphs are labeled (a), (b), (c), and (d).]

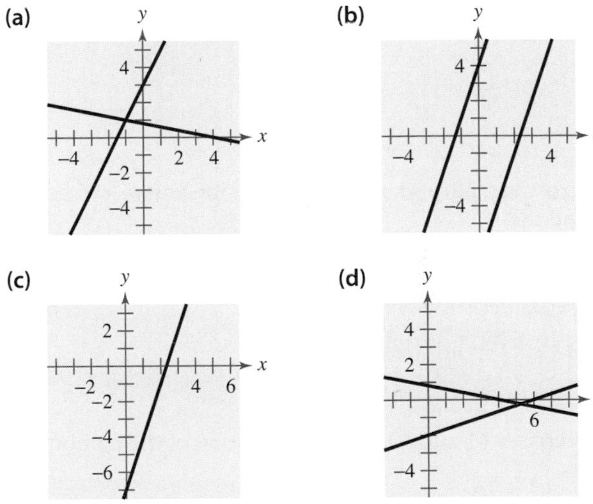

27. $\begin{cases} x + 5y = 4 \\ x - 3y = 6 \end{cases}$

28. $\begin{cases} -3x + y = -7 \\ 9x - 3y = 21 \end{cases}$

29. $\begin{cases} 3x - y = 7 \\ -6x + 2y = 8 \end{cases}$

30. $\begin{cases} 2x - y = -3 \\ x + 5y = 4 \end{cases}$

Supply and Demand **In Exercises 31 and 32, find the equilibrium point of demand and supply equations.**

	Demand	*Supply*
31.	$p = 37 - 0.0002x$	$p = 22 + 0.00001x$
32.	$p = 120 - 0.0001x$	$p = 45 + 0.0002x$

7.3 In Exercises 33 and 34, use back-substitution to solve the system of linear equations.

33. $\begin{cases} x - 4y + 3z = 3 \\ -y + z = -1 \\ z = -5 \end{cases}$

34. $\begin{cases} x - 7y + 8z = 85 \\ y - 9z = -35 \\ z = 3 \end{cases}$

In Exercises 35–38, use Gaussian elimination to solve the system of equations.

35. $\begin{cases} x + 2y + 6z = 4 \\ -3x + 2y - z = -4 \\ 4x + 2z = 16 \end{cases}$

36. $\begin{cases} x + 3y - z = 13 \\ 2x - 5z = 23 \\ 4x - y - 2z = 14 \end{cases}$

37. $\begin{cases} x - 2y + z = -6 \\ 2x - 3y = -7 \\ -x + 3y - 3z = 11 \end{cases}$

38. $\begin{cases} 2x + 6z = -9 \\ 3x - 2y + 11z = -16 \\ 3x - y + 7z = -11 \end{cases}$

In Exercises 39 and 40, solve the nonsquare system of equations.

39. $\begin{cases} 5x - 12y + 7z = 16 \\ 3x - 7y + 4z = 9 \end{cases}$

40. $\begin{cases} 2x + 5y - 19z = 34 \\ 3x + 8y - 31z = 54 \end{cases}$

In Exercises 41 and 42, find the equation of the parabola

$y = ax^2 + bx + c$

that passes through the points. To verify your result, use a graphing utility to plot the points and graph the parabola.

41.

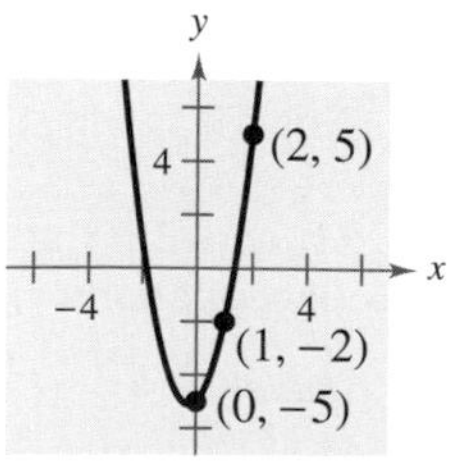

42.

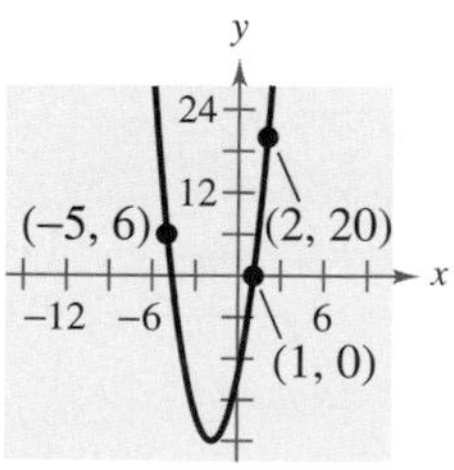

In Exercises 43 and 44, find the equation of the circle

$x^2 + y^2 + Dx + Ey + F = 0$

that passes through the points. To verify your result, use a graphing utility to plot the points and graph the circle.

43.

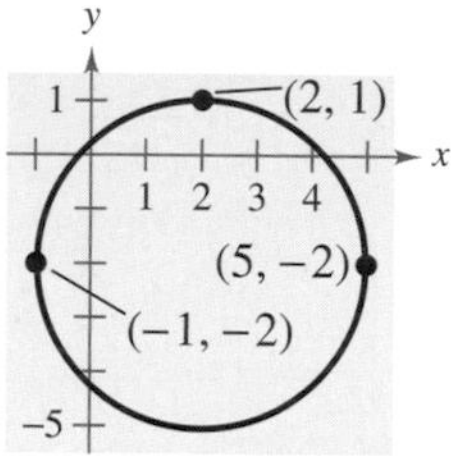

44.

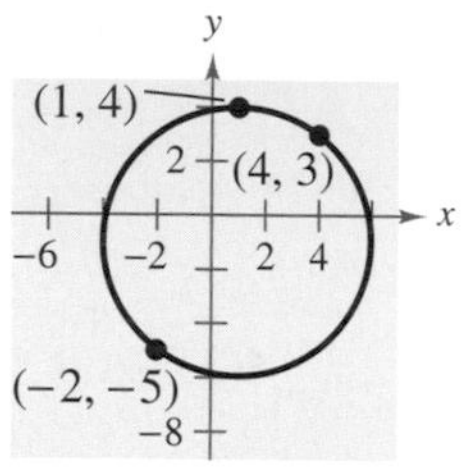

45. ***Data Analysis: Online Shopping*** The table shows the projected numbers y (in millions) of people shopping online in the United States from 2003 to 2005. (Source: eMarketer)

Year	Online shoppers, y
2003	101.7
2004	108.4
2005	121.1

(a) Use the technique demonstrated in Exercises 67–70 in Section 7.3 to set up a system of equations for the data and to find a least squares regression parabola that models the data. Let x represent the year, with $x = 3$ corresponding to 2003.

(b) Use a graphing utility to graph the parabola and the data in the same viewing window. How well does the model fit the data?

(c) Use the model to estimate the number of online shoppers in 2008. Does your answer seem reasonable?

46. ***Agriculture*** A mixture of 6 gallons of chemical A, 8 gallons of chemical B, and 13 gallons of chemical C is required to kill a destructive crop insect. Commercial spray X contains 1, 2, and 2 parts, respectively, of these chemicals. Commercial spray Y contains only chemical C. Commercial spray Z contains chemicals A, B, and C in equal amounts. How much of each type of commercial spray is needed to get the desired mixture?

47. ***Investment Analysis*** An inheritance of \$40,000 was divided among three investments yielding \$3500 in interest per year. The interest rates for the three investments were 7%, 9%, and 11%. Find the amount placed in each investment if the second and third were \$3000 and \$5000 less than the first, respectively.

48. ***Vertical Motion*** An object moving vertically is at the given heights at the specified times. Find the position equation $s = \frac{1}{2}at^2 + v_0t + s_0$ for the object.

(a) At $t = 1$ second, $s = 134$ feet
At $t = 2$ seconds, $s = 86$ feet
At $t = 3$ seconds, $s = 6$ feet

(b) At $t = 1$ second, $s = 184$ feet
At $t = 2$ seconds, $s = 116$ feet
At $t = 3$ seconds, $s = 16$ feet

7.4 In Exercises 49–52, write the form of the partial fraction decomposition for the rational expression. Do not solve for the constants.

49. $\dfrac{3}{x^2 + 20x}$

50. $\dfrac{x - 8}{x^2 - 3x - 28}$

51. $\dfrac{3x - 4}{x^3 - 5x^2}$

52. $\dfrac{x - 2}{x(x^2 + 2)^2}$

In Exercises 53–60, write the partial fraction decomposition of the rational expression.

53. $\dfrac{4 - x}{x^2 + 6x + 8}$

54. $\dfrac{-x}{x^2 + 3x + 2}$

55. $\dfrac{x^2}{x^2 + 2x - 15}$

56. $\dfrac{9}{x^2 - 9}$

57. $\dfrac{x^2 + 2x}{x^3 - x^2 + x - 1}$

58. $\dfrac{4x}{3(x - 1)^2}$

59. $\dfrac{3x^2 + 4x}{(x^2 + 1)^2}$

60. $\dfrac{4x^2}{(x - 1)(x^2 + 1)}$

7.5 In Exercises 61–64, sketch the graph of the inequality.

61. $y \le 5 - \frac{1}{2}x$

62. $3y - x \ge 7$

63. $y - 4x^2 > -1$

64. $y \le \dfrac{3}{x^2 + 2}$

In Exercises 65–72, sketch the graph and label the vertices of the solution set of the system of inequalities.

65. $\begin{cases} x + 2y \le 160 \\ 3x + y \le 180 \\ x \ge 0 \\ y \ge 0 \end{cases}$

66. $\begin{cases} 2x + 3y \le 24 \\ 2x + y \le 16 \\ x \ge 0 \\ y \ge 0 \end{cases}$

67. $\begin{cases} 3x + 2y \ge 24 \\ x + 2y \ge 12 \\ 2 \le x \le 15 \\ y \le 15 \end{cases}$

68. $\begin{cases} 2x + y \ge 16 \\ x + 3y \ge 18 \\ 0 \le x \le 25 \\ 0 \le y \le 25 \end{cases}$

69. $\begin{cases} y < x + 1 \\ y > x^2 - 1 \end{cases}$

70. $\begin{cases} y \le 6 - 2x - x^2 \\ y \ge x + 6 \end{cases}$

71. $\begin{cases} 2x - 3y \ge 0 \\ 2x - y \le 8 \\ y \ge 0 \end{cases}$

72. $\begin{cases} x^2 + y^2 \le 9 \\ (x - 3)^2 + y^2 \le 9 \end{cases}$

73. ***Inventory Costs*** A warehouse operator has 24,000 square feet of floor space in which to store two products. Each unit of product I requires 20 square feet of floor space and costs \$12 per day to store. Each unit of product II requires 30 square feet of floor space and costs \$8 per day to store. The total storage cost per day cannot exceed \$12,400. Find and graph a system of inequalities describing all possible inventory levels.

74. ***Nutrition*** A dietitian is asked to design a special dietary supplement using two different foods. Each ounce of food X contains 12 units of calcium, 10 units of iron, and 20 units of vitamin B. Each ounce of food Y contains 15 units of calcium, 20 units of iron, and 12 units of vitamin B. The minimum daily requirements of the diet are 300 units of calcium, 280 units of iron, and 300 units of vitamin B.

(a) Write a system of inequalities describing the different amounts of food X and food Y that can be used.

(b) Sketch a graph of the region in part (a).

(c) Find two solutions to the system and interpret their meanings in the context of the problem.

Supply and Demand **In Exercises 75 and 76, (a) graph the systems representing the consumer surplus and producer surplus for the supply and demand equations and (b) find the consumer surplus and producer surplus.**

	Demand	*Supply*
75.	$p = 160 - 0.0001x$	$p = 70 + 0.0002x$
76.	$p = 130 - 0.0002x$	$p = 30 + 0.0003x$

7.6 In Exercises 77–82, sketch the region determined by the constraints. Then find the minimum and maximum values of the objective function and where they occur, subject to the indicated restraints.

77. Objective function:
$z = 3x + 4y$
Constraints:
$x \ge 0$
$y \ge 0$
$2x + 5y \le 50$
$4x + y \le 28$

78. Objective function:
$z = 10x + 7y$
Constraints:
$x \ge 0$
$y \ge 0$
$2x + y \ge 100$
$x + y \ge 75$

79. Objective function:

$z = 1.75x + 2.25y$

Constraints:

$$\begin{aligned} x &\geq 0 \\ y &\geq 0 \\ 2x + y &\geq 25 \\ 3x + 2y &\geq 45 \end{aligned}$$

80. Objective function:

$z = 50x + 70y$

Constraints:

$$\begin{aligned} x &\geq 0 \\ y &\geq 0 \\ x + 2y &\leq 1500 \\ 5x + 2y &\leq 3500 \end{aligned}$$

81. Objective function:

$z = 5x + 11y$

Constraints:

$$\begin{aligned} x &\geq 0 \\ y &\geq 0 \\ x + 3y &\leq 12 \\ 3x + 2y &\leq 15 \end{aligned}$$

82. Objective function:

$z = -2x + y$

Constraints:

$$\begin{aligned} x &\geq 0 \\ y &\geq 0 \\ x + y &\geq 7 \\ 5x + 2y &\geq 20 \end{aligned}$$

83. ***Optimal Revenue*** A student is working part time as a hairdresser to pay college expenses. The student may work no more than 24 hours per week. Haircuts cost \$25 and require an average of 20 minutes, and permanents cost \$70 and require an average of 1 hour and 10 minutes. What combination of haircuts and/or permanents will yield an optimal revenue? What is the optimal revenue?

84. ***Optimal Profit*** A shoe manufacturer produces a walking shoe and a running shoe yielding profits of \$18 and \$24, respectively. Each shoe must go through three processes, for which the required times per unit are shown in the table.

	Process I	Process II	Process III
Hours for walking shoe	4	1	1
Hours for running shoe	2	2	1
Hours available per day	24	9	8

What is the optimal production level for each type of shoe? What is the optimal profit?

85. ***Optimal Cost*** A pet supply company mixes two brands of dry dog food. Brand X costs \$15 per bag and contains eight units of nutritional element A, one unit of nutritional element B, and two units of nutritional element C. Brand Y costs \$30 per bag and contains two units of nutritional element A, one unit of nutritional element B, and seven units of nutritional element C. Each bag of mixed dog food must contain at least 16 units, 5 units, and 20 units of nutritional elements A, B, and C, respectively. Find the numbers of bags of brands X and Y that should be mixed to produce a mixture meeting the minimum nutritional requirements and having an optimal cost. What is the optimal cost?

86. ***Optimal Cost*** Regular unleaded gasoline and premium unleaded gasoline have octane ratings of 87 and 93, respectively. For the week of January 3, 2005, regular unleaded gasoline in Houston, Texas averaged \$1.63 per gallon. For the same week, premium unleaded gasoline averaged \$1.83 per gallon. Determine the blend of regular and premium unleaded gasoline that results in an optimal cost of mid-grade unleaded (89-octane) gasoline. What is the optimal cost? (Source: Energy Information Administration)

Synthesis

True or False? **In Exercises 87 and 88, determine whether the statement is true or false. Justify your answer.**

87. The system

$$\begin{cases} y \leq 5 \\ y \geq -2 \\ y \geq \frac{7}{2}x - 9 \\ y \geq -\frac{7}{2}x + 26 \end{cases}$$

represents the region covered by an isosceles trapezoid.

88. It is possible for an objective function of a linear programming problem to have exactly 10 maximum value points.

In Exercises 89–92, find a system of linear equations having the ordered pair as a solution. (There are many correct answers.)

89. $(-6, 8)$

90. $(5, -4)$

91. $\left(\frac{4}{3}, 3\right)$

92. $\left(-1, \frac{9}{4}\right)$

In Exercises 93–96, find a system of linear equations having the ordered triple as a solution. (There are many answers.)

93. $(4, -1, 3)$

94. $(-3, 5, 6)$

95. $\left(5, \frac{3}{2}, 2\right)$

96. $\left(\frac{3}{4}, -2, 8\right)$

97. ***Writing*** Explain what is meant by an inconsistent system of linear equations.

98. How can you tell graphically that a system of linear equations in two variables has no solution? Give an example.

99. ***Writing*** Write a brief paragraph describing any advantages of substitution over the graphical method of solving a system of equations.

7 Chapter Test

Take this test as you would take a test in class. When you are finished, check your work against the answers given in the back of the book.

In Exercises 1–3, solve the system by the method of substitution.

1. $\begin{cases} x - y = -7 \\ 4x + 5y = 8 \end{cases}$ **2.** $\begin{cases} y = x - 1 \\ y = (x - 1)^3 \end{cases}$ **3.** $\begin{cases} 2x - y^2 = 0 \\ x - y = 4 \end{cases}$

In Exercises 4–6, solve the system graphically.

4. $\begin{cases} 2x - 3y = 0 \\ 2x + 3y = 12 \end{cases}$ **5.** $\begin{cases} y = 9 - x^2 \\ y = x + 3 \end{cases}$ **6.** $\begin{cases} y - \ln x = 12 \\ 7x - 2y + 11 = -6 \end{cases}$

In Exercises 7–10, solve the linear system by the method of elimination.

7. $\begin{cases} 2x + 3y = 17 \\ 5x - 4y = -15 \end{cases}$ **8.** $\begin{cases} 2.5x - y = 6 \\ 3x + 4y = 2 \end{cases}$

9. $\begin{cases} x - 2y + 3z = 11 \\ 2x - z = 3 \\ 3y + z = -8 \end{cases}$ **10.** $\begin{cases} 3x + 2y + z = 17 \\ -x + y + z = 4 \\ x - y - z = 3 \end{cases}$

In Exercises 11–14, write the partial fraction decomposition of the rational expression.

11. $\dfrac{2x + 5}{x^2 - x - 2}$ **12.** $\dfrac{3x^2 - 2x + 4}{x^2(2 - x)}$ **13.** $\dfrac{x^2 + 5}{x^3 - x}$ **14.** $\dfrac{x^2 - 4}{x^3 + 2x}$

In Exercises 15–17, sketch the graph and label the vertices of the solution of the system of inequalities.

15. $\begin{cases} 2x + y \le 4 \\ 2x - y \ge 0 \\ x \ge 0 \end{cases}$ **16.** $\begin{cases} y < -x^2 + x + 4 \\ y > 4x \end{cases}$ **17.** $\begin{cases} x^2 + y^2 \le 16 \\ x \ge 1 \\ y \ge -3 \end{cases}$

18. Find the maximum and minimum values of the objective function $z = 20x + 12y$ and where they occur, subject to the following constraints.

$$\left.\begin{array}{r} x \ge 0 \\ y \ge 0 \\ x + 4y \le 32 \\ 3x + 2y \le 36 \end{array}\right\} \quad \text{Constraints}$$

19. A total of \$50,000 is invested in two funds paying 8% and 8.5% simple interest. The yearly interest is \$4150. How much is invested at each rate?

20. Find the equation of the parabola $y = ax^2 + bx + c$ passing through the points $(0, 6)$, $(-2, 2)$, and $\left(3, \frac{9}{2}\right)$.

21. A manufacturer produces two types of television stands. The amounts (in hours) of time for assembling, staining, and packaging the two models are shown in the table at the left. The total amounts of time available for assembling, staining, and packaging are 4000, 8950, and 2650 hours, respectively. The profits per unit are \$30 (model I) and \$40 (model II). What is the optimal inventory level for each model? What is the optimal profit?

	Model I	Model II
Assembling	0.5	0.75
Staining	2.0	1.5
Packaging	0.5	0.5

TABLE FOR 21

Proofs in Mathematics

An **indirect proof** can be useful in proving statements of the form "p implies q." Recall that the conditional statement $p \rightarrow q$ is false only when p is true and q is false. To prove a conditional statement indirectly, assume that p is true and q is false. If this assumption leads to an impossibility, then you have proved that the conditional statement is true. An indirect proof is also called a **proof by contradiction.**

You can use an indirect proof to prove the following conditional statement,

"If a is a positive integer and a^2 is divisible by 2, then a is divisible by 2,"

as follows. First, assume that p, "a is a positive integer and a^2 is divisible by 2," is true and q, "a is divisible by 2," is false. This means that a is not divisible by 2. If so, a is odd and can be written as $a = 2n + 1$, where n is an integer.

$a = 2n + 1$ Definition of an odd integer

$a^2 = 4n^2 + 4n + 1$ Square each side.

$a^2 = 2(2n^2 + 2n) + 1$ Distributive Property

So, by the definition of an odd integer, a^2 is odd. This contradicts the assumption, and you can conclude that a is divisible by 2.

Example **Using an Indirect Proof**

Use an indirect proof to prove that $\sqrt{2}$ is an irrational number.

Solution

Begin by assuming that $\sqrt{2}$ is *not* an irrational number. Then $\sqrt{2}$ can be written as the quotient of two integers a and $b(b \neq 0)$ that have no common factors.

$\sqrt{2} = \dfrac{a}{b}$ Assume that $\sqrt{2}$ is a rational number.

$2 = \dfrac{a^2}{b^2}$ Square each side.

$2b^2 = a^2$ Multiply each side by b^2.

This implies that 2 is a factor of a^2. So, 2 is also a factor of a, and a can be written as $2c$, where c is an integer.

$2b^2 = (2c)^2$ Substitute $2c$ for a.

$2b^2 = 4c^2$ Simplify.

$b^2 = 2c^2$ Divide each side by 2.

This implies that 2 is a factor of b^2 and also a factor of b. So, 2 is a factor of both a and b. This contradicts the assumption that a and b have no common factors. So, you can conclude that $\sqrt{2}$ is an irrational number.

P.S. Problem Solving

This collection of thought-provoking and challenging exercises further explores and expands upon concepts learned in this chapter.

1. A theorem from geometry states that if a triangle is inscribed in a circle such that one side of the triangle is a diameter of the circle, then the triangle is a right triangle. Show that this theorem is true for the circle

$$x^2 + y^2 = 100$$

and the triangle formed by the lines

$$y = 0, \; y = \tfrac{1}{2}x + 5, \text{ and } y = -2x + 20.$$

2. Find k_1 and k_2 such that the system of equations has an infinite number of solutions.

$$\begin{cases} 3x - 5y = 8 \\ 2x + k_1 y = k_2 \end{cases}$$

3. Consider the following system of linear equations in x and y.

$$\begin{cases} ax + by = e \\ cx + dy = f \end{cases}$$

Under what conditions will the system have exactly one solution?

4. Graph the lines determined by each system of linear equations. Then use Gaussian elimination to solve each system. At each step of the elimination process, graph the corresponding lines. What do you observe?

(a) $\begin{cases} x - 4y = -3 \\ 5x - 6y = 13 \end{cases}$

(b) $\begin{cases} 2x - 3y = 7 \\ -4x + 6y = -14 \end{cases}$

5. A system of two equations in two unknowns is solved and has a finite number of solutions. Determine the maximum number of solutions of the system satisfying each condition.

(a) Both equations are linear.

(b) One equation is linear and the other is quadratic.

(c) Both equations are quadratic.

6. In the 2004 presidential election, approximately 118.304 million voters divided their votes among three presidential candidates. George W. Bush received 3,320,000 votes more than John Kerry. Ralph Nader received 0.3% of the votes. Write and solve a system of equations to find the total number of votes cast for each candidate. Let B represent the total votes cast for Bush, K the total votes cast for Kerry, and N the total votes cast for Nader. (Source: CNN.com)

7. The Vietnam Veterans Memorial (or "The Wall") in Washington, D.C. was designed by Maya Ying Lin when she was a student at Yale University. This monument has two vertical, triangular sections of black granite with a common side (see figure). The bottom of each section is level with the ground. The tops of the two sections can be approximately modeled by the equations

$$-2x + 50y = 505 \quad \text{and} \quad 2x + 50y = 505$$

when the x-axis is superimposed at the base of the wall. Each unit in the coordinate system represents 1 foot. How high is the memorial at the point where the two sections meet? How long is each section?

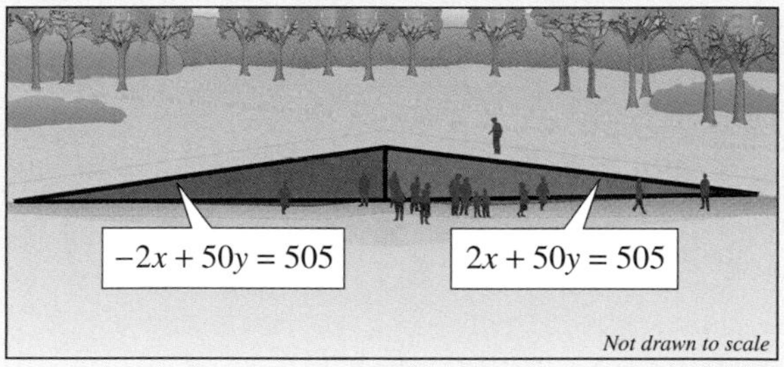

8. Weights of atoms and molecules are measured in atomic mass units (u). A molecule of C_2H_6 (ethane) is made up of two carbon atoms and six hydrogen atoms and weighs 30.07 u. A molecule of C_3H_8 (propane) is made up of three carbon atoms and eight hydrogen atoms and weighs 44.097 u. Find the weights of a carbon atom and a hydrogen atom.

9. To connect a DVD player to a television set, a cable with special connectors is required at both ends. You buy a six-foot cable for \$15.50 and a three-foot cable for \$10.25. Assuming that the cost of a cable is the sum of the cost of the two connectors and the cost of the cable itself, what is the cost of a four-foot cable? Explain your reasoning.

10. A hotel 35 miles from an airport runs a shuttle service to and from the airport. The 9:00 A.M. bus leaves for the airport traveling at 30 miles per hour. The 9:15 A.M. bus leaves for the airport traveling at 40 miles per hour. Write a system of linear equations that represents distance as a function of time for each bus. Graph and solve the system. How far from the airport will the 9:15 A.M. bus catch up to the 9:00 A.M. bus?

11. Solve each system of equations by letting $X = 1/x$, $Y = 1/y$, and $Z = 1/z$.

(a) $\begin{cases} \dfrac{12}{x} - \dfrac{12}{y} = 7 \\ \dfrac{3}{x} + \dfrac{4}{y} = 0 \end{cases}$

(b) $\begin{cases} \dfrac{2}{x} + \dfrac{1}{y} - \dfrac{3}{z} = 4 \\ \dfrac{4}{x} + \dfrac{2}{z} = 10 \\ -\dfrac{2}{x} + \dfrac{3}{y} - \dfrac{13}{z} = -8 \end{cases}$

12. What values should be given to a, b, and c so that the linear system shown has $(-1, 2, -3)$ as its only solution?

$$\begin{cases} x + 2y - 3z = a & \text{Equation 1} \\ -x - y + z = b & \text{Equation 2} \\ 2x + 3y - 2z = c & \text{Equation 3} \end{cases}$$

13. The following system has one solution: $x = 1$, $y = -1$, and $z = 2$.

$$\begin{cases} 4x - 2y + 5z = 16 \\ x + y = 0 \\ -x - 3y + 2z = 6 \end{cases}$$

Solve the system given by (a) Equation 1 and Equation 2, (b) Equation 1 and Equation 3, and (c) Equation 2 and Equation 3. (d) How many solutions does each of these systems have?

14. Solve the system of linear equations algebraically.

$$\begin{cases} x_1 - x_2 + 2x_3 + 2x_4 + 6x_5 = 6 \\ 3x_1 - 2x_2 + 4x_3 + 4x_4 + 12x_5 = 14 \\ -x_2 - x_3 - x_4 - 3x_5 = -3 \\ 2x_1 - 2x_2 + 4x_3 + 5x_4 + 15x_5 = 10 \\ 2x_1 - 2x_2 + 4x_3 + 4x_4 + 13x_5 = 13 \end{cases}$$

15. Each day, an average adult moose can process about 32 kilograms of terrestrial vegetation (twigs and leaves) and aquatic vegetation. From this food, it needs to obtain about 1.9 grams of sodium and 11,000 calories of energy. Aquatic vegetation has about 0.15 gram of sodium per kilogram and about 193 calories of energy per kilogram, whereas terrestrial vegetation has minimal sodium and about four times more energy than aquatic vegetation. Write and graph a system of inequalities that describes the amounts t and a of terrestrial and aquatic vegetation, respectively, for the daily diet of an average adult moose. (Source: Biology by Numbers)

16. For a healthy person who is 4 feet 10 inches tall, the recommended minimum weight is about 91 pounds and increases by about 3.7 pounds for each additional inch of height. The recommended maximum weight is about 119 pounds and increases by about 4.8 pounds for each additional inch of height. (Source: Dietary Guidelines Advisory Committee)

(a) Let x be the number of inches by which a person's height exceeds 4 feet 10 inches and let y be the person's weight in pounds. Write a system of inequalities that describes the possible values of x and y for a healthy person.

(b) Use a graphing utility to graph the system of inequalities from part (a).

(c) What is the recommended weight range for someone 6 feet tall?

17. The cholesterol in human blood is necessary, but too much cholesterol can lead to health problems. A blood cholesterol test gives three readings: LDL ("bad") cholesterol, HDL ("good") cholesterol, and total cholesterol (LDL + HDL). It is recommended that your LDL cholesterol level be less than 130 milligrams per deciliter, your HDL cholesterol level be at least 35 milligrams per deciliter, and your total cholesterol level be no more than 200 milligrams per deciliter. (Source: WebMD, Inc.)

(a) Write a system of linear inequalities for the recommended cholesterol levels. Let x represent HDL cholesterol and let y represent LDL cholesterol.

(b) Graph the system of inequalities from part (a). Label any vertices of the solution region.

(c) Are the following cholesterol levels within recommendations? Explain your reasoning.

LDL: 120 milligrams per deciliter

HDL: 90 milligrams per deciliter

Total: 210 milligrams per deciliter

(d) Give an example of cholesterol levels in which the LDL cholesterol level is too high but the HDL and total cholesterol levels are acceptable.

(e) Another recommendation is that the ratio of total cholesterol to HDL cholesterol be less than 4. Find a point in your solution region from part (b) that meets this recommendation, and explain why it meets the recommendation.

Matrices and Determinants

8

8.1 Matrices and Systems of Equations

8.2 Operations with Matrices

8.3 The Inverse of a Square Matrix

8.4 The Determinant of a Square Matrix

8.5 Applications of Matrices and Determinants

Matrices can be used to analyze financial information such as the profit a fruit farmer makes on two fruit crops.

Darren McCollester/Getty Images

SELECTED APPLICATIONS

Matrices have many real-life applications. The applications listed below represent a small sample of the applications in this chapter.

- Electrical Network, Exercise 82, page 585
- Data Analysis: Snowboarders, Exercise 90, page 585
- Agriculture, Exercise 61, page 599
- Profit, Exercise 67, page 600
- Investment Portfolio, Exercises 67–70, page 609
- Data Analysis: Supreme Court, Exercise 58, page 630
- Long-Distance Plans, Exercise 66, page 634

8.1 Matrices and Systems of Equations

What you should learn

- Write matrices and identify their orders.
- Perform elementary row operations on matrices.
- Use matrices and Gaussian elimination to solve systems of linear equations.
- Use matrices and Gauss-Jordan elimination to solve systems of linear equations.

Why you should learn it

You can use matrices to solve systems of linear equations in two or more variables. For instance, in Exercise 90 on page 585, you will use a matrix to find a model for the number of people who participated in snowboarding in the United States from 1997 to 2001.

Matrices

In this section, you will study a streamlined technique for solving systems of linear equations. This technique involves the use of a rectangular array of real numbers called a **matrix.** The plural of matrix is *matrices*.

Definition of Matrix

If m and n are positive integers, an $m \times n$ (read "m by n") matrix is a rectangular array

$$\begin{array}{c} \\ \text{Row 1} \\ \text{Row 2} \\ \text{Row 3} \\ \vdots \\ \text{Row } m \end{array} \begin{array}{c} \begin{array}{ccccc} \text{Column 1} & \text{Column 2} & \text{Column 3} & \cdots & \text{Column } n \end{array} \\ \begin{bmatrix} a_{11} & a_{12} & a_{13} & \cdots & a_{1n} \\ a_{21} & a_{22} & a_{23} & \cdots & a_{2n} \\ a_{31} & a_{32} & a_{33} & \cdots & a_{3n} \\ \vdots & \vdots & \vdots & & \vdots \\ a_{m1} & a_{m2} & a_{m3} & \cdots & a_{mn} \end{bmatrix} \end{array}$$

in which each **entry,** a_{ij}, of the matrix is a number. An $m \times n$ matrix has m rows and n columns. Matrices are usually denoted by capital letters.

The entry in the ith row and jth column is denoted by the *double subscript* notation a_{ij}. For instance, a_{23} refers to the entry in the second row, third column. A matrix having m rows and n columns is said to be of **order** $m \times n$. If $m = n$, the matrix is **square** of order n. For a square matrix, the entries $a_{11}, a_{22}, a_{33}, \ldots$ are the **main diagonal** entries.

Example 1 Order of Matrices

Determine the order of each matrix.

a. $[2]$ **b.** $\begin{bmatrix} 1 & -3 & 0 & \frac{1}{2} \end{bmatrix}$

c. $\begin{bmatrix} 0 & 0 \\ 0 & 0 \end{bmatrix}$ **d.** $\begin{bmatrix} 5 & 0 \\ 2 & -2 \\ -7 & 4 \end{bmatrix}$

Solution

a. This matrix has *one* row and *one* column. The order of the matrix is 1×1.
b. This matrix has *one* row and *four* columns. The order of the matrix is 1×4.
c. This matrix has *two* rows and *two* columns. The order of the matrix is 2×2.
d. This matrix has *three* rows and *two* columns. The order of the matrix is 3×2.

✓CHECKPOINT Now try Exercise 1.

A matrix that has only one row is called a **row matrix,** and a matrix that has only one column is called a **column matrix.**

A matrix derived from a system of linear equations (each written in standard form with the constant term on the right) is the **augmented matrix** of the system. Moreover, the matrix derived from the coefficients of the system (but not including the constant terms) is the **coefficient matrix** of the system.

System:
$$\begin{cases} x - 4y + 3z = 5 \\ -x + 3y - z = -3 \\ 2x \qquad - 4z = 6 \end{cases}$$

Augmented Matrix:
$$\begin{bmatrix} 1 & -4 & 3 & \vdots & 5 \\ -1 & 3 & -1 & \vdots & -3 \\ 2 & 0 & -4 & \vdots & 6 \end{bmatrix}$$

Coefficient Matrix:
$$\begin{bmatrix} 1 & -4 & 3 \\ -1 & 3 & -1 \\ 2 & 0 & -4 \end{bmatrix}$$

STUDY TIP

The vertical dots in an augmented matrix separate the coefficients of the linear system from the constant terms.

Note the use of 0 for the missing coefficient of the y-variable in the third equation, and also note the fourth column of constant terms in the augmented matrix.

When forming either the coefficient matrix or the augmented matrix of a system, you should begin by vertically aligning the variables in the equations and using zeros for the coefficients of the missing variables.

Example 2 Writing an Augmented Matrix

Write the augmented matrix for the system of linear equations.

$$\begin{cases} x + 3y - w = 9 \\ -y + 4z + 2w = -2 \\ x - 5z - 6w = 0 \\ 2x + 4y - 3z = 4 \end{cases}$$

What is the order of the augmented matrix?

Solution

Begin by rewriting the linear system and aligning the variables.

$$\begin{cases} x + 3y \qquad\qquad - w = 9 \\ \quad -y + 4z + 2w = -2 \\ x \qquad - 5z - 6w = 0 \\ 2x + 4y - 3z \qquad = 4 \end{cases}$$

Next, use the coefficients and constant terms as the matrix entries. Include zeros for the coefficients of the missing variables.

$$\begin{matrix} R_1 \\ R_2 \\ R_3 \\ R_4 \end{matrix} \begin{bmatrix} 1 & 3 & 0 & -1 & \vdots & 9 \\ 0 & -1 & 4 & 2 & \vdots & -2 \\ 1 & 0 & -5 & -6 & \vdots & 0 \\ 2 & 4 & -3 & 0 & \vdots & 4 \end{bmatrix}$$

The augmented matrix has four rows and five columns, so it is a 4×5 matrix. The notation R_n is used to designate each row in the matrix. For example, Row 1 is represented by R_1.

CHECKPOINT Now try Exercise 9.

Elementary Row Operations

In Section 7.3, you studied three operations that can be used on a system of linear equations to produce an equivalent system.

1. Interchange two equations.
2. Multiply an equation by a nonzero constant.
3. Add a multiple of an equation to another equation.

In matrix terminology, these three operations correspond to **elementary row operations.** An elementary row operation on an augmented matrix of a given system of linear equations produces a new augmented matrix corresponding to a new (but equivalent) system of linear equations. Two matrices are **row-equivalent** if one can be obtained from the other by a sequence of elementary row operations.

Elementary Row Operations

1. Interchange two rows.
2. Multiply a row by a nonzero constant.
3. Add a multiple of a row to another row.

Although elementary row operations are simple to perform, they involve a lot of arithmetic. Because it is easy to make a mistake, you should get in the habit of noting the elementary row operations performed in each step so that you can go back and check your work.

Example 3 Elementary Row Operations

a. Interchange the first and second rows of the original matrix.

Original Matrix *New Row-Equivalent Matrix*

$$\begin{bmatrix} 0 & 1 & 3 & 4 \\ -1 & 2 & 0 & 3 \\ 2 & -3 & 4 & 1 \end{bmatrix} \qquad \begin{matrix} R_2 \\ R_1 \\ \end{matrix} \begin{bmatrix} -1 & 2 & 0 & 3 \\ 0 & 1 & 3 & 4 \\ 2 & -3 & 4 & 1 \end{bmatrix}$$

b. Multiply the first row of the original matrix by $\frac{1}{2}$.

Original Matrix *New Row-Equivalent Matrix*

$$\begin{bmatrix} 2 & -4 & 6 & -2 \\ 1 & 3 & -3 & 0 \\ 5 & -2 & 1 & 2 \end{bmatrix} \qquad \begin{matrix} \frac{1}{2}R_1 \rightarrow \\ \\ \\ \end{matrix} \begin{bmatrix} 1 & -2 & 3 & -1 \\ 1 & 3 & -3 & 0 \\ 5 & -2 & 1 & 2 \end{bmatrix}$$

c. Add -2 times the first row of the original matrix to the third row.

Original Matrix *New Row-Equivalent Matrix*

$$\begin{bmatrix} 1 & 2 & -4 & 3 \\ 0 & 3 & -2 & -1 \\ 2 & 1 & 5 & -2 \end{bmatrix} \qquad \begin{matrix} \\ \\ -2R_1 + R_3 \rightarrow \end{matrix} \begin{bmatrix} 1 & 2 & -4 & 3 \\ 0 & 3 & -2 & -1 \\ 0 & -3 & 13 & -8 \end{bmatrix}$$

Note that the elementary row operation is written beside the row that is *changed*.

✓CHECKPOINT Now try Exercise 25.

Technology

Most graphing utilities can perform elementary row operations on matrices. Consult the user's guide for your graphing utility for specific keystrokes.

After performing a row operation, the new row-equivalent matrix that is displayed on your graphing utility is stored in the *answer* variable. You should use the *answer* variable and not the original matrix for subsequent row operations.

In Example 3 in Section 7.3, you used Gaussian elimination with back-substitution to solve a system of linear equations. The next example demonstrates the matrix version of Gaussian elimination. The two methods are essentially the same. The basic difference is that with matrices you do not need to keep writing the variables.

Example 4 **Comparing Linear Systems and Matrix Operations**

Linear System / *Associated Augmented Matrix*

$$\begin{cases} x - 2y + 3z = 9 \\ -x + 3y = -4 \\ 2x - 5y + 5z = 17 \end{cases} \qquad \begin{bmatrix} 1 & -2 & 3 & \vdots & 9 \\ -1 & 3 & 0 & \vdots & -4 \\ 2 & -5 & 5 & \vdots & 17 \end{bmatrix}$$

Add the first equation to the second equation. / Add the first row to the second row ($R_1 + R_2$).

$$\begin{cases} x - 2y + 3z = 9 \\ y + 3z = 5 \\ 2x - 5y + 5z = 17 \end{cases} \qquad \begin{matrix} \\ R_1 + R_2 \rightarrow \\ \\ \end{matrix} \begin{bmatrix} 1 & -2 & 3 & \vdots & 9 \\ 0 & 1 & 3 & \vdots & 5 \\ 2 & -5 & 5 & \vdots & 17 \end{bmatrix}$$

Add -2 times the first equation to the third equation. / Add -2 times the first row to the third row ($-2R_1 + R_3$).

$$\begin{cases} x - 2y + 3z = 9 \\ y + 3z = 5 \\ -y - z = -1 \end{cases} \qquad \begin{matrix} \\ \\ -2R_1 + R_3 \rightarrow \end{matrix} \begin{bmatrix} 1 & -2 & 3 & \vdots & 9 \\ 0 & 1 & 3 & \vdots & 5 \\ 0 & -1 & -1 & \vdots & -1 \end{bmatrix}$$

Add the second equation to the third equation. / Add the second row to the third row ($R_2 + R_3$).

$$\begin{cases} x - 2y + 3z = 9 \\ y + 3z = 5 \\ 2z = 4 \end{cases} \qquad \begin{matrix} \\ \\ R_2 + R_3 \rightarrow \end{matrix} \begin{bmatrix} 1 & -2 & 3 & \vdots & 9 \\ 0 & 1 & 3 & \vdots & 5 \\ 0 & 0 & 2 & \vdots & 4 \end{bmatrix}$$

Multiply the third equation by $\frac{1}{2}$. / Multiply the third row by $\frac{1}{2}$ ($\frac{1}{2}R_3$).

$$\begin{cases} x - 2y + 3z = 9 \\ y + 3z = 5 \\ z = 2 \end{cases} \qquad \begin{matrix} \\ \\ \frac{1}{2}R_3 \rightarrow \end{matrix} \begin{bmatrix} 1 & -2 & 3 & \vdots & 9 \\ 0 & 1 & 3 & \vdots & 5 \\ 0 & 0 & 1 & \vdots & 2 \end{bmatrix}$$

At this point, you can use back-substitution to find x and y.

$$y + 3(2) = 5 \qquad \text{Substitute 2 for } z.$$

$$y = -1 \qquad \text{Solve for } y.$$

$$x - 2(-1) + 3(2) = 9 \qquad \text{Substitute } -1 \text{ for } y \text{ and 2 for } z.$$

$$x = 1 \qquad \text{Solve for } x.$$

The solution is $x = 1$, $y = -1$, and $z = 2$.

✓CHECKPOINT Now try Exercise 27.

STUDY TIP

Remember that you should check a solution by substituting the values of x, y, and z into each equation of the original system. For example, you can check the solution to Example 4 as follows.

Equation 1:
$1 - 2(-1) + 3(2) = 9$ ✓

Equation 2:
$-1 + 3(-1) = -4$ ✓

Equation 3:
$2(1) - 5(-1) + 5(2) = 17$ ✓

The last matrix in Example 4 is said to be in **row-echelon form.** The term *echelon* refers to the stair-step pattern formed by the nonzero elements of the matrix. To be in this form, a matrix must have the following properties.

Row-Echelon Form and Reduced Row-Echelon Form

A matrix in **row-echelon form** has the following properties.

1. Any rows consisting entirely of zeros occur at the bottom of the matrix.
2. For each row that does not consist entirely of zeros, the first nonzero entry is 1 (called a **leading 1**).
3. For two successive (nonzero) rows, the leading 1 in the higher row is farther to the left than the leading 1 in the lower row.

A matrix in *row-echelon form* is in **reduced row-echelon form** if every column that has a leading 1 has zeros in every position above and below its leading 1.

Example 5 Row-Echelon Form

Determine whether each matrix is in row-echelon form. If it is, determine whether the matrix is in reduced row-echelon form.1

a. $\begin{bmatrix} 1 & 2 & -1 & 4 \\ 0 & 1 & 0 & 3 \\ 0 & 0 & 1 & -2 \end{bmatrix}$ **b.** $\begin{bmatrix} 1 & 2 & -1 & 2 \\ 0 & 0 & 0 & 0 \\ 0 & 1 & 2 & -4 \end{bmatrix}$

c. $\begin{bmatrix} 1 & -5 & 2 & -1 & 3 \\ 0 & 0 & 1 & 3 & -2 \\ 0 & 0 & 0 & 1 & 4 \\ 0 & 0 & 0 & 0 & 1 \end{bmatrix}$ **d.** $\begin{bmatrix} 1 & 0 & 0 & -1 \\ 0 & 1 & 0 & 2 \\ 0 & 0 & 1 & 3 \\ 0 & 0 & 0 & 0 \end{bmatrix}$

e. $\begin{bmatrix} 1 & 2 & -3 & 4 \\ 0 & 2 & 1 & -1 \\ 0 & 0 & 1 & -3 \end{bmatrix}$ **f.** $\begin{bmatrix} 0 & 1 & 0 & 5 \\ 0 & 0 & 1 & 3 \\ 0 & 0 & 0 & 0 \end{bmatrix}$

Solution

The matrices in (a), (c), (d), and (f) are in row-echelon form. The matrices in (d) and (f) are in *reduced* row-echelon form because every column that has a leading 1 has zeros in every position above and below its leading 1. The matrix in (b) is not in row-echelon form because a row of all zeros does not occur at the bottom of the matrix. The matrix in (e) is not in row-echelon form because the first nonzero entry in Row 2 is not a leading 1.

✓CHECKPOINT Now try Exercise 29.

Every matrix is row-equivalent to a matrix in row-echelon form. For instance, in Example 5, you can change the matrix in part (e) to row-echelon form by multiplying its second row by $\frac{1}{2}$.

Gaussian Elimination with Back-Substitution

Gaussian elimination with back-substitution works well for solving systems of linear equations by hand or with a computer. For this algorithm, the order in which the elementary row operations are performed is important. You should operate from left to right by columns, using elementary row operations to obtain zeros in all entries directly below the leading 1's.

Example 6 Gaussian Elimination with Back-Substitution

Solve the system
$$\begin{cases} y + z - 2w = -3 \\ x + 2y - z = 2 \\ 2x + 4y + z - 3w = -2 \\ x - 4y - 7z - w = -19 \end{cases}.$$

Solution

$$\begin{bmatrix} 0 & 1 & 1 & -2 & \vdots & -3 \\ 1 & 2 & -1 & 0 & \vdots & 2 \\ 2 & 4 & 1 & -3 & \vdots & -2 \\ 1 & -4 & -7 & -1 & \vdots & -19 \end{bmatrix}$$
Write augmented matrix.

$$\begin{matrix} R_2 \\ R_1 \\ \\ \\ \end{matrix} \begin{bmatrix} 1 & 2 & -1 & 0 & \vdots & 2 \\ 0 & 1 & 1 & -2 & \vdots & -3 \\ 2 & 4 & 1 & -3 & \vdots & -2 \\ 1 & -4 & -7 & -1 & \vdots & -19 \end{bmatrix}$$
Interchange R_1 and R_2 so first column has leading 1 in upper left corner.

$$\begin{matrix} \\ \\ -2R_1 + R_3 \rightarrow \\ -R_1 + R_4 \rightarrow \end{matrix} \begin{bmatrix} 1 & 2 & -1 & 0 & \vdots & 2 \\ 0 & 1 & 1 & -2 & \vdots & -3 \\ 0 & 0 & 3 & -3 & \vdots & -6 \\ 0 & -6 & -6 & -1 & \vdots & -21 \end{bmatrix}$$
Perform operations on R_3 and R_4 so first column has zeros below its leading 1.

$$\begin{matrix} \\ \\ \\ 6R_2 + R_4 \rightarrow \end{matrix} \begin{bmatrix} 1 & 2 & -1 & 0 & \vdots & 2 \\ 0 & 1 & 1 & -2 & \vdots & -3 \\ 0 & 0 & 3 & -3 & \vdots & -6 \\ 0 & 0 & 0 & -13 & \vdots & -39 \end{bmatrix}$$
Perform operations on R_4 so second column has zeros below its leading 1.

$$\begin{matrix} \\ \\ \frac{1}{3}R_3 \rightarrow \\ -\frac{1}{13}R_4 \rightarrow \end{matrix} \begin{bmatrix} 1 & 2 & -1 & 0 & \vdots & 2 \\ 0 & 1 & 1 & -2 & \vdots & -3 \\ 0 & 0 & 1 & -1 & \vdots & -2 \\ 0 & 0 & 0 & 1 & \vdots & 3 \end{bmatrix}$$
Perform operations on R_3 and R_4 so third and fourth columns have leading 1's.

The matrix is now in row-echelon form, and the corresponding system is

$$\begin{cases} x + 2y - z = 2 \\ y + z - 2w = -3 \\ z - w = -2 \\ w = 3 \end{cases}.$$

Using back-substitution, the solution is $x = -1$, $y = 2$, $z = 1$, and $w = 3$.

CHECKPOINT Now try Exercise 51.

The procedure for using Gaussian elimination with back-substitution is summarized below.

Gaussian Elimination with Back-Substitution

1. Write the augmented matrix of the system of linear equations.
2. Use elementary row operations to rewrite the augmented matrix in row-echelon form.
3. Write the system of linear equations corresponding to the matrix in row-echelon form, and use back-substitution to find the solution.

When solving a system of linear equations, remember that it is possible for the system to have no solution. If, in the elimination process, you obtain a row with zeros except for the last entry, it is unnecessary to continue the elimination process. You can simply conclude that the system has no solution, or is *inconsistent*.

Example 7 A System with No Solution

Solve the system $\begin{cases} x - y + 2z = 4 \\ x + z = 6 \\ 2x - 3y + 5z = 4 \\ 3x + 2y - z = 1 \end{cases}$.

Solution

$$\begin{bmatrix} 1 & -1 & 2 & \vdots & 4 \\ 1 & 0 & 1 & \vdots & 6 \\ 2 & -3 & 5 & \vdots & 4 \\ 3 & 2 & -1 & \vdots & 1 \end{bmatrix}$$ Write augmented matrix.

$$\begin{matrix} \\ -R_1 + R_2 \rightarrow \\ -2R_1 + R_3 \rightarrow \\ -3R_1 + R_4 \rightarrow \end{matrix} \begin{bmatrix} 1 & -1 & 2 & \vdots & 4 \\ 0 & 1 & -1 & \vdots & 2 \\ 0 & -1 & 1 & \vdots & -4 \\ 0 & 5 & -7 & \vdots & -11 \end{bmatrix}$$ Perform row operations.

$$\begin{matrix} \\ \\ R_2 + R_3 \rightarrow \\ \\ \end{matrix} \begin{bmatrix} 1 & -1 & 2 & \vdots & 4 \\ 0 & 1 & -1 & \vdots & 2 \\ 0 & 0 & 0 & \vdots & -2 \\ 0 & 5 & -7 & \vdots & -11 \end{bmatrix}$$ Perform row operations.

Note that the third row of this matrix consists of zeros except for the last entry. This means that the original system of linear equations is inconsistent. You can see why this is true by converting back to a system of linear equations.

$$\begin{cases} x - y + 2z = 4 \\ y - z = 2 \\ 0 = -2 \\ 5y - 7z = -11 \end{cases}$$

Because the third equation is not possible, the system has no solution.

✓CHECKPOINT Now try Exercise 57.

Gauss-Jordan Elimination

With Gaussian elimination, elementary row operations are applied to a matrix to obtain a (row-equivalent) row-echelon form of the matrix. A second method of elimination, called **Gauss-Jordan elimination,** after Carl Friedrich Gauss and Wilhelm Jordan (1842–1899), continues the reduction process until a *reduced* row-echelon form is obtained. This procedure is demonstrated in Example 8.

Example 8 Gauss-Jordan Elimination

Use Gauss-Jordan elimination to solve the system $\begin{cases} x - 2y + 3z = 9 \\ -x + 3y = -4. \\ 2x - 5y + 5z = 17 \end{cases}$

Solution

In Example 4, Gaussian elimination was used to obtain the row-echelon form of the linear system above.

$$\begin{bmatrix} 1 & -2 & 3 & \vdots & 9 \\ 0 & 1 & 3 & \vdots & 5 \\ 0 & 0 & 1 & \vdots & 2 \end{bmatrix}$$

Now, apply elementary row operations until you obtain zeros above each of the leading 1's, as follows.

$$\begin{matrix} 2R_2 + R_1 \rightarrow \\ \\ \\ \end{matrix} \begin{bmatrix} 1 & 0 & 9 & \vdots & 19 \\ 0 & 1 & 3 & \vdots & 5 \\ 0 & 0 & 1 & \vdots & 2 \end{bmatrix}$$

Perform operations on R_1 so second column has a zero above its leading 1.

$$\begin{matrix} -9R_3 + R_1 \rightarrow \\ -3R_3 + R_2 \rightarrow \\ \\ \end{matrix} \begin{bmatrix} 1 & 0 & 0 & \vdots & 1 \\ 0 & 1 & 0 & \vdots & -1 \\ 0 & 0 & 1 & \vdots & 2 \end{bmatrix}$$

Perform operations on R_1 and R_2 so third column has zeros above its leading 1.

The matrix is now in reduced row-echelon form. Converting back to a system of linear equations, you have

$$\begin{cases} x = 1 \\ y = -1. \\ z = 2 \end{cases}$$

Now you can simply read the solution, $x = 1$, $y = -1$, and $z = 2$, which can be written as the ordered triple $(1, -1, 2)$.

✓CHECKPOINT Now try Exercise 59.

The elimination procedures described in this section sometimes result in fractional coefficients. For instance, in the elimination procedure for the system

$$\begin{cases} 2x - 5y + 5z = 17 \\ 3x - 2y + 3z = 11 \\ -3x + 3y = -6 \end{cases}$$

you may be inclined to multiply the first row by $\frac{1}{2}$ to produce a leading 1, which will result in working with fractional coefficients. You can sometimes avoid fractions by judiciously choosing the order in which you apply elementary row operations.

Technology

For a demonstration of a graphical approach to Gauss-Jordan elimination on a 2 × 3 matrix, see the Visualizing Row Operations Program available for several models of graphing calculators at our website *college.hmco.com.*

STUDY TIP

The advantage of using Gauss-Jordan elimination to solve a system of linear equations is that the solution of the system is easily found without using back-substitution, as illustrated in Example 8.

Recall from Chapter 7 that when there are fewer equations than variables in a system of equations, then the system has either no solution or infinitely many solutions.

Example 9 A System with an Infinite Number of Solutions

Solve the system.

$$\begin{cases} 2x + 4y - 2z = 0 \\ 3x + 5y = 1 \end{cases}$$

Solution

$$\begin{bmatrix} 2 & 4 & -2 & \vdots & 0 \\ 3 & 5 & 0 & \vdots & 1 \end{bmatrix}$$

$$\tfrac{1}{2}R_1 \rightarrow \begin{bmatrix} 1 & 2 & -1 & \vdots & 0 \\ 3 & 5 & 0 & \vdots & 1 \end{bmatrix}$$

$$-3R_1 + R_2 \rightarrow \begin{bmatrix} 1 & 2 & -1 & \vdots & 0 \\ 0 & -1 & 3 & \vdots & 1 \end{bmatrix}$$

$$-R_2 \rightarrow \begin{bmatrix} 1 & 2 & -1 & \vdots & 0 \\ 0 & 1 & -3 & \vdots & -1 \end{bmatrix}$$

$$-2R_2 + R_1 \rightarrow \begin{bmatrix} 1 & 0 & 5 & \vdots & 2 \\ 0 & 1 & -3 & \vdots & -1 \end{bmatrix}$$

The corresponding system of equations is

$$\begin{cases} x + 5z = 2 \\ y - 3z = -1 \end{cases}.$$

Solving for x and y in terms of z, you have

$$x = -5z + 2 \qquad \text{and} \qquad y = 3z - 1.$$

To write a solution to the system that does not use any of the three variables of the system, let a represent any real number and let

$$z = a.$$

Now substitute a for z in the equations for x and y.

$$x = -5z + 2 = -5a + 2$$

$$y = 3z - 1 = 3a - 1$$

So, the solution set can be written as an ordered triple with the form

$$(-5a + 2, 3a - 1, a)$$

where a is any real number. Remember that a solution set of this form represents an infinite number of solutions. Try substituting values for a to obtain a few solutions. Then check each solution in the original equation.

✓CHECKPOINT Now try Exercise 65.

STUDY TIP

In Example 9, x and y are solved for in terms of the third variable z. To write a solution to the system that does not use any of the three variables of the system, let a represent any real number and let $z = a$. Then solve for x and y. The solution can then be written in terms of a, which is not one of the variables of the system.

It is worth noting that the row-echelon form of a matrix is not unique. That is, two different sequences of elementary row operations may yield different row-echelon forms. This is demonstrated in Example 10.

Example 10 Comparing Row-Echelon Forms

Compare the following row-echelon form with the one found in Example 4. Is it the same? Does it yield the same solution?

$$\begin{cases} x - 2y + 3z = 9 \\ -x + 3y \qquad = -4 \\ 2x - 5y + 5z = 17 \end{cases}$$

$$\begin{bmatrix} 1 & -2 & 3 & \vdots & 9 \\ -1 & 3 & 0 & \vdots & -4 \\ 2 & -5 & 5 & \vdots & 17 \end{bmatrix}$$

$$\begin{matrix} R_2 \\ R_1 \\ \end{matrix} \begin{bmatrix} -1 & 3 & 0 & \vdots & -4 \\ 1 & -2 & 3 & \vdots & 9 \\ 2 & -5 & 5 & \vdots & 17 \end{bmatrix}$$

$$\begin{matrix} -R_1 \rightarrow \\ \\ \end{matrix} \begin{bmatrix} 1 & -3 & 0 & \vdots & 4 \\ 1 & -2 & 3 & \vdots & 9 \\ 2 & -5 & 5 & \vdots & 17 \end{bmatrix}$$

$$\begin{matrix} \\ -R_1 + R_2 \rightarrow \\ -2R_1 + R_3 \rightarrow \end{matrix} \begin{bmatrix} 1 & -3 & 0 & \vdots & 4 \\ 0 & 1 & 3 & \vdots & 5 \\ 0 & 1 & 5 & \vdots & 9 \end{bmatrix}$$

$$\begin{matrix} \\ \\ -R_2 + R_3 \rightarrow \end{matrix} \begin{bmatrix} 1 & -3 & 0 & \vdots & 4 \\ 0 & 1 & 3 & \vdots & 5 \\ 0 & 0 & 2 & \vdots & 4 \end{bmatrix}$$

$$\begin{matrix} \\ \\ \frac{1}{2}R_3 \rightarrow \end{matrix} \begin{bmatrix} 1 & -3 & 0 & \vdots & 4 \\ 0 & 1 & 3 & \vdots & 5 \\ 0 & 0 & 1 & \vdots & 2 \end{bmatrix}$$

Solution

This row-echelon form is different from that obtained in Example 4. The corresponding system of linear equations for this row-echelon matrix is

$$\begin{cases} x - 3y \qquad = 4 \\ \qquad y + 3z = 5. \\ \qquad\qquad z = 2 \end{cases}$$

Using back-substitution on this system, you obtain the solution

$x = 1$, $y = -1$, and $z = 2$

which is the same solution that was obtained in Example 4.

CHECKPOINT Now try Exercise 77.

You have seen that the row-echelon form of a given matrix *is not* unique; however, the *reduced* row-echelon form of a given matrix *is* unique. Try applying Gauss-Jordan elimination to the row echelon matrix in Example 10 to see that you obtain the same reduced row-echelon form as in Example 8.

8.1 Exercises

VOCABULARY CHECK: Fill in the blanks.

1. A rectangular array of real numbers than can be used to solve a system of linear equations is called a ________.
2. A matrix is ________ if the number of rows equals the number of columns.
3. For a square matrix, the entries $a_{11}, a_{22}, a_{33}, \ldots, a_{nn}$ are the ________ ________ entries.
4. A matrix with only one row is called a ________ matrix and a matrix with only one column is called a ________ matrix.
5. The matrix derived from a system of linear equations is called the ________ matrix of the system.
6. The matrix derived from the coefficients of a system of linear equations is called the ________ matrix of the system.
7. Two matrices are called ________ if one of the matrices can be obtained from the other by a sequence of elementary row operations.
8. A matrix in row-echelon form is in ________ ________ ________ if every column that has a leading 1 has zeros in every position above and below its leading 1.
9. The process of using row operations to write a matrix in reduced row-echelon form is called ________ ________.

In Exercises 1–6, determine the order of the matrix.

1. $\begin{bmatrix} 7 & 0 \end{bmatrix}$

2. $\begin{bmatrix} 5 & -3 & 8 & 7 \end{bmatrix}$

3. $\begin{bmatrix} 2 \\ 36 \\ 3 \end{bmatrix}$

4. $\begin{bmatrix} -3 & 7 & 15 & 0 \\ 0 & 0 & 3 & 3 \\ 1 & 1 & 6 & 7 \end{bmatrix}$

5. $\begin{bmatrix} 33 & 45 \\ -9 & 20 \end{bmatrix}$

6. $\begin{bmatrix} -7 & 6 & 4 \\ 0 & -5 & 1 \end{bmatrix}$

In Exercises 7–12, write the augmented matrix for the system of linear equations.

7. $\begin{cases} 4x - 3y = -5 \\ -x + 3y = 12 \end{cases}$

8. $\begin{cases} 7x + 4y = 22 \\ 5x - 9y = 15 \end{cases}$

9. $\begin{cases} x + 10y - 2z = 2 \\ 5x - 3y + 4z = 0 \\ 2x + y = 6 \end{cases}$

10. $\begin{cases} -x - 8y + 5z = 8 \\ -7x - 15z = -38 \\ 3x - y + 8z = 20 \end{cases}$

11. $\begin{cases} 7x - 5y + z = 13 \\ 19x - 8z = 10 \end{cases}$

12. $\begin{cases} 9x + 2y - 3z = 20 \\ -25y + 11z = -5 \end{cases}$

In Exercises 13–18, write the system of linear equations represented by the augmented matrix. (Use variables *x*, *y*, *z*, and *w*, if applicable.)

13. $\left[\begin{array}{cc|c} 1 & 2 & 7 \\ 2 & -3 & 4 \end{array}\right]$

14. $\left[\begin{array}{cc|c} 7 & -5 & 0 \\ 8 & 3 & -2 \end{array}\right]$

15. $\left[\begin{array}{ccc|c} 2 & 0 & 5 & -12 \\ 0 & 1 & -2 & 7 \\ 6 & 3 & 0 & 2 \end{array}\right]$

16. $\left[\begin{array}{ccc|c} 4 & -5 & -1 & 18 \\ -11 & 0 & 6 & 25 \\ 3 & 8 & 0 & -29 \end{array}\right]$

17. $\left[\begin{array}{cccc|c} 9 & 12 & 3 & 0 & 0 \\ -2 & 18 & 5 & 2 & 10 \\ 1 & 7 & -8 & 0 & -4 \\ 3 & 0 & 2 & 0 & -10 \end{array}\right]$

18. $\left[\begin{array}{cccc|c} 6 & 2 & -1 & -5 & -25 \\ -1 & 0 & 7 & 3 & 7 \\ 4 & -1 & -10 & 6 & 23 \\ 0 & 8 & 1 & -11 & -21 \end{array}\right]$

In Exercises 19–22, fill in the blank(s) using elementary row operations to form a row-equivalent matrix.

19. $\begin{bmatrix} 1 & 4 & 3 \\ 2 & 10 & 5 \end{bmatrix}$

$\begin{bmatrix} 1 & 4 & 3 \\ 0 & \square & -1 \end{bmatrix}$

20. $\begin{bmatrix} 3 & 6 & 8 \\ 4 & -3 & 6 \end{bmatrix}$

$\begin{bmatrix} 1 & \square & \frac{8}{3} \\ 4 & -3 & 6 \end{bmatrix}$

21. $\begin{bmatrix} 1 & 1 & 4 & -1 \\ 3 & 8 & 10 & 3 \\ -2 & 1 & 12 & 6 \end{bmatrix}$

$\begin{bmatrix} 1 & 1 & 4 & -1 \\ 0 & 5 & \square & \square \\ 0 & 3 & \square & \square \end{bmatrix}$

$\begin{bmatrix} 1 & 1 & 4 & -1 \\ 0 & 1 & -\frac{2}{5} & \frac{6}{5} \\ 0 & 3 & \square & \square \end{bmatrix}$

22. $\begin{bmatrix} 2 & 4 & 8 & 3 \\ 1 & -1 & -3 & 2 \\ 2 & 6 & 4 & 9 \end{bmatrix}$

$\begin{bmatrix} 1 & \square & \square & \square \\ 1 & -1 & -3 & 2 \\ 2 & 6 & 4 & 9 \end{bmatrix}$

$\begin{bmatrix} 1 & 2 & 4 & \frac{3}{2} \\ 0 & \square & -7 & \frac{1}{2} \\ 0 & 2 & \square & \square \end{bmatrix}$

In Exercises 23–26, identify the elementary row operation(s) being performed to obtain the new row-equivalent matrix.

	Original Matrix	*New Row-Equivalent Matrix*
23.	$\begin{bmatrix} -2 & 5 & 1 \\ 3 & -1 & -8 \end{bmatrix}$	$\begin{bmatrix} 13 & 0 & -39 \\ 3 & -1 & -8 \end{bmatrix}$
24.	$\begin{bmatrix} 3 & -1 & -4 \\ -4 & 3 & 7 \end{bmatrix}$	$\begin{bmatrix} 3 & -1 & -4 \\ 5 & 0 & -5 \end{bmatrix}$
25.	$\begin{bmatrix} 0 & -1 & -5 & 5 \\ -1 & 3 & -7 & 6 \\ 4 & -5 & 1 & 3 \end{bmatrix}$	$\begin{bmatrix} -1 & 3 & -7 & 6 \\ 0 & -1 & -5 & 5 \\ 0 & 7 & -27 & 27 \end{bmatrix}$
26.	$\begin{bmatrix} -1 & -2 & 3 & -2 \\ 2 & -5 & 1 & -7 \\ 5 & 4 & -7 & 6 \end{bmatrix}$	$\begin{bmatrix} -1 & -2 & 3 & -2 \\ 0 & -9 & 7 & -11 \\ 0 & -6 & 8 & -4 \end{bmatrix}$

27. Perform the sequence of row operations on the matrix. What did the operations accomplish?

$$\begin{bmatrix} 1 & 2 & 3 \\ 2 & -1 & -4 \\ 3 & 1 & -1 \end{bmatrix}$$

(a) Add -2 times R_1 to R_2.
(b) Add -3 times R_1 to R_3.
(c) Add -1 times R_2 to R_3.
(d) Multiply R_2 by $-\frac{1}{5}$.
(e) Add -2 times R_2 to R_1.

28. Perform the sequence of row operations on the matrix. What did the operations accomplish?

$$\begin{bmatrix} 7 & 1 \\ 0 & 2 \\ -3 & 4 \\ 4 & 1 \end{bmatrix}$$

(a) Add R_3 to R_4.
(b) Interchange R_1 and R_4.
(c) Add 3 times R_1 to R_3.
(d) Add -7 times R_1 to R_4.
(e) Multiply R_2 by $\frac{1}{2}$.
(f) Add the appropriate multiples of R_2 to R_1, R_3, and R_4.

In Exercises 29–32, determine whether the matrix is in row-echelon form. If it is, determine if it is also in reduced row-echelon form.

29. $\begin{bmatrix} 1 & 0 & 0 & 0 \\ 0 & 1 & 1 & 5 \\ 0 & 0 & 0 & 0 \end{bmatrix}$

30. $\begin{bmatrix} 1 & 3 & 0 & 0 \\ 0 & 0 & 1 & 8 \\ 0 & 0 & 0 & 0 \end{bmatrix}$

31. $\begin{bmatrix} 2 & 0 & 4 & 0 \\ 0 & -1 & 3 & 6 \\ 0 & 0 & 1 & 5 \end{bmatrix}$

32. $\begin{bmatrix} 1 & 0 & 2 & 1 \\ 0 & 1 & -3 & 10 \\ 0 & 0 & 1 & 0 \end{bmatrix}$

In Exercises 33–36, write the matrix in row-echelon form. (Remember that the row-echelon form of a matrix is not unique.)

33. $\begin{bmatrix} 1 & 1 & 0 & 5 \\ -2 & -1 & 2 & -10 \\ 3 & 6 & 7 & 14 \end{bmatrix}$ **34.** $\begin{bmatrix} 1 & 2 & -1 & 3 \\ 3 & 7 & -5 & 14 \\ -2 & -1 & -3 & 8 \end{bmatrix}$

35. $\begin{bmatrix} 1 & -1 & -1 & 1 \\ 5 & -4 & 1 & 8 \\ -6 & 8 & 18 & 0 \end{bmatrix}$ **36.** $\begin{bmatrix} 1 & -3 & 0 & -7 \\ -3 & 10 & 1 & 23 \\ 4 & -10 & 2 & -24 \end{bmatrix}$

In Exercises 37–42, use the matrix capabilities of a graphing utility to write the matrix in *reduced* row-echelon form.

37. $\begin{bmatrix} 3 & 3 & 3 \\ -1 & 0 & -4 \\ 2 & 4 & -2 \end{bmatrix}$ **38.** $\begin{bmatrix} 1 & 3 & 2 \\ 5 & 15 & 9 \\ 2 & 6 & 10 \end{bmatrix}$

39. $\begin{bmatrix} 1 & 2 & 3 & -5 \\ 1 & 2 & 4 & -9 \\ -2 & -4 & -4 & 3 \\ 4 & 8 & 11 & -14 \end{bmatrix}$

40. $\begin{bmatrix} -2 & 3 & -1 & -2 \\ 4 & -2 & 5 & 8 \\ 1 & 5 & -2 & 0 \\ 3 & 8 & -10 & -30 \end{bmatrix}$

41. $\begin{bmatrix} -3 & 5 & 1 & 12 \\ 1 & -1 & 1 & 4 \end{bmatrix}$

42. $\begin{bmatrix} 5 & 1 & 2 & 4 \\ -1 & 5 & 10 & -32 \end{bmatrix}$

In Exercises 43–46, write the system of linear equations represented by the augmented matrix. Then use back-substitution to solve. (Use variables *x*, *y*, and *z*, if applicable.)

43. $\left[\begin{array}{rr|r} 1 & -2 & 4 \\ 0 & 1 & -3 \end{array}\right]$ **44.** $\left[\begin{array}{rr|r} 1 & 5 & 0 \\ 0 & 1 & -1 \end{array}\right]$

45. $\left[\begin{array}{rrr|r} 1 & -1 & 2 & 4 \\ 0 & 1 & -1 & 2 \\ 0 & 0 & 1 & -2 \end{array}\right]$

46. $\left[\begin{array}{rrr|r} 1 & 2 & -2 & -1 \\ 0 & 1 & 1 & 9 \\ 0 & 0 & 1 & -3 \end{array}\right]$

In Exercises 47–50, an augmented matrix that represents a system of linear equations (in variables *x*, *y*, and *z*, if applicable) has been reduced using Gauss-Jordan elimination. Write the solution represented by the augmented matrix.

47. $\begin{bmatrix} 1 & 0 & \vdots & 3 \\ 0 & 1 & \vdots & -4 \end{bmatrix}$

48. $\begin{bmatrix} 1 & 0 & \vdots & -6 \\ 0 & 1 & \vdots & 10 \end{bmatrix}$

49. $\begin{bmatrix} 1 & 0 & 0 & \vdots & -4 \\ 0 & 1 & 0 & \vdots & -10 \\ 0 & 0 & 1 & \vdots & 4 \end{bmatrix}$

50. $\begin{bmatrix} 1 & 0 & 0 & \vdots & 5 \\ 0 & 1 & 0 & \vdots & -3 \\ 0 & 0 & 1 & \vdots & 0 \end{bmatrix}$

In Exercises 51–70, use matrices to solve the system of equations (if possible). Use Gaussian elimination with back-substitution or Gauss-Jordan elimination.

51. $\begin{cases} x + 2y = 7 \\ 2x + y = 8 \end{cases}$

52. $\begin{cases} 2x + 6y = 16 \\ 2x + 3y = 7 \end{cases}$

53. $\begin{cases} 3x - 2y = -27 \\ x + 3y = 13 \end{cases}$

54. $\begin{cases} -x + y = 4 \\ 2x - 4y = -34 \end{cases}$

55. $\begin{cases} -2x + 6y = -22 \\ x + 2y = -9 \end{cases}$

56. $\begin{cases} 5x - 5y = -5 \\ -2x - 3y = 7 \end{cases}$

57. $\begin{cases} -x + 2y = 1.5 \\ 2x - 4y = 3 \end{cases}$

58. $\begin{cases} x - 3y = 5 \\ -2x + 6y = -10 \end{cases}$

59. $\begin{cases} x - 3z = -2 \\ 3x + y - 2z = 5 \\ 2x + 2y + z = 4 \end{cases}$

60. $\begin{cases} 2x - y + 3z = 24 \\ 2y - z = 14 \\ 7x - 5y = 6 \end{cases}$

61. $\begin{cases} -x + y - z = -14 \\ 2x - y + z = 21 \\ 3x + 2y + z = 19 \end{cases}$

62. $\begin{cases} 2x + 2y - z = 2 \\ x - 3y + z = -28 \\ -x + y = 14 \end{cases}$

63. $\begin{cases} x + 2y - 3z = -28 \\ 4y + 2z = 0 \\ -x + y - z = -5 \end{cases}$

64. $\begin{cases} 3x - 2y + z = 15 \\ -x + y + 2z = -10 \\ x - y - 4z = 14 \end{cases}$

65. $\begin{cases} x + y - 5z = 3 \\ x - 2z = 1 \\ 2x - y - z = 0 \end{cases}$

66. $\begin{cases} 2x + 3z = 3 \\ 4x - 3y + 7z = 5 \\ 8x - 9y + 15z = 9 \end{cases}$

67. $\begin{cases} x + 2y + z + 2w = 8 \\ 3x + 7y + 6z + 9w = 26 \end{cases}$

68. $\begin{cases} 4x + 12y - 7z - 20w = 22 \\ 3x + 9y - 5z - 28w = 30 \end{cases}$

69. $\begin{cases} -x + y = -22 \\ 3x + 4y = 4 \\ 4x - 8y = 32 \end{cases}$

70. $\begin{cases} x + 2y = 0 \\ x + y = 6 \\ 3x - 2y = 8 \end{cases}$

In Exercises 71–76, use the matrix capabilities of a graphing utility to reduce the augmented matrix corresponding to the system of equations, and solve the system.

71. $\begin{cases} 3x + 3y + 12z = 6 \\ x + y + 4z = 2 \\ 2x + 5y + 20z = 10 \\ -x + 2y + 8z = 4 \end{cases}$

72. $\begin{cases} 2x + 10y + 2z = 6 \\ x + 5y + 2z = 6 \\ x + 5y + z = 3 \\ -3x - 15y - 3z = -9 \end{cases}$

73. $\begin{cases} 2x + y - z + 2w = -6 \\ 3x + 4y + w = 1 \\ x + 5y + 2z + 6w = -3 \\ 5x + 2y - z - w = 3 \end{cases}$

74. $\begin{cases} x + 2y + 2z + 4w = 11 \\ 3x + 6y + 5z + 12w = 30 \\ x + 3y - 3z + 2w = -5 \\ 6x - y - z + w = -9 \end{cases}$

75. $\begin{cases} x + y + z + w = 0 \\ 2x + 3y + z - 2w = 0 \\ 3x + 5y + z = 0 \end{cases}$

76. $\begin{cases} x + 2y + z + 3w = 0 \\ x - y + w = 0 \\ y - z + 2w = 0 \end{cases}$

In Exercises 77–80, determine whether the two systems of linear equations yield the same solution. If so, find the solution using matrices.

77. (a) $\begin{cases} x - 2y + z = -6 \\ y - 5z = 16 \\ z = -3 \end{cases}$ (b) $\begin{cases} x + y - 2z = 6 \\ y + 3z = -8 \\ z = -3 \end{cases}$

78. (a) $\begin{cases} x - 3y + 4z = -11 \\ y - z = -4 \\ z = 2 \end{cases}$ (b) $\begin{cases} x + 4y = -11 \\ y + 3z = 4 \\ z = 2 \end{cases}$

79. (a) $\begin{cases} x - 4y + 5z = 27 \\ y - 7z = -54 \\ z = 8 \end{cases}$ (b) $\begin{cases} x - 6y + z = 15 \\ y + 5z = 42 \\ z = 8 \end{cases}$

80. (a) $\begin{cases} x + 3y - z = 19 \\ y + 6z = -18 \\ z = -4 \end{cases}$ (b) $\begin{cases} x - y + 3z = -15 \\ y - 2z = 14 \\ z = -4 \end{cases}$

81. Use the system

$$\begin{cases} x + 3y + z = 3 \\ x + 5y + 5z = 1 \\ 2x + 6y + 3z = 8 \end{cases}$$

to write two different matrices in row-echelon form that yield the same solution.

82. ***Electrical Network*** The currents in an electrical network are given by the solution of the system

$$\begin{cases} I_1 - I_2 + I_3 = 0 \\ 3I_1 + 4I_2 \qquad = 18 \\ I_2 + 3I_3 = 6 \end{cases}$$

where I_1, I_2, and I_3 are measured in amperes. Solve the system of equations using matrices.

83. ***Partial Fractions*** Use a system of equations to write the partial fraction decomposition of the rational expression. Solve the system using matrices.

$$\frac{4x^2}{(x+1)^2(x-1)} = \frac{A}{x-1} + \frac{B}{x+1} + \frac{C}{(x+1)^2}$$

84. ***Partial Fractions*** Use a system of equations to write the partial fraction decomposition of the rational expression. Solve the system using matrices.

$$\frac{8x^2}{(x-1)^2(x+1)} = \frac{A}{x+1} + \frac{B}{x-1} + \frac{C}{(x-1)^2}$$

85. ***Finance*** A small shoe corporation borrowed \$1,500,000 to expand its line of shoes. Some of the money was borrowed at 7%, some at 8%, and some at 10%. Use a system of equations to determine how much was borrowed at each rate if the annual interest was \$130,500 and the amount borrowed at 10% was 4 times the amount borrowed at 7%. Solve the system using matrices.

86. ***Finance*** A small software corporation borrowed \$500,000 to expand its software line. Some of the money was borrowed at 9%, some at 10%, and some at 12%. Use a system of equations to determine how much was borrowed at each rate if the annual interest was \$52,000 and the amount borrowed at 10% was $2\frac{1}{2}$ times the amount borrowed at 9%. Solve the system using matrices.

In Exercises 87 and 88, use a system of equations to find the specified equation that passes through the points. Solve the system using matrices. Use a graphing utility to verify your results.

87. Parabola:

$y = ax^2 + bx + c$

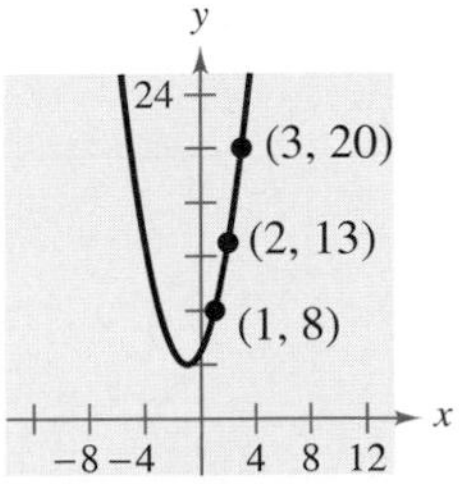

88. Parabola:

$y = ax^2 + bx + c$

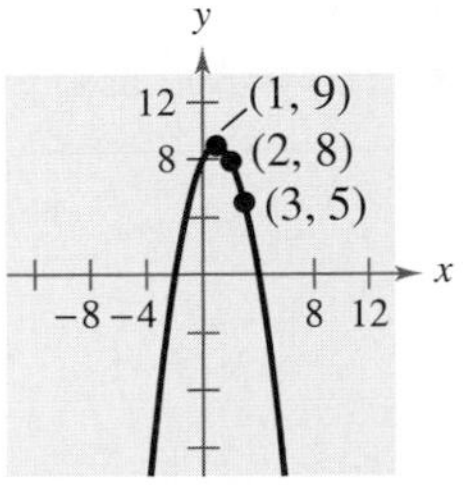

89. ***Mathematical Modeling*** A videotape of the path of a ball thrown by a baseball player was analyzed with a grid covering the TV screen. The tape was paused three times, and the position of the ball was measured each time. The coordinates obtained are shown in the table. (x and y are measured in feet.)

Horizontal distance, x	Height, y
0	5.0
15	9.6
30	12.4

(a) Use a system of equations to find the equation of the parabola $y = ax^2 + bx + c$ that passes through the three points. Solve the system using matrices.

(b) Use a graphing utility to graph the parabola.

(c) Graphically approximate the maximum height of the ball and the point at which the ball struck the ground.

(d) Analytically find the maximum height of the ball and the point at which the ball struck the ground.

(e) Compare your results from parts (c) and (d).

Model It

90. ***Data Analysis: Snowboarders*** The table shows the numbers of people y (in millions) in the United States who participated in snowboarding for selected years from 1997 to 2001. (Source: National Sporting Goods Association)

Year	Number, y
1997	2.8
1999	3.3
2001	5.3

(a) Use a system of equations to find the equation of the parabola $y = at^2 + bt + c$ that passes through the points. Let t represent the year, with $t = 7$ corresponding to 1997. Solve the system using matrices.

(b) Use a graphing utility to graph the parabola.

(c) Use the equation in part (a) to estimate the number of people who participated in snowboarding in 2003. How does this value compare with the actual 2003 value of 6.3 million?

(d) Use the equation in part (a) to estimate y in the year 2008. Is the estimate reasonable? Explain.

Network Analysis **In Exercises 91 and 92, answer the questions about the specified network. (In a network it is assumed that the total flow into each junction is equal to the total flow out of each junction.)**

91. Water flowing through a network of pipes (in thousands of cubic meters per hour) is shown in the figure.

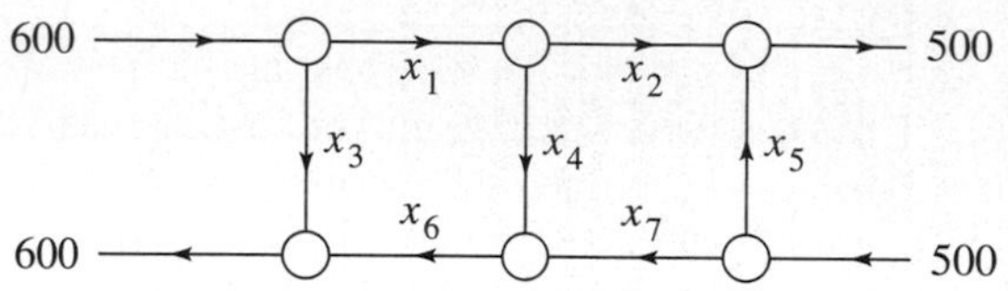

(a) Solve this system using matrices for the water flow represented by x_i, $i = 1, 2, \ldots, 7$.

(b) Find the network flow pattern when $x_6 = 0$ and $x_7 = 0$.

(c) Find the network flow pattern when $x_5 = 1000$ and $x_6 = 0$.

92. The flow of traffic (in vehicles per hour) through a network of streets is shown in the figure.

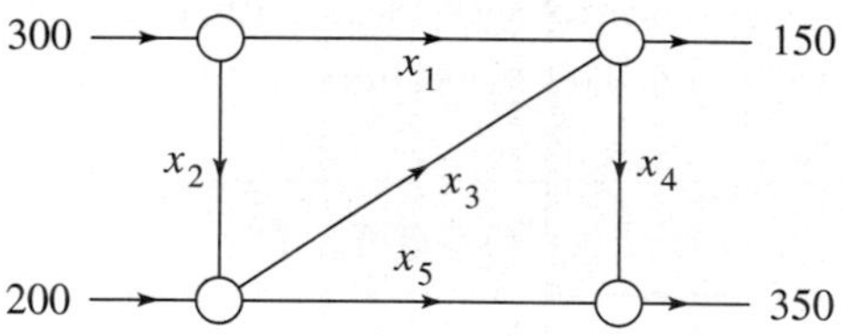

(a) Solve this system using matrices for the traffic flow represented by x_i, $i = 1, 2, \ldots, 5$.

(b) Find the traffic flow when $x_2 = 200$ and $x_3 = 50$.

(c) Find the traffic flow when $x_2 = 150$ and $x_3 = 0$.

Synthesis

True or False? **In Exercises 93–95, determine whether the statement is true or false. Justify your answer.**

93. $\begin{bmatrix} 5 & 0 & -2 & 7 \\ -1 & 3 & -6 & 0 \end{bmatrix}$ is a 4×2 matrix.

94. The matrix

$$\begin{bmatrix} 0 & 0 & 0 & 0 \\ 0 & 0 & 1 & -4 \\ 0 & 1 & 0 & 2 \\ 1 & 0 & 0 & 5 \end{bmatrix}$$

is in reduced row-echelon form.

95. The method of Gaussian elimination reduces a matrix until a reduced row-echelon form is obtained.

96. ***Think About It*** The augmented matrix represents a system of linear equations (in variables x, y, and z) that has been reduced using Gauss-Jordan elimination. Write a system of equations with nonzero coefficients that is represented by the reduced matrix. (There are many correct answers.)

$$\left[\begin{array}{ccc:c} 1 & 0 & 3 & -2 \\ 0 & 1 & 4 & 1 \\ 0 & 0 & 0 & 0 \end{array}\right]$$

97. ***Think About It***

(a) Describe the row-echelon form of an augmented matrix that corresponds to a system of linear equations that is inconsistent.

(b) Describe the row-echelon form of an augmented matrix that corresponds to a system of linear equations that has an infinite number of solutions.

98. Describe the three elementary row operations that can be performed on an augmented matrix.

99. What is the relationship between the three elementary row operations performed on an augmented matrix and the operations that lead to equivalent systems of equations?

100. ***Writing*** In your own words, describe the difference between a matrix in row-echelon form and a matrix in reduced row-echelon form.

Skills Review

In Exercises 101–106, sketch the graph of the function. Do not use a graphing utility.

101. $f(x) = \dfrac{2x^2 - 4x}{3x - x^2}$

102. $f(x) = \dfrac{x^2 - 2x + 1}{x^2 - 1}$

103. $f(x) = 2^{x-1}$

104. $g(x) = 3^{-x+2}$

105. $h(x) = \ln(x - 1)$

106. $f(x) = 3 + \ln x$

8.2 Operations with Matrices

What you should learn

- Decide whether two matrices are equal.
- Add and subtract matrices and multiply matrices by scalars.
- Multiply two matrices.
- Use matrix operations to model and solve real-life problems.

Why you should learn it

Matrix operations can be used to model and solve real-life problems. For instance, in Exercise 70 on page 601, matrix operations are used to analyze annual health care costs.

© Royalty-Free/Corbis

Equality of Matrices

In Section 8.1, you used matrices to solve systems of linear equations. There is a rich mathematical theory of matrices, and its applications are numerous. This section and the next two introduce some fundamentals of matrix theory. It is standard mathematical convention to represent matrices in any of the following three ways.

Representation of Matrices

1. A matrix can be denoted by an uppercase letter such as A, B, or C.
2. A matrix can be denoted by a representative element enclosed in brackets, such as $[a_{ij}]$, $[b_{ij}]$, or $[c_{ij}]$.
3. A matrix can be denoted by a rectangular array of numbers such as

$$A = [a_{ij}] = \begin{bmatrix} a_{11} & a_{12} & a_{13} & \cdots & a_{1n} \\ a_{21} & a_{22} & a_{23} & \cdots & a_{2n} \\ a_{31} & a_{32} & a_{33} & \cdots & a_{3n} \\ \vdots & \vdots & \vdots & & \vdots \\ a_{m1} & a_{m2} & a_{m3} & \cdots & a_{mn} \end{bmatrix}.$$

Two matrices $A = [a_{ij}]$ and $B = [b_{ij}]$ are **equal** if they have the same order $(m \times n)$ and $a_{ij} = b_{ij}$ for $1 \le i \le m$ and $1 \le j \le n$. In other words, two matrices are equal if their corresponding entries are equal.

Example 1 Equality of Matrices

Solve for a_{11}, a_{12}, a_{21}, and a_{22} in the following matrix equation.

$$\begin{bmatrix} a_{11} & a_{12} \\ a_{21} & a_{22} \end{bmatrix} = \begin{bmatrix} 2 & -1 \\ -3 & 0 \end{bmatrix}$$

Solution

Because two matrices are equal only if their corresponding entries are equal, you can conclude that

$$a_{11} = 2, \quad a_{12} = -1, \quad a_{21} = -3, \quad \text{and} \quad a_{22} = 0.$$

✓CHECKPOINT Now try Exercise 1.

Be sure you see that for two matrices to be equal, they must have the same order *and* their corresponding entries must be equal. For instance,

$$\begin{bmatrix} 2 & -1 \\ \sqrt{4} & \frac{1}{2} \end{bmatrix} = \begin{bmatrix} 2 & -1 \\ 2 & 0.5 \end{bmatrix} \quad \text{but} \quad \begin{bmatrix} 2 & -1 \\ 3 & 4 \\ 0 & 0 \end{bmatrix} \neq \begin{bmatrix} 2 & -1 \\ 3 & 4 \end{bmatrix}.$$

Matrix Addition and Scalar Multiplication

In this section, three basic matrix operations will be covered. The first two are matrix addition and scalar multiplication. With matrix addition, you can add two matrices (of the same order) by adding their corresponding entries.

The Granger Collection

Historical Note

Arthur Cayley (1821–1895), a British mathematician, invented matrices around 1858. Cayley was a Cambridge University graduate and a lawyer by profession. His groundbreaking work on matrices was begun as he studied the theory of transformations. Cayley also was instrumental in the development of determinants. Cayley and two American mathematicians, Benjamin Peirce (1809–1880) and his son Charles S. Peirce (1839–1914), are credited with developing "matrix algebra."

Definition of Matrix Addition

If $A = [a_{ij}]$ and $B = [b_{ij}]$ are matrices of order $m \times n$, their sum is the $m \times n$ matrix given by

$$A + B = [a_{ij} + b_{ij}].$$

The sum of two matrices of different orders is undefined.

Example 2 Addition of Matrices

a. $\begin{bmatrix} -1 & 2 \\ 0 & 1 \end{bmatrix} + \begin{bmatrix} 1 & 3 \\ -1 & 2 \end{bmatrix} = \begin{bmatrix} -1+1 & 2+3 \\ 0+(-1) & 1+2 \end{bmatrix}$

$= \begin{bmatrix} 0 & 5 \\ -1 & 3 \end{bmatrix}$

b. $\begin{bmatrix} 0 & 1 & -2 \\ 1 & 2 & 3 \end{bmatrix} + \begin{bmatrix} 0 & 0 & 0 \\ 0 & 0 & 0 \end{bmatrix} = \begin{bmatrix} 0 & 1 & -2 \\ 1 & 2 & 3 \end{bmatrix}$

c. $\begin{bmatrix} 1 \\ -3 \\ -2 \end{bmatrix} + \begin{bmatrix} -1 \\ 3 \\ 2 \end{bmatrix} = \begin{bmatrix} 0 \\ 0 \\ 0 \end{bmatrix}$

d. The sum of

$$A = \begin{bmatrix} 2 & 1 & 0 \\ 4 & 0 & -1 \\ 3 & -2 & 2 \end{bmatrix} \quad \text{and}$$

$$B = \begin{bmatrix} 0 & 1 \\ -1 & 3 \\ 2 & 4 \end{bmatrix}$$

is undefined because A is of order 3×3 and B is of order 3×2.

✓CHECKPOINT Now try Exercise 7(a).

In operations with matrices, numbers are usually referred to as **scalars.** In this text, scalars will always be real numbers. You can multiply a matrix A by a scalar c by multiplying each entry in A by c.

Definition of Scalar Multiplication

If $A = [a_{ij}]$ is an $m \times n$ matrix and c is a scalar, the **scalar multiple** of A by c is the $m \times n$ matrix given by

$$cA = [ca_{ij}].$$

The symbol $-A$ represents the negation of A, which is the scalar product $(-1)A$. Moreover, if A and B are of the same order, then $A - B$ represents the sum of A and $(-1)B$. That is,

$$A - B = A + (-1)B.$$ Subtraction of matrices

The order of operations for matrix expressions is similar to that for real numbers. In particular, you perform scalar multiplication before matrix addition and subtraction, as shown in Example 3(c).

Example 3 Scalar Multiplication and Matrix Subtraction

For the following matrices, find (a) $3A$, (b) $-B$, and (c) $3A - B$.

$$A = \begin{bmatrix} 2 & 2 & 4 \\ -3 & 0 & -1 \\ 2 & 1 & 2 \end{bmatrix} \quad \text{and} \quad B = \begin{bmatrix} 2 & 0 & 0 \\ 1 & -4 & 3 \\ -1 & 3 & 2 \end{bmatrix}$$

Solution

a. $$3A = 3\begin{bmatrix} 2 & 2 & 4 \\ -3 & 0 & -1 \\ 2 & 1 & 2 \end{bmatrix}$$ Scalar multiplication

$$= \begin{bmatrix} 3(2) & 3(2) & 3(4) \\ 3(-3) & 3(0) & 3(-1) \\ 3(2) & 3(1) & 3(2) \end{bmatrix}$$ Multiply each entry by 3.

$$= \begin{bmatrix} 6 & 6 & 12 \\ -9 & 0 & -3 \\ 6 & 3 & 6 \end{bmatrix}$$ Simplify.

b. $$-B = (-1)\begin{bmatrix} 2 & 0 & 0 \\ 1 & -4 & 3 \\ -1 & 3 & 2 \end{bmatrix}$$ Definition of negation

$$= \begin{bmatrix} -2 & 0 & 0 \\ -1 & 4 & -3 \\ 1 & -3 & -2 \end{bmatrix}$$ Multiply each entry by -1.

c. $$3A - B = \begin{bmatrix} 6 & 6 & 12 \\ -9 & 0 & -3 \\ 6 & 3 & 6 \end{bmatrix} - \begin{bmatrix} 2 & 0 & 0 \\ 1 & -4 & 3 \\ -1 & 3 & 2 \end{bmatrix}$$ Matrix subtraction

$$= \begin{bmatrix} 4 & 6 & 12 \\ -10 & 4 & -6 \\ 7 & 0 & 4 \end{bmatrix}$$ Subtract corresponding entries.

✓CHECKPOINT Now try Exercises 7(b), (c), and (d).

It is often convenient to rewrite the scalar multiple cA by factoring c out of every entry in the matrix. For instance, in the following example, the scalar $\frac{1}{2}$ has been factored out of the matrix.

$$\begin{bmatrix} \frac{1}{2} & -\frac{3}{2} \\ \frac{5}{2} & \frac{1}{2} \end{bmatrix} = \begin{bmatrix} \frac{1}{2}(1) & \frac{1}{2}(-3) \\ \frac{1}{2}(5) & \frac{1}{2}(1) \end{bmatrix} = \frac{1}{2}\begin{bmatrix} 1 & -3 \\ 5 & 1 \end{bmatrix}$$

Exploration

Consider matrices A, B, and C below. Perform the indicated operations and compare the results.

$$A = \begin{bmatrix} 3 & -1 \\ 4 & 7 \end{bmatrix}, \quad B = \begin{bmatrix} -2 & 0 \\ 8 & 1 \end{bmatrix},$$

$$C = \begin{bmatrix} 5 & 2 \\ 2 & -6 \end{bmatrix}$$

a. Find $A + B$ and $B + A$.

b. Find $A + B$, then add C to the resulting matrix. Find $B + C$, then add A to the resulting matrix.

c. Find $2A$ and $2B$, then add the two resulting matrices. Find $A + B$, then multiply the resulting matrix by 2.

The properties of matrix addition and scalar multiplication are similar to those of addition and multiplication of real numbers.

Properties of Matrix Addition and Scalar Multiplication

Let A, B, and C be $m \times n$ matrices and let c and d be scalars.

1. $A + B = B + A$ — Commutative Property of Matrix Addition
2. $A + (B + C) = (A + B) + C$ — Associative Property of Matrix Addition
3. $(cd)A = c(dA)$ — Associative Property of Scalar Multiplication
4. $1A = A$ — Scalar Identity Property
5. $c(A + B) = cA + cB$ — Distributive Property
6. $(c + d)A = cA + dA$ — Distributive Property

Note that the Associative Property of Matrix Addition allows you to write expressions such as $A + B + C$ without ambiguity because the same sum occurs no matter how the matrices are grouped. This same reasoning applies to sums of four or more matrices.

Example 4 Addition of More than Two Matrices

By adding corresponding entries, you obtain the following sum of four matrices.

$$\begin{bmatrix} 1 \\ 2 \\ -3 \end{bmatrix} + \begin{bmatrix} -1 \\ -1 \\ 2 \end{bmatrix} + \begin{bmatrix} 0 \\ 1 \\ 4 \end{bmatrix} + \begin{bmatrix} 2 \\ -3 \\ -2 \end{bmatrix} = \begin{bmatrix} 2 \\ -1 \\ 1 \end{bmatrix}$$

CHECKPOINT Now try Exercise 13.

Example 5 Using the Distributive Property

Perform the indicated matrix operations.

$$3\left(\begin{bmatrix} -2 & 0 \\ 4 & 1 \end{bmatrix} + \begin{bmatrix} 4 & -2 \\ 3 & 7 \end{bmatrix}\right)$$

Solution

$$3\left(\begin{bmatrix} -2 & 0 \\ 4 & 1 \end{bmatrix} + \begin{bmatrix} 4 & -2 \\ 3 & 7 \end{bmatrix}\right) = 3\begin{bmatrix} -2 & 0 \\ 4 & 1 \end{bmatrix} + 3\begin{bmatrix} 4 & -2 \\ 3 & 7 \end{bmatrix}$$

$$= \begin{bmatrix} -6 & 0 \\ 12 & 3 \end{bmatrix} + \begin{bmatrix} 12 & -6 \\ 9 & 21 \end{bmatrix}$$

$$= \begin{bmatrix} 6 & -6 \\ 21 & 24 \end{bmatrix}$$

CHECKPOINT Now try Exercise 15.

In Example 5, you could add the two matrices first and then multiply the matrix by 3, as follows. Notice that you obtain the same result.

$$3\left(\begin{bmatrix} -2 & 0 \\ 4 & 1 \end{bmatrix} + \begin{bmatrix} 4 & -2 \\ 3 & 7 \end{bmatrix}\right) = 3\begin{bmatrix} 2 & -2 \\ 7 & 8 \end{bmatrix} = \begin{bmatrix} 6 & -6 \\ 21 & 24 \end{bmatrix}$$

Technology

Most graphing utilities have the capability of performing matrix operations. Consult the user's guide for your graphing utility for specific keystrokes. Try using a graphing utility to find the sum of the matrices

$$A = \begin{bmatrix} 2 & -3 \\ -1 & 0 \end{bmatrix}$$

and

$$B = \begin{bmatrix} -1 & 4 \\ 2 & -5 \end{bmatrix}.$$

One important property of addition of real numbers is that the number 0 is the additive identity. That is, $c + 0 = c$ for any real number c. For matrices, a similar property holds. That is, if A is an $m \times n$ matrix and O is the $m \times n$ **zero matrix** consisting entirely of zeros, then $A + O = A$.

In other words, O is the **additive identity** for the set of all $m \times n$ matrices. For example, the following matrices are the additive identities for the set of all 2×3 and 2×2 matrices.

$$\underbrace{O = \begin{bmatrix} 0 & 0 & 0 \\ 0 & 0 & 0 \end{bmatrix}}_{2 \times 3 \text{ zero matrix}} \quad \text{and} \quad \underbrace{O = \begin{bmatrix} 0 & 0 \\ 0 & 0 \end{bmatrix}}_{2 \times 2 \text{ zero matrix}}$$

The algebra of real numbers and the algebra of matrices have many similarities. For example, compare the following solutions.

STUDY TIP

Remember that matrices are denoted by capital letters. So, when you solve for X, you are solving for a *matrix* that makes the matrix equation true.

Real Numbers (Solve for x.)	*m × n Matrices (Solve for X.)*
$x + a = b$	$X + A = B$
$x + a + (-a) = b + (-a)$	$X + A + (-A) = B + (-A)$
$x + 0 = b - a$	$X + O = B - A$
$x = b - a$	$X = B - A$

The algebra of real numbers and the algebra of matrices also have important differences, which will be discussed later.

Example 6 Solving a Matrix Equation

Solve for X in the equation $3X + A = B$, where

$$A = \begin{bmatrix} 1 & -2 \\ 0 & 3 \end{bmatrix} \quad \text{and} \quad B = \begin{bmatrix} -3 & 4 \\ 2 & 1 \end{bmatrix}.$$

Solution

Begin by solving the equation for X to obtain

$$3X = B - A$$

$$X = \frac{1}{3}(B - A).$$

Now, using the matrices A and B, you have

$$X = \frac{1}{3}\left(\begin{bmatrix} -3 & 4 \\ 2 & 1 \end{bmatrix} - \begin{bmatrix} 1 & -2 \\ 0 & 3 \end{bmatrix}\right) \qquad \text{Substitute the matrices.}$$

$$= \frac{1}{3}\begin{bmatrix} -4 & 6 \\ 2 & -2 \end{bmatrix} \qquad \text{Subtract matrix } A \text{ from matrix } B.$$

$$= \begin{bmatrix} -\frac{4}{3} & 2 \\ \frac{2}{3} & -\frac{2}{3} \end{bmatrix}. \qquad \text{Multiply the matrix by } \tfrac{1}{3}.$$

CHECKPOINT Now try Exercise 25.

Matrix Multiplication

The third basic matrix operation is **matrix multiplication.** At first glance, the definition may seem unusual. You will see later, however, that this definition of the product of two matrices has many practical applications.

Definition of Matrix Multiplication

If $A = [a_{ij}]$ is an $m \times n$ matrix and $B = [b_{ij}]$ is an $n \times p$ matrix, the product AB is an $m \times p$ matrix

$$AB = [c_{ij}]$$

where $c_{ij} = a_{i1}b_{1j} + a_{i2}b_{2j} + a_{i3}b_{3j} + \cdot \cdot \cdot + a_{in}b_{nj}$.

The definition of matrix multiplication indicates a *row-by-column* multiplication, where the entry in the ith row and jth column of the product AB is obtained by multiplying the entries in the ith row of A by the corresponding entries in the jth column of B and then adding the results. The general pattern for matrix multiplication is as follows.

$$\begin{bmatrix} a_{11} & a_{12} & a_{13} & \cdots & a_{1n} \\ a_{21} & a_{22} & a_{23} & \cdots & a_{2n} \\ a_{31} & a_{32} & a_{33} & \cdots & a_{3n} \\ \vdots & \vdots & \vdots & & \vdots \\ a_{i1} & a_{i2} & a_{i3} & \cdots & a_{in} \\ \vdots & \vdots & \vdots & & \vdots \\ a_{m1} & a_{m2} & a_{m3} & \cdots & a_{mn} \end{bmatrix} \begin{bmatrix} b_{11} & b_{12} & \cdots & b_{1j} & \cdots & b_{1p} \\ b_{21} & b_{22} & \cdots & b_{2j} & \cdots & b_{2p} \\ b_{31} & b_{32} & \cdots & b_{3j} & \cdots & b_{3p} \\ \vdots & \vdots & & \vdots & & \vdots \\ b_{n1} & b_{n2} & \cdots & b_{nj} & \cdots & b_{np} \end{bmatrix} = \begin{bmatrix} c_{11} & c_{12} & \cdots & c_{1j} & \cdots & c_{1p} \\ c_{21} & c_{22} & \cdots & c_{2j} & \cdots & c_{2p} \\ \vdots & \vdots & & \vdots & & \vdots \\ c_{i1} & c_{i2} & \cdots & c_{ij} & \cdots & c_{ip} \\ \vdots & \vdots & & \vdots & & \vdots \\ c_{m1} & c_{m2} & \cdots & c_{mj} & \cdots & c_{mp} \end{bmatrix}$$

$$a_{i1}b_{1j} + a_{i2}b_{2j} + a_{i3}b_{3j} + \cdot \cdot \cdot + a_{in}b_{nj} = c_{ij}$$

Example 7 **Finding the Product of Two Matrices**

First, note that the product AB is defined because the number of columns of A is equal to the number of rows of B. Moreover, the product AB has order 3×2. To find the entries of the product, multiply each row of A by each column of B, as follows.

$$AB = \begin{bmatrix} -1 & 3 \\ 4 & -2 \\ 5 & 0 \end{bmatrix} \begin{bmatrix} -3 & 2 \\ -4 & 1 \end{bmatrix}$$

$$= \begin{bmatrix} (-1)(-3) + (3)(-4) & (-1)(2) + (3)(1) \\ (4)(-3) + (-2)(-4) & (4)(2) + (-2)(1) \\ (5)(-3) + (0)(-4) & (5)(2) + (0)(1) \end{bmatrix}$$

$$= \begin{bmatrix} -9 & 1 \\ -4 & 6 \\ -15 & 10 \end{bmatrix}$$

CHECKPOINT Now try Exercise 29.

Be sure you understand that for the product of two matrices to be defined, the number of *columns* of the first matrix must equal the number of *rows* of the second matrix. That is, the middle two indices must be the same. The outside two indices give the order of the product, as shown below.

$$\underset{m \times n}{A} \quad \times \quad \underset{n \times p}{B} \quad = \quad \underset{m \times p}{AB}$$

Equal (the middle indices n and n)

Order of AB (the outside indices m and p)

Example 8 Finding the Product of Two Matrices

Find the product AB where

$$A = \begin{bmatrix} 1 & 0 & 3 \\ 2 & -1 & -2 \end{bmatrix} \quad \text{and} \quad B = \begin{bmatrix} -2 & 4 \\ 1 & 0 \\ -1 & 1 \end{bmatrix}.$$

Solution

Note that the order of A is 2×3 and the order of B is 3×2. So, the product AB has order 2×2.

$$AB = \begin{bmatrix} 1 & 0 & 3 \\ 2 & -1 & -2 \end{bmatrix}\begin{bmatrix} -2 & 4 \\ 1 & 0 \\ -1 & 1 \end{bmatrix}$$

$$= \begin{bmatrix} 1(-2) + 0(1) + 3(-1) & 1(4) + 0(0) + 3(1) \\ 2(-2) + (-1)(1) + (-2)(-1) & 2(4) + (-1)(0) + (-2)(1) \end{bmatrix}$$

$$= \begin{bmatrix} -5 & 7 \\ -3 & 6 \end{bmatrix}$$

CHECKPOINT Now try Exercise 31.

Example 9 Patterns in Matrix Multiplication

a. $$\underset{2 \times 2}{\begin{bmatrix} 3 & 4 \\ -2 & 5 \end{bmatrix}}\underset{2 \times 2}{\begin{bmatrix} 1 & 0 \\ 0 & 1 \end{bmatrix}} = \underset{2 \times 2}{\begin{bmatrix} 3 & 4 \\ -2 & 5 \end{bmatrix}}$$

b. $$\underset{3 \times 3}{\begin{bmatrix} 6 & 2 & 0 \\ 3 & -1 & 2 \\ 1 & 4 & 6 \end{bmatrix}}\underset{3 \times 1}{\begin{bmatrix} 1 \\ 2 \\ -3 \end{bmatrix}} = \underset{3 \times 1}{\begin{bmatrix} 10 \\ -5 \\ -9 \end{bmatrix}}$$

c. The product AB for the following matrices is not defined.

$$\underset{3 \times 2}{A = \begin{bmatrix} -2 & 1 \\ 1 & -3 \\ 1 & 4 \end{bmatrix}} \quad \text{and} \quad \underset{3 \times 4}{B = \begin{bmatrix} -2 & 3 & 1 & 4 \\ 0 & 1 & -1 & 2 \\ 2 & -1 & 0 & 1 \end{bmatrix}}$$

CHECKPOINT Now try Exercise 33.

Exploration

Use the following matrices to find AB, BA, $(AB)C$, and $A(BC)$. What do your results tell you about matrix multiplication, commutativity, and associativity?

$$A = \begin{bmatrix} 1 & 2 \\ 3 & 4 \end{bmatrix}, \quad B = \begin{bmatrix} 0 & 1 \\ 2 & 3 \end{bmatrix}, \quad C = \begin{bmatrix} 3 & 0 \\ 0 & 1 \end{bmatrix}$$

Example 10 **Patterns in Matrix Multiplication**

a. $\begin{bmatrix} 1 & -2 & -3 \end{bmatrix}\begin{bmatrix} 2 \\ -1 \\ 1 \end{bmatrix} = \begin{bmatrix} 1 \end{bmatrix}$ **b.** $\begin{bmatrix} 2 \\ -1 \\ 1 \end{bmatrix}\begin{bmatrix} 1 & -2 & -3 \end{bmatrix} = \begin{bmatrix} 2 & -4 & -6 \\ -1 & 2 & 3 \\ 1 & -2 & -3 \end{bmatrix}$

1×3 3×1 1×1 3×1 1×3 3×3

✓CHECKPOINT Now try Exercise 45.

In Example 10, note that the two products are different. Even if AB and BA are defined, matrix multiplication is not, in general, commutative. That is, for most matrices, $AB \neq BA$. This is one way in which the algebra of real numbers and the algebra of matrices differ.

Properties of Matrix Multiplication

Let A, B, and C be matrices and let c be a scalar.

1. $A(BC) = (AB)C$ Associative Property of Multiplication
2. $A(B + C) = AB + AC$ Distributive Property
3. $(A + B)C = AC + BC$ Distributive Property
4. $c(AB) = (cA)B = A(cB)$ Associative Property of Scalar Multiplication

Definition of Identity Matrix

The $n \times n$ matrix that consists of 1's on its main diagonal and 0's elsewhere is called the **identity matrix of order n** and is denoted by

$$I_n = \begin{bmatrix} 1 & 0 & 0 & \cdots & 0 \\ 0 & 1 & 0 & \cdots & 0 \\ 0 & 0 & 1 & \cdots & 0 \\ \vdots & \vdots & \vdots & & \vdots \\ 0 & 0 & 0 & \cdots & 1 \end{bmatrix}. \quad \text{Identity matrix}$$

Note that an identity matrix must be *square*. When the order is understood to be n, you can denote I_n simply by I.

If A is an $n \times n$ matrix, the identity matrix has the property that $AI_n = A$ and $I_nA = A$. For example,

$$\begin{bmatrix} 3 & -2 & 5 \\ 1 & 0 & 4 \\ -1 & 2 & -3 \end{bmatrix}\begin{bmatrix} 1 & 0 & 0 \\ 0 & 1 & 0 \\ 0 & 0 & 1 \end{bmatrix} = \begin{bmatrix} 3 & -2 & 5 \\ 1 & 0 & 4 \\ -1 & 2 & -3 \end{bmatrix} \quad AI = A$$

and

$$\begin{bmatrix} 1 & 0 & 0 \\ 0 & 1 & 0 \\ 0 & 0 & 1 \end{bmatrix}\begin{bmatrix} 3 & -2 & 5 \\ 1 & 0 & 4 \\ -1 & 2 & -3 \end{bmatrix} = \begin{bmatrix} 3 & -2 & 5 \\ 1 & 0 & 4 \\ -1 & 2 & -3 \end{bmatrix}. \quad IA = A$$

Applications

Matrix multiplication can be used to represent a system of linear equations. Note how the system

$$\begin{cases} a_{11}x_1 + a_{12}x_2 + a_{13}x_3 = b_1 \\ a_{21}x_1 + a_{22}x_2 + a_{23}x_3 = b_2 \\ a_{31}x_1 + a_{32}x_2 + a_{33}x_3 = b_3 \end{cases}$$

can be written as the matrix equation $AX = B$, where A is the *coefficient matrix* of the system, and X and B are column matrices.

$$\underbrace{\begin{bmatrix} a_{11} & a_{12} & a_{13} \\ a_{21} & a_{22} & a_{23} \\ a_{31} & a_{32} & a_{33} \end{bmatrix}}_{A} \times \underbrace{\begin{bmatrix} x_1 \\ x_2 \\ x_3 \end{bmatrix}}_{X} = \underbrace{\begin{bmatrix} b_1 \\ b_2 \\ b_3 \end{bmatrix}}_{B}$$

Example 11 **Solving a System of Linear Equations**

Consider the following system of linear equations.

$$\begin{cases} x_1 - 2x_2 + x_3 = -4 \\ \quad\quad x_2 + 2x_3 = 4 \\ 2x_1 + 3x_2 - 2x_3 = 2 \end{cases}$$

a. Write this system as a matrix equation, $AX = B$.

b. Use Gauss-Jordan elimination on the augmented matrix $[A \vdots B]$ to solve for the matrix X.

> **STUDY TIP**
>
> The notation $[A \vdots B]$ represents the augmented matrix formed when matrix B is adjoined to matrix A. The notation $[I \vdots X]$ represents the reduced row-echelon form of the augmented matrix that yields the *solution* to the system.

Solution

a. In matrix form, $AX = B$, the system can be written as follows.

$$\begin{bmatrix} 1 & -2 & 1 \\ 0 & 1 & 2 \\ 2 & 3 & -2 \end{bmatrix} \begin{bmatrix} x_1 \\ x_2 \\ x_3 \end{bmatrix} = \begin{bmatrix} -4 \\ 4 \\ 2 \end{bmatrix}$$

b. The augmented matrix is formed by adjoining matrix B to matrix A.

$$[A \vdots B] = \left[\begin{array}{ccc:c} 1 & -2 & 1 & -4 \\ 0 & 1 & 2 & 4 \\ 2 & 3 & -2 & 2 \end{array}\right]$$

Using Gauss-Jordan elimination, you can rewrite this equation as

$$[I \vdots X] = \left[\begin{array}{ccc:c} 1 & 0 & 0 & -1 \\ 0 & 1 & 0 & 2 \\ 0 & 0 & 1 & 1 \end{array}\right].$$

So, the solution of the system of linear equations is $x_1 = -1$, $x_2 = 2$, and $x_3 = 1$, and the solution of the matrix equation is

$$X = \begin{bmatrix} x_1 \\ x_2 \\ x_3 \end{bmatrix} = \begin{bmatrix} -1 \\ 2 \\ 1 \end{bmatrix}.$$

CHECKPOINT Now try Exercise 55.

Example 12 Softball Team Expenses

Two softball teams submit equipment lists to their sponsors.

	Women's Team	*Men's Team*
Bats	12	15
Balls	45	38
Gloves	15	17

Each bat costs \$80, each ball costs \$6, and each glove costs \$60. Use matrices to find the total cost of equipment for each team.

Solution

The equipment lists E and the costs per item C can be written in matrix form as

$$E = \begin{bmatrix} 12 & 15 \\ 45 & 38 \\ 15 & 17 \end{bmatrix}$$

and

$$C = \begin{bmatrix} 80 & 6 & 60 \end{bmatrix}.$$

The total cost of equipment for each team is given by the product

$$\begin{aligned} CE &= \begin{bmatrix} 80 & 6 & 60 \end{bmatrix} \begin{bmatrix} 12 & 15 \\ 45 & 38 \\ 15 & 17 \end{bmatrix} \\ &= \begin{bmatrix} 80(12) + 6(45) + 60(15) & 80(15) + 6(38) + 60(17) \end{bmatrix} \\ &= \begin{bmatrix} 2130 & 2448 \end{bmatrix}. \end{aligned}$$

So, the total cost of equipment for the women's team is \$2130 and the total cost of equipment for the men's team is \$2448. Notice that you cannot find the total cost using the product EC because EC is not defined. That is, the number of columns of E (2 columns) does not equal the number of rows of C (1 row).

✓CHECKPOINT Now try Exercise 63.

WRITING ABOUT MATHEMATICS

Problem Posing Write a matrix multiplication application problem that uses the matrix

$$A = \begin{bmatrix} 20 & 42 & 33 \\ 17 & 30 & 50 \end{bmatrix}.$$

Exchange problems with another student in your class. Form the matrices that represent the problem, and solve the problem. Interpret your solution in the context of the problem. Check with the creator of the problem to see if you are correct. Discuss other ways to represent and/or approach the problem.

8.2 Exercises

VOCABULARY CHECK:

In Exercises 1–4, fill in the blanks.

1. Two matrices are ________ if all of their corresponding entries are equal.
2. When performing matrix operations, real numbers are often referred to as ________.
3. A matrix consisting entirely of zeros is called a ________ matrix and is denoted by ________.
4. The $n \times n$ matrix consisting of 1's on its main diagonal and 0's elsewhere is called the ________ matrix of order n.

In Exercises 5 and 6, match the matrix property with the correct form. *A*, *B*, and *C* are matrices of order $m \times n$, and *c* and *d* are scalars.

5. (a) $1A = A$ — (i) Distributive Property
   (b) $A + (B + C) = (A + B) + C$ — (ii) Commutative Property of Matrix Addition
   (c) $(c + d)A = cA + dA$ — (iii) Scalar Identity Property
   (d) $(cd)A = c(dA)$ — (iv) Associative Property of Matrix Addition
   (e) $A + B = B + A$ — (v) Associative Property of Scalar Multiplication
6. (a) $A + O = A$ — (i) Distributive Property
   (b) $c(AB) = A(cB)$ — (ii) Additive Identity of Matrix Addition
   (c) $A(B + C) = AB + AC$ — (iii) Associative Property of Multiplication
   (d) $A(BC) = (AB)C$ — (iv) Associative Property of Scalar Multiplication

---

In Exercises 1–4, find *x* and *y*.

1. $\begin{bmatrix} x & -2 \\ 7 & y \end{bmatrix} = \begin{bmatrix} -4 & -2 \\ 7 & 22 \end{bmatrix}$

2. $\begin{bmatrix} -5 & x \\ y & 8 \end{bmatrix} = \begin{bmatrix} -5 & 13 \\ 12 & 8 \end{bmatrix}$

3. $\begin{bmatrix} 16 & 4 & 5 & 4 \\ -3 & 13 & 15 & 6 \\ 0 & 2 & 4 & 0 \end{bmatrix} = \begin{bmatrix} 16 & 4 & 2x+1 & 4 \\ -3 & 13 & 15 & 3x \\ 0 & 2 & 3y-5 & 0 \end{bmatrix}$

4. $\begin{bmatrix} x+2 & 8 & -3 \\ 1 & 2y & 2x \\ 7 & -2 & y+2 \end{bmatrix} = \begin{bmatrix} 2x+6 & 8 & -3 \\ 1 & 18 & -8 \\ 7 & -2 & 11 \end{bmatrix}$

In Exercises 5–12, if possible, find (a) *A* + *B*, (b) *A* − *B*, (c) 3*A*, and (d) 3*A* − 2*B*.

5. $A = \begin{bmatrix} 1 & -1 \\ 2 & -1 \end{bmatrix}, \quad B = \begin{bmatrix} 2 & -1 \\ -1 & 8 \end{bmatrix}$

6. $A = \begin{bmatrix} 1 & 2 \\ 2 & 1 \end{bmatrix}, \quad B = \begin{bmatrix} -3 & -2 \\ 4 & 2 \end{bmatrix}$

7. $A = \begin{bmatrix} 6 & -1 \\ 2 & 4 \\ -3 & 5 \end{bmatrix}, \quad B = \begin{bmatrix} 1 & 4 \\ -1 & 5 \\ 1 & 10 \end{bmatrix}$

8. $A = \begin{bmatrix} 2 & 1 & 1 \\ -1 & -1 & 4 \end{bmatrix}, \quad B = \begin{bmatrix} 2 & -3 & 4 \\ -3 & 1 & -2 \end{bmatrix}$

9. $A = \begin{bmatrix} 2 & 2 & -1 & 0 & 1 \\ 1 & 1 & -2 & 0 & -1 \end{bmatrix},$
   $B = \begin{bmatrix} 1 & 1 & -1 & 1 & 0 \\ -3 & 4 & 9 & -6 & -7 \end{bmatrix}$

10. $A = \begin{bmatrix} -1 & 4 & 0 \\ 3 & -2 & 2 \\ 5 & 4 & -1 \\ 0 & 8 & -6 \\ -4 & -1 & 0 \end{bmatrix}, \quad B = \begin{bmatrix} -3 & 5 & 1 \\ 2 & -4 & -7 \\ 10 & -9 & -1 \\ 3 & 2 & -4 \\ 0 & 1 & -2 \end{bmatrix}$

11. $A = \begin{bmatrix} 6 & 0 & 3 \\ -1 & -4 & 0 \end{bmatrix}, \quad B = \begin{bmatrix} 8 & -1 \\ 4 & -3 \end{bmatrix}$

12. $A = \begin{bmatrix} 3 \\ 2 \\ -1 \end{bmatrix}, \quad B = \begin{bmatrix} -4 & 6 & 2 \end{bmatrix}$

In Exercises 13–18, evaluate the expression.

13. $\begin{bmatrix} -5 & 0 \\ 3 & -6 \end{bmatrix} + \begin{bmatrix} 7 & 1 \\ -2 & -1 \end{bmatrix} + \begin{bmatrix} -10 & -8 \\ 14 & 6 \end{bmatrix}$

14. $\begin{bmatrix} 6 & 8 \\ -1 & 0 \end{bmatrix} + \begin{bmatrix} 0 & 5 \\ -3 & -1 \end{bmatrix} + \begin{bmatrix} -11 & -7 \\ 2 & -1 \end{bmatrix}$

15. $4\left(\begin{bmatrix} -4 & 0 & 1 \\ 0 & 2 & 3 \end{bmatrix} - \begin{bmatrix} 2 & 1 & -2 \\ 3 & -6 & 0 \end{bmatrix}\right)$

16. $\frac{1}{2}([5 \quad -2 \quad 4 \quad 0] + [14 \quad 6 \quad -18 \quad 9])$

17. $-3\left(\begin{bmatrix} 0 & -3 \\ 7 & 2 \end{bmatrix} + \begin{bmatrix} -6 & 3 \\ 8 & 1 \end{bmatrix}\right) - 2\begin{bmatrix} 4 & -4 \\ 7 & -9 \end{bmatrix}$

18. $-1\begin{bmatrix} 4 & 11 \\ -2 & -1 \\ 9 & 3 \end{bmatrix} + \frac{1}{6}\left(\begin{bmatrix} -5 & -1 \\ 3 & 4 \\ 0 & 13 \end{bmatrix} + \begin{bmatrix} 7 & 5 \\ -9 & -1 \\ 6 & -1 \end{bmatrix}\right)$

In Exercises 19–22, use the matrix capabilities of a graphing utility to evaluate the expression. Round your results to three decimal places, if necessary.

19. $\frac{3}{7}\begin{bmatrix} 2 & 5 \\ -1 & -4 \end{bmatrix} + 6\begin{bmatrix} -3 & 0 \\ 2 & 2 \end{bmatrix}$

20. $55\left(\begin{bmatrix} 14 & -11 \\ -22 & 19 \end{bmatrix} + \begin{bmatrix} -22 & 20 \\ 13 & 6 \end{bmatrix}\right)$

21. $-\begin{bmatrix} 3.211 & 6.829 \\ -1.004 & 4.914 \\ 0.055 & -3.889 \end{bmatrix} - \begin{bmatrix} -1.630 & -3.090 \\ 5.256 & 8.335 \\ -9.768 & 4.251 \end{bmatrix}$

22. $-12\left(\begin{bmatrix} 6 & 20 \\ 1 & -9 \\ -2 & 5 \end{bmatrix} + \begin{bmatrix} 14 & -15 \\ -8 & -6 \\ 7 & 0 \end{bmatrix} + \begin{bmatrix} -31 & -19 \\ 16 & 10 \\ 24 & -10 \end{bmatrix}\right)$

In Exercises 23–26, solve fo *X* in the equation, given

$$A = \begin{bmatrix} -2 & -1 \\ 1 & 0 \\ 3 & -4 \end{bmatrix} \quad \text{and} \quad B = \begin{bmatrix} 0 & 3 \\ 2 & 0 \\ -4 & -1 \end{bmatrix}.$$

23. $X = 3A - 2B$

24. $2X = 2A - B$

25. $2X + 3A = B$

26. $2A + 4B = -2X$

In Exercises 27–34, if possible, find *AB* and state the order of the result.

27. $A = \begin{bmatrix} 2 & 1 \\ -3 & 4 \\ 1 & 6 \end{bmatrix}, \quad B = \begin{bmatrix} 0 & -1 & 0 \\ 4 & 0 & 2 \\ 8 & -1 & 7 \end{bmatrix}$

28. $A = \begin{bmatrix} 1 & 0 & 3 & -2 \\ 6 & 13 & 8 & -17 \end{bmatrix}, \quad B = \begin{bmatrix} 1 & 6 \\ 4 & 2 \end{bmatrix}$

29. $A = \begin{bmatrix} 0 & -1 & 0 \\ 4 & 0 & 2 \\ 8 & -1 & 7 \end{bmatrix}, \quad B = \begin{bmatrix} 2 & 1 \\ -3 & 4 \\ 1 & 6 \end{bmatrix}$

30. $A = \begin{bmatrix} -1 & 3 \\ 4 & -5 \\ 0 & 2 \end{bmatrix}, \quad B = \begin{bmatrix} 1 & 2 \\ 0 & 7 \end{bmatrix}$

31. $A = \begin{bmatrix} 1 & 0 & 0 \\ 0 & 4 & 0 \\ 0 & 0 & -2 \end{bmatrix}, \quad B = \begin{bmatrix} 3 & 0 & 0 \\ 0 & -1 & 0 \\ 0 & 0 & 5 \end{bmatrix}$

32. $A = \begin{bmatrix} 5 & 0 & 0 \\ 0 & -8 & 0 \\ 0 & 0 & 7 \end{bmatrix}, \quad B = \begin{bmatrix} \frac{1}{5} & 0 & 0 \\ 0 & -\frac{1}{8} & 0 \\ 0 & 0 & \frac{1}{2} \end{bmatrix}$

33. $A = \begin{bmatrix} 0 & 0 & 5 \\ 0 & 0 & -3 \\ 0 & 0 & 4 \end{bmatrix}, \quad B = \begin{bmatrix} 6 & -11 & 4 \\ 8 & 16 & 4 \\ 0 & 0 & 0 \end{bmatrix}$

34. $A = \begin{bmatrix} 10 \\ 12 \end{bmatrix}, \quad B = [6 \quad -2 \quad 1 \quad 6]$

In Exercises 35–40, use the matrix capabilities of a graphing utility to find *AB*, if possible.

35. $A = \begin{bmatrix} 5 & 6 & -3 \\ -2 & 5 & 1 \\ 10 & -5 & 5 \end{bmatrix}, \quad B = \begin{bmatrix} 1 & -1 & 2 \\ 8 & 1 & 4 \\ 4 & -2 & 9 \end{bmatrix}$

36. $A = \begin{bmatrix} 11 & -12 & 4 \\ 14 & 10 & 12 \\ 6 & -2 & 9 \end{bmatrix}, \quad B = \begin{bmatrix} 12 & 10 \\ -5 & 12 \\ 15 & 16 \end{bmatrix}$

37. $A = \begin{bmatrix} -3 & 8 & -6 & 8 \\ -12 & 15 & 9 & 6 \\ 5 & -1 & 1 & 5 \end{bmatrix}, \quad B = \begin{bmatrix} 3 & 1 & 6 \\ 24 & 15 & 14 \\ 16 & 10 & 21 \\ 8 & -4 & 10 \end{bmatrix}$

38. $A = \begin{bmatrix} -2 & 4 & 8 \\ 21 & 5 & 6 \\ 13 & 2 & 6 \end{bmatrix}, \quad B = \begin{bmatrix} 2 & 0 \\ -7 & 15 \\ 32 & 14 \\ 0.5 & 1.6 \end{bmatrix}$

39. $A = \begin{bmatrix} 9 & 10 & -38 & 18 \\ 100 & -50 & 250 & 75 \end{bmatrix},$

$B = \begin{bmatrix} 52 & -85 & 27 & 45 \\ 40 & -35 & 60 & 82 \end{bmatrix}$

40. $A = \begin{bmatrix} 15 & -18 \\ -4 & 12 \\ -8 & 22 \end{bmatrix}, \quad B = \begin{bmatrix} -7 & 22 & 1 \\ 8 & 16 & 24 \end{bmatrix}$

In Exercises 41–46, if possible, find (a) *AB*, (b) *BA*, and (c) A^2. (*Note:* $A^2 = AA$.)

41. $A = \begin{bmatrix} 1 & 2 \\ 4 & 2 \end{bmatrix}, \quad B = \begin{bmatrix} 2 & -1 \\ -1 & 8 \end{bmatrix}$

42. $A = \begin{bmatrix} 2 & -1 \\ 1 & 4 \end{bmatrix}, \quad B = \begin{bmatrix} 0 & 0 \\ 3 & -3 \end{bmatrix}$

43. $A = \begin{bmatrix} 3 & -1 \\ 1 & 3 \end{bmatrix}, \quad B = \begin{bmatrix} 1 & -3 \\ 3 & 1 \end{bmatrix}$

44. $A = \begin{bmatrix} 1 & -1 \\ 1 & 1 \end{bmatrix}, \quad B = \begin{bmatrix} 1 & 3 \\ -3 & 1 \end{bmatrix}$

45. $A = \begin{bmatrix} 7 \\ 8 \\ -1 \end{bmatrix}, \quad B = [1 \quad 1 \quad 2]$

46. $A = [3 \quad 2 \quad 1], \quad B = \begin{bmatrix} 2 \\ 3 \\ 0 \end{bmatrix}$

In Exercises 47–50, evaluate the expression. Use the matrix capabilities of a graphing utility to verify your answer.

47. $\begin{bmatrix} 3 & 1 \\ 0 & -2 \end{bmatrix}\begin{bmatrix} 1 & 0 \\ -2 & 2 \end{bmatrix}\begin{bmatrix} 1 & 0 \\ 2 & 4 \end{bmatrix}$

48. $-3\left(\begin{bmatrix} 6 & 5 & -1 \\ 1 & -2 & 0 \end{bmatrix}\begin{bmatrix} 0 & 3 \\ -1 & -3 \\ 4 & 1 \end{bmatrix}\right)$

49. $\begin{bmatrix} 0 & 2 & -2 \\ 4 & 1 & 2 \end{bmatrix}\left(\begin{bmatrix} 4 & 0 \\ 0 & -1 \\ -1 & 2 \end{bmatrix} + \begin{bmatrix} -2 & 3 \\ -3 & 5 \\ 0 & -3 \end{bmatrix}\right)$

50. $\begin{bmatrix} 3 \\ -1 \\ 5 \\ 7 \end{bmatrix}([5 \quad -6] + [7 \quad -1] + [-8 \quad 9])$

In Exercises 51–58, (a) write the system of linear equations as a matrix equation, $AX = B$, and (b) use Gauss-Jordan elimination on the augmented matrix $[A \,\vdots\, B]$ to solve for the matrix X.

51. $\begin{cases} -x_1 + x_2 = 4 \\ -2x_1 + x_2 = 0 \end{cases}$

52. $\begin{cases} 2x_1 + 3x_2 = 5 \\ x_1 + 4x_2 = 10 \end{cases}$

53. $\begin{cases} -2x_1 - 3x_2 = -4 \\ 6x_1 + x_2 = -36 \end{cases}$

54. $\begin{cases} -4x_1 + 9x_2 = -13 \\ x_1 - 3x_2 = 12 \end{cases}$

55. $\begin{cases} x_1 - 2x_2 + 3x_3 = 9 \\ -x_1 + 3x_2 - x_3 = -6 \\ 2x_1 - 5x_2 + 5x_3 = 17 \end{cases}$

56. $\begin{cases} x_1 + x_2 - 3x_3 = 9 \\ -x_1 + 2x_2 = 6 \\ x_1 - x_2 + x_3 = -5 \end{cases}$

57. $\begin{cases} x_1 - 5x_2 + 2x_3 = -20 \\ -3x_1 + x_2 - x_3 = 8 \\ -2x_2 + 5x_3 = -16 \end{cases}$

58. $\begin{cases} x_1 - x_2 + 4x_3 = 17 \\ x_1 + 3x_2 = -11 \\ -6x_2 + 5x_3 = 40 \end{cases}$

59. ***Manufacturing*** A corporation has three factories, each of which manufactures acoustic guitars and electric guitars. The number of units of guitars produced at factory j in one day is represented by a_{ij} in the matrix

$$A = \begin{bmatrix} 70 & 50 & 25 \\ 35 & 100 & 70 \end{bmatrix}.$$

Find the production levels if production is increased by 20%.

60. ***Manufacturing*** A corporation has four factories, each of which manufactures sport utility vehicles and pickup trucks. The number of units of vehicle i produced at factory j in one day is represented by a_{ij} in the matrix

$$A = \begin{bmatrix} 100 & 90 & 70 & 30 \\ 40 & 20 & 60 & 60 \end{bmatrix}.$$

Find the production levels if production is increased by 10%.

61. ***Agriculture*** A fruit grower raises two crops, apples and peaches. Each of these crops is sent to three different outlets for sale. These outlets are The Farmer's Market, The Fruit Stand, and The Fruit Farm. The numbers of bushels of apples sent to the three outlets are 125, 100, and 75, respectively. The numbers of bushels of peaches sent to the three outlets are 100, 175, and 125, respectively. The profit per bushel for apples is \$3.50 and the profit per bushel for peaches is \$6.00.

(a) Write a matrix A that represents the number of bushels of each crop i that are shipped to each outlet j. State what each entry a_{ij} of the matrix represents.

(b) Write a matrix B that represents the profit per bushel of each fruit. State what each entry b_{ij} of the matrix represents.

(c) Find the product BA and state what each entry of the matrix represents.

62. ***Revenue*** A manufacturer of electronics produces three models of portable CD players, which are shipped to two warehouses. The number of units of model i that are shipped to warehouse j is represented by a_{ij} in the matrix

$$A = \begin{bmatrix} 5{,}000 & 4{,}000 \\ 6{,}000 & 10{,}000 \\ 8{,}000 & 5{,}000 \end{bmatrix}.$$

The prices per unit are represented by the matrix

$$B = [\$39.50 \quad \$44.50 \quad \$56.50].$$

Compute BA and interpret the result.

63. ***Inventory*** A company sells five models of computers through three retail outlets. The inventories are represented by S.

$$S = \overbrace{\begin{matrix} A & B & C & D & E \end{matrix}}^{\text{Model}} \quad S = \begin{bmatrix} 3 & 2 & 2 & 3 & 0 \\ 0 & 2 & 3 & 4 & 3 \\ 4 & 2 & 1 & 3 & 2 \end{bmatrix} \begin{matrix} 1 \\ 2 \\ 3 \end{matrix} \Big\} \text{ Outlet}$$

The wholesale and retail prices are represented by T.

$$T = \begin{bmatrix} \$840 & \$1100 \\ \$1200 & \$1350 \\ \$1450 & \$1650 \\ \$2650 & \$3000 \\ \$3050 & \$3200 \end{bmatrix} \begin{matrix} A \\ B \\ C \\ D \\ E \end{matrix} \Big\} \text{ Model}$$

(Columns: Price — Wholesale, Retail)

Compute ST and interpret the result.

64. ***Voting Preferences*** The matrix

$$P = \overset{\text{From}}{\overbrace{\begin{matrix} R & D & I \end{matrix}}} \\ P = \begin{bmatrix} 0.6 & 0.1 & 0.1 \\ 0.2 & 0.7 & 0.1 \\ 0.2 & 0.2 & 0.8 \end{bmatrix} \begin{matrix} R \\ D \\ I \end{matrix} \left.\vphantom{\begin{matrix} R \\ D \\ I \end{matrix}}\right\} \text{To}$$

is called a *stochastic matrix*. Each entry $p_{ij}\ (i \neq j)$ represents the proportion of the voting population that changes from party i to party j, and p_{ii} represents the proportion that remains loyal to the party from one election to the next. Compute and interpret P^2.

65. ***Voting Preferences*** Use a graphing utility to find P^3, P^4, P^5, P^6, P^7, and P^8 for the matrix given in Exercise 64. Can you detect a pattern as P is raised to higher powers?

66. ***Labor/Wage Requirements*** A company that manufactures boats has the following labor-hour and wage requirements.

Labor per boat

$$\overset{\text{Department}}{\overbrace{\begin{matrix} \text{Cutting} & \text{Assembly} & \text{Packaging} \end{matrix}}} \\ S = \begin{bmatrix} 1.0\text{ hr} & 0.5\text{ hr} & 0.2\text{ hr} \\ 1.6\text{ hr} & 1.0\text{ hr} & 0.2\text{ hr} \\ 2.5\text{ hr} & 2.0\text{ hr} & 1.4\text{ hr} \end{bmatrix} \begin{matrix} \text{Small} \\ \text{Medium} \\ \text{Large} \end{matrix} \left.\vphantom{\begin{matrix} a \\ b \\ c \end{matrix}}\right\} \text{Boat size}$$

Wages per hour

$$\overset{\text{Plant}}{\overbrace{\begin{matrix} A & B \end{matrix}}} \\ T = \begin{bmatrix} \$12 & \$10 \\ \$9 & \$8 \\ \$8 & \$7 \end{bmatrix} \begin{matrix} \text{Cutting} \\ \text{Assembly} \\ \text{Packaging} \end{matrix} \left.\vphantom{\begin{matrix} a \\ b \\ c \end{matrix}}\right\} \text{Department}$$

Compute ST and interpret the result.

67. ***Profit*** At a local dairy mart, the numbers of gallons of skim milk, 2% milk, and whole milk sold over the weekend are represented by A.

$$\begin{matrix} \text{Skim milk} & \text{2\% milk} & \text{Whole milk} \end{matrix} \\ A = \begin{bmatrix} 40 & 64 & 52 \\ 60 & 82 & 76 \\ 76 & 96 & 84 \end{bmatrix} \begin{matrix} \text{Friday} \\ \text{Saturday} \\ \text{Sunday} \end{matrix}$$

The selling prices (in dollars per gallon) and the profits (in dollars per gallon) for the three types of milk sold by the dairy mart are represented by B.

$$\begin{matrix} \text{Selling price} & \text{Profit} \end{matrix} \\ B = \begin{bmatrix} 2.65 & 0.65 \\ 2.85 & 0.70 \\ 3.05 & 0.85 \end{bmatrix} \begin{matrix} \text{Skim milk} \\ \text{2\% milk} \\ \text{Whole milk} \end{matrix}$$

(a) Compute AB and interpret the result.

(b) Find the dairy mart's total profit from milk sales for the weekend.

68. ***Profit*** At a convenience store, the numbers of gallons of 87-octane, 89-octane, and 93-octane gasoline sold over the weekend are represented by A.

$$\overset{\text{Octane}}{\overbrace{\begin{matrix} 87 & 89 & 93 \end{matrix}}} \\ A = \begin{bmatrix} 580 & 840 & 320 \\ 560 & 420 & 160 \\ 860 & 1020 & 540 \end{bmatrix} \begin{matrix} \text{Friday} \\ \text{Saturday} \\ \text{Sunday} \end{matrix}$$

The selling prices per gallon and the profits per gallon for the three grades of gasoline sold by the convenience store are represents by B.

$$\begin{matrix} \text{Selling price} & \text{Profit} \end{matrix} \\ B = \begin{bmatrix} 1.95 & 0.32 \\ 2.05 & 0.36 \\ 2.15 & 0.40 \end{bmatrix} \begin{matrix} 87 \\ 89 \\ 93 \end{matrix} \left.\vphantom{\begin{matrix} a \\ b \\ c \end{matrix}}\right\} \text{Octane}$$

(a) Compute AB and interpret the result.

(b) Find the convenience store's profit from gasoline sales for the weekend.

69. ***Exercise*** The numbers of calories burned by individuals of different body weights performing different types of aerobic exercises for a 20-minute time period are shown in matrix A.

$$\overset{\text{Calories burned}}{\overbrace{\begin{matrix} \text{120-lb person} & \text{150-lb person} \end{matrix}}} \\ A = \begin{bmatrix} 109 & 136 \\ 127 & 159 \\ 64 & 79 \end{bmatrix} \begin{matrix} \text{Bicycling} \\ \text{Jogging} \\ \text{Walking} \end{matrix}$$

(a) A 120-pound person and a 150-pound person bicycled for 40 minutes, jogged for 10 minutes, and walked for 60 minutes. Organize the time spent exercising in a matrix B.

(b) Compute BA and interpret the result.

Model It

70. ***Health Care*** The health care plans offered this year by a local manufacturing plant are as follows. For individuals, the comprehensive plan costs \$694.32, the HMO standard plan costs \$451.80, and the HMO Plus plan costs \$489.48. For families, the comprehensive plan costs \$1725.36, the HMO standard plan costs \$1187.76 and the HMO Plus plan costs \$1248.12. The plant expects the costs of the plans to change next year as follows. For individuals, the costs for the comprehensive, HMO standard, and HMO Plus plans will be \$683.91, \$463.10, and \$499.27, respectively. For families, the costs for the comprehensive, HMO standard, and HMO Plus plans will be \$1699.48, \$1217.45, and \$1273.08, respectively.

(a) Organize the information using two matrices A and B, where A represents the health care plan costs for this year and B represents the health care plan costs for next year. State what each entry of each matrix represents.

(b) Compute $A - B$ and interpret the result.

(c) The employees receive monthly paychecks from which the health care plan costs are deducted. Use the matrices from part (a) to write matrices that show how much will be deducted from each employees' paycheck this year and next year.

(d) Suppose the costs of each plan instead increase by 4% next year. Write a matrix that shows the new monthly payment.

Synthesis

True or False? **In Exercises 71 and 72, determine whether the statement is true or false. Justify your answer.**

71. Two matrices can be added only if they have the same order.

72. $\begin{bmatrix} -6 & -2 \\ 2 & -6 \end{bmatrix}\begin{bmatrix} 4 & 0 \\ 0 & -1 \end{bmatrix} = \begin{bmatrix} 4 & 0 \\ 0 & -1 \end{bmatrix}\begin{bmatrix} -6 & -2 \\ 2 & -6 \end{bmatrix}$

Think About It **In Exercises 73–80, let matrices A, B, C, and D be of orders 2×3, 2×3, 3×2, and 2×2, respectively. Determine whether the matrices are of proper order to perform the operation(s). If so, give the order of the answer.**

73. $A + 2C$

74. $B - 3C$

75. AB

76. BC

77. $BC - D$

78. $CB - D$

79. $D(A - 3B)$

80. $(BC - D)A$

81. ***Think About It*** If a, b, and c are real numbers such that $c \neq 0$ and $ac = bc$, then $a = b$. However, if A, B, and C are nonzero matrices such that $AC = BC$, then A is *not* necessarily equal to B. Illustrate this using the following matrices.

$$A = \begin{bmatrix} 0 & 1 \\ 0 & 1 \end{bmatrix}, \quad B = \begin{bmatrix} 1 & 0 \\ 1 & 0 \end{bmatrix}, \quad C = \begin{bmatrix} 2 & 3 \\ 2 & 3 \end{bmatrix}$$

82. ***Think About It*** If a and b are real numbers such that $ab = 0$, then $a = 0$ or $b = 0$. However, if A and B are matrices such that $AB = O$, it is *not* necessarily true that $A = O$ or $B = O$. Illustrate this using the following matrices.

$$A = \begin{bmatrix} 3 & 3 \\ 4 & 4 \end{bmatrix}, \quad B = \begin{bmatrix} 1 & -1 \\ -1 & 1 \end{bmatrix}$$

83. ***Exploration*** Let A and B be unequal diagonal matrices of the same order. (A **diagonal matrix** is a square matrix in which each entry not on the main diagonal is zero.) Determine the products AB for several pairs of such matrices. Make a conjecture about a quick rule for such products.

84. ***Exploration*** Let $i = \sqrt{-1}$ and let

$$A = \begin{bmatrix} i & 0 \\ 0 & i \end{bmatrix} \quad \text{and} \quad B = \begin{bmatrix} 0 & -i \\ i & 0 \end{bmatrix}.$$

(a) Find A^2, A^3, and A^4. Identify any similarities with i^2, i^3, and i^4.

(b) Find and identify B^2.

Skills Review

In Exercises 85–90, solve the equation.

85. $3x^2 + 20x - 32 = 0$

86. $8x^2 - 10x - 3 = 0$

87. $4x^3 + 10x^2 - 3x = 0$

88. $3x^3 + 22x^2 - 45x = 0$

89. $3x^3 - 12x^2 + 5x - 20 = 0$

90. $2x^3 - 5x^2 - 12x + 30 = 0$

In Exercises 91–94, solve the system of linear equations both graphically and algebraically.

91. $\begin{cases} -x + 4y = -9 \\ 5x - 8y = 39 \end{cases}$

92. $\begin{cases} 8x - 3y = -17 \\ -6x + 7y = 27 \end{cases}$

93. $\begin{cases} -x + 2y = -5 \\ -3x - y = -8 \end{cases}$

94. $\begin{cases} 6x - 13y = 11 \\ 9x + 5y = 41 \end{cases}$

8.3 The Inverse of a Square Matrix

What you should learn

- Verify that two matrices are inverses of each other.
- Use Gauss-Jordan elimination to find the inverses of matrices.
- Use a formula to find the inverses of 2×2 matrices.
- Use inverse matrices to solve systems of linear equations.

Why you should learn it

You can use inverse matrices to model and solve real-life problems. For instance, in Exercise 72 on page 610, an inverse matrix is used to find a linear model for the number of licensed drivers in the United States.

Jon Love/Getty Images

The Inverse of a Matrix

This section further develops the algebra of matrices. To begin, consider the real number equation $ax = b$. To solve this equation for x, multiply each side of the equation by a^{-1} (provided that $a \neq 0$).

$$ax = b$$
$$(a^{-1}a)x = a^{-1}b$$
$$(1)x = a^{-1}b$$
$$x = a^{-1}b$$

The number a^{-1} is called the *multiplicative inverse of a* because $a^{-1}a = 1$. The definition of the multiplicative **inverse of a matrix** is similar.

Definition of the Inverse of a Square Matrix

Let A be an $n \times n$ matrix and let I_n be the $n \times n$ identity matrix. If there exists a matrix A^{-1} such that

$$AA^{-1} = I_n = A^{-1}A$$

then A^{-1} is called the **inverse** of A. The symbol A^{-1} is read "A inverse."

Example 1 The Inverse of a Matrix

Show that B is the inverse of A, where

$$A = \begin{bmatrix} -1 & 2 \\ -1 & 1 \end{bmatrix} \quad \text{and} \quad B = \begin{bmatrix} 1 & -2 \\ 1 & -1 \end{bmatrix}.$$

Solution

To show that B is the inverse of A, show that $AB = I = BA$, as follows.

$$AB = \begin{bmatrix} -1 & 2 \\ -1 & 1 \end{bmatrix}\begin{bmatrix} 1 & -2 \\ 1 & -1 \end{bmatrix} = \begin{bmatrix} -1+2 & 2-2 \\ -1+1 & 2-1 \end{bmatrix} = \begin{bmatrix} 1 & 0 \\ 0 & 1 \end{bmatrix}$$

$$BA = \begin{bmatrix} 1 & -2 \\ 1 & -1 \end{bmatrix}\begin{bmatrix} -1 & 2 \\ -1 & 1 \end{bmatrix} = \begin{bmatrix} -1+2 & 2-2 \\ -1+1 & 2-1 \end{bmatrix} = \begin{bmatrix} 1 & 0 \\ 0 & 1 \end{bmatrix}$$

As you can see, $AB = I = BA$. This is an example of a square matrix that has an inverse. Note that not all square matrices have an inverse.

✓CHECKPOINT Now try Exercise 1.

Recall that it is not always true that $AB = BA$, even if both products are defined. However, if A and B are both square matrices and $AB = I_n$, it can be shown that $BA = I_n$. So, in Example 1, you need only to check that $AB = I_2$.

Finding Inverse Matrices

If a matrix A has an inverse, A is called **invertible** (or **nonsingular**); otherwise, A is called **singular.** A nonsquare matrix cannot have an inverse. To see this, note that if A is of order $m \times n$ and B is of order $n \times m$ (where $m \neq n$), the products AB and BA are of different orders and so cannot be equal to each other. Not all square matrices have inverses (see the matrix at the bottom of page 605). If, however, a matrix does have an inverse, that inverse is unique. Example 2 shows how to use a system of equations to find the inverse of a matrix.

Example 2 Finding the Inverse of a Matrix

Find the inverse of

$$A = \begin{bmatrix} 1 & 4 \\ -1 & -3 \end{bmatrix}.$$

Solution

To find the inverse of A, try to solve the matrix equation $AX = I$ for X.

$$\overset{A}{\begin{bmatrix} 1 & 4 \\ -1 & -3 \end{bmatrix}} \overset{X}{\begin{bmatrix} x_{11} & x_{12} \\ x_{21} & x_{22} \end{bmatrix}} = \overset{I}{\begin{bmatrix} 1 & 0 \\ 0 & 1 \end{bmatrix}}$$

$$\begin{bmatrix} x_{11} + 4x_{21} & x_{12} + 4x_{22} \\ -x_{11} - 3x_{21} & -x_{12} - 3x_{22} \end{bmatrix} = \begin{bmatrix} 1 & 0 \\ 0 & 1 \end{bmatrix}$$

Equating corresponding entries, you obtain two systems of linear equations.

$$\begin{cases} x_{11} + 4x_{21} = 1 \\ -x_{11} - 3x_{21} = 0 \end{cases}$$ Linear system with two variables, x_{11} and x_{21}.

$$\begin{cases} x_{12} + 4x_{22} = 0 \\ -x_{12} - 3x_{22} = 1 \end{cases}$$ Linear system with two variables, x_{12} and x_{22}.

Solve the first system using elementary row operations to determine that $x_{11} = -3$ and $x_{21} = 1$. From the second system you can determine that $x_{12} = -4$ and $x_{22} = 1$. Therefore, the inverse of A is

$$X = A^{-1}$$
$$= \begin{bmatrix} -3 & -4 \\ 1 & 1 \end{bmatrix}.$$

You can use matrix multiplication to check this result.

Check

$$AA^{-1} = \begin{bmatrix} 1 & 4 \\ -1 & -3 \end{bmatrix}\begin{bmatrix} -3 & -4 \\ 1 & 1 \end{bmatrix} = \begin{bmatrix} 1 & 0 \\ 0 & 1 \end{bmatrix} \quad ✓$$

$$A^{-1}A = \begin{bmatrix} -3 & -4 \\ 1 & 1 \end{bmatrix}\begin{bmatrix} 1 & 4 \\ -1 & -3 \end{bmatrix} = \begin{bmatrix} 1 & 0 \\ 0 & 1 \end{bmatrix} \quad ✓$$

✓CHECKPOINT Now try Exercise 13.

In Example 2, note that the two systems of linear equations have the *same coefficient matrix A*. Rather than solve the two systems represented by

$$\begin{bmatrix} 1 & 4 & \vdots & 1 \\ -1 & -3 & \vdots & 0 \end{bmatrix}$$

and

$$\begin{bmatrix} 1 & 4 & \vdots & 0 \\ -1 & -3 & \vdots & 1 \end{bmatrix}$$

separately, you can solve them *simultaneously* by *adjoining* the identity matrix to the coefficient matrix to obtain

$$\overbrace{\begin{bmatrix} 1 & 4 \\ -1 & -3 \end{bmatrix}}^{A} \begin{matrix} \vdots \\ \vdots \end{matrix} \overbrace{\begin{bmatrix} 1 & 0 \\ 0 & 1 \end{bmatrix}}^{I}.$$

This "doubly augmented" matrix can be represented as $[A \;\vdots\; I]$. By applying Gauss-Jordan elimination to this matrix, you can solve *both* systems with a single elimination process.

$$\begin{bmatrix} 1 & 4 & \vdots & 1 & 0 \\ -1 & -3 & \vdots & 0 & 1 \end{bmatrix}$$

$$\begin{matrix} \\ R_1 + R_2 \rightarrow \end{matrix} \begin{bmatrix} 1 & 4 & \vdots & 1 & 0 \\ 0 & 1 & \vdots & 1 & 1 \end{bmatrix}$$

$$\begin{matrix} -4R_2 + R_1 \rightarrow \\ \\ \end{matrix} \begin{bmatrix} 1 & 0 & \vdots & -3 & -4 \\ 0 & 1 & \vdots & 1 & 1 \end{bmatrix}$$

So, from the "doubly augmented" matrix $[A \;\vdots\; I]$, you obtain the matrix $[I \;\vdots\; A^{-1}]$.

$$\overbrace{\begin{bmatrix} 1 & 4 \\ -1 & -3 \end{bmatrix}}^{A} \begin{matrix} \vdots \\ \vdots \end{matrix} \overbrace{\begin{bmatrix} 1 & 0 \\ 0 & 1 \end{bmatrix}}^{I} \;\Rightarrow\; \overbrace{\begin{bmatrix} 1 & 0 \\ 0 & 1 \end{bmatrix}}^{I} \begin{matrix} \vdots \\ \vdots \end{matrix} \overbrace{\begin{bmatrix} -3 & -4 \\ 1 & 1 \end{bmatrix}}^{A^{-1}}$$

This procedure (or algorithm) works for any square matrix that has an inverse.

Technology

Most graphing utilities can find the inverse of a square matrix. To do so, you may have to use the inverse key $\boxed{x^{-1}}$. Consult the user's guide for your graphing utility for specific keystrokes.

Finding an Inverse Matrix

Let A be a square matrix of order n.

1. Write the $n \times 2n$ matrix that consists of the given matrix A on the left and the $n \times n$ identity matrix I on the right to obtain $[A \;\vdots\; I]$.
2. If possible, row reduce A to I using elementary row operations on the *entire* matrix $[A \;\vdots\; I]$. The result will be the matrix $[I \;\vdots\; A^{-1}]$. If this is not possible, A is not invertible.
3. Check your work by multiplying to see that $AA^{-1} = I = A^{-1}A$.

Example 3 Finding the Inverse of a Matrix

Find the inverse of $A = \begin{bmatrix} 1 & -1 & 0 \\ 1 & 0 & -1 \\ 6 & -2 & -3 \end{bmatrix}$.

Solution

Begin by adjoining the identity matrix to A to form the matrix

$$[A \vdots I] = \left[\begin{array}{ccc:ccc} 1 & -1 & 0 & 1 & 0 & 0 \\ 1 & 0 & -1 & 0 & 1 & 0 \\ 6 & -2 & -3 & 0 & 0 & 1 \end{array}\right].$$

Use elementary row operations to obtain the form $[I \vdots A^{-1}]$, as follows.

$$\begin{array}{r} \\ -R_1 + R_2 \rightarrow \\ -6R_1 + R_3 \rightarrow \end{array} \left[\begin{array}{ccc:ccc} 1 & -1 & 0 & 1 & 0 & 0 \\ 0 & 1 & -1 & -1 & 1 & 0 \\ 0 & 4 & -3 & -6 & 0 & 1 \end{array}\right]$$

$$\begin{array}{r} R_2 + R_1 \rightarrow \\ \\ -4R_2 + R_3 \rightarrow \end{array} \left[\begin{array}{ccc:ccc} 1 & 0 & -1 & 0 & 1 & 0 \\ 0 & 1 & -1 & -1 & 1 & 0 \\ 0 & 0 & 1 & -2 & -4 & 1 \end{array}\right]$$

$$\begin{array}{r} R_3 + R_1 \rightarrow \\ R_3 + R_2 \rightarrow \\ \\ \end{array} \left[\begin{array}{ccc:ccc} 1 & 0 & 0 & -2 & -3 & 1 \\ 0 & 1 & 0 & -3 & -3 & 1 \\ 0 & 0 & 1 & -2 & -4 & 1 \end{array}\right] = [I \vdots A^{-1}]$$

So, the matrix A is invertible and its inverse is

$$A^{-1} = \begin{bmatrix} -2 & -3 & 1 \\ -3 & -3 & 1 \\ -2 & -4 & 1 \end{bmatrix}.$$

Confirm this result by multiplying A and A^{-1} to obtain I, as follows.

Check

$$AA^{-1} = \begin{bmatrix} 1 & -1 & 0 \\ 1 & 0 & -1 \\ 6 & -2 & -3 \end{bmatrix} \begin{bmatrix} -2 & -3 & 1 \\ -3 & -3 & 1 \\ -2 & -4 & 1 \end{bmatrix} = \begin{bmatrix} 1 & 0 & 0 \\ 0 & 1 & 0 \\ 0 & 0 & 1 \end{bmatrix} = I$$

CHECKPOINT Now try Exercise 21.

STUDY TIP

Be sure to check your solution because it is easy to make algebraic errors when using elementary row operations.

The process shown in Example 3 applies to any $n \times n$ matrix A. When using this algorithm, if the matrix A does not reduce to the identity matrix, then A does not have an inverse. For instance, the following matrix has no inverse.

$$A = \begin{bmatrix} 1 & 2 & 0 \\ 3 & -1 & 2 \\ -2 & 3 & -2 \end{bmatrix}$$

To confirm that matrix A above has no inverse, adjoin the identity matrix to A to form $[A \vdots I]$ and perform elementary row operations on the matrix. After doing so, you will see that it is impossible to obtain the identity matrix I on the left. Therefore, A is not invertible.

Exploration

Use a graphing utility with matrix capabilities to find the inverse of the matrix

$$A = \begin{bmatrix} 1 & -3 \\ -2 & 6 \end{bmatrix}.$$

What message appears on the screen? Why does the graphing utility display this message?

The Inverse of a 2 × 2 Matrix

Using Gauss-Jordan elimination to find the inverse of a matrix works well (even as a computer technique) for matrices of order 3×3 or greater. For 2×2 matrices, however, many people prefer to use a formula for the inverse rather than Gauss-Jordan elimination. This simple formula, which works *only* for 2×2 matrices, is explained as follows. If A is a 2×2 matrix given by

$$A = \begin{bmatrix} a & b \\ c & d \end{bmatrix}$$

then A is invertible if and only if $ad - bc \neq 0$. Moreover, if $ad - bc \neq 0$, the inverse is given by

$$A^{-1} = \frac{1}{ad - bc}\begin{bmatrix} d & -b \\ -c & a \end{bmatrix}.$$ Formula for inverse of matrix A

The denominator $ad - bc$ is called the **determinant** of the 2×2 matrix A. You will study determinants in the next section.

Example 4 Finding the Inverse of a 2 × 2 Matrix

If possible, find the inverse of each matrix.

a. $A = \begin{bmatrix} 3 & -1 \\ -2 & 2 \end{bmatrix}$

b. $B = \begin{bmatrix} 3 & -1 \\ -6 & 2 \end{bmatrix}$

Solution

a. For the matrix A, apply the formula for the inverse of a 2×2 matrix to obtain

$$\begin{aligned} ad - bc &= (3)(2) - (-1)(-2) \\ &= 4. \end{aligned}$$

Because this quantity is not zero, the inverse is formed by interchanging the entries on the main diagonal, changing the signs of the other two entries, and multiplying by the scalar $\frac{1}{4}$, as follows.

$$A^{-1} = \frac{1}{4}\begin{bmatrix} 2 & 1 \\ 2 & 3 \end{bmatrix}$$ Substitute for a, b, c, d, and the determinant.

$$= \begin{bmatrix} \frac{1}{2} & \frac{1}{4} \\ \frac{1}{2} & \frac{3}{4} \end{bmatrix}$$ Multiply by the scalar $\frac{1}{4}$.

b. For the matrix B, you have

$$\begin{aligned} ad - bc &= (3)(2) - (-1)(-6) \\ &= 0 \end{aligned}$$

which means that B is not invertible.

✓CHECKPOINT Now try Exercise 39.

Systems of Linear Equations

You know that a system of linear equations can have exactly one solution, infinitely many solutions, or no solution. If the coefficient matrix A of a *square* system (a system that has the same number of equations as variables) is invertible, the system has a unique solution, which is defined as follows.

A System of Equations with a Unique Solution

If A is an invertible matrix, the system of linear equations represented by $AX = B$ has a unique solution given by

$$X = A^{-1}B.$$

Technology

To solve a system of equations with a graphing utility, enter the matrices A and B in the matrix editor. Then, using the inverse key, solve for X.

A [x^{-1}] B [ENTER]

The screen will display the solution, matrix X.

Example 5 Solving a System Using an Inverse

You are going to invest \$10,000 in AAA-rated bonds, AA-rated bonds, and B-rated bonds and want an annual return of \$730. The average yields are 6% on AAA bonds, 7.5% on AA bonds, and 9.5% on B bonds. You will invest twice as much in AAA bonds as in B bonds. Your investment can be represented as

$$\begin{cases} x + y + z = 10{,}000 \\ 0.06x + 0.075y + 0.095z = 730 \\ x - 2z = 0 \end{cases}$$

where x, y, and z represent the amounts invested in AAA, AA, and B bonds, respectively. Use an inverse matrix to solve the system.

Solution

Begin by writing the system in the matrix form $AX = B$.

$$\begin{bmatrix} 1 & 1 & 1 \\ 0.06 & 0.075 & 0.095 \\ 1 & 0 & -2 \end{bmatrix}\begin{bmatrix} x \\ y \\ z \end{bmatrix} = \begin{bmatrix} 10{,}000 \\ 730 \\ 0 \end{bmatrix}$$

Then, use Gauss-Jordan elimination to find A^{-1}.

$$A^{-1} = \begin{bmatrix} 15 & -200 & -2 \\ -21.5 & 300 & 3.5 \\ 7.5 & -100 & -1.5 \end{bmatrix}$$

Finally, multiply B by A^{-1} on the left to obtain the solution.

$$X = A^{-1}B$$

$$= \begin{bmatrix} 15 & -200 & -2 \\ -21.5 & 300 & 3.5 \\ 7.5 & -100 & -1.5 \end{bmatrix}\begin{bmatrix} 10{,}000 \\ 730 \\ 0 \end{bmatrix} = \begin{bmatrix} 4000 \\ 4000 \\ 2000 \end{bmatrix}$$

The solution to the system is $x = 4000$, $y = 4000$, and $z = 2000$. So, you will invest \$4000 in AAA bonds, \$4000 in AA bonds, and \$2000 in B bonds.

CHECKPOINT Now try Exercise 67.

8.3 Exercises

VOCABULARY CHECK: Fill in the blanks.

1. In a ________ matrix, the number of rows equals the number of columns.
2. If there exists an $n \times n$ matrix A^{-1} such that $AA^{-1} = I_n = A^{-1}A$, then A^{-1} is called the ________ of A.
3. If a matrix A has an inverse, it is called invertible or ________; if it does not have an inverse, it is called ________.
4. If A is an invertible matrix, the system of linear equations represented by $AX = B$ has a unique solution given by $X =$ ________.

In Exercises 1–10, show that *B* is the inverse of *A*.

1. $A = \begin{bmatrix} 2 & 1 \\ 5 & 3 \end{bmatrix}, B = \begin{bmatrix} 3 & -1 \\ -5 & 2 \end{bmatrix}$

2. $A = \begin{bmatrix} 1 & -1 \\ -1 & 2 \end{bmatrix}, B = \begin{bmatrix} 2 & 1 \\ 1 & 1 \end{bmatrix}$

3. $A = \begin{bmatrix} 1 & 2 \\ 3 & 4 \end{bmatrix}, B = \begin{bmatrix} -2 & 1 \\ \frac{3}{2} & -\frac{1}{2} \end{bmatrix}$

4. $A = \begin{bmatrix} 1 & -1 \\ 2 & 3 \end{bmatrix}, B = \begin{bmatrix} \frac{3}{5} & \frac{1}{5} \\ -\frac{2}{5} & \frac{1}{5} \end{bmatrix}$

5. $A = \begin{bmatrix} 2 & -17 & 11 \\ -1 & 11 & -7 \\ 0 & 3 & -2 \end{bmatrix}, B = \begin{bmatrix} 1 & 1 & 2 \\ 2 & 4 & -3 \\ 3 & 6 & -5 \end{bmatrix}$

6. $A = \begin{bmatrix} -4 & 1 & 5 \\ -1 & 2 & 4 \\ 0 & -1 & -1 \end{bmatrix}, B = \begin{bmatrix} -\frac{1}{2} & 1 & \frac{3}{2} \\ \frac{1}{4} & -1 & -\frac{11}{4} \\ -\frac{1}{4} & 1 & \frac{7}{4} \end{bmatrix}$

7. $A = \begin{bmatrix} 2 & 0 & 1 & 1 \\ 3 & 0 & 0 & 1 \\ -1 & 1 & -2 & 1 \\ 4 & -1 & 1 & 0 \end{bmatrix}, B = \begin{bmatrix} -1 & 2 & -1 & -1 \\ -4 & 9 & -5 & -6 \\ 0 & 1 & -1 & -1 \\ 3 & -5 & 3 & 3 \end{bmatrix}$

8. $A = \begin{bmatrix} -2 & 0 & 1 & 0 \\ 1 & -1 & -3 & 0 \\ -2 & -1 & 0 & -2 \\ 0 & 1 & 3 & -1 \end{bmatrix}, B = \begin{bmatrix} -3 & -3 & 1 & -2 \\ 12 & 14 & -5 & 10 \\ -5 & -6 & 2 & -4 \\ -3 & -4 & 1 & -3 \end{bmatrix}$

9. $A = \begin{bmatrix} -2 & 2 & 3 \\ 1 & -1 & 0 \\ 0 & 1 & 4 \end{bmatrix}, B = \frac{1}{3}\begin{bmatrix} -4 & -5 & 3 \\ -4 & -8 & 3 \\ 1 & 2 & 0 \end{bmatrix}$

10. $A = \begin{bmatrix} -1 & 1 & 0 & -1 \\ 1 & -1 & 1 & 0 \\ -1 & 1 & 2 & 0 \\ 0 & -1 & 1 & 1 \end{bmatrix},$

$B = \frac{1}{3}\begin{bmatrix} -3 & 1 & 1 & -3 \\ -3 & -1 & 2 & -3 \\ 0 & 1 & 1 & 0 \\ -3 & -2 & 1 & 0 \end{bmatrix}$

In Exercises 11–26, find the inverse of the matrix (if it exists).

11. $\begin{bmatrix} 2 & 0 \\ 0 & 3 \end{bmatrix}$

12. $\begin{bmatrix} 1 & 2 \\ 3 & 7 \end{bmatrix}$

13. $\begin{bmatrix} 1 & -2 \\ 2 & -3 \end{bmatrix}$

14. $\begin{bmatrix} -7 & 33 \\ 4 & -19 \end{bmatrix}$

15. $\begin{bmatrix} -1 & 1 \\ -2 & 1 \end{bmatrix}$

16. $\begin{bmatrix} 11 & 1 \\ -1 & 0 \end{bmatrix}$

17. $\begin{bmatrix} 2 & 4 \\ 4 & 8 \end{bmatrix}$

18. $\begin{bmatrix} 2 & 3 \\ 1 & 4 \end{bmatrix}$

19. $\begin{bmatrix} 2 & 7 & 1 \\ -3 & -9 & 2 \end{bmatrix}$

20. $\begin{bmatrix} -2 & 5 \\ 6 & -15 \\ 0 & 1 \end{bmatrix}$

21. $\begin{bmatrix} 1 & 1 & 1 \\ 3 & 5 & 4 \\ 3 & 6 & 5 \end{bmatrix}$

22. $\begin{bmatrix} 1 & 2 & 2 \\ 3 & 7 & 9 \\ -1 & -4 & -7 \end{bmatrix}$

23. $\begin{bmatrix} 1 & 0 & 0 \\ 3 & 4 & 0 \\ 2 & 5 & 5 \end{bmatrix}$

24. $\begin{bmatrix} 1 & 0 & 0 \\ 3 & 0 & 0 \\ 2 & 5 & 5 \end{bmatrix}$

25. $\begin{bmatrix} -8 & 0 & 0 & 0 \\ 0 & 1 & 0 & 0 \\ 0 & 0 & 4 & 0 \\ 0 & 0 & 0 & -5 \end{bmatrix}$

26. $\begin{bmatrix} 1 & 3 & -2 & 0 \\ 0 & 2 & 4 & 6 \\ 0 & 0 & -2 & 1 \\ 0 & 0 & 0 & 5 \end{bmatrix}$

In Exercises 27–38, use the matrix capabilities of a graphing utility to find the inverse of the matrix (if it exists).

27. $\begin{bmatrix} 1 & 2 & -1 \\ 3 & 7 & -10 \\ -5 & -7 & -15 \end{bmatrix}$

28. $\begin{bmatrix} 10 & 5 & -7 \\ -5 & 1 & 4 \\ 3 & 2 & -2 \end{bmatrix}$

29. $\begin{bmatrix} 1 & 1 & 2 \\ 3 & 1 & 0 \\ -2 & 0 & 3 \end{bmatrix}$

30. $\begin{bmatrix} 3 & 2 & 2 \\ 2 & 2 & 2 \\ -4 & 4 & 3 \end{bmatrix}$

31. $\begin{bmatrix} -\frac{1}{2} & \frac{3}{4} & \frac{1}{4} \\ 1 & 0 & -\frac{3}{2} \\ 0 & -1 & \frac{1}{2} \end{bmatrix}$

32. $\begin{bmatrix} -\frac{5}{6} & \frac{1}{3} & \frac{11}{6} \\ 0 & \frac{2}{3} & 2 \\ 1 & -\frac{1}{2} & -\frac{5}{2} \end{bmatrix}$

33. $\begin{bmatrix} 0.1 & 0.2 & 0.3 \\ -0.3 & 0.2 & 0.2 \\ 0.5 & 0.4 & 0.4 \end{bmatrix}$

34. $\begin{bmatrix} 0.6 & 0 & -0.3 \\ 0.7 & -1 & 0.2 \\ 1 & 0 & -0.9 \end{bmatrix}$

35. $\begin{bmatrix} 1 & 0 & 3 & 0 \\ 0 & 2 & 0 & 4 \\ 1 & 0 & 3 & 0 \\ 0 & 2 & 0 & 4 \end{bmatrix}$

36. $\begin{bmatrix} 4 & 8 & -7 & 14 \\ 2 & 5 & -4 & 6 \\ 0 & 2 & 1 & -7 \\ 3 & 6 & -5 & 10 \end{bmatrix}$

37. $\begin{bmatrix} -1 & 0 & 1 & 0 \\ 0 & 2 & 0 & -1 \\ 2 & 0 & -1 & 0 \\ 0 & -1 & 0 & 1 \end{bmatrix}$

38. $\begin{bmatrix} 1 & -2 & -1 & -2 \\ 3 & -5 & -2 & -3 \\ 2 & -5 & -2 & -5 \\ -1 & 4 & 4 & 11 \end{bmatrix}$

In Exercises 39–44, use the formula on page 606 to find the inverse of the 2×2 matrix (if it exists).

39. $\begin{bmatrix} 5 & -2 \\ 2 & 3 \end{bmatrix}$

40. $\begin{bmatrix} 7 & 12 \\ -8 & -5 \end{bmatrix}$

41. $\begin{bmatrix} -4 & -6 \\ 2 & 3 \end{bmatrix}$

42. $\begin{bmatrix} -12 & 3 \\ 5 & -2 \end{bmatrix}$

43. $\begin{bmatrix} \frac{7}{2} & -\frac{3}{4} \\ \frac{1}{5} & \frac{4}{5} \end{bmatrix}$

44. $\begin{bmatrix} -\frac{1}{4} & \frac{9}{4} \\ \frac{5}{3} & \frac{8}{9} \end{bmatrix}$

In Exercises 45–48, use the inverse matrix found in Exercise 13 to solve the system of linear equations.

45. $\begin{cases} x - 2y = 5 \\ 2x - 3y = 10 \end{cases}$

46. $\begin{cases} x - 2y = 0 \\ 2x - 3y = 3 \end{cases}$

47. $\begin{cases} x - 2y = 4 \\ 2x - 3y = 2 \end{cases}$

48. $\begin{cases} x - 2y = 1 \\ 2x - 3y = -2 \end{cases}$

In Exercises 49 and 50, use the inverse matrix found in Exercise 21 to solve the system of linear equations.

49. $\begin{cases} x + y + z = 0 \\ 3x + 5y + 4z = 5 \\ 3x + 6y + 5z = 2 \end{cases}$

50. $\begin{cases} x + y + z = -1 \\ 3x + 5y + 4z = 2 \\ 3x + 6y + 5z = 0 \end{cases}$

In Exercises 51 and 52, use the inverse matrix found in Exercise 38 to solve the system of linear equations.

51. $\begin{cases} x_1 - 2x_2 - x_3 - 2x_4 = 0 \\ 3x_1 - 5x_2 - 2x_3 - 3x_4 = 1 \\ 2x_1 - 5x_2 - 2x_3 - 5x_4 = -1 \\ -x_1 + 4x_2 + 4x_3 + 11x_4 = 2 \end{cases}$

52. $\begin{cases} x_1 - 2x_2 - x_3 - 2x_4 = 1 \\ 3x_1 - 5x_2 - 2x_3 - 3x_4 = -2 \\ 2x_1 - 5x_2 - 2x_3 - 5x_4 = 0 \\ -x_1 + 4x_2 + 4x_3 + 11x_4 = -3 \end{cases}$

In Exercises 53–60, use an inverse matrix to solve (if possible) the system of linear equations.

53. $\begin{cases} 3x + 4y = -2 \\ 5x + 3y = 4 \end{cases}$

54. $\begin{cases} 18x + 12y = 13 \\ 30x + 24y = 23 \end{cases}$

55. $\begin{cases} -0.4x + 0.8y = 1.6 \\ 2x - 4y = 5 \end{cases}$

56. $\begin{cases} 0.2x - 0.6y = 2.4 \\ -x + 1.4y = -8.8 \end{cases}$

57. $\begin{cases} -\frac{1}{4}x + \frac{3}{8}y = -2 \\ \frac{3}{2}x + \frac{3}{4}y = -12 \end{cases}$

58. $\begin{cases} \frac{5}{6}x - y = -20 \\ \frac{4}{3}x - \frac{7}{2}y = -51 \end{cases}$

59. $\begin{cases} 4x - y + z = -5 \\ 2x + 2y + 3z = 10 \\ 5x - 2y + 6z = 1 \end{cases}$

60. $\begin{cases} 4x - 2y + 3z = -2 \\ 2x + 2y + 5z = 16 \\ 8x - 5y - 2z = 4 \end{cases}$

In Exercises 61–66, use the matrix capabilities of a graphing utility to solve (if possible) the system of linear equations.

61. $\begin{cases} 5x - 3y + 2z = 2 \\ 2x + 2y - 3z = 3 \\ x - 7y + 8z = -4 \end{cases}$

62. $\begin{cases} 2x + 3y + 5z = 4 \\ 3x + 5y + 9z = 7 \\ 5x + 9y + 17z = 13 \end{cases}$

63. $\begin{cases} 3x - 2y + z = -29 \\ -4x + y - 3z = 37 \\ x - 5y + z = -24 \end{cases}$

64. $\begin{cases} -8x + 7y - 10z = -151 \\ 12x + 3y - 5z = 86 \\ 15x - 9y + 2z - 187 \end{cases}$

65. $\begin{cases} 7x - 3y + 2w = 41 \\ -2x + y - w = -13 \\ 4x + z - 2w = 12 \\ -x + y - w = -8 \end{cases}$

66. $\begin{cases} 2x + 5y + w = 11 \\ x + 4y + 2z - 2w = -7 \\ 2x - 2y + 5z + w = 3 \\ x - 3w = -1 \end{cases}$

Investment Portfolio **In Exercises 67–70, consider a person who invests in AAA-rated bonds, A-rated bonds, and B-rated bonds. The average yields are 6.5% on AAA bonds, 7% on A bonds, and 9% on B bonds. The person invests twice as much in B bonds as in A bonds. Let x, y, and z represent the amounts invested in AAA, A, and B bonds, respectively.**

$$\begin{cases} x + y + z = \text{(total investment)} \\ 0.065x + 0.07y + 0.09z = \text{(annual return)} \\ 2y - z = 0 \end{cases}$$

Use the inverse of the coefficient matrix of this system to find the amount invested in each type of bond.

	Total Investment	*Annual Return*
67.	\$10,000	\$705
68.	\$10,000	\$760
69.	\$12,000	\$835
70.	\$500,000	\$38,000

71. ***Circuit Analysis*** Consider the circuit shown in the figure. The currents I_1, I_2, and I_3, in amperes, are the solution of the system of linear equations

$$\begin{cases} 2I_1 \qquad\quad + 4I_3 = E_1 \\ \qquad I_2 + 4I_3 = E_2 \\ I_1 + I_2 - \; I_3 = 0 \end{cases}$$

where E_1 and E_2 are voltages. Use the inverse of the coefficient matrix of this system to find the unknown currents for the voltages.

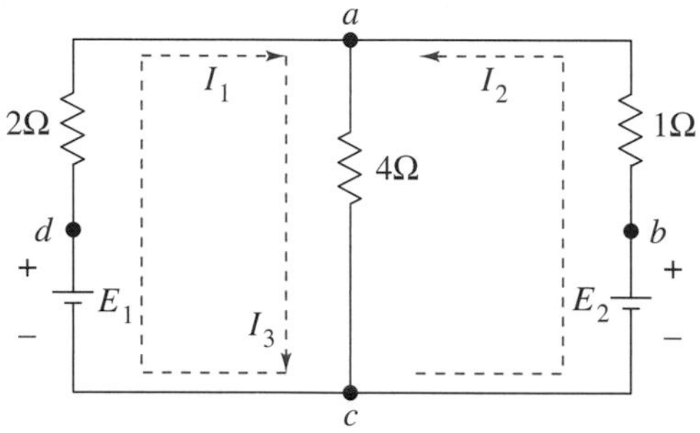

(a) $E_1 = 14$ volts, $E_2 = 28$ volts

(b) $E_1 = 24$ volts, $E_2 = 23$ volts

Model It

72. ***Data Analysis: Licensed Drivers*** The table shows the numbers y (in millions) of licensed drivers in the United States for selected years 1997 to 2001. (Source: U.S. Federal Highway Administration)

Year	Drivers, y
1997	182.7
1999	187.2
2001	191.3

(a) Use the technique demonstrated in Exercises 57–62 in Section 7.2 to create a system of linear equations for the data. Let t represent the year, with $t = 7$ corresponding to 1997.

(b) Use the matrix capabilities of a graphing utility to find an inverse matrix to solve the system from part (a) and find the least squares regression line $y = at + b$.

(c) Use the result of part (b) to estimate the number of licensed drivers in 2003.

(d) The actual number of licensed drivers in 2003 was 196.2 million. How does this value compare with your estimate from part (c)?

Model It (continued)

(e) Use the result of part (b) to estimate when the number of licensed drivers will reach 208 million.

Synthesis

True or False? **In Exercises 73 and 74, determine whether the statement is true or false. Justify your answer.**

73. Multiplication of an invertible matrix and its inverse is commutative.

74. If you multiply two square matrices and obtain the identity matrix, you can assume that the matrices are inverses of one another.

75. If A is a 2×2 matrix $A = \begin{bmatrix} a & b \\ c & d \end{bmatrix}$, then A is invertible if and only if $ad - bc \neq 0$. If $ad - bc \neq 0$, verify that the inverse is

$$A^{-1} = \frac{1}{ad - bc}\begin{bmatrix} d & -b \\ -c & a \end{bmatrix}.$$

76. ***Exploration*** Consider matrices of the form

$$A = \begin{bmatrix} a_{11} & 0 & 0 & 0 & \cdots & 0 \\ 0 & a_{22} & 0 & 0 & \cdots & 0 \\ 0 & 0 & a_{33} & 0 & \cdots & 0 \\ \vdots & \vdots & \vdots & \vdots & \cdots & \vdots \\ 0 & 0 & 0 & 0 & \cdots & a_{nn} \end{bmatrix}.$$

(a) Write a 2×2 matrix and a 3×3 matrix in the form of A. Find the inverse of each.

(b) Use the result of part (a) to make a conjecture about the inverses of matrices in the form of A.

Skills Review

In Exercises 77 and 78, solve the inequality and sketch the solution on the real number line.

77. $|x + 7| \geq 2$

78. $|2x - 1| < 3$

In Exercises 79–82, solve the equation. Approximate the result to three decimal places.

79. $3^{x/2} = 315$

80. $2000e^{-x/5} = 400$

81. $\log_2 x - 2 = 4.5$

82. $\ln x + \ln(x - 1) = 0$

83. **Make a Decision** To work an extended application analyzing the number of U.S. households with color televisions from 1985 to 2005, visit this text's website at *college.hmco.com*. *(Data Source: Nielsen Media Research)*

8.4 The Determinant of a Square Matrix

What you should learn

- Find the determinants of 2 × 2 matrices.
- Find minors and cofactors of square matrices.
- Find the determinants of square matrices.

Why you should learn it

Determinants are often used in other branches of mathematics. For instance, Exercises 79–84 on page 618 show some types of determinants that are useful when changes in variables are made in calculus.

The Determinant of a 2 × 2 Matrix

Every *square* matrix can be associated with a real number called its **determinant.** Determinants have many uses, and several will be discussed in this and the next section. Historically, the use of determinants arose from special number patterns that occur when systems of linear equations are solved. For instance, the system

$$\begin{cases} a_1x + b_1y = c_1 \\ a_2x + b_2y = c_2 \end{cases}$$

has a solution

$$x = \frac{c_1b_2 - c_2b_1}{a_1b_2 - a_2b_1} \quad \text{and} \quad y = \frac{a_1c_2 - a_2c_1}{a_1b_2 - a_2b_1}$$

provided that $a_1b_2 - a_2b_1 \neq 0$. Note that the denominators of the two fractions are the same. This denominator is called the *determinant* of the coefficient matrix of the system.

Coefficient Matrix	*Determinant*
$A = \begin{bmatrix} a_1 & b_1 \\ a_2 & b_2 \end{bmatrix}$	$\det(A) = a_1b_2 - a_2b_1$

The determinant of the matrix A can also be denoted by vertical bars on both sides of the matrix, as indicated in the following definition.

Definition of the Determinant of a 2 × 2 Matrix

The **determinant** of the matrix

$$A = \begin{bmatrix} a_1 & b_1 \\ a_2 & b_2 \end{bmatrix}$$

is given by

$$\det(A) = |A| = \begin{vmatrix} a_1 & b_1 \\ a_2 & b_2 \end{vmatrix} = a_1b_2 - a_2b_1.$$

In this text, $\det(A)$ and $|A|$ are used interchangeably to represent the determinant of A. Although vertical bars are also used to denote the absolute value of a real number, the context will show which use is intended.

A convenient method for remembering the formula for the determinant of a 2 × 2 matrix is shown in the following diagram.

$$\det(A) = \begin{vmatrix} a_1 & b_1 \\ a_2 & b_2 \end{vmatrix} = a_1b_2 - a_2b_1$$

Note that the determinant is the difference of the products of the two diagonals of the matrix.

Example 1 The Determinant of a 2 × 2 Matrix

Find the determinant of each matrix.

a. $A = \begin{bmatrix} 2 & -3 \\ 1 & 2 \end{bmatrix}$

b. $B = \begin{bmatrix} 2 & 1 \\ 4 & 2 \end{bmatrix}$

c. $C = \begin{bmatrix} 0 & \frac{3}{2} \\ 2 & 4 \end{bmatrix}$

Solution

a. $\det(A) = \begin{vmatrix} 2 & -3 \\ 1 & 2 \end{vmatrix}$

$= 2(2) - 1(-3)$

$= 4 + 3 = 7$

b. $\det(B) = \begin{vmatrix} 2 & 1 \\ 4 & 2 \end{vmatrix}$

$= 2(2) - 4(1)$

$= 4 - 4 = 0$

c. $\det(C) = \begin{vmatrix} 0 & \frac{3}{2} \\ 2 & 4 \end{vmatrix}$

$= 0(4) - 2\left(\frac{3}{2}\right)$

$= 0 - 3 = -3$

✓CHECKPOINT Now try Exercise 5.

Exploration

Use a graphing utility with matrix capabilities to find the determinant of the following matrix.

$$A = \begin{bmatrix} 1 & 2 \\ -1 & 0 \\ 3 & -2 \end{bmatrix}$$

What message appears on the screen? Why does the graphing utility display this message?

Notice in Example 1 that the determinant of a matrix can be positive, zero, or negative.

The determinant of a matrix of order 1×1 is defined simply as the entry of the matrix. For instance, if $A = [-2]$, then $\det(A) = -2$.

Technology

Most graphing utilities can evaluate the determinant of a matrix. For instance, you can evaluate the determinant of

$$A = \begin{bmatrix} 2 & -3 \\ 1 & 2 \end{bmatrix}$$

by entering the matrix as $[A]$ and then choosing the *determinant* feature. The result should be 7, as in Example 1(a). Try evaluating the determinants of other matrices. Consult the user's guide for your graphing utility for specific keystrokes.

Minors and Cofactors

To define the determinant of a square matrix of order 3×3 or higher, it is convenient to introduce the concepts of **minors** and **cofactors.**

Sign Pattern for Cofactors

$$\begin{bmatrix} + & - & + \\ - & + & - \\ + & - & + \end{bmatrix}$$

3×3 matrix

$$\begin{bmatrix} + & - & + & - \\ - & + & - & + \\ + & - & + & - \\ - & + & - & + \end{bmatrix}$$

4×4 matrix

$$\begin{bmatrix} + & - & + & - & + & \cdots \\ - & + & - & + & - & \cdots \\ + & - & + & - & + & \cdots \\ - & + & - & + & - & \cdots \\ + & - & + & - & + & \cdots \\ \vdots & \vdots & \vdots & \vdots & \vdots & \end{bmatrix}$$

$n \times n$ matrix

Minors and Cofactors of a Square Matrix

If A is a square matrix, the **minor** M_{ij} of the entry a_{ij} is the determinant of the matrix obtained by deleting the ith row and jth column of A. The **cofactor** C_{ij} of the entry a_{ij} is

$$C_{ij} = (-1)^{i+j} M_{ij}.$$

In the sign pattern for cofactors at the left, notice that *odd* positions (where $i + j$ is odd) have negative signs and *even* positions (where $i + j$ is even) have positive signs.

Example 2 Finding the Minors and Cofactors of a Matrix

Find all the minors and cofactors of

$$A = \begin{bmatrix} 0 & 2 & 1 \\ 3 & -1 & 2 \\ 4 & 0 & 1 \end{bmatrix}.$$

Solution

To find the minor M_{11}, delete the first row and first column of A and evaluate the determinant of the resulting matrix.

$$\begin{bmatrix} 0 & 2 & 1 \\ 3 & -1 & 2 \\ 4 & 0 & 1 \end{bmatrix}, \quad M_{11} = \begin{vmatrix} -1 & 2 \\ 0 & 1 \end{vmatrix} = -1(1) - 0(2) = -1$$

Similarly, to find M_{12}, delete the first row and second column.

$$\begin{bmatrix} 0 & 2 & 1 \\ 3 & -1 & 2 \\ 4 & 0 & 1 \end{bmatrix}, \quad M_{12} = \begin{vmatrix} 3 & 2 \\ 4 & 1 \end{vmatrix} = 3(1) - 4(2) = -5$$

Continuing this pattern, you obtain the minors.

$$\begin{array}{lll} M_{11} = -1 & M_{12} = -5 & M_{13} = 4 \\ M_{21} = 2 & M_{22} = -4 & M_{23} = -8 \\ M_{31} = 5 & M_{32} = -3 & M_{33} = -6 \end{array}$$

Now, to find the cofactors, combine these minors with the checkerboard pattern of signs for a 3×3 matrix shown at the upper left.

$$\begin{array}{lll} C_{11} = -1 & C_{12} = 5 & C_{13} = 4 \\ C_{21} = -2 & C_{22} = -4 & C_{23} = 8 \\ C_{31} = 5 & C_{32} = 3 & C_{33} = -6 \end{array}$$

✓CHECKPOINT Now try Exercise 27.

The Determinant of a Square Matrix

The definition below is called *inductive* because it uses determinants of matrices of order $n - 1$ to define determinants of matrices of order n.

Determinant of a Square Matrix

If A is a square matrix (of order 2×2 or greater), the determinant of A is the sum of the entries in any row (or column) of A multiplied by their respective cofactors. For instance, expanding along the first row yields

$$|A| = a_{11}C_{11} + a_{12}C_{12} + \cdot \cdot \cdot + a_{1n}C_{1n}.$$

Applying this definition to find a determinant is called **expanding by cofactors.**

Try checking that for a 2×2 matrix

$$A = \begin{bmatrix} a_1 & b_1 \\ a_2 & b_2 \end{bmatrix}$$

this definition of the determinant yields $|A| = a_1b_2 - a_2b_1$, as previously defined.

Example 3 The Determinant of a Matrix of Order 3 × 3

Find the determinant of

$$A = \begin{bmatrix} 0 & 2 & 1 \\ 3 & -1 & 2 \\ 4 & 0 & 1 \end{bmatrix}.$$

Solution

Note that this is the same matrix that was in Example 2. There you found the cofactors of the entries in the first row to be

$$C_{11} = -1, \quad C_{12} = 5, \quad \text{and} \quad C_{13} = 4.$$

So, by the definition of a determinant, you have

$$\begin{aligned} |A| &= a_{11}C_{11} + a_{12}C_{12} + a_{13}C_{13} && \text{First-row expansion} \\ &= 0(-1) + 2(5) + 1(4) \\ &= 14. \end{aligned}$$

CHECKPOINT Now try Exercise 37.

In Example 3, the determinant was found by expanding by the cofactors in the first row. You could have used any row or column. For instance, you could have expanded along the second row to obtain

$$\begin{aligned} |A| &= a_{21}C_{21} + a_{22}C_{22} + a_{23}C_{23} && \text{Second-row expansion} \\ &= 3(-2) + (-1)(-4) + 2(8) \\ &= 14. \end{aligned}$$

When expanding by cofactors, you do not need to find cofactors of zero entries, because zero times its cofactor is zero.

$$a_{ij}C_{ij} = (0)C_{ij} = 0$$

So, the row (or column) containing the most zeros is usually the best choice for expansion by cofactors. This is demonstrated in the next example.

Example 4 The Determinant of a Matrix of Order 4 × 4

Find the determinant of

$$A = \begin{bmatrix} 1 & -2 & 3 & 0 \\ -1 & 1 & 0 & 2 \\ 0 & 2 & 0 & 3 \\ 3 & 4 & 0 & 2 \end{bmatrix}.$$

Solution

After inspecting this matrix, you can see that three of the entries in the third column are zeros. So, you can eliminate some of the work in the expansion by using the third column.

$$|A| = 3(C_{13}) + 0(C_{23}) + 0(C_{33}) + 0(C_{43})$$

Because C_{23}, C_{33}, and C_{43} have zero coefficients, you need only find the cofactor C_{13}. To do this, delete the first row and third column of A and evaluate the determinant of the resulting matrix.

$$C_{13} = (-1)^{1+3}\begin{vmatrix} -1 & 1 & 2 \\ 0 & 2 & 3 \\ 3 & 4 & 2 \end{vmatrix}$$ Delete 1st row and 3rd column.

$$= \begin{vmatrix} -1 & 1 & 2 \\ 0 & 2 & 3 \\ 3 & 4 & 2 \end{vmatrix}$$ Simplify.

Expanding by cofactors in the second row yields

$$C_{13} = 0(-1)^3\begin{vmatrix} 1 & 2 \\ 4 & 2 \end{vmatrix} + 2(-1)^4\begin{vmatrix} -1 & 2 \\ 3 & 2 \end{vmatrix} + 3(-1)^5\begin{vmatrix} -1 & 1 \\ 3 & 4 \end{vmatrix}$$

$$= 0 + 2(1)(-8) + 3(-1)(-7)$$

$$= 5.$$

So, you obtain

$$|A| = 3C_{13}$$

$$= 3(5)$$

$$= 15.$$

CHECKPOINT Now try Exercise 47.

Try using a graphing utility to confirm the result of Example 4.

8.4 Exercises

VOCABULARY CHECK: Fill in the blanks.

1. Both $\det(A)$ and $|A|$ represent the ________ of the matrix A.
2. The ________ M_{ij} of the entry a_{ij} is the determinant of the matrix obtained by deleting the ith row and jth column of the square matrix A.
3. The ________ C_{ij} of the entry a_{ij} of the square matrix A is given by $(-1)^{i+j} M_{ij}$.
4. The method of finding the determinant of a matrix of order 2×2 or greater is called ________ by ________.

In Exercises 1–16, find the determinant of the matrix.

1. $[5]$

2. $[-8]$

3. $\begin{bmatrix} 2 & 1 \\ 3 & 4 \end{bmatrix}$

4. $\begin{bmatrix} -3 & 1 \\ 5 & 2 \end{bmatrix}$

5. $\begin{bmatrix} 5 & 2 \\ -6 & 3 \end{bmatrix}$

6. $\begin{bmatrix} 2 & -2 \\ 4 & 3 \end{bmatrix}$

7. $\begin{bmatrix} -7 & 0 \\ 3 & 0 \end{bmatrix}$

8. $\begin{bmatrix} 4 & -3 \\ 0 & 0 \end{bmatrix}$

9. $\begin{bmatrix} 2 & 6 \\ 0 & 3 \end{bmatrix}$

10. $\begin{bmatrix} 2 & -3 \\ -6 & 9 \end{bmatrix}$

11. $\begin{bmatrix} -3 & -2 \\ -6 & -1 \end{bmatrix}$

12. $\begin{bmatrix} 4 & 7 \\ -2 & 5 \end{bmatrix}$

13. $\begin{bmatrix} 9 & 0 \\ 7 & 8 \end{bmatrix}$

14. $\begin{bmatrix} 0 & 6 \\ -3 & 2 \end{bmatrix}$

15. $\begin{bmatrix} -\frac{1}{2} & \frac{1}{3} \\ -6 & \frac{1}{3} \end{bmatrix}$

16. $\begin{bmatrix} \frac{2}{3} & \frac{4}{3} \\ -1 & -\frac{1}{3} \end{bmatrix}$

In Exercises 17–22, use the matrix capabilities of a graphing utility to find the determinant of the matrix.

17. $\begin{bmatrix} 0.3 & 0.2 & 0.2 \\ 0.2 & 0.2 & 0.2 \\ -0.4 & 0.4 & 0.3 \end{bmatrix}$

18. $\begin{bmatrix} 0.1 & 0.2 & 0.3 \\ -0.3 & 0.2 & 0.2 \\ 0.5 & 0.4 & 0.4 \end{bmatrix}$

19. $\begin{bmatrix} 0.9 & 0.7 & 0 \\ -0.1 & 0.3 & 1.3 \\ -2.2 & 4.2 & 6.1 \end{bmatrix}$

20. $\begin{bmatrix} 0.1 & 0.1 & -4.3 \\ 7.5 & 6.2 & 0.7 \\ 0.3 & 0.6 & -1.2 \end{bmatrix}$

21. $\begin{bmatrix} 1 & 4 & -2 \\ 3 & 6 & -6 \\ -2 & 1 & 4 \end{bmatrix}$

22. $\begin{bmatrix} 2 & 3 & 1 \\ 0 & 5 & -2 \\ 0 & 0 & -2 \end{bmatrix}$

In Exercises 23–30, find all (a) minors and (b) cofactors of the matrix.

23. $\begin{bmatrix} 3 & 4 \\ 2 & -5 \end{bmatrix}$

24. $\begin{bmatrix} 11 & 0 \\ -3 & 2 \end{bmatrix}$

25. $\begin{bmatrix} 3 & 1 \\ -2 & -4 \end{bmatrix}$

26. $\begin{bmatrix} -6 & 5 \\ 7 & -2 \end{bmatrix}$

27. $\begin{bmatrix} 4 & 0 & 2 \\ -3 & 2 & 1 \\ 1 & -1 & 1 \end{bmatrix}$

28. $\begin{bmatrix} 1 & -1 & 0 \\ 3 & 2 & 5 \\ 4 & -6 & 4 \end{bmatrix}$

29. $\begin{bmatrix} 3 & -2 & 8 \\ 3 & 2 & -6 \\ -1 & 3 & 6 \end{bmatrix}$

30. $\begin{bmatrix} -2 & 9 & 4 \\ 7 & -6 & 0 \\ 6 & 7 & -6 \end{bmatrix}$

In Exercises 31–36, find the determinant of the matrix by the method of expansion by cofactors. Expand using the indicated row or column.

31. $\begin{bmatrix} -3 & 2 & 1 \\ 4 & 5 & 6 \\ 2 & -3 & 1 \end{bmatrix}$

(a) Row 1

(b) Column 2

32. $\begin{bmatrix} -3 & 4 & 2 \\ 6 & 3 & 1 \\ 4 & -7 & -8 \end{bmatrix}$

(a) Row 2

(b) Column 3

33. $\begin{bmatrix} 5 & 0 & -3 \\ 0 & 12 & 4 \\ 1 & 6 & 3 \end{bmatrix}$

(a) Row 2

(b) Column 2

34. $\begin{bmatrix} 10 & -5 & 5 \\ 30 & 0 & 10 \\ 0 & 10 & 1 \end{bmatrix}$

(a) Row 3

(b) Column 1

35. $\begin{bmatrix} 6 & 0 & -3 & 5 \\ 4 & 13 & 6 & -8 \\ -1 & 0 & 7 & 4 \\ 8 & 6 & 0 & 2 \end{bmatrix}$

(a) Row 2

(b) Column 2

36. $\begin{bmatrix} 10 & 8 & 3 & -7 \\ 4 & 0 & 5 & -6 \\ 0 & 3 & 2 & 7 \\ 1 & 0 & -3 & 2 \end{bmatrix}$

(a) Row 3

(b) Column 1

In Exercises 37–52, find the determinant of the matrix. Expand by cofactors on the row or column that appears to make the computations easiest.

37. $\begin{bmatrix} 2 & -1 & 0 \\ 4 & 2 & 1 \\ 4 & 2 & 1 \end{bmatrix}$

38. $\begin{bmatrix} -2 & 2 & 3 \\ 1 & -1 & 0 \\ 0 & 1 & 4 \end{bmatrix}$

39. $\begin{bmatrix} 6 & 3 & -7 \\ 0 & 0 & 0 \\ 4 & -6 & 3 \end{bmatrix}$

40. $\begin{bmatrix} 1 & 1 & 2 \\ 3 & 1 & 0 \\ -2 & 0 & 3 \end{bmatrix}$

41. $\begin{bmatrix} -1 & 2 & -5 \\ 0 & 3 & 4 \\ 0 & 0 & 3 \end{bmatrix}$

42. $\begin{bmatrix} 1 & 0 & 0 \\ -4 & -1 & 0 \\ 5 & 1 & 5 \end{bmatrix}$

43. $\begin{bmatrix} 1 & 4 & -2 \\ 3 & 2 & 0 \\ -1 & 4 & 3 \end{bmatrix}$

44. $\begin{bmatrix} 2 & -1 & 3 \\ 1 & 4 & 4 \\ 1 & 0 & 2 \end{bmatrix}$

45. $\begin{bmatrix} 2 & 4 & 6 \\ 0 & 3 & 1 \\ 0 & 0 & -5 \end{bmatrix}$

46. $\begin{bmatrix} -3 & 0 & 0 \\ 7 & 11 & 0 \\ 1 & 2 & 2 \end{bmatrix}$

47. $\begin{bmatrix} 2 & 6 & 6 & 2 \\ 2 & 7 & 3 & 6 \\ 1 & 5 & 0 & 1 \\ 3 & 7 & 0 & 7 \end{bmatrix}$

48. $\begin{bmatrix} 3 & 6 & -5 & 4 \\ -2 & 0 & 6 & 0 \\ 1 & 1 & 2 & 2 \\ 0 & 3 & -1 & -1 \end{bmatrix}$

49. $\begin{bmatrix} 5 & 3 & 0 & 6 \\ 4 & 6 & 4 & 12 \\ 0 & 2 & -3 & 4 \\ 0 & 1 & -2 & 2 \end{bmatrix}$

50. $\begin{bmatrix} 1 & 4 & 3 & 2 \\ -5 & 6 & 2 & 1 \\ 0 & 0 & 0 & 0 \\ 3 & -2 & 1 & 5 \end{bmatrix}$

51. $\begin{bmatrix} 3 & 2 & 4 & -1 & 5 \\ -2 & 0 & 1 & 3 & 2 \\ 1 & 0 & 0 & 4 & 0 \\ 6 & 0 & 2 & -1 & 0 \\ 3 & 0 & 5 & 1 & 0 \end{bmatrix}$

52. $\begin{bmatrix} 5 & 2 & 0 & 0 & -2 \\ 0 & 1 & 4 & 3 & 2 \\ 0 & 0 & 2 & 6 & 3 \\ 0 & 0 & 3 & 4 & 1 \\ 0 & 0 & 0 & 0 & 2 \end{bmatrix}$

In Exercises 53–60, use the matrix capabilities of a graphing utility to evaluate the determinant.

53. $\begin{vmatrix} 3 & 8 & -7 \\ 0 & -5 & 4 \\ 8 & 1 & 6 \end{vmatrix}$

54. $\begin{vmatrix} 5 & -8 & 0 \\ 9 & 7 & 4 \\ -8 & 7 & 1 \end{vmatrix}$

55. $\begin{vmatrix} 7 & 0 & -14 \\ -2 & 5 & 4 \\ -6 & 2 & 12 \end{vmatrix}$

56. $\begin{vmatrix} 3 & 0 & 0 \\ -2 & 5 & 0 \\ 12 & 5 & 7 \end{vmatrix}$

57. $\begin{vmatrix} 1 & -1 & 8 & 4 \\ 2 & 6 & 0 & -4 \\ 2 & 0 & 2 & 6 \\ 0 & 2 & 8 & 0 \end{vmatrix}$

58. $\begin{vmatrix} 0 & -3 & 8 & 2 \\ 8 & 1 & -1 & 6 \\ -4 & 6 & 0 & 9 \\ -7 & 0 & 0 & 14 \end{vmatrix}$

59. $\begin{vmatrix} 3 & -2 & 4 & 3 & 1 \\ -1 & 0 & 2 & 1 & 0 \\ 5 & -1 & 0 & 3 & 2 \\ 4 & 7 & -8 & 0 & 0 \\ 1 & 2 & 3 & 0 & 2 \end{vmatrix}$

60. $\begin{vmatrix} -2 & 0 & 0 & 0 & 0 \\ 0 & 3 & 0 & 0 & 0 \\ 0 & 0 & -1 & 0 & 0 \\ 0 & 0 & 0 & 2 & 0 \\ 0 & 0 & 0 & 0 & -4 \end{vmatrix}$

In Exercises 61–68, find (a) $|A|$, (b) $|B|$, (c) AB, and (d) $|AB|$.

61. $A = \begin{bmatrix} -1 & 0 \\ 0 & 3 \end{bmatrix}, \quad B = \begin{bmatrix} 2 & 0 \\ 0 & -1 \end{bmatrix}$

62. $A = \begin{bmatrix} -2 & 1 \\ 4 & -2 \end{bmatrix}, \quad B = \begin{bmatrix} 1 & 2 \\ 0 & -1 \end{bmatrix}$

63. $A = \begin{bmatrix} 4 & 0 \\ 3 & -2 \end{bmatrix}, \quad B = \begin{bmatrix} -1 & 1 \\ -2 & 2 \end{bmatrix}$

64. $A = \begin{bmatrix} 5 & 4 \\ 3 & -1 \end{bmatrix}, \quad B = \begin{bmatrix} 0 & 6 \\ 1 & -2 \end{bmatrix}$

65. $A = \begin{bmatrix} 0 & 1 & 2 \\ -3 & -2 & 1 \\ 0 & 4 & 1 \end{bmatrix}, \quad B = \begin{bmatrix} 3 & -2 & 0 \\ 1 & -1 & 2 \\ 3 & 1 & 1 \end{bmatrix}$

66. $A = \begin{bmatrix} 3 & 2 & 0 \\ -1 & -3 & 4 \\ -2 & 0 & 1 \end{bmatrix}, \quad B = \begin{bmatrix} -3 & 0 & 1 \\ 0 & 2 & -1 \\ -2 & -1 & 1 \end{bmatrix}$

67. $A = \begin{bmatrix} -1 & 2 & 1 \\ 1 & 0 & 1 \\ 0 & 1 & 0 \end{bmatrix}, \quad B = \begin{bmatrix} -1 & 0 & 0 \\ 0 & 2 & 0 \\ 0 & 0 & 3 \end{bmatrix}$

68. $A = \begin{bmatrix} 2 & 0 & 1 \\ 1 & -1 & 2 \\ 3 & 1 & 0 \end{bmatrix}, \quad B = \begin{bmatrix} 2 & -1 & 4 \\ 0 & 1 & 3 \\ 3 & -2 & 1 \end{bmatrix}$

In Exercises 69–74, evaluate the determinant(s) to verify the equation.

69. $\begin{vmatrix} w & x \\ y & z \end{vmatrix} = -\begin{vmatrix} y & z \\ w & x \end{vmatrix}$

70. $\begin{vmatrix} w & cx \\ y & cz \end{vmatrix} = c\begin{vmatrix} w & x \\ y & z \end{vmatrix}$

71. $\begin{vmatrix} w & x \\ y & z \end{vmatrix} = \begin{vmatrix} w & x + cw \\ y & z + cy \end{vmatrix}$

72. $\begin{vmatrix} w & x \\ cw & cx \end{vmatrix} = 0$

73. $\begin{vmatrix} 1 & x & x^2 \\ 1 & y & y^2 \\ 1 & z & z^2 \end{vmatrix} = (y - x)(z - x)(z - y)$

74. $\begin{vmatrix} a + b & a & a \\ a & a + b & a \\ a & a & a + b \end{vmatrix} = b^2(3a + b)$

In Exercises 75–78, solve for x.

75. $\begin{vmatrix} x - 1 & 2 \\ 3 & x - 2 \end{vmatrix} = 0$

76. $\begin{vmatrix} x - 2 & -1 \\ -3 & x \end{vmatrix} = 0$

77. $\begin{vmatrix} x + 3 & 2 \\ 1 & x + 2 \end{vmatrix} = 0$

78. $\begin{vmatrix} x + 4 & -2 \\ 7 & x - 5 \end{vmatrix} = 0$

In Exercises 79–84, evaluate the determinant in which the entries are functions. Determinants of this type occur when changes in variables are made in calculus.

79. $\begin{vmatrix} 4u & -1 \\ -1 & 2v \end{vmatrix}$

80. $\begin{vmatrix} 3x^2 & -3y^2 \\ 1 & 1 \end{vmatrix}$

81. $\begin{vmatrix} e^{2x} & e^{3x} \\ 2e^{2x} & 3e^{3x} \end{vmatrix}$

82. $\begin{vmatrix} e^{-x} & xe^{-x} \\ -e^{-x} & (1-x)e^{-x} \end{vmatrix}$

83. $\begin{vmatrix} x & \ln x \\ 1 & 1/x \end{vmatrix}$

84. $\begin{vmatrix} x & x \ln x \\ 1 & 1 + \ln x \end{vmatrix}$

Synthesis

True or False? **In Exercises 85 and 86, determine whether the statement is true or false. Justify your answer.**

85. If a square matrix has an entire row of zeros, the determinant will always be zero.

86. If two columns of a square matrix are the same, the determinant of the matrix will be zero.

87. ***Exploration*** Find square matrices A and B to demonstrate that $|A + B| \neq |A| + |B|$.

88. ***Exploration*** Consider square matrices in which the entries are consecutive integers. An example of such a matrix is

$$\begin{bmatrix} 4 & 5 & 6 \\ 7 & 8 & 9 \\ 10 & 11 & 12 \end{bmatrix}.$$

(a) Use a graphing utility to evaluate the determinants of four matrices of this type. Make a conjecture based on the results.

(b) Verify your conjecture.

89. ***Writing*** Write a brief paragraph explaining the difference between a square matrix and its determinant.

90. ***Think About It*** If A is a matrix of order 3×3 such that $|A| = 5$, is it possible to find $|2A|$? Explain.

Properties of Determinants **In Exercises 91–93, a property of determinants is given (A and B are square matrices). State how the property has been applied to the given determinants and use a graphing utility to verify the results.**

91. If B is obtained from A by interchanging two rows of A or interchanging two columns of A, then $|B| = -|A|$.

(a) $\begin{vmatrix} 1 & 3 & 4 \\ -7 & 2 & -5 \\ 6 & 1 & 2 \end{vmatrix} = -\begin{vmatrix} 1 & 4 & 3 \\ -7 & -5 & 2 \\ 6 & 2 & 1 \end{vmatrix}$

(b) $\begin{vmatrix} 1 & 3 & 4 \\ -2 & 2 & 0 \\ 1 & 6 & 2 \end{vmatrix} = -\begin{vmatrix} 1 & 6 & 2 \\ -2 & 2 & 0 \\ 1 & 3 & 4 \end{vmatrix}$

92. If B is obtained from A by adding a multiple of a row of A to another row of A or by adding a multiple of a column of A to another column of A, then $|B| = |A|$.

(a) $\begin{vmatrix} 1 & -3 \\ 5 & 2 \end{vmatrix} = \begin{vmatrix} 1 & -3 \\ 0 & 17 \end{vmatrix}$

(b) $\begin{vmatrix} 5 & 4 & 2 \\ 2 & -3 & 4 \\ 7 & 6 & 3 \end{vmatrix} = \begin{vmatrix} 1 & 10 & -6 \\ 2 & -3 & 4 \\ 7 & 6 & 3 \end{vmatrix}$

93. If B is obtained from A by multiplying a row by a nonzero constant c or by multiplying a column by a nonzero constant c, then $|B| = c|A|$.

(a) $\begin{vmatrix} 5 & 10 \\ 2 & -3 \end{vmatrix} = 5\begin{vmatrix} 1 & 2 \\ 2 & -3 \end{vmatrix}$

(b) $\begin{vmatrix} 1 & 8 & -3 \\ 3 & -12 & 6 \\ 7 & 4 & 3 \end{vmatrix} = 12\begin{vmatrix} 1 & 2 & -1 \\ 3 & -3 & 2 \\ 7 & 1 & 3 \end{vmatrix}$

94. ***Exploration*** A **diagonal matrix** is a square matrix with all zero entries above and below its main diagonal. Evaluate the determinant of each diagonal matrix. Make a conjecture based on your results.

(a) $\begin{vmatrix} 7 & 0 \\ 0 & 4 \end{vmatrix}$

(b) $\begin{vmatrix} -1 & 0 & 0 \\ 0 & 5 & 0 \\ 0 & 0 & 2 \end{vmatrix}$

(c) $\begin{vmatrix} 2 & 0 & 0 & 0 \\ 0 & -2 & 0 & 0 \\ 0 & 0 & 1 & 0 \\ 0 & 0 & 0 & 3 \end{vmatrix}$

Skills Review

In Exercises 95–100, find the domain of the function.

95. $f(x) = x^3 - 2x$

96. $g(x) = \sqrt[3]{x}$

97. $h(x) = \sqrt{16 - x^2}$

98. $A(x) = \dfrac{3}{36 - x^2}$

99. $g(t) = \ln(t - 1)$

100. $f(s) = 625e^{-0.5s}$

In Exercises 101 and 102, sketch the graph of the solution of the system of inequalities.

101. $\begin{cases} x + y \leq 8 \\ x \geq -3 \\ 2x - y < 5 \end{cases}$

102. $\begin{cases} -x - y > 4 \\ y \leq 1 \\ 7x + 4y \leq -10 \end{cases}$

In Exercises 103–106, find the inverse of the matrix (if it exists).

103. $\begin{bmatrix} -4 & 1 \\ 8 & -1 \end{bmatrix}$

104. $\begin{bmatrix} -5 & -8 \\ 3 & 6 \end{bmatrix}$

105. $\begin{bmatrix} -7 & 2 & 9 \\ 2 & -4 & -6 \\ 3 & 5 & 2 \end{bmatrix}$

106. $\begin{bmatrix} -6 & 2 & 0 \\ 1 & 3 & -2 \\ -2 & 0 & 1 \end{bmatrix}$

8.5 Applications of Matrices and Determinants

What you should learn

- Use Cramer's Rule to solve systems of linear equations.
- Use determinants to find the areas of triangles.
- Use a determinant to test for collinear points and find an equation of a line passing through two points.
- Use matrices to encode and decode messages.

Why you should learn it

You can use Cramer's Rule to solve real-life problems. For instance, in Exercise 58 on page 630, Cramer's Rule is used to find a quadratic model for the number of U.S. Supreme Court cases waiting to be tried.

Cramer's Rule

So far, you have studied three methods for solving a system of linear equations: substitution, elimination with equations, and elimination with matrices. In this section, you will study one more method, **Cramer's Rule,** named after Gabriel Cramer (1704–1752). This rule uses determinants to write the solution of a system of linear equations. To see how Cramer's Rule works, take another look at the solution described at the beginning of Section 8.4. There, it was pointed out that the system

$$\begin{cases} a_1x + b_1y = c_1 \\ a_2x + b_2y = c_2 \end{cases}$$

has a solution

$$x = \frac{c_1b_2 - c_2b_1}{a_1b_2 - a_2b_1} \quad \text{and} \quad y = \frac{a_1c_2 - a_2c_1}{a_1b_2 - a_2b_1}$$

provided that $a_1b_2 - a_2b_1 \neq 0$. Each numerator and denominator in this solution can be expressed as a determinant, as follows.

$$x = \frac{c_1b_2 - c_2b_1}{a_1b_2 - a_2b_1} = \frac{\begin{vmatrix} c_1 & b_1 \\ c_2 & b_2 \end{vmatrix}}{\begin{vmatrix} a_1 & b_1 \\ a_2 & b_2 \end{vmatrix}} \qquad y = \frac{a_1c_2 - a_2c_1}{a_1b_2 - a_2b_1} = \frac{\begin{vmatrix} a_1 & c_1 \\ a_2 & c_2 \end{vmatrix}}{\begin{vmatrix} a_1 & b_1 \\ a_2 & b_2 \end{vmatrix}}$$

Relative to the original system, the denominator for x and y is simply the determinant of the *coefficient* matrix of the system. This determinant is denoted by D. The numerators for x and y are denoted by D_x and D_y, respectively. They are formed by using the column of constants as replacements for the coefficients of x and y, as follows.

Coefficient Matrix	D	D_x	D_y
$\begin{bmatrix} a_1 & b_1 \\ a_2 & b_2 \end{bmatrix}$	$\begin{vmatrix} a_1 & b_1 \\ a_2 & b_2 \end{vmatrix}$	$\begin{vmatrix} c_1 & b_1 \\ c_2 & b_2 \end{vmatrix}$	$\begin{vmatrix} a_1 & c_1 \\ a_2 & c_2 \end{vmatrix}$

For example, given the system

$$\begin{cases} 2x - 5y = 3 \\ -4x + 3y = 8 \end{cases}$$

the coefficient matrix, D, D_x, and D_y are as follows.

Coefficient Matrix	D	D_x	D_y
$\begin{bmatrix} 2 & -5 \\ -4 & 3 \end{bmatrix}$	$\begin{vmatrix} 2 & -5 \\ -4 & 3 \end{vmatrix}$	$\begin{vmatrix} 3 & -5 \\ 8 & 3 \end{vmatrix}$	$\begin{vmatrix} 2 & 3 \\ -4 & 8 \end{vmatrix}$

Cramer's Rule generalizes easily to systems of n equations in n variables. The value of each variable is given as the quotient of two determinants. The denominator is the determinant of the coefficient matrix, and the numerator is the determinant of the matrix formed by replacing the column corresponding to the variable (being solved for) with the column representing the constants. For instance, the solution for x_3 in the following system is shown.

$$\begin{cases} a_{11}x_1 + a_{12}x_2 + a_{13}x_3 = b_1 \\ a_{21}x_1 + a_{22}x_2 + a_{23}x_3 = b_2 \\ a_{31}x_1 + a_{32}x_2 + a_{33}x_3 = b_3 \end{cases} \qquad x_3 = \frac{|A_3|}{|A|} = \frac{\begin{vmatrix} a_{11} & a_{12} & b_1 \\ a_{21} & a_{22} & b_2 \\ a_{31} & a_{32} & b_3 \end{vmatrix}}{\begin{vmatrix} a_{11} & a_{12} & a_{13} \\ a_{21} & a_{22} & a_{23} \\ a_{31} & a_{32} & a_{33} \end{vmatrix}}$$

Cramer's Rule

If a system of n linear equations in n variables has a coefficient matrix A with a nonzero determinant $|A|$, the solution of the system is

$$x_1 = \frac{|A_1|}{|A|}, \quad x_2 = \frac{|A_2|}{|A|}, \quad . . . , \quad x_n = \frac{|A_n|}{|A|}$$

where the ith column of A_i is the column of constants in the system of equations. If the determinant of the coefficient matrix is zero, the system has either no solution or infinitely many solutions.

Example 1 Using Cramer's Rule for a 2 × 2 System

Use Cramer's Rule to solve the system of linear equations.

$$\begin{cases} 4x - 2y = 10 \\ 3x - 5y = 11 \end{cases}$$

Solution

To begin, find the determinant of the coefficient matrix.

$$D = \begin{vmatrix} 4 & -2 \\ 3 & -5 \end{vmatrix} = -20 - (-6) = -14$$

Because this determinant is not zero, you can apply Cramer's Rule.

$$x = \frac{D_x}{D} = \frac{\begin{vmatrix} 10 & -2 \\ 11 & -5 \end{vmatrix}}{-14} = \frac{-50 - (-22)}{-14} = \frac{-28}{-14} = 2$$

$$y = \frac{D_y}{D} = \frac{\begin{vmatrix} 4 & 10 \\ 3 & 11 \end{vmatrix}}{-14} = \frac{44 - 30}{-14} = \frac{14}{-14} = -1$$

So, the solution is $x = 2$ and $y = -1$. Check this in the original system.

CHECKPOINT Now try Exercise 1.

Example 2 **Using Cramer's Rule for a 3 × 3 System**

Use Cramer's Rule to solve the system of linear equations.

$$\begin{cases} -x + 2y - 3z = 1 \\ 2x \qquad + z = 0 \\ 3x - 4y + 4z = 2 \end{cases}$$

Solution

To find the determinant of the coefficient matrix

$$\begin{bmatrix} -1 & 2 & -3 \\ 2 & 0 & 1 \\ 3 & -4 & 4 \end{bmatrix}$$

expand along the second row, as follows.

$$D = 2(-1)^3\begin{vmatrix} 2 & -3 \\ -4 & 4 \end{vmatrix} + 0(-1)^4\begin{vmatrix} -1 & -3 \\ 3 & 4 \end{vmatrix} + 1(-1)^5\begin{vmatrix} -1 & 2 \\ 3 & -4 \end{vmatrix}$$

$$= -2(-4) + 0 - 1(-2)$$

$$= 10$$

Because this determinant is not zero, you can apply Cramer's Rule.

$$x = \frac{D_x}{D} = \frac{\begin{vmatrix} 1 & 2 & -3 \\ 0 & 0 & 1 \\ 2 & -4 & 4 \end{vmatrix}}{10} = \frac{8}{10} = \frac{4}{5}$$

$$y = \frac{D_y}{D} = \frac{\begin{vmatrix} -1 & 1 & -3 \\ 2 & 0 & 1 \\ 3 & 2 & 4 \end{vmatrix}}{10} = \frac{-15}{10} = -\frac{3}{2}$$

$$z = \frac{D_z}{D} = \frac{\begin{vmatrix} -1 & 2 & 1 \\ 2 & 0 & 0 \\ 3 & -4 & 2 \end{vmatrix}}{10} = \frac{-16}{10} = -\frac{8}{5}$$

The solution is $\left(\frac{4}{5}, -\frac{3}{2}, -\frac{8}{5}\right)$. Check this in the original system as follows.

Check

$-\left(\frac{4}{5}\right) + 2\left(-\frac{3}{2}\right) - 3\left(-\frac{8}{5}\right) \stackrel{?}{=} 1$ Substitute into Equation 1.

$-\frac{4}{5} - 3 + \frac{24}{5} = 1$ Equation 1 checks. ✓

$2\left(\frac{4}{5}\right) + \left(-\frac{8}{5}\right) \stackrel{?}{=} 0$ Substitute into Equation 2.

$\frac{8}{5} - \frac{8}{5} = 0$ Equation 2 checks. ✓

$3\left(\frac{4}{5}\right) - 4\left(-\frac{3}{2}\right) + 4\left(-\frac{8}{5}\right) \stackrel{?}{=} 2$ Substitute into Equation 3.

$\frac{12}{5} + 6 - \frac{32}{5} = 2$ Equation 3 checks. ✓

✓CHECKPOINT Now try Exercise 7.

Remember that Cramer's Rule does not apply when the determinant of the coefficient matrix is zero. This would create division by zero, which is undefined.

Area of a Triangle

Another application of matrices and determinants is finding the area of a triangle whose vertices are given as points in a coordinate plane.

Area of a Triangle

The area of a triangle with vertices (x_1, y_1), (x_2, y_2), and (x_3, y_3) is

$$\text{Area} = \pm\frac{1}{2}\begin{vmatrix} x_1 & y_1 & 1 \\ x_2 & y_2 & 1 \\ x_3 & y_3 & 1 \end{vmatrix}$$

where the symbol $\pm$ indicates that the appropriate sign should be chosen to yield a positive area.

Example 3 **Finding the Area of a Triangle**

Find the area of a triangle whose vertices are $(1, 0)$, $(2, 2)$, and $(4, 3)$, as shown in Figure 8.1.

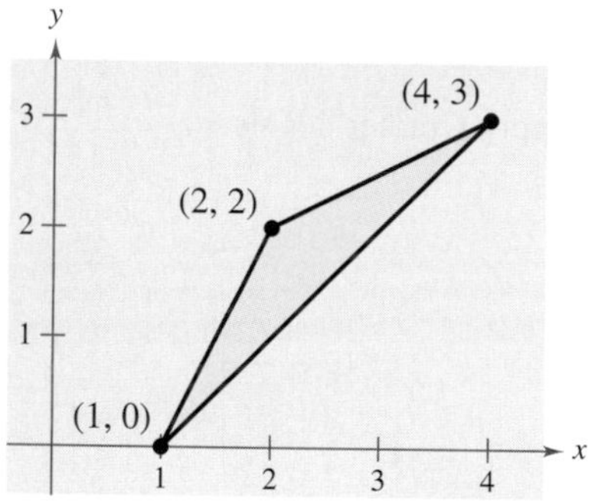

FIGURE 8.1

Solution

Let $(x_1, y_1) = (1, 0)$, $(x_2, y_2) = (2, 2)$, and $(x_3, y_3) = (4, 3)$. Then, to find the area of the triangle, evaluate the determinant.

$$\begin{vmatrix} x_1 & y_1 & 1 \\ x_2 & y_2 & 1 \\ x_3 & y_3 & 1 \end{vmatrix} = \begin{vmatrix} 1 & 0 & 1 \\ 2 & 2 & 1 \\ 4 & 3 & 1 \end{vmatrix}$$

$$= 1(-1)^2\begin{vmatrix} 2 & 1 \\ 3 & 1 \end{vmatrix} + 0(-1)^3\begin{vmatrix} 2 & 1 \\ 4 & 1 \end{vmatrix} + 1(-1)^4\begin{vmatrix} 2 & 2 \\ 4 & 3 \end{vmatrix}$$

$$= 1(-1) + 0 + 1(-2) = -3.$$

Using this value, you can conclude that the area of the triangle is

$$\text{Area} = -\frac{1}{2}\begin{vmatrix} 1 & 0 & 1 \\ 2 & 2 & 1 \\ 4 & 3 & 1 \end{vmatrix}$$ Choose $(-)$ so that the area is positive.

$$= -\frac{1}{2}(-3) = \frac{3}{2} \text{ square units.}$$

✓CHECKPOINT Now try Exercise 19.

Exploration

Use determinants to find the area of a triangle with vertices $(3, -1)$, $(7, -1)$, and $(7, 5)$. Confirm your answer by plotting the points in a coordinate plane and using the formula

$$\text{Area} = \tfrac{1}{2}(\text{base})(\text{height}).$$

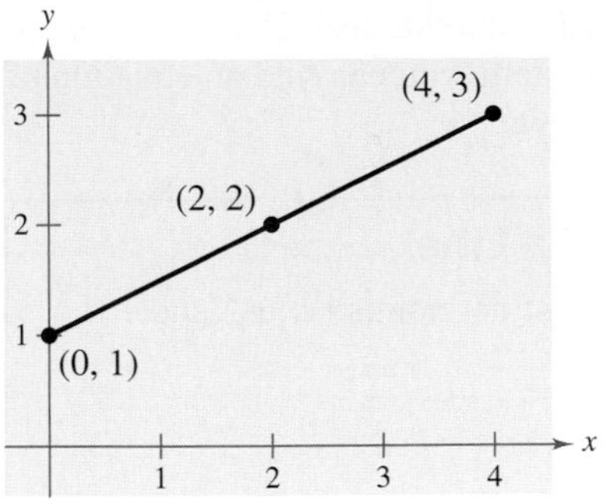

FIGURE 8.2

Lines in a Plane

What if the three points in Example 3 had been on the same line? What would have happened had the area formula been applied to three such points? The answer is that the determinant would have been zero. Consider, for instance, the three collinear points (0, 1), (2, 2), and (4, 3), as shown in Figure 8.2. The area of the "triangle" that has these three points as vertices is

$$\frac{1}{2}\begin{vmatrix} 0 & 1 & 1 \\ 2 & 2 & 1 \\ 4 & 3 & 1 \end{vmatrix} = \frac{1}{2}\left[0(-1)^2\begin{vmatrix} 2 & 1 \\ 3 & 1 \end{vmatrix} + 1(-1)^3\begin{vmatrix} 2 & 1 \\ 4 & 1 \end{vmatrix} + 1(-1)^4\begin{vmatrix} 2 & 2 \\ 4 & 3 \end{vmatrix}\right]$$

$$= \frac{1}{2}[0 - 1(-2) + 1(-2)]$$

$$= 0.$$

The result is generalized as follows.

> **Test for Collinear Points**
>
> Three points (x_1, y_1), (x_2, y_2), and (x_3, y_3) are **collinear** (lie on the same line) if and only if
>
> $$\begin{vmatrix} x_1 & y_1 & 1 \\ x_2 & y_2 & 1 \\ x_3 & y_3 & 1 \end{vmatrix} = 0.$$

Example 4 Testing for Collinear Points

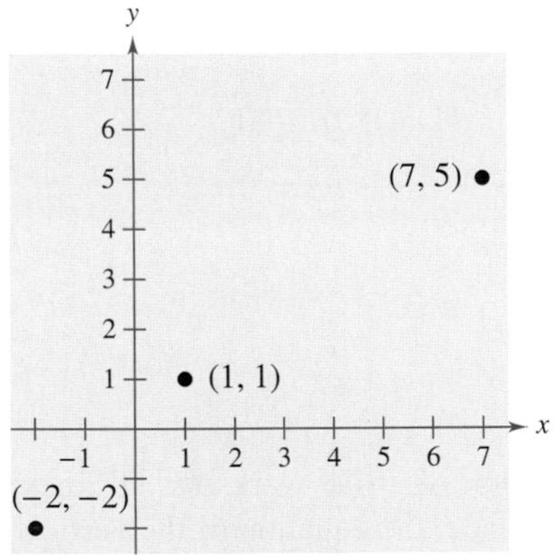

FIGURE 8.3

Determine whether the points $(-2, -2)$, (1, 1), and (7, 5) are collinear. (See Figure 8.3.)

Solution

Letting $(x_1, y_1) = (-2, -2)$, $(x_2, y_2) = (1, 1)$, and $(x_3, y_3) = (7, 5)$, you have

$$\begin{vmatrix} x_1 & y_1 & 1 \\ x_2 & y_2 & 1 \\ x_3 & y_3 & 1 \end{vmatrix} = \begin{vmatrix} -2 & -2 & 1 \\ 1 & 1 & 1 \\ 7 & 5 & 1 \end{vmatrix}$$

$$= -2(-1)^2\begin{vmatrix} 1 & 1 \\ 5 & 1 \end{vmatrix} + (-2)(-1)^3\begin{vmatrix} 1 & 1 \\ 7 & 1 \end{vmatrix} + 1(-1)^4\begin{vmatrix} 1 & 1 \\ 7 & 5 \end{vmatrix}$$

$$= -2(-4) + 2(-6) + 1(-2)$$

$$= -6.$$

Because the value of this determinant is *not* zero, you can conclude that the three points do not lie on the same line. Moreover, the area of the triangle with vertices at these points is $\left(-\frac{1}{2}\right)(-6) = 3$ square units.

CHECKPOINT Now try Exercise 31.

The test for collinear points can be adapted to another use. That is, if you are given two points on a rectangular coordinate system, you can find an equation of the line passing through the two points, as follows.

Two-Point Form of the Equation of a Line

An equation of the line passing through the distinct points (x_1, y_1) and (x_2, y_2) is given by

$$\begin{vmatrix} x & y & 1 \\ x_1 & y_1 & 1 \\ x_2 & y_2 & 1 \end{vmatrix} = 0.$$

Example 5 Finding an Equation of a Line

Find an equation of the line passing through the two points $(2, 4)$ and $(-1, 3)$, as shown in Figure 8.4.

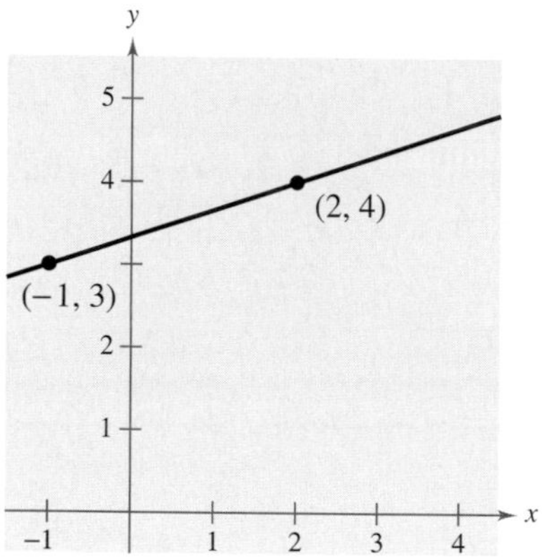

FIGURE 8.4

Solution

Let $(x_1, y_1) = (2, 4)$ and $(x_2, y_2) = (-1, 3)$. Applying the determinant formula for the equation of a line produces

$$\begin{vmatrix} x & y & 1 \\ 2 & 4 & 1 \\ -1 & 3 & 1 \end{vmatrix} = 0.$$

To evaluate this determinant, you can expand by cofactors along the first row to obtain the following.

$$x(-1)^2\begin{vmatrix} 4 & 1 \\ 3 & 1 \end{vmatrix} + y(-1)^3\begin{vmatrix} 2 & 1 \\ -1 & 1 \end{vmatrix} + 1(-1)^4\begin{vmatrix} 2 & 4 \\ -1 & 3 \end{vmatrix} = 0$$

$$x(1)(1) + y(-1)(3) + (1)(1)(10) = 0$$

$$x - 3y + 10 = 0$$

So, an equation of the line is

$$x - 3y + 10 = 0.$$

CHECKPOINT Now try Exercise 39.

Note that this method of finding the equation of a line works for all lines, including horizontal and vertical lines. For instance, the equation of the vertical line through $(2, 0)$ and $(2, 2)$ is

$$\begin{vmatrix} x & y & 1 \\ 2 & 0 & 1 \\ 2 & 2 & 1 \end{vmatrix} = 0$$

$$4 - 2x = 0$$

$$x = 2.$$

Cryptography

A **cryptogram** is a message written according to a secret code. (The Greek word *kryptos* means "hidden.") Matrix multiplication can be used to encode and decode messages. To begin, you need to assign a number to each letter in the alphabet (with 0 assigned to a blank space), as follows.

0 = _	9 = I	18 = R
1 = A	10 = J	19 = S
2 = B	11 = K	20 = T
3 = C	12 = L	21 = U
4 = D	13 = M	22 = V
5 = E	14 = N	23 = W
6 = F	15 = O	24 = X
7 = G	16 = P	25 = Y
8 = H	17 = Q	26 = Z

Then the message is converted to numbers and partitioned into **uncoded row matrices,** each having n entries, as demonstrated in Example 6.

Example 6 Forming Uncoded Row Matrices

Write the uncoded row matrices of order 1×3 for the message

MEET ME MONDAY.

Solution

Partitioning the message (including blank spaces, but ignoring punctuation) into groups of three produces the following uncoded row matrices.

$$[13 \quad 5 \quad 5] \ [20 \quad 0 \quad 13] \ [5 \quad 0 \quad 13] \ [15 \quad 14 \quad 4] \ [1 \quad 25 \quad 0]$$

M E E T M E M O N D A Y

Note that a blank space is used to fill out the last uncoded row matrix.

CHECKPOINT Now try Exercise 45.

To encode a message, use the techniques demonstrated in Section 8.3 to choose an $n \times n$ invertible matrix such as

$$A = \begin{bmatrix} 1 & -2 & 2 \\ -1 & 1 & 3 \\ 1 & -1 & -4 \end{bmatrix}$$

and multiply the uncoded row matrices by A (on the right) to obtain **coded row matrices.** Here is an example.

Uncoded Matrix *Encoding Matrix A* *Coded Matrix*

$$[13 \quad 5 \quad 5] \begin{bmatrix} 1 & -2 & 2 \\ -1 & 1 & 3 \\ 1 & -1 & -4 \end{bmatrix} = [13 \quad -26 \quad 21]$$

Example 7 **Encoding a Message**

Use the following invertible matrix to encode the message MEET ME MONDAY.

$$A = \begin{bmatrix} 1 & -2 & 2 \\ -1 & 1 & 3 \\ 1 & -1 & -4 \end{bmatrix}$$

Solution

The coded row matrices are obtained by multiplying each of the uncoded row matrices found in Example 6 by the matrix A, as follows.

Uncoded Matrix *Encoding Matrix A* *Coded Matrix*

$$[13 \quad 5 \quad 5] \begin{bmatrix} 1 & -2 & 2 \\ -1 & 1 & 3 \\ 1 & -1 & -4 \end{bmatrix} = [13 \quad -26 \quad 21]$$

$$[20 \quad 0 \quad 13] \begin{bmatrix} 1 & -2 & 2 \\ -1 & 1 & 3 \\ 1 & -1 & -4 \end{bmatrix} = [33 \quad -53 \quad -12]$$

$$[5 \quad 0 \quad 13] \begin{bmatrix} 1 & -2 & 2 \\ -1 & 1 & 3 \\ 1 & -1 & -4 \end{bmatrix} = [18 \quad -23 \quad -42]$$

$$[15 \quad 14 \quad 4] \begin{bmatrix} 1 & -2 & 2 \\ -1 & 1 & 3 \\ 1 & -1 & -4 \end{bmatrix} = [5 \quad -20 \quad 56]$$

$$[1 \quad 25 \quad 0] \begin{bmatrix} 1 & -2 & 2 \\ -1 & 1 & 3 \\ 1 & -1 & -4 \end{bmatrix} = [-24 \quad 23 \quad 77]$$

So, the sequence of coded row matrices is

$$[13 \; -26 \; 21]\,[33 \; -53 \; -12]\,[18 \; -23 \; -42]\,[5 \; -20 \; 56]\,[-24 \; 23 \; 77].$$

Finally, removing the matrix notation produces the following cryptogram.

$$13 \; -26 \; 21 \; 33 \; -53 \; -12 \; 18 \; -23 \; -42 \; 5 \; -20 \; 56 \; -24 \; 23 \; 77$$

CHECKPOINT Now try Exercise 47.

For those who do not know the encoding matrix A, decoding the cryptogram found in Example 7 is difficult. But for an authorized receiver who knows the encoding matrix A, decoding is simple. The receiver just needs to multiply the coded row matrices by A^{-1} (on the right) to retrieve the uncoded row matrices. Here is an example.

$$\underbrace{[13 \quad -26 \quad 21]}_{\text{Coded}} \underbrace{\begin{bmatrix} -1 & -10 & -8 \\ -1 & -6 & -5 \\ 0 & -1 & -1 \end{bmatrix}}_{A^{-1}} = \underbrace{[13 \quad 5 \quad 5]}_{\text{Uncoded}}$$

© Corbis

Historical Note

During World War II, Navajo soldiers created a code using their native language to send messages between battalions. Native words were assigned to represent characters in the English alphabet, and they created a number of expressions for important military terms, like *iron-fish* to mean *submarine*. Without the Navajo Code Talkers, the Second World War might have had a very different outcome.

Example 8 **Decoding a Message**

Use the inverse of the matrix

$$A = \begin{bmatrix} 1 & -2 & 2 \\ -1 & 1 & 3 \\ 1 & -1 & -4 \end{bmatrix}$$

to decode the cryptogram

13 −26 21 33 −53 −12 18 −23 −42 5 −20 56 −24 23 77.

Solution

First find A^{-1} by using the techniques demonstrated in Section 8.3. A^{-1} is the decoding matrix. Then partition the message into groups of three to form the coded row matrices. Finally, multiply each coded row matrix by A^{-1} (on the right).

Coded Matrix *Decoding Matrix* A^{-1} *Decoded Matrix*

$$[13 \quad -26 \quad 21]\begin{bmatrix} -1 & -10 & -8 \\ -1 & -6 & -5 \\ 0 & -1 & -1 \end{bmatrix} = [13 \quad 5 \quad 5]$$

$$[33 \quad -53 \quad -12]\begin{bmatrix} -1 & -10 & -8 \\ -1 & -6 & -5 \\ 0 & -1 & -1 \end{bmatrix} = [20 \quad 0 \quad 13]$$

$$[18 \quad -23 \quad -42]\begin{bmatrix} -1 & -10 & -8 \\ -1 & -6 & -5 \\ 0 & -1 & -1 \end{bmatrix} = [5 \quad 0 \quad 13]$$

$$[5 \quad -20 \quad 56]\begin{bmatrix} -1 & -10 & -8 \\ -1 & -6 & -5 \\ 0 & -1 & -1 \end{bmatrix} = [15 \quad 14 \quad 4]$$

$$[-24 \quad 23 \quad 77]\begin{bmatrix} -1 & -10 & -8 \\ -1 & -6 & -5 \\ 0 & -1 & -1 \end{bmatrix} = [1 \quad 25 \quad 0]$$

So, the message is as follows.

[13	5	5]	[20	0	13]	[5	0	13]	[15	14	4]	[1	25	0]
M	E	E	T		M	E		M	O	N	D	A	Y	

✓CHECKPOINT Now try Exercise 53.

WRITING ABOUT MATHEMATICS

Cryptography Use your school's library, the Internet, or some other reference source to research information about another type of cryptography. Write a short paragraph describing how mathematics is used to code and decode messages.

8.5 Exercises

VOCABULARY CHECK: Fill in the blanks.

1. The method of using determinants to solve a system of linear equations is called ________ ________.
2. Three points are ________ if the points lie on the same line.
3. The area A of a triangle with vertices (x_1, y_1), (x_2, y_2), and (x_3, y_3) is given by ________.
4. A message written according to a secret code is called a ________.
5. To encode a message, choose an invertible matrix A and multiply the ________ row matrices by A (on the right) to obtain ________ row matrices.

In Exercises 1–10, use Cramer's Rule to solve (if possible) the system of equations.

1. $\begin{cases} 3x + 4y = -2 \\ 5x + 3y = 4 \end{cases}$

2. $\begin{cases} -4x - 7y = 47 \\ -x + 6y = -27 \end{cases}$

3. $\begin{cases} 3x + 2y = -2 \\ 6x + 4y = 4 \end{cases}$

4. $\begin{cases} 6x - 5y = 17 \\ -13x + 3y = -76 \end{cases}$

5. $\begin{cases} -0.4x + 0.8y = 1.6 \\ 0.2x + 0.3y = 2.2 \end{cases}$

6. $\begin{cases} 2.4x - 1.3y = 14.63 \\ -4.6x + 0.5y = -11.51 \end{cases}$

7. $\begin{cases} 4x - y + z = -5 \\ 2x + 2y + 3z = 10 \\ 5x - 2y + 6z = 1 \end{cases}$

8. $\begin{cases} 4x - 2y + 3z = -2 \\ 2x + 2y + 5z = 16 \\ 8x - 5y - 2z = 4 \end{cases}$

9. $\begin{cases} x + 2y + 3z = -3 \\ -2x + y - z = 6 \\ 3x - 3y + 2z = -11 \end{cases}$

10. $\begin{cases} 5x - 4y + z = -14 \\ -x + 2y - 2z = 10 \\ 3x + y + z = 1 \end{cases}$

In Exercises 11–14, use a graphing utility and Cramer's Rule to solve (if possible) the system of equations.

11. $\begin{cases} 3x + 3y + 5z = 1 \\ 3x + 5y + 9z = 2 \\ 5x + 9y + 17z = 4 \end{cases}$

12. $\begin{cases} x + 2y - z = -7 \\ 2x - 2y - 2z = -8 \\ -x + 3y + 4z = 8 \end{cases}$

13. $\begin{cases} 2x + y + 2z = 6 \\ -x + 2y - 3z = 0 \\ 3x + 2y - z = 6 \end{cases}$

14. $\begin{cases} 2x + 3y + 5z = 4 \\ 3x + 5y + 9z = 7 \\ 5x + 9y + 17z = 13 \end{cases}$

In Exercises 15–24, use a determinant and the given vertices of a triangle to find the area of the triangle.

15.
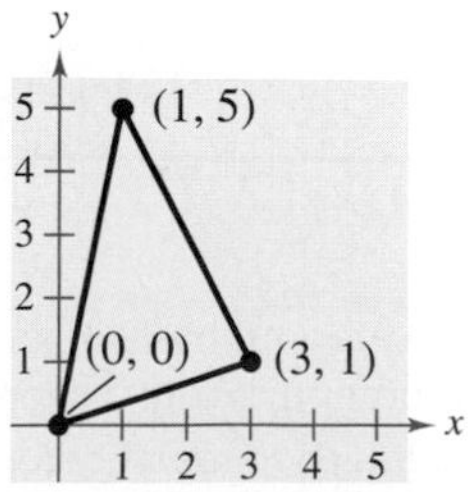

16.
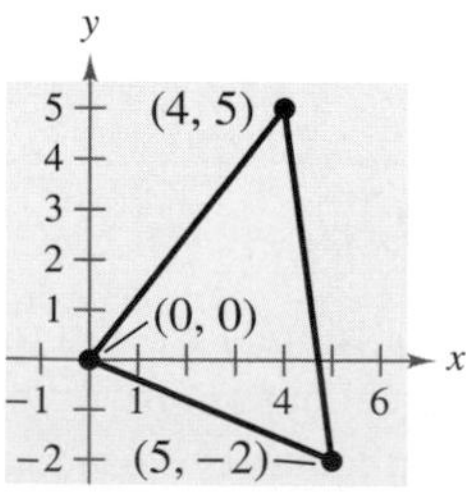

17.
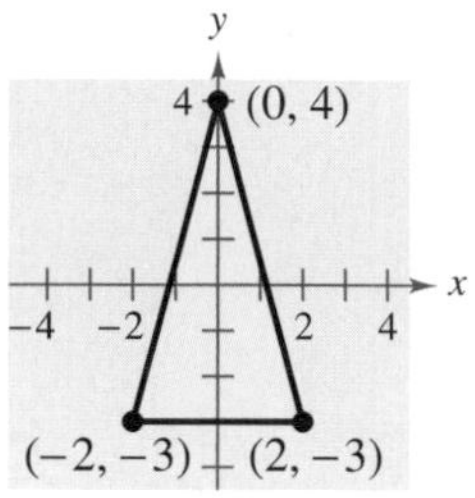

18.
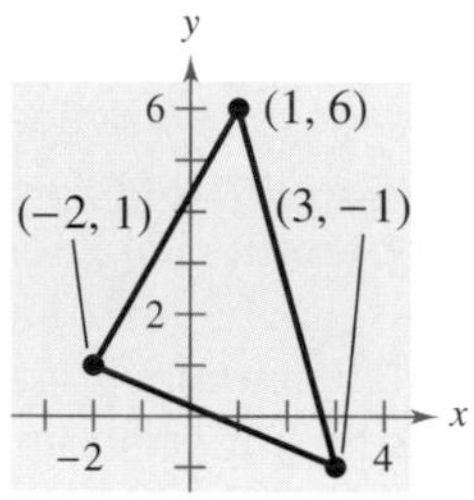

19.
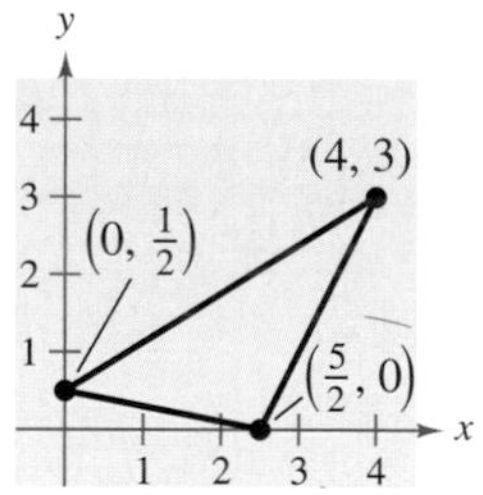

20.
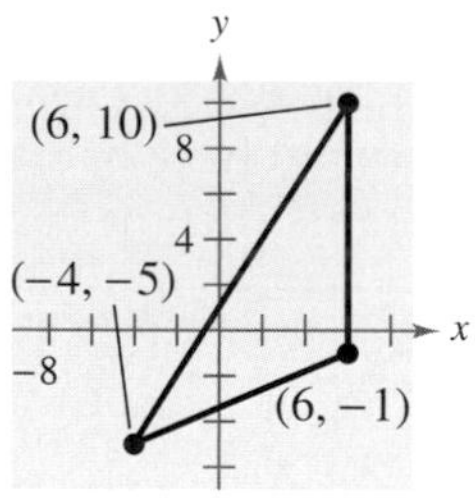

21. $(-2, 4), (2, 3), (-1, 5)$
22. $(0, -2), (-1, 4), (3, 5)$
23. $(-3, 5), (2, 6), (3, -5)$
24. $(-2, 4), (1, 5), (3, -2)$

In Exercises 25 and 26, find a value of y such that the triangle with the given vertices has an area of 4 square units.

25. $(-5, 1), (0, 2), (-2, y)$
26. $(-4, 2), (-3, 5), (-1, y)$

In Exercises 27 and 28, find a value of y such that the triangle with the given vertices has an area of 6 square units.

27. $(-2, -3), (1, -1), (-8, y)$
28. $(1, 0), (5, -3), (-3, y)$

29. ***Area of a Region*** A large region of forest has been infested with gypsy moths. The region is roughly triangular, as shown in the figure. From the northernmost vertex A of the region, the distances to the other vertices are 25 miles south and 10 miles east (for vertex B), and 20 miles south and 28 miles east (for vertex C). Use a graphing utility to approximate the number of square miles in this region.

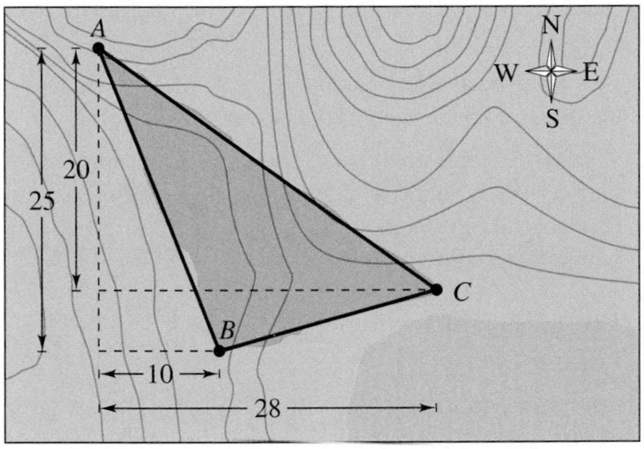

30. ***Area of a Region*** You own a triangular tract of land, as shown in the figure. To estimate the number of square feet in the tract, you start at one vertex, walk 65 feet east and 50 feet north to the second vertex, and then walk 85 feet west and 30 feet north to the third vertex. Use a graphing utility to determine how many square feet there are in the tract of land.

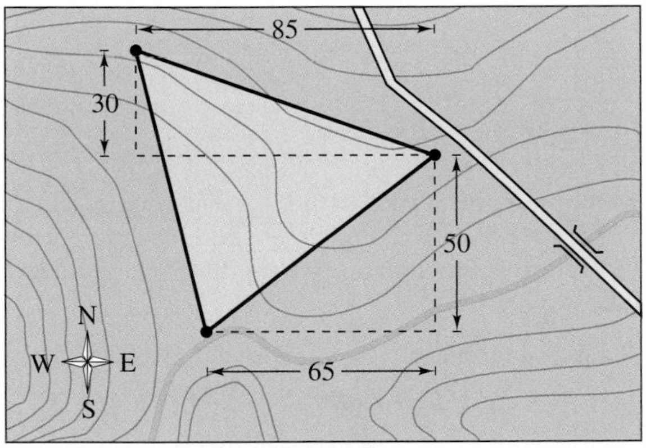

In Exercises 31–36, use a determinant to determine whether the points are collinear.

31. $(3, -1), (0, -3), (12, 5)$
32. $(-3, -5), (6, 1), (10, 2)$
33. $\left(2, -\frac{1}{2}\right), (-4, 4), (6, -3)$
34. $(0, 1), (4, -2), \left(-2, \frac{5}{2}\right)$
35. $(0, 2), (1, 2.4), (-1, 1.6)$
36. $(2, 3), (3, 3.5), (-1, 2)$

In Exercises 37 and 38, find y such that the points are collinear.

37. $(2, -5), (4, y), (5, -2)$
38. $(-6, 2), (-5, y), (-3, 5)$

In Exercises 39–44, use a determinant to find an equation of the line passing through the points.

39. $(0, 0), (5, 3)$
40. $(0, 0), (-2, 2)$
41. $(-4, 3), (2, 1)$
42. $(10, 7), (-2, -7)$
43. $\left(-\frac{1}{2}, 3\right), \left(\frac{5}{2}, 1\right)$
44. $\left(\frac{2}{3}, 4\right), (6, 12)$

In Exercises 45 and 46, find the uncoded 1×3 row matrices for the message. Then encode the message using the encoding matrix.

	Message	*Encoding Matrix*
45.	TROUBLE IN RIVER CITY	$\begin{bmatrix} 1 & -1 & 0 \\ 1 & 0 & -1 \\ -6 & 2 & 3 \end{bmatrix}$
46.	PLEASE SEND MONEY	$\begin{bmatrix} 4 & 2 & 1 \\ -3 & -3 & -1 \\ 3 & 2 & 1 \end{bmatrix}$

In Exercises 47–50, write a cryptogram for the message using the matrix A.

$$A = \begin{bmatrix} 1 & 2 & 2 \\ 3 & 7 & 9 \\ -1 & -4 & -7 \end{bmatrix}.$$

47. CALL AT NOON
48. ICEBERG DEAD AHEAD
49. HAPPY BIRTHDAY
50. OPERATION OVERLOAD

In Exercises 51–54, use A^{-1} to decode the cryptogram.

51. $A = \begin{bmatrix} 1 & 2 \\ 3 & 5 \end{bmatrix}$

11 21 64 112 25 50 29 53 23 46
40 75 55 92

52. $A = \begin{bmatrix} -5 & 2 \\ -7 & 3 \end{bmatrix}$

−136 58 −173 72 −120 51 −95 38
−178 73 −70 28 −242 101 −115 47
−90 36 −115 49 −199 82

53. $A = \begin{bmatrix} 1 & -1 & 0 \\ 1 & 0 & -1 \\ -6 & 2 & 3 \end{bmatrix}$

9 −1 −9 38 −19 −19 28 −9 −19 −80 25
41 −64 21 31 9 −5 −4

54. $A = \begin{bmatrix} 3 & -4 & 2 \\ 0 & 2 & 1 \\ 4 & -5 & 3 \end{bmatrix}$

112 −140 83 19 −25 13 72 −76 61 95
−118 71 20 21 38 35 −23 36 42 −48 32

In Exercises 55 and 56, decode the cryptogram by using the inverse of the matrix A.

$$A = \begin{bmatrix} 1 & 2 & 2 \\ 3 & 7 & 9 \\ -1 & -4 & -7 \end{bmatrix}$$

55. 20 17 −15 −12 −56 −104 1 −25 −65 62 143 181

56. 13 −9 −59 61 112 106 −17 −73 −131 11 24 29 65 144 172

57. The following cryptogram was encoded with a 2×2 matrix.

8 21 −15 −10 −13 −13 5 10 5 25 5 19 −1 6 20 40 −18 −18 1 16

The last word of the message is _RON. What is the message?

Model It

58. ***Data Analysis: Supreme Court*** The table shows the numbers y of U.S. Supreme Court cases waiting to be tried for the years 2000 through 2002. (Source: Office of the Clerk, Supreme Court of the United States)

Year	Number of cases, y
2000	8965
2001	9176
2002	9406

(a) Use the technique demonstrated in Exercises 67–70 in Section 7.3 to create a system of linear equations for the data. Let t represent the year, with $t = 0$ corresponding to 2000.

(b) Use Cramer's Rule to solve the system from part (a) and find the least squares regression parabola $y = at^2 + bt + c$.

(c) Use a graphing utility to graph the parabola from part (b).

(d) Use the graph from part (c) to estimate when the number of U.S. Supreme Court cases waiting to be tried will reach 10,000.

Synthesis

True or False? **In Exercises 59–61, determine whether the statement is true or false. Justify your answer.**

59. In Cramer's Rule, the numerator is the determinant of the coefficient matrix.

60. You cannot use Cramer's Rule when solving a system of linear equations if the determinant of the coefficient matrix is zero.

61. In a system of linear equations, if the determinant of the coefficient matrix is zero, the system has no solution.

62. ***Writing*** At this point in the text, you have learned several methods for solving systems of linear equations. Briefly describe which method(s) you find easiest to use and which method(s) you find most difficult to use.

Skills Review

In Exercises 63–66, use any method to solve the system of equations.

63. $\begin{cases} -x - 7y = -22 \\ 5x + y = -26 \end{cases}$

64. $\begin{cases} 3x + 8y = 11 \\ -2x + 12y = -16 \end{cases}$

65. $\begin{cases} -x - 3y + 5z = -14 \\ 4x + 2y - z = -1 \\ 5x - 3y + 2z = -11 \end{cases}$

66. $\begin{cases} 5x - y - z = 7 \\ -2x + 3y + z = -5 \\ 4x + 10y - 5z = -37 \end{cases}$

In Exercises 67 and 68, sketch the region determined by the constraints. Then find the minimum and maximum values of the objective function and where they occur, subject to the constraints.

67. Objective function:

$z = 6x + 4y$

Constraints:

$x \geq 0$

$y \geq 0$

$x + 6y \leq 30$

$6x + y \leq 40$

68. Objective function:

$z = 6x + 7y$

Constraints:

$x \geq 0$

$y \geq 0$

$4x + 3y \geq 24$

$x + 3y \geq 15$

8 Chapter Summary

What did you learn?

Section 8.1	Review Exercises
☐ Write matrices and identify their orders *(p. 572).*	1–8
☐ Perform elementary row operations on matrices *(p. 574).*	9, 10
☐ Use matrices and Gaussian elimination to solve systems of linear equations *(p. 577).*	11–24
☐ Use matrices and Gauss-Jordan elimination to solve systems of linear equations *(p. 579).*	25–30
Section 8.2	
☐ Decide whether two matrices are equal *(p. 587).*	31–34
☐ Add and subtract matrices and multiply matrices by scalars *(p. 588).*	35–48
☐ Multiply two matrices *(p. 592).*	49–62
☐ Use matrix operations to model and solve real-life problems *(p. 595).*	63–66
Section 8.3	
☐ Verify that two matrices are inverses of each other *(p. 602).*	67–70
☐ Use Gauss-Jordan elimination to find the inverses of matrices *(p. 603).*	71–78
☐ Use a formula to find the inverses of 2×2 matrices *(p. 606).*	79–82
☐ Use inverse matrices to solve systems of linear equations *(p. 607.*	83–94
Section 8.4	
☐ Find the determinants of 2×2 matrices *(p. 611).*	95–98
☐ Find minors and cofactors of square matrices *(p. 613).*	99–102
☐ Find the determinants of square matrices *(p. 614).*	103–106
Section 8.5	
☐ Use Cramer's Rule to solve systems of linear equations *(p. 619).*	107–110
☐ Use determinants to find the areas of triangles *(p. 622).*	111–114
☐ Use a determinant to test for collinear points and to find an equation of a line passing through two points *(p. 623).*	115–120
☐ Use matrices to encode and decode messages *(p. 625).*	121–124

8 Review Exercises

8.1 **In Exercises 1–4, determine the order of the matrix.**

1. $\begin{bmatrix} -4 \\ 0 \\ 5 \end{bmatrix}$ **2.** $\begin{bmatrix} 3 & -1 & 0 & 6 \\ -2 & 7 & 1 & 4 \end{bmatrix}$

3. $[3]$ **4.** $[6 \quad 2 \quad -5 \quad 8 \quad 0]$

In Exercises 5 and 6, write the augmented matrix for the system of linear equations.

5. $\begin{cases} 3x - 10y = 15 \\ 5x + 4y = 22 \end{cases}$ **6.** $\begin{cases} 8x - 7y + 4z = 12 \\ 3x - 5y + 2z = 20 \\ 5x + 3y - 3z = 26 \end{cases}$

In Exercises 7 and 8, write the system of linear equations represented by the augmented matrix. (Use variables *x*, *y*, *z*, and *w*, if applicable.)

7. $\left[\begin{array}{ccccc} 5 & 1 & 7 & \vdots & -9 \\ 4 & 2 & 0 & \vdots & 10 \\ 9 & 4 & 2 & \vdots & 3 \end{array}\right]$

8. $\left[\begin{array}{cccccc} 13 & 16 & 7 & 3 & \vdots & 2 \\ 1 & 21 & 8 & 5 & \vdots & 12 \\ 4 & 10 & -4 & 3 & \vdots & -1 \end{array}\right]$

In Exercises 9 and 10, write the matrix in row-echelon form. Remember that the row-echelon form of a matrix is not unique.

9. $\begin{bmatrix} 0 & 1 & 1 \\ 1 & 2 & 3 \\ 2 & 2 & 2 \end{bmatrix}$ **10.** $\begin{bmatrix} 4 & 8 & 16 \\ 3 & -1 & 2 \\ -2 & 10 & 12 \end{bmatrix}$

In Exercises 11–14, write the system of linear equations represented by the augmented matrix. Then use back-substitution to solve the system. (Use variables *x*, *y*, and *z*.)

11. $\left[\begin{array}{ccccc} 1 & 2 & 3 & \vdots & 9 \\ 0 & 1 & -2 & \vdots & 2 \\ 0 & 0 & 1 & \vdots & 0 \end{array}\right]$

12. $\left[\begin{array}{ccccc} 1 & 3 & -9 & \vdots & 4 \\ 0 & 1 & -1 & \vdots & 10 \\ 0 & 0 & 1 & \vdots & -2 \end{array}\right]$

13. $\left[\begin{array}{ccccc} 1 & -5 & 4 & \vdots & 1 \\ 0 & 1 & 2 & \vdots & 3 \\ 0 & 0 & 1 & \vdots & 4 \end{array}\right]$

14. $\left[\begin{array}{ccccc} 1 & -8 & 0 & \vdots & -2 \\ 0 & 1 & -1 & \vdots & -7 \\ 0 & 0 & 1 & \vdots & 1 \end{array}\right]$

In Exercises 15–24, use matrices and Gaussian elimination with back-substitution to solve the system of equations (if possible).

15. $\begin{cases} 5x + 4y = 2 \\ -x + y = -22 \end{cases}$ **16.** $\begin{cases} 2x - 5y = 2 \\ 3x - 7y = 1 \end{cases}$

17. $\begin{cases} 0.3x - 0.1y = -0.13 \\ 0.2x - 0.3y = -0.25 \end{cases}$

18. $\begin{cases} 0.2x - 0.1y = 0.07 \\ 0.4x - 0.5y = -0.01 \end{cases}$

19. $\begin{cases} 2x + 3y + z = 10 \\ 2x - 3y - 3z = 22 \\ 4x - 2y + 3z = -2 \end{cases}$

20. $\begin{cases} 2x + 3y + 3z = 3 \\ 6x + 6y + 12z = 13 \\ 12x + 9y - z = 2 \end{cases}$

21. $\begin{cases} 2x + y + 2z = 4 \\ 2x + 2y = 5 \\ 2x - y + 6z = 2 \end{cases}$

22. $\begin{cases} x + 2y + 6z = 1 \\ 2x + 5y + 15z = 4 \\ 3x + y + 3z = -6 \end{cases}$

23. $\begin{cases} 2x + y + z = 6 \\ -2y + 3z - w = 9 \\ 3x + 3y - 2z - 2w = -11 \\ x + z + 3w = 14 \end{cases}$

24. $\begin{cases} x + 2y + w = 3 \\ -3y + 3z = 0 \\ 4x + 4y + z + 2w = 0 \\ 2x + z = 3 \end{cases}$

In Exercises 25–28, use matrices and Gauss-Jordan elimination to solve the system of equations.

25. $\begin{cases} -x + y + 2z = 1 \\ 2x + 3y + z = -2 \\ 5x + 4y + 2z = 4 \end{cases}$

26. $\begin{cases} 4x + 4y + 4z = 5 \\ 4x - 2y - 8z = 1 \\ 5x + 3y + 8z = 6 \end{cases}$

27. $\begin{cases} 2x - y + 9z = -8 \\ -x - 3y + 4z = -15 \\ 5x + 2y - z = 17 \end{cases}$

28. $\begin{cases} -3x + y + 7z = -20 \\ 5x - 2y - z = 34 \\ -x + y + 4z = -8 \end{cases}$

In Exercises 29 and 30, use the matrix capabilities of a graphing utility to reduce the augmented matrix corresponding to the system of equations, and solve the system.

29. $\begin{cases} 3x - y + 5z - 2w = -44 \\ x + 6y + 4z - w = 1 \\ 5x - y + z + 3w = -15 \\ 4y - z - 8w = 58 \end{cases}$

30. $\begin{cases} 4x + 12y + 2z = 20 \\ x + 6y + 4z = 12 \\ x + 6y + z = 8 \\ -2x - 10y - 2z = -10 \end{cases}$

8.2 **In Exercises 31–34, find *x* and *y*.**

31. $\begin{bmatrix} -1 & x \\ y & 9 \end{bmatrix} = \begin{bmatrix} -1 & 12 \\ -7 & 9 \end{bmatrix}$

32. $\begin{bmatrix} -1 & 0 \\ x & 5 \\ -4 & y \end{bmatrix} = \begin{bmatrix} -1 & 0 \\ 8 & 5 \\ -4 & 0 \end{bmatrix}$

33. $\begin{bmatrix} x+3 & -4 & 4y \\ 0 & -3 & 2 \\ -2 & y+5 & 6x \end{bmatrix} = \begin{bmatrix} 5x-1 & -4 & 44 \\ 0 & -3 & 2 \\ -2 & 16 & 6 \end{bmatrix}$

34. $\begin{bmatrix} -9 & 4 & 2 & -5 \\ 0 & -3 & 7 & -4 \\ 6 & -1 & 1 & 0 \end{bmatrix} = \begin{bmatrix} -9 & 4 & x-10 & -5 \\ 0 & -3 & 7 & 2y \\ \frac{1}{2}x & -1 & 1 & 0 \end{bmatrix}$

In Exercises 35–38, if possible, find (a) *A* + *B*, (b) *A* − *B*, (c) 4*A*, and (d) *A* + 3*B*.

35. $A = \begin{bmatrix} 2 & -2 \\ 3 & 5 \end{bmatrix}, \quad B = \begin{bmatrix} -3 & 10 \\ 12 & 8 \end{bmatrix}$

36. $A = \begin{bmatrix} 5 & 4 \\ -7 & 2 \\ 11 & 2 \end{bmatrix}, \quad B = \begin{bmatrix} 4 & 12 \\ 20 & 40 \\ 15 & 30 \end{bmatrix}$

37. $A = \begin{bmatrix} 5 & 4 \\ -7 & 2 \\ 11 & 2 \end{bmatrix}, \quad B = \begin{bmatrix} 0 & 3 \\ 4 & 12 \\ 20 & 40 \end{bmatrix}$

38. $A = \begin{bmatrix} 6 & -5 & 7 \end{bmatrix}, \quad B = \begin{bmatrix} -1 \\ 4 \\ 8 \end{bmatrix}$

In Exercises 39–42, perform the matrix operations. If it is not possible, explain why.

39. $\begin{bmatrix} 7 & 3 \\ -1 & 5 \end{bmatrix} + \begin{bmatrix} 10 & -20 \\ 14 & -3 \end{bmatrix}$

40. $\begin{bmatrix} -11 & 16 & 19 \\ -7 & -2 & 1 \end{bmatrix} - \begin{bmatrix} 6 & 0 \\ 8 & -4 \\ -2 & 10 \end{bmatrix}$

41. $-2\begin{bmatrix} 1 & 2 \\ 5 & -4 \\ 6 & 0 \end{bmatrix} + 8\begin{bmatrix} 7 & 1 \\ 1 & 2 \\ 1 & 4 \end{bmatrix}$

42. $-\begin{bmatrix} 8 & -1 & 8 \\ -2 & 4 & 12 \\ 0 & -6 & 0 \end{bmatrix} - 5\begin{bmatrix} -2 & 0 & -4 \\ 3 & -1 & 1 \\ 6 & 12 & -8 \end{bmatrix}$

In Exercises 43 and 44, use the matrix capabilities of a graphing utility to evaluate the expression.

43. $3\begin{bmatrix} 8 & -2 & 5 \\ 1 & 3 & -1 \end{bmatrix} + 6\begin{bmatrix} 4 & -2 & -3 \\ 2 & 7 & 6 \end{bmatrix}$

44. $-5\begin{bmatrix} 2 & 0 \\ 7 & -2 \\ 8 & 2 \end{bmatrix} + 4\begin{bmatrix} 4 & -2 \\ 6 & 11 \\ -1 & 3 \end{bmatrix}$

In Exercises 45–48, solve for *X* in the equation given

$$A = \begin{bmatrix} -4 & 0 \\ 1 & -5 \\ -3 & 2 \end{bmatrix} \quad \text{and} \quad B = \begin{bmatrix} 1 & 2 \\ -2 & 1 \\ 4 & 4 \end{bmatrix}.$$

45. $X = 3A - 2B$

46. $6X = 4A + 3B$

47. $3X + 2A = B$

48. $2A - 5B = 3X$

In Exercises 49–52, find *AB*, if possible.

49. $A = \begin{bmatrix} 2 & -2 \\ 3 & 5 \end{bmatrix}, \quad B = \begin{bmatrix} -3 & 10 \\ 12 & 8 \end{bmatrix}$

50. $A = \begin{bmatrix} 5 & 4 \\ -7 & 2 \\ 11 & 2 \end{bmatrix}, \quad B = \begin{bmatrix} 4 & 12 \\ 20 & 40 \\ 15 & 30 \end{bmatrix}$

51. $A = \begin{bmatrix} 5 & 4 \\ -7 & 2 \\ 11 & 2 \end{bmatrix}, \quad B = \begin{bmatrix} 4 & 12 \\ 20 & 40 \end{bmatrix}$

52. $A = \begin{bmatrix} 6 & -5 & 7 \end{bmatrix}, \quad B = \begin{bmatrix} -1 \\ 4 \\ 8 \end{bmatrix}$

In Exercises 53–60, perform the matrix operations. If it is not possible, explain why.

53. $\begin{bmatrix} 1 & 2 \\ 5 & -4 \\ 6 & 0 \end{bmatrix}\begin{bmatrix} 6 & -2 & 8 \\ 4 & 0 & 0 \end{bmatrix}$

54. $\begin{bmatrix} 1 & 5 & 6 \\ 2 & -4 & 0 \end{bmatrix}\begin{bmatrix} 6 & -2 & 8 \\ 4 & 0 & 0 \end{bmatrix}$

55. $\begin{bmatrix} 1 & 5 & 6 \\ 2 & -4 & 0 \end{bmatrix}\begin{bmatrix} 6 & 4 \\ -2 & 0 \\ 8 & 0 \end{bmatrix}$

56. $\begin{bmatrix} 1 & 3 & 2 \\ 0 & 2 & -4 \\ 0 & 0 & 3 \end{bmatrix}\begin{bmatrix} 4 & -3 & 2 \\ 0 & 3 & -1 \\ 0 & 0 & 2 \end{bmatrix}$

57. $\begin{bmatrix} 4 \\ 6 \end{bmatrix}\begin{bmatrix} 6 & -2 \end{bmatrix}$

58. $\begin{bmatrix} 4 & -2 & 6 \end{bmatrix}\begin{bmatrix} -2 & 1 \\ 0 & -3 \\ 2 & 0 \end{bmatrix}$

59. $\begin{bmatrix} 2 & 1 \\ 6 & 0 \end{bmatrix}\left(\begin{bmatrix} 4 & 2 \\ -3 & 1 \end{bmatrix} + \begin{bmatrix} -2 & 4 \\ 0 & 4 \end{bmatrix}\right)$

60. $-3\begin{bmatrix} 1 & -1 \\ 4 & 2 \end{bmatrix}\left(\begin{bmatrix} 0 & 3 \\ 1 & 2 \end{bmatrix}\begin{bmatrix} 1 & 0 \\ 5 & -3 \end{bmatrix}\right)$

In Exercises 61 and 62, use the matrix capabilities of a graphing utility to find the product.

61. $\begin{bmatrix} 4 & 1 \\ 11 & -7 \\ 12 & 3 \end{bmatrix}\begin{bmatrix} 3 & -5 & 6 \\ 2 & -2 & -2 \end{bmatrix}$

62. $\begin{bmatrix} -2 & 3 & 10 \\ 4 & -2 & 2 \end{bmatrix}\begin{bmatrix} 1 & 1 \\ -5 & 2 \\ 3 & 2 \end{bmatrix}$

63. ***Manufacturing*** A tire corporation has three factories, each of which manufactures two products. The number of units of product i produced at factory j in one day is represented by a_{ij} in the matrix

$$A = \begin{bmatrix} 80 & 120 & 140 \\ 40 & 100 & 80 \end{bmatrix}.$$

Find the production levels if production is decreased by 5%.

64. ***Manufacturing*** A corporation has four factories, each of which manufactures three types of cordless power tools. The number of units of cordless power tools produced at factory j in one day is represented by a_{ij} in the matrix

$$A = \begin{bmatrix} 80 & 70 & 90 & 40 \\ 50 & 30 & 80 & 20 \\ 90 & 60 & 100 & 50 \end{bmatrix}.$$

Find the production levels if production is increased by 20%.

65. ***Manufacturing*** A manufacturing company produces three kinds of computer games that are shipped to two warehouses. The number of units of game i that are shipped to warehouse j is represented by a_{ij} in the matrix

$$A = \begin{bmatrix} 8200 & 7400 \\ 6500 & 9800 \\ 5400 & 4800 \end{bmatrix}.$$

The price per unit is represented by the matrix

$B = [\$10.25 \quad \$14.50 \quad \$17.75]$.

Compute BA and interpret the result.

66. ***Long-Distance Plans*** The charges (in dollars per minute) of two long-distance telephone companies for in-state, state-to-state, and international calls are represented by C.

$$C = \overset{\text{Company}}{\overset{\begin{matrix} \text{A} & \text{B} \end{matrix}}{\begin{bmatrix} 0.07 & 0.095 \\ 0.10 & 0.08 \\ 0.28 & 0.25 \end{bmatrix}}} \begin{matrix} \text{In-state} \\ \text{State-to-state} \\ \text{International} \end{matrix} \left.\vphantom{\begin{matrix} a \\ b \\ c \end{matrix}}\right\} \text{Type of call}$$

You plan to use 120 minutes on in-state calls, 80 minutes on state-to-state calls, and 20 minutes on international calls each month.

(a) Write a matrix T that represents the times spent on the phone for each type of call.

(b) Compute TC and interpret the result.

8.3 In Exercises 67–70, show that B is the inverse of A.

67. $A = \begin{bmatrix} -4 & -1 \\ 7 & 2 \end{bmatrix}, \quad B = \begin{bmatrix} -2 & -1 \\ 7 & 4 \end{bmatrix}$

68. $A = \begin{bmatrix} 5 & -1 \\ 11 & -2 \end{bmatrix}, \quad B = \begin{bmatrix} -2 & 1 \\ -11 & 5 \end{bmatrix}$

69. $A = \begin{bmatrix} 1 & 1 & 0 \\ 1 & 0 & 1 \\ 6 & 2 & 3 \end{bmatrix}, \quad B = \begin{bmatrix} -2 & -3 & 1 \\ 3 & 3 & -1 \\ 2 & 4 & -1 \end{bmatrix}$

70. $A = \begin{bmatrix} 1 & -1 & 0 \\ -1 & 0 & -1 \\ 8 & -4 & 2 \end{bmatrix}, \quad B = \begin{bmatrix} -2 & 1 & \frac{1}{2} \\ -3 & 1 & \frac{1}{2} \\ 2 & -2 & -\frac{1}{2} \end{bmatrix}$

In Exercises 71–74, find the inverse of the matrix (if it exists).

71. $\begin{bmatrix} -6 & 5 \\ -5 & 4 \end{bmatrix}$

72. $\begin{bmatrix} -3 & -5 \\ 2 & 3 \end{bmatrix}$

73. $\begin{bmatrix} -1 & -2 & -2 \\ 3 & 7 & 9 \\ 1 & 4 & 7 \end{bmatrix}$

74. $\begin{bmatrix} 0 & -2 & 1 \\ -5 & -2 & -3 \\ 7 & 3 & 4 \end{bmatrix}$

In Exercises 75–78, use the matrix capabilities of a graphing utility to find the inverse of the matrix (if it exists).

75. $\begin{bmatrix} 2 & 0 & 3 \\ -1 & 1 & 1 \\ 2 & -2 & 1 \end{bmatrix}$

76. $\begin{bmatrix} 1 & 4 & 6 \\ 2 & -3 & 1 \\ -1 & 18 & 16 \end{bmatrix}$

77. $\begin{bmatrix} 1 & 3 & 1 & 6 \\ 4 & 4 & 2 & 6 \\ 3 & 4 & 1 & 2 \\ -1 & 2 & -1 & -2 \end{bmatrix}$

78. $\begin{bmatrix} 8 & 0 & 2 & 8 \\ 4 & -2 & 0 & -2 \\ 1 & 2 & 1 & 4 \\ -1 & 4 & 1 & 1 \end{bmatrix}$

In Exercises 79–82, use the formula below to find the inverse of the matrix, it it exists.

$$A^{-1} = \frac{1}{ad - bc}\begin{bmatrix} d & -b \\ -c & a \end{bmatrix}$$

79. $\begin{bmatrix} -7 & 2 \\ -8 & 2 \end{bmatrix}$

80. $\begin{bmatrix} 10 & 4 \\ 7 & 3 \end{bmatrix}$

81. $\begin{bmatrix} -\frac{1}{2} & 20 \\ \frac{3}{10} & -6 \end{bmatrix}$

82. $\begin{bmatrix} -\frac{3}{4} & \frac{5}{2} \\ -\frac{4}{5} & -\frac{8}{3} \end{bmatrix}$

In Exercises 83–90, use an inverse matrix to solve (if possible) the system of linear equations.

83. $\begin{cases} -x + 4y = 8 \\ 2x - 7y = -5 \end{cases}$

84. $\begin{cases} 5x - y = 13 \\ -9x + 2y = -24 \end{cases}$

85. $\begin{cases} -3x + 10y = 8 \\ 5x - 17y = -13 \end{cases}$

86. $\begin{cases} 4x - 2y = -10 \\ -19x + 9y = 47 \end{cases}$

87. $\begin{cases} 3x + 2y - z = 6 \\ x - y + 2z = -1 \\ 5x + y + z = 7 \end{cases}$

88. $\begin{cases} -x + 4y - 2z = 12 \\ 2x - 9y + 5z = -25 \\ -x + 5y - 4z = 10 \end{cases}$

89. $\begin{cases} -2x + y + 2z = -13 \\ -x - 4y + z = -11 \\ -y - z = 0 \end{cases}$

90. $\begin{cases} 3x - y + 5z = -14 \\ -x + y + 6z = 8 \\ -8x + 4y - z = 44 \end{cases}$

In Exercises 91–94, use the matrix capabilities of a graphing utility to solve (if possible) the system of linear equations.

91. $\begin{cases} x + 2y = -1 \\ 3x + 4y = -5 \end{cases}$

92. $\begin{cases} x + 3y = 23 \\ -6x + 2y = -18 \end{cases}$

93. $\begin{cases} -3x - 3y - 4z = 2 \\ y + z = -1 \\ 4x + 3y + 4z = -1 \end{cases}$

94. $\begin{cases} x - 3y - 2z = 8 \\ -2x + 7y + 3z = -19 \\ x - y - 3z = 3 \end{cases}$

8.4 In Exercises 95–98, find the determinant of the matrix.

95. $\begin{bmatrix} 8 & 5 \\ 2 & -4 \end{bmatrix}$

96. $\begin{bmatrix} -9 & 11 \\ 7 & -4 \end{bmatrix}$

97. $\begin{bmatrix} 50 & -30 \\ 10 & 5 \end{bmatrix}$

98. $\begin{bmatrix} 14 & -24 \\ 12 & -15 \end{bmatrix}$

In Exercises 99–102, find all (a) minors and (b) cofactors of the matrix.

99. $\begin{bmatrix} 2 & -1 \\ 7 & 4 \end{bmatrix}$

100. $\begin{bmatrix} 3 & 6 \\ 5 & -4 \end{bmatrix}$

101. $\begin{bmatrix} 3 & 2 & -1 \\ -2 & 5 & 0 \\ 1 & 8 & 6 \end{bmatrix}$

102. $\begin{bmatrix} 8 & 3 & 4 \\ 6 & 5 & -9 \\ -4 & 1 & 2 \end{bmatrix}$

In Exercises 103–106, find the determinant of the matrix. Expand by cofactors on the row or column that appears to make the computations easiest.

103. $\begin{bmatrix} -2 & 4 & 1 \\ -6 & 0 & 2 \\ 5 & 3 & 4 \end{bmatrix}$

104. $\begin{bmatrix} 4 & 7 & -1 \\ 2 & -3 & 4 \\ -5 & 1 & -1 \end{bmatrix}$

105. $\begin{bmatrix} 3 & 0 & -4 & 0 \\ 0 & 8 & 1 & 2 \\ 6 & 1 & 8 & 2 \\ 0 & 3 & -4 & 1 \end{bmatrix}$

106. $\begin{bmatrix} -5 & 6 & 0 & 0 \\ 0 & 1 & -1 & 2 \\ -3 & 4 & -5 & 1 \\ 1 & 6 & 0 & 3 \end{bmatrix}$

8.5 In Exercises 107–110, use Cramer's Rule to solve (if possible) the system of equations.

107. $\begin{cases} 5x - 2y = 6 \\ -11x + 3y = -23 \end{cases}$

108. $\begin{cases} 3x + 8y = -7 \\ 9x - 5y = 37 \end{cases}$

109. $\begin{cases} -2x + 3y - 5z = -11 \\ 4x - y + z = -3 \\ -x - 4y + 6z = 15 \end{cases}$

110. $\begin{cases} 5x - 2y + z = 15 \\ 3x - 3y - z = -7 \\ 2x - y - 7z = -3 \end{cases}$

In Exercises 111–114, use a determinant and the given vertices of a triangle to find the area of the triangle.

111.

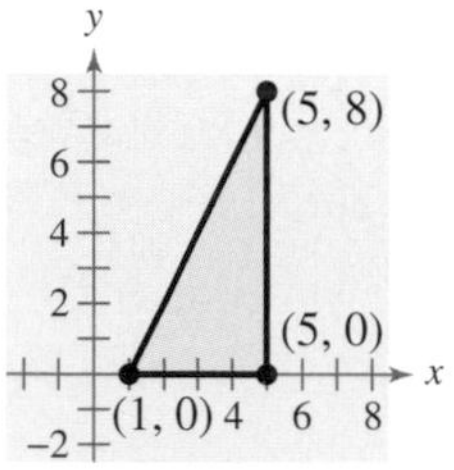

112.

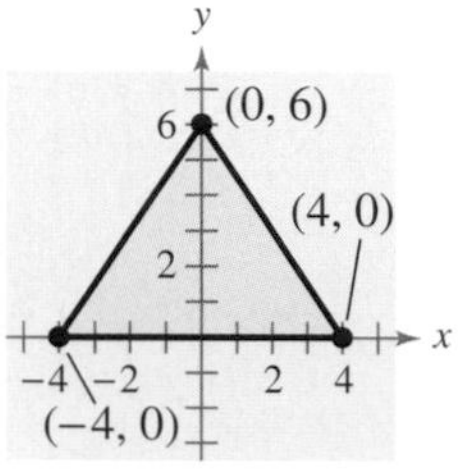

113.

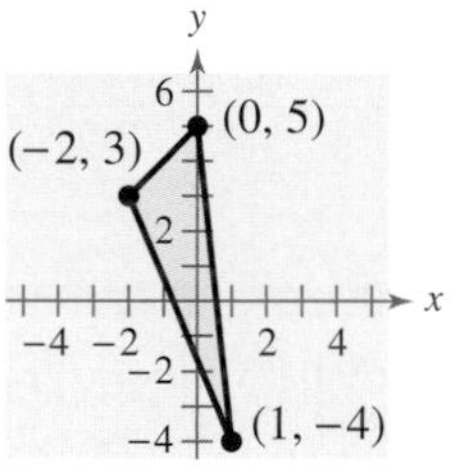

114.

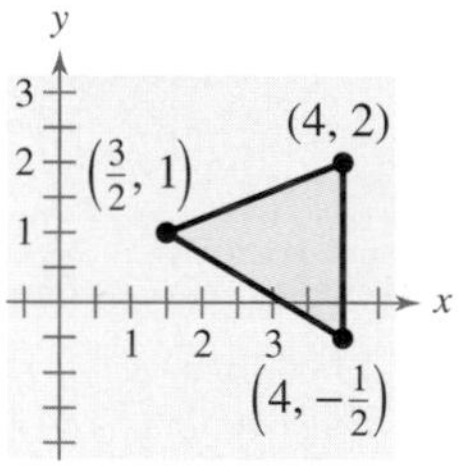

In Exercises 115 and 116, use a determinant to determine whether the points are collinear.

115. $(-1, 7), (3, -9), (-3, 15)$

116. $(0, -5), (-2, -6), (8, -1)$

In Exercises 117–120, use a determinant to find an equation of the line passing through the points.

117. $(-4, 0), (4, 4)$

118. $(2, 5), (6, -1)$

119. $\left(-\frac{5}{2}, 3\right), \left(\frac{7}{2}, 1\right)$

120. $(-0.8, 0.2), (0.7, 3.2)$

In Exercises 121 and 122, find the uncoded 1 × 3 row matrices for the message. Then encode the message using the encoding matrix.

	Message	*Encoding Matrix*
121.	LOOK OUT BELOW	$\begin{bmatrix} 2 & -2 & 0 \\ 3 & 0 & -3 \\ -6 & 2 & 3 \end{bmatrix}$
122.	RETURN TO BASE	$\begin{bmatrix} 2 & 1 & 0 \\ -6 & -6 & -2 \\ 3 & 2 & 1 \end{bmatrix}$

In Exercises 123 and 124, decode the cryptogram by using the inverse of the matrix

$$A = \begin{bmatrix} -5 & 4 & -3 \\ 10 & -7 & 6 \\ 8 & -6 & 5 \end{bmatrix}.$$

123. −5 11 −2 370 −265 225 −57 48 −33 32 −15 20 245 −171 147

124. 145 −105 92 264 −188 160 23 −16 15 129 −84 78 −9 8 −5 159 −118 100 219 −152 133 370 −265 225 −105 84 −63

Synthesis

True or False? **In Exercises 125 and 126, determine whether the statement is true or false. Justify your answer.**

125. It is possible to find the determinant of a 4 × 5 matrix.

126. $\begin{vmatrix} a_{11} & a_{12} & a_{13} \\ a_{21} & a_{22} & a_{23} \\ a_{31} + c_1 & a_{32} + c_2 & a_{33} + c_3 \end{vmatrix} =$

$$\begin{vmatrix} a_{11} & a_{12} & a_{13} \\ a_{21} & a_{22} & a_{23} \\ a_{31} & a_{32} & a_{33} \end{vmatrix} + \begin{vmatrix} a_{11} & a_{12} & a_{13} \\ a_{21} & a_{22} & a_{23} \\ c_1 & c_2 & c_3 \end{vmatrix}$$

127. Under what conditions does a matrix have an inverse?

128. ***Writing*** What is meant by the cofactor of an entry of a matrix? How are cofactors used to find the determinant of the matrix?

129. Three people were asked to solve a system of equations using an augmented matrix. Each person reduced the matrix to row-echelon form. The reduced matrices were

$$\begin{bmatrix} 1 & 2 & \vdots & 3 \\ 0 & 1 & \vdots & 1 \end{bmatrix},$$

$$\begin{bmatrix} 1 & 0 & \vdots & 1 \\ 0 & 1 & \vdots & 1 \end{bmatrix},$$

and

$$\begin{bmatrix} 1 & 2 & \vdots & 3 \\ 0 & 0 & \vdots & 0 \end{bmatrix}.$$

Can all three be right? Explain.

130. ***Think About It*** Describe the row-echelon form of an augmented matrix that corresponds to a system of linear equations that has a unique solution.

131. Solve the equation for λ.

$$\begin{vmatrix} 2 - \lambda & 5 \\ 3 & -8 - \lambda \end{vmatrix} = 0$$

8 Chapter Test

Take this test as you would take a test in class. When you are finished, check your work against the answers given in the back of the book.

In Exercises 1 and 2, write the matrix in reduced row-echelon form.

1. $\begin{bmatrix} 1 & -1 & 5 \\ 6 & 2 & 3 \\ 5 & 3 & -3 \end{bmatrix}$

2. $\begin{bmatrix} 1 & 0 & -1 & 2 \\ -1 & 1 & 1 & -3 \\ 1 & 1 & -1 & 1 \\ 3 & 2 & -3 & 4 \end{bmatrix}$

3. Write the augmented matrix corresponding to the system of equations and solve the system.

$$\begin{cases} 4x + 3y - 2z = 14 \\ -x - y + 2z = -5 \\ 3x + y - 4z = 8 \end{cases}$$

4. Find (a) $A - B$, (b) $3A$, (c) $3A - 2B$, and (d) AB (if possible).

$$A = \begin{bmatrix} 5 & 4 \\ -4 & -4 \end{bmatrix}, \quad B = \begin{bmatrix} 4 & -1 \\ -4 & 0 \end{bmatrix}$$

In Exercises 5 and 6, find the inverse of the matrix (if it exists).

5. $\begin{bmatrix} -6 & 4 \\ 10 & -5 \end{bmatrix}$

6. $\begin{bmatrix} -2 & 4 & -6 \\ 2 & 1 & 0 \\ 4 & -2 & 5 \end{bmatrix}$

7. Use the result of Exercise 5 to solve the system.

$$\begin{cases} -6x + 4y = 10 \\ 10x - 5y = 20 \end{cases}$$

In Exercises 8–10, evaluate the determinant of the matrix.

8. $\begin{bmatrix} -9 & 4 \\ 13 & 16 \end{bmatrix}$

9. $\begin{bmatrix} \frac{5}{2} & \frac{13}{4} \\ -8 & \frac{6}{5} \end{bmatrix}$

10. $\begin{bmatrix} 6 & -7 & 2 \\ 3 & -2 & 0 \\ 1 & 5 & 1 \end{bmatrix}$

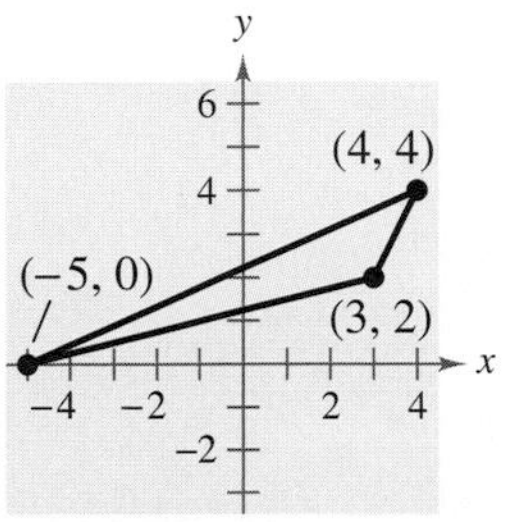

FIGURE FOR 13

In Exercises 11 and 12, use Cramer's Rule to solve (if possible) the system of equations.

11. $\begin{cases} 7x + 6y = 9 \\ -2x - 11y = -49 \end{cases}$

12. $\begin{cases} 6x - y + 2z = -4 \\ -2x + 3y - z = 10 \\ 4x - 4y + z = -18 \end{cases}$

13. Use a determinant to find the area of the triangle in the figure.

14. Find the uncoded 1×3 row matrices for the message KNOCK ON WOOD. Then encode the message using the matrix A below.

$$A = \begin{bmatrix} 1 & -1 & 0 \\ 1 & 0 & -1 \\ 6 & -2 & -3 \end{bmatrix}$$

15. One hundred liters of a 50% solution is obtained by mixing a 60% solution with a 20% solution. How many liters of each solution must be used to obtain the desired mixture?

Proofs in Mathematics

Proofs without words are pictures or diagrams that give a visual understanding of why a theorem or statement is true. They can also provide a starting point for writing a formal proof. The following proof shows that a 2×2 determinant is the area of a parallelogram.

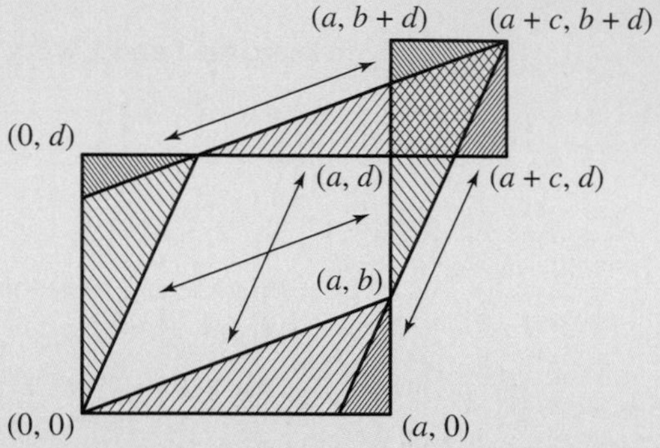

$\begin{vmatrix} a & b \\ c & d \end{vmatrix} = ad - bc =$ ‖▭‖ − ‖□‖ = ‖▱‖

The following is a color-coded version of the proof along with a brief explanation of why this proof works.

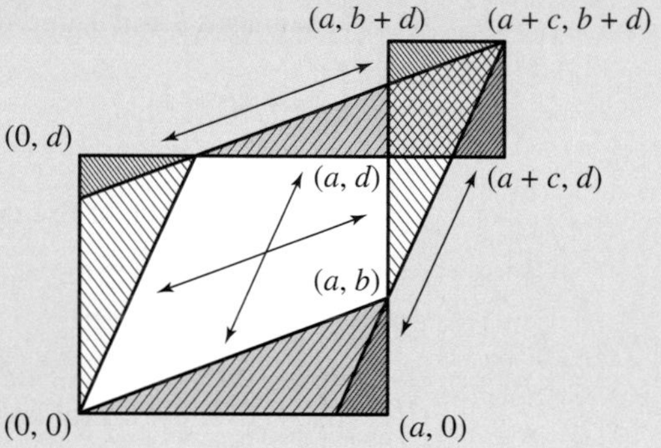

$\begin{vmatrix} a & b \\ c & d \end{vmatrix} = ad - bc =$ ‖▭‖ − ‖□‖ = ‖▱‖

Area of ▭ = Area of orange △ + Area of yellow △ + Area of blue △ + Area of pink △ + Area of white quadrilateral

Area of □ = Area of orange △ + Area of pink △ + Area of green quadrilateral

Area of ▱ = Area of white quadrilateral + Area of blue △ + Area of yellow △ − Area of green quadrilateral
= Area of ▭ − Area of □

From "Proof Without Words" by Solomon W. Golomb, *Mathematics Magazine*, March 1985. Vol. 58, No. 2, pg. 107. Reprinted with permission.

P.S. Problem Solving

This collection of thought-provoking and challenging exercises further explores and expands upon concepts learned in this chapter.

1. The columns of matrix T show the coordinates of the vertices of a triangle. Matrix A is a transformation matrix.

$$A = \begin{bmatrix} 0 & -1 \\ 1 & 0 \end{bmatrix} \quad T = \begin{bmatrix} 1 & 2 & 3 \\ 1 & 4 & 2 \end{bmatrix}$$

(a) Find AT and AAT. Then sketch the original triangle and the two transformed triangles. What transformation does A represent?

(b) Given the triangle determined by AAT, describe the transformation process that produces the triangle determined by AT and then the triangle determined by T.

2. The matrices show the number of people (in thousands) who lived in each region of the United States in 2000 and the number of people (in thousands) projected to live in each region in 2015. The regional populations are separated into three age categories. (Source: U.S. Census Bureau)

2000

	0–17	18–64	65 +
Northeast	13,049	33,175	7,372
Midwest	16,646	39,486	8,263
South	25,569	62,235	12,437
Mountain	4,935	11,210	2,031
Pacific	12,098	28,036	4,893

2015

	0–17	18–64	65 +
Northeast	12,589	34,081	8,165
Midwest	15,886	41,038	10,101
South	25,916	68,998	17,470
Mountain	5,226	12,626	3,270
Pacific	14,906	33,296	6,565

(a) The total population in 2000 was 281,435,000 and the projected total population in 2015 is 310,133,000. Rewrite the matrices to give the information as percents of the total population.

(b) Write a matrix that gives the projected change in the percent of the population in each region and age group from 2000 to 2015.

(c) Based on the result of part (b), which region(s) and age group(s) are projected to show relative growth from 2000 to 2015?

3. Determine whether the matrix is idempotent. A square matrix is **idempotent** if $A^2 = A$.

(a) $\begin{bmatrix} 1 & 0 \\ 0 & 0 \end{bmatrix}$ (b) $\begin{bmatrix} 0 & 1 \\ 1 & 0 \end{bmatrix}$

(c) $\begin{bmatrix} 2 & 3 \\ -1 & -2 \end{bmatrix}$ (d) $\begin{bmatrix} 2 & 3 \\ 1 & 2 \end{bmatrix}$

4. Let $A = \begin{bmatrix} 1 & 2 \\ -2 & 1 \end{bmatrix}$.

(a) Show that $A^2 - 2A + 5I = O$, where I is the identity matrix of order 2.

(b) Show that $A^{-1} = \frac{1}{5}(2I - A)$.

(c) Show in general that for any square matrix satisfying

$$A^2 - 2A + 5I = O$$

the inverse of A is given by

$$A^{-1} = \tfrac{1}{5}(2I - A).$$

5. Two competing companies offer cable television to a city with 100,000 households. Gold Cable Company has 25,000 subscribers and Galaxy Cable Company has 30,000 subscribers. (The other 45,000 households do not subscribe.) The percent changes in cable subscriptions each year are shown in the matrix below.

Percent Changes		From Gold	From Galaxy	From Nonsubscriber
Percent Changes	To Gold	0.70	0.15	0.15
	To Galaxy	0.20	0.80	0.15
	To Nonsubscriber	0.10	0.05	0.70

(a) Find the number of subscribers each company will have in 1 year using matrix multiplication. Explain how you obtained your answer.

(b) Find the number of subscribers each company will have in 2 years using matrix multiplication. Explain how you obtained your answer.

(c) Find the number of subscribers each company will have in 3 years using matrix multiplication. Explain how you obtained your answer.

(d) What is happening to the number of subscribers to each company? What is happening to the number of nonsubscribers?

6. Find x such that the matrix is equal to its own inverse.

$$A = \begin{bmatrix} 3 & x \\ -2 & -3 \end{bmatrix}$$

7. Find x such that the matrix is singular.

$$A = \begin{bmatrix} 4 & x \\ -2 & -3 \end{bmatrix}$$

8. Find an example of a singular 2×2 matrix satisfying $A^2 = A$.

9. Verify the following equation.

$$\begin{vmatrix} 1 & 1 & 1 \\ a & b & c \\ a^2 & b^2 & c^2 \end{vmatrix} = (a - b)(b - c)(c - a)$$

10. Verify the following equation.

$$\begin{vmatrix} 1 & 1 & 1 \\ a & b & c \\ a^3 & b^3 & c^3 \end{vmatrix} = (a - b)(b - c)(c - a)(a + b + c)$$

11. Verify the following equation.

$$\begin{vmatrix} x & 0 & c \\ -1 & x & b \\ 0 & -1 & a \end{vmatrix} = ax^2 + bx + c$$

12. Use the equation given in Exercise 11 as a model to find a determinant that is equal to $ax^3 + bx^2 + cx + d$.

13. The atomic masses of three compounds are shown in the table. Use a linear system and Cramer's Rule to find the atomic masses of sulfur (S), nitrogen (N), and fluorine (F).

Compound	Formula	Atomic mass
Tetrasulphur tetranitride	S_4N_4	184
Sulfur hexafluoride	SF_6	146
Dinitrogen tetrafluoride	N_2F_4	104

14. A walkway lighting package includes a transformer, a certain length of wire, and a certain number of lights on the wire. The price of each lighting package depends on the length of wire and the number of lights on the wire. Use the following information to find the cost of a transformer, the cost per foot of wire, and the cost of a light. Assume that the cost of each item is the same in each lighting package.

- A package that contains a transformer, 25 feet of wire, and 5 lights costs \$20.
- A package that contains a transformer, 50 feet of wire, and 15 lights costs \$35.
- A package that contains a transformer, 100 feet of wire, and 20 lights costs \$50.

15. The **transpose** of a matrix, denoted A^T, is formed by writing its columns as rows. Find the transpose of each matrix and verify that $(AB)^T = B^TA^T$.

$$A = \begin{bmatrix} -1 & 1 & -2 \\ 2 & 0 & 1 \end{bmatrix}, \quad B = \begin{bmatrix} -3 & 0 \\ 1 & 2 \\ 1 & -1 \end{bmatrix}$$

16. Use the inverse of matrix A to decode the cryptogram.

$$A = \begin{bmatrix} 1 & -2 & 2 \\ 1 & 1 & -3 \\ 1 & -1 & 4 \end{bmatrix}$$

23 13 −34 31 −34 63 25 −17 61
24 14 −37 41 −17 −8 20 −29 40
38 −56 116 13 −11 1 22 −3 −6
41 −53 85 28 −32 16

17. A code breaker intercepted the encoded message below.

45 −35 38 −30 18 −18 35 −30 81 −60
42 −28 75 −55 2 −2 22 −21 15
−10

Let

$$A^{-1} = \begin{bmatrix} w & x \\ y & z \end{bmatrix}.$$

(a) You know that $[45 \quad -35]A^{-1} = [10 \quad 15]$ and that $[38 \quad -30]A^{-1} = [8 \quad 14]$, where A^{-1} is the inverse of the encoding matrix A. Write and solve two systems of equations to find w, x, y, and z.

(b) Decode the message.

18. Let

$$A = \begin{bmatrix} 6 & 4 & 1 \\ 0 & 2 & 3 \\ 1 & 1 & 2 \end{bmatrix}.$$

Use a graphing utility to find A^{-1}. Compare $|A^{-1}|$ with $|A|$. Make a conjecture about the determinant of the inverse of a matrix.

19. Let A be an $n \times n$ matrix each of whose rows adds up to zero. Find $|A|$.

20. Consider matrices of the form

$$A = \begin{bmatrix} 0 & a_{12} & a_{13} & a_{14} & \cdots & a_{1n} \\ 0 & 0 & a_{23} & a_{24} & \cdots & a_{2n} \\ 0 & 0 & 0 & a_{34} & \cdots & a_{3n} \\ \vdots & \vdots & \vdots & \vdots & \cdots & \vdots \\ 0 & 0 & 0 & 0 & \cdots & a_{(n-1)n} \\ 0 & 0 & 0 & 0 & \cdots & 0 \end{bmatrix}$$

(a) Write a 2×2 matrix and a 3×3 matrix in the form of A.

(b) Use a graphing utility to raise each of the matrices to higher powers. Describe the result.

(c) Use the result of part (b) to make a conjecture about powers of A if A is a 4×4 matrix. Use a graphing utility to test your conjecture.

(d) Use the results of parts (b) and (c) to make a conjecture about powers of A if A is an $n \times n$ matrix.

Sequences, Series, and Probability

9

9.1 Sequences and Series

9.2 Arithmetic Sequences and Partial Sums

9.3 Geometric Sequences and Series

9.4 Mathematical Induction

9.5 The Binomial Theorem

9.6 Counting Principles

9.7 Probability

Poker has become a popular card game in recent years. You can use the probability theory developed in this chapter to calculate the likelihood of getting different poker hands.

Jeff Greenberg/PhotoEdit, Inc.

SELECTED APPLICATIONS

Sequences, series, and probability have many real-life applications. The applications listed below represent a small sample of the applications in this chapter.

- Federal Debt, Exercise 111, page 651
- Falling Object, Exercises 87 and 88, page 661
- Multiplier Effect, Exercises 113–116, page 671
- Data Analysis: Tax Returns, Exercise 61, page 682
- Child Support, Exercise 80, page 690
- Poker Hand Exercise 57, page 699
- Lottery, Exercise 65, page 700
- Defective Units, Exercise 47, page 711
- Population Growth, Exercise 139, page 718

9.1 Sequences and Series

What you should learn

- Use sequence notation to write the terms of sequences.
- Use factorial notation.
- Use summation notation to write sums.
- Find the sums of infinite series.
- Use sequences and series to model and solve real-life problems.

Why you should learn it

Sequences and series can be used to model real-life problems. For instance, in Exercise 109 on page 651, sequences are used to model the number of Best Buy stores from 1998 through 2003.

Scott Olson/Getty Images

Sequences

In mathematics, the word *sequence* is used in much the same way as in ordinary English. Saying that a collection is listed in *sequence* means that it is ordered so that it has a first member, a second member, a third member, and so on.

Mathematically, you can think of a sequence as a *function* whose domain is the set of positive integers.

$$f(1) = a_1,\ f(2) = a_2,\ f(3) = a_3,\ f(4) = a_4, \ldots, f(n) = a_n, \ldots$$

Rather than using function notation, however, sequences are usually written using subscript notation, as indicated in the following definition.

> **Definition of Sequence**
>
> An **infinite sequence** is a function whose domain is the set of positive integers. The function values
>
> $$a_1, a_2, a_3, a_4, \ldots, a_n, \ldots$$
>
> are the **terms** of the sequence. If the domain of the function consists of the first n positive integers only, the sequence is a **finite sequence.**

On occasion it is convenient to begin subscripting a sequence with 0 instead of 1 so that the terms of the sequence become $a_0, a_1, a_2, a_3, \ldots$.

Example 1 Writing the Terms of a Sequence

Write the first four terms of the sequences given by

a. $a_n = 3n - 2$ **b.** $a_n = 3 + (-1)^n$.

Solution

a. The first four terms of the sequence given by $a_n = 3n - 2$ are

$a_1 = 3(1) - 2 = 1$ 1st term

$a_2 = 3(2) - 2 = 4$ 2nd term

$a_3 = 3(3) - 2 = 7$ 3rd term

$a_4 = 3(4) - 2 = 10.$ 4th term

b. The first four terms of the sequence given by $a_n = 3 + (-1)^n$ are

$a_1 = 3 + (-1)^1 = 3 - 1 = 2$ 1st term

$a_2 = 3 + (-1)^2 = 3 + 1 = 4$ 2nd term

$a_3 = 3 + (-1)^3 = 3 - 1 = 2$ 3rd term

$a_4 = 3 + (-1)^4 = 3 + 1 = 4.$ 4th term

✓CHECKPOINT Now try Exercise 1.

Exploration

Write out the first five terms of the sequence whose nth term is

$$a_n = \frac{(-1)^{n+1}}{2n-1}.$$

Are they the same as the first five terms of the sequence in Example 2? If not, how do they differ?

Example 2 A Sequence Whose Terms Alternate in Sign

Write the first five terms of the sequence given by $a_n = \dfrac{(-1)^n}{2n-1}$.

Solution

The first five terms of the sequence are as follows.

$$a_1 = \frac{(-1)^1}{2(1)-1} = \frac{-1}{2-1} = -1 \qquad \text{1st term}$$

$$a_2 = \frac{(-1)^2}{2(2)-1} = \frac{1}{4-1} = \frac{1}{3} \qquad \text{2nd term}$$

$$a_3 = \frac{(-1)^3}{2(3)-1} = \frac{-1}{6-1} = -\frac{1}{5} \qquad \text{3rd term}$$

$$a_4 = \frac{(-1)^4}{2(4)-1} = \frac{1}{8-1} = \frac{1}{7} \qquad \text{4th term}$$

$$a_5 = \frac{(-1)^5}{2(5)-1} = \frac{-1}{10-1} = -\frac{1}{9} \qquad \text{5th term}$$

✓CHECKPOINT Now try Exercise 17.

Simply listing the first few terms is not sufficient to define a unique sequence—the nth term *must be given.* To see this, consider the following sequences, both of which have the same first three terms.

$$\frac{1}{2}, \frac{1}{4}, \frac{1}{8}, \frac{1}{16}, \ldots, \frac{1}{2^n}, \ldots$$

$$\frac{1}{2}, \frac{1}{4}, \frac{1}{8}, \frac{1}{15}, \ldots, \frac{6}{(n+1)(n^2-n+6)}, \ldots$$

Example 3 Finding the nth Term of a Sequence

Write an expression for the apparent nth term (a_n) of each sequence.

a. 1, 3, 5, 7, . . . **b.** 2, −5, 10, −17, . . .

Solution

a. *n:* 1 2 3 4 . . . n

Terms: 1 3 5 7 . . . a_n

Apparent pattern: Each term is 1 less than twice n, which implies that

$$a_n = 2n - 1.$$

b. *n:* 1 2 3 4 . . . n

Terms: 2 −5 10 −17 . . . a_n

Apparent pattern: The terms have alternating signs with those in the even positions being negative. Each term is 1 more than the square of n, which implies that

$$a_n = (-1)^{n+1}(n^2 + 1)$$

✓CHECKPOINT Now try Exercise 37.

Technology

To graph a sequence using a graphing utility, set the mode to *sequence* and *dot* and enter the sequence. The graph of the sequence in Example 3(a) is shown below. You can use the *trace* feature or *value* feature to identify the terms.

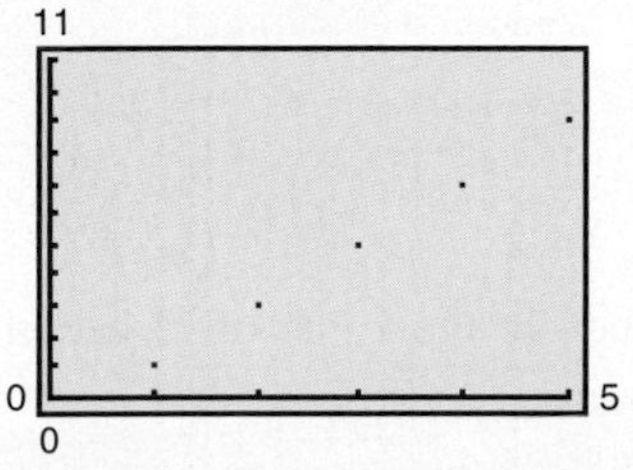

Some sequences are defined **recursively.** To define a sequence recursively, you need to be given one or more of the first few terms. All other terms of the sequence are then defined using previous terms. A well-known example is the Fibonacci sequence shown in Example 4.

Example 4 **The Fibonacci Sequence: A Recursive Sequence**

The Fibonacci sequence is defined recursively, as follows.

$$a_0 = 1,\ a_1 = 1,\ a_k = a_{k-2} + a_{k-1},\ \text{where } k \geq 2$$

Write the first six terms of this sequence.

Solution

$a_0 = 1$ 0th term is given.

$a_1 = 1$ 1st term is given.

$a_2 = a_{2-2} + a_{2-1} = a_0 + a_1 = 1 + 1 = 2$ Use recursion formula.

$a_3 = a_{3-2} + a_{3-1} = a_1 + a_2 = 1 + 2 = 3$ Use recursion formula.

$a_4 = a_{4-2} + a_{4-1} = a_2 + a_3 = 2 + 3 = 5$ Use recursion formula.

$a_5 = a_{5-2} + a_{5-1} = a_3 + a_4 = 3 + 5 = 8$ Use recursion formula.

✓CHECKPOINT Now try Exercise 51.

STUDY TIP

The subscripts of a sequence make up the domain of the sequence and they serve to identify the location of a term within the sequence. For example, a_4 is the fourth term of the sequence, and a_n is the nth term of the sequence. Any variable can be used as a subscript. The most commonly used variable subscripts in sequence and series notation are i, j, k, and n.

Factorial Notation

Some very important sequences in mathematics involve terms that are defined with special types of products called **factorials.**

Definition of Factorial

If n is a positive integer, ***n* factorial** is defined as

$$n! = 1 \cdot 2 \cdot 3 \cdot 4 \cdot \cdot \cdot (n - 1) \cdot n.$$

As a special case, zero factorial is defined as $0! = 1$.

Here are some values of $n!$ for the first several nonnegative integers. Notice that $0!$ is 1 by definition.

$0! = 1$

$1! = 1$

$2! = 1 \cdot 2 = 2$

$3! = 1 \cdot 2 \cdot 3 = 6$

$4! = 1 \cdot 2 \cdot 3 \cdot 4 = 24$

$5! = 1 \cdot 2 \cdot 3 \cdot 4 \cdot 5 = 120$

The value of n does not have to be very large before the value of $n!$ becomes extremely large. For instance, $10! = 3{,}628{,}800$.

Factorials follow the same conventions for order of operations as do exponents. For instance,

$$2n! = 2(n!) = 2(1 \cdot 2 \cdot 3 \cdot 4 \cdot \cdot \cdot n)$$

whereas $(2n)! = 1 \cdot 2 \cdot 3 \cdot 4 \cdot \cdot \cdot 2n$.

Example 5 Writing the Terms of a Sequence Involving Factorials

Write the first five terms of the sequence given by

$$a_n = \frac{2^n}{n!}.$$

Begin with $n = 0$. Then graph the terms on a set of coordinate axes.

Solution

$$a_0 = \frac{2^0}{0!} = \frac{1}{1} = 1 \qquad \text{0th term}$$

$$a_1 = \frac{2^1}{1!} = \frac{2}{1} = 2 \qquad \text{1st term}$$

$$a_2 = \frac{2^2}{2!} = \frac{4}{2} = 2 \qquad \text{2nd term}$$

$$a_3 = \frac{2^3}{3!} = \frac{8}{6} = \frac{4}{3} \qquad \text{3rd term}$$

$$a_4 = \frac{2^4}{4!} = \frac{16}{24} = \frac{2}{3} \qquad \text{4th term}$$

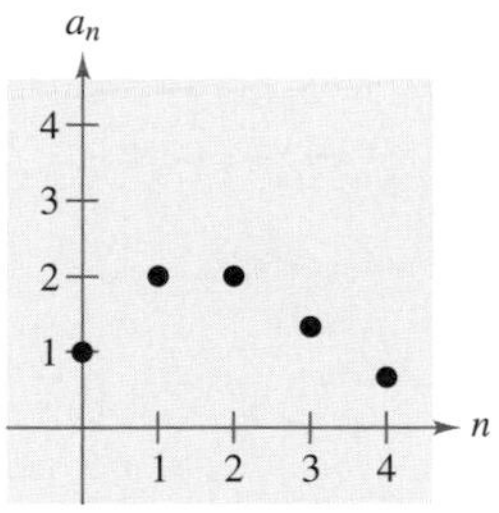

FIGURE 9.1

Figure 9.1 shows the first five terms of the sequence.

CHECKPOINT Now try Exercise 59.

When working with fractions involving factorials, you will often find that the fractions can be reduced to simplify the computations.

Example 6 Evaluating Factorial Expressions

Evaluate each factorial expression.

a. $\dfrac{8!}{2! \cdot 6!}$ **b.** $\dfrac{2! \cdot 6!}{3! \cdot 5!}$ **c.** $\dfrac{n!}{(n-1)!}$

Solution

a. $\dfrac{8!}{2! \cdot 6!} = \dfrac{\cancel{1 \cdot 2 \cdot 3 \cdot 4 \cdot 5 \cdot 6} \cdot 7 \cdot 8}{1 \cdot 2 \cdot \cancel{1 \cdot 2 \cdot 3 \cdot 4 \cdot 5 \cdot 6}} = \dfrac{7 \cdot 8}{2} = 28$

b. $\dfrac{2! \cdot 6!}{3! \cdot 5!} = \dfrac{\cancel{1 \cdot 2} \cdot \cancel{1 \cdot 2 \cdot 3 \cdot 4 \cdot 5} \cdot 6}{\cancel{1 \cdot 2} \cdot 3 \cdot \cancel{1 \cdot 2 \cdot 3 \cdot 4 \cdot 5}} = \dfrac{6}{3} = 2$

c. $\dfrac{n!}{(n-1)!} = \dfrac{\cancel{1 \cdot 2 \cdot 3 \cdots (n-1)} \cdot n}{\cancel{1 \cdot 2 \cdot 3 \cdots (n-1)}} = n$

CHECKPOINT Now try Exercise 69.

STUDY TIP

Note in Example 6(a) that you can simplify the computation as follows.

$$\frac{8!}{2! \cdot 6!} = \frac{8 \cdot 7 \cdot \cancel{6!}}{2! \cdot \cancel{6!}} = \frac{8 \cdot 7}{2 \cdot 1} = 28$$

Technology

Most graphing utilities are able to sum the first n terms of a sequence. Check your user's guide for a *sum sequence* feature or a *series* feature.

Summation Notation

There is a convenient notation for the sum of the terms of a finite sequence. It is called **summation notation** or **sigma notation** because it involves the use of the uppercase Greek letter sigma, written as Σ.

Definition of Summation Notation

The sum of the first n terms of a sequence is represented by

$$\sum_{i=1}^{n} a_i = a_1 + a_2 + a_3 + a_4 + \cdot \cdot \cdot + a_n$$

where i is called the **index of summation,** n is the **upper limit of summation,** and 1 is the **lower limit of summation.**

Example 7 Summation Notation for Sums

Find each sum.

a. $\sum_{i=1}^{5} 3i$ **b.** $\sum_{k=3}^{6} (1 + k^2)$ **c.** $\sum_{i=0}^{8} \frac{1}{i!}$

Solution

a.
$$\begin{aligned}\sum_{i=1}^{5} 3i &= 3(1) + 3(2) + 3(3) + 3(4) + 3(5)\\ &= 3(1 + 2 + 3 + 4 + 5)\\ &= 3(15)\\ &= 45\end{aligned}$$

b.
$$\begin{aligned}\sum_{k=3}^{6} (1 + k^2) &= (1 + 3^2) + (1 + 4^2) + (1 + 5^2) + (1 + 6^2)\\ &= 10 + 17 + 26 + 37\\ &= 90\end{aligned}$$

c.
$$\begin{aligned}\sum_{i=0}^{8} \frac{1}{i!} &= \frac{1}{0!} + \frac{1}{1!} + \frac{1}{2!} + \frac{1}{3!} + \frac{1}{4!} + \frac{1}{5!} + \frac{1}{6!} + \frac{1}{7!} + \frac{1}{8!}\\ &= 1 + 1 + \frac{1}{2} + \frac{1}{6} + \frac{1}{24} + \frac{1}{120} + \frac{1}{720} + \frac{1}{5040} + \frac{1}{40{,}320}\\ &\approx 2.71828\end{aligned}$$

For this summation, note that the sum is very close to the irrational number $e \approx 2.718281828$. It can be shown that as more terms of the sequence whose nth term is $1/n!$ are added, the sum becomes closer and closer to e.

CHECKPOINT Now try Exercise 73.

STUDY TIP

Summation notation is an instruction to add the terms of a sequence. From the definition at the right, the upper limit of summation tells you where to end the sum. Summation notation helps you generate the appropriate terms of the sequence prior to finding the actual sum, which may be unclear.

In Example 7, note that the lower limit of a summation does not have to be 1. Also note that the index of summation does not have to be the letter i. For instance, in part (b), the letter k is the index of summation.

STUDY TIP

Variations in the upper and lower limits of summation can produce quite different-looking summation notations for *the same sum*. For example, the following two sums have the same terms.

$$\sum_{i=1}^{3} 3(2^i) = 3(2^1 + 2^2 + 2^3)$$

$$\sum_{i=0}^{2} 3(2^{i+1}) = 3(2^1 + 2^2 + 2^3)$$

Properties of Sums

1. $\sum_{i=1}^{n} c = cn$, c is a constant.
2. $\sum_{i=1}^{n} ca_i = c\sum_{i=1}^{n} a_i$, c is a constant.
3. $\sum_{i=1}^{n} (a_i + b_i) = \sum_{i=1}^{n} a_i + \sum_{i=1}^{n} b_i$
4. $\sum_{i=1}^{n} (a_i - b_i) = \sum_{i=1}^{n} a_i - \sum_{i=1}^{n} b_i$

For proofs of these properties, see Proofs in Mathematics on page 722.

Series

Many applications involve the sum of the terms of a finite or infinite sequence. Such a sum is called a **series.**

Definition of Series

Consider the infinite sequence $a_1, a_2, a_3, \ldots, a_i, \ldots$.

1. The sum of the first n terms of the sequence is called a **finite series** or the ***n*th partial sum** of the sequence and is denoted by

$$a_1 + a_2 + a_3 + \cdots + a_n = \sum_{i=1}^{n} a_i.$$

2. The sum of all the terms of the infinite sequence is called an **infinite series** and is denoted by

$$a_1 + a_2 + a_3 + \cdots + a_i + \cdots = \sum_{i=1}^{\infty} a_i.$$

Example 8 Finding the Sum of a Series

For the series $\sum_{i=1}^{\infty} \frac{3}{10^i}$, find (a) the third partial sum and (b) the sum.

Solution

a. The third partial sum is

$$\sum_{i=1}^{3} \frac{3}{10^i} = \frac{3}{10^1} + \frac{3}{10^2} + \frac{3}{10^3} = 0.3 + 0.03 + 0.003 = 0.333.$$

b. The sum of the series is

$$\sum_{i=1}^{\infty} \frac{3}{10^i} = \frac{3}{10^1} + \frac{3}{10^2} + \frac{3}{10^3} + \frac{3}{10^4} + \frac{3}{10^5} + \cdots$$

$$= 0.3 + 0.03 + 0.003 + 0.0003 + 0.00003 + \cdots$$

$$= 0.33333\ldots = \frac{1}{3}.$$

✓CHECKPOINT Now try Exercise 99.

Application

Sequences have many applications in business and science. One such application is illustrated in Example 9.

Example 9 Population of the United States

For the years 1980 to 2003, the resident population of the United States can be approximated by the model

$$a_n = 226.9 + 2.05n + 0.035n^2, \qquad n = 0, 1, \ldots, 23$$

where a_n is the population (in millions) and n represents the year, with $n = 0$ corresponding to 1980. Find the last five terms of this finite sequence, which represent the U.S. population for the years 1999 to 2003. (Source: U.S. Census Bureau)

Solution

The last five terms of this finite sequence are as follows.

$$a_{19} = 226.9 + 2.05(19) + 0.035(19)^2 \approx 278.5 \qquad \text{1999 population}$$

$$a_{20} = 226.9 + 2.05(20) + 0.035(20)^2 = 281.9 \qquad \text{2000 population}$$

$$a_{21} = 226.9 + 2.05(21) + 0.035(21)^2 \approx 285.4 \qquad \text{2001 population}$$

$$a_{22} = 226.9 + 2.05(22) + 0.035(22)^2 \approx 288.9 \qquad \text{2002 population}$$

$$a_{23} = 226.9 + 2.05(23) + 0.035(23)^2 \approx 292.6 \qquad \text{2003 population}$$

✓CHECKPOINT Now try Exercise 111.

Exploration

A $3 \times 3 \times 3$ cube is created using 27 unit cubes (a unit cube has a length, width, and height of 1 unit) and only the faces of each cube that are visible are painted blue (see Figure 9.2). Complete the table below to determine how many unit cubes of the $3 \times 3 \times 3$ cube have 0 blue faces, 1 blue face, 2 blue faces, and 3 blue faces. Do the same for a $4 \times 4 \times 4$ cube, a $5 \times 5 \times 5$ cube, and a $6 \times 6 \times 6$ cube and add your results to the table below. What type of pattern do you observe in the table? Write a formula you could use to determine the column values for an $n \times n \times n$ cube.

Number of blue cube faces	0	1	2	3
$3 \times 3 \times 3$				

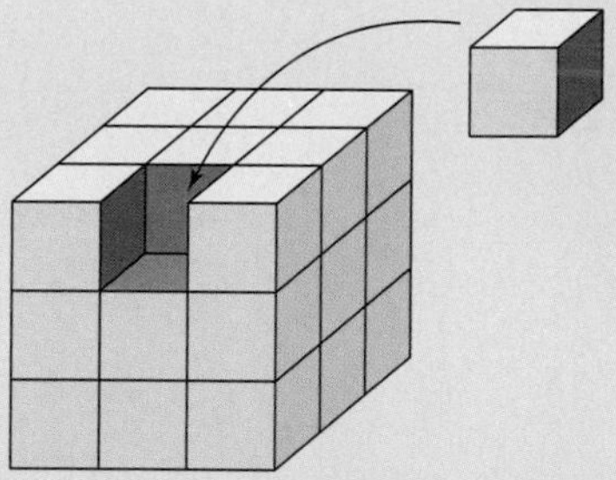

FIGURE 9.2

9.1 Exercises

VOCABULARY CHECK: Fill in the blanks.

1. An ________ ________ is a function whose domain is the set of positive integers.
2. The function values $a_1, a_2, a_3, a_4, \ldots$ are called the ________ of a sequence.
3. A sequence is a ________ sequence if the domain of the function consists of the first n positive integers.
4. If you are given one or more of the first few terms of a sequence, and all other terms of the sequence are defined using previous terms, then the sequence is said to be defined ________.
5. If n is a positive integer, n ________ is defined as $n! = 1 \cdot 2 \cdot 3 \cdot 4 \cdots (n-1) \cdot n$.
6. The notation used to represent the sum of the terms of a finite sequence is ________ ________ or sigma notation.
7. For the sum $\sum_{i=1}^{n} a_i$, i is called the ________ of summation, n is the ________ limit of summation, and 1 is the ________ limit of summation.
8. The sum of the terms of a finite or infinite sequence is called a ________.
9. The ________ ________ ________ of a sequence is the sum of the first n terms of the sequence.

In Exercises 1–22, write the first five terms of the sequence. (Assume that n begins with 1.)

1. $a_n = 3n + 1$
2. $a_n = 5n - 3$
3. $a_n = 2^n$
4. $a_n = \left(\frac{1}{2}\right)^n$
5. $a_n = (-2)^n$
6. $a_n = \left(-\frac{1}{2}\right)^n$
7. $a_n = \dfrac{n+2}{n}$
8. $a_n = \dfrac{n}{n+2}$
9. $a_n = \dfrac{6n}{3n^2 - 1}$
10. $a_n = \dfrac{3n^2 - n + 4}{2n^2 + 1}$
11. $a_n = \dfrac{1 + (-1)^n}{n}$
12. $a_n = 1 + (-1)^n$
13. $a_n = 2 - \dfrac{1}{3^n}$
14. $a_n = \dfrac{2^n}{3^n}$
15. $a_n = \dfrac{1}{n^{3/2}}$
16. $a_n = \dfrac{10}{n^{2/3}}$
17. $a_n = \dfrac{(-1)^n}{n^2}$
18. $a_n = (-1)^n\left(\dfrac{n}{n+1}\right)$
19. $a_n = \frac{2}{3}$
20. $a_n = 0.3$
21. $a_n = n(n-1)(n-2)$
22. $a_n = n(n^2 - 6)$

In Exercises 23–26, find the indicated term of the sequence.

23. $a_n = (-1)^n(3n - 2)$

    $a_{25} =$ ____
24. $a_n = (-1)^{n-1}[n(n-1)]$

    $a_{16} =$ ____
25. $a_n = \dfrac{4n}{2n^2 - 3}$

    $a_{11} =$ ____
26. $a_n = \dfrac{4n^2 - n + 3}{n(n-1)(n+2)}$

    $a_{13} =$ ____

In Exercises 27–32, use a graphing utility to graph the first 10 terms of the sequence. (Assume that n begins with 1.)

27. $a_n = \dfrac{3}{4}n$
28. $a_n = 2 - \dfrac{4}{n}$
29. $a_n = 16(-0.5)^{n-1}$
30. $a_n = 8(0.75)^{n-1}$
31. $a_n = \dfrac{2n}{n+1}$
32. $a_n = \dfrac{n^2}{n^2 + 2}$

In Exercises 33–36, match the sequence with the graph of its first 10 terms. [The graphs are labeled (a), (b), (c), and (d).]

(a)

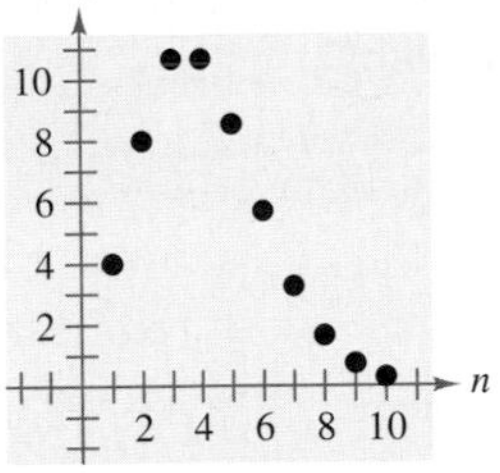

(b)

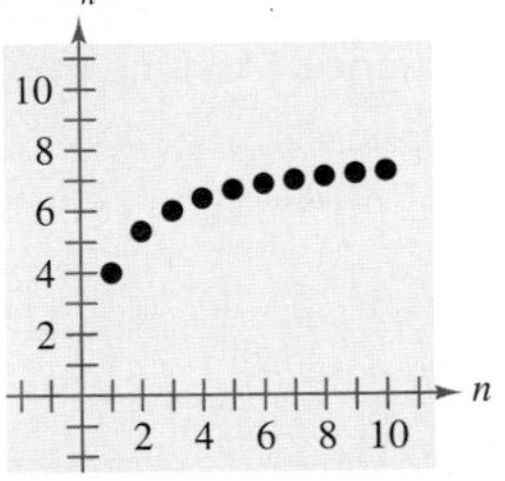

(c)

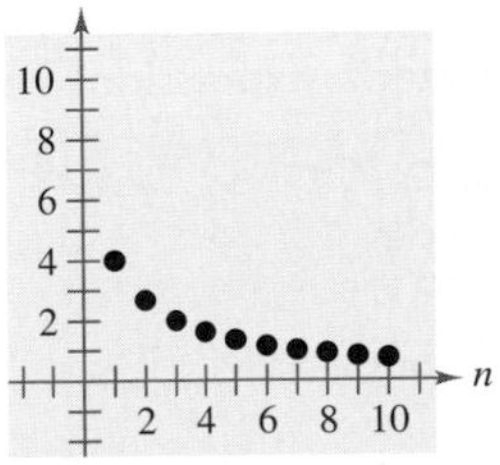

(d)

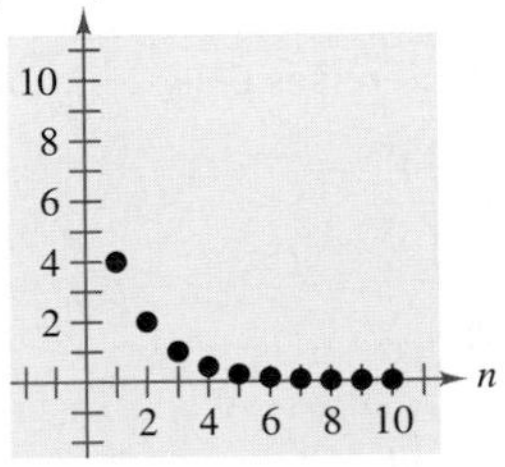

33. $a_n = \dfrac{8}{n+1}$
34. $a_n = \dfrac{8n}{n+1}$
35. $a_n = 4(0.5)^{n-1}$
36. $a_n = \dfrac{4^n}{n!}$

In Exercises 37–50, write an expression for the apparent *n*th term of the sequence. (Assume that *n* begins with 1.)

37. $1, 4, 7, 10, 13, \ldots$

38. $3, 7, 11, 15, 19, \ldots$

39. $0, 3, 8, 15, 24, \ldots$

40. $2, -4, 6, -8, 10, \ldots$

41. $\frac{-2}{3}, \frac{3}{4}, \frac{-4}{5}, \frac{5}{6}, \frac{-6}{7}, \ldots$

42. $\frac{1}{2}, \frac{-1}{4}, \frac{1}{8}, \frac{-1}{16}, \ldots$

43. $\frac{2}{1}, \frac{3}{3}, \frac{4}{5}, \frac{5}{7}, \frac{6}{9}, \ldots$

44. $\frac{1}{3}, \frac{2}{9}, \frac{4}{27}, \frac{8}{81}, \ldots$

45. $1, \frac{1}{4}, \frac{1}{9}, \frac{1}{16}, \frac{1}{25}, \ldots$

46. $1, \frac{1}{2}, \frac{1}{6}, \frac{1}{24}, \frac{1}{120}, \ldots$

47. $1, -1, 1, -1, 1, \ldots$

48. $1, 2, \frac{2^2}{2}, \frac{2^3}{6}, \frac{2^4}{24}, \frac{2^5}{120}, \ldots$

49. $1 + \frac{1}{1}, 1 + \frac{1}{2}, 1 + \frac{1}{3}, 1 + \frac{1}{4}, 1 + \frac{1}{5}, \ldots$

50. $1 + \frac{1}{2}, 1 + \frac{3}{4}, 1 + \frac{7}{8}, 1 + \frac{15}{16}, 1 + \frac{31}{32}, \ldots$

In Exercises 51–54, write the first five terms of the sequence defined recursively.

51. $a_1 = 28, \quad a_{k+1} = a_k - 4$

52. $a_1 = 15, \quad a_{k+1} = a_k + 3$

53. $a_1 = 3, \quad a_{k+1} = 2(a_k - 1)$

54. $a_1 = 32, \quad a_{k+1} = \frac{1}{2}a_k$

In Exercises 55–58, write the first five terms of the sequence defined recursively. Use the pattern to write the *n*th term of the sequence as a function of *n*. (Assume that *n* begins with 1.)

55. $a_1 = 6, \quad a_{k+1} = a_k + 2$

56. $a_1 = 25, \quad a_{k+1} = a_k - 5$

57. $a_1 = 81, \quad a_{k+1} = \frac{1}{3}a_k$

58. $a_1 = 14, \quad a_{k+1} = (-2)a_k$

In Exercises 59–64, write the first five terms of the sequence. (Assume that *n* begins with 0.)

59. $a_n = \dfrac{3^n}{n!}$

60. $a_n = \dfrac{n!}{n}$

61. $a_n = \dfrac{1}{(n+1)!}$

62. $a_n = \dfrac{n^2}{(n+1)!}$

63. $a_n = \dfrac{(-1)^{2n}}{(2n)!}$

64. $a_n = \dfrac{(-1)^{2n+1}}{(2n+1)!}$

In Exercises 65–72, simplify the factorial expression.

65. $\dfrac{4!}{6!}$

66. $\dfrac{5!}{8!}$

67. $\dfrac{10!}{8!}$

68. $\dfrac{25!}{23!}$

69. $\dfrac{(n+1)!}{n!}$

70. $\dfrac{(n+2)!}{n!}$

71. $\dfrac{(2n-1)!}{(2n+1)!}$

72. $\dfrac{(3n+1)!}{(3n)!}$

In Exercises 73–84, find the sum.

73. $\displaystyle\sum_{i=1}^{5}(2i+1)$

74. $\displaystyle\sum_{i=1}^{6}(3i-1)$

75. $\displaystyle\sum_{k=1}^{4}10$

76. $\displaystyle\sum_{k=1}^{5}5$

77. $\displaystyle\sum_{i=0}^{4}i^2$

78. $\displaystyle\sum_{i=0}^{5}2i^2$

79. $\displaystyle\sum_{k=0}^{3}\frac{1}{k^2+1}$

80. $\displaystyle\sum_{j=3}^{5}\frac{1}{j^2-3}$

81. $\displaystyle\sum_{k=2}^{5}(k+1)^2(k-3)$

82. $\displaystyle\sum_{i=1}^{4}[(i-1)^2+(i+1)^3]$

83. $\displaystyle\sum_{i=1}^{4}2^i$

84. $\displaystyle\sum_{j=0}^{4}(-2)^j$

In Exercises 85–88, use a calculator to find the sum.

85. $\displaystyle\sum_{j=1}^{6}(24-3j)$

86. $\displaystyle\sum_{j=1}^{10}\frac{3}{j+1}$

87. $\displaystyle\sum_{k=0}^{4}\frac{(-1)^k}{k+1}$

88. $\displaystyle\sum_{k=0}^{4}\frac{(-1)^k}{k!}$

In Exercises 89–98, use sigma notation to write the sum.

89. $\dfrac{1}{3(1)} + \dfrac{1}{3(2)} + \dfrac{1}{3(3)} + \cdots + \dfrac{1}{3(9)}$

90. $\dfrac{5}{1+1} + \dfrac{5}{1+2} + \dfrac{5}{1+3} + \cdots + \dfrac{5}{1+15}$

91. $\left[2\left(\frac{1}{8}\right)+3\right] + \left[2\left(\frac{2}{8}\right)+3\right] + \cdots + \left[2\left(\frac{8}{8}\right)+3\right]$

92. $\left[1-\left(\frac{1}{6}\right)^2\right] + \left[1-\left(\frac{2}{6}\right)^2\right] + \cdots + \left[1-\left(\frac{6}{6}\right)^2\right]$

93. $3 - 9 + 27 - 81 + 243 - 729$

94. $1 - \frac{1}{2} + \frac{1}{4} - \frac{1}{8} + \cdots - \frac{1}{128}$

95. $\dfrac{1}{1^2} - \dfrac{1}{2^2} + \dfrac{1}{3^2} - \dfrac{1}{4^2} + \cdots - \dfrac{1}{20^2}$

96. $\dfrac{1}{1\cdot 3} + \dfrac{1}{2\cdot 4} + \dfrac{1}{3\cdot 5} + \cdots + \dfrac{1}{10\cdot 12}$

97. $\frac{1}{4} + \frac{3}{8} + \frac{7}{16} + \frac{15}{32} + \frac{31}{64}$

98. $\frac{1}{2} + \frac{2}{4} + \frac{6}{8} + \frac{24}{16} + \frac{120}{32} + \frac{720}{64}$

In Exercises 99–102, find the indicated partial sum of the series.

99. $\displaystyle\sum_{i=1}^{\infty}5\left(\tfrac{1}{2}\right)^i$

Fourth partial sum

100. $\displaystyle\sum_{i=1}^{\infty}2\left(\tfrac{1}{3}\right)^i$

Fifth partial sum

101. $\displaystyle\sum_{n=1}^{\infty}4\left(-\tfrac{1}{2}\right)^n$

Third partial sum

102. $\displaystyle\sum_{n=1}^{\infty}8\left(-\tfrac{1}{4}\right)^n$

Fourth partial sum

In Exercises 103–106, find the sum of the infinite series.

103. $\sum_{i=1}^{\infty} 6\left(\frac{1}{10}\right)^i$

104. $\sum_{k=1}^{\infty} \left(\frac{1}{10}\right)^k$

105. $\sum_{k=1}^{\infty} 7\left(\frac{1}{10}\right)^k$

106. $\sum_{i=1}^{\infty} 2\left(\frac{1}{10}\right)^i$

107. ***Compound Interest*** A deposit of \$5000 is made in an account that earns 8% interest compounded quarterly. The balance in the account after n quarters is given by

$$A_n = 5000\left(1 + \frac{0.08}{4}\right)^n, \quad n = 1, 2, 3, \ldots.$$

(a) Write the first eight terms of this sequence.

(b) Find the balance in this account after 10 years by finding the 40th term of the sequence.

108. ***Compound Interest*** A deposit of \$100 is made each month in an account that earns 12% interest compounded monthly. The balance in the account after n months is given by

$$A_n = 100(101)[(1.01)^n - 1], \quad n = 1, 2, 3, \ldots.$$

(a) Write the first six terms of this sequence.

(b) Find the balance in this account after 5 years by finding the 60th term of the sequence.

(c) Find the balance in this account after 20 years by finding the 240th term of the sequence.

Model It

109. ***Data Analysis: Number of Stores*** The table shows the numbers a_n of Best Buy stores for the years 1998 to 2003. (Source: Best Buy Company, Inc.)

Year	Number of stores, a_n
1998	311
1999	357
2000	419
2001	481
2002	548
2003	608

Model It (continued)

(a) Use the *regression* feature of a graphing utility to find a linear sequence that models the data. Let n represent the year, with $n = 8$ corresponding to 1998.

(b) Use the *regression* feature of a graphing utility to find a quadratic sequence that models the data.

(c) Evaluate the sequences from parts (a) and (b) for $n = 8, 9, \ldots, 13$. Compare these values with those shown in the table. Which model is a better fit for the data? Explain.

(d) Which model do you think would better predict the number of Best Buy stores in the future? Use the model you chose to predict the number of Best Buy stores in 2008.

110. ***Medicine*** The numbers a_n (in thousands) of AIDS cases reported from 1995 to 2003 can be approximated by the model

$$a_n = 0.0457n^3 - 0.352n^2 - 9.05n + 121.4,$$
$$n = 5, 6, \ldots, 13$$

where n is the year, with $n = 5$ corresponding to 1995. (Source: U.S. Centers for Disease Control and Prevention)

(a) Find the terms of this finite sequence. Use the *statistical plotting* feature of a graphing utility to construct a bar graph that represents the sequence.

(b) What does the graph in part (a) say about reported cases of AIDS?

111. ***Federal Debt*** From 1990 to 2003, the federal debt of the United States rose from just over \$3 trillion to almost \$7 trillion. The federal debt a_n (in billions of dollars) from 1990 to 2003 is approximated by the model

$$a_n = 2.7698n^3 - 61.372n^2 + 600.00n + 3102.9,$$
$$n = 0, 1, \ldots, 13$$

where n is the year, with $n = 0$ corresponding to 1990. (Source: U.S. Office of Management and Budget)

(a) Find the terms of this finite sequence. Use the *statistical plotting* feature of a graphing utility to construct a bar graph that represents the sequence.

(b) What does the pattern in the bar graph in part (a) say about the future of the federal debt?

112. ***Revenue*** The revenues a_n (in millions of dollars) for Amazon.com for the years 1996 through 2003 are shown in the figure. The revenues can be approximated by the model

$$a_n = 46.609n^2 - 119.84n - 1125.8, \quad n = 6, 7, \ldots, 13$$

where n is the year, with $n = 6$ corresponding to 1996. Use this model to approximate the total revenue from 1996 through 2003. Compare this sum with the result of adding the revenues shown in the figure. (Source: Amazon.com)

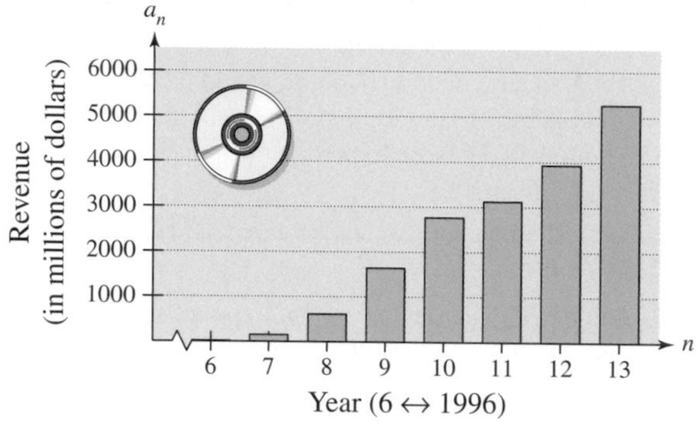

Synthesis

True or False? **In Exercises 113 and 114, determine whether the statement is true or false. Justify your answer.**

113. $\sum_{i=1}^{4}(i^2 + 2i) = \sum_{i=1}^{4} i^2 + 2\sum_{i=1}^{4} i$ **114.** $\sum_{j=1}^{4} 2^j = \sum_{j=3}^{6} 2^{j-2}$

Fibonacci Sequence **In Exercises 115 and 116, use the Fibonacci sequence. (See Example 4.)**

115. Write the first 12 terms of the Fibonacci sequence a_n and the first 10 terms of the sequence given by

$$b_n = \frac{a_{n+1}}{a_n}, \quad n \geq 1.$$

116. Using the definition for b_n in Exercise 115, show that b_n can be defined recursively by

$$b_n = 1 + \frac{1}{b_{n-1}}.$$

Arithmetic Mean **In Exercises 117–120, use the following definition of the arithmetic mean $\bar{x}$ of a set of n measurements $x_1, x_2, x_3, \ldots, x_n$.**

$$\bar{x} = \frac{1}{n}\sum_{i=1}^{n} x_i$$

117. Find the arithmetic mean of the six checking account balances \$327.15, \$785.69, \$433.04, \$265.38, \$604.12, and \$590.30. Use the statistical capabilities of a graphing utility to verify your result.

118. Find the arithmetic mean of the following prices per gallon for regular unleaded gasoline at five gasoline stations in a city: \$1.899, \$1.959, \$1.919, \$1.939, and \$1.999. Use the statistical capabilities of a graphing utility to verify your result.

119. ***Proof*** Prove that $\sum_{i=1}^{n}(x_i - \bar{x}) = 0$.

120. ***Proof*** Prove that $\sum_{i=1}^{n}(x_i - \bar{x})^2 = \sum_{i=1}^{n} x_i^2 - \frac{1}{n}\left(\sum_{i=1}^{n} x_i\right)^2$.

In Exercises 121–124, find the first five terms of the sequence.

121. $a_n = \dfrac{x^n}{n!}$ **122.** $a_n = \dfrac{(-1)^n x^{2n+1}}{2n + 1}$

123. $a_n = \dfrac{(-1)^n x^{2n}}{(2n)!}$ **124.** $a_n = \dfrac{(-1)^n x^{2n+1}}{(2n + 1)!}$

Skills Review

In Exercises 125–128, determine whether the function has an inverse function. If it does, find its inverse function.

125. $f(x) = 4x - 3$ **126.** $g(x) = \dfrac{3}{x}$

127. $h(x) = \sqrt{5x + 1}$ **128.** $f(x) = (x - 1)^2$

In Exercises 129–132, find (a) $A - B$, (b) $4B - 3A$, (c) AB, and (d) BA.

129. $A = \begin{bmatrix} 6 & 5 \\ 3 & 4 \end{bmatrix}, \quad B = \begin{bmatrix} -2 & 4 \\ 6 & -3 \end{bmatrix}$

130. $A = \begin{bmatrix} 10 & 7 \\ -4 & 6 \end{bmatrix}, \quad B = \begin{bmatrix} 0 & -12 \\ 8 & 11 \end{bmatrix}$

131. $A = \begin{bmatrix} -2 & -3 & 6 \\ 4 & 5 & 7 \\ 1 & 7 & 4 \end{bmatrix}, \quad B = \begin{bmatrix} 1 & 4 & 2 \\ 0 & 1 & 6 \\ 0 & 3 & 1 \end{bmatrix}$

132. $A = \begin{bmatrix} -1 & 4 & 0 \\ 5 & 1 & 2 \\ 0 & -1 & 3 \end{bmatrix}, \quad B = \begin{bmatrix} 0 & 4 & 0 \\ 3 & 1 & -2 \\ -1 & 0 & 2 \end{bmatrix}$

In Exercises 133–136, find the determinant of the matrix.

133. $A = \begin{bmatrix} 3 & 5 \\ -1 & 7 \end{bmatrix}$ **134.** $A = \begin{bmatrix} -2 & 8 \\ 12 & 15 \end{bmatrix}$

135. $A = \begin{bmatrix} 3 & 4 & 5 \\ 0 & 7 & 3 \\ 4 & 9 & -1 \end{bmatrix}$

136. $A = \begin{bmatrix} 16 & 11 & 10 & 2 \\ 9 & 8 & 3 & 7 \\ -2 & -1 & 12 & 3 \\ -4 & 6 & 2 & 1 \end{bmatrix}$

9.2 Arithmetic Sequences and Partial Sums

What you should learn

- Recognize, write, and find the *n*th terms of arithmetic sequences.
- Find *n*th partial sums of arithmetic sequences.
- Use arithmetic sequences to model and solve real-life problems.

Why you should learn it

Arithmetic sequences have practical real-life applications. For instance, in Exercise 83 on page 660, an arithmetic sequence is used to model the seating capacity of an auditorium.

© mediacolor's Alamy

Arithmetic Sequences

A sequence whose consecutive terms have a common difference is called an **arithmetic sequence.**

Definition of Arithmetic Sequence

A sequence is **arithmetic** if the differences between consecutive terms are the same. So, the sequence

$$a_1, a_2, a_3, a_4, \ldots, a_n, \ldots$$

is arithmetic if there is a number d such that

$$a_2 - a_1 = a_3 - a_2 = a_4 - a_3 = \cdots = d.$$

The number d is the **common difference** of the arithmetic sequence.

Example 1 **Examples of Arithmetic Sequences**

a. The sequence whose nth term is $4n + 3$ is arithmetic. For this sequence, the common difference between consecutive terms is 4.

$$\underbrace{7, 11}_{11-7=4}, 15, 19, \ldots, 4n + 3, \ldots \qquad \text{Begin with } n = 1.$$

b. The sequence whose nth term is $7 - 5n$ is arithmetic. For this sequence, the common difference between consecutive terms is -5.

$$\underbrace{2, -3}_{-3-2=-5}, -8, -13, \ldots, 7 - 5n, \ldots \qquad \text{Begin with } n = 1.$$

c. The sequence whose nth term is $\frac{1}{4}(n + 3)$ is arithmetic. For this sequence, the common difference between consecutive terms is $\frac{1}{4}$.

$$\underbrace{1, \frac{5}{4}}_{\frac{5}{4}-1=\frac{1}{4}}, \frac{3}{2}, \frac{7}{4}, \ldots, \frac{n+3}{4}, \ldots \qquad \text{Begin with } n = 1.$$

✓CHECKPOINT Now try Exercise 1.

The sequence 1, 4, 9, 16, . . . , whose nth term is n^2, is *not* arithmetic. The difference between the first two terms is

$$a_2 - a_1 = 4 - 1 = 3$$

but the difference between the second and third terms is

$$a_3 - a_2 = 9 - 4 = 5.$$

In Example 1, notice that each of the arithmetic sequences has an nth term that is of the form $dn + c$, where the common difference of the sequence is d. An arithmetic sequence may be thought of as a linear function whose domain is the set of natural numbers.

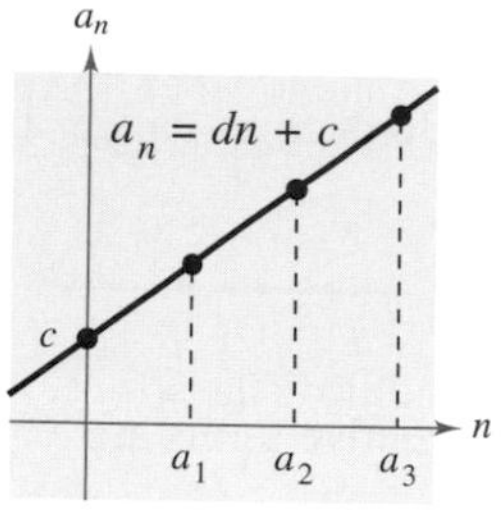

FIGURE 9.3

The nth Term of an Arithmetic Sequence

The nth term of an arithmetic sequence has the form

$$a_n = dn + c \qquad \text{Linear form}$$

where d is the common difference between consecutive terms of the sequence and $c = a_1 - d$. A graphical representation of this definition is shown in Figure 9.3. Substituting $a_1 - d$ for c in $a_n = dn + c$ yields an alternative *recursion* form for the nth term of an arithmetic sequence.

$$a_n = a_1 + (n - 1)\,d \qquad \text{Alternative form}$$

STUDY TIP

The alternative recursion form of the nth term of an arithmetic sequence can be derived from the pattern below.

$a_1 = a_1$ 1st term

$a_2 = a_1 + d$ 2nd term

$a_3 = a_1 + 2d$ 3rd term

$a_4 = a_1 + 3d$ 4th term

$a_5 = a_1 + 4d$ 5th term

1 less

⋮

$a_n = a_1 + (n - 1)\,d$ nth term

1 less

Example 2 **Finding the nth Term of an Arithmetic Sequence**

Find a formula for the nth term of the arithmetic sequence whose common difference is 3 and whose first term is 2.

Solution

Because the sequence is arithmetic, you know that the formula for the nth term is of the form $a_n = dn + c$. Moreover, because the common difference is $d = 3$, the formula must have the form

$$a_n = 3n + c. \qquad \text{Substitute 3 for } d.$$

Because $a_1 = 2$, it follows that

$$\begin{aligned} c &= a_1 - d \\ &= 2 - 3 \qquad \text{Substitute 2 for } a_1 \text{ and 3 for } d. \\ &= -1. \end{aligned}$$

So, the formula for the nth term is

$$a_n = 3n - 1.$$

The sequence therefore has the following form.

$$2, 5, 8, 11, 14, \ldots, 3n - 1, \ldots$$

✓CHECKPOINT Now try Exercise 21.

Another way to find a formula for the nth term of the sequence in Example 2 is to begin by writing the terms of the sequence.

a_1	a_2	a_3	a_4	a_5	a_6	a_7	. . .
2	2 + 3	5 + 3	8 + 3	11 + 3	14 + 3	17 + 3	. . .
2	5	8	11	14	17	20	. . .

From these terms, you can reason that the nth term is of the form

$$a_n = dn + c = 3n - 1.$$

STUDY TIP

You can find a_1 in Example 3 by using the alternative recursion form of the nth term of an arithmetic sequence, as follows.

$$a_n = a_1 + (n - 1)d$$
$$a_4 = a_1 + (4 - 1)d$$
$$20 = a_1 + (4 - 1)5$$
$$20 = a_1 + 15$$
$$5 = a_1$$

Example 3 Writing the Terms of an Arithmetic Sequence

The fourth term of an arithmetic sequence is 20, and the 13th term is 65. Write the first 11 terms of this sequence.

Solution

You know that $a_4 = 20$ and $a_{13} = 65$. So, you must add the common difference d nine times to the fourth term to obtain the 13th term. Therefore, the fourth and 13th terms of the sequence are related by

$$a_{13} = a_4 + 9d. \qquad a_4 \text{ and } a_{13} \text{ are nine terms apart.}$$

Using $a_4 = 20$ and $a_{13} = 65$, you can conclude that $d = 5$, which implies that the sequence is as follows.

a_1	a_2	a_3	a_4	a_5	a_6	a_7	a_8	a_9	a_{10}	a_{11} . . .
5	10	15	20	25	30	35	40	45	50	55 . . .

✓CHECKPOINT Now try Exercise 37.

If you know the nth term of an arithmetic sequence *and* you know the common difference of the sequence, you can find the $(n + 1)$th term by using the *recursion formula*

$$a_{n+1} = a_n + d. \qquad \text{Recursion formula}$$

With this formula, you can find any term of an arithmetic sequence, *provided* that you know the preceding term. For instance, if you know the first term, you can find the second term. Then, knowing the second term, you can find the third term, and so on.

Example 4 Using a Recursion Formula

Find the ninth term of the arithmetic sequence that begins with 2 and 9.

Solution

For this sequence, the common difference is $d = 9 - 2 = 7$. There are two ways to find the ninth term. One way is simply to write out the first nine terms (by repeatedly adding 7).

2, 9, 16, 23, 30, 37, 44, 51, 58

Another way to find the ninth term is to first find a formula for the nth term. Because the first term is 2, it follows that

$$c = a_1 - d = 2 - 7 = -5.$$

Therefore, a formula for the nth term is

$$a_n = 7n - 5$$

which implies that the ninth term is

$$a_9 = 7(9) - 5 = 58.$$

✓CHECKPOINT Now try Exercise 45.

The Sum of a Finite Arithmetic Sequence

There is a simple formula for the *sum* of a finite arithmetic sequence.

STUDY TIP

Note that this formula works only for *arithmetic* sequences.

The Sum of a Finite Arithmetic Sequence

The sum of a finite arithmetic sequence with n terms is

$$S_n = \frac{n}{2}(a_1 + a_n).$$

For a proof of the sum of a finite arithmetic sequence, see Proofs in Mathematics on page 723.

Example 5 Finding the Sum of a Finite Arithmetic Sequence

Find the sum: $1 + 3 + 5 + 7 + 9 + 11 + 13 + 15 + 17 + 19$.

Solution

To begin, notice that the sequence is arithmetic (with a common difference of 2). Moreover, the sequence has 10 terms. So, the sum of the sequence is

$$S_n = \frac{n}{2}(a_1 + a_n) \qquad \text{Formula for the sum of an arithmetic sequence}$$

$$= \frac{10}{2}(1 + 19) \qquad \text{Substitute 10 for } n, \text{ 1 for } a_1, \text{ and 19 for } a_n.$$

$$= 5(20) = 100. \qquad \text{Simplify.}$$

✓CHECKPOINT Now try Exercise 63.

Example 6 Finding the Sum of a Finite Arithmetic Sequence

Find the sum of the integers (a) from 1 to 100 and (b) from 1 to N.

Solution

a. The integers from 1 to 100 form an arithmetic sequence that has 100 terms. So, you can use the formula for the sum of an arithmetic sequence, as follows.

$$S_n = 1 + 2 + 3 + 4 + 5 + 6 + \cdot \cdot \cdot + 99 + 100$$

$$= \frac{n}{2}(a_1 + a_n) \qquad \text{Formula for sum of an arithmetic sequence}$$

$$= \frac{100}{2}(1 + 100) \qquad \text{Substitute 100 for } n, \text{ 1 for } a_1, \text{ 100 for } a_n.$$

$$= 50(101) = 5050 \qquad \text{Simplify.}$$

b. $S_n = 1 + 2 + 3 + 4 + \cdot \cdot \cdot + N$

$$= \frac{n}{2}(a_1 + a_n) \qquad \text{Formula for sum of an arithmetic sequence}$$

$$= \frac{N}{2}(1 + N) \qquad \text{Substitute } N \text{ for } n, \text{ 1 for } a_1, \text{ and } N \text{ for } a_n.$$

✓CHECKPOINT Now try Exercise 65.

The Granger Collection

Historical Note

A teacher of Carl Friedrich Gauss (1777–1855) asked him to add all the integers from 1 to 100. When Gauss returned with the correct answer after only a few moments, the teacher could only look at him in astounded silence. This is what Gauss did:

$$\begin{aligned} S_n &= 1 + 2 + 3 + \cdots + 100 \\ S_n &= 100 + 99 + 98 + \cdots + 1 \\ \hline 2S_n &= 101 + 101 + 101 + \cdots + 101 \end{aligned}$$

$$S_n = \frac{100 \times 101}{2} = 5050$$

The sum of the first n terms of an infinite sequence is the *nth partial sum*. The nth partial sum can be found by using the formula for the sum of a finite arithmetic sequence.

Example 7 **Finding a Partial Sum of an Arithmetic Sequence**

Find the 150th partial sum of the arithmetic sequence

$$5, 16, 27, 38, 49, \ldots.$$

Solution

For this arithmetic sequence, $a_1 = 5$ and $d = 16 - 5 = 11$. So,

$$c = a_1 - d = 5 - 11 = -6$$

and the nth term is $a_n = 11n - 6$. Therefore, $a_{150} = 11(150) - 6 = 1644$, and the sum of the first 150 terms is

$$S_{150} = \frac{n}{2}(a_1 + a_{150}) \qquad n\text{th partial sum formula}$$

$$= \frac{150}{2}(5 + 1644) \qquad \text{Substitute 150 for } n\text{, 5 for } a_1\text{, and 1644 for } a_{150}.$$

$$= 75(1649) \qquad \text{Simplify.}$$

$$= 123{,}675. \qquad n\text{th partial sum}$$

✓CHECKPOINT Now try Exercise 69.

Applications

Example 8 **Prize Money**

In a golf tournament, the 16 golfers with the lowest scores win cash prizes. First place receives a cash prize of \$1000, second place receives \$950, third place receives \$900, and so on. What is the total amount of prize money?

Solution

The cash prizes awarded form an arithmetic sequence in which the common difference is $d = -50$. Because

$$c = a_1 - d = 1000 - (-50) = 1050$$

you can determine that the formula for the nth term of the sequence is $a_n = -50n + 1050$. So, the 16th term of the sequence is $a_{16} = -50(16) + 1050 = 250$, and the total amount of prize money is

$$S_{16} = 1000 + 950 + 900 + \cdots + 250$$

$$S_{16} = \frac{n}{2}(a_1 + a_{16}) \qquad n\text{th partial sum formula}$$

$$= \frac{16}{2}(1000 + 250) \qquad \text{Substitute 16 for } n\text{, 1000 for } a_1\text{, and 250 for } a_{16}.$$

$$= 8(1250) = \$10{,}000. \qquad \text{Simplify.}$$

✓CHECKPOINT Now try Exercise 89.

Example 9 Total Sales

A small business sells $10,000 worth of skin care products during its first year. The owner of the business has set a goal of increasing annual sales by $7500 each year for 9 years. Assuming that this goal is met, find the total sales during the first 10 years this business is in operation.

Solution

The annual sales form an arithmetic sequence in which $a_1 = 10{,}000$ and $d = 7500$. So,

$$\begin{aligned} c &= a_1 - d \\ &= 10{,}000 - 7500 \\ &= 2500 \end{aligned}$$

and the nth term of the sequence is

$$a_n = 7500n + 2500.$$

This implies that the 10th term of the sequence is

$$\begin{aligned} a_{10} &= 7500(10) + 2500 \\ &= 77{,}500. \end{aligned}$$ See Figure 9.4.

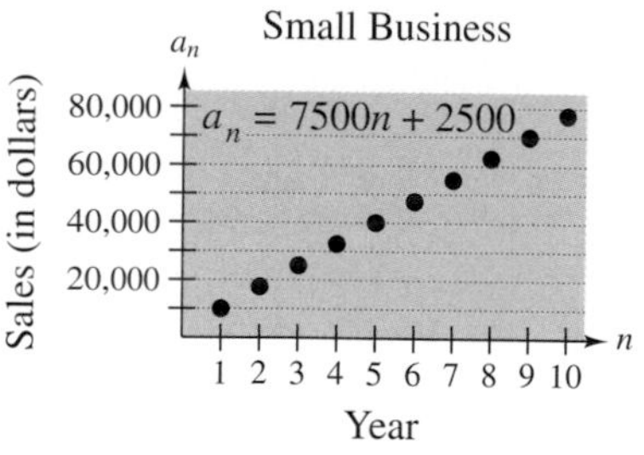

FIGURE 9.4

The sum of the first 10 terms of the sequence is

$$S_{10} = \frac{n}{2}(a_1 + a_{10})$$ nth partial sum formula

$$= \frac{10}{2}(10{,}000 + 77{,}500)$$ Substitute 10 for n, 10,000 for a_1, and 77,500 for a_{10}.

$$= 5(87{,}500)$$ Simplify.

$$= 437{,}500.$$ Simplify.

So, the total sales for the first 10 years will be $437,500.

CHECKPOINT Now try Exercise 91.

Writing about Mathematics

Numerical Relationships Decide whether it is possible to fill in the blanks in each of the sequences such that the resulting sequence is arithmetic. If so, find a recursion formula for the sequence.

a. -7, ___, ___, ___, ___, ___, 11

b. 17, ___, ___, ___, ___, ___, ___, ___, ___, 71

c. 2, 6, ___, ___, 162

d. 4, 7.5, ___, ___, ___, ___, ___, ___, ___, ___, 39

e. 8, 12, ___, ___, ___, 60.75

9.2 Exercises

VOCABULARY CHECK: Fill in the blanks.

1. A sequence is called an ________ sequence if the differences between two consecutive terms are the same. This difference is called the ________ difference.
2. The nth term of an arithmetic sequence has the form ________.
3. The formula $S_n = \frac{n}{2}(a_1 + a_n)$ can be used to find the sum of the first n terms of an arithmetic sequence, called the ________ of a ________ ________ ________.

In Exercises 1–10, determine whether the sequence is arithmetic. If so, find the common difference.

1. $10, 8, 6, 4, 2, \ldots$
2. $4, 7, 10, 13, 16, \ldots$
3. $1, 2, 4, 8, 16, \ldots$
4. $80, 40, 20, 10, 5, \ldots$
5. $\frac{9}{4}, 2, \frac{7}{4}, \frac{3}{2}, \frac{5}{4}, \ldots$
6. $3, \frac{5}{2}, 2, \frac{3}{2}, 1, \ldots$
7. $\frac{1}{3}, \frac{2}{3}, 1, \frac{4}{3}, \frac{5}{6}, \ldots$
8. $5.3, 5.7, 6.1, 6.5, 6.9, \ldots$
9. $\ln 1, \ln 2, \ln 3, \ln 4, \ln 5, \ldots$
10. $1^2, 2^2, 3^2, 4^2, 5^2, \ldots$

In Exercises 11–18, write the first five terms of the sequence. Determine whether the sequence is arithmetic. If so, find the common difference. (Assume that n begins with 1.)

11. $a_n = 5 + 3n$
12. $a_n = 100 - 3n$
13. $a_n = 3 - 4(n - 2)$
14. $a_n = 1 + (n - 1)4$
15. $a_n = (-1)^n$
16. $a_n = 2^{n-1}$
17. $a_n = \dfrac{(-1)^n 3}{n}$
18. $a_n = (2^n)n$

In Exercises 19–30, find a formula for a_n for the arithmetic sequence.

19. $a_1 = 1, d = 3$
20. $a_1 = 15, d = 4$
21. $a_1 = 100, d = -8$
22. $a_1 = 0, d = -\frac{2}{3}$
23. $a_1 = x, d = 2x$
24. $a_1 = -y, d = 5y$
25. $4, \frac{3}{2}, -1, -\frac{7}{2}, \ldots$
26. $10, 5, 0, -5, -10, \ldots$
27. $a_1 = 5, a_4 = 15$
28. $a_1 = -4, a_5 = 16$
29. $a_3 = 94, a_6 = 85$
30. $a_5 = 190, a_{10} = 115$

In Exercises 31–38, write the first five terms of the arithmetic sequence.

31. $a_1 = 5, d = 6$
32. $a_1 = 5, d = -\frac{3}{4}$
33. $a_1 = -2.6, d = -0.4$
34. $a_1 = 16.5, d = 0.25$
35. $a_1 = 2, a_{12} = 46$
36. $a_4 = 16, a_{10} = 46$
37. $a_8 = 26, a_{12} = 42$
38. $a_3 = 19, a_{15} = -1.7$

In Exercises 39–44, write the first five terms of the arithmetic sequence. Find the common difference and write the nth term of the sequence as a function of n.

39. $a_1 = 15, \quad a_{k+1} = a_k + 4$
40. $a_1 = 6, \quad a_{k+1} = a_k + 5$
41. $a_1 = 200, \quad a_{k+1} = a_k - 10$
42. $a_1 = 72, \quad a_{k+1} = a_k - 6$
43. $a_1 = \frac{5}{8}, \quad a_{k+1} = a_k - \frac{1}{8}$
44. $a_1 = 0.375, \quad a_{k+1} = a_k + 0.25$

In Exercises 45–48, the first two terms of the arithmetic sequence are given. Find the missing term.

45. $a_1 = 5, a_2 = 11, a_{10} =$ ▢
46. $a_1 = 3, a_2 = 13, a_9 =$ ▢
47. $a_1 = 4.2, a_2 = 6.6, a_7 =$ ▢
48. $a_1 = -0.7, a_2 = -13.8, a_8 =$ ▢

In Exercises 49–52, match the arithmetic sequence with its graph. [The graphs are labeled (a), (b), (c), and (d).]

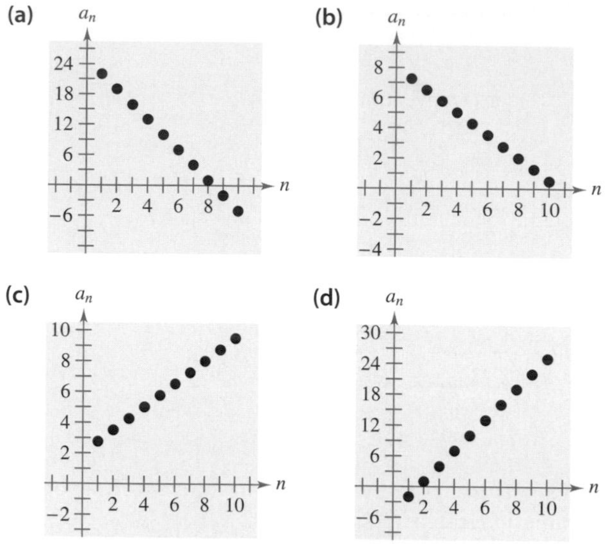

49. $a_n = -\frac{3}{4}n + 8$

50. $a_n = 3n - 5$

51. $a_n = 2 + \frac{3}{4}n$

52. $a_n = 25 - 3n$

In Exercises 53–56, use a graphing utility to graph the first 10 terms of the sequence. (Assume that *n* begins with 1.)

53. $a_n = 15 - \frac{3}{2}n$

54. $a_n = -5 + 2n$

55. $a_n = 0.2n + 3$

56. $a_n = -0.3n + 8$

In Exercises 57–64, find the indicated *n*th partial sum of the arithmetic sequence.

57. 8, 20, 32, 44, . . . , $n = 10$

58. 2, 8, 14, 20, . . . , $n = 25$

59. 4.2, 3.7, 3.2, 2.7, . . . , $n = 12$

60. 0.5, 0.9, 1.3, 1.7, . . . , $n = 10$

61. 40, 37, 34, 31, . . . , $n = 10$

62. 75, 70, 65, 60, . . . , $n = 25$

63. $a_1 = 100,\ a_{25} = 220,\ n = 25$

64. $a_1 = 15,\ a_{100} = 307,\ n = 100$

65. Find the sum of the first 100 positive odd integers.

66. Find the sum of the integers from -10 to 50.

In Exercises 67–74, find the partial sum.

67. $\sum_{n=1}^{50} n$

68. $\sum_{n=1}^{100} 2n$

69. $\sum_{n=10}^{100} 6n$

70. $\sum_{n=51}^{100} 7n$

71. $\sum_{n=11}^{30} n - \sum_{n=1}^{10} n$

72. $\sum_{n=51}^{100} n - \sum_{n=1}^{50} n$

73. $\sum_{n=1}^{400} (2n - 1)$

74. $\sum_{n=1}^{250} (1000 - n)$

In Exercises 75–80, use a graphing utility to find the partial sum.

75. $\sum_{n=1}^{20} (2n + 5)$

76. $\sum_{n=0}^{50} (1000 - 5n)$

77. $\sum_{n=1}^{100} \frac{n + 4}{2}$

78. $\sum_{n=0}^{100} \frac{8 - 3n}{16}$

79. $\sum_{i=1}^{60} \left(250 - \frac{8}{3}i\right)$

80. $\sum_{j=1}^{200} (4.5 + 0.025j)$

Job Offer **In Exercises 81 and 82, consider a job offer with the given starting salary and the given annual raise.**

(a) Determine the salary during the sixth year of employment.

(b) Determine the total compensation from the company through six full years of employment.

	Starting Salary	*Annual Raise*
81.	\$32,500	\$1500
82.	\$36,800	\$1750

83. ***Seating Capacity*** Determine the seating capacity of an auditorium with 30 rows of seats if there are 20 seats in the first row, 24 seats in the second row, 28 seats in the third row, and so on.

84. ***Seating Capacity*** Determine the seating capacity of an auditorium with 36 rows of seats if there are 15 seats in the first row, 18 seats in the second row, 21 seats in the third row, and so on.

85. ***Brick Pattern*** A brick patio has the approximate shape of a trapezoid (see figure). The patio has 18 rows of bricks. The first row has 14 bricks and the 18th row has 31 bricks. How many bricks are in the patio?

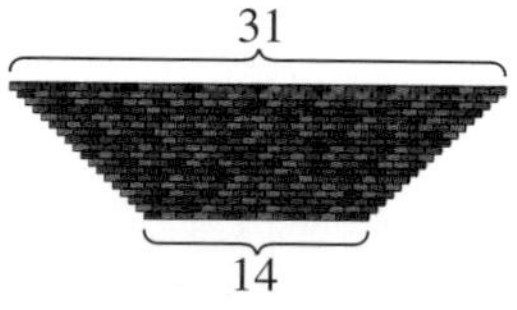

FIGURE FOR 85

FIGURE FOR 86

86. ***Brick Pattern*** A triangular brick wall is made by cutting some bricks in half to use in the first column of every other row. The wall has 28 rows. The top row is one-half brick wide and the bottom row is 14 bricks wide. How many bricks are used in the finished wall?

87. ***Falling Object*** An object with negligible air resistance is dropped from a plane. During the first second of fall, the object falls 4.9 meters; during the second second, it falls 14.7 meters; during the third second, it falls 24.5 meters; during the fourth second, it falls 34.3 meters. If this arithmetic pattern continues, how many meters will the object fall in 10 seconds?

88. ***Falling Object*** An object with negligible air resistance is dropped from the top of the Sears Tower in Chicago at a height of 1454 feet. During the first second of fall, the object falls 16 feet; during the second second, it falls 48 feet; during the third second, it falls 80 feet; during the fourth second, it falls 112 feet. If this arithmetic pattern continues, how many feet will the object fall in 7 seconds?

89. ***Prize Money*** A county fair is holding a baked goods competition in which the top eight bakers receive cash prizes. First places receives a cash prize of $200, second place receives $175, third place receives $150, and so on.

(a) Write a sequence a_n that represents the cash prize awarded in terms of the place n in which the baked good places.

(b) Find the total amount of prize money awarded at the competition.

90. ***Prize Money*** A city bowling league is holding a tournament in which the top 12 bowlers with the highest three-game totals are awarded cash prizes. First place will win $1200, second place $1100, third place $1000, and so on.

(a) Write a sequence a_n that represents the cash prize awarded in terms of the place n in which the bowler finishes.

(b) Find the total amount of prize money awarded at the tournament.

91. ***Total Profit*** A small snowplowing company makes a profit of $8000 during its first year. The owner of the company sets a goal of increasing profit by $1500 each year for 5 years. Assuming that this goal is met, find the total profit during the first 6 years of this business. What kinds of economic factors could prevent the company from meeting its profit goal? Are there any other factors that could prevent the company from meeting its goal? Explain.

92. ***Total Sales*** An entrepreneur sells $15,000 worth of sports memorabilia during one year and sets a goal of increasing annual sales by $5000 each year for 9 years. Assuming that this goal is met, find the total sales during the first 10 years of this business. What kinds of economic factors could prevent the business from meeting its goals?

93. ***Borrowing Money*** You borrowed $2000 from a friend to purchase a new laptop computer and have agreed to pay back the loan with monthly payments of $200 plus 1% interest on the unpaid balance.

(a) Find the first six monthly payments you will make, and the unpaid balance after each month.

(b) Find the total amount of interest paid over the term of the loan.

94. ***Borrowing Money*** You borrowed $5000 from your parents to purchase a used car. The arrangements of the loan are such that you will make payments of $250 per month plus 1% interest on the unpaid balance.

(a) Find the first year's monthly payments you will make, and the unpaid balance after each month.

(b) Find the total amount of interest paid over the term of the loan.

Model It

95. ***Data Analysis: Personal Income*** The table shows the per capita personal income a_n in the United States from 1993 to 2003. (Source: U.S. Bureau of Economic Analysis)

Year	Per capita personal income, a_n
1993	$21,356
1994	$22,176
1995	$23,078
1996	$24,176
1997	$25,334
1998	$26,880
1999	$27,933
2000	$29,848
2001	$30,534
2002	$30,913
2003	$31,633

(a) Find an arithmetic sequence that models the data. Let n represent the year, with $n = 3$ corresponding to 1993.

(b) Use the *regression* feature of a graphing utility to find a linear model for the data. How does this model compare with the arithmetic sequence you found in part (a)?

(c) Use a graphing utility to graph the terms of the finite sequence you found in part (a).

(d) Use the sequence from part (a) to estimate the per capita personal income in 2004 and 2005.

(e) Use your school's library, the Internet, or some other reference source to find the actual per capita personal income in 2004 and 2005, and compare these values with the estimates from part (d).

96. ***Data Analysis: Revenue*** The table shows the annual revenue a_n (in millions of dollars) for Nextel Communications, Inc. from 1997 to 2003. (Source: Nextel Communications, Inc.)

Year	Revenue, a_n
1997	739
1998	1847
1999	3326
2000	5714
2001	7689
2002	8721
2003	10,820

(a) Construct a bar graph showing the annual revenue from 1997 to 2003.

(b) Use the *linear regression* feature of a graphing utility to find an arithmetic sequence that approximates the annual revenue from 1997 to 2003.

(c) Use summation notation to represent the *total* revenue from 1997 to 2003. Find the total revenue.

(d) Use the sequence from part (b) to estimate the annual revenue in 2008.

Synthesis

True or False? **In Exercises 97 and 98, determine whether the statement is true or false. Justify your answer.**

97. Given an arithmetic sequence for which only the first two terms are known, it is possible to find the nth term.

98. If the only known information about a finite arithmetic sequence is its first term and its last term, then it is possible to find the sum of the sequence.

99. ***Writing*** In your own words, explain what makes a sequence arithmetic.

100. ***Writing*** Explain how to use the first two terms of an arithmetic sequence to find the nth term.

101. ***Exploration***

(a) Graph the first 10 terms of the arithmetic sequence $a_n = 2 + 3n$.

(b) Graph the equation of the line $y = 3x + 2$.

(c) Discuss any differences between the graph of

$a_n = 2 + 3n$

and the graph of

$y = 3x + 2$.

(d) Compare the slope of the line in part (b) with the common difference of the sequence in part (a). What can you conclude about the slope of a line and the common difference of an arithmetic sequence?

102. ***Pattern Recognition***

(a) Compute the following sums of positive odd integers.

$1 + 3 = \square$

$1 + 3 + 5 = \square$

$1 + 3 + 5 + 7 = \square$

$1 + 3 + 5 + 7 + 9 = \square$

$1 + 3 + 5 + 7 + 9 + 11 = \square$

(b) Use the sums in part (a) to make a conjecture about the sums of positive odd integers. Check your conjecture for the sum

$1 + 3 + 5 + 7 + 9 + 11 + 13 = \square$.

(c) Verify your conjecture algebraically.

103. ***Think About It*** The sum of the first 20 terms of an arithmetic sequence with a common difference of 3 is 650. Find the first term.

104. ***Think About It*** The sum of the first n terms of an arithmetic sequence with first term a_1 and common difference d is S_n. Determine the sum if each term is increased by 5. Explain.

Skills Review

In Exercises 105–108, find the slope and y-intercept (if possible) of the equation of the line. Sketch the line.

105. $2x - 4y = 3$

106. $9x + y = -8$

107. $x - 7 = 0$

108. $y + 11 = 0$

In Exercises 109 and 110, use Gauss-Jordan elimination to solve the system of equations.

109. $\begin{cases} 2x - y + 7z = -10 \\ 3x + 2y - 4z = 17 \\ 6x - 5y + z = -20 \end{cases}$

110. $\begin{cases} -x + 4y + 10z = 4 \\ 5x - 3y + z = 31 \\ 8x + 2y - 3z = -5 \end{cases}$

111. **Make a Decision** To work an extended application analyzing the median sales price of existing one-family homes in the United States from 1987 to 2003, visit this text's website at *college.hmco.com*. *(Data Source: National Association of Realtors)*

9.3 Geometric Sequences and Series

What you should learn

- Recognize, write, and find the *n*th terms of geometric sequences.
- Find *n*th partial sums of geometric sequences.
- Find the sum of an infinite geometric series.
- Use geometric sequences to model and solve real-life problems.

Why you should learn it

Geometric sequences can be used to model and solve real-life problems. For instance, in Exercise 99 on page 670, you will use a geometric sequence to model the population of China.

© Bob Krist/Corbis

Geometric Sequences

In Section 9.2, you learned that a sequence whose consecutive terms have a common *difference* is an arithmetic sequence. In this section, you will study another important type of sequence called a **geometric sequence.** Consecutive terms of a geometric sequence have a common *ratio*.

Definition of Geometric Sequence

A sequence is **geometric** if the ratios of consecutive terms are the same. So, the sequence $a_1, a_2, a_3, a_4, \ldots, a_n \ldots$ is geometric if there is a number r such that

$$\frac{a_2}{a_1} = r, \quad \frac{a_3}{a_2} = r, \quad \frac{a_4}{a_3} = r, \quad r \neq 0$$

and so the number r is the **common ratio** of the sequence.

Example 1 Examples of Geometric Sequences

a. The sequence whose nth term is 2^n is geometric. For this sequence, the common ratio of consecutive terms is 2.

$$\underbrace{2, 4,}_{\frac{4}{2} = 2} 8, 16, \ldots, 2^n, \ldots \qquad \text{Begin with } n = 1.$$

b. The sequence whose nth term is $4(3^n)$ is geometric. For this sequence, the common ratio of consecutive terms is 3.

$$\underbrace{12, 36,}_{\frac{36}{12} = 3} 108, 324, \ldots, 4(3^n), \ldots \qquad \text{Begin with } n = 1.$$

c. The sequence whose nth term is $\left(-\frac{1}{3}\right)^n$ is geometric. For this sequence, the common ratio of consecutive terms is $-\frac{1}{3}$.

$$\underbrace{-\frac{1}{3}, \frac{1}{9},}_{\frac{1/9}{-1/3} = -\frac{1}{3}} -\frac{1}{27}, \frac{1}{81}, \ldots, \left(-\frac{1}{3}\right)^n, \ldots \qquad \text{Begin with } n = 1.$$

✓CHECKPOINT Now try Exercise 1.

The sequence 1, 4, 9, 16, . . . , whose nth term is n^2, is *not* geometric. The ratio of the second term to the first term is

$$\frac{a_2}{a_1} = \frac{4}{1} = 4$$

but the ratio of the third term to the second term is $\frac{a_3}{a_2} = \frac{9}{4}$.

In Example 1, notice that each of the geometric sequences has an nth term that is of the form ar^n, where the common ratio of the sequence is r. A geometric sequence may be thought of as an exponential function whose domain is the set of natural numbers.

The nth Term of a Geometric Sequence

The nth term of a geometric sequence has the form

$$a_n = a_1 r^{n-1}$$

where r is the common ratio of consecutive terms of the sequence. So, every geometric sequence can be written in the following form.

$$\begin{array}{cccccccc} a_1, & a_2, & a_3, & a_4, & a_5, & \ldots, & a_n, & \ldots \\ \downarrow & \downarrow & \downarrow & \downarrow & \downarrow & & \downarrow & \\ a_1, & a_1 r, & a_1 r^2, & a_1 r^3, & a_1 r^4, & \ldots, & a_1 r^{n-1}, & \ldots \end{array}$$

If you know the nth term of a geometric sequence, you can find the $(n + 1)$th term by multiplying by r. That is, $a_{n+1} = ra_n$.

Example 2 Finding the Terms of a Geometric Sequence

Write the first five terms of the geometric sequence whose first term is $a_1 = 3$ and whose common ratio is $r = 2$. Then graph the terms on a set of coordinate axes.

Solution

Starting with 3, repeatedly multiply by 2 to obtain the following.

$a_1 = 3$	1st term
$a_2 = 3(2^1) = 6$	2nd term
$a_3 = 3(2^2) = 12$	3rd term
$a_4 = 3(2^3) = 24$	4th term
$a_5 = 3(2^4) = 48$	5th term

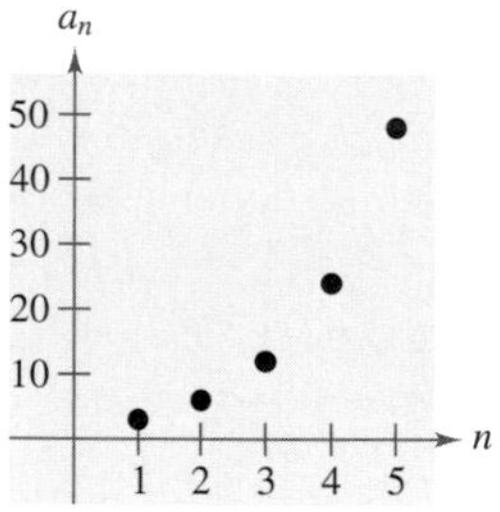

FIGURE 9.5

Figure 9.5 shows the first five terms of this geometric sequence.

CHECKPOINT Now try Exercise 11.

Example 3 Finding a Term of a Geometric Sequence

Find the 15th term of the geometric sequence whose first term is 20 and whose common ratio is 1.05.

Solution

$a_{15} = a_1 r^{n-1}$	Formula for geometric sequence
$= 20(1.05)^{15-1}$	Substitute 20 for a_1, 1.05 for r, and 15 for n.
≈ 39.599	Use a calculator.

CHECKPOINT Now try Exercise 27.

Example 4 Finding a Term of a Geometric Sequence

Find the 12th term of the geometric sequence

$5, 15, 45, \ldots .$

Solution

The common ratio of this sequence is

$$r = \frac{15}{5} = 3.$$

Because the first term is $a_1 = 5$, you can determine the 12th term $(n = 12)$ to be

$a_n = a_1 r^{n-1}$	Formula for geometric sequence
$a_{12} = 5(3)^{12-1}$	Substitute 5 for a_1, 3 for r, and 12 for n.
$= 5(177,147)$	Use a calculator.
$= 885,735.$	Simplify.

CHECKPOINT Now try Exercise 35.

If you know any two terms of a geometric sequence, you can use that information to find a formula for the nth term of the sequence.

Example 5 Finding a Term of a Geometric Sequence

The fourth term of a geometric sequence is 125, and the 10th term is 125/64. Find the 14th term. (Assume that the terms of the sequence are positive.)

Solution

The 10th term is related to the fourth term by the equation

$a_{10} = a_4 r^6.$ Multiply 4th term by r^{10-4}.

Because $a_{10} = 125/64$ and $a_4 = 125$, you can solve for r as follows.

$\frac{125}{64} = 125r^6$	Substitute $\frac{125}{64}$ for a_{10} and 125 for a_4.
$\frac{1}{64} = r^6$	Divide each side by 125.
$\frac{1}{2} = r$	Take the sixth root of each side.

You can obtain the 14th term by multiplying the 10th term by r^4.

$a_{14} = a_{10} r^4$	Multiply the 10th term by r^{14-10}.
$= \frac{125}{64}\left(\frac{1}{2}\right)^4$	Substitute $\frac{125}{64}$ for a_{10} and $\frac{1}{2}$ for r.
$= \frac{125}{1024}$	Simplify.

CHECKPOINT Now try Exercise 41.

STUDY TIP

Remember that r is the common ratio of consecutive terms of a geometric sequence. So, in Example 5,

$$a_{10} = a_1 r^9$$
$$= a_1 \cdot r \cdot r \cdot r \cdot r^6$$
$$= a_1 \cdot \frac{a_2}{a_1} \cdot \frac{a_3}{a_2} \cdot \frac{a_4}{a_3} \cdot r^6$$
$$= a_4 r^6.$$

The Sum of a Finite Geometric Sequence

The formula for the sum of a *finite* geometric sequence is as follows.

> **The Sum of a Finite Geometric Sequence**
>
> The sum of the finite geometric sequence
>
> $$a_1,\ a_1r,\ a_1r^2,\ a_1r^3,\ a_1r^4,\ .\ .\ .\ ,\ a_1r^{n-1}$$
>
> with common ratio $r \neq 1$ is given by $S_n = \sum_{i=1}^{n} a_1\, r^{i-1} = a_1\left(\frac{1 - r^n}{1 - r}\right)$.

For a proof of the sum of a finite geometric sequence, see Proofs in Mathematics on page 723.

Example 6 Finding the Sum of a Finite Geometric Sequence

Find the sum $\sum_{i=1}^{12} 4(0.3)^{i-1}$.

Solution

By writing out a few terms, you have

$$\sum_{i=1}^{12} 4(0.3)^{i-1} = 4(0.3)^0 + 4(0.3)^1 + 4(0.3)^2 + \cdot\cdot\cdot + 4(0.3)^{11}.$$

Now, because $a_1 = 4$, $r = 0.3$, and $n = 12$, you can apply the formula for the sum of a finite geometric sequence to obtain

$$S_n = a_1\left(\frac{1 - r^n}{1 - r}\right) \qquad \text{Formula for the sum of a sequence}$$

$$\sum_{i=1}^{12} 4(0.3)^{i=1} = 4\left[\frac{1 - (0.3)^{12}}{1 - 0.3}\right] \qquad \text{Substitute 4 for } a_1\text{, 0.3 for } r\text{, and 12 for } n.$$

$$\approx 5.714. \qquad \text{Use a calculator.}$$

CHECKPOINT Now try Exercise 57.

When using the formula for the sum of a finite geometric sequence, be careful to check that the sum is of the form

$$\sum_{i=1}^{n} a_1\, r^{i-1}. \qquad \text{Exponent for } r \text{ is } i - 1.$$

If the sum is not of this form, you must adjust the formula. For instance, if the sum in Example 6 were $\sum_{i=1}^{12} 4(0.3)^i$, then you would evaluate the sum as follows.

$$\sum_{i=1}^{12} 4(0.3)^i = 4(0.3) + 4(0.3)^2 + 4(0.3)^3 + \cdot\cdot\cdot + 4(0.3)^{12}$$

$$= 4(0.3) + [4(0.3)](0.3) + [4(0.3)](0.3)^2 + \cdot\cdot\cdot + [4(0.3)](0.3)^{11}$$

$$= 4(0.3)\left[\frac{1 - (0.3)^{12}}{1 - 0.3}\right] \approx 1.714. \qquad a_1 = 4(0.3),\ r = 0.3,\ n = 12$$

Exploration

Use a graphing utility to graph

$$y = \left(\frac{1 - r^x}{1 - r}\right)$$

for $r = \frac{1}{2}, \frac{2}{3}$, and $\frac{4}{5}$. What happens as $x \to \infty$?

Use a graphing utility to graph

$$y = \left(\frac{1 - r^x}{1 - r}\right)$$

for $r = 1.5$, 2, and 3. What happens as $x \to \infty$?

Geometric Series

The summation of the terms of an infinite geometric *sequence* is called an **infinite geometric series** or simply a **geometric series.**

The formula for the sum of a *finite* geometric *sequence* can, depending on the value of r, be extended to produce a formula for the sum of an *infinite* geometric *series*. Specifically, if the common ratio r has the property that $|r| < 1$, it can be shown that r^n becomes arbitrarily close to zero as n increases without bound. Consequently,

$$a_1\left(\frac{1 - r^n}{1 - r}\right) \longrightarrow a_1\left(\frac{1 - 0}{1 - r}\right) \quad \text{as} \quad n \longrightarrow \infty.$$

This result is summarized as follows.

The Sum of an Infinite Geometric Series

If $|r| < 1$, the infinite geometric series

$$a_1 + a_1r + a_1r^2 + a_1r^3 + \cdot \cdot \cdot + a_1r^{n-1} + \cdot \cdot \cdot$$

has the sum

$$S = \sum_{i=0}^{\infty} a_1r^i = \frac{a_1}{1 - r}.$$

Note that if $|r| \geq 1$, the series does not have a sum.

Example 7 Finding the Sum of an Infinite Geometric Series

Find each sum.

a. $\sum_{n=1}^{\infty} 4(0.6)^{n-1}$

b. $3 + 0.3 + 0.03 + 0.003 + \cdot \cdot \cdot$

Solution

a. $\sum_{n=1}^{\infty} 4(0.6)^{n-1} = 4 + 4(0.6) + 4(0.6)^2 + 4(0.6)^3 + \cdot \cdot \cdot + 4(0.6)^{n-1} + \cdot \cdot \cdot$

$$= \frac{4}{1 - 0.6} \qquad \frac{a_1}{1 - r}$$

$$= 10$$

b. $3 + 0.3 + 0.03 + 0.003 + \cdot \cdot \cdot = 3 + 3(0.1) + 3(0.1)^2 + 3(0.1)^3 + \cdot \cdot \cdot$

$$= \frac{3}{1 - 0.1} \qquad \frac{a_1}{1 - r}$$

$$= \frac{10}{3}$$

$$\approx 3.33$$

✓CHECKPOINT Now try Exercise 79.

Application

Example 8 **Increasing Annuity**

A deposit of \$50 is made on the first day of each month in a savings account that pays 6% compounded monthly. What is the balance at the end of 2 years? (This type of savings plan is called an **increasing annuity.**)

STUDY TIP

Recall from Section 3.1 that the formula for compound interest is

$$A = P\left(1 + \frac{r}{n}\right)^{nt}.$$

So, in Example 8, \$50 is the principal P, 0.06 is the interest rate r, 12 is the number of compoundings per year n, and 2 is the time t in years. If you substitute these values into the formula, you obtain

$$A = 50\left(1 + \frac{0.06}{12}\right)^{12(2)}$$
$$= 50\left(1 + \frac{0.06}{12}\right)^{24}.$$

Solution

The first deposit will gain interest for 24 months, and its balance will be

$$A_{24} = 50\left(1 + \frac{0.06}{12}\right)^{24}$$
$$= 50(1.005)^{24}.$$

The second deposit will gain interest for 23 months, and its balance will be

$$A_{23} = 50\left(1 + \frac{0.06}{12}\right)^{23}$$
$$= 50(1.005)^{23}.$$

The last deposit will gain interest for only 1 month, and its balance will be

$$A_1 = 50\left(1 + \frac{0.06}{12}\right)^{1}$$
$$= 50(1.005).$$

The total balance in the annuity will be the sum of the balances of the 24 deposits. Using the formula for the sum of a finite geometric sequence, with $A_1 = 50(1.005)$ and $r = 1.005$, you have

$$S_{24} = 50(1.005)\left[\frac{1 - (1.005)^{24}}{1 - 1.005}\right]$$ Substitute 50(1.005) for A_1, 1.005 for r, and 24 for n.

$$= \$1277.96.$$ Simplify.

CHECKPOINT Now try Exercise 107.

WRITING ABOUT MATHEMATICS

An Experiment You will need a piece of string or yarn, a pair of scissors, and a tape measure. Measure out any length of string at least 5 feet long. Double over the string and cut it in half. Take one of the resulting halves, double it over, and cut it in half. Continue this process until you are no longer able to cut a length of string in half. How many cuts were you able to make? Construct a sequence of the resulting string lengths after each cut, starting with the original length of the string. Find a formula for the nth term of this sequence. How many cuts could you theoretically make? Discuss why you were not able to make that many cuts.

9.3 Exercises

VOCABULARY CHECK: Fill in the blanks.

1. A sequence is called a ________ sequence if the ratios between consecutive terms are the same. This ratio is called the ________ ratio.
2. The nth term of a geometric sequence has the form ________.
3. The formula for the sum of a finite geometric sequence is given by ________.
4. The sum of the terms of an infinite geometric sequence is called a ________ ________.
5. The formula for the sum of an infinite geometric series is given by ________.

In Exercises 1–10, determine whether the sequence is geometric. If so, find the common ratio.

1. $5, 15, 45, 135, . . .$ **2.** $3, 12, 48, 192, . . .$

3. $3, 12, 21, 30, . . .$ **4.** $36, 27, 18, 9, . . .$

5. $1, -\frac{1}{2}, \frac{1}{4}, -\frac{1}{8}, . . .$ **6.** $5, 1, 0.2, 0.04, . . .$

7. $\frac{1}{8}, \frac{1}{4}, \frac{1}{2}, 1, . . .$ **8.** $9, -6, 4, -\frac{8}{3}, . . .$

9. $1, \frac{1}{2}, \frac{1}{3}, \frac{1}{4}, . . .$ **10.** $\frac{1}{5}, \frac{2}{7}, \frac{3}{9}, \frac{4}{11}, . . .$

In Exercises 11–20, write the first five terms of the geometric sequence.

11. $a_1 = 2, r = 3$ **12.** $a_1 = 6, r = 2$

13. $a_1 = 1, r = \frac{1}{2}$ **14.** $a_1 = 1, r = \frac{1}{3}$

15. $a_1 = 5, r = -\frac{1}{10}$ **16.** $a_1 = 6, r = -\frac{1}{4}$

17. $a_1 = 1, r = e$ **18.** $a_1 = 3, r = \sqrt{5}$

19. $a_1 = 2, r = \dfrac{x}{4}$ **20.** $a_1 = 5, r = 2x$

In Exercises 21–26, write the first five terms of the geometric sequence. Determine the common ratio and write the *n*th term of the sequence as a function of *n*.

21. $a_1 = 64, \quad a_{k+1} = \frac{1}{2}a_k$ **22.** $a_1 = 81, \quad a_{k+1} = \frac{1}{3}a_k$

23. $a_1 = 7, \quad a_{k+1} = 2a_k$ **24.** $a_1 = 5, \quad a_{k+1} = -2a_k$

25. $a_1 = 6, \quad a_{k+1} = -\frac{3}{2}a_k$ **26.** $a_1 = 48, \quad a_{k+1} = -\frac{1}{2}a_k$

In Exercises 27–34, write an expression for the *n*th term of the geometric sequence. Then find the indicated term.

27. $a_1 = 4, r = \frac{1}{2}, n = 10$ **28.** $a_1 = 5, r = \frac{3}{2}, n = 8$

29. $a_1 = 6, r = -\frac{1}{3}, n = 12$ **30.** $a_1 = 64, r = -\frac{1}{4}, n = 10$

31. $a_1 = 100, r = e^x, n = 9$

32. $a_1 = 1, r = \sqrt{3}, n = 8$

33. $a_1 = 500, r = 1.02, n = 40$

34. $a_1 = 1000, r = 1.005, n = 60$

In Exercises 35–42, find the indicated *n*th term of the geometric sequence.

35. 9th term: $7, 21, 63, . . .$

36. 7th term: $3, 36, 432, . . .$

37. 10th term: $5, 30, 180, . . .$

38. 22nd term: $4, 8, 16, . . .$

39. 3rd term: $a_1 = 16, a_4 = \frac{27}{4}$

40. 1st term: $a_2 = 3, a_5 = \frac{3}{64}$

41. 6th term: $a_4 = -18, a_7 = \frac{2}{3}$

42. 7th term: $a_3 = \frac{16}{3}, a_5 = \frac{64}{27}$

In Exercises 43–46, match the geometric sequence with its graph. [The graphs are labeled (a), (b), (c), and (d).]

(a)

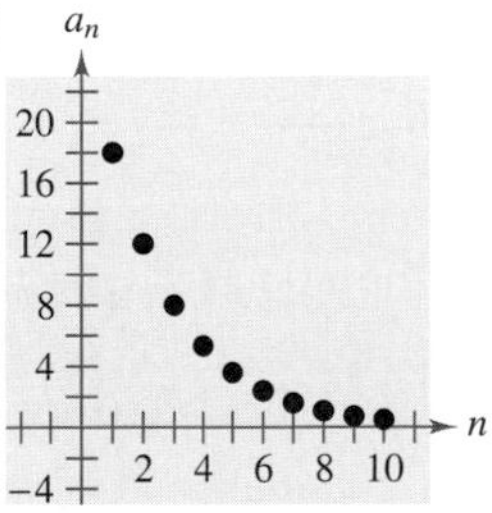

(b)

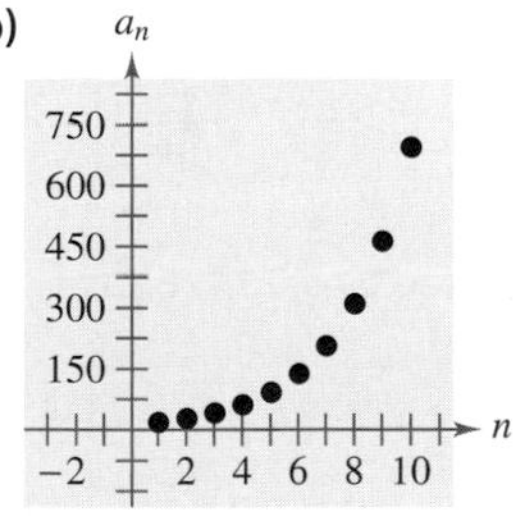

(c)

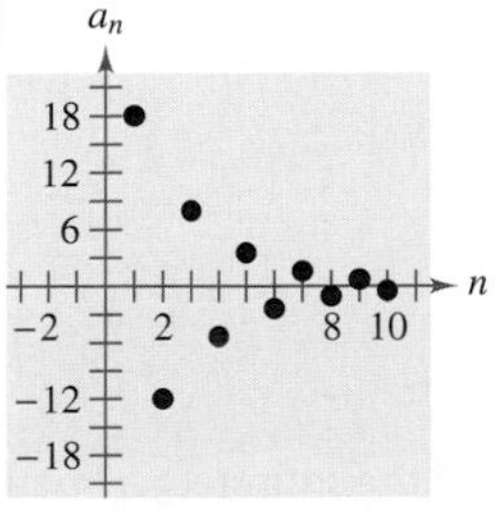

(d)

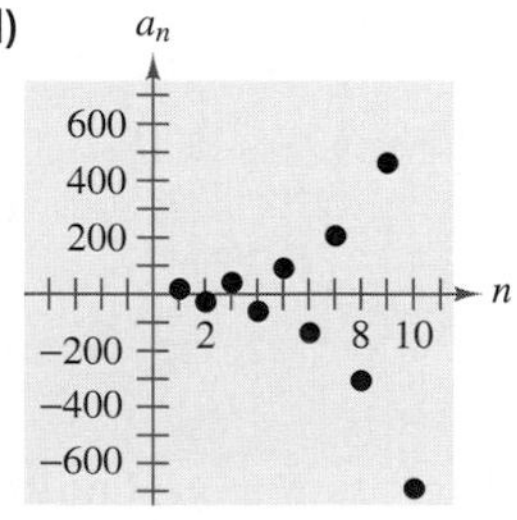

43. $a_n = 18\left(\frac{2}{3}\right)^{n-1}$ **44.** $a_n = 18\left(-\frac{2}{3}\right)^{n-1}$

45. $a_n = 18\left(\frac{3}{2}\right)^{n-1}$ **46.** $a_n = 18\left(-\frac{3}{2}\right)^{n-1}$

In Exercises 47–52, use a graphing utility to graph the first 10 terms of the sequence.

47. $a_n = 12(-0.75)^{n-1}$

48. $a_n = 10(1.5)^{n-1}$

49. $a_n = 12(-0.4)^{n-1}$

50. $a_n = 20(-1.25)^{n-1}$

51. $a_n = 2(1.3)^{n-1}$

52. $a_n = 10(1.2)^{n-1}$

In Exercises 53–72, find the sum of the finite geometric sequence.

53. $\sum_{n=1}^{9} 2^{n-1}$

54. $\sum_{n=1}^{10} \left(\frac{5}{2}\right)^{n-1}$

55. $\sum_{n=1}^{9} (-2)^{n-1}$

56. $\sum_{n=1}^{8} 5\left(-\frac{3}{2}\right)^{n-1}$

57. $\sum_{i=1}^{7} 64\left(-\frac{1}{2}\right)^{i-1}$

58. $\sum_{i=1}^{10} 2\left(\frac{1}{4}\right)^{i-1}$

59. $\sum_{i=1}^{6} 32\left(\frac{1}{4}\right)^{i-1}$

60. $\sum_{i=1}^{12} 16\left(\frac{1}{2}\right)^{i-1}$

61. $\sum_{n=0}^{20} 3\left(\frac{3}{2}\right)^{n}$

62. $\sum_{n=0}^{40} 5\left(\frac{3}{5}\right)^{n}$

63. $\sum_{n=0}^{15} 2\left(\frac{4}{3}\right)^{n}$

64. $\sum_{n=0}^{20} 10\left(\frac{1}{5}\right)^{n}$

65. $\sum_{n=0}^{5} 300(1.06)^{n}$

66. $\sum_{n=0}^{6} 500(1.04)^{n}$

67. $\sum_{n=0}^{40} 2\left(-\frac{1}{4}\right)^{n}$

68. $\sum_{n=0}^{50} 10\left(\frac{2}{3}\right)^{n-1}$

69. $\sum_{i=1}^{10} 8\left(-\frac{1}{4}\right)^{i-1}$

70. $\sum_{i=0}^{25} 8\left(-\frac{1}{2}\right)^{i}$

71. $\sum_{i=1}^{10} 5\left(-\frac{1}{3}\right)^{i-1}$

72. $\sum_{i=1}^{100} 15\left(\frac{2}{3}\right)^{i-1}$

In Exercises 73–78, use summation notation to write the sum.

73. $5 + 15 + 45 + \cdots + 3645$

74. $7 + 14 + 28 + \cdots + 896$

75. $2 - \frac{1}{2} + \frac{1}{8} - \cdots + \frac{1}{2048}$

76. $15 - 3 + \frac{3}{5} - \cdots - \frac{3}{625}$

77. $0.1 + 0.4 + 1.6 + \cdots + 102.4$

78. $32 + 24 + 18 + \cdots + 10.125$

In Exercises 79–92, find the sum of the infinite geometric series.

79. $\sum_{n=0}^{\infty} \left(\frac{1}{2}\right)^{n}$

80. $\sum_{n=0}^{\infty} 2\left(\frac{2}{3}\right)^{n}$

81. $\sum_{n=0}^{\infty} \left(-\frac{1}{2}\right)^{n}$

82. $\sum_{n=0}^{\infty} 2\left(-\frac{2}{3}\right)^{n}$

83. $\sum_{n=0}^{\infty} 4\left(\frac{1}{4}\right)^{n}$

84. $\sum_{n=0}^{\infty} \left(\frac{1}{10}\right)^{n}$

85. $\sum_{n=0}^{\infty} (0.4)^{n}$

86. $\sum_{n=0}^{\infty} 4(0.2)^{n}$

87. $\sum_{n=0}^{\infty} -3(0.9)^{n}$

88. $\sum_{n=0}^{\infty} -10(0.2)^{n}$

89. $8 + 6 + \frac{9}{2} + \frac{27}{8} + \cdots$

90. $9 + 6 + 4 + \frac{8}{3} + \cdots$

91. $\frac{1}{9} - \frac{1}{3} + 1 - 3 + \cdots$

92. $-\frac{125}{36} + \frac{25}{6} - 5 + 6 - \cdots$

In Exercises 93–96, find the rational number representation of the repeating decimal.

93. $0.\overline{36}$

94. $0.\overline{297}$

95. $0.3\overline{18}$

96. $1.3\overline{8}$

Graphical Reasoning **In Exercises 97 and 98, use a graphing utility to graph the function. Identify the horizontal asymptote of the graph and determine its relationship to the sum.**

97. $f(x) = 6\left[\dfrac{1 - (0.5)^x}{1 - (0.5)}\right], \quad \sum_{n=0}^{\infty} 6\left(\dfrac{1}{2}\right)^n$

98. $f(x) = 2\left[\dfrac{1 - (0.8)^x}{1 - (0.8)}\right], \quad \sum_{n=0}^{\infty} 2\left(\dfrac{4}{5}\right)^n$

Model It

99. ***Data Analysis: Population*** The table shows the population a_n of China (in millions) from 1998 through 2004. (Source: U.S. Census Bureau)

Year	Population, a_n
1998	1250.4
1999	1260.1
2000	1268.9
2001	1276.9
2002	1284.3
2003	1291.5
2004	1298.8

(a) Use the *exponential regression* feature of a graphing utility to find a geometric sequence that models the data. Let n represent the year, with $n = 8$ corresponding to 1998.

(b) Use the sequence from part (a) to describe the rate at which the population of China is growing.

Model It (continued)

(c) Use the sequence from part (a) to predict the population of China in 2010. The U.S. Census Bureau predicts the population of China will be 1374.6 million in 2010. How does this value compare with your prediction?

(d) Use the sequence from part (a) to determine when the population of China will reach 1.32 billion.

100. ***Compound Interest*** A principal of \$1000 is invested at 6% interest. Find the amount after 10 years if the interest is compounded (a) annually, (b) semiannually, (c) quarterly, (d) monthly, and (e) daily.

101. ***Compound Interest*** A principal of \$2500 is invested at 2% interest. Find the amount after 20 years if the interest is compounded (a) annually, (b) semiannually, (c) quarterly, (d) monthly, and (e) daily.

102. ***Depreciation*** A tool and die company buys a machine for \$135,000 and it depreciates at a rate of 30% per year. (In other words, at the end of each year the depreciated value is 70% of what it was at the beginning of the year.) Find the depreciated value of the machine after 5 full years.

103. ***Annuities*** A deposit of \$100 is made at the beginning of each month in an account that pays 6%, compounded monthly. The balance A in the account at the end of 5 years is

$$A = 100\left(1 + \frac{0.06}{12}\right)^1 + \cdot \cdot \cdot + 100\left(1 + \frac{0.06}{12}\right)^{60}.$$

Find A.

104. ***Annuities*** A deposit of \$50 is made at the beginning of each month in an account that pays 8%, compounded monthly. The balance A in the account at the end of 5 years is

$$A = 50\left(1 + \frac{0.08}{12}\right)^1 + \cdot \cdot \cdot + 50\left(1 + \frac{0.08}{12}\right)^{60}.$$

Find A.

105. ***Annuities*** A deposit of P dollars is made at the beginning of each month in an account earning an annual interest rate r, compounded monthly. The balance A after t years is

$$A = P\left(1 + \frac{r}{12}\right) + P\left(1 + \frac{r}{12}\right)^2 + \cdot \cdot \cdot + P\left(1 + \frac{r}{12}\right)^{12t}.$$

Show that the balance is

$$A = P\left[\left(1 + \frac{r}{12}\right)^{12t} - 1\right]\left(1 + \frac{12}{r}\right).$$

106. ***Annuities*** A deposit of P dollars is made at the beginning of each month in an account earning an annual interest rate r, compounded continuously. The balance A after t years is $A = Pe^{r/12} + Pe^{2r/12} + \cdot \cdot \cdot + Pe^{12tr/12}$. Show that the balance is

$$A = \frac{Pe^{r/12}(e^{rt} - 1)}{e^{r/12} - 1}.$$

Annuities **In Exercises 107–110, consider making monthly deposits of P dollars in a savings account earning an annual interest rate r. Use the results of Exercises 105 and 106 to find the balance A after t years if the interest is compounded (a) monthly and (b) continuously.**

107. $P = \$50,\ r = 7\%,\ t = 20$ years

108. $P = \$75,\ r = 3\%,\ t = 25$ years

109. $P = \$100,\ r = 10\%,\ t = 40$ years

110. $P = \$20,\ r = 6\%,\ t = 50$ years

111. ***Annuities*** Consider an initial deposit of P dollars in an account earning an annual interest rate r, compounded monthly. At the end of each month, a withdrawal of W dollars will occur and the account will be depleted in t years. The amount of the initial deposit required is

$$P = W\left(1 + \frac{r}{12}\right)^{-1} + W\left(1 + \frac{r}{12}\right)^{-2} + \cdot \cdot \cdot + W\left(1 + \frac{r}{12}\right)^{-12t}.$$

Show that the initial deposit is

$$P = W\left(\frac{12}{r}\right)\left[1 - \left(1 + \frac{r}{12}\right)^{-12t}\right].$$

112. ***Annuities*** Determine the amount required in a retirement account for an individual who retires at age 65 and wants an income of \$2000 from the account each month for 20 years. Use the result of Exercise 111 and assume that the account earns 9% compounded monthly.

Multiplier Effect **In Exercises 113–116, use the following information. A tax rebate has been given to property owners by the state government with the anticipation that each property owner spends approximately p% of the rebate, and in turn each recipient of this amount spends p% of what they receive, and so on. Economists refer to this exchange of money and its circulation within the economy as the "multiplier effect." The multiplier effect operates on the idea that the expenditures of one individual become the income of another individual. For the given tax rebate, find the total amount put back into the state's economy, if this effect continues without end.**

	Tax rebate	*p%*
113.	\$400	75%
114.	\$250	80%
115.	\$600	72.5%
116.	\$450	77.5%

117. ***Geometry*** The sides of a square are 16 inches in length. A new square is formed by connecting the midpoints of the sides of the original square, and two of the resulting triangles are shaded (see figure). If this process is repeated five more times, determine the total area of the shaded region.

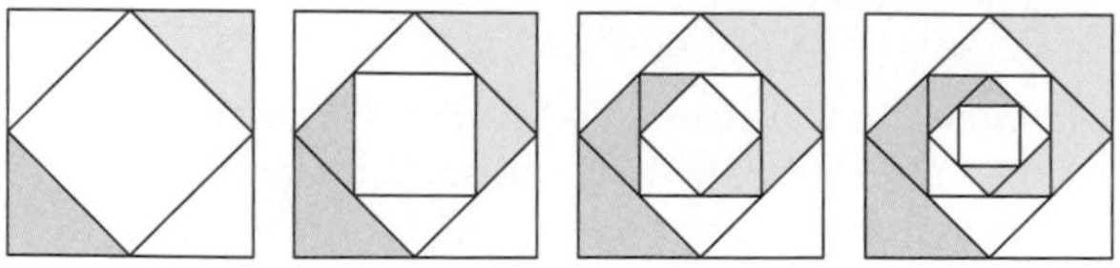

118. ***Sales*** The annual sales a_n (in millions of dollars) for Urban Outfitters for 1994 through 2003 can be approximated by the model

$$a_n = 54.6e^{0.172n}, \qquad n = 4, 5, \ldots, 13$$

where n represents the year, with $n = 4$ corresponding to 1994. Use this model and the formula for the sum of a finite geometric sequence to approximate the total sales earned during this 10-year period. (Source: Urban Outfitters Inc.)

119. ***Salary*** An investment firm has a job opening with a salary of \$30,000 for the first year. Suppose that during the next 39 years, there is a 5% raise each year. Find the total compensation over the 40-year period.

120. ***Distance*** A ball is dropped from a height of 16 feet. Each time it drops h feet, it rebounds $0.81h$ feet.

(a) Find the total vertical distance traveled by the ball.

(b) The ball takes the following times (in seconds) for each fall.

$$\begin{array}{ll} s_1 = -16t^2 + 16, & s_1 = 0 \text{ if } t = 1 \\ s_2 = -16t^2 + 16(0.81), & s_2 = 0 \text{ if } t = 0.9 \\ s_3 = -16t^2 + 16(0.81)^2, & s_3 = 0 \text{ if } t = (0.9)^2 \\ s_4 = -16t^2 + 16(0.81)^3, & s_4 = 0 \text{ if } t = (0.9)^3 \\ \vdots & \vdots \\ s_n = -16t^2 + 16(0.81)^{n-1}, & s_n = 0 \text{ if } t = (0.9)^{n-1} \end{array}$$

Beginning with s_2, the ball takes the same amount of time to bounce up as it does to fall, and so the total time elapsed before it comes to rest is

$$t = 1 + 2\sum_{n=1}^{\infty}(0.9)^n.$$

Find this total time.

Synthesis

True or False? **In Exercises 121 and 122, determine whether the statement is true or false. Justify your answer.**

121. A sequence is geometric if the ratios of consecutive differences of consecutive terms are the same.

122. You can find the nth term of a geometric sequence by multiplying its common ratio by the first term of the sequence raised to the $(n-1)$th power.

123. ***Writing*** Write a brief paragraph explaining why the terms of a geometric sequence decrease in magnitude when $-1 < r < 1$.

124. Find two different geometric series with sums of 4.

Skills Review

In Exercises 125–128, evaluate the function for $f(x) = 3x + 1$ and $g(x) = x^2 - 1$.

125. $g(x + 1)$

126. $f(x + 1)$

127. $f(g(x + 1))$

128. $g(f(x + 1))$

In Exercises 129–132, completely factor the expression.

129. $9x^3 - 64x$

130. $x^2 + 4x - 63$

131. $6x^2 - 13x - 5$

132. $16x^2 - 4x^4$

In Exercises 133–138, perform the indicated operation(s) and simplify.

133. $\dfrac{3}{x+3} \cdot \dfrac{x(x+3)}{x-3}$

134. $\dfrac{x-2}{x+7} \cdot \dfrac{2x(x+7)}{6x(x-2)}$

135. $\dfrac{x}{3} \div \dfrac{3x}{6x+3}$

136. $\dfrac{x-5}{x-3} \div \dfrac{10-2x}{2(3-x)}$

137. $5 + \dfrac{7}{x+2} + \dfrac{2}{x-2}$

138. $8 - \dfrac{x-1}{x+4} - \dfrac{4}{x-1} - \dfrac{x+4}{(x-1)(x+4)}$

139. **Make a Decision** To work an extended application analyzing the amounts spent on research and development in the United States from 1980 to 2003, visit this text's website at *college.hmco.com.* *(Data Source: U.S. National Science Foundation)*

9.4 Mathematical Induction

What you should learn

- Use mathematical induction to prove statements involving a positive integer *n*.
- Recognize patterns and write the *n*th term of a sequence.
- Find the sums of powers of integers.
- Find finite differences of sequences.

Why you should learn it

Finite differences can be used to determine what type of model can be used to represent a sequence. For instance, in Exercise 61 on page 682, you will use finite differences to find a model that represents the number of individual income tax returns filed in the United States from 1998 to 2003.

Mario Tama/Getty Images

Introduction

In this section, you will study a form of mathematical proof called **mathematical induction.** It is important that you see clearly the logical need for it, so take a closer look at the problem discussed in Example 5 in Section 9.2.

$$S_1 = 1 = 1^2$$

$$S_2 = 1 + 3 = 2^2$$

$$S_3 = 1 + 3 + 5 = 3^2$$

$$S_4 = 1 + 3 + 5 + 7 = 4^2$$

$$S_5 = 1 + 3 + 5 + 7 + 9 = 5^2$$

Judging from the pattern formed by these first five sums, it appears that the sum of the first n odd integers is

$$S_n = 1 + 3 + 5 + 7 + 9 + \cdot \cdot \cdot + (2n - 1) = n^2.$$

Although this particular formula *is* valid, it is important for you to see that recognizing a pattern and then simply *jumping to the conclusion* that the pattern must be true for all values of n is *not* a logically valid method of proof. There are many examples in which a pattern appears to be developing for small values of n and then at some point the pattern fails. One of the most famous cases of this was the conjecture by the French mathematician Pierre de Fermat (1601–1665), who speculated that all numbers of the form

$$F_n = 2^{2^n} + 1, \quad n = 0, 1, 2, . . .$$

are prime. For $n = 0, 1, 2, 3,$ and 4, the conjecture is true.

$$F_0 = 3$$

$$F_1 = 5$$

$$F_2 = 17$$

$$F_3 = 257$$

$$F_4 = 65{,}537$$

The size of the next Fermat number ($F_5 = 4{,}294{,}967{,}297$) is so great that it was difficult for Fermat to determine whether it was prime or not. However, another well-known mathematician, Leonhard Euler (1707–1783), later found the factorization

$$F_5 = 4{,}294{,}967{,}297$$
$$= 641(6{,}700{,}417)$$

which proved that F_5 is not prime and therefore Fermat's conjecture was false.

Just because a rule, pattern, or formula seems to work for several values of n, you cannot simply decide that it is valid for all values of n without going through a *legitimate proof*. Mathematical induction is one method of proof.

STUDY TIP

It is important to recognize that in order to prove a statement by induction, both parts of the Principle of Mathematical Induction are necessary.

The Principle of Mathematical Induction

Let P_n be a statement involving the positive integer n. If

1. P_1 is true, and
2. for every positive integer k, the truth of P_k implies the truth of P_{k+1}

then the statement P_n must be true for all positive integers n.

To apply the Principle of Mathematical Induction, you need to be able to determine the statement P_{k+1} for a given statement P_k. To determine P_{k+1}, substitute the quantity $k + 1$ for k in the statement P_k.

Example 1 A Preliminary Example

Find the statement P_{k+1} for each given statement P_k.

a. $P_k: S_k = \dfrac{k^2(k+1)^2}{4}$

b. $P_k: S_k = 1 + 5 + 9 + \cdot \cdot \cdot + [4(k-1) - 3] + (4k - 3)$

c. $P_k: k + 3 < 5k^2$

d. $P_k: 3^k \geq 2k + 1$

Solution

a. $P_{k+1}: S_{k+1} = \dfrac{(k+1)^2(k+1+1)^2}{4}$ Replace k by $k + 1$.

$= \dfrac{(k+1)^2(k+2)^2}{4}$ Simplify.

b. $P_{k+1}: S_{k+1} = 1 + 5 + 9 + \cdot \cdot \cdot + \{4[(k+1) - 1] - 3\} + [4(k+1) - 3]$

$= 1 + 5 + 9 + \cdot \cdot \cdot + (4k - 3) + (4k + 1)$

c. $P_{k+1}: (k+1) + 3 < 5(k+1)^2$

$k + 4 < 5(k^2 + 2k + 1)$

d. $P_{k+1}: 3^{k+1} \geq 2(k+1) + 1$

$3^{k+1} \geq 2k + 3$

CHECKPOINT Now try Exercise 1.

A well-known illustration used to explain why the Principle of Mathematical Induction works is the unending line of dominoes shown in Figure 9.6. If the line actually contains infinitely many dominoes, it is clear that you could not knock the entire line down by knocking down only *one domino* at a time. However, suppose it were true that each domino would knock down the next one as it fell. Then you could knock them all down simply by pushing the first one and starting a chain reaction. Mathematical induction works in the same way. If the truth of P_k implies the truth of P_{k+1} and if P_1 is true, the chain reaction proceeds as follows: P_1 implies P_2, P_2 implies P_3, P_3 implies P_4, and so on.

FIGURE 9.6

When using mathematical induction to prove a *summation* formula (such as the one in Example 2), it is helpful to think of S_{k+1} as

$$S_{k+1} = S_k + a_{k+1}$$

where a_{k+1} is the $(k + 1)$th term of the original sum.

Example 2 Using Mathematical Induction

Use mathematical induction to prove the following formula.

$$\begin{aligned} S_n &= 1 + 3 + 5 + 7 + \cdot \cdot \cdot + (2n - 1) \\ &= n^2 \end{aligned}$$

Solution

Mathematical induction consists of two distinct parts. First, you must show that the formula is true when $n = 1$.

1. When $n = 1$, the formula is valid, because

$$S_1 = 1 = 1^2.$$

The second part of mathematical induction has two steps. The first step is to *assume* that the formula is valid for some integer k. The second step is to use this assumption to prove that the formula is valid for the *next* integer, $k + 1$.

2. Assuming that the formula

$$\begin{aligned} S_k &= 1 + 3 + 5 + 7 + \cdot \cdot \cdot + (2k - 1) \\ &= k^2 \end{aligned}$$

is true, you must show that the formula $S_{k+1} = (k + 1)^2$ is true.

$$\begin{aligned} S_{k+1} &= 1 + 3 + 5 + 7 + \cdot \cdot \cdot + (2k - 1) + [2(k + 1) - 1] \\ &= [1 + 3 + 5 + 7 + \cdot \cdot \cdot + (2k - 1)] + (2k + 2 - 1) \\ &= S_k + (2k + 1) && \text{Group terms to form } S_k. \\ &= k^2 + 2k + 1 && \text{Replace } S_k \text{ by } k^2. \\ &= (k + 1)^2 \end{aligned}$$

Combining the results of parts (1) and (2), you can conclude by mathematical induction that the formula is valid for all positive integer values of n.

CHECKPOINT Now try Exercise 5.

It occasionally happens that a statement involving natural numbers is not true for the first $k - 1$ positive integers but is true for all values of $n \geq k$. In these instances, you use a slight variation of the Principle of Mathematical Induction in which you verify P_k rather than P_1. This variation is called the *extended principle of mathematical induction*. To see the validity of this, note from Figure 9.6 that all but the first $k - 1$ dominoes can be knocked down by knocking over the kth domino. This suggests that you can prove a statement P_n to be true for $n \geq k$ by showing that P_k is true and that P_k implies P_{k+1}. In Exercises 17–22 of this section, you are asked to apply this extension of mathematical induction.

Example 3 **Using Mathematical Induction**

Use mathematical induction to prove the formula

$$S_n = 1^2 + 2^2 + 3^2 + 4^2 + \cdot \cdot \cdot + n^2 = \frac{n(n + 1)(2n + 1)}{6}$$

for all integers $n \geq 1$.

Solution

1. When $n = 1$, the formula is valid, because

$$S_1 = 1^2 = \frac{1(2)(3)}{6}.$$

2. Assuming that

$$S_k = 1^2 + 2^2 + 3^2 + 4^2 + \cdot \cdot \cdot + k^2 \qquad a_k = k^2$$
$$= \frac{k(k + 1)(2k + 1)}{6}$$

you must show that

$$S_{k+1} = \frac{(k + 1)(k + 1 + 1)[2(k + 1) + 1]}{6}$$
$$= \frac{(k + 1)(k + 2)(2k + 3)}{6}.$$

To do this, write the following.

$$S_{k+1} = S_k + a_{k+1}$$
$$= (1^2 + 2^2 + 3^2 + 4^2 + \cdot \cdot \cdot + k^2) + (k + 1)^2 \qquad \text{Substitute for } S_k.$$
$$= \frac{k(k + 1)(2k + 1)}{6} + (k + 1)^2 \qquad \text{By assumption}$$
$$= \frac{k(k + 1)(2k + 1) + 6(k + 1)^2}{6} \qquad \text{Combine fractions.}$$
$$= \frac{(k + 1)[k(2k + 1) + 6(k + 1)]}{6} \qquad \text{Factor.}$$
$$= \frac{(k + 1)(2k^2 + 7k + 6)}{6} \qquad \text{Simplify.}$$
$$= \frac{(k + 1)(k + 2)(2k + 3)}{6} \qquad S_k \text{ implies } S_{k+1}.$$

Combining the results of parts (1) and (2), you can conclude by mathematical induction that the formula is valid for *all* integers $n \geq 1$.

CHECKPOINT Now try Exercise 11.

STUDY TIP

Remember that when adding rational expressions, you must first find the least common denominator (LCD). In Example 3, the LCD is 6.

When proving a formula using mathematical induction, the only statement that you *need* to verify is P_1. As a check, however, it is a good idea to try verifying some of the other statements. For instance, in Example 3, try verifying P_2 and P_3.

Example 4 **Proving an Inequality by Mathematical Induction**

Prove that $n < 2^n$ for all positive integers n.

Solution

1. For $n = 1$ and $n = 2$, the statement is true because

$$1 < 2^1 \quad \text{and} \quad 2 < 2^2.$$

2. Assuming that

$$k < 2^k$$

you need to show that $k + 1 < 2^{k+1}$. For $n = k$, you have

$$2^{k+1} = 2(2^k) > 2(k) = 2k. \qquad \text{By assumption}$$

Because $2k = k + k > k + 1$ for all $k > 1$, it follows that

$$2^{k+1} > 2k > k + 1 \quad \text{or} \quad k + 1 < 2^{k+1}.$$

Combining the results of parts (1) and (2), you can conclude by mathematical induction that $n < 2^n$ for all integers $n \geq 1$.

✓CHECKPOINT Now try Exercise 17.

STUDY TIP

To check a result that you have proved by mathematical induction, it helps to list the statement for several values of n. For instance, in Example 4, you could list

$$1 < 2^1 = 2, \quad 2 < 2^2 = 4,$$

$$2 < 2^3 = 8, \quad 4 < 2^4 = 16,$$

$$5 < 2^5 = 32, \quad 6 < 2^6 = 64,$$

From this list, your intuition confirms that the statement $n < 2^n$ is reasonable.

Example 5 **Proving Factors by Mathematical Induction**

Prove that 3 is a factor of $4^n - 1$ for all positive integers n.

Solution

1. For $n = 1$, the statement is true because

$$4^1 - 1 = 3.$$

So, 3 is a factor.

2. Assuming that 3 is a factor of $4^k - 1$, you must show that 3 is a factor of $4^{k+1} - 1$. To do this, write the following.

$$\begin{aligned} 4^{k+1} - 1 &= 4^{k+1} - 4^k + 4^k - 1 && \text{Subtract and add } 4^k. \\ &= 4^k(4 - 1) + (4^k - 1) && \text{Regroup terms.} \\ &= 4^k \cdot 3 + (4^k - 1) && \text{Simplify.} \end{aligned}$$

Because 3 is a factor of $4^k \cdot 3$ and 3 is also a factor of $4^k - 1$, it follows that 3 is a factor of $4^{k+1} - 1$. Combining the results of parts (1) and (2), you can conclude by mathematical induction that 3 is a factor of $4^n - 1$ for all positive integers n.

✓CHECKPOINT Now try Exercise 29.

Pattern Recognition

Although choosing a formula on the basis of a few observations does *not* guarantee the validity of the formula, pattern recognition *is* important. Once you have a pattern or formula that you think works, you can try using mathematical induction to prove your formula.

Finding a Formula for the nth Term of a Sequence

To find a formula for the nth term of a sequence, consider these guidelines.

1. Calculate the first several terms of the sequence. It is often a good idea to write the terms in both simplified and factored forms.
2. Try to find a recognizable pattern for the terms and write a formula for the nth term of the sequence. This is your *hypothesis* or *conjecture*. You might try computing one or two more terms in the sequence to test your hypothesis.
3. Use mathematical induction to prove your hypothesis.

Example 6 **Finding a Formula for a Finite Sum**

Find a formula for the finite sum and prove its validity.

$$\frac{1}{1 \cdot 2} + \frac{1}{2 \cdot 3} + \frac{1}{3 \cdot 4} + \frac{1}{4 \cdot 5} + \cdot \cdot \cdot + \frac{1}{n(n + 1)}$$

Solution

Begin by writing out the first few sums.

$$S_1 = \frac{1}{1 \cdot 2} = \frac{1}{2} = \frac{1}{1 + 1}$$

$$S_2 = \frac{1}{1 \cdot 2} + \frac{1}{2 \cdot 3} = \frac{4}{6} = \frac{2}{3} = \frac{2}{2 + 1}$$

$$S_3 = \frac{1}{1 \cdot 2} + \frac{1}{2 \cdot 3} + \frac{1}{3 \cdot 4} = \frac{9}{12} = \frac{3}{4} = \frac{3}{3 + 1}$$

$$S_4 = \frac{1}{1 \cdot 2} + \frac{1}{2 \cdot 3} + \frac{1}{3 \cdot 4} + \frac{1}{4 \cdot 5} = \frac{48}{60} = \frac{4}{5} = \frac{4}{4 + 1}$$

From this sequence, it appears that the formula for the kth sum is

$$S_k = \frac{1}{1 \cdot 2} + \frac{1}{2 \cdot 3} + \frac{1}{3 \cdot 4} + \frac{1}{4 \cdot 5} + \cdot \cdot \cdot + \frac{1}{k(k + 1)} = \frac{k}{k + 1}.$$

To prove the validity of this hypothesis, use mathematical induction. Note that you have already verified the formula for $n = 1$, so you can begin by assuming that the formula is valid for $n = k$ and trying to show that it is valid for $n = k + 1$.

$$S_{k+1} = \left[\frac{1}{1 \cdot 2} + \frac{1}{2 \cdot 3} + \frac{1}{3 \cdot 4} + \frac{1}{4 \cdot 5} + \cdot \cdot \cdot + \frac{1}{k(k + 1)}\right] + \frac{1}{(k + 1)(k + 2)}$$

$$= \frac{k}{k + 1} + \frac{1}{(k + 1)(k + 2)} \qquad \text{By assumption}$$

$$= \frac{k(k + 2) + 1}{(k + 1)(k + 2)} = \frac{k^2 + 2k + 1}{(k + 1)(k + 2)} = \frac{(k + 1)^2}{(k + 1)(k + 2)} = \frac{k + 1}{k + 2}$$

So, by mathematical induction, you can conclude that the hypothesis is valid.

CHECKPOINT Now try Exercise 35.

Sums of Powers of Integers

The formula in Example 3 is one of a collection of useful summation formulas. This and other formulas dealing with the sums of various powers of the first n positive integers are as follows.

Sums of Powers of Integers

1. $1 + 2 + 3 + 4 + \cdots + n = \dfrac{n(n+1)}{2}$

2. $1^2 + 2^2 + 3^2 + 4^2 + \cdots + n^2 = \dfrac{n(n+1)(2n+1)}{6}$

3. $1^3 + 2^3 + 3^3 + 4^3 + \cdots + n^3 = \dfrac{n^2(n+1)^2}{4}$

4. $1^4 + 2^4 + 3^4 + 4^4 + \cdots + n^4 = \dfrac{n(n+1)(2n+1)(3n^2+3n-1)}{30}$

5. $1^5 + 2^5 + 3^5 + 4^5 + \cdots + n^5 = \dfrac{n^2(n+1)^2(2n^2+2n-1)}{12}$

Example 7 **Finding a Sum of Powers of Integers**

Find each sum.

a. $\displaystyle\sum_{i=1}^{7} i^3 = 1^3 + 2^3 + 3^3 + 4^3 + 5^3 + 6^3 + 7^3$ **b.** $\displaystyle\sum_{i=1}^{4} (6i - 4i^2)$

Solution

a. Using the formula for the sum of the cubes of the first n positive integers, you obtain

$$\sum_{i=1}^{7} i^3 = 1^3 + 2^3 + 3^3 + 4^3 + 5^3 + 6^3 + 7^3$$

$$= \frac{7^2(7+1)^2}{4} = \frac{49(64)}{4} = 784. \qquad \text{Formula 3}$$

b. $\displaystyle\sum_{i=1}^{4} (6i - 4i^2) = \sum_{i=1}^{4} 6i - \sum_{i=1}^{4} 4i^2$

$$= 6\sum_{i=1}^{4} i - 4\sum_{i=1}^{4} i^2$$

$$= 6\left[\frac{4(4+1)}{2}\right] - 4\left[\frac{4(4+1)(8+1)}{6}\right] \qquad \text{Formula 1 and 2}$$

$$= 6(10) - 4(30)$$

$$= 60 - 120 = -60$$

✓CHECKPOINT Now try Exercise 47.

STUDY TIP

For a linear model, the *first* differences should be the same nonzero number. For a quadratic model, the *second* differences are the same nonzero number.

Finite Differences

The **first differences** of a sequence are found by subtracting consecutive terms. The **second differences** are found by subtracting consecutive first differences. The first and second differences of the sequence 3, 5, 8, 12, 17, 23, . . . are as follows.

n:	1		2		3		4		5		6
a_n:	3		5		8		12		17		23
First differences:		2		3		4		5		6	
Second differences:			1		1		1		1		

For this sequence, the second differences are all the same. When this happens, the sequence has a perfect *quadratic* model. If the first differences are all the same, the sequence has a *linear* model. That is, it is arithmetic.

Example 8 Finding a Quadratic Model

Find the quadratic model for the sequence

3, 5, 8, 12, 17, 23, ...

Solution

You know from the second differences shown above that the model is quadratic and has the form

$$a_n = an^2 + bn + c.$$

By substituting 1, 2, and 3 for n, you can obtain a system of three linear equations in three variables.

$a_1 = a(1)^2 + b(1) + c = 3$ Substitute 1 for n.

$a_2 = a(2)^2 + b(2) + c = 5$ Substitute 2 for n.

$a_3 = a(3)^2 + b(3) + c = 8$ Substitute 3 for n.

You now have a system of three equations in a, b, and c.

$$\begin{cases} a + b + c = 3 & \text{Equation 1} \\ 4a + 2b + c = 5 & \text{Equation 2} \\ 9a + 3b + c = 8 & \text{Equation 3} \end{cases}$$

Using the techniques discussed in Chapter 7, you can find the solution to be $a = \frac{1}{2}$, $b = \frac{1}{2}$, and $c = 2$. So, the quadratic model is

$$a_n = \frac{1}{2}n^2 + \frac{1}{2}n + 2.$$

Try checking the values of a_1, a_2, and a_3.

✓CHECKPOINT Now try Exercise 57.

9.4 Exercises

VOCABULARY CHECK: Fill in the blanks.

1. The first step in proving a formula by ________ ________ is to show that the formula is true when $n = 1$.
2. The ________ differences of a sequence are found by subtracting consecutive terms.
3. A sequence is an ________ sequence if the first differences are all the same nonzero number.
4. If the ________ differences of a sequence are all the same nonzero number, then the sequence has a perfect quadratic model.

In Exercises 1–4, find P_{k+1} for the given P_k.

1. $P_k = \dfrac{5}{k(k+1)}$
2. $P_k = \dfrac{1}{2(k+2)}$
3. $P_k = \dfrac{k^2(k+1)^2}{4}$
4. $P_k = \dfrac{k}{3}(2k+1)$

In Exercises 5–16, use mathematical induction to prove the formula for every positive integer n.

5. $2 + 4 + 6 + 8 + \cdots + 2n = n(n+1)$
6. $3 + 7 + 11 + 15 + \cdots + (4n-1) = n(2n+1)$
7. $2 + 7 + 12 + 17 + \cdots + (5n-3) = \dfrac{n}{2}(5n-1)$
8. $1 + 4 + 7 + 10 + \cdots + (3n-2) = \dfrac{n}{2}(3n-1)$
9. $1 + 2 + 2^2 + 2^3 + \cdots + 2^{n-1} = 2^n - 1$
10. $2(1 + 3 + 3^2 + 3^3 + \cdots + 3^{n-1}) = 3^n - 1$
11. $1 + 2 + 3 + 4 + \cdots + n = \dfrac{n(n+1)}{2}$
12. $1^3 + 2^3 + 3^3 + 4^3 + \cdots + n^3 = \dfrac{n^2(n+1)^2}{4}$
13. $\displaystyle\sum_{i=1}^{n} i^5 = \frac{n^2(n+1)^2(2n^2+2n-1)}{12}$
14. $\displaystyle\sum_{i=1}^{n} i^4 = \frac{n(n+1)(2n+1)(3n^2+3n-1)}{30}$
15. $\displaystyle\sum_{i=1}^{n} i(i+1) = \frac{n(n+1)(n+2)}{3}$
16. $\displaystyle\sum_{i=1}^{n} \frac{1}{(2i-1)(2i+1)} = \frac{n}{2n+1}$

In Exercises 17–22, prove the inequality for the indicated integer values of n.

17. $n! > 2^n, \quad n \geq 4$
18. $\left(\frac{4}{3}\right)^n > n, \quad n \geq 7$
19. $\dfrac{1}{\sqrt{1}} + \dfrac{1}{\sqrt{2}} + \dfrac{1}{\sqrt{3}} + \cdots + \dfrac{1}{\sqrt{n}} > \sqrt{n}, \quad n \geq 2$
20. $\left(\dfrac{x}{y}\right)^{n+1} < \left(\dfrac{x}{y}\right)^n, \quad n \geq 1$ and $0 < x < y$
21. $(1+a)^n \geq na, \quad n \geq 1$ and $a > 0$
22. $2n^2 > (n+1)^2, \quad n \geq 3$

In Exercises 23–34, use mathematical induction to prove the property for all positive integers n.

23. $(ab)^n = a^n b^n$
24. $\left(\dfrac{a}{b}\right)^n = \dfrac{a^n}{b^n}$
25. If $x_1 \neq 0, x_2 \neq 0, \ldots, x_n \neq 0$, then $(x_1 x_2 x_3 \cdots x_n)^{-1} = x_1^{-1} x_2^{-1} x_3^{-1} \cdots x_n^{-1}$.
26. If $x_1 > 0, x_2 > 0, \ldots, x_n > 0$, then $\ln(x_1 x_2 \cdots x_n) = \ln x_1 + \ln x_2 + \cdots + \ln x_n$.
27. Generalized Distributive Law: $x(y_1 + y_2 + \cdots + y_n) = xy_1 + xy_2 + \cdots + xy_n$
28. $(a + bi)^n$ and $(a - bi)^n$ are complex conjugates for all $n \geq 1$.
29. A factor of $(n^3 + 3n^2 + 2n)$ is 3.
30. A factor of $(n^3 - n + 3)$ is 3.
31. A factor of $(n^4 - n + 4)$ is 2.
32. A factor of $(2^{2n+1} + 1)$ is 3.
33. A factor of $(2^{4n-2} + 1)$ is 5.
34. A factor of $(2^{2n-1} + 3^{2n-1})$ is 5.

In Exercises 35–40, find a formula for the sum of the first n terms of the sequence.

35. $1, 5, 9, 13, \ldots$
36. $25, 22, 19, 16, \ldots$
37. $1, \frac{9}{10}, \frac{81}{100}, \frac{729}{1000}, \ldots$
38. $3, -\frac{9}{2}, \frac{27}{4}, -\frac{81}{8}, \ldots$
39. $\dfrac{1}{4}, \dfrac{1}{12}, \dfrac{1}{24}, \dfrac{1}{40}, \ldots, \dfrac{1}{2n(n+1)}, \ldots$
40. $\dfrac{1}{2 \cdot 3}, \dfrac{1}{3 \cdot 4}, \dfrac{1}{4 \cdot 5}, \dfrac{1}{5 \cdot 6}, \ldots, \dfrac{1}{(n+1)(n+2)}, \ldots$

In Exercises 41–50, find the sum using the formulas for the sums of powers of integers.

41. $\sum_{n=1}^{15} n$

42. $\sum_{n=1}^{30} n$

43. $\sum_{n=1}^{6} n^2$

44. $\sum_{n=1}^{10} n^3$

45. $\sum_{n=1}^{5} n^4$

46. $\sum_{n=1}^{8} n^5$

47. $\sum_{n=1}^{6} (n^2 - n)$

48. $\sum_{n=1}^{20} (n^3 - n)$

49. $\sum_{i=1}^{6} (6i - 8i^3)$

50. $\sum_{j=1}^{10} \left(3 - \frac{1}{2}j + \frac{1}{2}j^2\right)$

In Exercises 51–56, write the first six terms of the sequence beginning with the given term. Then calculate the first and second differences of the sequence. State whether the sequence has a linear model, a quadratic model, or neither.

51. $a_1 = 0$
$a_n = a_{n-1} + 3$

52. $a_1 = 2$
$a_n = a_{n-1} + 2$

53. $a_1 = 3$
$a_n = a_{n-1} - n$

54. $a_2 = -3$
$a_n = -2a_{n-1}$

55. $a_0 = 2$
$a_n = (a_{n-1})^2$

56. $a_0 = 0$
$a_n = a_{n-1} + n$

In Exercises 57–60, find a quadratic model for the sequence with the indicated terms.

57. $a_0 = 3,\ a_1 = 3,\ a_4 = 15$

58. $a_0 = 7,\ a_1 = 6,\ a_3 = 10$

59. $a_0 = -3,\ a_2 = 1,\ a_4 = 9$

60. $a_0 = 3,\ a_2 = 0,\ a_6 = 36$

Model It

61. ***Data Analysis: Tax Returns*** The table shows the number a_n (in millions) of individual tax returns filed in the United States from 1998 to 2003. (Source: Internal Revenue Service)

Year	Number of returns, a_n
1998	120.3
1999	122.5
2000	124.9
2001	127.1
2002	129.4
2003	130.3

Model It (continued)

(a) Find the first differences of the data shown in the table.

(b) Use your results from part (a) to determine whether a linear model can be used to approximate the data. If so, find a model algebraically. Let n represent the year, with $n = 8$ corresponding to 1998.

(c) Use the *regression* feature of a graphing utility to find a linear model for the data. Compare this model with the one from part (b).

(d) Use the models found in parts (b) and (c) to estimate the number of individual tax returns filed in 2008. How do these values compare?

Synthesis

62. ***Writing*** In your own words, explain what is meant by a proof by mathematical induction.

True or False? **In Exercises 63–66, determine whether the statement is true or false. Justify your answer.**

63. If the statement P_1 is true but the true statement P_6 does *not* imply that the statement P_7 is true, then P_n is not necessarily true for all positive integers n.

64. If the statement P_k is true and P_k implies P_{k+1}, then P_1 is also true.

65. If the second differences of a sequence are all zero, then the sequence is arithmetic.

66. A sequence with n terms has $n - 1$ second differences.

Skills Review

In Exercises 67–70, find the product.

67. $(2x^2 - 1)^2$

68. $(2x - y)^2$

69. $(5 - 4x)^3$

70. $(2x - 4y)^3$

In Exercises 71–74, (a) state the domain of the function, (b) identify all intercepts, (c) find any vertical and horizontal asymptotes, and (d) plot additional solution points as needed to sketch the graph of the rational function.

71. $f(x) = \dfrac{x}{x + 3}$

72. $g(x) = \dfrac{x^2}{x^2 - 4}$

73. $h(t) = \dfrac{t - 7}{t}$

74. $f(x) = \dfrac{5 + x}{1 - x}$

9.5 The Binomial Theorem

What you should learn

- Use the Binomial Theorem to calculate binomial coefficients.
- Use Pascal's Triangle to calculate binomial coefficients.
- Use binomial coefficients to write binomial expansions.

Why you should learn it

You can use binomial coefficients to model and solve real-life problems. For instance, in Exercise 80 on page 690, you will use binomial coefficients to write the expansion of a model that represents the amounts of child support collected in the U. S.

© Vince Streano/Corbis

Binomial Coefficients

Recall that a *binomial* is a polynomial that has two terms. In this section, you will study a formula that gives a quick method of raising a binomial to a power. To begin, look at the expansion of $(x + y)^n$ for several values of n.

$$(x + y)^0 = 1$$
$$(x + y)^1 = x + y$$
$$(x + y)^2 = x^2 + 2xy + y^2$$
$$(x + y)^3 = x^3 + 3x^2y + 3xy^2 + y^3$$
$$(x + y)^4 = x^4 + 4x^3y + 6x^2y^2 + 4xy^3 + y^4$$
$$(x + y)^5 = x^5 + 5x^4y + 10x^3y^2 + 10x^2y^3 + 5xy^4 + y^5$$

There are several observations you can make about these expansions.

1. In each expansion, there are $n + 1$ terms.
2. In each expansion, x and y have symmetrical roles. The powers of x decrease by 1 in successive terms, whereas the powers of y increase by 1.
3. The sum of the powers of each term is n. For instance, in the expansion of $(x + y)^5$, the sum of the powers of each term is 5.

$$(x + y)^5 = x^5 + \overbrace{5x^4y^1}^{4+1=5} + \overbrace{10x^3y^2}^{3+2=5} + 10x^2y^3 + 5x^1y^4 + y^5$$

4. The coefficients increase and then decrease in a symmetric pattern.

The coefficients of a binomial expansion are called **binomial coefficients.** To find them, you can use the **Binomial Theorem.**

The Binomial Theorem

In the expansion of $(x + y)^n$

$$(x + y)^n = x^n + nx^{n-1}y + \cdots + {}_nC_r\, x^{n-r}y^r + \cdots + nxy^{n-1} + y^n$$

the coefficient of $x^{n-r}y^r$ is

$${}_nC_r = \frac{n!}{(n-r)!r!}.$$

The symbol $\binom{n}{r}$ is often used in place of ${}_nC_r$ to denote binomial coefficients.

For a proof of the Binomial Theorem, see Proofs in Mathematics on page 724.

> **Technology**
>
> Most graphing calculators are programmed to evaluate ${}_nC_r$. Consult the user's guide for your calculator and then evaluate ${}_8C_5$. You should get an answer of 56.

Example 1 **Finding Binomial Coefficients**

Find each binomial coefficient.

a. ${}_8C_2$ **b.** $\binom{10}{3}$ **c.** ${}_7C_0$ **d.** $\binom{8}{8}$

Solution

a. $${}_8C_2 = \frac{8!}{6! \cdot 2!} = \frac{(8 \cdot 7) \cdot \cancel{6!}}{\cancel{6!} \cdot 2!} = \frac{8 \cdot 7}{2 \cdot 1} = 28$$

b. $$\binom{10}{3} = \frac{10!}{7! \cdot 3!} = \frac{(10 \cdot 9 \cdot 8) \cdot \cancel{7!}}{\cancel{7!} \cdot 3!} = \frac{10 \cdot 9 \cdot 8}{3 \cdot 2 \cdot 1} = 120$$

c. $${}_7C_0 = \frac{\cancel{7!}}{\cancel{7!} \cdot 0!} = 1$$ **d.** $$\binom{8}{8} = \frac{\cancel{8!}}{0! \cdot \cancel{8!}} = 1$$

CHECKPOINT Now try Exercise 1.

When $r \neq 0$ and $r \neq n$, as in parts (a) and (b) above, there is a simple pattern for evaluating binomial coefficients that works because there will always be factorial terms that divide out from the expression.

$${}_8C_2 = \frac{\overbrace{8 \cdot 7}^{2\text{ factors}}}{\underbrace{2 \cdot 1}_{2\text{ factors}}} \quad \text{and} \quad \binom{10}{3} = \frac{\overbrace{10 \cdot 9 \cdot 8}^{3\text{ factors}}}{\underbrace{3 \cdot 2 \cdot 1}_{3\text{ factors}}}$$

Example 2 **Finding Binomial Coefficients**

Find each binomial coefficient.

a. ${}_7C_3$ **b.** $\binom{7}{4}$ **c.** ${}_{12}C_1$ **d.** $\binom{12}{11}$

Solution

a. $${}_7C_3 = \frac{7 \cdot \cancel{6} \cdot 5}{\cancel{3} \cdot \cancel{2} \cdot 1} = 35$$

b. $$\binom{7}{4} = \frac{7 \cdot \cancel{6} \cdot 5 \cdot \cancel{4}}{\cancel{4} \cdot \cancel{3} \cdot \cancel{2} \cdot 1} = 35$$

c. $${}_{12}C_1 = \frac{12}{1} = 12$$

d. $$\binom{12}{11} = \frac{12!}{1! \cdot 11!} = \frac{(12) \cdot \cancel{11!}}{1! \cdot \cancel{11!}} = \frac{12}{1} = 12$$

CHECKPOINT Now try Exercise 7.

It is not a coincidence that the results in parts (a) and (b) of Example 2 are the same and that the results in parts (c) and (d) are the same. In general, it is true that

$${}_nC_r = {}_nC_{n-r}.$$

This shows the symmetric property of binomial coefficients that was identified earlier.

Pascal's Triangle

There is a convenient way to remember the pattern for binomial coefficients. By arranging the coefficients in a triangular pattern, you obtain the following array, which is called **Pascal's Triangle.** This triangle is named after the famous French mathematician Blaise Pascal (1623–1662).

1
1 1
1 2 1
1 3 3 1
1 4 6 4 1
1 5 10 10 5 1 $\quad 4 + 6 = 10$
1 6 15 20 15 6 1
1 7 21 35 35 21 7 1 $\quad 15 + 6 = 21$

The first and last numbers in each row of Pascal's Triangle are 1. Every other number in each row is formed by adding the two numbers immediately above the number. Pascal noticed that numbers in this triangle are precisely the same numbers that are the coefficients of binomial expansions, as follows.

$$(x + y)^0 = 1 \qquad \text{0th row}$$
$$(x + y)^1 = 1x + 1y \qquad \text{1st row}$$
$$(x + y)^2 = 1x^2 + 2xy + 1y^2 \qquad \text{2nd row}$$
$$(x + y)^3 = 1x^3 + 3x^2y + 3xy^2 + 1y^3 \qquad \text{3rd row}$$
$$(x + y)^4 = 1x^4 + 4x^3y + 6x^2y^2 + 4xy^3 + 1y^4 \qquad \vdots$$
$$(x + y)^5 = 1x^5 + 5x^4y + 10x^3y^2 + 10x^2y^3 + 5xy^4 + 1y^5$$
$$(x + y)^6 = 1x^6 + 6x^5y + 15x^4y^2 + 20x^3y^3 + 15x^2y^4 + 6xy^5 + 1y^6$$
$$(x + y)^7 = 1x^7 + 7x^6y + 21x^5y^2 + 35x^4y^3 + 35x^3y^4 + 21x^2y^5 + 7xy^6 + 1y^7$$

The top row in Pascal's Triangle is called the *zeroth row* because it corresponds to the binomial expansion $(x + y)^0 = 1$. Similarly, the next row is called the *first row* because it corresponds to the binomial expansion $(x + y)^1 = 1(x) + 1(y)$. In general, the *nth row* in Pascal's Triangle gives the coefficients of $(x + y)^n$.

Exploration

Complete the table and describe the result.

n	r	${}_nC_r$	${}_nC_{n-r}$
9	5		
7	1		
12	4		
6	0		
10	7		

What characteristic of Pascal's Triangle is illustrated by this table?

Example 3 Using Pascal's Triangle

Use the seventh row of Pascal's Triangle to find the binomial coefficients.

$${}_8C_0, {}_8C_1, {}_8C_2, {}_8C_3, {}_8C_4, {}_8C_5, {}_8C_6, {}_8C_7, {}_8C_8$$

Solution

1 7 21 35 35 21 7 1
1 8 28 56 70 56 28 8 1

${}_8C_0$ ${}_8C_1$ ${}_8C_2$ ${}_8C_3$ ${}_8C_4$ ${}_8C_5$ ${}_8C_6$ ${}_8C_7$ ${}_8C_8$

✓CHECKPOINT Now try Exercise 11.

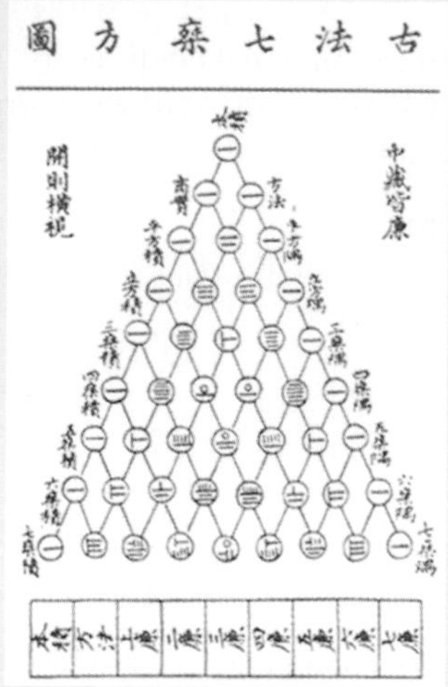

Historical Note

Precious Mirror "Pascal's" Triangle and forms of the Binomial Theorem were known in Eastern cultures prior to the Western "discovery" of the theorem. A Chinese text entitled *Precious Mirror* contains a triangle of binomial expansions through the eighth power.

Binomial Expansions

As mentioned at the beginning of this section, when you write out the coefficients for a binomial that is raised to a power, you are **expanding a binomial.** The formulas for binomial coefficients give you an easy way to expand binomials, as demonstrated in the next four examples.

Example 4 Expanding a Binomial

Write the expansion for the expression

$(x + 1)^3$.

Solution

The binomial coefficients from the third row of Pascal's Triangle are

1, 3, 3, 1.

So, the expansion is as follows.

$$(x + 1)^3 = (1)x^3 + (3)x^2(1) + (3)x(1^2) + (1)(1^3)$$
$$= x^3 + 3x^2 + 3x + 1$$

✓CHECKPOINT Now try Exercise 15.

To expand binomials representing *differences* rather than sums, you alternate signs. Here are two examples.

$$(x - 1)^3 = x^3 - 3x^2 + 3x - 1$$
$$(x - 1)^4 = x^4 - 4x^3 + 6x^2 - 4x + 1$$

Example 5 Expanding a Binomial

Write the expansion for each expression.

a. $(2x - 3)^4$ **b.** $(x - 2y)^4$

Solution

The binomial coefficients from the fourth row of Pascal's Triangle are

1, 4, 6, 4, 1.

Therefore, the expansions are as follows.

a. $(2x - 3)^4 = (1)(2x)^4 - (4)(2x)^3(3) + (6)(2x)^2(3^2) - (4)(2x)(3^3) + (1)(3^4)$

$= 16x^4 - 96x^3 + 216x^2 - 216x + 81$

b. $(x - 2y)^4 = (1)x^4 - (4)x^3(2y) + (6)x^2(2y)^2 - (4)x(2y)^3 + (1)(2y)^4$

$= x^4 - 8x^3y + 24x^2y^2 - 32xy^3 + 16y^4$

✓CHECKPOINT Now try Exercise 19.

Technology

You can use a graphing utility to check the expansion in Example 6. Graph the original binomial expression and the expansion in the same viewing window. The graphs should coincide as shown below.

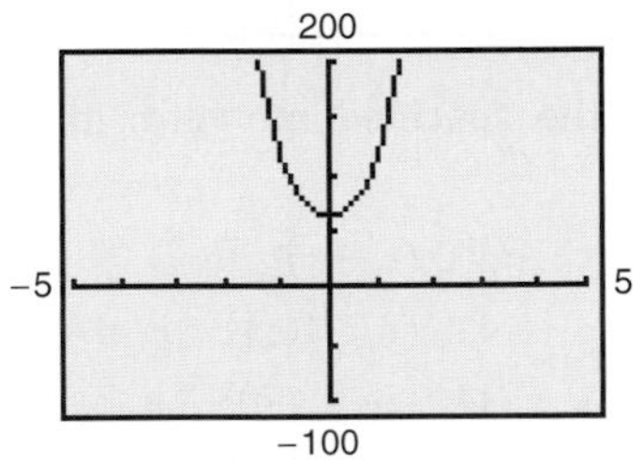

Example 6 Expanding a Binomial

Write the expansion for $(x^2 + 4)^3$.

Solution

Use the third row of Pascal's Triangle, as follows.

$$(x^2 + 4)^3 = (1)(x^2)^3 + (3)(x^2)^2(4) + (3)x^2(4^2) + (1)(4^3)$$
$$= x^6 + 12x^4 + 48x^2 + 64$$

✓CHECKPOINT Now try Exercise 29.

Sometimes you will need to find a specific term in a binomial expansion. Instead of writing out the entire expansion, you can use the fact that, from the Binomial Theorem, the $(r + 1)$th term is ${}_nC_r\, x^{n-r} y^r$.

Example 7 Finding a Term in a Binomial Expansion

a. Find the sixth term of $(a + 2b)^8$.

b. Find the coefficient of the term a^6b^5 in the expansion of $(3a - 2b)^{11}$.

Solution

a. Remember that the formula is for the $(r + 1)$th term, so r is one less than the number of the term you are looking for. So, to find the sixth term in this binomial expansion, use $r = 5$, $n = 8$, $x = a$, and $y = 2b$, as shown.

$${}_8C_5\, a^{8-5}(2b)^5 = 56 \cdot a^3 \cdot (2b)^5 = 56(2^5)a^3b^5 = 1792a^3b^5.$$

b. In this case, $n = 11$, $r = 5$, $x = 3a$, and $y = -2b$. Substitute these values to obtain

$${}_nC_r\, x^{n-r} y^r = {}_{11}C_5(3a)^6(-2b)^5$$
$$= (462)(729a^6)(-32b^5)$$
$$= -10{,}777{,}536a^6b^5.$$

So, the coefficient is $-10{,}777{,}536$.

✓CHECKPOINT Now try Exercise 41.

Writing about Mathematics

Error Analysis You are a math instructor and receive the following solutions from one of your students on a quiz. Find the error(s) in each solution. Discuss ways that your student could avoid the error(s) in the future.

a. Find the second term in the expansion of $(2x - 3y)^5$.

~~$5(2x)^4(3y)^2 = 720x^4y^2$~~

b. Find the fourth term in the expansion of $\left(\frac{1}{2}x + 7y\right)^6$.

~~${}_6C_4\left(\frac{1}{2}x\right)^2(7y)^4 = 9003.75x^2y^4$~~

9.5 Exercises

VOCABULARY CHECK: Fill in the blanks.

1. The coefficients of a binomial expansion are called ________ ________.
2. To find binomial coefficients, you can use the ________ ________ or ________ ________.
3. The notation used to denote a binomial coefficient is ________ or ________.
4. When you write out the coefficients for a binomial that is raised to a power, you are ________ a ________.

In Exercises 1–10, calculate the binomial coefficient.

1. ${}_5C_3$
2. ${}_8C_6$
3. ${}_{12}C_0$
4. ${}_{20}C_{20}$
5. ${}_{20}C_{15}$
6. ${}_{12}C_5$
7. $\binom{10}{4}$
8. $\binom{10}{6}$
9. $\binom{100}{98}$
10. $\binom{100}{2}$

In Exercises 11–14, evaluate using Pascal's Triangle.

11. $\binom{8}{5}$
12. $\binom{8}{7}$
13. ${}_7C_4$
14. ${}_6C_3$

In Exercises 15–34, use the Binomial Theorem to expand and simplify the expression.

15. $(x + 1)^4$
16. $(x + 1)^6$
17. $(a + 6)^4$
18. $(a + 5)^5$
19. $(y - 4)^3$
20. $(y - 2)^5$
21. $(x + y)^5$
22. $(c + d)^3$
23. $(r + 3s)^6$
24. $(x + 2y)^4$
25. $(3a - 4b)^5$
26. $(2x - 5y)^5$
27. $(2x + y)^3$
28. $(7a + b)^3$
29. $(x^2 + y^2)^4$
30. $(x^2 + y^2)^6$
31. $\left(\frac{1}{x} + y\right)^5$
32. $\left(\frac{1}{x} + 2y\right)^6$
33. $2(x - 3)^4 + 5(x - 3)^2$
34. $3(x + 1)^5 - 4(x + 1)^3$

In Exercises 35–38, expand the binomial by using Pascal's Triangle to determine the coefficients.

35. $(2t - s)^5$
36. $(3 - 2z)^4$
37. $(x + 2y)^5$
38. $(2v + 3)^6$

In Exercises 39–46, find the specified *n*th term in the expansion of the binomial.

39. $(x + y)^{10}, \quad n = 4$
40. $(x - y)^6, \quad n = 7$
41. $(x - 6y)^5, \quad n = 3$
42. $(x - 10z)^7, \quad n = 4$
43. $(4x + 3y)^9, \quad n = 8$
44. $(5a + 6b)^5, \quad n = 5$
45. $(10x - 3y)^{12}, \quad n = 9$
46. $(7x + 2y)^{15}, \quad n = 7$

In Exercises 47–54, find the coefficient *a* of the term in the expansion of the binomial.

Binomial	*Term*
47. $(x + 3)^{12}$	ax^5
48. $(x^2 + 3)^{12}$	ax^8
49. $(x - 2y)^{10}$	ax^8y^2
50. $(4x - y)^{10}$	ax^2y^8
51. $(3x - 2y)^9$	ax^4y^5
52. $(2x - 3y)^8$	ax^6y^2
53. $(x^2 + y)^{10}$	ax^8y^6
54. $(z^2 - t)^{10}$	az^4t^8

In Exercises 55–58, use the Binomial Theorem to expand and simplify the expression.

55. $(\sqrt{x} + 3)^4$
56. $(2\sqrt{t} - 1)^3$
57. $(x^{2/3} - y^{1/3})^3$
58. $(u^{3/5} + 2)^5$

In Exercises 59–62, expand the expression in the difference quotient and simplify.

$$\frac{f(x + h) - f(x)}{h} \qquad \text{Difference quotient}$$

59. $f(x) = x^3$
60. $f(x) = x^4$
61. $f(x) = \sqrt{x}$
62. $f(x) = \frac{1}{x}$

In Exercises 63–68, use the Binomial Theorem to expand the complex number. Simplify your result.

63. $(1 + i)^4$

64. $(2 - i)^5$

65. $(2 - 3i)^6$

66. $\left(5 + \sqrt{-9}\right)^3$

67. $\left(-\frac{1}{2} + \frac{\sqrt{3}}{2}i\right)^3$

68. $\left(5 - \sqrt{3}i\right)^4$

Approximation **In Exercises 69–72, use the Binomial Theorem to approximate the quantity accurate to three decimal places. For example, in Exercise 69, use the expansion**

$$(1.02)^8 = (1 + 0.02)^8 = 1 + 8(0.02) + 28(0.02)^2 + \cdot \cdot \cdot.$$

69. $(1.02)^8$

70. $(2.005)^{10}$

71. $(2.99)^{12}$

72. $(1.98)^9$

Graphical Reasoning **In Exercises 73 and 74, use a graphing utility to graph f and g in the same viewing window. What is the relationship between the two graphs? Use the Binomial Theorem to write the polynomial function g in standard form.**

73. $f(x) = x^3 - 4x, \quad g(x) = f(x + 4)$

74. $f(x) = -x^4 + 4x^2 - 1, \quad g(x) = f(x - 3)$

Probability **In Exercises 75–78, consider n independent trials of an experiment in which each trial has two possible outcomes: "success" or "failure." The probability of a success on each trial is p, and the probability of a failure is $q = 1 - p$. In this context, the term ${}_nC_k\, p^k q^{n-k}$ in the expansion of $(p + q)^n$ gives the probability of k successes in the n trials of the experiment.**

75. A fair coin is tossed seven times. To find the probability of obtaining four heads, evaluate the term

$${}_7C_4\left(\tfrac{1}{2}\right)^4\left(\tfrac{1}{2}\right)^3$$

in the expansion of $\left(\frac{1}{2} + \frac{1}{2}\right)^7$.

76. The probability of a baseball player getting a hit during any given time at bat is $\frac{1}{4}$. To find the probability that the player gets three hits during the next 10 times at bat, evaluate the term

$${}_{10}C_3\left(\tfrac{1}{4}\right)^3\left(\tfrac{3}{4}\right)^7$$

in the expansion of $\left(\frac{1}{4} + \frac{3}{4}\right)^{10}$.

77. The probability of a sales representative making a sale with any one customer is $\frac{1}{3}$. The sales representative makes eight contacts a day. To find the probability of making four sales, evaluate the term

$${}_8C_4\left(\tfrac{1}{3}\right)^4\left(\tfrac{2}{3}\right)^4$$

in the expansion of $\left(\frac{1}{3} + \frac{2}{3}\right)^8$.

78. To find the probability that the sales representative in Exercise 77 makes four sales if the probability of a sale with any one customer is $\frac{1}{2}$, evaluate the term

$${}_8C_4\left(\tfrac{1}{2}\right)^4\left(\tfrac{1}{2}\right)^4$$

in the expansion of $\left(\frac{1}{2} + \frac{1}{2}\right)^8$.

Model It

79. ***Data Analysis: Water Consumption*** The table shows the per capita consumption of bottled water $f(t)$ (in gallons) in the United States from 1990 through 2003. (Source: Economic Research Service, U.S. Department of Agriculture)

Year	Consumption, $f(t)$
1990	8.0
1991	8.0
1992	9.7
1993	10.3
1994	11.3
1995	12.1
1996	13.0
1997	13.9
1998	15.0
1999	16.4
2000	17.4
2001	18.8
2002	20.7
2003	22.0

(a) Use the *regression* feature of a graphing utility to find a cubic model for the data. Let t represent the year, with $t = 0$ corresponding to 1990.

(b) Use a graphing utility to plot the data and the model in the same viewing window.

(c) You want to adjust the model so that $t = 0$ corresponds to 2000 rather than 1990. To do this, you shift the graph of f 10 units *to the left* to obtain $g(t) = f(t + 10)$. Write $g(t)$ in standard form.

(d) Use a graphing utility to graph g in the same viewing window as f.

(e) Use both models to estimate the per capita consumption of bottled water in 2008. Do you obtain the same answer?

(f) Describe the overall trend in the data. What factors do you think may have contributed to the increase in the per capita consumption of bottled water?

80. ***Child Support*** The amounts $f(t)$ (in billions of dollars) of child support collected in the United States from 1990 to 2002 can be approximated by the model

$$f(t) = 0.031t^2 + 0.82t + 6.1, \quad 0 \le t \le 12$$

where t represents the year, with $t = 0$ corresponding to 1990 (see figure). (Source: U.S. Department of Health and Human Services)

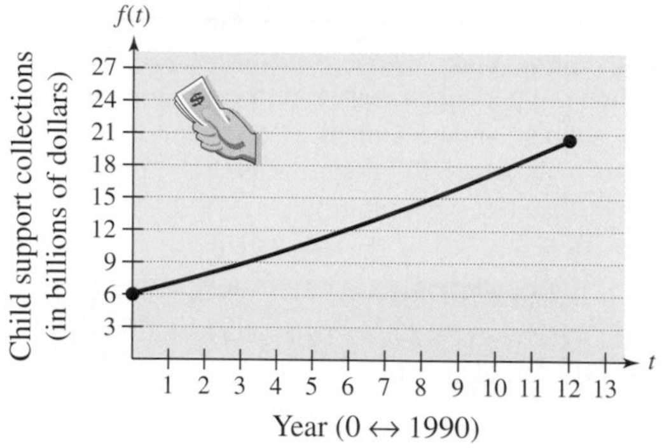

(a) You want to adjust the model so that $t = 0$ corresponds to 2000 rather than 1990. To do this, you shift the graph of f 10 units *to the left* and obtain $g(t) = f(t + 10)$. Write $g(t)$ in standard form.

(b) Use a graphing utility to graph f and g in the same viewing window.

(c) Use the graphs to estimate when the child support collections will exceed \$30 billion.

Synthesis

True or False? **In Exercises 81–83, determine whether the statement is true or false. Justify your answer.**

81. The Binomial Theorem could be used to produce each row of Pascal's Triangle.

82. A binomial that represents a difference cannot always be accurately expanded using the Binomial Theorem.

83. The x^{10}-term and the x^{14}-term of the expansion of $(x^2 + 3)^{12}$ have identical coefficients.

84. ***Writing*** In your own words, explain how to form the rows of Pascal's Triangle.

85. Form rows 8–10 of Pascal's Triangle.

86. ***Think About It*** How many terms are in the expansion of $(x + y)^n$?

87. ***Think About It*** How do the expansions of $(x + y)^n$ and $(x - y)^n$ differ?

88. ***Graphical Reasoning*** Which two functions have identical graphs, and why? Use a graphing utility to graph the functions in the given order and in the same viewing window. Compare the graphs.

(a) $f(x) = (1 - x)^3$

(b) $g(x) = 1 - x^3$

(c) $h(x) = 1 + 3x + 3x^2 + x^3$

(d) $k(x) = 1 - 3x + 3x^2 - x^3$

(e) $p(x) = 1 + 3x - 3x^2 + x^3$

Proof **In Exercises 89–92, prove the property for all integers r and n where $0 \le r \le n$.**

89. ${}_nC_r = {}_nC_{n-r}$

90. ${}_nC_0 - {}_nC_1 + {}_nC_2 - \cdots \pm {}_nC_n = 0$

91. ${}_{n+1}C_r = {}_nC_r + {}_nC_{r-1}$

92. The sum of the numbers in the nth row of Pascal's Triangle is 2^n.

Skills Review

In Exercises 93–96, the graph of $y = g(x)$ is shown. Graph f and use the graph to write an equation for the graph of g.

93. $f(x) = x^2$

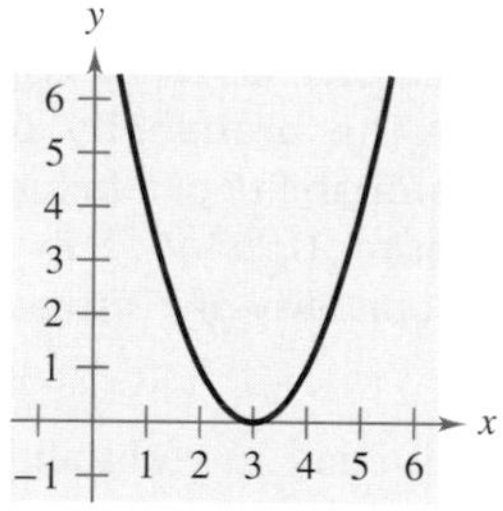

94. $f(x) = x^2$

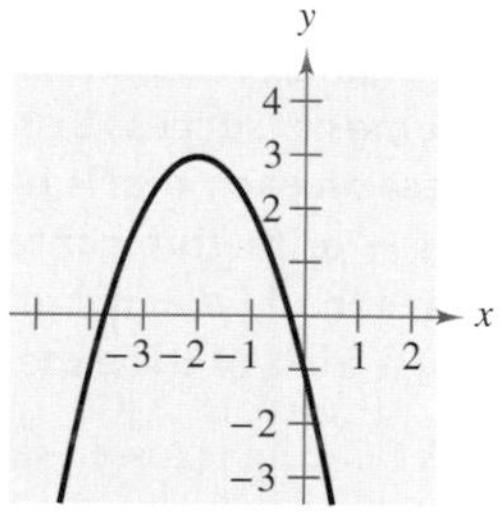

95. $f(x) = \sqrt{x}$

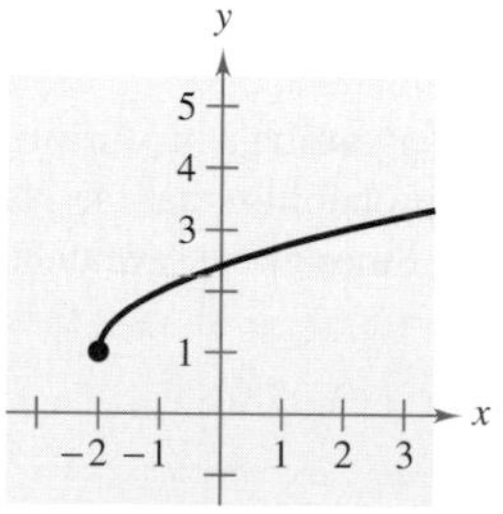

96. $f(x) = \sqrt{x}$

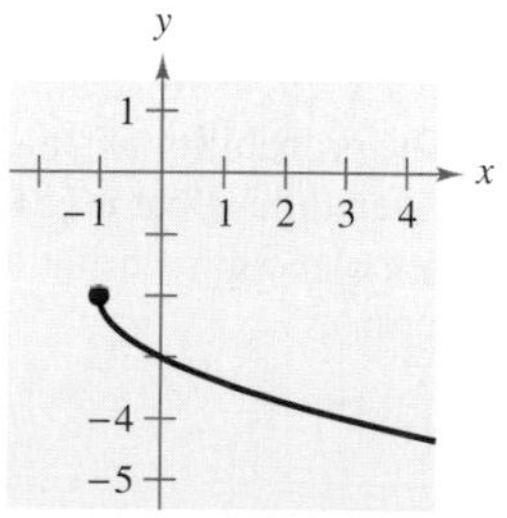

In Exercises 97 and 98, find the inverse of the matrix.

97. $\begin{bmatrix} -6 & 5 \\ -5 & 4 \end{bmatrix}$

98. $\begin{bmatrix} 1.2 & -2.3 \\ -2 & 4 \end{bmatrix}$

9.6 Counting Principles

What you should learn

- Solve simple counting problems.
- Use the Fundamental Counting Principle to solve counting problems.
- Use permutations to solve counting problems.
- Use combinations to solve counting problems.

Why you should learn it

You can use counting principles to solve counting problems that occur in real life. For instance, in Exercise 65 on page 700, you are asked to use counting principles to determine the number of possible ways of selecting the winning numbers in the Powerball lottery.

Simple Counting Problems

This section and Section 9.7 present a brief introduction to some of the basic counting principles and their application to probability. In Section 9.7, you will see that much of probability has to do with counting the number of ways an event can occur. The following two examples describe simple counting problems.

Example 1 Selecting Pairs of Numbers at Random

Eight pieces of paper are numbered from 1 to 8 and placed in a box. One piece of paper is drawn from the box, its number is written down, and the piece of paper is *replaced in the box*. Then, a second piece of paper is drawn from the box, and its number is written down. Finally, the two numbers are added together. How many different ways can a sum of 12 be obtained?

Solution

To solve this problem, count the different ways that a sum of 12 can be obtained using two numbers from 1 to 8.

First number	4	5	6	7	8
Second number	8	7	6	5	4

From this list, you can see that a sum of 12 can occur in five different ways.

✓CHECKPOINT Now try Exercise 5.

Example 2 Selecting Pairs of Numbers at Random

Eight pieces of paper are numbered from 1 to 8 and placed in a box. Two pieces of paper are drawn from the box *at the same time*, and the numbers on the pieces of paper are written down and totaled. How many different ways can a sum of 12 be obtained?

Solution

To solve this problem, count the different ways that a sum of 12 can be obtained *using two different numbers* from 1 to 8.

First number	4	5	7	8
Second number	8	7	5	4

So, a sum of 12 can be obtained in four different ways.

✓CHECKPOINT Now try Exercise 7.

The difference between the counting problems in Examples 1 and 2 can be described by saying that the random selection in Example 1 occurs **with replacement,** whereas the random selection in Example 2 occurs **without replacement,** which eliminates the possibility of choosing two 6's.

The Fundamental Counting Principle

Examples 1 and 2 describe simple counting problems in which you can *list* each possible way that an event can occur. When it is possible, this is always the best way to solve a counting problem. However, some events can occur in so many different ways that it is not feasible to write out the entire list. In such cases, you must rely on formulas and counting principles. The most important of these is the **Fundamental Counting Principle.**

> **Fundamental Counting Principle**
>
> Let E_1 and E_2 be two events. The first event E_1 can occur in m_1 different ways. After E_1 has occurred, E_2 can occur in m_2 different ways. The number of ways that the two events can occur is $m_1 \cdot m_2$.

The Fundamental Counting Principle can be extended to three or more events. For instance, the number of ways that three events E_1, E_2, and E_3 can occur is $m_1 \cdot m_2 \cdot m_3$.

Example 3 Using the Fundamental Counting Principle

How many different pairs of letters from the English alphabet are possible?

Solution

There are two events in this situation. The first event is the choice of the first letter, and the second event is the choice of the second letter. Because the English alphabet contains 26 letters, it follows that the number of two-letter pairs is $26 \cdot 26 = 676$.

CHECKPOINT Now try Exercise 13.

Example 4 Using the Fundamental Counting Principle

Telephone numbers in the United States currently have 10 digits. The first three are the *area code* and the next seven are the *local telephone number*. How many different telephone numbers are possible within each area code? (Note that at this time, a local telephone number cannot begin with 0 or 1.)

Solution

Because the first digit of a local telephone number cannot be 0 or 1, there are only eight choices for the first digit. For each of the other six digits, there are 10 choices.

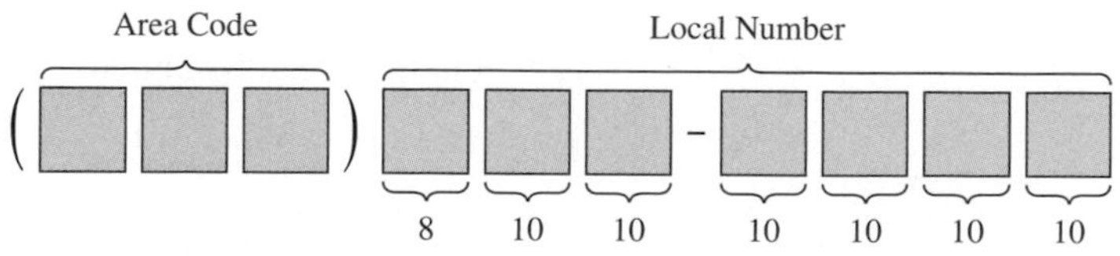

So, the number of local telephone numbers that are possible *within* each area code is $8 \cdot 10 \cdot 10 \cdot 10 \cdot 10 \cdot 10 \cdot 10 = 8{,}000{,}000$.

CHECKPOINT Now try Exercise 19.

Permutations

One important application of the Fundamental Counting Principle is in determining the number of ways that n elements can be arranged (in order). An ordering of n elements is called a **permutation** of the elements.

> **Definition of Permutation**
>
> A **permutation** of n different elements is an ordering of the elements such that one element is first, one is second, one is third, and so on.

Example 5 Finding the Number of Permutations of n Elements

How many permutations are possible for the letters A, B, C, D, E, and F?

Solution

Consider the following reasoning.

First position: Any of the *six* letters

Second position: Any of the remaining *five* letters

Third position: Any of the remaining *four* letters

Fourth position: Any of the remaining *three* letters

Fifth position: Any of the remaining *two* letters

Sixth position: The *one* remaining letter

So, the numbers of choices for the six positions are as follows.

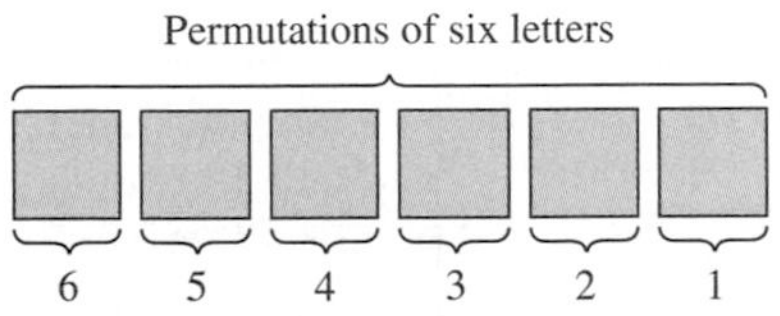

The total number of permutations of the six letters is

$$6! = 6 \cdot 5 \cdot 4 \cdot 3 \cdot 2 \cdot 1$$
$$= 720.$$

✓CHECKPOINT Now try Exercise 39.

> **Number of Permutations of n Elements**
>
> The number of permutations of n elements is
>
> $$n \cdot (n - 1) \cdot \cdot \cdot 4 \cdot 3 \cdot 2 \cdot 1 = n!.$$
>
> In other words, there are $n!$ different ways that n elements can be ordered.

Vaughn Youtz/Newsmakers/Getty Images

Eleven thoroughbred racehorses hold the title of Triple Crown winner for winning the Kentucky Derby, the Preakness, and the Belmont Stakes in the same year. Forty-nine horses have won two out of the three races.

Example 6 Counting Horse Race Finishes

Eight horses are running in a race. In how many different ways can these horses come in first, second, and third? (Assume that there are no ties.)

Solution

Here are the different possibilities.

Win (first position): *Eight* choices

Place (second position): *Seven* choices

Show (third position): *Six* choices

Using the Fundamental Counting Principle, multiply these three numbers together to obtain the following.

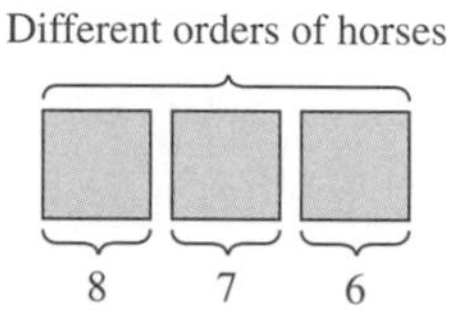

So, there are $8 \cdot 7 \cdot 6 = 336$ different orders.

✓CHECKPOINT Now try Exercise 43.

It is useful, on occasion, to order a *subset* of a collection of elements rather than the entire collection. For example, you might want to choose and order r elements out of a collection of n elements. Such an ordering is called a **permutation of n elements taken r at a time.**

Technology

Most graphing calculators are programmed to evaluate ${}_nP_r$. Consult the user's guide for your calculator and then evaluate ${}_8P_5$. You should get an answer of 6720.

Permutations of n Elements Taken r at a Time

The number of permutations of n elements taken r at a time is

$$\begin{aligned} {}_nP_r &= \frac{n!}{(n-r)!} \\ &= n(n-1)(n-2) \cdot \cdot \cdot (n-r+1). \end{aligned}$$

Using this formula, you can rework Example 6 to find that the number of permutations of eight horses taken three at a time is

$$\begin{aligned} {}_8P_3 &= \frac{8!}{(8-3)!} \\ &= \frac{8!}{5!} \\ &= \frac{8 \cdot 7 \cdot 6 \cdot \cancel{5!}}{\cancel{5!}} \\ &= 336 \end{aligned}$$

which is the same answer obtained in the example.

Remember that for permutations, order is important. So, if you are looking at the possible permutations of the letters A, B, C, and D taken three at a time, the permutations (A, B, D) and (B, A, D) are counted as different because the *order* of the elements is different.

Suppose, however, that you are asked to find the possible permutations of the letters A, A, B, and C. The total number of permutations of the four letters would be ${}_4P_4 = 4!$. However, not all of these arrangements would be *distinguishable* because there are two A's in the list. To find the number of distinguishable permutations, you can use the following formula.

Distinguishable Permutations

Suppose a set of n objects has n_1 of one kind of object, n_2 of a second kind, n_3 of a third kind, and so on, with

$$n = n_1 + n_2 + n_3 + \cdot \cdot \cdot + n_k.$$

Then the number of **distinguishable permutations** of the n objects is

$$\frac{n!}{n_1! \cdot n_2! \cdot n_3! \cdot \cdot \cdot \cdot \cdot n_k!}.$$

Example 7 Distinguishable Permutations

In how many distinguishable ways can the letters in BANANA be written?

Solution

This word has six letters, of which three are A's, two are N's, and one is a B. So, the number of distinguishable ways the letters can be written is

$$\frac{n!}{n_1! \cdot n_2! \cdot n_3!} = \frac{6!}{3! \cdot 2! \cdot 1!}$$

$$= \frac{6 \cdot 5 \cdot 4 \cdot \cancel{3!}}{\cancel{3!} \cdot 2!}$$

$$= 60.$$

The 60 different distinguishable permutations are as follows.

AAABNN	AAANBN	AAANNB	AABANN	AABNAN	AABNNA
AANABN	AANANB	AANBAN	AANBNA	AANNAB	AANNBA
ABAANN	ABANAN	ABANNA	ABNAAN	ABNANA	ABNNAA
ANAABN	ANAANB	ANABAN	ANABNA	ANANAB	ANANBA
ANBAAN	ANBANA	ANBNAA	ANNAAB	ANNABA	ANNBAA
BAAANN	BAANAN	BAANNA	BANAAN	BANANA	BANNAA
BNAAAN	BNAANA	BNANAA	BNNAAA	NAAABN	NAAANB
NAABAN	NAABNA	NAANAB	NAANBA	NABAAN	NABANA
NABNAA	NANAAB	NANABA	NANBAA	NBAAAN	NBAANA
NBANAA	NBNAAA	NNAAAB	NNAABA	NNABAA	NNBAAA

CHECKPOINT Now try Exercise 45.

Combinations

When you count the number of possible permutations of a set of elements, *order* is important. As a final topic in this section, you will look at a method of selecting subsets of a larger set in which order is *not* important. Such subsets are called **combinations of n elements taken r at a time.** For instance, the combinations

$$\{A, B, C\} \qquad \text{and} \qquad \{B, A, C\}$$

are equivalent because both sets contain the same three elements, and the order in which the elements are listed is not important. So, you would count only one of the two sets. A common example of how a combination occurs is a card game in which the player is free to reorder the cards after they have been dealt.

Example 8 Combinations of n Elements Taken r at a Time

In how many different ways can three letters be chosen from the letters A, B, C, D, and E? (The order of the three letters is not important.)

Solution

The following subsets represent the different combinations of three letters that can be chosen from the five letters.

$\{A, B, C\}$ $\{A, B, D\}$
$\{A, B, E\}$ $\{A, C, D\}$
$\{A, C, E\}$ $\{A, D, E\}$
$\{B, C, D\}$ $\{B, C, E\}$
$\{B, D, E\}$ $\{C, D, E\}$

From this list, you can conclude that there are 10 different ways that three letters can be chosen from five letters.

CHECKPOINT Now try Exercise 55.

Combinations of n Elements Taken r at a Time

The number of combinations of n elements taken r at a time is

$${}_nC_r = \frac{n!}{(n-r)!r!} \quad \text{which is equivalent to} \quad {}_nC_r = \frac{{}_nP_r}{r!}.$$

Note that the formula for ${}_nC_r$ is the same one given for binomial coefficients. To see how this formula is used, solve the counting problem in Example 8. In that problem, you are asked to find the number of combinations of five elements taken three at a time. So, $n = 5$, $r = 3$, and the number of combinations is

$${}_5C_3 = \frac{5!}{2!3!} = \frac{5 \cdot \overset{2}{\cancel{4}} \cdot \cancel{3!}}{\cancel{2} \cdot 1 \cdot \cancel{3!}} = 10$$

which is the same answer obtained in Example 8.

A ♥	A ♦	A ♣	A ♠
2 ♥	2 ♦	2 ♣	2 ♠
3 ♥	3 ♦	3 ♣	3 ♠
4 ♥	4 ♦	4 ♣	4 ♠
5 ♥	5 ♦	5 ♣	5 ♠
6 ♥	6 ♦	6 ♣	6 ♠
7 ♥	7 ♦	7 ♣	7 ♠
8 ♥	8 ♦	8 ♣	8 ♠
9 ♥	9 ♦	9 ♣	9 ♠
10 ♥	10 ♦	10 ♣	10 ♠
J ♥	J ♦	J ♣	J ♠
Q ♥	Q ♦	Q ♣	Q ♠
K ♥	K ♦	K ♣	K ♠

FIGURE 9.7 *Standard deck of playing cards*

Example 9 Counting Card Hands

A standard poker hand consists of five cards dealt from a deck of 52 (see Figure 9.7). How many different poker hands are possible? (After the cards are dealt, the player may reorder them, and so order is not important.)

Solution

You can find the number of different poker hands by using the formula for the number of combinations of 52 elements taken five at a time, as follows.

$$
\begin{aligned}
{}_{52}C_5 &= \frac{52!}{(52-5)!5!} \\
&= \frac{52!}{47!5!} \\
&= \frac{52 \cdot 51 \cdot 50 \cdot 49 \cdot 48 \cdot \cancel{47!}}{5 \cdot 4 \cdot 3 \cdot 2 \cdot 1 \cdot \cancel{47!}} \\
&= 2{,}598{,}960
\end{aligned}
$$

CHECKPOINT Now try Exercise 63.

Example 10 Forming a Team

You are forming a 12-member swim team from 10 girls and 15 boys. The team must consist of five girls and seven boys. How many different 12-member teams are possible?

Solution

There are ${}_{10}C_5$ ways of choosing five girls. The are ${}_{15}C_7$ ways of choosing seven boys. By the Fundamental Counting Principal, there are ${}_{10}C_5 \cdot {}_{15}C_7$ ways of choosing five girls and seven boys.

$$
\begin{aligned}
{}_{10}C_5 \cdot {}_{15}C_7 &= \frac{10!}{5! \cdot 5!} \cdot \frac{15!}{8! \cdot 7!} \\
&= 252 \cdot 6435 \\
&= 1{,}621{,}620
\end{aligned}
$$

So, there are 1,621,620 12-member swim teams possible.

CHECKPOINT Now try Exercise 65.

When solving problems involving counting principles, you need to be able to distinguish among the various counting principles in order to determine which is necessary to solve the problem correctly. To do this, ask yourself the following questions.

1. Is the order of the elements important? *Permutation*
2. Are the chosen elements a subset of a larger set in which order is not important? *Combination*
3. Does the problem involve two or more separate events? *Fundamental Counting Principle*

9.6 Exercises

VOCABULARY CHECK: Fill in the blanks.

1. The ________ ________ ________ states that if there are m_1 ways for one event to occur and m_2 ways for a second event to occur, there are $m_1 \cdot m_2$ ways for both events to occur.
2. An ordering of n elements is called a ________ of the elements.
3. The number of permutations of n elements taken r at a time is given by the formula ________.
4. The number of ________ ________ of n objects is given by $\dfrac{n!}{n_1!n_2!n_3! \cdot \cdot \cdot n_k!}$.
5. When selecting subsets of a larger set in which order is not important, you are finding the number of ________ of n elements taken r at a time.

Random Selection **In Exercises 1–8, determine the number of ways a computer can randomly generate one or more such integers from 1 through 12.**

1. An odd integer
2. An even integer
3. A prime integer
4. An integer that is greater than 9
5. An integer that is divisible by 4
6. An integer that is divisible by 3
7. Two *distinct* integers whose sum is 9
8. Two *distinct* integers whose sum is 8

9. ***Entertainment Systems*** A customer can choose one of three amplifiers, one of two compact disc players, and one of five speaker models for an entertainment system. Determine the number of possible system configurations.

10. ***Job Applicants*** A college needs two additional faculty members: a chemist and a statistician. In how many ways can these positions be filled if there are five applicants for the chemistry position and three applicants for the statistics position?

11. ***Course Schedule*** A college student is preparing a course schedule for the next semester. The student may select one of two mathematics courses, one of three science courses, and one of five courses from the social sciences and humanities. How many schedules are possible?

12. ***Aircraft Boarding*** Eight people are boarding an aircraft. Two have tickets for first class and board before those in the economy class. In how many ways can the eight people board the aircraft?

13. ***True-False Exam*** In how many ways can a six-question true-false exam be answered? (Assume that no questions are omitted.)

14. ***True-False Exam*** In how many ways can a 12-question true-false exam be answered? (Assume that no questions are omitted.)

15. ***License Plate Numbers*** In the state of Pennsylvania, each standard automobile license plate number consists of three letters followed by a four-digit number. How many distinct license plate numbers can be formed in Pennsylvania?

16. ***License Plate Numbers*** In a certain state, each automobile license plate number consists of two letters followed by a four-digit number. To avoid confusion between "O" and "zero" and between "I" and "one," the letters "O" and "I" are not used. How many distinct license plate numbers can be formed in this state?

17. ***Three-Digit Numbers*** How many three-digit numbers can be formed under each condition?
    (a) The leading digit cannot be zero.
    (b) The leading digit cannot be zero and no repetition of digits is allowed.
    (c) The leading digit cannot be zero and the number must be a multiple of 5.
    (d) The number is at least 400.

18. ***Four-Digit Numbers*** How many four-digit numbers can be formed under each condition?
    (a) The leading digit cannot be zero.
    (b) The leading digit cannot be zero and no repetition of digits is allowed.
    (c) The leading digit cannot be zero and the number must be less than 5000.
    (d) The leading digit cannot be zero and the number must be even.

19. ***Combination Lock*** A combination lock will open when the right choice of three numbers (from 1 to 40, inclusive) is selected. How many different lock combinations are possible?

20. ***Combination Lock*** A combination lock will open when the right choice of three numbers (from 1 to 50, inclusive) is selected. How many different lock combinations are possible?

21. ***Concert Seats*** Four couples have reserved seats in a row for a concert. In how many different ways can they be seated if

(a) there are no seating restrictions?

(b) the two members of each couple wish to sit together?

22. ***Single File*** In how many orders can four girls and four boys walk through a doorway single file if

(a) there are no restrictions?

(b) the girls walk through before the boys?

In Exercises 23–28, evaluate $_nP_r$.

23. $_4P_4$ **24.** $_5P_5$

25. $_8P_3$ **26.** $_{20}P_2$

27. $_5P_4$ **28.** $_7P_4$

In Exercises 29 and 30, solve for *n*.

29. $14 \cdot {_nP_3} = {_{n+2}P_4}$ **30.** ${_nP_5} = 18 \cdot {_{n-2}P_4}$

In Exercises 31–36, evaluate using a graphing utility.

31. $_{20}P_5$ **32.** $_{100}P_5$

33. $_{100}P_3$ **34.** $_{10}P_8$

35. $_{20}C_5$ **36.** $_{10}C_7$

37. ***Posing for a Photograph*** In how many ways can five children posing for a photograph line up in a row?

38. ***Riding in a Car*** In how many ways can six people sit in a six-passenger car?

39. ***Choosing Officers*** From a pool of 12 candidates, the offices of president, vice-president, secretary, and treasurer will be filled. In how many different ways can the offices be filled?

40. ***Assembly Line Production*** There are four processes involved in assembling a product, and these processes can be performed in any order. The management wants to test each order to determine which is the least time-consuming. How many different orders will have to be tested?

In Exercises 41–44, find the number of distinguishable permutations of the group of letters.

41. A, A, G, E, E, E, M **42.** B, B, B, T, T, T, T, T

43. A, L, G, E, B, R, A **44.** M, I, S, S, I, S, S, I, P, P, I

45. Write all permutations of the letters A, B, C, and D.

46. Write all permutations of the letters A, B, C, and D if the letters B and C must remain between the letters A and D.

47. ***Batting Order*** A baseball coach is creating a nine-player batting order by selecting from a team of 15 players. How many different batting orders are possible?

48. ***Athletics*** Six sprinters have qualified for the finals in the 100-meter dash at the NCAA national track meet. In how many ways can the sprinters come in first, second, and third? (Assume there are no ties.)

49. ***Jury Selection*** From a group of 40 people, a jury of 12 people is to be selected. In how many different ways can the jury be selected?

50. ***Committee Members*** As of January 2005, the U.S. Senate Committee on Indian Affairs had 14 members. Assuming party affiliation was not a factor in selection, how many different committees were possible from the 100 U.S. senators?

51. Write all possible selections of two letters that can be formed from the letters A, B, C, D, E, and F. (The order of the two letters is not important.)

52. ***Forming an Experimental Group*** In order to conduct an experiment, five students are randomly selected from a class of 20. How many different groups of five students are possible?

53. ***Lottery Choices*** In the Massachusetts Mass Cash game, a player chooses five distinct numbers from 1 to 35. In how many ways can a player select the five numbers?

54. ***Lottery Choices*** In the Louisiana Lotto game, a player chooses six distinct numbers from 1 to 40. In how many ways can a player select the six numbers?

55. ***Defective Units*** A shipment of 10 microwave ovens contains three defective units. In how many ways can a vending company purchase four of these units and receive (a) all good units, (b) two good units, and (c) at least two good units?

56. ***Interpersonal Relationships*** The complexity of interpersonal relationships increases dramatically as the size of a group increases. Determine the numbers of different two-person relationships in groups of people of sizes (a) 3, (b) 8, (c) 12, and (d) 20.

57. ***Poker Hand*** You are dealt five cards from an ordinary deck of 52 playing cards. In how many ways can you get (a) a full house and (b) a five-card combination containing two jacks and three aces? (A full house consists of three of one kind and two of another. For example, A-A-A-5-5 and K-K-K-10-10 are full houses.)

58. ***Job Applicants*** A toy manufacturer interviews eight people for four openings in the research and development department of the company. Three of the eight people are women. If all eight are qualified, in how many ways can the employer fill the four positions if (a) the selection is random and (b) exactly two selections are women?

59. ***Forming a Committee*** A six-member research committee at a local college is to be formed having one administrator, three faculty members, and two students. There are seven administrators, 12 faculty members, and 20 students in contention for the committee. How many six-member committees are possible?

60. ***Law Enforcement*** A police department uses computer imaging to create digital photographs of alleged perpetrators from eyewitness accounts. One software package contains 195 hairlines, 99 sets of eyes and eyebrows, 89 noses, 105 mouths, and 74 chins and cheek structures.

(a) Find the possible number of different faces that the software could create.

(b) A eyewitness can clearly recall the hairline and eyes and eyebrows of a suspect. How many different faces can be produced with this information?

Geometry **In Exercises 61–64, find the number of diagonals of the polygon. (A line segment connecting any two nonadjacent vertices is called a *diagonal* of the polygon.)**

61. Pentagon **62.** Hexagon

63. Octagon **64.** Decagon (10 sides)

Model It

65. ***Lottery*** Powerball is a lottery game that is operated by the Multi-State Lottery Association and is played in 27 states, Washington D.C., and the U.S. Virgin Islands. The game is played by drawing five white balls out of a drum of 53 white balls (numbered 1–53) and one red powerball out of a drum of 42 red balls (numbered 1–42). The jackpot is won by matching all five white balls in any order and the red powerball.

(a) Find the possible number of winning Powerball numbers.

(b) Find the possible number of winning Powerball numbers if the jackpot is won by matching all five white balls in order and the red power ball.

(c) Compare the results of part (a) with a state lottery in which a jackpot is won by matching six balls from a drum of 53 balls.

66. ***Permutations or Combinations?*** Decide whether each scenario should be counted using permutations or combinations. Explain your reasoning.

(a) Number of ways 10 people can line up in a row for concert tickets

(b) Number of different arrangements of three types of flowers from an array of 20 types

(c) Number of three-digit pin numbers for a debit card

(d) Number of two-scoop ice cream cones created from 31 different flavors

Synthesis

True or False? **In Exercises 67 and 68, determine whether the statement is true or false. Justify your answer.**

67. The number of letter pairs that can be formed in any order from any of the first 13 letters in the alphabet (A–M) is an example of a permutation.

68. The number of permutations of n elements can be determined by using the Fundamental Counting Principle.

69. What is the relationship between ${}_nC_r$ and ${}_nC_{n-r}$?

70. Without calculating the numbers, determine which of the following is greater. Explain.

(a) The number of combinations of 10 elements taken six at a time

(b) The number of permutations of 10 elements taken six at a time

Proof **In Exercises 71–74, prove the identity.**

71. ${}_nP_{n-1} = {}_nP_n$ **72.** ${}_nC_n = {}_nC_0$

73. ${}_nC_{n-1} = {}_nC_1$ **74.** ${}_nC_r = \dfrac{{}_nP_r}{r!}$

75. ***Think About It*** Can your calculator evaluate ${}_{100}P_{80}$? If not, explain why.

76. ***Writing*** Explain in words the meaning of ${}_nP_r$.

Skills Review

In Exercises 77–80, evaluate the function at each specified value of the independent variable and simplify.

77. $f(x) = 3x^2 + 8$

(a) $f(3)$ (b) $f(0)$ (c) $f(-5)$

78. $g(x) = \sqrt{x-3} + 2$

(a) $g(3)$ (b) $g(7)$ (c) $g(x+1)$

79. $f(x) = -|x-5| + 6$

(a) $f(-5)$ (b) $f(-1)$ (c) $f(11)$

80. $f(x) = \begin{cases} x^2 - 2x + 5, & x \le -4 \\ -x^2 - 2, & x > -4 \end{cases}$

(a) $f(-4)$ (b) $f(-1)$ (c) $f(-20)$

In Exercises 81–84, solve the equation. Round your answer to two decimal places, if necessary.

81. $\sqrt{x-3} = x - 6$ **82.** $\dfrac{4}{t} + \dfrac{3}{2t} = 1$

83. $\log_2(x-3) = 5$ **84.** $e^{x/3} = 16$

9.7 Probability

What you should learn

- Find the probabilities of events.
- Find the probabilities of mutually exclusive events.
- Find the probabilities of independent events.
- Find the probability of the complement of an event.

Why you should learn it

Probability applies to many games of chance. For instance, in Exercise 55, on page 712, you will calculate probabilities that relate to the game of roulette.

Hank de Lespinasse/The Image Bank

The Probability of an Event

Any happening for which the result is uncertain is called an **experiment.** The possible results of the experiment are **outcomes,** the set of all possible outcomes of the experiment is the **sample space** of the experiment, and any subcollection of a sample space is an **event.**

For instance, when a six-sided die is tossed, the sample space can be represented by the numbers 1 through 6. For this experiment, each of the outcomes is *equally likely*.

To describe sample spaces in such a way that each outcome is equally likely, you must sometimes distinguish between or among various outcomes in ways that appear artificial. Example 1 illustrates such a situation.

Example 1 Finding a Sample Space

Find the sample space for each of the following.

a. One coin is tossed.

b. Two coins are tossed.

c. Three coins are tossed.

Solution

a. Because the coin will land either heads up (denoted by H) or tails up (denoted by T), the sample space is

$$S = \{H, T\}.$$

b. Because either coin can land heads up or tails up, the possible outcomes are as follows.

HH = heads up on both coins

HT = heads up on first coin and tails up on second coin

TH = tails up on first coin and heads up on second coin

TT = tails up on both coins

So, the sample space is

$$S = \{HH, HT, TH, TT\}.$$

Note that this list distinguishes between the two cases HT and TH, even though these two outcomes appear to be similar.

c. Following the notation of part (b), the sample space is

$$S = \{HHH, HHT, HTH, HTT, THH, THT, TTH, TTT\}.$$

Note that this list distinguishes among the cases HHT, HTH, and THH, and among the cases HTT, THT, and TTH.

✓CHECKPOINT Now try Exercise 1.

Exploration

Toss two coins 100 times and write down the number of heads that occur on each toss (0, 1, or 2). How many times did two heads occur? How many times would you expect two heads to occur if you did the experiment 1000 times?

To calculate the probability of an event, count the number of outcomes in the event and in the sample space. The *number of outcomes* in event E is denoted by $n(E)$, and the number of outcomes in the sample space S is denoted by $n(S)$. The probability that event E will occur is given by $n(E)/n(S)$.

The Probability of an Event

If an event E has $n(E)$ equally likely outcomes and its sample space S has $n(S)$ equally likely outcomes, the **probability** of event E is

$$P(E) = \frac{n(E)}{n(S)}.$$

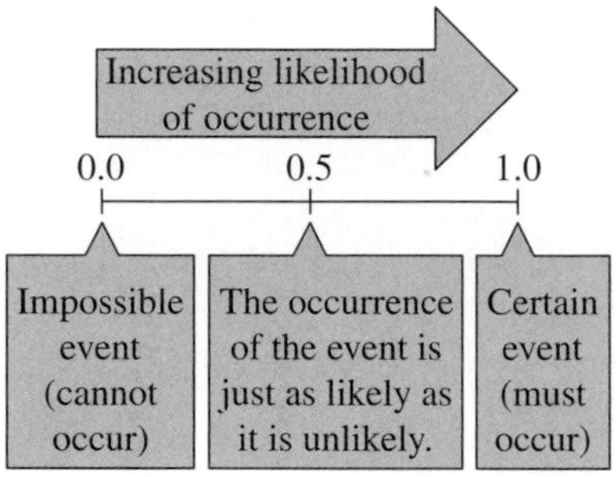

FIGURE 9.8

Because the number of outcomes in an event must be less than or equal to the number of outcomes in the sample space, the probability of an event must be a number between 0 and 1. That is,

$$0 \le P(E) \le 1$$

as indicated in Figure 9.8. If $P(E) = 0$, event E *cannot occur*, and E is called an **impossible event.** If $P(E) = 1$, event E *must occur*, and E is called a **certain event.**

Example 2 Finding the Probability of an Event

a. Two coins are tossed. What is the probability that both land heads up?

b. A card is drawn from a standard deck of playing cards. What is the probability that it is an ace?

Solution

a. Following the procedure in Example 1(b), let

$$E = \{HH\}$$

and

$$S = \{HH, HT, TH, TT\}.$$

The probability of getting two heads is

$$P(E) = \frac{n(E)}{n(S)} = \frac{1}{4}.$$

b. Because there are 52 cards in a standard deck of playing cards and there are four aces (one in each suit), the probability of drawing an ace is

$$P(E) = \frac{n(E)}{n(S)}$$

$$= \frac{4}{52}$$

$$= \frac{1}{13}.$$

CHECKPOINT Now try Exercise 11.

STUDY TIP

You can write a probability as a fraction, decimal, or percent. For instance, in Example 2(a), the probability of getting two heads can be written as $\frac{1}{4}$, 0.25, or 25%.

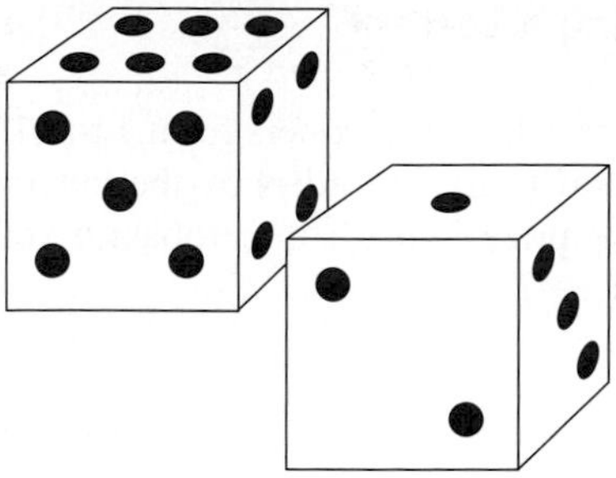

FIGURE 9.9

Example 3 **Finding the Probability of an Event**

Two six-sided dice are tossed. What is the probability that the total of the two dice is 7? (See Figure 9.9.)

Solution

Because there are six possible outcomes on each die, you can use the Fundamental Counting Principle to conclude that there are $6 \cdot 6$ or 36 different outcomes when two dice are tossed. To find the probability of rolling a total of 7, you must first count the number of ways in which this can occur.

First die	Second die
1	6
2	5
3	4
4	3
5	2
6	1

So, a total of 7 can be rolled in six ways, which means that the probability of rolling a 7 is

$$P(E) = \frac{n(E)}{n(S)} = \frac{6}{36} = \frac{1}{6}.$$

CHECKPOINT Now try Exercise 15.

STUDY TIP

You could have written out each sample space in Examples 2 and 3 and simply counted the outcomes in the desired events. For larger sample spaces, however, you should use the counting principles discussed in Section 9.6.

Example 4 **Finding the Probability of an Event**

Twelve-sided dice, as shown in Figure 9.10, can be constructed (in the shape of regular dodecahedrons) such that each of the numbers from 1 to 6 appears twice on each die. Prove that these dice can be used in any game requiring ordinary six-sided dice without changing the probabilities of different outcomes.

Solution

For an ordinary six-sided die, each of the numbers 1, 2, 3, 4, 5, and 6 occurs only once, so the probability of any particular number coming up is

$$P(E) = \frac{n(E)}{n(S)} = \frac{1}{6}.$$

For one of the 12-sided dice, each number occurs twice, so the probability of any particular number coming up is

$$P(E) = \frac{n(E)}{n(S)} = \frac{2}{12} = \frac{1}{6}.$$

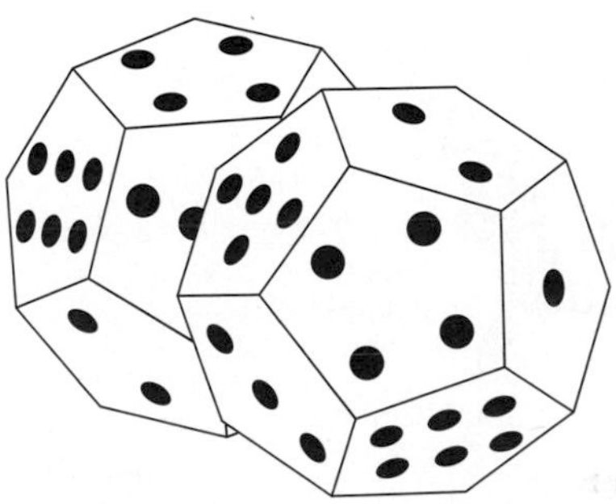

FIGURE 9.10

CHECKPOINT Now try Exercise 17.

Example 5 The Probability of Winning a Lottery

In the Arizona state lottery, a player chooses six different numbers from 1 to 41. If these six numbers match the six numbers drawn (in any order) by the lottery commission, the player wins (or shares) the top prize. What is the probability of winning the top prize if the player buys one ticket?

Solution

To find the number of elements in the sample space, use the formula for the number of combinations of 41 elements taken six at a time.

$$\begin{aligned} n(S) &= {}_{41}C_6 \\ &= \frac{41 \cdot 40 \cdot 39 \cdot 38 \cdot 37 \cdot 36}{6 \cdot 5 \cdot 4 \cdot 3 \cdot 2 \cdot 1} \\ &= 4{,}496{,}388 \end{aligned}$$

If a person buys only one ticket, the probability of winning is

$$P(E) = \frac{n(E)}{n(S)} = \frac{1}{4{,}496{,}388}.$$

CHECKPOINT Now try Exercise 21.

Example 6 Random Selection

The numbers of colleges and universities in various regions of the United States in 2003 are shown in Figure 9.11. One institution is selected at random. What is the probability that the institution is in one of the three southern regions? (Source: National Center for Education Statistics)

Solution

From the figure, the total number of colleges and universities is 4163. Because there are $700 + 284 + 386 = 1370$ colleges and universities in the three southern regions, the probability that the institution is in one of these regions is

$$P(E) = \frac{n(E)}{n(S)} = \frac{1370}{4163} \approx 0.329.$$

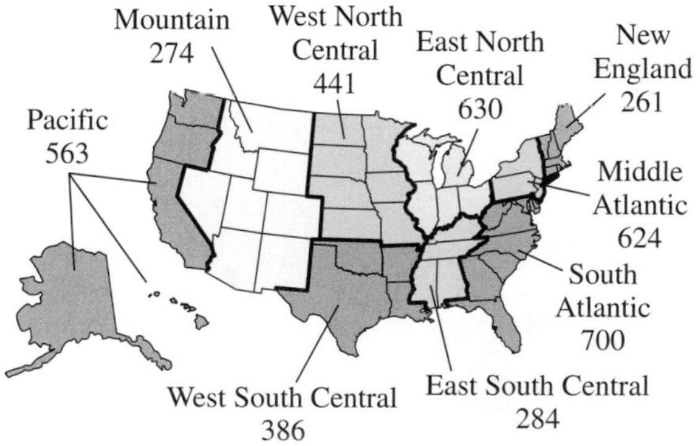

FIGURE 9.11

CHECKPOINT Now try Exercise 33.

Mutually Exclusive Events

Two events A and B (from the same sample space) are **mutually exclusive** if A and B have no outcomes in common. In the terminology of sets, the intersection of A and B is the empty set, which is written as

$$P(A \cap B) = 0.$$

For instance, if two dice are tossed, the event A of rolling a total of 6 and the event B of rolling a total of 9 are mutually exclusive. To find the probability that one or the other of two mutually exclusive events will occur, you can *add* their individual probabilities.

Probability of the Union of Two Events

If A and B are events in the same sample space, the probability of A or B occurring is given by

$$P(A \cup B) = P(A) + P(B) - P(A \cap B).$$

If A and B are mutually exclusive, then

$$P(A \cup B) = P(A) + P(B).$$

Example 7 **The Probability of a Union of Events**

One card is selected from a standard deck of 52 playing cards. What is the probability that the card is either a heart or a face card?

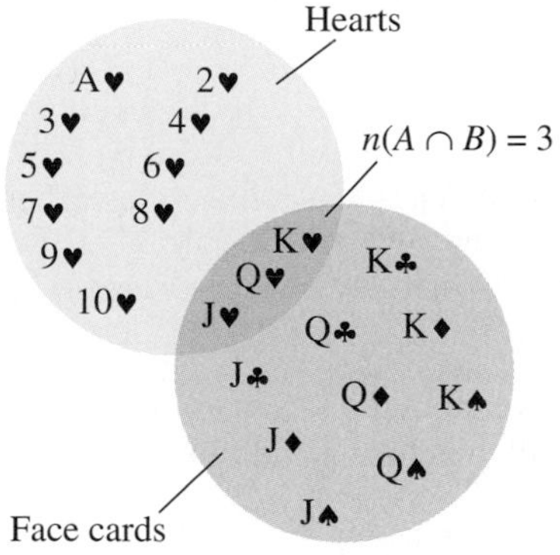

FIGURE 9.12

Solution

Because the deck has 13 hearts, the probability of selecting a heart (event A) is

$$P(A) = \frac{13}{52}.$$

Similarly, because the deck has 12 face cards, the probability of selecting a face card (event B) is

$$P(B) = \frac{12}{52}.$$

Because three of the cards are hearts *and* face cards (see Figure 9.12), it follows that

$$P(A \cap B) = \frac{3}{52}.$$

Finally, applying the formula for the probability of the union of two events, you can conclude that the probability of selecting a heart or a face card is

$$P(A \cup B) = P(A) + P(B) - P(A \cap B)$$

$$= \frac{13}{52} + \frac{12}{52} - \frac{3}{52} = \frac{22}{52} \approx 0.423.$$

✓CHECKPOINT Now try Exercise 45.

Example 8 Probability of Mutually Exclusive Events

The personnel department of a company has compiled data on the numbers of employees who have been with the company for various periods of time. The results are shown in the table.

Years of service	Number of employees
0–4	157
5–9	89
10–14	74
15–19	63
20–24	42
25–29	38
30–34	37
35–39	21
40–44	8

If an employee is chosen at random, what is the probability that the employee has (a) 4 or fewer years of service and (b) 9 or fewer years of service?

Solution

a. To begin, add the number of employees to find that the total is 529. Next, let event A represent choosing an employee with 0 to 4 years of service. Then the probability of choosing an employee who has 4 or fewer years of service is

$$P(A) = \frac{157}{529} \approx 0.297.$$

b. Let event B represent choosing an employee with 5 to 9 years of service. Then

$$P(B) = \frac{89}{529}.$$

Because event A from part (a) and event B have no outcomes in common, you can conclude that these two events are mutually exclusive and that

$$\begin{aligned} P(A \cup B) &= P(A) + P(B) \\ &= \frac{157}{529} + \frac{89}{529} \\ &= \frac{246}{529} \\ &\approx 0.465. \end{aligned}$$

So, the probability of choosing an employee who has 9 or fewer years of service is about 0.465.

CHECKPOINT Now try Exercise 47.

Independent Events

Two events are **independent** if the occurrence of one has no effect on the occurrence of the other. For instance, rolling a total of 12 with two six-sided dice has no effect on the outcome of future rolls of the dice. To find the probability that two independent events will occur, *multiply* the probabilities of each.

Probability of Independent Events

If A and B are independent events, the probability that both A and B will occur is

$$P(A \text{ and } B) = P(A) \cdot P(B).$$

Example 9 Probability of Independent Events

A random number generator on a computer selects three integers from 1 to 20. What is the probability that all three numbers are less than or equal to 5?

Solution

The probability of selecting a number from 1 to 5 is

$$P(A) = \frac{5}{20} = \frac{1}{4}.$$

So, the probability that all three numbers are less than or equal to 5 is

$$P(A) \cdot P(A) \cdot P(A) = \left(\frac{1}{4}\right)\left(\frac{1}{4}\right)\left(\frac{1}{4}\right)$$

$$= \frac{1}{64}.$$

CHECKPOINT Now try Exercise 48.

Example 10 Probability of Independent Events

In 2004, approximately 20% of the adult population of the United States got their news from the Internet every day. In a survey, 10 people were chosen at random from the adult population. What is the probability that all 10 got their news from the Internet every day? (Source: The Gallup Poll)

Solution

Let A represent choosing an adult who gets the news from the Internet every day. The probability of choosing an adult who got his or her news from the Internet every day is 0.20, the probability of choosing a second adult who got his or her news from the Internet every day is 0.20, and so on. Because these events are independent, you can conclude that the probability that all 10 people got their news from the Internet every day is

$$[P(A)]^{10} = (0.20)^{10} \approx 0.0000001.$$

CHECKPOINT Now try Exercise 49.

Exploration

You are in a class with 22 other people. What is the probability that at least two out of the 23 people will have a birthday on the same day of the year?

The complement of the probability that at least two people have the same birthday is the probability that all 23 birthdays are different. So, first find the probability that all 23 people have different birthdays and then find the complement.

Now, determine the probability that in a room with 50 people at least two people have the same birthday.

The Complement of an Event

The **complement of an event** A is the collection of all outcomes in the sample space that are *not* in A. The complement of event A is denoted by A'. Because $P(A \text{ or } A') = 1$ and because A and A' are mutually exclusive, it follows that $P(A) + P(A') = 1$. So, the probability of A' is

$$P(A') = 1 - P(A).$$

For instance, if the probability of *winning* a certain game is

$$P(A) = \frac{1}{4}$$

the probability of *losing* the game is

$$P(A') = 1 - \frac{1}{4}$$
$$= \frac{3}{4}.$$

Probability of a Complement

Let A be an event and let A' be its complement. If the probability of A is $P(A)$, the probability of the complement is

$$P(A') = 1 - P(A).$$

Example 11 Finding the Probability of a Complement

A manufacturer has determined that a machine averages one faulty unit for every 1000 it produces. What is the probability that an order of 200 units will have one or more faulty units?

Solution

To solve this problem as stated, you would need to find the probabilities of having exactly one faulty unit, exactly two faulty units, exactly three faulty units, and so on. However, using complements, you can simply find the probability that all units are perfect and then subtract this value from 1. Because the probability that any given unit is perfect is 999/1000, the probability that all 200 units are perfect is

$$P(A) = \left(\frac{999}{1000}\right)^{200}$$
$$\approx 0.819.$$

So, the probability that at least one unit is faulty is

$$P(A') = 1 - P(A)$$
$$\approx 1 - 0.819.$$
$$= 0.181$$

✓CHECKPOINT Now try Exercise 51.

9.7 Exercises

VOCABULARY CHECK:

In Exercises 1–7, fill in the blanks.

1. An ________ is an event whose result is uncertain, and the possible results of the event are called ________.
2. The set of all possible outcomes of an experiment is called the ________ ________.
3. To determine the ________ of an event, you can use the formula $P(E) = \frac{n(E)}{n(S)}$, where $n(E)$ is the number of outcomes in the event and $n(S)$ is the number of outcomes in the sample space.
4. If $P(E) = 0$, then E is an ________ event, and if $P(E) = 1$, then E is a ________ event.
5. If two events from the same sample space have no outcomes in common, then the two events are ________ ________.
6. If the occurrence of one event has no effect on the occurrence of a second event, then the events are ________.
7. The ________ of an event A is the collection of all outcomes in the sample space that are not in A.
8. Match the probability formula with the correct probability name.

(a) Probability of the union of two events	(i) $P(A \cup B) = P(A) + P(B)$
(b) Probability of mutually exclusive events	(ii) $P(A') = 1 - P(A)$
(c) Probability of independent events	(iii) $P(A \cup B) = P(A) + P(B) - P(A \cap B)$
(d) Probability of a complement	(iv) $P(A \text{ and } B) = P(A) \cdot P(B)$

In Exercises 1–6, determine the sample space for the experiment.

1. A coin and a six-sided die are tossed.
2. A six-sided die is tossed twice and the sum of the points is recorded.
3. A taste tester has to rank three varieties of yogurt, A, B, and C, according to preference.
4. Two marbles are selected from a bag containing two red marbles, two blue marbles, and one yellow marble. The color of each marble is recorded.
5. Two county supervisors are selected from five supervisors, A, B, C, D, and E, to study a recycling plan.
6. A sales representative makes presentations about a product in three homes per day. In each home, there may be a sale (denote by S) or there may be no sale (denote by F).

Tossing a Coin **In Exercises 7–10, find the probability for the experiment of tossing a coin three times. Use the sample space $S = \{HHH, HHT, HTH, HTT, THH, THT, TTH, TTT\}$.**

7. The probability of getting exactly one tail
8. The probability of getting a head on the first toss
9. The probability of getting at least one head
10. The probability of getting at least two heads

Drawing a Card **In Exercises 11–14, find the probability for the experiment of selecting one card from a standard deck of 52 playing cards.**

11. The card is a face card.
12. The card is not a face card.
13. The card is a red face card.
14. The card is a 6 or lower. (Aces are low.)

Tossing a Die **In Exercises 15–20, find the probability for the experiment of tossing a six-sided die twice.**

15. The sum is 4.
16. The sum is at least 7.
17. The sum is less than 11.
18. The sum is 2, 3, or 12.
19. The sum is odd and no more than 7.
20. The sum is odd or prime.

Drawing Marbles **In Exercises 21–24, find the probability for the experiment of drawing two marbles (without replacement) from a bag containing one green, two yellow, and three red marbles.**

21. Both marbles are red.
22. Both marbles are yellow.
23. Neither marble is yellow.
24. The marbles are of different colors.

In Exercises 25–28, you are given the probability that an event will happen. Find the probability that the event *will* not happen.

25. $P(E) = 0.7$

26. $P(E) = 0.36$

27. $P(E) = \frac{1}{4}$

28. $P(E) = \frac{2}{3}$

In Exercises 29–32, you are given the probability that an event *will not* happen. Find the probability that the event *will* happen.

29. $P(E') = 0.14$

30. $P(E') = 0.92$

31. $P(E') = \frac{17}{35}$

32. $P(E') = \frac{61}{100}$

33. ***Data Analysis*** A study of the effectiveness of a flu vaccine was conducted with a sample of 500 people. Some participants in the study were given no vaccine, some were given one injection, and some were given two injections. The results of the study are listed in the table.

	No vaccine	One injection	Two injections	Total
Flu	7	2	13	22
No flu	149	52	277	478
Total	156	54	290	500

A person is selected at random from the sample. Find the specified probability.

(a) The person had two injections.

(b) The person did not get the flu.

(c) The person got the flu and had one injection.

34. ***Data Analysis*** One hundred college students were interviewed to determine their political party affiliations and whether they favored a balanced-budget amendment to the Constitution. The results of the study are listed in the table, where D represents Democrat and R represents Republican.

	Favor	Not Favor	Unsure	Total
D	23	25	7	55
R	32	9	4	45
Total	55	34	11	100

A person is selected at random from the sample. Find the probability that the described person is selected.

(a) A person who doesn't favor the amendment

(b) A Republican

(c) A Democrat who favors the amendment

35. ***Graphical Reasoning*** The figure shows the results of a recent survey in which 1011 adults were asked to grade U.S. public schools. (Source: Phi Delta Kappa/Gallup Poll)

Grading Public Schools

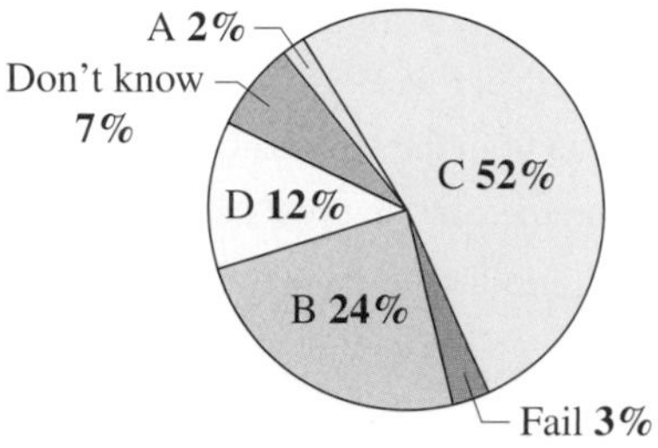

(a) Estimate the number of adults who gave U.S. public schools a B.

(b) An adult is selected at random. What is the probabilty that the adult will give the U.S. public schools an A?

(c) An adult is selected at random. What is the probabilty the adult will give the U.S. public schools a C or a D?

36. ***Graphical Reasoning*** The figure shows the results of a survey in which auto racing fans listed their favorite type of racing. (Source: ESPN Sports Poll/TNS Sports)

Favorite Type of Racing

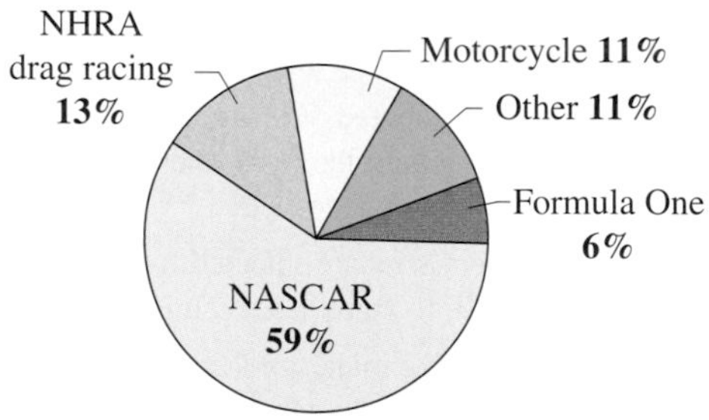

(a) What is the probability that an auto racing fan selected at random lists NASCAR racing as his or her favorite type of racing?

(b) What is the probability that an auto racing fan selected at random lists Formula One or motorcycle racing as his or her favorite type of racing?

(c) What is the probability that an auto racing fan selected at random does *not* list NHRA drag racing as his or her favorite type of racing?

37. ***Alumni Association*** A college sends a survey to selected members of the class of 2006. Of the 1254 people who graduated that year, 672 are women, of whom 124 went on to graduate school. Of the 582 male graduates, 198 went on to graduate school. An alumni member is selected at random. What are the probabilities that the person is (a) female, (b) male, and (c) female and did not attend graduate school?

38. ***Education*** In a high school graduating class of 202 students, 95 are on the honor roll. Of these, 71 are going on to college, and of the other 107 students, 53 are going on to college. A student is selected at random from the class. What are the probabilities that the person chosen is (a) going to college, (b) not going to college, and (c) on the honor roll, but not going to college?

39. ***Winning an Election*** Taylor, Moore, and Jenkins are candidates for public office. It is estimated that Moore and Jenkins have about the same probability of winning, and Taylor is believed to be twice as likely to win as either of the others. Find the probability of each candidate winning the election.

40. ***Winning an Election*** Three people have been nominated for president of a class. From a poll, it is estimated that the first candidate has a 37% chance of winning and the second candidate has a 44% chance of winning. What is the probability that the third candidate will win?

In Exercises 41–52, the sample spaces are large and you should use the counting principles discussed in Section 9.6.

41. ***Preparing for a Test*** A class is given a list of 20 study problems, from which 10 will be part of an upcoming exam. A student knows how to solve 15 of the problems. Find the probabilities that the student will be able to answer (a) all 10 questions on the exam, (b) exactly eight questions on the exam, and (c) at least nine questions on the exam.

42. ***Payroll Mix-Up*** Five paychecks and envelopes are addressed to five different people. The paychecks are randomly inserted into the envelopes. What are the probabilities that (a) exactly one paycheck will be inserted in the correct envelope and (b) at least one paycheck will be inserted in the correct envelope?

43. ***Game Show*** On a game show, you are given five digits to arrange in the proper order to form the price of a car. If you are correct, you win the car. What is the probability of winning, given the following conditions?
    (a) You guess the position of each digit.
    (b) You know the first digit and guess the positions of the other digits.

44. ***Card Game*** The deck of a card game is made up of 108 cards. Twenty-five each are red, yellow, blue, and green, and eight are wild cards. Each player is randomly dealt a seven-card hand.
    (a) What is the probability that a hand will contain exactly two wild cards?
    (b) What is the probability that a hand will contain two wild cards, two red cards, and three blue cards?

45. ***Drawing a Card*** One card is selected at random from an ordinary deck of 52 playing cards. Find the probabilities that (a) the card is an even-numbered card, (b) the card is a heart or a diamond, and (c) the card is a nine or a face card.

46. ***Poker Hand*** Five cards are drawn from an ordinary deck of 52 playing cards. What is the probability that the hand drawn is a full house? (A full house is a hand that consists of two of one kind and three of another kind.)

47. ***Defective Units*** A shipment of 12 microwave ovens contains three defective units. A vending company has ordered four of these units, and because each is identically packaged, the selection will be random. What are the probabilities that (a) all four units are good, (b) exactly two units are good, and (c) at least two units are good?

48. ***Random Number Generator*** Two integers from 1 through 40 are chosen by a random number generator. What are the probabilities that (a) the numbers are both even, (b) one number is even and one is odd, (c) both numbers are less than 30, and (d) the same number is chosen twice?

49. ***Flexible Work Hours*** In a survey, people were asked if they would prefer to work flexible hours—even if it meant slower career advancement—so they could spend more time with their families. The results of the survey are shown in the figure. Three people from the survey were chosen at random. What is the probability that all three people would prefer flexible work hours?

Flexible Work Hours

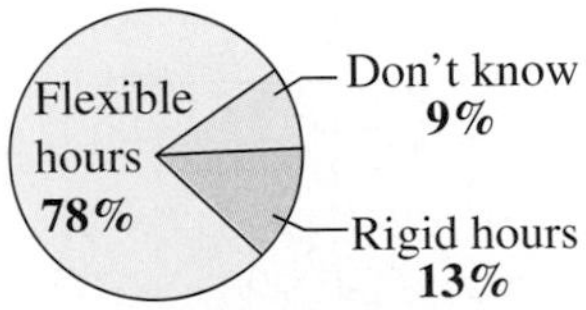

50. ***Consumer Awareness*** Suppose that the methods used by shoppers to pay for merchandise are as shown in the circle graph. Two shoppers are chosen at random. What is the probability that both shoppers paid for their purchases only in cash?

How Shoppers Pay for Merchandise

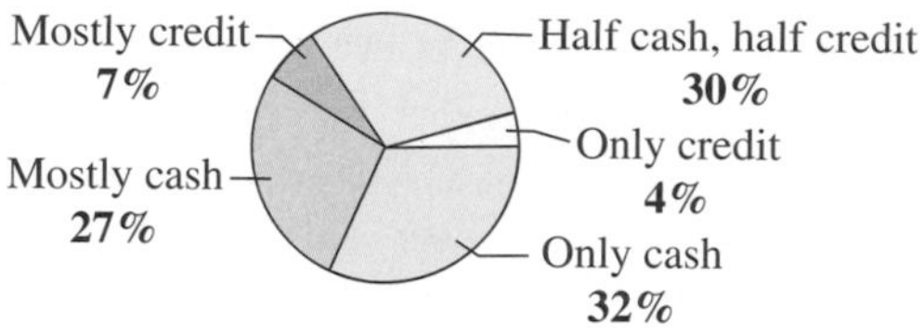

51. ***Backup System*** A space vehicle has an independent backup system for one of its communication networks. The probability that either system will function satisfactorily during a flight is 0.985. What are the probabilities that during a given flight (a) both systems function satisfactorily, (b) at least one system functions satisfactorily, and (c) both systems fail?

52. ***Backup Vehicle*** A fire company keeps two rescue vehicles. Because of the demand on the vehicles and the chance of mechanical failure, the probability that a specific vehicle is available when needed is 90%. The availability of one vehicle is *independent* of the availability of the other. Find the probabilities that (a) both vehicles are available at a given time, (b) neither vehicle is available at a given time, and (c) at least one vehicle is available at a given time.

53. ***A Boy or a Girl?*** Assume that the probability of the birth of a child of a particular sex is 50%. In a family with four children, what are the probabilities that (a) all the children are boys, (b) all the children are the same sex, and (c) there is at least one boy?

54. ***Geometry*** You and a friend agree to meet at your favorite fast-food restaurant between 5:00 and 6:00 P.M. The one who arrives first will wait 15 minutes for the other, and then will leave (see figure). What is the probability that the two of you will actually meet, assuming that your arrival times are random within the hour?

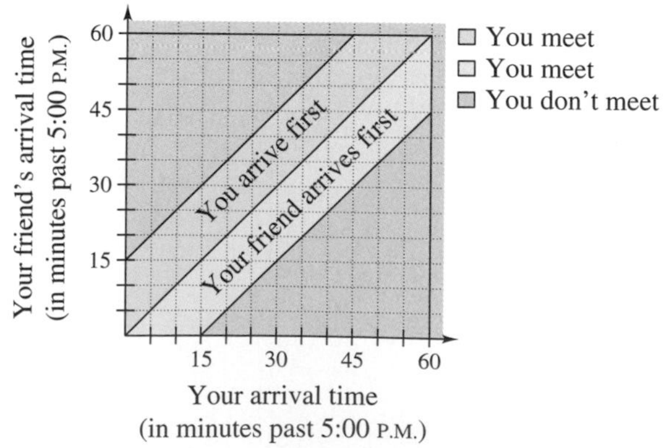

Model It

55. ***Roulette*** American roulette is a game in which a wheel turns on a spindle and is divided into 38 pockets. Thirty-six of the pockets are numbered 1–36, of which half are red and half are black. Two of the pockets are green and are numbered 0 and 00 (see figure). The dealer spins the wheel and a small ball in opposite directions. As the ball slows to a stop, it has an equal probability of landing in any of the numbered pockets.

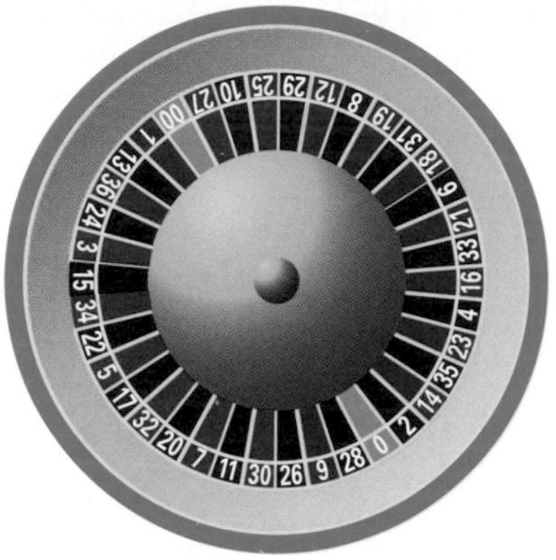

(a) Find the probability of landing in the number 00 pocket.

(b) Find the probability of landing in a red pocket.

(c) Find the probability of landing in a green pocket or a black pocket.

(d) Find the probability of landing in the number 14 pocket on two consecutive spins.

(e) Find the probability of landing in a red pocket on three consecutive spins.

(f) European roulette does not contain the 00 pocket. Repeat parts (a)–(e) for European roulette. How do the probabilities for European roulette compare with the probabilities for American roulette?

56. ***Estimating*** π A coin of diameter d is dropped onto a paper that contains a grid of squares d units on a side (see figure).

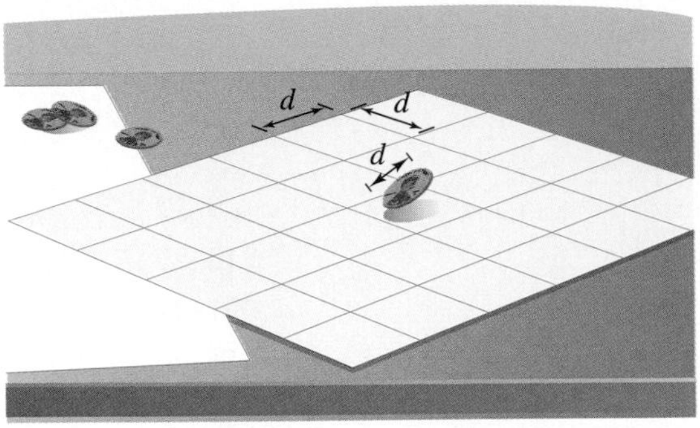

(a) Find the probability that the coin covers a vertex of one of the squares on the grid.

(b) Perform the experiment 100 times and use the results to approximate π.

Synthesis

True or False? **In Exercises 57 and 58, determine whether the statement is true or false. Justify your answer.**

57. If A and B are independent events with nonzero probabilities, then A can occur when B occurs.

58. Rolling a number less than 3 on a normal six-sided die has a probability of $\frac{1}{3}$. The complement of this event is to roll a number greater than 3, and its probability is $\frac{1}{2}$.

59. ***Pattern Recognition and Exploration*** Consider a group of n people.

(a) Explain why the following pattern gives the probabilities that the n people have distinct birthdays.

$$n = 2: \quad \frac{365}{365} \cdot \frac{364}{365} = \frac{365 \cdot 364}{365^2}$$

$$n = 3: \quad \frac{365}{365} \cdot \frac{364}{365} \cdot \frac{363}{365} = \frac{365 \cdot 364 \cdot 363}{365^3}$$

(b) Use the pattern in part (a) to write an expression for the probability that $n = 4$ people have distinct birthdays.

(c) Let P_n be the probability that the n people have distinct birthdays. Verify that this probability can be obtained recursively by

$$P_1 = 1 \text{ and } P_n = \frac{365 - (n - 1)}{365} P_{n-1}.$$

(d) Explain why $Q_n = 1 - P_n$ gives the probability that at least two people in a group of n people have the same birthday.

(e) Use the results of parts (c) and (d) to complete the table.

n	10	15	20	23	30	40	50
P_n							
Q_n							

(f) How many people must be in a group so that the probability of at least two of them having the same birthday is greater than $\frac{1}{2}$? Explain.

60. ***Think About It*** A weather forecast indicates that the probability of rain is 40%. What does this mean?

Skills Review

In Exercises 61–70, find all real solutions of the equation.

61. $6x^2 + 8 = 0$

62. $4x^2 + 6x - 12 = 0$

63. $x^3 - x^2 - 3x = 0$

64. $x^5 + x^3 - 2x = 0$

65. $\frac{12}{x} = -3$

66. $\frac{32}{x} = 2x$

67. $\frac{2}{x - 5} = 4$

68. $\frac{3}{2x + 3} - 4 = \frac{-1}{2x + 3}$

69. $\frac{3}{x - 2} + \frac{x}{x + 2} = 1$

70. $\frac{2}{x} - \frac{5}{x - 2} = \frac{-13}{x^2 - 2x}$

In Exercises 71–74, sketch the graph of the solution set of the system of inequalities.

71. $\begin{cases} y \geq -3 \\ x \geq -1 \\ -x - y \geq -8 \end{cases}$

72. $\begin{cases} x \leq 3 \\ y \leq 6 \\ 5x + 2y \geq 10 \end{cases}$

73. $\begin{cases} x^2 + y \geq -2 \\ y \geq x - 4 \end{cases}$

74. $\begin{cases} x^2 + y^2 \leq 4 \\ x + y \geq -2 \end{cases}$

9 Chapter Summary

What did you learn?

	Review Exercises
Section 9.1	
☐ Use sequence notation to write the terms of sequences *(p. 642).*	1–8
☐ Use factorial notation *(p. 644).*	9–12
☐ Use summation notation to write sums *(p. 646).*	13–20
☐ Find the sums of infinite series *(p. 647).*	21–24
☐ Use sequences and series to model and solve real-life problems *(p. 648).*	25, 26
Section 9.2	
☐ Recognize, write, and find the *n*th terms of arithmetic sequences *(p. 653).*	27–40
☐ Find *n*th partial sums of arithmetic sequences *(p. 656).*	41–46
☐ Use arithmetic sequences to model and solve real-life problems *(p. 657).*	47, 48
Section 9.3	
☐ Recognize, write, and find the *n*th terms of geometric sequences *(p. 663).*	49–60
☐ Find *n*th partial sums of geometric sequences *(p. 666).*	61–70
☐ Find sums of infinite geometric series *(p. 667).*	71–76
☐ Use geometric sequences to model and solve real-life problems *(p. 668).*	77, 78
Section 9.4	
☐ Use mathematical induction to prove statements involving a positive integer n *(p. 673).*	79–82
☐ Recognize patterns and write the *n*th term of a sequence *(p. 677).*	83–86
☐ Find the sums of powers of integers *(p. 679).*	87–90
☐ Find finite differences of sequences *(p. 680).*	91–94
Section 9.5	
☐ Use the Binomial Theorem to calculate binomial coefficients *(p. 683).*	95–98
☐ Use Pascal's Triangle to calculate binomial coefficients *(p. 685).*	99–102
☐ Use binomial coefficients to write binomial expansions *(p. 686).*	103–108
Section 9.6	
☐ Solve simple counting problems *(p. 691).*	109, 110
☐ Use the Fundamental Counting Principle to solve counting problems *(p. 692).*	111, 112
☐ Use permutations to solve counting problems *(p. 693).*	113, 114
☐ Use combinations to solve counting problems *(p. 696).*	115, 116
Section 9.7	
☐ Find the probabilities of events *(p. 701).*	117, 118
☐ Find the probabilities of mutually exclusive events *(p. 705).*	119, 120
☐ Find the probabilities of independent events *(p. 707).*	121, 122
☐ Find the probability of the complement of an event *(p. 708).*	123, 124

9 Review Exercises

9.1 In Exercises 1–4, write the first five terms of the sequence. (Assume that n begins with 1.)

1. $a_n = 2 + \dfrac{6}{n}$

2. $a_n = \dfrac{(-1)^n 5n}{2n - 1}$

3. $a_n = \dfrac{72}{n!}$

4. $a_n = n(n - 1)$

In Exercises 5–8, write an expression for the apparent nth term of the sequence. (Assume that n begins with 1.)

5. $-2, 2, -2, 2, -2, \ldots$

6. $-1, 2, 7, 14, 23, \ldots$

7. $4, 2, \frac{4}{3}, 1, \frac{4}{5}, \ldots$

8. $1, -\frac{1}{2}, \frac{1}{3}, -\frac{1}{4}, \frac{1}{5}, \ldots$

In Exercises 9–12, simplify the factorial expression.

9. $5!$

10. $3! \cdot 2!$

11. $\dfrac{3! \cdot 5!}{6!}$

12. $\dfrac{7! \cdot 6!}{6! \cdot 8!}$

In Exercises 13–18, find the sum.

13. $\sum_{i=1}^{6} 5$

14. $\sum_{k=2}^{5} 4k$

15. $\sum_{j=1}^{4} \dfrac{6}{j^2}$

16. $\sum_{i=1}^{8} \dfrac{i}{i + 1}$

17. $\sum_{k=1}^{10} 2k^3$

18. $\sum_{j=0}^{4} (j^2 + 1)$

In Exercises 19 and 20, use sigma notation to write the sum.

19. $\dfrac{1}{2(1)} + \dfrac{1}{2(2)} + \dfrac{1}{2(3)} + \cdots + \dfrac{1}{2(20)}$

20. $\dfrac{1}{2} + \dfrac{2}{3} + \dfrac{3}{4} + \cdots + \dfrac{9}{10}$

In Exercises 21–24, find the sum of the infinite series.

21. $\sum_{i=1}^{\infty} \dfrac{5}{10^i}$

22. $\sum_{i=1}^{\infty} \dfrac{3}{10^i}$

23. $\sum_{k=1}^{\infty} \dfrac{2}{100^k}$

24. $\sum_{k=2}^{\infty} \dfrac{9}{10^k}$

25. ***Compound Interest*** A deposit of \$10,000 is made in an account that earns 8% interest compounded monthly. The balance in the account after n months is given by

$$A_n = 10{,}000\left(1 + \frac{0.08}{12}\right)^n, \quad n = 1, 2, 3, \ldots$$

(a) Write the first 10 terms of this sequence.

(b) Find the balance in this account after 10 years by finding the 120th term of the sequence.

26. ***Education*** The enrollment a_n (in thousands) in Head Start programs in the United States from 1994 to 2002 can be approximated by the model

$$a_n = 1.07n^2 + 6.1n + 693, \quad n = 4, 5, \ldots, 12$$

where n is the year, with $n = 4$ corresponding to 1994. Find the terms of this finite sequence. Use a graphing utility to construct a bar graph that represents the sequence. (Source: U.S. Administration for Children and Families)

9.2 In Exercises 27–30, determine whether the sequence is arithmetic. If so, find the common difference.

27. $5, 3, 1, -1, -3, \ldots$

28. $0, 1, 3, 6, 10, \ldots$

29. $\frac{1}{2}, 1, \frac{3}{2}, 2, \frac{5}{2}, \ldots$

30. $\frac{9}{9}, \frac{8}{9}, \frac{7}{9}, \frac{6}{9}, \frac{5}{9}, \ldots$

In Exercises 31–34, write the first five terms of the arithmetic sequence.

31. $a_1 = 4, d = 3$

32. $a_1 = 6, d = -2$

33. $a_1 = 25, a_{k+1} = a_k + 3$

34. $a_1 = 4.2, a_{k+1} = a_k + 0.4$

In Exercises 35–40, find a formula for a_n for the arithmetic sequence.

35. $a_1 = 7, d = 12$

36. $a_1 = 25, d = -3$

37. $a_1 = y, d = 3y$

38. $a_1 = -2x, d = x$

39. $a_2 = 93, a_6 = 65$

40. $a_7 = 8, a_{13} = 6$

In Exercises 41–44, find the partial sum.

41. $\sum_{j=1}^{10} (2j - 3)$

42. $\sum_{j=1}^{8} (20 - 3j)$

43. $\sum_{k=1}^{11} \left(\frac{2}{3}k + 4\right)$

44. $\sum_{k=1}^{25} \left(\dfrac{3k + 1}{4}\right)$

45. Find the sum of the first 100 positive multiples of 5.

46. Find the sum of the integers from 20 to 80 (inclusive).

47. ***Job Offer*** The starting salary for an accountant is $34,000 with a guaranteed salary increase of $2250 per year. Determine (a) the salary during the fifth year and (b) the total compensation through 5 full years of employment.

48. ***Baling Hay*** In the first two trips baling hay around a large field, a farmer obtains 123 bales and 112 bales, respectively. Because each round gets shorter, the farmer estimates that the same pattern will continue. Estimate the total number of bales made if the farmer takes another six trips around the field.

9.3 **In Exercises 49–52, determine whether the sequence is geometric. If so, find the common ratio.**

49. 5, 10, 20, 40, . . .

50. 54, −18, 6, −2, . . .

51. $\frac{1}{3}, -\frac{2}{3}, \frac{4}{3}, -\frac{8}{3}, \ldots$

52. $\frac{1}{4}, \frac{2}{5}, \frac{3}{6}, \frac{4}{7}, \ldots$

In Exercises 53–56, write the first five terms of the geometric sequence.

53. $a_1 = 4,\ r = -\frac{1}{4}$

54. $a_1 = 2,\ r = 2$

55. $a_1 = 9,\ a_3 = 4$

56. $a_1 = 2,\ a_3 = 12$

In Exercises 57–60, write an expression for the *n*th term of the geometric sequence. Then find the 20th term of the sequence.

57. $a_1 = 16, a_2 = -8$

58. $a_3 = 6, a_4 = 1$

59. $a_1 = 100, r = 1.05$

60. $a_1 = 5, r = 0.2$

In Exercises 61–66, find the sum of the finite geometric sequence.

61. $\sum_{i=1}^{7} 2^{i-1}$

62. $\sum_{i=1}^{5} 3^{i-1}$

63. $\sum_{i=1}^{4} \left(\frac{1}{2}\right)^{i}$

64. $\sum_{i=1}^{6} \left(\frac{1}{3}\right)^{i-1}$

65. $\sum_{i=1}^{5} (2)^{i-1}$

66. $\sum_{i=1}^{4} 6(3)^{i}$

In Exercises 67–70, use a graphing utility to find the sum of the finite geometric sequence.

67. $\sum_{i=1}^{10} 10\left(\frac{3}{5}\right)^{i-1}$

68. $\sum_{i=1}^{15} 20(0.2)^{i-1}$

69. $\sum_{i=1}^{25} 100(1.06)^{i-1}$

70. $\sum_{i=1}^{20} 8\left(\frac{6}{5}\right)^{i-1}$

In Exercises 71–76, find the sum of the infinite geometric series.

71. $\sum_{i=1}^{\infty} \left(\frac{7}{8}\right)^{i-1}$

72. $\sum_{i=1}^{\infty} \left(\frac{1}{3}\right)^{i-1}$

73. $\sum_{i=1}^{\infty} (0.1)^{i-1}$

74. $\sum_{i=1}^{\infty} (0.5)^{i-1}$

75. $\sum_{k=1}^{\infty} 4\left(\frac{2}{3}\right)^{k-1}$

76. $\sum_{k=1}^{\infty} 1.3\left(\frac{1}{10}\right)^{k-1}$

77. ***Depreciation*** A paper manufacturer buys a machine for $120,000. During the next 5 years, it will depreciate at a rate of 30% per year. (That is, at the end of each year the depreciated value will be 70% of what it was at the beginning of the year.)

(a) Find the formula for the *n*th term of a geometric sequence that gives the value of the machine *t* full years after it was purchased.

(b) Find the depreciated value of the machine after 5 full years.

78. ***Annuity*** You deposit $200 in an account at the beginning of each month for 10 years. The account pays 6% compounded monthly. What will your balance be at the end of 10 years? What would the balance be if the interest were compounded continuously?

9.4 **In Exercises 79–82, use mathematical induction to prove the formula for every positive integer *n*.**

79. $3 + 5 + 7 + \cdots + (2n + 1) = n(n + 2)$

80. $1 + \frac{3}{2} + 2 + \frac{5}{2} + \cdots + \frac{1}{2}(n + 1) = \frac{n}{4}(n + 3)$

81. $\sum_{i=0}^{n-1} ar^{i} = \frac{a(1 - r^{n})}{1 - r}$

82. $\sum_{k=0}^{n-1} (a + kd) = \frac{n}{2}[2a + (n - 1)d]$

In Exercises 83–86, find a formula for the sum of the first *n* terms of the sequence.

83. 9, 13, 17, 21, . . .

84. 68, 60, 52, 44, . . .

85. $1, \frac{3}{5}, \frac{9}{25}, \frac{27}{125}, \ldots$

86. $12, -1, \frac{1}{12}, -\frac{1}{144}, \ldots$

In Exercises 87–90, find the sum using the formulas for the sums of powers of integers.

87. $\sum_{n=1}^{30} n$

88. $\sum_{n=1}^{10} n^2$

89. $\sum_{n=1}^{7} (n^4 - n)$

90. $\sum_{n=1}^{6} (n^5 - n^2)$

In Exercises 91–94, write the first five terms of the sequence beginning with the given term. Then calculate the first and second differences of the sequence. State whether the sequence has a linear model, a quadratic model, or neither.

91. $a_1 = 5$
$a_n = a_{n-1} + 5$

92. $a_1 = -3$
$a_n = a_{n-1} - 2n$

93. $a_1 = 16$
$a_n = a_{n-1} - 1$

94. $a_0 = 0$
$a_n = n - a_{n-1}$

9.5 In Exercises 95–98, use the Binomial Theorem to calculate the binomial coefficient.

95. ${}_6C_4$

96. ${}_{10}C_7$

97. ${}_8C_5$

98. ${}_{12}C_3$

In Exercises 99–102, use Pascal's Triangle to calculate the binomial coefficient.

99. $\binom{7}{3}$

100. $\binom{9}{4}$

101. $\binom{8}{6}$

102. $\binom{5}{3}$

In Exercises 103–108, use the Binomial Theorem to expand and simplify the expression. (Remember that $i = \sqrt{-1}$.)

103. $(x + 4)^4$

104. $(x - 3)^6$

105. $(a - 3b)^5$

106. $(3x + y^2)^7$

107. $(5 + 2i)^4$

108. $(4 - 5i)^3$

9.6 **109.** ***Numbers in a Hat*** Slips of paper numbered 1 through 14 are placed in a hat. In how many ways can you draw two numbers with replacement that total 12?

110. ***Home Theater Systems*** A customer in an electronics store can choose one of six speaker systems, one of five DVD players, and one of six plasma televisions to design a home theater system. How many systems can be designed?

111. ***Telephone Numbers*** The same three-digit prefix is used for all of the telephone numbers in a small town. How many different telephone numbers are possible by changing only the last four digits?

112. ***Course Schedule*** A college student is preparing a course schedule for the next semester. The student may select one of three mathematics courses, one of four science courses, and one of six history courses. How many schedules are possible?

113. ***Bike Race*** There are 10 bicyclists entered in a race. In how many different ways could the top three places be decided?

114. ***Jury Selection*** A group of potential jurors has been narrowed down to 32 people. In how many ways can a jury of 12 people be selected?

115. ***Apparel*** You have eight different suits to choose from to take on a trip. How many combinations of three suits could you take on your trip?

116. ***Menu Choices*** A local sub shop offers five different breads, seven different meats, three different cheeses, and six different vegetables. Find the total number of combinations of sandwiches possible.

9.7 **117.** ***Apparel*** A man has five pairs of socks, of which no two pairs are the same color. He randomly selects two socks from a drawer. What is the probability that he gets a matched pair?

118. ***Bookshelf Order*** A child returns a five-volume set of books to a bookshelf. The child is not able to read, and so cannot distinguish one volume from another. What is the probability that the books are shelved in the correct order?

119. ***Students by Class*** At a particular university, the numbers of students in the four classes are broken down by percents, as shown in the table.

Class	Percent
Freshmen	31
Sophomores	26
Juniors	25
Seniors	18

A single student is picked randomly by lottery for a cash scholarship. What is the probability that the scholarship winner is

(a) a junior or senior?

(b) a freshman, sophomore, or junior?

120. ***Data Analysis*** A sample of college students, faculty, and administration were asked whether they favored a proposed increase in the annual activity fee to enhance student life on campus. The results of the study are listed in the table.

	Students	Faculty	Admin.	Total
Favor	237	37	18	292
Oppose	163	38	7	208
Total	400	75	25	500

A person is selected at random from the sample. Find each specified probability.

(a) The person is not in favor of the proposal.

(b) The person is a student.

(c) The person is a faculty member and is in favor of the proposal.

121. ***Tossing a Die*** A six-sided die is tossed three times. What is the probability of getting a 6 on each roll?

122. ***Tossing a Die*** A six-sided die is tossed six times. What is the probability that each side appears exactly once?

123. ***Drawing a Card*** You randomly select a card from a 52-card deck. What is the probability that the card is *not* a club?

124. ***Tossing a Coin*** Find the probability of obtaining at least one tail when a coin is tossed five times.

Synthesis

True or False? **In Exercises 125–129, determine whether the statement is true or false. Justify your answer.**

125. $\dfrac{(n+2)!}{n!} = (n+2)(n+1)$

126. $\displaystyle\sum_{i=1}^{5}(i^3 + 2i) = \sum_{i=1}^{5} i^3 + \sum_{i=1}^{5} 2i$

127. $\displaystyle\sum_{k=1}^{8} 3k = 3\sum_{k=1}^{8} k$

128. $\displaystyle\sum_{j=1}^{6} 2^j = \sum_{j=3}^{8} 2^{j-2}$

129. The value of ${}_nP_r$ is always greater than the value of ${}_nC_r$.

130. ***Think About It*** An infinite sequence is a function. What is the domain of the function?

131. ***Think About It*** How do the two sequences differ?

(a) $a_n = \dfrac{(-1)^n}{n}$

(b) $a_n = \dfrac{(-1)^{n+1}}{n}$

132. ***Graphical Reasoning*** The graphs of two sequences are shown below. Identify each sequence as arithmetic or geometric. Explain your reasoning.

(a)

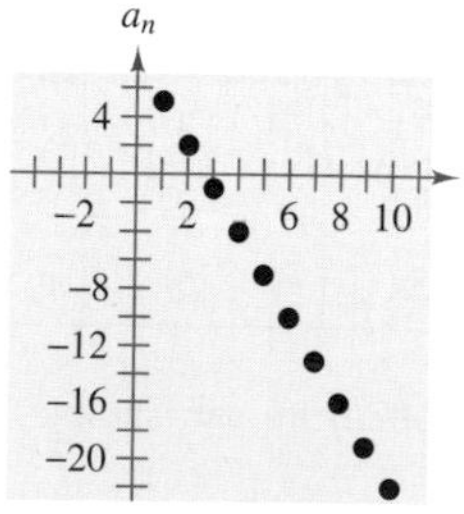

(b)

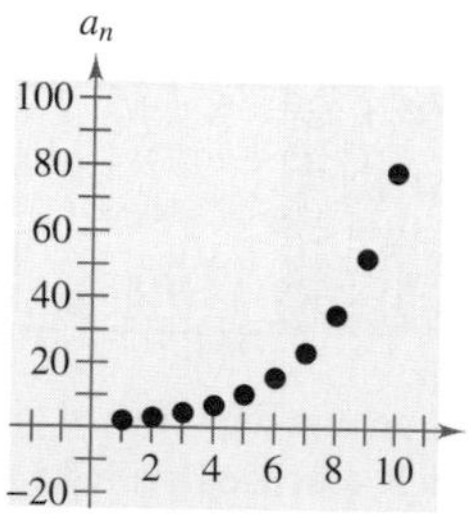

133. ***Writing*** Explain what is meant by a recursion formula.

134. ***Writing*** Explain why the terms of a geometric sequence decrease when $0 < r < 1$.

Graphical Reasoning **In Exercises 135–138, match the sequence or sum of a sequence with its graph without doing any calculations. Explain your reasoning. [The graphs are labeled (a), (b), (c), and (d).]**

(a)

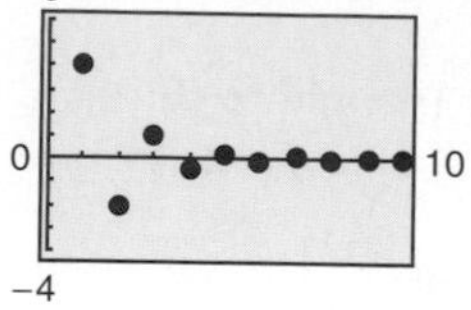

(b)

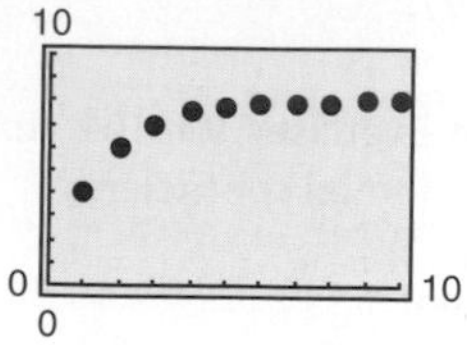

(c)

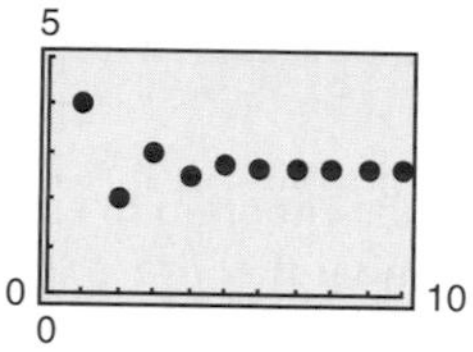

(d)

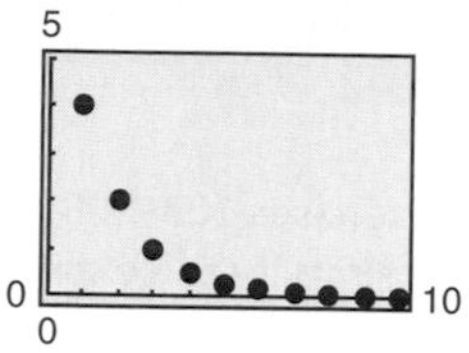

135. $a_n = 4\left(\frac{1}{2}\right)^{n-1}$

136. $a_n = 4\left(-\frac{1}{2}\right)^{n-1}$

137. $a_n = \displaystyle\sum_{k=1}^{n} 4\left(\frac{1}{2}\right)^{k-1}$

138. $a_n = \displaystyle\sum_{k=1}^{n} 4\left(-\frac{1}{2}\right)^{k-1}$

139. ***Population Growth*** Consider an idealized population with the characteristic that each member of the population produces one offspring at the end of every time period. If each member has a life span of three time periods and the population begins with 10 newborn members, then the following table shows the population during the first five time periods.

	Time Period				
Age Bracket	1	2	3	4	5
0–1	10	10	20	40	70
1–2		10	10	20	40
2–3			10	10	20
Total	10	20	40	70	130

The sequence for the total population has the property that

$S_n = S_{n-1} + S_{n-2} + S_{n-3}, \quad n > 3.$

Find the total population during the next five time periods.

140. The probability of an event must be a real number in what interval? Is the interval open or closed?

9 Chapter Test

Take this test as you would take a test in class. When you are finished, check your work against the answers given in the back of the book.

1. Write the first five terms of the sequence $a_n = \dfrac{(-1)^n}{3n+2}$. (Assume that n begins with 1.)

2. Write an expression for the nth term of the sequence.

$$\frac{3}{1!}, \frac{4}{2!}, \frac{5}{3!}, \frac{6}{4!}, \frac{7}{5!}, \ldots$$

3. Find the next three terms of the series. Then find the fifth partial sum of the series.

$$6 + 17 + 28 + 39 + \cdots$$

4. The fifth term of an arithmetic sequence is 5.4, and the 12th term is 11.0. Find the nth term.

5. Write the first five terms of the sequence $a_n = 5(2)^{n-1}$. (Assume that n begins with 1.)

In Exercises 6–8, find the sum.

6. $\displaystyle\sum_{i=1}^{50} (2i^2 + 5)$.

7. $\displaystyle\sum_{n=1}^{7} (8n - 5)$

8. $\displaystyle\sum_{i=1}^{\infty} 4\left(\frac{1}{2}\right)^i$.

9. Use mathematical induction to prove the formula.

$$5 + 10 + 15 + \cdots + 5n = \frac{5n(n+1)}{2}$$

10. Use the Binomial Theorem to expand the expression $(x + 2y)^4$.

11. Find the coefficient of the term $a^3 b^5$ in the expansion of $(2a - 3b)^8$.

In Exercises 12 and 13, evaluate each expression.

12. (a) ${}_{9}P_{2}$ (b) ${}_{70}P_{3}$

13. (a) ${}_{11}C_{4}$ (b) ${}_{66}C_{4}$

14. How many distinct license plates can be issued consisting of one letter followed by a three-digit number?

15. Eight people are going for a ride in a boat that seats eight people. The owner of the boat will drive, and only three of the remaining people are willing to ride in the two bow seats. How many seating arrangements are possible?

16. You attend a karaoke night and hope to hear your favorite song. The karaoke song book has 300 different songs (your favorite song is among the 300 songs). Assuming that the singers are equally likely to pick any song and no song is repeated, what is the probability that your favorite song is one of the 20 that you hear that night?

17. You are with seven of your friends at a party. Names of all of the 60 guests are placed in a hat and drawn randomly to award eight door prizes. Each guest is limited to one prize. What is the probability that you and your friends win all eight of the prizes?

18. The weather report calls for a 75% chance of snow. According to this report, what is the probability that it will *not* snow?

9 Cumulative Test for Chapters 7–9

Take this test to review the material from earlier chapters. When you are finished, check your work against the answers given in the back of the book.

In Exercises 1–4, solve the system by the specified method.

1. Substitution

$$\begin{cases} y = 3 - x^2 \\ 2(y - 2) = x - 1 \end{cases}$$

2. Elimination

$$\begin{cases} x + 3y = -1 \\ 2x + 4y = 0 \end{cases}$$

3. Elimination

$$\begin{cases} -2x + 4y - z = 3 \\ x - 2y + 2z = -6 \\ x - 3y - z = 1 \end{cases}$$

4. Gauss-Jordan Elimination

$$\begin{cases} x + 3y - 2z = -7 \\ -2x + y - z = -5 \\ 4x + y + z = 3 \end{cases}$$

In Exercises 5 and 6, sketch the graph of the solution set of the system of inequalities.

5. $\begin{cases} 2x + y \ge -3 \\ x - 3y \le 2 \end{cases}$

6. $\begin{cases} x - y > 6 \\ 5x + 2y < 10 \end{cases}$

7. Sketch the region determined by the constraints. Then find the minimum and maximum values, and where they occur, of the objective function $z = 3x + 2y$, subject to the indicated constraints.

$$\begin{aligned} x + 4y &\le 20 \\ 2x + y &\le 12 \\ x &\ge 0 \\ y &\ge 0 \end{aligned}$$

8. A custom-blend bird seed is to be mixed from seed mixtures costing \$0.75 per pound and \$1.25 per pound. How many pounds of each seed mixture are used to make 200 pounds of custom-blend bird seed costing \$0.95 per pound?

9. Find the equation of the parabola $y = ax^2 + bx + c$ passing through the points (0, 4), (3, 1), and (6, 4).

$$\begin{cases} -x + 2y - z = 9 \\ 2x - y + 2z = -9 \\ 3x + 3y - 4z = 7 \end{cases}$$

SYSTEM FOR 10 AND 11

In Exercises 10 and 11, use the system of equations at the left.

10. Write the augmented matrix corresponding to the system of equations.

11. Solve the system using the matrix found in Exercise 10 and Gauss-Jordan elimination.

In Exercises 12–15, use the following matrices to find each of the following, if possible.

$$A = \begin{bmatrix} 4 & 0 \\ -1 & 2 \end{bmatrix}, \quad B = \begin{bmatrix} -1 & 3 \\ 1 & 0 \end{bmatrix}$$

12. $A + B$

13. $-2B$

14. $A - 2B$

15. AB

$$\begin{bmatrix} 8 & 0 & -5 \\ 1 & 3 & -1 \\ -2 & 6 & 4 \end{bmatrix}$$

MATRIX FOR 16

16. Find the determinant of the matrix at the left.

17. Find the inverse of the matrix (if it exists): $\begin{bmatrix} 1 & 2 & -1 \\ 3 & 7 & -10 \\ -5 & -7 & -15 \end{bmatrix}$.

Age group	Gym shoes	Jogging shoes	Walking shoes
14–17	0.09	0.09	0.03
18–24	0.06	0.10	0.05
25–34	0.12	0.25	0.12

MATRIX FOR 18

18. The percents (by age group) of the total amounts spent on three types of footwear in a recent year are shown in the matrix. The total amounts (in millions) spent by each age group on the three types of footwear were \$442.20 (14–17 age group), \$466.57(18–24 age group), and \$1088.09 (25–34 age group). How many dollars worth of gym shoes, jogging shoes, and walking shoes were sold that year? (Source: National Sporting Goods Association)

In Exercises 19 and 20, use Cramer's Rule to solve the system of equations.

19. $\begin{cases} 8x - 3y = -52 \\ 3x + 5y = 5 \end{cases}$

20. $\begin{cases} 5x + 4y + 3z = 7 \\ -3x - 8y + 7z = -9 \\ 7x - 5y - 6z = -53 \end{cases}$

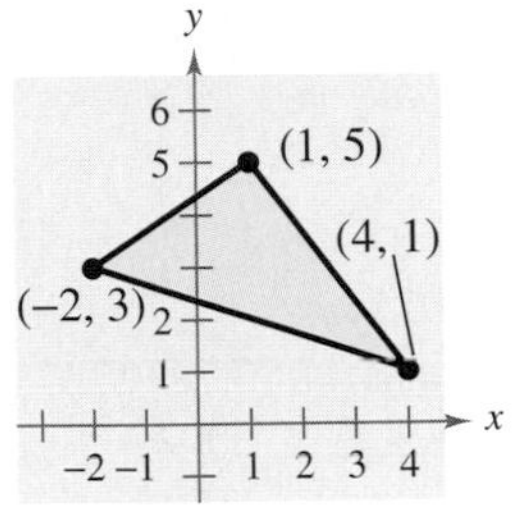

FIGURE FOR 21

21. Find the area of the triangle shown in the figure.

22. Write the first five terms of the sequence $a_n = \dfrac{(-1)^{n+1}}{2n + 3}$ (assume that n begins with 1).

23. Write an expression for the nth term of the sequence.

$\dfrac{2!}{4}, \dfrac{3!}{5}, \dfrac{4!}{6}, \dfrac{5!}{7}, \dfrac{6!}{8}, \ldots$

24. Find the sum of the first 20 terms of the arithmetic sequence 8, 12, 16, 20, ...

25. The sixth term of an arithmetic sequence is 20.6, and the ninth term is 30.2.

(a) Find the 20th term.

(b) Find the nth term.

26. Write the first five terms of the sequence $a_n = 3(2)^{n-1}$ (assume that n begins with 1).

27. Find the sum: $\displaystyle\sum_{i=0}^{\infty} 1.3\left(\tfrac{1}{10}\right)^{i-1}$.

28. Use mathematical induction to prove the formula

$3 + 7 + 11 + 15 + \cdots + (4n - 1) = n(2n + 1)$.

29. Use the Binomial Theorem to expand and simplify $(z - 3)^4$.

In Exercises 30–33, evaluate the expression.

30. ${}_7P_3$ **31.** ${}_{25}P_2$ **32.** $\binom{8}{4}$ **33.** ${}_{10}C_3$

In Exercises 34 and 35, find the number of distinguishable permutations of the group of letters.

34. B, A, S, K, E, T, B, A, L, L **35.** A, N, T, A, R, C, T, I, C, A

36. A personnel manager at a department store has 10 applicants to fill three different sales positions. In how many ways can this be done, assuming that all the applicants are qualified for any of the three positions?

37. On a game show, the digits 3, 4, and 5 must be arranged in the proper order to form the price of an appliance. If the digits are arranged correctly, the contestant wins the appliance. What is the probability of winning if the contestant knows that the price is at least \$400?

Proofs in Mathematics

Properties of Sums *(p. 647)*

1. $\sum_{i=1}^{n} c = cn,\quad c$ is a constant.

2. $\sum_{i=1}^{n} ca_i = c\sum_{i=1}^{n} a_i,\quad c$ is a constant.

3. $\sum_{i=1}^{n} (a_i + b_i) = \sum_{i=1}^{n} a_i + \sum_{i=1}^{n} b_i$

4. $\sum_{i=1}^{n} (a_i - b_i) = \sum_{i=1}^{n} a_i - \sum_{i=1}^{n} b_i$

Proof

Each of these properties follows directly from the properties of real numbers.

1. $\sum_{i=1}^{n} c = c + c + c + \cdots + c = cn \qquad n \text{ terms}$

The Distributive Property is used in the proof of Property 2.

2. $\sum_{i=1}^{n} ca_i = ca_1 + ca_2 + ca_3 + \cdots + ca_n$

$$= c(a_1 + a_2 + a_3 + \cdots + a_n) = c\sum_{i=1}^{n} a_i$$

The proof of Property 3 uses the Commutative and Associative Properties of Addition.

3.
$$\sum_{i=1}^{n} (a_i + b_i) = (a_1 + b_1) + (a_2 + b_2) + (a_3 + b_3) + \cdots + (a_n + b_n)$$
$$= (a_1 + a_2 + a_3 + \cdots + a_n) + (b_1 + b_2 + b_3 + \cdots + b_n)$$
$$= \sum_{i=1}^{n} a_i + \sum_{i=1}^{n} b_i$$

The proof of Property 4 uses the Commutative and Associative Properties of Addition and the Distributive Property.

4.
$$\sum_{i=1}^{n} (a_i - b_i) = (a_1 - b_1) + (a_2 - b_2) + (a_3 - b_3) + \cdots + (a_n - b_n)$$
$$= (a_1 + a_2 + a_3 + \cdots + a_n) + (-b_1 - b_2 - b_3 - \cdots - b_n)$$
$$= (a_1 + a_2 + a_3 + \cdots + a_n) - (b_1 + b_2 + b_3 + \cdots + b_n)$$
$$= \sum_{i=1}^{n} a_i - \sum_{i=1}^{n} b_i$$

Infinite Series

The study of infinite series was considered a novelty in the fourteenth century. Logician Richard Suiseth, whose nickname was Calculator, solved this problem.

If throughout the first half of a given time interval a variation continues at a certain intensity; throughout the next quarter of the interval at double the intensity; throughout the following eighth at triple the intensity and so ad infinitum; The average intensity for the whole interval will be the intensity of the variation during the second subinterval (or double the intensity).

This is the same as saying that the sum of the infinite series

$$\frac{1}{2} + \frac{2}{4} + \frac{3}{8} + \cdots + \frac{n}{2^n} + \cdots$$

is 2.

The Sum of a Finite Arithmetic Sequence *(p. 656)*

The sum of a finite arithmetic sequence with n terms is

$$S_n = \frac{n}{2}(a_1 + a_n).$$

Proof

Begin by generating the terms of the arithmetic sequence in two ways. In the first way, repeatedly add d to the first term to obtain

$$\begin{aligned} S_n &= a_1 + a_2 + a_3 + \cdot \cdot \cdot + a_{n-2} + a_{n-1} + a_n \\ &= a_1 + [a_1 + d] + [a_1 + 2d] + \cdot \cdot \cdot + [a_1 + (n - 1)d]. \end{aligned}$$

In the second way, repeatedly subtract d from the nth term to obtain

$$\begin{aligned} S_n &= a_n + a_{n-1} + a_{n-2} + \cdot \cdot \cdot + a_3 + a_2 + a_1 \\ &= a_n + [a_n - d] + [a_n - 2d] + \cdot \cdot \cdot + [a_n - (n - 1)d]. \end{aligned}$$

If you add these two versions of S_n, the multiples of d subtract out and you obtain

$$2S_n = (a_1 + a_n) + (a_1 + a_n) + (a_1 + a_n) + \cdot \cdot \cdot + (a_1 + a_n) \quad n \text{ terms}$$

$$2S_n = n(a_1 + a_n)$$

$$S_n = \frac{n}{2}(a_1 + a_n).$$

The Sum of a Finite Geometric Sequence *(p. 666)*

The sum of the finite geometric sequence

$$a_1,\ a_1r,\ a_1r^2,\ a_1r^3,\ a_1r^4,\ .\ .\ .\ ,\ a_1r^{n-1}$$

with common ratio $r \neq 1$ is given by $S_n = \sum_{i=1}^{n} a_1r^{i-1} = a_1\left(\frac{1 - r^n}{1 - r}\right)$.

Proof

$$S_n = a_1 + a_1r + a_1r^2 + \cdot \cdot \cdot + a_1r^{n-2} + a_1r^{n-1}$$

$$rS_n = a_1r + a_1r^2 + a_1r^3 + \cdot \cdot \cdot + a_1r^{n-1} + a_1r^n \qquad \text{Multiply by } r.$$

Subtracting the second equation from the first yields

$$S_n - rS_n = a_1 - a_1r^n.$$

So, $S_n(1 - r) = a_1(1 - r^n)$, and, because $r \neq 1$, you have $S_n = a_1\left(\frac{1 - r^n}{1 - r}\right)$.

The Binomial Theorem *(p. 683)*

In the expansion of $(x + y)^n$

$$(x + y)^n = x^n + nx^{n-1}y + \cdots + {}_nC_r\, x^{n-r}y^r + \cdots + nxy^{n-1} + y^n$$

the coefficient of $x^{n-r}y^r$ is

$${}_nC_r = \frac{n!}{(n-r)!r!}.$$

Proof

The Binomial Theorem can be proved quite nicely using mathematical induction. The steps are straightforward but look a little messy, so only an outline of the proof is presented.

1. If $n = 1$, you have $(x + y)^1 = x^1 + y^1 = {}_1C_0x + {}_1C_1y$, and the formula is valid.

2. Assuming that the formula is true for $n = k$, the coefficient of $x^{k-r}y^r$ is

$${}_kC_r = \frac{k!}{(k-r)!r!} = \frac{k(k-1)(k-2)\cdots(k-r+1)}{r!}.$$

To show that the formula is true for $n = k + 1$, look at the coefficient of $x^{k+1-r}y^r$ in the expansion of

$$(x + y)^{k+1} = (x + y)^k(x + y).$$

From the right-hand side, you can determine that the term involving $x^{k+1-r}y^r$ is the sum of two products.

$$({}_kC_rx^{k-r}y^r)(x) + ({}_kC_{r-1}x^{k+1-r}y^{r-1})(y)$$

$$= \left[\frac{k!}{(k-r)!r!} + \frac{k!}{(k+1-r)!(r-1)!}\right]x^{k+1-r}y^r$$

$$= \left[\frac{(k+1-r)k!}{(k+1-r)!r!} + \frac{k!r}{(k+1-r)!r!}\right]x^{k+1-r}y^r$$

$$= \left[\frac{k!(k+1-r+r)}{(k+1-r)!r!}\right]x^{k+1-r}y^r$$

$$= \left[\frac{(k+1)!}{(k+1-r)!r!}\right]x^{k+1-r}y^r$$

$$= {}_{k+1}C_rx^{k+1-r}y^r$$

So, by mathematical induction, the Binomial Theorem is valid for all positive integers n.

P.S. Problem Solving

This collection of thought-provoking and challenging exercises further explores and expands upon concepts learned in this chapter.

1. Let $x_0 = 1$ and consider the sequence x_n given by

$$x_n = \frac{1}{2}x_{n-1} + \frac{1}{x_{n-1}}, \quad n = 1, 2, . . .$$

Use a graphing utility to compute the first 10 terms of the sequence and make a conjecture about the value of x_n as n approaches infinity.

2. Consider the sequence

$$a_n = \frac{n+1}{n^2+1}.$$

(a) Use a graphing utility to graph the first 10 terms of the sequence.

(b) Use the graph from part (a) to estimate the value of a_n as n approaches infinity.

(c) Complete the table.

n	1	10	100	1000	10,000
a_n					

(d) Use the table from part (c) to determine (if possible) the value of a_n as n approaches infinity.

3. Consider the sequence

$$a_n = 3 + (-1)^n.$$

(a) Use a graphing utility to graph the first 10 terms of the sequence.

(b) Use the graph from part (a) to describe the behavior of the graph of the sequence.

(c) Complete the table.

n	1	10	101	1000	10,001
a_n					

(d) Use the table from part (c) to determine (if possible) the value of a_n as n approaches infinity.

4. The following operations are performed on each term of an arithmetic sequence. Determine if the resulting sequence is arithmetic, and if so, state the common difference.

(a) A constant C is added to each term.

(b) Each term is multiplied by a nonzero constant C.

(c) Each term is squared.

5. The following sequence of perfect squares is not arithmetic.

1, 4, 9, 16, 25, 36, 49, 64, 81, . . .

However, you can form a related sequence that is arithmetic by finding the differences of consecutive terms.

(a) Write the first eight terms of the related arithmetic sequence described above. What is the nth term of this sequence?

(b) Describe how you can find an arithmetic sequence that is related to the following sequence of perfect cubes.

1, 8, 27, 64, 125, 216, 343, 512, 729, . . .

(c) Write the first seven terms of the related sequence in part (b) and find the nth term of the sequence.

(d) Describe how you can find the arithmetic sequence that is related to the following sequence of perfect fourth powers.

1, 16, 81, 256, 625, 1296, 2401, 4096, 6561, . . .

(e) Write the first six terms of the related sequence in part (d) and find the nth term of the sequence.

6. Can the Greek hero Achilles, running at 20 feet per second, ever catch a tortoise, starting 20 feet ahead of Achilles and running at 10 feet per second? The Greek mathematician Zeno said no. When Achilles runs 20 feet, the tortoise will be 10 feet ahead. Then, when Achilles runs 10 feet, the tortoise will be 5 feet ahead. Achilles will keep cutting the distance in half but will never catch the tortoise. The table shows Zeno's reasoning. From the table you can see that both the distances and the times required to achieve them form infinite geometric series. Using the table, show that both series have finite sums. What do these sums represent?

Distance (in feet)	Time (in seconds)
20	1
10	0.5
5	0.25
2.5	0.125
1.25	0.0625
0.625	0.03125

7. Recall that a *fractal* is a geometric figure that consists of a pattern that is repeated infinitely on a smaller and smaller scale. A well-known fractal is called the *Sierpinski Triangle*. In the first stage, the midpoints of the three sides are used to create the vertices of a new triangle, which is then removed, leaving three triangles. The first three stages are shown on the next page. Note that each remaining triangle is similar to the original triangle. Assume that the length of each side of the original triangle is one unit.

Write a formula that describes the side length of the triangles that will be generated in the nth stage. Write a formula for the area of the triangles that will be generated in the nth stage.

FIGURE FOR 7

8. You can define a sequence using a piecewise formula. The following is an example of a piecewise-defined sequence.

$$a_1 = 7, \quad a_n = \begin{cases} \dfrac{a_{n-1}}{2}, & \text{if } a_{n-1} \text{ is even} \\ 3a_{n-1} + 1, & \text{if } a_{n-1} \text{ is odd} \end{cases}$$

(a) Write the first 10 terms of the sequence.

(b) Choose three different values for a_1 (other than $a_1 = 7$). For each value of a_1, find the first 10 terms of the sequence. What conclusions can you make about the behavior of this sequence?

9. The numbers 1, 5, 12, 22, 35, 51, . . . are called pentagonal numbers because they represent the numbers of dots used to make pentagons, as shown below. Use mathematical induction to prove that the nth pentagonal number P_n is given by

$$P_n = \frac{n(3n - 1)}{2}.$$

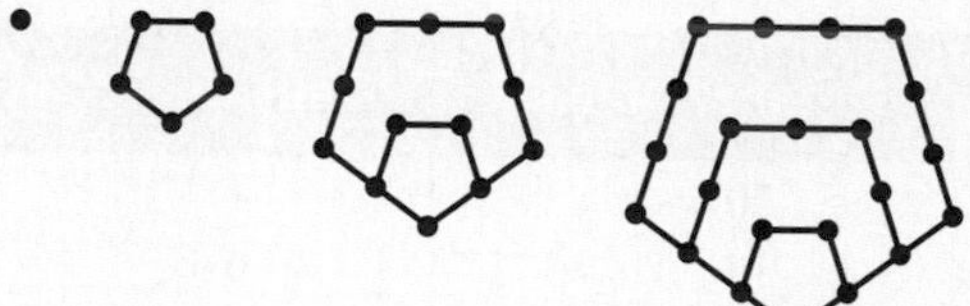

10. What conclusion can be drawn from the following information about the sequence of statements P_n?

(a) P_3 is true and P_k implies P_{k+1}.

(b) $P_1, P_2, P_3, \ldots, P_{50}$ are all true.

(c) P_1, P_2, and P_3 are all true, but the truth of P_k does not imply that P_{k+1} is true.

(d) P_2 is true and P_{2k} implies P_{2k+2}.

11. Let $f_1, f_2, \ldots, f_n, \ldots$ be the Fibonacci sequence.

(a) Use mathematical induction to prove that

$$f_1 + f_2 + \cdots + f_n = f_{n+2} - 1.$$

(b) Find the sum of the first 20 terms of the Fibonacci sequence.

12. The odds in favor of an event occurring are the ratio of the probability that the event will occur to the probability that the event will not occur. The reciprocal of this ratio represents the odds against the event occurring.

(a) Six marbles in a bag are red. The odds against choosing a red marble are 4 to 1. How many marbles are in the bag?

(b) A bag contains three blue marbles and seven yellow marbles. What are the odds in favor of choosing a blue marble? What are the odds against choosing a blue marble?

(c) Write a formula for converting the odds in favor of an event to the probability of the event.

(d) Write a formula for converting the probability of an event to the odds in favor of the event.

13. You are taking a test that contains only multiple choice questions (there are five choices for each question). You are on the last question and you know that the answer is not B or D, but you are not sure about answers A, C, and E. What is the probability that you will get the right answer if you take a guess?

14. A dart is thrown at the circular target shown below. The dart is equally likely to hit any point inside the target. What is the probability that it hits the region outside the triangle?

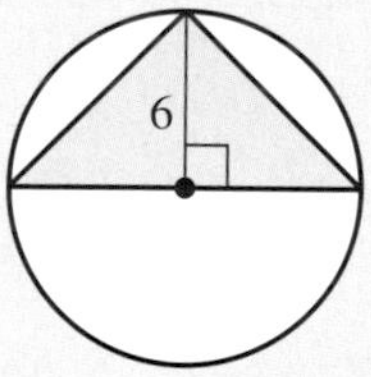

15. An event A has n possible outcomes, which have the values $x_1, x_2, \ldots, x_n$. The probabilities of the n outcomes occurring are $p_1, p_2, \ldots, p_n$. The **expected value** V of an event A is the sum of the products of the outcomes' probabilities and their values, $V = p_1x_1 + p_2x_2 + \cdots + p_nx_n$.

(a) To win California's Super Lotto Plus game, you must match five different numbers chosen from the numbers 1 to 47, plus one Mega number chosen from the numbers 1 to 27. You purchase a ticket for \$1. If the jackpot for the next drawing is \$12,000,000, what is the expected value for the ticket?

(b) You are playing a dice game in which you need to score 60 points to win. On each turn, you roll two six-sided dice. Your score for the turn is 0 if the dice do not show the same number, and the product of the numbers on the dice if they do show the same number. What is the expected value for each turn? How many turns will it take on average to score 60 points?

Topics in Analytic Geometry

10

10.1 **Lines**
10.2 **Introduction to Conics: Parabolas**
10.3 **Ellipses**
10.4 **Hyperbolas**
10.5 **Rotation of Conics**
10.6 **Parametric Equations**
10.7 **Polar Coordinates**
10.8 **Graphs of Polar Equations**
10.9 **Polar Equations of Conics**

The nine planets move about the sun in elliptical orbits. You can use the techniques presented in this chapter to determine the distances between the planets and the center of the sun.

Kauko Helavuo/Getty Images

SELECTED APPLICATIONS

Analytic geometry concepts have many real-life applications. The applications listed below represent a small sample of the applications in this chapter.

- Inclined Plane, Exercise 56, page 734
- Revenue, Exercise 59, page 741
- Architecture, Exercise 57, page 751
- Satellite Orbit, Exercise 60, page 752
- LORAN, Exercise 42, page 761
- Running Path, Exercise 44, page 762
- Projectile Motion, Exercises 57 and 58, page 777
- Planetary Motion, Exercises 51–56, page 798
- Locating an Explosion, Exercise 40, page 802

10.1 Lines

What you should learn

- Find the inclination of a line.
- Find the angle between two lines.
- Find the distance between a point and a line.

Why you should learn it

The inclination of a line can be used to measure heights indirectly. For instance, in Exercise 56 on page 734, the inclination of a line can be used to determine the change in elevation from the base to the top of the Johnstown Inclined Plane.

AP/Wide World Photos

Inclination of a Line

In Section 1.3, you learned that the graph of the linear equation

$$y = mx + b$$

is a nonvertical line with slope m and y-intercept $(0, b)$. There, the slope of a line was described as the rate of change in y with respect to x. In this section, you will look at the slope of a line in terms of the angle of inclination of the line.

Every nonhorizontal line must intersect the x-axis. The angle formed by such an intersection determines the **inclination** of the line, as specified in the following definition.

> **Definition of Inclination**
>
> The **inclination** of a nonhorizontal line is the positive angle θ (less than π) measured counterclockwise from the x-axis to the line. (See Figure 10.1.)

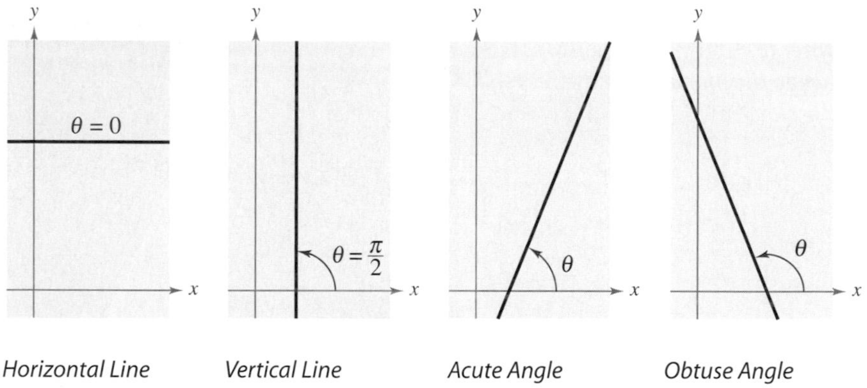

FIGURE 10.1

The inclination of a line is related to its slope in the following manner.

> **Inclination and Slope**
>
> If a nonvertical line has inclination θ and slope m, then
>
> $$m = \tan \theta.$$

For a proof of the relation between inclination and slope, see Proofs in Mathematics on page 806.

Example 1 Finding the Inclination of a Line

Find the inclination of the line $2x + 3y = 6$.

Solution

The slope of this line is $m = -\frac{2}{3}$. So, its inclination is determined from the equation

$$\tan \theta = -\frac{2}{3}.$$

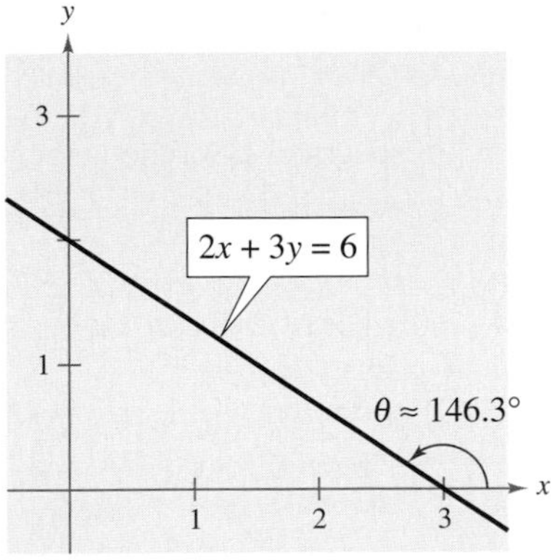

FIGURE 10.2

From Figure 10.2, it follows that $\frac{\pi}{2} < \theta < \pi$. This means that

$$\begin{aligned}\theta &= \pi + \arctan\left(-\frac{2}{3}\right)\\ &\approx \pi + (-0.588)\\ &= \pi - 0.588\\ &\approx 2.554.\end{aligned}$$

The angle of inclination is about 2.554 radians or about 146.3°.

CHECKPOINT Now try Exercise 19.

The Angle Between Two Lines

Two distinct lines in a plane are either parallel or intersecting. If they intersect and are nonperpendicular, their intersection forms two pairs of opposite angles. One pair is acute and the other pair is obtuse. The smaller of these angles is called the **angle between the two lines.** As shown in Figure 10.3, you can use the inclinations of the two lines to find the angle between the two lines. If two lines have inclinations θ_1 and θ_2, where $\theta_1 < \theta_2$ and $\theta_2 - \theta_1 < \pi/2$, the angle between the two lines is

$$\theta = \theta_2 - \theta_1.$$

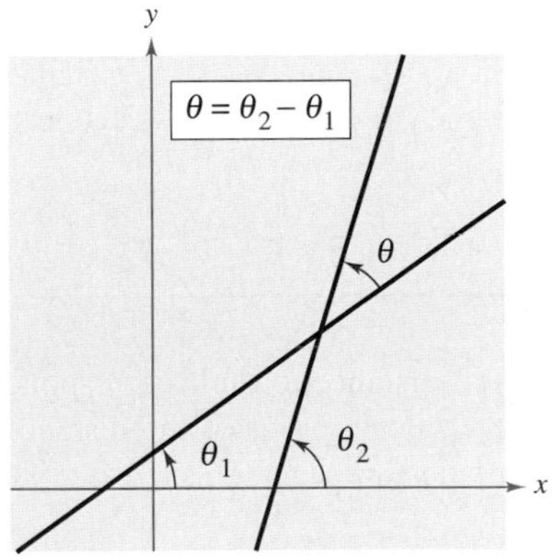

FIGURE 10.3

You can use the formula for the tangent of the difference of two angles

$$\begin{aligned}\tan \theta &= \tan(\theta_2 - \theta_1)\\ &= \frac{\tan \theta_2 - \tan \theta_1}{1 + \tan \theta_1 \tan \theta_2}\end{aligned}$$

to obtain the formula for the angle between two lines.

Angle Between Two Lines

If two nonperpendicular lines have slopes m_1 and m_2, the angle between the two lines is

$$\tan \theta = \left|\frac{m_2 - m_1}{1 + m_1 m_2}\right|.$$

Example 2 Finding the Angle Between Two Lines

Find the angle between the two lines.

Line 1: $2x - y - 4 = 0$ *Line 2:* $3x + 4y - 12 = 0$

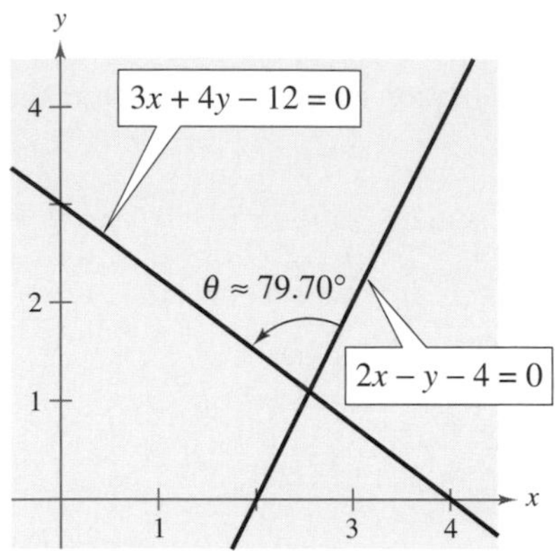

FIGURE 10.4

Solution

The two lines have slopes of $m_1 = 2$ and $m_2 = -\frac{3}{4}$, respectively. So, the tangent of the angle between the two lines is

$$\tan\theta = \left|\frac{m_2 - m_1}{1 + m_1 m_2}\right| = \left|\frac{(-3/4) - 2}{1 + (2)(-3/4)}\right| = \left|\frac{-11/4}{-2/4}\right| = \frac{11}{2}.$$

Finally, you can conclude that the angle is

$$\theta = \arctan\frac{11}{2} \approx 1.391 \text{ radians} \approx 79.70°$$

as shown in Figure 10.4.

CHECKPOINT Now try Exercise 27.

The Distance Between a Point and a Line

Finding the distance between a line and a point not on the line is an application of perpendicular lines. This distance is defined as the length of the perpendicular line segment joining the point and the line, as shown in Figure 10.5.

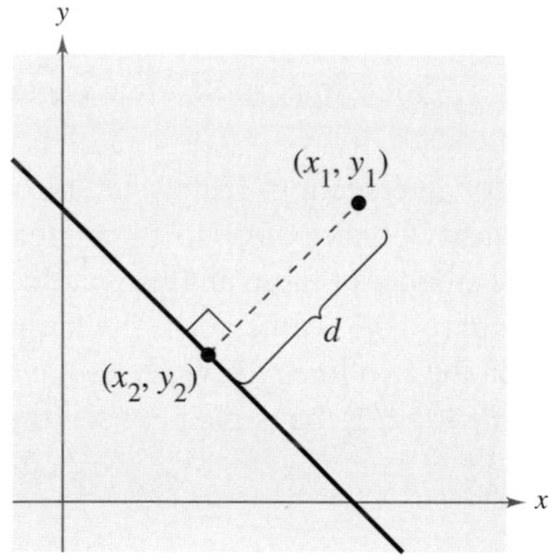

FIGURE 10.5

Distance Between a Point and a Line

The distance between the point (x_1, y_1) and the line $Ax + By + C = 0$ is

$$d = \frac{|Ax_1 + By_1 + C|}{\sqrt{A^2 + B^2}}.$$

Remember that the values of A, B, and C in this distance formula correspond to the general equation of a line, $Ax + By + C = 0$. For a proof of the distance between a point and a line, see Proofs in Mathematics on page 806.

Example 3 Finding the Distance Between a Point and a Line

Find the distance between the point $(4, 1)$ and the line $y = 2x + 1$.

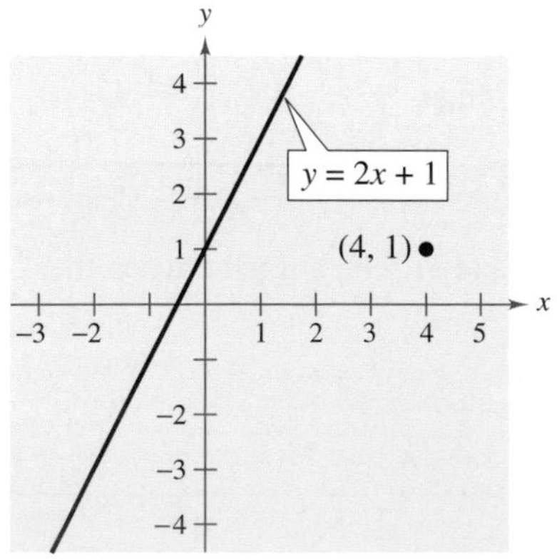

FIGURE 10.6

Solution

The general form of the equation is

$$-2x + y - 1 = 0.$$

So, the distance between the point and the line is

$$d = \frac{|-2(4) + 1(1) + (-1)|}{\sqrt{(-2)^2 + 1^2}} = \frac{8}{\sqrt{5}} \approx 3.58 \text{ units}.$$

The line and the point are shown in Figure 10.6.

CHECKPOINT Now try Exercise 39.

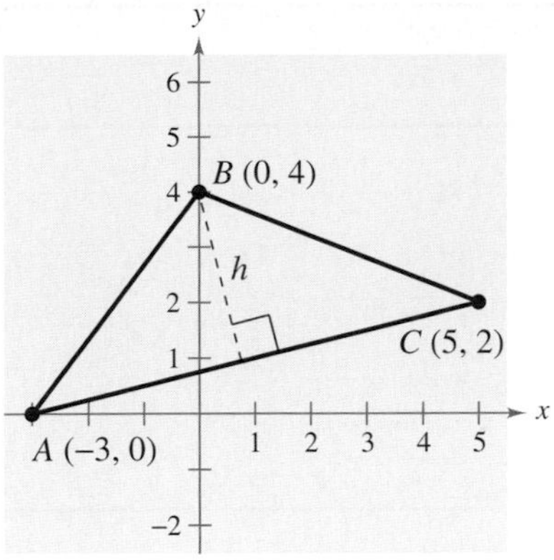

FIGURE 10.7

Example 4 **An Application of Two Distance Formulas**

Figure 10.7 shows a triangle with vertices $A(-3, 0)$, $B(0, 4)$, and $C(5, 2)$.

a. Find the altitude h from vertex B to side AC.

b. Find the area of the triangle.

Solution

a. To find the altitude, use the formula for the distance between line AC and the point $(0, 4)$. The equation of line AC is obtained as follows.

Slope: $m = \dfrac{2-0}{5-(-3)} = \dfrac{2}{8} = \dfrac{1}{4}$

Equation: $y - 0 = \dfrac{1}{4}(x + 3)$ — Point-slope form

$4y = x + 3$ — Multiply each side by 4.

$x - 4y + 3 = 0$ — General form

So, the distance between this line and the point $(0, 4)$ is

$$\text{Altitude} = h = \frac{|1(0) + (-4)(4) + 3|}{\sqrt{1^2 + (-4)^2}} = \frac{13}{\sqrt{17}} \text{ units.}$$

b. Using the formula for the distance between two points, you can find the length of the base AC to be

$b = \sqrt{[5-(-3)]^2 + (2-0)^2}$ — Distance Formula

$= \sqrt{8^2 + 2^2}$ — Simplify.

$= \sqrt{68}$ — Simplify.

$= 2\sqrt{17}$ units. — Simplify.

Finally, the area of the triangle in Figure 10.7 is

$A = \dfrac{1}{2}bh$ — Formula for the area of a triangle

$= \dfrac{1}{2}\left(2\sqrt{17}\right)\left(\dfrac{13}{\sqrt{17}}\right)$ — Substitute for b and h.

$= 13$ square units. — Simplify.

CHECKPOINT Now try Exercise 45.

WRITING ABOUT MATHEMATICS

Inclination and the Angle Between Two Lines Discuss why the inclination of a line can be an angle that is larger than $\pi/2$, but the angle between two lines cannot be larger than $\pi/2$. Decide whether the following statement is true or false: "The inclination of a line is the angle between the line and the x-axis." Explain.

10.1 Exercises

VOCABULARY CHECK: Fill in the blanks.

1. The ________ of a nonhorizontal line is the positive angle θ (less than π) measured counterclockwise from the x-axis to the line.
2. If a nonvertical line has inclination θ and slope m, then $m =$ ________ .
3. If two nonperpendicular lines have slopes m_1 and m_2, the angle between the two lines is $\tan \theta =$ ________ .
4. The distance between the point (x_1, y_1) and the line $Ax + By + C = 0$ is given by $d =$ ________ .

In Exercises 1–8, find the slope of the line with inclination θ.

1.
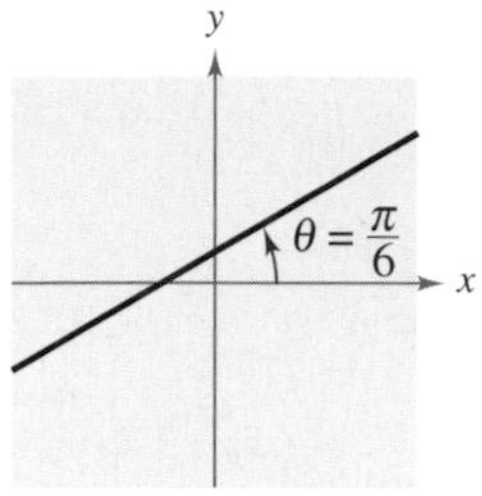

2.
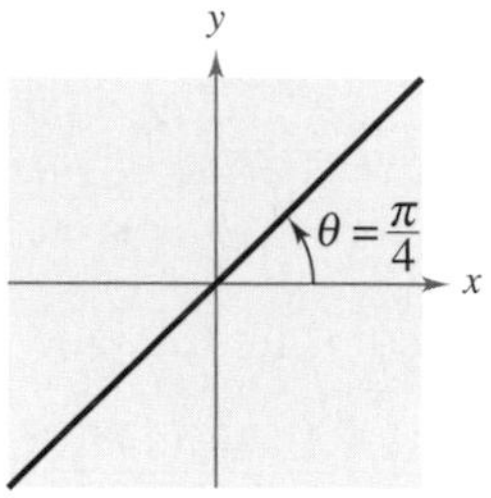

3.
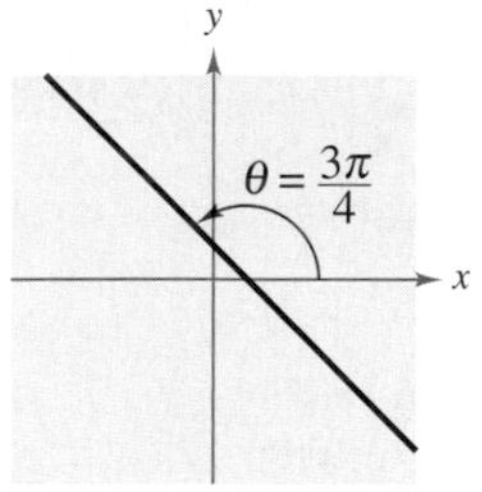

4.
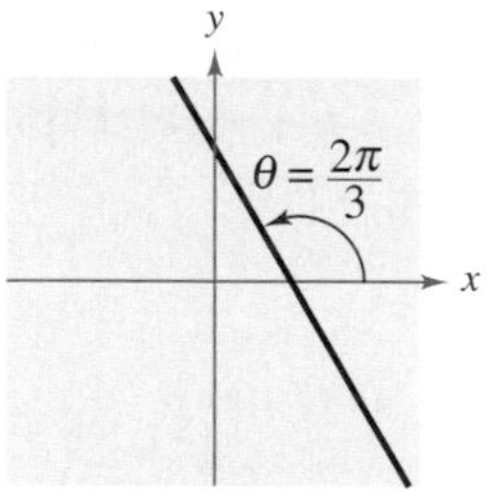

5. $\theta = \frac{\pi}{3}$ radians
6. $\theta = \frac{5\pi}{6}$ radians
7. $\theta = 1.27$ radians
8. $\theta = 2.88$ radians

In Exercises 9–14, find the inclination θ (in radians and degrees) of the line with a slope of m.

9. $m = -1$
10. $m = -2$
11. $m = 1$
12. $m = 2$
13. $m = \frac{3}{4}$
14. $m = -\frac{5}{2}$

In Exercises 15–18, find the inclination θ (in radians and degrees) of the line passing through the points.

15. $(6, 1), (10, 8)$
16. $(12, 8), (-4, -3)$
17. $(-2, 20), (10, 0)$
18. $(0, 100), (50, 0)$

In Exercises 19–22, find the inclination θ (in radians and degrees) of the line.

19. $6x - 2y + 8 = 0$
20. $4x + 5y - 9 = 0$
21. $5x + 3y = 0$
22. $x - y - 10 = 0$

In Exercises 23–32, find the angle θ (in radians and degrees) between the lines.

23. $3x + y = 3$
$x - y = 2$

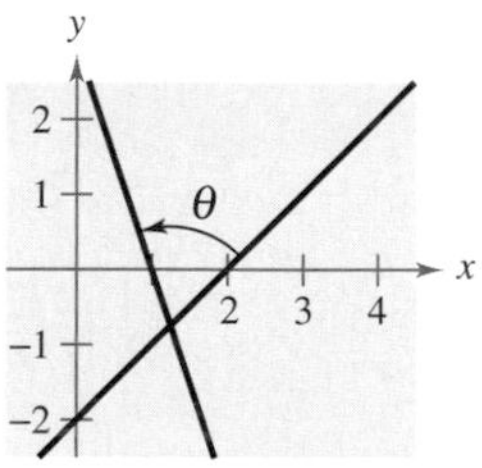

24. $x + 3y = 2$
$x - 2y = -3$

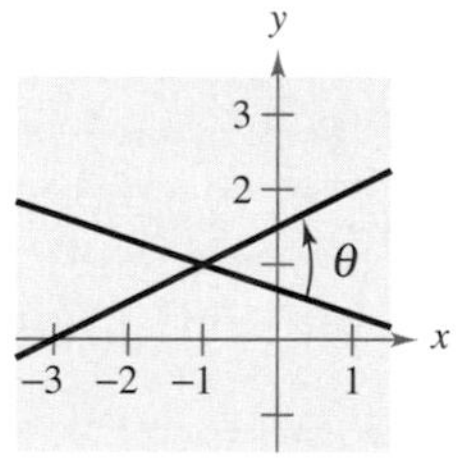

25. $x - y = 0$
$3x - 2y = -1$

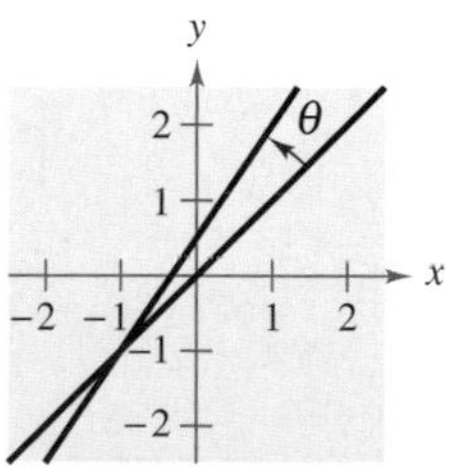

26. $2x - y = 2$
$4x + 3y = 24$

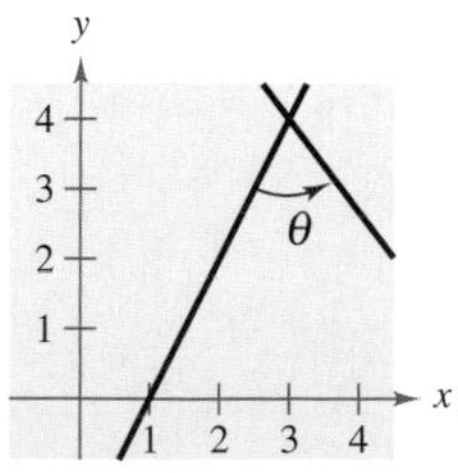

27. $x - 2y = 7$
$6x + 2y = 5$

28. $5x + 2y = 16$
$3x - 5y = -1$

29. $x + 2y = 8$
$x - 2y = 2$

30. $3x - 5y = 3$
$3x + 5y = 12$

31. $0.05x - 0.03y = 0.21$
$0.07x + 0.02y = 0.16$

32. $0.02x - 0.05y = -0.19$
$0.03x + 0.04y = 0.52$

Angle Measurement **In Exercises 33–36, find the slope of each side of the triangle and use the slopes to find the measures of the interior angles.**

33.

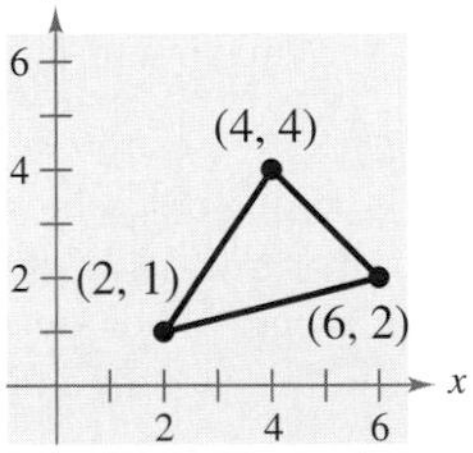

34.

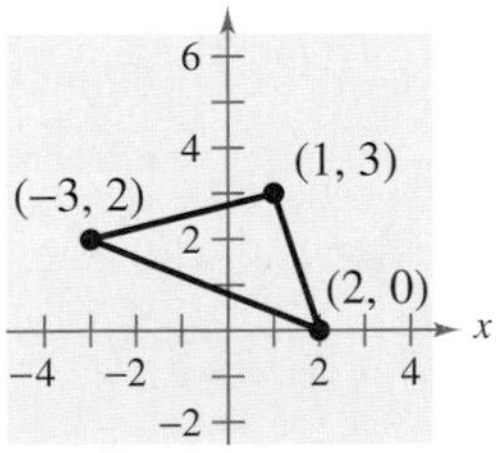

35.

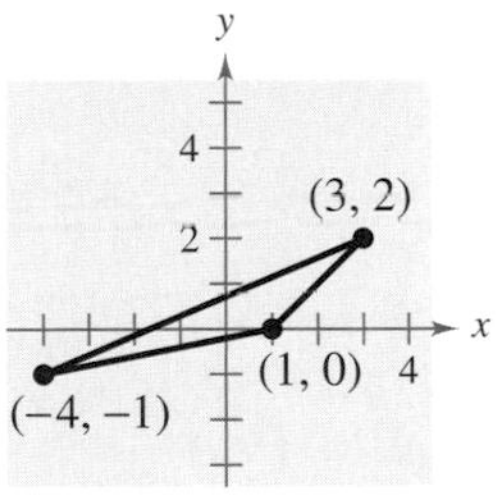

36.

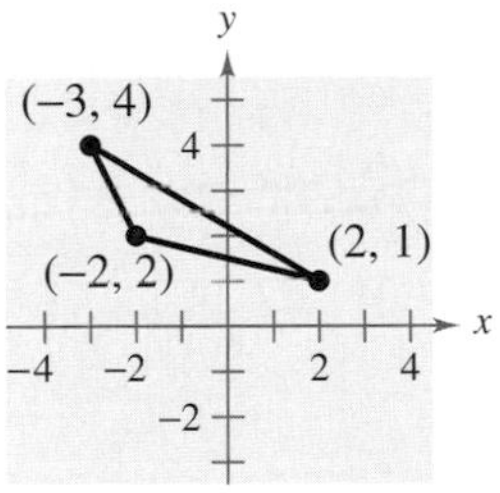

In Exercises 37–44, find the distance between the point and the line.

	Point	*Line*
37.	$(0, 0)$	$4x + 3y = 0$
38.	$(0, 0)$	$2x - y = 4$
39.	$(2, 3)$	$4x + 3y = 10$
40.	$(-2, 1)$	$x - y = 2$
41.	$(6, 2)$	$x + 1 = 0$
42.	$(10, 8)$	$y - 4 = 0$
43.	$(0, 8)$	$6x - y = 0$
44.	$(4, 2)$	$x - y = 20$

In Exercises 45–48, the points represent the vertices of a triangle. (a) Draw triangle *ABC* in the coordinate plane, (b) find the altitude from vertex *B* of the triangle to side *AC*, and (c) find the area of the triangle.

45. $A = (0, 0),\ B = (1, 4),\ C = (4, 0)$

46. $A = (0, 0),\ B = (4, 5),\ C = (5, -2)$

47. $A = \left(-\frac{1}{2}, \frac{1}{2}\right),\ B = (2, 3),\ C = \left(\frac{5}{2}, 0\right)$

48. $A = (-4, -5),\ B = (3, 10),\ C = (6, 12)$

In Exercises 49 and 50, find the distance between the parallel lines.

49. $x + y = 1$
$x + y = 5$

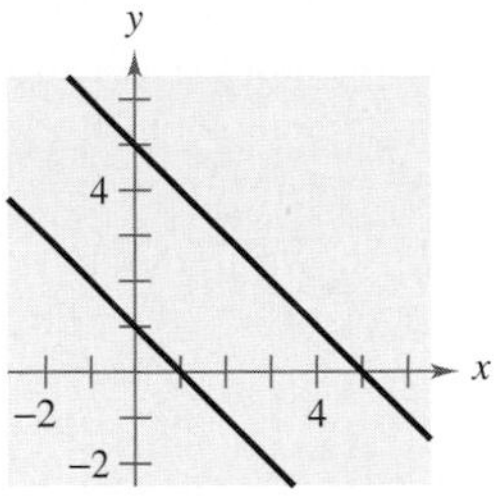

50. $3x - 4y = 1$
$3x - 4y = 10$

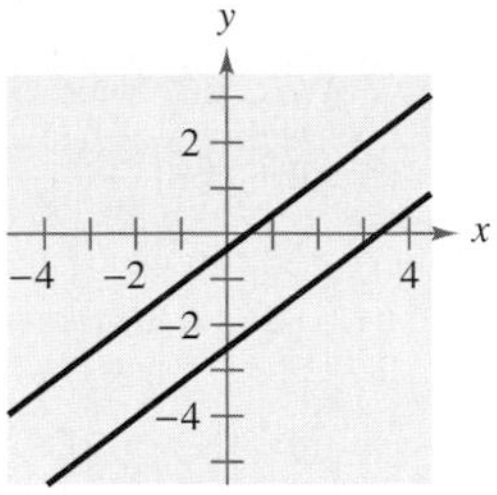

51. *Road Grade* A straight road rises with an inclination of 0.10 radian from the horizontal (see figure). Find the slope of the road and the change in elevation over a two-mile stretch of the road.

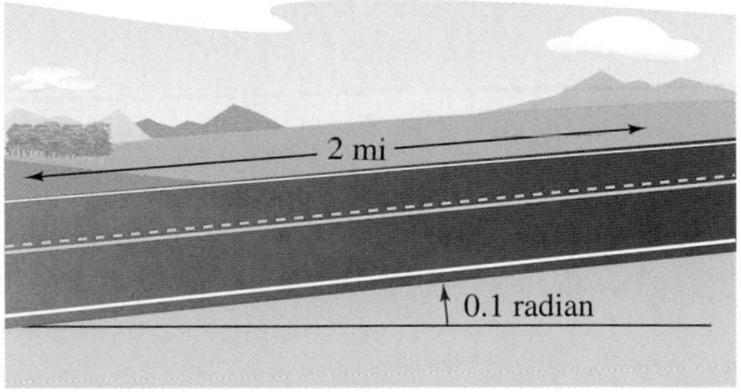

52. *Road Grade* A straight road rises with an inclination of 0.20 radian from the horizontal. Find the slope of the road and the change in elevation over a one-mile stretch of the road.

53. *Pitch of a Roof* A roof has a rise of 3 feet for every horizontal change of 5 feet (see figure). Find the inclination of the roof.

54. ***Conveyor Design*** A moving conveyor is built so that it rises 1 meter for each 3 meters of horizontal travel.

(a) Draw a diagram that gives a visual representation of the problem.

(b) Find the inclination of the conveyor.

(c) The conveyor runs between two floors in a factory. The distance between the floors is 5 meters. Find the length of the conveyor.

55. ***Truss*** Find the angles α and β shown in the drawing of the roof truss.

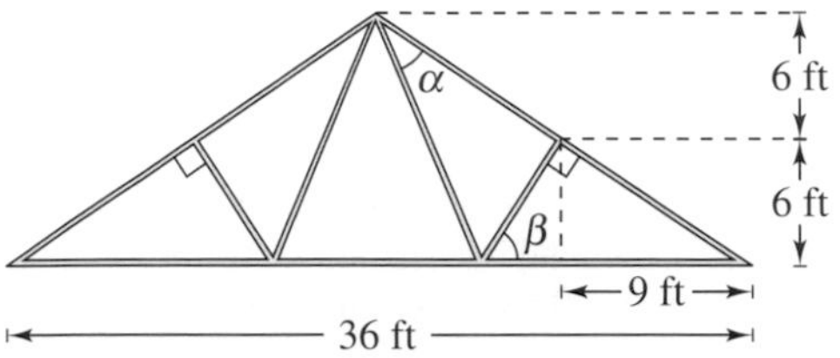

Model It

56. ***Inclined Plane*** The Johnstown Inclined Plane in Johnstown, Pennsylvania is an inclined railway that was designed to carry people to the hilltop community of Westmont. It also proved useful in carrying people and vehicles to safety during severe floods. The railway is 896.5 feet long with a 70.9% uphill grade (see figure).

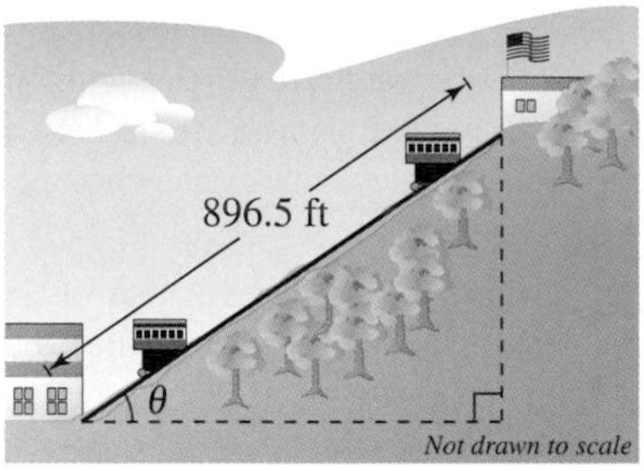

(a) Find the inclination θ of the railway.

(b) Find the change in elevation from the base to the top of the railway.

(c) Using the origin of a rectangular coordinate system as the base of the inclined plane, find the equation of the line that models the railway track.

(d) Sketch a graph of the equation you found in part (c).

Synthesis

True or False? **In Exercises 57 and 58, determine whether the statement is true or false. Justify your answer.**

57. A line that has an inclination greater than $\pi/2$ radians has a negative slope.

58. To find the angle between two lines whose angles of inclination θ_1 and θ_2 are known, substitute θ_1 and θ_2 for m_1 and m_2, respectively, in the formula for the angle between two lines.

59. ***Exploration*** Consider a line with slope m and y-intercept $(0, 4)$.

(a) Write the distance d between the origin and the line as a function of m.

(b) Graph the function in part (a).

(c) Find the slope that yields the maximum distance between the origin and the line.

(d) Find the asymptote of the graph in part (b) and interpret its meaning in the context of the problem.

60. ***Exploration*** Consider a line with slope m and y-intercept $(0, 4)$.

(a) Write the distance d between the point $(3, 1)$ and the line as a function of m.

(b) Graph the function in part (a).

(c) Find the slope that yields the maximum distance between the point and the line.

(d) Is it possible for the distance to be 0? If so, what is the slope of the line that yields a distance of 0?

(e) Find the asymptote of the graph in part (b) and interpret its meaning in the context of the problem.

Skills Review

In Exercises 61–66, find all x-intercepts and y-intercepts of the graph of the quadratic function.

61. $f(x) = (x - 7)^2$

62. $f(x) = (x + 9)^2$

63. $f(x) = (x - 5)^2 - 5$

64. $f(x) = (x + 11)^2 + 12$

65. $f(x) = x^2 - 7x - 1$

66. $f(x) = x^2 + 9x - 22$

In Exercises 67–72, write the quadratic function in standard form by completing the square. Identify the vertex of the function.

67. $f(x) = 3x^2 + 2x - 16$

68. $f(x) = 2x^2 - x - 21$

69. $f(x) = 5x^2 + 34x - 7$

70. $f(x) = -x^2 - 8x - 15$

71. $f(x) = 6x^2 - x - 12$

72. $f(x) = -8x^2 - 34x - 21$

In Exercises 73–76, graph the quadratic function.

73. $f(x) = (x - 4)^2 + 3$

74. $f(x) = 6 - (x + 1)^2$

75. $g(x) = 2x^2 - 3x + 1$

76. $g(x) = -x^2 + 6x - 8$

10.2 Introduction to Conics: Parabolas

What you should learn

- Recognize a conic as the intersection of a plane and a double-napped cone.
- Write equations of parabolas in standard form and graph parabolas.
- Use the reflective property of parabolas to solve real-life problems.

Why you should learn it

Parabolas can be used to model and solve many types of real-life problems. For instance, in Exercise 62 on page 742, a parabola is used to model the cables of the Golden Gate Bridge.

Cosmo Condina/Getty Images

Conics

Conic sections were discovered during the classical Greek period, 600 to 300 B.C. The early Greeks were concerned largely with the geometric properties of conics. It was not until the 17th century that the broad applicability of conics became apparent and played a prominent role in the early development of calculus.

A **conic section** (or simply **conic**) is the intersection of a plane and a double-napped cone. Notice in Figure 10.8 that in the formation of the four basic conics, the intersecting plane does not pass through the vertex of the cone. When the plane does pass through the vertex, the resulting figure is a **degenerate conic,** as shown in Figure 10.9.

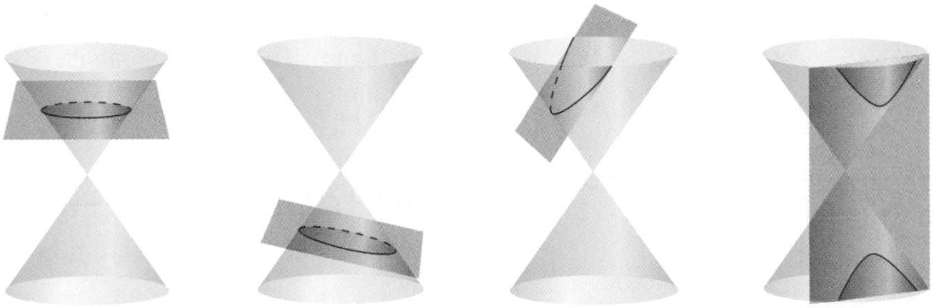

Circle *Ellipse* *Parabola* *Hyperbola*

FIGURE 10.8 *Basic Conics*

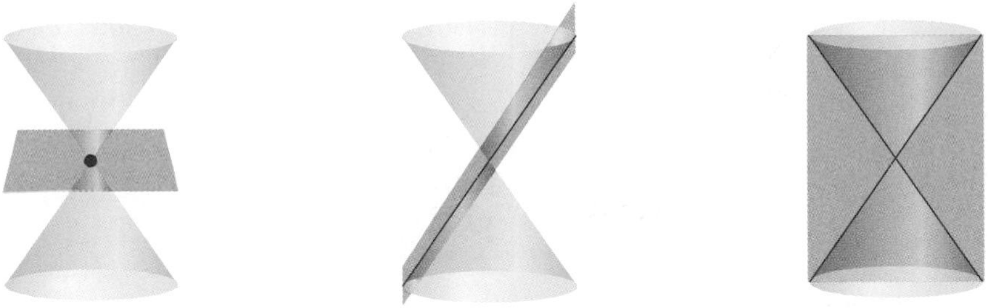

Point *Line* *Two Intersecting Lines*

FIGURE 10.9 *Degenerate Conics*

There are several ways to approach the study of conics. You could begin by defining conics in terms of the intersections of planes and cones, as the Greeks did, or you could define them algebraically, in terms of the general second-degree equation

$$Ax^2 + Bxy + Cy^2 + Dx + Ey + F = 0.$$

However, you will study a third approach, in which each of the conics is defined as a **locus** (collection) of points satisfying a geometric property. For example, in Section 1.2, you learned that a circle is defined as the collection of all points (x, y) that are equidistant from a fixed point (h, k). This leads to the standard form of the equation of a circle

$$(x - h)^2 + (y - k)^2 = r^2. \qquad \text{Equation of circle}$$

Parabolas

In Section 2.1, you learned that the graph of the quadratic function

$$f(x) = ax^2 + bx + c$$

is a parabola that opens upward or downward. The following definition of a parabola is more general in the sense that it is independent of the orientation of the parabola.

> **Definition of Parabola**
>
> A **parabola** is the set of all points (x, y) in a plane that are equidistant from a fixed line **(directrix)** and a fixed point **(focus)** not on the line.

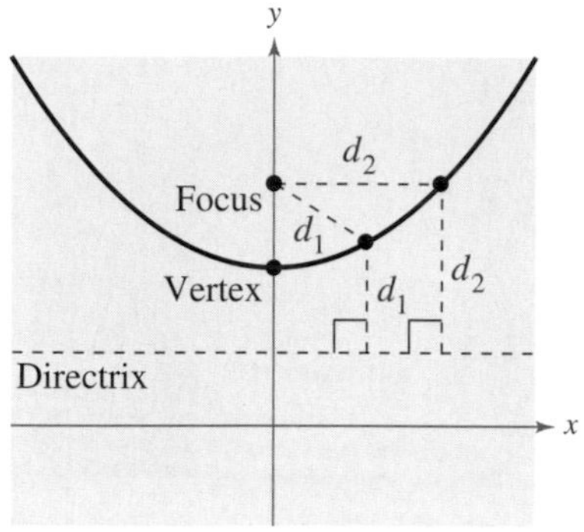

FIGURE 10.10 *Parabola*

The midpoint between the focus and the directrix is called the **vertex,** and the line passing through the focus and the vertex is called the **axis** of the parabola. Note in Figure 10.10 that a parabola is symmetric with respect to its axis. Using the definition of a parabola, you can derive the following **standard form** of the equation of a parabola whose directrix is parallel to the x-axis or to the y-axis.

> **Standard Equation of a Parabola**
>
> The **standard form of the equation of a parabola** with vertex at (h, k) is as follows.
>
> $(x - h)^2 = 4p(y - k),\ p \neq 0$ Vertical axis, directrix: $y = k - p$
>
> $(y - k)^2 = 4p(x - h),\ p \neq 0$ Horizontal axis, directrix: $x = h - p$
>
> The focus lies on the axis p units (*directed distance*) from the vertex. If the vertex is at the origin $(0, 0)$, the equation takes one of the following forms.
>
> $x^2 = 4py$ Vertical axis
>
> $y^2 = 4px$ Horizontal axis
>
> See Figure 10.11.

For a proof of the standard form of the equation of a parabola, see Proofs in Mathematics on page 807.

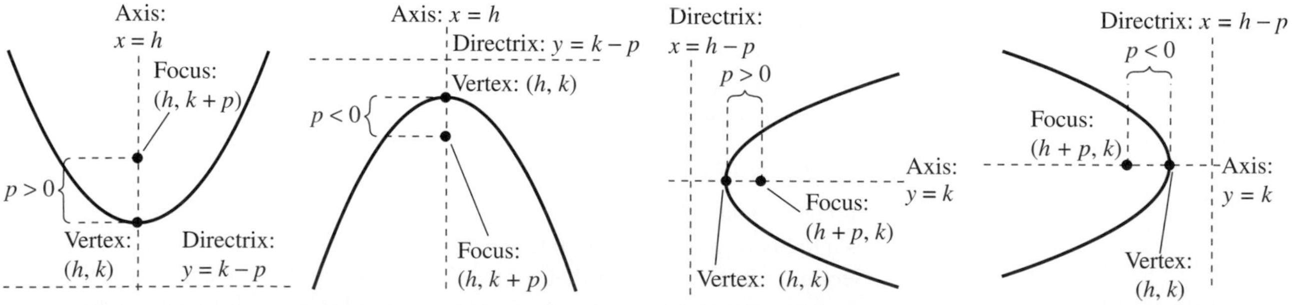

(a) $(x - h)^2 = 4p(y - k)$ **Vertical axis:** $p > 0$

(b) $(x - h)^2 = 4p(y - k)$ **Vertical axis:** $p < 0$

(c) $(y - k)^2 = 4p(x - h)$ **Horizontal axis:** $p > 0$

(d) $(y - k)^2 = 4p(x - h)$ **Horizontal axis:** $p < 0$

FIGURE 10.11

Technology

Use a graphing utility to confirm the equation found in Example 1. In order to graph the equation, you may have to use two separate equations:

$y_1 = \sqrt{8x}$ Upper part

and

$y_2 = -\sqrt{8x}.$ Lower part

STUDY TIP

You may want to review the technique of completing the square found in Appendix A.5, which will be used to rewrite each of the conics in standard form.

Example 1 Vertex at the Origin

Find the standard equation of the parabola with vertex at the origin and focus $(2, 0)$.

Solution

The axis of the parabola is horizontal, passing through $(0, 0)$ and $(2, 0)$, as shown in Figure 10.12.

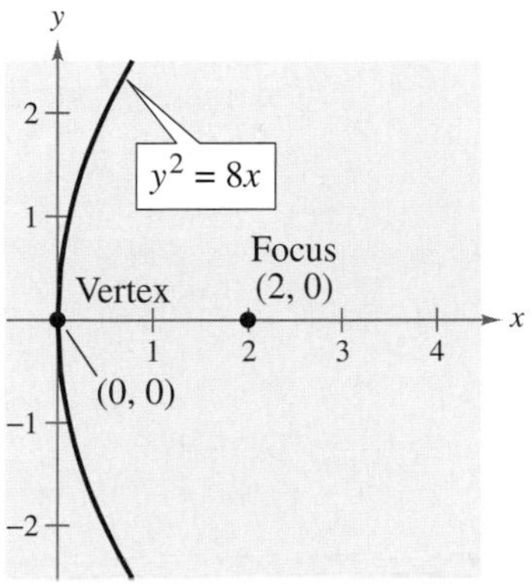

FIGURE 10.12

So, the standard form is $y^2 = 4px$, where $h = 0$, $k = 0$, and $p = 2$. So, the equation is $y^2 = 8x$.

CHECKPOINT Now try Exercise 33.

Example 2 Finding the Focus of a Parabola

Find the focus of the parabola given by $y = -\frac{1}{2}x^2 - x + \frac{1}{2}$.

Solution

To find the focus, convert to standard form by completing the square.

$y = -\frac{1}{2}x^2 - x + \frac{1}{2}$	Write original equation.
$-2y = x^2 + 2x - 1$	Multiply each side by –2.
$1 - 2y = x^2 + 2x$	Add 1 to each side.
$1 + 1 - 2y = x^2 + 2x + 1$	Complete the square.
$2 - 2y = x^2 + 2x + 1$	Combine like terms.
$-2(y - 1) = (x + 1)^2$	Standard form

Comparing this equation with

$$(x - h)^2 = 4p(y - k)$$

you can conclude that $h = -1, k = 1$, and $p = -\frac{1}{2}$. Because p is negative, the parabola opens downward, as shown in Figure 10.13. So, the focus of the parabola is $(h, k \mid p) = \left(-1, \frac{1}{2}\right)$.

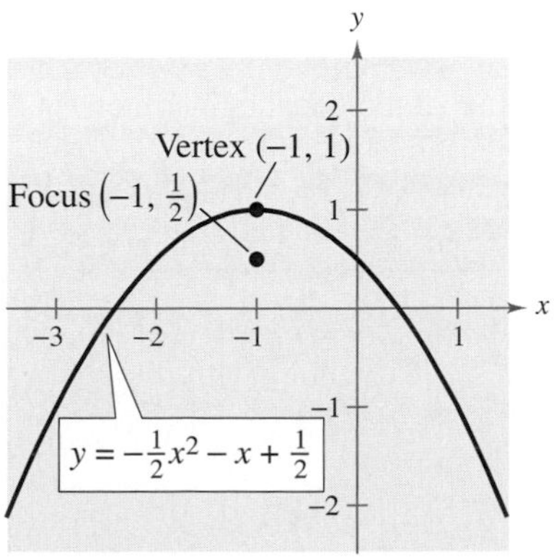

FIGURE 10.13

CHECKPOINT Now try Exercise 21.

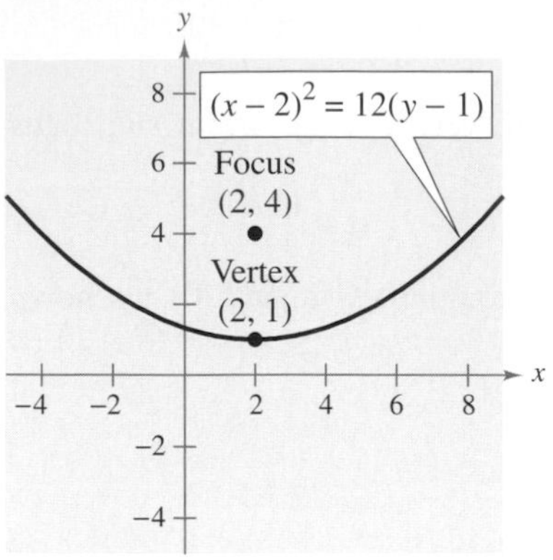

FIGURE 10.14

Example 3 Finding the Standard Equation of a Parabola

Find the standard form of the equation of the parabola with vertex (2, 1) and focus (2, 4).

Solution

Because the axis of the parabola is vertical, passing through (2, 1) and (2, 4), consider the equation

$$(x - h)^2 = 4p(y - k)$$

where $h = 2$, $k = 1$, and $p = 4 - 1 = 3$. So, the standard form is

$$(x - 2)^2 = 12(y - 1).$$

You can obtain the more common quadratic form as follows.

$$(x - 2)^2 = 12(y - 1) \qquad \text{Write original equation.}$$

$$x^2 - 4x + 4 = 12y - 12 \qquad \text{Multiply.}$$

$$x^2 - 4x + 16 = 12y \qquad \text{Add 12 to each side.}$$

$$\frac{1}{12}(x^2 - 4x + 16) = y \qquad \text{Divide each side by 12.}$$

The graph of this parabola is shown in Figure 10.14.

CHECKPOINT Now try Exercise 45.

Application

A line segment that passes through the focus of a parabola and has endpoints on the parabola is called a **focal chord.** The specific focal chord perpendicular to the axis of the parabola is called the **latus rectum.**

Parabolas occur in a wide variety of applications. For instance, a parabolic reflector can be formed by revolving a parabola around its axis. The resulting surface has the property that all incoming rays parallel to the axis are reflected through the focus of the parabola. This is the principle behind the construction of the parabolic mirrors used in reflecting telescopes. Conversely, the light rays emanating from the focus of a parabolic reflector used in a flashlight are all parallel to one another, as shown in Figure 10.15.

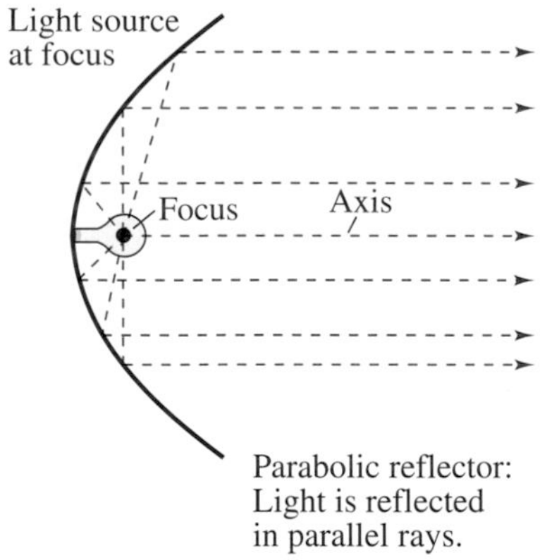

FIGURE 10.15

A line is **tangent** to a parabola at a point on the parabola if the line intersects, but does not cross, the parabola at the point. Tangent lines to parabolas have special properties related to the use of parabolas in constructing reflective surfaces.

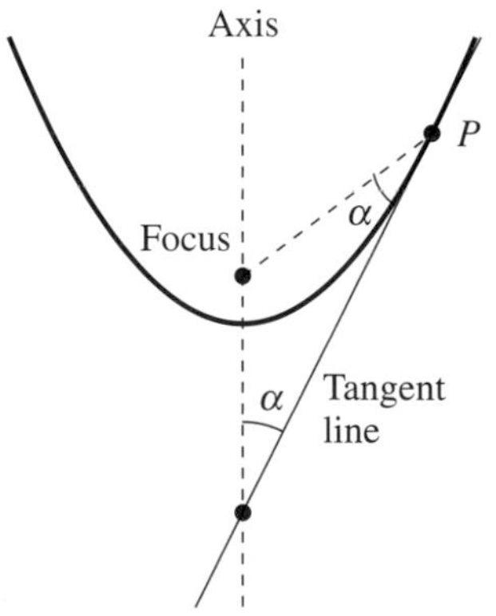

FIGURE 10.16

Reflective Property of a Parabola

The tangent line to a parabola at a point P makes equal angles with the following two lines (see Figure 10.16).

1. The line passing through P and the focus
2. The axis of the parabola

Example 4 Finding the Tangent Line at a Point on a Parabola

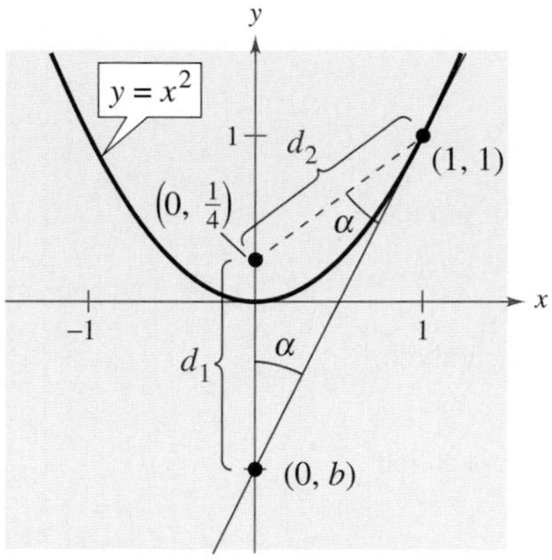

FIGURE 10.17

Find the equation of the tangent line to the parabola given by $y = x^2$ at the point $(1, 1)$.

Solution

For this parabola, $p = \frac{1}{4}$ and the focus is $\left(0, \frac{1}{4}\right)$, as shown in Figure 10.17. You can find the y-intercept $(0, b)$ of the tangent line by equating the lengths of the two sides of the isosceles triangle shown in Figure 10.17:

$$d_1 = \frac{1}{4} - b$$

and

$$d_2 = \sqrt{(1 - 0)^2 + \left[1 - \left(\frac{1}{4}\right)\right]^2} = \frac{5}{4}.$$

Note that $d_1 = \frac{1}{4} - b$ rather than $b - \frac{1}{4}$. The order of subtraction for the distance is important because the distance must be positive. Setting $d_1 = d_2$ produces

$$\frac{1}{4} - b = \frac{5}{4}$$

$$b = -1.$$

So, the slope of the tangent line is

$$m = \frac{1 - (-1)}{1 - 0} = 2$$

and the equation of the tangent line in slope-intercept form is

$$y = 2x - 1.$$

✓CHECKPOINT Now try Exercise 55.

Technology

Use a graphing utility to confirm the result of Example 4. By graphing

$y_1 = x^2$ and $y_2 = 2x - 1$

in the same viewing window, you should be able to see that the line touches the parabola at the point $(1, 1)$.

WRITING ABOUT MATHEMATICS

Television Antenna Dishes Cross sections of television antenna dishes are parabolic in shape. Use the figure shown to write a paragraph explaining why these dishes are parabolic.

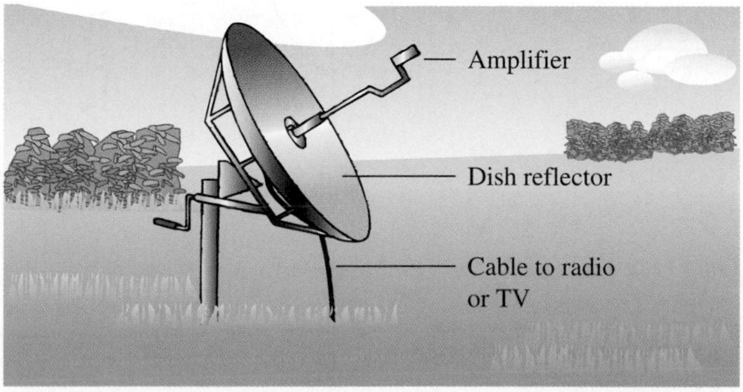

10.2 Exercises

VOCABULARY CHECK: Fill in the blanks.

1. A ________ is the intersection of a plane and a double-napped cone.
2. A collection of points satisfying a geometric property can also be referred to as a ________ of points.
3. A ________ is defined as the set of all points (x, y) in a plane that are equidistant from a fixed line, called the ________, and a fixed point, called the ________, not on the line.
4. The line that passes through the focus and vertex of a parabola is called the ________ of the parabola.
5. The ________ of a parabola is the midpoint between the focus and the directrix.
6. A line segment that passes through the focus of a parabola and has endpoints on the parabola is called a ________ ________ .
7. A line is ________ to a parabola at a point on the parabola if the line intersects, but does not cross, the parabola at the point.

In Exercises 1–4, describe in words how a plane could intersect with the double-napped cone shown to form the conic section.

1. Circle
2. Ellipse
3. Parabola
4. Hyperbola

In Exercises 5–10, match the equation with its graph. [The graphs are labeled (a), (b), (c), (d), (e), and (f).]

(a)

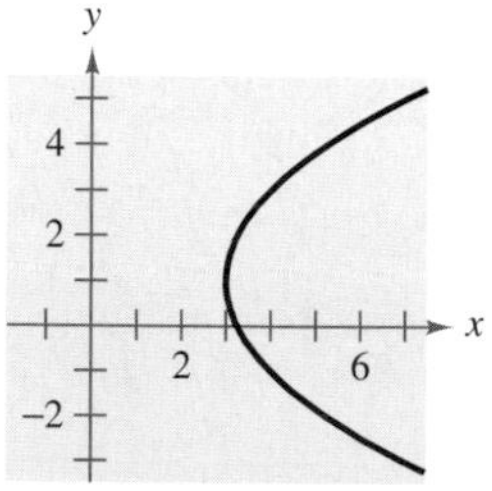

(b)

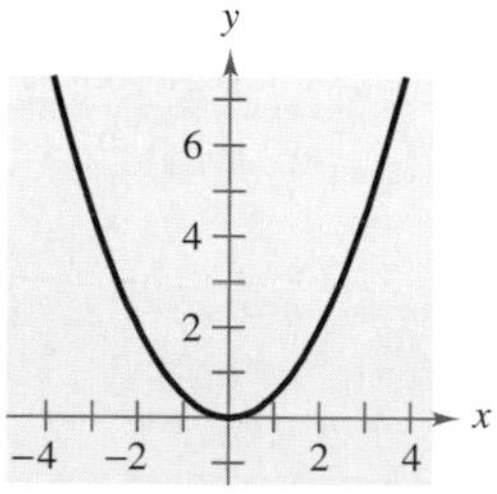

(c)

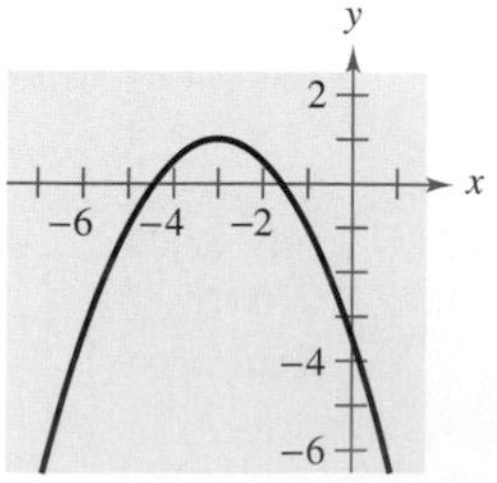

(d)

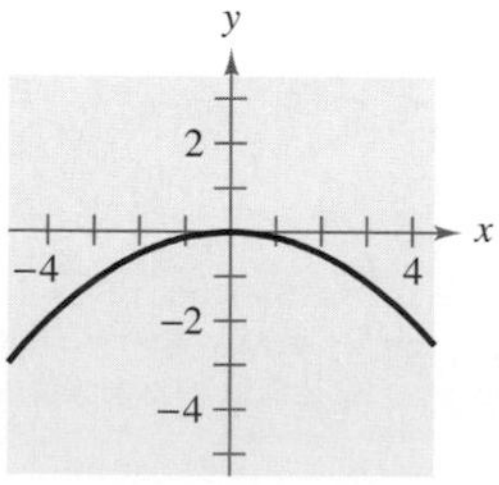

(e)

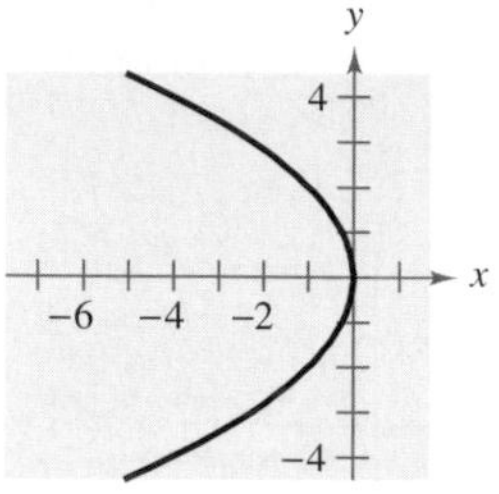

(f)

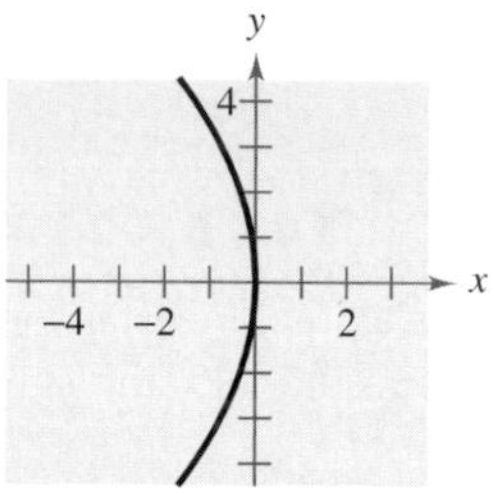

5. $y^2 = -4x$
6. $x^2 = 2y$
7. $x^2 = -8y$
8. $y^2 = -12x$
9. $(y - 1)^2 = 4(x - 3)$
10. $(x + 3)^2 = -2(y - 1)$

In Exercises 11–24, find the vertex, focus, and directrix of the parabola and sketch its graph.

11. $y = \frac{1}{2}x^2$
12. $y = -2x^2$
13. $y^2 = -6x$
14. $y^2 = 3x$
15. $x^2 + 6y = 0$
16. $x + y^2 = 0$
17. $(x - 1)^2 + 8(y + 2) = 0$
18. $(x + 5) + (y - 1)^2 = 0$
19. $\left(x + \frac{3}{2}\right)^2 = 4(y - 2)$
20. $\left(x + \frac{1}{2}\right)^2 = 4(y - 1)$
21. $y = \frac{1}{4}(x^2 - 2x + 5)$
22. $x = \frac{1}{4}(y^2 + 2y + 33)$
23. $y^2 + 6y + 8x + 25 = 0$
24. $y^2 - 4y - 4x = 0$

In Exercises 25–28, find the vertex, focus, and directrix of the parabola. Use a graphing utility to graph the parabola.

25. $x^2 + 4x + 6y - 2 = 0$
26. $x^2 - 2x + 8y + 9 = 0$
27. $y^2 + x + y = 0$
28. $y^2 - 4x - 4 = 0$

In Exercises 29–40, find the standard form of the equation of the parabola with the given characteristic(s) and vertex at the origin.

29.

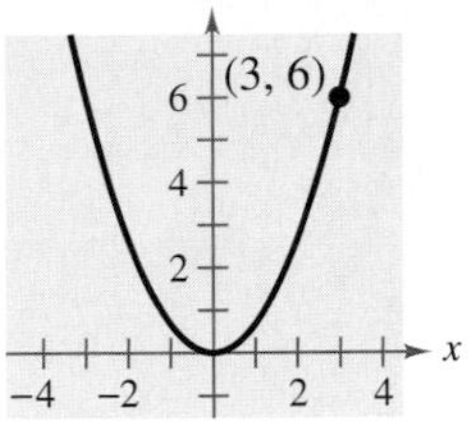

30.

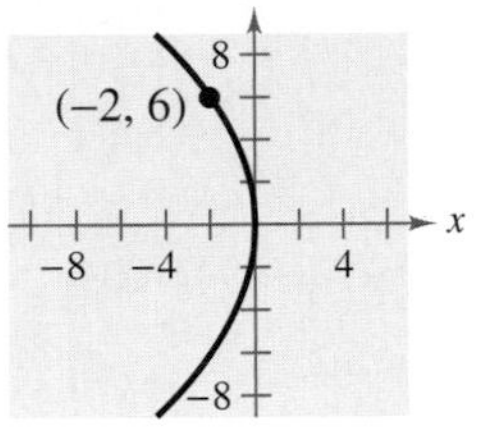

31. Focus: $\left(0, -\frac{3}{2}\right)$

32. Focus: $\left(\frac{5}{2}, 0\right)$

33. Focus: $(-2, 0)$

34. Focus: $(0, -2)$

35. Directrix: $y = -1$

36. Directrix: $y = 3$

37. Directrix: $x = 2$

38. Directrix: $x = -3$

39. Horizontal axis and passes through the point $(4, 6)$

40. Vertical axis and passes through the point $(-3, -3)$

In Exercises 41–50, find the standard form of the equation of the parabola with the given characteristics.

41.

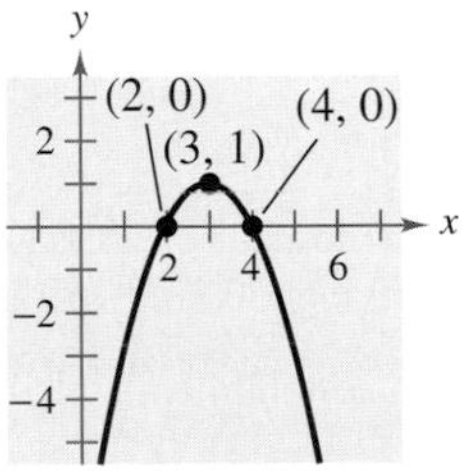

42.

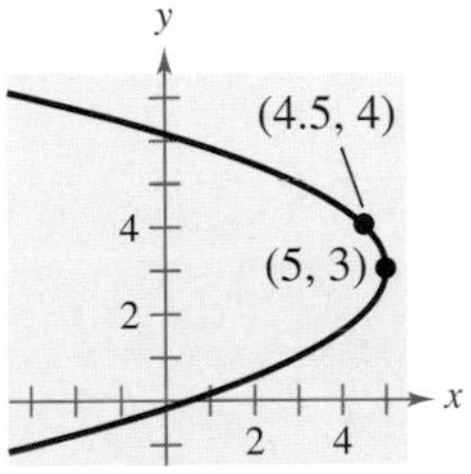

43.

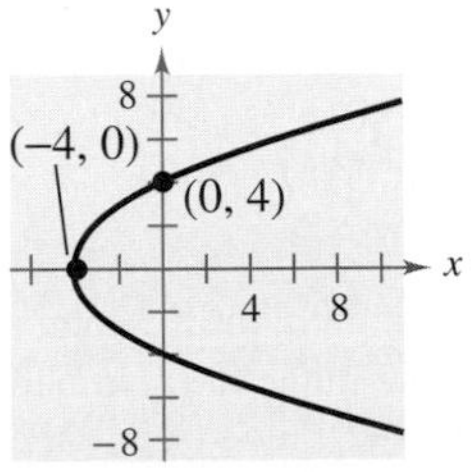

44.

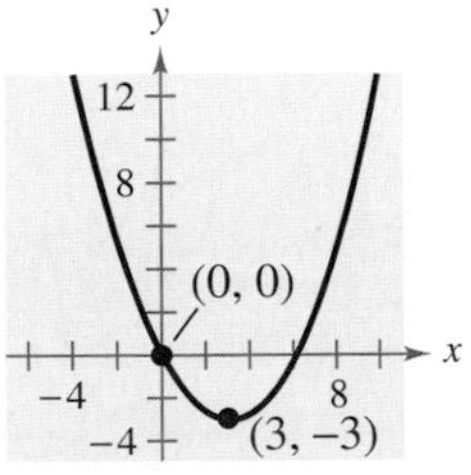

45. Vertex: $(5, 2)$; focus: $(3, 2)$

46. Vertex: $(-1, 2)$; focus: $(-1, 0)$

47. Vertex: $(0, 4)$; directrix: $y = 2$

48. Vertex: $(-2, 1)$; directrix: $x = 1$

49. Focus: $(2, 2)$; directrix: $x = -2$

50. Focus: $(0, 0)$; directrix: $y = 8$

In Exercises 51 and 52, change the equation of the parabola so that its graph matches the description.

51. $(y - 3)^2 = 6(x + 1)$; upper half of parabola

52. $(y + 1)^2 = 2(x - 4)$; lower half of parabola

In Exercises 53 and 54, the equations of a parabola and a tangent line to the parabola are given. Use a graphing utility to graph both equations in the same viewing window. Determine the coordinates of the point of tangency.

	Parabola	*Tangent Line*
53.	$y^2 - 8x = 0$	$x - y + 2 = 0$
54.	$x^2 + 12y = 0$	$x + y - 3 = 0$

In Exercises 55–58, find an equation of the tangent line to the parabola at the given point, and find the *x*-intercept of the line.

55. $x^2 = 2y$, $(4, 8)$

56. $x^2 = 2y$, $\left(-3, \frac{9}{2}\right)$

57. $y = -2x^2$, $(-1, -2)$

58. $y = -2x^2$, $(2, -8)$

59. ***Revenue*** The revenue R (in dollars) generated by the sale of x units of a patio furniture set is given by

$$(x - 106)^2 = -\frac{4}{5}(R - 14{,}045).$$

Use a graphing utility to graph the function and approximate the number of sales that will maximize revenue.

60. ***Revenue*** The revenue R (in dollars) generated by the sale of x units of a digital camera is given by

$$(x - 135)^2 = -\frac{5}{7}(R - 25{,}515).$$

Use a graphing utility to graph the function and approximate the number of sales that will maximize revenue.

61. ***Satellite Antenna*** The receiver in a parabolic television dish antenna is 4.5 feet from the vertex and is located at the focus (see figure). Write an equation for a cross section of the reflector. (Assume that the dish is directed upward and the vertex is at the origin.)

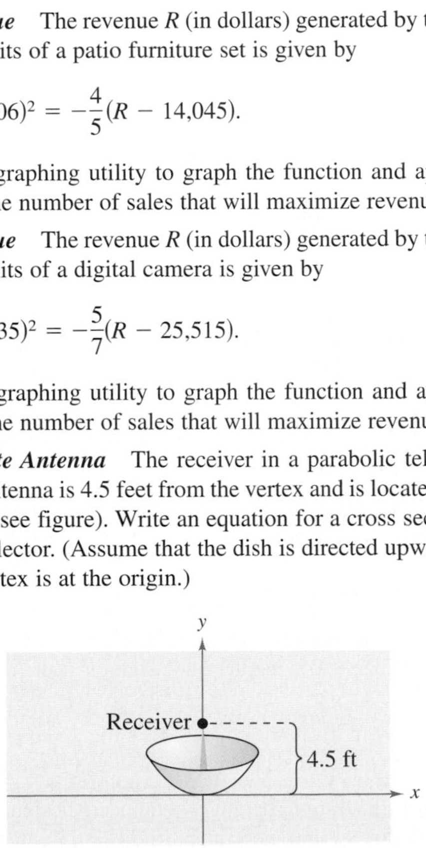

Model It

62. ***Suspension Bridge*** Each cable of the Golden Gate Bridge is suspended (in the shape of a parabola) between two towers that are 1280 meters apart. The top of each tower is 152 meters above the roadway. The cables touch the roadway midway between the towers.

(a) Draw a sketch of the bridge. Locate the origin of a rectangular coordinate system at the center of the roadway. Label the coordinates of the known points.

(b) Write an equation that models the cables.

(c) Complete the table by finding the height y of the suspension cables over the roadway at a distance of x meters from the center of the bridge.

Distance, x	Height, y
0	
250	
400	
500	
1000	

63. ***Road Design*** Roads are often designed with parabolic surfaces to allow rain to drain off. A particular road that is 32 feet wide is 0.4 foot higher in the center than it is on the sides (see figure).

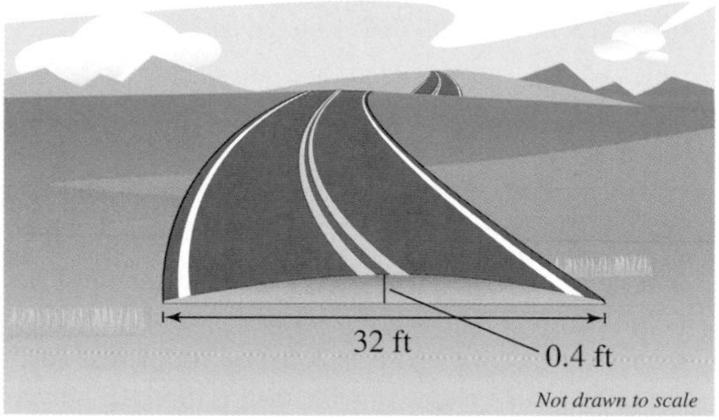

Cross section of road surface

(a) Find an equation of the parabola that models the road surface. (Assume that the origin is at the center of the road.)

(b) How far from the center of the road is the road surface 0.1 foot lower than in the middle?

64. ***Highway Design*** Highway engineers design a parabolic curve for an entrance ramp from a straight street to an interstate highway (see figure). Find an equation of the parabola.

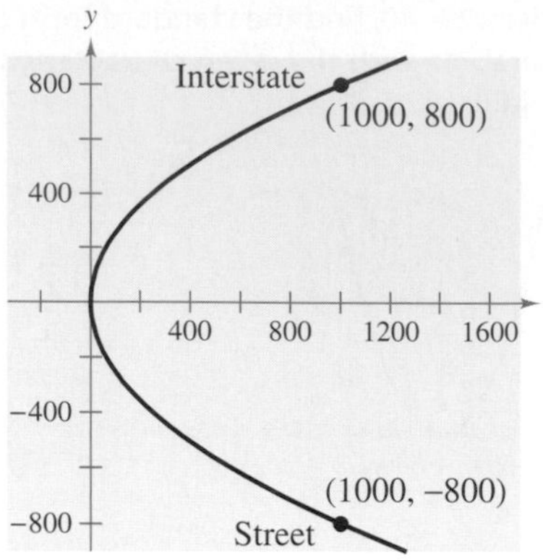

FIGURE FOR 64

65. ***Satellite Orbit*** A satellite in a 100-mile-high circular orbit around Earth has a velocity of approximately 17,500 miles per hour. If this velocity is multiplied by $\sqrt{2}$, the satellite will have the minimum velocity necessary to escape Earth's gravity and it will follow a parabolic path with the center of Earth as the focus (see figure).

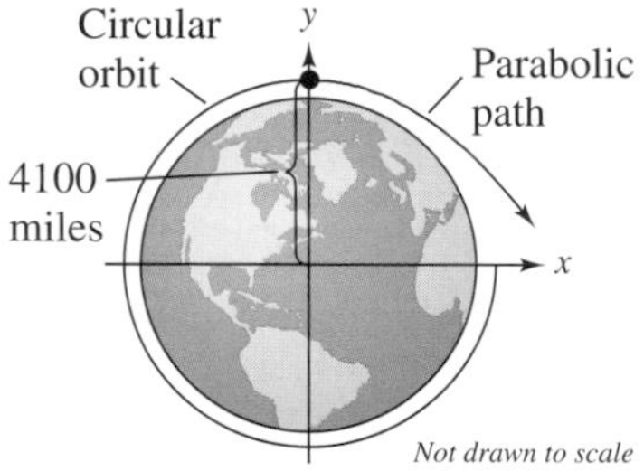

(a) Find the escape velocity of the satellite.

(b) Find an equation of the parabolic path of the satellite (assume that the radius of Earth is 4000 miles).

66. ***Path of a Softball*** The path of a softball is modeled by

$$-12.5(y - 7.125) = (x - 6.25)^2$$

where the coordinates x and y are measured in feet, with $x = 0$ corresponding to the position from which the ball was thrown.

(a) Use a graphing utility to graph the trajectory of the softball.

(b) Use the *trace* feature of the graphing utility to approximate the highest point and the range of the trajectory.

Projectile Motion **In Exercises 67 and 68, consider the path of a projectile projected horizontally with a velocity of v feet per second at a height of s feet, where the model for the path is**

$$x^2 = -\frac{v^2}{16}(y - s).$$

In this model (in which air resistance is disregarded), y is the height (in feet) of the projectile and x is the horizontal distance (in feet) the projectile travels.

67. A ball is thrown from the top of a 75-foot tower with a velocity of 32 feet per second.

(a) Find the equation of the parabolic path.

(b) How far does the ball travel horizontally before striking the ground?

68. A cargo plane is flying at an altitude of 30,000 feet and a speed of 540 miles per hour. A supply crate is dropped from the plane. How many *feet* will the crate travel horizontally before it hits the ground?

Synthesis

True or False? **In Exercises 69 and 70, determine whether the statement is true or false. Justify your answer.**

69. It is possible for a parabola to intersect its directrix.

70. If the vertex and focus of a parabola are on a horizontal line, then the directrix of the parabola is vertical.

71. ***Exploration*** Consider the parabola $x^2 = 4py$.

(a) Use a graphing utility to graph the parabola for $p = 1$, $p = 2$, $p = 3$, and $p = 4$. Describe the effect on the graph when p increases.

(b) Locate the focus for each parabola in part (a).

(c) For each parabola in part (a), find the length of the chord passing through the focus and parallel to the directrix (see figure). How can the length of this chord be determined directly from the standard form of the equation of the parabola?

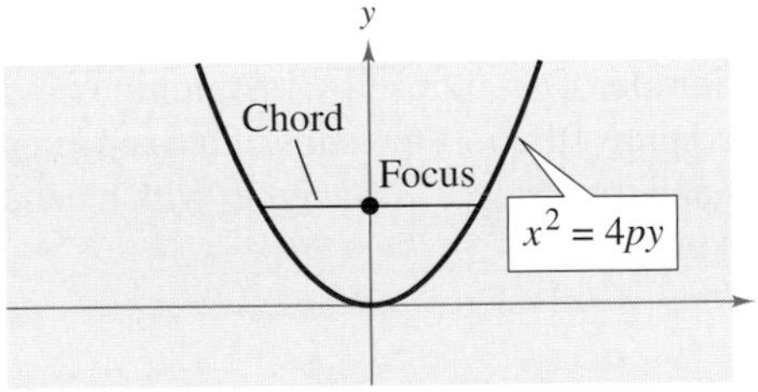

(d) Explain how the result of part (c) can be used as a sketching aid when graphing parabolas.

72. ***Geometry*** The area of the shaded region in the figure is

$$A = \frac{8}{3}p^{1/2}b^{3/2}.$$

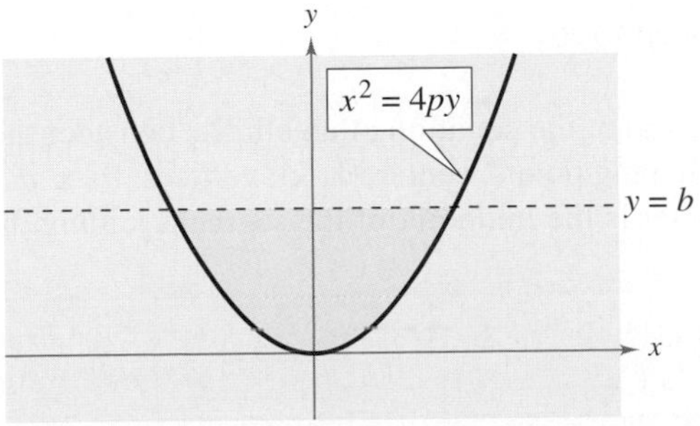

(a) Find the area when $p = 2$ and $b = 4$.

(b) Give a geometric explanation of why the area approaches 0 as p approaches 0.

73. ***Exploration*** Let (x_1, y_1) be the coordinates of a point on the parabola $x^2 = 4py$. The equation of the line tangent to the parabola at the point is

$$y - y_1 = \frac{x_1}{2p}(x - x_1).$$

What is the slope of the tangent line?

74. ***Writing*** In your own words, state the reflective property of a parabola.

Skills Review

In Exercises 75–78, list the possible rational zeros of f given by the Rational Zero Test.

75. $f(x) = x^3 - 2x^2 + 2x - 4$

76. $f(x) = 2x^3 + 4x^2 - 3x + 10$

77. $f(x) = 2x^5 + x^2 + 16$

78. $f(x) = 3x^3 - 12x + 22$

79. Find a polynomial with real coefficients that has the zeros $3, 2 + i$, and $2 - i$.

80. Find all the zeros of

$$f(x) = 2x^3 - 3x^2 + 50x - 75$$

if one of the zeros is $x = \frac{3}{2}$.

81. Find all the zeros of the function

$$g(x) = 6x^4 + 7x^3 - 29x^2 - 28x + 20$$

if two of the zeros are $x = \pm 2$.

82. Use a graphing utility to graph the function given by

$$h(x) = 2x^4 + x^3 - 19x^2 - 9x + 9.$$

Use the graph to approximate the zeros of h.

In Exercises 83–90, use the information to solve the triangle. Round your answers to two decimal places.

83. $A = 35°, a = 10, b = 7$

84. $B = 54°, b = 18, c = 11$

85. $A = 40°, B = 51°, c = 3$

86. $B = 26°, C = 104°, a = 19$

87. $a = 7, b = 10, c = 16$

88. $a = 58, b = 28, c = 75$

89. $A = 65°, b = 5, c = 12$

90. $B = 71°, a = 21, c = 29$

10.3 Ellipses

What you should learn

- Write equations of ellipses in standard form and graph ellipses.
- Use properties of ellipses to model and solve real-life problems.
- Find eccentricities of ellipses.

Why you should learn it

Ellipses can be used to model and solve many types of real-life problems. For instance, in Exercise 59 on page 751, an ellipse is used to model the orbit of Halley's comet.

Harvard College Observatory/ SPL/Photo Researchers, Inc.

Introduction

The second type of conic is called an **ellipse,** and is defined as follows.

> **Definition of Ellipse**
>
> An **ellipse** is the set of all points (x, y) in a plane, the sum of whose distances from two distinct fixed points **(foci)** is constant. See Figure 10.18.

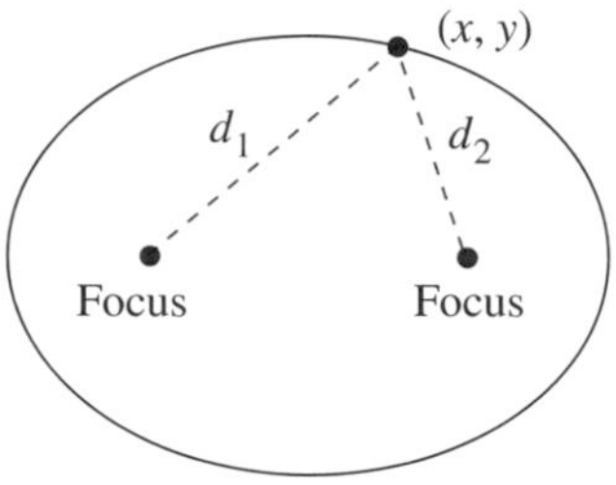

$d_1 + d_2$ is constant.
FIGURE 10.18

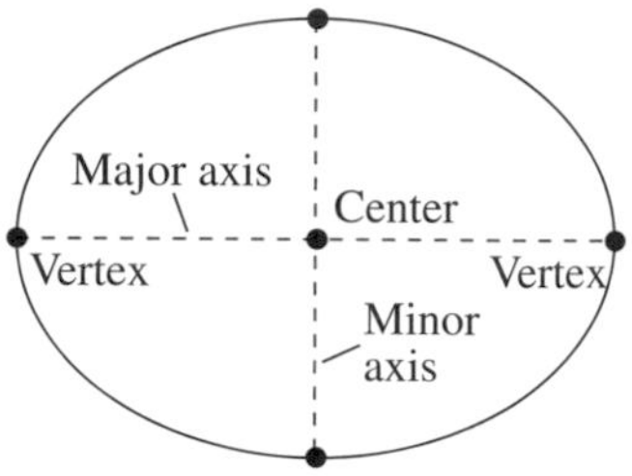

FIGURE 10.19

The line through the foci intersects the ellipse at two points called **vertices.** The chord joining the vertices is the **major axis,** and its midpoint is the **center** of the ellipse. The chord perpendicular to the major axis at the center is the **minor axis** of the ellipse. See Figure 10.19.

You can visualize the definition of an ellipse by imagining two thumbtacks placed at the foci, as shown in Figure 10.20. If the ends of a fixed length of string are fastened to the thumbtacks and the string is *drawn taut* with a pencil, the path traced by the pencil will be an ellipse.

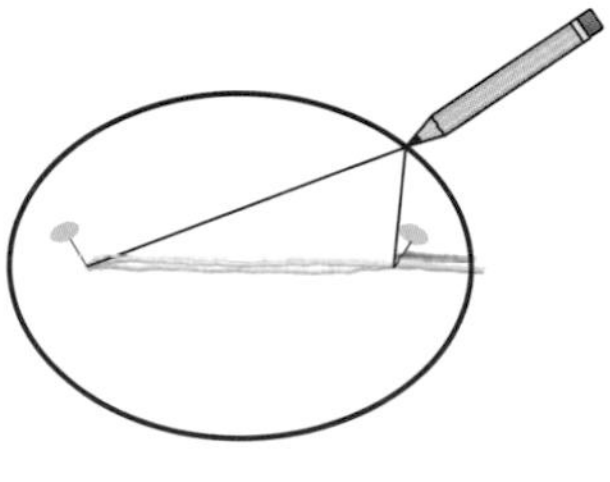

FIGURE 10.20

To derive the standard form of the equation of an ellipse, consider the ellipse in Figure 10.21 with the following points: center, (h, k); vertices, $(h \pm a, k)$; foci, $(h \pm c, k)$. Note that the center is the midpoint of the segment joining the foci.

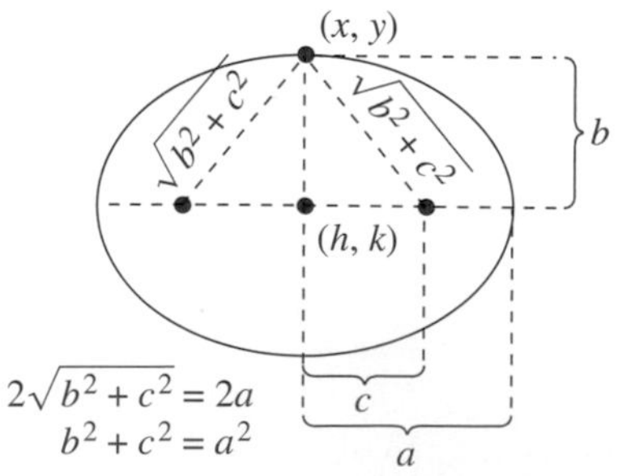

FIGURE 10.21

The sum of the distances from any point on the ellipse to the two foci is constant. Using a vertex point, this constant sum is

$$(a + c) + (a - c) = 2a \qquad \text{Length of major axis}$$

or simply the length of the major axis. Now, if you let (x, y) be *any* point on the ellipse, the sum of the distances between (x, y) and the two foci must also be $2a$. That is,

$$\sqrt{[x - (h - c)]^2 + (y - k)^2} + \sqrt{[x - (h + c)]^2 + (y - k)^2} = 2a.$$

Finally, in Figure 10.21, you can see that $b^2 = a^2 - c^2$, which implies that the equation of the ellipse is

$$b^2(x - h)^2 + a^2(y - k)^2 = a^2b^2$$

$$\frac{(x - h)^2}{a^2} + \frac{(y - k)^2}{b^2} = 1.$$

You would obtain a similar equation in the derivation by starting with a vertical major axis. Both results are summarized as follows.

STUDY TIP

Consider the equation of the ellipse

$$\frac{(x - h)^2}{a^2} + \frac{(y - k)^2}{b^2} = 1.$$

If you let $a = b$, then the equation can be rewritten as

$$(x - h)^2 + (y - k)^2 = a^2$$

which is the standard form of the equation of a circle with radius $r = a$ (see Section 1.2). Geometrically, when $a = b$ for an ellipse, the major and minor axes are of equal length, and so the graph is a circle.

Standard Equation of an Ellipse

The **standard form of the equation of an ellipse,** with center (h, k) and major and minor axes of lengths $2a$ and $2b$, respectively, where $0 < b < a$, is

$$\frac{(x - h)^2}{a^2} + \frac{(y - k)^2}{b^2} = 1 \qquad \text{Major axis is horizontal.}$$

$$\frac{(x - h)^2}{b^2} + \frac{(y - k)^2}{a^2} = 1. \qquad \text{Major axis is vertical.}$$

The foci lie on the major axis, c units from the center, with $c^2 = a^2 - b^2$. If the center is at the origin $(0, 0)$, the equation takes one of the following forms.

$$\frac{x^2}{a^2} + \frac{y^2}{b^2} = 1 \qquad \text{Major axis is horizontal.}$$

$$\frac{x^2}{b^2} + \frac{y^2}{a^2} = 1 \qquad \text{Major axis is vertical.}$$

Figure 10.22 shows both the horizontal and vertical orientations for an ellipse.

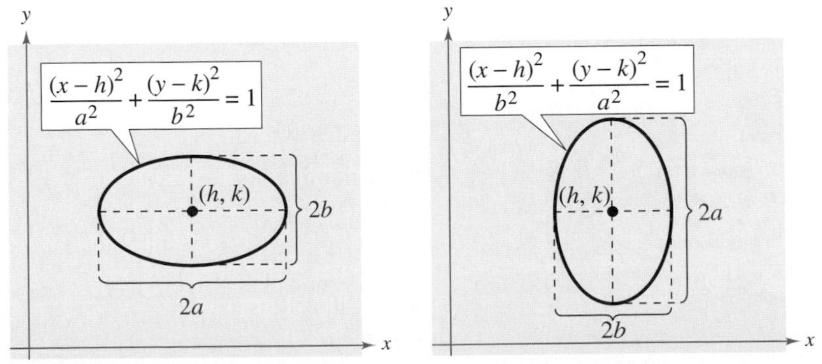

Major axis is horizontal. *Major axis is vertical.*

FIGURE 10.22

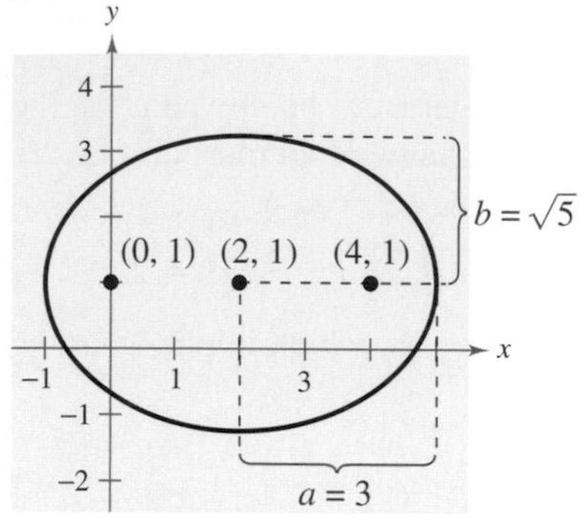

FIGURE 10.23

Example 1 Finding the Standard Equation of an Ellipse

Find the standard form of the equation of the ellipse having foci at (0, 1) and (4, 1) and a major axis of length 6, as shown in Figure 10.23.

Solution

Because the foci occur at (0, 1) and (4, 1), the center of the ellipse is (2, 1) and the distance from the center to one of the foci is $c = 2$. Because $2a = 6$, you know that $a = 3$. Now, from $c^2 = a^2 - b^2$, you have

$$b = \sqrt{a^2 - c^2} = \sqrt{3^2 - 2^2} = \sqrt{5}.$$

Because the major axis is horizontal, the standard equation is

$$\frac{(x-2)^2}{3^2} + \frac{(y-1)^2}{\left(\sqrt{5}\right)^2} = 1.$$

This equation simplifies to

$$\frac{(x-2)^2}{9} + \frac{(y-1)^2}{5} = 1.$$

CHECKPOINT Now try Exercise 49.

Example 2 Sketching an Ellipse

Sketch the ellipse given by $x^2 + 4y^2 + 6x - 8y + 9 = 0$.

Solution

Begin by writing the original equation in standard form. In the fourth step, note that 9 and 4 are added to *both* sides of the equation when completing the squares.

$$x^2 + 4y^2 + 6x - 8y + 9 = 0 \quad \text{Write original equation.}$$

$$\left(x^2 + 6x + \square\right) + \left(4y^2 - 8y + \square\right) = -9 \quad \text{Group terms.}$$

$$\left(x^2 + 6x + \square\right) + 4\left(y^2 - 2y + \square\right) = -9 \quad \text{Factor 4 out of } y\text{-terms.}$$

$$(x^2 + 6x + 9) + 4(y^2 - 2y + 1) = -9 + 9 + 4(1)$$

$$(x+3)^2 + 4(y-1)^2 = 4 \quad \text{Write in completed square form.}$$

$$\frac{(x+3)^2}{4} + \frac{(y-1)^2}{1} = 1 \quad \text{Divide each side by 4.}$$

$$\frac{(x+3)^2}{2^2} + \frac{(y-1)^2}{1^2} = 1 \quad \text{Write in standard form.}$$

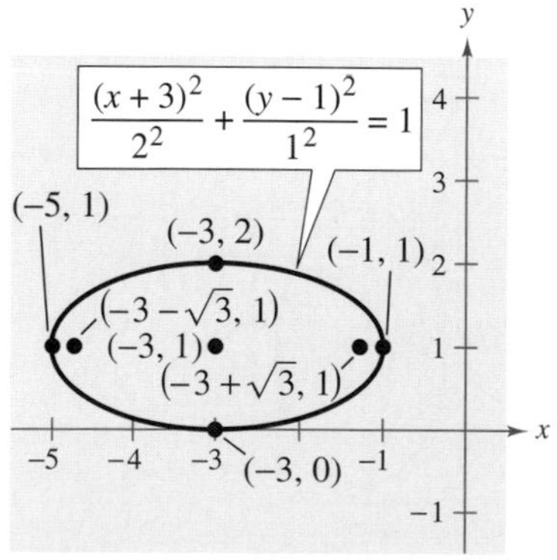

FIGURE 10.24

From this standard form, it follows that the center is $(h, k) = (-3, 1)$. Because the denominator of the x-term is $a^2 = 2^2$, the endpoints of the major axis lie two units to the right and left of the center. Similarly, because the denominator of the y-term is $b^2 = 1^2$, the endpoints of the minor axis lie one unit up and down from the center. Now, from $c^2 = a^2 - b^2$, you have $c = \sqrt{2^2 - 1^2} = \sqrt{3}$. So, the foci of the ellipse are $\left(-3 - \sqrt{3}, 1\right)$ and $\left(-3 + \sqrt{3}, 1\right)$. The ellipse is shown in Figure 10.24.

CHECKPOINT Now try Exercise 25.

Example 3 Analyzing an Ellipse

Find the center, vertices, and foci of the ellipse $4x^2 + y^2 - 8x + 4y - 8 = 0$.

Solution

By completing the square, you can write the original equation in standard form.

$$4x^2 + y^2 - 8x + 4y - 8 = 0 \qquad \text{Write original equation.}$$

$$(4x^2 - 8x + \square) + (y^2 + 4y + \square) = 8 \qquad \text{Group terms.}$$

$$4(x^2 - 2x + \square) + (y^2 + 4y + \square) = 8 \qquad \text{Factor 4 out of } x\text{-terms.}$$

$$4(x^2 - 2x + 1) + (y^2 + 4y + 4) = 8 + 4(1) + 4$$

$$4(x - 1)^2 + (y + 2)^2 = 16 \qquad \text{Write in completed square form.}$$

$$\frac{(x-1)^2}{4} + \frac{(y+2)^2}{16} = 1 \qquad \text{Divide each side by 16.}$$

$$\frac{(x-1)^2}{2^2} + \frac{(y+2)^2}{4^2} = 1 \qquad \text{Write in standard form.}$$

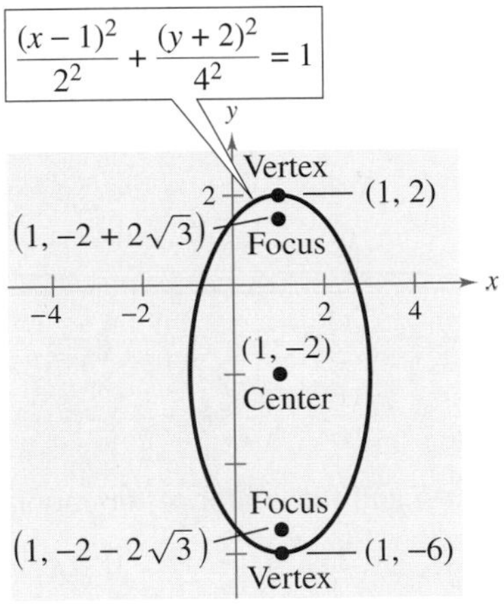

FIGURE 10.25

The major axis is vertical, where $h = 1$, $k = -2$, $a = 4$, $b = 2$, and

$$c = \sqrt{a^2 - b^2} = \sqrt{16 - 4} = \sqrt{12} = 2\sqrt{3}.$$

So, you have the following.

Center: $(1, -2)$ Vertices: $(1, -6)$, $(1, 2)$ Foci: $(1, -2 - 2\sqrt{3})$, $(1, -2 + 2\sqrt{3})$

The graph of the ellipse is shown in Figure 10.25.

✓CHECKPOINT Now try Exercise 29.

Technology

You can use a graphing utility to graph an ellipse by graphing the upper and lower portions in the same viewing window. For instance, to graph the ellipse in Example 3, first solve for y to get

$$y_1 = -2 + 4\sqrt{1 - \frac{(x-1)^2}{4}} \quad \text{and} \quad y_2 = -2 - 4\sqrt{1 - \frac{(x-1)^2}{4}}.$$

Use a viewing window in which $-6 \le x \le 9$ and $-7 \le y \le 3$. You should obtain the graph shown below.

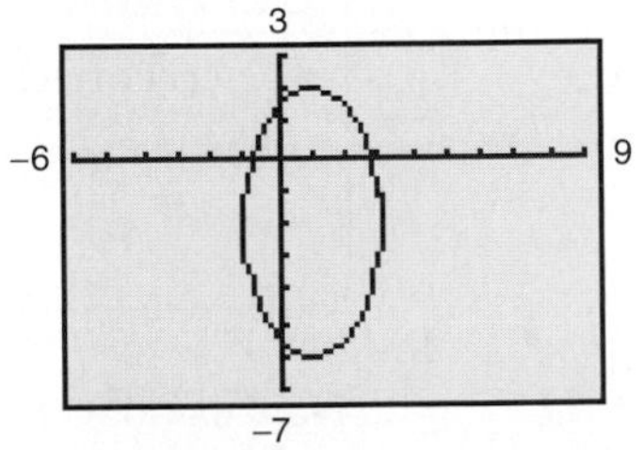

Application

Ellipses have many practical and aesthetic uses. For instance, machine gears, supporting arches, and acoustic designs often involve elliptical shapes. The orbits of satellites and planets are also ellipses. Example 4 investigates the elliptical orbit of the moon about Earth.

Example 4 An Application Involving an Elliptical Orbit

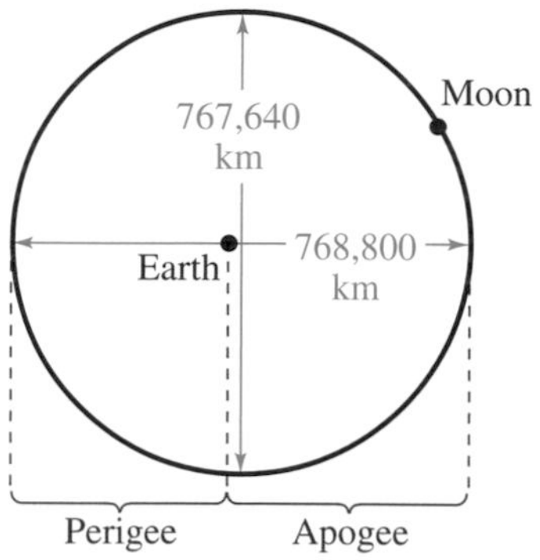

FIGURE 10.26

The moon travels about Earth in an elliptical orbit with Earth at one focus, as shown in Figure 10.26. The major and minor axes of the orbit have lengths of 768,800 kilometers and 767,640 kilometers, respectively. Find the greatest and smallest distances (the *apogee* and *perigee*), respectively from Earth's center to the moon's center.

Solution

Because $2a = 768{,}800$ and $2b = 767{,}640$, you have

$$a = 384{,}400 \text{ and } b = 383{,}820$$

which implies that

$$\begin{aligned} c &= \sqrt{a^2 - b^2} \\ &= \sqrt{384{,}400^2 - 383{,}820^2} \\ &\approx 21{,}108. \end{aligned}$$

So, the greatest distance between the center of Earth and the center of the moon is

$$a + c \approx 384{,}400 + 21{,}108 = 405{,}508 \text{ kilometers}$$

and the smallest distance is

$$a - c \approx 384{,}400 - 21{,}108 = 363{,}292 \text{ kilometers.}$$

✓CHECKPOINT Now try Exercise 59.

STUDY TIP

Note in Example 4 and Figure 10.26 that Earth *is not* the center of the moon's orbit.

Eccentricity

One of the reasons it was difficult for early astronomers to detect that the orbits of the planets are ellipses is that the foci of the planetary orbits are relatively close to their centers, and so the orbits are nearly circular. To measure the ovalness of an ellipse, you can use the concept of **eccentricity.**

Definition of Eccentricity

The **eccentricity** e of an ellipse is given by the ratio

$$e = \frac{c}{a}.$$

Note that $0 < e < 1$ for *every* ellipse.

To see how this ratio is used to describe the shape of an ellipse, note that because the foci of an ellipse are located along the major axis between the vertices and the center, it follows that

$$0 < c < a.$$

For an ellipse that is nearly circular, the foci are close to the center and the ratio c/a is small, as shown in Figure 10.27. On the other hand, for an elongated ellipse, the foci are close to the vertices, and the ratio c/a is close to 1, as shown in Figure 10.28.

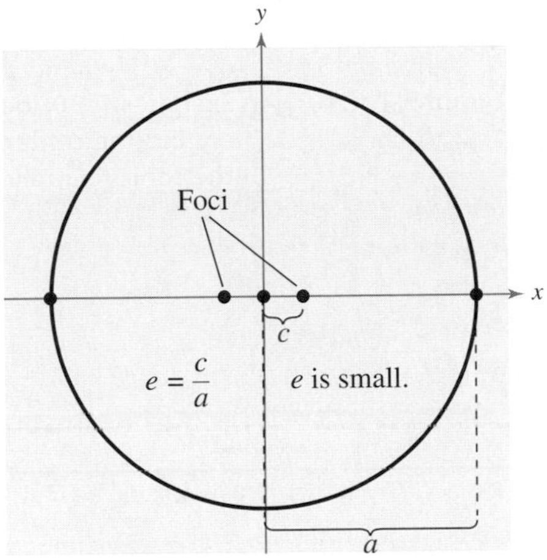

FIGURE 10.27

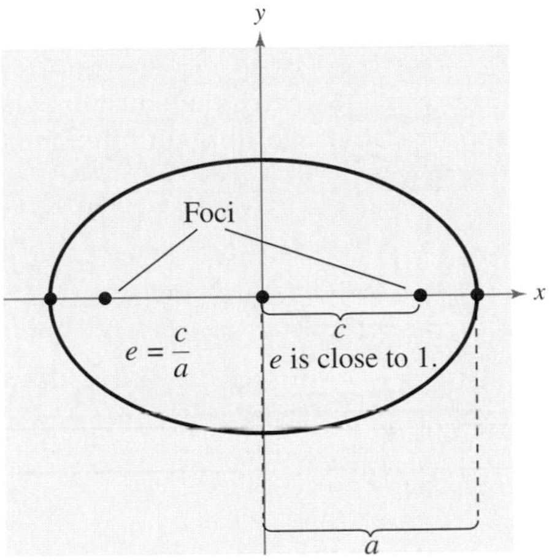

FIGURE 10.28

NASA

The time it takes Saturn to orbit the sun is equal to 29.4 Earth years.

The orbit of the moon has an eccentricity of $e \approx 0.0549$, and the eccentricities of the nine planetary orbits are as follows.

Mercury:	$e \approx 0.2056$	Saturn:	$e \approx 0.0542$
Venus:	$e \approx 0.0068$	Uranus:	$e \approx 0.0472$
Earth:	$e \approx 0.0167$	Neptune:	$e \approx 0.0086$
Mars:	$e \approx 0.0934$	Pluto:	$e \approx 0.2488$
Jupiter:	$e \approx 0.0484$		

Writing about Mathematics

Ellipses and Circles

a. Show that the equation of an ellipse can be written as

$$\frac{(x-h)^2}{a^2} + \frac{(y-k)^2}{a^2(1-e^2)} = 1.$$

b. For the equation in part (a), let $a = 4$, $h = 1$, and $k = 2$, and use a graphing utility to graph the ellipse for $e = 0.95$, $e = 0.75$, $e = 0.5$, $e = 0.25$, and $e = 0.1$. Discuss the changes in the shape of the ellipse as e approaches 0.

c. Make a conjecture about the shape of the graph in part (b) when $e = 0$. What is the equation of this ellipse? What is another name for an ellipse with an eccentricity of 0?

10.3 Exercises

VOCABULARY CHECK: Fill in the blanks.

1. An ________ is the set of all points (x, y) in a plane, the sum of whose distances from two distinct fixed points, called ________, is constant.
2. The chord joining the vertices of an ellipse is called the ________ ________, and its midpoint is the ________ of the ellipse.
3. The chord perpendicular to the major axis at the center of the ellipse is called the ________ ________ of the ellipse.
4. The concept of ________ is used to measure the ovalness of an ellipse.

In Exercises 1–6, match the equation with its graph. [The graphs are labeled (a), (b), (c), (d), (e), and (f).]

(a)

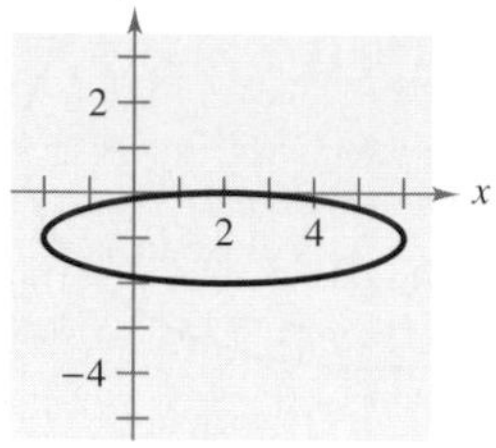

(b)

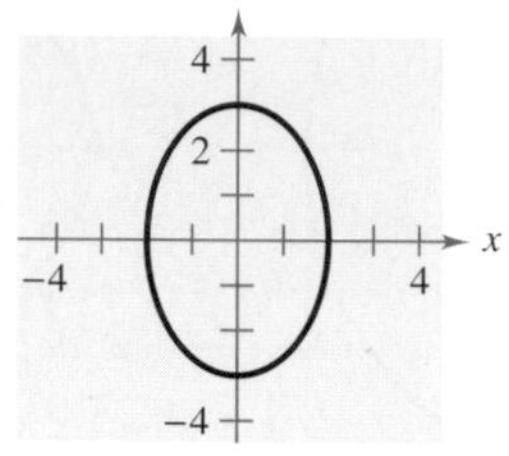

(c)

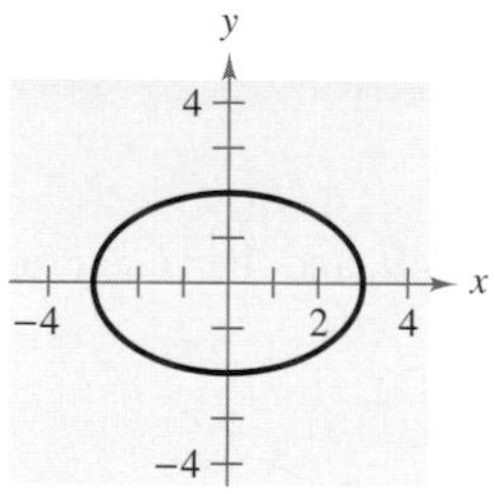

(d)

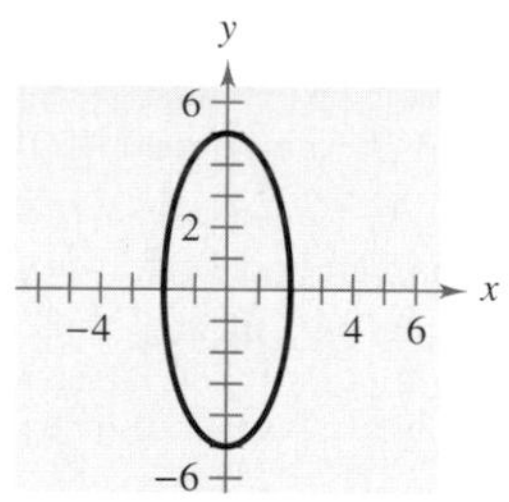

(e)

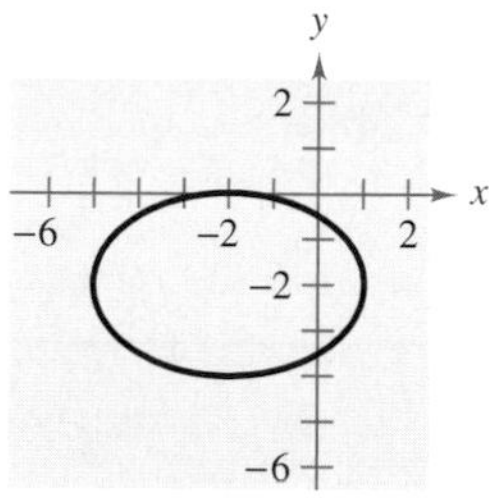

(f)

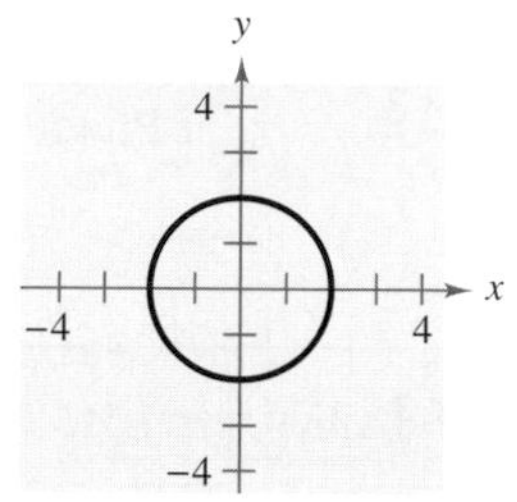

1. $\dfrac{x^2}{4} + \dfrac{y^2}{9} = 1$
2. $\dfrac{x^2}{9} + \dfrac{y^2}{4} = 1$
3. $\dfrac{x^2}{4} + \dfrac{y^2}{25} = 1$
4. $\dfrac{x^2}{4} + \dfrac{y^2}{4} = 1$
5. $\dfrac{(x - 2)^2}{16} + (y + 1)^2 = 1$
6. $\dfrac{(x + 2)^2}{9} + \dfrac{(y + 2)^2}{4} = 1$

In Exercises 7–30, identify the conic as a circle or an ellipse. Then find the center, radius, vertices, foci, and eccentricity of the conic (if applicable), and sketch its graph.

7. $\dfrac{x^2}{25} + \dfrac{y^2}{16} = 1$
8. $\dfrac{x^2}{81} + \dfrac{y^2}{144} = 1$
9. $\dfrac{x^2}{25} + \dfrac{y^2}{25} = 1$
10. $\dfrac{x^2}{9} + \dfrac{y^2}{9} = 1$
11. $\dfrac{x^2}{5} + \dfrac{y^2}{9} = 1$
12. $\dfrac{x^2}{64} + \dfrac{y^2}{28} = 1$
13. $\dfrac{(x + 3)^2}{16} + \dfrac{(y - 5)^2}{25} = 1$
14. $\dfrac{(x - 4)^2}{12} + \dfrac{(y + 3)^2}{16} = 1$
15. $\dfrac{x^2}{4/9} + \dfrac{(y + 1)^2}{4/9} = 1$
16. $\dfrac{(x + 5)^2}{9/4} + (y - 1)^2 = 1$
17. $(x + 2)^2 + \dfrac{(y + 4)^2}{1/4} = 1$
18. $\dfrac{(x - 3)^2}{25/4} + \dfrac{(y - 1)^2}{25/4} = 1$
19. $9x^2 + 4y^2 + 36x - 24y + 36 = 0$
20. $9x^2 + 4y^2 - 54x + 40y + 37 = 0$
21. $x^2 + y^2 - 2x + 4y - 31 = 0$
22. $x^2 + 5y^2 - 8x - 30y - 39 = 0$
23. $3x^2 + y^2 + 18x - 2y - 8 = 0$
24. $6x^2 + 2y^2 + 18x - 10y + 2 = 0$
25. $x^2 + 4y^2 - 6x + 20y - 2 = 0$
26. $x^2 + y^2 - 4x + 6y - 3 = 0$
27. $9x^2 + 9y^2 + 18x - 18y + 14 = 0$
28. $16x^2 + 25y^2 - 32x + 50y + 16 = 0$
29. $9x^2 + 25y^2 - 36x - 50y + 60 = 0$
30. $16x^2 + 16y^2 - 64x + 32y + 55 = 0$

In Exercises 31–34, use a graphing utility to graph the ellipse. Find the center, foci, and vertices. (Recall that it may be necessary to solve the equation for *y* and obtain two equations.)

31. $5x^2 + 3y^2 = 15$
32. $3x^2 + 4y^2 = 12$
33. $12x^2 + 20y^2 - 12x + 40y - 37 = 0$
34. $36x^2 + 9y^2 + 48x - 36y - 72 = 0$

In Exercises 35–42, find the standard form of the equation of the ellipse with the given characteristics and center at the origin.

35.

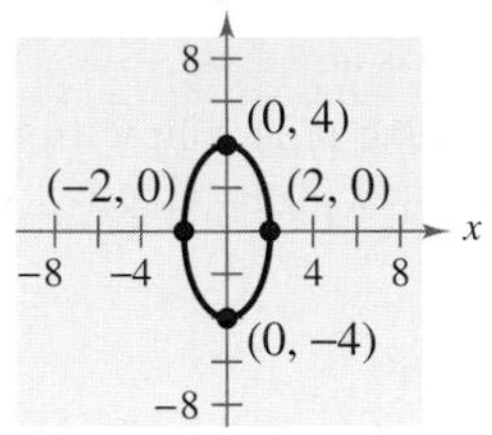

36.

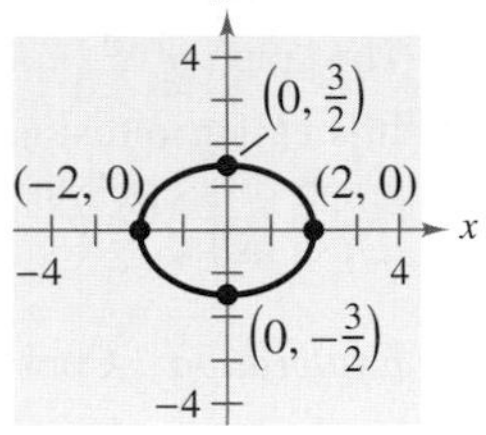

37. Vertices: $(\pm 6, 0)$; foci: $(\pm 2, 0)$

38. Vertices: $(0, \pm 8)$; foci: $(0, \pm 4)$

39. Foci: $(\pm 5, 0)$; major axis of length 12

40. Foci: $(\pm 2, 0)$; major axis of length 8

41. Vertices: $(0, \pm 5)$; passes through the point $(4, 2)$

42. Major axis vertical; passes through the points $(0, 4)$ and $(2, 0)$

In Exercises 43–54, find the standard form of the equation of the ellipse with the given characteristics.

43.

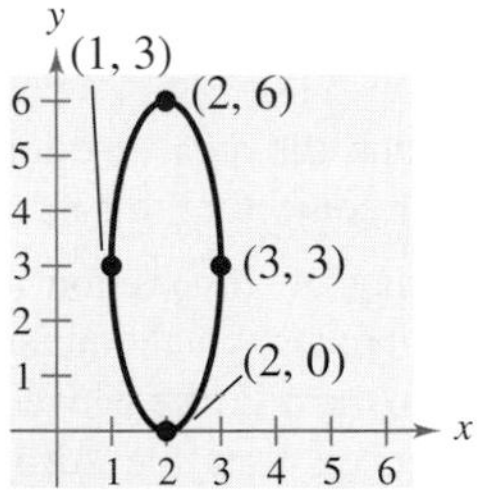

44.

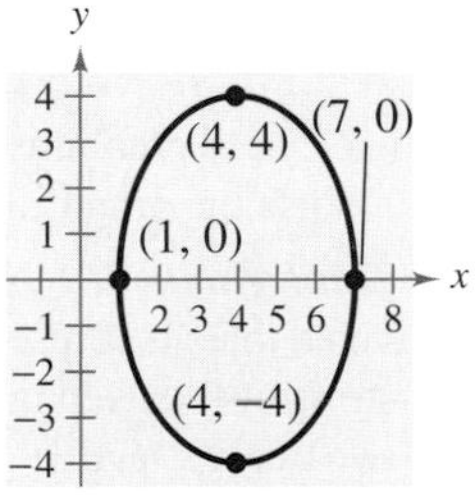

45.

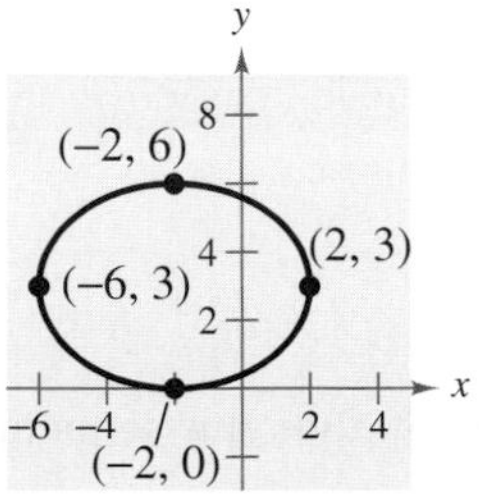

46.

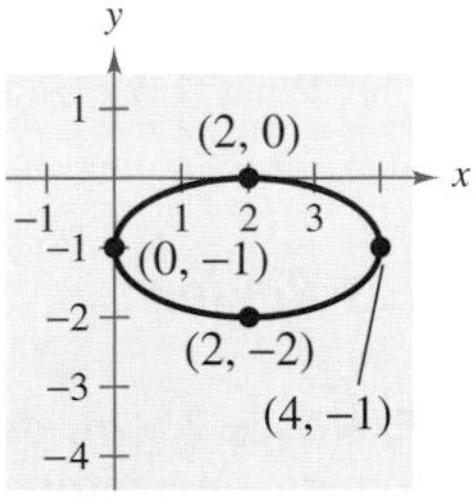

47. Vertices: $(0, 4), (4, 4)$; minor axis of length 2

48. Foci: $(0, 0), (4, 0)$; major axis of length 8

49. Foci: $(0, 0), (0, 8)$; major axis of length 16

50. Center: $(2, -1)$; vertex: $\left(2, \frac{1}{2}\right)$; minor axis of length 2

51. Center: $(0, 4)$; $a = 2c$; vertices: $(-4, 4), (4, 4)$

52. Center: $(3, 2)$; $a = 3c$; foci: $(1, 2), (5, 2)$

53. Vertices: $(0, 2), (4, 2)$; endpoints of the minor axis: $(2, 3), (2, 1)$

54. Vertices: $(5, 0), (5, 12)$; endpoints of the minor axis: $(1, 6), (9, 6)$

55. Find an equation of the ellipse with vertices $(\pm 5, 0)$ and eccentricity $e = \frac{3}{5}$.

56. Find an equation of the ellipse with vertices $(0, \pm 8)$ and eccentricity $e = \frac{1}{2}$.

57. ***Architecture*** A semielliptical arch over a tunnel for a one-way road through a mountain has a major axis of 50 feet and a height at the center of 10 feet.

(a) Draw a rectangular coordinate system on a sketch of the tunnel with the center of the road entering the tunnel at the origin. Identify the coordinates of the known points.

(b) Find an equation of the semielliptical arch over the tunnel.

(c) You are driving a moving truck that has a width of 8 feet and a height of 9 feet. Will the moving truck clear the opening of the arch?

58. ***Architecture*** A fireplace arch is to be constructed in the shape of a semiellipse. The opening is to have a height of 2 feet at the center and a width of 6 feet along the base (see figure). The contractor draws the outline of the ellipse using tacks as described at the beginning of this section. Give the required positions of the tacks and the length of the string.

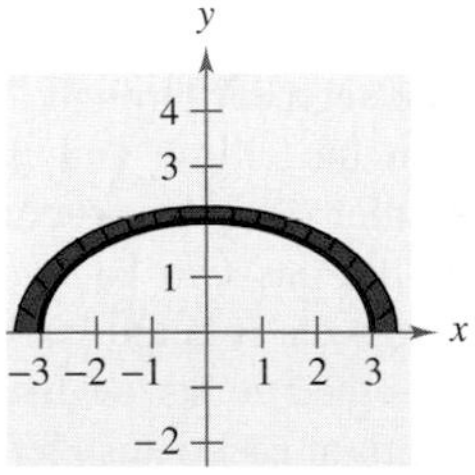

Model It

59. ***Comet Orbit*** Halley's comet has an elliptical orbit, with the sun at one focus. The eccentricity of the orbit is approximately 0.967. The length of the major axis of the orbit is approximately 35.88 astronomical units. (An astronomical unit is about 93 million miles.)

(a) Find an equation of the orbit. Place the center of the orbit at the origin, and place the major axis on the x-axis.

(b) Use a graphing utility to graph the equation of the orbit.

(c) Find the greatest (aphelion) and smallest (perihelion) distances from the sun's center to the comet's center.

60. ***Satellite Orbit*** The first artificial satellite to orbit Earth was Sputnik I (launched by the former Soviet Union in 1957). Its highest point above Earth's surface was 947 kilometers, and its lowest point was 228 kilometers (see figure). The center of Earth was the focus of the elliptical orbit, and the radius of Earth is 6378 kilometers. Find the eccentricity of the orbit.

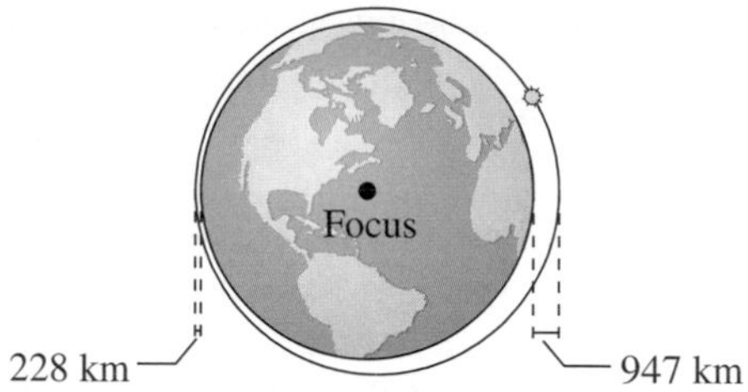

61. ***Motion of a Pendulum*** The relation between the velocity y (in radians per second) of a pendulum and its angular displacement θ from the vertical can be modeled by a semiellipse. A 12-centimeter pendulum crests $(y = 0)$ when the angular displacement is -0.2 radian and 0.2 radian. When the pendulum is at equilibrium $(\theta = 0)$, the velocity is -1.6 radians per second.

(a) Find an equation that models the motion of the pendulum. Place the center at the origin.

(b) Graph the equation from part (a).

(c) Which half of the ellipse models the motion of the pendulum?

62. ***Geometry*** A line segment through a focus of an ellipse with endpoints on the ellipse and perpendicular to the major axis is called a **latus rectum** of the ellipse. Therefore, an ellipse has two latera recta. Knowing the length of the latera recta is helpful in sketching an ellipse because it yields other points on the curve (see figure). Show that the length of each latus rectum is $2b^2/a$.

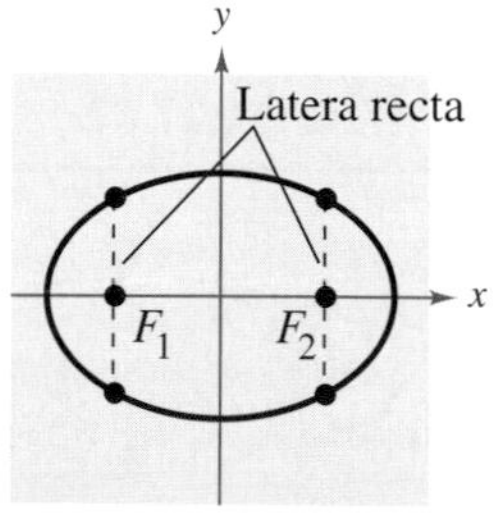

In Exercises 63–66, sketch the graph of the ellipse, using latera recta (see Exercise 62).

63. $\frac{x^2}{9} + \frac{y^2}{16} = 1$

64. $\frac{x^2}{4} + \frac{y^2}{1} = 1$

65. $5x^2 + 3y^2 = 15$

66. $9x^2 + 4y^2 = 36$

Synthesis

True or False? **In Exercises 67 and 68, determine whether the statement is true or false. Justify your answer.**

67. The graph of $x^2 + 4y^4 - 4 = 0$ is an ellipse.

68. It is easier to distinguish the graph of an ellipse from the graph of a circle if the eccentricity of the ellipse is large (close to 1).

69. ***Exploration*** Consider the ellipse

$$\frac{x^2}{a^2} + \frac{y^2}{b^2} = 1, \quad a + b = 20.$$

(a) The area of the ellipse is given by $A = \pi ab$. Write the area of the ellipse as a function of a.

(b) Find the equation of an ellipse with an area of 264 square centimeters.

(c) Complete the table using your equation from part (a), and make a conjecture about the shape of the ellipse with maximum area.

a	8	9	10	11	12	13
A						

(d) Use a graphing utility to graph the area function and use the graph to support your conjecture in part (c).

70. ***Think About It*** At the beginning of this section it was noted that an ellipse can be drawn using two thumbtacks, a string of fixed length (greater than the distance between the two tacks), and a pencil. If the ends of the string are fastened at the tacks and the string is drawn taut with a pencil, the path traced by the pencil is an ellipse.

(a) What is the length of the string in terms of a?

(b) Explain why the path is an ellipse.

Skills Review

In Exercises 71–74, determine whether the sequence is arithmetic, geometric, or neither.

71. 80, 40, 20, 10, 5, . . .

72. 66, 55, 44, 33, 22, . . .

73. $-\frac{1}{2}, \frac{1}{2}, \frac{3}{2}, \frac{5}{2}, \frac{7}{2}, \ldots$

74. $\frac{1}{4}, \frac{1}{2}, 1, 2, 4, \ldots$

In Exercises 75–78, find the sum.

75. $\sum_{n=0}^{6} (-3)^n$

76. $\sum_{n=0}^{6} 3^n$

77. $\sum_{n=0}^{10} 5\left(\frac{4}{3}\right)^n$

78. $\sum_{n=1}^{10} 4\left(\frac{3}{4}\right)^{n-1}$

10.4 Hyperbolas

What you should learn

- Write equations of hyperbolas in standard form.
- Find asymptotes of and graph hyperbolas.
- Use properties of hyperbolas to solve real-life problems.
- Classify conics from their general equations.

Why you should learn it

Hyperbolas can be used to model and solve many types of real-life problems. For instance, in Exercise 42 on page 761, hyperbolas are used in long distance radio navigation for aircraft and ships.

AP/Wide World Photos

Introduction

The third type of conic is called a **hyperbola.** The definition of a hyperbola is similar to that of an ellipse. The difference is that for an ellipse the *sum* of the distances between the foci and a point on the ellipse is fixed, whereas for a hyperbola the *difference* of the distances between the foci and a point on the hyperbola is fixed.

Definition of Hyperbola

A **hyperbola** is the set of all points (x, y) in a plane, the difference of whose distances from two distinct fixed points **(foci)** is a positive constant. See Figure 10.29.

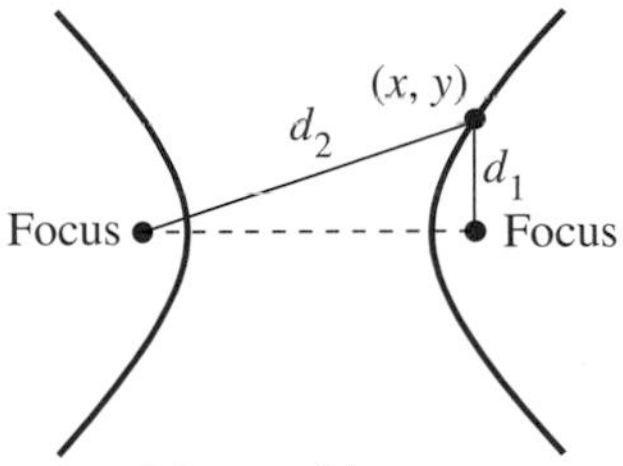

$d_2 - d_1$ is a positive constant.

FIGURE 10.29

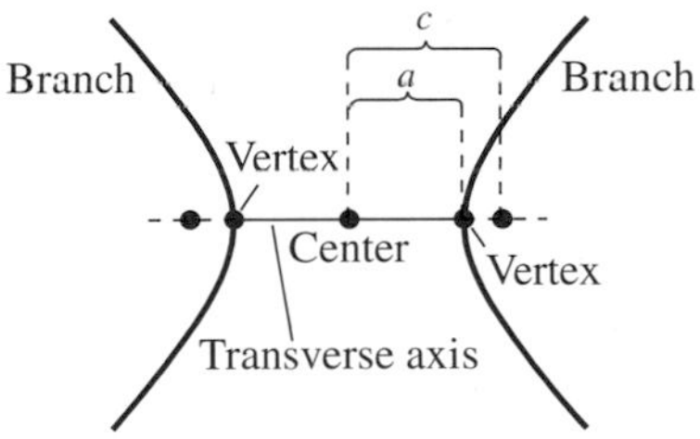

FIGURE 10.30

The graph of a hyperbola has two disconnected **branches.** The line through the two foci intersects the hyperbola at its two **vertices.** The line segment connecting the vertices is the **transverse axis,** and the midpoint of the transverse axis is the **center** of the hyperbola. See Figure 10.30. The development of the standard form of the equation of a hyperbola is similar to that of an ellipse. Note in the definition below that a, b, and c are related differently for hyperbolas than for ellipses.

Standard Equation of a Hyperbola

The **standard form of the equation of a hyperbola** with center (h, k) is

$$\frac{(x-h)^2}{a^2} - \frac{(y-k)^2}{b^2} = 1$$ Transverse axis is horizontal.

$$\frac{(y-k)^2}{a^2} - \frac{(x-h)^2}{b^2} = 1.$$ Transverse axis is vertical.

The vertices are a units from the center, and the foci are c units from the center. Moreover, $c^2 = a^2 + b^2$. If the center of the hyperbola is at the origin $(0, 0)$, the equation takes one of the following forms.

$$\frac{x^2}{a^2} - \frac{y^2}{b^2} = 1$$ Transverse axis is horizontal.

$$\frac{y^2}{a^2} - \frac{x^2}{b^2} = 1$$ Transverse axis is vertical.

Figure 10.31 shows both the horizontal and vertical orientations for a hyperbola.

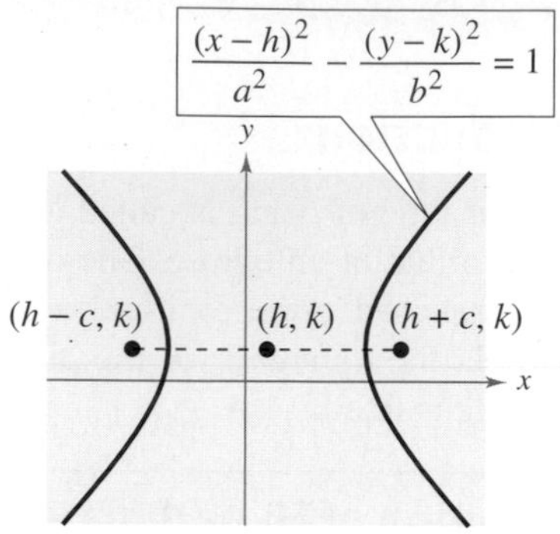

Transverse axis is horizontal.

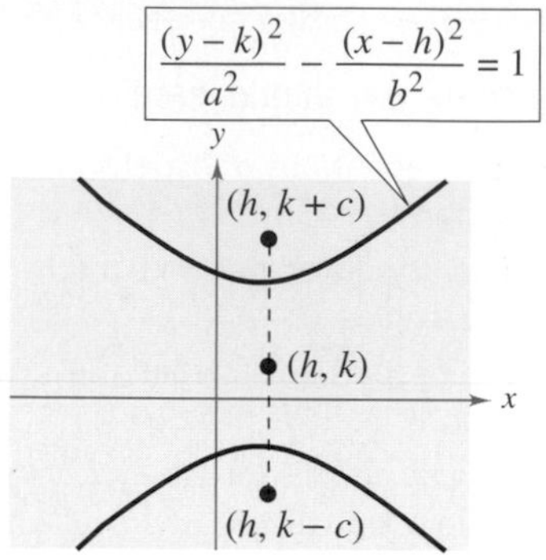

Transverse axis is vertical.

FIGURE 10.31

Example 1 Finding the Standard Equation of a Hyperbola

Find the standard form of the equation of the hyperbola with foci $(-1, 2)$ and $(5, 2)$ and vertices $(0, 2)$ and $(4, 2)$.

Solution

By the Midpoint Formula, the center of the hyperbola occurs at the point $(2, 2)$. Furthermore, $c = 5 - 2 = 3$ and $a = 4 - 2 = 2$, and it follows that

$$b = \sqrt{c^2 - a^2} = \sqrt{3^2 - 2^2} = \sqrt{9 - 4} = \sqrt{5}.$$

So, the hyperbola has a horizontal transverse axis and the standard form of the equation is

$$\frac{(x-2)^2}{2^2} - \frac{(y-2)^2}{(\sqrt{5})^2} = 1.$$ See Figure 10.32.

This equation simplifies to

$$\frac{(x-2)^2}{4} - \frac{(y-2)^2}{5} = 1.$$

> **STUDY TIP**
>
> When finding the standard form of the equation of any conic, it is helpful to sketch a graph of the conic with the given characteristics.

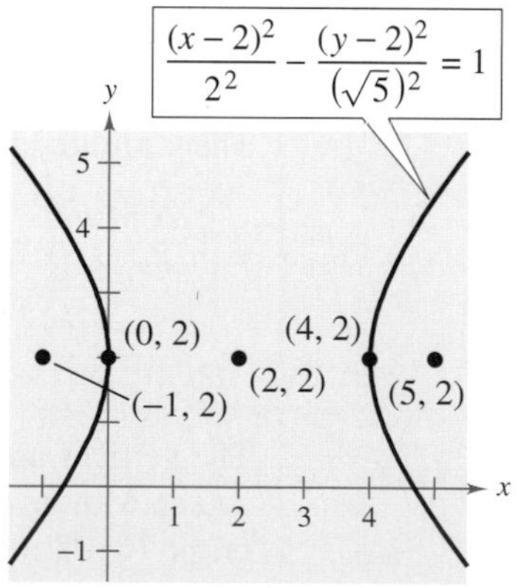

FIGURE 10.32

✓CHECKPOINT Now try Exercise 27.

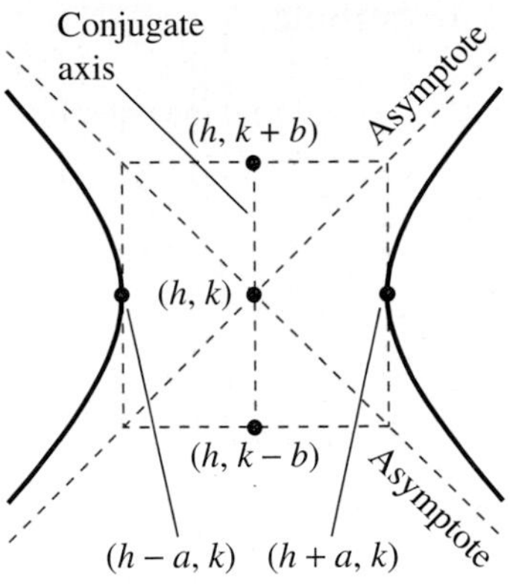

FIGURE 10.33

Asymptotes of a Hyperbola

Each hyperbola has two **asymptotes** that intersect at the center of the hyperbola, as shown in Figure 10.33. The asymptotes pass through the vertices of a rectangle of dimensions $2a$ by $2b$, with its center at (h, k). The line segment of length $2b$ joining $(h, k + b)$ and $(h, k - b)$ [or $(h + b, k)$ and $(h - b, k)$] is the **conjugate axis** of the hyperbola.

Asymptotes of a Hyperbola

The equations of the asymptotes of a hyperbola are

$$y = k \pm \frac{b}{a}(x - h) \qquad \text{Transverse axis is horizontal.}$$

$$y = k \pm \frac{a}{b}(x - h). \qquad \text{Transverse axis is vertical.}$$

Example 2 Using Asymptotes to Sketch a Hyperbola

Sketch the hyperbola whose equation is $4x^2 - y^2 = 16$.

Solution

Divide each side of the original equation by 16, and rewrite the equation in standard form.

$$\frac{x^2}{2^2} - \frac{y^2}{4^2} = 1 \qquad \text{Write in standard form.}$$

From this, you can conclude that $a = 2$, $b = 4$, and the transverse axis is horizontal. So, the vertices occur at $(-2, 0)$ and $(2, 0)$, and the endpoints of the conjugate axis occur at $(0, -4)$ and $(0, 4)$. Using these four points, you are able to sketch the rectangle shown in Figure 10.34. Now, from $c^2 = a^2 + b^2$, you have $c = \sqrt{2^2 + 4^2} = \sqrt{20} = 2\sqrt{5}$. So, the foci of the hyperbola are $\left(-2\sqrt{5}, 0\right)$ and $\left(2\sqrt{5}, 0\right)$. Finally, by drawing the asymptotes through the corners of this rectangle, you can complete the sketch shown in Figure 10.35. Note that the asymptotes are $y = 2x$ and $y = -2x$.

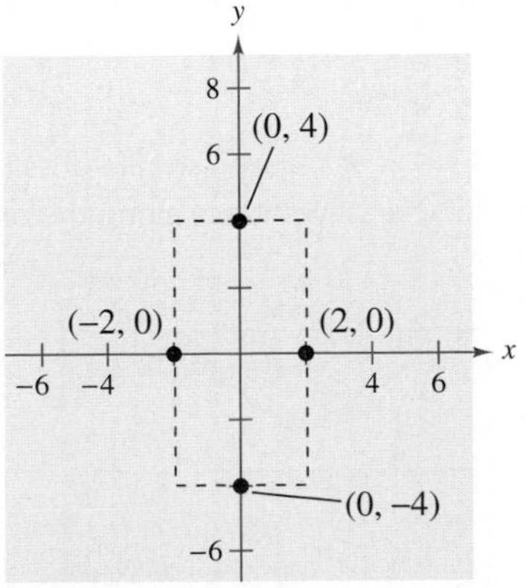

FIGURE 10.34

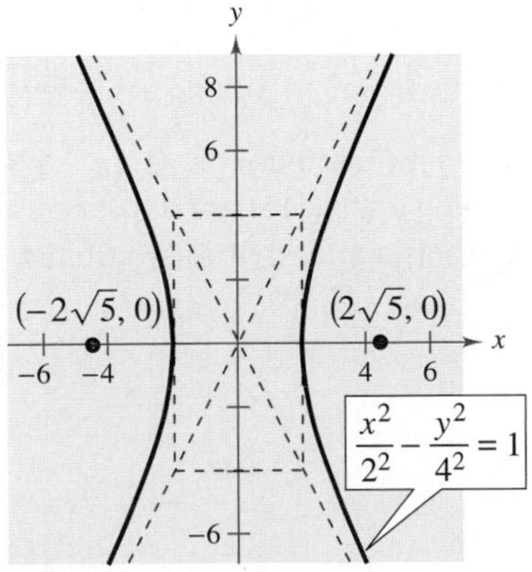

FIGURE 10.35

CHECKPOINT Now try Exercise 7.

Example 3 Finding the Asymptotes of a Hyperbola

Sketch the hyperbola given by $4x^2 - 3y^2 + 8x + 16 = 0$ and find the equations of its asymptotes and the foci.

Solution

$$4x^2 - 3y^2 + 8x + 16 = 0 \quad \text{Write original equation.}$$

$$(4x^2 + 8x) - 3y^2 = -16 \quad \text{Group terms.}$$

$$4(x^2 + 2x) - 3y^2 = -16 \quad \text{Factor 4 from } x\text{-terms.}$$

$$4(x^2 + 2x + 1) - 3y^2 = -16 + 4 \quad \text{Add 4 to each side.}$$

$$4(x + 1)^2 - 3y^2 = -12 \quad \text{Write in completed square form.}$$

$$-\frac{(x + 1)^2}{3} + \frac{y^2}{4} = 1 \quad \text{Divide each side by } -12.$$

$$\frac{y^2}{2^2} - \frac{(x + 1)^2}{(\sqrt{3})^2} = 1 \quad \text{Write in standard form.}$$

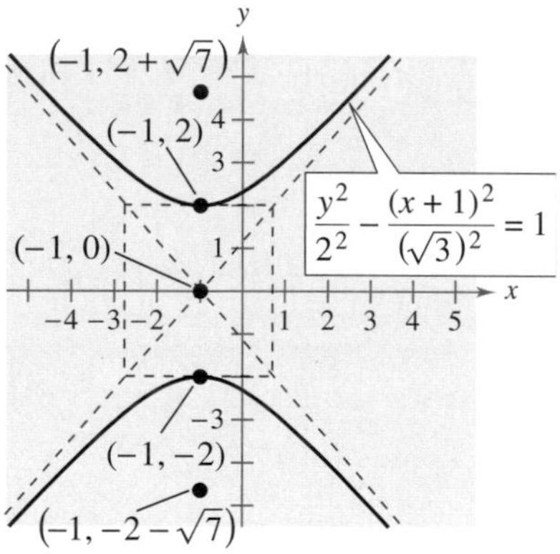

FIGURE 10.36

From this equation you can conclude that the hyperbola has a vertical transverse axis, centered at $(-1, 0)$, has vertices $(-1, 2)$ and $(-1, -2)$, and has a conjugate axis with endpoints $(-1 - \sqrt{3}, 0)$ and $(-1 + \sqrt{3}, 0)$. To sketch the hyperbola, draw a rectangle through these four points. The asymptotes are the lines passing through the corners of the rectangle. Using $a = 2$ and $b = \sqrt{3}$, you can conclude that the equations of the asymptotes are

$$y = \frac{2}{\sqrt{3}}(x + 1) \quad \text{and} \quad y = -\frac{2}{\sqrt{3}}(x + 1).$$

Finally, you can determine the foci by using the equation $c^2 = a^2 + b^2$. So, you have $c = \sqrt{2^2 + (\sqrt{3})^2} = \sqrt{7}$, and the foci are $(-1, -2 - \sqrt{7})$ and $(-1, -2 + \sqrt{7})$. The hyperbola is shown in Figure 10.36.

CHECKPOINT Now try Exercise 13.

Technology

You can use a graphing utility to graph a hyperbola by graphing the upper and lower portions in the same viewing window. For instance, to graph the hyperbola in Example 3, first solve for y to get

$$y_1 = 2\sqrt{1 + \frac{(x + 1)^2}{3}} \quad \text{and} \quad y_2 = -2\sqrt{1 + \frac{(x + 1)^2}{3}}.$$

Use a viewing window in which $-9 \le x \le 9$ and $-6 \le y \le 6$. You should obtain the graph shown below. Notice that the graphing utility does not draw the asymptotes. However, if you trace along the branches, you will see that the values of the hyperbola approach the asymptotes.

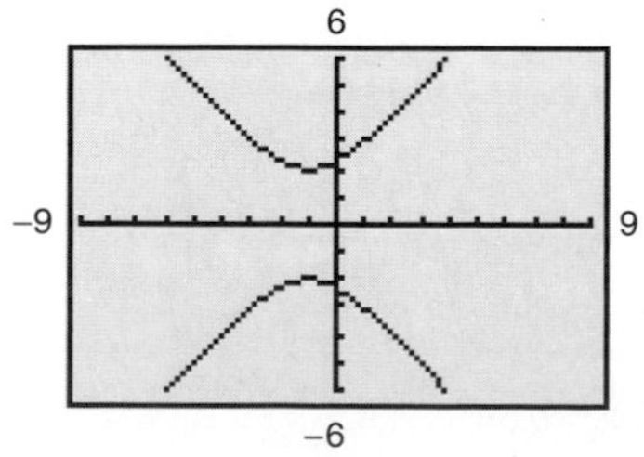

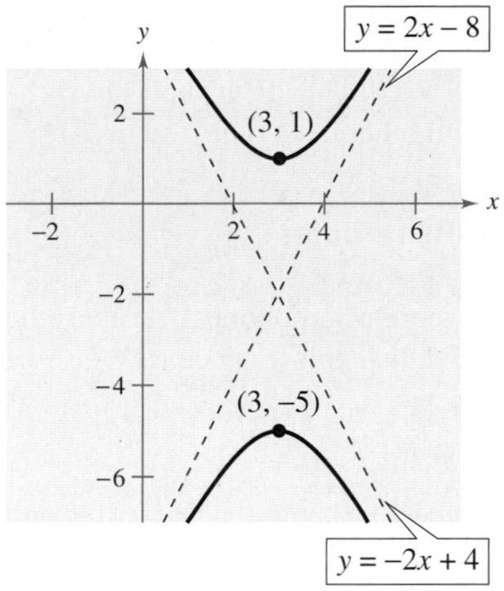

FIGURE 10.37

Example 4 Using Asymptotes to Find the Standard Equation

Find the standard form of the equation of the hyperbola having vertices $(3, -5)$ and $(3, 1)$ and having asymptotes

$$y = 2x - 8 \qquad \text{and} \qquad y = -2x + 4$$

as shown in Figure 10.37.

Solution

By the Midpoint Formula, the center of the hyperbola is $(3, -2)$. Furthermore, the hyperbola has a vertical transverse axis with $a = 3$. From the original equations, you can determine the slopes of the asymptotes to be

$$m_1 = 2 = \frac{a}{b} \qquad \text{and} \qquad m_2 = -2 = -\frac{a}{b}$$

and, because $a = 3$ you can conclude

$$2 = \frac{a}{b} \Rightarrow 2 = \frac{3}{b} \Rightarrow b = \frac{3}{2}.$$

So, the standard form of the equation is

$$\frac{(y+2)^2}{3^2} - \frac{(x-3)^2}{\left(\frac{3}{2}\right)^2} = 1.$$

CHECKPOINT Now try Exercise 35.

As with ellipses, the *eccentricity* of a hyperbola is

$$e = \frac{c}{a} \qquad \text{Eccentricity}$$

and because $c > a$, it follows that $e > 1$. If the eccentricity is large, the branches of the hyperbola are nearly flat, as shown in Figure 10.38. If the eccentricity is close to 1, the branches of the hyperbola are more narrow, as shown in Figure 10.39.

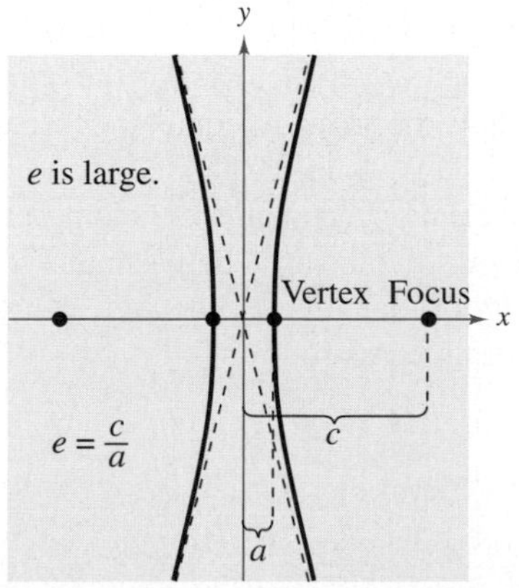

FIGURE 10.38

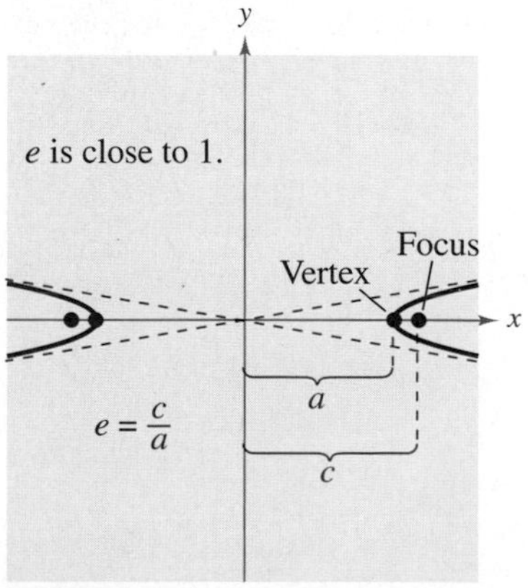

FIGURE 10.39

Applications

The following application was developed during World War II. It shows how the properties of hyperbolas can be used in radar and other detection systems.

Example 5 An Application Involving Hyperbolas

Two microphones, 1 mile apart, record an explosion. Microphone A receives the sound 2 seconds before microphone B. Where did the explosion occur? (Assume sound travels at 1100 feet per second.)

Solution

Assuming sound travels at 1100 feet per second, you know that the explosion took place 2200 feet farther from B than from A, as shown in Figure 10.40. The locus of all points that are 2200 feet closer to A than to B is one branch of the hyperbola

$$\frac{x^2}{a^2} - \frac{y^2}{b^2} = 1$$

where

$$c = \frac{5280}{2} = 2640$$

and

$$a = \frac{2200}{2} = 1100.$$

So, $b^2 = c^2 - a^2 = 2640^2 - 1100^2 = 5{,}759{,}600$, and you can conclude that the explosion occurred somewhere on the right branch of the hyperbola

$$\frac{x^2}{1{,}210{,}000} - \frac{y^2}{5{,}759{,}600} = 1.$$

CHECKPOINT Now try Exercise 41.

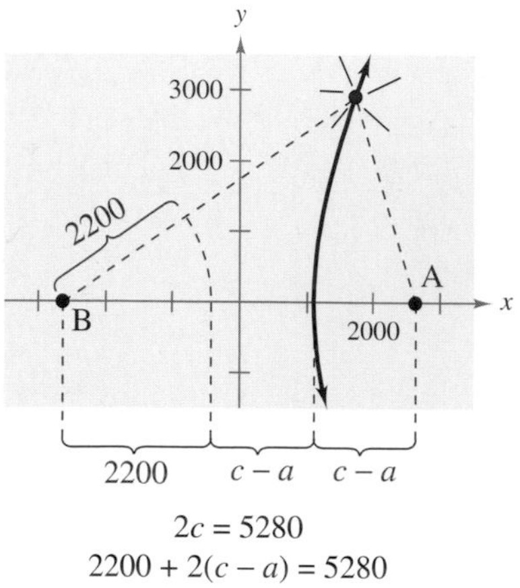

FIGURE 10.40

Another interesting application of conic sections involves the orbits of comets in our solar system. Of the 610 comets identified prior to 1970, 245 have elliptical orbits, 295 have parabolic orbits, and 70 have hyperbolic orbits. The center of the sun is a focus of each of these orbits, and each orbit has a vertex at the point where the comet is closest to the sun, as shown in Figure 10.41. Undoubtedly, there have been many comets with parabolic or hyperbolic orbits that were not identified. We only get to see such comets *once*. Comets with elliptical orbits, such as Halley's comet, are the only ones that remain in our solar system.

If p is the distance between the vertex and the focus (in meters), and v is the velocity of the comet at the vertex in (meters per second), then the type of orbit is determined as follows.

1. Ellipse: $v < \sqrt{2GM/p}$
2. Parabola: $v = \sqrt{2GM/p}$
3. Hyperbola: $v > \sqrt{2GM/p}$

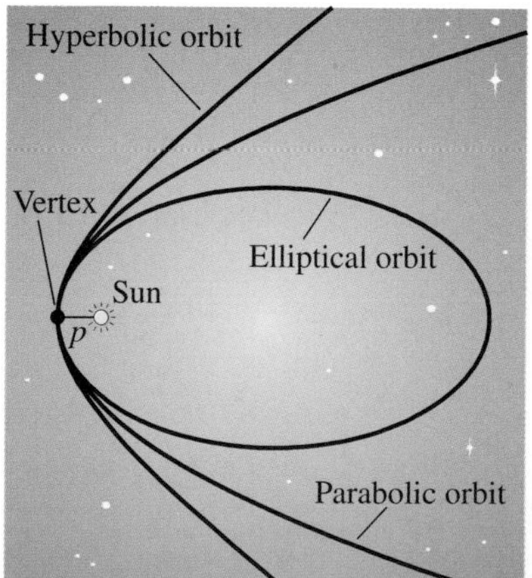

FIGURE 10.41

In each of these relations, $M = 1.989 \times 10^{30}$ kilograms (the mass of the sun) and $G \approx 6.67 \times 10^{-11}$ cubic meter per kilogram-second squared (the universal gravitational constant).

General Equations of Conics

Classifying a Conic from Its General Equation

The graph of $Ax^2 + Cy^2 + Dx + Ey + F = 0$ is one of the following.

1. *Circle:* $A = C$
2. *Parabola:* $AC = 0$ — $A = 0$ or $C = 0$, but not both.
3. *Ellipse:* $AC > 0$ — A and C have like signs.
4. *Hyperbola:* $AC < 0$ — A and C have unlike signs.

The test above is valid *if* the graph is a conic. The test does not apply to equations such as $x^2 + y^2 = -1$, whose graph is not a conic.

Example 6 Classifying Conics from General Equations

Classify the graph of each equation.

a. $4x^2 - 9x + y - 5 = 0$

b. $4x^2 - y^2 + 8x - 6y + 4 = 0$

c. $2x^2 + 4y^2 - 4x + 12y = 0$

d. $2x^2 + 2y^2 - 8x + 12y + 2 = 0$

Solution

a. For the equation $4x^2 - 9x + y - 5 = 0$, you have

$$AC = 4(0) = 0. \qquad \text{Parabola}$$

So, the graph is a parabola.

b. For the equation $4x^2 - y^2 + 8x - 6y + 4 = 0$, you have

$$AC = 4(-1) < 0. \qquad \text{Hyperbola}$$

So, the graph is a hyperbola.

c. For the equation $2x^2 + 4y^2 - 4x + 12y = 0$, you have

$$AC = 2(4) > 0. \qquad \text{Ellipse}$$

So, the graph is an ellipse.

d. For the equation $2x^2 + 2y^2 - 8x + 12y + 2 = 0$, you have

$$A = C = 2. \qquad \text{Circle}$$

So, the graph is a circle.

CHECKPOINT Now try Exercise 49.

Historical Note
Caroline Herschel (1750–1848) was the first woman to be credited with detecting a new comet. During her long life, this English astronomer discovered a total of eight new comets.

WRITING ABOUT MATHEMATICS

Sketching Conics Sketch each of the conics described in Example 6. Write a paragraph describing the procedures that allow you to sketch the conics efficiently.

10.4 Exercises

VOCABULARY CHECK: Fill in the blanks.

1. A ________ is the set of all points (x, y) in a plane, the difference of whose distances from two distinct fixed points, called ________, is a positive constant.
2. The graph of a hyperbola has two disconnected parts called ________.
3. The line segment connecting the vertices of a hyperbola is called the ________ ________, and the midpoint of the line segment is the ________ of the hyperbola.
4. Each hyperbola has two ________ that intersect at the center of the hyperbola.
5. The general form of the equation of a conic is given by ________.

In Exercises 1–4, match the equation with its graph. [The graphs are labeled (a), (b), (c), and (d).]

(a)

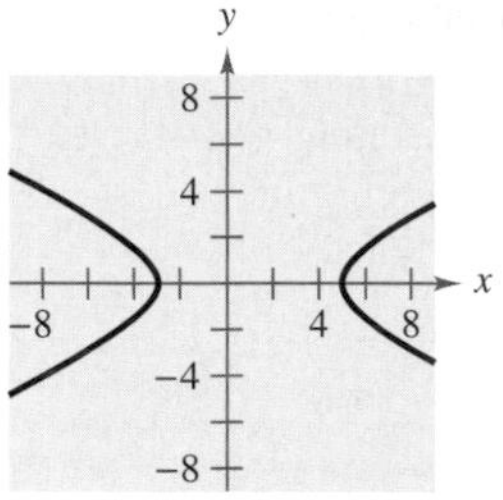

(b)

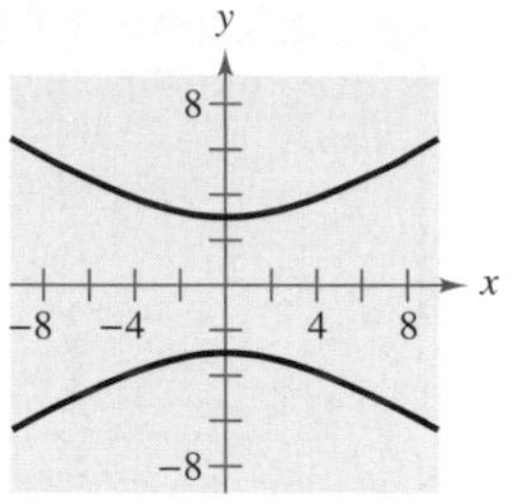

(c)

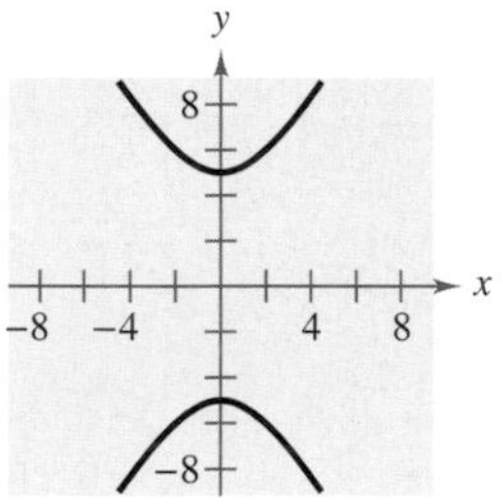

(d)

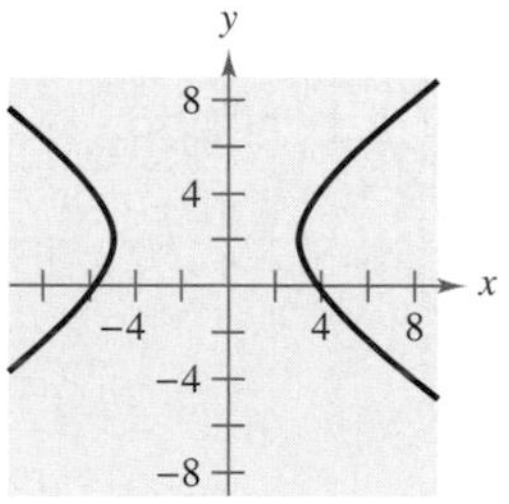

1. $\dfrac{y^2}{9} - \dfrac{x^2}{25} = 1$

2. $\dfrac{y^2}{25} - \dfrac{x^2}{9} = 1$

3. $\dfrac{(x-1)^2}{16} - \dfrac{y^2}{4} = 1$

4. $\dfrac{(x+1)^2}{16} - \dfrac{(y-2)^2}{9} = 1$

In Exercises 5–16, find the center, vertices, foci, and the equations of the asymptotes of the hyperbola, and sketch its graph using the asymptotes as an aid.

5. $x^2 - y^2 = 1$

6. $\dfrac{x^2}{9} - \dfrac{y^2}{25} = 1$

7. $\dfrac{y^2}{25} - \dfrac{x^2}{81} = 1$

8. $\dfrac{x^2}{36} - \dfrac{y^2}{4} = 1$

9. $\dfrac{(x-1)^2}{4} - \dfrac{(y+2)^2}{1} = 1$

10. $\dfrac{(x+3)^2}{144} - \dfrac{(y-2)^2}{25} = 1$

11. $\dfrac{(y+6)^2}{1/9} - \dfrac{(x-2)^2}{1/4} = 1$

12. $\dfrac{(y-1)^2}{1/4} - \dfrac{(x+3)^2}{1/16} = 1$

13. $9x^2 - y^2 - 36x - 6y + 18 = 0$

14. $x^2 - 9y^2 + 36y - 72 = 0$

15. $x^2 - 9y^2 + 2x - 54y - 80 = 0$

16. $16y^2 - x^2 + 2x + 64y + 63 = 0$

In Exercises 17–20, find the center, vertices, foci, and the equations of the asymptotes of the hyperbola. Use a graphing utility to graph the hyperbola and its asymptotes.

17. $2x^2 - 3y^2 = 6$
18. $6y^2 - 3x^2 = 18$
19. $9y^2 - x^2 + 2x + 54y + 62 = 0$
20. $9x^2 - y^2 + 54x + 10y + 55 = 0$

In Exercises 21–26, find the standard form of the equation of the hyperbola with the given characteristics and center at the origin.

21. Vertices: $(0, \pm 2)$; foci: $(0, \pm 4)$
22. Vertices: $(\pm 4, 0)$; foci: $(\pm 6, 0)$
23. Vertices: $(\pm 1, 0)$; asymptotes: $y = \pm 5x$
24. Vertices: $(0, \pm 3)$; asymptotes: $y = \pm 3x$
25. Foci: $(0, \pm 8)$; asymptotes: $y = \pm 4x$
26. Foci: $(\pm 10, 0)$; asymptotes: $y = \pm \frac{3}{4}x$

In Exercises 27–38, find the standard form of the equation of the hyperbola with the given characteristics.

27. Vertices: $(2, 0)$, $(6, 0)$; foci: $(0, 0)$, $(8, 0)$
28. Vertices: $(2, 3)$, $(2, -3)$; foci: $(2, 6)$, $(2, -6)$

29. Vertices: $(4, 1), (4, 9)$; foci: $(4, 0), (4, 10)$

30. Vertices: $(-2, 1), (2, 1)$; foci: $(-3, 1), (3, 1)$

31. Vertices: $(2, 3), (2, -3)$;
passes through the point $(0, 5)$

32. Vertices: $(-2, 1), (2, 1)$;
passes through the point $(5, 4)$

33. Vertices: $(0, 4), (0, 0)$;
passes through the point $(\sqrt{5}, -1)$

34. Vertices: $(1, 2), (1, -2)$;
passes through the point $(0, \sqrt{5})$

35. Vertices: $(1, 2), (3, 2)$;
asymptotes: $y = x$, $y = 4 - x$

36. Vertices: $(3, 0), (3, 6)$;
asymptotes: $y = 6 - x$, $y = x$

37. Vertices: $(0, 2), (6, 2)$;
asymptotes: $y = \frac{2}{3}x$, $y = 4 - \frac{2}{3}x$

38. Vertices: $(3, 0), (3, 4)$;
asymptotes: $y = \frac{2}{3}x$, $y = 4 - \frac{2}{3}x$

39. ***Art*** A sculpture has a hyperbolic cross section (see figure).

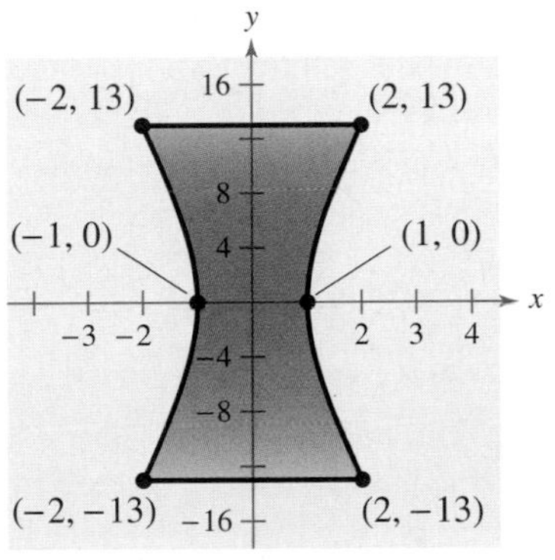

(a) Write an equation that models the curved sides of the sculpture.

(b) Each unit in the coordinate plane represents 1 foot. Find the width of the sculpture at a height of 5 feet.

40. ***Sound Location*** You and a friend live 4 miles apart (on the same "east-west" street) and are talking on the phone. You hear a clap of thunder from lightning in a storm, and 18 seconds later your friend hears the thunder. Find an equation that gives the possible places where the lightning could have occurred. (Assume that the coordinate system is measured in feet and that sound travels at 1100 feet per second.)

41. ***Sound Location*** Three listening stations located at $(3300, 0)$, $(3300, 1100)$, and $(-3300, 0)$ monitor an explosion. The last two stations detect the explosion 1 second and 4 seconds after the first, respectively. Determine the coordinates of the explosion. (Assume that the coordinate system is measured in feet and that sound travels at 100 feet per second.)

Model It

42. ***LORAN*** Long distance radio navigation for aircraft and ships uses synchronized pulses transmitted by widely separated transmitting stations. These pulses travel at the speed of light (186,000 miles per second). The difference in the times of arrival of these pulses at an aircraft or ship is constant on a hyperbola having the transmitting stations as foci. Assume that two stations, 300 miles apart, are positioned on the rectangular coordinate system at points with coordinates $(-150, 0)$ and $(150, 0)$, and that a ship is traveling on a hyperbolic path with coordinates $(x, 75)$ (see figure).

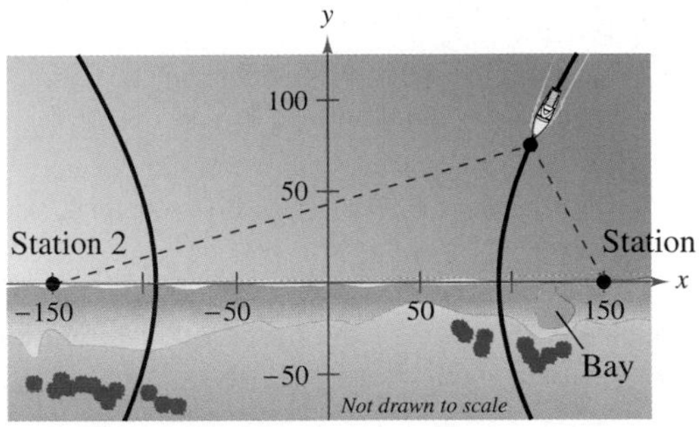

(a) Find the x-coordinate of the position of the ship if the time difference between the pulses from the transmitting stations is 1000 microseconds (0.001 second).

(b) Determine the distance between the ship and station 1 when the ship reaches the shore.

(c) The ship wants to enter a bay located between the two stations. The bay is 30 miles from station 1. What should the time difference be between the pulses?

(d) The ship is 60 miles offshore when the time difference in part (c) is obtained. What is the position of the ship?

43. ***Hyperbolic Mirror*** A hyperbolic mirror (used in some telescopes) has the property that a light ray directed at a focus will be reflected to the other focus. The focus of a hyperbolic mirror (see figure) has coordinates (24, 0). Find the vertex of the mirror if the mount at the top edge of the mirror has coordinates (24, 24).

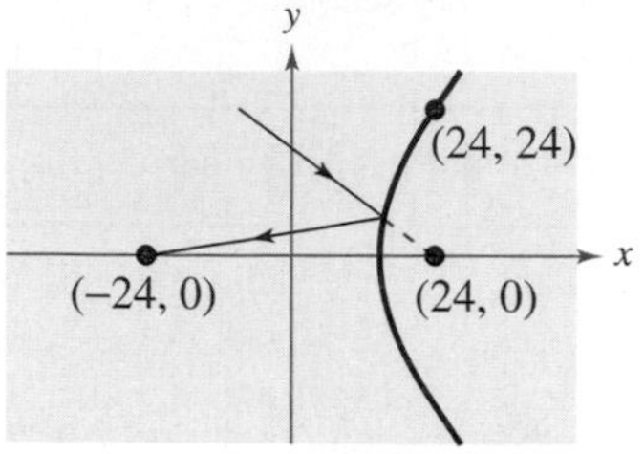

44. ***Running Path*** Let (0, 0) represent a water fountain located in a city park. Each day you run through the park along a path given by

$$x^2 + y^2 - 200x - 52{,}500 = 0$$

where x and y are measured in meters.

(a) What type of conic is your path? Explain your reasoning.

(b) Write the equation of the path in standard form. Sketch a graph of the equation.

(c) After you run, you walk to the water fountain. If you stop running at $(-100, 150)$, how far must you walk for a drink of water?

In Exercises 45–60, classify the graph of the equation as a circle, a parabola, an ellipse, or a hyperbola.

45. $x^2 + y^2 - 6x + 4y + 9 = 0$

46. $x^2 + 4y^2 - 6x + 16y + 21 = 0$

47. $4x^2 - y^2 - 4x - 3 = 0$

48. $y^2 - 6y - 4x + 21 = 0$

49. $y^2 - 4x^2 + 4x - 2y - 4 = 0$

50. $x^2 + y^2 - 4x + 6y - 3 = 0$

51. $x^2 - 4x - 8y + 2 = 0$

52. $4x^2 + y^2 - 8x + 3 = 0$

53. $4x^2 + 3y^2 + 8x - 24y + 51 = 0$

54. $4y^2 - 2x^2 - 4y - 8x - 15 = 0$

55. $25x^2 - 10x - 200y - 119 = 0$

56. $4y^2 + 4x^2 - 24x + 35 = 0$

57. $4x^2 + 16y^2 - 4x - 32y + 1 = 0$

58. $2y^2 + 2x + 2y + 1 = 0$

59. $100x^2 + 100y^2 - 100x + 400y + 409 = 0$

60. $4x^2 - y^2 + 4x + 2y - 1 = 0$

Synthesis

True or False? **In Exercises 61 and 62, determine whether the statement is true or false. Justify your answer.**

61. In the standard form of the equation of a hyperbola, the larger the ratio of b to a, the larger the eccentricity of the hyperbola.

62. In the standard form of the equation of a hyperbola, the trivial solution of two intersecting lines occurs when $b = 0$.

63. Consider a hyperbola centered at the origin with a horizontal transverse axis. Use the definition of a hyperbola to derive its standard form.

64. ***Writing*** Explain how the central rectangle of a hyperbola can be used to sketch its asymptotes.

65. ***Think About It*** Change the equation of the hyperbola so that its graph is the bottom half of the hyperbola.

$$9x^2 - 54x - 4y^2 + 8y + 41 = 0$$

66. ***Exploration*** A circle and a parabola can have 0, 1, 2, 3, or 4 points of intersection. Sketch the circle given by $x^2 + y^2 = 4$. Discuss how this circle could intersect a parabola with an equation of the form $y = x^2 + C$. Then find the values of C for each of the five cases described below. Use a graphing utility to verify your results.

(a) No points of intersection

(b) One point of intersection

(c) Two points of intersection

(d) Three points of intersection

(e) Four points of intersection

Skills Review

In Exercises 67–72, factor the polynomial completely.

67. $x^3 - 16x$

68. $x^2 + 14x + 49$

69. $2x^3 - 24x^2 + 72x$

70. $6x^3 - 11x^2 - 10x$

71. $16x^3 + 54$

72. $4 - x + 4x^2 - x^3$

In Exercises 73–76, sketch a graph of the function. Include two full periods.

73. $y = 2\cos x + 1$

74. $y = \sin \pi x$

75. $y = \tan 2x$

76. $y = -\frac{1}{2}\sec x$

10.5 Rotation of Conics

What you should learn

- Rotate the coordinate axes to eliminate the xy-term in equations of conics.
- Use the discriminant to classify conics.

Why you should learn it

As illustrated in Exercises 7–18 on page 769, rotation of the coordinate axes can help you identify the graph of a general second-degree equation.

Rotation

In the preceding section, you learned that the equation of a conic with axes parallel to one of the coordinate axes has a standard form that can be written in the general form

$$Ax^2 + Cy^2 + Dx + Ey + F = 0. \qquad \text{Horizontal or vertical axis}$$

In this section, you will study the equations of conics whose axes are rotated so that they are not parallel to either the x-axis or the y-axis. The general equation for such conics contains an xy-term.

$$Ax^2 + Bxy + Cy^2 + Dx + Ey + F = 0 \qquad \text{Equation in } xy\text{-plane}$$

To eliminate this xy-term, you can use a procedure called **rotation of axes.** The objective is to rotate the x- and y-axes until they are parallel to the axes of the conic. The rotated axes are denoted as the x'-axis and the y'-axis, as shown in Figure 10.42.

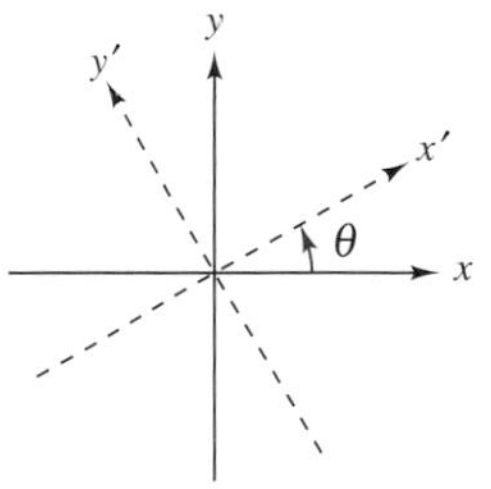

FIGURE 10.42

After the rotation, the equation of the conic in the new $x'y'$-plane will have the form

$$A'(x')^2 + C'(y')^2 + D'x' + E'y' + F' = 0. \qquad \text{Equation in } x'y'\text{-plane}$$

Because this equation has no xy-term, you can obtain a standard form by completing the square. The following theorem identifies how much to rotate the axes to eliminate the xy-term and also the equations for determining the new coefficients A', C', D', E', and F'.

Rotation of Axes to Eliminate an xy-Term

The general second-degree equation $Ax^2 + Bxy + Cy^2 + Dx + Ey + F = 0$ can be rewritten as

$$A'(x')^2 + C'(y')^2 + D'x' + E'y' + F' = 0$$

by rotating the coordinate axes through an angle θ, where

$$\cot 2\theta = \frac{A - C}{B}.$$

The coefficients of the new equation are obtained by making the substitutions $x = x' \cos \theta - y' \sin \theta$ and $y = x' \sin \theta + y' \cos \theta$.

STUDY TIP

Remember that the substitutions

$$x = x'\cos\theta - y'\sin\theta$$

and

$$y = x'\sin\theta + y'\cos\theta$$

were developed to eliminate the $x'y'$-term in the rotated system. You can use this as a check on your work. In other words, if your final equation contains an $x'y'$-term, you know that you made a mistake.

Example 1 Rotation of Axes for a Hyperbola

Write the equation $xy - 1 = 0$ in standard form.

Solution

Because $A = 0$, $B = 1$, and $C = 0$, you have

$$\cot 2\theta = \frac{A - C}{B} = 0 \quad \Rightarrow \quad 2\theta = \frac{\pi}{2} \quad \Rightarrow \quad \theta = \frac{\pi}{4}$$

which implies that

$$\begin{aligned} x &= x'\cos\frac{\pi}{4} - y'\sin\frac{\pi}{4} \\ &= x'\left(\frac{1}{\sqrt{2}}\right) - y'\left(\frac{1}{\sqrt{2}}\right) \\ &= \frac{x' - y'}{\sqrt{2}} \end{aligned}$$

and

$$\begin{aligned} y &= x'\sin\frac{\pi}{4} + y'\cos\frac{\pi}{4} \\ &= x'\left(\frac{1}{\sqrt{2}}\right) + y'\left(\frac{1}{\sqrt{2}}\right) \\ &= \frac{x' + y'}{\sqrt{2}}. \end{aligned}$$

The equation in the $x'y'$-system is obtained by substituting these expressions in the equation $xy - 1 = 0$.

$$\left(\frac{x' - y'}{\sqrt{2}}\right)\left(\frac{x' + y'}{\sqrt{2}}\right) - 1 = 0$$

$$\frac{(x')^2 - (y')^2}{2} - 1 = 0$$

$$\frac{(x')^2}{(\sqrt{2})^2} - \frac{(y')^2}{(\sqrt{2})^2} = 1 \qquad \text{Write in standard form.}$$

In the $x'y'$-system, this is a hyperbola centered at the origin with vertices at $(\pm\sqrt{2}, 0)$, as shown in Figure 10.43. To find the coordinates of the vertices in the xy-system, substitute the coordinates $(\pm\sqrt{2}, 0)$ in the equations

$$x = \frac{x' - y'}{\sqrt{2}} \quad \text{and} \quad y = \frac{x' + y'}{\sqrt{2}}.$$

This substitution yields the vertices $(1, 1)$ and $(-1, -1)$ in the xy-system. Note also that the asymptotes of the hyperbola have equations $y' = \pm x'$, which correspond to the original x- and y-axes.

CHECKPOINT Now try Exercise 7.

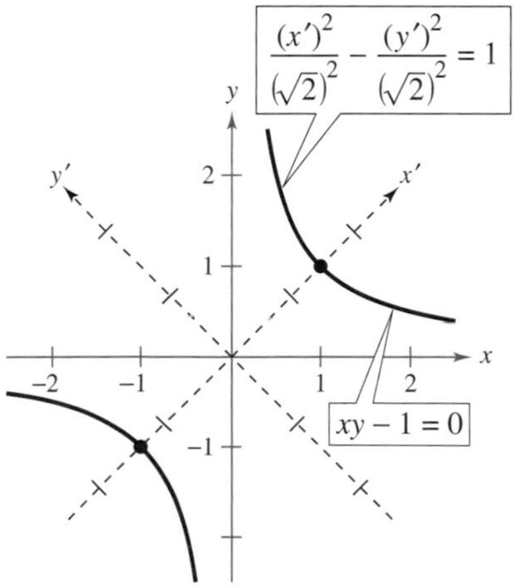

Vertices:
In x′y′-system: $(\sqrt{2}, 0), (-\sqrt{2}, 0)$
In xy-system: $(1, 1), (-1, -1)$
FIGURE 10.43

Example 2 Rotation of Axes for an Ellipse

Sketch the graph of $7x^2 - 6\sqrt{3}xy + 13y^2 - 16 = 0$.

Solution

Because $A = 7$, $B = -6\sqrt{3}$, and $C = 13$, you have

$$\cot 2\theta = \frac{A - C}{B} = \frac{7 - 13}{-6\sqrt{3}} = \frac{1}{\sqrt{3}}$$

which implies that $\theta = \pi/6$. The equation in the $x'y'$-system is obtained by making the substitutions

$$x = x' \cos\frac{\pi}{6} - y' \sin\frac{\pi}{6}$$
$$= x'\left(\frac{\sqrt{3}}{2}\right) - y'\left(\frac{1}{2}\right)$$
$$= \frac{\sqrt{3}x' - y'}{2}$$

and

$$y = x' \sin\frac{\pi}{6} + y' \cos\frac{\pi}{6}$$
$$= x'\left(\frac{1}{2}\right) + y'\left(\frac{\sqrt{3}}{2}\right)$$
$$= \frac{x' + \sqrt{3}y'}{2}$$

in the original equation. So, you have

$$7x^2 - 6\sqrt{3}xy + 13y^2 - 16 = 0$$
$$7\left(\frac{\sqrt{3}x' - y'}{2}\right)^2 - 6\sqrt{3}\left(\frac{\sqrt{3}x' - y'}{2}\right)\left(\frac{x' + \sqrt{3}y'}{2}\right)$$
$$+ 13\left(\frac{x' + \sqrt{3}y'}{2}\right)^2 - 16 = 0$$

which simplifies to

$$4(x')^2 + 16(y')^2 - 16 = 0$$
$$4(x')^2 + 16(y')^2 = 16$$
$$\frac{(x')^2}{4} + \frac{(y')^2}{1} = 1$$
$$\frac{(x')^2}{2^2} + \frac{(y')^2}{1^2} = 1. \qquad \text{Write in standard form.}$$

This is the equation of an ellipse centered at the origin with vertices $(\pm 2, 0)$ in the $x'y'$-system, as shown in Figure 10.44.

✓CHECKPOINT Now try Exercise 13.

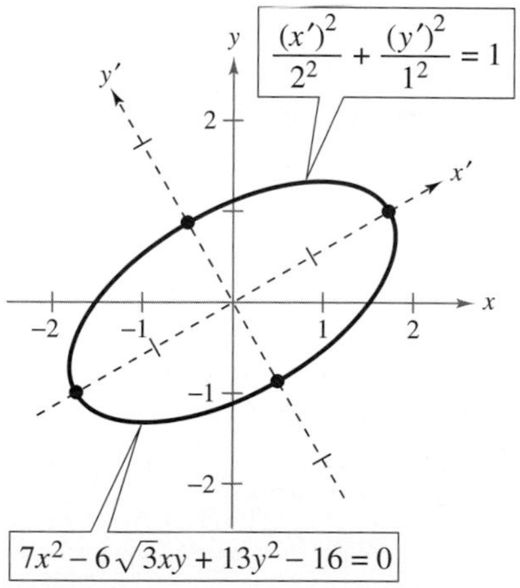

Vertices:
In x'y'-system: $(\pm 2, 0)$, $(0, \pm 1)$
In xy-system: $(\sqrt{3}, 1)$, $(-\sqrt{3}, -1)$, $\left(\frac{1}{2}, -\frac{\sqrt{3}}{2}\right)$, $\left(-\frac{1}{2}, \frac{\sqrt{3}}{2}\right)$

FIGURE 10.44

Example 3 Rotation of Axes for a Parabola

Sketch the graph of $x^2 - 4xy + 4y^2 + 5\sqrt{5}y + 1 = 0$.

Solution

Because $A = 1$, $B = -4$, and $C = 4$, you have

$$\cot 2\theta = \frac{A - C}{B} = \frac{1 - 4}{-4} = \frac{3}{4}.$$

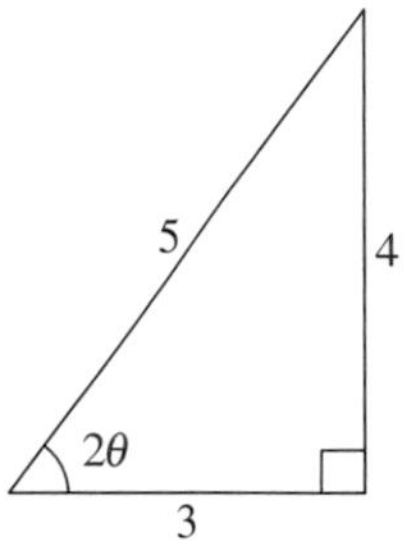

FIGURE 10.45

Using this information, draw a right triangle as shown in Figure 10.45. From the figure, you can see that $\cos 2\theta = \frac{3}{5}$. To find the values of $\sin\theta$ and $\cos\theta$, you can use the half-angle formulas in the forms

$$\sin\theta = \sqrt{\frac{1 - \cos 2\theta}{2}} \quad \text{and} \quad \cos\theta = \sqrt{\frac{1 + \cos 2\theta}{2}}.$$

So,

$$\sin\theta = \sqrt{\frac{1 - \cos 2\theta}{2}} = \sqrt{\frac{1 - \frac{3}{5}}{2}} = \sqrt{\frac{1}{5}} = \frac{1}{\sqrt{5}}$$

$$\cos\theta = \sqrt{\frac{1 + \cos 2\theta}{2}} = \sqrt{\frac{1 + \frac{3}{5}}{2}} = \sqrt{\frac{4}{5}} = \frac{2}{\sqrt{5}}.$$

Consequently, you use the substitutions

$$x = x'\cos\theta - y'\sin\theta$$
$$= x'\left(\frac{2}{\sqrt{5}}\right) - y'\left(\frac{1}{\sqrt{5}}\right) = \frac{2x' - y'}{\sqrt{5}}$$

$$y = x'\sin\theta + y'\cos\theta$$
$$= x'\left(\frac{1}{\sqrt{5}}\right) + y'\left(\frac{2}{\sqrt{5}}\right) = \frac{x' + 2y'}{\sqrt{5}}.$$

Substituting these expressions in the original equation, you have

$$x^2 - 4xy + 4y^2 + 5\sqrt{5}y + 1 = 0$$

$$\left(\frac{2x' - y'}{\sqrt{5}}\right)^2 - 4\left(\frac{2x' - y'}{\sqrt{5}}\right)\left(\frac{x' + 2y'}{\sqrt{5}}\right) + 4\left(\frac{x' + 2y'}{\sqrt{5}}\right)^2 + 5\sqrt{5}\left(\frac{x' + 2y'}{\sqrt{5}}\right) + 1 = 0$$

which simplifies as follows.

$$5(y')^2 + 5x' + 10y' + 1 = 0$$

$$5[(y')^2 + 2y'] = -5x' - 1 \qquad \text{Group terms.}$$

$$5(y' + 1)^2 = -5x' + 4 \qquad \text{Write in completed square form.}$$

$$(y' + 1)^2 = (-1)\left(x' - \frac{4}{5}\right) \qquad \text{Write in standard form.}$$

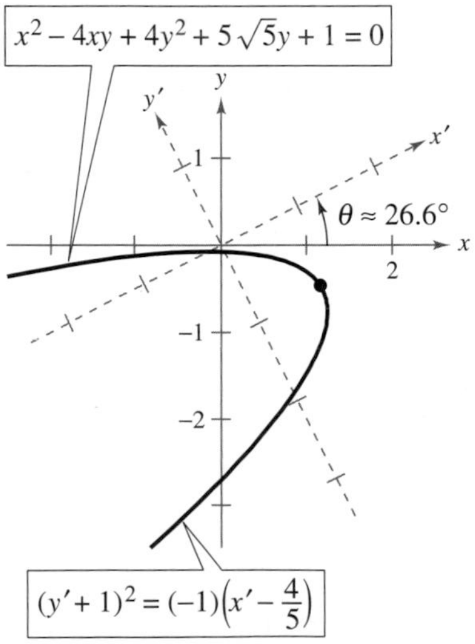

Vertex:
In x′y′-system: $\left(\frac{4}{5}, -1\right)$
In xy-system: $\left(\frac{13}{5\sqrt{5}}, -\frac{6}{5\sqrt{5}}\right)$

FIGURE 10.46

The graph of this equation is a parabola with vertex $\left(\frac{4}{5}, -1\right)$. Its axis is parallel to the x'-axis in the $x'y'$-system, and because $\sin\theta = 1/\sqrt{5}$, $\theta \approx 26.6°$, as shown in Figure 10.46.

✓CHECKPOINT Now try Exercise 17.

Invariants Under Rotation

In the rotation of axes theorem listed at the beginning of this section, note that the constant term is the same in both equations, $F' = F$. Such quantities are **invariant under rotation.** The next theorem lists some other rotation invariants.

Rotation Invariants

The rotation of the coordinate axes through an angle θ that transforms the equation $Ax^2 + Bxy + Cy^2 + Dx + Ey + F = 0$ into the form

$$A'(x')^2 + C'(y')^2 + D'x' + E'y' + F' = 0$$

has the following rotation invariants.

1. $F = F'$

2. $A + C = A' + C'$

3. $B^2 - 4AC = (B')^2 - 4A'C'$

STUDY TIP

If there is an xy-term in the equation of a conic, you should realize then that the conic is rotated. Before rotating the axes, you should use the discriminant to classify the conic.

You can use the results of this theorem to classify the graph of a second-degree equation *with* an xy-term in much the same way you do for a second-degree equation *without* an xy-term. Note that because $B' = 0$, the invariant $B^2 - 4AC$ reduces to

$$B^2 - 4AC = -4A'C'. \quad \text{Discriminant}$$

This quantity is called the **discriminant** of the equation

$$Ax^2 + Bxy + Cy^2 + Dx + Ey + F = 0.$$

Now, from the classification procedure given in Section 10.4, you know that the sign of $A'C'$ determines the type of graph for the equation

$$A'(x')^2 + C'(y')^2 + D'x' + E'y' + F' = 0.$$

Consequently, the sign of $B^2 - 4AC$ will determine the type of graph for the original equation, as given in the following classification.

Classification of Conics by the Discriminant

The graph of the equation $Ax^2 + Bxy + Cy^2 + Dx + Ey + F = 0$ is, except in degenerate cases, determined by its discriminant as follows.

1. *Ellipse or circle:* $B^2 - 4AC < 0$

2. *Parabola:* $B^2 - 4AC = 0$

3. *Hyperbola:* $B^2 - 4AC > 0$

For example, in the general equation

$$3x^2 + 7xy + 5y^2 - 6x - 7y + 15 = 0$$

you have $A = 3$, $B = 7$, and $C = 5$. So the discriminant is

$$B^2 - 4AC = 7^2 - 4(3)(5) = 49 - 60 = -11.$$

Because $-11 < 0$, the graph of the equation is an ellipse or a circle.

Example 4 Rotation and Graphing Utilities

For each equation, classify the graph of the equation, use the Quadratic Formula to solve for y, and then use a graphing utility to graph the equation.

a. $2x^2 - 3xy + 2y^2 - 2x = 0$ **b.** $x^2 - 6xy + 9y^2 - 2y + 1 = 0$

c. $3x^2 + 8xy + 4y^2 - 7 = 0$

Solution

a. Because $B^2 - 4AC = 9 - 16 < 0$, the graph is a circle or an ellipse. Solve for y as follows.

$$2x^2 - 3xy + 2y^2 - 2x = 0 \quad \text{Write original equation.}$$

$$2y^2 - 3xy + (2x^2 - 2x) = 0 \quad \text{Quadratic form } ay^2 + by + c = 0$$

$$y = \frac{-(-3x) \pm \sqrt{(-3x)^2 - 4(2)(2x^2 - 2x)}}{2(2)}$$

$$y = \frac{3x \pm \sqrt{x(16 - 7x)}}{4}$$

Graph both of the equations to obtain the ellipse shown in Figure 10.47.

$$y_1 = \frac{3x + \sqrt{x(16 - 7x)}}{4} \quad \text{Top half of ellipse}$$

$$y_2 = \frac{3x - \sqrt{x(16 - 7x)}}{4} \quad \text{Bottom half of ellipse}$$

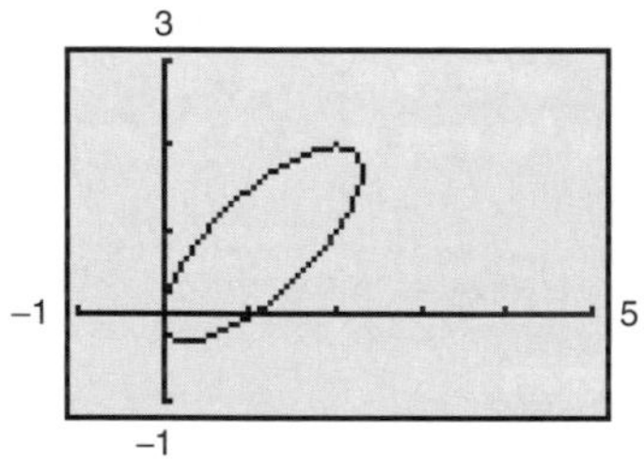

FIGURE 10.47

b. Because $B^2 - 4AC = 36 - 36 = 0$, the graph is a parabola.

$$x^2 - 6xy + 9y^2 - 2y + 1 = 0 \quad \text{Write original equation.}$$

$$9y^2 - (6x + 2)y + (x^2 + 1) = 0 \quad \text{Quadratic form } ay^2 + by + c = 0$$

$$y = \frac{(6x + 2) \pm \sqrt{(6x + 2)^2 - 4(9)(x^2 + 1)}}{2(9)}$$

Graphing both of the equations to obtain the parabola shown in Figure 10.48.

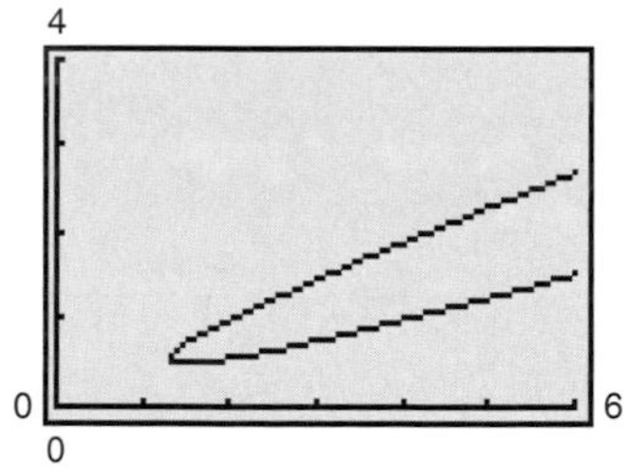

FIGURE 10.48

c. Because $B^2 - 4AC = 64 - 48 > 0$, the graph is a hyperbola.

$$3x^2 + 8xy + 4y^2 - 7 = 0 \quad \text{Write original equation.}$$

$$4y^2 + 8xy + (3x^2 - 7) = 0 \quad \text{Quadratic form } ay^2 + by + c = 0$$

$$y = \frac{-8x \pm \sqrt{(8x)^2 - 4(4)(3x^2 - 7)}}{2(4)}$$

The graphs of these two equations yield the hyperbola shown in Figure 10.49.

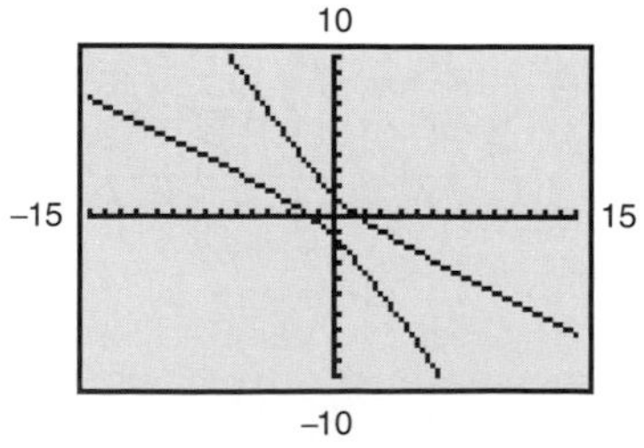

FIGURE 10.49

CHECKPOINT Now try Exercise 33.

Writing about Mathematics

Classifying a Graph as a Hyperbola In Section 2.6, it was mentioned that the graph of $f(x) = 1/x$ is a hyperbola. Use the techniques in this section to verify this, and justify each step. Compare your results with those of another student.

10.5 Exercises

VOCABULARY CHECK: Fill in the blanks.

1. The procedure used to eliminate the xy-term in a general second-degree equation is called ________ of ________.
2. After rotating the coordinate axes through an angle θ, the general second-degree equation in the new $x'y'$-plane will have the form ________.
3. Quantities that are equal in both the original equation of a conic and the equation of the rotated conic are ________ ________ ________.
4. The quantity $B^2 - 4AC$ is called the ________ of the equation $Ax^2 + Bxy + Cy^2 + Dx + Ey + F = 0$.

In Exercises 1–6, the $x'y'$-coordinate system has been rotated θ degrees from the xy-coordinate system. The coordinates of a point in the xy-coordinate system are given. Find the coordinates of the point in the rotated coordinate system.

1. $\theta = 90°, (0, 3)$
2. $\theta = 45°, (3, 3)$
3. $\theta = 30°, (1, 3)$
4. $\theta = 60°, (3, 1)$
5. $\theta = 45°, (2, 1)$
6. $\theta = 30°, (2, 4)$

In Exercises 7–18, rotate the axes to eliminate the xy-term in the equation. Then write the equation in standard form. Sketch the graph of the resulting equation, showing both sets of axes.

7. $xy + 1 = 0$
8. $xy - 2 = 0$
9. $x^2 - 2xy + y^2 - 1 = 0$
10. $xy + x - 2y + 3 = 0$
11. $xy - 2y - 4x = 0$
12. $2x^2 - 3xy - 2y^2 + 10 = 0$
13. $5x^2 - 6xy + 5y^2 - 12 = 0$
14. $13x^2 + 6\sqrt{3}xy + 7y^2 - 16 = 0$
15. $3x^2 - 2\sqrt{3}xy + y^2 + 2x + 2\sqrt{3}y = 0$
16. $16x^2 - 24xy + 9y^2 - 60x - 80y + 100 = 0$
17. $9x^2 + 24xy + 16y^2 + 90x - 130y = 0$
18. $9x^2 + 24xy + 16y^2 + 80x - 60y = 0$

In Exercises 19–26, use a graphing utility to graph the conic. Determine the angle θ through which the axes are rotated. Explain how you used the graphing utility to obtain the graph.

19. $x^2 + 2xy + y^2 = 20$
20. $x^2 - 4xy + 2y^2 = 6$
21. $17x^2 + 32xy - 7y^2 = 75$
22. $40x^2 + 36xy + 25y^2 = 52$
23. $32x^2 + 48xy + 8y^2 = 50$
24. $24x^2 + 18xy + 12y^2 = 34$
25. $4x^2 - 12xy + 9y^2 + (4\sqrt{13} - 12)x - (6\sqrt{13} + 8)y = 91$
26. $6x^2 - 4xy + 8y^2 + (5\sqrt{5} - 10)x - (7\sqrt{5} + 5)y = 80$

In Exercises 27–32, match the graph with its equation. [The graphs are labeled (a), (b), (c), (d), (e), and (f).]

(a)
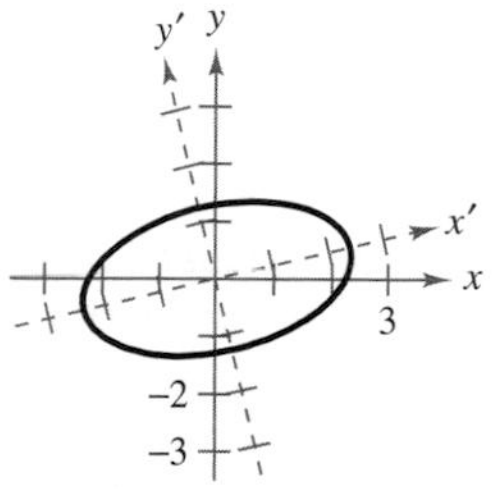

(b)
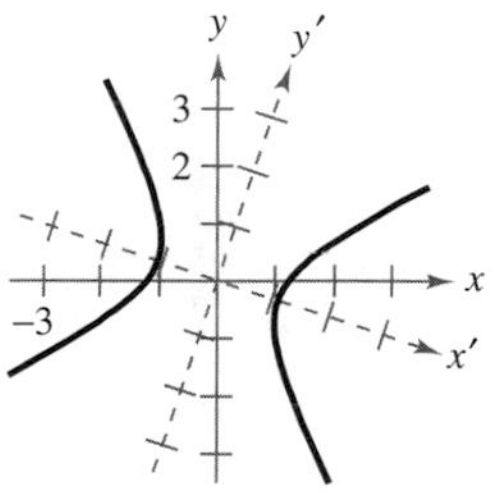

(c)
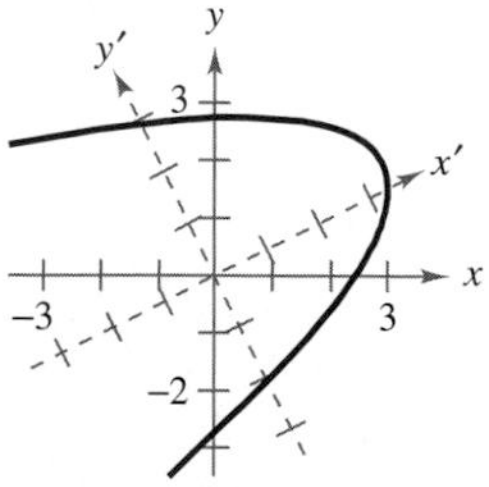

(d)
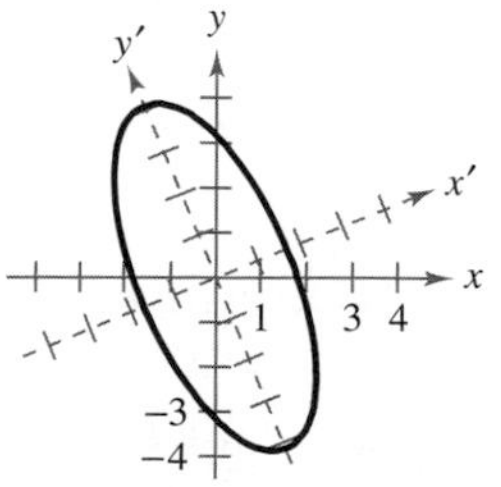

(e)
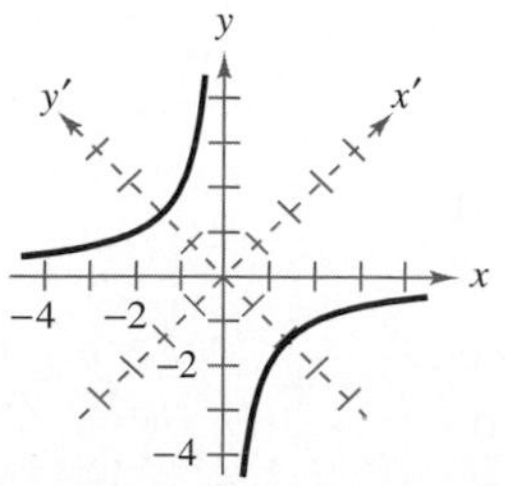

(f)
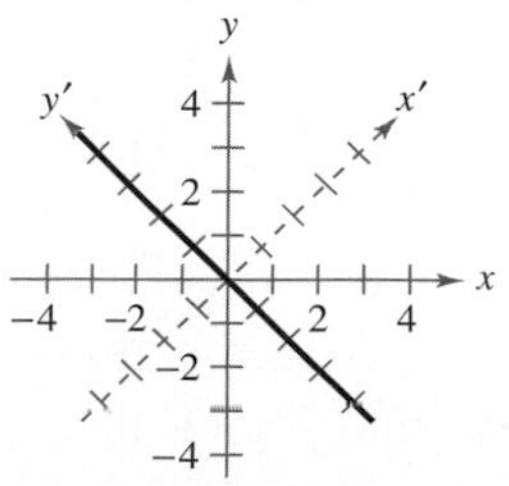

27. $xy + 2 = 0$

28. $x^2 + 2xy + y^2 = 0$

29. $-2x^2 + 3xy + 2y^2 + 3 = 0$

30. $x^2 - xy + 3y^2 - 5 = 0$

31. $3x^2 + 2xy + y^2 - 10 = 0$

32. $x^2 - 4xy + 4y^2 + 10x - 30 = 0$

In Exercises 33–40, (a) use the discriminant to classify the graph, (b) use the Quadratic Formula to solve for *y*, and (c) use a graphing utility to graph the equation.

33. $16x^2 - 8xy + y^2 - 10x + 5y = 0$

34. $x^2 - 4xy - 2y^2 - 6 = 0$

35. $12x^2 - 6xy + 7y^2 - 45 = 0$

36. $2x^2 + 4xy + 5y^2 + 3x - 4y - 20 = 0$

37. $x^2 - 6xy - 5y^2 + 4x - 22 = 0$

38. $36x^2 - 60xy + 25y^2 + 9y = 0$

39. $x^2 + 4xy + 4y^2 - 5x - y - 3 = 0$

40. $x^2 + xy + 4y^2 + x + y - 4 = 0$

In Exercises 41–44, sketch (if possible) the graph of the degenerate conic.

41. $y^2 - 9x^2 = 0$

42. $x^2 + y^2 - 2x + 6y + 10 = 0$

43. $x^2 + 2xy + y^2 - 1 = 0$

44. $x^2 - 10xy + y^2 = 0$

In Exercises 45–58, find any points of intersection of the graphs algebraically and then verify using a graphing utility.

45. $-x^2 + y^2 + 4x - 6y + 4 = 0$
$x^2 + y^2 - 4x - 6y + 12 = 0$

46. $-x^2 - y^2 - 8x + 20y - 7 = 0$
$x^2 + 9y^2 + 8x + 4y + 7 = 0$

47. $-4x^2 - y^2 - 16x + 24y - 16 = 0$
$4x^2 + y^2 + 40x - 24y + 208 = 0$

48. $x^2 - 4y^2 - 20x - 64y - 172 = 0$
$16x^2 + 4y^2 - 320x + 64y + 1600 = 0$

49. $x^2 - y^2 - 12x + 16y - 64 = 0$
$x^2 + y^2 - 12x - 16y + 64 = 0$

50. $x^2 + 4y^2 - 2x - 8y + 1 = 0$
$-x^2 + 2x - 4y - 1 = 0$

51. $-16x^2 - y^2 + 24y - 80 = 0$
$16x^2 + 25y^2 - 400 = 0$

52. $16x^2 - y^2 + 16y - 128 = 0$
$y^2 - 48x - 16y - 32 = 0$

53. $x^2 + y^2 - 4 = 0$
$3x - y^2 = 0$

54. $4x^2 + 9y^2 - 36y = 0$
$x^2 + 9y - 27 = 0$

55. $x^2 + 2y^2 - 4x + 6y - 5 = 0$
$-x + y - 4 = 0$

56. $x^2 + 2y^2 - 4x + 6y - 5 = 0$
$x^2 - 4x - y + 4 = 0$

57. $xy + x - 2y + 3 = 0$
$x^2 + 4y^2 - 9 = 0$

58. $5x^2 - 2xy + 5y^2 - 12 = 0$
$x + y - 1 = 0$

Synthesis

True or False? **In Exercises 59 and 60, determine whether the statement is true or false. Justify your answer.**

59. The graph of the equation

$$x^2 + xy + ky^2 + 6x + 10 = 0$$

where k is any constant less than $\frac{1}{4}$, is a hyperbola.

60. After a rotation of axes is used to eliminate the xy-term from an equation of the form

$$Ax^2 + Bxy + Cy^2 + Dx + Ey + F = 0$$

the coefficients of the x^2- and y^2-terms remain A and C, respectively.

61. Show that the equation

$$x^2 + y^2 = r^2$$

is invariant under rotation of axes.

62. Find the lengths of the major and minor axes of the ellipse graphed in Exercise 14.

Skills Review

In Exercises 63–70, graph the function.

63. $f(x) = |x + 3|$

64. $f(x) = |x - 4| + 1$

65. $g(x) = \sqrt{4 - x^2}$

66. $g(x) = \sqrt{3x - 2}$

67. $h(t) = -(t - 2)^3 + 3$

68. $h(t) = \frac{1}{2}(t + 4)^3$

69. $f(t) = [\![t - 5]\!] + 1$

70. $f(t) = -2[\![t]\!] + 3$

In Exercises 71–74, find the area of the triangle.

71. $C = 110°, a = 8, b = 12$

72. $B = 70°, a = 25, c = 16$

73. $a = 11, b = 18, c = 10$

74. $a = 23, b = 35, c = 27$

10.6 Parametric Equations

What you should learn

- Evaluate sets of parametric equations for given values of the parameter.
- Sketch curves that are represented by sets of parametric equations.
- Rewrite sets of parametric equations as single rectangular equations by eliminating the parameter.
- Find sets of parametric equations for graphs.

Why you should learn it

Parametric equations are useful for modeling the path of an object. For instance, in Exercise 59 on page 777, you will use a set of parametric equations to model the path of a baseball.

Jed Jacobsohn/Getty Images

Plane Curves

Up to this point you have been representing a graph by a single equation involving the *two* variables x and y. In this section, you will study situations in which it is useful to introduce a *third* variable to represent a curve in the plane.

To see the usefulness of this procedure, consider the path followed by an object that is propelled into the air at an angle of 45°. If the initial velocity of the object is 48 feet per second, it can be shown that the object follows the parabolic path

$$y = -\frac{x^2}{72} + x \qquad \text{Rectangular equation}$$

as shown in Figure 10.50. However, this equation does not tell the whole story. Although it does tell you *where* the object has been, it doesn't tell you *when* the object was at a given point (x, y) on the path. To determine this time, you can introduce a third variable t, called a **parameter.** It is possible to write both x and y as functions of t to obtain the **parametric equations**

$$x = 24\sqrt{2}t \qquad \text{Parametric equation for } x$$

$$y = -16t^2 + 24\sqrt{2}t. \qquad \text{Parametric equation for } y$$

From this set of equations you can determine that at time $t = 0$, the object is at the point $(0, 0)$. Similarly, at time $t = 1$, the object is at the point $(24\sqrt{2}, 24\sqrt{2} - 16)$, and so on, as shown in Figure 10.50.

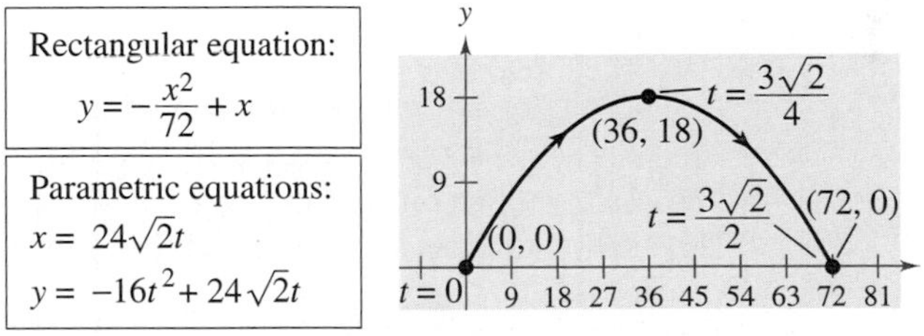

Curvilinear Motion: Two Variables for Position, One Variable for Time

FIGURE 10.50

For this particular motion problem, x and y are continuous functions of t, and the resulting path is a **plane curve.** (Recall that a *continuous function* is one whose graph can be traced without lifting the pencil from the paper.)

Definition of Plane Curve

If f and g are continuous functions of t on an interval I, the set of ordered pairs $(f(t), g(t))$ is a **plane curve** C. The equations

$$x = f(t) \qquad \text{and} \qquad y = g(t)$$

are **parametric equations** for C, and t is the **parameter.**

Sketching a Plane Curve

When sketching a curve represented by a pair of parametric equations, you still plot points in the xy-plane. Each set of coordinates (x, y) is determined from a value chosen for the parameter t. Plotting the resulting points in the order of *increasing* values of t traces the curve in a specific direction. This is called the **orientation** of the curve.

Example 1 Sketching a Curve

Sketch the curve given by the parametric equations

$$x = t^2 - 4 \quad \text{and} \quad y = \frac{t}{2}, \quad -2 \le t \le 3.$$

Solution

Using values of t in the interval, the parametric equations yield the points (x, y) shown in the table.

t	x	y
-2	0	-1
-1	-3	$-1/2$
0	-4	0
1	-3	$1/2$
2	0	1
3	5	$3/2$

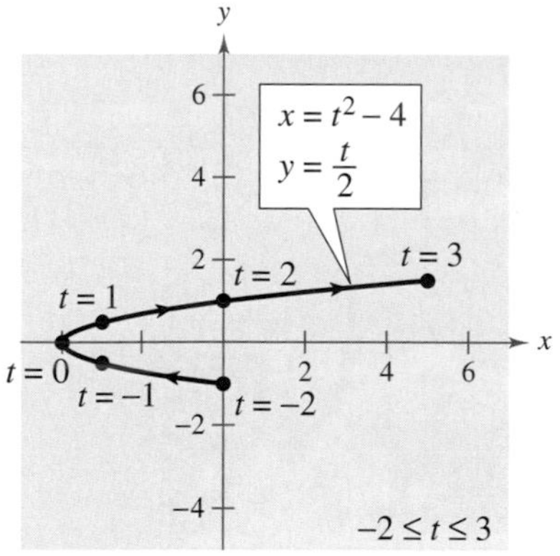

FIGURE 10.51

By plotting these points in the order of increasing t, you obtain the curve C shown in Figure 10.51. Note that the arrows on the curve indicate its orientation as t increases from -2 to 3. So, if a particle were moving on this curve, it would start at $(0, -1)$ and then move along the curve to the point $\left(5, \frac{3}{2}\right)$.

CHECKPOINT Now try Exercises 1(a) and (b).

Note that the graph shown in Figure 10.51 does not define y as a function of x. This points out one benefit of parametric equations—they can be used to represent graphs that are more general than graphs of functions.

It often happens that two different sets of parametric equations have the same graph. For example, the set of parametric equations

$$x = 4t^2 - 4 \quad \text{and} \quad y = t, \quad -1 \le t \le \frac{3}{2}$$

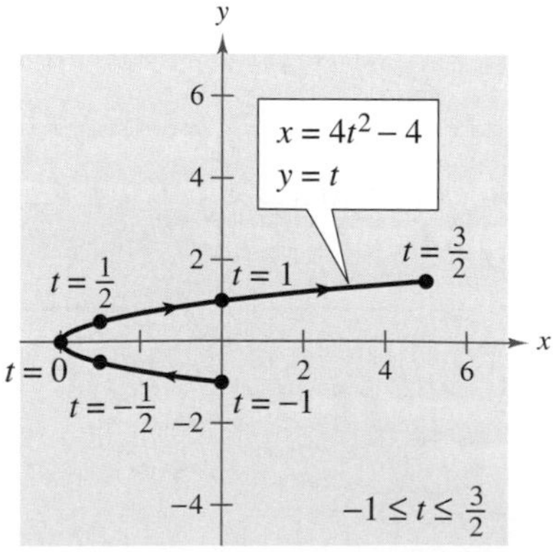

FIGURE 10.52

has the same graph as the set given in Example 1. However, by comparing the values of t in Figures 10.51 and 10.52, you see that this second graph is traced out more *rapidly* (considering t as time) than the first graph. So, in applications, different parametric representations can be used to represent various *speeds* at which objects travel along a given path.

Eliminating the Parameter

Example 1 uses simple point plotting to sketch the curve. This tedious process can sometimes be simplified by finding a rectangular equation (in x and y) that has the same graph. This process is called **eliminating the parameter.**

Parametric equations	→	Solve for t in one equation.	→	Substitute in other equation.	→	Rectangular equation
$x = t^2 - 4$ $y = t/2$		$t = 2y$		$x = (2y)^2 - 4$		$x = 4y^2 - 4$

Now you can recognize that the equation $x = 4y^2 - 4$ represents a parabola with a horizontal axis and vertex $(-4, 0)$.

When converting equations from parametric to rectangular form, you may need to alter the domain of the rectangular equation so that its graph matches the graph of the parametric equations. Such a situation is demonstrated in Example 2.

Exploration

Most graphing utilities have a *parametric* mode. If yours does, enter the parametric equations from Example 2. Over what values should you let t vary to obtain the graph shown in Figure 10.53?

Example 2 Eliminating the Parameter

Sketch the curve represented by the equations

$$x = \frac{1}{\sqrt{t+1}} \quad \text{and} \quad y = \frac{t}{t+1}$$

by eliminating the parameter and adjusting the domain of the resulting rectangular equation.

Solution

Solving for t in the equation for x produces

$$x = \frac{1}{\sqrt{t+1}} \quad \Rightarrow \quad x^2 = \frac{1}{t+1}$$

which implies that

$$t = \frac{1 - x^2}{x^2}.$$

Now, substituting in the equation for y, you obtain the rectangular equation

$$y = \frac{t}{t+1} = \frac{\frac{(1-x^2)}{x^2}}{\left[\frac{(1-x^2)}{x^2}\right] + 1} = \frac{\frac{1-x^2}{x^2}}{\frac{1-x^2}{x^2} + 1} \cdot \frac{x^2}{x^2} = 1 - x^2.$$

From this rectangular equation, you can recognize that the curve is a parabola that opens downward and has its vertex at $(0, 1)$. Also, this rectangular equation is defined for all values of x, but from the parametric equation for x you can see that the curve is defined only when $t > -1$. This implies that you should restrict the domain of x to positive values, as shown in Figure 10.53.

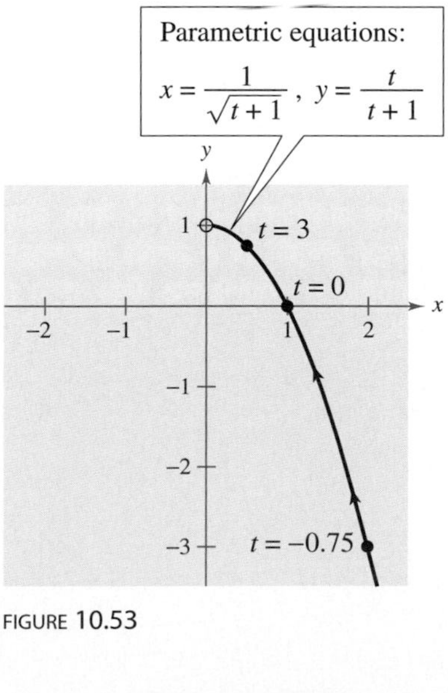

FIGURE 10.53

CHECKPOINT Now try Exercise 1(c).

STUDY TIP

To eliminate the parameter in equations involving trigonometric functions, try using the identities

$$\sin^2 \theta + \cos^2 \theta = 1$$

$$\sec^2 \theta - \tan^2 \theta = 1$$

as shown in Example 3.

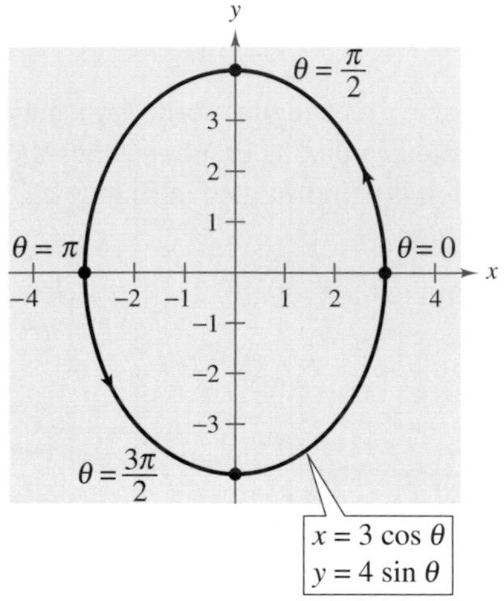

FIGURE 10.54

It is not necessary for the parameter in a set of parametric equations to represent time. The next example uses an *angle* as the parameter.

Example 3 Eliminating an Angle Parameter

Sketch the curve represented by

$$x = 3 \cos \theta \quad \text{and} \quad y = 4 \sin \theta, \quad 0 \le \theta \le 2\pi$$

by eliminating the parameter.

Solution

Begin by solving for $\cos \theta$ and $\sin \theta$ in the equations.

$$\cos \theta = \frac{x}{3} \quad \text{and} \quad \sin \theta = \frac{y}{4}$$ Solve for $\cos \theta$ and $\sin \theta$.

Use the identity $\sin^2 \theta + \cos^2 \theta = 1$ to form an equation involving only x and y.

$$\cos^2 \theta + \sin^2 \theta = 1$$ Pythagorean identity

$$\left(\frac{x}{3}\right)^2 + \left(\frac{y}{4}\right)^2 = 1$$ Substitute $\frac{x}{3}$ for $\cos \theta$ and $\frac{y}{4}$ for $\sin \theta$.

$$\frac{x^2}{9} + \frac{y^2}{16} = 1$$ Rectangular equation

From this rectangular equation, you can see that the graph is an ellipse centered at $(0, 0)$, with vertices $(0, 4)$ and $(0, -4)$ and minor axis of length $2b = 6$, as shown in Figure 10.54. Note that the elliptic curve is traced out *counterclockwise* as θ varies from 0 to 2π.

CHECKPOINT Now try Exercise 13.

In Examples 2 and 3, it is important to realize that eliminating the parameter is primarily an *aid to curve sketching*. If the parametric equations represent the path of a moving object, the graph alone is not sufficient to describe the object's motion. You still need the parametric equations to tell you the *position*, *direction*, and *speed* at a given time.

Finding Parametric Equations for a Graph

You have been studying techniques for sketching the graph represented by a set of parametric equations. Now consider the *reverse* problem—that is, how can you find a set of parametric equations for a given graph or a given physical description? From the discussion following Example 1, you know that such a representation is not unique. That is, the equations

$$x = 4t^2 - 4 \quad \text{and} \quad y = t, \; -1 \le t \le \frac{3}{2}$$

produced the same graph as the equations

$$x = t^2 - 4 \quad \text{and} \quad y = \frac{t}{2}, \; -2 \le t \le 3.$$

This is further demonstrated in Example 4.

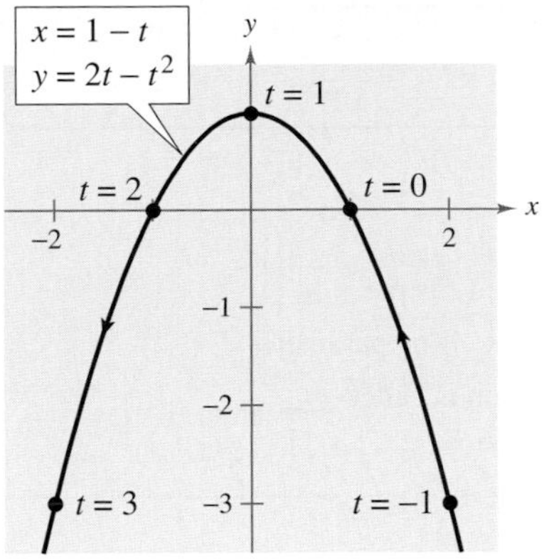

FIGURE 10.55

Example 4 Finding Parametric Equations for a Graph

Find a set of parametric equations to represent the graph of $y = 1 - x^2$, using the following parameters.

a. $t = x$ **b.** $t = 1 - x$

Solution

a. Letting $t = x$, you obtain the parametric equations

$$x = t \quad \text{and} \quad y = 1 - x^2 = 1 - t^2.$$

b. Letting $t = 1 - x$, you obtain the parametric equations

$$x = 1 - t \quad \text{and} \quad y = 1 - x^2 = 1 - (1 - t)^2 = 2t - t^2.$$

In Figure 10.55, note how the resulting curve is oriented by the increasing values of t. For part (a), the curve would have the opposite orientation.

✓CHECKPOINT Now try Exercise 37.

Example 5 Parametric Equations for a Cycloid

Describe the **cycloid** traced out by a point P on the circumference of a circle of radius a as the circle rolls along a straight line in a plane.

Solution

As the parameter, let θ be the measure of the circle's rotation, and let the point $P = (x, y)$ begin at the origin. When $\theta = 0$, P is at the origin; when $\theta = \pi$, P is at a maximum point $(\pi a, 2a)$; and when $\theta = 2\pi$, P is back on the x-axis at $(2\pi a, 0)$. From Figure 10.56, you can see that $\angle APC = 180° - \theta$. So, you have

$$\sin\theta = \sin(180° - \theta) = \sin(\angle APC) = \frac{AC}{a} = \frac{BD}{a}$$

$$\cos\theta = -\cos(180° - \theta) = -\cos(\angle APC) = \frac{AP}{-a}$$

which implies that $AP = -a\cos\theta$ and $BD = a\sin\theta$. Because the circle rolls along the x-axis, you know that $OD = \overparen{PD} = a\theta$. Furthermore, because $BA = DC = a$, you have

$$x = OD - BD = a\theta - a\sin\theta \quad \text{and} \quad y = BA + AP = a - a\cos\theta.$$

So, the parametric equations are $x = a(\theta - \sin\theta)$ and $y = a(1 - \cos\theta)$.

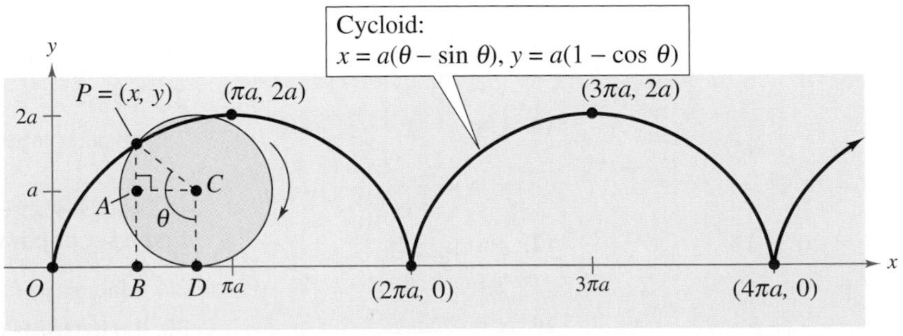

FIGURE 10.56

✓CHECKPOINT Now try Exercise 63.

STUDY TIP

In Example 5, $\overparen{PD}$ represents the arc of the circle between points P and D.

Technology

Use a graphing utility in *parametric* mode to obtain a graph similar to Figure 10.56 by graphing the following equations.

$X_{1T} = T - \sin T$

$Y_{1T} = 1 - \cos T$

10.6 Exercises

VOCABULARY CHECK: Fill in the blanks.

1. If f and g are continuous functions of t on an interval I, the set of ordered pairs $(f(t), g(t))$ is a ________ ________ C. The equations $x = f(t)$ and $y = g(t)$ are ________ equations for C, and t is the ________.
2. The ________ of a curve is the direction in which the curve is traced out for increasing values of the parameter.
3. The process of converting a set of parametric equations to a corresponding rectangular equation is called ________ the ________.

---

1. Consider the parametric equations $x = \sqrt{t}$ and $y = 3 - t$.
   (a) Create a table of x- and y-values using $t = 0, 1, 2, 3,$ and 4.
   (b) Plot the points (x, y) generated in part (a), and sketch a graph of the parametric equations.
   (c) Find the rectangular equation by eliminating the parameter. Sketch its graph. How do the graphs differ?
2. Consider the parametric equations $x = 4\cos^2\theta$ and $y = 2\sin\theta$.
   (a) Create a table of x- and y-values using $\theta = -\pi/2, -\pi/4, 0, \pi/4,$ and $\pi/2$.
   (b) Plot the points (x, y) generated in part (a), and sketch a graph of the parametric equations.
   (c) Find the rectangular equation by eliminating the parameter. Sketch its graph. How do the graphs differ?

In Exercises 3–22, (a) sketch the curve represented by the parametric equations (indicate the orientation of the curve) and (b) eliminate the parameter and write the corresponding rectangular equation whose graph represents the curve. Adjust the domain of the resulting rectangular equation if necessary.

3. $x = 3t - 3$, $y = 2t + 1$
4. $x = 3 - 2t$, $y = 2 + 3t$
5. $x = \frac{1}{4}t$, $y = t^2$
6. $x = t$, $y = t^3$
7. $x = t + 2$, $y = t^2$
8. $x = \sqrt{t}$, $y = 1 - t$
9. $x = t + 1$, $y = \dfrac{t}{t + 1}$
10. $x = t - 1$, $y = \dfrac{t}{t - 1}$
11. $x = 2(t + 1)$, $y = |t - 2|$
12. $x = |t - 1|$, $y = t + 2$
13. $x = 3\cos\theta$, $y = 3\sin\theta$
14. $x = 2\cos\theta$, $y = 3\sin\theta$
15. $x = 4\sin 2\theta$, $y = 2\cos 2\theta$
16. $x = \cos\theta$, $y = 2\sin 2\theta$
17. $x = 4 + 2\cos\theta$, $y = -1 + \sin\theta$
18. $x = 4 + 2\cos\theta$, $y = 2 + 3\sin\theta$
19. $x = e^{-t}$, $y = e^{3t}$
20. $x = e^{2t}$, $y = e^t$
21. $x = t^3$, $y = 3\ln t$
22. $x = \ln 2t$, $y = 2t^2$

In Exercises 23 and 24, determine how the plane curves differ from each other.

23. (a) $x = t$, $y = 2t + 1$
    (b) $x = \cos\theta$, $y = 2\cos\theta + 1$
    (c) $x = e^{-t}$, $y = 2e^{-t} + 1$
    (d) $x = e^t$, $y = 2e^t + 1$
24. (a) $x = t$, $y = t^2 - 1$
    (b) $x = t^2$, $y = t^4 - 1$
    (c) $x = \sin t$, $y = \sin^2 t - 1$
    (d) $x = e^t$, $y = e^{2t} - 1$

In Exercises 25–28, eliminate the parameter and obtain the standard form of the rectangular equation.

25. Line through (x_1, y_1) and (x_2, y_2):
    $x = x_1 + t(x_2 - x_1),\ y = y_1 + t(y_2 - y_1)$
26. Circle: $x = h + r\cos\theta,\ y = k + r\sin\theta$
27. Ellipse: $x = h + a\cos\theta,\ y = k + b\sin\theta$
28. Hyperbola: $x = h + a\sec\theta,\ y = k + b\tan\theta$

In Exercises 29–36, use the results of Exercises 25–28 to find a set of parametric equations for the line or conic.

29. Line: passes through $(0, 0)$ and $(6, -3)$
30. Line: passes through $(2, 3)$ and $(6, -3)$
31. Circle: center: $(3, 2)$; radius: 4

32. Circle: center: $(-3, 2)$; radius: 5

33. Ellipse: vertices: $(\pm 4, 0)$; foci: $(\pm 3, 0)$

34. Ellipse: vertices: $(4, 7), (4, -3)$;
foci: $(4, 5), (4, -1)$

35. Hyperbola: vertices: $(\pm 4, 0)$; foci: $(\pm 5, 0)$

36. Hyperbola: vertices: $(\pm 2, 0)$; foci: $(\pm 4, 0)$

In Exercises 37–44, find a set of parametric equations for the rectangular equation using (a) $t = x$ and (b) $t = 2 - x$.

37. $y = 3x - 2$

38. $x = 3y - 2$

39. $y = x^2$

40. $y = x^3$

41. $y = x^2 + 1$

42. $y = 2 - x$

43. $y = \dfrac{1}{x}$

44. $y = \dfrac{1}{2x}$

In Exercises 45–52, use a graphing utility to graph the curve represented by the parametric equations.

45. Cycloid: $x = 4(\theta - \sin\theta),\ y = 4(1 - \cos\theta)$

46. Cycloid: $x = \theta + \sin\theta,\ y = 1 - \cos\theta$

47. Prolate cycloid: $x = \theta - \frac{3}{2}\sin\theta,\ y = 1 - \frac{3}{2}\cos\theta$

48. Prolate cycloid: $x = 2\theta - 4\sin\theta,\ y = 2 - 4\cos\theta$

49. Hypocycloid: $x = 3\cos^3\theta,\ y = 3\sin^3\theta$

50. Curtate cycloid: $x = 8\theta - 4\sin\theta,\ y = 8 - 4\cos\theta$

51. Witch of Agnesi: $x = 2\cot\theta,\ y = 2\sin^2\theta$

52. Folium of Descartes: $x = \dfrac{3t}{1 + t^3},\ y = \dfrac{3t^2}{1 + t^3}$

In Exercises 53–56, match the parametric equations with the correct graph and describe the domain and range. [The graphs are labeled (a), (b), (c), and (d).]

(a)

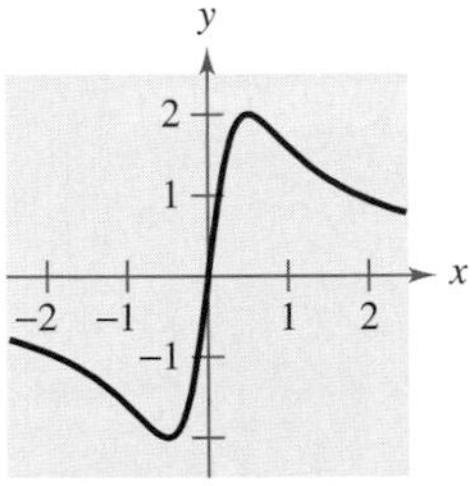

(b)

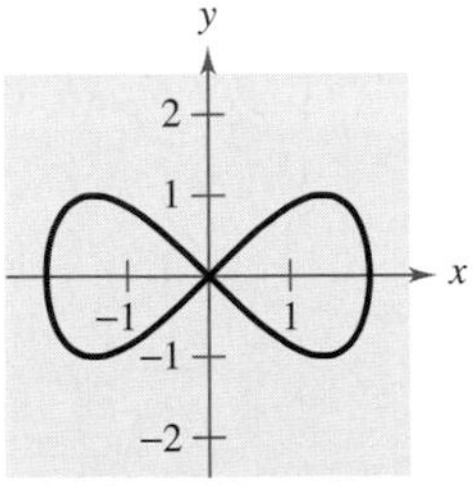

(c)

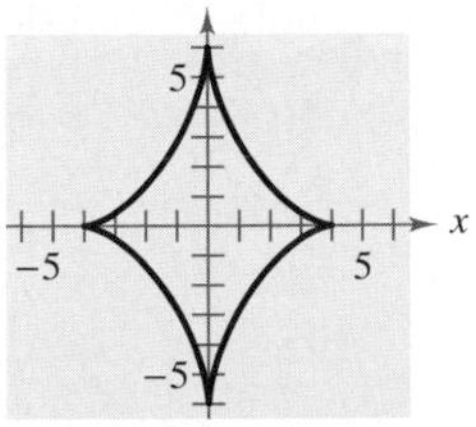

(d)

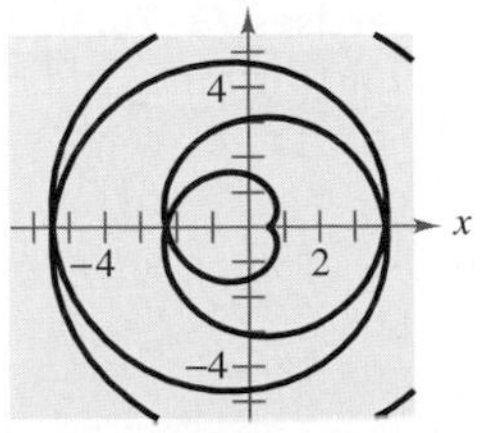

53. Lissajous curve: $x = 2\cos\theta,\ y = \sin 2\theta$

54. Evolute of ellipse: $x = 4\cos^3\theta,\ y = 6\sin^3\theta$

55. Involute of circle: $x = \frac{1}{2}(\cos\theta + \theta\sin\theta)$
$y = \frac{1}{2}(\sin\theta - \theta\cos\theta)$

56. Serpentine curve: $x = \frac{1}{2}\cot\theta,\ y = 4\sin\theta\cos\theta$

Projectile Motion **A projectile is launched at a height of h feet above the ground at an angle of θ with the horizontal. The initial velocity is v_0 feet per second and the path of the projectile is modeled by the parametric equations**

$$x = (v_0\cos\theta)t \quad \text{and} \quad y = h + (v_0\sin\theta)t - 16t^2.$$

In Exercises 57 and 58, use a graphing utility to graph the paths of a projectile launched from ground level at each value of θ and v_0. For each case, use the graph to approximate the maximum height and the range of the projectile.

57. (a) $\theta = 60°$, $v_0 = 88$ feet per second
(b) $\theta = 60°$, $v_0 = 132$ feet per second
(c) $\theta = 45°$, $v_0 = 88$ feet per second
(d) $\theta = 45°$, $v_0 = 132$ feet per second

58. (a) $\theta = 15°$, $v_0 = 60$ feet per second
(b) $\theta = 15°$, $v_0 = 100$ feet per second
(c) $\theta = 30°$, $v_0 = 60$ feet per second
(d) $\theta = 30°$, $v_0 = 100$ feet per second

Model It

59. *Sports* The center field fence in Yankee Stadium is 7 feet high and 408 feet from home plate. A baseball is hit at a point 3 feet above the ground. It leaves the bat at an angle of θ degrees with the horizontal at a speed of 100 miles per hour (see figure).

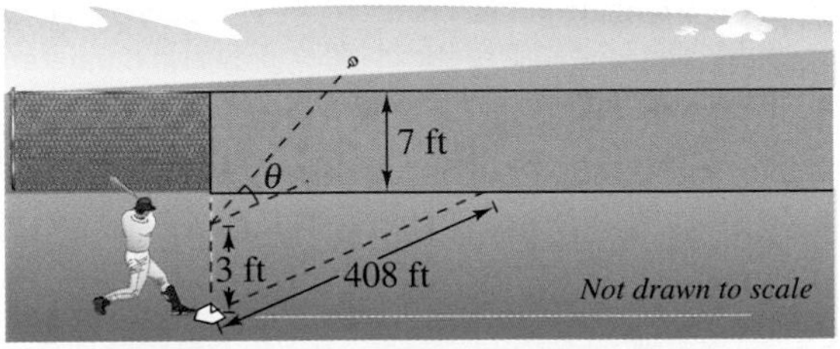

(a) Write a set of parametric equations that model the path of the baseball.

(b) Use a graphing utility to graph the path of the baseball when $\theta = 15°$. Is the hit a home run?

(c) Use a graphing utility to graph the path of the baseball when $\theta = 23°$. Is the hit a home run?

(d) Find the minimum angle required for the hit to be a home run.

60. ***Sports*** An archer releases an arrow from a bow at a point 5 feet above the ground. The arrow leaves the bow at an angle of 10° with the horizontal and at an initial speed of 240 feet per second.

(a) Write a set of parametric equations that model the path of the arrow.

(b) Assuming the ground is level, find the distance the arrow travels before it hits the ground. (Ignore air resistance.)

(c) Use a graphing utility to graph the path of the arrow and approximate its maximum height.

(d) Find the total time the arrow is in the air.

61. ***Projectile Motion*** Eliminate the parameter t from the parametric equations

$$x = (v_0 \cos \theta)t \quad \text{and} \quad y = h + (v_0 \sin \theta)t - 16t^2$$

for the motion of a projectile to show that the rectangular equation is

$$y = -\frac{16 \sec^2 \theta}{v_0^2}x^2 + (\tan \theta)x + h.$$

62. ***Path of a Projectile*** The path of a projectile is given by the rectangular equation

$$y = 7 + x - 0.02x^2.$$

(a) Use the result of Exercise 61 to find h, v_0, and θ. Find the parametric equations of the path.

(b) Use a graphing utility to graph the rectangular equation for the path of the projectile. Confirm your answer in part (a) by sketching the curve represented by the parametric equations.

(c) Use a graphing utility to approximate the maximum height of the projectile and its range.

63. ***Curtate Cycloid*** A wheel of radius a units rolls along a straight line without slipping. The curve traced by a point P that is b units from the center ($b < a$) is called a **curtate cycloid** (see figure). Use the angle θ shown in the figure to find a set of parametric equations for the curve.

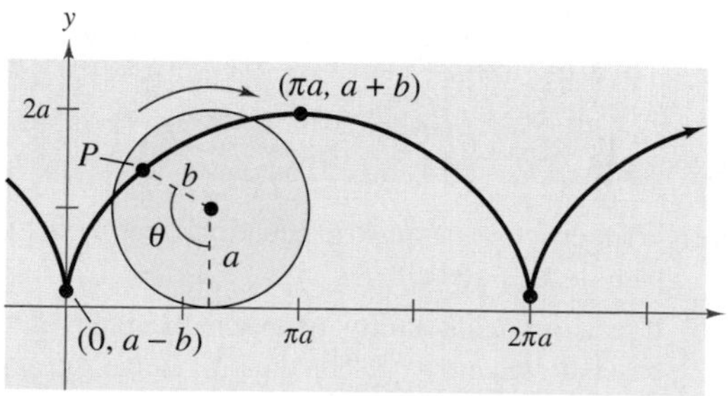

64. ***Epicycloid*** A circle of radius one unit rolls around the outside of a circle of radius two units without slipping. The curve traced by a point on the circumference of the smaller circle is called an **epicycloid** (see figure). Use the angle θ shown in the figure to find a set of parametric equations for the curve.

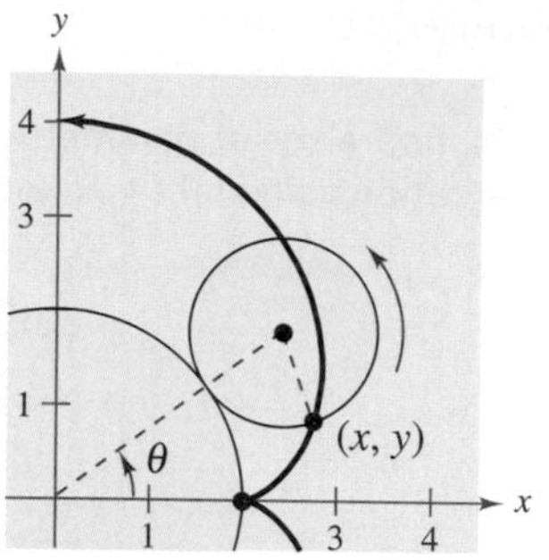

Synthesis

True or False? **In Exercises 65 and 66, determine whether the statement is true or false. Justify your answer.**

65. The two sets of parametric equations $x = t$, $y = t^2 + 1$ and $x = 3t$, $y = 9t^2 + 1$ have the same rectangular equation.

66. The graph of the parametric equations $x = t^2$ and $y = t^2$ is the line $y = x$.

67. ***Writing*** Write a short paragraph explaining why parametric equations are useful.

68. ***Writing*** Explain the process of sketching a plane curve given by parametric equations. What is meant by the orientation of the curve?

Skills Review

In Exercises 69–72, solve the system of equations.

69. $\begin{cases} 5x - 7y = 11 \\ -3x + y = -13 \end{cases}$

70. $\begin{cases} 3x + 5y = 9 \\ 4x - 2y = -14 \end{cases}$

71. $\begin{cases} 3a - 2b + c = 8 \\ 2a + b - 3c = -3 \\ a - 3b + 9c = 16 \end{cases}$

72. $\begin{cases} 5u + 7v + 9w = 4 \\ u - 2v - 3w = 7 \\ 8u - 2v + w = 20 \end{cases}$

In Exercises 73–76, find the reference angle θ', and sketch θ and θ' in standard position.

73. $\theta = 105°$

74. $\theta = 230°$

75. $\theta = -\dfrac{2\pi}{3}$

76. $\theta = \dfrac{5\pi}{6}$

10.7 Polar Coordinates

What you should learn

- Plot points on the polar coordinate system.
- Convert points from rectangular to polar form and vice versa.
- Convert equations from rectangular to polar form and vice versa.

Why you should learn it

Polar coordinates offer a different mathematical perspective on graphing. For instance, in Exercises 1–8 on page 783, you are asked to find multiple representations of polar coordinates.

Introduction

So far, you have been representing graphs of equations as collections of points (x, y) on the rectangular coordinate system, where x and y represent the directed distances from the coordinate axes to the point (x, y). In this section, you will study a different system called the **polar coordinate system.**

To form the polar coordinate system in the plane, fix a point O, called the **pole** (or **origin**), and construct from O an initial ray called the **polar axis,** as shown in Figure 10.57. Then each point P in the plane can be assigned **polar coordinates** (r, θ) as follows.

1. $r =$ *directed distance* from O to P

2. $\theta =$ *directed angle*, counterclockwise from polar axis to segment $\overline{OP}$

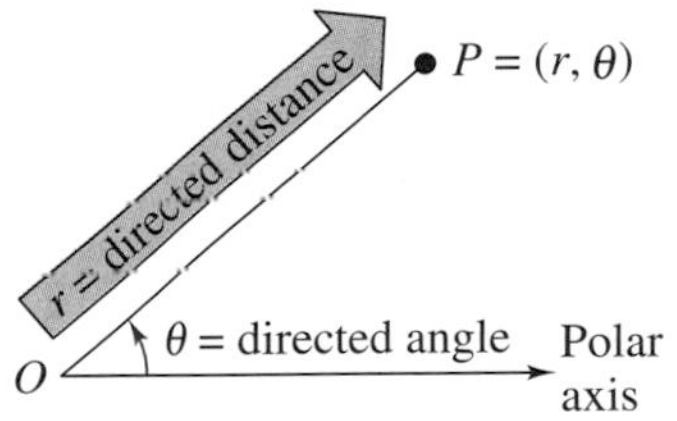

FIGURE 10.57

Example 1 Plotting Points on the Polar Coordinate System

a. The point $(r, \theta) = (2, \pi/3)$ lies two units from the pole on the terminal side of the angle $\theta = \pi/3$, as shown in Figure 10.58.

b. The point $(r, \theta) = (3, -\pi/6)$ lies three units from the pole on the terminal side of the angle $\theta = -\pi/6$, as shown in Figure 10.59.

c. The point $(r, \theta) = (3, 11\pi/6)$ coincides with the point $(3, -\pi/6)$, as shown in Figure 10.60.

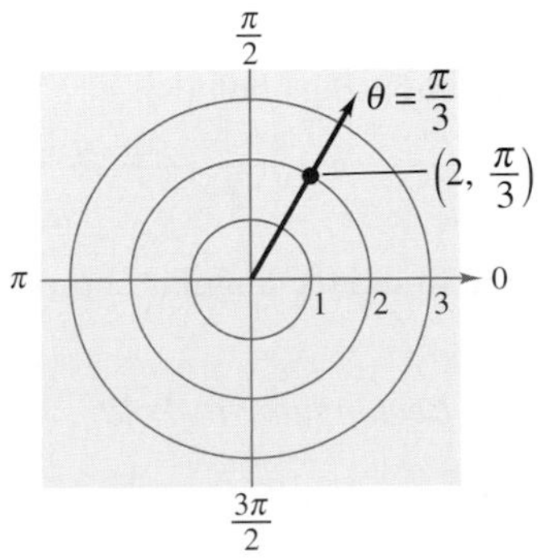

FIGURE 10.58

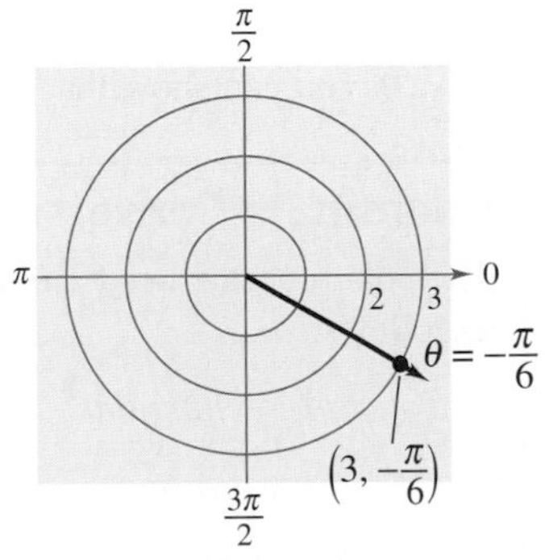

FIGURE 10.59

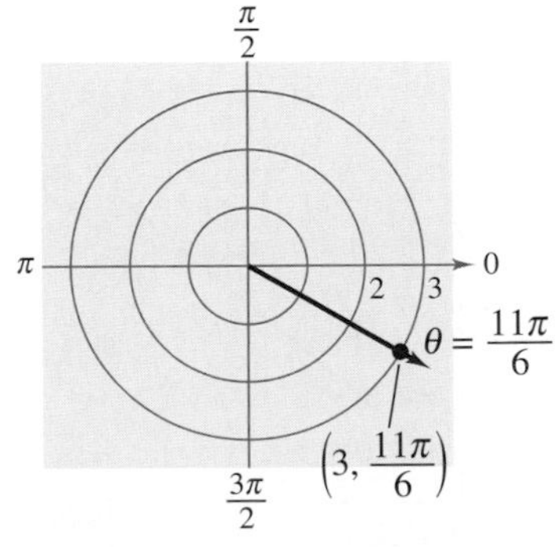

FIGURE 10.60

✓CHECKPOINT Now try Exercise 1.

Exploration

Most graphing calculators have a *polar* graphing mode. If yours does, graph the equation $r = 3$. (Use a setting in which $-6 \le x \le 6$ and $-4 \le y \le 4$.) You should obtain a circle of radius 3.

a. Use the *trace* feature to cursor around the circle. Can you locate the point $(3, 5\pi/4)$?

b. Can you find other polar representations of the point $(3, 5\pi/4)$? If so, explain how you did it.

In rectangular coordinates, each point (x, y) has a unique representation. This is not true for polar coordinates. For instance, the coordinates (r, θ) and $(r, \theta + 2\pi)$ represent the same point, as illustrated in Example 1. Another way to obtain multiple representations of a point is to use negative values for r. Because r is a *directed distance*, the coordinates (r, θ) and $(-r, \theta + \pi)$ represent the same point. In general, the point (r, θ) can be represented as

$$(r, \theta) = (r, \theta \pm 2n\pi) \quad \text{or} \quad (r, \theta) = (-r, \theta \pm (2n + 1)\pi)$$

where n is any integer. Moreover, the pole is represented by $(0, \theta)$, where θ is any angle.

Example 2 **Multiple Representations of Points**

Plot the point $(3, -3\pi/4)$ and find three additional polar representations of this point, using $-2\pi < \theta < 2\pi$.

Solution

The point is shown in Figure 10.61. Three other representations are as follows.

$$\left(3, -\frac{3\pi}{4} + 2\pi\right) = \left(3, \frac{5\pi}{4}\right) \qquad \text{Add } 2\pi \text{ to } \theta.$$

$$\left(-3, -\frac{3\pi}{4} - \pi\right) = \left(-3, -\frac{7\pi}{4}\right) \qquad \text{Replace } r \text{ by } -r\text{; subtract } \pi \text{ from } \theta.$$

$$\left(-3, -\frac{3\pi}{4} + \pi\right) = \left(-3, \frac{\pi}{4}\right) \qquad \text{Replace } r \text{ by } -r\text{; add } \pi \text{ to } \theta.$$

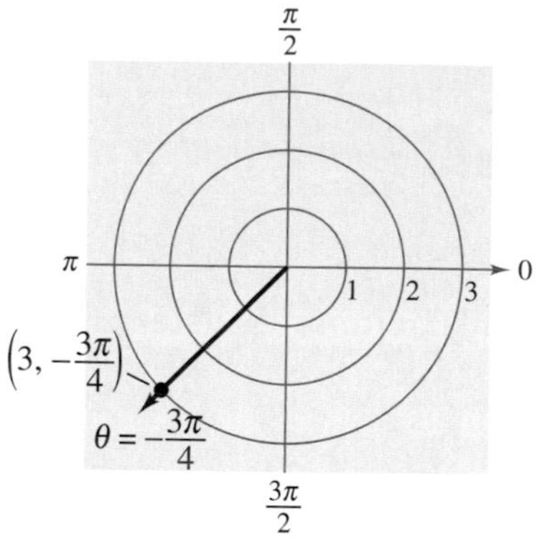

$\left(3, -\frac{3\pi}{4}\right) = \left(3, \frac{5\pi}{4}\right) = \left(-3, -\frac{7\pi}{4}\right) = \left(-3, \frac{\pi}{4}\right) = \ldots$

FIGURE 10.61

✓CHECKPOINT Now try Exercise 3.

Coordinate Conversion

To establish the relationship between polar and rectangular coordinates, let the polar axis coincide with the positive x-axis and the pole with the origin, as shown in Figure 10.62. Because (x, y) lies on a circle of radius r, it follows that $r^2 = x^2 + y^2$. Moreover, for $r > 0$, the definitions of the trigonometric functions imply that

$$\tan \theta = \frac{y}{x}, \qquad \cos \theta = \frac{x}{r}, \qquad \text{and} \qquad \sin \theta = \frac{y}{r}.$$

If $r < 0$, you can show that the same relationships hold.

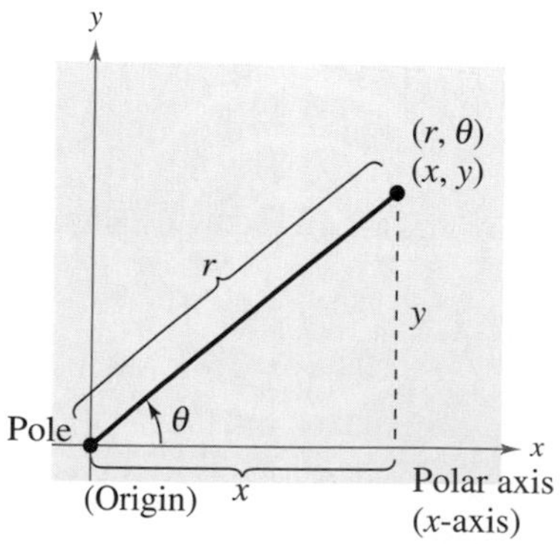

FIGURE 10.62

Coordinate Conversion

The polar coordinates (r, θ) are related to the rectangular coordinates (x, y) as follows.

Polar-to-Rectangular	*Rectangular-to-Polar*
$x = r \cos \theta$	$\tan \theta = \frac{y}{x}$
$y = r \sin \theta$	$r^2 = x^2 + y^2$

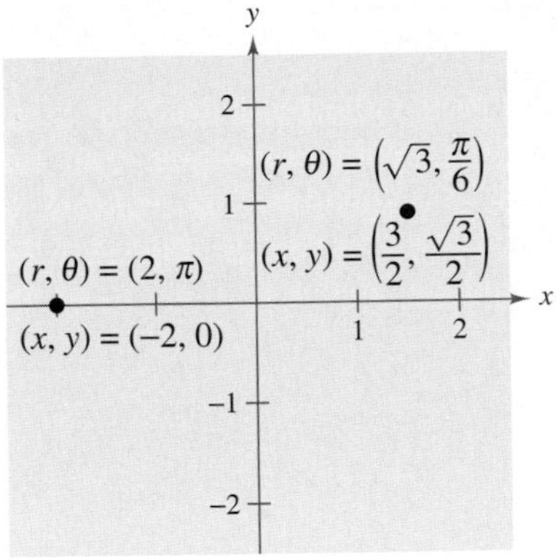

FIGURE 10.63

Example 3 Polar-to-Rectangular Conversion

Convert each point to rectangular coordinates.

a. $(2, \pi)$ **b.** $\left(\sqrt{3}, \frac{\pi}{6}\right)$

Solution

a. For the point $(r, \theta) = (2, \pi)$, you have the following.

$$x = r\cos\theta = 2\cos\pi = -2$$

$$y = r\sin\theta = 2\sin\pi = 0$$

The rectangular coordinates are $(x, y) = (-2, 0)$. (See Figure 10.63.)

b. For the point $(r, \theta) = \left(\sqrt{3}, \frac{\pi}{6}\right)$, you have the following.

$$x = \sqrt{3}\cos\frac{\pi}{6} = \sqrt{3}\left(\frac{\sqrt{3}}{2}\right) = \frac{3}{2}$$

$$y = \sqrt{3}\sin\frac{\pi}{6} = \sqrt{3}\left(\frac{1}{2}\right) = \frac{\sqrt{3}}{2}$$

The rectangular coordinates are $(x, y) = \left(\frac{3}{2}, \frac{\sqrt{3}}{2}\right)$.

CHECKPOINT Now try Exercise 13.

Example 4 Rectangular-to-Polar Conversion

Convert each point to polar coordinates.

a. $(-1, 1)$ **b.** $(0, 2)$

Solution

a. For the second-quadrant point $(x, y) = (-1, 1)$, you have

$$\tan\theta = \frac{y}{x} = -1$$

$$\theta = \frac{3\pi}{4}.$$

Because θ lies in the same quadrant as (x, y), use positive r.

$$r = \sqrt{x^2 + y^2} = \sqrt{(-1)^2 + (1)^2} = \sqrt{2}$$

So, *one* set of polar coordinates is $(r, \theta) = (\sqrt{2}, 3\pi/4)$, as shown in Figure 10.64.

b. Because the point $(x, y) = (0, 2)$ lies on the positive y-axis, choose

$$\theta = \frac{\pi}{2} \quad \text{and} \quad r = 2.$$

This implies that *one* set of polar coordinates is $(r, \theta) = (2, \pi/2)$, as shown in Figure 10.65.

CHECKPOINT Now try Exercise 19.

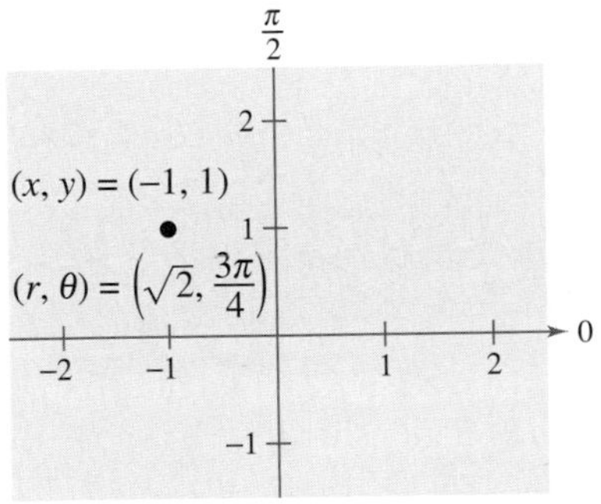

FIGURE 10.64

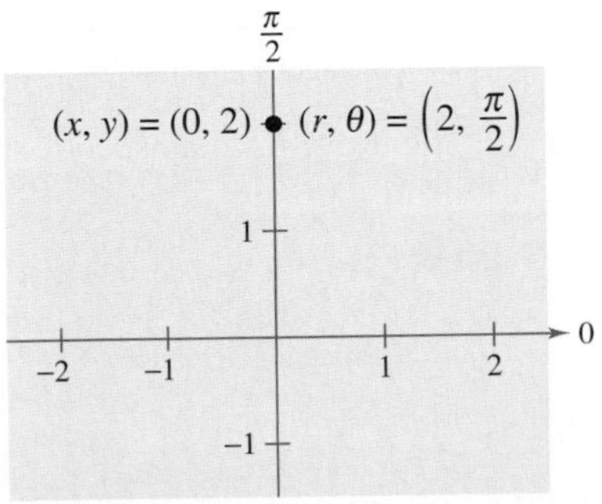

FIGURE 10.65

Equation Conversion

By comparing Examples 3 and 4, you can see that point conversion from the polar to the rectangular system is straightforward, whereas point conversion from the rectangular to the polar system is more involved. For equations, the opposite is true. To convert a rectangular equation to polar form, you simply replace x by $r\cos\theta$ and y by $r\sin\theta$. For instance, the rectangular equation $y = x^2$ can be written in polar form as follows.

$$y = x^2 \qquad \text{Rectangular equation}$$

$$r\sin\theta = (r\cos\theta)^2 \qquad \text{Polar equation}$$

$$r = \sec\theta\tan\theta \qquad \text{Simplest form}$$

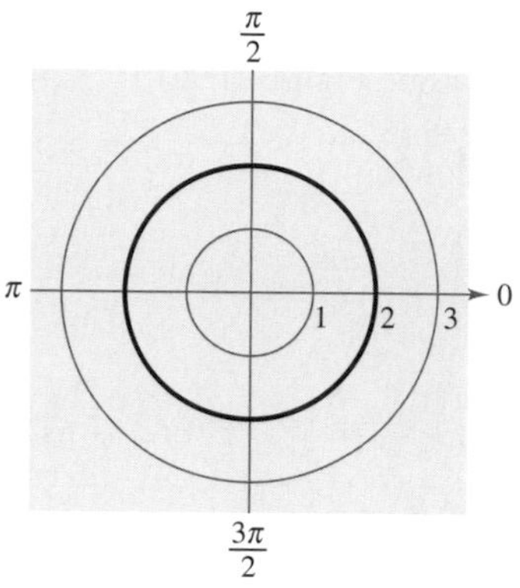

FIGURE 10.66

On the other hand, converting a polar equation to rectangular form requires considerable ingenuity.

Example 5 demonstrates several polar-to-rectangular conversions that enable you to sketch the graphs of some polar equations.

Example 5 Converting Polar Equations to Rectangular Form

Describe the graph of each polar equation and find the corresponding rectangular equation.

a. $r = 2$ **b.** $\theta = \dfrac{\pi}{3}$ **c.** $r = \sec\theta$

Solution

a. The graph of the polar equation $r = 2$ consists of all points that are two units from the pole. In other words, this graph is a circle centered at the origin with a radius of 2, as shown in Figure 10.66. You can confirm this by converting to rectangular form, using the relationship $r^2 = x^2 + y^2$.

$$\underbrace{r = 2}_{\text{Polar equation}} \quad \Rightarrow \quad r^2 = 2^2 \quad \Rightarrow \quad \underbrace{x^2 + y^2 = 2^2}_{\text{Rectangular equation}}$$

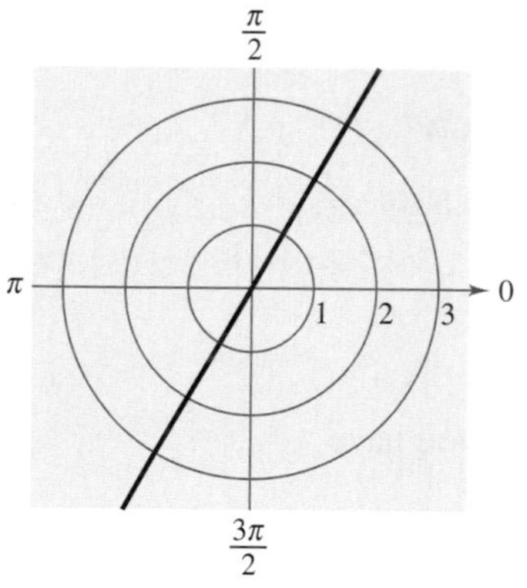

FIGURE 10.67

b. The graph of the polar equation $\theta = \pi/3$ consists of all points on the line that makes an angle of $\pi/3$ with the positive polar axis, as shown in Figure 10.67. To convert to rectangular form, make use of the relationship $\tan\theta = y/x$.

$$\underbrace{\theta = \frac{\pi}{3}}_{\text{Polar equation}} \quad \Rightarrow \quad \tan\theta = \sqrt{3} \quad \Rightarrow \quad \underbrace{y = \sqrt{3}x}_{\text{Rectangular equation}}$$

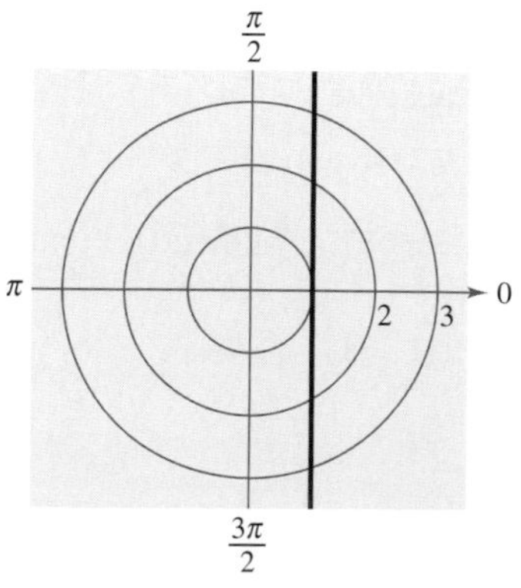

FIGURE 10.68

c. The graph of the polar equation $r = \sec\theta$ is not evident by simple inspection, so convert to rectangular form by using the relationship $r\cos\theta = x$.

$$\underbrace{r = \sec\theta}_{\text{Polar equation}} \quad \Rightarrow \quad r\cos\theta = 1 \quad \Rightarrow \quad \underbrace{x = 1}_{\text{Rectangular equation}}$$

Now you see that the graph is a vertical line, as shown in Figure 10.68.

✓CHECKPOINT Now try Exercise 65.

10.7 Exercises

VOCABULARY CHECK: Fill in the blanks.

1. The origin of the polar coordinate system is called the ________.
2. For the point (r, θ), r is the ________ ________ from O to P and θ is the ________ ________ counterclockwise from the polar axis to the line segment $\overline{OP}$.
3. To plot the point (r, θ), use the ________ coordinate system.
4. The polar coordinates (r, θ) are related to the rectangular coordinates (x, y) as follows:

$x =$ ________ $\tan\theta =$ ________

$y =$ ________ $r^2 =$ ________

In Exercises 1–8, plot the point given in polar coordinates and find two additional polar representations of the point, using $-2\pi < \theta < 2\pi$.

1. $\left(4, -\frac{\pi}{3}\right)$
2. $\left(-1, -\frac{3\pi}{4}\right)$
3. $\left(0, -\frac{7\pi}{6}\right)$
4. $\left(16, \frac{5\pi}{2}\right)$
5. $\left(\sqrt{2}, 2.36\right)$
6. $(-3, -1.57)$
7. $\left(2\sqrt{2}, 4.71\right)$
8. $(-5, -2.36)$

In Exercises 9–16, a point in polar coordinates is given. Convert the point to rectangular coordinates.

9. $\left(3, \frac{\pi}{2}\right)$

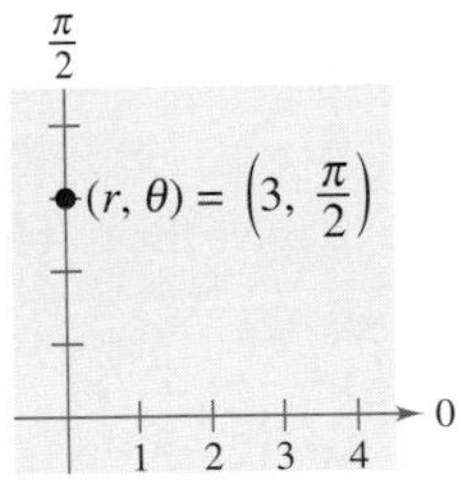

10. $\left(3, \frac{3\pi}{2}\right)$

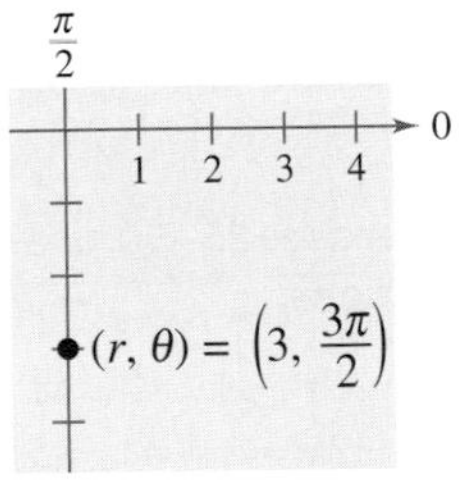

11. $\left(-1, \frac{5\pi}{4}\right)$

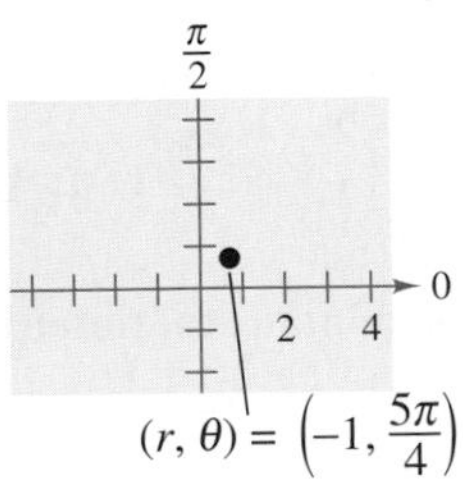

12. $(0, -\pi)$

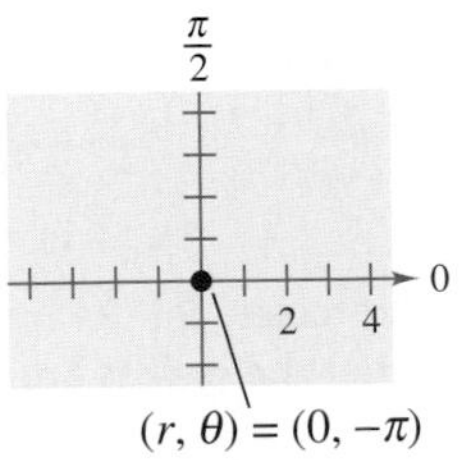

13. $\left(2, \frac{3\pi}{4}\right)$
14. $\left(-2, \frac{7\pi}{6}\right)$
15. $(-2.5, 1.1)$
16. $(8.25, 3.5)$

In Exercises 17–26, a point in rectangular coordinates is given. Convert the point to polar coordinates.

17. $(1, 1)$
18. $(-3, -3)$
19. $(-6, 0)$
20. $(0, -5)$
21. $(-3, 4)$
22. $(3, -1)$
23. $\left(-\sqrt{3}, -\sqrt{3}\right)$
24. $\left(\sqrt{3}, -1\right)$
25. $(6, 9)$
26. $(5, 12)$

In Exercises 27–32, use a graphing utility to find one set of polar coordinates for the point given in rectangular coordinates.

27. $(3, -2)$
28. $(-5, 2)$
29. $\left(\sqrt{3}, 2\right)$
30. $\left(3, \sqrt{2}, 3\sqrt{2}\right)$
31. $\left(\frac{5}{2}, \frac{4}{3}\right)$
32. $\left(\frac{7}{4}, \frac{3}{2}\right)$

In Exercises 33–48, convert the rectangular equation to polar form. Assume $a > 0$.

33. $x^2 + y^2 = 9$
34. $x^2 + y^2 = 16$
35. $y = 4$
36. $y = x$
37. $x = 10$
38. $x = 4a$
39. $3x - y + 2 = 0$
40. $3x + 5y - 2 = 0$
41. $xy = 16$
42. $2xy = 1$
43. $y^2 - 8x - 16 = 0$
44. $(x^2 + y^2)^2 = 9(x^2 - y^2)$
45. $x^2 + y^2 = a^2$
46. $x^2 + y^2 = 9a^2$
47. $x^2 + y^2 - 2ax = 0$
48. $x^2 + y^2 - 2ay = 0$

In Exercises 49–64, convert the polar equation to rectangular form.

49. $r = 4 \sin \theta$

50. $r = 2 \cos \theta$

51. $\theta = \dfrac{2\pi}{3}$

52. $\theta = \dfrac{5\pi}{3}$

53. $r = 4$

54. $r = 10$

55. $r = 4 \csc \theta$

56. $r = -3 \sec \theta$

57. $r^2 = \cos \theta$

58. $r^2 = \sin 2\theta$

59. $r = 2 \sin 3\theta$

60. $r = 3 \cos 2\theta$

61. $r = \dfrac{2}{1 + \sin \theta}$

62. $r = \dfrac{1}{1 - \cos \theta}$

63. $r = \dfrac{6}{2 - 3 \sin \theta}$

64. $r = \dfrac{6}{2 \cos \theta - 3 \sin \theta}$

In Exercises 65–70, describe the graph of the polar equation and find the corresponding rectangular equation. Sketch its graph.

65. $r = 6$

66. $r = 8$

67. $\theta = \dfrac{\pi}{6}$

68. $\theta = \dfrac{3\pi}{4}$

69. $r = 3 \sec \theta$

70. $r = 2 \csc \theta$

Synthesis

True or False? **In Exercises 71 and 72, determine whether the statement is true or false. Justify your answer.**

71. If $\theta_1 = \theta_2 + 2\pi n$ for some integer n, then (r, θ_1) and (r, θ_2) represent the same point on the polar coordinate system.

72. If $|r_1| = |r_2|$, then (r_1, θ) and (r_2, θ) represent the same point on the polar coordinate system.

73. Convert the polar equation $r = 2(h \cos \theta + k \sin \theta)$ to rectangular form and verify that it is the equation of a circle. Find the radius of the circle and the rectangular coordinates of the center of the circle.

74. Convert the polar equation $r = \cos \theta + 3 \sin \theta$ to rectangular form and identify the graph.

75. ***Think About It***
   (a) Show that the distance between the points (r_1, θ_1) and (r_2, θ_2) is $\sqrt{r_1^2 + r_2^2 - 2r_1r_2 \cos(\theta_1 - \theta_2)}$.
   (b) Describe the positions of the points relative to each other for $\theta_1 = \theta_2$. Simplify the Distance Formula for this case. Is the simplification what you expected? Explain.
   (c) Simplify the Distance Formula for $\theta_1 - \theta_2 = 90°$. Is the simplification what you expected? Explain.
   (d) Choose two points on the polar coordinate system and find the distance between them. Then choose different polar representations of the same two points and apply the Distance Formula again. Discuss the result.

76. ***Exploration***
   (a) Set the window format of your graphing utility on rectangular coordinates and locate the cursor at any position off the coordinate axes. Move the cursor horizontally and observe any changes in the displayed coordinates of the points. Explain the changes in the coordinates. Now repeat the process moving the cursor vertically.
   (b) Set the window format of your graphing utility on polar coordinates and locate the cursor at any position off the coordinate axes. Move the cursor horizontally and observe any changes in the displayed coordinates of the points. Explain the changes in the coordinates. Now repeat the process moving the cursor vertically.
   (c) Explain why the results of parts (a) and (b) are not the same.

Skills Review

In Exercises 77–80, use the properties of logarithms to expand the expression as a sum, difference, and/or constant multiple of logarithms. (Assume all variables are positive.)

77. $\log_6 \dfrac{x^2z}{3y}$

78. $\log_4 \dfrac{\sqrt{2x}}{y}$

79. $\ln x(x + 4)^2$

80. $\ln 5x^2(x^2 + 1)$

In Exercises 81–84, condense the expression to the logarithm of a single quantity.

81. $\log_7 x - \log_7 3y$

82. $\log_5 a + 8 \log_5(x + 1)$

83. $\dfrac{1}{2} \ln x + \ln(x - 2)$

84. $\ln 6 + \ln y - \ln(x - 3)$

In Exercises 85–90, use Cramer's Rule to solve the system of equations.

85. $\begin{cases} 5x - 7y = -11 \\ -3x + y = -3 \end{cases}$

86. $\begin{cases} 3x - 5y = 10 \\ 4x - 2y = -5 \end{cases}$

87. $\begin{cases} 3a - 2b + c = 0 \\ 2a + b - 3c = 0 \\ a - 3b + 9c = 8 \end{cases}$

88. $\begin{cases} 5u + 7v + 9w = 15 \\ u - 2v - 3w = 7 \\ 8u - 2v + w = 0 \end{cases}$

89. $\begin{cases} -x + y + 2z = 1 \\ 2x + 3y + z = -2 \\ 5x + 4y + 2z = 4 \end{cases}$

90. $\begin{cases} 2x_1 + x_2 + 2x_3 = 4 \\ 2x_1 + 2x_2 = 5 \\ 2x_1 - x_2 + 6x_3 = 2 \end{cases}$

In Exercises 91–94, use a determinant to determine whether the points are collinear.

91. $(4, -3), (6, -7), (-2, -1)$

92. $(-2, 4), (0, 1), (4, -5)$

93. $(-6, -4), (-1, -3), (1.5, -2.5)$

94. $(-2.3, 5), (-0.5, 0), (1.5, -3)$

10.8 Graphs of Polar Equations

What you should learn

- Graph polar equations by point plotting.
- Use symmetry to sketch graphs of polar equations.
- Use zeros and maximum r-values to sketch graphs of polar equations.
- Recognize special polar graphs.

Why you should learn it

Equations of several common figures are simpler in polar form than in rectangular form. For instance, Exercise 6 on page 791 shows the graph of a circle and its polar equation.

Introduction

In previous chapters, you spent a lot of time learning how to sketch graphs on rectangular coordinate systems. You began with the basic point-plotting method, which was then enhanced by sketching aids such as symmetry, intercepts, asymptotes, periods, and shifts. This section approaches curve sketching on the polar coordinate system similarly, beginning with a demonstration of point plotting.

Example 1 **Graphing a Polar Equation by Point Plotting**

Sketch the graph of the polar equation $r = 4 \sin \theta$.

Solution

The sine function is periodic, so you can get a full range of r-values by considering values of θ in the interval $0 \le \theta \le 2\pi$, as shown in the following table.

θ	0	$\frac{\pi}{6}$	$\frac{\pi}{3}$	$\frac{\pi}{2}$	$\frac{2\pi}{3}$	$\frac{5\pi}{6}$	π	$\frac{7\pi}{6}$	$\frac{3\pi}{2}$	$\frac{11\pi}{6}$	2π
r	0	2	$2\sqrt{3}$	4	$2\sqrt{3}$	2	0	-2	-4	-2	0

If you plot these points as shown in Figure 10.69, it appears that the graph is a circle of radius 2 whose center is at the point $(x, y) = (0, 2)$.

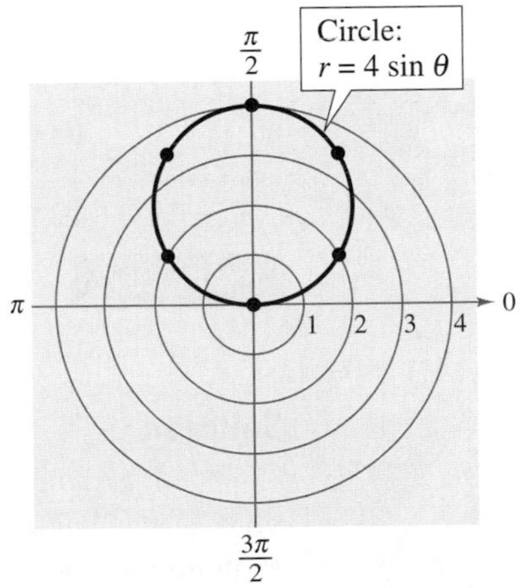

FIGURE 10.69

CHECKPOINT Now try Exercise 21.

You can confirm the graph in Figure 10.69 by converting the polar equation to rectangular form and then sketching the graph of the rectangular equation. You can also use a graphing utility set to *polar* mode and graph the polar equation or set the graphing utility to *parametric* mode and graph a parametric representation.

Symmetry

In Figure 10.69, note that as θ increases from 0 to 2π the graph is traced out twice. Moreover, note that the graph is *symmetric with respect to the line* $\theta = \pi/2$. Had you known about this symmetry and retracing ahead of time, you could have used fewer points.

Symmetry with respect to the line $\theta = \pi/2$ is one of three important types of symmetry to consider in polar curve sketching. (See Figure 10.70.)

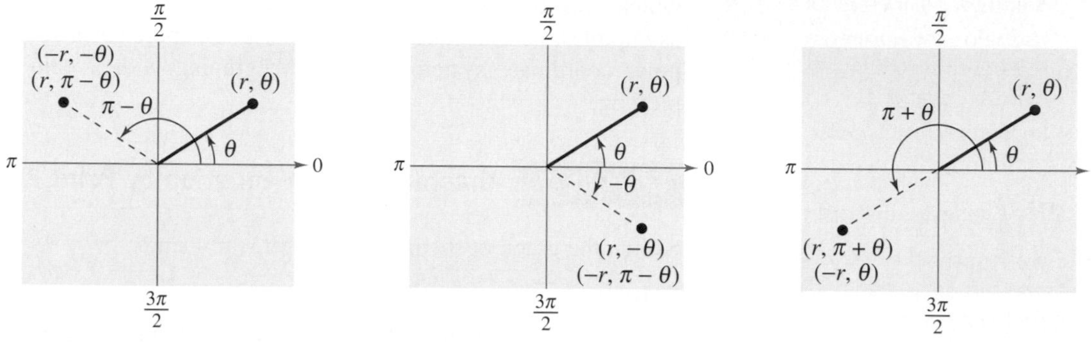

Symmetry with Respect to the Line $\theta = \frac{\pi}{2}$ *Symmetry with Respect to the Polar Axis* *Symmetry with Respect to the Pole*

FIGURE 10.70

STUDY TIP

Note in Example 2 that $\cos(-\theta) = \cos\theta$. This is because the cosine function is *even*. Recall from Section 4.2 that the cosine function is even and the sine function is odd. That is, $\sin(-\theta) = -\sin\theta$.

Tests for Symmetry in Polar Coordinates

The graph of a polar equation is symmetric with respect to the following if the given substitution yields an equivalent equation.

1. *The line* $\theta = \pi/2$: Replace (r, θ) by $(r, \pi - \theta)$ or $(-r, -\theta)$.
2. *The polar axis:* Replace (r, θ) by $(r, -\theta)$ or $(-r, \pi - \theta)$.
3. *The pole:* Replace (r, θ) by $(r, \pi + \theta)$ or $(-r, \theta)$.

Example 2 Using Symmetry to Sketch a Polar Graph

Use symmetry to sketch the graph of $r = 3 + 2\cos\theta$.

Solution

Replacing (r, θ) by $(r, -\theta)$ produces $r = 3 + 2\cos(-\theta) = 3 + 2\cos\theta$. So, you can conclude that the curve is symmetric with respect to the polar axis. Plotting the points in the table and using polar axis symmetry, you obtain the graph shown in Figure 10.71. This graph is called a **limaçon.**

θ	0	$\frac{\pi}{3}$	$\frac{\pi}{2}$	$\frac{2\pi}{3}$	π
r	5	4	3	2	1

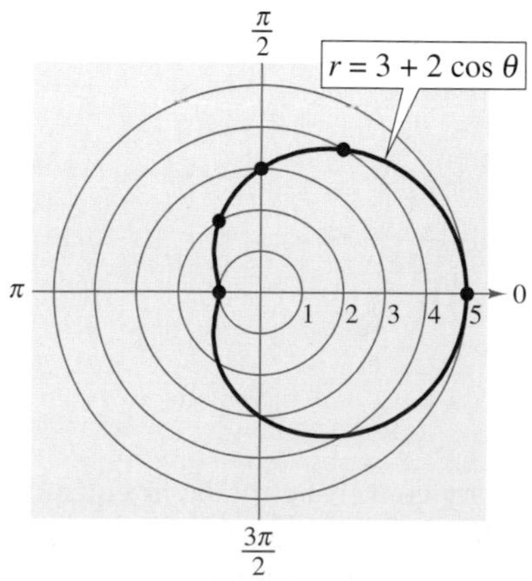

FIGURE 10.71

✓CHECKPOINT Now try Exercise 27.

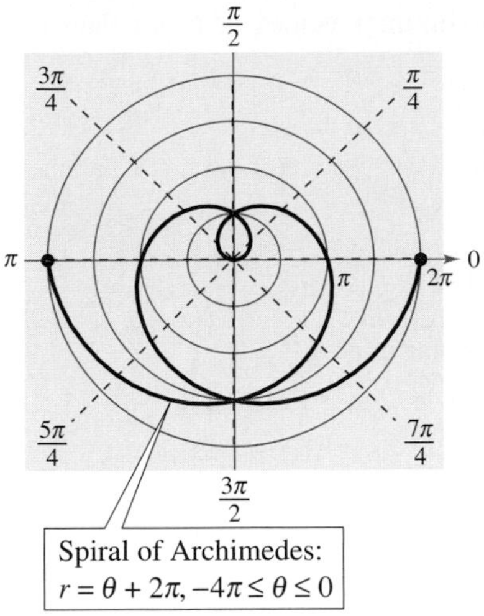

FIGURE 10.72

The three tests for symmetry in polar coordinates listed on page 786 are sufficient to guarantee symmetry, but they are not necessary. For instance, Figure 10.72 shows the graph of $r = \theta + 2\pi$ to be symmetric with respect to the line $\theta = \pi/2$, and yet the tests on page 786 fail to indicate symmetry because neither of the following replacements yields an equivalent equation.

Original Equation	*Replacement*	*New Equation*
$r = \theta + 2\pi$	(r, θ) by $(-r, -\theta)$	$-r = -\theta + 2\pi$
$r = \theta + 2\pi$	(r, θ) by $(r, \pi - \theta)$	$r = -\theta + 3\pi$

The equations discussed in Examples 1 and 2 are of the form

$r = 4 \sin \theta = f(\sin \theta)$ and $r = 3 + 2 \cos \theta = g(\cos \theta)$.

The graph of the first equation is symmetric with respect to the line $\theta = \pi/2$, and the graph of the second equation is symmetric with respect to the polar axis. This observation can be generalized to yield the following tests.

Quick Tests for Symmetry in Polar Coordinates

1. The graph of $r = f(\sin \theta)$ is symmetric with respect to the line $\theta = \dfrac{\pi}{2}$.
2. The graph of $r = g(\cos \theta)$ is symmetric with respect to the polar axis.

Zeros and Maximum *r*-Values

Two additional aids to graphing of polar equations involve knowing the θ-values for which $|r|$ is maximum and knowing the θ-values for which $r = 0$. For instance, in Example 1, the maximum value of $|r|$ for $r = 4 \sin \theta$ is $|r| = 4$, and this occurs when $\theta = \pi/2$, as shown in Figure 10.69. Moreover, $r = 0$ when $\theta = 0$.

Example 3 Sketching a Polar Graph

Sketch the graph of $r = 1 - 2 \cos \theta$.

Solution

From the equation $r = 1 - 2 \cos \theta$, you can obtain the following.

Symmetry: With respect to the polar axis

Maximum value of $|r|$: $r = 3$ when $\theta = \pi$

Zero of r: $r = 0$ when $\theta = \pi/3$

The table shows several θ-values in the interval $[0, \pi]$. By plotting the corresponding points, you can sketch the graph shown in Figure 10.73.

θ	0	$\frac{\pi}{6}$	$\frac{\pi}{3}$	$\frac{\pi}{2}$	$\frac{2\pi}{3}$	$\frac{5\pi}{6}$	π
r	-1	-0.73	0	1	2	2.73	3

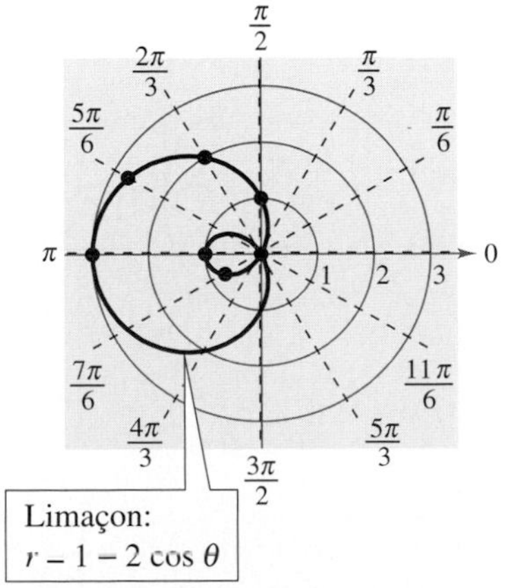

FIGURE 10.73

Note how the negative r-values determine the *inner loop* of the graph in Figure 10.73. This graph, like the one in Figure 10.71, is a limaçon.

✓CHECKPOINT Now try Exercise 29.

Some curves reach their zeros and maximum r-values at more than one point, as shown in Example 4.

Example 4 Sketching a Polar Graph

Sketch the graph of $r = 2 \cos 3\theta$.

Solution

Symmetry: With respect to the polar axis

Maximum value of $|r|$: $|r| = 2$ when $3\theta = 0, \pi, 2\pi, 3\pi$ or $\theta = 0, \pi/3, 2\pi/3, \pi$

Zeros of r: $r = 0$ when $3\theta = \pi/2, 3\pi/2, 5\pi/2$ or $\theta = \pi/6, \pi/2, 5\pi/6$

θ	0	$\frac{\pi}{12}$	$\frac{\pi}{6}$	$\frac{\pi}{4}$	$\frac{\pi}{3}$	$\frac{5\pi}{12}$	$\frac{\pi}{2}$
r	2	$\sqrt{2}$	0	$-\sqrt{2}$	-2	$-\sqrt{2}$	0

By plotting these points and using the specified symmetry, zeros, and maximum values, you can obtain the graph shown in Figure 10.74. This graph is called a **rose curve,** and each of the loops on the graph is called a *petal* of the rose curve. Note how the entire curve is generated as θ increases from 0 to π.

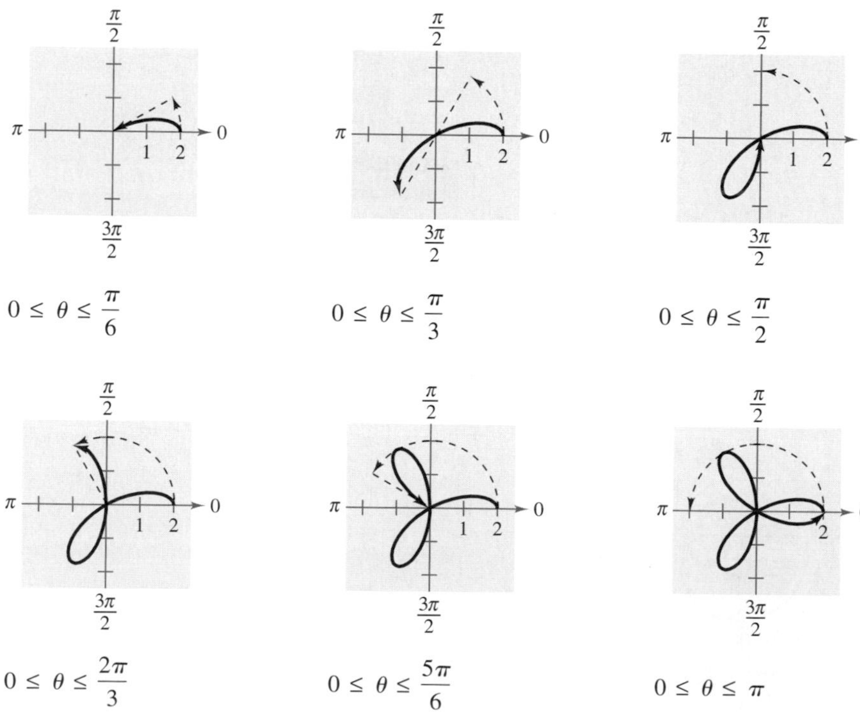

FIGURE 10.74

✓CHECKPOINT Now try Exercise 33.

Exploration

Notice that the rose curve in Example 4 has three petals. How many petals do the rose curves given by $r = 2 \cos 4\theta$ and $r = 2 \sin 3\theta$ have? Determine the numbers of petals for the curves given by $r = 2 \cos n\theta$ and $r = 2 \sin n\theta$, where n is a positive integer.

Technology

Use a graphing utility in *polar* mode to verify the graph of $r = 2 \cos 3\theta$ shown in Figure 10.74.

Special Polar Graphs

Several important types of graphs have equations that are simpler in polar form than in rectangular form. For example, the circle

$$r = 4 \sin \theta$$

in Example 1 has the more complicated rectangular equation

$$x^2 + (y - 2)^2 = 4.$$

Several other types of graphs that have simple polar equations are shown below.

Limaçons

$r = a \pm b \cos \theta$

$r = a \pm b \sin \theta$

$(a > 0, b > 0)$

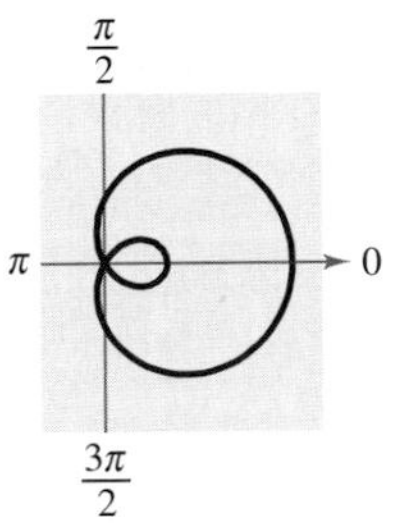

$\frac{a}{b} < 1$

Limaçon with inner loop

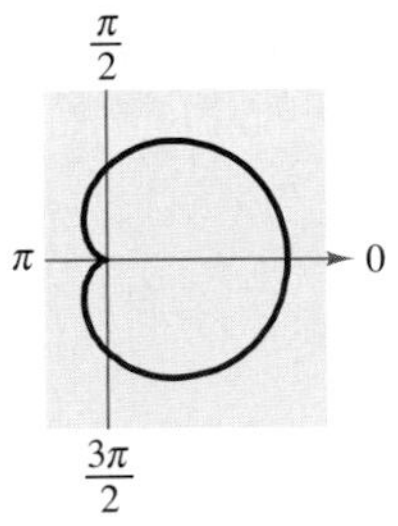

$\frac{a}{b} = 1$

Cardioid (heart-shaped)

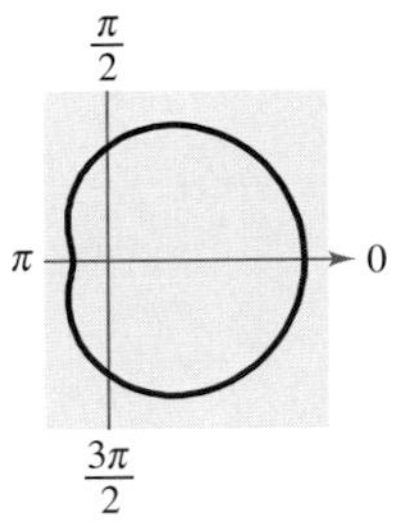

$1 < \frac{a}{b} < 2$

Dimpled limaçon

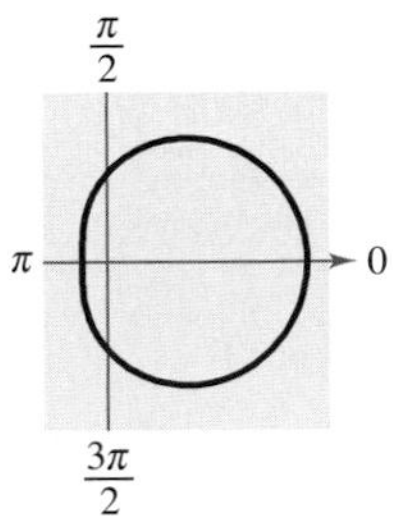

$\frac{a}{b} \geq 2$

Convex limaçon

Rose Curves

n petals if n is odd,
$2n$ petals if n is even
$(n \geq 2)$

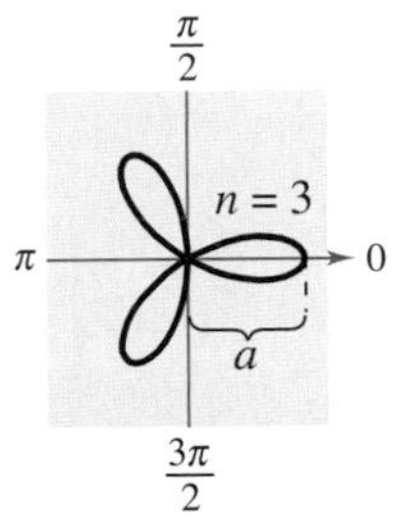

$r = a \cos n\theta$

Rose curve

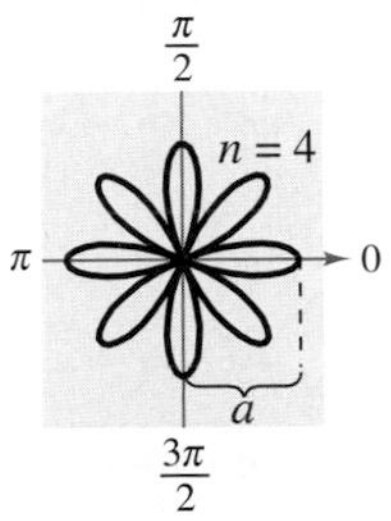

$r = a \cos n\theta$

Rose curve

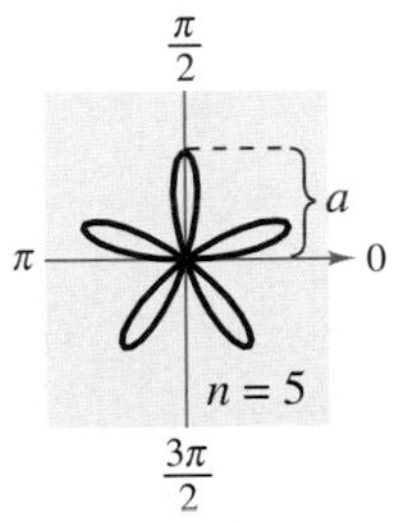

$r = a \sin n\theta$

Rose curve

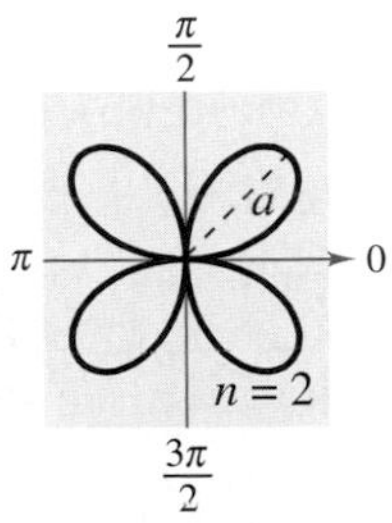

$r = a \sin n\theta$

Rose curve

Circles and Lemniscates

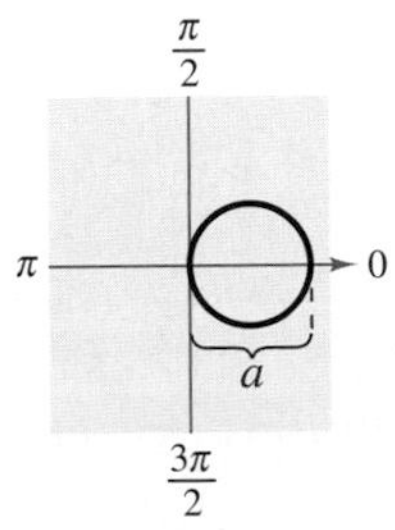

$r = a \cos \theta$

Circle

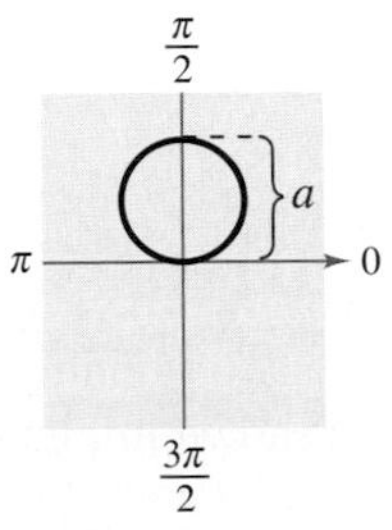

$r = a \sin \theta$

Circle

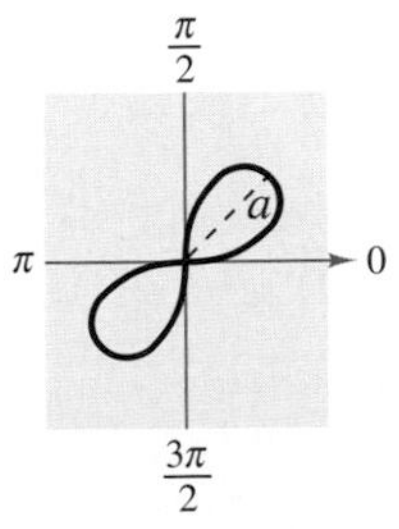

$r^2 = a^2 \sin 2\theta$

Lemniscate

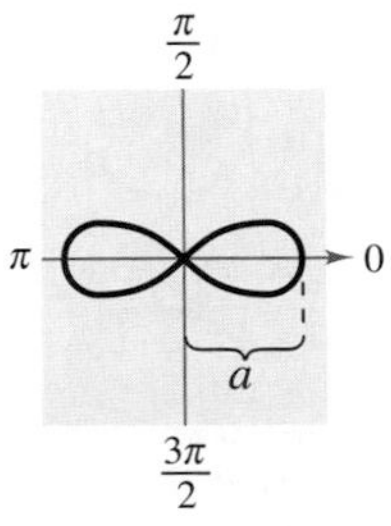

$r^2 = a^2 \cos 2\theta$

Lemniscate

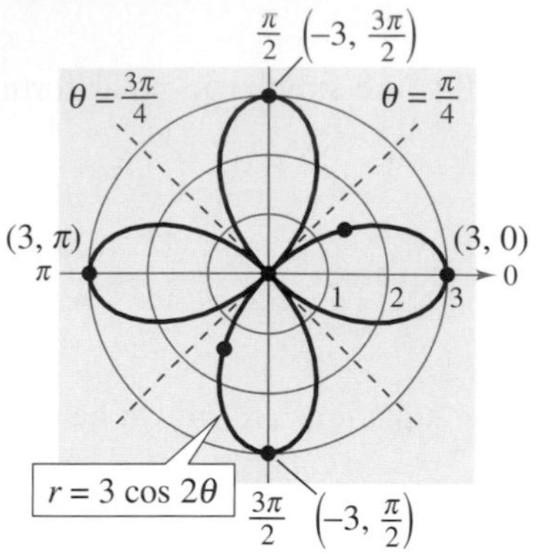

FIGURE 10.75

Example 5 Sketching a Rose Curve

Sketch the graph of $r = 3\cos 2\theta$.

Solution

Type of curve: Rose curve with $2n = 4$ petals

Symmetry: With respect to polar axis, the line $\theta = \pi/2$, and the pole

Maximum value of $|r|$: $|r| = 3$ when $\theta = 0, \pi/2, \pi, 3\pi/2$

Zeros of r: $r = 0$ when $\theta = \pi/4, 3\pi/4$

Using this information together with the additional points shown in the following table, you obtain the graph shown in Figure 10.75.

θ	0	$\frac{\pi}{6}$	$\frac{\pi}{4}$	$\frac{\pi}{3}$
r	3	$\frac{3}{2}$	0	$-\frac{3}{2}$

CHECKPOINT Now try Exercise 35.

Example 6 Sketching a Lemniscate

Sketch the graph of $r^2 = 9\sin 2\theta$.

Solution

Type of curve: Lemniscate

Symmetry: With respect to the pole

Maximum value of $|r|$: $|r| = 3$ when $\theta = \frac{\pi}{4}$

Zeros of r: $r = 0$ when $\theta = 0, \frac{\pi}{2}$

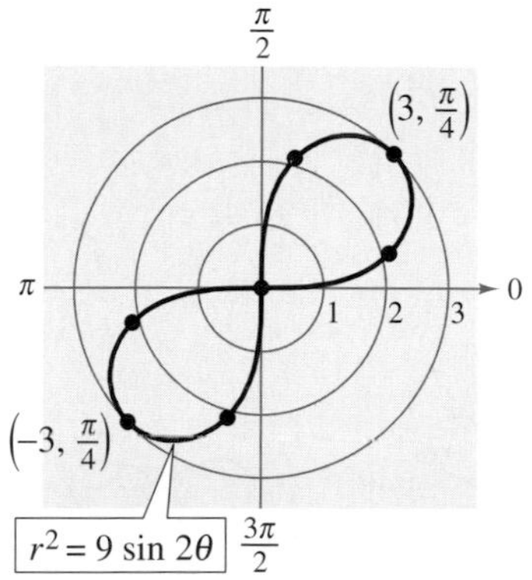

FIGURE 10.76

If $\sin 2\theta < 0$, this equation has no solution points. So, you restrict the values of θ to those for which $\sin 2\theta \geq 0$.

$$0 \leq \theta \leq \frac{\pi}{2} \quad \text{or} \quad \pi \leq \theta \leq \frac{3\pi}{2}$$

Moreover, using symmetry, you need to consider only the first of these two intervals. By finding a few additional points (see table below), you can obtain the graph shown in Figure 10.76.

θ	0	$\frac{\pi}{12}$	$\frac{\pi}{4}$	$\frac{5\pi}{12}$	$\frac{\pi}{2}$
$r = \pm 3\sqrt{\sin 2\theta}$	0	$\frac{\pm 3}{\sqrt{2}}$	± 3	$\frac{\pm 3}{\sqrt{2}}$	0

CHECKPOINT Now try Exercise 39.

10.8 Exercises

VOCABULARY CHECK: Fill in the blanks.

1. The graph of $r = f(\sin\theta)$ is symmetric with respect to the line ________.
2. The graph of $r = g(\cos\theta)$ is symmetric with respect to the ________ ________.
3. The equation $r = 2 + \cos\theta$ represents a ________ ________.
4. The equation $r = 2\cos\theta$ represents a ________.
5. The equation $r^2 = 4\sin 2\theta$ represents a ________.
6. The equation $r = 1 + \sin\theta$ represents a ________.

In Exercises 1–6, identify the type of polar graph.

1.

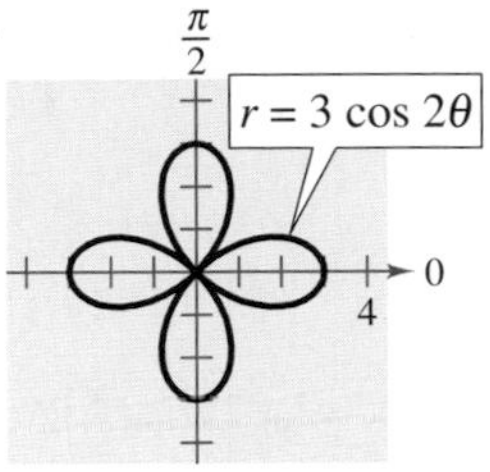

2.

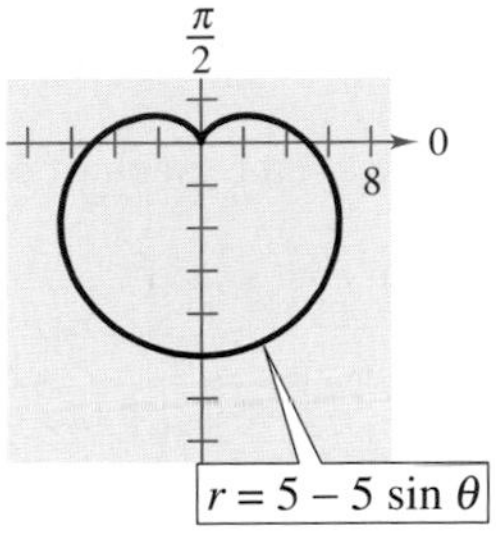

3.

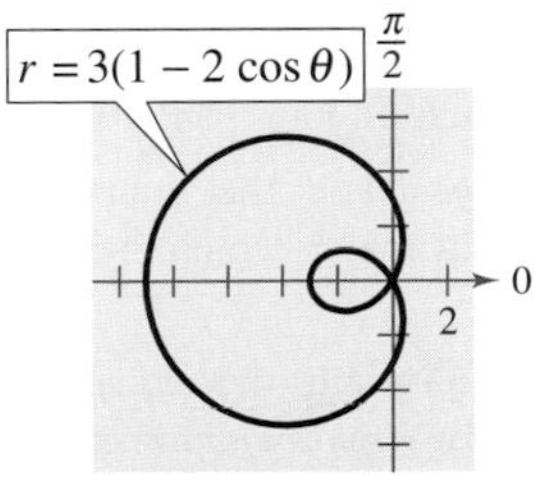

4.

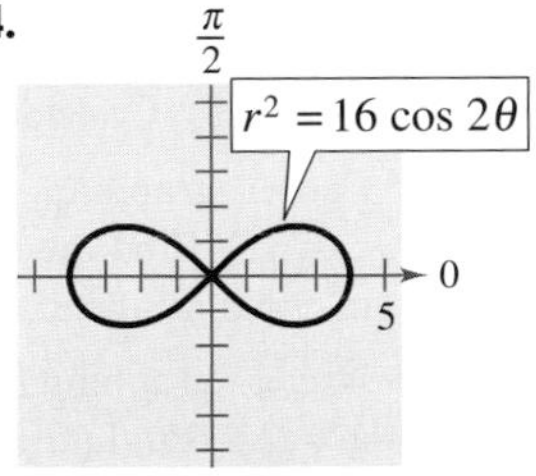

5.

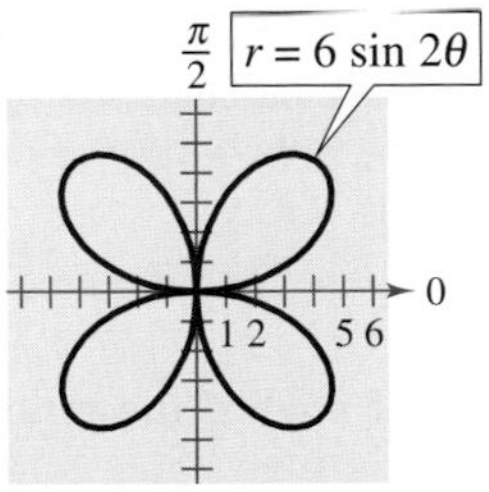

6.

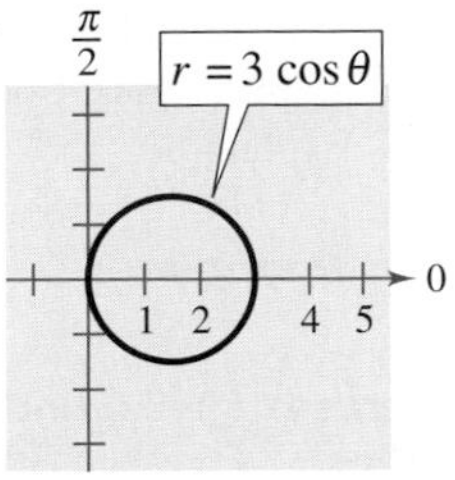

In Exercises 7–12, test for symmetry with respect to $\theta = \pi/2$, the polar axis, and the pole.

7. $r = 5 + 4\cos\theta$

8. $r = 16\cos 3\theta$

9. $r = \dfrac{2}{1 + \sin\theta}$

10. $r = \dfrac{3}{2 + \cos\theta}$

11. $r^2 = 16\cos 2\theta$

12. $r^2 = 36\sin 2\theta$

In Exercises 13–16, find the maximum value of $|r|$ and any zeros of r.

13. $r = 10(1 - \sin\theta)$

14. $r = 6 + 12\cos\theta$

15. $r = 4\cos 3\theta$

16. $r = 3\sin 2\theta$

In Exercises 17–40, sketch the graph of the polar equation using symmetry, zeros, maximum r-values, and any other additional points.

17. $r = 5$

18. $r = 2$

19. $r = \dfrac{\pi}{6}$

20. $r = -\dfrac{3\pi}{4}$

21. $r = 3\sin\theta$

22. $r = 4\cos\theta$

23. $r = 3(1 - \cos\theta)$

24. $r = 4(1 - \sin\theta)$

25. $r = 4(1 + \sin\theta)$

26. $r = 2(1 + \cos\theta)$

27. $r = 3 + 6\sin\theta$

28. $r = 4 - 3\sin\theta$

29. $r = 1 - 2\sin\theta$

30. $r = 1 - 2\cos\theta$

31. $r = 3 - 4\cos\theta$

32. $r = 4 + 3\cos\theta$

33. $r = 5\sin 2\theta$

34. $r = 3\cos 2\theta$

35. $r = 2\sec\theta$

36. $r = 5\csc\theta$

37. $r = \dfrac{3}{\sin\theta - 2\cos\theta}$

38. $r = \dfrac{6}{2\sin\theta - 3\cos\theta}$

39. $r^2 = 9\cos 2\theta$

40. $r^2 = 4\sin\theta$

In Exercises 41–46, use a graphing utility to graph the polar equation. Describe your viewing window.

41. $r = 8\cos\theta$

42. $r = \cos 2\theta$

43. $r = 3(2 - \sin\theta)$

44. $r = 2\cos(3\theta - 2)$

45. $r = 8\sin\theta\cos^2\theta$

46. $r = 2\csc\theta + 5$

In Exercises 47–52, use a graphing utility to graph the polar equation. Find an interval for θ for which the graph is traced *only once*.

47. $r = 3 - 4\cos\theta$

48. $r = 5 + 4\cos\theta$

49. $r = 2\cos\left(\dfrac{3\theta}{2}\right)$

50. $r = 3\sin\left(\dfrac{5\theta}{2}\right)$

51. $r^2 = 9\sin 2\theta$

52. $r^2 = \dfrac{1}{\theta}$

In Exercises 53–56, use a graphing utility to graph the polar equation and show that the indicated line is an asymptote of the graph.

	Name of Graph	*Polar Equation*	*Asymptote*
53.	Conchoid	$r = 2 - \sec\theta$	$x = -1$
54.	Conchoid	$r = 2 + \csc\theta$	$y = 1$
55.	Hyperbolic spiral	$r = \dfrac{3}{\theta}$	$y = 3$
56.	Strophoid	$r = 2\cos 2\theta\sec\theta$	$x = -2$

Synthesis

True or False? **In Exercises 57 and 58, determine whether the statement is true or false. Justify your answer.**

57. In the polar coordinate system, if a graph that has symmetry with respect to the polar axis were folded on the line $\theta = 0$, the portion of the graph above the polar axis would coincide with the portion of the graph below the polar axis.

58. In the polar coordinate system, if a graph that has symmetry with respect to the pole were folded on the line $\theta = 3\pi/4$, the portion of the graph on one side of the fold would coincide with the portion of the graph on the other side of the fold.

59. ***Exploration*** Sketch the graph of $r = 6\cos\theta$ over each interval. Describe the part of the graph obtained in each case.

(a) $0 \le \theta \le \dfrac{\pi}{2}$ (b) $\dfrac{\pi}{2} \le \theta \le \pi$

(c) $-\dfrac{\pi}{2} \le \theta \le \dfrac{\pi}{2}$ (d) $\dfrac{\pi}{4} \le \theta \le \dfrac{3\pi}{4}$

60. ***Graphical Reasoning*** Use a graphing utility to graph the polar equation $r = 6[1 + \cos(\theta - \phi)]$ for (a) $\phi = 0$, (b) $\phi = \pi/4$, and (c) $\phi = \pi/2$. Use the graphs to describe the effect of the angle ϕ. Write the equation as a function of $\sin\theta$ for part (c).

61. The graph of $r = f(\theta)$ is rotated about the pole through an angle ϕ. Show that the equation of the rotated graph is $r = f(\theta - \phi)$.

62. Consider the graph of $r = f(\sin\theta)$.

(a) Show that if the graph is rotated counterclockwise $\pi/2$ radians about the pole, the equation of the rotated graph is $r = f(-\cos\theta)$.

(b) Show that if the graph is rotated counterclockwise π radians about the pole, the equation of the rotated graph is $r = f(-\sin\theta)$.

(c) Show that if the graph is rotated counterclockwise $3\pi/2$ radians about the pole, the equation of the rotated graph is $r = f(\cos\theta)$.

In Exercises 63–66, use the results of Exercises 61 and 62.

63. Write an equation for the limaçon $r = 2 - \sin\theta$ after it has been rotated through the given angle.

(a) $\dfrac{\pi}{4}$ (b) $\dfrac{\pi}{2}$ (c) π (d) $\dfrac{3\pi}{2}$

64. Write an equation for the rose curve $r = 2\sin 2\theta$ after it has been rotated through the given angle.

(a) $\dfrac{\pi}{6}$ (b) $\dfrac{\pi}{2}$ (c) $\dfrac{2\pi}{3}$ (d) π

65. Sketch the graph of each equation.

(a) $r = 1 - \sin\theta$ (b) $r = 1 - \sin\left(\theta - \dfrac{\pi}{4}\right)$

66. Sketch the graph of each equation.

(a) $r = 3\sec\theta$ (b) $r = 3\sec\left(\theta - \dfrac{\pi}{4}\right)$

(c) $r = 3\sec\left(\theta + \dfrac{\pi}{3}\right)$ (d) $r = 3\sec\left(\theta - \dfrac{\pi}{2}\right)$

67. ***Exploration*** Use a graphing utility to graph and identify $r = 2 + k\sin\theta$ for $k = 0, 1, 2,$ and 3.

68. ***Exploration*** Consider the equation $r = 3\sin k\theta$.

(a) Use a graphing utility to graph the equation for $k = 1.5$. Find the interval for θ over which the graph is traced only once.

(b) Use a graphing utility to graph the equation for $k = 2.5$. Find the interval for θ over which the graph is traced only once.

(c) Is it possible to find an interval for θ over which the graph is traced only once for any rational number k? Explain.

Skills Review

In Exercises 69–72, find the zeros (if any) of the rational function.

69. $f(x) = \dfrac{x^2 - 9}{x + 1}$

70. $f(x) = 6 + \dfrac{4}{x^2 + 4}$

71. $f(x) = 5 - \dfrac{3}{x - 2}$

72. $f(x) = \dfrac{x^3 - 27}{x^2 + 4}$

In Exercises 73 and 74, find the standard form of the equation of the ellipse with the given characteristics. Then sketch the ellipse.

73. Vertices: $(-4, 2), (2, 2)$; minor axis of length 4

74. Foci: $(3, 2), (3, -4)$; major axis of length 8

10.9 Polar Equations of Conics

What you should learn

- Define conics in terms of eccentricity.
- Write and graph equations of conics in polar form.
- Use equations of conics in polar form to model real-life problems.

Why you should learn it

The orbits of planets and satellites can be modeled with polar equations. For instance, in Exercise 58 on page 798, a polar equation is used to model the orbit of a satellite.

Alternative Definition of Conic

In Sections 10.3 and 10.4, you learned that the rectangular equations of ellipses and hyperbolas take simple forms when the origin lies at their *centers*. As it happens, there are many important applications of conics in which it is more convenient to use one of the *foci* as the origin. In this section, you will learn that polar equations of conics take simple forms if one of the foci lies at the pole.

To begin, consider the following alternative definition of conic that uses the concept of eccentricity.

Alternative Definition of Conic

The locus of a point in the plane that moves so that its distance from a fixed point (focus) is in a constant ratio to its distance from a fixed line (directrix) is a **conic.** The constant ratio is the **eccentricity** of the conic and is denoted by e. Moreover, the conic is an **ellipse** if $e < 1$, a **parabola** if $e = 1$, and a **hyperbola** if $e > 1$. (See Figure 10.77.)

In Figure 10.77, note that for each type of conic, the focus is at the pole.

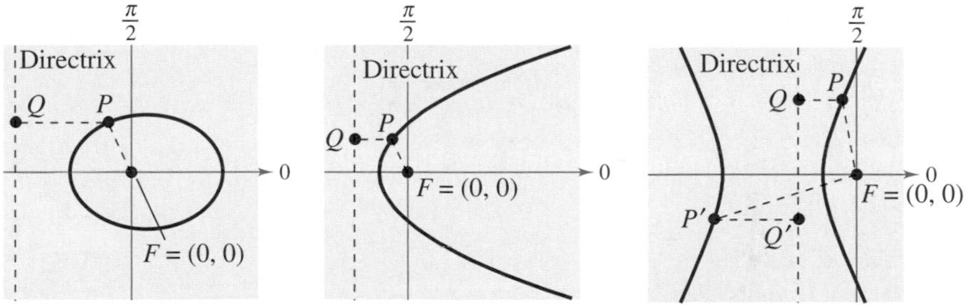

Ellipse: $0 < e < 1$ $\frac{PF}{PQ} < 1$

Parabola: $e = 1$ $\frac{PF}{PQ} = 1$

Hyperbola $e > 1$ $\frac{PF}{PQ} = \frac{P'F}{P'Q'} > 1$

FIGURE 10.77

Polar Equations of Conics

The benefit of locating a focus of a conic at the pole is that the equation of the conic takes on a simpler form. For a proof of the polar equations of conics, see Proofs in Mathematics on page 808.

Polar Equations of Conics

The graph of a polar equation of the form

1. $r = \dfrac{ep}{1 \pm e \cos \theta}$ or **2.** $r = \dfrac{ep}{1 \pm e \sin \theta}$

is a conic, where $e > 0$ is the eccentricity and $|p|$ is the distance between the focus (pole) and the directrix.

Equations of the form

$$r = \frac{ep}{1 \pm e \cos \theta} = g(\cos \theta) \qquad \text{Vertical directrix}$$

correspond to conics with a vertical directrix and symmetry with respect to the polar axis. Equations of the form

$$r = \frac{ep}{1 \pm e \sin \theta} = g(\sin \theta) \qquad \text{Horizontal directrix}$$

correspond to conics with a horizontal directrix and symmetry with respect to the line $\theta = \pi/2$. Moreover, the converse is also true—that is, any conic with a focus at the pole and having a horizontal or vertical directrix can be represented by one of the given equations.

Example 1 Identifying a Conic from Its Equation

Identify the type of conic represented by the equation $r = \dfrac{15}{3 - 2 \cos \theta}$.

Algebraic Solution

To identify the type of conic, rewrite the equation in the form $r = (ep)/(1 \pm e \cos \theta)$.

$$r = \frac{15}{3 - 2 \cos \theta} \qquad \text{Write original equation.}$$

$$= \frac{5}{1 - (2/3) \cos \theta} \qquad \text{Divide numerator and denominator by 3.}$$

Because $e = \frac{2}{3} < 1$, you can conclude that the graph is an ellipse.

CHECKPOINT Now try Exercise 11.

Graphical Solution

You can start sketching the graph by plotting points from $\theta = 0$ to $\theta = \pi$. Because the equation is of the form $r = g(\cos \theta)$, the graph of r is symmetric with respect to the polar axis. So, you can complete the sketch, as shown in Figure 10.78. From this, you can conclude that the graph is an ellipse.

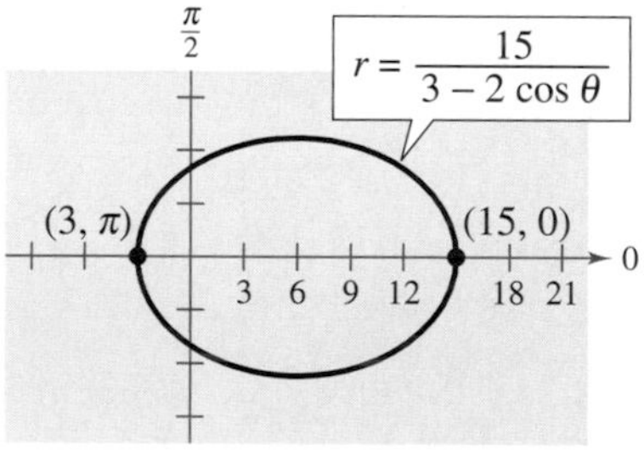

FIGURE 10.78

For the ellipse in Figure 10.78, the major axis is horizontal and the vertices lie at $(15, 0)$ and $(3, \pi)$. So, the length of the *major* axis is $2a = 18$. To find the length of the *minor* axis, you can use the equations $e = c/a$ and $b^2 = a^2 - c^2$ to conclude that

$$\begin{aligned} b^2 &= a^2 - c^2 \\ &= a^2 - (ea)^2 \\ &= a^2(1 - e^2). \qquad \text{Ellipse} \end{aligned}$$

Because $e = \frac{2}{3}$, you have $b^2 = 9^2\left[1 - \left(\frac{2}{3}\right)^2\right] = 45$, which implies that $b = \sqrt{45} = 3\sqrt{5}$. So, the length of the minor axis is $2b = 6\sqrt{5}$. A similar analysis for hyperbolas yields

$$\begin{aligned} b^2 &= c^2 - a^2 \\ &= (ea)^2 - a^2 \\ &= a^2(e^2 - 1). \qquad \text{Hyperbola} \end{aligned}$$

Example 2 Sketching a Conic from Its Polar Equation

Identify the conic $r = \dfrac{32}{3 + 5\sin\theta}$ and sketch its graph.

Solution

Dividing the numerator and denominator by 3, you have

$$r = \frac{32/3}{1 + (5/3)\sin\theta}.$$

Because $e = \frac{5}{3} > 1$, the graph is a hyperbola. The transverse axis of the hyperbola lies on the line $\theta = \pi/2$, and the vertices occur at $(4, \pi/2)$ and $(-16, 3\pi/2)$. Because the length of the transverse axis is 12, you can see that $a = 6$. To find b, write

$$b^2 = a^2(e^2 - 1) = 6^2\left[\left(\frac{5}{3}\right)^2 - 1\right] = 64.$$

So, $b = 8$. Finally, you can use a and b to determine that the asymptotes of the hyperbola are $y = 10 \pm \frac{3}{4}x$. The graph is shown in Figure 10.79.

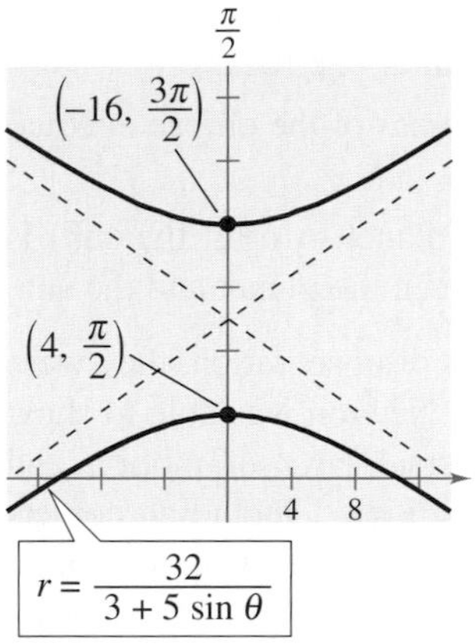

FIGURE 10.79

CHECKPOINT Now try Exercise 19.

Technology

Use a graphing utility set in *polar* mode to verify the four orientations shown at the right. Remember that *e* must be positive, but *p* can be positive or negative.

In the next example, you are asked to find a polar equation of a specified conic. To do this, let p be the distance between the pole and the directrix.

1. *Horizontal directrix above the pole:* $r = \dfrac{ep}{1 + e\sin\theta}$
2. *Horizontal directrix below the pole:* $r = \dfrac{ep}{1 - e\sin\theta}$
3. *Vertical directrix to the right of the pole:* $r = \dfrac{ep}{1 + e\cos\theta}$
4. *Vertical directrix to the left of the pole:* $r = \dfrac{ep}{1 - e\cos\theta}$

Example 3 Finding the Polar Equation of a Conic

Find the polar equation of the parabola whose focus is the pole and whose directrix is the line $y = 3$.

Solution

From Figure 10.80, you can see that the directrix is horizontal and above the pole, so you can choose an equation of the form

$$r = \frac{ep}{1 + e\sin\theta}.$$

Moreover, because the eccentricity of a parabola is $e = 1$ and the distance between the pole and the directrix is $p = 3$, you have the equation

$$r = \frac{3}{1 + \sin\theta}.$$

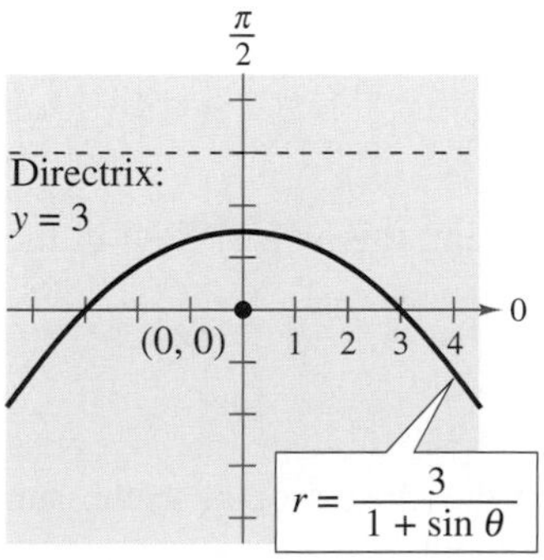

FIGURE 10.80

CHECKPOINT Now try Exercise 33.

Applications

Kepler's Laws (listed below), named after the German astronomer Johannes Kepler (1571–1630), can be used to describe the orbits of the planets about the sun.

1. Each planet moves in an elliptical orbit with the sun at one focus.
2. A ray from the sun to the planet sweeps out equal areas of the ellipse in equal times.
3. The square of the period (the time it takes for a planet to orbit the sun) is proportional to the cube of the mean distance between the planet and the sun.

Although Kepler simply stated these laws on the basis of observation, they were later validated by Isaac Newton (1642–1727). In fact, Newton was able to show that each law can be deduced from a set of universal laws of motion and gravitation that govern the movement of all heavenly bodies, including comets and satellites. This is illustrated in the next example, which involves the comet named after the English mathematician and physicist Edmund Halley (1656–1742).

If you use Earth as a reference with a period of 1 year and a distance of 1 astronomical unit (an *astronomical unit* is defined as the mean distance between Earth and the sun, or about 93 million miles), the proportionality constant in Kepler's third law is 1. For example, because Mars has a mean distance to the sun of $d = 1.524$ astronomical units, its period P is given by $d^3 = P^2$. So, the period of Mars is $P \approx 1.88$ years.

Example 4 Halley's Comet

Halley's comet has an elliptical orbit with an eccentricity of $e \approx 0.967$. The length of the major axis of the orbit is approximately 35.88 astronomical units. Find a polar equation for the orbit. How close does Halley's comet come to the sun?

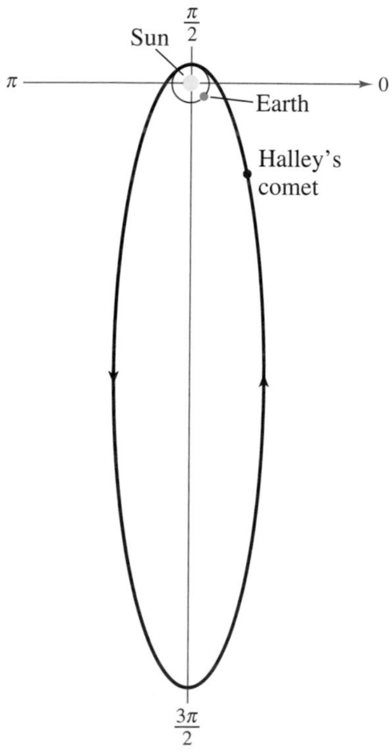

FIGURE 10.81

Solution

Using a vertical axis, as shown in Figure 10.81, choose an equation of the form $r = ep/(1 + e\sin\theta)$. Because the vertices of the ellipse occur when $\theta = \pi/2$ and $\theta = 3\pi/2$, you can determine the length of the major axis to be the sum of the r-values of the vertices. That is,

$$2a = \frac{0.967p}{1 + 0.967} + \frac{0.967p}{1 - 0.967} \approx 29.79p \approx 35.88.$$

So, $p \approx 1.204$ and $ep \approx (0.967)(1.204) \approx 1.164$. Using this value of ep in the equation, you have

$$r = \frac{1.164}{1 + 0.967\sin\theta}$$

where r is measured in astronomical units. To find the closest point to the sun (the focus), substitute $\theta = \pi/2$ in this equation to obtain

$$r = \frac{1.164}{1 + 0.967\sin(\pi/2)} \approx 0.59 \text{ astronomical unit} \approx 55{,}000{,}000 \text{ miles}.$$

CHECKPOINT Now try Exercise 57.

10.9 Exercises

VOCABULARY CHECK:

In Exercises 1–3, fill in the blanks.

1. The locus of a point in the plane that moves so that its distance from a fixed point (focus) is in a constant ratio to its distance from a fixed line (directrix) is a ________.
2. The constant ratio is the ________ of the conic and is denoted by ________.
3. An equation of the form $r = \dfrac{ep}{1 + e\cos\theta}$ has a ________ directrix to the ________ of the pole.
4. Match the conic with its eccentricity.

   (a) $e < 1$ (b) $e = 1$ (c) $e > 1$

   (i) parabola (ii) hyperbola (iii) ellipse

In Exercises 1–4, write the polar equation of the conic for $e = 1$, $e = 0.5$, and $e = 1.5$. Identify the conic for each equation. Verify your answers with a graphing utility.

1. $r = \dfrac{4e}{1 + e\cos\theta}$
2. $r = \dfrac{4e}{1 - e\cos\theta}$
3. $r = \dfrac{4e}{1 - e\sin\theta}$
4. $r = \dfrac{4e}{1 + e\sin\theta}$

In Exercises 5–10, match the polar equation with its graph. [The graphs are labeled (a), (b), (c), (d), (e), and (f).]

(a)

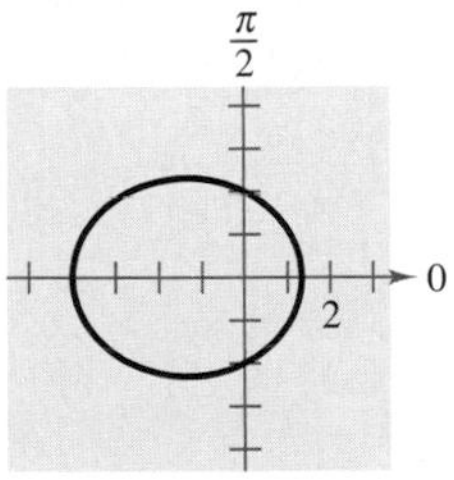

(b)

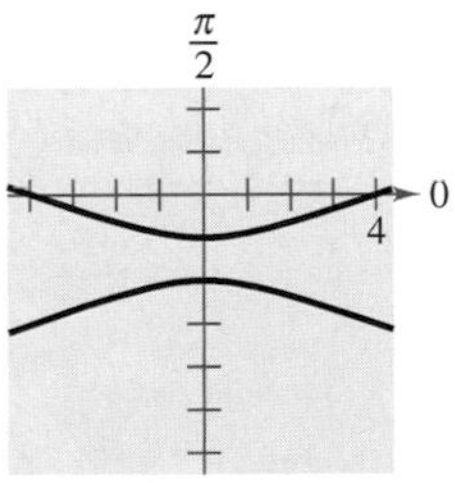

(c)

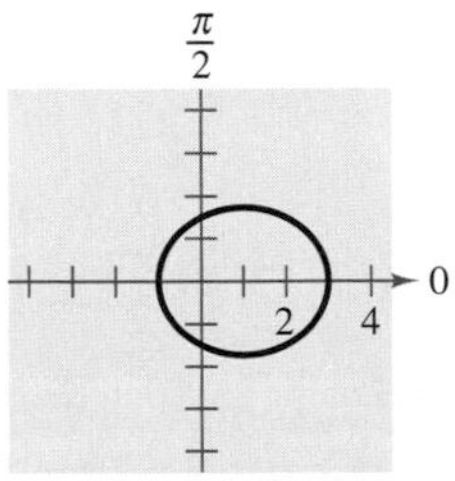

(d)

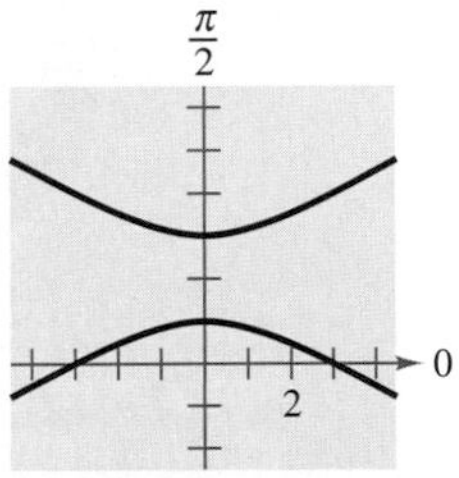

(e)

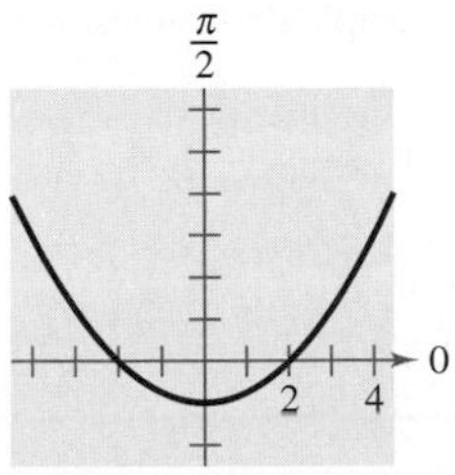

(f)

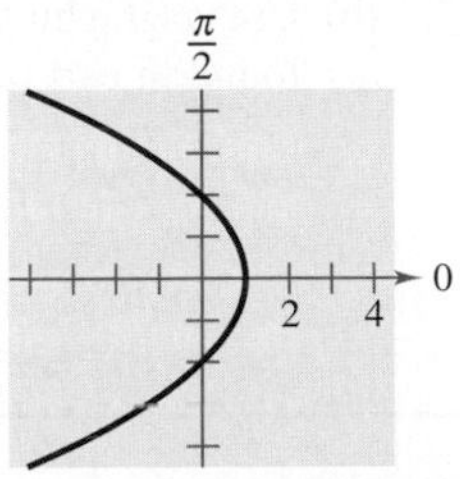

5. $r = \dfrac{2}{1 + \cos\theta}$
6. $r = \dfrac{3}{2 - \cos\theta}$
7. $r = \dfrac{3}{1 + 2\sin\theta}$
8. $r = \dfrac{2}{1 - \sin\theta}$
9. $r = \dfrac{4}{2 + \cos\theta}$
10. $r = \dfrac{4}{1 - 3\sin\theta}$

In Exercises 11–24, identify the conic and sketch its graph.

11. $r = \dfrac{2}{1 - \cos\theta}$
12. $r = \dfrac{3}{1 + \sin\theta}$
13. $r = \dfrac{5}{1 + \sin\theta}$
14. $r = \dfrac{6}{1 + \cos\theta}$
15. $r = \dfrac{2}{2 - \cos\theta}$
16. $r = \dfrac{3}{3 + \sin\theta}$
17. $r = \dfrac{6}{2 + \sin\theta}$
18. $r = \dfrac{9}{3 - 2\cos\theta}$
19. $r = \dfrac{3}{2 + 4\sin\theta}$
20. $r = \dfrac{5}{-1 + 2\cos\theta}$
21. $r = \dfrac{3}{2 - 6\cos\theta}$
22. $r = \dfrac{3}{2 + 6\sin\theta}$
23. $r = \dfrac{4}{2 - \cos\theta}$
24. $r = \dfrac{2}{2 + 3\sin\theta}$

In Exercises 25–28, use a graphing utility to graph the polar equation. Identify the graph.

25. $r = \dfrac{-1}{1 - \sin\theta}$
26. $r = \dfrac{-5}{2 + 4\sin\theta}$
27. $r = \dfrac{3}{-4 + 2\cos\theta}$
28. $r = \dfrac{4}{1 - 2\cos\theta}$

In Exercises 29–32, use a graphing utility to graph the rotated conic.

29. $r = \dfrac{2}{1 - \cos(\theta - \pi/4)}$ (See Exercise 11.)

30. $r = \dfrac{3}{3 + \sin(\theta - \pi/3)}$ (See Exercise 16.)

31. $r = \dfrac{6}{2 + \sin(\theta + \pi/6)}$ (See Exercise 17.)

32. $r = \dfrac{5}{-1 + 2\cos(\theta + 2\pi/3)}$ (See Exercise 20.)

In Exercises 33–48, find a polar equation of the conic with its focus at the pole.

	Conic	*Eccentricity*	*Directrix*
33.	Parabola	$e = 1$	$x = -1$
34.	Parabola	$e = 1$	$y = -2$
35.	Ellipse	$e = \frac{1}{2}$	$y = 1$
36.	Ellipse	$e = \frac{3}{4}$	$y = -3$
37.	Hyperbola	$e = 2$	$x = 1$
38.	Hyperbola	$e = \frac{3}{2}$	$x = -1$

	Conic	*Vertex or Vertices*
39.	Parabola	$(1, -\pi/2)$
40.	Parabola	$(6, 0)$
41.	Parabola	$(5, \pi)$
42.	Parabola	$(10, \pi/2)$
43.	Ellipse	$(2, 0), (10, \pi)$
44.	Ellipse	$(2, \pi/2), (4, 3\pi/2)$
45.	Ellipse	$(20, 0), (4, \pi)$
46.	Hyperbola	$(2, 0), (8, 0)$
47.	Hyperbola	$(1, 3\pi/2), (9, 3\pi/2)$
48.	Hyperbola	$(4, \pi/2), (1, \pi/2)$

49. ***Planetary Motion*** The planets travel in elliptical orbits with the sun at one focus. Assume that the focus is at the pole, the major axis lies on the polar axis, and the length of the major axis is $2a$ (see figure). Show that the polar equation of the orbit is $r = a(1 - e^2)/(1 - e\cos\theta)$ where e is the eccentricity.

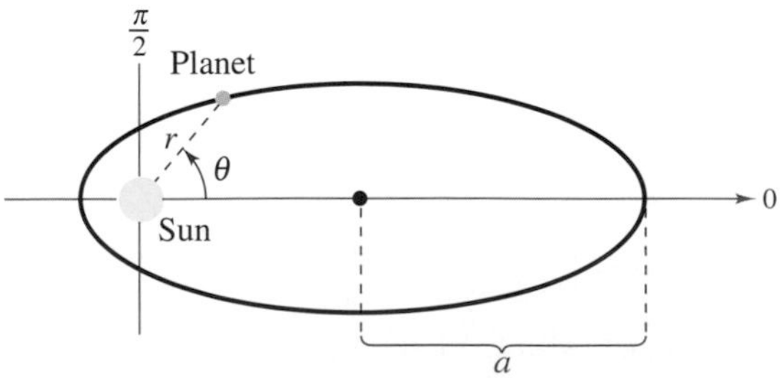

50. ***Planetary Motion*** Use the result of Exercise 49 to show that the minimum distance (*perihelion distance*) from the sun to the planet is $r = a(1 - e)$ and the maximum distance (*aphelion distance*) is $r = a(1 + e)$.

Planetary Motion **In Exercises 51–56, use the results of Exercises 49 and 50 to find the polar equation of the planet's orbit and the perihelion and aphelion distances.**

51.	Earth	$a = 95.956 \times 10^6$ miles, $e = 0.0167$
52.	Saturn	$a = 1.427 \times 10^9$ kilometers, $e = 0.0542$
53.	Venus	$a = 108.209 \times 10^6$ kilometers, $e = 0.0068$
54.	Mercury	$a = 35.98 \times 10^6$ miles, $e = 0.2056$
55.	Mars	$a = 141.63 \times 10^6$ miles, $e = 0.0934$
56.	Jupiter	$a = 778.41 \times 10^6$ kilometers, $e = 0.0484$

57. ***Astronomy*** The comet Encke has an elliptical orbit with an eccentricity of $e \approx 0.847$. The length of the major axis of the orbit is approximately 4.42 astronomical units. Find a polar equation for the orbit. How close does the comet come to the sun?

Model It

58. ***Satellite Tracking*** A satellite in a 100-mile-high circular orbit around Earth has a velocity of approximately 17,500 miles per hour. If this velocity is multiplied by $\sqrt{2}$, the satellite will have the minimum velocity necessary to escape Earth's gravity and it will follow a parabolic path with the center of Earth as the focus (see figure).

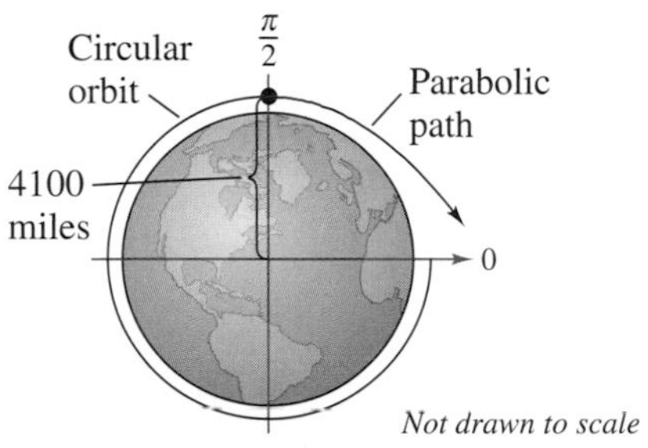

(a) Find a polar equation of the parabolic path of the satellite (assume the radius of Earth is 4000 miles).

(b) Use a graphing utility to graph the equation you found in part (a).

(c) Find the distance between the surface of the Earth and the satellite when $\theta = 30°$.

(d) Find the distance between the surface of Earth and the satellite when $\theta = 60°$.

Synthesis

True or False? **In Exercises 59–61, determine whether the statement is true or false. Justify your answer.**

59. For a given value of $e > 1$ over the interval $\theta = 0$ to $\theta = 2\pi$, the graph of

$$r = \frac{ex}{1 - e\cos\theta}$$

is the same as the graph of

$$r = \frac{e(-x)}{1 + e\cos\theta}.$$

60. The graph of

$$r = \frac{4}{-3 - 3\sin\theta}$$

has a horizontal directrix above the pole.

61. The conic represented by the following equation is an ellipse.

$$r^2 = \frac{16}{9 - 4\cos\left(\theta + \frac{\pi}{4}\right)}$$

62. ***Writing*** In your own words, define the term *eccentricity* and explain how it can be used to classify conics.

63. Show that the polar equation of the ellipse

$$\frac{x^2}{a^2} + \frac{y^2}{b^2} = 1 \quad \text{is} \quad r^2 = \frac{b^2}{1 - e^2\cos^2\theta}.$$

64. Show that the polar equation of the hyperbola

$$\frac{x^2}{a^2} - \frac{y^2}{b^2} = 1 \quad \text{is} \quad r^2 = \frac{-b^2}{1 - e^2\cos^2\theta}.$$

In Exercises 65–70, use the results of Exercises 63 and 64 to write the polar form of the equation of the conic.

65. $\dfrac{x^2}{169} + \dfrac{y^2}{144} = 1$

66. $\dfrac{x^2}{25} + \dfrac{y^2}{16} = 1$

67. $\dfrac{x^2}{9} - \dfrac{y^2}{16} = 1$

68. $\dfrac{x^2}{36} - \dfrac{y^2}{4} = 1$

69. Hyperbola One focus: $(5, \pi/2)$
Vertices: $(4, \pi/2), (4, -\pi/2)$

70. Ellipse One focus: $(4, 0)$
Vertices: $(5, 0), (5, \pi)$

71. ***Exploration*** Consider the polar equation

$$r = \frac{4}{1 - 0.4\cos\theta}.$$

(a) Identify the conic without graphing the equation.

(b) Without graphing the following polar equations, describe how each differs from the given polar equation.

$$r_1 = \frac{4}{1 + 0.4\cos\theta}, \quad r_2 = \frac{4}{1 - 0.4\sin\theta}$$

(c) Use a graphing utility to verify your results in part (b).

72. ***Exploration*** The equation

$$r = \frac{ep}{1 \pm e\sin\theta}$$

is the equation of an ellipse with $e < 1$. What happens to the lengths of both the major axis and the minor axis when the value of e remains fixed and the value of p changes? Use an example to explain your reasoning.

Skills Review

In Exercises 73–78, solve the trigonometric equation.

73. $4\sqrt{3}\tan\theta - 3 = 1$

74. $6\cos x - 2 = 1$

75. $12\sin^2\theta = 9$

76. $9\csc^2 x \quad 10 = 2$

77. $2\cot x = 5\cos\dfrac{\pi}{2}$

78. $\sqrt{2}\sec\theta = 2\csc\dfrac{\pi}{4}$

In Exercises 79–82, find the exact value of the trigonometric function given that u and v are in Quadrant IV and $\sin u = -\frac{3}{5}$ and $\cos v = 1/\sqrt{2}$.

79. $\cos(u + v)$

80. $\sin(u + v)$

81. $\cos(u - v)$

82. $\sin(u - v)$

In Exercises 83 and 84, find the exact values of $\sin 2u$, $\cos 2u$, and $\tan 2u$ using the double-angle formulas.

83. $\sin u = \dfrac{4}{5}, \ \dfrac{\pi}{2} < u < \pi$

84. $\tan u = -\sqrt{3}, \ \dfrac{3\pi}{2} < u < 2\pi$

In Exercises 85–88, find a formula for a_n for the arithmetic sequence.

85. $a_1 = 0, d = -\frac{1}{4}$

86. $a_1 = 13, d = 3$

87. $a_3 = 27, a_8 = 72$

88. $a_1 = 5, a_4 = 9.5$

In Exercises 89–92, evaluate the expression. Do not use a calculator.

89. ${}_{12}C_9$

90. ${}_{18}C_{16}$

91. ${}_{10}P_3$

92. ${}_{29}P_2$

10 Chapter Summary

What did you learn?

	Review Exercises
Section 10.1	
☐ Find the inclination of a line *(p. 728)*.	1–4
☐ Find the angle between two lines *(p. 729)*.	5–8
☐ Find the distance between a point and a line *(p. 730)*.	9, 10
Section 10.2	
☐ Recognize a conic as the intersection of a plane and a double-napped cone *(p. 735)*.	11, 12
☐ Write equations of parabolas in standard form and graph parabolas *(p. 736)*.	13–16
☐ Use the reflective property of parabolas to solve real-life problems *(p. 738)*.	17–20
Section 10.3	
☐ Write equations of ellipses in standard form and graph ellipses *(p. 744)*.	21–24
☐ Use properties of ellipses to model and solve real-life problems *(p. 748)*.	25, 26
☐ Find the eccentricities of ellipses *(p. 748)*.	27–30
Section 10.4	
☐ Write equations of hyperbolas in standard form *(p. 753)*.	31–34
☐ Find asymptotes of and graph hyperbolas *(p. 755)*.	35–38
☐ Use properties of hyperbolas to solve real-life problems *(p. 758)*.	39, 40
☐ Classify conics from their general equations *(p. 759)*.	41–44
Section 10.5	
☐ Rotate the coordinate axes to eliminate the *xy*-term in equations of conics *(p. 763)*.	45–48
☐ Use the discriminant to classify conics *(p. 767)*.	49–52
Section 10.6	
☐ Evaluate sets of parametric equations for given values of the parameter *(p. 771)*.	53, 54
☐ Sketch curves that are represented by sets of parametric equations *(p. 772)*. and rewrite the equations as single rectangular equations *(p. 773)*.	55–60
☐ Find sets of parametric equations for graphs *(p. 774)*.	61–64
Section 10.7	
☐ Plot points on the polar coordinate system *(p. 779)*.	65–68
☐ Convert points from rectangular to polar form and vice versa *(p. 780)*.	69–76
☐ Convert equations from rectangular to polar form and vice versa *(p. 782)*.	77–88
Section 10.8	
☐ Graph polar equations by point plotting *(p. 785)*.	89–98
☐ Use symmetry *(p. 786)*, zeros, and maximum *r*-values *(p. 787)* to sketch graphs of polar equations.	89–98
☐ Recognize special polar graphs *(p. 789)*.	99–102
Section 10.9	
☐ Define conics in terms of eccentricity and write and graph equations of conics in polar form *(p. 793)*.	103–110
☐ Use equations of conics in polar form to model real-life problems *(p. 796)*.	111, 112

10 Review Exercises

10.1 In Exercises 1–4, find the inclination θ (in radians and degrees) of the line with the given characteristics.

1. Passes through the points $(-1, 2)$ and $(2, 5)$
2. Passes through the points $(3, 4)$ and $(-2, 7)$
3. Equation: $y = 2x + 4$
4. Equation: $6x - 7y - 5 = 0$

In Exercises 5–8, find the angle θ (in radians and degrees) between the lines.

5. $4x + y = 2$
   $-5x + y = -1$

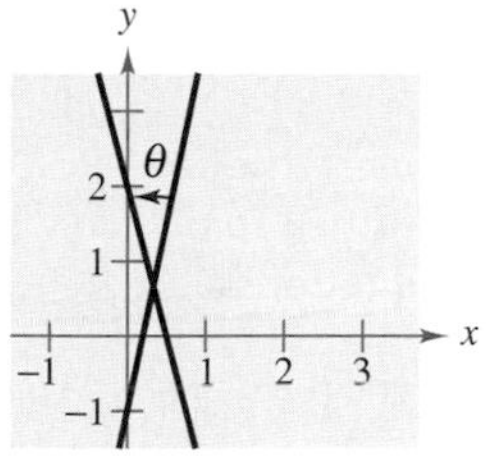

6. $-5x + 3y = 3$
   $-2x + 3y = 1$

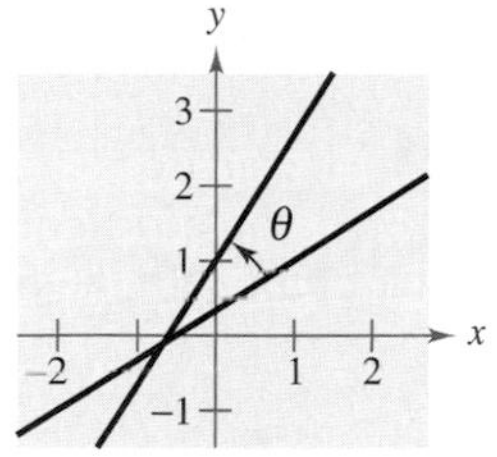

7. $2x - 7y = 8$
   $0.4x + y = 0$

8. $0.02x + 0.07y = 0.18$
   $0.09x - 0.04y = 0.17$

In Exercises 9 and 10, find the distance between the point and the line.

	Point	*Line*
9.	$(1, 2)$	$x - y - 3 = 0$
10.	$(0, 4)$	$x + 2y - 2 = 0$

10.2 In Exercises 11 and 12, state what type of conic is formed by the intersection of the plane and the double-napped cone.

11.

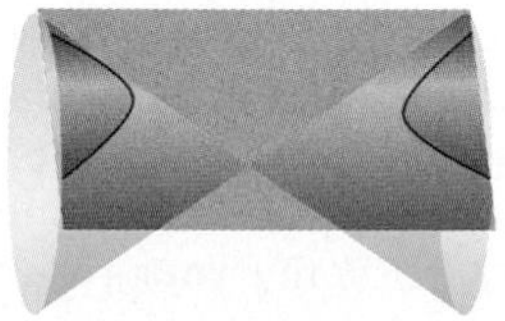

12.

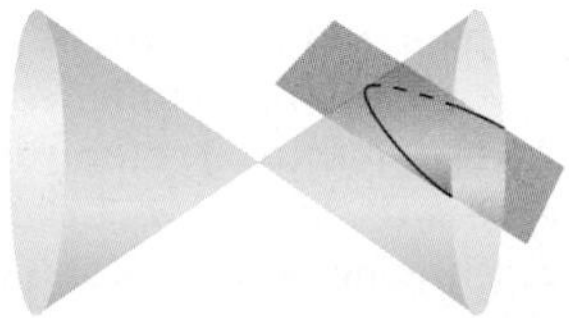

In Exercises 13–16, find the standard form of the equation of the parabola with the given characteristics. Then graph the parabola.

13. Vertex: $(0, 0)$
    Focus: $(4, 0)$

14. Vertex: $(2, 0)$
    Focus: $(0, 0)$

15. Vertex: $(0, 2)$
    Directrix: $x = -3$

16. Vertex: $(2, 2)$
    Directrix: $y = 0$

In Exercises 17 and 18, find an equation of the tangent line to the parabola at the given point, and find the x-intercept of the line.

17. $x^2 = -2y,\ (2, -2)$
18. $x^2 = -2y,\ (-4, -8)$

19. ***Architecture*** A parabolic archway is 12 meters high at the vertex. At a height of 10 meters, the width of the archway is 8 meters (see figure). How wide is the archway at ground level?

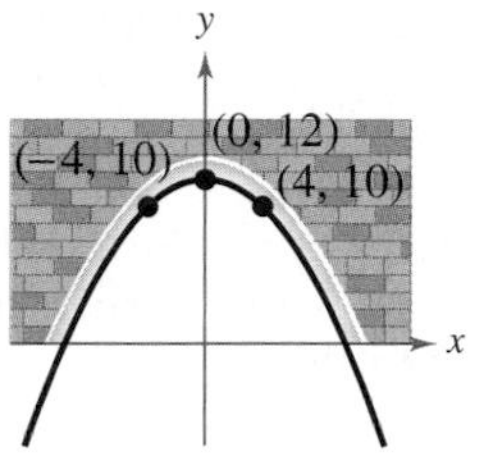

FIGURE FOR 19

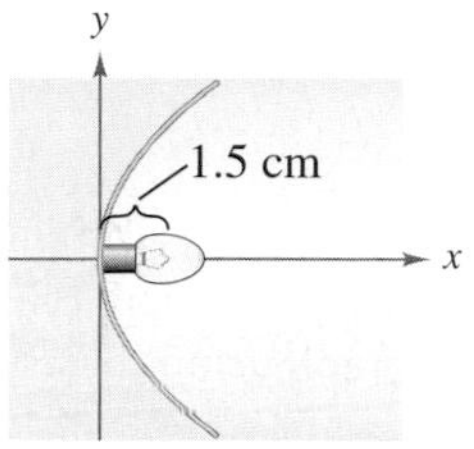

FIGURE FOR 20

20. ***Flashlight*** The light bulb in a flashlight is at the focus of its parabolic reflector, 1.5 centimeters from the vertex of the reflector (see figure). Write an equation of a cross section of the flashlight's reflector with its focus on the positive x-axis and its vertex at the origin.

10.3 In Exercises 21–24, find the standard form of the equation of the ellipse with the given characteristics. Then graph the ellipse.

21. Vertices: $(-3, 0), (7, 0)$; foci: $(0, 0), (4, 0)$
22. Vertices: $(2, 0), (2, 4)$; foci: $(2, 1), (2, 3)$
23. Vertices: $(0, 1), (4, 1)$; endpoints of the minor axis: $(2, 0), (2, 2)$
24. Vertices: $(-4, -1), (-4, 11)$; endpoints of the minor axis: $(-6, 5), (-2, 5)$

25. ***Architecture*** A semielliptical archway is to be formed over the entrance to an estate. The arch is to be set on pillars that are 10 feet apart and is to have a height (atop the pillars) of 4 feet. Where should the foci be placed in order to sketch the arch?

26. ***Wading Pool*** You are building a wading pool that is in the shape of an ellipse. Your plans give an equation for the elliptical shape of the pool measured in feet as

$$\frac{x^2}{324} + \frac{y^2}{196} = 1.$$

Find the longest distance across the pool, the shortest distance, and the distance between the foci.

In Exercises 27–30, find the center, vertices, foci, and eccentricity of the ellipse.

27. $\dfrac{(x+2)^2}{81} + \dfrac{(y-1)^2}{100} = 1$

28. $\dfrac{(x-5)^2}{1} + \dfrac{(y+3)^2}{36} = 1$

29. $16x^2 + 9y^2 - 32x + 72y + 16 = 0$

30. $4x^2 + 25y^2 + 16x - 150y + 141 = 0$

10.4 In Exercises 31–34, find the standard form of the equation of the hyperbola with the given characteristics.

31. Vertices: $(0, \pm 1)$; foci: $(0, \pm 3)$

32. Vertices: $(2, 2), (-2, 2)$; foci: $(4, 2), (-4, 2)$

33. Foci: $(0, 0), (8, 0)$; asymptotes: $y = \pm 2(x - 4)$

34. Foci: $(3, \pm 2)$; asymptotes: $y = \pm 2(x - 3)$

In Exercises 35–38, find the center, vertices, foci, and the equations of the asymptotes of the hyperbola, and sketch its graph using the asymptotes as an aid.

35. $\dfrac{(x-3)^2}{16} - \dfrac{(y+5)^2}{4} = 1$

36. $\dfrac{(y-1)^2}{4} - x^2 = 1$

37. $9x^2 - 16y^2 - 18x - 32y - 151 = 0$

38. $-4x^2 + 25y^2 - 8x + 150y + 121 = 0$

39. ***LORAN*** Radio transmitting station A is located 200 miles east of transmitting station B. A ship is in an area to the north and 40 miles west of station A. Synchronized radio pulses transmitted at 186,000 miles per second by the two stations are received 0.0005 second sooner from station A than from station B. How far north is the ship?

40. ***Locating an Explosion*** Two of your friends live 4 miles apart and on the same "east-west" street, and you live halfway between them. You are having a three-way phone conversation when you hear an explosion. Six seconds later, your friend to the east hears the explosion, and your friend to the west hears it 8 seconds after you do. Find equations of two hyperbolas that would locate the explosion. (Assume that the coordinate system is measured in feet and that sound travels at 1100 feet per second.)

In Exercises 41–44, classify the graph of the equation as a circle, a parabola, an ellipse, or a hyperbola.

41. $5x^2 - 2y^2 + 10x - 4y + 17 = 0$

42. $-4y^2 + 5x + 3y + 7 = 0$

43. $3x^2 + 2y^2 - 12x + 12y + 29 = 0$

44. $4x^2 + 4y^2 - 4x + 8y - 11 = 0$

10.5 In Exercises 45–48, rotate the axes to eliminate the *xy*-term in the equation. Then write the equation in standard form. Sketch the graph of the resulting equation, showing both sets of axes.

45. $xy - 4 = 0$

46. $x^2 - 10xy + y^2 + 1 = 0$

47. $5x^2 - 2xy + 5y^2 - 12 = 0$

48. $4x^2 + 8xy + 4y^2 + 7\sqrt{2}x + 9\sqrt{2}y = 0$

In Exercises 49–52, (a) use the discriminant to classify the graph, (b) use the Quadratic Formula to solve for *y*, and (c) use a graphing utility to graph the equation.

49. $16x^2 - 24xy + 9y^2 - 30x - 40y = 0$

50. $13x^2 - 8xy + 7y^2 - 45 = 0$

51. $x^2 + y^2 + 2xy + 2\sqrt{2}x - 2\sqrt{2}y + 2 = 0$

52. $x^2 - 10xy + y^2 + 1 = 0$

10.6 In Exercises 53 and 54, complete the table for each set of parametric equations. Plot the points (x, y) and sketch a graph of the parametric equations.

53. $x = 3t - 2$ and $y = 7 - 4t$

t	-3	-2	-1	0	1	2	3
x							
y							

54. $x = \dfrac{1}{5}t$ and $y = \dfrac{4}{t-1}$

t	-1	0	2	3	4	5
x						
y						

In Exercises 55–60, (a) sketch the curve represented by the parametric equations (indicate the orientation of the curve) and (b) eliminate the parameter and write the corresponding rectangular equation whose graph represents the curve. Adjust the domain of the resulting rectangular equation, if necessary. (c) Verify your result with a graphing utility.

55. $x = 2t$
$y = 4t$

56. $x = 1 + 4t$
$y = 2 - 3t$

57. $x = t^2$
$y = \sqrt{t}$

58. $x = t + 4$
$y = t^2$

59. $x = 6\cos\theta$
$y = 6\sin\theta$

60. $x = 3 + 3\cos\theta$
$y = 2 + 5\sin\theta$

61. Find a parametric representation of the circle with center $(5, 4)$ and radius 6.

62. Find a parametric representation of the ellipse with center $(-3, 4)$, major axis horizontal and eight units in length, and minor axis six units in length.

63. Find a parametric representation of the hyperbola with vertices $(0, \pm 4)$ and foci $(0, \pm 5)$.

64. ***Involute of a Circle*** The *involute* of a circle is described by the endpoint P of a string that is held taut as it is unwound from a spool (see figure). The spool does not rotate. Show that a parametric representation of the involute of a circle is

$$x = r(\cos\theta + \theta\sin\theta)$$

$$y = r(\sin\theta - \theta\cos\theta).$$

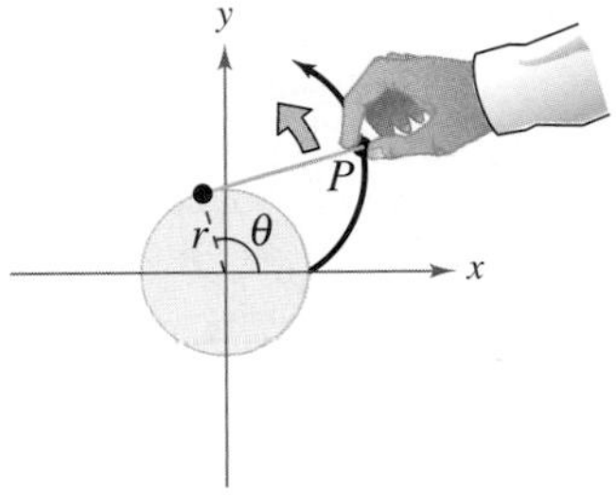

10.7 **In Exercises 65–68, plot the point given in polar coordinates and find two additional polar representations of the point, using $-2\pi < \theta < 2\pi$.**

65. $\left(2, \dfrac{\pi}{4}\right)$

66. $\left(-5, -\dfrac{\pi}{3}\right)$

67. $(-7, 4.19)$

68. $(\sqrt{3}, 2.62)$

In Exercises 69–72, a point in polar coordinates is given. Convert the point to rectangular coordinates.

69. $\left(-1, \dfrac{\pi}{3}\right)$ **70.** $\left(2, \dfrac{5\pi}{4}\right)$

71. $\left(3, \dfrac{3\pi}{4}\right)$ **72.** $\left(0, \dfrac{\pi}{2}\right)$

In Exercises 73–76, a point in rectangular coordinates is given. Convert the point to polar coordinates.

73. $(0, 2)$

74. $(-\sqrt{5}, \sqrt{5})$

75. $(4, 6)$

76. $(3, -4)$

In Exercises 77–82, convert the rectangular equation to polar form.

77. $x^2 + y^2 = 49$ **78.** $x^2 + y^2 = 20$

79. $x^2 + y^2 - 6y = 0$ **80.** $x^2 + y^2 - 4x = 0$

81. $xy = 5$ **82.** $xy = -2$

In Exercises 83–88, convert the polar equation to rectangular form.

83. $r = 5$ **84.** $r = 12$

85. $r = 3\cos\theta$ **86.** $r = 8\sin\theta$

87. $r^2 = \sin\theta$ **88.** $r^2 = \cos 2\theta$

10.8 **In Exercises 89–98, determine the symmetry of r, the maximum value of $|r|$, and any zeros of r. Then sketch the graph of the polar equation (plot additional points if necessary).**

89. $r = 4$ **90.** $r = 11$

91. $r = 4\sin 2\theta$ **92.** $r = \cos 5\theta$

93. $r = -2(1 + \cos\theta)$ **94.** $r = 3 - 4\cos\theta$

95. $r = 2 + 6\sin\theta$ **96.** $r = 5 - 5\cos\theta$

97. $r = -3\cos 2\theta$ **98.** $r = \cos 2\theta$

In Exercises 99–102, identify the type of polar graph and use a graphing utility to graph the equation.

99. $r = 3(2 - \cos\theta)$

100. $r = 3(1 - 2\cos\theta)$

101. $r = 4\cos 3\theta$

102. $r^2 = 9\cos 2\theta$

10.9 **In Exercises 103–106, identify the conic and sketch its graph.**

103. $r = \dfrac{1}{1 + 2\sin\theta}$

104. $r = \dfrac{2}{1 + \sin\theta}$

105. $r = \dfrac{4}{5 - 3\cos\theta}$

106. $r = \dfrac{16}{4 + 5\cos\theta}$

In Exercises 107–110, find a polar equation of the conic with its focus at the pole.

107. Parabola Vertex: $(2, \pi)$

108. Parabola Vertex: $(2, \pi/2)$

109. Ellipse Vertices: $(5, 0), (1, \pi)$

110. Hyperbola Vertices: $(1, 0), (7, 0)$

111. ***Explorer 18*** On November 26, 1963, the United States launched Explorer 18. Its low and high points above the surface of Earth were 119 miles and 122,800 miles, respectively (see figure). The center of Earth was at one focus of the orbit. Find the polar equation of the orbit and find the distance between the surface of Earth (assume Earth has a radius of 4000 miles) and the satellite when $\theta = \pi/3$.

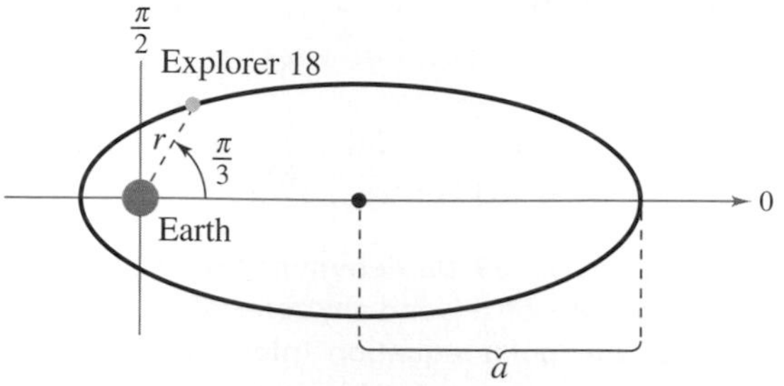

112. ***Asteroid*** An asteroid takes a parabolic path with Earth as its focus. It is about 6,000,000 miles from Earth at its closest approach. Write the polar equation of the path of the asteroid with its vertex at $\theta = \pi/2$. Find the distance between the asteroid and Earth when $\theta = -\pi/3$.

Synthesis

True or False? **In Exercises 113–116, determine whether the statement is true or false. Justify your answer.**

113. When $B = 0$ in an equation of the form

$$Ax^2 + Bxy + Cy^2 + Dx + Ey + F = 0$$

the graph of the equation can be a parabola only if $C = 0$ also.

114. The graph of $\frac{1}{4}x^2 - y^4 = 1$ is a hyperbola.

115. Only one set of parametric equations can represent the line $y = 3 - 2x$.

116. There is a unique polar coordinate representation of each point in the plane.

117. Consider an ellipse with the major axis horizontal and 10 units in length. The number b in the standard form of the equation of the ellipse must be less than what real number? Explain the change in the shape of the ellipse as b approaches this number.

118. The graph of the parametric equations $x = 2 \sec t$ and $y = 3 \tan t$ is shown in the figure. How would the graph change for the equations $x = 2 \sec(-t)$ and $y = 3 \tan(-t)$?

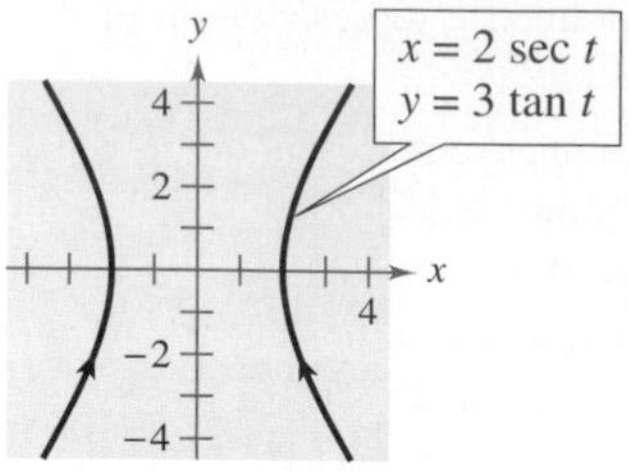

FIGURE FOR 118

119. A moving object is modeled by the parametric equations $x = 4 \cos t$ and $y = 3 \sin t$, where t is time (see figure). How would the path change for the following?

(a) $x = 4 \cos 2t, \quad y = 3 \sin 2t$

(b) $x = 5 \cos t, \quad y = 3 \sin t$

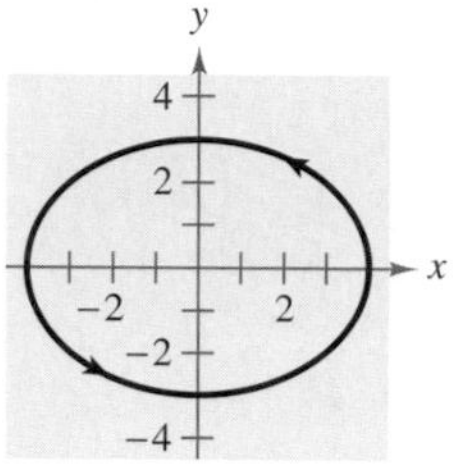

120. Identify the type of symmetry each of the following polar points has with the point in the figure.

(a) $\left(-4, \frac{\pi}{6}\right)$ (b) $\left(4, -\frac{\pi}{6}\right)$ (c) $\left(-4, -\frac{\pi}{6}\right)$

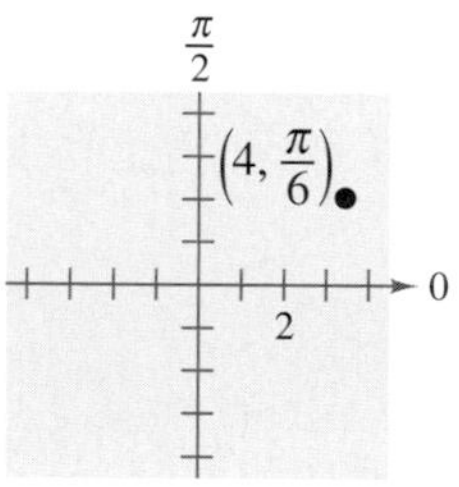

121. What is the relationship between the graphs of the rectangular and polar equations?

(a) $x^2 + y^2 = 25, \quad r = 5$ (b) $x - y = 0, \quad \theta = \frac{\pi}{4}$

122. ***Geometry*** The area of the ellipse in the figure is twice the area of the circle. What is the length of the major axis? (*Hint:* The area of an ellipse is $A = \pi ab$.)

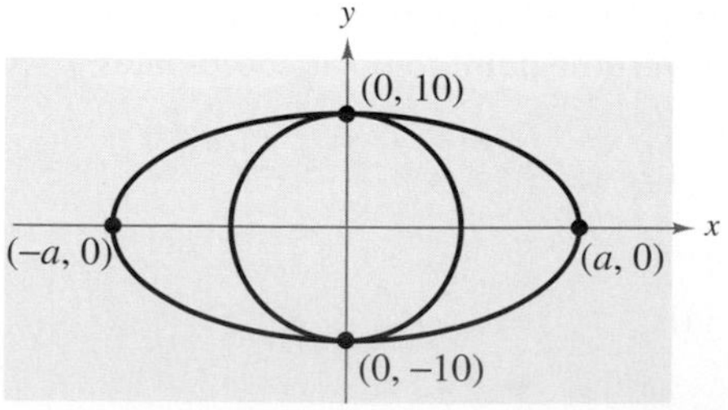

10 Chapter Test

Take this test as you would take a test in class. When you are finished, check your work against the answers given in the back of the book.

1. Find the inclination of the line $2x - 7y + 3 = 0$.
2. Find the angle between the lines $3x + 2y - 4 = 0$ and $4x - y + 6 = 0$.
3. Find the distance between the point $(7, 5)$ and the line $y = 5 - x$.

In Exercises 4–7, classify the conic and write the equation in standard form. Identify the center, vertices, foci, and asymptotes (if applicable). Then sketch the graph of the conic.

4. $y^2 - 4x + 4 = 0$
5. $x^2 - 4y^2 - 4x = 0$
6. $9x^2 + 16y^2 + 54x - 32y - 47 = 0$
7. $2x^2 + 2y^2 - 8x - 4y + 9 = 0$

8. Find the standard form of the equation of the parabola with vertex $(3, -2)$, with a vertical axis, and passing through the point $(0, 4)$.
9. Find the standard form of the equation of the hyperbola with foci $(0, 0)$ and $(0, 4)$ and asymptotes $y = \pm\frac{1}{2}x + 2$.
10. (a) Determine the number of degrees the axis must be rotated to eliminate the xy-term of the conic $x^2 + 6xy + y^2 - 6 = 0$.

    (b) Graph the conic from part (a) and use a graphing utility to confirm your result.
11. Sketch the curve represented by the parametric equations $x = 2 + 3 \cos \theta$ and $y = 2 \sin \theta$. Eliminate the parameter and write the corresponding rectangular equation.
12. Find a set of parametric equations of the line passing through the points $(2, -3)$ and $(6, 4)$. (There are many correct answers.)
13. Convert the polar coordinate $\left(-2, \frac{5\pi}{6}\right)$ to rectangular form.
14. Convert the rectangular coordinate $(2, -2)$ to polar form and find two additional polar representations of this point.
15. Convert the rectangular equation $x^2 + y^2 - 4y = 0$ to polar form.

In Exercises 16–19, sketch the graph of the polar equation. Identify the type of graph.

16. $r = \dfrac{4}{1 + \cos \theta}$
17. $r = \dfrac{4}{2 + \cos \theta}$
18. $r = 2 + 3 \sin \theta$
19. $r = 3 \sin 2\theta$

20. Find a polar equation of the ellipse with focus at the pole, eccentricity $e = \frac{1}{4}$, and directrix $y = 4$.
21. A straight road rises with an inclination of 0.15 radian from the horizontal. Find the slope of the road and the change in elevation over a one-mile stretch of the road.
22. A baseball is hit at a point 3 feet above the ground toward the left field fence. The fence is 10 feet high and 375 feet from home plate. The path of the baseball can be modeled by the parametric equations $x = (115 \cos \theta)t$ and $y = 3 + (115 \sin \theta)t - 16t^2$. Will the baseball go over the fence if it is hit at an angle of $\theta = 30°$? Will the baseball go over the fence if $\theta = 35°$?

Proofs in Mathematics

Inclination and Slope *(p. 728)*

If a nonvertical line has inclination θ and slope m, then $m = \tan\theta$.

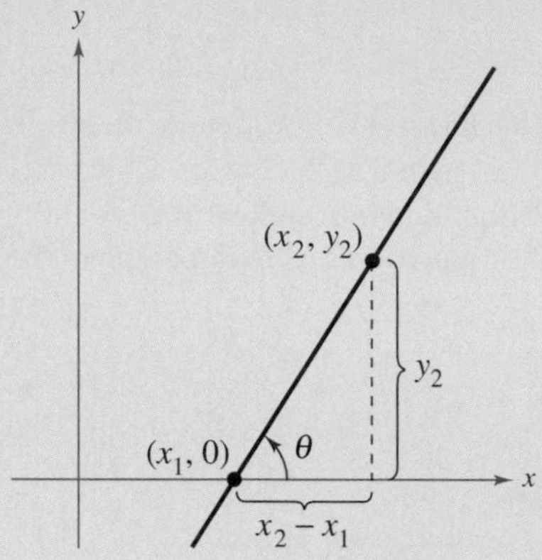

Proof

If $m = 0$, the line is horizontal and $\theta = 0$. So, the result is true for horizontal lines because $m = 0 = \tan 0$.

If the line has a positive slope, it will intersect the x-axis. Label this point $(x_1, 0)$, as shown in the figure. If (x_2, y_2) is a second point on the line, the slope is

$$m = \frac{y_2 - 0}{x_2 - x_1} = \frac{y_2}{x_2 - x_1} = \tan\theta.$$

The case in which the line has a negative slope can be proved in a similar manner.

Distance Between a Point and a Line *(p. 730)*

The distance between the point (x_1, y_1) and the line $Ax + By + C = 0$ is

$$d = \frac{|Ax_1 + By_1 + C|}{\sqrt{A^2 + B^2}}.$$

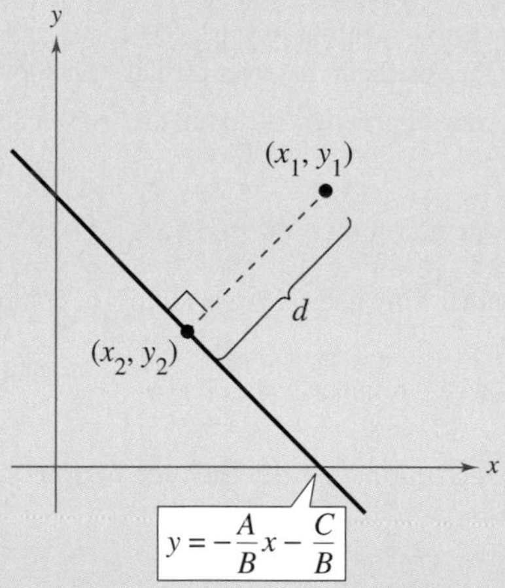

Proof

For simplicity's sake, assume that the given line is neither horizontal nor vertical (see figure). By writing the equation $Ax + By + C = 0$ in slope-intercept form

$$y = -\frac{A}{B}x - \frac{C}{B}$$

you can see that the line has a slope of $m = -A/B$. So, the slope of the line passing through (x_1, y_1) and perpendicular to the given line is B/A, and its equation is $y - y_1 = (B/A)(x - x_1)$. These two lines intersect at the point (x_2, y_2), where

$$x_2 = \frac{B(Bx_1 - Ay_1) - AC}{A^2 + B^2} \quad \text{and} \quad y_2 = \frac{A(-Bx_1 + Ay_1) - BC}{A^2 + B^2}.$$

Finally, the distance between (x_1, y_1) and (x_2, y_2) is

$$\begin{aligned} d &= \sqrt{(x_2 - x_1)^2 + (y_2 - y_1)^2} \\ &= \sqrt{\left(\frac{B^2x_1 - ABy_1 - AC}{A^2 + B^2} - x_1\right)^2 + \left(\frac{-ABx_1 + A^2y_1 - BC}{A^2 + B^2} - y_1\right)^2} \\ &= \sqrt{\frac{A^2(Ax_1 + By_1 + C)^2 + B^2(Ax_1 + By_1 + C)^2}{(A^2 + B^2)^2}} \\ &= \frac{|Ax_1 + By_1 + C|}{\sqrt{A^2 + B^2}}. \end{aligned}$$

Parabolic Paths

There are many natural occurrences of parabolas in real life. For instance, the famous astronomer Galileo discovered in the 17th century that an object that is projected upward and obliquely to the pull of gravity travels in a parabolic path. Examples of this are the center of gravity of a jumping dolphin and the path of water molecules in a drinking fountain.

Standard Equation of a Parabola *(p. 736)*

(p. 736)

The standard form of the equation of a parabola with vertex at (h, k) is as follows.

$(x - h)^2 = 4p(y - k), \quad p \neq 0$ — Vertical axis, directrix: $y = k - p$

$(y - k)^2 = 4p(x - h), \quad p \neq 0$ — Horizontal axis, directrix: $x = h - p$

The focus lies on the axis p units (*directed distance*) from the vertex. If the vertex is at the origin $(0, 0)$, the equation takes one of the following forms.

$x^2 = 4py$ — Vertical axis

$y^2 = 4px$ — Horizontal axis

Proof

For the case in which the directrix is parallel to the x-axis and the focus lies above the vertex, as shown in the top figure, if (x, y) is any point on the parabola, then, by definition, it is equidistant from the focus $(h, k + p)$ and the directrix $y = k - p$. So, you have

$$\sqrt{(x - h)^2 + [y - (k + p)]^2} = y - (k - p)$$

$$(x - h)^2 + [y - (k + p)]^2 = [y - (k - p)]^2$$

$$(x - h)^2 + y^2 - 2y(k + p) + (k + p)^2 = y^2 - 2y(k - p) + (k - p)^2$$

$$(x - h)^2 + y^2 - 2ky - 2py + k^2 + 2pk + p^2 = y^2 - 2ky + 2py + k^2 - 2pk + p^2$$

$$(x - h)^2 - 2py + 2pk = 2py - 2pk$$

$$(x - h)^2 = 4p(y - k).$$

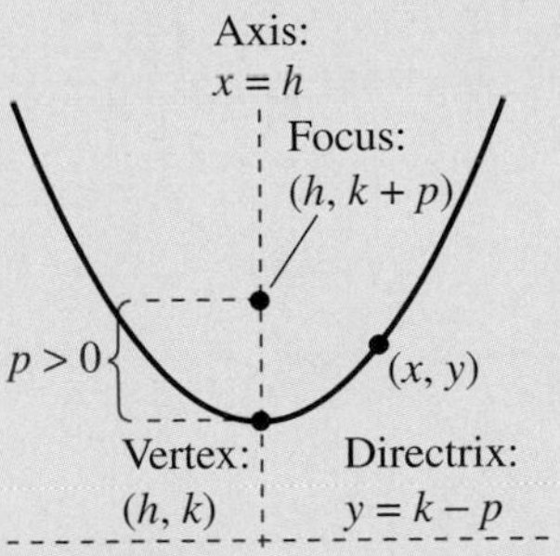

Parabola with vertical axis

For the case in which the directrix is parallel to the y-axis and the focus lies to the right of the vertex, as shown in the bottom figure, if (x, y) is any point on the parabola, then, by definition, it is equidistant from the focus $(h + p, k)$ and the directrix $x = h - p$. So, you have

$$\sqrt{[x - (h + p)]^2 + (y - k)^2} = x - (h - p)$$

$$[x - (h + p)]^2 + (y - k)^2 = [x - (h - p)]^2$$

$$x^2 - 2x(h + p) + (h + p)^2 + (y - k)^2 = x^2 - 2x(h - p) + (h - p)^2$$

$$x^2 - 2hx - 2px + h^2 + 2ph + p^2 + (y - k)^2 = x^2 - 2hx + 2px + h^2 - 2ph + p^2$$

$$-2px + 2ph + (y - k)^2 = 2px - 2ph$$

$$(y - k)^2 = 4p(x - h).$$

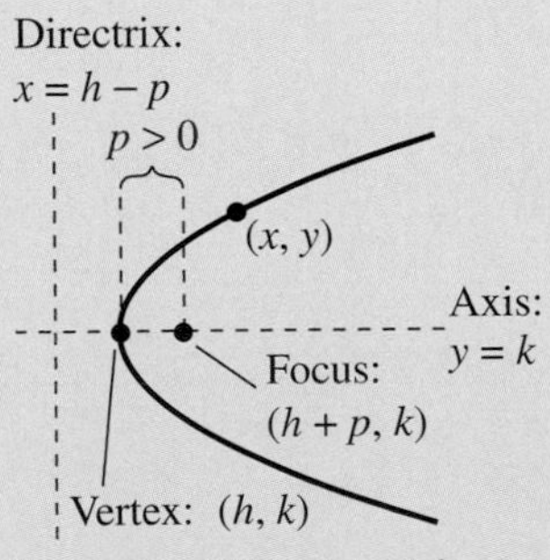

Parabola with horizontal axis

Note that if a parabola is centered at the origin, then the two equations above would simplify to $x^2 = 4py$ and $y^2 = 4px$, respectively.

Polar Equations of Conics *(p. 793)*

The graph of a polar equation of the form

1. $r = \dfrac{ep}{1 \pm e \cos \theta}$

or

2. $r = \dfrac{ep}{1 \pm e \sin \theta}$

is a conic, where $e > 0$ is the eccentricity and $|p|$ is the distance between the focus (pole) and the directrix.

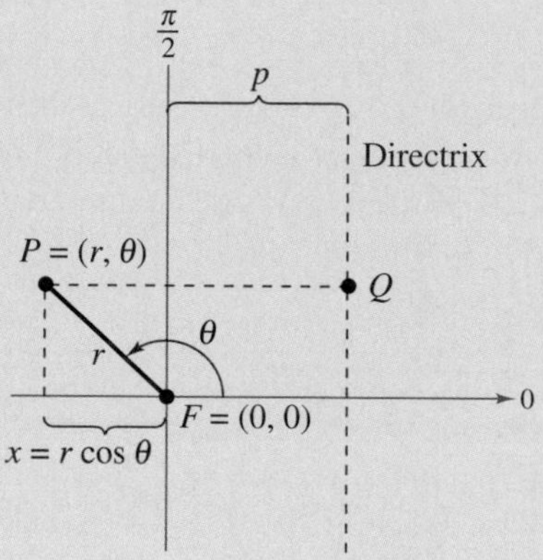

Proof

A proof for $r = ep/(1 + e \cos \theta)$ with $p > 0$ is shown here. The proofs of the other cases are similar. In the figure, consider a vertical directrix, p units to the right of the focus $F = (0, 0)$. If $P = (r, \theta)$ is a point on the graph of

$$r = \frac{ep}{1 + e \cos \theta}$$

the distance between P and the directrix is

$$\begin{aligned} PQ &= |p - x| \\ &= |p - r \cos \theta| \\ &= \left| p - \left(\frac{ep}{1 + e \cos \theta} \right) \cos \theta \right| \\ &= \left| p \left(1 - \frac{e \cos \theta}{1 + e \cos \theta} \right) \right| \\ &= \left| \frac{p}{1 + e \cos \theta} \right| \\ &= \left| \frac{r}{e} \right|. \end{aligned}$$

Moreover, because the distance between P and the pole is simply $PF = |r|$, the ratio of PF to PQ is

$$\begin{aligned} \frac{PF}{PQ} &= \frac{|r|}{\left| \frac{r}{e} \right|} \\ &= |e| \\ &= e \end{aligned}$$

and, by definition, the graph of the equation must be a conic.

P.S. Problem Solving

This collection of thought-provoking and challenging exercises further explores and expands upon concepts learned in this chapter.

1. Several mountain climbers are located in a mountain pass between two peaks. The angles of elevation to the two peaks are 0.84 radian and 1.10 radians. A range finder shows that the distances to the peaks are 3250 feet and 6700 feet, respectively (see figure).

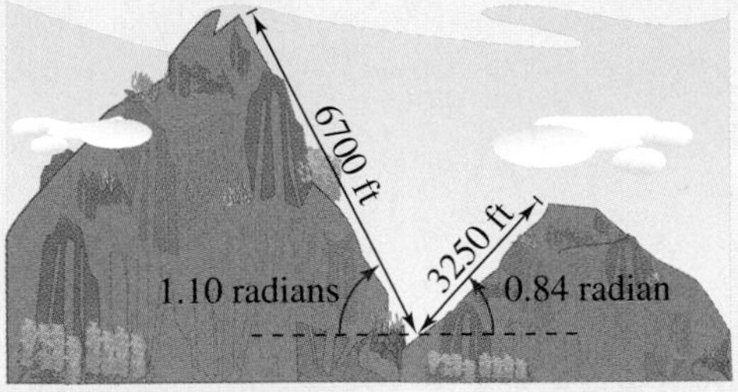

(a) Find the angle between the two lines of sight to the peaks.

(b) Approximate the amount of vertical climb that is necessary to reach the summit of each peak.

2. Statuary Hall is an elliptical room in the United States Capitol in Washington D.C. The room is also called the Whispering Gallery because a person standing at one focus of the room can hear even a whisper spoken by a person standing at the other focus. This occurs because any sound that is emitted from one focus of an ellipse will reflect off the side of the ellipse to the other focus. Statuary Hall is 46 feet wide and 97 feet long.

(a) Find an equation that models the shape of the room.

(b) How far apart are the two foci?

(c) What is the area of the floor of the room? (The area of an ellipse is $A = \pi ab$.)

3. Find the equation(s) of all parabolas that have the x-axis as the axis of symmetry and focus at the origin.

4. Find the area of the square inscribed in the ellipse below.

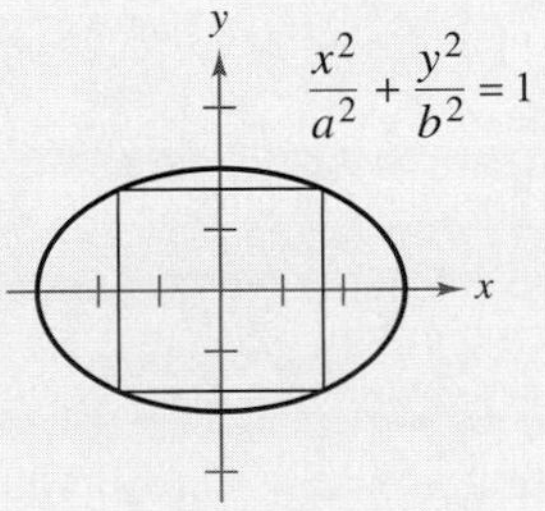

5. A tour boat travels between two islands that are 12 miles apart (see figure). For a trip between the islands, there is enough fuel for a 20-mile trip.

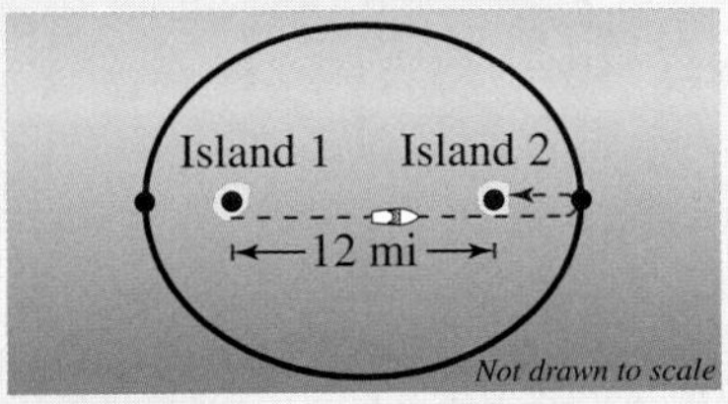

(a) Explain why the region in which the boat can travel is bounded by an ellipse.

(b) Let $(0, 0)$ represent the center of the ellipse. Find the coordinates of each island.

(c) The boat travels from one island, straight past the other island to the vertex of the ellipse, and back to the second island. How many miles does the boat travel? Use your answer to find the coordinates of the vertex.

(d) Use the results from parts (b) and (c) to write an equation for the ellipse that bounds the region in which the boat can travel.

6. Find an equation of the hyperbola such that for any point on the hyperbola, the difference between its distances from the points $(2, 2)$ and $(10, 2)$ is 6.

7. Prove that the graph of the equation

$$Ax^2 + Cy^2 + Dx + Ey + F = 0$$

is one of the following (except in degenerate cases).

Conic	*Condition*
(a) Circle	$A = C$
(b) Parabola	$A = 0$ or $C = 0$ (but not both)
(c) Ellipse	$AC > 0$
(d) Hyperbola	$AC < 0$

8. The following sets of parametric equations model projectile motion.

$$x = (v_0 \cos \theta)t \qquad x = (v_0 \cos \theta)t$$

$$y = (v_0 \sin \theta)t \qquad y = h + (v_0 \sin \theta)t - 16t^2$$

(a) Under what circumstances would you use each model?

(b) Eliminate the parameter for each set of equations.

(c) In which case is the path of the moving object not affected by a change in the velocity v? Explain.

9. As t increases, the ellipse given by the parametric equations

$$x = \cos t \text{ and } y = 2 \sin t$$

is traced out *counterclockwise*. Find a parametric representation for which the same ellipse is traced out *clockwise*.

10. A **hypocycloid** has the parametric equations

$$x = (a - b) \cos t + b \cos\left(\frac{a - b}{b} t\right)$$

and

$$y = (a - b) \sin t - b \sin\left(\frac{a - b}{b} t\right).$$

Use a graphing utility to graph the hypocycloid for each value of a and b. Describe each graph.

(a) $a = 2, b = 1$ (b) $a = 3, b = 1$

(c) $a = 4, b = 1$ (d) $a = 10, b = 1$

(e) $a = 3, b = 2$ (f) $a = 4, b = 3$

11. The curve given by the parametric equations

$$x = \frac{1 - t^2}{1 + t^2}$$

and

$$y = \frac{t(1 - t^2)}{1 + t^2}$$

is called a **strophoid.**

(a) Find a rectangular equation of the strophoid.

(b) Find a polar equation of the strophoid.

(c) Use a graphing utility to graph the strophoid.

12. The rose curves described in this chapter are of the form

$$r = a \cos n\theta \qquad \text{or} \qquad r = a \sin n\theta$$

where n is a positive integer that is greater than or equal to 2. Use a graphing utility to graph $r = a \cos n\theta$ and $r = a \sin n\theta$ for some noninteger values of n. Describe the graphs.

13. What conic section is represented by the polar equation

$$r = a \sin \theta + b \cos \theta?$$

14. The graph of the polar equation

$$r = e^{\cos \theta} - 2 \cos 4\theta + \sin^5\left(\frac{\theta}{12}\right)$$

is called the *butterfly curve*, as shown in the figure.

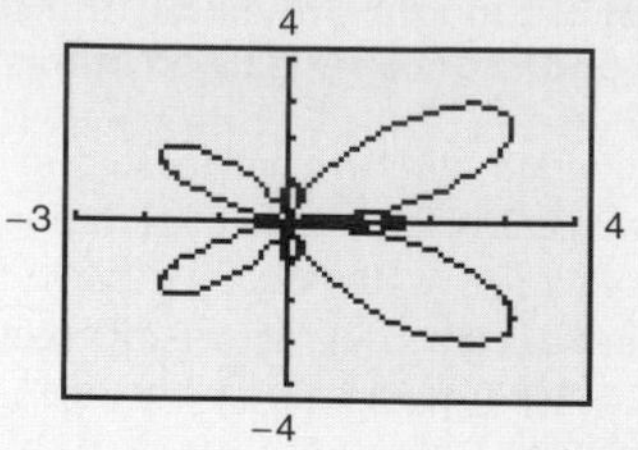

$r = e^{\cos \theta} - 2 \cos 4\theta + \sin^5\left(\frac{\theta}{12}\right)$

FIGURE FOR 14

(a) The graph above was produced using $0 \le \theta \le 2\pi$. Does this show the entire graph? Explain your reasoning.

(b) Approximate the maximum r-value of the graph. Does this value change if you use $0 \le \theta \le 4\pi$ instead of $0 \le \theta \le 2\pi$? Explain.

15. Use a graphing utility to graph the polar equation

$$r = \cos 5\theta + n \cos \theta$$

for $0 \le \theta \le \pi$ for the integers $n = -5$ to $n = 5$. As you graph these equations, you should see the graph change shape from a heart to a bell. Write a short paragraph explaining what values of n produce the heart portion of the curve and what values of n produce the bell portion.

16. The planets travel in elliptical orbits with the sun at one focus. The polar equation of the orbit of a planet with one focus at the pole and major axis of length $2a$ is

$$r = \frac{(1 - e^2)a}{1 - e \cos \theta}$$

where e is the eccentricity. The minimum distance (perihelion) from the sun to a planet is $r = a(1 - e)$ and the maximum distance (aphelion) is $r = a(1 + e)$. The length of the major axis for the planet Neptune is $a = 9.000 \times 10^9$ kilometers and the eccentricity is $e = 0.0086$. The length of the major axis for the planet Pluto is $a = 10.813 \times 10^9$ kilometers and the eccentricity is $e = 0.2488$.

(a) Find the polar equation of the orbit of each planet.

(b) Find the perihelion and aphelion distances for each planet.

(c) Use a graphing utility to graph the polar equation of each planet's orbit in the same viewing window.

(d) Do the orbits of the two planets intersect? Will the two planets ever collide? Why or why not?

(e) Is Pluto ever closer to the sun than Neptune? Why is Pluto called the ninth planet and Neptune the eighth planet?

Analytic Geometry in Three Dimensions

11

11.1 The Three-Dimensional Coordinate System
11.2 Vectors in Space
11.3 The Cross Product of Two Vectors
11.4 Lines and Planes in Space

The three-dimensional coordinate system is used in chemistry to help understand the structure of crystals. For example, isometric crystals are shaped like cubes

Arnold Fisher/Photo Researchers, Inc.

SELECTED APPLICATIONS

Three-dimensional analytic geometry concepts have many real-life applications. The applications listed below represent a small sample of the applications in this chapter.

- Crystals, Exercise 63, page 818
- Geography, Exercise 66, page 819
- Tension, Exercise 43, page 826
- Torque, Exercise 43, page 833
- Data Analysis: Milk Consumption, Exercise 47, page 842
- Mechanical Design, Exercise 48, page 842
- Moment of a Force, Exercise 12, page 849

11.1 The Three-Dimensional Coordinate System

What you should learn

- Plot points in the three-dimensional coordinate system.
- Find distances between points in space and find midpoints of line segments joining points in space.
- Write equations of spheres in standard form and find traces of surfaces in space.

Why you should learn it

The three-dimensional coordinate system can be used to graph equations that model surfaces in space, such as the spherical shape of Earth, as shown in Exercise 66 on page 819.

NASA

The Three-Dimensional Coordinate System

Recall that the Cartesian plane is determined by two perpendicular number lines called the x-axis and the y-axis. These axes, together with their point of intersection (the origin), allow you to develop a two-dimensional coordinate system for identifying points in a plane. To identify a point in space, you must introduce a third dimension to the model. The geometry of this three-dimensional model is called **solid analytic geometry.**

You can construct a **three-dimensional coordinate system** by passing a z-axis perpendicular to both the x- and y-axes at the origin. Figure 11.1 shows the positive portion of each coordinate axis. Taken as pairs, the axes determine three **coordinate planes:** the ***xy*-plane,** the ***xz*-plane,** and the ***yz*-plane.** These three coordinate planes separate the three-dimensional coordinate system into eight **octants.** The first octant is the one in which all three coordinates are positive. In this three-dimensional system, a point P in space is determined by an ordered triple (x, y, z), where x, y, and z are as follows.

$x =$ directed distance from yz-plane to P

$y =$ directed distance from xz-plane to P

$z =$ directed distance from xy-plane to P

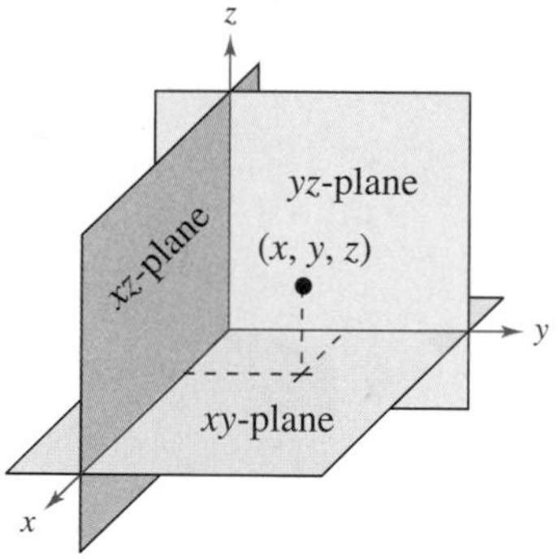

FIGURE 11.1

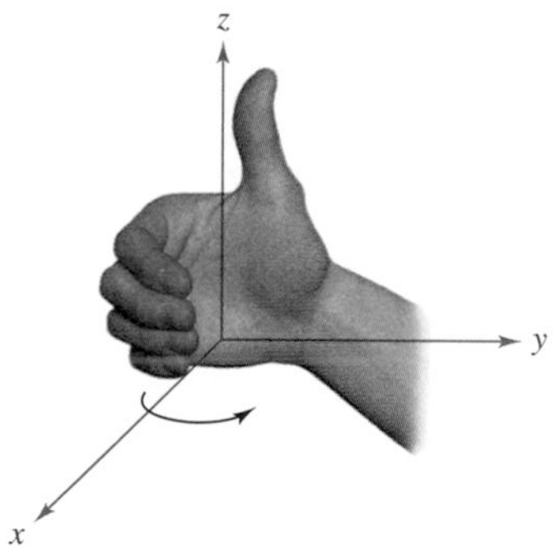

FIGURE 11.2

A three-dimensional coordinate system can have either a **left-handed** or a **right-handed** orientation. In this text, you will work exclusively with right-handed systems, as illustrated in Figure 11.2. In a right-handed system, Octants II, III, and IV are found by rotating counterclockwise around the positive z-axis. Octant V is vertically below Octant I. Octants VI, VII, and VIII are then found by rotating counterclockwise around the negative z-axis. See Figure 11.3.

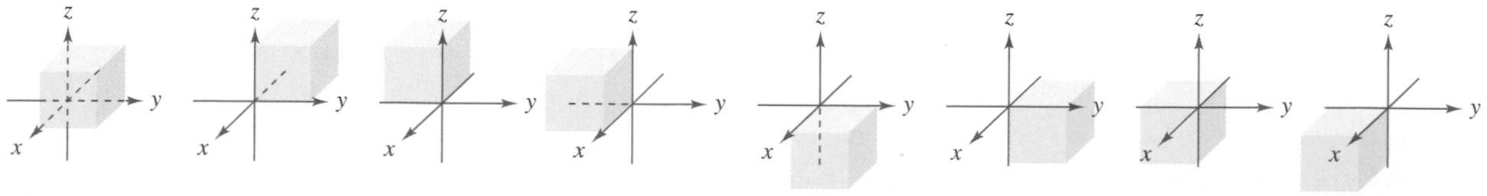

Octant I Octant II Octant III Octant IV Octant V Octant VI Octant VII Octant VIII

FIGURE 11.3

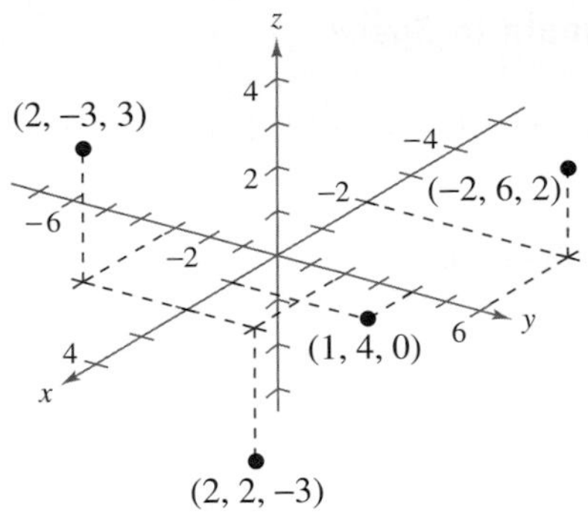

FIGURE 11.4

Example 1 Plotting Points in Space

Plot each point in space.

a. $(2, -3, 3)$ **b.** $(-2, 6, 2)$ **c.** $(1, 4, 0)$ **d.** $(2, 2, -3)$

Solution

To plot the point $(2, -3, 3)$, notice that $x = 2$, $y = -3$, and $z = 3$. To help visualize the point, locate the point $(2, -3)$ in the xy-plane (denoted by a cross in Figure 11.4). The point $(2, -3, 3)$ lies three units above the cross. The other three points are also shown in Figure 11.4.

CHECKPOINT Now try Exercise 5.

The Distance and Midpoint Formulas

Many of the formulas established for the two-dimensional coordinate system can be extended to three dimensions. For example, to find the distance between two points in space, you can use the Pythagorean Theorem twice, as shown in Figure 11.5. Note that $a = x_2 - x_1$, $b = y_2 - y_1$, and $c = z_2 - z_1$.

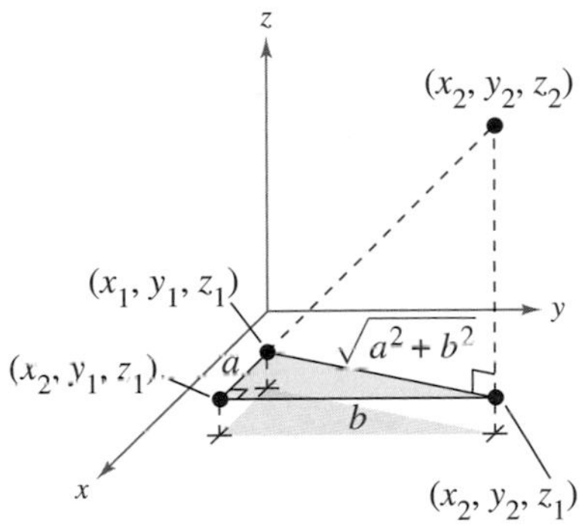

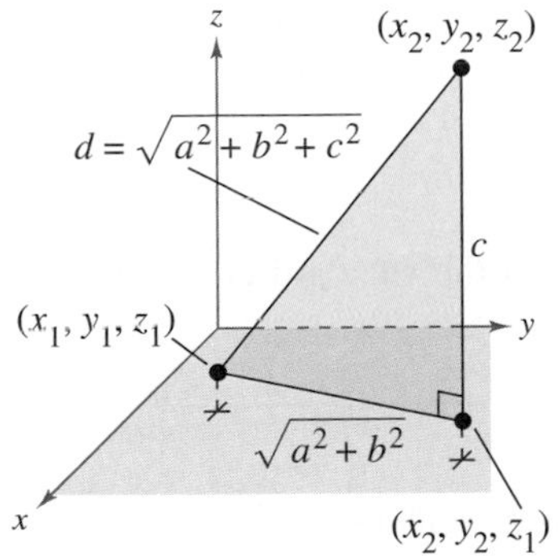

FIGURE 11.5

Distance Formula in Space

The distance between the points (x_1, y_1, z_1) and (x_2, y_2, z_2) given by the Distance Formula in Space is

$$d = \sqrt{(x_2 - x_1)^2 + (y_2 - y_1)^2 + (z_2 - z_1)^2}.$$

Example 2 Finding the Distance Between Two Points in Space

Find the distance between $(1, 0, 2)$ and $(2, 4, -3)$.

Solution

$$d = \sqrt{(x_2 - x_1)^2 + (y_2 - y_1)^2 + (z_2 - z_1)^2} \quad \text{Distance Formula in Space}$$

$$= \sqrt{(2 - 1)^2 + (4 - 0)^2 + (-3 - 2)^2} \quad \text{Substitute.}$$

$$= \sqrt{1 + 16 + 25} = \sqrt{42} \quad \text{Simplify.}$$

CHECKPOINT Now try Exercise 17.

Notice the similarity between the Distance Formulas in the plane and in space. The Midpoint Formulas in the plane and in space are also similar.

Midpoint Formula in Space

The midpoint of the line segment joining the points (x_1, y_1, z_1) and (x_2, y_2, z_2) given by the Midpoint Formula in Space is

$$\left(\frac{x_1 + x_2}{2}, \frac{y_1 + y_2}{2}, \frac{z_1 + z_2}{2}\right).$$

Example 3 **Using the Midpoint Formula in Space**

Find the midpoint of the line segment joining $(5, -2, 3)$ and $(0, 4, 4)$.

Solution

Using the Midpoint Formula in Space, the midpoint is

$$\left(\frac{5+0}{2}, \frac{-2+4}{2}, \frac{3+4}{2}\right) = \left(\frac{5}{2}, 1, \frac{7}{2}\right)$$

as shown in Figure 11.6.

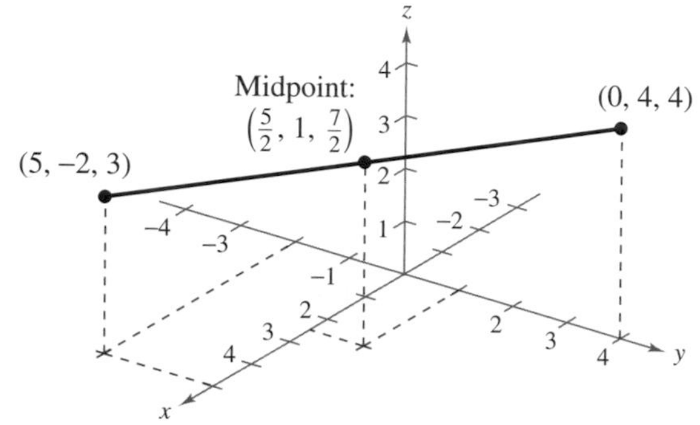

FIGURE 11.6

✓CHECKPOINT Now try Exercise 31.

The Equation of a Sphere

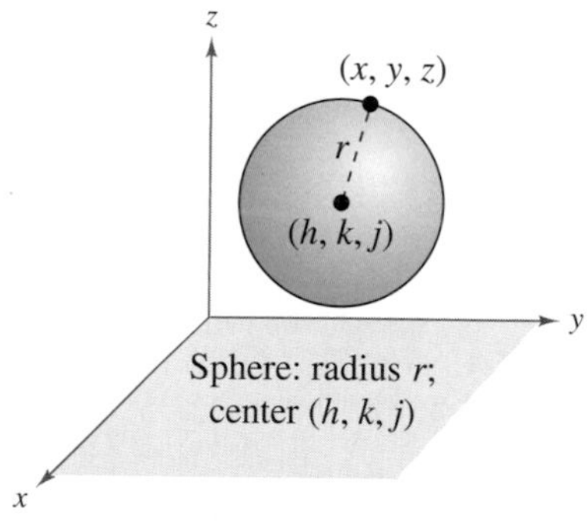

FIGURE 11.7

A **sphere** with center (h, k, j) and radius r is defined as the set of all points (x, y, z) such that the distance between (x, y, z) and (h, k, j) is r, as shown in Figure 11.7. Using the Distance Formula, this condition can be written as

$$\sqrt{(x-h)^2 + (y-k)^2 + (z-j)^2} = r.$$

By squaring each side of this equation, you obtain the standard equation of a sphere.

Standard Equation of a Sphere

The **standard equation of a sphere** with center (h, k, j) and radius r is given by

$$(x-h)^2 + (y-k)^2 + (z-j)^2 = r^2.$$

Notice the similarity of this formula to the equation of a circle in the plane.

$$(x-h)^2 + (y-k)^2 + (z-j)^2 = r^2 \quad \text{Equation of sphere in space}$$

$$(x-h)^2 + (y-k)^2 = r^2 \quad \text{Equation of circle in the plane}$$

As is true with the equation of a circle, the equation of a sphere is simplified when the center lies at the origin. In this case, the equation is

$$x^2 + y^2 + z^2 = r^2. \quad \text{Sphere with center at origin}$$

Example 4 Finding the Equation of a Sphere

Find the standard equation of the sphere with center $(2, 4, 3)$ and radius 3. Does this sphere intersect the xy-plane?

Solution

$$(x - h)^2 + (y - k)^2 + (z - j)^2 = r^2 \quad \text{Standard equation}$$

$$(x - 2)^2 + (y - 4)^2 + (z - 3)^2 = 3^2 \quad \text{Substitute.}$$

From the graph shown in Figure 11.8, you can see that the center of the sphere lies three units above the xy-plane. Because the sphere has a radius of 3, you can conclude that it does intersect the xy-plane—at the point $(2, 4, 0)$.

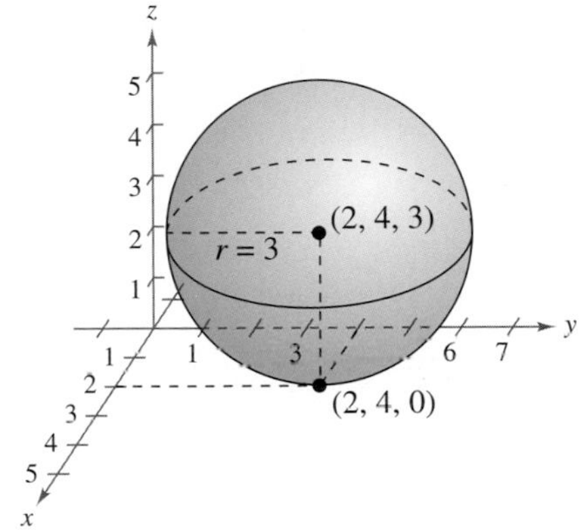

FIGURE 11.8

CHECKPOINT Now try Exercise 39.

Exploration

Find the equation of the sphere that has the points $(3, -2, 6)$ and $(-1, 4, 2)$ as endpoints of a diameter. Explain how this problem gives you a chance to use all three formulas discussed so far in this section: the Distance Formula in Space, the Midpoint Formula in Space, and the standard equation of a sphere.

Example 5 Finding the Center and Radius of a Sphere

Find the center and radius of the sphere given by

$$x^2 + y^2 + z^2 - 2x + 4y - 6z + 8 = 0.$$

Solution

To obtain the standard equation of this sphere, complete the square as follows.

$$x^2 + y^2 + z^2 - 2x + 4y - 6z + 8 = 0$$

$$(x^2 - 2x + \square) + (y^2 + 4y + \square) + (z^2 - 6z + \square) = -8$$

$$(x^2 - 2x + 1) + (y^2 + 4y + 4) + (z^2 - 6z + 9) = -8 + 1 + 4 + 9$$

$$(x - 1)^2 + (y + 2)^2 + (z - 3)^2 = (\sqrt{6})^2$$

So, the center of the sphere is $(1, -2, 3)$, and its radius is $\sqrt{6}$. See Figure 11.9.

CHECKPOINT Now try Exercise 49.

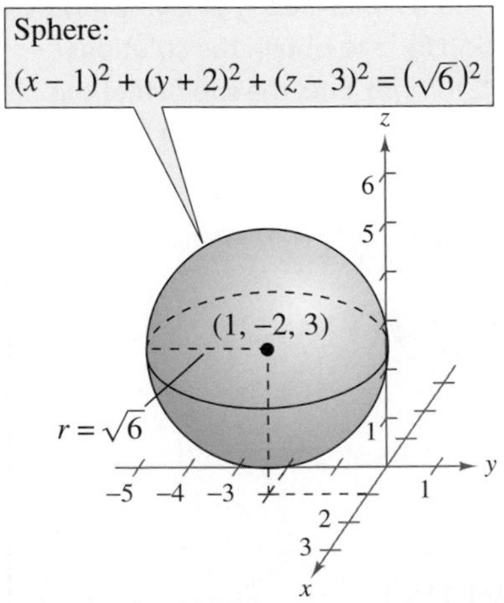

FIGURE 11.9

Note in Example 5 that the points satisfying the equation of the sphere are "surface points," not "interior points." In general, the collection of points satisfying an equation involving x, y, and z is called a **surface in space.**

Finding the intersection of a surface with one of the three coordinate planes (or with a plane parallel to one of the three coordinate planes) helps one visualize the surface. Such an intersection is called a **trace** of the surface. For example, the xy-trace of a surface consists of all points that are common to both the surface *and* the xy-plane. Similarly, the xz-trace of a surface consists of all points that are common to both the surface and the xz-plane.

Example 6 Finding a Trace of a Surface

Sketch the xy-trace of the sphere given by $(x-3)^2+(y-2)^2+(z+4)^2=5^2$.

Solution

To find the xy-trace of this surface, use the fact that every point in the xy-plane has a z-coordinate of zero. By substituting $z=0$ into the original equation, the resulting equation will represent the intersection of the surface with the xy-plane.

$$(x-3)^2+(y-2)^2+(z+4)^2=5^2$$ Write original equation.

$$(x-3)^2+(y-2)^2+(0+4)^2=5^2$$ Substitute 0 for z.

$$(x-3)^2+(y-2)^2+16=25$$ Simplify.

$$(x-3)^2+(y-2)^2=9$$ Subtract 16 from each side.

$$(x-3)^2+(y-2)^2=3^2$$ Equation of circle

You can see that the xy-trace is a circle of radius 3, as shown in Figure 11.10.

CHECKPOINT Now try Exercise 57.

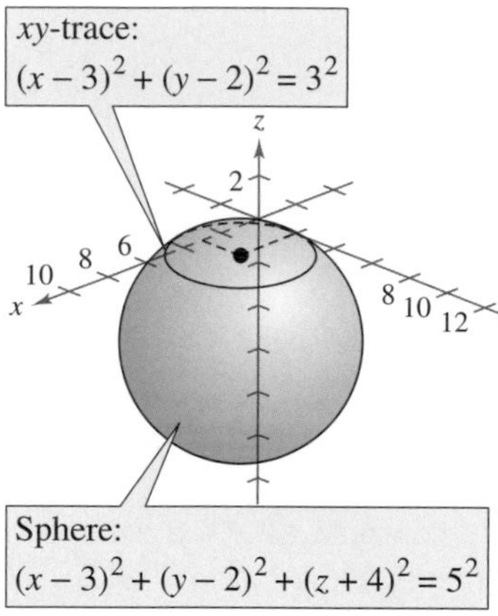

FIGURE 11.10

Technology

Most three-dimensional graphing utilities and computer algebra systems represent *surfaces* by sketching several traces of the surface. The traces are usually taken in equally spaced parallel planes. To graph an equation involving x, y, and z with a three-dimensional "function grapher," you must first set the graphing mode to *three-dimensional* and solve the equation for z. After entering the equation, you need to specify a rectangular viewing cube (the three-dimensional analog of a viewing window). For instance, to graph the top half of the sphere from Example 6, solve the equation for z to obtain the solutions $z=-4\pm\sqrt{25-(x-3)^2-(y-2)^2}$. The equation $z=-4+\sqrt{25-(x-3)^2-(y-2)^2}$ represents the top half of the sphere. Enter this equation, as shown in Figure 11.11. Next, use the viewing cube shown in Figure 11.12. Finally, you can display the graph, as shown in Figure 11.13.

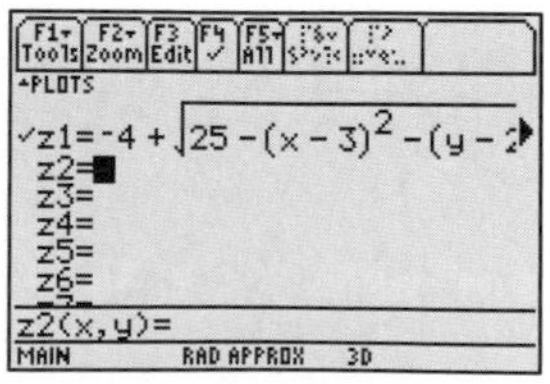

FIGURE 11.11

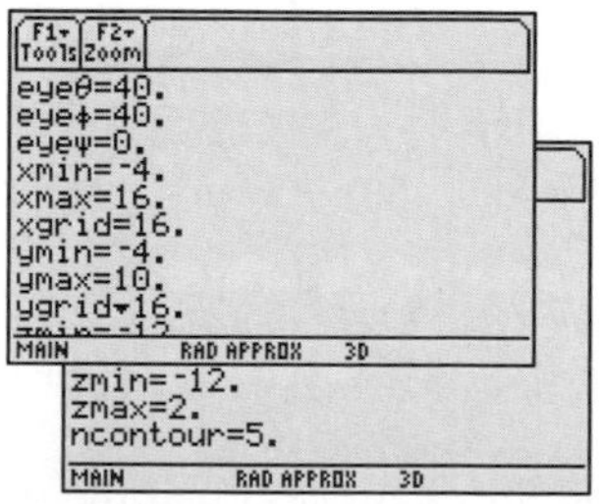

FIGURE 11.12

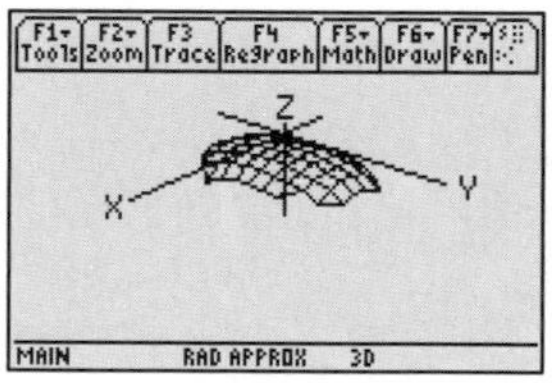

FIGURE 11.13

11.1 Exercises

VOCABULARY CHECK: Fill in the blanks.

1. A _______ coordinate system can be formed by passing a z-axis perpendicular to both the x-axis and the y-axis at the origin.
2. The three coordinate planes of a three-dimensional coordinate system are the _______, the _______, and the _______.
3. The coordinate planes of a three-dimensional coordinate system separate the coordinate system into eight _______.
4. The distance between the points (x_1, y_1, z_1) and (x_2, y_2, z_2) can be found using the _______ _______ in Space.
5. The midpoint of the line segment joining the points (x_1, y_1, z_1) and (x_2, y_2, z_2) given by the Midpoint Formula in Space is _______.
6. A _______ is the set of all points (x, y, z) such that the distance between (x, y, z) and a fixed point (h, k, j) is r.
7. A _______ in _______ is the collection of points satisfying an equation involving x, y, and z.
8. The intersection of a surface with one of the three coordinate planes is called a _______ of the surface.

In Exercises 1 and 2, approximate the coordinates of the points.

1.

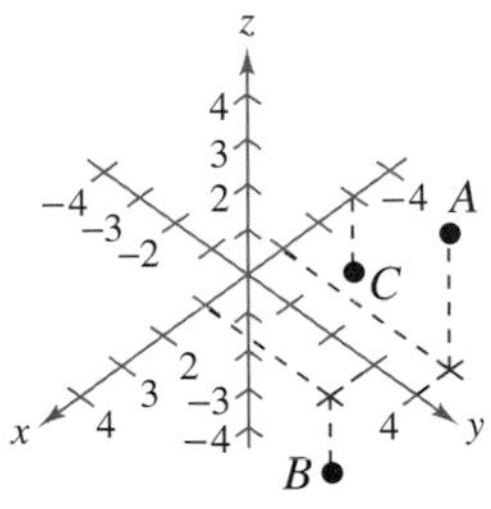

2.

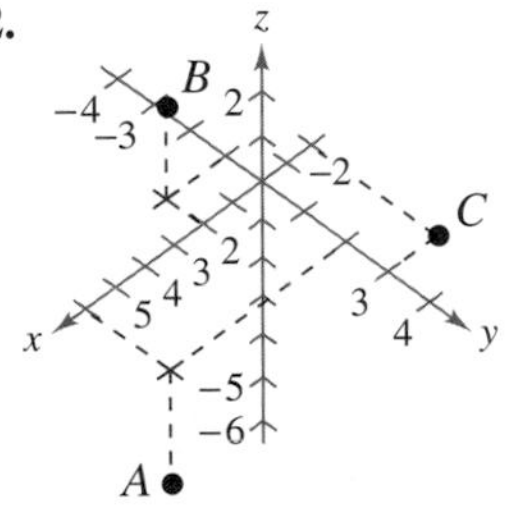

In Exercises 3–6, plot each point in the same three-dimensional coordinate system.

3. (a) $(2, 1, 3)$ (b) $(-1, 2, 1)$

4. (a) $(3, 0, 0)$ (b) $(-3, -2, -1)$

5. (a) $(3, -1, 0)$ (b) $(-4, 2, 2)$

6. (a) $(0, 4, -3)$ (b) $(4, 0, 4)$

In Exercises 7–10, find the coordinates of the point.

7. The point is located three units behind the yz-plane, three units to the right of the xz-plane, and four units above the xy-plane.

8. The point is located six units in front of the yz-plane, one unit to the left of the xz-plane, and one unit below the xy-plane.

9. The point is located on the x-axis, 10 units in front of the yz-plane.

10. The point is located in the yz-plane, two units to the right of the xz-plane, and eight units above the xy-plane.

In Exercises 11–16, determine the octant(s) in which (x, y, z) is located so that the condition(s) is (are) satisfied.

11. $x > 0, y < 0, z > 0$

12. $x < 0, y > 0, z < 0$

13. $z > 0$

14. $y < 0$

15. $xy < 0$

16. $yz > 0$

In Exercises 17–24, find the distance between the points.

17. $(0, 0, 0), (5, 2, 6)$

18. $(1, 0, 0), (7, 0, 4)$

19. $(3, 2, 5), (7, 4, 8)$

20. $(4, 1, 9), (2, 1, 6)$

21. $(-1, 4, -2), (6, 0, -9)$

22. $(1, 1, -7), (-2, -3, -7)$

23. $(0, -3, 0), (1, 0, -10)$

24. $(2, -4, 0), (0, 6, -3)$

In Exercises 25–28, find the lengths of the sides of the right triangle. Show that these lengths satisfy the Pythagorean Theorem.

25.
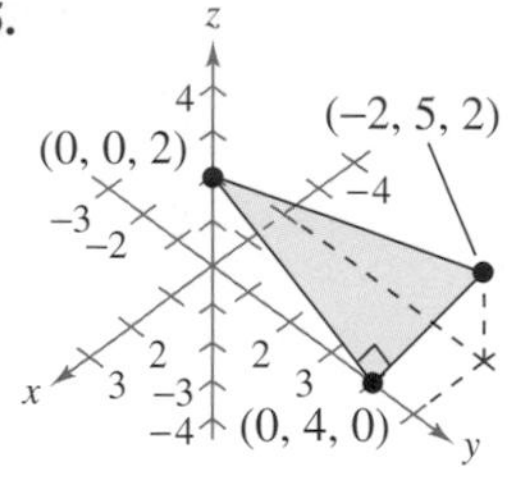

26.
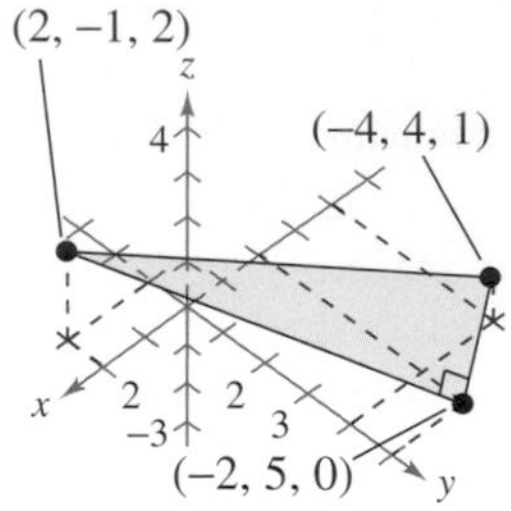

27. (0, 0, 0), (2, 2, 1), (2, −4, 4)

28. (1, 0, 1), (1, 3, 1), (1, 0, 3)

In Exercises 29 and 30, find the lengths of the sides of the triangle with the indicated vertices, and determine whether the triangle is a right triangle, an isosceles triangle, or neither.

29. (1, −3, −2), (5, −1, 2), (−1, 1, 2)

30. (5, 3, 4), (7, 1, 3), (3, 5, 3)

In Exercises 31–38, find the midpoint of the line segment joining the points.

31. (0, 0, 0), (3, −2, 4)

32. (1, 5, −1), (2, 2, 2)

33. (3, −6, 10), (−3, 4, 4)

34. (−1, 5, −3), (3, 7, −1)

35. (6, −2, 5), (−4, 2, 6)

36. (−3, 5, 5), (−6, 4, 8)

37. (−2, 8, 10), (7, −4, 2)

38. (9, −5, 1), (9, −2, −4)

In Exercises 39–46, find the standard form of the equation of the sphere with the given characteristics.

39.
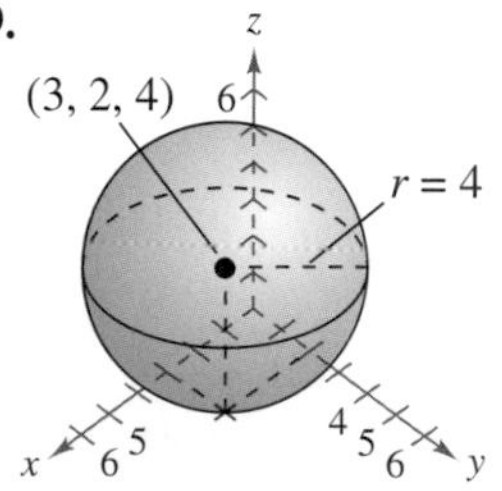

40.
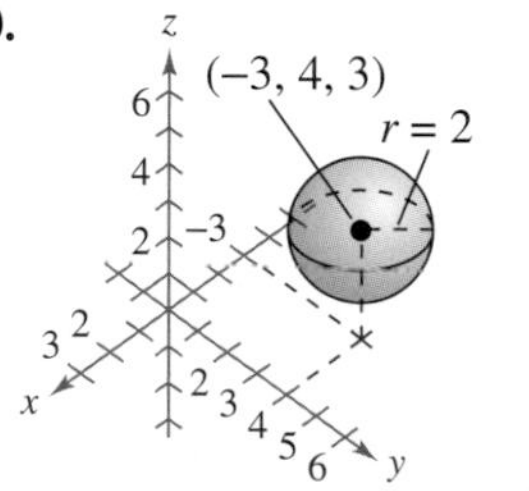

41. Center: (0, 4, 3); radius: 3

42. Center: (2, −1, 8); radius: 6

43. Center: (−3, 7, 5); diameter: 10

44. Center: (0, 5, −9); diameter: 8

45. Endpoints of a diameter: (3, 0, 0), (0, 0, 6)

46. Endpoints of a diameter: (2, −2, 2), (−1, 4, 6)

In Exercises 47–56, find the center and radius of the sphere.

47. $x^2 + y^2 + z^2 - 5x = 0$

48. $x^2 + y^2 + z^2 - 8y = 0$

49. $x^2 + y^2 + z^2 - 4x + 2y - 6z + 10 = 0$

50. $x^2 + y^2 + z^2 - 6x + 4y + 9 = 0$

51. $x^2 + y^2 + z^2 + 4x - 8z + 19 = 0$

52. $x^2 + y^2 + z^2 - 8y - 6z + 13 = 0$

53. $9x^2 + 9y^2 + 9z^2 - 18x - 6y - 72z + 73 = 0$

54. $2x^2 + 2y^2 + 2z^2 - 2x - 6y - 4z + 5 = 0$

55. $9x^2 + 9y^2 + 9z^2 - 6x + 18y + 1 = 0$

56. $4x^2 + 4y^2 + 4z^2 - 4x - 32y + 8z + 33 = 0$

In Exercises 57–60, sketch the graph of the equation and sketch the specified trace.

57. $(x - 1)^2 + y^2 + z^2 = 36$; xz-trace

58. $x^2 + (y + 3)^2 + z^2 = 25$; yz-trace

59. $(x + 2)^2 + (y - 3)^2 + z^2 = 9$; yz-trace

60. $x^2 + (y - 1)^2 + (z + 1)^2 = 4$; xy-trace

In Exercises 61 and 62, use a three-dimensional graphing utility to graph the sphere.

61. $x^2 + y^2 + z^2 - 6x - 8y - 10z + 46 = 0$

62. $x^2 + y^2 + z^2 + 6y - 8z + 21 = 0$

63. ***Crystals*** Crystals are classified according to their symmetry. Crystals shaped like cubes are classified as isometric. The vertices of an isometric crystal mapped onto a three-dimensional coordinate system are shown in the figure. Determine (x, y, z).

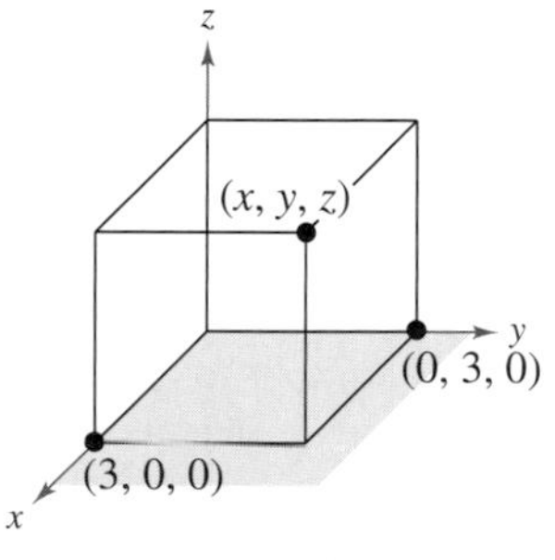

FIGURE FOR 63

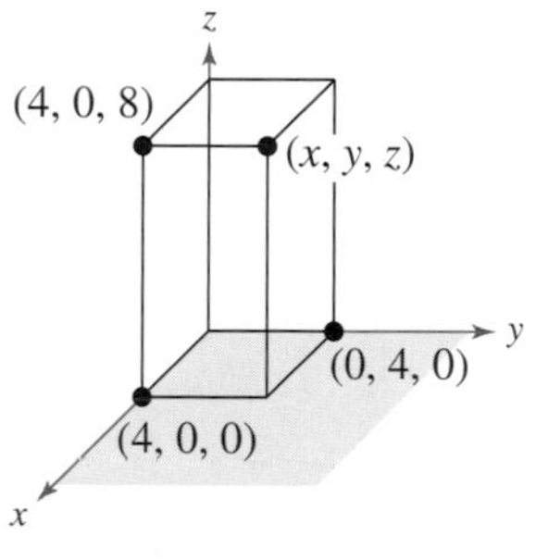

FIGURE FOR 64

64. ***Crystals*** Crystals shaped like rectangular prisms are classified as tetragonal. The vertices of a tetragonal crystal mapped onto a three-dimensional coordinate system are shown in the figure. Determine (x, y, z).

65. ***Architecture*** A spherical building has a diameter of 165 feet. The center of the building is placed at the origin of a three-dimensional coordinate system. What is the equation of the sphere?

Model It

66. ***Geography*** Assume that Earth is a sphere with a radius of 3963 miles. The center of Earth is placed at the origin of a three-dimensional coordinate system (see figure).

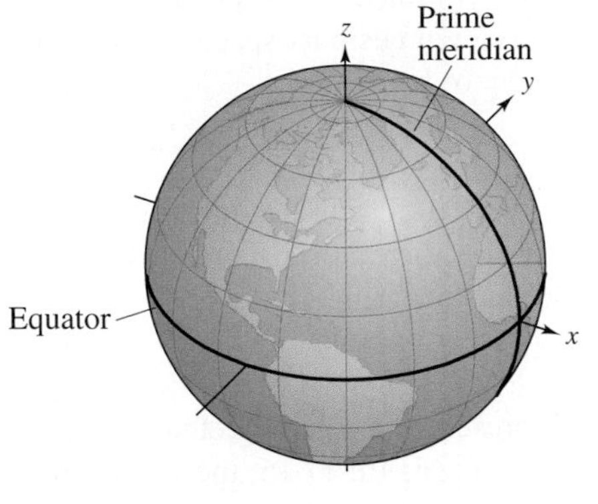

(a) What is the equation of the sphere?

(b) Lines of longitude that run north-south could be represented by what trace(s)? What shape would each of these traces form?

(c) Lines of latitude that run east-west could be represented by what trace(s)? What shape would each of these traces form?

(d) The prime meridian would represent what trace of the equation of the sphere from part (a)?

(e) The equator would represent what trace of the equation of the sphere from part (a)?

Synthesis

True or False? **In Exercises 67 and 68, determine whether the statement is true or false. Justify your answer.**

67. In the ordered triple (x, y, z) that represents point P in space, x is the directed distance from the xy-plane to P.

68. The surface consisting of all points (x, y, z) in space that are the same distance r from the point (h, j, k) has a circle as its xy-trace.

69. ***Think About It*** What is the z-coordinate of any point in the xy-plane? What is the y-coordinate of any point in the xz-plane? What is the x-coordinate of any point in the yz-plane?

70. ***Writing*** In two-dimensional coordinate geometry, the graph of the equation $ax + by + c = 0$ is a line. In three-dimensional coordinate geometry, what is the graph of the equation $ax + by + cz = 0$? Is it a line? Explain your reasoning.

71. A sphere intersects the yz-plane. Describe the trace.

72. A plane intersects the xy-plane. Describe the trace.

73. A line segment has (x_1, y_1, z_1) as one endpoint and (x_m, y_m, z_m) as its midpoint. Find the other endpoint (x_2, y_2, z_2) of the line segment in terms of x_1, y_1, z_1, x_m, y_m, and z_m.

74. Use the result of Exercise 73 to find the coordinates of the endpoint of a line segment if the coordinates of the other endpoint and the midpoint are $(3, 0, 2)$ and $(5, 8, 7)$, respectively.

Skills Review

In Exercises 75–80, solve the quadratic equation by completing the square.

75. $v^2 + 3v - 2 = 0$

76. $z^2 - 7z - 19 = 0$

77. $x^2 - 5x + 5 = 0$

78. $x^2 + 3x - 1 = 0$

79. $4y^2 + 4y - 9 = 0$

80. $2x^2 + 5x - 8 = 0$

In Exercises 81–84, find the magnitude and direction angle of the vector v.

81. $\mathbf{v} = 3\mathbf{i} - 3\mathbf{j}$

82. $\mathbf{v} = -\mathbf{i} + 2\mathbf{j}$

83. $\mathbf{v} = 4\mathbf{i} + 5\mathbf{j}$

84. $\mathbf{v} = 10\mathbf{i} - 7\mathbf{j}$

In Exercises 85 and 86, find the dot product of u and v.

85. $\mathbf{u} = \langle -4, 1 \rangle$
$\mathbf{v} = \langle 3, 5 \rangle$

86. $\mathbf{u} = \langle -1, 0 \rangle$
$\mathbf{v} = \langle -2, -6 \rangle$

In Exercises 87–90, write the first five terms of the sequence beginning with the given term. Then calculate the first and second differences of the sequence. State whether the sequence has a linear model, a quadratic model, or neither.

87. $a_0 = 1$
$a_n = a_{n-1} + n^2$

88. $a_0 = 0$
$a_n = a_{n-1} - 1$

89. $a_1 = -1$
$a_n = a_{n-1} + 3$

90. $a_1 = 4$
$a_n = a_{n-1} - 2n$

In Exercises 91–98, find the standard form of the equation of the conic with the given characteristics.

91. Circle: center: $(-5, 1)$; radius: 7

92. Circle: center: $(3, -6)$; radius: 9

93. Parabola: vertex: $(4, 1)$; focus: $(1, 1)$

94. Parabola: vertex: $(-2, 5)$; focus: $(-2, 0)$

95. Ellipse: vertices: $(0, 3)$, $(6, 3)$; minor axis of length 4

96. Ellipse: foci: $(0, 0)$, $(0, 6)$; major axis of length 9

97. Hyperbola: vertices: $(4, 0)$, $(8, 0)$; foci: $(0, 0)$, $(12, 0)$

98. Hyperbola: vertices: $(3, 1)$, $(3, 9)$; foci: $(3, 0)$, $(3, 10)$

11.2 Vectors in Space

What you should learn

- Find the component forms of the unit vectors in the same direction of, the magnitudes of, the dot products of, and the angles between vectors in space.
- Determine whether vectors in space are parallel or orthogonal.
- Use vectors in space to solve real-life problems.

Why you should learn it

Vectors in space can be used to represent many physical forces, such as tension in the cables used to support auditorium lights, as shown in Exercise 44 on page 826.

SuperStock

Vectors in Space

Physical forces and velocities are not confined to the plane, so it is natural to extend the concept of vectors from two-dimensional space to three-dimensional space. In space, vectors are denoted by ordered triples

$$\mathbf{v} = \langle v_1, v_2, v_3 \rangle. \qquad \text{Component form}$$

The **zero vector** is denoted by $\mathbf{0} = \langle 0, 0, 0 \rangle$. Using the unit vectors $\mathbf{i} = \langle 1, 0, 0 \rangle$, $\mathbf{j} = \langle 0, 1, 0 \rangle$, and $\mathbf{k} = \langle 0, 0, 1 \rangle$ in the direction of the positive z-axis, the **standard unit vector notation** for $\mathbf{v}$ is

$$\mathbf{v} = v_1\mathbf{i} + v_2\mathbf{j} + v_3\mathbf{k} \qquad \text{Unit vector form}$$

as shown in Figure 11.14. If $\mathbf{v}$ is represented by the directed line segment from $P(p_1, p_2, p_3)$ to $Q(q_1, q_2, q_3)$, as shown in Figure 11.15, the **component form** of $\mathbf{v}$ is produced by subtracting the coordinates of the initial point from the corresponding coordinates of the terminal point

$$\mathbf{v} = \langle v_1, v_2, v_3 \rangle = \langle q_1 - p_1, q_2 - p_2, q_3 - p_3 \rangle.$$

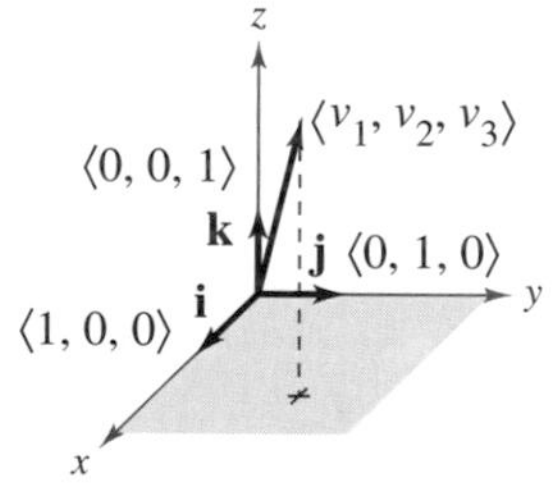

FIGURE 11.14

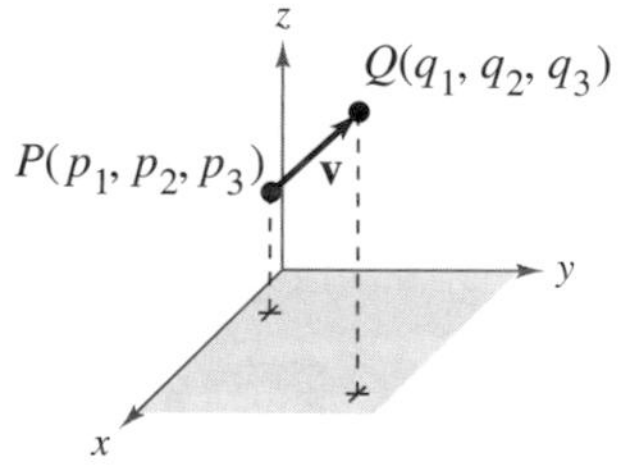

FIGURE 11.15

Vectors in Space

1. Two vectors are **equal** if and only if their corresponding components are equal.
2. The **magnitude** (or **length**) of $\mathbf{u} = \langle u_1, u_2, u_3 \rangle$ is $\|\mathbf{u}\| = \sqrt{u_1^2 + u_2^2 + u_3^2}$.
3. A **unit vector u** in the direction of $\mathbf{v}$ is $\mathbf{u} = \dfrac{\mathbf{v}}{\|\mathbf{v}\|}$, $\mathbf{v} \neq \mathbf{0}$.
4. The **sum** of $\mathbf{u} = \langle u_1, u_2, u_3 \rangle$ and $\mathbf{v} = \langle v_1, v_2, v_3 \rangle$ is
$$\mathbf{u} + \mathbf{v} = \langle u_1 + v_1, u_2 + v_2, u_3 + v_3 \rangle. \qquad \text{Vector addition}$$
5. The **scalar multiple** of the real number c and $\mathbf{u} = \langle u_1, u_2, u_3 \rangle$ is
$$c\mathbf{u} = \langle cu_1, cu_2, cu_3 \rangle. \qquad \text{Scalar multiplication}$$
6. The **dot product** of $\mathbf{u} = \langle u_1, u_2, u_3 \rangle$ and $\mathbf{v} = \langle v_1, v_2, v_3 \rangle$ is
$$\mathbf{u} \cdot \mathbf{v} = u_1v_1 + u_2v_2 + u_3v_3. \qquad \text{Dot product}$$

Example 1 Finding the Component Form of a Vector

Find the component form and magnitude of the vector **v** having initial point (3, 4, 2) and terminal point (3, 6, 4). Then find a unit vector in the direction of **v**.

Solution

The component form of **v** is

$$\mathbf{v} = \langle 3 - 3, 6 - 4, 4 - 2 \rangle = \langle 0, 2, 2 \rangle$$

which implies that its magnitude is

$$\|\mathbf{v}\| = \sqrt{0^2 + 2^2 + 2^2} = \sqrt{8} = 2\sqrt{2}.$$

The unit vector in the direction of **v** is

$$\mathbf{u} = \frac{\mathbf{v}}{\|\mathbf{v}\|} = \frac{1}{2\sqrt{2}}\langle 0, 2, 2 \rangle = \left\langle 0, \frac{1}{\sqrt{2}}, \frac{1}{\sqrt{2}} \right\rangle = \left\langle 0, \frac{\sqrt{2}}{2}, \frac{\sqrt{2}}{2} \right\rangle.$$

✓CHECKPOINT Now try Exercise 3.

Example 2 Finding the Dot Product of Two Vectors

Find the dot product of $\langle 0, 3, -2 \rangle$ and $\langle 4, -2, 3 \rangle$.

Solution

$$\langle 0, 3, -2 \rangle \cdot \langle 4, -2, 3 \rangle = 0(4) + 3(-2) + (-2)(3)$$
$$= 0 - 6 - 6 = -12$$

Note that the dot product of two vectors is a real number, not a vector.

✓CHECKPOINT Now try Exercise 19.

Technology

Some graphing utilities have the capability to perform vector operations, such as the dot product. Consult the user's guide for your graphing utility for specific instructions.

As was discussed in Section 6.4, the **angle between two nonzero vectors** is the angle θ, $0 \le \theta \le \pi$, between their respective standard position vectors, as shown in Figure 11.16. This angle can be found using the dot product. (Note that the angle between the zero vector and another vector is not defined.)

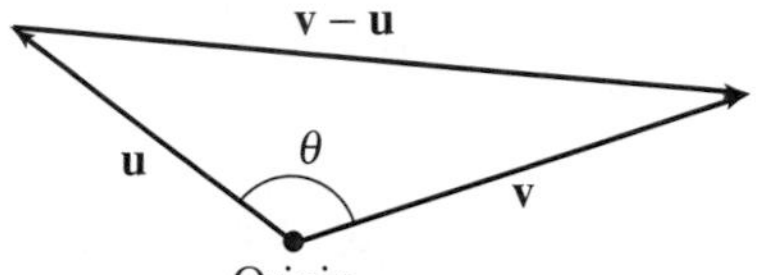

FIGURE 11.16

Angle Between Two Vectors

If θ is the angle between two nonzero vectors **u** and **v**, then $\cos\theta = \dfrac{\mathbf{u} \cdot \mathbf{v}}{\|\mathbf{u}\|\,\|\mathbf{v}\|}$.

If the dot product of two nonzero vectors is zero, the angle between the vectors is 90° (recall that $\cos 90° = 0$). Such vectors are called **orthogonal.** For instance, the standard unit vectors **i**, **j**, and **k** are orthogonal to each other.

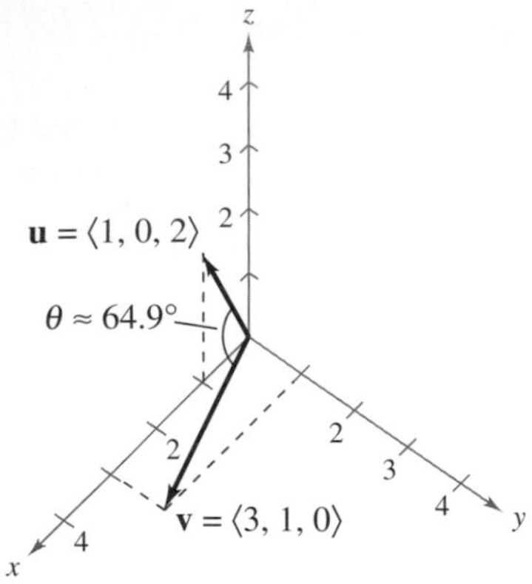

FIGURE 11.17

Example 3 Finding the Angle Between Two Vectors

Find the angle between $\mathbf{u} = \langle 1, 0, 2 \rangle$ and $\mathbf{v} = \langle 3, 1, 0 \rangle$.

Solution

$$\cos \theta = \frac{\mathbf{u} \cdot \mathbf{v}}{\|\mathbf{u}\| \, \|\mathbf{v}\|} = \frac{\langle 1, 0, 2 \rangle \cdot \langle 3, 1, 0 \rangle}{\|\langle 1, 0, 2 \rangle\| \, \|\langle 3, 1, 0 \rangle\|} = \frac{3}{\sqrt{50}}$$

This implies that the angle between the two vectors is

$$\theta = \arccos \frac{3}{\sqrt{50}} \approx 64.9^\circ$$

as shown in Figure 11.17.

CHECKPOINT Now try Exercise 23.

Parallel Vectors

Recall from the definition of scalar multiplication that positive scalar multiples of a nonzero vector $\mathbf{v}$ have the same direction as $\mathbf{v}$, whereas negative multiples have the direction opposite that of $\mathbf{v}$. In general, two nonzero vectors $\mathbf{u}$ and $\mathbf{v}$ are **parallel** if there is some scalar c such that $\mathbf{u} = c\mathbf{v}$. For example, in Figure 11.18, the vectors $\mathbf{u}$, $\mathbf{v}$, and $\mathbf{w}$ are parallel because $\mathbf{u} = 2\mathbf{v}$ and $\mathbf{w} = -\mathbf{v}$.

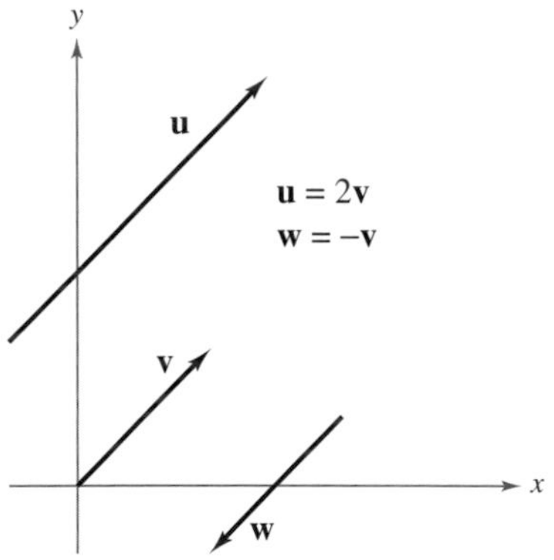

FIGURE 11.18

Example 4 Parallel Vectors

Vector $\mathbf{w}$ has initial point $(1, -2, 0)$ and terminal point $(3, 2, 1)$. Which of the following vectors is parallel to $\mathbf{w}$?

a. $\mathbf{u} = \langle 4, 8, 2 \rangle$ **b.** $\mathbf{v} = \langle 4, 8, 4 \rangle$

Solution

Begin by writing $\mathbf{w}$ in component form.

$$\mathbf{w} = \langle 3 - 1, 2 - (-2), 1 - 0 \rangle = \langle 2, 4, 1 \rangle$$

a. Because

$$\begin{aligned} \mathbf{u} &= \langle 4, 8, 2 \rangle \\ &= 2\langle 2, 4, 1 \rangle \\ &= 2\mathbf{w}, \end{aligned}$$

you can conclude that $\mathbf{u}$ *is* parallel to $\mathbf{w}$.

b. In this case, you need to find a scalar c such that

$$\langle 4, 8, 4 \rangle = c\langle 2, 4, 1 \rangle.$$

However, equating corresponding components produces $c = 2$ for the first two components and $c = 4$ for the third. So, the equation has no solution, and the vectors $\mathbf{v}$ and $\mathbf{w}$ are *not* parallel.

CHECKPOINT Now try Exercise 27.

You can use vectors to determine whether three points are collinear (lie on the same line). The points P, Q, and R are **collinear** if and only if the vectors $\overrightarrow{PQ}$ and $\overrightarrow{PR}$ are parallel.

Example 5 Using Vectors to Determine Collinear Points

Determine whether the points $P(2, -1, 4)$, $Q(5, 4, 6)$, and $R(-4, -11, 0)$ are collinear.

Solution

The component forms of $\overrightarrow{PQ}$ and $\overrightarrow{PR}$ are

$$\overrightarrow{PQ} = \langle 5 - 2, 4 - (-1), 6 - 4 \rangle = \langle 3, 5, 2 \rangle$$

and

$$\overrightarrow{PR} = \langle -4 - 2, -11 - (-1), 0 - 4 \rangle = \langle -6, -10, -4 \rangle.$$

Because $\overrightarrow{PR} = -2\overrightarrow{PQ}$, you can conclude that they are parallel. Therefore, the points P, Q, and R lie on the same line, as shown in Figure 11.19.

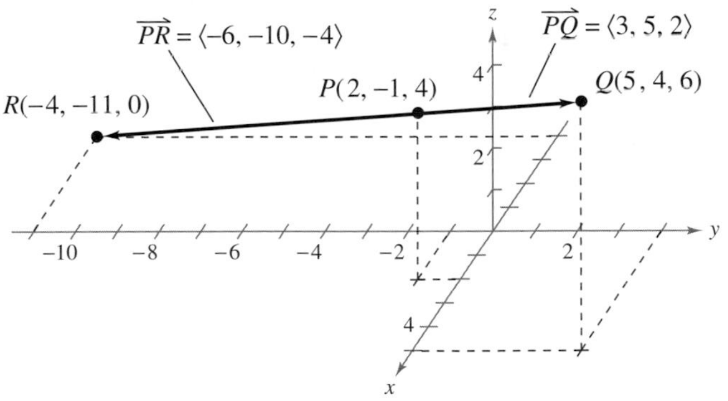

FIGURE 11.19

✓CHECKPOINT Now try Exercise 31.

Example 6 Finding the Terminal Point of a Vector

The initial point of the vector $\mathbf{v} = \langle 4, 2, -1 \rangle$ is $P(3, -1, 6)$. What is the terminal point of this vector?

Solution

Using the component form of the vector whose initial point is $P(3, -1, 6)$ and whose terminal point is $Q(q_1, q_2, q_3)$, you can write

$$\begin{aligned}\overrightarrow{PQ} &= \langle q_1 - p_1, q_2 - p_2, q_3 - p_3 \rangle \\ &= \langle q_1 - 3, q_2 + 1, q_3 - 6 \rangle = \langle 4, 2, -1 \rangle.\end{aligned}$$

This implies that $q_1 - 3 = 4$, $q_2 + 1 = 2$, and $q_3 - 6 = -1$. The solutions of these three equations are $q_1 = 7$, $q_2 = 1$, and $q_3 = 5$. So, the terminal point is $Q(7, 1, 5)$.

✓CHECKPOINT Now try Exercise 35.

Application

In Section 6.3, you saw how to use vectors to solve an equilibrium problem in a plane. The next example shows how to use vectors to solve an equilibrium problem in space.

Example 7 Solving an Equilibrium Problem

A weight of 480 pounds is supported by three ropes. As shown in Figure 11.20, the weight is located at $S(0, 2, -1)$. The ropes are tied to the points $P(2, 0, 0)$, $Q(0, 4, 0)$, and $R(-2, 0, 0)$. Find the force (or tension) on each rope.

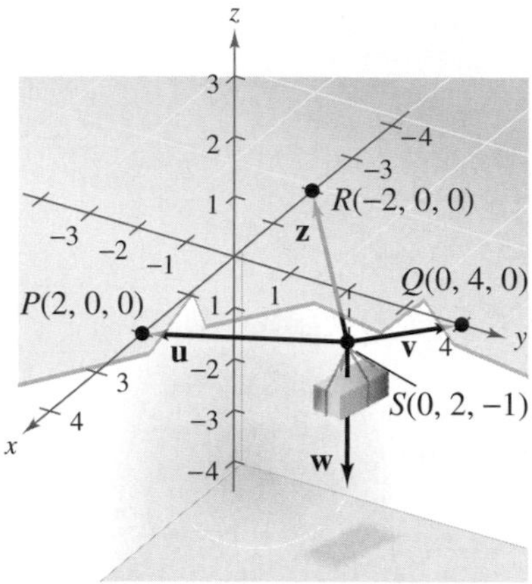

FIGURE 11.20

Solution

The (downward) force of the weight is represented by the vector

$$\mathbf{w} = \langle 0, 0, -480 \rangle.$$

The force vectors corresponding to the ropes are as follows.

$$\mathbf{u} = \|\mathbf{u}\|\frac{\overrightarrow{SP}}{\|\overrightarrow{SP}\|} = \|\mathbf{u}\|\frac{\langle 2-0, 0-2, 0-(-1)\rangle}{3} = \|\mathbf{u}\|\left\langle \frac{2}{3}, -\frac{2}{3}, \frac{1}{3}\right\rangle$$

$$\mathbf{v} = \|\mathbf{v}\|\frac{\overrightarrow{SQ}}{\|\overrightarrow{SQ}\|} = \|\mathbf{v}\|\frac{\langle 0-0, 4-2, 0-(-1)\rangle}{\sqrt{5}} = \|\mathbf{v}\|\left\langle 0, \frac{2}{\sqrt{5}}, \frac{1}{\sqrt{5}}\right\rangle$$

$$\mathbf{z} = \|\mathbf{z}\|\frac{\overrightarrow{SR}}{\|\overrightarrow{SR}\|} = \|\mathbf{z}\|\frac{\langle -2-0, 0-2, 0-(-1)\rangle}{3} = \|\mathbf{z}\|\left\langle -\frac{2}{3}, -\frac{2}{3}, \frac{1}{3}\right\rangle$$

For the system to be in equilibrium, it must be true that

$$\mathbf{u} + \mathbf{v} + \mathbf{z} + \mathbf{w} = \mathbf{0} \quad \text{or} \quad \mathbf{u} + \mathbf{v} + \mathbf{z} = -\mathbf{w}.$$

This yields the following system of linear equations.

$$\begin{cases} \frac{2}{3}\|\mathbf{u}\| \qquad\qquad\qquad - \frac{2}{3}\|\mathbf{z}\| = 0 \\ -\frac{2}{3}\|\mathbf{u}\| + \frac{2}{\sqrt{5}}\|\mathbf{v}\| - \frac{2}{3}\|\mathbf{z}\| = 0 \\ \frac{1}{3}\|\mathbf{u}\| + \frac{1}{\sqrt{5}}\|\mathbf{v}\| + \frac{1}{3}\|\mathbf{z}\| = 480 \end{cases}$$

Using the techniques demonstrated in Chapter 7, you can find the solution of the system to be

$$\|\mathbf{u}\| = 360.0$$

$$\|\mathbf{v}\| \approx 536.7$$

$$\|\mathbf{z}\| = 360.0.$$

So, the rope attached at point P has 360 pounds of tension, the rope attached at point Q has about 536.7 pounds of tension, and the rope attached at point R has 360 pounds of tension.

CHECKPOINT Now try Exercise 43.

11.2 Exercises

VOCABULARY CHECK: Fill in the blanks.

1. The _______ vector is denoted by $\mathbf{0} = \langle 0, 0, 0 \rangle$.
2. The standard unit vector notation for a vector $\mathbf{v}$ is given by _______ .
3. The _______ _______ of a vector $\mathbf{v}$ is produced by subtracting the coordinates of the initial point from the corresponding coordinates of the terminal point.
4. If the dot product of two nonzero vectors is zero, the angle between the vectors is 90° and the vectors are called _______ .
5. Two nonzero vectors $\mathbf{u}$ and $\mathbf{v}$ are _______ if there is some scalar c such that $\mathbf{u} = c\mathbf{v}$.

In Exercises 1 and 2, (a) find the component form of the vector v and (b) sketch the vector with its initial point at the origin.

1.

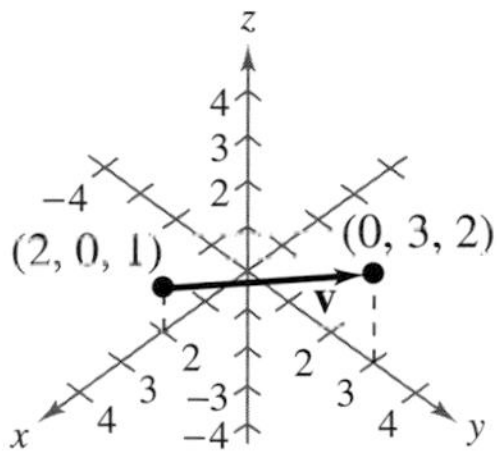

2.

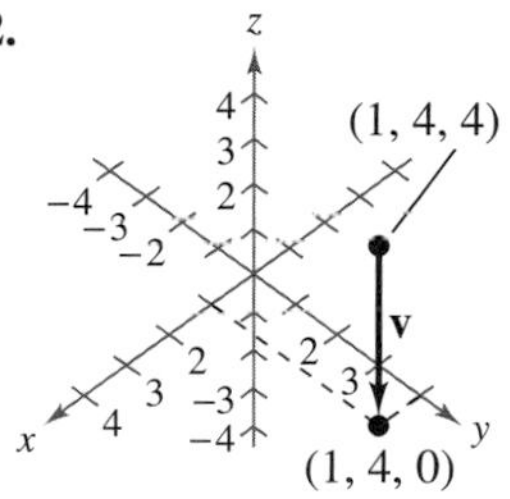

In Exercises 3 and 4, (a) write the component form of the vector v, (b) find the magnitude of v, and (c) find a unit vector in the direction of v.

3. Initial point: $(-6, 4, -2)$
   Terminal point: $(1, -1, 3)$
4. Initial point: $(-7, 3, 5)$
   Terminal point: $(0, 0, 2)$

In Exercises 5 and 6, sketch each scalar multiple of v.

5. $\mathbf{v} = \langle 1, 1, 3 \rangle$
   (a) $2\mathbf{v}$ (b) $-\mathbf{v}$ (c) $\frac{3}{2}\mathbf{v}$ (d) $0\mathbf{v}$
6. $\mathbf{v} = \langle -1, 2, 2 \rangle$
   (a) $-\mathbf{v}$ (b) $2\mathbf{v}$ (c) $\frac{1}{2}\mathbf{v}$ (d) $\frac{5}{2}\mathbf{v}$

In Exercises 7–10, find the vector z, given $\mathbf{u} = \langle -1, 3, 2 \rangle$, $\mathbf{v} = \langle 1, -2, -2 \rangle$, and $\mathbf{w} = \langle 5, 0, -5 \rangle$.

7. $\mathbf{z} = \mathbf{u} - 2\mathbf{v}$
8. $\mathbf{z} = 7\mathbf{u} + \mathbf{v} - \frac{1}{5}\mathbf{w}$
9. $2\mathbf{z} - 4\mathbf{u} = \mathbf{w}$
10. $\mathbf{u} + \mathbf{v} + \mathbf{z} = \mathbf{0}$

In Exercises 11–16, find the magnitude of v.

11. $\mathbf{v} = \langle 7, 8, 7 \rangle$
12. $\mathbf{v} = \langle -2, 0, -5 \rangle$
13. $\mathbf{v} = 4\mathbf{i} - 3\mathbf{j} - 7\mathbf{k}$
14. $\mathbf{v} = 2\mathbf{i} - \mathbf{j} + 6\mathbf{k}$
15. Initial point: $(1, -3, 4)$
    Terminal point: $(1, 0, -1)$
16. Initial point: $(0, -1, 0)$
    Terminal point: $(1, 2, -2)$

In Exercises 17 and 18, find a unit vector (a) in the direction of u and (b) in the direction opposite of u.

17. $\mathbf{u} = 8\mathbf{i} + 3\mathbf{j} - \mathbf{k}$
18. $\mathbf{u} = -3\mathbf{i} + 5\mathbf{j} + 10\mathbf{k}$

In Exercises 19–22, find the dot product of u and v.

19. $\mathbf{u} = \langle 4, 4, -1 \rangle$
    $\mathbf{v} = \langle 2, -5, -8 \rangle$
20. $\mathbf{u} = \langle 3, -1, 6 \rangle$
    $\mathbf{v} = \langle 4, -10, 1 \rangle$
21. $\mathbf{u} = 2\mathbf{i} - 5\mathbf{j} + 3\mathbf{k}$
    $\mathbf{v} = 9\mathbf{i} + 3\mathbf{j} - \mathbf{k}$
22. $\mathbf{u} = 3\mathbf{j} - 6\mathbf{k}$
    $\mathbf{v} = 6\mathbf{i} - 4\mathbf{j} - 2\mathbf{k}$

In Exercises 23–26, find the angle θ between the vectors.

23. $\mathbf{u} = \langle 0, 2, 2 \rangle$
    $\mathbf{v} = \langle 3, 0, -4 \rangle$
24. $\mathbf{u} = \langle -1, 3, 0 \rangle$
    $\mathbf{v} = \langle 1, 2, -1 \rangle$
25. $\mathbf{u} = 10\mathbf{i} + 40\mathbf{j}$
    $\mathbf{v} = -3\mathbf{j} + 8\mathbf{k}$
26. $\mathbf{u} = 8\mathbf{j} - 20\mathbf{k}$
    $\mathbf{v} = 10\mathbf{i} - 5\mathbf{k}$

In Exercises 27–30, determine whether u and v are orthogonal, parallel, or neither.

27. $\mathbf{u} = \langle -12, 6, 15 \rangle$
$\mathbf{v} = \langle 8, -4, -10 \rangle$

28. $\mathbf{u} = \langle -1, 3, -1 \rangle$
$\mathbf{v} = \langle 2, -1, 5 \rangle$

29. $\mathbf{u} = \frac{3}{4}\mathbf{i} - \frac{1}{2}\mathbf{j} + 2\mathbf{k}$
$\mathbf{v} = 4\mathbf{i} + 10\mathbf{j} + \mathbf{k}$

30. $\mathbf{u} = -\mathbf{i} + \frac{1}{2}\mathbf{j} - \mathbf{k}$
$\mathbf{v} = 8\mathbf{i} - 4\mathbf{j} + 8\mathbf{k}$

In Exercises 31–34, use vectors to determine whether the points are collinear.

31. $(5, 4, 1), (7, 3, -1), (4, 5, 3)$

32. $(-2, 7, 4), (-4, 8, 1), (0, 6, 7)$

33. $(1, 3, 2), (-1, 2, 5), (3, 4, -1)$

34. $(0, 4, 4), (-1, 5, 6), (-2, 6, 7)$

In Exercises 35–38, the vector v and its initial point are given. Find the terminal point.

35. $\mathbf{v} = \langle 2, -4, 7 \rangle$
Initial point: $(1, 5, 0)$

36. $\mathbf{v} = \langle 4, -1, -1 \rangle$
Initial point: $(6, -4, 3)$

37. $\mathbf{v} = \left\langle 4, \frac{3}{2}, -\frac{1}{4} \right\rangle$
Initial point: $\left(2, 1, -\frac{3}{2}\right)$

38. $\mathbf{v} = \left\langle \frac{5}{2}, -\frac{1}{2}, 4 \right\rangle$
Initial point: $\left(3, 2, -\frac{1}{2}\right)$

39. Determine the values of c such that $\|c\mathbf{u}\| = 3$, where $\mathbf{u} = \mathbf{i} + 2\mathbf{j} + 3\mathbf{k}$.

40. Determine the values of c such that $\|c\mathbf{u}\| = 12$, where $\mathbf{u} = -2\mathbf{i} + 2\mathbf{j} - 4\mathbf{k}$.

In Exercises 41 and 42, write the component form of v.

41. $\mathbf{v}$ lies in the yz-plane, has magnitude 4, and makes an angle of 45° with the positive y-axis.

42. $\mathbf{v}$ lies in the xz-plane, has magnitude 10, and makes an angle of 60° with the positive z-axis.

43. ***Tension*** The weight of a crate is 500 newtons. Find the tension in each of the supporting cables shown in the figure.

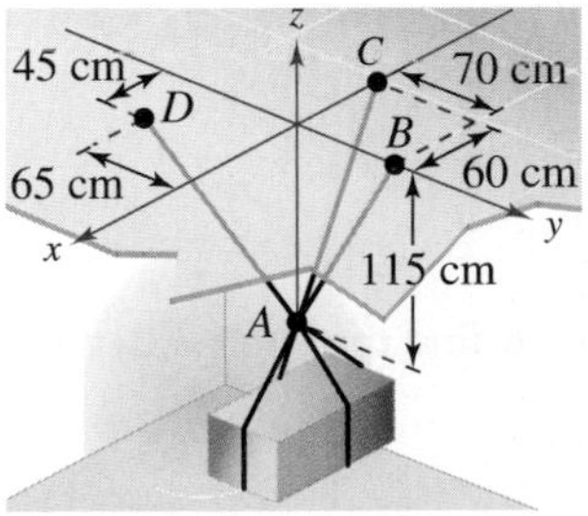

Model It

44. ***Tension*** The lights in an auditorium are 24-pound disks of radius 18 inches. Each disk is supported by three equally spaced cables that are L inches long (see figure).

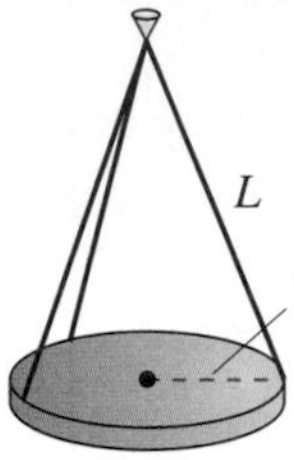

(a) Write the tension T in each cable as a function of L. Determine the domain of the function.

(b) Use the function from part (a) to complete the table.

L	20	25	30	35	40	45	50
T							

(c) Use a graphing utility to graph the function in part (a). What are the asymptotes of the graph? Interpret their meaning in the context of the problem.

(d) Determine the minimum length of each cable if a cable can carry a maximum load of 10 pounds.

Synthesis

True or False? **In Exercises 45 and 46, determine whether the statement is true or false. Justify your answer.**

45. If the dot product of two nonzero vectors is zero, then the angle between the vectors is a right angle.

46. If AB and AC are parallel vectors, then points A, B, and C are collinear.

47. What is known about the nonzero vectors $\mathbf{u}$ and $\mathbf{v}$ if $\mathbf{u} \cdot \mathbf{v} < 0$? Explain.

48. ***Writing*** Consider the two nonzero vectors $\mathbf{u}$ and $\mathbf{v}$. Describe the geometric figure generated by the terminal points of the vectors $t\mathbf{v}$, $\mathbf{u} + t\mathbf{v}$, and $s\mathbf{u} + t\mathbf{v}$, where s and t represent real numbers.

Skills Review

In Exercises 49–52, find a set of parametric equations for the rectangular equation using (a) $t = x$ and (b) $t = x + 1$.

49. $y = 3x + 2$

50. $y = \dfrac{2}{x}$

51. $y = x^2 - 8$

52. $y = 4x^3$

11.3 The Cross Product of Two Vectors

What you should learn

- Find cross products of vectors in space.
- Use geometric properties of cross products of vectors in space.
- Use triple scalar products to find volumes of parallelepipeds.

Why you should learn it

The cross product of two vectors in space has many applications in physics and engineering. For instance, in Exercise 43 on page 833, the cross product is used to find the torque on the crank of a bicycle's brake.

Carl Schneider/Getty Images

The Cross Product

Many applications in physics, engineering, and geometry involve finding a vector in space that is orthogonal to two given vectors. In this section, you will study a product that will yield such a vector. It is called the **cross product**, and it is conveniently defined and calculated using the standard unit vector form.

Definition of Cross Product of Two Vectors in Space

Let

$$\mathbf{u} = u_1\mathbf{i} + u_2\mathbf{j} + u_3\mathbf{k} \quad \text{and} \quad \mathbf{v} = v_1\mathbf{i} + v_2\mathbf{j} + v_3\mathbf{k}$$

be vectors in space. The cross product of $\mathbf{u}$ and $\mathbf{v}$ is the vector

$$\mathbf{u} \times \mathbf{v} = (u_2v_3 - u_3v_2)\mathbf{i} - (u_1v_3 - u_3v_1)\mathbf{j} + (u_1v_2 - u_2v_1)\mathbf{k}.$$

It is important to note that this definition applies only to three-dimensional vectors. The cross product is not defined for two-dimensional vectors.

A convenient way to calculate $\mathbf{u} \times \mathbf{v}$ is to use the following *determinant form* with cofactor expansion. (This 3×3 determinant form is used simply to help remember the formula for the cross product—it is technically not a determinant because the entries of the corresponding matrix are not all real numbers.)

$$\mathbf{u} \times \mathbf{v} = \begin{vmatrix} \mathbf{i} & \mathbf{j} & \mathbf{k} \\ u_1 & u_2 & u_3 \\ v_1 & v_2 & v_3 \end{vmatrix}$$

Put $\mathbf{u}$ in Row 2.

Put $\mathbf{v}$ in Row 3.

$$= \begin{vmatrix} u_2 & u_3 \\ v_2 & v_3 \end{vmatrix}\mathbf{i} - \begin{vmatrix} u_1 & u_3 \\ v_1 & v_3 \end{vmatrix}\mathbf{j} + \begin{vmatrix} u_1 & u_2 \\ v_1 & v_2 \end{vmatrix}\mathbf{k}$$

$$= (u_2v_3 - u_3v_2)\mathbf{i} - (u_1v_3 - u_3v_1)\mathbf{j} + (u_1v_2 - u_2v_1)\mathbf{k}$$

Note the minus sign in front of the $\mathbf{j}$-component. Recall from Section 8.4 that each of the three 2×2 determinants can be evaluated by using the following pattern.

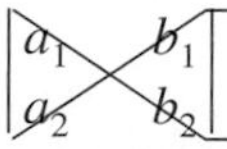

$$\begin{vmatrix} a_1 & b_1 \\ a_2 & b_2 \end{vmatrix} = a_1b_2 - a_2b_1$$

Exploration

Find each cross product. What can you conclude?

a. $\mathbf{i} \times \mathbf{j}$ **b.** $\mathbf{i} \times \mathbf{k}$ **c.** $\mathbf{j} \times \mathbf{k}$

Technology

Some graphing utilities have the capability to perform vector operations, such as the cross product. Consult the user's guide for your graphing utility for specific instructions.

Exploration

Calculate $\mathbf{u} \times \mathbf{v}$ and $-(\mathbf{v} \times \mathbf{u})$ for several values of $\mathbf{u}$ and $\mathbf{v}$. What do your results imply? Interpret your results geometrically.

Example 1 Finding Cross Products

Given $\mathbf{u} = \mathbf{i} + 2\mathbf{j} + \mathbf{k}$ and $\mathbf{v} = 3\mathbf{i} + \mathbf{j} + 2\mathbf{k}$, find each cross product.

a. $\mathbf{u} \times \mathbf{v}$ **b.** $\mathbf{v} \times \mathbf{u}$ **c.** $\mathbf{v} \times \mathbf{v}$

Solution

$$\textbf{a. } \mathbf{u} \times \mathbf{v} = \begin{vmatrix} \mathbf{i} & \mathbf{j} & \mathbf{k} \\ 1 & 2 & 1 \\ 3 & 1 & 2 \end{vmatrix}$$

$$= \begin{vmatrix} 2 & 1 \\ 1 & 2 \end{vmatrix}\mathbf{i} - \begin{vmatrix} 1 & 1 \\ 3 & 2 \end{vmatrix}\mathbf{j} + \begin{vmatrix} 1 & 2 \\ 3 & 1 \end{vmatrix}\mathbf{k}$$

$$= (4 - 1)\mathbf{i} - (2 - 3)\mathbf{j} + (1 - 6)\mathbf{k}$$

$$= 3\mathbf{i} + \mathbf{j} - 5\mathbf{k}$$

$$\textbf{b. } \mathbf{v} \times \mathbf{u} = \begin{vmatrix} \mathbf{i} & \mathbf{j} & \mathbf{k} \\ 3 & 1 & 2 \\ 1 & 2 & 1 \end{vmatrix}$$

$$= \begin{vmatrix} 1 & 2 \\ 2 & 1 \end{vmatrix}\mathbf{i} - \begin{vmatrix} 3 & 2 \\ 1 & 1 \end{vmatrix}\mathbf{j} + \begin{vmatrix} 3 & 1 \\ 1 & 2 \end{vmatrix}\mathbf{k}$$

$$= (1 - 4)\mathbf{i} - (3 - 2)\mathbf{j} + (6 - 1)\mathbf{k}$$

$$= -3\mathbf{i} - \mathbf{j} + 5\mathbf{k}$$

$$\textbf{c. } \mathbf{v} \times \mathbf{v} = \begin{vmatrix} \mathbf{i} & \mathbf{j} & \mathbf{k} \\ 3 & 1 & 2 \\ 3 & 1 & 2 \end{vmatrix} = \mathbf{0}$$

CHECKPOINT Now try Exercise 9.

The results obtained in Example 1 suggest some interesting algebraic properties of the cross product. For instance,

$$\mathbf{u} \times \mathbf{v} = -(\mathbf{v} \times \mathbf{u}) \quad \text{and} \quad \mathbf{v} \times \mathbf{v} = \mathbf{0}.$$

These properties, and several others, are summarized in the following list.

Algebraic Properties of the Cross Product

Let $\mathbf{u}$, $\mathbf{v}$, and $\mathbf{w}$ be vectors in space and let c be a scalar.

1. $\mathbf{u} \times \mathbf{v} = -(\mathbf{v} \times \mathbf{u})$
2. $\mathbf{u} \times (\mathbf{v} + \mathbf{w}) = (\mathbf{u} \times \mathbf{v}) + (\mathbf{u} \times \mathbf{w})$
3. $c(\mathbf{u} \times \mathbf{v}) = (c\mathbf{u}) \times \mathbf{v} = \mathbf{u} \times (c\mathbf{v})$
4. $\mathbf{u} \times \mathbf{0} = \mathbf{0} \times \mathbf{u} = \mathbf{0}$
5. $\mathbf{u} \times \mathbf{u} = \mathbf{0}$
6. $\mathbf{u} \cdot (\mathbf{v} \times \mathbf{w}) = (\mathbf{u} \times \mathbf{v}) \cdot \mathbf{w}$

For proofs of the Algebraic Properties of the Cross Product, see Proofs in Mathematics on page 847.

Geometric Properties of the Cross Product

The first property listed on the preceding page indicates that the cross product is *not commutative*. In particular, this property indicates that the vectors $\mathbf{u} \times \mathbf{v}$ and $\mathbf{v} \times \mathbf{u}$ have equal lengths but opposite directions. The following list gives some other *geometric* properties of the cross product of two vectors.

Geometric Properties of the Cross Product

Let $\mathbf{u}$ and $\mathbf{v}$ be nonzero vectors in space, and let θ be the angle between $\mathbf{u}$ and $\mathbf{v}$.

1. $\mathbf{u} \times \mathbf{v}$ is orthogonal to both $\mathbf{u}$ and $\mathbf{v}$.
2. $\|\mathbf{u} \times \mathbf{v}\| = \|\mathbf{u}\| \, \|\mathbf{v}\| \sin \theta$
3. $\mathbf{u} \times \mathbf{v} = \mathbf{0}$ if and only if $\mathbf{u}$ and $\mathbf{v}$ are scalar multiples of each other.
4. $\|\mathbf{u} \times \mathbf{v}\| =$ area of parallelogram having $\mathbf{u}$ and $\mathbf{v}$ as adjacent sides.

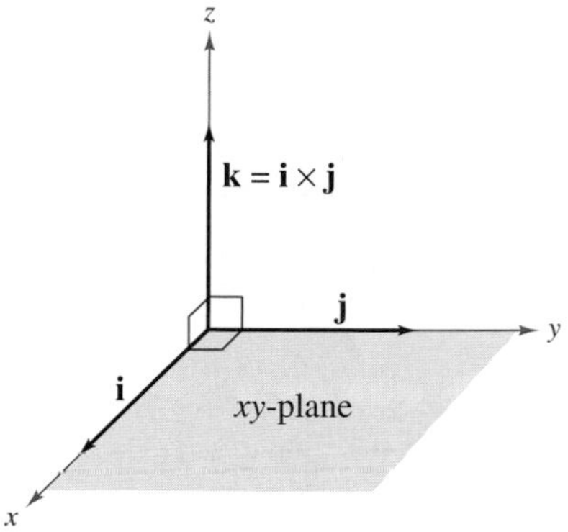

FIGURE 11.21

For proofs of the Geometric Properties of the Cross Product, see Proofs in Mathematics on page 848.

Both $\mathbf{u} \times \mathbf{v}$ and $\mathbf{v} \times \mathbf{u}$ are perpendicular to the plane determined by $\mathbf{u}$ and $\mathbf{v}$. One way to remember the orientations of the vectors $\mathbf{u}$, $\mathbf{v}$, and $\mathbf{u} \times \mathbf{v}$ is to compare them with the unit vectors $\mathbf{i}$, $\mathbf{j}$, and $\mathbf{k} = \mathbf{i} \times \mathbf{j}$, as shown in Figure 11.21. The three vectors $\mathbf{u}$, $\mathbf{v}$, and $\mathbf{u} \times \mathbf{v}$ form a *right-handed system*.

Example 2 Using the Cross Product

Find a unit vector that is orthogonal to both

$$\mathbf{u} = 3\mathbf{i} - 4\mathbf{j} + \mathbf{k} \quad \text{and} \quad \mathbf{v} = -3\mathbf{i} + 6\mathbf{j}.$$

Solution

The cross product $\mathbf{u} \times \mathbf{v}$, as shown in Figure 11.22, is orthogonal to both $\mathbf{u}$ and $\mathbf{v}$.

$$\mathbf{u} \times \mathbf{v} = \begin{vmatrix} \mathbf{i} & \mathbf{j} & \mathbf{k} \\ 3 & -4 & 1 \\ -3 & 6 & 0 \end{vmatrix}$$

$$= -6\mathbf{i} - 3\mathbf{j} + 6\mathbf{k}$$

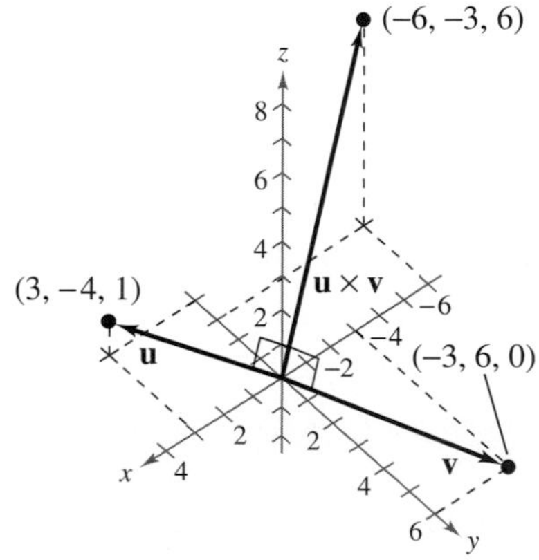

FIGURE 11.22

Because

$$\|\mathbf{u} \times \mathbf{v}\| = \sqrt{(-6)^2 + (-3)^2 + 6^2}$$

$$= \sqrt{81}$$

$$= 9$$

a unit vector orthogonal to both $\mathbf{u}$ and $\mathbf{v}$ is

$$\frac{\mathbf{u} \times \mathbf{v}}{\|\mathbf{u} \times \mathbf{v}\|} = -\frac{2}{3}\mathbf{i} - \frac{1}{3}\mathbf{j} + \frac{2}{3}\mathbf{k}.$$

CHECKPOINT Now try Exercise 15.

In Example 2, note that you could have used the cross product $\mathbf{v} \times \mathbf{u}$ to form a unit vector that is orthogonal to both $\mathbf{u}$ and $\mathbf{v}$. With that choice, you would have obtained the *negative* of the unit vector found in the example.

The fourth geometric property of the cross product states that $\|\mathbf{u} \times \mathbf{v}\|$ is the area of the parallelogram that has $\mathbf{u}$ and $\mathbf{v}$ as adjacent sides. A simple example of this is given by the unit square with adjacent sides of $\mathbf{i}$ and $\mathbf{j}$. Because

$$\mathbf{i} \times \mathbf{j} = \mathbf{k}$$

and $\|\mathbf{k}\| = 1$, it follows that the square has an area of 1. This geometric property of the cross product is illustrated further in the next example.

Example 3 Geometric Application of the Cross Product

Show that the quadrilateral with vertices at the following points is a parallelogram. Then find the area of the parallelogram. Is the parallelogram a rectangle?

$$A(5, 2, 0), \quad B(2, 6, 1), \quad C(2, 4, 7), \quad D(5, 0, 6)$$

Solution

From Figure 11.23 you can see that the sides of the quadrilateral correspond to the following four vectors.

$$\overrightarrow{AB} = -3\mathbf{i} + 4\mathbf{j} + \mathbf{k}$$

$$\overrightarrow{CD} = 3\mathbf{i} - 4\mathbf{j} - \mathbf{k} = -\overrightarrow{AB}$$

$$\overrightarrow{AD} = 0\mathbf{i} - 2\mathbf{j} + 6\mathbf{k}$$

$$\overrightarrow{CB} = 0\mathbf{i} + 2\mathbf{j} - 6\mathbf{k} = -\overrightarrow{AD}$$

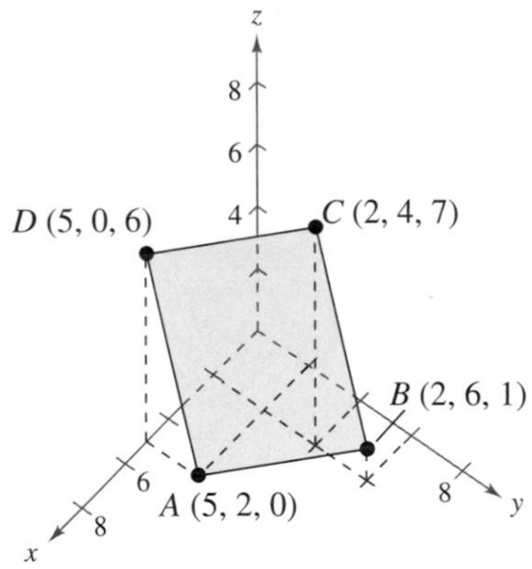

FIGURE 11.23

Because $\overrightarrow{CD} = -\overrightarrow{AB}$ and $\overrightarrow{CB} = -\overrightarrow{AD}$, you can conclude that $\overrightarrow{AB}$ is parallel to $\overrightarrow{CD}$ and $\overrightarrow{AD}$ is parallel to $\overrightarrow{CB}$. It follows that the quadrilateral is a parallelogram with $\overrightarrow{AB}$ and $\overrightarrow{AD}$ as adjacent sides. Moreover, because

$$\overrightarrow{AB} \times \overrightarrow{AD} = \begin{vmatrix} \mathbf{i} & \mathbf{j} & \mathbf{k} \\ -3 & 4 & 1 \\ 0 & -2 & 6 \end{vmatrix} = 26\mathbf{i} + 18\mathbf{j} + 6\mathbf{k}$$

the area of the parallelogram is

$$\|\overrightarrow{AB} \times \overrightarrow{AD}\| = \sqrt{26^2 + 18^2 + 6^2} = \sqrt{1036} \approx 32.19.$$

You can tell whether the parallelogram is a rectangle by finding the angle between the vectors $\overrightarrow{AB}$ and $\overrightarrow{AD}$.

$$\sin\theta = \frac{\|\overrightarrow{AB} \times \overrightarrow{AD}\|}{\|\overrightarrow{AB}\|\,\|\overrightarrow{AD}\|}$$

$$= \frac{\sqrt{1036}}{\sqrt{26}\sqrt{40}} \approx 0.998$$

$$\theta = \arcsin 0.998$$

$$\theta \approx 86.4°$$

Because $\theta \neq 90°$, the parallelogram is not a rectangle.

CHECKPOINT Now try Exercise 27.

Exploration

If you connect the terminal points of two vectors **u** and **v** that have the same initial points, a triangle is formed. Is it possible to use the cross product $\mathbf{u} \times \mathbf{v}$ to determine the area of the triangle? Explain. Verify your conclusion using two vectors from Example 3.

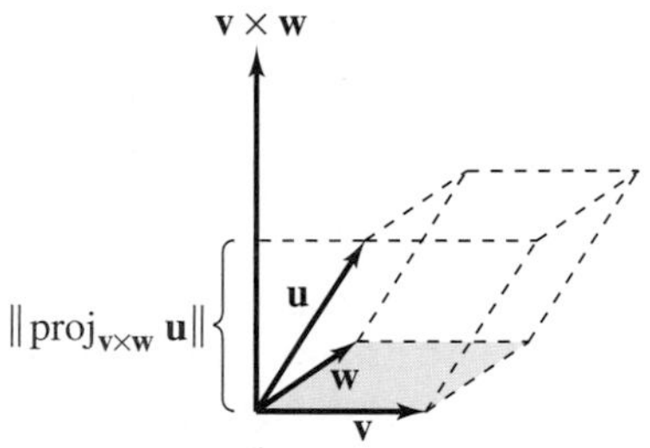

Area of base $= \|\mathbf{v} \times \mathbf{w}\|$
Volume of parallelepiped $= |\mathbf{u} \cdot (\mathbf{v} \times \mathbf{w})|$
FIGURE 11.24

The Triple Scalar Product

For the vectors **u**, **v**, and **w** in space, the dot product of **u** and $\mathbf{v} \times \mathbf{w}$ is called the triple scalar product of **u**, **v**, and **w**.

The Triple Scalar Product

For $\mathbf{u} = u_1\mathbf{i} + u_2\mathbf{j} + u_3\mathbf{k}$, $\mathbf{v} = v_1\mathbf{i} + v_2\mathbf{j} + v_3\mathbf{k}$, and $\mathbf{w} = w_1\mathbf{i} + w_2\mathbf{j} + w_3\mathbf{k}$, the **triple scalar product** is given by

$$\mathbf{u} \cdot (\mathbf{v} \times \mathbf{w}) = \begin{vmatrix} u_1 & u_2 & u_3 \\ v_1 & v_2 & v_3 \\ w_1 & w_2 & w_3 \end{vmatrix}.$$

If the vectors **u**, **v**, and **w** do not lie in the same plane, the triple scalar product $\mathbf{u} \cdot (\mathbf{v} \times \mathbf{w})$ can be used to determine the volume of the parallelepiped (a polyhedron, all of whose faces are parallelograms) with **u**, **v**, and **w** as adjacent edges, as shown in Figure 11.24.

Geometric Property of Triple Scalar Product

The volume V of a parallelepiped with vectors **u**, **v**, and **w** as adjacent edges is given by

$$V = |\mathbf{u} \cdot (\mathbf{v} \times \mathbf{w})|.$$

Example 4 Volume by the Triple Scalar Product

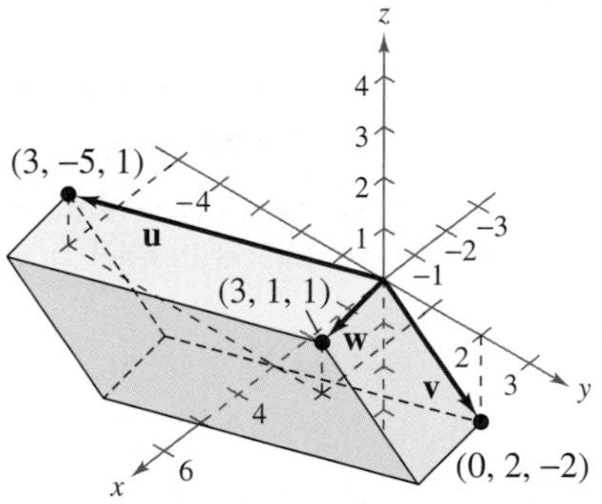

FIGURE 11.25

Find the volume of the parallelepiped having

$$\mathbf{u} = 3\mathbf{i} - 5\mathbf{j} + \mathbf{k}, \quad \mathbf{v} = 2\mathbf{j} - 2\mathbf{k}, \quad \text{and} \quad \mathbf{w} = 3\mathbf{i} + \mathbf{j} + \mathbf{k}$$

as adjacent edges, as shown in Figure 11.25.

Solution

The value of the triple scalar product is

$$\mathbf{u} \cdot (\mathbf{v} \times \mathbf{w}) = \begin{vmatrix} 3 & -5 & 1 \\ 0 & 2 & -2 \\ 3 & 1 & 1 \end{vmatrix}$$

$$= 3\begin{vmatrix} 2 & -2 \\ 1 & 1 \end{vmatrix} - (-5)\begin{vmatrix} 0 & -2 \\ 3 & 1 \end{vmatrix} + 1\begin{vmatrix} 0 & 2 \\ 3 & 1 \end{vmatrix}$$

$$= 3(4) + 5(6) + 1(-6)$$

$$= 36.$$

So, the volume of the parallelepiped is

$$|\mathbf{u} \cdot (\mathbf{v} \times \mathbf{w})| = |36| = 36.$$

CHECKPOINT Now try Exercise 39.

11.3 Exercises

VOCABULARY CHECK: Fill in the blanks.

1. To find a vector in space that is orthogonal to two given vectors, find the _______ _______ of the two vectors.
2. $\mathbf{u} \times \mathbf{u} =$ _______
3. $\|\mathbf{u} \times \mathbf{v}\| =$ _______
4. The dot product of **u** and $\mathbf{v} \times \mathbf{w}$ is called the _______ _______ _______ of **u**, **v**, and **w**.

In Exercises 1–4, find the cross product of the unit vectors and sketch the result.

1. $\mathbf{j} \times \mathbf{i}$
2. $\mathbf{k} \times \mathbf{j}$
3. $\mathbf{i} \times \mathbf{k}$
4. $\mathbf{k} \times \mathbf{i}$

In Exercises 5–14, find $\mathbf{u} \times \mathbf{v}$ and show that it is orthogonal to both u and v.

5. $\mathbf{u} = \langle 3, -2, 5 \rangle$, $\mathbf{v} = \langle 0, -1, 1 \rangle$
6. $\mathbf{u} = \langle 6, 8, 3 \rangle$, $\mathbf{v} = \langle 4, -1, -4 \rangle$
7. $\mathbf{u} = \langle -10, 0, 6 \rangle$, $\mathbf{v} = \langle 7, 0, 0 \rangle$
8. $\mathbf{u} = \langle -5, 5, 11 \rangle$, $\mathbf{v} = \langle 2, 2, 3 \rangle$
9. $\mathbf{u} = 6\mathbf{i} + 2\mathbf{j} + \mathbf{k}$, $\mathbf{v} = \mathbf{i} + 3\mathbf{j} - 2\mathbf{k}$
10. $\mathbf{u} = \mathbf{i} + \frac{3}{2}\mathbf{j} - \frac{5}{2}\mathbf{k}$, $\mathbf{v} = \frac{1}{2}\mathbf{i} - \frac{3}{4}\mathbf{j} + \frac{1}{4}\mathbf{k}$
11. $\mathbf{u} = 6\mathbf{k}$, $\mathbf{v} = -\mathbf{i} + 3\mathbf{j} + \mathbf{k}$
12. $\mathbf{u} = \frac{2}{3}\mathbf{i}$, $\mathbf{v} = \frac{1}{3}\mathbf{j} - 3\mathbf{k}$
13. $\mathbf{u} = -\mathbf{i} + \mathbf{k}$, $\mathbf{v} = \mathbf{j} - 2\mathbf{k}$
14. $\mathbf{u} = \mathbf{i} - 2\mathbf{k}$, $\mathbf{v} = -\mathbf{j} + \mathbf{k}$

In Exercises 15–20, find a unit vector orthogonal to u and v.

15. $\mathbf{u} = 3\mathbf{i} + \mathbf{j}$, $\mathbf{v} = \mathbf{j} + \mathbf{k}$
16. $\mathbf{u} = \mathbf{i} + 2\mathbf{j}$, $\mathbf{v} = \mathbf{i} - 3\mathbf{k}$
17. $\mathbf{u} = -3\mathbf{i} + 2\mathbf{j} - 5\mathbf{k}$, $\mathbf{v} = \frac{1}{2}\mathbf{i} - \frac{3}{4}\mathbf{j} + \frac{1}{10}\mathbf{k}$
18. $\mathbf{u} = 7\mathbf{i} - 14\mathbf{j} + 5\mathbf{k}$, $\mathbf{v} = 14\mathbf{i} + 28\mathbf{j} - 15\mathbf{k}$
19. $\mathbf{u} = \mathbf{i} + \mathbf{j} - \mathbf{k}$, $\mathbf{v} = \mathbf{i} + \mathbf{j} + \mathbf{k}$
20. $\mathbf{u} = \mathbf{i} - 2\mathbf{j} + 2\mathbf{k}$, $\mathbf{v} = 2\mathbf{i} - \mathbf{j} - 2\mathbf{k}$

In Exercises 21–26, find the area of the parallelogram that has the vectors as adjacent sides.

21. $\mathbf{u} = \mathbf{k}$, $\mathbf{v} = \mathbf{i} + \mathbf{k}$
22. $\mathbf{u} = \mathbf{i} + 2\mathbf{j} + 2\mathbf{k}$, $\mathbf{v} = \mathbf{i} + \mathbf{k}$
23. $\mathbf{u} = 3\mathbf{i} + 4\mathbf{j} + 6\mathbf{k}$, $\mathbf{v} = 2\mathbf{i} - \mathbf{j} + 5\mathbf{k}$
24. $\mathbf{u} = -2\mathbf{i} + 3\mathbf{j} + 2\mathbf{k}$, $\mathbf{v} = \mathbf{i} + 2\mathbf{j} + 4\mathbf{k}$
25. $\mathbf{u} = \langle 2, 2, -3 \rangle$, $\mathbf{v} = \langle 0, 2, 3 \rangle$
26. $\mathbf{u} = \langle 4, -3, 2 \rangle$, $\mathbf{v} = \langle 5, 0, 1 \rangle$

In Exercises 27 and 28, (a) verify that the points are the vertices of a parallelogram, (b) find its area, and (c) determine whether the parallelogram is a rectangle.

27. $A(2, -1, 4)$, $B(3, 1, 2)$, $C(0, 5, 6)$, $D(-1, 3, 8)$
28. $A(1, 1, 1)$, $B(2, 3, 4)$, $C(6, 5, 2)$, $D(7, 7, 5)$

In Exercises 29–32, find the area of the triangle with the given vertices. (The area A of the triangle having u and v as adjacent sides is given by $A = \frac{1}{2}\|\mathbf{u} \times \mathbf{v}\|$.)

29. $(0, 0, 0)$, $(1, 2, 3)$, $(-3, 0, 0)$
30. $(1, -4, 3)$, $(2, 0, 2)$, $(-2, 2, 0)$
31. $(2, 3, -5)$, $(-2, -2, 0)$, $(3, 0, 6)$
32. $(2, 4, 0)$, $(-2, -4, 0)$, $(0, 0, 4)$

In Exercises 33–36, find the triple scalar product.

33. $\mathbf{u} = \langle 2, 3, 3 \rangle$, $\mathbf{v} = \langle 4, 4, 0 \rangle$, $\mathbf{w} = \langle 0, 0, 4 \rangle$
34. $\mathbf{u} = \langle 2, 0, 1 \rangle$, $\mathbf{v} = \langle 0, 3, 0 \rangle$, $\mathbf{w} = \langle 0, 0, 1 \rangle$
35. $\mathbf{u} = 2\mathbf{i} + 3\mathbf{j} + \mathbf{k}$, $\mathbf{v} = \mathbf{i} - \mathbf{j}$, $\mathbf{w} = 4\mathbf{i} + 3\mathbf{j} + \mathbf{k}$
36. $\mathbf{u} = \mathbf{i} + 4\mathbf{j} - 7\mathbf{k}$, $\mathbf{v} = 2\mathbf{i} + 4\mathbf{k}$, $\mathbf{w} = -3\mathbf{j} + 6\mathbf{k}$

In Exercises 37–40, use the triple scalar product to find the volume of the parallelepiped having adjacent edges u, v, and w.

37. $\mathbf{u} = \mathbf{i} + \mathbf{j}$, $\mathbf{v} = \mathbf{j} + \mathbf{k}$, $\mathbf{w} = \mathbf{i} + \mathbf{k}$

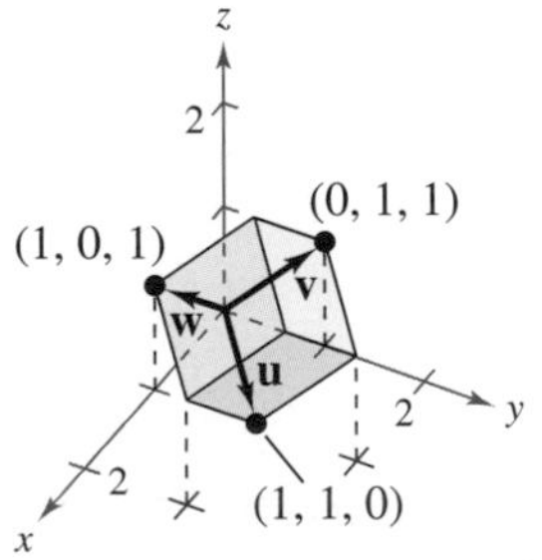

38. $\mathbf{u} = \mathbf{i} + \mathbf{j} + 3\mathbf{k}$, $\mathbf{v} = 3\mathbf{j} + 3\mathbf{k}$, $\mathbf{w} = 3\mathbf{i} + 3\mathbf{k}$

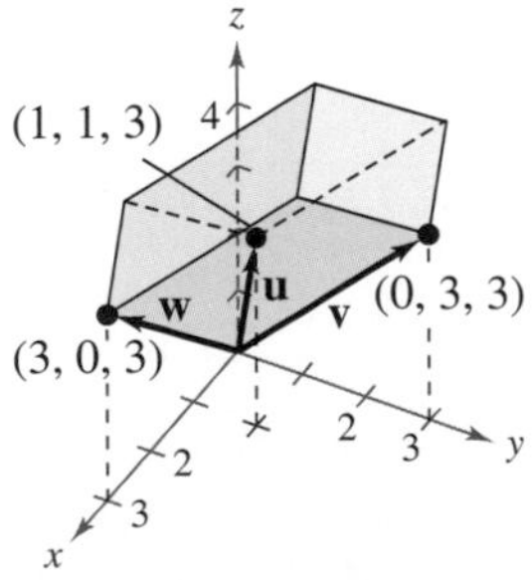

39. $\mathbf{u} = \langle 0, 2, 2 \rangle$
$\mathbf{v} = \langle 0, 0, -2 \rangle$
$\mathbf{w} = \langle 3, 0, 2 \rangle$

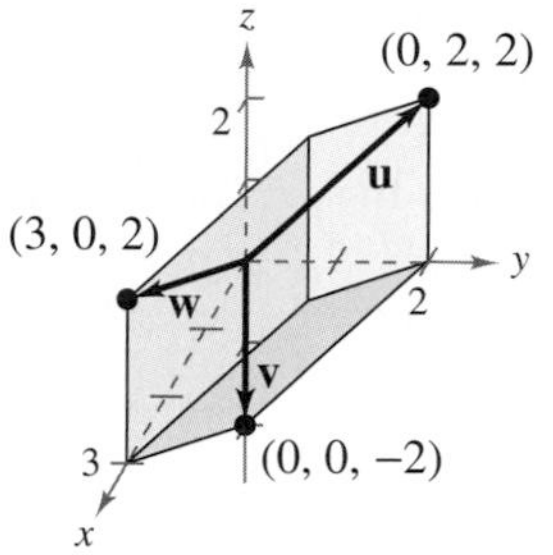

40. $\mathbf{u} = \langle 1, 2, -1 \rangle$
$\mathbf{v} = \langle -1, 2, 2 \rangle$
$\mathbf{w} = \langle 2, 0, 1 \rangle$

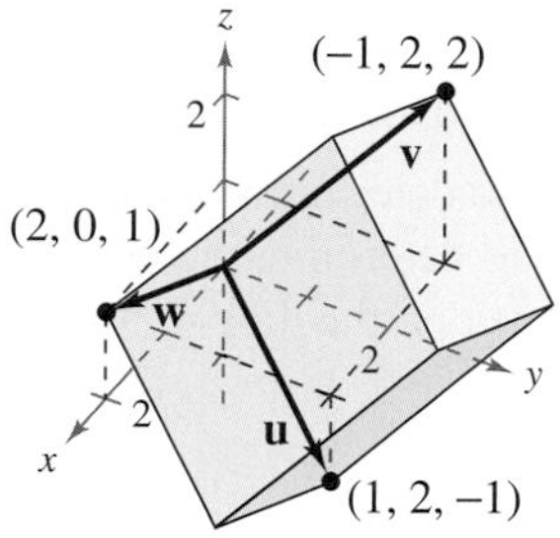

In Exercises 41 and 42, find the volume of the parallelepiped with the given vertices.

41. $A(0, 0, 0)$, $B(4, 0, 0)$, $C(4, -2, 3)$, $D(0, -2, 3)$, $E(4, 5, 3)$, $F(0, 5, 3)$, $G(0, 3, 6)$, $H(4, 3, 6)$

42. $A(0, 0, 0)$, $B(1, 1, 0)$, $C(1, 0, 2)$, $D(0, 1, 1)$, $E(2, 1, 2)$, $F(1, 1, 3)$, $G(1, 2, 1)$, $H(2, 2, 3)$

Model It

43. ***Torque*** The brakes on a bicycle are applied by using a downward force of p pounds on the pedal when the six-inch crank makes a 40° angle with the horizontal (see figure). Vectors representing the position of the crank and the force are $\mathbf{V} = \frac{1}{2}(-\cos 40°\mathbf{j} - \sin 40°\mathbf{k})$ and $\mathbf{F} = -p\mathbf{k}$, respectively.

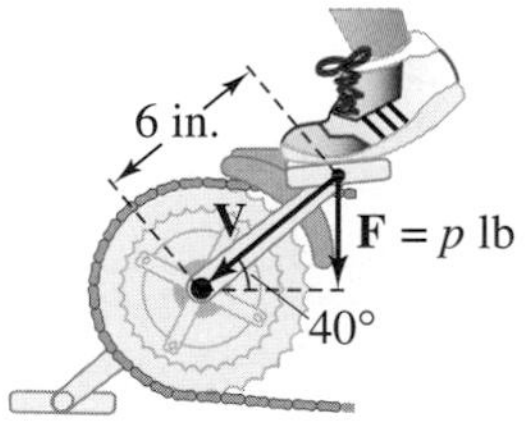

(a) The magnitude of the torque on the crank is given by $\|V \times F\|$. Using the given information, write the torque T on the crank as a function of p.

(b) Use the function from part (a) to complete the table.

p	15	20	25	30	35	40	45
T							

44. ***Torque*** Both the magnitude and direction of the force on a crankshaft change as the crankshaft rotates. Use the technique given in Exercise 43 to find the magnitude of the torque on the crankshaft using the position and data shown in the figure.

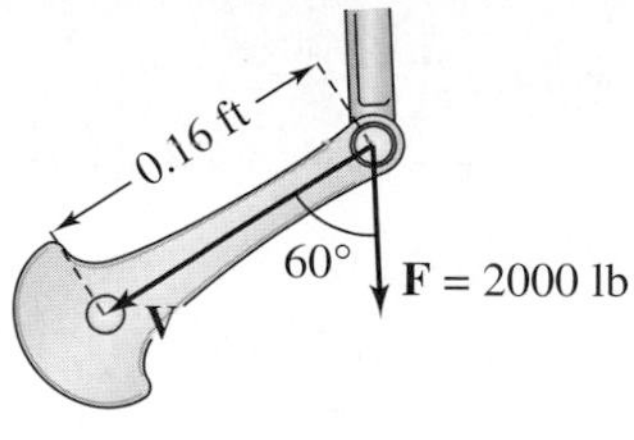

FIGURE FOR 44

Synthesis

True or False? **In Exercises 45 and 46, determine whether the statement is true or false. Justify your answer.**

45. The cross product is not defined for vectors in the plane.

46. If $\mathbf{u}$ and $\mathbf{v}$ are vectors in space that are nonzero and nonparallel, then $\mathbf{u} \times \mathbf{v} = \mathbf{v} \times \mathbf{u}$.

47. ***Think About It*** If the magnitudes of two vectors are doubled, how will the magnitude of the cross product of the vectors change?

48. ***Proof*** Consider the vectors $\mathbf{u} = \langle \cos \alpha, \sin \alpha, 0 \rangle$ and $\mathbf{v} = \langle \cos \beta, \sin \beta, 0 \rangle$, where $\alpha > \beta$. Find the cross product of the vectors and use the result to prove the identity

$$\sin(\alpha - \beta) = \sin \alpha \cos \beta - \cos \alpha \sin \beta.$$

Skills Review

In Exercises 49–56, evaluate the expression without using a calculator.

49. $\cos 480°$

50. $\tan 300°$

51. $\sin 690°$

52. $\cos 930°$

53. $\sin \dfrac{19\pi}{6}$

54. $\cos \dfrac{17\pi}{6}$

55. $\tan \dfrac{15\pi}{4}$

56. $\tan \dfrac{10\pi}{3}$

In Exercises 57 and 58, sketch the region determined by the constraints. Then find the minimum and maximum values of the objective function and where they occur, subject to the indicated constraints.

57. Objective function:
$z = 6x + 4y$
Constraints:
$x + 6y \leq 30$
$6x + y \leq 40$
$x \geq 0$
$y \geq 0$

58. Objective function:
$z = 6x + 7y$
Constraints:
$4x + 3y \geq 24$
$x + 3y \geq 15$
$x \geq 0$
$y \geq 0$

11.4 Lines and Planes in Space

What you should learn

- Find parametric and symmetric equations of lines in space.
- Find equations of planes in space.
- Sketch planes in space.
- Find distances between points and planes in space.

Why you should learn it

Equations in three variables can be used to model real-life data. For instance, in Exercise 47 on page 842, you will determine how changes in the consumption of two types of milk affect the consumption of a third type of milk.

Lines in Space

In the plane, *slope* is used to determine an equation of a line. In space, it is more convenient to use *vectors* to determine the equation of a line.

In Figure 11.26, consider the line L through the point $P(x_1, y_1, z_1)$ and parallel to the vector

$$\mathbf{v} = \langle a, b, c \rangle. \qquad \text{Direction vector for } L$$

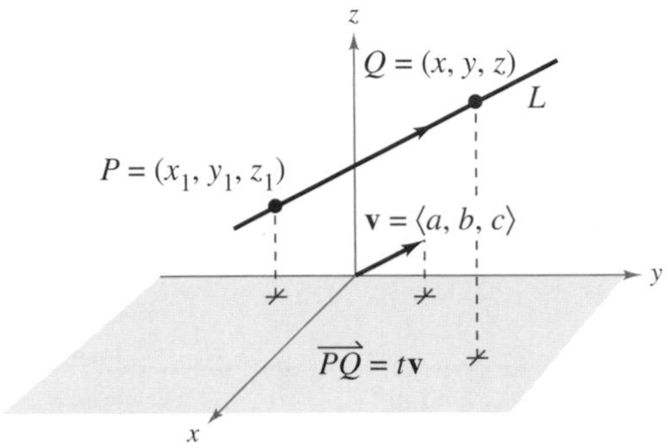

FIGURE 11.26

The vector $\mathbf{v}$ is the **direction vector** for the line L, and a, b, and c are the **direction numbers.** One way of describing the line L is to say that it consists of all points $Q(x, y, z)$ for which the vector $\overrightarrow{PQ}$ is parallel to $\mathbf{v}$. This means that $\overrightarrow{PQ}$ is a scalar multiple of $\mathbf{v}$, and you can write $\overrightarrow{PQ} = t\mathbf{v}$, where t is a scalar.

$$\begin{aligned} \overrightarrow{PQ} &= \langle x - x_1, y - y_1, z - z_1 \rangle \\ &= \langle at, bt, ct \rangle \\ &= t\mathbf{v} \end{aligned}$$

By equating corresponding components, you can obtain the **parametric equations of a line in space.**

> **Parametric Equations of a Line in Space**
>
> A line L parallel to the vector $\mathbf{v} = \langle a, b, c \rangle$ and passing through the point $P(x_1, y_1, z_1)$ is represented by the parametric equations
>
> $$x = x_1 + at, \qquad y = y_1 + bt, \qquad \text{and} \qquad z = z_1 + ct.$$

If the direction numbers a, b, and c are all nonzero, you can eliminate the parameter t to obtain the **symmetric equations** of a line.

$$\frac{x - x_1}{a} = \frac{y - y_1}{b} = \frac{z - z_1}{c} \qquad \text{Symmetric equations}$$

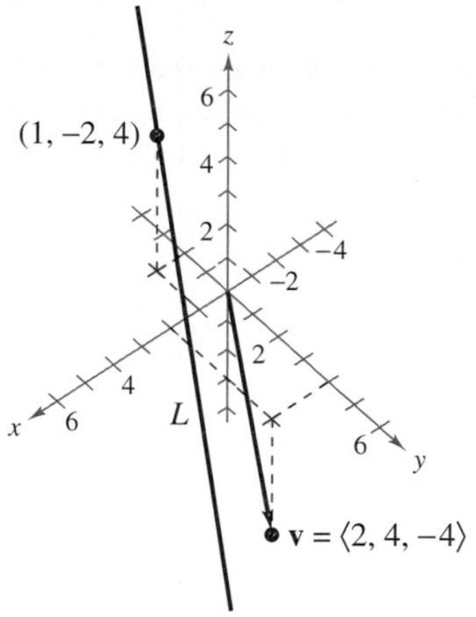

FIGURE 11.27

Example 1 Finding Parametric and Symmetric Equations

Find parametric and symmetric equations of the line L that passes through the point $(1, -2, 4)$ and is parallel to $\mathbf{v} = \langle 2, 4, -4 \rangle$.

Solution

To find a set of parametric equations of the line, use the coordinates $x_1 = 1$, $y_1 = -2$, and $z_1 = 4$ and direction numbers $a = 2$, $b = 4$, and $c = -4$ (see Figure 11.27).

$$x = 1 + 2t, \qquad y = -2 + 4t, \qquad z = 4 - 4t \qquad \text{Parametric equations}$$

Because a, b, and c are all nonzero, a set of symmetric equations is

$$\frac{x-1}{2} = \frac{y+2}{4} = \frac{z-4}{-4}. \qquad \text{Symmetric equations}$$

CHECKPOINT Now try Exercise 1.

Neither the parametric equations nor the symmetric equations of a given line are unique. For instance, in Example 1, by letting $t = 1$ in the parametric equations you would obtain the point $(3, 2, 0)$. Using this point with the direction numbers $a = 2$, $b = 4$, and $c = -4$ produces the parametric equations

$$x = 3 + 2t, \qquad y = 2 + 4t, \quad \text{and} \quad z = -4t.$$

STUDY TIP

To check the answer to Example 2, verify that the two original points lie on the line. To see this, substitute $t = 0$ and $t = 1$ in the parametric equations as follows.

$t = 0$:

$x = -2 + 3(0) = -2$

$y = 1 + 2(0) = 1$

$z = 5(0) = 0$

$t = 1$:

$x = -2 + 3(1) = 1$

$y = 1 + 2(1) = 3$

$z = 5(1) = 5$

Example 2 Parametric and Symmetric Equations of a Line Through Two Points

Find a set of parametric and symmetric equations of the line that passes through the points $(-2, 1, 0)$ and $(1, 3, 5)$.

Solution

Begin by letting $P = (-2, 1, 0)$ and $Q = (1, 3, 5)$. Then a direction vector for the line passing through P and Q is

$$\begin{aligned}\mathbf{v} &= \overrightarrow{PQ} \\ &= \langle 1 - (-2), 3 - 1, 5 - 0 \rangle \\ &= \langle 3, 2, 5 \rangle \\ &= \langle a, b, c \rangle.\end{aligned}$$

Using the direction numbers $a = 3$, $b = 2$, and $c = 5$ with the initial point $P(-2, 1, 0)$, you can obtain the parametric equations

$$x = -2 + 3t, \qquad y = 1 + 2t, \quad \text{and} \quad z = 5t. \qquad \text{Parametric equations}$$

Because a, b, and c are all nonzero, a set of symmetric equations is

$$\frac{x+2}{3} = \frac{y-1}{2} = \frac{z}{5}. \qquad \text{Symmetric equations}$$

CHECKPOINT Now try Exercise 7.

Planes in Space

You have seen how an equation of a line in space can be obtained from a point on the line and a vector *parallel* to it. You will now see that an equation of a plane in space can be obtained from a point in the plane and a vector *normal* (perpendicular) to the plane.

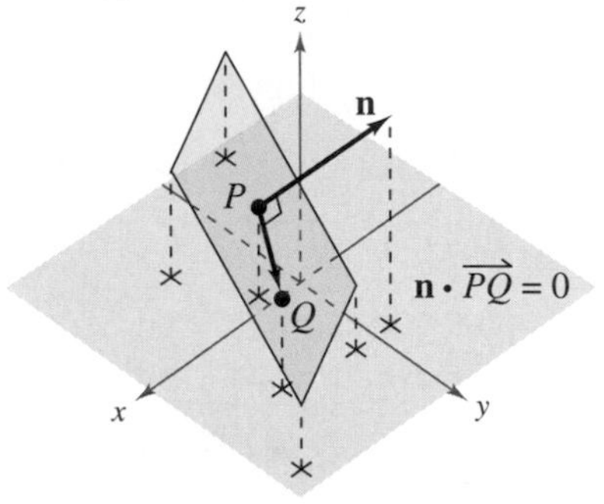

FIGURE 11.28

Consider the plane containing the point $P(x_1, y_1, z_1)$ having a nonzero normal vector $\mathbf{n} = \langle a, b, c\rangle$, as shown in Figure 11.28. This plane consists of all points $Q(x, y, z)$ for which the vector $\overrightarrow{PQ}$ is orthogonal to **n**. Using the dot product, you can write the following.

$$\mathbf{n} \cdot \overrightarrow{PQ} = 0 \qquad \overrightarrow{PQ} \text{ is orthogonal to } \mathbf{n}.$$

$$\langle a, b, c\rangle \cdot \langle x - x_1, y - y_1, z - z_1\rangle = 0$$

$$a(x - x_1) + b(y - y_1) + c(z - z_1) = 0$$

The third equation of the plane is said to be in standard form.

Standard Equation of a Plane in Space

The plane containing the point (x_1, y_1, z_1) and having normal vector $\mathbf{n} = \langle a, b, c\rangle$ can be represented by the **standard form of the equation of a plane** $a(x - x_1) + b(y - y_1) + c(z - z_1) = 0$.

Regrouping terms yields the **general form of the equation of a plane** in space

$$ax + by + cz + d = 0. \qquad \text{General form of equation of plane}$$

Given the general form of the equation of a plane, it is easy to find a normal vector to the plane. Use the coefficients of x, y, and z to write $\mathbf{n} = \langle a, b, c\rangle$.

Exploration

Consider the following four planes.

$$2x + 3y - z = 2 \qquad 4x + 6y - 2z = 5$$

$$-2x - 3y + z = -2 \qquad -6x - 9y + 3z = 11$$

What are the normal vectors for each plane? What can you say about the relative positions of these planes in space?

Example 3 Finding an Equation of a Plane in Three-Space

Find the general form of the equation of the plane passing through the points $(2, 1, 1)$, $(0, 4, 1)$, and $(-2, 1, 4)$.

Solution

To find the equation of the plane, you need a point in the plane and a vector that is normal to the plane. There are three choices for the point, but no normal vector is given. To obtain a normal vector, use the cross product of vectors **u** and **v** extending from the point $(2, 1, 1)$ to the points $(0, 4, 1)$ and $(-2, 1, 4)$, as shown in Figure 11.29. The component forms of **u** and **v** are

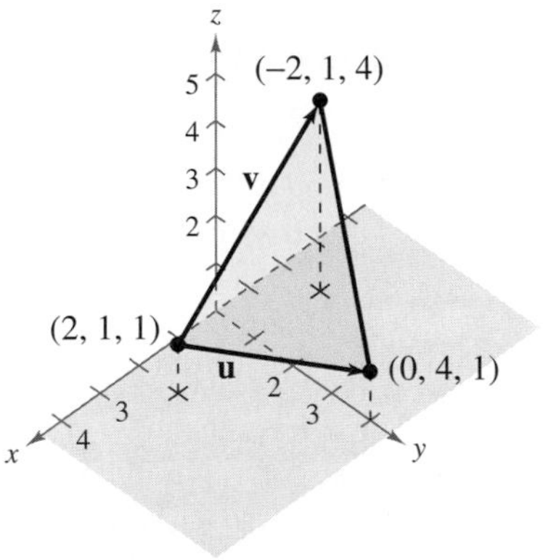

FIGURE 11.29

$$\mathbf{u} = \langle 0 - 2, 4 - 1, 1 - 1 \rangle = \langle -2, 3, 0 \rangle$$

$$\mathbf{v} = \langle -2 - 2, 1 - 1, 4 - 1 \rangle = \langle -4, 0, 3 \rangle$$

and it follows that

$$\mathbf{n} = \mathbf{u} \times \mathbf{v} = \begin{vmatrix} \mathbf{i} & \mathbf{j} & \mathbf{k} \\ -2 & 3 & 0 \\ -4 & 0 & 3 \end{vmatrix}$$

$$= 9\mathbf{i} + 6\mathbf{j} + 12\mathbf{k}$$

$$= \langle a, b, c \rangle$$

is normal to the given plane. Using the direction numbers for **n** and the initial point $(x_1, y_1, z_1) = (2, 1, 1)$, you can determine an equation of the plane to be

$$a(x - x_1) + b(y - y_1) + c(z - z_1) = 0$$

$$9(x - 2) + 6(y - 1) + 12(z - 1) = 0 \qquad \text{Standard form}$$

$$9x + 6y + 12z - 36 = 0$$

$$3x + 2y + 4z - 12 = 0. \qquad \text{General form}$$

Check that each of the three points satisfies the equation $3x + 2y + 4z - 12 = 0$.

CHECKPOINT Now try Exercise 25.

Two distinct planes in three-space either are parallel or intersect in a line. If they intersect, you can determine the angle θ $(0 \le \theta \le 90°)$ between them from the angle between their normal vectors, as shown in Figure 11.30. Specifically, if vectors $\mathbf{n}_1$ and $\mathbf{n}_2$ are normal to two intersecting planes, the angle θ between the normal vectors is equal to the **angle between the two planes** and is given by

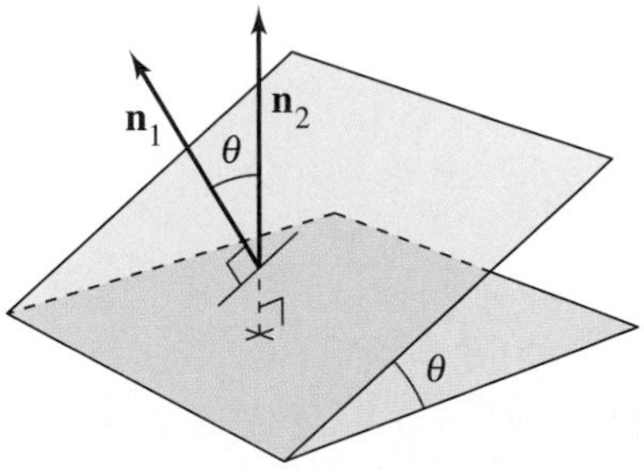

FIGURE 11.30

$$\cos\theta = \frac{|\mathbf{n}_1 \cdot \mathbf{n}_2|}{\|\mathbf{n}_1\|\,\|\mathbf{n}_2\|}. \qquad \text{Angle between two planes}$$

Consequently, two planes with normal vectors $\mathbf{n}_1$ and $\mathbf{n}_2$ are

1. *perpendicular* if $\mathbf{n}_1 \cdot \mathbf{n}_2 = 0$.
2. *parallel* if $\mathbf{n}_1$ is a scalar multiple of $\mathbf{n}_2$.

Example 4 Finding the Line of Intersection of Two Planes

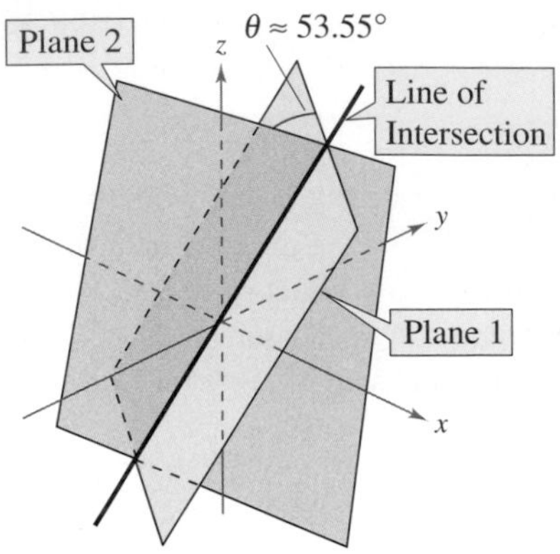

FIGURE 11.31

Find the angle between the two planes given by

$$x - 2y + z = 0 \qquad \text{Equation for plane 1}$$

$$2x + 3y - 2z = 0 \qquad \text{Equation for plane 2}$$

and find parametric equations of their line of intersection (see Figure 11.31).

Solution

The normal vectors for the planes are $\mathbf{n}_1 = \langle 1, -2, 1 \rangle$ and $\mathbf{n}_2 = \langle 2, 3, -2 \rangle$. Consequently, the angle between the two planes is determined as follows.

$$\cos\theta = \frac{|\mathbf{n}_1 \cdot \mathbf{n}_2|}{\|\mathbf{n}_1\|\,\|\mathbf{n}_2\|} = \frac{|-6|}{\sqrt{6}\sqrt{17}} = \frac{6}{\sqrt{102}} \approx 0.59409.$$

This implies that the angle between the two planes is $\theta \approx 53.55°$. You can find the line of intersection of the two planes by simultaneously solving the two linear equations representing the planes. One way to do this is to multiply the first equation by -2 and add the result to the second equation.

$$\begin{array}{r} x - 2y + z = 0 \\ \underline{2x + 3y - 2z = 0} \end{array} \quad \Longrightarrow \quad \begin{array}{r} -2x + 4y - 2z = 0 \\ \underline{2x + 3y - 2z = 0} \\ 7y - 4z = 0 \end{array} \quad \Longrightarrow \quad y = \frac{4z}{7}$$

Substituting $y = 4z/7$ back into one of the original equations, you can determine that $x = z/7$. Finally, by letting $t = z/7$, you obtain the parametric equations

$$x = t = x_1 + at, \qquad y = 4t = y_1 + bt, \qquad z = 7t = z_1 + ct.$$

Because $(x_1, y_1, z_1) = (0, 0, 0)$ lies in both planes, you can substitute for x_1, y_1, and z_1 in these parametric equations, which indicates that $a = 1$, $b = 4$, and $c = 7$ are direction numbers for the line of intersection.

CHECKPOINT Now try Exercise 33.

Note that the direction numbers in Example 4 can also be obtained from the cross product of the two normal vectors as follows.

$$\mathbf{n}_1 \times \mathbf{n}_2 = \begin{vmatrix} \mathbf{i} & \mathbf{j} & \mathbf{k} \\ 1 & -2 & 1 \\ 2 & 3 & -2 \end{vmatrix}$$

$$= \begin{vmatrix} -2 & 1 \\ 3 & -2 \end{vmatrix}\mathbf{i} - \begin{vmatrix} 1 & 1 \\ 2 & -2 \end{vmatrix}\mathbf{j} + \begin{vmatrix} 1 & -2 \\ 2 & 3 \end{vmatrix}\mathbf{k}$$

$$= \mathbf{i} + 4\mathbf{j} + 7\mathbf{k}$$

This means that the *line of intersection of the two planes is parallel to the cross product of their normal vectors.*

Sketching Planes in Space

Technology

Most three-dimensional graphing utilities and computer algebra systems can graph a plane in space. Consult the user's guide for your utility for specific instructions.

As discussed in Section 11.1, if a plane in space intersects one of the coordinate planes, the line of intersection is called the *trace* of the given plane in the coordinate plane. To sketch a plane in space, it is helpful to find its points of intersection with the coordinate axes and its traces in the coordinate planes. For example, consider the plane

$$3x + 2y + 4z = 12. \qquad \text{Equation of plane}$$

You can find the xy-trace by letting $z = 0$ and sketching the line

$$3x + 2y = 12 \qquad xy\text{-trace}$$

in the xy-plane. This line intersects the x-axis at $(4, 0, 0)$ and the y-axis at $(0, 6, 0)$. In Figure 11.32, this process is continued by finding the yz-trace and the xz-trace and then shading the triangular region lying in the first octant.

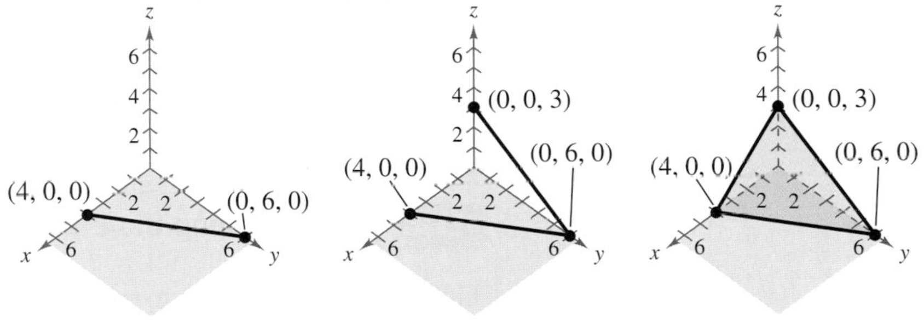

(a) *xy-trace* $(z = 0)$: $3x + 2y = 12$ (b) *yz-trace* $(x = 0)$: $2y + 4z = 12$ (c) *xz-trace* $(y = 0)$: $3x + 4z = 12$

FIGURE 11.32

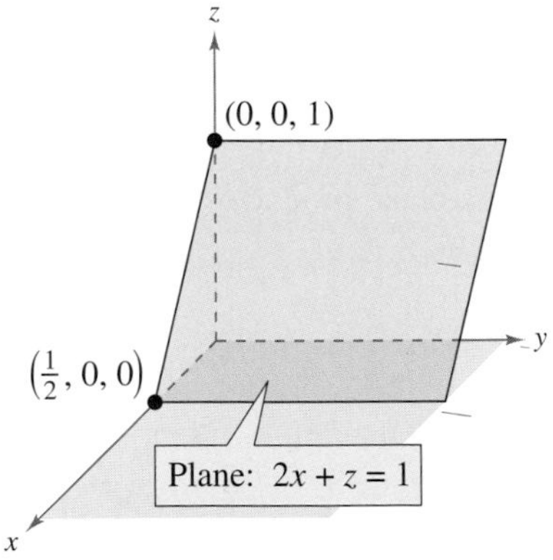

Plane is parallel to y-axis

FIGURE 11.33

If the equation of a plane has a missing variable, such as $2x + z = 1$, the plane must be *parallel to the axis* represented by the missing variable, as shown in Figure 11.33. If two variables are missing from the equation of a plane, then it is *parallel to the coordinate* plane represented by the missing variables, as shown in Figure 11.34.

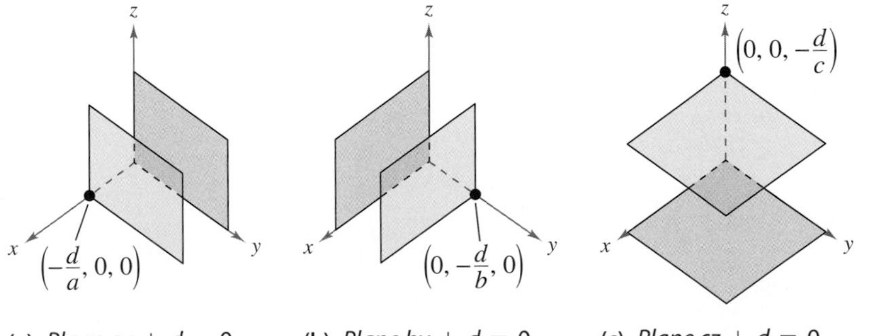

(a) *Plane* $ax + d = 0$ *is parallel to yz-plane.* (b) *Plane* $by + d = 0$ *is parallel to xz-plane.* (c) *Plane* $cz + d = 0$ *is parallel to xy-plane.*

FIGURE 11.34

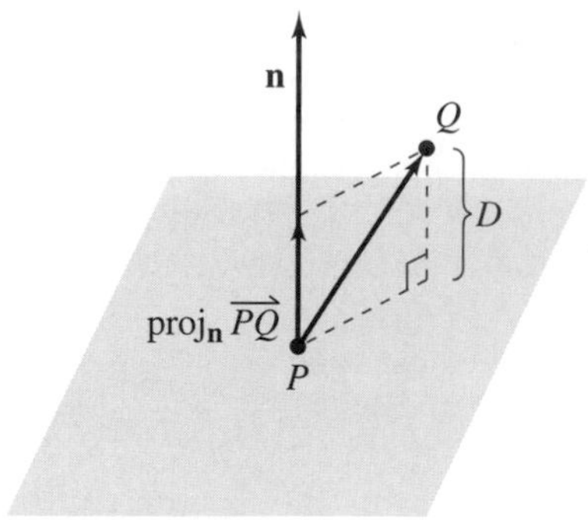

$D = \|\text{proj}_{\mathbf{n}}\overrightarrow{PQ}\|$
FIGURE 11.35

Distance Between a Point and a Plane

The distance D between a point Q and a plane is the length of the shortest line segment connecting Q to the plane, as shown in Figure 11.35. If P is *any* point in the plane, you can find this distance by projecting the vector $\overrightarrow{PQ}$ onto the normal vector $\mathbf{n}$. The length of this projection is the desired distance.

Distance Between a Point and a Plane

The **distance between a plane and a point Q** (not in the plane) is

$$D = \|\text{proj}_{\mathbf{n}}\overrightarrow{PQ}\|$$
$$= \frac{|\overrightarrow{PQ} \cdot \mathbf{n}|}{\|\mathbf{n}\|}$$

where P is a point in the plane and $\mathbf{n}$ is normal to the plane.

To find a point in the plane given by $ax + by + cz + d = 0$, where $a \neq 0$, let $y = 0$ and $z = 0$. Then, from the equation $ax + d = 0$, you can conclude that the point $(-d/a, 0, 0)$ lies in the plane.

Example 5 Finding the Distance Between a Point and a Plane

Find the distance between the point $Q(1, 5, -4)$ and the plane $3x - y + 2z = 6$.

Solution

You know that $\mathbf{n} = \langle 3, -1, 2\rangle$ is normal to the given plane. To find a point in the plane, let $y = 0$ and $z = 0$, and obtain the point $P(2, 0, 0)$. The vector from P to Q is

$$\overrightarrow{PQ} = \langle 1 - 2, 5 - 0, -4 - 0\rangle$$
$$= \langle -1, 5, -4\rangle.$$

The formula for the distance between a point and a plane produces

$$D = \frac{|\overrightarrow{PQ} \cdot \mathbf{n}|}{\|\mathbf{n}\|}$$
$$= \frac{|\langle -1, 5, -4\rangle \cdot \langle 3, -1, 2\rangle|}{\sqrt{9 + 1 + 4}}$$
$$= \frac{|-3 - 5 - 8|}{\sqrt{14}}$$
$$= \frac{16}{\sqrt{14}}.$$

CHECKPOINT Now try Exercise 45.

The choice of the point P in Example 5 is arbitrary. Try choosing a different point to verify that you obtain the same distance.

11.4 Exercises

VOCABULARY CHECK: Fill in the blanks.

1. The _______ vector for a line L is given by $\mathbf{v} =$ _______ .
2. The _______ _______ of a line in space are given by $x = x_1 + at$, $y = y_1 + bt$, and $z = z_1 + ct$.
3. If the direction numbers a, b, and c of the vector $\mathbf{v} = \langle a, b, c\rangle$ are all nonzero, you can eliminate the parameter to obtain the _______ _______ of a line.
4. A vector that is perpendicular to a plane is called _______ .
5. The standard form of the equation of a plane is given by _______ .

In Exercises 1–6, find a set of (a) parametric equations and (b) symmetric equations for the line through the point and parallel to the specified vector or line. (For each line, write the direction numbers as integers.)

	Point	*Parallel to*
1.	$(0, 0, 0)$	$\mathbf{v} = \langle 1, 2, 3\rangle$
2.	$(3, -5, 1)$	$\mathbf{v} = \langle 3, -7, -10\rangle$
3.	$(-4, 1, 0)$	$\mathbf{v} = \frac{1}{2}\mathbf{i} + \frac{4}{3}\mathbf{j} - \mathbf{k}$
4.	$(5, 0, 10)$	$\mathbf{v} = 4\mathbf{i} + 3\mathbf{k}$
5.	$(2, -3, 5)$	$x = 5 + 2t,\ y = 7 - 3t,\ z = -2 + t$
6.	$(1, 0, 1)$	$x = 3 + 3t,\ y = 5 - 2t,\ z = -7 + t$

In Exercises 7–14, find (a) a set of parametric equations and (b) if possible, a set of symmetric equations of the line that passes through the given points. (For each line, write the direction numbers as integers.)

7. $(2, 0, 2), (1, 4, -3)$

8. $(2, 3, 0), (10, 8, 12)$

9. $(-3, 8, 15), (1, -2, 16)$

10. $(2, 3, -1), (1, -5, 3)$

11. $(3, 1, 2), (-1, 1, 5)$

12. $(2, -1, 5), (2, 1, -3)$

13. $\left(-\frac{1}{2}, 2, \frac{1}{2}\right), \left(1, -\frac{1}{2}, 0\right)$

14. $\left(-\frac{3}{2}, \frac{3}{2}, 2\right), (3, -5, -4)$

In Exercises 15 and 16, sketch a graph of the line.

15. $x = 2t,\ y = 2 + t,$
$z = 1 + \frac{1}{2}t$

16. $x = 5 - 2t,\ y = 1 + t,$
$z = 5 - \frac{1}{2}t$

In Exercises 17–22, find the general form of the equation of the plane passing through the point and perpendicular to the specified vector or line.

	Point	*Perpendicular to*
17.	$(2, 1, 2)$	$\mathbf{n} = \mathbf{i}$
18.	$(1, 0, -3)$	$\mathbf{n} = \mathbf{k}$
19.	$(5, 6, 3)$	$\mathbf{n} = -2\mathbf{i} + \mathbf{j} - 2\mathbf{k}$
20.	$(0, 0, 0)$	$\mathbf{n} = -3\mathbf{j} + 5\mathbf{k}$
21.	$(2, 0, 0)$	$x = 3 - t,\ y = 2 - 2t,\ z = 4 + t$
22.	$(0, 0, 6)$	$x = 1 - t,\ y = 2 + t,\ z = 4 - 2t$

In Exercises 23–26, find the general form of the equation of the plane passing through the three points.

23. $(0, 0, 0), (1, 2, 3), (-2, 3, 3)$

24. $(4, -1, 3), (2, 5, 1), (-1, 2, 1)$

25. $(2, 3, -2), (3, 4, 2), (1, -1, 0)$

26. $(5, -1, 4), (1, -1, 2), (2, 1, -3)$

In Exercises 27 and 28, find the general form of the equation of the plane with the given characteristics.

27. The plane passes through the point $(2, 5, 3)$ and is parallel to the xz-plane.

28. The plane passes through the points $(2, 2, 1)$ and $(-1, 1, -1)$ and is perpendicular to the plane $2x - 3y + z = 3$.

In Exercises 29–32, determine whether the planes are parallel, orthogonal, or neither. If they are neither parallel nor orthogonal, find the angle of intersection.

29. $5x - 3y + z = 4$
$x + 4y + 7z = 1$

30. $3x + y - 4z = 3$
$-9x - 3y + 12z = 4$

31. $2x - z = 1$
$4x + y + 8z = 10$

32. $x - 5y - z = 1$
$5x - 25y - 5z = -3$

In Exercises 33–36, (a) find the angle between the two planes and (b) find parametric equations of their line of intersection.

33. $3x - 4y + 5z = 6$
$x + y - z = 2$

34. $x - 3y + z = -2$
$2x + 5z + 3 = 0$

35. $x + y - z = 0$
$2x - 5y - z = 1$

36. $2x + 4y - 2z = 1$
$-3x - 6y + 3z = 10$

In Exercises 37–42, plot the intercepts and sketch a graph of the plane.

37. $x + 2y + 3z = 6$

38. $2x - y + 4z = 4$

39. $x + 2y = 4$

40. $y + z = 5$

41. $3x + 2y - z = 6$

42. $x - 3z = 6$

In Exercises 43–46, find the distance between the point and the plane.

43. $(0, 0, 0)$
$8x - 4y + z = 8$

44. $(3, 2, 1)$
$x - y + 2z = 4$

45. $(4, -2, -2)$
$2x - y + z = 4$

46. $(-1, 2, 5)$
$2x + 3y + z = 12$

Model It

47. ***Data Analysis: Milk Consumption*** The table shows the per capita milk consumptions (in gallons) of different types of plain milk in the United States from 1999 to 2003. Consumption of light and skim milks, reduced-fat milk, and whole milk are represented by the variables x, y, and z, respectively. (Source: U.S. Department of Agriculture)

Year	x	y	z
1999	6.2	7.3	7.8
2000	6.1	7.1	7.7
2001	5.9	7.0	7.4
2002	5.7	7.0	7.3
2003	5.6	6.9	7.2

A model for the data is given by

$-0.81x - 0.36y + z = 0.2.$

(a) Complete a fifth column in the table using the model to approximate z for the given values of x and y.

(b) Compare the approximations from part (a) with the actual values of z.

(c) According to this model, any increases or decreases in consumption of two types of milk will have what effect on the consumption of the third type of milk?

48. ***Mechanical Design*** A chute at the top of a grain elevator of a combine funnels the grain into a bin as shown in the figure. Find the angle between two adjacent sides.

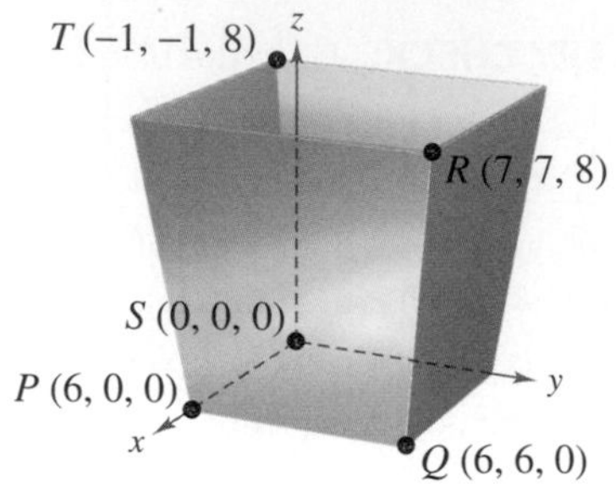

Synthesis

True or False? **In Exercises 49 and 50, determine whether the statement is true or false. Justify your answer.**

49. Every two lines in space are either intersecting or parallel.

50. Two nonparallel planes in space will always intersect.

51. The direction numbers of two distinct lines in space are 10, -18, 20, and -15, 27, -30. What is the relationship between the lines? Explain.

52. ***Exploration***

(a) Describe and find an equation for the surface generated by all points (x, y, z) that are two units from the point $(4, -1, 1)$.

(b) Describe and find an equation for the surface generated by all points (x, y, z) that are two units from the plane $4x - 3y + z = 10$.

Skills Review

In Exercises 53–56, convert the polar equation to rectangular form.

53. $r = 10$

54. $\theta = \frac{3\pi}{4}$

55. $r = 3 \cos \theta$

56. $r = \frac{1}{2 - \cos \theta}$

In Exercises 57–60, convert the rectangular equation to polar form.

57. $x^2 + y^2 = 49$

58. $x^2 + y^2 - 4x = 0$

59. $y = 5$

60. $2x - y + 1 = 0$

11 Chapter Summary

What did you learn?

	Review Exercises
Section 11.1	
☐ Plot points in the three-dimensional coordinate system *(p. 812)*.	1–4
☐ Find distances between points in space and find midpoints of line segments joining points in space *(p. 813)*.	5–12
☐ Write equations of spheres in standard form and find traces of surfaces in space *(p. 814)*.	13–20
Section 11.2	
☐ Find the component forms of, the unit vectors in the same direction of, the magnitudes of, the dot products of, and the angles between vectors in space *(p. 820)*.	21–30
☐ Determine whether vectors in space are parallel or orthogonal *(p. 822)*.	31–34
☐ Use vectors in space to solve real-life problems *(p. 824)*.	35, 36
Section 11.3	
☐ Find cross products of vectors in space *(p. 827)*.	37, 38
☐ Use geometric properties of cross products of vectors in space *(p. 829)*.	39–42
☐ Use triple scalar products to find volumes of parallelepipeds *(p. 831)*.	43, 44
Section 11.4	
☐ Find parametric and symmetric equations of lines in space *(p. 834)*.	45–48
☐ Find equations of planes in space *(p. 836)*.	49–52
☐ Sketch planes in space *(p. 839)*.	53–56
☐ Find distances between points and planes in space *(p. 840)*.	57–60

11 Review Exercises

11.1 In Exercises 1 and 2, plot each point in the same three-dimensional coordinate system.

1. (a) $(5, -1, 2)$
   (b) $(-3, 3, 0)$
2. (a) $(2, 4, -3)$
   (b) $(0, 0, 5)$

3. Find the coordinates of the point in the xy-plane four units to the right of the xz-plane and five units behind the yz-plane.
4. Find the coordinates of the point located on the y-axis and seven units to the left of the xz-plane.

In Exercises 5 and 6, find the distance between the points.

5. $(4, 0, 7), (5, 2, 1)$
6. $(2, 3, -4), (-1, -3, 0)$

In Exercises 7 and 8, find the lengths of the sides of the right triangle. Show that these lengths satisfy the Pythagorean Theorem.

7. 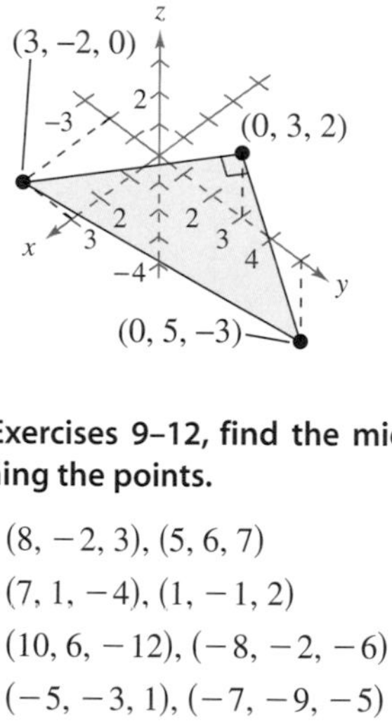

8. 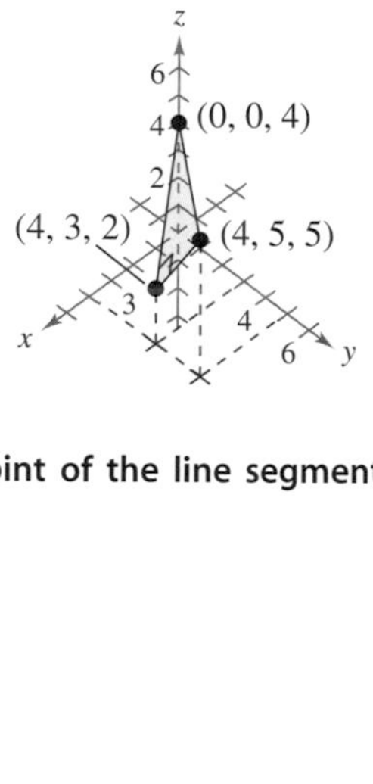

In Exercises 9–12, find the midpoint of the line segment joining the points.

9. $(8, -2, 3), (5, 6, 7)$
10. $(7, 1, -4), (1, -1, 2)$
11. $(10, 6, -12), (-8, -2, -6)$
12. $(-5, -3, 1), (-7, -9, -5)$

In Exercises 13–16, find the standard form of the equation of the sphere with the given characteristics.

13. Center: $(2, 3, 5)$; radius: 1
14. Center: $(3, -2, 4)$; radius: 4
15. Center: $(1, 5, 2)$; diameter: 12
16. Center: $(0, 4, -1)$; diameter: 15

In Exercises 17 and 18, find the center and radius of the sphere.

17. $x^2 + y^2 + z^2 - 4x - 6y + 4 = 0$
18. $x^2 + y^2 + z^2 - 10x + 6y - 4z + 34 = 0$

In Exercises 19 and 20, sketch the graph of the equation and sketch the specified trace.

19. $x^2 + (y - 3)^2 + z^2 = 16$
    (a) xz-trace (b) yz-trace
20. $(x + 2)^2 + (y - 1)^2 + z^2 = 9$
    (a) xy-trace (b) yz-trace

11.2 In Exercises 21–24, (a) write the component form of the vector v, (b) find the magnitude of v, and (c) find a unit vector in the direction of v.

21. Initial point: $(2, -1, 4)$
    Terminal point: $(3, 3, 0)$
22. Initial point: $(2, -1, 2)$
    Terminal point: $(-3, 2, 3)$
23. Initial point: $(7, -4, 3)$
    Terminal point: $(-3, 2, 10)$
24. Initial point: $(0, 3, -1)$
    Terminal point: $(5, -8, 6)$

In Exercises 25–28, find the dot product of u and v.

25. $\mathbf{u} = \langle -1, 4, 3 \rangle$
    $\mathbf{v} = \langle 0, -6, 5 \rangle$
26. $\mathbf{u} = \langle 8, -4, 2 \rangle$
    $\mathbf{v} = \langle 2, 5, 2 \rangle$
27. $\mathbf{u} = 2\mathbf{i} - \mathbf{j} + \mathbf{k}$
    $\mathbf{v} = \mathbf{i} - \mathbf{k}$
28. $\mathbf{u} = 2\mathbf{i} + \mathbf{j} - 2\mathbf{k}$
    $\mathbf{v} = \mathbf{i} - 3\mathbf{j} + 2\mathbf{k}$

In Exercises 29 and 30, find the angle θ between the vectors.

29. $\mathbf{u} - \langle 2\sqrt{2}, -4, 4 \rangle$
    $\mathbf{v} = \langle -\sqrt{2}, 1, 2 \rangle$
30. $\mathbf{u} = \langle 3, 1, -1 \rangle$
    $\mathbf{v} = \langle 4, 5, 2 \rangle$

In Exercises 31 and 32, determine whether u and v are orthogonal, parallel, or neither.

31. $\mathbf{u} = \langle 39, -12, 21 \rangle$
    $\mathbf{v} = \langle -26, 8, -14 \rangle$
32. $\mathbf{u} = \langle 8, 5, -8 \rangle$
    $\mathbf{v} = \langle -2, 4, \frac{1}{2} \rangle$

In Exercises 33 and 34, use vectors to determine whether the points are collinear.

33. $(5, 2, 0), (2, 6, 1), (2, 4, 7)$

34. $(6, 3, -1), (5, 8, 3), (7, -2, -5)$

35. ***Tension*** A load of 300 pounds is supported by three cables, as shown in the figure. Find the tension in each of the supporting cables.

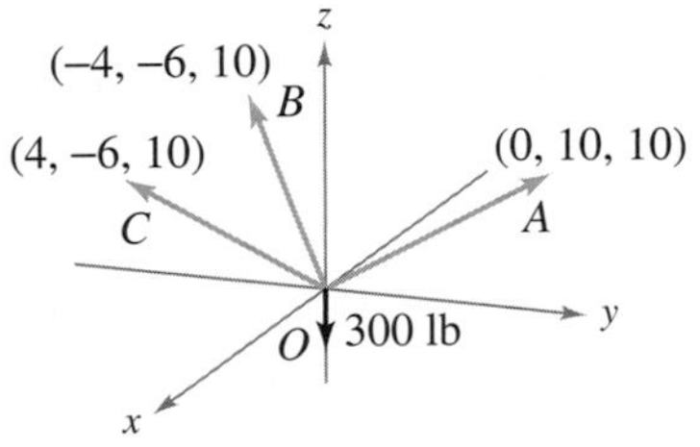

36. ***Tension*** Determine the tension in each of the supporting cables in Exercise 35 if the load is 200 pounds.

11.3 In Exercises 37 and 38, find u × v.

37. $\mathbf{u} = \langle -2, 8, 2\rangle$
$\mathbf{v} = \langle 1, 1, -1\rangle$

38. $\mathbf{u} = \langle 10, 15, 5\rangle$
$\mathbf{v} = \langle 5, -3, 0\rangle$

In Exercises 39 and 40, find a unit vector orthogonal to u and v.

39. $\mathbf{u} = -3\mathbf{i} + 2\mathbf{j} - 5\mathbf{k}$
$\mathbf{v} = 10\mathbf{i} - 15\mathbf{j} + 2\mathbf{k}$

40. $\mathbf{u} = 4\mathbf{k}$
$\mathbf{v} = \mathbf{i} + 12\mathbf{k}$

In Exercises 41 and 42, verify that the points are the vertices of a parallelogram and find its area.

41. $(2, -1, 1), (5, 1, 4), (0, 1, 1), (3, 3, 4)$

42. $(0, 4, 0), (1, 4, 1), (0, 6, 0), (1, 6, 1)$

In Exercises 43 and 44, find the volume of the parallelepiped with the given vertices.

43. $A(0, 0, 0), B(3, 0, 0), C(0, 5, 1), D(3, 5, 1),$
$E(2, 0, 5), F(5, 0, 5), G(2, 5, 6), H(5, 5, 6)$

44. $A(0, 0, 0), B(2, 0, 0), C(2, 4, 0), D(0, 4, 0),$
$E(0, 0, 6), F(2, 0, 6), G(2, 4, 6), H(0, 4, 6)$

11.4 In Exercises 45–48, find a set of (a) parametric equations and (b) symmetric equations for the specified line.

45. The line passes through the points $(-1, 3, 5)$ and $(3, 6, -1)$.

46. The line passes through the points $(0, -10, 3)$ and $(5, 10, 0)$.

47. The line passes through the point $(0, 0, 0)$ and is parallel to the vector $\mathbf{v} = \left\langle -2, \frac{5}{2}, 1\right\rangle$.

48. The line passes through the point $(3, 2, 1)$ and is parallel to the line given by $x = y = z$.

In Exercises 49–52, find the general form of the equation of the specified plane.

49. The plane passes through the points $(0, 0, 0), (5, 0, 2)$, and $(2, 3, 8)$.

50. The plane passes through the points $(-1, 3, 4), (4, -2, 2)$, and $(2, 8, 6)$.

51. The plane passes through the point $(5, 3, 2)$ and is parallel to the xy-plane.

52. The plane passes through the point $(0, 0, 6)$ and is perpendicular to the line given by $x = 1 - t$, $y = 2 + t$, and $z = 4 - 2t$.

In Exercises 53–56, plot the intercepts and sketch a graph of the plane.

53. $3x - 2y + 3z = 6$

54. $5x - y - 5z = 5$

55. $2x - 3z = 6$

56. $4y - 3z = 12$

In Exercises 57–60, find the distance between the point and the plane.

57. $(2, 3, 10)$
$2x - 20y + 6z = 6$

58. $(1, 2, 3)$
$2x - y + z = 4$

59. $(0, 0, 0)$
$x - 10y + 3z = 2$

60. $(0, 0, 0)$
$2x + 3y + z = 12$

Synthesis

True or False? **In Exercises 61 and 62, determine whether the statement is true or false. Justify your answer.**

61. The cross product is commutative.

62. The triple scalar product of three vectors in space is a scalar.

In Exercises 63–66, let $\mathbf{u} = \langle 3, -2, 1\rangle$, $\mathbf{v} = \langle 2, -4, -3\rangle$, and $\mathbf{w} = \langle -1, 2, 2\rangle$.

63. Show that $\mathbf{u} \cdot \mathbf{u} = \|\mathbf{u}\|^2$.

64. Show that $\mathbf{u} \times \mathbf{v} = -(\mathbf{v} \times \mathbf{u})$.

65. Show that $\mathbf{u} \cdot (\mathbf{v} + \mathbf{w}) = \mathbf{u} \cdot \mathbf{v} + \mathbf{u} \cdot \mathbf{w}$.

66. Show that $\mathbf{u} \times (\mathbf{v} + \mathbf{w}) = (\mathbf{u} \times \mathbf{v}) + (\mathbf{u} \times \mathbf{w})$.

11 Chapter Test

Take this test as you would take a test in class. After you are finished, check your work against the answers given in the back of the book.

1. Plot each point in the same three-dimensional coordinate system.
   (a) $(5, -2, 3)$ (b) $(-2, -2, 3)$

In Exercises 2–4, use the points $A(8, -2, 5)$, $B(6, 4, -1)$, and $C(-4, 3, 0)$, to solve the problem.

2. Consider the triangle with vertices A, B, and C. Is it a right triangle? Explain.
3. Find the coordinates of the midpoint of the line segment joining points A and B.
4. Find the standard form of the equation of the sphere for which A and B are the endpoints of a diameter. Sketch the sphere and its xz-trace.

In Exercises 5–8, let u and v be the vectors from $A(8, -2, 5)$ to $B(6, 4, -1)$ and A to $C(-4, 3, 0)$, respectively.

5. Write $\mathbf{u}$ and $\mathbf{v}$ in component form.
6. Find (a) $\|\mathbf{v}\|$, (b) $\mathbf{u} \cdot \mathbf{v}$, and (c) $\mathbf{u} \times \mathbf{v}$.
7. Find the angle between $\mathbf{u}$ and $\mathbf{v}$.
8. Find a set of (a) parametric equations and (b) symmetric equations for the line through points A and B.

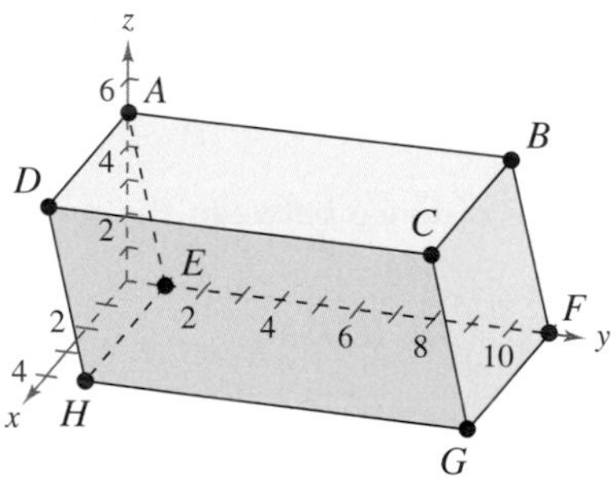

FIGURE FOR 13

In Exercises 9 and 10, determine whether u and v are orthogonal, parallel, or neither.

9. $\mathbf{u} = \mathbf{i} - 2\mathbf{j} - \mathbf{k}$
   $\mathbf{v} = \mathbf{j} + 6\mathbf{k}$
10. $\mathbf{u} = 2\mathbf{i} - 3\mathbf{j} + \mathbf{k}$
    $\mathbf{v} = -\mathbf{i} - \mathbf{j} - \mathbf{k}$

11. Verify that the points $(2, -3, 1)$, $(6, 5, -1)$, $(3, -6, 4)$, and $(7, 2, 2)$ are the vertices of a parallelogram, and find its area.
12. Find the general form of the equation of the plane passing through the points $(-3, -4, 2)$, $(-3, 4, 1)$, and $(1, 1, -2)$.
13. Find the volume of the parallelepiped at the left with the given vertices.
    $A(0, 0, 5)$, $B(0, 10, 5)$, $C(4, 10, 5)$, $D(4, 0, 5)$,
    $E(0, 1, 0)$, $F(0, 11, 0)$, $G(4, 11, 0)$, $H(4, 1, 0)$

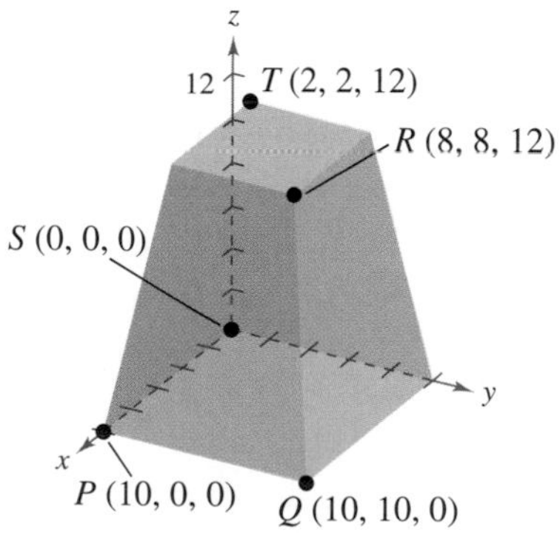

FIGURE FOR 17

In Exercises 14 and 15, plot the intercepts and sketch a graph of the plane.

14. $2x + 3y + 4z = 12$
15. $5x - y - 2z = 10$

16. Find the distance between the point $(2, -1, 6)$ and the plane $3x - 2y + z = 6$.
17. A tractor fuel tank has the shape and dimensions shown in the figure. In fabricating the tank, it is necessary to know the angle between two adjacent sides. Find this angle.

Proofs in Mathematics

Notation for Dot and Cross Products

The notation for the dot product and cross product of vectors was first introduced by the American physicist Josiah Willard Gibbs (1839–1903). In the early 1880s, Gibbs built a system to represent physical quantities called *vector analysis*. The system was a departure from William Hamilton's theory of quaternions.

Algebraic Properties of the Cross Product *(p. 828)*

Let $\mathbf{u}$, $\mathbf{v}$, and $\mathbf{w}$ be vectors in space and let c be a scalar.

1. $\mathbf{u} \times \mathbf{v} = -(\mathbf{v} \times \mathbf{u})$
2. $\mathbf{u} \times (\mathbf{v} + \mathbf{w}) = (\mathbf{u} \times \mathbf{v}) + (\mathbf{u} \times \mathbf{w})$
3. $c(\mathbf{u} \times \mathbf{v}) = (c\mathbf{u}) \times \mathbf{v} = \mathbf{u} \times (c\mathbf{v})$
4. $\mathbf{u} \times \mathbf{0} = \mathbf{0} \times \mathbf{u} = \mathbf{0}$
5. $\mathbf{u} \times \mathbf{u} = \mathbf{0}$
6. $\mathbf{u} \cdot (\mathbf{v} \times \mathbf{w}) = (\mathbf{u} \times \mathbf{v}) \cdot \mathbf{w}$

Proof

Let $\mathbf{u} = u_1\mathbf{i} + u_2\mathbf{j} + u_3\mathbf{k}$, $\mathbf{v} = v_1\mathbf{i} + v_2\mathbf{j} + v_3\mathbf{k}$, $\mathbf{w} = w_1\mathbf{i} + w_2\mathbf{j} + w_3\mathbf{k}$, $\mathbf{0} = 0\mathbf{i} + 0\mathbf{j} + 0\mathbf{k}$, and let c be a scalar.

1. $$\mathbf{u} \times \mathbf{v} = (u_2v_3 - u_3v_2)\mathbf{i} - (u_1v_3 - u_3v_1)\mathbf{j} + (u_1v_2 - u_2v_1)\mathbf{k}$$
$$\mathbf{v} \times \mathbf{u} = (v_2u_3 - v_3u_2)\mathbf{i} - (v_1u_3 - v_3u_1)\mathbf{j} + (v_1u_2 - v_2u_1)\mathbf{k}$$

So, this implies $\mathbf{u} \times \mathbf{v} = -(\mathbf{v} \times \mathbf{u})$.

2. $$\begin{aligned}\mathbf{u} \times (\mathbf{v} + \mathbf{w}) &= [u_2(v_3 + w_3) - u_3(v_2 + w_2)]\mathbf{i} - [u_1(v_3 + w_3) - \\ &\quad u_3(v_1 + w_1)]\mathbf{j} + [u_1(v_2 + w_2) - u_2(v_1 + w_1)]\mathbf{k} \\ &= (u_2v_3 - u_3v_2)\mathbf{i} - (u_1v_3 - u_3v_1)\mathbf{j} + (u_1v_2 - u_2v_1)\mathbf{k} + \\ &\quad (u_2w_3 - u_3w_2)\mathbf{i} - (u_1w_3 - u_3w_1)\mathbf{j} + (u_1w_2 - u_2w_1)\mathbf{k} \\ &= (\mathbf{u} \times \mathbf{v}) + (\mathbf{u} \times \mathbf{w})\end{aligned}$$

3. $$\begin{aligned}(c\mathbf{u}) \times \mathbf{v} &= (cu_2v_3 - cu_3v_2)\mathbf{i} - (cu_1v_3 - cu_3v_1)\mathbf{j} + (cu_1v_2 - cu_2v_1)\mathbf{k} \\ &= c[u_2v_3 - u_3v_2)\mathbf{i} - (u_1v_3 - u_3v_1)\mathbf{j} + (u_1v_2 - u_2v_1)\mathbf{k}] = c(\mathbf{u} \times \mathbf{v})\end{aligned}$$

4. $$\begin{aligned}\mathbf{u} \times \mathbf{0} &= (u_2 \cdot 0 - u_3 \cdot 0)\mathbf{i} - (u_1 \cdot 0 - u_3 \cdot 0)\mathbf{j} + (u_1 \cdot 0 - u_2 \cdot 0)\mathbf{k} \\ &= 0\mathbf{i} + 0\mathbf{j} + 0\mathbf{k} = \mathbf{0} \\ \mathbf{0} \times \mathbf{u} &= (0 \cdot u_3 - 0 \cdot u_2)\mathbf{i} - (0 \cdot u_3 - 0 \cdot u_1)\mathbf{j} + (0 \cdot u_2 - 0 \cdot u_1)\mathbf{k} \\ &= 0\mathbf{i} + 0\mathbf{j} + 0\mathbf{k} = \mathbf{0}\end{aligned}$$

So, this implies $\mathbf{u} \times \mathbf{0} = \mathbf{0} \times \mathbf{u} = \mathbf{0}$.

5. $$\mathbf{u} \times \mathbf{u} = (u_2u_3 - u_3u_2)\mathbf{i} - (u_1u_3 - u_3u_1)\mathbf{j} + (u_1u_2 - u_2u_1)\mathbf{k} = \mathbf{0}$$

6. $$\mathbf{u} \cdot (\mathbf{v} \times \mathbf{w}) = \begin{vmatrix} u_1 & u_2 & u_3 \\ v_1 & v_2 & v_3 \\ w_1 & w_2 & w_3 \end{vmatrix} \text{ and}$$

$$(\mathbf{u} \times \mathbf{v}) \cdot \mathbf{w} = \mathbf{w} \cdot (\mathbf{u} \times \mathbf{v}) = \begin{vmatrix} w_1 & w_2 & w_3 \\ u_1 & u_2 & u_3 \\ v_1 & v_2 & v_3 \end{vmatrix}$$

$$\begin{aligned}\mathbf{u} \cdot (\mathbf{v} \times \mathbf{w}) &= u_1(v_2w_3 - w_2v_3) - u_2(v_1w_3 - w_1v_3) + u_3(v_1w_2 - w_1v_2) \\ &= u_1v_2w_3 - u_1w_2v_3 - u_2v_1w_3 + u_2w_1v_3 + u_3v_1w_2 - u_3w_1v_2 \\ &= u_2w_1v_3 - u_3w_1v_2 - u_1w_2v_3 + u_3v_1w_2 + u_1v_2w_3 - u_2v_1w_3 \\ &= w_1(u_2v_3 - v_2u_3) - w_2(u_1v_3 - v_1u_3) + w_3(u_1v_2 - v_1u_2) \\ &= (\mathbf{u} \times \mathbf{v}) \cdot \mathbf{w}\end{aligned}$$

Geometric Properties of the Cross Product *(p. 829)*

Let **u** and **v** be nonzero vectors in space, and let θ be the angle between **u** and **v**.

1. $\mathbf{u} \times \mathbf{v}$ is orthogonal to both **u** and **v**.
2. $\|\mathbf{u} \times \mathbf{v}\| = \|\mathbf{u}\|\,\|\mathbf{v}\| \sin \theta$.
3. $\mathbf{u} \times \mathbf{v} = \mathbf{0}$ if and only if **u** and **v** are scalar multiples of each other.
4. $\|\mathbf{u} \times \mathbf{v}\| =$ area of parallelogram having **u** and **v** as adjacent sides.

Proof

Let $\mathbf{u} = u_1\mathbf{i} + u_2\mathbf{j} + u_3\mathbf{k}$, $\mathbf{v} = v_1\mathbf{i} + v_2\mathbf{j} + v_3\mathbf{k}$, and $\mathbf{0} = 0\mathbf{i} + 0\mathbf{j} + 0\mathbf{k}$.

1.

$$\begin{aligned}
\mathbf{u} \times \mathbf{v} &= (u_2v_3 - u_3v_2)\mathbf{i} - (u_1v_3 - u_3v_1)\mathbf{j} + (u_1v_2 - u_2v_1)\mathbf{k}\\
(\mathbf{u} \times \mathbf{v}) \cdot \mathbf{u} &= (u_2v_3 - u_3v_2)u_1 - (u_1v_3 - u_3v_1)u_2 + (u_1v_2 - u_2v_1)u_3\\
&= u_1u_2v_3 - u_1u_3v_2 - u_1u_2v_3 + u_2u_3v_1 + u_1u_3v_2 - u_2u_3v_1 = 0\\
(\mathbf{u} \times \mathbf{v}) \cdot \mathbf{v} &= (u_2v_3 - u_3v_2)v_1 - (u_1v_3 - u_3v_1)v_2 + (u_1v_2 - u_2v_1)v_3\\
&= u_2v_1v_3 - u_3v_1v_2 - u_1v_2v_3 + u_3v_1v_2 + u_1v_2v_3 - u_2v_1v_3 = 0
\end{aligned}$$

Because two vectors are orthogonal if their dot product is zero, it follows that $\mathbf{u} \times \mathbf{v}$ is orthogonal to both **u** and **v**.

2. Note that $\cos \theta = \dfrac{\mathbf{u} \cdot \mathbf{v}}{\|\mathbf{u}\|\,\|\mathbf{v}\|}$. Therefore,

$$\begin{aligned}
\|\mathbf{u}\|\,\|\mathbf{v}\| \sin \theta &= \|\mathbf{u}\|\,\|\mathbf{v}\| \sqrt{1 - \cos^2 \theta}\\
&= \|\mathbf{u}\|\,\|\mathbf{v}\| \sqrt{1 - \frac{(\mathbf{u} \cdot \mathbf{v})^2}{\|\mathbf{u}\|^2\,\|\mathbf{v}\|^2}}\\
&= \sqrt{\|\mathbf{u}\|^2\|\mathbf{v}\|^2 - (\mathbf{u} \cdot \mathbf{v})^2}\\
&= \sqrt{(u_1^2 + u_2^2 + u_3^2)(v_1^2 + v_2^2 + v_3^2) - (u_1v_1 + u_2v_2 + u_3v_3)^2}\\
&= \sqrt{(u_2v_3 - u_3v_2)^2 + (u_1v_3 - u_3v_1)^2 + (u_1v_2 - u_2v_1)^2} = \|\mathbf{u} \times \mathbf{v}\|.
\end{aligned}$$

3. If **u** and **v** are scalar multiples of each other, then $\mathbf{u} = c\mathbf{v}$ for some scalar c.

$$\mathbf{u} \times \mathbf{v} = (c\mathbf{v}) \times \mathbf{v} = c(\mathbf{v} \times \mathbf{v}) = c(\mathbf{0}) = \mathbf{0}$$

If $\mathbf{u} \times \mathbf{v} = \mathbf{0}$, then $\|\mathbf{u}\|\,\|\mathbf{v}\| \sin \theta = 0$. (Assume $\mathbf{u} \neq \mathbf{0}$ and $\mathbf{v} \neq \mathbf{0}$.) So, $\sin \theta = 0$, and $\theta = 0$ or $\theta = \pi$. In either case, because θ is the angle between the vectors, **u** and **v** are parallel. Therefore, $\mathbf{u} = c\mathbf{v}$ for some scalar c.

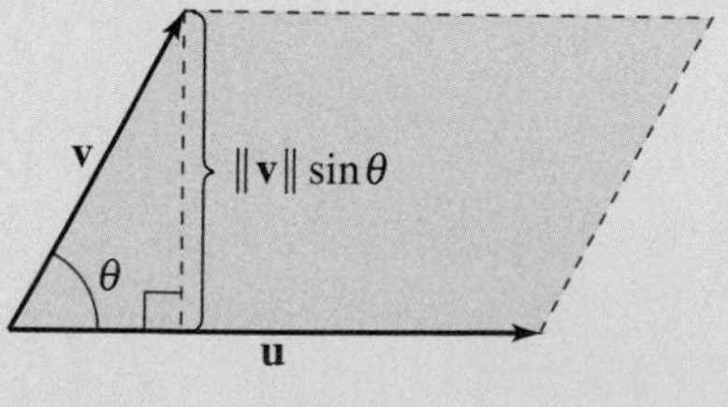

4. The figure at the left is a parallelogram having **v** and **u** as adjacent sides. Because the height of the parallelogram is $\|\mathbf{v}\| \sin \theta$, the area is

$$\begin{aligned}
\text{Area} &= (\text{base})(\text{height})\\
&= \|\mathbf{u}\|\,\|\mathbf{v}\| \sin \theta\\
&= \|\mathbf{u} \times \mathbf{v}\|.
\end{aligned}$$

P.S. Problem Solving

This collection of thought-provoking and challenging exercises further explores and expands upon concepts learned in this chapter.

1. Let $\mathbf{u} = \mathbf{i} + \mathbf{j}$, $\mathbf{v} = \mathbf{j} + \mathbf{k}$, and $\mathbf{w} = a\mathbf{u} + b\mathbf{v}$.

(a) Sketch $\mathbf{u}$ and $\mathbf{v}$.

(b) If $\mathbf{w} = \mathbf{0}$, show that a and b must both be zero.

(c) Find a and b such that $\mathbf{w} = \mathbf{i} + 2\mathbf{j} + \mathbf{k}$.

(d) Show that no choice of a and b yields $\mathbf{w} = \mathbf{i} + 2\mathbf{j} + 3\mathbf{k}$.

2. The initial and terminal points of $\mathbf{v}$ are (x_1, y_1, z_1) and (x, y, z), respectively. Describe the set of all points (x, y, z) such that $\|\mathbf{v}\| = 4$.

3. You are given the component forms of the vectors $\mathbf{u}$ and $\mathbf{v}$. Write a program for a graphing utility in which the output is (a) the component form of $\mathbf{u} + \mathbf{v}$, (b) $\|\mathbf{u} + \mathbf{v}\|$, (c) $\|\mathbf{u}\|$, and (d) $\|\mathbf{v}\|$.

4. Run the program you wrote in Exercise 3 for the vectors $\mathbf{u} = \langle -1, 3, 4\rangle$ and $\mathbf{v} = \langle 5, 4.5, -6\rangle$.

5. The vertices of a triangle are given. Determine whether the triangle is an acute triangle, an obtuse triangle, or a right triangle. Explain your reasoning.

(a) $(1, 2, 0), (0, 0, 0), (-2, 1, 0)$

(b) $(-3, 0, 0), (0, 0, 0), (1, 2, 3)$

(c) $(2, -3, 4), (0, 1, 2), (-1, 2, 0)$

(d) $(2, -7, 3), (-1, 5, 8), (4, 6, -1)$

6. A television camera weighing 120 pounds is supported by a tripod (see figure). Represent the force exerted on each leg of the tripod as a vector.

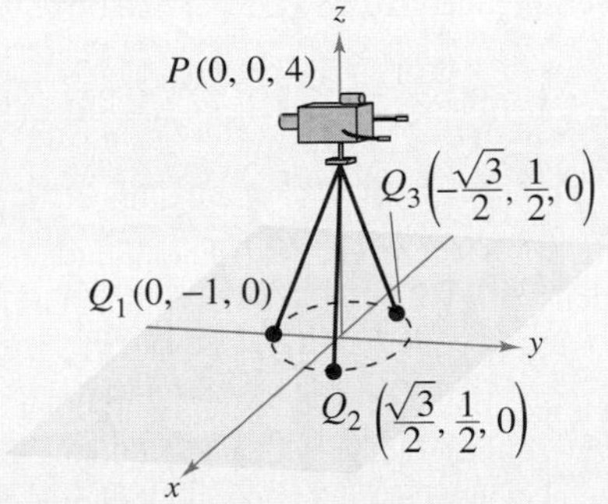

7. A precast concrete wall is temporarily kept in its vertical position by ropes (see figure). Find the total force exerted on the pin at position A. The tensions in AB and AC are 420 pounds and 650 pounds, respectively.

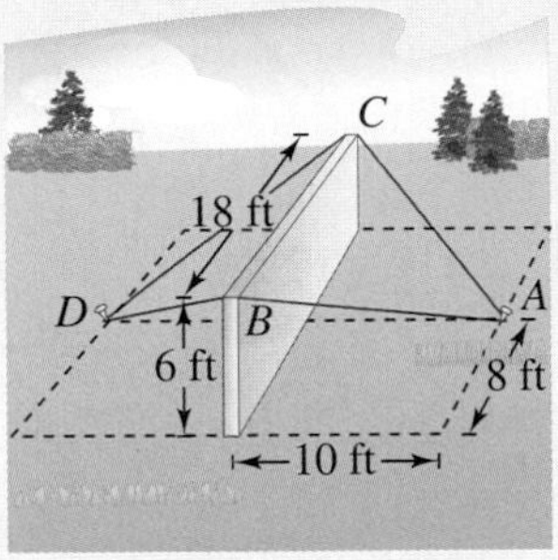

FIGURE FOR 7

8. Prove $\|\mathbf{u} \times \mathbf{v}\| = \|\mathbf{u}\|\,\|\mathbf{v}\|$ if $\mathbf{u}$ and $\mathbf{v}$ are orthogonal.

9. Prove $\mathbf{u} \times (\mathbf{v} \times \mathbf{w}) = (\mathbf{u} \cdot \mathbf{w})\mathbf{v} - (\mathbf{u} \cdot \mathbf{v})\mathbf{w}$.

10. Prove that the triple scalar product of $\mathbf{u}$, $\mathbf{v}$, and $\mathbf{w}$ is given by

$$\mathbf{u} \cdot (\mathbf{v} \times \mathbf{w}) = \begin{vmatrix} u_1 & u_2 & u_3 \\ v_1 & v_2 & v_3 \\ w_1 & w_2 & w_3 \end{vmatrix}.$$

11. Prove that the volume V of a parallelepiped with vectors $\mathbf{u}$, $\mathbf{v}$, and $\mathbf{w}$ as adjacent edges is given by $V = |\mathbf{u} \cdot (\mathbf{v} \times \mathbf{w})|$.

12. In physics, the cross product can be used to measure **torque,** or the **moment M** of a force $\mathbf{F}$ about a point P. If the point of application of the force is Q, the moment of $\mathbf{F}$ about P is given by $\mathbf{M} = \overrightarrow{PQ} \times \mathbf{F}$. A force of 60 pounds acts on the pipe wrench shown in the figure.

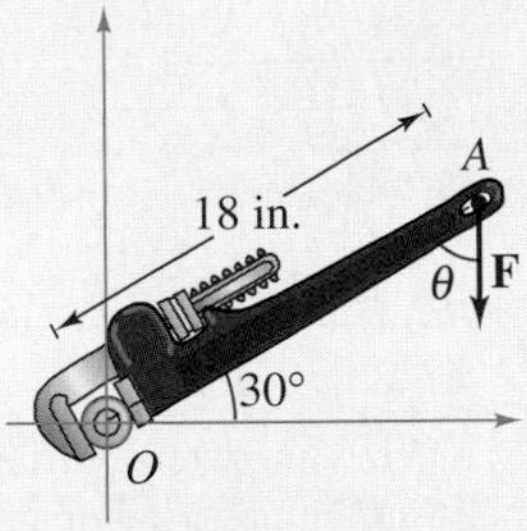

(a) Find the magnitude of the moment about O. Use a graphing utility to graph the resulting function of θ.

(b) Use the result of part (a) to determine the magnitude of the moment when $\theta = 45°$.

(c) Use the result of part (a) to determine the angle θ when the magnitude of the moment is maximum. Is the answer what you expected? Why or why not?

13. A force of 200 pounds acts on a bracket shown in the figure.

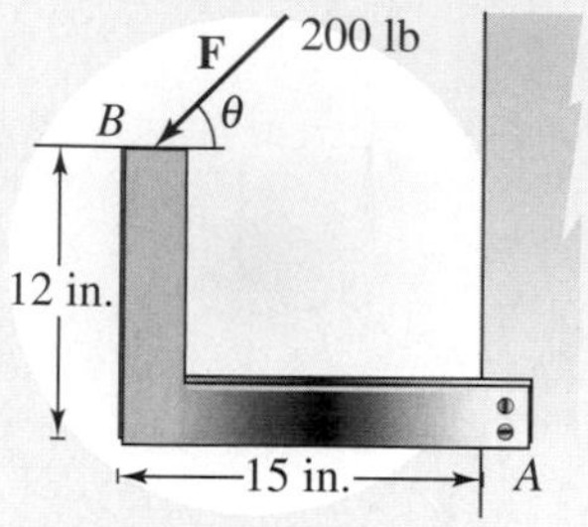

(a) Determine the vector $\overrightarrow{AB}$ and the vector $\mathbf{F}$ representing the force. ($\mathbf{F}$ will be in terms of θ.)

(b) Find the magnitude of the moment (torque) about A by evaluating $\|\overrightarrow{AB} \times \mathbf{F}\|$. Use a graphing utility to graph the resulting function of θ for $0° \le \theta \le 180°$.

(c) Use the result of part (b) to determine the magnitude of the moment when $\theta = 30°$.

(d) Use the result of part (b) to determine the angle θ when the magnitude of the moment is maximum.

(e) Use the graph in part (b) to approximate the zero of the function. Interpret the meaning of the zero in the context of the problem.

14. Using vectors, prove the Law of Sines: If **a**, **b**, and **c** are three sides of the triangle shown in the figure, then

$$\frac{\sin A}{\|\mathbf{a}\|} = \frac{\sin B}{\|\mathbf{b}\|} = \frac{\sin C}{\|\mathbf{c}\|}.$$

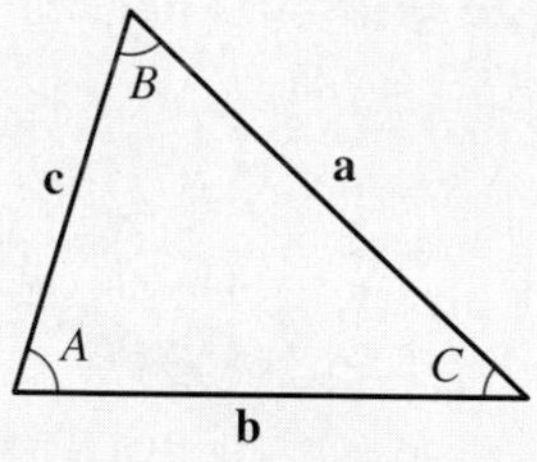

15. Two insects are crawling along different lines in three-space. At time t (in minutes), the first insect is at the point (x, y, z) on the line given by

$$x = 6 + t, \ y = 8 - t, \ z = 3 + t.$$

Also, at time t, the second insect is at the point (x, y, z) on the line given by

$$x = 1 + t, \ y = 2 + t, \ z = 2t.$$

Assume distances are given in inches.

(a) Find the distance between the two insects at time $t = 0$.

(b) Use a graphing utility to graph the distance between the insects from $t = 0$ to $t = 10$.

(c) Using the graph from part (b), what can you conclude about the distance between the insects?

(d) Using the graph from part (b), determine how close the insects get to each other.

16. The distance between a point Q and a line in space is given by

$$D = \frac{\|\overrightarrow{PQ} \times \mathbf{u}\|}{\|\mathbf{u}\|}$$

where u is a direction vector for the line and P is a point on the line. Find the distance between the point and the line given by the set of parametric equations.

(a) $(1, 5, -2)$

$$x = -2 + 4t, \ y = 3, \ z = 1 - t$$

(b) $(1, -2, 4)$

$$x = 2t, \ y = -3 + t, \ z = 2 + 2t$$

17. Use the formula given in Exercise 16.

(a) Find the shortest distance between the point $Q(2, 0, 0)$ and the line determined by the points $P_1(0, 0, 1)$ and $P_2(0, 1, 2)$.

(b) Find the shortest distance between the point $Q(2, 0, 0)$ and the line segment joining the points $P_1(0, 0, 1)$ and $P_2(0, 1, 2)$.

18. Consider the line given by the parametric equations

$$x = -t + 3, \ y = \frac{1}{2}t + 1, \ z = 2t - 1$$

and the point $(4, 3, s)$ for any real number s.

(a) Write the distance between the point and the line as a function of s. (*Hint:* Use the formula given in Exercise 16.)

(b) Use a graphing utility to graph the function from part (a). Use the graph to find the value of s such that the distance between the point and the line is a minimum.

(c) Use the *zoom* feature of the graphing utility to zoom out several times on the graph in part (b). Does it appear that the graph has slant asymptotes? Explain. If it appears to have slant asymptotes, find them.

Limits and an Introduction to Calculus

12

12.1 Introduction to Limits

12.2 Techniques for Evaluating Limits

12.3 The Tangent Line Problem

12.4 Limits at Infinity and Limits of Sequences

12.5 The Area Problem

The fundamental concept of integral calculus is the calculation of the area of a plane region bounded by the graph of a function. In surveying, civil engineers use integration to estimate the areas of irregular plots of real estate.

SELECTED APPLICATIONS

Limit concepts have many real-life applications. The applications listed below represent a small sample of the applications in this chapter.

- Geometry, Exercise 1, page 860
- Free-Falling Object, Exercises 67 and 68, page 871
- Consumer Awareness, Exercise 72, page 872
- Market Research, Exercise 52, page 881
- Path of a Ball, Exercise 53, page 882
- Oxygen Level, Exercise 47, page 890
- Data Analysis: Social Security, Exercise 51, page 890
- Civil Engineering, Exercise 36, page 899

12.1 Introduction to Limits

What you should learn

- Use the definition of a limit to estimate limits.
- Determine whether limits of functions exist.
- Use properties of limits and direct substitution to evaluate limits.

Why you should learn it

The concept of a limit is useful in applications involving maximization. For instance, in Exercise 1 on page 860, the concept of a limit is used to verify the maximum volume of an open box.

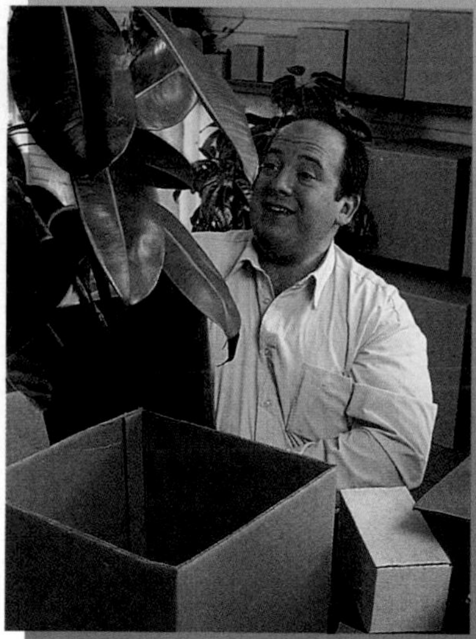

Dick Lurial/FPG International

The Limit Concept

The notion of a limit is a *fundamental* concept of calculus. In this chapter, you will learn how to evaluate limits and how they are used in the two basic problems of calculus: the tangent line problem and the area problem.

Example 1 Finding a Rectangle of Maximum Area

You are given 24 inches of wire and are asked to form a rectangle whose area is as large as possible. Determine the dimensions of the rectangle that will produce a maximum area.

Solution

Let w represent the width of the rectangle and let l represent the length of the rectangle. Because

$$2w + 2l = 24 \qquad \text{Perimeter is 24.}$$

it follows that $l = 12 - w$, as shown in Figure 12.1. So, the area of the rectangle is

$$A = lw \qquad \text{Formula for area}$$

$$= (12 - w)w \qquad \text{Substitute } 12 - w \text{ for } l.$$

$$= 12w - w^2. \qquad \text{Simplify.}$$

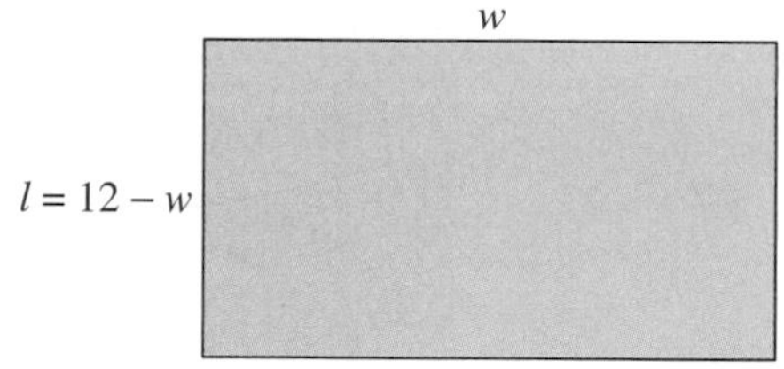

FIGURE 12.1

Using this model for area, you can experiment with different values of w to see how to obtain the maximum area. After trying several values, it appears that the maximum area occurs when $w = 6$, as shown in the table.

Width, w	5.0	5.5	5.9	6.0	6.1	6.5	7.0
Area, A	35.00	35.75	35.99	36.00	35.99	35.75	35.00

In limit terminology, you can say that "the limit of A as w approaches 6 is 36." This is written as

$$\lim_{w \to 6} A = \lim_{w \to 6} (12w - w^2) = 36.$$

CHECKPOINT Now try Exercise 1.

STUDY TIP

An alternative notation for $\lim_{x \to c} f(x) = L$ is

$$f(x) \to L \text{ as } x \to c$$

which is read as "$f(x)$ approaches L as x approaches c."

Definition of Limit

Definition of Limit

If $f(x)$ becomes arbitrarily close to a unique number L as x approaches c from either side, the limit of $f(x)$ as x approaches c is L. This is written as

$$\lim_{x \to c} f(x) = L.$$

Example 2 Estimating a Limit Numerically

Use a table to estimate numerically the limit: $\lim_{x \to 2} (3x - 2)$.

Solution

Let $f(x) = 3x - 2$. Then construct a table that shows values of $f(x)$ for two sets of x-values—one set that approaches 2 from the left and one that approaches 2 from the right.

x	1.9	1.99	1.999	2.0	2.001	2.01	2.1
$f(x)$	3.700	3.970	3.997	?	4.003	4.030	4.300

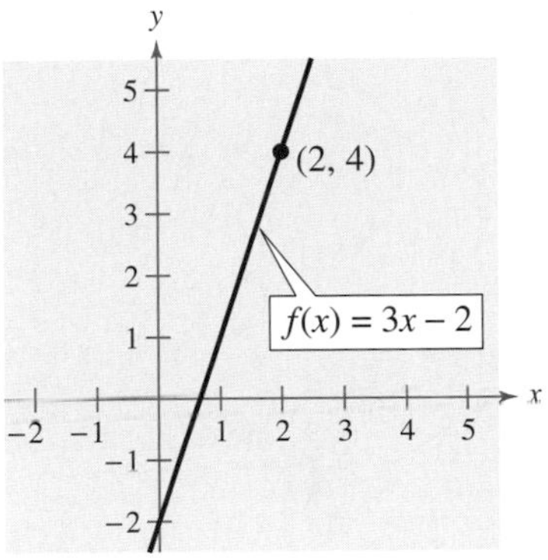

FIGURE 12.2

From the table, it appears that the closer x gets to 2, the closer $f(x)$ gets to 4. So, you can estimate the limit to be 4. Figure 12.2 adds further support for this conclusion.

CHECKPOINT Now try Exercise 3.

In Figure 12.2, note that the graph of $f(x) = 3x - 2$ is continuous. For graphs that are not continuous, finding a limit can be more difficult.

Example 3 Estimating a Limit Numerically

Use a table to estimate numerically the limit: $\lim_{x \to 0} \dfrac{x}{\sqrt{x+1} - 1}$.

Solution

Let $f(x) = x/\left(\sqrt{x+1} - 1\right)$. Then construct a table that shows values of $f(x)$ for two sets of x-values—one set that approaches 0 from the left and one that approaches 0 from the right.

x	−0.01	−0.001	−0.0001	0	0.0001	0.001	0.01
$f(x)$	1.99499	1.99949	1.99995	?	2.00005	2.00050	2.00499

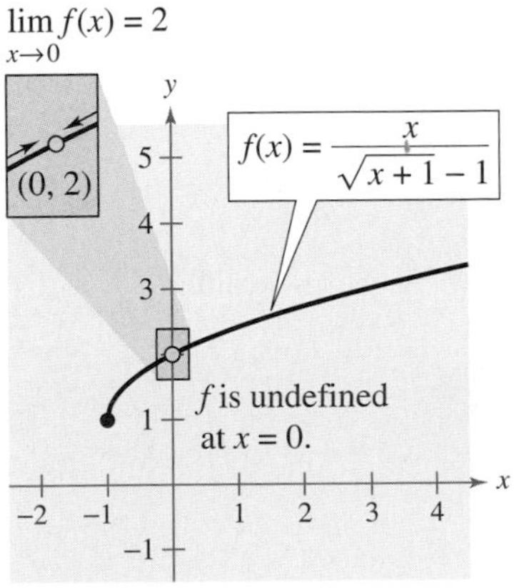

FIGURE 12.3

From the table, it appears that the limit is 2. The graph shown in Figure 12.3 verifies that the limit is 2.

CHECKPOINT Now try Exercise 5.

In Example 3, note that $f(x)$ has a limit when $x \to 0$ even though the function is not defined when $x = 0$. This often happens, and it is important to realize that *the existence or nonexistence of* $f(x)$ *at* $x = c$ *has no bearing on the existence of the limit of* $f(x)$ *as* x *approaches* c.

Example 4 Estimating a Limit

Estimate the limit: $\lim_{x \to 1} \dfrac{x^3 - x^2 + x - 1}{x - 1}$.

Numerical Solution

Let $f(x) = (x^3 - x^2 + x - 1)/(x - 1)$. Then construct a table that shows values of $f(x)$ for two sets of x-values—one set that approaches 1 from the left and one that approaches 1 from the right.

x	0.9	0.99	0.999	1.0
$f(x)$	1.8100	1.9801	1.9980	?

x	1.0	1.001	1.01	1.1
$f(x)$	?	2.0020	2.0201	2.2100

From the tables, it appears that the limit is 2.

CHECKPOINT Now try Exercise 7.

Graphical Solution

Let $f(x) = (x^3 - x^2 + x - 1)/(x - 1)$. Then sketch a graph of the function, as shown in Figure 12.4. From the graph, it appears that as x approaches 1 from either side, $f(x)$ approaches 2. So, you can estimate the limit to be 2.

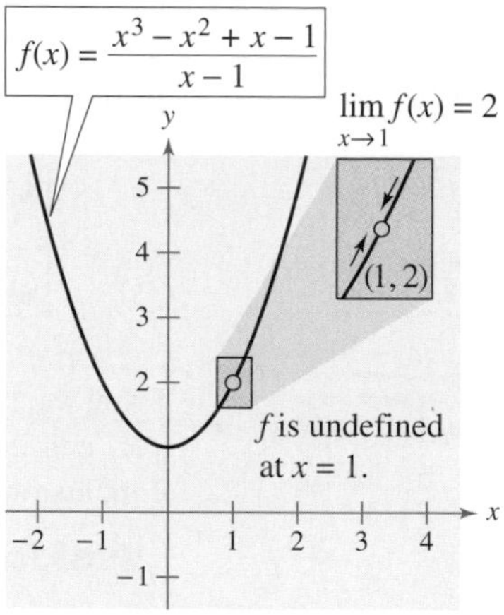

FIGURE 12.4

Example 5 Using a Graph to Find a Limit

Find the limit of $f(x)$ as x approaches 3, where f is defined as

$$f(x) = \begin{cases} 2, & x \neq 3 \\ 0, & x = 3 \end{cases}.$$

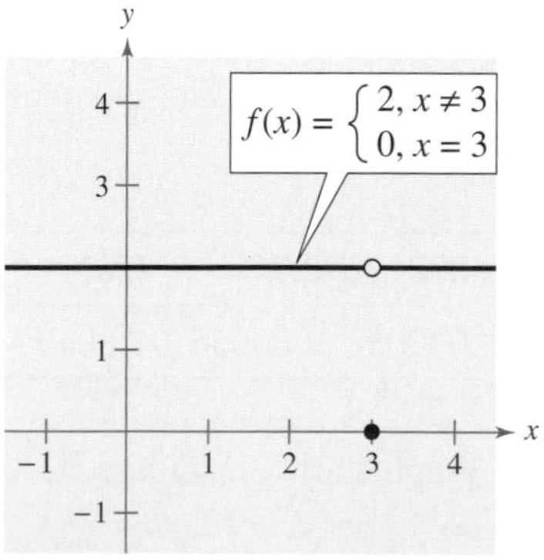

FIGURE 12.5

Solution

Because $f(x) = 2$ for all x other than $x = 3$ and because the value of $f(3)$ is immaterial, it follows that the limit is 2 (see Figure 12.5). So, you can write

$$\lim_{x \to 3} f(x) = 2.$$

The fact that $f(3) = 0$ has no bearing on the existence or value of the limit as x approaches 3. For instance, if the function were defined as

$$f(x) = \begin{cases} 2, & x \neq 3 \\ 4, & x = 3 \end{cases}$$

the limit as x approaches 3 would be the same.

CHECKPOINT Now try Exercise 15.

Limits That Fail to Exist

Next, you will examine some functions for which limits do not exist.

Example 6 **Comparing Left and Right Behavior**

Show that the limit does not exist.

$$\lim_{x\to 0} \frac{|x|}{x}$$

Solution

Consider the graph of the function given by $f(x) = |x|/x$. From Figure 12.6, you can see that for positive x-values

$$\frac{|x|}{x} = 1, \qquad x > 0$$

and for negative x-values

$$\frac{|x|}{x} = -1, \qquad x < 0.$$

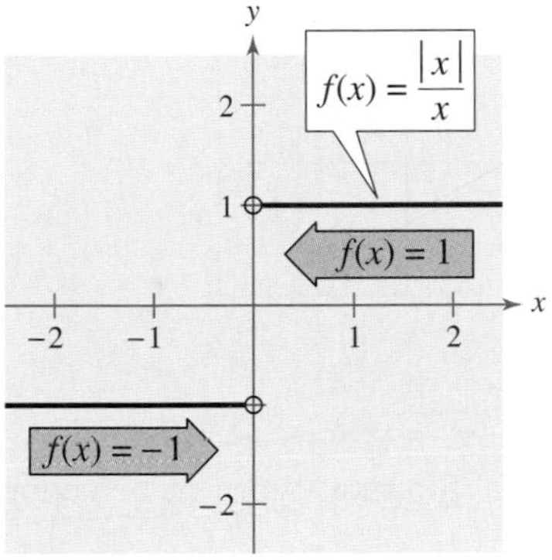

FIGURE 12.6

This means that no matter how close x gets to 0, there will be both positive and negative x-values that yield $f(x) = 1$ and $f(x) = -1$. This implies that the limit does not exist.

✓CHECKPOINT Now try Exercise 19.

Example 7 **Unbounded Behavior**

Discuss the existence of the limit.

$$\lim_{x\to 0} \frac{1}{x^2}$$

Solution

Let $f(x) = 1/x^2$. In Figure 12.7, note that as x approaches 0 from either the right or the left, $f(x)$ increases without bound. This means that by choosing x close enough to 0, you can force $f(x)$ to be as large as you want. For instance, $f(x)$ will be larger than 100 if you choose x that is within $\frac{1}{10}$ of 0. That is,

$$0 < |x| < \frac{1}{10} \quad \Rightarrow \quad f(x) = \frac{1}{x^2} > 100.$$

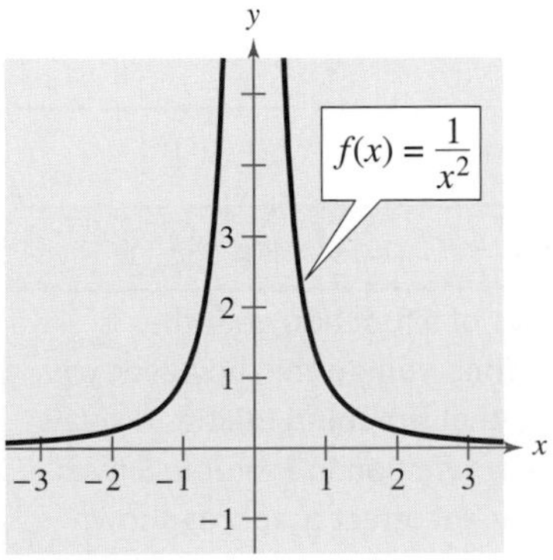

FIGURE 12.7

Similarly, you can force $f(x)$ to be larger than 1,000,000, as follows.

$$0 < |x| < \frac{1}{1000} \quad \Rightarrow \quad f(x) = \frac{1}{x^2} > 1{,}000{,}000$$

Because $f(x)$ is not approaching a unique real number L as x approaches 0, you can conclude that the limit does not exist.

✓CHECKPOINT Now try Exercise 20.

Example 8 Oscillating Behavior

Discuss the existence of the limit.

$$\lim_{x \to 0} \sin\left(\frac{1}{x}\right)$$

Solution

Let $f(x) = \sin(1/x)$. In Figure 12.8, you can see that as x approaches 0, $f(x)$ oscillates between -1 and 1. Therefore, the limit does not exist because no matter how close you are to 0, it is possible to choose values of x_1 and x_2 such that $\sin(1/x_1) = 1$ and $\sin(1/x_2) = -1$, as indicated in the table.

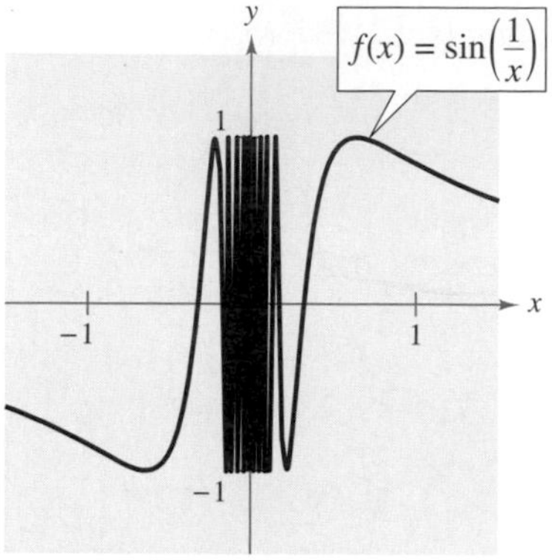

FIGURE 12.8

x	$-\frac{2}{\pi}$	$-\frac{2}{3\pi}$	$-\frac{2}{5\pi}$	0	$\frac{2}{5\pi}$	$\frac{2}{3\pi}$	$\frac{2}{\pi}$
$\sin\left(\frac{1}{x}\right)$	-1	1	-1	?	1	-1	1

CHECKPOINT Now try Exercise 21.

Examples 6, 7, and 8 show three of the most common types of behavior associated with the *nonexistence* of a limit.

Conditions Under Which Limits Do Not Exist

The limit of $f(x)$ as $x \to c$ does not exist if any of the following conditions are true.

1. $f(x)$ approaches a different number from the right side of c than it approaches from the left side of c. — Example 6
2. $f(x)$ increases or decreases without bound as x approaches c. — Example 7
3. $f(x)$ oscillates between two fixed values as x approaches c. — Example 8

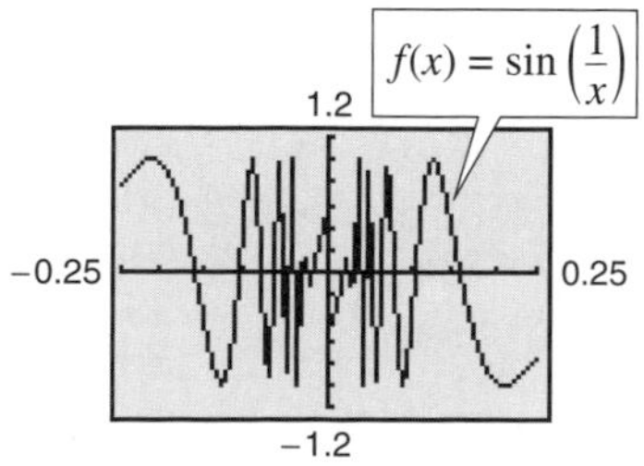

FIGURE 12.9

Technology

A graphing utility can help you discover the behavior of a function near the x-value at which you are trying to evaluate a limit. When you do this, however, you should realize that you can't always trust the graphs that graphing utilities display. For instance, if you use a graphing utility to graph the function in Example 8 over an interval containing 0, you will most likely obtain an incorrect graph, as shown in Figure 12.9. The reason that a graphing utility can't show the correct graph is that the graph has infinitely many oscillations over any interval that contains 0.

Exploration

Use a graphing utility to graph the tangent function. What are $\lim_{x \to 0} \tan x$ and $\lim_{x \to \pi/4} \tan x$? What can you say about the existence of the limit $\lim_{x \to \pi/2} \tan x$?

Properties of Limits and Direct Substitution

You have seen that sometimes the limit of $f(x)$ as $x \to c$ is simply $f(c)$, as shown in Example 2. In such cases, it is said that the limit can be evaluated by **direct substitution.** That is,

$$\lim_{x \to c} f(x) = f(c). \qquad \text{Substitute } c \text{ for } x.$$

There are many "well-behaved" functions, such as polynomial functions and rational functions with nonzero denominators, that have this property. Some of the basic ones are included in the following list.

Basic Limits

Let b and c be real numbers and let n be a positive integer.

1. $\lim_{x \to c} b = b$ — Limit of a constant function
2. $\lim_{x \to c} x = c$ — Limit of the identity function
3. $\lim_{x \to c} x^n = c^n$ — Limit of a power function
4. $\lim_{x \to c} \sqrt[n]{x} = \sqrt[n]{c}$, for n even and $c > 0$ — Limit of a radical function

For a proof of the limit of a power function, see Proofs in Mathematics on page 907.

Trigonometric functions can also be included in this list. For instance,

$$\lim_{x \to \pi} \sin x = \sin \pi = 0$$

and

$$\lim_{x \to 0} \cos x = \cos 0 = 1.$$

By combining the basic limits with the following operations, you can find limits for a wide variety of functions.

Properties of Limits

Let b and c be real numbers, let n be a positive integer, and let f and g be functions with the following limits.

$$\lim_{x \to c} f(x) = L \quad \text{and} \quad \lim_{x \to c} g(x) = K$$

1. Scalar multiple: $\lim_{x \to c} [bf(x)] = bL$
2. Sum or difference: $\lim_{x \to c} [f(x) \pm g(x)] = L \pm K$
3. Product: $\lim_{x \to c} [f(x)g(x)] = LK$
4. Quotient: $\lim_{x \to c} \dfrac{f(x)}{g(x)} = \dfrac{L}{K}$, provided $K \neq 0$
5. Power: $\lim_{x \to c} [f(x)]^n = L^n$

Example 9 Direct Substitution and Properties of Limits

Find each limit.

a. $\lim_{x \to 4} x^2$ **b.** $\lim_{x \to 4} 5x$ **c.** $\lim_{x \to \pi} \frac{\tan x}{x}$

d. $\lim_{x \to 9} \sqrt{x}$ **e.** $\lim_{x \to \pi} (x \cos x)$ **f.** $\lim_{x \to 3} (x + 4)^2$

Solution

You can use the properties of limits and direct substitution to evaluate each limit.

a. $\lim_{x \to 4} x^2 = (4)^2$

$= 16$

b. $\lim_{x \to 4} 5x = 5 \lim_{x \to 4} x$ Property 1

$= 5(4) = 20$

c. $\lim_{x \to \pi} \frac{\tan x}{x} = \frac{\lim_{x \to \pi} \tan x}{\lim_{x \to \pi} x}$ Property 4

$= \frac{0}{\pi} = 0$

d. $\lim_{x \to 9} \sqrt{x} = \sqrt{9} = 3$

e. $\lim_{x \to \pi} (x \cos x) = \left(\lim_{x \to \pi} x\right)\left(\lim_{x \to \pi} \cos x\right)$ Property 3

$= \pi(\cos \pi)$

$= -\pi$

f. $\lim_{x \to 3} (x + 4)^2 = \left[\left(\lim_{x \to 3} x\right) + \left(\lim_{x \to 3} 4\right)\right]^2$ Properties 2 and 5

$= (3 + 4)^2$

$= 7^2 = 49$

CHECKPOINT Now try Exercise 35.

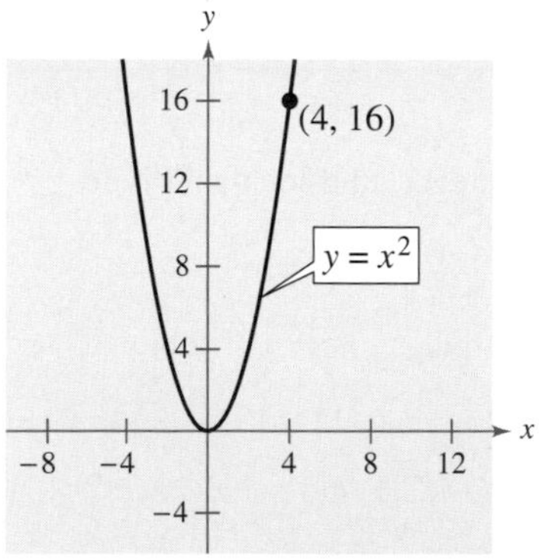

FIGURE 12.10

When evaluating limits, remember that there are several ways to solve most problems. Often, a problem can be solved *numerically*, *graphically*, or *algebraically*. The limits in Example 9 were found algebraically. You can verify the solutions numerically and/or graphically. For instance, to verify the limit in Example 9(a) numerically, create a table that shows values of x^2 for two sets of x-values—one set that approaches 4 from the left and one that approaches 4 from the right, as shown below. From the table, you can see that the limit as x approaches 4 is 16. Now, to verify the limit graphically, sketch the graph of $y = x^2$. From the graph shown in Figure 12.10, you can determine that the limit as x approaches 4 is 16.

x	3.9	3.99	3.999	4.0	4.001	4.01	4.1
x^2	15.2100	15.9201	15.9920	?	16.0080	16.0801	16.8100

The results of using direct substitution to evaluate limits of polynomial and rational functions are summarized as follows.

Limits of Polynomial and Rational Functions

1. If p is a polynomial function and c is a real number, then

$$\lim_{x \to c} p(x) = p(c).$$

2. If r is a rational function given by $r(x) = p(x)/q(x)$, and c is a real number such that $q(c) \neq 0$, then

$$\lim_{x \to c} r(x) = r(c) = \frac{p(c)}{q(c)}.$$

Exploration

Use a graphing utility to graph the function given by

$$f(x) = \frac{x^2 - 3x - 10}{x - 5}.$$

Use the *trace* feature to approximate $\lim_{x \to 4} f(x)$. What do you think $\lim_{x \to 5} f(x)$ equals? Is f defined at $x = 5$? Does this affect the existence of the limit as x approaches 5?

For a proof of the limit of a polynomial function, see Proofs in Mathematics on page 907.

Example 10 Evaluating Limits by Direct Substitution

Find each limit.

a. $\lim_{x \to -1} (x^2 + x - 6)$ **b.** $\lim_{x \to -1} \dfrac{x^2 + x - 6}{x + 3}$

Solution

The first function is a polynomial function and the second is a rational function (with a nonzero denominator at $x = -1$). So, you can evaluate the limits by direct substitution.

a.
$$\lim_{x \to -1} (x^2 + x - 6) = (-1)^2 + (-1) - 6 = -6$$

b.
$$\lim_{x \to -1} \frac{x^2 + x - 6}{x + 3} = \frac{(-1)^2 + (-1) - 6}{-1 + 3} = -\frac{6}{2} = -3$$

✓CHECKPOINT Now try Exercise 39.

Writing About Mathematics

Graphs with Holes Sketch the graph of each function. Then find the limits of each function as x approaches 1 and as x approaches 2. What conclusions can you make?

a. $f(x) = x + 1$ **b.** $g(x) = \dfrac{x^2 - 1}{x - 1}$ **c.** $h(x) = \dfrac{x^3 - 2x^2 - x + 2}{x^2 - 3x + 2}$

Use a graphing utility to graph each function above. Does the graphing utility distinguish among the three graphs? Write a short explanation of your findings.

12.1 Exercises

VOCABULARY CHECK: Fill in the blanks.

1. If $f(x)$ becomes arbitrarily close to a unique number L as x approaches c from either side, the _______ of $f(x)$ as x approaches c is L.
2. The limit of $f(x)$ as $x \to c$ does not exist if $f(x)$ _______ between two fixed values.
3. To evaluate the limit of a polynomial function, use _______ _______.

Model It

1. ***Geometry*** You create an open box from a square piece of material, 24 centimeters on a side. You cut equal squares from the corners and turn up the sides.
   (a) Draw and label a diagram that represents the box.
   (b) Verify that the volume V of the box is given by $V = 4x(12 - x)^2$.
   (c) The box has a maximum volume when $x = 4$. Use a graphing utility to complete the table and observe the behavior of the function as x approaches 4. Use the table to find $\lim_{x \to 4} V$.

x	3	3.5	3.9	4	4.1	4.5	5
V							

   (d) Use a graphing utility to graph the volume function. Verify that the volume is maximum when $x = 4$.

2. ***Geometry*** You are given wire and are asked to form a right triangle with a hypotenuse of $\sqrt{18}$ inches whose area is as large as possible.
   (a) Draw and label a diagram that shows the base x and height y of the triangle.
   (b) Verify that the area A of the triangle is given by $A = \frac{1}{2}x\sqrt{18 - x^2}$.
   (c) The triangle has a maximum area when $x = 3$ inches. Use a graphing utility to complete the table and observe the behavior of the function as x approaches 3. Use the table to find $\lim_{x \to 3} A$.

x	2	2.5	2.9	3	3.1	3.5	4
A							

   (d) Use a graphing utility to graph the area function. Verify that the area is maximum when $x = 3$ inches.

In Exercises 3–6, complete the table and use the result to estimate the limit numerically. Determine whether or not the limit can be reached.

3. $\lim_{x \to 2} (5x + 4)$

x	1.9	1.99	1.999	2	2.001	2.01	2.1
$f(x)$				?			

4. $\lim_{x \to 2} (x^2 - 3x + 1)$

x	1.9	1.99	1.999	2	2.001	2.01	2.1
$f(x)$				?			

5. $\lim_{x \to 3} \dfrac{x - 3}{x^2 - 9}$

x	2.9	2.99	2.999	3	3.001	3.01	3.1
$f(x)$				?			

6. $\lim_{x \to -1} \dfrac{x + 1}{x^2 - x - 2}$

x	−1.1	−1.01	−1.001	−1	−0.999
$f(x)$				?	

x	−0.99	−0.9
$f(x)$		

In Exercises 7–14, create a table of values for the function and use the result to estimate the limit numerically. Use a graphing utility to graph the corresponding function to confirm your result graphically.

7. $\lim_{x \to 1} \dfrac{x - 1}{x^2 + 2x - 3}$

8. $\lim_{x \to -2} \dfrac{x + 2}{x^2 + 5x + 6}$

9. $\lim_{x \to 0} \dfrac{\sqrt{x + 5} - \sqrt{5}}{x}$

10. $\lim_{x \to -3} \dfrac{\sqrt{1 - x} - 2}{x + 3}$

11. $\lim_{x \to -4} \dfrac{\dfrac{x}{x + 2} - 2}{x + 4}$

12. $\lim_{x \to 2} \dfrac{\dfrac{1}{x + 2} - \dfrac{1}{4}}{x - 2}$

13. $\lim_{x \to 0} \dfrac{\sin x}{x}$

14. $\lim_{x \to 0} \dfrac{\cos x - 1}{x}$

In Exercises 15 and 16, graph the function and find the limit (if it exists) as x approaches 2.

15. $f(x) = \begin{cases} 2x + 1, & x < 2 \\ x + 3, & x \geq 2 \end{cases}$

16. $f(x) = \begin{cases} -2x, & x \leq 2 \\ x^2 - 4x + 1, & x > 2 \end{cases}$

In Exercises 17–22, use the graph to find the limit (if it exists). If the limit does not exist, explain why.

17. $\lim_{x \to -4} (x^2 - 3)$

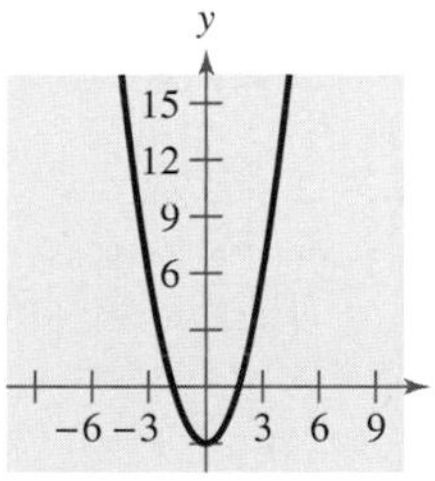

18. $\lim_{x \to 2} \dfrac{3x^2 - 12}{x - 2}$

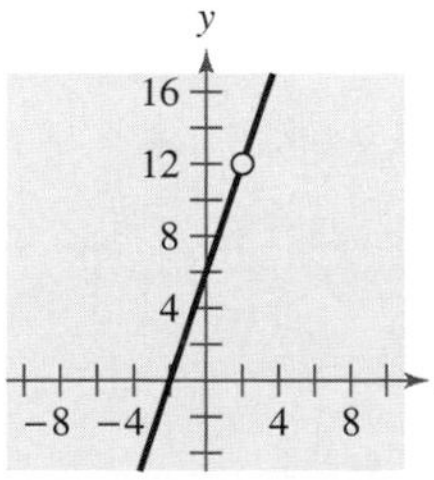

19. $\lim_{x \to -2} \dfrac{|x + 2|}{x + 2}$

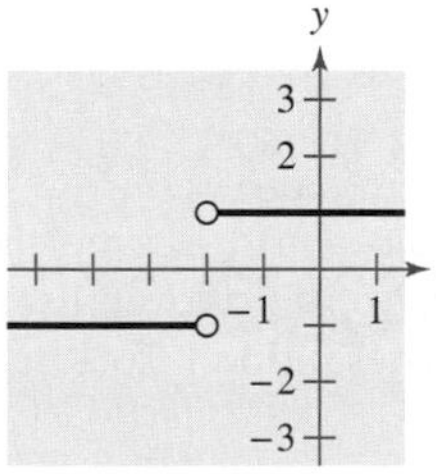

20. $\lim_{x \to 1} \dfrac{1}{x - 1}$

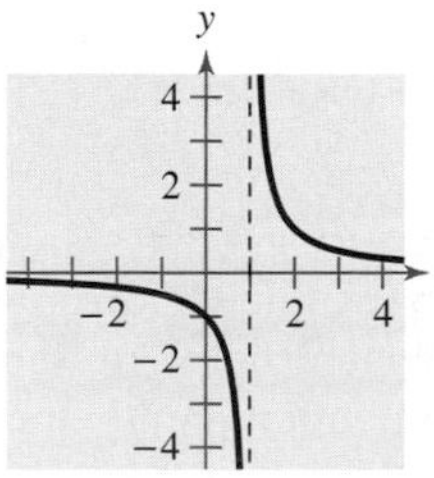

21. $\lim_{x \to 0} 2 \cos \dfrac{\pi}{x}$

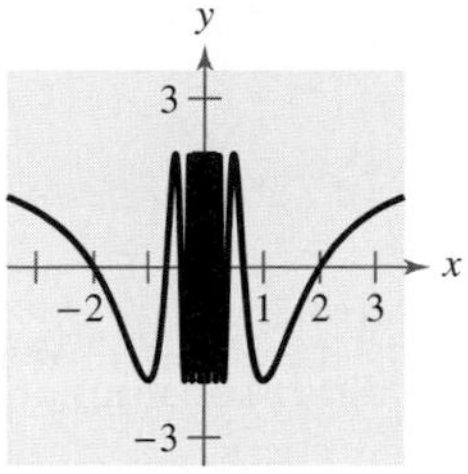

22. $\lim_{x \to -1} \sin \dfrac{\pi x}{2}$

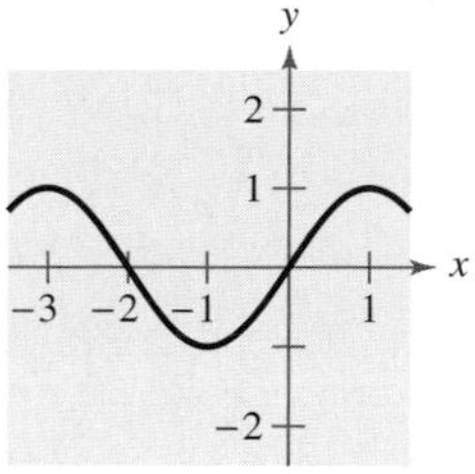

In Exercises 23–32, use a graphing utility to graph the function and use the graph to determine whether the limit exists. If the limit does not exist, explain why.

23. $f(x) = \dfrac{5}{2 + e^{1/x}}, \quad \lim_{x \to 0} f(x)$

24. $f(x) = \dfrac{e^x - 1}{x}, \quad \lim_{x \to 0} f(x)$

25. $f(x) = \cos \dfrac{1}{x}, \quad \lim_{x \to 0} f(x)$

26. $f(x) = \sin \pi x, \quad \lim_{x \to 1} f(x)$

27. $f(x) = \dfrac{\sqrt{x + 3} - 1}{x - 4}, \quad \lim_{x \to 4} f(x)$

28. $f(x) = \dfrac{\sqrt{x + 5} - 4}{x - 2}, \quad \lim_{x \to 2} f(x)$

29. $f(x) = \dfrac{x - 1}{x^2 - 4x + 3}, \quad \lim_{x \to 1} f(x)$

30. $f(x) = \dfrac{7}{x - 3}, \quad \lim_{x \to 3} f(x)$

31. $f(x) = \ln(x + 3), \quad \lim_{x \to 4} f(x)$

32. $f(x) = \ln(7 - x), \quad \lim_{x \to -1} f(x)$

In Exercises 33 and 34, use the given information to evaluate each limit.

33. $\lim_{x \to c} f(x) = 3, \quad \lim_{x \to c} g(x) = 6$

(a) $\lim_{x \to c} [-2g(x)]$

(b) $\lim_{x \to c} [f(x) + g(x)]$

(c) $\lim_{x \to c} \dfrac{f(x)}{g(x)}$

(d) $\lim_{x \to c} \sqrt{f(x)}$

34. $\lim_{x \to c} f(x) = 5, \quad \lim_{x \to c} g(x) = -2$

(a) $\lim_{x \to c} [f(x) + g(x)]^2$

(b) $\lim_{x \to c} [6f(x)g(x)]$

(c) $\lim_{x \to c} \dfrac{5g(x)}{4f(x)}$

(d) $\lim_{x \to c} \dfrac{1}{\sqrt{f(x)}}$

In Exercises 35 and 36, find (a) $\lim_{x\to 2} f(x)$, (b) $\lim_{x\to 2} g(x)$, (c) $\lim_{x\to 2} [f(x)g(x)]$, and (d) $\lim_{x\to 2} [g(x) - f(x)]$.

35. $f(x) = x^3, \quad g(x) = \dfrac{\sqrt{x^2+5}}{2x^2}$

36. $f(x) = \dfrac{x}{3-x}, \quad g(x) = \sin \pi x$

In Exercises 37–56, find the limit by direct substitution.

37. $\lim_{x\to 5} (10 - x^2)$

38. $\lim_{x\to -2} \left(\frac{1}{2}x^3 - 5x\right)$

39. $\lim_{x\to -3} (2x^2 + 4x + 1)$

40. $\lim_{x\to -2} (x^3 - 6x + 5)$

41. $\lim_{x\to 3} \left(-\dfrac{9}{x}\right)$

42. $\lim_{x\to -5} \dfrac{6}{x+2}$

43. $\lim_{x\to -3} \dfrac{3x}{x^2+1}$

44. $\lim_{x\to 4} \dfrac{x-1}{x^2+2x+3}$

45. $\lim_{x\to -2} \dfrac{5x+3}{2x-9}$

46. $\lim_{x\to 3} \dfrac{x^2+1}{x}$

47. $\lim_{x\to -1} \sqrt{x+2}$

48. $\lim_{x\to 3} \sqrt[3]{x^2-1}$

49. $\lim_{x\to 7} \dfrac{5x}{\sqrt{x+2}}$

50. $\lim_{x\to 8} \dfrac{\sqrt{x+1}}{x-4}$

51. $\lim_{x\to 3} e^x$

52. $\lim_{x\to e} \ln x$

53. $\lim_{x\to \pi} \sin 2x$

54. $\lim_{x\to \pi} \tan x$

55. $\lim_{x\to 1/2} \arcsin x$

56. $\lim_{x\to 1} \arccos \dfrac{x}{2}$

Synthesis

True or False? **In Exercises 57 and 58, determine whether the statement is true or false. Justify your answer.**

57. The limit of a function as x approaches c does not exist if the function approaches -3 from the left of c and 3 from the right of c.

58. The limit of the product of two functions is equal to the product of the limits of the two functions.

59. ***Think About It*** From Exercises 3 to 6, select a limit that can be reached and one that cannot be reached.

 (a) Use a graphing utility to graph the corresponding functions using a standard viewing window. Do the graphs reveal whether or not the limit can be reached? Explain.

 (b) Use a graphing utility to graph the corresponding functions using a *decimal* setting. Do the graphs reveal whether or not the limit can be reached? Explain.

60. ***Think About It*** Use the results of Exercise 59 to draw a conclusion as to whether or not you can use the graph generated by a graphing utility to determine reliably if a limit can be reached.

61. ***Think About It***

 (a) If $f(2) = 4$, can you conclude anything about $\lim_{x\to 2} f(x)$? Explain your reasoning.

 (b) If $\lim_{x\to 2} f(x) = 4$, can you conclude anything about $f(2)$? Explain your reasoning.

62. ***Writing*** Write a brief description of the meaning of the notation $\lim_{x\to 5} f(x) = 12$.

Writing **In Exercises 63 and 64, (a) use a graphing utility to graph the function and estimate the limit (if it exists). (b) Use the graph in part (a) to determine the domain of the function. (c) Determine the domain of the function algebraically. How do the domains compare? (d) Write a short paragraph about the importance of examining a function algebraically as well as graphically.**

63. $f(x) = \dfrac{x-9}{\sqrt{x}-3}$

 $\lim_{x\to 9} f(x)$

64. $f(x) = \dfrac{x-3}{x^2-9}$

 $\lim_{x\to 3} f(x)$

Skills Review

In Exercises 65–70, simplify the rational expression.

65. $\dfrac{5-x}{3x-15}$

66. $\dfrac{x^2-81}{9-x}$

67. $\dfrac{15x^2+7x-4}{15x^2+x-2}$

68. $\dfrac{x^2-12x+36}{x^2-7x+6}$

69. $\dfrac{x^3+27}{x^2+x-6}$

70. $\dfrac{x^3-8}{x^2-4}$

In Exercises 71–74, (a) plot the points in the same three-dimensional coordinate system, (b) find the distance between the points, and (c) find the midpoint of the line segment joining the points.

71. $(3, 2, 7), (3, 2, 8)$

72. $(1, 0, 3), (5, 2, 6)$

73. $(3, -3, 0), (0, 5, -5)$

74. $(0, -4, 0), (2, 0, -9)$

12.2 Techniques for Evaluating Limits

What you should learn

- Use the dividing out technique to evaluate limits of functions.
- Use the rationalizing technique to evaluate limits of functions.
- Approximate limits of functions graphically and numerically.
- Evaluate one-sided limits of functions.
- Evaluate limits of difference quotients from calculus.

Why you should learn it

Limits can be applied in real-life situations. For instance, in Exercise 72 on page 872, you will determine limits involving the costs of making photocopies.

Michael Krasowitz/Getty Images

Dividing Out Technique

In Section 12.1, you studied several types of functions whose limits can be evaluated by direct substitution. In this section, you will study several techniques for evaluating limits of functions for which direct substitution fails.

Suppose you were asked to find the following limit.

$$\lim_{x \to -3} \frac{x^2 + x - 6}{x + 3}$$

Direct substitution produces 0 in both the numerator and denominator.

$$(-3)^2 + (-3) - 6 = 0 \qquad \text{Numerator is 0 when } x = -3.$$

$$-3 + 3 = 0 \qquad \text{Denominator is 0 when } x = -3.$$

The resulting fraction, $\frac{0}{0}$, has no meaning as a real number. It is called an **indeterminate form** because you cannot, from the form alone, determine the limit. By using a table, however, it appears that the limit of the function as $x \to -3$ is -5.

x	-3.01	-3.001	-3.0001	-3	-2.9999	-2.999	-2.99
$\frac{x^2 + x - 6}{x + 3}$	-5.01	-5.001	-5.0001	?	-4.9999	-4.999	-4.99

When you try to evaluate a limit of a rational function by direct substitution and encounter the indeterminate form $\frac{0}{0}$, you can conclude that the numerator and denominator must have a common factor. After factoring and dividing out, you should try direct substitution again. Example 1 shows how you can use the **dividing out technique** to evaluate limits of these types of functions.

Example 1 Dividing Out Technique

Find the limit: $\lim_{x \to -3} \frac{x^2 + x - 6}{x + 3}$.

Solution

From the discussion above, you know that direct substitution fails. So, begin by factoring the numerator and dividing out any common factors.

$$\lim_{x \to -3} \frac{x^2 + x - 6}{x + 3} = \lim_{x \to -3} \frac{(x - 2)(x + 3)}{x + 3} \qquad \text{Factor numerator.}$$

$$= \lim_{x \to -3} \frac{(x - 2)\cancel{(x + 3)}}{\cancel{x + 3}} \qquad \text{Divide out common factor.}$$

$$= \lim_{x \to -3} (x - 2) \qquad \text{Simplify.}$$

$$= -3 - 2 = -5 \qquad \text{Direct substitution and simplify.}$$

✓CHECKPOINT Now try Exercise 7.

The validity of the dividing out technique stems from the fact that if two functions agree at all but a single number c, they must have identical limit behavior at $x = c$. In Example 1, the functions given by

$$f(x) = \frac{x^2 + x - 6}{x + 3} \quad \text{and} \quad g(x) = x - 2$$

agree at all values of x other than $x = -3$. So, you can use $g(x)$ to find the limit of $f(x)$.

Example 2 Dividing Out Technique

Find the limit.

$$\lim_{x \to 1} \frac{x - 1}{x^3 - x^2 + x - 1}$$

Solution

Begin by substituting $x = 1$ into the numerator and denominator.

$$1 - 1 = 0 \qquad \text{Numerator is 0 when } x = 1.$$

$$1^3 - 1^2 + 1 - 1 = 0 \qquad \text{Denominator is 0 when } x = 1.$$

Because both the numerator and denominator are zero when $x = 1$, direct substitution will not yield the limit. To find the limit, you should factor the numerator and denominator, divide out any common factors, and then try direct substitution again.

$$\lim_{x \to 1} \frac{x - 1}{x^3 - x^2 + x - 1} = \lim_{x \to 1} \frac{x - 1}{(x - 1)(x^2 + 1)} \qquad \text{Factor denominator.}$$

$$= \lim_{x \to 1} \frac{\cancel{x - 1}}{\cancel{(x - 1)}(x^2 + 1)} \qquad \text{Divide out common factor.}$$

$$= \lim_{x \to 1} \frac{1}{x^2 + 1} \qquad \text{Simplify.}$$

$$= \frac{1}{1^2 + 1} \qquad \text{Direct substitution}$$

$$= \frac{1}{2} \qquad \text{Simplify.}$$

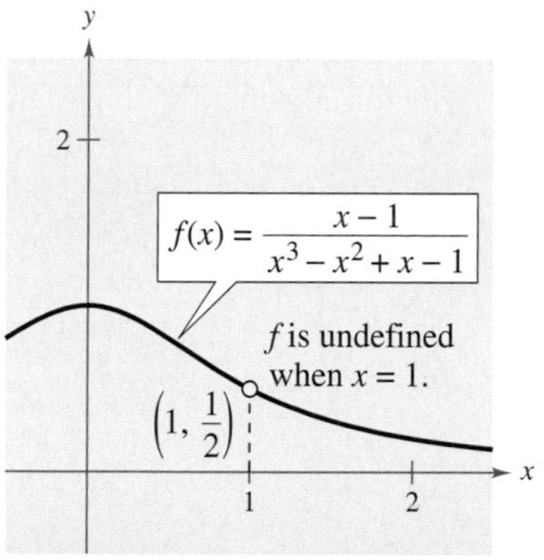

FIGURE 12.11

This result is shown graphically in Figure 12.11.

CHECKPOINT Now try Exercise 9.

In Example 2, the factorization of the denominator can be obtained by dividing by $(x - 1)$ or by grouping as follows.

$$x^3 - x^2 + x - 1 = x^2(x - 1) + (x - 1)$$

$$= (x - 1)(x^2 + 1)$$

Rationalizing Technique

Another way to find the limits of some functions is first to rationalize the numerator of the function. This is called the **rationalizing technique.** Recall that rationalizing the numerator means multiplying the numerator and denominator by the conjugate of the numerator. For instance, the conjugate of $\sqrt{x} + 4$ is $\sqrt{x} - 4$.

Example 3 Rationalizing Technique

Find the limit: $\lim_{x \to 0} \frac{\sqrt{x+1} - 1}{x}$.

Solution

By direct substitution, you obtain the indeterminate form $\frac{0}{0}$.

$$\lim_{x \to 0} \frac{\sqrt{x+1} - 1}{x} = \frac{\sqrt{0+1} - 1}{0} = \frac{0}{0} \qquad \text{Indeterminate form}$$

In this case, you can rewrite the fraction by rationalizing the numerator.

$$\frac{\sqrt{x+1} - 1}{x} = \left(\frac{\sqrt{x+1} - 1}{x}\right)\left(\frac{\sqrt{x+1} + 1}{\sqrt{x+1} + 1}\right)$$

$$= \frac{(x+1) - 1}{x\left(\sqrt{x+1} + 1\right)} \qquad \text{Multiply.}$$

$$= \frac{x}{x\left(\sqrt{x+1} + 1\right)} \qquad \text{Simplify.}$$

$$= \frac{\not{x}}{\not{x}\left(\sqrt{x+1} + 1\right)} \qquad \text{Divide out common factor.}$$

$$= \frac{1}{\sqrt{x+1} + 1}, \quad x \neq 0 \qquad \text{Simplify.}$$

Now you can evaluate the limit by direct substitution.

$$\lim_{x \to 0} \frac{\sqrt{x+1} - 1}{x} = \lim_{x \to 0} \frac{1}{\sqrt{x+1} + 1} = \frac{1}{\sqrt{0+1} + 1} = \frac{1}{1+1} = \frac{1}{2}$$

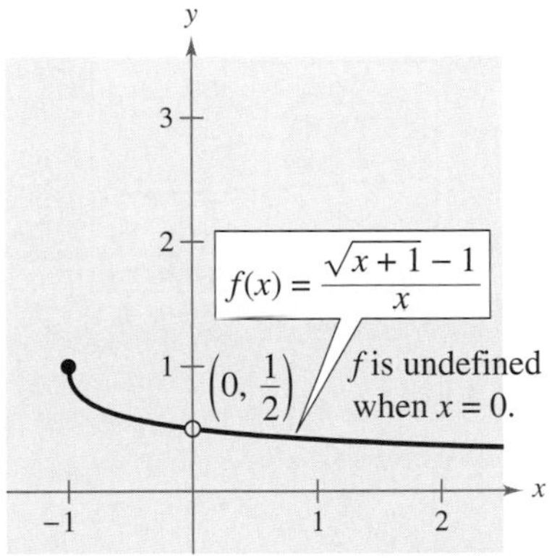

FIGURE 12.12

You can reinforce your conclusion that the limit is $\frac{1}{2}$ by constructing a table, as shown below, or by sketching a graph, as shown in Figure 12.12.

x	-0.1	-0.01	-0.001	0	0.001	0.01	0.1
$f(x)$	0.5132	0.5013	0.5001	?	0.4999	0.4988	0.4881

✓CHECKPOINT Now try Exercise 17.

The rationalizing technique for evaluating limits is based on multiplication by a convenient form of 1. In Example 3, the convenient form is

$$1 = \frac{\sqrt{x+1} + 1}{\sqrt{x+1} + 1}.$$

Using Technology

The dividing out and rationalizing techniques may not work well for finding limits of nonalgebraic functions. You often need to use more sophisticated analytic techniques to find limits of these types of functions.

Example 4 Approximating a Limit

Approximate the limit: $\lim_{x \to 0} (1 + x)^{1/x}$.

Numerical Solution

Let $f(x) = (1 + x)^{1/x}$. Because you are finding the limit when $x = 0$, use the *table* feature of a graphing utility to create a table that shows the value of f for x starting at $x = -0.01$ and has a step of 0.001, as shown in Figure 12.13. Because 0 is halfway between -0.001 and 0.001, use the average of the values of f at these two x-coordinates to estimate the limit as follows.

$$\lim_{x \to 0} (1 + x)^{1/x} \approx \frac{2.7196 + 2.7169}{2} = 2.71825$$

The actual limit can be found algebraically to be $e \approx 2.71828$.

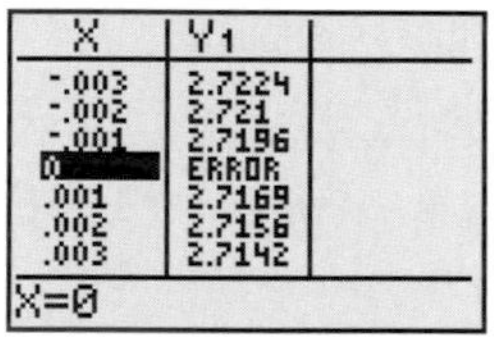

FIGURE 12.13

CHECKPOINT Now try Exercise 27.

Graphical Solution

To approximate the limit graphically, graph the function $f(x) = (1 + x)^{1/x}$, as shown in Figure 12.14. Using the *zoom* and *trace* features of the graphing utility, choose two points on the graph of f, such as

$$(-0.00017, 2.7185) \quad \text{and} \quad (0.00017, 2.7181)$$

as shown in Figure 12.15. Because the x-coordinates of these two points are equidistant from 0, you can approximate the limit to be the average of the y-coordinates. That is,

$$\lim_{x \to 0} (1 + x)^{1/x} \approx \frac{2.7185 + 2.7181}{2} = 2.7183.$$

The actual limit can be found algebraically to be $e \approx 2.71828$.

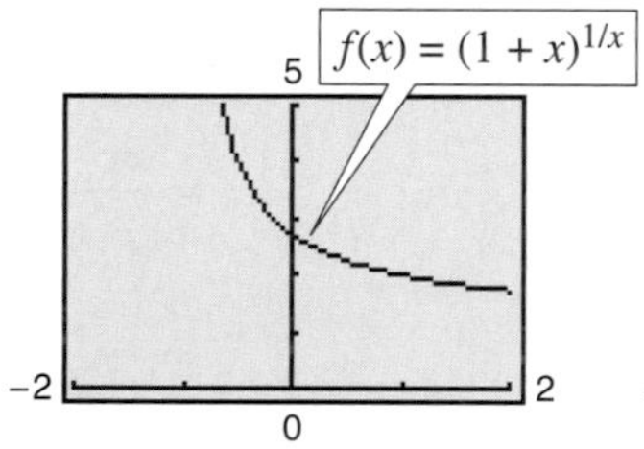

FIGURE 12.14

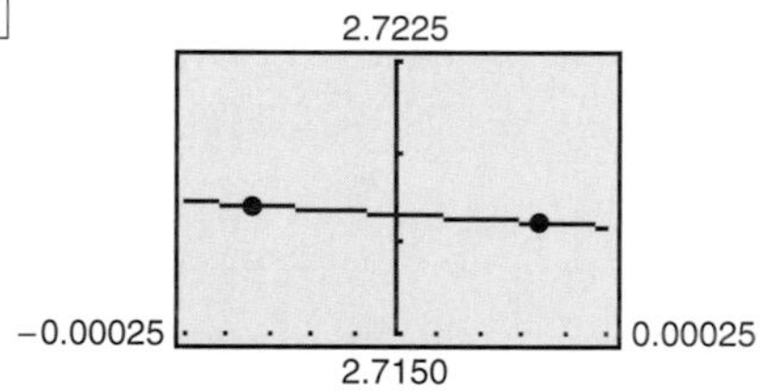

FIGURE 12.15

Example 5 Approximating a Limit Graphically

Approximate the limit: $\lim_{x \to 0} \frac{\sin x}{x}$.

Solution

Direct substitution produces the indeterminate form $\frac{0}{0}$. To approximate the limit, begin by using a graphing utility to graph $f(x) = (\sin x)/x$, as shown in Figure 12.16. Then use the *zoom* and *trace* features of the graphing utility to choose a point on each side of 0, such as $(-0.0012467, 0.9999997)$ and $(0.0012467, 0.9999997)$. Finally, approximate the limit as the average of the y-coordinates of these two points, $\lim_{x \to 0} (\sin x)/x \approx 0.9999997$. It can be shown algebraically that this limit is exactly 1.

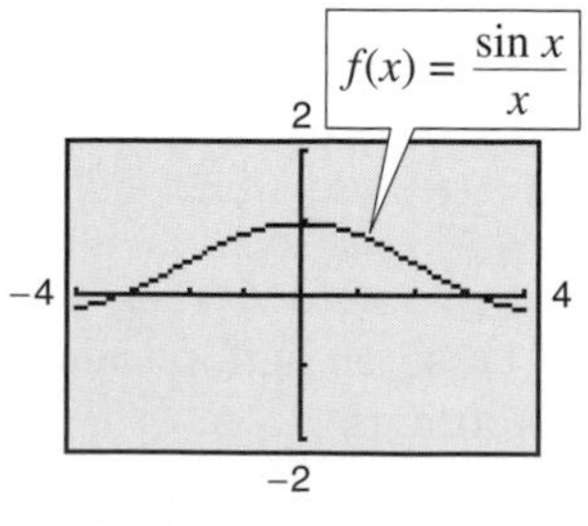

FIGURE 12.16

CHECKPOINT Now try Exercise 31.

Technology

The graphs shown in Figures 12.14 and 12.16 appear to be continuous at $x = 0$. However, when you try to use the *trace* or the *value* feature of a graphing utility to determine the value of y when $x = 0$, there is no value given. Some graphing utilities can show breaks or holes in a graph when an appropriate viewing window is used. Because the holes in the graphs in Figures 12.14 and 12.16 occur on the y-axis, the holes are not visible.

One-Sided Limits

In Section 12.1, you saw that one way in which a limit can fail to exist is when a function approaches a different value from the left side of c than it approaches from the right side of c. This type of behavior can be described more concisely with the concept of a **one-sided limit.**

$$\lim_{x \to c^-} f(x) = L_1 \text{ or } f(x) \to L_1 \text{ as } x \to c^- \qquad \text{Limit from the left}$$

$$\lim_{x \to c^+} f(x) = L_2 \text{ or } f(x) \to L_2 \text{ as } x \to c^+ \qquad \text{Limit from the right}$$

Example 6 Evaluating One-Sided Limits

Find the limit as $x \to 0$ from the left and the limit as $x \to 0$ from the right for

$$f(x) = \frac{|2x|}{x}.$$

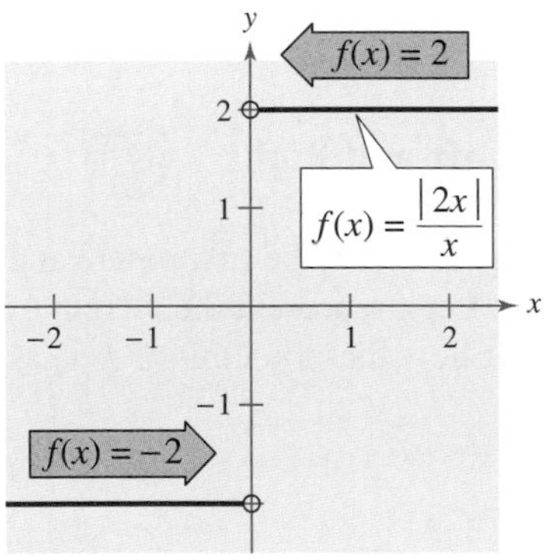

FIGURE 12.17

Solution

From the graph of f, shown in Figure 12.17, you can see that $f(x) = -2$ for all $x < 0$. Therefore, the limit from the left is

$$\lim_{x \to 0^-} \frac{|2x|}{x} = -2. \qquad \text{Limit from the left: } f(x) \to -2 \text{ as } x \to 0^-$$

Because $f(x) = 2$ for all $x > 0$, the limit from the right is

$$\lim_{x \to 0^+} \frac{|2x|}{x} = 2. \qquad \text{Limit from the right: } f(x) \to 2 \text{ as } x \to 0^+$$

✓CHECKPOINT Now try Exercise 43.

In Example 6, note that the function approaches different limits from the left and from the right. In such cases, the limit of $f(x)$ as $x \to c$ does not exist. For the limit of a function to exist as $x \to c$, it must be true that both one-sided limits exist and are equal.

Existence of a Limit

If f is a function and c and L are real numbers, then

$$\lim_{x \to c} f(x) = L$$

if and only if both the left and right limits *exist* and are *equal* to L.

Example 7 Finding One-Sided Limits

Find the limit of $f(x)$ as x approaches 1.

$$f(x) = \begin{cases} 4 - x, & x < 1 \\ 4x - x^2, & x > 1 \end{cases}$$

Solution

Remember that you are concerned about the value of f near $x = 1$ rather than at $x = 1$. So, for $x < 1$, $f(x)$ is given by $4 - x$, and you can use direct substitution to obtain

$$\begin{aligned} \lim_{x \to 1^-} f(x) &= \lim_{x \to 1^-} (4 - x) \\ &= 4 - 1 \\ &= 3. \end{aligned}$$

For $x > 1$, $f(x)$ is given by $4x - x^2$, and you can use direct substitution to obtain

$$\begin{aligned} \lim_{x \to 1^+} f(x) &= \lim_{x \to 1^+} (4x - x^2) \\ &= 4(1) - 1^2 \\ &= 3. \end{aligned}$$

Because the one-sided limits both exist and are equal to 3, it follows that

$$\lim_{x \to 1} f(x) = 3.$$

The graph in Figure 12.18 confirms this conclusion.

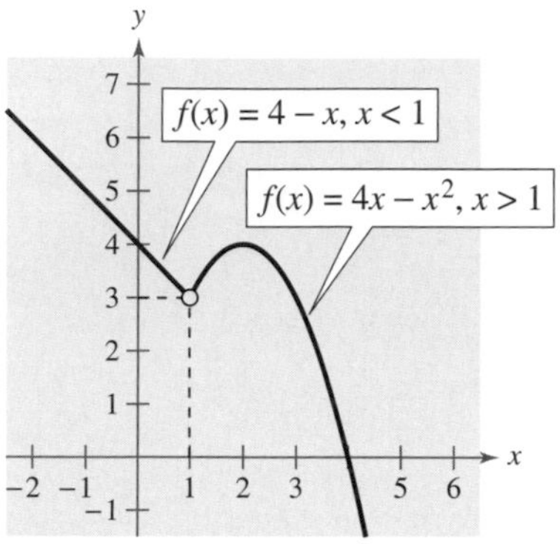

FIGURE 12.18

CHECKPOINT Now try Exercise 47.

Example 8 Comparing Limits from the Left and Right

To ship a package overnight, a delivery service charges \$8 for the first pound and \$2 for each additional pound or portion of a pound. Let x represent the weight of a package and let $f(x)$ represent the shipping cost. Show that the limit of $f(x)$ as $x \to 2$ does not exist.

$$f(x) = \begin{cases} 8, & 0 < x \le 1 \\ 10, & 1 < x \le 2 \\ 12, & 2 < x \le 3 \end{cases}$$

Solution

The graph of f is shown in Figure 12.19. The limit of $f(x)$ as x approaches 2 from the left is

$$\lim_{x \to 2^-} f(x) = 10$$

whereas the limit of $f(x)$ as x approaches 2 from the right is

$$\lim_{x \to 2^+} f(x) = 12.$$

Because these one-sided limits are not equal, the limit of $f(x)$ as $x \to 2$ does not exist.

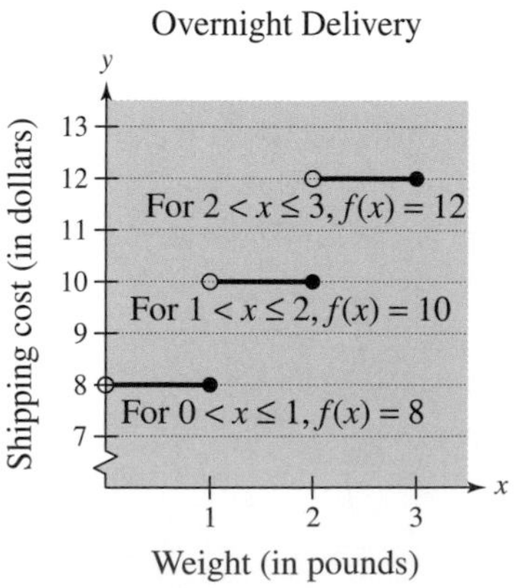

FIGURE 12.19

CHECKPOINT Now try Exercise 69.

A Limit from Calculus

In the next section, you will study an important type of limit from calculus—the limit of a **difference quotient.**

Example 9 Evaluating a Limit from Calculus

For the function given by $f(x) = x^2 - 1$, find

$$\lim_{h \to 0} \frac{f(3 + h) - f(3)}{h}.$$

Solution

Direct substitution produces an indeterminate form.

$$\lim_{h \to 0} \frac{f(3 + h) - f(3)}{h} = \lim_{h \to 0} \frac{[(3 + h)^2 - 1] - [(3)^2 - 1]}{h}$$

$$= \lim_{h \to 0} \frac{9 + 6h + h^2 - 1 - 9 + 1}{h}$$

$$= \lim_{h \to 0} \frac{6h + h^2}{h}$$

$$= \frac{0}{0}$$

By factoring and dividing out, you obtain the following.

$$\lim_{h \to 0} \frac{f(3 + h) - f(3)}{h} = \lim_{h \to 0} \frac{6h + h^2}{h} = \lim_{h \to 0} \frac{\cancel{h}(6 + h)}{\cancel{h}}$$

$$= \lim_{h \to 0} (6 + h)$$

$$= 6 + 0$$

$$= 6$$

So, the limit is 6.

CHECKPOINT Now try Exercise 63.

Note that for any x-value, the limit of a difference quotient is an expression of the form

$$\lim_{h \to 0} \frac{f(x + h) - f(x)}{h}.$$

Direct substitution into the difference quotient always produces the indeterminate form $\frac{0}{0}$. For instance,

$$\lim_{h \to 0} \frac{f(x + h) - f(x)}{h} = \frac{f(x + 0) - f(x)}{0}$$

$$= \frac{f(x) - f(x)}{0}$$

$$= \frac{0}{0}.$$

STUDY TIP

For a review of evaluating difference quotients, refer to Section 1.4.

12.2 Exercises

VOCABULARY CHECK: Fill in the blanks.

1. To evaluate the limit of a rational function that has common factors in its numerator and denominator, use the _______ _______ _______ .
2. The fraction $\frac{0}{0}$ has no meaning as a real number and therefore is called an _______ _______ .
3. The limit $\lim\limits_{x\to c^-} f(x) = L_1$ is an example of a _______ _______ .
4. The limit of a _______ _______ is an expression of the form $\lim\limits_{h\to 0} \dfrac{f(x+h) - f(x)}{h}$.

In Exercises 1–4, use the graph to determine each limit visually (if it exists). Then identify another function that agrees with the given function at all but one point.

1. $g(x) = \dfrac{-2x^2 + x}{x}$

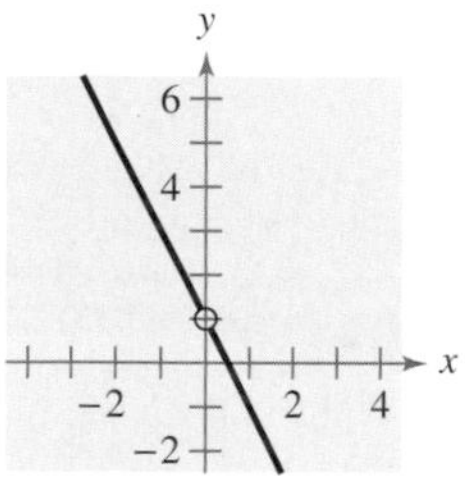

(a) $\lim\limits_{x\to 0} g(x)$

(b) $\lim\limits_{x\to -1} g(x)$

(c) $\lim\limits_{x\to -2} g(x)$

2. $h(x) = \dfrac{x^2 - 3x}{x}$

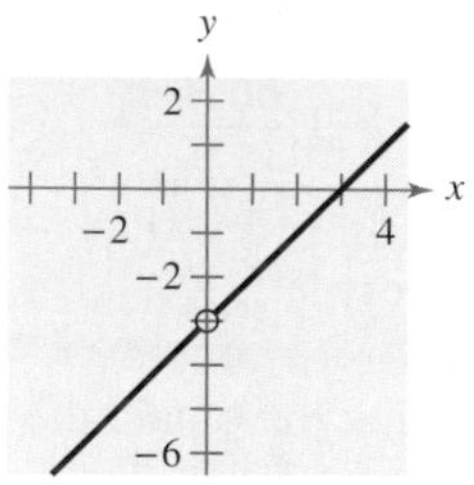

(a) $\lim\limits_{x\to -2} h(x)$

(b) $\lim\limits_{x\to 0} h(x)$

(c) $\lim\limits_{x\to 3} h(x)$

3. $g(x) = \dfrac{x^3 - x}{x - 1}$

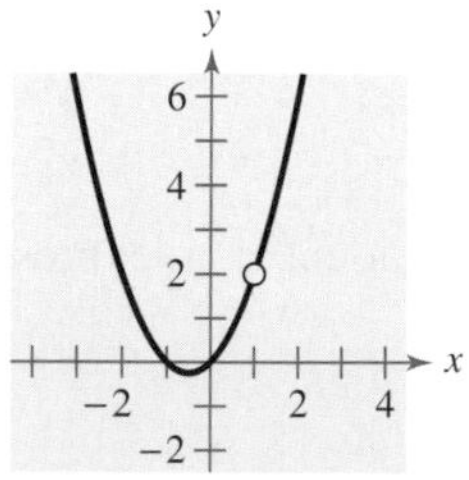

(a) $\lim\limits_{x\to 1} g(x)$

(b) $\lim\limits_{x\to -1} g(x)$

(c) $\lim\limits_{x\to 0} g(x)$

4. $f(x) = \dfrac{x^2 - 1}{x + 1}$

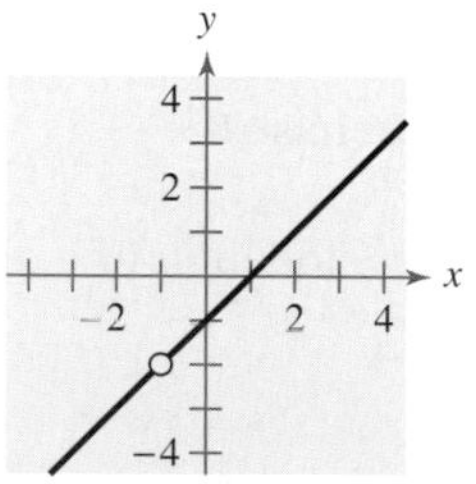

(a) $\lim\limits_{x\to 1} f(x)$

(b) $\lim\limits_{x\to 2} f(x)$

(c) $\lim\limits_{x\to -1} f(x)$

In Exercises 5–26, find the limit (if it exists). Use a graphing utility to verify your result graphically.

5. $\lim\limits_{x\to 6} \dfrac{x - 6}{x^2 - 36}$

6. $\lim\limits_{x\to 5} \dfrac{5 - x}{x^2 - 25}$

7. $\lim\limits_{x\to -1} \dfrac{1 - 2x - 3x^2}{1 + x}$

8. $\lim\limits_{x\to -2} \dfrac{2x^2 + 3x - 2}{x + 2}$

9. $\lim\limits_{t\to 2} \dfrac{t^3 - 8}{t - 2}$

10. $\lim\limits_{t\to -3} \dfrac{t^3 + 27}{t + 3}$

11. $\lim\limits_{x\to 2} \dfrac{x^5 - 32}{x - 2}$

12. $\lim\limits_{x\to 1} \dfrac{x^4 - 1}{x - 1}$

13. $\lim\limits_{y\to 0} \dfrac{\sqrt{5 + y} - \sqrt{5}}{y}$

14. $\lim\limits_{z\to 0} \dfrac{\sqrt{7 - z} - \sqrt{7}}{z}$

15. $\lim\limits_{x\to 0} \dfrac{\sqrt{x + 3} - \sqrt{3}}{x}$

16. $\lim\limits_{x\to 0} \dfrac{\sqrt{x + 4} - 2}{x}$

17. $\lim\limits_{x\to 0} \dfrac{\sqrt{2x + 1} - 1}{x}$

18. $\lim\limits_{x\to 9} \dfrac{3 - \sqrt{x}}{x - 9}$

19. $\lim\limits_{x\to -3} \dfrac{\sqrt{x + 7} - 2}{x + 3}$

20. $\lim\limits_{x\to 2} \dfrac{4 - \sqrt{18 - x}}{x - 2}$

21. $\lim\limits_{x\to 0} \dfrac{\dfrac{1}{x + 1} - 1}{x}$

22. $\lim\limits_{x\to 0} \dfrac{\dfrac{1}{4 - x} - \dfrac{1}{4}}{x}$

23. $\lim\limits_{x\to 0} \dfrac{\dfrac{1}{x + 4} - \dfrac{1}{4}}{x}$

24. $\lim\limits_{x\to 0} \dfrac{\dfrac{1}{2 + x} - \dfrac{1}{2}}{x}$

25. $\lim\limits_{x\to 0} \dfrac{\sec x}{\tan x}$

26. $\lim\limits_{x\to \pi/2} \dfrac{1 - \sin x}{\cos x}$

In Exercises 27–38, use a graphing utility to graph the function and approximate the limit accurate to three decimal places.

27. $\lim_{x\to 0} \dfrac{e^{2x} - 1}{x}$
28. $\lim_{x\to 0} \dfrac{1 - e^{-x}}{x}$
29. $\lim_{x\to 0^+} (x \ln x)$
30. $\lim_{x\to 0^+} (x^2 \ln x)$
31. $\lim_{x\to 0} \dfrac{\sin 2x}{x}$
32. $\lim_{x\to 0} \dfrac{\sin 3x}{x}$
33. $\lim_{x\to 0} \dfrac{\tan x}{x}$
34. $\lim_{x\to 0} \dfrac{1 - \cos 2x}{x}$
35. $\lim_{x\to 1} \dfrac{1 - \sqrt[3]{x}}{1 - x}$
36. $\lim_{x\to 1} \dfrac{\sqrt[3]{x} - x}{x - 1}$
37. $\lim_{x\to 0} (1 - x)^{2/x}$
38. $\lim_{x\to 0} (1 + 2x)^{1/x}$

Graphical, Numerical, and Algebraic Analysis **In Exercises 39–42, (a) graphically approximate the limit (if it exists) by using a graphing utility to graph the function, (b) numerically approximate the limit (if it exists) by using the *table* feature of a graphing utility to create a table, and (c) algebraically evaluate the limit (if it exists) by the appropriate technique(s).**

39. $\lim_{x\to 1^-} \dfrac{x - 1}{x^2 - 1}$
40. $\lim_{x\to 5^+} \dfrac{5 - x}{25 - x^2}$
41. $\lim_{x\to 16^+} \dfrac{4 - \sqrt{x}}{x - 16}$
42. $\lim_{x\to 0^-} \dfrac{\sqrt{x + 2} - \sqrt{2}}{x}$

In Exercises 43–50, graph the function. Determine the limit (if it exists) by evaluating the corresponding one-sided limits.

43. $\lim_{x\to 6} \dfrac{|x - 6|}{x - 6}$
44. $\lim_{x\to 2} \dfrac{|x - 2|}{x - 2}$
45. $\lim_{x\to 1} \dfrac{1}{x^2 + 1}$
46. $\lim_{x\to 1} \dfrac{1}{x^2 - 1}$
47. $\lim_{x\to 2} f(x)$ where $f(x) = \begin{cases} x - 1, & x \le 2 \\ 2x - 3, & x > 2 \end{cases}$
48. $\lim_{x\to 1} f(x)$ where $f(x) = \begin{cases} 2x + 1, & x < 1 \\ 4 - x^2, & x \ge 1 \end{cases}$
49. $\lim_{x\to 1} f(x)$ where $f(x) = \begin{cases} 4 - x^2, & x \le 1 \\ 3 - x, & x > 1 \end{cases}$
50. $\lim_{x\to 0} f(x)$ where $f(x) = \begin{cases} 4 - x^2, & x \le 0 \\ x + 4, & x > 0 \end{cases}$

In Exercises 51–56, use a graphing utility to graph the function and the equations $y = x$ and $y = -x$ in the same viewing window. Use the graph to find $\lim_{x\to 0} f(x)$.

51. $f(x) = x \cos x$
52. $f(x) = |x \sin x|$
53. $f(x) = |x| \sin x$
54. $f(x) = |x| \cos x$
55. $f(x) = x \sin \dfrac{1}{x}$
56. $f(x) = x \cos \dfrac{1}{x}$

In Exercises 57 and 58, state which limit can be evaluated by using direct substitution. Then evaluate or approximate each limit.

57. (a) $\lim_{x\to 0} x^2 \sin x^2$ (b) $\lim_{x\to 0} \dfrac{\sin x^2}{x^2}$
58. (a) $\lim_{x\to 0} \dfrac{x}{\cos x}$ (b) $\lim_{x\to 0} \dfrac{1 - \cos x}{x}$

In Exercises 59–66, find $\lim_{h\to 0} \dfrac{f(x + h) - f(x)}{h}$.

59. $f(x) = 3x - 1$
60. $f(x) = 5 - 6x$
61. $f(x) = \sqrt{x}$
62. $f(x) = \sqrt{x - 2}$
63. $f(x) = x^2 - 3x$
64. $f(x) = 4 - 2x - x^2$
65. $f(x) = \dfrac{1}{x + 2}$
66. $f(x) = \dfrac{1}{x - 1}$

Free-Falling Object **In Exercises 67 and 68, use the position function $s(t) = -16t^2 + 128$, which gives the height (in feet) of a free-falling object. The velocity at time $t = a$ seconds is given by $\lim_{t\to a} [s(a) - s(t)]/(a - t)$.**

67. Find the velocity when $t = 1$ second.
68. Find the velocity when $t = 2$ seconds.

69. ***Salary Contract*** A union contract guarantees a 10% salary increase yearly for 3 years. For a current salary of \$28,000, the salary $f(t)$ (in thousands of dollars) for the next 3 years is given by

$$f(t) = \begin{cases} 28.00, & 0 < t \le 1 \\ 30.80, & 1 < t \le 2 \\ 33.88, & 2 < t \le 3 \end{cases}$$

where t represents the time in years. Show that the limit of f as $t \to 2$ does not exist.

70. ***Consumer Awareness*** The cost of sending a package overnight is \$10.75 for the first pound and \$3.95 for each additional pound or portion of a pound. A plastic mailing bag can hold up to 3 pounds. The cost $f(x)$ of sending a package in a plastic mailing bag is given by

$$f(x) = \begin{cases} 10.75, & 0 < x \le 1 \\ 14.70, & 1 < x \le 2 \\ 18.65, & 2 < x \le 3 \end{cases}$$

where x represents the weight of the package (in pounds). Show that the limit of f as $x \to 1$ does not exist.

71. ***Communications*** The cost of a telephone call between two cities is \$0.75 for the first minute and \$0.50 for each additional minute or portion of a minute. A model for the cost C is given by $C(t) = 0.75 - 0.50[\![-(t - 1)]\!]$ where t is the time in minutes. (Recall from Section 1.6 that $f(x) = [\![x]\!] =$ the greatest integer less than or equal to x.)

(a) Sketch the graph of C for $0 < t \leq 5$.

(b) Complete the table and observe the behavior of C as t approaches 3.5. Use the graph from part (a) and the table to find $\lim_{t \to 3.5} C(t)$.

t	3	3.3	3.4	3.5	3.6	3.7	4
C				?			

(c) Complete the table and observe the behavior of C as t approaches 3. Does the limit of $C(t)$ as t approaches 3 exist? Explain.

t	2	2.5	2.9	3	3.1	3.5	4
C				?			

Model It

72. ***Consumer Awareness*** The cost C (in dollars) of making x photocopies at a copy shop is given by the function

$$C(x) = \begin{cases} 0.15x, & 0 < x \leq 25 \\ 0.10x, & 25 < x \leq 100 \\ 0.07x, & 100 < x \leq 500 \\ 0.05x, & x > 500 \end{cases}$$

(a) Sketch a graph of the function.

(b) Find each limit and interpret your result in the context of the situation.

(i) $\lim_{x \to 15} C(x)$ (ii) $\lim_{x \to 99} C(x)$ (iii) $\lim_{x \to 305} C(x)$

(c) Create a table of values to show numerically that each limit does not exist.

(i) $\lim_{x \to 25} C(x)$ (ii) $\lim_{x \to 100} C(x)$ (iii) $\lim_{x \to 500} C(x)$

(d) Explain how you can use the graph in part (a) to verify that the limits in part (c) do not exist.

Synthesis

True or False? **In Exercises 73 and 74, determine whether the statement is true or false. Justify your answer.**

73. When your attempt to find the limit of a rational function yields the indeterminate form $\frac{0}{0}$, the rational function's numerator and denominator have a common factor.

74. If $f(c) = L$, then $\lim_{x \to c} f(x) = L$.

75. ***Think About It***

(a) Sketch the graph of a function for which $f(2)$ is defined but for which the limit of $f(x)$ as x approaches 2 does not exist.

(b) Sketch the graph of a function for which the limit of $f(x)$ as x approaches 1 is 4 but for which $f(1) \neq 4$.

76. ***Writing*** Consider the limit of the rational function given by $p(x)/q(x)$. What conclusion can you make if direct substitution produces each expression? Write a short paragraph explaining your reasoning.

(a) $\lim_{x \to c} \frac{p(x)}{q(x)} = \frac{0}{1}$ (b) $\lim_{x \to c} \frac{p(x)}{q(x)} = \frac{1}{1}$

(c) $\lim_{x \to c} \frac{p(x)}{q(x)} = \frac{1}{0}$ (d) $\lim_{x \to c} \frac{p(x)}{q(x)} = \frac{0}{0}$

Skills Review

77. Write an equation of the line that passes through $(6, -10)$ and is perpendicular to the line that passes through $(4, -6)$ and $(3, -4)$.

78. Write an equation of the line that passes through $(1, -1)$ and is parallel to the line that passes through $(3, -3)$ and $(5, -2)$.

79. ***Arc Length*** Find the length of the arc on a circle with a radius of 8.5 inches intercepted by a central angle of 45°.

80. ***Arc Length*** Find the length of the arc on a circle with a radius of 26 millimeters intercepted by a central angle of 101°.

81. ***Circular Sector*** Find the area of the sector of a circle with a radius of 9 centimeters and central angle $\theta = 135°$.

82. ***Circular Sector*** Find the area of the sector of a circle with a radius of 3.4 feet and central angle $\theta = 81°$.

In Exercises 83–88, identify the type of conic algebraically. Then use a graphing utility to graph the conic.

83. $r = \frac{3}{1 + \cos\theta}$

84. $r = \frac{12}{3 + 2\sin\theta}$

85. $r = \frac{9}{2 + 3\cos\theta}$

86. $r = \frac{4}{4 + \cos\theta}$

87. $r = \frac{5}{1 - \sin\theta}$

88. $r = \frac{6}{3 - 4\sin\theta}$

In Exercises 89–92, determine whether the vectors are orthogonal, parallel, or neither.

89. $\langle 7, -2, 3\rangle, \langle -1, 4, 5\rangle$

90. $\langle 5, 5, 0\rangle, \langle 0, 5, 1\rangle$

91. $\langle -4, 3, -6\rangle, \langle 12, -9, 18\rangle$

92. $\langle 2, -3, 1\rangle, \langle -2, 2, 2\rangle$

12.3 The Tangent Line Problem

What you should learn

- Use a tangent line to approximate the slope of a graph at a point.
- Use the limit definition of slope to find exact slopes of graphs.
- Find derivatives of functions and use derivatives to find slopes of graphs.

Why you should learn it

The slope of the graph of a function can be used to analyze rates of change at particular points on the graph. For instance, in Exercise 52 on page 881, the slope of the graph is used to analyze the rate of change in book sales for particular selling prices.

© Bettman/Corbis

Tangent Line to a Graph

Calculus is a branch of mathematics that studies rates of change of functions. If you go on to take a course in calculus, you will learn that rates of change have many applications in real life.

Earlier in the text, you learned how the slope of a line indicates the rate at which a line rises or falls. For a line, this rate (or slope) is the same at every point on the line. For graphs other than lines, the rate at which the graph rises or falls changes from point to point. For instance, in Figure 12.20, the parabola is rising more quickly at the point (x_1, y_1) than it is at the point (x_2, y_2). At the vertex (x_3, y_3), the graph levels off, and at the point (x_4, y_4), the graph is falling.

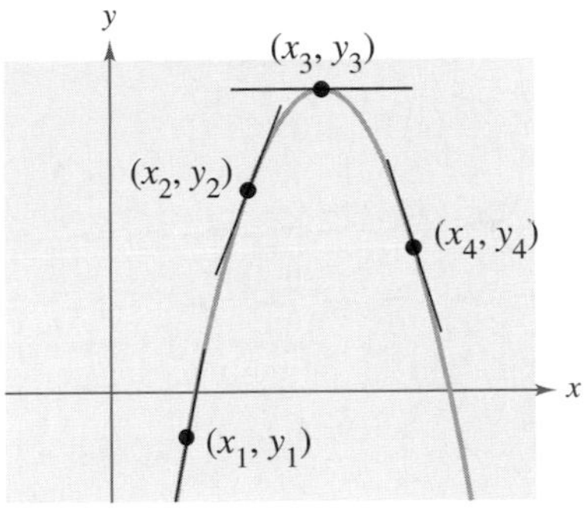

FIGURE 12.20

To determine the rate at which a graph rises or falls at a *single point*, you can find the slope of the tangent line at that point. In simple terms, the **tangent line** to the graph of a function f at a point $P(x_1, y_1)$ is the line that best approximates the slope of the graph at the point. Figure 12.21 shows other examples of tangent lines.

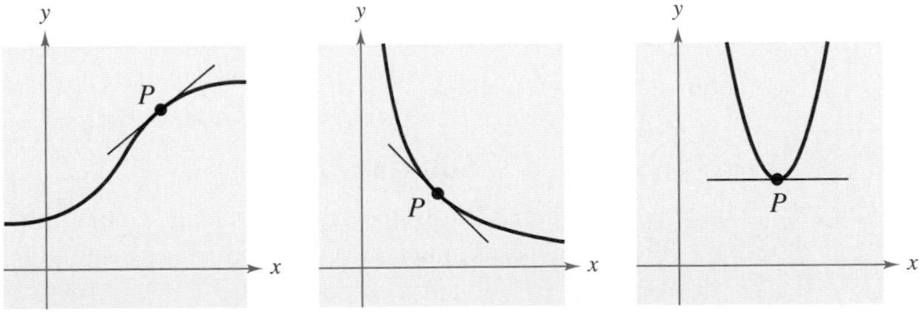

FIGURE 12.21

From geometry, you know that a line is tangent to a circle if the line intersects the circle at only one point. Tangent lines to noncircular graphs, however, can intersect the graph at more than one point. For instance, in the first graph in Figure 12.21, if the tangent line were extended, it would intersect the graph at a point other than the point of tangency.

Slope of a Graph

Because a tangent line approximates the slope of the graph at a point, the problem of finding the slope of a graph at a point is the same as finding the slope of the tangent line at the point.

Example 1 Visually Approximating the Slope of a Graph

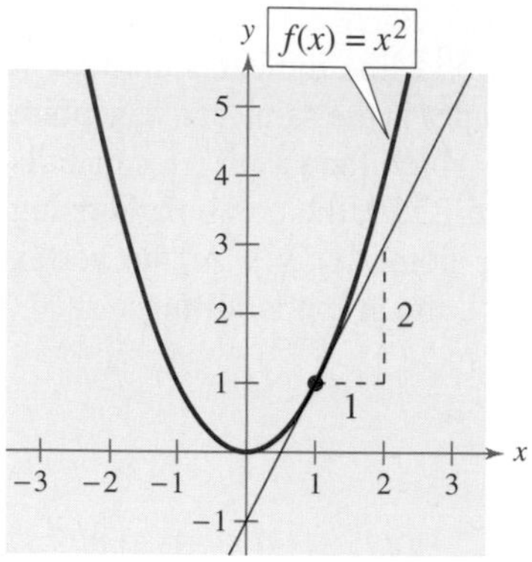

FIGURE 12.22

Use the graph in Figure 12.22 to approximate the slope of the graph of $f(x) = x^2$ at the point $(1, 1)$.

Solution

From the graph of $f(x) = x^2$, you can see that the tangent line at $(1, 1)$ rises approximately two units for each unit change in x. So, you can estimate the slope of the tangent line at $(1, 1)$ to be

$$\text{Slope} = \frac{\text{change in } y}{\text{change in } x}$$

$$\approx \frac{2}{1}$$

$$= 2.$$

Because the tangent line at the point $(1, 1)$ has a slope of about 2, you can conclude that the graph of f has a slope of about 2 at the point $(1, 1)$.

CHECKPOINT Now try Exercise 1.

When you are visually approximating the slope of a graph, remember that the scales on the horizontal and vertical axes may differ. When this happens (as it frequently does in applications), the slope of the tangent line is distorted, and you must be careful to account for the difference in scales.

Example 2 Approximating the Slope of a Graph

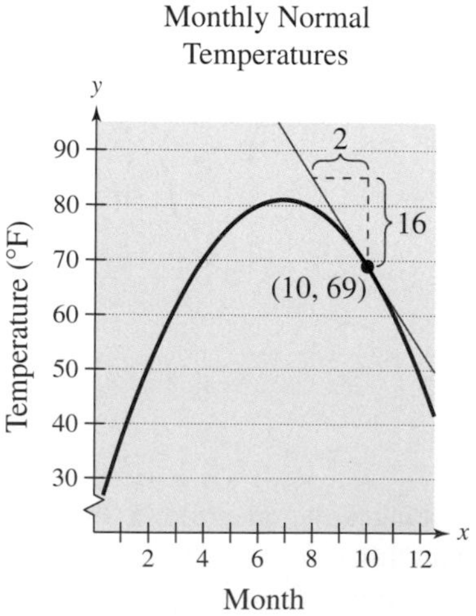

FIGURE 12.23

Figure 12.23 graphically depicts the monthly normal temperatures (in degrees Fahrenheit) for Dallas, Texas. Approximate the slope of this graph at the indicated point and give a physical interpretation of the result. (Source: National Climatic Data Center)

Solution

From the graph, you can see that the tangent line at the given point falls approximately 16 units for each two-unit change in x. So, you can estimate the slope at the given point to be

$$\text{Slope} = \frac{\text{change in } y}{\text{change in } x} \approx \frac{-16}{2} = -8 \text{ degrees per month.}$$

This means that you can expect the monthly normal temperature in November to be about 8 degrees lower than the normal temperature in October.

CHECKPOINT Now try Exercise 3.

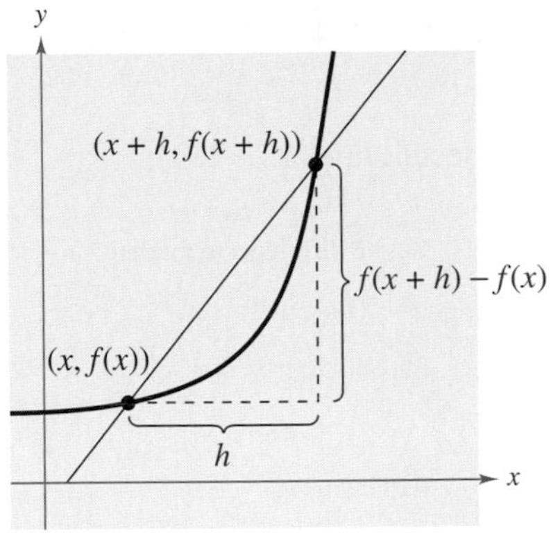

FIGURE 12.24

Slope and the Limit Process

In Examples 1 and 2, you approximated the slope of a graph at a point by creating a graph and then "eyeballing" the tangent line at the point of tangency. A more precise method of approximating tangent lines makes use of a **secant line** through the point of tangency and a second point on the graph, as shown in Figure 12.24. If $(x, f(x))$ is the point of tangency and $(x + h, f(x + h))$ is a second point on the graph of f, the slope of the secant line through the two points is given by

$$m_{\text{sec}} = \frac{\text{change in } y}{\text{change in } x} = \frac{f(x + h) - f(x)}{h}. \qquad \text{Slope of secant line}$$

The right side of this equation is called the **difference quotient.** The denominator h is the *change in x*, and the numerator is the *change in y*. The beauty of this procedure is that you obtain more and more accurate approximations of the slope of the tangent line by choosing points closer and closer to the point of tangency, as shown in Figure 12.25.

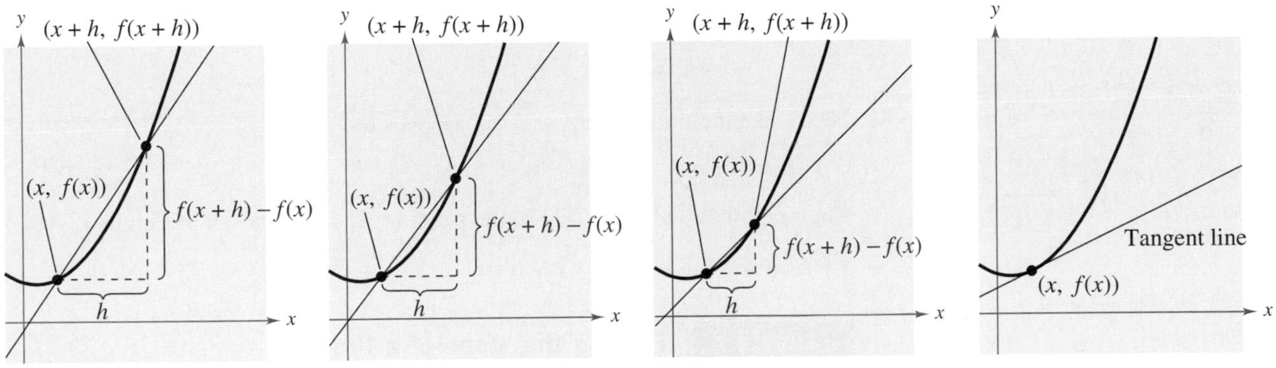

As h approaches 0, the secant line approaches the tangent line.

FIGURE 12.25

Using the limit process, you can find the *exact* slope of the tangent line at $(x, f(x))$.

> **Definition of the Slope of a Graph**
>
> The **slope** m of the graph of f at the point $(x, f(x))$ is equal to the slope of its tangent line at $(x, f(x))$, and is given by
>
> $$m = \lim_{h \to 0} m_{\text{sec}} = \lim_{h \to 0} \frac{f(x + h) - f(x)}{h}$$
>
> provided this limit exists.

From the definition above and from Section 12.2, you can see that the difference quotient is used frequently in calculus. Using the difference quotient to find the slope of a tangent line to a graph is a major concept of calculus.

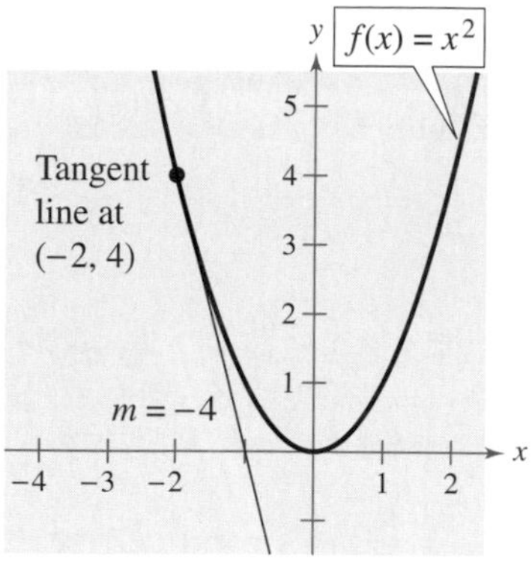

FIGURE 12.26

Example 3 Finding the Slope of a Graph

Find the slope of the graph of $f(x) = x^2$ at the point $(-2, 4)$.

Solution

Find an expression that represents the slope of a secant line at $(-2, 4)$.

$$m_{sec} = \frac{f(-2+h) - f(-2)}{h} \qquad \text{Set up difference quotient.}$$

$$= \frac{(-2+h)^2 - (-2)^2}{h} \qquad \text{Substitute in } f(x) = x^2.$$

$$= \frac{4 - 4h + h^2 - 4}{h} \qquad \text{Expand terms.}$$

$$= \frac{-4h + h^2}{h} \qquad \text{Simplify.}$$

$$= \frac{\cancel{h}(-4+h)}{\cancel{h}} \qquad \text{Factor and divide out.}$$

$$= -4 + h, \quad h \neq 0 \qquad \text{Simplify.}$$

Next, take the limit of m_{sec} as h approaches 0.

$$m = \lim_{h \to 0} m_{sec} = \lim_{h \to 0} (-4 + h) = -4$$

The graph has a slope of -4 at the point $(-2, 4)$, as shown in Figure 12.26.

CHECKPOINT Now try Exercise 5.

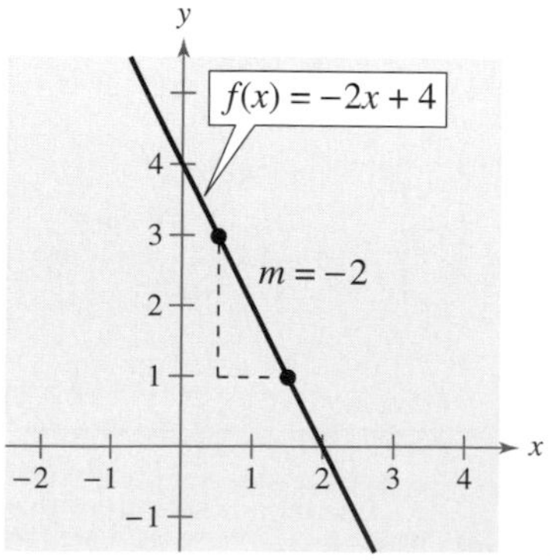

FIGURE 12.27

Example 4 Finding the Slope of a Graph

Find the slope of $f(x) = -2x + 4$.

Solution

$$m = \lim_{h \to 0} \frac{f(x+h) - f(x)}{h} \qquad \text{Set up difference quotient.}$$

$$= \lim_{h \to 0} \frac{[-2(x+h) + 4] - (-2x + 4)}{h} \qquad \text{Substitute in } f(x) = -2x + 4.$$

$$= \lim_{h \to 0} \frac{-2x - 2h + 4 + 2x - 4}{h} \qquad \text{Expand terms.}$$

$$= \lim_{h \to 0} \frac{-2\cancel{h}}{\cancel{h}} \qquad \text{Divide out.}$$

$$= -2 \qquad \text{Simplify.}$$

You know from your study of linear functions that the line given by $f(x) = -2x + 4$ has a slope of -2, as shown in Figure 12.27. This conclusion is consistent with that obtained by the limit definition of slope, as shown above.

CHECKPOINT Now try Exercise 7.

It is important that you see the difference between the ways the difference quotients were set up in Examples 3 and 4. In Example 3, you were finding the slope of a graph at a specific point $(c, f(c))$. To find the slope in such a case, you can use the following form of the difference quotient.

$$m = \lim_{h \to 0} \frac{f(c + h) - f(c)}{h}$$ Slope at specific point

In Example 4, however, you were finding a *formula* for the slope at *any* point on the graph. In such cases, you should use x, rather than c, in the difference quotient.

$$m = \lim_{h \to 0} \frac{f(x + h) - f(x)}{h}$$ Formula for slope

Except for linear functions, this form will always produce a function of x, which can then be evaluated to find the slope at any desired point.

Technology

Try verifying the result in Example 5 by using a graphing utility to graph the function and the tangent lines at $(-1, 2)$ and $(2, 5)$ as

$y_1 = x^2 + 1$

$y_2 = -2x$

$y_3 = 4x - 3$

in the same viewing window. Some graphing utilities even have a *tangent* feature that automatically graphs the tangent line to a curve at a given point. If you have such a graphing utility, try verifying Example 5 using this feature.

Example 5 Finding a Formula for the Slope of a Graph

Find a formula for the slope of the graph of $f(x) = x^2 + 1$. What are the slopes at the points $(-1, 2)$ and $(2, 5)$?

Solution

$$m_{sec} = \frac{f(x + h) - f(x)}{h}$$ Set up difference quotient.

$$= \frac{[(x + h)^2 + 1] - (x^2 + 1)}{h}$$ Substitute in $f(x) = x^2 + 1$.

$$= \frac{x^2 + 2xh + h^2 + 1 - x^2 - 1}{h}$$ Expand terms.

$$= \frac{2xh + h^2}{h}$$ Simplify.

$$= \frac{\cancel{h}(2x + h)}{\cancel{h}}$$ Factor and divide out.

$$= 2x + h, \quad h \neq 0$$ Simplify.

Next, take the limit of m_{sec} as h approaches 0.

$$m = \lim_{h \to 0} m_{sec} = \lim_{h \to 0} (2x + h) = 2x$$ Formula for finding slope

Using the formula $m = 2x$ for the slope at $(x, f(x))$, you can find the slope at the specified points. At $(-1, 2)$, the slope is

$$m = 2(-1) = -2$$

and at $(2, 5)$, the slope is

$$m = 2(2) = 4.$$

The graph of f is shown in Figure 12.28.

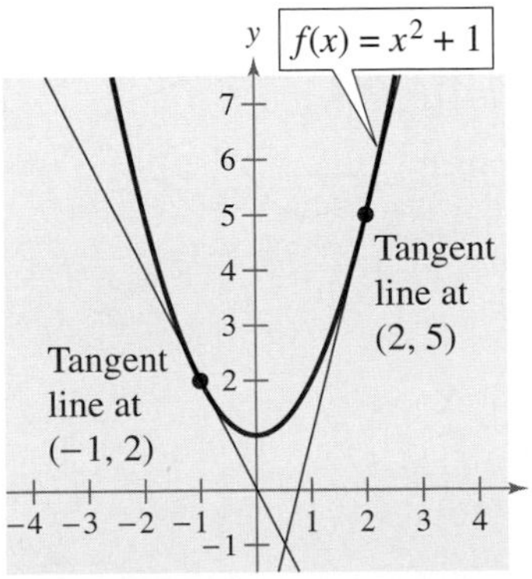

FIGURE 12.28

CHECKPOINT Now try Exercise 13.

The Derivative of a Function

In Example 5, you started with the function $f(x) = x^2 + 1$ and used the limit process to derive another function, $m = 2x$, that represents the slope of the graph of f at the point $(x, f(x))$. This derived function is called the **derivative** of f at x. It is denoted by $f'(x)$, which is read as "f prime of x."

Definition of the Derivative

The **derivative** of f at x is given by

$$f'(x) = \lim_{h \to 0} \frac{f(x+h) - f(x)}{h}$$

provided this limit exists.

Remember that the derivative $f'(x)$ is a formula for the slope of the tangent line to the graph of f at the point $(x, f(x))$.

Example 6 Finding a Derivative

Find the derivative of $f(x) = 3x^2 - 2x$.

Solution

$$\begin{aligned} f'(x) &= \lim_{h \to 0} \frac{f(x+h) - f(x)}{h} \\ &= \lim_{h \to 0} \frac{[3(x+h)^2 - 2(x+h)] - (3x^2 - 2x)}{h} \\ &= \lim_{h \to 0} \frac{3x^2 + 6xh + 3h^2 - 2x - 2h - 3x^2 + 2x}{h} \\ &= \lim_{h \to 0} \frac{6xh + 3h^2 - 2h}{h} \\ &= \lim_{h \to 0} \frac{\cancel{h}(6x + 3h - 2)}{\cancel{h}} \\ &= \lim_{h \to 0} (6x + 3h - 2) \\ &= 6x - 2 \end{aligned}$$

So, the derivative of $f(x) = 3x^2 - 2x$ is

$$f'(x) = 6x - 2.$$

CHECKPOINT Now try Exercise 29.

Exploration

Use a graphing utility to graph the function $f(x) = 3x^2 - 2x$. Use the *trace* feature to approximate the coordinates of the vertex of this parabola. Then use the derivative of $f(x) = 3x^2 - 2x$ to find the slope of the tangent line at the vertex. Make a conjecture about the slope of the tangent line at the vertex of an arbitrary parabola.

Note that in addition to $f'(x)$, other notations can be used to denote the derivative of $y = f(x)$. The most common are

$$\frac{dy}{dx}, \quad y', \quad \frac{d}{dx}[f(x)], \quad \text{and} \quad D_x[y].$$

Example 7 **Using the Derivative**

Find $f'(x)$ for $f(x) = \sqrt{x}$. Then find the slopes of the graph of f at the points $(1, 1)$ and $(4, 2)$.

Solution

$$f'(x) = \lim_{h \to 0} \frac{f(x+h) - f(x)}{h}$$

$$= \lim_{h \to 0} \frac{\sqrt{x+h} - \sqrt{x}}{h}$$

Because direct substitution yields the indeterminate form $\frac{0}{0}$, you should use the rationalizing technique discussed in Section 12.2 to find the limit.

$$= \lim_{h \to 0} \left(\frac{\sqrt{x+h} - \sqrt{x}}{h}\right)\left(\frac{\sqrt{x+h} + \sqrt{x}}{\sqrt{x+h} + \sqrt{x}}\right)$$

$$= \lim_{h \to 0} \frac{(x+h) - x}{h(\sqrt{x+h} + \sqrt{x})}$$

$$= \lim_{h \to 0} \frac{\not{h}}{\not{h}(\sqrt{x+h} + \sqrt{x})}$$

$$= \lim_{h \to 0} \frac{1}{\sqrt{x+h} + \sqrt{x}} = \frac{1}{2\sqrt{x}}$$

At the point $(1, 1)$, the slope is

$$f'(1) = \frac{1}{2\sqrt{1}} = \frac{1}{2}.$$

At the point $(4, 2)$, the slope is

$$f'(4) = \frac{1}{2\sqrt{4}} = \frac{1}{4}.$$

The graph of f is shown in Figure 12.29.

CHECKPOINT Now try Exercise 35.

STUDY TIP

Remember that in order to rationalize the numerator of an expression, you must multiply the numerator and denominator by the conjugate of the numerator.

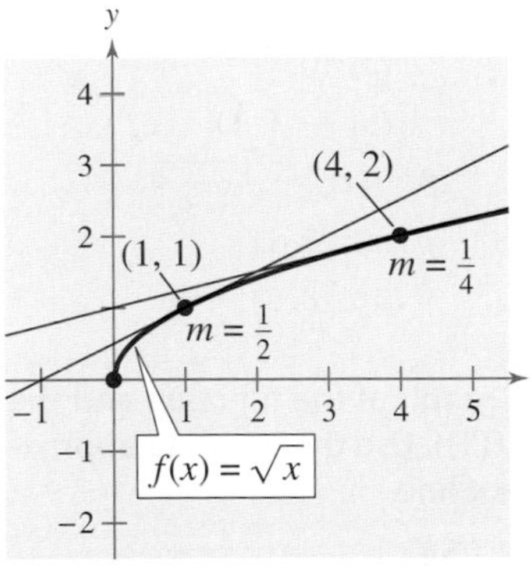

FIGURE 12.29

WRITING ABOUT MATHEMATICS

Using a Derivative to Find Slope In many applications, it is convenient to use a variable other than x as the independent variable. Complete the following limit process to find the derivative of $f(t) = 3/t$. Then use the result to find the slope of the graph of $f(t) = 3/t$ at the point $(3, 1)$.

$$f'(t) = \lim_{h \to 0} \frac{f(t+h) - f(t)}{h} = \lim_{h \to 0} \frac{\frac{3}{t+h} - \frac{3}{t}}{h} = \ldots$$

Write a short paragraph summarizing your findings.

12.3 Exercises

VOCABULARY CHECK: Fill in the blanks.

1. _______ is the study of the rates of change of functions.
2. The _______ _______ to the graph of a function at a point is the line that best approximates the slope of the graph at the point.
3. A _______ _______ is a line through the point of tangency and a second point on the graph.
4. The slope of the tangent line to a graph at $(x, f(x))$ is given by _______ .
5. The _______ of a function f at x represents the slope of the graph of f at the point $(x, f(x))$.

In Exercises 1–4, use the figure to approximate the slope of the curve at the point (x, y).

1.
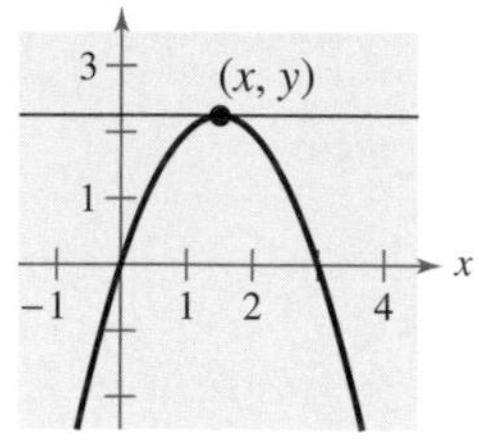

2.
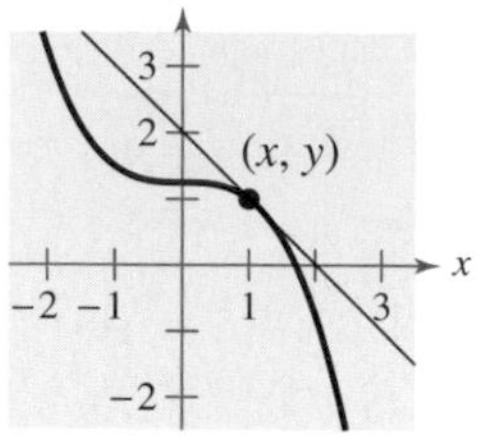

3.
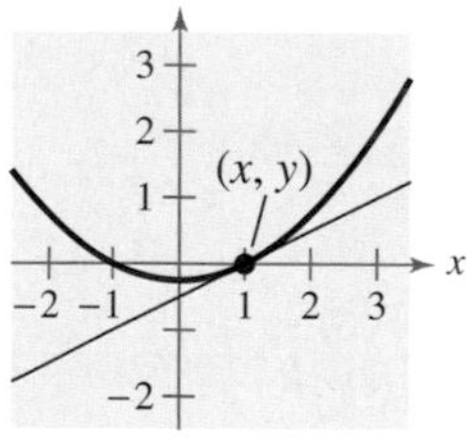

4.
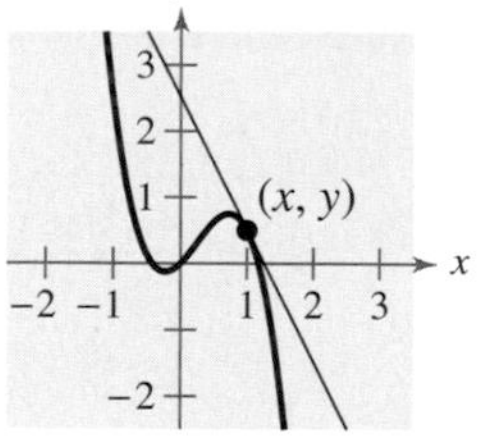

In Exercises 5–12, use the limit process to find the slope of the graph of the function at the specified point. Use a graphing utility to confirm your result.

5. $g(x) = x^2 - 4x, \quad (3, -3)$
6. $f(x) = 10x - 2x^2, \quad (3, 12)$
7. $g(x) = 5 - 2x, \quad (1, 3)$
8. $h(x) = 2x + 5, \quad (-1, -3)$
9. $g(x) = \dfrac{4}{x}, \quad (2, 2)$
10. $g(x) = \dfrac{1}{x - 2}, \quad \left(4, \dfrac{1}{2}\right)$
11. $h(x) = \sqrt{x}, \quad (9, 3)$
12. $h(x) = \sqrt{x + 10}, \quad (-1, 3)$

In Exercises 13–18, find a formula for the slope of the graph of f at the point $(x, f(x))$. Then use it to find the slope at the two given points.

13. $f(x) = 4 - x^2$
    (a) $(0, 4)$
    (b) $(-1, 3)$
14. $f(x) = x^3$
    (a) $(1, 1)$
    (b) $(-2, -8)$
15. $f(x) = \dfrac{1}{x + 4}$
    (a) $\left(0, \frac{1}{4}\right)$
    (b) $\left(-2, \frac{1}{2}\right)$
16. $f(x) = \dfrac{1}{x + 2}$
    (a) $\left(0, \frac{1}{2}\right)$
    (b) $(-1, 1)$
17. $f(x) = \sqrt{x - 1}$
    (a) $(5, 2)$
    (b) $(10, 3)$
18. $f(x) = \sqrt{x - 4}$
    (a) $(5, 1)$
    (b) $(8, 2)$

In Exercises 19–24, sketch a graph of the function and the tangent line at the point $(1, f(1))$. Use the graph to approximate the slope of the tangent line.

19. $f(x) = x^2 - 2$
20. $f(x) = x^2 - 2x + 1$
21. $f(x) = \sqrt{2 - x}$
22. $f(x) = \sqrt{x + 3}$
23. $f(x) = \dfrac{4}{x + 1}$
24. $f(x) = \dfrac{3}{2 - x}$

In Exercises 25–34, find the derivative of the function.

25. $f(x) = 5$
26. $f(x) = -1$
27. $g(x) = 9 - \frac{1}{3}x$
28. $f(x) = -5x + 2$
29. $f(x) = 4 - 3x^2$
30. $f(x) = x^2 - 3x + 4$
31. $f(x) = \dfrac{1}{x^2}$
32. $f(x) = \dfrac{1}{x^3}$
33. $f(x) = \dfrac{1}{\sqrt{x - 9}}$
34. $h(s) = \dfrac{1}{\sqrt{s + 1}}$

In Exercises 35–38, (a) find the slope of the graph of f at the given point, (b) use the result of part (a) to find an equation of the tangent line to the graph at the point, and (c) graph the function and the tangent line.

35. $f(x) = x^2 - 1, \quad (2, 3)$

36. $f(x) = x^3 - x, \quad (2, 6)$

37. $f(x) = \sqrt{x + 1}, \quad (3, 2)$

38. $f(x) = \sqrt{x - 2}, \quad (3, 1)$

In Exercises 39–42, use a graphing utility to graph f over the interval $[-2, 2]$ and complete the table. Compare the value of the first derivative with a visual approximation of the slope of the graph.

x	-2	-1.5	-1	-0.5	0	0.5	1	1.5	2
$f(x)$									
$f'(x)$									

39. $f(x) = \frac{1}{2}x^2$

40. $f(x) = \frac{1}{4}x^3$

41. $f(x) = \sqrt{x + 3}$

42. $f(x) = \dfrac{x^2 - 4}{x + 4}$

In Exercises 43–46, find an equation of the line that is tangent to the graph of f and parallel to the given line.

	Function	*Line*
43.	$f(x) = -\frac{1}{4}x^2$	$x + y = 0$
44.	$f(x) = x^2 + 1$	$2x + y = 0$
45.	$f(x) = -\frac{1}{2}x^3$	$6x + y + 4 = 0$
46.	$f(x) = x^2 - x$	$x + 2y - 6 = 0$

In Exercises 47–50, find the derivative of f. Use the derivative to determine any points on the graph of f at which the tangent line is horizontal. Use a graphing utility to verify your results.

47. $f(x) = x^2 - 4x + 3$

48. $f(x) = x^3 + 3x$

49. $f(x) = 3x^3 - 9x$

50. $f(x) = 3x^4 + 4x^3$

51. ***Revenue*** The table shows the revenue y (in millions of dollars) for Blockbuster, Inc. from 1999 to 2004. (Source: Blockbuster, Inc.)

Year	Revenue, y
1999	4463.5
2000	4960.1
2001	5156.7
2002	5565.9
2003	5911.7
2004	6053.2

(a) Use the *regression* feature of a graphing utility to find a quadratic model for the data. Let x represent the time in years, with $x = 9$ corresponding to 1999.

(b) Use a graphing utility to graph the model found in part (a). Estimate the slope of the graph when $x = 12$ and give an interpretation of the result.

(c) Use a graphing utility to graph the tangent line to the model when $x = 12$. Compare the slope given by the graphing utility with the estimate in part (b).

Model It

52. ***Market Research*** The data in the table show the number N (in thousands) of books sold when the price per book is p (in dollars).

Price, p	Number of books, N
\$10	900
\$15	630
\$20	396
\$25	227
\$30	102
\$35	36

(a) Use the *regression* feature of a graphing utility to find a quadratic model for the data.

(b) Use a graphing utility to graph the model found in part (a). Estimate the slopes of the graph when $p = \$15$ and $p = \$30$.

(c) Use a graphing utility to graph the tangent lines to the model when $p = \$15$ and $p = \$30$. Compare the slopes given by the graphing utility with your estimates in part (b).

(d) The slopes of the tangent lines at $p = \$15$ and $p = \$30$ are not the same. Explain what this means to the company selling the books.

53. ***Path of a Ball*** The path of a ball thrown by a child is modeled by

$$y = -x^2 + 5x + 2$$

where y is the height of the ball (in feet) and x is the horizontal distance (in feet) from the point from which the ball was thrown. Using your knowledge of the slopes of tangent lines, show that the height of the ball is increasing on the interval $[0, 2]$ and decreasing on the interval $[4, 6]$. Explain your reasoning.

54. ***Profit*** The profit P (in hundreds of dollars) that a company makes depends on the amount x (in hundreds of dollars) the company spends on advertising. The profit function is given by

$$P(x) = 200 + 30x - 0.5x^2.$$

Using your knowledge of the slopes of tangent lines, show that the profit is increasing on the interval $[0, 20]$ and decreasing on the interval $[40, 60]$.

Synthesis

True or False? **In Exercises 55 and 56, determine whether the statement is true or false. Justify your answer.**

55. The slope of the graph of $y = x^2$ is different at every point on the graph of f.

56. A tangent line to a graph can intersect the graph only at the point of tangency.

In Exercises 57–60, match the function with the graph of its *derivative*. It is not necessary to find the derivative of the function. [The graphs are labeled (a), (b), (c), and (d).]

(a)

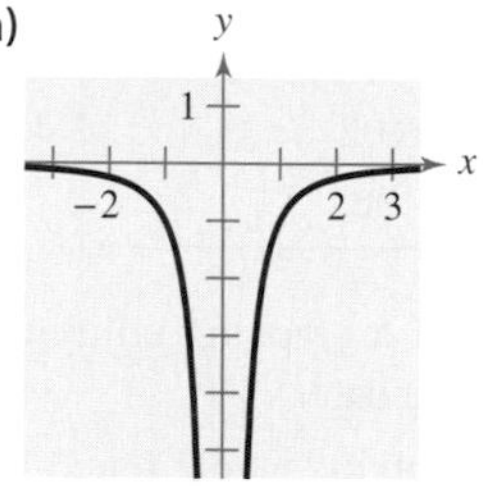

(b)

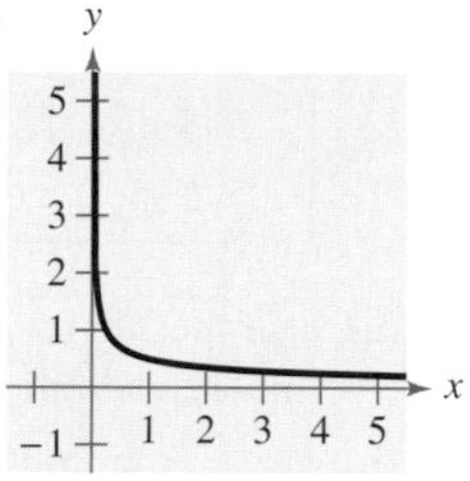

(c)

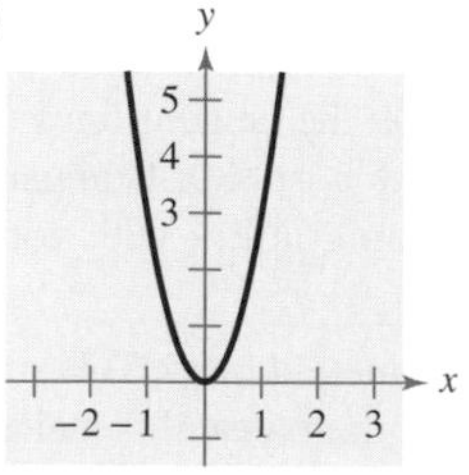

(d)

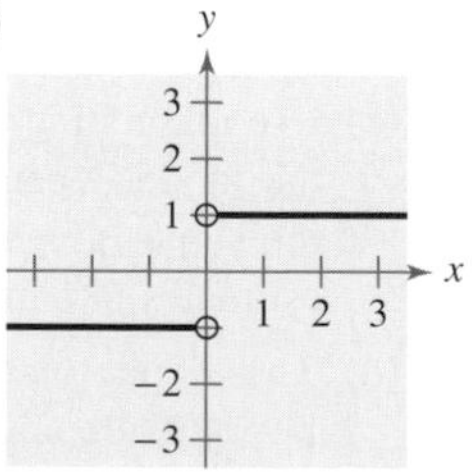

57. $f(x) = \sqrt{x}$

58. $f(x) = \dfrac{1}{x}$

59. $f(x) = |x|$

60. $f(x) = x^3$

61. ***Think About It*** Sketch the graph of a function whose derivative is always positive.

62. ***Think About It*** Sketch the graph of a function whose derivative is always negative.

63. ***Think About It*** Sketch the graph of a function for which $f'(x) < 0$ for $x < 1$, $f'(x) \geq 0$ for $x > 1$, and $f'(1) = 0$.

64. ***Conjecture*** Consider the functions $f(x) = x^2$ and $g(x) = x^3$.

(a) Sketch the graphs of f and f' on the same set of coordinate axes.

(b) Sketch the graphs of g and g' on the same set of coordinate axes.

(c) Identify any pattern between the functions f and g and their respective derivatives. Use the pattern to make a conjecture about $h'(x)$ if $h(x) = x^n$, where n is an integer and $n \geq 2$.

Skills Review

In Exercises 65–68, sketch the graph of the rational function. As sketching aids, check for intercepts, vertical asymptotes, and horizontal asymptotes. Use a graphing utility to verify your graph.

65. $f(x) = \dfrac{1}{x^2 - x - 2}$

66. $f(x) = \dfrac{x - 2}{x^2 - 4x + 3}$

67. $f(x) = \dfrac{x^2 - x - 2}{x - 2}$

68. $f(x) = \dfrac{x^2 - 16}{x + 4}$

In Exercises 69–72, find the cross product of the vectors.

69. $\langle 1, 1, 1 \rangle, \langle 2, 1, -1 \rangle$

70. $\langle -10, 0, 6 \rangle, \langle 7, 0, 0 \rangle$

71. $\langle -4, 10, 0 \rangle, \langle 4, -1, 0 \rangle$

72. $\langle 8, -7, 14 \rangle, \langle -1, 8, 4 \rangle$

73. **Make a Decision** To work an extended application analyzing the amount spent on advertising in the United States, visit this text's website at *college.hmco.com*. *(Data Source: Universal McCann)*

12.4 Limits at Infinity and Limits of Sequences

What you should learn

- Evaluate limits of functions at infinity.
- Find limits of sequences.

Why you should learn it

Finding limits at infinity is useful in many types of real-life applications. For instance, in Exercise 52 on page 891, you are asked to find a limit at infinity to determine the number of military reserve personnel in the future.

© Karen Kasmauski/Corbis

Limits at Infinity and Horizontal Asymptotes

As pointed out at the beginning of this chapter, there are two basic problems in calculus: finding **tangent lines** and finding the area of a region. In Section 12.3, you saw how limits can be used to solve the tangent line problem. In this section and the next, you will see how a different type of limit, a *limit at infinity*, can be used to solve the area problem. To get an idea of what is meant by a limit at infinity, consider the function given by

$$f(x) = \frac{x+1}{2x}.$$

The graph of f is shown in Figure 12.30. From earlier work, you know that $y = \frac{1}{2}$ is a horizontal asymptote of the graph of this function. Using limit notation, this can be written as follows.

$$\lim_{x\to-\infty} f(x) = \frac{1}{2} \qquad \text{Horizontal asymptote to the left}$$

$$\lim_{x\to\infty} f(x) = \frac{1}{2} \qquad \text{Horizontal asymptote to the right}$$

These limits mean that the value of $f(x)$ gets arbitrarily close to $\frac{1}{2}$ as x decreases or increases without bound.

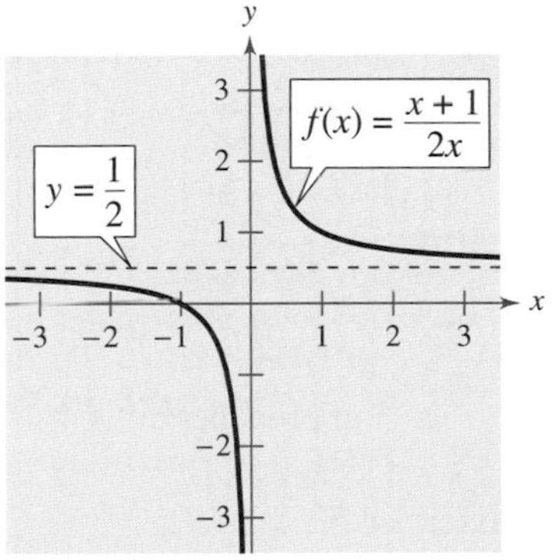

FIGURE 12.30

Definition of Limits at Infinity

If f is a function and L_1 and L_2 are real numbers, the statements

$$\lim_{x\to-\infty} f(x) = L_1 \qquad \text{Limit as } x \text{ approaches } -\infty$$

and

$$\lim_{x\to\infty} f(x) = L_2 \qquad \text{Limit as } x \text{ approaches } \infty$$

denote the **limits at infinity.** The first statement is read "*the limit of $f(x)$ as x approaches $-\infty$ is L_1*," and the second is read "*the limit of $f(x)$ as x approaches ∞ is L_2*."

To help evaluate limits at infinity, you can use the following definition.

Limits at Infinity

If r is a positive real number, then

$$\lim_{x \to \infty} \frac{1}{x^r} = 0. \qquad \text{Limit toward the right}$$

Furthermore, if x^r is defined when $x < 0$, then

$$\lim_{x \to -\infty} \frac{1}{x^r} = 0. \qquad \text{Limit toward the left}$$

Limits at infinity share many of the properties of limits listed in Section 12.1. Some of these properties are demonstrated in the next example.

Exploration

Use a graphing utility to graph the two functions given by

$$y_1 = \frac{1}{\sqrt{x}} \quad \text{and} \quad y_2 = \frac{1}{\sqrt[3]{x}}$$

in the same viewing window. Why doesn't y_1 appear to the left of the y-axis? How does this relate to the statement at the right about the infinite limit

$$\lim_{x \to -\infty} \frac{1}{x^r}?$$

Example 1 Evaluating a Limit at Infinity

Find the limit.

$$\lim_{x \to \infty} \left(4 - \frac{3}{x^2}\right)$$

Algebraic Solution

Use the properties of limits listed in Section 12.1.

$$\begin{aligned} \lim_{x \to \infty} \left(4 - \frac{3}{x^2}\right) &= \lim_{x \to \infty} 4 - \lim_{x \to \infty} \frac{3}{x^2} \\ &= \lim_{x \to \infty} 4 - 3\left(\lim_{x \to \infty} \frac{1}{x^2}\right) \\ &= 4 - 3(0) \\ &= 4 \end{aligned}$$

So, the limit of $f(x) = 4 - \dfrac{3}{x^2}$ as x approaches ∞ is 4.

CHECKPOINT Now try Exercise 5.

Graphical Solution

Use a graphing utility to graph $y = 4 - 3/x^2$. Then use the *trace* feature to determine that as x gets larger and larger, y gets closer and closer to 4, as shown in Figure 12.31. Note that the line $y = 4$ is a horizontal asymptote to the right.

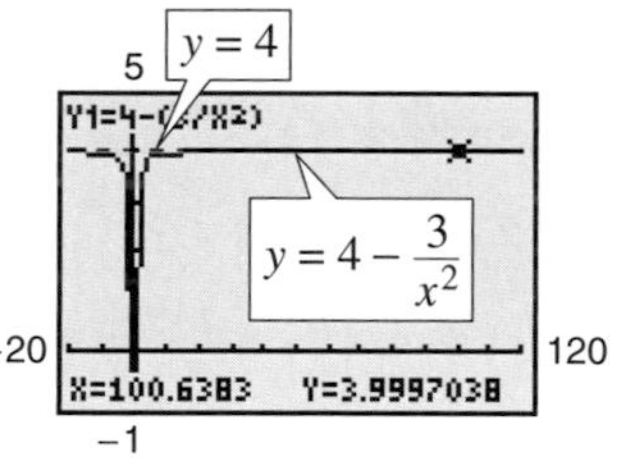

FIGURE 12.31

In Figure 12.31, it appears that the line $y = 4$ is also a horizontal asymptote *to the left*. You can verify this by showing that

$$\lim_{x \to -\infty} \left(4 - \frac{3}{x^2}\right) = 4.$$

The graph of a rational function need not have a horizontal asymptote. If it does, however, its left and right horizontal asymptotes must be the same.

When evaluating limits at infinity for more complicated rational functions, divide the numerator and denominator by the *highest-powered term* in the denominator. This enables you to evaluate each limit using the limits at infinity at the top of the page.

Exploration

Use a graphing utility to complete the table below to verify that

$$\lim_{x\to\infty} \frac{1}{x} = 0.$$

x	10^0	10^1	10^2
$\frac{1}{x}$			

x	10^3	10^4	10^5
$\frac{1}{x}$			

Make a conjecture about

$$\lim_{x\to 0} \frac{1}{x}.$$

Example 2 Comparing Limits at Infinity

Find the limit as x approaches ∞ for each function.

a. $f(x) = \dfrac{-2x + 3}{3x^2 + 1}$ **b.** $f(x) = \dfrac{-2x^2 + 3}{3x^2 + 1}$ **c.** $f(x) = \dfrac{-2x^3 + 3}{3x^2 + 1}$

Solution

In each case, begin by dividing both the numerator and denominator by x^2, the highest-powered term in the denominator.

a.
$$\lim_{x\to\infty} \frac{-2x + 3}{3x^2 + 1} = \lim_{x\to\infty} \frac{-\frac{2}{x} + \frac{3}{x^2}}{3 + \frac{1}{x^2}} = \frac{-0 + 0}{3 + 0} = 0$$

b.
$$\lim_{x\to\infty} \frac{-2x^2 + 3}{3x^2 + 1} = \lim_{x\to\infty} \frac{-2 + \frac{3}{x^2}}{3 + \frac{1}{x^2}} = \frac{-2 + 0}{3 + 0} = -\frac{2}{3}$$

c.
$$\lim_{x\to\infty} \frac{-2x^3 + 3}{3x^2 + 1} = \lim_{x\to\infty} \frac{-2x + \frac{3}{x^2}}{3 + \frac{1}{x^2}}$$

In this case, you can conclude that the limit does not exist because the numerator decreases without bound as the denominator approaches 3.

CHECKPOINT Now try Exercise 13.

In Example 2, observe that when the degree of the numerator is less than the degree of the denominator, as in part (a), the limit is 0. When the degrees of the numerator and denominator are equal, as in part (b), the limit is the ratio of the coefficients of the highest-powered terms. When the degree of the numerator is greater than the degree of the denominator, as in part (c), the limit does not exist.

This result seems reasonable when you realize that for large values of x, the highest-powered term of a polynomial is the most "influential" term. That is, a polynomial tends to behave as its highest-powered term behaves as x approaches positive or negative infinity.

Limits at Infinity for Rational Functions

Consider the rational function $f(x) = N(x)/D(x)$, where

$$N(x) = a_n x^n + \cdot\cdot\cdot + a_0 \quad \text{and} \quad D(x) = b_m x^m + \cdot\cdot\cdot + b_0.$$

The limit of $f(x)$ as x approaches positive or negative infinity is as follows.

$$\lim_{x \to \pm\infty} f(x) = \begin{cases} 0, & n < m \\ \dfrac{a_n}{b_m}, & n = m \end{cases}$$

If $n > m$, the limit does not exist.

Example 3 **Finding the Average Cost**

You are manufacturing greeting cards that cost \$0.50 per card to produce. Your initial investment is \$5000, which implies that the total cost C of producing x cards is given by $C = 0.50x + 5000$. The average cost $\overline{C}$ per card is given by

$$\overline{C} = \frac{C}{x} = \frac{0.50x + 5000}{x}.$$

Find the average cost per card when (a) $x = 1000$, (b) $x = 10{,}000$, and (c) $x = 100{,}000$. (d) What is the limit of $\overline{C}$ as x approaches infinity?

Solution

a. When $x = 1000$, the average cost per card is

$$\overline{C} = \frac{0.50(1000) + 5000}{1000} \qquad x = 1000$$

$$= \$5.50.$$

b. When $x = 10{,}000$, the average cost per card is

$$\overline{C} = \frac{0.50(10{,}000) + 5000}{10{,}000} \qquad x = 10{,}000$$

$$= \$1.00.$$

c. When $x = 100{,}000$, the average cost per card is

$$\overline{C} = \frac{0.50(100{,}000) + 5000}{100{,}000} \qquad x = 100{,}000$$

$$= \$0.55.$$

d. As x approaches infinity, the limit of $\overline{C}$ is

$$\lim_{x \to \infty} \frac{0.50x + 5000}{x} = \$0.50. \qquad x \to \infty$$

The graph of $\overline{C}$ is shown in Figure 12.32.

CHECKPOINT Now try Exercise 49.

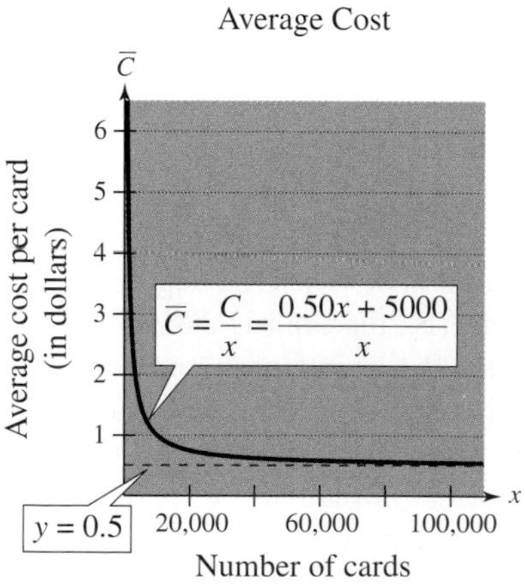

As $x \to \infty$, the average cost per card approaches \$0.50.

FIGURE 12.32

Limits of Sequences

Limits of sequences have many of the same properties as limits of functions. For instance, consider the sequence whose nth term is $a_n = 1/2^n$.

$$\frac{1}{2}, \frac{1}{4}, \frac{1}{8}, \frac{1}{16}, \frac{1}{32}, \ldots$$

As n increases without bound, the terms of this sequence get closer and closer to 0, and the sequence is said to **converge** to 0. Using limit notation, you can write

$$\lim_{n \to \infty} \frac{1}{2^n} = 0.$$

The following relationship shows how limits of functions of x can be used to evaluate the limit of a sequence.

Technology

There are a number of ways to use a graphing utility to generate the terms of a sequence. For instance, you can display the first 10 terms of the sequence

$$a_n = \frac{1}{2^n}$$

using the *sequence* feature or the *table* feature.

Limit of a Sequence

Let f be a function of a real variable such that

$$\lim_{x \to \infty} f(x) = L.$$

If $\{a_n\}$ is a sequence such that $f(n) = a_n$ for every positive integer n, then

$$\lim_{n \to \infty} a_n = L.$$

A sequence that does not converge is said to **diverge.** For instance, the terms of the sequence $1, -1, 1, -1, 1, \ldots$ oscillate between 1 and -1. Therefore, the sequence diverges because it does not approach a unique number.

Example 4 Finding the Limit of a Sequence

Find the limit of each sequence. (Assume n begins with 1.)

a. $a_n = \dfrac{2n + 1}{n + 4}$

b. $b_n = \dfrac{2n + 1}{n^2 + 4}$

c. $c_n = \dfrac{2n^2 + 1}{4n^2}$

Solution

a. $\displaystyle\lim_{n \to \infty} \frac{2n + 1}{n + 4} = 2$ $\quad \frac{3}{5}, \frac{5}{6}, \frac{7}{7}, \frac{9}{8}, \frac{11}{9}, \frac{13}{10}, \ldots \to 2$

b. $\displaystyle\lim_{n \to \infty} \frac{2n + 1}{n^2 + 4} = 0$ $\quad \frac{3}{5}, \frac{5}{8}, \frac{7}{13}, \frac{9}{20}, \frac{11}{29}, \frac{13}{40}, \ldots \to 0$

c. $\displaystyle\lim_{n \to \infty} \frac{2n^2 + 1}{4n^2} = \frac{1}{2}$ $\quad \frac{3}{4}, \frac{9}{16}, \frac{19}{36}, \frac{33}{64}, \frac{51}{100}, \frac{73}{144}, \ldots \to \frac{1}{2}$

✓CHECKPOINT Now try Exercise 33.

STUDY TIP

You can use the definition of limits at infinity for rational functions on page 886 to verify the limits of the sequences in Example 4.

In the next section, you will encounter limits of sequences such as that shown in Example 5. A strategy for evaluating such limits is to begin by writing the nth term in standard rational function form. Then you can determine the limit by comparing the degrees of the numerator and denominator, as shown on page 886.

Example 5 Finding the Limit of a Sequence

Find the limit of the sequence whose nth term is

$$a_n = \frac{8}{n^3}\left[\frac{n(n+1)(2n+1)}{6}\right].$$

Algebraic Solution

Begin by writing the nth term in standard rational function form—as the ratio of two polynomials.

$$a_n = \frac{8}{n^3}\left[\frac{n(n+1)(2n+1)}{6}\right] \qquad \text{Write original } n\text{th term.}$$

$$= \frac{8(n)(n+1)(2n+1)}{6n^3} \qquad \text{Multiply fractions.}$$

$$= \frac{8n^3 + 12n^2 + 4n}{3n^3} \qquad \text{Write in standard rational form.}$$

From this form, you can see that the degree of the numerator is equal to the degree of the denominator. So, the limit of the sequence is the ratio of the coefficients of the highest-powered terms.

$$\lim_{n\to\infty} \frac{8n^3 + 12n^2 + 4n}{3n^3} = \frac{8}{3}$$

CHECKPOINT Now try Exercise 43.

Numerical Solution

Construct a table that shows the value of a_n as n becomes larger and larger, as shown below.

n	a_n
1	8
10	3.08
100	2.707
1000	2.671
10,000	2.667

From the table, you can estimate that as n approaches ∞, a_n gets closer and closer to $2.667 \approx \frac{8}{3}$.

Writing about Mathematics

Comparing Rates of Convergence In the table in Example 5 above, the value of a_n approaches its limit of $\frac{8}{3}$ rather slowly. (The first term to be accurate to three decimal places is $a_{4801} \approx 2.667$.) Each of the following sequences converges to 0. Which converges the quickest? Which converges the slowest? Why? Write a short paragraph discussing your conclusions.

a. $a_n = \dfrac{1}{n}$ **b.** $b_n = \dfrac{1}{n^2}$ **c.** $c_n = \dfrac{1}{2^n}$

d. $d_n = \dfrac{1}{n!}$ **e.** $h_n = \dfrac{2^n}{n!}$

12.4 Exercises

VOCABULARY CHECK: Fill in the blanks.

1. A________ at ________ can be used to solve the area problem in calculus.
2. A sequence that has a limit is said to ________.
3. A sequence that does not have a limit is said to ________.

In Exercises 1–4, match the function with its graph, using horizontal asymptotes as aids. [The graphs are labeled (a), (b), (c), and (d).]

(a)

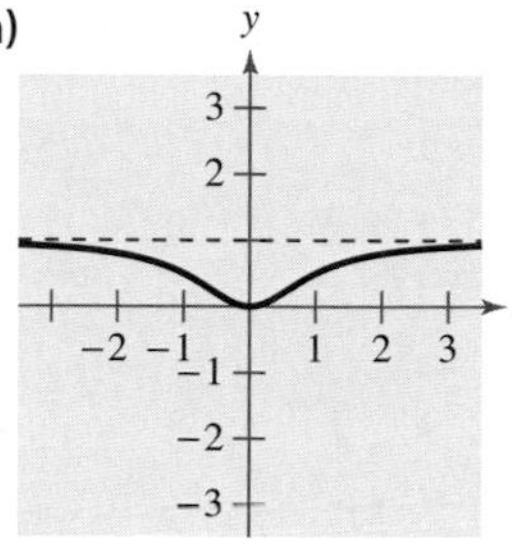

(b)

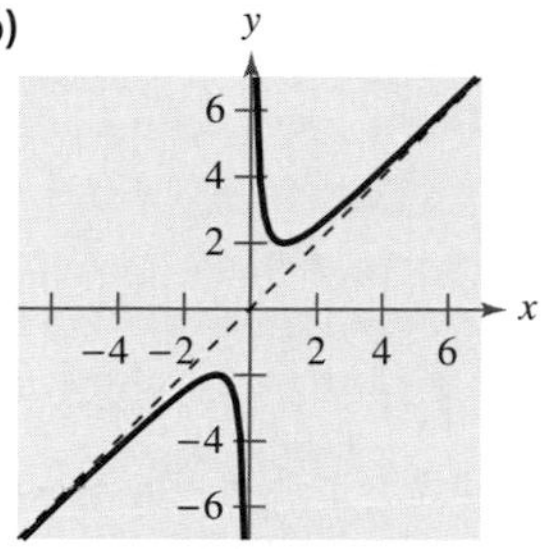

(c)

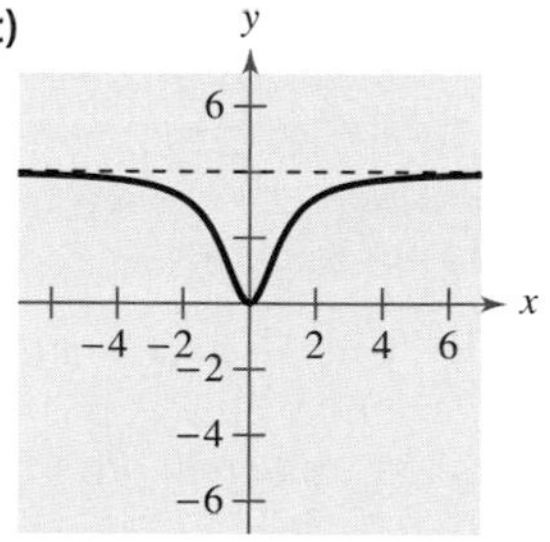

(d)

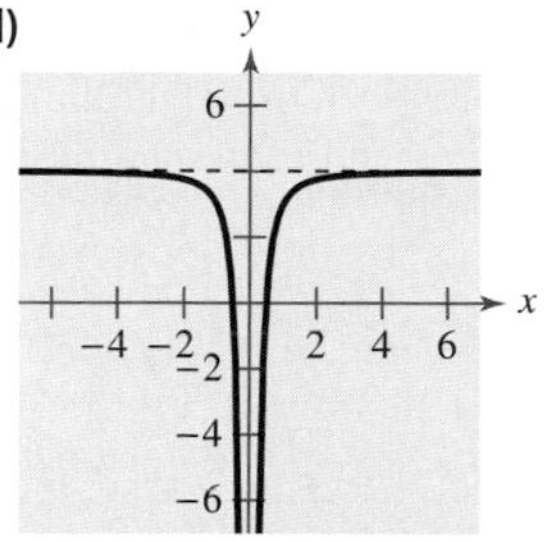

1. $f(x) = \dfrac{4x^2}{x^2 + 1}$
2. $f(x) = \dfrac{x^2}{x^2 + 1}$
3. $f(x) = 4 - \dfrac{1}{x^2}$
4. $f(x) = x + \dfrac{1}{x}$

In Exercises 5–22, find the limit (if it exists). If the limit does not exist, explain why. Use a graphing utility to verify your result graphically.

5. $\lim\limits_{x\to\infty} \dfrac{3}{x^2}$
6. $\lim\limits_{x\to\infty} \dfrac{5}{2x}$
7. $\lim\limits_{x\to\infty} \dfrac{3 + x}{3 - x}$
8. $\lim\limits_{x\to\infty} \dfrac{1 - 6x}{1 + 5x}$
9. $\lim\limits_{x\to-\infty} \dfrac{4x - 3}{2x + 1}$
10. $\lim\limits_{x\to\infty} \dfrac{1 - 2x}{x + 2}$
11. $\lim\limits_{x\to-\infty} \dfrac{3x^2 - 4}{1 - x^2}$
12. $\lim\limits_{x\to-\infty} \dfrac{3x^2 + 1}{4x^2 - 5}$
13. $\lim\limits_{t\to\infty} \dfrac{t^2}{t + 3}$
14. $\lim\limits_{y\to\infty} \dfrac{4y^4}{y^2 + 3}$
15. $\lim\limits_{t\to\infty} \dfrac{1 - 2t + 6t^2}{5 + 3t - 4t^2}$
16. $\lim\limits_{x\to-\infty} \dfrac{2x^2 - 5x - 12}{1 - 6x - 8x^2}$
17. $\lim\limits_{x\to-\infty} \dfrac{-(x^2 + 3)}{(2 - x)^2}$
18. $\lim\limits_{x\to\infty} \dfrac{2x^2 - 6}{(x - 1)^2}$
19. $\lim\limits_{x\to-\infty} \left[\dfrac{x}{(x + 1)^2} - 4\right]$
20. $\lim\limits_{x\to\infty} \left[7 + \dfrac{2x^2}{(x + 3)^2}\right]$
21. $\lim\limits_{t\to\infty} \left(\dfrac{1}{3t^2} - \dfrac{5t}{t + 2}\right)$
22. $\lim\limits_{x\to\infty} \left[\dfrac{x}{2x + 1} + \dfrac{3x^2}{(x - 3)^2}\right]$

In Exercises 23–28, use a graphing utility to graph the function and verify that the horizontal asymptote corresponds to the limit at infinity.

23. $y = \dfrac{3x}{1 - x}$
24. $y = \dfrac{x^2}{x^2 + 4}$
25. $y = \dfrac{2x}{1 - x^2}$
26. $y = \dfrac{2x + 1}{x^2 - 1}$
27. $y = 1 - \dfrac{3}{x^2}$
28. $y = 2 + \dfrac{1}{x}$

Numerical and Graphical Analysis **In Exercises 29–32, (a) complete the table and numerically estimate the limit as x approaches infinity, and (b) use a graphing utility to graph the function and estimate the limit graphically.**

x	10^0	10^1	10^2	10^3	10^4	10^5	10^6
$f(x)$							

29. $f(x) = x - \sqrt{x^2 + 2}$
30. $f(x) = 3x - \sqrt{9x^2 + 1}$
31. $f(x) = 3\left(2x - \sqrt{4x^2 + x}\right)$
32. $f(x) - 4\left(4x - \sqrt{16x^2 - x}\right)$

In Exercises 33–42, write the first five terms of the sequence and find the limit of the sequence (if it exists). If the limit does not exist, explain why. Assume n begins with 1.

33. $a_n = \dfrac{n+1}{n^2+1}$

34. $a_n = \dfrac{n}{n^2+1}$

35. $a_n = \dfrac{n}{2n+1}$

36. $a_n = \dfrac{4n-1}{n+3}$

37. $a_n = \dfrac{n^2}{3n+2}$

38. $a_n = \dfrac{4n^2+1}{2n}$

39. $a_n = \dfrac{(n+1)!}{n!}$

40. $a_n = \dfrac{(3n-1)!}{(3n+1)!}$

41. $a_n = \dfrac{(-1)^n}{n}$

42. $a_n = \dfrac{(-1)^{n+1}}{n^2}$

In Exercises 43–46, find the limit of the sequence. Then verify the limit numerically by using a graphing utility to complete the table.

n	10^0	10^1	10^2	10^3	10^4	10^5	10^6
a_n							

43. $a_n = \dfrac{1}{n}\left(n + \dfrac{1}{n}\left[\dfrac{n(n+1)}{2}\right]\right)$

44. $a_n = \dfrac{4}{n}\left(n + \dfrac{4}{n}\left[\dfrac{n(n+1)}{2}\right]\right)$

45. $a_n = \dfrac{16}{n^3}\left[\dfrac{n(n+1)(2n+1)}{6}\right]$

46. $a_n = \dfrac{n(n+1)}{n^2} - \dfrac{1}{n^4}\left[\dfrac{n(n+1)}{2}\right]^2$

47. ***Oxygen Level*** Suppose that $f(t)$ measures the level of oxygen in a pond, where $f(t) = 1$ is the normal (unpolluted) level and the time t is measured in weeks. When $t = 0$, organic waste is dumped into the pond, and as the waste material oxidizes, the level of oxygen in the pond is given by

$$f(t) = \frac{t^2 - t + 1}{t^2 + 1}.$$

(a) What is the limit of this function as t approaches infinity?

(b) Use a graphing utility to graph the function and verify the result of part (a).

(c) Explain the meaning of the limit in the context of the problem.

48. ***Typing Speed*** The average typing speed S (in words per minute) for a student after t weeks of lessons is given by

$$S = \frac{100t^2}{65 + t^2}, \quad t > 0.$$

(a) What is the limit of this function as t approaches infinity?

(b) Use a graphing utility to graph the function and verify the result of part (a).

(c) Explain the meaning of the limit in the context of the problem.

49. ***Average Cost*** The cost function for a certain model of personal digital assistant (PDA) is given by $C = 13.50x + 45{,}750$, where C is measured in dollars and x is the number of PDAs produced.

(a) Write a model for the average cost per unit produced.

(b) Find the average costs per unit when $x = 100$ and $x = 1000$.

(c) Determine the limit of the average cost function as x approaches infinity. Explain the meaning of the limit in the context of the problem.

50. ***Average Cost*** The cost function for a company to recycle x tons of material is given by $C = 1.25x + 10{,}500$, where C is measured in dollars.

(a) Write a model for the average cost per ton of material recycled.

(b) Find the average costs of recycling 100 tons of material and 1000 tons of material.

(c) Determine the limit of the average cost function as x approaches infinity. Explain the meaning of the limit in the context of the problem.

51. ***Data Analysis: Social Security*** The table shows the average monthly Social Security benefits B (in dollars) for retired workers aged 62 or over from 1997 to 2003. (Source: U.S. Social Security Administration)

Year	Benefit, B
1997	765
1998	780
1999	804
2000	844
2001	874
2002	895
2003	922

A model for the data is given by

$$B = \frac{199.0 + 999.46t}{1.0 + 1.43t - 0.032t^2}, \quad 7 \le t \le 13$$

where t represents the year, with $t = 7$ corresponding to 1997.

(a) Use a graphing utility to create a scatter plot of the data and graph the model in the same viewing window. How well does the model fit the data?

(b) Use the model to predict the average monthly benefit in 2006.

(c) Discuss why this model should not be used to predict the average monthly Social Security benefits in future years.

Model It

52. ***Data Analysis: Military*** The table shows the numbers N (in thousands) of U.S. military reserve personnel for the years 1997 through 2003. (Source: U.S. Department of Defense)

Year	Number, N
1997	1474
1998	1382
1999	1317
2000	1277
2001	1249
2002	1222
2003	1189

A model for the data is given by

$$N = \frac{632.8 - 283.17t}{1.0 - 0.27t}, \quad 7 \le t \le 13$$

where t represents the year, with $t = 7$ corresponding to 1997.

(a) Use a graphing utility to create a scatter plot of the data and graph the model in the same viewing window. How well does the model fit the data?

(b) Use the model to predict the number of military reserve personnel in 2006.

(c) What is the limit of the function as t approaches infinity? Explain the meaning of the limit in the context of the problem. Do you think the limit is realistic? Explain.

Synthesis

True or False? **In Exercises 53–56, determine whether the statement is true or false. Justify your answer.**

53. Every rational function has a horizontal asymptote.

54. If $f(x)$ increases without bound as x approaches c, then the limit of $f(x)$ exists.

55. If a sequence converges, then it has a limit.

56. When the degrees of the numerator and denominator of a rational function are equal, the limit does not exist.

57. ***Think About It*** Find the functions f and g such that both $f(x)$ and $g(x)$ increase without bound as x approaches c, but $\lim_{x\to c} [f(x) - g(x)] \neq \infty$.

58. ***Think About It*** Use a graphing utility to graph the function given by

$$f(x) = \frac{x}{\sqrt{x^2 + 1}}.$$

How many horizontal asymptotes does the function appear to have? What are the horizontal asymptotes?

Exploration **In Exercises 59–62, create a scatter plot of the terms of the sequence. Determine whether the sequence converges or diverges. If it converges, estimate its limit.**

59. $a_n = 4\left(\frac{2}{3}\right)^n$

60. $a_n = 3\left(\frac{3}{2}\right)^n$

61. $a_n = \dfrac{3[1 - (1.5)^n]}{1 - 1.5}$

62. $a_n = \dfrac{3[1 - (0.5)^n]}{1 - 0.5}$

Skills Review

In Exercises 63 and 64, sketch the graphs of y and each transformation on the same rectangular coordinate system.

63. $y = x^4$

(a) $f(x) = (x + 3)^4$

(b) $f(x) = x^4 - 1$

(c) $f(x) = -2 + x^4$

(d) $f(x) = \frac{1}{2}(x - 4)^4$

64. $y = x^3$

(a) $f(x) = (x + 2)^3$

(b) $f(x) = 3 + x^3$

(c) $f(x) = 2 - \frac{1}{4}x^3$

(d) $f(x) = 3(x + 1)^3$

In Exercises 65–68, divide using long division.

65. $(x^4 + 2x^3 - 3x^2 - 8x - 4) \div (x^2 - 4)$

66. $(2x^5 - 8x^3 + 4x - 1) \div (x^2 - 2x + 1)$

67. $(3x^4 + 17x^3 + 10x^2 - 9x - 8) \div (3x + 2)$

68. $(10x^3 + 51x^2 + 48x - 28) \div (5x - 2)$

In Exercises 69–72, find all the real zeros of the polynomial function. Use a graphing utility to graph the function and verify that the real zeros are the x-intercepts of the graph of the function.

69. $f(x) = x^4 - x^3 - 20x^2$

70. $f(x) = x^5 + x^3 - 6x$

71. $f(x) = x^3 - 3x^2 + 2x - 6$

72. $f(x) = x^3 - 4x^2 - 25x + 100$

In Exercises 73–76, find the sum.

73. $\displaystyle\sum_{i=1}^{6} (2i + 3)$

74. $\displaystyle\sum_{i=0}^{4} 5i^2$

75. $\displaystyle\sum_{k=1}^{10} 15$

76. $\displaystyle\sum_{k=0}^{8} \frac{3}{k^2 + 1}$

12.5 The Area Problem

What you should learn

- Find limits of summations.
- Use rectangles to approximate areas of plane regions.
- Use limits of summations to find areas of plane regions.

Why you should learn it

The limits of summations are useful in determining areas of plane regions. For instance, in Exercise 36 on page 899, you are asked to find the limit of a summation to determine the area of a parcel of land bounded by a stream and two roads.

Limits of Summations

Earlier in the text, you used the concept of a limit to obtain a formula for the sum S of an infinite geometric series

$$S = a_1 + a_1 r + a_1 r^2 + \cdot \cdot \cdot = \sum_{i=1}^{\infty} a_1 r^{i-1} = \frac{a_1}{1-r}, \quad |r| < 1.$$

Using limit notation, this sum can be written as

$$S = \lim_{n\to\infty} \sum_{i=1}^{n} a_1 r^{i-1} = \lim_{n\to\infty} \frac{a_1(1-r^n)}{1-r} = \frac{a_1}{1-r}. \qquad \lim_{n\to\infty} r^n = 0 \text{ for } |r| < 1$$

The following summation formulas and properties are used to evaluate finite and infinite summations.

Summation Formulas and Properties

1. $\sum_{i=1}^{n} c = cn$, c is a constant.
2. $\sum_{i=1}^{n} i = \frac{n(n+1)}{2}$
3. $\sum_{i=1}^{n} i^2 = \frac{n(n+1)(2n+1)}{6}$
4. $\sum_{i=1}^{n} i^3 = \frac{n^2(n+1)^2}{4}$
5. $\sum_{i=1}^{n} (a_i \pm b_i) = \sum_{i=1}^{n} a_i \pm \sum_{i=1}^{n} b_i$
6. $\sum_{i=1}^{n} ka_i = k\sum_{i=1}^{n} a_i$, k is a constant.

Example 1 Evaluating a Summation

Evaluate the summation.

$$\sum_{i=1}^{200} i = 1 + 2 + 3 + 4 + \cdot \cdot \cdot + 200$$

Solution

Using the second summation formula with $n = 200$, you can write

$$\sum_{i=1}^{n} i = \frac{n(n+1)}{2}$$

$$\sum_{i=1}^{200} i = \frac{200(200+1)}{2}$$

$$= \frac{40{,}200}{2}$$

$$= 20{,}100.$$

CHECKPOINT Now try Exercise 1.

STUDY TIP

Recall from Section 9.3 that the sum of a finite geometric sequence is given by

$$\sum_{i=1}^{n} a_1 r^{i-1} = a_1\left(\frac{1-r^n}{1-r}\right).$$

Furthermore, if $0 < |r| < 1$, then $r^n \to 0$ as $n \to \infty$.

> **Technology**
>
> Some graphing utilities have a *sum sequence* feature that is useful for computing summations. Consult the user's guide for your graphing utility for the required keystrokes.

Example 2 **Evaluating a Summation**

Evaluate the summation

$$S = \sum_{i=1}^{n} \frac{i+2}{n^2} = \frac{3}{n^2} + \frac{4}{n^2} + \frac{5}{n^2} + \cdots + \frac{n+2}{n^2}$$

for $n = 10, 100, 1000$, and $10{,}000$.

Solution

Begin by applying summation formulas and properties to simplify S. In the second line of the solution, note that $1/n^2$ can be factored out of the sum because n is considered to be constant. You could not factor i out of the summation because i is the (variable) index of summation.

$$S = \sum_{i=1}^{n} \frac{i+2}{n^2}$$ Write original form of summation.

$$= \frac{1}{n^2}\sum_{i=1}^{n}(i+2)$$ Factor constant $1/n^2$ out of sum.

$$= \frac{1}{n^2}\left(\sum_{i=1}^{n} i + \sum_{i=1}^{n} 2\right)$$ Write as two sums.

$$= \frac{1}{n^2}\left[\frac{n(n+1)}{2} + 2n\right]$$ Apply Formulas 1 and 2.

$$= \frac{1}{n^2}\left(\frac{n^2+5n}{2}\right)$$ Add fractions.

$$= \frac{n+5}{2n}$$ Simplify.

Now you can evaluate the sum by substituting the appropriate values of n, as shown in the following table.

n	10	100	1000	10,000
$\sum_{i=1}^{n} \frac{i+2}{n^2} = \frac{n+5}{2n}$	0.75	0.525	0.5025	0.50025

✓CHECKPOINT Now try Exercise 9.

In Example 2, note that the sum appears to approach a limit as n increases. To find the limit of

$$\frac{n+5}{2n}$$

as n approaches infinity, you can use the techniques from Section 12.4 to write

$$\lim_{n\to\infty} \frac{n+5}{2n} = \frac{1}{2}.$$

Be sure you notice the strategy used in Example 2. Rather than separately evaluating the sums

$$\sum_{i=1}^{10} \frac{i+2}{n^2}, \quad \sum_{i=1}^{100} \frac{i+2}{n^2}, \quad \sum_{i=1}^{1000} \frac{i+2}{n^2}, \quad \sum_{i=1}^{10,000} \frac{i+2}{n^2}$$

it was more efficient first to convert to rational form using the summation formulas and properties listed on page 892.

$$S = \underbrace{\sum_{i=1}^{n} \frac{i+2}{n^2}}_{\text{Summation form}} = \underbrace{\frac{n+5}{2n}}_{\text{Rational form}}$$

With this rational form, each sum can be evaluated by simply substituting appropriate values of n.

Example 3 Finding the Limit of a Summation

Find the limit of $S(n)$ as $n \to \infty$.

$$S(n) = \sum_{i=1}^{n} \left(1 + \frac{i}{n}\right)^2 \left(\frac{1}{n}\right)$$

Solution

Begin by rewriting the summation in rational form.

$$S(n) = \sum_{i=1}^{n} \left(1 + \frac{i}{n}\right)^2 \left(\frac{1}{n}\right)$$ Write original form of summation.

$$= \sum_{i=1}^{n} \left(\frac{n^2 + 2ni + i^2}{n^2}\right) \left(\frac{1}{n}\right)$$ Square $(1 + i/n)$ and write as a single fraction.

$$= \frac{1}{n^3} \sum_{i=1}^{n} (n^2 + 2ni + i^2)$$ Factor constant $1/n^3$ out of the sum.

$$= \frac{1}{n^3} \left(\sum_{i=1}^{n} n^2 + \sum_{i=1}^{n} 2ni + \sum_{i=1}^{n} i^2 \right)$$ Write as three sums.

$$= \frac{1}{n^3} \left\{ n^3 + 2n\left[\frac{n(n+1)}{2}\right] + \frac{n(n+1)(2n+1)}{6} \right\}$$ Use summation formulas.

$$= \frac{14n^3 + 9n^2 + n}{6n^3}$$ Simplify.

In this rational form, you can now find the limit as $n \to \infty$.

$$\lim_{n \to \infty} S(n) = \lim_{n \to \infty} \frac{14n^3 + 9n^2 + n}{6n^3} = \frac{14}{6} = \frac{7}{3}$$

✓CHECKPOINT Now try Exercise 11.

STUDY TIP

As you can see from Example 3, there is a lot of algebra involved in rewriting a summation in rational form. You may want to review simplifying rational expressions if you are having difficulty with this procedure.

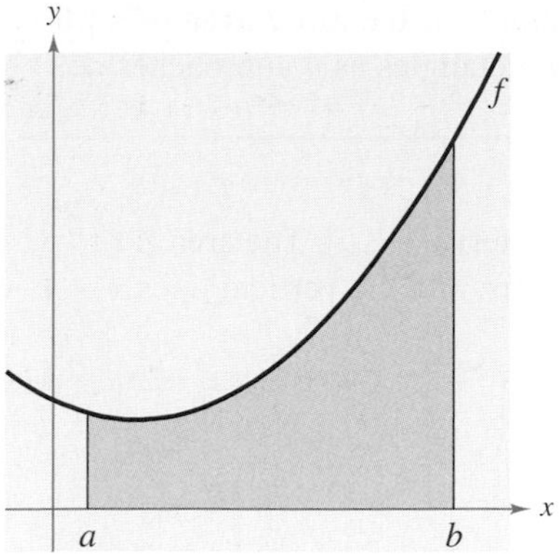

FIGURE 12.33

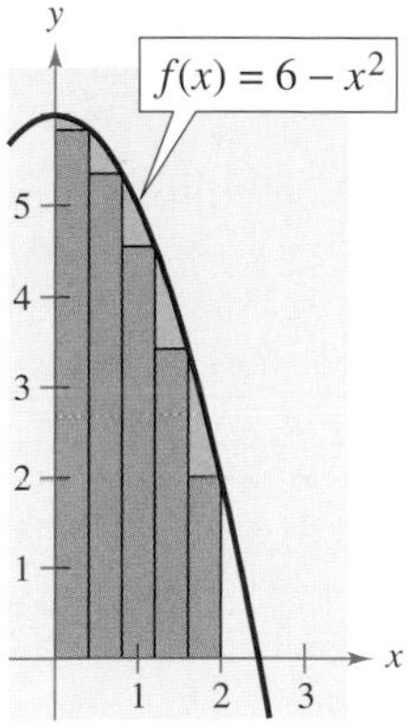

FIGURE 12.34

The Area Problem

You now have the tools needed to solve the second basic problem of calculus: the area problem. The problem is to find the *area* of the region R bounded by the graph of a nonnegative, continuous function f, the x-axis, and the vertical lines $x = a$ and $x = b$, as shown in Figure 12.33.

If the region R is a square, a triangle, a trapezoid, or a semicircle, you can find its area by using a geometric formula. For more general regions, however, you must use a different approach—one that involves the limit of a summation. The basic strategy is to use a collection of rectangles of equal width that approximates the region R, as illustrated in Example 4.

Example 4 Approximating the Area of a Region

Use the five rectangles in Figure 12.34 to approximate the area of the region bounded by the graph of $f(x) = 6 - x^2$, the x-axis, and the lines $x = 0$ and $x = 2$.

Solution

Because the length of the interval along the x-axis is 2 and there are five rectangles, the width of each rectangle is $\frac{2}{5}$. The height of each rectangle can be obtained by evaluating f at the right endpoint of each interval. The five intervals are as follows.

$$\left[0, \frac{2}{5}\right], \quad \left[\frac{2}{5}, \frac{4}{5}\right], \quad \left[\frac{4}{5}, \frac{6}{5}\right], \quad \left[\frac{6}{5}, \frac{8}{5}\right], \quad \left[\frac{8}{5}, \frac{10}{5}\right]$$

Notice that the right endpoint of each interval is $\frac{2}{5}i$ for $i = 1, 2, 3, 4, 5$. The sum of the areas of the five rectangles is

$$\sum_{i=1}^{5} \overbrace{f\left(\frac{2i}{5}\right)}^{\text{Height}} \overbrace{\left(\frac{2}{5}\right)}^{\text{Width}} = \sum_{i=1}^{5} \left[6 - \left(\frac{2i}{5}\right)^2\right]\left(\frac{2}{5}\right)$$

$$= \frac{2}{5}\left(\sum_{i=1}^{5} 6 - \frac{4}{25}\sum_{i=1}^{5} i^2\right) = \frac{2}{5}\left[6(5) - \frac{4}{25} \cdot \frac{5(5+1)(10+1)}{6}\right]$$

$$= \frac{2}{5}\left(30 - \frac{44}{5}\right) = \frac{212}{25} = 8.48.$$

So, you can approximate the area of R as 8.48 square units.

CHECKPOINT Now try Exercise 17.

By increasing the number of rectangles used in Example 4, you can obtain closer and closer approximations of the area of the region. For instance, using 25 rectangles of width $\frac{2}{25}$ each, you can approximate the area to be $A \approx 9.17$ square units. The following table shows even better approximations.

n	5	25	100	1000	5000
Approximate area	8.48	9.17	9.29	9.33	9.33

Based on the procedure illustrated in Example 4, the *exact* **area of a plane region** R is given by the limit of the sum of n rectangles as n approaches ∞.

Area of a Plane Region

Let f be continuous and nonnegative on the interval $[a, b]$. The area A of the region bounded by the graph of f, the x-axis, and the vertical lines $x = a$ and $x = b$ is given by

$$A = \lim_{n\to\infty} \sum_{i=1}^{n} \underbrace{f\left(a + \frac{(b-a)i}{n}\right)}_{\text{Height}} \underbrace{\left(\frac{b-a}{n}\right)}_{\text{Width}}.$$

Example 5 Finding the Area of a Region

Find the area of the region bounded by the graph of $f(x) = x^2$ and the x-axis between $x = 0$ and $x = 1$, as shown in Figure 12.35.

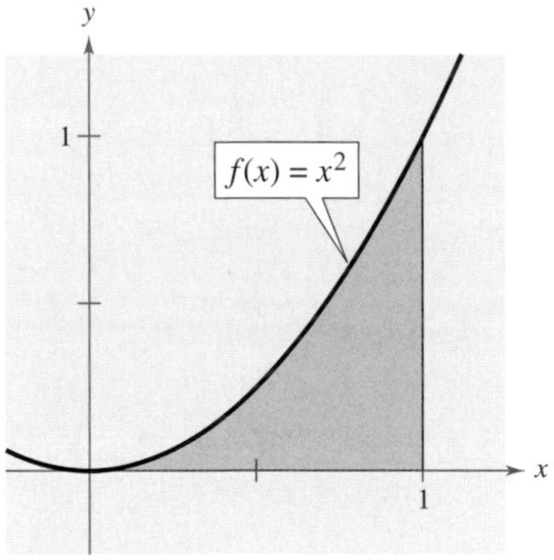

FIGURE 12.35

Solution

Begin by finding the dimensions of the rectangles.

$$\textit{Width: } \frac{b-a}{n} = \frac{1-0}{n} = \frac{1}{n}$$

$$\textit{Height: } f\left(a + \frac{(b-a)i}{n}\right) = f\left(0 + \frac{(1-0)i}{n}\right) = f\left(\frac{i}{n}\right) = \frac{i^2}{n^2}$$

Next, approximate the area as the sum of the areas of n rectangles.

$$A \approx \sum_{i=1}^{n} f\left(a + \frac{(b-a)i}{n}\right)\left(\frac{b-a}{n}\right)$$

$$= \sum_{i=1}^{n} \left(\frac{i^2}{n^2}\right)\left(\frac{1}{n}\right) \quad \text{Summation form}$$

$$= \sum_{i=1}^{n} \frac{i^2}{n^3}$$

$$= \frac{1}{n^3}\sum_{i=1}^{n} i^2$$

$$= \frac{1}{n^3}\left[\frac{n(n+1)(2n+1)}{6}\right]$$

$$= \frac{2n^3 + 3n^2 + n}{6n^3} \quad \text{Rational form}$$

Finally, find the exact area by taking the limit as n approaches ∞.

$$A = \lim_{n\to\infty} \frac{2n^3 + 3n^2 + n}{6n^3} = \frac{1}{3}$$

CHECKPOINT Now try Exercise 23.

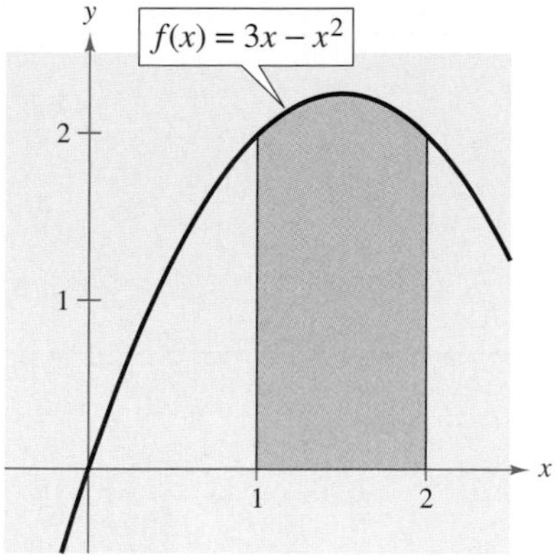

FIGURE 12.36

Example 6 **Finding the Area of a Region**

Find the area of the region bounded by the graph of $f(x) = 3x - x^2$ and the x-axis between $x = 1$ and $x = 2$, as shown in Figure 12.36.

Solution

Begin by finding the dimensions of the rectangles.

$$\textit{Width: } \frac{b-a}{n} = \frac{2-1}{n} = \frac{1}{n}$$

$$\begin{aligned}\textit{Height: } f\left(a + \frac{(b-a)i}{n}\right) &= f\left(1 + \frac{i}{n}\right)\\ &= 3\left(1 + \frac{i}{n}\right) - \left(1 + \frac{i}{n}\right)^2\\ &= 3 + \frac{3i}{n} - \left(1 + \frac{2i}{n} + \frac{i^2}{n^2}\right)\\ &= 2 + \frac{i}{n} - \frac{i^2}{n^2}\end{aligned}$$

Next, approximate the area as the sum of the areas of n rectangles.

$$\begin{aligned}A &\approx \sum_{i=1}^{n} f\left(a + \frac{(b-a)i}{n}\right)\left(\frac{b-a}{n}\right)\\ &= \sum_{i=1}^{n}\left(2 + \frac{i}{n} - \frac{i^2}{n^2}\right)\left(\frac{1}{n}\right)\\ &= \frac{1}{n}\sum_{i=1}^{n} 2 + \frac{1}{n^2}\sum_{i=1}^{n} i - \frac{1}{n^3}\sum_{i=1}^{n} i^2\\ &= \frac{1}{n}(2n) + \frac{1}{n^2}\left[\frac{n(n+1)}{2}\right] - \frac{1}{n^3}\left[\frac{n(n+1)(2n+1)}{6}\right]\\ &= 2 + \frac{n^2+n}{2n^2} - \frac{2n^3+3n^2+n}{6n^3}\\ &= 2 + \frac{1}{2} + \frac{1}{2n} - \frac{1}{3} - \frac{1}{2n} - \frac{1}{6n^2}\\ &= \frac{13}{6} - \frac{1}{6n^2}\end{aligned}$$

Finally, find the exact area by taking the limit as n approaches ∞.

$$\begin{aligned}A &= \lim_{n\to\infty}\left(\frac{13}{6} - \frac{1}{6n^2}\right)\\ &= \frac{13}{6}\end{aligned}$$

CHECKPOINT Now try Exercise 29.

12.5 Exercises

VOCABULARY CHECK: Fill in the blanks.

1. $\sum_{i=1}^{n} i =$ _______ 2. $\sum_{i=1}^{n} i^3 =$ _______

3. The exact _______ of a plane region R is given by the limit of the sum of n rectangles as n approaches ∞.

In Exercises 1–6, evaluate the sum using the summation formulas and properties.

1. $\sum_{i=1}^{60} 7$

2. $\sum_{i=1}^{30} i^2$

3. $\sum_{k=1}^{20} (k^3 + 2)$

4. $\sum_{k=1}^{50} (2k + 1)$

5. $\sum_{j=1}^{25} (j^2 + j)$

6. $\sum_{j=1}^{10} (j^3 - 3j^2)$

In Exercises 7–14, (a) rewrite the sum as a rational function $S(n)$, (b) use $S(n)$ to complete the table, and (c) find $\lim_{n\to\infty} S(n)$.

n	10^0	10^1	10^2	10^3	10^4
$S(n)$					

7. $\sum_{i=1}^{n} \frac{i^3}{n^4}$

8. $\sum_{i=1}^{n} \frac{i}{n^2}$

9. $\sum_{i=1}^{n} \frac{3}{n^3}(1 + i^2)$

10. $\sum_{i=1}^{n} \frac{2i + 3}{n^2}$

11. $\sum_{i=1}^{n} \left(\frac{i^2}{n^3} + \frac{2}{n}\right)\left(\frac{1}{n}\right)$

12. $\sum_{i=1}^{n} \left[3 - 2\left(\frac{i}{n}\right)\right]\left(\frac{1}{n}\right)$

13. $\sum_{i=1}^{n} \left[1 - \left(\frac{i}{n}\right)^2\right]\left(\frac{1}{n}\right)$

14. $\sum_{i=1}^{n} \left[\frac{4}{n} + \left(\frac{2i}{n^2}\right)\right]\left(\frac{2i}{n}\right)$

In Exercises 15–18, approximate the area of the region using the indicated number of rectangles of equal width.

15. $f(x) = x + 4$

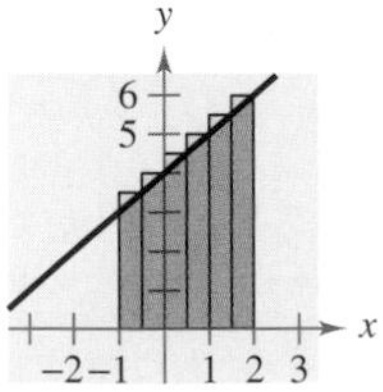

16. $f(x) = 2 - x^2$

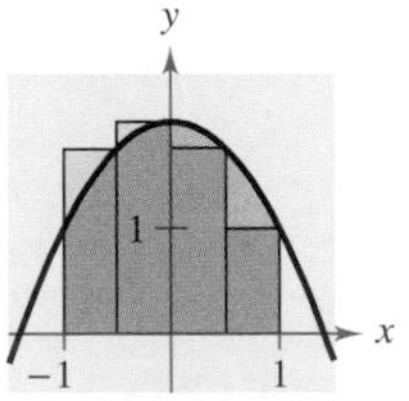

17. $f(x) = \frac{1}{4}x^3$

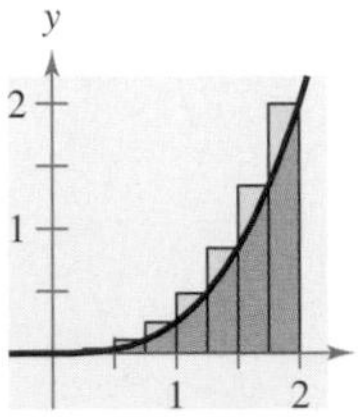

18. $f(x) = \frac{1}{2}(x - 1)^3$

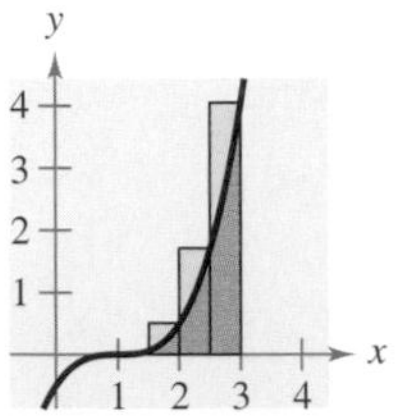

In Exercises 19–22, complete the table showing the approximate area of the region in the graph using n rectangles of equal width.

n	4	8	20	50
Approximate area				

19. $f(x) = -\frac{1}{3}x + 4$

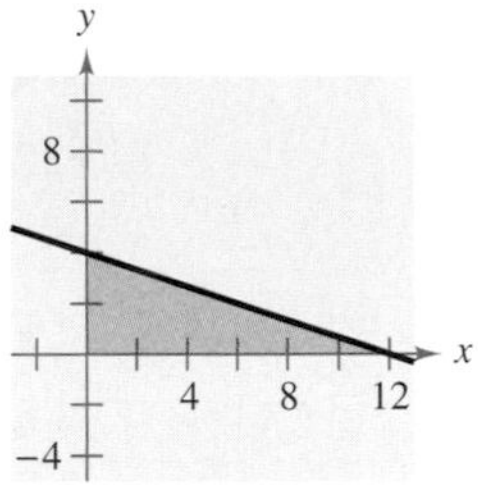

20. $f(x) = 9 - x^2$

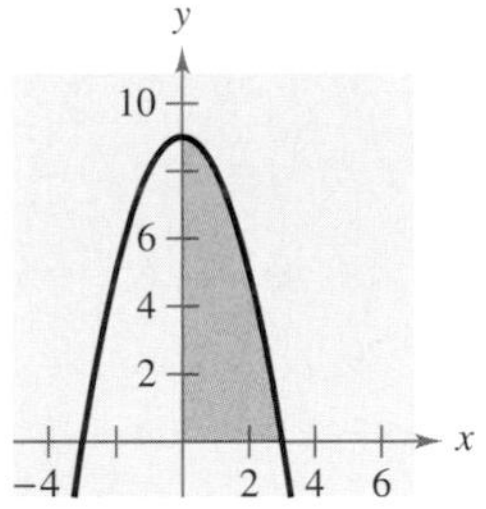

21. $f(x) = \frac{1}{9}x^3$

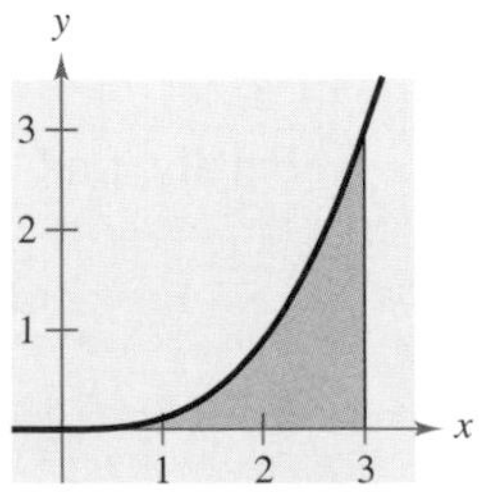

22. $f(x) = 3 - \frac{1}{4}x^3$

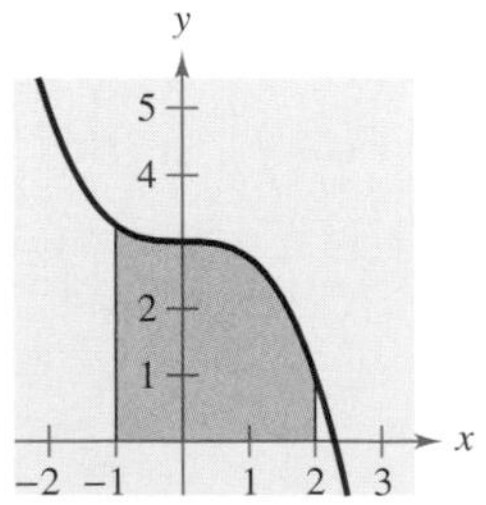

In Exercises 23–34, use the limit process to find the area of the region between the graph of the function and the x-axis over the specified interval.

	Function	*Interval*
23.	$f(x) = 4x + 1$	$[0, 1]$
24.	$f(x) = 3x + 2$	$[0, 2]$
25.	$f(x) = -2x + 3$	$[0, 1]$
26.	$f(x) = 3x - 4$	$[2, 5]$
27.	$f(x) = 2 - x^2$	$[-1, 1]$
28.	$f(x) = x^2 + 2$	$[0, 1]$
29.	$g(x) = 8 - x^3$	$[1, 2]$
30.	$g(x) = 64 - x^3$	$[1, 4]$
31.	$g(x) = 2x - x^3$	$[0, 1]$
32.	$g(x) = 4x - x^3$	$[0, 2]$
33.	$f(x) = \frac{1}{4}(x^2 + 4x)$	$[1, 4]$
34.	$f(x) = x^2 - x^3$	$[-1, 1]$

35. ***Civil Engineering*** The boundaries of a parcel of land are two edges modeled by the coordinate axes and a stream modeled by the equation

$$y = (-3.0 \times 10^{-6})x^3 + 0.002x^2 - 1.05x + 400.$$

Use a graphing utility to graph the equation. Find the area of the property. Assume all distances are measured in feet.

Model It

36. ***Civil Engineering*** The table shows the measurements (in feet) of a lot bounded by a stream and two straight roads that meet at right angles (see figure).

x	0	50	100	150	200	250	300
y	450	362	305	268	245	156	0

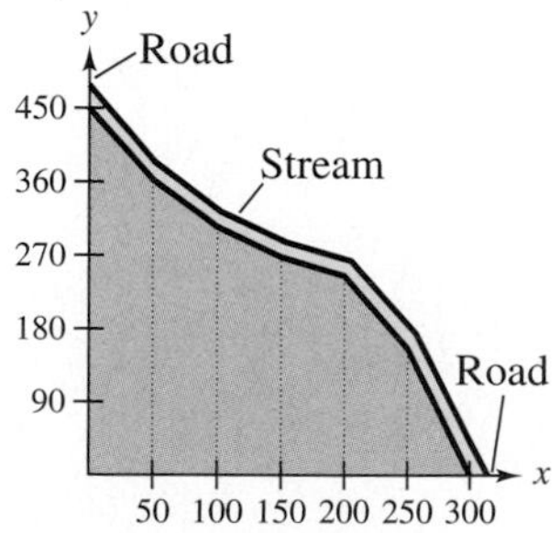

(a) Use the *regression* feature of a graphing utility to find a model of the form

$$y = ax^3 + bx^2 + cx + d.$$

Model It (continued)

(b) Use a graphing utility to plot the data and graph the model in the same viewing window.

(c) Use the model in part (a) to estimate the area of the lot.

Synthesis

True or False? **In Exercises 37 and 38, determine whether the statement is true or false. Justify your answer.**

37. The sum of the first n positive integers is $n(n + 1)/2$.

38. The exact area of a region is given by the limit of the sum of n rectangles as n approaches 0.

39. ***Writing*** Describe the process of finding the area of a region bounded by the graph of a nonnegative, continuous function f, the x-axis, and the vertical lines $x = a$ and $x = b$.

40. ***Think About It*** Determine which value best approximates the area of the region shown in the graph. (Make your selection on the basis of the sketch of the region and *not* by performing any calculations.)

(a) -2 (b) 1 (c) 4 (d) 6 (e) 9

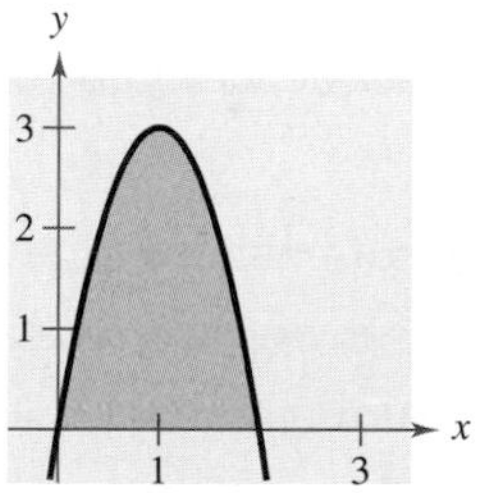

Skills Review

In Exercises 41–46, solve the equation.

41. $\sin 2x - \sqrt{3} \sin x = 0$

42. $\sin 2x + \sqrt{2} \cos x = 0$

43. $2 \tan x = \tan 2x$

44. $\cos 2x - 3 \sin x = 2$

45. $2 \cot x = 5 \cos \dfrac{\pi}{2}$

46. $\sqrt{2} \sec x = 2 \csc \dfrac{\pi}{4}$

In Exercises 47–50, use the vectors $\mathbf{u} = \langle 4, -5 \rangle$ and $\mathbf{v} = \langle -1, -2 \rangle$ to find the indicated quantity.

47. $(\mathbf{u} \cdot \mathbf{v})\mathbf{u}$

48. $3\mathbf{u} \cdot \mathbf{v}$

49. $\|\mathbf{v}\| - 2$

50. $\|\mathbf{u}\|^2 - \|\mathbf{v}\|^2$

12 Chapter Summary

What did you learn?

Section 12.1	Review Exercises
☐ Use the definition of a limit to estimate limits *(p. 853).*	1, 2
☐ Determine whether limits of functions exist *(p. 855).*	3–6
☐ Use properties of limits and direct substitution to evaluate limits *(p. 857).*	7–20
Section 12.2	
☐ Use the dividing out technique to evaluate limits of functions *(p. 863).*	21–28
☐ Use the rationalizing technique to evaluate limits of functions *(p. 865).*	29–32
☐ Approximate limits of functions graphically and numerically *(p. 866).*	33–40
☐ Evaluate one-sided limits of functions *(p. 867).*	41–48
☐ Evaluate limits of difference quotients from calculus *(p. 869).*	49–52
Section 12.3	
☐ Use a tangent line to approximate the slope of a graph at a point *(p. 874).*	53–58
☐ Use the limit definition of slope to find exact slopes of graphs *(p. 875).*	59–62
☐ Find derivatives of functions and use derivatives to find slopes of graphs *(p. 878).*	63–74
Section 12.4	
☐ Evaluate limits of functions at infinity *(p. 883).*	75–82
☐ Find limits of sequences *(p. 887).*	83–86
Section 12.5	
☐ Find limits of summations *(p. 892).*	87, 88
☐ Use rectangles to approximate areas of plane regions *(p. 895).*	89–92
☐ Use limits of summations to find areas of plane regions *(p. 895).*	93–99

12 Review Exercises

12.1 In Exercises 1 and 2, complete the table and use the result to estimate the limit numerically. Determine whether or not the limit can be reached.

1. $\lim_{x \to 3} (6x - 1)$

x	2.9	2.99	2.999	3	3.001	3.01	3.1
$f(x)$				?			

2. $\lim_{x \to 2} \dfrac{x - 2}{3x^2 - 4x - 4}$

x	1.9	1.99	1.999	2	2.001	2.01	2.1
$f(x)$				?			

In Exercises 3–6, use the graph to find the limit (if it exists). If the limit does not exist, explain why.

3. $\lim_{x \to 1} (3 - x)$

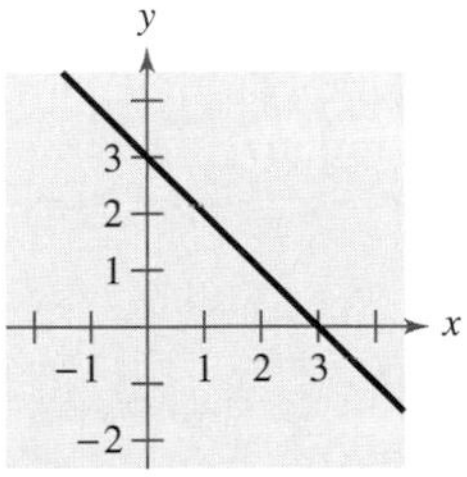

4. $\lim_{x \to 2} \dfrac{1}{x - 2}$

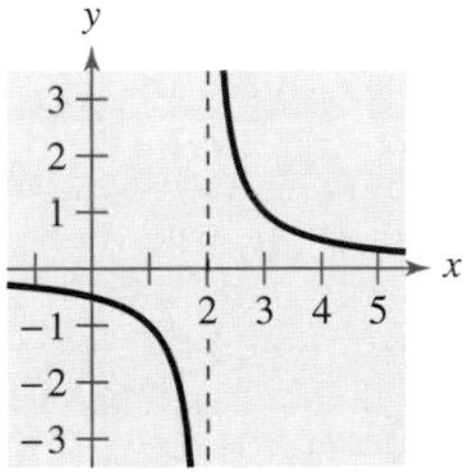

5. $\lim_{x \to 1} \dfrac{x^2 - 1}{x - 1}$

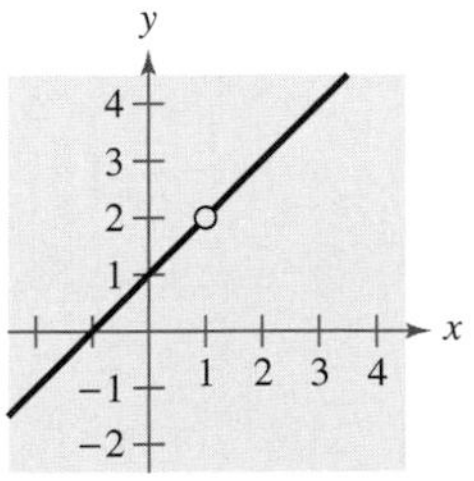

6. $\lim_{x \to -1} (2x^2 + 1)$

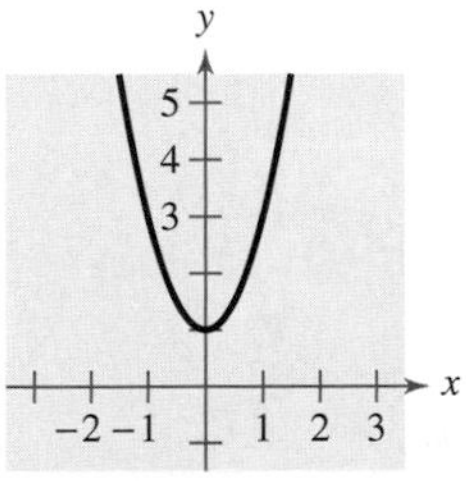

In Exercises 7 and 8, use the given information to evaluate each limit.

7. $\lim_{x \to c} f(x) = 4, \ \lim_{x \to c} g(x) = 5$

(a) $\lim_{x \to c} [f(x)]^3$ (b) $\lim_{x \to c} [3f(x) - g(x)]$

(c) $\lim_{x \to c} [f(x)g(x)]$ (d) $\lim_{x \to c} \dfrac{f(x)}{g(x)}$

8. $\lim_{x \to c} f(x) = 27, \ \lim_{x \to c} g(x) = 12$

(a) $\lim_{x \to c} \sqrt[3]{f(x)}$ (b) $\lim_{x \to c} \dfrac{f(x)}{18}$

(c) $\lim_{x \to c} [f(x)g(x)]$ (d) $\lim_{x \to c} [f(x) - 2g(x)]$

In Exercises 9–20, find the limit by direct substitution.

9. $\lim_{x \to 4} \left(\frac{1}{2}x + 3\right)$
10. $\lim_{x \to -1} \sqrt{5 - x}$
11. $\lim_{x \to 2} \dfrac{x^2 - 1}{x^3 + 2}$
12. $\lim_{x \to e} 7$
13. $\lim_{x \to \pi} \sin 3x$
14. $\lim_{x \to 0} \tan x$
15. $\lim_{x \to 3} (5x - 4)$
16. $\lim_{x \to -2} (5 - 2x - x^2)$
17. $\lim_{x \to 2} (5x - 3)(3x + 5)$
18. $\lim_{x \to -3} (x^3 - 6x^2 + 3x - 1)$
19. $\lim_{t \to 3} \dfrac{t^2 + 1}{t}$
20. $\lim_{x \to 2} \dfrac{3x + 5}{5x - 3}$

12.2 In Exercises 21–32, find the limit (if it exists). Use a graphing utility to verify your result graphically.

21. $\lim_{t \to -2} \dfrac{t + 2}{t^2 - 4}$
22. $\lim_{t \to 3} \dfrac{t^2 - 9}{t - 3}$
23. $\lim_{x \to 5} \dfrac{x - 5}{x^2 + 5x - 50}$
24. $\lim_{x \to -1} \dfrac{x + 1}{x^2 - 5x - 6}$
25. $\lim_{x \to -2} \dfrac{x^2 - 4}{x^3 + 8}$
26. $\lim_{x \to 4} \dfrac{x^3 - 64}{x^2 - 16}$
27. $\lim_{x \to -1} \dfrac{\dfrac{1}{x + 2} - 1}{x + 1}$
28. $\lim_{x \to 0} \dfrac{\dfrac{1}{x + 1} - 1}{x}$
29. $\lim_{u \to 0} \dfrac{\sqrt{4 + u} - 2}{u}$
30. $\lim_{v \to 0} \dfrac{\sqrt{v + 9} - 3}{v}$
31. $\lim_{x \to 5} \dfrac{\sqrt{x - 1} - 2}{x - 5}$
32. $\lim_{x \to 1} \dfrac{\sqrt{3} - \sqrt{x + 2}}{1 - x}$

Graphical and Numerical Analysis **In Exercises 33–40, (a) graphically approximate the limit (if it exists) by using a graphing utility to graph the function, and (b) numerically approximate the limit (if it exists) by using the *table* feature of a graphing utility to create a table.**

33. $\lim_{x \to 3} \dfrac{x - 3}{x^2 - 9}$
34. $\lim_{x \to 4} \dfrac{4 - x}{16 - x^2}$
35. $\lim_{x \to 0} e^{-2/x}$
36. $\lim_{x \to 0} e^{-4/x^2}$

37. $\lim_{x\to 0} \frac{\sin 4x}{2x}$

38. $\lim_{x\to 0} \frac{\tan 2x}{x}$

39. $\lim_{x\to 1^+} \frac{\sqrt{2x+1}-\sqrt{3}}{x-1}$

40. $\lim_{x\to 1^+} \frac{1-\sqrt{x}}{x-1}$

In Exercises 41–48, graph the function. Determine the limit (if it exists) by evaluating the corresponding one-sided limits.

41. $\lim_{x\to 3} \frac{|x-3|}{x-3}$

42. $\lim_{x\to 8} \frac{|8-x|}{8-x}$

43. $\lim_{x\to 2} \frac{2}{x^2-4}$

44. $\lim_{x\to -3} \frac{1}{x^2+9}$

45. $\lim_{x\to 5} \frac{|x-5|}{x-5}$

46. $\lim_{x\to -2} \frac{|x+2|}{x+2}$

47. $\lim_{x\to 2} f(x)$ where $f(x) = \begin{cases} 5-x, & x \le 2 \\ x^2-3, & x > 2 \end{cases}$

48. $\lim_{x\to 0} f(x)$ where $f(x) = \begin{cases} x-6, & x \ge 0 \\ x^2-4, & x < 0 \end{cases}$

In Exercises 49–52, find $\lim_{h\to 0} \frac{f(x+h)-f(x)}{h}$.

49. $f(x) = 4x + 3$

50. $f(x) = 11 - 2x$

51. $f(x) = 3x - x^2$

52. $f(x) = x^2 - 5x - 2$

12.3 In Exercises 53 and 54, approximate the slope of the tangent line to the graph at the point (x, y).

53.

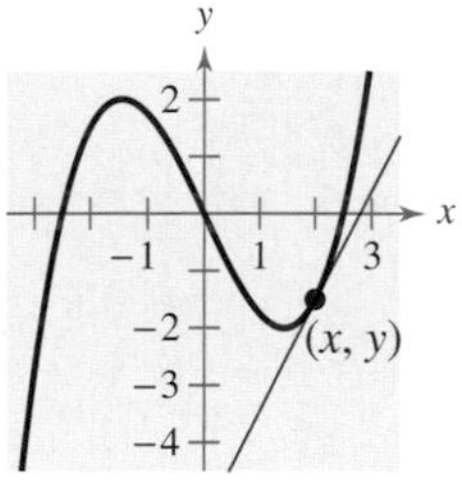

54.

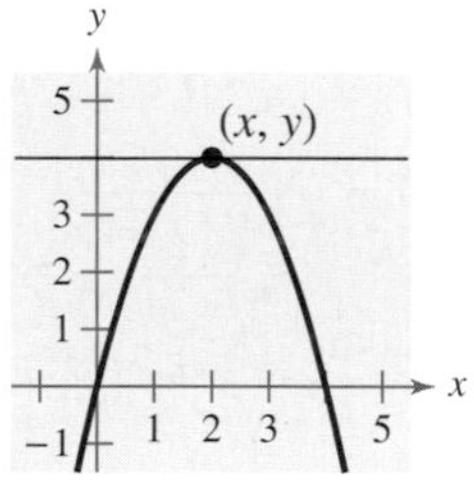

In Exercises 55–58, sketch a graph of the function and the tangent line at the point $(2, f(2))$. Use the graph to approximate the slope of the tangent line.

55. $f(x) = x^2 - 2x$

56. $f(x) = 6 - x^2$

57. $f(x) = \sqrt{x+2}$

58. $f(x) = \sqrt{x^2+5}$

In Exercises 59–62, find a formula for the slope of the graph of f at the point $(x, f(x))$. Then use it to find the slope at the two given points.

59. $f(x) = x^2 - 4x$

(a) $(0, 0)$ (b) $(5, 5)$

60. $f(x) = \frac{1}{4}x^4$

(a) $(-2, 4)$ (b) $\left(1, \frac{1}{4}\right)$

61. $f(x) = \frac{4}{x-6}$

(a) $(7, 4)$ (b) $(8, 2)$

62. $f(x) = \sqrt{x}$

(a) $(1, 1)$ (b) $(4, 2)$

In Exercises 63–72, find the derivative of the function.

63. $f(x) = 5$

64. $g(x) = -3$

65. $h(x) = 5 - \frac{1}{2}x$

66. $f(x) = 3x$

67. $g(x) = 2x^2 - 1$

68. $f(x) = -x^3 + 4x$

69. $f(t) = \sqrt{t+5}$

70. $f(x) = \frac{1}{\sqrt{12-x}}$

71. $g(s) = \frac{4}{s+5}$

72. $g(t) = \frac{6}{5-t}$

In Exercises 73 and 74, (a) find the slope of the graph of f at the given point, (b) use the result of part (a) to find an equation of the tangent line to the graph at the point, and (c) graph the function and the tangent line.

73. $f(x) = 2x^2 - 1, (0, -1)$

74. $f(x) = x^2 + 10, (2, 14)$

12.4 In Exercises 75–82, find the limit (if it exists). If the limit does not exist, explain why. Use a graphing utility to verify your result graphically.

75. $\lim_{x\to\infty} \frac{4x}{2x-3}$

76. $\lim_{x\to\infty} \frac{7x}{14x+2}$

77. $\lim_{x\to-\infty} \frac{2x}{x^2-25}$

78. $\lim_{x\to-\infty} \frac{6x}{(x-2)^3}$

79. $\lim_{x\to\infty} \frac{x^2}{2x+3}$

80. $\lim_{y\to\infty} \frac{3y^4}{y^2+1}$

81. $\lim_{x\to\infty} \left[\frac{x}{(x-2)^2} + 3\right]$

82. $\lim_{x\to\infty} \left[2 - \frac{2x^2}{(x+1)^2}\right]$

In Exercises 83–86, write the first five terms of the sequence and find the limit of the sequence (if it exists). If the limit does not exist, explain why. Assume n begins with 1.

83. $a_n = \dfrac{3n - 1}{2n + 1}$

84. $a_n = \dfrac{n}{n^2 + 1}$

85. $a_n = \dfrac{1}{2n^2}[3 - 2n(n + 1)]$

86. $a_n = \left(\dfrac{2}{n}\right)\left\{n + \dfrac{2}{n}\left[\dfrac{n(n - 1)}{2} - n\right]\right\}$

12.5 In Exercises 87 and 88, (a) use the summation formulas and properties to rewrite the sum as a rational function $S(n)$, (b) use $S(n)$ to complete the table, and (c) find $\lim_{n\to\infty} S(n)$.

n	10^0	10^1	10^2	10^3	10^4
$S(n)$					

87. $\displaystyle\sum_{i=1}^{n}\left(\frac{4i^2}{n^2} - \frac{i}{n}\right)\left(\frac{1}{n}\right)$

88. $\displaystyle\sum_{i=1}^{n}\left[4 - \left(\frac{3i}{n}\right)^2\right]\left(\frac{3i}{n^2}\right)$

In Exercises 89 and 90, approximate the area of the region using the indicated number of rectangles of equal width.

89. $f(x) = 4 - x$

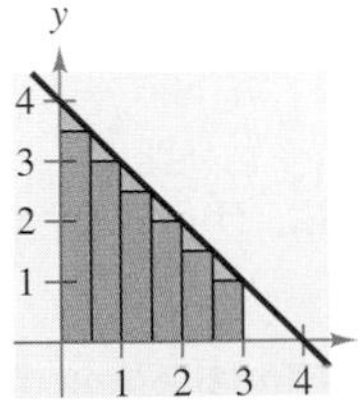

90. $f(x) = 4 - x^2$

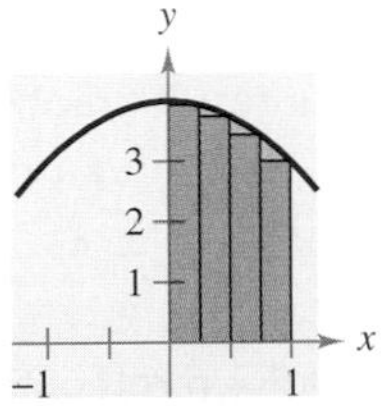

In Exercises 91 and 92, complete the table showing the approximate area of the region in the graph using n rectangles of equal width.

n	4	8	20	50
Approximate area				

91. $f(x) = \frac{1}{4}x^2$

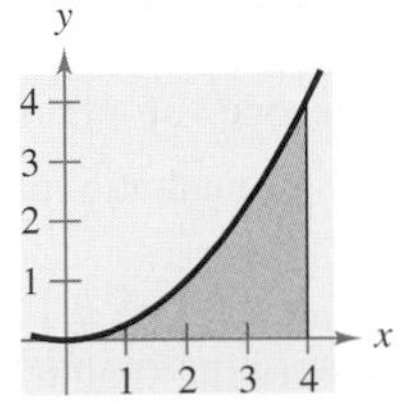

92. $f(x) = 4x - x^2$

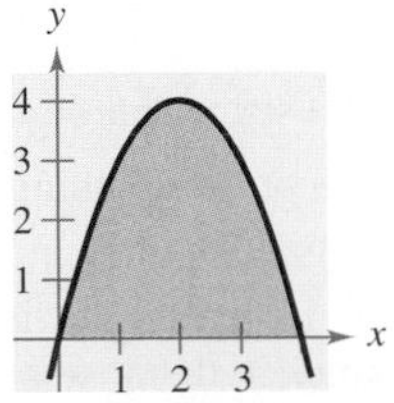

In Exercises 93–98, use the limit process to find the area of the region between the graph of the function and the x-axis over the specified interval.

	Function	*Interval*
93.	$f(x) = 10 - x$	$[0, 10]$
94.	$f(x) = 2x - 6$	$[3, 6]$
95.	$f(x) = x^2 + 4$	$[-1, 2]$
96.	$f(x) = 8(x - x^2)$	$[0, 1]$
97.	$f(x) = 2(x^2 - x^3)$	$[-1, 1]$
98.	$f(x) = 4 - (x - 2)^2$	$[0, 4]$

99. ***Civil Engineering*** The table shows the measurements (in feet) of a lot bounded by a stream and two straight roads that meet at right angles (see figure).

x	0	100	200	300	400	500
y	125	125	120	112	90	90

x	600	700	800	900	1000
y	95	88	75	35	0

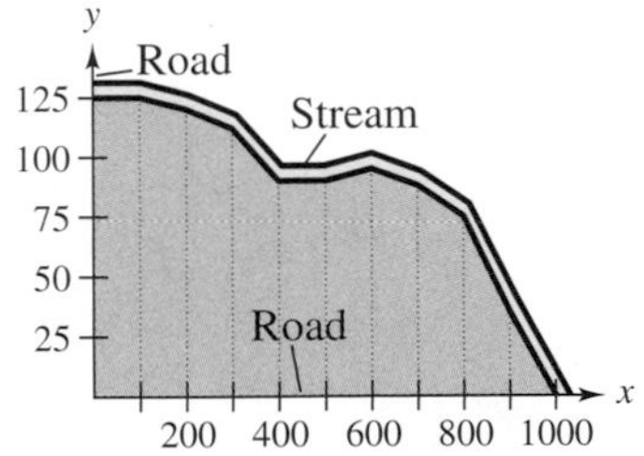

(a) Use the *regression* feature of a graphing utility to find a model of the form $y = ax^3 + bx^2 + cx + d$.

(b) Use a graphing utility to plot the data and graph the model in the same viewing window.

(c) Use the model in part (a) to estimate the area of the lot.

Synthesis

True or False? **In Exercises 100 and 101, determine whether the statement is true or false. Justify your answer.**

100. The limit of the sum of two functions is the sum of the limits of the two functions.

101. If the degree of the numerator $N(x)$ of a rational function $f(x) = N(x)/D(x)$ is greater than the degree of its denominator $D(x)$, then the limit of the rational function as x approaches ∞ is 0.

102. ***Writing*** Write a short paragraph explaining several reasons why the limit of a function may not exist.

12 Chapter Test

Take this test as you would take a test in class. When you are finished, check your work against the answers given in the back of the book.

In Exercises 1–3, sketch a graph of the function and approximate the limit (if it exists). Then find the limit (if it exists) algebraically by using appropriate techniques.

1. $\lim_{x \to -2} \frac{x^2 - 1}{2x}$ **2.** $\lim_{x \to -1} \frac{2x^2 - x - 3}{x + 1}$ **3.** $\lim_{x \to 5} \frac{\sqrt{x} - 2}{x - 5}$

In Exercises 4 and 5, use a graphing utility to graph the function and approximate the limit. Write an approximation that is accurate to four decimal places. Then create a table to verify your limit numerically.

4. $\lim_{x \to 0} \frac{\sin 3x}{x}$ **5.** $\lim_{x \to 0} \frac{e^{2x} - 1}{x}$

6. Find a formula for the slope of the graph of f at the point $(x, f(x))$. Then use it to find the slope at the given point.

(a) $f(x) = 3x^2 - 5x - 2$, $(2, 0)$ (b) $f(x) = 2x^3 + 6x$, $(-1, -8)$

In Exercises 7–9, find the derivative of the function.

7. $f(x) = 4 - \frac{3}{4}x$ **8.** $f(x) = 2x^2 + 4x - 1$ **9.** $f(x) = \frac{1}{x + 3}$

In Exercises 10–12, find the limit (if it exists). If the limit does not exist, explain why. Use a graphing utility to verify your result graphically.

10. $\lim_{x \to \infty} \frac{6}{5x - 1}$ **11.** $\lim_{x \to \infty} \frac{1 - 3x^2}{x^2 - 5}$ **12.** $\lim_{x \to -\infty} \frac{3x^3}{x + 2}$

In Exercises 13 and 14, write the first five terms of the sequence and find the limit of the sequence (if it exists). If the limit does not exist, explain why. Assume *n* begins with 1.

13. $a_n = \frac{n^2 + 3n - 4}{2n^2 + n - 2}$ **14.** $a_n = \frac{1 + (-1)^n}{n}$

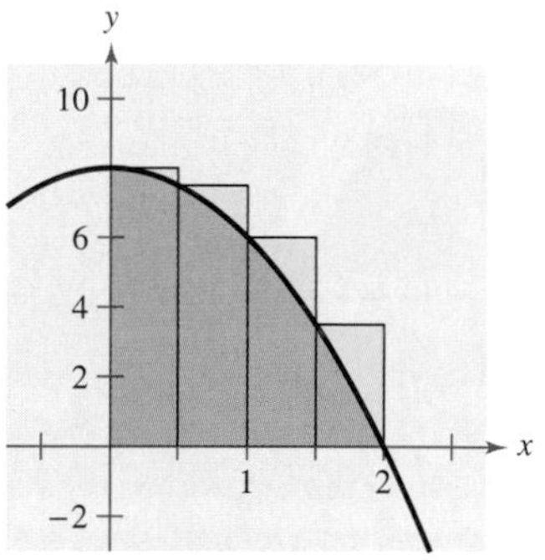

FIGURE FOR 15

15. Approximate the area of the region bounded by the graph of $f(x) = 8 - 2x^2$ shown at the left using the indicated number of rectangles of equal width.

In Exercises 16 and 17, use the limit process to find the area of the region between the graph of the function and the *x*-axis over the specified interval.

16. $f(x) = x + 2$; interval: $[-2, 2]$ **17.** $f(x) = 1 - x^3$; interval: $[0, 1]$

18. The table shows the altitude of a space shuttle during its first 5 seconds of motion.

(a) Use the regression feature of a graphing utility to find a quadratic model $y = ax^2 + bx + c$ for the data.

(b) The value of the derivative of the model is the rate of change of altitude with respect to time, or the velocity, at that instant. Find the velocity of the shuttle after 5 seconds.

Time (seconds), x	Altitude (feet), y
0	0
1	1
2	23
3	60
4	115
5	188

TABLE FOR 18

12 Cumulative Test for Chapters 10-12

Take this test to review the material from earlier chapters. When you are finished, check your work against the answers given in the back of the book.

In Exercises 1 and 2, identify the conic and sketch its graph.

1. $\dfrac{(x-2)^2}{4} + \dfrac{(y+1)^2}{9} = 1$

2. $x^2 + y^2 - 2x - 4y + 1 = 0$

3. Find the standard form of the equation of the ellipse with vertices $(0, 0)$ and $(0, 4)$ and endpoints of the minor axis $(1, 2)$ and $(-1, 2)$.

4. Determine the number of degrees through which the axis must be rotated to eliminate the xy-term of the conic $x^2 - 4xy + 2y^2 = 6$. Then graph the conic.

5. Sketch the curve represented by the parametric equations $x = 4 \ln t$ and $y = \frac{1}{2}t^2$. Then eliminate the parameter and write the corresponding rectangular equation whose graph represents the curve.

6. Plot the point $(-2, -3\pi/4)$ and find three additional polar representations for $-2\pi < \theta < 2\pi$.

7. Convert the rectangular equation $-8x - 3y + 5 = 0$ to polar form.

8. Convert the polar equation $r = \dfrac{2}{4 - 5\cos\theta}$ to rectangular form.

In Exercises 9–11, sketch the graph of the polar equation. Identify the type of graph.

9. $r = -\dfrac{\pi}{6}$

10. $r = 3 - 2\sin\theta$

11. $r = 2 + 5\cos\theta$

In Exercises 12 and 13, find the coordinates of the point.

12. The point is located six units behind the yz-plane, one unit to the right of the xz-plane, and three units above the xy-plane.

13. The point is located on the y-axis, four units to the left of the xz-plane.

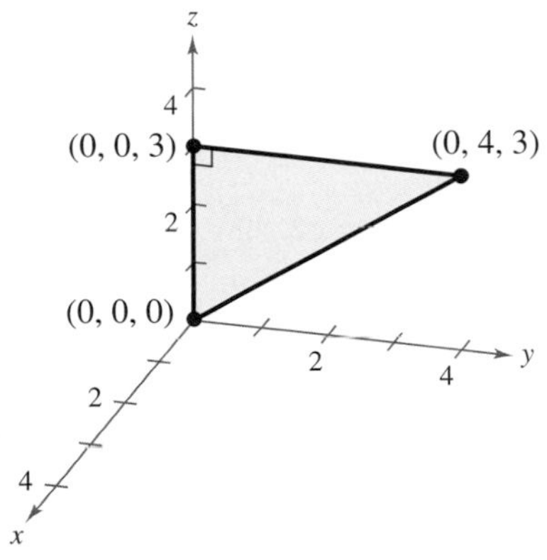

FIGURE FOR 15

14. Find the distance between the points $(-2, 3, -6)$ and $(4, -5, 1)$.

15. Find the lengths of the sides of the right triangle at the left. Show that these lengths satisfy the Pythagorean Theorem.

16. Find the coordinates of the midpoint of the line segment joining $(3, 4, -1)$ and $(-5, 0, 2)$.

17. Find an equation of the sphere for which the endpoints of a diameter are $(0, 0, 0)$ and $(4, 4, 8)$.

18. Sketch the graph of the equation $(x - 2)^2 + (y + 1)^2 + z^2 = 4$, and sketch the xy-trace and the yz-trace.

19. For the vectors $\mathbf{u} = \langle 2, -6, 0\rangle$ and $\mathbf{v} = \langle -4, 5, 3\rangle$, find $\mathbf{u} \cdot \mathbf{v}$ and $\mathbf{u} \times \mathbf{v}$.

In Exercises 20–22, determine whether u and v are orthogonal, parallel, or neither.

20. $\mathbf{u} = \langle 4, 4, 0\rangle$
$\mathbf{v} = \langle 0, -8, 6\rangle$

21. $\mathbf{u} = \langle 4, -2, 10\rangle$
$\mathbf{v} = \langle -2, 6, 2\rangle$

22. $\mathbf{u} = \langle -1, 6, -3\rangle$
$\mathbf{v} = \langle 3, -18, 9\rangle$

23. Find the volume of the parallelepiped with the vertices $A(1, 3, 2,)$, $B(3, 4, 2)$, $C(3, 2, 2)$, $D(1, 1, 2)$, $E(1, 3, 5)$, $F(3, 4, 5)$, $G(3, 2, 5)$, and $H(1, 1, 5)$.

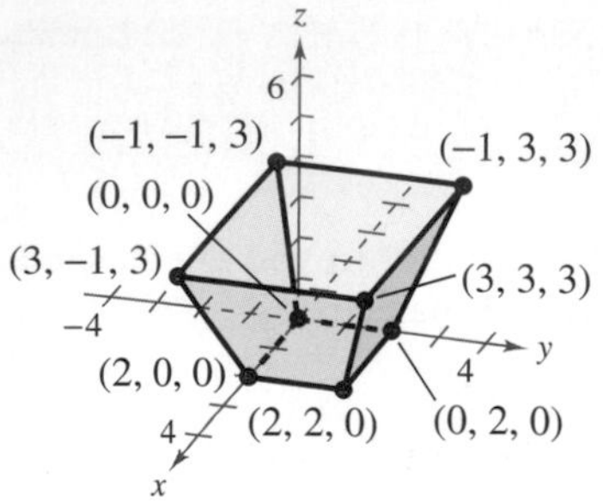

FIGURE FOR 28

24. Find sets of (a) parametric equations and (b) symmetric equations for the line passing through the points $(-2, 3, 0)$ and $(5, 8, 25)$.

25. Find an equation of the plane passing through the points $(0, 0, 0)$, $(-2, 3, 0)$, and $(5, 8, 25)$.

26. Label the intercepts and sketch the graph of the plane given by $3x - 6y - 12z = 24$.

27. Find the distance between the point $(0, 0, 25)$ and the plane $2x - 5y + z = 10$.

28. A plastic wastebasket has the shape and dimensions shown in the figure. In fabricating a mold for making the wastebasket, it is necessary to know the angle between two adjacent sides. Find the angle.

In Exercises 29–34, find the limit (if it exists). If the limit does not exist, explain why. Use a graphing utility to verify your result graphically.

29. $\lim_{x \to 4} (5x - x^2)$

30. $\lim_{x \to -2^+} \dfrac{x + 2}{x^2 + x - 2}$

31. $\lim_{x \to 7} \dfrac{x - 7}{x^2 - 49}$

32. $\lim_{x \to 0} \dfrac{\sqrt{x + 4} - 2}{x}$

33. $\lim_{x \to 4^-} \dfrac{|x - 4|}{x - 4}$

34. $\lim_{x \to 0} \sin\left(\dfrac{\pi}{x}\right)$

In Exercises 35–38, find a formula for the slope of the graph of *f* at the point $(x, f(x))$. Then use it to find the slope at the given point.

35. $f(x) = 3 - x^2$, $(1, 2)$

36. $f(x) = \sqrt{x + 3}$, $(-2, 1)$

37. $f(x) = \dfrac{1}{x + 3}$, $\left(1, \dfrac{1}{4}\right)$

38. $f(x) = x^4$, $(-1, 1)$

In Exercises 39–42, find the limit (if it exists). If the limit does not exist, explain why. Use a graphing utility to verify your result graphically.

39. $\lim_{x \to \infty} \dfrac{2x^4 - x^3 + 4}{x^2 - 9}$

40. $\lim_{x \to \infty} \dfrac{3 - 7x}{x + 4}$

41. $\lim_{x \to \infty} \dfrac{3x^2 + 1}{x^2 + 4}$

42. $\lim_{x \to \infty} \dfrac{2x}{x^2 + 3x - 2}$

In Exercises 43–45, evaluate the sum using the summation formulas and properties.

43. $\sum_{i=1}^{50} (1 - i^2)$

44. $\sum_{k=1}^{20} (3k^2 - 2k)$

45. $\sum_{i=1}^{40} (12 + i^3)$

In Exercises 46 and 47, approximate the area of the region using the indicated number of rectangles of equal width.

46.

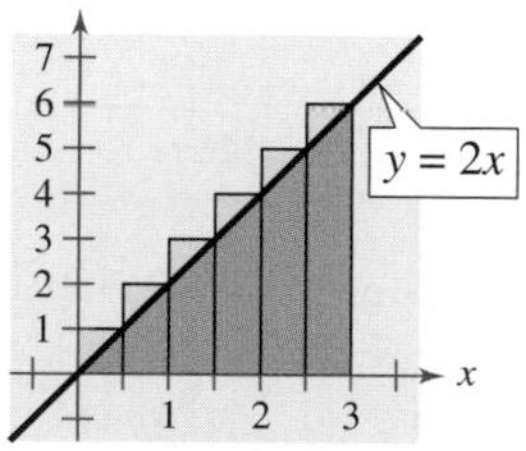

47.

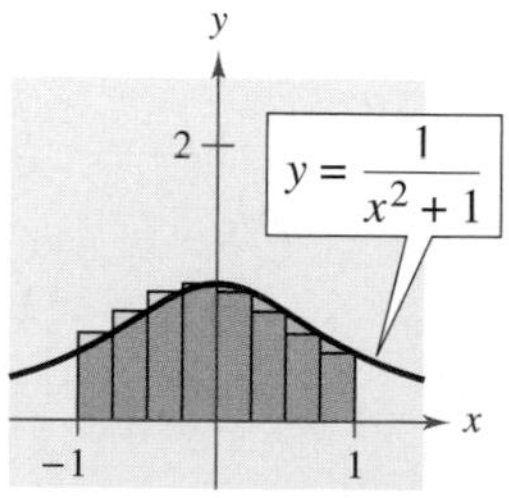

In Exercises 48–50, use the limit process to find the area of the region between the graph of the function and the *x*-axis over the specified interval.

48. $f(x) = 1 - x^3$
Interval: $[0, 1]$

49. $f(x) = x + 3$
Interval: $[-3, 3]$

50. $f(x) = x^2$
Interval: $[-1, 1]$

Proofs in Mathematics

Many of the proofs of the definitions and properties presented in this chapter are beyond the scope of this text. Included below are simple proofs for the limit of a power function and the limit of a polynomial function.

Proving Limits

To prove most of the definitions and properties from this chapter, you must use the *formal* definition of a limit. This definition is called the epsilon-delta definition and was first introduced by Karl Weierstrass (1815–1897). If you go on to take a course in calculus, you will use this definition of a limit extensively.

Limit of a Power Function *(p. 857)*

$\lim_{x \to c} x^n = c^n$, c is a real number and n is a positive integer.

Proof

$$\begin{aligned}
\lim_{x \to c} x^n &= \lim_{x \to c} \underbrace{(x \cdot x \cdot x \cdot \cdots \cdot x)}_{n \text{ factors}} \\
&= \underbrace{\lim_{x \to c} x \cdot \lim_{x \to c} x \cdot \lim_{x \to c} x \cdot \cdots \cdot \lim_{x \to c} x}_{n \text{ factors}} && \text{Product Property of Limits} \\
&= \underbrace{c \cdot c \cdot c \cdot \cdots \cdot c}_{n \text{ factors}} && \text{Limit of the identity function} \\
&= c^n && \text{Exponential form}
\end{aligned}$$

Limit of a Polynomial Function *(p. 859)*

If p is a polynomial function and c is a real number, then

$$\lim_{x \to c} p(x) = p(c).$$

Proof

Let p be a polynomial function such that

$$p(x) = a_n x^n + a_{n-1} x^{n-1} + \cdot \cdot \cdot + a_2 x^2 + a_1 x + a_0.$$

Because a polynomial function is the sum of monomial functions, you can write the following.

$$\begin{aligned}
\lim_{x \to c} p(x) &= \lim_{x \to c} (a_n x^n + a_{n-1} x^{n-1} + \cdot \cdot \cdot + a_2 x^2 + a_1 x + a_0) \\
&= \lim_{x \to c} a_n x^n + \lim_{x \to c} a_{n-1} x^{n-1} + \cdot \cdot \cdot + \lim_{x \to c} a_2 x^2 + \lim_{x \to c} a_1 x + \lim_{x \to c} a_0 \\
&= a_n c^n + a_{n-1} c^{n-1} + \cdot \cdot \cdot + a_2 c^2 + a_1 c + a_0 && \text{Scalar Multiple Property of Limits and limit of a power function} \\
&= p(c) && p \text{ evaluated at } c
\end{aligned}$$

P.S. Problem Solving

This collection of thought-provoking and challenging exercises further explores and expands upon concepts learned in this chapter.

1. Consider the graphs of the four functions g_1, g_2, g_3, and g_4.

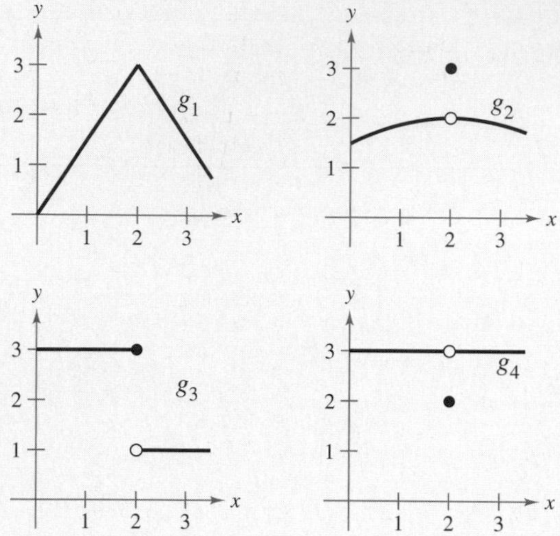

For each given condition of the function f, which of the graphs could be the graph of f?

(a) $\lim_{x \to 2} f(x) = 3$ (b) $\lim_{x \to 2^-} f(x) = 3$

(c) $\lim_{x \to 2^+} f(x) = 3$

2. Sketch the graph of the function given by $f(x) = [\![x]\!] + [\![-x]\!]$.

(a) Evaluate $f(1), f(0), f\left(\frac{1}{2}\right)$, and $f(-2.7)$.

(b) Evaluate the following limits.

$\lim_{x \to 1^-} f(x)$, $\lim_{x \to 1^+} f(x)$, $\lim_{x \to 1/2} f(x)$

3. Sketch the graph of the function given by $f(x) = \left[\!\!\left[\frac{1}{x}\right]\!\!\right]$.

(a) Evaluate $f\left(\frac{1}{4}\right), f(3)$, and $f(1)$.

(b) Evaluate the following limits.

$\lim_{x \to 1^-} f(x)$, $\lim_{x \to 1^+} f(x)$, $\lim_{x \to (1/2)^-} f(x)$, $\lim_{x \to (1/2)^+} f(x)$

4. Let $P(3, 4)$ be a point on the circle $x^2 + y^2 = 25$ (see figure).

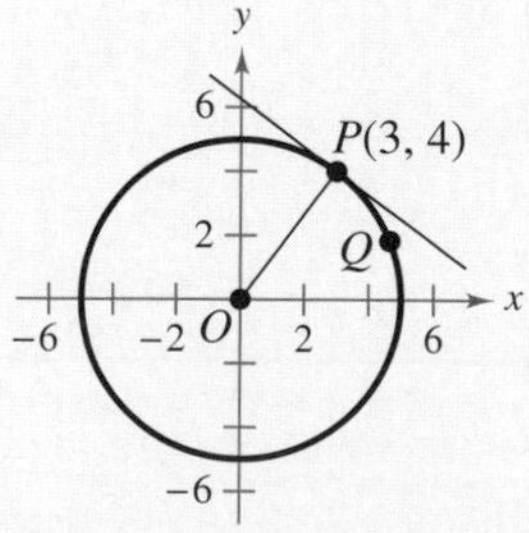

(a) What is the slope of the line joining P and $O(0, 0)$?

(b) Find an equation of the tangent line to the circle at P.

(c) Let $Q(x, y)$ be another point on the circle in the first quadrant. Find the slope m_x of the line joining P and Q in terms of x.

(d) Evaluate $\lim_{x \to 3} m_x$. How does this number relate to your answer in part (b)?

5. Find the values of the constants a and b such that

$$\lim_{x \to 0} \frac{\sqrt{a + bx} - \sqrt{3}}{x} = \sqrt{3}.$$

6. Consider the function given by

$$f(x) = \frac{\sqrt{3 + x^{1/3}} - 2}{x - 1}.$$

(a) Find the domain of f.

(b) Use a graphing utility to graph the function.

(c) Evaluate $\lim_{x \to -27^+} f(x)$. Verify your result using the graph in part (b).

(d) Evaluate $\lim_{x \to 1} f(x)$. Verify your result using the graph in part (b).

7. Let

$$f(x) = \begin{cases} 0, & \text{if } x \text{ is rational} \\ 1, & \text{if } x \text{ is irrational} \end{cases}$$

and

$$g(x) = \begin{cases} 0, & \text{if } x \text{ is rational} \\ x, & \text{if } x \text{ is irrational} \end{cases}.$$

Find (if possible) $\lim_{x \to 0} f(x)$ and $\lim_{x \to 0} g(x)$. Explain your reasoning.

8. Graph the two parabolas $y = x^2$ and $y = -x^2 + 2x - 5$ in the same coordinate plane. Find equations of the two lines that are simultaneously tangent to both parabolas.

9. Find a function of the form $f(x) = a + b\sqrt{x}$ that is tangent to the line $2y - 3x = 5$ at the point $(1, 4)$.

10. (a) Find an equation of the tangent line to the parabola $y = x^2$ at the point $(2, 4)$.

(b) Find an equation of the normal line to $y = x^2$ at the point $(2, 4)$. (The **normal line** is perpendicular to the tangent line). Where does this line intersect the parabola a second time?

(c) Find equations of the tangent line and normal line to $y = x^2$ at the point $(0, 0)$.

11. A line with slope m passes through the point (0, 4).

(a) Recall that the distance d between a point (x_1, y_1) and the line $Ax + By + C = 0$ is given by

$$d = \frac{|Ax_1 + By_1 + C|}{\sqrt{A^2 + B^2}}.$$

Write the distance d between the line and the point (3, 1) as a function of m.

(b) Use a graphing utility to graph the function from part (a).

(c) Find $\lim_{m\to\infty} d(m)$ and $\lim_{m\to-\infty} d(m)$. Give a geometric interpretation of the results.

12. A heat probe is attached to the heat exchanger of a heating system. The temperature T (in degrees Celsius) is recorded t seconds after the furnace is started. The results for the first 2 minutes are recorded in the table.

t	T
0	25.2°
15	36.9°
30	45.5°
45	51.4°
60	56.0°
75	59.6°
90	62.0°
105	64.0°
120	65.2°

(a) Use the *regression* feature of a graphing utility to find a model of the form $T_1 = at^2 + bt + c$ for the data.

(b) Use a graphing utility to graph T_1 with the original data. How well does the model fit the data?

(c) A rational model for the data is given by

$$T_2 = \frac{86t + 1451}{t + 58}.$$

Use a graphing utility to graph T_2 with the original data. How well does the model fit the data?

(d) Evaluate $T_1(0)$ and $T_2(0)$.

(e) Find $\lim_{t\to\infty} T_2$. Verify your result using the graph in part (c).

(f) Interpret the result of part (e) in the context of the problem. Is it possible to do this type of analysis using T_1? Explain your reasoning.

13. When using a graphing utility to generate a table to approximate

$$\lim_{x\to 0} \frac{\tan 2x}{x}$$

a student concluded that the limit was 0.03491 rather than 2. Determine the probable cause of the error.

14. Let $P(x, y)$ be a point on the parabola $y = x^2$ in the first quadrant. Consider the triangle PAO formed by P, $A(0, 1)$, and the origin $O(0, 0)$, and the triangle PBO formed by P, $B(1, 0)$, and the origin (see figure).

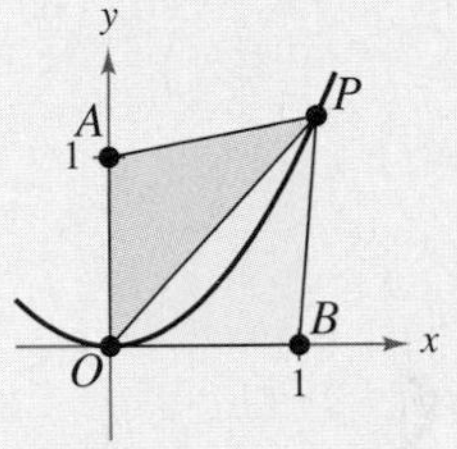

(a) Write the perimeter of each triangle in terms of x.

(b) Complete the table. Let $r(x)$ be the ratio of the perimeters of the two triangles.

$$r(x) = \frac{\text{Perimeter } \triangle PAO}{\text{Perimeter } \triangle PBO}$$

x	4	2	1	0.1	0.01
Perimeter $\triangle PAO$					
Perimeter $\triangle PBO$					
$r(x)$					

(c) Find $\lim_{x\to 0^+} r(x)$.

15. Archimedes showed that the area of a parabolic arch is equal to $\frac{2}{3}$ the product of the base and the height (see figure).

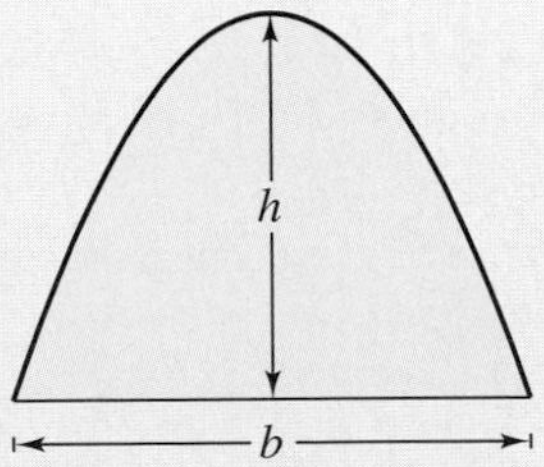

(a) Graph the parabolic arch bounded by $y = 9 - x^2$ and the x-axis.

(b) Use the limit process to find the area of the parabolic arch.

(c) Find the base and height of the arch and verify Archimedes's formula.

Appendix A Review of Fundamental Concepts of Algebra

A.1 Real Numbers and Their Properties

What you should learn

- Represent and classify real numbers.
- Order real numbers and use inequalities.
- Find the absolute values of real numbers and find the distance between two real numbers.
- Evaluate algebraic expressions.
- Use the basic rules and properties of algebra.

Why you should learn it

Real numbers are used to represent many real-life quantities. For example, in Exercise 65 on page A9, you will use real numbers to represent the federal deficit.

Real Numbers

Real numbers are used in everyday life to describe quantities such as age, miles per gallon, and population. Real numbers are represented by symbols such as

$$-5, 9, 0, \frac{4}{3}, 0.666 \ldots, 28.21, \sqrt{2}, \pi, \text{ and } \sqrt[3]{-32}.$$

Here are some important **subsets** (each member of subset B is also a member of set A) of the real numbers. The three dots, called *ellipsis points*, indicate that the pattern continues indefinitely.

$\{1, 2, 3, 4, \ldots\}$ Set of natural numbers

$\{0, 1, 2, 3, 4, \ldots\}$ Set of whole numbers

$\{\ldots, -3, -2, -1, 0, 1, 2, 3, \ldots\}$ Set of integers

A real number is **rational** if it can be written as the ratio p/q of two integers, where $q \neq 0$. For instance, the numbers

$$\frac{1}{3} = 0.3333 \ldots = 0.\overline{3}, \frac{1}{8} = 0.125, \text{ and } \frac{125}{111} = 1.126126 \ldots = 1.\overline{126}$$

are rational. The decimal representation of a rational number either repeats $\left(\text{as in } \frac{173}{55} = 3.1\overline{45}\right)$ or terminates $\left(\text{as in } \frac{1}{2} = 0.5\right)$. A real number that cannot be written as the ratio of two integers is called **irrational.** Irrational numbers have infinite nonrepeating decimal representations. For instance, the numbers

$$\sqrt{2} = 1.4142135 \ldots \approx 1.41 \quad \text{and} \quad \pi = 3.1415926 \ldots \approx 3.14$$

are irrational. (The symbol $\approx$ means "is approximately equal to.") Figure A.1 shows subsets of real numbers and their relationships to each other.

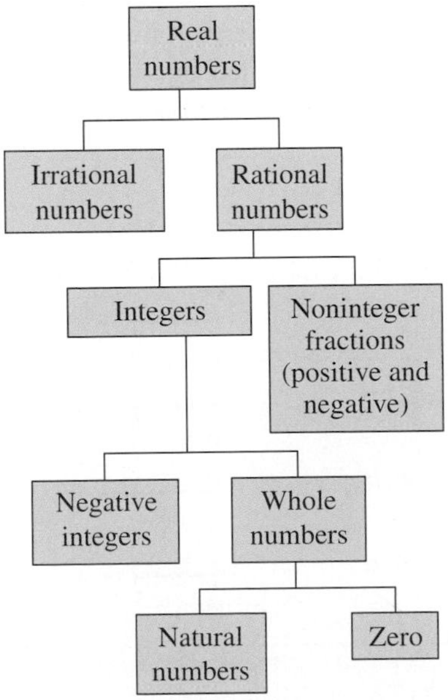

FIGURE A.1 *Subsets of real numbers*

Real numbers are represented graphically by a **real number line.** The point 0 on the real number line is the **origin.** Numbers to the right of 0 are positive, and numbers to the left of 0 are negative, as shown in Figure A.2. The term **nonnegative** describes a number that is either positive or zero.

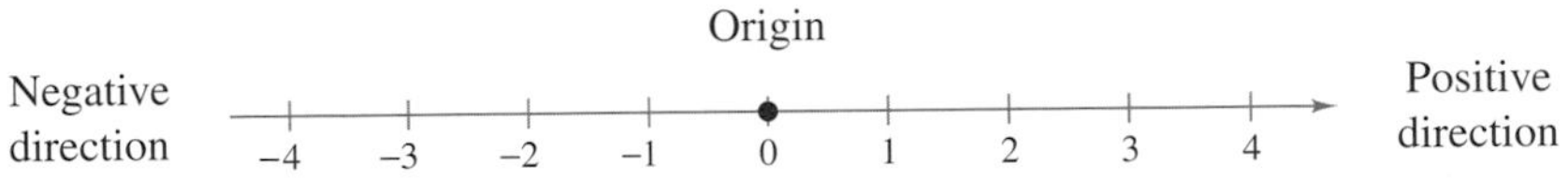

FIGURE A.2 *The real number line*

As illustrated in Figure A.3, there is a *one-to-one correspondence* between real numbers and points on the real number line.

Every real number corresponds to exactly one point on the real number line.

Every point on the real number line corresponds to exactly one real number.

FIGURE A.3 *One-to-one*

Ordering Real Numbers

One important property of real numbers is that they are *ordered*.

Definition of Order on the Real Number Line

If a and b are real numbers, a is less than b if $b - a$ is positive. The **order** of a and b is denoted by the **inequality** $a < b$. This relationship can also be described by saying that b is *greater than* a and writing $b > a$. The inequality $a \leq b$ means that a is *less than or equal to* b, and the inequality $b \geq a$ means that b is *greater than or equal to* a. The symbols $<$, $>$, $\leq$, and $\geq$ are *inequality symbols.*

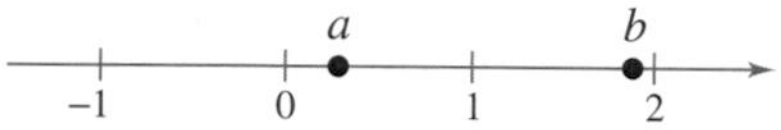

FIGURE A.4 *$a < b$ if and only if a lies to the left of b.*

Geometrically, this definition implies that $a < b$ if and only if a lies to the *left* of b on the real number line, as shown in Figure A.4.

Example 1 Interpreting Inequalities

Describe the subset of real numbers represented by each inequality.

a. $x \leq 2$ **b.** $-2 \leq x < 3$

Solution

a. The inequality $x \leq 2$ denotes all real numbers less than or equal to 2, as shown in Figure A.5.

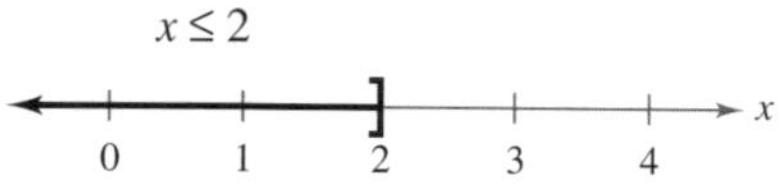

FIGURE A.5

b. The inequality $-2 \leq x < 3$ means that $x \geq -2$ *and* $x < 3$. This "double inequality" denotes all real numbers between -2 and 3, including -2 but not including 3, as shown in Figure A.6.

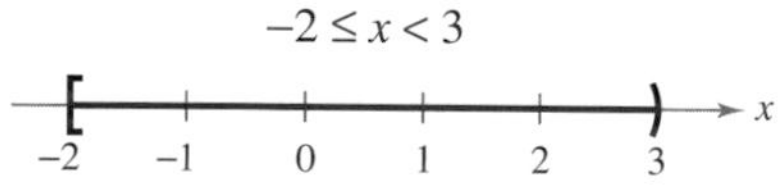

FIGURE A.6

CHECKPOINT Now try Exercise 19.

Inequalities can be used to describe subsets of real numbers called **intervals.** In the bounded intervals below, the real numbers a and b are the **endpoints** of each interval. The endpoints of a closed interval are included in the interval, whereas the endpoints of an open interval are not included in the interval.

Bounded Intervals on the Real Number Line

Notation	*Interval Type*	*Inequality*	*Graph*
$[a, b]$	Closed	$a \leq x \leq b$	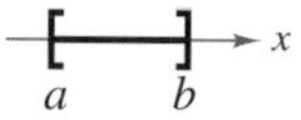
(a, b)	Open	$a < x < b$	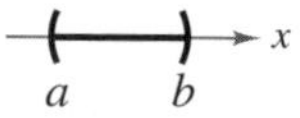
$[a, b)$		$a \leq x < b$	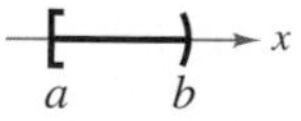
$(a, b]$		$a < x \leq b$	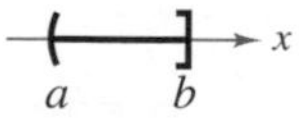

STUDY TIP

The reason that the four types of intervals at the right are called *bounded* is that each has a finite length. An interval that does not have a finite length is *unbounded* (see page A3).

The symbols ∞, **positive infinity,** and $-\infty$, **negative infinity,** do not represent real numbers. They are simply convenient symbols used to describe the unboundedness of an interval such as $(1, \infty)$ or $(-\infty, 3]$.

> **STUDY TIP**
>
> Note that whenever you write intervals containing ∞ or $-\infty$, you always use a parenthesis and never a bracket. This is because these symbols are never an endpoint of an interval and therefore not included in the interval.

Unbounded Intervals on the Real Number Line

Notation	*Interval Type*	*Inequality*	*Graph*
$[a, \infty)$		$x \geq a$	
(a, ∞)	Open	$x > a$	
$(-\infty, b]$		$x \leq b$	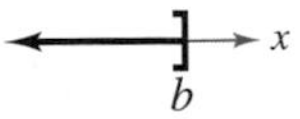
$(-\infty, b)$	Open	$x < b$	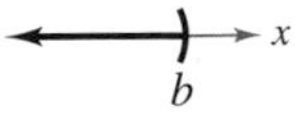
$(-\infty, \infty)$	Entire real line	$-\infty < x < \infty$	

Example 2 **Using Inequalities to Represent Intervals**

Use inequality notation to describe each of the following.

a. c is at most 2. **b.** m is at least -3.

c. All x in the interval $(-3, 5]$

Solution

a. The statement "c is at most 2" can be represented by $c \leq 2$.

b. The statement "m is at least -3" can be represented by $m \geq -3$.

c. "All x in the interval $(-3, 5]$" can be represented by $-3 < x \leq 5$.

CHECKPOINT Now try Exercise 31.

Example 3 **Interpreting Intervals**

Give a verbal description of each interval.

a. $(-1, 0)$ **b.** $[2, \infty)$ **c.** $(-\infty, 0)$

Solution

a. This interval consists of all real numbers that are greater than -1 and less than 0.

b. This interval consists of all real numbers that are greater than or equal to 2.

c. This interval consists of all negative real numbers.

CHECKPOINT Now try Exercise 29.

The **Law of Trichotomy** states that for any two real numbers a and b, *precisely* one of three relationships is possible:

$a = b, \quad a < b, \quad \text{or} \quad a > b.$ Law of Trichotomy

Absolute Value and Distance

The **absolute value** of a real number is its *magnitude*, or the distance between the origin and the point representing the real number on the real number line.

Definition of Absolute Value

If a is a real number, then the absolute value of a is

$$|a| = \begin{cases} a, & \text{if } a \geq 0 \\ -a, & \text{if } a < 0 \end{cases}.$$

Notice in this definition that the absolute value of a real number is never negative. For instance, if $a = -5$, then $|-5| = -(-5) = 5$. The absolute value of a real number is either positive or zero. Moreover, 0 is the only real number whose absolute value is 0. So, $|0| = 0$.

Example 4 Evaluating the Absolute Value of a Number

Evaluate $\dfrac{|x|}{x}$ for (a) $x > 0$ and (b) $x < 0$.

Solution

a. If $x > 0$, then $|x| = x$ and $\dfrac{|x|}{x} = \dfrac{x}{x} = 1$.

b. If $x < 0$, then $|x| = -x$ and $\dfrac{|x|}{x} = \dfrac{-x}{x} = -1$.

✓CHECKPOINT Now try Exercise 47.

Properties of Absolute Values

1. $|a| \geq 0$ **2.** $|-a| = |a|$

3. $|ab| = |a||b|$ **4.** $\left|\dfrac{a}{b}\right| = \dfrac{|a|}{|b|}, \quad b \neq 0$

Absolute value can be used to define the distance between two points on the real number line. For instance, the distance between -3 and 4 is

$$|-3 - 4| = |-7|$$
$$= 7$$

as shown in Figure A.7.

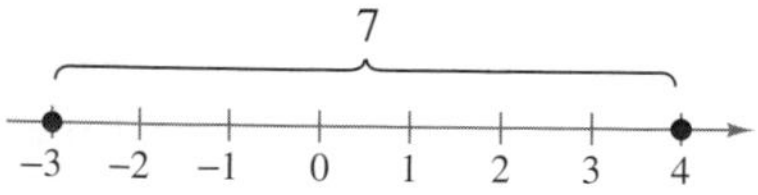

FIGURE A.7 *The distance between −3 and 4 is 7.*

Distance Between Two Points on the Real Number Line

Let a and b be real numbers. The **distance between a and b** is

$$d(a, b) = |b - a| = |a - b|.$$

Algebraic Expressions

One characteristic of algebra is the use of letters to represent numbers. The letters are **variables,** and combinations of letters and numbers are **algebraic expressions.** Here are a few examples of algebraic expressions.

$$5x, \qquad 2x - 3, \qquad \frac{4}{x^2 + 2}, \qquad 7x + y$$

Definition of an Algebraic Expression

An **algebraic expression** is a collection of letters **(variables)** and real numbers **(constants)** combined using the operations of addition, subtraction, multiplication, division, and exponentiation.

The **terms** of an algebraic expression are those parts that are separated by *addition*. For example,

$$x^2 - 5x + 8 = x^2 + (-5x) + 8$$

has three terms: x^2 and $-5x$ are the **variable terms** and 8 is the **constant term.** The numerical factor of a variable term is the **coefficient** of the variable term. For instance, the coefficient of $-5x$ is -5, and the coefficient of x^2 is 1.

To **evaluate** an algebraic expression, substitute numerical values for each of the variables in the expression. Here are two examples.

Expression	*Value of Variable*	*Substitute*	*Value of Expression*
$-3x + 5$	$x = 3$	$-3(3) + 5$	$-9 + 5 = -4$
$3x^2 + 2x - 1$	$x = -1$	$3(-1)^2 + 2(-1) - 1$	$3 - 2 - 1 = 0$

When an algebraic expression is evaluated, the **Substitution Principle** is used. It states that "If $a = b$, then a can be replaced by b in any expression involving a." In the first evaluation shown above, for instance, 3 is *substituted* for x in the expression $-3x + 5$.

Basic Rules of Algebra

There are four arithmetic operations with real numbers: *addition*, *multiplication*, *subtraction*, and *division*, denoted by the symbols $+$, $\times$ or $\cdot$, $-$, and $\div$ or /. Of these, addition and multiplication are the two primary operations. Subtraction and division are the inverse operations of addition and multiplication, respectively.

Definitions of Subtraction and Division

Subtraction: Add the opposite.

$$a - b = a + (-b)$$

Division: Multiply by the reciprocal.

If $b \neq 0$, then $a/b = a\left(\frac{1}{b}\right) = \frac{a}{b}$.

In these definitions, $-b$ is the **additive inverse** (or opposite) of b, and $1/b$ is the **multiplicative inverse** (or reciprocal) of b. In the fractional form a/b, a is the **numerator** of the fraction and b is the **denominator.**

Because the properties of real numbers below are true for variables and algebraic expressions as well as for real numbers, they are often called the **Basic Rules of Algebra.** Try to formulate a verbal description of each property. For instance, the first property states that *the order in which two real numbers are added does not affect their sum.*

Basic Rules of Algebra

Let a, b, and c be real numbers, variables, or algebraic expressions.

Property		*Example*
Commutative Property of Addition:	$a + b = b + a$	$4x + x^2 = x^2 + 4x$
Commutative Property of Multiplication:	$ab = ba$	$(4 - x)x^2 = x^2(4 - x)$
Associative Property of Addition:	$(a + b) + c = a + (b + c)$	$(x + 5) + x^2 = x + (5 + x^2)$
Associative Property of Multiplication:	$(ab)c = a(bc)$	$(2x \cdot 3y)(8) = (2x)(3y \cdot 8)$
Distributive Properties:	$a(b + c) = ab + ac$	$3x(5 + 2x) = 3x \cdot 5 + 3x \cdot 2x$
	$(a + b)c = ac + bc$	$(y + 8)y = y \cdot y + 8 \cdot y$
Additive Identity Property:	$a + 0 = a$	$5y^2 + 0 = 5y^2$
Multiplicative Identity Property:	$a \cdot 1 = a$	$(4x^2)(1) = 4x^2$
Additive Inverse Property:	$a + (-a) = 0$	$5x^3 + (-5x^3) = 0$
Multiplicative Inverse Property:	$a \cdot \frac{1}{a} = 1, \quad a \neq 0$	$(x^2 + 4)\left(\frac{1}{x^2 + 4}\right) = 1$

Because subtraction is defined as "adding the opposite," the Distributive Properties are also true for subtraction. For instance, the "subtraction form" of $a(b + c) = ab + ac$ is $a(b - c) = ab - ac$.

Properties of Negation and Equality

Let a and b be real numbers, variables, or algebraic expressions.

Property	*Example*
1. $(-1)a = -a$	$(-1)7 = -7$
2. $-(-a) = a$	$-(-6) = 6$
3. $(-a)b = -(ab) = a(-b)$	$(-5)3 = -(5 \cdot 3) = 5(-3)$
4. $(-a)(-b) = ab$	$(-2)(-x) = 2x$
5. $-(a + b) = (-a) + (-b)$	$-(x + 8) = (-x) + (-8)$
	$= -x - 8$
6. If $a = b$, then $a \pm c = b \pm c$.	$\frac{1}{2} + 3 = 0.5 + 3$
7. If $a = b$, then $ac = bc$.	$4^2 \cdot 2 = 16 \cdot 2$
8. If $a \pm c = b \pm c$, then $a = b$.	$1.4 - 1 = \frac{7}{5} - 1 \Rightarrow 1.4 = \frac{7}{5}$
9. If $ac = bc$ and $c \neq 0$, then $a = b$.	$3x = 3 \cdot 4 \Rightarrow x = 4$

STUDY TIP

Notice the difference between the *opposite of a number* and a *negative number*. If a is already negative, then its opposite, $-a$, is positive. For instance, if $a = -5$, then

$$-a = -(-5) = 5.$$

STUDY TIP

The "or" in the Zero-Factor Property includes the possibility that either or both factors may be zero. This is an **inclusive or,** and it is the way the word "or" is generally used in mathematics.

Properties of Zero

Let a and b be real numbers, variables, or algebraic expressions.

1. $a + 0 = a$ and $a - 0 = a$

2. $a \cdot 0 = 0$

3. $\dfrac{0}{a} = 0, \quad a \neq 0$

4. $\dfrac{a}{0}$ is undefined.

5. Zero-Factor Property: If $ab = 0$, then $a = 0$ or $b = 0$.

Properties and Operations of Fractions

Let a, b, c, and d be real numbers, variables, or algebraic expressions such that $b \neq 0$ and $d \neq 0$.

1. Equivalent Fractions: $\dfrac{a}{b} = \dfrac{c}{d}$ if and only if $ad = bc$.

2. Rules of Signs: $-\dfrac{a}{b} = \dfrac{-a}{b} = \dfrac{a}{-b}$ and $\dfrac{-a}{-b} = \dfrac{a}{b}$

3. Generate Equivalent Fractions: $\dfrac{a}{b} = \dfrac{ac}{bc}, \quad c \neq 0$

4. Add or Subtract with Like Denominators: $\dfrac{a}{b} \pm \dfrac{c}{b} = \dfrac{a \pm c}{b}$

5. Add or Subtract with Unlike Denominators: $\dfrac{a}{b} \pm \dfrac{c}{d} = \dfrac{ad \pm bc}{bd}$

6. Multiply Fractions: $\dfrac{a}{b} \cdot \dfrac{c}{d} = \dfrac{ac}{bd}$

7. Divide Fractions: $\dfrac{a}{b} \div \dfrac{c}{d} = \dfrac{a}{b} \cdot \dfrac{d}{c} = \dfrac{ad}{bc}, \quad c \neq 0$

STUDY TIP

In Property 1 of fractions, the phrase "if and only if" implies two statements. One statement is: If $a/b = c/d$, then $ad = bc$. The other statement is: If $ad = bc$, where $b \neq 0$ and $d \neq 0$, then $a/b = c/d$.

Example 5 Properties and Operations of Fractions

a. Equivalent fractions: $\dfrac{x}{5} = \dfrac{3 \cdot x}{3 \cdot 5} = \dfrac{3x}{15}$

b. Divide fractions: $\dfrac{7}{x} \div \dfrac{3}{2} = \dfrac{7}{x} \cdot \dfrac{2}{3} = \dfrac{14}{3x}$

c. Add fractions with unlike denominators: $\dfrac{x}{3} + \dfrac{2x}{5} = \dfrac{5 \cdot x + 3 \cdot 2x}{3 \cdot 5} = \dfrac{11x}{15}$

✓CHECKPOINT Now try Exercise 103.

If a, b, and c are integers such that $ab = c$, then a and b are **factors** or **divisors** of c. A **prime number** is an integer that has exactly two positive factors—itself and 1—such as 2, 3, 5, 7, and 11. The numbers 4, 6, 8, 9, and 10 are **composite** because each can be written as the product of two or more prime numbers. The number 1 is neither prime nor composite. The **Fundamental Theorem of Arithmetic** states that every positive integer greater than 1 can be written as the product of prime numbers in precisely one way (disregarding order). For instance, the *prime factorization* of 24 is $24 = 2 \cdot 2 \cdot 2 \cdot 3$.

A.1 Exercises

VOCABULARY CHECK: Fill in the blanks.

1. A real number is ________ if it can be written as the ratio $\frac{p}{q}$ of two integers, where $q \neq 0$.
2. ________ numbers have infinite nonrepeating decimal representations.
3. The distance between a point on the real number line and the origin is the ________ ________ of the real number.
4. A number that can be written as the product of two or more prime numbers is called a ________ number.
5. An integer that has exactly two positive factors, the integer itself and 1, is called a ________ number.
6. An algebraic expression is a collection of letters called ________ and real numbers called ________.
7. The ________ of an algebraic expression are those parts separated by addition.
8. The numerical factor of a variable term is the ________ of the variable term.
9. The ________ ________ states that if $ab = 0$, then $a = 0$ or $b = 0$.

In Exercises 1–6, determine which numbers in the set are (a) natural numbers, (b) whole numbers, (c) integers, (d) rational numbers, and (e) irrational numbers.

1. $-9, -\frac{7}{2}, 5, \frac{2}{3}, \sqrt{2}, 0, 1, -4, 2, -11$
2. $\sqrt{5}, -7, -\frac{7}{3}, 0, 3.12, \frac{5}{4}, -3, 12, 5$
3. $2.01, 0.666 \ldots, -13, 0.010110111 \ldots, 1, -6$
4. $2.3030030003 \ldots, 0.7575, -4.63, \sqrt{10}, -75, 4$
5. $-\pi, -\frac{1}{3}, \frac{6}{3}, \frac{1}{2}\sqrt{2}, -7.5, -1, 8, -22$
6. $25, -17, -\frac{12}{5}, \sqrt{9}, 3.12, \frac{1}{2}\pi, 7, -11.1, 13$

In Exercises 7–10, use a calculator to find the decimal form of the rational number. If it is a nonterminating decimal, write the repeating pattern.

7. $\frac{5}{8}$
8. $\frac{1}{3}$
9. $\frac{41}{333}$
10. $\frac{6}{11}$

In Exercises 11 and 12, approximate the numbers and place the correct symbol (< or >) between them.

11. 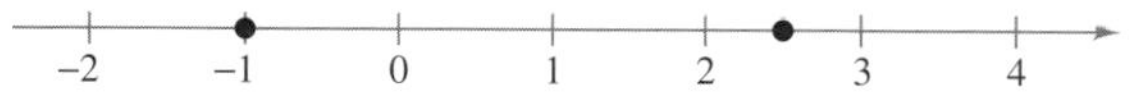

12. 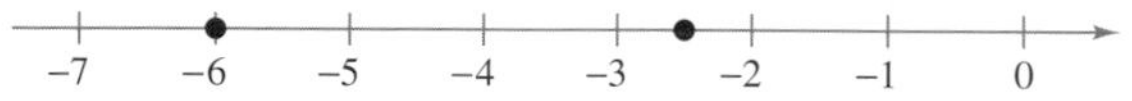

In Exercises 13–18, plot the two real numbers on the real number line. Then place the appropriate inequality symbol (< or >) between them.

13. $-4, -8$
14. $-3.5, 1$
15. $\frac{3}{2}, 7$
16. $1, \frac{16}{3}$
17. $\frac{5}{6}, \frac{2}{3}$
18. $-\frac{8}{7}, -\frac{3}{7}$

In Exercises 19–30, (a) give a verbal description of the subset of real numbers represented by the inequality or the interval, (b) sketch the subset on the real number line, and (c) state whether the interval is bounded or unbounded.

19. $x \leq 5$
20. $x \geq -2$
21. $x < 0$
22. $x > 3$
23. $[4, \infty)$
24. $(-\infty, 2)$
25. $-2 < x < 2$
26. $0 \leq x \leq 5$
27. $-1 \leq x < 0$
28. $0 < x \leq 6$
29. $[-2, 5)$
30. $(-1, 2]$

In Exercises 31–38, use inequality notation to describe the set.

31. All x in the interval $(-2, 4]$
32. All y in the interval $[-6, 0)$
33. y is nonnegative.
34. y is no more than 25.
35. t is at least 10 and at most 22.
36. k is less than 5 but no less than -3.
37. The dog's weight W is more than 65 pounds.
38. The annual rate of inflation r is expected to be at least 2.5% but no more than 5%.

In Exercises 39–48, evaluate the expression.

39. $|-10|$
40. $|0|$
41. $|3 - 8|$
42. $|4 - 1|$
43. $|-1| - |-2|$
44. $-3 - |-3|$
45. $\dfrac{-5}{|-5|}$
46. $-3|-3|$
47. $\dfrac{|x + 2|}{x + 2}, \quad x < -2$
48. $\dfrac{|x - 1|}{x - 1}, \quad x > 1$

In Exercises 49–54, place the correct symbol (<, >, or =) between the pair of real numbers.

49. $|-3| \quad \square \quad -|-3|$

50. $|-4| \quad \square \quad |4|$

51. $-5 \quad \square \quad -|5|$

52. $-|-6| \quad \square \quad |-6|$

53. $-|-2| \quad \square \quad -|2|$

54. $-(-2) \quad \square \quad -2$

In Exercises 55–60, find the distance between *a* and *b*.

55. $a = 126, b = 75$

56. $a = -126, b = -75$

57. $a = -\frac{5}{2}, b = 0$

58. $a = \frac{1}{4}, b = \frac{11}{4}$

59. $a = \frac{16}{5}, b = \frac{112}{75}$

60. $a = 9.34, b = -5.65$

Budget Variance **In Exercises 61–64, the accounting department of a sports drink bottling company is checking to see whether the actual expenses of a department differ from the budgeted expenses by more than \$500 or by more than 5%. Fill in the missing parts of the table, and determine whether each actual expense passes the "budget variance test."**

	Budgeted Expense, b	*Actual Expense, a*	$\lvert a - b \rvert$	$0.05b$
61. Wages	\$112,700	\$113,356		
62. Utilities	\$9,400	\$9,772		
63. Taxes	\$37,640	\$37,335		
64. Insurance	\$2,575	\$2,613		

65. ***Federal Deficit*** The bar graph shows the federal government receipts (in billions of dollars) for selected years from 1960 through 2000. (Source: U.S. Office of Management and Budget)

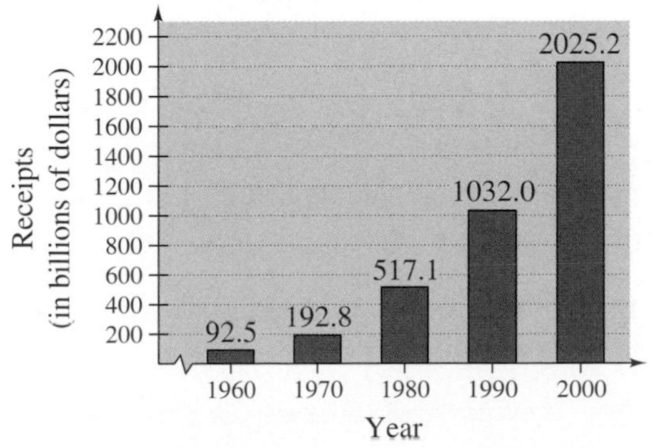

(a) Complete the table. (*Hint:* Find $|\text{Receipts} - \text{Expenditures}|$.)

Year	Expenditures (in billions)	Surplus or deficit (in billions)
1960	\$92.2	
1970	\$195.6	
1980	\$590.9	
1990	\$1253.2	
2000	\$1788.8	

(b) Use the table in part (a) to construct a bar graph showing the magnitude of the surplus or deficit for each year.

66. ***Veterans*** The table shows the number of living veterans (in thousands) in the United States in 2002 by age group. Construct a circle graph showing the percent of living veterans by age group as a fraction of the total number of living veterans. (Source: Department of Veteran Affairs)

Age group	Number of veterans
Under 35	2213
35–44	3290
45–54	4666
55–64	5665
65 and older	9784

In Exercises 67–72, use absolute value notation to describe the situation.

67. The distance between x and 5 is no more than 3.

68. The distance between x and -10 is at least 6.

69. y is at least six units from 0.

70. y is at most two units from a.

71. While traveling on the Pennsylvania Turnpike, you pass milepost 326 near Valley Forge, then milepost 351 near Philadelphia. How many miles do you travel during that time period?

72. The temperature in Chicago, Illinois was 48° last night at midnight, then 82° at noon today. What was the change in temperature over the 12-hour period?

In Exercises 73–78, identify the terms. Then identify the coefficients of the variable terms of the expression.

73. $7x + 4$

74. $6x^3 - 5x$

75. $\sqrt{3}x^2 - 8x - 11$

76. $3\sqrt{3}x^2 + 1$

77. $4x^3 + \frac{x}{2} - 5$

78. $3x^4 - \frac{x^2}{4}$

In Exercises 79–84, evaluate the expression for each value of *x*. (If not possible, state the reason.)

	Expression	*Values*	
79.	$4x - 6$	(a) $x = -1$	(b) $x = 0$
80.	$9 - 7x$	(a) $x = -3$	(b) $x = 3$
81.	$x^2 - 3x + 4$	(a) $x = -2$	(b) $x = 2$
82.	$-x^2 + 5x - 4$	(a) $x = -1$	(b) $x = 1$
83.	$\frac{x+1}{x-1}$	(a) $x = 1$	(b) $x = -1$
84.	$\frac{x}{x+2}$	(a) $x = 2$	(b) $x = -2$

In Exercises 85–96, identify the rule(s) of algebra illustrated by the statement.

85. $x + 9 = 9 + x$

86. $2\left(\frac{1}{2}\right) = 1$

87. $\frac{1}{h+6}(h + 6) = 1, \quad h \neq -6$

88. $(x + 3) - (x + 3) = 0$

89. $2(x + 3) = 2 \cdot x + 2 \cdot 3$

90. $(z - 2) + 0 = z - 2$

91. $1 \cdot (1 + x) = 1 + x$

92. $(z + 5)x = z \cdot x + 5 \cdot x$

93. $x + (y + 10) = (x + y) + 10$

94. $x(3y) = (x \cdot 3)y = (3x)y$

95. $3(t - 4) = 3 \cdot t - 3 \cdot 4$

96. $\frac{1}{7}(7 \cdot 12) = \left(\frac{1}{7} \cdot 7\right)12 = 1 \cdot 12 = 12$

In Exercises 97–104, perform the operation(s). (Write fractional answers in simplest form.)

97. $\frac{3}{16} + \frac{5}{16}$

98. $\frac{6}{7} - \frac{4}{7}$

99. $\frac{5}{8} - \frac{5}{12} + \frac{1}{6}$

100. $\frac{10}{11} + \frac{6}{33} - \frac{13}{66}$

101. $12 \div \frac{1}{4}$

102. $-\left(6 \cdot \frac{4}{8}\right)$

103. $\frac{2x}{3} - \frac{x}{4}$

104. $\frac{5x}{6} \cdot \frac{2}{9}$

105. (a) Use a calculator to complete the table.

n	1	0.5	0.01	0.0001	0.000001
$5/n$					

(b) Use the result from part (a) to make a conjecture about the value of $5/n$ as n approaches 0.

106. (a) Use a calculator to complete the table.

n	1	10	100	10,000	100,000
$5/n$					

(b) Use the result from part (a) to make a conjecture about the value of $5/n$ as n increases without bound.

Synthesis

True or False? **In Exercises 107 and 108, determine whether the statement is true or false. Justify your answer.**

107. If $a < b$, then $\frac{1}{a} < \frac{1}{b}$, where $a \neq b \neq 0$.

108. Because $\frac{a+b}{c} = \frac{a}{c} + \frac{b}{c}$, then $\frac{c}{a+b} = \frac{c}{a} + \frac{c}{b}$.

109. ***Exploration*** Consider $|u + v|$ and $|u| + |v|$, where $u \neq v \neq 0$.

(a) Are the values of the expressions always equal? If not, under what conditions are they unequal?

(b) If the two expressions are not equal for certain values of u and v, is one of the expressions always greater than the other? Explain.

110. ***Think About It*** Is there a difference between saying that a real number is positive and saying that a real number is nonnegative? Explain.

111. ***Think About It*** Because every even number is divisible by 2, is it possible that there exist any even prime numbers? Explain.

112. ***Writing*** Describe the differences among the sets of natural numbers, whole numbers, integers, rational numbers, and irrational numbers.

In Exercises 113 and 114, use the real numbers *A*, *B*, and *C* shown on the number line. Determine the sign of each expression.

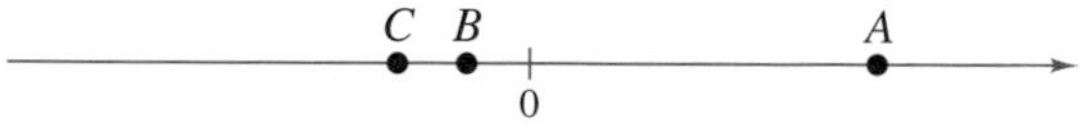

113. (a) $-A$ (b) $B - A$

114. (a) $-C$ (b) $A - C$

115. ***Writing*** Can it ever be true that $|a| = -a$ for a real number a? Explain.

A.2 Exponents and Radicals

What you should learn

- Use properties of exponents.
- Use scientific notation to represent real numbers.
- Use properties of radicals.
- Simplify and combine radicals.
- Rationalize denominators and numerators.
- Use properties of rational exponents.

Why you should learn it

Real numbers and algebraic expressions are often written with exponents and radicals. For instance, in Exercise 105 on page A22, you will use an expression involving rational exponents to find the time required for a funnel to empty for different water heights.

Integer Exponents

Repeated *multiplication* can be written in **exponential form.**

Repeated Multiplication	*Exponential Form*
$a \cdot a \cdot a \cdot a \cdot a$	a^5
$(-4)(-4)(-4)$	$(-4)^3$
$(2x)(2x)(2x)(2x)$	$(2x)^4$

Exponential Notation

If a is a real number and n is a positive integer, then

$$a^n = \underbrace{a \cdot a \cdot a \cdot \cdot \cdot a}_{n \text{ factors}}$$

where n is the **exponent** and a is the **base.** The expression a^n is read "a to the nth **power.**"

An exponent can also be negative. In Property 3 below, be sure you see how to use a negative exponent.

Properties of Exponents

Let a and b be real numbers, variables, or algebraic expressions, and let m and n be integers. (All denominators and bases are nonzero.)

Property	*Example*
1. $a^m a^n = a^{m+n}$	$3^2 \cdot 3^4 = 3^{2+4} = 3^6 = 729$
2. $\dfrac{a^m}{a^n} = a^{m-n}$	$\dfrac{x^7}{x^4} = x^{7-4} = x^3$
3. $a^{-n} = \dfrac{1}{a^n} = \left(\dfrac{1}{a}\right)^n$	$y^{-4} = \dfrac{1}{y^4} = \left(\dfrac{1}{y}\right)^4$
4. $a^0 = 1, \quad a \neq 0$	$(x^2+1)^0 = 1$
5. $(ab)^m = a^m b^m$	$(5x)^3 = 5^3x^3 = 125x^3$
6. $(a^m)^n = a^{mn}$	$(y^3)^{-4} = y^{3(-4)} = y^{-12} = \dfrac{1}{y^{12}}$
7. $\left(\dfrac{a}{b}\right)^m = \dfrac{a^m}{b^m}$	$\left(\dfrac{2}{x}\right)^3 = \dfrac{2^3}{x^3} = \dfrac{8}{x^3}$
8. $\lvert a^2 \rvert = \lvert a \rvert^2 = a^2$	$\lvert(-2)^2\rvert = \lvert -2 \rvert^2 = (2)^2 = 4$

Technology

You can use a calculator to evaluate exponential expressions. When doing so, it is important to know when to use parentheses because the calculator follows the order of operations. For instance, evaluate $(-2)^4$ as follows

Scientific:

(2 +/−) y^x 4 =

Graphing:

((−) 2) ^ 4 ENTER

The display will be 16. If you omit the parentheses, the display will be -16.

It is important to recognize the difference between expressions such as $(-2)^4$ and -2^4. In $(-2)^4$, the parentheses indicate that the exponent applies to the negative sign as well as to the 2, but in $-2^4 = -(2^4)$, the exponent applies only to the 2. So, $(-2)^4 = 16$ and $-2^4 = -16$.

The properties of exponents listed on the preceding page apply to *all* integers m and n, not just to positive integers as shown in the examples in this section.

Example 1 Using Properties of Exponents

Use the properties of exponents to simplify each expression.

a. $(-3ab^4)(4ab^{-3})$ **b.** $(2xy^2)^3$ **c.** $3a(-4a^2)^0$ **d.** $\left(\dfrac{5x^3}{y}\right)^2$

Solution

a. $(-3ab^4)(4ab^{-3}) = (-3)(4)(a)(a)(b^4)(b^{-3}) = -12a^2b$

b. $(2xy^2)^3 = 2^3(x)^3(y^2)^3 = 8x^3y^6$

c. $3a(-4a^2)^0 = 3a(1) = 3a, \quad a \neq 0$

d. $\left(\dfrac{5x^3}{x}\right)^2 = \dfrac{5^2(x^3)^2}{y^2} = \dfrac{25x^6}{y^2}$

CHECKPOINT Now try Exercise 25.

Example 2 Rewriting with Positive Exponents

Rewrite each expression with positive exponents.

a. x^{-1} **b.** $\dfrac{1}{3x^{-2}}$ **c.** $\dfrac{12a^3b^{-4}}{4a^{-2}b}$ **d.** $\left(\dfrac{3x^2}{y}\right)^{-2}$

Solution

a. $x^{-1} = \dfrac{1}{x}$ Property 3

b. $\dfrac{1}{3x^{-2}} = \dfrac{1(x^2)}{3} = \dfrac{x^2}{3}$ The exponent -2 does not apply to 3.

c. $\dfrac{12a^3b^{-4}}{4a^{-2}b} = \dfrac{12a^3 \cdot a^2}{4b \cdot b^4} = \dfrac{3a^5}{b^5}$ Properties 3 and 1

d. $\left(\dfrac{3x^2}{y}\right)^{-2} = \dfrac{3^{-2}(x^2)^{-2}}{y^{-2}}$ Properties 5 and 7

$= \dfrac{3^{-2}x^{-4}}{y^{-2}}$ Property 6

$= \dfrac{y^2}{3^2x^4}$ Property 3

$= \dfrac{y^2}{9x^4}$ Simplify.

CHECKPOINT Now try Exercise 33.

STUDY TIP

Rarely in algebra is there only one way to solve a problem. Don't be concerned if the steps you use to solve a problem are not exactly the same as the steps presented in this text. The important thing is to use steps that you understand and, of course, steps that are justified by the rules of algebra. For instance, you might prefer the following steps for Example 2(d).

$$\left(\frac{3x^2}{y}\right)^{-2} = \left(\frac{y}{3x^2}\right)^2 = \frac{y^2}{9x^4}$$

Note how Property 3 is used in the first step of this solution. The fractional form of this property is

$$\left(\frac{a}{b}\right)^{-m} = \left(\frac{b}{a}\right)^m.$$

Scientific Notation

Exponents provide an efficient way of writing and computing with very large (or very small) numbers. For instance, there are about 359 billion billion gallons of water on Earth—that is, 359 followed by 18 zeros.

$$359{,}000{,}000{,}000{,}000{,}000{,}000$$

It is convenient to write such numbers in **scientific notation.** This notation has the form $\pm c \times 10^n$, where $1 \le c < 10$ and n is an integer. So, the number of gallons of water on Earth can be written in scientific notation as

$$3.59 \times 100{,}000{,}000{,}000{,}000{,}000{,}000 = 3.59 \times 10^{20}.$$

The *positive* exponent 20 indicates that the number is *large* (10 or more) and that the decimal point has been moved 20 places. A *negative* exponent indicates that the number is *small* (less than 1). For instance, the mass (in grams) of one electron is approximately

$$9.0 \times 10^{-28} = 0.\underbrace{0000000000000000000000000009}_{\text{28 decimal places}}.$$

Example 3 Scientific Notation

Write each number in scientific notation.

a. 0.0000782 **b.** 836,100,000

Solution

a. $0.0000782 = 7.82 \times 10^{-5}$ **b.** $836{,}100{,}000 = 8.361 \times 10^{8}$

✓CHECKPOINT Now try Exercise 37.

Example 4 Decimal Notation

Write each number in decimal notation.

a. 9.36×10^{-6} **b.** 1.345×10^{2}

Solution

a. $9.36 \times 10^{-6} = 0.00000936$ **b.** $1.345 \times 10^{2} = 134.5$

✓CHECKPOINT Now try Exercise 41.

Technology

Most calculators automatically switch to scientific notation when they are showing large (or small) numbers that exceed the display range.

To *enter* numbers in scientific notation, your calculator should have an exponential entry key labeled

[EE] or [EXP].

Consult the user's guide for your calculator for instructions on keystrokes and how numbers in scientific notation are displayed.

Radicals and Their Properties

A **square root** of a number is one of its two equal factors. For example, 5 is a square root of 25 because 5 is one of the two equal factors of 25. In a similar way, a **cube root** of a number is one of its three equal factors, as in $125 = 5^3$.

Definition of *n*th Root of a Number

Let a and b be real numbers and let $n \geq 2$ be a positive integer. If

$$a = b^n$$

then b is an ***n*th root of *a*.** If $n = 2$, the root is a **square root.** If $n = 3$, the root is a **cube root.**

Some numbers have more than one nth root. For example, both 5 and -5 are square roots of 25. The *principal square root* of 25, written as $\sqrt{25}$, is the positive root, 5. The **principal *n*th root** of a number is defined as follows.

Principal *n*th Root of a Number

Let a be a real number that has at least one nth root. The **principal *n*th root of *a*** is the nth root that has the same sign as a. It is denoted by a **radical symbol**

$$\sqrt[n]{a}. \qquad \text{Principal } n\text{th root}$$

The positive integer n is the **index** of the radical, and the number a is the **radicand.** If $n = 2$, omit the index and write $\sqrt{a}$ rather than $\sqrt[2]{a}$. (The plural of index is *indices.*)

A common misunderstanding is that the square root sign implies both negative and positive roots. This is not correct. The square root sign implies only a positive root. When a negative root is needed, you must use the negative sign with the square root sign.

Incorrect: ~~$\sqrt{4} = \pm 2$~~ *Correct:* $-\sqrt{4} = -2$ *and* $\sqrt{4} = 2$

Example 5 Evaluating Expressions Involving Radicals

a. $\sqrt{36} = 6$ because $6^2 = 36$.

b. $-\sqrt{36} = -6$ because $-(\sqrt{36}) = -(\sqrt{6^2}) = -(6) = -6$.

c. $\sqrt[3]{\dfrac{125}{64}} = \dfrac{5}{4}$ because $\left(\dfrac{5}{4}\right)^3 = \dfrac{5^3}{4^3} = \dfrac{125}{64}$.

d. $\sqrt[5]{-32} = -2$ because $(-2)^5 = -32$.

e. $\sqrt[4]{-81}$ is not a real number because there is no real number that can be raised to the fourth power to produce -81.

CHECKPOINT Now try Exercise 51.

Here are some generalizations about the nth roots of real numbers.

Generalizations About nth Roots of Real Numbers			
Real Number a	Integer n	Root(s) of a	Example
$a > 0$	$n > 0$, is even.	$\sqrt[n]{a},\ -\sqrt[n]{a}$	$\sqrt[4]{81} = 3,\ -\sqrt[4]{81} = -3$
$a > 0$ or $a < 0$	n is odd.	$\sqrt[n]{a}$	$\sqrt[3]{-8} = -2$
$a < 0$	n is even.	No real roots	$\sqrt{-4}$ is not a real number.
$a = 0$	n is even or odd.	$\sqrt[n]{0} = 0$	$\sqrt[5]{0} = 0$

Integers such as 1, 4, 9, 16, 25, and 36 are called **perfect squares** because they have integer square roots. Similarly, integers such as 1, 8, 27, 64, and 125 are called **perfect cubes** because they have integer cube roots.

Properties of Radicals

Let a and b be real numbers, variables, or algebraic expressions such that the indicated roots are real numbers, and let m and n be positive integers.

Property	*Example*
1. $\sqrt[n]{a^m} = \left(\sqrt[n]{a}\right)^m$	$\sqrt[3]{8^2} = \left(\sqrt[3]{8}\right)^2 = (2)^2 = 4$
2. $\sqrt[n]{a} \cdot \sqrt[n]{b} = \sqrt[n]{ab}$	$\sqrt{5} \cdot \sqrt{7} = \sqrt{5 \cdot 7} = \sqrt{35}$
3. $\dfrac{\sqrt[n]{a}}{\sqrt[n]{b}} = \sqrt[n]{\dfrac{a}{b}}, \quad b \neq 0$	$\dfrac{\sqrt[4]{27}}{\sqrt[4]{9}} = \sqrt[4]{\dfrac{27}{9}} = \sqrt[4]{3}$
4. $\sqrt[m]{\sqrt[n]{a}} = \sqrt[mn]{a}$	$\sqrt[3]{\sqrt{10}} = \sqrt[6]{10}$
5. $\left(\sqrt[n]{a}\right)^n = a$	$\left(\sqrt{3}\right)^2 = 3$
6. For n even, $\sqrt[n]{a^n} = \lvert a \rvert$.	$\sqrt{(-12)^2} = \lvert -12 \rvert = 12$
For n odd, $\sqrt[n]{a^n} = a$.	$\sqrt[3]{(-12)^3} = -12$

A common special case of Property 6 is $\sqrt{a^2} = \lvert a \rvert$.

Example 6 Using Properties of Radicals

Use the properties of radicals to simplify each expression.

a. $\sqrt{8} \cdot \sqrt{2}$ **b.** $\left(\sqrt[3]{5}\right)^3$ **c.** $\sqrt[3]{x^3}$ **d.** $\sqrt[6]{y^6}$

Solution

a. $\sqrt{8} \cdot \sqrt{2} = \sqrt{8 \cdot 2} = \sqrt{16} = 4$

b. $\left(\sqrt[3]{5}\right)^3 = 5$

c. $\sqrt[3]{x^3} = x$

d. $\sqrt[6]{y^6} = \lvert y \rvert$

CHECKPOINT Now try Exercise 61.

Simplifying Radicals

An expression involving radicals is in **simplest form** when the following conditions are satisfied.

1. All possible factors have been removed from the radical.
2. All fractions have radical-free denominators (accomplished by a process called *rationalizing the denominator*).
3. The index of the radical is reduced.

To simplify a radical, factor the radicand into factors whose exponents are multiples of the index. The roots of these factors are written outside the radical, and the "leftover" factors make up the new radicand.

STUDY TIP

When you simplify a radical, it is important that both expressions are defined for the same values of the variable. For instance, in Example 7(b), $\sqrt{75x^3}$ and $5x\sqrt{3x}$ are both defined only for nonnegative values of x. Similarly, in Example 7(c), $\sqrt[4]{(5x)^4}$ and $5|x|$ are both defined for all real values of x.

Example 7 Simplifying Even Roots

(Perfect 4th power: 16; Leftover factor: 3)

a. $\sqrt[4]{48} = \sqrt[4]{16 \cdot 3} = \sqrt[4]{2^4 \cdot 3} = 2\sqrt[4]{3}$

(Perfect square: $25x^2$; Leftover factor: $3x$)

b. $\sqrt{75x^3} = \sqrt{25x^2 \cdot 3x}$ Find largest square factor.

$= \sqrt{(5x)^2 \cdot 3x}$

$= 5x\sqrt{3x}$ Find root of perfect square.

c. $\sqrt[4]{(5x)^4} = |5x| = 5|x|$

✓CHECKPOINT Now try Exercise 63(a).

Example 8 Simplifying Odd Roots

(Perfect cube: 8; Leftover factor: 3)

a. $\sqrt[3]{24} = \sqrt[3]{8 \cdot 3} = \sqrt[3]{2^3 \cdot 3} = 2\sqrt[3]{3}$

(Perfect cube: $8a^3$; Leftover factor: $3a$)

b. $\sqrt[3]{24a^4} = \sqrt[3]{8a^3 \cdot 3a}$ Find largest cube factor.

$= \sqrt[3]{(2a)^3 \cdot 3a}$

$= 2a\sqrt[3]{3a}$ Find root of perfect cube.

c. $\sqrt[3]{-40x^6} = \sqrt[3]{(-8x^6) \cdot 5}$ Find largest cube factor.

$= \sqrt[3]{(-2x^2)^3 \cdot 5}$

$= -2x^2\sqrt[3]{5}$ Find root of perfect cube.

✓CHECKPOINT Now try Exercise 63(b).

Radical expressions can be combined (added or subtracted) if they are **like radicals**—that is, if they have the same index and radicand. For instance, $\sqrt{2}$, $3\sqrt{2}$, and $\frac{1}{2}\sqrt{2}$ are like radicals, but $\sqrt{3}$ and $\sqrt{2}$ are unlike radicals. To determine whether two radicals can be combined, you should first simplify each radical.

Example 9 **Combining Radicals**

a. $2\sqrt{48} - 3\sqrt{27} = 2\sqrt{16 \cdot 3} - 3\sqrt{9 \cdot 3}$ Find square factors.

$= 8\sqrt{3} - 9\sqrt{3}$ Find square roots and multiply by coefficients.

$= (8 - 9)\sqrt{3}$ Combine like terms.

$= -\sqrt{3}$ Simplify.

b. $\sqrt[3]{16x} - \sqrt[3]{54x^4} = \sqrt[3]{8 \cdot 2x} - \sqrt[3]{27 \cdot x^3 \cdot 2x}$ Find cube factors.

$= 2\sqrt[3]{2x} - 3x\sqrt[3]{2x}$ Find cube roots.

$= (2 - 3x)\sqrt[3]{2x}$ Combine like terms.

CHECKPOINT Now try Exercise 71.

Rationalizing Denominators and Numerators

To rationalize a denominator or numerator of the form $a - b\sqrt{m}$ or $a + b\sqrt{m}$, multiply both numerator and denominator by a **conjugate:** $a + b\sqrt{m}$ and $a - b\sqrt{m}$ are conjugates of each other. If $a = 0$, then the rationalizing factor for $\sqrt{m}$ is itself, $\sqrt{m}$. For cube roots, choose a rationalizing factor that generates a perfect cube.

Example 10 **Rationalizing Single-Term Denominators**

Rationalize the denominator of each expression.

a. $\dfrac{5}{2\sqrt{3}}$ **b.** $\dfrac{2}{\sqrt[3]{5}}$

Solution

a. $\dfrac{5}{2\sqrt{3}} = \dfrac{5}{2\sqrt{3}} \cdot \dfrac{\sqrt{3}}{\sqrt{3}}$ $\sqrt{3}$ is rationalizing factor.

$= \dfrac{5\sqrt{3}}{2(3)}$ Multiply.

$= \dfrac{5\sqrt{3}}{6}$ Simplify.

b. $\dfrac{2}{\sqrt[3]{5}} = \dfrac{2}{\sqrt[3]{5}} \cdot \dfrac{\sqrt[3]{5^2}}{\sqrt[3]{5^2}}$ $\sqrt[3]{5^2}$ is rationalizing factor.

$= \dfrac{2\sqrt[3]{5^2}}{\sqrt[3]{5^3}}$ Multiply.

$= \dfrac{2\sqrt[3]{25}}{5}$ Simplify.

CHECKPOINT Now try Exercise 79.

Example 11 Rationalizing a Denominator with Two Terms

$$\frac{2}{3+\sqrt{7}} = \frac{2}{3+\sqrt{7}} \cdot \frac{3-\sqrt{7}}{3-\sqrt{7}}$$ Multiply numerator and denominator by conjugate of denominator.

$$= \frac{2(3-\sqrt{7})}{3(3)+3(-\sqrt{7})+\sqrt{7}(3)-(\sqrt{7})(\sqrt{7})}$$ Use Distributive Property.

$$= \frac{2(3-\sqrt{7})}{(3)^2-(\sqrt{7})^2}$$ Simplify.

$$= \frac{2(3-\sqrt{7})}{9-7}$$ Square terms of denominator.

$$= \frac{2(3-\sqrt{7})}{2} = 3-\sqrt{7}$$ Simplify.

CHECKPOINT Now try Exercise 81.

Sometimes it is necessary to rationalize the numerator of an expression. For instance, in Appendix A.4 you will use the technique shown in the next example to rationalize the numerator of an expression from calculus.

STUDY TIP

Do not confuse the expression $\sqrt{5}+\sqrt{7}$ with the expression $\sqrt{5+7}$. In general, $\sqrt{x+y}$ does not equal $\sqrt{x}+\sqrt{y}$. Similarly, $\sqrt{x^2+y^2}$ does not equal $x+y$.

Example 12 Rationalizing a Numerator

$$\frac{\sqrt{5}-\sqrt{7}}{2} = \frac{\sqrt{5}-\sqrt{7}}{2} \cdot \frac{\sqrt{5}+\sqrt{7}}{\sqrt{5}+\sqrt{7}}$$ Multiply numerator and denominator by conjugate of numerator.

$$= \frac{(\sqrt{5})^2-(\sqrt{7})^2}{2(\sqrt{5}+\sqrt{7})}$$ Simplify.

$$= \frac{5-7}{2(\sqrt{5}+\sqrt{7})}$$ Square terms of numerator.

$$= \frac{-2}{2(\sqrt{5}+\sqrt{7})} = \frac{-1}{\sqrt{5}+\sqrt{7}}$$ Simplify.

CHECKPOINT Now try Exercise 85.

Rational Exponents

Definition of Rational Exponents

If a is a real number and n is a positive integer such that the principal nth root of a exists, then $a^{1/n}$ is defined as

$$a^{1/n} = \sqrt[n]{a}, \text{ where } 1/n \text{ is the } \textbf{rational exponent} \text{ of } a.$$

Moreover, if m is a positive integer that has no common factor with n, then

$$a^{m/n} = (a^{1/n})^m = (\sqrt[n]{a})^m \quad \text{and} \quad a^{m/n} = (a^m)^{1/n} = \sqrt[n]{a^m}.$$

The symbol ∫ indicates an example or exercise that highlights algebraic techniques specifically used in calculus.

STUDY TIP

Rational exponents can be tricky, and you must remember that the expression $b^{m/n}$ is not defined unless $\sqrt[n]{b}$ is a real number. This restriction produces some unusual-looking results. For instance, the number $(-8)^{1/3}$ is defined because $\sqrt[3]{-8} = -2$, but the number $(-8)^{2/6}$ is undefined because $\sqrt[6]{-8}$ is not a real number.

The numerator of a rational exponent denotes the *power* to which the base is raised, and the denominator denotes the *index* or the *root* to be taken.

Power

Index

$$b^{m/n} = \left(\sqrt[n]{b}\right)^m = \sqrt[n]{b^m}$$

When you are working with rational exponents, the properties of integer exponents still apply. For instance,

$$2^{1/2}2^{1/3} = 2^{(1/2)+(1/3)} = 2^{5/6}.$$

Example 13 Changing from Radical to Exponential Form

a. $\sqrt{3} = 3^{1/2}$

b. $\sqrt{(3xy)^5} = \sqrt[2]{(3xy)^5} = (3xy)^{(5/2)}$

c. $2x\sqrt[4]{x^3} = (2x)(x^{3/4}) = 2x^{1+(3/4)} = 2x^{7/4}$

✓CHECKPOINT Now try Exercise 87.

Technology

There are four methods of evaluating radicals on most graphing calculators. For square roots, you can use the *square root key* $\boxed{\sqrt{\ }}$. For cube roots, you can use the *cube root key* $\boxed{\sqrt[3]{\ }}$. For other roots, you can first convert the radical to exponential form and then use the *exponential key* $\boxed{\wedge}$, or you can use the *xth root key* $\boxed{\sqrt[x]{\ }}$. Consult the user's guide for your calculator for specific keystrokes.

Example 14 Changing from Exponential to Radical Form

a. $(x^2 + y^2)^{3/2} = \left(\sqrt{x^2 + y^2}\right)^3 = \sqrt{(x^2 + y^2)^3}$

b. $2y^{3/4}z^{1/4} = 2(y^3z)^{1/4} = 2\sqrt[4]{y^3z}$

c. $a^{-3/2} = \dfrac{1}{a^{3/2}} = \dfrac{1}{\sqrt{a^3}}$ **d.** $x^{0.2} = x^{1/5} = \sqrt[5]{x}$

✓CHECKPOINT Now try Exercise 89.

Rational exponents are useful for evaluating roots of numbers on a calculator, for reducing the index of a radical, and for simplifying expressions in calculus.

Example 15 Simplifying with Rational Exponents

a. $(-32)^{-4/5} = \left(\sqrt[5]{-32}\right)^{-4} = (-2)^{-4} = \dfrac{1}{(-2)^4} = \dfrac{1}{16}$

b. $(-5x^{5/3})(3x^{-3/4}) = -15x^{(5/3)-(3/4)} = -15x^{11/12}, \quad x \neq 0$

c. $\sqrt[9]{a^3} = a^{3/9} = a^{1/3} = \sqrt[3]{a}$ Reduce index.

d. $\sqrt[3]{\sqrt{125}} = \sqrt[6]{125} = \sqrt[6]{(5)^3} = 5^{3/6} = 5^{1/2} = \sqrt{5}$

e. $(2x - 1)^{4/3}(2x - 1)^{-1/3} = (2x - 1)^{(4/3)-(1/3)}$

$$= 2x - 1, \quad x \neq \frac{1}{2}$$

f. $\dfrac{x - 1}{(x - 1)^{-1/2}} = \dfrac{x - 1}{(x - 1)^{-1/2}} \cdot \dfrac{(x - 1)^{1/2}}{(x - 1)^{1/2}}$

$$= \frac{(x - 1)^{3/2}}{(x - 1)^0}$$

$$= (x - 1)^{3/2}, \quad x \neq 1$$

✓CHECKPOINT Now try Exercise 99.

A.2 Exercises

VOCABULARY CHECK: Fill in the blanks.

1. In the exponential form a^n, n is the ________ and a is the ________.
2. A convenient way of writing very large or very small numbers is called ________ ________.
3. One of the two equal factors of a number is called a __________ __________ of the number.
4. The ________ ________ ________ of a number is the nth root that has the same sign as a, and is denoted by $\sqrt[n]{a}$.
5. In the radical form, $\sqrt[n]{a}$ the positive integer n is called the ________ of the radical and the number a is called the ________.
6. When an expression involving radicals has all possible factors removed, radical-free denominators, and a reduced index, it is in ________ ________.
7. The expressions $a + b\sqrt{m}$ and $a - b\sqrt{m}$ are ________ of each other.
8. The process used to create a radical-free denominator is know as ________ the denominator.
9. In the expression $b^{m/n}$, m denotes the ________ to which the base is raised and n denotes the ________ or root to be taken.

In Exercises 1 and 2, write the expression as a repeated multiplication problem.

1. 8^5 2. $(-2)^7$

In Exercises 3 and 4, write the expression using exponential notation.

3. $(4.9)(4.9)(4.9)(4.9)(4.9)(4.9)$
4. $(-10)(-10)(-10)(-10)(-10)$

In Exercises 5–12, evaluate each expression.

5. (a) $3^2 \cdot 3$ (b) $3 \cdot 3^3$
6. (a) $\dfrac{5^5}{5^2}$ (b) $\dfrac{3^2}{3^4}$
7. (a) $(3^3)^0$ (b) -3^2
8. (a) $(2^3 \cdot 3^2)^2$ (b) $\left(-\frac{3}{5}\right)^3\left(\frac{5}{3}\right)^2$
9. (a) $\dfrac{3 \cdot 4^{-4}}{3^{-4} \cdot 4^{-1}}$ (b) $32(-2)^{-5}$
10. (a) $\dfrac{4 \cdot 3^{-2}}{2^{-2} \cdot 3^{-1}}$ (b) $(-2)^0$
11. (a) $2^{-1} + 3^{-1}$ (b) $(2^{-1})^{-2}$
12. (a) $3^{-1} + 2^{-2}$ (b) $(3^{-2})^2$

In Exercises 13–16, use a calculator to evaluate the expression. (If necessary, round your answer to three decimal places.)

13. $(-4)^3(5^2)$ 14. $(8^{-4})(10^3)$
15. $\dfrac{3^6}{7^3}$ 16. $\dfrac{4^3}{3^{-4}}$

In Exercises 17–24, evaluate the expression for the given value of x.

	Expression	*Value*
17.	$-3x^3$	$x = 2$
18.	$7x^{-2}$	$x = 4$
19.	$6x^0$	$x = 10$
20.	$5(-x)^3$	$x = 3$
21.	$2x^3$	$x = -3$
22.	$-3x^4$	$x = -2$
23.	$4x^2$	$x = -\frac{1}{2}$
24.	$5(-x)^3$	$x = -\frac{1}{3}$

In Exercises 25–30, simplify each expression.

25. (a) $(-5z)^3$ (b) $5x^4(x^2)$
26. (a) $(3x)^2$ (b) $(4x^3)^0$
27. (a) $6y^2(2y^0)^2$ (b) $\dfrac{3x^5}{x^3}$
28. (a) $(-z)^3(3z^4)$ (b) $\dfrac{25y^8}{10y^4}$
29. (a) $\dfrac{7x^2}{x^3}$ (b) $\dfrac{12(x + y)^3}{9(x + y)}$
30. (a) $\dfrac{r^4}{r^6}$ (b) $\left(\dfrac{4}{y}\right)^3\left(\dfrac{3}{y}\right)^4$

In Exercises 31–36, rewrite each expression with positive exponents and simplify.

31. (a) $(x + 5)^0, \quad x \neq -5$ (b) $(2x^2)^{-2}$
32. (a) $(2x^5)^0, \quad x \neq 0$ (b) $(z + 2)^{-3}(z + 2)^{-1}$

33. (a) $(-2x^2)^3(4x^3)^{-1}$ (b) $\left(\dfrac{x}{10}\right)^{-1}$

34. (a) $(4y^{-2})(8y^4)$ (b) $\left(\dfrac{x^{-3}y^4}{5}\right)^{-3}$

35. (a) $3^n \cdot 3^{2n}$ (b) $\left(\dfrac{a^{-2}}{b^{-2}}\right)\left(\dfrac{b}{a}\right)^3$

36. (a) $\dfrac{x^2 \cdot x^n}{x^3 \cdot x^n}$ (b) $\left(\dfrac{a^{-3}}{b^{-3}}\right)\left(\dfrac{a}{b}\right)^3$

In Exercises 37–40, write the number in scientific notation.

37. Land area of Earth: 57,300,000 square miles

38. Light year: 9,460,000,000,000 kilometers

39. Relative density of hydrogen: 0.0000899 gram per cubic centimeter

40. One micron (millionth of a meter): 0.00003937 inch

In Exercises 41–44, write the number in decimal notation.

41. Worldwide daily consumption of Coca-Cola: 4.568×10^9 ounces (Source: The Coca-Cola Company)

42. Interior temperature of the sun: 1.5×10^7 degrees Celsius

43. Charge of an electron: 1.6022×10^{-19} coulomb

44. Width of a human hair: 9.0×10^{-5} meter

In Exercises 45 and 46, evaluate each expression without using a calculator.

45. (a) $\sqrt{25 \times 10^8}$ (b) $\sqrt[3]{8 \times 10^{15}}$

46. (a) $(1.2 \times 10^7)(5 \times 10^{-3})$ (b) $\dfrac{(6.0 \times 10^8)}{(3.0 \times 10^{-3})}$

In Exercises 47–50, use a calculator to evaluate each expression. (Round your answer to three decimal places.)

47. (a) $750\left(1 + \dfrac{0.11}{365}\right)^{800}$

(b) $\dfrac{67{,}000{,}000 + 93{,}000{,}000}{0.0052}$

48. (a) $(9.3 \times 10^6)^3(6.1 \times 10^{-4})$

(b) $\dfrac{(2.414 \times 10^4)^6}{(1.68 \times 10^5)^5}$

49. (a) $\sqrt{4.5 \times 10^9}$ (b) $\sqrt[3]{6.3 \times 10^4}$

50. (a) $(2.65 \times 10^{-4})^{1/3}$ (b) $\sqrt{9 \times 10^{-4}}$

In Exercises 51–56, evaluate each expression without using a calculator.

51. (a) $\sqrt{9}$ (b) $\sqrt[3]{\frac{27}{8}}$

52. (a) $27^{1/3}$ (b) $36^{3/2}$

53. (a) $32^{-3/5}$ (b) $\left(\frac{16}{81}\right)^{-3/4}$

54. (a) $100^{-3/2}$ (b) $\left(\frac{9}{4}\right)^{-1/2}$

55. (a) $\left(-\dfrac{1}{64}\right)^{-1/3}$ (b) $\left(\dfrac{1}{\sqrt{32}}\right)^{-2/5}$

56. (a) $\left(-\dfrac{125}{27}\right)^{-1/3}$ (b) $-\left(\dfrac{1}{125}\right)^{-4/3}$

In Exercises 57–60, use a calculator to approximate the number. (Round your answer to three decimal places.)

57. (a) $\sqrt{57}$ (b) $\sqrt[5]{-27^3}$

58. (a) $\sqrt[3]{45^2}$ (b) $\sqrt[6]{125}$

59. (a) $(-12.4)^{-1.8}$ (b) $(5\sqrt{3})^{-2.5}$

60. (a) $\dfrac{7 - (4.1)^{-3.2}}{2}$ (b) $\left(\dfrac{13}{3}\right)^{-3/2} - \left(-\dfrac{3}{2}\right)^{13/3}$

In Exercises 61 and 62, use the properties of radicals to simplify each expression.

61. (a) $(\sqrt[3]{4})^3$ (b) $\sqrt[5]{96x^5}$

62. (a) $\sqrt{12} \cdot \sqrt{3}$ (b) $\sqrt[4]{(3x^2)^4}$

In Exercises 63–74, simplify each radical expression.

63. (a) $\sqrt{8}$ (b) $\sqrt[3]{54}$

64. (a) $\sqrt[3]{\frac{16}{27}}$ (b) $\sqrt{\frac{75}{4}}$

65. (a) $\sqrt{72x^3}$ (b) $\sqrt{\dfrac{18^2}{z^3}}$

66. (a) $\sqrt{54xy^4}$ (b) $\sqrt{\dfrac{32a^4}{b^2}}$

67. (a) $\sqrt[3]{16x^5}$ (b) $\sqrt{75x^2y^{-4}}$

68. (a) $\sqrt[4]{3x^4y^2}$ (b) $\sqrt[5]{160x^8z^4}$

69. (a) $2\sqrt{50} + 12\sqrt{8}$ (b) $10\sqrt{32} - 6\sqrt{18}$

70. (a) $4\sqrt{27} - \sqrt{75}$ (b) $\sqrt[3]{16} + 3\sqrt[3]{54}$

71. (a) $5\sqrt{x} - 3\sqrt{x}$ (b) $-2\sqrt{9y} + 10\sqrt{y}$

72. (a) $8\sqrt{49x} - 14\sqrt{100x}$ (b) $-3\sqrt{48x^2} + 7\sqrt{75x^2}$

73. (a) $3\sqrt{x+1} + 10\sqrt{x+1}$ (b) $7\sqrt{80x} - 2\sqrt{125x}$

74. (a) $-\sqrt{x^3 - 7} + 5\sqrt{x^3 - 7}$ (b) $11\sqrt{245x^3} - 9\sqrt{45x^3}$

In Exercises 75–78, complete the statement with <, =, or >.

75. $\sqrt{5} + \sqrt{3}$ ☐ $\sqrt{5 + 3}$

76. $\sqrt{\dfrac{3}{11}}$ ☐ $\dfrac{\sqrt{3}}{\sqrt{11}}$

77. 5 ☐ $\sqrt{3^2 + 2^2}$

78. 5 ☐ $\sqrt{3^2 + 4^2}$

In Exercises 79–82, rationalize the denominator of the expression. Then simplify your answer.

79. $\dfrac{1}{\sqrt{3}}$

80. $\dfrac{5}{\sqrt{10}}$

81. $\dfrac{2}{5 - \sqrt{3}}$ **82.** $\dfrac{3}{\sqrt{5} + \sqrt{6}}$

In Exercises 83–86, rationalize the numerator of the expression. Then simplify your answer.

83. $\dfrac{\sqrt{8}}{2}$ **84.** $\dfrac{\sqrt{2}}{3}$

85. $\dfrac{\sqrt{5} + \sqrt{3}}{3}$ **86.** $\dfrac{\sqrt{7} - 3}{4}$

In Exercises 87–94, fill in the missing form of the expression.

	Radical Form	*Rational Exponent Form*
87.	$\sqrt{9}$	
88.	$\sqrt[3]{64}$	
89.		$32^{1/5}$
90.		$-(144^{1/2})$
91.	$\sqrt[3]{-216}$	
92.		$(-243)^{1/5}$
93.	$(\sqrt[4]{81})^3$	
94.		$16^{5/4}$

In Exercises 95–98, perform the operations and simplify.

95. $\dfrac{(2x^2)^{3/2}}{2^{1/2}x^4}$ **96.** $\dfrac{x^{4/3}y^{2/3}}{(xy)^{1/3}}$

97. $\dfrac{x^{-3} \cdot x^{1/2}}{x^{3/2} \cdot x^{-1}}$ **98.** $\dfrac{5^{-1/2} \cdot 5x^{5/2}}{(5x)^{3/2}}$

In Exercises 99 and 100, reduce the index of each radical.

99. (a) $\sqrt[4]{3^2}$ (b) $\sqrt[6]{(x + 1)^4}$

100. (a) $\sqrt[6]{x^3}$ (b) $\sqrt[4]{(3x^2)^4}$

In Exercises 101 and 102, write each expression as a single radical. Then simplify your answer.

101. (a) $\sqrt{\sqrt{32}}$ (b) $\sqrt{\sqrt[4]{2x}}$

102. (a) $\sqrt{\sqrt{243(x + 1)}}$ (b) $\sqrt{\sqrt[3]{10a^7b}}$

103. ***Period of a Pendulum*** The period T (in seconds) of a pendulum is

$$T = 2\pi\sqrt{\frac{L}{32}}$$

where L is the length of the pendulum (in feet). Find the period of a pendulum whose length is 2 feet.

104. ***Erosion*** A stream of water moving at the rate of v feet per second can carry particles of size $0.03\sqrt{v}$ inches. Find the size of the largest particle that can be carried by a stream flowing at the rate of $\frac{3}{4}$ foot per second.

105. ***Mathematical Modeling*** A funnel is filled with water to a height of h centimeters. The formula

$$t = 0.03[12^{5/2} - (12 - h)^{5/2}], \quad 0 \le h \le 12$$

represents the amount of time t (in seconds) that it will take for the funnel to empty.

(a) Use the table feature of a graphing utility to find the times required for the funnel to empty for water heights of $h = 0$, $h = 1$, $h = 2$, . . . $h = 12$ centimeters.

(b) What value does t appear to be approaching as the height of the water becomes closer and closer to 12 centimeters?

106. ***Speed of Light*** The speed of light is approximately 11,180,000 miles per minute. The distance from the sun to Earth is approximately 93,000,000 miles. Find the time for light to travel from the sun to Earth.

Synthesis

True or False? **In Exercises 107 and 108, determine whether the statement is true or false. Justify your answer.**

107. $\dfrac{x^{k+1}}{x} = x^k$ **108.** $(a^n)^k = a^{n^k}$

109. Verify that $a^0 = 1$, $a \neq 0$. (*Hint:* Use the property of exponents $a^m/a^n = a^{m-n}$.)

110. Explain why each of the following pairs is not equal.

(a) $(3x)^{-1} \neq \dfrac{3}{x}$ (b) $y^3 \cdot y^2 \neq y^6$

(c) $(a^2b^3)^4 \neq a^6b^7$ (d) $(a + b)^2 \neq a^2 + b^2$

(e) $\sqrt{4x^2} \neq 2x$ (f) $\sqrt{2} + \sqrt{3} \neq \sqrt{5}$

111. ***Exploration*** List all possible digits that occur in the units place of the square of a positive integer. Use that list to determine whether $\sqrt{5233}$ is an integer.

112. ***Think About It*** Square the real number $2/\sqrt{5}$ and note that the radical is eliminated from the denominator. Is this equivalent to rationalizing the denominator? Why or why not?

The symbol $\int$ indicates an example or exercise that highlights algebraic techniques specifically used in calculus.

The symbol [graphing utility icon] indicates an exercise or a part of an exercise in which you are instructed to use a graphing utility.

A.3 Polynomials and Factoring

What you should learn

- Write polynomials in standard form.
- Add, subtract, and multiply polynomials.
- Use special products to multiply polynomials.
- Remove common factors from polynomials.
- Factor special polynomial forms.
- Factor trinomials as the product of two binomials.
- Factor polynomials by grouping.

Why you should learn it

Polynomials can be used to model and solve real-life problems. For instance, in Exercise 210 on page A34, a polynomial is used to model the stopping distance of an automobile.

Polynomials

The most common type of algebraic expression is the **polynomial.** Some examples are $2x + 5$, $3x^4 - 7x^2 + 2x + 4$, and $5x^2y^2 - xy + 3$. The first two are *polynomials in x* and the third is a *polynomial in x and y*. The terms of a polynomial in x have the form ax^k, where a is the **coefficient** and k is the **degree** of the term. For instance, the polynomial

$$2x^3 - 5x^2 + 1 = 2x^3 + (-5)x^2 + (0)x + 1$$

has coefficients 2, -5, 0, and 1.

Definition of a Polynomial in x

Let $a_0, a_1, a_2, \ldots, a_n$ be real numbers and let n be a nonnegative integer. A polynomial in x is an expression of the form

$$a_nx^n + a_{n-1}x^{n-1} + \cdots + a_1x + a_0$$

where $a_n \neq 0$. The polynomial is of **degree** n, a_n is the **leading coefficient,** and a_0 is the **constant term.**

Polynomials with one, two, and three terms are called **monomials, binomials,** and **trinomials,** respectively. In **standard form,** a polynomial is written with descending powers of x.

Example 1 Writing Polynomials in Standard Form

	Polynomial	*Standard Form*	*Degree*
a.	$4x^2 - 5x^7 - 2 + 3x$	$-5x^7 + 4x^2 + 3x - 2$	7
b.	$4 - 9x^2$	$-9x^2 + 4$	2
c.	8	$8 \ (8 = 8x^0)$	0

✓CHECKPOINT Now try Exercise 11.

A polynomial that has all zero coefficients is called the zero polynomial, denoted by 0. No degree is assigned to this particular polynomial. For polynomials in more than one variable, the degree of a *term* is the sum of the exponents of the variables in the term. The degree of the *polynomial* is the highest degree of its terms. For instance, the degree of the polynomial $-2x^3y^6 + 4xy - x^7y^4$ is 11 because the sum of the exponents in the last term is the greatest. The leading coefficient of the polynomial is the coefficient of the highest-degree term. Expressions are not polynomials if a variable is underneath a radical or if a polynomial expression (with degree greater than 0) is in the denominator of a term. The following expressions are not polynomials.

$x^3 - \sqrt{3x} = x^3 - (3x)^{1/2}$ The exponent "1/2" is not an integer.

$x^2 + \dfrac{5}{x} = x^2 + 5x^{-1}$ The exponent "-1" is not a nonnegative integer.

Operations with Polynomials

You can add and subtract polynomials in much the same way you add and subtract real numbers. Simply add or subtract the *like terms* (terms having the same variables to the same powers) by adding their coefficients. For instance, $-3xy^2$ and $5xy^2$ are like terms and their sum is

$$\begin{aligned} -3xy^2 + 5xy^2 &= (-3 + 5)xy^2 \\ &= 2xy^2. \end{aligned}$$

STUDY TIP

When an expression inside parentheses is preceded by a negative sign, remember to distribute the negative sign to each term inside the parentheses, as shown.

$$\begin{aligned} &-(x^2 - x + 3) \\ &\quad = -x^2 + x - 3 \end{aligned}$$

Example 2 Sums and Differences of Polynomials

a. $(5x^3 - 7x^2 - 3) + (x^3 + 2x^2 - x + 8)$

$= (5x^3 + x^3) + (-7x^2 + 2x^2) - x + (-3 + 8)$ Group like terms.

$= 6x^3 - 5x^2 - x + 5$ Combine like terms.

b. $(7x^4 - x^2 - 4x + 2) - (3x^4 - 4x^2 + 3x)$

$= 7x^4 - x^2 - 4x + 2 - 3x^4 + 4x^2 - 3x$ Distributive Property

$= (7x^4 - 3x^4) + (-x^2 + 4x^2) + (-4x - 3x) + 2$ Group like terms.

$= 4x^4 + 3x^2 - 7x + 2$ Combine like terms.

✓CHECKPOINT Now try Exercise 33.

To find the *product* of two polynomials, use the left and right Distributive Properties. For example, if you treat $5x + 7$ as a single quantity, you can multiply $3x - 2$ by $5x + 7$ as follows.

$$\begin{aligned} (3x - 2)(5x + 7) &= 3x(5x + 7) - 2(5x + 7) \\ &= (3x)(5x) + (3x)(7) - (2)(5x) - (2)(7) \\ &= 15x^2 + 21x - 10x - 14 \end{aligned}$$

Product of First terms | Product of Outer terms | Product of Inner terms | Product of Last terms

$$= 15x^2 + 11x - 14$$

Note in this **FOIL Method** (which can only be used to multiply two binomials) that the outer (O) and inner (I) terms are like terms and can be combined.

Example 3 Finding a Product by the FOIL Method

Use the FOIL Method to find the product of $2x - 4$ and $x + 5$.

Solution

F O I L

$$\begin{aligned} (2x - 4)(x + 5) &= 2x^2 + 10x - 4x - 20 \\ &= 2x^2 + 6x - 20 \end{aligned}$$

✓CHECKPOINT Now try Exercise 47.

Special Products

Some binomial products have special forms that occur frequently in algebra. You do not need to memorize these formulas because you can use the Distributive Property to multiply. However, becoming familiar with these formulas will enable you to manipulate the algebra more quickly.

Special Products

Let u and v be real numbers, variables, or algebraic expressions.

Special Product	*Example*
Sum and Difference of Same Terms	
$(u + v)(u - v) = u^2 - v^2$	$(x + 4)(x - 4) = x^2 - 4^2$ $= x^2 - 16$
Square of a Binomial	
$(u + v)^2 = u^2 + 2uv + v^2$	$(x + 3)^2 = x^2 + 2(x)(3) + 3^2$ $= x^2 + 6x + 9$
$(u - v)^2 = u^2 - 2uv + v^2$	$(3x - 2)^2 = (3x)^2 - 2(3x)(2) + 2^2$ $= 9x^2 - 12x + 4$
Cube of a Binomial	
$(u + v)^3 = u^3 + 3u^2v + 3uv^2 + v^3$	$(x + 2)^3 = x^3 + 3x^2(2) + 3x(2^2) + 2^3$ $= x^3 + 6x^2 + 12x + 8$
$(u - v)^3 = u^3 - 3u^2v + 3uv^2 - v^3$	$(x - 1)^3 = x^3 - 3x^2(1) + 3x(1^2) - 1^3$ $= x^3 - 3x^2 + 3x - 1$

Example 4 Special Products

Find each product.

a. $5x + 9$ and $5x - 9$ **b.** $x + y - 2$ and $x + y + 2$

Solution

a. The product of a sum and a difference of the *same* two terms has no middle term and takes the form $(u + v)(u - v) = u^2 - v^2$.

$$(5x + 9)(5x - 9) = (5x)^2 - 9^2 = 25x^2 - 81$$

b. By grouping $x + y$ in parentheses, you can write the product of the trinomials as a special product.

$$(x + y - 2)(x + y + 2) = [\underset{\text{Difference}}{(x + y) - 2}][\underset{\text{Sum}}{(x + y) + 2}]$$

$$= (x + y)^2 - 2^2 \quad \text{Sum and difference of same terms}$$

$$= x^2 + 2xy + y^2 - 4$$

✓CHECKPOINT Now try Exercise 67.

Polynomials with Common Factors

The process of writing a polynomial as a product is called **factoring.** It is an important tool for solving equations and for simplifying rational expressions.

Unless noted otherwise, when you are asked to factor a polynomial, you can assume that you are looking for factors with integer coefficients. If a polynomial cannot be factored using integer coefficients, then it is **prime** or **irreducible over the integers.** For instance, the polynomial $x^2 - 3$ is irreducible over the integers. Over the *real numbers*, this polynomial can be factored as

$$x^2 - 3 = (x + \sqrt{3})(x - \sqrt{3}).$$

A polynomial is **completely factored** when each of its factors is prime. For instance

$$x^3 - x^2 + 4x - 4 = (x - 1)(x^2 + 4)$$ Completely factored

is completely factored, but

$$x^3 - x^2 - 4x + 4 = (x - 1)(x^2 - 4)$$ Not completely factored

is not completely factored. Its complete factorization is

$$x^3 - x^2 - 4x + 4 = (x - 1)(x + 2)(x - 2).$$

The simplest type of factoring involves a polynomial that can be written as the product of a monomial and another polynomial. The technique used here is the Distributive Property, $a(b + c) = ab + ac$, in the *reverse* direction.

$$ab + ac = a(b + c)$$ a is a common factor.

Removing (factoring out) any common factors is the first step in completely factoring a polynomial.

Example 5 Removing Common Factors

Factor each expression.

a. $6x^3 - 4x$

b. $-4x^2 + 12x - 16$

c. $(x - 2)(2x) + (x - 2)(3)$

Solution

a. $6x^3 - 4x = 2x(3x^2) - 2x(2)$ $2x$ is a common factor.

$= 2x(3x^2 - 2)$

b. $-4x^2 + 12x - 16 = -4(x^2) + (-4)(-3x) + (-4)4$ -4 is a common factor.

$= -4(x^2 - 3x + 4)$

c. $(x - 2)(2x) + (x - 2)(3) = (x - 2)(2x + 3)$ $(x - 2)$ is a common factor.

CHECKPOINT Now try Exercise 91.

Factoring Special Polynomial Forms

Some polynomials have special forms that arise from the special product forms on page A25. You should learn to recognize these forms so that you can factor such polynomials easily.

Factoring Special Polynomial Forms

Factored Form	*Example*
Difference of Two Squares	
$u^2 - v^2 = (u + v)(u - v)$	$9x^2 - 4 = (3x)^2 - 2^2 = (3x + 2)(3x - 2)$
Perfect Square Trinomial	
$u^2 + 2uv + v^2 = (u + v)^2$	$x^2 + 6x + 9 = x^2 + 2(x)(3) + 3^2 = (x + 3)^2$
$u^2 - 2uv + v^2 = (u - v)^2$	$x^2 - 6x + 9 = x^2 - 2(x)(3) + 3^2 = (x - 3)^2$
Sum or Difference of Two Cubes	
$u^3 + v^3 = (u + v)(u^2 - uv + v^2)$	$x^3 + 8 = x^3 + 2^3 = (x + 2)(x^2 - 2x + 4)$
$u^3 - v^3 = (u - v)(u^2 + uv + v^2)$	$27x^3 - 1 = (3x)^3 - 1^3 = (3x - 1)(9x^2 + 3x + 1)$

One of the easiest special polynomial forms to factor is the difference of two squares. The factored form is always a set of *conjugate pairs*.

$$u^2 - v^2 = (u + v)(u - v) \qquad \text{Conjugate pairs}$$

Difference (arrow to the minus sign in $u^2 - v^2$)   Opposite signs (arrows to the signs in $(u + v)(u - v)$)

To recognize perfect square terms, look for coefficients that are squares of integers and variables raised to *even powers*.

STUDY TIP

In Example 6, note that the first step in factoring a polynomial is to check for any common factors. Once the common factors are removed, it is often possible to recognize patterns that were not immediately obvious.

Example 6 **Removing a Common Factor First**

$$3 - 12x^2 = 3(1 - 4x^2) \qquad \text{3 is a common factor.}$$
$$= 3[1^2 - (2x)^2]$$
$$= 3(1 + 2x)(1 - 2x) \qquad \text{Difference of two squares}$$

✓CHECKPOINT Now try Exercise 105.

Example 7 **Factoring the Difference of Two Squares**

a. $(x + 2)^2 - y^2 = [(x + 2) + y][(x + 2) - y]$
$$= (x + 2 + y)(x + 2 - y)$$

b. $16x^4 - 81 = (4x^2)^2 - 9^2$
$$= (4x^2 + 9)(4x^2 - 9) \qquad \text{Difference of two squares}$$
$$= (4x^2 + 9)[(2x)^2 - 3^2]$$
$$= (4x^2 + 9)(2x + 3)(2x - 3) \qquad \text{Difference of two squares}$$

✓CHECKPOINT Now try Exercise 109.

A **perfect square trinomial** is the square of a binomial, and it has the following form.

$$u^2 + 2uv + v^2 = (u + v)^2 \qquad \text{or} \qquad u^2 - 2uv + v^2 = (u - v)^2$$

Like signs   Like signs

Note that the first and last terms are squares and the middle term is twice the product of u and v.

Example 8 Factoring Perfect Square Trinomials

Factor each trinomial.

a. $x^2 - 10x + 25$

b. $16x^2 + 24x + 9$

Solution

a. $x^2 - 10x + 25 = x^2 - 2(x)(5) + 5^2 = (x - 5)^2$

b. $16x^2 + 24x + 9 = (4x)^2 + 2(4x)(3) + 3^2 = (4x + 3)^2$

CHECKPOINT Now try Exercise 115.

The next two formulas show the sums and differences of cubes. Pay special attention to the signs of the terms.

Like signs   Like signs

$$u^3 + v^3 = (u + v)(u^2 - uv + v^2) \qquad u^3 - v^3 = (u - v)(u^2 + uv + v^2)$$

Unlike signs   Unlike signs

Example 9 Factoring the Difference of Cubes

Factor $x^3 - 27$.

Solution

$x^3 - 27 = x^3 - 3^3$ Rewrite 27 as 3^3.

$= (x - 3)(x^2 + 3x + 9)$ Factor.

CHECKPOINT Now try Exercise 123.

Example 10 Factoring the Sum of Cubes

a. $y^3 + 8 = y^3 + 2^3$ Rewrite 8 as 2^3.

$= (y + 2)(y^2 - 2y + 4)$ Factor.

b. $3(x^3 + 64) = 3(x^3 + 4^3)$ Rewrite 64 as 4^3.

$= 3(x + 4)(x^2 - 4x + 16)$ Factor.

CHECKPOINT Now try Exercise 125.

Trinomials with Binomial Factors

To factor a trinomial of the form $ax^2 + bx + c$, use the following pattern.

Factors of a

$$ax^2 + bx + c = (\square x + \square)(\square x + \square)$$

Factors of c

The goal is to find a combination of factors of a and c such that the outer and inner products add up to the middle term bx. For instance, in the trinomial $6x^2 + 17x + 5$, you can write all possible factorizations and determine which one has outer and inner products that add up to $17x$.

$$(6x + 5)(x + 1),\ (6x + 1)(x + 5),\ (2x + 1)(3x + 5),\ (2x + 5)(3x + 1)$$

You can see that $(2x + 5)(3x + 1)$ is the correct factorization because the outer (O) and inner (I) products add up to $17x$.

$$\overset{}{(2x + 5)(3x + 1)} = \underset{\text{F}}{6x^2} + \underset{\text{O}}{2x} + \underset{\text{I}}{15x} + \underset{\text{L}}{5} = 6x^2 + \underset{\text{O + I}}{17x} + 5.$$

Example 11 **Factoring a Trinomial: Leading Coefficient Is 1**

Factor $x^2 - 7x + 12$.

Solution

The possible factorizations are

$$(x - 2)(x - 6), \quad (x - 1)(x - 12), \quad \text{and} \quad (x - 3)(x - 4).$$

Testing the middle term, you will find the correct factorization to be

$$x^2 - 7x + 12 = (x - 3)(x - 4).$$

✓CHECKPOINT Now try Exercise 131.

Example 12 **Factoring a Trinomial: Leading Coefficient Is Not 1**

Factor $2x^2 + x - 15$.

Solution

The eight possible factorizations are as follows.

$$(2x - 1)(x + 15) \qquad (2x + 1)(x - 15)$$
$$(2x - 3)(x + 5) \qquad (2x + 3)(x - 5)$$
$$(2x - 5)(x + 3) \qquad (2x + 5)(x - 3)$$
$$(2x - 15)(x + 1) \qquad (2x + 15)(x - 1)$$

Testing the middle term, you will find the correct factorization to be

$$2x^2 + x - 15 = (2x - 5)(x + 3). \qquad \text{O + I} = 6x - 5x = x$$

✓CHECKPOINT Now try Exercise 139.

STUDY TIP

Factoring a trinomial can involve trial and error. However, once you have produced the factored form, it is an easy matter to check your answer. For instance, you can verify the factorization in Example 11 by multiplying out the expression $(x - 3)(x - 4)$ to see that you obtain the original trinomial, $x^2 - 7x + 12$.

Factoring by Grouping

Sometimes polynomials with more than three terms can be factored by a method called **factoring by grouping.** It is not always obvious which terms to group, and sometimes several different groupings will work.

Example 13 Factoring by Grouping

Use factoring by grouping to factor $x^3 - 2x^2 - 3x + 6$.

Solution

$$x^3 - 2x^2 - 3x + 6 = (x^3 - 2x^2) - (3x - 6) \quad \text{Group terms.}$$
$$= x^2(x - 2) - 3(x - 2) \quad \text{Factor each group.}$$
$$= (x - 2)(x^2 - 3) \quad \text{Distributive Property}$$

CHECKPOINT Now try Exercise 147.

STUDY TIP

Another way to factor the polynomial in Example 13 is to group the terms as follows.

$$x^3 - 2x^2 - 3x + 6$$
$$= (x^3 - 3x) - (2x^2 - 6)$$
$$= x(x^2 - 3) - 2(x^2 - 3)$$
$$= (x^2 - 3)(x - 2)$$

As you can see, you obtain the same result as in Example 13.

Factoring a trinomial can involve quite a bit of trial and error. Some of this trial and error can be lessened by using factoring by grouping. The key to this method of factoring is knowing how to rewrite the middle term. In general, to factor a trinomial $ax^2 + bx + c$ by grouping, choose factors of the product ac that add up to b and use these factors to rewrite the middle term. This technique is illustrated in Example 14.

Example 14 Factoring a Trinomial by Grouping

Use factoring by grouping to factor $2x^2 + 5x - 3$.

Solution

In the trinomial $2x^2 + 5x - 3$, $a = 2$ and $c = -3$, which implies that the product ac is -6. Now, -6 factors as $(6)(-1)$ and $6 - 1 = 5 = b$. So, you can rewrite the middle term as $5x = 6x - x$. This produces the following.

$$2x^2 + 5x - 3 = 2x^2 + 6x - x - 3 \quad \text{Rewrite middle term.}$$
$$= (2x^2 + 6x) - (x + 3) \quad \text{Group terms.}$$
$$= 2x(x + 3) - (x + 3) \quad \text{Factor groups.}$$
$$= (x + 3)(2x - 1) \quad \text{Distributive Property}$$

So, the trinomial factors as $2x^2 + 5x - 3 = (x + 3)(2x - 1)$.

CHECKPOINT Now try Exercise 153.

Guidelines for Factoring Polynomials

1. Factor out any common factors using the Distributive Property.
2. Factor according to one of the special polynomial forms.
3. Factor as $ax^2 + bx + c = (mx + r)(nx + s)$.
4. Factor by grouping.

A.3 Exercises

VOCABULARY CHECK: Fill in the blanks.

1. For the polynomial $a_nx^n + a_{n-1}x^{n-1} + \cdots + a_1x + a_0$, the degree is ________, the leading coefficient is ________, and the constant term is ________.
2. A polynomial in x in standard form is written with ________ powers of x.
3. A polynomial with one term is called a ________, while a polynomial with two terms is called a ________, and a polynomial with three terms is called a ________.
4. To add or subtract polynomials, add or subtract the ________ ________ by adding their coefficients.
5. The letters in "FOIL" stand for the following.
   F ________ O ________ I ________ L ________
6. The process of writing a polynomial as a product is called ________.
7. A polynomial is ________ ________ when each of its factors is prime.

In Exercises 1–6, match the polynomial with its description. [The polynomials are labeled (a), (b), (c), (d), (e), and (f).]

(a) $3x^2$ (b) $1 - 2x^3$
(c) $x^3 + 3x^2 + 3x + 1$ (d) 12
(e) $-3x^5 + 2x^3 + x$ (f) $\frac{2}{3}x^4 + x^2 + 10$

1. A polynomial of degree 0
2. A trinomial of degree 5
3. A binomial with leading coefficient -2
4. A monomial of positive degree
5. A trinomial with leading coefficient $\frac{2}{3}$
6. A third-degree polynomial with leading coefficient 1

In Exercises 7–10, write a polynomial that fits the description. (There are many correct answers.)

7. A third-degree polynomial with leading coefficient -2
8. A fifth-degree polynomial with leading coefficient 6
9. A fourth-degree binomial with a negative leading coefficient
10. A third-degree binomial with an even leading coefficient

In Exercises 11–22, (a) write the polynomial in standard form, (b) identify the degree and leading coefficient of the polynomial, and (c) state whether the polynomial is a monomial, a binomial, or a trinomial.

11. $14x - \frac{1}{2}x^5$
12. $2x^2 - x + 1$
13. $-3x^4 + 2x^2 - 5$
14. $7x$
15. $x^5 - 1$
16. $-y + 25y^2 + 1$
17. 3
18. $t^2 + 9$
19. $1 + 6x^4 - 4x^5$
20. $3 + 2x$
21. $4x^3y$
22. $-x^5y + 2x^2y^2 + xy^4$

In Exercises 23–28, determine whether the expression is a polynomial. If so, write the polynomial in standard form.

23. $2x - 3x^3 + 8$
24. $2x^3 + x - 3x^{-1}$
25. $\dfrac{3x + 4}{x}$
26. $\dfrac{x^2 + 2x - 3}{2}$
27. $y^2 - y^4 + y^3$
28. $\sqrt{y^2 - y^4}$

In Exercises 29–46, perform the operation and write the result in standard form.

29. $(6x + 5) - (8x + 15)$
30. $(2x^2 + 1) - (x^2 - 2x + 1)$
31. $-(x^3 - 2) + (4x^3 - 2x)$
32. $-(5x^2 - 1) - (-3x^2 + 5)$
33. $(15x^2 - 6) - (-8.3x^3 - 14.7x^2 - 17)$
34. $(15.2x^4 - 18x - 19.1) - (13.9x^4 - 9.6x + 15)$
35. $5z - [3z - (10z + 8)]$
36. $(y^3 + 1) - [(y^2 + 1) + (3y - 7)]$
37. $3x(x^2 - 2x + 1)$
38. $y^2(4y^2 + 2y - 3)$
39. $-5z(3z - 1)$
40. $(-3x)(5x + 2)$
41. $(1 - x^3)(4x)$
42. $-4x(3 - x^3)$
43. $(2.5x^2 + 3)(3x)$
44. $(2 - 3.5y)(2y^3)$
45. $-4x(\frac{1}{8}x + 3)$
46. $2y(4 - \frac{7}{8}y)$

In Exercises 47–84, multiply or find the special product.

47. $(x + 3)(x + 4)$
48. $(x - 5)(x + 10)$
49. $(3x - 5)(2x + 1)$
50. $(7x - 2)(4x - 3)$
51. $(x^2 - x + 1)(x^2 + x + 1)$
52. $(x^2 + 3x - 2)(x^2 - 3x - 2)$
53. $(x + 10)(x - 10)$ **54.** $(2x + 3)(2x - 3)$
55. $(x + 2y)(x - 2y)$ **56.** $(2x + 3y)(2x - 3y)$
57. $(2x + 3)^2$ **58.** $(4x + 5)^2$
59. $(2x - 5y)^2$ **60.** $(5 - 8x)^2$
61. $(x + 1)^3$ **62.** $(x - 2)^3$
63. $(2x - y)^3$ **64.** $(3x + 2y)^3$
65. $(4x^3 - 3)^2$ **66.** $(8x + 3)^2$
67. $[(m - 3) + n][(m - 3) - n]$
68. $[(x + y) + 1][(x + y) - 1]$
69. $[(x - 3) + y]^2$ **70.** $[(x + 1) - y]^2$
71. $(2r^2 - 5)(2r^2 + 5)$ **72.** $(3a^3 - 4b^2)(3a^3 + 4b^2)$
73. $\left(\frac{1}{2}x - 3\right)^2$ **74.** $\left(\frac{2}{3}t + 5\right)^2$
75. $\left(\frac{1}{3}x - 2\right)\left(\frac{1}{3}x + 2\right)$ **76.** $\left(2x + \frac{1}{5}\right)\left(2x - \frac{1}{5}\right)$
77. $(1.2x + 3)^2$ **78.** $(1.5y - 3)^2$
79. $(1.5x - 4)(1.5x + 4)$ **80.** $(2.5y + 3)(2.5y - 3)$
81. $5x(x + 1) - 3x(x + 1)$
82. $(2x - 1)(x + 3) + 3(x + 3)$
83. $(u + 2)(u - 2)(u^2 + 4)$
84. $(x + y)(x - y)(x^2 + y^2)$

In Exercises 85–88, find the product. (The expressions are not polynomials, but the formulas can still be used.)

85. $(\sqrt{x} + \sqrt{y})(\sqrt{x} - \sqrt{y})$ **86.** $(5 + \sqrt{x})(5 - \sqrt{x})$
87. $(x - \sqrt{5})^2$ **88.** $(x + \sqrt{3})^2$

In Exercises 89–96, factor out the common factor.

89. $3x + 6$ **90.** $5y - 30$
91. $2x^3 - 6x$ **92.** $4x^3 - 6x^2 + 12x$
93. $x(x - 1) + 6(x - 1)$ **94.** $3x(x + 2) - 4(x + 2)$
95. $(x + 3)^2 - 4(x + 3)$ **96.** $(3x - 1)^2 + (3x - 1)$

In Exercises 97–102, find the greatest common factor such that the remaining factors have only integer coefficients.

97. $\frac{1}{2}x + 4$ **98.** $\frac{1}{3}y + 5$
99. $\frac{1}{2}x^3 + 2x^2 - 5x$ **100.** $\frac{1}{3}y^4 - 5y^2 + 2y$
101. $\frac{2}{3}x(x - 3) - 4(x - 3)$ **102.** $\frac{4}{5}y(y + 1) - 2(y + 1)$

In Exercises 103–112, completely factor the difference of two squares.

103. $x^2 - 81$
104. $x^2 - 49$
105. $32y^2 - 18$
106. $4 - 36y^2$
107. $16x^2 - \frac{1}{9}$
108. $\frac{4}{25}y^2 - 64$
109. $(x - 1)^2 - 4$ **110.** $25 - (z + 5)^2$
111. $9u^2 - 4v^2$ **112.** $25x^2 - 16y^2$

In Exercises 113–122, factor the perfect square trinomial.

113. $x^2 - 4x + 4$ **114.** $x^2 + 10x + 25$
115. $4t^2 + 4t + 1$ **116.** $9x^2 - 12x + 4$
117. $25y^2 - 10y + 1$ **118.** $36y^2 - 108y + 81$
119. $9u^2 + 24uv + 16v^2$ **120.** $4x^2 - 4xy + y^2$
121. $x^2 - \frac{4}{3}x + \frac{4}{9}$ **122.** $z^2 + z + \frac{1}{4}$

In Exercises 123–130, factor the sum or difference of cubes.

123. $x^3 - 8$ **124.** $x^3 - 27$
125. $y^3 + 64$ **126.** $z^3 + 125$
127. $8t^3 - 1$ **128.** $27x^3 + 8$
129. $u^3 + 27v^3$ **130.** $64x^3 - y^3$

In Exercises 131–144, factor the trinomial.

131. $x^2 + x - 2$ **132.** $x^2 + 5x + 6$
133. $s^2 - 5s + 6$ **134.** $t^2 - t - 6$
135. $20 - y - y^2$ **136.** $24 + 5z - z^2$
137. $x^2 - 30x + 200$ **138.** $x^2 - 13x + 42$
139. $3x^2 - 5x + 2$ **140.** $2x^2 - x - 1$
141. $5x^2 + 26x + 5$ **142.** $12x^2 + 7x + 1$
143. $-9z^2 + 3z + 2$ **144.** $-5u^2 - 13u + 6$

In Exercises 145–152, factor by grouping.

145. $x^3 - x^2 + 2x - 2$ **146.** $x^3 + 5x^2 - 5x - 25$
147. $2x^3 - x^2 - 6x + 3$ **148.** $5x^3 - 10x^2 + 3x - 6$
149. $6 + 2x - 3x^3 - x^4$ **150.** $x^5 + 2x^3 + x^2 + 2$
151. $6x^3 - 2x + 3x^2 - 1$ **152.** $8x^5 - 6x^2 + 12x^3 - 9$

In Exercises 153–158, factor the trinomial by grouping.

153. $3x^2 + 10x + 8$ **154.** $2x^2 + 9x + 9$
155. $6x^2 + x - 2$ **156.** $6x^2 - x - 15$
157. $15x^2 - 11x + 2$ **158.** $12x^2 - 13x + 1$

In Exercises 159–192, completely factor the expression.

159. $6x^2 - 54$

160. $12x^2 - 48$

161. $x^3 - 4x^2$

162. $x^3 - 9x$

163. $x^2 - 2x + 1$

164. $16 + 6x - x^2$

165. $1 - 4x + 4x^2$

166. $-9x^2 + 6x - 1$

167. $2x^2 + 4x - 2x^3$

168. $2y^3 - 7y^2 - 15y$

169. $9x^2 + 10x + 1$

170. $13x + 6 + 5x^2$

171. $\frac{1}{81}x^2 + \frac{2}{9}x - 8$

172. $\frac{1}{8}x^2 - \frac{1}{96}x - \frac{1}{16}$

173. $3x^3 + x^2 + 15x + 5$

174. $5 - x + 5x^2 - x^3$

175. $x^4 - 4x^3 + x^2 - 4x$

176. $3u - 2u^2 + 6 - u^3$

177. $\frac{1}{4}x^3 + 3x^2 + \frac{3}{4}x + 9$

178. $\frac{1}{5}x^3 + x^2 - x - 5$

179. $(t - 1)^2 - 49$

180. $(x^2 + 1)^2 - 4x^2$

181. $(x^2 + 8)^2 - 36x^2$

182. $2t^3 - 16$

183. $5x^3 + 40$

184. $4x(2x - 1) + (2x - 1)^2$

185. $5(3 - 4x)^2 - 8(3 - 4x)(5x - 1)$

186. $2(x + 1)(x - 3)^2 - 3(x + 1)^2(x - 3)$

187. $7(3x + 2)^2(1 - x)^2 + (3x + 2)(1 - x)^3$

188. $7x(2)(x^2 + 1)(2x) - (x^2 + 1)^2(7)$

189. $3(x - 2)^2(x + 1)^4 + (x - 2)^3(4)(x + 1)^3$

190. $2x(x - 5)^4 - x^2(4)(x - 5)^3$

191. $5(x^6 + 1)^4(6x^5)(3x + 2)^3 + 3(3x + 2)^2(3)(x^6 + 1)^5$

192. $\frac{x^2}{2}(x^2 + 1)^4 - (x^2 + 1)^5$

In Exercises 193–196, find all values of *b* for which the trinomial can be factored.

193. $x^2 + bx - 15$

194. $x^2 + bx + 50$

195. $x^2 + bx - 12$

196. $x^2 + bx + 24$

In Exercises 197–200, find two integer values of *c* such that the trinomial can be factored. (There are many correct answers.)

197. $2x^2 + 5x + c$

198. $3x^2 - 10x + c$

199. $3x^2 - x + c$

200. $2x^2 + 9x + c$

201. ***Cost, Revenue, and Profit*** An electronics manufacturer can produce and sell x radios per week. The total cost C (in dollars) of producing x radios is

$C = 73x + 25{,}000$

and the total revenue R (in dollars) is

$R = 95x.$

(a) Find the profit P in terms of x.

(b) Find the profit obtained by selling 5000 radios per week.

202. ***Cost, Revenue, and Profit*** An artisan can produce and sell x hats per month. The total cost C (in dollars) of producing x hats is

$C = 460 + 12x$

and the total revenue R (in dollars) is

$R = 36x.$

(a) Find the profit P in terms of x.

(b) Find the profit obtained by selling 42 hats per month.

203. ***Compound Interest*** After 2 years, an investment of \$500 compounded annually at an interest rate r will yield an amount of $500(1 + r)^2$.

(a) Write this polynomial in standard form.

(b) Use a calculator to evaluate the polynomial for the values of r shown in the table.

r	$2\frac{1}{2}\%$	3%	4%	$4\frac{1}{2}\%$	5%
$500(1 + r)^2$					

(c) What conclusion can you make from the table?

204. ***Compound Interest*** After 3 years, an investment of \$1200 compounded annually at an interest rate r will yield an amount of $1200(1 + r)^3$.

(a) Write this polynomial in standard form.

(b) Use a calculator to evaluate the polynomial for the values of r shown in the table.

r	2%	3%	$3\frac{1}{2}\%$	4%	$4\frac{1}{2}\%$
$1200(1 + r)^3$					

(c) What conclusion can you make from the table?

205. ***Volume of a Box*** A take-out fast-food restaurant is constructing an open box by cutting squares from the corners of a piece of cardboard that is 18 centimeters by 26 centimeters (see figure). The edge of each cut-out square is x centimeters.

(a) Find the volume of the box in terms of x.

(b) Find the volume when $x = 1$, $x = 2$, and $x = 3$.

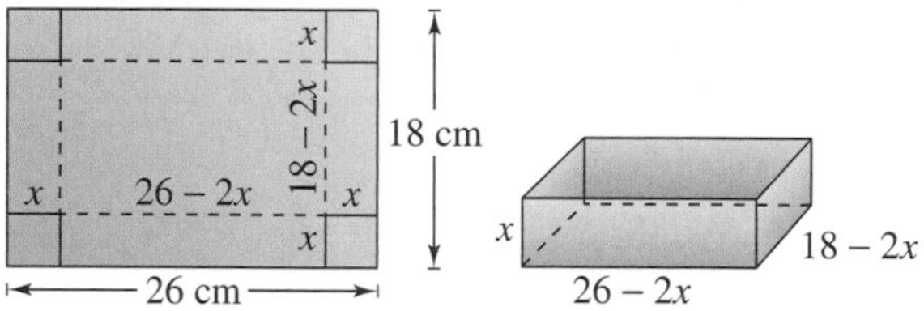

206. ***Volume of a Box*** An overnight shipping company is designing a closed box by cutting along the solid lines and folding along the broken lines on the rectangular piece of corrugated cardboard shown in the figure. The length and width of the rectangle are 45 centimeters and 15 centimeters, respectively.

(a) Find the volume of the shipping box in terms of x.

(b) Find the volume when $x = 3$, $x = 5$, and $x = 7$.

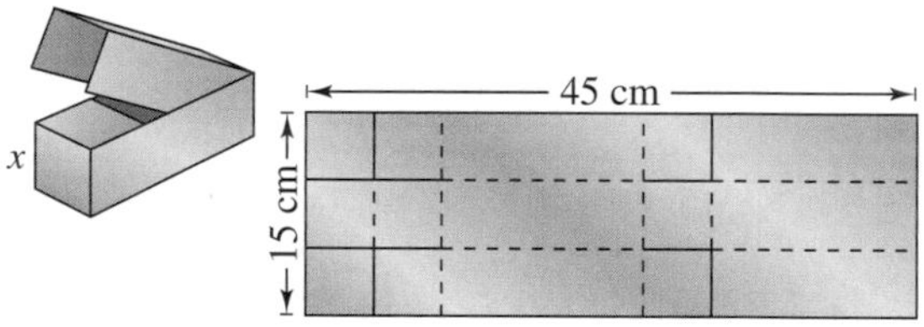

Geometry **In Exercises 207 and 208, find a polynomial that represents the total number of square feet for the floor plan shown in the figure.**

207.

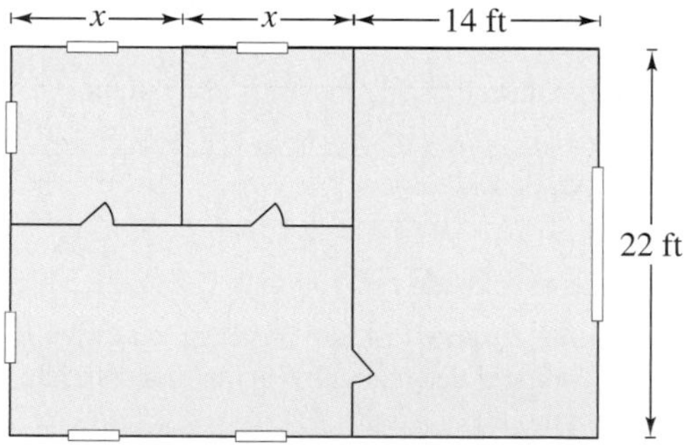

208.

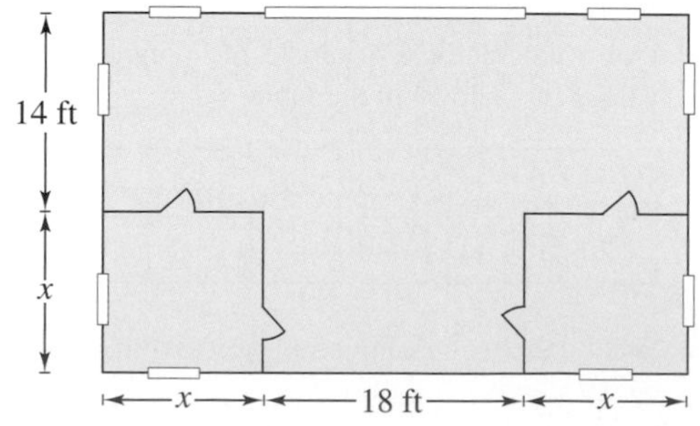

209. ***Geometry*** Find the area of the shaded region in each figure. Write your result as a polynomial in standard form.

(a)

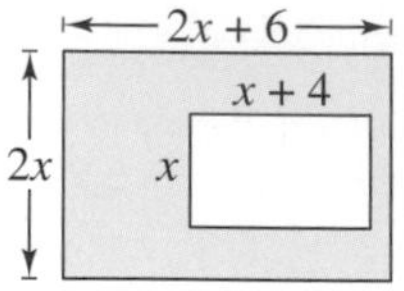

(b)

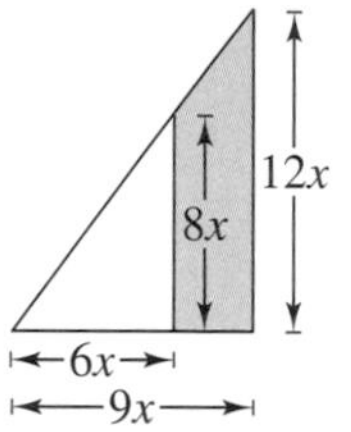

210. ***Stopping Distance*** The stopping distance of an automobile is the distance traveled during the driver's reaction time plus the distance traveled after the brakes are applied. In an experiment, these distances were measured (in feet) when the automobile was traveling at a speed of x miles per hour on dry, level pavement, as shown in the bar graph. The distance traveled during the reaction time R was

$$R = 1.1x$$

and the braking distance B was

$$B = 0.0475x^2 - 0.001x + 0.23.$$

(a) Determine the polynomial that represents the total stopping distance T.

(b) Use the result of part (a) to estimate the total stopping distance when $x = 30$, $x = 40$, and $x = 55$ miles per hour.

(c) Use the bar graph to make a statement about the total stopping distance required for increasing speeds.

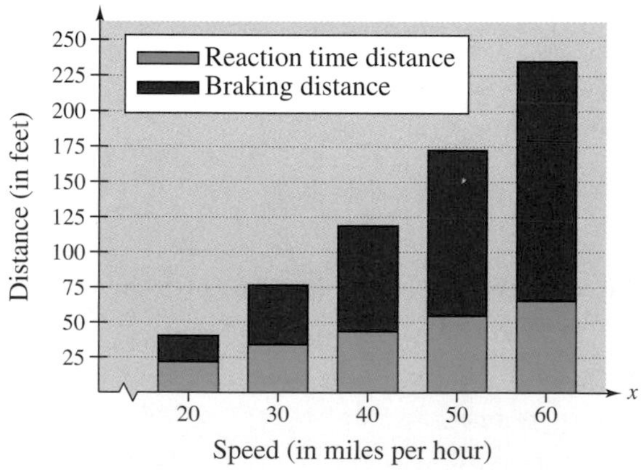

Geometric Modeling **In Exercises 211–214, draw a "geometric factoring model" to represent the factorization. For instance, a factoring model for**

$$2x^2 + 3x + 1 = (2x + 1)(x + 1)$$

is shown in the figure.

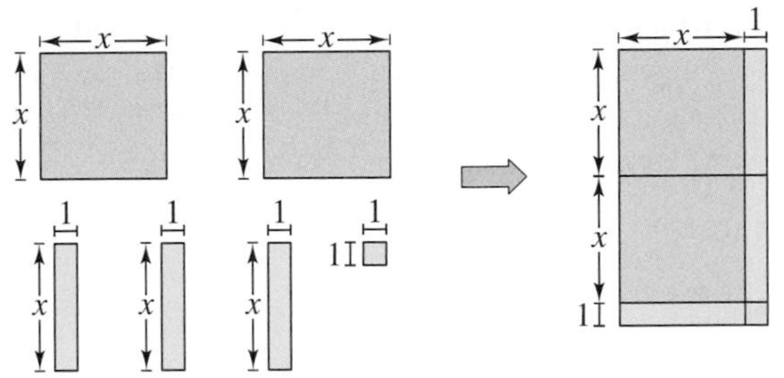

211. $3x^2 + 7x + 2 = (3x + 1)(x + 2)$

212. $x^2 + 4x + 3 = (x + 3)(x + 1)$

213. $2x^2 + 7x + 3 = (2x + 1)(x + 3)$

214. $x^2 + 3x + 2 = (x + 2)(x + 1)$

Geometry **In Exercises 215–218, write an expression in factored form for the area of the shaded portion of the figure.**

215.

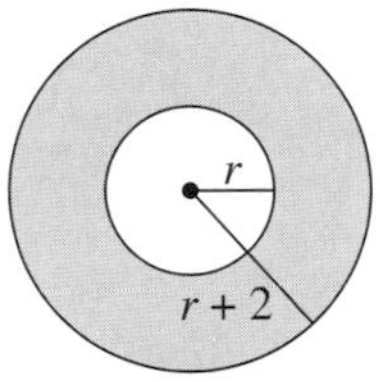

216.

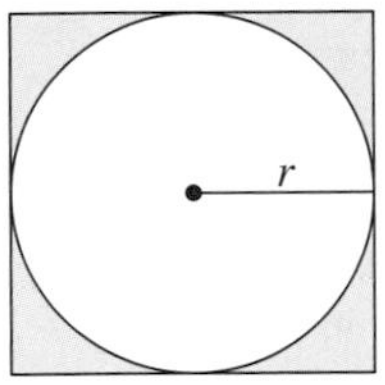

217.

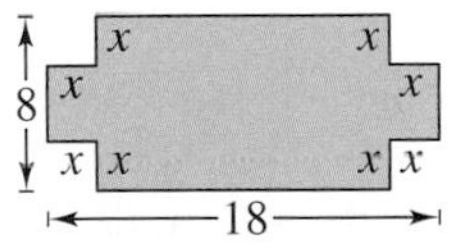

218.

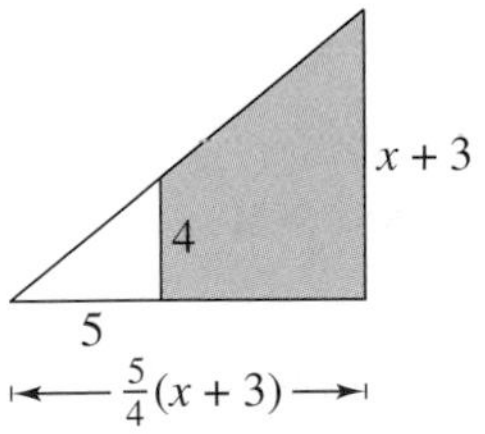

219. ***Geometry*** The volume V of concrete used to make the cylindrical concrete storage tank shown in the figure is $V = \pi R^2 h - \pi r^2 h$ where R is the outside radius, r is the inside radius, and h is the height of the storage tank.

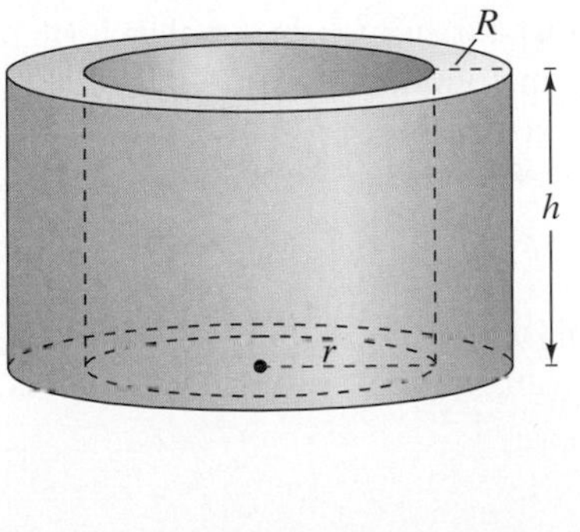

(a) Factor the expression for the volume.

(b) From the result of part (a), show that the volume of concrete is

$$2\pi(\text{average radius})(\text{thickness of the tank})h.$$

220. ***Chemistry*** The rate of change of an autocatalytic chemical reaction is $kQx - kx^2$, where Q is the amount of the original substance, x is the amount of substance formed, and k is a constant of proportionality. Factor the expression.

Synthesis

True or False? **In Exercises 221–224, determine whether the statement is true or false. Justify your answer.**

221. The product of two binomials is always a second-degree polynomial.

222. The sum of two binomials is always a binomial.

223. The difference of two perfect squares can be factored as the product of conjugate pairs.

224. The sum of two perfect squares can be factored as the binomial sum squared.

225. Find the degree of the product of two polynomials of degrees m and n.

226. Find the degree of the sum of two polynomials of degrees m and n if $m < n$.

227. ***Think About It*** When the polynomial

$$-x^3 + 3x^2 + 2x - 1$$

is subtracted from an unknown polynomial, the difference is

$$5x^2 + 8.$$

If it is possible, find the unknown polynomial.

228. ***Logical Reasoning*** Verify that $(x + y)^2$ is not equal to $x^2 + y^2$ by letting $x = 3$ and $y = 4$ and evaluating both expressions. Are there any values of x and y for which $(x + y)^2 = x^2 + y^2$? Explain.

229. Factor $x^{2n} - y^{2n}$ completely.

230. Factor $x^{3n} + y^{3n}$ completely.

231. Factor $x^{3n} - y^{2n}$ completely.

232. ***Writing*** Explain what is meant when it is said that a polynomial is in factored form.

233. Give an example of a polynomial that is prime with respect to the integers.

A.4 Rational Expressions

What you should learn

- Find domains of algebraic expressions.
- Simplify rational expressions.
- Add, subtract, multiply, and divide rational expressions.
- Simplify complex fractions and rewrite difference quotients.

Why you should learn it

Rational expressions can be used to solve real-life problems. For instance, in Exercise 84 on page A45, a rational expression is used to model the projected number of households banking and paying bills online from 2002 through 2007.

Domain of an Algebraic Expression

The set of real numbers for which an algebraic expression is defined is the **domain** of the expression. Two algebraic expressions are **equivalent** if they have the same domain and yield the same values for all numbers in their domain. For instance, $(x + 1) + (x + 2)$ and $2x + 3$ are equivalent because

$$\begin{aligned}(x + 1) + (x + 2) &= x + 1 + x + 2\\ &= x + x + 1 + 2\\ &= 2x + 3.\end{aligned}$$

Example 1 **Finding the Domain of an Algebraic Expression**

a. The domain of the polynomial

$$2x^3 + 3x + 4$$

is the set of all real numbers. In fact, the domain of any polynomial is the set of all real numbers, unless the domain is specifically restricted.

b. The domain of the radical expression

$$\sqrt{x - 2}$$

is the set of real numbers greater than or equal to 2, because the square root of a negative number is not a real number.

c. The domain of the expression

$$\frac{x + 2}{x - 3}$$

is the set of all real numbers except $x = 3$, which would result in division by zero, which is undefined.

✓CHECKPOINT Now try Exercise 1.

The quotient of two algebraic expressions is a *fractional expression*. Moreover, the quotient of two *polynomials* such as

$$\frac{1}{x}, \qquad \frac{2x - 1}{x + 1}, \qquad \text{or} \qquad \frac{x^2 - 1}{x^2 + 1}$$

is a **rational expression.** Recall that a fraction is in simplest form if its numerator and denominator have no factors in common aside from ± 1. To write a fraction in simplest form, divide out common factors.

$$\frac{a \cdot \cancel{c}}{b \cdot \cancel{c}} = \frac{a}{b}, \quad c \neq 0$$

The key to success in simplifying rational expressions lies in your ability to *factor* polynomials.

Simplifying Rational Expressions

When simplifying rational expressions, be sure to factor each polynomial completely before concluding that the numerator and denominator have no factors in common.

In this text, when a rational expression is written, the domain is usually not listed with the expression. It is *implied* that the real numbers that make the denominator zero are excluded from the expression. Also, when performing operations with rational expressions, this text follows the convention of listing *by the simplified expression* all values of x that must be specifically excluded from the domain in order to make the domains of the simplified and original expressions agree.

STUDY TIP

In Example 2, do not make the mistake of trying to simplify further by dividing out terms.

$$\frac{x+6}{3} = \frac{x+6}{3} = x+2$$

Remember that to simplify fractions, divide out common *factors*, not terms.

Example 2 Simplifying a Rational Expression

Write $\dfrac{x^2 + 4x - 12}{3x - 6}$ in simplest form.

Solution

$$\frac{x^2 + 4x - 12}{3x - 6} = \frac{(x+6)\cancel{(x-2)}}{3\cancel{(x-2)}} \qquad \text{Factor completely.}$$

$$= \frac{x+6}{3}, \quad x \neq 2 \qquad \text{Divide out common factors.}$$

Note that the original expression is undefined when $x = 2$ (because division by zero is undefined). To make sure that the simplified expression is *equivalent* to the original expression, you must restrict the domain of the simplified expression by excluding the value $x = 2$.

✓CHECKPOINT Now try Exercise 19.

Sometimes it may be necessary to change the sign of a factor to simplify a rational expression, as shown in Example 3.

Example 3 Simplifying Rational Expressions

Write $\dfrac{12 + x - x^2}{2x^2 - 9x + 4}$ in simplest form.

Solution

$$\frac{12 + x - x^2}{2x^2 - 9x + 4} = \frac{(4-x)(3+x)}{(2x-1)(x-4)} \qquad \text{Factor completely.}$$

$$= \frac{-\cancel{(x-4)}(3+x)}{(2x-1)\cancel{(x-4)}} \qquad (4-x) = -(x-4)$$

$$= -\frac{3+x}{2x-1}, \quad x \neq 4 \qquad \text{Divide out common factors.}$$

✓CHECKPOINT Now try Exercise 25.

Operations with Rational Expressions

To multiply or divide rational expressions, use the properties of fractions discussed in Appendix A.1. Recall that to divide fractions, you invert the divisor and multiply.

Example 4 Multiplying Rational Expressions

$$\frac{2x^2 + x - 6}{x^2 + 4x - 5} \cdot \frac{x^3 - 3x^2 + 2x}{4x^2 - 6x} = \frac{\cancel{(2x - 3)}(x + 2)}{(x + 5)\cancel{(x - 1)}} \cdot \frac{\cancel{x}(x - 2)\cancel{(x - 1)}}{2\cancel{x}\cancel{(2x - 3)}}$$

$$= \frac{(x + 2)(x - 2)}{2(x + 5)}, \qquad x \neq 0, x \neq 1, x \neq \tfrac{3}{2}$$

CHECKPOINT Now try Exercise 39.

In Example 4 the restrictions $x \neq 0$, $x \neq 1$, and $x \neq \frac{3}{2}$ are listed with the simplified expression in order to make the two domains agree. Note that the value $x = -5$ is excluded from both domains, so it is not necessary to list this value.

Example 5 Dividing Rational Expressions

$$\frac{x^3 - 8}{x^2 - 4} \div \frac{x^2 + 2x + 4}{x^3 + 8} = \frac{x^3 - 8}{x^2 - 4} \cdot \frac{x^3 + 8}{x^2 + 2x + 4} \qquad \text{Invert and multiply.}$$

$$= \frac{\cancel{(x - 2)}\cancel{(x^2 + 2x + 4)}}{\cancel{(x + 2)}\cancel{(x - 2)}} \cdot \frac{\cancel{(x + 2)}(x^2 - 2x + 4)}{\cancel{(x^2 + 2x + 4)}}$$

$$= x^2 - 2x + 4, \qquad x \neq \pm 2 \qquad \text{Divide out common factors.}$$

CHECKPOINT Now try Exercise 41.

To add or subtract rational expressions, you can use the LCD (least common denominator) method or the *basic definition*

$$\frac{a}{b} \pm \frac{c}{d} = \frac{ad \pm bc}{bd}, \qquad b \neq 0, d \neq 0. \qquad \text{Basic definition}$$

This definition provides an efficient way of adding or subtracting *two* fractions that have no common factors in their denominators.

Example 6 Subtracting Rational Expressions

$$\frac{x}{x - 3} - \frac{2}{3x + 4} = \frac{x(3x + 4) - 2(x - 3)}{(x - 3)(3x + 4)} \qquad \text{Basic definition}$$

$$= \frac{3x^2 + 4x - 2x + 6}{(x - 3)(3x + 4)} \qquad \text{Distributive Property}$$

$$= \frac{3x^2 + 2x + 6}{(x - 3)(3x + 4)} \qquad \text{Combine like terms.}$$

CHECKPOINT Now try Exercise 49.

STUDY TIP

When subtracting rational expressions, remember to distribute the negative sign to all the terms in the quantity that is being subtracted.

For three or more fractions, or for fractions with a repeated factor in the denominators, the LCD method works well. Recall that the least common denominator of several fractions consists of the product of all prime factors in the denominators, with each factor given the highest power of its occurrence in any denominator. Here is a numerical example.

$$\frac{1}{6} + \frac{3}{4} - \frac{2}{3} = \frac{1 \cdot 2}{6 \cdot 2} + \frac{3 \cdot 3}{4 \cdot 3} - \frac{2 \cdot 4}{3 \cdot 4}$$ The LCD is 12.

$$= \frac{2}{12} + \frac{9}{12} - \frac{8}{12}$$

$$= \frac{3}{12}$$

$$= \frac{1}{4}$$

Sometimes the numerator of the answer has a factor in common with the denominator. In such cases the answer should be simplified. For instance, in the example above, $\frac{3}{12}$ was simplified to $\frac{1}{4}$.

Example 7 Combining Rational Expressions: The LCD Method

Perform the operations and simplify.

$$\frac{3}{x-1} - \frac{2}{x} + \frac{x+3}{x^2-1}$$

Solution

Using the factored denominators $(x - 1)$, x, and $(x + 1)(x - 1)$, you can see that the LCD is $x(x + 1)(x - 1)$.

$$\frac{3}{x-1} - \frac{2}{x} + \frac{x+3}{(x+1)(x-1)}$$

$$= \frac{3(x)(x+1)}{x(x+1)(x-1)} - \frac{2(x+1)(x-1)}{x(x+1)(x-1)} + \frac{(x+3)(x)}{x(x+1)(x-1)}$$

$$= \frac{3(x)(x+1) - 2(x+1)(x-1) + (x+3)(x)}{x(x+1)(x-1)}$$

$$= \frac{3x^2 + 3x - 2x^2 + 2 + x^2 + 3x}{x(x+1)(x-1)}$$ Distributive Property

$$= \frac{3x^2 - 2x^2 + x^2 + 3x + 3x + 2}{x(x+1)(x-1)}$$ Group like terms.

$$= \frac{2x^2 + 6x + 2}{x(x+1)(x-1)}$$ Combine like terms.

$$= \frac{2(x^2 + 3x + 1)}{x(x+1)(x-1)}$$ Factor.

✓CHECKPOINT Now try Exercise 51.

Complex Fractions and the Difference Quotient

Fractional expressions with separate fractions in the numerator, denominator, or both are called **complex fractions.** Here are two examples.

$$\frac{\left(\frac{1}{x}\right)}{x^2+1} \quad \text{and} \quad \frac{\left(\frac{1}{x}\right)}{\left(\frac{1}{x^2+1}\right)}$$

A complex fraction can be simplified by combining the fractions in its numerator into a single fraction and then combining the fractions in its denominator into a single fraction. Then invert the denominator and multiply.

Example 8 **Simplifying a Complex Fraction**

$$\frac{\left(\frac{2}{x}-3\right)}{\left(1-\frac{1}{x-1}\right)} = \frac{\left[\frac{2-3(x)}{x}\right]}{\left[\frac{1(x-1)-1}{x-1}\right]} \qquad \text{Combine fractions.}$$

$$= \frac{\left(\frac{2-3x}{x}\right)}{\left(\frac{x-2}{x-1}\right)} \qquad \text{Simplify.}$$

$$= \frac{2-3x}{x} \cdot \frac{x-1}{x-2} \qquad \text{Invert and multiply.}$$

$$= \frac{(2-3x)(x-1)}{x(x-2)}, \quad x \neq 1$$

✓CHECKPOINT Now try Exercise 57.

Another way to simplify a complex fraction is to multiply its numerator and denominator by the LCD of all fractions in its numerator and denominator. This method is applied to the fraction in Example 8 as follows.

$$\frac{\left(\frac{2}{x}-3\right)}{\left(1-\frac{1}{x-1}\right)} = \frac{\left(\frac{2}{x}-3\right)}{\left(1-\frac{1}{x-1}\right)} \cdot \frac{x(x-1)}{x(x-1)} \qquad \text{LCD is } x(x-1).$$

$$= \frac{\left(\frac{2-3x}{\cancel{x}}\right) \cdot \cancel{x}(x-1)}{\left(\frac{x-2}{\cancel{x-1}}\right) \cdot x(\cancel{x-1})}$$

$$= \frac{(2-3x)(x-1)}{x(x-2)}, \quad x \neq 1$$

The next three examples illustrate some methods for simplifying rational expressions involving negative exponents and radicals. These types of expressions occur frequently in calculus.

To simplify an expression with negative exponents, one method is to begin by factoring out the common factor with the *smaller* exponent. Remember that when factoring, you *subtract* exponents. For instance, in $3x^{-5/2} + 2x^{-3/2}$ the smaller exponent is $-\frac{5}{2}$ and the common factor is $x^{-5/2}$.

$$\begin{aligned} 3x^{-5/2} + 2x^{-3/2} &= x^{-5/2}[3(1) + 2x^{-3/2-(-5/2)}] \\ &= x^{-5/2}(3 + 2x^1) \\ &= \frac{3 + 2x}{x^{5/2}} \end{aligned}$$

Example 9 **Simplifying an Expression**

Simplify the following expression containing negative exponents.

$$x(1 - 2x)^{-3/2} + (1 - 2x)^{-1/2}$$

Solution

Begin by factoring out the common factor with the *smaller exponent.*

$$\begin{aligned} x(1 - 2x)^{-3/2} + (1 - 2x)^{-1/2} &= (1 - 2x)^{-3/2}[x + (1 - 2x)^{(-1/2)-(-3/2)}] \\ &= (1 - 2x)^{-3/2}[x + (1 - 2x)^1] \\ &= \frac{1 - x}{(1 - 2x)^{3/2}} \end{aligned}$$

CHECKPOINT Now try Exercise 65.

A second method for simplifying an expression with negative exponents is shown in the next example.

Example 10 **Simplifying an Expression with Negative Exponents**

$$\begin{aligned} &\frac{(4 - x^2)^{1/2} + x^2(4 - x^2)^{-1/2}}{4 - x^2} \\ &\quad = \frac{(4 - x^2)^{1/2} + x^2(4 - x^2)^{-1/2}}{4 - x^2} \cdot \frac{(4 - x^2)^{1/2}}{(4 - x^2)^{1/2}} \\ &\quad = \frac{(4 - x^2)^1 + x^2(4 - x^2)^0}{(4 - x^2)^{3/2}} \\ &\quad = \frac{4 - x^2 + x^2}{(4 - x^2)^{3/2}} \\ &\quad = \frac{4}{(4 - x^2)^{3/2}} \end{aligned}$$

CHECKPOINT Now try Exercise 67.

Example 11 **Rewriting a Difference Quotient**

The following expression from calculus is an example of a *difference quotient*.

$$\frac{\sqrt{x+h}-\sqrt{x}}{h}$$

Rewrite this expression by rationalizing its numerator.

Solution

$$\begin{aligned}\frac{\sqrt{x+h}-\sqrt{x}}{h} &= \frac{\sqrt{x+h}-\sqrt{x}}{h} \cdot \frac{\sqrt{x+h}+\sqrt{x}}{\sqrt{x+h}+\sqrt{x}} \\ &= \frac{\left(\sqrt{x+h}\right)^2-\left(\sqrt{x}\right)^2}{h\left(\sqrt{x+h}+\sqrt{x}\right)} \\ &= \frac{h}{h\left(\sqrt{x+h}+\sqrt{x}\right)} \\ &= \frac{1}{\sqrt{x+h}+\sqrt{x}}, \qquad h \neq 0\end{aligned}$$

Notice that the original expression is undefined when $h = 0$. So, you must exclude $h = 0$ from the domain of the simplified expression so that the expressions are equivalent.

CHECKPOINT Now try Exercise 73.

Difference quotients, such as that in Example 11, occur frequently in calculus. Often, they need to be rewritten in an equivalent form that can be evaluated when $h = 0$. Note that the equivalent form is not simpler than the original form, but it has the advantage that it is defined when $h = 0$.

A.4 Exercises

VOCABULARY CHECK: Fill in the blanks.

1. The set of real numbers for which an algebraic expression is defined is the ________ of the expression.

2. The quotient of two algebraic expressions is a fractional expression and the quotient of two polynomials is a ________ ________.

3. Fractional expressions with separate fractions in the numerator, denominator, or both are called ________ fractions.

4. To simplify an expression with negative exponents, it is possible to begin by factoring out the common factor with the ________ exponent.

5. Two algebraic expressions that have the same domain and yield the same values for all numbers in their domains are called ________.

6. An important rational expression, such as $\frac{(x+h)^2 - x^2}{h}$, that occurs in calculus is called a ________ ________.

In Exercises 1–8, find the domain of the expression.

1. $3x^2 - 4x + 7$
2. $2x^2 + 5x - 2$
3. $4x^3 + 3, \quad x \geq 0$
4. $6x^2 - 9, \quad x > 0$
5. $\dfrac{1}{x - 2}$
6. $\dfrac{x + 1}{2x + 1}$
7. $\sqrt{x + 1}$
8. $\sqrt{6 - x}$

In Exercises 9 and 10, find the missing factor in the numerator such that the two fractions are equivalent.

9. $\dfrac{5}{2x} = \dfrac{5(\quad)}{6x^2}$
10. $\dfrac{3}{4} = \dfrac{3(\quad)}{4(x + 1)}$

In Exercises 11–28, write the rational expression in simplest form.

11. $\dfrac{15x^2}{10x}$
12. $\dfrac{18y^2}{60y^5}$
13. $\dfrac{3xy}{xy + x}$
14. $\dfrac{2x^2y}{xy - y}$
15. $\dfrac{4y - 8y^2}{10y - 5}$
16. $\dfrac{9x^2 + 9x}{2x + 2}$
17. $\dfrac{x - 5}{10 - 2x}$
18. $\dfrac{12 - 4x}{x - 3}$
19. $\dfrac{y^2 - 16}{y + 4}$
20. $\dfrac{x^2 - 25}{5 - x}$
21. $\dfrac{x^3 + 5x^2 + 6x}{x^2 - 4}$
22. $\dfrac{x^2 + 8x - 20}{x^2 + 11x + 10}$
23. $\dfrac{y^2 - 7y + 12}{y^2 + 3y - 18}$
24. $\dfrac{x^2 - 7x + 6}{x^2 + 11x + 10}$
25. $\dfrac{2 - x + 2x^2 - x^3}{x^2 - 4}$
26. $\dfrac{x^2 - 9}{x^3 + x^2 - 9x - 9}$
27. $\dfrac{z^3 - 8}{z^2 + 2z + 4}$
28. $\dfrac{y^3 - 2y^2 - 3y}{y^3 + 1}$

In Exercises 29 and 30, complete the table. What can you conclude?

29.

x	0	1	2	3	4	5	6
$\dfrac{x^2 - 2x - 3}{x - 3}$							
$x + 1$							

30.

x	0	1	2	3	4	5	6
$\dfrac{x - 3}{x^2 - x - 6}$							
$\dfrac{1}{x + 2}$							

31. ***Error Analysis*** Describe the error.

$$\frac{5x^3}{2x^3 + 4} = \frac{5x^3}{2x^3 + 4} = \frac{5}{2 + 4} = \frac{5}{6}$$

32. ***Error Analysis*** Describe the error.

$$\frac{x^3 + 25x}{x^2 - 2x - 15} = \frac{x(x^2 + 25)}{(x - 5)(x + 3)} = \frac{x(x + 5)(x - 5)}{(x - 5)(x + 3)} = \frac{x(x + 5)}{x + 3}$$

Geometry **In Exercises 33 and 34, find the ratio of the area of the shaded portion of the figure to the total area of the figure.**

33.

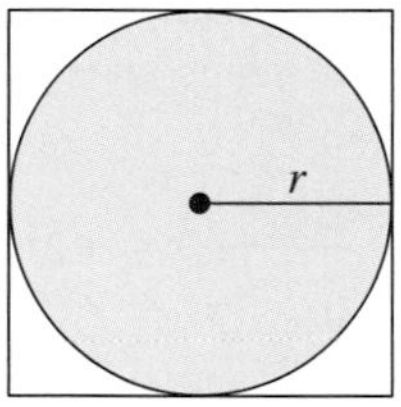

34.

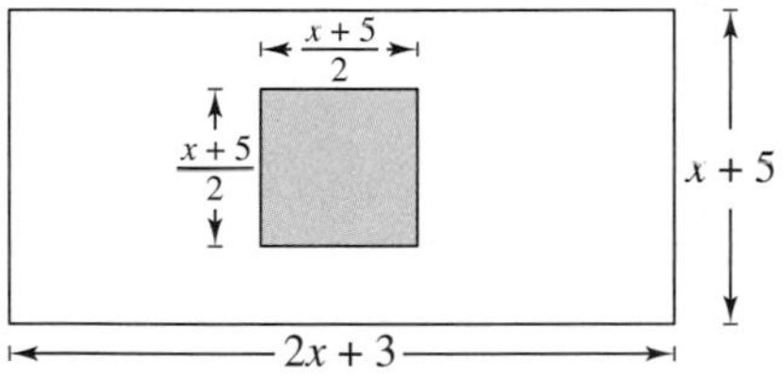

In Exercises 35–42, perform the multiplication or division and simplify.

35. $\dfrac{5}{x - 1} \cdot \dfrac{x - 1}{25(x - 2)}$
36. $\dfrac{x + 13}{x^3(3 - x)} \cdot \dfrac{x(x - 3)}{5}$
37. $\dfrac{r}{r - 1} \cdot \dfrac{r^2 - 1}{r^2}$
38. $\dfrac{4y - 16}{5y + 15} \cdot \dfrac{2y + 6}{4 - y}$
39. $\dfrac{t^2 - t - 6}{t^2 + 6t + 9} \cdot \dfrac{t + 3}{t^2 - 4}$
40. $\dfrac{x^2 + xy - 2y^2}{x^3 + x^2y} \cdot \dfrac{x}{x^2 + 3xy + 2y^2}$
41. $\dfrac{x^2 - 36}{x} \div \dfrac{x^3 - 6x^2}{x^2 + x}$
42. $\dfrac{x^2 - 14x + 49}{x^2 - 49} \div \dfrac{3x - 21}{x + 7}$

In Exercises 43–52, perform the addition or subtraction and simplify.

43. $\dfrac{5}{x-1}+\dfrac{x}{x-1}$

44. $\dfrac{2x-1}{x+3}+\dfrac{1-x}{x+3}$

45. $6-\dfrac{5}{x+3}$

46. $\dfrac{3}{x-1}-5$

47. $\dfrac{3}{x-2}+\dfrac{5}{2-x}$

48. $\dfrac{2x}{x-5}-\dfrac{5}{5-x}$

49. $\dfrac{1}{x^2-x-2}-\dfrac{x}{x^2-5x+6}$

50. $\dfrac{2}{x^2-x-2}+\dfrac{10}{x^2+2x-8}$

51. $-\dfrac{1}{x}+\dfrac{2}{x^2+1}+\dfrac{1}{x^3+x}$

52. $\dfrac{2}{x+1}+\dfrac{2}{x-1}+\dfrac{1}{x^2-1}$

Error Analysis **In Exercises 53 and 54, describe the error.**

53. $\dfrac{x+4}{x+2}-\dfrac{3x-8}{x+2}=\dfrac{x+4-3x-8}{x+2}=\dfrac{-2x-4}{x+2}=\dfrac{-2(x+2)}{x+2}=-2$

54. $\dfrac{6-x}{x(x+2)}+\dfrac{x+2}{x^2}+\dfrac{8}{x^2(x+2)}=\dfrac{x(6-x)+(x+2)^2+8}{x^2(x+2)}=\dfrac{6x-x^2+x^2+4+8}{x^2(x+2)}=\dfrac{6(x+2)}{x^2(x+2)}=\dfrac{6}{x^2}$

In Exercises 55–60, simplify the complex fraction.

55. $\dfrac{\left(\dfrac{x}{2}-1\right)}{(x-2)}$

56. $\dfrac{(x-4)}{\left(\dfrac{x}{4}-\dfrac{4}{x}\right)}$

57. $\dfrac{\left[\dfrac{x^2}{(x+1)^2}\right]}{\left[\dfrac{x}{(x+1)^3}\right]}$

58. $\dfrac{\left(\dfrac{x^2-1}{x}\right)}{\left[\dfrac{(x-1)^2}{x}\right]}$

59. $\dfrac{\left(\sqrt{x}-\dfrac{1}{2\sqrt{x}}\right)}{\sqrt{x}}$

60. $\dfrac{\left(\dfrac{t^2}{\sqrt{t^2+1}}-\sqrt{t^2+1}\right)}{t^2}$

In Exercises 61–66, factor the expression by removing the common factor with the smaller exponent.

61. x^5-2x^{-2}

62. x^5-5x^{-3}

63. $x^2(x^2+1)^{-5}-(x^2+1)^{-4}$

64. $2x(x-5)^{-3}-4x^2(x-5)^{-4}$

65. $2x^2(x-1)^{1/2}-5(x-1)^{-1/2}$

66. $4x^3(2x-1)^{3/2}-2x(2x-1)^{-1/2}$

In Exercises 67 and 68, simplify the expression.

67. $\dfrac{3x^{1/3}-x^{-2/3}}{3x^{-2/3}}$

68. $\dfrac{-x^3(1-x^2)^{-1/2}-2x(1-x^2)^{1/2}}{x^4}$

In Exercises 69–72, simplify the difference quotient.

69. $\dfrac{\left(\dfrac{1}{x+h}-\dfrac{1}{x}\right)}{h}$

70. $\dfrac{\left[\dfrac{1}{(x+h)^2}-\dfrac{1}{x^2}\right]}{h}$

71. $\dfrac{\left(\dfrac{1}{x+h-4}-\dfrac{1}{x-4}\right)}{h}$

72. $\dfrac{\left(\dfrac{x+h}{x+h+1}-\dfrac{x}{x+1}\right)}{h}$

In Exercises 73–76, simplify the difference quotient by rationalizing the numerator.

73. $\dfrac{\sqrt{x+2}-\sqrt{x}}{2}$

74. $\dfrac{\sqrt{z-3}-\sqrt{z}}{3}$

75. $\dfrac{\sqrt{x+h+1}-\sqrt{x+1}}{h}$

76. $\dfrac{\sqrt{x+h-2}-\sqrt{x-2}}{h}$

Probability **In Exercises 77 and 78, consider an experiment in which a marble is tossed into a box whose base is shown in the figure. The probability that the marble will come to rest in the shaded portion of the box is equal to the ratio of the shaded area to the total area of the figure. Find the probability.**

77.

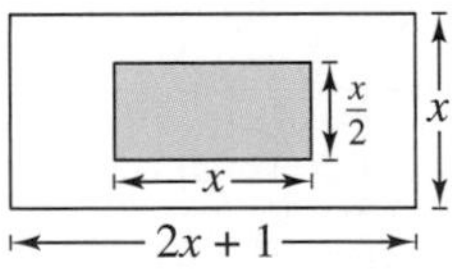

78.

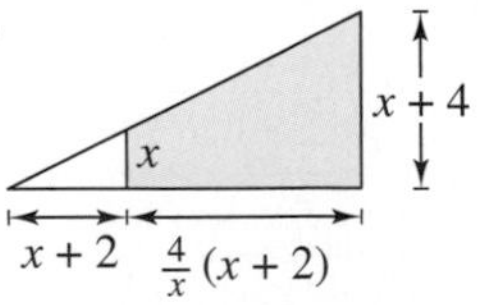

79. ***Rate*** A photocopier copies at a rate of 16 pages per minute.

(a) Find the time required to copy one page.

(b) Find the time required to copy x pages.

(c) Find the time required to copy 60 pages.

80. ***Rate*** After working together for t hours on a common task, two workers have done fractional parts of the job equal to $t/3$ and $t/5$, respectively. What fractional part of the task has been completed?

Finance **In Exercises 81 and 82, the formula that approximates the annual interest rate r of a monthly installment loan is given by**

$$r = \frac{\left[\frac{24(NM - P)}{N}\right]}{\left(P + \frac{NM}{12}\right)}$$

where N is the total number of payments, M is the monthly payment, and P is the amount financed.

81. (a) Approximate the annual interest rate for a four-year car loan of \$16,000 that has monthly payments of \$400.

(b) Simplify the expression for the annual interest rate r, and then rework part (a).

82. (a) Approximate the annual interest rate for a five-year car loan of \$28,000 that has monthly payments of \$525.

(b) Simplify the expression for the annual interest rate r, and then rework part (a).

83. ***Refrigeration*** When food (at room temperature) is placed in a refrigerator, the time required for the food to cool depends on the amount of food, the air circulation in the refrigerator, the original temperature of the food, and the temperature of the refrigerator. The model that gives the temperature of food that has an original temperature of 75°F and is placed in a 40°F refrigerator is

$$T = 10\left(\frac{4t^2 + 16t + 75}{t^2 + 4t + 10}\right)$$

where T is the temperature (in degrees Fahrenheit) and t is the time (in hours).

(a) Complete the table.

t	0	2	4	6	8	10
T						

t	12	14	16	18	20	22
T						

(b) What value of T does the mathematical model appear to be approaching?

84. ***Interactive Money Management*** The table shows the projected numbers of U.S. households (in millions) banking online and paying bills online for the years 2002 through 2007. (Source: eMarketer; Forrester Research)

Year	Banking	Paying Bills
2002	21.9	13.7
2003	26.8	17.4
2004	31.5	20.9
2005	35.0	23.9
2006	40.0	26.7
2007	45.0	29.1

Mathematical models for these data are

$$\text{Number banking online} = \frac{-0.728t^2 + 23.81t - 0.3}{-0.049t^2 + 0.61t + 1.0}$$

and

$$\text{Number paying bills online} = \frac{4.39t + 5.5}{0.002t^2 + 0.01t + 1.0}$$

where t represents the year, with $t = 2$ corresponding to 2002.

(a) Using the models, create a table to estimate the projected number of households banking online and the projected number of households paying bills online for the given years.

(b) Compare the values given by the models with the actual data.

(c) Determine a model for the ratio of the projected number of households paying bills online to the projected number of households banking online.

(d) Use the model from part (c) to find the ratio over the given years. Interpret your results.

Synthesis

True or False? **In Exercises 85 and 86, determine whether the statement is true or false. Justify your answer.**

85. $\dfrac{x^{2n} - 1^{2n}}{x^n - 1^n} = x^n + 1^n$

86. $\dfrac{x^2 - 3x + 2}{x - 1} = x - 2$, for all values of x.

87. ***Think About It*** How do you determine whether a rational expression is in simplest form?

A.5 Solving Equations

What you should learn

- Identify different types of equations.
- Solve linear equations in one variable and equations that lead to linear equations.
- Solve quadratic equations by factoring, extracting square roots, completing the square, and using the Quadratic Formula.
- Solve polynomial equations of degree three or greater.
- Solve equations involving radicals.
- Solve equations with absolute values.

Why you should learn it

Linear equations are used in many real-life applications. For example, in Exercise 185 on page A58, linear equations can be used to model the relationship between the length of a thigh-bone and the height of a person, helping researchers learn about ancient cultures.

Equations and Solutions of Equations

An **equation** in x is a statement that two algebraic expressions are equal. For example

$$3x - 5 = 7,\ x^2 - x - 6 = 0, \text{ and } \sqrt{2x} = 4$$

are equations. To **solve** an equation in x means to find all values of x for which the equation is true. Such values are **solutions.** For instance, $x = 4$ is a solution of the equation

$$3x - 5 = 7$$

because $3(4) - 5 = 7$ is a true statement.

The solutions of an equation depend on the kinds of numbers being considered. For instance, in the set of rational numbers, $x^2 = 10$ has no solution because there is no rational number whose square is 10. However, in the set of real numbers, the equation has the two solutions $x = \sqrt{10}$ and $x = -\sqrt{10}$.

An equation that is true for *every* real number in the *domain* of the variable is called an **identity.** The domain is the set of all real numbers for which the equation is defined. For example

$$x^2 - 9 = (x + 3)(x - 3) \qquad \text{Identity}$$

is an identity because it is a true statement for any real value of x. The equation

$$\frac{x}{3x^2} = \frac{1}{3x} \qquad \text{Identity}$$

where $x \neq 0$, is an identity because it is true for any nonzero real value of x.

An equation that is true for just *some* (or even none) of the real numbers in the domain of the variable is called a **conditional equation.** For example, the equation

$$x^2 - 9 = 0 \qquad \text{Conditional equation}$$

is conditional because $x = 3$ and $x = -3$ are the only values in the domain that satisfy the equation. The equation $2x - 4 = 2x + 1$ is conditional because there are no real values of x for which the equation is true. Learning to solve conditional equations is the primary focus of this section.

Linear Equations in One Variable

Definition of a Linear Equation

A **linear equation in one variable** x is an equation that can be written in the standard form

$$ax + b = 0$$

where a and b are real numbers with $a \neq 0$.

A linear equation has exactly one solution. To see this, consider the following steps. (Remember that $a \neq 0$.)

$ax + b = 0$	Write original equation.
$ax = -b$	Subtract b from each side.
$x = -\dfrac{b}{a}$	Divide each side by a.

To solve a conditional equation in x, isolate x on one side of the equation by a sequence of **equivalent** (and usually simpler) **equations,** each having the same solution(s) as the original equation. The operations that yield equivalent equations come from the Substitution Principle (see Appendix A.1) and simplification techniques.

Generating Equivalent Equations

An equation can be transformed into an *equivalent equation* by one or more of the following steps.

	Given Equation	*Equivalent Equation*
1. Remove symbols of grouping, combine like terms, or simplify fractions on one or both sides of the equation.	$2x - x = 4$	$x = 4$
2. Add (or subtract) the same quantity to (from) *each* side of the equation.	$x + 1 = 6$	$x = 5$
3. Multiply (or divide) *each* side of the equation by the same *nonzero* quantity.	$2x = 6$	$x = 3$
4. Interchange the two sides of the equation.	$2 = x$	$x = 2$

Example 1 Solving a Linear Equation

a. $3x - 6 = 0$	Original equation
$3x = 6$	Add 6 to each side.
$x = 2$	Divide each side by 3.
b. $5x + 4 = 3x - 8$	Original equation
$2x + 4 = -8$	Subtract $3x$ from each side.
$2x = -12$	Subtract 4 from each side.
$x = -6$	Divide each side by 2.

✓CHECKPOINT Now try Exercise 13.

STUDY TIP

After solving an equation, you should check each solution in the original equation. For instance, you can check the solution to Example 1(a) as follows.

$3x - 6 = 0$	Write original equation.
$3(2) - 6 \stackrel{?}{=} 0$	Substitute 2 for x.
$0 = 0$	Solution checks. ✓

Try checking the solution to Example 1(b).

To solve an equation involving fractional expressions, find the least common denominator (LCD) of all terms and multiply every term by the LCD. This process will clear the original equation of fractions and produce a simpler equation to work with.

STUDY TIP

An equation with a *single fraction* on each side can be cleared of denominators by **cross multiplying,** which is equivalent to multiplying by the LCD and then dividing out. To do this, multiply the left numerator by the right denominator and the right numerator by the left denominator as follows.

$\frac{a}{b} = \frac{c}{d}$ LCD is bd.

$\frac{a}{b} \cdot bd = \frac{c}{d} \cdot bd$ Multiply by LCD.

$ad = cb$ Divide out common factors.

Example 2 An Equation Involving Fractional Expressions

Solve $\frac{x}{3} + \frac{3x}{4} = 2$.

Solution

$\frac{x}{3} + \frac{3x}{4} = 2$ Write original equation.

$(12)\frac{x}{3} + (12)\frac{3x}{4} = (12)2$ Multiply each term by the LCD of 12.

$4x + 9x = 24$ Divide out and multiply.

$13x = 24$ Combine like terms.

$x = \frac{24}{13}$ Divide each side by 13.

The solution is $x = \frac{24}{13}$. Check this in the original equation.

CHECKPOINT Now try Exercise 21.

When multiplying or dividing an equation by a *variable* quantity, it is possible to introduce an extraneous solution. An **extraneous solution** is one that does not satisfy the original equation. Therefore, it is essential that you check your solutions.

Example 3 An Equation with an Extraneous Solution

Solve $\frac{1}{x-2} = \frac{3}{x+2} - \frac{6x}{x^2-4}$.

Solution

The LCD is $x^2 - 4$, or $(x + 2)(x - 2)$. Multiply each term by this LCD.

$$\frac{1}{x-2}(x+2)(x-2) = \frac{3}{x+2}(x+2)(x-2) - \frac{6x}{x^2-4}(x+2)(x-2)$$

$$x + 2 = 3(x - 2) - 6x, \quad x \neq \pm 2$$

$$x + 2 = 3x - 6 - 6x$$

$$x + 2 = -3x - 6$$

$$4x = -8 \quad \Rightarrow \quad x = -2 \qquad \text{Extraneous solution}$$

In the original equation, $x = -2$ yields a denominator of zero. So, $x = -2$ is an extraneous solution, and the original equation has *no solution.*

CHECKPOINT Now try Exercise 37.

STUDY TIP

Recall that the least common denominator of two or more fractions consists of the product of all prime factors in the denominators, with each factor given the highest power of its occurrence in any denominator. For instance, in Example 3, by factoring each denominator you can determine that the LCD is $(x + 2)(x - 2)$.

Quadratic Equations

A **quadratic equation** in x is an equation that can be written in the general form

$$ax^2 + bx + c = 0$$

where a, b, and c are real numbers, with $a \neq 0$. A quadratic equation in x is also known as a **second-degree polynomial equation** in x.

You should be familiar with the following four methods of solving quadratic equations.

Solving a Quadratic Equation

Factoring: If $ab = 0$, then $a = 0$ or $b = 0$.

Example:

$$x^2 - x - 6 = 0$$
$$(x - 3)(x + 2) = 0$$
$$x - 3 = 0 \quad \Rightarrow \quad x = 3$$
$$x + 2 = 0 \quad \Rightarrow \quad x = -2$$

Square Root Principle: If $u^2 = c$, where $c > 0$, then $u = \pm\sqrt{c}$.

Example:

$$(x + 3)^2 = 16$$
$$x + 3 = \pm 4$$
$$x = -3 \pm 4$$
$$x = 1 \quad \text{or} \quad x = -7$$

Completing the Square: If $x^2 + bx = c$, then

$$x^2 + bx + \left(\frac{b}{2}\right)^2 = c + \left(\frac{b}{2}\right)^2 \qquad \text{Add } \left(\frac{b}{2}\right)^2 \text{ to each side.}$$
$$\left(x + \frac{b}{2}\right)^2 = c + \frac{b^2}{4}.$$

Example:

$$x^2 + 6x = 5$$
$$x^2 + 6x + 3^2 = 5 + 3^2 \qquad \text{Add } \left(\frac{6}{2}\right)^2 \text{ to each side.}$$
$$(x + 3)^2 = 14$$
$$x + 3 = \pm\sqrt{14}$$
$$x = -3 \pm \sqrt{14}$$

Quadratic Formula: If $ax^2 + bx + c = 0$, then $x = \dfrac{-b \pm \sqrt{b^2 - 4ac}}{2a}$.

Example:

$$2x^2 + 3x - 1 = 0$$
$$x = \frac{-3 \pm \sqrt{3^2 - 4(2)(-1)}}{2(2)}$$
$$= \frac{-3 \pm \sqrt{17}}{4}$$

STUDY TIP

The Square Root Principle is also referred to as *extracting square roots*.

STUDY TIP

You can solve every quadratic equation by completing the square or using the Quadratic Formula.

Example 4 Solving a Quadratic Equation by Factoring

a. $2x^2 + 9x + 7 = 3$ — Original equation

$2x^2 + 9x + 4 = 0$ — Write in general form.

$(2x + 1)(x + 4) = 0$ — Factor.

$2x + 1 = 0 \implies x = -\frac{1}{2}$ — Set 1st factor equal to 0.

$x + 4 = 0 \implies x = -4$ — Set 2nd factor equal to 0.

The solutions are $x = -\frac{1}{2}$ and $x = -4$. Check these in the original equation.

b. $6x^2 - 3x = 0$ — Original equation

$3x(2x - 1) = 0$ — Factor.

$3x = 0 \implies x = 0$ — Set 1st factor equal to 0.

$2x - 1 = 0 \implies x = \frac{1}{2}$ — Set 2nd factor equal to 0.

The solutions are $x = 0$ and $x = \frac{1}{2}$. Check these in the original equation.

CHECKPOINT Now try Exercise 57.

Note that the method of solution in Example 4 is based on the Zero-Factor Property from Appendix A.1. Be sure you see that this property works *only* for equations written in general form (in which the right side of the equation is zero). So, all terms must be collected on one side *before* factoring. For instance, in the equation $(x - 5)(x + 2) = 8$, it is *incorrect* to set each factor equal to 8. Try to solve this equation correctly.

Example 5 Extracting Square Roots

Solve each equation by extracting square roots.

a. $4x^2 = 12$ **b.** $(x - 3)^2 = 7$

Solution

a. $4x^2 = 12$ — Write original equation.

$x^2 = 3$ — Divide each side by 4.

$x = \pm\sqrt{3}$ — Extract square roots.

When you take the square root of a variable expression, you must account for both positive and negative solutions. So, the solutions are $x = \sqrt{3}$ and $x = -\sqrt{3}$. Check these in the original equation.

b. $(x - 3)^2 = 7$ — Write original equation.

$x - 3 = \pm\sqrt{7}$ — Extract square roots.

$x = 3 \pm \sqrt{7}$ — Add 3 to each side.

The solutions are $x = 3 \pm \sqrt{7}$. Check these in the original equation.

CHECKPOINT Now try Exercise 77.

When solving quadratic equations by completing the square, you must add $(b/2)^2$ to *each side* in order to maintain equality. If the leading coefficient is *not* 1, you must divide each side of the equation by the leading coefficient *before* completing the square, as shown in Example 7.

Example 6 Completing the Square: Leading Coefficient Is 1

Solve $x^2 + 2x - 6 = 0$ by completing the square.

Solution

$$x^2 + 2x - 6 = 0 \qquad \text{Write original equation.}$$

$$x^2 + 2x = 6 \qquad \text{Add 6 to each side.}$$

$$x^2 + 2x + 1^2 = 6 + 1^2 \qquad \text{Add } 1^2 \text{ to each side.}$$

$$(\text{half of } 2)^2$$

$$(x + 1)^2 = 7 \qquad \text{Simplify.}$$

$$x + 1 = \pm\sqrt{7} \qquad \text{Take square root of each side.}$$

$$x = -1 \pm \sqrt{7} \qquad \text{Subtract 1 from each side.}$$

The solutions are $x = -1 \pm \sqrt{7}$. Check these in the original equation.

CHECKPOINT Now try Exercise 85.

Example 7 Completing the Square: Leading Coefficient Is Not 1

$$3x^2 - 4x - 5 = 0 \qquad \text{Original equation}$$

$$3x^2 - 4x = 5 \qquad \text{Add 5 to each side.}$$

$$x^2 - \frac{4}{3}x = \frac{5}{3} \qquad \text{Divide each side by 3.}$$

$$x^2 - \frac{4}{3}x + \left(-\frac{2}{3}\right)^2 = \frac{5}{3} + \left(-\frac{2}{3}\right)^2 \qquad \text{Add } \left(-\tfrac{2}{3}\right)^2 \text{ to each side.}$$

$$\left(\text{half of } -\tfrac{4}{3}\right)^2$$

$$x^2 - \frac{4}{3}x + \frac{4}{9} = \frac{19}{9} \qquad \text{Simplify.}$$

$$\left(x - \frac{2}{3}\right)^2 = \frac{19}{9} \qquad \text{Perfect square trinomial.}$$

$$x - \frac{2}{3} = \pm\frac{\sqrt{19}}{3} \qquad \text{Extract square roots.}$$

$$x = \frac{2}{3} \pm \frac{\sqrt{19}}{3} \qquad \text{Solutions}$$

CHECKPOINT Now try Exercise 91.

STUDY TIP

When using the Quadratic Formula, remember that *before* the formula can be applied, you must first write the quadratic equation in general form.

Example 8 **The Quadratic Formula: Two Distinct Solutions**

Use the Quadratic Formula to solve $x^2 + 3x = 9$.

Solution

$$x^2 + 3x = 9$$ Write original equation.

$$x^2 + 3x - 9 = 0$$ Write in general form.

$$x = \frac{-b \pm \sqrt{b^2 - 4ac}}{2a}$$ Quadratic Formula

$$x = \frac{-3 \pm \sqrt{(3)^2 - 4(1)(-9)}}{2(1)}$$ Substitute $a = 1$, $b = 3$, and $c = -9$.

$$x = \frac{-3 \pm \sqrt{45}}{2}$$ Simplify.

$$x = \frac{-3 \pm 3\sqrt{5}}{2}$$ Simplify.

The equation has two solutions:

$$x = \frac{-3 + 3\sqrt{5}}{2} \quad \text{and} \quad x = \frac{-3 - 3\sqrt{5}}{2}.$$

Check these in the original equation.

CHECKPOINT Now try Exercise 101.

Example 9 **The Quadratic Formula: One Solution**

Use the Quadratic Formula to solve $8x^2 - 24x + 18 = 0$.

Solution

$$8x^2 - 24x + 18 = 0$$ Write original equation.

$$4x^2 - 12x + 9 = 0$$ Divide out common factor of 2.

$$x = \frac{-b \pm \sqrt{b^2 - 4ac}}{2a}$$ Quadratic Formula

$$x = \frac{-(-12) \pm \sqrt{(-12)^2 - 4(4)(9)}}{2(4)}$$ Substitute $a = 4$, $b = -12$, and $c = 9$.

$$x = \frac{12 \pm \sqrt{0}}{8} = \frac{3}{2}$$ Simplify.

This quadratic equation has only one solution: $x = \frac{3}{2}$. Check this in the original equation.

CHECKPOINT Now try Exercise 105.

Note that Example 9 could have been solved without first dividing out a common factor of 2. Substituting $a = 8$, $b = -24$, and $c = 18$ into the Quadratic Formula produces the same result.

STUDY TIP

A common mistake that is made in solving an equation such as that in Example 10 is to divide each side of the equation by the variable factor x^2. This loses the solution $x = 0$. When solving an equation, always write the equation in general form, then factor the equation and set each factor equal to zero. Do not divide each side of an equation by a variable factor in an attempt to simplify the equation.

Polynomial Equations of Higher Degree

The methods used to solve quadratic equations can sometimes be extended to solve polynomial equations of higher degree.

Example 10 Solving a Polynomial Equation by Factoring

Solve $3x^4 = 48x^2$.

Solution

First write the polynomial equation in general form with zero on one side, factor the other side, and then set each factor equal to zero and solve.

$3x^4 = 48x^2$ Write original equation.

$3x^4 - 48x^2 = 0$ Write in general form.

$3x^2(x^2 - 16) = 0$ Factor out common factor.

$3x^2(x + 4)(x - 4) = 0$ Write in factored form.

$3x^2 = 0 \Rightarrow x = 0$ Set 1st factor equal to 0.

$x + 4 = 0 \Rightarrow x = -4$ Set 2nd factor equal to 0.

$x - 4 = 0 \Rightarrow x = 4$ Set 3rd factor equal to 0.

You can check these solutions by substituting in the original equation, as follows.

Check

$3(0)^4 = 48(0)^2$ 0 checks. ✓

$3(-4)^4 = 48(-4)^2$ −4 checks. ✓

$3(4)^4 = 48(4)^2$ 4 checks. ✓

So, you can conclude that the solutions are $x = 0$, $x = -4$, and $x = 4$.

✓CHECKPOINT Now try Exercise 135.

Example 11 Solving a Polynomial Equation by Factoring

Solve $x^3 - 3x^2 - 3x + 9 = 0$.

Solution

$x^3 - 3x^2 - 3x + 9 = 0$ Write original equation.

$x^2(x - 3) - 3(x - 3) = 0$ Factor by grouping.

$(x - 3)(x^2 - 3) = 0$ Distributive Property

$x - 3 = 0 \Rightarrow x = 3$ Set 1st factor equal to 0.

$x^2 - 3 = 0 \Rightarrow x = \pm\sqrt{3}$ Set 2nd factor equal to 0.

The solutions are $x = 3$, $x = \sqrt{3}$, and $x = -\sqrt{3}$. Check these in the original equation.

✓CHECKPOINT Now try Exercise 143.

Equations Involving Radicals

Operations such as squaring each side of an equation, raising each side of an equation to a rational power, and multiplying each side of an equation by a variable quantity all can introduce extraneous solutions. So, when you use any of these operations, checking your solutions is crucial.

Example 12 Solving Equations Involving Radicals

a.

$\sqrt{2x+7} - x = 2$	Original equation
$\sqrt{2x+7} = x + 2$	Isolate radical.
$2x + 7 = x^2 + 4x + 4$	Square each side.
$0 = x^2 + 2x - 3$	Write in general form.
$0 = (x+3)(x-1)$	Factor.
$x + 3 = 0 \Rightarrow x = -3$	Set 1st factor equal to 0.
$x - 1 = 0 \Rightarrow x = 1$	Set 2nd factor equal to 0.

By checking these values, you can determine that the only solution is $x = 1$.

b.

$\sqrt{2x-5} - \sqrt{x-3} = 1$	Original equation
$\sqrt{2x-5} = \sqrt{x-3} + 1$	Isolate $\sqrt{2x-5}$.
$2x - 5 = x - 3 + 2\sqrt{x-3} + 1$	Square each side.
$2x - 5 = x - 2 + 2\sqrt{x-3}$	Combine like terms.
$x - 3 = 2\sqrt{x-3}$	Isolate $2\sqrt{x-3}$.
$x^2 - 6x + 9 = 4(x-3)$	Square each side.
$x^2 - 10x + 21 = 0$	Write in general form.
$(x-3)(x-7) = 0$	Factor.
$x - 3 = 0 \Rightarrow x = 3$	Set 1st factor equal to 0.
$x - 7 = 0 \Rightarrow x = 7$	Set 2nd factor equal to 0.

The solutions are $x = 3$ and $x = 7$. Check these in the original equation.

STUDY TIP

When an equation contains two radicals, it may not be possible to isolate both. In such cases, you may have to raise each side of the equation to a power at *two* different stages in the solution, as shown in Example 12(b).

✓CHECKPOINT Now try Exercise 155.

Example 13 Solving an Equation Involving a Rational Exponent

$(x-4)^{2/3} = 25$	Original equation
$\sqrt[3]{(x-4)^2} = 25$	Rewrite in radical form.
$(x-4)^2 = 15{,}625$	Cube each side.
$x - 4 = \pm 125$	Take square root of each side.
$x = 129, \quad x = -121$	Add 4 to each side.

✓CHECKPOINT Now try Exercise 163.

Equations with Absolute Values

To solve an equation involving an absolute value, remember that the expression inside the absolute value signs can be positive or negative. This results in *two* separate equations, each of which must be solved. For instance, the equation

$$|x - 2| = 3$$

results in the two equations $x - 2 = 3$ and $-(x - 2) = 3$, which implies that the equation has two solutions: $x = 5$ and $x = -1$.

Example 14 Solving an Equation Involving Absolute Value

Solve $|x^2 - 3x| = -4x + 6$.

Solution

Because the variable expression inside the absolute value signs can be positive or negative, you must solve the following two equations.

First Equation

$x^2 - 3x = -4x + 6$ — Use positive expression.

$x^2 + x - 6 = 0$ — Write in general form.

$(x + 3)(x - 2) = 0$ — Factor.

$x + 3 = 0 \Rightarrow x = -3$ — Set 1st factor equal to 0.

$x - 2 = 0 \Rightarrow x = 2$ — Set 2nd factor equal to 0.

Second Equation

$-(x^2 - 3x) = -4x + 6$ — Use negative expression.

$x^2 - 7x + 6 = 0$ — Write in general form.

$(x - 1)(x - 6) = 0$ — Factor.

$x - 1 = 0 \Rightarrow x = 1$ — Set 1st factor equal to 0.

$x - 6 = 0 \Rightarrow x = 6$ — Set 2nd factor equal to 0.

Check

$|(-3)^2 - 3(-3)| \stackrel{?}{=} -4(-3) + 6$ — Substitute -3 for x.

$18 = 18$ — -3 checks. ✓

$|(2)^2 - 3(2)| \stackrel{?}{=} -4(2) + 6$ — Substitute 2 for x.

$2 \neq -2$ — 2 does not check.

$|(1)^2 - 3(1)| \stackrel{?}{=} -4(1) + 6$ — Substitute 1 for x.

$2 = 2$ — 1 checks. ✓

$|(6)^2 - 3(6)| \stackrel{?}{=} -4(6) + 6$ — Substitute 6 for x.

$18 \neq -18$ — 6 does not check.

The solutions are $x = -3$ and $x = 1$.

✓CHECKPOINT Now try Exercise 181.

A.5 Exercises

VOCABULARY CHECK: Fill in the blanks.

1. An ________ is a statement that equates two algebraic expressions.
2. To find all values that satisfy an equation is to ________ the equation.
3. There are two types of equations, ________ and ________ equations.
4. A linear equation in one variable is an equation that can be written in the standard from ________.
5. When solving an equation, it is possible to introduce an ________ solution, which is a value that does not satisfy the original equation.
6. An equation of the form $ax^2 + bx + c = 0$, $a \neq 0$ is a ________ ________, or a second-degree polynomial equation in x.
7. The four methods that can be used to solve a quadratic equation are ________, ________, ________, and the ________.

In Exercises 1–10, determine whether the equation is an identity or a conditional equation.

1. $2(x - 1) = 2x - 2$
2. $3(x + 2) = 5x + 4$
3. $-6(x - 3) + 5 = -2x + 10$
4. $3(x + 2) - 5 = 3x + 1$
5. $4(x + 1) - 2x = 2(x + 2)$
6. $-7(x - 3) + 4x = 3(7 - x)$
7. $x^2 - 8x + 5 = (x - 4)^2 - 11$
8. $x^2 + 2(3x - 2) = x^2 + 6x - 4$
9. $3 + \dfrac{1}{x + 1} = \dfrac{4x}{x + 1}$
10. $\dfrac{5}{x} + \dfrac{3}{x} = 24$

In Exercises 11–26, solve the equation and check your solution.

11. $x + 11 = 15$
12. $7 - x = 19$
13. $7 - 2x = 25$
14. $7x + 2 = 23$
15. $8x - 5 = 3x + 20$
16. $7x + 3 = 3x - 17$
17. $2(x + 5) - 7 = 3(x - 2)$
18. $3(x + 3) = 5(1 - x) - 1$
19. $x - 3(2x + 3) = 8 - 5x$
20. $9x - 10 = 5x + 2(2x - 5)$
21. $\dfrac{5x}{4} + \dfrac{1}{2} = x - \dfrac{1}{2}$
22. $\dfrac{x}{5} - \dfrac{x}{2} = 3 + \dfrac{3x}{10}$

23 $\frac{3}{2}(z + 5) - \frac{1}{4}(z + 24) = 0$

24. $\dfrac{3x}{2} + \dfrac{1}{4}(x - 2) = 10$
25. $0.25x + 0.75(10 - x) = 3$
26. $0.60x + 0.40(100 - x) = 50$

In Exercises 27–48, solve the equation and check your solution. (If not possible, explain why.)

27. $x + 8 = 2(x - 2) - x$
28. $8(x + 2) - 3(2x + 1) = 2(x + 5)$
29. $\dfrac{100 - 4x}{3} = \dfrac{5x + 6}{4} + 6$
30. $\dfrac{17 + y}{y} + \dfrac{32 + y}{y} = 100$
31. $\dfrac{5x - 4}{5x + 4} = \dfrac{2}{3}$
32. $\dfrac{10x + 3}{5x + 6} = \dfrac{1}{2}$
33. $10 - \dfrac{13}{x} = 4 + \dfrac{5}{x}$
34. $\dfrac{15}{x} - 4 = \dfrac{6}{x} + 3$
35. $3 = 2 + \dfrac{2}{z + 2}$
36. $\dfrac{1}{x} + \dfrac{2}{x - 5} = 0$
37. $\dfrac{x}{x + 4} + \dfrac{4}{x + 4} + 2 = 0$
38. $\dfrac{7}{2x + 1} - \dfrac{8x}{2x - 1} = -4$
39. $\dfrac{2}{(x - 4)(x - 2)} = \dfrac{1}{x - 4} + \dfrac{2}{x - 2}$
40. $\dfrac{4}{x - 1} + \dfrac{6}{3x + 1} = \dfrac{15}{3x + 1}$
41. $\dfrac{1}{x - 3} + \dfrac{1}{x + 3} = \dfrac{10}{x^2 - 9}$
42. $\dfrac{1}{x - 2} + \dfrac{3}{x + 3} = \dfrac{4}{x^2 + x - 6}$
43. $\dfrac{3}{x^2 - 3x} + \dfrac{4}{x} = \dfrac{1}{x - 3}$
44. $\dfrac{6}{x} - \dfrac{2}{x + 3} = \dfrac{3(x + 5)}{x^2 + 3x}$

45. $(x + 2)^2 + 5 = (x + 3)^2$

46. $(x + 1)^2 + 2(x - 2) = (x + 1)(x - 2)$

47. $(x + 2)^2 - x^2 = 4(x + 1)$

48. $(2x + 1)^2 = 4(x^2 + x + 1)$

In Exercises 49–54, write the quadratic equation in general form.

49. $2x^2 = 3 - 8x$

50. $x^2 = 16x$

51. $(x - 3)^2 = 3$

52. $13 - 3(x + 7)^2 = 0$

53. $\frac{1}{5}(3x^2 - 10) = 18x$

54. $x(x + 2) = 5x^2 + 1$

In Exercises 55–68, solve the quadratic equation by factoring.

55. $6x^2 + 3x = 0$

56. $9x^2 - 1 = 0$

57. $x^2 - 2x - 8 = 0$

58. $x^2 - 10x + 9 = 0$

59. $x^2 + 10x + 25 = 0$

60. $4x^2 + 12x + 9 = 0$

61. $3 + 5x - 2x^2 = 0$

62. $2x^2 = 19x + 33$

63. $x^2 + 4x = 12$

64. $-x^2 + 8x = 12$

65. $\frac{3}{4}x^2 + 8x + 20 = 0$

66. $\frac{1}{8}x^2 - x - 16 = 0$

67. $x^2 + 2ax + a^2 = 0$, a is a real number

68. $(x + a)^2 - b^2 = 0$, a and b are real numbers

In Exercises 69–82, solve the equation by extracting square roots.

69. $x^2 = 49$

70. $x^2 = 169$

71. $x^2 = 11$

72. $x^2 = 32$

73. $3x^2 = 81$

74. $9x^2 = 36$

75. $(x - 12)^2 = 16$

76. $(x + 13)^2 = 25$

77. $(x + 2)^2 = 14$

78. $(x - 5)^2 = 30$

79. $(2x - 1)^2 = 18$

80. $(4x + 7)^2 = 44$

81. $(x - 7)^2 = (x + 3)^2$

82. $(x + 5)^2 = (x + 4)^2$

In Exercises 83–92, solve the quadratic equation by completing the square.

83. $x^2 + 4x - 32 = 0$

84. $x^2 - 2x - 3 = 0$

85. $x^2 + 12x + 25 = 0$

86. $x^2 + 8x + 14 = 0$

87. $9x^2 - 18x = -3$

88. $9x^2 - 12x = 14$

89. $8 + 4x - x^2 = 0$

90. $-x^2 + x - 1 = 0$

91. $2x^2 + 5x - 8 = 0$

92. $4x^2 - 4x - 99 = 0$

In Exercises 93–116, use the Quadratic Formula to solve the equation.

93. $2x^2 + x - 1 = 0$

94. $2x^2 - x - 1 = 0$

95. $16x^2 + 8x - 3 = 0$

96. $25x^2 - 20x + 3 = 0$

97. $2 + 2x - x^2 = 0$

98. $x^2 - 10x + 22 = 0$

99. $x^2 + 14x + 44 = 0$

100. $6x = 4 - x^2$

101. $x^2 + 8x - 4 = 0$

102. $4x^2 - 4x - 4 = 0$

103. $12x - 9x^2 = -3$

104. $16x^2 + 22 = 40x$

105. $9x^2 + 24x + 16 = 0$

106. $36x^2 + 24x - 7 = 0$

107. $4x^2 + 4x = 7$

108. $16x^2 - 40x + 5 = 0$

109. $28x - 49x^2 = 4$

110. $3x + x^2 - 1 = 0$

111. $8t = 5 + 2t^2$

112. $25h^2 + 80h + 61 = 0$

113. $(y - 5)^2 = 2y$

114. $(z + 6)^2 = -2z$

115. $\frac{1}{2}x^2 + \frac{3}{8}x = 2$

116. $(\frac{5}{7}x - 14)^2 = 8x$

In Exercises 117–124, use the Quadratic Formula to solve the equation. (Round your answer to three decimal places.)

117. $5.1x^2 - 1.7x - 3.2 = 0$

118. $2x^2 - 2.50x - 0.42 = 0$

119. $-0.067x^2 - 0.852x + 1.277 = 0$

120. $-0.005x^2 + 0.101x - 0.193 = 0$

121. $422x^2 - 506x - 347 = 0$

122. $1100x^2 + 326x - 715 = 0$

123. $12.67x^2 + 31.55x + 8.09 = 0$

124. $-3.22x^2 - 0.08x + 28.651 = 0$

In Exercises 125–134, solve the equation using any convenient method.

125. $x^2 - 2x - 1 = 0$

126. $11x^2 + 33x = 0$

127. $(x + 3)^2 = 81$

128. $x^2 - 14x + 49 = 0$

129. $x^2 - x - \frac{11}{4} = 0$

130. $x^2 + 3x - \frac{3}{4} = 0$

131. $(x + 1)^2 = x^2$

132. $a^2x^2 - b^2 = 0$, a and b are real numbers

133. $3x + 4 = 2x^2 - 7$

134. $4x^2 + 2x + 4 = 2x + 8$

In Exercises 135–152, find all solutions of the equation. Check your solutions in the original equation.

135. $4x^4 - 18x^2 = 0$

136. $20x^3 - 125x = 0$

137. $x^4 - 81 = 0$

138. $x^6 - 64 = 0$

139. $x^3 + 216 = 0$

140. $27x^3 - 512 = 0$

141. $5x^3 + 30x^2 + 45x = 0$

142. $9x^4 - 24x^3 + 16x^2 = 0$

143. $x^3 - 3x^2 - x + 3 = 0$

144. $x^3 + 2x^2 + 3x + 6 = 0$

145. $x^4 - x^3 + x - 1 = 0$

146. $x^4 + 2x^3 - 8x - 16 = 0$

147. $x^4 - 4x^2 + 3 = 0$

148. $x^4 + 5x^2 - 36 = 0$

149. $4x^4 - 65x^2 + 16 = 0$

150. $36t^4 + 29t^2 - 7 = 0$

151. $x^6 + 7x^3 - 8 = 0$

152. $x^6 + 3x^3 + 2 = 0$

In Exercises 153–184, find all solutions of the equation. Check your solutions in the original equation.

153. $\sqrt{2x} - 10 = 0$

154. $4\sqrt{x} - 3 = 0$

155. $\sqrt{x - 10} - 4 = 0$

156. $\sqrt{5 - x} - 3 = 0$

157. $\sqrt[3]{2x + 5} + 3 = 0$

158. $\sqrt[3]{3x + 1} - 5 = 0$

159. $-\sqrt{26 - 11x} + 4 = x$

160. $x + \sqrt{31 - 9x} = 5$

161. $\sqrt{x + 1} = \sqrt{3x + 1}$

162. $\sqrt{x + 5} = \sqrt{x - 5}$

163. $(x - 5)^{3/2} = 8$

164. $(x + 3)^{3/2} = 8$

165. $(x + 3)^{2/3} = 8$

166. $(x + 2)^{2/3} = 9$

167. $(x^2 - 5)^{3/2} = 27$

168. $(x^2 - x - 22)^{3/2} = 27$

169. $3x(x - 1)^{1/2} + 2(x - 1)^{3/2} = 0$

170. $4x^2(x - 1)^{1/3} + 6x(x - 1)^{4/3} = 0$

171. $x = \dfrac{3}{x} + \dfrac{1}{2}$

172. $\dfrac{4}{x} - \dfrac{5}{3} = \dfrac{x}{6}$

173. $\dfrac{1}{x} - \dfrac{1}{x + 1} = 3$

174. $\dfrac{4}{x + 1} - \dfrac{3}{x + 2} = 1$

175. $\dfrac{20 - x}{x} = x$

176. $4x + 1 = \dfrac{3}{x}$

177. $\dfrac{x}{x^2 - 4} + \dfrac{1}{x + 2} = 3$

178. $\dfrac{x + 1}{3} - \dfrac{x + 1}{x + 2} = 0$

179. $|2x - 1| = 5$

180. $|3x + 2| = 7$

181. $|x| = x^2 + x - 3$

182. $|x^2 + 6x| = 3x + 18$

183. $|x + 1| = x^2 - 5$

184. $|x - 10| = x^2 - 10x$

185. ***Anthropology*** The relationship between the length of an adult's femur (thigh bone) and the height of the adult can be approximated by the linear equations

$y = 0.432x - 10.44$ Female

$y = 0.449x - 12.15$ Male

where y is the length of the femur in inches and x is the height of the adult in inches (see figure).

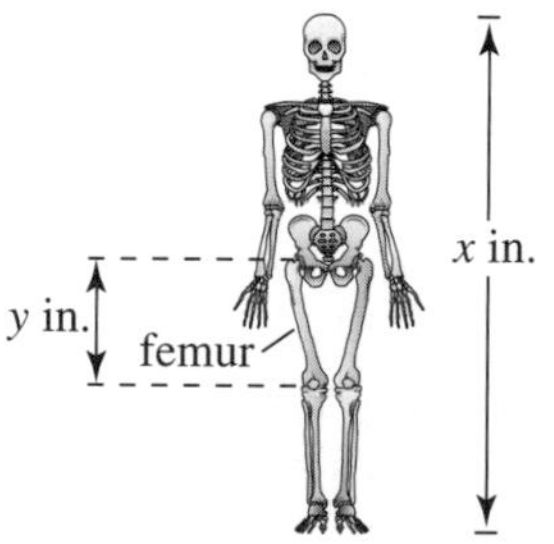

(a) An anthropologist discovers a femur belonging to an adult human female. The bone is 16 inches long. Estimate the height of the female.

(b) From the foot bones of an adult human male, an anthropologist estimates that the person's height was 69 inches. A few feet away from the site where the foot bones were discovered, the anthropologist discovers a male adult femur that is 19 inches long. Is it likely that both the foot bones and the thigh bone came from the same person?

(c) Complete the table to determine if there is a height of an adult for which an anthropologist would not be able to determine whether the femur belonged to a male or a female.

Height, x	Female femur length, y	Male femur length, y
60		
70		
80		
90		
100		
110		

186. ***Operating Cost*** A delivery company has a fleet of vans. The annual operating cost C per van is

$C = 0.32m + 2500$

where m is the number of miles traveled by a van in a year. What number of miles will yield an annual operating cost of \$10,000?

187. ***Flood Control*** A river has risen 8 feet above its flood stage. The water begins to recede at a rate of 3 inches per hour. Write a mathematical model that shows the number of feet above flood stage after t hours. If the water continually recedes at this rate, when will the river be 1 foot above its flood stage?

188. ***Floor Space*** The floor of a one-story building is 14 feet longer than it is wide. The building has 1632 square feet of floor space.

(a) Draw a diagram that gives a visual representation of the floor space. Represent the width as w and show the length in terms of w.

(b) Write a quadratic equation in terms of w.

(c) Find the length and width of the floor of the building.

189. ***Packaging*** An open box with a square base (see figure) is to be constructed from 84 square inches of material. The height of the box is 2 inches. What are the dimensions of the box? (*Hint:* The surface area is $S = x^2 + 4xh$.)

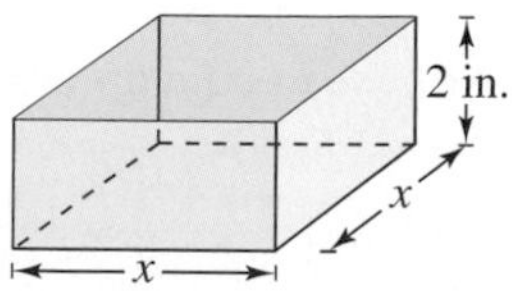

190. ***Geometry*** The hypotenuse of an isosceles right triangle is 5 centimeters long. How long are its sides?

191. ***Geometry*** An equilateral triangle has a height of 10 inches. How long is one of its sides? (*Hint:* Use the height of the triangle to partition the triangle into two congruent right triangles.)

192. ***Flying Speed*** Two planes leave simultaneously from Chicago's O'Hare Airport, one flying due north and the other due east (see figure). The northbound plane is flying 50 miles per hour faster than the eastbound plane. After 3 hours, the planes are 2440 miles apart. Find the speed of each plane.

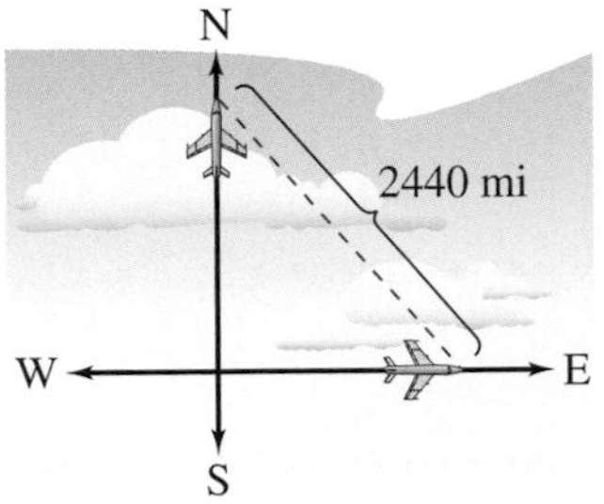

193. ***Voting Population*** The total voting-age population P (in millions) in the United States from 1990 to 2002 can be modeled by

$$P = \frac{182.45 - 3.189t}{1.00 - 0.026t}, \quad 0 \le t \le 12$$

where t represents the year, with $t = 0$ corresponding to 1990. (Source: U.S. Census Bureau)

(a) In which year did the total voting-age population reach 200 million?

(b) Use the model to predict when the total voting-age population will reach 230 million. Is this prediction reasonable? Explain.

194. ***Airline Passengers*** An airline offers daily flights between Chicago and Denver. The total monthly cost C (in millions of dollars) of these flights is $C = \sqrt{0.2x + 1}$ where x is the number of passengers (in thousands). The total cost of the flights for June is 2.5 million dollars. How many passengers flew in June?

195. ***Demand*** The demand equation for a video game is modeled by $p = 40 - \sqrt{0.01x + 1}$ where x is the number of units demanded per day and p is the price per unit. Approximate the demand when the price is \$37.55.

196. ***Demand*** The demand equation for a high definition television set is modeled by

$$p = 800 - \sqrt{0.01x + 1}$$

where x is the number of units demanded per month and p is the price per unit. Approximate the demand when the price is \$750.

Synthesis

True or False? **In Exercises 197–200, determine whether the statement is true or false. Justify your answer.**

197. The equation $x(3 - x) = 10$ is a linear equation.

198. If $(2x - 3)(x + 5) = 8$, then either $2x - 3 = 8$ or $x + 5 = 8$.

199. An equation can never have more than one extraneous solution.

200. When solving an absolute value equation, you will always have to check more than one solution.

201. ***Think About It*** What is meant by *equivalent equations*? Give an example of two equivalent equations.

202. ***Writing*** Describe the steps used to transform an equation into an equivalent equation.

203. To solve the equation $2x^2 + 3x = 15x$, a student divides each side by x and solves the equation $2x + 3 = 15$. The resulting solution $(x = 6)$ satisfies the original equation. Is there an error? Explain.

204. Solve $3(x + 4)^2 + (x + 4) - 2 = 0$ in two ways.

(a) Let $u = x + 4$, and solve the resulting equation for u. Then solve the u-solution for x.

(b) Expand and collect like terms in the equation, and solve the resulting equation for x.

(c) Which method is easier? Explain.

Think About It **In Exercises 205–210, write a quadratic equation that has the given solutions. (There are many correct answers.)**

205. -3 and 6

206. -4 and -11

207. 8 and 14

208. $\frac{1}{6}$ and $-\frac{2}{5}$

209. $1 + \sqrt{2}$ and $1 - \sqrt{2}$

210. $-3 + \sqrt{5}$ and $-3 - \sqrt{5}$

In Exercises 211 and 212, consider an equation of the form $x + |x - a| = b$, where a and b are constants.

211. Find a and b when the solution of the equation is $x = 9$. (There are many correct answers.)

212. ***Writing*** Write a short paragraph listing the steps required to solve this equation involving absolute values and explain why it is important to check your solutions.

213. Solve each equation, given that a and b are not zero.

(a) $ax^2 + bx = 0$

(b) $ax^2 - ax = 0$

A.6 Linear Inequalities in One Variable

What you should learn

- Represent solutions of linear inequalities in one variable.
- Solve linear inequalities in one variable.
- Solve inequalities involving absolute values.
- Use inequalities to model and solve real-life problems.

Why you should learn it

Inequalities can be used to model and solve real-life problems. For instance, in Exercise 101 on page A68, you will use a linear inequality to analyze the average salary for elementary school teachers.

Introduction

Simple inequalities were discussed in Appendix A.1. There, you used the inequality symbols $<$, $\leq$, $>$, and $\geq$ to compare two numbers and to denote subsets of real numbers. For instance, the simple inequality

$$x \geq 3$$

denotes all real numbers x that are greater than or equal to 3.

Now, you will expand your work with inequalities to include more involved statements such as

$$5x - 7 < 3x + 9$$

and

$$-3 \leq 6x - 1 < 3.$$

As with an equation, you **solve an inequality** in the variable x by finding all values of x for which the inequality is true. Such values are **solutions** and are said to **satisfy** the inequality. The set of all real numbers that are solutions of an inequality is the **solution set** of the inequality. For instance, the solution set of

$$x + 1 < 4$$

is all real numbers that are less than 3.

The set of all points on the real number line that represent the solution set is the **graph of the inequality.** Graphs of many types of inequalities consist of intervals on the real number line. See Appendix A.1 to review the nine basic types of intervals on the real number line. Note that each type of interval can be classified as *bounded* or *unbounded.*

Example 1 Intervals and Inequalities

Write an inequality to represent each interval, and state whether the interval is bounded or unbounded.

a. $(-3, 5]$

b. $(-3, \infty)$

c. $[0, 2]$

d. $(-\infty, \infty)$

Solution

a. $(-3, 5]$ corresponds to $-3 < x \leq 5$. Bounded

b. $(-3, \infty)$ corresponds to $-3 < x$. Unbounded

c. $[0, 2]$ corresponds to $0 \leq x \leq 2$. Bounded

d. $(-\infty, \infty)$ corresponds to $-\infty < x < \infty$. Unbounded

CHECKPOINT Now try Exercise 1.

Properties of Inequalities

The procedures for solving linear inequalities in one variable are much like those for solving linear equations. To isolate the variable, you can make use of the **Properties of Inequalities.** These properties are similar to the properties of equality, but there are two important exceptions. When each side of an inequality is multiplied or divided by a negative number, the direction of the inequality symbol must be reversed. Here is an example.

$$-2 < 5 \qquad \text{Original inequality}$$

$$(-3)(-2) > (-3)(5) \qquad \text{Multiply each side by } -3 \text{ and reverse inequality.}$$

$$6 > -15 \qquad \text{Simplify.}$$

Notice that if the inequality was not reversed you would obtain the false statement $6 < -15$.

Two inequalities that have the same solution set are **equivalent.** For instance, the inequalities

$$x + 2 < 5$$

and

$$x < 3$$

are equivalent. To obtain the second inequality from the first, you can subtract 2 from each side of the inequality. The following list describes the operations that can be used to create equivalent inequalities.

Properties of Inequalities

Let a, b, c, and d be real numbers.

1. Transitive Property

$$a < b \text{ and } b < c \implies a < c$$

2. Addition of Inequalities

$$a < b \text{ and } c < d \implies a + c < b + d$$

3. Addition of a Constant

$$a < b \implies a + c < b + c$$

4. Multiplication by a Constant

$$\text{For } c > 0,\ a < b \implies ac < bc$$

$$\text{For } c < 0,\ a < b \implies ac > bc \qquad \text{Reverse the inequality.}$$

Each of the properties above is true if the symbol $<$ is replaced by $\le$ and the symbol $>$ is replaced by $\ge$. For instance, another form of the multiplication property would be as follows.

$$\text{For } c > 0,\ a \le b \implies ac \le bc$$

$$\text{For } c < 0,\ a \le b \implies ac \ge bc$$

Solving a Linear Inequality in One Variable

The simplest type of inequality is a **linear inequality** in one variable. For instance, $2x + 3 > 4$ is a linear inequality in x.

In the following examples, pay special attention to the steps in which the inequality symbol is reversed. Remember that when you multiply or divide by a negative number, you must reverse the inequality symbol.

Example 2 Solving Linear Inequalities

Solve each inequality.

a. $5x - 7 > 3x + 9$

b. $1 - \frac{3x}{2} \geq x - 4$

STUDY TIP

Checking the solution set of an inequality is not as simple as checking the solutions of an equation. You can, however, get an indication of the validity of a solution set by substituting a few convenient values of x.

Solution

a. $5x - 7 > 3x + 9$ Write original inequality.

$2x - 7 > 9$ Subtract $3x$ from each side.

$2x > 16$ Add 7 to each side.

$x > 8$ Divide each side by 2.

The solution set is all real numbers that are greater than 8, which is denoted by $(8, \infty)$. The graph of this solution set is shown in Figure A.8. Note that a parenthesis at 8 on the real number line indicates that 8 *is not* part of the solution set.

Solution interval: $(8, \infty)$

FIGURE A.8

b. $1 - \frac{3x}{2} \geq x - 4$ Write original inequality.

$2 - 3x \geq 2x - 8$ Multiply each side by 2.

$2 - 5x \geq -8$ Subtract $2x$ from each side.

$-5x \geq -10$ Subtract 2 from each side.

$x \leq 2$ Divide each side by -5 and reverse the inequality.

The solution set is all real numbers that are less than or equal to 2, which is denoted by $(-\infty, 2]$. The graph of this solution set is shown in Figure A.9. Note that a bracket at 2 on the real number line indicates that 2 *is* part of the solution set.

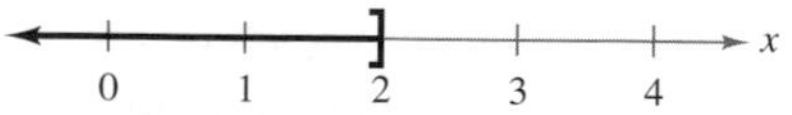

Solution interval: $(-\infty, 2]$

FIGURE A.9

CHECKPOINT Now try Exercise 25.

Sometimes it is possible to write two inequalities as a **double inequality.** For instance, you can write the two inequalities $-4 \le 5x - 2$ and $5x - 2 < 7$ more simply as

$$-4 \le 5x - 2 < 7. \qquad \text{Double inequality}$$

This form allows you to solve the two inequalities together, as demonstrated in Example 3.

Example 3 Solving a Double Inequality

To solve a double inequality, you can isolate x as the middle term.

$$-3 \le 6x - 1 < 3 \qquad \text{Original inequality}$$

$$-3 + 1 \le 6x - 1 + 1 < 3 + 1 \qquad \text{Add 1 to each part.}$$

$$-2 \le 6x < 4 \qquad \text{Simplify.}$$

$$\frac{-2}{6} \le \frac{6x}{6} < \frac{4}{6} \qquad \text{Divide each part by 6.}$$

$$-\frac{1}{3} \le x < \frac{2}{3} \qquad \text{Simplify.}$$

The solution set is all real numbers that are greater than or equal to $-\frac{1}{3}$ and less than $\frac{2}{3}$, which is denoted by $\left[-\frac{1}{3}, \frac{2}{3}\right)$. The graph of this solution set is shown in Figure A.10.

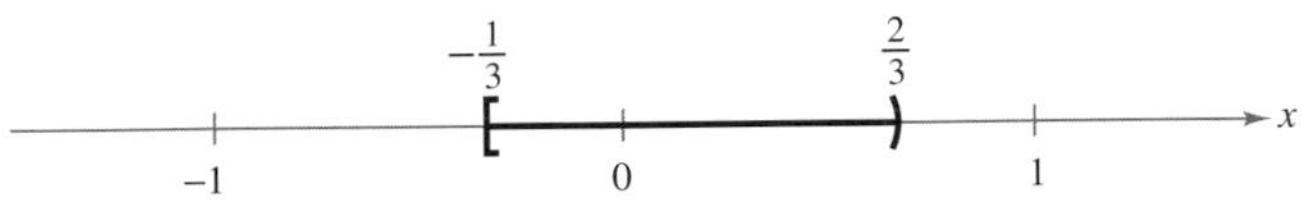

Solution interval: $\left[-\frac{1}{3}, \frac{2}{3}\right)$

FIGURE A.10

✓CHECKPOINT Now try Exercise 37.

The double inequality in Example 3 could have been solved in two parts as follows.

$$-3 \le 6x - 1 \quad \text{and} \quad 6x - 1 < 3$$

$$-2 \le 6x \qquad\qquad 6x < 4$$

$$-\frac{1}{3} \le x \qquad\qquad x < \frac{2}{3}$$

The solution set consists of all real numbers that satisfy *both* inequalities. In other words, the solution set is the set of all values of x for which

$$-\frac{1}{3} \le x < \frac{2}{3}.$$

When combining two inequalities to form a double inequality, be sure that the inequalities satisfy the Transitive Property. For instance, it is *incorrect* to combine the inequalities $3 < x$ and $x \le -1$ as $3 < x \le -1$. This "inequality" is wrong because 3 is not less than -1.

Technology

A graphing utility can be used to identify the solution set of the graph of an inequality. For instance, to find the solution set of $|x - 5| < 2$ (see Example 4), rewrite the inequality as $|x - 5| - 2 < 0$, enter

Y1 = abs (X − 5) − 2,

and press the *graph* key. The graph should look like the one shown below.

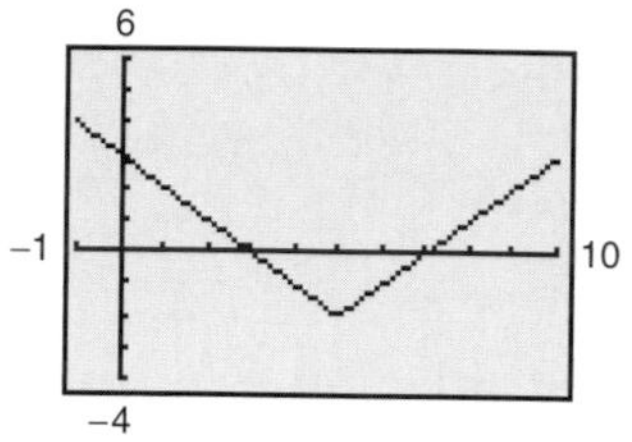

Notice that the graph is below the x-axis on the interval $(3, 7)$.

Inequalities Involving Absolute Values

Solving an Absolute Value Inequality

Let x be a variable or an algebraic expression and let a be a real number such that $a \geq 0$.

1. The solutions of $|x| < a$ are all values of x that lie between $-a$ and a.

   $|x| < a$ if and only if $-a < x < a$. Double inequality

2. The solutions of $|x| > a$ are all values of x that are less than $-a$ or greater than a.

   $|x| > a$ if and only if $x < -a$ or $x > a$. Compound inequality

These rules are also valid if $<$ is replaced by $\leq$ and $>$ is replaced by $\geq$.

Example 4 **Solving an Absolute Value Inequality**

Solve each inequality.

a. $|x - 5| < 2$ **b.** $|x + 3| \geq 7$

Solution

a. $|x - 5| < 2$ Write original inequality.

$-2 < x - 5 < 2$ Write equivalent inequalities.

$-2 + 5 < x - 5 + 5 < 2 + 5$ Add 5 to each part.

$3 < x < 7$ Simplify.

The solution set is all real numbers that are greater than 3 and less than 7, which is denoted by $(3, 7)$. The graph of this solution set is shown in Figure A.11.

b. $|x + 3| \geq 7$ Write original inequality.

$x + 3 \leq -7$ or $x + 3 \geq 7$ Write equivalent inequalities.

$x + 3 - 3 \leq -7 - 3$ $x + 3 - 3 \geq 7 - 3$ Subtract 3 from each side.

$x \leq -10$ $x \geq 4$ Simplify.

The solution set is all real numbers that are less than or equal to -10 *or* greater than or equal to 4. The interval notation for this solution set is $(-\infty, -10] \cup [4, \infty)$. The symbol $\cup$ is called a *union* symbol and is used to denote the combining of two sets. The graph of this solution set is shown in Figure A.12.

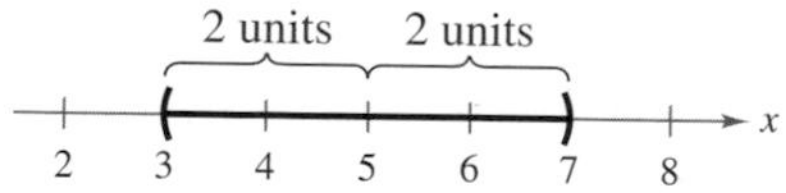

$|x - 5| < 2$: *Solutions lie inside* $(3, 7)$

FIGURE A.11

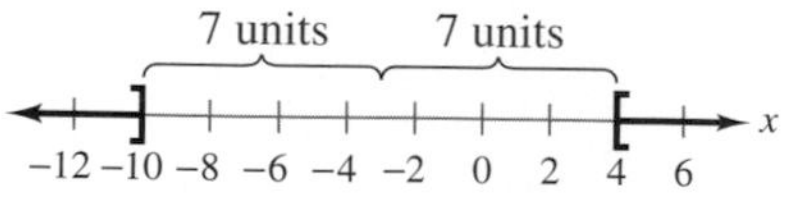

$|x + 3| \geq 7$: *Solutions lie outside* $(-10, 4)$

FIGURE A.12

CHECKPOINT Now try Exercise 49.

STUDY TIP

Note that the graph of the inequality $|x - 5| < 2$ can be described as all real numbers *within* two units of 5, as shown in Figure A.11.

Applications

A problem-solving plan can be used to model and solve real-life problems that involve inequalities, as illustrated in Example 5.

Example 5 Comparative Shopping

You are choosing between two different cell phone plans. Plan A costs \$49.99 per month for 500 minutes plus \$0.40 for each additional minute. Plan B costs \$45.99 per month for 500 minutes plus \$0.45 for each additional minute. How many *additional* minutes must you use in one month for plan B to cost more than plan A?

Solution

Verbal Model: Monthly cost for plan B > Monthly cost for plan A

Labels: Minutes used (over 500) in one month $= m$ (minutes)
Monthly cost for plan A $= 0.40m + 49.99$ (dollars)
Monthly cost for plan B $= 0.45m + 45.99$ (dollars)

Inequality: $0.45m + 45.99 > 0.40m + 49.99$

$$0.05m > 4$$

$$m > 80 \text{ minutes}$$

Plan B costs more if you use more than 80 additional minutes in one month.

✓CHECKPOINT Now try Exercise 91.

Example 6 Accuracy of a Measurement

You go to a candy store to buy chocolates that cost \$9.89 per pound. The scale that is used in the store has a state seal of approval that indicates the scale is accurate to within half an ounce (or $\frac{1}{32}$ of a pound). According to the scale, your purchase weighs one-half pound and costs \$4.95. How much might you have been undercharged or overcharged as a result of inaccuracy in the scale?

Solution

Let x represent the *true* weight of the candy. Because the scale is accurate to within half an ounce (or $\frac{1}{32}$ of a pound), the difference between the exact weight (x) and the scale weight $\left(\frac{1}{2}\right)$ is less than or equal to $\frac{1}{32}$ of a pound. That is, $\left|x - \frac{1}{2}\right| \leq \frac{1}{32}$. You can solve this inequality as follows.

$$-\frac{1}{32} \leq x - \frac{1}{2} \leq \frac{1}{32}$$

$$\frac{15}{32} \leq x \leq \frac{17}{32}$$

$$0.46875 \leq x \leq 0.53125$$

In other words, your "one-half pound" of candy could have weighed as little as 0.46875 pound (which would have cost \$4.64) or as much as 0.53125 pound (which would have cost \$5.25). So, you could have been overcharged by as much as \$0.31 or undercharged by as much as \$0.30.

✓CHECKPOINT Now try Exercise 105.

A.6 Exercises

VOCABULARY CHECK: Fill in the blanks.

1. The set of all real numbers that are solutions to an inequality is the ________ ________ of the inequality.
2. The set of all points on the real number line that represent the solution set of an inequality is the ________ of the inequality.
3. To solve a linear inequality in one variable, you can use the properties of inequalities, which are identical to those used to solve equations, with the exception of multiplying or dividing each side by a ________ number.
4. Two inequalities that have the same solution set are ________ ________.
5. It is sometimes possible to write two inequalities as one inequality, called a ________ inequality.
6. The symbol $\cup$ is called a ________ symbol and is used to denote the combining of two sets.

In Exercises 1–6, (a) write an inequality that represents the interval and (b) state whether the interval is bounded or unbounded.

1. $[-1, 5]$ **2.** $(2, 10]$

3. $(11, \infty)$ **4.** $[-5, \infty)$

5. $(-\infty, -2)$ **6.** $(-\infty, 7]$

In Exercises 7–12, match the inequality with its graph. [The graphs are labeled (a), (b), (c), (d), (e), and (f).]

(a)
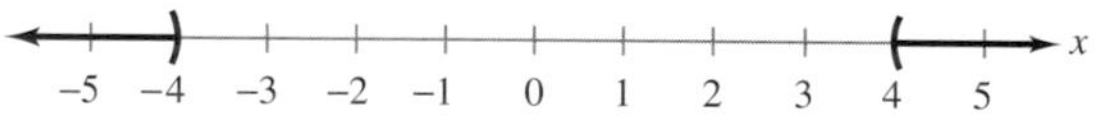

(b)
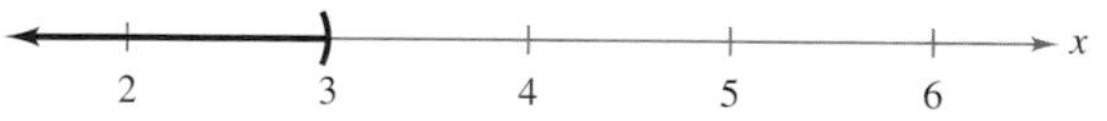

(c)
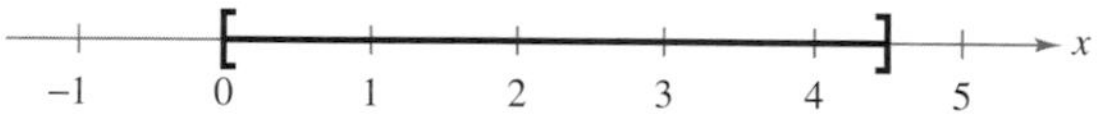

(d)
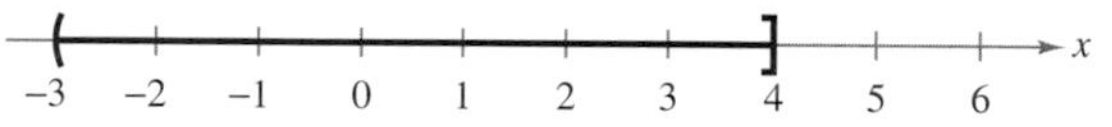

(e)
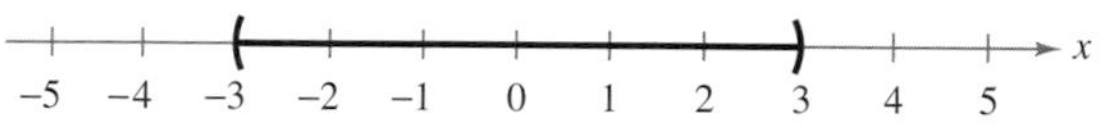

(f)
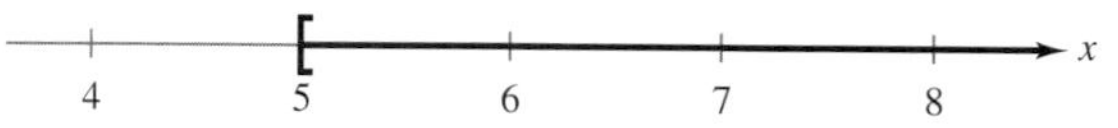

7. $x < 3$ **8.** $x \geq 5$

9. $-3 < x \leq 4$ **10.** $0 \leq x \leq \frac{9}{2}$

11. $|x| < 3$ **12.** $|x| > 4$

In Exercises 13–18, determine whether each value of *x* is a solution of the inequality.

Inequality	*Values*	
13. $5x - 12 > 0$	(a) $x = 3$	(b) $x = -3$
	(c) $x = \frac{5}{2}$	(d) $x = \frac{3}{2}$
14. $2x + 1 < -3$	(a) $x = 0$	(b) $x = -\frac{1}{4}$
	(c) $x = -4$	(d) $x = -\frac{3}{2}$
15. $0 < \dfrac{x - 2}{4} < 2$	(a) $x = 4$	(b) $x = 10$
	(c) $x = 0$	(d) $x = \frac{7}{2}$
16. $-1 < \dfrac{3 - x}{2} \leq 1$	(a) $x = 0$	(b) $x = -5$
	(c) $x = 1$	(d) $x = 5$
17. $\lvert x - 10\rvert \geq 3$	(a) $x = 13$	(b) $x = -1$
	(c) $x = 14$	(d) $x = 9$
18. $\lvert 2x - 3\rvert < 15$	(a) $x = -6$	(b) $x = 0$
	(c) $x = 12$	(d) $x = 7$

In Exercises 19–44, solve the inequality and sketch the solution on the real number line. (Some inequalities have no solutions.)

19. $4x < 12$ **20.** $10x < -40$

21. $-2x > -3$ **22.** $-6x > 15$

23. $x - 5 \geq 7$

24. $x + 7 \leq 12$

25. $2x + 7 < 3 + 4x$

26. $3x + 1 \geq 2 + x$

27. $2x - 1 \geq 1 - 5x$

28. $6x - 4 \leq 2 + 8x$

29. $4 - 2x < 3(3 - x)$

30. $4(x + 1) < 2x + 3$

31. $\frac{3}{4}x - 6 \leq x - 7$

32. $3 + \frac{2}{7}x > x - 2$

33. $\frac{1}{2}(8x + 1) \geq 3x + \frac{5}{2}$

34. $9x - 1 < \frac{3}{4}(16x - 2)$

35. $3.6x + 11 \geq -3.4$

36. $15.6 - 1.3x < -5.2$

37. $1 < 2x + 3 < 9$

38. $-8 \leq -(3x + 5) < 13$

39. $-4 < \dfrac{2x-3}{3} < 4$

40. $0 \le \dfrac{x+3}{2} < 5$

41. $\frac{3}{4} > x + 1 > \frac{1}{4}$

42. $-1 < 2 - \dfrac{x}{3} < 1$

43. $3.2 \le 0.4x - 1 \le 4.4$

44. $4.5 > \dfrac{1.5x+6}{2} > 10.5$

In Exercises 45–60, solve the inequality and sketch the solution on the real number line. (Some inequalities have no solution.)

45. $|x| < 6$

46. $|x| > 4$

47. $\left|\dfrac{x}{2}\right| > 1$

48. $\left|\dfrac{x}{5}\right| > 3$

49. $|x-5| < -1$

50. $|x-7| < -5$

51. $|x-20| \le 6$

52. $|x-8| \ge 0$

53. $|3-4x| \ge 9$

54. $|1-2x| < 5$

55. $\left|\dfrac{x-3}{2}\right| \ge 4$

56. $\left|1 - \dfrac{2x}{3}\right| < 1$

57. $|9-2x| - 2 < -1$

58. $|x+14| + 3 > 17$

59. $2|x+10| \ge 9$

60. $3|4-5x| \le 9$

Graphical Analysis **In Exercises 61–68, use a graphing utility to graph the inequality and identify the solution set.**

61. $6x > 12$

62. $3x - 1 \le 5$

63. $5 - 2x \ge 1$

64. $3(x+1) < x + 7$

65. $|x-8| \le 14$

66. $|2x+9| > 13$

67. $2|x+7| \ge 13$

68. $\frac{1}{2}|x+1| \le 3$

Graphical Analysis **In Exercises 69–74, use a graphing utility to graph the equation. Use the graph to approximate the values of x that satisfy each inequality.**

Equation	*Inequalities*	
69. $y = 2x - 3$	(a) $y \ge 1$	(b) $y \le 0$
70. $y = \frac{2}{3}x + 1$	(a) $y \le 5$	(b) $y \ge 0$
71. $y = -\frac{1}{2}x + 2$	(a) $0 \le y \le 3$	(b) $y \ge 0$
72. $y = -3x + 8$	(a) $-1 \le y \le 3$	(b) $y \le 0$
73. $y = \|x-3\|$	(a) $y \le 2$	(b) $y \ge 4$
74. $y = \left\|\frac{1}{2}x + 1\right\|$	(a) $y \le 4$	(b) $y \ge 1$

In Exercises 75–80, find the interval(s) on the real number line for which the radicand is nonnegative.

75. $\sqrt{x-5}$ **76.** $\sqrt{x-10}$

77. $\sqrt{x+3}$ **78.** $\sqrt{3-x}$

79. $\sqrt[4]{7-2x}$ **80.** $\sqrt[4]{6x+15}$

81. ***Think About It*** The graph of $|x-5| < 3$ can be described as all real numbers within three units of 5. Give a similar description of $|x-10| < 8$.

82. ***Think About It*** The graph of $|x-2| > 5$ can be described as all real numbers more than five units from 2. Give a similar description of $|x-8| > 4$.

In Exercises 83–90, use absolute value notation to define the interval (or pair of intervals) on the real number line.

83. 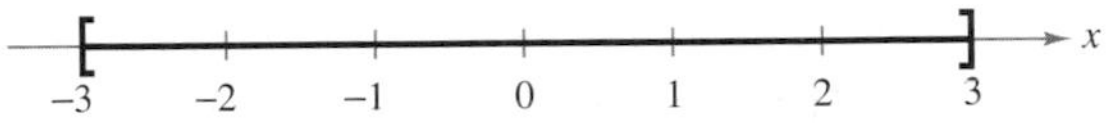

84. 

85. 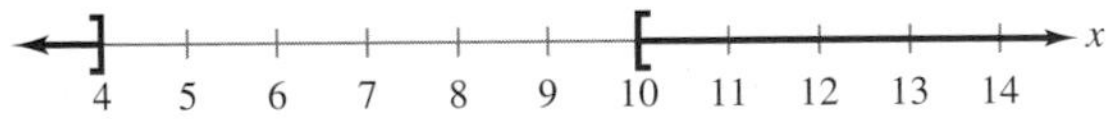

86. 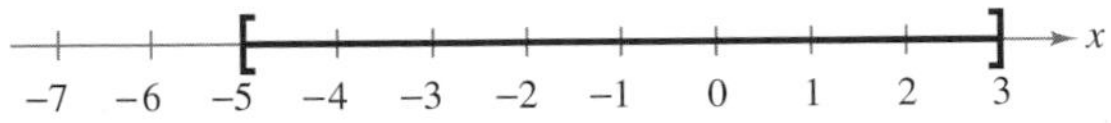

87. All real numbers within 10 units of 12

88. All real numbers at least five units from 8

89. All real numbers more than four units from -3

90. All real numbers no more than seven units from -6

91. ***Checking Account*** You can choose between two types of checking accounts at your local bank. Type A charges a monthly service fee of \$6 plus \$0.25 for each check written. Type B charges a monthly service fee of \$4.50 plus \$0.50 for each check written. How many checks must you write in a month in order for the monthly charges for type A to be less than that for type B?

92. ***Copying Costs*** Your department sends its copying to the photocopy center of your company. The center bills your department \$0.10 per page. You have investigated the possibility of buying a departmental copier for \$3000. With your own copier, the cost per page would be \$0.03. The expected life of the copier is 4 years. How many copies must you make in the four-year period to justify buying the copier?

93. ***Investment*** In order for an investment of \$1000 to grow to more than \$1062.50 in 2 years, what must the annual interest rate be? $[A = P(1 + rt)]$

94. ***Investment*** In order for an investment of \$750 to grow to more than \$825 in 2 years, what must the annual interest rate be? $[A = P(1 + rt)]$

95. ***Cost, Revenue, and Profit*** The revenue for selling x units of a product is $R = 115.95x$. The cost of producing x units is

$$C = 95x + 750.$$

To obtain a profit, the revenue must be greater than the cost. For what values of x will this product return a profit?

96. ***Cost, Revenue, and Profit*** The revenue for selling x units of a product is $R = 24.55x$. The cost of producing x units is

$$C = 15.4x + 150{,}000.$$

To obtain a profit, the revenue must be greater than the cost. For what values of x will this product return a profit?

97. ***Daily Sales*** A doughnut shop sells a dozen doughnuts for \$2.95. Beyond the fixed costs (rent, utilities, and insurance) of \$150 per day, it costs \$1.45 for enough materials (flour, sugar, and so on) and labor to produce a dozen doughnuts. The daily profit from doughnut sales varies between \$50 and \$200. Between what levels (in dozens) do the daily sales vary?

98. ***Weight Loss Program*** A person enrolls in a diet and exercise program that guarantees a loss of at least $1\frac{1}{2}$ pounds per week. The person's weight at the beginning of the program is 164 pounds. Find the maximum number of weeks before the person attains a goal weight of 128 pounds.

99. ***Data Analysis: IQ Scores and GPA*** The admissions office of a college wants to determine whether there is a relationship between IQ scores x and grade-point averages y after the first year of school. An equation that models the data the admissions office obtained is

$$y = 0.067x - 5.638.$$

(a) Use a graphing utility to graph the model.

(b) Use the graph to estimate the values of x that predict a grade-point average of at least 3.0.

100. ***Data Analysis: Weightlifting*** You want to determine whether there is a relationship between an athlete's weight x (in pounds) and the athlete's maximum bench-press weight y (in pounds). The table shows a sample of data from 12 athletes.

(a) Use a graphing utility to plot the data.

Athlete's weight, x	Bench-press weight, y
165	170
184	185
150	200
210	255
196	205
240	295
202	190
170	175
185	195
190	185
230	250
160	155

(b) A model for the data is $y = 1.3x - 36$. Use a graphing utility to graph the model in the same viewing window used in part (a).

(c) Use the graph to estimate the values of x that predict a maximum bench-press weight of at least 200 pounds.

(d) Verify your estimate from part (c) algebraically.

(e) Use the graph to write a statement about the accuracy of the model. If you think the graph indicates that an athlete's weight is not a particularly good indicator of the athlete's maximum bench-press weight, list other factors that might influence an individual's maximum bench-press weight.

101. ***Teachers' Salaries*** The average salary S (in thousands of dollars) for elementary school teachers in the United States from 1990 to 2002 is approximated by the model

$$S = 1.05t + 31.0, \quad 0 \le t \le 12$$

where t represents the year, with $t = 0$ corresponding to 1990. (Source: National Education Association)

(a) According to this model, when was the average salary at least \$32,000, but not more than \$42,000?

(b) According to this model, when will the average salary exceed \$48,000?

102. ***Egg Production*** The number of eggs E (in billions) produced in the United States from 1990 to 2002 can be modeled by

$$E = 1.64t + 67.2, \quad 0 \le t \le 12$$

where t represents the year, with $t = 0$ corresponding to 1990. (Source: U.S. Department of Agriculture)

(a) According to this model, when was the annual egg production 70 billion, but no more than 80 billion?

(b) According to this model, when will the annual egg production exceed 95 billion?

103. ***Geometry*** The side of a square is measured as 10.4 inches with a possible error of $\frac{1}{16}$ inch. Using these measurements, determine the interval containing the possible areas of the square.

104. ***Geometry*** The side of a square is measured as 24.2 centimeters with a possible error of 0.25 centimeter. Using these measurements, determine the interval containing the possible areas of the square.

105. ***Accuracy of Measurement*** You stop at a self-service gas station to buy 15 gallons of 87-octane gasoline at \$1.89 a gallon. The gas pump is accurate to within $\frac{1}{10}$ of a gallon. How much might you be undercharged or overcharged?

106. ***Accuracy of Measurement*** You buy six T-bone steaks that cost \$14.99 per pound. The weight that is listed on the package is 5.72 pounds. The scale that weighed the package is accurate to within $\frac{1}{2}$ ounce. How much might you be undercharged or overcharged?

107. ***Time Study*** A time study was conducted to determine the length of time required to perform a particular task in a manufacturing process. The times required by approximately two-thirds of the workers in the study satisfied the inequality

$$\left|\frac{t - 15.6}{1.9}\right| < 1$$

where t is time in minutes. Determine the interval on the real number line in which these times lie.

108. ***Height*** The heights h of two-thirds of the members of a population satisfy the inequality

$$\left|\frac{h - 68.5}{2.7}\right| \le 1$$

where h is measured in inches. Determine the interval on the real number line in which these heights lie.

109. ***Meteorology*** An electronic device is to be operated in an environment with relative humidity h in the interval defined by $|h - 50| \le 30$. What are the minimum and maximum relative humidities for the operation of this device?

110. ***Music*** Michael Kasha of Florida State University used physics and mathematics to design a new classical guitar. He used the model for the frequency of the vibrations on a circular plate

$$v = \frac{2.6t}{d^2}\sqrt{\frac{E}{\rho}}$$

where v is the frequency (in vibrations per second), t is the plate thickness (in millimeters), d is the diameter of the plate, E is the elasticity of the plate material, and ρ is the density of the plate material. For fixed values of d, E, and ρ, the graph of the equation is a line (see figure).

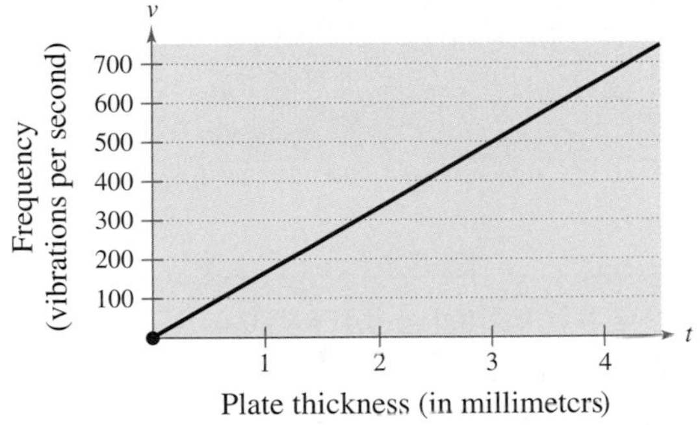

(a) Estimate the frequency when the plate thickness is 2 millimeters.

(b) Estimate the plate thickness when the frequency is 600 vibrations per second.

(c) Approximate the interval for the plate thickness when the frequency is between 200 and 400 vibrations per second.

(d) Approximate the interval for the frequency when the plate thickness is less than 3 millimeters.

Synthesis

True or False? **In Exercises 111 and 112, determine whether the statement is true or false. Justify your answer.**

111. If a, b, and c are real numbers, and $a \le b$, then $ac \le bc$.

112. If $-10 \le x \le 8$, then $-10 \ge -x$ and $-x \ge -8$.

113. Identify the graph of the inequality $|x - a| \ge 2$.

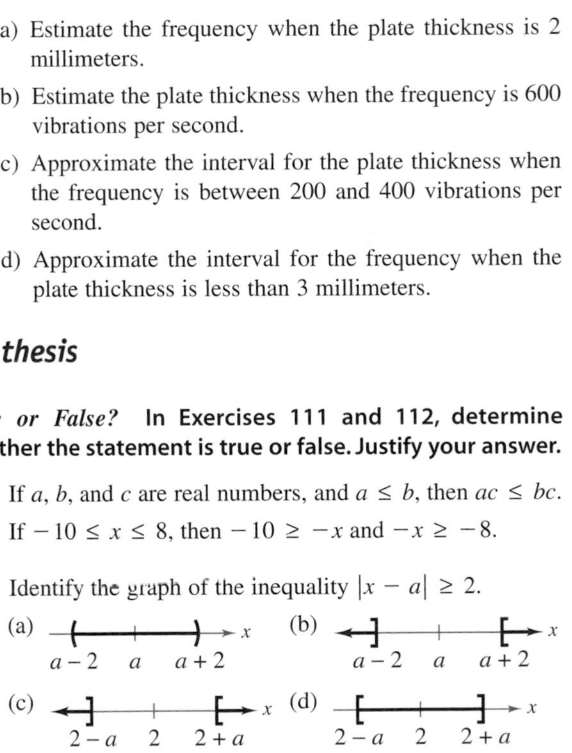

114. Find sets of values of a, b, and c such that $0 \le x \le 10$ is a solution of the inequality $|ax - b| \le c$.

A.7 Errors and the Algebra of Calculus

What you should learn

- Avoid common algebraic errors.
- Recognize and use algebraic techniques that are common in calculus.

Why you should learn it

An efficient command of algebra is critical in mastering this course and in the study of calculus.

Algebraic Errors to Avoid

This section contains five lists of common algebraic errors: errors involving parentheses, errors involving fractions, errors involving exponents, errors involving radicals, and errors involving dividing out. Many of these errors are made because they seem to be the *easiest* things to do. For instance, the operations of subtraction and division are often believed to be commutative and associative. The following examples illustrate the fact that subtraction and division are neither commutative nor associative.

Not commutative	*Not associative*
$4 - 3 \neq 3 - 4$	$8 - (6 - 2) \neq (8 - 6) - 2$
$15 \div 5 \neq 5 \div 15$	$20 \div (4 \div 2) \neq (20 \div 4) \div 2$

Errors Involving Parentheses

Potential Error	*Correct Form*	*Comment*
~~$a - (x - b) = a - x - b$~~	$a - (x - b) = a - x + b$	Change all signs when distributing minus sign.
~~$(a + b)^2 = a^2 + b^2$~~	$(a + b)^2 = a^2 + 2ab + b^2$	Remember the middle term when squaring binomials.
~~$\left(\frac{1}{2}a\right)\left(\frac{1}{2}b\right) = \frac{1}{2}(ab)$~~	$\left(\frac{1}{2}a\right)\left(\frac{1}{2}b\right) = \frac{1}{4}(ab) = \frac{ab}{4}$	$\frac{1}{2}$ occurs twice as a factor.
~~$(3x + 6)^2 = 3(x + 2)^2$~~	$(3x + 6)^2 = [3(x + 2)]^2 = 3^2(x + 2)^2$	When factoring, apply exponents to all factors.

Errors Involving Fractions

Potential Error	*Correct Form*	*Comment*
~~$\frac{a}{x + b} = \frac{a}{x} + \frac{a}{b}$~~	Leave as $\frac{a}{x + b}$.	Do not add denominators when adding fractions.
~~$\frac{\left(\frac{x}{a}\right)}{b} = \frac{bx}{a}$~~	$\frac{\left(\frac{x}{a}\right)}{b} = \left(\frac{x}{a}\right)\left(\frac{1}{b}\right) = \frac{x}{ab}$	Multiply by the reciprocal when dividing fractions.
~~$\frac{1}{a} + \frac{1}{b} = \frac{1}{a + b}$~~	$\frac{1}{a} + \frac{1}{b} = \frac{b + a}{ab}$	Use the property for adding fractions.
~~$\frac{1}{3x} = \frac{1}{3}x$~~	$\frac{1}{3x} = \frac{1}{3} \cdot \frac{1}{x}$	Use the property for multiplying fractions.
~~$(1/3)x = \frac{1}{3x}$~~	$(1/3)x = \frac{1}{3} \cdot x = \frac{x}{3}$	Be careful when using a slash to denote division.
~~$(1/x) + 2 = \frac{1}{x + 2}$~~	$(1/x) + 2 = \frac{1}{x} + 2 = \frac{1 + 2x}{x}$	Be careful when using a slash to denote division and be sure to find a common denominator before you add fractions.

Errors Involving Exponents

Potential Error	*Correct Form*	*Comment*
$(x^2)^3 = x^5$	$(x^2)^3 = x^{2 \cdot 3} = x^6$	Multiply exponents when raising a power to a power.
$x^2 \cdot x^3 = x^6$	$x^2 \cdot x^3 = x^{2+3} = x^5$	Add exponents when multiplying powers with like bases.
$2x^3 = (2x)^3$	$2x^3 = 2(x^3)$	Exponents have priority over coefficients.
$\frac{1}{x^2 - x^3} = x^{-2} - x^{-3}$	Leave as $\frac{1}{x^2 - x^3}$.	Do not move term-by-term from denominator to numerator.

Errors Involving Radicals

Potential Error	*Correct Form*	*Comment*
$\sqrt{5x} = 5\sqrt{x}$	$\sqrt{5x} = \sqrt{5}\sqrt{x}$	Radicals apply to every factor inside the radical.
$\sqrt{x^2 + a^2} = x + a$	Leave as $\sqrt{x^2 + a^2}$.	Do not apply radicals term-by-term.
$\sqrt{-x + a} = -\sqrt{x - a}$	Leave as $\sqrt{-x + a}$.	Do not factor minus signs out of square roots.

Errors Involving Dividing Out

Potential Error	*Correct Form*	*Comment*
$\frac{a + bx}{a} = 1 + bx$	$\frac{a + bx}{a} = \frac{a}{a} + \frac{bx}{a} = 1 + \frac{b}{a}x$	Divide out common factors, not common terms.
$\frac{a + ax}{a} = a + x$	$\frac{a + ax}{a} = \frac{a(1 + x)}{a} = 1 + x$	Factor before dividing out.
$1 + \frac{x}{2x} = 1 + \frac{1}{x}$	$1 + \frac{x}{2x} = 1 + \frac{1}{2} = \frac{3}{2}$	Divide out common factors.

A good way to avoid errors is to *work slowly*, *write neatly*, and *talk to yourself*. Each time you write a step, ask yourself why the step is algebraically legitimate. You can justify the step below because *dividing the numerator and denominator by the same nonzero number produces an equivalent fraction*.

$$\frac{2x}{6} = \frac{\cancel{2} \cdot x}{\cancel{2} \cdot 3} = \frac{x}{3}$$

Example 1 Using the Property for Adding Fractions

Describe and correct the error. $\frac{1}{2x} + \frac{1}{3x} = \frac{1}{5x}$

Solution

When adding fractions, use the property for adding fractions: $\frac{1}{a} + \frac{1}{b} = \frac{b + a}{ab}$.

$$\frac{1}{2x} + \frac{1}{3x} = \frac{3x + 2x}{6x^2} = \frac{5x}{6x^2} = \frac{5}{6x}$$

✓CHECKPOINT Now try Exercise 17.

Some Algebra of Calculus

In calculus it is often necessary to take a simplified algebraic expression and "unsimplify" it. See the following lists, taken from a standard calculus text.

Unusual Factoring

Expression	*Useful Calculus Form*	*Comment*
$\dfrac{5x^4}{8}$	$\dfrac{5}{8}x^4$	Write with fractional coefficient.
$\dfrac{x^2+3x}{-6}$	$-\dfrac{1}{6}(x^2+3x)$	Write with fractional coefficient.
$2x^2-x-3$	$2\left(x^2-\dfrac{x}{2}-\dfrac{3}{2}\right)$	Factor out the leading coefficient.
$\dfrac{x}{2}(x+1)^{-1/2}+(x+1)^{1/2}$	$\dfrac{(x+1)^{-1/2}}{2}[x+2(x+1)]$	Factor out factor with lowest power.

Writing with Negative Exponents

Expression	*Useful Calculus Form*	*Comment*
$\dfrac{9}{5x^3}$	$\dfrac{9}{5}x^{-3}$	Move the factor to the numerator and change the sign of the exponent.
$\dfrac{7}{\sqrt{2x-3}}$	$7(2x-3)^{-1/2}$	Move the factor to the numerator and change the sign of the exponent.

Writing a Fraction as a Sum

Expression	*Useful Calculus Form*	*Comment*
$\dfrac{x+2x^2+1}{\sqrt{x}}$	$x^{1/2}+2x^{3/2}+x^{-1/2}$	Divide each term by $x^{1/2}$.
$\dfrac{1+x}{x^2+1}$	$\dfrac{1}{x^2+1}+\dfrac{x}{x^2+1}$	Rewrite the fraction as the sum of fractions.
$\dfrac{2x}{x^2+2x+1}$	$\dfrac{2x+2-2}{x^2+2x+1}$	Add and subtract the same term.
	$=\dfrac{2x+2}{x^2+2x+1}-\dfrac{2}{(x+1)^2}$	Rewrite the fraction as the difference of fractions.
$\dfrac{x^2-2}{x+1}$	$x-1-\dfrac{1}{x+1}$	Use long division. (See Section 2.3.)
$\dfrac{x+7}{x^2-x-6}$	$\dfrac{2}{x-3}-\dfrac{1}{x+2}$	Use the method of partial fractions. (See Section 7.4.)

Inserting Factors and Terms

Expression	*Useful Calculus Form*	*Comment*
$(2x - 1)^3$	$\frac{1}{2}(2x - 1)^3(2)$	Multiply and divide by 2.
$7x^2(4x^3 - 5)^{1/2}$	$\frac{7}{12}(4x^3 - 5)^{1/2}(12x^2)$	Multiply and divide by 12.
$\frac{4x^2}{9} - 4y^2 = 1$	$\frac{x^2}{9/4} - \frac{y^2}{1/4} = 1$	Write with fractional denominators.
$\frac{x}{x + 1}$	$\frac{x + 1 - 1}{x + 1} = 1 - \frac{1}{x + 1}$	Add and subtract the same term.

The next five examples demonstrate many of the steps in the preceding lists.

Example 2 **Factors Involving Negative Exponents**

Factor $x(x + 1)^{-1/2} + (x + 1)^{1/2}$.

Solution

When multiplying factors with like bases, you add exponents. When factoring, you are undoing multiplication, and so you *subtract* exponents.

$$\begin{aligned} x(x + 1)^{-1/2} + (x + 1)^{1/2} &= (x + 1)^{-1/2}[x(x + 1)^0 + (x + 1)^1] \\ &= (x + 1)^{-1/2}[x + (x + 1)] \\ &= (x + 1)^{-1/2}(2x + 1) \end{aligned}$$

CHECKPOINT Now try Exercise 23.

Another way to simplify the expression in Example 2 is to multiply the expression by a fractional form of 1 and then use the Distributive Property.

$$\begin{aligned} x(x + 1)^{-1/2} + (x + 1)^{1/2} &= [x(x + 1)^{-1/2} + (x + 1)^{1/2}] \cdot \frac{(x + 1)^{1/2}}{(x + 1)^{1/2}} \\ &= \frac{x(x + 1)^0 + (x + 1)^1}{(x + 1)^{1/2}} = \frac{2x + 1}{\sqrt{x + 1}} \end{aligned}$$

Example 3 **Inserting Factors in an Expression**

Insert the required factor: $\frac{x + 2}{(x^2 + 4x - 3)^2} = (\quad)\frac{1}{(x^2 + 4x - 3)^2}(2x + 4)$.

Solution

The expression on the right side of the equation is twice the expression on the left side. To make both sides equal, insert a factor of $\frac{1}{2}$.

$$\frac{x + 2}{(x^2 + 4x - 3)^2} = \left(\frac{1}{2}\right)\frac{1}{(x^2 + 4x - 3)^2}(2x + 4)$$

Right side is multiplied and divided by 2.

CHECKPOINT Now try Exercise 25.

Example 4 **Rewriting Fractions**

Explain why the two expressions are equivalent.

$$\frac{4x^2}{9} - 4y^2 = \frac{x^2}{\frac{9}{4}} - \frac{y^2}{\frac{1}{4}}$$

Solution

To write the expression on the left side of the equation in the form given on the right side, multiply the numerators and denominators of both terms by $\frac{1}{4}$.

$$\frac{4x^2}{9} - 4y^2 = \frac{4x^2}{9}\left(\frac{\frac{1}{4}}{\frac{1}{4}}\right) - 4y^2\left(\frac{\frac{1}{4}}{\frac{1}{4}}\right) = \frac{x^2}{\frac{9}{4}} - \frac{y^2}{\frac{1}{4}}$$

CHECKPOINT Now try Exercise 29.

Example 5 **Rewriting with Negative Exponents**

Rewrite each expression using negative exponents.

a. $\dfrac{-4x}{(1 - 2x^2)^2}$ **b.** $\dfrac{2}{5x^3} - \dfrac{1}{\sqrt{x}} + \dfrac{3}{5(4x)^2}$

Solution

a. $\dfrac{-4x}{(1 - 2x^2)^2} = -4x(1 - 2x^2)^{-2}$

b. Begin by writing the second term in exponential form.

$$\frac{2}{5x^3} - \frac{1}{\sqrt{x}} + \frac{3}{5(4x)^2} = \frac{2}{5x^3} - \frac{1}{x^{1/2}} + \frac{3}{5(4x)^2}$$

$$= \frac{2}{5}x^{-3} - x^{-1/2} + \frac{3}{5}(4x)^{-2}$$

CHECKPOINT Now try Exercise 39.

Example 6 **Writing a Fraction as a Sum of Terms**

Rewrite each fraction as the sum of three terms.

a. $\dfrac{x^2 - 4x + 8}{2x}$ **b.** $\dfrac{x + 2x^2 + 1}{\sqrt{x}}$

Solution

a. $\dfrac{x^2 - 4x + 8}{2x} = \dfrac{x^2}{2x} - \dfrac{4x}{2x} + \dfrac{8}{2x}$

$= \dfrac{x}{2} - 2 + \dfrac{4}{x}$

b. $\dfrac{x + 2x^2 + 1}{\sqrt{x}} = \dfrac{x}{x^{1/2}} + \dfrac{2x^2}{x^{1/2}} + \dfrac{1}{x^{1/2}}$

$= x^{1/2} + 2x^{3/2} + x^{-1/2}$

CHECKPOINT Now try Exercise 43.

A.7 Exercises

VOCABULARY CHECK: Fill in the blanks.

1. To write the expression $\frac{2}{\sqrt{x}}$ with negative exponents, move $\sqrt{x}$ to the ________ and change the sign of the exponent.

2. When dividing fractions, multiply by the ________.

In Exercises 1–18, describe and correct the error.

1. $2x - (3y + 4) = 2x - 3y + 4$
2. $5z + 3(x - 2) = 5z + 3x - 2$
3. $\frac{4}{16x - (2x + 1)} = \frac{4}{14x + 1}$
4. $\frac{1 - x}{(5 - x)(-x)} = \frac{x - 1}{x(x - 5)}$
5. $(5z)(6z) = 30z$
6. $x(yz) = (xy)(xz)$
7. $a\left(\frac{x}{y}\right) = \frac{ax}{ay}$
8. $(4x)^2 = 4x^2$
9. $\sqrt{x + 9} = \sqrt{x} + 3$
10. $\sqrt{25 - x^2} = 5 - x$
11. $\frac{2x^2 + 1}{5x} = \frac{2x + 1}{5}$
12. $\frac{6x + y}{6x - y} = \frac{x + y}{x - y}$
13. $\frac{1}{a^{-1} + b^{-1}} = \left(\frac{1}{a + b}\right)^{-1}$
14. $\frac{1}{x + y^{-1}} = \frac{y}{x + 1}$
15. $(x^2 + 5x)^{1/2} = x(x + 5)^{1/2}$
16. $x(2x - 1)^2 = (2x^2 - x)^2$
17. $\frac{3}{x} + \frac{4}{y} = \frac{7}{x + y}$
18. $\frac{1}{2y} = (1/2)y$

In Exercises 19–38, insert the required factor in the parentheses.

19. $\frac{3x + 2}{5} = \frac{1}{5}(\quad)$
20. $\frac{7x^2}{10} = \frac{7}{10}(\quad)$
21. $\frac{2}{3}x^2 + \frac{1}{3}x + 5 = \frac{1}{3}(\quad)$
22. $\frac{3}{4}x + \frac{1}{2} = \frac{1}{4}(\quad)$
23. $x^2(x^3 - 1)^4 = (\quad)(x^3 - 1)^4(3x^2)$
24. $x(1 - 2x^2)^3 = (\quad)(1 - 2x^2)^3(-4x)$
25. $\frac{4x + 6}{(x^2 + 3x + 7)^3} = (\quad)\frac{1}{(x^2 + 3x + 7)^3}(2x + 3)$
26. $\frac{x + 1}{(x^2 + 2x - 3)^2} = (\quad)\frac{1}{(x^2 + 2x - 3)^2}(2x + 2)$
27. $\frac{3}{x} + \frac{5}{2x^2} - \frac{3}{2}x = (\quad)(6x + 5 - 3x^3)$
28. $\frac{(x - 1)^2}{169} + (y + 5)^2 = \frac{(x - 1)^3}{169(\quad)} + (y + 5)^2$
29. $\frac{9x^2}{25} + \frac{16y^2}{49} = \frac{x^2}{(\quad)} + \frac{y^2}{(\quad)}$
30. $\frac{3x^2}{4} - \frac{9y^2}{16} = \frac{x^2}{(\quad)} - \frac{y^2}{(\quad)}$
31. $\frac{x^2}{1/12} - \frac{y^2}{2/3} = \frac{12x^2}{(\quad)} - \frac{3y^2}{(\quad)}$
32. $\frac{x^2}{4/9} + \frac{y^2}{7/8} = \frac{9x^2}{(\quad)} + \frac{8y^2}{(\quad)}$
33. $x^{1/3} - 5x^{4/3} = x^{1/3}(\quad)$
34. $3(2x + 1)x^{1/2} + 4x^{3/2} = x^{1/2}(\quad)$
35. $(1 - 3x)^{4/3} - 4x(1 - 3x)^{1/3} = (1 - 3x)^{1/3}(\quad)$
36. $\frac{1}{2\sqrt{x}} + 5x^{3/2} - 10x^{5/2} = \frac{1}{2\sqrt{x}}(\quad)$
37. $\frac{1}{10}(2x + 1)^{5/2} - \frac{1}{6}(2x + 1)^{3/2} = \frac{(2x + 1)^{3/2}}{15}(\quad)$
38. $\frac{3}{7}(t + 1)^{7/3} - \frac{3}{4}(t + 1)^{4/3} = \frac{3(t + 1)^{4/3}}{28}(\quad)$

In Exercises 39–42, write the expression using negative exponents.

39. $\frac{3x^2}{(2x - 1)^3}$
40. $\frac{x + 1}{x(6 - x)^{1/2}}$
41. $\frac{4}{3x} + \frac{4}{x^4} - \frac{7x}{\sqrt[3]{2x}}$
42. $\frac{x}{x - 2} + \frac{1}{x^2} + \frac{8}{3(9x)^3}$

In Exercises 43–48, write the fraction as a sum of two or more terms.

43. $\frac{16 - 5x - x^2}{x}$
44. $\frac{x^3 - 5x^2 + 4}{x^2}$
45. $\frac{4x^3 - 7x^2 + 1}{x^{1/3}}$
46. $\frac{2x^5 - 3x^3 + 5x - 1}{x^{3/2}}$
47. $\frac{3 - 5x^2 - x^4}{\sqrt{x}}$
48. $\frac{x^3 - 5x^4}{3x^2}$

In Exercises 49–60, simplify the expression.

49. $\frac{-2(x^2 - 3)^{-3}(2x)(x + 1)^3 - 3(x + 1)^2(x^2 - 3)^{-2}}{[(x + 1)^3]^2}$
50. $\frac{x^5(-3)(x^2 + 1)^{-4}(2x) - (x^2 + 1)^{-3}(5)x^4}{(x^5)^2}$
51. $\frac{(6x + 1)^3(27x^2 + 2) - (9x^3 + 2x)(3)(6x + 1)^2(6)}{[(6x + 1)^3]^2}$

52. $\dfrac{(4x^2+9)^{1/2}(2)-(2x+3)\left(\frac{1}{2}\right)(4x^2+9)^{-1/2}(8x)}{[(4x^2+9)^{1/2}]^2}$

53. $\dfrac{(x+2)^{3/4}(x+3)^{-2/3}-(x+3)^{1/3}(x+2)^{-1/4}}{[(x+2)^{3/4}]^2}$

54. $(2x-1)^{1/2}-(x+2)(2x-1)^{-1/2}$

55. $\dfrac{2(3x-1)^{1/3}-(2x+1)\left(\frac{1}{3}\right)(3x-1)^{-2/3}(3)}{(3x-1)^{2/3}}$

56. $\dfrac{(x+1)\left(\frac{1}{2}\right)(2x-3x^2)^{-1/2}(2-6x)-(2x-3x^2)^{1/2}}{(x+1)^2}$

57. $\dfrac{1}{(x^2+4)^{1/2}}\cdot\dfrac{1}{2}(x^2+4)^{-1/2}(2x)$

58. $\dfrac{1}{x^2-6}(2x)+\dfrac{1}{2x+5}(2)$

59. $(x^2+5)^{1/2}\left(\frac{3}{2}\right)(3x-2)^{1/2}(3)$
$\quad + (3x-2)^{3/2}\left(\frac{1}{2}\right)(x^2+5)^{-1/2}(2x)$

60. $(3x+2)^{-1/2}(3)(x-6)^{1/2}(1)$
$\quad + (x-6)^3\left(-\frac{1}{2}\right)(3x+2)^{-3/2}(3)$

61. ***Athletics*** An athlete has set up a course for training as part of her regimen in preparation for an upcoming triathlon. She is dropped off by a boat 2 miles from the nearest point on shore. The finish line is 4 miles down the coast and 2 miles inland (see figure). She can swim 2 miles per hour and run 6 miles per hour. The time t (in hours) required for her to reach the finish line can be approximated by the model

$$t=\frac{\sqrt{x^2+4}}{2}+\frac{\sqrt{(4-x)^2+4}}{6}$$

where x is the distance down the coast (in miles) to which she swims and then leaves the water to start her run.

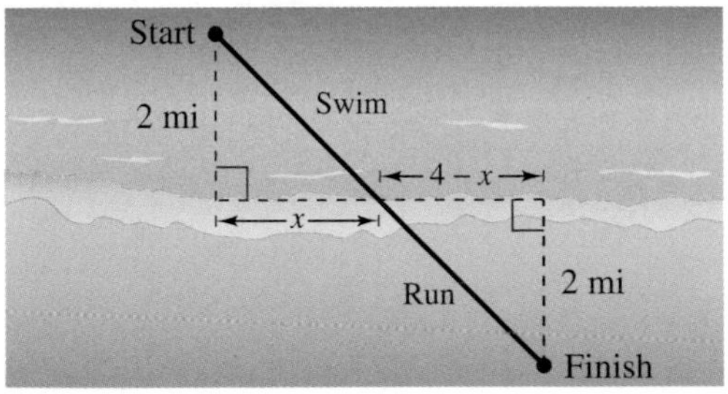

(a) Find the times required for the triathlete to finish when she swims to the points $x = 0.5$, $x = 1.0, \ldots,$ $x = 3.5$, and $x = 4.0$ miles down the coast.

(b) Use your results from part (a) to determine the distance down the coast that will yield the minimum amount of time required for the triathlete to reach the finish line.

(c) The expression below was obtained using calculus. It can be used to find the minimum amount of time required for the triathlete to reach the finish line. Simplify the expression.

$$\tfrac{1}{2}x(x^2+4)^{-1/2}+\tfrac{1}{6}(x-4)(x^2-8x+20)^{-1/2}$$

62. (a) Verify that $y_1 = y_2$ analytically.

$$y_1 = x^2\left(\frac{1}{3}\right)(x^2+1)^{-2/3}(2x)+(x^2+1)^{1/3}(2x)$$

$$y_2=\frac{2x(4x^2+3)}{3(x^2+1)^{2/3}}$$

(b) Complete the table and demonstrate the equality in part (a) numerically.

x	-2	-1	$-\frac{1}{2}$	0	1	2	$\frac{5}{2}$
y_1							
y_2							

Synthesis

True or False? **In Exercises 63–66, determine whether the statement is true or false. Justify your answer.**

63. $x^{-1}+y^{-2}=\dfrac{y^2+x}{xy^2}$

64. $\dfrac{1}{x^{-2}+y^{-1}}=x^2+y$

65. $\dfrac{1}{\sqrt{x}+4}=\dfrac{\sqrt{x}-4}{x-16}$

66. $\dfrac{x^2-9}{\sqrt{x}-3}=\sqrt{x}+3$

In Exercises 67–70, find and correct any errors. If the problem is correct, state that it is correct.

67. $x^n\cdot x^{3n}=x^{3n^2}$

68. $(x^n)^{2n}+(x^{2n})^n=2x^{2n^2}$

69. $x^{2n}+y^{2n}=(x^n+y^n)^2$

70. $\dfrac{x^{2n}\cdot x^{3n}}{x^{3n}+x^2}=\dfrac{x^{5n}}{x^{3n}+x^2}$

71. ***Think About It*** You are taking a course in calculus, and for one of the homework problems you obtain the following answer.

$$\frac{1}{10}(2x-1)^{5/2}+\frac{1}{6}(2x-1)^{3/2}$$

The answer in the back of the book is $\frac{1}{15}(2x-1)^{3/2}(3x+1)$. Show how the second answer can be obtained from the first. Then use the same technique to simplify each of the following expressions.

(a) $\dfrac{2}{3}x(2x-3)^{3/2}-\dfrac{2}{15}(2x-3)^{5/2}$

(b) $\dfrac{2}{3}x(4+x)^{3/2}-\dfrac{2}{15}(4+x)^{5/2}$

Answers to Odd-Numbered Exercises and Tests

Chapter 1

Section 1.1 *(page 9)*

Vocabulary Check *(page 9)*

1. (a) v (b) vi (c) i (d) iv (e) iii (f) ii
2. Cartesian **3.** Distance Formula
4. Midpoint Formula

1. A: (2, 6), B: (−6, −2), C: (4, −4), D: (−3, 2)

3.

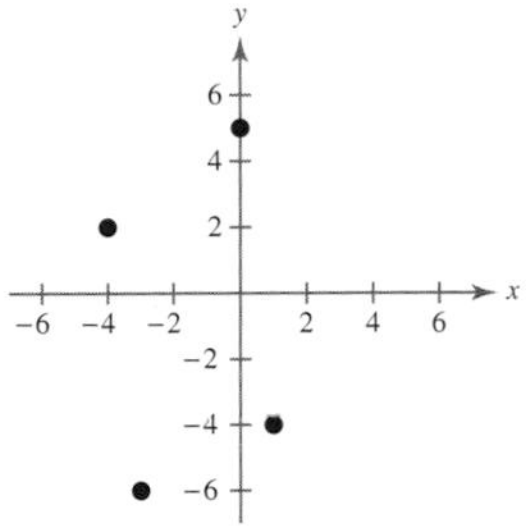

5.

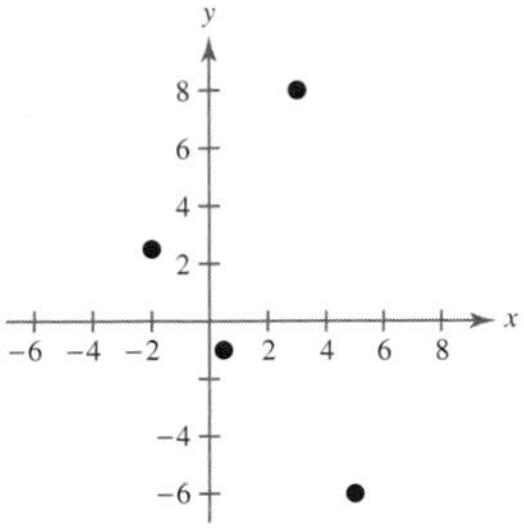

7. (−3, 4) **9.** (−5, −5) **11.** Quadrant IV
13. Quadrant II **15.** Quadrant III or IV
17. Quadrant III **19.** Quadrant I or III

21.

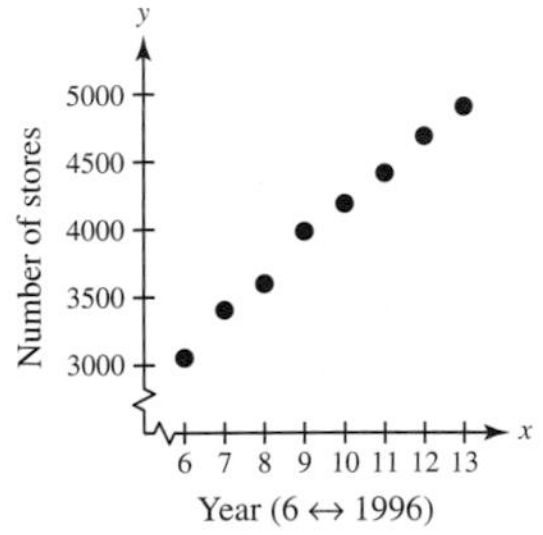

23. 8 **25.** 5

27. (a) 4, 3, 5 (b) $4^2 + 3^2 = 5^2$

29. (a) 10, 3, $\sqrt{109}$ (b) $10^2 + 3^2 = (\sqrt{109})^2$

31. (a)

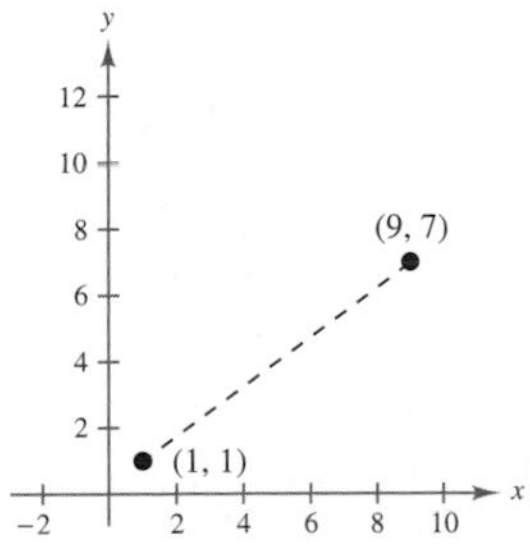

(b) 10
(c) (5, 4)

33. (a)

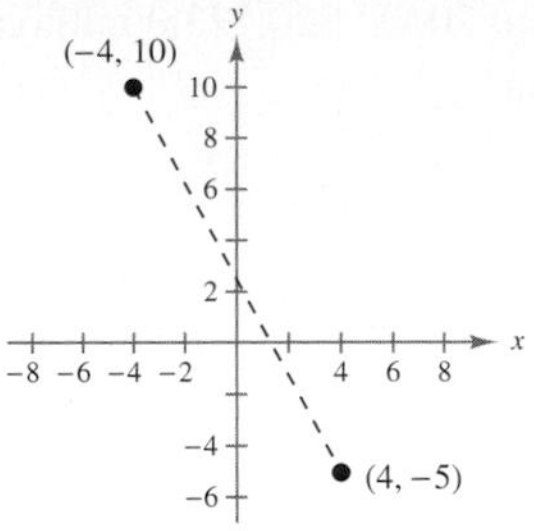

(b) 17
(c) $\left(0, \frac{5}{2}\right)$

35. (a)

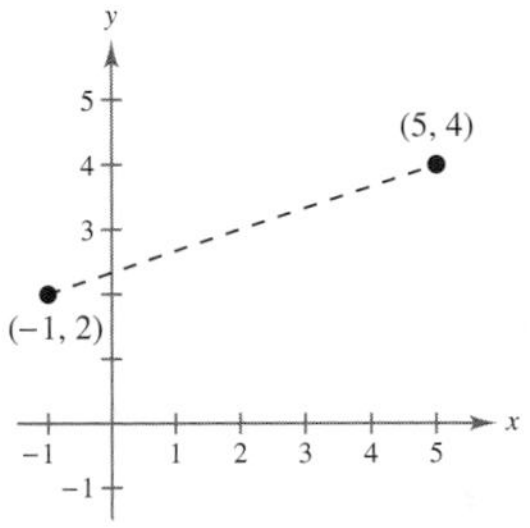

(b) $2\sqrt{10}$
(c) (2, 3)

37. (a)

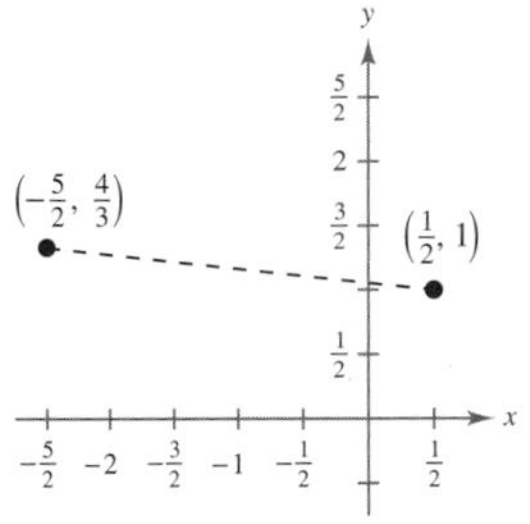

(b) $\dfrac{\sqrt{82}}{3}$
(c) $\left(-1, \frac{7}{6}\right)$

39. (a)

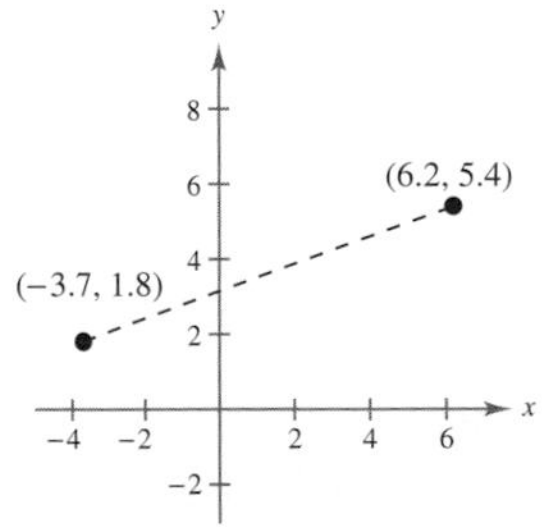

(b) $\sqrt{110.97}$
(c) (1.25, 3.6)

41. $(\sqrt{5})^2 + (\sqrt{45})^2 = (\sqrt{50})^2$

43. $(2x_m - x_1, 2y_m - y_1)$

45. $\left(\dfrac{3x_1 + x_2}{4}, \dfrac{3y_1 + y_2}{4}\right), \left(\dfrac{x_1 + x_2}{2}, \dfrac{y_1 + y_2}{2}\right),$
$\left(\dfrac{x_1 + 3x_2}{4}, \dfrac{y_1 + 3y_2}{4}\right)$

47. $2\sqrt{505} \approx 45$ yards **49.** \$3803.5 million

51. (0, 1), (4, 2), (1, 4) **53.** (−3, 6), (2, 10), (2, 4), (−3, 4)

55. \$3.31 per pound; 2001 **57.** ≈ 250%

59. (a) The number of artists elected each year seems to be nearly steady except for the first few years. From six to eight artists will be elected in 2008.
(b) The Rock and Roll Hall of Fame was opened in 1986.

61. 1998: \$19,384.5 million; 2000: \$20,223.0 million; 2002: \$21,061.5 million

63. $\sqrt[3]{\dfrac{4.47}{\pi}} \approx 1.12$ inches

65. Length of side = 43 centimeters; area = 800.64 square centimeters

67. (a)

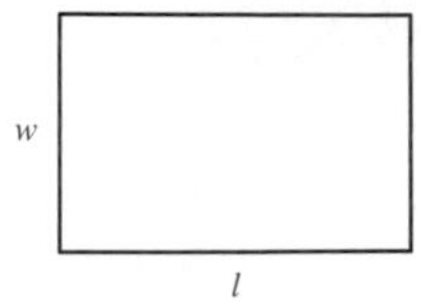

(b) $l = 1.5w$; $p = 5w$
(c) 7.5 meters × 5 meters

69. (a)

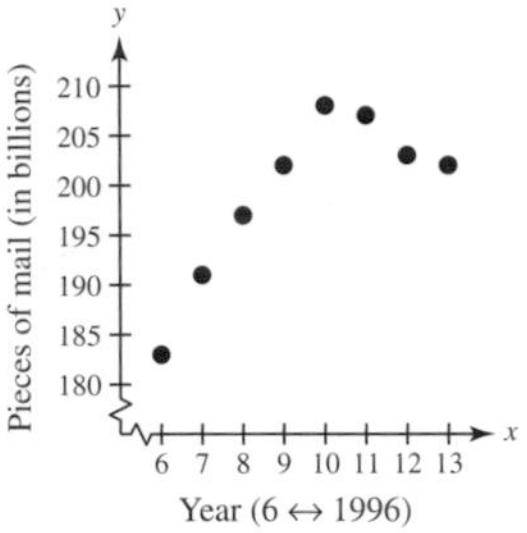

(b) 2002
(c) Answers will vary. Sample answer: Technology now enables us to transport information in many ways other than by mail. The Internet is one example.

71.

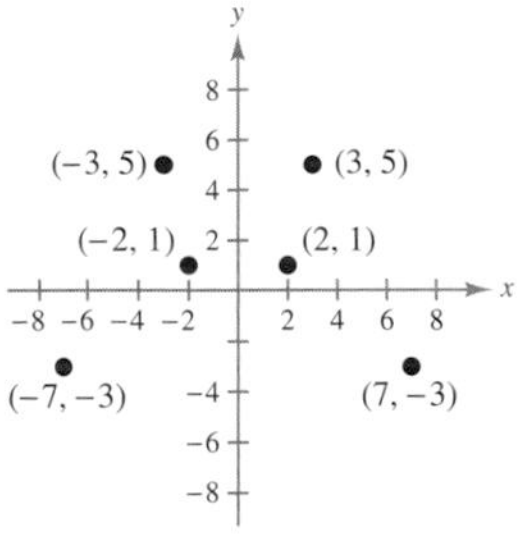

(a) The point is reflected through the y-axis.
(b) The point is reflected through the x-axis.
(c) The point is reflected through the origin.

73. False. The Midpoint Formula would be used 15 times.

75. No. It depends on the magnitudes of the quantities measured.

77. b **78.** c **79.** d **80.** a **81.** $x = 1$

83. $x = 2 \pm \sqrt{11}$ **85.** $x < \frac{3}{5}$ **87.** $14 < x < 22$

Section 1.2 *(page 22)*

Vocabulary Check *(page 22)*

1. solution or solution point 2. graph
3. intercepts 4. y-axis 5. circle; (h, k); r
6. numerical

1. (a) Yes (b) Yes **3.** (a) No (b) Yes

5.

x	-1	0	1	2	$\frac{5}{2}$
y	7	5	3	1	0
(x, y)	$(-1, 7)$	$(0, 5)$	$(1, 3)$	$(2, 1)$	$\left(\frac{5}{2}, 0\right)$

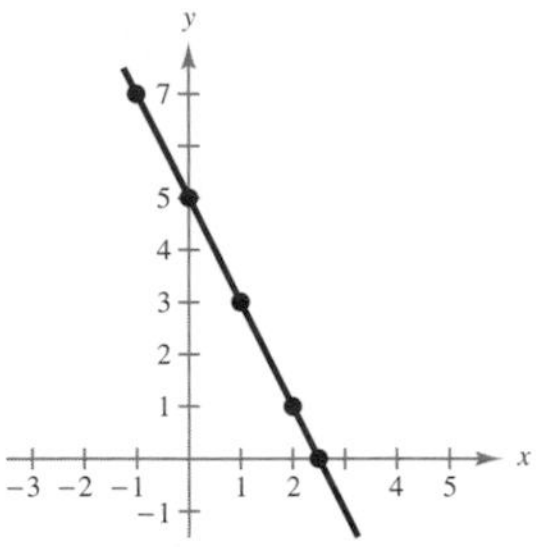

7.

x	-1	0	1	2	3
y	4	0	-2	-2	0
(x, y)	$(-1, 4)$	$(0, 0)$	$(1, -2)$	$(2, -2)$	$(3, 0)$

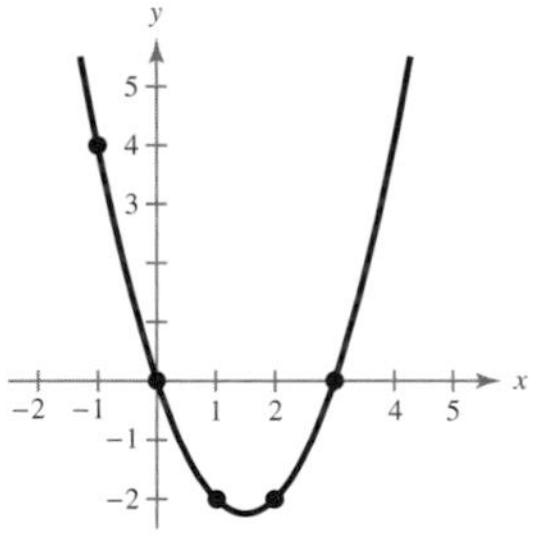

9. x-intercepts: $(\pm 2, 0)$
y-intercept: $(0, 16)$

11. x-intercept: $\left(\frac{6}{5}, 0\right)$
y-intercept: $(0, -6)$

13. x-intercept: $(-4, 0)$
y-intercept: $(0, 2)$

15. x-intercept: $\left(\frac{7}{3}, 0\right)$
y-intercept: $(0, 7)$

17. x-intercepts: $(0, 0)$, $(2, 0)$
y-intercept: $(0, 0)$

19. x-intercept: $(6, 0)$
y-intercepts: $\left(0, \pm\sqrt{6}\right)$

21.

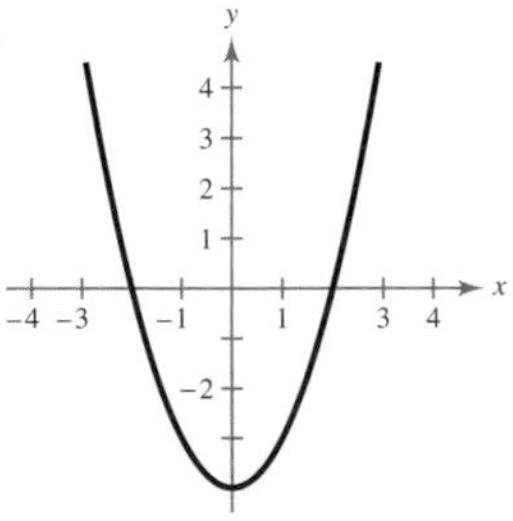

23.

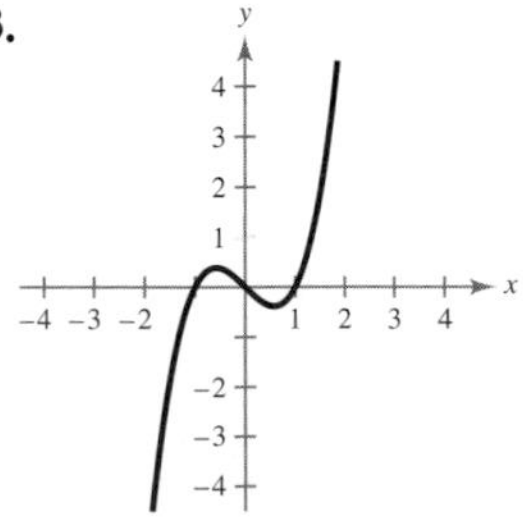

25. y-axis symmetry **27.** Origin symmetry
29. Origin symmetry **31.** x-axis symmetry

33.
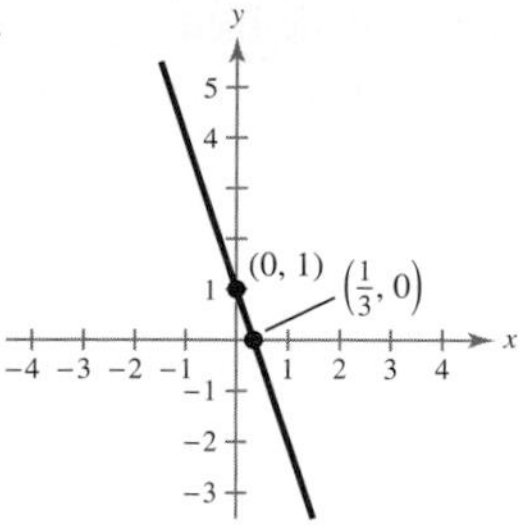

35.
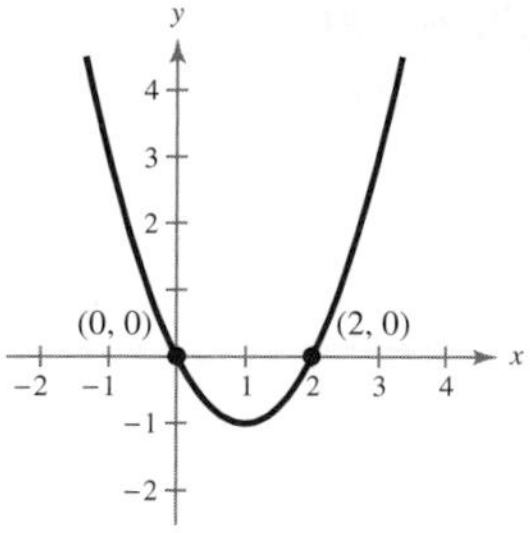

37.
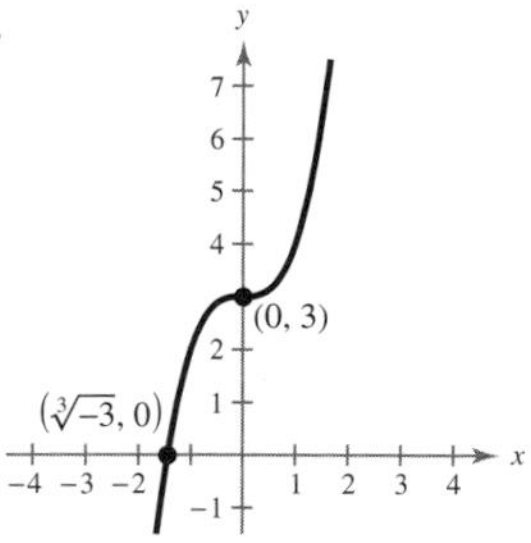

39.
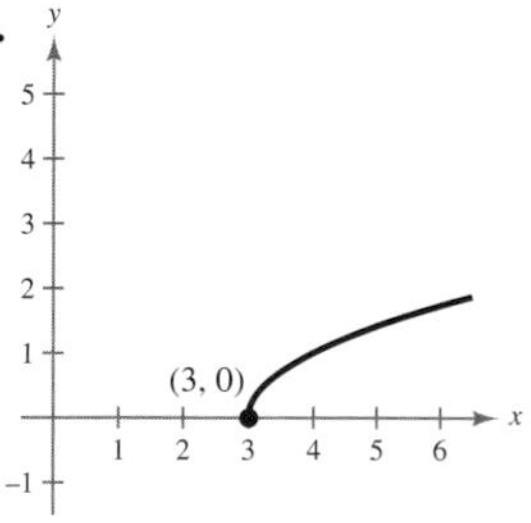

41.
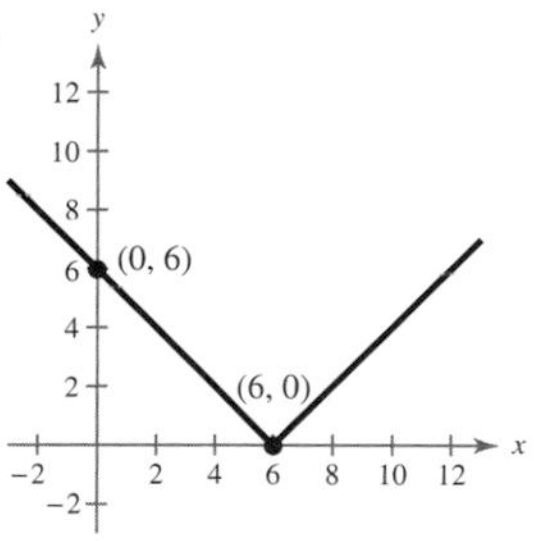

43.
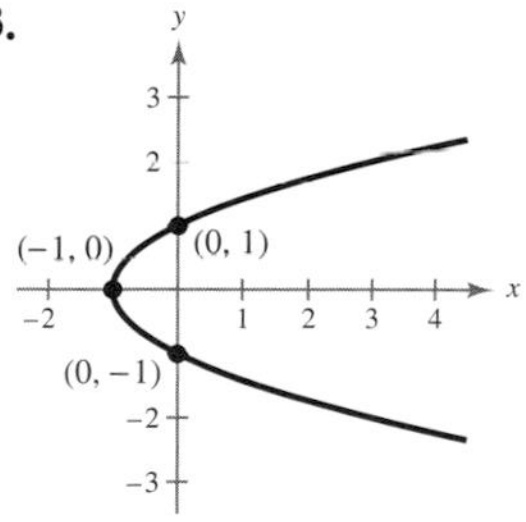

45.
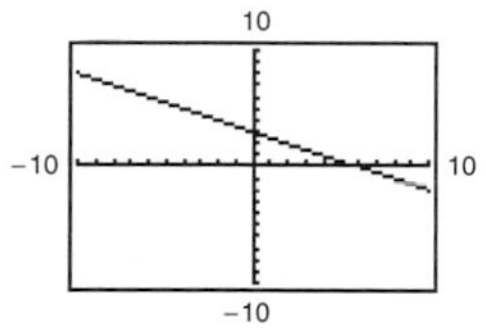

Intercepts: (6, 0), (0, 3)

47.
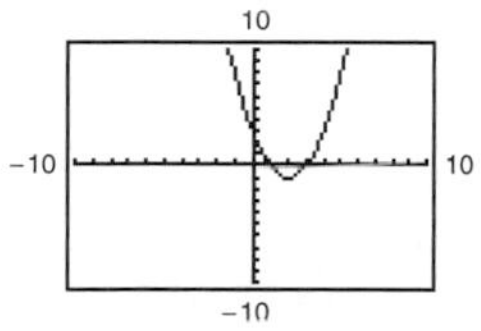

Intercepts: (3, 0), (1, 0), (0, 3)

49.
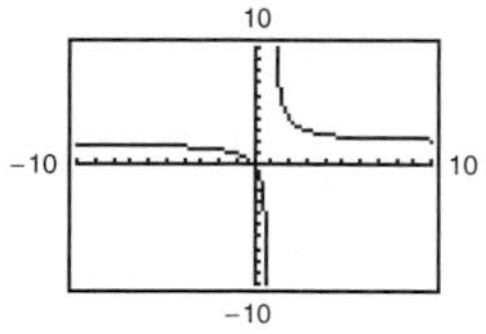

Intercept: (0, 0)

51.
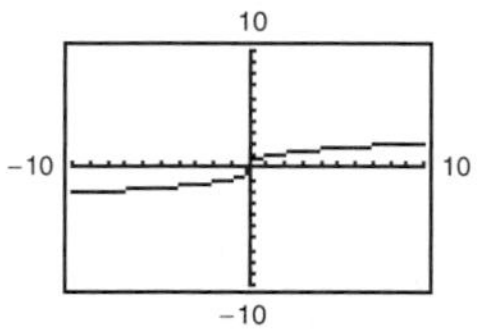

Intercept: (0, 0)

53.
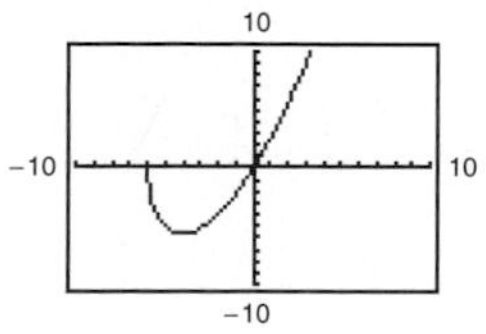

Intercepts: (0, 0), (−6, 0)

55.
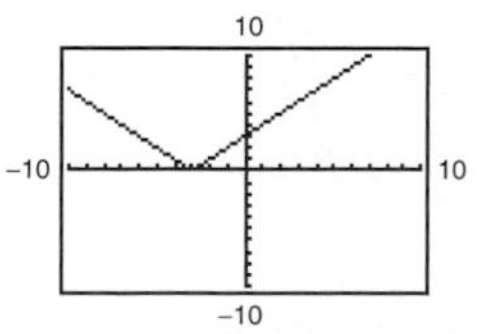

Intercepts: (−3, 0), (0, 3)

57. $x^2 + y^2 = 16$ **59.** $(x - 2)^2 + (y + 1)^2 = 16$

61. $(x + 1)^2 + (y - 2)^2 = 5$

63. $(x - 3)^2 + (y - 4)^2 = 25$

65. Center: (0, 0); Radius: 5

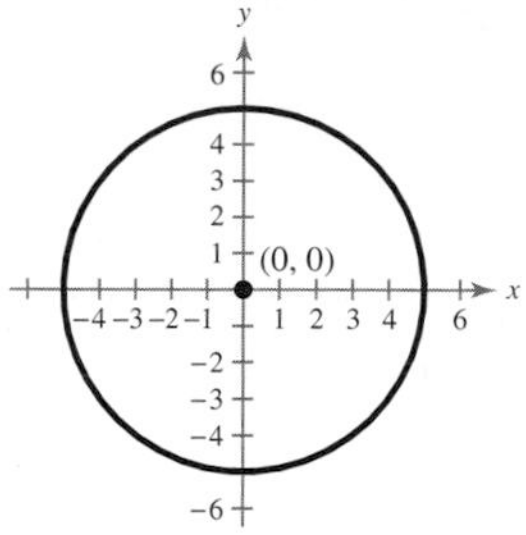

67. Center: (1, −3); Radius: 3

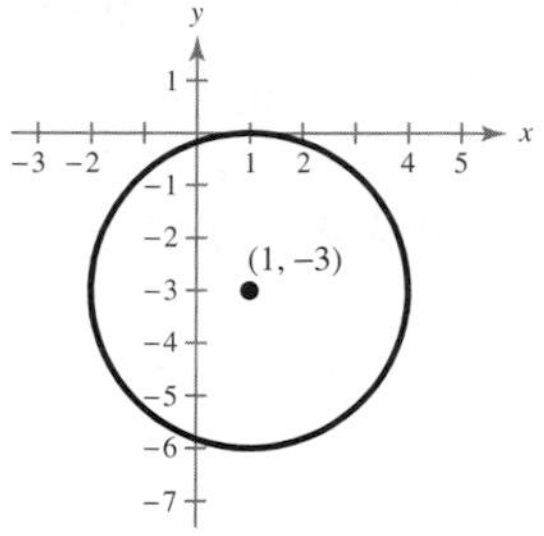

69. Center: $\left(\frac{1}{2}, \frac{1}{2}\right)$; Radius: $\frac{3}{2}$

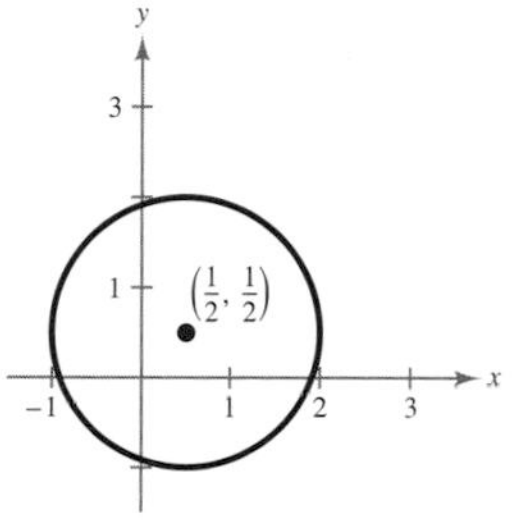

71.

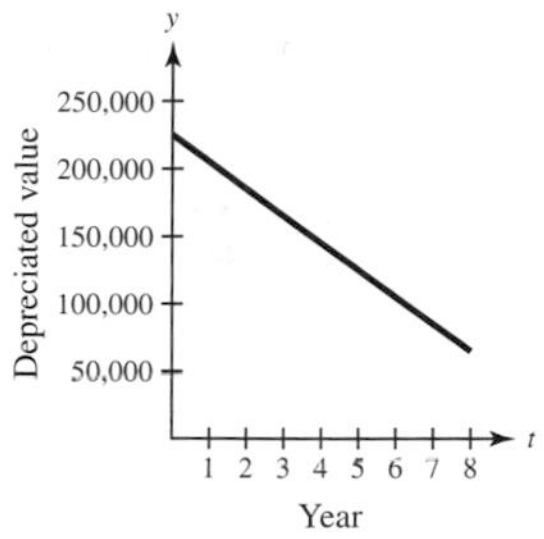

73. (a)
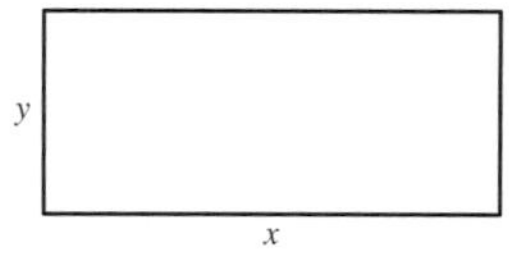

(b) Answers will vary.

(c)
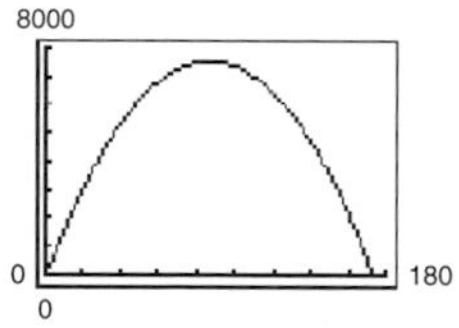

(d) $x = 86\frac{2}{3}$, $y = 86\frac{2}{3}$

(e) A regulation NFL playing field is 120 yards long and $53\frac{1}{3}$ yards wide. The actual area is 6400 square yards.

75. (a) and (b)
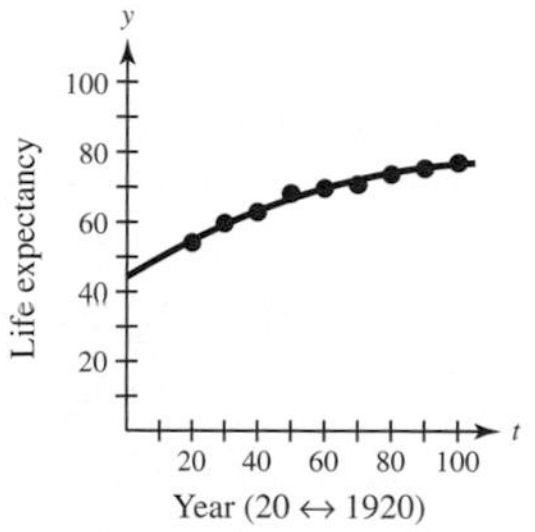

(c) 66.0 years (d) 2005: 77.0 years; 2010: 77.1 years

(e) Answers will vary.

CHAPTER 1

77. False. A graph is symmetric with respect to the x-axis if, whenever (x, y) is on the graph $(x, -y)$ is also on the graph.

79. The viewing window is incorrect. Change the viewing window. Answers will vary.

81. $9x^5,\ 4x^3,\ -7$ **83.** $2\sqrt{2x}$

85. $\dfrac{10\sqrt{7x}}{x}$ **87.** $\sqrt[3]{|t|}$

Section 1.3 *(page 34)*

Vocabulary Check *(page 34)*

1. linear **2.** slope **3.** parallel
4. perpendicular **5.** rate or rate of change
6. linear extrapolation
7. a. iii b. i c. v d. ii e. iv

1. (a) L_2 (b) L_3 (c) L_1

3.

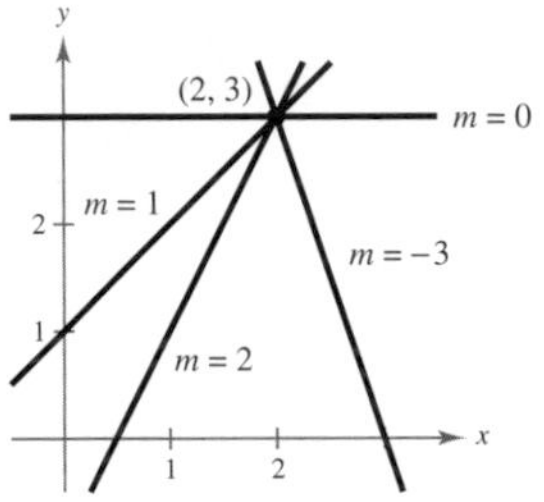

5. $\frac{3}{2}$ **7.** -4

9. $m = 5$;
y-intercept: $(0, 3)$

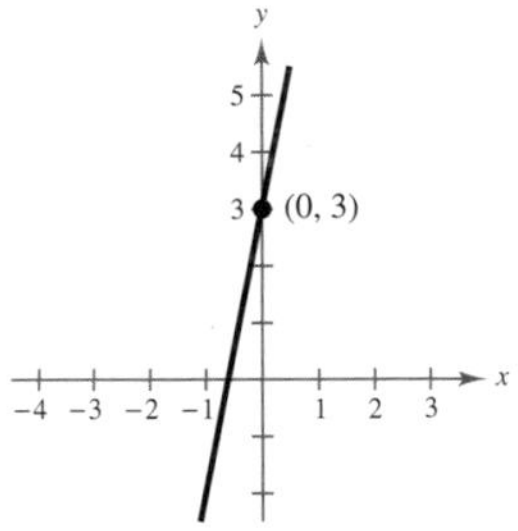

11. $m = -\frac{1}{2}$;
y-intercept: $(0, 4)$

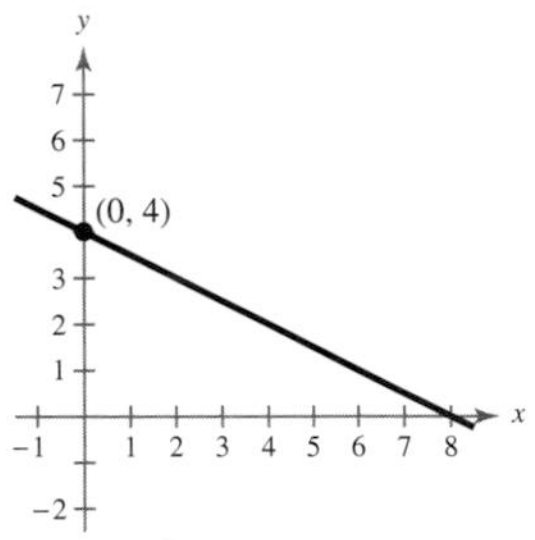

13. m is undefined.
There is no y-intercept.

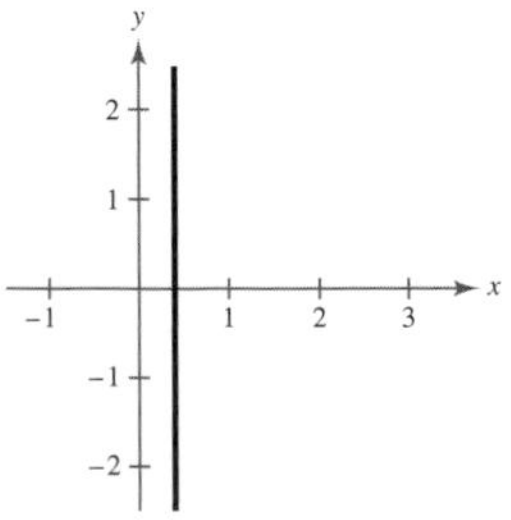

15. $m = -\frac{7}{6}$;
y-intercept: $(0, 5)$

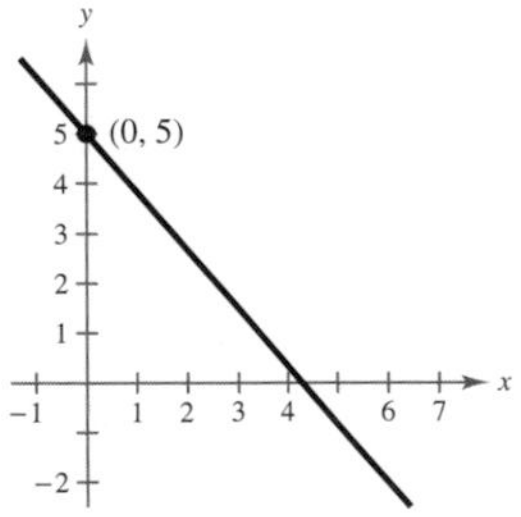

17. $m = 0$;
y-intercept: $(0, 3)$

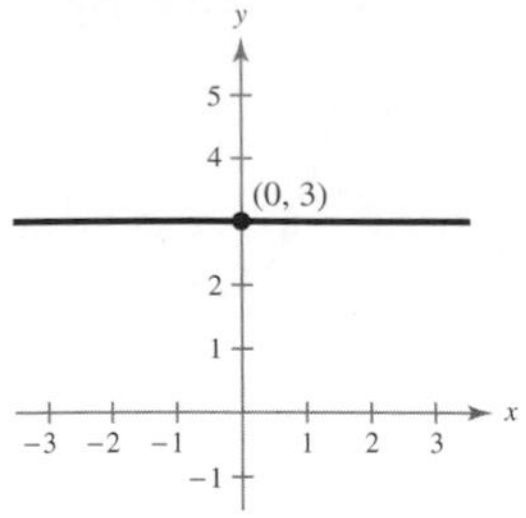

19. m is undefined.
There is no y-intercept.

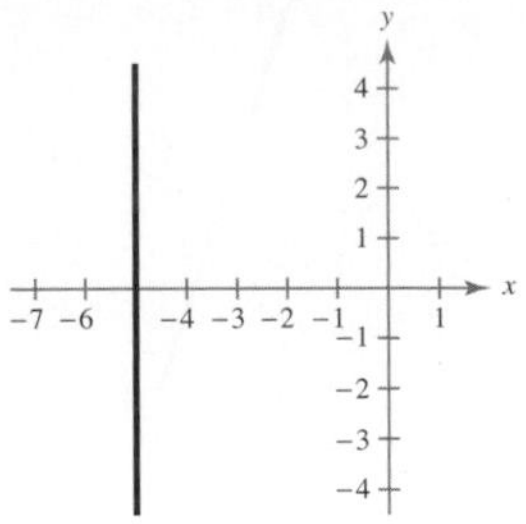

21.

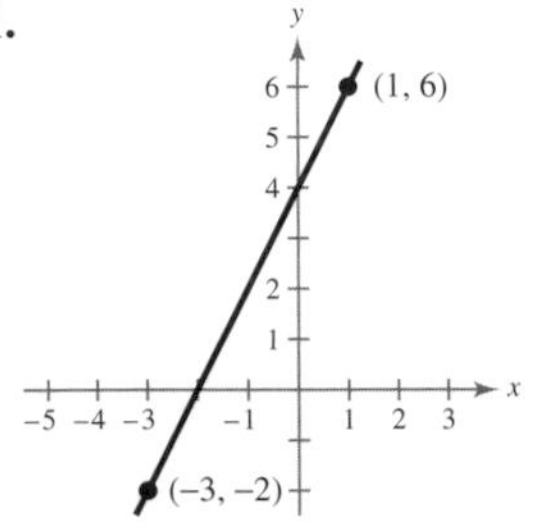

$m = 2$

23.

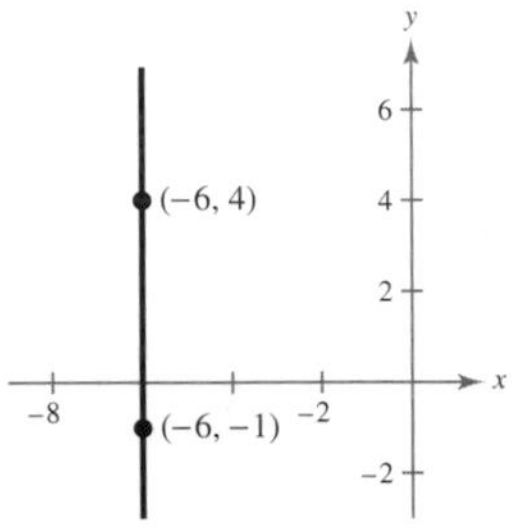

m is undefined.

25.

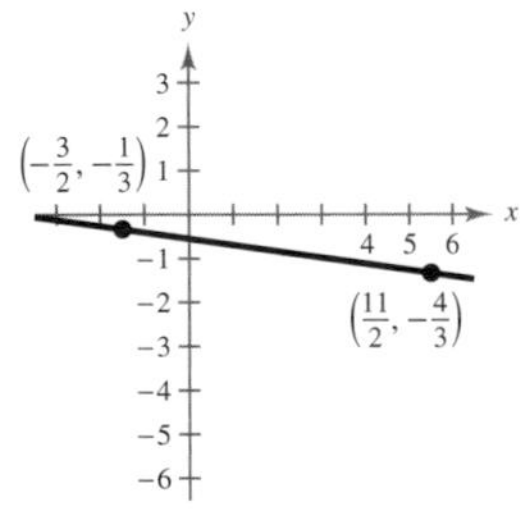

$m = -\frac{1}{7}$

27.

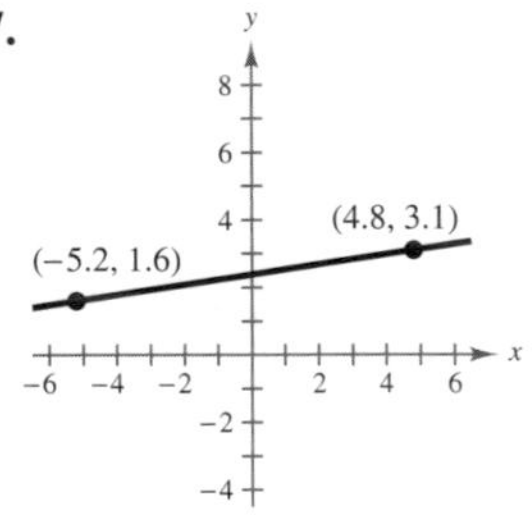

$m = 0.15$

29. $(0, 1), (3, 1), (-1, 1)$

31. $(6, -5), (7, -4), (8, -3)$

33. $(-8, 0), (-8, 2), (-8, 3)$

35. $(-4, 6), (-3, 8), (-2, 10)$

37. $(9, -1), (11, 0), (13, 1)$

39. $y = 3x - 2$

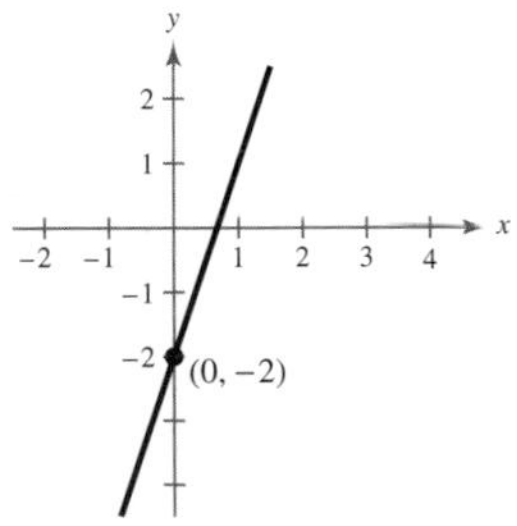

41. $y = -2x$

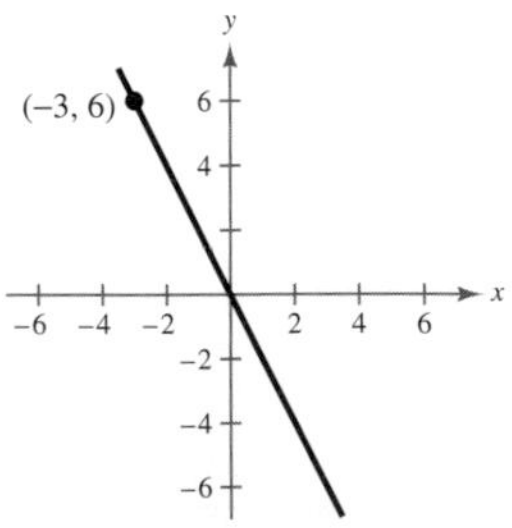

43. $y = -\frac{1}{3}x + \frac{4}{3}$

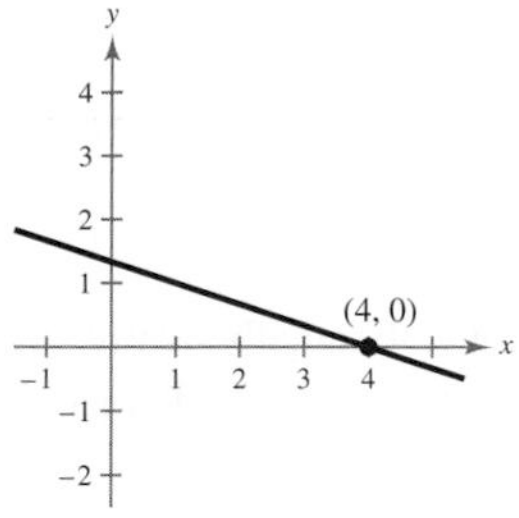

45. $x = 6$

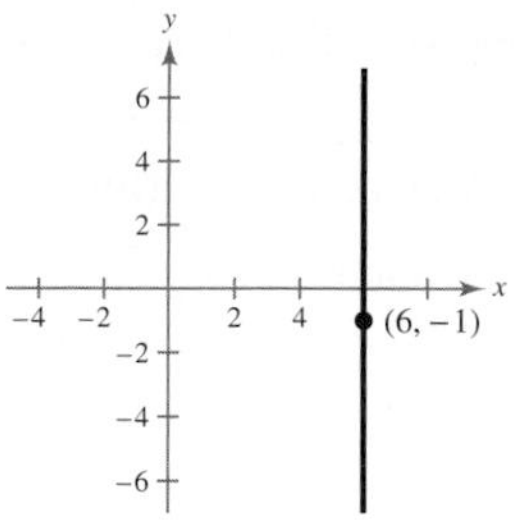

47. $y = \frac{5}{2}$

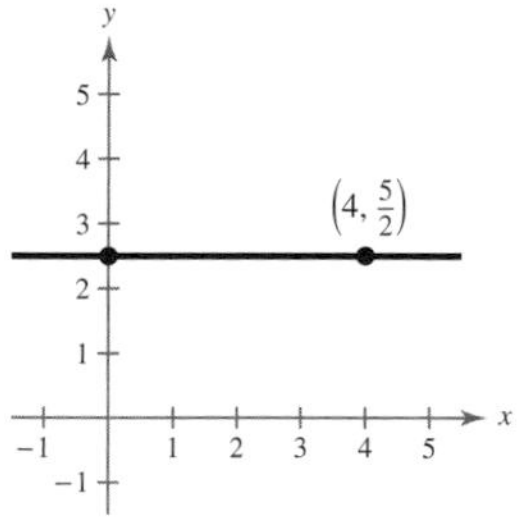

49. $y = 5x + 27.3$

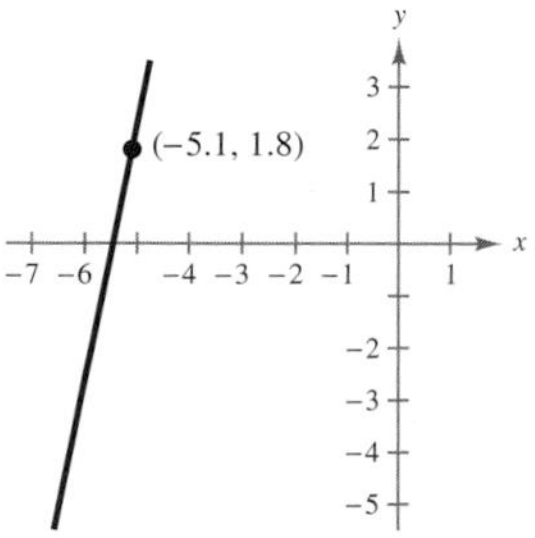

51. $y = -\frac{3}{5}x + 2$

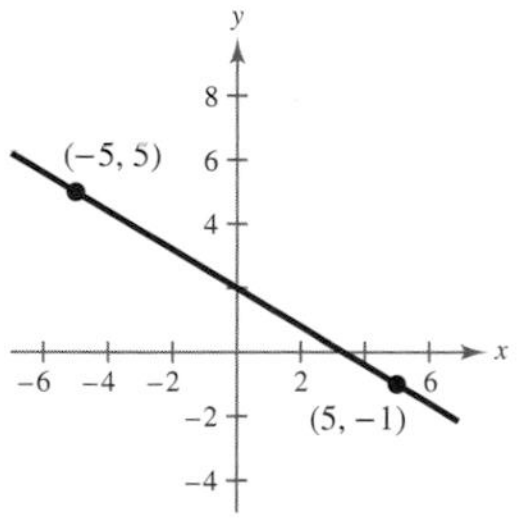

53. $x = -8$

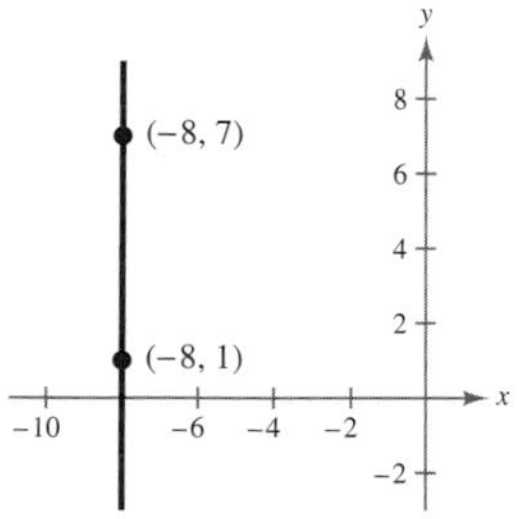

55. $y = -\frac{1}{2}x + \frac{3}{2}$

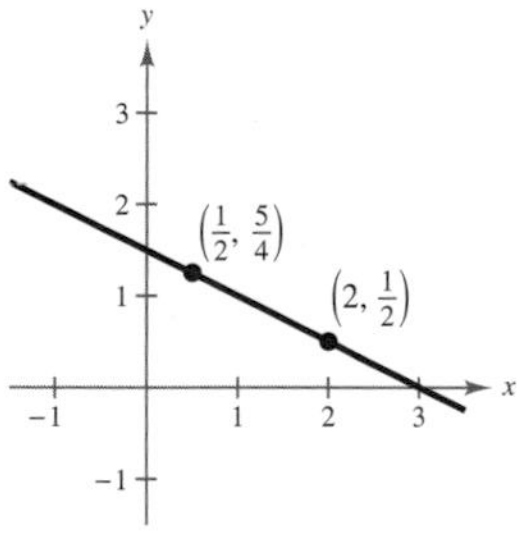

57. $y = -\frac{6}{5}x - \frac{18}{25}$

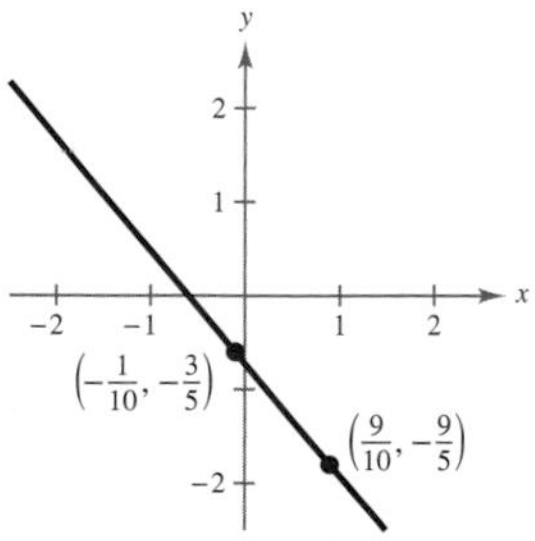

59. $y = 0.4x + 0.2$

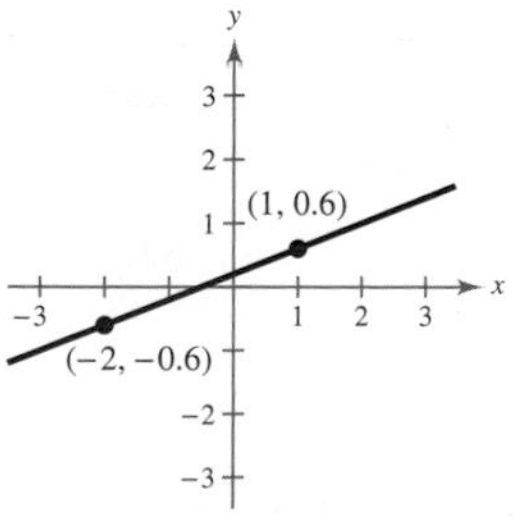

61. $y = -1$

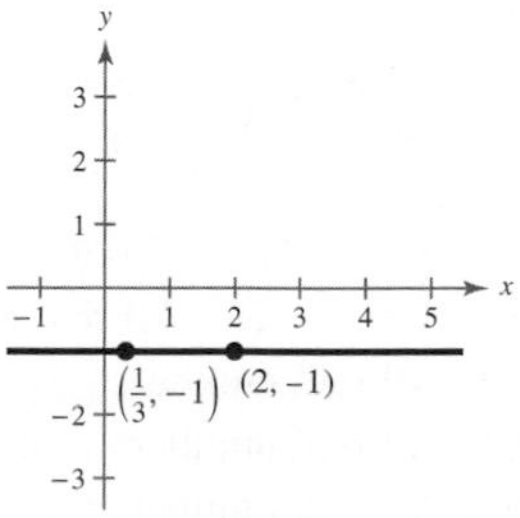

63. $x = \frac{7}{3}$

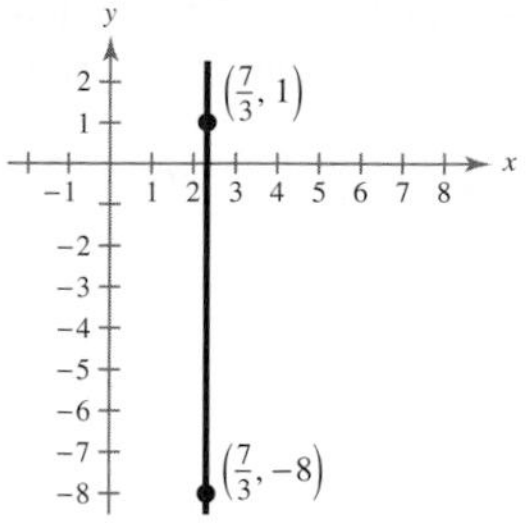

65. Perpendicular **67.** Parallel

69. (a) $y = 2x - 3$ (b) $y = -\frac{1}{2}x + 2$

71. (a) $y = -\frac{3}{4}x + \frac{3}{8}$ (b) $y = \frac{4}{3}x + \frac{127}{72}$

73. (a) $y = 0$ (b) $x = -1$

75. (a) $x = 2$ (b) $y = 5$

77. (a) $y = x + 4.3$ (b) $y = -x + 9.3$

79. $3x + 2y - 6 = 0$ **81.** $12x + 3y + 2 = 0$

83. $x + y - 3 = 0$

85. Line (b) is perpendicular to line (c).

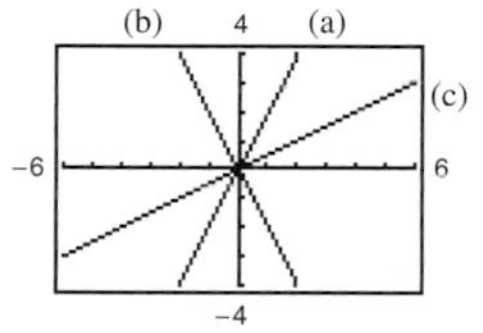

87. Line (a) is parallel to line (b).
Line (c) is perpendicular to line (a) and line (b).

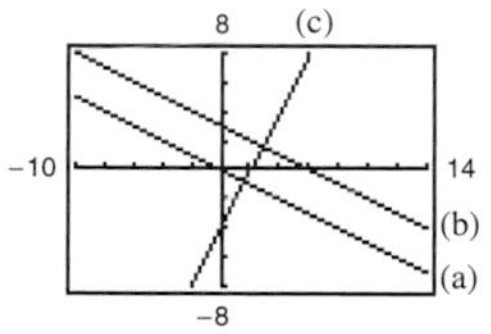

89. $3x - 2y - 1 = 0$ **91.** $80x + 12y + 139 = 0$

93. (a) Sales increasing 135 units per year
(b) No change in sales
(c) Sales decreasing 40 units per year

95. (a) Salary increased greatest from 1990 to 1992; Least from 1992 to 1994
(b) Slope of line from 1990 to 2002 is about 2351.83
(c) Salary increased an average of \$2351.83 over the 12 years between 1990 and 2002

97. 12 feet **99.** $V(t) = 3165 - 125t$

101. b; The slope is -20, which represents the decrease in the amount of the loan each week. The y-intercept is (0, 200) which represents the original amount of the loan.

102. c; The slope is 2, which represents the hourly wage per unit produced. The y-intercept is (0, 8.50) which represents the initial hourly wage.

103. a; The slope is 0.32, which represents the increase in travel cost for each mile driven. The y-intercept is (0, 30) which represents the amount per day for food.

104. d; The slope is -100, which represents the decrease in the value of the word processor each year. The y-intercept is $(0, 750)$ which represents the initial purchase price of the computer.

105. $y = 0.4825t - 2.2325$; $y(18) \approx \$6.45$; $y(20) \approx \$7.42$

107. $V = -175t + 875$

109. (a) $y(t) = 179.5t + 40{,}571$
(b) $y(8) = 42{,}007$; $y(10) = 42{,}366$ (c) $m = 179.5$

111. $S = 0.85L$

113. (a) $C = 16.75t + 36{,}500$ (b) $R = 27t$
(c) $P = 10.25t - 36{,}500$ (d) $t \approx 3561$ hours

115. (a)

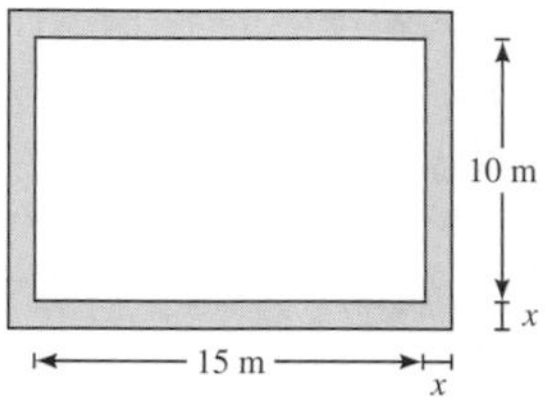

(b) $y = 8x + 50$

(c)

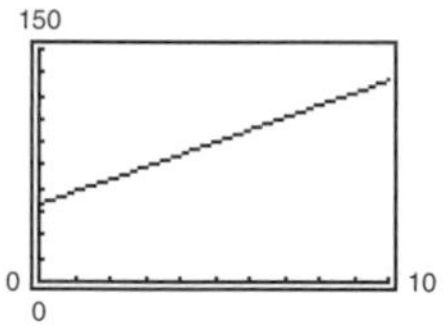

(d) $m = 8$, 8 meters

117. $C = 0.38x + 120$

119. (a) and (b)

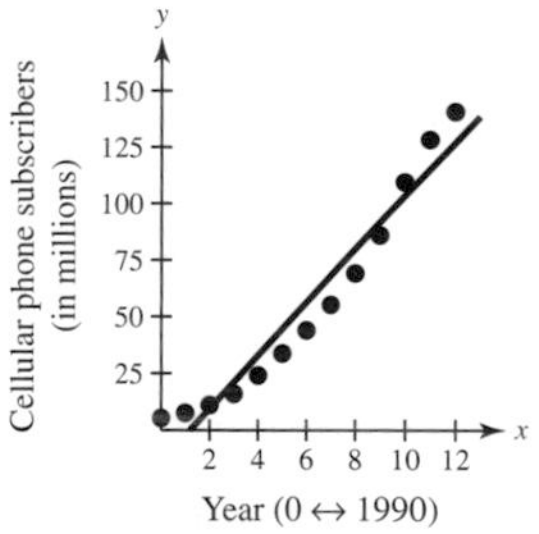

(c) Answers will vary. Sample answer: $y = 11.72x - 14.1$
(d) Answers will vary. Sample answer: The y-intercept indicates that initially there were -14.1 million subscribers which doesn't make sense in the context of this problem. Each year, the number of cellular phone subscribers increases by 11.72 million.
(e) The model is accurate.
(f) Answers will vary. Sample answer: 196.9 million

121. False. The slope with the greatest magnitude corresponds to the steepest line.

123. Find the distance between each two points and use the Pythagorean Theorem.

125. No. The slope cannot be determined without knowing the scale on the y-axis. The slopes could be the same.

127. V-intercept: initial cost; Slope: annual depreciation

129. d **130.** c **131.** a **132.** b

133. -1 **135.** $\frac{7}{2}, 7$ **137.** No solution

139. Answers will vary.

Section 1.4 *(page 48)*

Vocabulary Check *(page 48)*

1. domain; range; function
2. verbally; numerically; graphically; algebraically
3. independent; dependent **4.** piecewise-defined
5. implied domain **6.** difference quotient

1. Yes **3.** No

5. Yes, each input value has exactly one output value.

7. No, the input values of 7 and 10 each have two different output values.

9. (a) Function
(b) Not a function, because the element 1 in A corresponds to two elements, -2 and 1, in B.
(c) Function
(d) Not a function, because not every element in A is matched with an element in B.

11. Each is a function. For each year there corresponds one and only one circulation.

13. Not a function **15.** Function **17.** Function

19. Not a function **21.** Function **23.** Not a function

25. (a) -1 (b) -9 (c) $2x - 5$

27. (a) 36π (b) $\frac{9}{2}\pi$ (c) $\frac{32}{3}\pi r^3$

29. (a) 1 (b) 2.5 (c) $3 - 2|x|$

31. (a) $-\frac{1}{9}$ (b) Undefined (c) $\dfrac{1}{y^2 + 6y}$

33. (a) 1 (b) -1 (c) $\dfrac{|x - 1|}{x - 1}$

35. (a) -1 (b) 2 (c) 6

37. (a) -7 (b) 4 (c) 9

39.

x	-2	-1	0	1	2
$f(x)$	1	-2	-3	-2	1

41.

t	-5	-4	-3	-2	-1
$h(t)$	1	$\frac{1}{2}$	0	$\frac{1}{2}$	1

43.

x	-2	-1	0	1	2
$f(x)$	5	$\frac{9}{2}$	4	1	0

45. 5 **47.** $\frac{4}{3}$ **49.** ± 3 **51.** $0, \pm 1$ **53.** $2, -1$

55. 3, 0 **57.** All real numbers

59. All real numbers t except $t = 0$

61. All real numbers y such that $y \geq 0$

63. All real numbers x such that $-1 \leq x \leq 1$

65. All real numbers x except $x = 0, -2$

67. All real numbers s such that $s \geq 1$ except $s = 4$
69. All real numbers x such that $x > 0$
71. $\{(-2, 4), (-1, 1), (0, 0), (1, 1), (2, 4)\}$
73. $\{(-2, 4), (-1, 3), (0, 2), (1, 3), (2, 4)\}$
75. $g(x) = cx^2; c = -2$ **76.** $f(x) = cx; c = \frac{1}{4}$
77. $r(x) = \frac{c}{x}; c = 32$ **78.** $h(x) = c\sqrt{|x|}; c = 3$
79. $3 + h, h \neq 0$ **81.** $3x^2 + 3xh + h^2 + 3, h \neq 0$
83. $-\frac{x+3}{9x^2}, x \neq 3$ **85.** $\frac{\sqrt{5x} - 5}{x - 5}$ **87.** $A = \frac{P^2}{16}$
89. (a) The maximum volume is 1024 cubic centimeters.
(b)
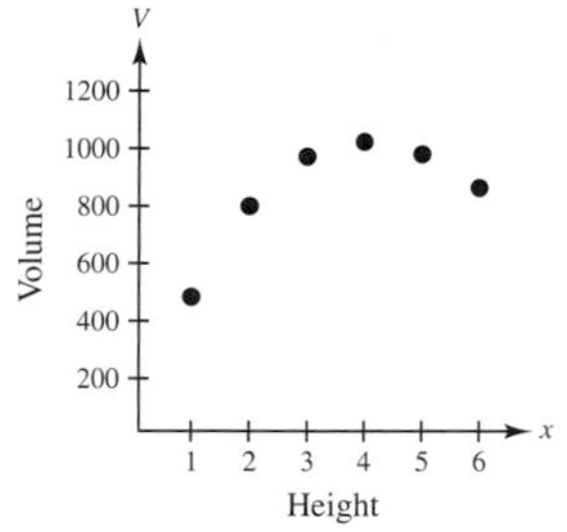

Yes, V is a function of x.
(c) $V = x(24 - 2x)^2, 0 < x < 12$
91. $A = \frac{x^2}{2(x - 2)}, x > 2$
93. Yes, the ball will be at a height of 6 feet.
95. 1990: \$27,300
1991: \$28,052
1992: \$29,168
1993: \$30,648
1994: \$32,492
1995: \$34,700
1996: \$37,272
1997: \$40,208
1998: \$41,300
1999: \$43,800
2000: \$46,300
2001: \$48,800
2002: \$51,300
97. (a) $C = 12.30x + 98{,}000$
(b) $R = 17.98x$
(c) $P = 5.68x - 98{,}000$
99. (a) $R = \frac{240n - n^2}{20}, n \geq 80$
(b)

n	90	100	110	120	130	140	150
$R(n)$	\$675	\$700	\$715	\$720	\$715	\$700	\$675

The revenue is maximum when 120 people take the trip.

101. (a)
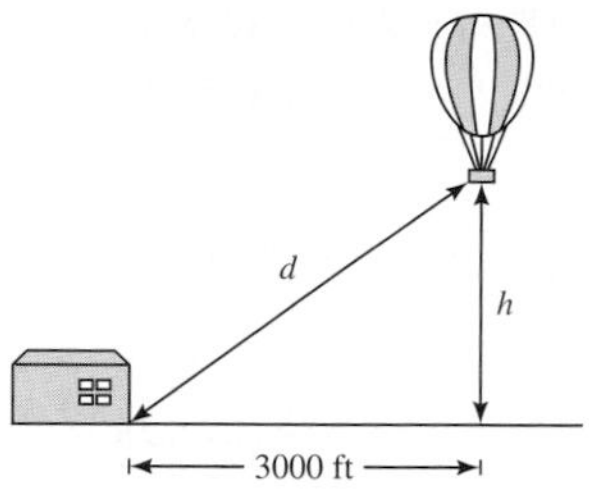

(b) $h = \sqrt{d^2 - 3000^2}, d \geq 3000$
103. False. The range is $[-1, \infty)$.
105. The domain is the set of inputs of the function, and the range is the set of outputs.
107. (a) Yes. The amount you pay in sales tax will increase as the price of the item purchased increases.
(b) No. The length of time that you study will not necessarily determine how well you do on an exam.
109. $\frac{15}{8}$ **111.** $-\frac{1}{5}$ **113.** $2x - 3y - 11 = 0$
115. $10x + 9y + 15 = 0$

Section 1.5 *(page 61)*

Vocabulary Check *(page 61)*

1. ordered pairs **2.** Vertical Line Test
3. zeros **4.** decreasing
5. maximum **6.** average rate of change; secant
7. odd **8.** even

1. Domain: $(-\infty, -1], [1, \infty)$
Range: $[0, \infty)$
3. Domain: $[-4, 4]$
Range: $[0, 4]$
5. (a) 0 (b) -1 (c) 0 (d) -2
7. (a) -3 (b) 0 (c) 1 (d) -3 **9.** Function
11. Not a function **13.** Function **15.** $-\frac{5}{2}, 6$
17. 0 **19.** $0, \pm\sqrt{2}$ **21.** $\pm\frac{1}{2}, 6$ **23.** $\frac{1}{2}$
25.
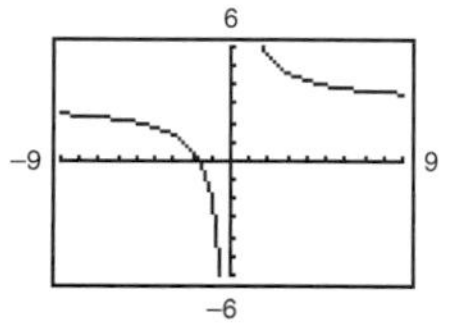

$-\frac{5}{3}$
27.
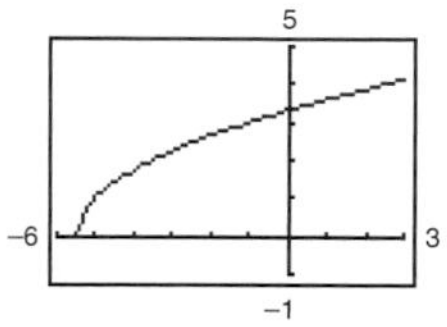

$-\frac{11}{2}$
29.
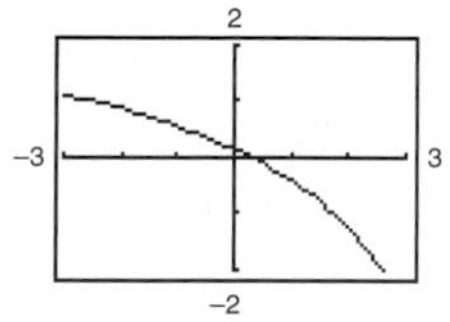

$\frac{1}{3}$
31. Increasing on $(-\infty, \infty)$
33. Increasing on $(-\infty, 0)$ and $(2, \infty)$
Decreasing on $(0, 2)$

CHAPTER 1

35. Increasing on $(-\infty, 0)$ and $(2, \infty)$; Constant on $(0, 2)$

37. Increasing on $(1, \infty)$; Decreasing on $(-\infty, -1)$
Constant on $(-1, 1)$

39.

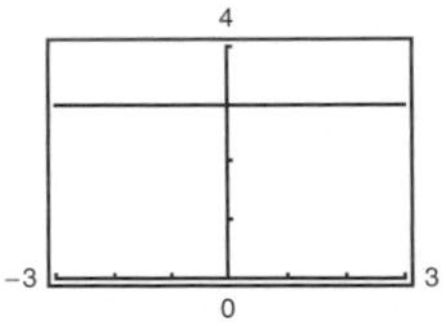

Constant on $(-\infty, \infty)$

41.

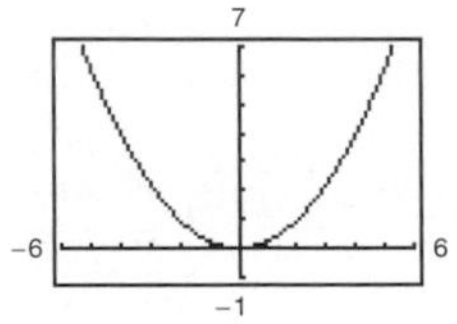

Decreasing on $(-\infty, 0)$
Increasing on $(0, \infty)$

43.

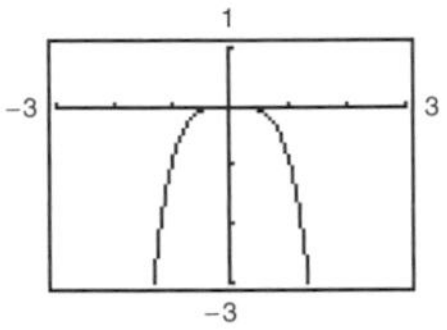

Increasing on $(-\infty, 0)$
Decreasing on $(0, \infty)$

45.

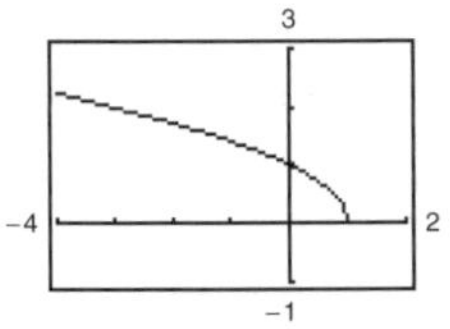

Decreasing on $(-\infty, 1)$

47.

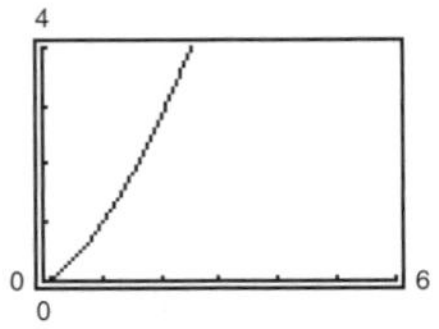

Increasing on $(0, \infty)$

49.

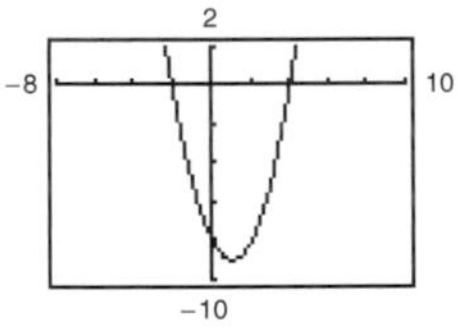

Relative minimum:
$(1, -9)$

51.

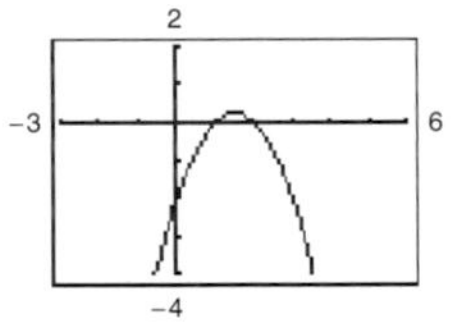

Relative maximum:
$(1.5, 0.25)$

53.

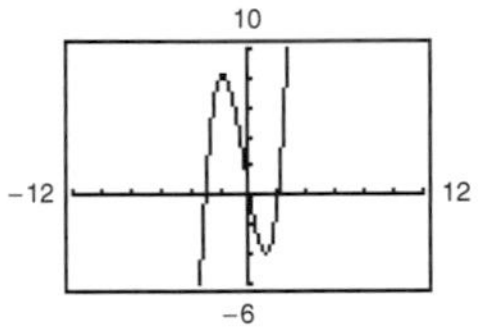

Relative maximum: $(-1.79, 8.21)$
Relative minimum: $(1.12, -4.06)$

55.

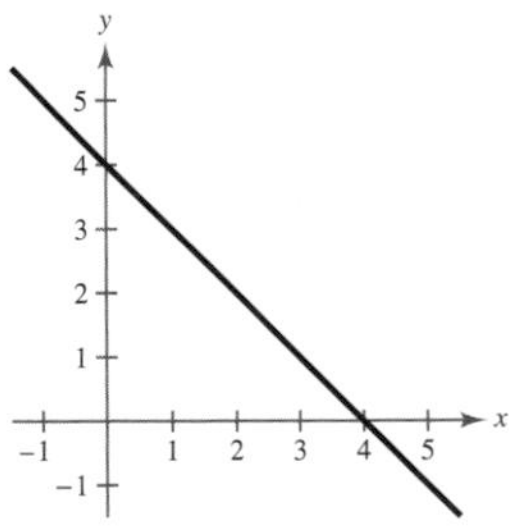

$(-\infty, 4]$

57.

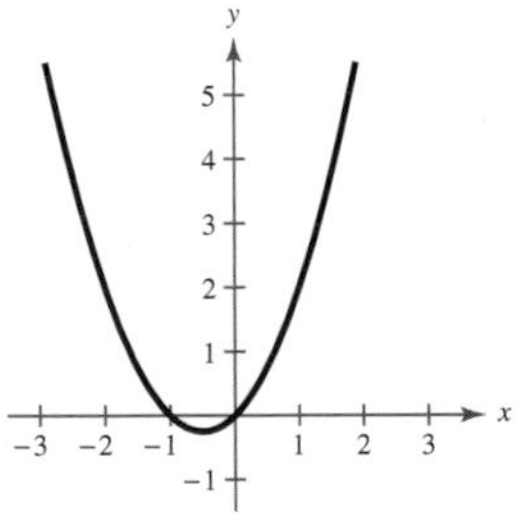

$(-\infty, -1], [0, \infty)$

59.

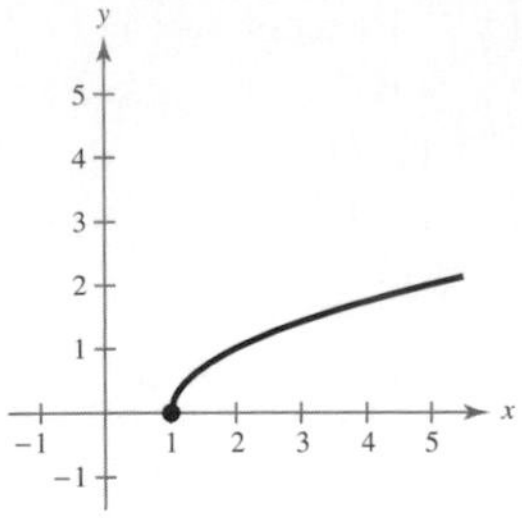

$[1, \infty)$

61.

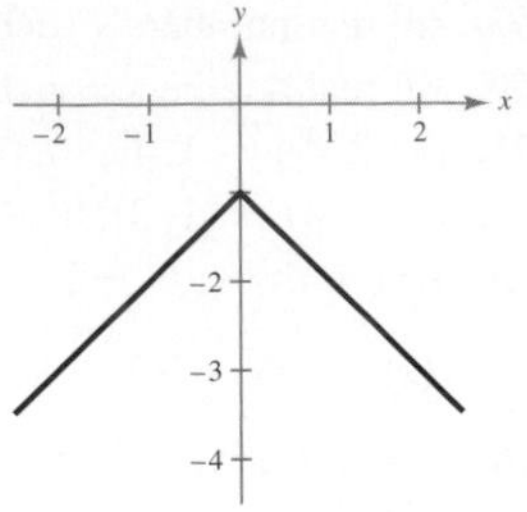

$f(x) < 0$ for all x

63. The average rate of change from $x_1 = 0$ to $x_2 = 3$ is -2.

65. The average rate of change from $x_1 = 1$ to $x_2 = 5$ is 18.

67. The average rate of change from $x_1 = 1$ to $x_2 = 3$ is 0.

69. The average rate of change from $x_1 = 3$ to $x_2 = 11$ is $-\frac{1}{4}$.

71. Even; y-axis symmetry **73.** Odd; origin symmetry

75. Neither even nor odd; no symmetry

77. $h = -x^2 + 4x - 3$ **79.** $h = 2x - x^2$

81. $L = \frac{1}{2}y^2$ **83.** $L = 4 - y^2$

85. (a)

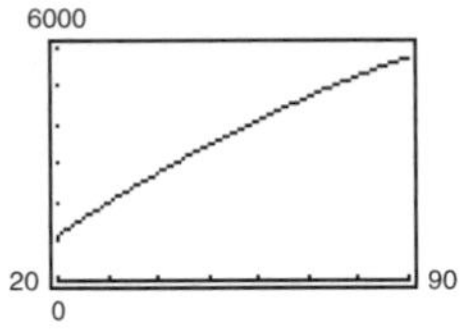

(b) 30 watts

87. (a) Ten thousands (b) Ten millions (c) Percents

89. (a)

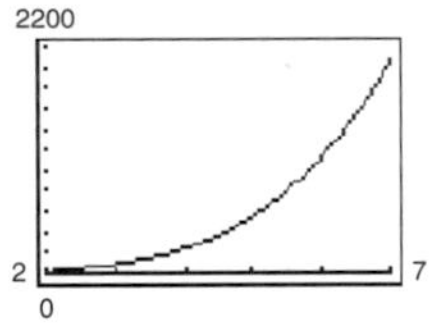

(b) The average rate of change from 2002 to 2007 is 408.56. The estimated revenue is increasing each year at a fast pace.

91. (a) $s = -16t^2 + 64t + 6$

(b)

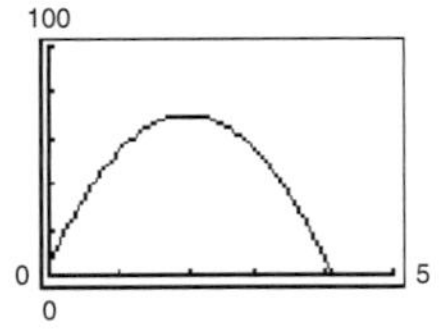

(c) Average rate of change = 16

(d) The slope of the secant line is positive.

(e) Secant line: $16t + 6$

(f)

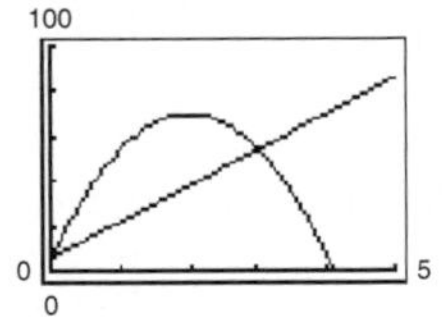

93. (a) $s = -16t^2 + 120t$

(b)

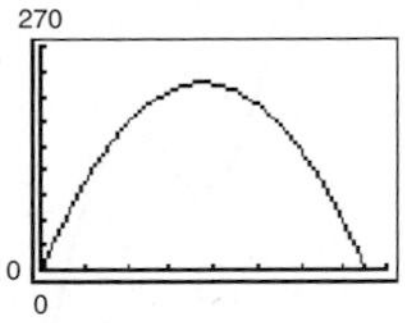

(c) Average rate of change $= -8$

(d) The slope of the secant line is negative.

(e) Secant line: $-8t + 240$

(f)

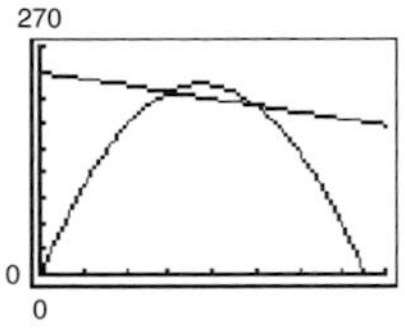

95. (a) $s = -16t^2 + 120$

(b)

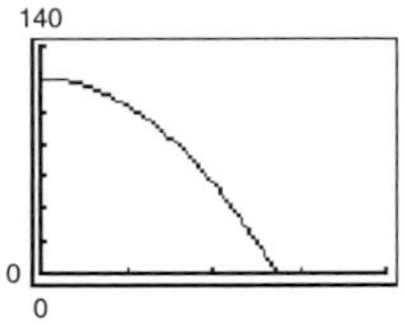

(c) Average rate of change $= -32$

(d) The slope of the secant line is negative.

(e) Secant line: $-32t + 120$

(f)

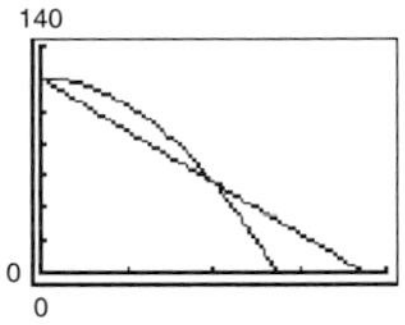

97. False. The function $f(x) = \sqrt{x^2 + 1}$ has a domain of all real numbers.

99. (a) Even. The graph is a reflection in the x-axis.

(b) Even. The graph is a reflection in the y-axis.

(c) Even. The graph is a vertical translation of f.

(d) Neither. The graph is a horizontal translation of f.

101. (a) $\left(\frac{3}{2}, 4\right)$ (b) $\left(\frac{3}{2}, -4\right)$

103. (a) $(-4, 9)$ (b) $(-4, -9)$

105. (a)

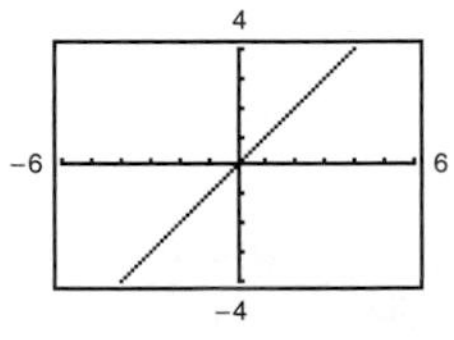

(b)

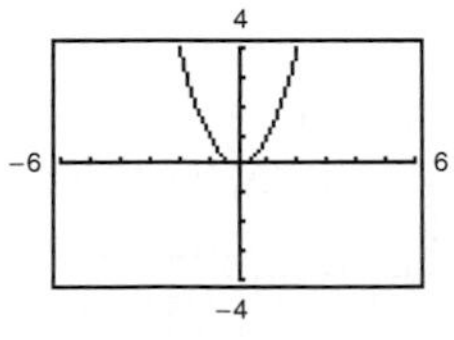

(c)

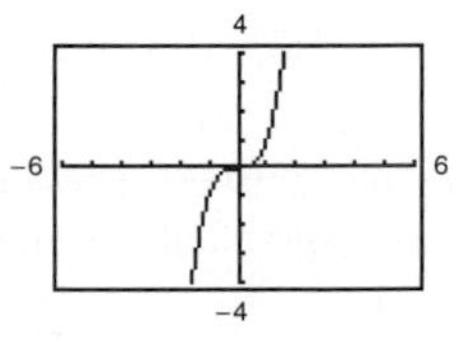

(d)

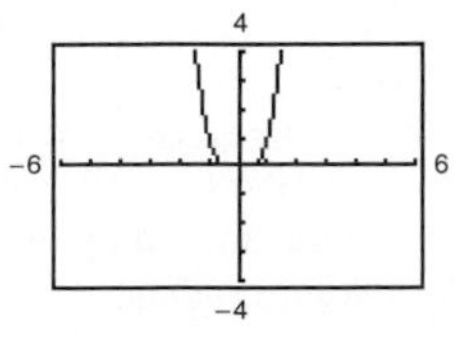

(e)

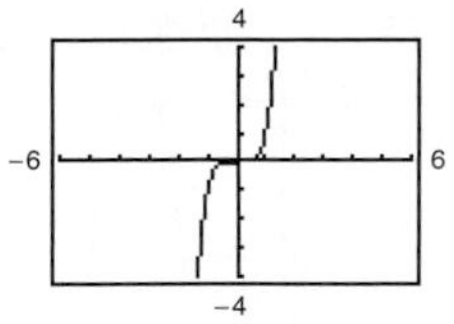

(f)

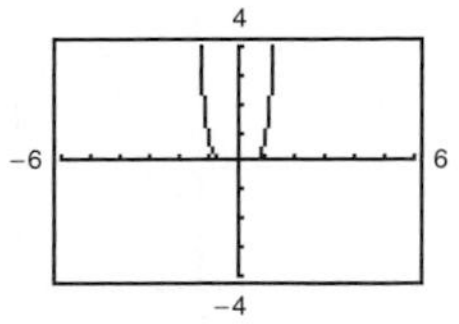

All the graphs pass through the origin. The graphs of the odd powers of x are symmetric with respect to the origin, and the graphs of the even powers are symmetric with respect to the y-axis. As the powers increase, the graphs become flatter in the interval $-1 < x < 1$.

107. 0, 10 **109.** $0, \pm 1$

111. (a) 37 (b) -28 (c) $5x - 43$

113. (a) -9 (b) $2\sqrt{7} - 9$

(c) The given value is not in the domain of the function.

115. $h + 4,\ h \neq 0$

Section 1.6 *(page 71)*

Vocabulary Check *(page 71)*

1. g **2.** i **3.** h **4.** a **5.** b
6. e **7.** f **8.** c **9.** d

1. (a) $f(x) = -2x + 6$

(b)

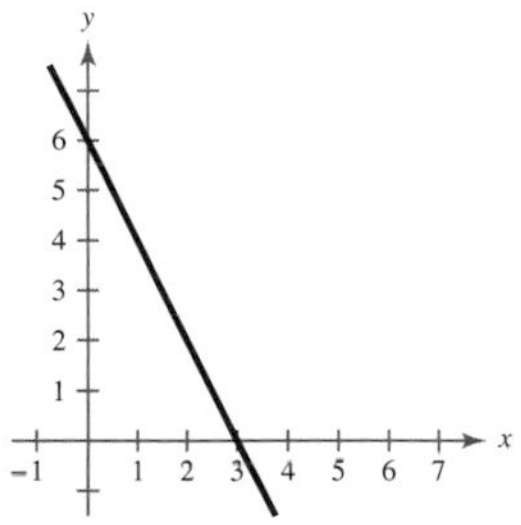

3. (a) $f(x) = -3x + 11$

(b)

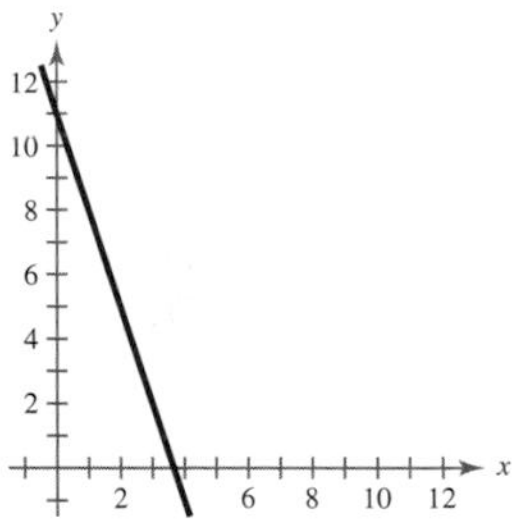

5. (a) $f(x) = -1$

(b)

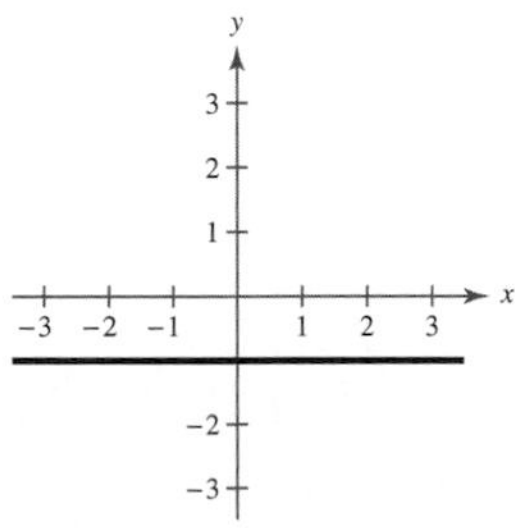

7. (a) $f(x) = \frac{6}{7}x - \frac{45}{7}$

(b)

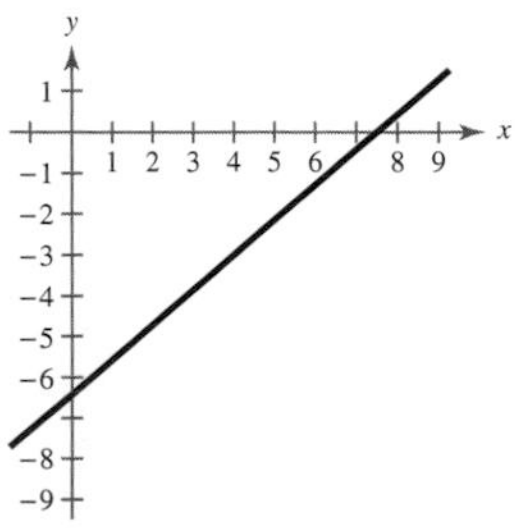

9.

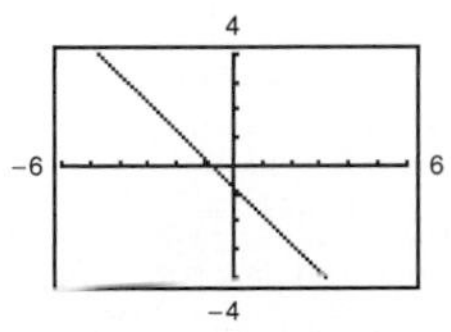

11.

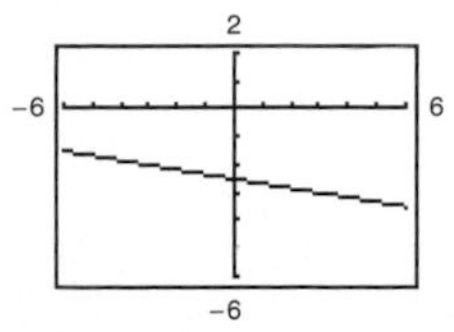

13.
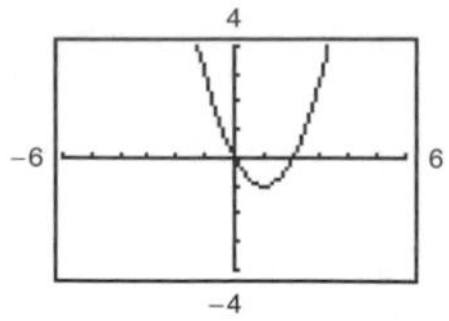

15.
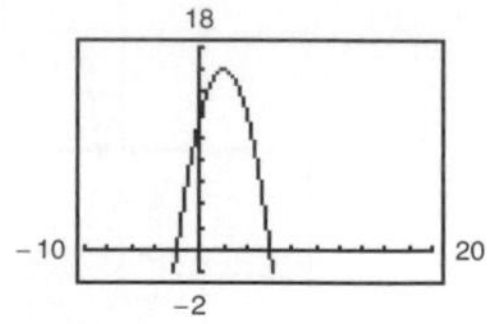

17.
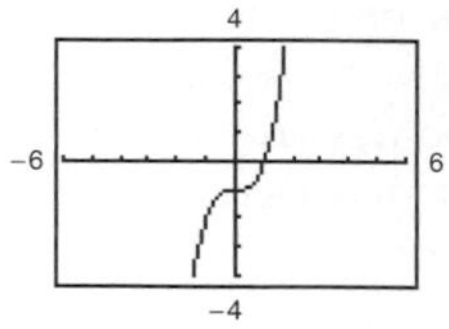

19.
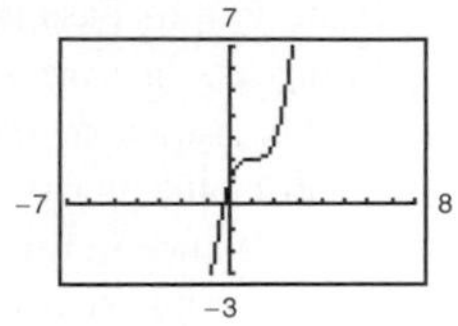

21.
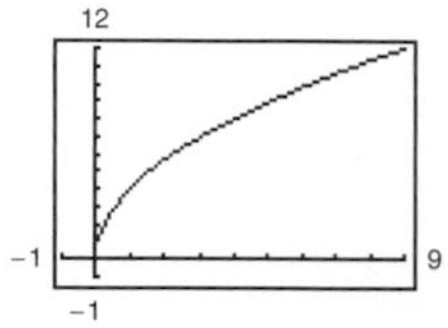

23.
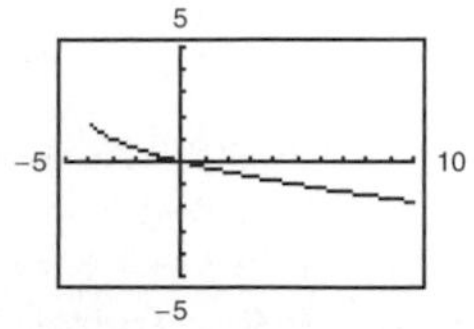

25.
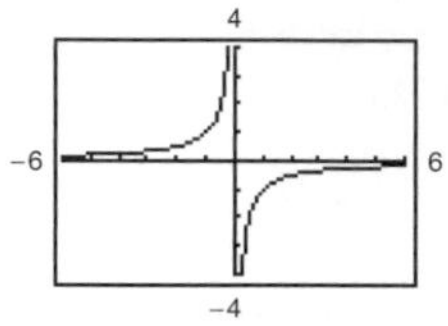

27.
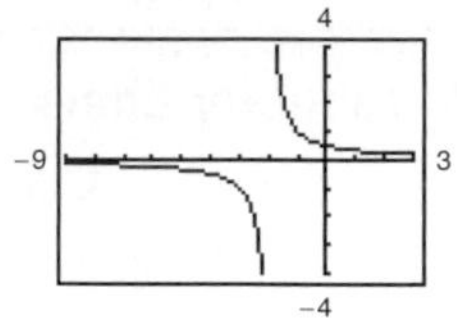

29. (a) 2 (b) 2 (c) -4 (d) 3

31. (a) 1 (b) 3 (c) 7 (d) -19

33. (a) 6 (b) -11 (c) 6 (d) -22

35. (a) -10 (b) -4 (c) -1 (d) 41

37.
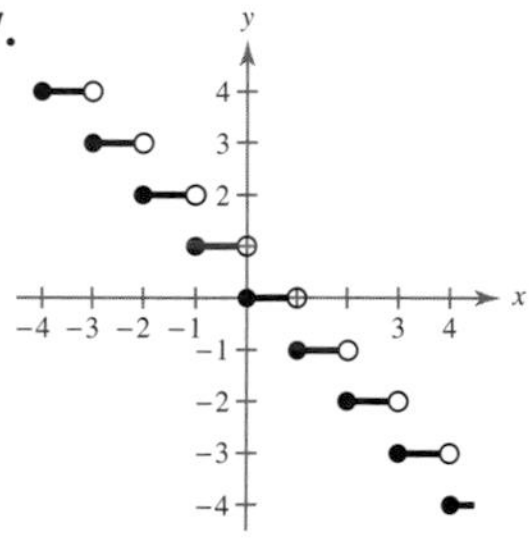

39.
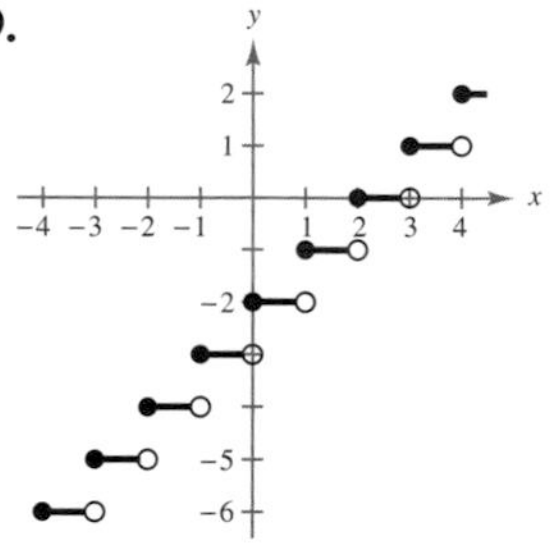

41.
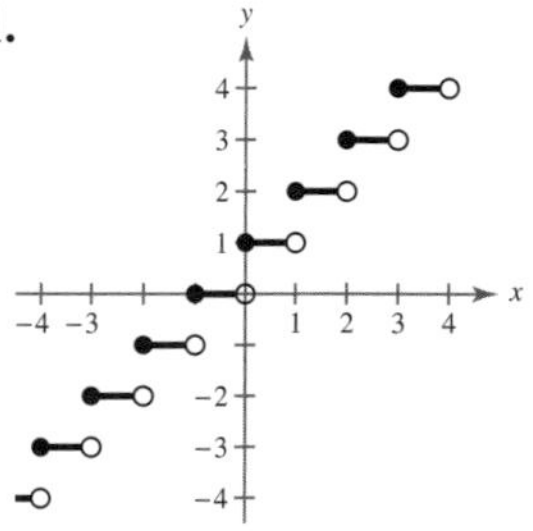

43.
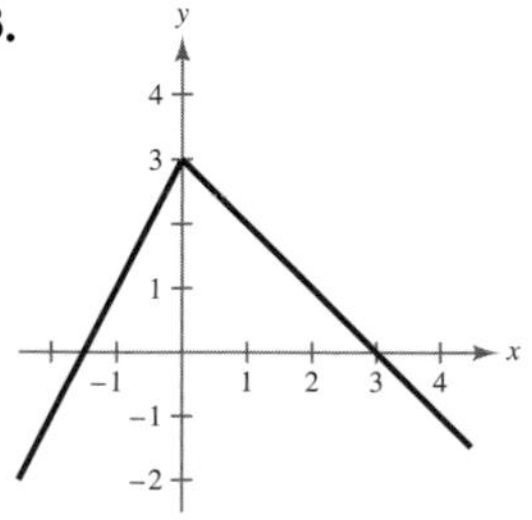

45.
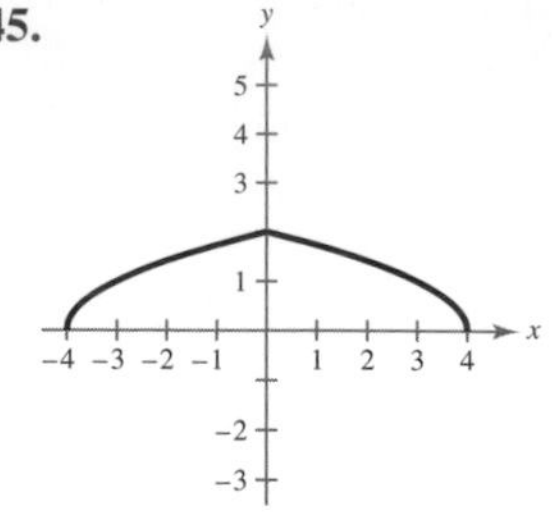

47.
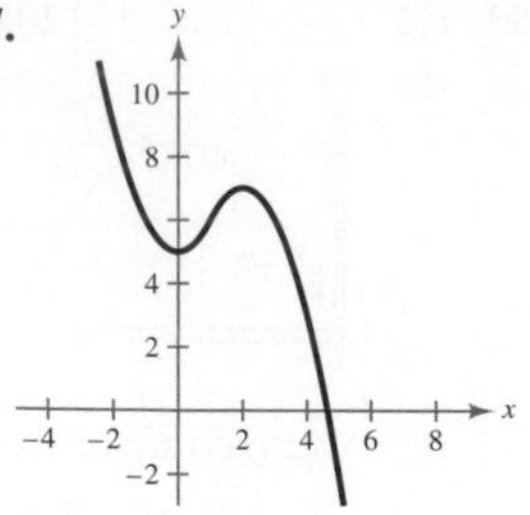

49.
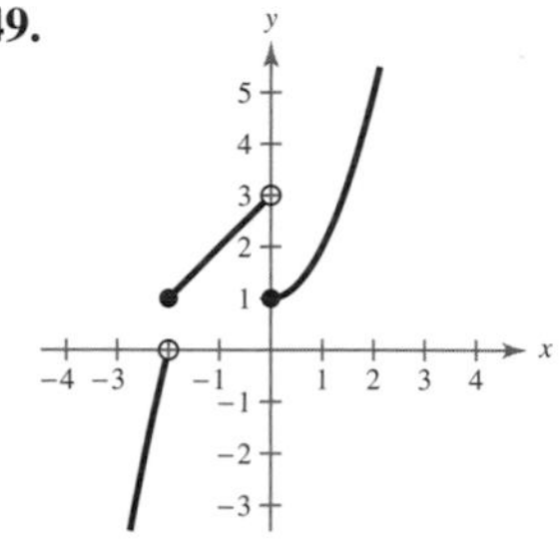

51. (a)
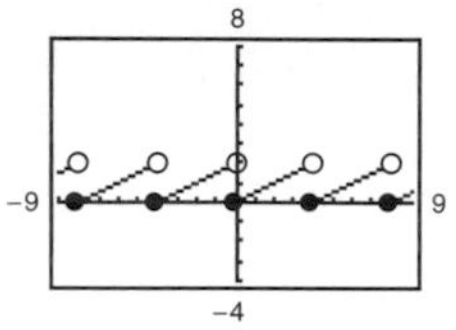

(b) Domain: $(-\infty, \infty)$; Range: $[0, 2)$

(c) Sawtooth pattern

53. (a) $f(x) = |x|$ (b) $g(x) = |x + 2| - 1$

55. (a) $f(x) = x^3$ (b) $g(x) = (x - 1)^3 - 2$

57. (a) $f(x) = 2$ (b) $g(x) = 2$

59. (a) $f(x) = x$ (b) $g(x) = x - 2$

61. (a)
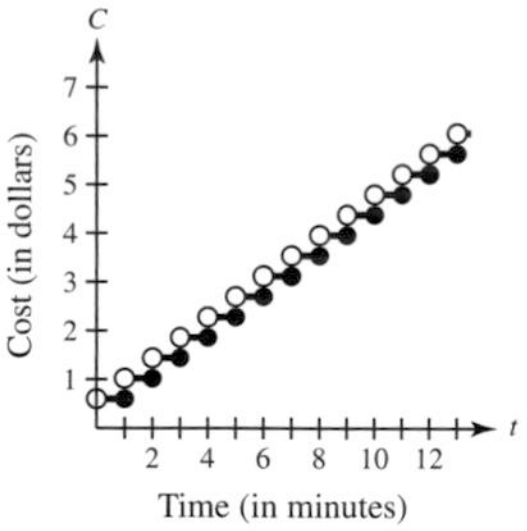

(b) \$5.64

63. (a)
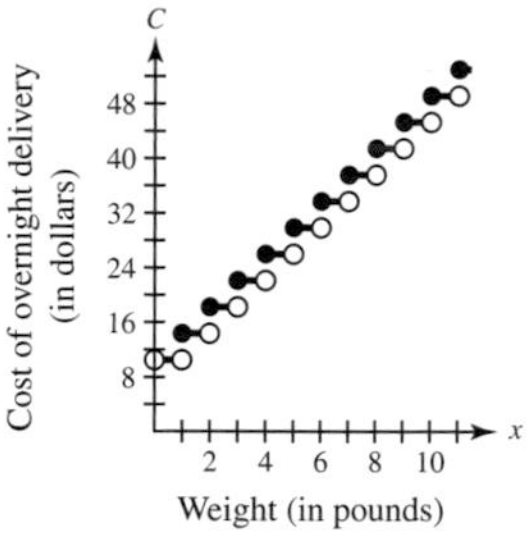

(b) \$50.25

65. (a) $W(30) = 360$; $W(40) = 480$; $W(45) = 570$; $W(50) = 660$

(b) $W(h) = \begin{cases} 12h, & 0 < h \le 45 \\ 18(h - 45) + 540, & h > 45 \end{cases}$

67. (a) $f(x) = \begin{cases} 0.505x^2 - 1.47x + 6.3, & 1 \le x \le 6 \\ -1.97x + 26.3, & 6 < x \le 12 \end{cases}$

Answers will vary. Sample answer: The domain is determined by inspection of a graph of the data with the two models.

(b)

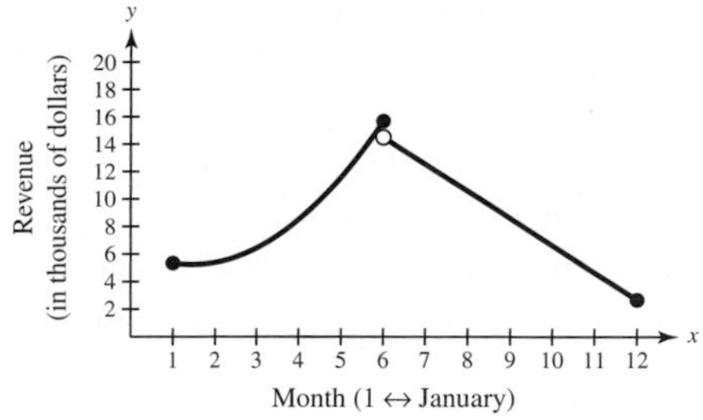

(c) $f(5) = 11.575, f(11) = 4.63$; These values represent the revenue for the months of May and November, respectively.

(d) These values are quite close to the actual data values.

69. False. A piecewise-defined function is a function that is defined by two or more equations over a specified domain. That domain may or may not include x- and y-intercepts.

71. $f(x) = \begin{cases} -\frac{4}{3}x + 6, & 0 \le x \le 3 \\ -\frac{2}{5}x + \frac{16}{5}, & 3 < x \le 8 \end{cases}$

73. $x \le 1$

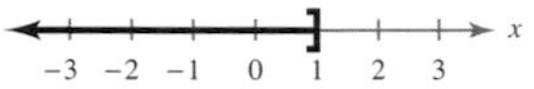

75. Neither

Section 1.7 *(page 79)*

Vocabulary Check *(page 79)*

1. rigid **2.** $-f(x); f(-x)$ **3.** nonrigid
4. horizontal shrink; horizontal stretch
5. vertical stretch; vertical shrink
6. (a) iv (b) ii (c) iii (d) i

1. (a)

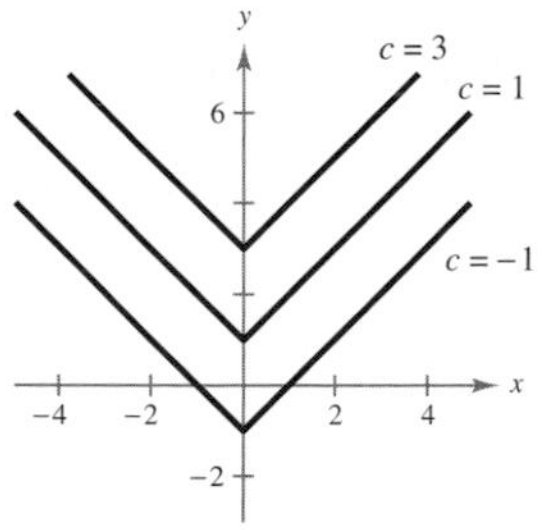

(b)

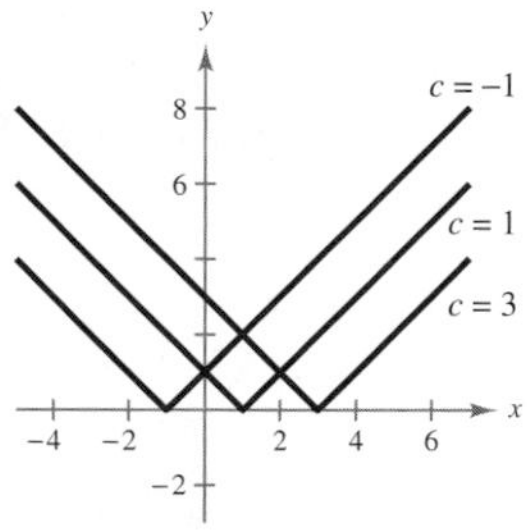

(c)

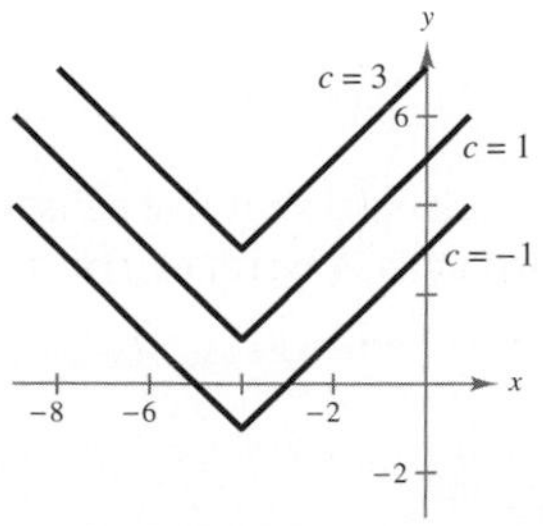

3. (a)

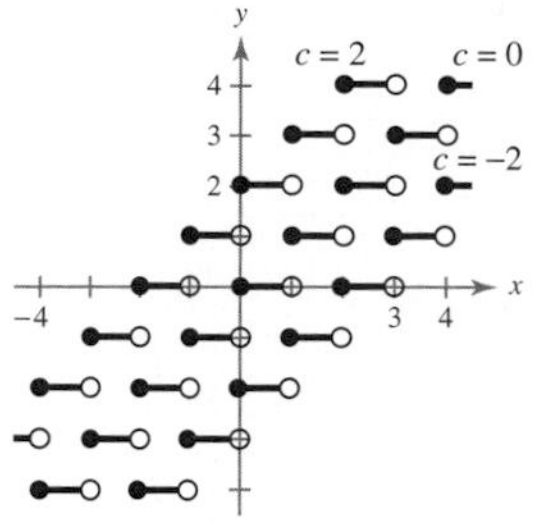

(b)

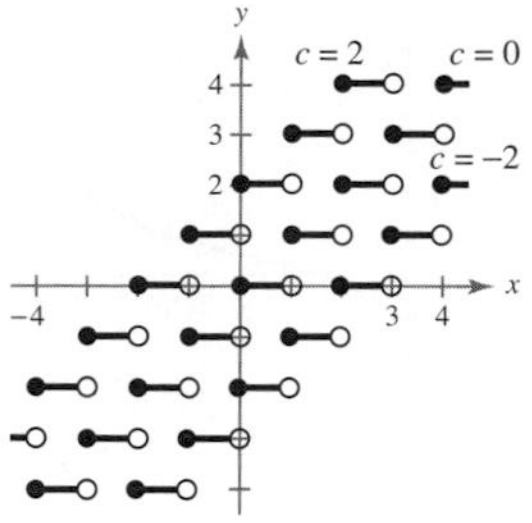

(c)

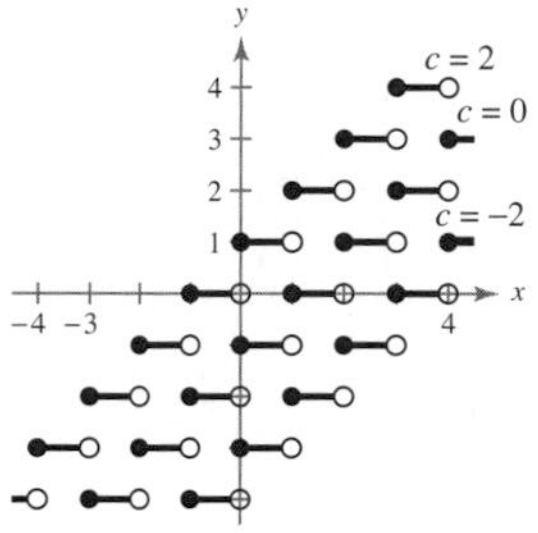

5. (a)

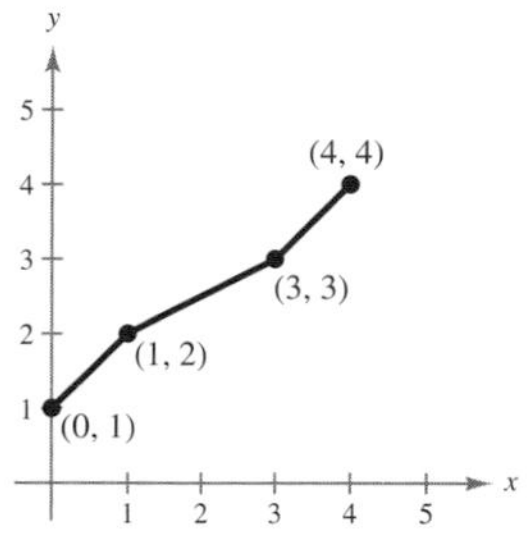

(b)

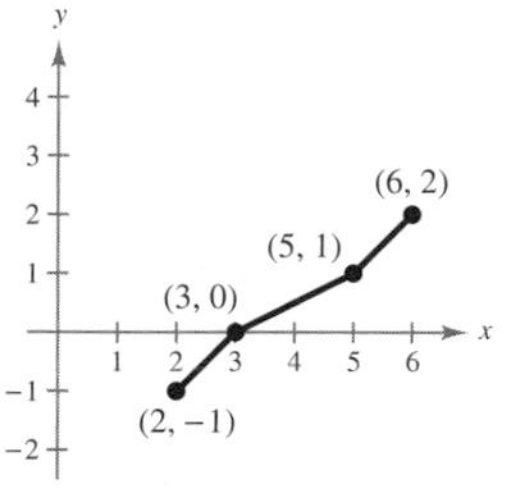

(c)

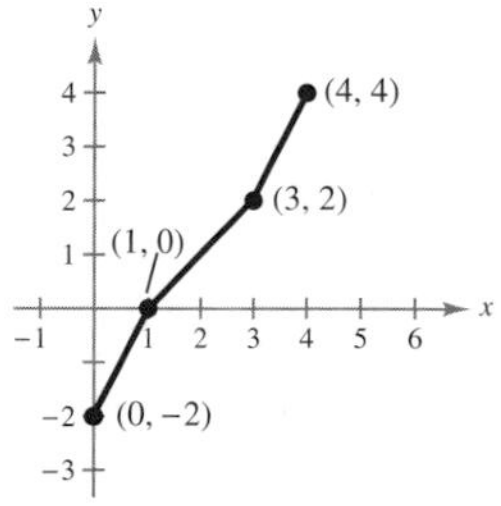

(d)

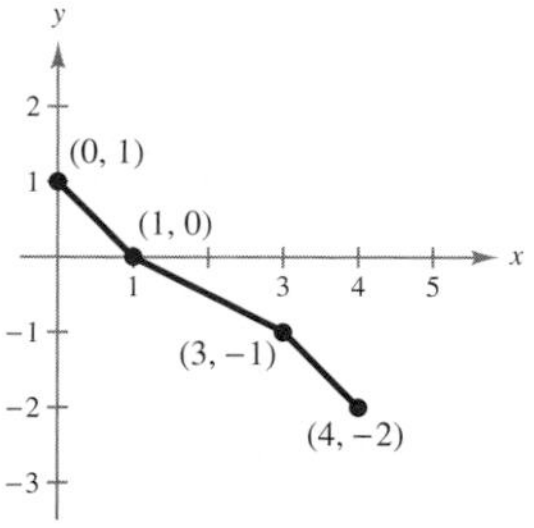

(e)

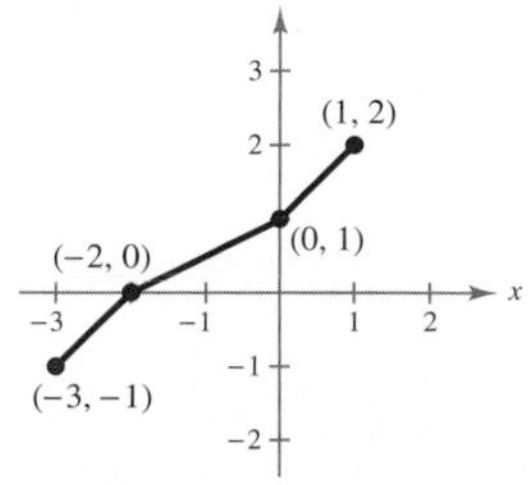

(f)

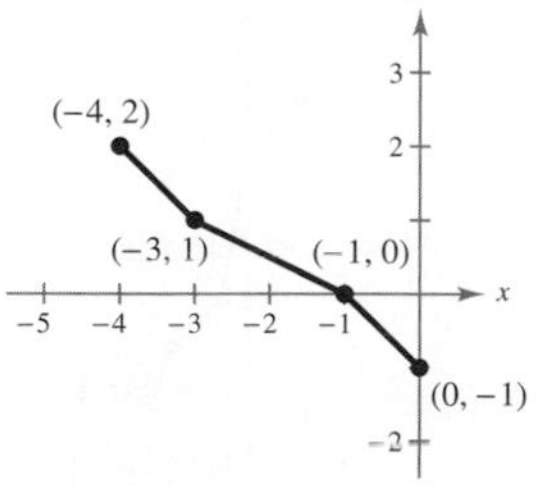

(g)

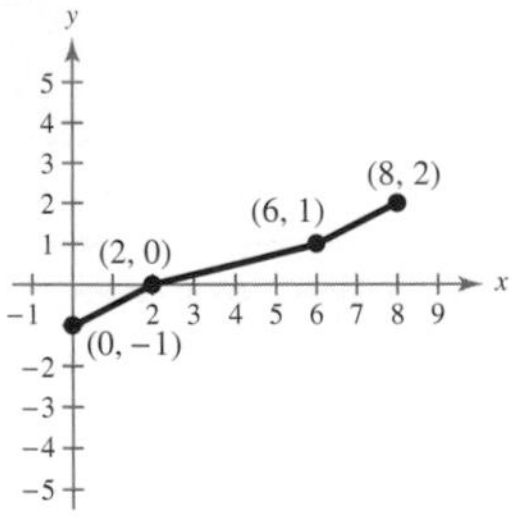

7. (a)

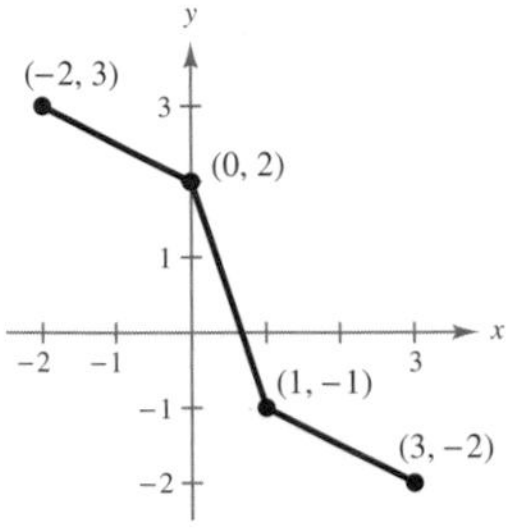

(b)

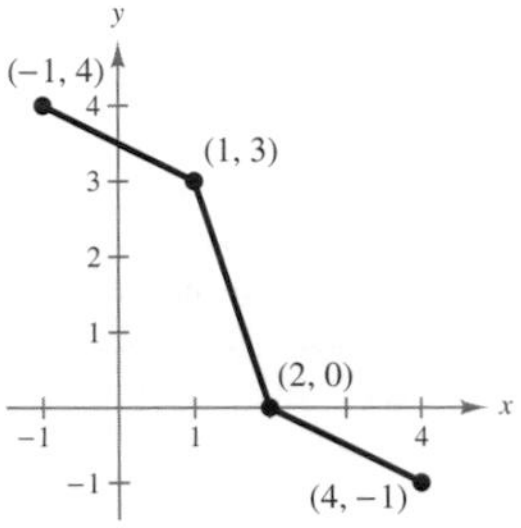

(c)

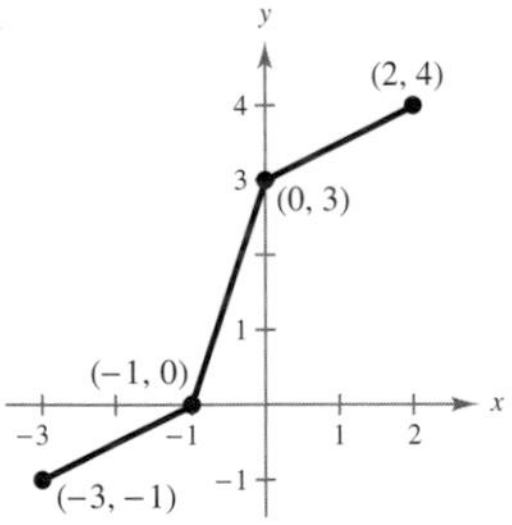

(d)

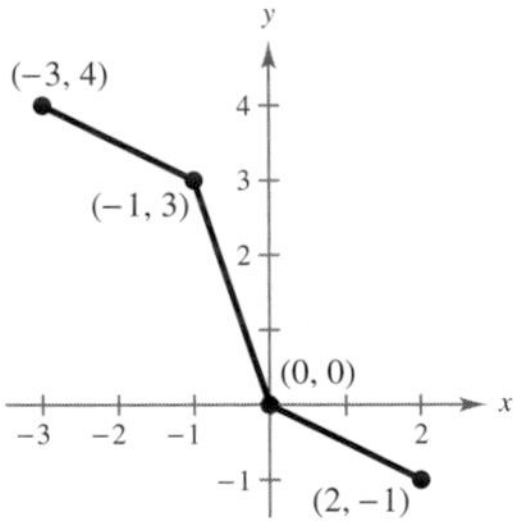

(e)

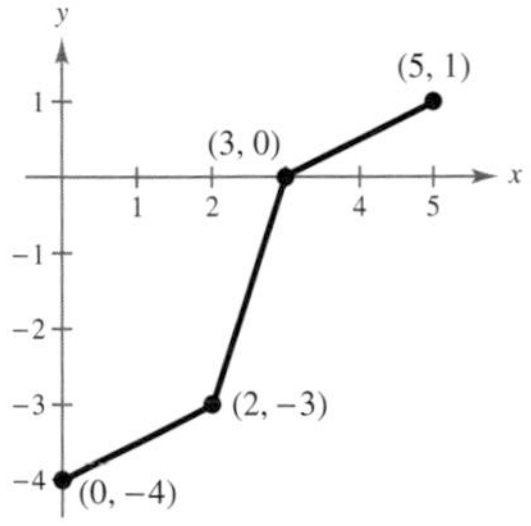

(f)

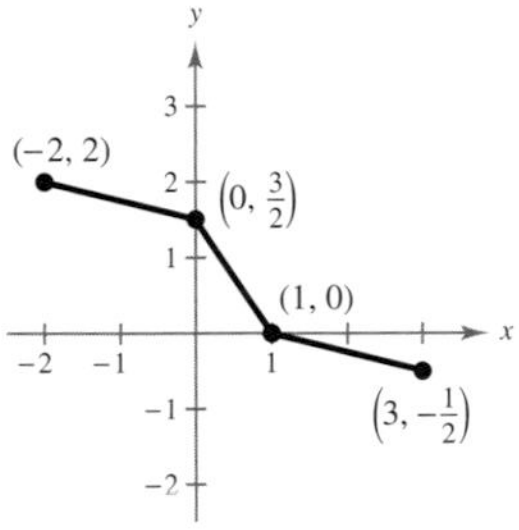

(g)

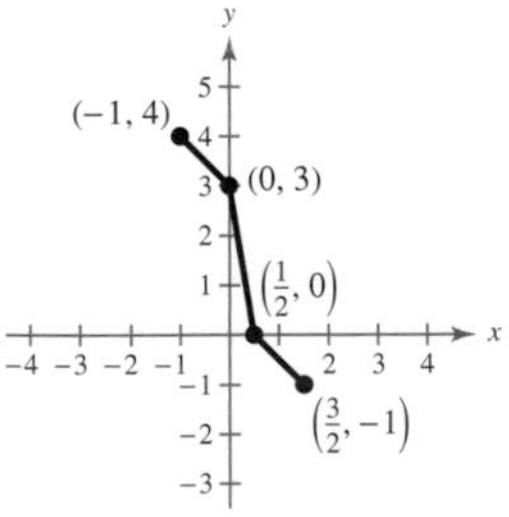

9. (a) $y = x^2 - 1$ (b) $y = 1 - (x + 1)^2$
(c) $y = -(x - 2)^2 + 6$ (d) $y = (x - 5)^2 - 3$

11. (a) $y = |x| + 5$ (b) $y = -|x + 3|$
(c) $y = |x - 2| - 4$ (d) $y = -|x - 6| - 1$

13. Horizontal shift of $y = x^3$; $y = (x - 2)^3$

15. Reflection in the x-axis of $y = x^2$; $y = -x^2$

17. Reflection in the x-axis and vertical shift of $y = \sqrt{x}$; $y = 1 - \sqrt{x}$

19. (a) $f(x) = x^2$
(b) Reflection in the x-axis, and vertical shift 12 units upward, of $f(x) = x^2$
(c)

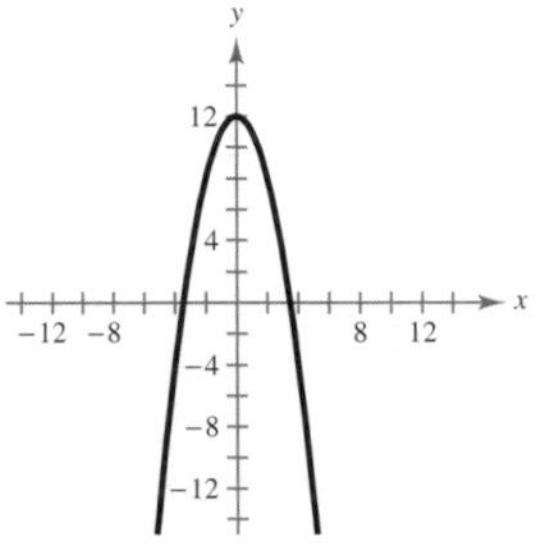

(d) $g(x) = 12 - f(x)$

21. (a) $f(x) = x^3$
(b) Vertical shift seven units upward, of $f(x) = x^3$
(c)

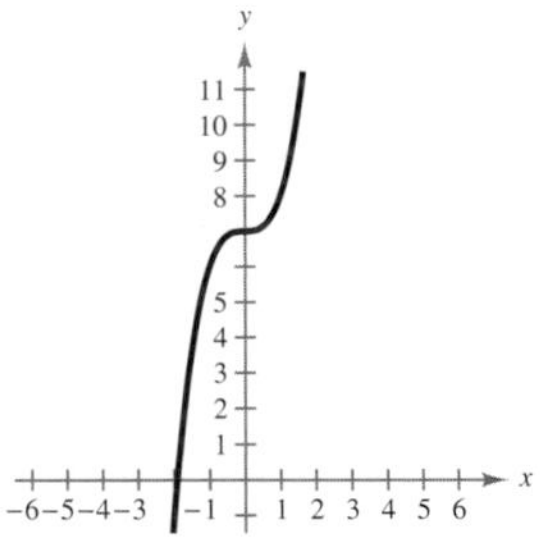

(d) $g(x) = f(x) + 7$

23. (a) $f(x) = x^2$
(b) Vertical shrink of two-thirds, and vertical shift four units upward, of $f(x) = x^2$
(c)

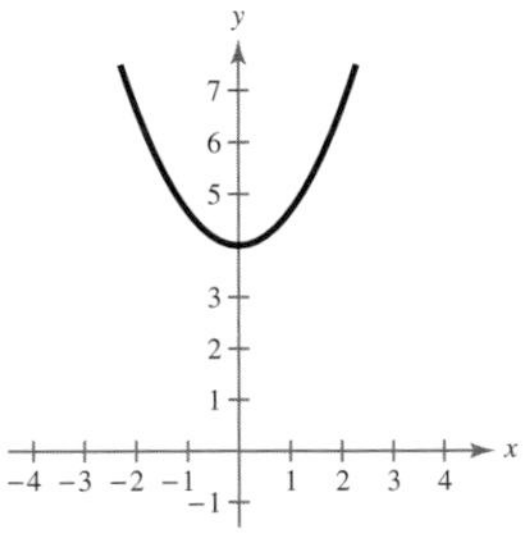

(d) $g(x) = \frac{2}{3}f(x) + 4$

25. (a) $f(x) = x^2$
(b) Reflection in the x-axis, horizontal shift five units to the left, and vertical shift two units upward, of $f(x) = x^2$

(c)

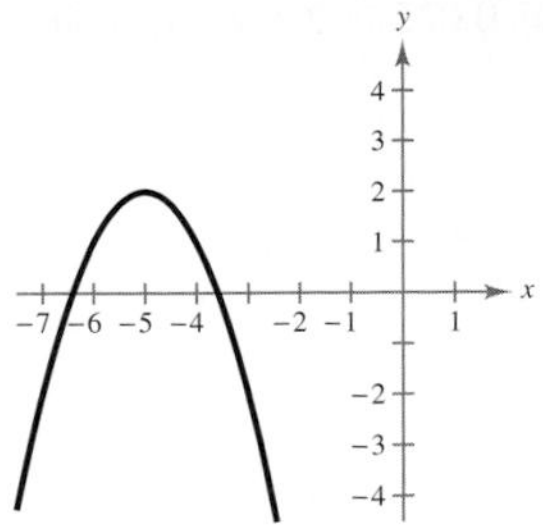

(d) $g(x) = 2 - f(x + 5)$

27. (a) $f(x) = \sqrt{x}$

(b) Horizontal shrink of $\frac{1}{3}$, of $f(x) = \sqrt{x}$

(c)

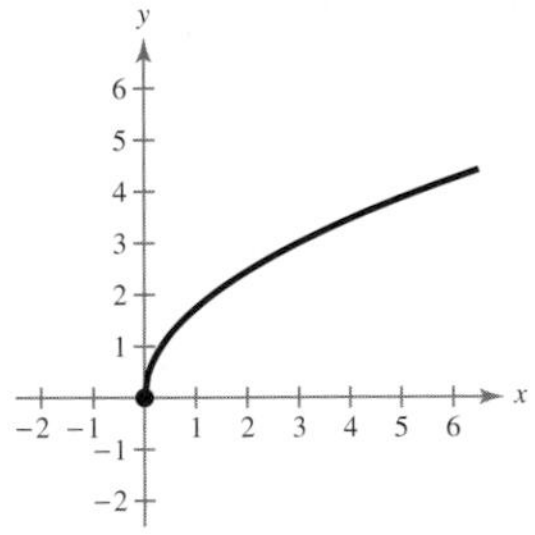

(d) $g(x) = f(3x)$

29. (a) $f(x) = x^3$

(b) Vertical shift two units upward, and horizontal shift one unit to the right, of $f(x) = x^3$

(c)

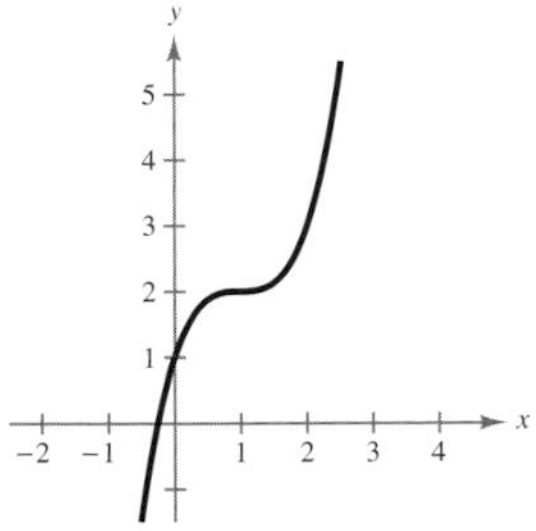

(d) $g(x) = f(x - 1) + 2$

31. (a) $f(x) = |x|$

(b) Reflection in the x-axis, and vertical shift two units downward, of $f(x) = |x|$

(c)

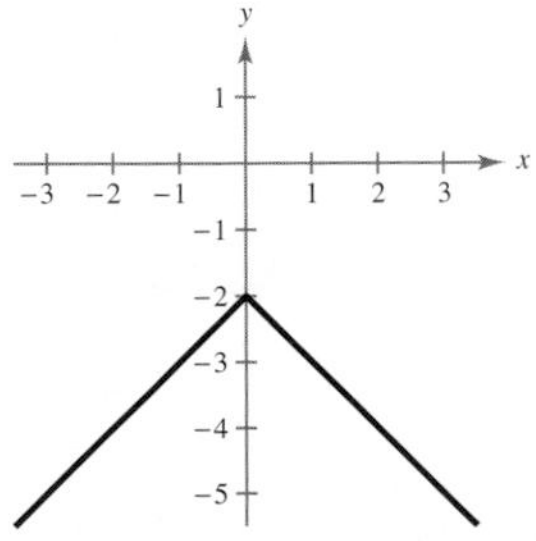

(d) $g(x) = -f(x) - 2$

33. (a) $f(x) = |x|$

(b) Reflection in the x-axis, horizontal shift four units to the left, and vertical shift eight units upward, of $f(x) = |x|$

(c)

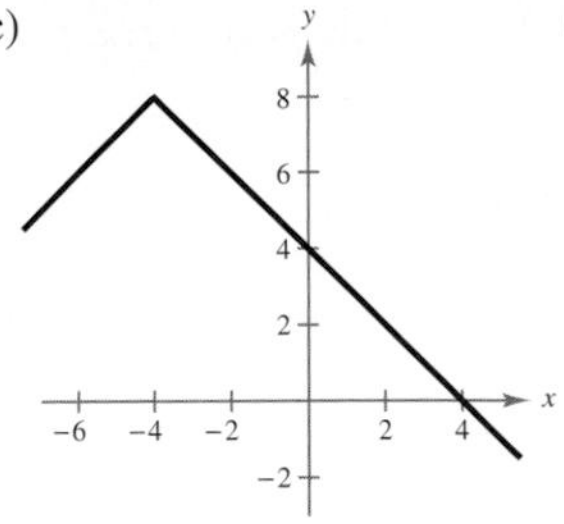

(d) $g(x) = -f(x + 4) + 8$

35. (a) $f(x) = [\![x]\!]$

(b) Reflection in the x-axis, and vertical shift three units upward, of $f(x) = [\![x]\!]$

(c)

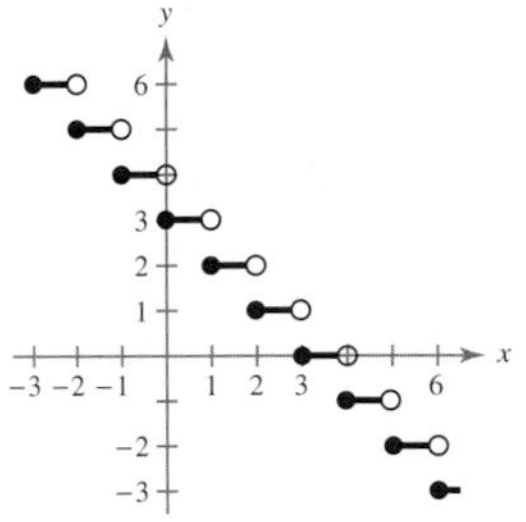

(d) $g(x) = 3 - f(x)$

37. (a) $f(x) = \sqrt{x}$

(b) Horizontal shift of nine units to the right, of $f(x) = \sqrt{x}$

(c)

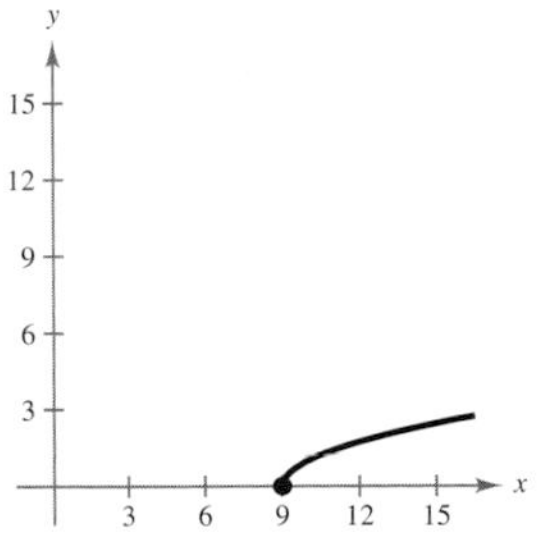

(d) $g(x) = f(x - 9)$

39. (a) $f(x) = \sqrt{x}$

(b) Reflection in the y-axis, horizontal shift of seven units to the right, and vertical shift two units downward, of $f(x) = \sqrt{x}$

(c)

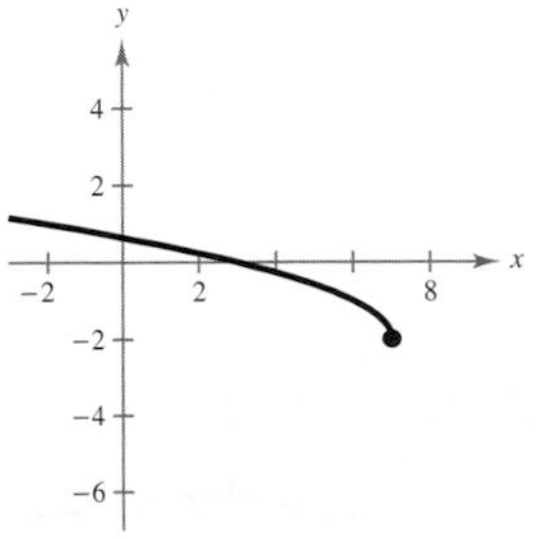

(d) $g(x) = f(7 - x) - 2$

41. (a) $f(x) = \sqrt{x}$

(b) Horizontal stretch, and vertical shift four units downward, of $f(x) = \sqrt{x}$

CHAPTER 1

(c)

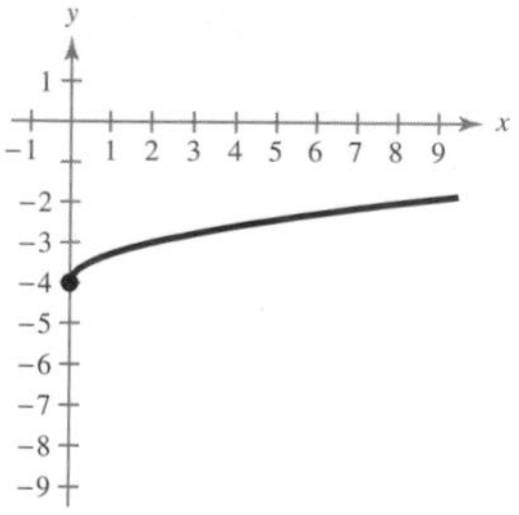

(d) $g(x) = f\left(\frac{1}{2}x\right) - 4$

43. $f(x) = (x - 2)^2 - 8$ **45.** $f(x) = (x - 13)^3$

47. $f(x) = -|x| - 10$ **49.** $f(x) = -\sqrt{-x + 6}$

51. (a) $y = -3x^2$ (b) $y = 4x^2 + 3$

53. (a) $y = -\frac{1}{2}|x|$ (b) $y = 3|x| - 3$

55. Vertical stretch of $y = x^3$; $y = 2x^3$

57. Reflection in the x-axis and vertical shrink of $y = x^2$; $y = -\frac{1}{2}x^2$

59. Reflection in the y-axis and vertical shrink of $y = \sqrt{x}$; $y = \frac{1}{2}\sqrt{-x}$

61. $y = -(x - 2)^3 + 2$ **63.** $y = -\sqrt{x} - 3$

65. (a)

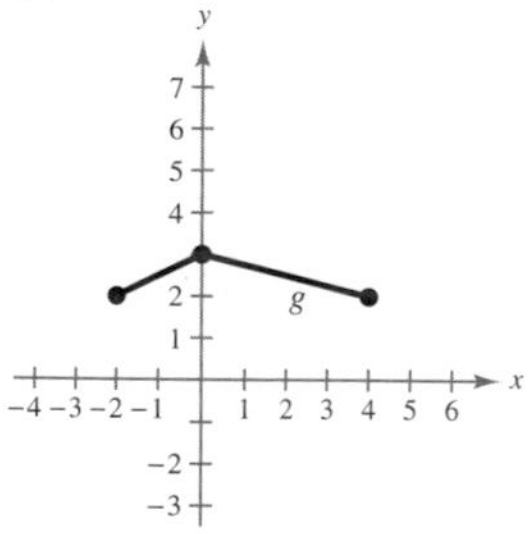

(b)

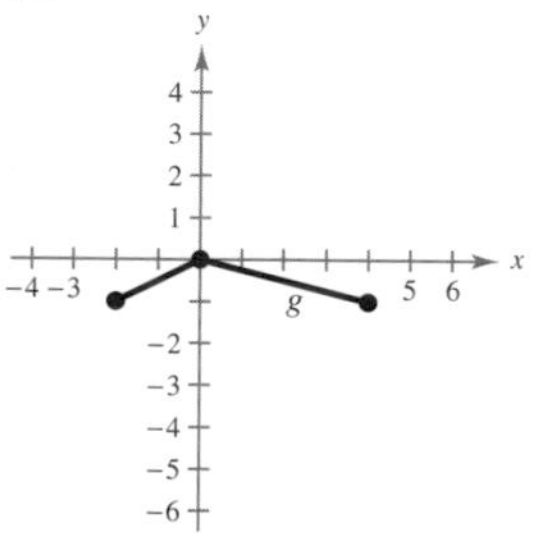

(c)

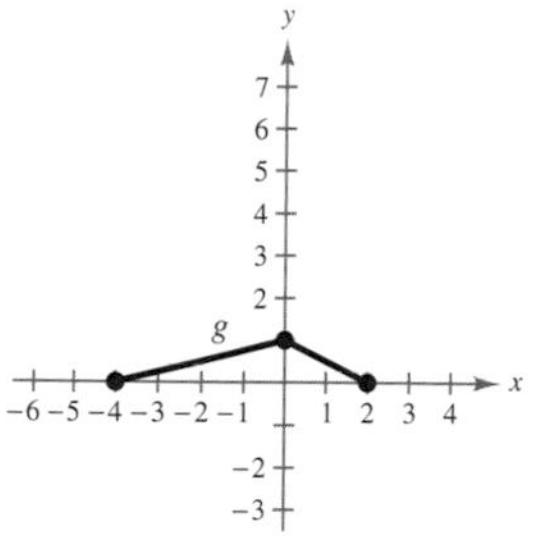

(d)

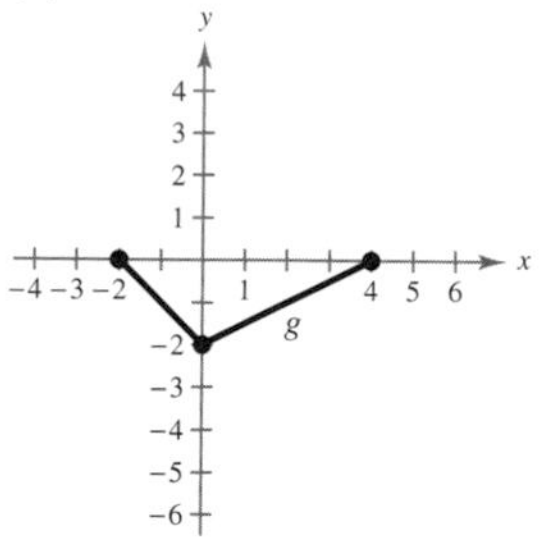

(e)

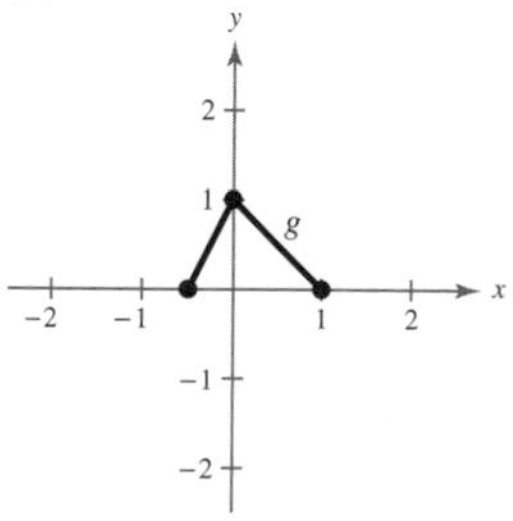

(f)

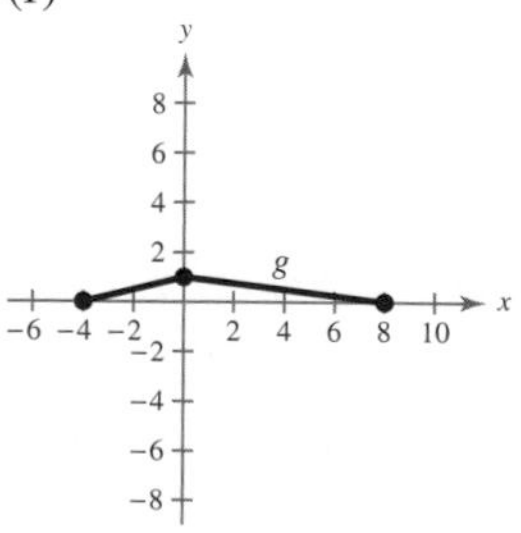

67. (a) Horizontal stretch of 0.035 and a vertical shift of 20.6 units upward.

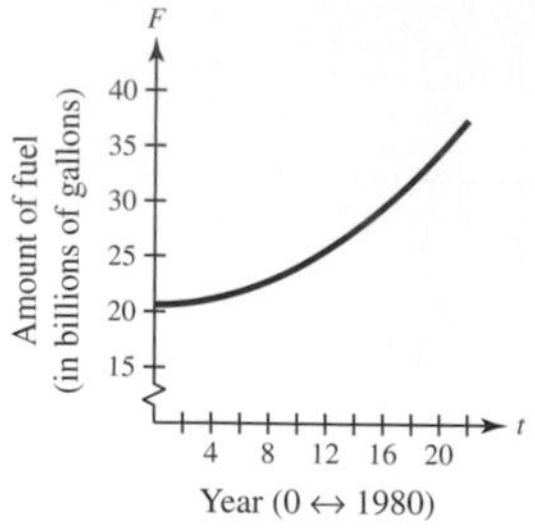

(b) 0.77-billion-gallon increase in fuel usage by trucks each year

(c) $f(t) = 20.6 + 0.035(t + 10)^2$. The graph is shifted 10 units to the left.

(d) 52.1 billion gallons. Yes.

69. True. $|-x| = |x|$

71. (a) $g(t) = \frac{3}{4}f(t)$ (b) $g(t) = f(t) + 10{,}000$
(c) $g(t) = f(t - 2)$

73. $(-2, 0), (-1, 1), (0, 2)$ **75.** $\dfrac{4}{x(1 - x)}$

77. $\dfrac{3x - 2}{x(x - 1)}$ **79.** $\dfrac{(x - 4)\sqrt{x^2 - 4}}{x^2 - 4}$

81. $5(x - 3),\ x \neq -3$

83. (a) 38 (b) $\frac{57}{4}$ (c) $x^2 - 12x + 38$

85. All real numbers x except $x = 1$

87. All real numbers x such that $-9 \leq x \leq 9$

Section 1.8 *(page 89)*

Vocabulary Check *(page 89)*

1. addition; subtraction; multiplication; division
2. composition **3.** $g(x)$ **4.** inner; outer

1.

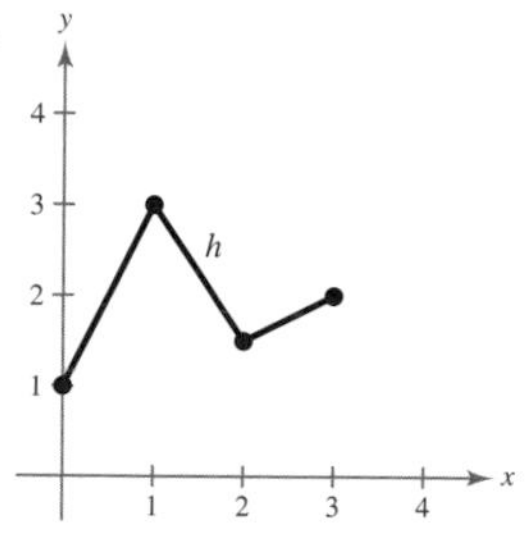

3.

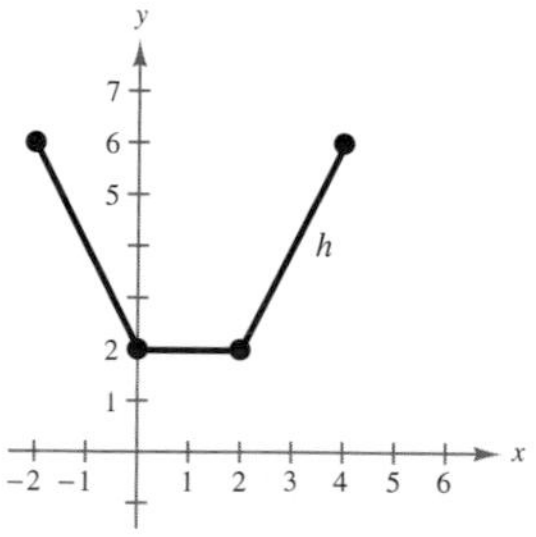

5. (a) $2x$ (b) 4 (c) $x^2 - 4$

(d) $\dfrac{x + 2}{x - 2}$; all real numbers x except $x = 2$

7. (a) $x^2 + 4x - 5$ (b) $x^2 - 4x + 5$ (c) $4x^3 - 5x^2$

(d) $\dfrac{x^2}{4x - 5}$; all real numbers x except $x = \dfrac{5}{4}$

9. (a) $x^2 + 6 + \sqrt{1 - x}$ (b) $x^2 + 6 - \sqrt{1 - x}$
(c) $(x^2 + 6)\sqrt{1 - x}$
(d) $\dfrac{(x^2 + 6)\sqrt{1 - x}}{1 - x}$; all real numbers x such that $x < 1$

11. (a) $\dfrac{x + 1}{x^2}$ (b) $\dfrac{x - 1}{x^2}$ (c) $\dfrac{1}{x^3}$
(d) x; all real numbers x except $x = 0$

13. 3 **15.** 5 **17.** $9t^2 - 3t + 5$ **19.** 74

21. 26 **23.** $\frac{3}{5}$

25.

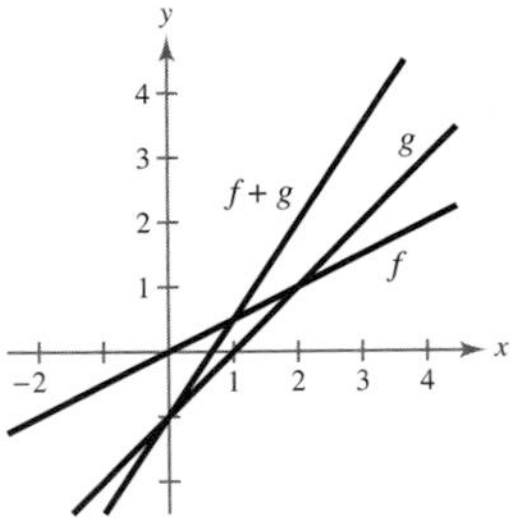

27.

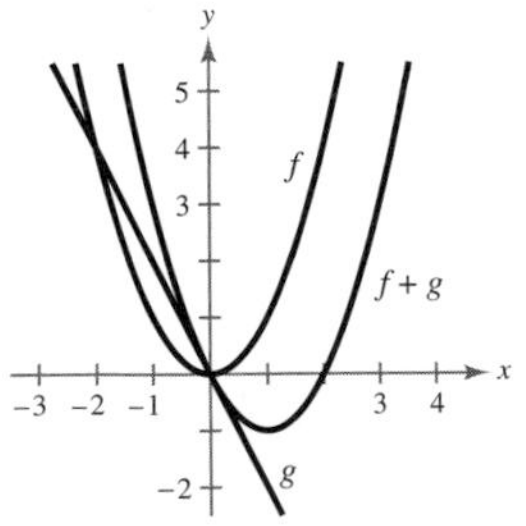

29.

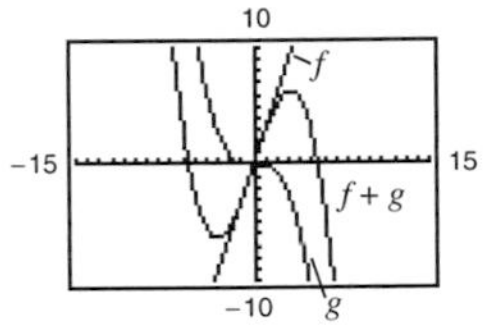

$f(x), g(x)$

31. (a) $(x - 1)^2$ (b) $x^2 - 1$ (c) x^4

33. (a) x (b) x (c) $\sqrt[3]{\sqrt[3]{x - 1} - 1}$

35. (a) $\sqrt{x^2 + 4}$ (b) $x + 4$
Domains of f and $g \circ f$: $x \geq -4$
Domains of g and $f \circ g$: all real numbers

37. (a) $x + 1$ (b) $\sqrt{x^2 + 1}$
Domains of f and $g \circ f$: all real numbers
Domains of g and $f \circ g$: all real numbers x such that $x \geq 0$

39. (a) $|x + 6|$ (b) $|x| + 6$
Domains of f, g, $f \circ g$, and $g \circ f$: all real numbers

41. (a) $\dfrac{1}{x + 3}$ (b) $\dfrac{1}{x} + 3$
Domains of f and $g \circ f$: all real numbers x except $x = 0$
Domains of g: all real numbers
Domains of $f \circ g$: all real numbers x except $x = -3$

43. (a) 3 (b) 0 **45.** (a) 0 (b) 4

47. $f(x) = x^2$, $g(x) = 2x + 1$

49. $f(x) = \sqrt[3]{x}$, $g(x) = x^2 - 4$

51. $f(x) = \dfrac{1}{x}$, $g(x) = x + 2$

53. $f(x) = \dfrac{x + 3}{4 + x}$, $g(x) = -x^2$

55. $T = \frac{3}{4}x + \frac{1}{15}x^2$

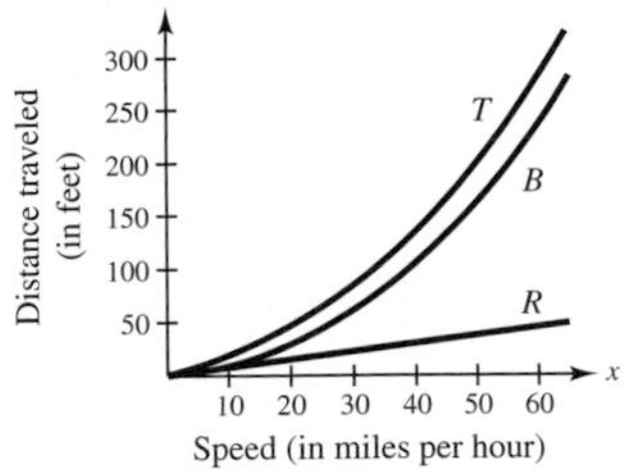

57. (a) $c(t) = \dfrac{p(t) + b(t) - d(t)}{p(t)} \times 100$
(b) $c(5)$ is the population change in the year 2005.

59. (a) $(A + N)(t) = 5.31t^2 - 102.0t + 1338$
$(A + N)(4) = 1014.96$
$(A + N)(8) = 861.84$
$(A + N)(12) = 878.64$
(b) $(A - N)(t) = 1.41t^2 - 17.6t + 132$
$(A - N)(4) = 84.16$
$(A - N)(8) = 81.44$
$(A - N)(12) = 123.84$

61. (a) $y_1 = 10.20t + 92.7$
$y_2 = 3.357t^2 - 26.46t + 379.5$
$y_3 = -0.465t^2 + 9.71t + 7.4$
(b) $y_1 + y_2 + y_3 = 2.892t^2 - 6.55t + 479.6$; this amount represents the amount spent on health care in the United States.
(c)

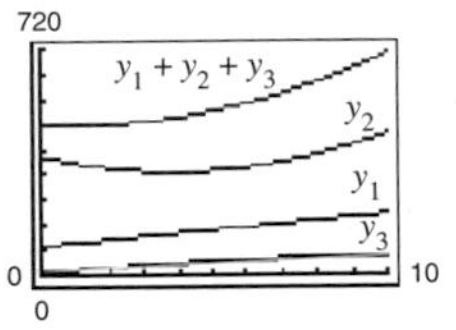

(d) In 2008, \$1298.708 billion is estimated to be spent on health services and supplies, and in 2010, \$1505.4 billion is estimated.

63. (a) $r(x) = \dfrac{x}{2}$ (b) $A(r) = \pi r^2$
(c) $(A \circ r)(x) = \pi\left(\dfrac{x}{2}\right)^2$; $(A \circ r)(x)$ represents the area of the circular base of the tank on the square foundation with side length x.

65. (a) $N(T(t)) = 30(3t^2 + 2t + 20)$ This represents the number of bacteria in the food as a function of time.
(b) $t = 2.846$ hours

67. $g(f(x))$ represents 3 percent of an amount over \$500,000.

69. False. $(f \circ g)(x) = 6x + 1$ and $(g \circ f)(x) = 6x + 6$

71. Answers will vary. **73.** 3 **75.** $\dfrac{-4}{x(x + h)}$

77. $3x - y - 10 = 0$

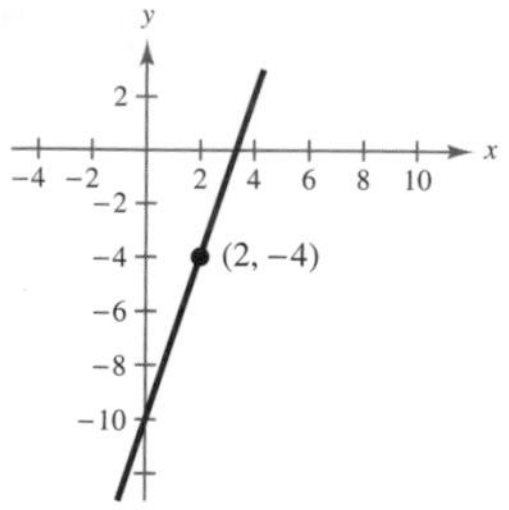

79. $3x + 2y - 22 = 0$

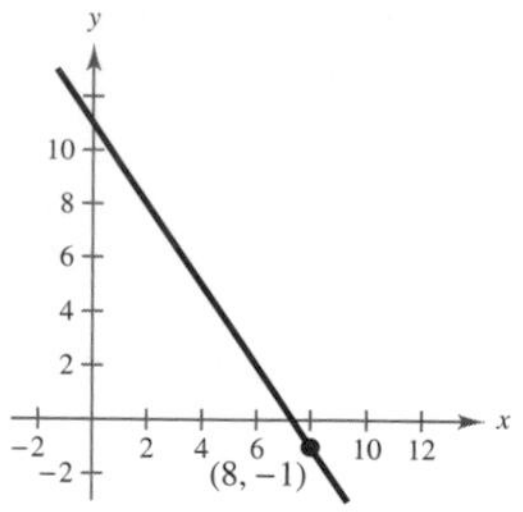

Section 1.9 *(page 99)*

Vocabulary Check *(page 99)*

1. inverse; f-inverse **2.** range; domain
3. $y = x$ **4.** one-to-one **5.** horizontal

1. $f^{-1}(x) = \frac{1}{6}x$ **3.** $f^{-1}(x) = x - 9$

5. $f^{-1}(x) = \dfrac{x-1}{3}$ **7.** $f^{-1}(x) = x^3$

9. c **10.** b **11.** a **12.** d

13. (a) $f(g(x)) = f\left(\dfrac{x}{2}\right) = 2\left(\dfrac{x}{2}\right) = x$

$g(f(x)) = g(2x) = \dfrac{(2x)}{2} = x$

(b)

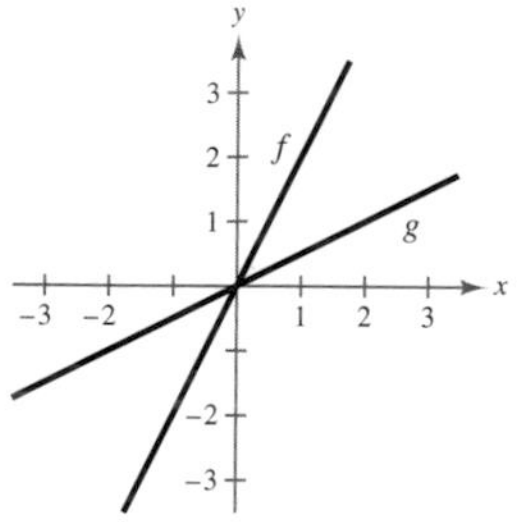

15. (a) $f(g(x)) = f\left(\dfrac{x-1}{7}\right) = 7\left(\dfrac{x-1}{7}\right) + 1 = x$

$g(f(x)) = g(7x+1) = \dfrac{(7x+1)-1}{7} = x$

(b)

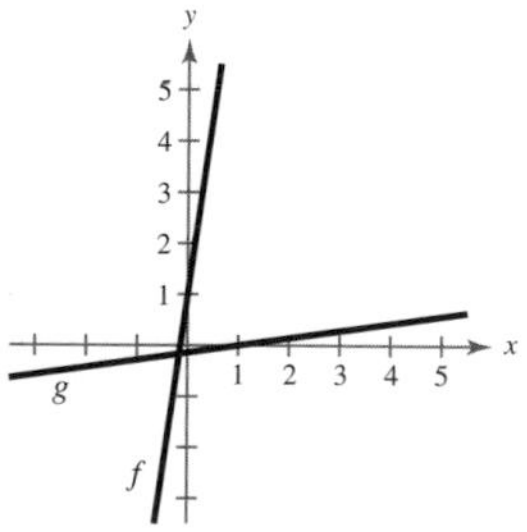

17. (a) $f(g(x)) = f\left(\sqrt[3]{8x}\right) = \dfrac{\left(\sqrt[3]{8x}\right)^3}{8} = x$

$g(f(x)) = g\left(\dfrac{x^3}{8}\right) = \sqrt[3]{8\left(\dfrac{x^3}{8}\right)} = x$

(b)

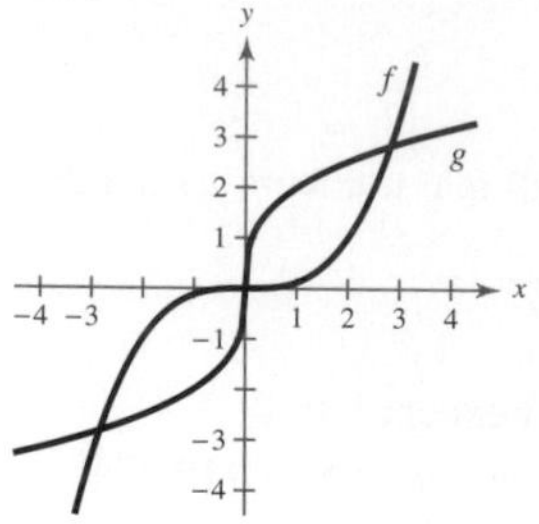

19. (a) $f(g(x)) = f(x^2 + 4),\ x \ge 0$

$= \sqrt{(x^2+4) - 4} = x$

$g(f(x)) = g\left(\sqrt{x-4}\right)$

$= \left(\sqrt{x-4}\right)^2 + 4 = x$

(b)

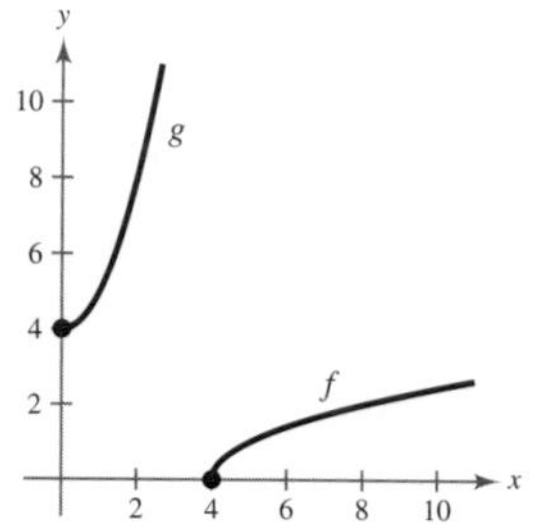

21. (a) $f(g(x)) = f\left(\sqrt{9-x}\right),\ x \le 9$

$= 9 - \left(\sqrt{9-x}\right)^2 = x$

$g(f(x)) = g(9 - x^2),\ x \ge 0$

$= \sqrt{9 - (9 - x^2)} = x$

(b)

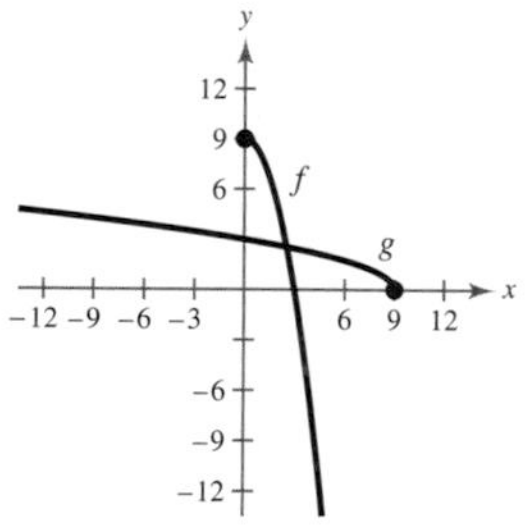

23. (a) $f(g(x)) = f\left(-\dfrac{5x+1}{x-1}\right) = \dfrac{-\left(\dfrac{5x+1}{x-1}\right) - 1}{-\left(\dfrac{5x+1}{x-1}\right) + 5}$

$= \dfrac{-5x - 1 - x + 1}{-5x - 1 + 5x - 5} = x$

$g(f(x)) = g\left(\dfrac{x-1}{x+5}\right) = \dfrac{-5\left(\dfrac{x-1}{x+5}\right) - 1}{\dfrac{x-1}{x+5} - 1}$

$= \dfrac{-5x + 5 - x - 5}{x - 1 - x - 5} = x$

(b)

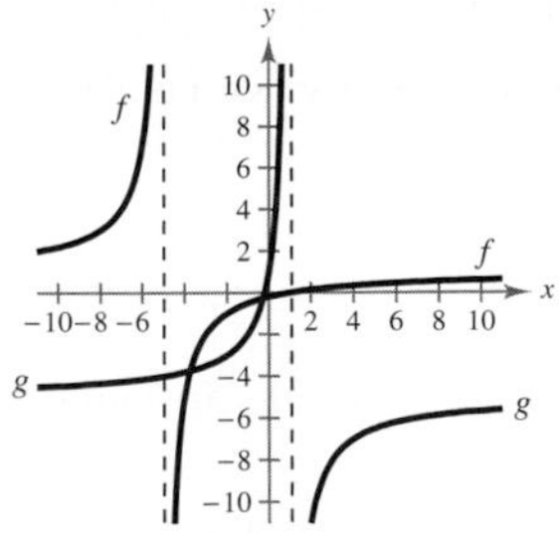

25. No **27.**

x	-2	0	2	4	6	8
$f^{-1}(x)$	-2	-1	0	1	2	3

29. Yes **31.** No

33.

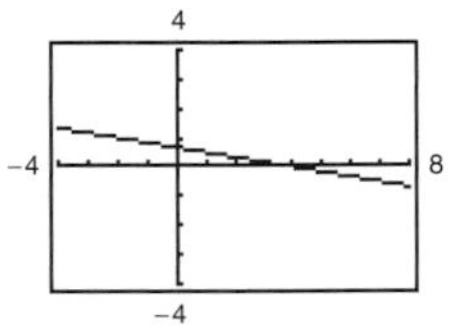

The function has an inverse.

35.

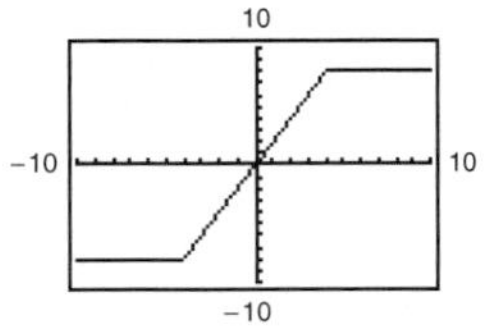

The function does not have an inverse.

37.

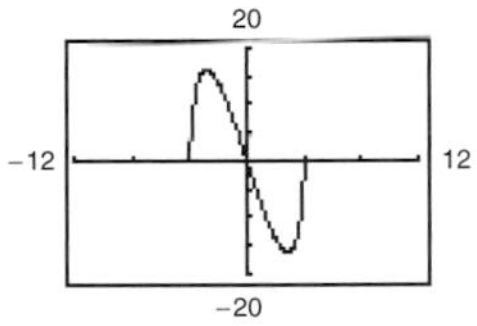

The function does not have an inverse.

39. (a) $f^{-1}(x) = \dfrac{x+3}{2}$

(b)

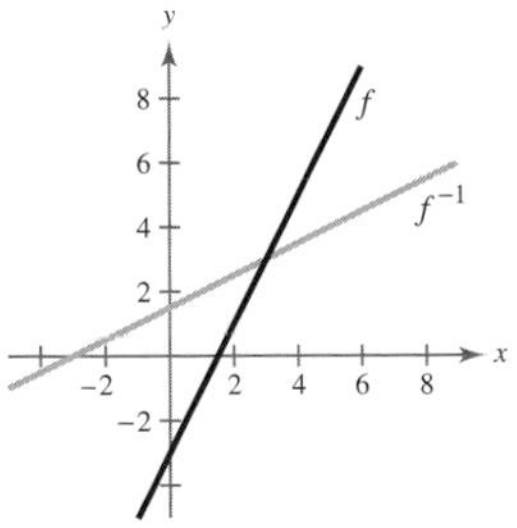

(c) The graph of f^{-1} is the reflection of the graph of f in the line $y = x$.

(d) The domains and ranges of f and f^{-1} are all real numbers.

41. (a) $f^{-1}(x) = \sqrt[5]{x+2}$

(b)

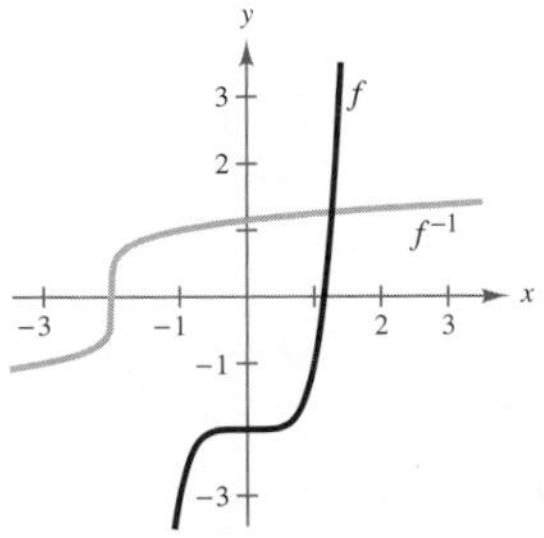

(c) The graph of f^{-1} is the reflection of the graph of f in the line $y = x$.

(d) The domains and ranges of f and f^{-1} are all real numbers.

43. (a) $f^{-1}(x) = x^2,\ x \ge 0$

(b)

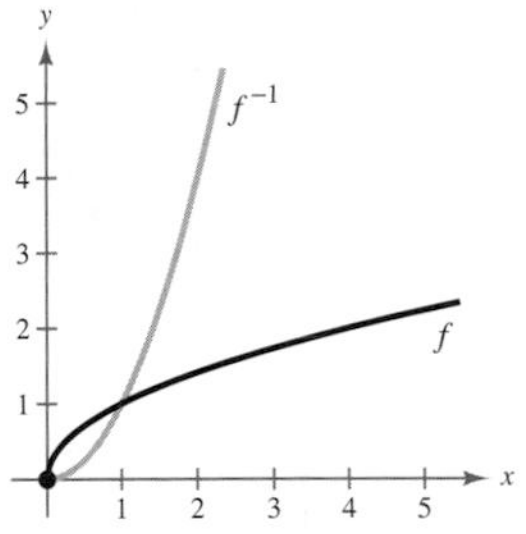

(c) The graph of f^{-1} is the reflection of the graph of f in the line $y = x$.

(d) The domains and ranges of f and f^{-1} are all real numbers x such that $x \ge 0$.

45. (a) $f^{-1}(x) = \sqrt{4 - x^2},\ 0 \le x \le 2$

(b)

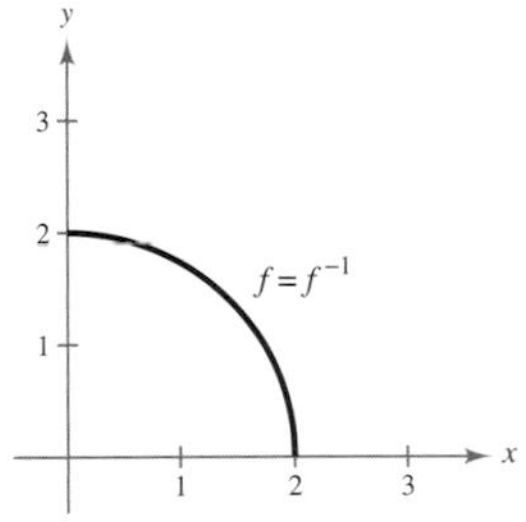

(c) The graph of f^{-1} is the same as the graph of f.

(d) The domains and ranges of f and f^{-1} are all real numbers x such that $0 \le x \le 2$.

47. (a) $f^{-1}(x) = \dfrac{4}{x}$

(b)

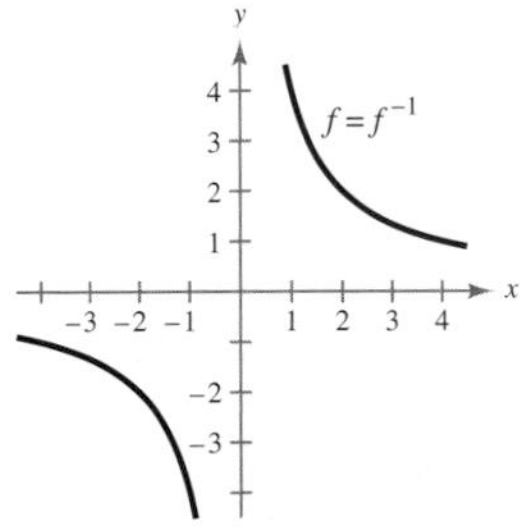

(c) The graph of f^{-1} is the same as the graph of f.

(d) The domains and ranges of f and f^{-1} are all real numbers x except $x = 0$.

49. (a) $f^{-1}(x) = \dfrac{2x+1}{x-1}$

(b)

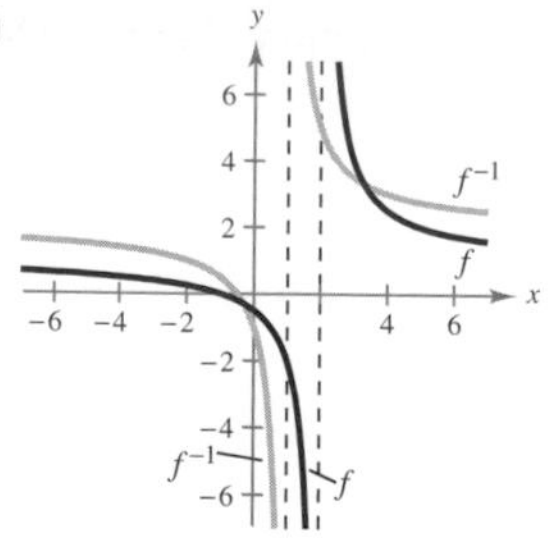

(c) The graph of f^{-1} is the reflection of the graph of f in the line $y = x$.

(d) The domain of f and the range of f^{-1} are all real numbers x except $x = 2$. The domain of f^{-1} and the range of f are all real numbers x except $x = 1$.

51. (a) $f^{-1}(x) = x^3 + 1$

(b)

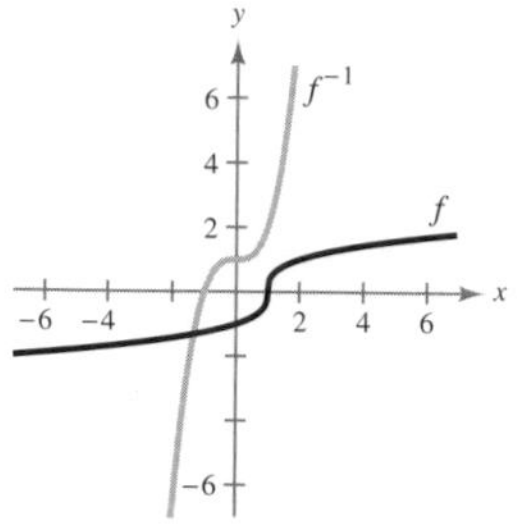

(c) The graph of f^{-1} is the reflection of the graph of f in the line $y = x$.

(d) The domains and ranges of f and f^{-1} are all real numbers.

53. (a) $f^{-1}(x) = \dfrac{5x - 4}{6 - 4x}$

(b)

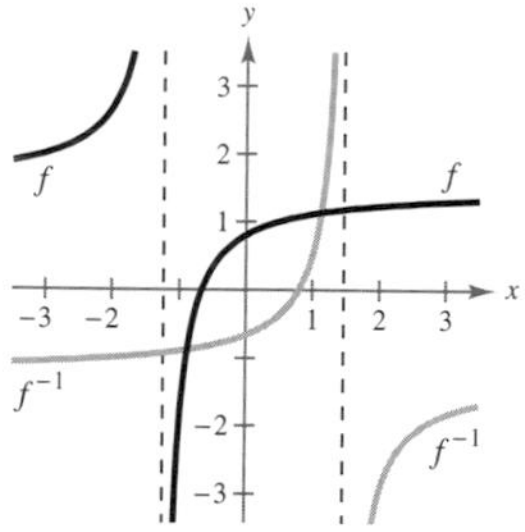

(c) The graph of f^{-1} is the reflection of the graph of f in the line $y = x$.

(d) The domain of f and the range of f^{-1} are all real numbers x except $x = -\frac{5}{4}$. The domain of f^{-1} and the range of f are all real numbers x except $x = \frac{3}{2}$.

55. No inverse **57.** $g^{-1}(x) = 8x$ **59.** No inverse

61. $f^{-1}(x) = \sqrt{x} - 3$ **63.** No inverse

65. No inverse **67.** $f^{-1}(x) = \dfrac{x^2 - 3}{2}, \quad x \geq 0$

69. 32 **71.** 600 **73.** $2\sqrt[3]{x + 3}$

75. $\dfrac{x + 1}{2}$ **77.** $\dfrac{x + 1}{2}$

79. (a) $f^{-1}(108{,}209) = 11$

(b) f^{-1} represents the year for a given number of households in the United States.

(c) $y = 1578.68t + 90{,}183.63$

(d) $f^{-1} = \dfrac{t - 90{,}183.63}{1578.68}$ (e) $f^{-1}(117{,}022) = 17$

(f) $f^{-1}(108{,}209) = 11.418$; the results are similar.

81. (a) Yes

(b) f^{-1} yields the year for a given number of miles traveled by motor vehicles.

(c) $f^{-1}(2632) = 8$

(d) No. $f(t)$ would not pass the Horizontal Line Test.

83. (a) $y = \sqrt{\dfrac{x - 245.50}{0.03}}, \quad 245.5 < x < 545.5$

x = degrees Fahrenheit; y = % load

(b)

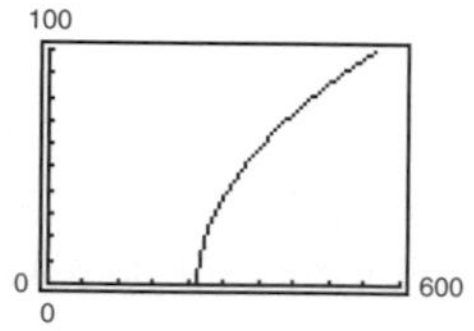

(c) $0 < x < 92.11$

85. False. $f(x) = x^2$ has no inverse.

87. Answers will vary.

89.

x	1	3	4	6
y	1	2	6	7

x	1	2	6	7
$f^{-1}(x)$	1	3	4	6

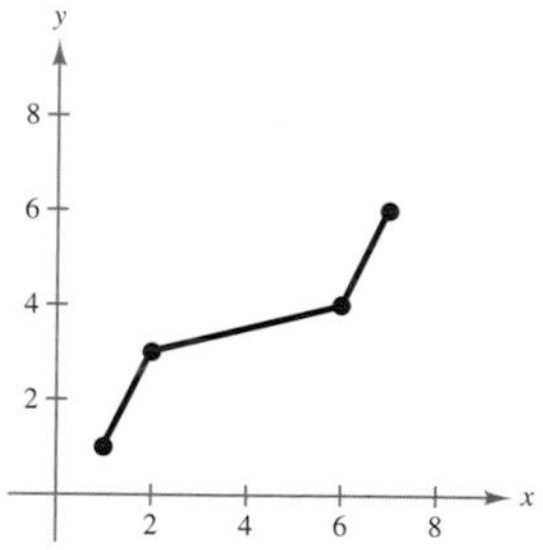

91.

x	−2	−1	3	4
y	6	0	−2	−3

x	−3	−2	0	6
$f^{-1}(x)$	4	3	−1	−2

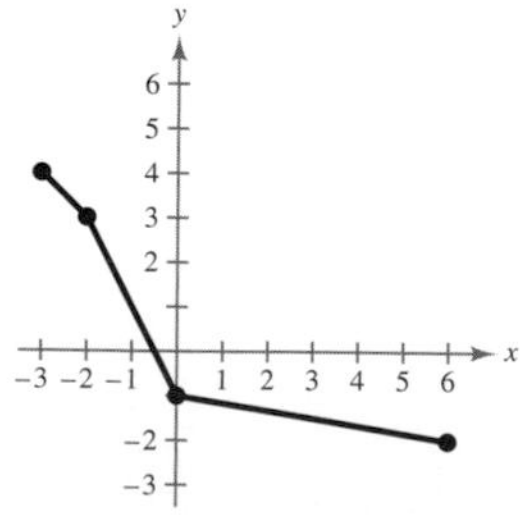

93. $k = \frac{1}{4}$ **95.** ± 8 **97.** $\frac{3}{2}$ **99.** $3 \pm \sqrt{5}$
101. $5, -\frac{10}{3}$ **103.** 16, 18

Section 1.10 *(page 109)*

Vocabulary Check *(page 109)*

1. variation; regression **2.** sum of square differences
3. correlation coefficient **4.** directly proportional
5. constant of variation **6.** directly proportional
7. inverse **8.** combined **9.** jointly proportional

1.

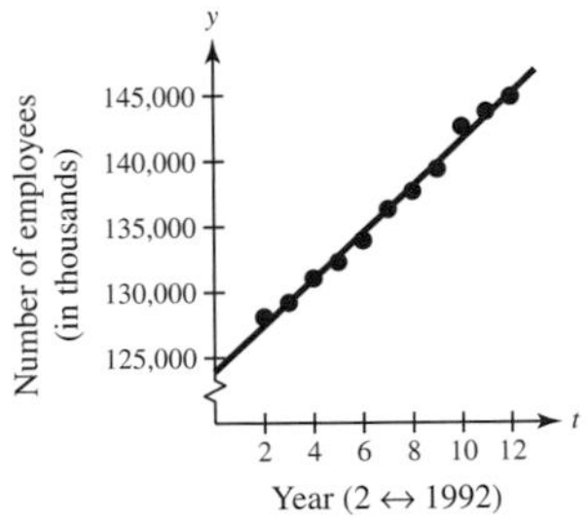

The model is a good fit for the actual data.

3.

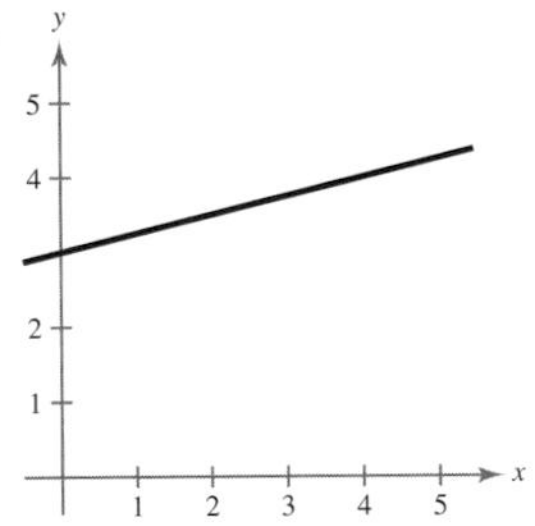

$y = \frac{1}{4}x + 3$

5.

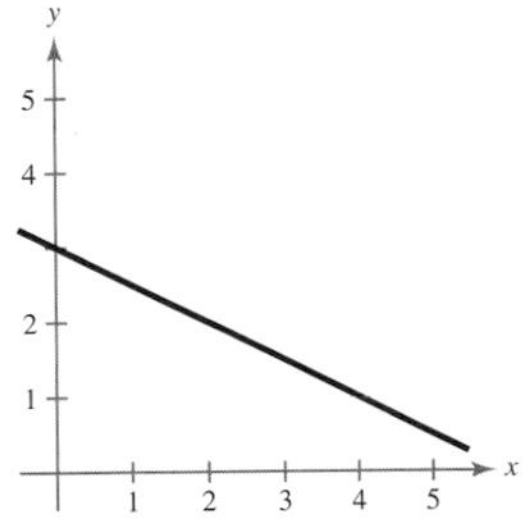

$y = -\frac{1}{2}x + 3$

7. (a) and (b)

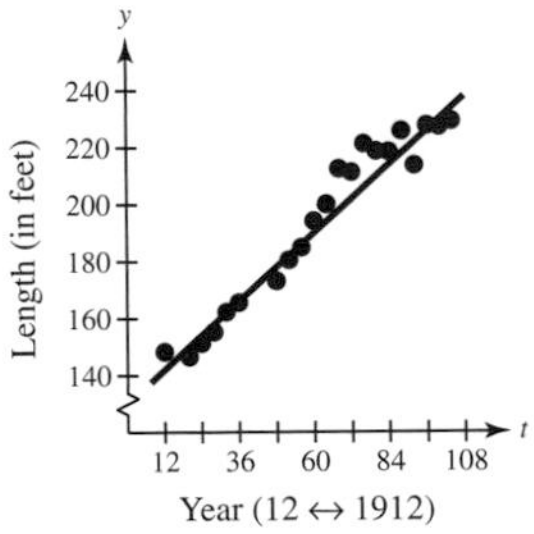

(c) $y = 1.03t + 130.27$ (d) The models are similar.
(e) Part (b): 238 feet; Part (c): 241.51 feet
(f) Answers will vary.

9. (a)

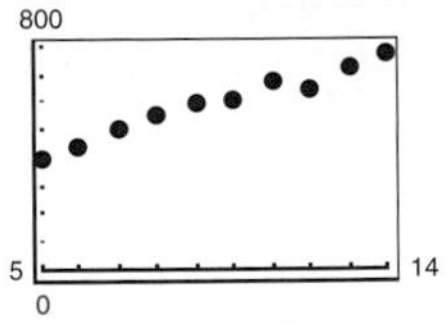

(b) $S = 38.4t + 224$

(c)

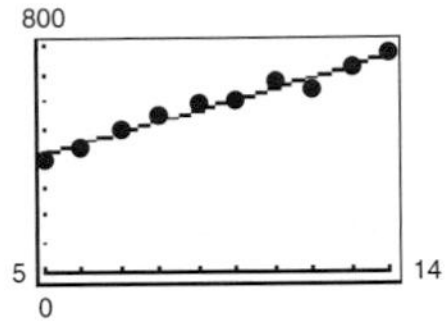

The model is a good fit.
(d) 2005: \$800 million; 2007: \$876.8 million
(e) Each year the annual gross ticket sales for Broadway shows in New York City increase by \$38.4 million.

11. Inversely

13.

x	2	4	6	8	10
$y = kx^2$	4	16	36	64	100

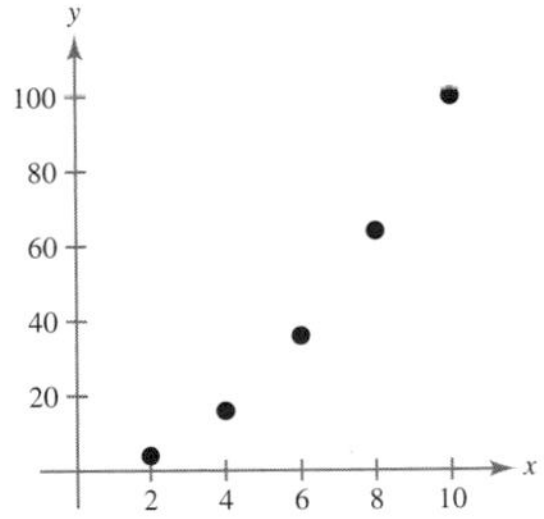

15.

x	2	4	6	8	10
$y = kx^2$	2	8	18	32	50

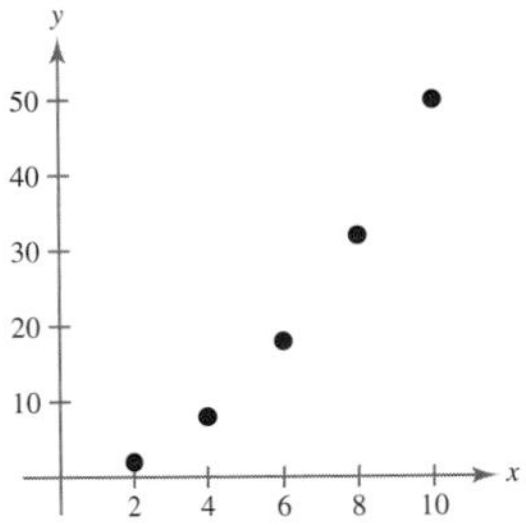

17.

x	2	4	6	8	10
$y = k/x^2$	$\frac{1}{2}$	$\frac{1}{8}$	$\frac{1}{18}$	$\frac{1}{32}$	$\frac{1}{50}$

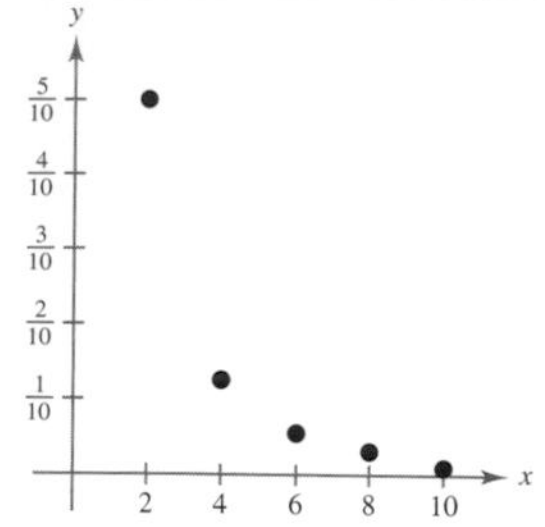

19.

x	2	4	6	8	10
$y = k/x^2$	$\frac{5}{2}$	$\frac{5}{8}$	$\frac{5}{18}$	$\frac{5}{32}$	$\frac{1}{10}$

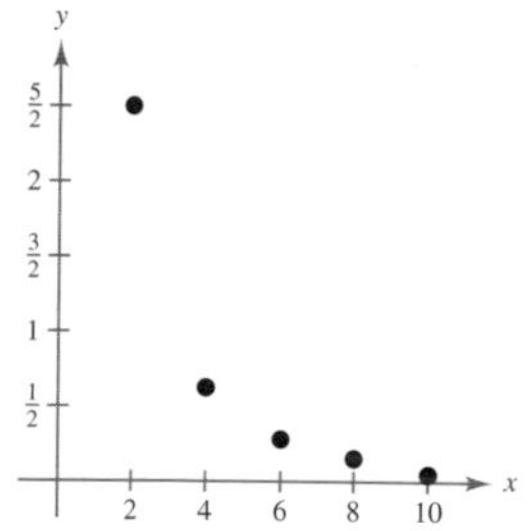

21. $y = \dfrac{5}{x}$ **23.** $y = -\dfrac{7}{10}x$ **25.** $y = \dfrac{12}{5}x$

27. $y = 205x$ **29.** $I = 0.035P$

31. Model: $y = \frac{33}{13}x$; 25.4 centimeters, 50.8 centimeters

33. $y = 0.0368x$; \$7360

35. (a) 0.05 meter (b) $176\frac{2}{3}$ newtons

37. 39.47 pounds **39.** $A = kr^2$ **41.** $y = \dfrac{k}{x^2}$

43. $F = \dfrac{kg}{r^2}$ **45.** $P = \dfrac{k}{V}$ **47.** $F = \dfrac{km_1m_2}{r^2}$

49. The area of a triangle is jointly proportional to its base and height.

51. The volume of a sphere varies directly as the cube of its radius.

53. Average speed is directly proportional to the distance and inversely proportional to the time.

55. $A = \pi r^2$ **57.** $y = \dfrac{28}{x}$ **59.** $F = 14rs^3$

61. $z = \dfrac{2x^2}{3y}$ **63.** ≈ 0.61 mile per hour **65.** 506 feet

67. 1470 joules **69.** The velocity is increased by one-third.

71. (a)

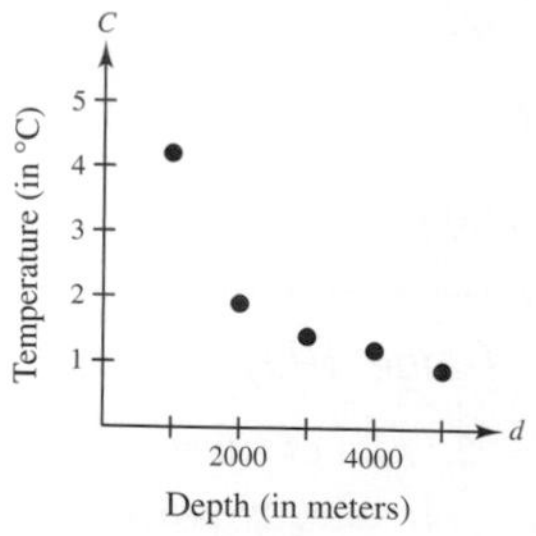

(b) Yes. $k_1 = 4200, k_2 = 3800, k_3 = 4200,$ $k_4 = 4800, k_5 = 4500$

(c) $C = \dfrac{4300}{d}$

(d)

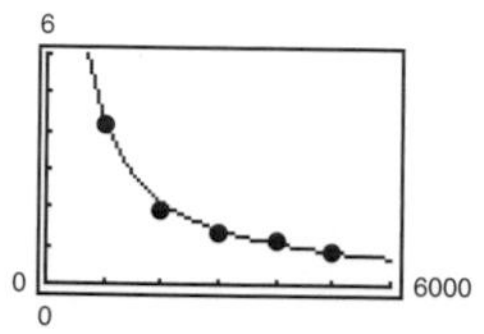

(e) ≈ 1433 meters

73. (a)

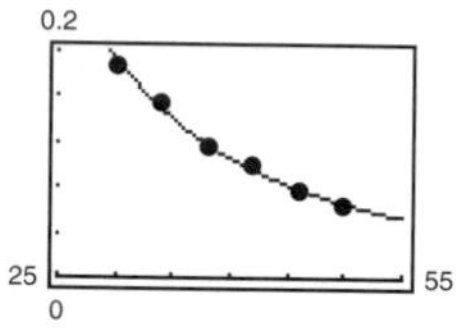

(b) 0.2857 microwatt per square centimeter

75. False. y will increase if k is positive and y will decrease if k is negative.

77. True. The closer the value of $|r|$ is to 1, the better the fit.

79. The accuracy is questionable when based on such limited data.

81. $x > 5$

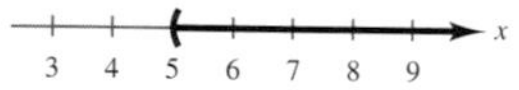

83. $-4 < x < 5$

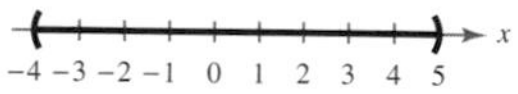

85. (a) $-\frac{5}{3}$ (b) $-\frac{7}{3}$ (c) 21 **87.** Answers will vary.

Review Exercises *(page 117)*

1.

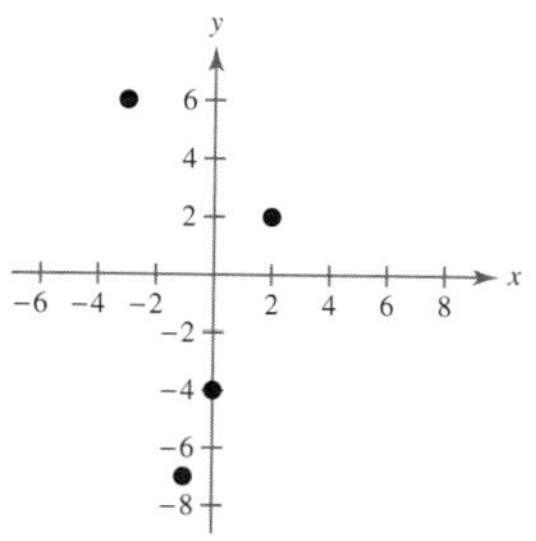

3. Quadrant IV

5. (a)

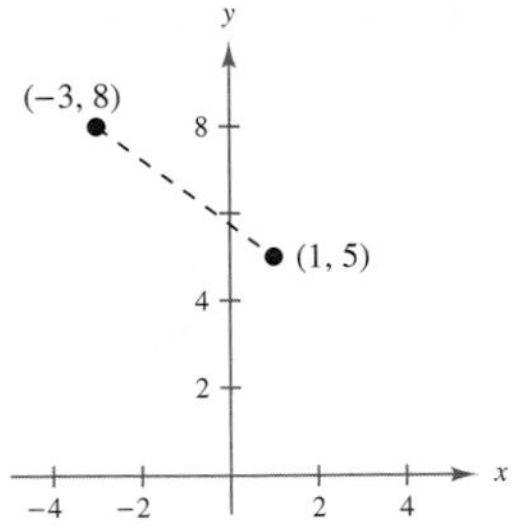

(b) 5

(c) $\left(-1, \frac{13}{2}\right)$

7. (a)

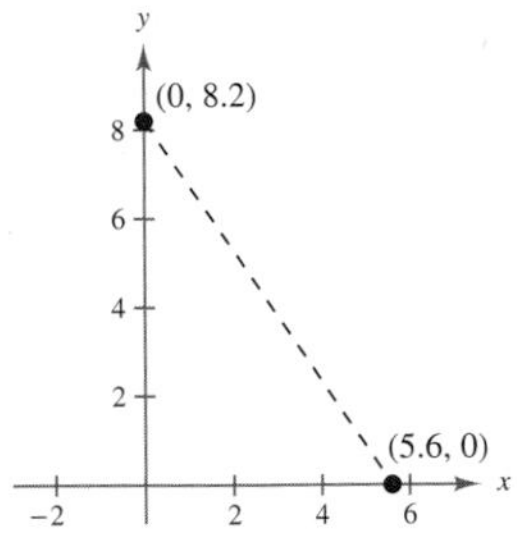

(b) 9.9

(c) (2.8, 4.1)

9. (2, 5), (4, 5), (2, 0), (4, 0)

11. \$656.45 million

13. Radius ≈ 22.5 centimeters

15.

x	−2	−1	0	1	2
y	−11	−8	−5	−2	1

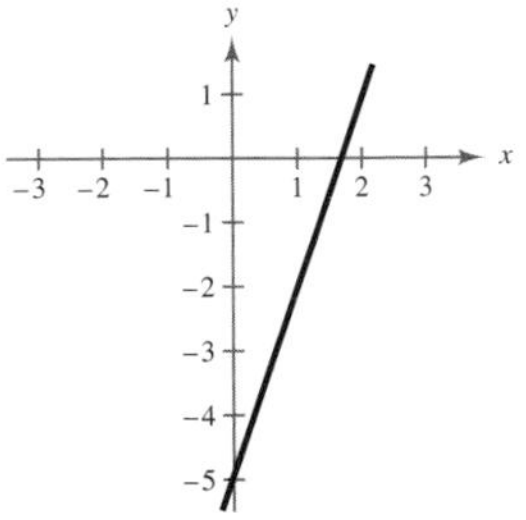

17.

x	−1	0	1	2	3	4
y	4	0	−2	−2	0	4

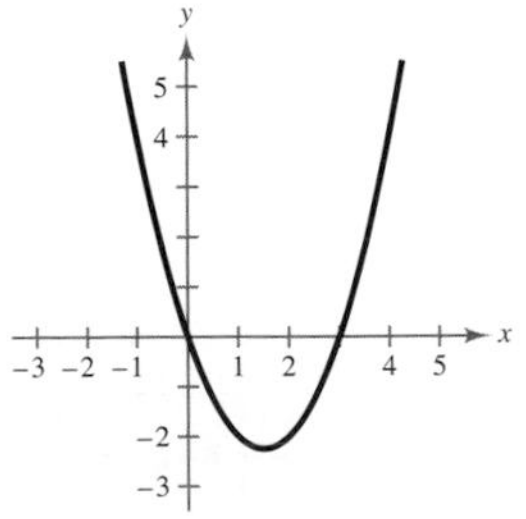

19.

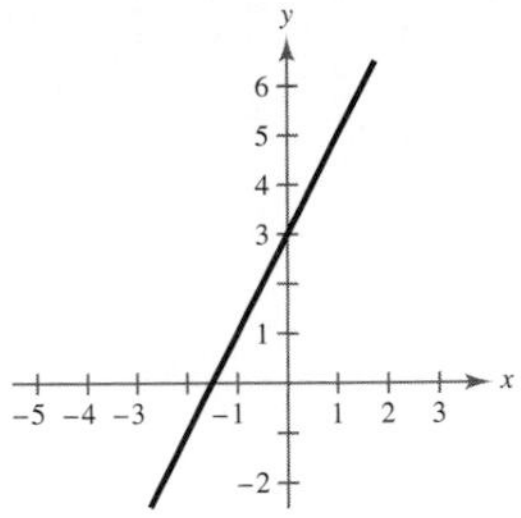

21.

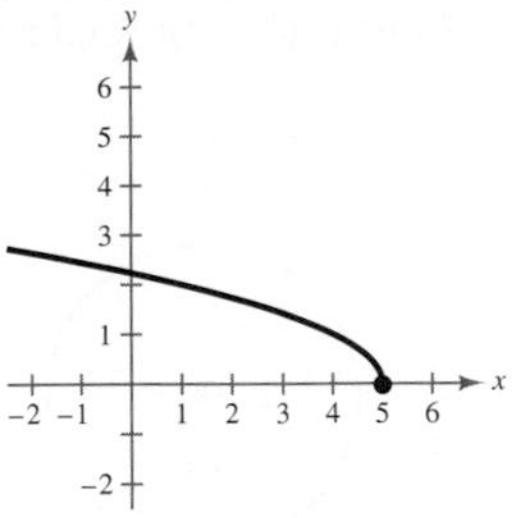

23.

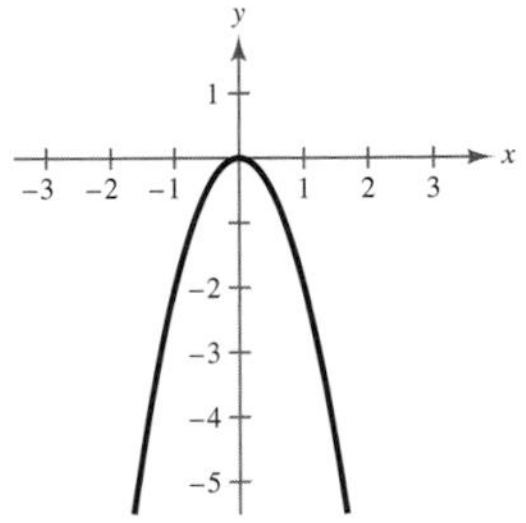

25. x-intercept: $\left(-\frac{7}{2}, 0\right)$
y-intercept: (0, 7)

27. x-intercepts: (1, 0), (5, 0)
y-intercept: (0, 5)

29. No symmetry

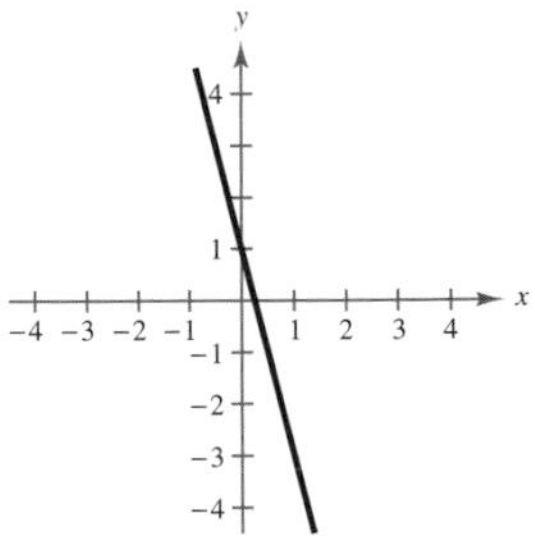

31. y-axis symmetry

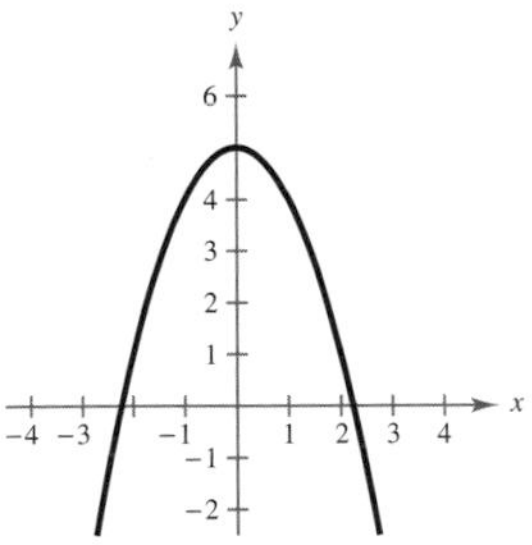

33. No symmetry

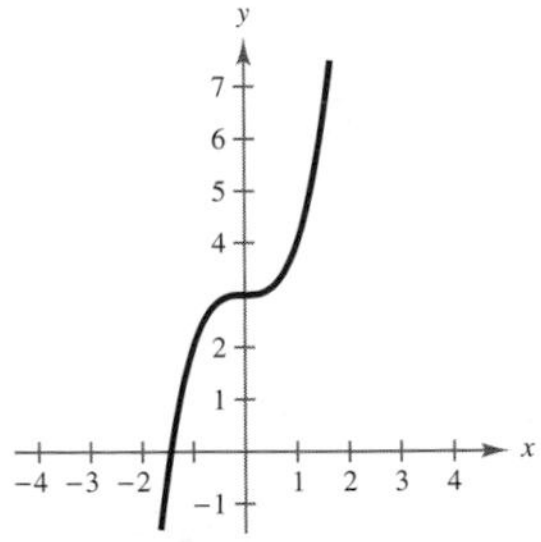

35. No symmetry

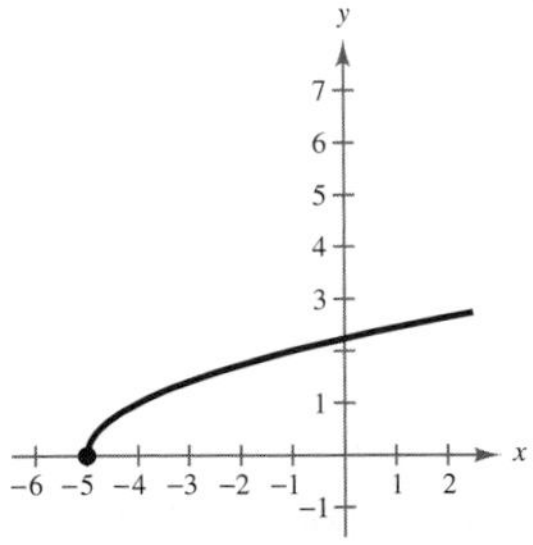

37. Center: (0, 0); Radius: 3

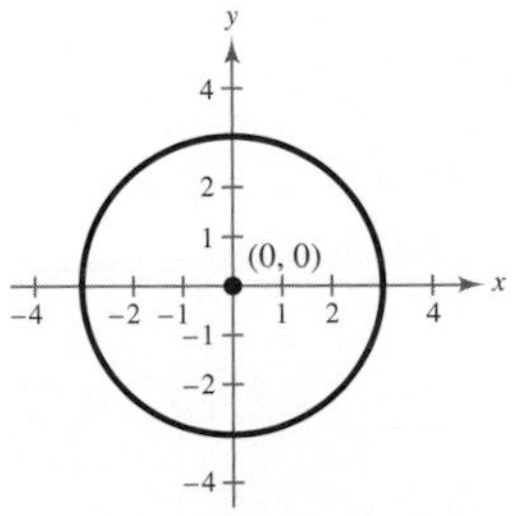

39. Center: (−2, 0); Radius: 4

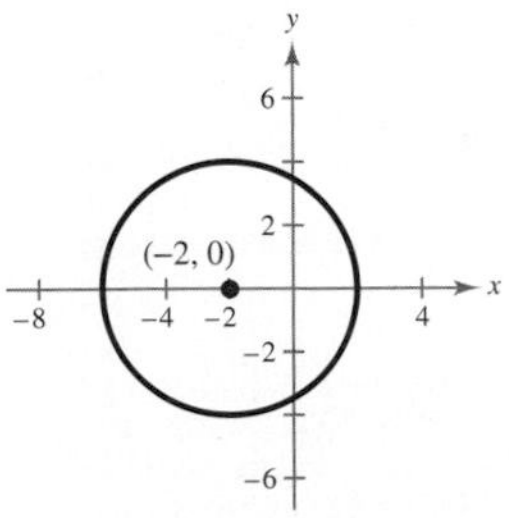

41. Center: $\left(\frac{1}{2}, -1\right)$; Radius: 6

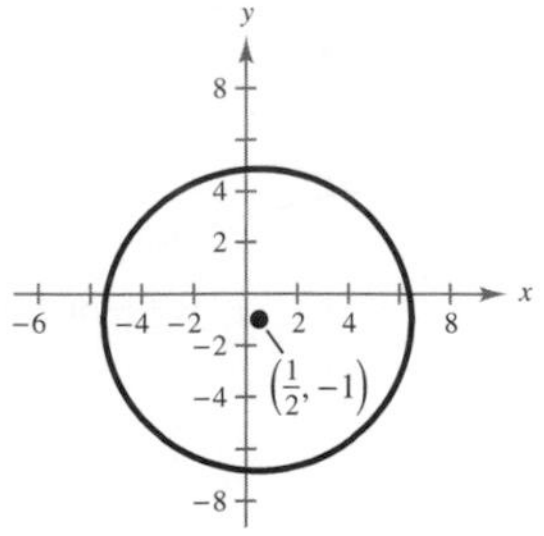

43. $(x - 2)^2 + (y + 3)^2 = 13$

45. (a)

x	0	4	8	12	16	20
F	0	5	10	15	20	25

(b)

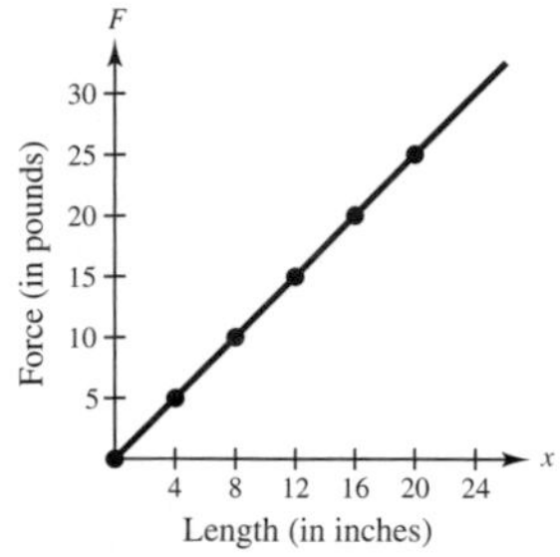

(c) 12.5 pounds

47. slope: 0
y-intercept: 6

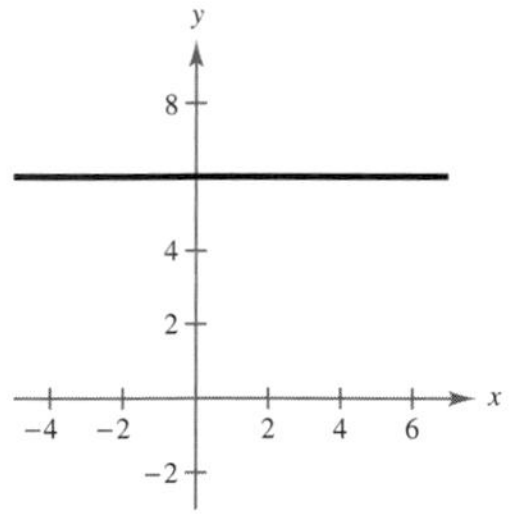

49. slope: 3
y-intercept: 13

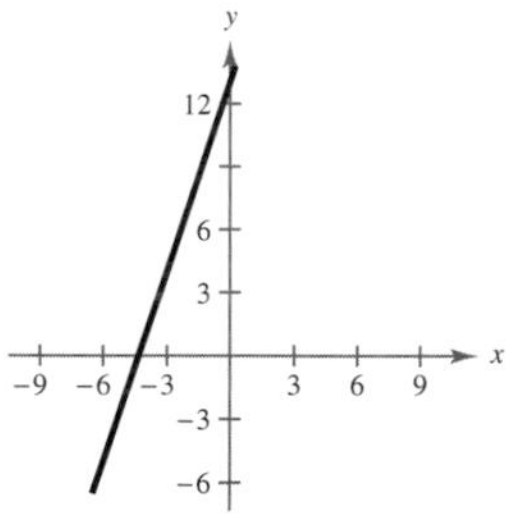

51.

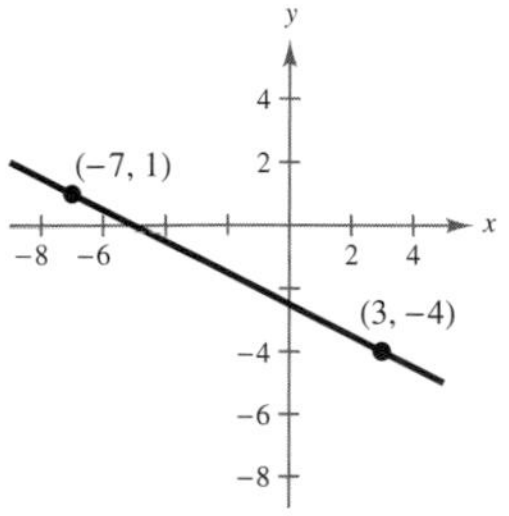

$m = -\frac{1}{2}$

53.

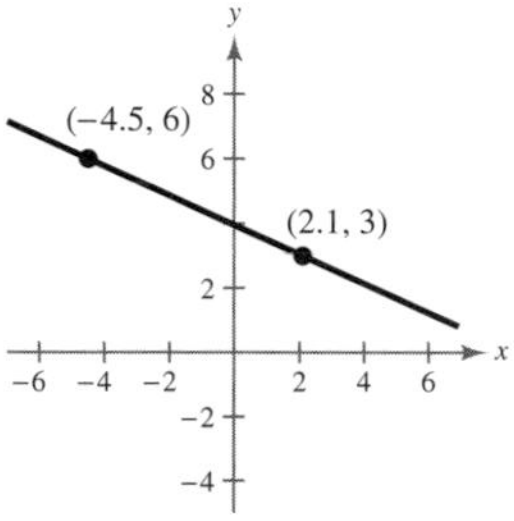

$m = -\frac{5}{11}$

55. $y = \frac{3}{2}x - 5$

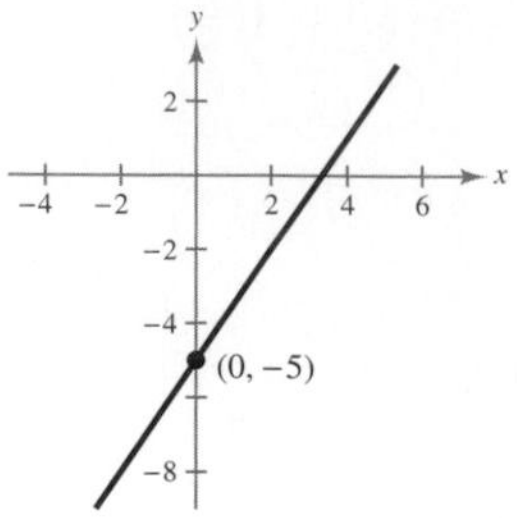

57. $y = -\frac{1}{2}x + 2$

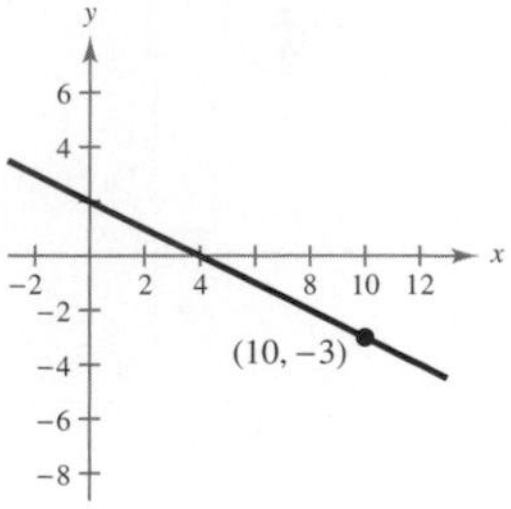

59. $x = 0$ **61.** $y = -\frac{4}{3}x + \frac{8}{3}$

63. (a) $y = \frac{5}{4}x - \frac{23}{4}$ (b) $y = -\frac{4}{5}x + \frac{2}{5}$

65. $V = 850t + 7400,\ 6 \le t \le 11$ **67.** No **69.** Yes

71. (a) 5 (b) 17 (c) $t^4 + 1$ (d) $t^2 + 2t + 2$

73. All real numbers x such that $-5 \le x \le 5$

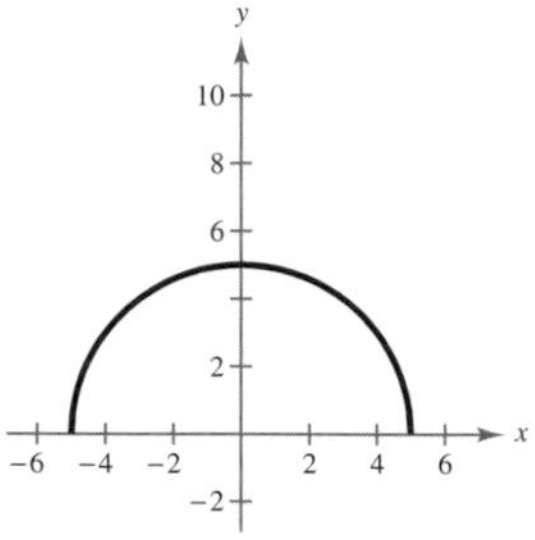

75. All real numbers x except $x = 3, -2$

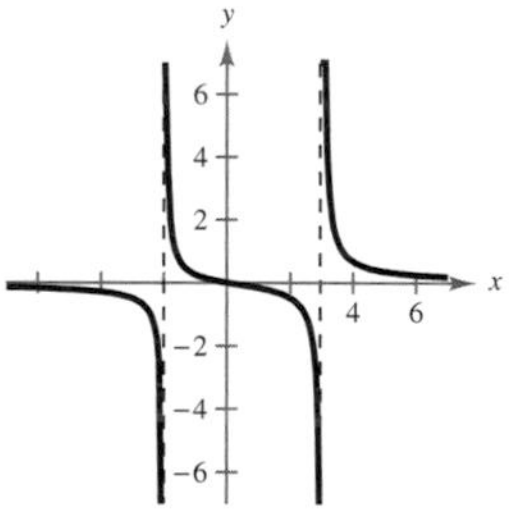

77. (a) 16 feet per second (b) 1.5 seconds
(c) -16 feet per second

79. $4x + 2h + 3,\quad h \neq 0$ **81.** Function

83. Not a function **85.** $\frac{7}{3}$, 3 **87.** $-\frac{3}{8}$

89. Increasing on $(0, \infty)$
Decreasing on $(-\infty, -1)$
Constant on $(-1, 0)$

91.

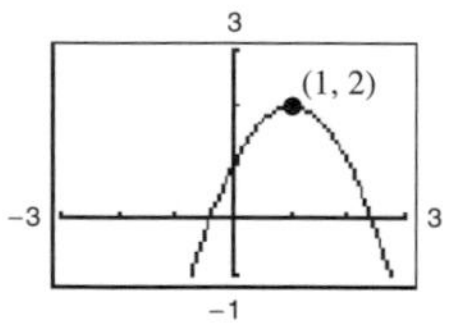

93.

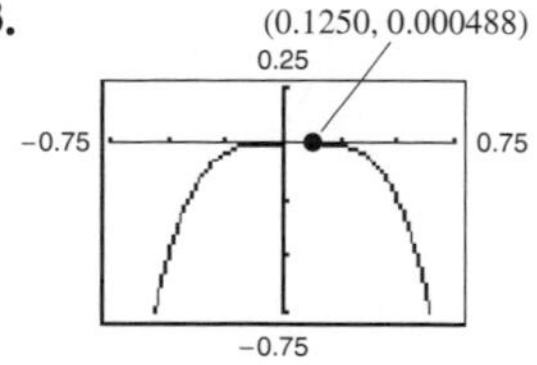

95. 4 **97.** $\frac{1 - \sqrt{2}}{2}$ **99.** Neither even nor odd

101. Odd

103. $f(x) = -3x$

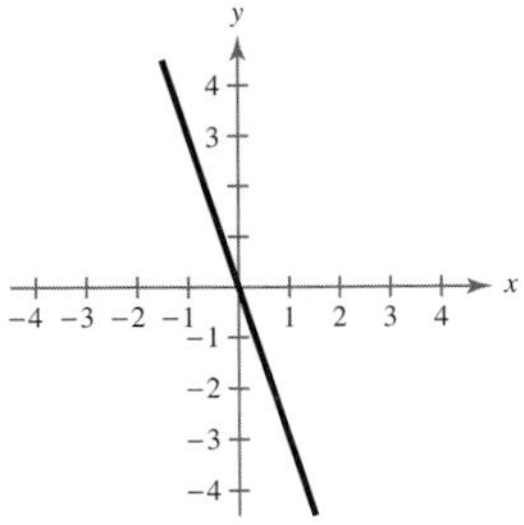

105.

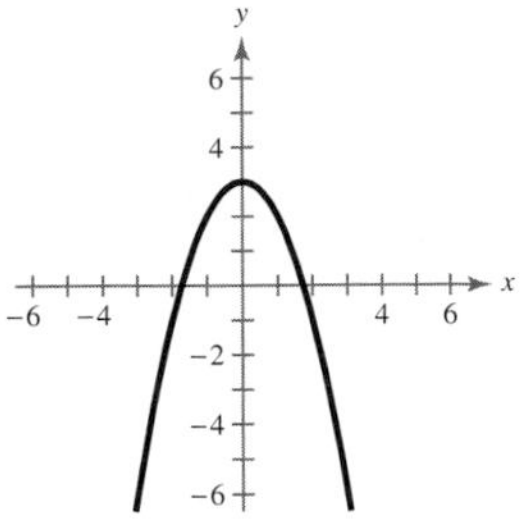

107.

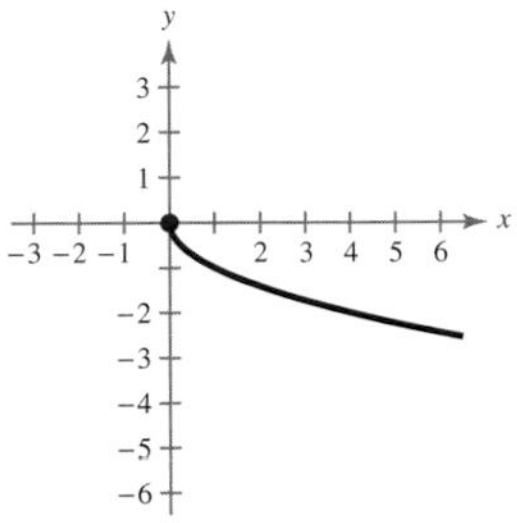

109.

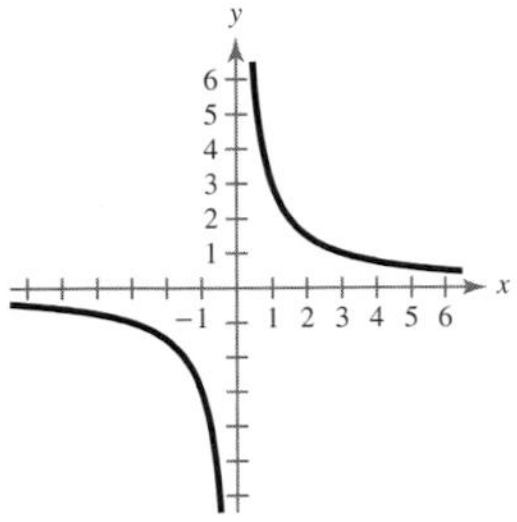

111.

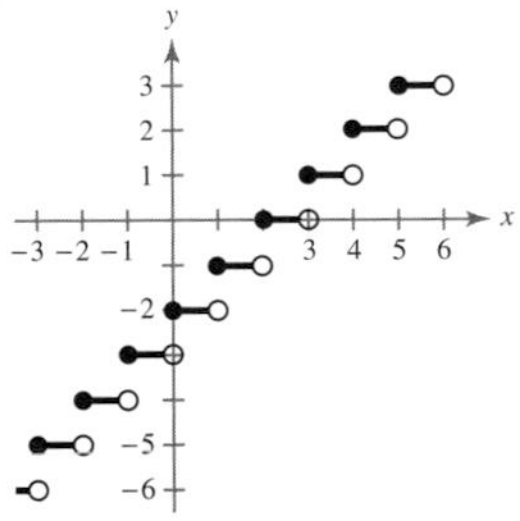

113.

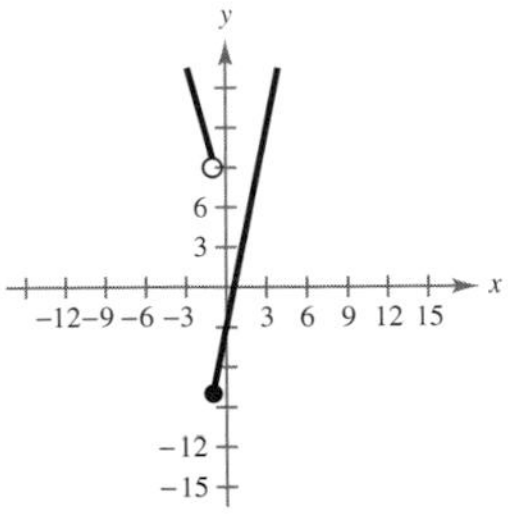

115. $y = x^3$

117. (a) $f(x) = x^2$

(b) Vertical shift of nine units downward

(c)

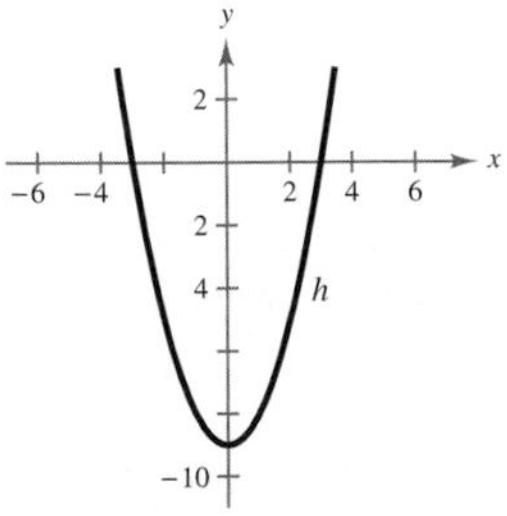

(d) $h(x) = f(x) - 9$

119. (a) $f(x) = \sqrt{x}$

(b) Horizontal shift of seven units to the right

(c)

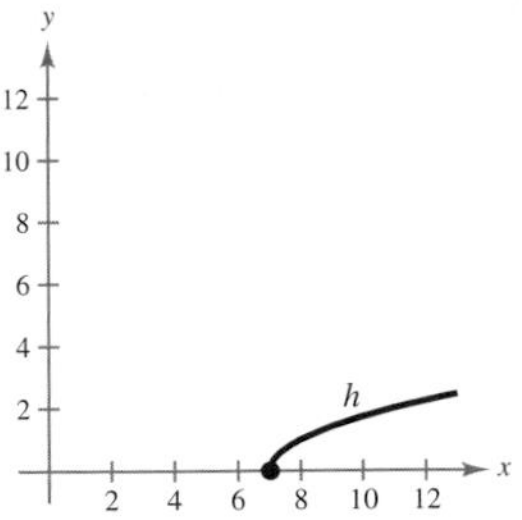

(d) $h(x) = f(x - 7)$

121. (a) $f(x) = x^2$

(b) Reflection in the x-axis, horizontal shift of three units to the left, and vertical shift of one unit upward

(c)

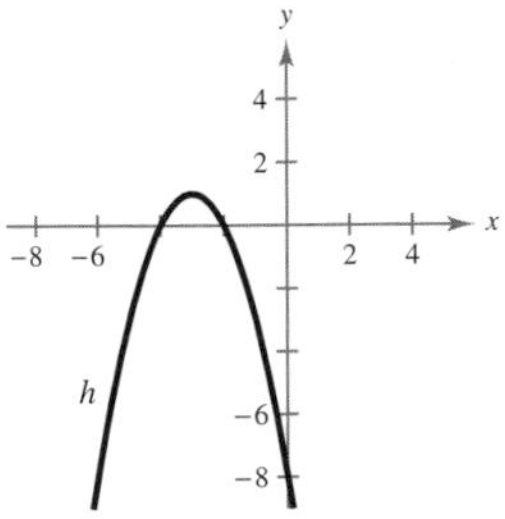

(d) $h(x) = -f(x + 3) + 1$

123. (a) $f(x) = [\![x]\!]$

(b) Reflection in the x-axis and vertical shift of six units upward

(c)

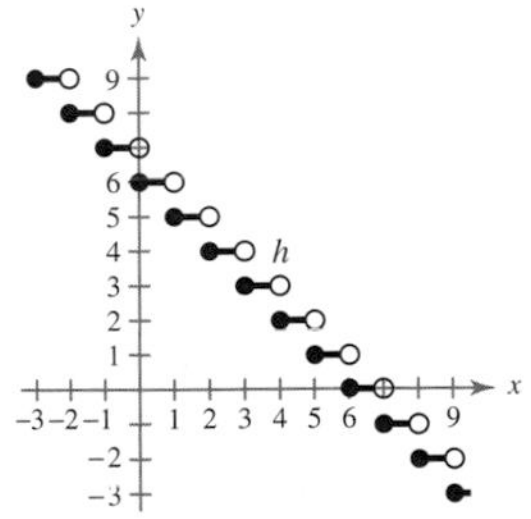

(d) $h(x) = -f(x) + 6$

125. (a) $f(x) = |x|$

(b) Reflections in the x-axis and the y-axis, horizontal shift of four units to the right, and vertical shift of six units upward

(c)

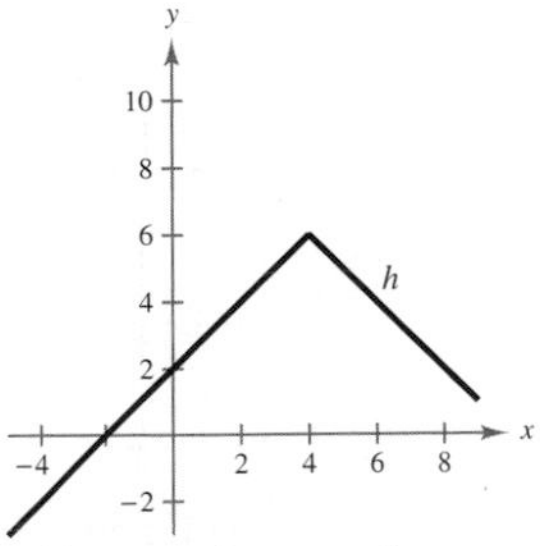

(d) $h(x) = -f(-x + 4) + 6$

CHAPTER 1

127. (a) $f(x) = [\![x]\!]$
(b) Horizontal shift of nine units to the right and vertical stretch
(c)
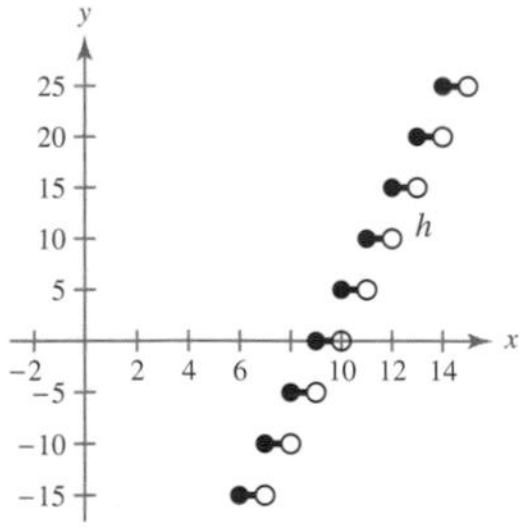

(d) $h(x) = 5f(x - 9)$

129. (a) $f(x) = \sqrt{x}$
(b) Reflection in the x-axis, vertical stretch, and horizontal shift of four units to the right
(c)
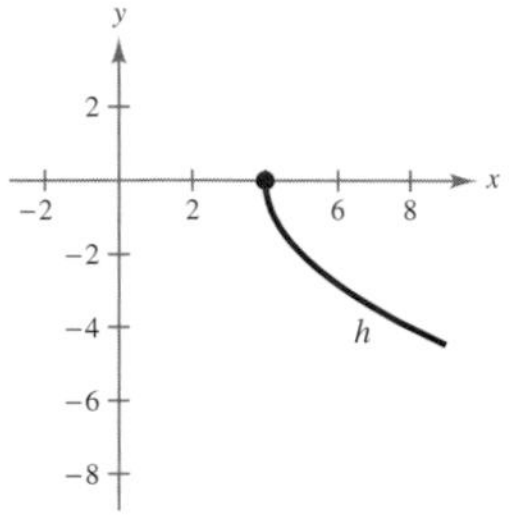

(d) $h(x) = -2f(x - 4)$

131. (a) $x^2 + 2x + 2$ (b) $x^2 - 2x + 4$
(c) $2x^3 - x^2 + 6x - 3$
(d) $\dfrac{x^2 + 3}{2x - 1}$; all real numbers x except $x = \dfrac{1}{2}$

133. (a) $x - \frac{8}{3}$ (b) $x - 8$
Domains of $f, g, f \circ g$, and $g \circ f$: all real numbers

135. $f(x) = x^3,\ g(x) = 6x - 5$

137. (a) $(v + d)(t) = -36.04t^2 + 804.6t - 1112$
(b)
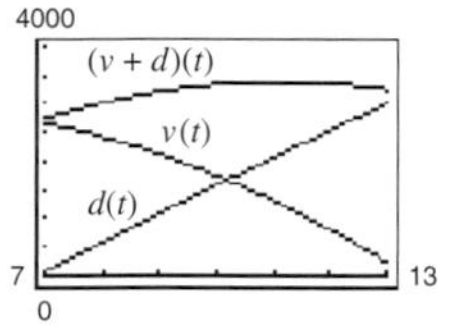

(c) $(v + d)(10) = 3330$

139. $f^{-1}(x) = x + 7$ **141.** The function has an inverse.

143.
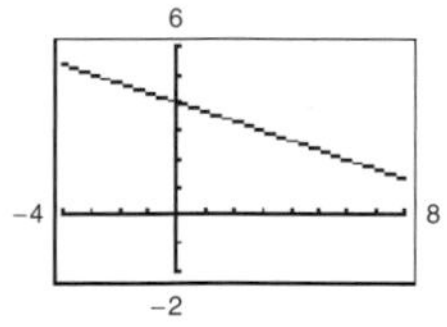

The function has an inverse.

145.
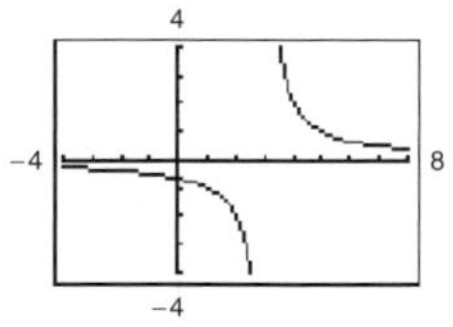

The function has an inverse.

147. (a) $f^{-1}(x) = 2x + 6$
(b)
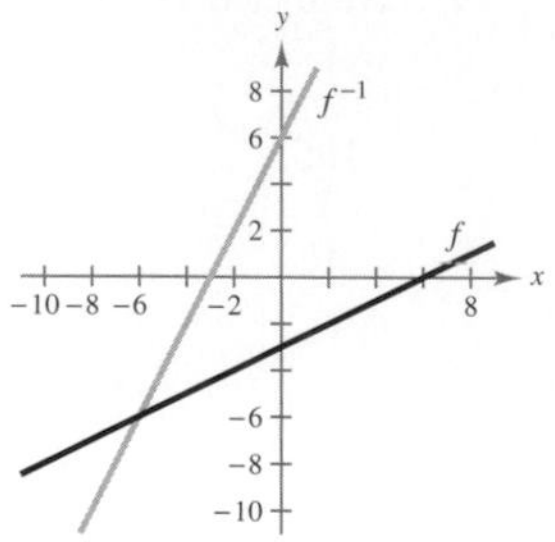

(c) The graph of f^{-1} is the reflection of the graph of f in the line $y = x$.
(d) Both f and f^{-1} have domains and ranges that are all real numbers.

149. (a) $f^{-1}(x) = x^2 - 1,\ x \geq 0$
(b)
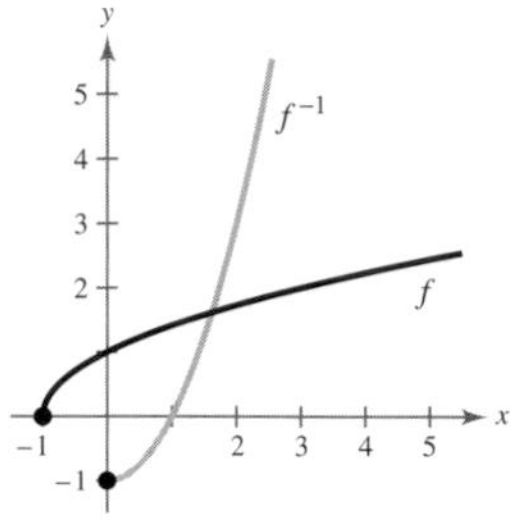

(c) The graph of f^{-1} is the reflection of the graph of f in the line $y = x$.
(d) f has a domain of $[-1, \infty)$ and a range of $[0, \infty)$; f^{-1} has a domain of $[0, \infty)$ and a range of $[-1, \infty)$.

151. $x \geq 4;\ f^{-1}(x) = \sqrt{\dfrac{x}{2}} + 4$

153. (a)
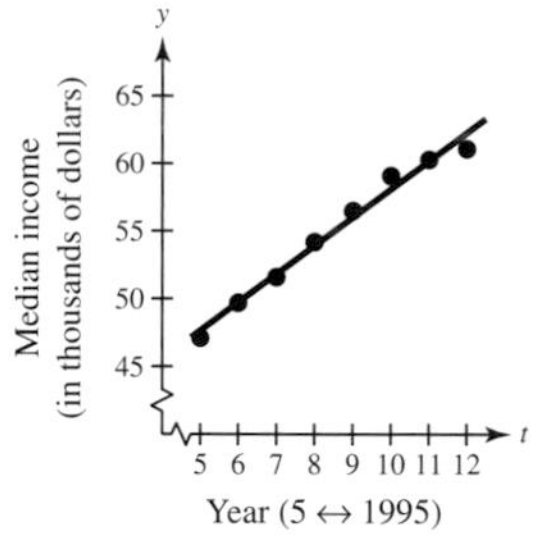

(b) The model is a good fit for the actual data.

155. Model: $m = \frac{8}{5}k$; 3.2 kilometers, 16 kilometers

157. A factor of 4 **159.** $\approx$ 2 hours, 26 minutes

161. False. The graph is reflected in the x-axis, shifted nine units to the left, and then shifted 13 units downward.

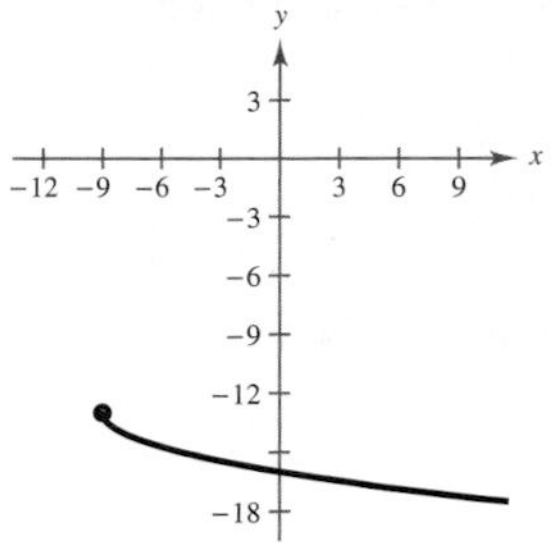

163. True. If y is directly proportional to x, then $y = kx$, so $x = (1/k)y$. Therefore, x is directly proportional to y.

165. A function from a set A to a set B is a relation that assigns to each element x in the set A exactly one element y in the set B.

Chapter Test *(page 123)*

1.

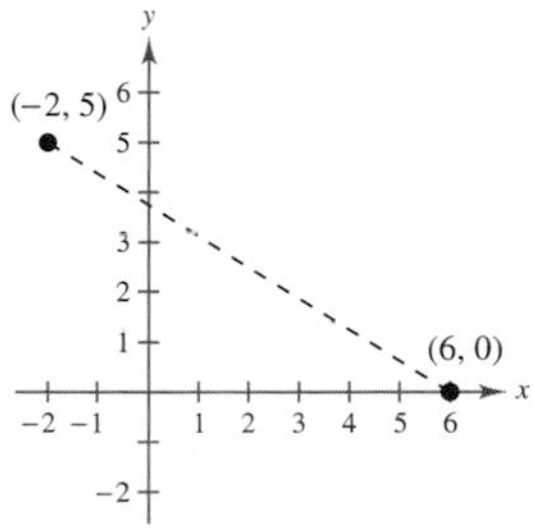

Midpoint: $\left(2, \frac{5}{2}\right)$; Distance: $\sqrt{89}$

2. $\approx$ 11.937 centimeters

3. No symmetry

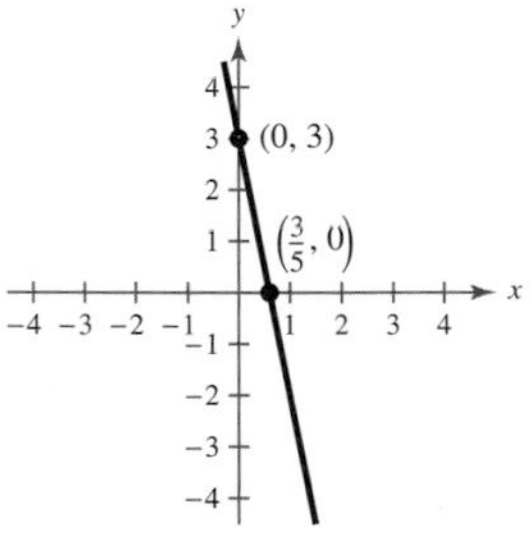

4. y-axis symmetry

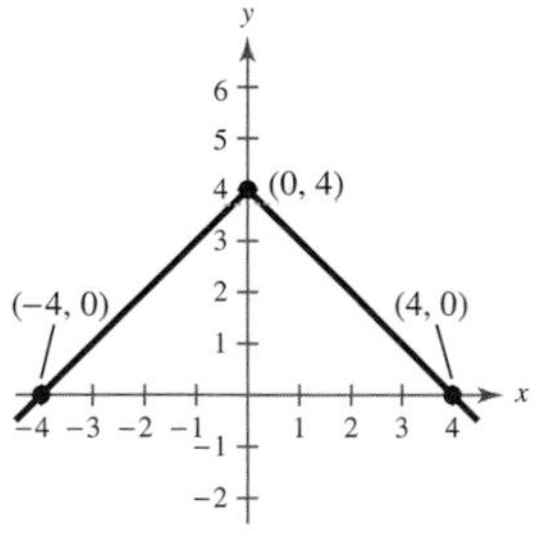

5. y-axis symmetry

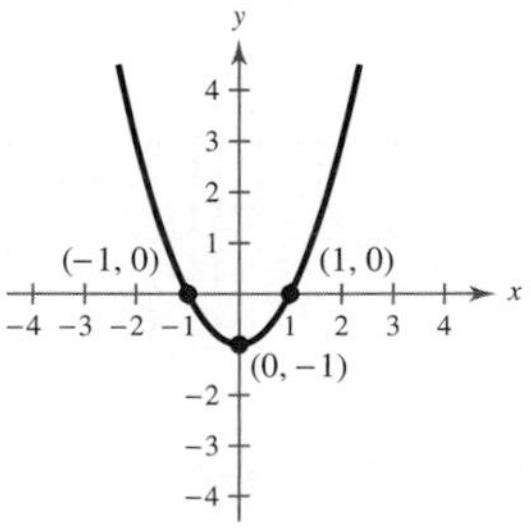

6. $(x - 1)^2 + (y - 3)^2 = 16$

7. $2x + y - 1 = 0$

8. $17x + 10y - 59 = 0$

9. (a) $4x - 7y + 44 = 0$ (b) $7x + 4y - 53 = 0$

10. (a) $-\dfrac{1}{8}$ (b) $-\dfrac{1}{28}$ (c) $\dfrac{\sqrt{x}}{x^2 - 18x}$

11. $-10 \le x \le 10$

12. (a) $0, \pm 0.4314$

(b)

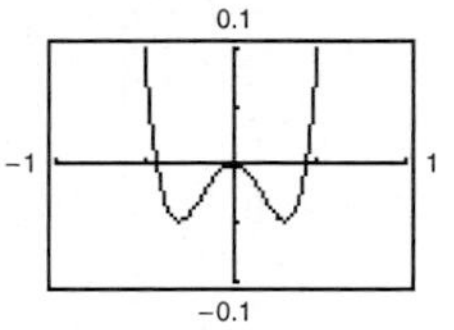

(c) Increasing on $(-0.31, 0), (0.31, \infty)$
Decreasing on $(-\infty, -0.31), (0, 0.31)$

(d) Even

13. (a) 0, 3

(b)

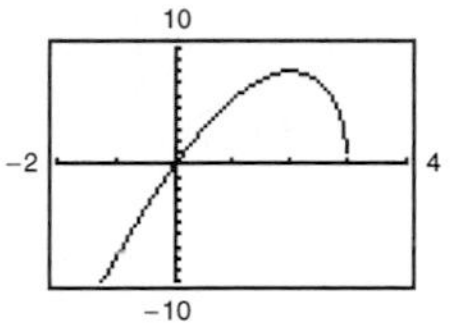

(c) Increasing on $(-\infty, 2)$
Decreasing on $(2, 3)$

(d) Neither even nor odd

14. (a) -5

(b)

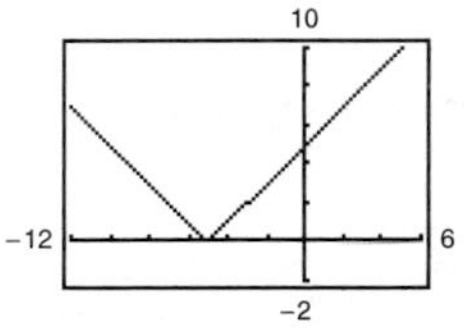

(c) Increasing on $(-5, \infty)$
Decreasing on $(-\infty, -5)$

(d) Neither even nor odd

15.

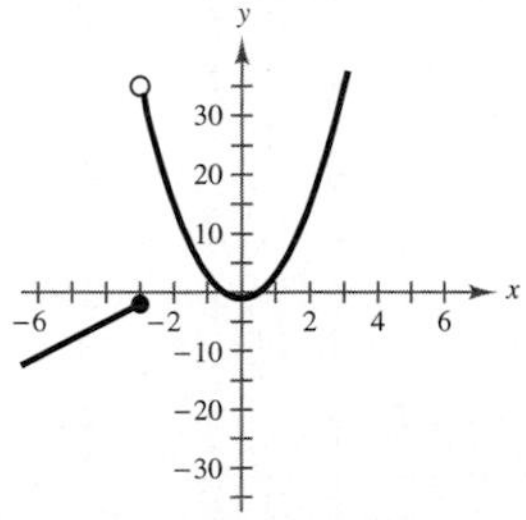

16. Reflection in the x-axis of $y = [\![x]\!]$

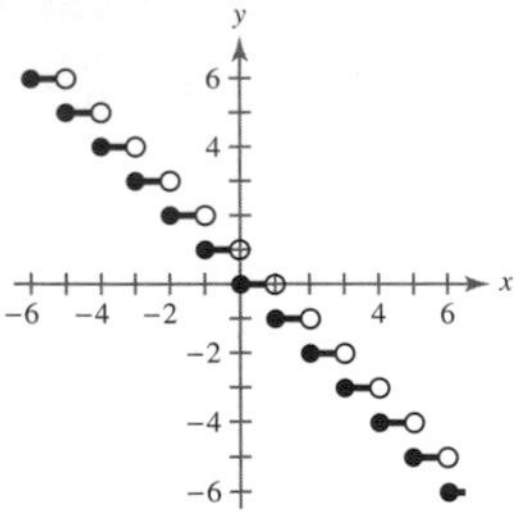

17. Reflection in the x-axis, horizontal shift, and vertical shift of $y = \sqrt{x}$

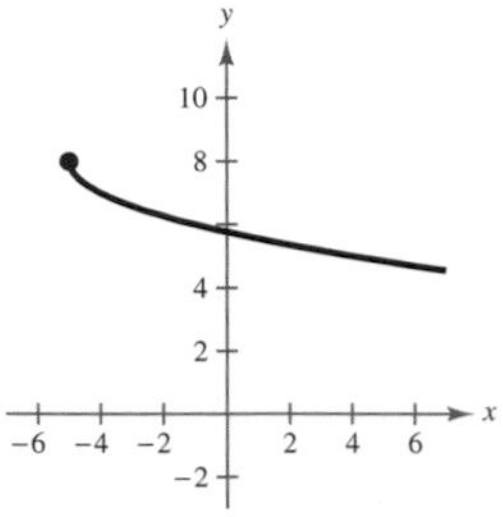

18. (a) $2x^2 - 4x - 2$ (b) $4x^2 + 4x - 12$
(c) $-3x^4 - 12x^3 + 22x^2 + 28x - 35$
(d) $\dfrac{3x^2 - 7}{-x^2 - 4x + 5}, \quad x \neq -5, 1$
(e) $3x^4 + 24x^3 + 18x^2 - 120x + 68$
(f) $-9x^4 + 30x^2 - 16$

19. (a) $\dfrac{1 + 2x^{3/2}}{x}, \quad x > 0$ (b) $\dfrac{1 - 2x^{3/2}}{x}, \quad x > 0$
(c) $\dfrac{2\sqrt{x}}{x}, \quad x > 0$ (d) $\dfrac{1}{2x^{3/2}}, \quad x > 0$
(e) $\dfrac{\sqrt{x}}{2x}, \quad x > 0$ (f) $\dfrac{2\sqrt{x}}{x}, \quad x > 0$

20. $f^{-1}(x) = \sqrt[3]{x - 8}$ **21.** No inverse

22. $f^{-1}(x) = \left(\frac{1}{3}x\right)^{2/3}, \ x \geq 0$ **23.** $v = 6\sqrt{s}$

24. $A = \dfrac{25}{6}xy$ **25.** $b = \dfrac{48}{a}$

Problem Solving *(page 125)*

1. (a) $W_1 = 2000 + 0.07S$ (b) $W_2 = 2300 + 0.05S$
(c)

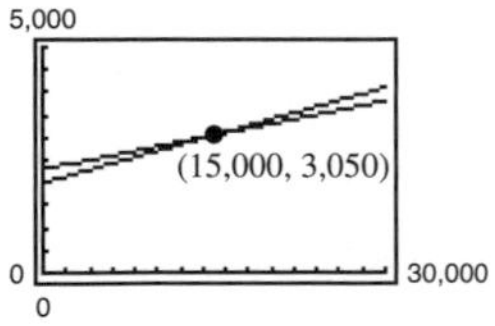

Both jobs pay the same monthly salary if sales equal \$15,000.

(d) No. Job 1 would pay \$3400 and job 2 would pay \$3300.

3. (a) The function will be even.
(b) The function will be odd.
(c) The function will be neither even nor odd.

5. $f(x) = a_{2n}x^{2n} + a_{2n-2}x^{2n-2} + \cdot \cdot \cdot + a_2x^2 + a_0$
$f(-x) = a_{2n}(-x)^{2n} + a_{2n-2}(-x)^{2n-2} + \cdot \cdot \cdot + a_2(-x)^2 + a_0$
$= f(x)$

7. (a) $81\frac{2}{3}$ hours (b) $25\frac{5}{7}$ miles per hour
(c) $y = \dfrac{-180}{7}x + 3400$

Domain: $0 \leq x \leq \dfrac{1190}{9}$

Range: $0 \leq y \leq 3400$

(d)

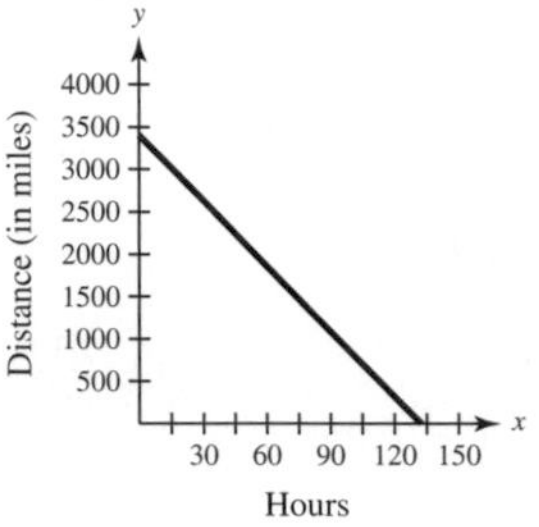

9. (a) $(f \circ g)(x) = 4x + 24$ (b) $(f \circ g)^{-1}(x) = \frac{1}{4}x - 6$
(c) $f^{-1}(x) = \frac{1}{4}x; g^{-1}(x) = x - 6$
(d) $(g^{-1} \circ f^{-1})(x) = \frac{1}{4}x - 6$
(e) $(f \circ g)(x) = 8x^3 + 1; (f \circ g)^{-1}(x) = \frac{1}{2}\sqrt[3]{x - 1};$
$f^{-1}(x) = \sqrt[3]{x - 1}; g^{-1}(x) = \frac{1}{2}x;$
$(g^{-1} \circ f^{-1})(x) = \frac{1}{2}\sqrt[3]{x - 1}$
(f) Answers will vary. (g) $(f \circ g)^{-1}(x) = (g^{-1} \circ f^{-1})(x)$

11. (a)

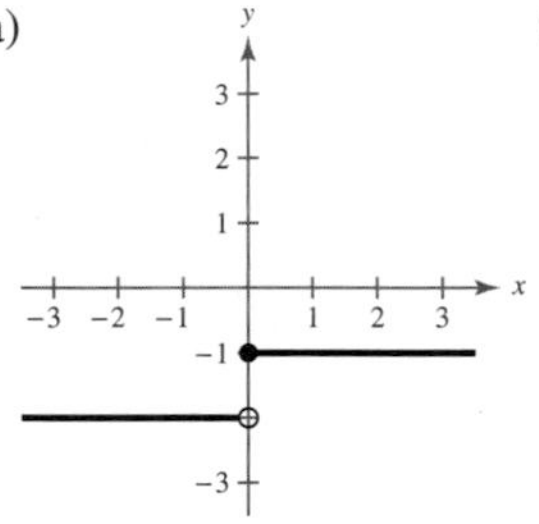

(b)

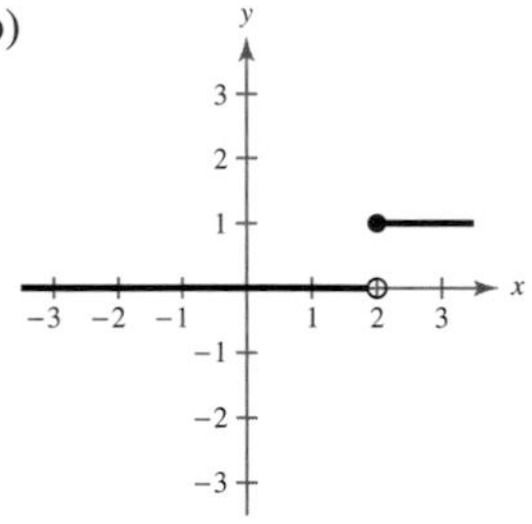

(c)

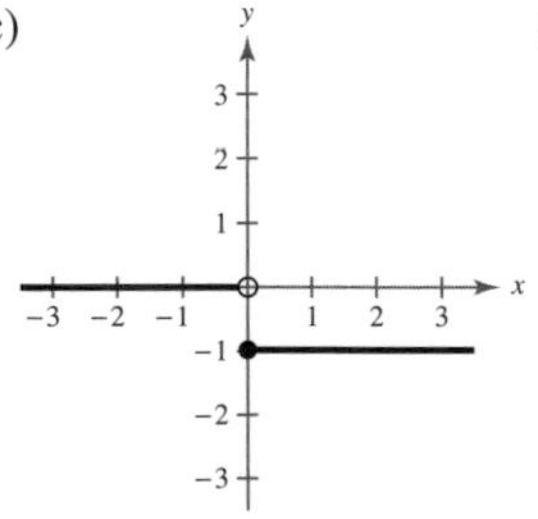

(d)

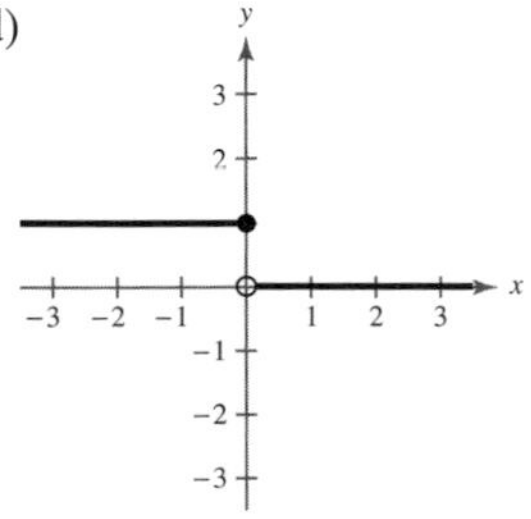

(e)

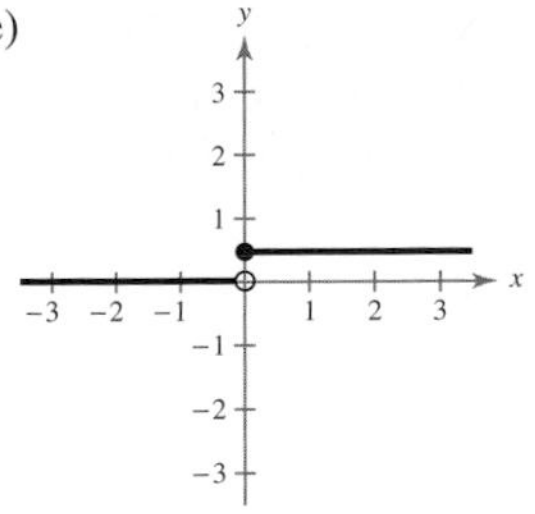

(f)

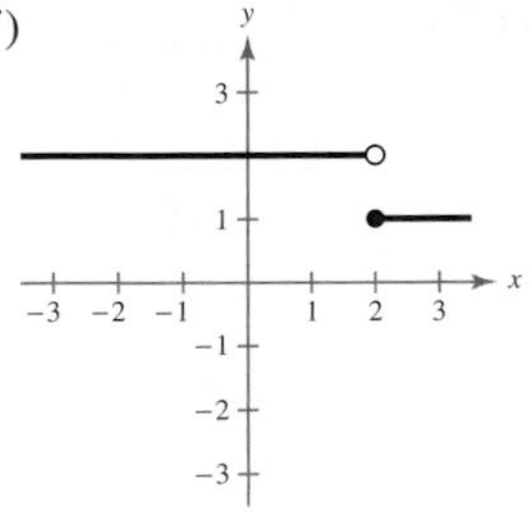

13. Proof

15. (a)

x	-4	-2	0	4
$f(f^{-1}(x))$	-4	-2	0	4

(b)

x	-3	-2	0	1
$(f+f^{-1})(x)$	5	1	-3	-5

(c)

x	-3	-2	0	1
$(f \circ f^{-1})(x)$	4	0	2	6

(d)

x	-4	-3	0	4
$\lvert f^{-1}(x) \rvert$	2	1	1	3

Chapter 2

Section 2.1 *(page 134)*

Vocabulary Check *(page 134)*

1. nonnegative integer; real **2.** quadratic; parabola
3. axis **4.** positive; minimum
5. negative; maximum

1. g **2.** c **3.** b **4.** h
5. f **6.** a **7.** e **8.** d

9. (a)

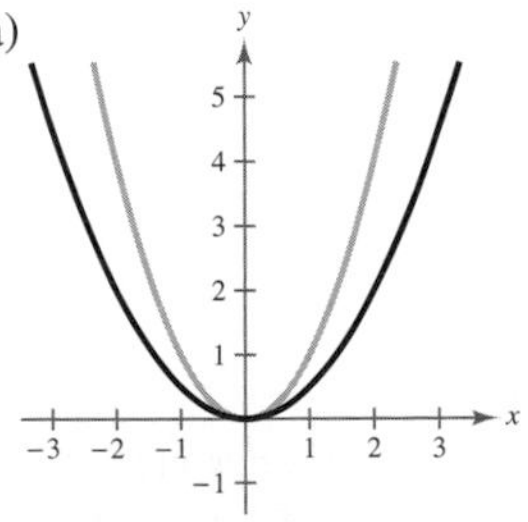

Vertical shrink

(b)

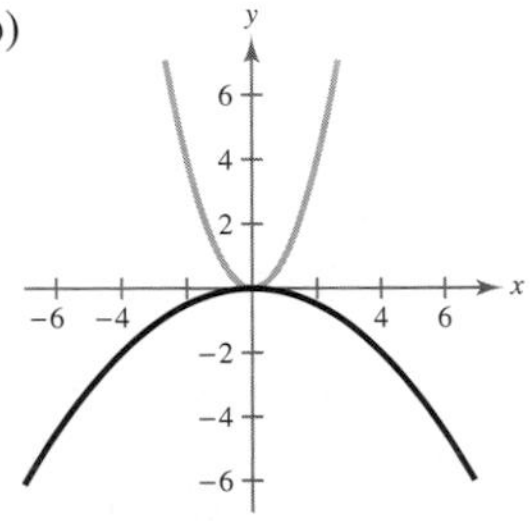

Vertical shrink and reflection in the x-axis

(c)

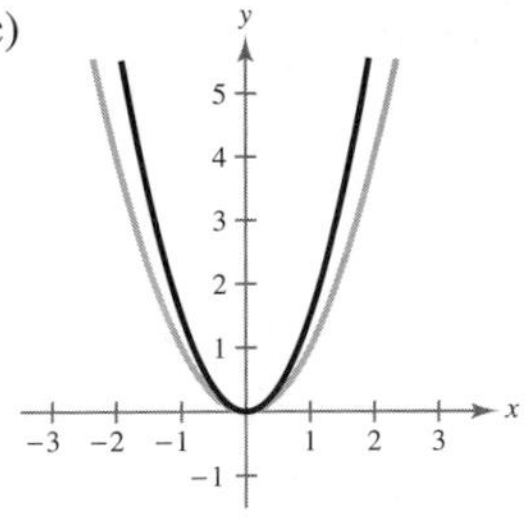

Vertical stretch

(d)

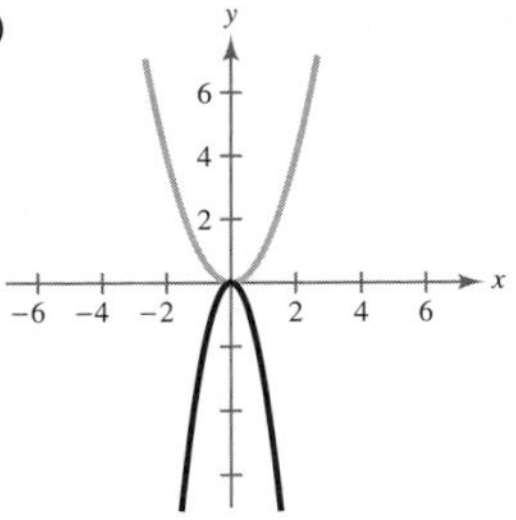

Vertical stretch and reflection in the x-axis

11. (a)

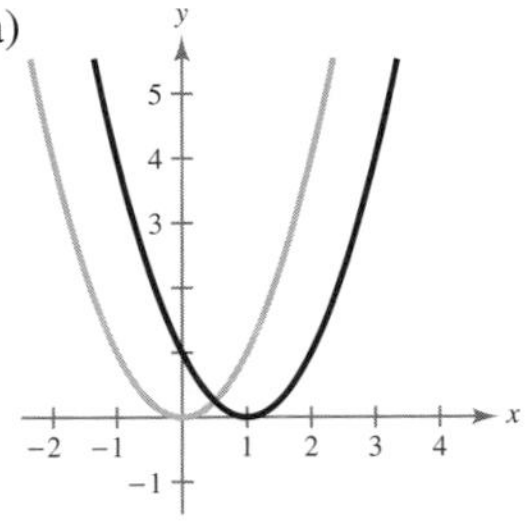

Horizontal shift

(b)

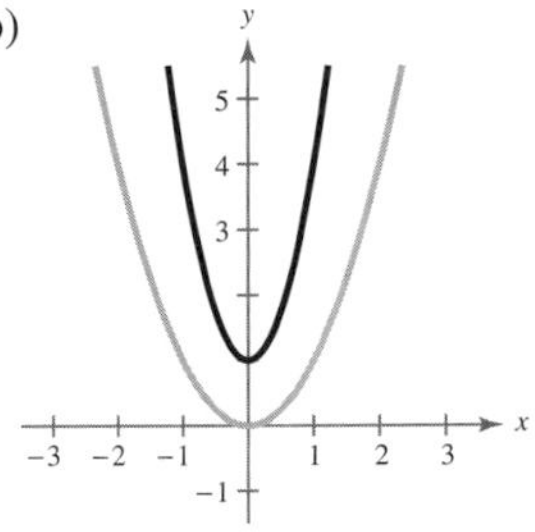

Horizontal shrink and vertical shift

(c)

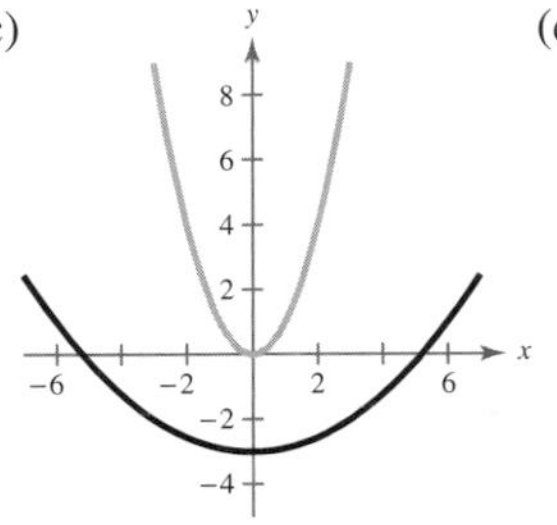

Horizontal stretch and vertical shift

(d)

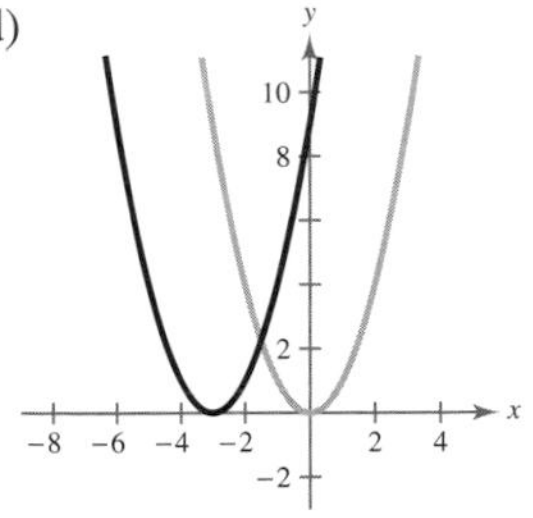

Horizontal shift

13.

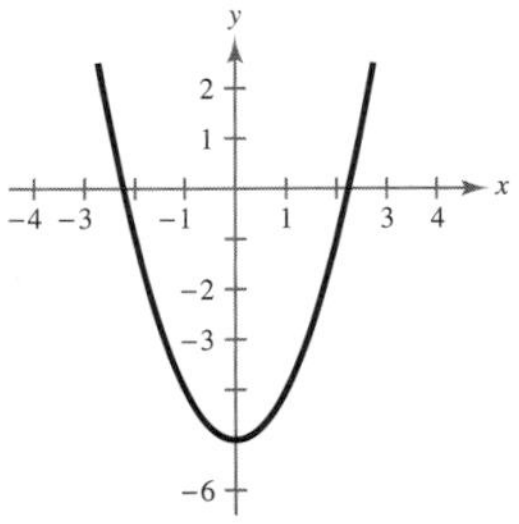

Vertex: $(0, -5)$
Axis of symmetry: y-axis
x-intercepts: $(\pm\sqrt{5}, 0)$

15.

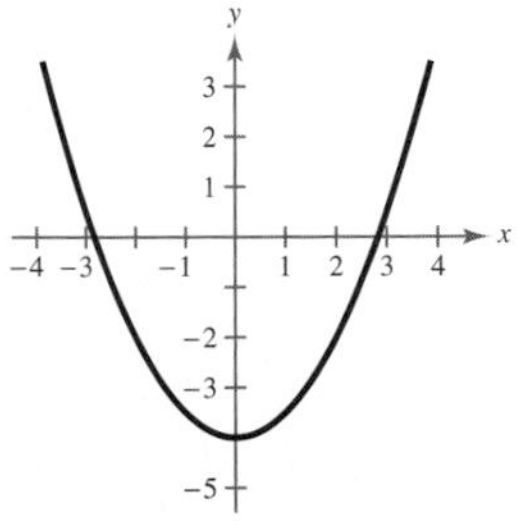

Vertex: $(0, -4)$
Axis of symmetry: y-axis
x-intercepts: $(\pm 2\sqrt{2}, 0)$

CHAPTER 2

17.

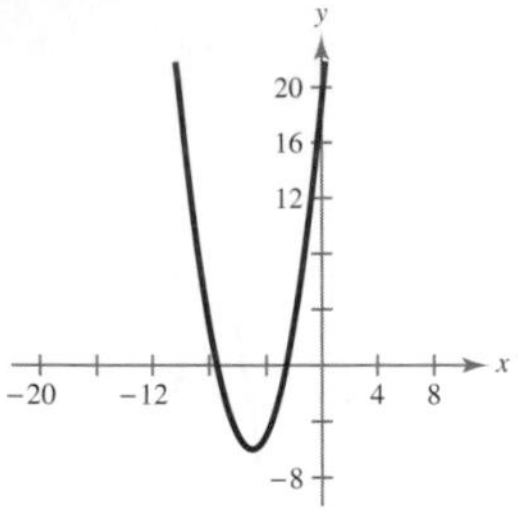

Vertex: $(-5, -6)$
Axis of symmetry: $x = -5$
x-intercepts: $(-5 \pm \sqrt{6}, 0)$

19.

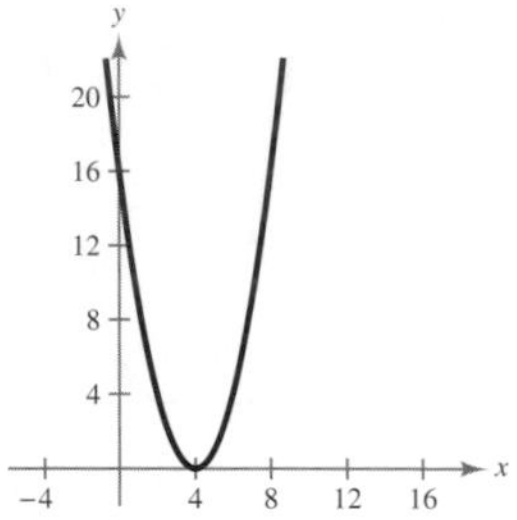

Vertex: $(4, 0)$
Axis of symmetry: $x = 4$
x-intercept: $(4, 0)$

21.

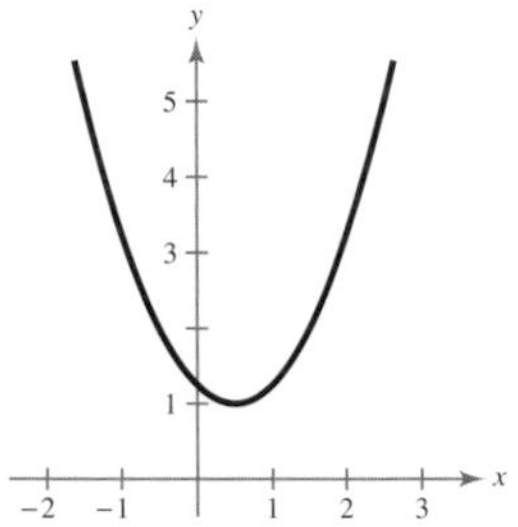

Vertex: $\left(\frac{1}{2}, 1\right)$
Axis of symmetry: $x = \frac{1}{2}$
No x-intercept

23.

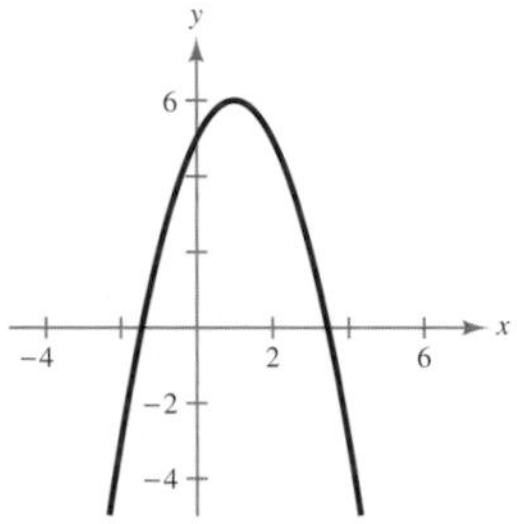

Vertex: $(1, 6)$
Axis of symmetry: $x = 1$
x-intercepts: $(1 \pm \sqrt{6}, 0)$

25.

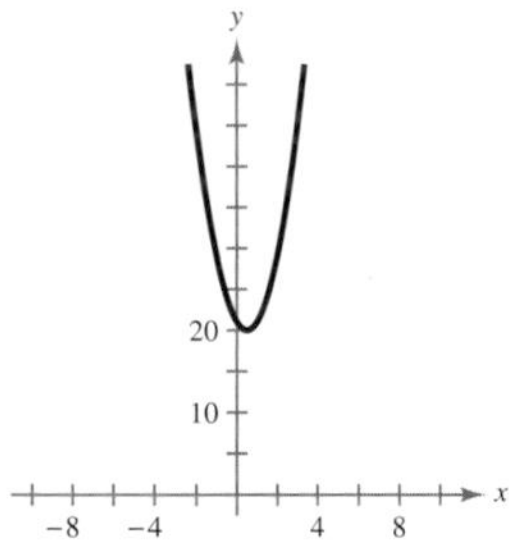

Vertex: $\left(\frac{1}{2}, 20\right)$
Axis of symmetry: $x = \frac{1}{2}$
No x-intercept

27.

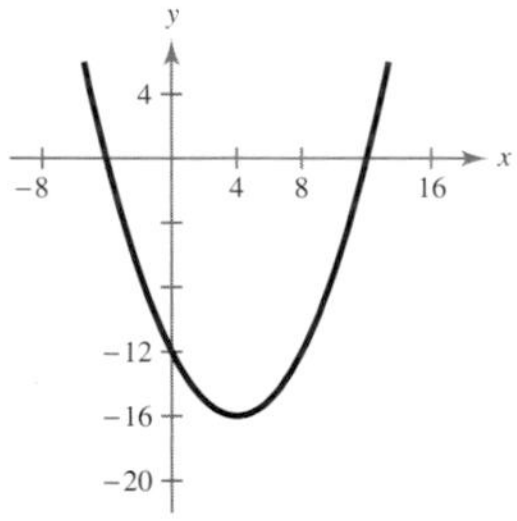

Vertex: $(4, -16)$
Axis of symmetry: $x = 4$
x-intercepts: $(-4, 0), (12, 0)$

29.

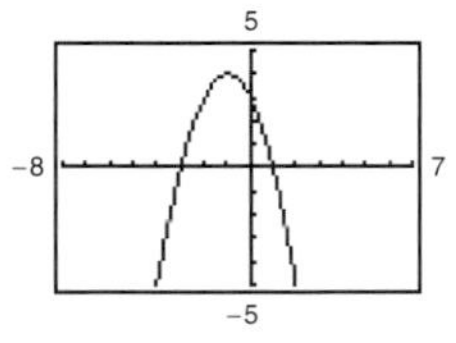

Vertex: $(-1, 4)$
Axis of symmetry: $x = -1$
x-intercepts: $(1, 0), (-3, 0)$

31.

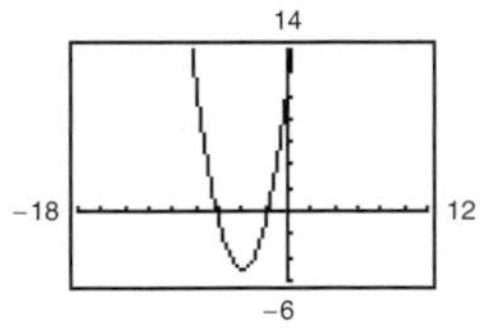

Vertex: $(-4, -5)$
Axis of symmetry: $x = -4$
x-intercepts: $(-4 \pm \sqrt{5}, 0)$

33.

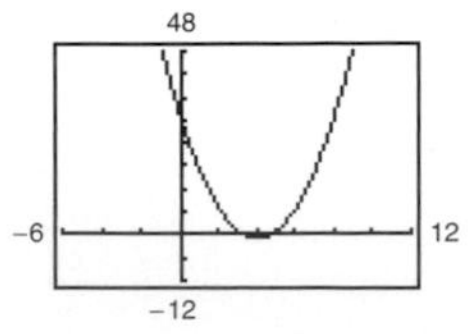

Vertex: $(4, -1)$
Axis of symmetry: $x = 4$
x-intercepts: $\left(4 \pm \frac{1}{2}\sqrt{2}, 0\right)$

35.

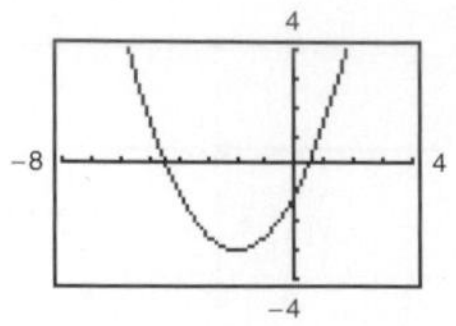

Vertex: $(-2, -3)$
Axis of symmetry: $x = -2$
x-intercepts: $(-2 \pm \sqrt{6}, 0)$

37. $y = (x - 1)^2$ **39.** $y = -(x + 1)^2 + 4$
41. $y = -2(x + 2)^2 + 2$ **43.** $f(x) = (x + 2)^2 + 5$
45. $f(x) = -\frac{1}{2}(x - 3)^2 + 4$ **47.** $f(x) = \frac{3}{4}(x - 5)^2 + 12$
49. $f(x) = -\frac{24}{49}\left(x + \frac{1}{4}\right)^2 + \frac{3}{2}$ **51.** $f(x) = -\frac{16}{3}\left(x + \frac{5}{2}\right)^2$
53. $(\pm 4, 0)$ **55.** $(5, 0), (-1, 0)$

57.

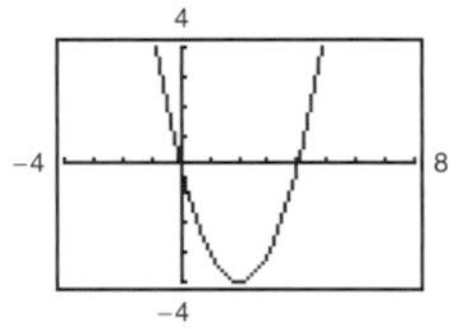

$(0, 0), (4, 0)$

59.

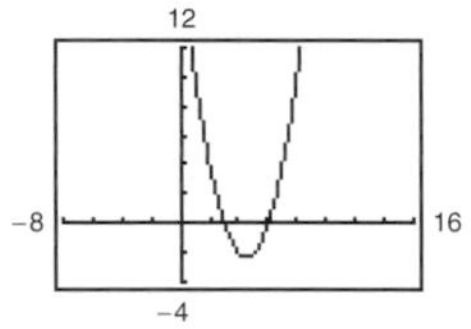

$(3, 0), (6, 0)$

61.

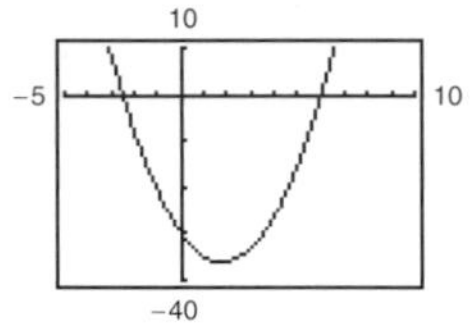

$\left(-\frac{5}{2}, 0\right), (6, 0)$

63.

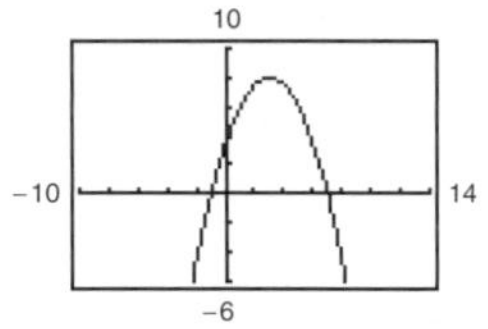

$(7, 0), (-1, 0)$

65. $f(x) = x^2 - 2x - 3$
$g(x) = -x^2 + 2x + 3$
67. $f(x) = x^2 - 10x$
$g(x) = -x^2 + 10x$
69. $f(x) = 2x^2 + 7x + 3$
$g(x) = -2x^2 - 7x - 3$
71. 55, 55 **73.** 12, 6
75. (a) $A = \dfrac{8x(50 - x)}{3}$

(b)

x	5	10	15	20	25	30
A	600	1067	1400	1600	1667	1600

$x = 25$ feet, $y = 33\frac{1}{3}$ feet

(c)

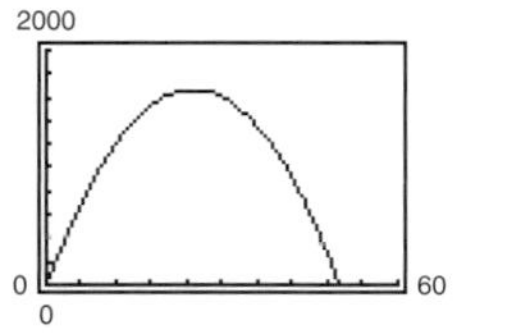

$x = 25$ feet, $y = 33\frac{1}{3}$ feet

(d) $A = -\frac{8}{3}(x - 25)^2 + \frac{5000}{3}$ (e) They are identical.

77. 16 feet **79.** 20 fixtures **81.** 350,000 units
83. (a) \$14,000,000; \$14,375,000; \$13,500,000
(b) 24; \$14,400
85. (a)

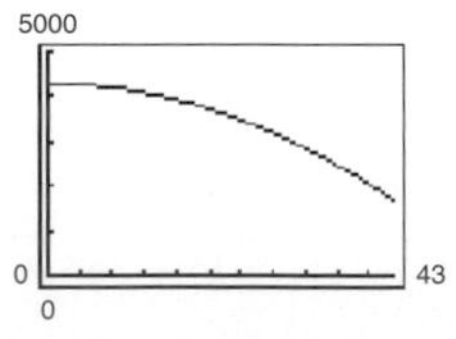

(b) 4299; answers will vary.
(c) 8879; 24

87. (a)

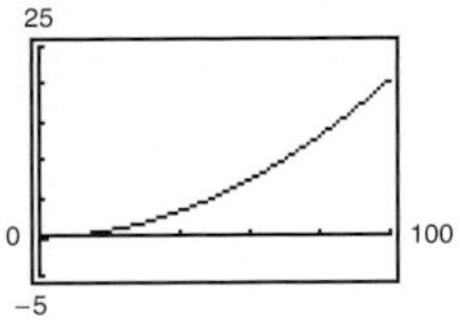

(b) 69.6 miles per hour

89. True. The equation has no real solutions, so the graph has no x-intercepts.

91. $f(x) = a\left(x + \frac{b}{2a}\right)^2 + \frac{4ac - b^2}{4a}$

93. Yes. A graph of a quadratic equation whose vertex is on the x-axis has only one x-intercept.

95. $y = -\frac{1}{3}x + \frac{5}{3}$ **97.** $y = \frac{5}{4}x + 3$ **99.** 27

101. $-\frac{1408}{49}$ **103.** 109 **105.** Answers will vary.

Section 2.2 *(page 148)*

Vocabulary Check *(page 148)*

1. continuous **2.** Leading Coefficient Test
3. n; $n - 1$ **4.** (a) solution; (b) $(x - a)$; (c) x-intercept
5. touches; crosses **6.** standard
7. Intermediate Value

1. c **2.** g **3.** h **4.** f
5. a **6.** e **7.** d **8.** b

9. (a)

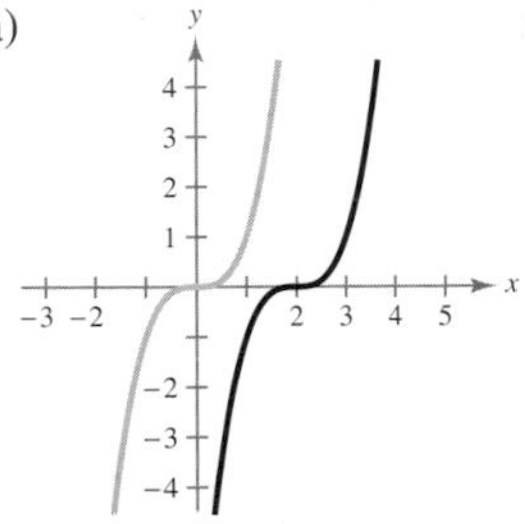

(b)

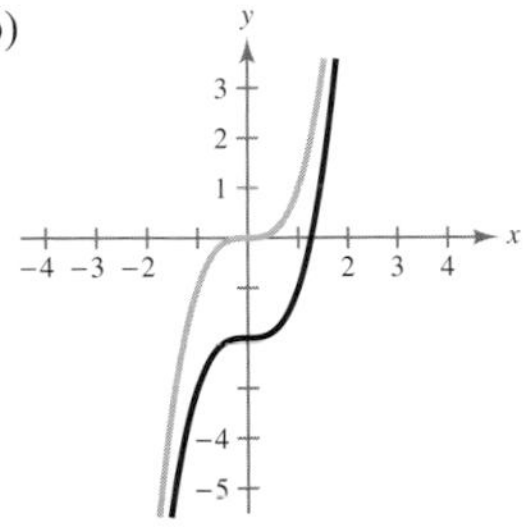

(c)

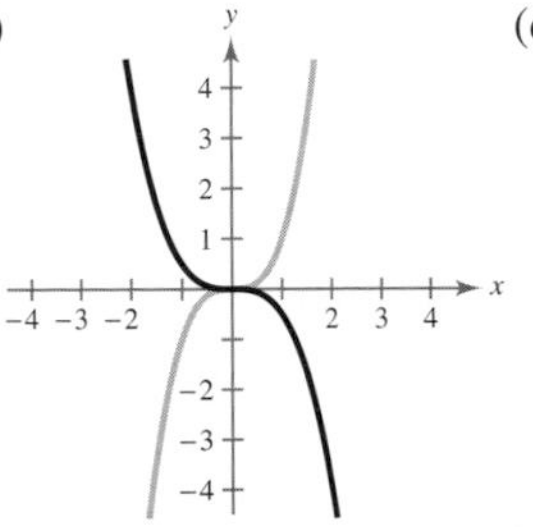

(d)

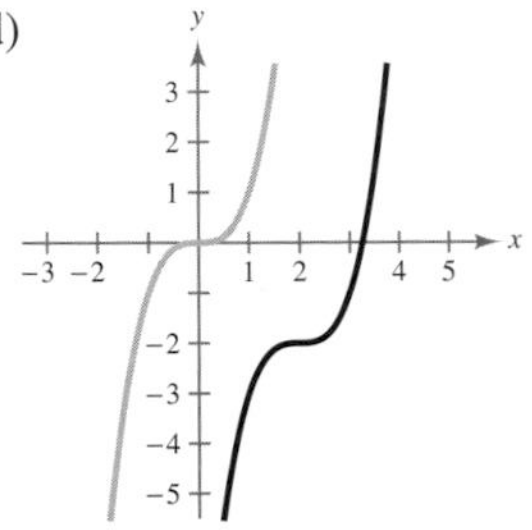

11. (a)

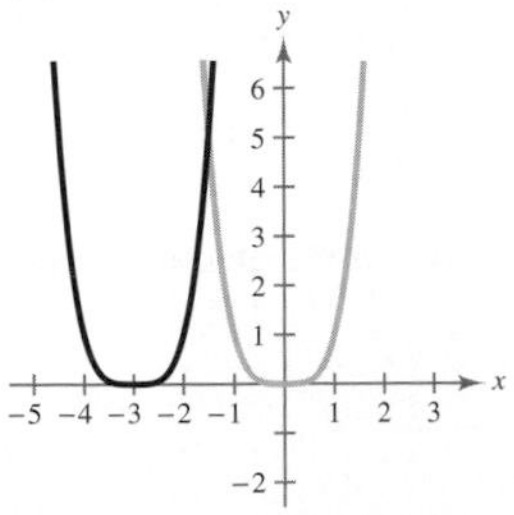

(b)

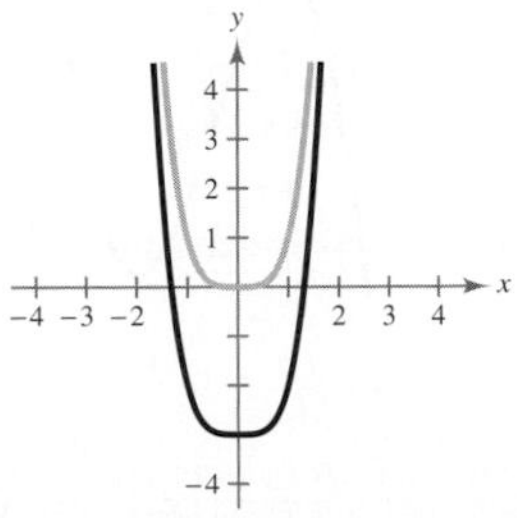

(c)

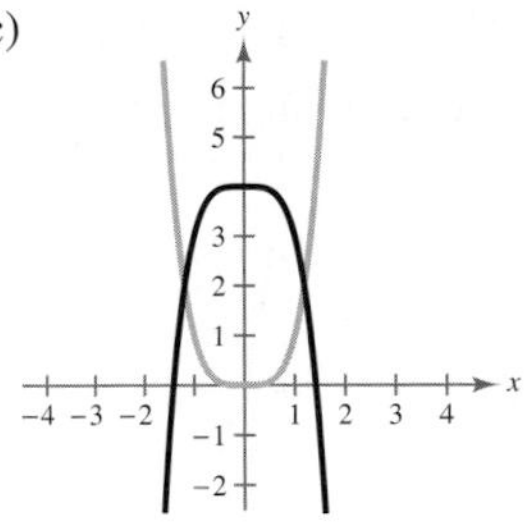

(d)

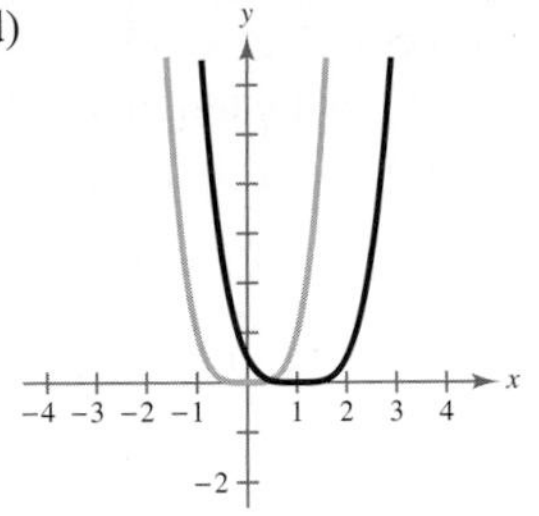

(e)

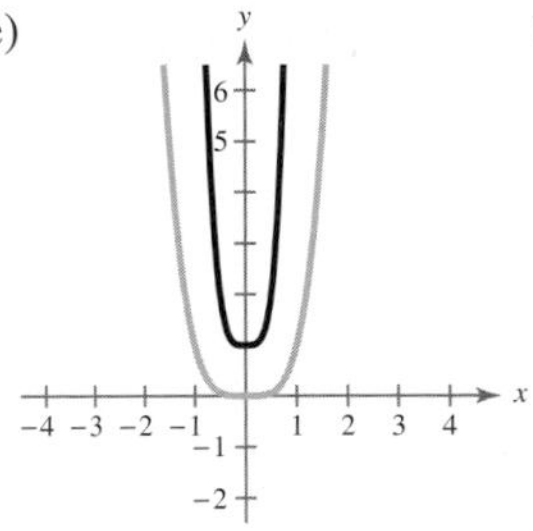

(f)

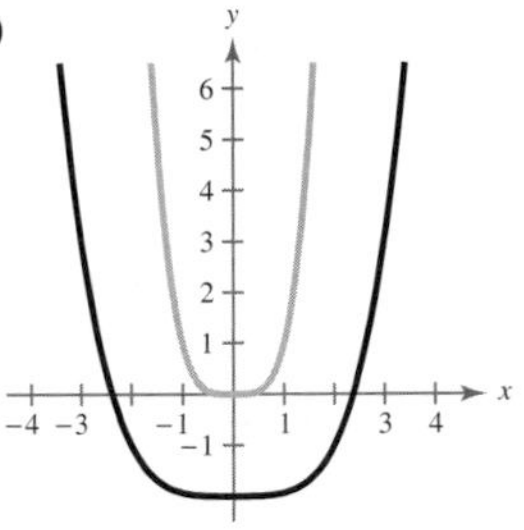

13. Falls to the left, rises to the right
15. Falls to the left, falls to the right
17. Rises to the left, falls to the right
19. Rises to the left, falls to the right
21. Falls to the left, falls to the right

23.

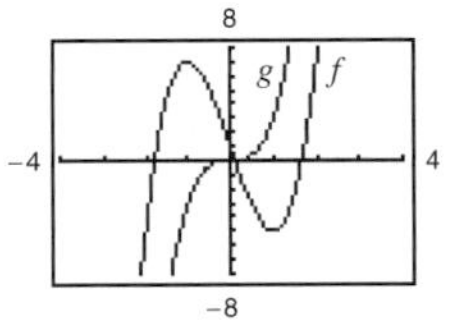

25.

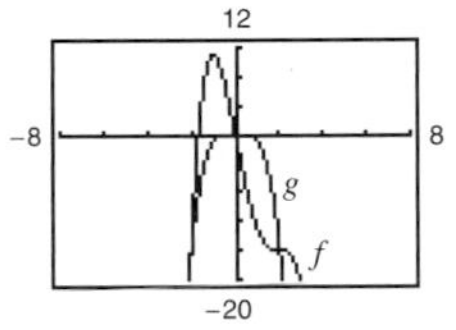

27. (a) ± 5
(b) odd multiplicity; number of turning points: 1
(c)

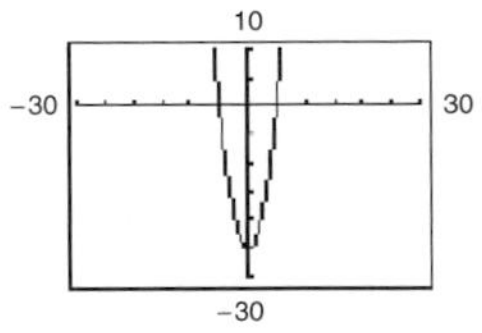

29. (a) 3
(b) even multiplicity; number of turning points: 1
(c)

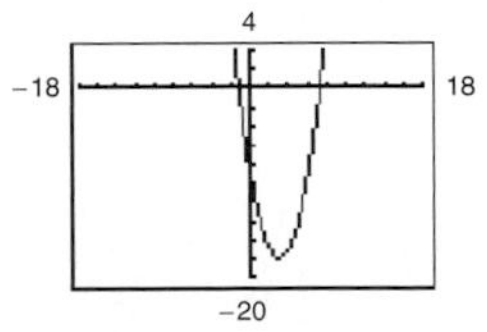

31. (a) $-2, 1$
(b) odd multiplicity; number of turning points: 1
(c)

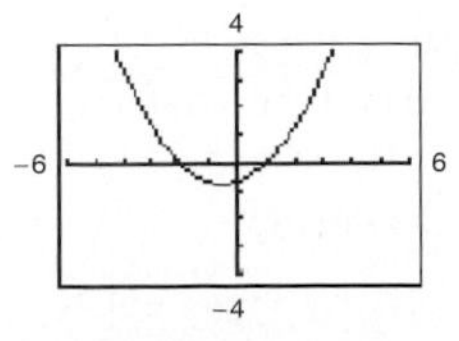

33. (a) $0, 2 \pm \sqrt{3}$
(b) odd multiplicity; number of turning points: 2
(c)
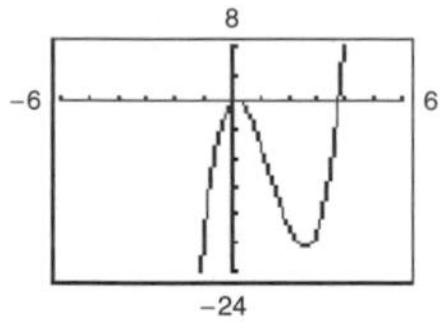

35. (a) 0, 2
(b) 0, odd multiplicity; 2, even multiplicity; number of turning points: 2
(c)
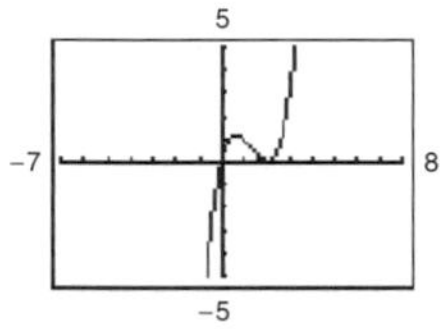

37. (a) $0, \pm\sqrt{3}$
(b) 0, odd multiplicity; $\pm\sqrt{3}$, even multiplicity; number of turning points: 4
(c)
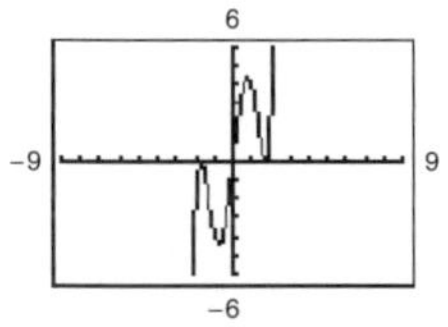

39. (a) No real zeros
(b) number of turning points: 1
(c)
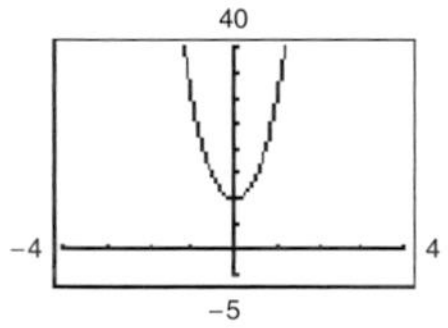

41. (a) $\pm 2, -3$
(b) odd multiplicity; number of turning points: 2
(c)
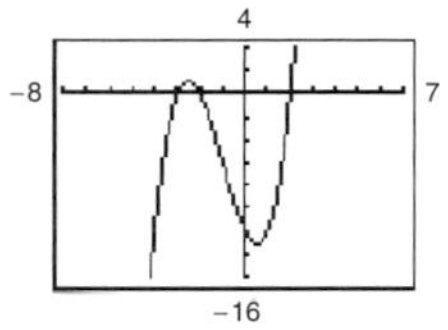

43. (a)
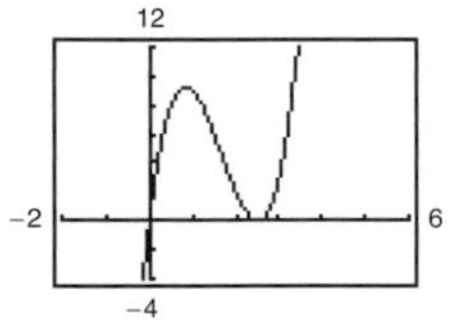

(b) x-intercepts: $(0, 0), \left(\frac{5}{2}, 0\right)$ (c) $x = 0, \frac{5}{2}$
(d) The answers in part (c) match the x-intercepts.

45. (a)
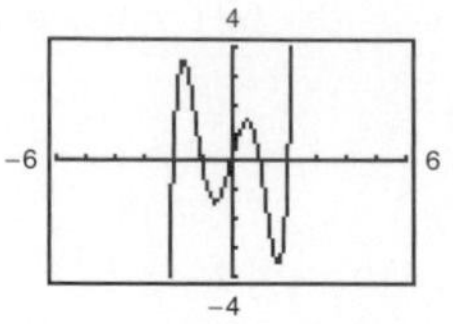

(b) x-intercepts: $(0, 0), (\pm 1, 0), (\pm 2, 0)$
(c) $x = 0, 1, -1, 2, -2$
(d) The answers in part (c) match the x-intercepts.

47. $f(x) = x^2 - 10x$ **49.** $f(x) = x^2 + 4x - 12$
51. $f(x) = x^3 + 5x^2 + 6x$
53. $f(x) = x^4 - 4x^3 - 9x^2 + 36x$
55. $f(x) = x^2 - 2x - 2$ **57.** $f(x) = x^2 + 4x + 4$
59. $f(x) = x^3 + 2x^2 - 3x$ **61.** $f(x) = x^3 - 3x$
63. $f(x) = x^4 + x^3 - 15x^2 + 23x - 10$
65. $f(x) = x^5 + 16x^4 + 96x^3 + 256x^2 + 256x$

67. (a) Falls to the left, rises to the right
(b) $0, \pm 3$ (c) Answers will vary.
(d)
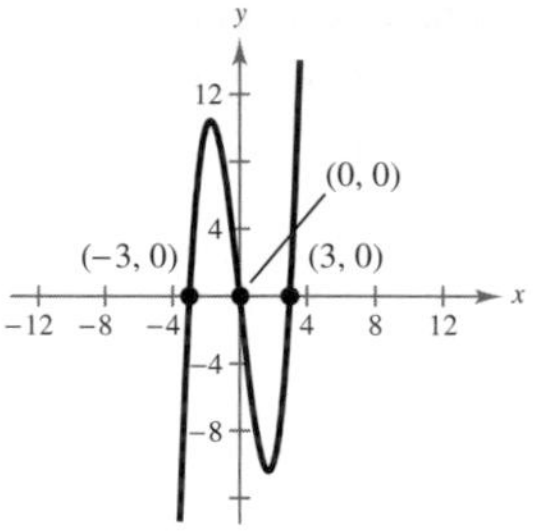

69. (a) Rises to the left, rises to the right
(b) No zeros (c) Answers will vary.
(d)
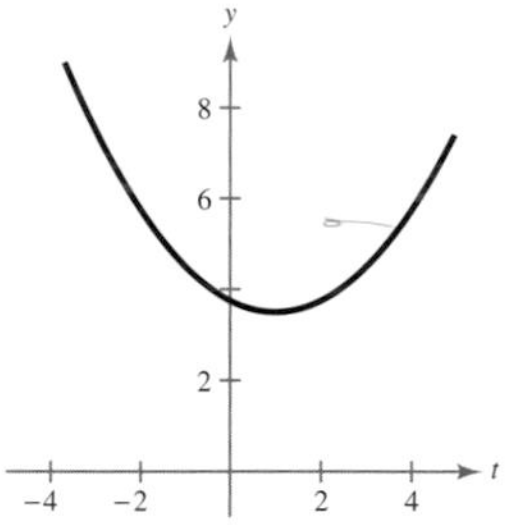

71. (a) Falls to the left, rises to the right
(b) 0, 3 (c) Answers will vary.
(d)
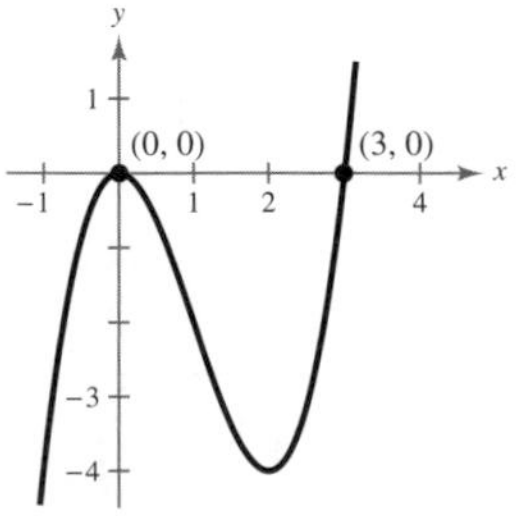

73. (a) Falls to the left, rises to the right
(b) 0, 2, 3 (c) Answers will vary.
(d)
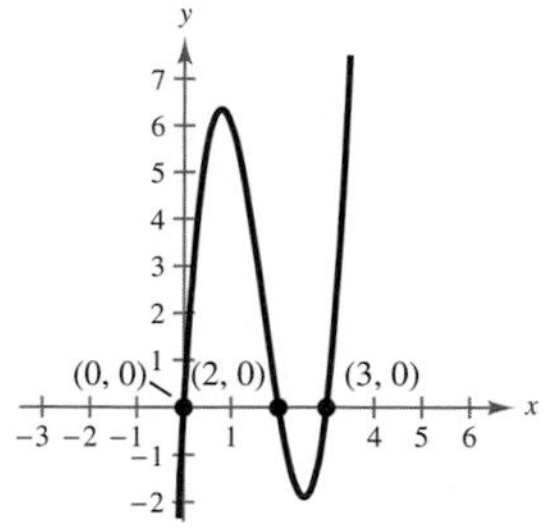

75. (a) Rises to the left, falls to the right
(b) $-5, 0$ (c) Answers will vary.
(d)
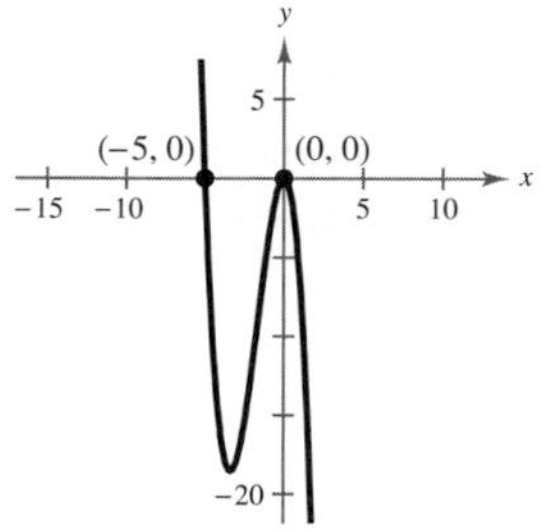

77. (a) Falls to the left, rises to the right
(b) 0, 4 (c) Answers will vary.
(d)
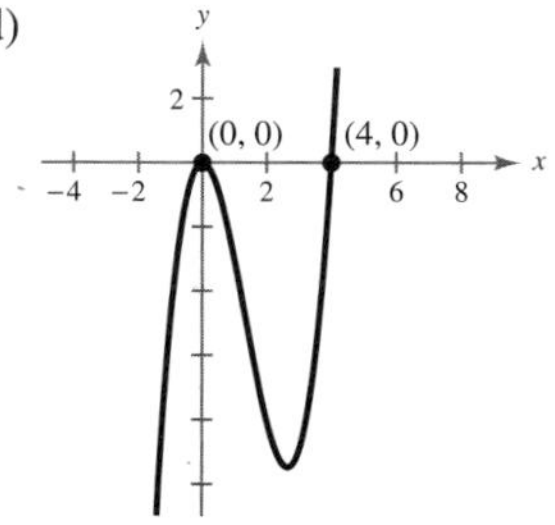

79. (a) Falls to the left, falls to the right
(b) ± 2 (c) Answers will vary.
(d)
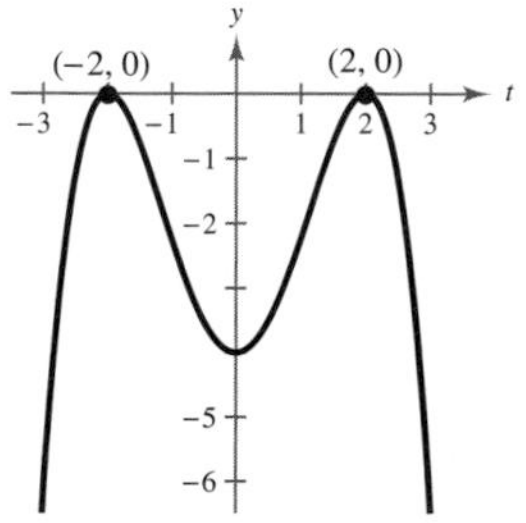

81.
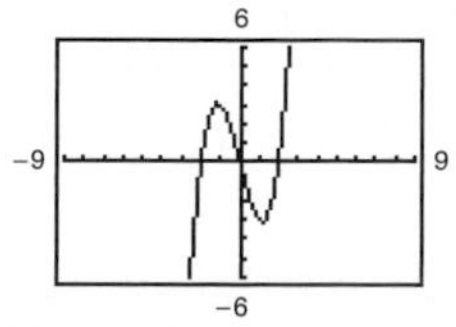

Zeros: $0, \pm 2$,
odd multiplicity

83.
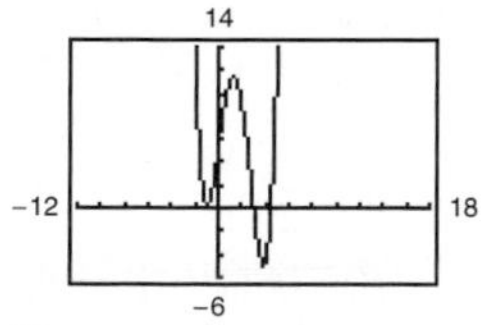

Zeros: -1,
even multiplicity;
$3, \frac{9}{2}$, odd multiplicity

85. $[-1, 0], [1, 2], [2, 3]$; $\approx -0.879, 1.347, 2.532$

87. $[-2, -1], [0, 1]$; $\approx -1.585, 0.779$

89. (a) $V = l \times w \times h$
$= (36 - 2x)(36 - 2x)x$
$= x(36 - 2x)^2$

(b) Domain: $0 < x < 18$

(c)

x	1	2	3	4	5	6	7
V	1156	2048	2700	3136	3380	3456	3388

6 inches × 24 inches × 24 inches

(d)
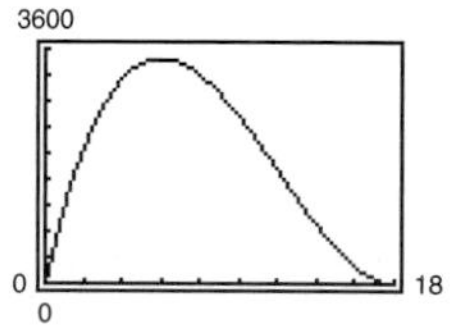

$x = 6$

91. (a) $A = -2x^2 + 12x$ (b) $V = -384x^2 + 2304x$
(c) 0 inches $< x <$ 6 inches
(d)
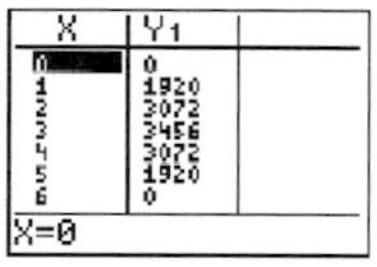

When $x = 3$, the volume is maximum at $V = 3456$; dimensions of gutter are 3 inches × 6 inches × 3 inches.

(e)
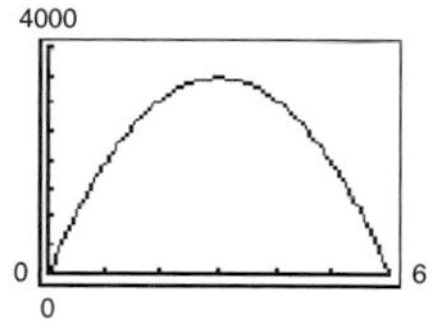

The maximum value is the same.
(f) No. Answers will vary.

93.
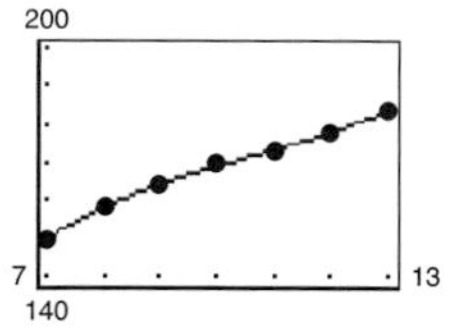

The model is a good fit.

95. Region 1: 259,370
Region 2: 223,470
Answers will vary.

97. (a)
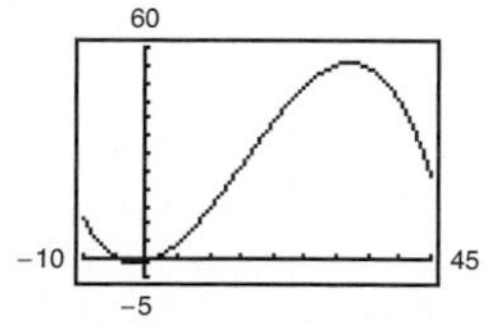

(b) $t \approx 15$ (c) Vertex: (15.22, 2.54)
(d) The results are approximately equal.

99. False. A fifth-degree polynomial can have at most four turning points.

101. True. The degree of the function is odd and its leading coefficient is negative, so the graph rises to the left and falls to the right.

103.

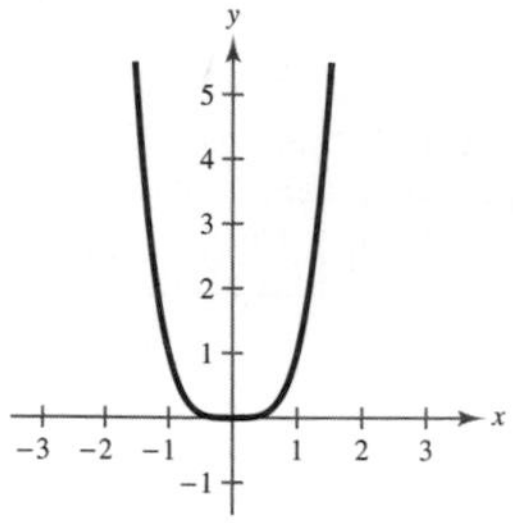

(a) Vertical shift of two units; Even
(b) Horizontal shift of two units; Neither even nor odd
(c) Reflection in the y-axis; Even
(d) Reflection in the x-axis; Even
(e) Horizontal stretch; Even
(f) Vertical shrink; Even
(g) $g(x) = x^3$; Neither odd nor even
(h) $g(x) = x^{16}$; Even

105. $(5x - 8)(x + 3)$ **107.** $x^2(4x + 5)(x - 3)$

109. $-\frac{7}{2}, 4$ **111.** $-\frac{5}{4}, \frac{1}{3}$ **113.** $1 \pm \sqrt{22}$

115. $\dfrac{-5 \pm \sqrt{185}}{4}$

117. Horizontal translation four units to the left of $y = x^2$

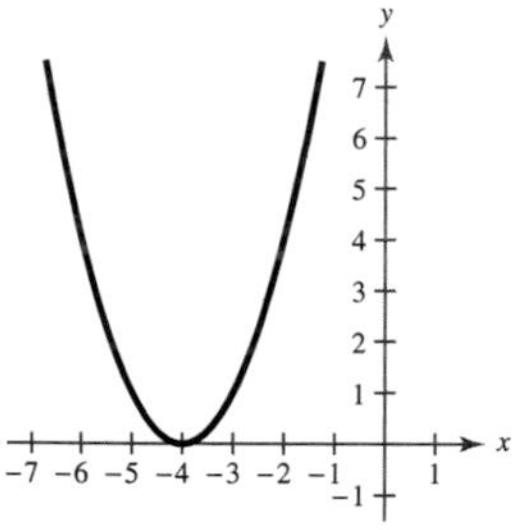

119. Horizontal translation one unit left and vertical translation five units down of $y = \sqrt{x}$

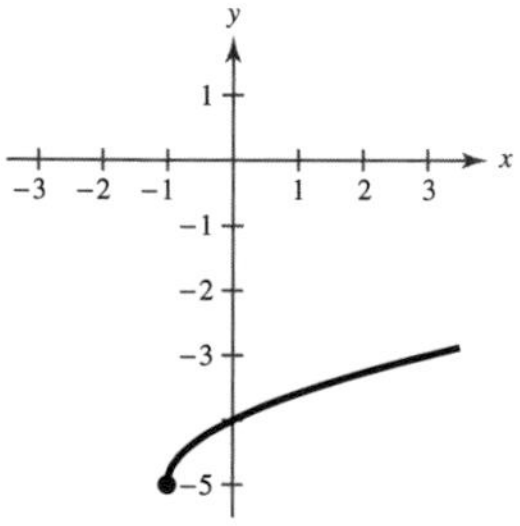

121. Vertical stretch by a factor of 2 and vertical translation nine units up of $y = [\![x]\!]$

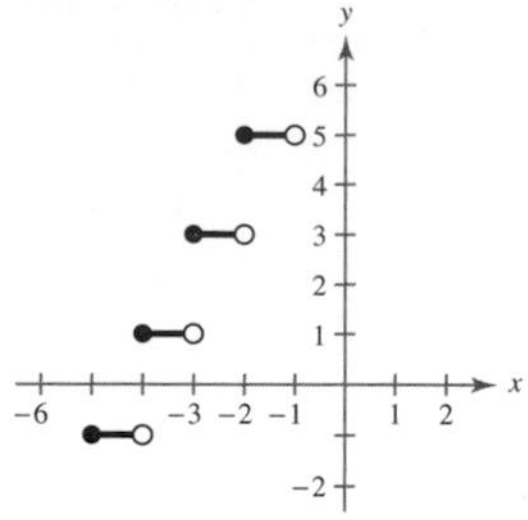

Section 2.3 *(page 159)*

Vocabulary Check *(page 159)*

1. dividend; divisor; quotient; remainder
2. improper; proper **3.** synthetic division
4. factor **5.** remainder

1. Answers will vary.

3.

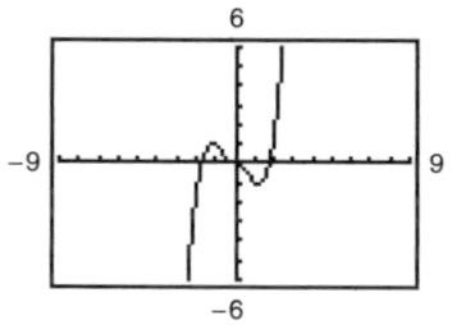

5. $2x + 4$

7. $x^2 - 3x + 1$ **9.** $x^3 + 3x^2 - 1$ **11.** $7 - \dfrac{11}{x + 2}$

13. $3x + 5 - \dfrac{2x - 3}{2x^2 + 1}$ **15.** $x^2 + 2x + 4 + \dfrac{2x - 11}{x^2 - 2x + 3}$

17. $x + 3 + \dfrac{6x^2 - 8x + 3}{(x - 1)^3}$ **19.** $3x^2 - 2x + 5$

21. $4x^2 - 9$ **23.** $-x^2 + 10x - 25$

25. $5x^2 + 14x + 56 + \dfrac{232}{x - 4}$

27. $10x^3 + 10x^2 + 60x + 360 + \dfrac{1360}{x - 6}$

29. $x^2 - 8x + 64$

31. $-3x^3 - 6x^2 - 12x - 24 - \dfrac{48}{x - 2}$

33. $-x^3 - 6x^2 - 36x - 36 - \dfrac{216}{x - 6}$

35. $4x^2 + 14x - 30$

37. $f(x) = (x - 4)(x^2 + 3x - 2) + 3,\ f(4) = 3$

39. $f(x) = \left(x + \frac{2}{3}\right)(15x^3 - 6x + 4) + \frac{34}{3},\ f\left(-\frac{2}{3}\right) = \frac{34}{3}$

41. $f(x) = \left(x - \sqrt{2}\right)\left[x^2 + \left(3 + \sqrt{2}\right)x + 3\sqrt{2}\right] - 8,$
$f\left(\sqrt{2}\right) = -8$

43. $f(x) = \left(x - 1 + \sqrt{3}\right)\left[-4x^2 + \left(2 + 4\sqrt{3}\right)x + \left(2 + 2\sqrt{3}\right)\right],$
$f\left(1 - \sqrt{3}\right) = 0$

45. (a) 1 (b) 4 (c) 4 (d) 1954

47. (a) 97 (b) $-\frac{5}{3}$ (c) 17 (d) -199

49. $(x - 2)(x + 3)(x - 1)$; Zeros: $2, -3, 1$

51. $(2x - 1)(x - 5)(x - 2)$; Zeros: $\frac{1}{2}, 5, 2$

53. $(x + \sqrt{3})(x - \sqrt{3})(x + 2)$; Zeros: $-\sqrt{3}, \sqrt{3}, -2$

55. $(x - 1)(x - 1 - \sqrt{3})(x - 1 + \sqrt{3})$;
Zeros: $1, 1 + \sqrt{3}, 1 - \sqrt{3}$

57. (a) Answers will vary. (b) $2x - 1$
(c) $f(x) = (2x - 1)(x + 2)(x - 1)$ (d) $\frac{1}{2}, -2, 1$
(e)

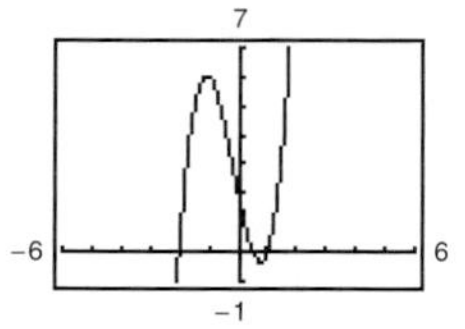

59. (a) Answers will vary. (b) $(x - 1), (x - 2)$
(c) $f(x) = (x - 1)(x - 2)(x - 5)(x + 4)$
(d) $1, 2, 5, -4$
(e)

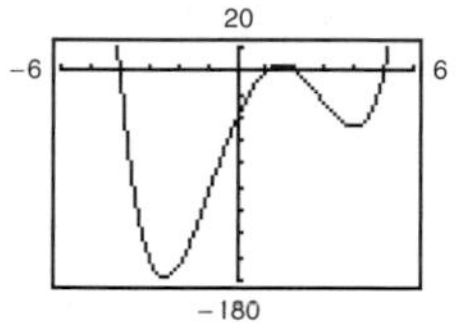

61. (a) Answers will vary. (b) $x + 7$
(c) $f(x) = (x + 7)(2x + 1)(3x - 2)$
(d) $-7, -\frac{1}{2}, \frac{2}{3}$
(e)

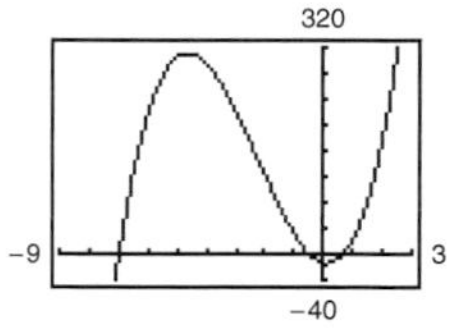

63. (a) Answers will vary. (b) $(x - \sqrt{5})$
(c) $f(x) = (x - \sqrt{5})(x + \sqrt{5})(2x - 1)$ (d) $\pm\sqrt{5}, \frac{1}{2}$
(e)

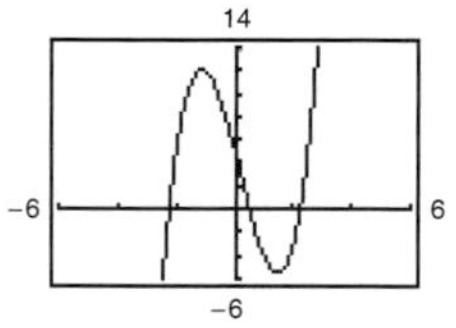

65. (a) Zeros are 2 and $\approx \pm 2.236$.
(b) $x = 2$ (c) $f(x) = (x - 2)(x - \sqrt{5})(x + \sqrt{5})$

67. (a) Zeros are -2, ≈ 0.268, and ≈ 3.732.
(b) $x = -2$
(c) $h(t) = (t + 2)[t - (2 + \sqrt{3})][t - (2 - \sqrt{3})]$

69. $2x^2 - x - 1, \ x \neq \frac{3}{2}$ **71.** $x^2 + 3x, \ x \neq -2, -1$

73. (a) and (b)

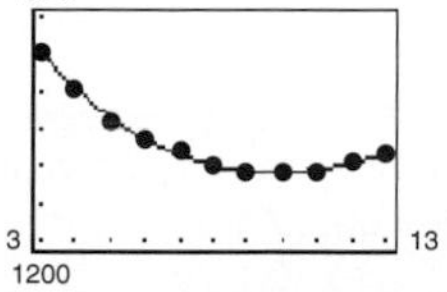

$M = -0.242x^3 + 12.43x^2 - 173.4x + 2118$

(c)

t	3	4	5	6	7	8
$M(t)$	1703	1608	1531	1473	1430	1402

t	9	10	11	12	13
$M(t)$	1388	1385	1392	1409	1433

Answers will vary.

(d) 1614 thousand. No, because the model will approach negative infinity quickly.

75. False. $-\frac{4}{7}$ is a zero of f.

77. True. The degree of the numerator is greater than the degree of the denominator.

79. $x^{2n} + 6x^n + 9$ **81.** The remainder is 0.

83. $c = -210$ **85.** 0; $x + 3$ is a factor of f.

87. $\pm\dfrac{5}{3}$ **89.** $-\dfrac{7}{5}, 2$ **91.** $\dfrac{-3 \pm \sqrt{3}}{2}$

93. $f(x) = x^3 - 7x^2 + 12x$

95. $f(x) = x^3 + x^2 - 7x - 3$

Section 2.4 *(page 167)*

Vocabulary Check *(page 167)*

1. (a) iii (b) i (c) ii **2.** $\sqrt{-1}; -1$
3. complex numbers; $a + bi$ **4.** principal square
5. complex conjugates

1. $a = -10, \ b = 6$ **3.** $a = 6, \ b = 5$ **5.** $4 + 3i$

7. $2 - 3\sqrt{3}i$ **9.** $5\sqrt{3}i$ **11.** 8

13. $-1 - 6i$ **15.** $0.3i$ **17.** $11 - i$ **19.** 4

21. $3 - 3\sqrt{2}i$ **23.** $-14 + 20i$ **25.** $\frac{1}{6} + \frac{7}{6}i$

27. $5 + i$ **29.** $12 + 30i$ **31.** 24 **33.** $-9 + 40i$

35. -10 **37.** $6 - 3i$, 45 **39.** $-1 + \sqrt{5}i$, 6

41. $-2\sqrt{5}i$, 20 **43.** $\sqrt{8}$, 8 **45.** $-5i$

47. $\frac{8}{41} + \frac{10}{41}i$ **49.** $\frac{4}{5} + \frac{3}{5}i$ **51.** $-5 - 6i$

53. $-\frac{120}{1681} - \frac{27}{1681}i$ **55.** $-\frac{1}{2} - \frac{5}{2}i$ **57.** $\frac{62}{949} + \frac{297}{949}i$

59. $-2\sqrt{3}$ **61.** -10

63. $(21 + 5\sqrt{2}) + (7\sqrt{5} - 3\sqrt{10})i$ **65.** $1 \pm i$

67. $-2 \pm \dfrac{1}{2}i$ **69.** $-\dfrac{5}{2}, -\dfrac{3}{2}$ **71.** $2 \pm \sqrt{2}i$

73. $\dfrac{5}{7} \pm \dfrac{5\sqrt{15}}{7}$ **75.** $-1 + 6i$

77. $-5i$ **79.** $-375\sqrt{3}i$ **81.** i

83. (a) $z_1 = 9 + 16i, z_2 = 20 - 10i$
(b) $z = \dfrac{11{,}240}{877} + \dfrac{4630}{877}i$

85. (a) 16 (b) 16 (c) 16 (d) 16

87. False. If the complex number is real, the number equals its conjugate.

89. False.
$i^{44} + i^{150} - i^{74} - i^{109} + i^{61} = 1 - 1 + 1 - i + i = 1$

91. Proof **93.** $-x^2 - 3x + 12$ **95.** $3x^2 + \frac{23}{2}x - 2$

97. -31 **99.** $\dfrac{27}{2}$ **101.** $a = \dfrac{\sqrt{3V\pi b}}{2\pi b}$ **103.** 1 liter

Section 2.5 *(page 179)*

Vocabulary Check *(page 179)*

1. Fundamental Theorem of Algebra
2. Linear Factorization Theorem **3.** Rational Zero
4. conjugate **5.** irreducible over the reals
6. Descartes' Rule of Signs **7.** lower; upper

1. 0, 6 **3.** $2, -4$ **5.** $-6, \pm i$ **7.** $\pm 1, \pm 3$

9. $\pm 1, \pm 3, \pm 5, \pm 9, \pm 15, \pm 45, \pm\frac{1}{2}, \pm\frac{3}{2}, \pm\frac{5}{2}, \pm\frac{9}{2}, \pm\frac{15}{2}, \pm\frac{45}{2}$

11. 1, 2, 3 **13.** $1, -1, 4$ **15.** $-1, -10$ **17.** $\frac{1}{2}, -1$

19. $-2, 3, \pm\frac{2}{3}$ **21.** $-1, 2$ **23.** $-6, \frac{1}{2}, 1$

25. (a) $\pm 1, \pm 2, \pm 4$
(b)

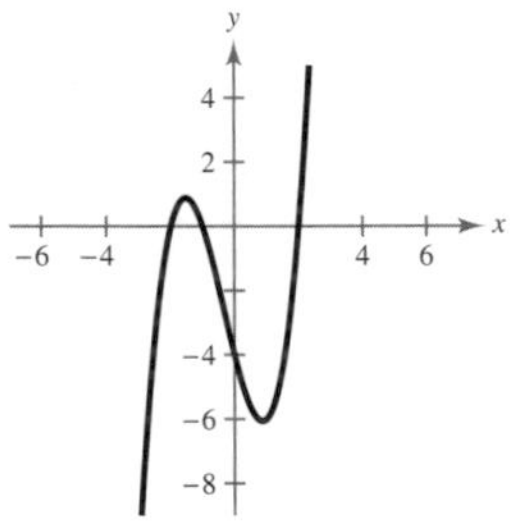

(c) $-2, -1, 2$

27. (a) $\pm 1, \pm 3, \pm\frac{1}{2}, \pm\frac{3}{2}, \pm\frac{1}{4}, \pm\frac{3}{4}$
(b)

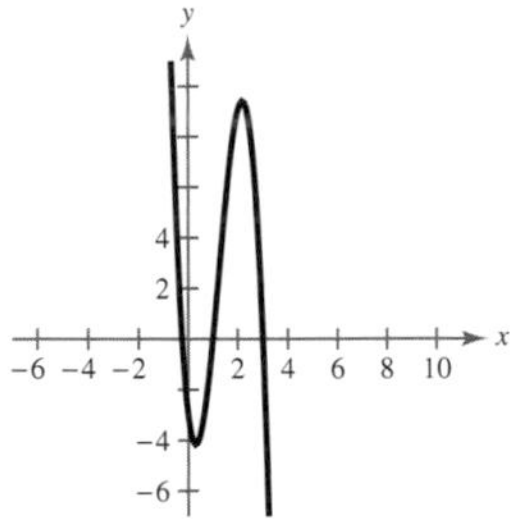

(c) $-\frac{1}{4}, 1, 3$

29. (a) $\pm 1, \pm 2, \pm 4, \pm 8, \pm\frac{1}{2}$
(b)

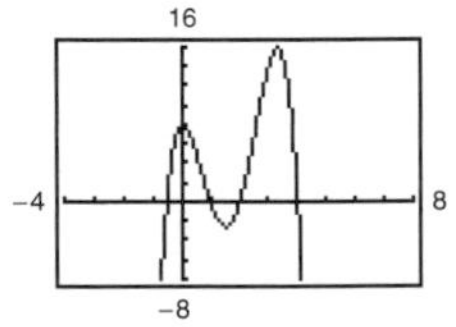

(c) $-\frac{1}{2}, 1, 2, 4$

31. (a) $\pm 1, \pm 3, \pm\frac{1}{2}, \pm\frac{3}{2}, \pm\frac{1}{4}, \pm\frac{3}{4}, \pm\frac{1}{8}, \pm\frac{3}{8}, \pm\frac{1}{16}, \pm\frac{3}{16}, \pm\frac{1}{32}, \pm\frac{3}{32}$
(b)

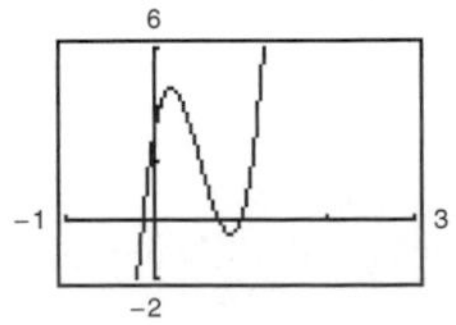

(c) $1, \frac{3}{4}, -\frac{1}{8}$

33. (a) $\pm 1, \approx \pm 1.414$
(b) $f(x) = (x + 1)(x - 1)(x + \sqrt{2})(x - \sqrt{2})$

35. (a) $0, 3, 4, \approx \pm 1.414$
(b) $h(x) = x(x - 3)(x - 4)(x + \sqrt{2})(x - \sqrt{2})$

37. $x^3 - x^2 + 25x - 25$ **39.** $x^3 + 4x^2 - 31x - 174$

41. $3x^4 - 17x^3 + 25x^2 + 23x - 22$

43. (a) $(x^2 + 9)(x^2 - 3)$
(b) $(x^2 + 9)(x + \sqrt{3})(x - \sqrt{3})$
(c) $(x + 3i)(x - 3i)(x + \sqrt{3})(x - \sqrt{3})$

45. (a) $(x^2 - 2x - 2)(x^2 - 2x + 3)$
(b) $(x - 1 + \sqrt{3})(x - 1 - \sqrt{3})(x^2 - 2x + 3)$
(c) $(x - 1 + \sqrt{3})(x - 1 - \sqrt{3})(x - 1 + \sqrt{2}i)$
$(x - 1 - \sqrt{2}i)$

47. $-\frac{3}{2}, \pm 5i$ **49.** $\pm 2i, 1, -\frac{1}{2}$ **51.** $-3 \pm i, \frac{1}{4}$

53. $2, -3 \pm \sqrt{2}i, 1$ **55.** $\pm 5i$; $(x + 5i)(x - 5i)$

57. $2 \pm \sqrt{3}$; $(x - 2 - \sqrt{3})(x - 2 + \sqrt{3})$

59. $\pm 3, \pm 3i$; $(x + 3)(x - 3)(x + 3i)(x - 3i)$

61. $1 \pm i$; $(z - 1 + i)(z - 1 - i)$

63. $2, 2 \pm i$; $(x - 2)(x - 2 + i)(x - 2 - i)$

65. $-2, 1 \pm \sqrt{2}i$; $(x + 2)(x - 1 + \sqrt{2}i)(x - 1 - \sqrt{2}i)$

67. $-\frac{1}{5}, 1 \pm \sqrt{5}i$; $(5x + 1)(x - 1 + \sqrt{5}i)(x - 1 - \sqrt{5}i)$

69. $2, \pm 2i$; $(x - 2)^2(x + 2i)(x - 2i)$

71. $\pm i, \pm 3i$; $(x + i)(x - i)(x + 3i)(x - 3i)$

73. $-10, -7 \pm 5i$ **75.** $-\frac{3}{4}, 1 \pm \frac{1}{2}i$

77. $-2, -\frac{1}{2}, \pm i$ **79.** No real zeros

81. No real zeros **83.** One positive zero

85. One or three positive zeros

87. Answers will vary. **89.** Answers will vary.

91. $1, -\frac{1}{2}$ **93.** $-\frac{3}{4}$ **95.** $\pm 2, \pm\frac{3}{2}$ **97.** $\pm 1, \frac{1}{4}$

99. d **100.** a **101.** b **102.** c

103. (a)

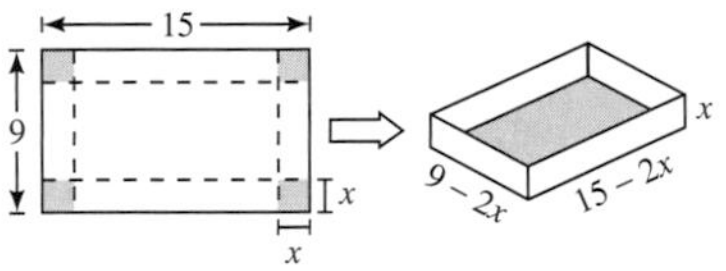

(b) $V = x(9 - 2x)(15 - 2x)$
Domain: $0 < x < \frac{9}{2}$

(c)

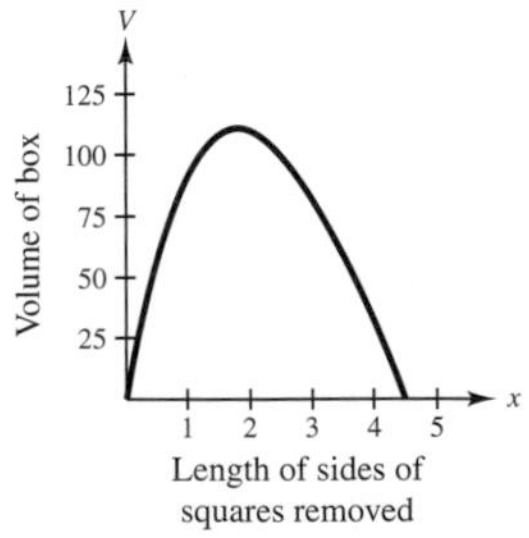

1.82 centimeters × 5.36 centimeters × 11.36 centimeters
(d) $\frac{1}{2}, \frac{7}{2}, 8$; 8 is not in the domain of V.

105. $x \approx 38.4$, or \$384,000

107. (a) $V = x^3 + 9x^2 + 26x + 24 = 120$
(b) 4 feet by 5 feet by 6 feet

109. $x \approx 40$, or 4000 units

111. No. Setting $p = 9{,}000{,}000$ and solving the resulting equation yields imaginary roots.

113. False. The most complex zeros it can have is two, and the Linear Factorization Theorem guarantees that there are three linear factors, so one zero must be real.

115. r_1, r_2, r_3 **117.** $5 + r_1, 5 + r_2, 5 + r_3$

119. The zeros cannot be determined.

121. (a) $0 < k < 4$ (b) $k = 4$ (c) $k < 0$ (d) $k > 4$

123. Answers will vary. There are infinitely many possible functions for f. Sample equation and graph:
$f(x) = -2x^3 + 3x^2 + 11x - 6$

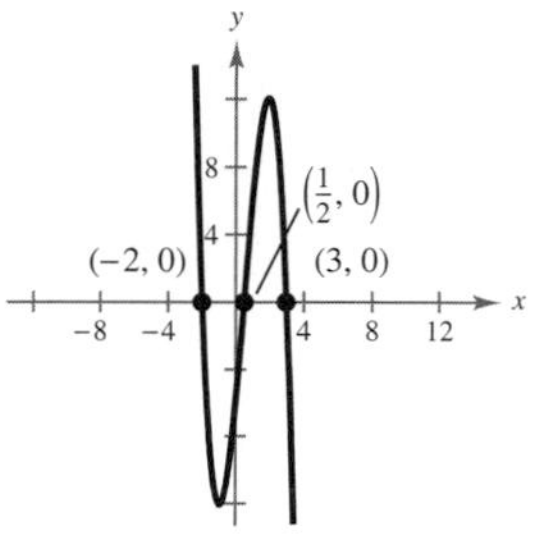

125. Answers will vary.

127. (a) $x^2 + b$ (b) $x^2 - 2ax + a^2 + b^2$

129. $-11 + 9i$ **131.** $20 + 40i$

133.

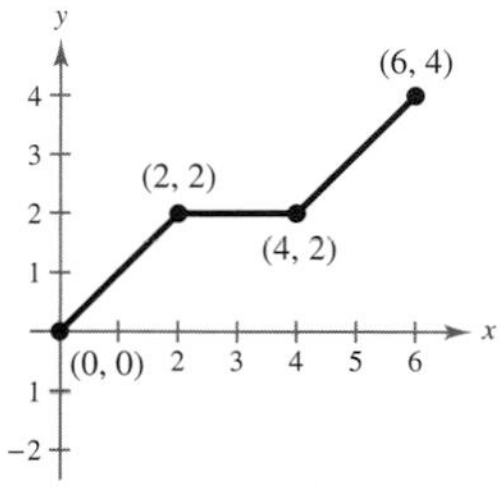

135.

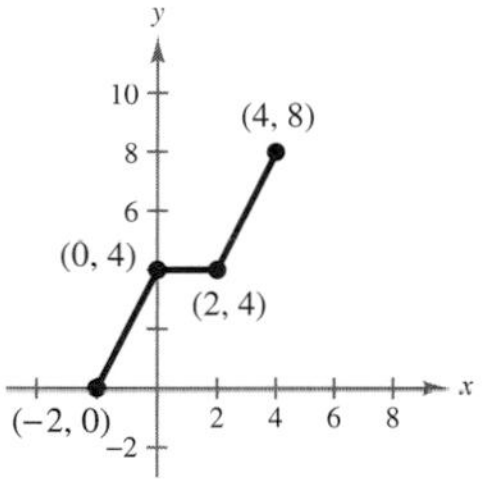

137.

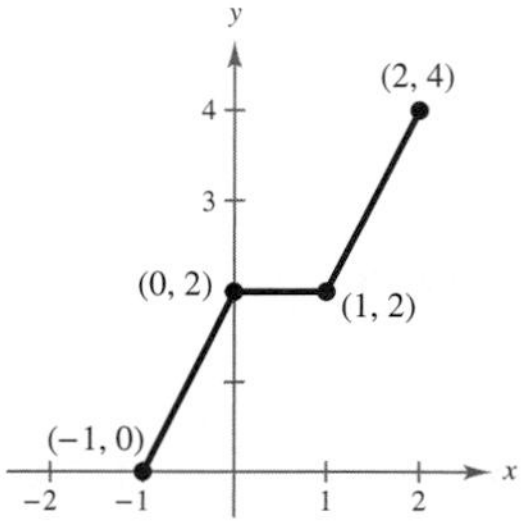

Section 2.6 *(page 193)*

Vocabulary Check *(page 193)*

1. rational functions **2.** vertical asymptote
3. horizontal asymptote **4.** slant asymptote

1. (a)

x	$f(x)$
0.5	−2
0.9	−10
0.99	−100
0.999	−1000

x	$f(x)$
1.5	2
1.1	10
1.01	100
1.001	1000

x	$f(x)$
5	0.25
10	$0.\overline{1}$
100	$0.\overline{01}$
1000	$0.\overline{001}$

(b) Vertical asymptote: $x = 1$
Horizontal asymptote: $y = 0$
(c) Domain: all real numbers x except $x = 1$

3. (a)

x	$f(x)$
0.5	−1
0.9	−12.79
0.99	−147.8
0.999	−1498

x	$f(x)$
1.5	5.4
1.1	17.29
1.01	152.3
1.001	1502

x	$f(x)$
5	3.125
10	$3.\overline{03}$
100	$3.\overline{0003}$
1000	3

(b) Vertical asymptotes: $x = \pm 1$
Horizontal asymptote: $y = 3$
(c) Domain: all real numbers x except $x = \pm 1$

5. Domain: all real numbers x except $x = 0$
Vertical asymptote: $x = 0$
Horizontal asymptote: $y = 0$

7. Domain: all real numbers x except $x = 2$
Vertical asymptote: $x = 2$
Horizontal asymptote: $y = -1$

9. Domain: all real numbers x except $x = \pm 1$
Vertical asymptotes: $x = \pm 1$

11. Domain: all real numbers x
Horizontal asymptote: $y = 3$

13. d **14.** a **15.** c **16.** b

17. 1 **19.** 6

21. Domain: all real numbers x except $x = \pm 4$;
Vertical asymptote: $x = -4$; horizontal asymptote: $y = 0$

23. Domain: all real numbers x except $x = -1, 3$;
Vertical asymptote: $x = 3$; horizontal asymptote: $y = 1$

25. Domain: all real numbers x except $x = -1, \frac{1}{2}$;
Vertical asymptote: $x = \frac{1}{2}$; horizontal asymptote: $y = \frac{1}{2}$

27. (a) Domain: all real numbers x except $x = -2$
(b) y-intercept: $\left(0, \frac{1}{2}\right)$
(c) Vertical asymptote: $x = -2$
Horizontal asymptote: $y = 0$

CHAPTER 2

(d)

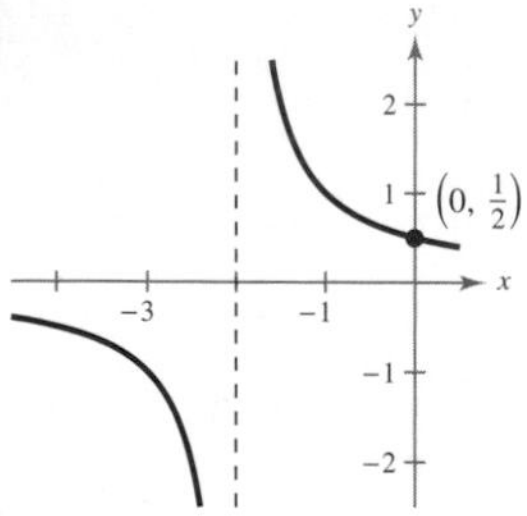

29. (a) Domain: all real numbers x except $x = -2$

(b) y-intercept: $\left(0, -\frac{1}{2}\right)$

(c) Vertical asymptote: $x = -2$

Horizontal asymptote: $y = 0$

(d)

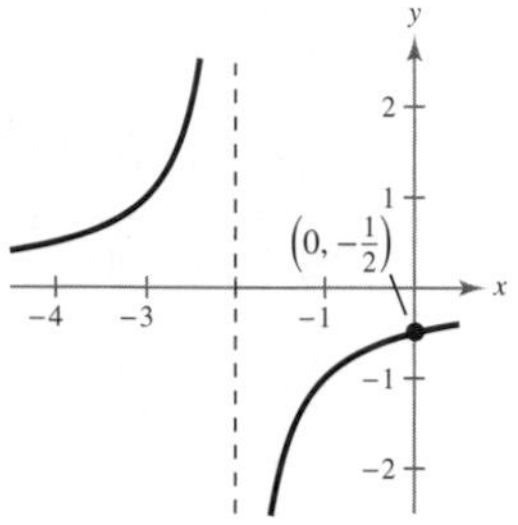

31. (a) Domain: all real numbers x except $x = -1$

(b) x-intercept: $\left(-\frac{5}{2}, 0\right)$

y-intercept: $(0, 5)$

(c) Vertical asymptote: $x = -1$

Horizontal asymptote: $y = 2$

(d)

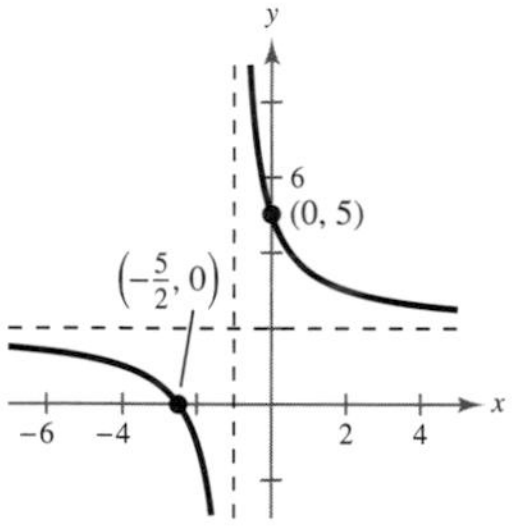

33. (a) Domain: all real numbers x

(b) Intercept: $(0, 0)$

(c) Horizontal asymptote: $y = 1$

(d)

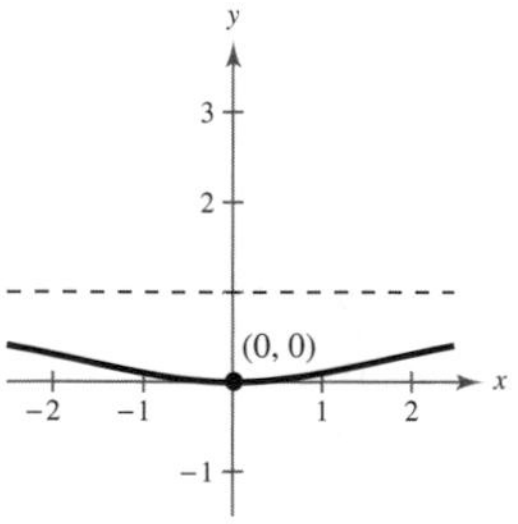

35. (a) Domain: all real numbers s

(b) Intercept: $(0, 0)$ (c) Horizontal asymptote: $y = 0$

(d)

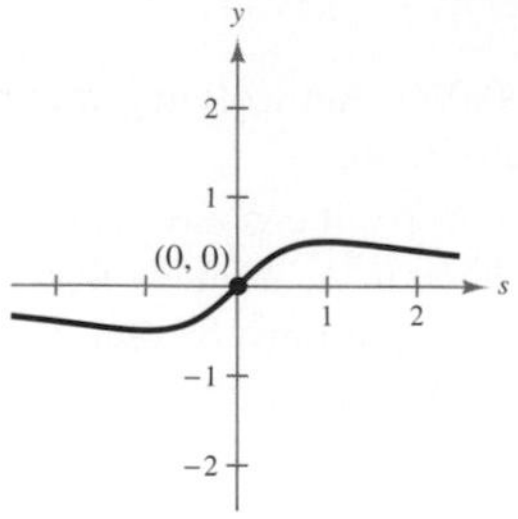

37. (a) Domain: all real numbers x except $x = \pm 2$

(b) x-intercepts: $(1, 0)$ and $(4, 0)$

y-intercept: $(0, -1)$

(c) Vertical asymptotes: $x = \pm 2$

Horizontal asymptote: $y = 1$

(d)

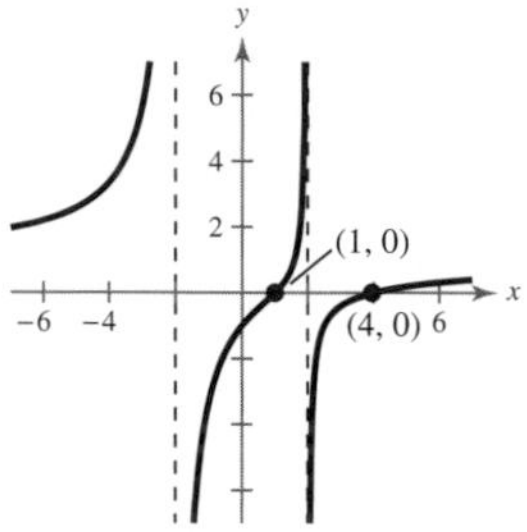

39. (a) Domain: all real numbers x except $x = \pm 1, 2$

(b) x-intercept: $(3, 0), \left(-\frac{1}{2}, 0\right)$

y-intercept: $\left(0, -\frac{3}{2}\right)$

(c) Vertical asymptotes: $x = 2, x = \pm 1$

Horizontal asymptote: $y = 0$

(d)

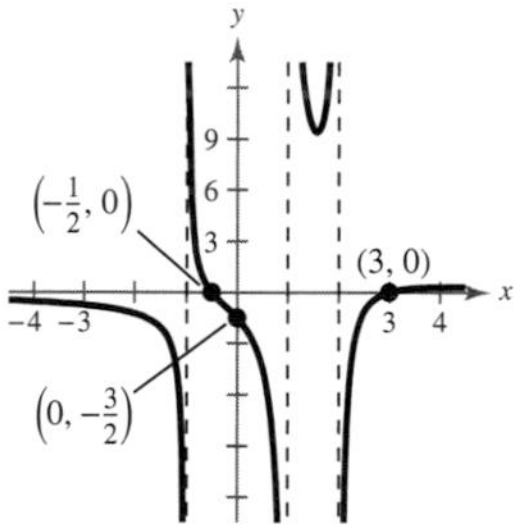

41. (a) Domain: all real numbers x except $x = 2, -3$

(b) Intercept: $(0, 0)$

(c) Vertical asymptote: $x = 2$

Horizontal asymptote: $y = 1$

(d)

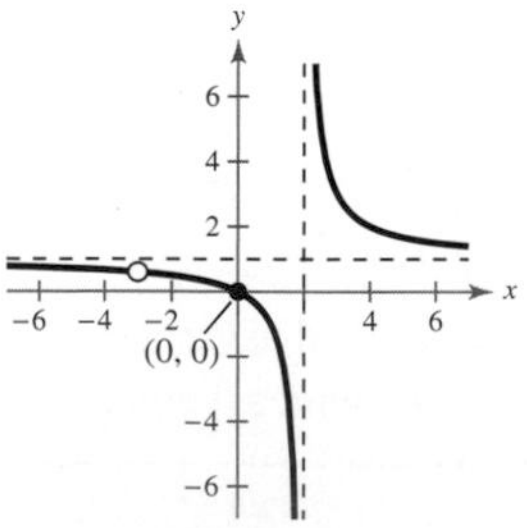

43. (a) Domain: all real numbers x except $x = -\frac{3}{2}, 2$
(b) x-intercept: $\left(\frac{1}{2}, 0\right)$
y-intercept: $\left(0, \frac{1}{3}\right)$
(c) Vertical asymptote: $x = -\frac{3}{2}$
Horizontal asymptote: $y = 1$
(d)

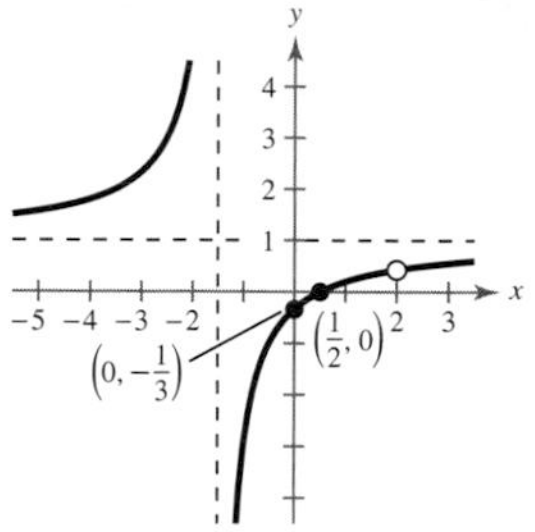

45. (a) Domain: all real numbers t except $t = -1$
(b) t-intercept: $(1, 0)$
y-intercept: $(0, -1)$
(c) Vertical asymptote: None
Horizontal asymptote: None
(d)

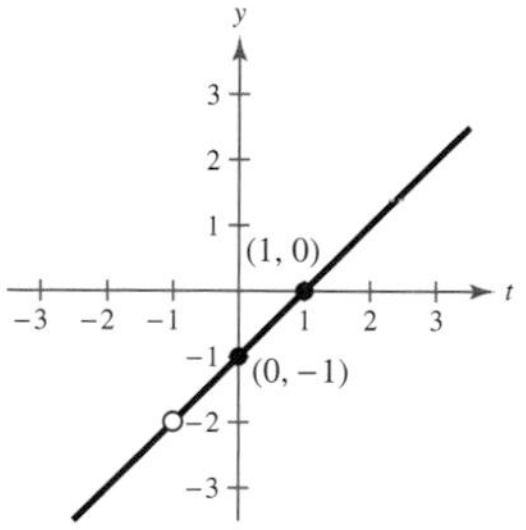

47. (a) Domain of f: all real numbers x except $x = -1$
Domain of g: all real numbers x
(b) $x - 1$; Vertical asymptotes: none
(c)

x	-3	-2	-1.5	-1	-0.5	0	1
$f(x)$	-4	-3	-2.5	Undef.	-1.5	-1	0
$g(x)$	-4	-3	-2.5	-2	-1.5	-1	0

(d)

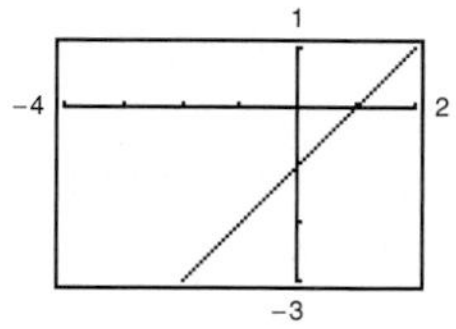

(e) Because there are only a finite number of pixels, the graphing utility may not attempt to evaluate the function where it does not exist.

49. (a) Domain of f: all real numbers x except $x = 0, 2$
Domain of g: all real numbers x except $x = 0$
(b) $\frac{1}{x}$; Vertical asymptote: $x = 0$
(c)

x	-0.5	0	0.5	1	1.5	2	3
$f(x)$	-2	Undef.	2	1	$\frac{2}{3}$	Undef.	$\frac{1}{3}$
$g(x)$	-2	Undef.	2	1	$\frac{2}{3}$	$\frac{1}{2}$	$\frac{1}{3}$

(d)

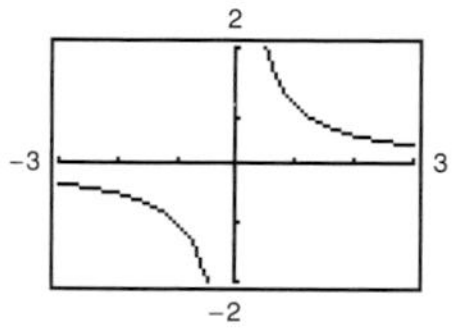

(e) Because there are only a finite number of pixels, the graphing utility may not attempt to evaluate the function where it does not exist.

51. (a) Domain: all real numbers x except $x = 0$
(b) x-intercepts: $(2, 0), (-2, 0)$
(c) Vertical asymptote: $x = 0$
Slant asymptote: $y = x$
(d)

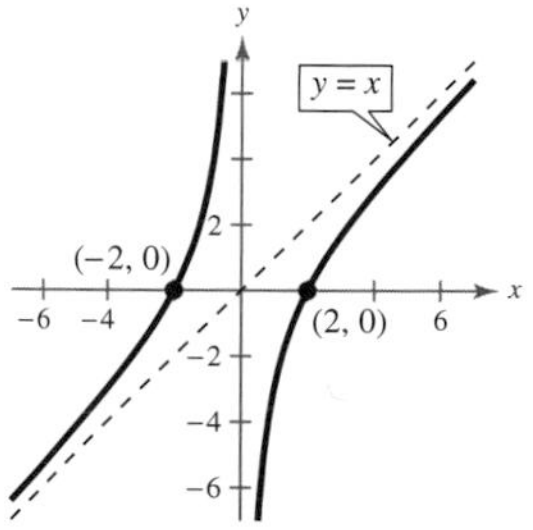

53. (a) Domain: all real numbers x except $x = 0$
(b) No intercepts
(c) Vertical asymptote: $x = 0$
Slant asymptote: $y = 2x$
(d)

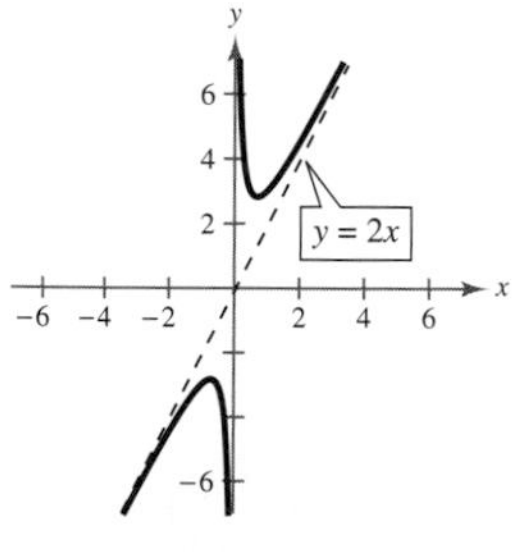

55. (a) Domain: all real numbers x except $x = 0$
(b) No intercepts
(c) Vertical asymptote: $x = 0$
Slant asymptote: $y = x$

CHAPTER 2

(d)

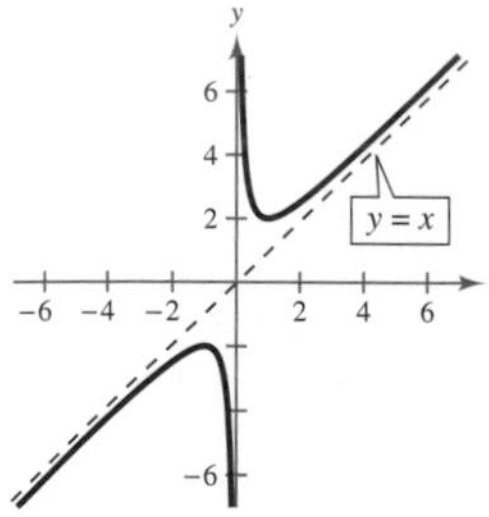

57. (a) Domain: all real numbers t except $t = -5$
(b) y-intercept: $(0, -0.2)$
(c) Vertical asymptote: $t = -5$
Slant asymptote: $y = -t + 5$
(d)

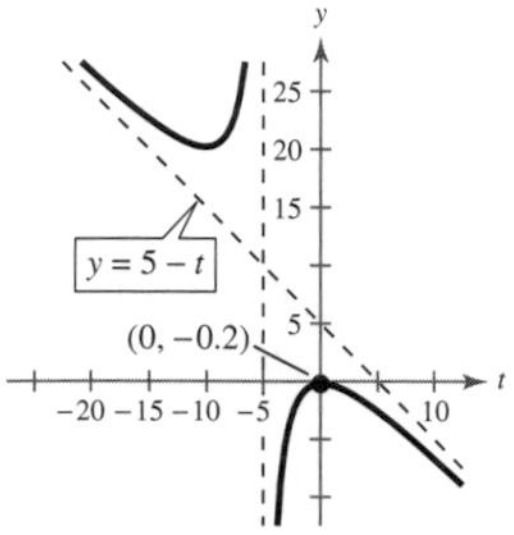

59. (a) Domain: all real numbers x except $x = \pm 1$
(b) Intercept: $(0, 0)$
(c) Vertical asymptotes: $x = \pm 1$
Slant asymptote: $y = x$
(d)

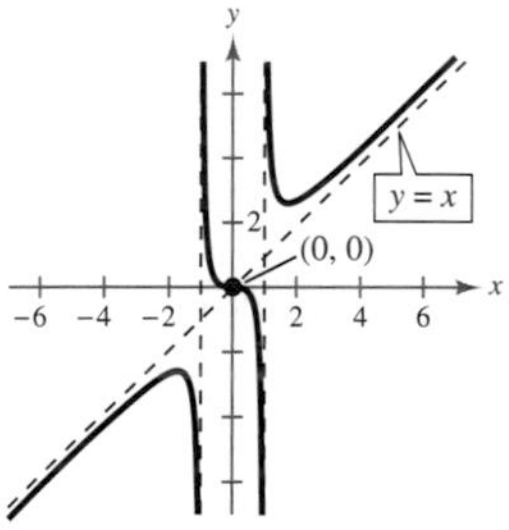

61. (a) Domain: all real numbers x except $x = 1$
(b) y-intercept: $(0, -1)$
(c) Vertical asymptote: $x = 1$
Slant asymptote: $y = x$
(d)

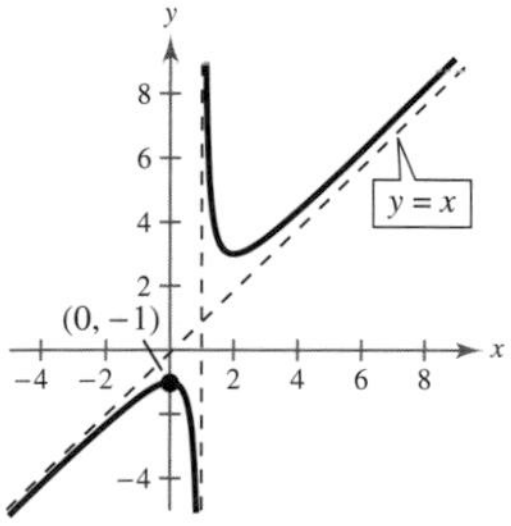

63. (a) Domain: all real numbers x except $x = -1, -2$
(b) y-intercept: $(0, 0.5)$
x-intercepts: $(0.5, 0)$, $(1, 0)$
(c) Vertical asymptote: $x = -2$
Slant asymptote: $y = 2x - 7$
(d)

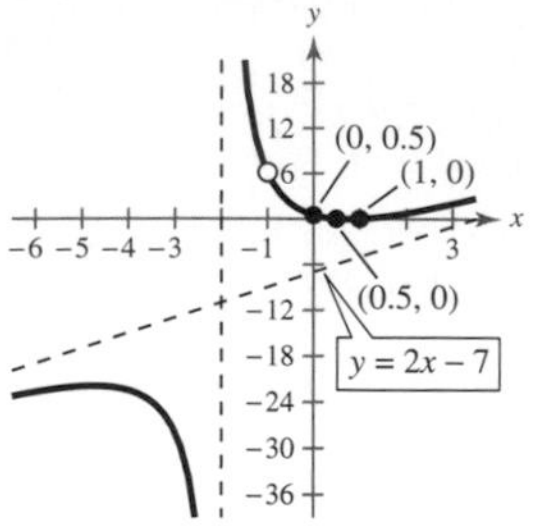

65.

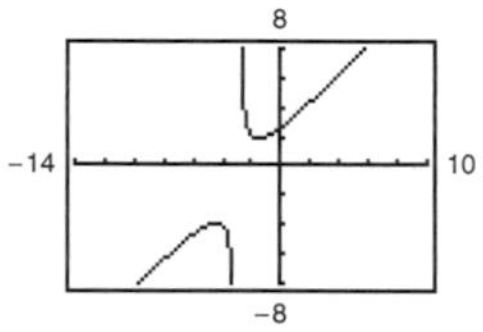

Domain: all real numbers x except $x = -3$
Vertical asymptote: $x = -3$
Slant asymptote: $y = x + 2$
$y = x + 2$

67.

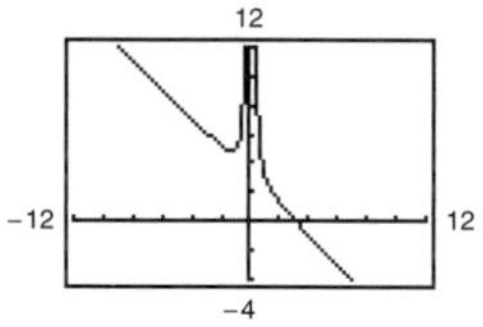

Domain: all real numbers x except $x = 0$
Vertical asymptote: $x = 0$
Slant asymptote: $y = -x + 3$
$y = -x + 3$

69. (a) $(-1, 0)$ (b) -1

71. (a) $(1, 0)$, $(-1, 0)$ (b) ± 1

73. (a)

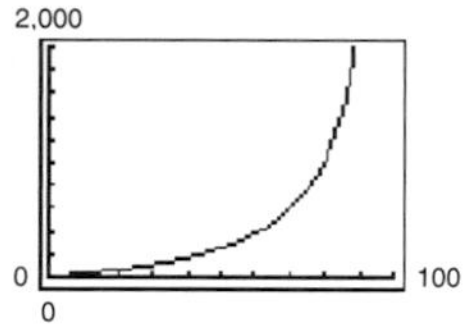

(b) \$28.33 million; \$170 million; \$765 million
(c) No. The function is undefined at $p = 100$.

75. (a) 333 deer, 500 deer, 800 deer (b) 1500 deer

77. (a) Answers will vary. (b) $(4, \infty)$
(c)

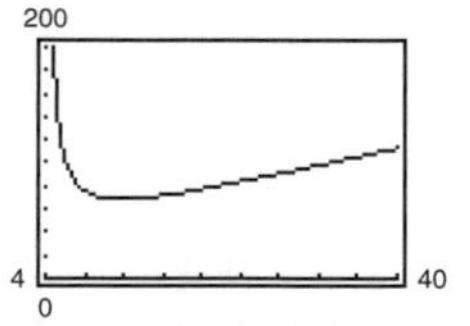

11.75 inches × 5.87 inches

79. (a) Answers will vary.
(b) Vertical asymptote: $x = 25$
Horizontal asymptote: $y = 25$
(c)
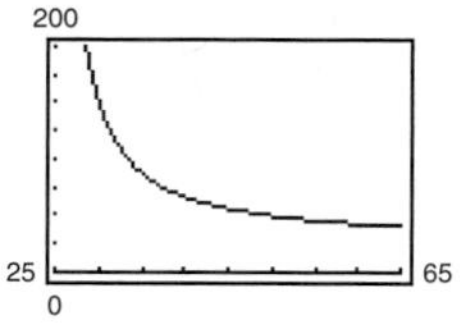

(d)

x	30	35	40	45	50	55	60
y	150	87.5	66.7	56.3	50	45.8	42.9

(e) Yes. You would expect the average speed for the round trip to be the average of the average speeds for the two parts of the trip.
(f) No. At 20 miles per hour you would use more time in one direction than is required for the round trip at an average speed of 50 miles per hour.

81. False. Polynomials do not have vertical asymptotes.

83. Answers will vary. Sample answer: $f(x) = \dfrac{2x^2}{x^2 + 1}$

85. $(x - 7)(x - 8)$

87. $(x - 5)(x + 2i)(x - 2i)$

89. $x \geq \frac{10}{3}$
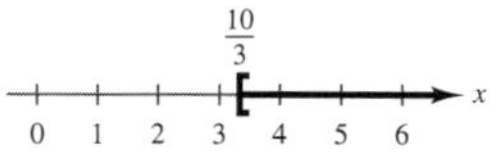

91. $-3 < x < 7$
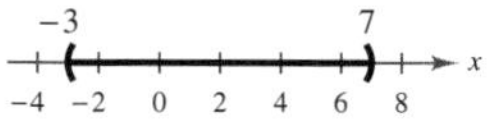

93. Answers will vary.

Section 2.7 *(page 204)*

Vocabulary Check *(page 204)*

1. critical; test intervals **2.** zeros; undefined values
3. $P = R - C$

1. (a) No (b) Yes (c) Yes (d) No
3. (a) Yes (b) No (c) No (d) Yes
5. $2, -\frac{3}{2}$ **7.** $\frac{7}{2}, 5$

9. $[-3, 3]$
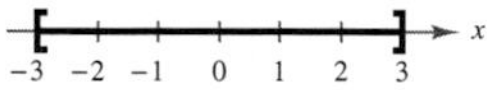

11. $(-7, 3)$
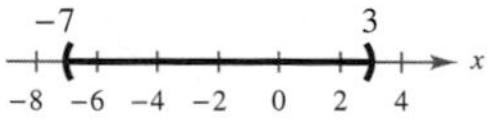

13. $(-\infty, -5] \cup [1, \infty)$
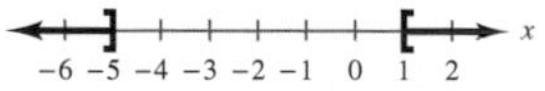

15. $(-3, 2)$
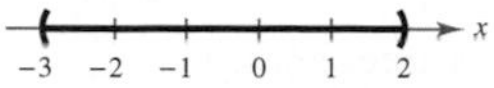

17. $(-3, 1)$
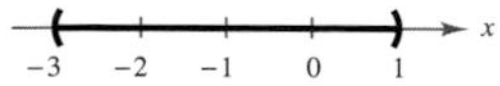

19. $(-\infty, -4 - \sqrt{21}] \cup [-4 + \sqrt{21}, \infty)$
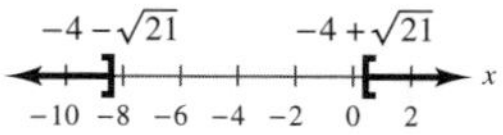

21. $(-1, 1) \cup (3, \infty)$
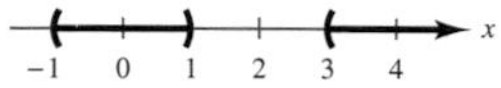

23. $[-3, 2] \cup [3, \infty)$
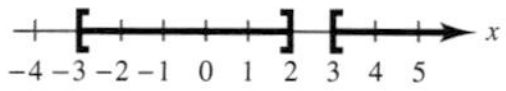

25. $x = \frac{1}{2}$
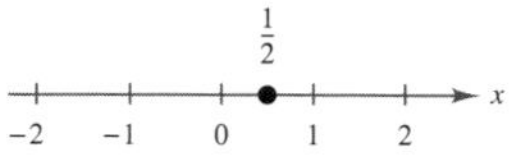

27. $(-\infty, 0) \cup \left(0, \frac{3}{2}\right)$

29. $[-2, 0] \cup [2, \infty)$ **31.** $[-2, \infty)$

33.
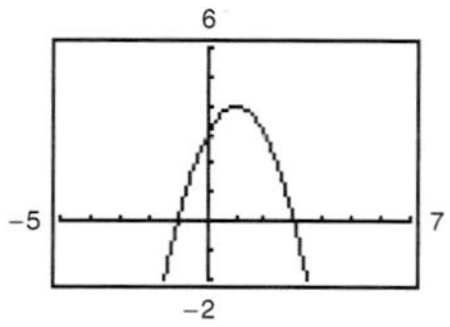

(a) $x \leq -1, x \geq 3$
(b) $0 \leq x \leq 2$

35.
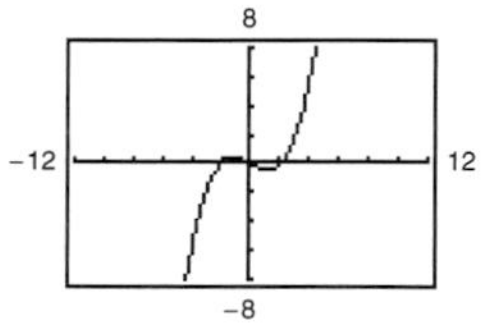

(a) $-2 \leq x \leq 0$,
$2 \leq x < \infty$
(b) $x \leq 4$

37. $(-\infty, -1) \cup (0, 1)$
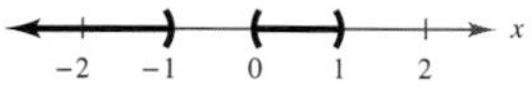

39. $(-\infty, -1) \cup (4, \infty)$
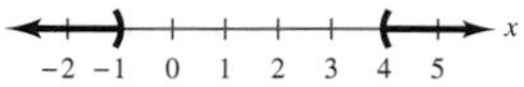

41. $(5, 15)$
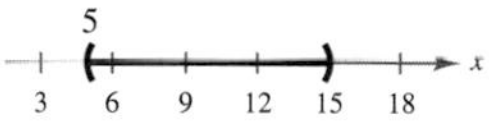

43. $\left(-5, -\frac{3}{2}\right) \cup (-1, \infty)$
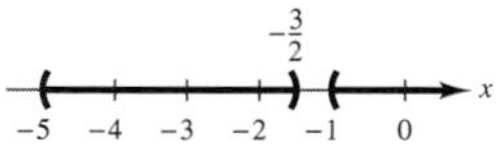

45. $\left(-\frac{3}{4}, 3\right) \cup [6, \infty)$
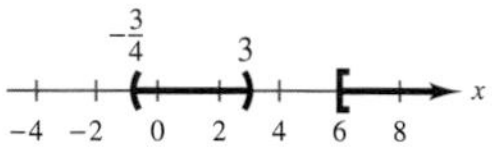

47. $(-3, -2] \cup [0, 3)$
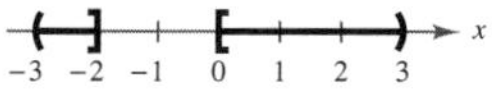

49. $(-\infty, -1) \cup \left(-\frac{2}{3}, 1\right) \cup (3, \infty)$

51.
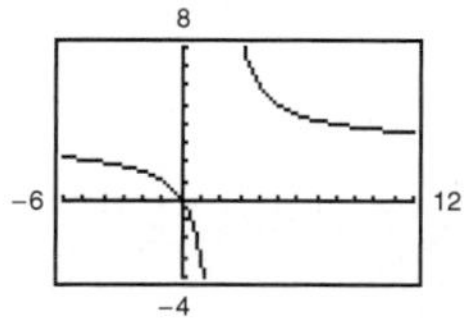

(a) $0 \leq x < 2$
(b) $2 < x \leq 4$

53.
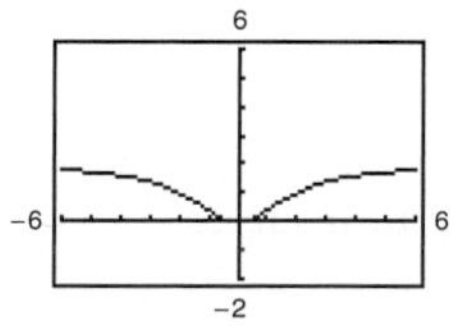

(a) $|x| \geq 2$
(b) $-\infty < x < \infty$

55. $[-2, 2]$ **57.** $(-\infty, 3] \cup [4, \infty)$

59. $(-5, 0] \cup (7, \infty)$ **61.** $(-3.51, 3.51)$

63. $(-0.13, 25.13)$ **65.** $(2.26, 2.39)$

67. (a) $t = 10$ seconds (b) 4 seconds $< t <$ 6 seconds

69. 13.8 meters $\leq L \leq$ 36.2 meters

71. $40{,}000 \leq x \leq 50{,}000$; $50.00 \leq p \leq 55.00$

73. (a)

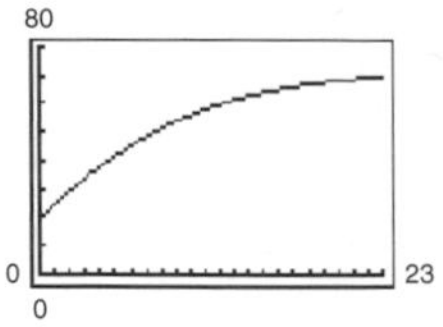

(b)

t	24	26	28	30	32	34
C	70.5	71.6	72.9	74.6	76.8	79.6

2011

(c) $t \approx 31$

(d)

t	36	37	38	39
C	83.2	85.4	87.8	90.5

t	40	41	42	43
C	93.5	96.8	100.4	104.4

2016 to 2021

(e) $37 \leq t \leq 41$ (f) Answers will vary.

75. $R_1 \geq 2$ ohms

77. True. The test intervals are $(-\infty, -3)$, $(-3, 1)$, $(1, 4)$, and $(4, \infty)$.

79. $(-\infty, -4] \cup [4, \infty)$ **81.** $\left(-\infty, -2\sqrt{30}\right] \cup \left[2\sqrt{30}, \infty\right)$

83. (a) If $a > 0$ and $c \leq 0$, b can be any real number. If $a > 0$ and $c > 0$, $b < -2\sqrt{ac}$ or $b > 2\sqrt{ac}$.

(b) 0

85. $(2x + 5)^2$ **87.** $(x + 3)(x + 2)(x - 2)$ **89.** $2x^2 + x$

Review Exercises *(page 208)*

1. (a)

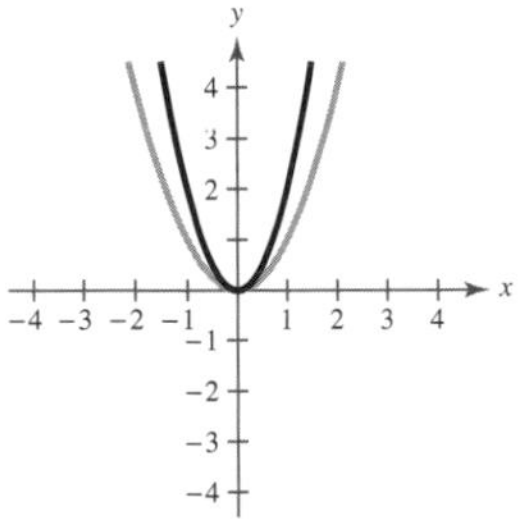

Vertical stretch

(b)

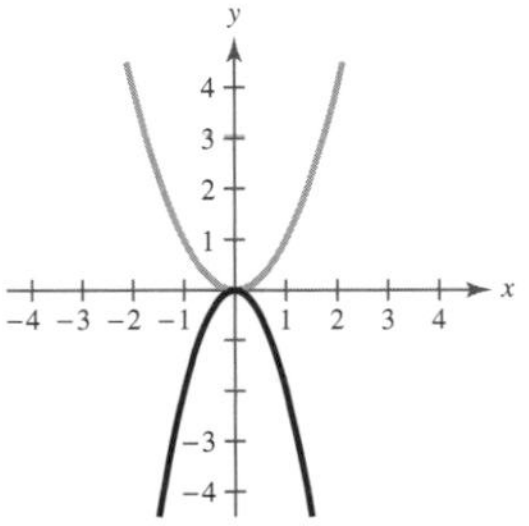

Vertical stretch and reflection in the x-axis

(c)

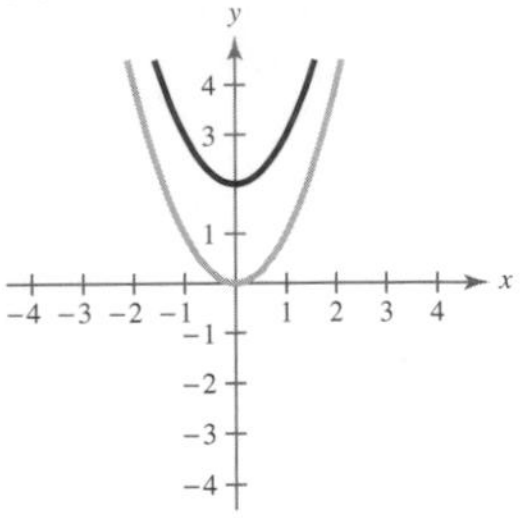

Vertical shift

(d)

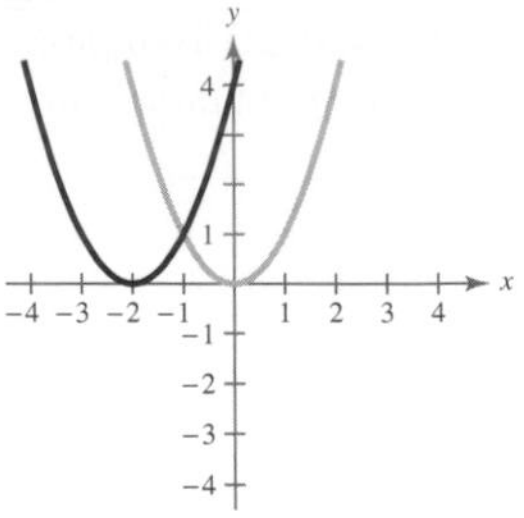

Horizontal shift

3. $g(x) = (x - 1)^2 - 1$

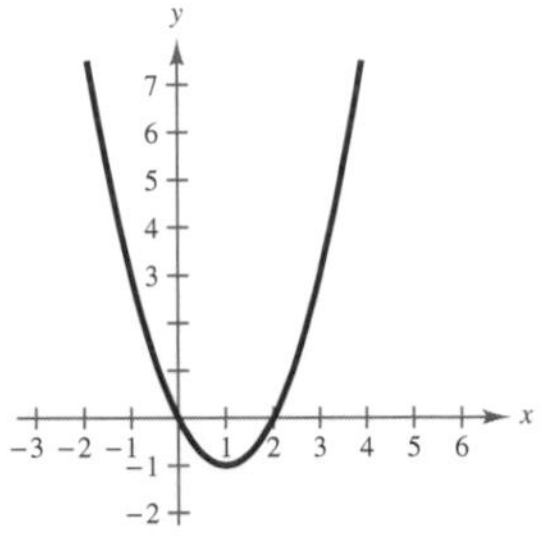

Vertex: $(1, -1)$
Axis of symmetry: $x = 1$
x-intercepts: $(0, 0)$, $(2, 0)$

5. $f(x) = (x + 4)^2 - 6$

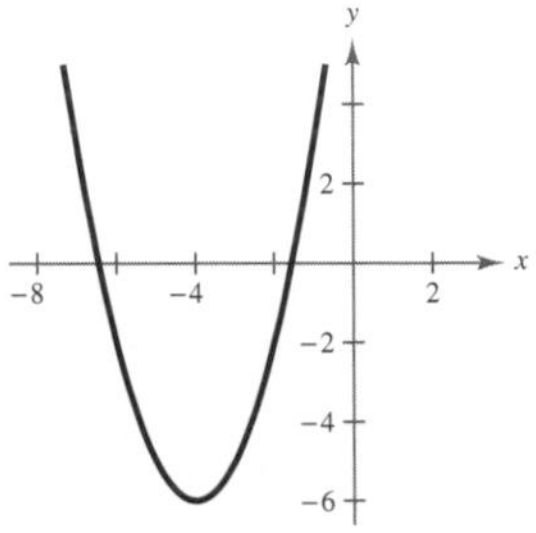

Vertex: $(-4, -6)$
Axis of symmetry: $x = -4$
x-intercepts: $\left(-4 \pm \sqrt{6}, 0\right)$

7. $f(t) = -2(t - 1)^2 + 3$

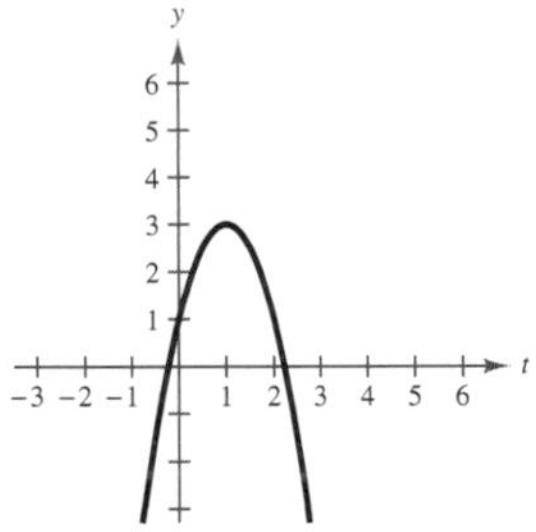

Vertex: $(1, 3)$
Axis of symmetry: $t = 1$
t-intercepts: $\left(1 \pm \dfrac{\sqrt{6}}{2}, 0\right)$

9. $h(x) = 4\left(x + \frac{1}{2}\right)^2 + 12$

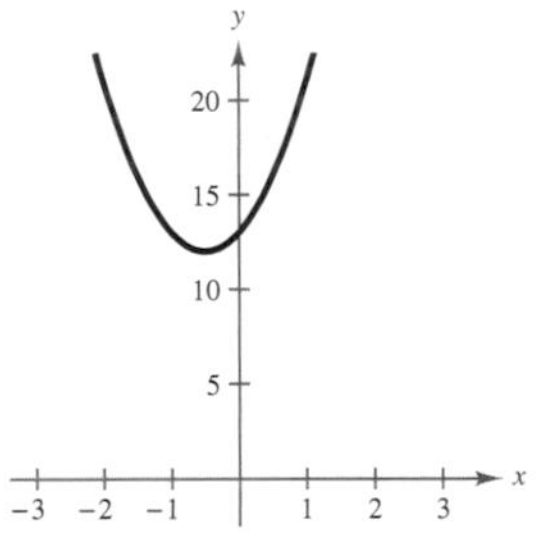

Vertex: $\left(-\frac{1}{2}, 12\right)$
Axis of symmetry: $x = -\frac{1}{2}$
No x-intercept

11. $h(x) = \left(x + \frac{5}{2}\right)^2 - \frac{41}{4}$

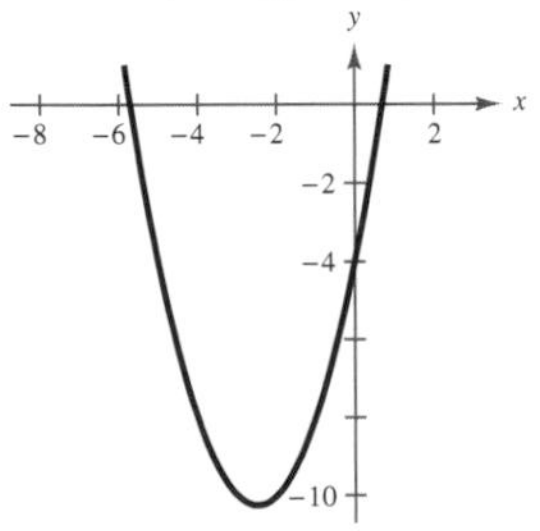

Vertex: $\left(-\frac{5}{2}, -\frac{41}{4}\right)$
Axis of symmetry: $x = -\frac{5}{2}$
x-intercepts: $\left(\dfrac{\pm\sqrt{41} - 5}{2}, 0\right)$

13. $f(x) = \frac{1}{3}\left(x + \frac{5}{2}\right)^2 - \frac{41}{12}$

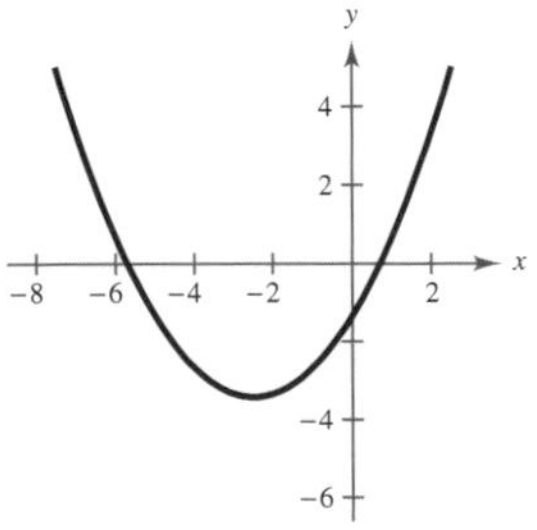

Vertex: $\left(-\frac{5}{2}, -\frac{41}{12}\right)$
Axis of symmetry: $x = -\frac{5}{2}$
x-intercepts: $\left(\dfrac{\pm\sqrt{41} - 5}{2}, 0\right)$

15. $f(x) = -\frac{1}{2}(x - 4)^2 + 1$

17. $f(x) = (x - 1)^2 - 4$

19. (a)

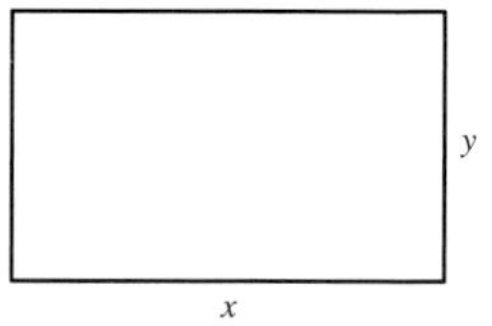

(b) $y = 100 - x$
$A = 100x - x^2$

(c) $x = 50,\ y = 50$

21. 1091 units

23.

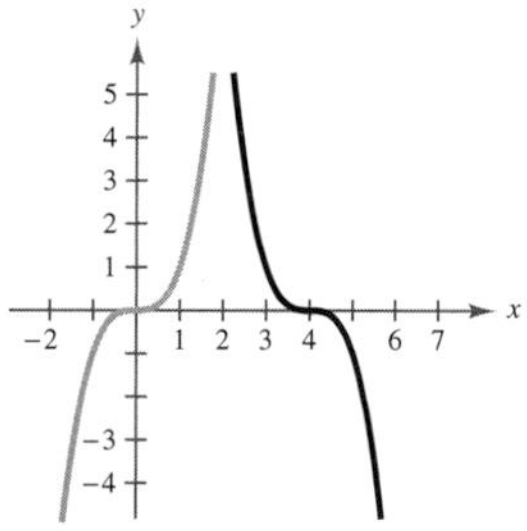

25.

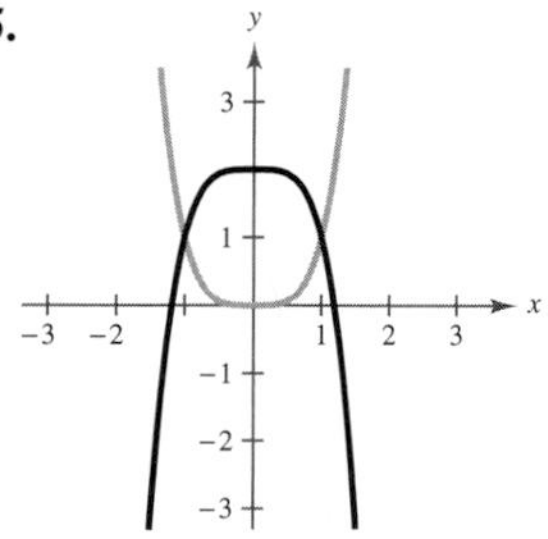

27.

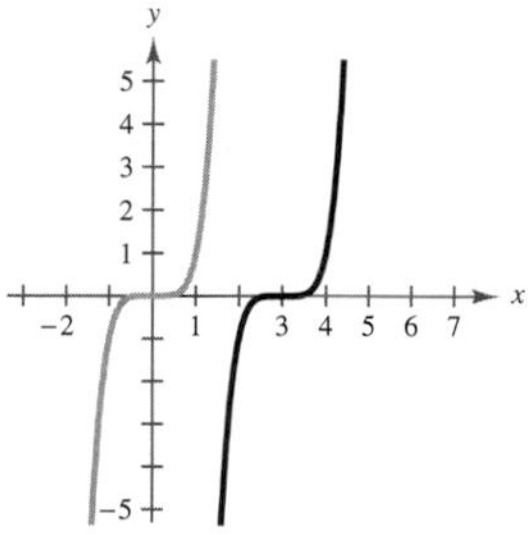

29. Falls to the left, falls to the right

31. Rises to the left, rises to the right

33. $-7, \frac{3}{2}$, odd multiplicity; turning point: 1

35. $0, \pm\sqrt{3}$, odd multiplicity; turning points: 2

37. 0, even multiplicity; $\frac{5}{3}$, odd multiplicity; turning points: 2

39. (a) Rises to the left, falls to the right (b) -1

(c) Answers will vary.

(d)

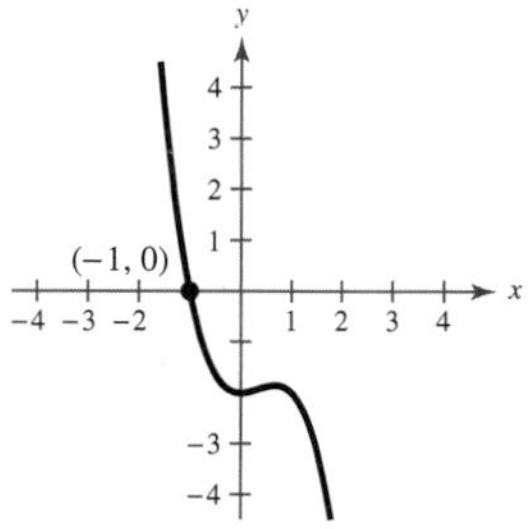

41. (a) Rises to the right, rises to the left (b) $-3, 0, 1$

(c) Answers will vary.

(d)

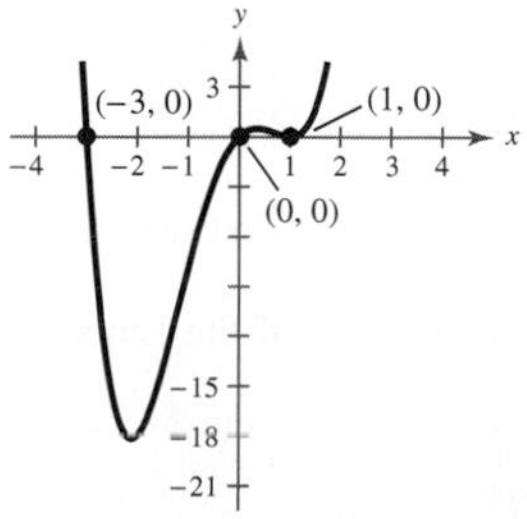

43. (a) $[-1, 0]$ (b) ≈ -0.900

45. (a) $[-1, 0], [1, 2]$ (b) $\approx -0.200, \approx 1.772$

47. $8x + 5 + \dfrac{2}{3x - 2}$ **49.** $5x + 2$

51. $x^2 - 3x + 2 - \dfrac{1}{x^2 + 2}$

53. $6x^3 + 8x^2 - 11x - 4 - \dfrac{8}{x - 2}$

55. $2x^2 - 11x - 6$

57. (a) Yes (b) Yes (c) Yes (d) No

59. (a) -421 (b) -9

61. (a) Answers will vary. (b) $(x + 7), (x + 1)$

(c) $f(x) = (x + 7)(x + 1)(x - 4)$ (d) $-7, -1, 4$

(e)

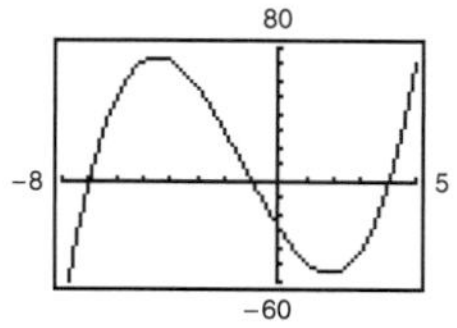

63. (a) Answers will vary. (b) $(x + 1), (x - 4)$

(c) $f(x) = (x + 1)(x - 4)(x + 2)(x - 3)$

(d) $-2, -1, 3, 4$

(e)

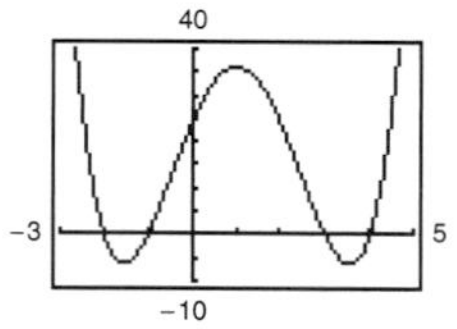

65. $6 + 2i$ **67.** $-1 + 3i$ **69.** $3 + 7i$

71. $40 + 65i$ **73.** $-4 - 46i$ **75.** $\frac{23}{17} + \frac{10}{17}i$

77. $\frac{21}{13} - \frac{1}{13}i$ **79.** $\pm\dfrac{\sqrt{3}}{3}i$ **81.** $1 \pm 3i$

83. 0, 2 **85.** 8, 1 **87.** $-4, 6, \pm 2i$

89. $\pm 1, \pm 3, \pm 5, \pm 15, \pm\frac{1}{2}, \pm\frac{3}{2}, \pm\frac{5}{2}, \pm\frac{15}{2}, \pm\frac{1}{4}, \pm\frac{3}{4}, \pm\frac{5}{4}, \pm\frac{15}{4}$

91. $-1, -3, 6$ **93.** 1, 8 **95.** $-4, 3$

97. $3x^4 - 14x^3 + 17x^2 - 42x + 24$

99. $4, \pm i$ **101.** $-3, \frac{1}{2}, 2 \pm i$

103. $0, 1, -5;\ f(x) = x(x - 1)(x + 5)$

105. $-4, 2 \pm 3i;\ g(x) = (x + 4)^2(x - 2 - 3i)(x - 2 + 3i)$

107. Two or no positive zeros, one negative zero

109. Answers will vary.

111. Domain: all real numbers x except $x = -12$

113. Domain: all real numbers x except $x = 6, 4$

115. Vertical asymptote: $x = -3$
Horizontal asymptote: $y = 0$

117. Vertical asymptote: $x = -3$
Horizontal asymptote: $y = 0$

119. (a) Domain: all real numbers x except $x = 0$

(b) No intercepts

(c) Vertical asymptote: $x = 0$
Horizontal asymptote: $y = 0$

(d)

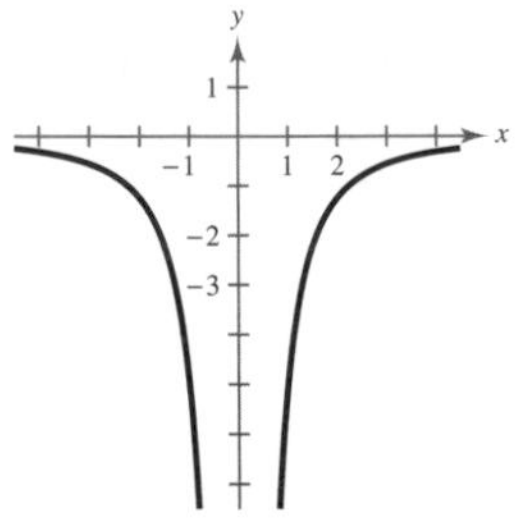

121. (a) Domain: all real numbers x except $x = 1$
(b) x-intercept: $(-2, 0)$
y-intercept: $(0, 2)$
(c) Vertical asymptote: $x = 1$
Horizontal asymptote: $y = -1$
(d)

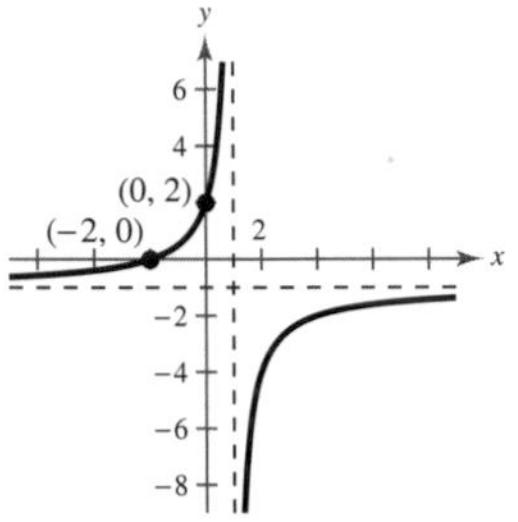

123. (a) Domain: all real numbers x (b) Intercept: $(0, 0)$
(c) Horizontal asymptote: $y = 1$
(d)

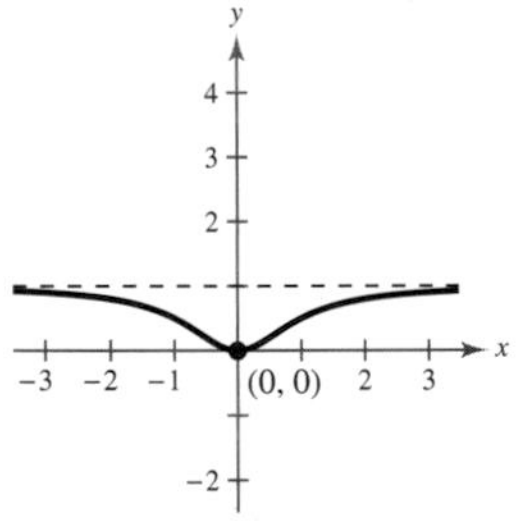

125. (a) Domain: all real numbers x (b) Intercept: $(0, 0)$
(c) Horizontal asymptote: $y = 0$
(d)

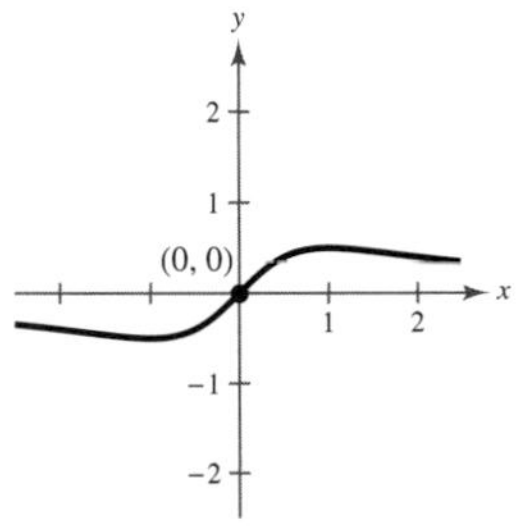

127. (a) Domain: all real numbers x (b) Intercept: $(0, 0)$
(c) Horizontal asymptote: $y = -6$

(d)

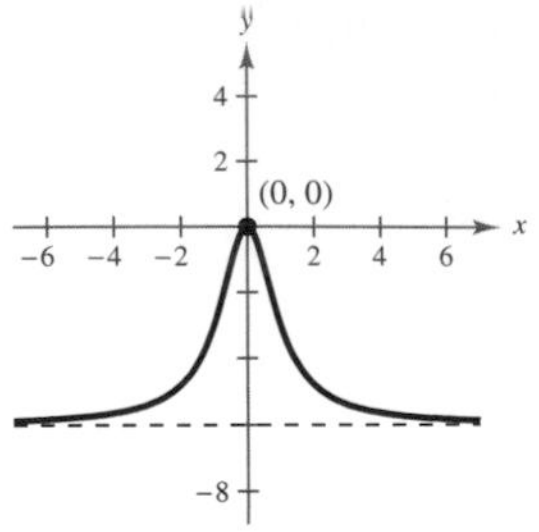

129. (a) Domain: all real numbers x except $x = 0, \frac{1}{3}$
(b) x-intercept: $(1.5, 0)$
(c) Vertical asymptote: $x = 0$
Horizontal asymptote: $y = 2$
(d)

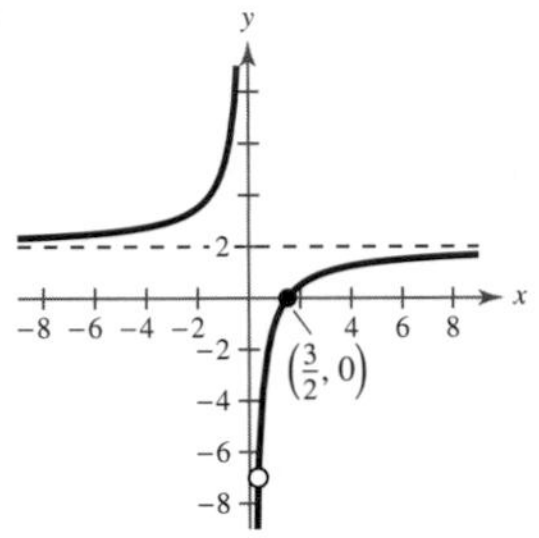

131. (a) Domain: all real numbers x
(b) Intercept: $(0, 0)$ (c) Slant asymptote: $y = 2x$
(d)

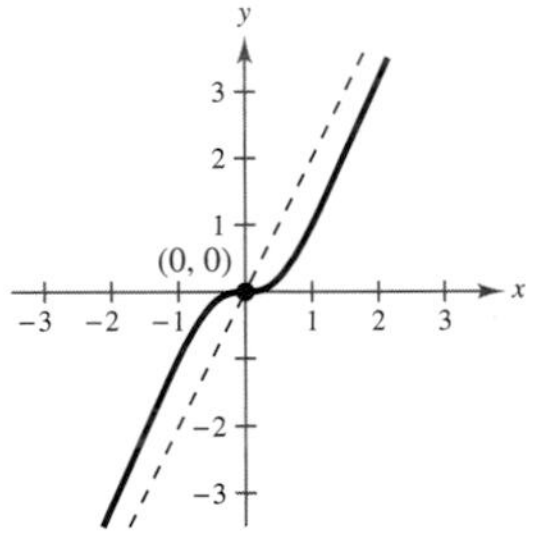

133. (a) Domain: all real numbers x except $x = \frac{4}{3}$
(b) y-intercept: $(0, -0.5)$
x-intercepts: $\left(\frac{2}{3}, 0\right)$, $(1, 0)$
(c) Vertical asymptote: $x = \frac{4}{3}$
Slant asymptote: $y = x - \frac{1}{3}$
(d)

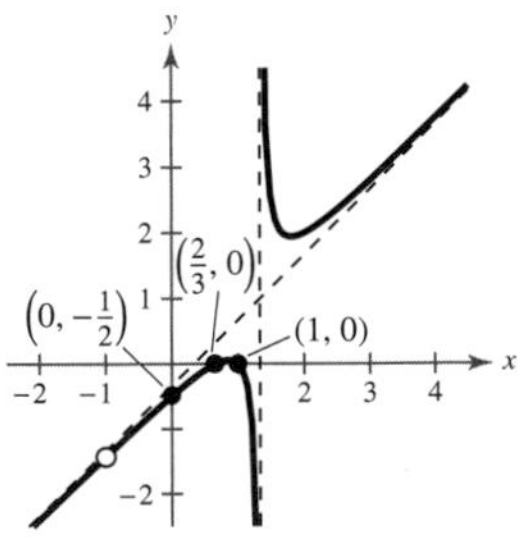

135. \$0.50 is the horizontal asymptote of the function.

137. (a)

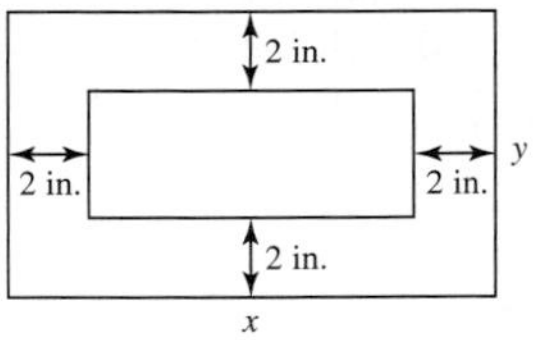

(b) $(x - 4)(y - 4) = 30$

$$y = \frac{4x + 14}{x - 4}$$

$$\text{Area} = x\left(\frac{4x + 14}{x - 4}\right) = \frac{2x(2x + 7)}{x - 4}$$

(c) $4 < x < \infty$

(d)

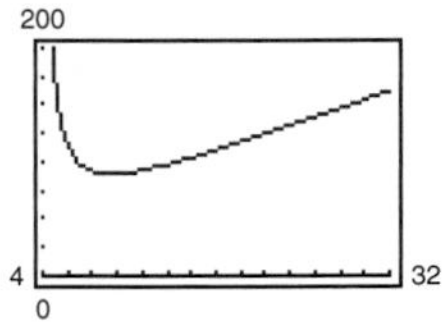

9.48 inches × 9.48 inches

139. $\left(-\frac{4}{3}, \frac{1}{2}\right)$ **141.** $[-4, 0] \cup [4, \infty)$

143. $[-5, -1) \cup (1, \infty)$ **145.** $[-4, -3] \cup (0, \infty)$

147. 4.9%

149. False. A fourth-degree polynomial can have at most four zeros, and complex zeros occur in conjugate pairs.

151. Find the vertex of the quadratic function and write the function in standard form. If the leading coefficient is positive, the vertex is a minimum. If the leading coefficient is negative, the vertex is a maximum.

153. An asymptote of a graph is a line to which the graph becomes arbitrarily close as x increases or decreases without bound.

Chapter Test *(page 212)*

1. (a) Reflection in the x-axis followed by a vertical translation

(b) Horizontal translation

2. $y = (x - 3)^2 - 6$

3. (a) 50 feet

(b) 5. Yes, changing the constant term results in a vertical translation of the graph and therefore changes the maximum height.

4. Rises to the left, falls to the right

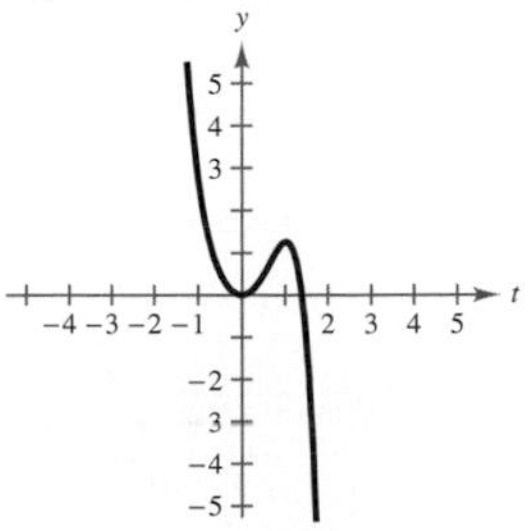

5. $3x + \dfrac{x - 1}{x^2 + 1}$ **6.** $2x^3 + 4x^2 + 3x + 6 + \dfrac{9}{x - 2}$

7. $(4x - 1)(x - \sqrt{3})(x + \sqrt{3})$;
Solutions: $\frac{1}{4}, \pm\sqrt{3}$

8. (a) $-3 + 5i$ (b) 7 **9.** $2 - i$

10. $f(x) = x^4 - 9x^3 + 28x^2 - 30x$

11. $f(x) = x^4 - 6x^3 + 16x^2 - 24x + 16$

12. $-2, \pm\sqrt{5}i$ **13.** $-2, 4, -1 \pm \sqrt{2}i$

14. x-intercepts: $(-2, 0), (2, 0)$
No y-intercept
Vertical asymptote: $x = 0$
Horizontal asymptote: $y = -1$

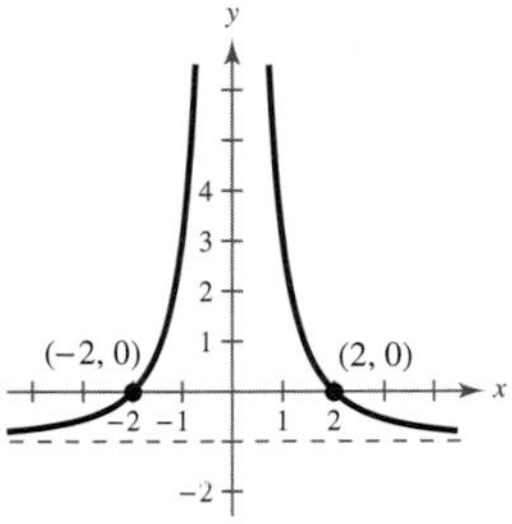

15. x-intercept: $(-1.5, 0)$
y-intercept: $(0, 0.75)$
Vertical asymptote: $x = -4$
Horizontal asymptote: $y = 2$

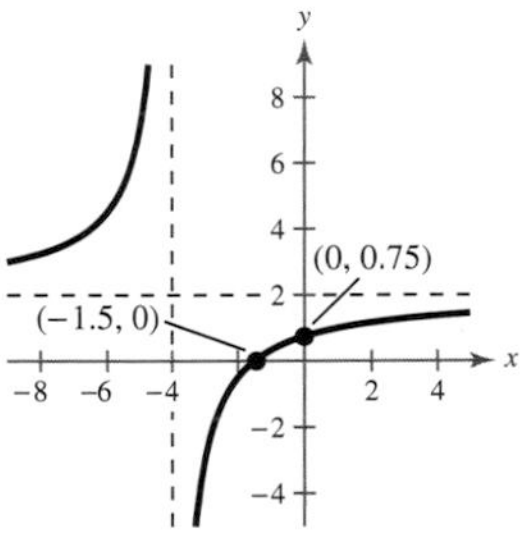

16. No x-intercept
y-intercept: $(0, -2)$
Vertical asymptote: $x = 1$
Slant asymptote: $y = x + 1$

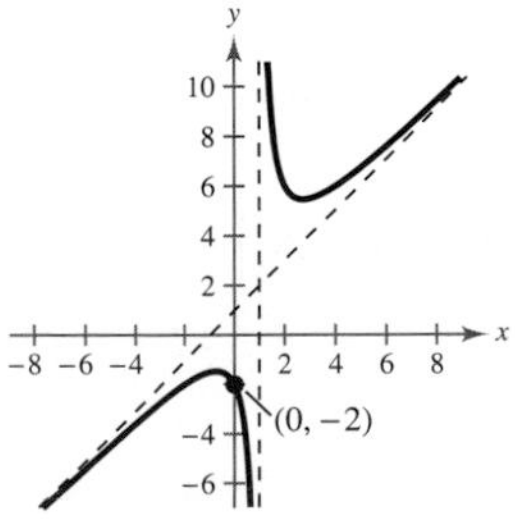

17. $x < -4$ or $x > \frac{3}{2}$

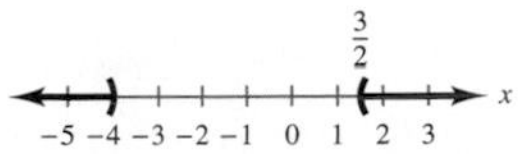

18. $x < -6$ or $0 < x < 4$

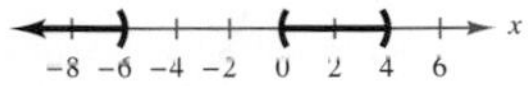

CHAPTER 2

Problem Solving (page 215)

1. Answers will vary.
3. 2 inches × 2 inches × 5 inches
5. (a) and (b) $y = -x^2 + 5x - 4$
7. (a) $f(x) = (x - 2)x^2 + 5 = x^3 - 2x^2 + 5$
   (b) $f(x) = -(x + 3)x^2 + 1 = -x^3 - 3x^2 + 1$
9. $(a + bi)(a - bi) = a^2 + abi - abi - b^2i^2$
   $= a^2 + b^2$
11. (a) As $|a|$ increases, the graph stretches vertically. For $a < 0$, the graph is reflected in the x-axis.
    (b) As $|b|$ increases, the vertical asymptote is translated. For $b > 0$, the graph is translated to the right. For $b < 0$, the graph is reflected in the x-axis and is translated to the left.

Chapter 3

Section 3.1 (page 226)

Vocabulary Check (page 226)

1. algebraic 2. transcendental
3. natural exponential; natural 4. $A = P\left(1 + \frac{r}{n}\right)^{nt}$
5. $A = Pe^{rt}$

1. 946.852 3. 0.006 5. 1767.767
7. d 8. c 9. a 10. b

11.

x	-2	-1	0	1	2
$f(x)$	4	2	1	0.5	0.25

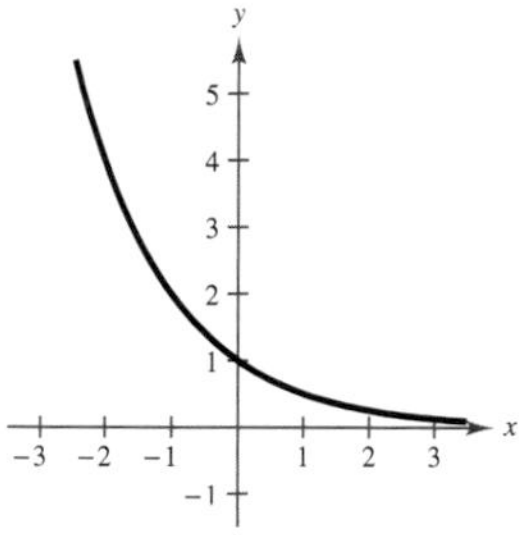

13.

x	-2	-1	0	1	2
$f(x)$	36	6	1	0.167	0.028

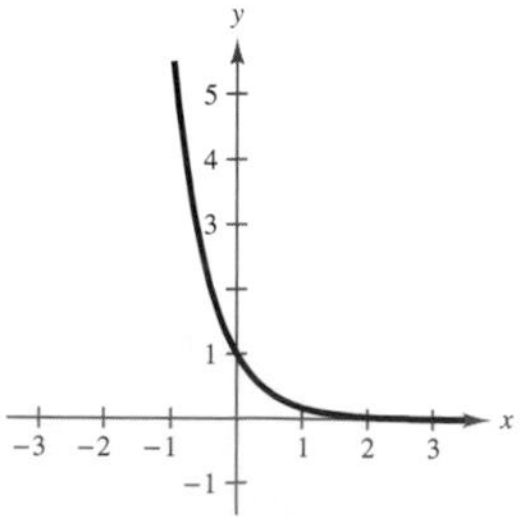

15.

x	-2	-1	0	1	2
$f(x)$	0.125	0.25	0.5	1	2

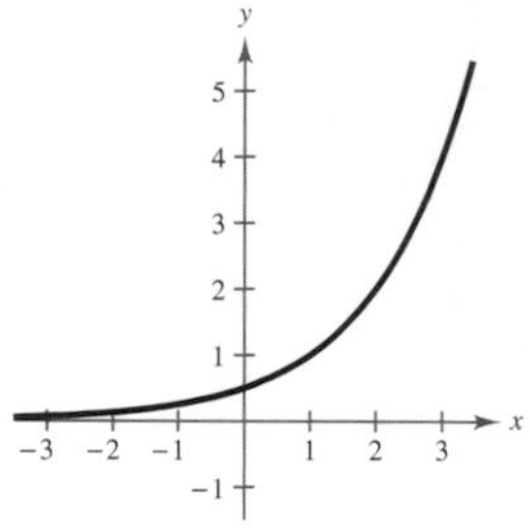

17. Shift the graph of f four units to the right.
19. Shift the graph of f five units upward.
21. Reflect the graph of f in the x-axis and y-axis and shift six units to the right.

23.

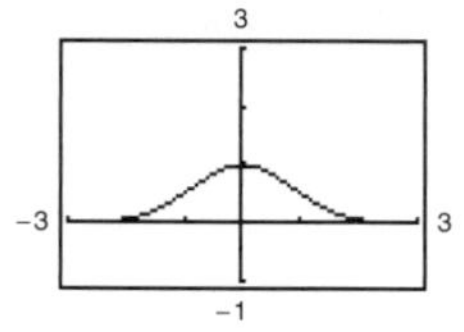

25.

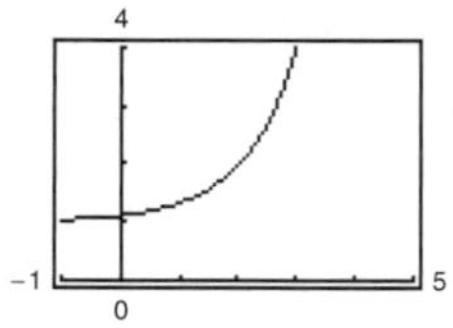

27. 0.472 29. 3.857×10^{-22} 31. 7166.647

33.

x	-2	-1	0	1	2
$f(x)$	0.135	0.368	1	2.718	7.389

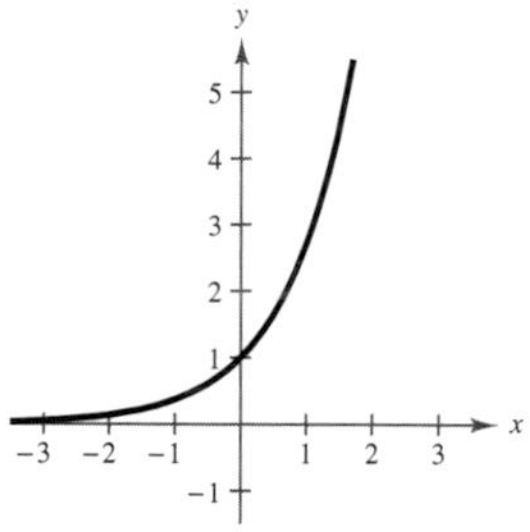

35.

x	-8	-7	-6	-5	-4
$f(x)$	0.055	0.149	0.406	1.104	3

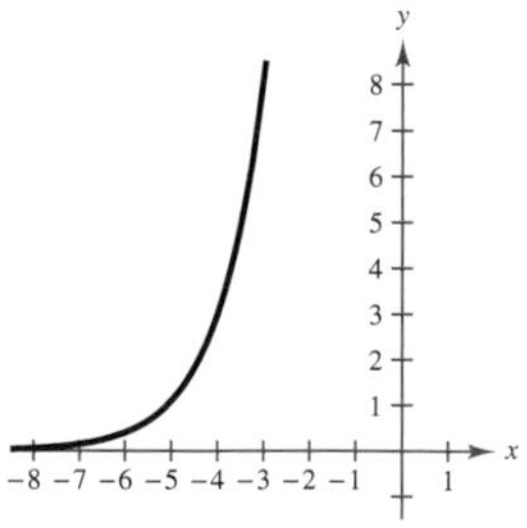

37.

x	-2	-1	0	1	2
$f(x)$	4.037	4.100	4.271	4.736	6

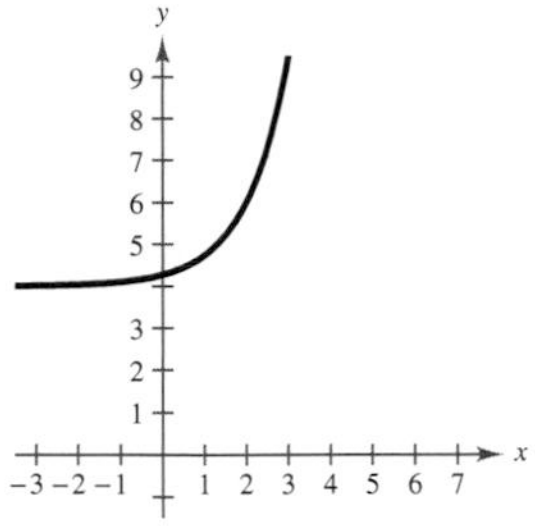

39.

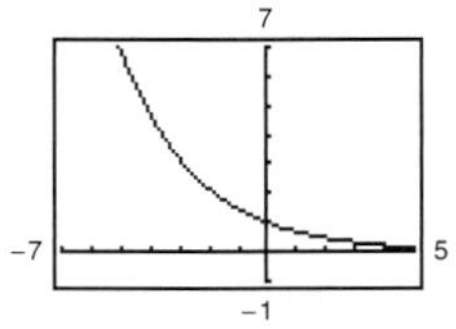

41.

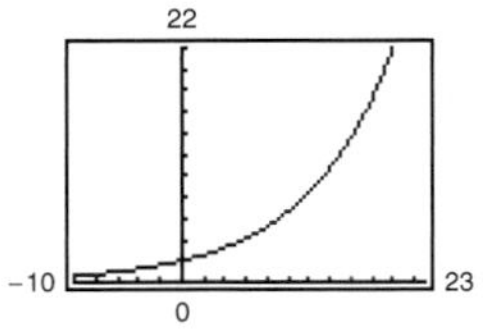

43.

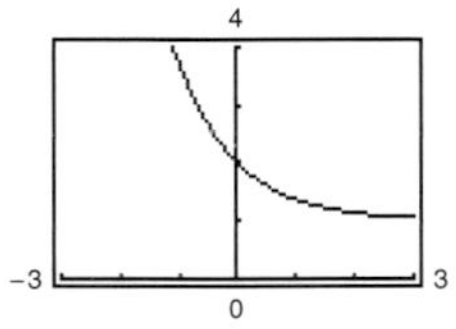

45. $x = 2$ **47.** $x = -3$ **49.** $x = \frac{1}{3}$ **51.** $x = 3, -1$

53.

n	1	2	4
A	\$3200.21	\$3205.09	\$3207.57

n	12	365	Continuous
A	\$3209.23	\$3210.06	\$3210.06

55.

n	1	2	4
A	\$4515.28	\$4535.05	\$4545.11

n	12	365	Continuous
A	\$4551.89	\$4555.18	\$4555.30

57.

t	10	20	30
A	\$17,901.90	\$26,706.49	\$39,841.40

t	40	50
A	\$59,436.39	\$88,668.67

59.

t	10	20	30
A	\$22,986.49	\$44,031.56	\$84,344.25

t	40	50
A	\$161,564.86	\$309,484.08

61. \$222,822.57 **63.** \$35.45

65. (a) $V(1) = 10{,}000.298$ (b) $V(1.5) = 100{,}004.47$
(c) $V(2) = 1{,}000{,}059.6$

67. (a) 25 grams (b) 16.21 grams
(c)

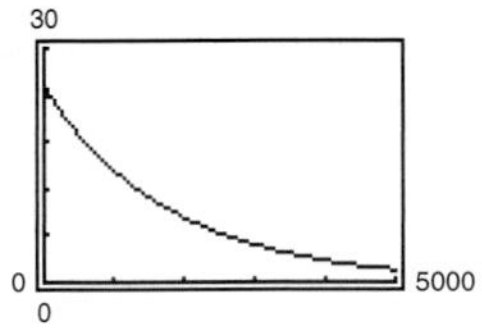

69. (a)

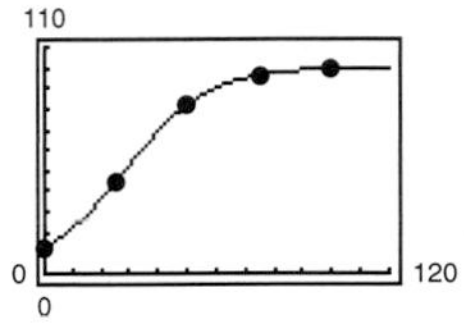

(b)

x	0	25	50	75	100
Model	12.5	44.5	81.82	96.19	99.3
Actual	12	44	81	96	99

(c) 63.14% (d) 38 masses

71. True. As $x \to -\infty$, $f(x) \to -2$ but never reaches -2.

73. $f(x) = h(x)$ **75.** $f(x) = g(x) = h(x)$

77. (a) $x < 0$ (b) $x > 0$

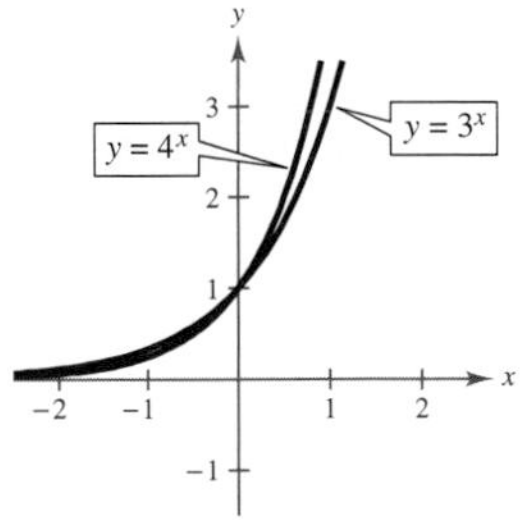

79.

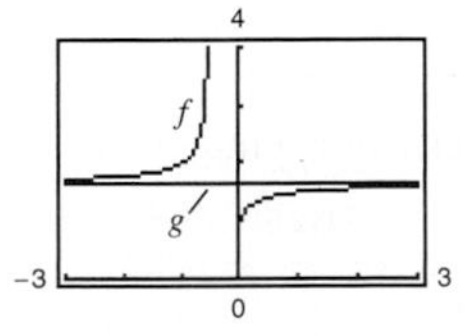

As $x \to \infty$, $f(x) \to g(x)$.
As $x \to -\infty$, $f(x) \to g(x)$.

81. $y = \pm\sqrt{25 - x^2}$

CHAPTER 3

83.

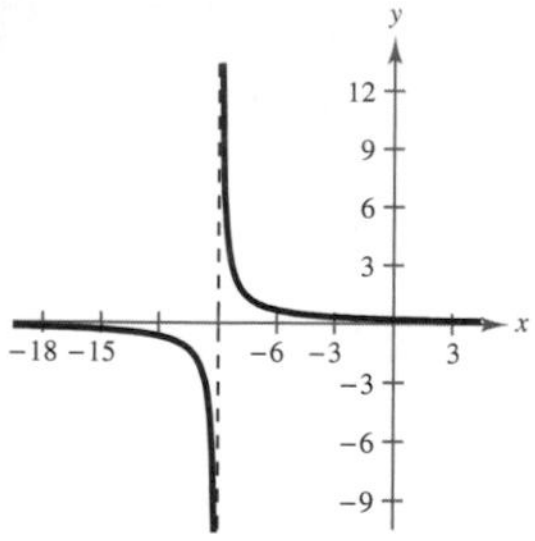

85. Answers will vary.

Section 3.2 *(page 236)*

Vocabulary Check *(page 236)*

1. logarithmic **2.** 10 **3.** natural; e
4. $a^{\log_a x} = x$ **5.** $x = y$

1. $4^3 = 64$ **3.** $7^{-2} = \frac{1}{49}$ **5.** $32^{2/5} = 4$
7. $36^{1/2} = 6$ **9.** $\log_5 125 = 3$ **11.** $\log_{81} 3 = \frac{1}{4}$
13. $\log_6 \frac{1}{36} = -2$ **15.** $\log_7 1 = 0$ **17.** 4 **19.** 0
21. 2 **23.** -0.0972 **25.** 1.097 **27.** 4 **29.** 1

31.

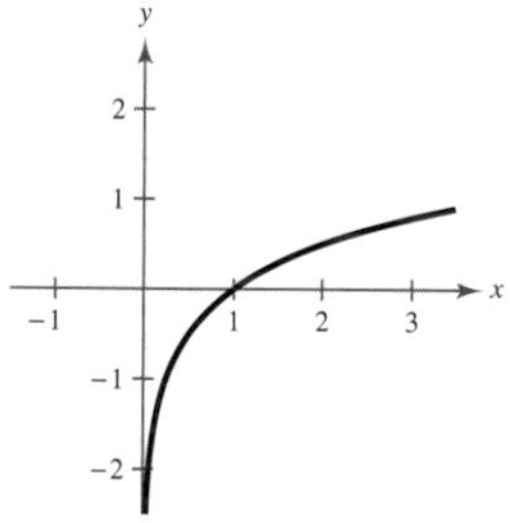

Domain: $(0, \infty)$
x-intercept: $(1, 0)$
Vertical asymptote: $x = 0$

33.

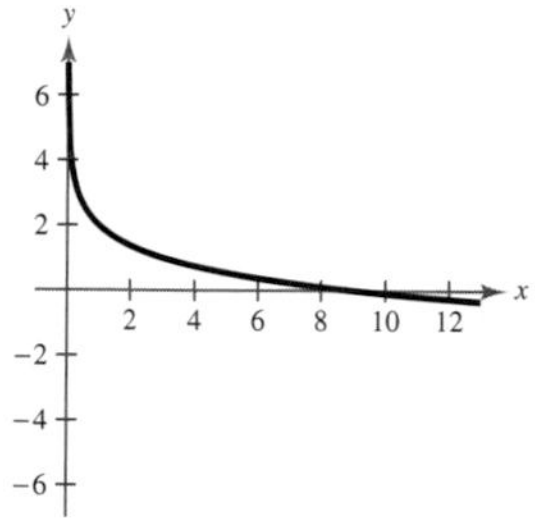

Domain: $(0, \infty)$
x-intercept: $(9, 0)$
Vertical asymptote: $x = 0$

35.

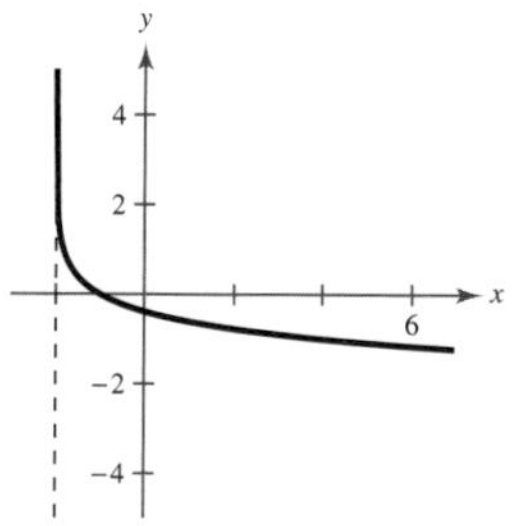

Domain: $(-2, \infty)$
x-intercept: $(-1, 0)$
Vertical asymptote: $x = -2$

37.

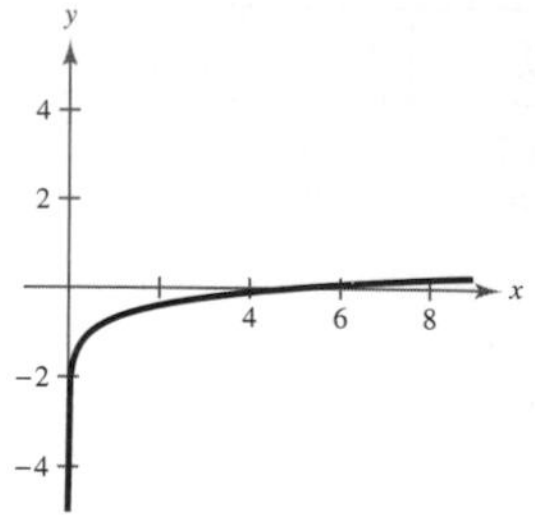

Domain: $(0, \infty)$
x-intercept: $(5, 0)$
Vertical asymptote: $x = 0$

39. c **40.** f **41.** d **42.** e **43.** b **44.** a
45. $e^{-0.693\ldots} = \frac{1}{2}$ **47.** $e^{1.386\ldots} = 4$
49. $e^{5.521\ldots} = 250$ **51.** $e^0 = 1$
53. $\ln 20.0855\ldots = 3$ **55.** $\ln 1.6487\ldots = \frac{1}{2}$
57. $\ln 0.6065\ldots = -0.5$ **59.** $\ln 4 = x$ **61.** 2.913
63. -0.575 **65.** 3 **67.** $-\frac{2}{3}$

69.

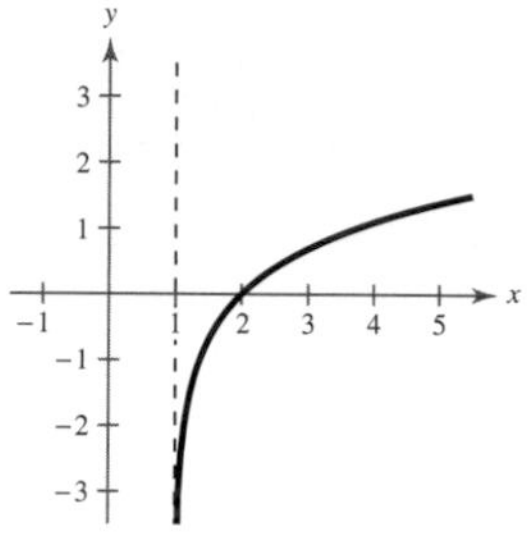

Domain: $(1, \infty)$
x-intercept: $(2, 0)$
Vertical asymptote: $x = 1$

71.

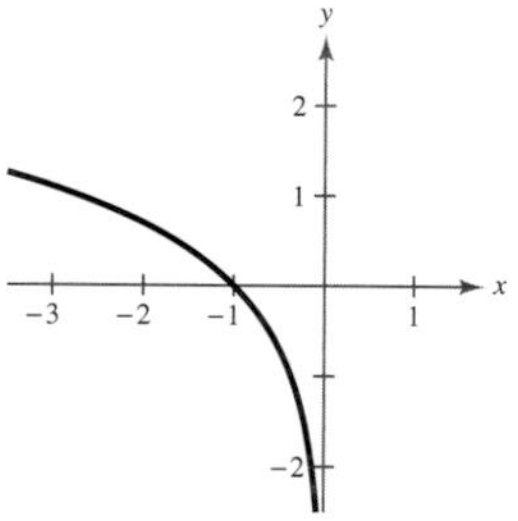

Domain: $(-\infty, 0)$
x-intercept: $(-1, 0)$
Vertical asymptote: $x = 0$

73.

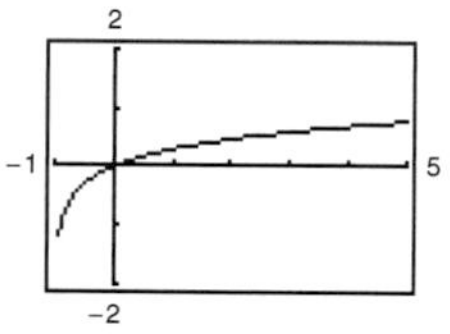

75.

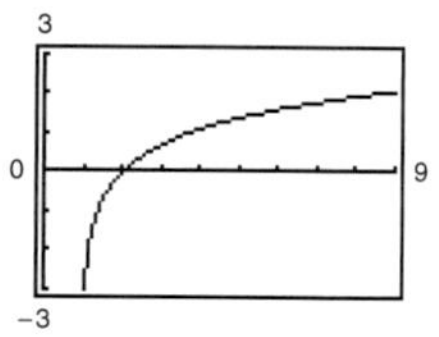

77.

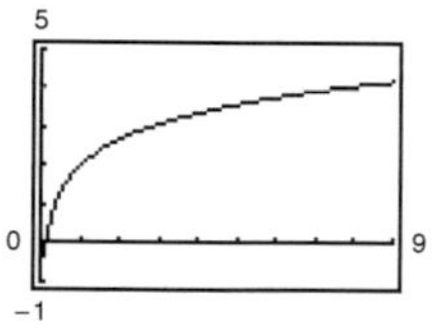

79. $x = 3$ **81.** $x = 7$ **83.** $x = 4$ **85.** $x = -5, 5$
87. (a) 30 years; 20 years (b) \$396,234; \$301,123.20
(c) \$246,234; \$151,123.20
(d) $x = 1000$; The monthly payment must be greater than \$1000.

89. (a)
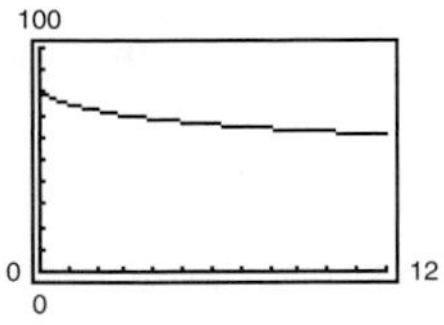

(b) 80
(c) 68.1
(d) 62.3

91. False. Reflecting $g(x)$ about the line $y = x$ will determine the graph of $f(x)$.

93.
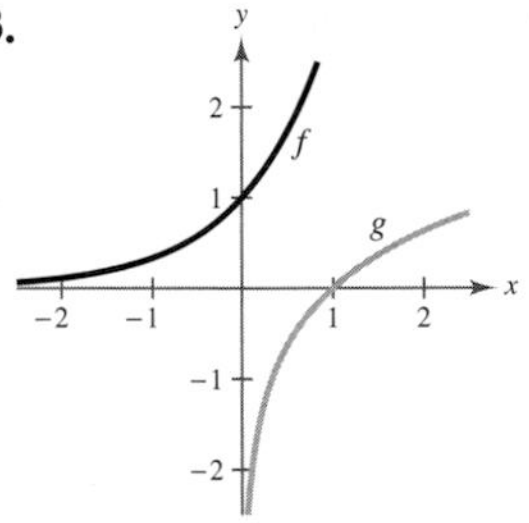

The functions f and g are inverses.

95.
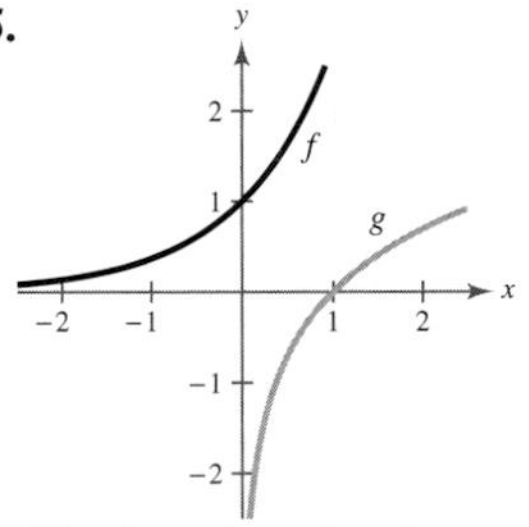

The functions f and g are inverses.

97. (a)
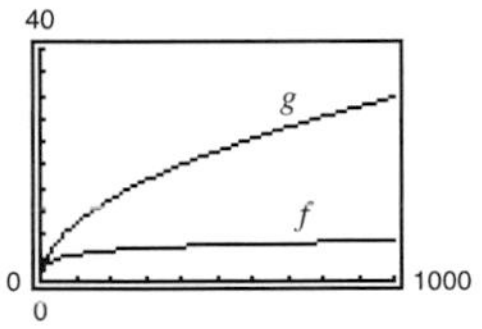

$g(x)$; The natural log function grows at a slower rate than the square root function.

(b)
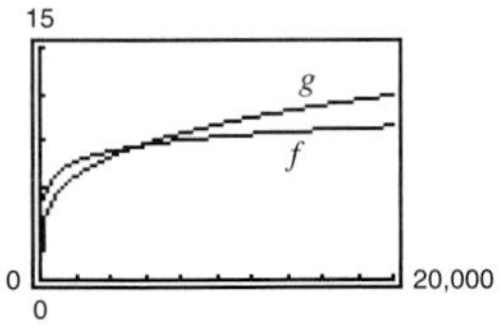

$g(x)$; The natural log function grows at a slower rate than the fourth root function.

99. (a) False (b) True (c) True (d) False

101. (a)
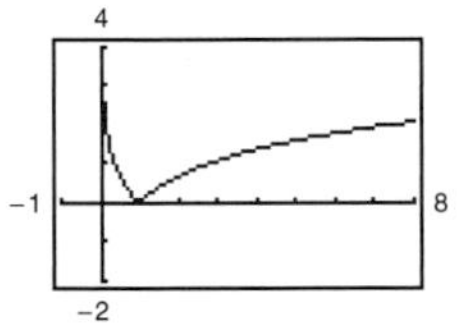

(b) Increasing: $(1, \infty)$
Decreasing: $(0, 1)$

(c) Relative minimum: $(1, 0)$

103. 15 **105.** 4300 **107.** 1028

Section 3.3 *(page 243)*

Vocabulary Check *(page 243)*

1. change-of-base **2.** $\dfrac{\log x}{\log a} = \dfrac{\ln x}{\ln a}$

3. c **4.** a **5.** b

1. (a) $\dfrac{\log x}{\log 5}$ (b) $\dfrac{\ln x}{\ln 5}$ **3.** (a) $\dfrac{\log x}{\log \frac{1}{5}}$ (b) $\dfrac{\ln x}{\ln \frac{1}{5}}$

5. (a) $\dfrac{\log \frac{3}{10}}{\log x}$ (b) $\dfrac{\ln \frac{3}{10}}{\ln x}$ **7.** (a) $\dfrac{\log x}{\log 2.6}$ (b) $\dfrac{\ln x}{\ln 2.6}$

9. 1.771 **11.** -2.000 **13.** -0.417 **15.** 2.633

17. $\frac{3}{2}$ **19.** $-3 - \log_5 2$ **21.** $6 + \ln 5$ **23.** 2

25. $\frac{3}{4}$ **27.** 2.4 **29.** -9 is not in the domain of $\log_3 x$.

31. 4.5 **33.** $-\frac{1}{2}$ **35.** 7 **37.** 2

39. $\log_4 5 + \log_4 x$ **41.** $4 \log_8 x$ **43.** $1 - \log_5 x$

45. $\frac{1}{2} \ln z$ **47.** $\ln x + \ln y + 2 \ln z$

49. $\ln z + 2 \ln(z - 1)$ **51.** $\frac{1}{2} \log_2(a - 1) - 2 \log_2 3$

53. $\frac{1}{3} \ln x - \frac{1}{3} \ln y$ **55.** $4 \ln x + \frac{1}{2} \ln y - 5 \ln z$

57. $2 \log_5 x - 2 \log_5 y - 3 \log_5 z$

59. $\dfrac{3}{4} \ln x + \dfrac{1}{4} \ln(x^2 + 3)$ **61.** $\ln 3x$ **63.** $\log_4 \dfrac{z}{y}$

65. $\log_2(x + 4)^2$ **67.** $\log_3 \sqrt[4]{5x}$ **69.** $\ln \dfrac{x}{(x + 1)^3}$

71. $\log \dfrac{xz^3}{y^2}$ **73.** $\ln \dfrac{x}{(x^2 - 4)^4}$ **75.** $\ln \sqrt[3]{\dfrac{x(x + 3)^2}{x^2 - 1}}$

77. $\log_8 \dfrac{\sqrt[3]{y(y + 4)^2}}{y - 1}$

79. $\log_2 \frac{32}{4} = \log_2 32 - \log_2 4$; Property 2

81. $\beta = 10(\log I + 12)$; 60 dB **83.** ≈ 3

85. $y = 256.24 - 20.8 \ln x$

87. False. $\ln 1 = 0$ **89.** False. $\ln(x - 2) \neq \ln x - \ln 2$

91. False. $u = v^2$ **93.** Answers will vary.

95. $f(x) = \dfrac{\log x}{\log 2} = \dfrac{\ln x}{\ln 2}$

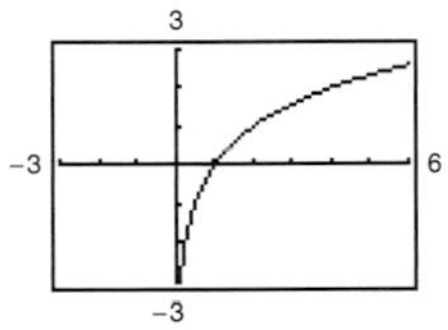

97. $f(x) = \dfrac{\log x}{\log \frac{1}{2}} = \dfrac{\ln x}{\ln \frac{1}{2}}$

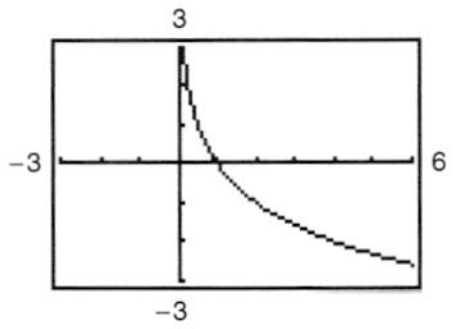

99. $f(x) = \dfrac{\log x}{\log 11.8} = \dfrac{\ln x}{\ln 11.8}$

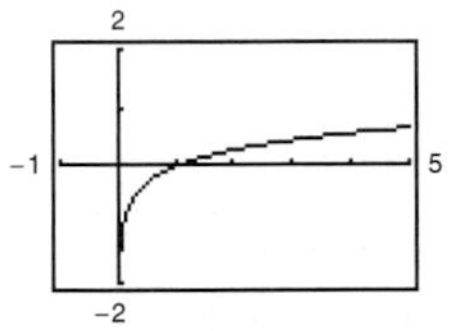

101. $f(x) = h(x)$; Property 2

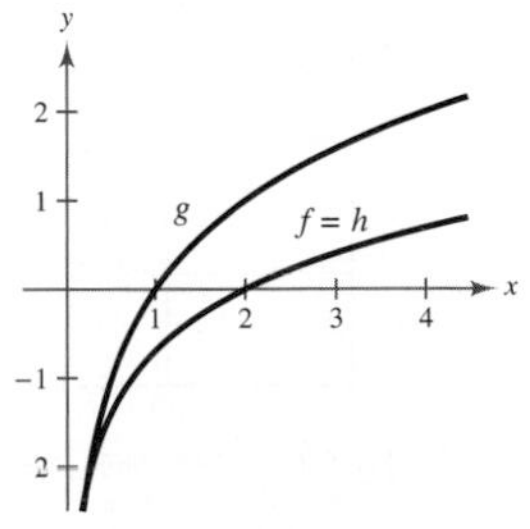

103. $\frac{3x^4}{2y^3}, x \neq 0$ **105.** $1, x \neq 0, y \neq 0$

107. $-1, \frac{1}{3}$ **109.** $\frac{-1 \pm \sqrt{97}}{6}$

Section 3.4 *(page 253)*

Vocabulary Check *(page 253)*

1. solve
2. (a) $x = y$ (b) $x = y$ (c) x (d) x
3. extraneous

1. (a) Yes (b) No
3. (a) No (b) Yes (c) Yes, approximate
5. (a) Yes, approximate (b) No (c) Yes
7. (a) No (b) Yes (c) Yes, approximate
9. 2 **11.** -5 **13.** 2 **15.** $\ln 2 \approx 0.693$
17. $e^{-1} \approx 0.368$ **19.** 64 **21.** (3, 8) **23.** (9, 2)
25. $2, -1$ **27.** $\approx 1.618, \approx -0.618$
29. $\frac{\ln 5}{\ln 3} \approx 1.465$ **31.** $\ln 5 \approx 1.609$ **33.** $\ln 28 \approx 3.332$
35. $\frac{\ln 80}{2 \ln 3} \approx 1.994$ **37.** 2 **39.** 4
41. $3 - \frac{\ln 565}{\ln 2} \approx -6.142$ **43.** $\frac{1}{3}\log\left(\frac{3}{2}\right) \approx 0.059$
45. $1 + \frac{\ln 7}{\ln 5} \approx 2.209$ **47.** $\frac{\ln 12}{3} \approx 0.828$
49. $-\ln\frac{3}{5} \approx 0.511$ **51.** 0 **53.** $\frac{\ln \frac{8}{3}}{3 \ln 2} + \frac{1}{3} \approx 0.805$
55. $\ln 5 \approx 1.609$ **57.** $\ln 4 \approx 1.386$
59. $2 \ln 75 \approx 8.635$ **61.** $\frac{1}{2} \ln 1498 \approx 3.656$
63. $\frac{\ln 4}{365 \ln\left(1 + \frac{0.065}{365}\right)} \approx 21.330$
65. $\frac{\ln 2}{12 \ln\left(1 + \frac{0.10}{12}\right)} \approx 6.960$

67.
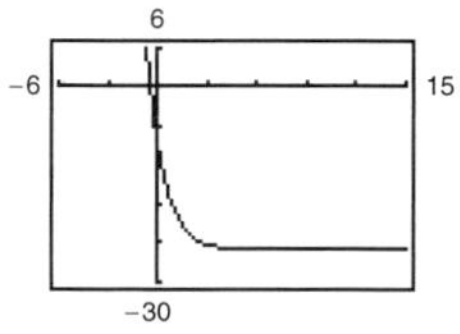

-0.427

69.
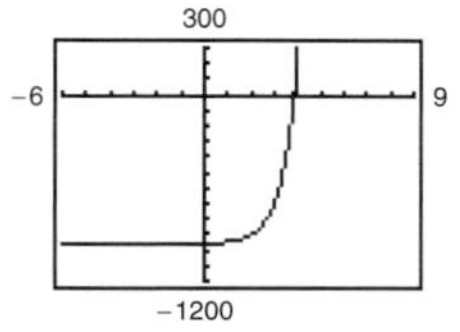

3.847

71.
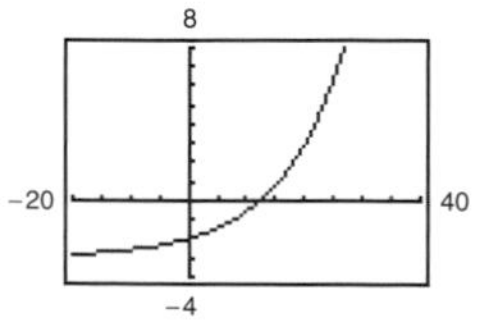

12.207

73.
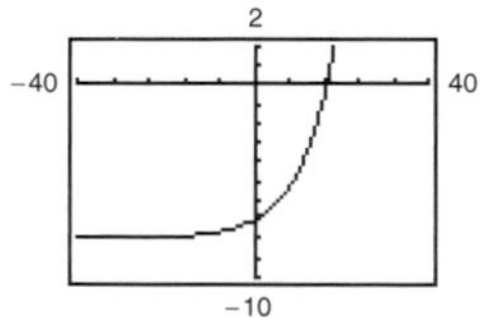

16.636

75. $e^{-3} \approx 0.050$ **77.** $\frac{e^{2.4}}{2} \approx 5.512$ **79.** 1,000,000
81. $\frac{e^{10/3}}{5} \approx 5.606$ **83.** $e^2 - 2 \approx 5.389$
85. $e^{-2/3} \approx 0.513$ **87.** $2(3^{11/6}) \approx 14.988$
89. No solution **91.** $1 + \sqrt{1 + e} \approx 2.928$
93. No solution **95.** 7 **97.** $\frac{-1 + \sqrt{17}}{2} \approx 1.562$
99. 2 **101.** $\frac{725 + 125\sqrt{33}}{8} \approx 180.384$

103.
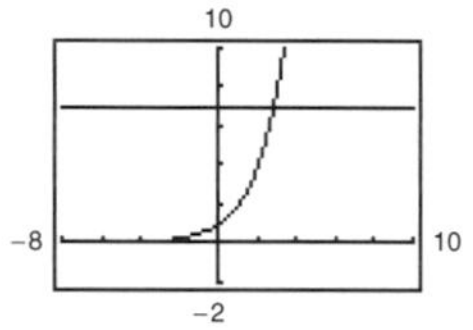

2.807

105.
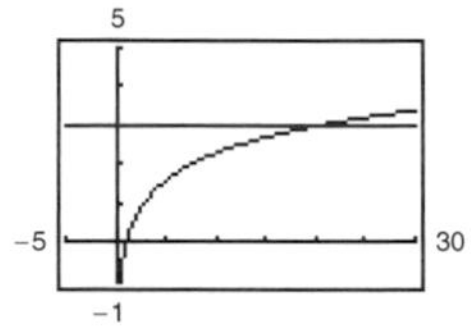

20.086

107. (a) 8.2 years (b) 12.9 years
109. (a) 1426 units (b) 1498 units
111. (a)
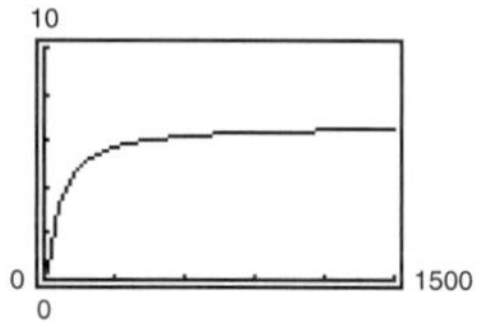

(b) $V = 6.7$; The yield will approach 6.7 million cubic feet per acre.
(c) 29.3 years

113. 2001
115. (a) $y = 100$ and $y = 0$; The range falls between 0% and 100%.
(b) Males: 69.71 inches Females: 64.51 inches
117. (a)

x	0.2	0.4	0.6	0.8	1.0
y	162.6	78.5	52.5	40.5	33.9

(b)
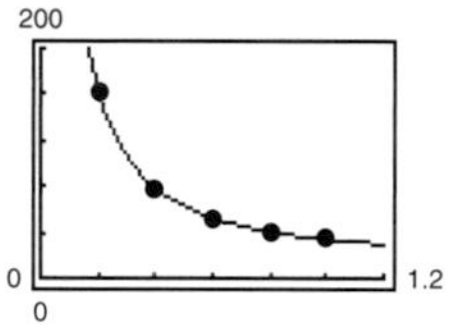

The model appears to fit the data well.
(c) 1.2 meters
(d) No. According to the model, when the number of g's is less than 23, x is between 2.276 meters and 4.404 meters, which isn't realistic in most vehicles.
119. $\log_b uv = \log_b u + \log_b v$
True by Property 1 in Section 5.3.
121. $\log_b(u - v) = \log_b u - \log_b v$
False.
$1.95 \approx \log(100 - 10) \neq \log 100 - \log 10 = 1$
123. Yes. See Exercise 93.
125. Yes. Time to double: $t = \frac{\ln 2}{r}$;
Time to quadruple: $t = \frac{\ln 4}{r} = 2\left(\frac{\ln 2}{r}\right)$

127. $4|x|y^2\sqrt{3y}$ **129.** $5\sqrt[3]{3}$

131.

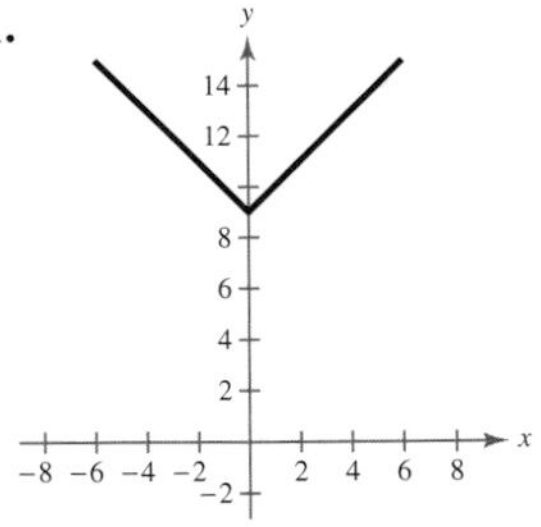

133.

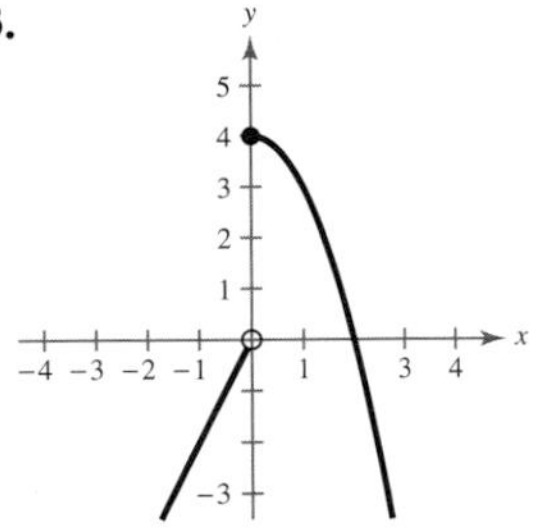

135. 1.226 **137.** -5.595

Section 3.5 *(page 264)*

Vocabulary Check *(page 264)*

1. $y = ae^{bx}$; $y = ae^{-bx}$
2. $y = a + b\ln x$; $y = a + b\log x$
3. normally distributed **4.** bell; average value
5. sigmoidal

1. c **2.** e **3.** b **4.** a **5.** d **6.** f

	Initial Investment	*Annual % Rate*	*Time to Double*	*Amount After 10 years*
7.	\$1000	3.5%	19.8 yr	\$1419.07
9.	\$750	8.9438%	7.75 yr	\$1834.36
11.	\$500	11.0%	6.3 yr	\$1505.00
13.	\$6376.28	4.5%	15.4 yr	\$10,000.00

15. \$112,087.09

17. (a) 6.642 years (b) 6.330 years
(c) 6.302 years (d) 6.301 years

19.

r	2%	4%	6%	8%	10%	12%
t	54.93	27.47	18.31	13.73	10.99	9.16

21.

r	2%	4%	6%	8%	10%	12%
t	55.48	28.01	18.85	14.27	11.53	9.69

23.

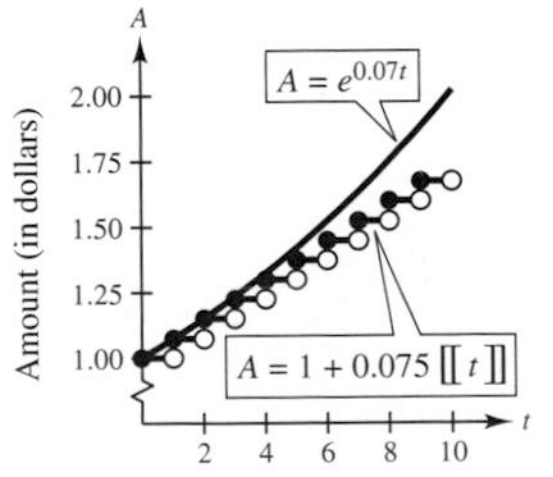

Continuous compounding

	Half-life (years)	*Initial Quantity*	*Amount After 1000 Years*
25.	1599	10 g	6.48 g
27.	5715	2.26 g	2 g
29.	24,100	2.16 g	2.1 g

31. $y = e^{0.7675x}$ **33.** $y = 5e^{-0.4024x}$

35. (a) Decreasing due to the negative exponent.
(b) 2000: population of 2430 thousand
2003: population of 2408.95 thousand
(c) 2018

37. $k = 0.2988$; $\approx 5{,}309{,}734$ hits **39.** 3.15 hours

41. (a) $\approx 12{,}180$ years old (b) ≈ 4797 years old

43. (a) $V = -6394t + 30{,}788$ (b) $V = 30{,}788e^{-0.268t}$
(c)

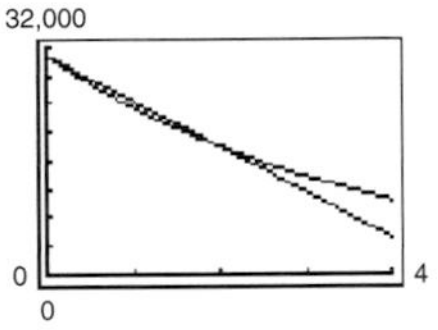

The exponential model depreciates faster.

(d)

t	1	3
$V = -6394t + 30{,}788$	24,394	11,606
$V = 30{,}788e^{-0.268t}$	23,550	13,779

(e) Answers will vary.

45. (a) $S(t) = 100(1 - e^{-0.1625t})$
(b)

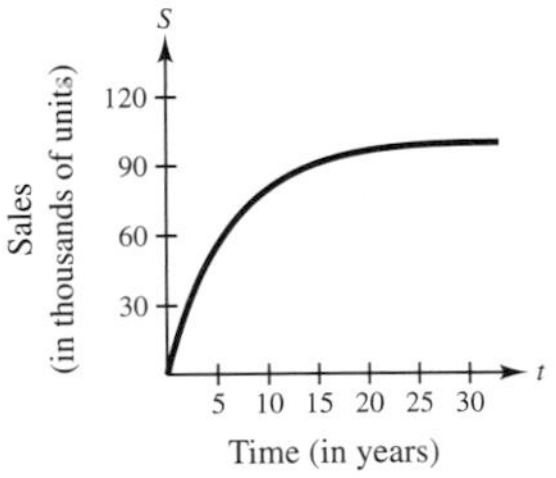

(c) 55,625

47. (a)

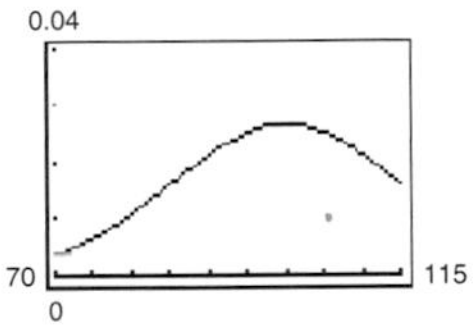

(b) 100

49. (a) 203 animals (b) 13 years
(c)

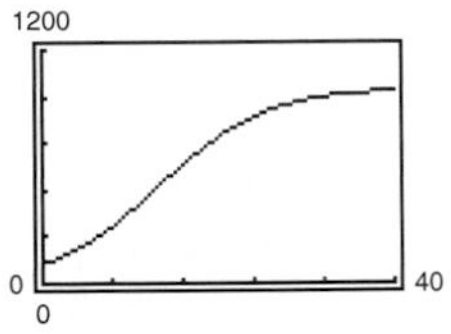

Horizontal asymptotes: $y = 0$, $y = 1000$. The population size will approach 1000 as time increases.

51. (a) $10^{7.9} \approx 79{,}432{,}823$ (b) $10^{8.3} \approx 199{,}526{,}231$
(c) $10^{4.2} \approx 15{,}849$

53. (a) 20 decibels (b) 70 decibels
(c) 40 decibels (d) 120 decibels

55. 95% **57.** 4.64 **59.** 1.58×10^{-6} moles per liter

61. $10^{5.1}$ **63.** 3:00 A.M.

65. (a)

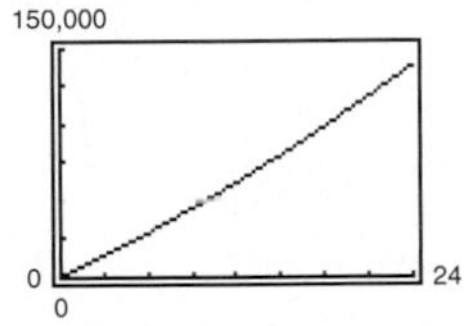

(b) ≈ 21 years; Yes

CHAPTER 3

67. False. The domain can be the set of real numbers for a logistic growth function.

69. False. The graph of $f(x)$ is the graph of $g(x)$ shifted upward five units.

71. (a) Logarithmic (b) Logistic (c) Exponential (d) Linear (e) None of the above (f) Exponential

73. (a)

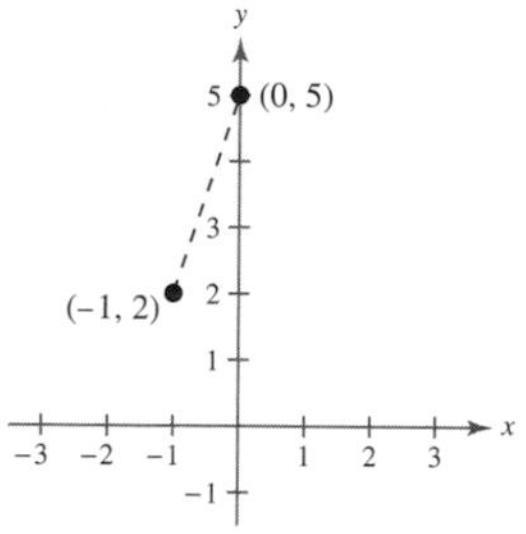

(b) $\sqrt{10}$
(c) $\left(-\frac{1}{2}, \frac{7}{2}\right)$
(d) 3

75. (a)

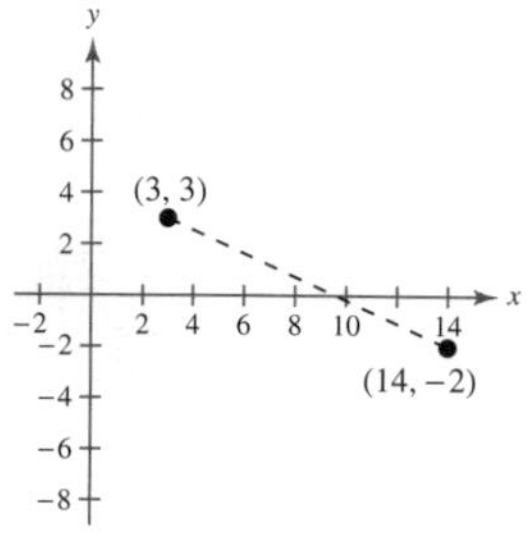

(b) $\sqrt{146}$
(c) $\left(\frac{17}{2}, \frac{1}{2}\right)$
(d) $-\frac{5}{11}$

77. (a)

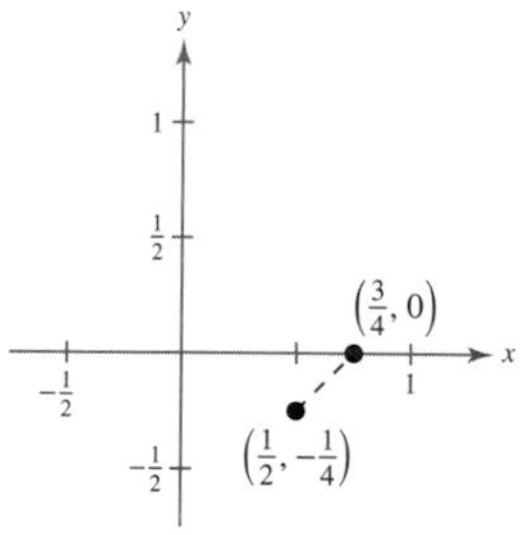

(b) $\sqrt{\frac{1}{8}}$
(c) $\left(\frac{5}{8}, -\frac{1}{8}\right)$
(d) 1

79.

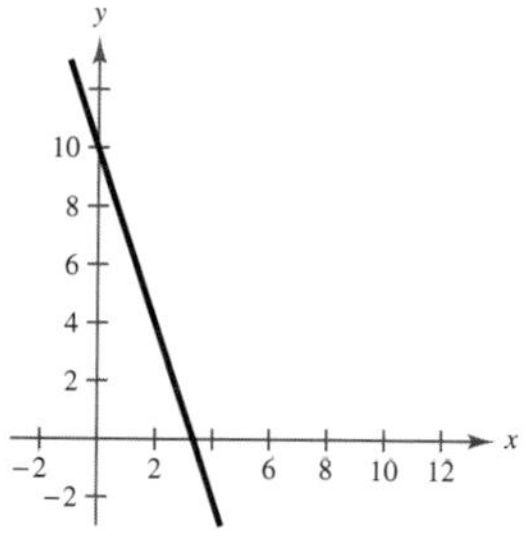

81.

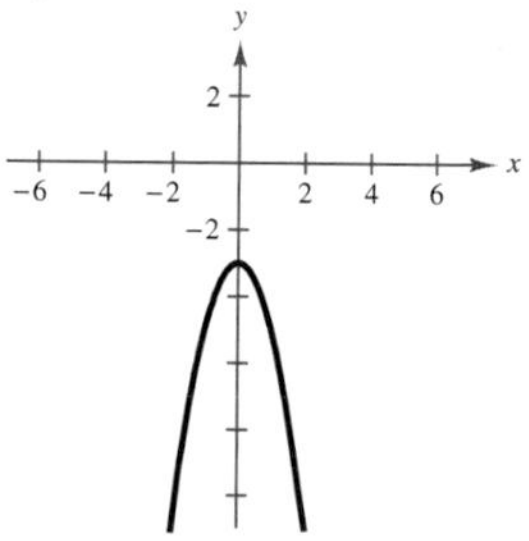

83.

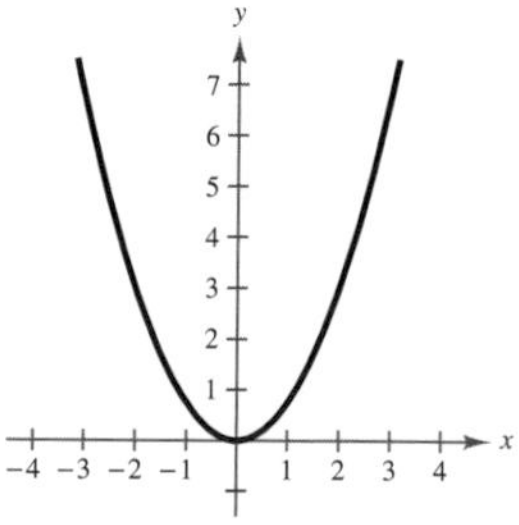

85.

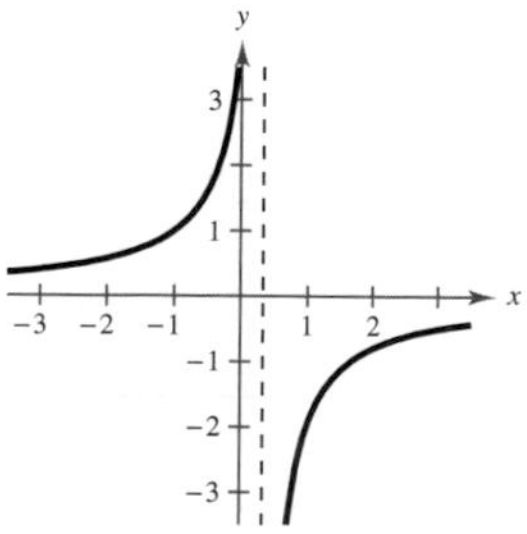

87.

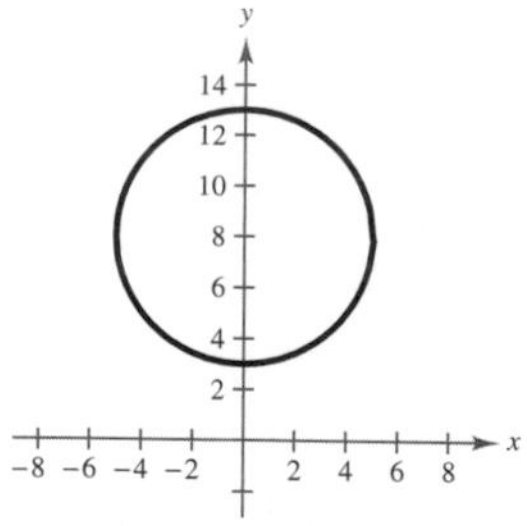

89.

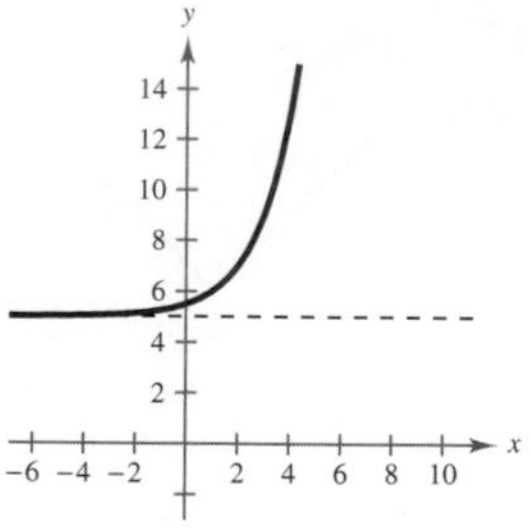

91.

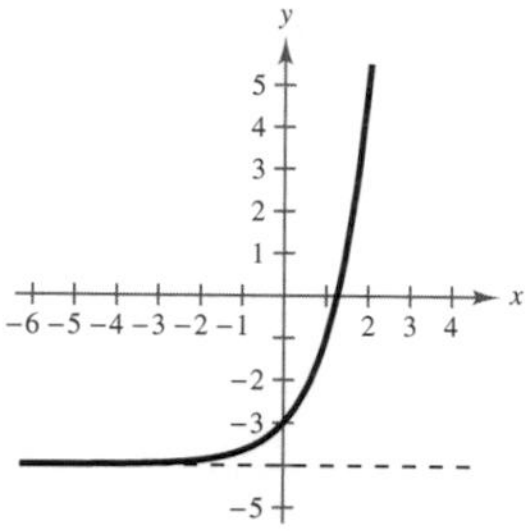

93. Answers will vary.

Review Exercises *(page 271)*

1. 76.699 **3.** 0.337 **5.** 1456.529

7. c **8.** d **9.** a **10.** b

11. Shift the graph of f one unit to the right.

13. Reflect f in the x-axis and shift two units to the left.

15.

x	-1	0	1	2	3
$f(x)$	8	5	4.25	4.063	4.016

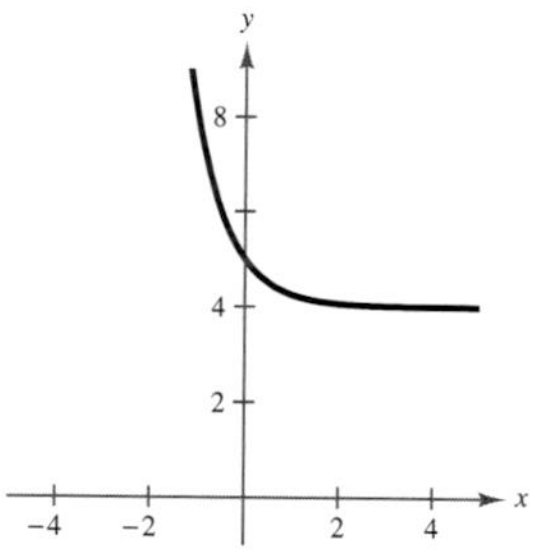

17.

x	-2	-1	0	1	2
$f(x)$	-0.377	-1	-2.65	-7.023	-18.61

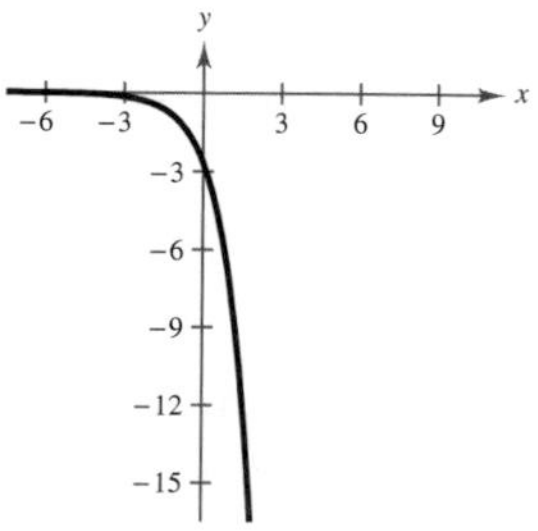

19.

x	-1	0	1	2	3
$f(x)$	4.008	4.04	4.2	5	9

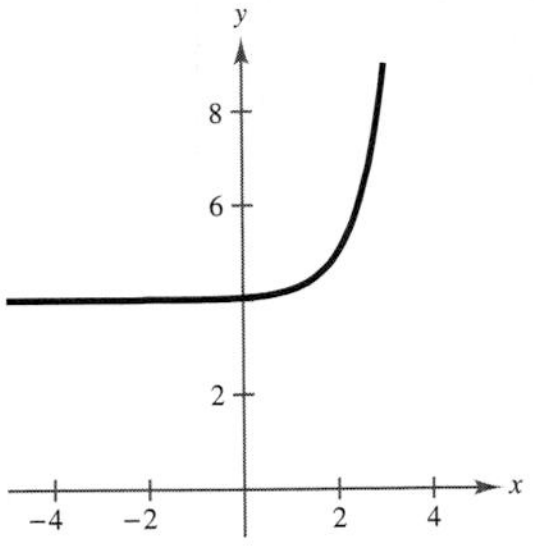

21.

x	-2	-1	0	1	2
$f(x)$	3.25	3.5	4	5	7

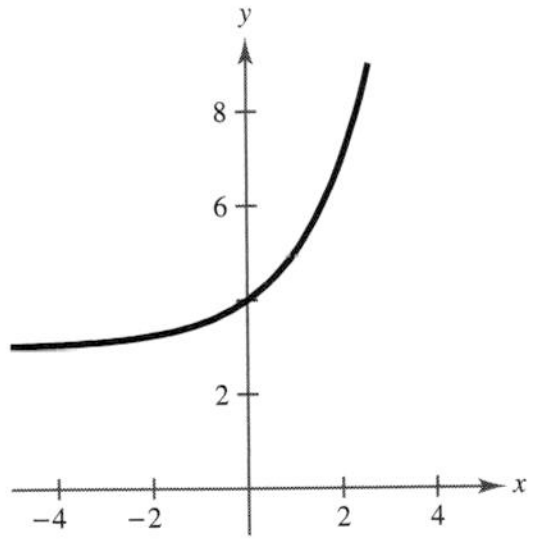

23. $x = -4$ **25.** $x = \frac{22}{5}$ **27.** 2980.958 **29.** 0.183

31.

x	-2	-1	0	1	2
$h(x)$	2.72	1.65	1	0.61	0.37

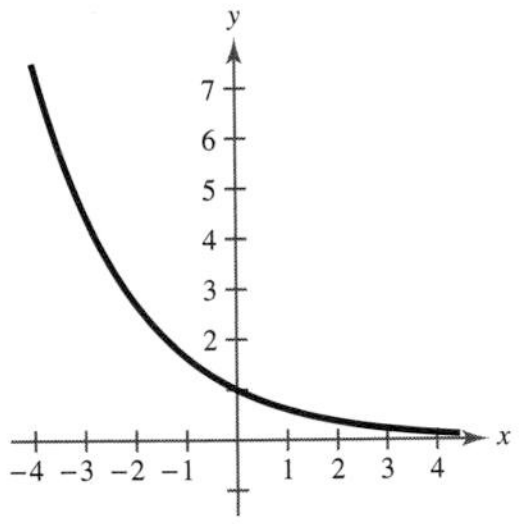

33.

x	-3	-2	-1	0	1
$f(x)$	0.37	1	2.72	7.39	20.09

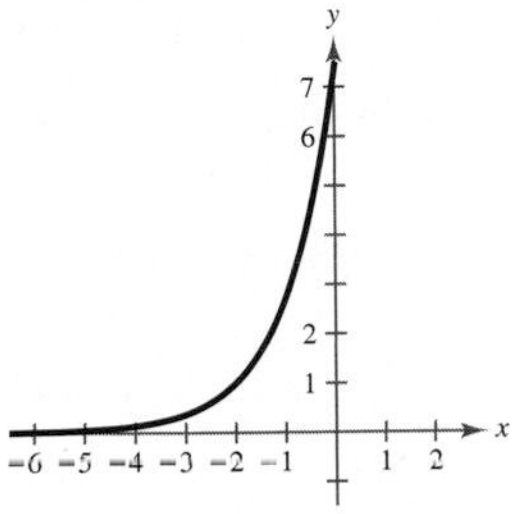

35.

n	1	2	4	12
A	\$6569.98	\$6635.43	\$6669.46	\$6692.64

n	365	Continuous
A	\$6704.00	\$6704.39

37. (a) 0.154 (b) 0.487 (c) 0.811

39. (a) \$1,069,047.14 (b) 7.9 years

41. $\log_4 64 = 3$ **43.** $\ln 2.2255\ldots = 0.8$

45. 3 **47.** -3 **49.** $x = 7$ **51.** $x = -5$

53. Domain: $(0, \infty)$
x-intercept: $(1, 0)$
Vertical asymptote: $x = 0$

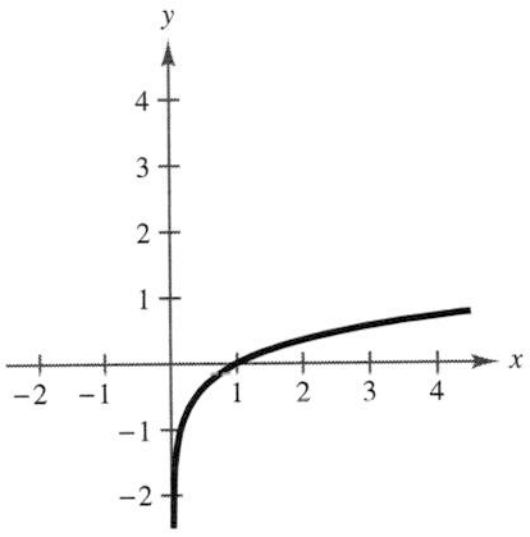

55. Domain: $(0, \infty)$
x-intercept: $(3, 0)$
Vertical asymptote: $x = 0$

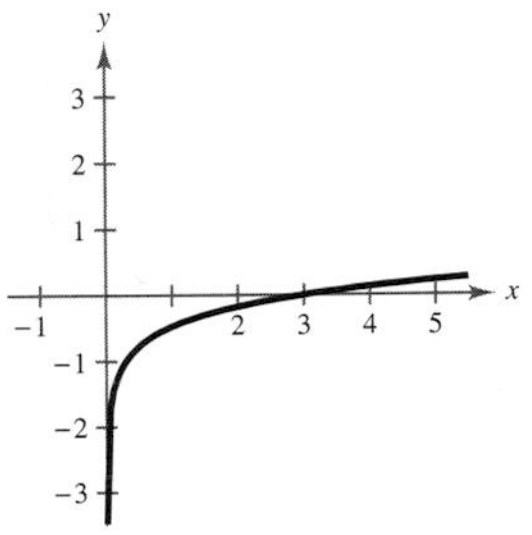

57. Domain: $(-5, \infty)$
x-intercept: $(9995, 0)$
Vertical asymptote: $x = -5$

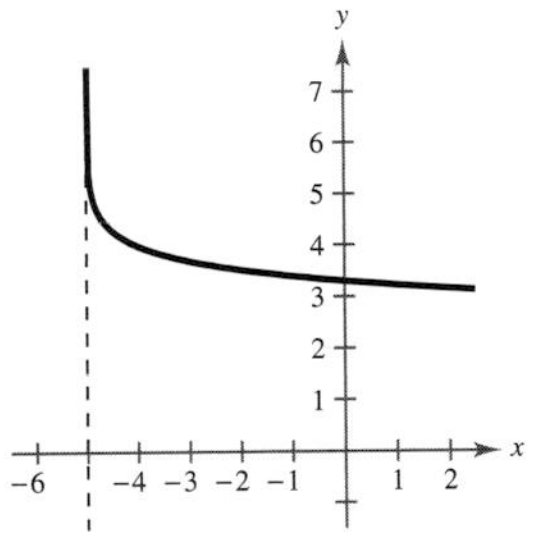

59. 3.118 **61.** -12 **63.** 2.034

65. Domain: $(0, \infty)$
x-intercept: $(e^{-3}, 0)$
Vertical asymptote: $x = 0$

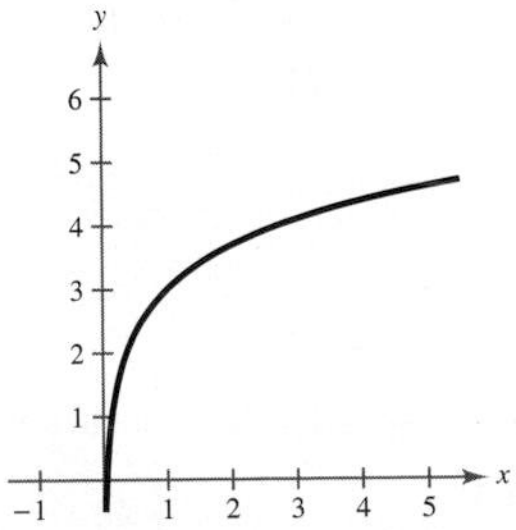

67. Domain: $(-\infty, 0), (0, \infty)$
x-intercept: $(\pm 1, 0)$
Vertical asymptote: $x = 0$

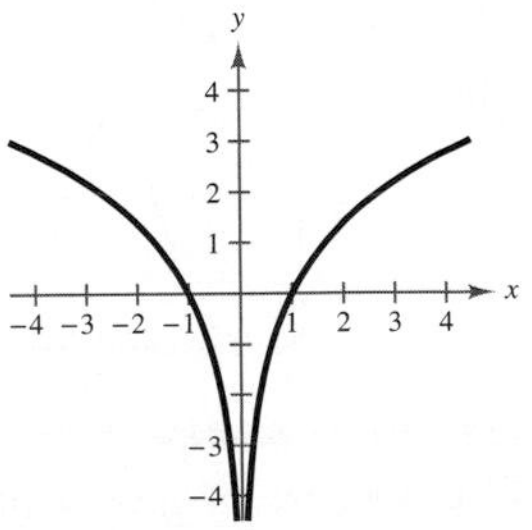

69. 53.4 inches **71.** 1.585 **73.** -2.322

75. $\log 2 + 2 \log 3 \approx 1.255$ **77.** $2 \ln 2 + \ln 5 \approx 2.996$

79. $1 + 2\log_5 x$ **81.** $1 + \log_3 2 - \frac{1}{3}\log_3 x$
83. $2\ln x + 2\ln y + \ln z$ **85.** $\ln(x + 3) - \ln x - \ln y$
87. $\log_2 5x$ **89.** $\ln \dfrac{x}{\sqrt[4]{y}}$ **91.** $\log_8 y^7 \sqrt[3]{x + 4}$
93. $\ln \dfrac{\sqrt{2x - 1}}{(x + 1)^2}$
95. (a) $0 \le h < 18{,}000$
(b)

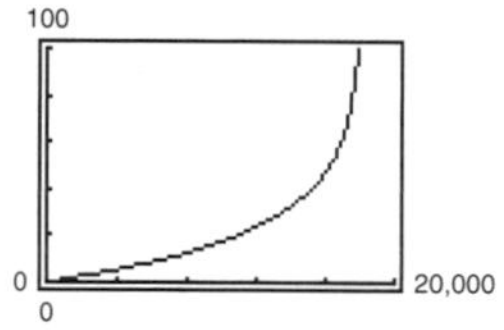

Vertical asymptote: $h = 18{,}000$

(c) The plane is climbing at a slower rate, so the time required increases.
(d) 5.46 minutes

97. 3 **99.** $\ln 3 \approx 1.099$ **101.** 16
103. $e^4 \approx 54.598$ **105.** $\ln 12 \approx 2.485$ **107.** $x = 1, 3$
109. $\dfrac{\ln 22}{\ln 2} \approx 4.459$ **111.** $\dfrac{\ln 17}{\ln 5} \approx 1.760$
113. $\ln 2 \approx 0.693$, $\ln 5 \approx 1.609$
115.

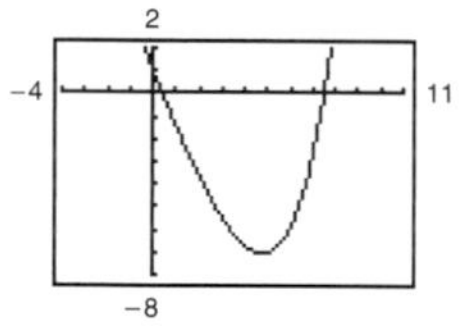

7.480; 0.392

117.

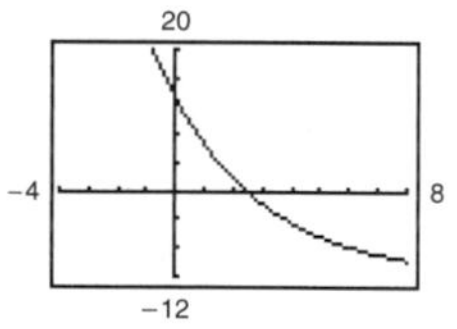

2.447

119. $\frac{1}{3}e^{8.2} \approx 1213.650$ **121.** $\frac{1}{4}e^{7.5} \approx 452.011$
123. $3e^2 \approx 22.167$ **125.** $e^4 - 1 \approx 53.598$
127. No solution **129.** 0.900
131.

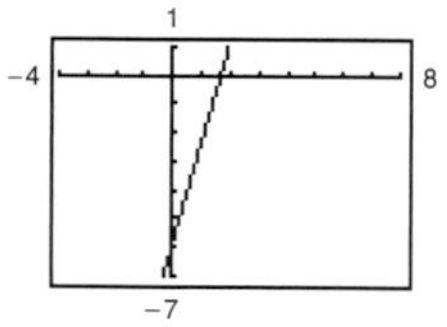

1.643

133.

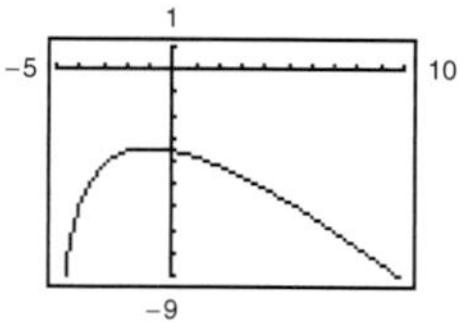

No solution

135. 15.2 years **137.** e **138.** b **139.** f
140. d **141.** a **142.** c **143.** $y = 2e^{0.1014x}$
145. 2008 **147.** (a) 13.8629% (b) $11,486.98
149. (a)

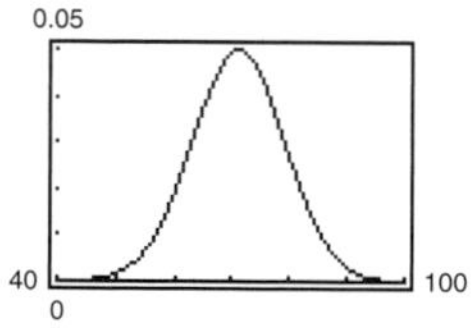

(b) 71

151. $10^{-3.5}$ watt per square centimeter
153. True by the inverse properties
155. b and d are negative.
a and c are positive.
Answers will vary.

Chapter Test *(page 275)*

1. 1123.690 **2.** 687.291 **3.** 0.497 **4.** 22.198

5.

x	-1	$-\frac{1}{2}$	0	$\frac{1}{2}$	1
$f(x)$	10	3.162	1	0.316	0.1

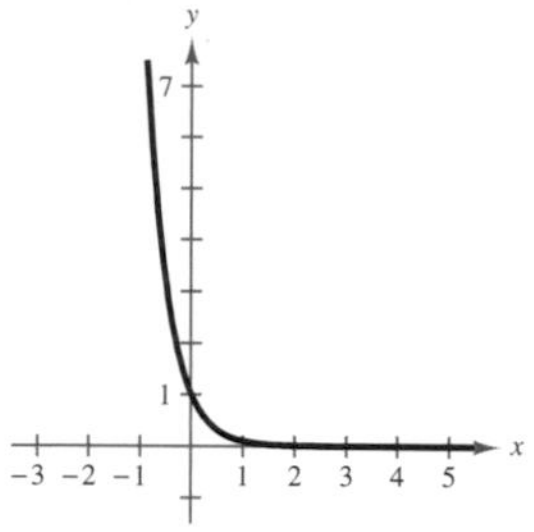

6.

x	-1	0	1	2	3
$f(x)$	-0.005	-0.028	-0.167	-1	-6

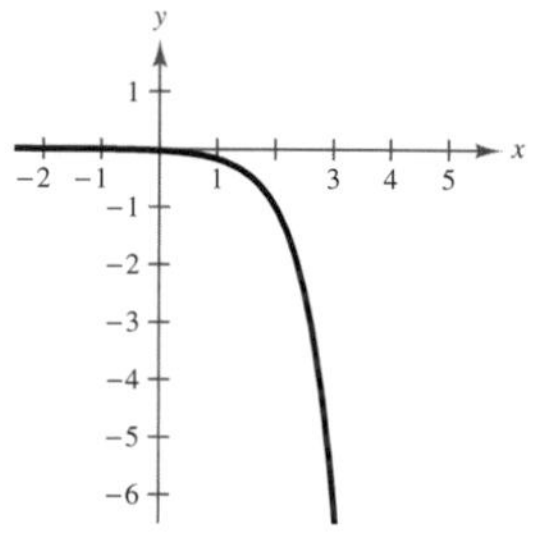

7.

x	-1	$-\frac{1}{2}$	0	$\frac{1}{2}$	1
$f(x)$	0.865	0.632	0	-1.718	-6.389

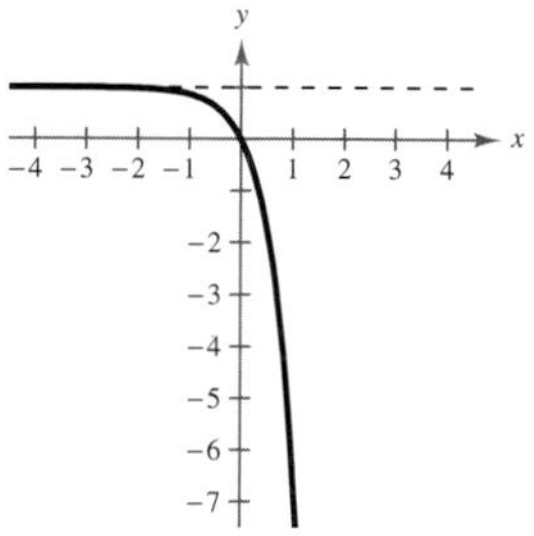

8. (a) -0.89 (b) 9.2

9.

x	$\frac{1}{2}$	1	$\frac{3}{2}$	2	4
$f(x)$	-5.699	-6	-6.176	-6.301	-6.602

Vertical asymptote: $x = 0$

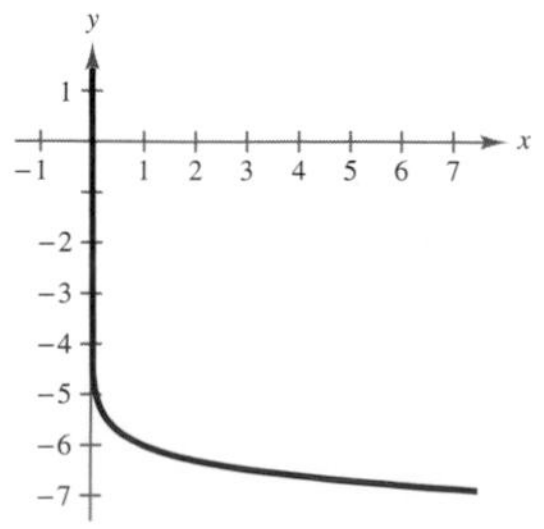

10.

x	5	7	9	11	13
$f(x)$	0	1.099	1.609	1.946	2.197

Vertical asymptote: $x = 4$

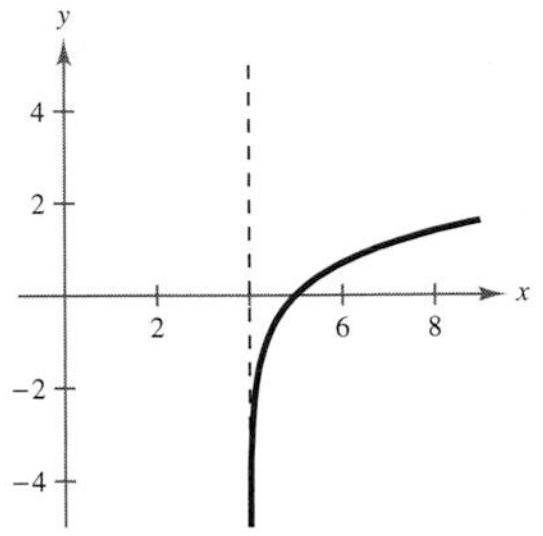

11.

x	-5	-3	-1	0	1
$f(x)$	1	2.099	2.609	2.792	2.946

Vertical asymptote: $x = -6$

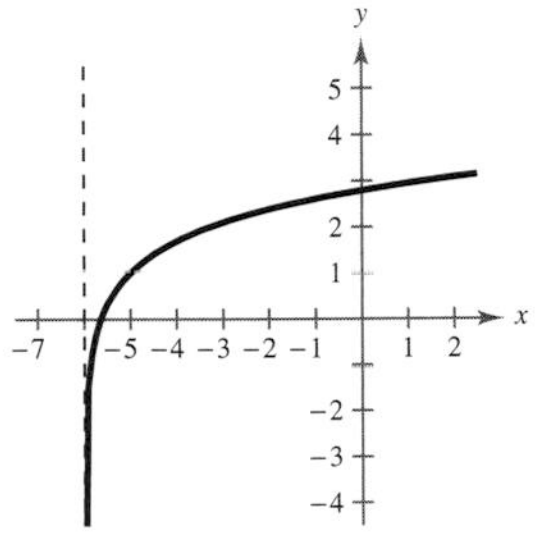

12. 1.945 **13.** 0.115 **14.** 1.328

15. $\log_2 3 + 4 \log_2 |a|$ **16.** $\ln 5 + \frac{1}{2}\ln x - \ln 6$

17. $(\log 7 + 2 \log x) - (\log y + 3 \log z)$

18. $\log_3 13y$ **19.** $\ln \dfrac{x^4}{y^4}$ **20.** $\ln \dfrac{x^2(x-5)}{y^3}$

21. $x = -2$ **22.** $x = \dfrac{\ln 44}{-5} \approx -0.757$

23. $\dfrac{\ln 197}{4} \approx 1.321$ **24.** $e^{1/2} \approx 1.649$

25. $e^{-11/4} \approx 0.0639$ **26.** $\frac{800}{501} \approx 1.597$

27. $y = 2745e^{0.1570x}$ **28.** 55%

29. (a)

x	$\frac{1}{4}$	1	2	4	5	6
H	58.720	75.332	86.828	103.43	110.59	117.38

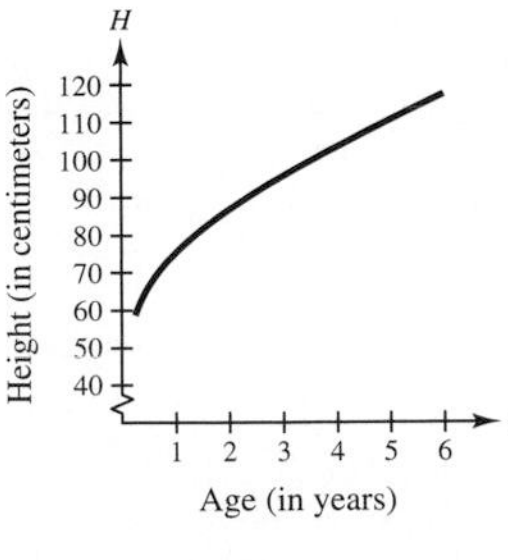

(b) 103 centimeters; 103.43 centimeters

Cumulative Test for Chapters 1–3 *(page 276)*

1. (a) Midpoint: $\left(1, \frac{3}{2}\right)$; Distance: $\sqrt{41}$

2.

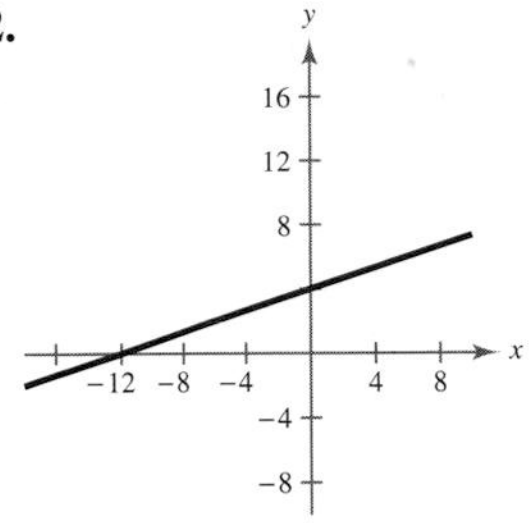

3.

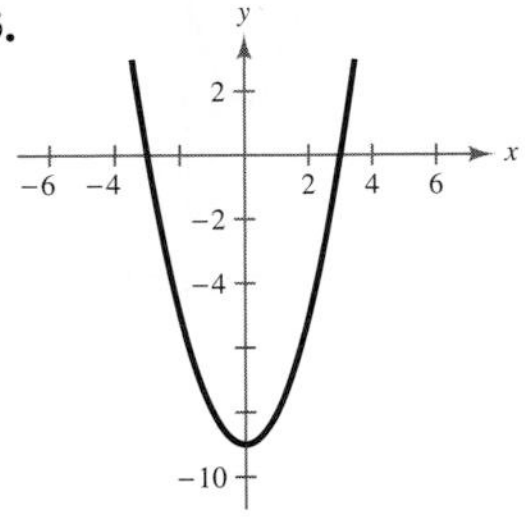

4.

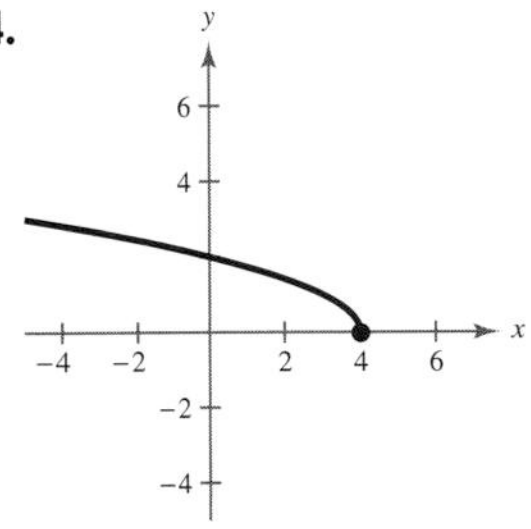

5. $y = 2x + 2$

6. For some values of x there correspond two values of y.

7. (a) $\dfrac{3}{2}$ (b) Division by 0 is undefined. (c) $\dfrac{s+2}{s}$

8. (a) Vertical shrink by $\frac{1}{2}$
(b) Vertical shift of two units upward
(c) Horizontal shift of two units to the left

9. (a) $5x - 2$ (b) $-3x - 4$ (c) $4x^2 - 11x - 3$
(d) $\dfrac{x-3}{4x+1}$; Domain: all real numbers x except $x = -\dfrac{1}{4}$

10. (a) $\sqrt{x-1} + x^2 + 1$ (b) $\sqrt{x-1} - x^2 - 1$
(c) $x^2\sqrt{x-1} + \sqrt{x-1}$
(d) $\dfrac{\sqrt{x-1}}{x^2+1}$; Domain: all real numbers x such that $x > 1$

11. (a) $2x + 12$ (b) $\sqrt{2x^2 + 6}$
Domain of $f \circ g$: all real numbers x such that $x \geq -6$
Domain of $g \circ f$: all real numbers

12. (a) $|x| - 2$ (b) $|x - 2|$
Domain of $f \circ g$ and $g \circ f$: all real numbers

13. Yes; $h^{-1}(x) = \frac{1}{5}(x + 2)$ **14.** 2438.65 kilowatts

15. $y = -\frac{3}{4}(x + 8)^2 + 5$

16.

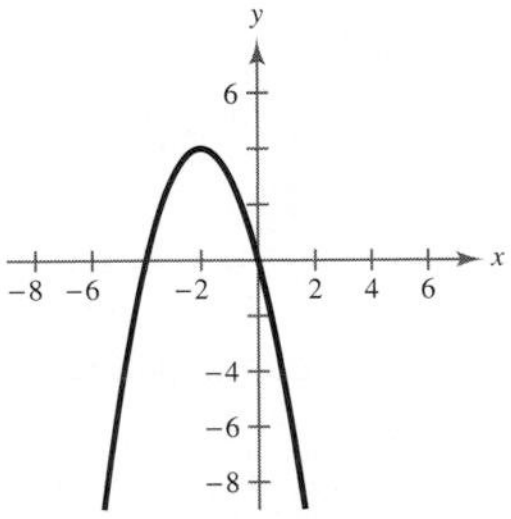

17.

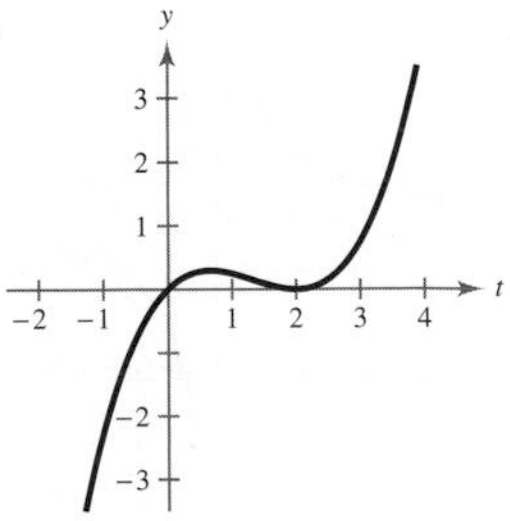

18.

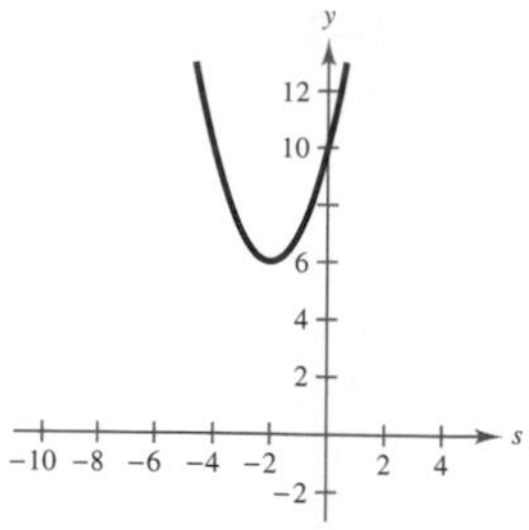

19. $-2, \pm 2i$; $(x + 2)(x + 2i)(x - 2i)$

20. $-7, 0, 3$; $x(x)(x - 3)(x + 7)$

21. $4, -\frac{1}{2}, 1 \pm 3i$; $(x - 4)(2x + 1)(x - 1 + 3i)(x - 1 - 3i)$

22. $3x - 2 - \dfrac{3x - 2}{2x^2 + 1}$

23. $2x^3 - x^2 + 2x - 10 + \dfrac{25}{x + 2}$

24.

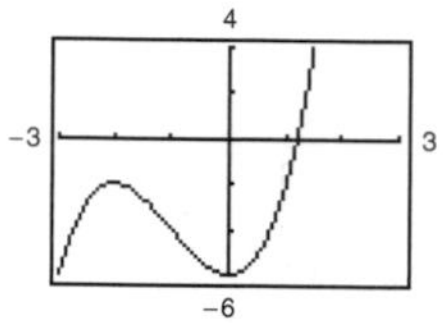

Interval: $[1, 2]$; 1.20

25. Intercept: $(0, 0)$
Vertical asymptotes: $x = \pm 3$
Horizontal asymptote: $y = 0$

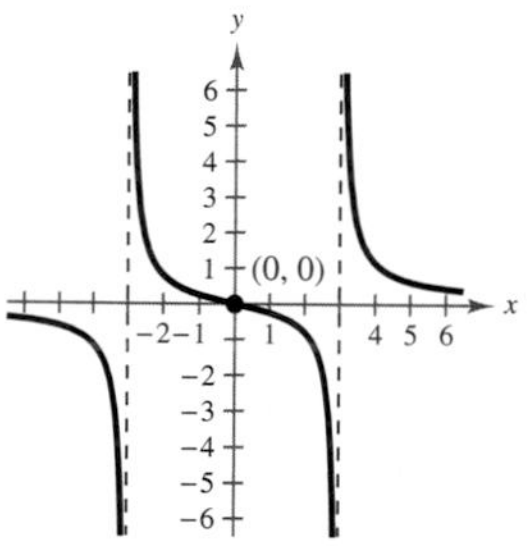

26. y-intercept: $(0, -1)$
x-intercept: $(1, 0)$
Horizontal asymptote: $y = 1$
Vertical asymptote: $x = -1$

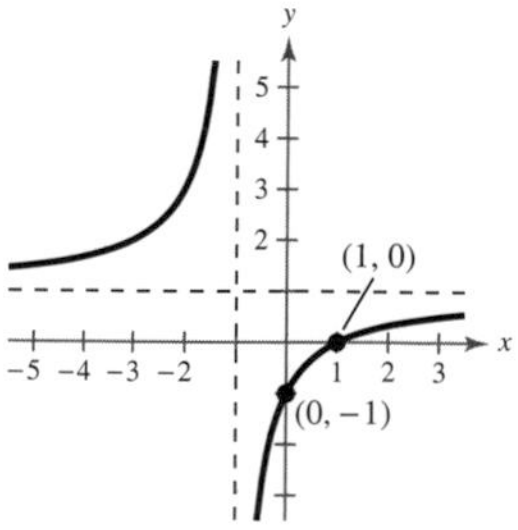

27. y-intercept: $(0, 6)$
x-intercepts: $(-2, 0), (-3, 0)$
Slant asymptote: $y = x + 4$
Vertical asymptote: $x = -1$

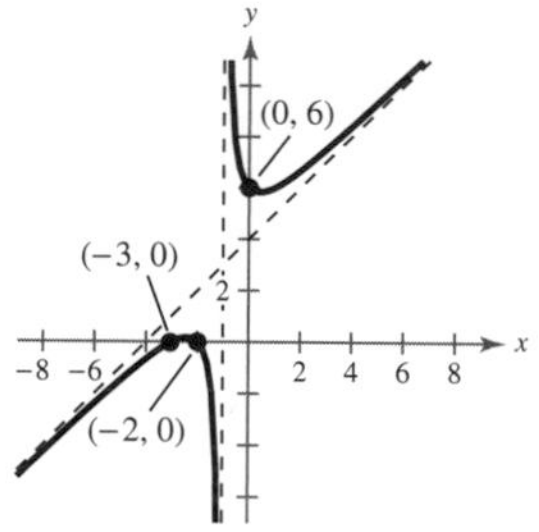

28. $x \leq -2$ or $0 \leq x \leq 2$

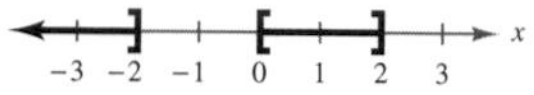

29. All real numbers x such that $x < -5$ or $x > -1$

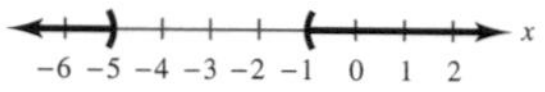

30. Reflect f in the x-axis and y-axis, and shift three units to the right.

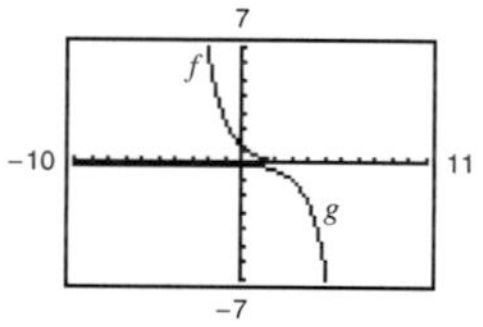

31. Reflect f in the x-axis, and shift four units upward.

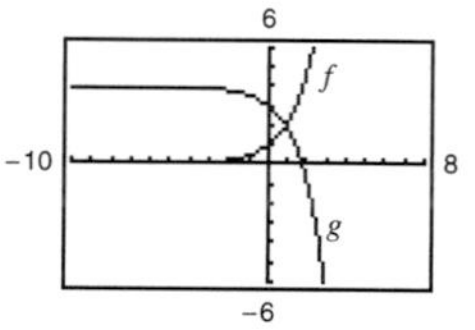

32. 1.991 **33.** -0.067 **34.** 1.717 **35.** 0.281

36. $\ln(x + 4) + \ln(x - 4) - 4 \ln x, x > 4$

37. $\ln \dfrac{x^2}{\sqrt{x + 5}}, x > 0$ **38.** $x = \dfrac{\ln 12}{2} \approx 1.242$

39. $\ln 3 \approx 1.099$ or $3 \ln 2 \approx 2.079$

40. $e^6 - 2 \approx 401.429$

41. (a)

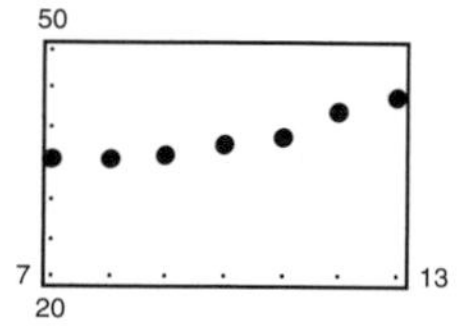

(b) $S = 0.274t^2 - 4.08t + 50.6$

(c) 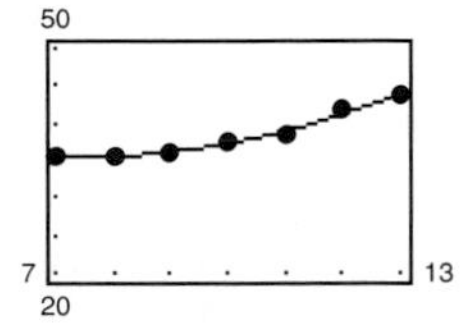

The model is a good fit for the data.

(d) 65.9 Yes, this is a reasonable answer.

Problem Solving (page 279)

1. 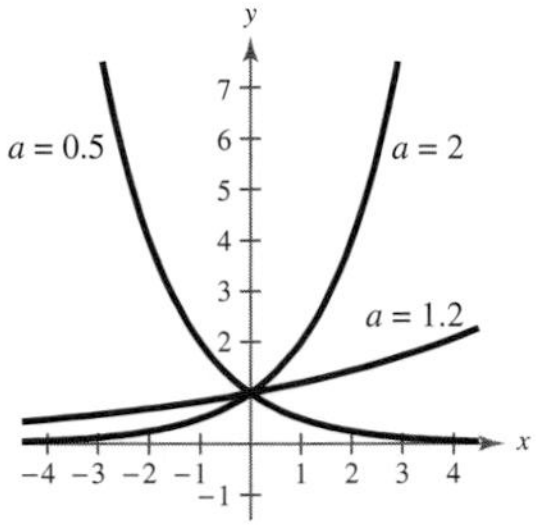

$y = 0.5^x$ and $y = 1.2^x$

$0 \le a \le 1.44$

3. As $x \to \infty$, the graph of e^x increases at a greater rate than the graph of x^n.

5. Answers will vary.

7. (a) 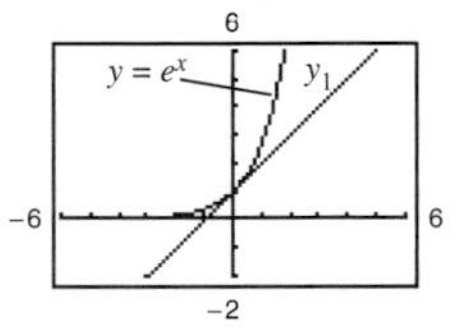

(b) 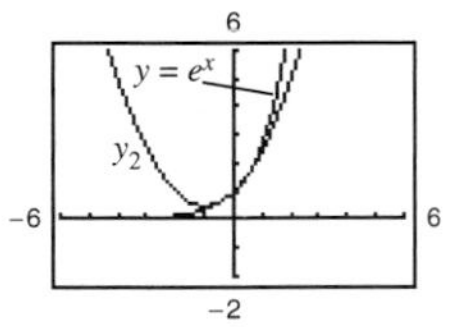

(c) 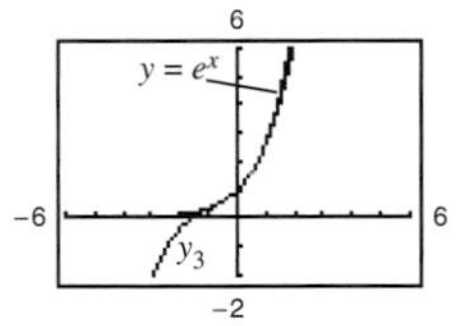

9. 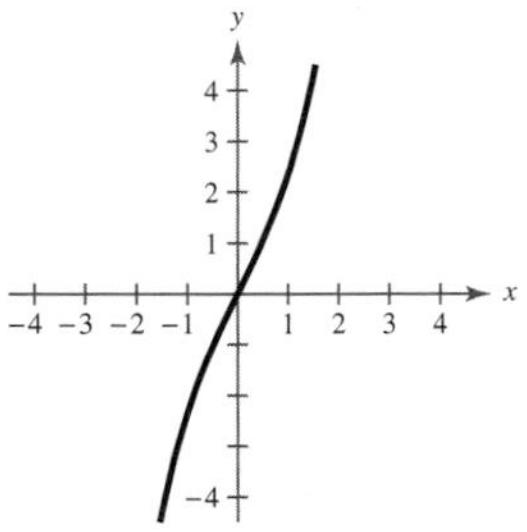

$f^{-1}(x) = \ln\left(\frac{x + \sqrt{x^2 + 4}}{2}\right)$

11. c **13.** $t = \dfrac{\ln c_1 - \ln c_2}{\left(\frac{1}{k_2} - \frac{1}{k_1}\right)\ln\frac{1}{2}}$

15. (a) $y_1 = 252{,}606(1.0310)^t$

(b) $y_2 = 400.88t^2 - 1464.6t + 291{,}782$

(c) 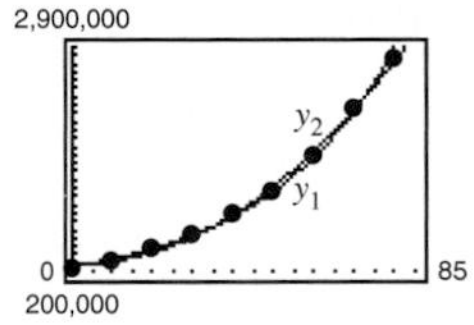

(d) The exponential model is a better fit. No, because the model is rapidly approaching infinity.

17. $1, e^2$

19. $y_4 = (x - 1) - \frac{1}{2}(x - 1)^2 + \frac{1}{3}(x - 1)^3 - \frac{1}{4}(x - 1)^4$

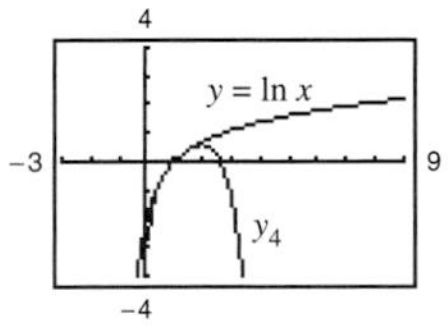

The pattern implies that

$\ln x = (x - 1) - \frac{1}{2}(x - 1)^2 + \frac{1}{3}(x - 1)^3 - \cdots.$

21. 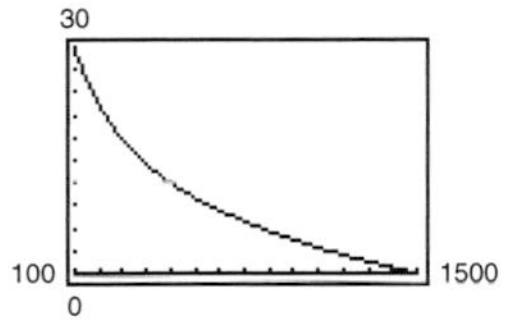

17.7 cubic feet per minute

23. (a) 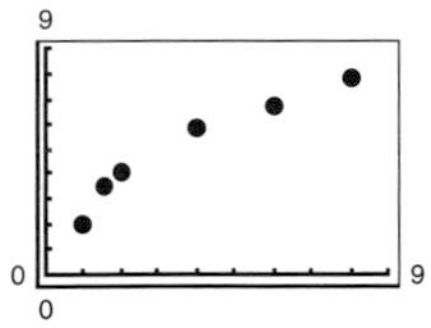

(b)–(e) Answers will vary.

25. (a) 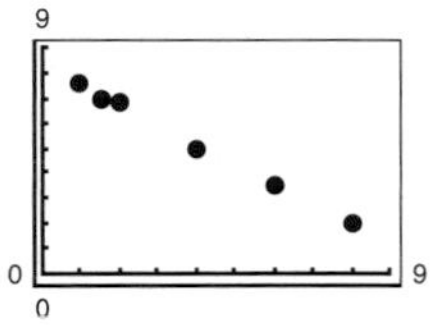

(b)–(e) Answers will vary.

Chapter 4

Section 4.1 (page 290)

Vocabulary Check (page 290)

1. Trigonometry **2.** angle **3.** coterminal
4. radian **5.** acute; obtuse
6. complementary; supplementary **7.** degree
8. linear **9.** angular **10.** $A = \frac{1}{2}r^2\theta$

1. 2 radians **3.** -3 radians **5.** 1 radian

7. (a) Quadrant I (b) Quadrant III

9. (a) Quadrant IV (b) Quadrant III

11. (a) Quadrant III (b) Quadrant II

13. (a)

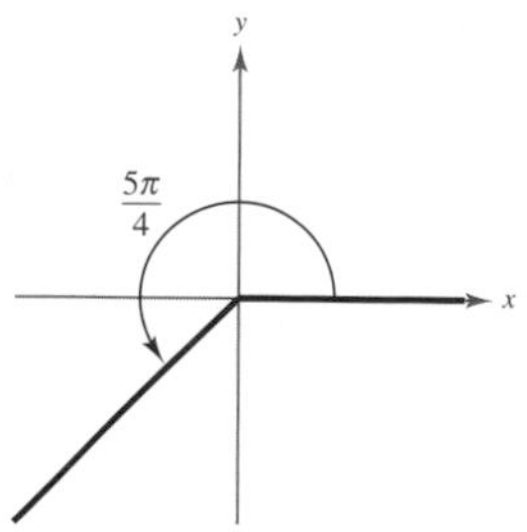

(b)

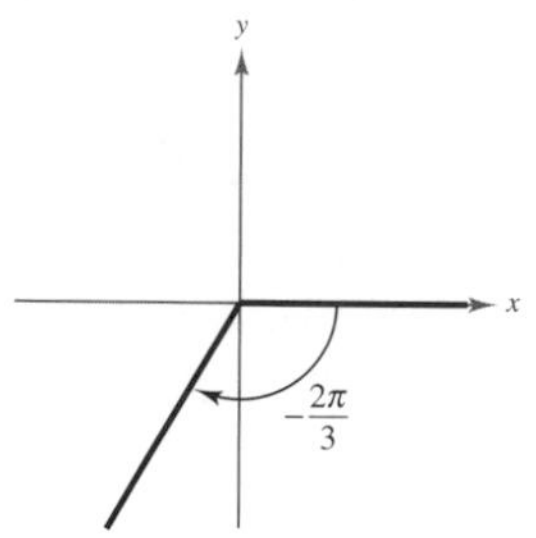

15. (a)

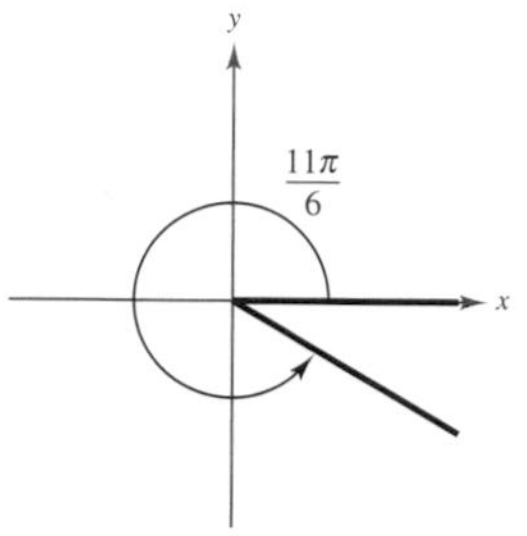

(b)

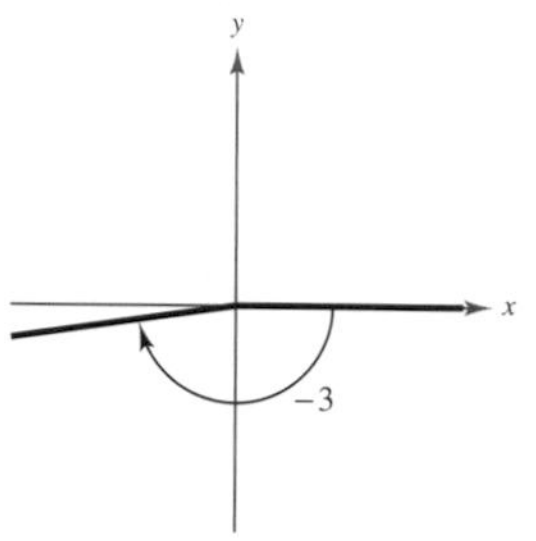

17. (a) $\frac{13\pi}{6}, -\frac{11\pi}{6}$ (b) $\frac{17\pi}{6}, -\frac{7\pi}{6}$

19. (a) $\frac{8\pi}{3}, -\frac{4\pi}{3}$ (b) $\frac{25\pi}{12}, -\frac{23\pi}{12}$

21. (a) Complement: $\frac{\pi}{6}$; Supplement: $\frac{2\pi}{3}$

(b) Complement: none; Supplement: $\frac{\pi}{4}$

23. (a) Complement: $\frac{\pi}{2} - 1 \approx 0.57$;

Supplement: $\pi - 1 \approx 2.14$

(b) Complement: none; Supplement: $\pi - 2 \approx 1.14$

25. 210° **27.** −60° **29.** 165°

31. (a) Quadrant II (b) Quadrant IV

33. (a) Quadrant III (b) Quadrant I

35. (a)

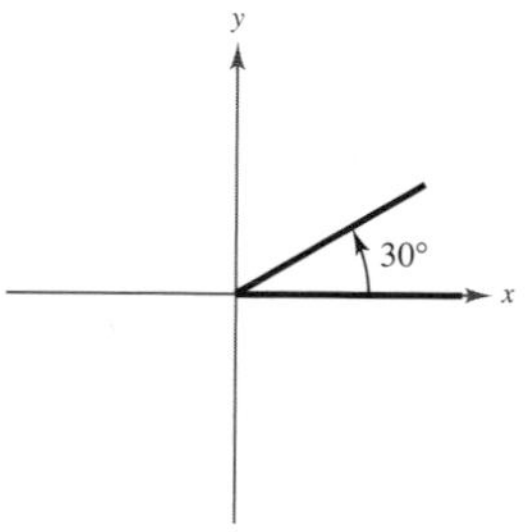

(b)

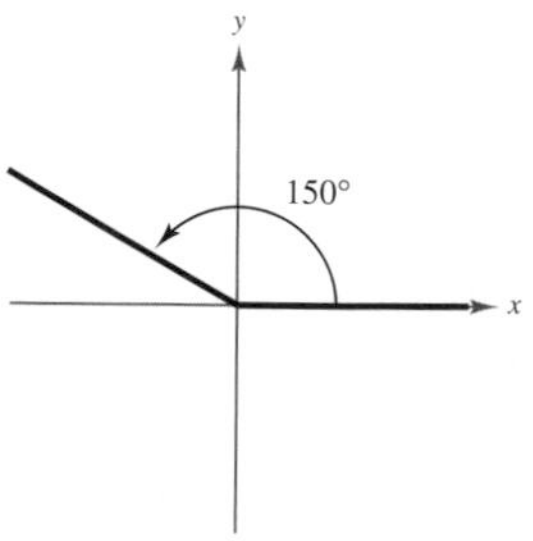

37. (a)

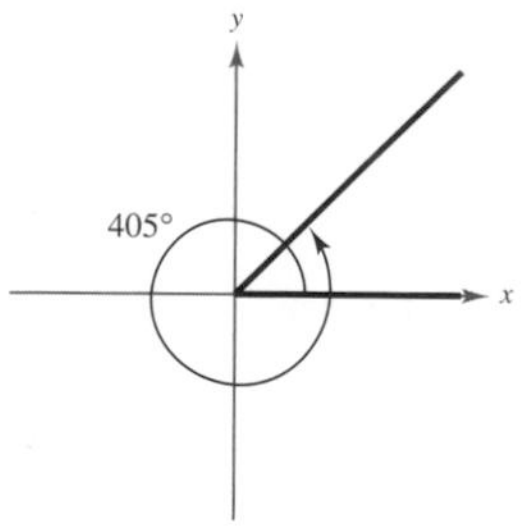

(b)

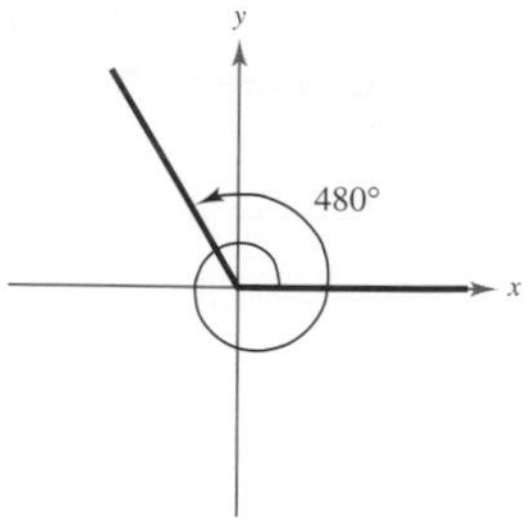

39. (a) 405°, −315° (b) 324°, −396°

41. (a) 600°, −120° (b) 180°, −540°

43. (a) Complement: 72°; Supplement: 162°

(b) Complement: none; Supplement: 65°

45. (a) Complement: 11°; Supplement: 101°

(b) Complement: none; Supplement: 30°

47. (a) $\frac{\pi}{6}$ (b) $\frac{5\pi}{6}$ **49.** (a) $-\frac{\pi}{9}$ (b) $-\frac{4\pi}{3}$

51. (a) 270° (b) 210° **53.** (a) 420° (b) −66°

55. 2.007 **57.** −3.776 **59.** 9.285 **61.** −0.014

63. 25.714° **65.** 337.500° **67.** −756.000°

69. −114.592° **71.** (a) 54.75° (b) −128.5°

73. (a) 85.308° (b) 330.007°

75. (a) 240° 36′ (b) −145° 48′

77. (a) 2° 30′ (b) −3° 34′ 48″

79. $\frac{6}{5}$ radians **81.** $\frac{32}{7}$ radians **83.** $\frac{2}{9}$ radian

85. $\frac{50}{29}$ radians **87.** 15π inches ≈ 47.12 inches

89. 3 meters **91.** $\frac{8\pi}{3}$ square inches ≈ 8.38 square inches

93. 12.27 square feet **95.** 591.3 miles

97. 0.071 radian ≈ 4.04° **99.** $\frac{5}{12}$ radian

101. (a) 728.3 revolutions per minute

(b) 4576 radians per minute

103. (a) $10{,}400\pi$ radians per minute

≈ 32,672.56 radians per minute

(b) $9425\pi/3$ feet per minute ≈ 9869.84 feet per minute

105. (a) $[400\pi, 1000\pi]$ radians per minute

(b) $[2400\pi, 6000\pi]$ centimeters per minute

107.

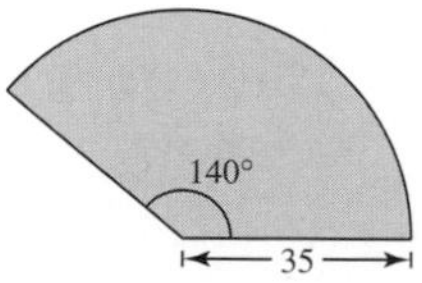

$A = 476.39\pi$ square meters ≈ 1496.62 square meters

109. False. A measurement of 4π radians corresponds to two complete revolutions from the initial to the terminal side of an angle.

111. False. The terminal side of the angle lies on the x-axis.
113. Increases. The linear velocity is proportional to the radius.
115. The arc length is increasing. If θ is constant, the length of the arc is proportional to the radius ($s = r\theta$).

117. $\frac{\sqrt{2}}{2}$ **119.** $2\sqrt{10}$

121.

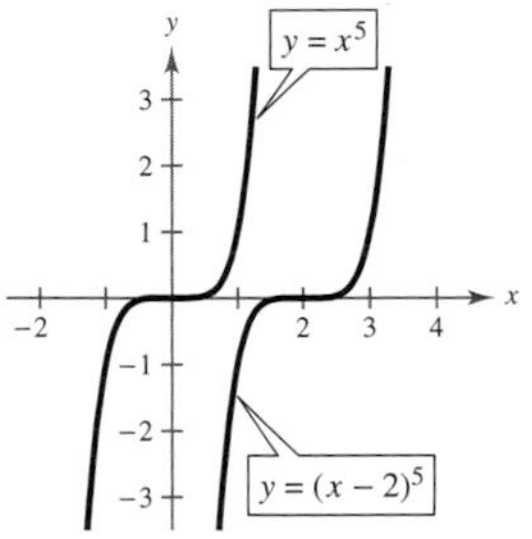

123.

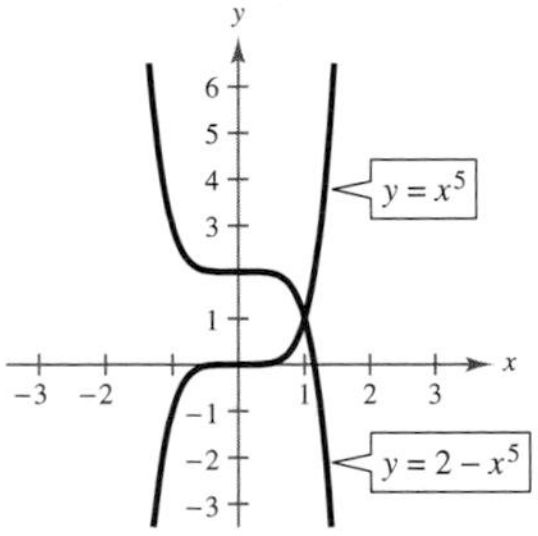

Section 4.2 *(page 299)*

Vocabulary Check *(page 299)*

1. unit circle **2.** periodic
3. period **4.** odd; even

1. $\sin\theta = \frac{15}{17}$ $\csc\theta = \frac{17}{15}$
$\cos\theta = -\frac{8}{17}$ $\sec\theta = -\frac{17}{8}$
$\tan\theta = -\frac{15}{8}$ $\cot\theta = -\frac{8}{15}$

3. $\sin\theta = -\frac{5}{13}$ $\csc\theta = -\frac{13}{5}$
$\cos\theta = \frac{12}{13}$ $\sec\theta = \frac{13}{12}$
$\tan\theta = -\frac{5}{12}$ $\cot\theta = -\frac{12}{5}$

5. $\left(\frac{\sqrt{2}}{2}, \frac{\sqrt{2}}{2}\right)$ **7.** $\left(-\frac{\sqrt{3}}{2}, -\frac{1}{2}\right)$ **9.** $\left(-\frac{1}{2}, -\frac{\sqrt{3}}{2}\right)$

11. $(0, -1)$

13. $\sin\frac{\pi}{4} = \frac{\sqrt{2}}{2}$
$\cos\frac{\pi}{4} = \frac{\sqrt{2}}{2}$
$\tan\frac{\pi}{4} = 1$

15. $\sin\left(-\frac{\pi}{6}\right) = -\frac{1}{2}$
$\cos\left(-\frac{\pi}{6}\right) = \frac{\sqrt{3}}{2}$
$\tan\left(-\frac{\pi}{6}\right) = -\frac{\sqrt{3}}{3}$

17. $\sin\left(-\frac{7\pi}{4}\right) = \frac{\sqrt{2}}{2}$
$\cos\left(-\frac{7\pi}{4}\right) = \frac{\sqrt{2}}{2}$
$\tan\left(-\frac{7\pi}{4}\right) = 1$

19. $\sin\frac{11\pi}{6} = -\frac{1}{2}$
$\cos\frac{11\pi}{6} = \frac{\sqrt{3}}{2}$
$\tan\frac{11\pi}{6} = -\frac{\sqrt{3}}{3}$

21. $\sin\left(-\frac{3\pi}{2}\right) = 1$
$\cos\left(-\frac{3\pi}{2}\right) = 0$
$\tan\left(-\frac{3\pi}{2}\right)$ is undefined.

23. $\sin\frac{3\pi}{4} = \frac{\sqrt{2}}{2}$ $\csc\frac{3\pi}{4} = \sqrt{2}$
$\cos\frac{3\pi}{4} = -\frac{\sqrt{2}}{2}$ $\sec\frac{3\pi}{4} = -\sqrt{2}$
$\tan\frac{3\pi}{4} = -1$ $\cot\frac{3\pi}{4} = -1$

25. $\sin\left(-\frac{\pi}{2}\right) = -1$ $\csc\left(-\frac{\pi}{2}\right) = -1$
$\cos\left(-\frac{\pi}{2}\right) = 0$ $\sec\left(-\frac{\pi}{2}\right)$ is undefined.
$\tan\left(-\frac{\pi}{2}\right)$ is undefined. $\cot\left(-\frac{\pi}{2}\right) = 0$

27. $\sin\left(\frac{4\pi}{3}\right) = -\frac{\sqrt{3}}{2}$ $\csc\left(\frac{4\pi}{3}\right) = -\frac{2\sqrt{3}}{3}$
$\cos\left(\frac{4\pi}{3}\right) = -\frac{1}{2}$ $\sec\left(\frac{4\pi}{3}\right) = -2$
$\tan\left(\frac{4\pi}{3}\right) = \sqrt{3}$ $\cot\left(\frac{4\pi}{3}\right) = \frac{\sqrt{3}}{3}$

29. $\sin 5\pi = \sin \pi = 0$ **31.** $\cos\frac{8\pi}{3} = \cos\frac{2\pi}{3} = -\frac{1}{2}$

33. $\cos\left(-\frac{15\pi}{2}\right) = \cos\frac{\pi}{2} = 0$

35. $\sin\left(-\frac{9\pi}{4}\right) = \sin\frac{7\pi}{4} = -\frac{\sqrt{2}}{2}$

37. (a) $-\frac{1}{3}$ (b) -3 **39.** (a) $-\frac{1}{5}$ (b) -5
41. (a) $\frac{4}{5}$ (b) $-\frac{4}{5}$ **43.** 0.7071 **45.** 1.0378
47. -0.1288 **49.** 1.3940 **51.** -1.4486
53. (a) -1 (b) -0.4
55. (a) 0.25 or 2.89 (b) 1.82 or 4.46
57. (a)

t	0	$\frac{1}{4}$	$\frac{1}{2}$	$\frac{3}{4}$	1
y	0.25	0.0138	-0.1501	-0.0249	0.0883

(b) $t \approx 5.5$ (c) The displacement decreases.

59. False. $\sin(-t) = -\sin t$ means that the function is odd, not that the sine of a negative angle is a negative number.
61. (a) y-axis symmetry (b) $\sin t_1 = \sin(\pi - t_1)$
(c) $\cos(\pi - t_1) = -\cos t_1$
63. $f^{-1}(x) = \frac{2}{3}(x + 1)$ **65.** $f^{-1}(x) = \sqrt{x^2 + 4}$, $x \geq 0$

67.

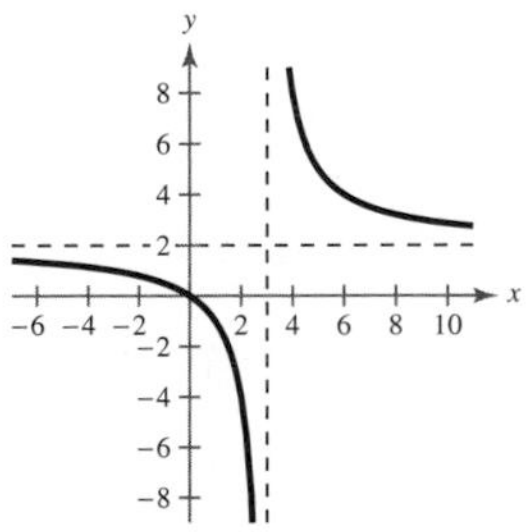

69.

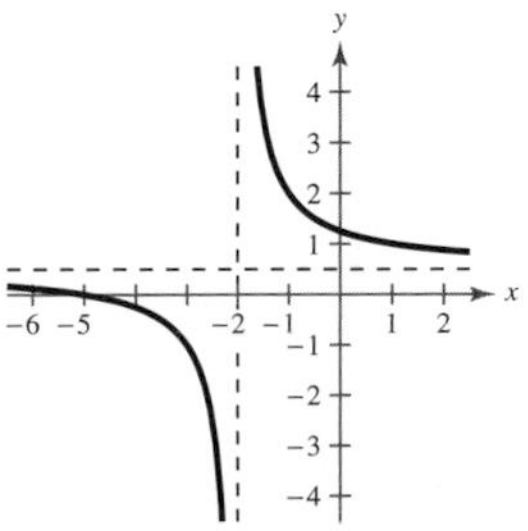

Section 4.3 *(page 308)*

Vocabulary Check *(page 308)*

1. (a) v (b) iv (c) vi (d) iii (e) i (f) ii
2. opposite; adjacent; hypotenuse
3. elevation; depression

1. $\sin\theta = \frac{3}{5}$ $\csc\theta = \frac{5}{3}$
$\cos\theta = \frac{4}{5}$ $\sec\theta = \frac{5}{4}$
$\tan\theta = \frac{3}{4}$ $\cot\theta = \frac{4}{3}$

3. $\sin\theta = \frac{9}{41}$ $\csc\theta = \frac{41}{9}$
$\cos\theta = \frac{40}{41}$ $\sec\theta = \frac{41}{40}$
$\tan\theta = \frac{9}{40}$ $\cot\theta = \frac{40}{9}$

5. $\sin\theta = \dfrac{1}{3}$ $\csc\theta = 3$
$\cos\theta = \dfrac{2\sqrt{2}}{3}$ $\sec\theta = \dfrac{3\sqrt{2}}{4}$
$\tan\theta = \dfrac{\sqrt{2}}{4}$ $\cot\theta = 2\sqrt{2}$
The triangles are similar, and corresponding sides are proportional.

7. $\sin\theta = \frac{3}{5}$ $\csc\theta = \frac{5}{3}$
$\cos\theta = \frac{4}{5}$ $\sec\theta = \frac{5}{4}$
$\tan\theta = \frac{3}{4}$ $\cot\theta = \frac{4}{3}$
The triangles are similar, and corresponding sides are proportional.

9.

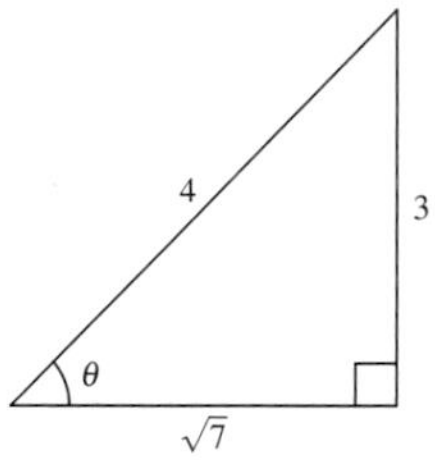

$\cos\theta = \dfrac{\sqrt{7}}{4}$ $\sec\theta = \dfrac{4\sqrt{7}}{7}$
$\tan\theta = \dfrac{3\sqrt{7}}{7}$ $\cot\theta = \dfrac{\sqrt{7}}{3}$
$\csc\theta = \dfrac{4}{3}$

11.

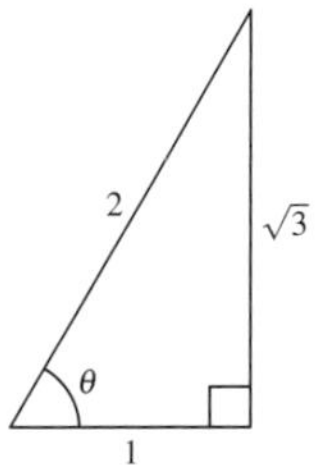

$\sin\theta = \dfrac{\sqrt{3}}{2}$ $\csc\theta = \dfrac{2\sqrt{3}}{3}$
$\cos\theta = \dfrac{1}{2}$ $\cot\theta = \dfrac{\sqrt{3}}{3}$
$\tan\theta = \sqrt{3}$

13.

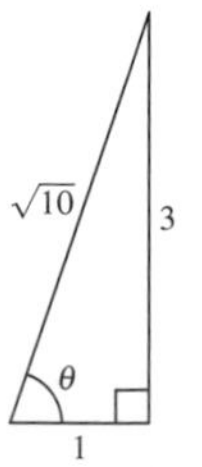

$\sin\theta = \dfrac{3\sqrt{10}}{10}$ $\sec\theta = \sqrt{10}$
$\cos\theta = \dfrac{\sqrt{10}}{10}$ $\cot\theta = \dfrac{1}{3}$
$\csc\theta = \dfrac{\sqrt{10}}{3}$

15.

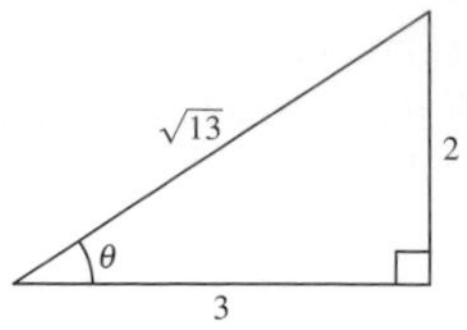

$\sin\theta = \dfrac{2\sqrt{13}}{13}$ $\csc\theta = \dfrac{\sqrt{13}}{2}$
$\cos\theta = \dfrac{3\sqrt{13}}{13}$ $\sec\theta = \dfrac{\sqrt{13}}{3}$
$\tan\theta = \dfrac{2}{3}$

17. $\dfrac{\pi}{6}; \dfrac{1}{2}$ **19.** $60°; \sqrt{3}$ **21.** $60°; \dfrac{\pi}{3}$ **23.** $30°; \dfrac{\sqrt{3}}{2}$

25. $45°; \dfrac{\pi}{4}$ **27.** (a) $\sqrt{3}$ (b) $\dfrac{1}{2}$ (c) $\dfrac{\sqrt{3}}{2}$ (d) $\dfrac{\sqrt{3}}{3}$

29. (a) $\dfrac{2\sqrt{13}}{13}$ (b) $\dfrac{3\sqrt{13}}{13}$ (c) $\dfrac{2}{3}$ (d) $\dfrac{\sqrt{13}}{2}$

31. (a) 3 (b) $\dfrac{2\sqrt{2}}{3}$ (c) $\dfrac{\sqrt{2}}{4}$ (d) $\dfrac{1}{3}$

33–41. Answers will vary. **43.** (a) 0.1736 (b) 0.1736
45. (a) 0.2815 (b) 3.5523
47. (a) 1.3499 (b) 1.3432
49. (a) 5.0273 (b) 0.1989
51. (a) 1.8527 (b) 0.9817

53. (a) $30° = \dfrac{\pi}{6}$ (b) $30° = \dfrac{\pi}{6}$

55. (a) $60° = \dfrac{\pi}{3}$ (b) $45° = \dfrac{\pi}{4}$

57. (a) $60° = \dfrac{\pi}{3}$ (b) $45° = \dfrac{\pi}{4}$

59. $30\sqrt{3}$ **61.** $\dfrac{32\sqrt{3}}{3}$

63. 443.2 meters; 323.3 meters **65.** $30° = \dfrac{\pi}{6}$

67. (a) 371.1 feet (b) 341.6 feet
(c) Moving down line at 61.8 feet per second
Dropping vertically at 24.2 feet per second

69. $(x_1, y_1) = (28\sqrt{3}, 28)$
$(x_2, y_2) = (28, 28\sqrt{3})$

71. (a)

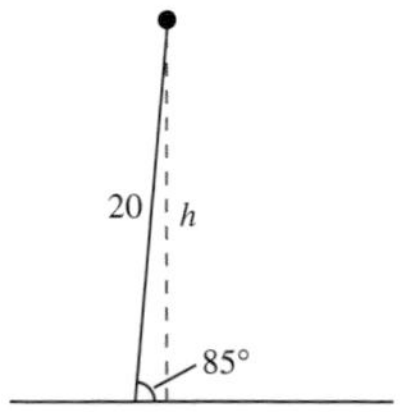

(b) $\sin 85° = \dfrac{h}{20}$
(c) 19.9 meters
(d) The side of the triangle labeled h will become shorter.
(e)

Angle, θ	80°	70°	60°	50°
Height	19.7	18.8	17.3	15.3

Angle, θ	40°	30°	20°	10°
Height	12.9	10.0	6.8	3.5

(f) As $\theta \to 0°, h \to 0$.

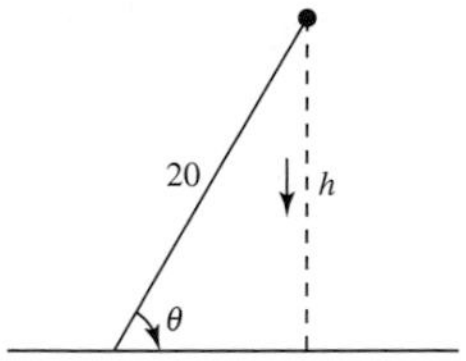

73. True, $\csc x = \dfrac{1}{\sin x}$. **75.** False, $\dfrac{\sqrt{2}}{2} + \dfrac{\sqrt{2}}{2} \neq 1$.

77. False, $1.7321 \neq 0.0349$.

79. Corresponding sides of similar triangles are proportional.

81. (a)

θ	0.1	0.2	0.3	0.4	0.5
$\sin\theta$	0.0998	0.1987	0.2955	0.3894	0.4794

(b) θ (c) As θ approaches 0, $\sin\theta$ approaches 0.

83. $\dfrac{x}{x-2}$, $x \neq \pm 6$ **85.** $\dfrac{2(x^2 - 5x - 10)}{(x-2)(x+2)^2}$

Section 4.4 *(page 318)*

Vocabulary Check *(page 318)*

1. $\dfrac{y}{r}$ **2.** $\csc\theta$ **3.** $\dfrac{y}{x}$ **4.** $\dfrac{r}{x}$ **5.** $\cos\theta$

6. $\cot\theta$ **7.** reference

1. (a) $\sin\theta = \frac{3}{5}$, $\cos\theta = \frac{4}{5}$, $\tan\theta = \frac{3}{4}$, $\csc\theta = \frac{5}{3}$, $\sec\theta = \frac{5}{4}$, $\cot\theta = \frac{4}{3}$

(b) $\sin\theta = -\frac{15}{17}$, $\cos\theta = \frac{8}{17}$, $\tan\theta = -\frac{15}{8}$, $\csc\theta = -\frac{17}{15}$, $\sec\theta = \frac{17}{8}$, $\cot\theta = -\frac{8}{15}$

3. (a) $\sin\theta = -\dfrac{1}{2}$, $\cos\theta = -\dfrac{\sqrt{3}}{2}$, $\tan\theta = \dfrac{\sqrt{3}}{3}$, $\csc\theta = -2$, $\sec\theta = -\dfrac{2\sqrt{3}}{3}$, $\cot\theta = \sqrt{3}$

(b) $\sin\theta = \dfrac{\sqrt{17}}{17}$, $\cos\theta = -\dfrac{4\sqrt{17}}{17}$, $\tan\theta = -\dfrac{1}{4}$, $\csc\theta = \sqrt{17}$, $\sec\theta = -\dfrac{\sqrt{17}}{4}$, $\cot\theta = -4$

5. $\sin\theta = \frac{24}{25}$ $\csc\theta = \frac{25}{24}$
$\cos\theta = \frac{7}{25}$ $\sec\theta = \frac{25}{7}$
$\tan\theta = \frac{24}{7}$ $\cot\theta = \frac{7}{24}$

7. $\sin\theta = \dfrac{5\sqrt{29}}{29}$ $\csc\theta = \dfrac{\sqrt{29}}{5}$
$\cos\theta = -\dfrac{2\sqrt{29}}{29}$ $\sec\theta = -\dfrac{\sqrt{29}}{2}$
$\tan\theta = -\dfrac{5}{2}$ $\cot\theta = -\dfrac{2}{5}$

9. $\sin\theta = \dfrac{68\sqrt{5849}}{5849}$ $\csc\theta = \dfrac{\sqrt{5849}}{68}$
$\cos\theta = -\dfrac{35\sqrt{5849}}{5849}$ $\sec\theta = -\dfrac{\sqrt{5849}}{35}$
$\tan\theta = -\dfrac{68}{35}$ $\cot\theta = -\dfrac{35}{68}$

11. Quadrant III **13.** Quadrant II

15. $\sin\theta = \frac{3}{5}$ $\csc\theta = \frac{5}{3}$
$\cos\theta = -\frac{4}{5}$ $\sec\theta = -\frac{5}{4}$
$\tan\theta = -\frac{3}{4}$ $\cot\theta = -\frac{4}{3}$

17. $\sin\theta = -\frac{15}{17}$ $\csc\theta = -\frac{17}{15}$
$\cos\theta = \frac{8}{17}$ $\sec\theta = \frac{17}{8}$
$\tan\theta = -\frac{15}{8}$ $\cot\theta = -\frac{8}{15}$

19. $\sin\theta = -\dfrac{\sqrt{10}}{10}$ $\csc\theta = -\sqrt{10}$
$\cos\theta = \dfrac{3\sqrt{10}}{10}$ $\sec\theta = \dfrac{\sqrt{10}}{3}$
$\tan\theta = -\dfrac{1}{3}$ $\cot\theta = -3$

21. $\sin\theta = \dfrac{\sqrt{3}}{2}$ $\csc\theta = \dfrac{2\sqrt{3}}{3}$
$\cos\theta = -\dfrac{1}{2}$ $\sec\theta = -2$
$\tan\theta = -\sqrt{3}$ $\cot\theta = -\dfrac{\sqrt{3}}{3}$

23. $\sin\theta = 0$ $\csc\theta$ is undefined.
$\cos\theta = -1$ $\sec\theta = -1$
$\tan\theta = 0$ $\cot\theta$ is undefined.

25. $\sin\theta = \dfrac{\sqrt{2}}{2}$ $\csc\theta = \sqrt{2}$
$\cos\theta = -\dfrac{\sqrt{2}}{2}$ $\sec\theta = -\sqrt{2}$
$\tan\theta = -1$ $\cot\theta = -1$

27. $\sin\theta = -\dfrac{2\sqrt{5}}{5}$ $\csc\theta = -\dfrac{\sqrt{5}}{2}$
$\cos\theta = -\dfrac{\sqrt{5}}{5}$ $\sec\theta = -\sqrt{5}$
$\tan\theta = 2$ $\cot\theta = \dfrac{1}{2}$

29. 0 **31.** Undefined **33.** 1 **35.** Undefined

37. $\theta' = 23°$

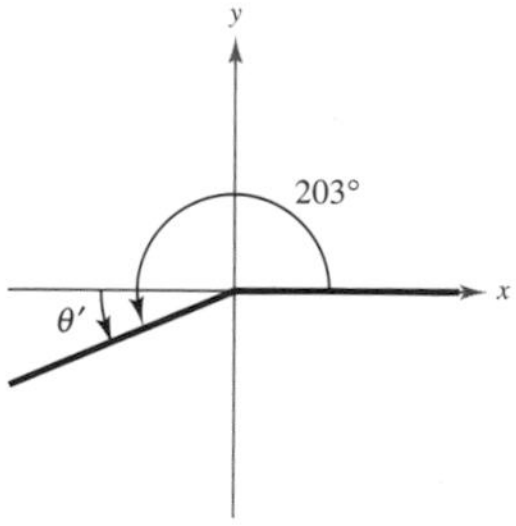

39. $\theta' = 65°$

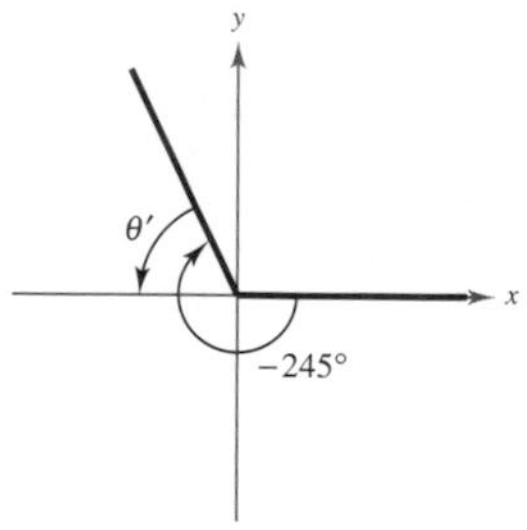

41. $\theta' = \dfrac{\pi}{3}$

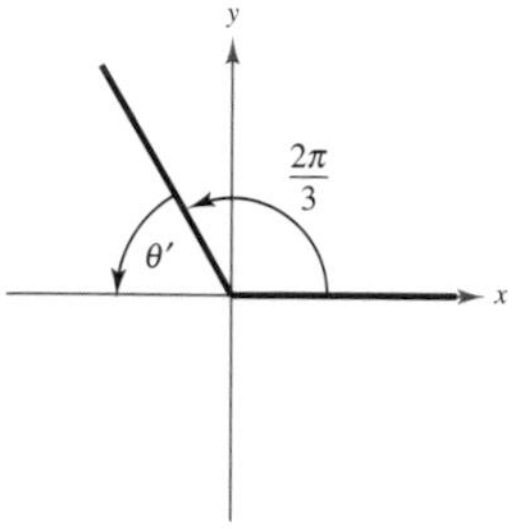

43. $\theta' = 3.5 - \pi$

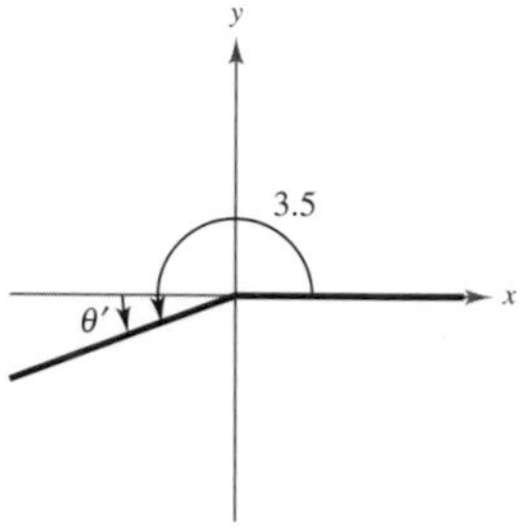

45. $\sin 225° = -\dfrac{\sqrt{2}}{2}$

$\cos 225° = -\dfrac{\sqrt{2}}{2}$

$\tan 225° = 1$

47. $\sin 750° = \dfrac{1}{2}$

$\cos 750° = \dfrac{\sqrt{3}}{2}$

$\tan 750° = \dfrac{\sqrt{3}}{3}$

49. $\sin(-150°) = -\dfrac{1}{2}$

$\cos(-150°) = -\dfrac{\sqrt{3}}{2}$

$\tan(-150°) = \dfrac{\sqrt{3}}{3}$

51. $\sin\dfrac{4\pi}{3} = -\dfrac{\sqrt{3}}{2}$

$\cos\dfrac{4\pi}{3} = -\dfrac{1}{2}$

$\tan\dfrac{4\pi}{3} = \sqrt{3}$

53. $\sin\left(-\dfrac{\pi}{6}\right) = -\dfrac{1}{2}$

$\cos\left(-\dfrac{\pi}{6}\right) = \dfrac{\sqrt{3}}{2}$

$\tan\left(-\dfrac{\pi}{6}\right) = -\dfrac{\sqrt{3}}{3}$

55. $\sin\dfrac{11\pi}{4} = \dfrac{\sqrt{2}}{2}$

$\cos\dfrac{11\pi}{4} = -\dfrac{\sqrt{2}}{2}$

$\tan\dfrac{11\pi}{4} = -1$

57. $\sin\left(-\dfrac{3\pi}{2}\right) = 1$

$\cos\left(-\dfrac{3\pi}{2}\right) = 0$

$\tan\left(-\dfrac{3\pi}{2}\right)$ is undefined.

59. $\dfrac{4}{5}$ **61.** $-\dfrac{\sqrt{13}}{2}$ **63.** $\dfrac{8}{5}$ **65.** 0.1736

67. −0.3420 **69.** −1.4826 **71.** 3.2361

73. 4.6373 **75.** 0.3640 **77.** −0.6052

79. −0.4142

81. (a) $30° = \dfrac{\pi}{6}$, $150° = \dfrac{5\pi}{6}$ (b) $210° = \dfrac{7\pi}{6}$, $330° = \dfrac{11\pi}{6}$

83. (a) $60° = \dfrac{\pi}{3}$, $120° = \dfrac{2\pi}{3}$ (b) $135° = \dfrac{3\pi}{4}$, $315° = \dfrac{7\pi}{4}$

85. (a) $45° = \dfrac{\pi}{4}$, $225° = \dfrac{5\pi}{4}$ (b) $150° = \dfrac{5\pi}{6}$, $330° = \dfrac{11\pi}{6}$

87. (a) $N = 22.099 \sin(0.522t - 2.219) + 55.008$
$F = 36.641 \sin(0.502t - 1.831) + 25.610$

(b) February: $N = 34.6°$, $F = -1.4°$
March: $N = 41.6°$, $F = 13.9°$
May: $N = 63.4°$, $F = 48.6°$
June: $N = 72.5°$, $F = 59.5°$
August: $N = 75.5°$, $F = 55.6°$
September: $N = 68.6°$, $F = 41.7°$
November: $N = 46.8°$, $F = 6.5°$

(c) Answers will vary.

89. (a) 2 centimeters (b) 0.14 centimeter
(c) −1.98 centimeters

91. 0.79 ampere

93. False. In each of the four quadrants, the signs of the secant function and cosine function will be the same, because these functions are reciprocals of each other.

95. As θ increases from 0° to 90°, x decreases from 12 cm to 0 cm and y increases from 0 cm to 12 cm. Therefore, $\sin\theta = y/12$ increases from 0 to 1 and $\cos\theta = x/12$ decreases from 1 to 0. Thus, $\tan\theta = y/x$ and increases without bound. When $\theta = 90°$, the tangent is undefined.

97.

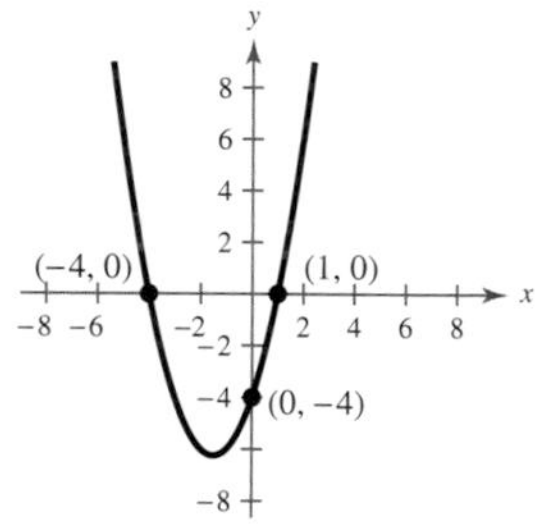

x-intercepts: $(1, 0)$, $(-4, 0)$
y-intercept: $(0, -4)$
Domain: all real numbers x

99.

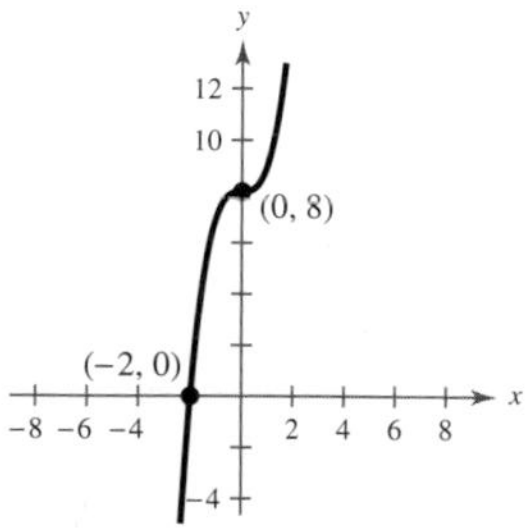

x-intercept: $(-2, 0)$
y-intercept: $(0, 8)$
Domain: all real numbers x

101.

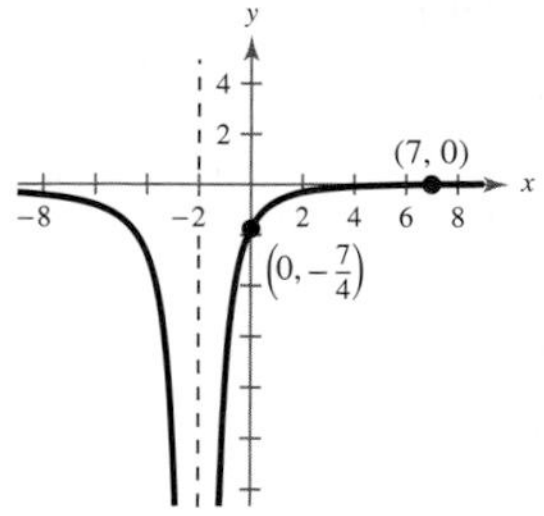

x-intercept: $(7, 0)$
y-intercept: $\left(0, -\frac{7}{4}\right)$
Vertical asymptote: $x = -2$
Horizontal asymptote: $y = 0$
Domain: all real numbers x except $x = -2$

103.

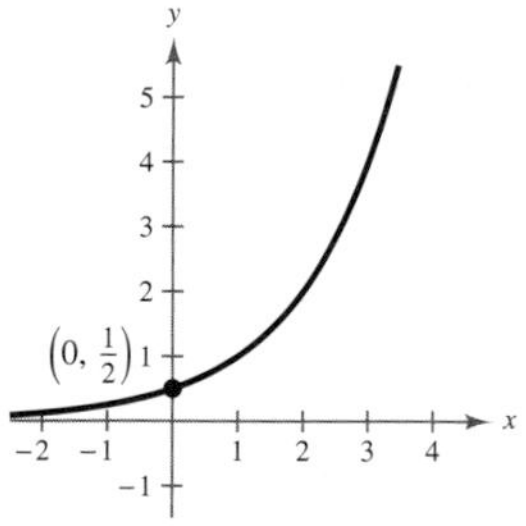

y-intercept: $\left(0, \frac{1}{2}\right)$
Horizontal asymptote: $y = 0$
Domain: all real numbers x

105.

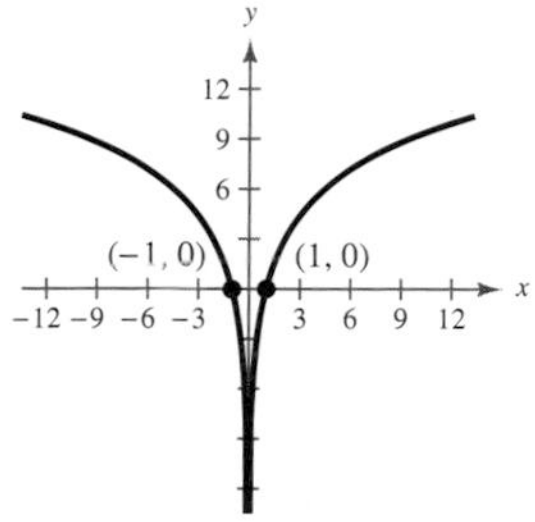

x-intercepts: $(\pm 1, 0)$
Vertical asymptote: $x = 0$
Domain: all real numbers x except $x = 0$

Section 4.5 *(page 328)*

Vocabulary Check *(page 328)*

1. cycle **2.** amplitude **3.** $\dfrac{2\pi}{b}$
4. phase shift **5.** vertical shift

1. Period: π
Amplitude: 3

3. Period: 4π
Amplitude: $\frac{5}{2}$

5. Period: 6
Amplitude: $\frac{1}{2}$

7. Period: 2π
Amplitude: 3

9. Period: $\dfrac{\pi}{5}$
Amplitude: 3

11. Period: 3π
Amplitude: $\frac{1}{2}$

13. Period: 1
Amplitude: $\frac{1}{4}$

15. g is a shift of f π units to the right.
17. g is a reflection of f in the x-axis.
19. The period of f is twice the period of g.
21. g is a shift of f three units upward.
23. The graph of g has twice the amplitude of the graph of f.
25. The graph of g is a horizontal shift of the graph of f π units to the right.

27.

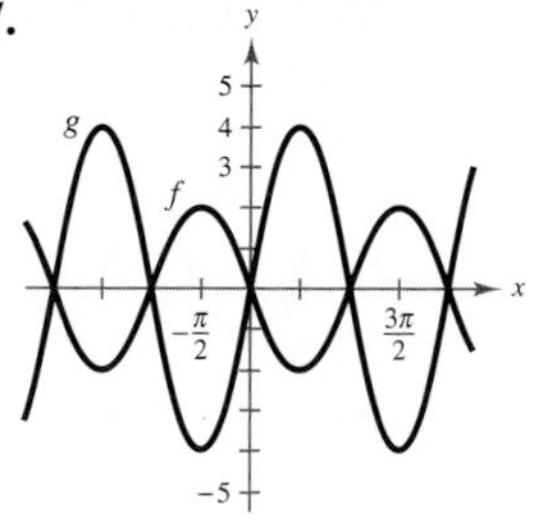

29.

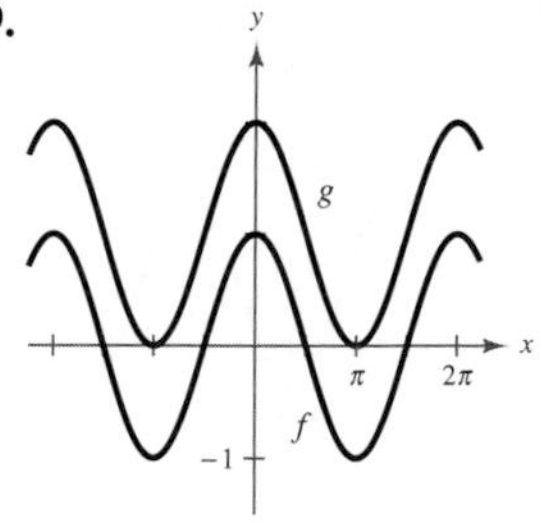

31.

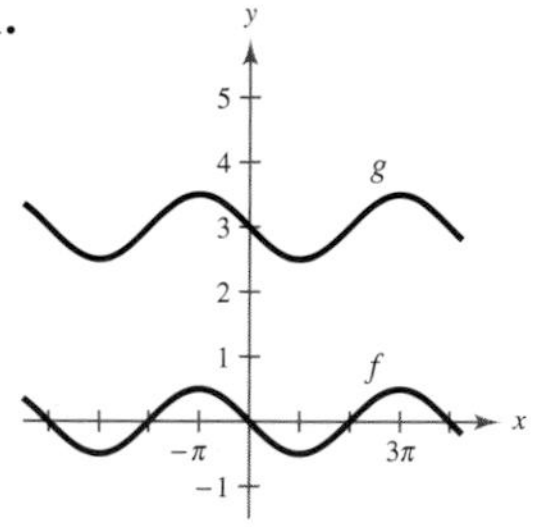

33.

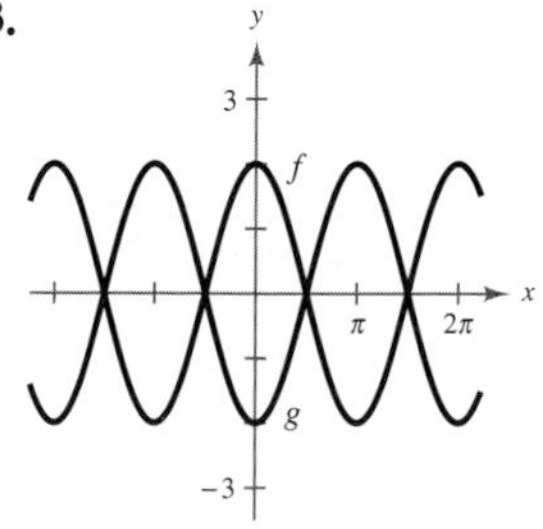

35.

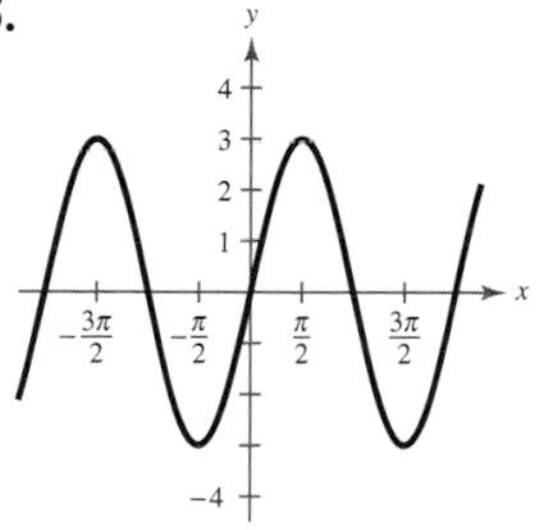

37.

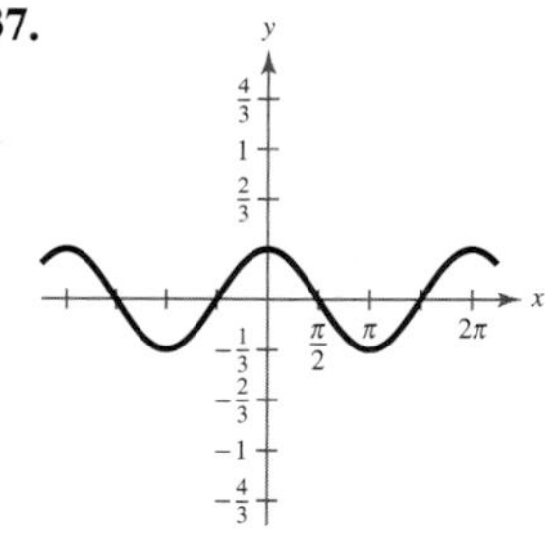

39.

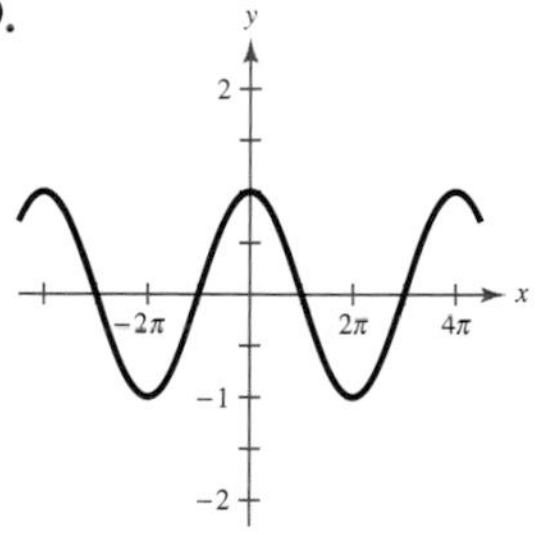

41.

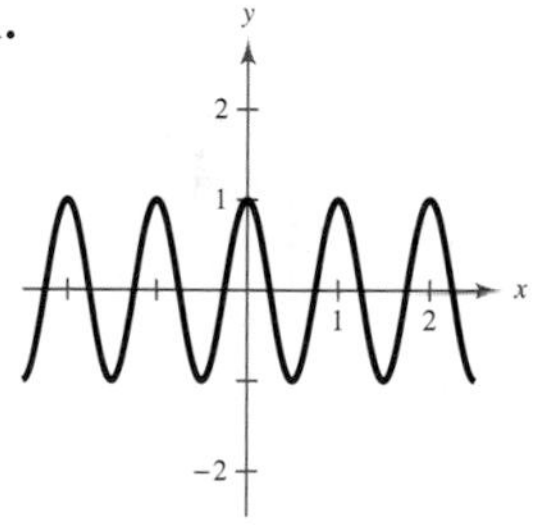

43.

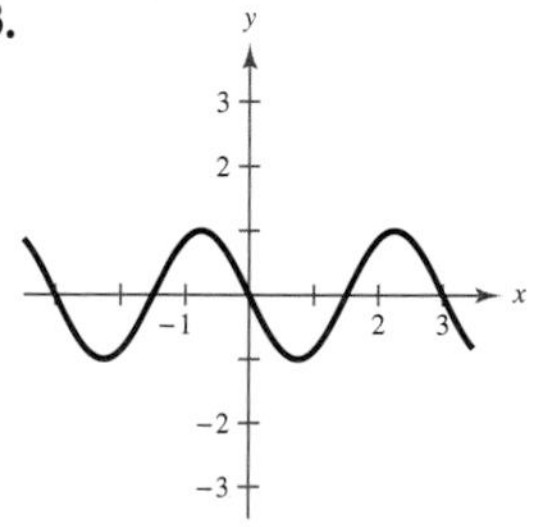

45.

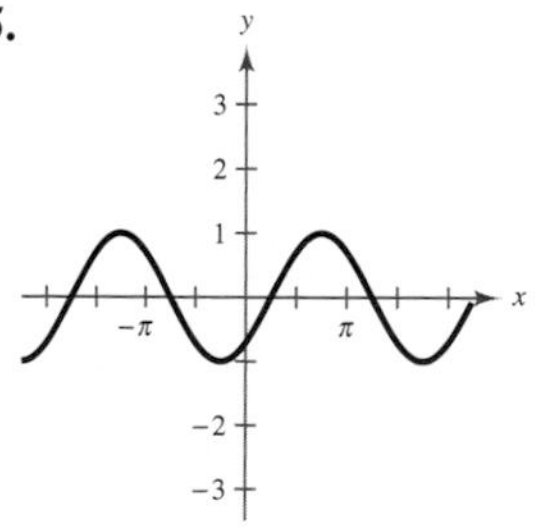

47.

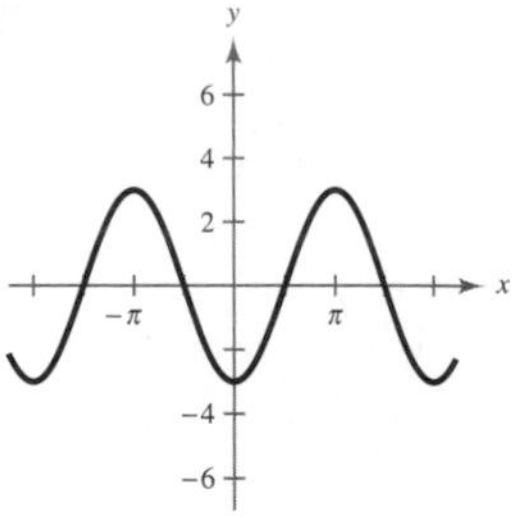

49.

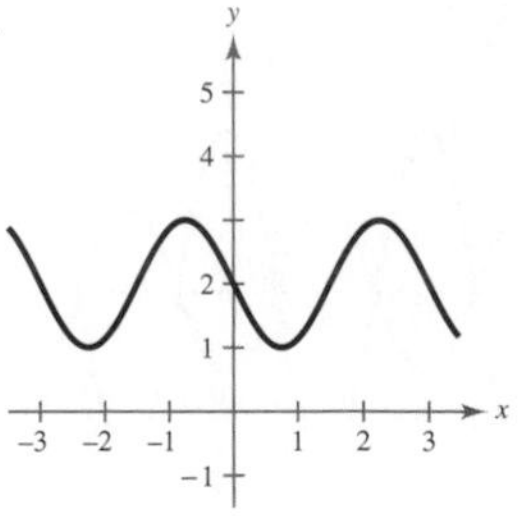

51.

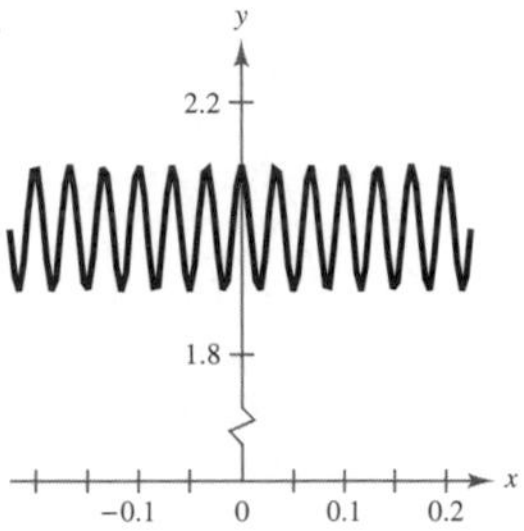

53.

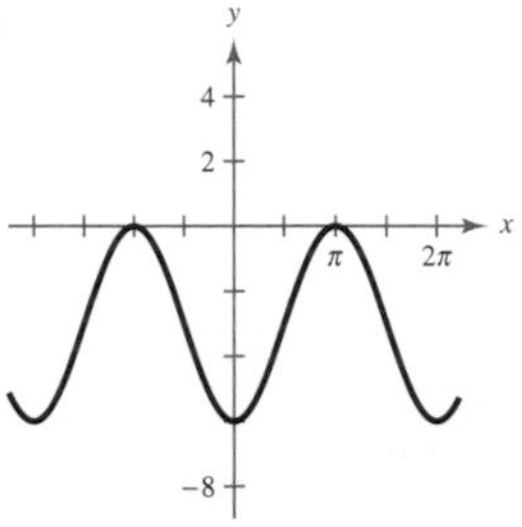

55.

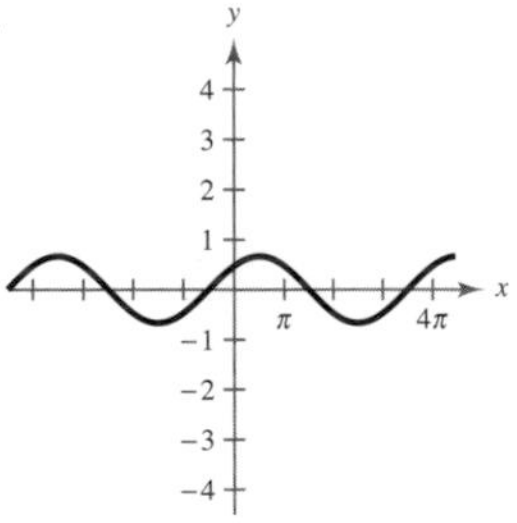

57.

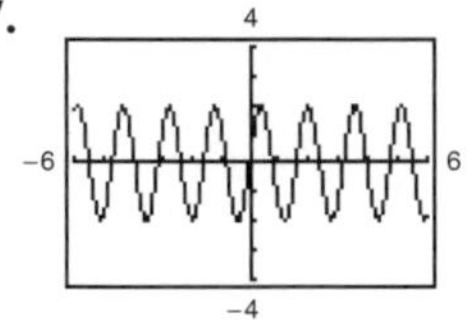

59.

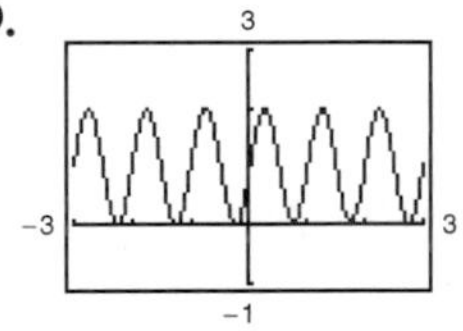

61.

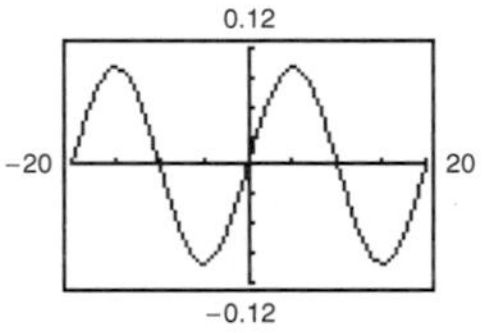

63. $a = 2, d = 1$ **65.** $a = -4, d = 4$

67. $a = -3, b = 2, c = 0$ **69.** $a = 2, b = 1, c = -\frac{\pi}{4}$

71.

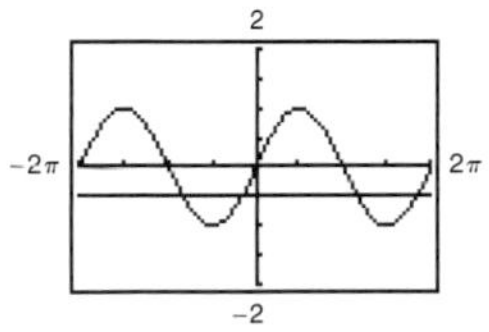

$x = -\frac{\pi}{6}, -\frac{5\pi}{6}, \frac{7\pi}{6}, \frac{11\pi}{6}$

73. (a) 6 seconds (b) 10 cycles per minute

(c)

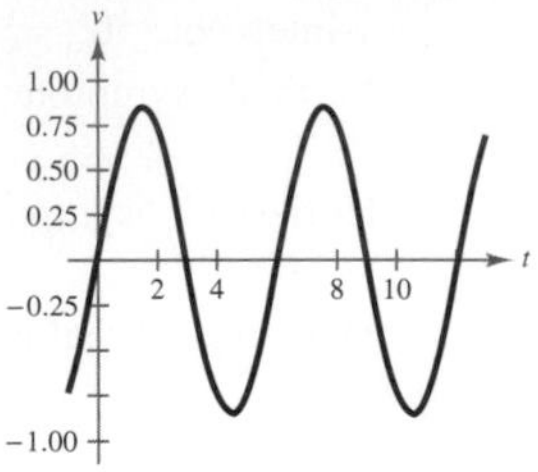

75. (a) $C(t) = 56.55 + 26.95 \cos\left(\frac{\pi}{6}t - 3.67\right)$

(b)

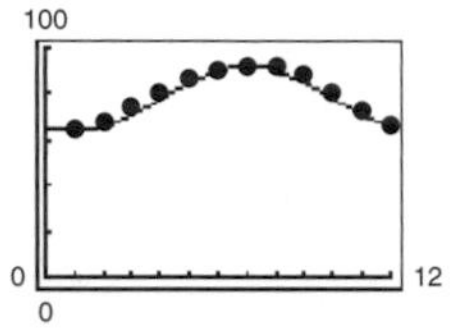

The model is a good fit.

(c)

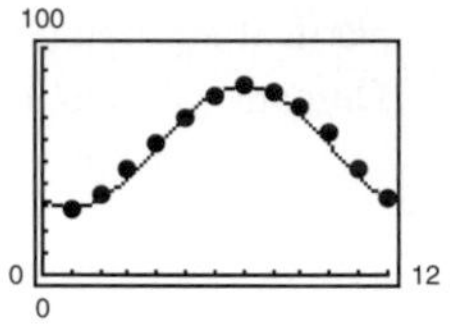

The model is a good fit.

(d) Tallahassee: 77.90°; Chicago: 56.55°

The constant term gives the annual average temperature.

(e) 12; yes; one full period is one year.

(f) Chicago; amplitude; the greater the amplitude, the greater the variability in temperature.

77. (a) $\frac{1}{440}$ second (b) 440 cycles per second

79. (a) 365; answers will vary.

(b) 30.3 gallons; the constant term

(c) $124 < t < 252$

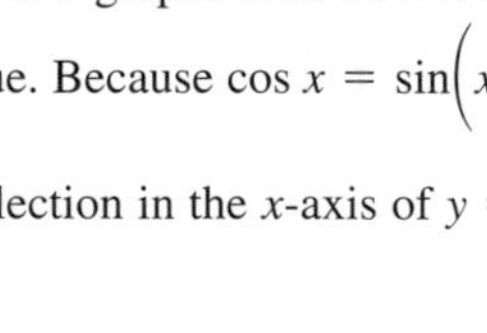

81. False. The graph of $f(x) = \sin(x + 2\pi)$ translates the graph of $f(x) = \sin x$ exactly one period to the left so that the two graphs look identical.

83. True. Because $\cos x = \sin\left(x + \frac{\pi}{2}\right)$, $y = -\cos x$ is a reflection in the x-axis of $y = \sin\left(x + \frac{\pi}{2}\right)$.

85.

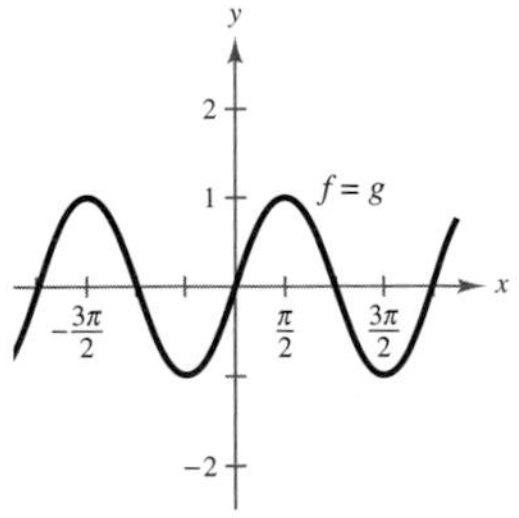

Conjecture: $\sin x = \cos\left(x - \frac{\pi}{2}\right)$

87. (a)

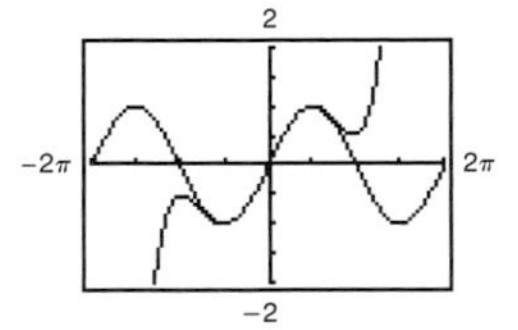

The graphs appear to coincide from $-\frac{\pi}{2}$ to $\frac{\pi}{2}$.

(b)

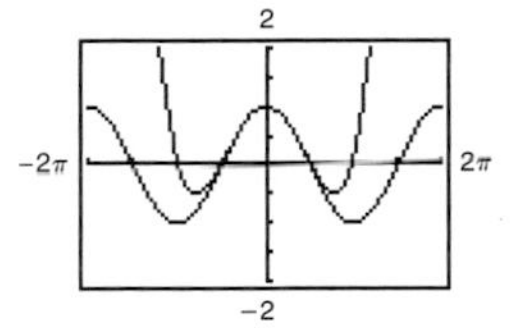

The graphs appear to coincide from $-\frac{\pi}{2}$ to $\frac{\pi}{2}$.

(c) $-\frac{x^7}{7!}, -\frac{x^6}{6!}$

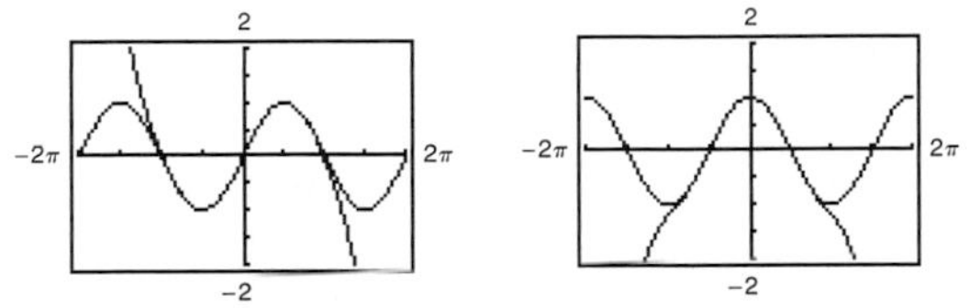

The interval of accuracy increased.

89. $\frac{1}{2}\log_{10}(x - 2)$ **91.** $3 \ln t - \ln(t - 1)$

93. $\log_{10} \sqrt{xy}$ **95.** $\ln \frac{3x}{y^4}$ **97.** Answers will vary.

Section 4.6 *(page 339)*

Vocabulary Check *(page 339)*

1. vertical **2.** reciprocal **3.** damping
4. π **5.** $x \neq n\pi$ **6.** $(-\infty, -1] \cup [1, \infty)$
7. 2π

1. e, π **2.** c, 2π **3.** a, 1 **4.** d, 2π
5. f, 4 **6.** b, 4

7.

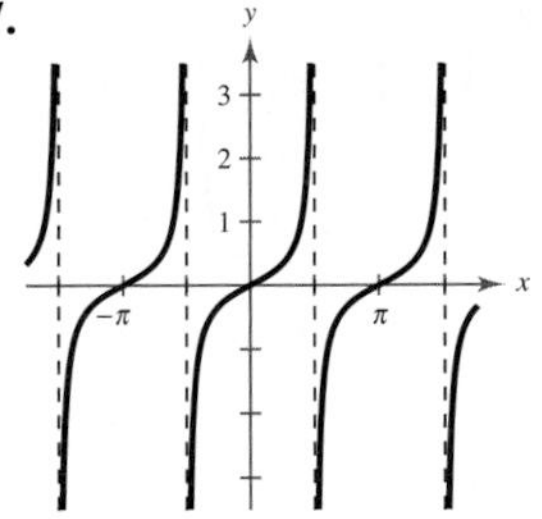

9.

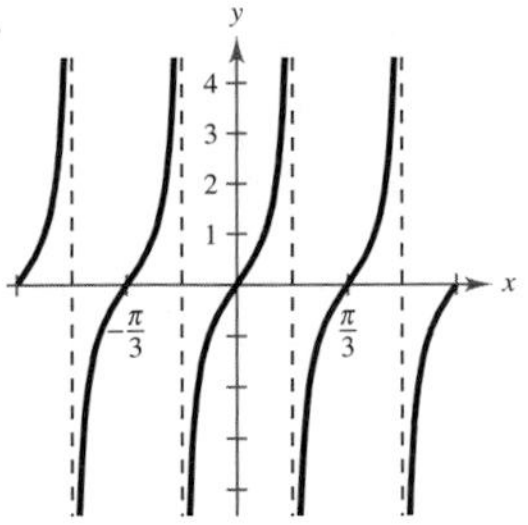

11.

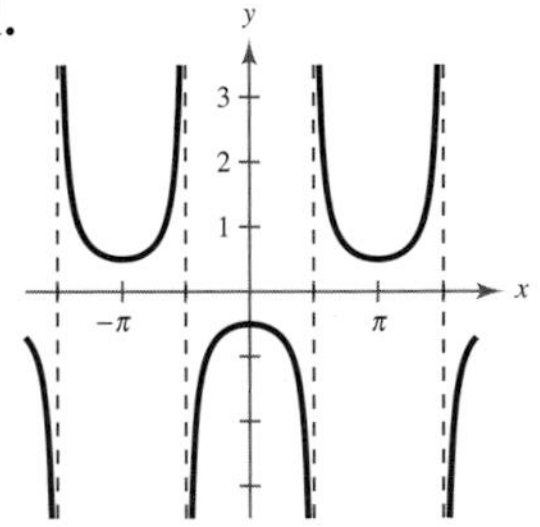

13.

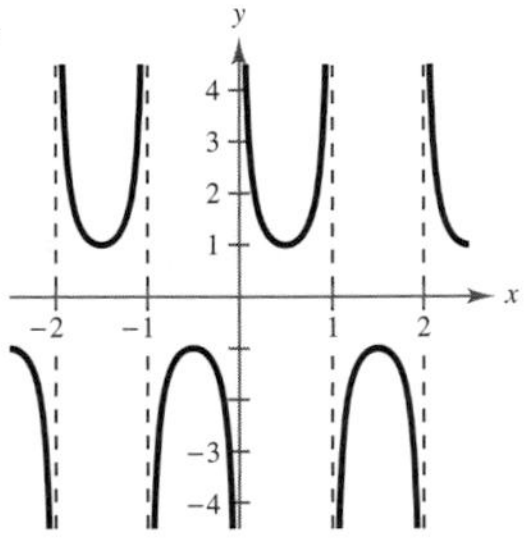

15.

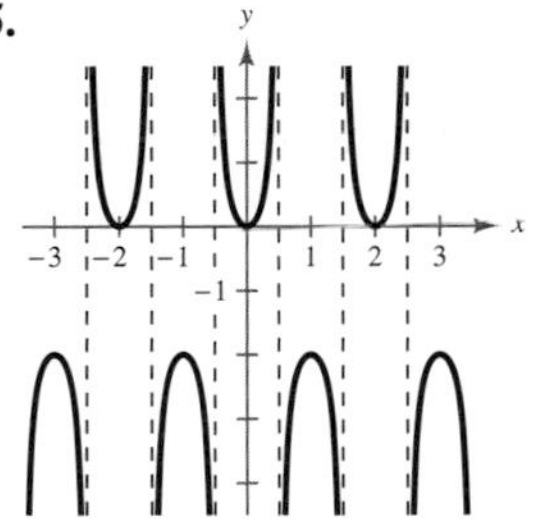

17.

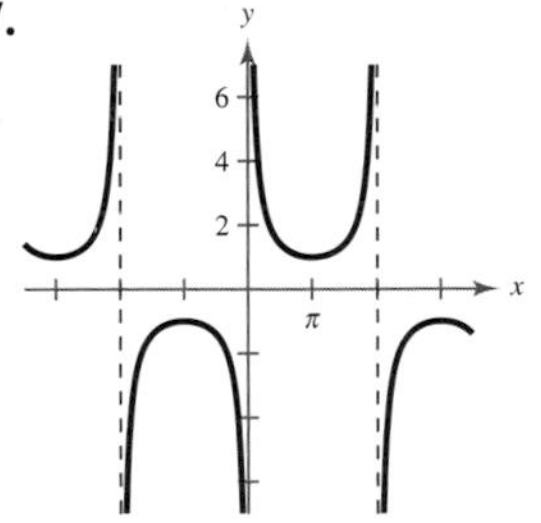

19.

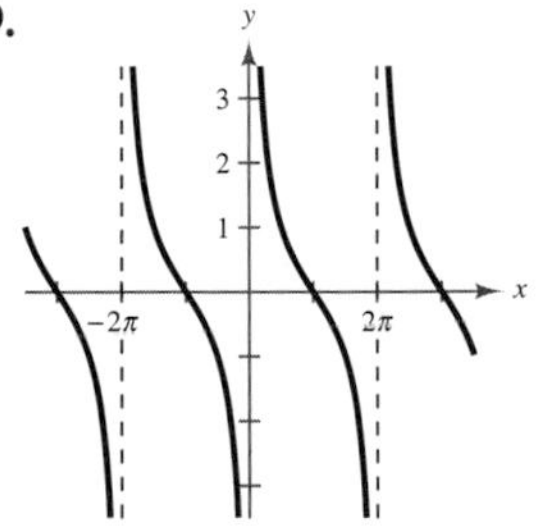

21.

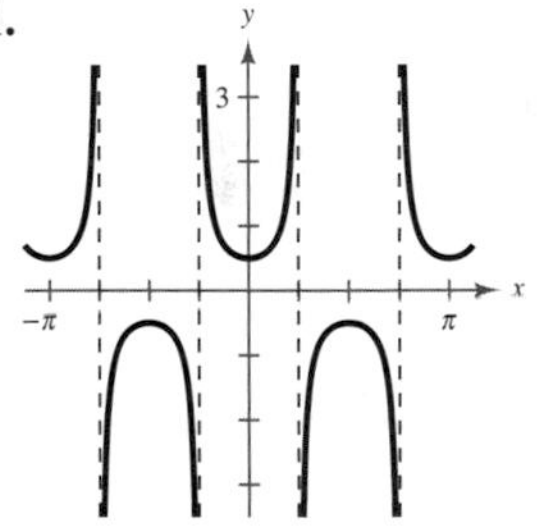

23.

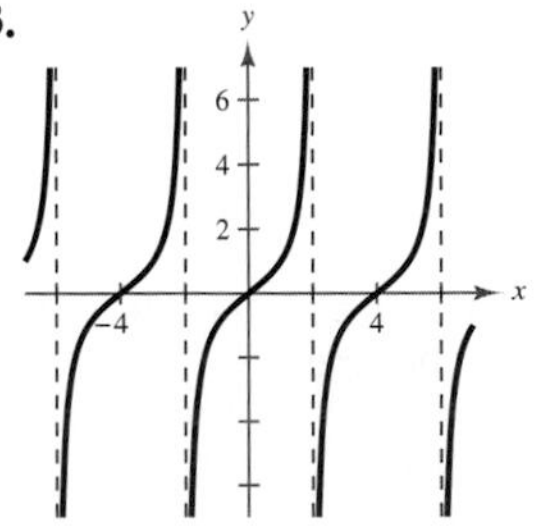

25.

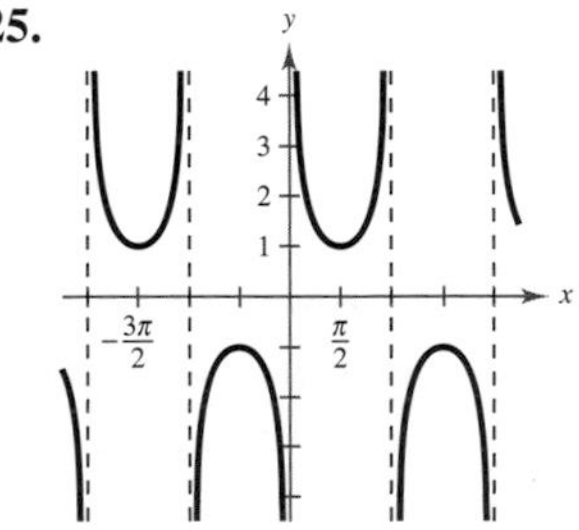

CHAPTER 4

27.

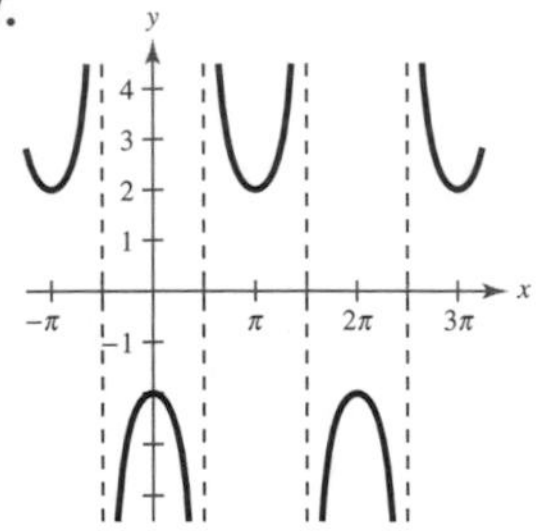

29.

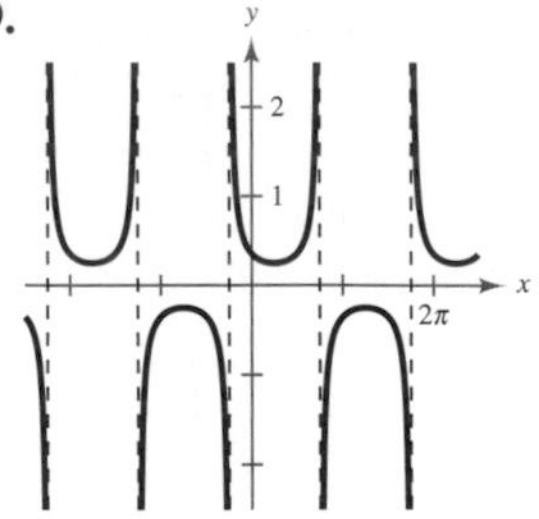

31.

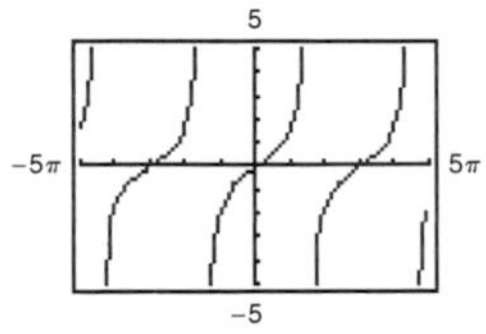

33.

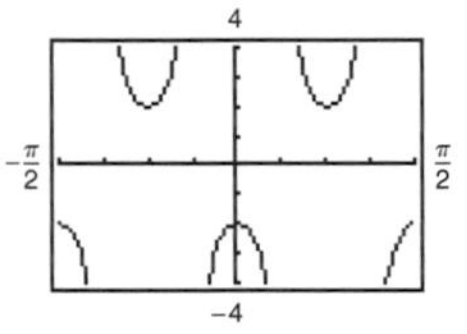

35.

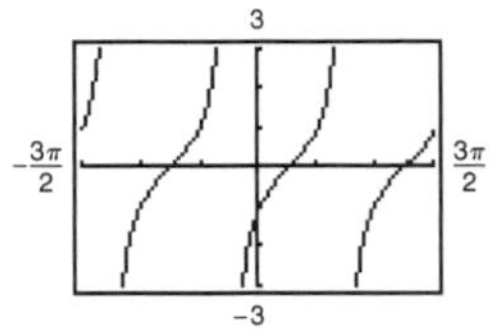

37.

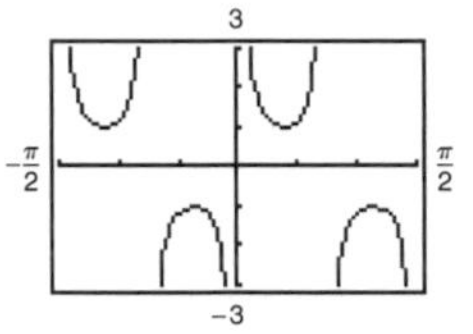

39.

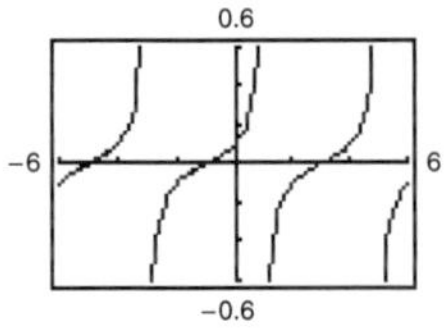

41. $-\frac{7\pi}{4}, -\frac{3\pi}{4}, \frac{\pi}{4}, \frac{5\pi}{4}$

43. $-\frac{4\pi}{3}, -\frac{\pi}{3}, \frac{2\pi}{3}, \frac{5\pi}{3}$

45. $-\frac{4\pi}{3}, -\frac{2\pi}{3}, \frac{2\pi}{3}, \frac{4\pi}{3}$

47. $-\frac{7\pi}{4}, -\frac{5\pi}{4}, \frac{\pi}{4}, \frac{3\pi}{4}$

49. Even

51. (a)

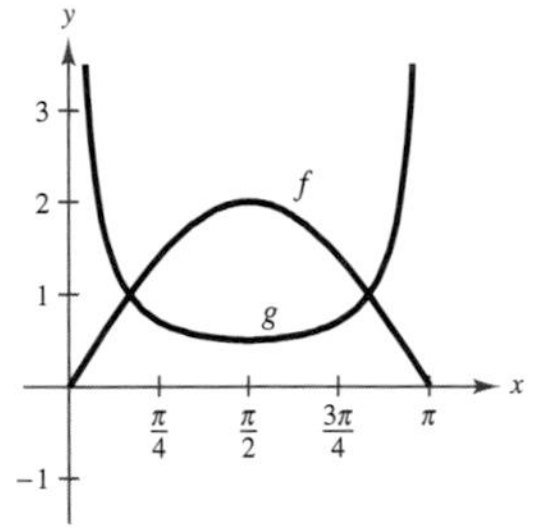

(b) $\frac{\pi}{6} < x < \frac{5\pi}{6}$

(c) f approaches 0 and g approaches $+\infty$ because the cosecant is the reciprocal of the sine.

53.

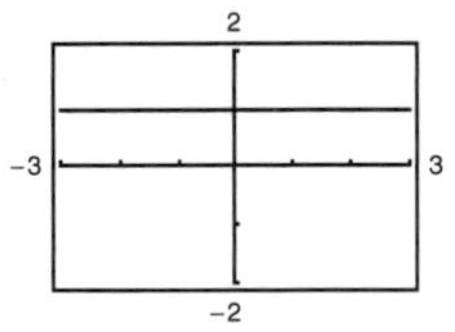

The expressions are equivalent except that when $\sin x = 0$, y_1 is undefined.

55.

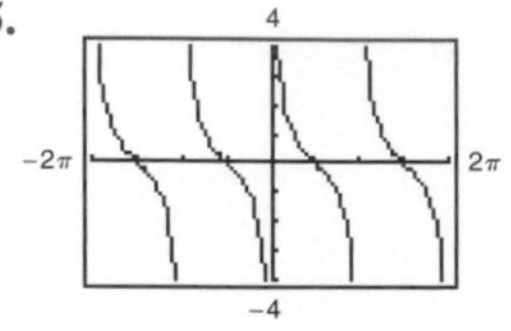

The expressions are equivalent.

57. d, $f \to 0$ as $x \to 0$. **58.** a, $f \to 0$ as $x \to 0$.

59. b, $g \to 0$ as $x \to 0$. **60.** c, $g \to 0$ as $x \to 0$.

61.

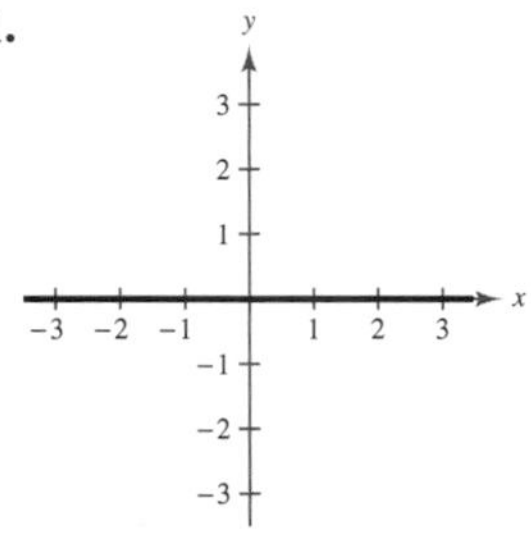

The functions are equal.

63.

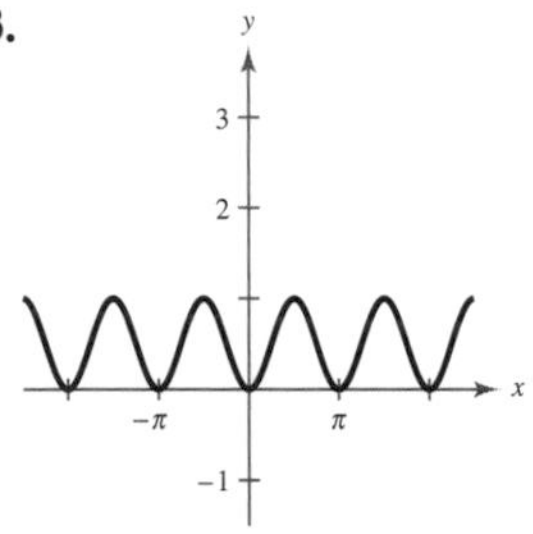

The functions are equal.

65.

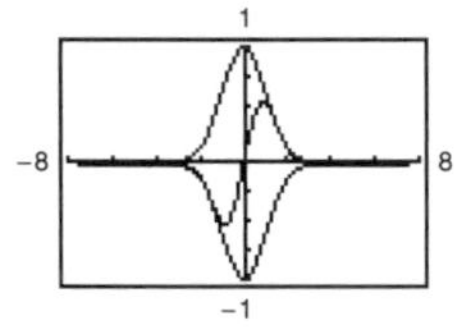

As $x \to \infty$, $g(x) \to 0$.

67.

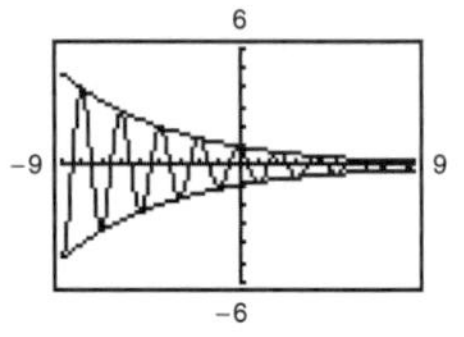

As $x \to \infty$, $f(x) \to 0$.

69.

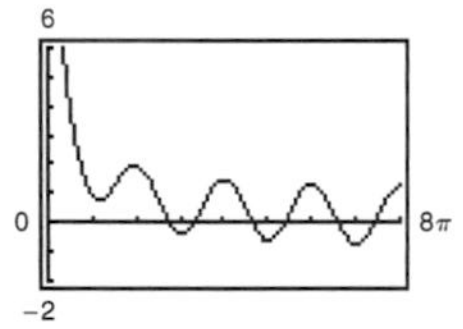

As $x \to 0$, $y \to \infty$.

71.

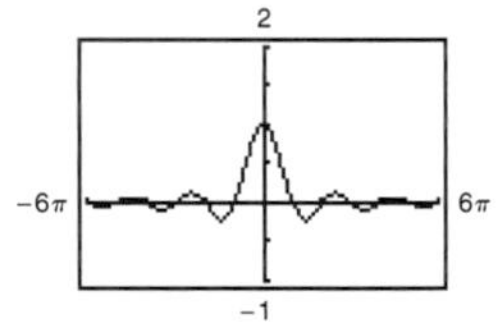

As $x \to 0$, $g(x) \to 1$.

73.

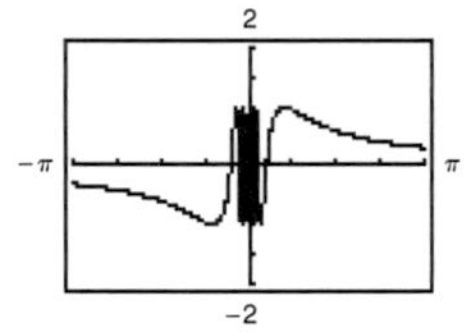

As $x \to 0$, $f(x)$ oscillates between 1 and -1.

75. $d = 7 \cot x$

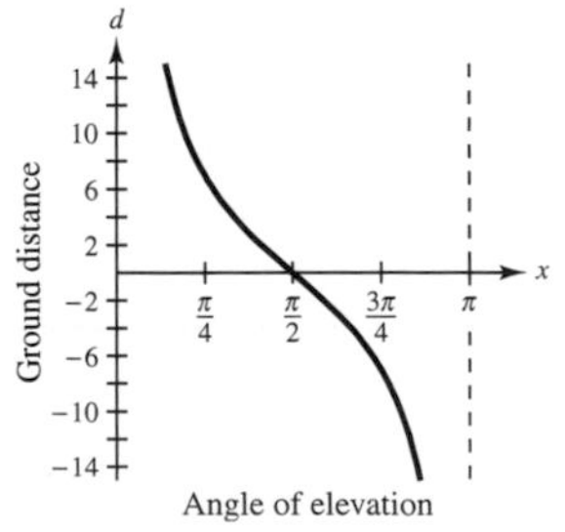

77. (a)

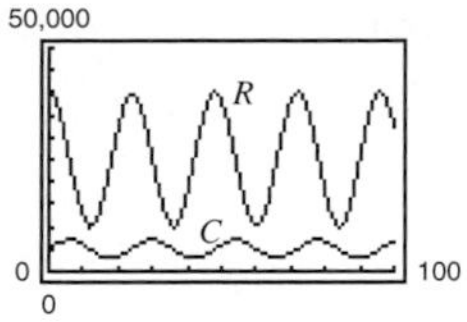

(b) As the predator population increases, the number of prey decreases. When the number of prey is small, the number of predators decreases.

(c) C: 24 months; R: 24 months

79. (a) H: 12 months; L: 12 months

(b) Summer; winter (c) 1 month

81. True. For a given value of x, the y-coordinate of $\csc x$ is the reciprocal of the y-coordinate of $\sin x$.

83. As x approaches $\pi/2$ from the left, f approaches ∞. As x approaches $\pi/2$ from the right, f approaches $-\infty$.

85. (a)

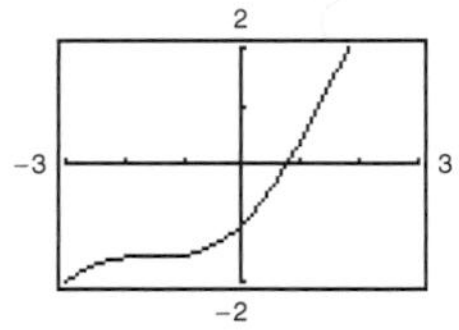

0.7391

(b) 1, 0.5403, 0.8576, 0.6543, 0.7935, 0.7014, 0.7640, 0.7221, 0.7504, 0.7314, . . . ; 0.7391

87.

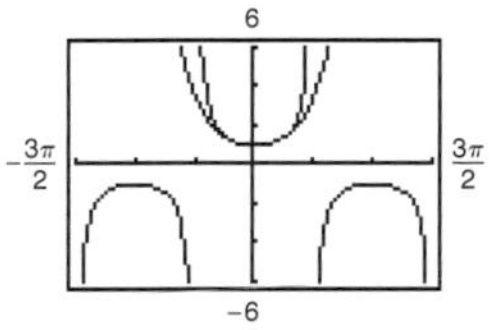

The graphs appear to coincide on the interval $-1.1 \le x \le 1.1$.

89. $\dfrac{\ln 54}{2} \approx 1.994$ **91.** $-\ln 2 \approx -0.693$

93. $\dfrac{2 + e^{73}}{3} \approx 1.684 \times 10^{31}$

95. $\pm\sqrt{e^{3.2} - 1} \approx \pm 4.851$ **97.** 2

Section 4.7 *(page 349)*

Vocabulary Check *(page 349)*

1. $y = \sin^{-1} x;\ -1 \le x \le 1$

2. $y = \arccos x;\ 0 \le y \le \pi$

3. $y = \tan^{-1} x;\ -\infty < x < \infty;\ -\dfrac{\pi}{2} < y < \dfrac{\pi}{2}$

1. $\dfrac{\pi}{6}$ **3.** $\dfrac{\pi}{3}$ **5.** $\dfrac{\pi}{6}$ **7.** $\dfrac{5\pi}{6}$ **9.** $-\dfrac{\pi}{3}$

11. $\dfrac{2\pi}{3}$ **13.** $\dfrac{\pi}{3}$ **15.** 0

17.

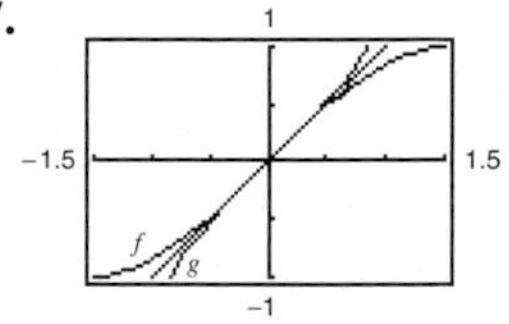

19. 1.29 **21.** −0.85 **23.** −1.25 **25.** 0.32

27. 1.99 **29.** 0.74 **31.** 0.85 **33.** 1.29

35. $-\dfrac{\pi}{3}, -\dfrac{\sqrt{3}}{3}, 1$ **37.** $\theta = \arctan \dfrac{x}{4}$

39. $\theta = \arcsin \dfrac{x+2}{5}$ **41.** $\theta = \arccos \dfrac{x+3}{2x}$

43. 0.3 **45.** −0.1 **47.** 0 **49.** $\dfrac{3}{5}$ **51.** $\dfrac{\sqrt{5}}{5}$

53. $\dfrac{12}{13}$ **55.** $\dfrac{\sqrt{34}}{5}$ **57.** $\dfrac{\sqrt{5}}{3}$ **59.** $\dfrac{1}{x}$

61. $\sqrt{1 - 4x^2}$ **63.** $\sqrt{1 - x^2}$ **65.** $\dfrac{\sqrt{9 - x^2}}{x}$

67. $\dfrac{\sqrt{x^2 + 2}}{x}$

69.

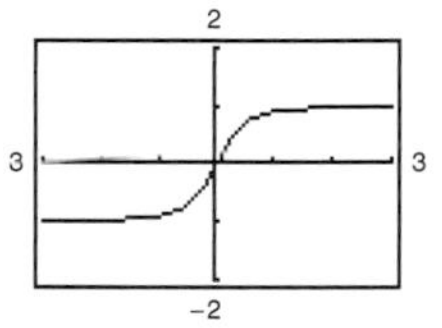

Asymptotes: $y = \pm 1$

71. $\dfrac{9}{\sqrt{x^2 + 81}},\ x > 0;\ \dfrac{-9}{\sqrt{x^2 + 81}},\ x < 0$

73. $\dfrac{|x - 1|}{\sqrt{x^2 - 2x + 10}}$

75.

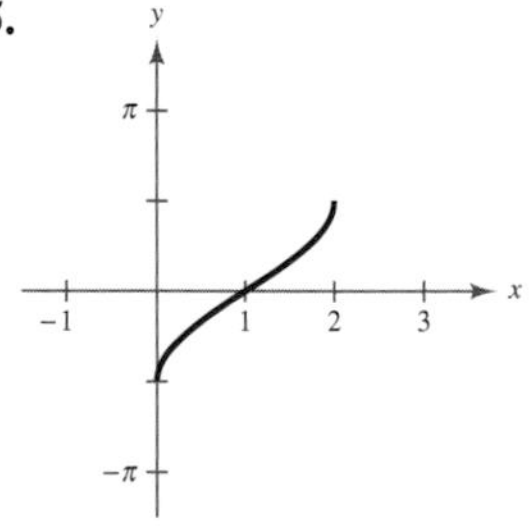

77.

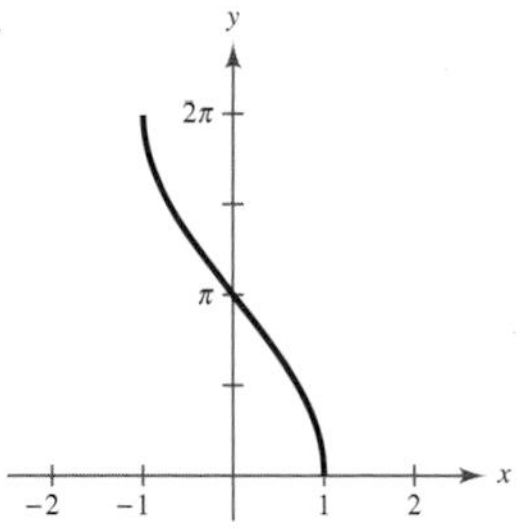

The graph of g is a horizontal shift one unit to the right of f.

79.

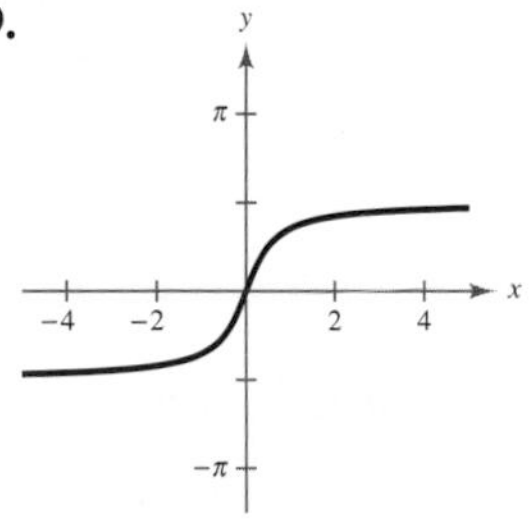

81.

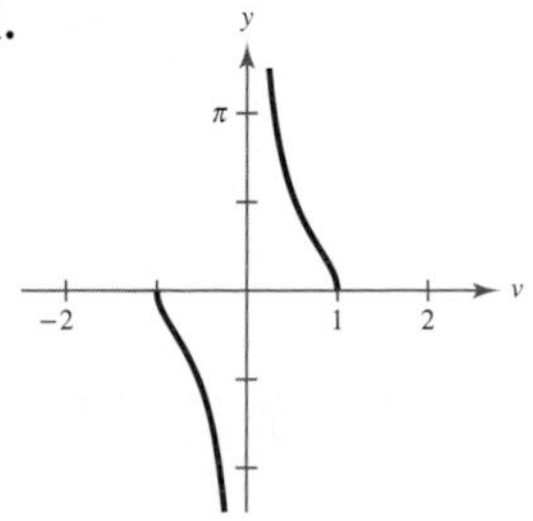

83.

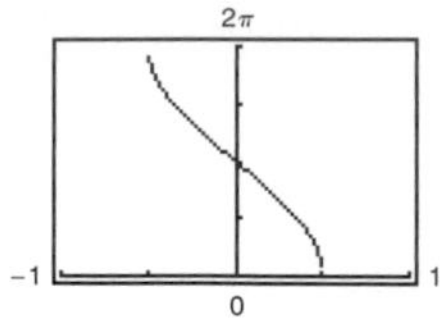

85.

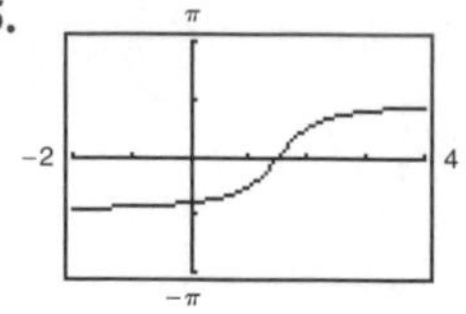

87.

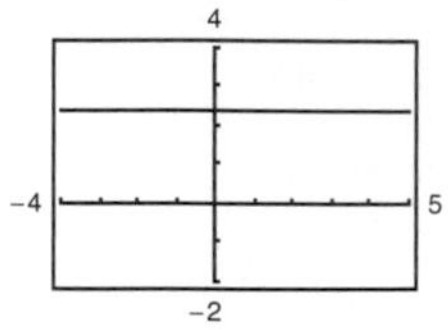

89. $3\sqrt{2}\sin\left(2t + \frac{\pi}{4}\right)$

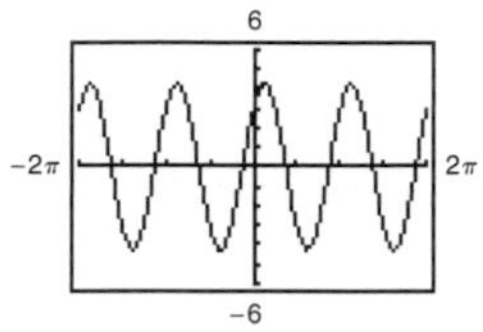

The graph implies that the identity is true.

91. (a) $\theta = \arcsin \frac{5}{s}$ (b) 0.13, 0.25

93. (a)

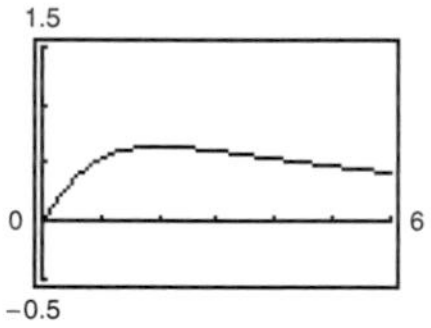

(b) 2 feet (c) $\beta = 0$; As x increases, β approaches 0.

95. (a) $\theta \approx 26.0°$ (b) 24.4 feet

97. (a) $\theta = \arctan \frac{x}{20}$ (b) 14.0°, 31.0°

99. False. $\frac{5\pi}{4}$ is not in the range of the arctangent.

101. Domain: $(-\infty, \infty)$
Range: $(0, \pi)$

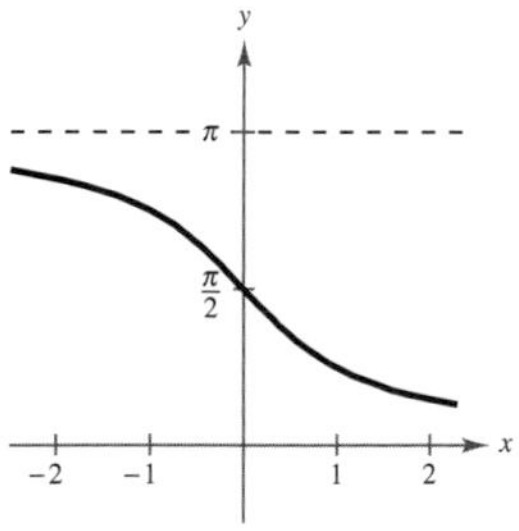

103. Domain: $(-\infty, -1] \cup [1, \infty)$
Range: $[-\pi/2, 0) \cup (0, \pi/2]$

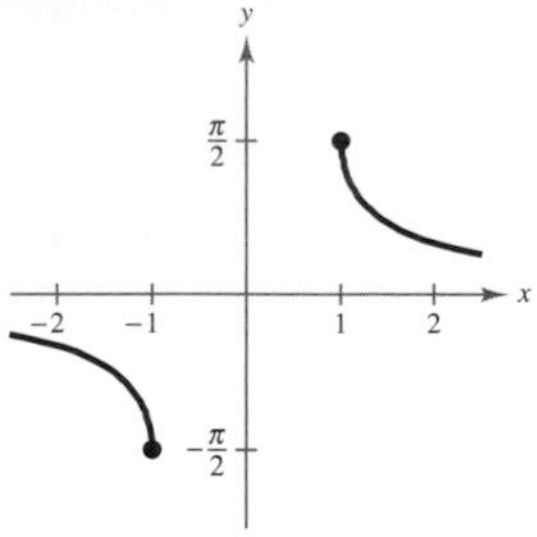

105. (a) $\frac{\pi}{4}$ (b) $\frac{\pi}{2}$ (c) 1.25 (d) 2.03

107. (a) $f \circ f^{-1}$ $f^{-1} \circ f$

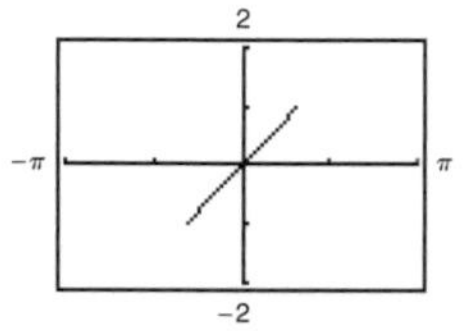

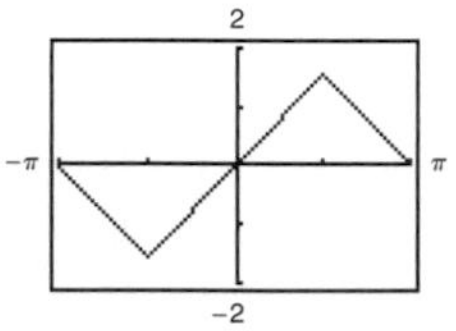

(b) The domains and ranges of the functions are restricted. The graphs of $f \circ f^{-1}$ and $f^{-1} \circ f$ differ because of the domains and ranges of f and f^{-1}.

109. 1279.284 **111.** 117.391

113.

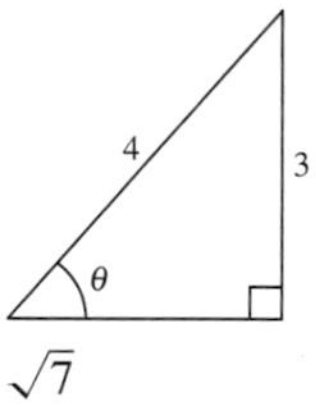

$\cos\theta = \frac{\sqrt{7}}{4}$ $\sec\theta = \frac{4\sqrt{7}}{7}$

$\tan\theta = \frac{3\sqrt{7}}{7}$ $\cot\theta = \frac{\sqrt{7}}{3}$

$\csc\theta = \frac{4}{3}$

115.

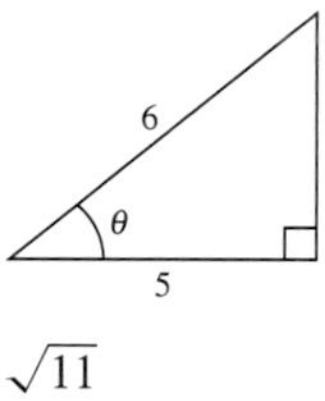

$\sin\theta = \frac{\sqrt{11}}{6}$ $\sec\theta = \frac{6}{5}$

$\tan\theta = \frac{\sqrt{11}}{5}$ $\cot\theta = \frac{5\sqrt{11}}{11}$

$\csc\theta = \frac{6\sqrt{11}}{11}$

117. Eight people

119. (a) \$21,253.63 (b) \$21,275.17
(c) \$21,285.66 (d) \$21,286.01

Section 4.8 *(page 359)*

Vocabulary Check *(page 359)*

1. elevation; depression **2.** bearing
3. harmonic motion

1. $a \approx 3.64$
$c \approx 10.64$
$B = 70°$

3. $a \approx 8.26$
$c \approx 25.38$
$A = 19°$

5. $c \approx 11.66$
$A \approx 30.96°$
$B \approx 59.04°$

7. $a \approx 49.48$
$A \approx 72.08°$
$B \approx 17.92°$

9. $a \approx 91.34$
$b \approx 420.70$
$B = 77°45'$

11. 2.56 inches

13. 19.99 inches **15.** 107.2 feet **17.** 19.7 feet

19. (a)

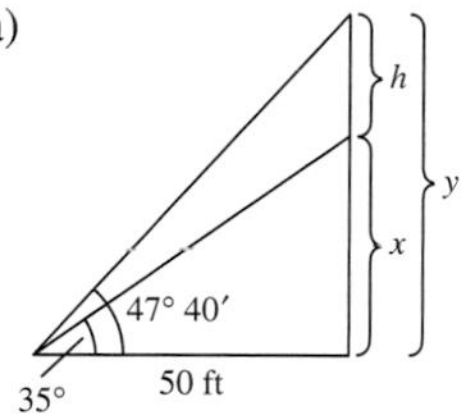

(b) $h = 50(\tan 47°40' - \tan 35°)$ (c) 19.9 feet

21. 2236.8 feet

23. (a)

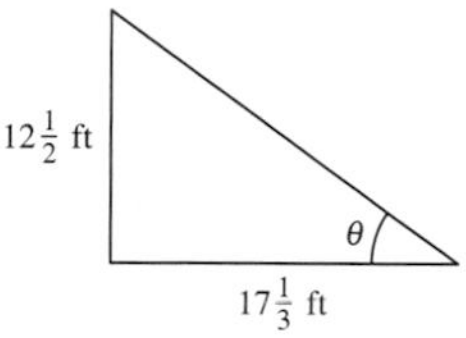

(b) $\tan \theta = \frac{12\frac{1}{2}}{17\frac{1}{3}}$ (c) 35.8°

25. 2.06° **27.** 0.73 mile

29. 554 miles north; 709 miles east

31. (a) 58.18 nautical miles west;
104.95 nautical miles south
(b) S 36.7° W; distance = 130.9 nautical miles

33. (a) N 58° E (b) 68.82 meters

35. N 56.31° W **37.** 1933.3 feet

39. $\approx$ 3.23 miles or $\approx$ 17,054 feet

41. 78.7° **43.** 35.3° **45.** 29.4 inches

47. $y = \sqrt{3}r$ **49.** $a \approx 12.2, b \approx 7$

51. $d = 4\sin(\pi t)$ **53.** $d = 3\cos\left(\frac{4\pi t}{3}\right)$

55. (a) 4 (b) 4 (c) 4 (d) $\frac{1}{16}$

57. (a) $\frac{1}{16}$ (b) 60 (c) 0 (d) $\frac{1}{120}$ **59.** $\omega = 528\pi$

61. (a)

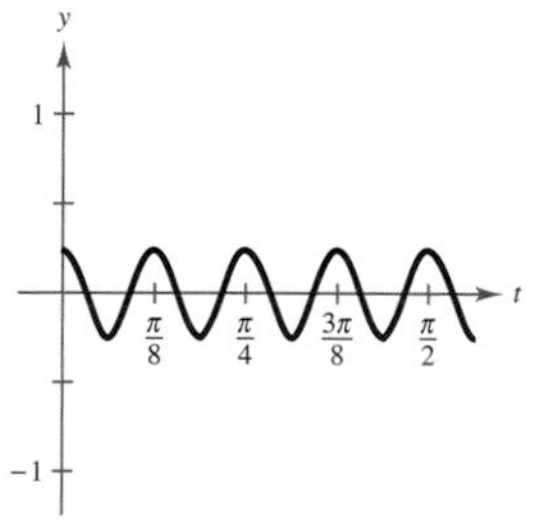

(b) $\frac{\pi}{8}$ (c) $\frac{\pi}{32}$

63. (a)

Base 1	Base 2	Altitude	Area
8	8 + 16 cos 30°	8 sin 30°	59.7
8	8 + 16 cos 40°	8 sin 40°	72.7
8	8 + 16 cos 50°	8 sin 50°	80.5
8	8 + 16 cos 60°	8 sin 60°	83.1
8	8 + 16 cos 70°	8 sin 70°	80.7
8	8 + 16 cos 80°	8 sin 80°	74.0
8	8 + 16 cos 90°	8 sin 90°	64.0

(b)

Base 1	Base 2	Altitude	Area
8	8 + 16 cos 56°	8 sin 56°	82.73
8	8 + 16 cos 58°	8 sin 58°	83.04
8	8 + 16 cos 59°	8 sin 59°	83.11
8	8 + 16 cos 60°	8 sin 60°	83.14
8	8 + 16 cos 61°	8 sin 61°	83.11
8	8 + 16 cos 62°	8 sin 62°	83.04

83.14 square feet

(c) $A = 64(1 + \cos\theta)(\sin\theta)$

(d)

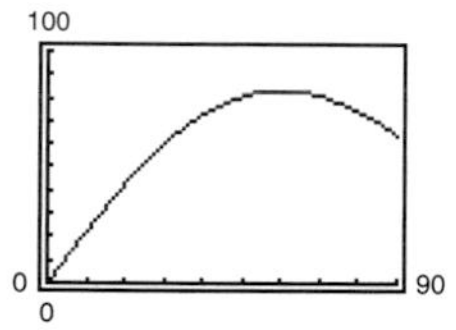

$\approx$ 83.1 square feet when $\theta = 60°$
The answers are the same.

65. False. The tower is leaning, so it is not perfectly vertical and does not form a right angle with the ground.

67. No. N 24° E means 24 degrees east of north.

69. $y = 4x + 6$

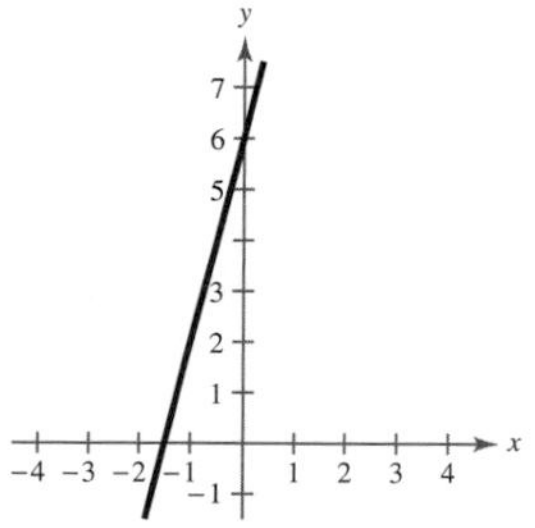

71. $y = -\frac{4}{5}x + \frac{22}{5}$

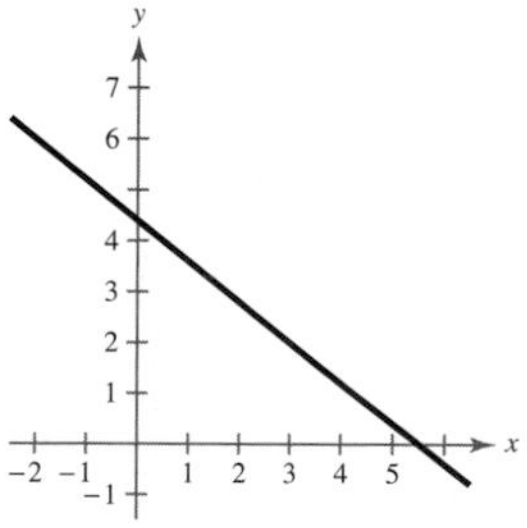

Review Exercises *(page 365)*

1. 0.5 radian

3. (a)

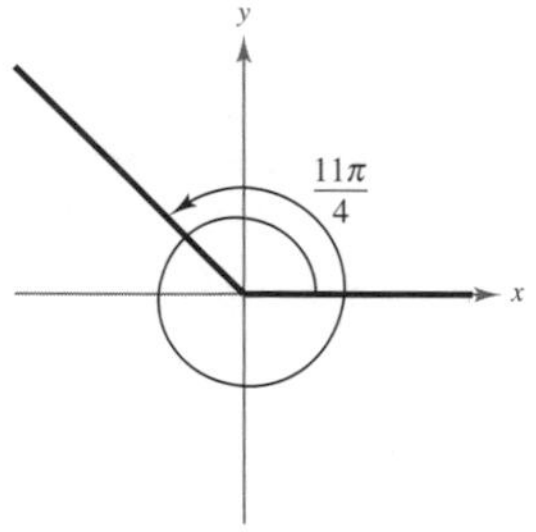

(b) Quadrant II

(c) $\frac{3\pi}{4}, -\frac{5\pi}{4}$

5. (a)

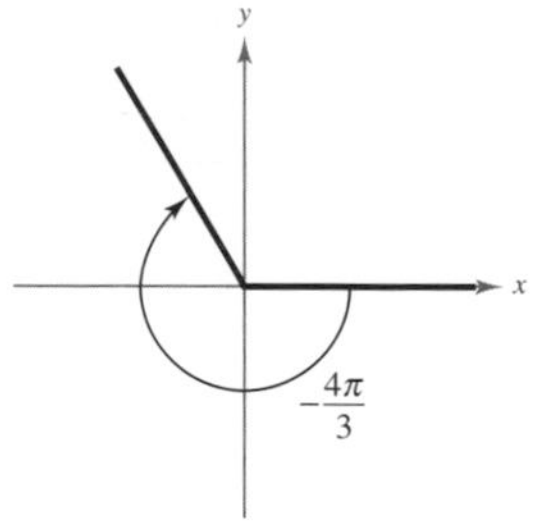

(b) Quadrant II

(c) $\frac{2\pi}{3}, -\frac{10\pi}{3}$

7. (a)

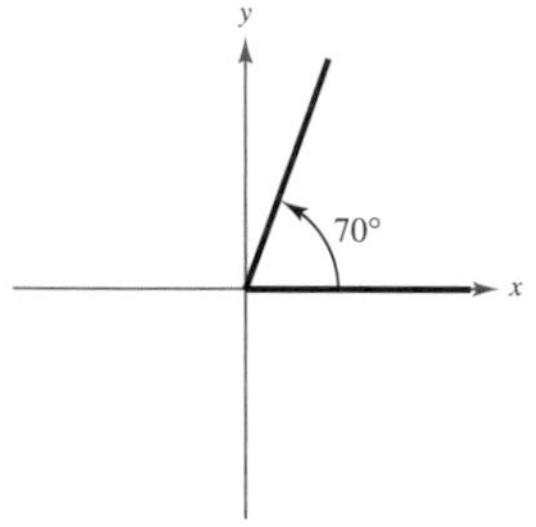

(b) Quadrant I

(c) 430°, −290°

9. (a)

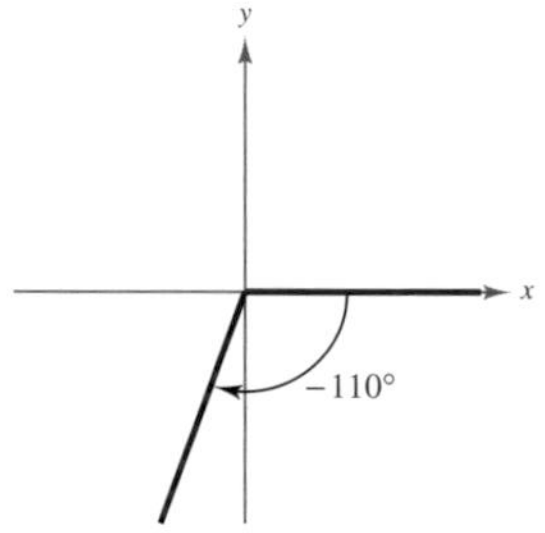

(b) Quadrant III

(c) 250°, −470°

11. 8.378 **13.** −0.589 **15.** 128.571°

17. −200.535° **19.** 478.17 inches

21. (a) $66\frac{2}{3}\pi$ radians per minute

(b) 400π inches per minute

23. Area = 339.28 square inches

25. $\left(-\frac{1}{2}, \frac{\sqrt{3}}{2}\right)$ **27.** $\left(-\frac{\sqrt{3}}{2}, \frac{1}{2}\right)$

29. $\sin\frac{7\pi}{6} = -\frac{1}{2}$ $\csc\frac{7\pi}{6} = -2$

$\cos\frac{7\pi}{6} = -\frac{\sqrt{3}}{2}$ $\sec\frac{7\pi}{6} = -\frac{2\sqrt{3}}{3}$

$\tan\frac{7\pi}{6} = \frac{\sqrt{3}}{3}$ $\cot\frac{7\pi}{6} = \sqrt{3}$

31. $\sin\left(-\frac{2\pi}{3}\right) = -\frac{\sqrt{3}}{2}$ $\csc\left(-\frac{2\pi}{3}\right) = -\frac{2\sqrt{3}}{3}$

$\cos\left(-\frac{2\pi}{3}\right) = -\frac{1}{2}$ $\sec\left(-\frac{2\pi}{3}\right) = -2$

$\tan\left(-\frac{2\pi}{3}\right) = \sqrt{3}$ $\cot\left(-\frac{2\pi}{3}\right) = \frac{\sqrt{3}}{3}$

33. $\sin\frac{11\pi}{4} = \sin\frac{3\pi}{4} = \frac{\sqrt{2}}{2}$

35. $\sin\left(-\frac{17\pi}{6}\right) = \sin\frac{7\pi}{6} = -\frac{1}{2}$

37. −75.3130 **39.** 3.2361

41. $\sin\theta = \frac{4\sqrt{41}}{41}$

$\cos\theta = \frac{5\sqrt{41}}{41}$

$\tan\theta = \frac{4}{5}$

$\csc\theta = \frac{\sqrt{41}}{4}$

$\sec\theta = \frac{\sqrt{41}}{5}$

$\cot\theta = \frac{5}{4}$

43. $\sin\theta = \frac{\sqrt{3}}{2}$

$\cos\theta = \frac{1}{2}$

$\tan\theta = \sqrt{3}$

$\csc\theta = \frac{2\sqrt{3}}{3}$

$\sec\theta = 2$

$\cot\theta = \frac{\sqrt{3}}{3}$

45. (a) 3 (b) $\frac{2\sqrt{2}}{3}$ (c) $\frac{3\sqrt{2}}{4}$ (d) $\frac{\sqrt{2}}{4}$

47. (a) $\frac{1}{4}$ (b) $\frac{\sqrt{15}}{4}$ (c) $\frac{4\sqrt{15}}{15}$ (d) $\frac{\sqrt{15}}{15}$

49. 0.6494 **51.** 0.5621 **53.** 3.6722 **55.** 71.3 meters

57. $\sin\theta = \frac{4}{5}$ $\csc\theta = \frac{5}{4}$

$\cos\theta = \frac{3}{5}$ $\sec\theta = \frac{5}{3}$

$\tan\theta = \frac{4}{3}$ $\cot\theta = \frac{3}{4}$

59. $\sin\theta = \frac{15\sqrt{241}}{241}$ $\csc\theta = \frac{\sqrt{241}}{15}$

$\cos\theta = \frac{4\sqrt{241}}{241}$ $\sec\theta = \frac{\sqrt{241}}{4}$

$\tan\theta = \frac{15}{4}$ $\cot\theta = \frac{4}{15}$

61. $\sin\theta = \frac{9\sqrt{82}}{82}$ $\csc\theta = \frac{\sqrt{82}}{9}$

$\cos\theta = \frac{-\sqrt{82}}{82}$ $\sec\theta = -\sqrt{82}$

$\tan\theta = -9$ $\cot\theta = -\frac{1}{9}$

63. $\sin\theta = \frac{4\sqrt{17}}{17}$ $\csc\theta = \frac{\sqrt{17}}{4}$

$\cos\theta = \frac{\sqrt{17}}{17}$ $\sec\theta = \sqrt{17}$

$\tan\theta = 4$ $\cot\theta = \frac{1}{4}$

65. $\sin\theta = -\frac{\sqrt{11}}{6}$

$\cos\theta = \frac{5}{6}$

$\tan\theta = -\frac{\sqrt{11}}{5}$

$\csc\theta = -\frac{6\sqrt{11}}{11}$

$\cot\theta = -\frac{5\sqrt{11}}{11}$

67. $\cos\theta = -\frac{\sqrt{55}}{8}$

$\tan\theta = -\frac{3\sqrt{55}}{55}$

$\csc\theta = \frac{8}{3}$

$\sec\theta = -\frac{8\sqrt{55}}{55}$

$\cot\theta = -\frac{\sqrt{55}}{3}$

69. $\sin\theta = \dfrac{\sqrt{21}}{5}$

$\tan\theta = -\dfrac{\sqrt{21}}{2}$

$\csc\theta = \dfrac{5\sqrt{21}}{21}$

$\sec\theta = -\dfrac{5}{2}$

$\cot\theta = -\dfrac{2\sqrt{21}}{21}$

71. $\theta' = 84°$

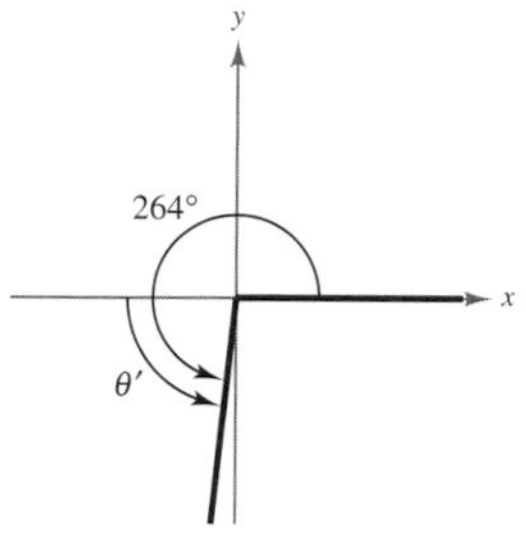

73. $\theta' = \dfrac{\pi}{5}$

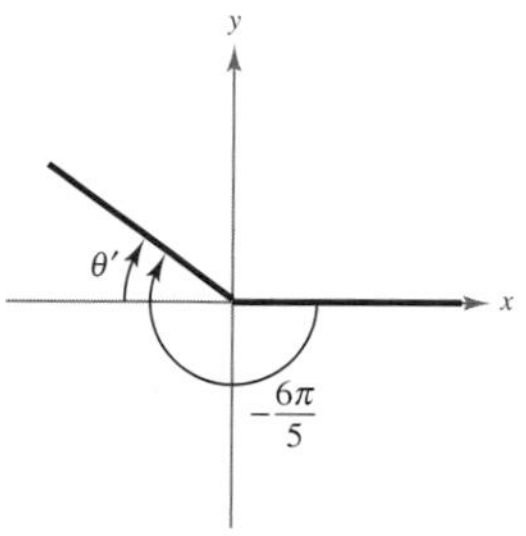

75. $\sin\dfrac{\pi}{3} = \dfrac{\sqrt{3}}{2}$; $\cos\dfrac{\pi}{3} = \dfrac{1}{2}$; $\tan\dfrac{\pi}{3} = \sqrt{3}$

77. $\sin\left(-\dfrac{7\pi}{3}\right) = -\dfrac{\sqrt{3}}{2}$; $\cos\left(-\dfrac{7\pi}{3}\right) = \dfrac{1}{2}$;

$\tan\left(-\dfrac{7\pi}{3}\right) = -\sqrt{3}$

79. $\sin 495° = \dfrac{\sqrt{2}}{2}$; $\cos 495° = -\dfrac{\sqrt{2}}{2}$; $\tan 495° = -1$

81. $\sin(-240°) = \dfrac{\sqrt{3}}{2}$; $\cos(-240°) = -\dfrac{1}{2}$;

$\tan(-240°) = -\sqrt{3}$

83. -0.7568 **85.** 0.0584 **87.** 3.2361

89.

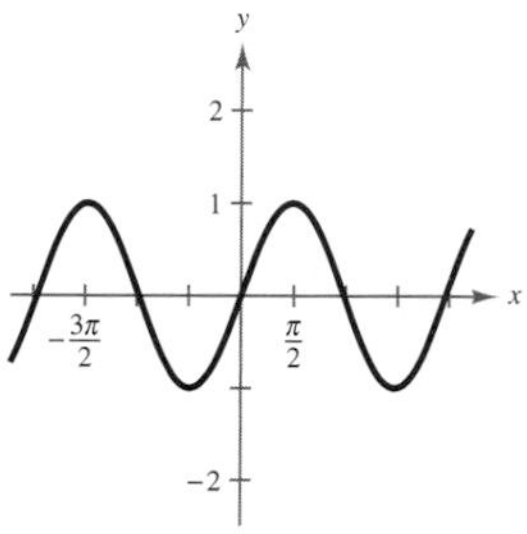

91.

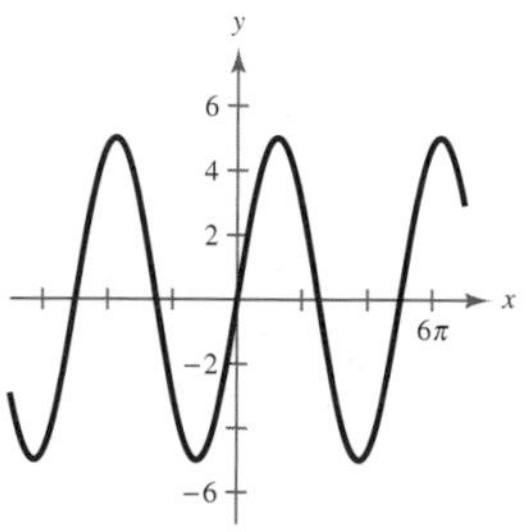

93.

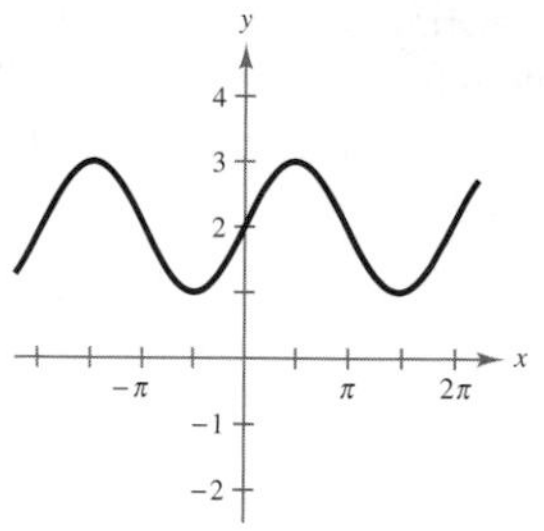

95.

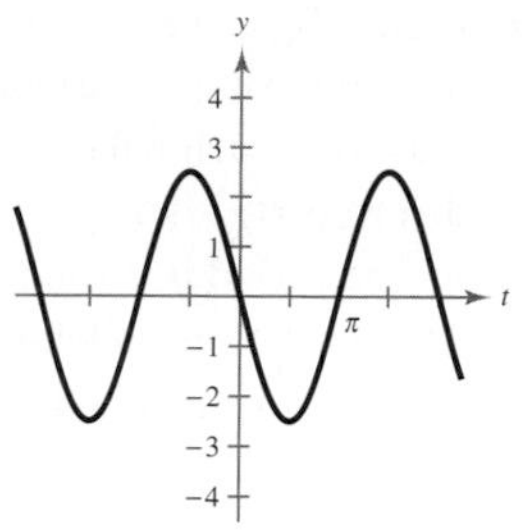

97. (a) $y = 2\sin 528\pi x$ (b) 264 cycles per second

99.

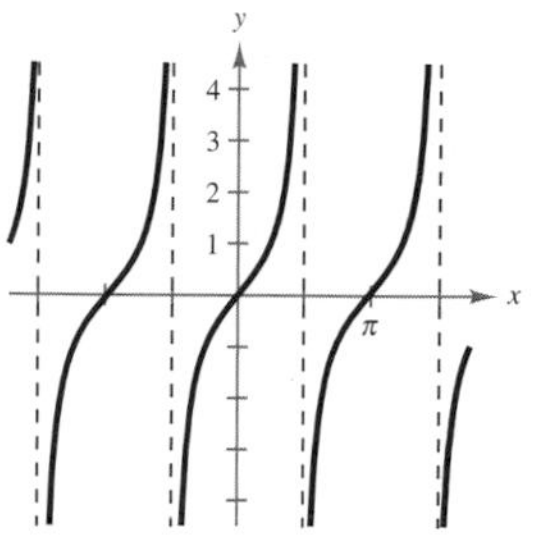

101.

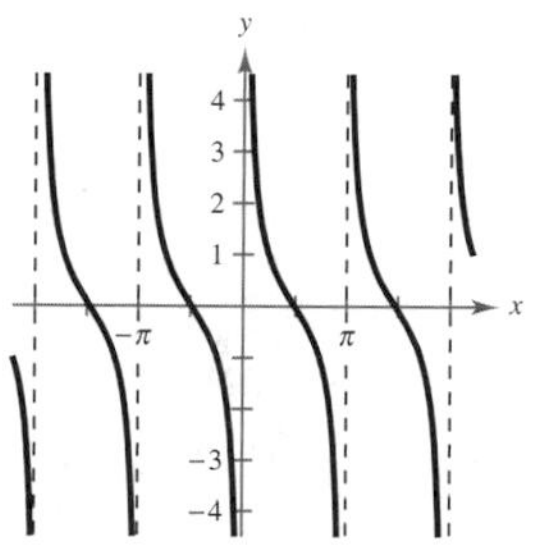

103.

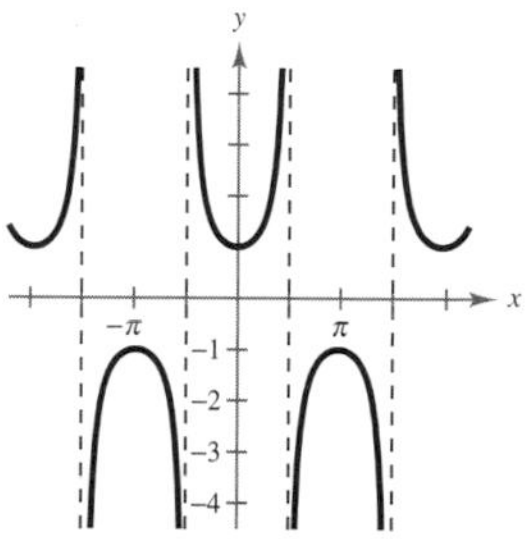

105.

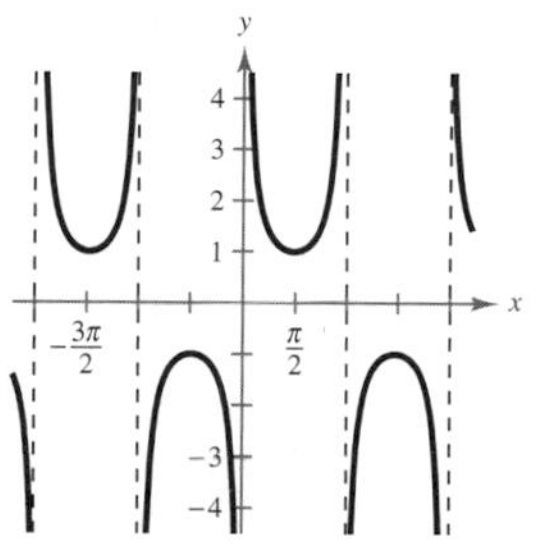

107.

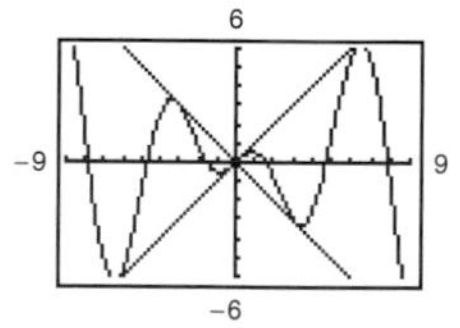

As $x \to +\infty, f(x) \to +\infty$

109. $-\dfrac{\pi}{6}$ **111.** 0.41 **113.** -0.46 **115.** $\dfrac{\pi}{6}$

117. π **119.** 1.24 **121.** -0.98

123.

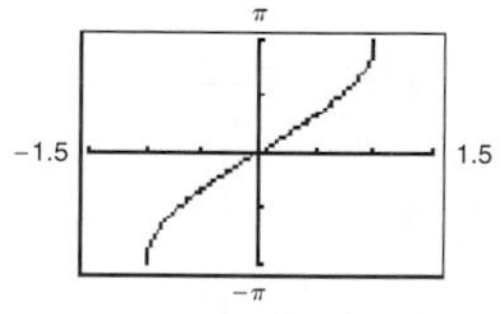

125.

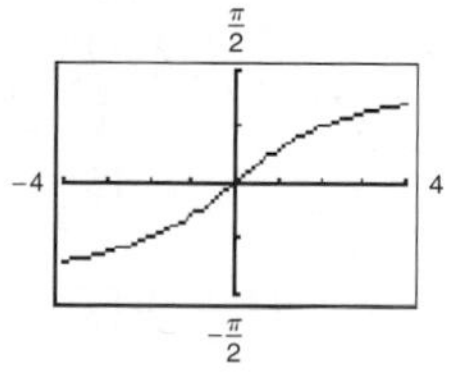

127. $\dfrac{4}{5}$ **129.** $\dfrac{13}{5}$ **131.** $\dfrac{\sqrt{4 - x^2}}{x}$ **133.** $66.8°$

135. 1221 miles, 85.6°

137. False. The sine or cosine function is often useful for modeling simple harmonic motion.

139. False. For each θ there corresponds exactly one value of y.

141. d; The period is 2π and the amplitude is 3.

143. b; The period is 2 and the amplitude is 2.

145. The function is undefined because $\sec\theta = 1/\cos\theta$.

147. The ranges of the other four trigonometric functions are $(-\infty, \infty)$ or $(-\infty, -1] \cup [1, \infty)$.

149. (a) $A = 0.4r^2, r > 0$; $s = 0.8r, r > 0$ (b) $A = 50\theta, \theta > 0$; $s = 10\theta, \theta > 0$

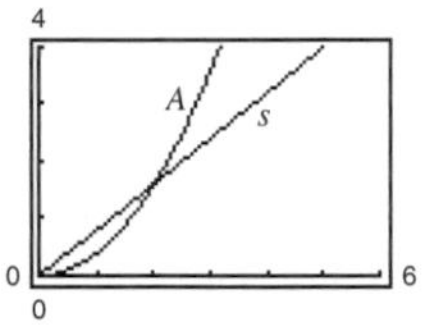

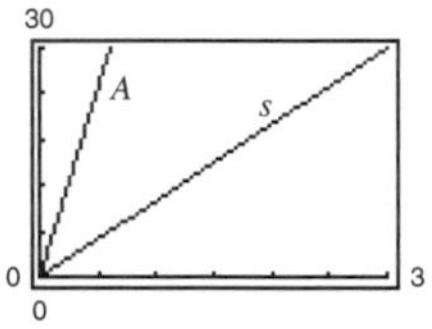

The area function increases more rapidly.

Chapter Test (page 369)

1. (a)

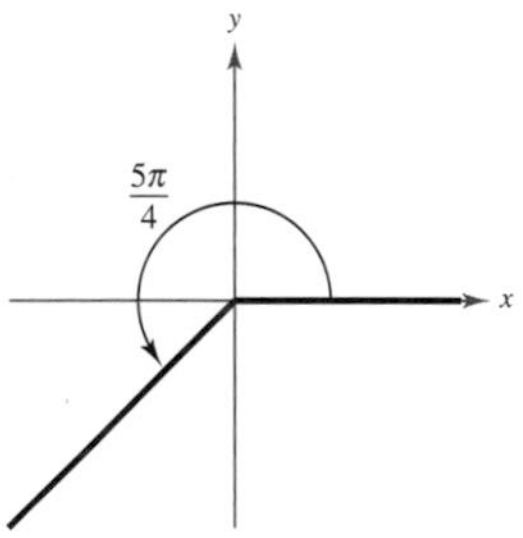

(b) $\frac{13\pi}{4}, -\frac{3\pi}{4}$

(c) 225°

2. 3000 radians per minute **3.** $\approx$ 709.04 square feet

4. $\sin\theta = \frac{3\sqrt{10}}{10}$ $\csc\theta = \frac{\sqrt{10}}{3}$

$\cos\theta = -\frac{\sqrt{10}}{10}$ $\sec\theta = -\sqrt{10}$

$\tan\theta = -3$ $\cot\theta = -\frac{1}{3}$

5. For $0 \le \theta < \frac{\pi}{2}$: For $\pi \le \theta < \frac{3\pi}{2}$:

$\sin\theta = \frac{3\sqrt{13}}{13}$ $\sin\theta = -\frac{3\sqrt{13}}{13}$

$\cos\theta = \frac{2\sqrt{13}}{13}$ $\cos\theta = -\frac{2\sqrt{13}}{13}$

$\csc\theta = \frac{\sqrt{13}}{3}$ $\csc\theta = -\frac{\sqrt{13}}{3}$

$\sec\theta = \frac{\sqrt{13}}{2}$ $\sec\theta = -\frac{\sqrt{13}}{2}$

$\cot\theta = \frac{2}{3}$ $\cot\theta = \frac{2}{3}$

6. $\theta' = 70°$

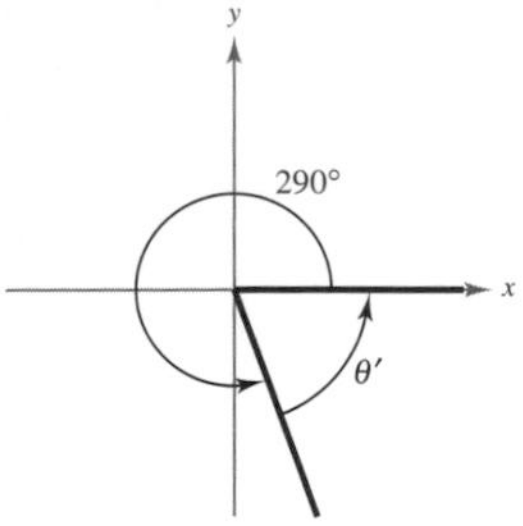

7. Quadrant III **8.** 150°, 210° **9.** 1.33, 1.81

10. $\sin\theta = -\frac{4}{5}$ **11.** $\sin\theta = \frac{15}{17}$

$\tan\theta = -\frac{4}{3}$ $\cos\theta = -\frac{8}{17}$

$\csc\theta = -\frac{5}{4}$ $\tan\theta = -\frac{15}{8}$

$\sec\theta = \frac{5}{3}$ $\csc\theta = \frac{17}{15}$

$\cot\theta = -\frac{3}{4}$ $\cot\theta = -\frac{8}{15}$

12.

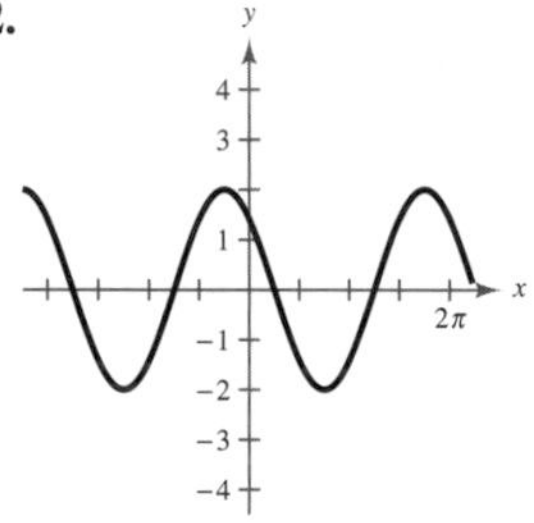

13.

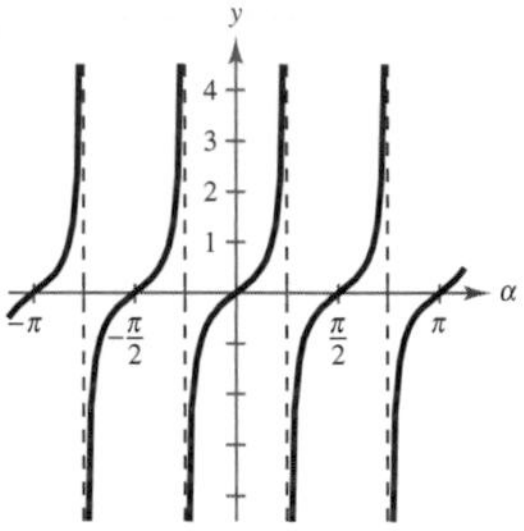

14.

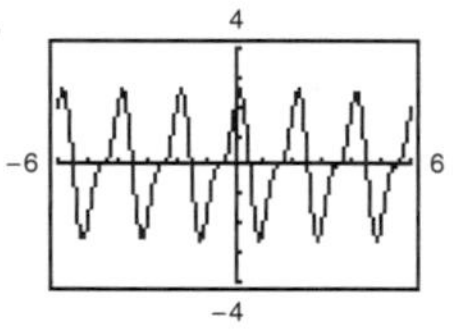

Period: 2

15.

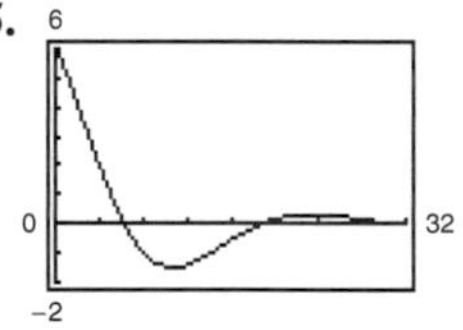

Not periodic

16. $a = -2, b = \frac{1}{2}, c = -\frac{\pi}{4}$ **17.** $\frac{\sqrt{5}}{2}$

18.

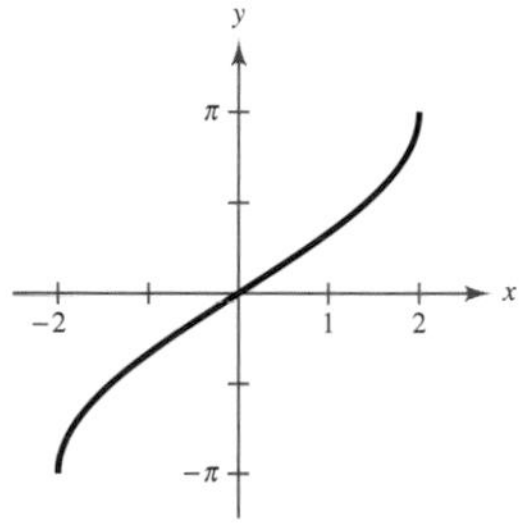

19. 310.1° **20.** $d = -6\cos\pi t$

Problem Solving (page 371)

1. (a) $\frac{11\pi}{2}$ radians or 990° (b) $\approx$ 816.42 feet

3. (a) 4767 feet (b) 3705 feet
(c) $w = 2183$ feet,
$$\tan 63° = \frac{w + 3705}{3000}$$

5. (a)

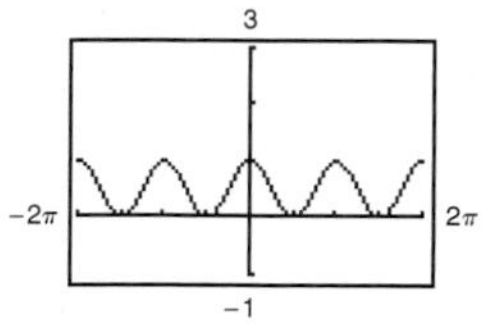

Even

(b)

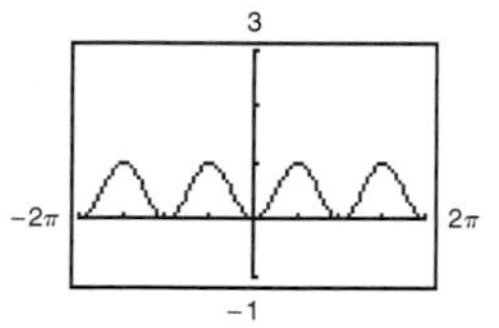

Even

7. $h = 51 - 50\sin\left(8\pi t + \frac{\pi}{2}\right)$

9. (a)

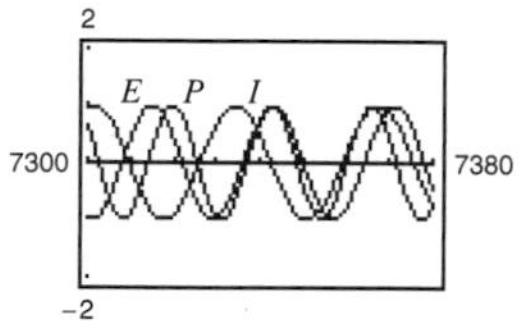

(b)

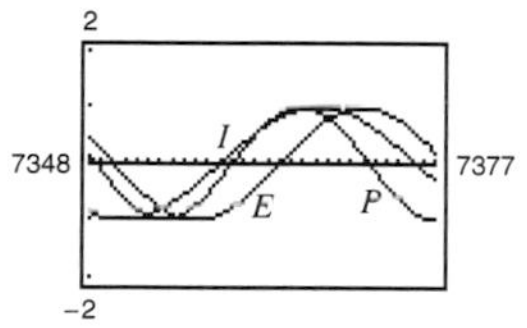

(c) $P(7369) = 0.631$
$E(7369) = 0.901$
$I(7369) = 0.945$

11. (a) 3.35, 7.35 (b) -0.65
(c) Yes. There is a difference of nine periods between the values.

13. (a) 40.5° (b) $x \approx 1.71$ feet; $y \approx 3.46$ feet
(c) ≈ 1.75 feet
(d) As you move closer to the rock, d must get smaller and smaller. The angles θ_1 and θ_2 will decrease along with the distance y, so d will decrease.

Chapter 5

Section 5.1 *(page 379)*

Vocabulary Check *(page 379)*

1. $\tan u$ **2.** $\cos u$ **3.** $\cot u$ **4.** $\csc u$
5. $\cot^2 u$ **6.** $\sec^2 u$ **7.** $\cos u$ **8.** $\csc u$
9. $\cos u$ **10.** $-\tan u$

1. $\sin x = \frac{\sqrt{3}}{2}$
$\cos x = -\frac{1}{2}$
$\tan x = -\sqrt{3}$
$\csc x = \frac{2\sqrt{3}}{3}$
$\sec x = -2$
$\cot x = -\frac{\sqrt{3}}{3}$

3. $\sin \theta = -\frac{\sqrt{2}}{2}$
$\cos \theta = \frac{\sqrt{2}}{2}$
$\tan \theta = -1$
$\sec \theta = \sqrt{2}$
$\csc \theta = -\sqrt{2}$
$\cot \theta = -1$

5. $\sin x = -\frac{5}{13}$
$\cos x = -\frac{12}{13}$
$\tan x = \frac{5}{12}$
$\sec x = -\frac{13}{12}$
$\csc x = -\frac{13}{5}$
$\cot x = \frac{12}{5}$

7. $\sin \phi = -\frac{\sqrt{5}}{3}$
$\cos \phi = \frac{2}{3}$
$\tan \phi = -\frac{\sqrt{5}}{2}$
$\sec \phi = \frac{3}{2}$
$\csc \phi = -\frac{3\sqrt{5}}{5}$
$\cot \phi = -\frac{2\sqrt{5}}{5}$

9. $\sin x = \frac{1}{3}$
$\cos x = -\frac{2\sqrt{2}}{3}$
$\tan x = -\frac{\sqrt{2}}{4}$
$\csc x = 3$
$\sec x = -\frac{3\sqrt{2}}{4}$
$\cot x = -2\sqrt{2}$

11. $\sin \theta = -\frac{2\sqrt{5}}{5}$
$\cos \theta = -\frac{\sqrt{5}}{5}$
$\tan \theta = 2$
$\csc \theta = -\frac{\sqrt{5}}{2}$
$\sec \theta = -\sqrt{5}$
$\cot \theta = \frac{1}{2}$

13. $\sin \theta = -1$
$\cos \theta = 0$
$\tan \theta$ is undefined.
$\cot \theta = 0$
$\csc \theta = -1$
$\sec \theta$ is undefined.

15. d **16.** a **17.** b **18.** f **19.** e **20.** c
21. b **22.** c **23.** f **24.** a **25.** e **26.** d
27. $\csc \theta$ **29.** $\cos^2 \phi$ **31.** $\cos x$ **33.** $\sin^2 x$
35. 1 **37.** $\tan x$ **39.** $1 + \sin y$ **41.** $\sec \beta$
43. $\cos u + \sin u$ **45.** $\sin^2 x$ **47.** $\sin^2 x \tan^2 x$
49. $\sec x + 1$ **51.** $\sec^4 x$ **53.** $\sin^2 x - \cos^2 x$
55. $\cot^2 x(\csc x - 1)$ **57.** $1 + 2\sin x \cos x$
59. $4\cot^2 x$ **61.** $2\csc^2 x$ **63.** $2\sec x$
65. $1 + \cos y$ **67.** $3(\sec x + \tan x)$

69.

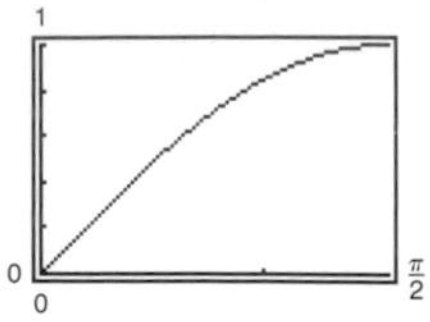

x	0.2	0.4	0.6	0.8	1.0
y_1	0.1987	0.3894	0.5646	0.7174	0.8415
y_2	0.1987	0.3894	0.5646	0.7174	0.8415

x	1.2	1.4
y_1	0.9320	0.9854
y_2	0.9320	0.9854

$y_1 = y_2$

71.

x	0.2	0.4	0.6	0.8	1.0
y_1	1.2230	1.5085	1.8958	2.4650	3.4082
y_2	1.2230	1.5085	1.8958	2.4650	3.4082

x	1.2	1.4
y_1	5.3319	11.6814
y_2	5.3319	11.6814

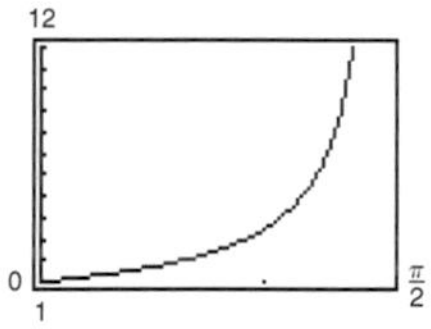

$y_1 = y_2$

73. $\csc x$ **75.** $\tan x$ **77.** $3 \sin \theta$ **79.** $3 \tan \theta$

81. $5 \sec \theta$ **83.** $3 \cos \theta = 3$; $\sin \theta = 0$; $\cos \theta = 1$

85. $4 \sin \theta = 2\sqrt{2}$; $\sin \theta = \dfrac{\sqrt{2}}{2}$; $\cos \theta = \dfrac{\sqrt{2}}{2}$

87. $0 \le \theta \le \pi$ **89.** $0 \le \theta < \dfrac{\pi}{2}, \dfrac{3\pi}{2} < \theta < 2\pi$

91. $\ln|\cot x|$ **93.** $\ln|\csc t \sec t|$

95. (a) $\csc^2 132° - \cot^2 132° \approx 1.8107 - 0.8107 = 1$

(b) $\csc^2 \dfrac{2\pi}{7} - \cot^2 \dfrac{2\pi}{7} \approx 1.6360 - 0.6360 = 1$

97. (a) $\cos(90° - 80°) = \sin 80° \approx 0.9848$

(b) $\cos\left(\dfrac{\pi}{2} - 0.8\right) = \sin 0.8 \approx 0.7174$

99. $\mu = \tan \theta$

101. True. For example, $\sin(-x) = -\sin x$.

103. 1, 1 **105.** ∞, 0

107. Not an identity because $\cos \theta = \pm\sqrt{1 - \sin^2 \theta}$

109. Not an identity because $\dfrac{\sin k\theta}{\cos k\theta} = \tan k\theta$

111. An identity because $\sin \theta \cdot \dfrac{1}{\sin \theta} = 1$

113. Answers will vary. **115.** $x - 25$

117. $\dfrac{x^2 + 6x - 8}{(x + 5)(x - 8)}$ **119.** $\dfrac{-5x^2 + 8x + 28}{(x^2 - 4)(x + 4)}$

121.

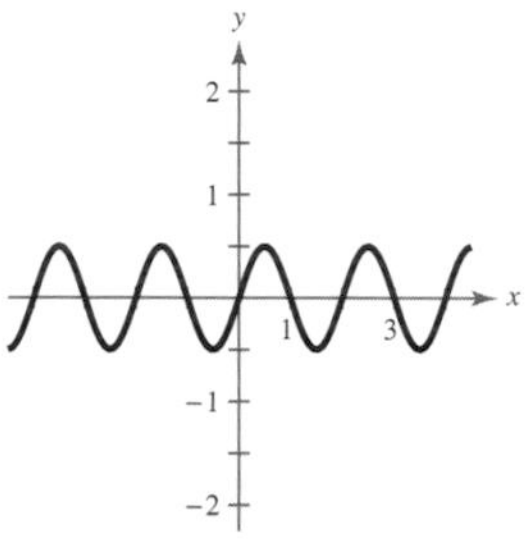

123.

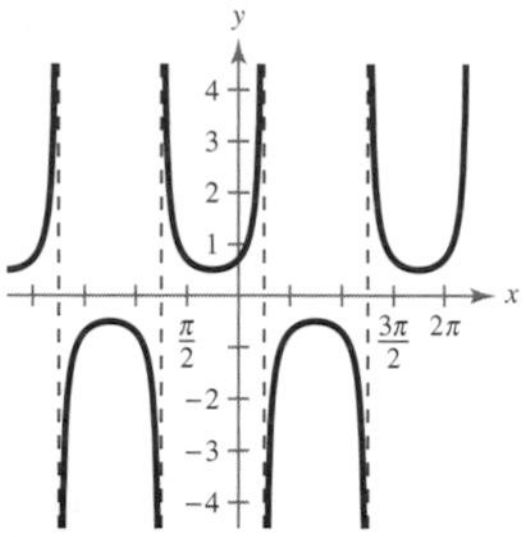

Section 5.2 *(page 387)*

Vocabulary Check *(page 387)*

1. identity **2.** conditional equation **3.** $\tan u$
4. $\cot u$ **5.** $\cos^2 u$ **6.** $\sin u$ **7.** $-\csc u$
8. $\sec u$

1–37. Answers will vary.

39. (a)

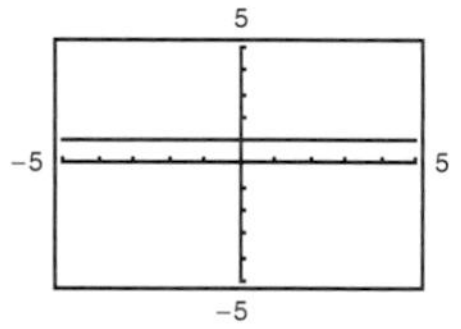

(b)

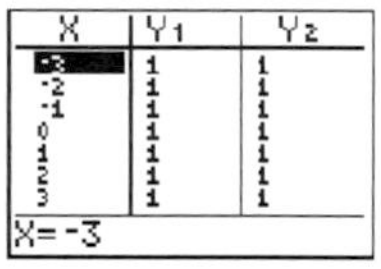

Identity

(c) Answers will vary.

41. (a)

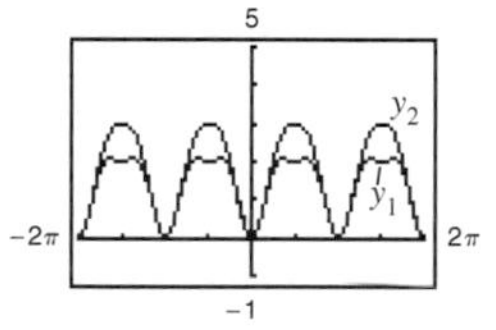

(b)

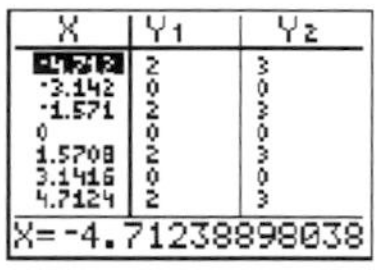

Not an identity

(c) Answers will vary.

43. (a)

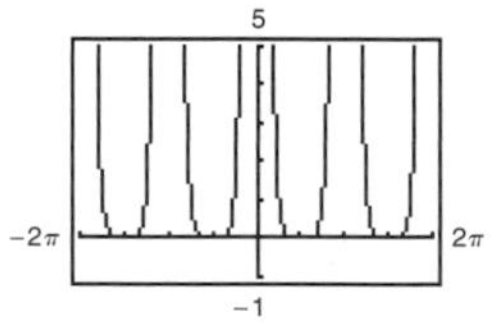

(b)

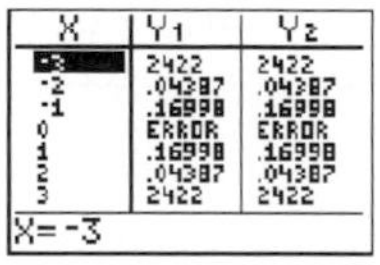

Identity

(c) Answers will vary.

45. (a)

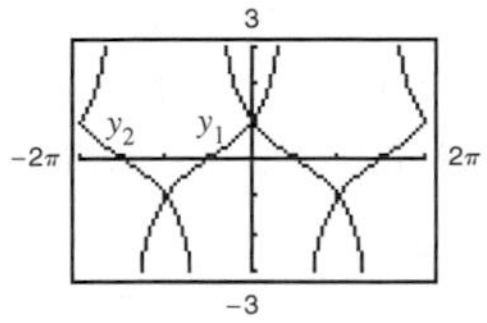

(b)

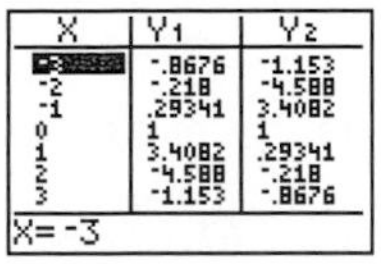

X	Y1	Y2
-3	-.8676	-1.153
-2	-.218	-4.588
-1	.29341	3.4082
0	1	1
1	3.4082	.29341
2	-4.588	-.218
3	-1.153	-.8676

X=-3

Not an identity

(c) Answers will vary.

47 and 49. Answers will vary. **51.** 1 **53.** 2

55. Answers will vary.

57. False. An identity is an equation that is true for all real values of θ.

59. The equation is not an identity because $\sin\theta = \pm\sqrt{1-\cos^2\theta}$.

Possible answer: $\dfrac{7\pi}{4}$

61. $2 + (3 - \sqrt{26})i$ **63.** $-8 + 4i$

65. $-3 \pm \sqrt{21}$ **67.** $1 \pm \sqrt{5}$

Section 5.3 *(page 396)*

Vocabulary Check *(page 396)*

1. general **2.** quadratic **3.** extraneous

1–5. Answers will vary. **7.** $\dfrac{2\pi}{3} + 2n\pi, \dfrac{4\pi}{3} + 2n\pi$

9. $\dfrac{\pi}{3} + 2n\pi, \dfrac{2\pi}{3} + 2n\pi$ **11.** $\dfrac{\pi}{6} + n\pi, \dfrac{5\pi}{6} + n\pi$

13. $n\pi, \dfrac{3\pi}{2} + 2n\pi$ **15.** $\dfrac{\pi}{3} + n\pi, \dfrac{2\pi}{3} + n\pi$

17. $\dfrac{\pi}{8} + \dfrac{n\pi}{2}, \dfrac{3\pi}{8} + \dfrac{n\pi}{2}$ **19.** $\dfrac{n\pi}{3}, \dfrac{\pi}{4} + n\pi$

21. $0, \dfrac{\pi}{2}, \pi, \dfrac{3\pi}{2}$ **23.** $0, \pi, \dfrac{\pi}{6}, \dfrac{5\pi}{6}, \dfrac{7\pi}{6}, \dfrac{11\pi}{6}$

25. $\dfrac{\pi}{3}, \dfrac{5\pi}{3}, \pi$ **27.** No solution **29.** $\pi, \dfrac{\pi}{3}, \dfrac{5\pi}{3}$

31. $\dfrac{\pi}{6}, \dfrac{5\pi}{6}, \dfrac{7\pi}{6}, \dfrac{11\pi}{6}$ **33.** $\dfrac{\pi}{2}$ **35.** $\dfrac{\pi}{6} + n\pi, \dfrac{5\pi}{6} + n\pi$

37. $\dfrac{\pi}{12} + \dfrac{n\pi}{3}$ **39.** $\dfrac{\pi}{2} + 4n\pi, \dfrac{7\pi}{2} + 4n\pi$ **41.** $-1 + 4n$

43. $-2 + 6n, 2 + 6n$ **45.** 2.678, 5.820

47. 1.047, 5.236 **49.** 0.860, 3.426

51. 0, 2.678, 3.142, 5.820

53. 0.983, 1.768, 4.124, 4.910

55. 0.3398, 0.8481, 2.2935, 2.8018

57. 1.9357, 2.7767, 5.0773, 5.9183

59. $\dfrac{\pi}{4}, \dfrac{5\pi}{4}$, arctan 5, arctan $5 + \pi$ **61.** $\dfrac{\pi}{3}, \dfrac{5\pi}{3}$

63. (a)

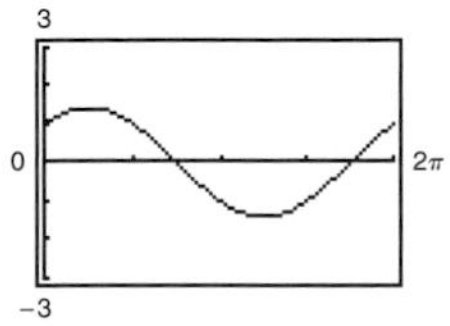

(b) $\dfrac{\pi}{4} \approx 0.7854$

$\dfrac{5\pi}{4} \approx 3.9270$

Maximum: (0.7854, 1.4142)

Minimum: (3.9270, −1.4142)

65. 1

67. (a) All real numbers x except $x = 0$

(b) y-axis symmetry; Horizontal asymptote: $y = 1$

(c) Oscillates (d) Infinitely many solutions

(e) Yes, 0.6366

69. 0.04 second, 0.43 second, 0.83 second

71. February, March, and April **73.** 36.9°, 53.1°

75. (a) Between $t = 8$ seconds and $t = 24$ seconds

(b) 5 times: $t = 16, 48, 80, 112, 144$ seconds

77. (a)

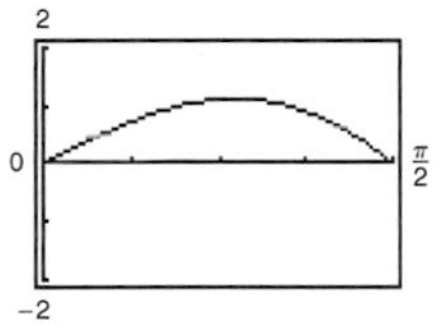

(b) $0.6 < x < 1.1$

$A \approx 1.12$

79. True. The first equation has a smaller period than the second equation, so it will have more solutions in the interval $[0, 2\pi)$.

81. 1 **83.** $C = 24°$

$a \approx 54.8$

$b \approx 50.1$

85. $\sin 390° = \dfrac{1}{2}$

$\cos 390° = \dfrac{\sqrt{3}}{2}$

$\tan 390° = \dfrac{\sqrt{3}}{3}$

87. $\sin(-1845°) = -\dfrac{\sqrt{2}}{2}$

$\cos(-1845°) = \dfrac{\sqrt{2}}{2}$

$\tan(-1845°) = -1$

89. 1.36° **91.** Answers will vary.

Section 5.4 *(page 404)*

Vocabulary Check *(page 404)*

1. $\sin u \cos v - \cos u \sin v$

2. $\cos u \cos v - \sin u \sin v$ **3.** $\dfrac{\tan u + \tan v}{1 - \tan u \tan v}$

4. $\sin u \cos v + \cos u \sin v$

5. $\cos u \cos v + \sin u \sin v$ **6.** $\dfrac{\tan u - \tan v}{1 + \tan u \tan v}$

1. (a) $\dfrac{-\sqrt{2} - \sqrt{6}}{4}$ (b) $\dfrac{-1 + \sqrt{2}}{2}$

3. (a) $\dfrac{\sqrt{2}-\sqrt{6}}{4}$ (b) $\dfrac{\sqrt{2}+1}{2}$

5. (a) $\dfrac{1}{2}$ (b) $\dfrac{-\sqrt{3}-1}{2}$

7. $\sin 105° = \dfrac{\sqrt{2}}{4}\left(\sqrt{3}+1\right)$

$\cos 105° = \dfrac{\sqrt{2}}{4}\left(1-\sqrt{3}\right)$

$\tan 105° = -2-\sqrt{3}$

9. $\sin 195° = \dfrac{\sqrt{2}}{4}\left(1-\sqrt{3}\right)$

$\cos 195° = -\dfrac{\sqrt{2}}{4}\left(\sqrt{3}+1\right)$

$\tan 195° = 2-\sqrt{3}$

11. $\sin\dfrac{11\pi}{12} = \dfrac{\sqrt{2}}{4}\left(\sqrt{3}-1\right)$

$\cos\dfrac{11\pi}{12} = -\dfrac{\sqrt{2}}{4}\left(\sqrt{3}+1\right)$

$\tan\dfrac{11\pi}{12} = -2+\sqrt{3}$

13. $\sin\dfrac{17\pi}{12} = -\dfrac{\sqrt{2}}{4}\left(\sqrt{3}+1\right)$

$\cos\dfrac{17\pi}{12} = \dfrac{\sqrt{2}}{4}\left(1-\sqrt{3}\right)$

$\tan\dfrac{17\pi}{12} = 2+\sqrt{3}$

15. $\sin 285° = -\dfrac{\sqrt{2}}{4}\left(\sqrt{3}+1\right)$

$\cos 285° = \dfrac{\sqrt{2}}{4}\left(\sqrt{3}-1\right)$

$\tan 285° = -\left(2+\sqrt{3}\right)$

17. $\sin(-165°) = -\dfrac{\sqrt{2}}{4}\left(\sqrt{3}-1\right)$

$\cos(-165°) = -\dfrac{\sqrt{2}}{4}\left(1+\sqrt{3}\right)$

$\tan(-165°) = 2-\sqrt{3}$

19. $\sin\dfrac{13\pi}{12} = \dfrac{\sqrt{2}}{4}\left(1-\sqrt{3}\right)$

$\cos\dfrac{13\pi}{12} = -\dfrac{\sqrt{2}}{4}\left(1+\sqrt{3}\right)$

$\tan\dfrac{13\pi}{12} = 2-\sqrt{3}$

21. $\sin\left(-\dfrac{13\pi}{12}\right) = \dfrac{\sqrt{2}}{4}\left(\sqrt{3}-1\right)$

$\cos\left(-\dfrac{13\pi}{12}\right) = -\dfrac{\sqrt{2}}{4}\left(\sqrt{3}+1\right)$

$\tan\left(-\dfrac{13\pi}{12}\right) = -2+\sqrt{3}$

23. $\cos 40°$ **25.** $\tan 239°$ **27.** $\sin 1.8$ **29.** $\tan 3x$

31. $-\dfrac{\sqrt{3}}{2}$ **33.** $\dfrac{\sqrt{3}}{2}$ **35.** -1 **37.** $-\dfrac{63}{65}$

39. $\frac{16}{65}$ **41.** $-\frac{63}{16}$ **43.** $\frac{65}{56}$ **45.** $\frac{3}{5}$ **47.** $-\frac{44}{117}$

49. $\frac{5}{3}$ **51.** 1 **53.** 0 **55–63.** Answers will vary.

65. $-\sin x$ **67.** $-\cos\theta$ **69.** $\dfrac{\pi}{2}$ **71.** $\dfrac{5\pi}{4}, \dfrac{7\pi}{4}$

73. $\dfrac{\pi}{4}, \dfrac{7\pi}{4}$

75. (a) $y = \dfrac{5}{12}\sin(2t + 0.6435)$

(b) $\dfrac{5}{12}$ feet (c) $\dfrac{1}{\pi}$ cycle per second

77. False. $\sin(u \pm v) = \sin u \cos v \pm \cos u \sin v$

79. False.

$\cos\left(x - \dfrac{\pi}{2}\right) = \cos x \cos\dfrac{\pi}{2} + \sin x \sin\dfrac{\pi}{2} = \sin x$

81–83. Answers will vary.

85. (a) $\sqrt{2}\sin\left(\theta + \dfrac{\pi}{4}\right)$ (b) $\sqrt{2}\cos\left(\theta - \dfrac{\pi}{4}\right)$

87. (a) $13\sin(3\theta + 0.3948)$ (b) $13\cos(3\theta - 1.1760)$

89. $2\cos\theta$ **91.** Proof **93.** 15°

95.

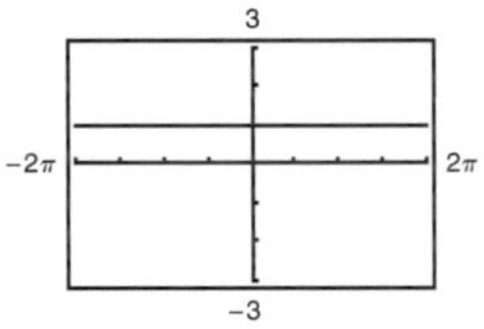

$\sin^2\left(\theta + \dfrac{\pi}{4}\right) + \sin^2\left(\theta - \dfrac{\pi}{4}\right) = 1$

97. $f^{-1}(x) = \dfrac{x+15}{5}$

99. Because f is not one-to-one, f^{-1} does not exist.

101. $4x - 3$ **103.** $6x - 3$

Section 5.5 *(page 415)*

Vocabulary Check *(page 415)*

1. $2\sin u\cos u$ **2.** $\cos^2 u$

3. $\cos^2 u - \sin^2 u = 2\cos^2 u - 1 = 1 - 2\sin^2 u$

4. $\tan^2 u$ **5.** $\pm\sqrt{\dfrac{1-\cos u}{2}}$

6. $\dfrac{1-\cos u}{\sin u} = \dfrac{\sin u}{1+\cos u}$

7. $\frac{1}{2}[\cos(u-v) + \cos(u+v)]$

8. $\frac{1}{2}[\sin(u+v) + \sin(u-v)]$

9. $2\sin\left(\dfrac{u+v}{2}\right)\cos\left(\dfrac{u-v}{2}\right)$

10. $-2\sin\left(\dfrac{u+v}{2}\right)\sin\left(\dfrac{u-v}{2}\right)$

1. $\frac{\sqrt{17}}{17}$ **3.** $\frac{15}{17}$ **5.** $\frac{8}{15}$ **7.** $\frac{17}{8}$ **9.** $0, \frac{\pi}{3}, \pi, \frac{5\pi}{3}$

11. $\frac{\pi}{12}, \frac{5\pi}{12}, \frac{13\pi}{12}, \frac{17\pi}{12}$ **13.** $0, \frac{2\pi}{3}, \frac{4\pi}{3}$

15. $\frac{\pi}{2}, \frac{\pi}{6}, \frac{5\pi}{6}, \frac{7\pi}{6}, \frac{3\pi}{2}, \frac{11\pi}{6}$ **17.** $0, \frac{\pi}{2}, \pi, \frac{3\pi}{2}$

19. $3 \sin 2x$ **21.** $4 \cos 2x$

23. $\sin 2u = \frac{24}{25}$
$\cos 2u = -\frac{7}{25}$
$\tan 2u = -\frac{24}{7}$

25. $\sin 2u = \frac{24}{25}$
$\cos 2u = \frac{7}{25}$
$\tan 2u = \frac{24}{7}$

27. $\sin 2u = -\frac{4\sqrt{21}}{25}$
$\cos 2u = -\frac{17}{25}$
$\tan 2u = \frac{4\sqrt{21}}{17}$

29. $\frac{1}{8}(3 + 4 \cos 2x + \cos 4x)$

31. $\frac{1}{8}(1 - \cos 4x)$

33. $\frac{1}{16}(1 + \cos 2x - \cos 4x - \cos 2x \cos 4x)$

35. $\frac{4\sqrt{17}}{17}$ **37.** $\frac{1}{4}$ **39.** $\sqrt{17}$

41. $\sin 75° = \frac{1}{2}\sqrt{2 + \sqrt{3}}$
$\cos 75° = \frac{1}{2}\sqrt{2 - \sqrt{3}}$
$\tan 75° = 2 + \sqrt{3}$

43. $\sin 112° 30' = \frac{1}{2}\sqrt{2 + \sqrt{2}}$
$\cos 112° 30' = -\frac{1}{2}\sqrt{2 - \sqrt{2}}$
$\tan 112° 30' = -1 - \sqrt{2}$

45. $\sin \frac{\pi}{8} = \frac{1}{2}\sqrt{2 - \sqrt{2}}$
$\cos \frac{\pi}{8} = \frac{1}{2}\sqrt{2 + \sqrt{2}}$
$\tan \frac{\pi}{8} = \sqrt{2} - 1$

47. $\sin \frac{3\pi}{8} = \frac{1}{2}\sqrt{2 + \sqrt{2}}$
$\cos \frac{3\pi}{8} = \frac{1}{2}\sqrt{2 - \sqrt{2}}$
$\tan \frac{3\pi}{8} = \sqrt{2} + 1$

49. $\sin \frac{u}{2} = \frac{5\sqrt{26}}{26}$
$\cos \frac{u}{2} = \frac{\sqrt{26}}{26}$
$\tan \frac{u}{2} = 5$

51. $\sin \frac{u}{2} = \sqrt{\frac{89 - 8\sqrt{89}}{178}}$
$\cos \frac{u}{2} = -\sqrt{\frac{89 + 8\sqrt{89}}{178}}$
$\tan \frac{u}{2} = \frac{8 - \sqrt{89}}{5}$

53. $\sin \frac{u}{2} = \frac{3\sqrt{10}}{10}$
$\cos \frac{u}{2} = -\frac{\sqrt{10}}{10}$
$\tan \frac{u}{2} = -3$

55. $|\sin 3x|$ **57.** $-|\tan 4x|$

59. π

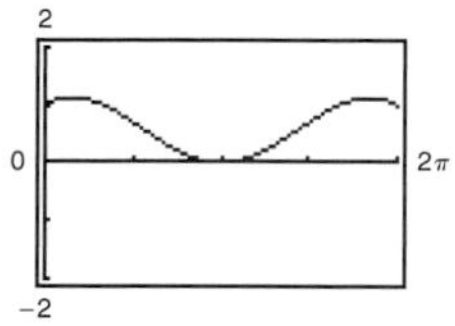

61. $\frac{\pi}{3}, \pi, \frac{5\pi}{3}$

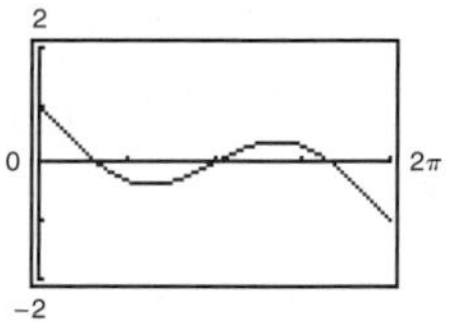

63. $3\left(\sin \frac{\pi}{2} + \sin 0\right)$ **65.** $5(\cos 60° + \cos 90°)$

67. $\frac{1}{2}(\sin 10\theta + \sin 2\theta)$ **69.** $\frac{5}{2}(\cos 8\beta + \cos 2\beta)$

71. $\frac{1}{2}(\cos 2y - \cos 2x)$ **73.** $\frac{1}{2}(\sin 2\theta + \sin 2\pi)$

75. $2 \cos 4\theta \sin \theta$ **77.** $2 \cos 4x \cos 2x$

79. $2 \cos \alpha \sin \beta$ **81.** $-2 \sin \theta \sin \frac{\pi}{2}$

83. $\frac{\sqrt{3} + 1}{2}$ **85.** $-\sqrt{2}$

87. $0, \frac{\pi}{4}, \frac{\pi}{2}, \frac{3\pi}{4}, \pi, \frac{5\pi}{4}, \frac{3\pi}{2}, \frac{7\pi}{4}$

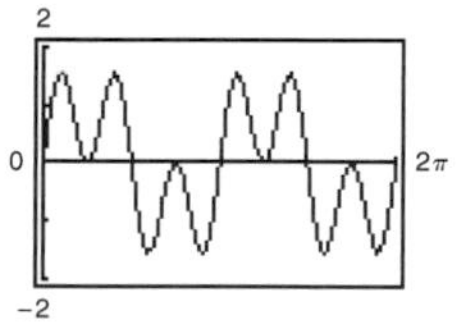

89. $\frac{\pi}{6}, \frac{5\pi}{6}$

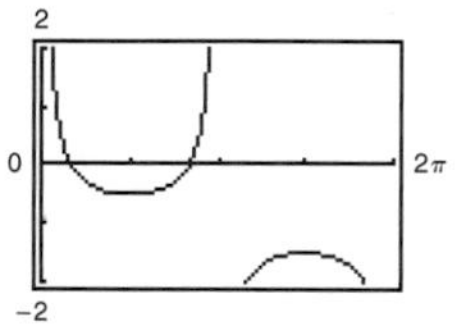

91. $\frac{25}{169}$ **93.** $\frac{4}{13}$ **95–109.** Answers will vary.

111.

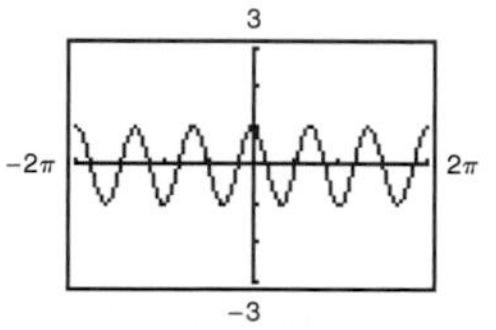

113.

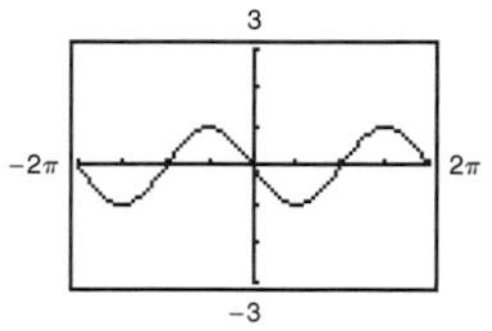

115.

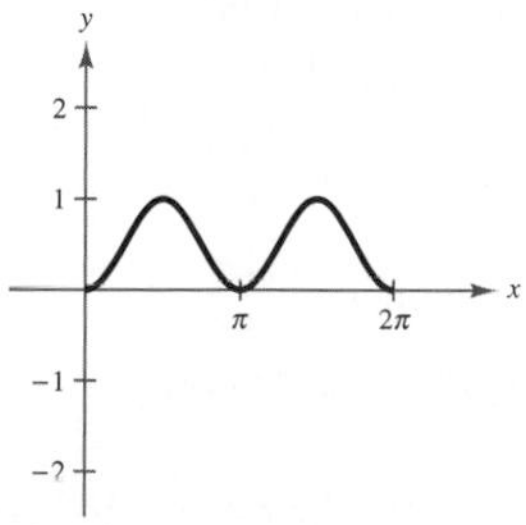

117. $2x\sqrt{1-x^2}$ **119.** $23.85°$

121. (a) π (b) 0.4482
(c) 760 miles per hour; 3420 miles per hour
(d) $\theta = 2\sin^{-1}\left(\frac{1}{M}\right)$

123. False. For $u < 0$,
$\sin 2u = -\sin(-2u)$
$= -2\sin(-u)\cos(-u)$
$= -2(-\sin u)\cos u$
$= 2\sin u \cos u.$

125. (a)

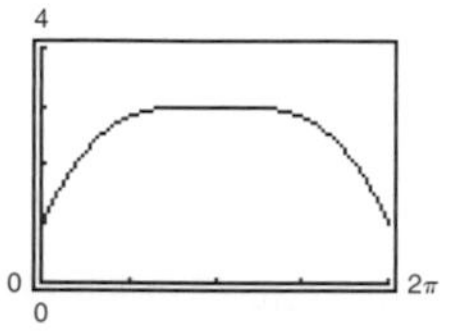

(b) π

Maximum: $(\pi, 3)$

127. (a) $\frac{1}{4}(3 + \cos 4x)$ (b) $2\cos^4 x - 2\cos^2 x + 1$
(c) $1 - 2\sin^2 x\cos^2 x$ (d) $1 - \frac{1}{2}\sin^2 2x$
(e) No. There is often more than one way to rewrite a trigonometric expression.

129. (a)

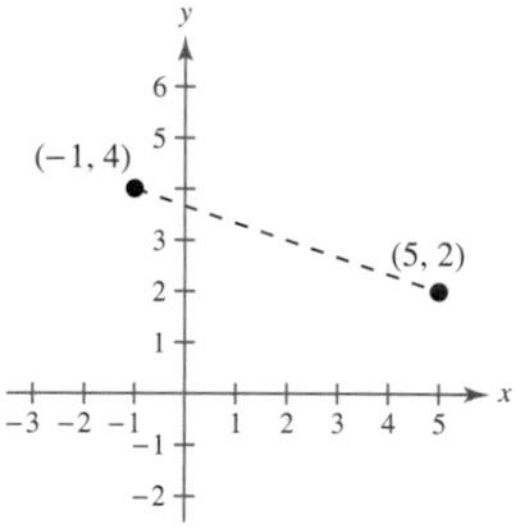

(b) Distance $= 2\sqrt{10}$ (c) Midpoint: $(2, 3)$

131. (a)

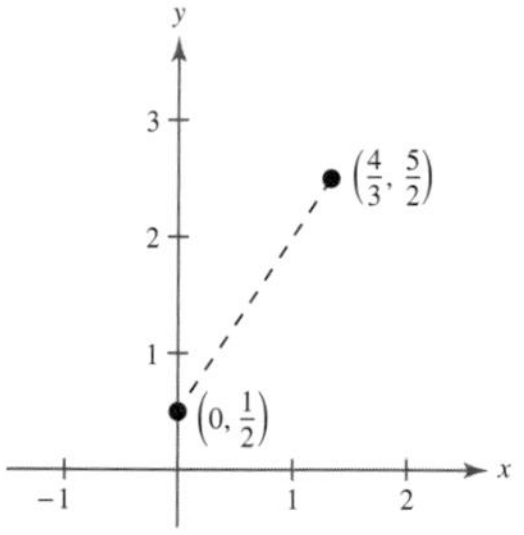

(b) Distance $= \frac{2}{3}\sqrt{13}$ (c) Midpoint: $\left(\frac{2}{3}, \frac{3}{2}\right)$

133. (a) Complement: 35°; supplement: 125°
(b) No complement; supplement: 18°

135. (a) Complement: $\frac{4\pi}{9}$; supplement: $\frac{17\pi}{18}$
(b) Complement: $\frac{\pi}{20}$; supplement: $\frac{11\pi}{20}$

137. September: \$235,000; October: \$272,600

139. ≈ 127 feet

Review Exercises *(page 420)*

1. $\sec x$ **3.** $\cos x$ **5.** $\cot x$

7. $\tan x = \frac{3}{4}$
$\csc x = \frac{5}{3}$
$\sec x = \frac{5}{4}$
$\cot x = \frac{4}{3}$

9. $\cos x = \frac{\sqrt{2}}{2}$
$\tan x = -1$
$\csc x = -\sqrt{2}$
$\sec x = \sqrt{2}$
$\cot x = -1$

11. $\sin^2 x$ **13.** 1 **15.** $\cot\theta$ **17.** $\cot^2 x$

19. $\sec x + 2\sin x$ **21.** $-2\tan^2\theta$

23–31. Answers will vary.

33. $\frac{\pi}{3} + 2n\pi, \frac{2\pi}{3} + 2n\pi$ **35.** $\frac{\pi}{6} + n\pi$

37. $\frac{\pi}{3} + n\pi, \frac{2\pi}{3} + n\pi$ **39.** $0, \frac{2\pi}{3}, \frac{4\pi}{3}$ **41.** $0, \frac{\pi}{2}, \pi$

43. $\frac{\pi}{8}, \frac{3\pi}{8}, \frac{9\pi}{8}, \frac{11\pi}{8}$

45. $0, \frac{\pi}{8}, \frac{3\pi}{8}, \frac{5\pi}{8}, \frac{7\pi}{8}, \frac{9\pi}{8}, \frac{11\pi}{8}, \frac{13\pi}{8}, \frac{15\pi}{8}$ **47.** $0, \pi$

49. $\arctan(-4) + \pi, \arctan(-4) + 2\pi, \arctan 3,$
$\pi + \arctan 3$

51. $\sin 285° = -\frac{\sqrt{2}}{4}(\sqrt{3} + 1)$
$\cos 285° = \frac{\sqrt{2}}{4}(\sqrt{3} - 1)$
$\tan 285° = -2 - \sqrt{3}$

53. $\sin\frac{25\pi}{12} = \frac{\sqrt{2}}{4}(\sqrt{3} - 1)$
$\cos\frac{25\pi}{12} = \frac{\sqrt{2}}{4}(\sqrt{3} + 1)$
$\tan\frac{25\pi}{12} = 2 - \sqrt{3}$

55. $\sin 15°$ **57.** $\tan 35°$ **59.** $-\frac{3}{52}(5 + 4\sqrt{7})$

61. $\frac{1}{52}(5\sqrt{7} + 36)$ **63.** $\frac{1}{52}(5\sqrt{7} - 36)$

65–69. Answers will vary. **71.** $\frac{\pi}{4}, \frac{7\pi}{4}$ **73.** $\frac{\pi}{6}, \frac{11\pi}{6}$

75. $\sin 2u = \frac{24}{25}$
$\cos 2u = -\frac{7}{25}$
$\tan 2u = -\frac{24}{7}$

77.

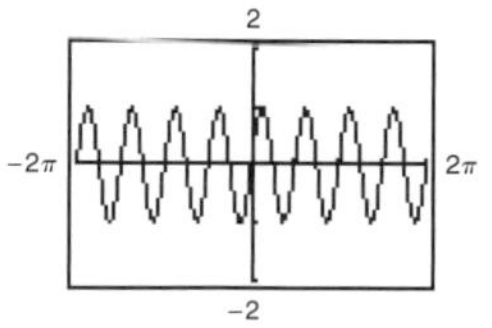

79. $\frac{1 - \cos 4x}{1 + \cos 4x}$ **81.** $\frac{3 - 4\cos 2x + \cos 4x}{4(1 + \cos 2x)}$

83. $\sin(-75°) = -\frac{1}{2}\sqrt{2 + \sqrt{3}}$
$\cos(-75°) = \frac{1}{2}\sqrt{2 - \sqrt{3}}$
$\tan(-75°) = -2 - \sqrt{3}$

85. $\sin \frac{19\pi}{12} = -\frac{1}{2}\sqrt{2 + \sqrt{3}}$
$\cos \frac{19\pi}{12} = \frac{1}{2}\sqrt{2 - \sqrt{3}}$
$\tan \frac{19\pi}{12} = -2 - \sqrt{3}$

87. $\sin \frac{u}{2} = \frac{\sqrt{10}}{10}$
$\cos \frac{u}{2} = \frac{3\sqrt{10}}{10}$
$\tan \frac{u}{2} = \frac{1}{3}$

89. $\sin \frac{u}{2} = \frac{3\sqrt{14}}{14}$
$\cos \frac{u}{2} = \frac{\sqrt{70}}{14}$
$\tan \frac{u}{2} = \frac{3\sqrt{5}}{5}$

91. $-|\cos 5x|$

93. $\frac{1}{2} \sin \frac{\pi}{3}$ **95.** $\frac{1}{2}(\cos 2\theta + \cos 8\theta)$ **97.** $2 \cos 3\theta \sin \theta$

99. $-2 \sin x \sin \frac{\pi}{6}$ **101.** $\theta = 15^\circ$ or $\frac{\pi}{12}$

103.
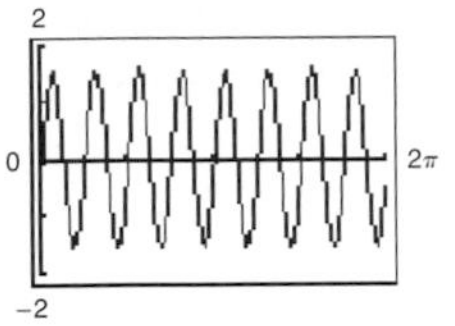

105. $\frac{1}{2}\sqrt{10}$ feet

107. False. If $(\pi/2) < \theta < \pi$, then $\cos(\theta/2) > 0$. The sign of $\cos(\theta/2)$ depends on the quadrant in which $\theta/2$ lies.

109. True. $4 \sin(-x) \cos(-x) = 4(-\sin x) \cos x$
$= -4 \sin x \cos x$
$= -2(2 \sin x \cos x)$
$= -2 \sin 2x$

111. Reciprocal identities:

$\sin \theta = \frac{1}{\csc \theta}$, $\cos \theta = \frac{1}{\sec \theta}$, $\tan \theta = \frac{1}{\cot \theta}$,

$\csc \theta = \frac{1}{\sin \theta}$, $\sec \theta = \frac{1}{\cos \theta}$, $\cot \theta = \frac{1}{\tan \theta}$

Quotient identities: $\tan \theta = \frac{\sin \theta}{\cos \theta}$, $\cot \theta = \frac{\cos \theta}{\sin \theta}$

Pythagorean identities: $\sin^2 \theta + \cos^2 \theta = 1$,
$1 + \tan^2 \theta = \sec^2 \theta$, $1 + \cot^2 \theta = \csc^2 \theta$

113. $-1 \le \sin x \le 1$ for all x **115.** $y_1 = y_2 + 1$

117. $-1.8431, 2.1758, 3.9903, 8.8935, 9.8820$

Chapter Test *(page 423)*

1. $\sin \theta = -\frac{3\sqrt{13}}{13}$
$\cos \theta = -\frac{2\sqrt{13}}{13}$
$\csc \theta = -\frac{\sqrt{13}}{3}$
$\sec \theta = -\frac{\sqrt{13}}{2}$
$\cot \theta = \frac{2}{3}$

2. 1 **3.** 1 **4.** $\csc \theta \sec \theta$

5. $\theta = 0, \frac{\pi}{2} < \theta \le \pi, \frac{3\pi}{2} < \theta < 2\pi$

6.
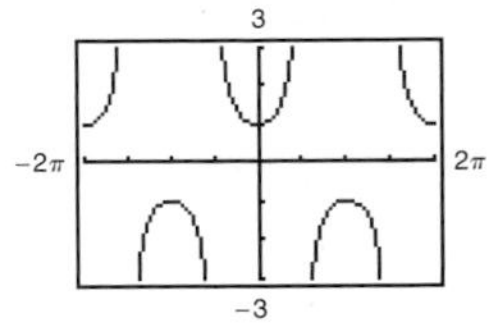

$y_1 = y_2$

7–12. Answers will vary.

13. $\frac{1}{16}\left(\frac{10 - 15 \cos 2x + 6 \cos 4x - \cos 6x}{1 + \cos 2x}\right)$ **14.** $\tan 2\theta$

15. $2(\sin 6\theta + \sin 2\theta)$ **16.** $-2 \cos \frac{7\theta}{2} \sin \frac{\theta}{2}$

17. $0, \frac{3\pi}{4}, \pi, \frac{7\pi}{4}$ **18.** $\frac{\pi}{6}, \frac{\pi}{2}, \frac{5\pi}{6}, \frac{3\pi}{2}$

19. $\frac{\pi}{6}, \frac{5\pi}{6}, \frac{7\pi}{6}, \frac{11\pi}{6}$ **20.** $\frac{\pi}{6}, \frac{5\pi}{6}, \frac{3\pi}{2}$

21. $-2.938, -2.663, 1.170$ **22.** $\frac{\sqrt{2} - \sqrt{6}}{4}$

23. $\sin 2u = \frac{4}{5}$, $\tan 2u = -\frac{4}{3}$, $\cos 2u = -\frac{3}{5}$

24. Day 123 to day 223

25. $t = 0.26$ minute
0.58 minute
0.89 minute
1.20 minutes
1.52 minutes
1.83 minutes

Problem Solving *(page 427)*

1. (a) $\cos \theta = \pm\sqrt{1 - \sin^2 \theta}$
$\tan \theta = \pm \frac{\sin \theta}{\sqrt{1 - \sin^2 \theta}}$
$\cot \theta = \pm \frac{\sqrt{1 - \sin^2 \theta}}{\sin \theta}$
$\sec \theta = \pm \frac{1}{\sqrt{1 - \sin^2 \theta}}$
$\csc \theta = \frac{1}{\sin \theta}$

(b) $\sin \theta = \pm\sqrt{1 - \cos^2 \theta}$
$\tan \theta = \pm\frac{\sqrt{1 - \cos^2 \theta}}{\cos \theta}$
$\csc \theta = \pm\frac{1}{\sqrt{1 - \cos^2 \theta}}$
$\sec \theta = \frac{1}{\cos \theta}$
$\cot \theta = \pm\frac{\cos \theta}{\sqrt{1 - \cos^2 \theta}}$

3. Answers will vary. **5.** $u + v = w$

7. $\sin\frac{\theta}{2} = \sqrt{\frac{1-\cos\theta}{2}}$

$\cos\frac{\theta}{2} = \sqrt{\frac{1+\cos\theta}{2}}$

$\tan\frac{\theta}{2} = \frac{\sin\theta}{1+\cos\theta}$

9. (a)

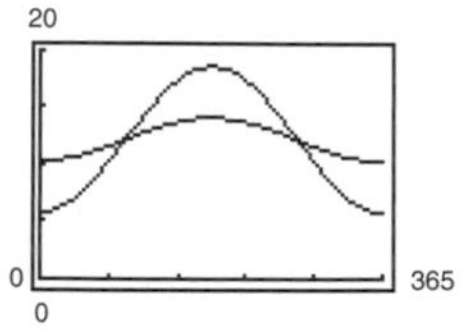

(b) $t = 91, t = 274$; Spring Equinox and Fall Equinox

(c) Seward; The amplitudes: 6.4 and 1.9

(d) 365.2 days

11. (a) $\frac{\pi}{6} \le x \le \frac{5\pi}{6}$ (b) $\frac{2\pi}{3} \le x \le \frac{4\pi}{3}$

(c) $\frac{\pi}{2} < x < \pi, \frac{3\pi}{2} < x < 2\pi$

(d) $0 \le x \le \frac{\pi}{4}, \frac{5\pi}{4} \le x \le 2\pi$

13. (a) $\sin(u+v+w)$

$= \sin u \cos v \cos w - \sin u \sin v \sin w$

$+ \cos u \sin v \cos w + \cos u \cos v \sin w$

(b) $\tan(u+v+w)$

$= \frac{\tan u + \tan v + \tan w - \tan u \tan v \tan w}{1 - \tan u \tan v - \tan u \tan w - \tan v \tan w}$

15. (a)

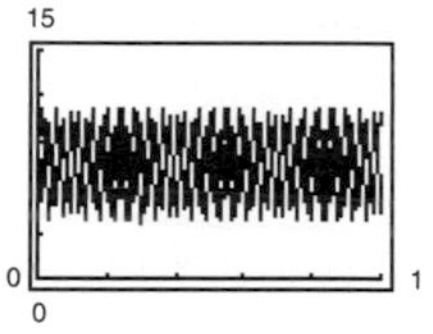

(b) 233.3 times per second

Chapter 6

Section 6.1 *(page 436)*

Vocabulary Check *(page 436)*

1. oblique **2.** $\frac{b}{\sin B}$ **3.** $\frac{1}{2}ac \sin B$

1. $C = 105°, b \approx 28.28, c \approx 38.64$

3. $C = 120°, b \approx 4.75, c \approx 7.17$

5. $B \approx 21.55°, C \approx 122.45°, c \approx 11.49$

7. $B = 60.9°, b \approx 19.32, c \approx 6.36$

9. $B = 42°4', a \approx 22.05, b \approx 14.88$

11. $A \approx 10°11', C \approx 154°19', c \approx 11.03$

13. $A \approx 25.57°, B \approx 9.43°, a \approx 10.53$

15. $B \approx 18°13', C \approx 51°32', c \approx 40.06$

17. $C = 83°, a \approx 0.62, b \approx 0.51$

19. $B \approx 48.74°, C \approx 21.26°, c \approx 48.23$

21. No solution

23. Two solutions:

$B \approx 72.21°, C \approx 49.79°, c \approx 10.27$

$B \approx 107.79°, C \approx 14.21°, c \approx 3.30$

25. (a) $b \le 5, b = \frac{5}{\sin 36°}$ (b) $5 < b < \frac{5}{\sin 36°}$

(c) $b > \frac{5}{\sin 36°}$

27. (a) $b \le 10.8, b = \frac{10.8}{\sin 10°}$ (b) $10.8 < b < \frac{10.8}{\sin 10°}$

(c) $b > \frac{10.8}{\sin 10°}$

29. 10.4 **31.** 1675.2 **33.** 3204.5 **35.** 15.3 meters

37. 16.1° **39.** 77 meters

41. (a)

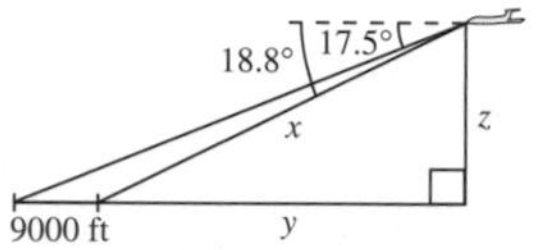

(b) 22.6 miles

(c) 21.4 miles

(d) 7.3 miles

43. 3.2 miles

45. True. If an angle of a triangle is obtuse (greater than 90°), then the other two angles must be acute and therefore less than 90°. The triangle is oblique.

47. (a) $\alpha = \arcsin(0.5 \sin\beta)$

(b)

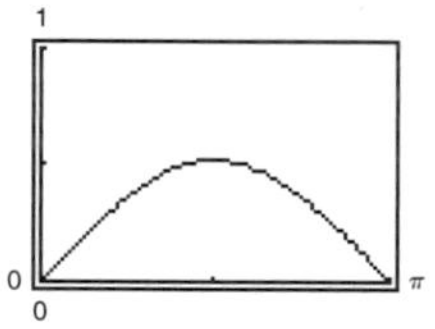

Domain: $0 < \beta < \pi$

Range: $0 < \alpha < \frac{\pi}{6}$

(c) $c = \frac{18 \sin[\pi - \beta - \arcsin(0.5 \sin\beta)]}{\sin\beta}$

(d)

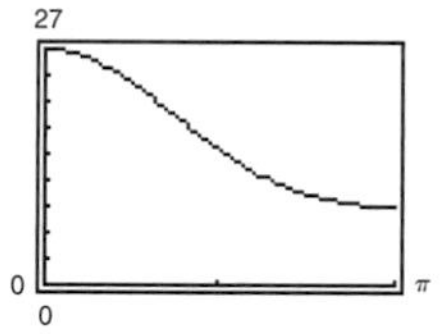

Domain: $0 < \beta < \pi$

Range: $9 < c < 27$

(e)

β	0.4	0.8	1.2	1.6
α	0.1960	0.3669	0.4848	0.5234
c	25.95	23.07	19.19	15.33

β	2.0	2.4	2.8
α	0.4720	0.3445	0.1683
c	12.29	10.31	9.27

As β increases from 0 to π, α increases and then decreases, and c decreases from 27 to 9.

49. $\cos x$ **51.** $\sin^2 x$

Section 6.2 *(page 443)*

Vocabulary Check *(page 443)*

1. Cosines **2.** $b^2 = a^2 + c^2 - 2ac \cos B$
3. Heron's Area Formula

1. $A \approx 23.07°, B \approx 34.05°, C \approx 122.88°$
3. $B \approx 23.79°, C \approx 126.21°, a \approx 18.59$
5. $A \approx 31.99°, B \approx 42.39°, C \approx 105.63°$
7. $A \approx 92.94°, B \approx 43.53°, C \approx 43.53°$
9. $B \approx 13.45°, C \approx 31.55°, a \approx 12.16$
11. $A \approx 141°45', C \approx 27°40', b \approx 11.87$
13. $A = 27°10', C = 27°10', b \approx 56.94$
15. $A \approx 33.80°, B \approx 103.20°, c \approx 0.54$

	a	b	c	d	θ	ϕ
17.	5	8	12.07	5.69	45°	135.1°
19.	10	14	20	13.86	68.2°	111.8°
21.	15	16.96	25	20	77.2°	102.8°

23. 16.25 **25.** 10.4 **27.** 52.11

29.
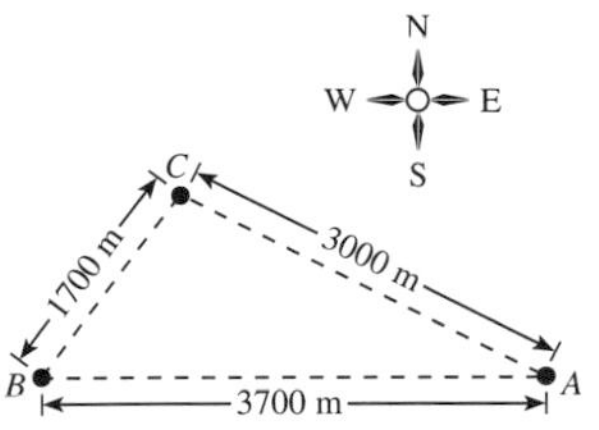

N 37.1° E, S 63.1° E

31. 373.3 meters **33.** 72.3° **35.** 43.3 miles
37. (a) N 58.4° W (b) S 81.5° W **39.** 63.7 feet
41. 24.2 miles
43. $\overline{PQ} \approx 9.4, \overline{QS} = 5, \overline{RS} \approx 12.8$

45.

d (inches)	9	10	12	13	14
θ (degrees)	60.9°	69.5°	88.0°	98.2°	109.6°
s (inches)	20.88	20.28	18.99	18.28	17.48

d (inches)	15	16
θ (degrees)	122.9°	139.8°
s (inches)	16.55	15.37

47. 46,837.5 square feet **49.** \$83,336.37
51. False. For s to be the average of the lengths of the three sides of the triangle, s would be equal to $(a + b + c)/3$.
53. False. The three side lengths do not form a triangle.
55. (a) 570.60 (b) 5910 (c) 177
57. Answers will vary.

59. $-\frac{\pi}{2}$ **61.** $\frac{\pi}{3}$ **63.** $-\frac{\pi}{3}$

65. $\frac{1}{\sqrt{1 - 4x^2}}$ **67.** $\frac{1}{x - 2}$

69. $\cos \theta = 1$
$\sec \theta = 1$
$\csc \theta$ is undefined.

71. $\tan \theta = -\frac{\sqrt{3}}{3}$
$\sec \theta = \frac{2\sqrt{3}}{3}$
$\csc \theta = -2$

73. $-2 \sin \frac{7\pi}{12} \sin \frac{\pi}{4}$

Section 6.3 *(page 456)*

Vocabulary Check *(page 456)*

1. directed line segment **2.** initial; terminal
3. magnitude **4.** vector
5. standard position **6.** unit vector
7. multiplication; addition **8.** resultant
9. linear combination; horizontal; vertical

1. $\|\mathbf{u}\| = \|\mathbf{v}\| = \sqrt{17}$, $\text{slope}_{\mathbf{u}} = \text{slope}_{\mathbf{v}} = \frac{1}{4}$
u and **v** have the same magnitude and direction, so they are equal.
3. $\mathbf{v} = \langle 3, 2 \rangle; \|\mathbf{v}\| = \sqrt{13}$ **5.** $\mathbf{v} = \langle -3, 2 \rangle; \|\mathbf{v}\| = \sqrt{13}$
7. $\mathbf{v} = \langle 0, 5 \rangle; \|\mathbf{v}\| = 5$ **9.** $\mathbf{v} = \langle 16, 7 \rangle; \|\mathbf{v}\| = \sqrt{305}$
11. $\mathbf{v} = \langle 8, 6 \rangle; \|\mathbf{v}\| = 10$ **13.** $\mathbf{v} = \langle -9, -12 \rangle; \|\mathbf{v}\| = 15$

15.
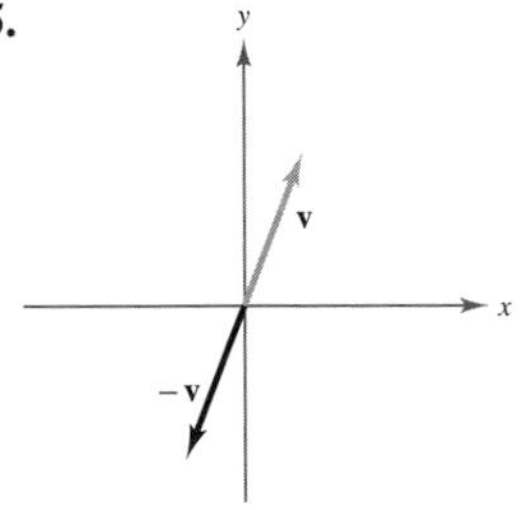

17.
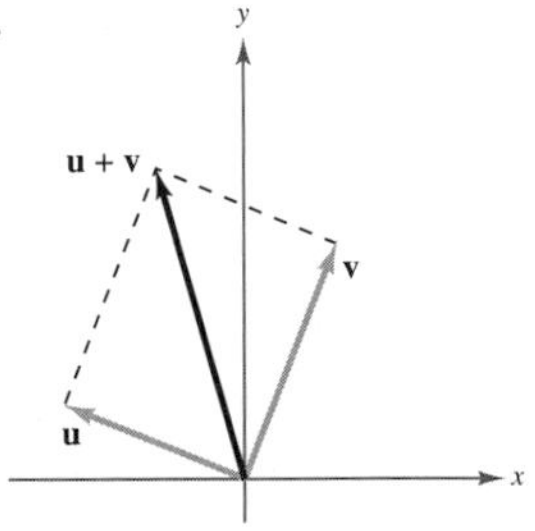

19.
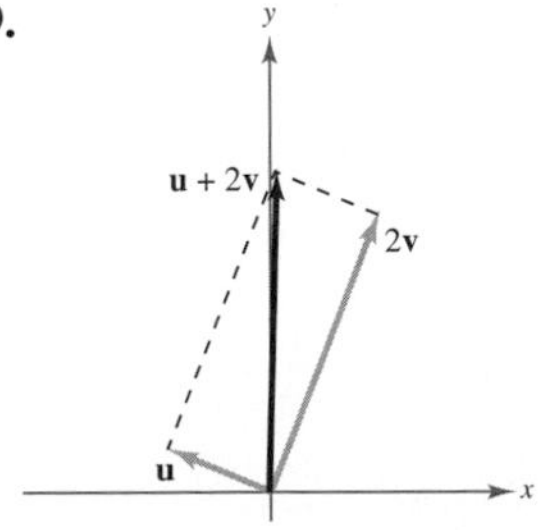

21. (a) $\langle 3, 4\rangle$

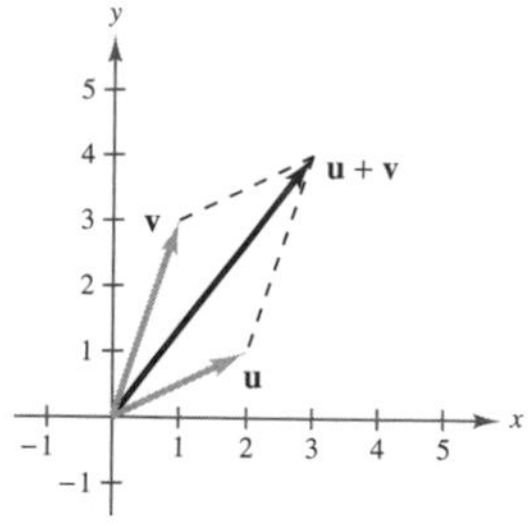

(b) $\langle 1, -2\rangle$

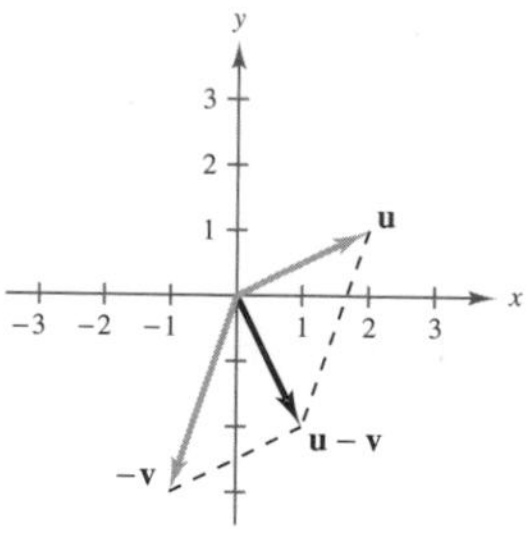

(c) $\langle 1, -7\rangle$

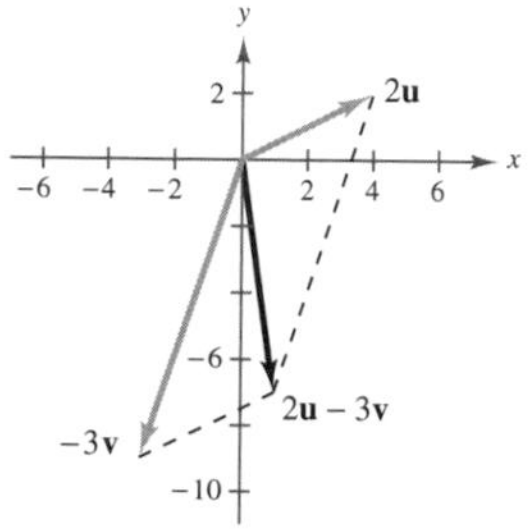

23. (a) $\langle -5, 3\rangle$

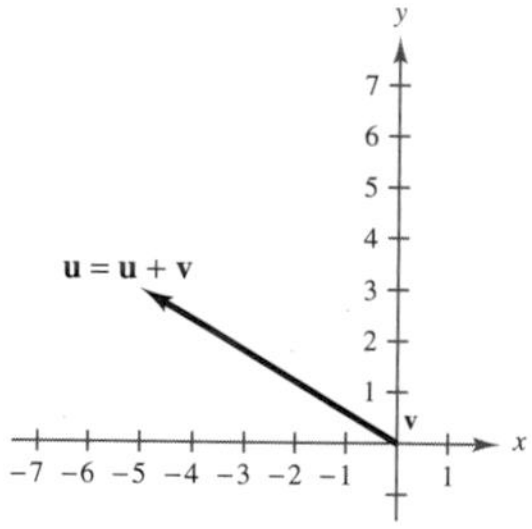

(b) $\langle -5, 3\rangle$

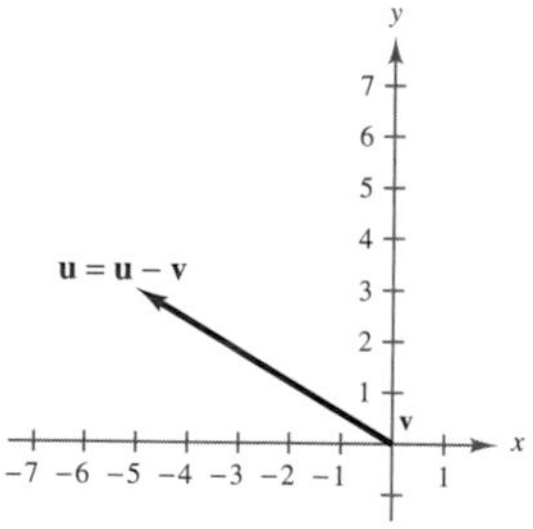

(c) $\langle -10, 6\rangle$

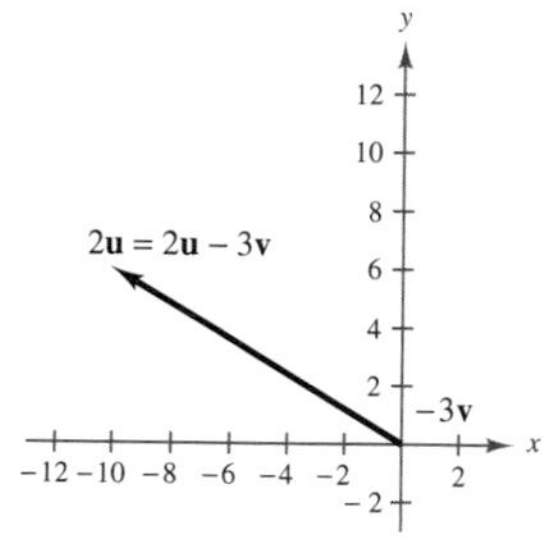

25. (a) $3\mathbf{i} - 2\mathbf{j}$

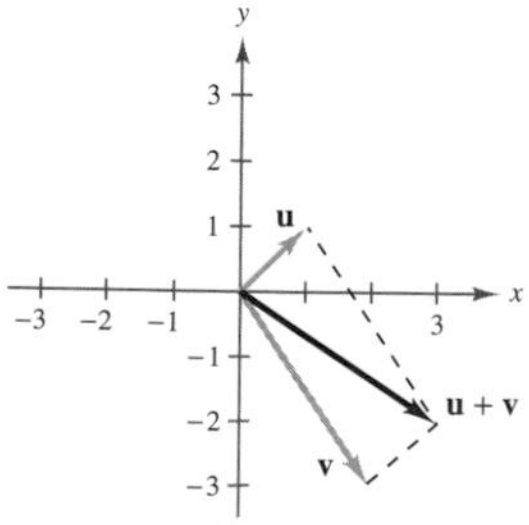

(b) $-\mathbf{i} + 4\mathbf{j}$

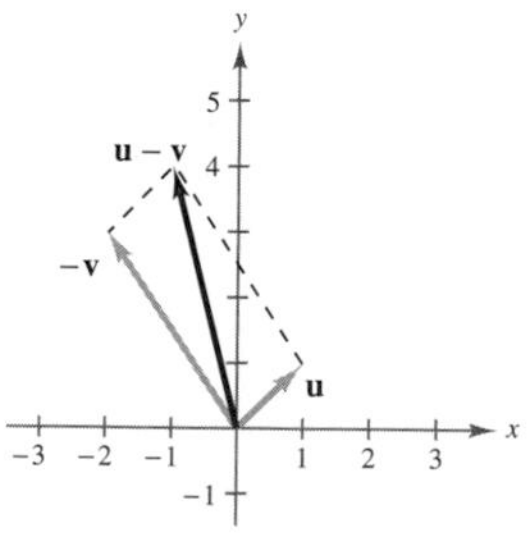

(c) $-4\mathbf{i} + 11\mathbf{j}$

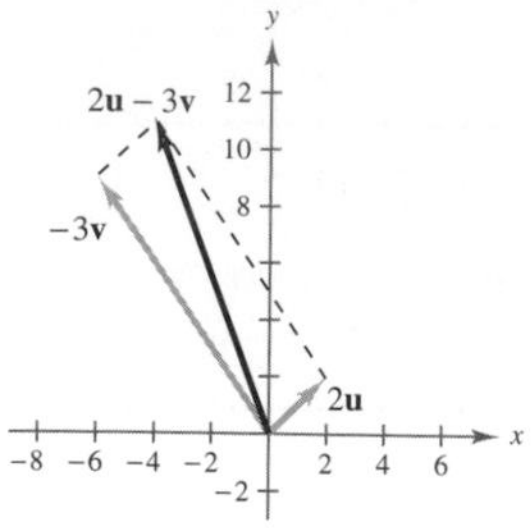

27. (a) $2\mathbf{i} + \mathbf{j}$

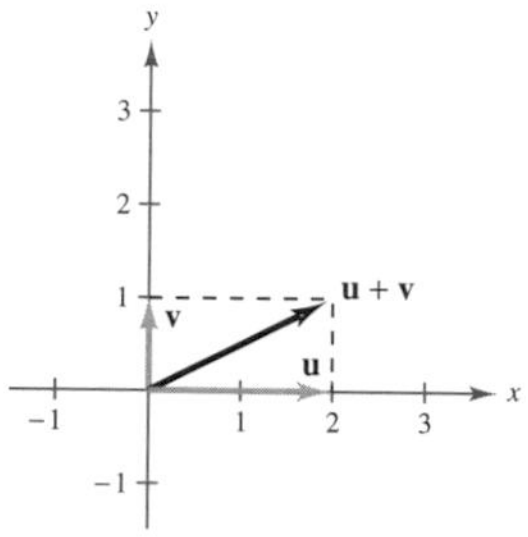

(b) $2\mathbf{i} - \mathbf{j}$

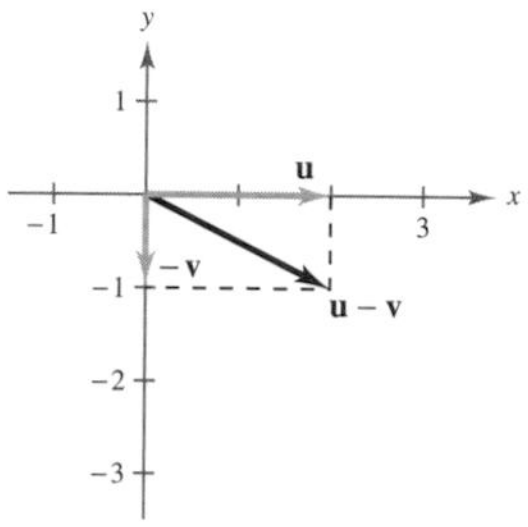

(c) $4\mathbf{i} - 3\mathbf{j}$

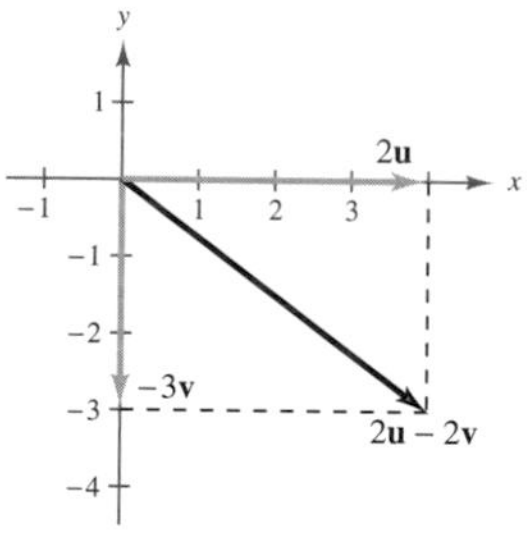

29. $\langle 1, 0\rangle$ **31.** $\left\langle -\frac{\sqrt{2}}{2}, \frac{\sqrt{2}}{2}\right\rangle$ **33.** $\frac{3\sqrt{10}}{10}\mathbf{i} - \frac{\sqrt{10}}{10}\mathbf{j}$

35. $\mathbf{j}$ **37.** $\frac{\sqrt{5}}{5}\mathbf{i} - \frac{2\sqrt{5}}{5}\mathbf{j}$ **39.** $\left\langle \frac{5\sqrt{2}}{2}, \frac{5\sqrt{2}}{2}\right\rangle$

41. $\left\langle \frac{18\sqrt{29}}{29}, \frac{45\sqrt{29}}{29}\right\rangle$ **43.** $7\mathbf{i} + 4\mathbf{j}$ **45.** $3\mathbf{i} + 8\mathbf{j}$

47. $\mathbf{v} = \left\langle 3, -\frac{3}{2}\right\rangle$

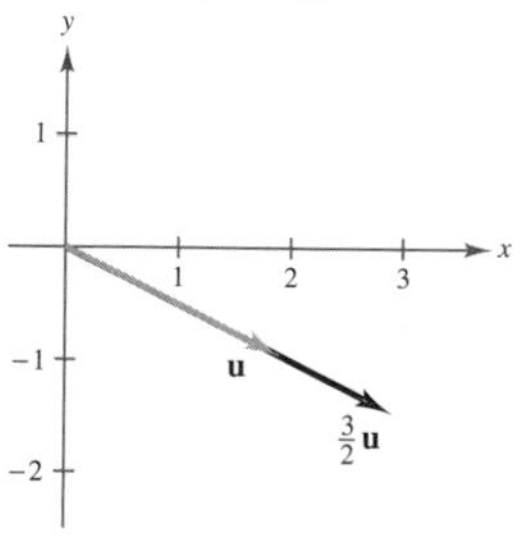

49. $\mathbf{v} = \langle 4, 3 \rangle$

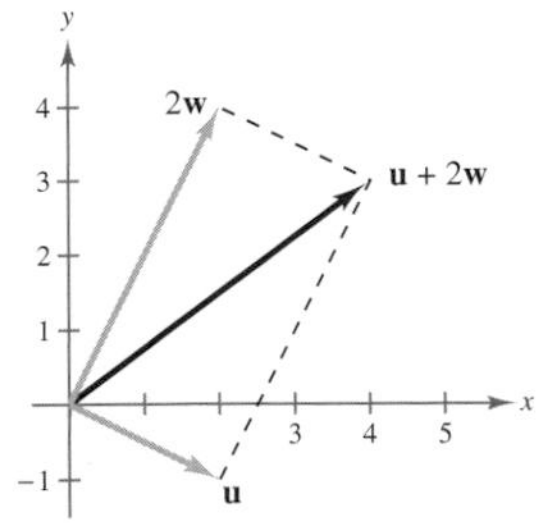

51. $\mathbf{v} = \langle \frac{7}{2}, -\frac{1}{2} \rangle$

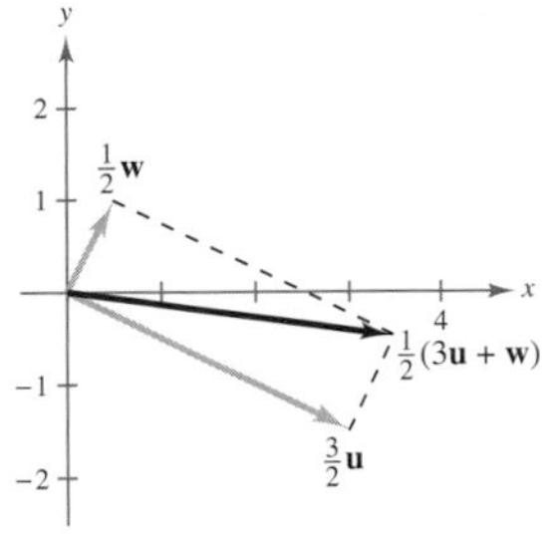

53. $\|\mathbf{v}\| = 3;\ \theta = 60°$ **55.** $\|\mathbf{v}\| = 6\sqrt{2};\ \theta = 315°$

57. $\mathbf{v} = \langle 3, 0 \rangle$ **59.** $\mathbf{v} = \left\langle -\frac{7\sqrt{3}}{4}, \frac{7}{4} \right\rangle$

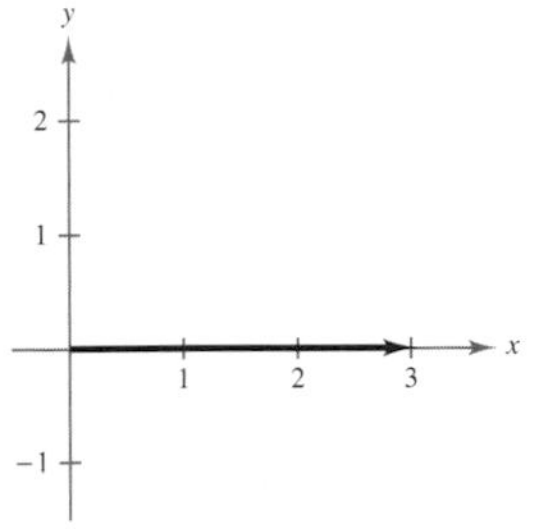

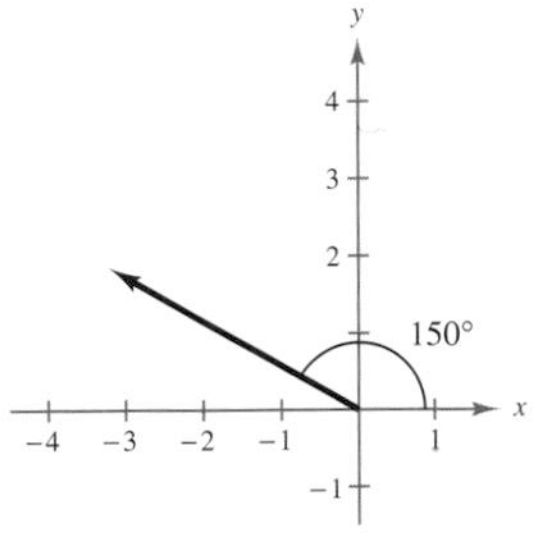

61. $\mathbf{v} = \left\langle -\frac{3\sqrt{6}}{2}, \frac{3\sqrt{2}}{2} \right\rangle$ **63.** $\mathbf{v} = \left\langle \frac{\sqrt{10}}{5}, \frac{3\sqrt{10}}{5} \right\rangle$

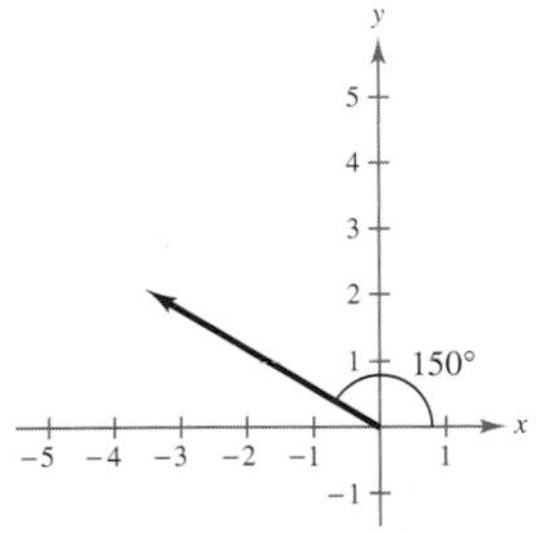

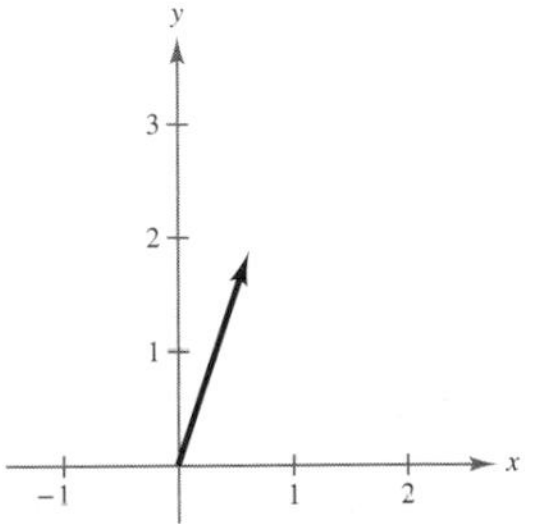

65. $\langle 5, 5 \rangle$ **67.** $\langle 10\sqrt{2} - 50, 10\sqrt{2} \rangle$ **69.** $90°$

71. $62.7°$ **73.** $12.8°$; 398.32 newtons

75. $71.3°$; 228.5 pounds

77. Vertical component: $70 \sin 35° \approx 40.15$ feet per second
Horizontal component: $70 \cos 35° \approx 57.34$ feet per second

79. $T_{AC} \approx 1758.8$ pounds **81.** 3154.4 pounds
$T_{BC} \approx 1305.4$ pounds

83. N 21.4° E; 138.7 kilometers per hour

85. 1928.4 foot-pounds **87.** True. See Example 1.

89. (a) $0°$ (b) $180°$
(c) No. The magnitude is at most equal to the sum when the angle between the vectors is $0°$.

91. Answers will vary. **93.** $\langle 1, 3 \rangle$ or $\langle -1, -3 \rangle$

95. $8 \tan \theta$ **97.** $6 \sec \theta$

99. $\frac{\pi}{2} + n\pi,\ \pi + 2n\pi$ **101.** $n\pi,\ \frac{\pi}{6} + 2n\pi,\ \frac{11\pi}{6} + 2n\pi$

Section 6.4 *(page 467)*

Vocabulary Check *(page 467)*

1. dot product **2.** $\frac{\mathbf{u} \cdot \mathbf{v}}{\|\mathbf{u}\| \|\mathbf{v}\|}$ **3.** orthogonal

4. $\left(\frac{\mathbf{u} \cdot \mathbf{v}}{\|\mathbf{v}\|^2}\right)\mathbf{v}$ **5.** $\|\text{proj}_{\overrightarrow{PQ}} \mathbf{F}\| \|\overrightarrow{PQ}\|;\ \mathbf{F} \cdot \overrightarrow{PQ}$

1. -9 **3.** -11 **5.** 6 **7.** -12 **9.** 8; scalar

11. $\langle -6, 8 \rangle$; vector **13.** $\langle -66, -66 \rangle$; vector

15. $\sqrt{5} - 1$; scalar **17.** 4; scalar **19.** 13

21. $5\sqrt{41}$ **23.** 6 **25.** $90°$ **27.** $143.13°$

29. $60.26°$ **31.** $90°$ **33.** $\frac{5\pi}{12}$

35.

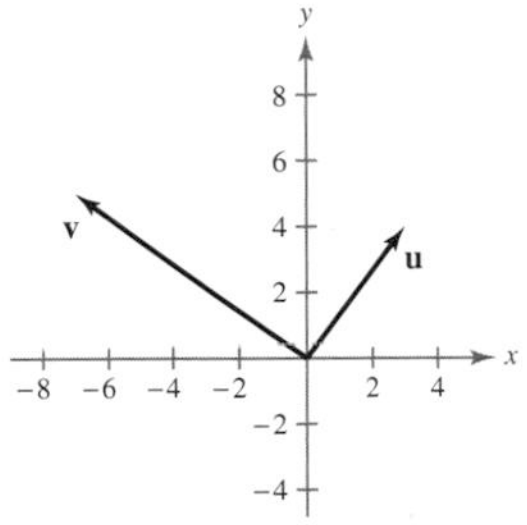

$\approx 91.33°$

37.

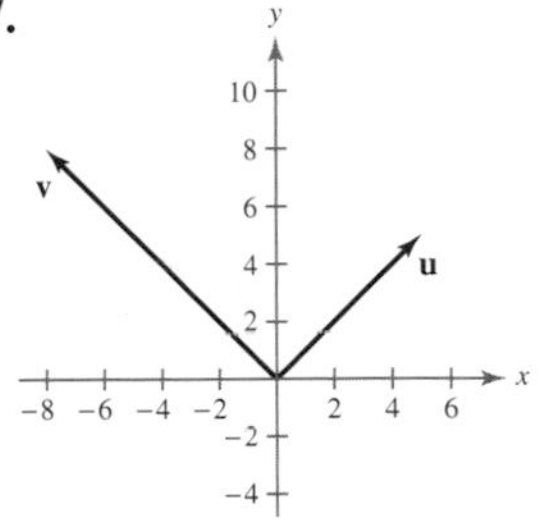

$90°$

39. $26.57°, 63.43°, 90°$ **41.** $41.63°, 53.13°, 85.24°$

43. -20 **45.** -229.1 **47.** Parallel **49.** Neither

51. Orthogonal **53.** $\frac{1}{37}\langle 84, 14 \rangle, \frac{1}{37}\langle -10, 60 \rangle$

55. $\frac{45}{229}\langle 2, 15 \rangle, \frac{6}{229}\langle -15, 2 \rangle$ **57.** 0

59. $\langle -5, 3 \rangle, \langle 5, -3 \rangle$ **61.** $\frac{2}{3}\mathbf{i} + \frac{1}{2}\mathbf{j},\ -\frac{2}{3}\mathbf{i} - \frac{1}{2}\mathbf{j}$ **63.** 32

65. (a) \$58,762.50; This value gives the total revenue that can be earned by selling all of the units.
(b) $1.05\mathbf{v}$

67. (a) Force $= 30{,}000 \sin d$
(b)

d	$0°$	$1°$	$2°$	$3°$	$4°$	$5°$
Force	0	523.6	1047.0	1570.1	2092.7	2614.7

d	$6°$	$7°$	$8°$	$9°$	$10°$
Force	3135.9	3656.1	4175.2	4693.0	5209.4

(c) 29,885.8 pounds

69. 735 newton-meters **71.** 779.4 foot-pounds

73. 21,650.64 foot-pounds

75. False. Work is represented by a scalar.

77. (a) $\theta = \frac{\pi}{2}$ (b) $0 \le \theta < \frac{\pi}{2}$ (c) $\frac{\pi}{2} < \theta \le \pi$

79. Answers will vary.

81. $12\sqrt{7}$ **83.** $-2\sqrt{6}$

85. $0, \frac{\pi}{6}, \pi, \frac{11\pi}{6}$ **87.** $0, \pi$ **89.** $-\frac{253}{325}$ **91.** $\frac{204}{325}$

Section 6.5 *(page 478)*

Vocabulary Check *(page 478)*

1. absolute value
2. trigonometric form; modulus; argument
3. DeMoivre's **4.** *n*th root

1.

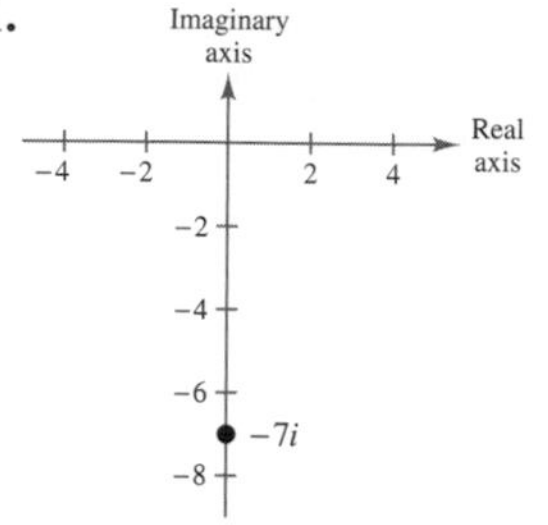

7

3.

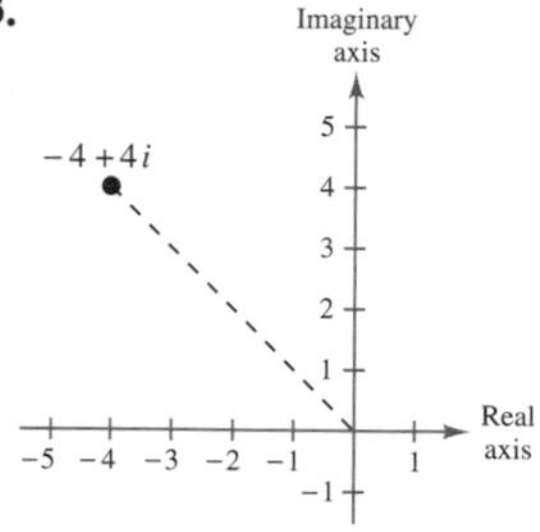

$4\sqrt{2}$

5.

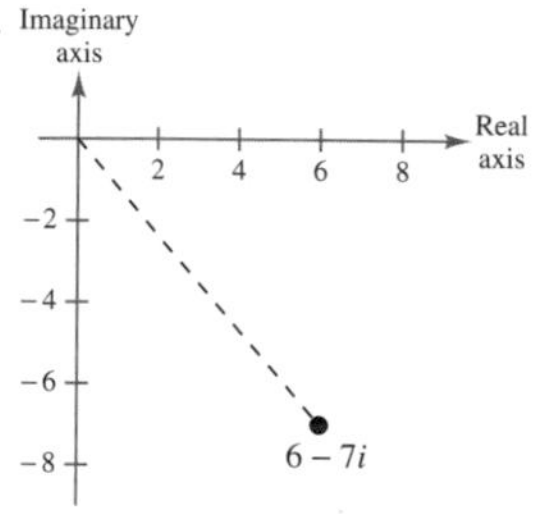

$\sqrt{85}$

7. $3\left(\cos\frac{\pi}{2} + i\sin\frac{\pi}{2}\right)$

9. $\sqrt{10}(\cos 5.96 + i\sin 5.96)$

11.

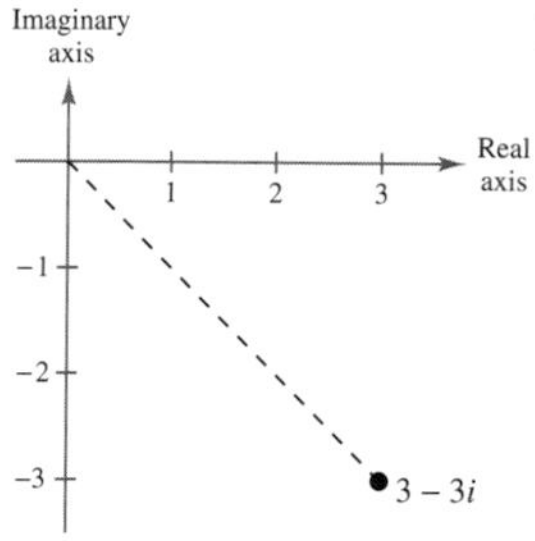

$3\sqrt{2}\left(\cos\frac{7\pi}{4} + i\sin\frac{7\pi}{4}\right)$

13.

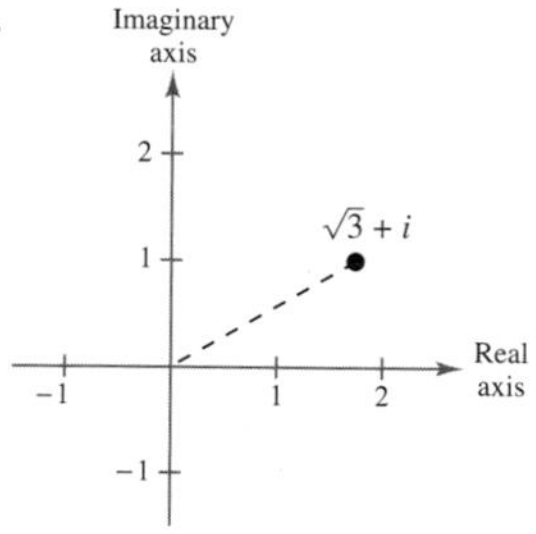

$2\left(\cos\frac{\pi}{6} + i\sin\frac{\pi}{6}\right)$

15.

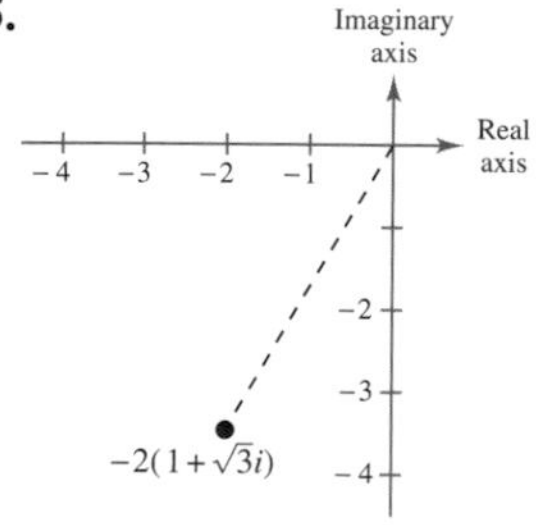

$4\left(\cos\frac{4\pi}{3} + i\sin\frac{4\pi}{3}\right)$

17.

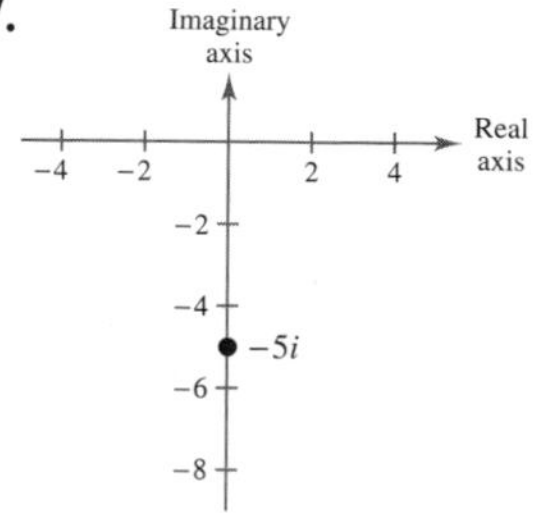

$5\left(\cos\frac{3\pi}{2} + i\sin\frac{3\pi}{2}\right)$

19.

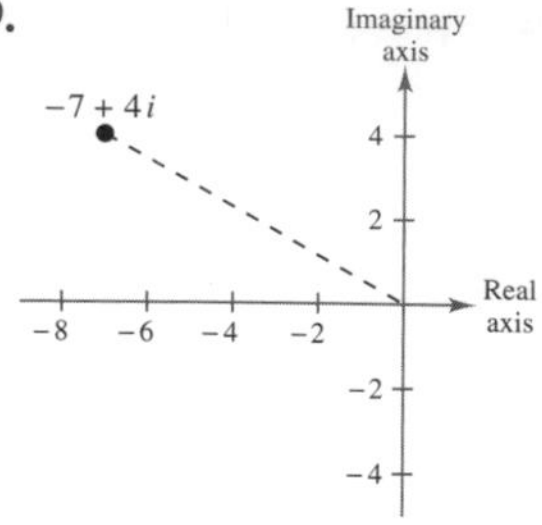

$\sqrt{65}(\cos 2.62 + i\sin 2.62)$

21.

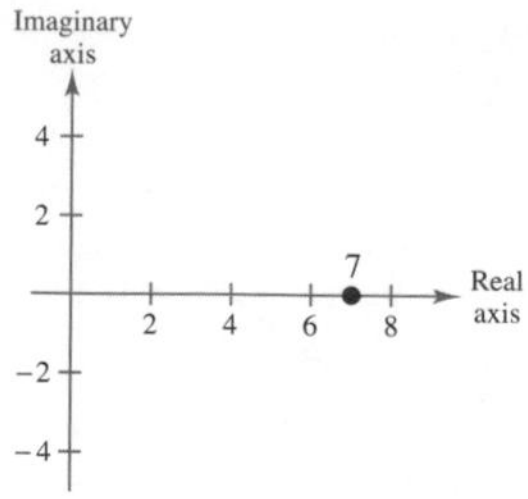

$7(\cos 0 + i\sin 0)$

23.

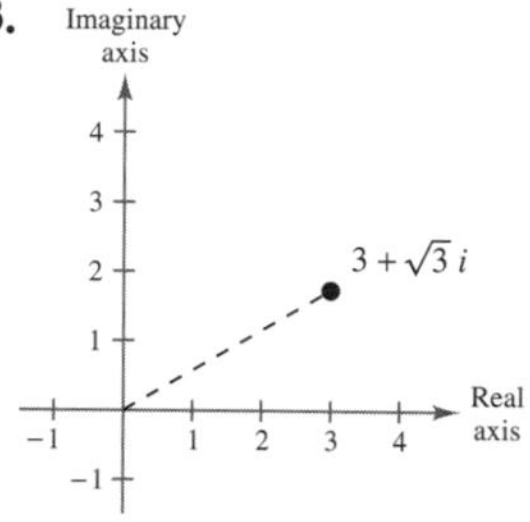

$2\sqrt{3}\left(\cos\frac{\pi}{6} + i\sin\frac{\pi}{6}\right)$

25.

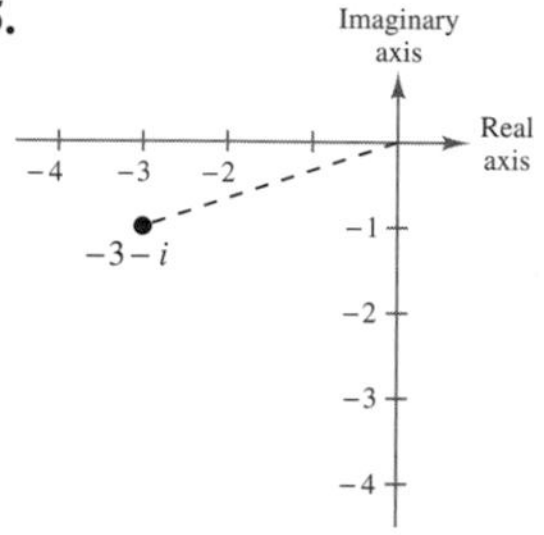

$\sqrt{10}(\cos 3.46 + i\sin 3.46)$

27.

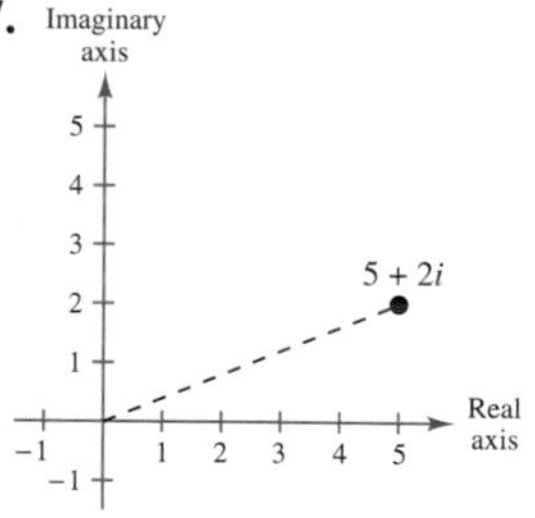

$\sqrt{29}(\cos 0.38 + i\sin 0.38)$

29.

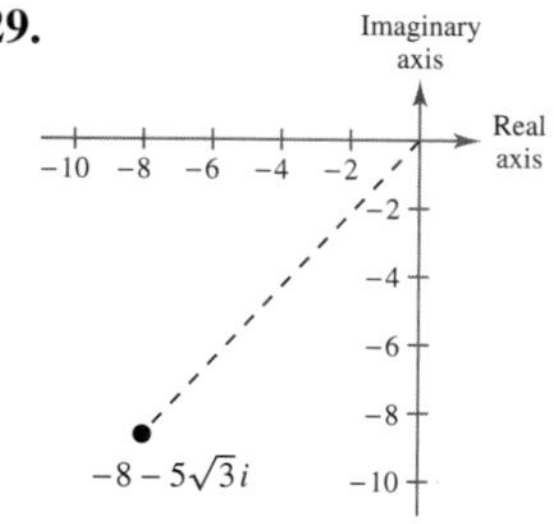

$\sqrt{139}(\cos 3.97 + i\sin 3.97)$

31.

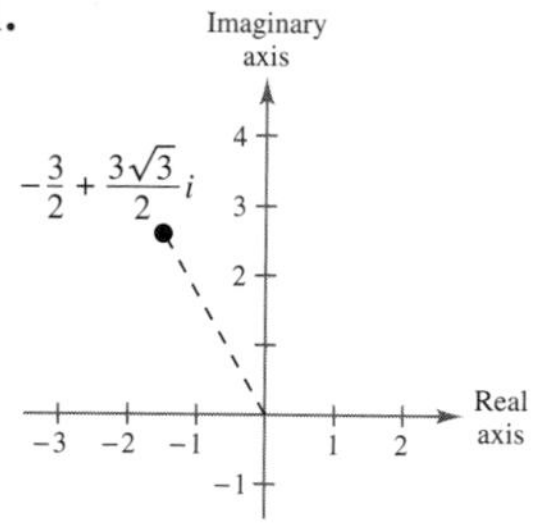

$-\frac{3}{2} + \frac{3\sqrt{3}}{2}i$

33.

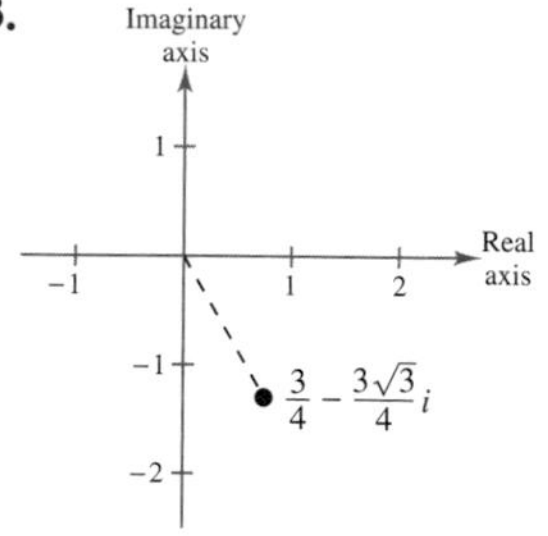

$\frac{3}{4} - \frac{3\sqrt{3}}{4}i$

35.

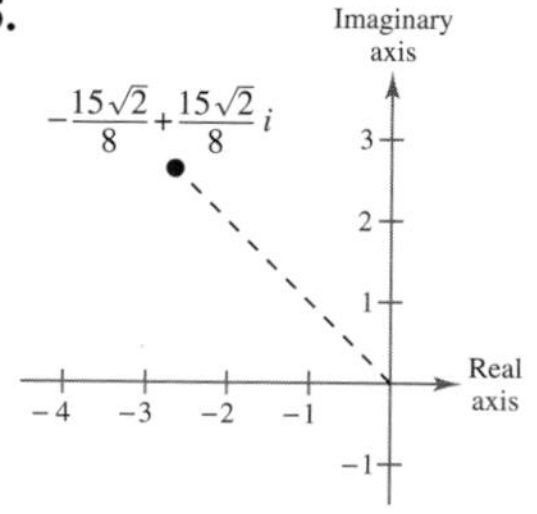

$-\frac{15\sqrt{2}}{8} + \frac{15\sqrt{2}}{8}i$

37.

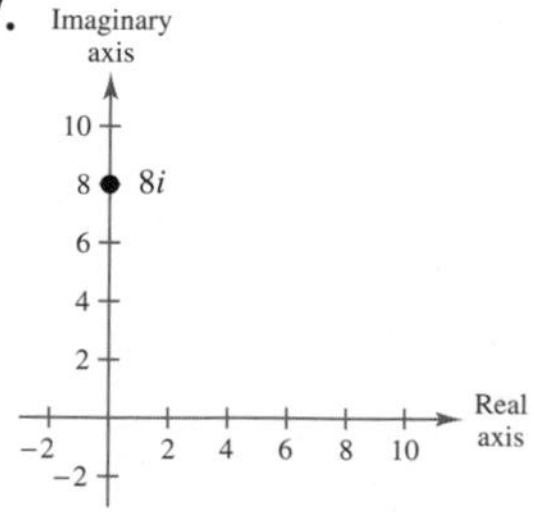

$8i$

39. 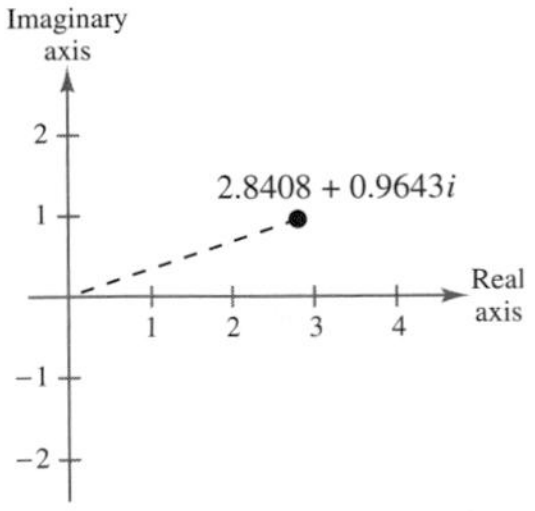

$2.8408 + 0.9643i$

41. $4.6985 + 1.7101i$ **43.** $-2.9044 + 0.7511i$

45. 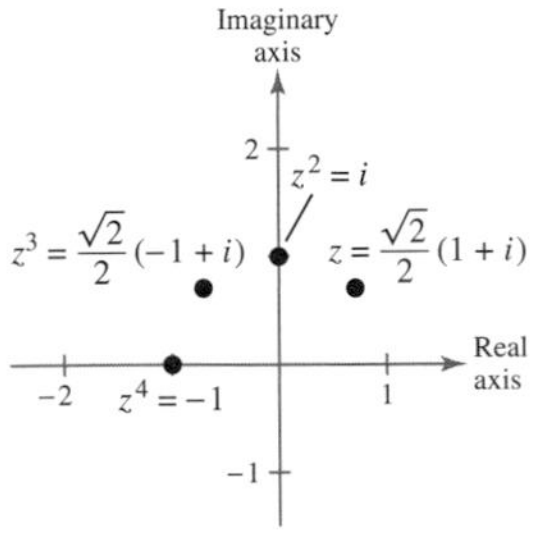

The absolute value of each is 1.

47. $12\left(\cos\frac{\pi}{3} + i\sin\frac{\pi}{3}\right)$ **49.** $\frac{10}{9}(\cos 200° + i\sin 200°)$

51. $0.27(\cos 150° + i\sin 150°)$ **53.** $\cos 30° + i\sin 30°$

55. $\cos\frac{2\pi}{3} + i\sin\frac{2\pi}{3}$ **57.** $4(\cos 302° + i\sin 302°)$

59. (a) $\left[2\sqrt{2}\left(\cos\frac{\pi}{4} + i\sin\frac{\pi}{4}\right)\right]\left[\sqrt{2}\left(\cos\frac{7\pi}{4} + i\sin\frac{7\pi}{4}\right)\right]$

(b) $4(\cos 0 + i\sin 0) = 4$ (c) 4

61. (a) $\left[2\left(\cos\frac{3\pi}{2} + i\sin\frac{3\pi}{2}\right)\right]\left[\sqrt{2}\left(\cos\frac{\pi}{4} + i\sin\frac{\pi}{4}\right)\right]$

(b) $2\sqrt{2}\left(\cos\frac{7\pi}{4} + i\sin\frac{7\pi}{4}\right) = 2 - 2i$

(c) $-2i - 2i^2 = -2i + 2 = 2 - 2i$

63. (a) $[5(\cos 0.93 + i\sin 0.93)] \div \left[2\left(\cos\frac{5\pi}{3} + i\sin\frac{5\pi}{3}\right)\right]$

(b) $\frac{5}{2}(\cos 1.97 + i\sin 1.97) \approx -0.982 + 2.299i$

(c) $\approx -0.982 + 2.299i$

65. (a) $[5(\cos 0 + i\sin 0)] \div \left[\sqrt{13}(\cos 0.98 + i\sin 0.98)\right]$

(b) $\frac{5}{\sqrt{13}}(\cos 5.30 + i\sin 5.30) \approx 0.769 - 1.154i$

(c) $\frac{10}{13} - \frac{15}{13}i \approx 0.769 - 1.154i$

67. 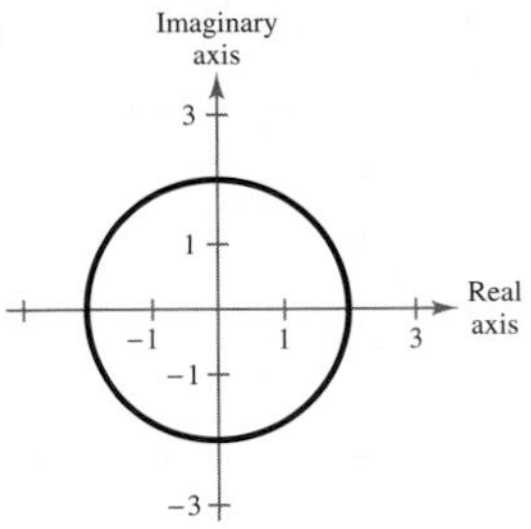

69. 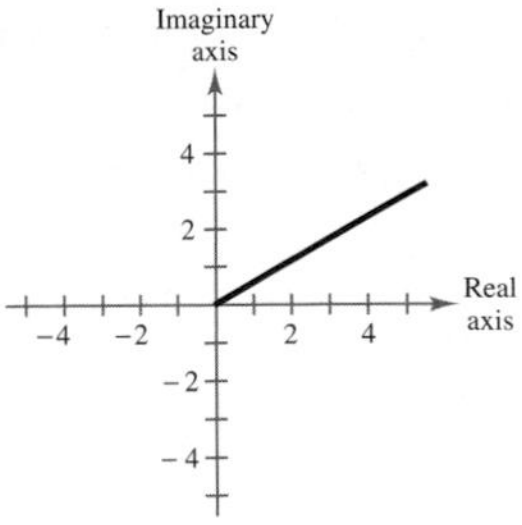

71. $-4 - 4i$ **73.** $-32i$ **75.** $-128\sqrt{3} - 128i$

77. $\frac{125}{2} + \frac{125\sqrt{3}}{2}i$ **79.** -1

81. $608.0 + 144.7i$ **83.** $-597 - 122i$

85. $\frac{81}{2} + \frac{81\sqrt{3}}{2}i$ **87.** $32i$

89. (a) $\sqrt{5}(\cos 60° + i\sin 60°)$
$\sqrt{5}(\cos 240° + i\sin 240°)$

(b) 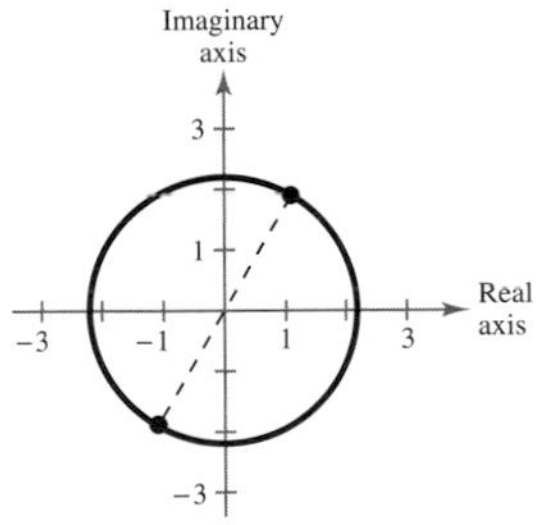

(c) $\frac{\sqrt{5}}{2} + \frac{\sqrt{15}}{2}i,\ -\frac{\sqrt{5}}{2} - \frac{\sqrt{15}}{2}i$

91. (a) $2\left(\cos\frac{2\pi}{9} + i\sin\frac{2\pi}{9}\right)$
$2\left(\cos\frac{8\pi}{9} + i\sin\frac{8\pi}{9}\right)$
$2\left(\cos\frac{14\pi}{9} + i\sin\frac{14\pi}{9}\right)$

(b) 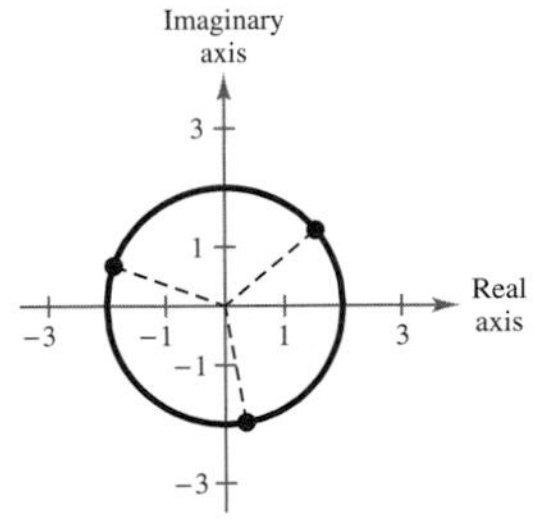

(c) $1.5321 + 1.2856i,\ -1.8794 + 0.6840i,$
$0.3473 - 1.9696i$

CHAPTER 6

93. (a) $5\left(\cos \frac{3\pi}{4} + i \sin \frac{3\pi}{4}\right)$

$5\left(\cos \frac{7\pi}{4} + i \sin \frac{7\pi}{4}\right)$

(b)

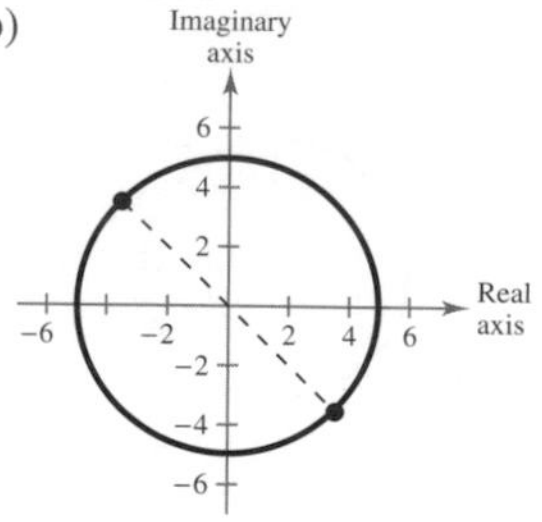

(c) $-\frac{5\sqrt{2}}{2} + \frac{5\sqrt{2}}{2}i$

$\frac{5\sqrt{2}}{2} - \frac{5\sqrt{2}}{2}i$

95. (a) $5\left(\cos \frac{4\pi}{9} + i \sin \frac{4\pi}{9}\right)$

$5\left(\cos \frac{10\pi}{9} + i \sin \frac{10\pi}{9}\right)$

$5\left(\cos \frac{16\pi}{9} + i \sin \frac{16\pi}{9}\right)$

(b)

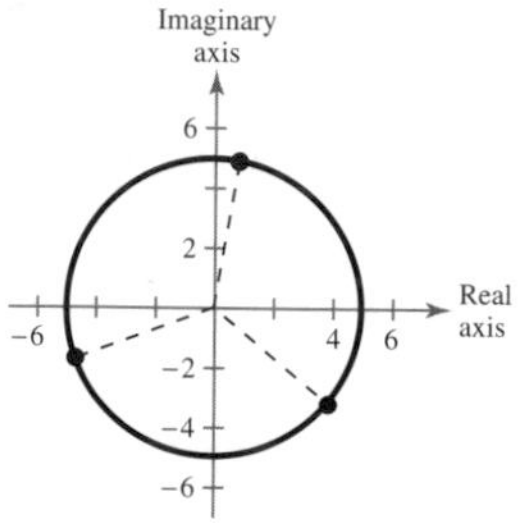

(c) $0.8682 + 4.9240i$,
$-4.6985 - 1.7101i$,
$3.8302 - 3.2140i$

97. (a) $2(\cos 0 + i \sin 0)$

$2\left(\cos \frac{\pi}{2} + i \sin \frac{\pi}{2}\right)$

$2(\cos \pi + i \sin \pi)$

$2\left(\cos \frac{3\pi}{2} + i \sin \frac{3\pi}{2}\right)$

(b)

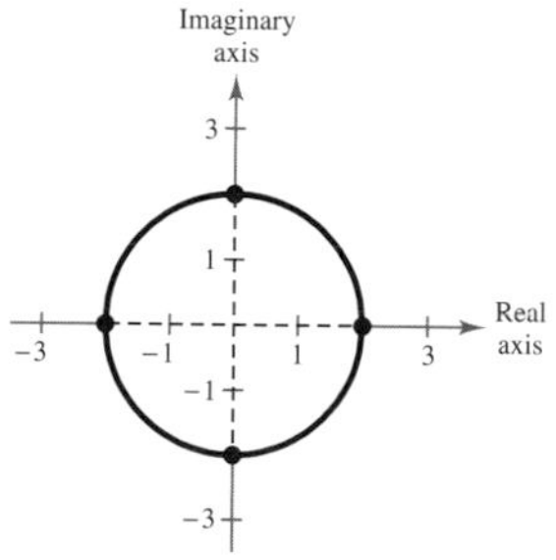

(c) $2, 2i, -2, -2i$

99. (a) $\cos 0 + i \sin 0$

$\cos \frac{2\pi}{5} + i \sin \frac{2\pi}{5}$

$\cos \frac{4\pi}{5} + i \sin \frac{4\pi}{5}$

$\cos \frac{6\pi}{5} + i \sin \frac{6\pi}{5}$

$\cos \frac{8\pi}{5} + i \sin \frac{8\pi}{5}$

(b)

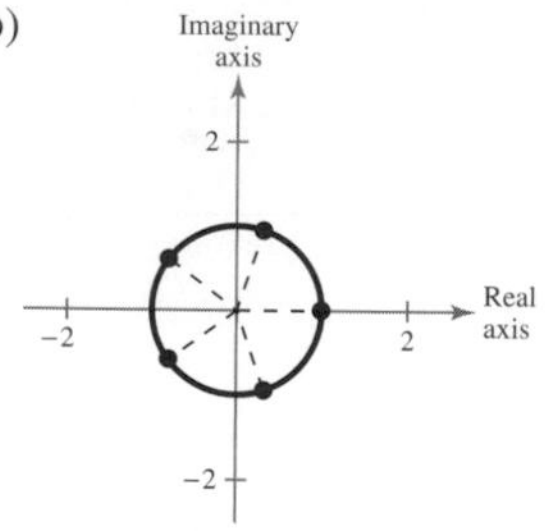

(c) $1, 0.3090 + 0.9511i$,
$-0.8090 + 0.5878i, -0.8090 - 0.5878i$,
$0.3090 - 0.9511i$

101. (a) $5\left(\cos \frac{\pi}{3} + i \sin \frac{\pi}{3}\right)$

$5(\cos \pi + i \sin \pi)$

$5\left(\cos \frac{5\pi}{3} + i \sin \frac{5\pi}{3}\right)$

(b)

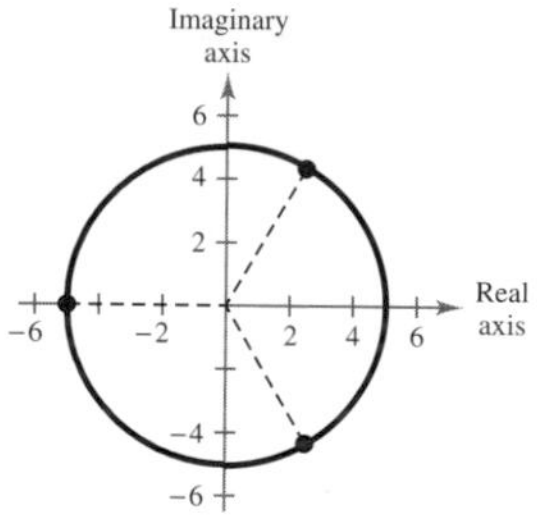

(c) $\frac{5}{2} + \frac{5\sqrt{3}}{2}i, -5, \frac{5}{2} - \frac{5\sqrt{3}}{2}i$

103. (a) $2\sqrt{2}\left(\cos \frac{3\pi}{20} + i \sin \frac{3\pi}{20}\right)$

$2\sqrt{2}\left(\cos \frac{11\pi}{20} + i \sin \frac{11\pi}{20}\right)$

$2\sqrt{2}\left(\cos \frac{19\pi}{20} + i \sin \frac{19\pi}{20}\right)$

$2\sqrt{2}\left(\cos \frac{27\pi}{20} + i \sin \frac{27\pi}{20}\right)$

$2\sqrt{2}\left(\cos \frac{7\pi}{4} + i \sin \frac{7\pi}{4}\right)$

(b)

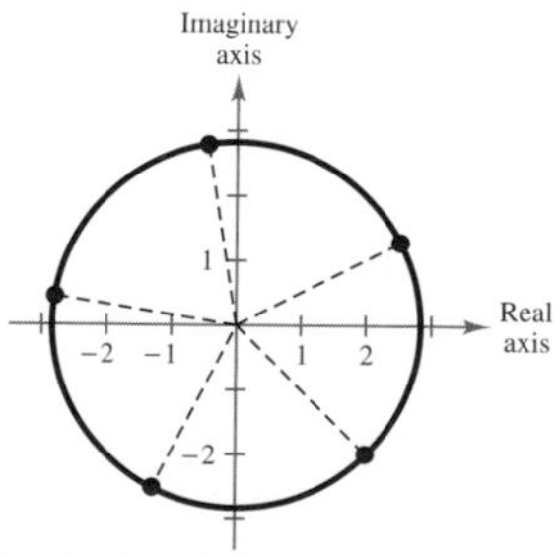

(c) $2.5201 + 1.2841i, -0.4425 + 2.7936i$,
$-2.7936 + 0.4425i, -1.2841 - 2.5201i, 2 - 2i$

105. $\cos\frac{3\pi}{8} + i\sin\frac{3\pi}{8}$

$\cos\frac{7\pi}{8} + i\sin\frac{7\pi}{8}$

$\cos\frac{11\pi}{8} + i\sin\frac{11\pi}{8}$

$\cos\frac{15\pi}{8} + i\sin\frac{15\pi}{8}$

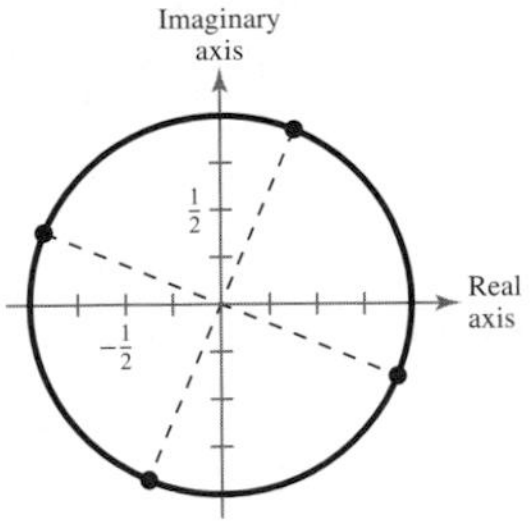

107. $3\left(\cos\frac{\pi}{5} + i\sin\frac{\pi}{5}\right)$

$3\left(\cos\frac{3\pi}{5} + i\sin\frac{3\pi}{5}\right)$

$3(\cos\pi + i\sin\pi)$

$3\left(\cos\frac{7\pi}{5} + i\sin\frac{7\pi}{5}\right)$

$3\left(\cos\frac{9\pi}{5} + i\sin\frac{9\pi}{5}\right)$

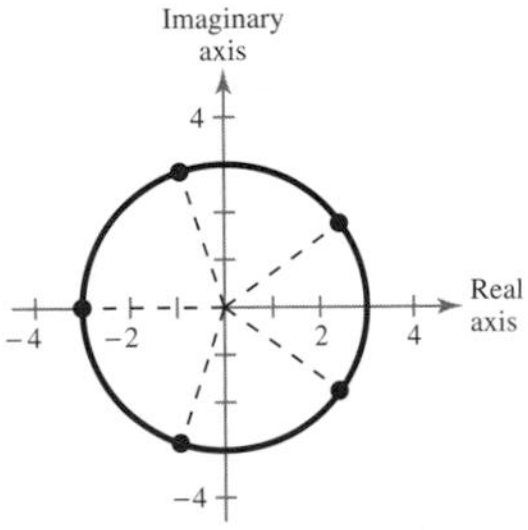

109. $2\left(\cos\frac{3\pi}{8} + i\sin\frac{3\pi}{8}\right)$

$2\left(\cos\frac{7\pi}{8} + i\sin\frac{7\pi}{8}\right)$

$2\left(\cos\frac{11\pi}{8} + i\sin\frac{11\pi}{8}\right)$

$2\left(\cos\frac{15\pi}{8} + i\sin\frac{15\pi}{8}\right)$

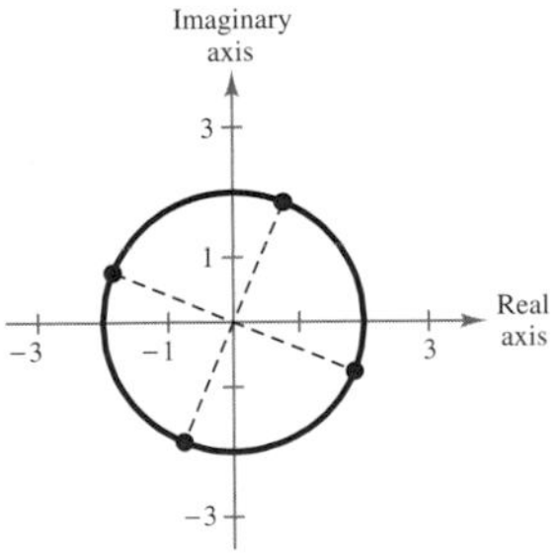

111. $\sqrt[6]{2}\left(\cos\frac{7\pi}{12} + i\sin\frac{7\pi}{12}\right)$

$\sqrt[6]{2}\left(\cos\frac{5\pi}{4} + i\sin\frac{5\pi}{4}\right)$

$\sqrt[6]{2}\left(\cos\frac{23\pi}{12} + i\sin\frac{23\pi}{12}\right)$

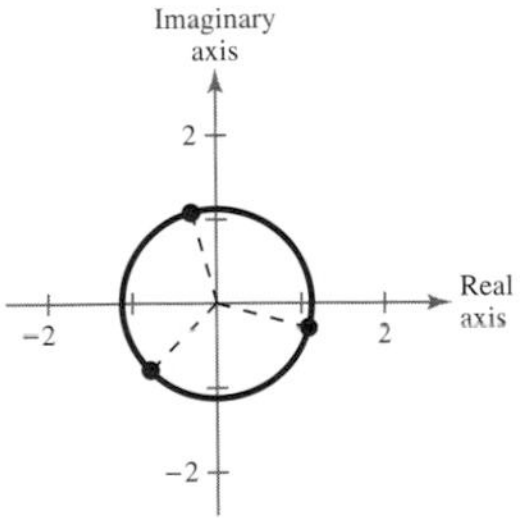

113. True, by the definition of the absolute value of a complex number.

115. True. $z_1z_2 = r_1r_2[\cos(\theta_1 + \theta_2) + i\sin(\theta_1 + \theta_2)] = 0$ if and only if $r_1 = 0$ and/or $r_2 = 0$.

117. Answers will vary.

119. (a) r^2 (b) $\cos 2\theta + i\sin 2\theta$

121. Answers will vary.

123. (a) $2(\cos 30° + i\sin 30°)$ (b) $8i$
$2(\cos 150° + i\sin 150°)$
$2(\cos 270° + i\sin 270°)$

125. $B = 68°, b \approx 19.80, c \approx 21.36$

127. $B = 60°, a \approx 65.01, c \approx 130.02$

129. $B = 47°45', a \approx 7.53, b \approx 8.29$

131. 16; 2 **133.** $\frac{1}{16}$; $\frac{4}{5}$ **135.** $3(\sin 11\theta + \sin 5\theta)$

Review Exercises *(page 482)*

1. $C = 74°, b \approx 13.19, c \approx 13.41$

3. $A = 26°, a \approx 24.89, c \approx 56.23$

5. $C = 66°, a \approx 2.53, b \approx 9.11$

7. $B = 108°, a \approx 11.76, c \approx 21.49$

9. $A \approx 20.41°, C \approx 9.59°, a \approx 20.92$

11. $B \approx 39.48°, C \approx 65.52°, c \approx 48.24$

13. 7.9 **15.** 33.5

17. 31.1 meters **19.** 31.01 feet

21. $A \approx 29.69°, B \approx 52.41°, C \approx 97.90°$

23. $A \approx 29.92°, B \approx 86.18°, C \approx 63.90°$

25. $A = 35°, C = 35°, b \approx 6.55$

27. $A \approx 45.76°, B \approx 91.24°, c \approx 21.42$

29. $\approx$ 4.3 feet, $\approx$ 12.6 feet

31. 615.1 meters **33.** 9.80 **35.** 8.36

37. $\|\mathbf{u}\| = \|\mathbf{v}\| = \sqrt{61}$, $\text{slope}_\mathbf{u} = \text{slope}_\mathbf{v} = \frac{5}{6}$

39. $\langle 7, -5\rangle$ **41.** $\langle 7, -7\rangle$ **43.** $\langle -4, 4\sqrt{3}\rangle$

45. (a) $\langle -4, 3\rangle$ (b) $\langle 2, -9\rangle$ (c) $\langle -3, -9\rangle$
(d) $\langle -11, -3\rangle$

47. (a) $\langle -1, 6\rangle$ (b) $\langle -9, -2\rangle$ (c) $\langle -15, 6\rangle$
(d) $\langle -17, 18\rangle$

49. (a) $7\mathbf{i} + 2\mathbf{j}$ (b) $-3\mathbf{i} - 4\mathbf{j}$ (c) $6\mathbf{i} - 3\mathbf{j}$
(d) $20\mathbf{i} + \mathbf{j}$

51. (a) $3\mathbf{i} + 6\mathbf{j}$ (b) $5\mathbf{i} - 6\mathbf{j}$ (c) $12\mathbf{i}$ (d) $18\mathbf{i} + 12\mathbf{j}$

53. $\langle 22, -7\rangle$

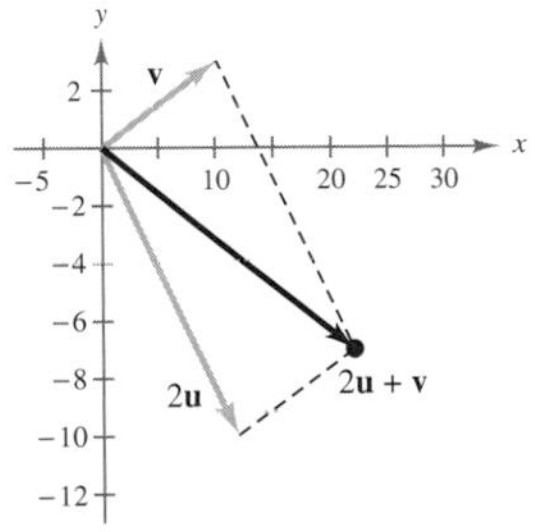

55. $\langle 30, 9\rangle$

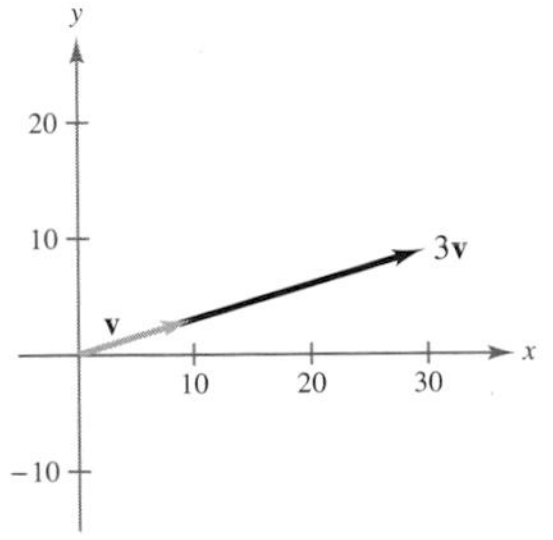

57. $-3\mathbf{i} + 4\mathbf{j}$ **59.** $6\mathbf{i} + 4\mathbf{j}$

61. $10\sqrt{2}(\cos 135°\mathbf{i} + \sin 135°\mathbf{j})$

63. $\|\mathbf{v}\| = 7$; $\theta = 60°$ **65.** $\|\mathbf{v}\| = \sqrt{41}$; $\theta = 38.7°$

67. $\|\mathbf{v}\| = 3\sqrt{2}$; $\theta = 225°$

69. The resultant force is 133.92 pounds and 5.6° from the 85-pound force.

71. 422.30 miles per hour; 130.4° **73.** 45

75. -2 **77.** 50; scalar **79.** $\langle 6, -8\rangle$; vector

81. $\frac{11\pi}{12}$ **83.** 160.5°

85. Orthogonal **87.** Neither

89. $-\frac{13}{17}\langle 4, 1\rangle, \frac{16}{17}\langle -1, 4\rangle$ **91.** $\frac{5}{2}\langle -1, 1\rangle, \frac{9}{2}\langle 1, 1\rangle$

93. 48 **95.** 72,000 foot-pounds

97.

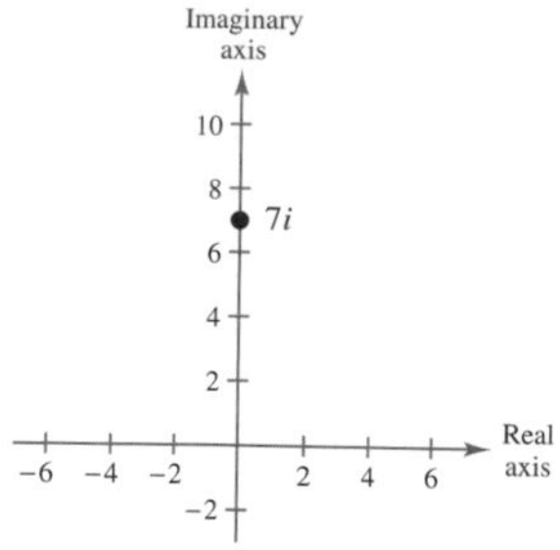

7

99.

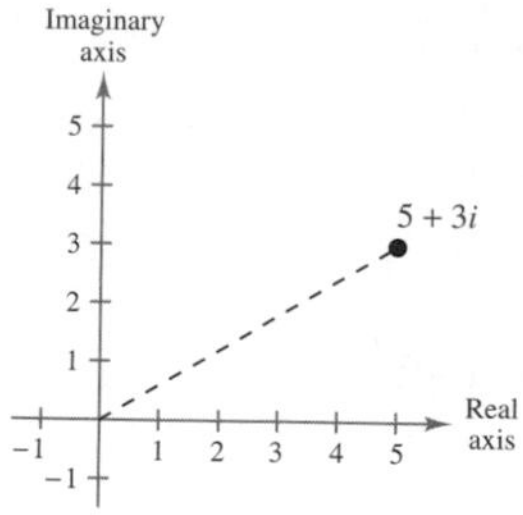

$\sqrt{34}$

101. $5\sqrt{2}\left(\cos\frac{7\pi}{4} + i\sin\frac{7\pi}{4}\right)$

103. $6\left(\cos\frac{5\pi}{6} + i\sin\frac{5\pi}{6}\right)$

105. (a) $z_1 = 4\left(\cos\frac{11\pi}{6} + i\sin\frac{11\pi}{6}\right)$

$z_2 = 10\left(\cos\frac{3\pi}{2} + i\sin\frac{3\pi}{2}\right)$

(b) $z_1 z_2 = 40\left(\cos\frac{10\pi}{3} + i\sin\frac{10\pi}{3}\right)$

$\frac{z_1}{z_2} = \frac{2}{5}\left(\cos\frac{\pi}{3} + i\sin\frac{\pi}{3}\right)$

107. $\frac{625}{2} + \frac{625\sqrt{3}}{2}i$ **109.** $2035 - 828i$

111. (a) $3\left(\cos\frac{\pi}{4} + i\sin\frac{\pi}{4}\right)$

$3\left(\cos\frac{7\pi}{12} + i\sin\frac{7\pi}{12}\right)$

$3\left(\cos\frac{11\pi}{12} + i\sin\frac{11\pi}{12}\right)$

$3\left(\cos\frac{5\pi}{4} + i\sin\frac{5\pi}{4}\right)$

$3\left(\cos\frac{19\pi}{12} + i\sin\frac{19\pi}{12}\right)$

$3\left(\cos\frac{23\pi}{12} + i\sin\frac{23\pi}{12}\right)$

(b)

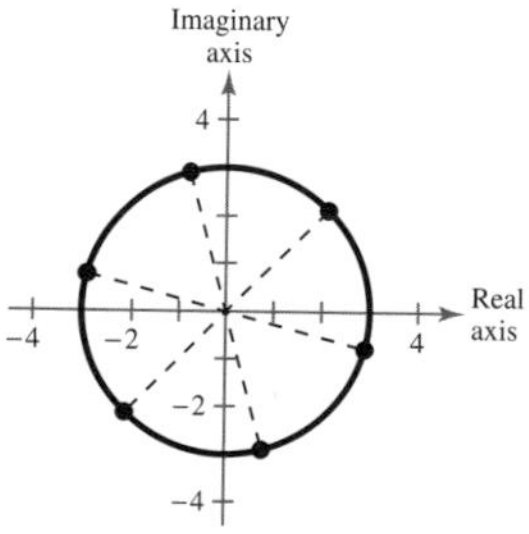

(c) $\frac{3\sqrt{2}}{2} + \frac{3\sqrt{2}}{2}i$, $-0.7765 + 2.898i$, $-2.898 + 0.7765i$, $-\frac{3\sqrt{2}}{2} - \frac{3\sqrt{2}}{2}i$, $0.7765 - 2.898i$, $2.898 - 0.7765i$

113. (a) $2(\cos 0 + i\sin 0)$

$2\left(\cos\frac{2\pi}{3} + i\sin\frac{2\pi}{3}\right)$

$2\left(\cos\frac{4\pi}{3} + i\sin\frac{4\pi}{3}\right)$

(b)

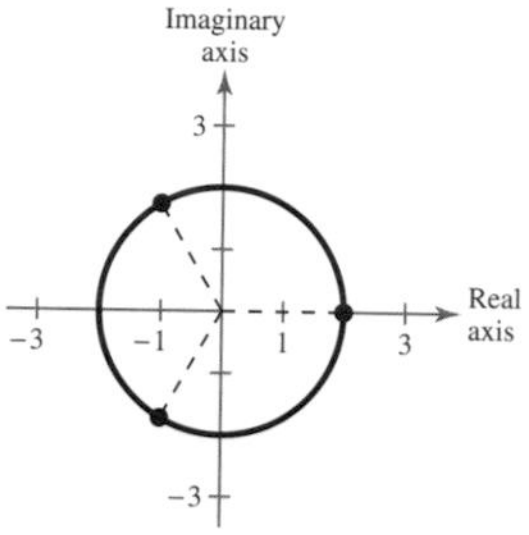

(c) $2, -1 + \sqrt{3}i, -1 - \sqrt{3}i$

115. $3\left(\cos\frac{\pi}{4} + i\sin\frac{\pi}{4}\right) = \frac{3\sqrt{2}}{2} + \frac{3\sqrt{2}}{2}i$

$3\left(\cos\frac{3\pi}{4} + i\sin\frac{3\pi}{4}\right) = -\frac{3\sqrt{2}}{2} + \frac{3\sqrt{2}}{2}i$

$3\left(\cos\frac{5\pi}{4} + i\sin\frac{5\pi}{4}\right) = -\frac{3\sqrt{2}}{2} - \frac{3\sqrt{2}}{2}i$

$3\left(\cos\frac{7\pi}{4} + i\sin\frac{7\pi}{4}\right) = \frac{3\sqrt{2}}{2} - \frac{3\sqrt{2}}{2}i$

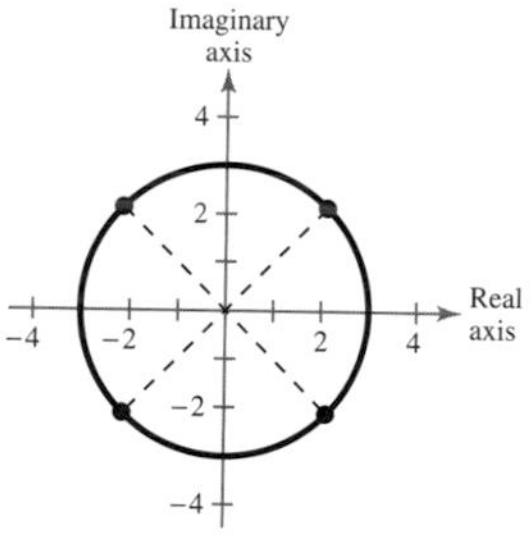

117. $2\left(\cos\frac{\pi}{2} + i\sin\frac{\pi}{2}\right) = 2i$

$2\left(\cos\frac{7\pi}{6} + i\sin\frac{7\pi}{6}\right) = -\sqrt{3} - i$

$2\left(\cos\frac{11\pi}{6} + i\sin\frac{11\pi}{6}\right) = \sqrt{3} - i$

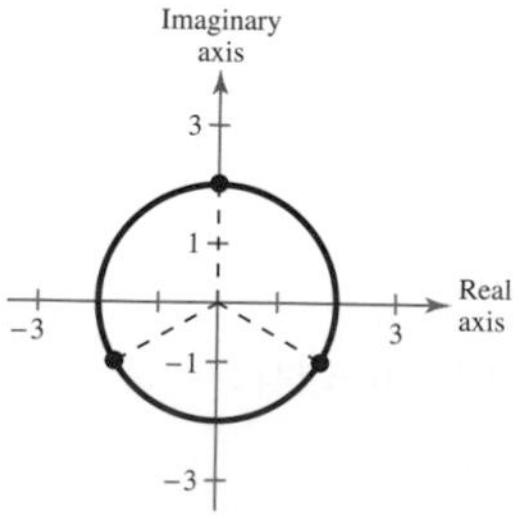

119. True. sin 90° is defined in the Law of Sines.

121. True. By definition, $\mathbf{u} = \dfrac{\mathbf{v}}{\|\mathbf{v}\|}$, so $\mathbf{v} = \|\mathbf{v}\|\mathbf{u}$.

123. False. The solutions to $x^2 - 8i = 0$ are $x = 2 + 2i$ and $x = -2 - 2i$.

125. $a^2 = b^2 + c^2 - 2bc \cos A$, $b^2 = a^2 + c^2 - 2ac \cos B$, $c^2 = a^2 + b^2 - 2ab \cos C$

127. **A** and **C**

129. If $k > 0$, the direction is the same and the magnitude is k times as great.
If $k < 0$, the result is a vector in the opposite direction and the magnitude is $|k|$ times as great.

131. (a) $4(\cos 60° + i \sin 60°)$
$4(\cos 180° + i \sin 180°)$
$4(\cos 300° + i \sin 300°)$
(b) -64

133. $z_1z_2 = -4$; $\dfrac{z_1}{z_2} = \cos(2\theta - \pi) + i\sin(2\theta - \pi)$
$= -\cos 2\theta - i \sin 2\theta$

Chapter Test *(page 486)*

1. $C = 88°$, $b \approx 27.81$, $c \approx 29.98$

2. $A = 43°$, $b \approx 25.75$, $c \approx 14.45$

3. Two solutions:
$B \approx 29.12°$, $C \approx 126.88°$, $c \approx 22.03$
$B \approx 150.88°$, $C \approx 5.12°$, $c \approx 2.46$

4. No solution **5.** $A \approx 39.96°$, $C \approx 40.04°$, $c \approx 15.02$

6. $A \approx 23.43°$, $B \approx 33.57°$, $c \approx 86.46$

7. 2052.5 square meters **8.** 606.3 miles; 29.1°

9. $\langle 14, -23 \rangle$ **10.** $\left\langle \dfrac{18\sqrt{34}}{17}, -\dfrac{30\sqrt{34}}{17} \right\rangle$

11. $\langle -4, 6 \rangle$

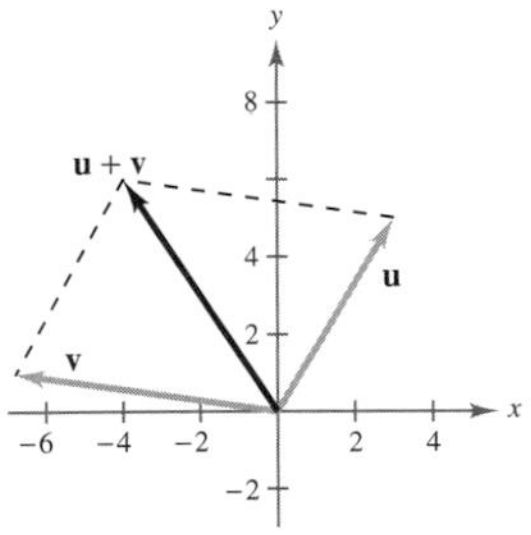

12. $\langle 10, 4 \rangle$

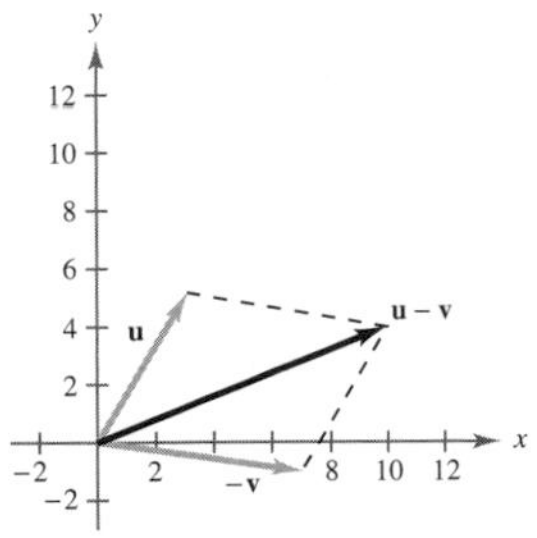

13. $\langle 36, 22 \rangle$

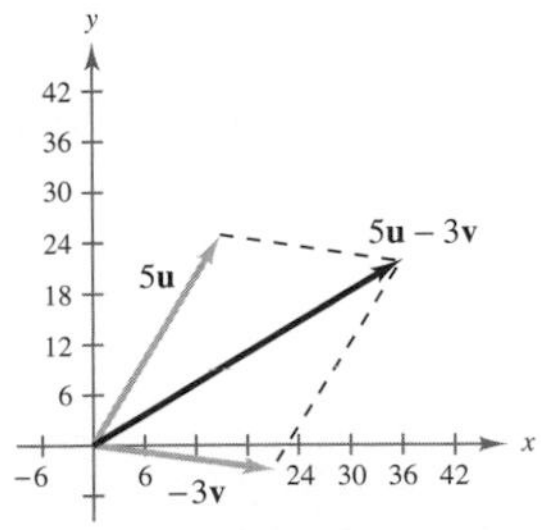

14. $\left\langle \frac{4}{5}, -\frac{3}{5} \right\rangle$

15. 14.9°; 250.15 pounds **16.** 135° **17.** No

18. $\frac{37}{26}\langle 5, 1 \rangle$; $\frac{29}{26}\langle -1, 5 \rangle$ **19.** ≈ 104 pounds

20. $5\sqrt{2}\left(\cos \dfrac{7\pi}{4} + i \sin \dfrac{7\pi}{4}\right)$ **21.** $-3 + 3\sqrt{3}i$

22. $-\dfrac{6561}{2} - \dfrac{6561\sqrt{3}}{2}i$ **23.** $5832i$

24. $4\sqrt[4]{2}\left(\cos \dfrac{\pi}{12} + i \sin \dfrac{\pi}{12}\right)$
$4\sqrt[4]{2}\left(\cos \dfrac{7\pi}{12} + i \sin \dfrac{7\pi}{12}\right)$
$4\sqrt[4]{2}\left(\cos \dfrac{13\pi}{12} + i \sin \dfrac{13\pi}{12}\right)$
$4\sqrt[4]{2}\left(\cos \dfrac{19\pi}{12} + i \sin \dfrac{19\pi}{12}\right)$

25. $3\left(\cos \dfrac{\pi}{6} + i \sin \dfrac{\pi}{6}\right)$
$3\left(\cos \dfrac{5\pi}{6} + i \sin \dfrac{5\pi}{6}\right)$
$3\left(\cos \dfrac{3\pi}{2} + i \sin \dfrac{3\pi}{2}\right)$

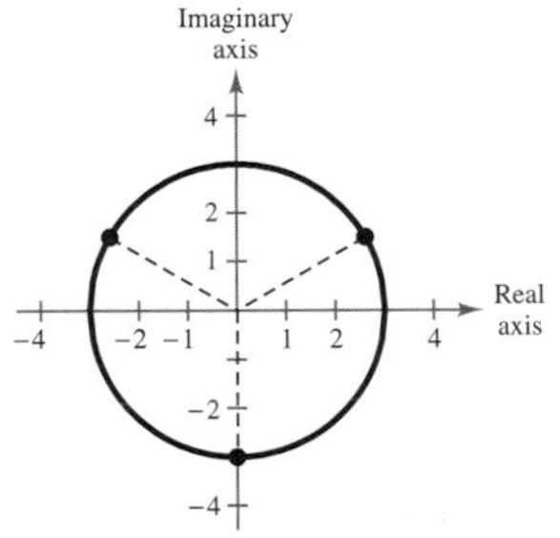

Cumulative Test for Chapters 4–6 *(page 487)*

1. (a)

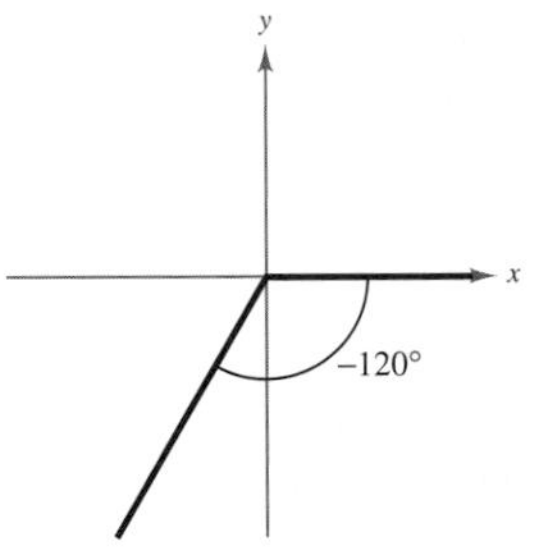

(b) 240°
(c) $-\dfrac{2\pi}{3}$
(d) 60°

(e) $\sin(-120°) = -\dfrac{\sqrt{3}}{2}$ $\csc(-120°) = -\dfrac{2\sqrt{3}}{3}$
$\cos(-120°) = -\dfrac{1}{2}$ $\sec(-120°) = -2$
$\tan(-120°) = \sqrt{3}$ $\cot(-120°) = \dfrac{\sqrt{3}}{3}$

2. 134.6° **3.** $\frac{3}{5}$

CHAPTER 6

4.

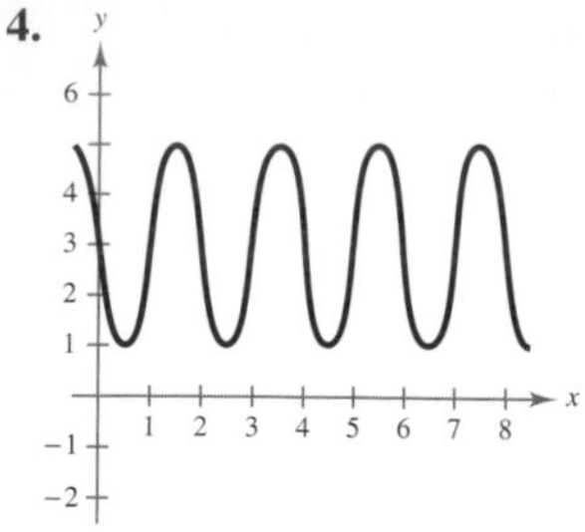

5.

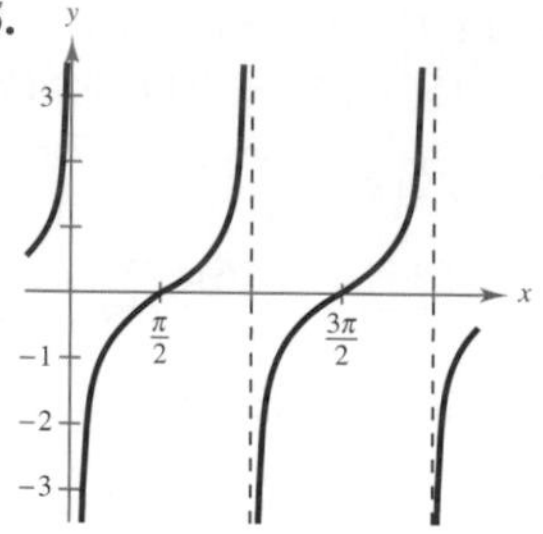

6.

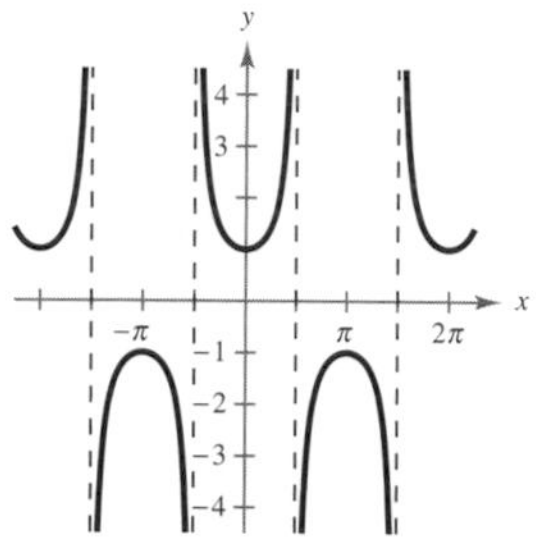

7. $a = -3, b = \pi, c = 0$

8.

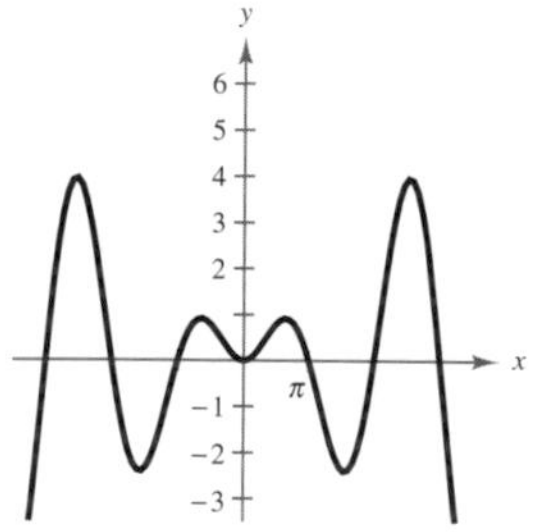

9. 6.7 **10.** $\frac{3}{4}$

11. $\sqrt{1 - 4x^2}$ **12.** 1 **13.** $2 \tan \theta$

14–16. Answers will vary. **17.** $\frac{\pi}{3}, \frac{\pi}{2}, \frac{3\pi}{2}, \frac{5\pi}{3}$

18. $\frac{\pi}{6}, \frac{5\pi}{6}, \frac{7\pi}{6}, \frac{11\pi}{6}$ **19.** $\frac{3\pi}{2}$ **20.** $\frac{16}{63}$ **21.** $\frac{4}{3}$

22. $\frac{\sqrt{5}}{5}, \frac{2\sqrt{5}}{5}$ **23.** $\frac{5}{2}\left(\sin \frac{5\pi}{2} - \sin \pi\right)$

24. $2 \cos 6x \cos 2x$

25. $B \approx 26.39°, C \approx 123.61°, c \approx 15.0$

26. $B \approx 52.48°, C \approx 97.52°, a \approx 5.04$

27. $B = 60°, a \approx 5.77, c \approx 11.55$

28. $A = 26.38°, B \approx 62.72°, C \approx 90.90°$

29. 36.4 square inches **30.** 85.2 square inches

31. $3\mathbf{i} + 5\mathbf{j}$ **32.** $\left\langle \frac{\sqrt{2}}{2}, \frac{\sqrt{2}}{2} \right\rangle$ **33.** -5

34. $-\frac{1}{13}\langle 1, 5 \rangle; \frac{21}{13}\langle 5, -1 \rangle$

35. $2\sqrt{2}\left(\cos \frac{3\pi}{4} + i \sin \frac{3\pi}{4}\right)$ **36.** $-12\sqrt{3} + 12i$

37. $\cos 0 + i \sin 0 = 1$

$\cos \frac{2\pi}{3} + i \sin \frac{2\pi}{3} = -\frac{1}{2} + \frac{\sqrt{3}}{2}i$

$\cos \frac{4\pi}{3} + i \sin \frac{4\pi}{3} = -\frac{1}{2} - \frac{\sqrt{3}}{2}i$

38. $3\left(\cos \frac{\pi}{5} + i \sin \frac{\pi}{5}\right)$

$3\left(\cos \frac{3\pi}{5} + i \sin \frac{3\pi}{5}\right)$

$3(\cos \pi + i \sin \pi)$

$3\left(\cos \frac{7\pi}{5} + i \sin \frac{7\pi}{5}\right)$

$3\left(\cos \frac{9\pi}{5} + i \sin \frac{9\pi}{5}\right)$

39. $\approx$ 395.8 radians per minute; $\approx$ 8312.6 inches per minute

40. Area = 63.67 square yards **41.** 5 feet **42.** 22.6°

43. $d = 4 \cos \frac{\pi}{4}t$ **44.** 32.6°; 543.9 kilometers per hour

45. 425 foot-pounds

Problem Solving *(page 493)*

1. 2.01 feet

3. (a)

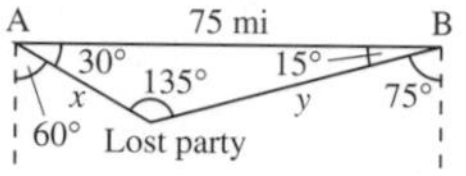

(b) Station A: 27.45 miles; Station B: 53.03 miles

(c) 11.03 miles; S 21.7° E

5. (a) (i) $\sqrt{2}$ (ii) $\sqrt{5}$ (iii) 1
(iv) 1 (v) 1 (vi) 1

(b) (i) 1 (ii) $3\sqrt{2}$ (iii) $\sqrt{13}$
(iv) 1 (v) 1 (vi) 1

(c) (i) $\frac{\sqrt{5}}{2}$ (ii) $\sqrt{13}$ (iii) $\frac{\sqrt{85}}{2}$
(iv) 1 (v) 1 (vi) 1

(d) (i) $2\sqrt{5}$ (ii) $5\sqrt{2}$ (iii) $5\sqrt{2}$
(iv) 1 (v) 1 (vi) 1r

7. $\mathbf{w} = \frac{1}{2}(\mathbf{u} + \mathbf{v}); \mathbf{w} = \frac{1}{2}(\mathbf{v} - \mathbf{u})$

9. (a)

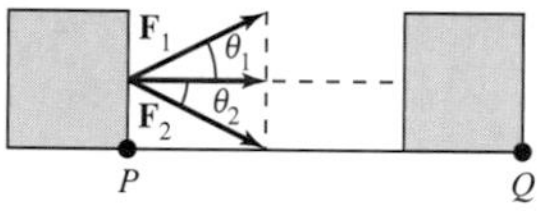

The amount of work done by $\mathbf{F}_1$ is equal to the amount of work done by $\mathbf{F}_2$.

(b)

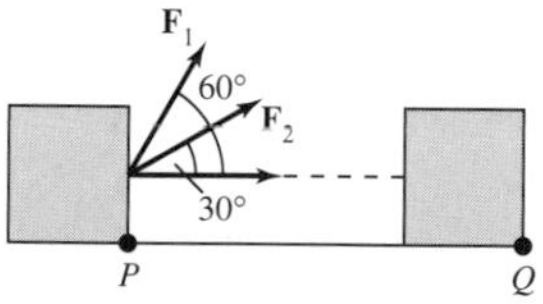

The amount of work done by $\mathbf{F}_2$ is $\sqrt{3}$ times as great as the amount of work done by $\mathbf{F}_1$.

Chapter 7

Section 7.1 *(page 503)*

Vocabulary Check *(page 503)*

1. system of equations **2.** solution
3. solving **4.** substitution
5. point of intersection **6.** break-even

1. (a) No (b) No (c) No (d) Yes
3. (a) No (b) Yes (c) No (d) No
5. $(2, 2)$ **7.** $(2, 6), (-1, 3)$
9. $(0, -5), (4, 3)$ **11.** $(0, 0), (2, -4)$
13. $(0, 1), (1, -1), (3, 1)$ **15.** $(5, 5)$ **17.** $\left(\frac{1}{2}, 3\right)$
19. $(1, 1)$ **21.** $\left(\frac{20}{3}, \frac{40}{3}\right)$ **23.** No solution
25. $(-2, 4), (0, 0)$ **27.** No solution **29.** $(4, 3)$
31. $\left(\frac{5}{2}, \frac{3}{2}\right)$ **33.** $(2, 2), (4, 0)$ **35.** $(1, 4), (4, 7)$
37. $\left(4, -\frac{1}{2}\right)$ **39.** No solution **41.** $(4, 3), (-4, 3)$

43.

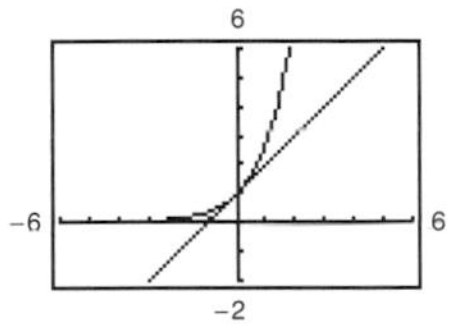

$(0, 1)$

45.

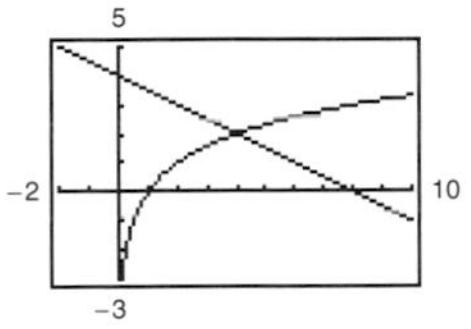

$(4, 2)$

47.

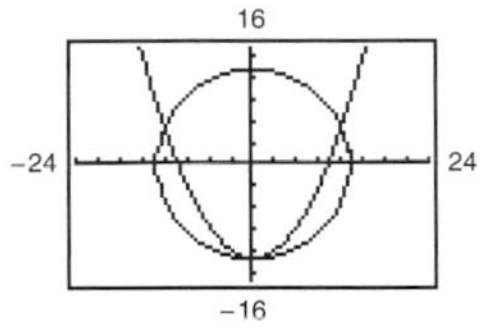

$(0, -13), (\pm 12, 5)$

49. $(1, 2)$ **51.** $(-2, 0), \left(\frac{29}{10}, \frac{21}{10}\right)$ **53.** No solution
55. $(0.287, 1.751)$ **57.** $(-1, 0), (0, 1), (1, 0)$
59. $\left(\frac{1}{2}, 2\right), \left(-4, -\frac{1}{4}\right)$ **61.** 192 units
63. (a) 781 units (b) 3708 units
65. (a) 8 weeks
(b)

	1	2	3	4
$360 - 24x$	336	312	228	264
$24 + 18x$	42	60	78	96

	5	6	7	8
$360 - 24x$	240	216	192	168
$24 + 18x$	114	132	150	168

67. More than \$11,666.67

69. (a) $\begin{cases} x + y = 25{,}000 \\ 0.06x + 0.085y = 2{,}000 \end{cases}$
(b)

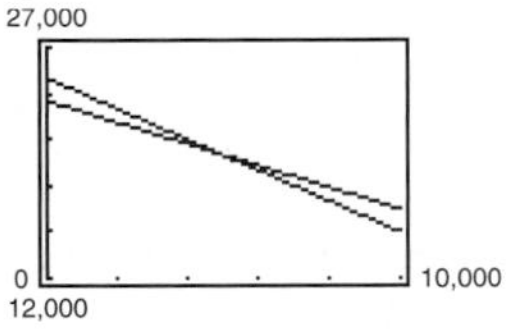

Decreases; Interest is fixed.
(c) \$5000

71. (a) Solar: $0.1429t^2 - 4.46t + 96.8$
Wind: $16.371t - 102.7$
(b)

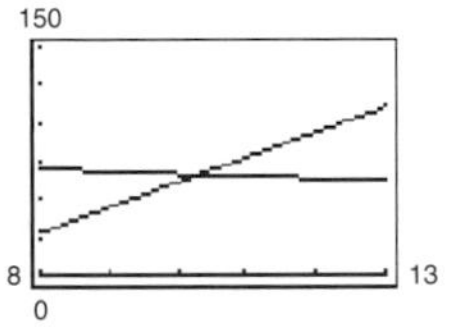

(c) Point of intersection: $(10.3, 66.01)$. Consumption of solar and wind energy are equal at this point in time in the year 2000.
(d) $t = 10.3, 135.47$
(e) The results are the same, but due to the given parameters, $t = 135.47$ is not of significance.
(f) Answers will vary.

73. 6 meters × 9 meters **75.** 9 inches × 12 inches
77. 8 kilometers × 12 kilometers
79. False. To solve a system of equations by substitution, you can solve for either variable in one of the two equations and then back-substitute.
81. 1. *Solve* one of the equations for one variable in terms of the other.
2. *Substitute* the expression found in Step 1 into the other equation to obtain an equation in one variable.
3. *Solve* the equation obtained in Step 2.
4. *Back-substitute* the value obtained in Step 3 into the expression obtained in Step 1 to find the value of the other variable.
5. *Check* that the solution satisfies *each* of the original equations.

83. (a) $y = 2x$ (b) $y = 0$ (c) $y = x - 2$
85. $2x + 7y - 45 = 0$ **87.** $y - 3 = 0$
89. $30x - 17y - 18 = 0$
91. Domain: All real numbers x except $x = 6$
Horizontal asymptote: $y = 0$
Vertical asymptote: $x = 6$
93. Domain: All real numbers x except $x = \pm 4$
Horizontal asymptote: $y = 1$
Vertical asymptotes: $x = \pm 4$

Section 7.2 *(page 515)*

Vocabulary Check *(page 515)*

1. elimination **2.** equivalent
3. consistent; inconsistent **4.** equilibrium point

1. (2, 1)

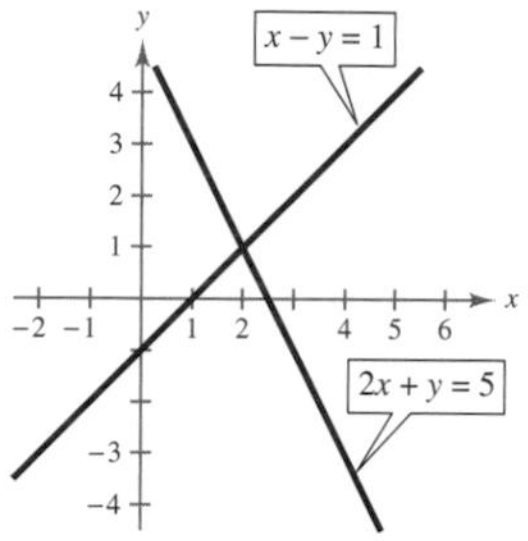

3. (1, −1)

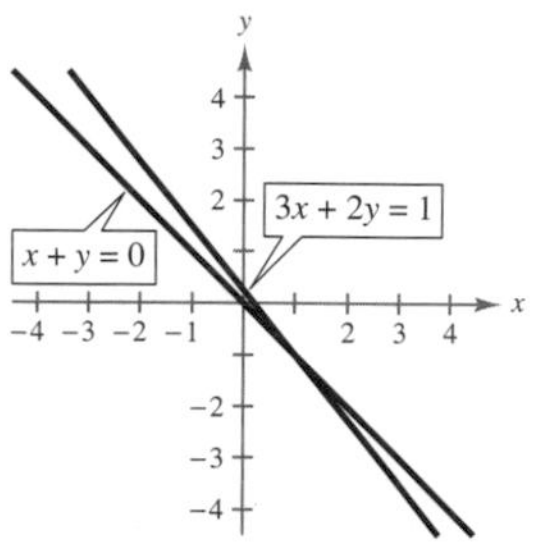

5. No solution

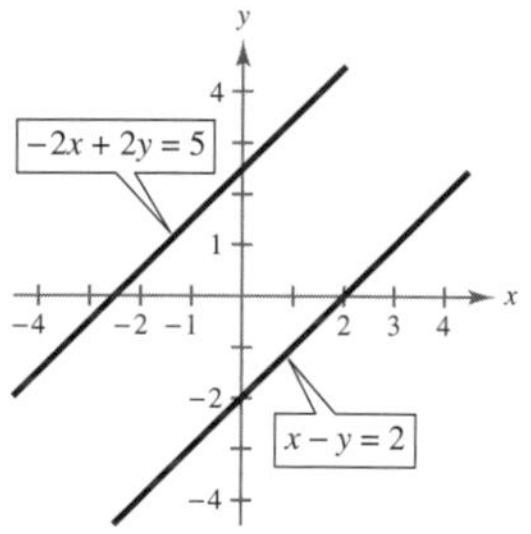

7. $\left(a, \frac{3}{2}a - \frac{5}{2}\right)$

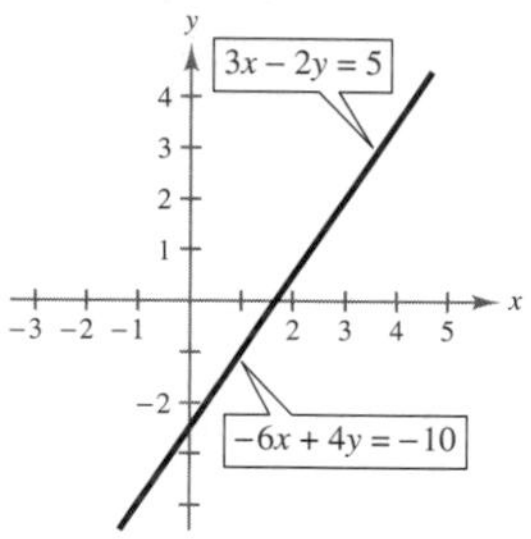

9. $\left(\frac{1}{3}, -\frac{2}{3}\right)$

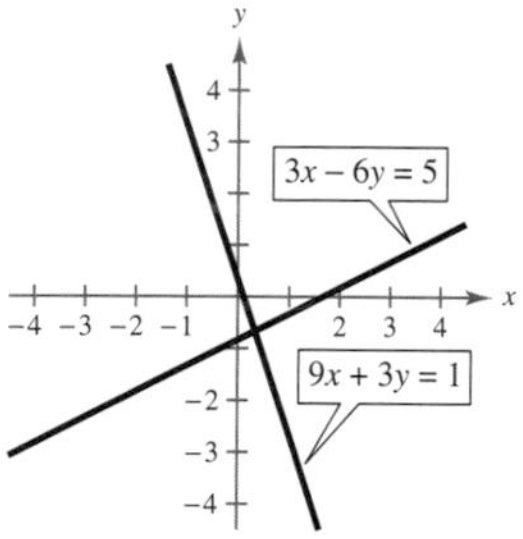

11. $\left(\frac{5}{2}, \frac{3}{4}\right)$ **13.** (3, 4) **15.** (4, −1) **17.** $\left(\frac{12}{7}, \frac{18}{7}\right)$
19. No solution **21.** $\left(\frac{18}{5}, \frac{3}{5}\right)$
23. Infinitely many solutions: $\left(a, -\frac{1}{2} + \frac{5}{6}a\right)$
25. $\left(\frac{90}{31}, -\frac{67}{31}\right)$ **27.** $\left(-\frac{6}{35}, \frac{43}{35}\right)$ **29.** (5, −2)
31. b; one solution; consistent
32. a; infinitely many solutions; consistent
33. c; one solution; consistent
34. d; no solutions; inconsistent
35. (4, 1) **37.** (2, −1) **39.** (6, −3) **41.** $\left(\frac{43}{6}, \frac{25}{6}\right)$
43. 550 miles per hour, 50 miles per hour
45. (80, 10) **47.** (2,000,000, 100)
49. Cheeseburger: 310 calories; fries: 230 calories
51. (a) $\begin{cases} x + y = 10 \\ 0.2x + 0.5y = 3 \end{cases}$
(b)

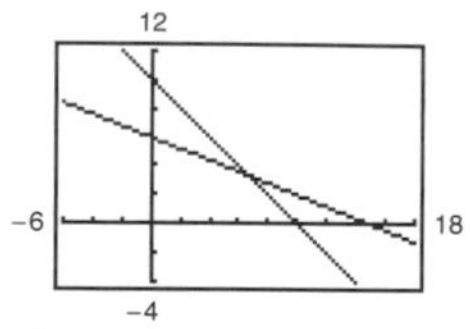

Decreases

(c) 20% solution: $6\frac{2}{3}$ liters
50% solution: $3\frac{1}{3}$ liters

53. $6000 **55.** 400 adult, 1035 student
57. $y = 0.97x + 2.1$ **59.** $y = 0.32x + 4.1$
61. $y = -2x + 4$
63. (a) $y = 14x + 19$ (b) 41.4 bushels per acre
65. False. Two lines that coincide have infinitely many points of intersection.
67. No. Two lines will intersect only once or will coincide, and if they coincide the system will have infinitely many solutions.
69. (39,600, 398). It is necessary to change the scale on the axes to see the point of intersection.
71. $k = -4$
73. $x \le -\frac{22}{3}$

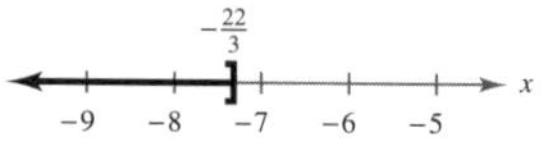

75. $x \le \frac{19}{16}$

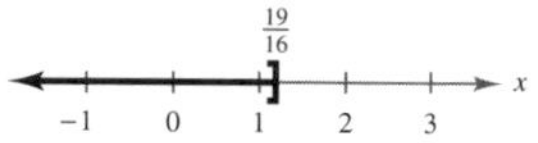

77. $-2 < x < 18$

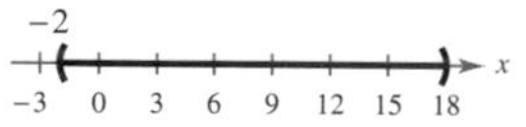

79. $-5 < x < \frac{7}{2}$

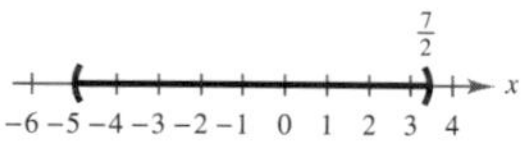

81. $\ln 6x$ **83.** $\log_9 \frac{12}{x}$ **85.** No solution
87. Answers will vary.

Section 7.3 *(page 527)*

Vocabulary Check *(page 527)*

1. row-echelon **2.** ordered triple
3. Gaussian **4.** row operation
5. nonsquare **6.** position

1. (a) No (b) No (c) No (d) Yes
3. (a) No (b) No (c) Yes (d) No
5. (1, −2, 4) **7.** (3, 10, 2) **9.** $\left(\frac{1}{2}, -2, 2\right)$
11. $\begin{cases} x - 2y + 3z = 5 \\ y - 2z = 9 \\ 2x - 3z = 0 \end{cases}$
First step in putting the system in row-echelon form
13. (1, 2, 3) **15.** (−4, 8, 5) **17.** (5, −2, 0)
19. No solution **21.** $\left(-\frac{1}{2}, 1, \frac{3}{2}\right)$
23. $(-3a + 10, 5a - 7, a)$ **25.** $(-a + 3, a + 1, a)$
27. $(2a, 21a - 2, 8a)$ **29.** $\left(-\frac{3}{2}a + \frac{1}{2}, -\frac{2}{3}a + 1, a\right)$

31. $(1, 1, 1, 1)$ **33.** No solution **35.** $(0, 0, 0)$

37. $(9a, -35a, 67a)$ **39.** $s = -16t^2 + 144$

41. $s = -16t^2 - 32t + 500$

43. $y = \frac{1}{2}x^2 - 2x$

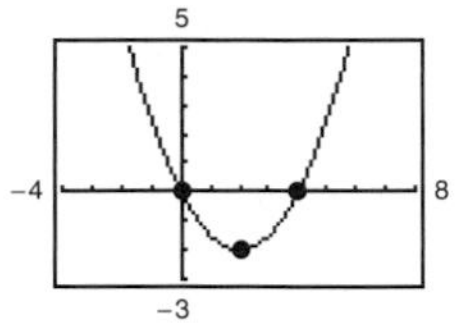

45. $y = x^2 - 6x + 8$

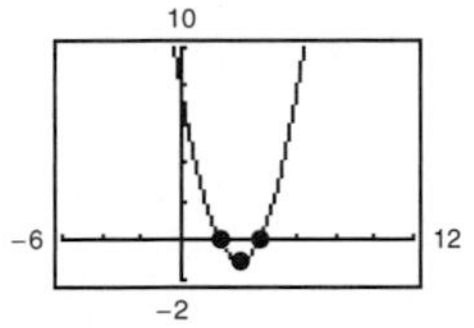

47. $x^2 + y^2 - 4x = 0$

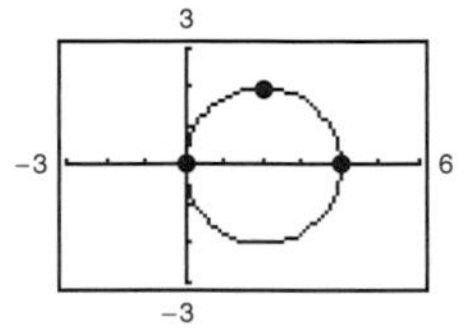

49. $x^2 + y^2 + 6x - 8y = 0$

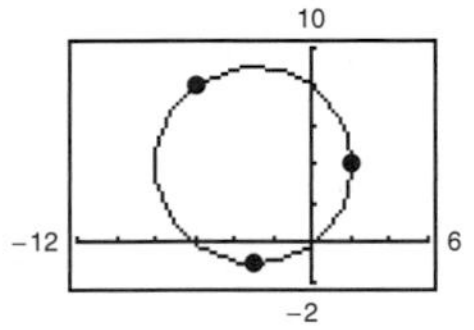

51. 6 touchdowns, 6 extra-point kicks, and 1 field goal

53. \$300,000 at 8%
\$400,000 at 9%
\$75,000 at 10%

55. $250{,}000 - \frac{1}{2}s$ in certificates of deposit
$125{,}000 + \frac{1}{2}s$ in municipal bonds
$125{,}000 - s$ in blue-chip stocks
s in growth stocks

57. Brand X = 4 lb
Brand Y = 9 lb
Brand Z = 9 lb

59. Vanilla = 2 lb
Hazelnut = 4 lb
French Roast = 4 lb

61. Television = 30 ads
Radio = 10 ads
Newspaper = 20 ads

63. (a) Not possible
(b) No gallons of 10%, 6 gallons of 15%, 6 gallons of 25%
(c) 4 gallons of 10%, No gallons of 15%, 8 gallons of 25%

65. $I_1 = 1, I_2 = 2, I_3 = 1$

67. $y = x^2 - x$ **69.** $y = -\frac{5}{24}x^2 - \frac{3}{10}x + \frac{41}{6}$

71. (a) $y = -0.0075x^2 + 1.3x + 20$
(b)

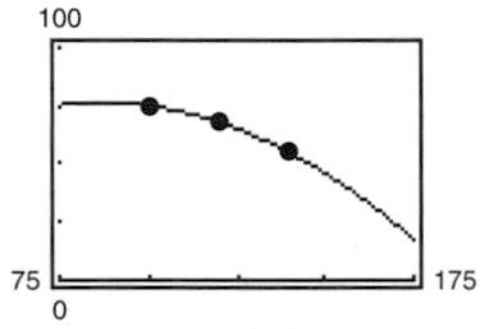

(c)

x	100	120	140
y	75	68	55

The values are the same.
(d) 24.25% (e) 156 females

73. Touchdowns = 8; Field goals = 2;
Two-point conversions = 1; Extra-point kicks = 5

75. $x = 5$
$y = 5$
$\lambda = -5$

77. $x = \pm\sqrt{2}/2$ or $x = 0$
$y = \frac{1}{2}$ $\quad y = 0$
$\lambda = 1$ $\quad \lambda = 0$

79. False. Equation 2 does not have a leading coefficient of 1.

81. No. Answers will vary.

83. $\begin{cases} 3x + y - z = 9 \\ x + 2y - z = 0 \\ -x + y + 3z = 1 \end{cases}$ $\begin{cases} x + y + z = 5 \\ x - 2z = 0 \\ 2y + z = 0 \end{cases}$

85. $\begin{cases} x + 2y - 4z = -5 \\ -x - 4y + 8z = 13 \\ x + 6y + 4z = 7 \end{cases}$ $\begin{cases} x + 2y + 4z = 9 \\ y + 2z = 3 \\ x - 4z = -4 \end{cases}$

87. 6.375 **89.** 80,000 **91.** $11 + i$

93. $22 + 3i$ **95.** $\frac{7}{2} + \frac{7}{2}i$

97. (a) $-4, 0, 3$
(b)

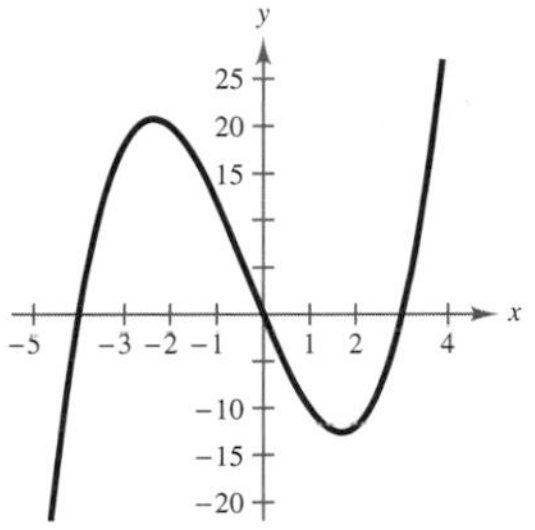

99. (a) $-4, -\frac{3}{2}, 3$
(b)

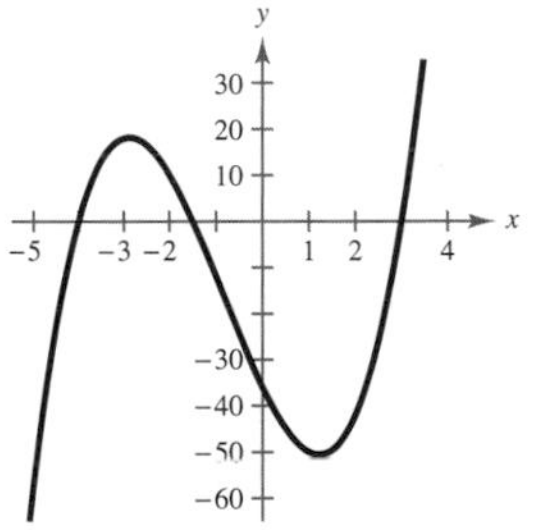

101.

x	-2	0	2	4	5
y	-5	-4.996	-4.938	-4	-1

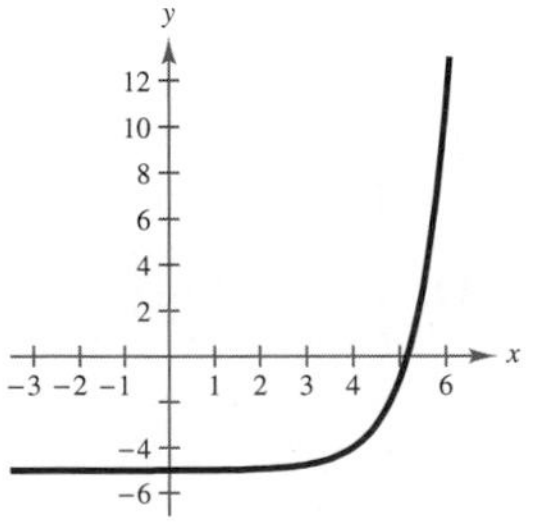

103.

x	-2	-1	0	1	2
y	5.793	4.671	4	3.598	3.358

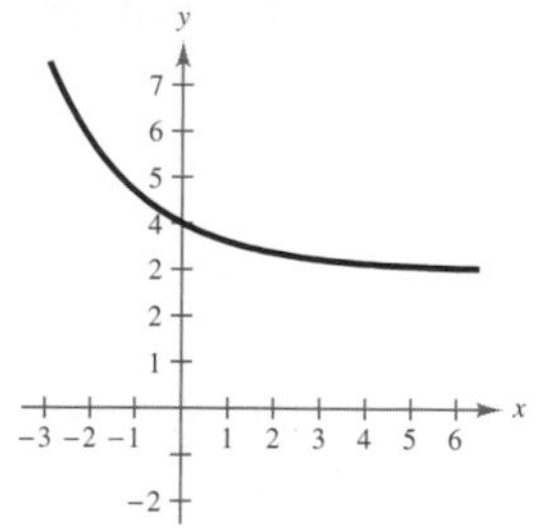

105. (40, 40) **107.** Answers will vary.

Section 7.4 *(page 539)*

Vocabulary Check *(page 539)*

1. partial fraction decomposition **2.** improper
3. linear; quadratic; irreducible **4.** basic equation

1. b **2.** c **3.** d **4.** a

5. $\frac{A}{x} + \frac{B}{x - 14}$ **7.** $\frac{A}{x} + \frac{B}{x^2} + \frac{C}{x - 10}$

9. $\frac{A}{x - 5} + \frac{B}{(x - 5)^2} + \frac{C}{(x - 5)^3}$ **11.** $\frac{A}{x} + \frac{Bx + C}{x^2 + 10}$

13. $\frac{A}{x} + \frac{Bx + C}{x^2 + 1} + \frac{Dx + E}{(x^2 + 1)^2}$ **15.** $\frac{1}{2}\left(\frac{1}{x - 1} - \frac{1}{x + 1}\right)$

17. $\frac{1}{x} - \frac{1}{x + 1}$ **19.** $\frac{1}{x} - \frac{2}{2x + 1}$

21. $\frac{1}{x - 1} - \frac{1}{x + 2}$ **23.** $-\frac{3}{x} - \frac{1}{x + 2} + \frac{5}{x - 2}$

25. $\frac{3}{x} - \frac{1}{x^2} + \frac{1}{x + 1}$ **27.** $\frac{3}{x - 3} + \frac{9}{(x - 3)^2}$

29. $-\frac{1}{x} + \frac{2x}{x^2 + 1}$ **31.** $-\frac{1}{x - 1} + \frac{x + 2}{x^2 - 2}$

33. $\frac{1}{6}\left(\frac{2}{x^2 + 2} - \frac{1}{x + 2} + \frac{1}{x - 2}\right)$

35. $\frac{1}{8}\left(\frac{1}{2x + 1} + \frac{1}{2x - 1} - \frac{4x}{4x^2 + 1}\right)$

37. $\frac{1}{x + 1} + \frac{2}{x^2 - 2x + 3}$ **39.** $1 - \frac{2x + 1}{x^2 + x + 1}$

41. $2x - 7 + \frac{17}{x + 2} + \frac{1}{x + 1}$

43. $x + 3 + \frac{6}{x - 1} + \frac{4}{(x - 1)^2} + \frac{1}{(x - 1)^3}$

45. $\frac{3}{2x - 1} - \frac{2}{x + 1}$ **47.** $\frac{2}{x} - \frac{1}{x^2} - \frac{2}{x + 1}$

49. $\frac{1}{x^2 + 2} + \frac{x}{(x^2 + 2)^2}$ **51.** $2x + \frac{1}{2}\left(\frac{3}{x - 4} - \frac{1}{x + 2}\right)$

53. (a) $\frac{3}{x} - \frac{2}{x - 4}$

$y = \frac{x - 12}{x(x - 4)}$

$y = \frac{3}{x}, y = -\frac{2}{x - 4}$

(b)

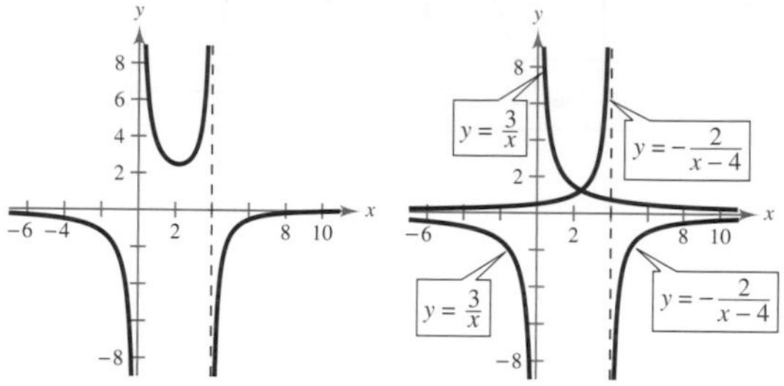

(c) The vertical asymptotes are the same.

55. (a) $\frac{3}{x - 3} + \frac{5}{x + 3}$

$y = \frac{2(4x - 3)}{x^2 - 9}$

$y = \frac{3}{x - 3}, y = \frac{5}{x + 3}$

(b)

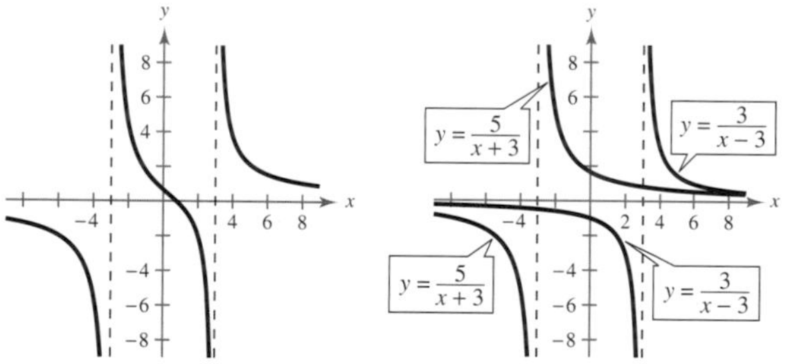

(c) The vertical asymptotes are the same.

57. (a) $\frac{2000}{7 - 4x} - \frac{2000}{11 - 7x}, \quad 0 < x \le 1$

(b) $\text{Ymax} = \left|\frac{2000}{7 - 4x}\right|$

$\text{Ymin} = \left|\frac{-2000}{11 - 7x}\right|$

(c)

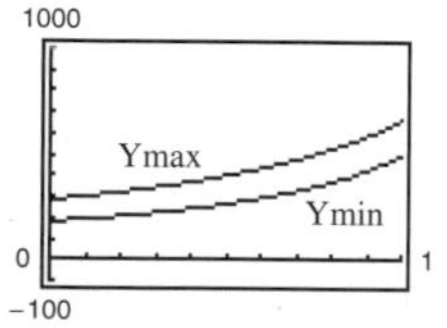

(d) Maximum: 400°F
Minimum: 266.7°F

59. False. The partial fraction decomposition is

$\frac{A}{x + 10} + \frac{B}{x - 10} + \frac{C}{(x - 10)^2}.$

61. $\frac{1}{2a}\left(\frac{1}{a + x} + \frac{1}{a - x}\right)$ **63.** $\frac{1}{a}\left(\frac{1}{y} + \frac{1}{a - y}\right)$

65.
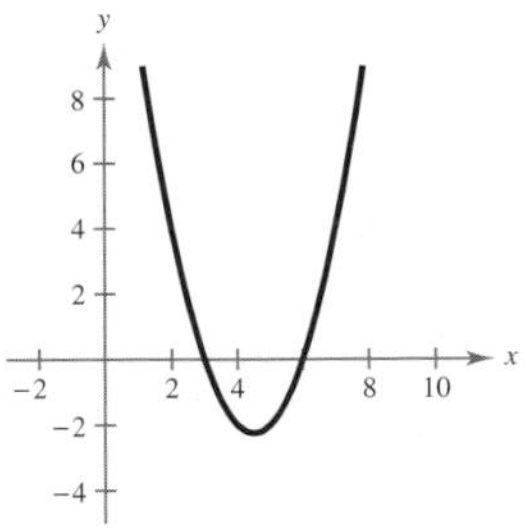

67.
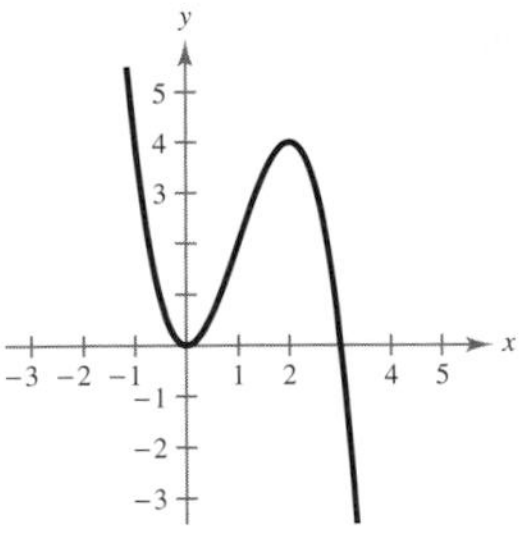

69.
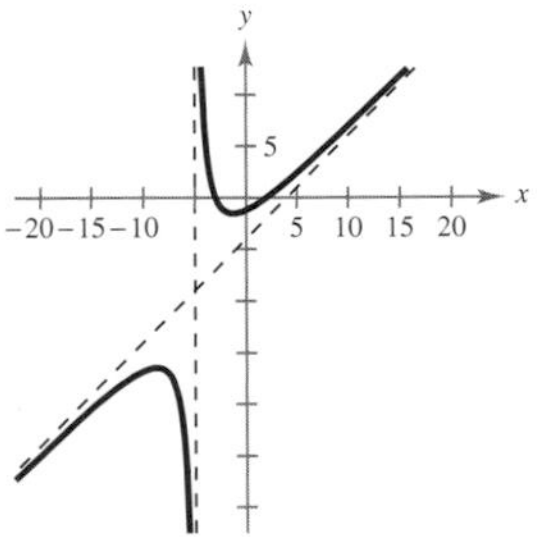

Section 7.5 *(page 548)*

Vocabulary Check *(page 548)*

1. solution **2.** graph **3.** linear
4. solution **5.** consumer surplus

1.
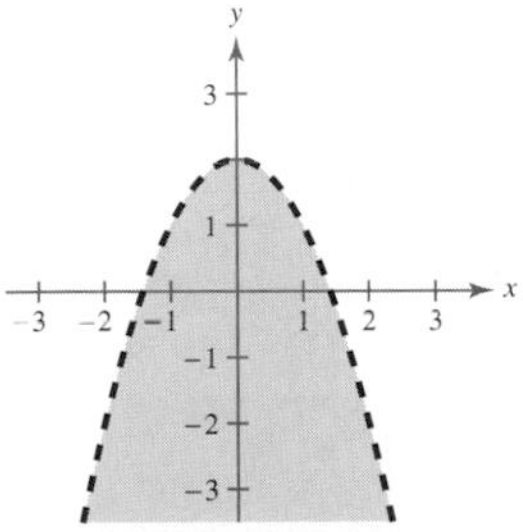

3.
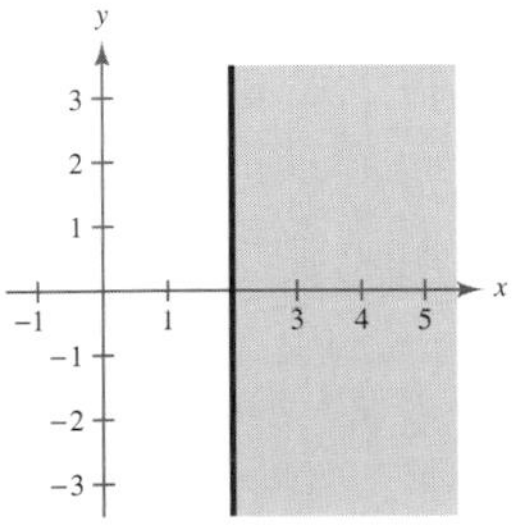

5.
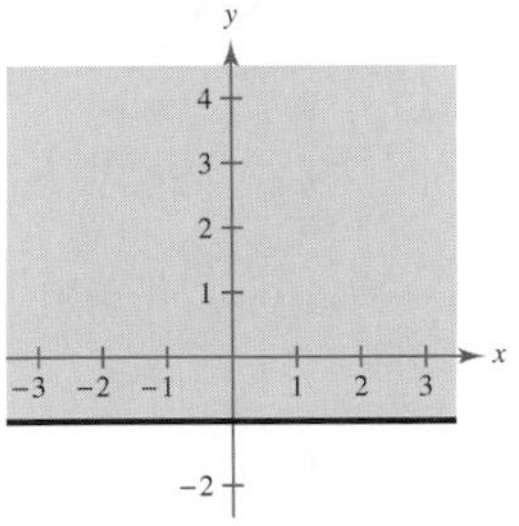

7.
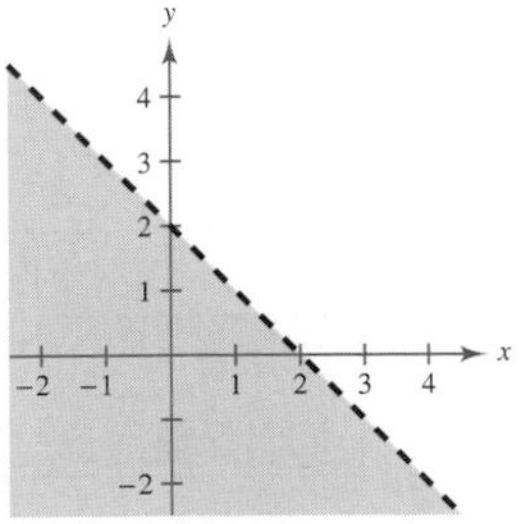

9.
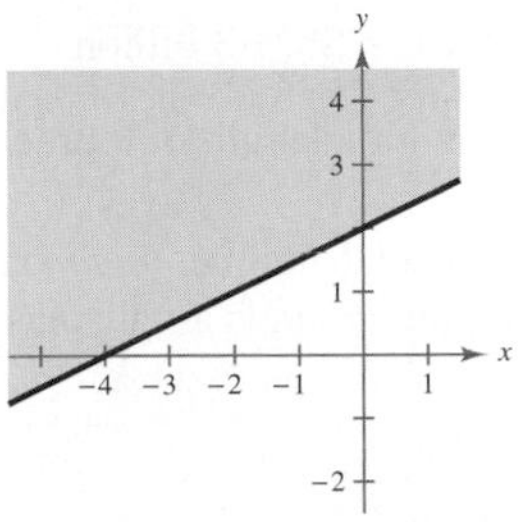

11.
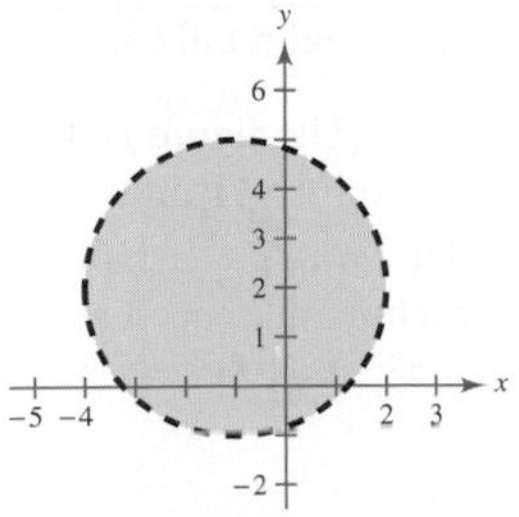

13.
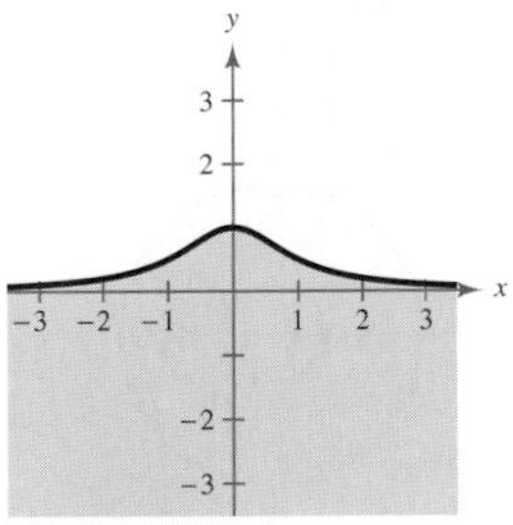

15.
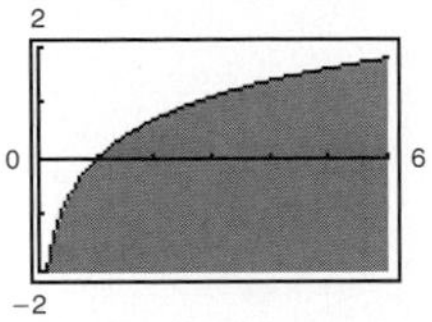

17.
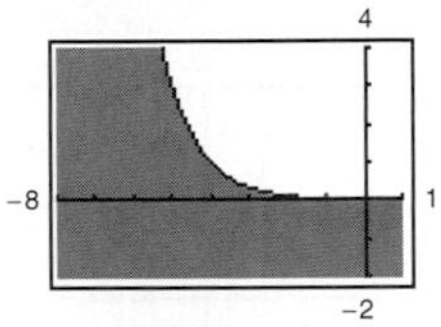

19.
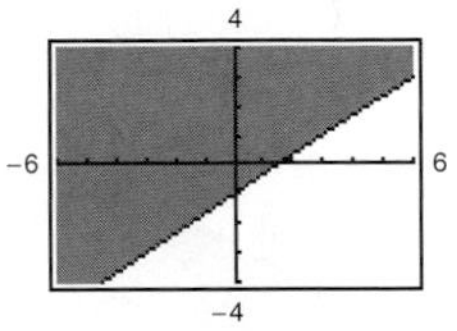

21.
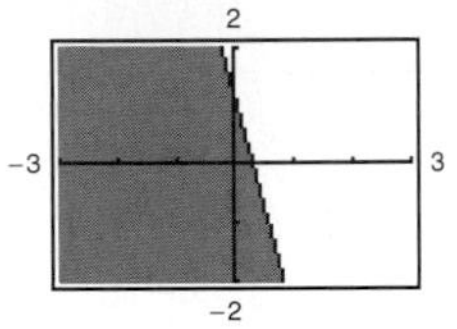

23.
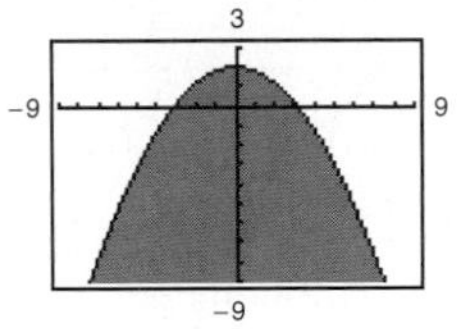

25.
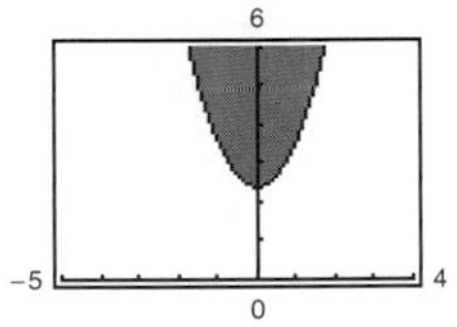

27. $y \le \frac{1}{2}x + 2$

29. $y \ge -\frac{2}{3}x + 2$

31. (a) No (b) No (c) Yes (d) Yes

33. (a) Yes (b) No (c) Yes (d) Yes

35.
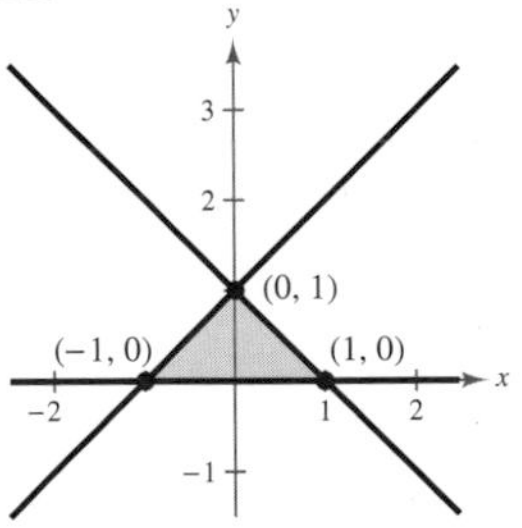

37.
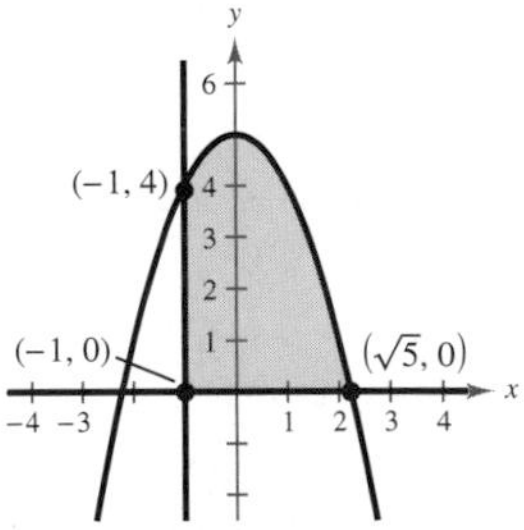

39.
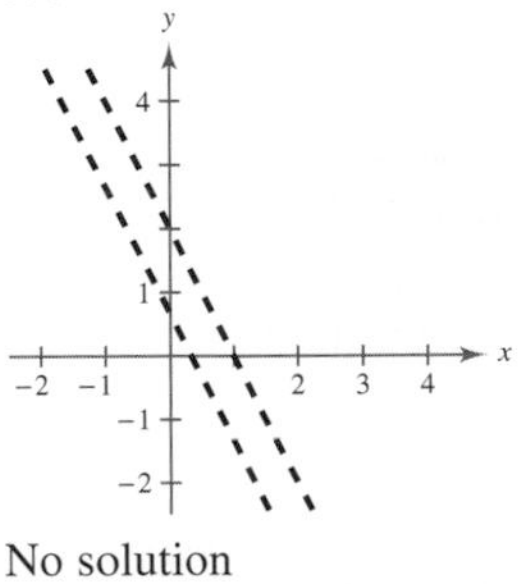

No solution

41.
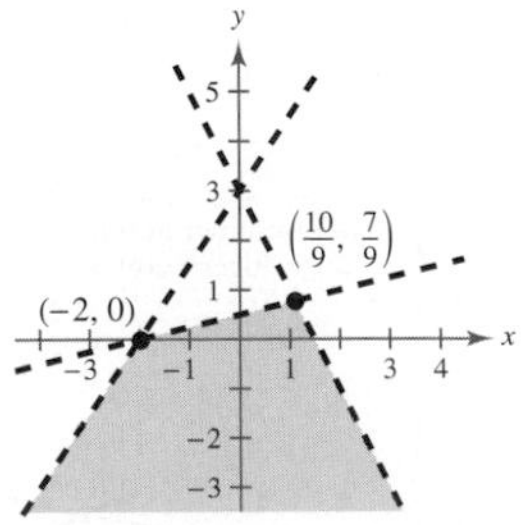

CHAPTER 7

43.

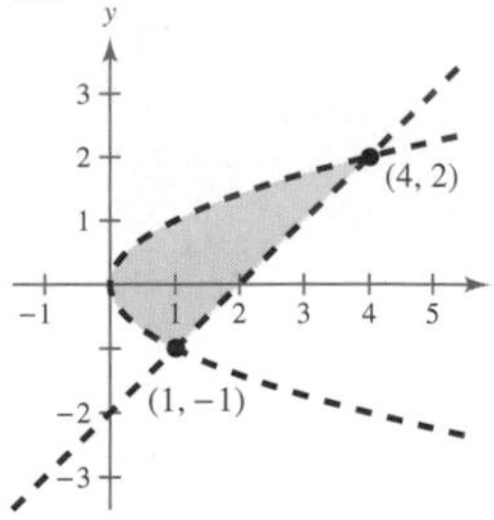

45.

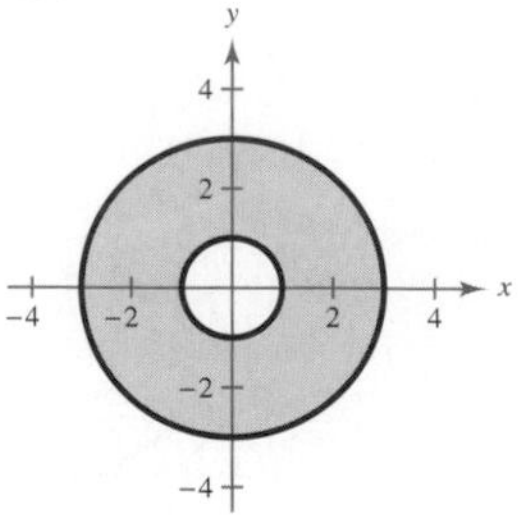

47.

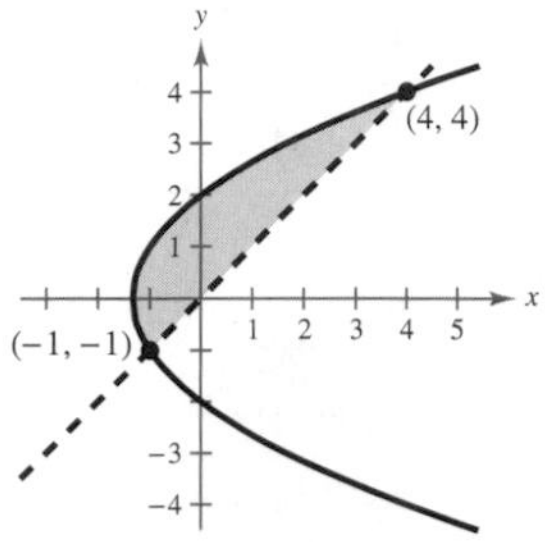

49.

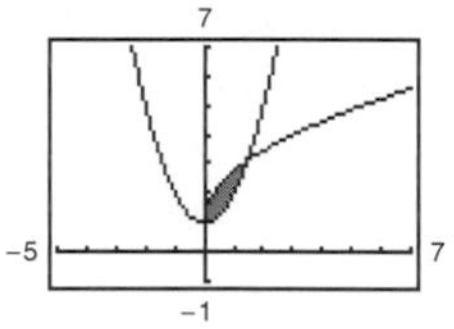

51.

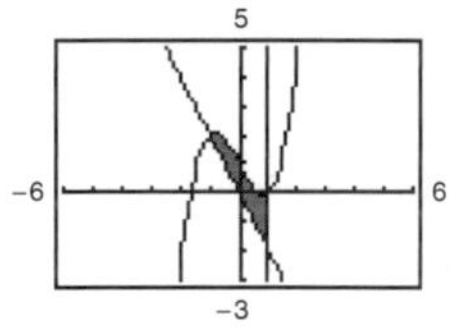

53.

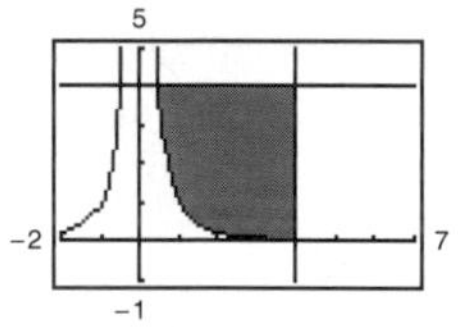

55. $\begin{cases} y \le 4 - x \\ x \ge 0 \\ y \ge 0 \end{cases}$ **57.** $\begin{cases} y \ge 4 - x \\ y \ge 2 - \frac{1}{4}x \\ x \ge 0,\ y \ge 0 \end{cases}$

59. $\begin{cases} x^2 + y^2 \le 16 \\ x \ge 0 \\ y \ge 0 \end{cases}$ **61.** $\begin{cases} 2 \le x \le 5 \\ 1 \le y \le 7 \end{cases}$ **63.** $\begin{cases} y \le \frac{3}{2}x \\ y \le -x + 5 \\ y \ge 0 \end{cases}$

65. (a)

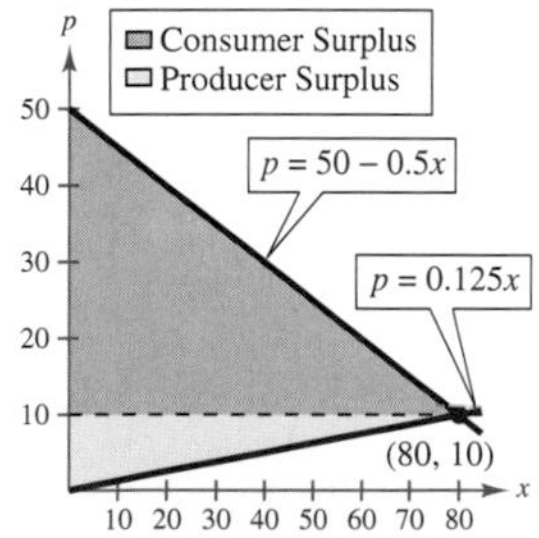

(b) Consumer surplus: \$1600
Producer surplus: \$400

67. (a)

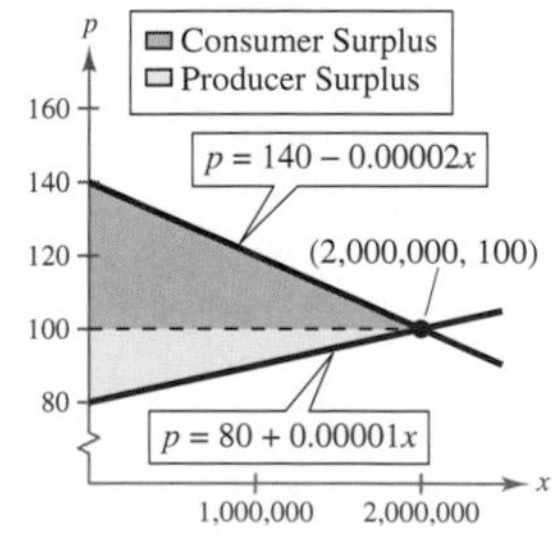

(b) Consumer surplus: \$40,000,000
Producer surplus: \$20,000,000

69. $\begin{cases} x + \frac{3}{2}y \le 12 \\ \frac{4}{3}x + \frac{3}{2}y \le 15 \\ x \ge 0 \\ y \ge 0 \end{cases}$

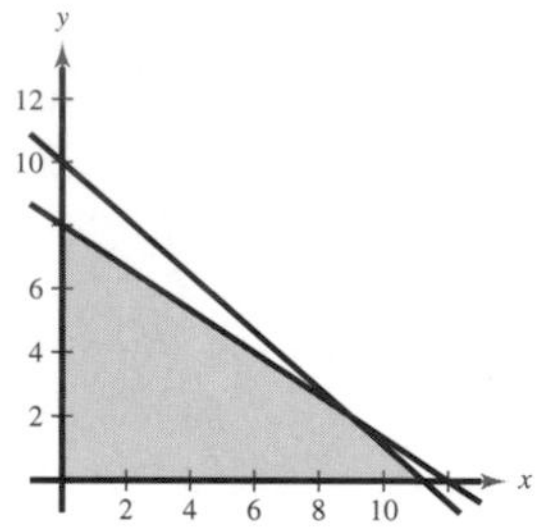

71. $\begin{cases} x + y \le 20{,}000 \\ y \ge 2x \\ x \ge 5{,}000 \\ y \ge 5{,}000 \end{cases}$

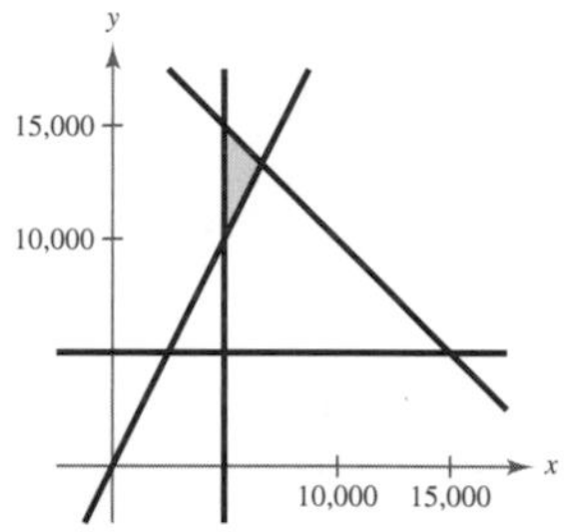

73. $\begin{cases} 55x + 70y \le 7500 \\ x \ge 50 \\ y \ge 40 \end{cases}$

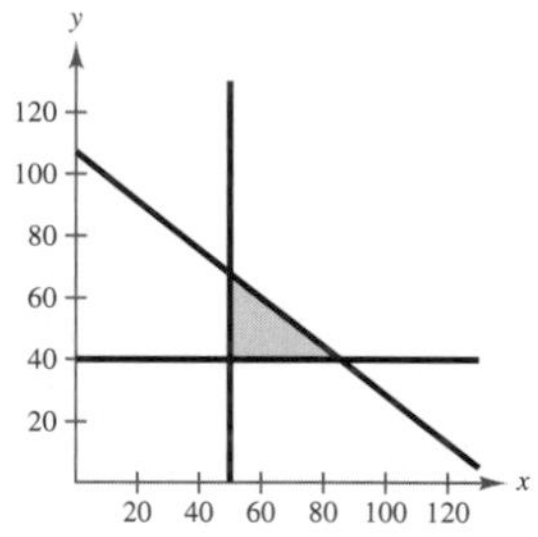

75. (a) $\begin{cases} 20x + 10y \ge 300 \\ 15x + 10y \ge 150 \\ 10x + 20y \ge 200 \\ x \ge 0 \\ y \ge 0 \end{cases}$ (b)

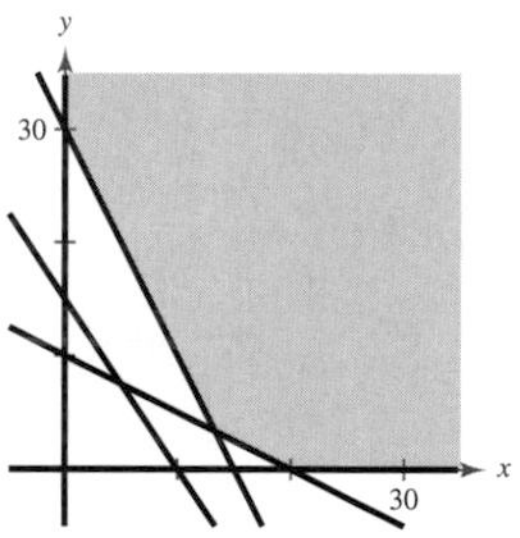

(c) Answers will vary.

77. (a) $y = 19.17t - 46.61$
(b)

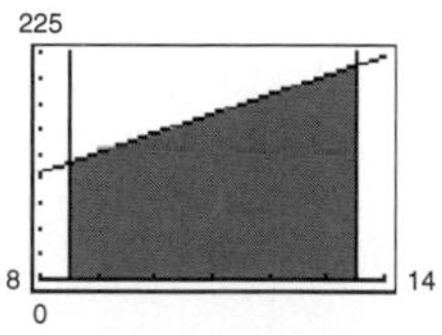

(c) Total retail sales $= \dfrac{h}{2}(a + b) = \$821.3$ billion

79. True. The figure is a rectangle with a length of 9 units and a width of 11 units.

81. The graph is a half-line on the real number line; on the rectangular coordinate system, the graph is a half-plane.

83. (a) $\begin{cases} \pi y^2 - \pi x^2 \geq 10 \\ y > x \\ x > 0 \end{cases}$ (b)

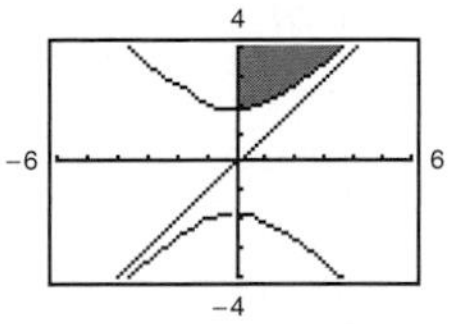

(c) The line is an asymptote to the boundary. The larger the circles, the closer the radii can be and the constraint will still be satisfied.

85. d **86.** b **87.** c **88.** a

89. $5x + 3y - 8 = 0$ **91.** $28x + 17y + 13 = 0$

93. $x + y + 1.8 = 0$

95. (a) $y_1 = 2.17t + 22.5$

$y_2 = -0.241t^2 + 7.23t - 3.4$

$y_3 = 27(1.05^t)$

(b)

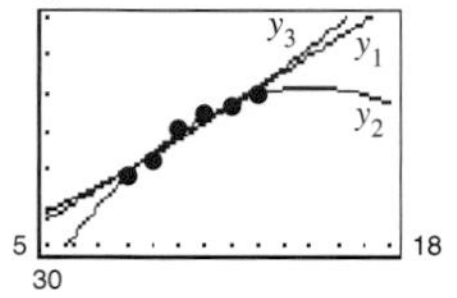

(c) The quadratic model is the best fit for the data.

(d) $48.66

Section 7.6 *(page 558)*

Vocabulary Check *(page 558)*

1. optimization **2.** linear programming

3. objective **4.** constraints; feasible solutions

5. vertex

1. Minimum at (0, 0): 0
Maximum at (5, 0): 20

3. Minimum at (0, 0): 0
Maximum at (0, 5): 40

5. Minimum at (0, 0): 0
Maximum at (3, 4): 17

7. Minimum at (0, 0): 0
Maximum at (4, 0): 20

9. Minimum at (0, 0): 0
Maximum at (60, 20): 740

11. Minimum at (0, 0): 0
Maximum at any point on the line segment connecting (60, 20) and (30, 45): 2100

13.

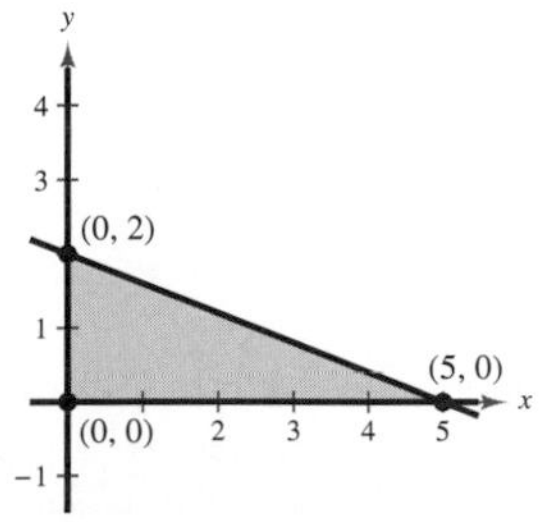

Minimum at (0, 0): 0
Maximum at (5, 0): 30

15.

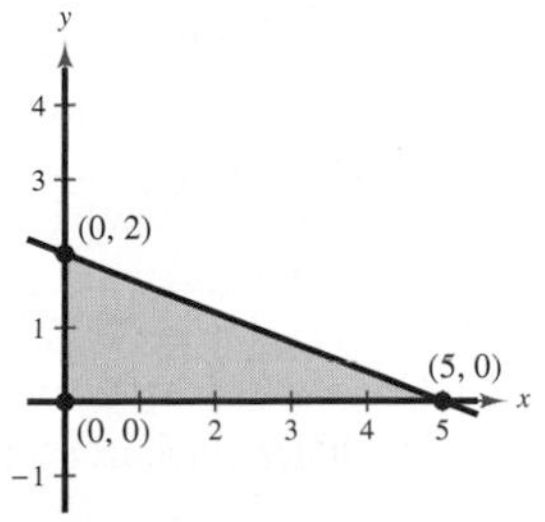

Minimum at (0, 0): 0
Maximum at (0, 2): 48

17.

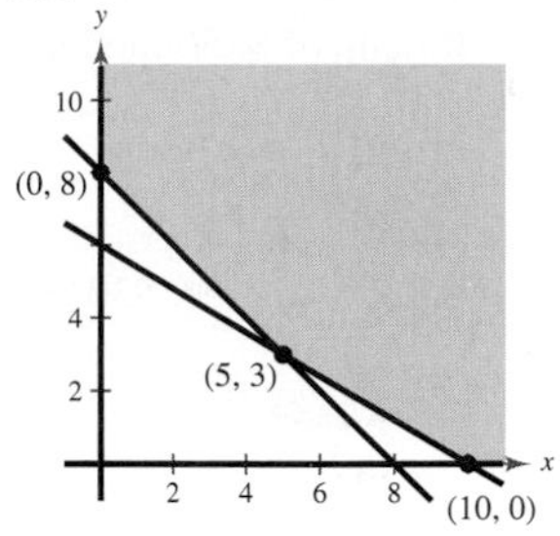

Minimum at (5, 3): 35
No maximum

19.

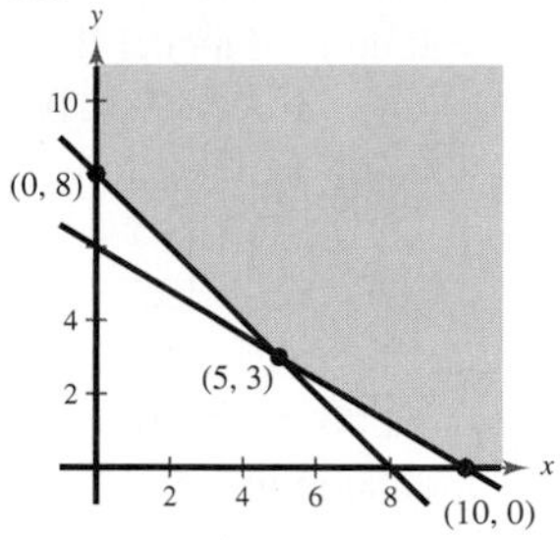

Minimum at (10, 0): 20
No maximum

21.

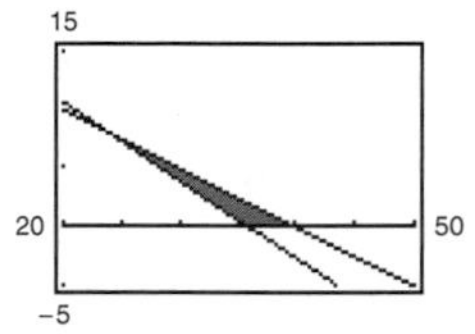

Minimum at (24, 8): 104
Maximum at (40, 0): 160

23.

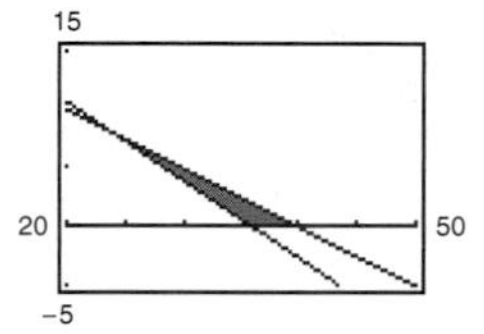

Minimum at (36, 0): 36
Maximum at (24, 8): 56

25. Maximum at (3, 6): 12 **27.** Maximum at (0, 10): 10

29. Maximum at (0, 5): 25 **31.** Maximum at $\left(\frac{22}{3}, \frac{19}{6}\right)$: $\frac{271}{6}$

33.

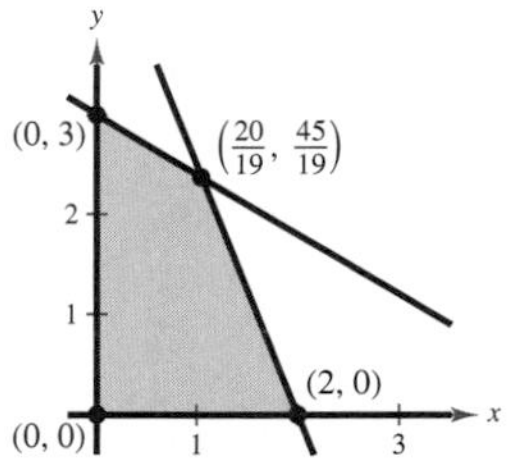

The maximum, 5, occurs at any point on the line segment connecting (2, 0) and $\left(\frac{20}{19}, \frac{45}{19}\right)$.

35.

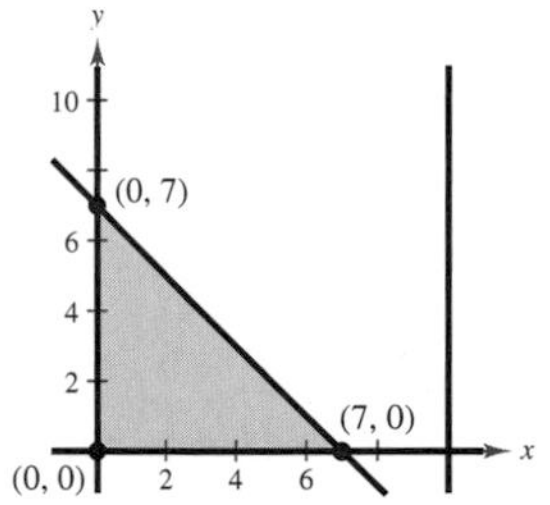

The constraint $x \leq 10$ is extraneous. Maximum at (0, 7): 14

37.

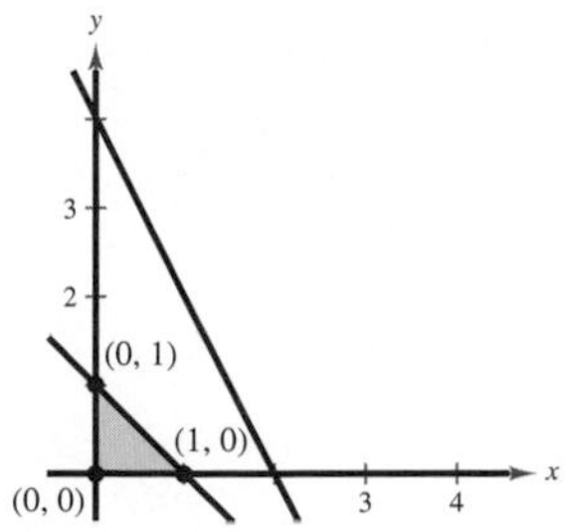

The constraint $2x + y \leq 4$ is extraneous.
Maximum at (0, 1): 4

CHAPTER 7

39. 750 units of model A
1000 units of model B
Optimal profit: $83,750

41. 216 units of $300 model
0 units of $250 model
Optimal profit: $8640

43. Three bags of brand X
Six bags of brand Y
Optimal cost: $195

45. 0 tax returns
12 audits
Optimal revenue: $30,000

47. $62,500 to type A
$187,500 to type B
Optimal return: $23,750

49. True. The objective function has a maximum value at any point on the line segment connecting the two vertices.

51. (a) $t \geq 9$ (b) $\frac{3}{4} \leq t \leq 9$

53. $z = x + 5y$ **55.** $z = 4x + y$ **57.** $\dfrac{9}{2(x+3)},\ x \neq 0$

59. $\dfrac{x^2 + 2x - 13}{x(x-2)},\ x \neq \pm 3$ **61.** $\ln 3 \approx 1.099$

63. $4 \ln 38 \approx 14.550$ **65.** $\frac{1}{3}e^{12/7} \approx 1.851$

67. $(-4, 3, -7)$

Review Exercises *(page 563)*

1. $(1, 1)$ **3.** $(0.25, 0.625)$ **5.** $(5, 4)$

7. $(0, 0), (2, 8), (-2, 8)$ **9.** $(4, -2)$

11. $(1.41, -0.66), (-1.41, 10.66)$

13.

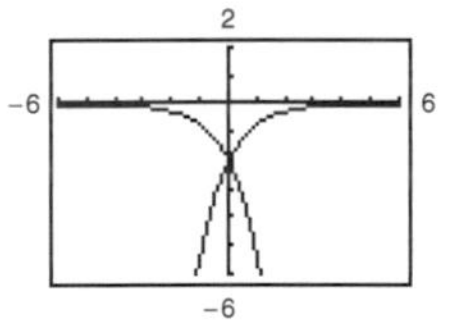

$(0, -2)$

15. 3847 units **17.** 96 meters × 144 meters **19.** $\left(\frac{5}{2}, 3\right)$

21. $(-0.5, 0.8)$ **23.** $(0, 0)$ **25.** $\left(\frac{8}{5}a + \frac{14}{5}, a\right)$

27. d, one solution, consistent

28. c, infinite solutions, consistent

29. b, no solution, inconsistent

30. a, one solution, consistent

31. $\left(\dfrac{500{,}000}{7}, \dfrac{159}{7}\right)$ **33.** $(2, -4, -5)$

35. $\left(\dfrac{24}{5}, \dfrac{22}{5}, -\dfrac{8}{5}\right)$ **37.** $(3a + 4, 2a + 5, a)$

39. $(a - 4, a - 3, a)$ **41.** $y = 2x^2 + x - 5$

43. $x^2 + y^2 - 4x + 4y - 1 = 0$

45. (a) $y = 3x^2 - 14.3x + 117.6$

(b)

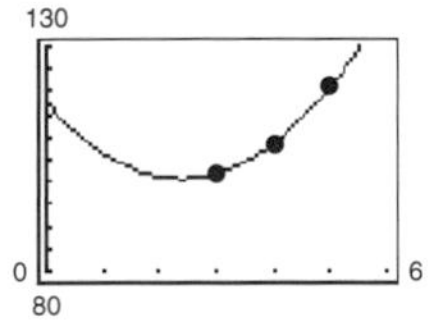

The model is a good fit.

(c) 195.2; yes.

47. $16,000 at 7%
$13,000 at 9%
$11,000 at 11%

49. $\dfrac{A}{x} + \dfrac{B}{x + 20}$ **51.** $\dfrac{A}{x} + \dfrac{B}{x^2} + \dfrac{C}{x - 5}$

53. $\dfrac{3}{x + 2} - \dfrac{4}{x + 4}$ **55.** $1 - \dfrac{25}{8(x + 5)} + \dfrac{9}{8(x - 3)}$

57. $\dfrac{1}{2}\left(\dfrac{3}{x - 1} - \dfrac{x - 3}{x^2 + 1}\right)$ **59.** $\dfrac{3x}{x^2 + 1} + \dfrac{x}{(x^2 + 1)^2}$

61.

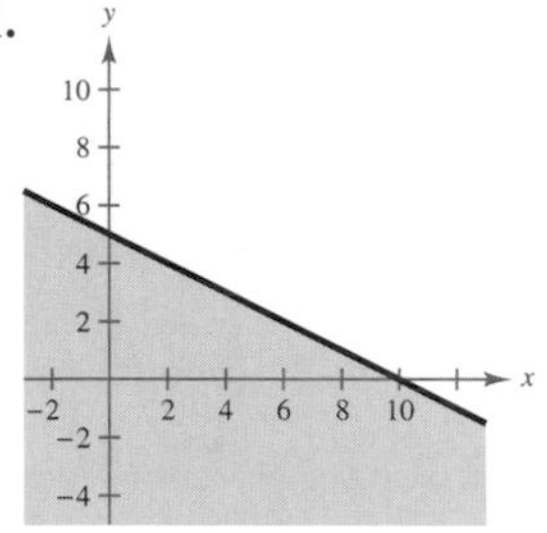

63.

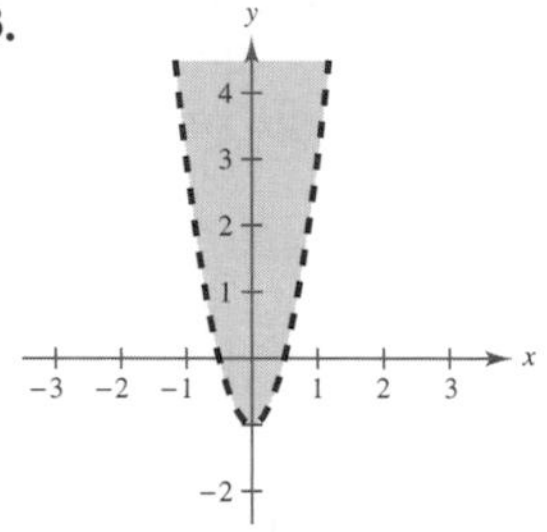

65.

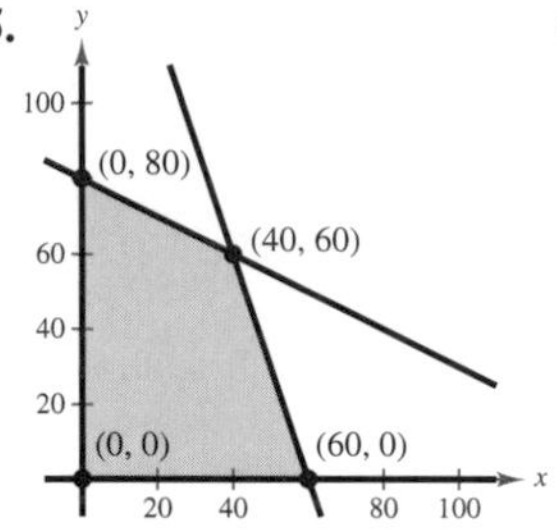

67.

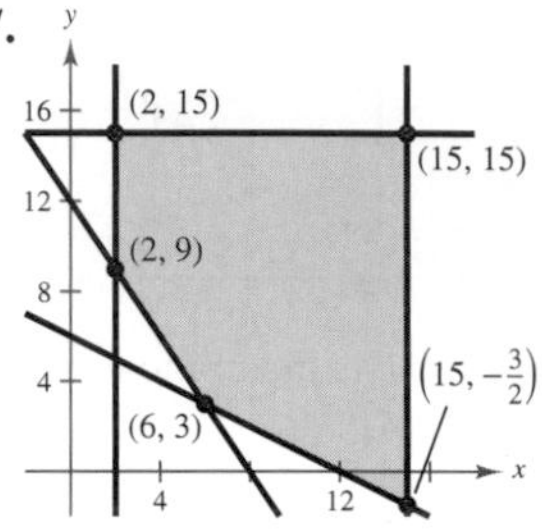

69.

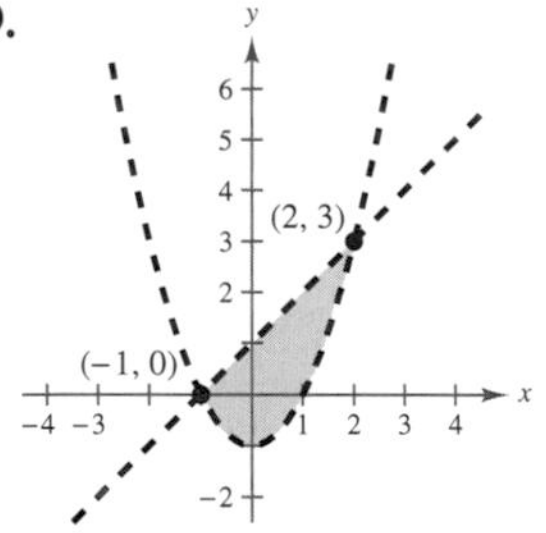

71.

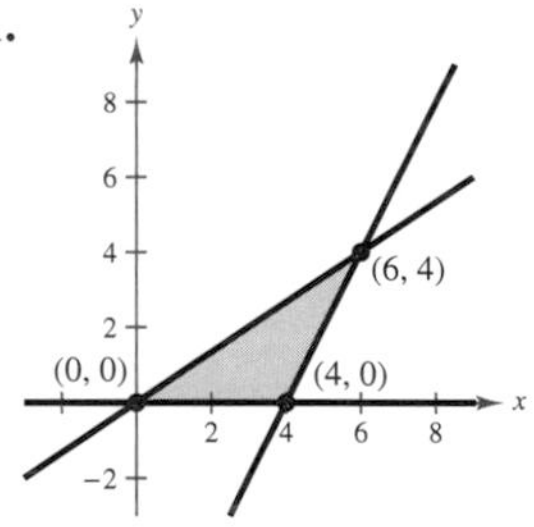

73. $\begin{cases} 20x + 30y \leq 24{,}000 \\ 12x + 8y \leq 12{,}400 \\ x \geq 0 \\ y \geq 0 \end{cases}$

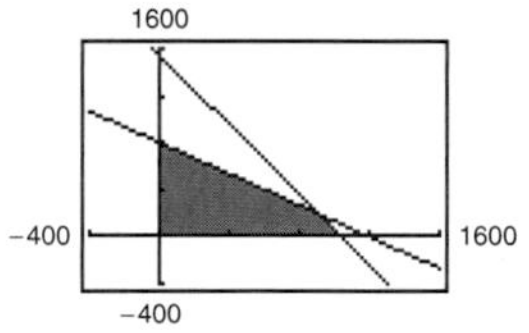

75. (a)

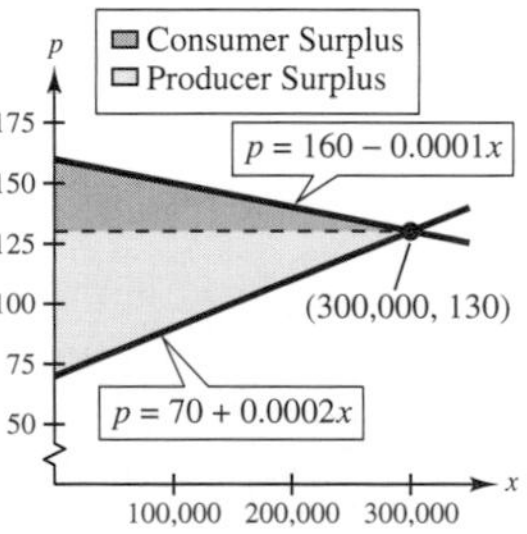

(b) Consumer surplus: $4,500,000
Producer surplus: $9,000,000

77.

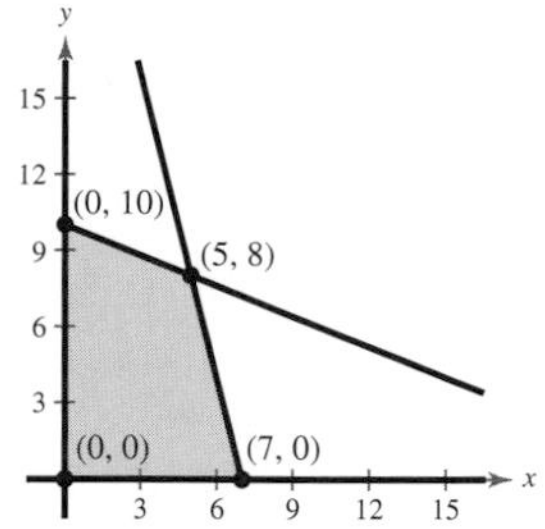

Minimum at $(0, 0)$: 0
Maximum at $(5, 8)$: 47

79.

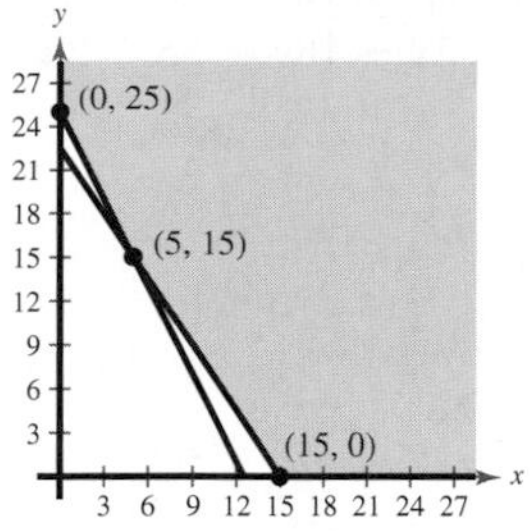

Minimum at $(15, 0)$: 26.25
No maximum

81.

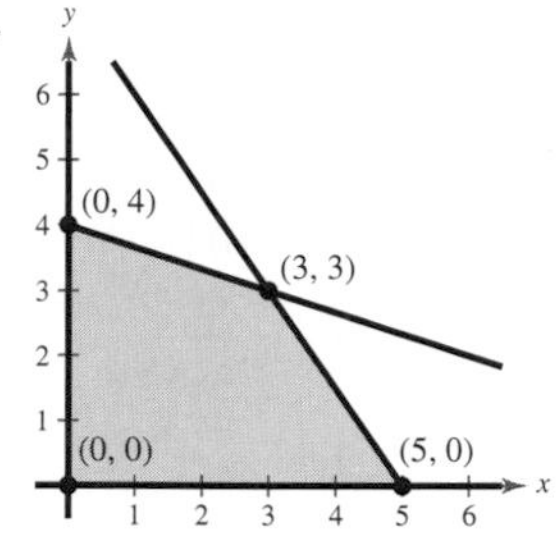

Minimum at $(0, 0)$: 0
Maximum at $(3, 3)$: 48

83. 72 haircuts
0 permanents
Optimal revenue: \$1800

85. Three bags of brand X
Two bags of brand Y
Optimal cost: \$105

87. False. To represent a region covered by an isosceles trapezoid, the last two inequality signs should be $\le$.

89. $\begin{cases} x + y = 2 \\ x - y = -14 \end{cases}$ **91.** $\begin{cases} 3x + y = 7 \\ -6x + 3y = 1 \end{cases}$

93. $\begin{cases} x + y + z = 6 \\ x + y - z = 0 \\ x - y - z = 2 \end{cases}$ **95.** $\begin{cases} 2x + 2y - 3z = 7 \\ x - 2y + z = 4 \\ -x + 4y - z = -1 \end{cases}$

97. An inconsistent system of linear equations has no solution.

99. Answers will vary.

Chapter Test *(page 567)*

1. $(-3, 4)$ **2.** $(0, -1)$, $(1, 0)$, $(2, 1)$

3. $(8, 4)$, $(2, -2)$

4.

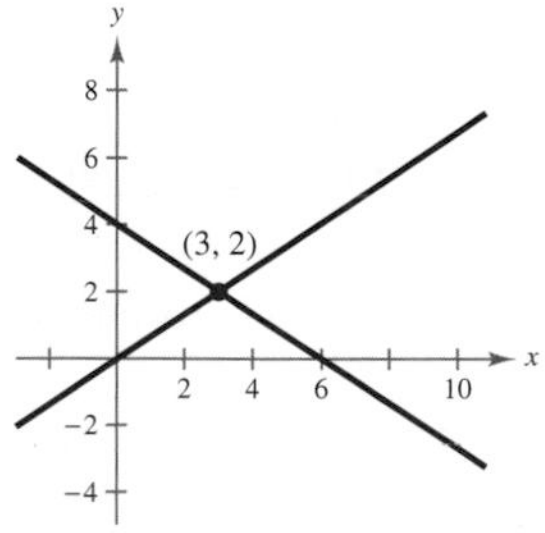

$(3, 2)$

5.

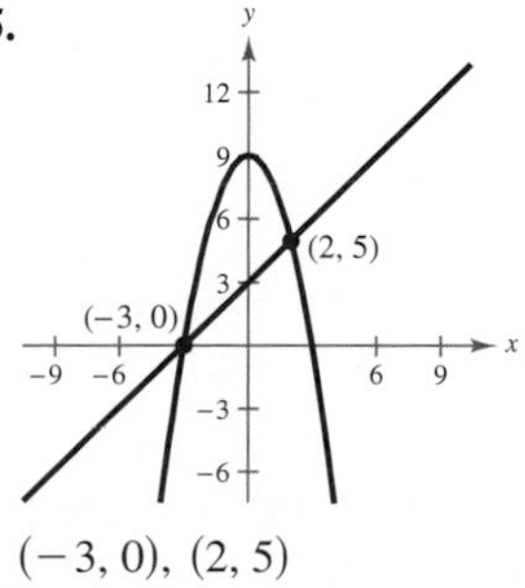

$(-3, 0)$, $(2, 5)$

6.

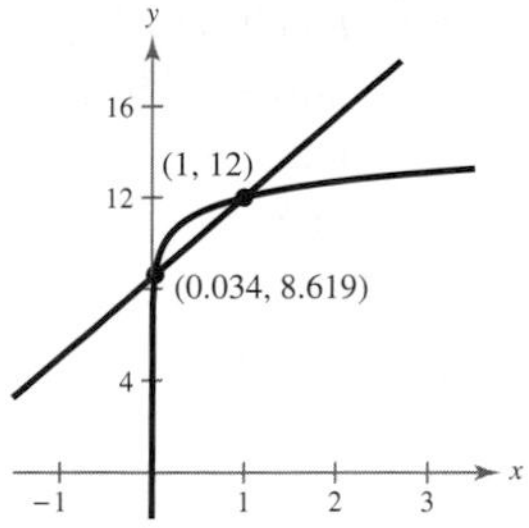

$(1, 12)$, $(0.034, 8.619)$

7. $(1, 5)$ **8.** $(2, -1)$ **9.** $(2, -3, 1)$ **10.** No solution

11. $-\dfrac{1}{x + 1} + \dfrac{3}{x - 2}$ **12.** $\dfrac{2}{x^2} + \dfrac{3}{2 - x}$

13. $-\dfrac{5}{x} + \dfrac{3}{x + 1} + \dfrac{3}{x - 1}$ **14.** $-\dfrac{2}{x} + \dfrac{3x}{x^2 + 2}$

15.

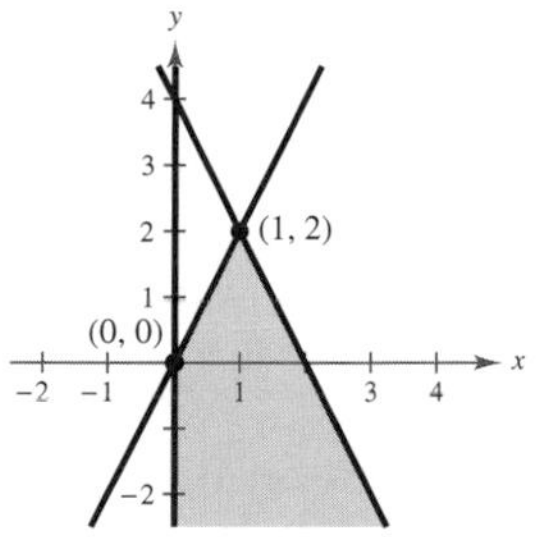

16.

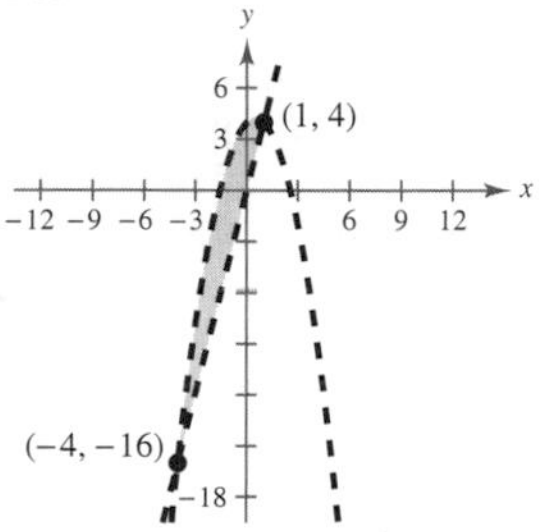

17.

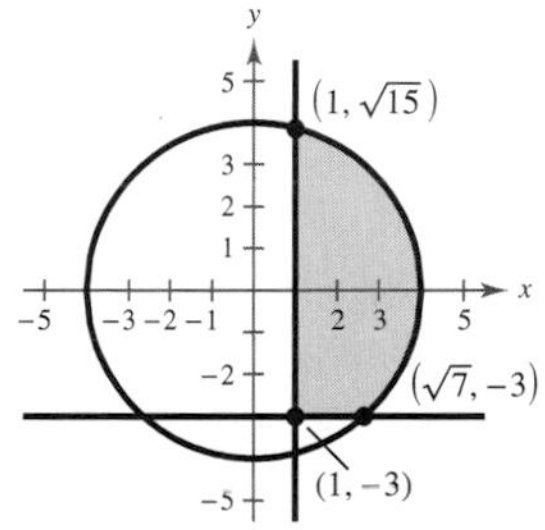

18. Maximum at $(12, 0)$: 240
Minimum at $(0, 0)$: 0

19. 8%: \$20,000
8.5%: \$30,000

20. $y = -\frac{1}{2}x^2 + x + 6$

21. 0 units of model I, 5300 units of model II
Optimal profit: \$212,000

Problem Solving *(page 569)*

1.

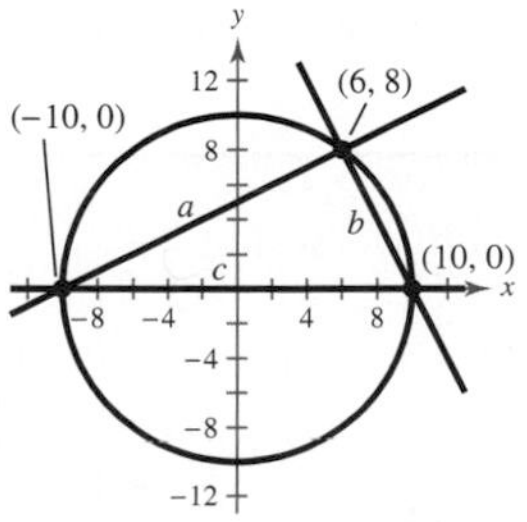

$a = 8\sqrt{5}$, $b = 4\sqrt{5}$, $c = 20$
$(8\sqrt{5})^2 + (4\sqrt{5})^2 = 20^2$
Therefore, the triangle is a right triangle.

3. $ad \neq bc$ **5.** (a) One (b) Two (c) Four

7. 10.1 feet high; $\approx$ 252.7 feet long **9.** \$12.00

11. (a) $(3, -4)$ (b) $\left(\dfrac{2}{-a+5}, \dfrac{1}{4a-1}, \dfrac{1}{a}\right)$

13. (a) $\left(\dfrac{-5a+16}{6}, \dfrac{5a-16}{6}, a\right)$

(b) $\left(\dfrac{-11a+36}{14}, \dfrac{13a-40}{14}, a\right)$

(c) $(-a+3, a-3, a)$ (d) Infinitely many

15. $\begin{cases} a + t \le 32 \\ 0.15a \ge 1.9 \\ 193a + 772t \ge 11{,}000 \end{cases}$

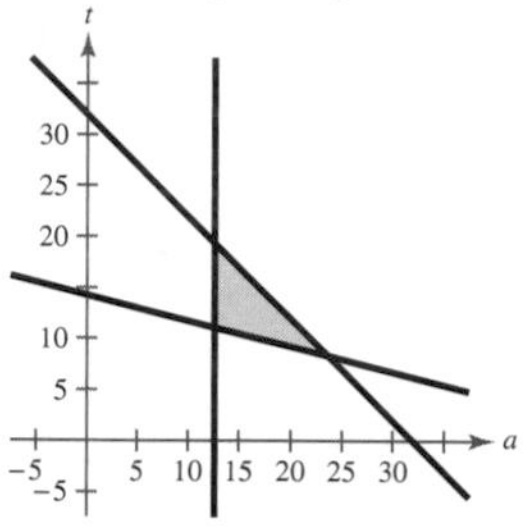

17. (a) $\begin{cases} x + y \le 200 \\ x \ge 35 \\ 0 < y \le 130 \end{cases}$ (b)

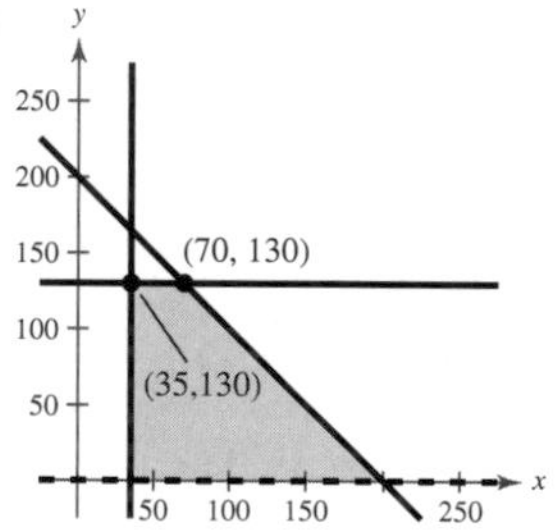

(c) No, because the total cholesterol is greater than 200 milligrams per deciliter.

(d) LDL: 140 milligrams per deciliter
HDL: 50 milligrams per deciliter
Total: 190 milligrams per deciliter

(e) $(50, 120)$; $\frac{170}{50} = 3.4 < 4$; answers will vary.

Chapter 8

Section 8.1 *(page 582)*

Vocabulary Check *(page 582)*

1. matrix **2.** square **3.** main diagonal
4. row; column **5.** augmented **6.** coefficient
7. row-equivalent **8.** reduced row-echelon form
9. Gauss-Jordan elimination

1. 1×2 **3.** 3×1 **5.** 2×2

7. $\left[\begin{array}{cc:c} 4 & -3 & -5 \\ -1 & 3 & 12 \end{array}\right]$ **9.** $\left[\begin{array}{ccc:c} 1 & 10 & -2 & 2 \\ 5 & -3 & 4 & 0 \\ 2 & 1 & 0 & 6 \end{array}\right]$

11. $\left[\begin{array}{ccc:c} 7 & -5 & 1 & 13 \\ 19 & 0 & -8 & 10 \end{array}\right]$ **13.** $\begin{cases} x + 2y = 7 \\ 2x - 3y = 4 \end{cases}$

15. $\begin{cases} 2x + 5z = -12 \\ y - 2z = 7 \\ 6x + 3y = 2 \end{cases}$

17. $\begin{cases} 9x + 12y + 3z = 0 \\ -2x + 18y + 5z + 2w = 10 \\ x + 7y - 8z = -4 \\ 3x + 2z = -10 \end{cases}$

19. $\begin{bmatrix} 1 & 4 & 3 \\ 0 & 2 & -1 \end{bmatrix}$

21. $\begin{bmatrix} 1 & 1 & 4 & -1 \\ 0 & 5 & -2 & 6 \\ 0 & 3 & 20 & 4 \end{bmatrix}\begin{bmatrix} 1 & 1 & 4 & -1 \\ 0 & 1 & -\frac{2}{5} & \frac{6}{5} \\ 0 & 3 & 20 & 4 \end{bmatrix}$

23. Add 5 times Row 2 to Row 1.

25. Interchange Row 1 and Row 2.
Add 4 times new Row 1 to Row 3.

27. (a) $\begin{bmatrix} 1 & 2 & 3 \\ 0 & -5 & -10 \\ 3 & 1 & -1 \end{bmatrix}$ (b) $\begin{bmatrix} 1 & 2 & 3 \\ 0 & -5 & -10 \\ 0 & -5 & -10 \end{bmatrix}$

(c) $\begin{bmatrix} 1 & 2 & 3 \\ 0 & -5 & -10 \\ 0 & 0 & 0 \end{bmatrix}$ (d) $\begin{bmatrix} 1 & 2 & 3 \\ 0 & 1 & 2 \\ 0 & 0 & 0 \end{bmatrix}$

(e) $\begin{bmatrix} 1 & 0 & -1 \\ 0 & 1 & 2 \\ 0 & 0 & 0 \end{bmatrix}$

The matrix is in reduced row-echelon form.

29. Reduced row-echelon form

31. Not in row-echelon form

33. $\begin{bmatrix} 1 & 1 & 0 & 5 \\ 0 & 1 & 2 & 0 \\ 0 & 0 & 1 & -1 \end{bmatrix}$ **35.** $\begin{bmatrix} 1 & -1 & -1 & 1 \\ 0 & 1 & 6 & 3 \\ 0 & 0 & 0 & 0 \end{bmatrix}$

37. $\begin{bmatrix} 1 & 0 & 0 \\ 0 & 1 & 0 \\ 0 & 0 & 1 \end{bmatrix}$ **39.** $\begin{bmatrix} 1 & 2 & 0 & 0 \\ 0 & 0 & 1 & 0 \\ 0 & 0 & 0 & 1 \\ 0 & 0 & 0 & 0 \end{bmatrix}$

41. $\begin{bmatrix} 1 & 0 & 3 & 16 \\ 0 & 1 & 2 & 12 \end{bmatrix}$ **43.** $\begin{cases} x - 2y = 4 \\ y = -3 \end{cases}$
$(-2, -3)$

45. $\begin{cases} x - y + 2z = 4 \\ y - z = 2 \\ z = -2 \end{cases}$
$(8, 0, -2)$

47. $(3, -4)$ **49.** $(-4, -10, 4)$ **51.** $(3, 2)$

53. $(-5, 6)$ **55.** $(-1, -4)$ **57.** Inconsistent

59. $(4, -3, 2)$ **61.** $(7, -3, 4)$ **63.** $(-4, -3, 6)$

65. $(2a + 1, 3a + 2, a)$

67. $(4 + 5b + 4a, 2 - 3b - 3a, b, a)$ **69.** Inconsistent

71. $(0, 2 - 4a, a)$ **73.** $(1, 0, 4, -2)$

75. $(-2a, a, a, 0)$ **77.** Yes; $(-1, 1, -3)$ **79.** No

81. $\left[\begin{array}{ccc:c} 1 & 3 & \frac{3}{2} & 4 \\ 0 & 1 & \frac{7}{4} & -\frac{3}{2} \\ 0 & 0 & 1 & 2 \end{array}\right], \left[\begin{array}{ccc:c} 1 & 3 & 1 & 3 \\ 0 & 1 & 2 & -1 \\ 0 & 0 & 1 & 2 \end{array}\right]$

83. $\dfrac{4x^2}{(x+1)^2(x-1)} = \dfrac{1}{x-1} + \dfrac{3}{x+1} - \dfrac{2}{(x+1)^2}$

85. \$150,000 at 7%
\$750,000 at 8%
\$600,000 at 10%

87. $y = x^2 + 2x + 5$

89. (a) $y = -0.004x^2 + 0.367x + 5$

(b)

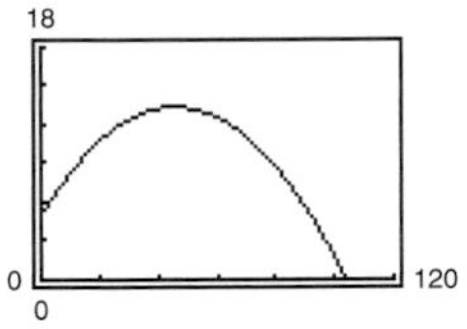

(c) 13 feet, 104 feet (d) 13.418 feet, 103.793 feet

(e) The results are similar.

91. (a) $x_1 = s,\ x_2 = t,\ x_3 = 600 - s,\ x_4 = s - t,\ x_5 = 500 - t,\ x_6 = s,\ x_7 = t$

(b) $x_1 = 0,\ x_2 = 0,\ x_3 = 600,\ x_4 = 0,\ x_5 = 500,\ x_6 = 0,\ x_7 = 0$

(c) $x_1 = 0,\ x_2 = -500,\ x_3 = 600,\ x_4 = 500,\ x_5 = 1000,\ x_6 = 0,\ x_7 = -500$

93. False. It is a 2×4 matrix.

95. False. Gaussian elimination reduces a matrix until a row-echelon form is obtained; Gauss-Jordan elimination reduces a matrix until a reduced row-echelon form is obtained.

97. (a) There exists a row with all zeros except for the entry in the last column.

(b) There are fewer rows with nonzero entries than there are variables and no rows as in (a).

99. They are the same.

101.

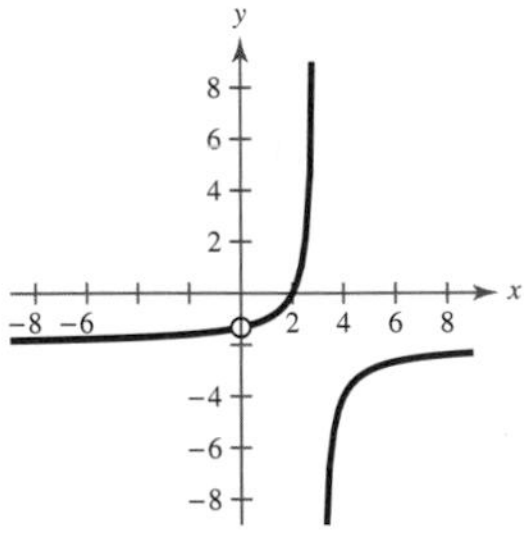

103.

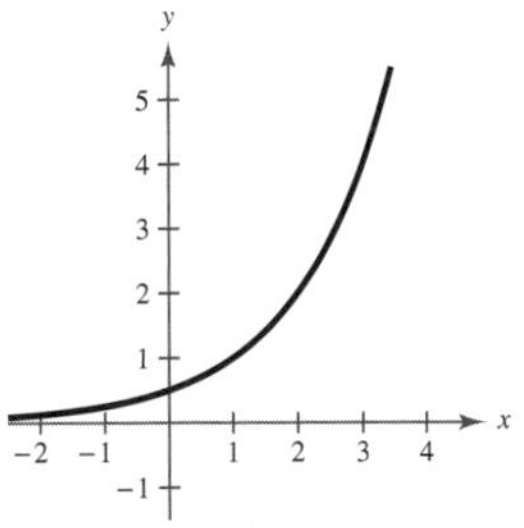

105.

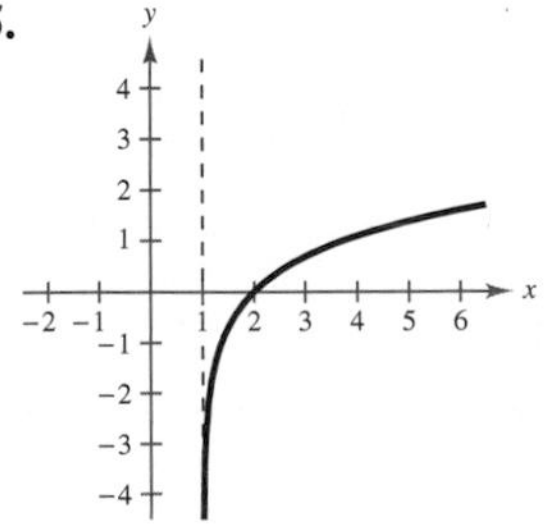

Section 8.2 *(page 597)*

Vocabulary Check *(page 597)*

1. equal **2.** scalars **3.** zero; O **4.** identity
5. (a) iii (b) iv (c) i (d) v (e) ii
6. (a) ii (b) iv (c) i (d) iii

1. $x = -4,\ y = 22$ **3.** $x = 2,\ y = 3$

5. (a) $\begin{bmatrix} 3 & -2 \\ 1 & 7 \end{bmatrix}$ (b) $\begin{bmatrix} -1 & 0 \\ 3 & -9 \end{bmatrix}$ (c) $\begin{bmatrix} 3 & -3 \\ 6 & -3 \end{bmatrix}$

(d) $\begin{bmatrix} -1 & -1 \\ 8 & -19 \end{bmatrix}$

7. (a) $\begin{bmatrix} 7 & 3 \\ 1 & 9 \\ -2 & 15 \end{bmatrix}$ (b) $\begin{bmatrix} 5 & -5 \\ 3 & -1 \\ -4 & -5 \end{bmatrix}$ (c) $\begin{bmatrix} 18 & -3 \\ 6 & 12 \\ -9 & 15 \end{bmatrix}$

(d) $\begin{bmatrix} 16 & -11 \\ 8 & 2 \\ -11 & -5 \end{bmatrix}$

9. (a) $\begin{bmatrix} 3 & 3 & -2 & 1 & 1 \\ -2 & 5 & 7 & -6 & -8 \end{bmatrix}$

(b) $\begin{bmatrix} 1 & 1 & 0 & -1 & 1 \\ 4 & -3 & -11 & 6 & 6 \end{bmatrix}$

(c) $\begin{bmatrix} 6 & 6 & -3 & 0 & 3 \\ 3 & 3 & -6 & 0 & -3 \end{bmatrix}$

(d) $\begin{bmatrix} 4 & 4 & -1 & -2 & 3 \\ 9 & -5 & -24 & 12 & 11 \end{bmatrix}$

11. (a), (b), and (d) not possible

(c) $\begin{bmatrix} 18 & 0 & 9 \\ -3 & -12 & 0 \end{bmatrix}$

13. $\begin{bmatrix} -8 & -7 \\ 15 & -1 \end{bmatrix}$ **15.** $\begin{bmatrix} -24 & -4 & 12 \\ -12 & 32 & 12 \end{bmatrix}$

17. $\begin{bmatrix} 10 & 8 \\ -59 & 9 \end{bmatrix}$ **19.** $\begin{bmatrix} -17.143 & 2.143 \\ 11.571 & 10.286 \end{bmatrix}$

21. $\begin{bmatrix} -1.581 & -3.739 \\ -4.252 & -13.249 \\ 9.713 & -0.362 \end{bmatrix}$ **23.** $\begin{bmatrix} -6 & -9 \\ -1 & 0 \\ 17 & -10 \end{bmatrix}$

25. $\begin{bmatrix} 3 & 3 \\ -\frac{1}{2} & 0 \\ -\frac{13}{2} & \frac{11}{2} \end{bmatrix}$ **27.** Not possible

29. $\begin{bmatrix} 3 & -4 \\ 10 & 16 \\ 26 & 46 \end{bmatrix}$ Order: 3×2

31. $\begin{bmatrix} 3 & 0 & 0 \\ 0 & -4 & 0 \\ 0 & 0 & -10 \end{bmatrix}$ Order: 3×3

33. $\begin{bmatrix} 0 & 0 & 0 \\ 0 & 0 & 0 \\ 0 & 0 & 0 \end{bmatrix}$ **35.** $\begin{bmatrix} 41 & 7 & 7 \\ 42 & 5 & 25 \\ -10 & -25 & 45 \end{bmatrix}$

Order: 3×3

37. $\begin{bmatrix} 151 & 25 & 48 \\ 516 & 279 & 387 \\ 47 & -20 & 87 \end{bmatrix}$ **39.** Not possible

41. (a) $\begin{bmatrix} 0 & 15 \\ 6 & 12 \end{bmatrix}$ (b) $\begin{bmatrix} -2 & 2 \\ 31 & 14 \end{bmatrix}$ (c) $\begin{bmatrix} 9 & 6 \\ 12 & 12 \end{bmatrix}$

43. (a) $\begin{bmatrix} 0 & -10 \\ 10 & 0 \end{bmatrix}$ (b) $\begin{bmatrix} 0 & -10 \\ 10 & 0 \end{bmatrix}$ (c) $\begin{bmatrix} 8 & -6 \\ 6 & 8 \end{bmatrix}$

45. (a) $\begin{bmatrix} 7 & 7 & 14 \\ 8 & 8 & 16 \\ -1 & -1 & -2 \end{bmatrix}$ (b) $[13]$ (c) Not possible

47. $\begin{bmatrix} 5 & 8 \\ -4 & -16 \end{bmatrix}$ **49.** $\begin{bmatrix} -4 & 10 \\ 3 & 14 \end{bmatrix}$

51. (a) $\begin{bmatrix} -1 & 1 \\ -2 & 1 \end{bmatrix}\begin{bmatrix} x_1 \\ x_2 \end{bmatrix} = \begin{bmatrix} 4 \\ 0 \end{bmatrix}$ (b) $\begin{bmatrix} 4 \\ 8 \end{bmatrix}$

53. (a) $\begin{bmatrix} -2 & -3 \\ 6 & 1 \end{bmatrix}\begin{bmatrix} x_1 \\ x_2 \end{bmatrix} = \begin{bmatrix} -4 \\ -36 \end{bmatrix}$ (b) $\begin{bmatrix} -7 \\ 6 \end{bmatrix}$

55. (a) $\begin{bmatrix} 1 & -2 & 3 \\ -1 & 3 & -1 \\ 2 & -5 & 5 \end{bmatrix}\begin{bmatrix} x_1 \\ x_2 \\ x_3 \end{bmatrix} = \begin{bmatrix} 9 \\ -6 \\ 17 \end{bmatrix}$ (b) $\begin{bmatrix} 1 \\ -1 \\ 2 \end{bmatrix}$

57. (a) $\begin{bmatrix} 1 & -5 & 2 \\ -3 & 1 & -1 \\ 0 & -2 & 5 \end{bmatrix}\begin{bmatrix} x_1 \\ x_2 \\ x_3 \end{bmatrix} = \begin{bmatrix} -20 \\ 8 \\ -16 \end{bmatrix}$ (b) $\begin{bmatrix} -1 \\ 3 \\ -2 \end{bmatrix}$

59. $\begin{bmatrix} 84 & 60 & 30 \\ 42 & 120 & 84 \end{bmatrix}$

61. (a) $A = \begin{bmatrix} 125 & 100 & 75 \\ 100 & 175 & 125 \end{bmatrix}$

The entries represent the numbers of bushels of each crop that are shipped to each outlet.

(b) $B = [\$3.50 \quad \$6.00]$

The entries represent the profits per bushel of each crop.

(c) $BA = [\$1037.50 \quad \$1400 \quad \$1012.50]$

The entries represent the profits from both crops at each of the three outlets.

63. $\begin{bmatrix} \$15{,}770 & \$18{,}300 \\ \$26{,}500 & \$29{,}250 \\ \$21{,}260 & \$24{,}150 \end{bmatrix}$

The entries represent the wholesale and retail values of the inventories at the three outlets.

65. $P^3 = \begin{bmatrix} 0.300 & 0.175 & 0.175 \\ 0.308 & 0.433 & 0.217 \\ 0.392 & 0.392 & 0.608 \end{bmatrix}$

$P^4 = \begin{bmatrix} 0.250 & 0.188 & 0.188 \\ 0.315 & 0.377 & 0.248 \\ 0.435 & 0.435 & 0.565 \end{bmatrix}$

$P^5 = \begin{bmatrix} 0.225 & 0.194 & 0.194 \\ 0.314 & 0.345 & 0.267 \\ 0.461 & 0.461 & 0.539 \end{bmatrix}$

$P^6 = \begin{bmatrix} 0.213 & 0.197 & 0.197 \\ 0.311 & 0.326 & 0.280 \\ 0.477 & 0.477 & 0.523 \end{bmatrix}$

$P^7 = \begin{bmatrix} 0.206 & 0.198 & 0.198 \\ 0.308 & 0.316 & 0.288 \\ 0.486 & 0.486 & 0.514 \end{bmatrix}$

$P^8 = \begin{bmatrix} 0.203 & 0.199 & 0.199 \\ 0.305 & 0.309 & 0.292 \\ 0.492 & 0.492 & 0.508 \end{bmatrix}$

Approaches the matrix

$\begin{bmatrix} 0.2 & 0.2 & 0.2 \\ 0.3 & 0.3 & 0.3 \\ 0.5 & 0.5 & 0.5 \end{bmatrix}$

67. (a) Sales \$ Profit (b) \$464

$\begin{bmatrix} 447 & 115 \\ 624.5 & 161 \\ 731.2 & 188 \end{bmatrix}$

The entries represent the total sales and profits for each type of milk.

69. (a) $[2 \quad 0.5 \quad 3]$

(b) 120 lb 150 lb

$[473.5 \quad 588.5]$

The entries represent the total calories burned.

71. True. The sum of two matrices of different orders is undefined.

73. Not possible **75.** Not possible **77.** 2×2

79. 2×3 **81.** $AC = BC = \begin{bmatrix} 2 & 3 \\ 2 & 3 \end{bmatrix}$

83. AB is a diagonal matrix whose entries are the products of the corresponding entries of A and B.

85. $-8, \frac{4}{3}$ **87.** $0, \frac{-5 \pm \sqrt{37}}{4}$ **89.** $4, \pm\frac{\sqrt{15}}{3}i$

91. $\left(7, -\frac{1}{2}\right)$ **93.** $(3, -1)$

Section 8.3 *(page 608)*

Vocabulary Check *(page 608)*

1. square **2.** inverse

3. nonsingular; singular **4.** $A^{-1}B$

1–9. $AB = I$ and $BA = I$

11. $\begin{bmatrix} \frac{1}{2} & 0 \\ 0 & \frac{1}{3} \end{bmatrix}$ **13.** $\begin{bmatrix} -3 & 2 \\ -2 & 1 \end{bmatrix}$ **15.** $\begin{bmatrix} 1 & -1 \\ 2 & -1 \end{bmatrix}$

17. Does not exist **19.** Does not exist

21. $\begin{bmatrix} 1 & 1 & -1 \\ -3 & 2 & -1 \\ 3 & -3 & 2 \end{bmatrix}$ **23.** $\begin{bmatrix} 1 & 0 & 0 \\ -\frac{3}{4} & \frac{1}{4} & 0 \\ \frac{7}{20} & -\frac{1}{4} & \frac{1}{5} \end{bmatrix}$

25. $\begin{bmatrix} -\frac{1}{8} & 0 & 0 & 0 \\ 0 & 1 & 0 & 0 \\ 0 & 0 & \frac{1}{4} & 0 \\ 0 & 0 & 0 & -\frac{1}{5} \end{bmatrix}$ **27.** $\begin{bmatrix} -175 & 37 & -13 \\ 95 & -20 & 7 \\ 14 & -3 & 1 \end{bmatrix}$

29. $\begin{bmatrix} -1.5 & 1.5 & 1 \\ 4.5 & -3.5 & -3 \\ -1 & 1 & 1 \end{bmatrix}$ **31.** $\begin{bmatrix} -12 & -5 & -9 \\ -4 & -2 & -4 \\ -8 & -4 & -6 \end{bmatrix}$

33. $\begin{bmatrix} 0 & -1.\overline{81} & 0.\overline{90} \\ -10 & 5 & 5 \\ 10 & -2.\overline{72} & -3.\overline{63} \end{bmatrix}$ **35.** Does not exist

37. $\begin{bmatrix} 1 & 0 & 1 & 0 \\ 0 & 1 & 0 & 1 \\ 2 & 0 & 1 & 0 \\ 0 & 1 & 0 & 2 \end{bmatrix}$ **39.** $\begin{bmatrix} \frac{3}{19} & \frac{2}{19} \\ -\frac{2}{19} & \frac{5}{19} \end{bmatrix}$

41. Does not exist **43.** $\begin{bmatrix} \frac{16}{59} & \frac{15}{59} \\ -\frac{4}{59} & \frac{70}{59} \end{bmatrix}$

45. $(5, 0)$ **47.** $(-8, -6)$ **49.** $(3, 8, -11)$

51. $(2, 1, 0, 0)$ **53.** $(2, -2)$ **55.** No solution

57. $(-4, -8)$ **59.** $(-1, 3, 2)$

61. $\left(\frac{5}{16}a + \frac{13}{16}, \frac{19}{16}a + \frac{11}{16}, a\right)$ **63.** $(-7, 3, -2)$

65. $(5, 0, -2, 3)$

67. \$7000 in AAA-rated bonds
\$1000 in A-rated bonds
\$2000 in B-rated bonds

69. \$9000 in AAA-rated bonds
\$1000 in A-rated bonds
\$2000 in B-rated bonds

71. (a) $I_1 = -3$ amperes (b) $I_1 = 2$ amperes
$I_2 = 8$ amperes $I_2 = 3$ amperes
$I_3 = 5$ amperes $I_3 = 5$ amperes

73. True. If B is the inverse of A, then $AB = I = BA$.

75. Answers will vary.

77. $x \ge -5$ or $x \le -9$

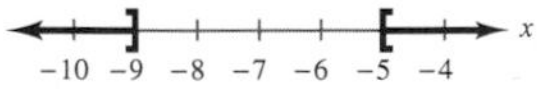

79. $\frac{2 \ln 315}{\ln 3} \approx 10.472$ **81.** $2^{6.5} \approx 90.510$

83. Answers will vary.

Section 8.4 *(page 616)*

Vocabulary Check *(page 616)*

1. determinant **2.** minor
3. cofactor **4.** expanding by cofactors

1. 5 **3.** 5 **5.** 27 **7.** 0 **9.** 6 **11.** -9

13. 72 **15.** $\frac{11}{6}$ **17.** -0.002 **19.** -4.842 **21.** 0

23. (a) $M_{11} = -5, M_{12} = 2, M_{21} = 4, M_{22} = 3$
(b) $C_{11} = -5, C_{12} = -2, C_{21} = -4, C_{22} = 3$

25. (a) $M_{11} = -4, M_{12} = -2, M_{21} = 1, M_{22} = 3$
(b) $C_{11} = -4, C_{12} = 2, C_{21} = -1, C_{22} = 3$

27. (a) $M_{11} = 3, M_{12} = -4, M_{13} = 1, M_{21} = 2, M_{22} = 2,$
$M_{23} = -4, M_{31} = -4, M_{32} = 10, M_{33} = 8$
(b) $C_{11} = 3, C_{12} = 4, C_{13} = 1, C_{21} = -2, C_{22} = 2,$
$C_{23} = 4, C_{31} = -4, C_{32} = -10, C_{33} = 8$

29. (a) $M_{11} = 30, M_{12} = 12, M_{13} = 11, M_{21} = -36,$
$M_{22} = 26, M_{23} = 7, M_{31} = -4, M_{32} = -42, M_{33} = 12$
(b) $C_{11} = 30, C_{12} = -12, C_{13} = 11, C_{21} = 36, C_{22} = 26,$
$C_{23} = -7, C_{31} = -4, C_{32} = 42, C_{33} = 12$

31. (a) -75 (b) -75 **33.** (a) 96 (b) 96

35. (a) 170 (b) 170 **37.** 0 **39.** 0 **41.** -9

43. -58 **45.** -30 **47.** -168 **49.** 0

51. 412 **53.** -126 **55.** 0 **57.** -336 **59.** 410

61. (a) -3 (b) -2 (c) $\begin{bmatrix} -2 & 0 \\ 0 & -3 \end{bmatrix}$ (d) 6

63. (a) -8 (b) 0 (c) $\begin{bmatrix} -4 & 4 \\ 1 & -1 \end{bmatrix}$ (d) 0

65. (a) -21 (b) -19 (c) $\begin{bmatrix} 7 & 1 & 4 \\ -8 & 9 & -3 \\ 7 & -3 & 9 \end{bmatrix}$ (d) 399

67. (a) 2 (b) -6 (c) $\begin{bmatrix} 1 & 4 & 3 \\ -1 & 0 & 3 \\ 0 & 2 & 0 \end{bmatrix}$ (d) -12

69–73. Answers will vary. **75.** $-1, 4$ **77.** $-1, -4$

79. $8uv - 1$ **81.** e^{5x} **83.** $1 - \ln x$

85. True. If an entire row is zero, then each cofactor in the expansion is multiplied by zero.

87. Answers will vary.

89. A square matrix is a square array of numbers. The determinant of a square matrix is a real number.

91. (a) Columns 2 and 3 of A were interchanged.
$|A| = -115 = -|B|$
(b) Rows 1 and 3 of A were interchanged.
$|A| = -40 = -|B|$

93. (a) Multiply Row 1 by 5.
(b) Multiply Column 2 by 4 and Column 3 by 3.

95. All real numbers x

97. All real numbers x such that $-4 \le x \le 4$

99. All real numbers t such that $t > 1$

101.

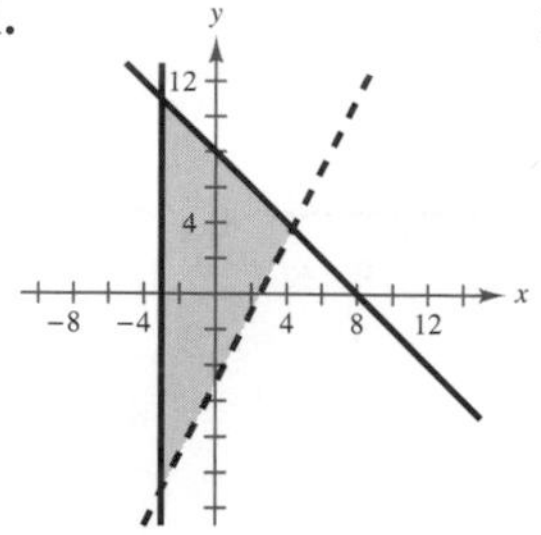

103. $\begin{bmatrix} \frac{1}{4} & \frac{1}{4} \\ 2 & 1 \end{bmatrix}$

105. Does not exist

Section 8.5 *(page 628)*

Vocabulary Check *(page 628)*

1. Cramer's Rule **2.** collinear

3. $A = \pm\frac{1}{2}\begin{vmatrix} x_1 & y_1 & 1 \\ x_2 & y_2 & 1 \\ x_3 & y_3 & 1 \end{vmatrix}$ **4.** cryptogram

5. uncoded; coded

1. $(2, -2)$ **3.** Not possible **5.** $\left(\frac{32}{7}, \frac{30}{7}\right)$

7. $(-1, 3, 2)$ **9.** $(-2, 1, -1)$ **11.** $\left(0, -\frac{1}{2}, \frac{1}{2}\right)$

13. $(1, 2, 1)$ **15.** 7 **17.** 14 **19.** $\frac{33}{8}$ **21.** $\frac{5}{2}$

23. 28 **25.** $y = \frac{16}{5}$ or $y = 0$

27. $y = -3$ or $y = -11$ **29.** 250 square miles

31. Collinear **33.** Not collinear **35.** Collinear

37. $y = -3$ **39.** $3x - 5y = 0$ **41.** $x + 3y - 5 = 0$

43. $2x + 3y - 8 = 0$

45. Uncoded: [20 18 15], [21 2 12], [5 0 9], [14 0 18], [9 22 5], [18 0 3], [9 20 25]

Encoded: −52 10 27 −49 3 34 −49 13 27 −94 22 54 1 1 −7 0 −12 9 −121 41 55

47. −6 −35 −69 11 20 17 6 −16 −58 46 79 67

49. −5 −41 −87 91 207 257 11 −5 −41 40 80 84 76 177 227

51. HAPPY NEW YEAR

53. CLASS IS CANCELED

55. SEND PLANES **57.** MEET ME TONIGHT RON

59. False. The denominator is the determinant of the coefficient matrix.

61. False. If the determinant of the coefficient matrix is zero, the system has either no solution or infinitely many solutions.

63. $(-6, 4)$ **65.** $(-1, 0, -3)$

67.

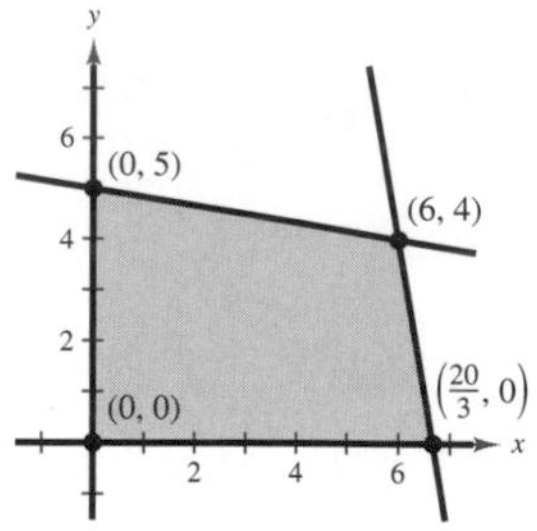

Minimum at (0, 0): 0

Maximum at (6, 4): 52

Review Exercises *(page 632)*

1. 3×1 **3.** 1×1 **5.** $\left[\begin{array}{cc|c} 3 & -10 & 15 \\ 5 & 4 & 22 \end{array}\right]$

7. $\begin{cases} 5x + y + 7z = -9 \\ 4x + 2y = 10 \\ 9x + 4y + 2z = 3 \end{cases}$ **9.** $\begin{bmatrix} 1 & 2 & 3 \\ 0 & 1 & 1 \\ 0 & 0 & 1 \end{bmatrix}$

11. $\begin{cases} x + 2y + 3z = 9 \\ y - 2z = 2 \\ z = 0 \end{cases}$ $(5, 2, 0)$ **13.** $\begin{cases} x - 5y + 4z = 1 \\ y + 2z = 3 \\ z = 4 \end{cases}$ $(-40, -5, 4)$

15. $(10, -12)$ **17.** $\left(-\frac{1}{5}, \frac{7}{10}\right)$ **19.** $(5, 2, -6)$

21. $\left(-2a + \frac{3}{2}, 2a + 1, a\right)$ **23.** $(1, 0, 4, 3)$

25. $(2, -3, 3)$ **27.** $(2, 3, -1)$ **29.** $(2, 6, -10, -3)$

31. $x = 12, y = -7$ **33.** $x = 1, y = 11$

35. (a) $\begin{bmatrix} -1 & 8 \\ 15 & 13 \end{bmatrix}$ (b) $\begin{bmatrix} 5 & -12 \\ -9 & -3 \end{bmatrix}$

(c) $\begin{bmatrix} 8 & -8 \\ 12 & 20 \end{bmatrix}$ (d) $\begin{bmatrix} -7 & 28 \\ 39 & 29 \end{bmatrix}$

37. (a) $\begin{bmatrix} 5 & 7 \\ -3 & 14 \\ 31 & 42 \end{bmatrix}$ (b) $\begin{bmatrix} 5 & 1 \\ -11 & -10 \\ -9 & -38 \end{bmatrix}$

(c) $\begin{bmatrix} 20 & 16 \\ -28 & 8 \\ 44 & 8 \end{bmatrix}$ (d) $\begin{bmatrix} 5 & 13 \\ 5 & 38 \\ 71 & 122 \end{bmatrix}$

39. $\begin{bmatrix} 17 & -17 \\ 13 & 2 \end{bmatrix}$ **41.** $\begin{bmatrix} 54 & 4 \\ -2 & 24 \\ -4 & 32 \end{bmatrix}$

43. $\begin{bmatrix} 48 & -18 & -3 \\ 15 & 51 & 33 \end{bmatrix}$ **45.** $\begin{bmatrix} -14 & -4 \\ 7 & -17 \\ -17 & -2 \end{bmatrix}$

47. $\begin{bmatrix} 3 & \frac{2}{3} \\ -\frac{4}{3} & \frac{11}{3} \\ \frac{10}{3} & 0 \end{bmatrix}$ **49.** $\begin{bmatrix} -30 & 4 \\ 51 & 70 \end{bmatrix}$

51. $\begin{bmatrix} 100 & 220 \\ 12 & -4 \\ 84 & 212 \end{bmatrix}$ **53.** $\begin{bmatrix} 14 & -2 & 8 \\ 14 & -10 & 40 \\ 36 & -12 & 48 \end{bmatrix}$

55. $\begin{bmatrix} 44 & 4 \\ 20 & 8 \end{bmatrix}$ **57.** $\begin{bmatrix} 24 & -8 \\ 36 & -12 \end{bmatrix}$ **59.** $\begin{bmatrix} 1 & 17 \\ 12 & 36 \end{bmatrix}$

61. $\begin{bmatrix} 14 & -22 & 22 \\ 19 & -41 & 80 \\ 42 & -66 & 66 \end{bmatrix}$ **63.** $\begin{bmatrix} 76 & 114 & 133 \\ 38 & 95 & 76 \end{bmatrix}$

65. [$274,150 $303,150]
The merchandise shipped to warehouse 1 is worth $274,150 and the merchandise shipped to warehouse 2 is worth $303,150.

67–69. $AB = I$ and $BA = I$

71. $\begin{bmatrix} 4 & -5 \\ 5 & -6 \end{bmatrix}$ **73.** $\begin{bmatrix} 13 & 6 & -4 \\ -12 & -5 & 3 \\ 5 & 2 & -1 \end{bmatrix}$

75. $\begin{bmatrix} \frac{1}{2} & -1 & -\frac{1}{2} \\ \frac{1}{2} & -\frac{2}{3} & -\frac{5}{6} \\ 0 & \frac{2}{3} & \frac{1}{3} \end{bmatrix}$ **77.** $\begin{bmatrix} -3 & 6 & -5.5 & 3.5 \\ 1 & -2 & 2 & -1 \\ 7 & -15 & 14.5 & -9.5 \\ -1 & 2.5 & -2.5 & 1.5 \end{bmatrix}$

79. $\begin{bmatrix} 1 & -1 \\ 4 & -\frac{7}{2} \end{bmatrix}$ **81.** $\begin{bmatrix} 2 & \frac{20}{3} \\ \frac{1}{10} & \frac{1}{6} \end{bmatrix}$ **83.** $(36, 11)$

85. $(-6, -1)$ **87.** $(2, -1, -2)$ **89.** $(6, 1, -1)$

91. $(-3, 1)$ **93.** $(1, 1, -2)$ **95.** -42 **97.** 550

99. (a) $M_{11} = 4, M_{12} = 7, M_{21} = -1, M_{22} = 2$
(b) $C_{11} = 4, C_{12} = -7, C_{21} = 1, C_{22} = 2$

101. (a) $M_{11} = 30, M_{12} = -12, M_{13} = -21,$
$M_{21} = 20, M_{22} = 19, M_{23} = 22, M_{31} = 5,$
$M_{32} = -2, M_{33} = 19$
(b) $C_{11} = 30, C_{12} = 12, C_{13} = -21,$
$C_{21} = -20, C_{22} = 19, C_{23} = -22,$
$C_{31} = 5, C_{32} = 2, C_{33} = 19$

103. 130 **105.** 279 **107.** $(4, 7)$ **109.** $(-1, 4, 5)$

111. 16 **113.** 10 **115.** Collinear

117. $x - 2y + 4 = 0$ **119.** $2x + 6y - 13 = 0$

121. Uncoded: [12 15 15], [11 0 15], [21 20 0], [2 5 12], [15 23 0]
Encoded: -21 6 0 -68 8 45 102 -42 -60 -53 20 21 99 -30 -69

123. SEE YOU FRIDAY

125. False. The matrix must be square.

127. The matrix must be square and its determinant nonzero.

129. No. The first two matrices describe a system of equations with one solution. The third matrix describes a system with infinitely many solutions.

131. $\lambda = \pm 2\sqrt{10} - 3$

Chapter Test *(page 637)*

1. $\begin{bmatrix} 1 & 0 & 0 \\ 0 & 1 & 0 \\ 0 & 0 & 1 \end{bmatrix}$

2. $\begin{bmatrix} 1 & 0 & -1 & 2 \\ 0 & 1 & 0 & -1 \\ 0 & 0 & 0 & 0 \\ 0 & 0 & 0 & 0 \end{bmatrix}$

3. $\left[\begin{array}{ccc:c} 4 & 3 & -2 & 14 \\ -1 & -1 & 2 & -5 \\ 3 & 1 & -4 & 8 \end{array}\right], \left(1, 3, -\frac{1}{2}\right)$

4. (a) $\begin{bmatrix} 1 & 5 \\ 0 & -4 \end{bmatrix}$
(b) $\begin{bmatrix} 15 & 12 \\ -12 & -12 \end{bmatrix}$
(c) $\begin{bmatrix} 7 & 14 \\ -4 & -12 \end{bmatrix}$
(d) $\begin{bmatrix} 4 & -5 \\ 0 & 4 \end{bmatrix}$

5. $\begin{bmatrix} \frac{1}{2} & \frac{2}{5} \\ 1 & \frac{3}{5} \end{bmatrix}$

6. $\begin{bmatrix} -\frac{5}{2} & 4 & -3 \\ 5 & -7 & 6 \\ 4 & -6 & 5 \end{bmatrix}$

7. $(13, 22)$ **8.** -196 **9.** 29 **10.** 43

11. $(-3, 5)$ **12.** $(-2, 4, 6)$ **13.** 7

14. Uncoded: [11 14 15], [3 11 0], [15 14 0], [23 15 15], [4 0 0]
Encoded: 115 -41 -59 14 -3 -11 29 -15 -14 128 -53 -60 4 -4 0

15. 75 liters of 60% solution
25 liters of 20% solution

Problem Solving *(page 639)*

1. (a) $AT = \begin{bmatrix} -1 & -4 & -2 \\ 1 & 2 & 3 \end{bmatrix}$
$AAT = \begin{bmatrix} -1 & -2 & -3 \\ -1 & -4 & -2 \end{bmatrix}$

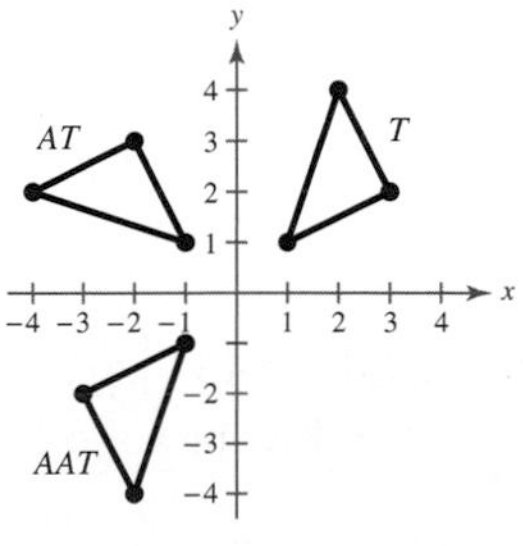

A represents a counterclockwise rotation.
(b) AAT is rotated clockwise 90° to obtain AT. AT is then rotated clockwise 90° to obtain T.

3. (a) Yes (b) No (c) No (d) No

5. (a) Gold Cable Company: 28,750 subscribers
Galaxy Cable Company: 35,750 subscribers
Nonsubscribers: 35,500
Answers will vary.
(b) Gold Cable Company: 30,813 subscribers
Galaxy Cable Company: 39,675 subscribers
Nonsubscribers: 29,513
Answers will vary.
(c) Gold Cable Company: 31,947 subscribers
Galaxy Cable Company: 42,329 subscribers
Nonsubscribers: 25,724
Answers will vary.
(d) Cable companies are increasing the number of subscribers, while the nonsubscribers are decreasing.

7. $x = 6$ **9–11.** Answers will vary.

13. Sulfur: 32 atomic mass units
Nitrogen: 14 atomic mass units
Fluorine: 19 atomic mass units

15. $A^T = \begin{bmatrix} -1 & 2 \\ 1 & 0 \\ -2 & 1 \end{bmatrix}$ $B^T = \begin{bmatrix} -3 & 1 & 1 \\ 0 & 2 & -1 \end{bmatrix}$

$(AB)^T = \begin{bmatrix} 2 & -5 \\ 4 & -1 \end{bmatrix} = B^T A^T$

17. (a) $A^{-1} = \begin{bmatrix} 1 & -2 \\ 1 & -3 \end{bmatrix}$
(b) JOHN RETURN TO BASE

19. $|A| = 0$

Chapter 9

Section 9.1 *(page 649)*

Vocabulary Check *(page 649)*

1. infinite sequence **2.** terms **3.** finite
4. recursively **5.** factorial
6. summation notation **7.** index; upper; lower
8. series **9.** nth partial sum

1. 4, 7, 10, 13, 16 **3.** 2, 4, 8, 16, 32

5. $-2, 4, -8, 16, -32$ **7.** $3, 2, \frac{5}{3}, \frac{3}{2}, \frac{7}{5}$

9. $3, \frac{12}{11}, \frac{9}{13}, \frac{24}{47}, \frac{15}{37}$ **11.** $0, 1, 0, \frac{1}{2}, 0$ **13.** $\frac{5}{3}, \frac{17}{9}, \frac{53}{27}, \frac{161}{81}, \frac{485}{243}$

15. $1, \frac{1}{2^{3/2}}, \frac{1}{3^{3/2}}, \frac{1}{8}, \frac{1}{5^{3/2}}$ **17.** $-1, \frac{1}{4}, -\frac{1}{9}, \frac{1}{16}, -\frac{1}{25}$

19. $\frac{2}{3}, \frac{2}{3}, \frac{2}{3}, \frac{2}{3}, \frac{2}{3}$ **21.** 0, 0, 6, 24, 60 **23.** -73 **25.** $\frac{44}{239}$

27.

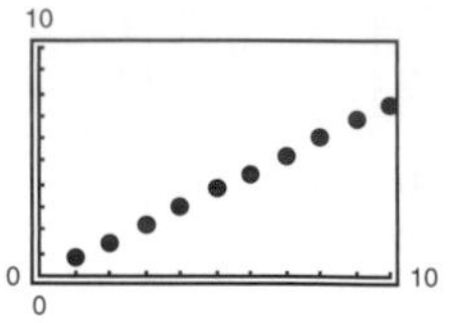

29.

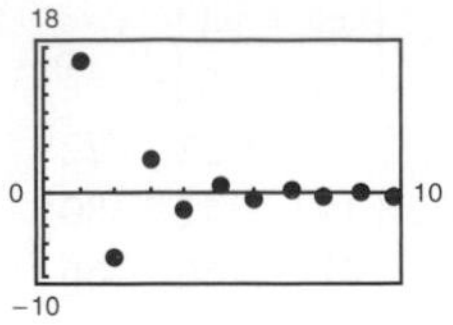

31.

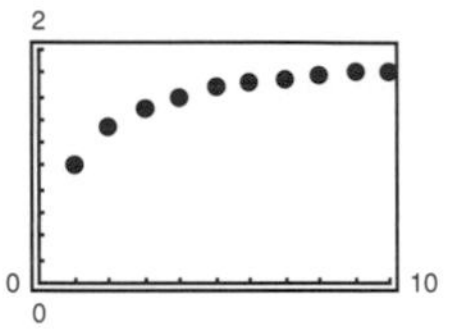

33. c **34.** b **35.** d **36.** a **37.** $a_n = 3n - 2$

39. $a_n = n^2 - 1$ **41.** $a_n = \frac{(-1)^n(n+1)}{n+2}$

43. $a_n = \frac{n+1}{2n-1}$ **45.** $a_n = \frac{1}{n^2}$ **47.** $a_n = (-1)^{n+1}$

49. $a_n = 1 + \frac{1}{n}$ **51.** 28, 24, 20, 16, 12

53. 3, 4, 6, 10, 18 **55.** 6, 8, 10, 12, 14
$a_n = 2n + 4$

57. 81, 27, 9, 3, 1
$a_n = \frac{243}{3^n}$
59. $1, 3, \frac{9}{2}, \frac{9}{2}, \frac{27}{8}$

61. $1, \frac{1}{2}, \frac{1}{6}, \frac{1}{24}, \frac{1}{120}$ **63.** $1, \frac{1}{2}, \frac{1}{24}, \frac{1}{720}, \frac{1}{40{,}320}$

65. $\frac{1}{30}$ **67.** 90 **69.** $n + 1$

71. $\frac{1}{2n(2n+1)}$ **73.** 35 **75.** 40 **77.** 30

79. $\frac{9}{5}$ **81.** 88 **83.** 30 **85.** 81 **87.** $\frac{47}{60}$

89. $\sum_{i=1}^{9} \frac{1}{3i}$ **91.** $\sum_{i=1}^{8} \left[2\left(\frac{i}{8}\right) + 3\right]$ **93.** $\sum_{i=1}^{6} (-1)^{i+1} 3^i$

95. $\sum_{i=1}^{20} \frac{(-1)^{i+1}}{i^2}$ **97.** $\sum_{i=1}^{5} \frac{2^i - 1}{2^{i+1}}$ **99.** $\frac{75}{16}$ **101.** $-\frac{3}{2}$

103. $\frac{2}{3}$ **105.** $\frac{7}{9}$

107. (a) $A_1 = \$5100.00$, $A_2 = \$5202.00$, $A_3 = \$5306.04$, $A_4 = \$5412.16$, $A_5 = \$5520.40$, $A_6 = \$5630.81$, $A_7 = \$5743.43$, $A_8 = \$5858.30$
(b) $A_{40} = \$11{,}040.20$

109. (a) $b_n = 60.57n - 182$
(b) $c_n = 1.61n^2 + 26.8n - 9.5$
(c)

n	8	9	10	11	12	13
a_n	311	357	419	481	548	608
b_n	303	363	424	484	545	605
c_n	308	362	420	480	544	611

The quadratic model is a better fit.
(d) The quadratic model; 995

111. (a) $a_0 = \$3102.9, a_1 = \$3644.3, a_2 = \$4079.6,$
$a_3 = \$4425.3, a_4 = \$4698.2, a_5 = \$4914.8,$
$a_6 = \$5091.8, a_7 = \$5245.7, a_8 = \$5393.2,$
$a_9 = \$5550.9, a_{10} = \$5735.5, a_{11} = \$5963.5,$
$a_{12} = \$6251.5, a_{13} = \$6616.3$

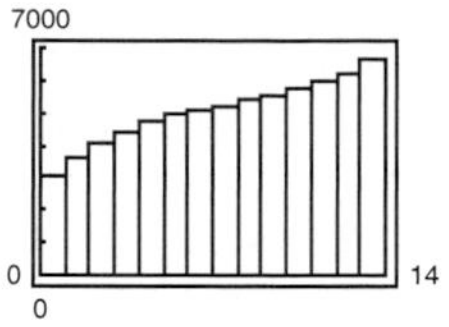

(b) The federal debt is increasing.

113. True by the Properties of Sums

115. 1, 1, 2, 3, 5, 8, 13, 21, 34, 55, 89, 144
$1, 2, \frac{3}{2}, \frac{5}{3}, \frac{8}{5}, \frac{13}{8}, \frac{21}{13}, \frac{34}{21}, \frac{55}{34}, \frac{89}{55}$

117. \$500.95 **119.** Answers will vary.

121. $x, \frac{x^2}{2}, \frac{x^3}{6}, \frac{x^4}{24}, \frac{x^5}{120}$

123. $-\frac{x^2}{2}, \frac{x^4}{24}, -\frac{x^6}{720}, \frac{x^8}{40{,}320}, -\frac{x^{10}}{3{,}628{,}800}$

125. $f^{-1}(x) = \frac{x+3}{4}$ **127.** $h^{-1}(x) = \frac{x^2-1}{5}, x \geq 0$

129. (a) $\begin{bmatrix} 8 & 1 \\ -2 & 6 \end{bmatrix}$ (b) $\begin{bmatrix} -26 & 1 \\ 12 & -21 \end{bmatrix}$
(c) $\begin{bmatrix} 18 & 9 \\ 10 & 7 \end{bmatrix}$ (d) $\begin{bmatrix} 4 & 2 \\ 24 & 21 \end{bmatrix}$

131. (a) $\begin{bmatrix} -3 & -7 & 4 \\ 4 & 4 & 1 \\ 1 & 4 & 3 \end{bmatrix}$ (b) $\begin{bmatrix} 10 & 25 & -10 \\ -12 & -11 & 3 \\ -3 & -9 & -8 \end{bmatrix}$
(c) $\begin{bmatrix} -2 & 7 & -16 \\ 4 & 42 & 45 \\ 1 & 23 & 48 \end{bmatrix}$ (d) $\begin{bmatrix} 16 & 31 & 42 \\ 10 & 47 & 31 \\ 13 & 22 & 25 \end{bmatrix}$

133. 26 **135.** -194

Section 9.2 *(page 659)*

Vocabulary Check *(page 659)*

1. arithmetic; common **2.** $a_n = dn + c$
3. sum of a finite arithmetic sequence

1. Arithmetic sequence, $d = -2$
3. Not an arithmetic sequence
5. Arithmetic sequence, $d = -\frac{1}{4}$
7. Not an arithmetic sequence
9. Not an arithmetic sequence
11. 8, 11, 14, 17, 20
Arithmetic sequence, $d = 3$
13. 7, 3, -1, -5, -9
Arithmetic sequence, $d = -4$
15. $-1, 1, -1, 1, -1$
Not an arithmetic sequence
17. $-3, \frac{3}{2}, -1, \frac{3}{4}, -\frac{3}{5}$
Not an arithmetic sequence
19. $a_n = 3n - 2$ **21.** $a_n = -8n + 108$
23. $a_n = 2xn - x$ **25.** $a_n = -\frac{5}{2}n + \frac{13}{2}$
27. $a_n = \frac{10}{3}n + \frac{5}{3}$ **29.** $a_n = -3n + 103$
31. 5, 11, 17, 23, 29 **33.** $-2.6, -3.0, -3.4, -3.8, -4.2$
35. 2, 6, 10, 14, 18 **37.** $-2, 2, 6, 10, 14$
39. 15, 19, 23, 27, 31; $d = 4$; $a_n = 4n + 11$
41. 200, 190, 180, 170, 160; $d = -10$; $a_n = -10n + 210$
43. $\frac{5}{8}, \frac{1}{2}, \frac{3}{8}, \frac{1}{4}, \frac{1}{8}$; $d = -\frac{1}{8}$; $a_n = -\frac{1}{8}n + \frac{3}{4}$
45. 59 **47.** 18.6 **49.** b **50.** d **51.** c **52.** a

53.

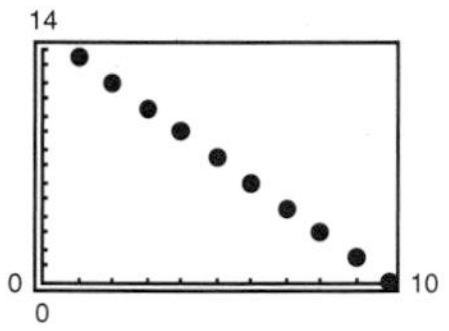

55.

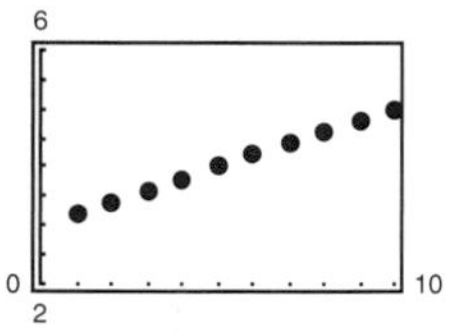

57. 620 **59.** 17.4 **61.** 265 **63.** 4000
65. 10,000 **67.** 1275 **69.** 30,030 **71.** 355
73. 160,000 **75.** 520 **77.** 2725 **79.** 10,120
81. (a) \$40,000 (b) \$217,500 **83.** 2340 seats
85. 405 bricks **87.** 490 meters
89. (a) $a_n = -25n + 225$ (b) \$900
91. \$70,500; answers will vary.
93. (a)

Month	1	2	3	4	5	6
Monthly payment	\$220	\$218	\$216	\$214	\$212	\$210
Unpaid balance	\$1800	\$1600	\$1400	\$1200	\$1000	\$800

(b) \$110

95. (a) $a_n = 1098n + 17{,}588$
(b) $a_n = 1114.9n + 17{,}795$; the models are similar.
(c)

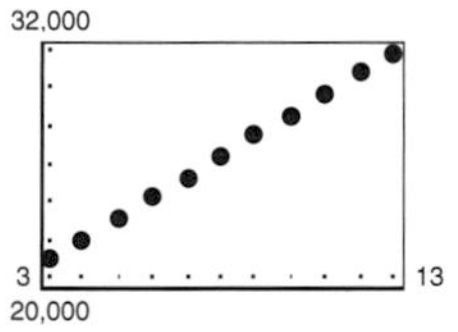

(d) 2004: \$32,960
2005: \$34,058

(e) Answers will vary.

97. True. Given a_1 and a_2, $d = a_2 - a_1$ and $a_n = a_1 + (n-1)d$.
99. Answers will vary.

101. (a) 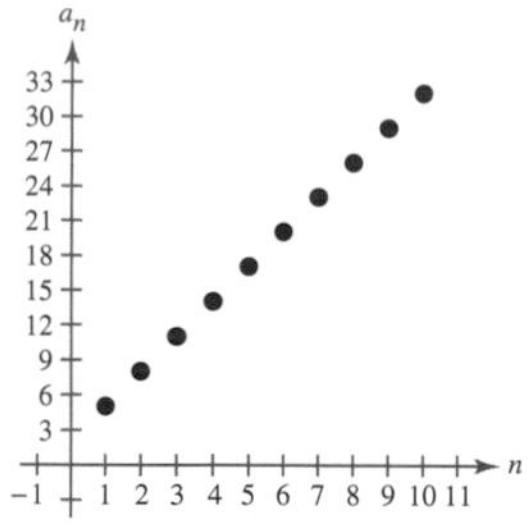
(b) 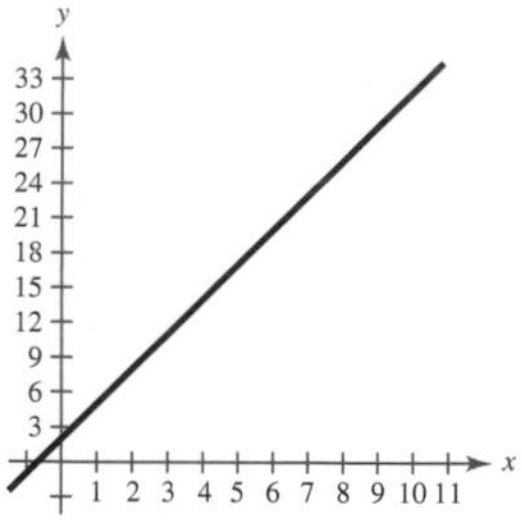

(c) The graph of $y = 3x + 2$ contains all points on the line. The graph of $a_n = 2 + 3n$ contains only points at the positive integers.

(d) The slope of the line and the common difference of the arithmetic sequence are equal.

103. 4

105. Slope: $\frac{1}{2}$;
y-intercept: $\left(0, -\frac{3}{4}\right)$

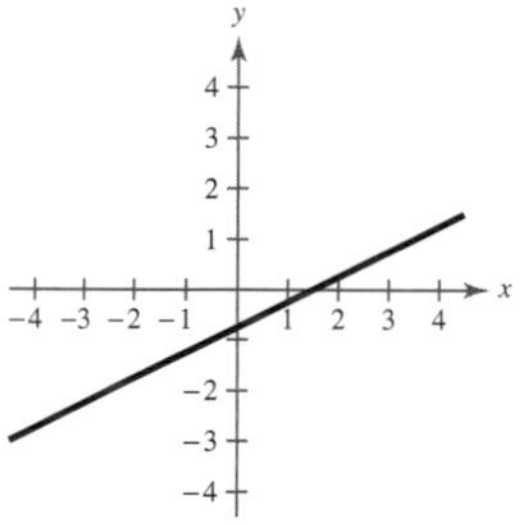

107. Slope: undefined;
No y-intercept

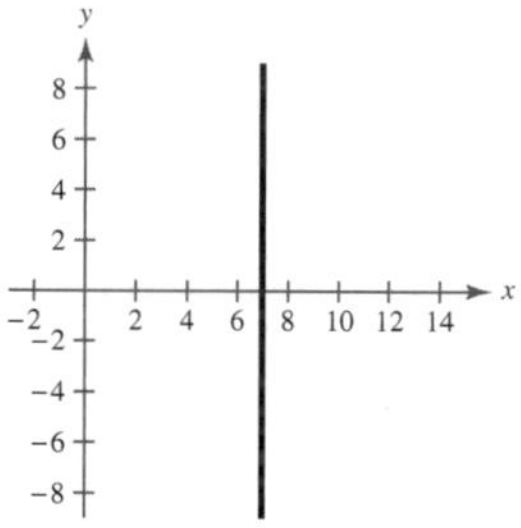

109. $x = 1, y = 5, z = -1$ **111.** Answers will vary.

Section 9.3 *(page 669)*

Vocabulary Check *(page 669)*

1. geometric; common
2. $a_n = a_1 r^{n-1}$
3. $S_n = a_1\left(\dfrac{1 - r^n}{1 - r}\right)$
4. geometric series
5. $S = \dfrac{a_1}{1 - r}$

1. Geometric sequence, $r = 3$
3. Not a geometric sequence
5. Geometric sequence, $r = -\frac{1}{2}$
7. Geometric sequence, $r = 2$
9. Not a geometric sequence
11. 2, 6, 18, 54, 162 **13.** $1, \frac{1}{2}, \frac{1}{4}, \frac{1}{8}, \frac{1}{16}$
15. $5, -\frac{1}{2}, \frac{1}{20}, -\frac{1}{200}, \frac{1}{2000}$ **17.** $1, e, e^2, e^3, e^4$
19. $2, \dfrac{x}{2}, \dfrac{x^2}{8}, \dfrac{x^3}{32}, \dfrac{x^4}{128}$
21. 64, 32, 16, 8, 4; $r = \frac{1}{2}$; $a_n = 128\left(\frac{1}{2}\right)^n$
23. 7, 14, 28, 56, 112; $r = 2$; $a_n = \frac{7}{2}(2)^n$
25. $6, -9, \frac{27}{2}, -\frac{81}{4}, \frac{243}{8}$; $r = -\frac{3}{2}$; $a_n = -4\left(-\frac{3}{2}\right)^n$
27. $a_n = 4\left(\dfrac{1}{2}\right)^{n-1}$; $\dfrac{1}{128}$ **29.** $a_n = 6\left(-\dfrac{1}{3}\right)^{n-1}$; $-\dfrac{2}{3^{10}}$
31. $a_n = 100e^{x(n-1)}$; $100e^{8x}$
33. $a_n = 500(1.02)^{n-1}$; ≈ 1082.372 **35.** 45,927
37. 50,388,480 **39.** $a_3 = 9$ **41.** $a_6 = -2$
43. a **44.** c **45.** b **46.** d

47. 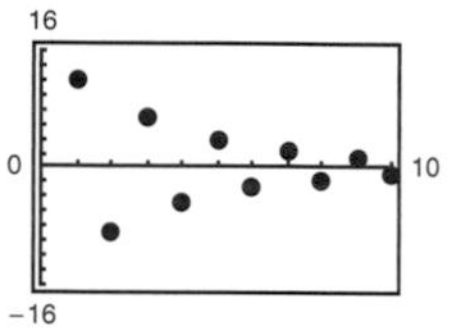

49. 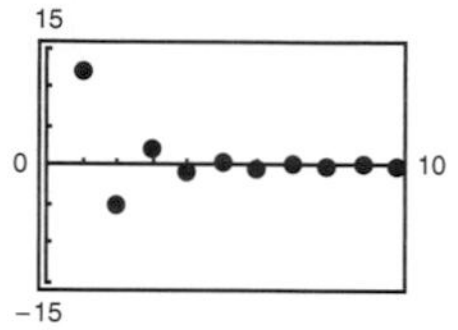

51. 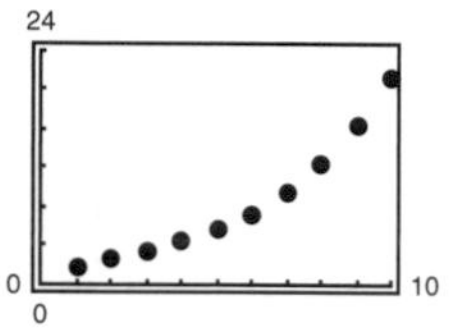

53. 511 **55.** 171 **57.** 43 **59.** $\frac{1365}{32}$
61. 29,921.311 **63.** 592.647 **65.** 2092.596
67. $\frac{8}{5}$ **69.** 6.400 **71.** 3.750
73. $\sum_{n=1}^{7} 5(3)^{n-1}$ **75.** $\sum_{n=1}^{7} 2\left(-\frac{1}{4}\right)^{n-1}$ **77.** $\sum_{n=1}^{6} 0.1(4)^{n-1}$
79. 2 **81.** $\frac{2}{3}$ **83.** $\frac{16}{3}$ **85.** $\frac{5}{3}$ **87.** -30
89. 32 **91.** Undefined **93.** $\frac{4}{11}$ **95.** $\frac{7}{22}$

97. 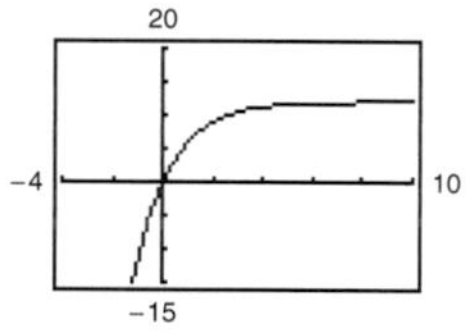

Horizontal asymptote: $y = 12$
Corresponds to the sum of the series

99. (a) $a_n = 1190.88(1.006)^n$
(b) The population is growing at a rate of 0.6% per year.
(c) 1342.2 million. This value is close to the prediction.
(d) 2007

101. (a) \$3714.87 (b) \$3722.16 (c) \$3725.85
(d) \$3728.32 (e) \$3729.52

103. \$7011.89 **105.** Answers will vary.
107. (a) \$26,198.27 (b) \$26,263.88
109. (a) \$118,590.12 (b) \$118,788.73
111. Answers will vary. **113.** \$1600
115. $\approx$ \$2181.82 **117.** 126 square inches
119. \$3,623,993.23
121. False. A sequence is geometric if the ratios of consecutive terms are the same.
123. Given a real number r between -1 and 1, as the exponent n increases, r^n approaches zero.

125. $x^2 + 2x$ **127.** $3x^2 + 6x + 1$

129. $x(3x + 8)(3x - 8)$ **131.** $(3x + 1)(2x - 5)$

133. $\dfrac{3x}{x - 3}, \ x \neq -3$ **135.** $\dfrac{2x + 1}{3}, \ x \neq 0, -\dfrac{1}{2}$

137. $\dfrac{5x^2 + 9x - 30}{(x + 2)(x - 2)}$ **139.** Answers will vary.

Section 9.4 *(page 681)*

> **Vocabulary Check** *(page 681)*
>
> **1.** mathematical induction **2.** first
>
> **3.** arithmetic **4.** second

1. $\dfrac{5}{(k + 1)(k + 2)}$ **3.** $\dfrac{(k + 1)^2(k + 2)^2}{4}$

5–33. Answers will vary. **35.** $S_n = n(2n - 1)$

37. $S_n = 10 - 10\left(\dfrac{9}{10}\right)^n$ **39.** $S_n = \dfrac{n}{2(n + 1)}$

41. 120 **43.** 91 **45.** 979 **47.** 70 **49.** -3402

51. 0, 3, 6, 9, 12, 15
First differences: 3, 3, 3, 3, 3
Second differences: 0, 0, 0, 0
Linear

53. 3, 1, -2, -6, -11, -17
First differences: -2, -3, -4, -5, -6
Second differences: -1, -1, -1, -1
Quadratic

55. 2, 4, 16, 256, 65,536, 4,294,967,296
First differences: 2, 12, 240, 65,280, 4,294,901,760
Second differences: 10, 228, 65,040, 4,294,836,480
Neither

57. $a_n = n^2 - n + 3$ **59.** $a_n = \frac{1}{2}n^2 + n - 3$

61. (a) 2.2, 2.4, 2.2, 2.3, 0.9
(b) A linear model can be used.
$a_n = 2.2n + 102.7$
(c) $a_n = 2.08n + 103.9$
(d) Part b: $a_n = 142.3$; Part c: $a_n = 141.34$
These are very similar.

63. True. P_7 may be false.

65. True. If the second differences are all zero, then the first differences are all the same and the sequence is arithmetic.

67. $4x^4 - 4x^2 + 1$ **69.** $-64x^3 + 240x^2 - 300x + 125$

71. (a) Domain: all real numbers x except $x = -3$
(b) Intercept: $(0, 0)$
(c) Vertical asymptote: $x = -3$
Horizontal asymptote: $y = 1$
(d)

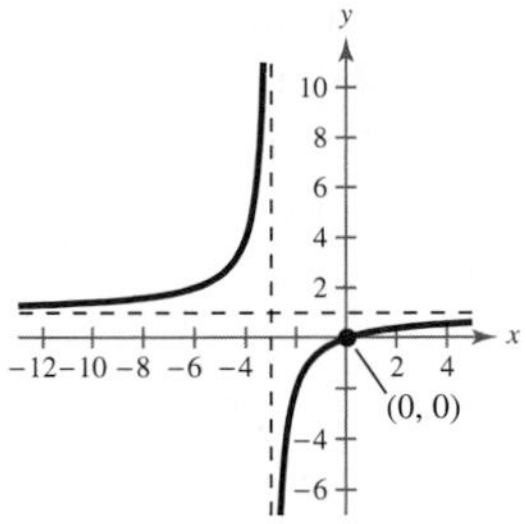

73. (a) Domain: all real numbers t except $t = 0$
(b) t-intercept: $(7, 0)$
(c) Vertical asymptote: $t = 0$
Horizontal asymptote: $y = 1$
(d)

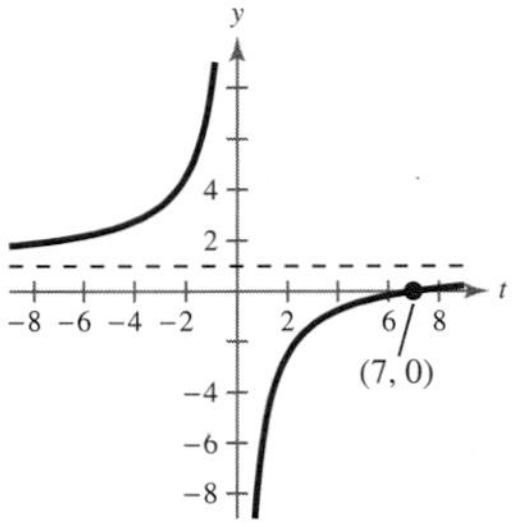

Section 9.5 *(page 688)*

> **Vocabulary Check** *(page 688)*
>
> **1.** binomial coefficients
>
> **2.** Binomial Theorem; Pascal's Triangle
>
> **3.** $\dbinom{n}{r}$; ${}_nC_r$ **4.** expanding a binomial

1. 10 **3.** 1 **5.** 15,504 **7.** 210 **9.** 4950

11. 56 **13.** 35 **15.** $x^4 + 4x^3 + 6x^2 + 4x + 1$

17. $a^4 + 24a^3 + 216a^2 + 864a + 1296$

19. $y^3 - 12y^2 + 48y - 64$

21. $x^5 + 5x^4y + 10x^3y^2 + 10x^2y^3 + 5xy^4 + y^5$

23. $r^6 + 18r^5s + 135r^4s^2 + 540r^3s^3 + 1215r^2s^4 + 1458rs^5 + 729s^6$

25. $243a^5 - 1620a^4b + 4320a^3b^2 - 5760a^2b^3 + 3840ab^4 - 1024b^5$

27. $8x^3 + 12x^2y + 6xy^2 + y^3$

29. $x^8 + 4x^6y^2 + 6x^4y^4 + 4x^2y^6 + y^8$

31. $\dfrac{1}{x^5} + \dfrac{5y}{x^4} + \dfrac{10y^2}{x^3} + \dfrac{10y^3}{x^2} + \dfrac{5y^4}{x} + y^5$

33. $2x^4 - 24x^3 + 113x^2 - 246x + 207$

35. $32t^5 - 80t^4s + 80t^3s^2 - 40t^2s^3 + 10ts^4 - s^5$

37. $x^5 + 10x^4y + 40x^3y^2 + 80x^2y^3 + 80xy^4 + 32y^5$

39. $120x^7y^3$ **41.** $360x^3y^2$ **43.** $1{,}259{,}712x^2y^7$

45. $32{,}476{,}950{,}000x^4y^8$ **47.** 1,732,104

49. 180 **51.** $-326{,}592$ **53.** 210

55. $x^2 + 12x^{3/2} + 54x + 108x^{1/2} + 81$

57. $x^2 - 3x^{4/3}y^{1/3} + 3x^{2/3}y^{2/3} - y$

59. $3x^2 + 3xh + h^2, h \neq 0$ **61.** $\dfrac{1}{\sqrt{x+h} + \sqrt{x}}, h \neq 0$

63. -4 **65.** $2035 + 828i$ **67.** 1

69. 1.172 **71.** 510,568.785

73.

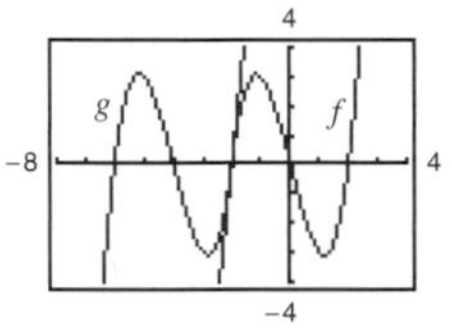

g is shifted four units to the left of f.

$g(x) = x^3 + 12x^2 + 44x + 48$

75. 0.273 **77.** 0.171

79. (a) $f(t) = 0.0025t^3 - 0.015t^2 + 0.88t + 7.7$

(b)

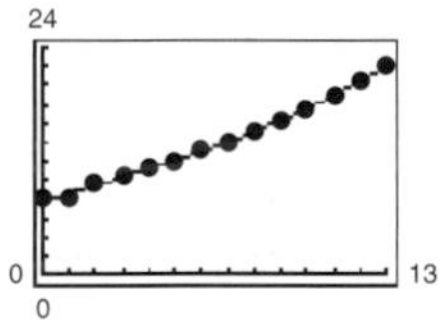

(c) $g(t) = 0.0025t^3 + 0.06t^2 + 1.33t + 17.5$

(d)

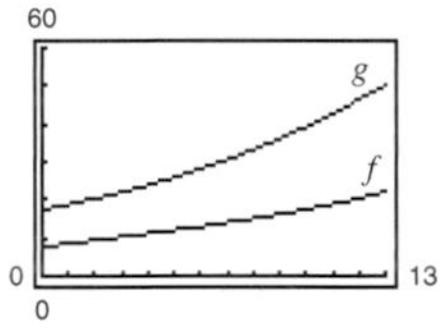

(e) $f(t)$: 33.26 gallons; $g(t)$: 33.26 gallons; yes

(f) The trend is for the per capita consumption of bottled water to increase. This may be due to the increasing concern with contaminants in tap water.

81. True. The coefficients from the Binomial Theorem can be used to find the numbers in Pascal's Triangle.

83. False. The coefficient of the x^{10}-term is 1,732,104 and the coefficient of the x^{14}-term is 192,456.

85.

1 8 28 56 70 56 28 8 1

1 9 36 84 126 126 84 36 9 1

1 10 45 120 210 252 210 120 45 10 1

87. The signs of the terms in the expansion of $(x - y)^n$ alternate between positive and negative.

89–91. Answers will vary.

93.

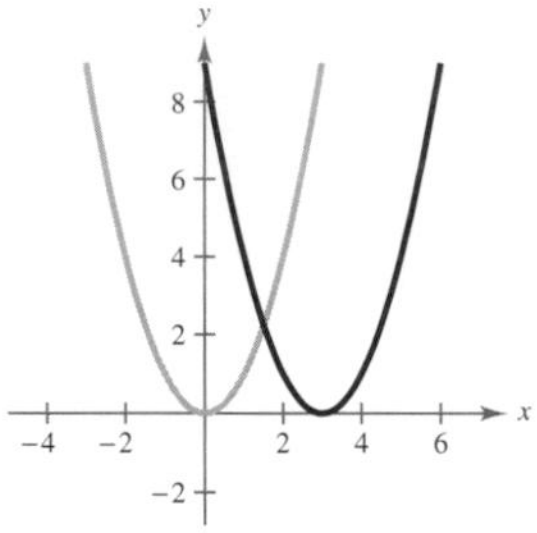

$g(x) = (x - 3)^2$

95.

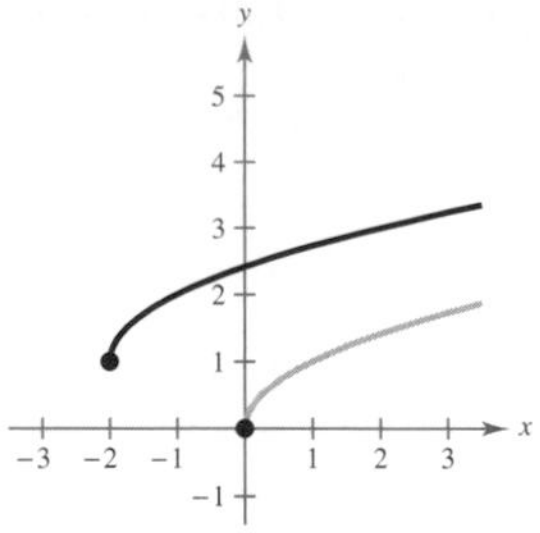

$g(x) = \sqrt{x + 2} + 1$

97. $\begin{bmatrix} 4 & -5 \\ 5 & -6 \end{bmatrix}$

Section 9.6 *(page 698)*

Vocabulary Check *(page 698)*

1. Fundamental Counting Principle **2.** permutation

3. ${}_nP_r = \dfrac{n!}{(n-r)!}$ **4.** distinguishable permutations

5. combinations

1. 6 **3.** 5 **5.** 3 **7.** 8 **9.** 30 **11.** 30

13. 64 **15.** 175,760,000

17. (a) 900 (b) 648 (c) 180 (d) 600

19. 64,000 **21.** (a) 40,320 (b) 384 **23.** 24

25. 336 **27.** 120 **29.** $n = 5$ or $n = 6$

31. 1,860,480 **33.** 970,200 **35.** 15,504 **37.** 120

39. 11,880 **41.** 420 **43.** 2520

45. ABCD, ABDC, ACBD, ACDB, ADBC, ADCB, BACD, BADC, CABD, CADB, DABC, DACB, BCAD, BDAC, CBAD, CDAB, DBAC, DCAB, BCDA, BDCA, CBDA, CDBA, DBCA, DCBA

47. 1,816,214,400 **49.** 5,586,853,480

51. AB, AC, AD, AE, AF, BC, BD, BE, BF, CD, CE, CF, DE, DF, EF

53. 324,632 **55.** (a) 35 (b) 63 (c) 203

57. (a) 3744 (b) 24 **59.** 292,600

61. 5 **63.** 20

65. (a) 146,107,962

(b) If the jackpot is won, there is only one winning number.

(c) There are 28,989,675 possible winning numbers in the state lottery, which is considerably less than the possible number of winning Powerball numbers.

67. False. It is an example of a combination.

69. They are equal.

71–73. Proof

75. No. For some calculators the number is too great.

77. (a) 35 (b) 8 (c) 83

79. (a) -4 (b) 0 (c) 0 **81.** 8.30 **83.** 35

Section 9.7 *(page 709)*

Vocabulary Check *(page 709)*

1. experiment; outcomes **2.** sample space
3. probability **4.** impossible; certain
5. mutually exclusive **6.** independent
7. complement **8.** (a) iii (b) i (c) iv (d) ii

1. $\{(H, 1), (H, 2), (H, 3), (H, 4), (H, 5), (H, 6), (T, 1), (T, 2), (T, 3), (T, 4), (T, 5), (T, 6)\}$
3. {ABC, ACB, BAC, BCA, CAB, CBA}
5. {AB, AC, AD, AE, BC, BD, BE, CD, CE, DE}
7. $\frac{3}{8}$ **9.** $\frac{7}{8}$ **11.** $\frac{3}{13}$ **13.** $\frac{3}{26}$ **15.** $\frac{1}{12}$ **17.** $\frac{11}{12}$
19. $\frac{1}{3}$ **21.** $\frac{1}{5}$ **23.** $\frac{2}{5}$ **25.** 0.3 **27.** $\frac{3}{4}$ **29.** 0.86
31. $\frac{18}{35}$ **33.** (a) 58% (b) 95.6% (c) 0.4%
35. (a) 243 (b) $\frac{1}{50}$ (c) $\frac{16}{25}$
37. (a) $\frac{112}{209}$ (b) $\frac{97}{209}$ (c) $\frac{274}{627}$
39. $P(\{\text{Taylor wins}\}) = \frac{1}{2}$
$P(\{\text{Moore wins}\}) = P(\{\text{Jenkins wins}\}) = \frac{1}{4}$
41. (a) $\frac{21}{1292}$ (b) $\frac{225}{646}$ (c) $\frac{49}{323}$
43. (a) $\frac{1}{120}$ (b) $\frac{1}{24}$ **45.** (a) $\frac{5}{13}$ (b) $\frac{1}{2}$ (c) $\frac{4}{13}$
47. (a) $\frac{14}{55}$ (b) $\frac{12}{55}$ (c) $\frac{54}{55}$ **49.** 0.4746
51. (a) 0.9702 (b) 0.9998 (c) 0.0002
53. (a) $\frac{1}{16}$ (b) $\frac{1}{8}$ (c) $\frac{15}{16}$
55. (a) $\frac{1}{38}$ (b) $\frac{9}{19}$ (c) $\frac{10}{19}$ (d) $\frac{1}{1444}$ (e) $\frac{729}{6859}$
(f) The probabilities are slightly better in European roulette.
57. True. Two events are independent if the occurrence of one has no effect on the occurrence of the other.
59. (a) As you consider successive people with distinct birthdays, the probabilities must decrease to take into account the birth dates already used. Because the birth dates of people are independent events, multiply the respective probabilities of distinct birthdays.
(b) $\frac{365}{365} \cdot \frac{364}{365} \cdot \frac{363}{365} \cdot \frac{362}{365}$ (c) Answers will vary.
(d) Q_n is the probability that the birthdays are *not* distinct, which is equivalent to at least two people having the same birthday.
(e)

n	10	15	20	23	30	40	50
P_n	0.88	0.75	0.59	0.49	0.29	0.11	0.03
Q_n	0.12	0.25	0.41	0.51	0.71	0.89	0.97

(f) 23
61. No real solution **63.** $0, \dfrac{1 \pm \sqrt{13}}{2}$ **65.** -4
67. $\frac{11}{2}$ **69.** -10

71.
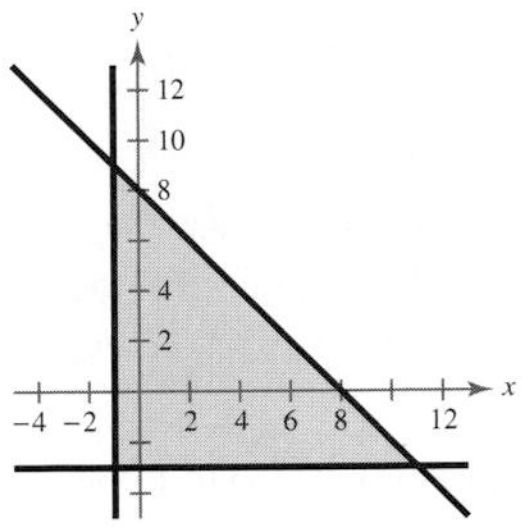
73.
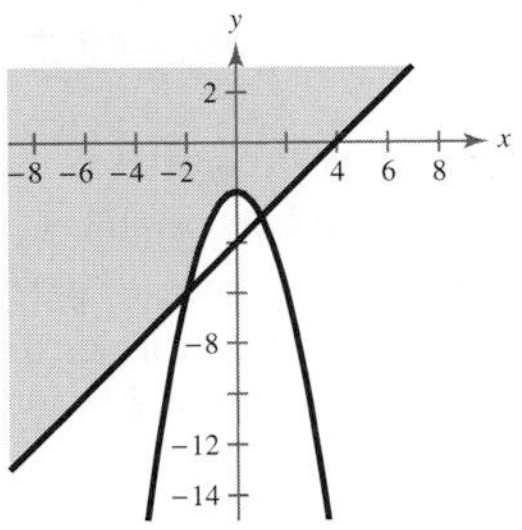

Review Exercises *(page 715)*

1. $8, 5, 4, \frac{7}{2}, \frac{16}{5}$ **3.** $72, 36, 12, 3, \frac{3}{5}$ **5.** $a_n = 2(-1)^n$
7. $a_n = \dfrac{4}{n}$ **9.** 120 **11.** 1 **13.** 30 **15.** $\dfrac{205}{24}$
17. 6050 **19.** $\displaystyle\sum_{k=1}^{20} \frac{1}{2k}$ **21.** $\dfrac{5}{9}$ **23.** $\dfrac{2}{99}$
25. (a) $A_1 = \$10{,}067$, $A_2 = \$10{,}134$, $A_3 = \$10{,}201$, $A_4 = \$10{,}269$, $A_5 = \$10{,}338$, $A_6 = \$10{,}407$, $A_7 = \$10{,}476$, $A_8 = \$10{,}546$, $A_9 = \$10{,}616$, $A_{10} = \$10{,}687$
(b) $A_{120} = \$22{,}196.40$
27. Arithmetic sequence, $d = -2$
29. Arithmetic sequence, $d = \frac{1}{2}$ **31.** 4, 7, 10, 13, 16
33. 25, 28, 31, 34, 37 **35.** $a_n = 12n - 5$
37. $a_n = 3ny - 2y$ **39.** $a_n = -7n + 107$
41. 80 **43.** 88 **45.** 25,250
47. (a) \$43,000 (b) \$192,500
49. Geometric sequence, $r = 2$
51. Geometric sequence, $r = -2$ **53.** $4, -1, \frac{1}{4}, -\frac{1}{16}, \frac{1}{64}$
55. $9, 6, 4, \frac{8}{3}, \frac{16}{9}$ or $9, -6, 4, -\frac{8}{3}, \frac{16}{9}$
57. $a_n = 16\left(-\frac{1}{2}\right)^{n-1}$; $\approx -3.052 \times 10^{-5}$
59. $a_n = 100(1.05)^{n-1}$; ≈ 252.695
61. 127 **63.** $\frac{15}{16}$ **65.** 31 **67.** 24.85
69. 5486.45 **71.** 8 **73.** $\frac{10}{9}$ **75.** 12
77. (a) $a_t = 120{,}000(0.7)^t$ (b) \$20,168.40
79–81. Answers will vary. **83.** $S_n = n(2n + 7)$
85. $S_n = \frac{5}{2}\left[1 - \left(\frac{3}{5}\right)^n\right]$ **87.** 465 **89.** 4648
91. 5, 10, 15, 20, 25
First differences: 5, 5, 5, 5
Second differences: 0, 0, 0
Linear
93. 16, 15, 14, 13, 12
First differences: $-1, -1, -1, -1$
Second differences: 0, 0, 0
Linear
95. 15 **97.** 56 **99.** 35 **101.** 28
103. $x^4 + 16x^3 + 96x^2 + 256x + 256$
105. $a^5 - 15a^4b + 90a^3b^2 - 270a^2b^3 + 405ab^4 - 243b^5$
107. $41 + 840i$ **109.** 11 **111.** 10,000 **113.** 720
115. 56 **117.** $\frac{1}{9}$ **119.** (a) 43% (b) 82%

121. $\frac{1}{216}$ **123.** $\frac{3}{4}$

125. True. $\dfrac{(n+2)!}{n!} = \dfrac{(n+2)(n+1)n!}{n!} = (n+2)(n+1)$

127. True by Properties of Sums

129. False. When r equals 0 or 1, then the results are the same.

131. In the sequence in part (a), the odd-numbered terms are negative, whereas in the sequence in part (b), the even-numbered terms are negative.

133. Each term of the sequence is defined in terms of preceding terms.

135. d **136.** a **137.** b **138.** c

139. 240, 440, 810, 1490, 2740

Chapter Test *(page 719)*

1. $-\frac{1}{5}, \frac{1}{8}, -\frac{1}{11}, \frac{1}{14}, -\frac{1}{17}$ **2.** $a_n = \dfrac{n+2}{n!}$

3. 50, 61, 72; 140 **4.** $a_n = 0.8n + 1.4$

5. 5, 10, 20, 40, 80 **6.** 86,100 **7.** 189

8. 4 **9.** Answers will vary.

10. $x^4 + 8x^3y + 24x^2y^2 + 32xy^3 + 16y^4$ **11.** $-108{,}864$

12. (a) 72 (b) 328,440 **13.** (a) 330 (b) 720,720

14. 26,000 **15.** 720 **16.** $\frac{1}{15}$ **17.** 3.908×10^{-10}

18. 25%

Cumulative Test for Chapters 7–9 *(page 720)*

1. $(1, 2), \left(-\frac{3}{2}, \frac{3}{4}\right)$ **2.** $(2, -1)$

3. $(4, 2, -3)$ **4.** $(1, -2, 1)$

5.

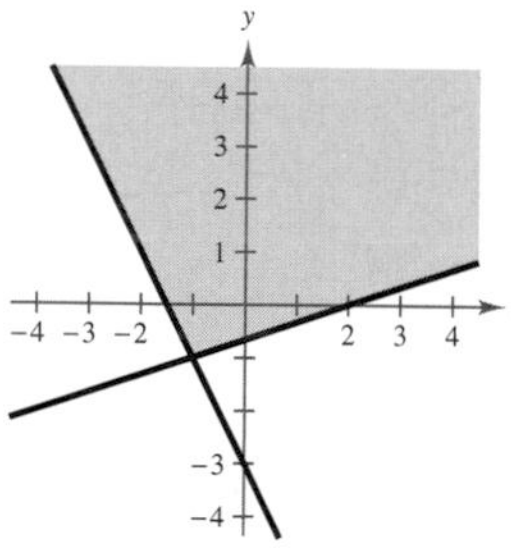

6.

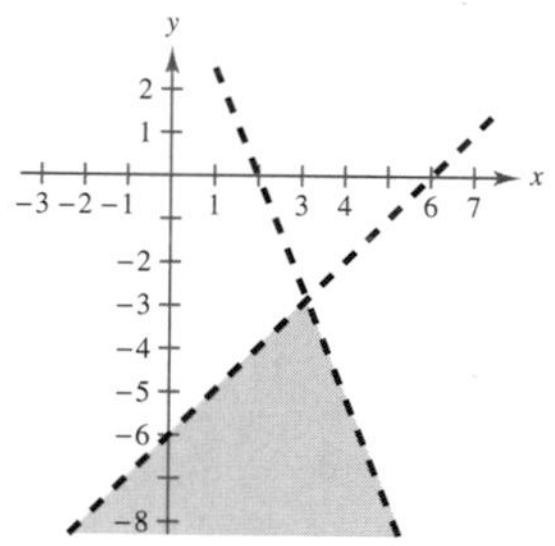

7.

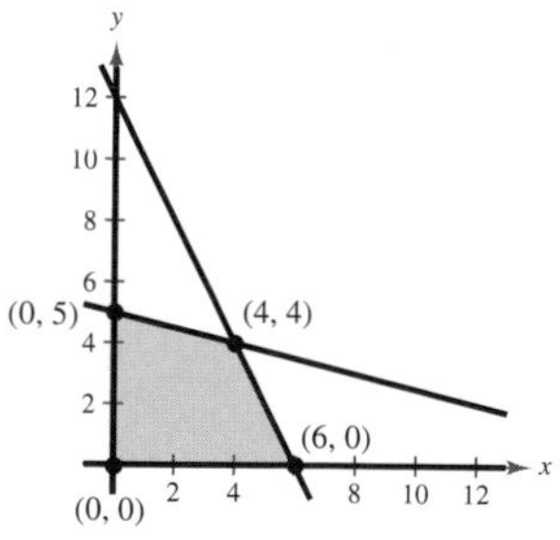

Maximum at (4, 4): $z = 20$

Minimum at (0, 0): $z = 0$

8. \$0.75 mixture: 120 pounds; \$1.25 mixture: 80 pounds

9. $y = \frac{1}{3}x^2 - 2x + 4$

10. $\left[\begin{array}{ccc|c} -1 & 2 & -1 & 9 \\ 2 & -1 & 2 & -9 \\ 3 & 3 & -4 & 7 \end{array}\right]$ **11.** $(-2, 3, -1)$

12. $\begin{bmatrix} 3 & 3 \\ 0 & 2 \end{bmatrix}$ **13.** $\begin{bmatrix} 2 & -6 \\ -2 & 0 \end{bmatrix}$ **14.** $\begin{bmatrix} 6 & -6 \\ -3 & 2 \end{bmatrix}$

15. $\begin{bmatrix} -4 & 12 \\ 3 & -3 \end{bmatrix}$ **16.** 84 **17.** $\begin{bmatrix} -175 & 37 & -13 \\ 95 & -20 & 7 \\ 14 & -3 & 1 \end{bmatrix}$

18. Gym shoes: \$198.36 million
Jogging shoes: \$358.48 million
Walking shoes: \$167.17 million

19. $(-5, 4)$ **20.** $(-3, 4, 2)$ **21.** 9

22. $\frac{1}{5}, -\frac{1}{7}, \frac{1}{9}, -\frac{1}{11}, \frac{1}{13}$ **23.** $a_n = \dfrac{(n+1)!}{n+3}$

24. 920 **25.** (a) 65.4 (b) $a_n = 3.2n + 1.4$

26. 3, 6, 12, 24, 48 **27.** $\frac{13}{9}$ **28.** Answers will vary.

29. $z^4 - 12z^3 + 54z^2 - 108z + 81$ **30.** 210 **31.** 600

32. 70 **33.** 120 **34.** 453,600 **35.** 151,200

36. 720 **37.** $\frac{1}{4}$

Problem Solving *(page 725)*

1. 1, 1.5, $1.41\overline{6}$, 1.414215686, 1.414213562, 1.414213562, . . .
x_n approaches $\sqrt{2}$.

3. (a)

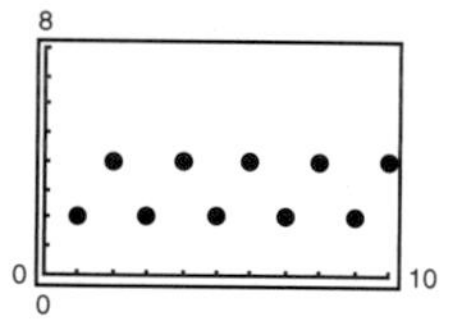

(b) If n is odd, $a_n = 2$, and if n is even, $a_n = 4$.

(c)

n	1	10	101	1000	10,001
a_n	2	4	2	4	2

(d) It is not possible to find the value of a_n as n approaches infinity.

5. (a) 3, 5, 7, 9, 11, 13, 15, 17; $a_n = 2n + 1$

(b) To obtain the arithmetic sequence, find the differences of consecutive terms of the sequence of perfect cubes. Then find the differences of consecutive terms of this sequence.

(c) 12, 18, 24, 30, 36, 42, 48; $a_n = 6n + 6$

(d) To obtain the arithmetic sequence, find the third sequence obtained by taking differences of consecutive terms in consecutive sequences.

(e) 60, 84, 108, 132, 156, 180; $a_n = 24n + 36$

7. $s_n = \left(\frac{1}{2}\right)^{n-1}$

$a_n = \dfrac{\sqrt{3}}{4}s_n^{\,2}$

9. Answers will vary.

11. (a) Answers will vary. (b) 17,710

13. $\frac{1}{3}$ **15.** (a) $-\$0.71$ (b) 2.53, 24 turns

Chapter 10

Section 10.1 (page 732)

Vocabulary Check (page 732)

1. inclination 2. $\tan\theta$
3. $\left|\dfrac{m_2 - m_1}{1 + m_1 m_2}\right|$ 4. $\dfrac{|Ax_1 + By_1 + C|}{\sqrt{A^2 + B^2}}$

1. $\dfrac{\sqrt{3}}{3}$ **3.** -1 **5.** $\sqrt{3}$ **7.** 3.2236

9. $\dfrac{3\pi}{4}$ radians, 135° **11.** $\dfrac{\pi}{4}$ radian, 45°

13. 0.6435 radian, 36.9° **15.** 1.0517 radians, 60.3°

17. 2.1112 radians, 121.0° **19.** 1.2490 radians, 71.6°

21. 2.1112 radians, 121.0° **23.** 1.1071 radians, 63.4°

25. 0.1974 radian, 11.3° **27.** 1.4289 radians, 81.9°

29. 0.9273 radian, 53.1° **31.** 0.8187 radian, 46.9°

33. $(2, 1) \leftrightarrow (4, 4)$: slope $= \frac{3}{2}$
$(4, 4) \leftrightarrow (6, 2)$: slope $= -1$
$(6, 2) \leftrightarrow (2, 1)$: slope $= \frac{1}{4}$
$(2, 1)$: 42.3°; $(4, 4)$: 78.7°; $(6, 2)$: 59.0°

35. $(-4, -1) \leftrightarrow (3, 2)$: slope $= \frac{3}{7}$
$(3, 2) \leftrightarrow (1, 0)$: slope $= 1$
$(1, 0) \leftrightarrow (-4, -1)$: slope $= \frac{1}{5}$
$(-4, -1)$: 11.9°; $(3, 2)$: 21.8°; $(1, 0)$: 146.3°

37. 0 **39.** $\dfrac{7}{5}$ **41.** 7 **43.** $\dfrac{8\sqrt{37}}{37} \approx 1.3152$

45.
(a)
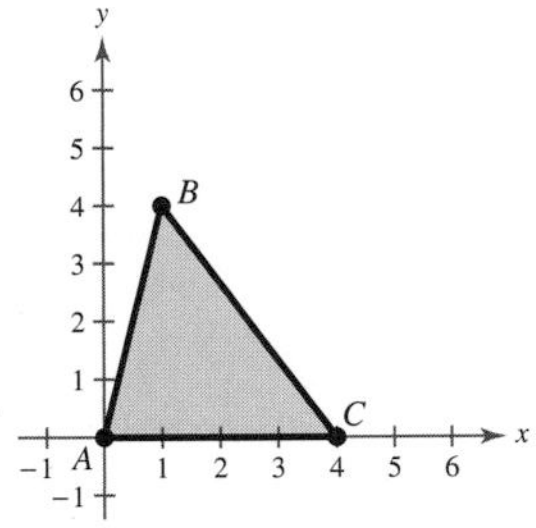

(b) 4 (c) 8

47.
(a)
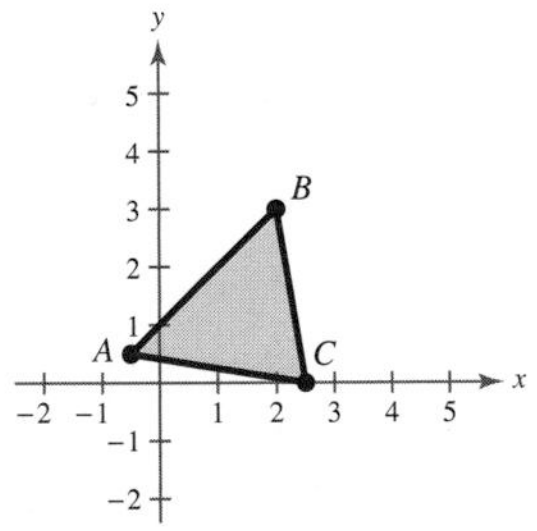

(b) $\dfrac{35\sqrt{37}}{74}$ (c) $\dfrac{35}{8}$

49. $2\sqrt{2}$ **51.** 0.1003, 1054 feet **53.** 31.0°

55. $\alpha \approx 33.69°$; $\beta \approx 56.31°$

57. True. The inclination of a line is related to its slope by $m = \tan\theta$. If the angle is greater than $\pi/2$ but less than π, then the angle is in the second quadrant, where the tangent function is negative.

59. (a) $d = \dfrac{4}{\sqrt{m^2 + 1}}$

(b)
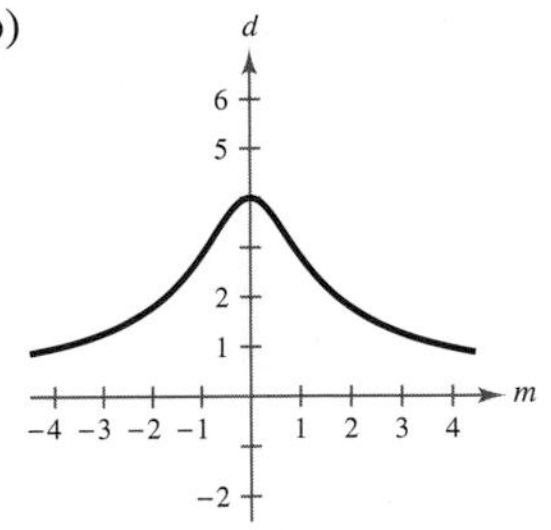

(c) $m = 0$

(d) The graph has a horizontal asymptote at $d = 0$. As the slope becomes larger, the distance between the origin and the line $y = mx + 4$, becomes smaller and approaches 0.

61. x-intercept: $(7, 0)$
y-intercept: $(0, 49)$

63. x-intercepts: $(5 \pm \sqrt{5}, 0)$
y-intercept: $(0, 20)$

65. x-intercepts: $\left(\dfrac{7 \pm \sqrt{53}}{2}, 0\right)$
y-intercept: $(0, -1)$

67. $f(x) = 3\left(x + \frac{1}{3}\right)^2 - \frac{49}{3}$
Vertex: $\left(-\frac{1}{3}, -\frac{49}{3}\right)$

69. $f(x) = 5\left(x + \frac{17}{5}\right)^2 - \frac{324}{5}$
Vertex: $\left(-\frac{17}{5}, -\frac{324}{5}\right)$

71. $f(x) = 6\left(x - \frac{1}{12}\right)^2 - \frac{289}{24}$
Vertex: $\left(\frac{1}{12}, -\frac{289}{24}\right)$

73.
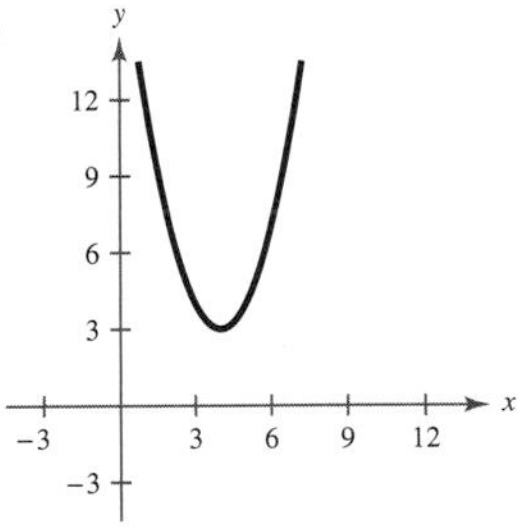

75.
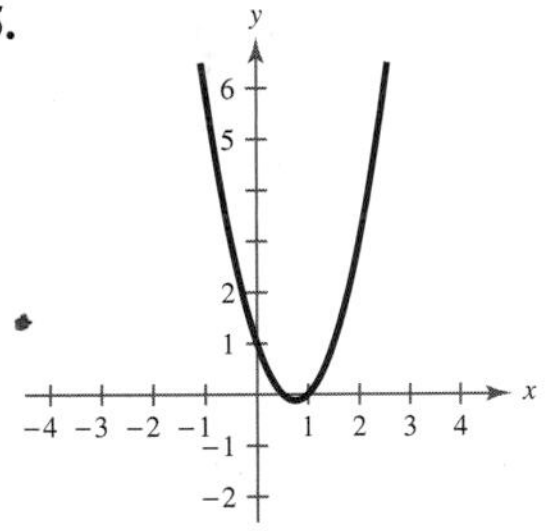

Section 10.2 (page 740)

Vocabulary Check (page 740)

1. conic 2. locus 3. parabola; directrix; focus
4. axis 5. vertex 6. focal chord 7. tangent

1. A circle is formed when a plane intersects the top or bottom half of a double-napped cone and is perpendicular to the axis of the cone.

3. A parabola is formed when a plane intersects the top or bottom half of a double-napped cone, is parallel to the side of the cone, and does not intersect the vertex.

5. e **6.** b **7.** d **8.** f **9.** a **10.** c

11. Vertex: $(0, 0)$
Focus: $\left(0, \frac{1}{2}\right)$
Directrix: $y = -\frac{1}{2}$

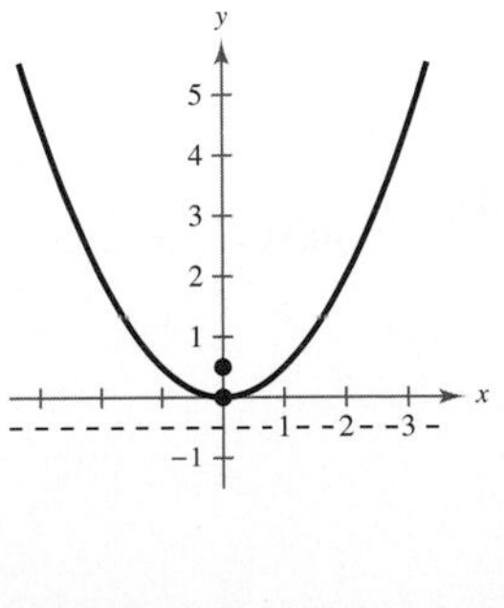

13. Vertex: $(0, 0)$
Focus: $\left(-\frac{3}{2}, 0\right)$
Directrix: $x = \frac{3}{2}$

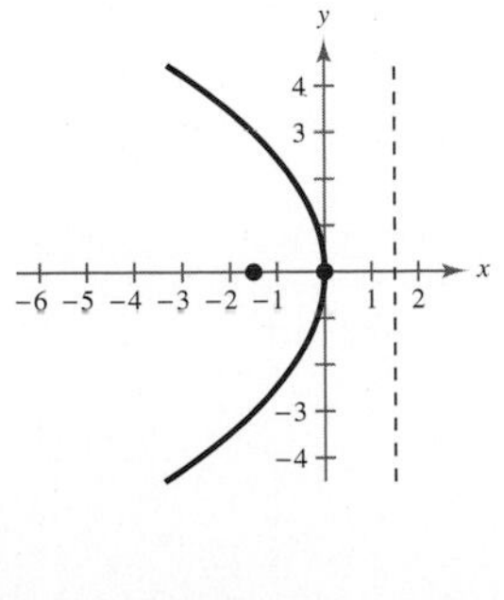

CHAPTER 10

15. Vertex: $(0, 0)$
Focus: $\left(0, -\frac{3}{2}\right)$
Directrix: $y = \frac{3}{2}$

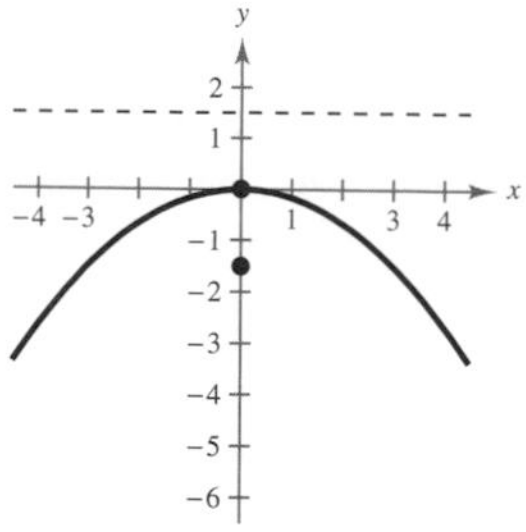

17. Vertex: $(1, -2)$
Focus: $(1, -4)$
Directrix: $y = 0$

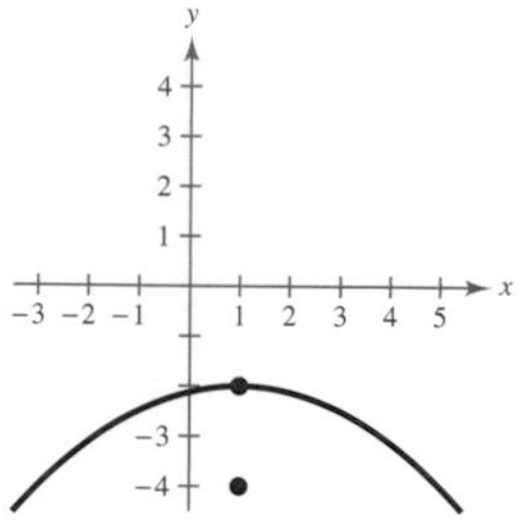

19. Vertex: $\left(-\frac{3}{2}, 2\right)$
Focus: $\left(-\frac{3}{2}, 3\right)$
Directrix: $y = 1$

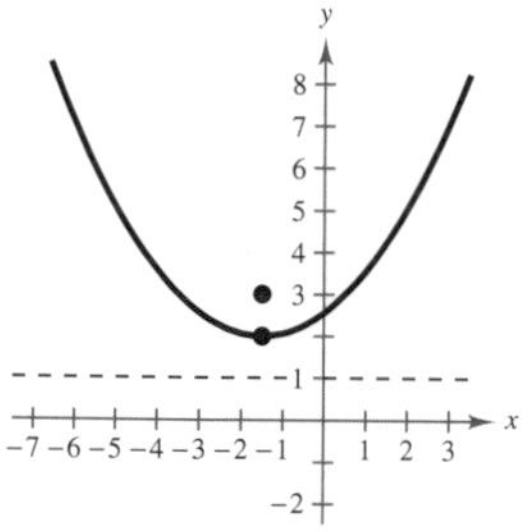

21. Vertex: $(1, 1)$
Focus: $(1, 2)$
Directrix: $y = 0$

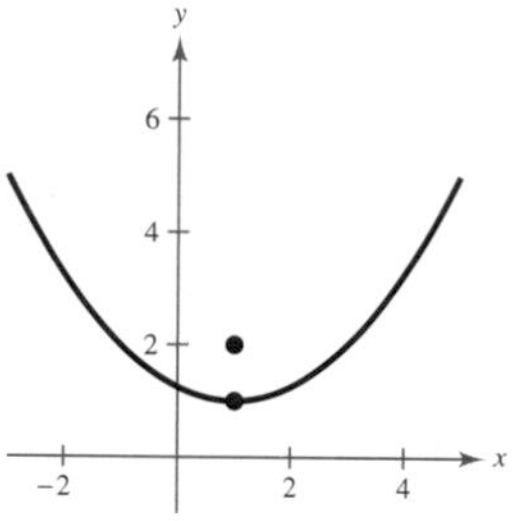

23. Vertex: $(-2, -3)$
Focus: $(-4, -3)$
Directrix: $x = 0$

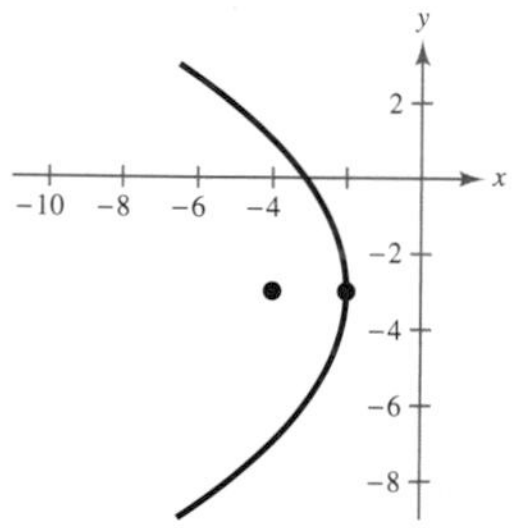

25. Vertex: $(-2, 1)$
Focus: $\left(-2, -\frac{1}{2}\right)$
Directrix: $x = -2$

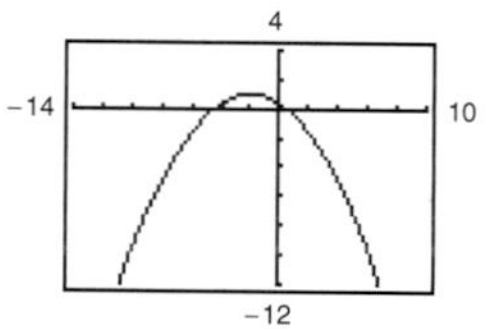

27. Vertex: $\left(\frac{1}{4}, -\frac{1}{2}\right)$
Focus: $\left(0, -\frac{1}{2}\right)$
Directrix: $x = \frac{1}{2}$

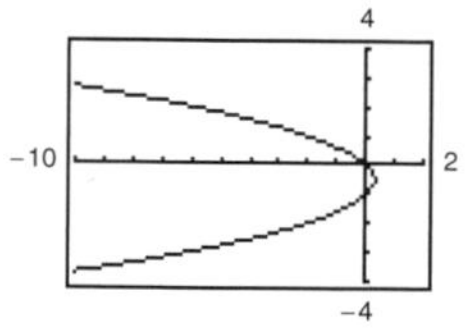

29. $x^2 = \frac{3}{2}y$ **31.** $x^2 = -6y$ **33.** $y^2 = -8x$
35. $x^2 = 4y$ **37.** $y^2 = -8x$ **39.** $y^2 = 9x$
41. $(x - 3)^2 = -(y - 1)$ **43.** $y^2 = 4(x + 4)$
45. $(y - 2)^2 = -8(x - 5)$ **47.** $x^2 = 8(y - 4)$
49. $(y - 2)^2 = 8x$ **51.** $y = \sqrt{6(x + 1)} + 3$
53.

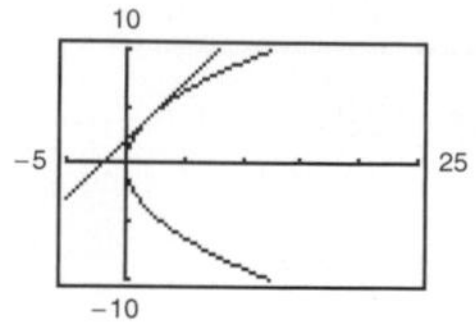

$(2, 4)$

55. $4x - y - 8 = 0$; $(2, 0)$ **57.** $4x - y + 2 = 0$; $\left(-\frac{1}{2}, 0\right)$
59.

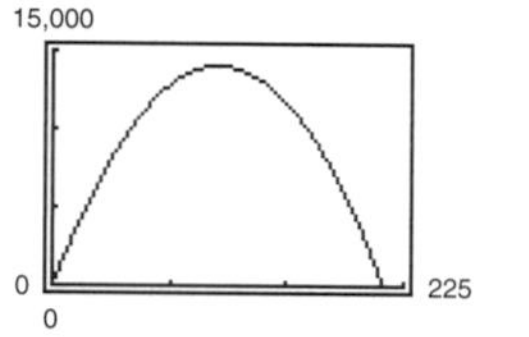

$x = 106$ units

61. $y = \frac{1}{18}x^2$
63. (a) $y = -\frac{1}{640}x^2$ (b) 8 feet
65. (a) $17{,}500\sqrt{2}$ miles per hour $\approx 24{,}750$ miles per hour
(b) $x^2 = -16{,}400(y - 4100)$
67. (a) $x^2 = -64(y - 75)$ (b) 69.3 feet
69. False. If the graph crossed the directrix, there would exist points closer to the directrix than the focus.
71. (a)

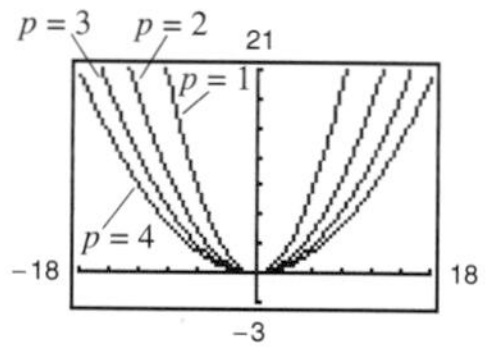

As p increases, the graph becomes wider.
(b) $(0, 1)$, $(0, 2)$, $(0, 3)$, $(0, 4)$ (c) 4, 8, 12, 16; $4|p|$
(d) Easy way to determine two additional points on the graph

73. $m = \dfrac{x_1}{2p}$ **75.** $\pm 1, \pm 2, \pm 4$
77. $\pm\frac{1}{2}, \pm 1, \pm 2, \pm 4, \pm 8, \pm 16$
79. $f(x) = x^3 - 7x^2 + 17x - 15$ **81.** $\frac{1}{2}, -\frac{5}{3}, \pm 2$
83. $B \approx 23.67°$, $C \approx 121.33°$, $c \approx 14.89$
85. $C = 89°$, $a \approx 1.93$, $b \approx 2.33$
87. $A \approx 16.39°$, $B \approx 23.77°$, $C \approx 139.84°$
89. $B \approx 24.62°$, $C \approx 90.38°$, $a \approx 10.88$

Section 10.3 *(page 750)*

Vocabulary Check *(page 750)*

1. ellipse; foci **2.** major axis; center
3. minor axis **4.** eccentricity

1. b **2.** c **3.** d **4.** f **5.** a **6.** e

7. Ellipse
Center: $(0, 0)$
Vertices: $(\pm 5, 0)$
Foci: $(\pm 3, 0)$
Eccentricity: $\frac{3}{5}$

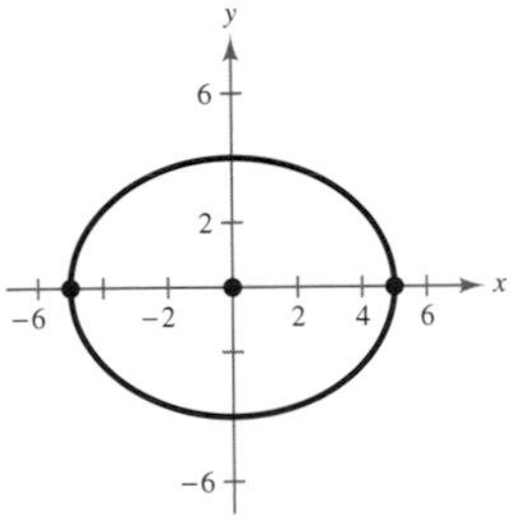

9. Circle
Center: $(0, 0)$
Radius: 5

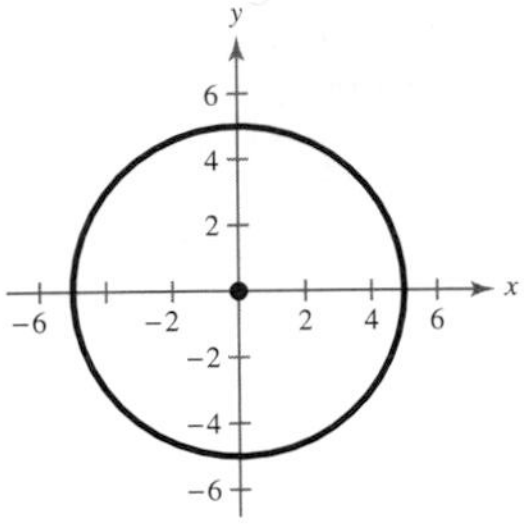

11. Ellipse
Center: $(0, 0)$
Vertices: $(0, \pm 3)$
Foci: $(0, \pm 2)$
Eccentricity: $\frac{2}{3}$

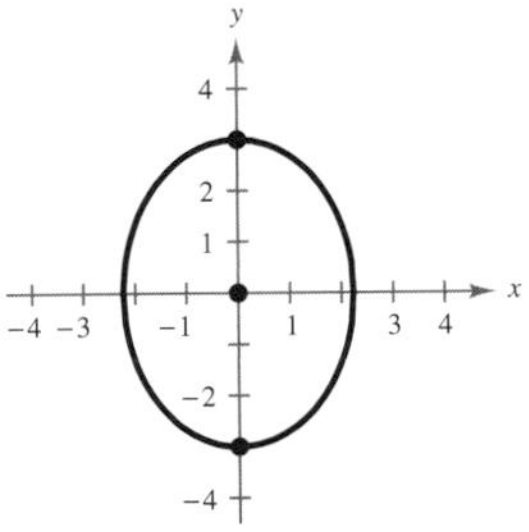

13. Ellipse
Center: $(-3, 5)$
Vertices:
$(-3, 10), (-3, 0)$
Foci: $(-3, 8), (-3, 2)$
Eccentricity: $\frac{3}{5}$

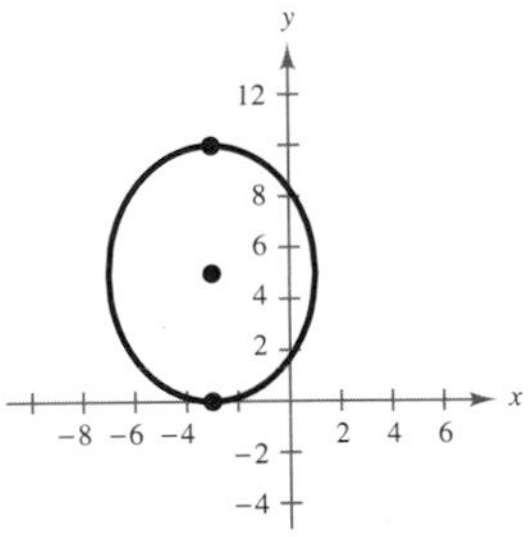

15. Circle
Center: $(0, -1)$
Radius: $\frac{2}{3}$

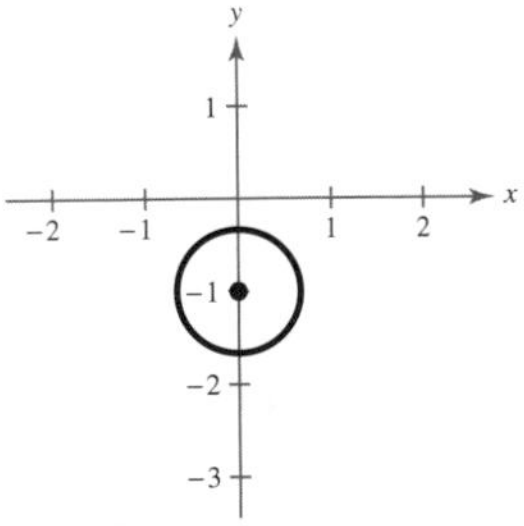

17. Ellipse
Center: $(-2, -4)$
Vertices:
$(-3, -4), (-1, -4)$
Foci: $\left(\frac{-4 \pm \sqrt{3}}{2}, -4\right)$
Eccentricity: $\frac{\sqrt{3}}{2}$

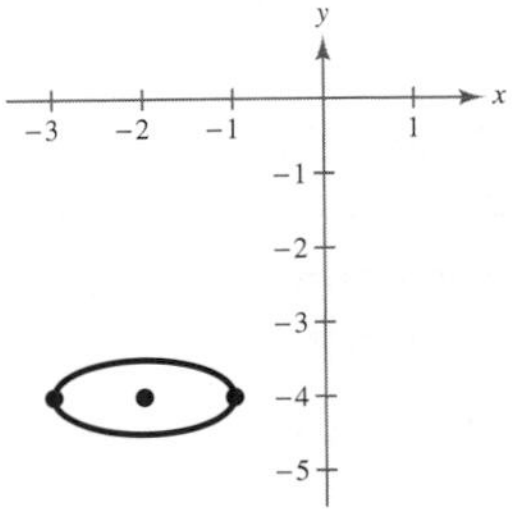

19. Ellipse
Center: $(-2, 3)$
Vertices: $(-2, 6), (-2, 0)$
Foci: $\left(-2, 3 \pm \sqrt{5}\right)$
Eccentricity: $\frac{\sqrt{5}}{3}$

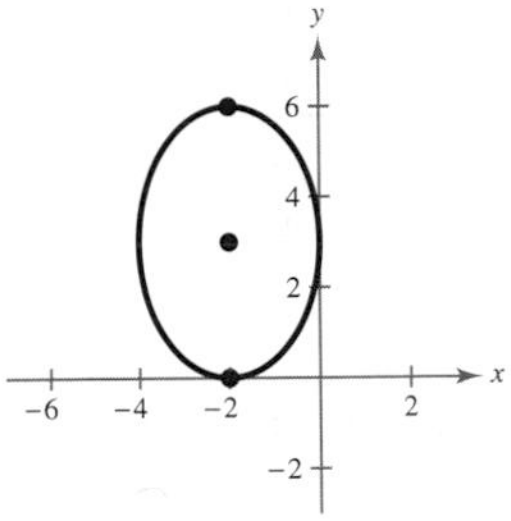

21. Circle
Center: $(1, -2)$
Radius: 6

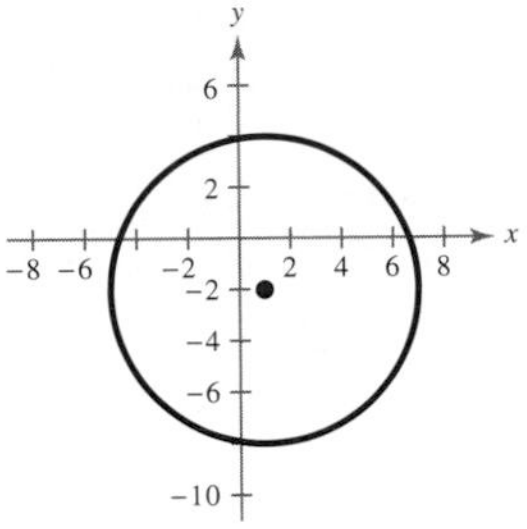

23. Ellipse
Center: $(-3, 1)$
Vertices: $(-3, 7), (-3, -5)$
Foci: $\left(-3, 1 \pm 2\sqrt{6}\right)$
Eccentricity: $\frac{\sqrt{6}}{3}$

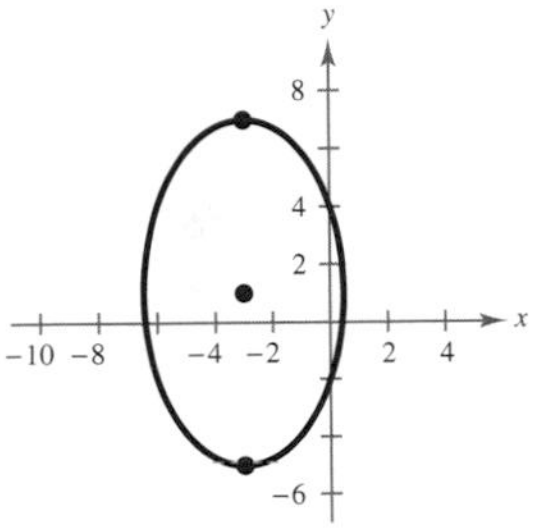

25. Ellipse
Center: $\left(3, -\frac{5}{2}\right)$
Vertices: $\left(9, -\frac{5}{2}\right), \left(-3, -\frac{5}{2}\right)$
Foci: $\left(3 \pm 3\sqrt{3}, -\frac{5}{2}\right)$
Eccentricity: $\frac{\sqrt{3}}{2}$

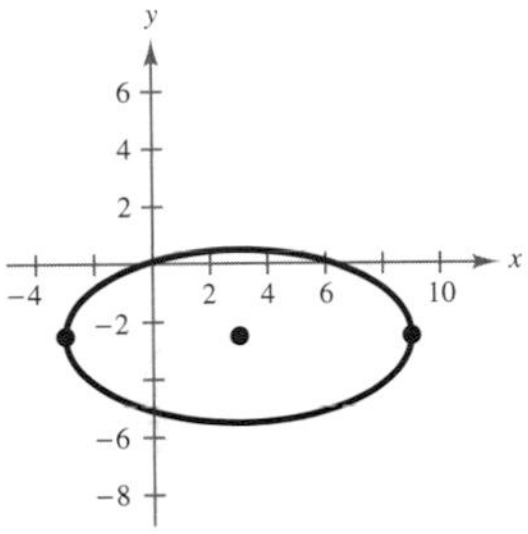

27. Circle
Center: $(-1, 1)$
Radius: $\frac{2}{3}$

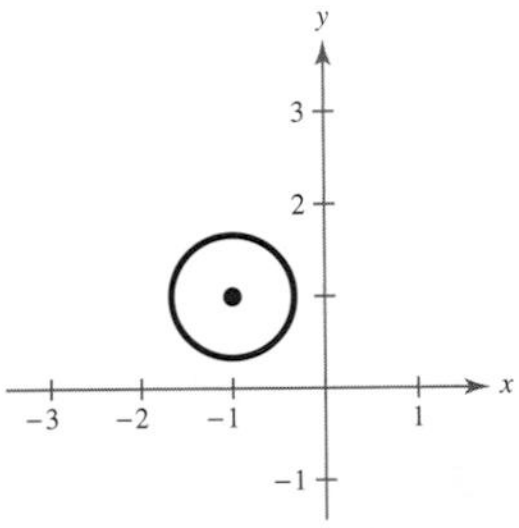

29. Ellipse
Center: $(2, 1)$
Vertices: $\left(\frac{7}{3}, 1\right), \left(\frac{5}{3}, 1\right)$
Foci: $\left(\frac{34}{15}, 1\right), \left(\frac{26}{15}, 1\right)$
Eccentricity: $\frac{4}{5}$

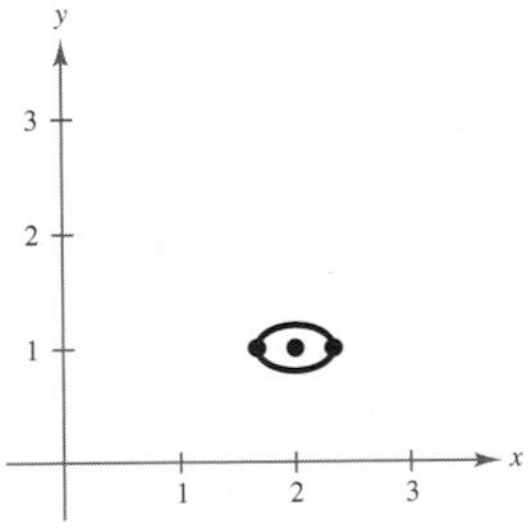

31.

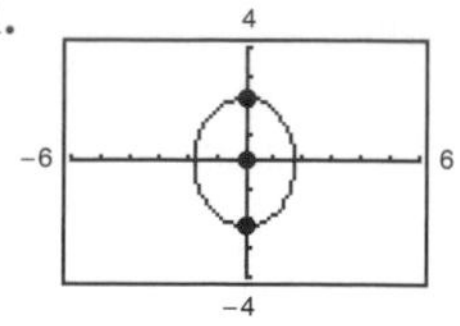

Center: $(0, 0)$
Vertices: $(0, \pm\sqrt{5})$
Foci: $(0, \pm\sqrt{2})$

33.

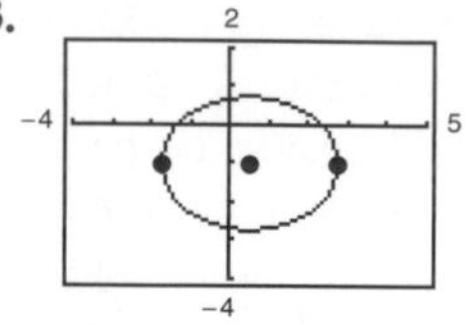

Center: $\left(\frac{1}{2}, -1\right)$
Vertices: $\left(\frac{1}{2} \pm \sqrt{5}, -1\right)$
Foci: $\left(\frac{1}{2} \pm \sqrt{2}, -1\right)$

35. $\dfrac{x^2}{4} + \dfrac{y^2}{16} = 1$ **37.** $\dfrac{x^2}{36} + \dfrac{y^2}{32} = 1$ **39.** $\dfrac{x^2}{36} + \dfrac{y^2}{11} = 1$

41. $\dfrac{21x^2}{400} + \dfrac{y^2}{25} = 1$ **43.** $\dfrac{(x-2)^2}{1} + \dfrac{(y-3)^2}{9} = 1$

45. $\dfrac{(x+2)^2}{16} + \dfrac{(y-3)^2}{9} = 1$

47. $\dfrac{(x-2)^2}{4} + \dfrac{(y-4)^2}{1} = 1$ **49.** $\dfrac{x^2}{48} + \dfrac{(y-4)^2}{64} = 1$

51. $\dfrac{x^2}{16} + \dfrac{(y-4)^2}{12} = 1$ **53.** $\dfrac{(x-2)^2}{4} + \dfrac{(y-2)^2}{1} = 1$

55. $\dfrac{x^2}{25} + \dfrac{y^2}{16} = 1$

57. (a)

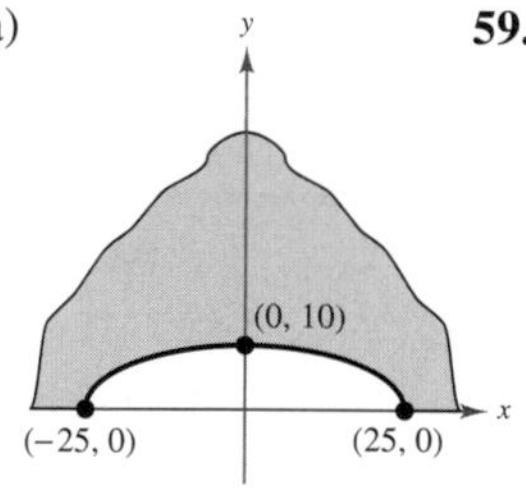

(b) $\dfrac{x^2}{625} + \dfrac{y^2}{100} = 1$

(c) Yes

59. (a) $\dfrac{x^2}{321.84} + \dfrac{y^2}{20.89} = 1$

(b)

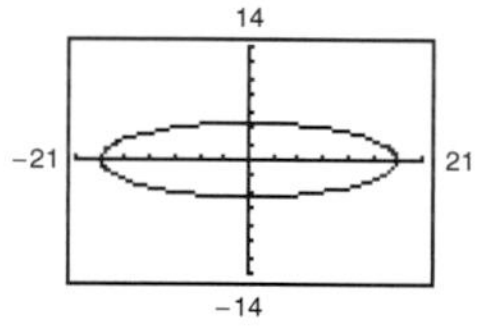

(c) Aphelion: 35.29 astronomical units
Perihelion: 0.59 astronomical unit

61. (a) $\dfrac{x^2}{0.04} + \dfrac{y^2}{2.56} = 1$

(b)

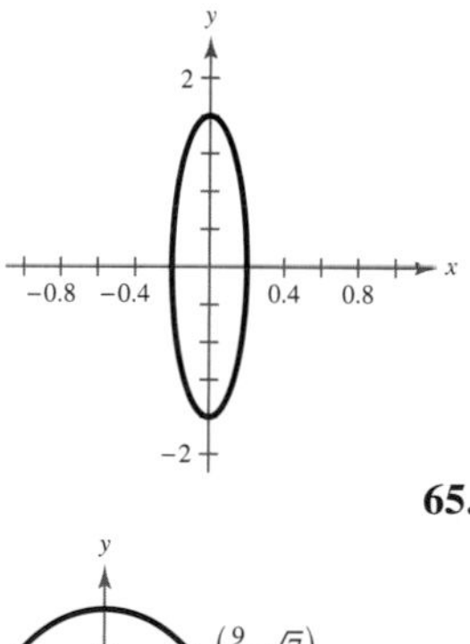

(c) The bottom half

63.

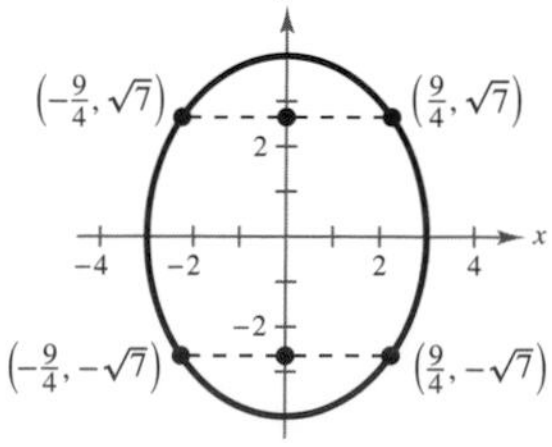

65.

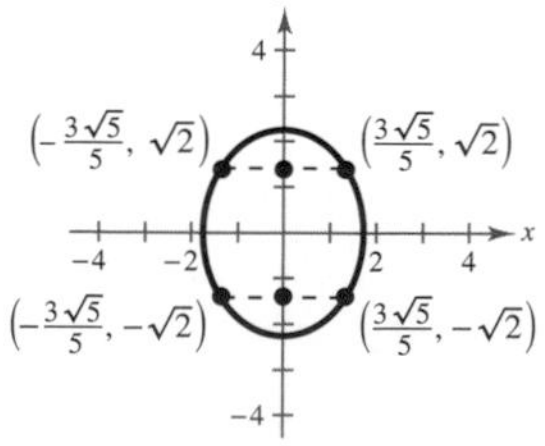

67. False. The graph of $x^2/4 + y^4 = 1$ is not an ellipse. The degree of y is 4, not 2.

69. (a) $A = \pi a(20 - a)$ (b) $\dfrac{x^2}{196} + \dfrac{y^2}{36} = 1$

(c)

a	8	9	10	11	12	13
A	301.6	311.0	314.2	311.0	301.6	285.9

$a = 10$, circle

(d)

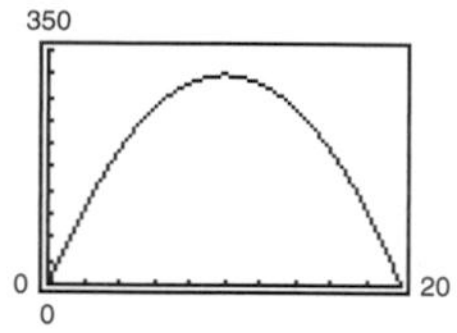

The shape of an ellipse with a maximum area is a circle. The maximum area is found when $a = 10$ (verified in part c) and therefore $b = 10$, so the equation produces a circle.

71. Geometric **73.** Arithmetic **75.** 547 **77.** 340.15

Section 10.4 *(page 760)*

Vocabulary Check *(page 760)*

1. hyperbola; foci **2.** branches
3. transverse axis; center **4.** asymptotes
5. $Ax^2 + Cy^2 + Dx + Ey + F = 0$

1. b **2.** c **3.** a **4.** d

5. Center: $(0, 0)$
Vertices: $(\pm 1, 0)$
Foci: $(\pm\sqrt{2}, 0)$
Asymptotes: $y = \pm x$

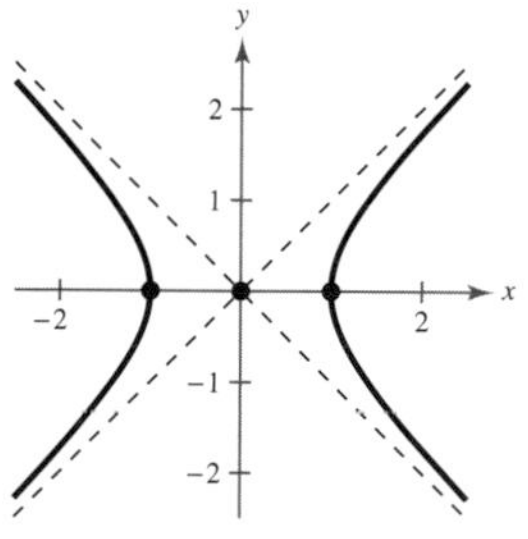

7. Center: $(0, 0)$
Vertices: $(0, \pm 5)$
Foci: $(0, \pm\sqrt{106})$
Asymptotes: $y = \pm\frac{5}{9}x$

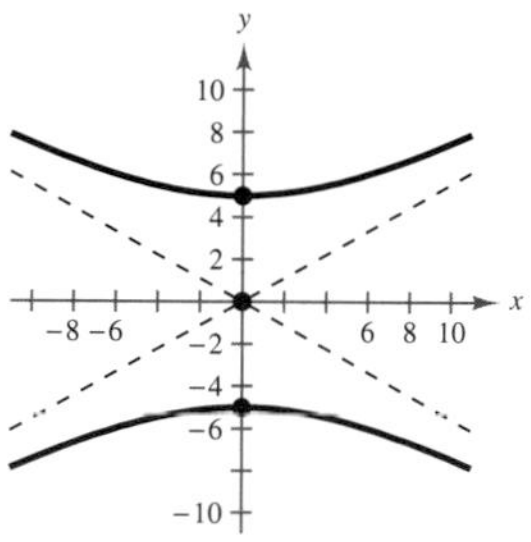

9. Center: $(1, -2)$
Vertices: $(3, -2), (-1, -2)$
Foci: $(1 \pm \sqrt{5}, -2)$
Asymptotes:
$y = -2 \pm \frac{1}{2}(x - 1)$

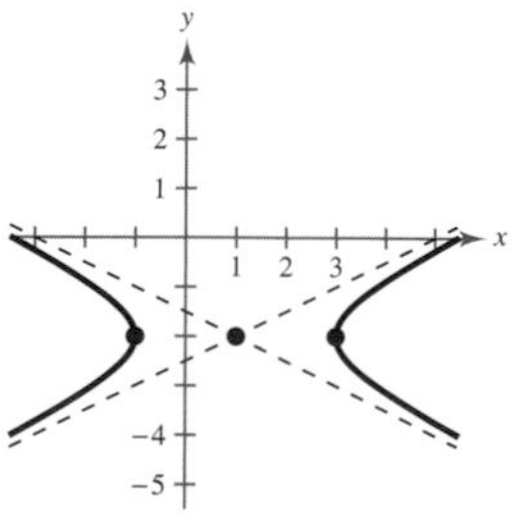

11. Center: $(2, -6)$

Vertices: $\left(2, -\frac{17}{3}\right), \left(2, -\frac{19}{3}\right)$

Foci: $\left(2, -6 \pm \frac{\sqrt{13}}{6}\right)$

Asymptotes:

$y = -6 \pm \frac{2}{3}(x - 2)$

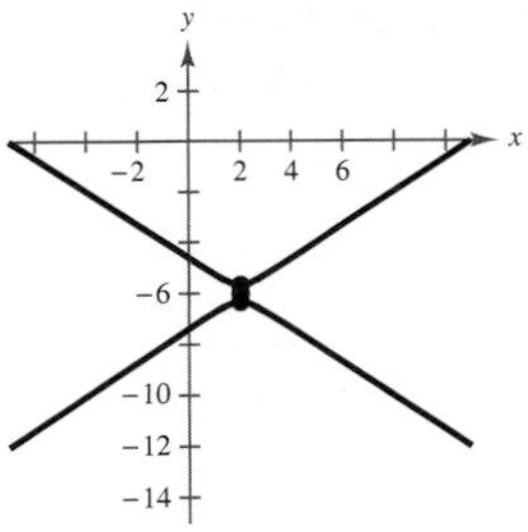

13. Center: $(2, -3)$

Vertices: $(3, -3), (1, -3)$

Foci: $(2 \pm \sqrt{10}, -3)$

Asymptotes:

$y = -3 \pm 3(x - 2)$

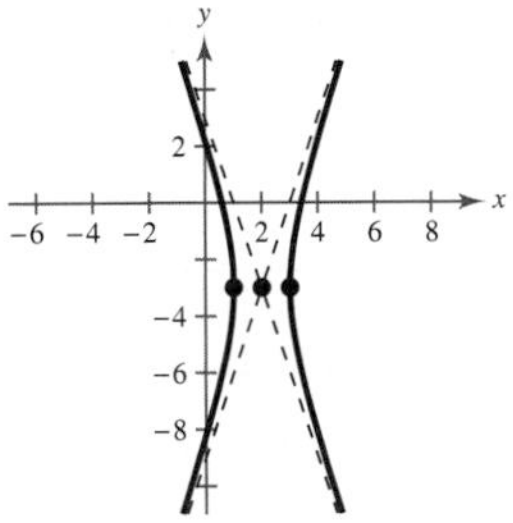

15. The graph of this equation is two lines intersecting at $(-1, -3)$.

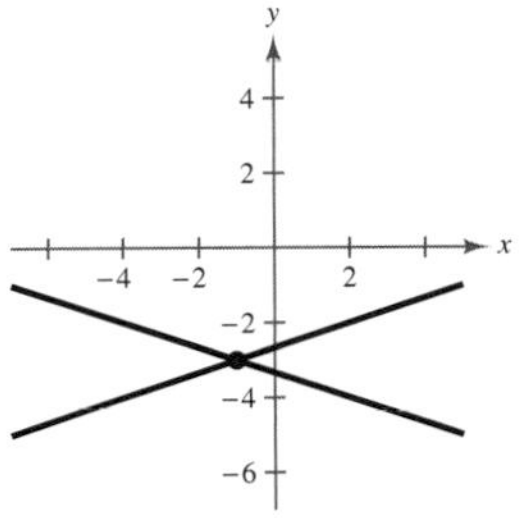

17. Center: $(0, 0)$

Vertices: $(\pm\sqrt{3}, 0)$

Foci: $(\pm\sqrt{5}, 0)$

Asymptotes: $y = \pm\frac{\sqrt{6}}{3}x$

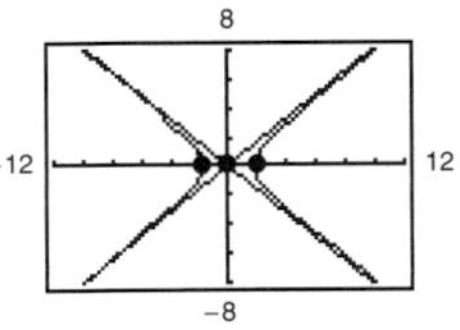

19. Center: $(1, -3)$

Vertices: $(1, -3 \pm \sqrt{2})$

Foci: $(1, -3 \pm 2\sqrt{5})$

Asymptotes:

$y = -3 \pm \frac{1}{3}(x - 1)$

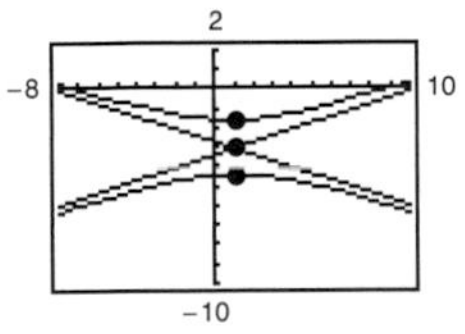

21. $\frac{y^2}{4} - \frac{x^2}{12} = 1$ **23.** $\frac{x^2}{1} - \frac{y^2}{25} = 1$

25. $\frac{17y^2}{1024} - \frac{17x^2}{64} = 1$ **27.** $\frac{(x - 4)^2}{4} - \frac{y^2}{12} = 1$

29. $\frac{(y - 5)^2}{16} - \frac{(x - 4)^2}{9} = 1$ **31.** $\frac{y^2}{9} - \frac{4(x - 2)^2}{9} = 1$

33. $\frac{(y - 2)^2}{4} - \frac{x^2}{4} = 1$ **35.** $\frac{(x - 2)^2}{1} - \frac{(y - 2)^2}{1} = 1$

37. $\frac{(x - 3)^2}{9} - \frac{(y - 2)^2}{4} = 1$

39. (a) $\frac{x^2}{1} - \frac{y^2}{169/3} = 1$ (b) ≈ 2.403 feet

41. $(3300, -2750)$ **43.** $(12(\sqrt{5} - 1), 0) \approx (14.83, 0)$

45. Circle **47.** Hyperbola **49.** Hyperbola

51. Parabola **53.** Ellipse **55.** Parabola

57. Ellipse **59.** Circle

61. True. For a hyperbola, $c^2 = a^2 + b^2$. The larger the ratio of b to a, the larger the eccentricity of the hyperbola, $e = c/a$.

63. Answers will vary.

65. $y = 1 - 3\sqrt{\frac{(x - 3)^2}{4} - 1}$ **67.** $x(x + 4)(x - 4)$

69. $2x(x - 6)^2$ **71.** $2(2x + 3)(4x^2 - 6x + 9)$

73.

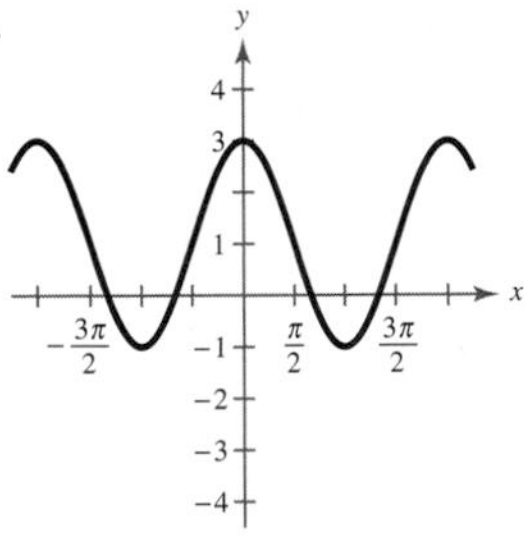

75.

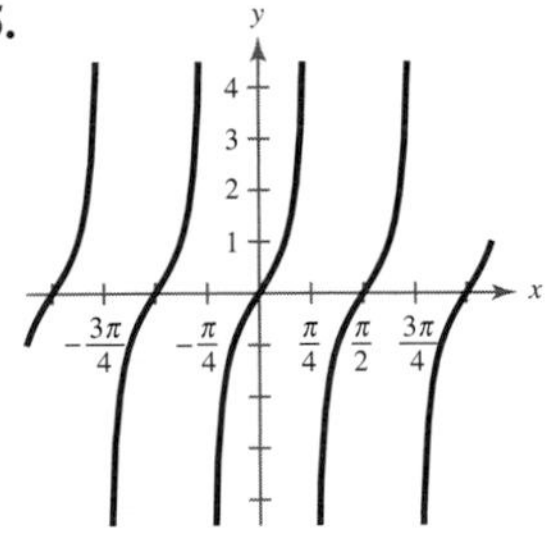

Section 10.5 *(page 769)*

> ### Vocabulary Check *(page 769)*
>
> **1.** rotation of axes
>
> **2.** $A'(x')^2 + C'(y')^2 + D'x' + E'y' + F' = 0$
>
> **3.** invariant under rotation **4.** discriminant

1. $(3, 0)$ **3.** $\left(\frac{3 + \sqrt{3}}{2}, \frac{3\sqrt{3} - 1}{2}\right)$ **5.** $\left(\frac{3\sqrt{2}}{2}, -\frac{\sqrt{2}}{2}\right)$

7. $\frac{(y')^2}{2} - \frac{(x')^2}{2} = 1$ **9.** $y' = \pm\frac{\sqrt{2}}{2}$

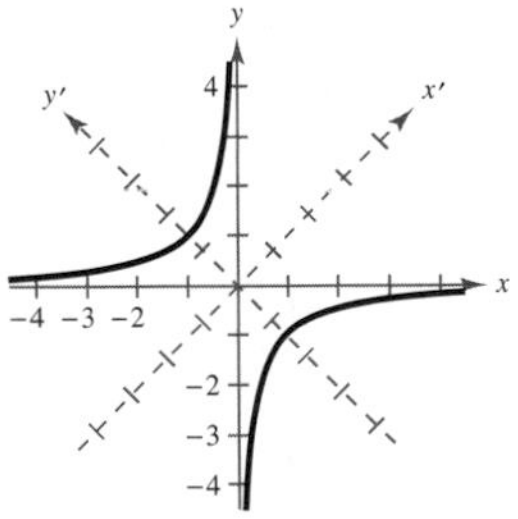

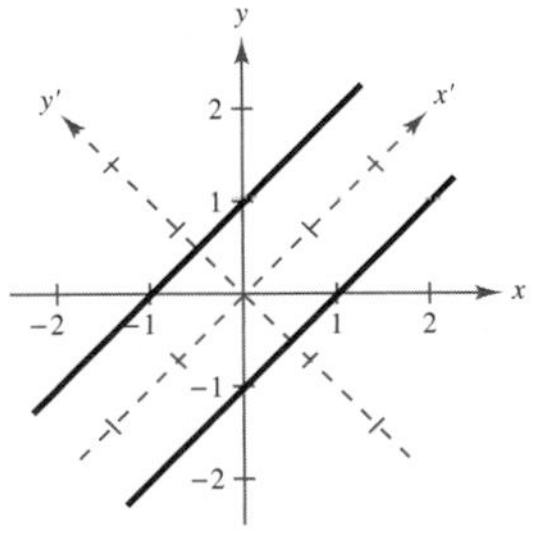

11. $\frac{(x' - 3\sqrt{2})^2}{16} - \frac{(y' - \sqrt{2})^2}{16} = 1$

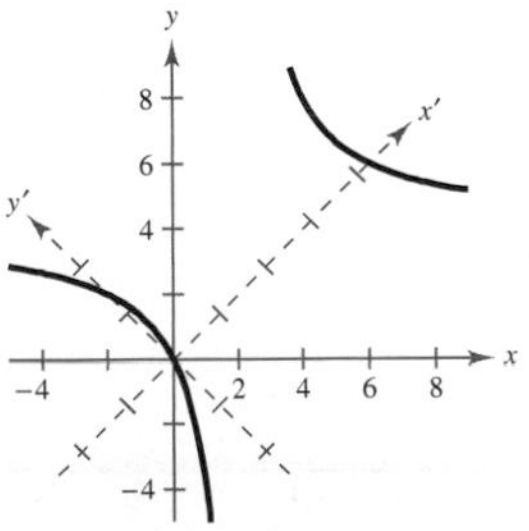

13. $\dfrac{(x')^2}{6} + \dfrac{(y')^2}{\frac{3}{2}} = 1$

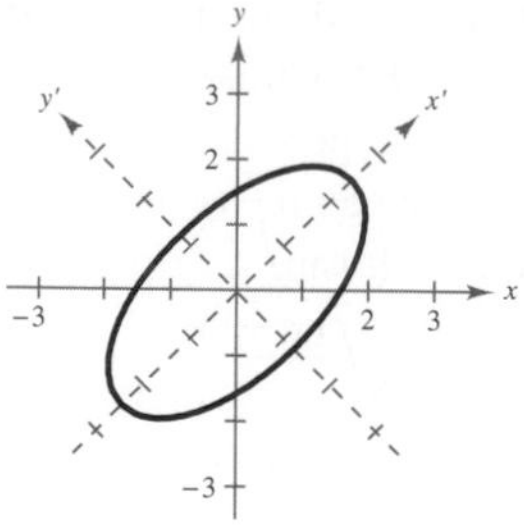

15. $(y')^2 = -x'$

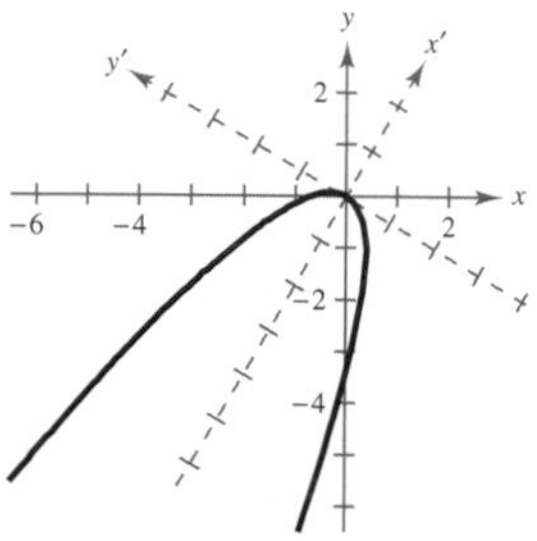

17. $(x' - 1)^2 = 6\left(y' + \frac{1}{6}\right)$

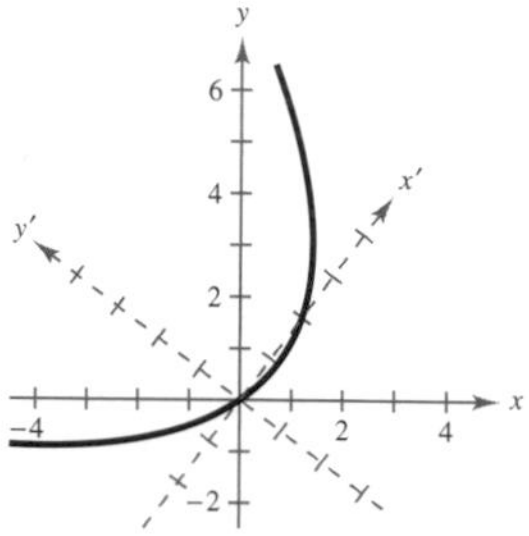

19.

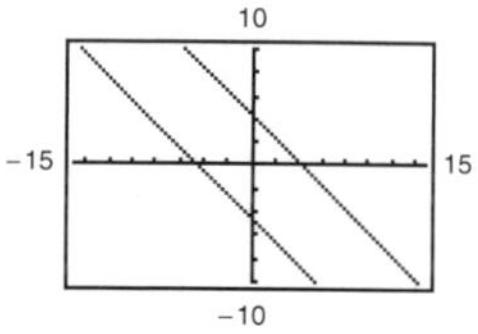

$\theta = 45°$

21.

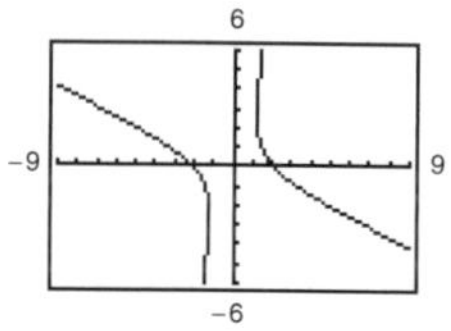

$\theta \approx 26.57°$

23.

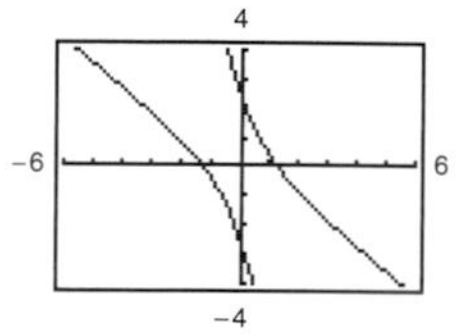

$\theta \approx 31.72°$

25.

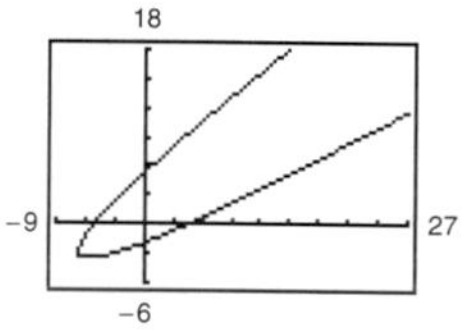

$\theta \approx 33.69°$

27. e **28.** f **29.** b **30.** a **31.** d **32.** c

33. (a) Parabola

(b) $y = \dfrac{(8x - 5) \pm \sqrt{(8x - 5)^2 - 4(16x^2 - 10x)}}{2}$

(c)

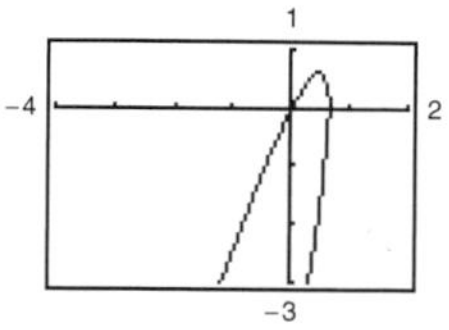

35. (a) Ellipse

(b) $y = \dfrac{6x \pm \sqrt{36x^2 - 28(12x^2 - 45)}}{14}$

(c)

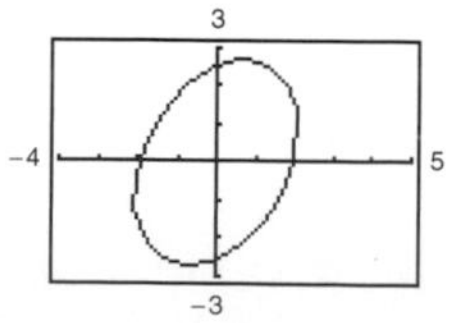

37. (a) Hyperbola

(b) $y = \dfrac{6x \pm \sqrt{36x^2 + 20(x^2 + 4x - 22)}}{-10}$

(c)

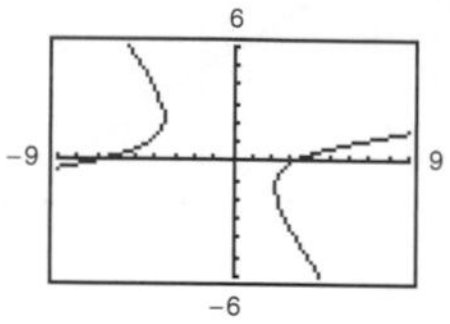

39. (a) Parabola

(b) $y = \dfrac{-(4x - 1) \pm \sqrt{(4x - 1)^2 - 16(x^2 - 5x - 3)}}{8}$

(c)

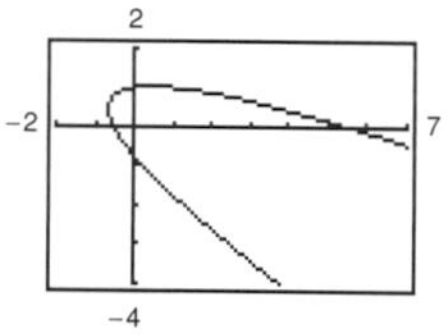

41.

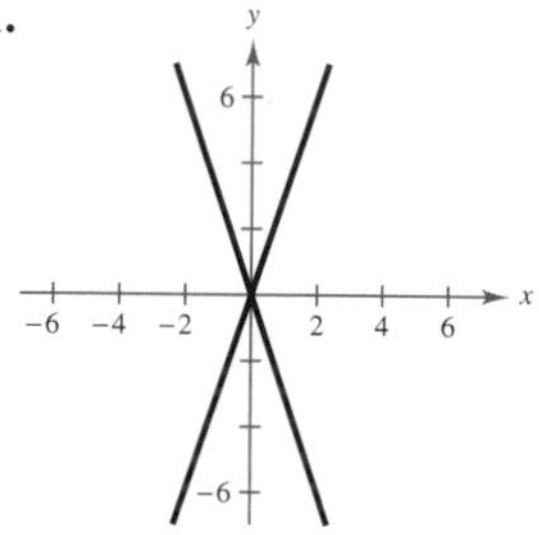

43.

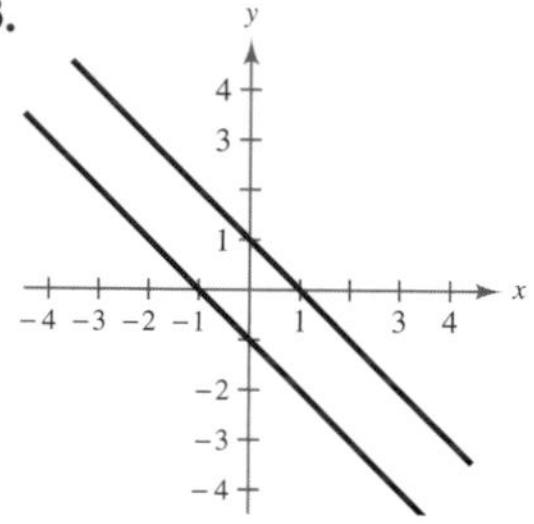

45. (2, 2), (2, 4) **47.** (−8, 12) **49.** (0, 8), (12, 8)

51. (0, 4) **53.** $(1, \sqrt{3}), (1, -\sqrt{3})$ **55.** No solution

57. $\left(0, \frac{3}{2}\right), (-3, 0)$

59. True. The graph of the equation can be classified by finding the discriminant. For a graph to be a hyperbola, the discriminant must be greater than zero. If $k \geq \frac{1}{4}$, then the discriminant would be less than or equal to zero.

61. Answers will vary.

63.

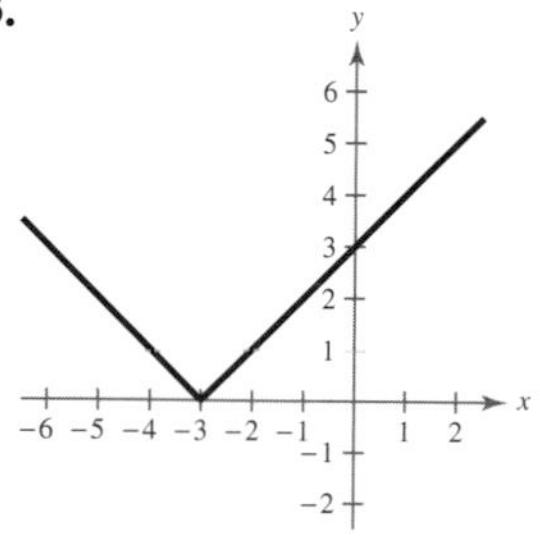

65.

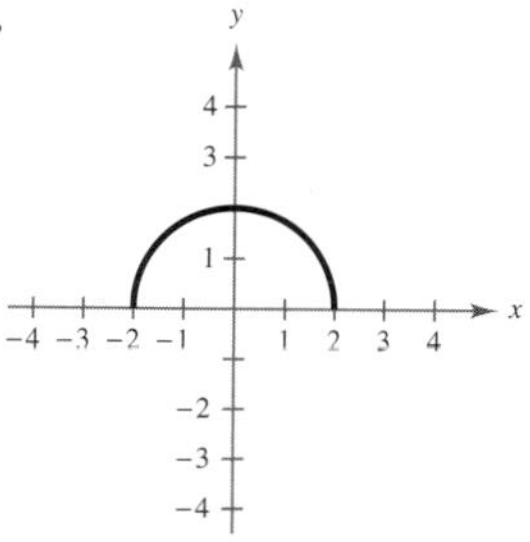

67.

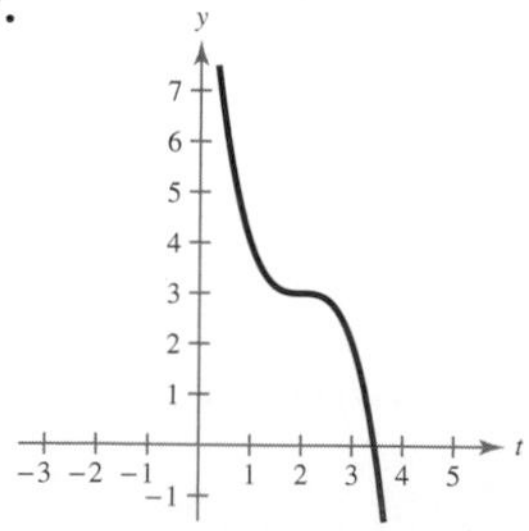

69.

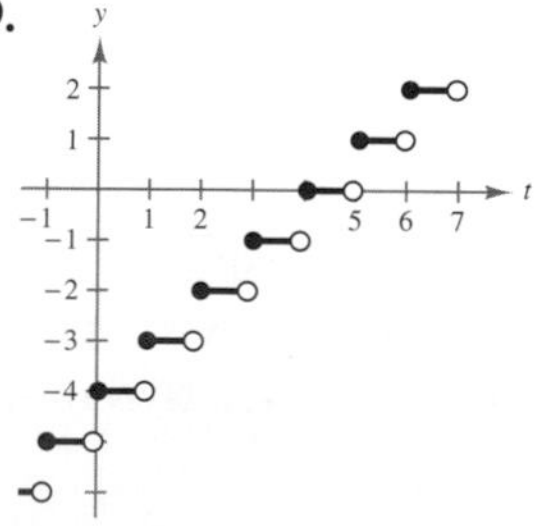

71. Area = 45.11 square units

73. Area = 48.60 square units

Section 10.6 *(page 776)*

Vocabulary Check *(page 776)*

1. plane curve; parametric; parameter
2. orientation **3.** eliminating the parameter

1. (a)

t	0	1	2	3	4
x	0	1	$\sqrt{2}$	$\sqrt{3}$	2
y	3	2	1	0	-1

(b)

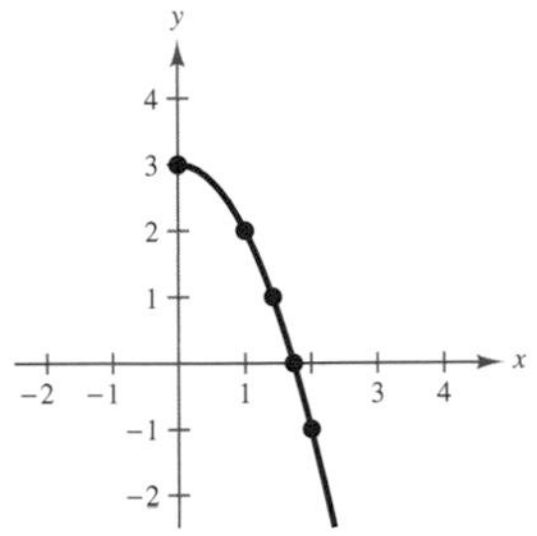

(c) $y = 3 - x^2$

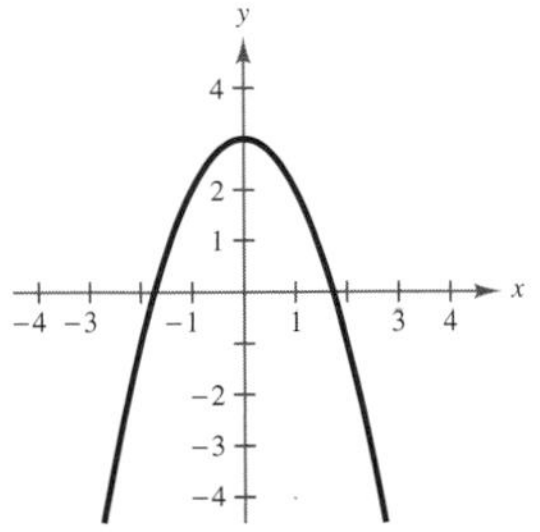

The graph of the rectangular equation shows the entire parabola rather than just the right half.

The graph of the rectangular equation continues the graph into the second and third quadrants.

3. (a)

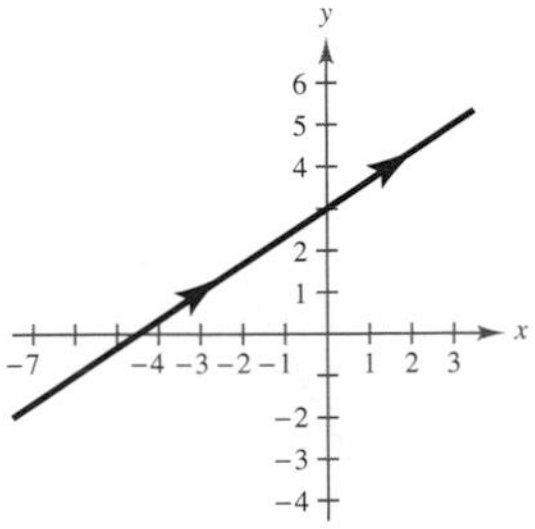

(b) $y = \frac{2}{3}x + 3$

5. (a)

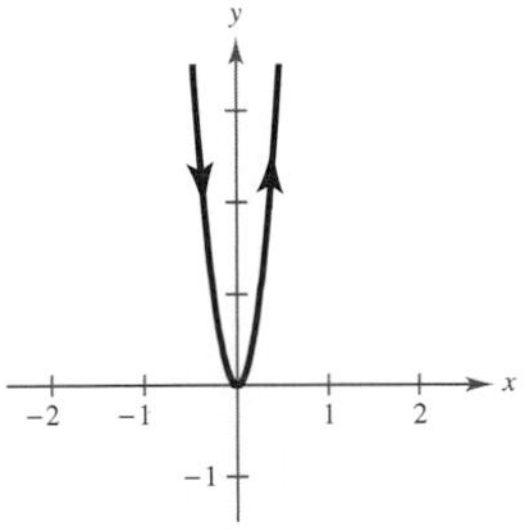

(b) $y = 16x^2$

7. (a)

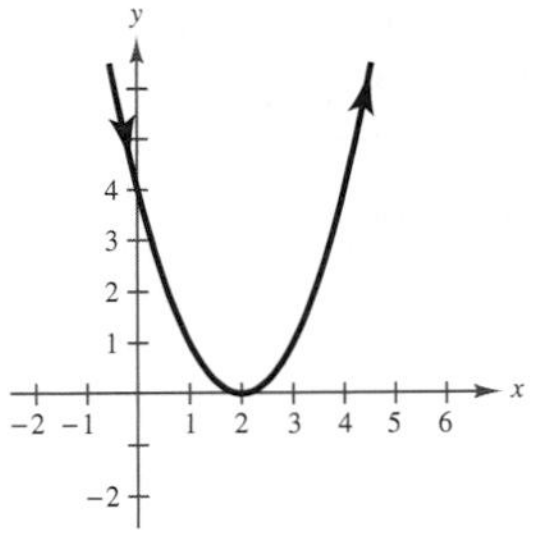

(b) $y = x^2 - 4x + 4$

9. (a)

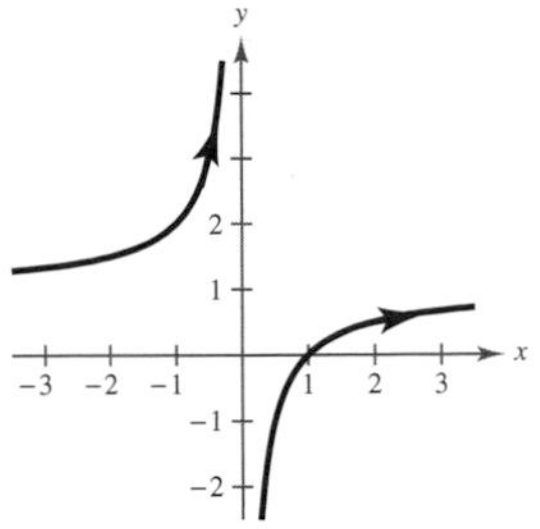

(b) $y = \dfrac{(x - 1)}{x}$

11. (a)

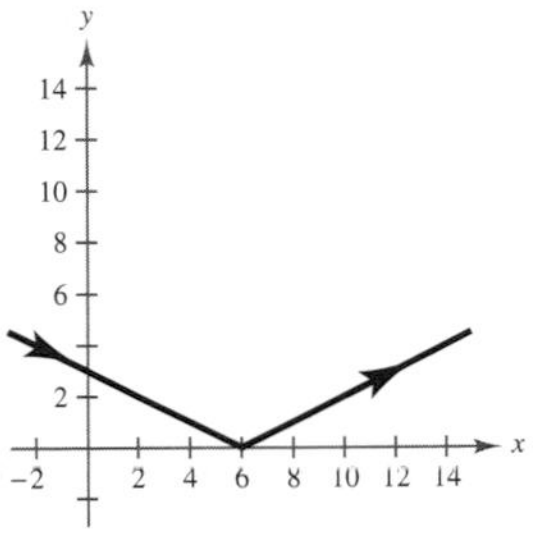

(b) $y = \left|\dfrac{x}{2} - 3\right|$

13. (a)

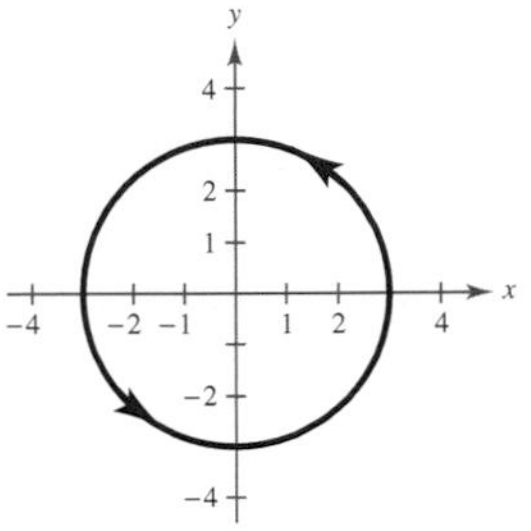

(b) $\dfrac{y^2}{9} + \dfrac{x^2}{9} = 1$

15. (a)

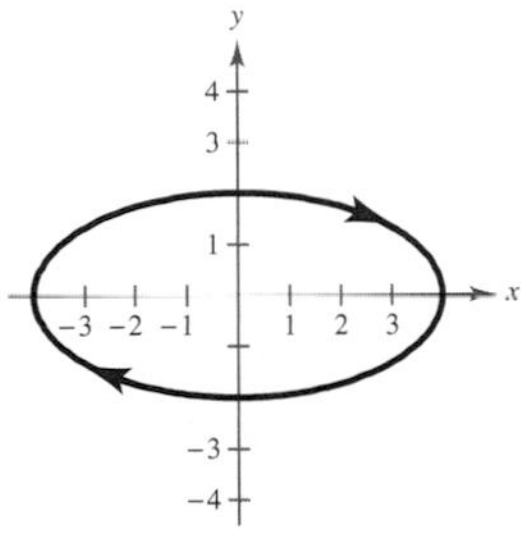

(b) $\dfrac{x^2}{16} + \dfrac{y^2}{4} = 1$

17. (a)

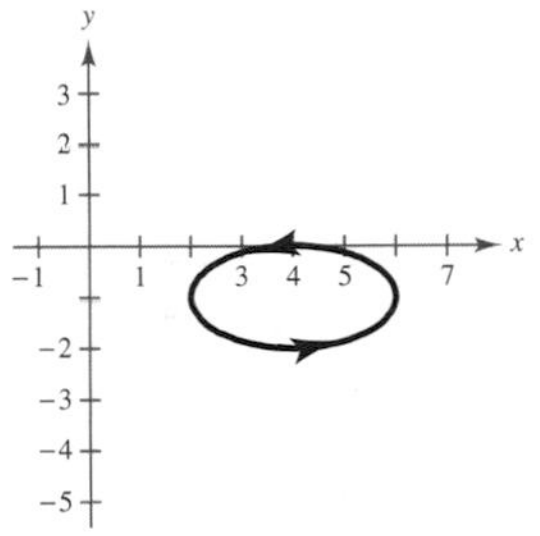

(b) $\dfrac{(x - 4)^2}{4} + (y + 1)^2 = 1$

19. (a)

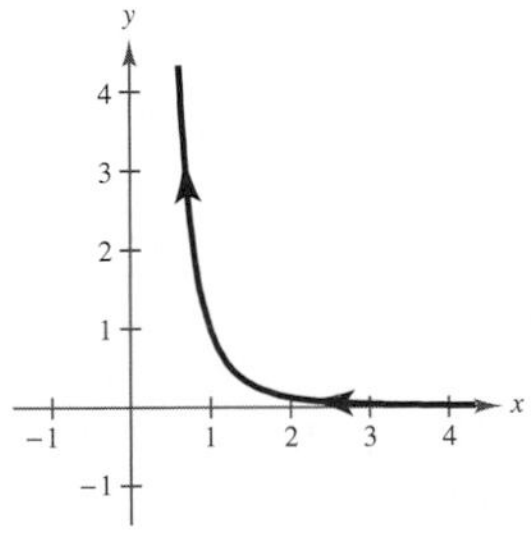

(b) $y = \dfrac{1}{x^3}$

21. (a)

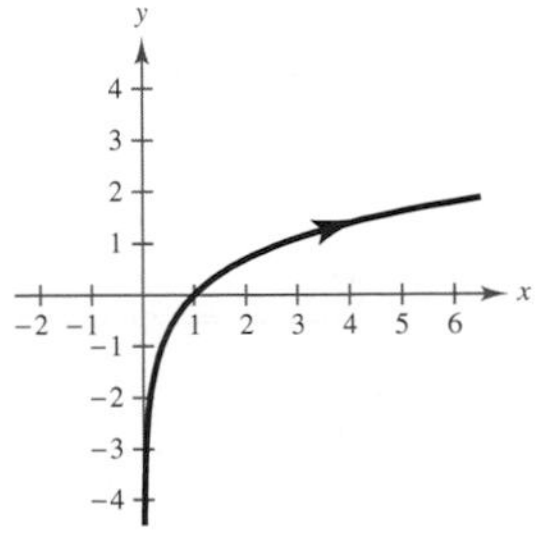

(b) $y = \ln x$

23. Each curve represents a portion of the line $y = 2x + 1$.

	Domain	*Orientation*
(a)	$(-\infty, \infty)$	Left to right
(b)	$[-1, 1]$	Depends on θ
(c)	$(0, \infty)$	Right to left
(d)	$(0, \infty)$	Left to right

25. $y - y_1 = m(x - x_1)$ **27.** $\dfrac{(x-h)^2}{a^2} + \dfrac{(y-k)^2}{b^2} = 1$

29. $x = 6t$
$y = -3t$

31. $x = 3 + 4\cos\theta$
$y = 2 + 4\sin\theta$

33. $x = 4\cos\theta$
$y = \sqrt{7}\sin\theta$

35. $x = 4\sec\theta$
$y = 3\tan\theta$

37. (a) $x = t,\ y = 3t - 2$ (b) $x = -t + 2,\ y = -3t + 4$

39. (a) $x = t, y = t^2$ (b) $x = -t + 2, y = t^2 - 4t + 4$

41. (a) $x = t, y = t^2 + 1$ (b) $x = -t + 2, y = t^2 - 4t + 5$

43. (a) $x = t, y = \dfrac{1}{t}$ (b) $x = -t + 2, y = -\dfrac{1}{t-2}$

45.
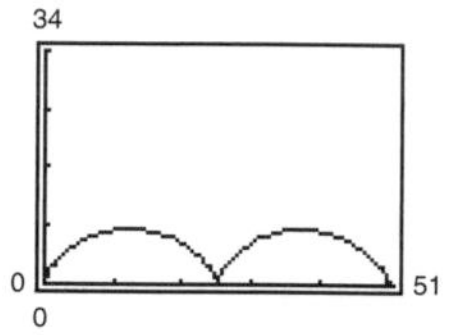

47.
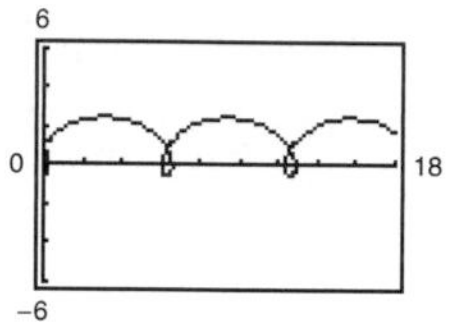

49.
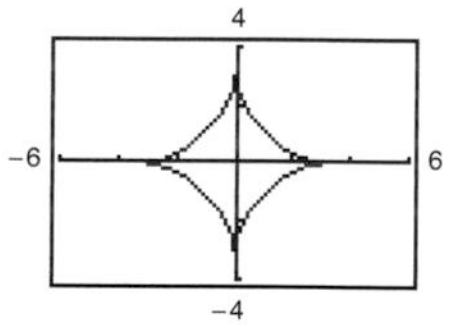

51.
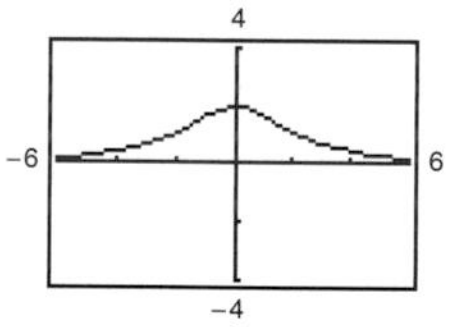

53. b
Domain: $[-2, 2]$
Range: $[-1, 1]$

55. d
Domain: $(-\infty, \infty)$
Range: $(-\infty, \infty)$

57. (a)
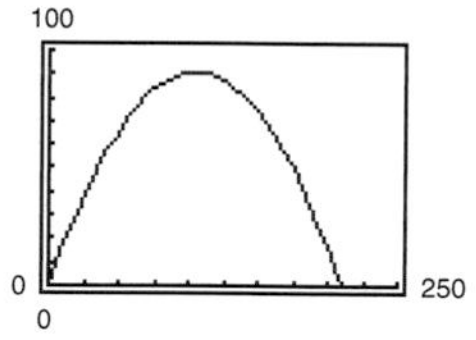

Maximum height: 90.7 feet
Range: 209.6 feet

(b)
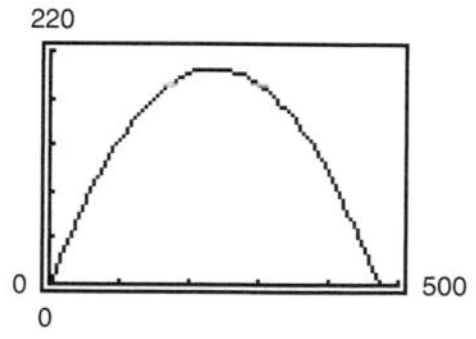

Maximum height: 204.2 feet
Range: 471.6 feet

(c)
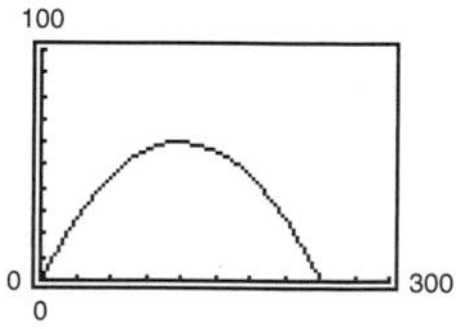

Maximum height: 60.5 feet
Range: 242.0 feet

(d)
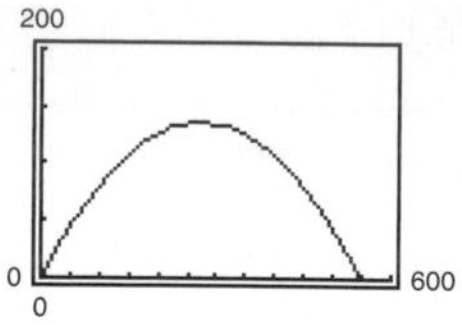

Maximum height: 136.1 feet
Range: 544.5 feet

59. (a) $x = (146.67\cos\theta)t$
$y = 3 + (146.67\sin\theta)t - 16t^2$

(b)
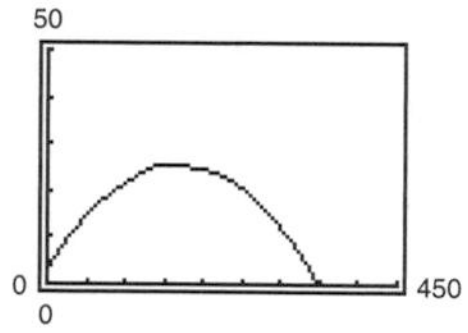

No

(c)
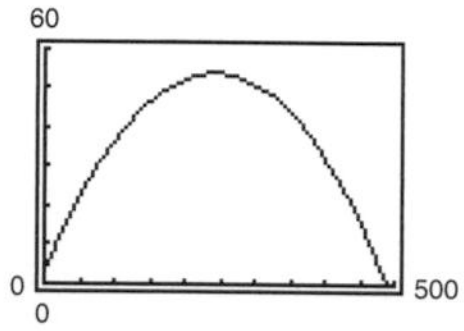

Yes

(d) 19.3°

61. Answers will vary.

63. $x = a\theta - b\sin\theta$
$y = a - b\cos\theta$

65. True
$x = t$
$y = t^2 + 1 \Rightarrow y = x^2 + 1$
$x = 3t$
$y = 9t^2 + 1 \Rightarrow y = x^2 + 1$

67. Parametric equations are useful when graphing two functions simultaneously on the same coordinate system. For example, they are useful when tracking the path of an object so that the position and the time associated with that position can be determined.

69. (5, 2) **71.** (1, −2, 1)

73. $\theta' = 75°$

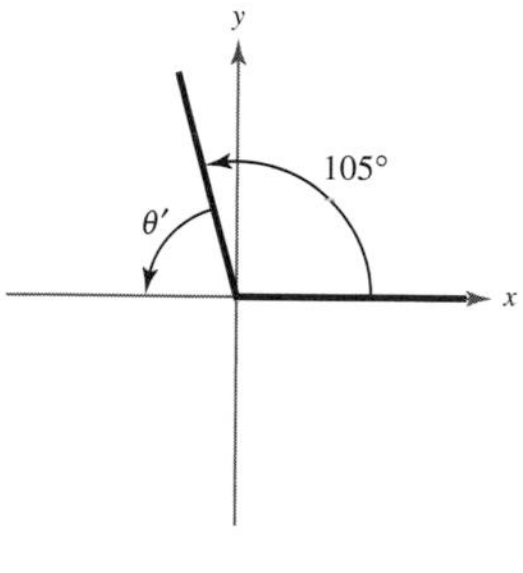

75. $\theta' = \dfrac{\pi}{3}$

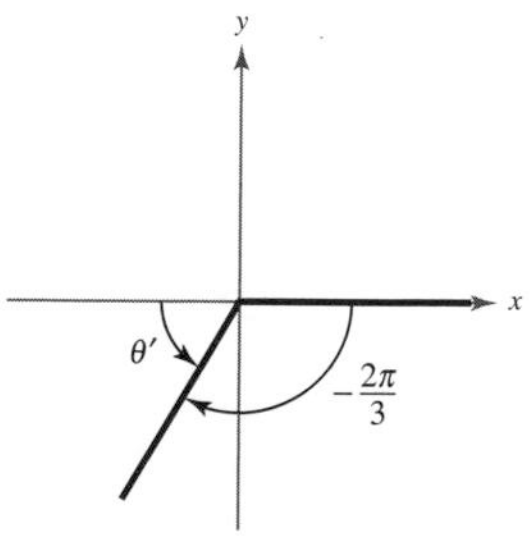

Section 10.7 *(page 783)*

Vocabulary Check *(page 783)*

1. pole **2.** directed distance; directed angle

3. polar **4.** $x = r\cos\theta$ $\quad \tan\theta = \dfrac{y}{x}$

$y = r\sin\theta \quad r^2 = x^2 + y^2$

1.

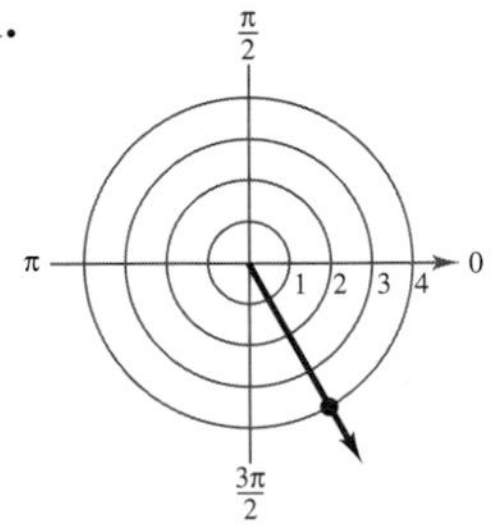

$\left(4, \frac{5\pi}{3}\right), \left(-4, -\frac{4\pi}{3}\right)$

3.

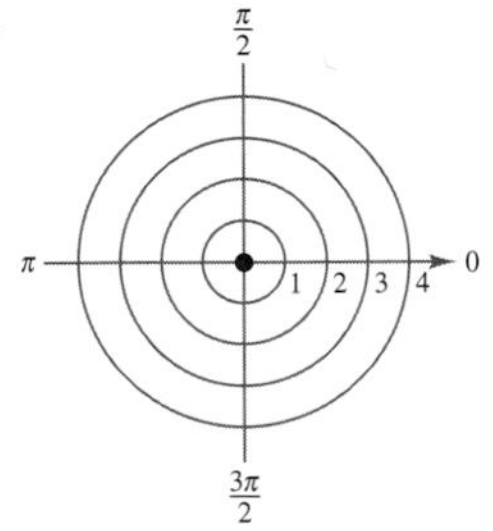

$\left(0, \frac{5\pi}{6}\right), \left(0, -\frac{13\pi}{6}\right)$

5.

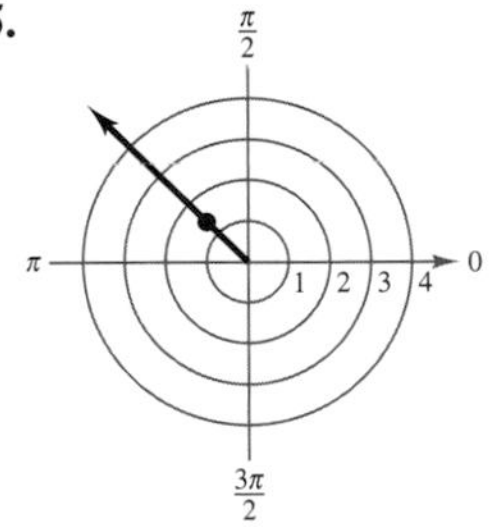

$(\sqrt{2}, 8.64), (-\sqrt{2}, -0.78)$

7.

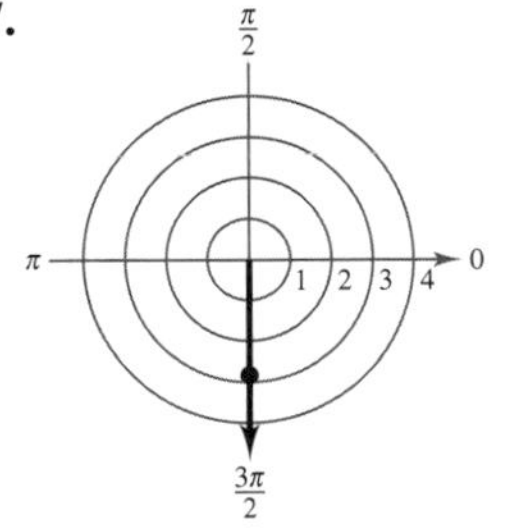

$(2\sqrt{2}, 10.99), (-2\sqrt{2}, 7.85)$

9. $(0, 3)$ **11.** $\left(\frac{\sqrt{2}}{2}, \frac{\sqrt{2}}{2}\right)$ **13.** $(-\sqrt{2}, \sqrt{2})$

15. $(-1.1340, -2.2280)$ **17.** $\left(\sqrt{2}, \frac{\pi}{4}\right)$ **19.** $(6, \pi)$

21. $(5, 2.2143)$ **23.** $\left(\sqrt{6}, \frac{5\pi}{4}\right)$ **25.** $(3\sqrt{13}, 0.9828)$

27. $(\sqrt{13}, 5.6952)$ **29.** $(\sqrt{7}, 0.8571)$

31. $\left(\frac{17}{6}, 0.4900\right)$ **33.** $r = 3$ **35.** $r = 4\csc\theta$

37. $r = 10\sec\theta$ **39.** $r = \dfrac{-2}{3\cos\theta - \sin\theta}$

41. $r^2 = 16\sec\theta\csc\theta = 32\csc 2\theta$

43. $r = \dfrac{4}{1 - \cos\theta}$ or $-\dfrac{4}{1 + \cos\theta}$

45. $r = a$ **47.** $r = 2a\cos\theta$ **49.** $x^2 + y^2 - 4y = 0$

51. $\sqrt{3}x + y = 0$ **53.** $x^2 + y^2 = 16$

55. $y = 4$ **57.** $x^2 + y^2 - x^{2/3} = 0$

59. $(x^2 + y^2)^2 = 6x^2y - 2y^3$ **61.** $x^2 + 4y - 4 = 0$

63. $4x^2 - 5y^2 - 36y - 36 = 0$

65. The graph of the polar equation consists of all points that are six units from the pole.
$x^2 + y^2 = 36$

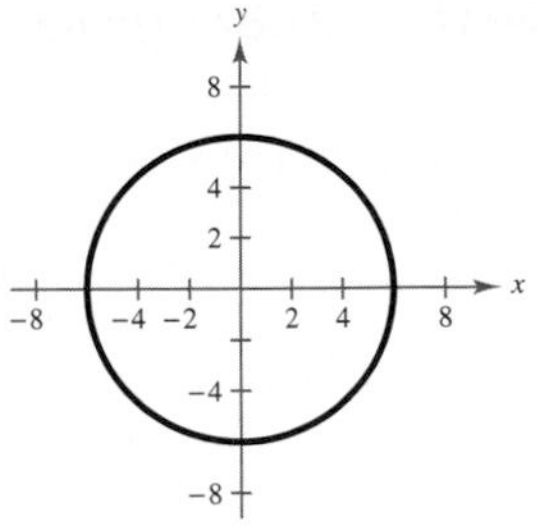

67. The graph of the polar equation consists of all points on the line that make an angle of $\pi/6$ with the positive polar axis.
$-\sqrt{3}x + 3y = 0$

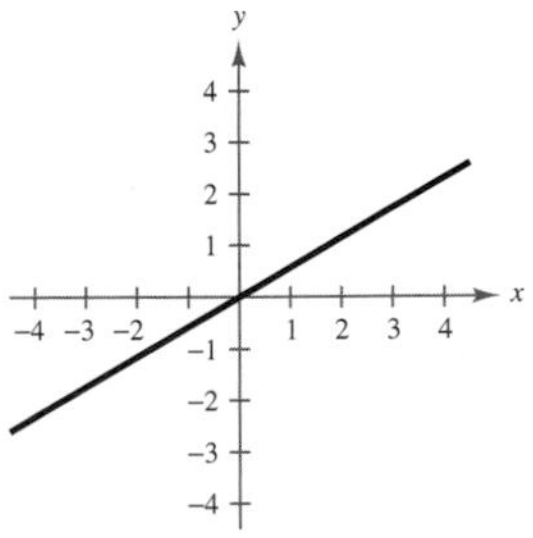

69. The graph of the polar equation is not evident by simple inspection, so convert to rectangular form.
$x - 3 = 0$

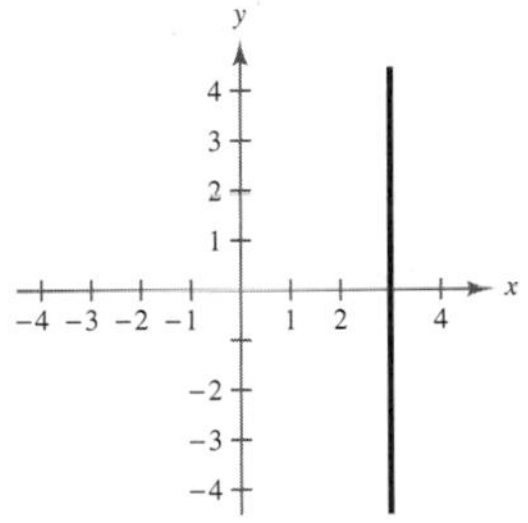

71. True. Because r is a directed distance, the point (r, θ) can be represented as $(r, \theta \pm 2\pi n)$.

73. $(x - h)^2 + (y - k)^2 = h^2 + k^2$
Radius: $\sqrt{h^2 + k^2}$
Center: (h, k)

75. (a) Answers will vary.
(b) (r_1, θ_1), (r_2, θ_2) and the pole are collinear.
$d = \sqrt{r_1^2 + r_2^2 - 2r_1r_2} = |r_1 - r_2|$
This represents the distance between two points on the line $\theta = \theta_1 = \theta_2$.
(c) $d = \sqrt{r_1^2 + r_2^2}$
This is the result of the Pythagorean Theorem.
(d) Answers will vary. For example:
Points: $(3, \pi/6)$, $(4, \pi/3)$
Distance: 2.053
Points: $(-3, 7\pi/6)$, $(-4, 4\pi/3)$
Distance: 2.053

77. $2\log_6 x + \log_6 z - \log_6 3 - \log_6 y$

79. $\ln x + 2\ln(x + 4)$ **81.** $\log_7 \dfrac{x}{3y}$ **83.** $\ln\sqrt{x}(x - 2)$

85. $(2, 3)$ **87.** $\left(\frac{8}{7}, \frac{88}{35}, \frac{8}{5}\right)$ **89.** $(2, -3, 3)$

91. Not collinear **93.** Collinear

Section 10.8 *(page 791)*

Vocabulary Check *(page 791)*

1. $\theta = \dfrac{\pi}{2}$ **2.** polar axis **3.** convex limaçon
4. circle **5.** lemniscate **6.** cardioid

1. Rose curve with 4 petals **3.** Limaçon with inner loop
5. Rose curve with 4 petals **7.** Polar axis

9. $\theta = \dfrac{\pi}{2}$ **11.** $\theta = \dfrac{\pi}{2}$, polar axis, pole

13. Maximum: $|r| = 20$ when $\theta = \dfrac{3\pi}{2}$

Zero: $r = 0$ when $\theta = \dfrac{\pi}{2}$

15. Maximum: $|r| = 4$ when $\theta = 0, \dfrac{\pi}{3}, \dfrac{2\pi}{3}$

Zero: $r = 0$ when $\theta = \dfrac{\pi}{6}, \dfrac{\pi}{2}, \dfrac{5\pi}{6}$

17.
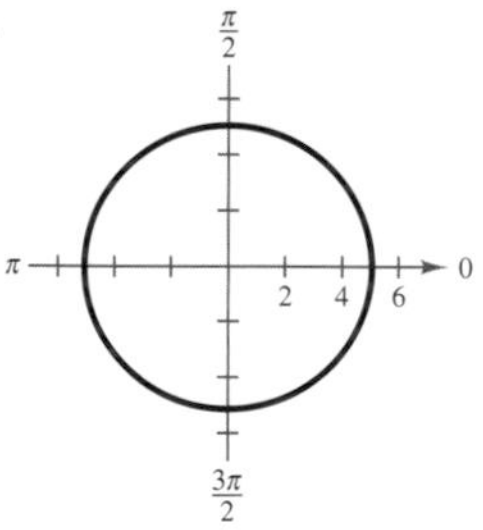

19.
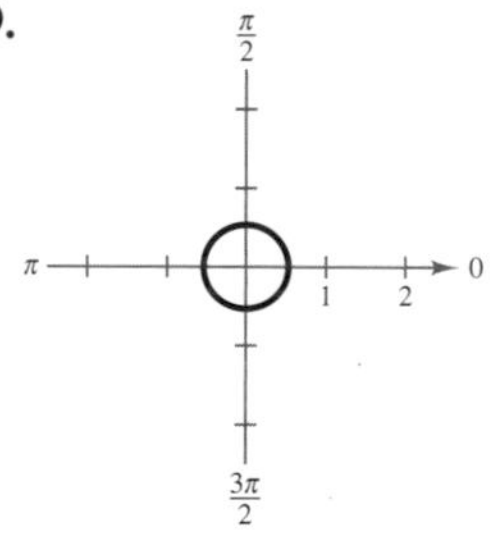

21.
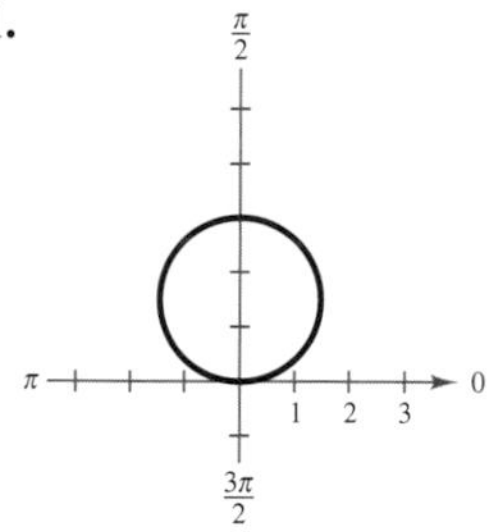

23.
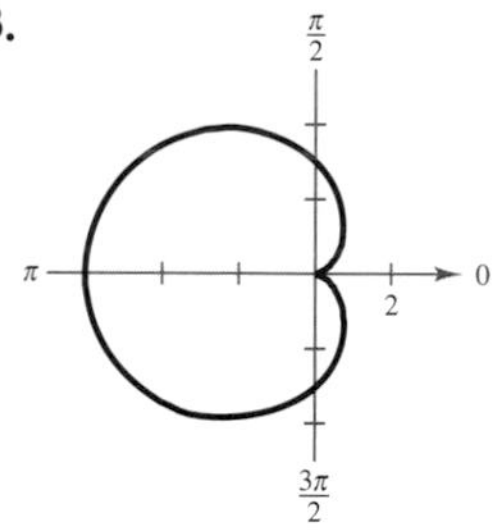

25.
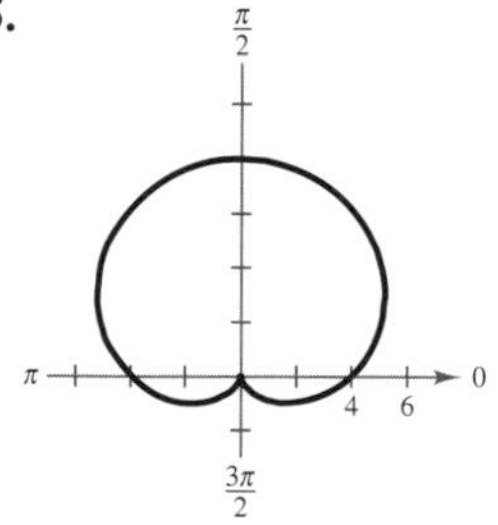

27.
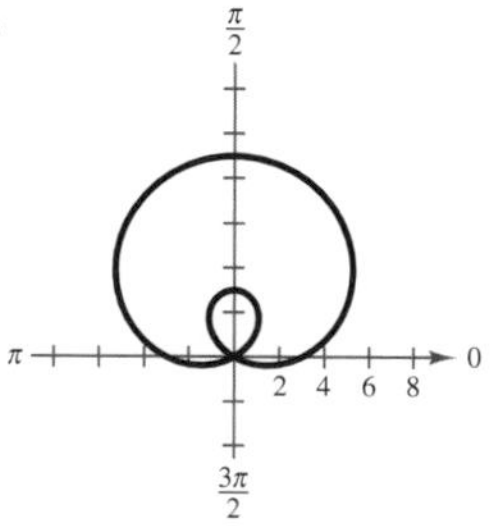

29.
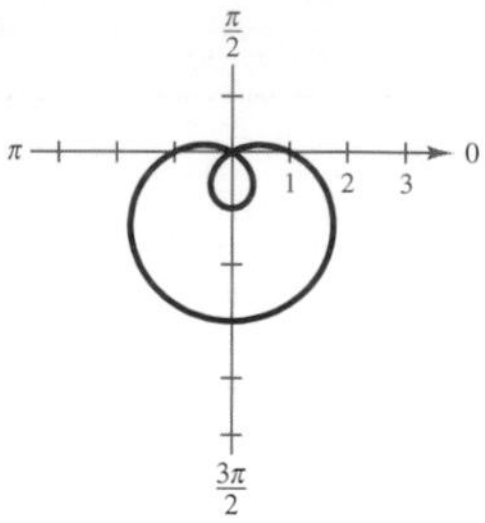

31.
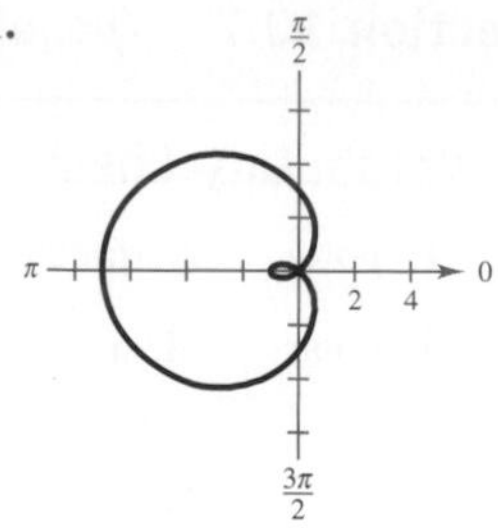

33.
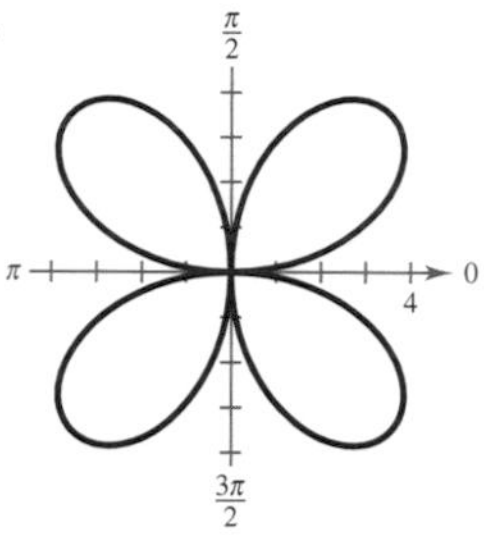

35.
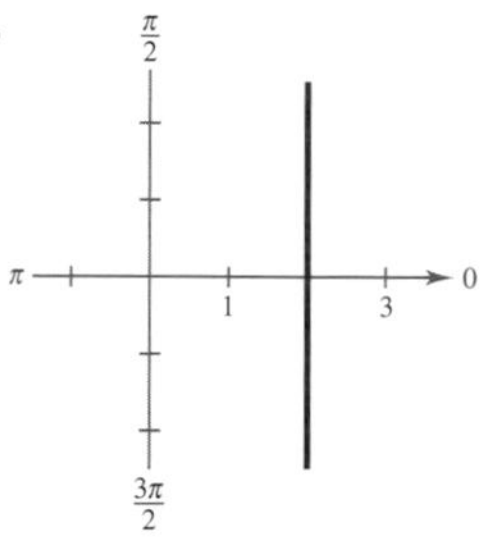

37.
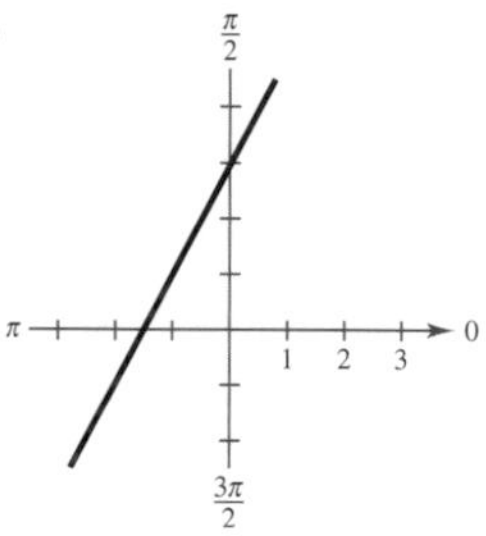

39.
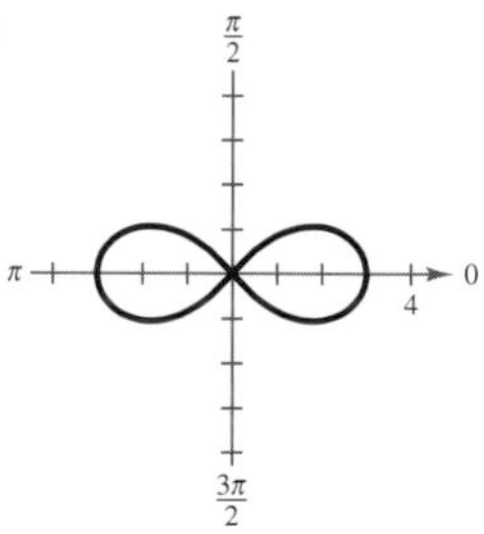

41.
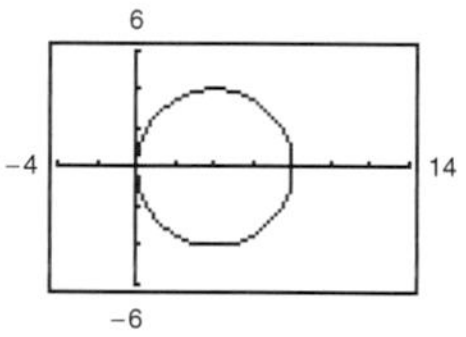

43.
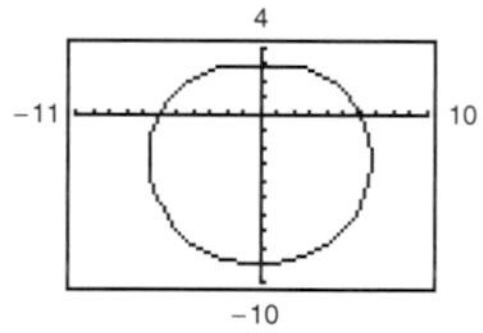

45.
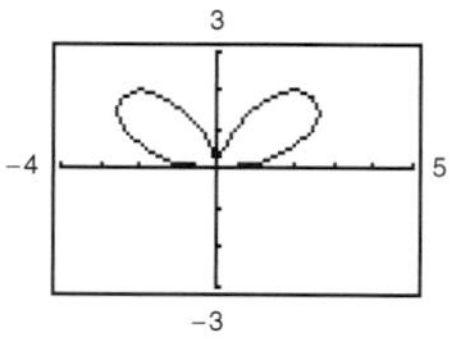

47.
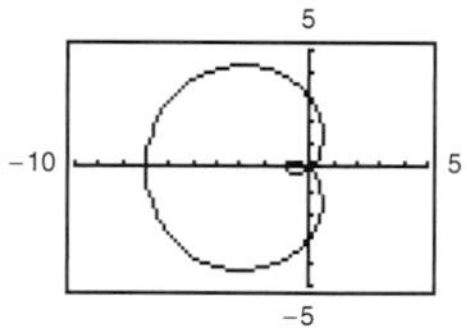

$0 \le \theta < 2\pi$

49.
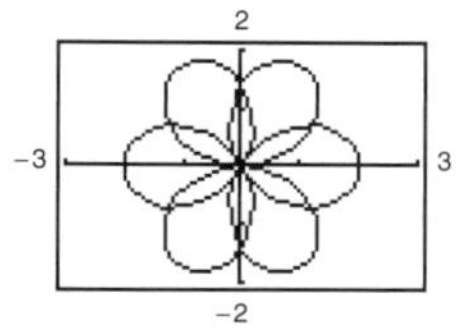

$0 \le \theta < 4\pi$

51.
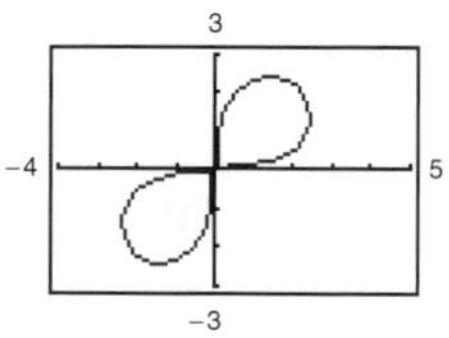

$0 \le \theta < \pi$

53.

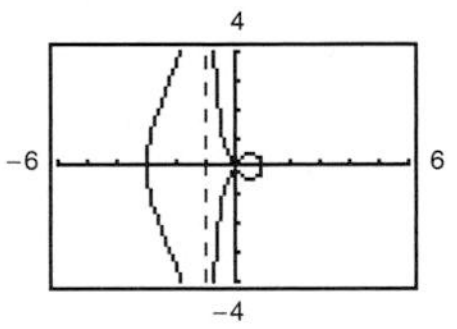

55.

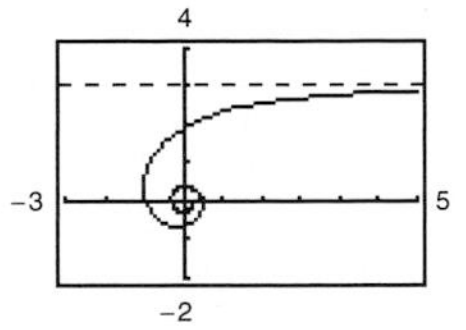

57. True. For a graph to have polar axis symmetry, replace (r, θ) by $(r, -\theta)$ or $(-r, \pi - \theta)$.

59. (a)

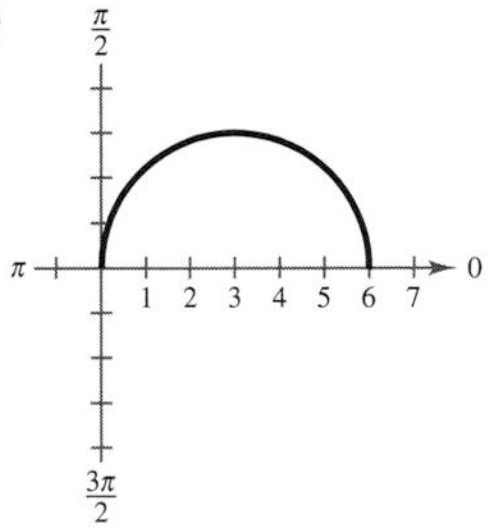

Upper half of circle

(b)

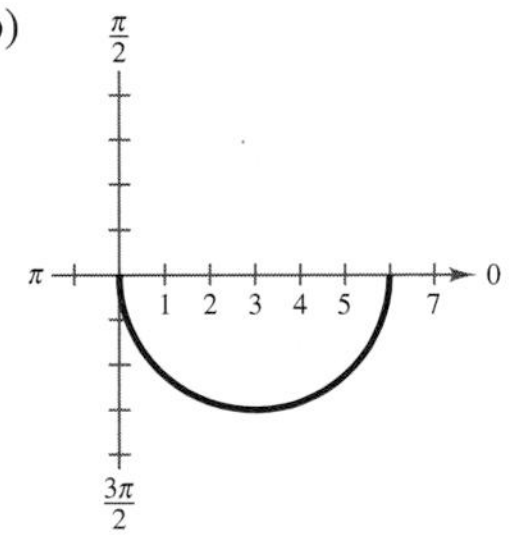

Lower half of circle

(c)

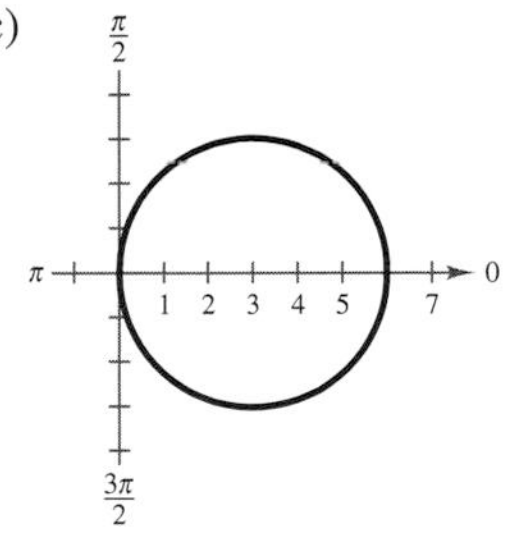

Full circle

(d)

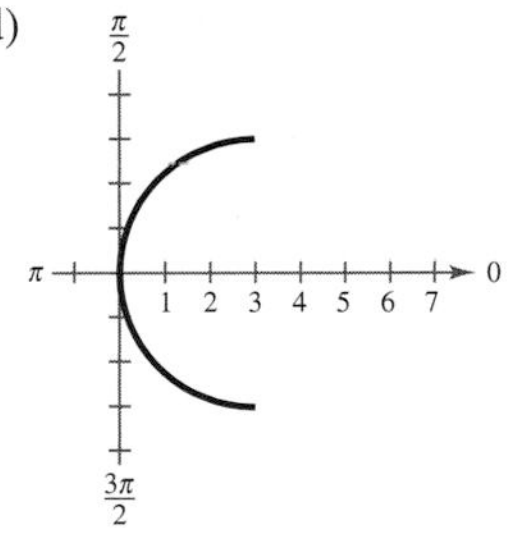

Left half of circle

61. Answers will vary.

63. (a) $r = 2 - \dfrac{\sqrt{2}}{2}(\sin\theta - \cos\theta)$ (b) $r = 2 + \cos\theta$

(c) $r = 2 + \sin\theta$ (d) $r = 2 - \cos\theta$

65. (a)

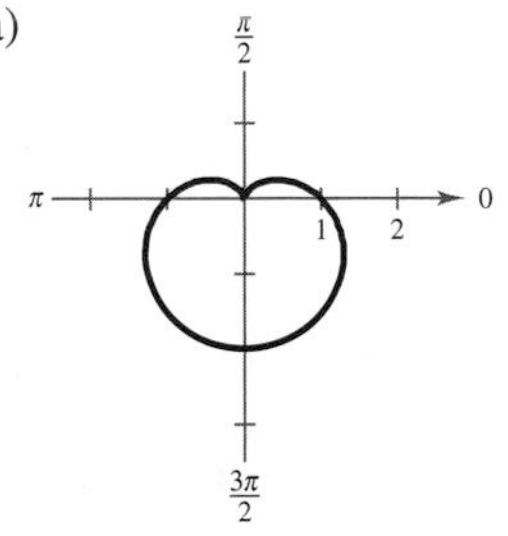

(b)

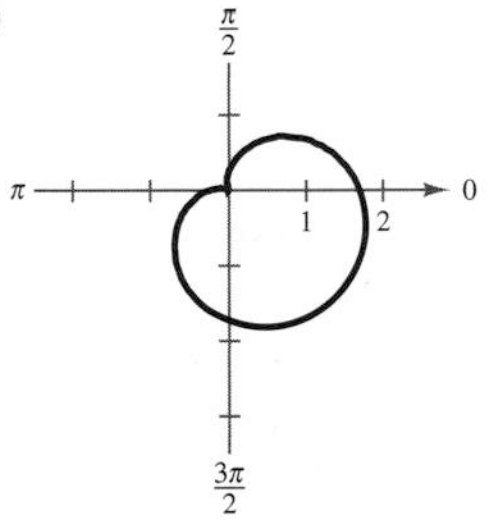

67.

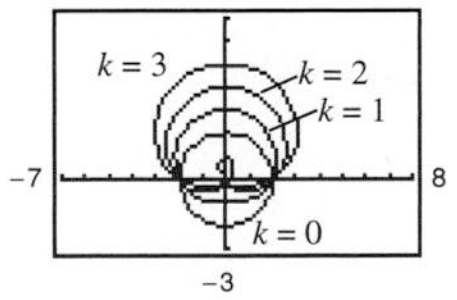

$k = 0$, circle
$k = 1$, convex limaçon
$k = 2$, cardioid
$k = 3$, limaçon with inner loop

69. ± 3 **71.** $\frac{13}{5}$

73. $\dfrac{(x + 1)^2}{9} + \dfrac{(y - 2)^2}{4} = 1$

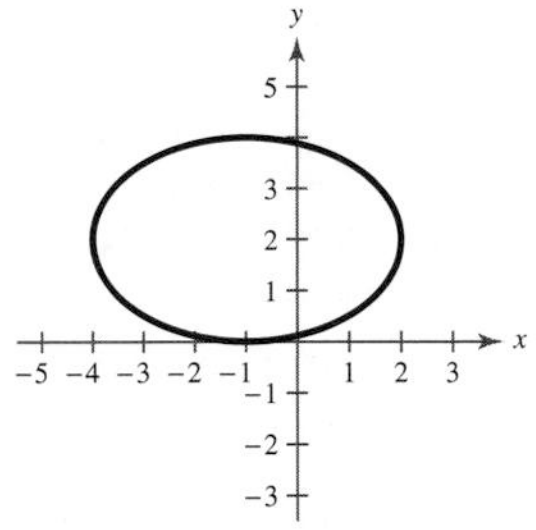

Section 10.9 *(page 797)*

Vocabulary Check *(page 797)*

1. conic **2.** eccentricity; e **3.** vertical; right
4. (a) iii (b) i (c) ii

1. $e = 1$: $r = \dfrac{4}{1 + \cos\theta}$, parabola

$e = 0.5$: $r = \dfrac{2}{1 + 0.5\cos\theta}$, ellipse

$e = 1.5$: $r = \dfrac{6}{1 + 1.5\cos\theta}$, hyperbola

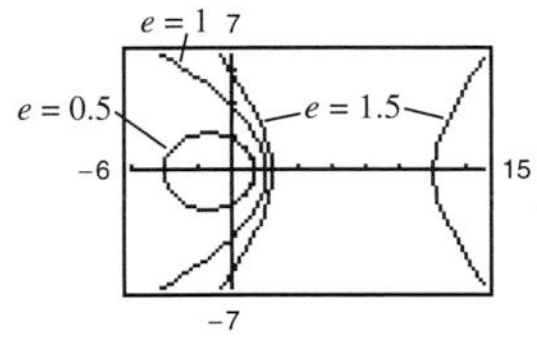

3. $e = 1$: $r = \dfrac{4}{1 - \sin\theta}$, parabola

$e = 0.5$: $r = \dfrac{2}{1 - 0.5\sin\theta}$, ellipse

$e = 1.5$: $r = \dfrac{6}{1 - 1.5\sin\theta}$, hyperbola

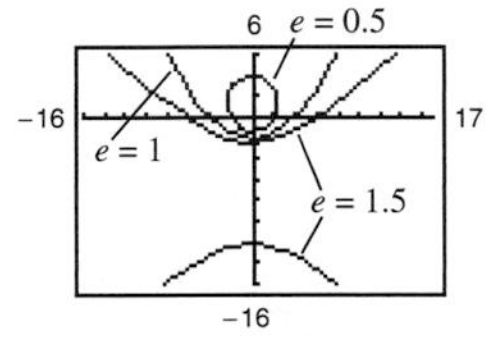

5. f **6.** c **7.** d **8.** e **9.** a **10.** b

11. Parabola

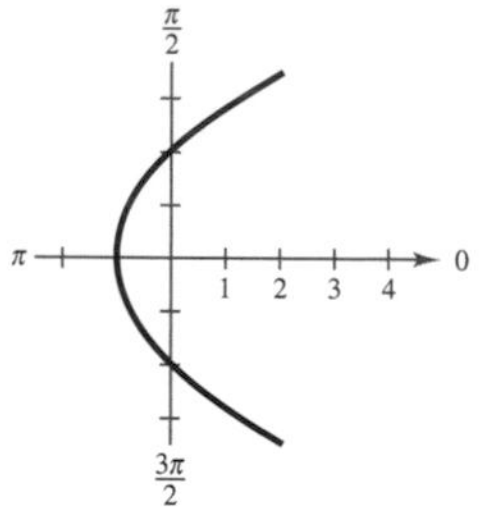

13. Parabola

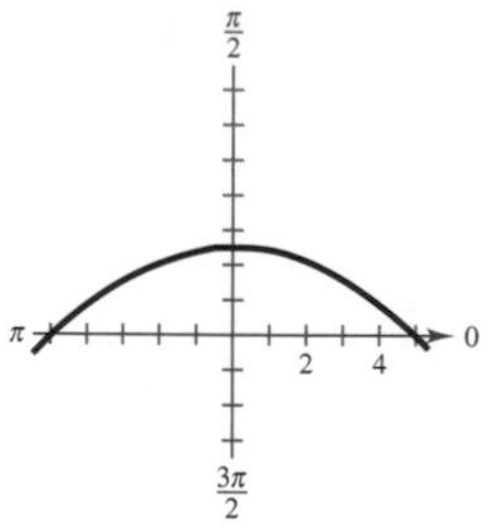

15. Ellipse

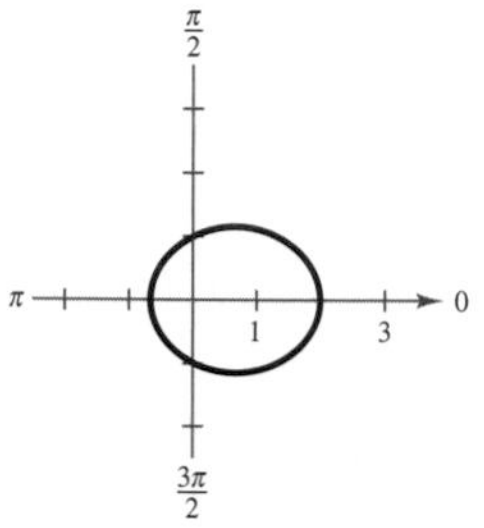

17. Ellipse

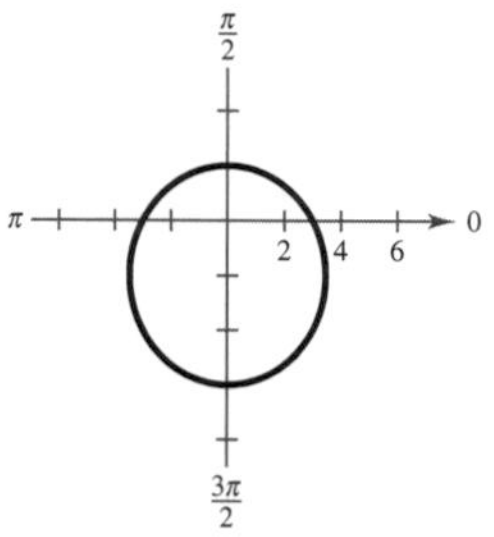

19. Hyperbola

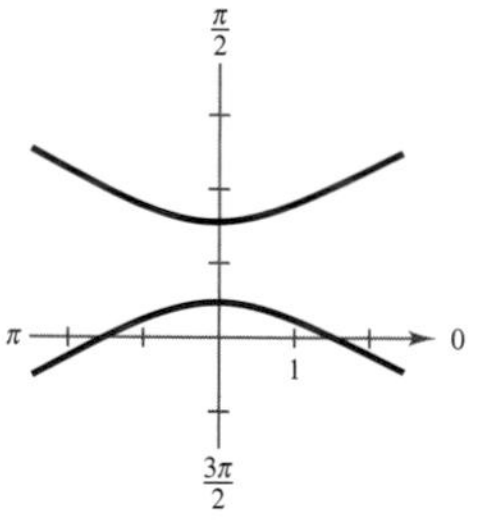

21. Hyperbola

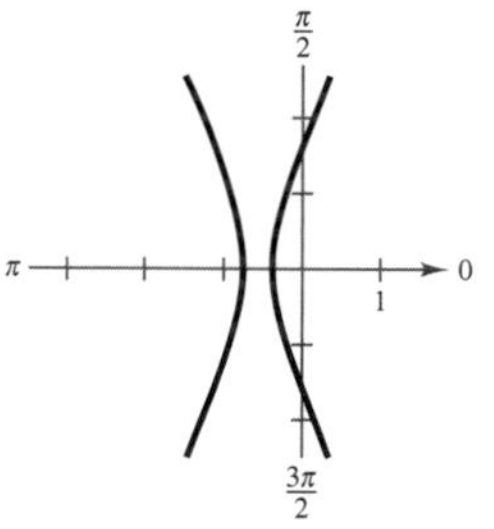

23. Ellipse

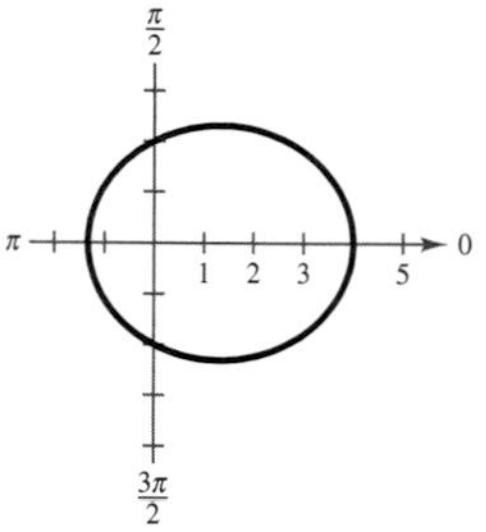

25.

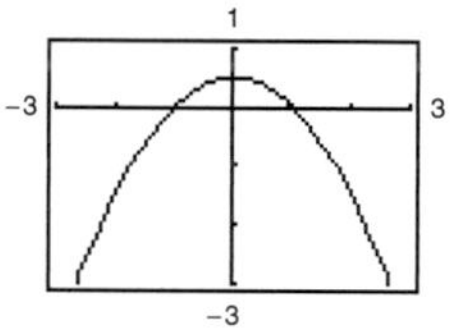

Parabola

27.

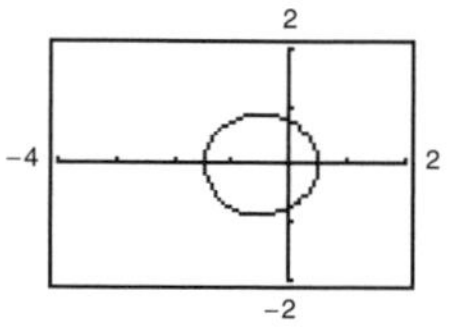

Ellipse

29.

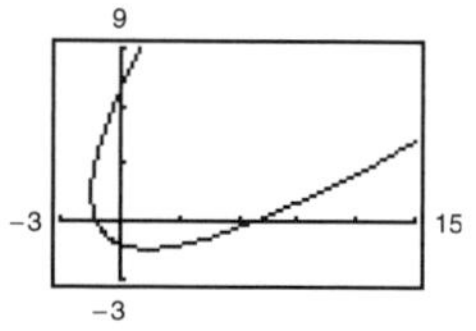

31.

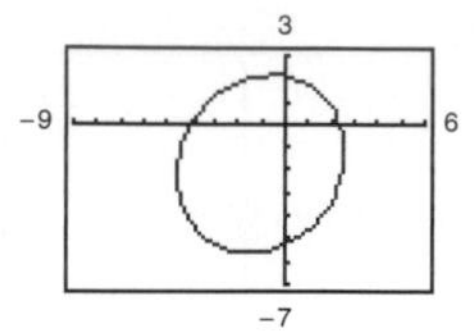

33. $r = \dfrac{1}{1 - \cos\theta}$ **35.** $r = \dfrac{1}{2 + \sin\theta}$

37. $r = \dfrac{2}{1 + 2\cos\theta}$ **39.** $r = \dfrac{2}{1 - \sin\theta}$

41. $r = \dfrac{10}{1 - \cos\theta}$ **43.** $r = \dfrac{10}{3 + 2\cos\theta}$

45. $r = \dfrac{20}{3 - 2\cos\theta}$ **47.** $r = \dfrac{9}{4 - 5\sin\theta}$

49. Answers will vary.

51. $r = \dfrac{9.5929 \times 10^7}{1 - 0.0167\cos\theta}$

Perihelion: 9.4354×10^7 miles

Aphelion: 9.7558×10^7 miles

53. $r = \dfrac{1.0820 \times 10^8}{1 - 0.0068\cos\theta}$

Perihelion: 1.0747×10^8 kilometers

Aphelion: 1.0894×10^8 kilometers

55. $r = \dfrac{1.4039 \times 10^8}{1 - 0.0934\cos\theta}$

Perihelion: 1.2840×10^8 miles

Aphelion: 1.5486×10^8 miles

57. $r = \dfrac{0.624}{1 + 0.847\sin\pi/2}$; $r = 0.338$ astronomical unit

59. True. The graphs represent the same hyperbola.

61. True. The conic is an ellipse because the eccentricity is less than 1.

63. Answers will vary. **65.** $r^2 = \dfrac{24{,}336}{169 - 25\cos^2\theta}$

67. $r^2 = \dfrac{144}{25\cos^2\theta - 9}$ **69.** $r^2 = \dfrac{144}{25\sin^2\theta - 16}$

71. (a) Ellipse

(b) The given polar equation, r, has a vertical directrix to the left of the pole. The equation, r_1, has a vertical directrix to the right of the pole, and the equation, r_2, has a horizontal directrix below the pole.

(c)

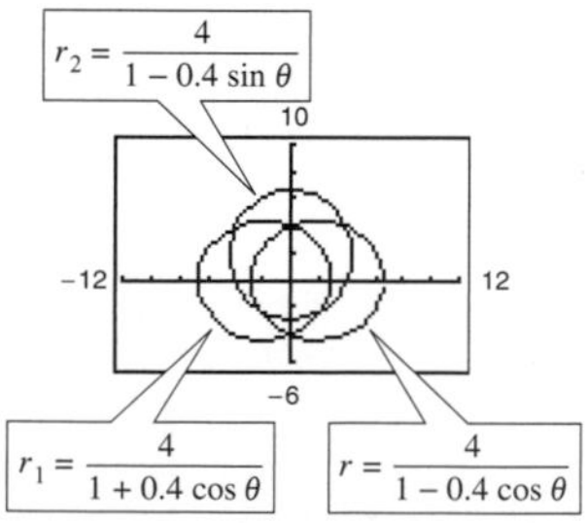

73. $\frac{\pi}{6} + n\pi$ **75.** $\frac{\pi}{3} + n\pi, \frac{2\pi}{3} + n\pi$

77. $\frac{\pi}{2} + n\pi$ **79.** $\frac{\sqrt{2}}{10}$ **81.** $\frac{7\sqrt{2}}{10}$

83. $\sin 2u = -\frac{24}{25}$

$\cos 2u = -\frac{7}{25}$

$\tan 2u = \frac{24}{7}$

85. $a_n = -\frac{1}{4}n + \frac{1}{4}$ **87.** $a_n = 9n$ **89.** 220 **91.** 720

Review Exercises *(page 801)*

1. $\frac{\pi}{4}$ radian, 45° **3.** 1.1071 radians, 63.43°

5. 0.4424 radian, 25.35° **7.** 0.6588 radian, 37.75°

9. $2\sqrt{2}$ **11.** Hyperbola

13. $y^2 = 16x$

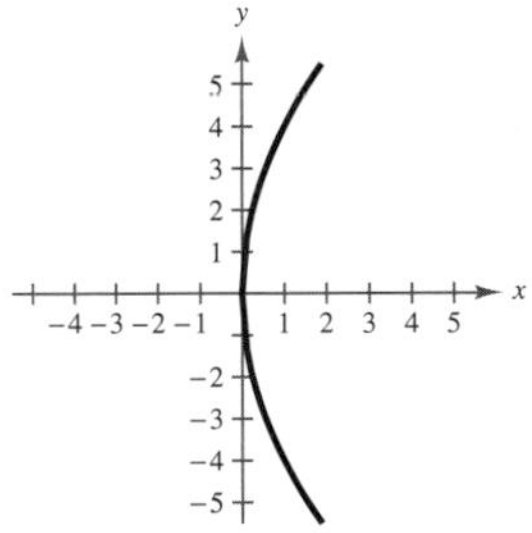

15. $(y - 2)^2 = 12x$

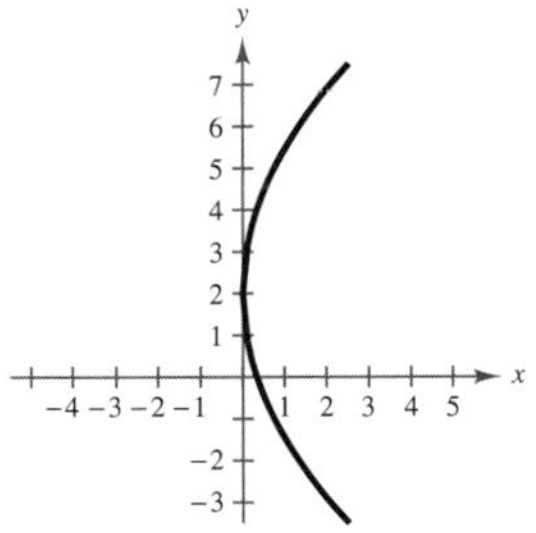

17. $y = -2x + 2$; (1, 0) **19.** $8\sqrt{6}$ meters

21. $\frac{(x-2)^2}{25} + \frac{y^2}{21} = 1$

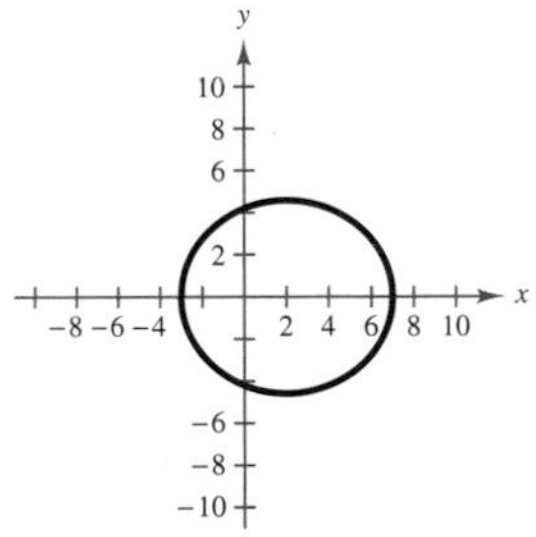

23. $\frac{(x-2)^2}{4} + (y-1)^2 = 1$

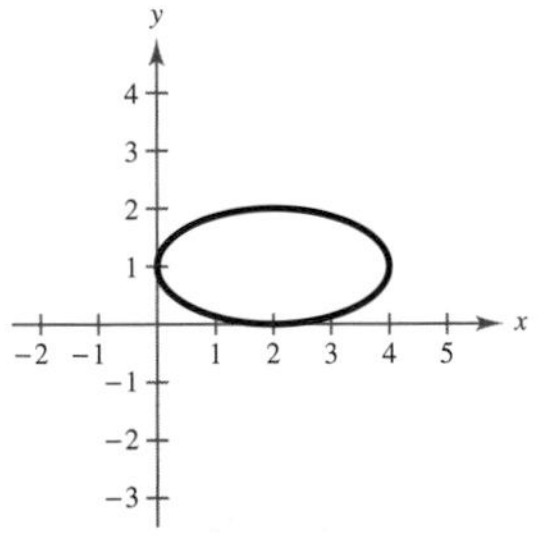

25. The foci occur 3 feet from the center of the arch on a line connecting the tops of the pillars.

27. Center: $(-2, 1)$
Vertices: $(-2, 11), (-2, -9)$
Foci: $\left(-2, 1 \pm \sqrt{19}\right)$
Eccentricity: $\frac{\sqrt{19}}{10}$

29. Center: $(1, -4)$
Vertices: $(1, 0), (1, -8)$
Foci: $\left(1, -4 \pm \sqrt{7}\right)$
Eccentricity: $\frac{\sqrt{7}}{4}$

31. $y^2 - \frac{x^2}{8} = 1$ **33.** $\frac{5(x-4)^2}{16} - \frac{5y^2}{64} = 1$

35. Center: $(3, -5)$
Vertices: $(7, -5), (-1, -5)$
Foci: $\left(3 \pm 2\sqrt{5}, -5\right)$
Asymptotes:
$y = -5 \pm \frac{1}{2}(x - 3)$

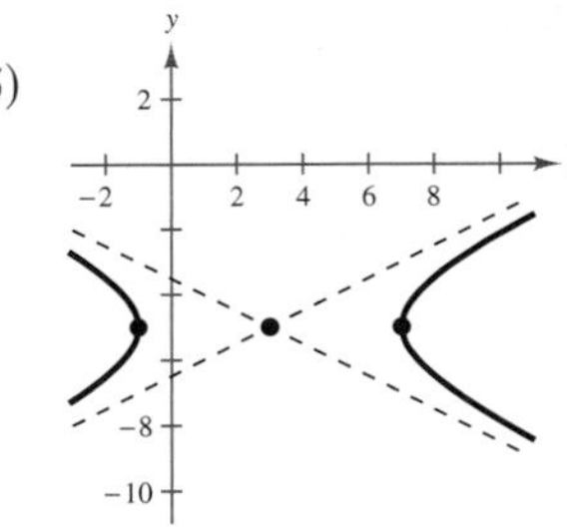

37. Center: $(1, -1)$
Vertices: $(5, -1), (-3, -1)$
Foci: $(6, -1), (-4, -1)$
Asymptotes:
$y = -1 \pm \frac{3}{4}(x - 1)$

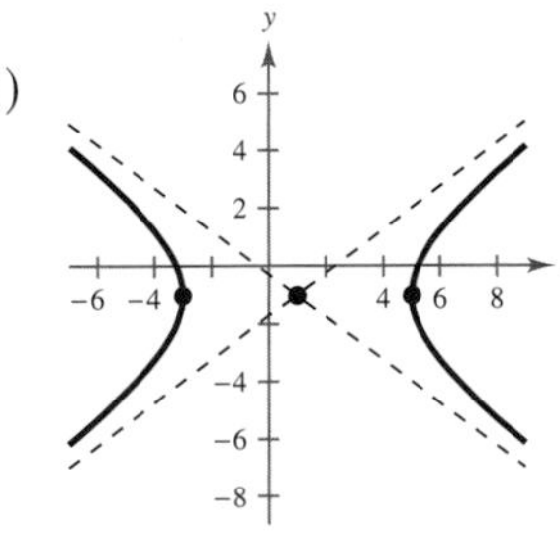

39. 72 miles **41.** Hyperbola **43.** Ellipse

45. $\frac{(x')^2}{8} - \frac{(y')^2}{8} = 1$

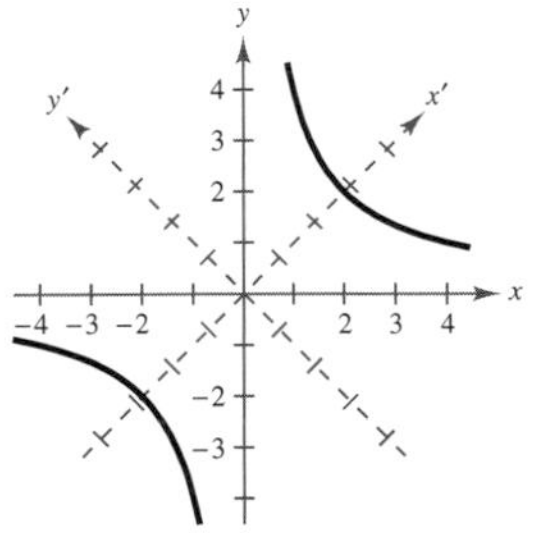

47. $\frac{(x')^2}{3} + \frac{(y')^2}{2} = 1$

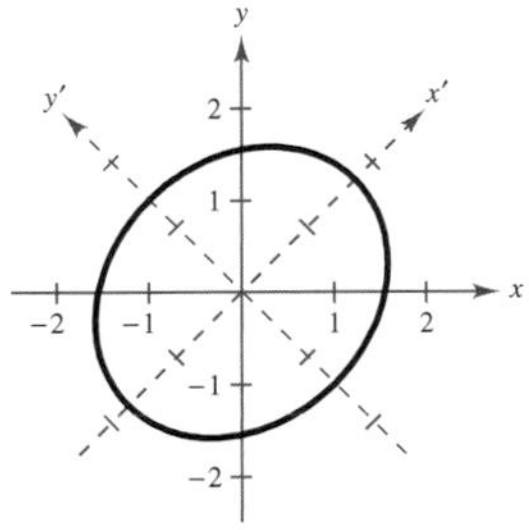

49. (a) Parabola

(b) $y = \frac{24x + 40 \pm \sqrt{(24x + 40)^2 - 36(16x^2 - 30x)}}{18}$

(c)

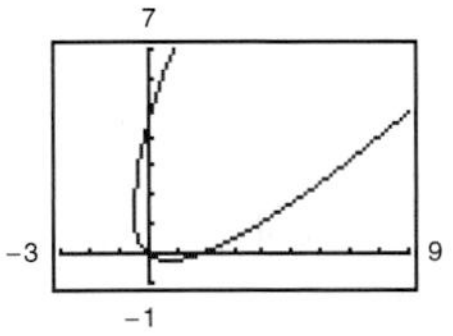

51. (a) Parabola

(b)

$y = \frac{-\left(2x - 2\sqrt{2}\right) \pm \sqrt{\left(2x - 2\sqrt{2}\right)^2 - 4\left(x^2 + 2\sqrt{2}x + 2\right)}}{2}$

(c)

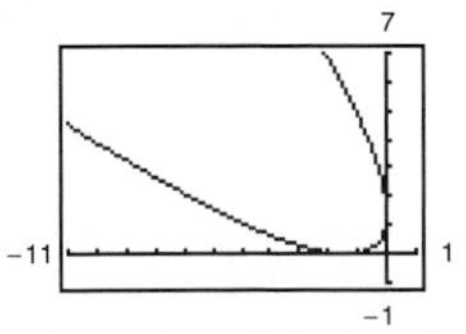

CHAPTER 10

53.

t	-3	-2	-1	0	1	2	3
x	-11	-8	-5	-2	1	4	7
y	19	15	11	7	3	-1	-5

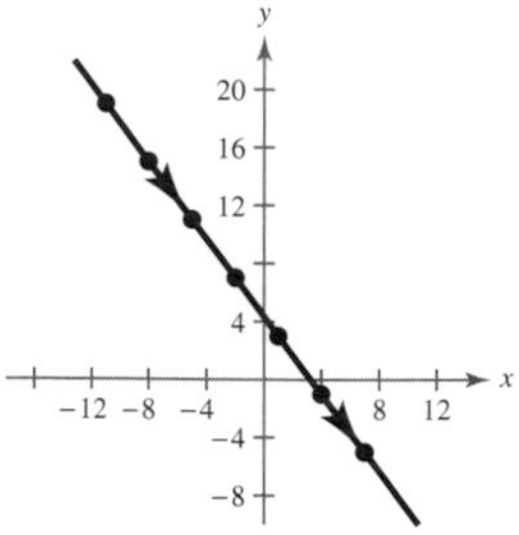

55. (a)

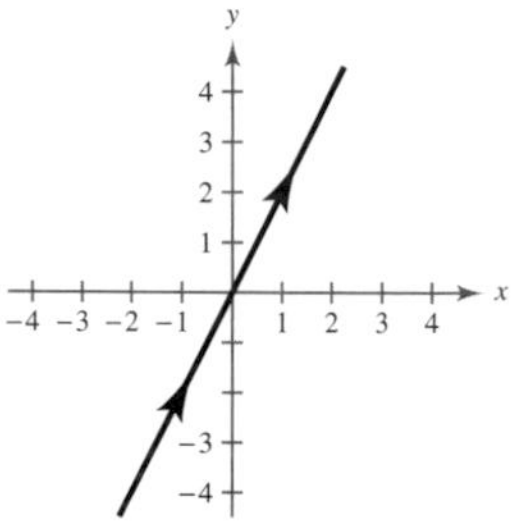

(b) $y = 2x$

57. (a)

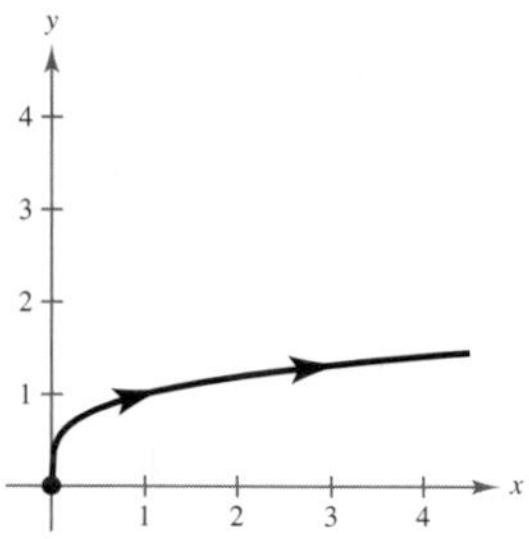

(b) $y = \sqrt[4]{x}$

59. (a)

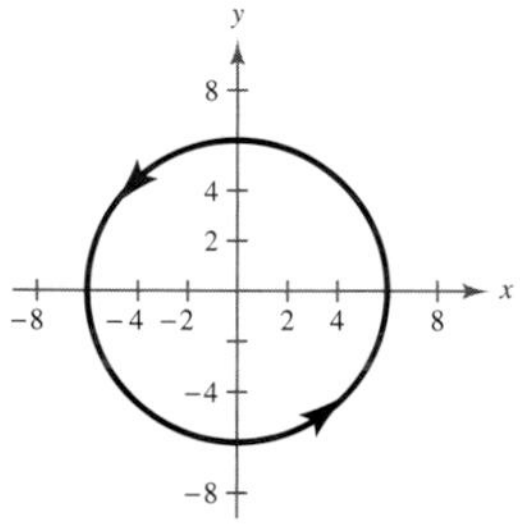

(b) $x^2 + y^2 = 36$

61. $x = 5 + 6 \cos \theta$
$y = 4 + 6 \sin \theta$

63. $x = 3 \tan \theta$
$y = 4 \sec \theta$

65.

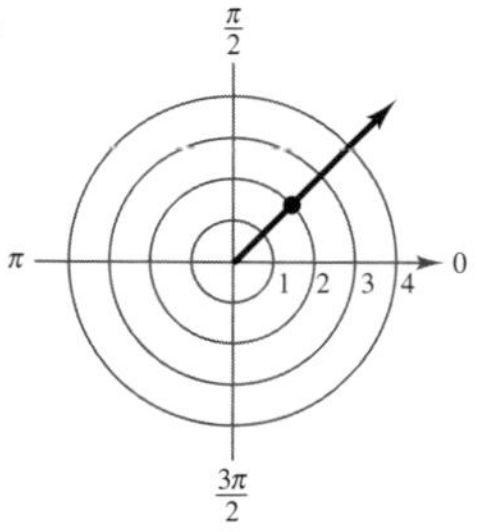

$\left(2, \frac{9\pi}{4}\right), \left(-2, \frac{5\pi}{4}\right)$

67.

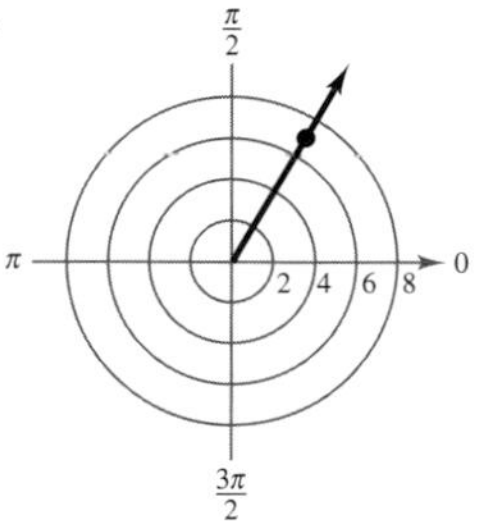

$(7, 1.05), (-7, 10.47)$

69. $\left(-\frac{1}{2}, -\frac{\sqrt{3}}{2}\right)$ **71.** $\left(-\frac{3\sqrt{2}}{2}, \frac{3\sqrt{2}}{2}\right)$ **73.** $\left(2, \frac{\pi}{2}\right)$

75. $\left(2\sqrt{13}, 0.9828\right)$ **77.** $r = 7$ **79.** $r = 6 \sin \theta$

81. $r^2 = 10 \csc 2\theta$ **83.** $x^2 + y^2 = 25$

85. $x^2 + y^2 = 3x$ **87.** $x^2 + y^2 = y^{2/3}$

89. Symmetry: $\theta = \frac{\pi}{2}$, polar axis, pole

Maximum value of $|r|$: $|r| = 4$ for all values of θ

No zeros of r

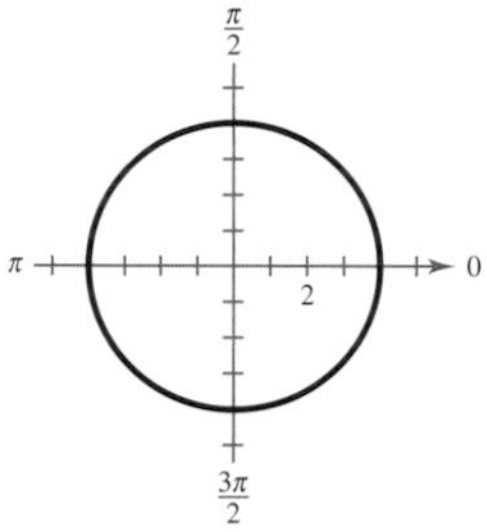

91. Symmetry: $\theta = \frac{\pi}{2}$, polar axis, pole

Maximum value of $|r|$: $|r| = 4$ when $\theta = \frac{\pi}{4}, \frac{3\pi}{4}, \frac{5\pi}{4}, \frac{7\pi}{4}$

Zeros of r: $r = 0$ when $\theta = 0, \frac{\pi}{2}, \pi, \frac{3\pi}{2}$

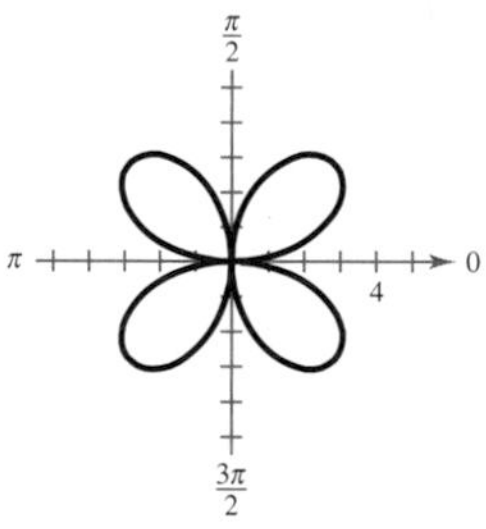

93. Symmetry: polar axis

Maximum value of $|r|$: $|r| = 4$ when $\theta = 0$

Zeros of r: $r = 0$ when $\theta = \pi$

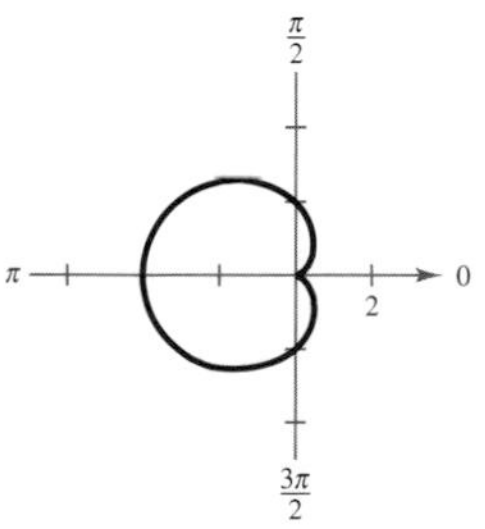

95. Symmetry: $\theta = \frac{\pi}{2}$

Maximum value of $|r|$: $|r| = 8$ when $\theta = \frac{\pi}{2}$

Zeros of r: $r = 0$ when $\theta = 3.4814, 5.9433$

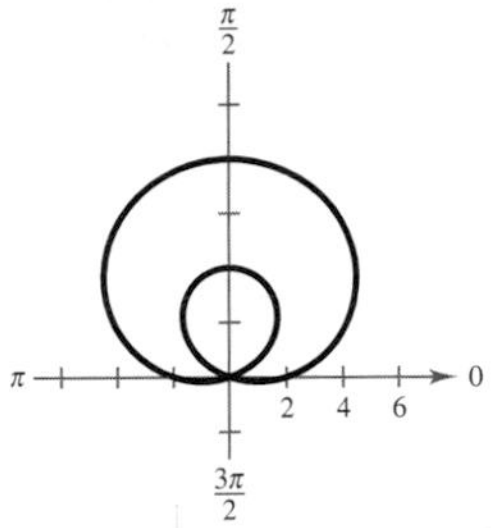

97. Symmetry: $\theta = \frac{\pi}{2}$, polar axis, pole

Maximum value of $|r|$: $|r| = 3$ when $\theta = 0, \frac{\pi}{2}, \pi, \frac{3\pi}{2}$

Zeros of r: $r = 0$ when $\theta = \frac{\pi}{4}, \frac{3\pi}{4}, \frac{5\pi}{4}, \frac{7\pi}{4}$

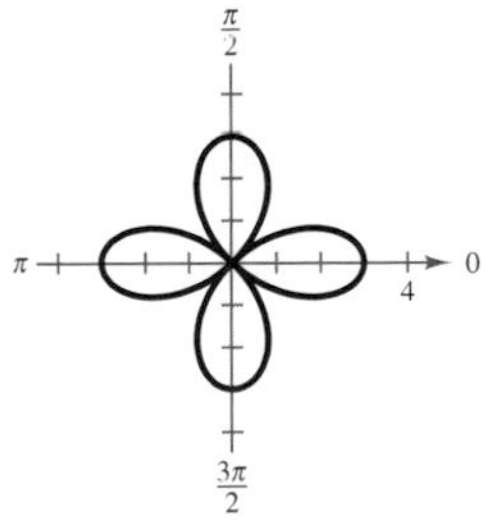

99. Limaçon

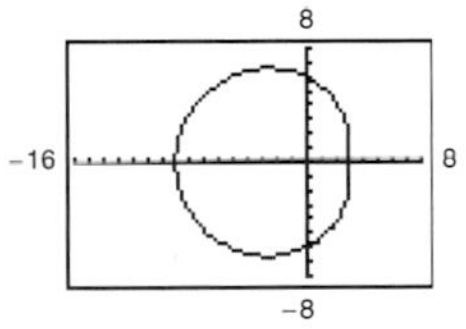

101. Rose curve

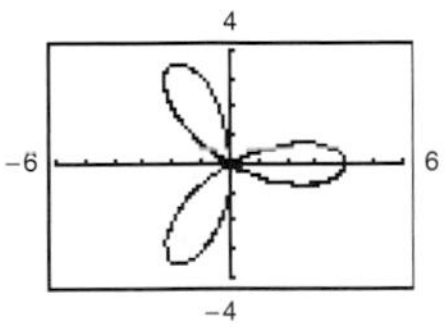

103. Hyperbola

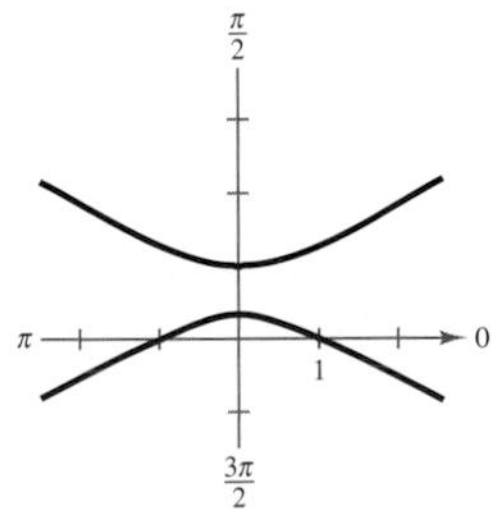

105. Ellipse

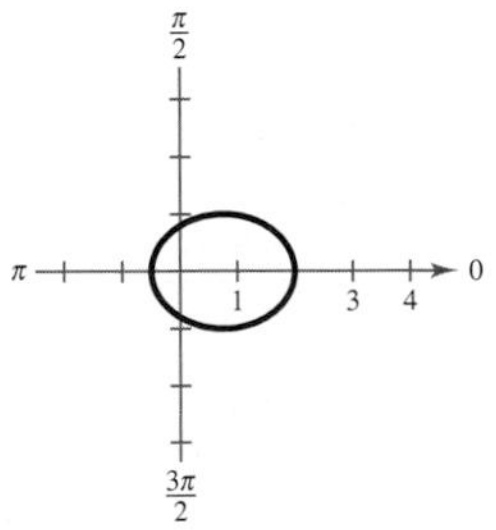

107. $r = \frac{4}{1 - \cos\theta}$

109. $r = \frac{5}{3 - 2\cos\theta}$

111. $r = \frac{7978.81}{1 - 0.937\cos\theta}$; 11,011.87 miles

113. False. When classifying an equation of the form $Ax^2 + Bxy + Cy^2 + Dx + Ey + F = 0$, its graph can be determined by its discriminant. For a graph to be a parabola, its discriminant, $B^2 - 4AC$, must equal zero. So, if $B = 0$, then A or C equals 0.

115. False. The following are two sets of parametric equations for the line.

$x = t,\ y = 3 - 2t$

$x = 3t,\ y = 3 - 6t$

117. 5. The ellipse becomes more circular and approaches a circle of radius 5.

119. (a) The speed would double.

(b) The elliptical orbit would be flatter; the length of the major axis would be greater.

121. (a) The graphs are the same.

(b) The graphs are the same.

Chapter Test *(page 805)*

1. 0.2783 radian, 15.9°

2. 0.8330 radian, 47.7°

3. $\frac{7\sqrt{2}}{2}$

4. Parabola: $y^2 = 4(x - 1)$

Vertex: $(1, 0)$

Focus: $(2, 0)$

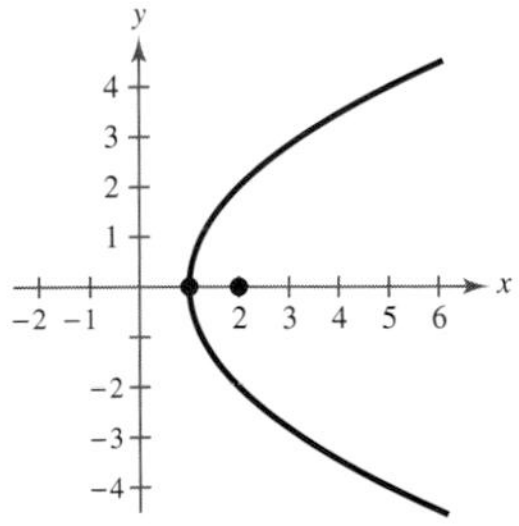

5. Hyperbola: $\frac{(x - 2)^2}{4} - y^2 = 1$

Center: $(2, 0)$

Vertices: $(0, 0), (4, 0)$

Foci: $\left(2 \pm \sqrt{5}, 0\right)$

Asymptotes: $y = \pm\frac{1}{2}(x - 2)$

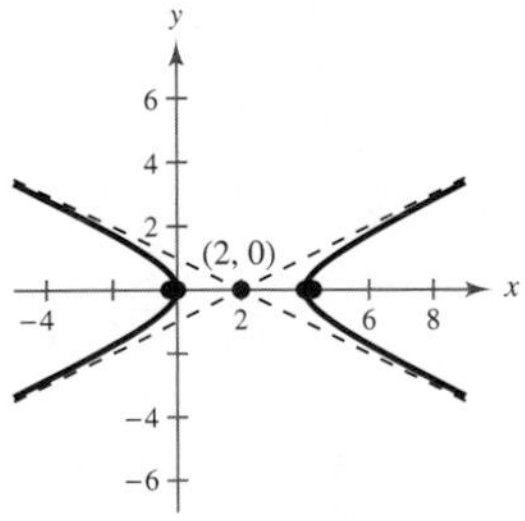

6. Ellipse: $\dfrac{(x+3)^2}{16} + \dfrac{(y-1)^2}{9} = 1$

Center: $(-3, 1)$

Vertices: $(1, 1), (-7, 1)$

Foci: $\left(-3 \pm \sqrt{7}, 1\right)$

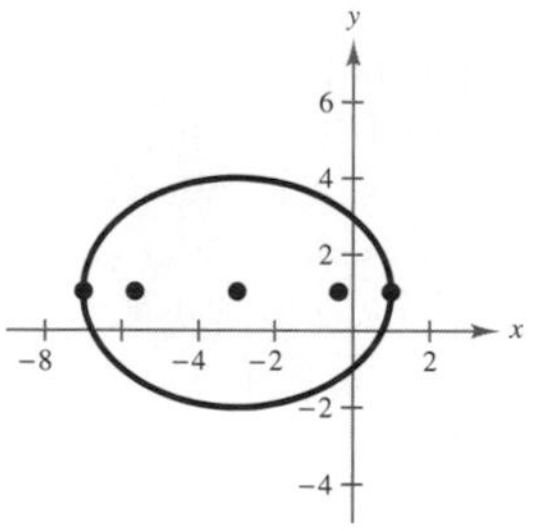

7. Circle: $(x-2)^2 + (y-1)^2 = \frac{1}{2}$

Center: $(2, 1)$

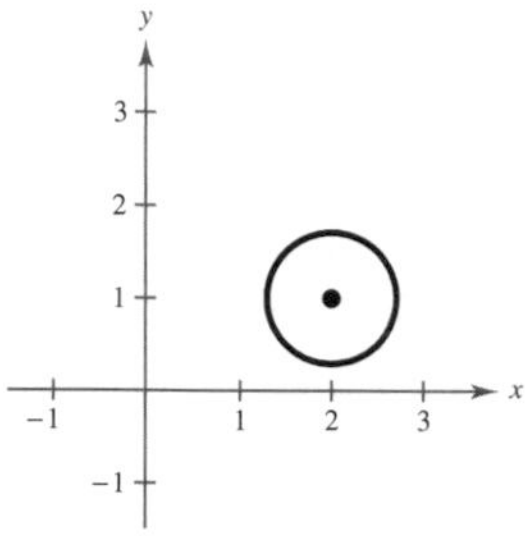

8. $(x-3)^2 = \dfrac{3}{2}(y+2)$ **9.** $\dfrac{5(y-2)^2}{4} - \dfrac{5x^2}{16} = 1$

10. (a) $45°$

(b)

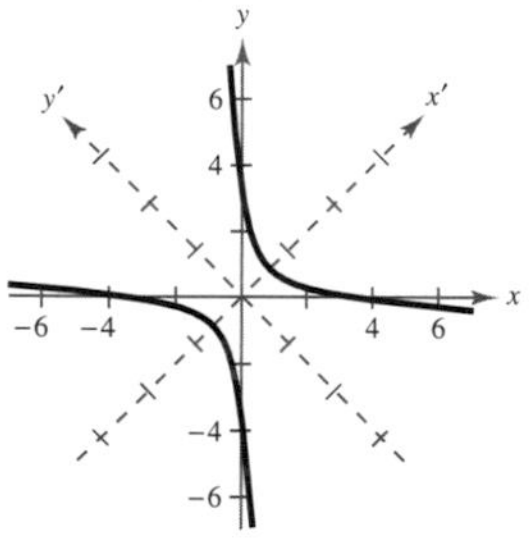

11.

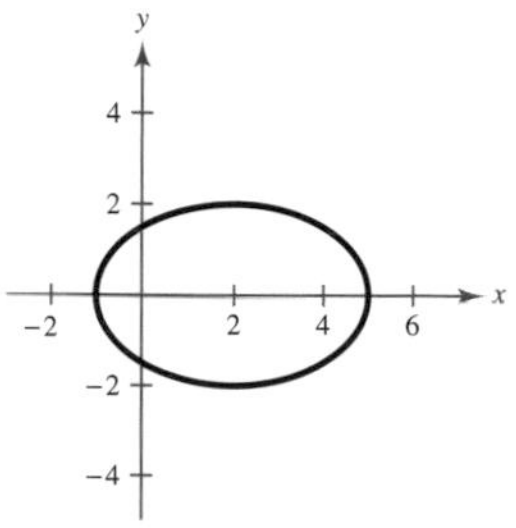

$\dfrac{(x-2)^2}{9} + \dfrac{y^2}{4} = 1$

12. $x = 6 + 4t$
$y = 4 + 7t$

13. $\left(\sqrt{3}, -1\right)$

14. $\left(2\sqrt{2}, \dfrac{7\pi}{4}\right), \left(-2\sqrt{2}, \dfrac{3\pi}{4}\right), \left(2\sqrt{2}, -\dfrac{\pi}{4}\right)$

15. $r = 4 \sin \theta$

16.

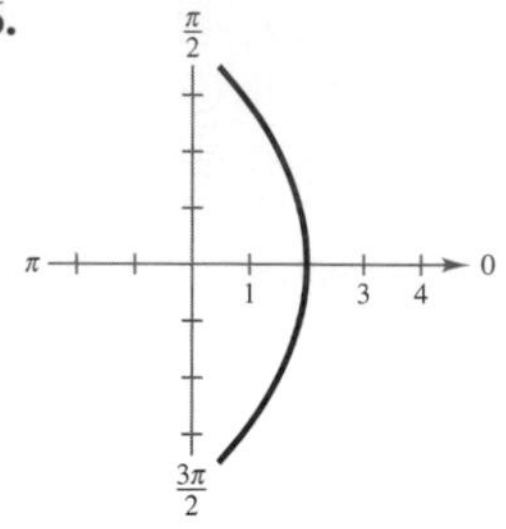

Parabola

17.

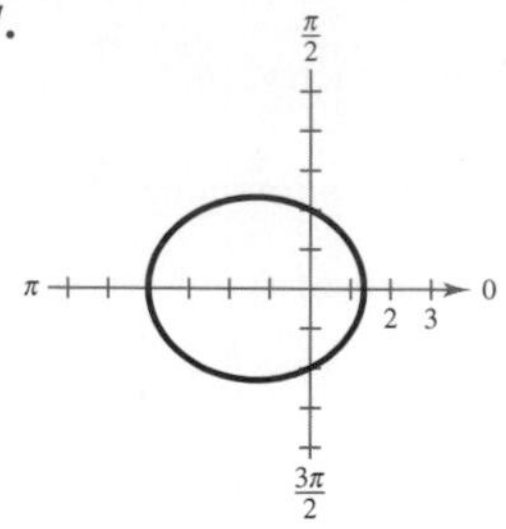

Ellipse

18.

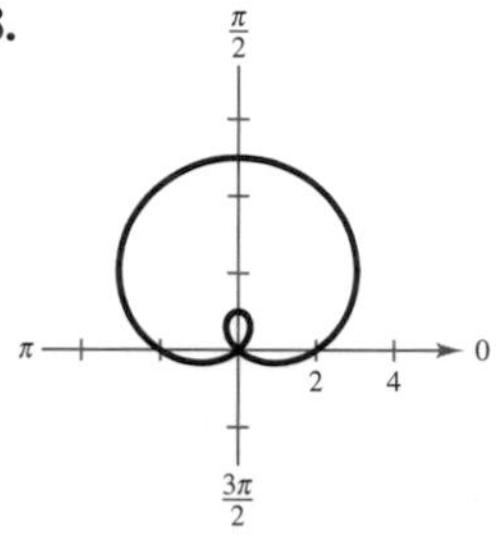

Limaçon with inner loop

19.

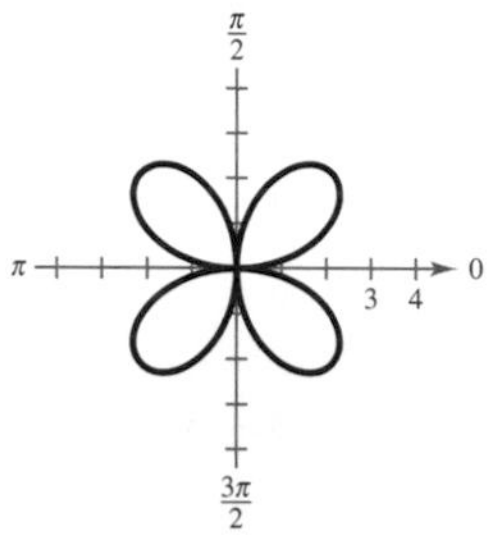

Rose curve

20. Answers will vary. For example: $r = \dfrac{1}{1 + 0.25 \sin \theta}$

21. Slope: 0.1511; Change in elevation: 789 feet

22. No; Yes

Problem Solving *(page 809)*

1. (a) 1.2016 radians (b) 2420 feet, 5971 feet

3. $y^2 = 4p(x + p)$

5. (a) Since $d_1 + d_2 \le 20$, by definition, the outer bound that the boat can travel is an ellipse. The islands are the foci.

(b) Island 1: $(-6, 0)$;
Island 2: $(6, 0)$

(c) 20 miles; Vertex: $(10, 0)$

(d) $\dfrac{x^2}{100} + \dfrac{y^2}{64} = 1$

7. Answers will vary.

9. Answers will vary. For example:
$x = \cos(-t)$
$y = 2 \sin(-t)$

11. (a) $y^2 = x^2\left(\dfrac{1-x}{1+x}\right)$ (b) $r = \cos 2\theta \sec \theta$

(c)

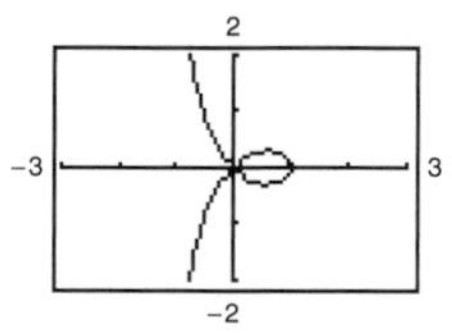

13. Circle

15.

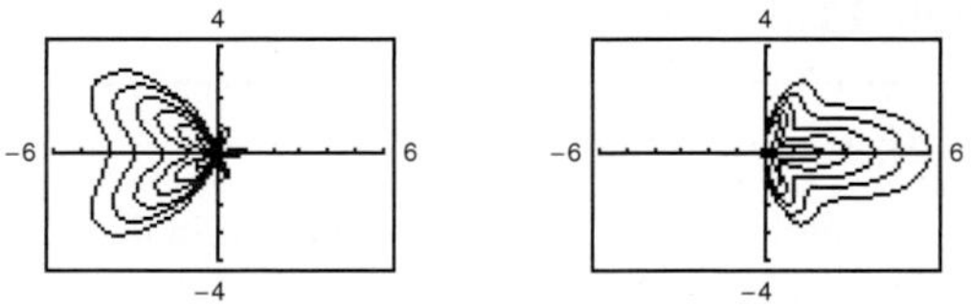

For $n \geq 1$, a bell is produced.

For $n \leq -1$, a heart is produced.

For $n = 0$, a rose curve is produced.

Chapter 11

Section 11.1 *(page 817)*

Vocabulary Check *(page 817)*

1. three-dimensional

2. *xy*-plane, *xz*-plane, *yz*-plane **3.** octants

4. Distance Formula **5.** $\left(\frac{x_1 + x_2}{2}, \frac{y_1 + y_2}{2}, \frac{z_1 + z_2}{2}\right)$

6. sphere **7.** surface, space **8.** trace

1. A: $(-1, 4, 4)$, B: $(1, 3, -2)$, C: $(-3, 0, -2)$

3.

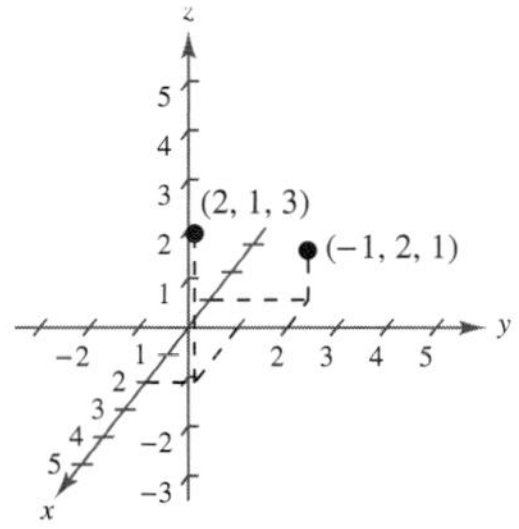

5.

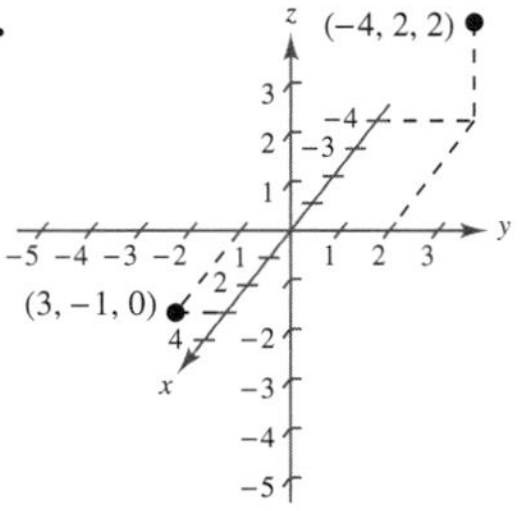

7. $(-3, 3, 4)$ **9.** $(10, 0, 0)$ **11.** Octant IV

13. Octants I, II, III, and IV

15. Octants II, IV, VI, and VIII **17.** $\sqrt{65}$ units

19. $\sqrt{29}$ units **21.** $\sqrt{114}$ units **23.** $\sqrt{110}$ units

25. $(2\sqrt{5})^2 + 3^2 = (\sqrt{29})^2$ **27.** $3^2 + 6^2 = (3\sqrt{5})^2$

29. 6, 6, $2\sqrt{10}$; isosceles triangle **31.** $\left(\frac{3}{2}, -1, 2\right)$

33. $(0, -1, 7)$ **35.** $(1, 0, 5.5)$ **37.** $(2.5, 2, 6)$

39. $(x - 3)^2 + (y - 2)^2 + (z - 4)^2 = 16$

41. $x^2 + (y - 4)^2 + (z - 3)^2 = 9$

43. $(x + 3)^2 + (y - 7)^2 + (z - 5)^2 = 25$

45. $\left(x - \frac{3}{2}\right)^2 + y^2 + (z - 3)^2 = \frac{45}{4}$

47. Center: $\left(\frac{5}{2}, 0, 0\right)$; radius: $\frac{5}{2}$

49. Center: $(2, -1, 3)$; radius: 2

51. Center: $(-2, 0, 4)$; radius: 1

53. Center: $\left(1, \frac{1}{3}, 4\right)$; radius: 3

55. Center: $\left(\frac{1}{3}, -1, 0\right)$; radius: 1

57.

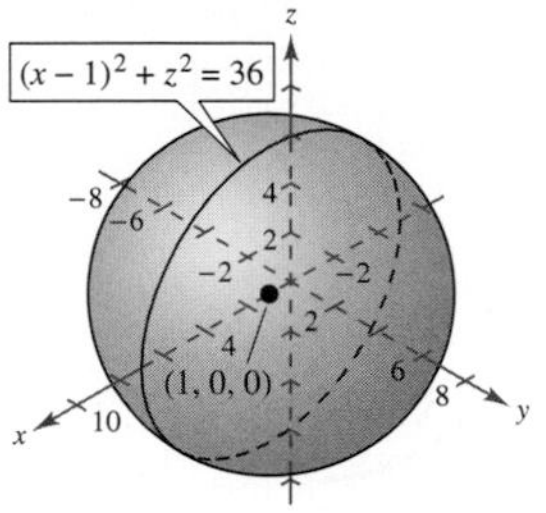

59.

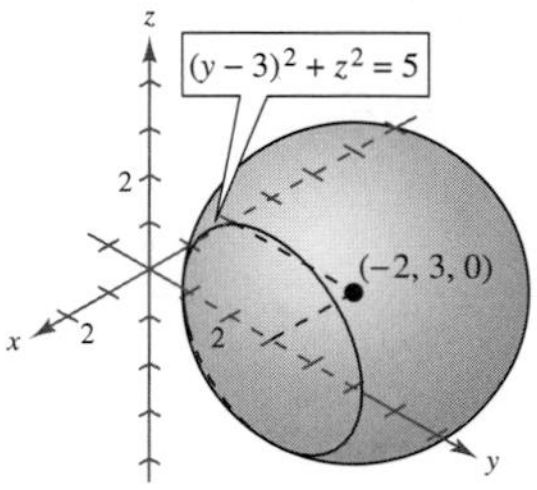

61.

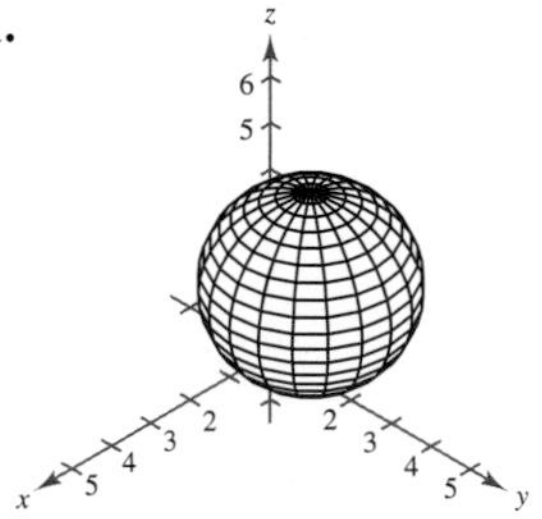

63. $(3, 3, 3)$ **65.** $x^2 + y^2 + z^2 = \frac{165^2}{4}$

67. False. z is the directed distance from the *xy*-plane to P.

69. 0; 0; 0

71. A point or a circle (where the sphere and the *yz*-plane meet)

73. $(x_2, y_2, z_2) = (2x_m - x_1, 2y_m - y_1, 2z_m - z_1)$

75. $v = -\frac{3 \pm \sqrt{17}}{2}$ **77.** $x = \frac{5 \pm \sqrt{5}}{2}$

79. $y = -\frac{1 \pm \sqrt{10}}{2}$ **81.** $3\sqrt{2}, \frac{7\pi}{4}$

83. $\sqrt{41}$, 51.34° **85.** -7

87. 1, 2, 6, 15, 31

First differences: 1, 4, 9, 16

Second differences: 3, 5, 7

Neither

89. -1, 2, 5, 8, 11

First differences: 3, 3, 3, 3

Second differences: 0, 0, 0

Linear

91. $(x + 5)^2 + (y - 1)^2 = 49$

93. $(y - 1)^2 = -12(x - 4)$

95. $\frac{(x - 3)^2}{9} + \frac{(y - 3)^2}{4} = 1$ **97.** $\frac{(x - 6)^2}{4} - \frac{y^2}{32} = 1$

Section 11.2 *(page 825)*

Vocabulary Check *(page 825)*

1. zero **2.** $\mathbf{v} = v_1\mathbf{i} + v_2\mathbf{j} + v_3\mathbf{k}$

3. component form **4.** orthogonal **5.** parallel

1. (a) $\langle -2, 3, 1\rangle$
(b)

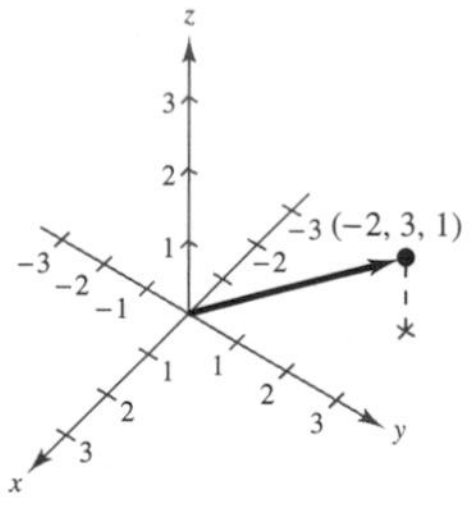

3. (a) $\langle 7, -5, 5\rangle$ (b) $3\sqrt{11}$ (c) $\frac{\sqrt{11}}{33}\langle 7, -5, 5\rangle$

5. (a)

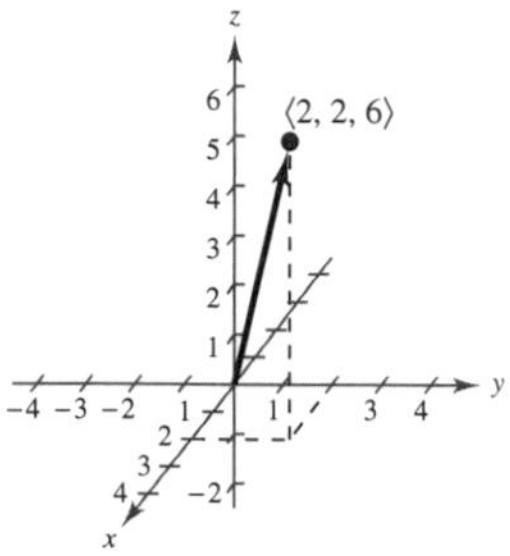

(b)

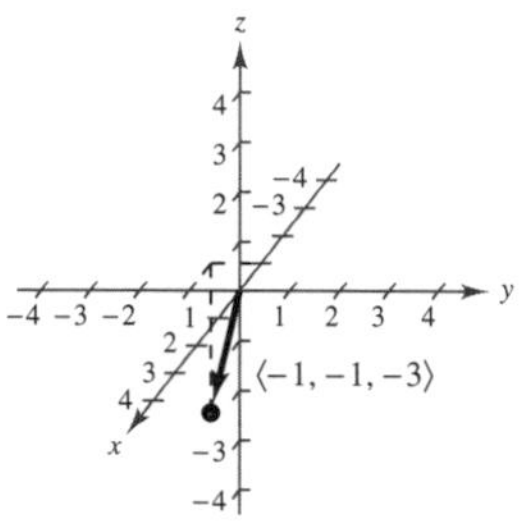

(c)

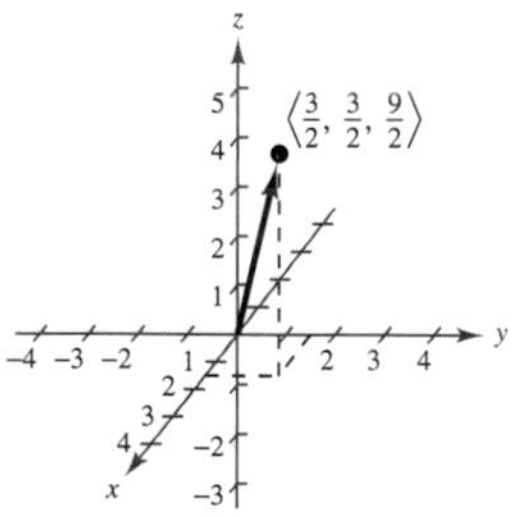

(d)

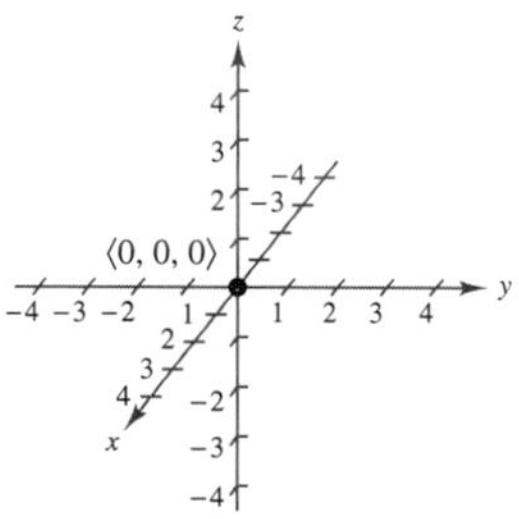

7. $\mathbf{z} = \langle -3, 7, 6\rangle$ **9.** $\mathbf{z} = \left\langle \frac{1}{2}, 6, \frac{3}{2}\right\rangle$ **11.** $9\sqrt{2}$

13. $\sqrt{74}$ **15.** $\sqrt{34}$

17. (a) $\frac{\sqrt{74}}{74}(8\mathbf{i} + 3\mathbf{j} - \mathbf{k})$ (b) $-\frac{\sqrt{74}}{74}(8\mathbf{i} + 3\mathbf{j} - \mathbf{k})$

19. -4 **21.** 0 **23.** $\approx 124.45°$ **25.** $\approx 109.92°$

27. Parallel **29.** Orthogonal **31.** Not collinear

33. Collinear **35.** $(3, 1, 7)$ **37.** $\left(6, \frac{5}{2}, -\frac{7}{4}\right)$

39. $\pm\frac{3\sqrt{14}}{14}$ **41.** $\left\langle 0, 2\sqrt{2}, 2\sqrt{2}\right\rangle$ or $\left\langle 0, 2\sqrt{2}, -2\sqrt{2}\right\rangle$

43. 226.52 newtons, 202.92 newtons, 157.91 newtons

45. True

47. The angle between **u** and **v** is an obtuse angle.

49. (a) $x = t$, $y = 3t + 2$ (b) $x = t - 1$, $y = 3t - 1$

51. (a) $x = t$, $y = t^2 - 8$ (b) $x = t - 1$, $y = t^2 - 2t - 7$

Section 11.3 (page 832)

Vocabulary Check (page 832)

1. cross product **2.** 0 **3.** $\|\mathbf{u}\|\,\|\mathbf{v}\|\sin\theta$
4. triple scalar product

1. $-\mathbf{k}$

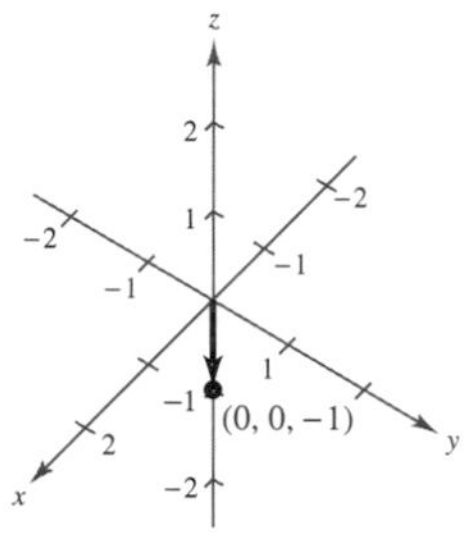

3. $-\mathbf{j}$

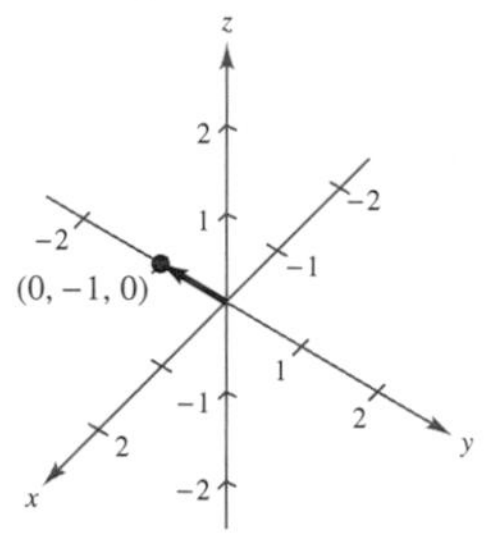

5. $\langle 3, -3, -3\rangle$ **7.** $\langle 0, 42, 0\rangle$

9. $-7\mathbf{i} + 13\mathbf{j} + 16\mathbf{k}$ **11.** $-18\mathbf{i} - 6\mathbf{j}$

13. $-\mathbf{i} - 2\mathbf{j} - \mathbf{k}$ **15.** $\frac{\sqrt{19}}{19}(\mathbf{i} - 3\mathbf{j} + 3\mathbf{k})$

17. $\frac{\sqrt{7602}}{7602}(-71\mathbf{i} - 44\mathbf{j} + 25\mathbf{k})$ **19.** $\frac{\sqrt{2}}{2}(\mathbf{i} - \mathbf{j})$

21. 1 **23.** $\sqrt{806}$ **25.** 14

27. (a) $\overrightarrow{AB} = \langle 1, 2, -2\rangle$ and is parallel to $\overrightarrow{DC} = \langle 1, 2, -2\rangle$. $\overrightarrow{AD} = \langle -3, 4, 4\rangle$ and is parallel to $\overrightarrow{BC} = \langle -3, 4, 4\rangle$.
(b) Area is $\|\overrightarrow{AB} \times \overrightarrow{AD}\| = 6\sqrt{10}$.
(c) The dot product is not 0 and therefore the parallelogram is not a rectangle.

29. $\frac{3\sqrt{13}}{2}$ **31.** $\frac{1}{2}\sqrt{4290}$ **33.** -16 **35.** 2

37. 2 **39.** 12 **41.** 84

43. (a) $T = \frac{p}{2}\cos 40°$

(b)

p	15	20	25	30	35	40	45
T	5.75	7.66	9.58	11.49	13.41	15.32	17.24

45. True. The cross product is not defined for two-dimensional vectors.

47. The magnitude of the cross product will be four times as large.

49. $-\frac{1}{2}$ **51.** $-\frac{1}{2}$ **53.** $-\frac{1}{2}$ **55.** -1

57.

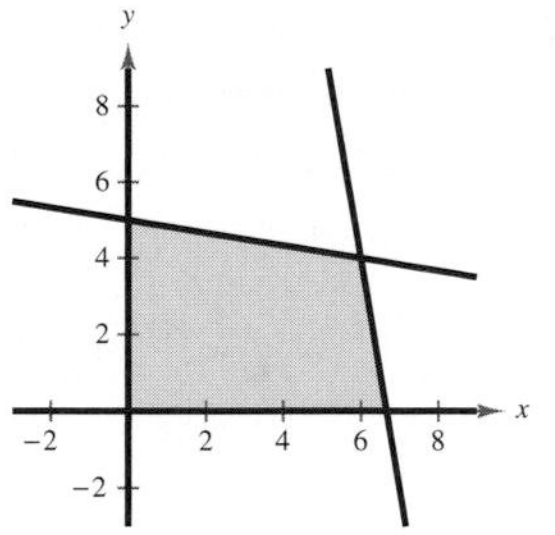

The minimum value of z is 0 and found at point $(0, 0)$.
The maximum value of z is 52 and found at point $(6, 4)$.

Section 11.4 *(page 841)*

Vocabulary Check *(page 841)*

1. direction, $\dfrac{\overrightarrow{PQ}}{t}$ **2.** parametric equations
3. symmetric equations **4.** normal
5. $a(x - x_1) + b(y - y_1) + c(z - z_1) = 0$

1. (a) $x = t,\ y = 2t,\ z = 3t$
(b) $x = \dfrac{y}{2} = \dfrac{z}{3}$

3. (a) $x = -4 + 3t,\ y = 1 + 8t,\ z = -6t$
(b) $\dfrac{x + 4}{3} = \dfrac{y - 1}{8} = \dfrac{z}{-6}$

5. (a) $x = 2 + 2t,\ y = -3 - 3t,\ z = 5 + t$
(b) $\dfrac{x - 2}{2} = \dfrac{y + 3}{-3} = z - 5$

7. (a) $x = 2 - t,\ y = 4t,\ z = 2 - 5t$
(b) $\dfrac{x - 2}{-1} = \dfrac{y}{4} = \dfrac{z - 2}{-5}$

9. (a) $x = -3 + 4t,\ y = 8 - 10t,\ z = 15 + t$
(b) $\dfrac{x + 3}{4} = \dfrac{y - 8}{-10} = z - 15$

11. (a) $x = 3 - 4t, y = 1, z = 2 + 3t$
(b) No symmetric equations

13. (a) $x = -\dfrac{1}{2} + 3t, y = 2 - 5t, z = \dfrac{1}{2} - t$
(b) $\dfrac{2x + 1}{3} = -\dfrac{2y - 4}{5} = \dfrac{2z - 1}{-1}$

15.

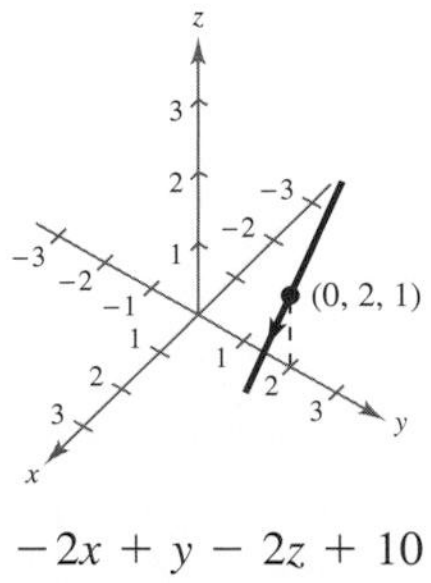

17. $x - 2 = 0$

19. $-2x + y - 2z + 10 = 0$ **21.** $-x - 2y + z + 2 = 0$

23. $-3x - 9y + 7z = 0$ **25.** $6x - 2y - z - 8 = 0$

27. $y - 5 = 0$ **29.** Orthogonal **31.** Orthogonal

33. (a) $60.7°$ (b) $x = -t + 2,\ y = 8t,\ z = 7t$

35. (a) $77.8°$ (b) $x = 6t + 1,\ y = t,\ z = 7t + 1$

37.

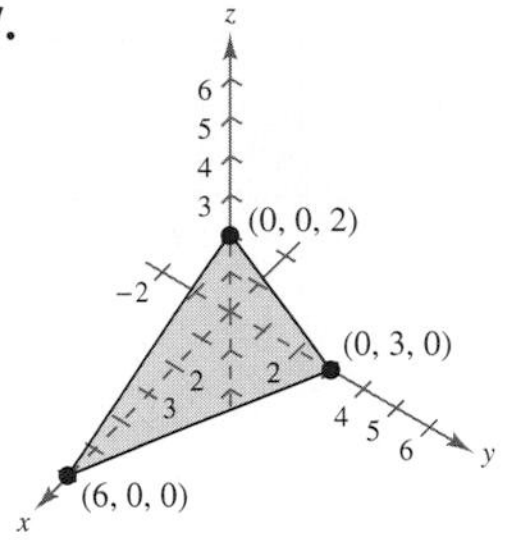

39.

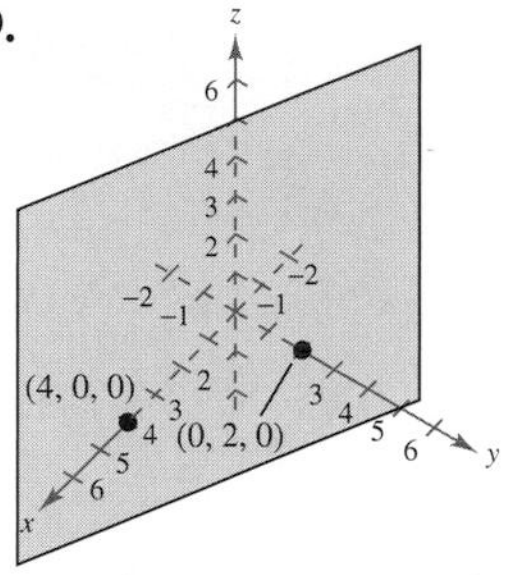

41.

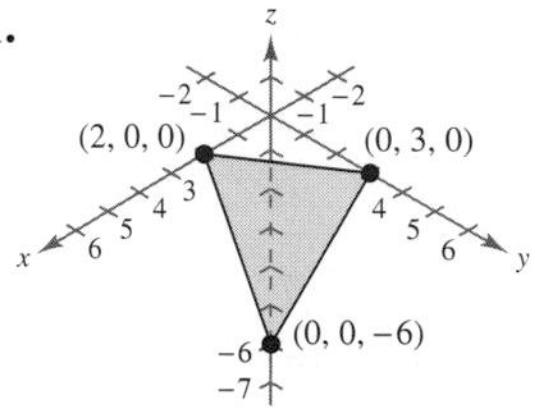

43. $\dfrac{8}{9}$ **45.** $\dfrac{4}{\sqrt{6}} = \dfrac{2\sqrt{6}}{3}$

47. (a)

Year	z
1999	7.85
2000	7.70
2001	7.50
2002	7.34
2003	7.22

(b) The approximations are very similar to the actual values of z.
(c) Answers will vary.

49. False. Lines that do not intersect and are not in the same plane may not be parallel.

51. Parallel. $\langle 10, -18, 20\rangle$ is a scalar multiple of $\langle -15, 27, -30\rangle$.

53. $x^2 + y^2 = 100$ **55.** $x^2 + y^2 - 3x = 0$

57. $r = 7$ **59.** $r = 5 \csc \theta$

Review Exercises *(page 844)*

1.

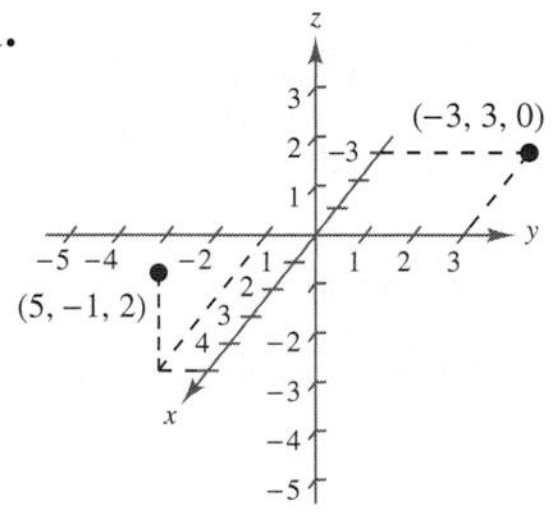

3. $(-5, 4, 0)$ **5.** $\sqrt{41}$

7. $\sqrt{29}, \sqrt{38}, \sqrt{67}$
$(\sqrt{29})^2 + (\sqrt{38})^2 = (\sqrt{67})^2$

9. $\left(\frac{13}{2}, 2, 5\right)$ **11.** $(1, 2, -9)$

13. $(x-2)^2 + (y-3)^2 + (z-5)^2 = 1$

15. $(x-1)^2 + (y-5)^2 + (z-2)^2 = 36$

17. Center: $(2, 3, 0)$; radius: 3

19. (a) (b)

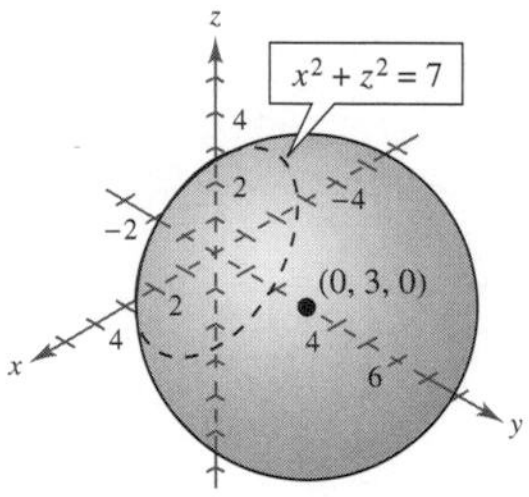

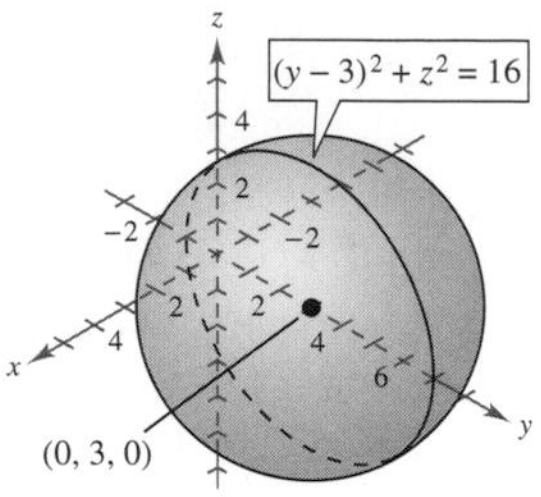

21. (a) $\langle 1, 4, -4\rangle$ (b) $\sqrt{33}$

(c) $\left\langle \frac{\sqrt{33}}{33}, \frac{4\sqrt{33}}{33}, \frac{-4\sqrt{33}}{33}\right\rangle$

23. (a) $\langle -10, 6, 7\rangle$ (b) $\sqrt{185}$

(c) $\left\langle \frac{-2\sqrt{185}}{37}, \frac{6\sqrt{185}}{185}, \frac{7\sqrt{185}}{185}\right\rangle$

25. -9 **27.** 1 **29.** $90°$ **31.** Parallel

33. Not collinear

35. *A*: 159.1 pounds of tension
B: 115.6 pounds of tension
C: 115.6 pounds of tension

37. $\langle -10, 0, -10\rangle$

39. $-\frac{71\sqrt{7602}}{7602}\mathbf{i} - \frac{22\sqrt{7602}}{3801}\mathbf{j} + \frac{25\sqrt{7602}}{7602}\mathbf{k}$

41. Area $= \sqrt{172} = 2\sqrt{43} \approx 13.11$ **43.** 75

45. (a) $x = -1 + 4t,\ y = 3 + 3t,\ z = 5 - 6t$

(b) $\frac{x+1}{4} = \frac{y-3}{3} = \frac{z-5}{-6}$

47. (a) $x = -2t,\ y = \frac{5}{2}t,\ z = t$ (b) $\frac{x}{-2} = \frac{y}{5/2} = z$

49. $-2x - 12y + 5z = 0$ **51.** $z - 2 = 0$

53.

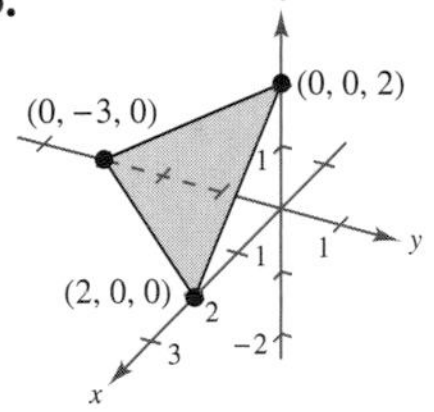

55.

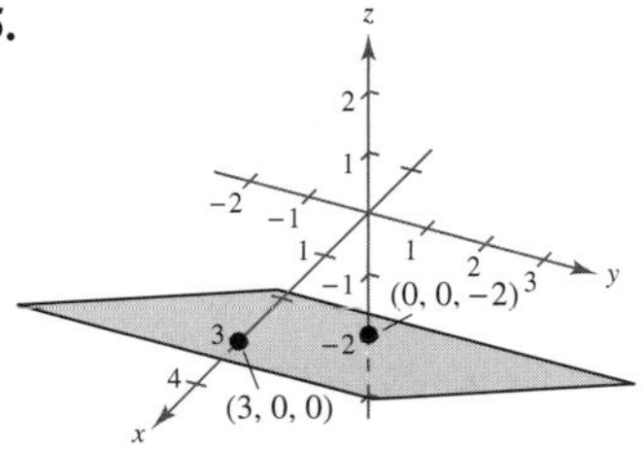

57. $\frac{\sqrt{110}}{110}$ **59.** $\frac{\sqrt{110}}{55}$

61. False. $\mathbf{u} \times \mathbf{v} = -(\mathbf{v} \times \mathbf{u})$ **63–65.** Answers will vary.

Chapter Test *(page 846)*

1.

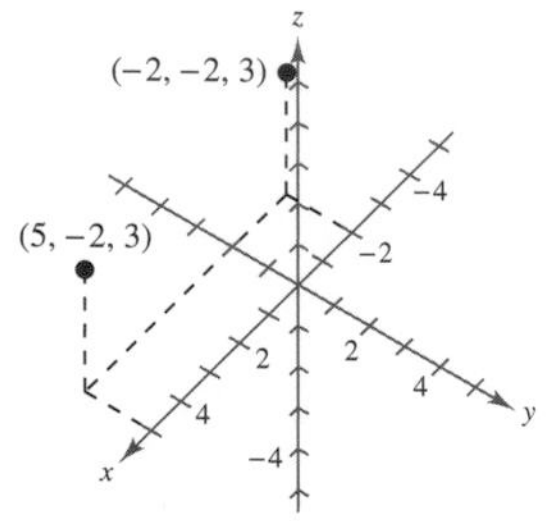

2. No. $\left(\sqrt{76}\right)^2 + \left(\sqrt{102}\right)^2 \neq \left(\sqrt{194}\right)^2$ **3.** $(7, 1, 2)$

4. $(x-7)^2 + (y-1)^2 + (z-2)^2 = 19$

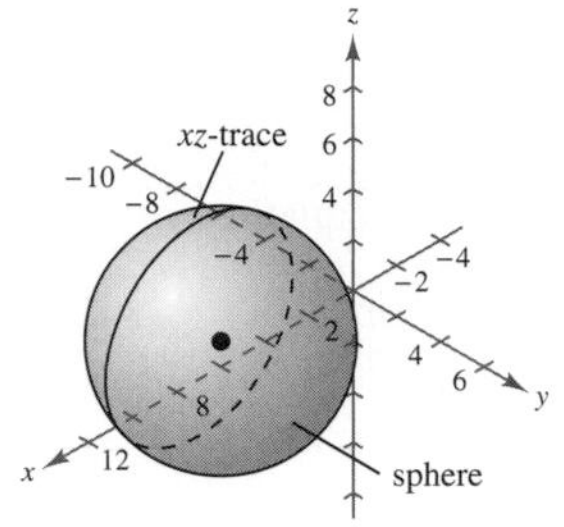

5. $\mathbf{u} = \langle -2, 6, -6\rangle$, $\mathbf{v} = \langle -12, 5, -5\rangle$

6. (a) $\sqrt{194}$ (b) 84 (c) $\langle 0, 62, 62\rangle$ **7.** $46.23°$

8. (a) $x = 8 - 2t,\ y = -2 + 6t,\ z = 5 - 6t$

(b) $\frac{x-8}{-2} = \frac{y+2}{6} = \frac{z-5}{-6}$

9. Neither **10.** Orthogonal

11. $\overrightarrow{AB}$ is parallel to $\overrightarrow{CD} = \langle 4, 8, -2\rangle$.
$\overrightarrow{AC}$ is parallel to $\overrightarrow{BD} = \langle 1, -3, 3\rangle$.
Area $= 2\sqrt{230}$

12. $27x + 4y + 32z + 33 = 0$ **13.** 200

14.

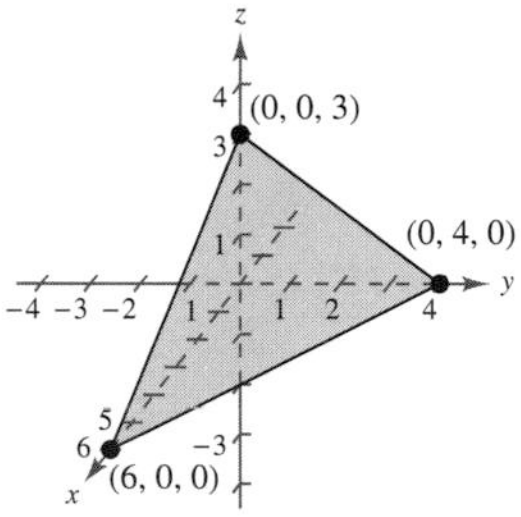

15.

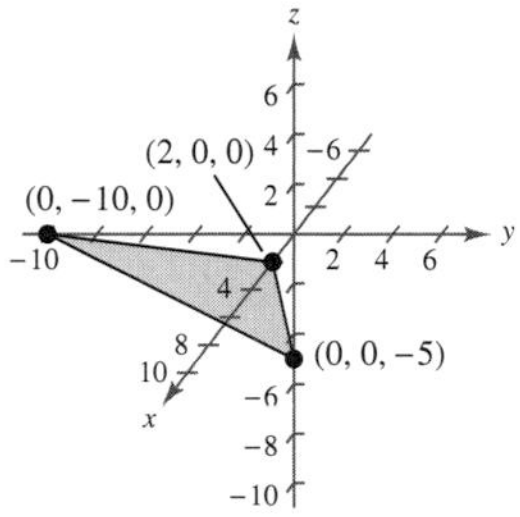

16. $\frac{8}{\sqrt{14}} = \frac{4\sqrt{14}}{7}$ **17.** $88.5°$

Problem Solving *(page 849)*

1. (a)

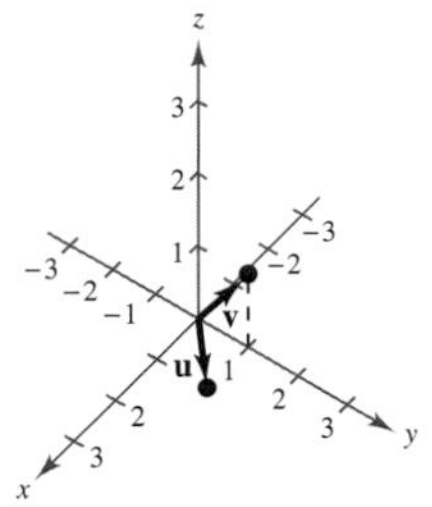

(b) Answers will vary.

(c) $a = b = 1$

(d) Answers will vary.

3. Answers will vary. See online website.

5. (a) Right triangle (b) Obtuse triangle

(c) Obtuse triangle (d) Acute triangle

7. $\|F\| \cong 860.0$ lbs **9–11.** Proof

13. (a) $\overrightarrow{AB} = -\frac{5}{4}\mathbf{j} + \mathbf{k}$, $\mathbf{F} = -200(\cos\theta\mathbf{j} + \sin\theta\mathbf{k})$

(b) $\|\overrightarrow{AB} \times \mathbf{F}\| = 25|10\sin\theta + 8\cos\theta|$

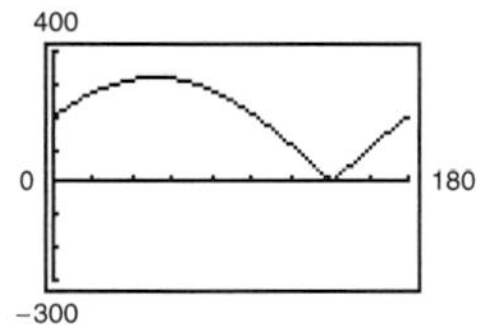

(c) $\|\overrightarrow{AB} \times \mathbf{F}\| \cong 298.2$ when $\theta = 30°$.

(d) $\theta \approx 51.34°$

(e) The zero is $\theta \approx 141.34°$; the angle making $\overrightarrow{AB}$ parallel to $\mathbf{F}$.

15. (a) $d = \sqrt{70}$ when $t = 0$.

(b)

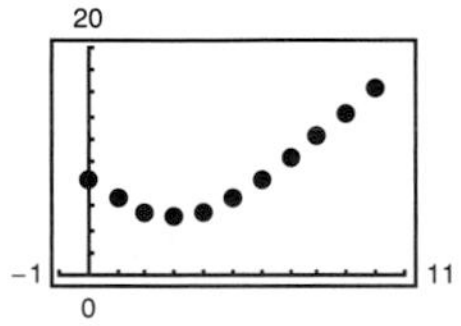

(c) The distance between the two insects appears to lessen in the first 3 seconds but then begins to increase with time.

(d) The insects get within 5 inches of each other.

17. (a) $D = \dfrac{3\sqrt{2}}{2}$ (b) $D = \sqrt{5}$

Chapter 12

Section 12.1 *(page 860)*

Vocabulary Check *(page 860)*

1. limit **2.** oscillates **3.** direct substitution

1. (a)

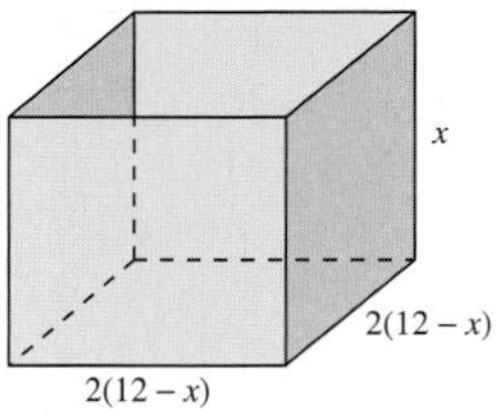

(b) $V = lwh$

$= 2(12 - x) \cdot 2(12 - x) \cdot x$

$= 4x(12 - x)^2$

(c)

x	3	3.5	3.9	4
V	972	1011.5	1023.5	1024

x	4.1	4.5	5
V	1023.5	1012.5	980

$\lim_{x \to 4} V = 1024$

(d)

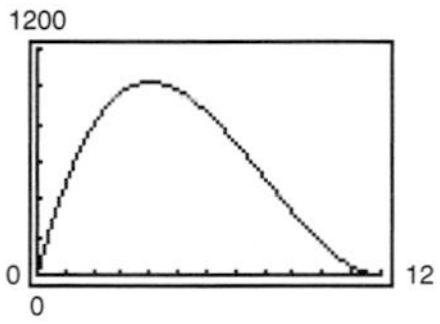

3.

x	1.9	1.99	1.999	2	2.001	2.01	2.1
$f(x)$	13.5	13.95	13.995	14	14.005	14.05	14.5

14; Yes

5.

x	2.9	2.99	2.999	3
$f(x)$	0.1695	0.1669	0.1667	Error

x	3.001	3.01	3.1
$f(x)$	0.1666	0.1664	0.1639

$\frac{1}{6}$; No

7.

x	0.9	0.99	0.999	1
$f(x)$	0.2564	0.2506	0.2501	Error

x	1.001	1.01	1.1
$f(x)$	0.2499	0.2494	0.2439

$\frac{1}{4}$;

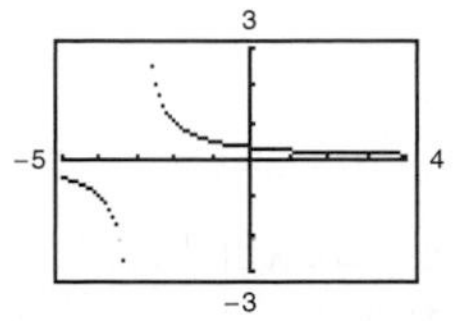

9.

x	-0.1	-0.01	-0.001	0
$f(x)$	0.2247	0.2237	0.2236	Error

x	0.001	0.01	0.1
$f(x)$	0.2236	0.2235	0.2225

0.2236;

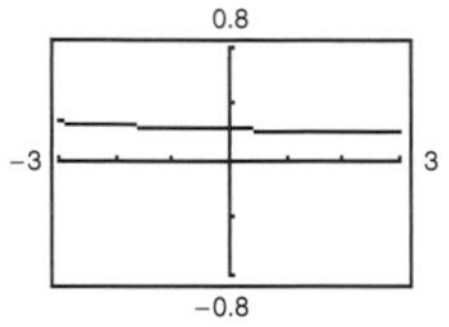

11.

x	-4.1	-4.01	-4.001	-4
$f(x)$	0.4762	0.4975	0.4998	Error

x	-3.999	-3.99	-3.9
$f(x)$	0.5003	0.5025	0.5263

$\frac{1}{2}$;

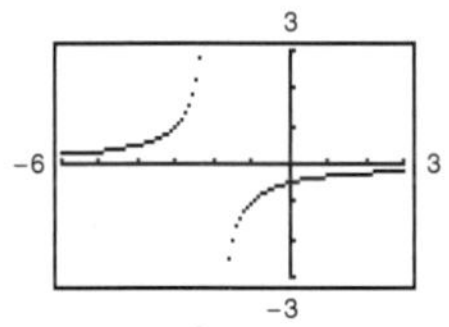

13.

x	-0.1	-0.01	-0.001	0
$f(x)$	0.9983	0.99998	0.9999998	Error

x	0.001	0.01	0.1
$f(x)$	0.9999998	0.99998	0.9983

1;

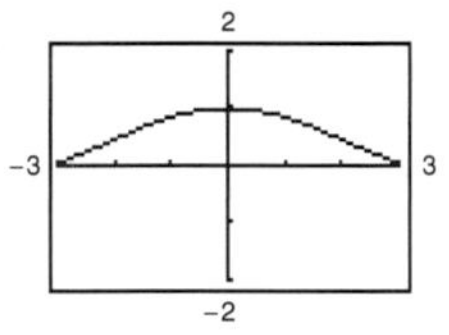

15.

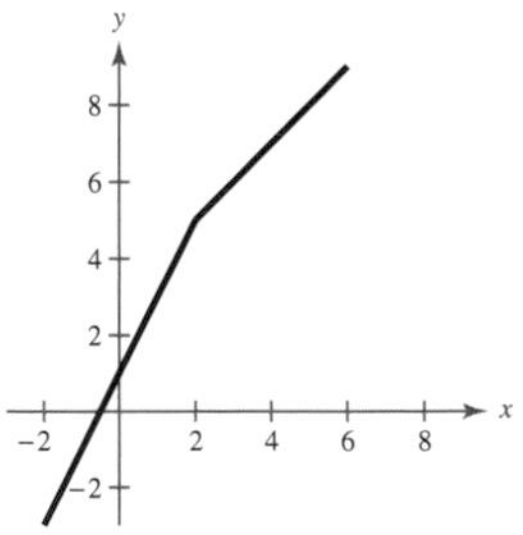

5

17. 13 **19.** Does not exist. Answers will vary.

21. Does not exist. Answers will vary.

23.

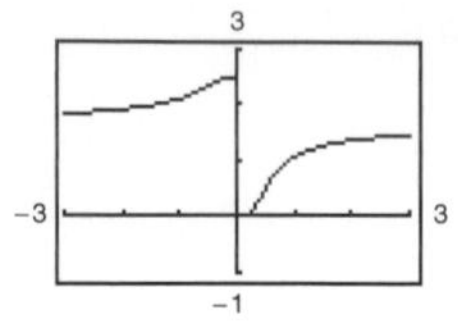

No. Answers will vary.

25.

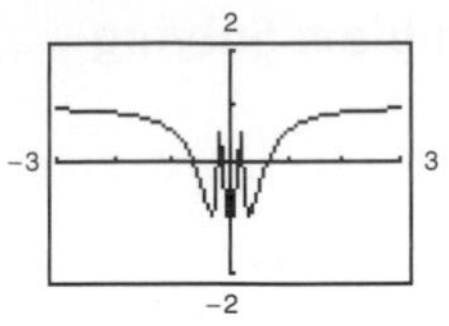

No. Answers will vary.

27.

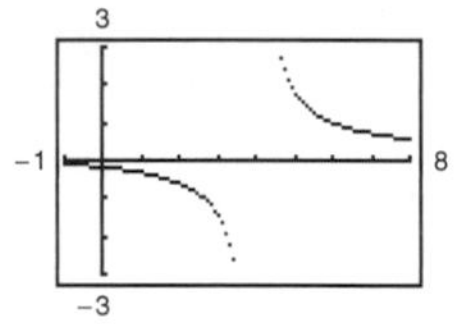

No. Answers will vary.

29.

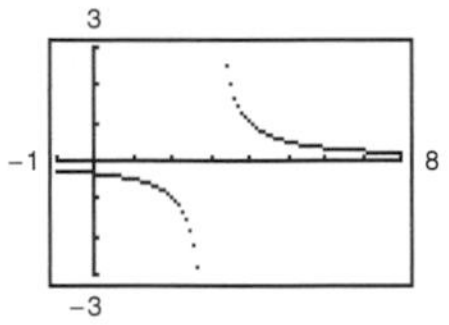

Yes

31.

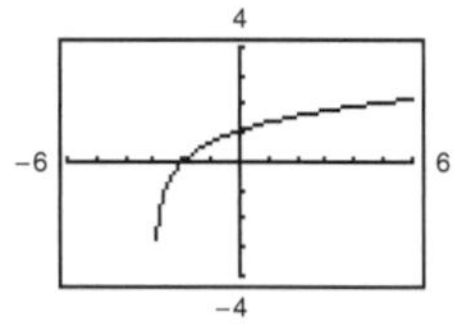

Yes

33. (a) -12 (b) 9 (c) $\frac{1}{2}$ (d) $\sqrt{3}$

35. (a) 8 (b) $\frac{3}{8}$ (c) 3 (d) $-\frac{61}{8}$

37. -15 **39.** 7 **41.** -3 **43.** $-\frac{9}{10}$ **45.** $\frac{7}{13}$

47. 1 **49.** $\frac{35}{3}$ **51.** $e^3 \approx 20.09$ **53.** 0

55. $\frac{\pi}{6}$ **57.** True **59.** (a) and (b) Answers will vary.

61. (a) No. The function may approach different values from the right and left of 2. For example,

$$f(x) = \begin{cases} 0, & x < 2 \\ 4, & x = 2 \\ 6, & x > 2 \end{cases}$$

implies $f(2) = 4$, but $\lim_{x \to 2} f(x) \neq 4$.

(b) No. The function may approach 4 as x approaches 2, but the function could be undefined at $x = 2$. For example, in the function $f(x) = \dfrac{4 \sin(x - 2)}{x - 2}$, the limit is 4 as x approaches 2, but $f(2)$ is not defined.

63. (a)

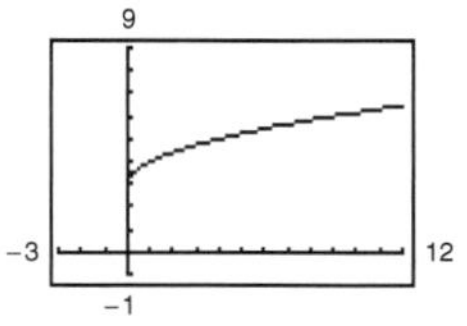

6

(b) Domain: all real numbers x such that $x \geq 0$

(c) Domain: all real numbers x such that $x \geq 0$ except $x = 9$

(d) It may not be clear from a graph that a function is not defined at a single point. Examining a function graphically and algebraically ensures that you will find all points at which the function is not defined.

65. $-\frac{1}{3},\ x \neq 5$ **67.** $\frac{5x+4}{5x+2},\ x \neq \frac{1}{3}$

69. $\frac{x^2 - 3x + 9}{x - 2},\ x \neq -3$

71. (a)

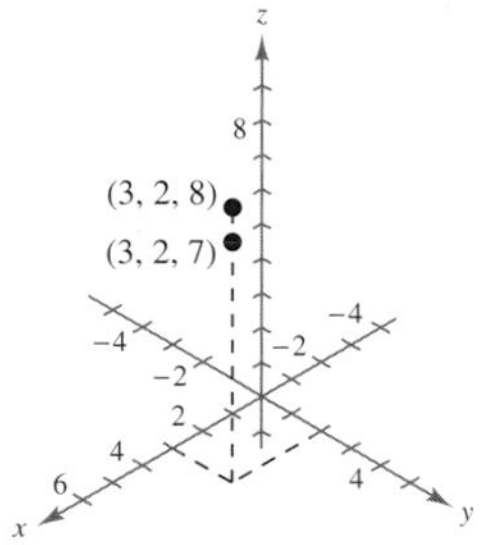

(b) 1 (c) $\left(3, 2, \frac{15}{2}\right)$

73. (a)

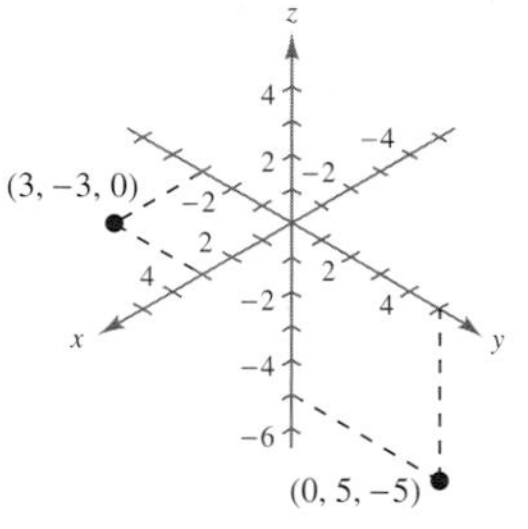

(b) $7\sqrt{2}$ (c) $\left(\frac{3}{2}, 1, -\frac{5}{2}\right)$

Section 12.2 *(page 870)*

Vocabulary Check *(page 870)*

1. dividing out technique **2.** indeterminate form
3. one-sided limit **4.** difference quotient

1. (a) 1 (b) 3 (c) 5
$g_2(x) = -2x + 1$

3. (a) 2 (b) 0 (c) 0
$g_2(x) = x(x + 1)$

5. $\frac{1}{12}$ **7.** 4 **9.** 12 **11.** 80 **13.** $\frac{\sqrt{5}}{10}$

15. $\frac{\sqrt{3}}{6}$ **17.** 1 **19.** $\frac{1}{4}$ **21.** -1

23. $-\frac{1}{16}$ **25.** Does not exist

27.

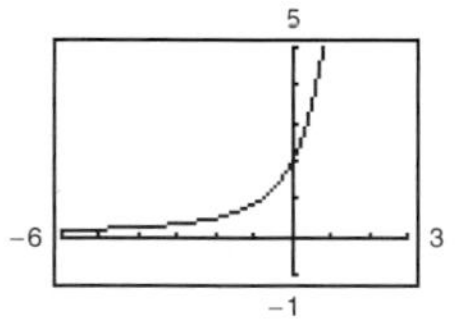

2.000

29.

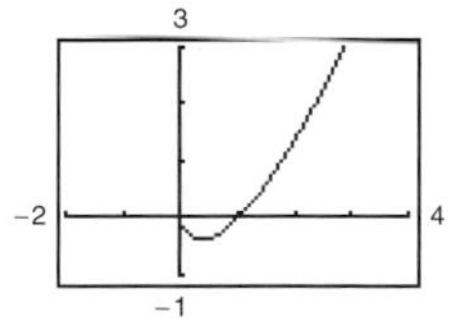

0

31.

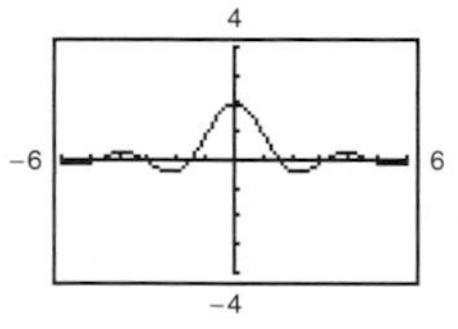

2.000

33.

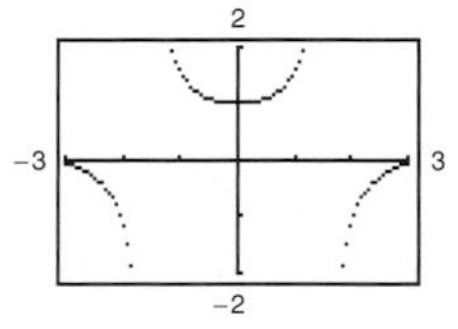

1.000

35.

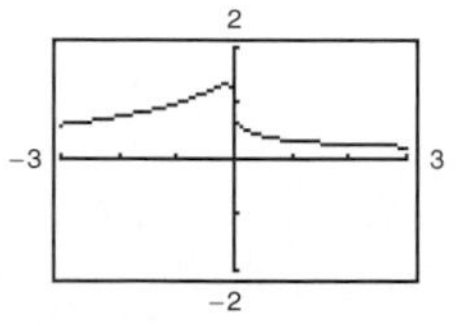

0.333

37.

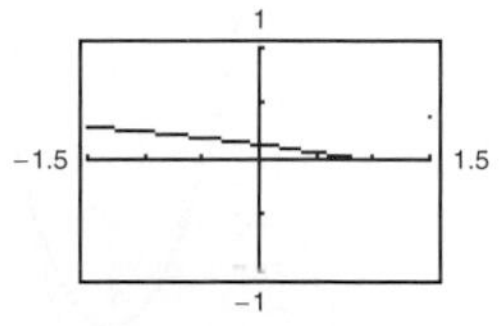

0.135

39. (a)

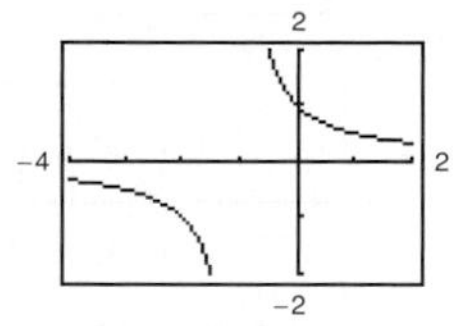

(b)

x	0.9	0.99	0.999	0.9999
$f(x)$	0.5263	0.5025	0.5003	0.5000

(c) $\lim_{x \to 1^-} \frac{(x-1)}{(x^2-1)} = 0.5$

41. (a)

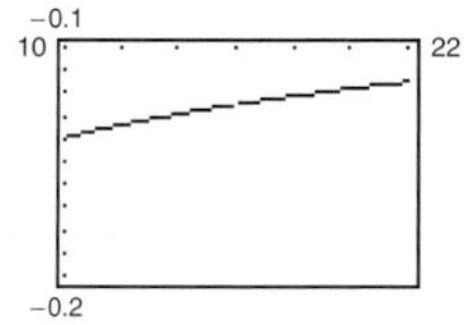

(b)

x	16.1	16.01	16.001	16.0001
$f(x)$	-0.12481	-0.12498	-0.124998	-0.1249998

(c) $\lim_{x \to 16^+} \frac{4 - \sqrt{x}}{x - 16} = -0.125$

43.

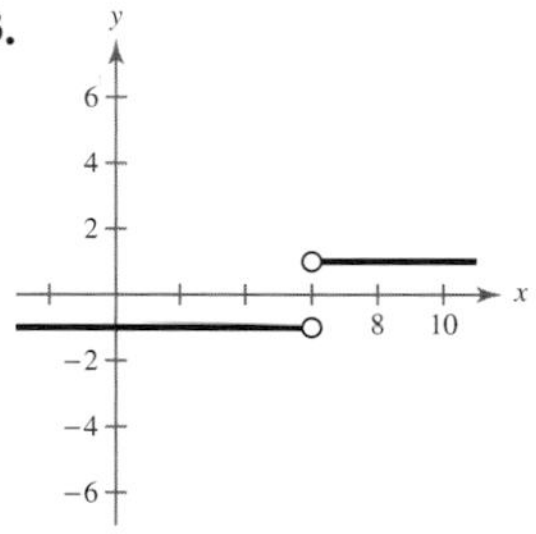

The limit does not exist.

45.

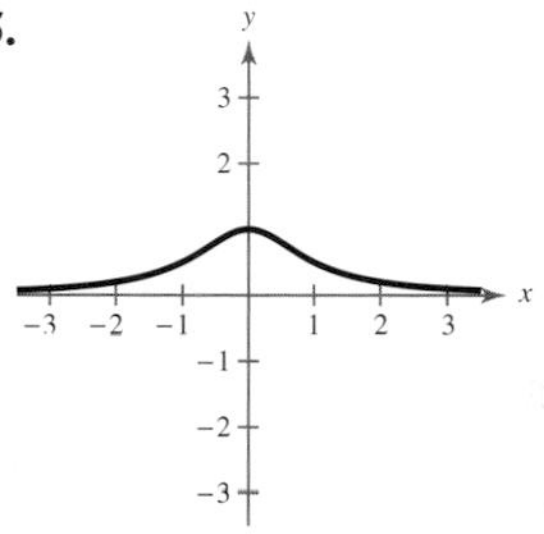

$\lim_{x \to 1} \frac{1}{x^2 + 1} = \frac{1}{2}$

47.

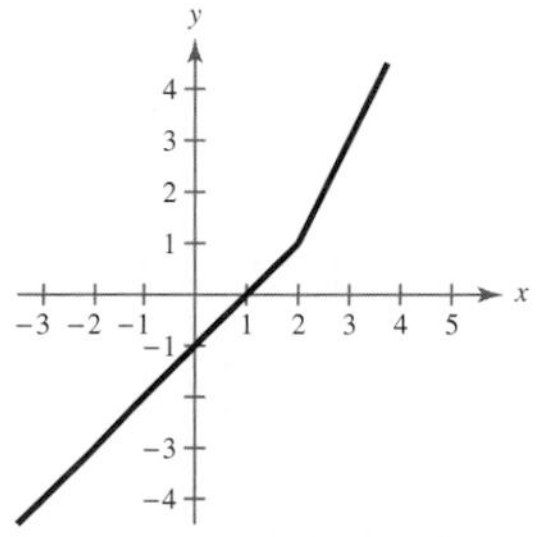

$\lim_{x \to 2} f(x)$ where $f(x) = \begin{cases} x - 1, & x \leq 2 \\ 2x - 3, & x > 2 \end{cases} = 1$

49.

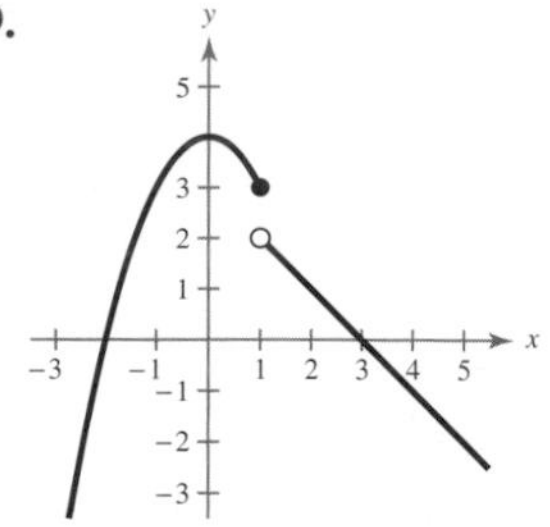

The limit does not exist.

51.

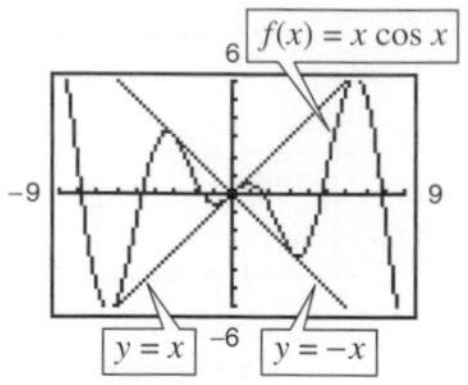

$\lim_{x\to 0} x\cos x = 0$

53.

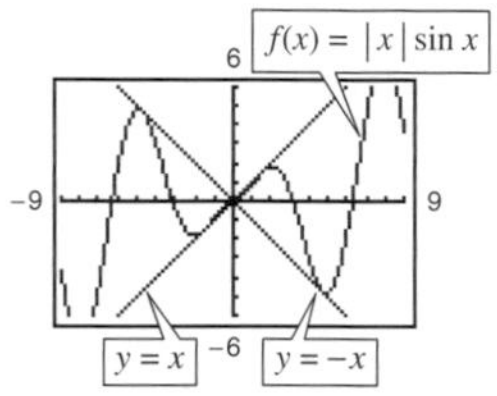

$\lim_{x\to 0} |x|\sin x = 0$

55.

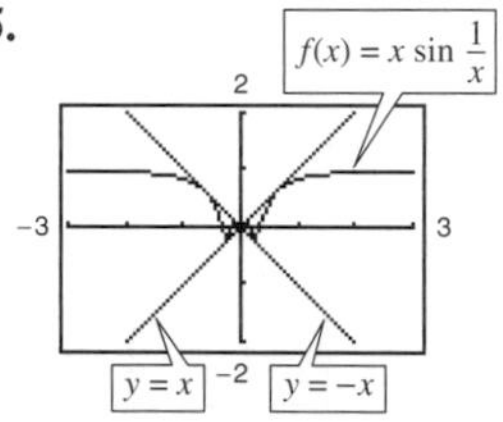

$\lim_{x\to 0} x\sin\frac{1}{x} = 0$

57. Limit (a) can be evaluated by direct substitution.
(a) 0 (b) 1

59. 3 **61.** $\frac{1}{2\sqrt{x}}$ **63.** $2x - 3$ **65.** $-\frac{1}{(x+2)^2}$

67. -32 feet per second **69.** Answers will vary.

71. (a)

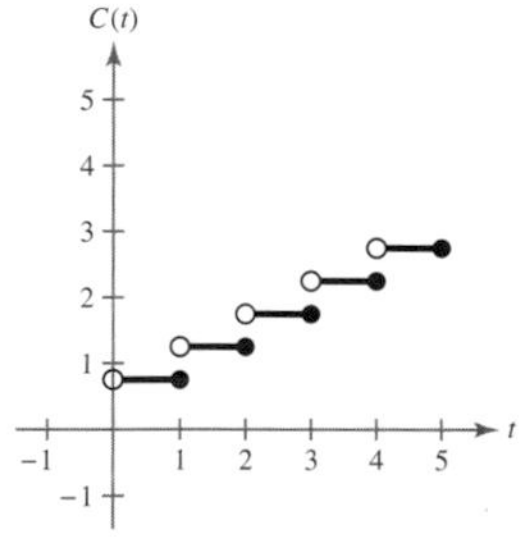

(b)

t	3	3.3	3.4	3.5	3.6	3.7	4
C	1.75	2.25	2.25	2.25	2.25	2.25	2.25

$\lim_{t\to 3.5} C(t) = 2.25$

(c)

t	2	2.5	2.9	3	3.1	3.5	4
C	1.25	1.75	1.75	1.75	2.25	2.25	2.25

The limit does not exist.

73. True **75.** (a) and (b) Graphs will vary.

77. $x - 2y - 26 = 0$ **79.** $s = 2.125\pi$ inches

81. $A = 30.375\pi$ square centimeters

83. Parabola

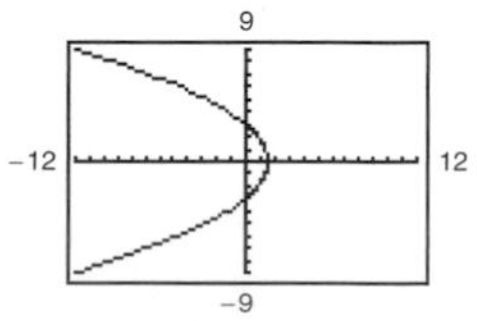

85. Hyperbola

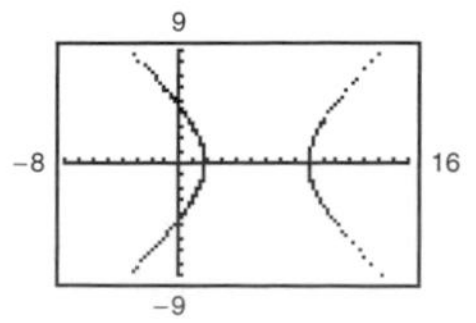

87. Parabola

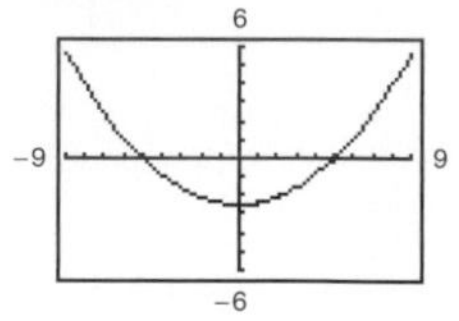

89. Orthogonal **91.** Parallel

Section 12.3 *(page 880)*

Vocabulary Check *(page 880)*

1. Calculus **2.** tangent line **3.** secant line
4. limit of a difference quotient **5.** derivative

1. 0 **3.** $\frac{1}{2}$ **5.** 2 **7.** -2 **9.** -1 **11.** $\frac{1}{6}$

13. $m = -2x$; (a) 0 (b) 2

15. $m = -\frac{1}{(x+4)^2}$; (a) $-\frac{1}{16}$ (b) $-\frac{1}{4}$

17. $m = \frac{1}{2\sqrt{x-1}}$; (a) $\frac{1}{4}$ (b) $\frac{1}{6}$

19.

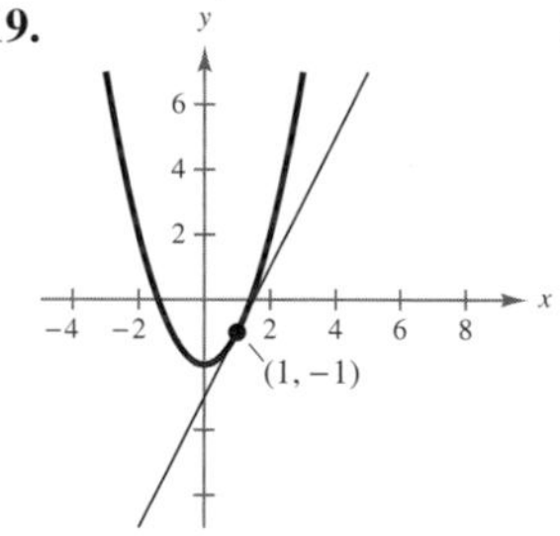

2

21.

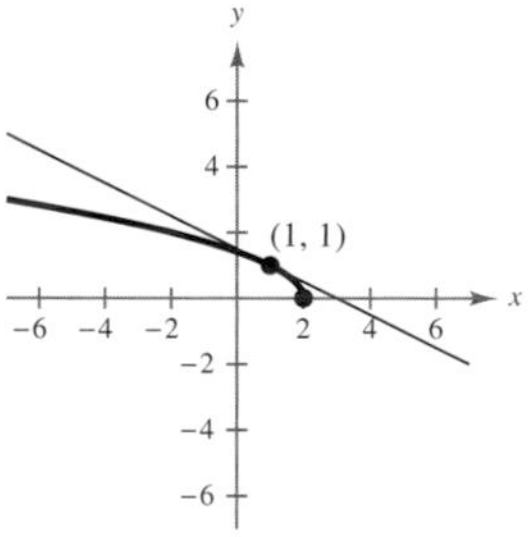

$-\frac{1}{2}$

23.

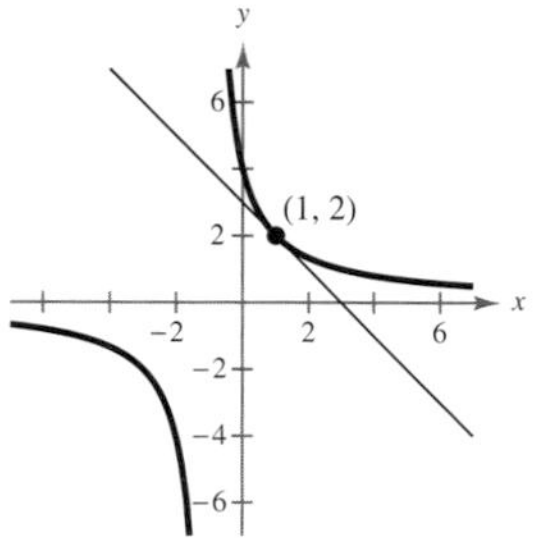

-1

25. 0 **27.** $-\frac{1}{3}$

29. $-6x$ **31.** $-\frac{2}{x^3}$ **33.** $-\frac{1}{2(x-9)^{3/2}}$

35. (a) 4 (b) $y = 4x - 5$
(c)

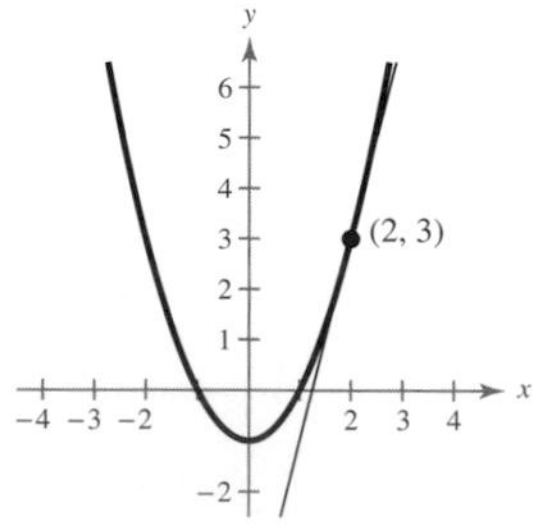

37. (a) $\frac{1}{4}$ (b) $y = \frac{1}{4}x + \frac{5}{4}$

(c)

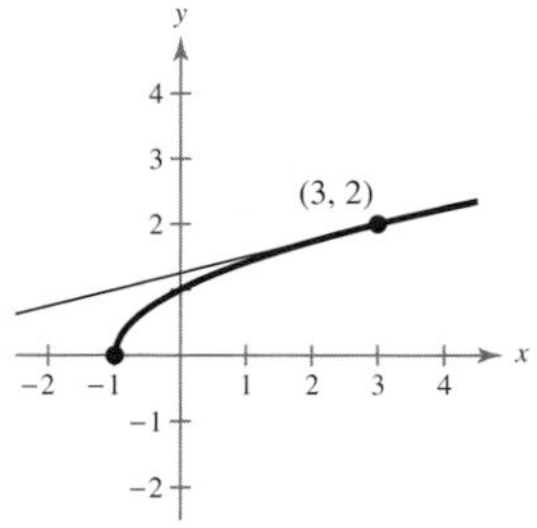

39.

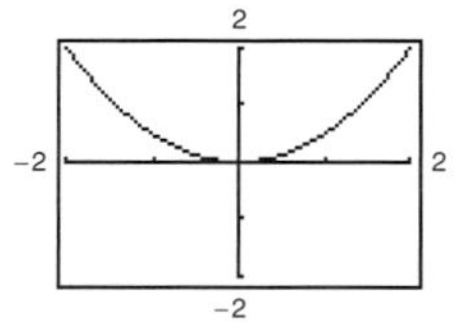

They appear to be the same.

x	-2	-1.5	-1	-0.5	0
$f(x)$	2	1.125	0.5	0.125	0
$f'(x)$	-2	-1.5	-1	-0.5	0

x	0.5	1	1.5	2
$f(x)$	0.125	0.5	1.125	2
$f'(x)$	0.5	1	1.5	2

41.

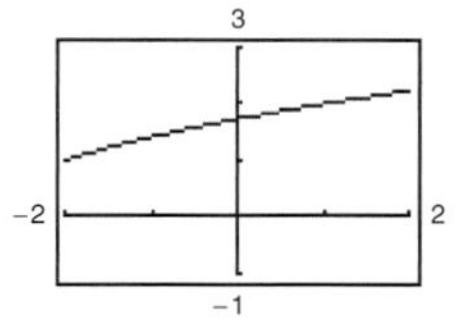

x	-2	-1.5	-1	-0.5	0
$f(x)$	1	1.225	1.414	1.581	1.732
$f'(x)$	0.5	0.408	0.354	0.316	0.289

x	0.5	1	1.5	2
$f(x)$	1.871	2	2.121	2.236
$f'(x)$	0.267	0.25	0.236	0.224

They appear to be the same.

43. $y = -x + 1$ **45.** $y = -6x \pm 8$

47. $f'(x) = 2x - 4$; horizontal tangent at $(2, -1)$

49. $f'(x) = 9x^2 - 9$; horizontal tangents at $(-1, 6)$ and $(1, -6)$

51. (a) $y = -21.048x^2 + 804.47x - 1054.5$

(b)

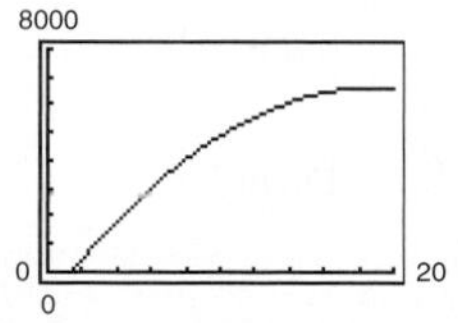

Slope when $x = 12$ is 299.31. This represents \$299.31 million and the rate of change of revenue in 2002.

(c)

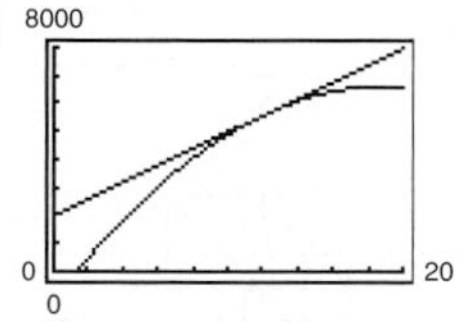

53. Answers will vary.

55. True. The slope is dependent on x.

57. b **58.** a **59.** d **60.** c

61. Answers will vary. Example: a sketch of any linear function with positive slope

63. Answers will vary. Example: a sketch of any quadratic function of the form $y = a(x - 1)^2 + k$, where $a > 0$.

65.

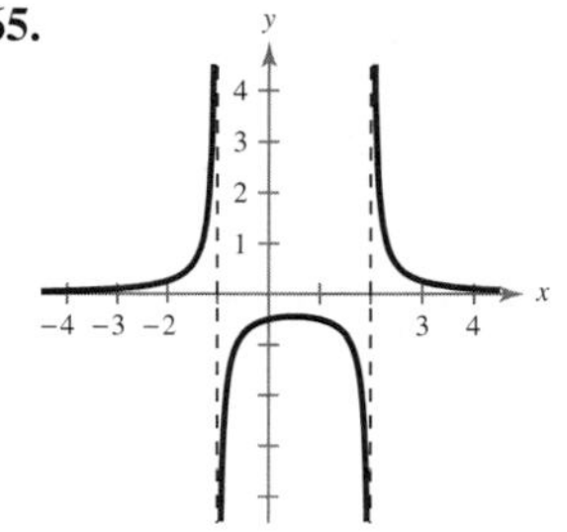

67.

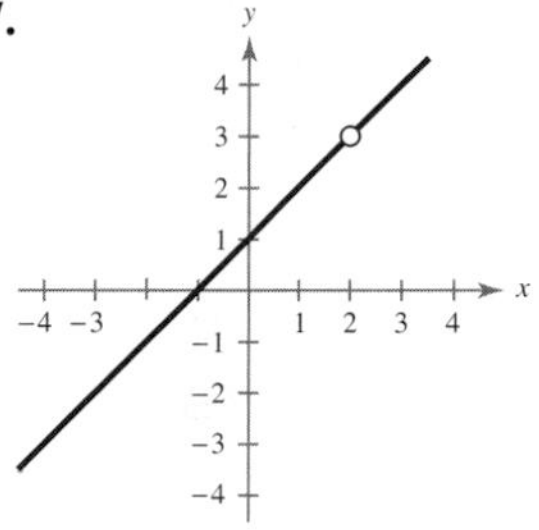

69. $\langle -2, 3, -1 \rangle$ **71.** $\langle 0, 0, -36 \rangle$

Section 12.4 *(page 889)*

Vocabulary Check *(page 889)*

1. limit, infinity **2.** converge **3.** diverge

1. c **2.** a **3.** d **4.** b **5.** 0

7. -1 **9.** 2 **11.** -3 **13.** Does not exist

15. $-\frac{3}{2}$ **17.** -1 **19.** -4 **21.** -5

23.

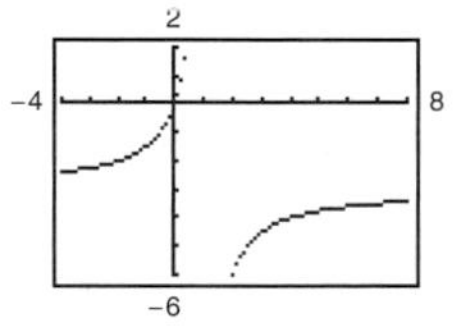

Horizontal asymptote: $y = -3$

25.

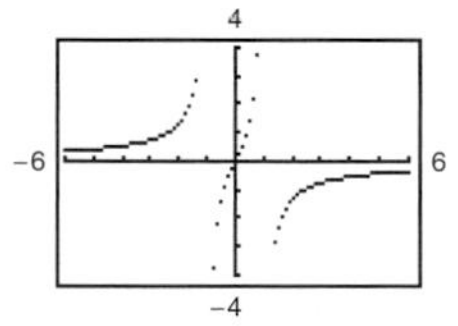

Horizontal asymptote: $y = 0$

27.

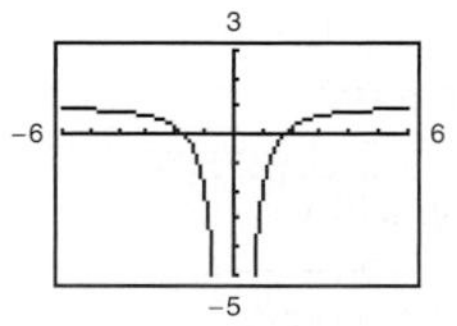

Horizontal asymptote: $y = 1$

29. (a)

x	10^0	10^1	10^2	10^3
$f(x)$	-0.7321	-0.0995	-0.0100	-0.0010

x	10^4	10^5	10^6
$f(x)$	-1.0×10^{-4}	-1.0×10^{-5}	-1.0×10^{-6}

(b)

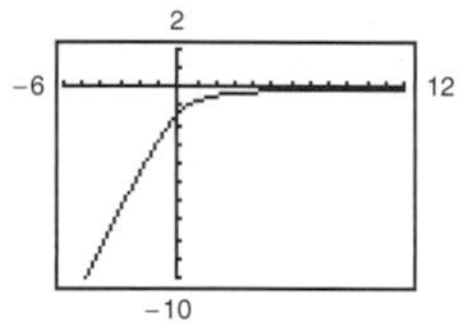

$\lim_{x\to\infty} f(x) = 0$

31. (a)

x	10^0	10^1	10^2	10^3
$f(x)$	-0.7082	-0.7454	-0.7495	-0.74995

x	10^4	10^5	10^6
$f(x)$	-0.749995	-0.7499995	-0.75

(b)

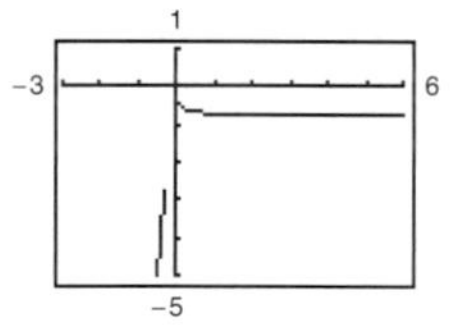

$\lim_{x\to\infty} f(x) = -\frac{3}{4}$

33. $1, \frac{3}{5}, \frac{2}{5}, \frac{5}{17}, \frac{3}{13}$
Limit: 0

35. $\frac{1}{3}, \frac{2}{5}, \frac{3}{7}, \frac{4}{9}, \frac{5}{11}$
Limit: $\frac{1}{2}$

37. $\frac{1}{5}, \frac{1}{2}, \frac{9}{11}, \frac{8}{7}, \frac{25}{17}$
Limit does not exist.

39. 2, 3, 4, 5, 6
Limit does not exist.

41. $-1, \frac{1}{2}, -\frac{1}{3}, \frac{1}{4}, -\frac{1}{5}$
Limit: 0

43. $\lim_{n\to\infty} a_n = \frac{3}{2}$

n	10^0	10^1	10^2	10^3
a_n	2	1.55	1.505	1.5005

n	10^4	10^5	10^6
a_n	1.50005	1.500005	1.5000005

45. $\lim_{n\to\infty} a_n = \frac{16}{3}$

n	10^0	10^1	10^2	10^3
a_n	16	6.16	5.4136	5.3413

n	10^4	10^5	10^6
a_n	5.3341	5.33341	5.333341

47. (a) 1

(b)

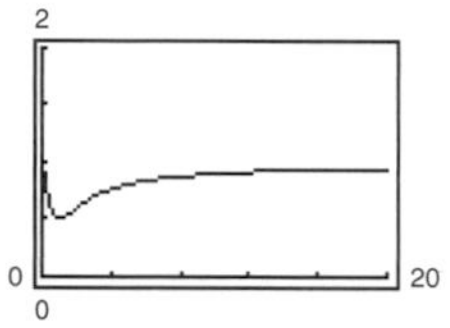

(c) Over a long period of time, the level of the oxygen in the pond is normal.

49. (a) $\overline{C}(x) = \dfrac{13.50x + 45{,}750}{x}$

(b) \$471; \$59.25

(c) \$13.50. As the number of PDAs gets very large, the average cost approaches \$13.50.

51. (a)

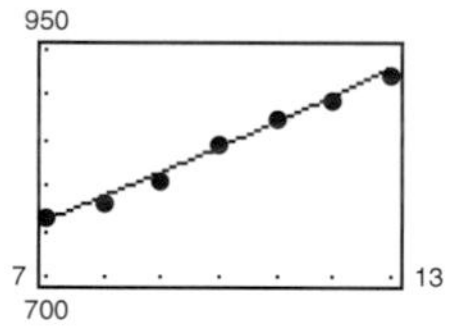

The model is a good fit to the data.

(b) 1032 dollars

(c) When t is slightly greater than 45, a vertical asymptote is found.

53. False. Graph $y = \dfrac{x^2}{x+1}$.

55. True. If the sequence converges, then the limit exists.

57. Let $f(x) = \dfrac{1}{x^2}$, $g(x) = \dfrac{1}{x^2}$, and $c = 0$. Now

$\lim_{x\to 0} \dfrac{1}{x^2} = \infty$, and $\lim_{x\to 0}[f(x) - g(x)] = 0$.

59.

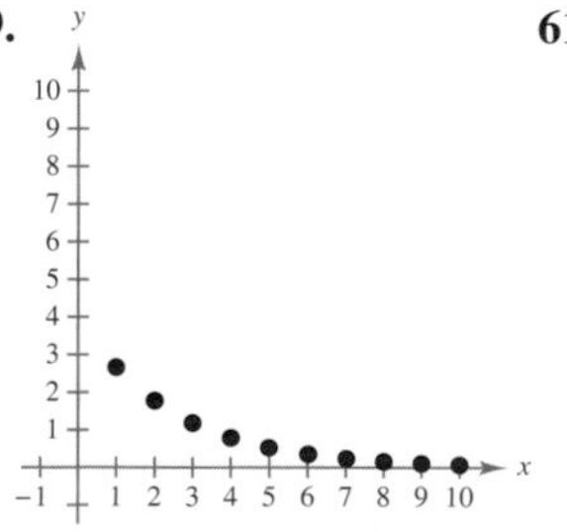

Converges to 0

61.

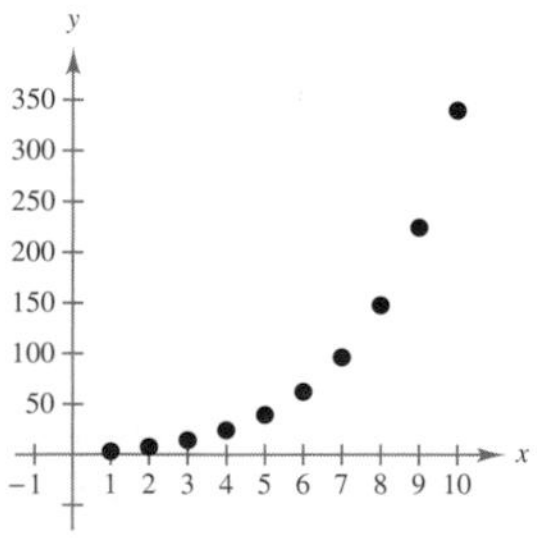

Diverges

63.

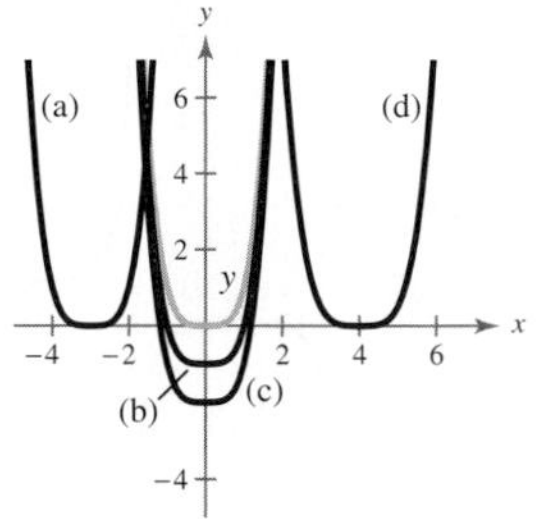

65. $x^2 + 2x + 1$

67. $x^3 + 5x^2 - 3 - \dfrac{2}{3x + 2}$

69. $-4, 5, 0, 0$

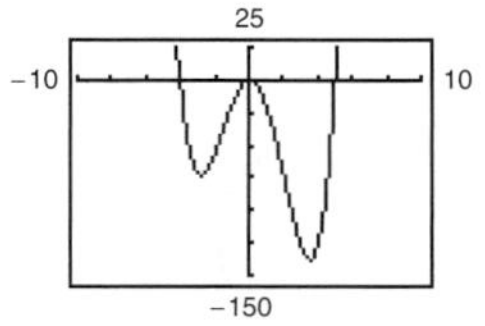

71. 3

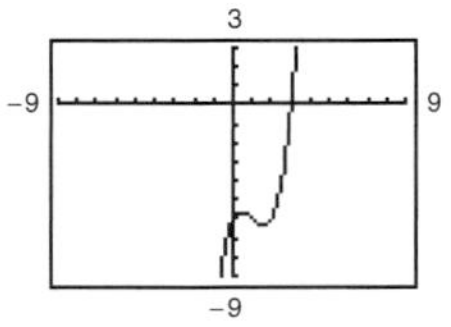

73. 60 **75.** 150

Section 12.5 *(page 898)*

Vocabulary Check *(page 898)*

1. $\dfrac{n(n+1)}{2}$ **2.** $\dfrac{n^2(n+1)^2}{4}$ **3.** area

1. 420 **3.** 44,140 **5.** 5850

7. (a) $S(n) = \dfrac{n^2 + 2n + 1}{4n^2}$

(b)

n	10^0	10^1	10^2	10^3	10^4
$S(n)$	1	0.3025	0.25503	0.25050	0.25005

(c) Limit: $\frac{1}{4}$

9. (a) $S(n) = \dfrac{2n^2 + 3n + 7}{2n^2}$

(b)

n	10^0	10^1	10^2	10^3	10^4
$S(n)$	6	1.185	1.0154	1.0015	1.00015

(c) Limit: 1

11. (a) $S(n) = \dfrac{14n^2 + 3n + 1}{6n^3}$

(b)

n	10^0	10^1	10^2	10^3	10^4
$S(n)$	3	0.2385	0.02338	0.002334	0.000233

(c) Limit: 0

13. (a) $S(n) = \dfrac{4n^2 - 3n - 1}{6n^2}$

(b)

n	10^0	10^1	10^2	10^3	10^4
$S(n)$	0	0.615	0.66165	0.666167	0.666617

(c) Limit: $\frac{2}{3}$

15. 14.25 square units **17.** 1.2656 square units

19.

n	4	8	20	50
Approximate area	18	21	22.8	23.52

21.

n	4	8	20	50
Approximate area	3.52	2.85	2.48	2.34

23. 3 square units **25.** 2 square units
27. $\frac{10}{3}$ square units **29.** $\frac{17}{4}$ square units
31. $\frac{3}{4}$ square unit **33.** $\frac{51}{4}$ square units

35.

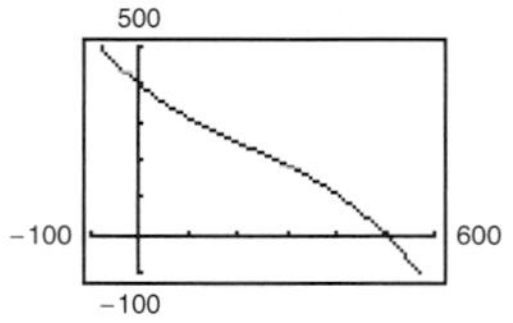

Area is 105,208.33 square feet $\approx$ 2.4153 acres

37. True **39.** Answers will vary.

41. $n\pi, \dfrac{\pi}{6} + 2n\pi, \dfrac{11\pi}{6} + 2n\pi$ **43.** $n\pi$

45. $\dfrac{\pi}{2} + n\pi$ **47.** $\langle 24, -30 \rangle$ **49.** $\sqrt{5} - 2$

Review Exercises *(page 901)*

1.

x	2.9	2.99	2.999	3
$f(x)$	16.4	16.94	16.994	17

x	3.001	3.01	3.1
$f(x)$	17.006	17.06	17.6

$\lim_{x \to 3} (6x - 1) = 17$; the limit can be reached.

3. 2 **5.** 2 **7.** (a) 64 (b) 7 (c) 20 (d) $\frac{4}{5}$
9. 5 **11.** $\frac{3}{10}$ **13.** 0 **15.** 11 **17.** 77 **19.** $\frac{10}{3}$
21. $-\frac{1}{4}$ **23.** $\frac{1}{15}$ **25.** $-\frac{1}{3}$ **27.** -1 **29.** $\frac{1}{4}$ **31.** $\frac{1}{4}$

33. (a)

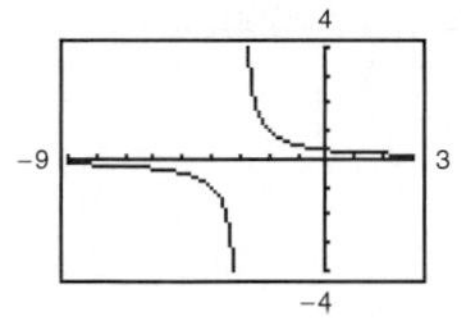

$\frac{1}{6}$

CHAPTER 12

(b)

x	2.9	2.99	3	3.01	3.1
$f(x)$	0.1695	0.1669	Error	0.1664	0.1639

0.166

35. (a)

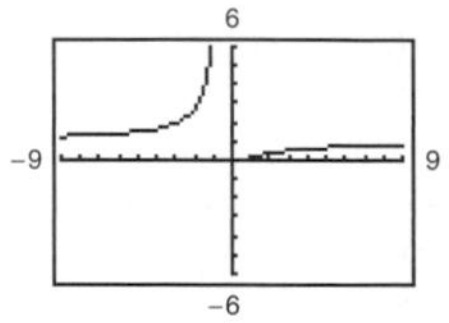

Limit does not exist.

(b)

x	-0.1	-0.01	-0.001	0
$f(x)$	4.85E8	7.2E86	Error	Error

x	0.001	0.01	0.1
$f(x)$	0	1E$-$87	2.1E$-$9

Limit does not exist.

37. (a)

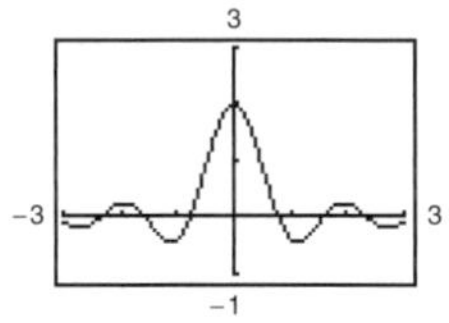

2

(b)

x	-0.1	-0.01	-0.001	0
$f(x)$	1.94709	1.99947	2	Error

x	0.001	0.01	0.1
$f(x)$	2	1.99947	1.94709

2

39. (a)

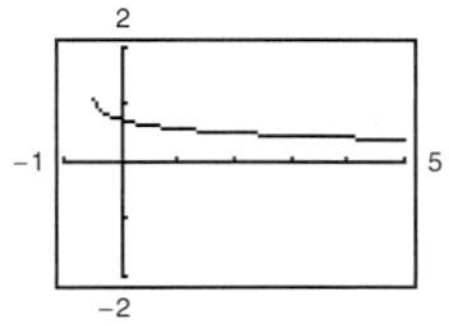

≈ 0.575

(b)

x	1.1	1.01	1.001	1.0001
$f(x)$	0.5680	0.5764	0.5773	0.5773

≈ 0.577 $\left(\text{Actual limit is } \dfrac{\sqrt{3}}{3}.\right)$

41.

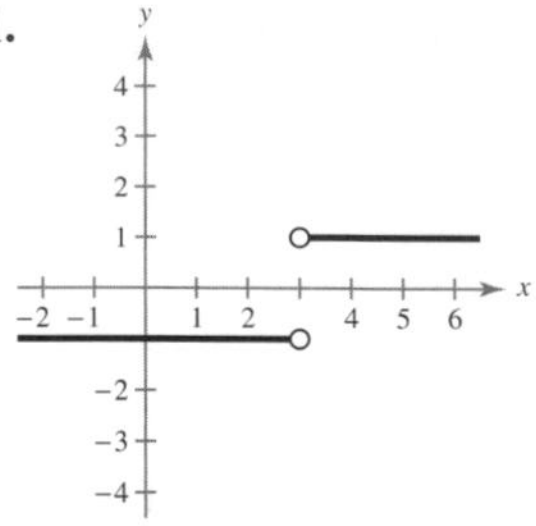

Limit does not exist.

43.

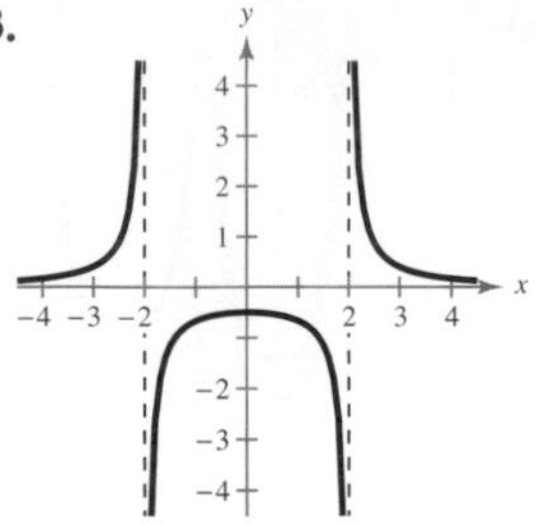

Limit does not exist.

45.

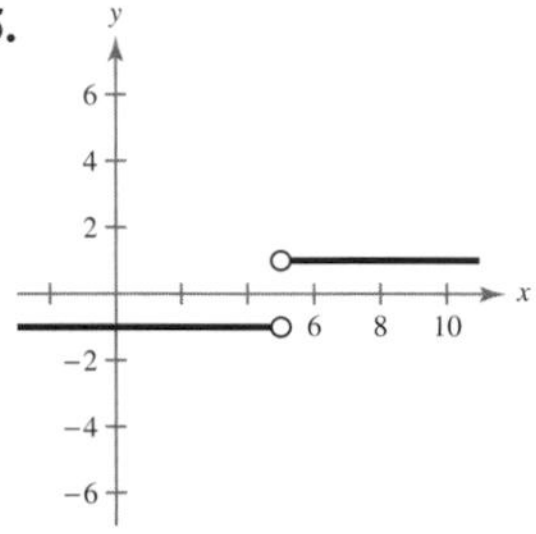

Limit does not exist.

47.

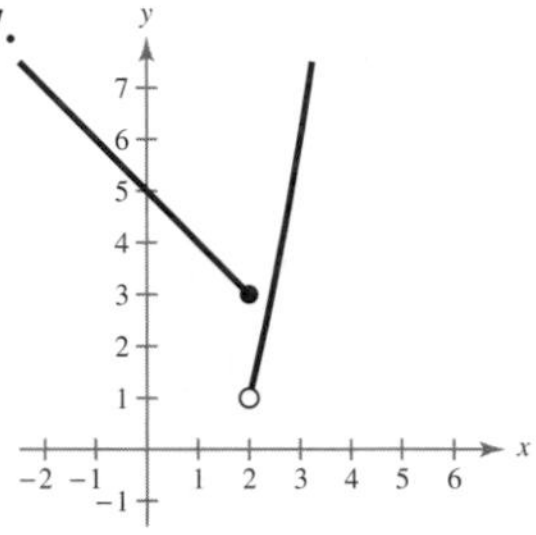

Limit does not exist.

49. 4 **51.** $3 - 2x$ **53.** 2

55.

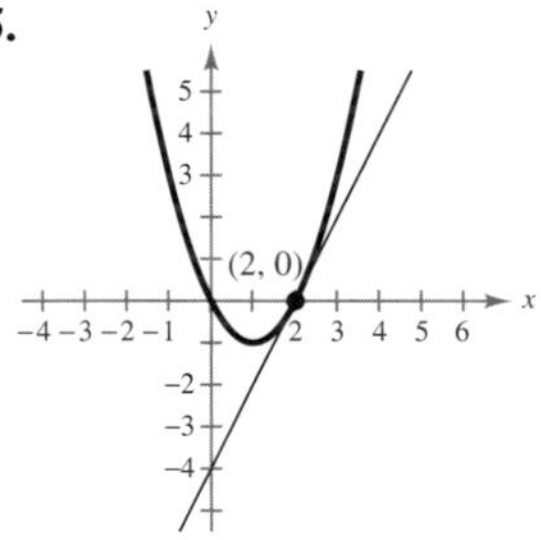

2

57.

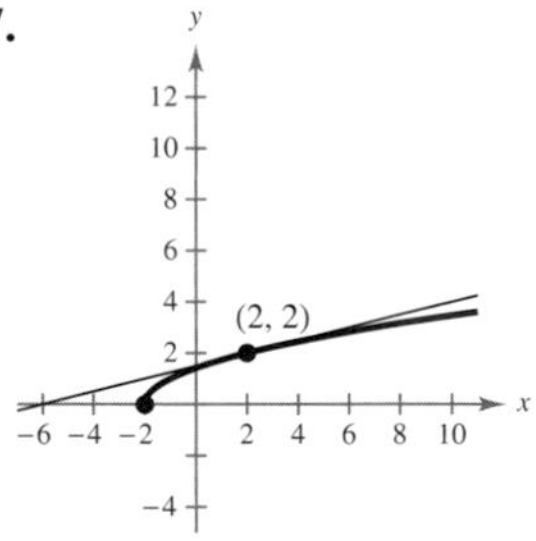

$\frac{1}{4}$

59. $m = 2x - 4$; (a) -4 (b) 6

61. $m = -\dfrac{4}{(x-6)^2}$; (a) -4 (b) -1

63. $f'(x) = 0$ **65.** $h'(x) = -\frac{1}{2}$ **67.** $g'(x) = 4x$

69. $f'(t) = \dfrac{1}{2\sqrt{t+5}}$ **71.** $g'(s) = -\dfrac{4}{(s+5)^2}$

73. (a) 0 (b) $y = -1$

(c)

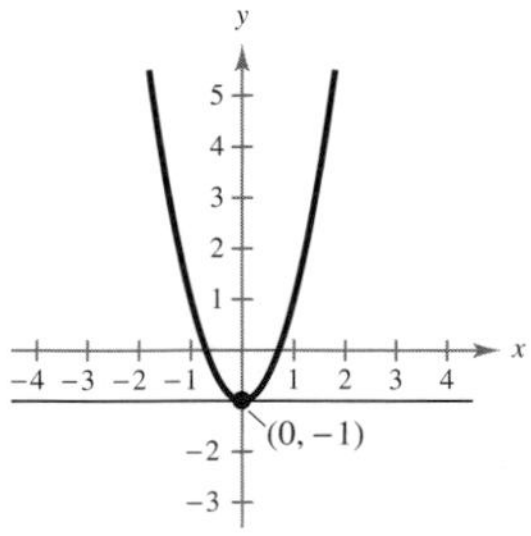

75. 2 **77.** 0 **79.** Limit does not exist. **81.** 3

83. $\frac{2}{3}, 1, \frac{8}{7}, \frac{11}{9}, \frac{14}{11}$
Limit: $\frac{3}{2}$

85. $-\frac{1}{2}, -\frac{9}{8}, -\frac{7}{6}, -\frac{37}{32}, -\frac{57}{50}$
Limit: -1

87. (a) $S(n) = \dfrac{(n+1)(5n+4)}{6n^2}$

(b)

n	10^0	10^1	10^2	10^3	10^4
$S(n)$	3	0.99	0.8484	0.8348	0.8335

(c) Limit: $\frac{5}{6}$

89. $\frac{27}{4} \approx 6.75$ square units

91.

n	4	8	20	50
Approximate area	7.5	6.375	5.74	5.4944

93. 50 square units **95.** 15 square units

97. $\frac{4}{3}$ square units

99. (a) $y = (-3.376068 \times 10^{-7})x^3 + (3.7529 \times 10^{-4})x^2 - 0.17x + 132$

(b)

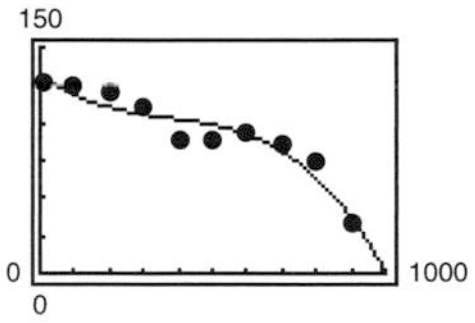

(c) $\approx 87{,}695.0$ square feet (Answers will vary.)

101. False. The limit of the rational function as x approaches ∞ does not exist.

Chapter Test *(page 904)*

1.

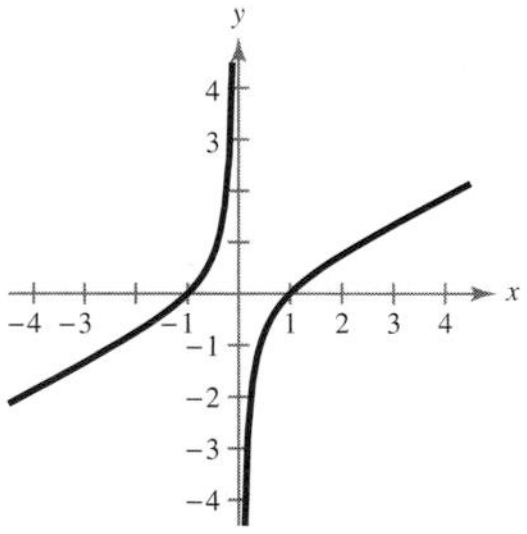

$\lim_{x \to -2} \dfrac{x^2 - 1}{2x} = -\dfrac{3}{4}$

2.

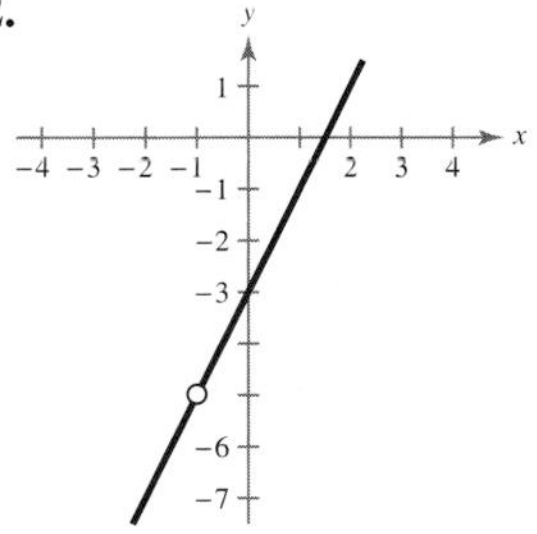

$\lim_{x \to -1} \dfrac{2x^2 - x - 3}{x + 1} = -5$

3.

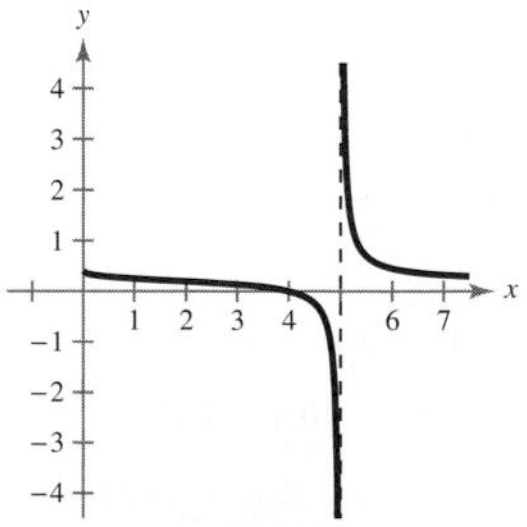

The limit does not exist.

4.

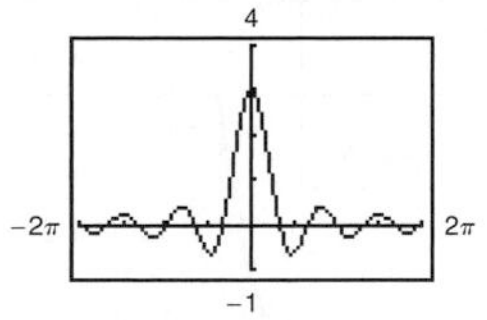

$\lim_{x \to 0} \dfrac{\sin 3x}{x} \approx 3$

x	-0.02	-0.01	0	0.01	0.02
$f(x)$	2.9982	2.9996	Error	2.9996	2.9982

5.

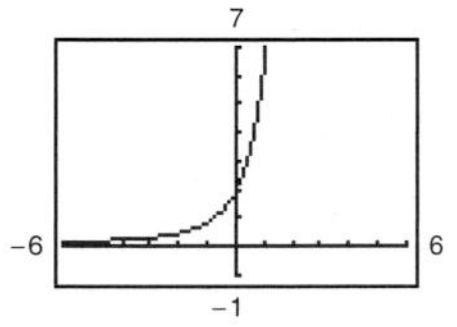

$\lim_{x \to 0} \dfrac{e^{2x} - 1}{x} \approx 2$

x	-0.004	-0.003	-0.002	-0.001	0
$f(x)$	1.9920	1.9940	1.9960	1.9980	Error

6. (a) $m = 6x - 5;\ 7$ (b) $m = 6x^2 + 6;\ 12$

7. $f'(x) = -\frac{3}{4}$ **8.** $f'(x) = 4x + 4$

9. $f'(x) = -\dfrac{1}{(x+3)^2}$ **10.** 0 **11.** -3

12. Does not exist

13. $0, \frac{3}{4}, \frac{14}{19}, \frac{12}{17}, \frac{36}{53}$
Limit: $\frac{1}{2}$

14. $0, 1, 0, \frac{1}{2}, 0$
Limit: 0

15. $\frac{25}{2}$ square units **16.** 8 square units

17. $\frac{3}{4}$ squarc unit

18. (a) $y = 8.79x^2 - 6.2x - 0.4$
(b) 81.7 feet per second

Cumulative Test for Chapters 10–12 *(page 905)*

1. Ellipse

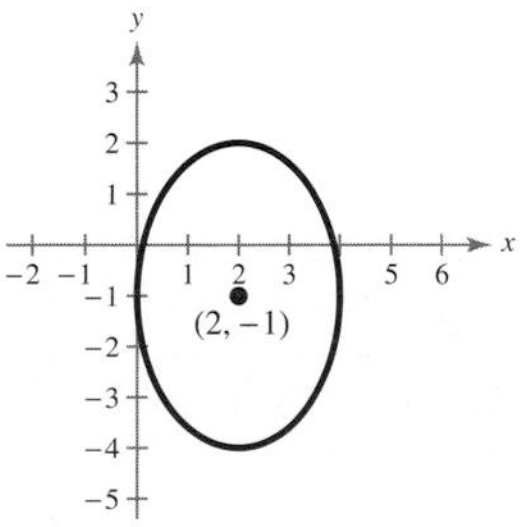

2. Circle

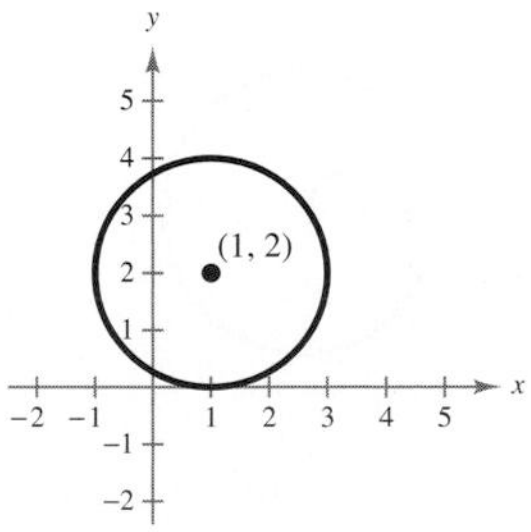

3. $\dfrac{x^2}{1} + \dfrac{(y-2)^2}{4} = 1$

4. $\theta = 37.98°$

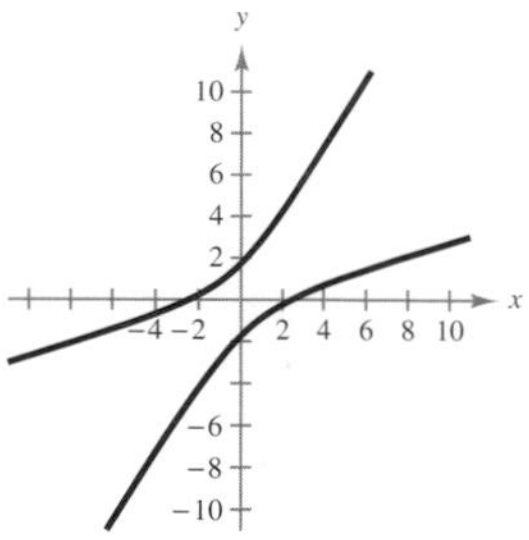

5.

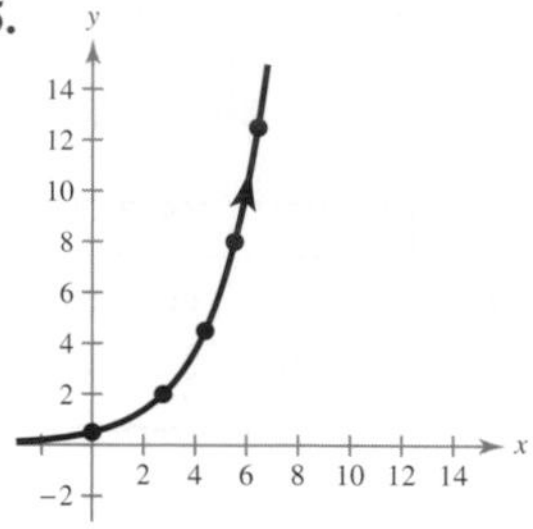

The corresponding rectangular equation is $y = \sqrt{e^x}/2$.

6.

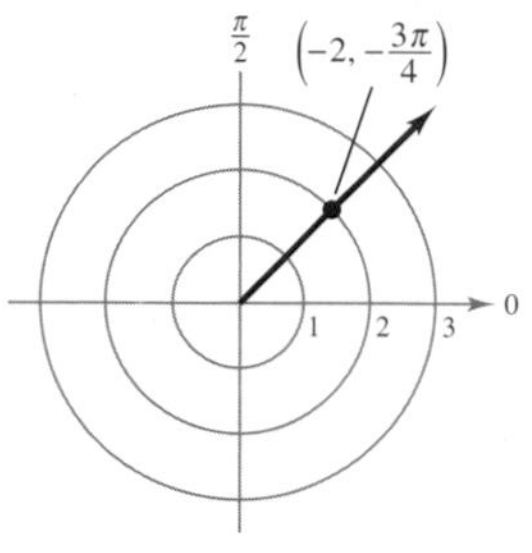

$\left(-2, \frac{5\pi}{4}\right), \left(2, -\frac{7\pi}{4}\right), \left(2, \frac{\pi}{4}\right)$

7. $-8r\cos\theta - 3r\sin\theta + 5 = 0$ or $r = \dfrac{5}{8\cos\theta + 3\sin\theta}$

8. $9x^2 + 20x - 16y^2 + 4 = 0$

9.

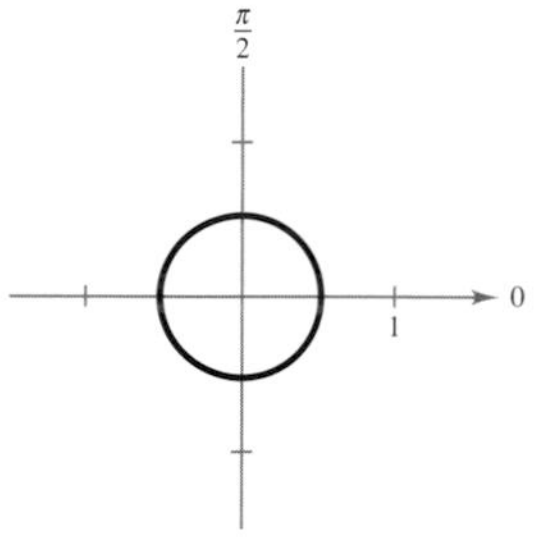

Circle

10.

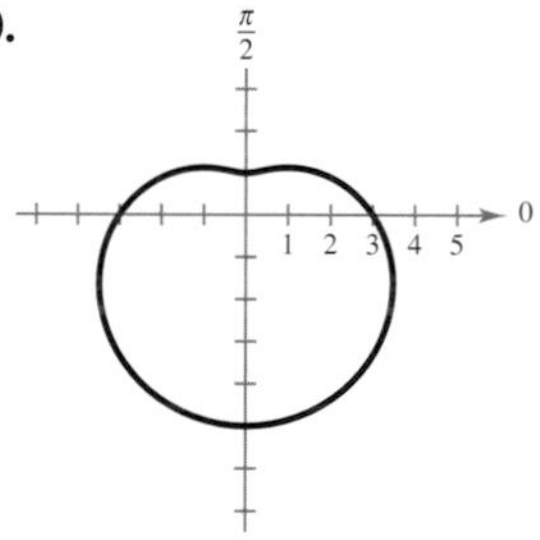

Dimpled limaçon

11.

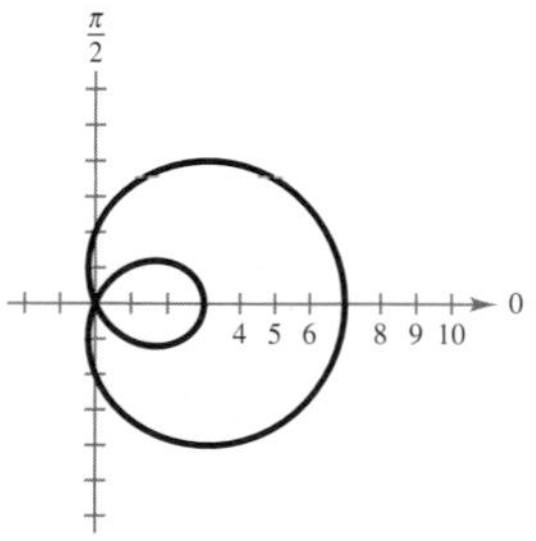

Limaçon with an open loop

12. $(-6, 1, 3)$ **13.** $(0, -4, 0)$ **14.** $\sqrt{149}$

15. 3, 4, 5

$$3^2 + 4^2 \stackrel{?}{=} 5^2$$
$$9 + 16 \stackrel{?}{=} 25$$
$$25 = 25$$

16. $\left(-1, 2, \frac{1}{2}\right)$ **17.** $(x - 2)^2 + (y - 2)^2 + (z - 4)^2 = 24$

18.

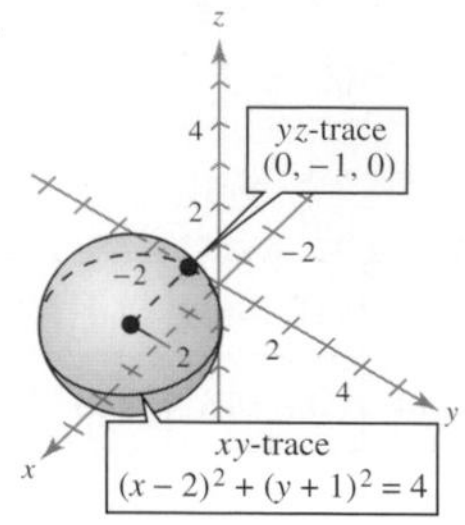

19. $\mathbf{u} \cdot \mathbf{v} = -38$

$\mathbf{u} \times \mathbf{v} = \langle -18, -6, -14 \rangle$

20. Neither **21.** Orthogonal **22.** Parallel

23. 12 cubic units

24. (a) $x = -2 + 7t,\ y = 3 + 5t,\ z = 25t$

(b) $\dfrac{x + 2}{7} = \dfrac{y - 3}{5} = \dfrac{z}{25}$

25. $75x + 50y - 31z = 0$

26.

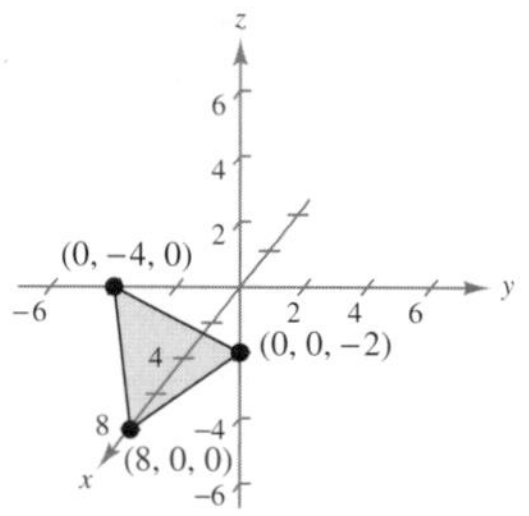

27. $\dfrac{\sqrt{30}}{2} \approx 2.74$

28. 84.26° **29.** 4 **30.** $-\frac{1}{3}$ **31.** $\frac{1}{14}$ **32.** $\frac{1}{4}$

33. -1 **34.** Limit does not exist.

35. $m = -2x;\ -2$ **36.** $m = \frac{1}{2}(x + 3)^{-1/2};\ \frac{1}{2}$

37. $m = -(x + 3)^{-2};\ -\frac{1}{16}$ **38.** $m = 4x^3;\ -4$

39. Limit does not exist. **40.** -7 **41.** 3

42. 0 **43.** $-42{,}875$ **44.** 8190 **45.** 672,880

46. $A = 10.5$ square units **47.** $A \approx 1.566$ square units

48. $\frac{3}{4}$ square unit **49.** 18 square units **50.** $\frac{2}{3}$ square unit

P.S. Problem Solving *(page 908)*

1. (a) g_1, g_4 (b) g_1, g_3, g_4 (c) g_1, g_4

3.

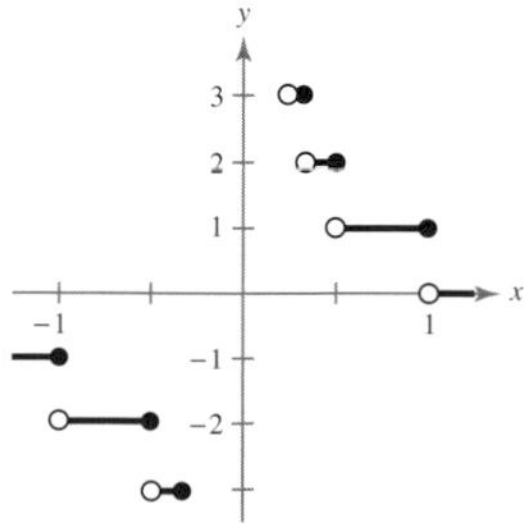

(a) $f\left(\frac{1}{4}\right) = [\![4]\!] = 4$

$f(3) = \left[\!\left[\frac{1}{3}\right]\!\right] = 0$

$f(1) = [\![1]\!] = 1$

(b) $\lim_{x \to 1^-} f(x) = 1$

$\lim_{x \to 1^+} f(x) = 0$

$\lim_{x \to (1/2)^-} f(x) = 2$

$\lim_{x \to (1/2)^+} f(x) = 1$

5. $a = 3, b = 6$

7. $\lim_{x\to 0} f(x)$ does not exist. No matter how close x is to 0, there are still an infinite number of rational and irrational numbers, so $\lim_{x\to 0} f(x)$ does not exist.

$\lim_{x\to 0} g(x) = 0$. When x is close to 0, both parts of the function are close to 0.

9. $y = 1 + 3\sqrt{x}$

11. (a) $d(m) = \dfrac{|-3m - 3|}{\sqrt{m^2 + 1}}$

(b)

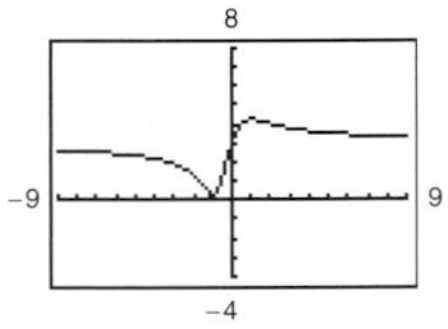

(c) $\lim_{x\to\infty} d(m) = 3, \lim_{x\to -\infty} d(m) = 3$. This indicates that the distance between the point and the line approaches 3 as the slope approaches positive or negative infinity.

13. The error was probably due to the calculator being in degree mode rather than radian mode.

15. (a)

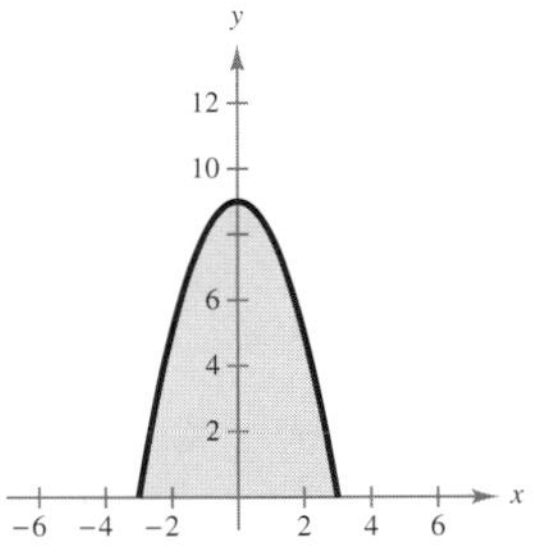

(b) $A = 36$

(c) Base $= 6$, height $= 9$; Area $= \frac{2}{3}bh = 36$

Appendix A

Appendix A.1 *(page A8)*

Vocabulary Check *(page A8)*

1. rational **2.** irrational **3.** absolute value
4. composite **5.** prime **6.** variables; constants
7. terms **8.** coefficient **9.** Zero-Factor Property

1. (a) 5, 1, 2 (b) 0, 5, 1, 2
(c) $-9, 5, 0, 1, -4, 2, -11$
(d) $-\frac{7}{2}, \frac{2}{3}, -9, 5, 0, 1, -4, 2, -11$ (e) $\sqrt{2}$

3. (a) 1 (b) 1 (c) $-13, 1, -6$
(d) $2.01, -13, 1, -6, 0.666\ldots$
(e) $0.010110111\ldots$

5. (a) $\frac{6}{3}, 8$ (b) $\frac{6}{3}, 8$ (c) $\frac{6}{3}, -1, 8, -22$
(d) $-\frac{1}{3}, \frac{6}{3}, -7.5, -1, 8, -22$ (e) $-\pi, \frac{1}{2}\sqrt{2}$

7. 0.625 **9.** $0.\overline{123}$ **11.** $-1 < 2.5$

13.

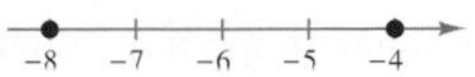

$-4 > -8$

15.

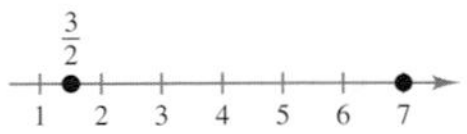

$\frac{3}{2} < 7$

17.

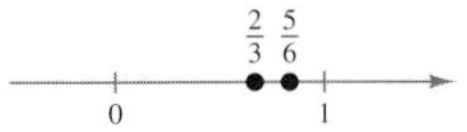

$\frac{5}{6} > \frac{2}{3}$

19. (a) $x \le 5$ denotes the set of all real numbers less than or equal to 5.

(b)

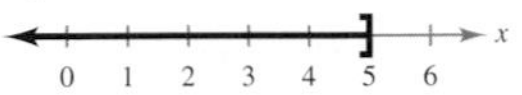

(c) Unbounded

21. (a) $x < 0$ denotes the set of all real numbers less than 0.

(b)

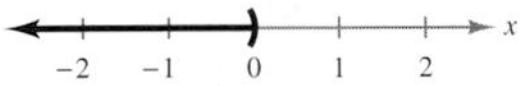

(c) Unbounded

23. (a) $[4, \infty)$ denotes the set of all real numbers greater than or equal to 4.

(b)

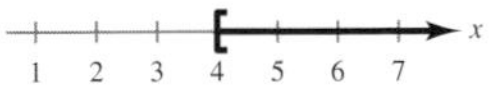

(c) Unbounded

25. (a) $-2 < x < 2$ denotes the set of all real numbers greater than -2 and less than 2.

(b)

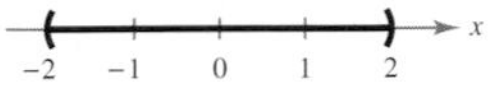

(c) Bounded

27. (a) $-1 \le x < 0$ denotes the set of all real numbers greater than or equal to -1 and less than 0.

(b)

(c) Bounded

29. (a) $[-2, 5)$ denotes the set of all real numbers greater than or equal to -2 and less than 5.

(b)

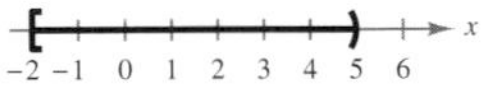

(c) Bounded

31. $-2 < x \le 4$ **33.** $y \ge 0$ **35.** $10 \le t \le 22$
37. $W > 65$ **39.** 10 **41.** 5 **43.** -1 **45.** -1
47. -1 **49.** $|-3| > -|-3|$ **51.** $-5 = -|5|$
53. $-|-2| = -|2|$ **55.** 51 **57.** $\frac{5}{2}$ **59.** $\frac{128}{75}$

61. $|\$113{,}356 - \$112{,}700| = \$656 > \$500$
$0.05(\$112{,}700) = \$5635$
Because the actual expenses differ from the budget by more than \$500, there is failure to meet the "budget variance test."

63. $|\$37{,}335 - \$37{,}640| = \$305 < \$500$
$0.05(\$37{,}640) = \$1882$
Because the difference between the actual expenses and the budget is less than \$500 and less than 5% of the budgeted amount, there is compliance with the "budget variance test."

65. (a)

Year	Expenditures (in billions)	Surplus or deficit (in billions)
1960	\$92.2	\$0.3 (s)
1970	\$195.6	\$2.8 (d)
1980	\$590.9	\$73.8 (d)
1990	\$1253.2	\$221.2 (d)
2000	\$1788.8	\$236.4 (s)

(b)

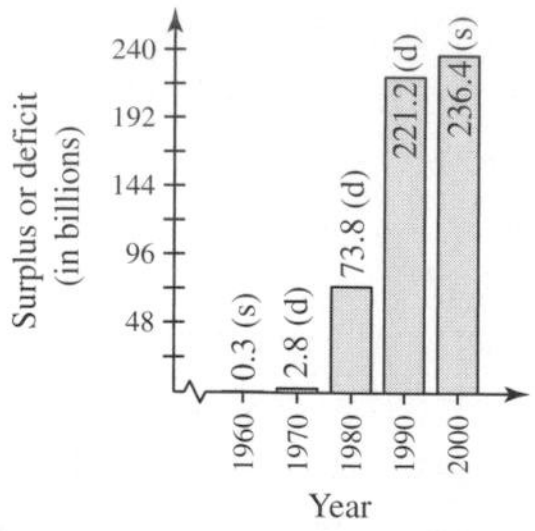

67. $|x - 5| \le 3$ **69.** $|y| \ge 6$

71. $|326 - 351| = 25$ miles

73. $7x$ and 4 are the terms; 7 is the coefficient.

75. $\sqrt{3}x^2$, $-8x$, and -11 are the terms; $\sqrt{3}$ and -8 are the coefficients.

77. $4x^3$, $x/2$, and -5 are the terms; 4 and $\frac{1}{2}$ are the coefficients.

79. (a) -10 (b) -6 **81.** (a) 14 (b) 2

83. (a) Division by 0 is undefined. (b) 0

85. Commutative Property of Addition

87. Multiplicative Inverse Property

89. Distributive Property

91. Multiplicative Identity Property

93. Associative Property of Addition

95. Distributive Property

97. $\dfrac{1}{2}$ **99.** $\dfrac{3}{8}$ **101.** 48 **103.** $\dfrac{5x}{12}$

105. (a)

n	1	0.5	0.01	0.0001	0.000001
$5/n$	5	10	500	50,000	5,000,000

(b) The value of $5/n$ approaches infinity as n approaches 0.

107. False. If $a < b$, then $\dfrac{1}{a} > \dfrac{1}{b}$, where $a \ne b \ne 0$.

109. (a) No. If one variable is negative and the other is positive, the expressions are unequal.

(b) $|u + v| \le |u| + |v|$

The expressions are equal when u and v have the same sign. If u and v differ in sign, $|u + v|$ is less than $|u| + |v|$.

111. The only even prime number is 2, because its only factors are itself and 1.

113. (a) Negative **115.** Yes. $|a| = -a$ if $a < 0$.

(b) Negative

Appendix A.2 *(page A20)*

Vocabulary Check *(page A20)*

1. exponent; base **2.** scientific notation

3. square root **4.** principle nth root

5. index; radicand **6.** simplest form

7. conjugates **8.** rationalizing

9. power; index

1. $8 \times 8 \times 8 \times 8 \times 8$ **3.** 4.9^6 **5.** (a) 27 (b) 81

7. (a) 1 (b) -9 **9.** (a) $\frac{243}{64}$ (b) -1

11. (a) $\frac{5}{6}$ (b) 4 **13.** -1600 **15.** 2.125

17. -24 **19.** 6 **21.** -54 **23.** 1

25. (a) $-125z^3$ (b) $5x^6$ **27.** (a) $24y^2$ (b) $3x^2$

29. (a) $\dfrac{7}{x}$ (b) $\dfrac{4}{3}(x + y)^2$ **31.** (a) 1 (b) $\dfrac{1}{4x^4}$

33. (a) $-2x^3$ (b) $\dfrac{10}{x}$ **35.** (a) 3^{3n} (b) $\dfrac{b^5}{a^5}$

37. 5.73×10^7 square miles

39. 8.99×10^{-5} gram per cubic centimeter

41. 4,568,000,000 ounces

43. 0.00000000000000000016022 coulomb

45. (a) 50,000 (b) 200,000

47. (a) 954.448 (b) 3.077×10^{10}

49. (a) 67,082.039 (b) 39.791

51. (a) 3 (b) $\frac{3}{2}$ **53.** (a) $\frac{1}{8}$ (b) $\frac{27}{8}$

55. (a) -4 (b) 2 **57.** (a) 7.550 (b) -7.225

59. (a) -0.011 (b) 0.005 **61.** (a) 4 (b) $2\sqrt[3]{3x}$

63. (a) $2\sqrt{2}$ (b) $3\sqrt[3]{2}$ **65.** (a) $6x\sqrt{2x}$ (b) $\dfrac{18\sqrt{z}}{z^2}$

67. (a) $2x\sqrt[3]{2x^2}$ (b) $\dfrac{5|x|\sqrt{3}}{y^2}$

69. (a) $34\sqrt{2}$ (b) $22\sqrt{2}$ **71.** (a) $2\sqrt{x}$ (b) $4\sqrt{y}$

73. (a) $13\sqrt{x + 1}$ (b) $18\sqrt{5x}$

75. $\sqrt{5} + \sqrt{3} > \sqrt{5 + 3}$ **77.** $5 > \sqrt{3^2 + 2^2}$

79. $\dfrac{\sqrt{3}}{3}$ **81.** $\dfrac{5 + \sqrt{3}}{11}$ **83.** $\dfrac{2}{\sqrt{2}}$ **85.** $\dfrac{2}{3(\sqrt{5} - \sqrt{3})}$

87. $9^{1/2}$ **89.** $\sqrt[5]{32}$ **91.** $(-216)^{1/3}$

93. $81^{3/4}$ **95.** $\dfrac{2}{x}$ **97.** $\dfrac{1}{x^3}$, $x > 0$

99. (a) $\sqrt{3}$ (b) $\sqrt[3]{(x + 1)^2}$

101. (a) $2\sqrt[4]{2}$ (b) $\sqrt[8]{2x}$ **103.** $\dfrac{\pi}{2} \approx 1.57$ seconds

105. (a)

h	0	1	2	3	4	5	6
t	0	2.93	5.48	7.67	9.53	11.08	12.32

h	7	8	9	10	11	12
t	13.29	14.00	14.50	14.80	14.93	14.96

(b) $t \to 8.64\sqrt{3} \approx 14.96$

107. True. When dividing variables, you subtract exponents.

109. $a^0 = 1$, $a \ne 0$, using the property $\dfrac{a^m}{a^n} = a^{m-n}$:

$\dfrac{a^m}{a^m} = a^{m-m} = a^0 = 1.$

111. When any positive integer is squared, the units digit is 0, 1, 4, 5, 6, or 9. Therefore, $\sqrt{5233}$ is not an integer.

Appendix A.3 *(page A31)*

Vocabulary Check *(page A31)*

1. n; a_n; a_0 **2.** descending
3. monomial; binomial; trinomial **4.** like terms
5. First terms; Outer terms; Inner terms; Last terms
6. factoring **7.** completely factored

1. d **2.** e **3.** b **4.** a **5.** f **6.** c
7. $-2x^3 + 4x^2 - 3x + 20$ **9.** $-15x^4 + 1$
11. (a) $-\frac{1}{2}x^5 + 14x$
(b) Degree: 5; Leading coefficient: $-\frac{1}{2}$
(c) Binomial
13. (a) $-3x^4 + 2x^2 - 5$
(b) Degree: 4; Leading coefficient: -3
(c) Trinomial
15. (a) $x^5 - 1$
(b) Degree: 5; Leading coefficient: 1
(c) Binomial
17. (a) 3
(b) Degree: 0; Leading coefficient: 3
(c) Monomial
19. (a) $-4x^5 + 6x^4 + 1$
(b) Degree: 5; Leading coefficient: -4
(c) Trinomial
21. (a) $4x^3y$
(b) Degree: 3; Leading coefficient: 4
(c) Monomial
23. Polynomial: $-3x^3 + 2x + 8$
25. Not a polynomial because it includes a term with a negative exponent
27. Polynomial: $-y^4 + y^3 + y^2$ **29.** $-2x - 10$
31. $3x^3 - 2x + 2$ **33.** $8.3x^3 + 29.7x^2 + 11$
35. $12z + 8$ **37.** $3x^3 - 6x^2 + 3x$ **39.** $-15z^2 + 5z$
41. $-4x^4 + 4x$ **43.** $7.5x^3 + 9x$ **45.** $-\frac{1}{2}x^2 - 12x$
47. $x^2 + 7x + 12$ **49.** $6x^2 - 7x - 5$
51. $x^4 + x^2 + 1$ **53.** $x^2 - 100$ **55.** $x^2 - 4y^2$
57. $4x^2 + 12x + 9$ **59.** $4x^2 - 20xy + 25y^2$
61. $x^3 + 3x^2 + 3x + 1$ **63.** $8x^3 - 12x^2y + 6xy^2 - y^3$
65. $16x^6 - 24x^3 + 9$ **67.** $m^2 - n^2 - 6m + 9$
69. $x^2 + 2xy + y^2 - 6x - 6y + 9$ **71.** $4r^4 - 25$
73. $\frac{1}{4}x^2 - 3x + 9$ **75.** $\frac{1}{9}x^2 - 4$
77. $1.44x^2 + 7.2x + 9$ **79.** $2.25x^2 - 16$
81. $2x^2 + 2x$ **83.** $u^4 - 16$ **85.** $x - y$
87. $x^2 - 2\sqrt{5}x + 5$ **89.** $3(x + 2)$ **91.** $2x(x^2 - 3)$
93. $(x - 1)(x + 6)$ **95.** $(x + 3)(x - 1)$
97. $\frac{1}{2}(x + 8)$ **99.** $\frac{1}{2}x(x^2 + 4x - 10)$
101. $\frac{2}{3}(x - 6)(x - 3)$ **103.** $(x + 9)(x - 9)$
105. $2(4y - 3)(4y + 3)$ **107.** $\left(4x + \frac{1}{3}\right)\left(4x - \frac{1}{3}\right)$
109. $(x + 1)(x - 3)$ **111.** $(3u + 2v)(3u - 2v)$
113. $(x - 2)^2$ **115.** $(2t + 1)^2$ **117.** $(5y - 1)^2$
119. $(3u + 4v)^2$ **121.** $\left(x - \frac{2}{3}\right)^2$
123. $(x - 2)(x^2 + 2x + 4)$ **125.** $(y + 4)(y^2 - 4y + 16)$
127. $(2t - 1)(4t^2 + 2t + 1)$
129. $(u + 3v)(u^2 - 3uv + 9v^2)$ **131.** $(x + 2)(x - 1)$
133. $(s - 3)(s - 2)$ **135.** $-(y + 5)(y - 4)$
137. $(x - 20)(x - 10)$ **139.** $(3x - 2)(x - 1)$
141. $(5x + 1)(x + 5)$ **143.** $-(3z - 2)(3z + 1)$
145. $(x - 1)(x^2 + 2)$ **147.** $(2x - 1)(x^2 - 3)$
149. $(3 + x)(2 - x^3)$ **151.** $(3x^2 - 1)(2x + 1)$
153. $(x + 2)(3x + 4)$ **155.** $(2x - 1)(3x + 2)$
157. $(3x - 1)(5x - 2)$ **159.** $6(x + 3)(x - 3)$
161. $x^2(x - 4)$ **163.** $(x - 1)^2$ **165.** $(1 - 2x)^2$
167. $-2x(x + 1)(x - 2)$ **169.** $(9x + 1)(x + 1)$
171. $\frac{1}{81}(x + 36)(x - 18)$ **173.** $(3x + 1)(x^2 + 5)$
175. $x(x - 4)(x^2 + 1)$ **177.** $\frac{1}{4}(x^2 + 3)(x + 12)$
179. $(t + 6)(t - 8)$ **181.** $(x + 2)(x + 4)(x - 2)(x - 4)$
183. $5(x + 2)(x^2 - 2x + 4)$ **185.** $(3 - 4x)(23 - 60x)$
187. $5(1 - x)^2(3x + 2)(4x + 3)$
189. $(x - 2)^2(x + 1)^3(7x - 5)$
191. $3(x^6 + 1)^4(3x + 2)^2(33x^6 + 20x^5 + 3)$
193. $-14, 14, -2, 2$ **195.** $-11, 11, -4, 4, -1, 1$
197. Two possible answers: $2, -12$
199. Two possible answers: $-2, -4$
201. (a) $P = 22x - 25{,}000$ (b) \$85,000
203. (a) $500r^2 + 1000r + 500$
(b)

r	$2\frac{1}{2}\%$	3%	4%
$500(1 + r)^2$	\$525.31	\$530.45	\$540.80

r	$4\frac{1}{2}\%$	5%
$500(1 + r)^2$	\$546.01	\$551.25

(c) The amount increases with increasing r.
205. (a) $V = 4x^3 - 88x^2 + 468x$
(b)

x (cm)	1	2	3
V (cm³)	384	616	720

207. $44x + 308$ **209.** (a) $3x^2 + 8x$ (b) $30x^2$
211.

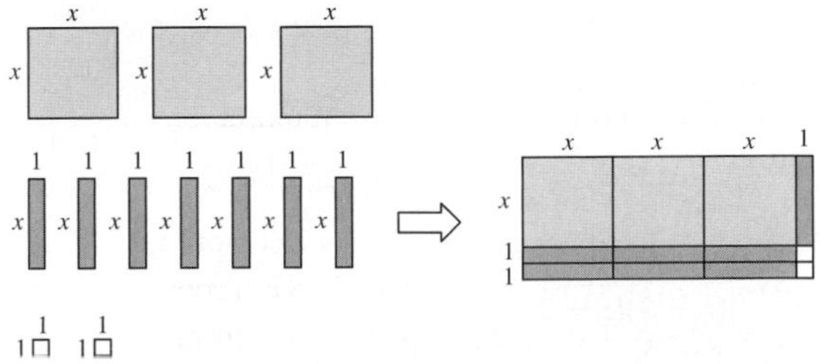

213.

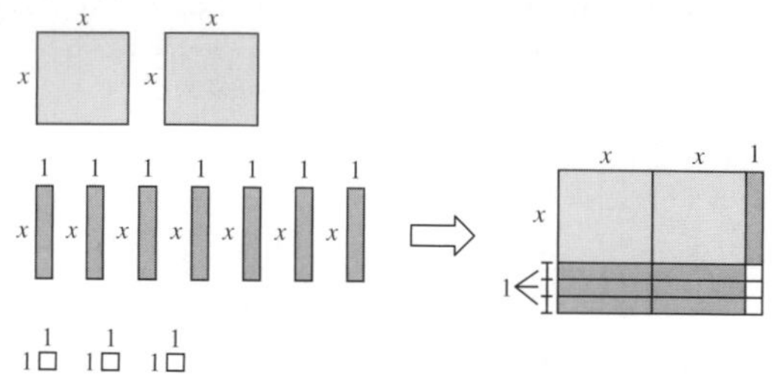

215. $4\pi(r + 1)$ **217.** $4(6 - x)(6 + x)$

219. (a) $\pi h(R - r)(R + r)$ (b) $V = 2\pi\left[\left(\frac{R + r}{2}\right)(R - r)\right]h$

221. False. $(4x^2 + 1)(3x + 1) = 12x^3 + 4x^2 + 3x + 1$

223. True. $a^2 - b^2 = (a + b)(a - b)$ **225.** $m + n$

227. $-x^3 + 8x^2 + 2x + 7$ **229.** $(x^n + y^n)(x^n - y^n)$

231. $x^{3n} - y^{2n}$ is completely factored.

233. Answers will vary. Sample answer: $x^2 - 3$

Appendix A.4 *(page A42)*

Vocabulary Check *(page A42)*

1. domain **2.** rational expression **3.** complex
4. smaller **5.** equivalent **6.** difference quotient

1. All real numbers **3.** All nonnegative real numbers

5. All real numbers x such that $x \neq 2$

7. All real numbers x such that $x \geq -1$ **9.** $3x,\ x \neq 0$

11. $\frac{3x}{2},\ x \neq 0$ **13.** $\frac{3y}{y + 1},\ x \neq 0$ **15.** $\frac{-4y}{5},\ y \neq \frac{1}{2}$

17. $-\frac{1}{2},\ x \neq 5$ **19.** $y - 4,\ y \neq -4$

21. $\frac{x(x + 3)}{x - 2},\ x \neq -2$ **23.** $\frac{y - 4}{y + 6},\ y \neq 3$

25. $\frac{-(x^2 + 1)}{(x + 2)},\ x \neq 2$ **27.** $z - 2$

29.

x	0	1	2	3	4	5	6
$\frac{x^2 - 2x - 3}{x - 3}$	1	2	3	Undef.	5	6	7
$x + 1$	1	2	3	4	5	6	7

The expressions are equivalent except at $x = 3$.

31. The expression cannot be simplified. **33.** $\frac{\pi}{4},\ r \neq 0$

35. $\frac{1}{5(x - 2)},\ x \neq 1$ **37.** $\frac{r + 1}{r},\ r \neq 1$

39. $\frac{t - 3}{(t + 3)(t - 2)},\ t \neq -2$ **41.** $\frac{(x + 6)(x + 1)}{x^2},\ x \neq 6$

43. $\frac{x + 5}{x - 1}$ **45.** $\frac{6x + 13}{x + 3}$ **47.** $-\frac{2}{x - 2}$

49. $-\frac{x^2 + 3}{(x + 1)(x - 2)(x - 3)}$ **51.** $\frac{2 - x}{x^2 + 1},\ x \neq 0$

53. The error was incorrect subtraction in the numerator.

55. $\frac{1}{2},\ x \neq 2$ **57.** $x(x + 1),\ x \neq -1, 0$

59. $\frac{2x - 1}{2x},\ x > 0$ **61.** $\frac{x^7 - 2}{x^2}$ **63.** $\frac{-1}{(x^2 + 1)^5}$

65. $\frac{2x^3 - 2x^2 - 5}{(x - 1)^{1/2}}$ **67.** $\frac{3x - 1}{3},\ x \neq 0$

69. $\frac{-1}{x(x + h)},\ h \neq 0$ **71.** $\frac{-1}{(x - 4)(x + h - 4)},\ h \neq 0$

73. $\frac{1}{\sqrt{x + 2} + \sqrt{x}}$ **75.** $\frac{1}{\sqrt{x + h + 1} + \sqrt{x + 1}},\ h \neq 0$

77. $\frac{x}{2(2x + 1)},\ x \neq 0$

79. (a) $\frac{1}{16}$ minute (b) $\frac{x}{16}$ minute(s) (c) $\frac{60}{16} = \frac{15}{4}$ minutes

81. (a) 9.09% (b) $\frac{288(MN - P)}{N(MN + 12P)}$; 9.09%

83. (a)

t	0	2	4	6	8	10
T	75	55.9	48.3	45	43.3	42.3

t	12	14	16	18	20	22
T	41.7	41.3	41.1	40.9	40.7	40.6

(b) The model is approaching a T-value of 40.

85. False. In order for the simplified expression to be equivalent to the original expression, the domain of the simplified expression needs to be restricted. If n is even, $x \neq -1, 1$. If n is odd, $x \neq 1$.

87. Completely factor each polynomial in the numerator and in the denominator. Then conclude that there are no common factors.

Appendix A.5 *(page A56)*

Vocabulary Check *(page A56)*

1. equation **2.** solve **3.** identities; conditional
4. $ax + b = 0$ **5.** extraneous
6. quadratic equation
7. factoring; extracting square roots; completing the square; Quadratic Formula

1. Identity **3.** Conditional equation **5.** Identity

7. Identity **9.** Conditional equation

11. 4 **13.** -9 **15.** 5 **17.** 9 **19.** No solution

21. -4 **23.** $-\frac{6}{5}$ **25.** 9

27. No solution. The x-terms sum to zero. **29.** 10

31. 4 **33.** 3 **35.** 0

37. No solution. The variable is divided out.
39. No solution. The solution is extraneous. **41.** 2
43. No solution. The solution is extraneous.
45. 0 **47.** All real numbers x
49. $2x^2 + 8x - 3 = 0$ **51.** $x^2 - 6x + 6 = 0$
53. $3x^2 - 90x - 10 = 0$ **55.** $0, -\frac{1}{2}$ **57.** $4, -2$
59. -5 **61.** $3, -\frac{1}{2}$ **63.** $2, -6$ **65.** $-\frac{20}{3}, -4$
67. $-a$ **69.** ± 7 **71.** $\pm\sqrt{11}$ **73.** $\pm 3\sqrt{3}$
75. 8, 16 **77.** $-2 \pm \sqrt{14}$ **79.** $\dfrac{1 \pm 3\sqrt{2}}{2}$
81. 2 **83.** $4, -8$ **85.** $\sqrt{11} - 6, -\sqrt{11} - 6$
87. $1 \pm \dfrac{\sqrt{6}}{3}$ **89.** $2 \pm 2\sqrt{3}$ **91.** $\dfrac{-5 \pm \sqrt{89}}{4}$
93. $\frac{1}{2}, -1$ **95.** $\frac{1}{4}, -\frac{3}{4}$ **97.** $1 \pm \sqrt{3}$
99. $-7 \pm \sqrt{5}$ **101.** $-4 \pm 2\sqrt{5}$ **103.** $\dfrac{2}{3} \pm \dfrac{\sqrt{7}}{3}$
105. $-\dfrac{4}{3}$ **107.** $-\dfrac{1}{2} \pm \sqrt{2}$ **109.** $\dfrac{2}{7}$
111. $2 \pm \dfrac{\sqrt{6}}{2}$ **113.** $6 \pm \sqrt{11}$ **115.** $-\dfrac{3}{8} \pm \dfrac{\sqrt{265}}{8}$
117. $0.976, -0.643$ **119.** $1.355, -14.071$
121. $1.687, -0.488$ **123.** $-0.290, -2.200$
125. $1 \pm \sqrt{2}$ **127.** $6, -12$ **129.** $\frac{1}{2} \pm \sqrt{3}$
131. $-\dfrac{1}{2}$ **133.** $\dfrac{3}{4} \pm \dfrac{\sqrt{97}}{4}$ **135.** $0, \pm\dfrac{3\sqrt{2}}{2}$
137. ± 3 **139.** -6 **141.** $-3, 0$ **143.** $3, 1, -1$
145. ± 1 **147.** $\pm\sqrt{3}, \pm 1$ **149.** $\pm\frac{1}{2}, \pm 4$ **151.** $1, -2$
153. 50 **155.** 26 **157.** -16 **159.** $2, -5$
161. 0 **163.** 9 **165.** $-3 \pm 16\sqrt{2}$
167. $\pm\sqrt{14}$ **169.** 1 **171.** $2, -\frac{3}{2}$
173. $\dfrac{-3 \pm \sqrt{21}}{6}$ **175.** $4, -5$ **177.** $\dfrac{1 \pm \sqrt{31}}{3}$
179. $3, -2$ **181.** $\sqrt{3}, -3$ **183.** $3, \dfrac{-1 - \sqrt{17}}{2}$
185. (a) 61.2 inches
(b) Yes. The estimated height of a male with a 19-inch femur is 69.4 inches.
(c)

Height, x	Female femur length	Male femur length
60	15.48	14.79
70	19.80	19.28
80	24.12	23.77
90	28.44	28.26
100	32.76	32.75
110	37.08	37.24

100 inches
(d) $x \approx 100.59$; There would not be a problem because it is not likely for either a male or a female to be 100 inches tall (which is 8 feet 4 inches tall).
187. $y = -0.25t + 8$; after about 28 hours
189. 6 inches × 6 inches × 2 inches
191. $\dfrac{20\sqrt{3}}{3} \approx 11.55$ inches
193. (a) 1998 (b) During 2007 **195.** 500 units
197. False. $x(3 - x) = 10$
$3x - x^2 = 10$
The equation cannot be written in the form $ax + b = 0$.
199. False. See Example 14 on page A55.
201. Equivalent equations have the same solution set, and one is derived from the other by steps for generating equivalent equations.
$2x = 5,\ 2x + 3 = 8$
203. Yes. The student should have subtracted $15x$ from both sides to make the right side of the equation equal to zero. Factoring out an x shows that there are two solutions, $x = 0$ and $x = 6$.
205. $x^2 - 3x - 18 = 0$ **207.** $x^2 - 22x + 112 = 0$
209. $x^2 - 2x - 1 = 0$ **211.** $a = 9, b = 9$
213. (a) $x = 0, -\dfrac{b}{a}$ (b) $x = 0, 1$

Appendix A.6 *(page A66)*

Vocabulary Check *(page A66)*

1. solution set **2.** graph **3.** negative
4. solution set **5.** double **6.** union

1. $-1 \leq x \leq 5$. Bounded **3.** $x > 11$. Unbounded
5. $x < -2$. Unbounded
7. b **8.** f **9.** d **10.** c **11.** e **12.** a
13. (a) Yes (b) No (c) Yes (d) No
15. (a) Yes (b) No (c) No (d) Yes
17. (a) Yes (b) Yes (c) Yes (d) No
19. $x < 3$

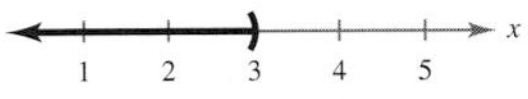

21. $x < \frac{3}{2}$

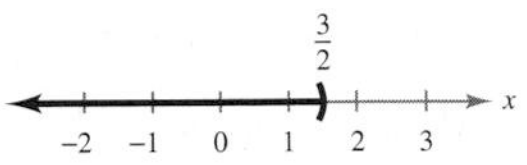

23. $x \geq 12$

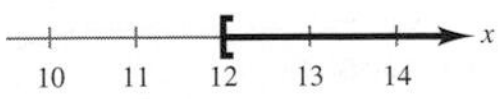

25. $x > 2$

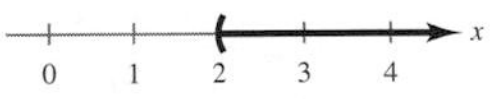

27. $x \geq \frac{2}{7}$

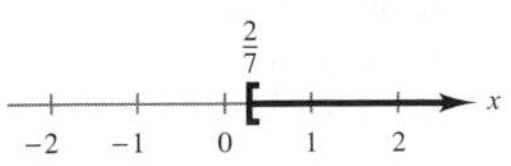

29. $x < 5$

31. $x \geq 4$

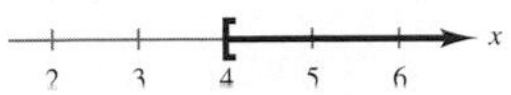

33. $x \geq 2$

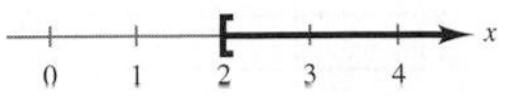

35. $x \geq -4$

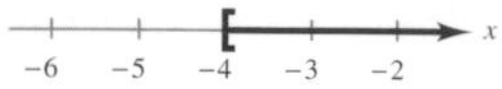

37. $-1 < x < 3$

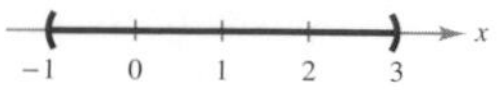

39. $-\frac{9}{2} < x < \frac{15}{2}$

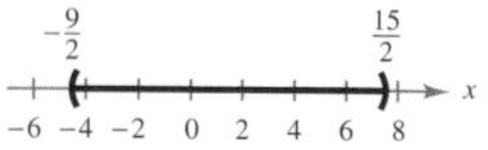

41. $-\frac{3}{4} < x < -\frac{1}{4}$

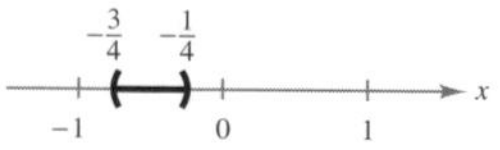

43. $10.5 \leq x \leq 13.5$

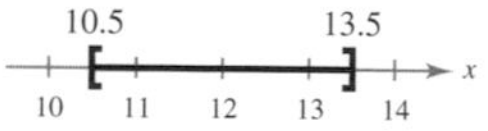

45. $-6 < x < 6$

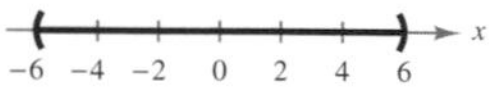

47. $x < -2, x > 2$

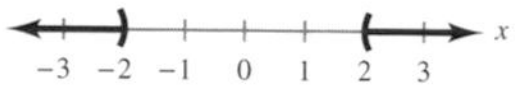

49. No solution

51. $14 \leq x \leq 26$

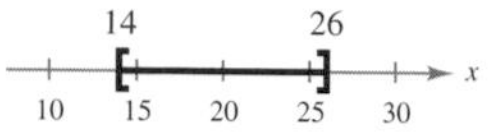

53. $x \leq -\frac{3}{2}, x \geq 3$

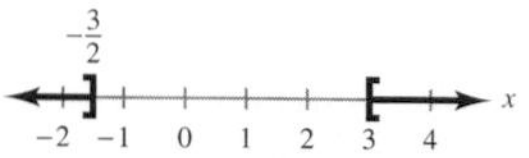

55. $x \leq -5,\ x \geq 11$

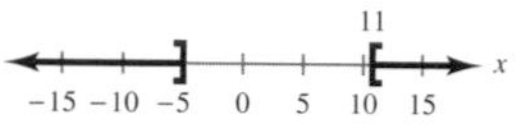

57. $4 < x < 5$

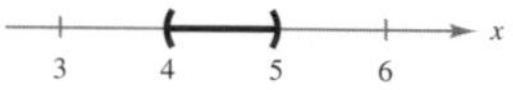

59. $x \leq -\frac{29}{2},\ x \geq -\frac{11}{2}$

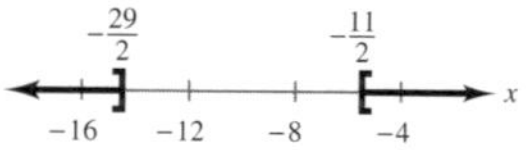

61.

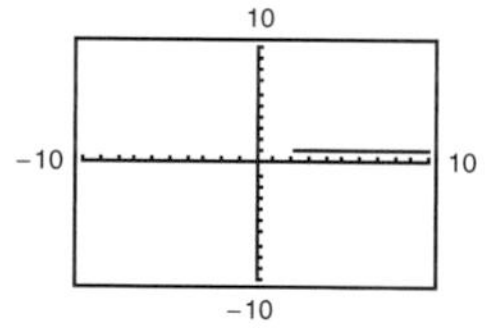

$x > 2$

63.

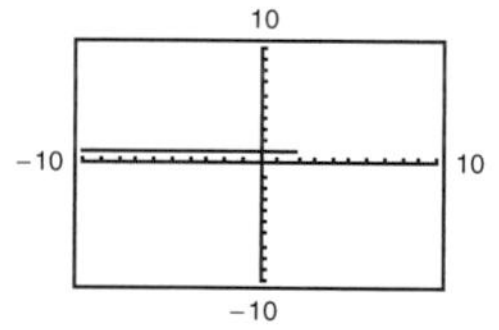

$x \leq 2$

65.

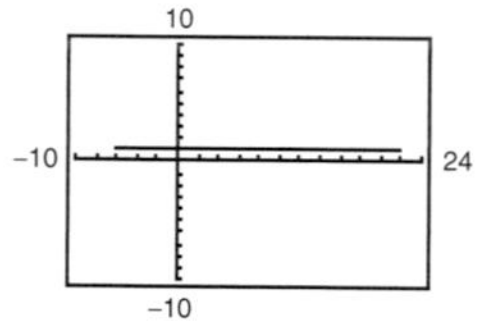

$-6 \leq x \leq 22$

67.

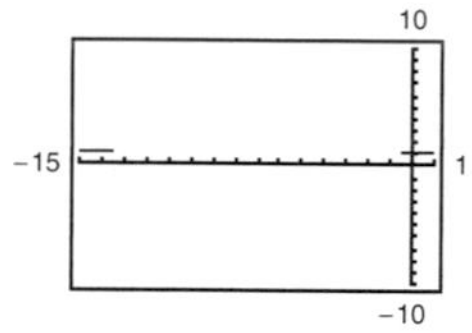

$x \leq -\frac{27}{2}, x \geq -\frac{1}{2}$

69.

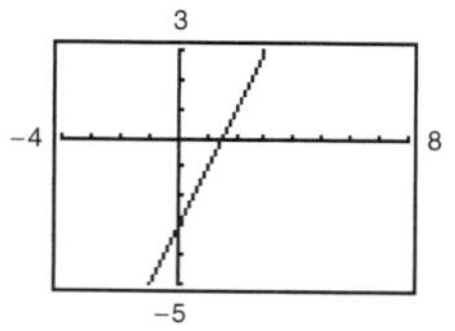

(a) $x \geq 2$

(b) $x \leq \frac{3}{2}$

71.

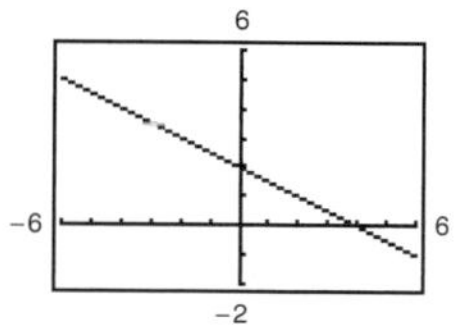

(a) $-2 \leq x \leq 4$

(b) $x \leq 4$

73.

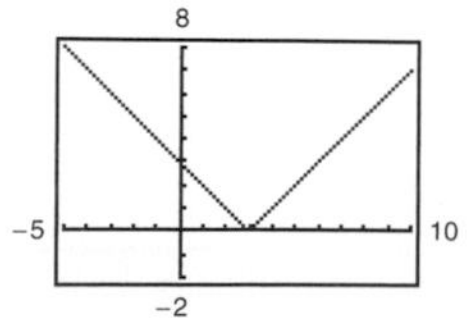

(a) $1 \leq x \leq 5$

(b) $x \leq -1,\ x \geq 7$

75. $[5, \infty)$ **77.** $[-3, \infty)$ **79.** $\left(-\infty, \frac{7}{2}\right]$

81. All real numbers within eight units of 10

83. $|x| \leq 3$ **85.** $|x - 7| \geq 3$ **87.** $|x - 12| < 10$

89. $|x + 3| > 4$ **91.** $x > 6$ **93.** $r > 3.125\%$

95. $x \geq 36$ **97.** $134 \leq x \leq 234$

99. (a)

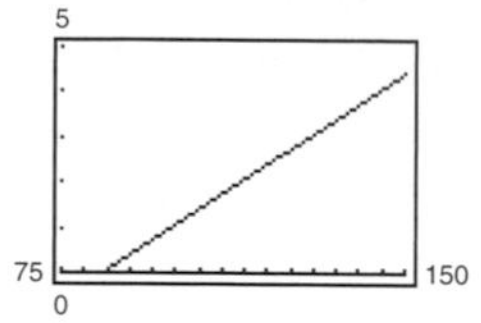

(b) $x \geq 129$

101. (a) $1 \leq t \leq 10$ (b) $t > 16$

103. 106.864 square inches $\leq$ area $\leq$ 109.464 square inches

105. Might be undercharged or overcharged by \$0.19.

107. $13.7 < t < 17.5$ **109.** $20 \leq h \leq 80$

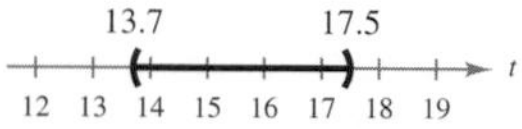

111. False. c has to be greater than zero. **113.** b

Appendix A.7 *(page A75)*

Vocabulary Check *(page A75)*

1. numerator **2.** reciprocal

1. Change all signs when distributing the minus sign.
$2x - (3y + 4) = 2x - 3y - 4$

3. Change all signs when distributing the minus sign.
$$\frac{4}{16x - (2x + 1)} = \frac{4}{14x - 1}$$

5. z occurs twice as a factor.
$(5z)(6z) = 30z^2$

7. The fraction as a whole is multiplied by a, not the numerator and denominator separately.
$$a\left(\frac{x}{y}\right) = \frac{ax}{y}$$

9. $\sqrt{x + 9}$ cannot be simplified.

11. Divide out common factors, not common terms.
$\frac{2x^2 + 1}{5x}$ cannot be simplified.

13. To get rid of negative exponents:
$$\frac{1}{a^{-1} + b^{-1}} = \frac{1}{a^{-1} + b^{-1}} \cdot \frac{ab}{ab} = \frac{ab}{b + a}.$$

15. Factor within grouping symbols before applying exponent to each factor.
$(x^2 + 5x)^{1/2} = [x(x + 5)]^{1/2} = x^{1/2}(x + 5)^{1/2}$

17. To add fractions, first find a common denominator.
$$\frac{3}{x} + \frac{4}{y} = \frac{3y + 4x}{xy}$$

19. $3x + 2$ **21.** $2x^2 + x + 15$ **23.** $\frac{1}{3}$ **25.** 2

27. $\dfrac{1}{2x^2}$ **29.** $\dfrac{25}{9}, \dfrac{49}{16}$ **31.** 1, 2 **33.** $1 - 5x$

35. $1 - 7x$ **37.** $3x - 1$ **39.** $3x^2(2x - 1)^{-3}$

41. $\dfrac{4}{3}x^{-1} + 4x^{-4} - 7x(2x)^{-1/3}$ **43.** $\dfrac{16}{x} - 5 - x$

45. $4x^{8/3} - 7x^{5/3} + \dfrac{1}{x^{1/3}}$ **47.** $\dfrac{3}{x^{1/2}} - 5x^{3/2} - x^{7/2}$

49. $\dfrac{-7x^2 - 4x + 9}{(x^2 - 3)^3(x + 1)^4}$ **51.** $\dfrac{27x^2 - 24x + 2}{(6x + 1)^4}$

53. $\dfrac{-1}{(x + 3)^{2/3}(x + 2)^{7/4}}$ **55.** $\dfrac{4x - 3}{(3x - 1)^{4/3}}$

57. $\dfrac{x}{x^2 + 4}$ **59.** $\dfrac{(3x - 2)^{1/2}(15x^2 - 4x + 45)}{2(x^2 + 5)^{1/2}}$

61. (a)

x	0.5	1.0	1.5	2.0
t	1.70	1.72	1.78	1.89

x	2.5	3.0	3.5	4.0
t	2.02	2.18	2.36	2.57

(b) $x = 0.5$ mile

(c) $\dfrac{3x\sqrt{x^2 - 8x + 20} + (x \quad 4)\sqrt{x^2 + 4}}{6\sqrt{x^2 + 4}\sqrt{x^2 - 8x + 20}}$

63. True. $x^{-1} + y^{-2} = \dfrac{1}{x} + \dfrac{1}{y^2} = \dfrac{y^2 + x}{xy^2}$

65. True. $\dfrac{1}{\sqrt{x} + 4} = \dfrac{1}{\sqrt{x} + 4} \cdot \dfrac{\sqrt{x} - 4}{\sqrt{x} - 4} = \dfrac{\sqrt{x} - 4}{x - 16}$

67. Add exponents when multiplying powers with like bases.
$x^n \cdot x^{3n} = x^{4n}$

69. When a binomial is squared, there is also a middle term.
$(x^n + y^n)^2 = x^{2n} + 2x^ny^n + y^{2n} \neq x^{2n} + y^{2n}$

71. The two answers are equivalent and can be obtained by factoring.

$\frac{1}{10}(2x - 1)^{5/2} + \frac{1}{6}(2x - 1)^{3/2}$
$= \frac{1}{60}(2x - 1)^{3/2}[6(2x - 1) + 10]$
$= \frac{1}{60}(2x - 1)^{3/2}(12x + 4)$
$= \frac{4}{60}(2x - 1)^{3/2}(3x + 1)$
$= \frac{1}{15}(2x - 1)^{3/2}(3x + 1)$

(a) $\frac{2}{5}(2x - 3)^{3/2}(x + 1)$ (b) $\frac{8}{15}(4 + x)^{3/2}(x - 1)$

Index

A

Absolute value
of a complex number, 470
inequality, solution of, A63
properties of, A4
of a real number, A4
Acute angle, 283
Addition
of a complex number, 163
of fractions
with like denominators, A7
with unlike denominators, A7
of matrices, 588
vector, 449
properties of, 451
resultant of, 449
Additive identity
for a complex number, 163
for a matrix, 591
for a real number, A6
Additive inverse, A5
for a complex number, 163
for a real number, A6
Adjacent side of a right triangle, 301
Adjoining matrices, 604
Algebraic expression, A5
domain of, A36
equivalent, A36
evaluate, A5
term of, A5
Algebraic function, 218
Algebraic properties of the cross product, 828, 847
Algebraic tests for symmetry, 19
Alternative definition of conic, 793
Alternative form of Law of Cosines, 439, 490
Amplitude of sine and cosine curves, 323
Angle(s), 282
acute, 283
between two lines, 729
between two planes, 837
between two vectors, 461, 492
in space, 821
central, 283
complementary, 285
conversions between radians and degrees, 286
coterminal, 282
degree, 285
of depression, 306
of elevation, 306
initial side, 282
measure of, 283
negative, 282
obtuse, 283
positive, 282
radian, 283
reference, 314
of repose, 351
standard position, 282
supplementary, 285
terminal side, 282
vertex, 282
Angular speed, 287
Aphelion distance, 798
Arc length, 287
Arccosine function, 345
Arcsine function, 343, 345
Arctangent function, 345
Area
common formulas for, 7
of an oblique triangle, 434
of a plane region, 896
of a region, 883
of a sector of a circle, 289
of a triangle, 622
Heron's Area Formula, 442, 491
Argument of a complex number, 471
Arithmetic combination, 84
Arithmetic sequence, 653
common difference of, 653
*n*th partial sum, 657
*n*th term of, 654
recursion form, 654
sum of a finite, 656, 723
Associative Property of Addition
for complex numbers, 164
for matrices, 590
for real numbers, A6
Associative Property of Multiplication
for complex numbers, 164
for matrices, 590, 594
for real numbers, A6
Associative Property of scalar multiplication for matrices, 594
Astronomical unit, 796
Asymptote(s)
horizontal, 185
of a hyperbola, 755
oblique, 190
of a rational function, 186
slant, 190
vertical, 185
Augmented matrix, 573
Average rate of change, 59
Average value of a population, 261
Axis (axes)
imaginary, 470
of a parabola, 129, 736
polar, 779
real, 470
rotation of, 763
of symmetry, 129

B

Back-substitution, 497
Base, A11
natural, 222
Basic equation, 534
guidelines for solving, 538
Basic limits, 857
Basic Rules of Algebra, A6
Bearings, 355
Bell-shaped curve, 261
Binomial, 683, A23
coefficient, 683
cube of, A25
expanding, 686
square of, A25
Binomial Theorem, 683, 724
Book value, 32
Bounded, A60
Bounded intervals, A2
Branches of a hyperbola, 753
Break-even point, 501
Butterfly curve, 810

C

Calculus, 873
area of a region, 883
tangent line, 883
Cardioid, 789
Cartesian plane, 2
Center
of a circle, 20
of an ellipse, 744
of a hyperbola, 753
Central angle of a circle, 283
Change-of-base formula, 239

Characteristics of a function from set *A* to set *B*, 40
Circle, 20, 789
arc length of, 287
center of, 20
central angle, 283
classifying
by the discriminant, 767
by general equation, 759
radius of, 20
sector of, 289
area of, 289
standard form of the equation of, 20
unit, 294
Circumference, common formulas for, 7
Classification of conics
by the discriminant, 767
by general equation, 759
Coded row matrices, 625
Coefficient
binomial, 683
correlation, 104
equating, 536
leading, A23
of a polynomial, A23
of a variable term, A5
Coefficient matrix, 573
Cofactor(s)
expanding by, 614
of a matrix, 613
Cofunction identities, 374
Collinear points, 13, 623, 823
test for, 623
Column matrix, 572
Combination of *n* elements taken *r* at a time, 696
Combined variation, 107
Common difference, 653
Common formulas
area, 7
circumference, 7
perimeter, 7
volume, 7
Common logarithmic function, 230
Common ratio, 663
Commutative Property of Addition
for complex numbers, 164
for matrices, 590
for real numbers, A6
Commutative Property of Multiplication
for complex numbers, 164
for real numbers, A6
Complement
of an event, 708
probability of, 708
Complementary angles, 285
Completely factored, A26
Completing the square, A49
Complex conjugates, 165
Complex fraction, A40
Complex number(s), 162
absolute value of, 470
addition of, 163
additive identity, 163
additive inverse, 163
argument of, 471
Associative Property of Addition, 164
Associative Property of Multiplication, 164
Commutative Property of Addition, 164
Commutative Property of Multiplication, 164
Distributive Property, 164
equality of, 162
imaginary part of, 162
modulus of, 471
*n*th root of, 475, 476
*n*th roots of unity, 477
polar form, 471
product of two, 472
quotient of two, 472
real part of, 162
standard form of, 162
subtraction of, 163
trigonometric form of, 471
Complex plane, 470
imaginary axis, 470
real axis, 470
Complex zeros occur in conjugate pairs, 173
Component form
of a vector in space, 820
of a vector **v**, 448
Components, vector, 463, 464
Composite number, A7
Composition, 86
Compound interest
continuous compounding, 223
formulas for, 224
Conditional equation, A46
Conditions under which limits do not exist, 856
Conic(s) or conic section(s), 735
alternative definition, 793
classifying
by the discriminant, 767
by general equation, 759
degenerate, 735
eccentricity of, 793
locus of, 735
polar equations of, 793, 808
rotation of axes, 763
Conjugate, 173, A17
of a complex number, 165
Conjugate axis of a hyperbola, 755
Consistent system of linear equations, 510
Constant, A5
function, 57, 67
limit of, 857
of proportionality, 105
term, A5, A23
of variation, 105
Constraints, 552
Consumer surplus, 546
Continuous compounding, 223
Continuous function, 139, 771
Converge, 887
Conversions between degrees and radians, 286
Convex limaçon, 789
Coordinate(s), 2
polar, 779
Coordinate axes, reflection in, 76
Coordinate conversion, 780
Coordinate planes, 812
xy-plane, 812
xz-plane, 812
yz-plane, 812
Coordinate system
polar, 779
three-dimensional, 812
Correlation coefficient, 104
Correspondence, one-to-one, A1
Cosecant function, 295, 301
of any angle, 312
graph of, 335, 338
Cosine curve, amplitude of, 323
Cosine function, 295, 301
of any angle, 312
common angles, 315
domain of, 297
graph of, 325, 338
inverse, 345
period of, 324
range of, 297
special angles, 303
Cotangent function, 295, 301
of any angle, 312
graph of, 334, 338
Coterminal angles, 282
Cramer's Rule, 619, 620
Critical numbers, 197, 201
Cross multiplying, A48

Cross product
algebraic properties of, 828, 847
determinant form of, 827
geometric properties of, 829, 848
of two vectors in space, 827
Cryptogram, 625
Cube of a binomial, A25
Cube root, A14
Cubic function, 68
Curtate cycloid, 778
Curve
butterfly, 810
plane, 771
rose, 788, 789
sine, 321
Cycloid, 775
curtate, 778

D

Damping factor, 337
Decreasing function, 57
Defined, 47
Definitions of trigonometric functions of any angle, 312
Degenerate conic, 735
Degree, 285
conversion to radians, 286
of a polynomial, A23
DeMoivre's Theorem, 474
Denominator, A5
rationalizing, 384, A16, A17
Dependent system of linear equations, 510
Dependent variable, 42, 47
Depreciated costs, 32
Derivative, 878
Descartes's Rule of Signs, 176
Determinant
of a matrix, 606, 611, 614
of a 2×2 matrix, 611
Determinant form of the cross product, 827
Diagonal matrix, 601, 618
Diagonal of a polygon, 700
Difference
common, 653
of functions, 84
of limits, 857
quotient, 46, 869, 875, A42
of two squares, A27
of vectors, 449
Differences
first, 680
second, 680
Dimpled limaçon, 789
Direct substitution, 857
Direct variation, 105
as an nth power, 106
Directed line segment, 447
initial point, 447
length of, 447
magnitude, 447
terminal point, 447
Direction angle of a vector, 453
Direction numbers, 834
Direction vector, 834
Directly proportional, 105
to the nth power, 106
Directrix of a parabola, 736
Discrete mathematics, 41
Discriminant, 767
classification of conics by, 767
Distance
between a point and a line, 730, 806
between a point and a plane, 840
between two points
in the plane, 4
on the real number line, A4
Distance Formula, 4
in space, 813
Distinguishable permutations, 695
Distributive Property
for complex numbers, 164
for matrices, 590, 594
for real numbers, A6
Diverge, 887
Dividing out technique, 863
Division
of fractions, A7
long, 153
of real numbers, A5
synthetic, 156
Division Algorithm, 154
Divisors, A7
Domain
of an algebraic expression, A36
of cosine function, 297
of a function, 40, 47
implied, 44, 47
of a rational function, 184
of sine function, 297
Dot product, 460
properties of, 460, 492
of vectors in space, 820
Double-angle formulas, 407, 425
Double inequality, A63
Doyle Log Rule, 505

E

Eccentricity
of a conic, 793
of an ellipse, 748, 793
of a hyperbola, 793
of a parabola, 793
Effective yield, 251
Elementary row operations, 574
Eliminating the parameter, 773
Elimination
Gaussian, 520
with back-substitution, 578
Gauss-Jordan, 579
method of, 507, 508
Ellipse, 744, 793
center of, 744
classifying
by the discriminant, 767
by general equation, 759
eccentricity of, 748, 793
foci of, 744
latus rectum of, 752
major axis of, 744
minor axis of, 744
standard form of the equation of, 745
vertices of, 744
Endpoints of an interval, A2
Entry of a matrix, 572
main diagonal, 572
Epicycloid, 778
Equal matrices, 587
Equality
of complex numbers, 162
properties of, A6
of vectors, 448
in space, 820
Equating the coefficients, 536
Equation(s), 14, A46
basic, 534
conditional, A46
equivalent, A47
generating, A47
graph of, 14
identity, A46
of a line, 25
general form, 33
intercept form, 36
point-slope form, 29, 33
slope-intercept form, 25, 33
summary of, 33
two-point form, 29, 33, 624
linear, 16
in one variable, A46
in two variables, 25

parametric, 771
of a plane
general form, 836
standard form, 836
position, 525
quadratic, 16, A49
second-degree polynomial, A49
solution of, 14, A46
solution point, 14
sphere, standard form, 814
symmetric, 834
system of, 496
in two variables, 14
Equilibrium point, 514, 546
Equivalent
equations, A47
generating, A47
expressions, A36
fractions, A7
generating, A7
inequalities, A61
systems, 509
operations that produce, 520
Evaluate an algebraic expression, A5
Evaluating trigonometric functions of any angle, 315
Even function, 60
trigonometric functions, 298
Even/odd identities, 374
Event(s), 701
complement of, 708
probability of, 708
independent, 707
probability of, 707
mutually exclusive, 705
probability of, 702
the union of two, 705
Existence of a limit, 867
Existence theorems, 169
Expanding
a binomial, 686
by cofactors, 614
Expected value, 726
Experiment, 701
outcome of, 701
sample space of, 701
Exponent(s), A11
properties of, A11
rational, A18
Exponential decay model, 257
Exponential equation, solving, 246
Exponential form, A11
Exponential function, 218
f with base *a*, 218
natural, 222
one-to-one property, 220
Exponential growth model, 257
Exponential notation, A11
Exponentiating, 249
Expression
algebraic, A5
fractional, A36
rational, A36
Extended principle of mathematical induction, 675
Extracting square roots, A49
Extraneous solution, A48, A54

F

Factor Theorem, 157, 213
Factorial, 644
Factoring, A26
completely, A26
by grouping, A30
polynomials, guidelines for, A30
solving a quadratic equation by, A49
special polynomial forms, A27
Factors
of an integer, A7
of a polynomial, 173, 214
Family of functions, 75
Far point, 216
Feasible solutions, 552
Finding a formula for the *n*th term of a sequence, 678
Finding intercepts of a graph, 17
Finding an inverse function, 97
Finding an inverse matrix, 604
Finding test intervals for a polynomial, 197
Finite sequence, 642
Finite series, 647
First differences, 680
Fixed cost, 31
Fixed point, 397
Focal chord
latus rectum, 738
of a parabola, 738
Focus (foci)
of an ellipse, 744
of a hyperbola, 753
of a parabola, 736
FOIL Method, A24
Formula(s)
change-of-base, 239
for compound interest, 224
double-angle, 407, 425
half-angle, 410
Heron's Area, 442, 491
for the *n*th term of a sequence, 678
power-reducing, 409, 425
product-to-sum, 411
Quadratic, A49
reduction, 402
sum and difference, 400, 424
summation, 892
sum-to-product, 412, 426
Four ways to represent a function, 41
Fractal, 726
Fraction(s)
addition of
with like denominators, A7
with unlike denominators, A7
complex, A40
division of, A7
equivalent, A7
generating, A7
multiplication of, A7
operations of, A7
partial, 533
decomposition, 533
properties of, A7
rules of signs for, A7
subtraction of
with like denominators, A7
with unlike denominators, A7
Fractional expression, A36
Frequency, 356
Function(s), 40, 47
algebraic, 218
arithmetic combination of, 84
characteristics of, 40
common logarithmic, 230
composition, 86
constant, 57, 67
continuous, 139, 771
cosecant, 295, 301
cosine, 295, 301
cotangent, 295, 301
cubic, 68
decreasing, 57
defined, 47
derivative of, 878
difference of, 84
domain of, 40, 47
even, 60
exponential, 218
family of, 75
four ways to represent, 41
graph of, 54
greatest integer, 69
of half-angles, 407
Heaviside, 126
identity, 67

implied domain of, 44, 47
increasing, 57
inverse, 93, 94
cosine, 345
sine, 343, 345
tangent, 345
trigonometric, 345
linear, 66
logarithmic, 229
of multiple angles, 407
name of, 42, 47
natural exponential, 222
natural logarithmic, 233
notation, 42, 47
objective, 552
odd, 60
one-to-one, 96
period of, 297
periodic, 297
piecewise-defined, 43
polynomial, 128
power, 140
product of, 84
quadratic, 128
quotient of, 84
range of, 40, 47
rational, 184
reciprocal, 68
secant, 295, 301
sine, 295, 301
square root, 68
squaring, 67
step, 69
sum of, 84
summary of terminology, 47
tangent, 295, 301
transcendental, 218
trigonometric, 295, 301, 312
undefined, 47
value of, 42, 47
Vertical Line Test, 55
zero of, 56
Fundamental Counting Principle, 692
Fundamental Theorem
of Algebra, 169
of Arithmetic, A7
Fundamental trigonometric identities, 304, 374

G

Gaussian elimination, 520
with back-substitution, 578
Gaussian model, 257
Gauss-Jordan elimination, 579
General form
of the equation of a line, 33
of the equation of a plane, 836
Generalizations about *n*th roots of real numbers, A15
Generating equivalent equations, A47
Generating equivalent fractions, A7
Geometric properties of the cross product, 829, 848
Geometric property of the triple scalar product, 831
Geometric sequence, 663
common ratio of, 663
*n*th term of, 664
sum of a finite, 666, 723
Geometric series, 667
sum of an infinite, 667
Graph, 14
of cosecant function, 335, 338
of cosine function, 325, 338
of cotangent function, 334, 338
of an equation, 14
of a function, 54
of an inequality, 541, A60
in two variables, 541
intercepts of, 17
of inverse cosine function, 345
of an inverse function, 95
of inverse sine function, 345
of inverse tangent function, 345
of a line, 25
point-plotting method, 15
of a rational function, guidelines for analyzing, 187
of secant function, 335, 338
of sine function, 325, 338
slope of, 875
special polar, 789
symmetry, 18
of tangent function, 332, 338
Graphical interpretations of solutions, 510
Graphical method, 500
Graphical tests for symmetry, 18
Greatest integer function, 69
Guidelines
for analyzing graphs of rational functions, 187
for factoring polynomials, A30
for solving the basic equation, 538
for verifying trigonometric identities, 382

H

Half-angle formulas, 410
Half-life, 225
Harmonic motion, simple, 356, 357
Heaviside function, 126
Heron's Area Formula, 442, 491
Horizontal asymptote, 185
Horizontal components of v, 452
Horizontal line, 33
Horizontal Line Test, 96
Horizontal shift, 74
Horizontal shrink, 78
of a trigonometric function, 324
Horizontal stretch, 78
of a trigonometric function, 324
Horizontal translation of a trigonometric function, 325
Human memory model, 235
Hyperbola, 185, 753, 793
asymptotes of, 755
branches of, 753
center of, 753
classifying
by the discriminant, 767
by general equation, 759
conjugate axis of, 755
eccentricity of, 793
foci of, 753
standard form of the equation of, 753
transverse axis of, 753
vertices of, 753
Hypocycloid, 810
Hypotenuse of a right triangle, 301

I

Idempotent square matrix, 639
Identity, A46
function, 67
limit of, 857
matrix of order *n*, 594
Imaginary axis of the complex plane, 470
Imaginary number, 162
pure, 162
Imaginary part of a complex number, 162
Imaginary unit *i*, 162
Implied domain, 44, 47
Improper rational expression, 154
Inclination, 728
and slope, 728, 806
Inclusive or, A7
Inconsistent system of linear equations, 510
Increasing annuity, 668
Increasing function, 57

Independent events, 707
  probability of, 707
Independent system of linear equations, 510
Independent variable, 42, 47
Indeterminate form, 863
Index
  of a radical, A14
  of summation, 646
Indirect proof, 568
Inductive, 614
Inequality (inequalities), A2
  absolute value, solution of, A63
  double, A63
  equivalent, A61
  graph of, 541, A60
  linear, 542, A62
  properties of, A61
  satisfy, A60
  solution of, 541, A60
  solution set of, A60
  symbol, A2
Infinite geometric series, 667
  sum of, 667
Infinite sequence, 642
Infinite series, 647
Infinite wedge, 545
Infinity
  limit at, 883, 884
    rational functions, 886
  negative, A3
  positive, A3
Initial point, 447
Initial side of an angle, 282
Integer(s)
  divisors of, A7
  factors of, A7
  irreducible over, A26
Intercept form of the equation of a line, 36
Intercepts, 17
  finding, 17
Intermediate Value Theorem, 146
Interval(s)
  bounded, A2
  on the real number line, A2
  unbounded, A3
Invariant under rotation, 767
Inverse
  additive, A5
  multiplicative, A5
Inverse function, 93
  cosine, 345
  definition of, 94
  finding, 97
  graph of, 95
  Horizontal Line Test, 96
  sine, 343, 345
  tangent, 345
Inverse of a matrix, 602
  finding an, 604
Inverse properties
  of logarithms, 230
  of natural logarithms, 234
  of trigonometric functions, 347
Inverse trigonometric functions, 345
Inverse variation, 107
Inversely proportional, 107
Invertible matrix, 603
Irrational number, A1
Irreducible
  over the integers, A26
  over the rationals, 174
  over the reals, 174

J

Joint variation, 108
Jointly proportional, 108

K

Kepler's Laws, 796
Key points
  of the graph of a trigonometric function, 322
  intercepts, 322
  maximum points, 322
  minimum points, 322

L

Latus rectum
  of an ellipse, 752
  of a parabola, 738
Law of Cosines, 439, 490
  alternative form of, 439, 490
  standard form of, 439, 490
Law of Sines, 430, 489
Law of Trichotomy, A3
Leading coefficient of a polynomial, A23
Leading Coefficient Test, 141
Least squares regression line, 104
Left-handed orientation, 812
Lemniscate, 789
Length of a directed line segment, 447
Length of a vector, 448
  in space, 820
Like radicals, A17
Like terms of a polynomial, A24
Limaçon, 786, 789
  convex, 789
  dimpled, 789
  with inner loop, 789
Limit(s), 853
  basic, 857
  of a constant function, 857
  converge, 887
  difference of, 857
  diverge, 887
  evaluating
    direct substitution, 857
    dividing out technique, 863
    rationalizing technique, 865
  existence of, 867
  of the identity function, 857
  indeterminate form, 863
  at infinity, 883, 884
    rational functions, 886
  nonexistence of, 856
  one-sided, 867
  of a polynomial function, 749
  of polynomial and rational functions, 907
  power of, 857
  of a power function, 857, 907
  product of, 857
  properties of, 857
  quotient of, 857
  of a radical function, 857
  of a rational function, 749
  scalar multiple of, 857
  of a sequence, 887
  sum of, 857
Line in space
  parametric equations of, 834
  symmetric, 834
Line(s) in the plane
  graph of, 25
  horizontal, 33
  inclination of, 728
  least squares regression, 104
  normal, 908
  parallel, 30
  perpendicular, 30
  secant, 875
  slope of, 25, 27
  tangent, 873, 883
  vertical, 33
Linear combination of vectors, 452
Linear depreciation, 32
Linear equation, 16
  general form, 33
  intercept form, 36
  in one variable, A46
  point-slope form, 29, 33
  slope-intercept form, 25, 33

summary of, 33
two-point form, 29, 182, 624
in two variables, 25
Linear extrapolation, 33
Linear Factorization Theorem, 169, 214
Linear function, 66
Linear inequality, 542, A62
Linear interpolation, 33
Linear programming, 552
problem, solving, 553
Linear speed, 287
Local maximum, 58
Local minimum, 58
Locus, 735
Logarithm(s)
change-of-base formula, 239
natural, properties of, 234, 240, 278
inverse, 234
one-to-one, 234
power, 278
product, 240, 278
quotient, 240, 278
properties of, 230, 240, 278
inverse, 230
one-to-one, 230
power, 240, 278
product, 240, 278
quotient, 240, 278
Logarithmic equation, solving, 246
Logarithmic function, 229
with base *a*, 229
common, 230
natural, 233
Logarithmic model, 257
Logistic
curve, 262
growth model, 257
Long division, 153
Lower bound, 177
Lower limit of summation, 646

M

Magnitude
of a directed line segment, 447
of a vector, 448
in space, 820
Main diagonal of a square matrix, 572
Major axis of an ellipse, 744
Marginal cost, 31
Mathematical induction, 673
extended principle of, 675
Principle of, 674
Matrix (matrices), 572
addition, 588
properties of, 590
additive identity, 591
adjoining, 604
augmented, 573
coded row, 625
coefficient, 573
cofactor of, 613
column, 572
determinant of, 606, 611, 614
diagonal, 601, 618
elementary row operations, 574
entry of a, 572
equal, 587
idempotent, 639
identity, 594
inverse of, 602
invertible, 603
minor of, 613
multiplication, 592
properties of, 594
nonsingular, 603
order of a, 572
in reduced row-echelon form, 576
representation of, 587
row, 572
in row-echelon form, 576
row-equivalent, 574
scalar identity, 590
scalar multiplication, 588
singular, 603
square, 572
stochastic, 599
transpose of, 640
uncoded row, 625
zero, 591
Measure of an angle, 283
degree, 285
radian, 283
Method
of elimination, 507, 508
of substitution, 496
Midpoint Formula, 5, 124
in space, 813
Midpoint of a line segment, 5
Minor axis of an ellipse, 744
Minor of a matrix, 613
Minors and cofactors of a square matrix, 613
Modulus of a complex number, 471
Moment, 849
Monomial, A23
Multiplication
of fractions, A7
of matrices, 592
scalar, 588
Multiplicative identity of a real number, A6
Multiplicative inverse, A5
for a matrix, 602
of a real number, A6
Multiplicity, 143
Multiplier effect, 671
Mutually exclusive events, 705

N

n factorial, 644
Name of a function, 42, 47
Natural base, 222
Natural exponential function, 222
Natural logarithm
properties of, 234, 240, 278
inverse, 234
one-to-one, 234
power, 240, 278
product, 240, 278
quotient, 240, 278
Natural logarithmic function, 233
Near point, 216
Negation, properties of, A6
Negative
angle, 282
infinity, A3
of a vector, 449
Newton's Law of Cooling, 268
Nonexistence of a limit, 856
Nonnegative number, A1
Nonrigid transformation, 78
Nonsingular matrix, 603
Nonsquare system of linear equations, 524
Normal line, 908
Normal vector, 836
Normally distributed, 261
Notation
exponential, A11
function, 42, 47
scientific, A13
sigma, 646
summation, 646
*n*th partial sum, 647
of an arithmetic sequence, 657
*n*th root(s)
of *a*, A14
of a complex number, 475, 476
generalizations about, A15
principal, A14
of unity, 477
*n*th term
of an arithmetic sequence, 654
recursion form, 654

of a geometric sequence, 664
of a sequence, finding a formula for, 678
Number(s)
complex, 162
composite, A7
critical, 197, 201
direction, 834
imaginary, 162
pure, 162
irrational, A1
nonnegative, A1
prime, A7
rational, A1
real, A1
Number of permutations of *n* elements, 693
taken *r* at a time, 694
Number of solutions of a linear system, 522
Numerator, A5

O

Objective function, 552
Oblique asymptote, 190
Oblique triangles, 430
area of, 434
Obtuse angle, 283
Octant, 812
Odd function, 60
trigonometric functions, 298
One cycle of a sine curve, 321
One-sided limit, 867
One-to-one correspondence, A1
One-to-one function, 96
One-to-one property
of exponential functions, 220
of logarithms, 230
of natural logarithms, 234
Operations of fractions, A7
Operations that produce equivalent systems, 520
Opposite side of a right triangle, 301
Optimal solution of a linear programming problem, 552
Optimization, 552
Order of a matrix, 572
Order on the real number line, A2
Ordered pair, 2
Ordered triple, 519
Orientation of a curve, 772
Origin, 2
of the polar coordinate system, 779
of the real number line, A1
symmetry, 18
Orthogonal vectors, 462
in space, 821
Outcome, 701

P

Parabola, 128, 736, 793
axis of, 129, 736
classifying
by the discriminant, 767
by general equation, 759
directrix of, 736
eccentricity of, 793
focal chord of, 738
focus of, 736
latus rectum of, 738
reflective property, 738
standard form of the equation of, 736, 807
tangent line, 738
vertex of, 129, 133, 736
Parallel lines, 30
Parallel vectors in space, 822
Parallelogram law, 449
Parameter, 771
eliminating the, 773
Parametric equations, 771
of a line in space, 834
Partial fraction, 533
decomposition, 533
Pascal's Triangle, 685
Perfect
cube, A15
square, A15
square trinomial, A27, A28
Perihelion distance, 798
Perimeter, common formulas for, 7
Period
of a function, 297
of sine and cosine functions, 324
Periodic function, 297
Permutation, 693
distinguishable, 695
of *n* elements, 693
taken *r* at a time, 694
Perpendicular lines, 30
Phase shift, 325
Piecewise-defined function, 43
Plane(s)
angle between two, 837
general form of the equation of, 836
standard form of the equation of, 836
trace of, 839
Plane curve, 771
orientation of, 772
Point
of diminishing returns, 151
equilibrium, 514, 546
Point-plotting method, 15
Point-slope form, 29, 33
Points of intersection, 500
Polar axis, 779
Polar coordinate system, 779
origin of, 779
pole, 779
Polar coordinates, 779
conversion to rectangular, 780
quick tests for symmetry in, 787
test for symmetry in, 786
Polar equations of conics, 793, 808
Polar form of a complex number, 471
Pole, 779
Polynomial(s), A23
coefficient of, A23
completely factored, A26
constant term, A23
degree of, A23
equation, second-degree, A49
factors of, 173, 214
finding test intervals for, 197
guidelines for factoring, A30
irreducible, A26
leading coefficient of, A23
like terms, A24
long division of, 153
prime, A26
prime factor, 174
standard form of, A23
synthetic division, 156
test intervals for, 144
Polynomial function, 128
limit of, 749, 907
real zeros of, 143
standard form of, 142
of *x* with degree *n*, 128
Polynomial inequality, test intervals, 197
Position equation, 525
Positive
angle, 282
infinity, A3
Power, A11
Power function, 140
limit of, 857, 907
Power of a limit, 857
Power property
of logarithms, 240, 278
of natural logarithms, 240, 278
Power-reducing formulas, 409, 425

Prime
factor of a polynomial, 174
factorization, A7
number, A7
polynomial, A26
Principal *n*th root
of *a*, A14
of a number, A14
Principal square root of a negative number, 166
Principle of Mathematical Induction, 674
Probability
of a complement, 708
of an event, 702
of independent events, 707
of the union of two events, 705
Producer surplus, 546
Product
of functions, 84
of limits, 857
of trigonometric functions, 407
of two complex numbers, 472
Product property
of logarithms, 240, 278
of natural logarithms, 240, 278
Product-to-sum formulas, 411
Projection, of a vector, 464
Proof, 124
by contradiction, 568
indirect, 568
without words, 638
Proper rational expression, 154
Properties
of absolute value, A4
of the cross product
algebraic, 828, 847
geometric, 829, 848
of the dot product, 460, 492
of equality, A6
of exponents, A11
of fractions, A7
of inequalities, A61
of inverse trigonometric functions, 347
of limits, 857
of logarithms, 230, 240, 278
inverse, 230
one-to-one, 230
power, 240, 278
product, 240, 278
quotient, 240, 278
of matrix addition and scalar multiplication, 590
of matrix multiplication, 594
of natural logarithms, 234, 240, 278
inverse, 234
one-to-one, 234
power, 240, 278
product, 240, 278
quotient, 240, 278
of negation, A6
one-to-one, exponential functions, 220
of radicals, A15
reflective, 738
summation, 892
of sums, 646, 722
of vector addition and scalar multiplication, 451
of zero, A7
Pure imaginary number, 162
Pythagorean identities, 304, 374
Pythagorean Theorem, 4, 370

Q

Quadrant, 2
Quadratic equation, 16, A49
solving
by completing the square, A49
by extracting square roots, A49
by factoring, A49
using the Quadratic Formula, A49
using the Square Root Principle, A49
Quadratic Formula, A49
Quadratic function, 128
standard form of, 131
Quick tests for symmetry in polar coordinates, 787
Quotient
difference, 46, 869, 875
of functions, 84
of limits, 857
of two complex numbers, 472
Quotient identities, 304, 374
Quotient property
of logarithms, 240, 278
of natural logarithms, 240, 278

R

Radian, 283
conversion to degrees, 286
Radical
index of, A14
like, A17
properties of, A15
simplest form, A16
symbol, A14
Radical function, limit of, 857
Radicand, A14
Radius of a circle, 20
Random selection
with replacement, 691
without replacement, 691
Range of a function, 40, 47
Rate, 31
Rate of change, 31
average, 59
Ratio, 31
Rational exponent, A18
Rational expression(s), A36
improper, 154
proper, 154
Rational function, 184
asymptotes of, 186
domain of, 184
graph of, guidelines for analyzing, 187
limit of, 749
at infinity, 886
test intervals for, 187
Rational inequality, test intervals, 201
Rational number, A1
Rational Zero Test, 170
Rationalizing a denominator, 384, A16, A17
Rationalizing technique, 865
Real axis of the complex plane, 470
Real number(s), A1
absolute value of, A4
division of, A5
subset of, A1
subtraction of, A5
Real number line, A1
bounded intervals on, A2
distance between two points, A4
interval on, A2
order on, A2
origin, A1
unbounded intervals on, A3
Real part of a complex number, 162
Real zeros of polynomial functions, 143
Reciprocal function, 68
Reciprocal identities, 304, 374
Rectangular coordinate system, 2
Rectangular coordinates, conversion to polar, 780
Recursion form of the *n*th term of an arithmetic sequence, 654
Recursion formula, 655
Recursive sequence, 644
Reduced row-echelon form, of a matrix, 576
Reducible over the reals, 174
Reduction formulas, 402

Reference angle, 314
Reflection, 76
  of a trigonometric function, 324
Reflective property of a parabola, 738
Relation, 40
Relative maximum, 58
Relative minimum, 58
Remainder Theorem, 157, 213
Repeated zero, 143
Representation of matrices, 587
Resultant of vector addition, 449
Right-handed orientation, 812
Right triangle
  definitions of trigonometric functions, 301
  hypotenuse of, 301
  opposite side of, 301
  right side of, 301
  solving, 306
Rigid transformation, 78
Root(s)
  of a complex number, 475, 476
  cube, A14
  principal *n*th, A14
  square, A14
Rose curve, 788, 789
Rotation
  of axes, 763
    to eliminate an *xy*-term, 763
  invariants, 767
Row-echelon form, 519
  of a matrix, 576
  reduced, 576
Row-equivalent, 574
Row matrix, 572
Row operations, 520
Rules of signs for fractions, A7

S

Sample space, 701
Satisfy the inequality, A60
Scalar, 588
  identity, 590
Scalar multiple, 588
  of a limit, 857
  of a vector in space, 820
Scalar multiplication, 588
  properties of, 590
  of a vector, 449
    properties of, 451
Scatter plot, 3
Scientific notation, A13
Scribner Log Rule, 505
Secant function, 295, 301
  of any angle, 312
  graph of, 335, 338
Secant line, 59, 875
Second-degree polynomial equation, A49
Second differences, 680
Sector of a circle, 289
  area of, 289
Sequence, 642
  arithmetic, 653
  finite, 642
  first differences of, 680
  geometric, 663
  infinite, 642
  limit of, 887
  *n*th partial sum, 647
  recursive, 644
  second differences of, 680
  terms of, 642
Series, 647
  finite, 647
  geometric, 667
  infinite, 647
    geometric, 667
Sierpinski Triangle, 726
Sigma notation, 646
Sigmoidal curve, 262
Simple harmonic motion, 356, 357
  frequency, 356
Simplest form, A16
Sine curve, 321
  amplitude of, 323
  one cycle of, 321
Sine function, 295, 301
  of any angle, 312
  common angles, 315
  curve, 321
  domain of, 297
  graph of, 325, 338
  inverse, 343, 345
  period of, 324
  range of, 297
  special angles, 303
Sines, cosines, and tangents of special angles, 303
Singular matrix, 603
Sketching the graph of an equation by point plotting, 15
Sketching the graph of an inequality in two variables, 541
Slant asymptote, 190
Slope, 834
  of a graph, 875
  inclination, 728, 806
  of a line, 25, 27
Slope-intercept form, 25, 33
Solid analytic geometry, 812
Solution(s)
  of an absolute value inequality, A63
  of an equation, 14, A46
  extraneous, A48, A54
  of an inequality, 541, A60
  of a system of equations, 496
    graphical interpretations, 510
  of a system of inequalities, 543
Solution point, 14
Solution set, A60
Solving
  an absolute value inequality, A63
  an equation, A46
  exponential and logarithmic equations, 246
  an inequality, A60
  a linear programming problem, 553
  right triangles, 306
  a system of equations, 496
    Gaussian elimination with back-substitution, 578
    Gauss-Jordan elimination, 579
    graphical method, 500
    method of elimination, 507, 508
    method of substitution, 496
  a system of linear equations
    Cramer's Rule, 619, 620
    Gaussian elimination, 520
Space
  Distance Formula in, 813
  Midpoint Formula in, 813
  surface in, 815
  vector in, 820
Special products, A25
Sphere, 814
  standard equation of, 814
Square
  of a binomial, A25
  of trigonometric functions, 407
Square matrix, 572
  determinant of, 614
  idempotent, 639
  main diagonal of, 572
  minors and cofactors of, 613
Square root(s), A14
  extracting, A49
  function, 68
  of a negative number, 166
Square Root Principle, A49
Square system of linear equations, 524
Squaring function, 67
Standard equation of a sphere, 814
Standard form
  of a complex number, 162
  of the equation of a circle, 20

of the equation of an ellipse, 745
of the equation of a hyperbola, 753
of the equation of a parabola, 736, 807
of the equation of a plane, 836
of the Law of Cosines, 439, 490
of a polynomial, A23
of a polynomial function, 142
of a quadratic function, 131
Standard position
of an angle, 282
of a vector, 448
Standard unit vector, 452
notation in space, 820
Step function, 69
Stochastic matrix, 599
Straight-line depreciation, 32
Strategies for solving exponential and logarithmic equations, 246
Strophoid, 810
Subset, A1
Substitution, method of, 496
Substitution Principle, A5
Subtraction
of a complex number, 163
of fractions
with like denominators, A7
with unlike denominators, A7
of real numbers, A5
Sum(s)
of a finite arithmetic sequence, 656, 723
of a finite geometric sequence, 666, 723
of functions, 84
of an infinite geometric series, 667
of limits, 857
*n*th partial, 647
of powers of integers, 679
properties of, 646, 722
of square differences, 104
of vectors in space, 820
Sum and difference formulas, 400, 424
Sum and difference of same terms, A25
Sum or difference of two cubes, A27
Summary
of equations of lines, 33
of function terminology, 47
Summation
formulas and properties, 892
index of, 646
lower limit of, 646
notation, 646
upper limit of, 646
Sum-to-product formulas, 412, 426
Supplementary angles, 285
Surface in space, 815
trace of, 816
Surplus
consumer, 546
producer, 546
Symmetric equations of a line in space, 834
Symmetry, 18
algebraic tests for, 19
graphical tests for, 18
quick tests for, in polar coordinates, 787
test for, in polar coordinates, 786
with respect to the origin, 18
with respect to the *x*-axis, 18
with respect to the *y*-axis, 18
Synthetic division, 156
uses of the remainder, 158
System of equations, 496
equivalent, 509
solution of, 496
with a unique solution, 607
System of inequalities, solution of, 543
System of linear equations
consistent, 510
dependent, 510
inconsistent, 510
independent, 510
nonsquare, 524
number of solutions, 522
row-echelon form, 519
row operations, 520
square, 524

T

Tangent function, 295, 301
of any angle, 312
common angles, 315
graph of, 332, 338
inverse, 345
special angles, 303
Tangent line, 873, 883
to a parabola, 738
Term
of an algebraic expression, A5
constant, A5, A23
of a sequence, 642
variable, A5
Terminal point, 447
Terminal side of an angle, 282
Test
for collinear points, 623
intervals
for a polynomial, 144
for a polynomial inequality, 197
for a rational function, 187
for a rational inequality, 201
for symmetry in polar coordinates, 786
Three-dimensional coordinate system, 812
left-handed orientation, 812
octant, 812
right-handed orientation, 812
Torque, 849
Trace
of a plane, 839
of a surface, 816
Transcendental function, 218
Transformation
nonrigid, 78
rigid, 78
Transpose of a matrix, 640
Transverse axis of a hyperbola, 753
Triangle
area of, 622
oblique, 430
area of, 434
Trigonometric form
argument of, 471
of a complex number, 471
modulus of, 471
Trigonometric function
of any angle, 312
evaluating, 315
cosecant, 295, 301
cosine, 295, 301
cotangent, 295, 301
even and odd, 298
horizontal shrink of, 324
horizontal stretch of, 324
horizontal translation of, 325
inverse properties of, 347
key points, 322
intercepts, 322
maximum points, 322
minimum points, 322
product of, 407
reflection of, 324
right triangle definitions of, 301
secant, 295, 301
sine, 295, 301
square of, 407
tangent, 295, 301
unit circle definitions of, 295
Trigonometric identities
cofunction identities, 374
even/odd identities, 374

fundamental identities, 304, 374
guidelines for verifying, 382
Pythagorean identities, 304, 374
quotient identities, 304, 374
reciprocal identities, 304, 374
Trigonometric values of common angles, 315
Trigonometry, 282
Trinomial, A23
perfect square, A27, A28
Triple scalar product, 831
geometric property of, 831
Two-point form of the equation of a line, 29, 33, 624

U

Unbounded, A60
Unbounded intervals, A3
Uncoded row matrices, 625
Undefined, 47
Unit circle, 294
definitions of trigonometric functions, 295
Unit vector, 448, 621
in the direction of v, 451
in space, in the direction of **v**, 820
standard, 452
Upper bound, 177
Upper limit of summation, 646
Upper and Lower Bound Rules, 177
Uses of the remainder in synthetic division, 158

V

Value of a function, 42, 47
Variable, A5
dependent, 42, 47
independent, 42, 47
term, A5
Variation
combined, 107
constant of, 105
direct, 105
as an *n*th power, 106
inverse, 107
joint, 108
in sign, 176
Vary directly, 105
as *n*th power, 106
Vary inversely, 107
Vary jointly, 108
Vector(s), 834
addition, 449
properties of, 451
resultant of, 449
angle between two, 461, 492
component form of, 448
components of, 463, 464
difference of, 449
directed line segment of, 447
direction of, 834
direction angle of, 453
dot product of, 460
properties of, 460, 492
equality of, 448
horizontal component of, 452
length of, 448
linear combination of, 452
magnitude of, 448
negative of, 449
normal, 836
orthogonal, 462
parallelogram law, 449
projection, 464
resultant, 449
scalar multiplication of, 449
properties of, 451
in space, 820
angle between two, 821
component form of, 820
cross product of, 827
dot product of, 820
equality of, 820
length of, 820
magnitude of, 820
orthogonal, 821
parallel, 822
scalar multiple of, 820
standard unit, 820
sum of, 820
unit, in the direction of **v**, 820
zero, 820
standard position of, 448
unit, 448, 621
in the direction of **v**, 451
standard, 452
v in the plane, 447
vertical component of, 452
zero, 448
Vertex (vertices)
of an angle, 282
of an ellipse, 744
of a hyperbola, 753
of a parabola, 129, 133, 736
Vertical asymptote, 185
Vertical components of **v**, 452
Vertical line, 33
Vertical Line Test, 55
Vertical shift, 74
Vertical shrink, 78
Vertical stretch, 78
Volume, common formulas for, 7

W

With replacement, 691
Without replacement, 691
Work, 466

X

x-axis, 2
symmetry, 18
x-coordinate, 2
xy-plane, 812
xz-plane, 812

Y

y-axis, 2
symmetry, 18
y-coordinate, 2
yz-plane, 812

Z

Zero(s)
of a function, 56
matrix, 591
multiplicity of, 143
of a polynomial function, 143
bounds for, 177
real, 143
properties of, A7
repeated, 143
vector, 448
in space, 820
Zero-Factor Property, A7

GRAPHS OF PARENT FUNCTIONS

Linear Function

$f(x) = mx + b$

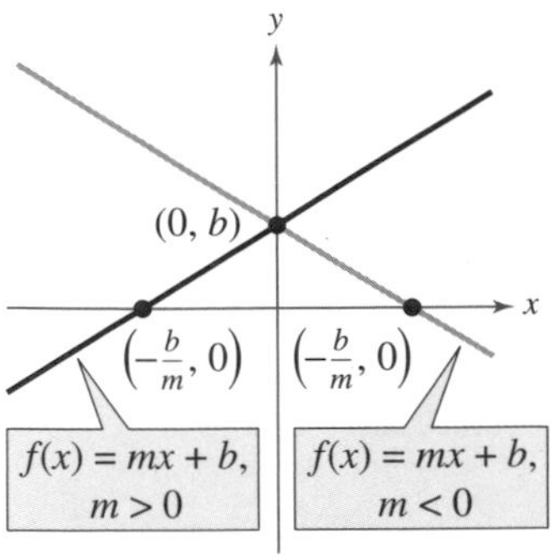

Domain: $(-\infty, \infty)$
Range: $(-\infty, \infty)$
x-intercept: $(-b/m, 0)$
y-intercept: $(0, b)$
Increasing when $m > 0$
Decreasing when $m < 0$

Absolute Value Function

$$f(x) = |x| = \begin{cases} x, & x \ge 0 \\ -x, & x < 0 \end{cases}$$

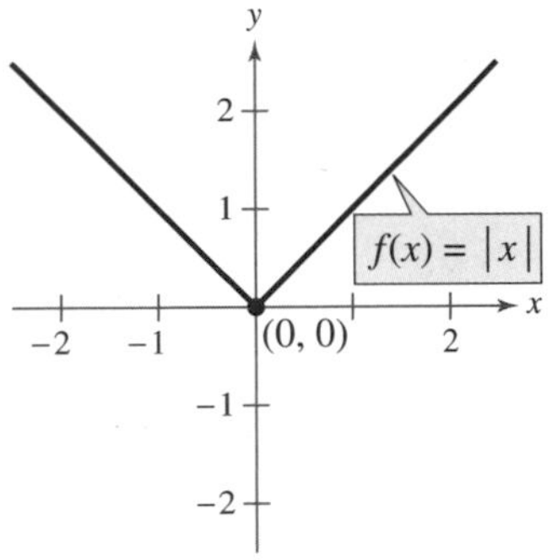

Domain: $(-\infty, \infty)$
Range: $[0, \infty)$
Intercept: $(0, 0)$
Decreasing on $(-\infty, 0)$
Increasing on $(0, \infty)$
Even function
y-axis symmetry

Square Root Function

$f(x) = \sqrt{x}$

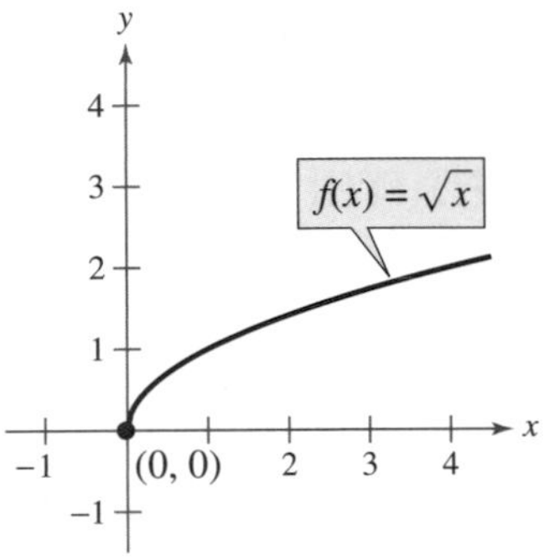

Domain: $[0, \infty)$
Range: $[0, \infty)$
Intercept: $(0, 0)$
Increasing on $(0, \infty)$

Greatest Integer Function

$f(x) = [\![x]\!]$

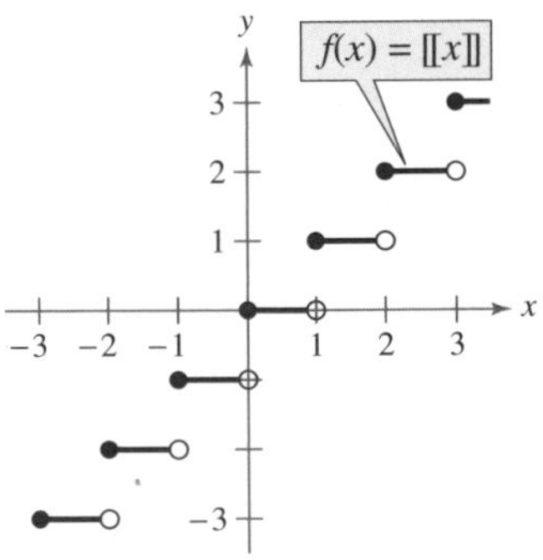

Domain: $(-\infty, \infty)$
Range: the set of integers
x-intercepts: in the interval $[0, 1)$
y-intercept: $(0, 0)$
Constant between each pair of consecutive integers
Jumps vertically one unit at each integer value

Quadratic (Squaring) Function

$f(x) = ax^2$

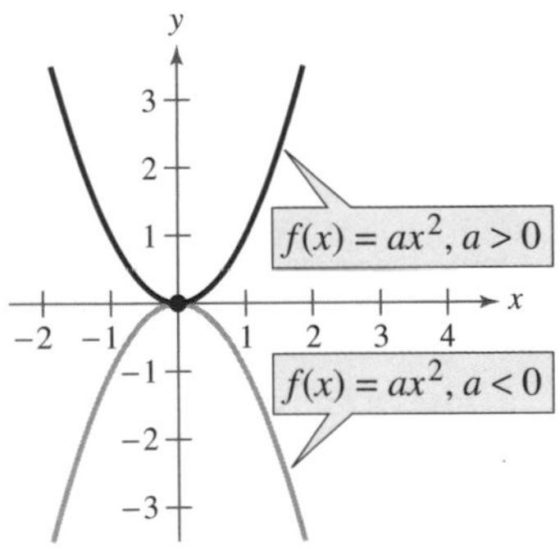

Domain: $(-\infty, \infty)$
Range $(a > 0)$: $[0, \infty)$
Range $(a < 0)$: $(-\infty, 0]$
Intercept: $(0, 0)$
Decreasing on $(-\infty, 0)$ for $a > 0$
Increasing on $(0, \infty)$ for $a > 0$
Increasing on $(-\infty, 0)$ for $a < 0$
Decreasing on $(0, \infty)$ for $a < 0$
Even function
y-axis symmetry
Relative minimum $(a > 0)$, relative maximum $(a < 0)$, or vertex: $(0, 0)$

Cubic Function

$f(x) = x^3$

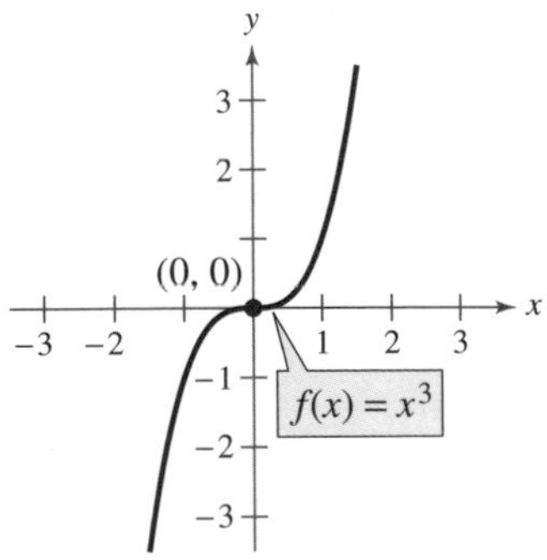

Domain: $(-\infty, \infty)$
Range: $(-\infty, \infty)$
Intercept: $(0, 0)$
Increasing on $(-\infty, \infty)$
Odd function
Origin symmetry

Rational (Reciprocal) Function

$f(x) = \dfrac{1}{x}$

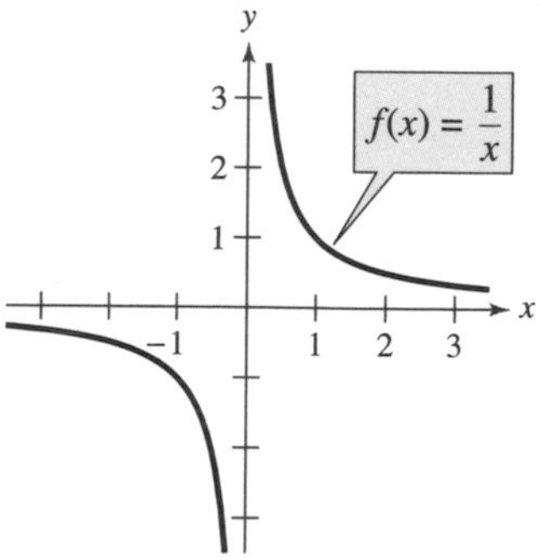

Domain: $(-\infty, 0) \cup (0, \infty)$
Range: $(-\infty, 0) \cup (0, \infty)$
No intercepts
Decreasing on $(-\infty, 0)$ and $(0, \infty)$
Odd function
Origin symmetry
Vertical asymptote: y-axis
Horizontal asymptote: x-axis

Exponential Function

$f(x) = a^x,\ a > 0,\ a \neq 1$

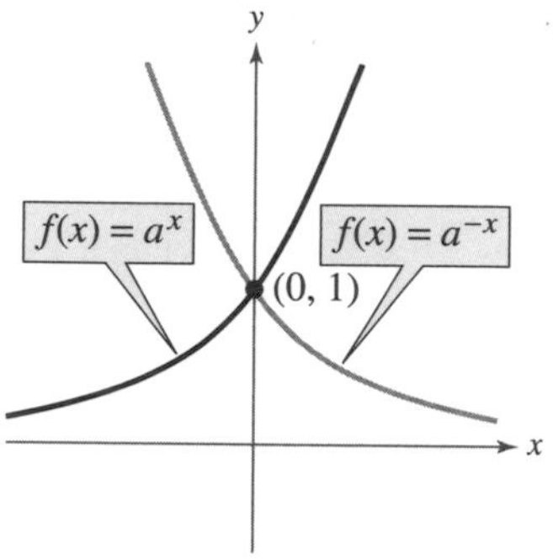

Domain: $(-\infty, \infty)$
Range: $(0, \infty)$
Intercept: $(0, 1)$
Increasing on $(-\infty, \infty)$
 for $f(x) = a^x$
Decreasing on $(-\infty, \infty)$
 for $f(x) = a^{-x}$
Horizontal asymptote: x-axis
Continuous

Logarithmic Function

$f(x) = \log_a x,\ a > 0,\ a \neq 1$

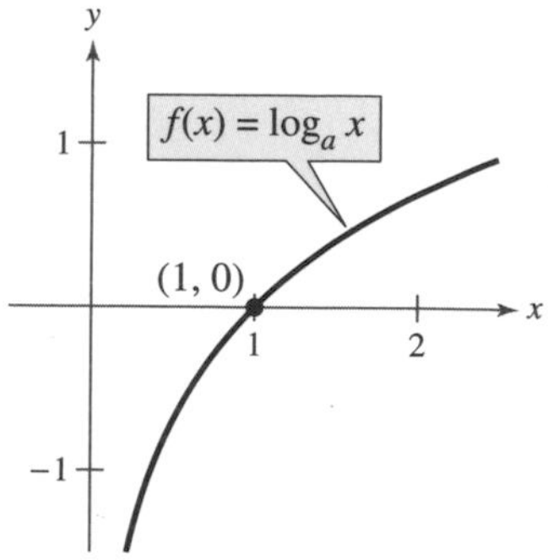

Domain: $(0, \infty)$
Range: $(-\infty, \infty)$
Intercept: $(1, 0)$
Increasing on $(0, \infty)$
Vertical asymptote: y-axis
Continuous
Reflection of graph of $f(x) = a^x$
 in the line $y = x$

Sine Function

$f(x) = \sin x$

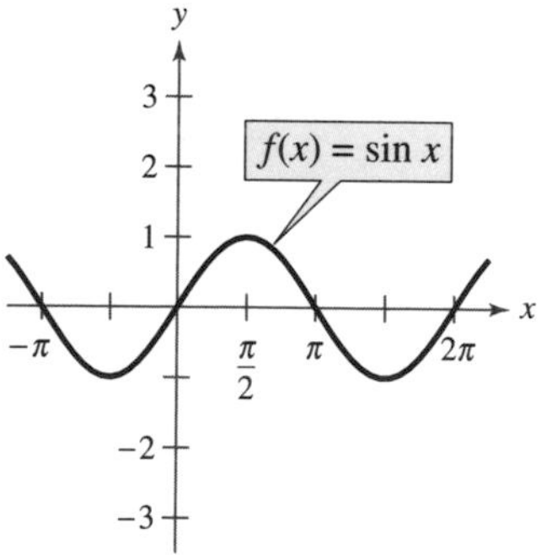

Domain: $(-\infty, \infty)$
Range: $[-1, 1]$
Period: 2π
x-intercepts: $(n\pi, 0)$
y-intercept: $(0, 0)$
Odd function
Origin symmetry

Cosine Function

$f(x) = \cos x$

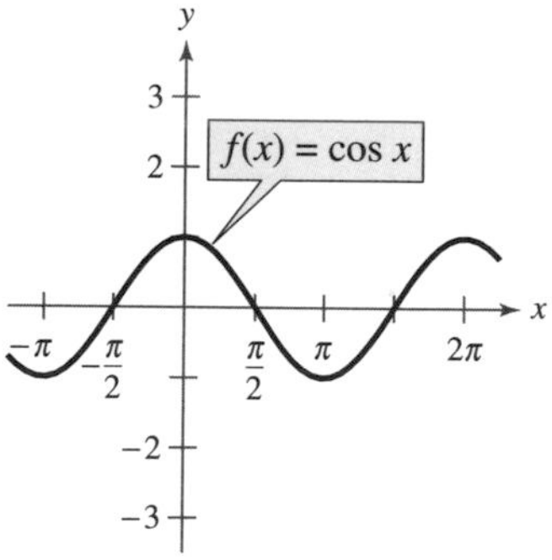

Domain: $(-\infty, \infty)$
Range: $[-1, 1]$
Period: 2π
x-intercepts: $\left(\dfrac{\pi}{2} + n\pi, 0\right)$
y-intercept: $(0, 1)$
Even function
y-axis symmetry

Tangent Function

$f(x) = \tan x$

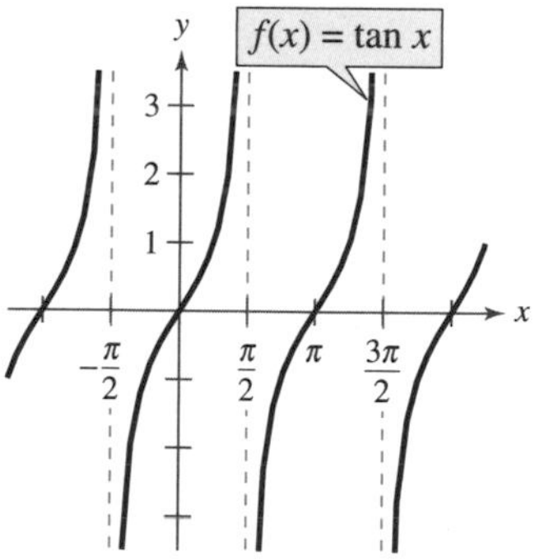

Domain: all $x \neq \dfrac{\pi}{2} + n\pi$
Range: $(-\infty, \infty)$
Period: π
x-intercepts: $(n\pi, 0)$
y-intercept: $(0, 0)$
Vertical asymptotes:

$$x = \frac{\pi}{2} + n\pi$$

Odd function
Origin symmetry